SCOTT FORESMAN-ADDISON WESLEY

Biology

SECOND EDITION

The Web of Life

Teacher's Edition

ERIC STRAUSS • MARYLIN LISOWSKI

Scott Foresman
Addison Wesley

Editorial Offices: Glenview, Illinois • New York, New York
Sales Offices: Reading, Massachusetts • Duluth, Georgia • Glenview, Illinois
Carrollton, Texas • Menlo Park, California

1-800-552-2259

http://www.sf.aw.com
http://www.biosurf.com

Second Edition

Cover design: Design Office

Front cover photographs: Tim Davis/Davis-Lynn Images

About the cover: Wolves and aspen trees are just two of the millions of species that comprise the web of life. The effects of the wolf's removal from and reintroduction to ecosystems demonstrate the delicate and complex connections among living things.

GeoSystems Global Corporation and Addison Wesley Longman are the publishers of the maps included in this textbook. The information contained in these maps is derived from a variety of sources, the publishers assume no responsibility for inconsistencies or inaccuracies in the data nor liability for any damages of any type arising from errors or omissions.

Printed in the United States of America
Published simultaneously in Canada

ISBN 0-201-33441-0

1 2 3 4 5 6 7 8 9 10 - VH - 03 02 01 00 99

Teacher's Edition Contents

Biology

The Web of Life

The program you need • for the course you want to teach!

As we developed *Biology: The Web of Life,* we asked teachers what they wanted in a biology program. The answer we got, in a word, was OPTIONS. So that's just what we delivered. This outstanding program gives you the choices you need to teach biology *your way.*

Authors

Marylin Lisowski

Marylin Lisowski is a professor of science education at Eastern Illinois University in Charleston. In addition to teaching biology and earth, environmental, and middle level science, Dr. Lisowski has lead international expeditions and field programs for high school students and teachers. She has been recognized as an Ohio Science Teacher of the Year, a Florida Honor Science Teacher, Illinois Environmental Educator of the Year, and Distinguished Professor of the Year.

Eric Strauss

Eric Strauss is Director of the Environmental Studies Program at Boston College in Chestnut Hill, Massachusetts. A dynamic and popular professor, Dr. Strauss draws on his background in both science and in mass communications to inspire students with exciting multimedia presentations. In addition to education, Dr. Strauss boasts an extensive background in science research and professional service. He currently runs a Cape Cod research station with his former high school teacher.

What teachers told us...

We responded with...

I need a program that will **reach and teach** all the students.

An abundance of engaging, **student-oriented features** and a **varied pedagogical format** to accommodate all student learning styles.

Every year there is **more content and less time.** I need a text that has it all but makes it easy for me to **pick and choose.**

Comprehensive content organized for **maximum flexibility** to allow you to quickly identify what you want to cover.

With local and national curricula, **standards, and testing,** I want to make certain students leave my course knowing the **basic concepts of biology** and how they are **interrelated.**

The **fundamental principles** of biology clearly **identified and connected** so that students do not "lose the forest for the trees."

Today, learning science is all about "doing science." I need a program that provides plenty of opportunities for **hands-on learning** with activities and labs of different types and lengths.

A **multitude of activities** and labs ranging from 5 minutes to a whole class period, that develop varied **learning and laboratory skills.**

Technology is great, but my needs are very specific—and changing.

Technology options— **videos, videodiscs, CD-ROMs, a website**—for every budget, hardware configuration, and staff experience level—current and future.

Program Components

Flexible and effective materials save you work and time, and offer your students exciting new dimensions in learning...

Student Edition
Reach and teach all your students with a text focused on the Big Ideas of Biology.

Teacher's Edition
Chapter Planning Guides and wraparound notes give you easy-to-access support.

Lab Manual
- 63 labs
- 14 lab skills exercises

Teacher's Resource Package

Unit Review Modules
- Section Reviews
- Vocabulary Reviews
- Interpreting Graphics Exercises
- Activity Recordsheets
- Critical Thinking Exercises
- Enrichment Topics
- Standard and Performance-based Chapter Tests
- Chapter Planning Guides
- Lab Practicals (one per unit)

Lab Manual Teacher's Edition
- 63 labs
- 14 lab skill exercises

Consumer Applications
Biology out of the classroom and into students' everyday lives.

Issues & Decision Making
Critical thinking about controversial, relevant issues in science.

Biotechnology Manual
- 17 labs
- 8 concepts and essays
- 4 Critical Thinking Exercises

Teacher's Curriculum Guide
Resource material for optional curricula pathways, and correlations.

Super Read!
Reading strategies and accompanying worksheets to help students be more efficient readers.

Spanish Reviews
Complete Spanish translation of all the chapter reviews and unit reviews.

Interpreting and Developing Graphics
Worksheets designed to help students interpret, analyze, and graph data.

Guide to Block Scheduling
An overview of block scheduling, and daily lesson plans.

Overhead Transparency Package
- 96 overheads with an instructional booklet

Animated Biological Concepts Videodisc Worksheets

Interactive Biology Simulations Worksheets

Technology Components

Videos

Biology Alive! Video Series
This five-part series, featuring *Biology: The Web Of Life* author and professor Dr. Eric Strauss, illustrates major biological concepts with fascinating examples culled from Dr. Strauss's field research station. Titles include *Signs of Life, The Continuity of Life, The Domain of Life, Conflict and Cooperation,* and *Life's Fragile Balance.*

Rewind: The Web of Life Reteach Videos
Contains selected Student Text narrative and illustrations from *Biology: The Web of Life* for review or make-up work. Ideal for ESL students and auditory learners.

Videodiscs

Animated Biological Concepts Videodiscs
This two-disc set uses spectacular computer animation to illuminate over 40 of the most difficult-to-teach concepts of biology. Includes comparative anatomy animations perfect for dissection-free classrooms. Comes with barcode directory and barcoded student worksheets.

Options for every budget, hardware configuration, and staff-experience level

CD-ROM's

TestWorks CD-ROM
Traditional and alternative testing for *Biology: The Web Of Life* provided in an easy-to-use-and-edit CD-ROM for Windows and Macintosh.

Interactive Biological Simulations CD-ROM
These in-depth simulations enable students to interact with biological processes, such as mitosis and protein synthesis, in ways not possible in the classroom or lab. Student worksheets included.

Teacher's Resource Planner CD-ROM
The complete Teacher's Resource Package available in a customizable CD-ROM format, PLUS an integrated comprehensive lesson planner. Supplements can be viewed either by individual item or by text chapter. Planning can be done for a day, week, term, or year for regular or block schedules.

Biología: la telaraña de la vida CD-ROM
Complete Spanish translation of *Biology: The Web of Life* Student Text.

Internet Sites

Provides a wealth of frequently updated Internet resources for students and teachers using *Biology: The Web of Life.* Includes additional activities, as well as information on careers in biology, critical thinking exercises, project ideas, and other text-related items, as well as links to other Internet sites.

The premier Internet biology site for students and teachers! Includes the latest biology research presented by the site's prestigious resident faculty, extensive learning activities, members' forum, links to Scientific American articles, and more.

Published by Peregrine Publishers, Inc.

Teacher's Edition
Chapter Planning Guide

Quickly determine what topics you want to cover and what resources are available.

Begin your chapter planning here. In this one handy location, you'll find the following useful information for every section in the chapter: objectives, activities, features, and appropriate Teacher's Resource Package print material.

PLANNING GUIDE

Section	Student Activities/Features	Teacher's Resour
6.1 Patterns of Inheritance **Objectives** ■ Distinguish between dominant traits and recessive traits ■ Analyze the results of Mendel's experiments with three generations of garden peas	**Lab Zone Discover It!** *Find Characteristics That Are Inherited,* p. 129 **Everyday Biology** *Bloodlines,* p. 130	**Unit 2 Review Module** ■ Section Review 6.1 ■ Enrichment Topics 6-
6.2 Principles of Inheritance **Objectives** ■ Explain the chromosome theory of heredity ■ Summarize Mendel's laws	**Lab Zone Think About It!** *Predicting Parakeet Color,* p. 135 **Lab Zone Do It!** *Can You Illustrate the Law of Dominance?* p. 137	**Unit 2 Review Module** ■ Section Review 6.2 ■ Activity Recordshee
6.3 Genetics and Predictions **Objectives** ■ Explain how probability is used in genetic predictions ■ Construct a Punnett square for monohybrid and dihybrid crosses ■ Infer genotype by using a test cross	**Lab Zone Do It!** *How Is Genetics Related to Probability?* p. 139	**Unit 2 Review Modu** ■ Section Review 6. ■ Activity Recordsh ■ Interpreting Grap **Consumer Applica** **Laboratory Manua** and Chance" **Interpreting and** **Graphics** 16, 17, 1
6.4 Predictions and People **Objectives** ■ Interpret pedigrees and understand their purpose ■ Contrast dominant and recessive genetic disorders ■ Identify some methods used to determine the likelihood of a genetic disorder occurring in offspring	**STS: Frontiers in Biology** *Genetic Counseling,* p. 144 **Everyday Biology** *Ears to You!* p. 145 **Lab Zone Investigate It!** *Using a Pedigree,* p. 146	**Unit 2 Review Mo** ■ Section Review ■ Activity Record ■ Critical Thinki ■ Enrichment T **Laboratory Mar** "Pedigree Analy **Biotechnology** "Assessing Gen Humans" **Issues and Dec**
6.5 Difficult Predictions **Objectives** ■ Compare and contrast patterns of inheritance that do not follow Mendel's laws ■ Explain how traits are influenced by the environment	**Everyday Biology** *Hold the Eggs,* p. 148 **In the Community** *Blood Drive,* p. 148 **STS: Issues in Biology** *The Genetics of Behavior,* p. 152	**Unit 2 Review** ■ Section Rev ■ Enrichmen ■ Vocabulary ■ Chapter 6 **Issues and D** **Spanish Rev**

Planning to integrate technology? This list of the technology opportunities in the chapter will help you do it with ease.

Technology Resources

Internet Connections

Within this chapter, you will see the (bioSURF) logo. If you and your students have access to the Internet, the following URL address will provide various Internet connections that are related to topics and features presented in this chapter:

http://genetics.biosurf.com

You can also find relevant chapter material at **The Biology Place** address:

http://www.biology.com

CD-ROMs

Biología: la telaraña de la vida, (Spanish Student Edition) Chapter 6
Teacher Resource Planner, Chapter 6
  Supplements
Interactive Biological Simulations
  ■ Punnett Squares
TestWorks CD-ROM
  ■ Chapter 6 Tests

Videodiscs

Animated Biological Concepts Videodiscs
  ■ Segregation of Chromosomes

Overhead Transparencies

  ■ Punnett Square, #14
  ■ Dihybrid Cross, #15

Videotapes

Biology Alive! Video Series
Rewind: The Web of Life Reteach Videos

Planning for Activities

STUDENT EDITION
Lab Zone
Discover It! p. 129
  ■ pencil
  ■ paper
  ■ graph paper

Lab Zone Do It! p. 137
  ■ buttons: two different
    colors
  ■ paper
  ■ pencil

Lab Zone Do It! p. 139
  ■ coins
  ■ pencil
  ■ paper

TEACHER'S EDITION
Class Activity, p. 131
Diagramming the parts of a flower
  ■ variety of flowers

Teacher Demo, p. 134
Modeling chromosome pairs
  ■ black and red plastic
    disks

Class Activity, p. 135
Dominant and recessive alleles
  ■ permanent marker
  ■ paper

Teacher Demo, p. 147
Testing for dominance
  ■ bottle
  ■ red beads
  ■ white beads

Teacher Demo, p. 148
Expressing incomplete dominance
  ■ plastic plates
  ■ variously-colored beans

Don't scramble for supplies at the last minute! Consult this list of the necessary materials for all chapter activities and labs.

Teacher's Edition Features

On page support where and when you need it!

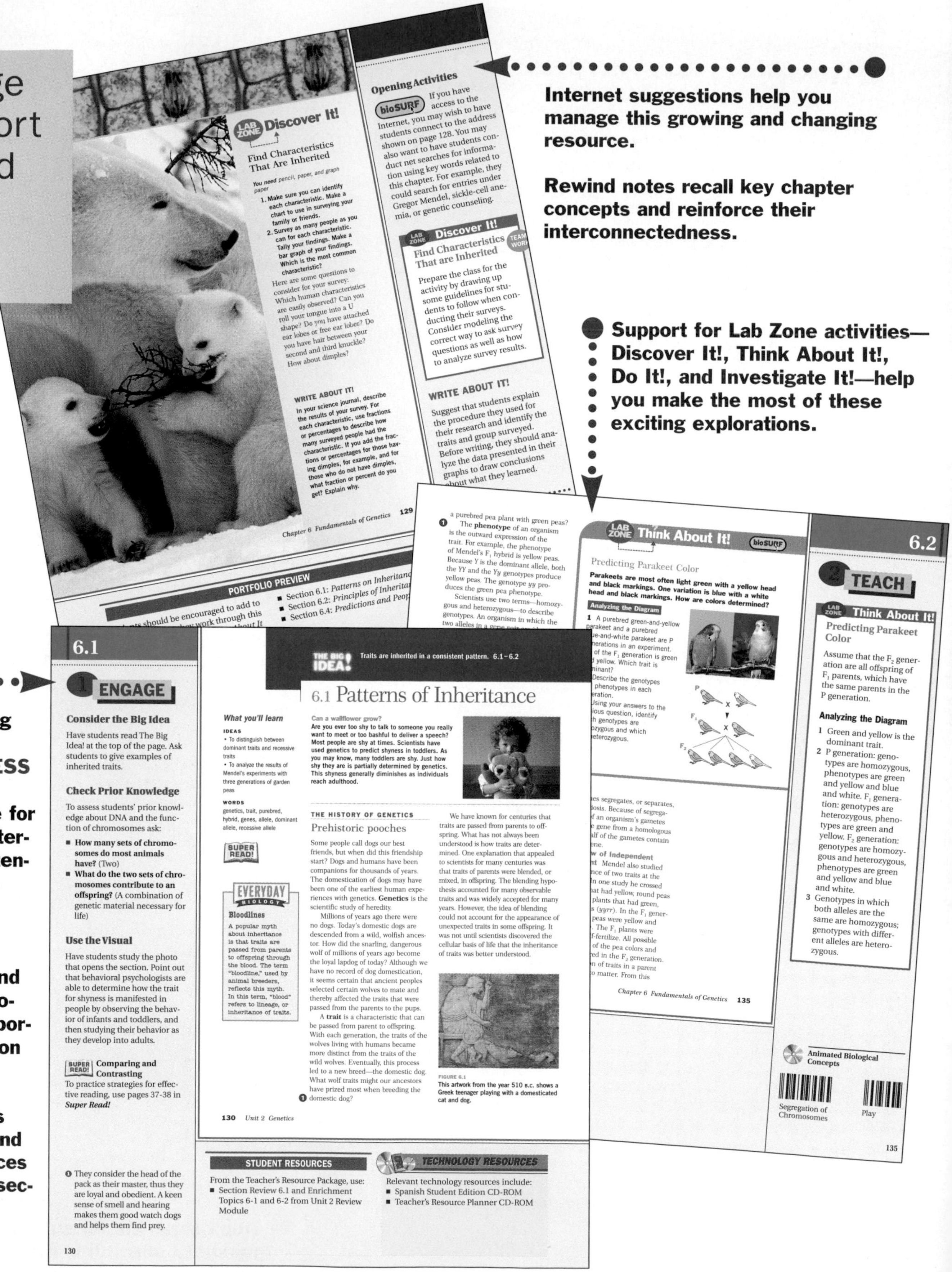

Internet suggestions help you manage this growing and changing resource.

Rewind notes recall key chapter concepts and reinforce their interconnectedness.

Support for Lab Zone activities—Discover It!, Think About It!, Do It!, and Investigate It!—help you make the most of these exciting explorations.

Three-step learning cycle of ENGAGE, TEACH, and ASSESS provides a simple, effective structure for presenting and determining student retention of the section content.

Quick Activities, Teacher Demos, and Class Activities provide numerous opportunities for hands-on learning.

Convenient listings of available print and technology resources accompany every section opener page.

LAB ZONE Discover It!

Find Characteristics That Are Inherited

You need pencil, paper, and graph paper.

1. Make sure you can identify each characteristic. Make a chart to use in surveying your family or friends.
2. Survey as many people as you can for each characteristic. Tally your findings. Make a bar graph of your findings. Which is the most common characteristic?

Here are some questions to consider for your survey: Which human characteristics are easily observed? Can you roll your tongue into a U shape? Do you have attached ear lobes or free ear lobes? Do you have hair between your second and third knuckle? How about dimples?

WRITE ABOUT IT!
In your science journal, describe the results of your survey. For each characteristic, use fractions or percentages to describe how many surveyed people had the characteristic. If you add the fractions or percentages for those having dimples, for example, and for those who do not have dimples, what fraction or percent do you get? Explain why.

Chapter 6 Fundamentals of Genetics 129

Opening Activities

bioSURF If you have access to the Internet, you may wish to have students connect to the address shown on page 128. You may also want to have students conduct net searches for information using key words related to this chapter. For example, they could search for entries under Gregor Mendel, sickle-cell anemia, or genetic counseling.

LAB ZONE Discover It! (TEAM WORK)

Find Characteristics That are Inherited

Prepare the class for the activity by drawing up some guidelines for students to follow when conducting their surveys. Consider modeling the correct way to ask survey questions as well as how to analyze survey results.

WRITE ABOUT IT!
Suggest that students explain the procedure they used for their research and identify the traits and group surveyed. Before writing, they should analyze the data presented in their graphs to draw conclusions about what they learned.

PORTFOLIO PREVIEW

...ts should be encouraged to add to... ...ey work through this... ...bout It...

- Section 6.1: Patterns on Inheritance
- Section 6.2: Principles of Inheritance
- Section 6.4: Predictions and People

---

a purebred pea plant with green peas?

The **phenotype** of an organism is the outward expression of the trait. For example, the phenotype of Mendel's F_1 hybrid is yellow peas. Because Y is the dominant allele, both the YY and the Yy genotypes produce yellow peas. The genotype yy produces the green pea phenotype.

Scientists use two terms—homozygous and heterozygous—to describe genotypes. An organism in which the two alleles in a gene pair...

...es segregates, or separates,... ...osis. Because of segrega-... ...f an organism's gametes... ...gene from a homologous... ...alf of the gametes contain... ...ene.

...w of Independent ...nt Mendel also studied ...nce of two traits at the ...n in one study he crossed ...at had yellow, round peas ...plants that had green, ...s ($yyrr$). In the F_1 gener-...peas were yellow and ...s. The F_1 plants were ...f-fertilize. All possible ...of the pea colors and ...ed in the F_2 generation. ...n of traits in a parent ...no matter. From this

---

LAB ZONE Think About It! bioSURF

Predicting Parakeet Color

Parakeets are most often light green with a yellow head and black markings. One variation is blue with a white head and black markings. How are colors determined?

Analyzing the Diagram

1. A purebred green-and-yellow parakeet and a purebred ...ue-and-white parakeet are P ...nerations in an experiment. ...t of the F_1 generation is green ...d yellow. Which trait is ...minant?
2. ...Describe the genotypes ...d phenotypes in each ...eration.
3. ...Using your answers to the ...ious question, identify ...ch genotypes are ...ozygous and which ...heterozygous.

6.1

1 ENGAGE

Consider the Big Idea

Have students read The Big Idea! at the top of the page. Ask students to give examples of inherited traits.

Check Prior Knowledge

To assess students' prior knowledge about DNA and the function of chromosomes ask:

- How many sets of chromosomes do most animals have? (Two)
- What do the two sets of chromosomes contribute to an offspring? (A combination of genetic material necessary for life)

Use the Visual

Have students study the photo that opens the section. Point out that behavioral psychologists are able to determine how the trait for shyness is manifested in people by observing the behavior of infants and toddlers, and then studying their behavior as they develop into adults.

SUPER READ! Comparing and Contrasting

To practice strategies for effective reading, use pages 37-38 in *Super Read!*

6.1

What you'll learn

IDEAS
- To distinguish between dominant traits and recessive traits
- To analyze the results of Mendel's experiments with three generations of garden peas

WORDS
genetics, trait, purebred, hybrid, genes, allele, dominant allele, recessive allele

SUPER READ!

EVERYDAY BIOLOGY

Bloodlines
A popular myth about inheritance is that traits are passed from parents to offspring through the blood. The term "bloodline," used by animal breeders, reflects this myth. In this term, "blood" refers to lineage, or inheritance of traits.

THE BIG IDEA!   Traits are inherited in a consistent pattern. 6.1–6.2

6.1 Patterns of Inheritance

Can a wallflower grow?
Are you ever too shy to talk to someone you really want to meet or too bashful to deliver a speech? Most people are shy at times. Scientists have used genetics to predict shyness in toddlers. As you may know, many toddlers are shy. Just how shy they are is partially determined by genetics. This shyness generally diminishes as individuals reach adulthood.

THE HISTORY OF GENETICS
Prehistoric pooches

Some people call dogs our best friends, but when did this friendship start? dogs and humans have been companions for thousands of years. The domestication of dogs may have been one of the earliest human experiences with genetics. **Genetics** is the scientific study of heredity.

Millions of years ago there were no dogs. Today's domestic dogs are descended from a wild, wolfish ancestor. How did the snarling, dangerous wolf of millions of years ago become the loyal lapdog of today? Although we have no record of dog domestication, it seems certain that ancient peoples selected certain wolves to mate and thereby affected the traits that were passed from the parents to the pups.

A **trait** is a characteristic that can be passed from parent to offspring. With each generation, the traits of the wolves living with humans became more distinct from the traits of the wild wolves. Eventually, this process led to a new breed—the domestic dog. What wolf traits might our ancestors have prized most when breeding the domestic dog?

We have known for centuries that traits are passed from parents to offspring. What has not always been understood is how traits are determined. One explanation that appealed to scientists for many centuries was that traits of parents were blended, or mixed, in offspring. The blending hypothesis accounted for many observable traits and was widely accepted for many years. However, the idea of blending could not account for the appearance of unexpected traits in some offspring. It was not until scientists discovered the cellular basis of life that the inheritance of traits was better understood.

FIGURE 6.1
This artwork from the year 510 B.C. shows a Greek teenager playing with a domesticated cat and dog.

130 *Unit 2 Genetics*

6.2

2 TEACH

LAB ZONE Think About It!

Predicting Parakeet Color

Assume that the F_2 generation are all offspring of F_1 parents, which have the same parents in the P generation.

Analyzing the Diagram

1. Green and yellow is the dominant trait.
2. P generation: genotypes are homozygous, phenotypes are green and yellow and blue and white. F_1 generation: genotypes are heterozygous, phenotypes are green and yellow. F_2 generation: genotypes are homozygous and heterozygous, phenotypes are green and yellow and blue and white.
3. Genotypes in which both alleles are the same are homozygous; genotypes with different alleles are heterozygous.

Animated Biological Concepts

Segregation of Chromosomes   Play

Chapter 6 Fundamentals of Genetics 135

135

STUDENT RESOURCES
From the Teacher's Resource Package, use:
- Section Review 6.1 and Enrichment Topics 6-1 and 6-2 from Unit 2 Review Module

TECHNOLOGY RESOURCES
Relevant technology resources include:
- Spanish Student Edition CD-ROM
- Teacher's Resource Planner CD-ROM

They consider the head of the pack as their master, thus they are loyal and obedient. A keen sense of smell and hearing makes them good watch dogs and helps them find prey.

Program Philosophy

Biology for All Students

Biology is a fascinating, dynamic, and exciting area of study. A successful high school biology course must reflect these characteristics. It must open the door to a lifetime of understanding and appreciation of the marvels of the natural world. It must also prepare students to take active roles in that world. For too many high school students, however, the study of biology is little more than hundreds of unrelated details and vocabulary words!

Biology: The Web of Life is a departure from the traditional programs that approach the subject in this way. It presents the fundamental content and concepts of biology structured around the "big ideas." Such a "big picture" perspective enhances student comprehension of the basic understanding of life. The following goals guided the efforts of all those involved in the program.

- To motivate, instruct, and excite students about the science of biology

- To emphasize the interconnectedness of core concepts and the interactions among living things

- To provide comprehensive scope and in-depth coverage of major topics appropriate for a high school biology course

- To address the spirit and specifics of the National Science Standards in a clear and comprehensive manner

- To build a framework of "big ideas" within which content and concepts can be explored

- To emphasize process and higher-order thinking skills in ways that engage and reward students

- To use real, familiar, and frequent examples of biological concepts that involve students in learning and ensure their success

- To provide a unique and attractive design that enhances content presentation, concept development, and visual-learning opportunities

- To support heterogeneous student populations and diverse teaching styles with a wide range of instructional tools

- To incorporate a full-spectrum technology program into the product.

"Doing" Science

Studies have shown that comprehension and retention increase dramatically when the instructional focus is shifted from the role of the student as a passive receptor of facts to that of an active participant in the discovery process.

Toward this goal, *Biology: The Web of Life* provides a variety of opportunities to develop and practice the art of doing science. In each chapter, Lab Zone activities allow students to experience biology both as a process and as a body of knowledge. The *Laboratory Manual* and *Project Biology* extend the hands-on experience by providing more than one hundred opportunities for active learning.

Skills Development

When educators discuss the skills that should be taught in the science classroom, they usually include the skills needed to conduct scientific research, such as observing, measuring, and graphing. Yet surveys of the biotechnology industry indicate that employers in the field consider writing and communication skills to be far more important than course work or grades. *Biology: The Web of Life* provides ample opportunities for the student to develop science process skills, as well as writing and communication skills. Numerous and varied suggestions for activities expand the range of skill-building by encouraging students to conduct independent research, deliver oral presentations, design visual displays, express themselves in a range of written modes, and delve deeply into specific subject areas.

Interest and Readability

No textbook, no matter how well planned, can effectively reach its audience if it is not written in a manner that is friendly, inviting, readable, and understandable. The goal of *Biology: The Web of Life* is to engage the interest of *all* students, and encourage them to learn biology because it is exciting, interesting, useful, relevant, and *fun!* Current and compelling stories, humorous and enlightening introductions, playful and informative openers, and connections among content blocks help draw the student into the subject. Features expand the scope of the text, making biology fascinating and real. In all ways, *Biology: The Web of Life* puts the *life* back into biology for all students.

Themes in Biology

Themes in science are like the framework of a building—they provide structure and support. By using a thematic approach to teaching, you can help students relate science concepts to their lives both in and out of the classroom. The goal of using themes to teach science is to help students understand the important ideas in science, the connections between those ideas, and how the ideas relate to their everyday lives.

Defining Themes

Using a thematic approach to teaching is not new, but different teachers may have different definitions of the word *theme*. Themes are sometimes defined as topics, as when someone describes the theme of a lesson as "insects." This topical approach can be very useful to students and teachers. In this textbook, however, themes are defined as links between the major concepts in science. A list of the textbook's major themes and their descriptions is shown in the chart below.

Using a Thematic Approach

The volume of scientific information has grown so large that it is impossible to teach students every fact that has been discovered. Too often, however, science is presented as a long string of unconnected facts and activities. A thematic approach to science allows students to derive a sense of how the main ideas in science relate to one another. You may wish to use themes to help students integrate different branches of science, to connect science concepts with other disciplines, or to relate science to their lives and society.

In *Biology: The Web of Life,* the themes are woven into the material and into the Big Ideas. The seven themes used throughout the textbook are correlated to relevant chapters in the chart on page T13. It is important to note that these themes do not represent all of the possible themes.

Theme	Description	Theme	Description
Scale and Structure	Scientists study the natural world at the microscopic and macroscopic levels. While much analysis is done by observing the smallest parts of objects, it is often necessary to observe structures as parts of systems.	**Patterns of Change/ Cycles**	Change is an essential part of the natural world. Change occurs in trends or in cycles. Not all change is predictable. Trends are relatively steady patterns; cycles are repeating patterns.
Energy	The theme of energy is a central concept in science. Life processes, physical and chemical changes, interactions, and the forces that cause natural cycles all involve energy.	**Stability and Equilibrium**	Stability and equilibrium are terms that describe situations that do not change or situations in which all forces are balanced.
Evolution	In its most general sense, evolution can be defined as change over time. Both living and nonliving things evolve.	**Systems and Interactions**	Natural systems include chemical systems, body systems, ecosystems, and the solar system. Within each system there are many kinds of interactions that involve two or more system components.
Unity and Diversity	Throughout the sciences, diverse kinds of structures in both living and nonliving are described. Yet despite great diversity or underlying sameness, there is unity.		

A Thematic Approach

Chapter	Scale and Structure	Energy	Evolution	Unity and Diversity	Patterns of Change/Cycles	Stability and Equilibrium	Systems and Interactions
1	X		X	X			X
2	X	X		X	X	X	X
3	X	X		X		X	X
4	X	X			X		
5	X	X			X		X
6	X		X	X	X		X
7	X		X		X	X	X
8	X			X	X	X	X
9	X		X	X	X		X
10				X	X	X	X
11	X	X	X	X	X	X	X
12	X			X	X		
13				X	X		
14	X	X	X	X	X	X	X
15	X	X		X	X	X	X
16	X	X	X	X	X	X	X
17	X			X		X	X
18	X	X		X	X		X
19	X			X	X		X
20			X	X	X		X
21	X	X	X	X	X		X
22	X	X	X	X			X
23	X	X	X	X	X		X
24	X	X	X	X	X		X
25	X	X		X	X	X	X
26	X	X	X	X	X		X
27	X	X	X	X	X		
28				X			X
29	X	X		X		X	X
30	X	X			X	X	X
31	X	X		X	X	X	X
32	X			X	X	X	X
33	X			X	X	X	X
34	X	X		X	X	X	X
35				X	X	X	X
36	X			X	X	X	X
37	X	X			X	X	X
38	X	X		X	X	X	X

The Lesson Cycle

Learning is an ongoing process that occurs in cycles. Similarly, each lesson should follow a cycle that encourages and enhances the learning process. In the Teacher's Edition, the lesson cycle of engage, teach, and assess helps make learning fun, meaningful, and enduring.

Engage

In the first step of the lesson cycle, the teacher engages the student's interest and inspires curiosity. Students are encouraged to activate prior knowledge and ask what they can learn about the new topic. During this stage of the lesson, misconceptions are explored and the teacher can identify target areas on which to focus. *Biology: The Web of Life* Teacher's Edition employs the following techniques to engage the students in the first step of the lesson cycle:

Consider the Big Idea corresponds to the Big Idea given in the student text. The Big Idea sets the stage, pointing out what the student will learn in the upcoming section or sections of the text.

Use the Visual provides suggestions for launching discussions or lessons using the photograph that introduces the text section.

Check Prior Knowledge, which appears in most section openers, helps to determine students' previous knowledge of the subject to be studied. This feature allows the teacher to assess the students' background and unveil misconceptions.

Teacher Demo or **Quick Activity** serves to pique students' interest with a relevant, active experience. The activity inspires the students to seek ways to answer questions of "how" and "why," rather than to simply acquire information or seek the "right answer."

Teach

During the second step of the lesson cycle, the teacher serves as a guide while the students explore phenomena, attempt to answer questions raised during the first step of the cycle, and begin to construct an understanding of a concept through hands-on participation. The teacher helps students to develop understanding through communication, construction of models, and critical thinking. Connections are made to other disciplines as well as to social and community issues.

Explain prompts the teacher to briefly point out pertinent background information that allows students to begin from a common starting point.

Discuss presents topics that relate to or reinforce the concepts in the student text and provides suggested topics for discussion among students.

Clarify Misconceptions demystifies common misconceptions related to the text material, explaining confusing terms, exposing illogical ideas, and clearing away misinformation that could stand in the way of new learning.

Use the Visual provides suggestions for incorporating a photograph, diagram, or illustration into the lesson, helping to engage the visual, spatial, or nonverbal learner in concept development.

Apply prompts students to apply newly acquired knowledge to a new or familiar situation.

Teacher Demo and **Class Activity** provide an opportunity for students to witness or experience the concepts described in the text. All students should participate in class activities, which may include the use of manipulatives or role playing.

Build Writing Skills helps teachers to encourage writing activities as an integral part of learning. Writing activities may include research, letters to the media and creative writing projects.

Think Critically encourages students to think beyond what is written on the page. This feature may present a problem or provide a series of questions to help guide a student.

Connections to other sciences and disciplines are extended parts of the learning cycle throughout many sections. These strategies give teachers an opportunity to integrate a variety of sciences and other disciplines into their curriculum.

Assess

During the assessment step of the lesson cycle, students demonstrate their understanding and mastery of concepts and skills by answering questions based on their observations and experiences during the lesson. This allows teachers to identify areas needing further clarification, and allows the students to evaluate their own success in achieving learning goals.

Evaluate Understanding uses questioning, student participation, written explanations, and student-generated materials to demonstrate learning.

Reteach presents the teacher with an alternative strategy to reinforce section content and concepts.

Cooperative Learning

Cooperative learning is an organizational scheme for the learning environment that requires students to work collaboratively to carry out structured activities. Rather than stressing individual or competitive accountability in which students work alone or against one another, cooperative learning emphasizes group responsibility, mastery, respect, and success. Students work in small groups to solve a problem or create a product to which each group member contributes and for which each member is held equally accountable. Interdependence is essential for the group to be successful in achieving its designated goal.

The cooperative learning approach provides an opportunity for students to develop positive social interaction skills that are beneficial in everyday life as well as in the classroom. Process and critical thinking skills are extended as students become aware of alternative problem solving methods. In addition, students often find that by sharing information with team members they come to a better understanding of the concepts they are studying.

Cooperative Learning Groups

Cooperative learning groups should range in number from two to six members and should be heterogeneous with respect to gender, ethnicity, and ability. Once a group is established, it should remain together until the activity is completed. Do not dissolve a group that is having difficulty working together socially or staying on task. Keeping the group intact helps students learn the social interaction skills needed to solve problems and complete tasks through cooperation and collaboration.

Collaborative/Social Skills

The development and enrichment of social skills are basic to successful collaboration and cooperation. For each cooperative learning activity, you should assign a specific social skill. Social skills include listening carefully, taking turns, sharing resources, encouraging participation, treating others with respect, providing constructive feedback, resolving conflict, reaching consensus, and explaining and helping without simply giving answers.

Self-Evaluation

In cooperative learning environments, students should be encouraged to become involved in the evaluation process. You can accomplish this by giving them adequate time to reflect on the activity. You should remind students that for any project all members of a group should be prepared to explain what the group has done.

Suggested Roles in Cooperative Groups

Members of a cooperative learning group must assume a variety of roles for the group to collaborate effectively. The roles will be determined primarily by the nature of the project. Some suggested roles are:

- **Principal Investigator** The Principal Investigator manages the tasks within the activity and insures that all members understand activity goals and content. The Principal Investigator serves as a liaison between the teacher and the group, reads instructions, checks results, and facilitates group discussions.
- **Primary Researcher** The Primary Researcher assumes the role of group manager for activities involving research. The Primary Researcher should explain tasks and identify resources.
- **Materials Manager** The Materials Manager assembles and distributes the materials and equipment. The Materials Manager is responsible for operating equipment, checking the results of the activity, and ensuring that all equipment is returned clean and in good working order. The Materials Manager also reports damaged or unsafe equipment.
- **Data Collector** The Data Collector is responsible for gathering, recording, analyzing, and organizing the group's data into the presentation format.
- **Data Organizer** The Data Organizer coordinates the group data and certifies each group member's contributions to the activity.
- **Presenter** The Presenter reports the results of an activity. The Presenter may field questions posed by classmates about the group's activity or delegate specific types of questions to other members of the group.
- **Timekeeper** The Timekeeper is responsible for keeping track of time, monitoring noise level, checking the results of an activity for accuracy, and making sure proper safety precautions are observed.

Concept Mapping

Concept mapping helps students learn in a more meaningful way by making key concepts and abstract information more understandable and useful. A concept map links together main ideas in a format that emphasizes interactions, interrelationships, pathways, and hierarchies. Concept mapping relies on a basic learning principle: People learn best by incorporating new information into what they already know. Using concept maps, students can assimilate new information, grasp new relationships, and perceive new connections.

Concept mapping helps students to:

- Link new ideas with previously learned material
- Organize information and establish relationships between ideas
- Find new meaning in the things they are learning.

Concept mapping helps teachers to

- Introduce new concepts to students in an interesting way
- Determine student misconceptions

Most important, concept mapping can give both students and teacher new insights into biology.

Constructing a Concept Map

Here are some suggestions for creating concept maps.

- Place the main concept in an oval at the top of the map.
- Draw branches from the main concept to subordinate concepts also in ovals.
- Draw branches from the subordinate concepts to specific examples.
- Use each concept only once in the map.
- Write the concepts as nouns or short phrases.
- Link the nouns by verbs, adverbs, and prepositions.
- Link every concept to at least one other concept.
- Do not let linking lines intersect.
- Make sure linking lines between concepts run in different directions on the map.
- Make certain that any two concepts and their linking words form a complete thought.

Teaching Concept Mapping Skills

The best way to teach students about concept mapping is to provide plenty of practice. Every chapter of *Biology: The Web of Life* has a concept mapping exercise in the Chapter Review. In the early chapters the concept mapping exercise consists of an incomplete map with blanks and a word list. Students write the missing concepts and linking words in the blanks. In later chapters, students prepare their own concept maps, first from a list of words and then entirely on their own.

To encourage students, show them examples of good maps. Good maps link concepts in a logical arrangement and do not contain misconceptions. However, remind students that concept maps are intended to be flexible tools for learning: There is no single correct way to do a concept map because there are many different ways to represent the same ideas.

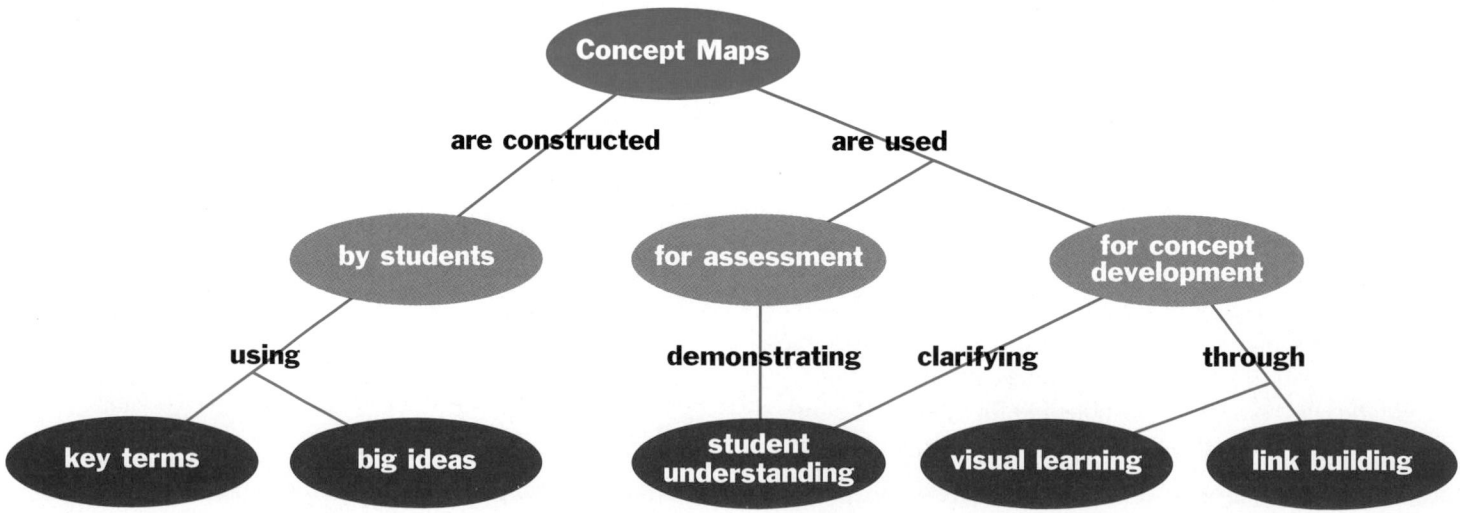

Students with Individual Needs

Today's science teachers must structure their teaching to accommodate a student population with diverse abilities, interests, and learning styles that span a broader range than ever before. A science classroom should be a positive learning environment, with optimum opportunities for all students to achieve success. Challenges such as visual, physical, or hearing impairments, limited English proficiency (LEP), and different levels of learning can be addressed through specific teaching strategies. General strategies that will help you prepare for the challenge of teaching diverse student populations are presented here. Specific tips for applying these strategies and accommodating students' needs appear throughout every chapter in the Teacher's Edition.

Learning Styles

Even among students with similar abilities and skills, there is a variety of cognitive and behavior patterns with which students approach the task of learning. Some students learn by visualizing spatial and physical relationships. Others learn through understanding patterns, rhythms, or motion. Some students prefer to work alone, while others are more successful in groups or cooperative situations.

To accommodate the wide variety of learning styles that are likely to comprise the population of any science classroom, it is essential that the instructional program be flexible and varied. A mixture of techniques should be used within each lesson to give all students an equal opportunity to succeed. Class time should include a blend of lecture, demonstration, and hands-on and minds-on inquiry, as well as the use of text and multimedia resources.

Students "At Risk"

Certain students, due to their ability levels, behavioral or emotional challenges, or previous educational experiences, are at greater risk than others for failing to achieve success. To main-tain a positive learning environment, emphasis should be placed on reinforcing success and minimizing failure.

Concepts should be presented in several different ways, using relevant, common examples. Learning goals should be presented frequently, at a pace that enables success to be achieved. *Biology: The Web of Life* provides a pacing guide to help you identify the essential concepts and text selections to construct a basic curriculum. Other general strategies for teaching at-risk students include:

- Provide clear, specific instruction, assignments, and learning goals that students can achieve.

- Use hands-on activities and demonstrations to reinforce concepts. Provide opportunities to repeat and practice new skills.

- Check for understanding frequently. Provide students with a variety of choices for demonstrating their learning, including speaking, writing, drawing, and multimedia presentations.

- Use Section Review Worksheets and Skills Worksheets (provided in the Teacher's Resource Package) to build and reinforce comprehension.

Physical, Visual, or Hearing Impairments

Students with a wide variety of impairments are now able to share in the process of learning science alongside their nonimpaired classmates. Teachers are faced with the task of ensuring that these students participate in the learning activities and have an equal opportunity to succeed. The nature and severity of the impairment will determine which classroom techniques will need to be adjusted to include all students. It is essential that the teacher work closely with the students, the parents, and the school guidance counselor to determine how best to address the students' individual needs.

- Encourage independence and help nonimpaired students and adults to understand the students' special needs.

- Make sure the physical arrangement of classroom furniture and other objects can accommodate wheelchairs, guide dogs, or other equipment. Materials should be within reach and accessible to all students.

- If appropriate, enlist the aid of one or two students to assist the challenged student as necessary, such as reading aloud, acting as a sight peer during lab work, or providing physical assistance.

- During physical activities, provide physically challenged students with roles in which they can participate in a nonphysical way, such as Timekeeper or Materials Manager.

- Seat students with limited hearing or visual problems near the front of the classroom. Face the class when speaking.

Limited English Proficiency (LEP) Students

Students who speak English as a second language face a variety of challenges in the science classroom. In addition to the challenge of achieving mastery in science, students must overcome a language barrier and discrepancies in educational background, as well as the social concerns resulting from cultural differences. It is difficult to grasp complex and abstract concepts when vocabulary and pronunciation provide barriers. The following suggestions will help your students to thrive in their new homeland:

- Speak clearly, using body language and gestures for emphasis.

- Have students create their own "dictionary" of key terms and unfamiliar words that includes a term in English, the term in their native language, and a brief definition.

- Use illustrations and other visual learning resources to help students grasp concepts. Provide labeling and vocabulary exercises to help build word power.

- Provide newspapers and magazines to make connections between the science content and cultural issues. Incorporate examples from various cultures into discussions and encourage student participation.

- Encourage students to make use of English-language dictionaries.

- Provide audiocassettes of lectures and/or text materials to reinforce classroom learning and to provide model language patterns.

- Have picture dictionaries, wall charts, and other visual learning resources available.

Gifted Students

Providing resources and enriched learning opportunities for the gifted student can be as important as accommodating impaired students. When learning is no longer challenging and stimulating, educational opportunities can easily be missed. Although gifted students can sometimes provide assistance in developing other students' comprehension, the activities of the gifted student must focus on maximizing his or her own educational opportunities.

- Provide students with the opportunity to work on independent projects of interest to the student. If possible, make arrangements for the student to accelerate his or her progress in selected subjects.

- Encourage students to use public resources, such as materials provided by government agencies, and to become involved in community activities.

- Emphasize the use of high-level cognitive skills, such as developing analogies, synthesizing new concepts, and analyzing relationships within and beyond the science disciplines. Encourage students to take intellectual "risks."

Skills in Biology

As with all sciences, mastering biology involves more than just acquiring a knowledge foundation. Instead, the study of biology offers students opportunities to learn, practice, and master skills that are relevant to their everyday world and their professional goals.

Biology is more than a collection of information to be read, discussed, tested, and assessed for a numerical grade. Content mastery can no longer be evaluated by students' abilities to recall vocabulary terms, memorize unrelated facts, or repeat a theory without understanding how the content and concepts are interconnected. Inquiry, discovery, and investigation must also be a part of each student's science experience. Students need to develop process skills and thinking skills.

Throughout the *Biology: The Web of Life* program, there are opportunities for students to learn, practice, and master a variety of skills. These skills include thinking skills, science process skills, and communication skills—all essential to academic, personal, and professional success.

Thinking Skills

Critical thinking is a process that uses a variety of skills including analyzing and solving problems, making decisions, and evaluating reasoning. Throughout this program, students are provided with opportunities to develop reasonable conclusions, evaluate information, make decisions, and assess issues with facts and reasoned judgment. Critical thinking and process skills can be found in the following features of the *Biology: The Web of Life* program: *Hit or Myth; Checkpoint; Think About It!; Chapter Review; Science, Technology, and Society (STS); Unit Review.*

Process Skills

Process skills are those skills usually associated with gathering, recording, organizing, interpreting, and analyzing information about the natural world. While the process skills are often identified as *science* skills, they are also used in many other settings to make decisions and to assess situations. As students use process skills, they will also use thinking skills—and a pattern emerges linking the two types of skills. Students have ample opportunities to learn and practice process skills throughout the *Biology: The Web of Life* program. A wide variety of activities helps the students to develop the following skills: classifying; measuring; predicting; observing; estimating; inferring; modeling; hypothesizing; collecting and recording data; organizing and analyzing data.

Communication Skills

The ability to communicate effectively is of paramount importance in today's world. Communication skills such as writing, reading, speaking, and listening are prerequisites to acquiring, analyzing, and applying information. In *Biology: The Web of Life* communication skills are an integral part of the Student Edition and other components.

Reading In a society that transmits an ever-increasing amount of information, reading is an essential life skill. Students must be effective readers who can read with understanding. Because the number of new terms in biology may be formidable, reading and comprehending the content and concepts can be difficult for many students. However, it is essential that students develop a working knowledge of the content-specific terms.

Writing Writing is a powerful tool for learning. Competency in writing is necessary for success in the classroom and throughout life. Writing uses a number of process and critical thinking skills. It involves collecting, recording, and organizing information, as well as sequencing, establishing relationships among ideas, ordering and organizing paragraphs, and revising written materials until a final polished draft has been completed.

To help all students develop effective reading and writing skills, numerous and varied pedagogical tools have been incorporated into *Biology: The Web of Life*. They include *What you'll learn; Key Terms; Concept Maps; Lab Zone* activities; *Write About It!; Critic's Corner;* and *bioSURF.*

Skills Matrix

Chapter	1	2	3	4	5	6	7	8	9	10	11	12	13	14	15	16	17	18
Describe		X	X	X			X	X	X	X	X		X	X	X	X	X	X
Identify	X	X		X	X	X		X		X	X	X	X	X		X	X	
Measure							X				X						X	
Record Data		X	X	X	X	X	X	X		X	X	X			X	X		X
Calculate					X					X								
Explain	X	X	X	X	X	X	X	X	X	X	X		X	X	X		X	X
Interpret	X	X	X	X	X	X	X	X	X	X	X	X	X	X	X	X	X	X
Summarize	X		X	X	X	X		X				X	X				X	
Apply	X	X			X			X		X	X					X		X
Organize Data													X					
Graph										X								
Model					X		X	X	X	X				X	X			
Analyze	X	X	X	X	X	X	X	X	X	X	X	X	X	X	X	X	X	X
Infer			X	X		X						X						
Compare and Contrast	X	X	X	X	X	X	X		X	X	X	X	X	X	X	X	X	X
Classify								X	X				X					
Hypothesize		X	X	X	X			X	X		X				X			X
Predict						X	X				X				X	X		
Evaluate											X	X						
Discuss																X		
Observe	X	X	X	X	X	X	X				X		X		X	X	X	X
Writing Connection	X	X	X	X	X	X	X	X	X	X	X	X	X	X	X	X	X	X
Distinguish		X			X	X	X	X	X				X		X			
Define							X											

19	20	21	22	23	24	25	26	27	28	29	30	31	32	33	34	35	36	37	38
X	X	X	X	X	X	X	X	X	X		X	X	X	X	X	X	X	X	X
X	X	X	X	X			X			X	X	X	X	X	X	X		X	X
X	X											X				X	X	X	
	X	X	X		X	X	X	X	X	X	X	X	X	X	X	X	X	X	X
		X										X	X	X	X		X		
X	X	X	X	X	X	X	X	X	X	X	X	X	X	X	X	X		X	X
X	X	X	X	X	X	X	X	X	X	X	X	X	X	X	X	X	X	X	X
						X	X			X						X			
X	X					X	X	X	X	X	X	X	X	X	X	X	X	X	X
														X					
X	X						X			X			X	X		X	X		
					X			X			X		X			X		X	
X	X	X	X	X	X	X	X	X	X	X	X	X	X	X	X	X	X	X	X
		X																	
X	X	X	X	X	X	X	X	X	X	X	X	X	X	X	X	X			X
					X		X	X		X									
	X			X	X						X						X		
		X	X			X				X				X		X			
										X	X							X	
	X																		
X	X	X	X	X	X	X	X	X	X	X	X	X	X	X	X	X	X	X	X
X	X	X	X	X	X	X	X	X	X	X	X	X	X	X	X	X	X	X	X
		X			X				X	X					X	X	X	X	
											X				X	X	X	X	

Pacing Guide

Scientific knowledge is constantly changing and expanding, and the field of biology is no exception. Most biology teachers are faced with the challenge of educating students of varied academic abilities. It takes careful planning to map out a method by which students can best be exposed to the major topics in the high school biology curriculum.

The organization of *Biology: The Web of Life* makes it suitable for a variety of student and teacher needs. The textbook is comprehensive enough to satisfy the most comprehensive high school biology curriculum, while remaining readable, interesting, and accessible to less-academically motivated students. In addition, the division of chapters into manageable numbered sections provides today's teachers with the flexibility needed to teach classes comprised of students with diverse learning levels.

Planning a Curriculum that Meets the Needs of Your Students

The following pages contain a pacing guide to assist teachers in designing lessons that meet the needs of *all* their students.

• **The Core Curriculum (C)** is designed for use by teachers whose classroom population is comprised largely of students with below-average academic abilities in both reading comprehension and general scholastic achievement. This core curriculum allows for material to be covered at a slower pace than that suitable for more advanced students. The pacing guide suggests topics to omit from the curriculum because they may be beyond the reach of these students. Students who study the core curriculum will be prepared to become scientifically literate citizens.

• **The Standard Curriculum (S)** is designed for use by teachers whose classroom populations are comprised largely of students considered average in ability and achievement levels. These students should have little difficulty reading and understanding most of the material presented. Some sections address abstract biological concepts that may not be necessary parts of your curriculum, or may be beyond the ability level of the average student. Suggestions for omitting such sections have been included in the pacing guide. Students who study the standard curriculum will be prepared for other science courses as well as to become scientifically literate citizens.

• **The Extended Standard Curriculum (ES)** is designed for use by teachers whose classroom population is comprised largely of students who are above average in their reading comprehension and general scholastic abilities. Students in this population will be able to read and comprehend the entire textbook with some degree of ease. In order to adequately challenge these students and provide them with the fullest course of study, it is recommended they be required to read the entire text, and complete many of the enrichment activities suggested in the Teacher's Edition and Teacher's Resource Package. Students who study the extended standard curriculum will be prepared for other advanced science courses as well as to become scientifically literate citizens.

		(C)	(S)	(ES)
1	**Study of Life**			
1.1	Similarities Among Living Things	•	•	•
1.2	The Evolving Earth		•	•
1.3	Doing the Science of Biology	•	•	•
2	**Chemical Basis of Life**			
2.1	Chemicals in Organisms	•	•	•
2.2	Basics of Chemistry	•	•	•
2.3	Chemicals at Work	•	•	•
2.4	Chemistry in Life Processes	•	•	•
2.5	Water and Solutions	•	•	•
3	**Cell Structure and Function**			
3.1	A Look at Cells	•	•	•
3.2	Basic Cell Structures	•	•	•
3.3	Cell Organelles	•	•	•
3.4	Cell Diversity	•	•	•
3.5	Cells and Their Environment	•	•	•

		(C)	(S)	(ES)
4	**Photosynthesis and Cellular Respiration**			
4.1	Energy and ATP	•	•	•
4.2	Photosynthesis		•	•
4.3	Cellular Respiration		•	•
4.4	Energy Flow in the Biosphere	•	•	•
5	**Cell Division**			
5.1	When Do Cells Divide?	•	•	•
5.2	How Do Cells Divide?	•	•	•
5.3	What Is Meiosis?	•	•	•
5.4	New Chromosome Combinations	•	•	•
6	**Fundamentals of Genetics**			
6.1	Patterns of Inheritance	•	•	•
6.2	Principles of Inheritance	•	•	•
6.3	Genetics and Predictions		•	•
6.4	Predictions and People	•	•	•
6.5	Difficult Predictions		•	•

		(C)	(S)	(ES)
7	**DNA, Genes, and Chromosomes**			
7.1	Molecule of Heredity		•	•
7.2	DNA Structure and Replication	•	•	•
7.3	Linked Genes		•	•
7.4	Sex Linkage		•	•
7.5	The Human Gene Map	•	•	•
8	**Protein Synthesis**			
8.1	From Genotype to Phenotype	•	•	•
8.2	Protein and Phenotype			•
8.3	Changes in Chromosomes	•	•	•
8.4	Genes and Cancer	•	•	•
9	**The Biotechnology Revolution**			
9.1	Breeding	•	•	•
9.2	Genetic Engineering			•
9.3	Applications of Genetic Engineering	•	•	•
9.4	Safety and Ethics of Biotechnology	•	•	•

43 (-11) 44 (-6) 42 (-42) 105/168

Assessing Student Progress

Learning Styles

Learning occurs at a variety of levels. Similarly, students process new information using different learning styles. The learning style of a student refers to the way in which the student is best able to learn and retain information. Some students learn best by reading, others by listening or seeing a visual presentation. Still other students learn best by touching and manipulating objects as in a laboratory environment. To ensure student success, it is important to provide opportunities to use each of these learning styles.

Assessing Opportunities

Just as there are different styles of learning, there are different methods for assessing student progress and understanding. These methods, which can be formal or informal, include the following: questions for student self-assessment; traditional paper-and-pencil tests; classroom discussions; performance assessment; presentations and discussions; portfolios; journals; interviews; projects; investigations.

The *Biology: The Web of Life* program includes the following assessment devices which can be used either informally or formally.

• **Checkpoint** Each section concludes with several questions that can be used as a self-check for students, a class-discussion exercise, or a written homework assignment. Included in these questions are a critical thinking question and a question that relates concepts by having students build on what they already know.

• **Chapter Review** Each chapter concludes with a Chapter Review. The review provides students with an opportunity to check their understanding of key vocabulary terms, content, and concepts. In addition, each Chapter Review includes a concept mapping activity, critical thinking questions, STS exercises, and suggestions for projects and reports that integrate biology with other sciences and disciplines.

• **Concept Mapping** Concept maps provide students with a visual study tool that shows relationships among ideas. Concept mapping is an open-ended assessment tool. Because different students learn and relate ideas in different ways, there is no single correct way to organize a concept map. As such, organization of individual concept maps may vary widely.

• **Creative Writing** Throughout the program, students are asked to express their ideas in a variety of creative writing exercises. The creative writing assignments provide opportunities for students to develop and enhance their writing skills as they communicate their knowledge about a topic. In assessing students' writing, you should ask yourself two questions: Does the information presented reflect an understanding of the concepts being discussed? and is the student communicating in a clear and effective way?

• **Portfolios** Portfolios are collections of representative work done by students during the year. Portfolios encourage students to communicate their knowledge in both traditional and creative ways; to assess and revise their own work; to develop the ability to identify their own strengths and weaknesses; and to set goals for learning. The decision to use portfolios requires input from teachers, administrators, and members of the community. Portfolios require a significant amount of time for planning and managing.

Many kinds of student work can be included in portfolios: photographs, artwork, videotapes, audiotapes, computer programs, research reports, projects, lab reports, journals, experimental models or designs, stages in a "work in progress." Students can select what they want to include in their portfolios within guidelines set by the teacher or the student, or by the nature of the content. Periodic portfolio reviews help to identify a student's strengths and weaknesses, assess a student's progress, and adjust instruction to meet individual needs.

• **Section Reviews** The Teacher's Resource Package includes Unit Modules containing Section Review worksheets for every section of every chapter. The worksheets can be used by students for informal review or by teachers as quizzes.

• **Tests** Also included in the Unit Modules is a comprehensive testing program with two different tests for each chapter. One chapter test consists of multiple-choice questions. The other test has performance-based assessment questions. The two testing formats provide maximum flexibility for teachers. The Unit Modules also include nine lab practical exams, one for each unit in the textbook. A comprehensive testing program is also available in the TestWorks CD-ROM.

Laboratory Opportunities

Student Edition

Throughout *Biology: The Web of Life,* there are numerous and diverse laboratory opportunities for students. The laboratory activities, all found under the umbrella head of **Lab Zone,** were developed to give students hands-on and minds-on experiences.

Lab Zone Discover It! activities are quick hands-on or paper-and-pencil activities found on each Chapter Opener page. They can be used as an exploration tool and to stimulate students' interest in the upcoming chapter material.

Lab Zone Think About It! activities provide mental practice in applying concepts. They are mainly paper-and-pencil activities, often accompanied by charts, graphs, and tables. Many require students to interpret information and think critically.

Lab Zone Do It! activities provide quick and effective applications of both concepts and scientific method. All require minimal equipment and are found near concepts that are connected to and enhanced by the activities.

Lab Zone Investigate It! are full-page activities that give students an opportunity to conduct more formal laboratory experiments. There are 27 Lab Zone Investigate It! activities that are more structured, or directed, and 11 activities that are more open-ended. All the labs, however, can be adapted to fit the needs of any classroom. Students use a variety of process skills and critical thinking skills as they work through each lab. The labs have been developed so that teachers do not need extensive laboratory equipment to complete them.

Laboratory Manual

The laboratory manual for *Biology: The Web of Life* includes at least one laboratory investigation per chapter of the student textbook. In addition, there are four optional dissection activities for those who choose to include dissections in their lab program. And for students who have had little prior laboratory experience or need to review basic lab skills and procedures, there are 14 laboratory skills activities at the beginning of the manual. These can be done at the beginning of the lab course to evaluate lab skills or in conjunction with relevant labs during the year.

Project Biology

This supplement, offered on-line through the Scott Foresman-Addison Wesley Web Site bioSURF, offers projects in which students can extend their laboratory skills and applications beyond the classroom and into the field. A variety of projects is provided with suggestions for implementing each project with different learning levels and adapting the projects to the type of environment in which students live.

Assessing Laboratory Skills

Many teachers regularly assess the laboratory skills of their students. Some states provide guidelines to assess laboratory skills. The items on the list below can be used as criteria for laboratory skills assessment. You may want to devise a list with different criteria for your students.

You may also wish to assess students' laboratory skills using the Lab Practical Exams provided in each Unit Review Module in the Teacher's Resource Package. The Lab Practical Exams offer complete performance-based testing of laboratory methods that students learn throughout the *Biology: The Web of Life* program.

Laboratory Skills

- Defines a problem and develops a testable hypothesis
- Selects lab material and makes observations for a defined problem
- Distinguishes between the controls and the variables in an experiment
- Uses microscope skills and techniques and uses measuring instruments
- Collects, organizes, and graphs data from observations
- Makes conclusions from experimental data
- Determines the accuracy of the observations and data

Laboratory Safety

Good planning and common sense can make the biology classroom and laboratory safe and enjoyable learning environments. Safety should always be of prime importance. Although students must be made aware of safe and appropriate laboratory behavior, accountability for student safety rests with the teacher and school administrators. It is imperative that you, the classroom teacher, are aware that accidental injury can occur in the classroom or laboratory at any time. By making yourself and your students aware of potentially dangerous situations, the risk of accidental injuries can be minimized.

Safety regulations vary from state to state, district to district, and school to school. Before any demonstration or laboratory investigation is performed, you must familiarize yourself with all federal, state, and local safety regulations, as well as specific guidelines established by your district or school. These guidelines will provide you with information about materials that are prohibited for use in the classroom and those that require special handling. Such guidelines provide instruction about ventilation, chemical storage and disposal procedures, and the appropriate procedures for handling accidents and emergencies.

General Safety Information

At the beginning of the school year and periodically throughout the year, review with students what to do in case of fire. Display a list of these instructions, along with a map showing the locations of fire exits, in a prominent location. Make sure students are instructed on the proper use of emergency equipment and know the locations of the following:

- fire alarm
- fire blanket
- first-aid kit
- eyewash facilities
- evacuation route
- dry-chemical fire extinguisher

In addition, make available to *each* student certain items of protective clothing. Review with students how and when each article of protective clothing should be used.

- safety goggles
- laboratory gloves
- laboratory apron

Caution students about wearing appropriate attire in the laboratory. Loose-fitting clothing should be properly confined. When open flames are in use, long hair should be tied back.

Encourage students to report all accidents immediately, no matter how minor. Students should be instructed to report any conditions that may pose a safety risk, such as broken glassware, damaged cords, or obstructed aisles.

Never permit students to work in a laboratory without supervision. Students should not have access to chemicals or other equipment unless they are properly supervised. In addition, make sure students understand that the laboratory is a place for serious study where playful behavior is inappropriate and will not be tolerated. Students should never be allowed to mix chemicals, alter equipment, or conduct experiments without guidance or permission.

Safety Symbols and Guidelines

A variety of safety symbols is used in the Laboratory Program to alert students to potential hazards. Remind students of proper laboratory procedures. Review with students the safety notes included in the Laboratory Program. Make sure students become familiar with the meanings of the safety symbols.

Before students begin to perform any in-text activity or laboratory investigation, review any caution statements that appear in the investigation. The teacher's notes for the in-text activities include a heading titled **Safety First!** Use this information to remind students of potentially dangerous situations or general safety procedures that should be followed in a given activity.

Field Study/Trip Safety

Field studies and trips can be exciting and valuable teaching tools in biology. However, as in a laboratory environment, field activities can pose dangers to students. Before students conduct field studies or go on field trips, it is suggested that teachers do the following:

- Find out if any students have medical conditions that may be aggravated by outdoor activities.
- Inform parents of the intended trip and obtain consent forms that permits each student to participate.
- Visit the site and look for potential dangers before taking students into the field.
- Warn students to avoid touching poisonous plants, such as poison ivy, oak, or sumac. Also instruct students not to try to touch or catch animals they may encounter.
- Carry a first-aid kit.

Use of Live Animals

When appropriate, responsible, and humane care are provided, the direct study of living organisms in the classroom gives students a unique perspective on biology and life processes.

Direct study of living things in the classroom is an appropriate and valuable part of teaching of biological science. Such study can provide students with an understanding of biological principles and interactions that cannot be provided by textbook instruction alone. Both the National Science Teachers Association (NSTA) and the National Association of Biology Teachers (NABT) have developed guidelines concerning the appropriate use of live animals in the classroom. The position statement of the NSTA regarding guidelines for responsible use of animals in the classroom is presented here. After you familiarize yourself with these guidelines, it is recommended that you also obtain and read the guidelines prepared by the NABT.

An NSTA Position Statement*

Guidelines for Responsible Use of Animals in the Classroom

These guidelines are recommended by the National Science Teachers Association for use by science educators and students. They apply, in particular, to the use of nonhuman animals in instructional activities planned and/or supervised by teachers of science at the precollege level.

Observation and experimentation with living organisms give students unique perspectives of life processes that are not provided by other modes of instruction. Studying animals in the classroom enables students to develop skills of observation and comparison, a sense of stewardship, and an appreciation for the unity, interrelationships, and complexity of life. This study, however, requires appropriate, humane care of the organisms. Teachers are expected to be knowledgeable about the proper care of organisms under study and the safety of their students.

*Published by the National Science Teachers Association, 1742 Connecticut Avenue NW, Washington, DC 20009. Reprinted with permission.

These are the guidelines recommended by NSTA concerning the responsible use of animals in the classroom laboratory:

- Acquisition and care of the animals must be appropriate to the species.

- Student classwork and science projects involving animals must be under the supervision of a science teacher or other trained professional.

- Teachers sponsoring or supervising the use of animals in instructional activities—including acquisition, care, and disposition—will adhere to local, state, and national laws, policies, and regulations regarding the organisms.

- Teachers must instruct students on safety precautions for handling live animals or animal specimens.

- Plans for the future care or disposition of animals at the conclusion of the study must be developed and implemented.

- Laboratory and dissection activities must be conducted with consideration and appreciation for the organism.

- Laboratory and dissection activities must be conducted in a clean and organized work space with care and laboratory precision.

- Laboratory and dissection activities must be based on carefully planned objectives.

- Laboratory and dissection objectives must be appropriate to the maturity level of the student.

- Student views or beliefs sensitive to dissection must be considered: the teacher will respond appropriately.

—Adopted by the NSTA Board of Directors in July, 1991

Supplies

For Laboratory Activities

Item	Quantity (Per Group)	Chapter
Agar plates	3	14
Apple	1	2, 19, 32, 35
Aquarium	2	26
Aspartic acid	0.5 g	11
Baby food jars	6	2, 36
	1	32
Bags, plastic	2	16
	4	19, 27
Baking soda	10 g	2
Balance, metric	1	1, 2
Balloons	3	4
	1	25, 31
Bananas	1	2
	3	19
Beakers		
100 mL	3	10
250 mL	3	4, 35
	1	7, 24, 31
500 mL	1	11, 25, 27
1000 mL	1	25
Beans, dry	250	10
Beef suet	2 pieces	2
Bird feeder	1	28
Blender	1	7
Bowl	1	4, 30, 38
	2	25
Boxes, small	several	23
Bread, sliced	2 slices	16
	1 slice	37
Brush	1	17
Buttons	4	6
Carbohydrates	2 samples	4
Cardboard		
carton	1	19
corrugated	3 18 cm X 3 cm strips	8
Cellophane		
clear	1 piece	4
	2 pieces	18
red, blue, yellow, and green	1 piece	4
Cheesecloth	2 pieces	7, 23
Cheese, Roquefort	2 oz	37
Chicken		
bone	7 cm	29
wing	1	29

Item	Quantity (Per Group)	Chapter
Clams, fresh	several	22
Clamp	1	25
Clay	40 mL	35
Cleaning product, abrasive	1	15
Clock	1	10, 14, 31, 34
Coins	2	6
Compost pile	1	26
Container, plastic	1	2, 5, 23, 26
	3	18
Cornmeal	6 oz	23
Coverslips	1	11
	3	18, 20, 21, 22
	6	36
Daphnia culture	1	21
Dictionary	1	15
Dill pickle	1 piece	37
Dishwashing liquid	6 mL	30
Dissecting pins	6	29
Dissecting probe	1	21
Dissecting tray	1	29
Dropper, medicine	1	3, 7, 11, 18, 23
		30, 32, 36
	2	21
Earthworms, live	2	22
Echinoderm specimens, preserved	several	24
Eggbeater	1	38
Egg, raw	1	3, 26
Elodea plant	1 leaf	3
Erlenmeyer flasks		
250 mL	2	11
Ethanol, 95%	60 mL	7
Euglena culture	1	15
Flashlight	1	22, 35
Feather		
contour	1	26
downy	1	26
Fern frond	1	16, 20
Field guide	1	13
Fish net	1	25
Flashlight	1	28
Flower pot	4	19
Food coloring	2 colors	18

Item	Quantity (Per Group)	Chapter
1 color	32	
Food wrap	15 cm X 15 cm	32
Forceps	1	3, 7, 10, 15, 29
	2	16
Frog, live	1	26
Funnel	1	4
	3	35
Gloves, disposable	1 pair	29, 32
Glucose solution	15 mL	30
Glucose test strips	5	30
Glue	1	5
Glutamic acid	0.5 g	11
Glycine	0.5 g	11
Goldfish	1	25
Graduated cylinder		
25 mL	1	7, 11, 36
	3	10
100 mL	1	35
Grapes	2	35
	4	37
Grease pencil	1	21, 32, 35, 36, 37
Ham	2 pieces	2
Hand lens	1	3, 13, 14, 17, 20, 23, 37, 38
Hot plate	1	11
Houseplant	1	37
Human hair	2 cm	3
Hydra culture	1	21
Ice cream container	1	15
Iced tea, dark, instant	1 packet	2
Insects, dead	several	23
Iodine solution	100–200 mL	4
Index card	1	15
Ink pad	1	9
Jar with lid	3	2
	1	3, 29
	5	4
	6	35
Jigsaw puzzle	25 pieces	12
Key	8–10	25
Knife	1	2, 17
Lamp	1	28
Laundry starch, liquid	6 oz	38
Leaves	1	4, 18
	6–10 different	13, 28
Lemon	1	2
Lights, growth	1	20
Limewater	12 oz	31
Liquid soap	10 mL	7
Liver, beef	2 cm strip	7
Lizard, live	1	26

Item	Quantity (Per Group)	Chapter
Loam	40 mL	35
Magnifying glass	1	1
Marbles	3	30
Marker, permanent	1	2, 4, 8, 9, 19, 23, 34
Mealworm larvae	1	23
Measuring stick	1	1
Meat tenderizer	1	2
Methyl cellulose	2 oz	15
Metric ruler	1	1, 8, 13, 15, 19, 20, 23, 34
Microscope		
compound	1	3, 5, 11, 14, 15, 16, 18, 20, 22, 23, 26, 36
dissecting	1	21
Milk	200 mL	2
	15 mL	30
Milk treatment product	10 mL	30
Modeling clay	6 oz	5, 7
Molasses solution, 10%	40 mL	36
Mushrooms, live	several	16
NaCl solution, 1%	5 mL	11
Nail	1	34
Newspaper	6 sheets	38
Notebook	1	26
Oranges	1	2, 37
Oven mitts	1 pair	11
Pan		
glass	1	22
square	1	38
Paper		
black	1 sheet	17
blotting	6 sheets	37
	4 sheets	38
colored	4 sheets	8
filter	3 sheets	35
graph	1 sheet	6, 9
	2 sheets	12
tissue	4 sheets	24
tracing	1 sheet	9
Paper clips	6	5
	1	25
Paper towel	5 sheets	2, 4
	3 sheets	18
	2 sheets	18, 19
Paramecium culture	1	15
Pasta, rotini	2 pieces	2
Peat pots	2	20

Item	Quantity (Per Group)	Chapter
Pennies	6	12
Petri dishes with lids	5	37, 38
Petroleum jelly	6 oz	18, 38
pH paper	5 pieces	2
Phenol red indicator	10 mL	32
Pinecones, female	2	20
Pipe cleaners	6	5
Plant	1	1, 5, 18
	6	17, 20
bean	1	18
flowering	1	17
	2	18
illustrations	6	17
spider runner	1	19
tomato	1	17
Pond water	25 mL	15
Potatoes	1	2
Posterboard	15 cm X 15 cm	28
Pushpins	36	8
Raisins	2	35
Razor blade, single-edged	1	16
Ring stand	1	11
Rocks	4	28
Rolling pin	1	38
Safety goggles	1	11, 32
Safranine stain	10 mL	18
Saline solution	10 mL	7
Salt	50 g	1
	200 g	35
Sand	40 g	1, 28, 35
Sandpaper	15 cm X 15 cm	28
Scale	1	4
Scalpel	1	7, 18, 20, 29
Scissors	1	5, 7, 9, 28, 29, 37
Screen	1	38
Seeds		
Brassica rapa	4	20
bean	10	4
	14	19
corn	10	19
radish	10	18
Shoe box with lid	1	28
Skeletons, mammal	3	27
Slides, glass	1	3, 11, 18, 20, 22
	2	16, 21, 30
	3	18
	4	15
	5	38
	6	36

Item	Quantity (Per Group)	Chapter
Slides, prepared:		
bacterium, various	3	14
human cheek cells	1	3
onion root tip mitosis	1	5
Snake, live	1	26
Soil	16 oz	20, 22, 28
	1 oz	22
Sow bugs, live	10	28
Specimen dish	1	23
Sponges	2	28
Spoon	1	23
Stakes, wooden	4	1
	2	20
Stapler	1	19
Stirring rod, glass	1	7, 11
Stock solution	10 mL	32
Straw, drinking	1	31
String	4 m	1
	1 m	5, 7
Sugar	50 g	1
Sweeteners	various	4
Tadpoles	10	25
Tape, cellophane	1	2
Tape measure, metric	1	4, 31
Teaspoon	3	10
Test tubes	4	27
Thermometer	1	25, 26, 27
Timer	1	25, 27
Tongs	1	11
Toothpaste carton	1	15
Toothpicks	6	5, 16, 20
	20	7
	2	15
	1	21
Tubing, rubber	30 cm	30
Tweezers	1	26
Vegetable		
oil	10 mL	30
shortening	6 oz	27
Vinegar, white	10 mL	2
	250 mL	3
	500 mL	29
Wood	various products	17
World globe	1	35
Yarn	6 cm	7
Yeast		
dried	1/2 tsp	4
solution	60 mL	36

Suppliers
of Equipment and Materials

The following companies supply biological materials or chemicals to schools.

Carolina Biological Supply Co.
2700 York Rd.
Burlington, NC 27215
800-334-5551

Central Scientific Co.
3300 CENCO Parkway
Franklin Park, IL 60131
800-262-3626

Connecticut Valley Biological
Supply Co., Inc.
P.O. Box 326
Southampton, MA 01073
800-628-7748

Edmund Scientific Co.
101 E. Gloucester Pike
Barrington, NJ 08007
609-547-3488

Fisher Scientific Educational
Materials Division
4901 W. Le Moyne St.
Chicago, IL 60651
800-955-1177

Hubbard Scientific
1120 Halbleib
Chippewa Falls, WI 54729
800-289-9299

Lab Safety Supply Inc.
401 S. Wright Rd.
Janesville, WI 53546-8729
800-356-0783

Nasco West Inc.
P.O. Box 3837
Modesto, CA 95352-3837
800-558-9595

Sargent-Welch Scientific Co.
P.O. Box 1026
Skokie, IL 60076-8026
800-727-4368

Scientific Kit® and Boreal® Laboratories
777 East Park Dr.
Tonawanda, NY 14150
716-874-6020

Ward's Natural Science Establishment Inc.
5100 West Henrietta Rd.
P.O. Box 92912
Rochester, NY 14692-9012
800-962-2660

Audiovisual Suppliers
The following companies supply audiovisual resources to schools.

Bullfrog Films
P.O. Box 149
Oley, PA 19547

Carolina Biological Supply Co.
2700 York Rd.
Burlington, NC 27215

Coronet/MTI Film and Video
108 Wilmot Rd.
Deerfield, IL 60015-9925

Encyclopedia Britannica
Educational Corporation
Learning Materials
310 South Michigan Ave.
Chicago, IL 60604-9839

Films for the Humanities and Sciences
P.O. Box 2053
Princeton, NJ 08543-2053

International Film Bureau
332 South Michigan Ave.
Chicago, IL 60604

National Geographic Society
Educational Services
P.O. Box 98019
Washington, D.C. 20090-8019

Optical Data Corporation
30 Technology Dr.
Warren, NJ 07059
800-524-2481
908-668-0022

Ward's Natural Science Establishment Inc.
5100 West Henrietta Rd.
P.O. Box 92912
Rochester, NY 14692-9012

Computer Software Suppliers
You may find some of the following programs helpful for the computer activities that are suggested in some chapter reviews in the Student Edition.

Distributors:
Claris Corporation
5201 Patrick Henry Drive
Santa Clara, CA 95052-8168
800-747-7483

Lotus Development Corporation
55 Cambridge Parkway
Cambridge, MA 02142
800-568-8712

Microsoft Corporation
One Microsoft Way
Redmond, WA 98052-6399
800-426-9400

Sunburst Communications
101 Castleton St.
Pleasantville, NY 10570
800-321-7511

Houghton Mifflin Company
925 East Meadow Dr.
Palo Alto, CA 94303
800-258-9773

Queue/HRM Software
338 Commerce Dr.
Fairfield, CT 06430
800-232-2224

Scholastic Software
2931 East McCarty Street
P.O. Box 7502
Jefferson City, MO 65102-9968
800-541-5513

Quality Computers
20200 Nine Mile Road
St. Claire Shores, MI 48080
800-443-6697

SCOTT FORESMAN-ADDISON WESLEY

*"We did not weave the web of life,
we are merely a strand in it.
Whatever we do to the web, we do
to ourselves."* –Chief Seattle

Biology

The Web of Life

Second Edition

ERIC STRAUSS • MARYLIN LISOWSKI

Scott Foresman
Addison Wesley

Editorial Offices: Glenview, Illinois • New York, New York
Sales Offices: Reading, Massachusetts • Duluth, Georgia • Glenview, Illinois
Carrollton, Texas • Menlo Park, California

1-800-552-2259

http://www.sf.aw.com
http://www.biosurf.com

SCOTT FORESMAN-ADDISON WESLEY

Biology
The Web of Life

Program Components

STUDENT EDITION

TEACHER'S EDITION

TEACHER'S RESOURCE PACKAGE

Laboratory Manual
(Teacher's Edition)
Unit Review Modules
Consumer Applications
Issues and Decision Making
Biotechnology Manual
Overhead Transparency Preview
Teacher's Curriculum Guide
Super Read! Strategies for
Effective Reading in Biology
Interpreting and Developing
Graphics
Guide to Block Scheduling
Spanish Reviews

LABORATORY MANUAL

Student Edition

OVERHEAD TRANSPARENCY
PACKAGE

TECHNOLOGY

Biology Alive! Video Series
Rewind: *The Web of Life*
Reteach Videos
Animated Biological Concepts
Videodiscs and Worksheets
TestWorks CD-ROM
Interactive Biological Simulations
CD-ROM and Worksheets
Teacher's Resource Planner
CD-ROM
Biología: la telaraña de la vida
CD-ROM (Spanish Student
Edition)
bioSURF Internet Site
The Biology Place Internet Site
Published by Peregrine Publishers, Inc.

Second Edition

Cover photograph: Tim Davis/Davis-Lynn Images

About the cover: Wolves and aspen trees are just two of the millions of species that comprise the web of life. The effects of the wolf's removal from and reintroduction to ecosystems demonstrate the delicate and complex connections among living things.

GeoSystems Global Corporation and Addison Wesley Longman are the publishers of the maps included in this textbook. The information contained in these maps is derived from a variety of sources. While every effort has been made to verify the information contained in such sources, the publishers assume no responsibility for inconsistencies or inaccuracies in the data nor liability for any damages of any type arising from errors or omissions.

ISBN 0-201-33440-2

1 2 3 4 5 6 7 8 9 10 - VH - 03 02 01 00 99

Brief Contents

iii

Contents

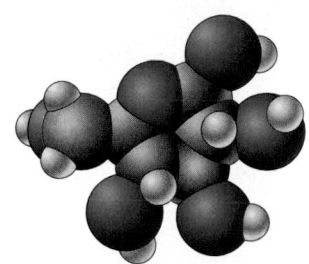
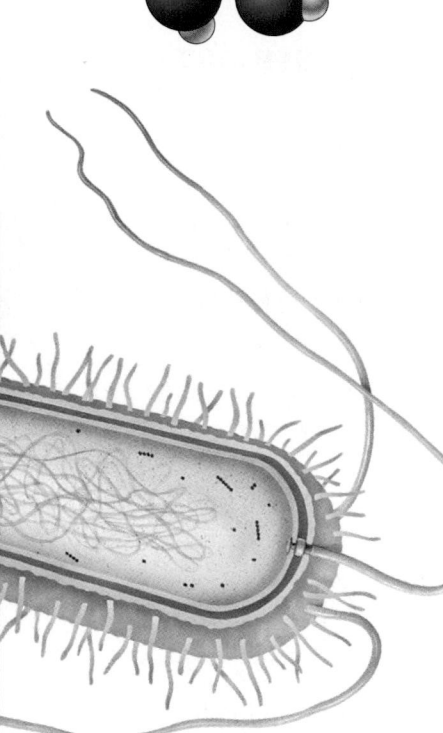

Unit 2 Genetics 126–225

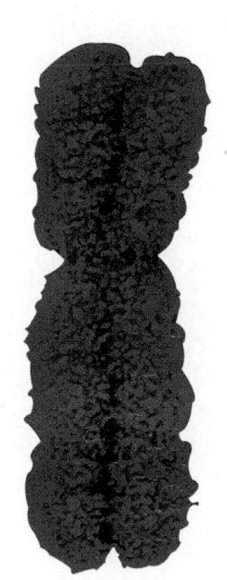

v

Unit 3 Change and Diversity 226-321

Unit 4 Monerans, Protists, and Fungi 322–393

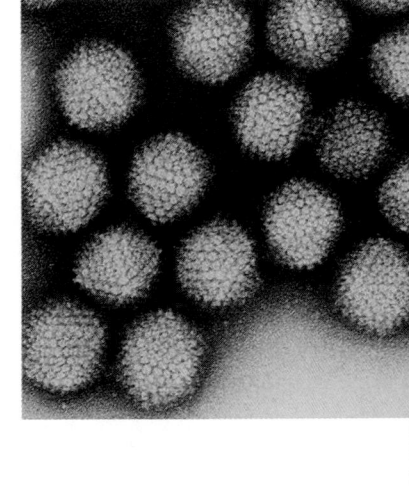

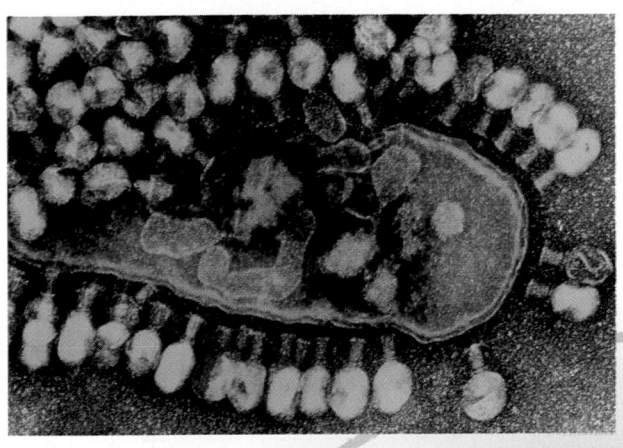

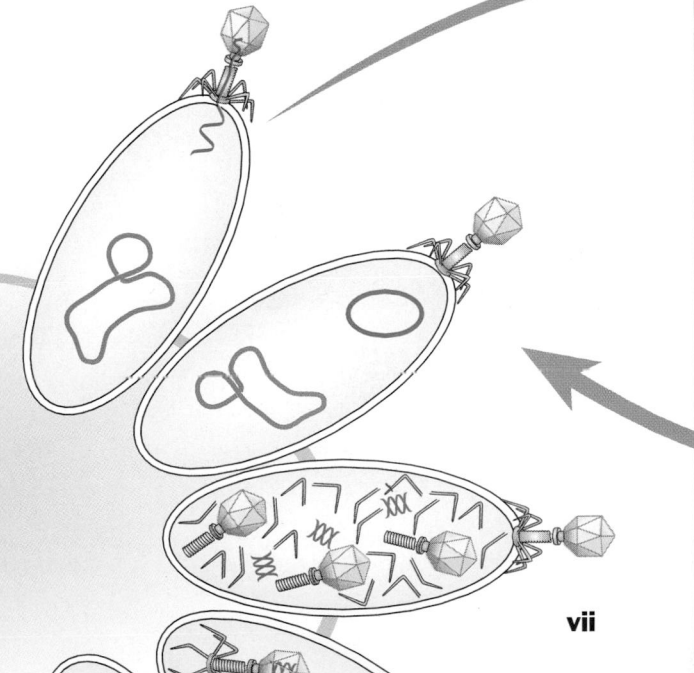

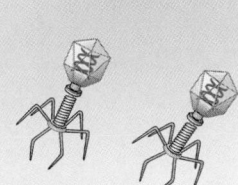

Unit 5 Plants 394–495

Unit 6 Invertebrate Animals 496–587

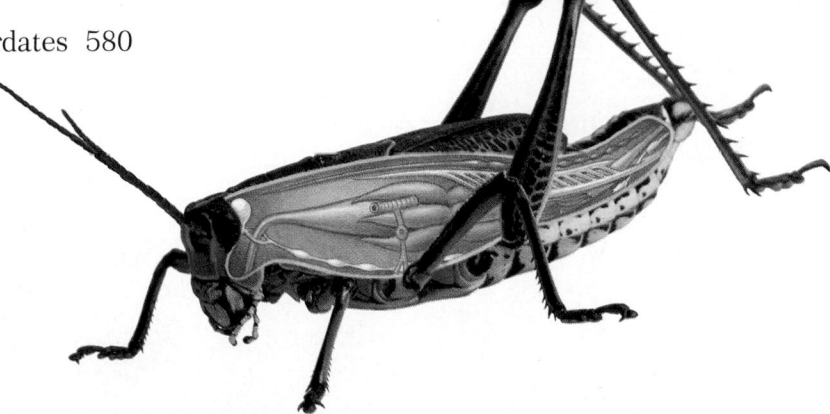

Unit 7 Vertebrate Animals 588–687

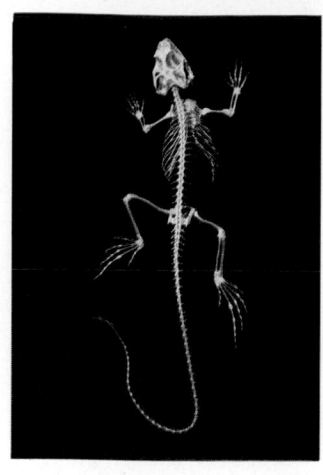

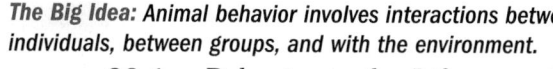

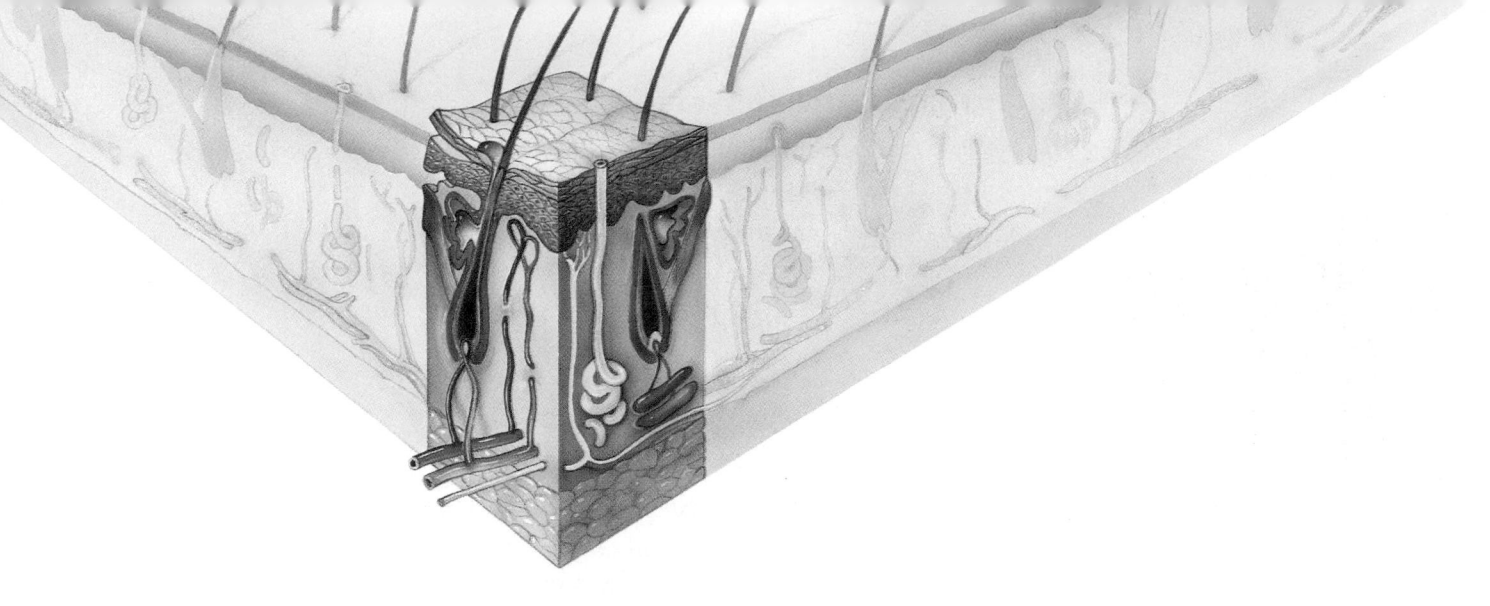

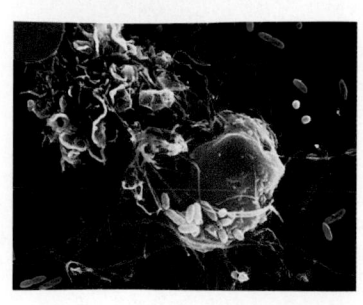
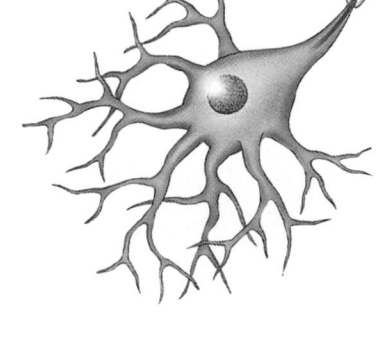

References and Resources

Big Ideas

There is much to learn in every chapter of this textbook. The Big Ideas! will help you organize and understand the essential knowledge and skills that comprise biology. Build a framework of biology by learning and connecting these Big Ideas.

Unit 1 The Basis of Life

- Living things share many characteristics, including organization and adaptation. 1.1–1.2

- Scientists use careful observation and controlled experiments to study the natural world. 1.3

- Living things are made of chemicals with characteristic structures and functions. 2.1–2.2

- Life processes depend on breaking and forming chemical bonds in chemical reactions. 2.3–2.4

- Life processes depend on the properties of water and the characteristics of solutions. 2.5

- Cell structures of living organisms perform life functions. 3.1–3.3

- Cells of major groups of organisms can be distinguished by their structural differences. 3.4

- Cells exchange materials with their environment by chemical and physical processes. 3.5

- All organisms get energy by breaking down the chemical compounds in food and making ATP and other molecules. 4.1–4.3

- Energy from sunlight passes through a series of living organisms. 4.4

- Cell division is the basis of reproduction and development 5.1–5.2

- Chromosome number is reduced in meiosis. 5.3–5.4

Unit 2 Genetics

- Traits are inherited in a consistent pattern. 6.1–6.2

- There are patterns of inheritance that make some traits predictable. 6.3–6.5

- The structure of DNA, the molecule of heredity, enables the molecule to copy itself. 7.1–7.2

- Genes, sections of DNA that code for a specific trait, are linked together on chromosomes. 7.3–7.5

- Genes are sequences of DNA bases that can be translated into proteins or parts of proteins when they are activated. 8.1–8.2

- Changes in DNA can cause changes in phenotype. 8.3–8.4

- Genotypes can be changed through selective breeding and genetic engineering. 9.1–9.2

- Technology enables us to find out about genotype and use this knowledge to affect phenotype. 9.3–9.4

Unit 3 Change and Diversity

- Populations change over time through natural selection. 10.1–10.2

- Scientific analysis of fossils and modern organisms supports the theory of evolution. 10.3

- New species can originate through natural selection and other changes in a population's gene pool. 10.4–10.5

- Evidence indicates that organic molecules and cells may have formed spontaneously on ancient Earth. 11.1

- Our planet and the organisms that inhabit it have changed greatly over time. 11.2–11.3

- Primates are mammals with binocular vision and dexterous hands and arms. 12.1

- There have been many different hominid species over time, each species with its own unique characteristics. 12.2–12.3

- Scientists classify organisms into a hierarchy of groups based on evolutionary relationships. 13.1–13.2

- Classification has numerous applications, including identifying species. 13.3

Unit 4 Monerans, Protists, and Fungi

- Viruses are particles that depend on living things to replicate. 14.1–14.3

- Monerans are microscopic organisms that lack a membrane-bound nucleus and membrane-bound organelles. 14.4–14.6

- Protists are a diverse group of eukaryotes that include unicellular and multicellular organisms. 15.1

- Protists can be classified into three groups—protozoans, algae, and molds. 15.2–15.4

- Protists have a major ecological impact as food sources, decomposers, and infectious agents. 15.5

- Fungi are stationary organisms that live as heterotrophs. 16.1–16.2

- Fungi act as decomposers and symbiotic partners of humans and many other organisms. 16.3

Unit 5 Plants

- Most plants have structures that enable them to survive on land and produce food. 17.1–17.3

- Key features can be used to classify plants. 17.4

- Plants perform life processes using specialized structures. 18.1–18.2

- The parts of most plants grow from specialized tissues. 18.3

- Plants respond to and affect the environment. 19.1–19.2
- Plants reproduce both asexually and sexually. 19.3–19.5
- Plants are multicellular organisms with adaptations for life on land. 20.1–20.2
- Ferns have vascular systems and reproduce by means of spores. 20.3
- Seed plants do not require water for fertilization and have therefore colonized extensive areas of land. 20.4–20.5

Unit 6 Invertebrate Animals

- Animals have evolved a number of adaptations enabling them to perform essential functions of life. 21.1
- Sponges are sessile animals without specialized tissues and organs. 21.2–21.3
- Cnidarians are radially symmetrical animals with specialized tissues and stinging tentacles. 21.4–21.5
- Sponges and cnidarians provide food and protection for a large number of organisms. 21.6
- Flatworms and roundworms have bilateral symmetry and specialized tissues. 22.1
- Mollusks share a common body plan that includes a muscular foot, a visceral mass, and a mantle. 22.2
- Annelids are wormlike animals with a segmented body. 22.3
- Arthropods are segmented invertebrates with jointed appendages and an exoskeleton. 23.1
- In general, arthropods are classified by the number of body segments they have and the structure of their appendages. 23.2–23.4
- Arthropods, as members of the largest phylum, have many important roles in the biosphere. 23.5
- Echinoderms are marine animals with spiny skin, an endoskeleton, and a water vascular system. 24.1
- Invertebrate chordates represent possible evolutionary links between invertebrates and vertebrates. 24.2

Unit 7 Vertebrate Animals

- Vertebrates are animals with backbones. 25.1
- Fishes are a diverse group of vertebrates that are adapted for life in the water. 25.2–25.4
- Although amphibians share some fish traits, they are adapted to life on land. 25.5–25.7
- Reptiles represent the first vertebrates with adaptations that enable them to live their entire lives out of water. 26.1–26.3
- With the development of feathers, birds were the first vertebrates able to maintain a constant body temperature. 26.4–26.6
- Although different species have unique adaptations, all mammals are endothermic vertebrates with hair and mammary glands. 27.1–27.2
- Mammals live almost everywhere on Earth and play important roles in ecosystems. 27.3
- Animal behaviors are adaptations that maximize survival and reproductive fitness. 28.1–28.3
- Animal behavior involves interactions between individuals, between groups, and with the environment. 28.4

Unit 8 Human Biology

- The human body consists of twelve systems. 29.1
- The body's skeleton provides support and protection. 29.2–29.3
- Muscles contract to move the body. 29.4–29.5
- The skin covers and protects the body's internal organs. 29.6
- The digestive system breaks down food into usable compounds. 30.1–30.3
- The excretory system eliminates nitrogen-containing wastes and helps maintain homeostasis. 30.4–30.5
- The vital exchange of oxygen and carbon dioxide occurs in the respiratory systems of animals. 31.1–31.3
- Circulatory systems transport materials necessary for life. 31.4–31.6
- The immune system protects the body from harmful organisms and substances. 32.1
- The immune system consists of specialized cells, organs, and organ systems that respond to the presence of a pathogen. 32.2–32.3
- A healthy immune system requires a healthy lifestyle. 32.4
- The endocrine system controls long-lasting internal changes. 33.1–33.3
- Reproductive systems make possible the continuation of life. 33.4–33.6
- Nervous systems control our detection of and response to the environment. 34.1
- The human nervous system consists of the brain, spinal cord, nerves, and sensory organs. 34.2–34.4
- The health of the nervous system can be affected by injury, disease, and substance abuse. 34.5

Unit 9 Organisms and the Environment

- Life depends on the relationships between living and nonliving parts of the environment. 35.1–35.2
- Regions of the biosphere have distinguishing characteristics. 35.3–35.4
- The size of a population is affected by living and nonliving factors. 36.1–36.2
- How populations interact determines the structure and characteristics of a community. 36.3
- Biotic and abiotic changes in a community alter the community structure. 36.4
- In an ecosystem, the flow of energy moves in one direction. 37.1–37.2
- Nutrients are recycled in ecosystems. 37.3
- Human use of essential natural resources can affect the web of life. 38.1
- Land, water, and air are invaluable natural resources. 38.2–38.4
- Humans can affect the future of the biosphere in a positive way. 38.5

Labs and Activities

Discover It!

Think About It!

Features

bioSURF

Internet references are included in Chapter Openers, in some Do It! and Think About It! activities, in the Community features, and Spotlight on Careers features.

Discover

The Web of Life

You are about to explore the amazing and wondrous web of life. Your textbook will serve as a valuable tool for your journey through the world of living things. Use the next few pages to become familiar with the organization and features of this textbook. Then begin your travels and enjoy biology!

Hit or Myth?

The amazing stories of **Hit or Myth**—sometimes fact and sometimes fiction—reflect the relevance of biology to today's world.

bioSURF

Connect the *Web of Life* to the World Wide Web using the **bioSURF** internet site.

Chapter Opener

We introduce you to the chapter with a story that puts the content in context. Use the **LAB ZONE Discover It!** activity to begin your exploration of the chapter material. Practice expressing your knowledge, ideas, and experiences as you **WRITE ABOUT IT!**

Super Read This logo refers to additional **Super Read** activities that can be used to practice reading skills.

Identify and Connect

The Big Idea

There is much to learn in every chapter of this textbook. **THE BIG IDEA!** will help you identify and connect major biology concepts.

What you'll learn

The **objectives** describe what you should be able to do after you have read the section. New **key terms** are listed at the beginning and shown in bold type so that you can recognize them easily. Each key term is accompanied by a definition.

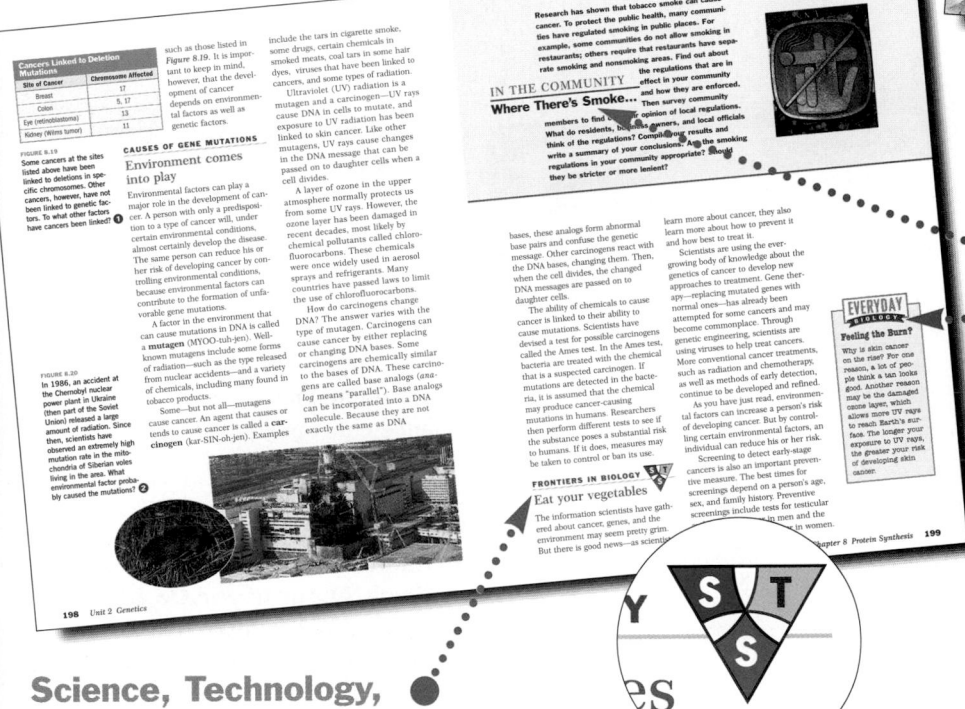

Everyday Biology and In the Community

Recognize that biology is everywhere by doing an activity in **In the Community** and by reading the often surprising and always interesting information in **Everyday Biology**.

Science, Technology, and Society

Information about the role of biology in your life and the lives of others is identified and categorized as **Environmental Awareness**, **Issues in Biology**, and **Frontiers in Biology**.

Visual Learning

Develop an understanding of the processes, cycles, and diversity of life by analyzing the **visual learning** figures found throughout the textbook. You can even see the illustrations "come to life" by viewing the **Animated Biological Concepts** and **Interactive Biological Simulations CD-ROM.**

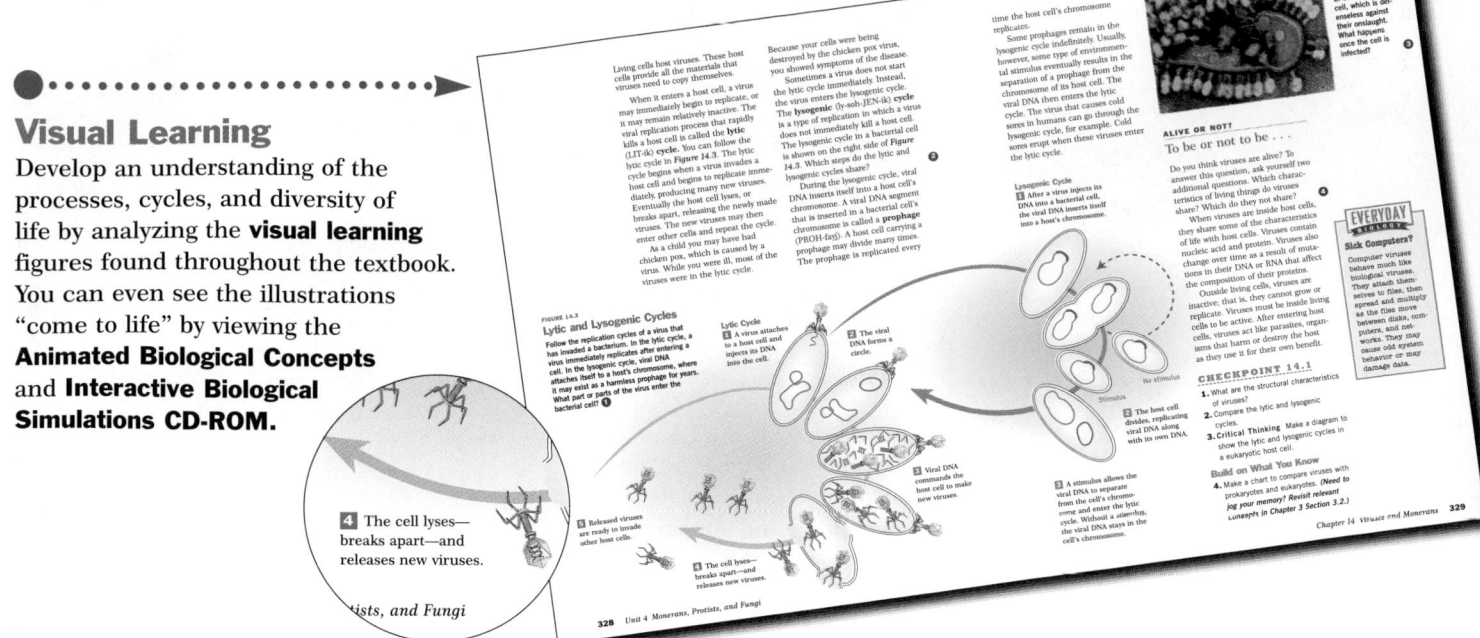

4 The cell lyses—breaks apart—and releases new viruses.

Interact and Explore

Lab Zone Activities

LAB ZONE Investigate It! activities give you an opportunity to experiment in much the same way a biologist does: You will use a variety of skills to hypothesize, experiment, observe, analyze, conclude, and apply your conclusions to other situations.

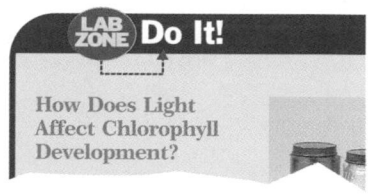

LAB ZONE Do It! activities provide quick and effective hands-on applications of science concepts and skills.

bioSURF In each chapter, there are references for bioSURF in the **Think About It!** and **Do It!** activities. When you see this logo, go to the **bioSURF** internet site to find additional related activities.

LAB ZONE Discover It!

Ripening Green Bananas

LAB ZONE Discover It! activities provide opportunities to explore ideas and discover characteristics of life—before you read about them.

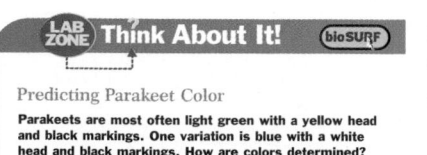

Think About It! **bioSURF**

Predicting Parakeet Color

Parakeets are most often light green with a yellow head and black markings. One variation is blue with a white head and black markings. How are colors determined?

Analyzing the Diagram

LAB ZONE Think About It! activities provide practice in analyzing and applying concepts.

Review and Extend

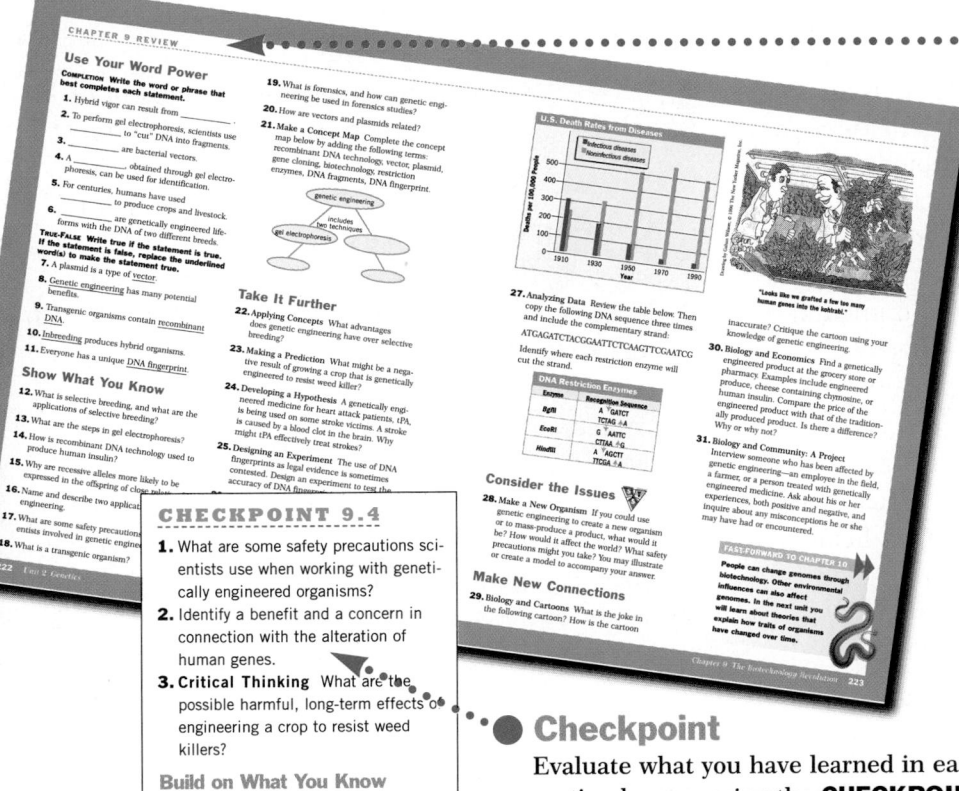

Chapter Review

Test your knowledge of the **words** and **ideas** presented in the chapter by answering questions. Challenge your understanding by answering the **critical thinking** questions in **Take It Further.** Use the questions in **Consider the Issues** and **Make New Connections** to extend the Chapter content.

Checkpoint

Evaluate what you have learned in each section by answering the **CHECKPOINT** questions. A **critical thinking** question gives you an opportunity to demonstrate your understanding. And the **Build on What You Know** question connects concepts in different chapters.

Unit Review

Integrate all the concepts you have learned throughout each unit by answering the questions and doing the activities in the **Unit Review**. Read a student's review of a book, film, or CD-ROM in **The Critic's Corner**. And through **Spotlight on Careers**, meet people whose lives exemplify biology in action.

The Authors...

Eric Strauss

In the years he has been teaching at Boston College, Eric Strauss has quadrupled enrollment in an introductory biology course for non-science majors. In addition, Eric helped start the Boston College Environmental Studies program and serves as the program director. His dynamic approach to teaching biology extends beyond the college classroom. High school students, college undergraduates, and graduate students conduct original research on animal behavior and ecology at a Cape Cod field research station run by Eric and his former high school teacher.

Marylin Lisowski

Before becoming professor of science education at Eastern Illinois University, Marylin taught Biology, Environmental Science, and Middle Level Science. She also directed a marine research station. Marylin shares her research experience with high-school teachers and students as she leads international expeditions and field programs. Dedicated to improving science education, Marylin has been the recipient of dozens of awards, including Ohio Science Teacher of the Year, Florida Honor Science Teacher, and Illinois Environmental Educator of the Year.

and others

who have helped us

Content Reviewers

David M. Armstrong, Ph.D.
*University of Colorado,
Boulder, CO*

John Ebinger, Ph.D.
*Eastern Illinois University
Charleston, IL*

Paul R. Ecklund, Ph.D.
*Cornell University
Ithaca, NY*

Dana M. García, Ph.D.
*Southwest Texas
State University
San Marcos, TX*

Alison Hill, Ph.D.
*University of
North Carolina
Chapel Hill, NC*

Rebecca A. Pyles, Ph.D.
*East Tennessee
State University
Johnson City, TN*

Gerald Skoog, Ed.D.
*Texas Tech University
Lubbock, TX*

Teacher Reviewers

George Bacon
*Crystal River
High School
Crystal River, FL*

Mary Bonetati
*Klein ISD
Spring, TX*

Bob Hembree
*Newman-Smith
High School
Carrollton, TX*

Michael Lopatka
*Edgewater High
School
Orlando, FL*

John Madden
*Mountain View
High School
Tucson, AZ*

Kim Mosely
*The Colony
High School
The Colony, TX*

Anne Tweed
*Eaglecrest
High School
Aurora, CO*

Jill Wallace
*Lewisville High
School
Lewisville, TX*

Dear Student Biologist:

Welcome to biology. We are delighted that you will be joining us in this exploration of life. Your teacher, your classmates, and this text-book are all part of a team that will guide you through the web of life. As biologists, we are excited by and inspired about the living world. As authors, we hope that you will come to share our excitement and inspiration.

Biology, like all of the sciences, is a process of discovery. It is a process with an impressive history and an incredible future. We want you to understand and appreciate the contributions of the past—as well as recognize and respond to the numerous possibilities that lie ahead. The biologists of today started their journey in a classroom similar to yours. Our program weaves current research and discoveries with insights made hundreds of years ago. Throughout your study, you will have the opportunity to make your own discoveries.

Many of these discoveries will apply to your everyday life. This may not surprise you: Biology is closely connected with all aspects of our day-to-day activities. Biology is also closely connected with the decisions you will be making about your future and the future of the planet Earth. It is our hope that your experience with this textbook and the "stuff" of biology will make you aware of and sensitive to the living world around you.

This is an exciting time to be learning biology. So, welcome aboard. Enjoy your discoveries. And, have fun!

Eric G. Strauss

Marylin Lisowski

1

PLANNING GUIDE

Section	Student Activities/Features	Teacher's Resource Package
1.1 Similarities Among Living Things **Objectives** ■ Compare different theories of the origins of life ■ Summarize the properties of life	**Lab Zone Discover It!** *Observing Ants*, p. 3 **Everyday Biology,** *Measurement Made Easy*, p. 5 **Lab Zone Do It!** *Comparing Living and Nonliving Things*, p. 9 **Everyday Biology,** *Get Organized*, p. 11	**Unit 1 Review Module** ■ Section Review 1.1 ■ Activity Recordsheet 1-1 **Laboratory Manual,** Lab 1: "What's Alive?" **Consumer Applications** 1-1 **Interpreting and Developing Graphics** 1
1.2 Adaptation and Interdependence **Objectives** ■ Explain how organisms respond and adapt to their environment ■ Compare the various interdependent relationships of organisms ■ Summarize the role of humans in the ecosystem	**Everyday Biology** *Fossil Walls*, p. 13 **STS: Environmental Awareness** *Humans and the Web of Life*, p. 16 **Lab Zone Do It!** *Observing Biodiversity*, p. 18	**Unit 1 Review Module** ■ Section Review 1.2 ■ Activity Recordsheet 1-2 ■ Enrichment Topic 1-1 **Interpreting and Developing Graphics** 2
1.3 Doing the Science of Biology **Objectives** ■ Summarize the scientific method ■ Explain the role of science in society	**Everyday Biology** *Pasteur's Process*, p. 22 **Lab Zone Think About It!** *Identifying Experimental Controls and Variables*, p. 23 **STS: Issues in Biology** *Science and Society*, p. 23 **In the Community** *Science in the News*, p. 24 **Lab Zone Investigate It!** *Designing a Scientific Experiment*, p. 26	**Unit 1 Review Module** ■ Section Review 1.3 ■ Activity Recordsheet 1-3 ■ Interpreting Graphics 1 ■ Critical Thinking Exercise 1 ■ Enrichment Topic 1-2 and 1-3 ■ Vocabulary Review 1 ■ Chapter 1 Tests **Laboratory Manual:** Lab Skills 1-14 **Issues and Decision Making** 1-2 **Consumer Applications** 1-2 **Interpreting and Developing Graphics** 3 **Spanish Reviews** Chapter 1

Technology Resources

Internet Connections

Within this chapter, you will see the **bioSURF** logo. If you and your students have access to the Internet, the following URL address will provide various Internet connections that are related to topics and features presented in this chapter:

http://basis_of_life.biosurf.com

You can also find relevant chapter material at **The Biology Place** address:

http://www.biology.com

CD-ROMs

Biología: la telaraña de la vida,
  (Spanish Student Edition) Chapter 1
Teacher's Resource Planner, Chapter 1
  Supplements
Interactive Biological Simulations
■ Scientific Method
TestWorks CD-ROM
■ Chapter 1 Tests

Overhead Transparencies

■ Redi's Experiment, #1
■ Pasteur's Experiment, #2

Videotapes

Biology Alive! Video Series
■ Signs of Life Video
■ The Domain of Life Video
■ The Continuity of Life Video
■ Conflict and Cooperation Video
■ Life's Fragile Balance Video
Rewind: The Web of Life Reteach Videos

Planning for Activities

STUDENT EDITION
Lab Zone
Discover It! p. 3
- small amount of sugar and salt
- sand or very small pebbles

Lab Zone Do It! p. 9
- two substances from teacher
- magnifying glass
- ruler
- balance
- small bowl
- stirring rod

Lab Zone Do It! p. 18
- park, woodland, or other unpaved outdoor location
- nails or pegs
- measuring stick
- string

Lab Zone
Investigate It! p. 26
- living plants or seeds
- measuring instruments

TEACHER'S EDITION
Teacher Demo, p. 4
Organisms and their environments
- photographs of organisms that live in air, water, and on land

Class Activity, p. 6
Living or nonliving
- photographs of living and nonliving things showing properties of life

Teacher Demo, p. 7
Metamorphosis
- photographs showing life cycles of frogs, butterflies, and humans

Teacher Demo, p. 8
Plant stimuli response
- mimosa plant or Venus' flytrap

Class Activity, p. 9
Examining cells
- microscopes
- prepared cells of different kinds of cells

Quick Activity, p. 12
Change over time
- photographs or drawings of dinosaurs in natural environments

Class Activity, p. 14
Identifying symbiotic relationships
- visuals, a movie, or videotape illustrating symbiotic relationships

Teacher Demo, p. 16
Dependency on other organisms
- variety of common products—plastics, wood, food products, clothing, medicines

Quick Activity, p. 19
Introducing the scientific method
- flashlights

Teacher Demo, p. 20
Science in everyday life
- newspaper and magazine articles of science-related topics

Teacher Demo, p. 20
Tools used in biology
- metric ruler
- hand lens
- microscope
- graduated cylinder
- litmus paper

Chapter Objectives

Students will learn the main concepts of this chapter as they complete the following objectives.

- Compare different theories of the origins of life
- Summarize the properties of life
- Explain how organisms respond and adapt to their environment
- Compare the various inter-dependent relationships of organisms
- Summarize the role of humans in the ecosystem
- Summarize the scientific method
- Explain the role of science in society

Key Words

1.1 *biosphere, organisms, spontaneous generation, biogenesis, cells, tissues, organs*

1.2 *predator, prey*

1.3 *scientific method, hypothesis, variable, control setup, theory*

The Opening Story

Have students discuss how they think the story relates to the content of this chapter. Point out that the origin of the word *science* is the Latin *scientia* meaning "knowledge" and the scientific method is a procedure for pursuing knowledge. Invite students to share what they would like to know about living organisms, life processes, and the world around them.

CHAPTER 1

The Study of Life

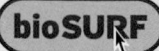

You can find out more about the study of life by exploring the following Internet address: *http://basis_of_life.biosurf.com*

In this chapter . . .

FEATURES

Everyday Biology
- Measurement Made Easy
- Get Organized!
- Fossil Walls
- Pasteur's Process

In the Community
Science in the News

 Environmental Awareness
Humans and the Web of LIfe

Issues in Biology
Science and Society

LAB ZONES

Discover It!
- Observing Ants

Do It!
- Comparing Living and Nonliving Things
- Observing Biodiversity

Think About It!
- Identifying Experimental Controls and Variables

Investigate It!
- Designing a Scientific Experiment

2   *Chapter 1 The Study of Life*

A CLOSER LOOK

All scientific knowledge begins with a search for answers to questions about our world. For example, imagine that you are on a central Texas plain where you notice a group of red insects. You kneel down to take a closer look. What do you see? There are two large ants and some smaller ones, as well as fine bits of gravel and things that appear to be eggs. Your observations leave you with many questions to be answered: What are the ants doing? Are they building something? Are they eating? Why are two ants so much larger than the others?

In science, the process of finding answers often leads to more questions. And each major scientific advance, such as the invention of the microscope, provides a new way of looking at our world that may lead to as many mysteries as it solves. Science is human curiosity at work, and biology is human curiosity about life. What do you, the biologist, see in the living world around you that you would like to know more about?

A microscopic view of an ant

LAB ZONE Discover It!

Observing Ants

You need *a small amount of sugar and salt, and some sand or very small pebbles*

1. Locate an ant colony. (Be careful—some ants bite!) Some places to hunt are along cracks in pavement and in sandy areas in lawns or along streets. By observing carefully you should be able to find the main entrance to the nest. Observe the ants' activity.
2. Sprinkle some sugar near the nest and some salt in another area near the nest. Did the sugar and salt affect the ants' activity? If so, how?
3. Now drop several pebbles or some sand into the nest opening. What happens? After recording your observations, remove the salt, sugar, and pebbles.

Ants live in highly organized social groups. They respond as a group to threats to their safety and to new sources of food. They mark trails chemically, and the trails can easily be disrupted by objects or events.

WRITE ABOUT IT!

Imagine that you, as a human and a member of society, are responding to threats from creatures the size of huge buildings. Write a story that describes how you would feel and react.

3

Opening Activities

bioSURF If you have access to the Internet in your classroom or school, you may wish to have students connect to the address shown on page 2. You may also want to have students conduct net searches for information using key words related to this chapter. For example, they could search for entries under cellular biology, ecosystem, Louis Pasteur, or biodiversity.

LAB ZONE Discover It!

Observing Ants   TEAM WORK

Before students begin this chapter, have them do the suggested activity either as a homework assignment or as a class field trip. Caution students not to touch the ants and to leave the colony as they found it. Some students may want to use a hand lens and wear gloves while doing the activity.

WRITE ABOUT IT!

Encourage students to use vivid sensory language to describe how they might respond. Suggest that they begin by jotting down feelings and reactions portrayed in science fiction stories or movies with a similar theme. Encourage students to illustrate their stories.

PORTFOLIO PREVIEW

Students should be encouraged to add to their portfolios as they work through this chapter. In addition to the *Write About It* opportunity, the following sections are excellent opportunities for portfolio entries:

- Section 1.1: *Similarities Between Living Things*
- Section 1.3: *Doing the Science of Biology*

THE BIG IDEA! Living things share many characteristics, including organization and adaptation. 1.1–1.2

① ENGAGE

Consider the Big Idea

Have students read The Big Idea! at the top of the page. Explain that living things are classified according to their level of organization and that successful organisms adapt to a changing environment.

Use the Visual

Have students study the photograph that opens the section. Explain that alchemists may have been misguided, but they developed important scientific procedures and tools. Ask:

■ **What scientific instruments are the alchemists using?**
(Flasks, tubes, and other chemistry paraphernalia)

Teacher Demo

Display photographs of familiar organisms that live in air, water, and on land. Ask students to identify each organism and describe its environment. Point out that all organisms live in the Earth's biosphere—the thin layer of air, and the water and land that is capable of supporting living things. Ask:

■ **What other characteristics do all living things have in common?**
(Energy, growth, response, reproduction, adaptation)

THE BIG IDEA! Living things share many characteristics, including organization and adaptation. 1.1–1.2

1.1 Similarities Among Living Things

What you'll learn

IDEAS
• To compare different theories of the origins of life
• To summarize the properties of life

WORDS
biosphere, organisms, spontaneous generation, biogenesis, cell, tissues, organs

A recipe for life?
Practiced in medieval times, alchemy was a blend of philosophy, early science, and magic. By following the right steps, alchemists thought they could transform common materials into precious metals or even create a formula for immortality. Of course, they never managed to make lead into gold or find the secret of life. However, alchemists did develop many of the first scientific instruments and techniques.

WHAT IS LIFE?

A very special status

We live in a part of Earth called the biosphere. The **biosphere** is the thin layer of air, land, and water that is home to all living things on Earth. Within the biosphere, the planet teems with life—from the microscopic bacteria that live on your skin to the huge humpback whales that cruise the Atlantic Ocean. The biosphere makes up much less than one percent of Earth's mass, yet when it comes to a discussion of life, this is where the action is!

All living things are called **organisms**. Organisms obey the same laws of physics and chemistry as do nonliving things. So what makes life special? How can we clearly recognize some things as being alive and other things as not? For most people, this distinction usually seems obvious. But this was not always so.

During much of human history, most cultures believed in a

FIGURE 1.1
Before spontaneous generation was disproven, people actually wrote recipes for living things. The Roman poet Virgil wrote this recipe for bees.

Recipe for Bees
1. Kill a bull during the first thaw of winter.
2. Build a shed.
3. Place the dead bull on branches and herbs inside the shed.
4. Wait for summer. The decaying body of the bull will produce bees.

view of life called vitalism. According to this view, living things exist because they have been filled with special forces called ethers, which bring nonliving things to life. The Greek philosopher and scholar Aristotle, who lived 2300 years ago, held this view of life. Vitalism dominated Western culture for nearly 2000 years. During the Dark Ages in Europe, it gave rise to the idea of spontaneous generation.

Spontaneous generation is the process by which life begins when ethers enter nonliving things. You can see one example of a spontaneous generation "recipe" in *Figure 1.1*. In addition to this belief about the origin of bees, mice were thought to come from discarded rags, geese from the mud banks of rivers, and salamanders from wood and fire. Although these ideas may seem foolish now, they were accepted as facts many years ago.

In 1668 the Italian physician Francesco Redi performed two experiments to test spontaneous generation. His experiments involved maggots, wormlike larvae that develop into flies. According to the theory of spontaneous

---

STUDENT RESOURCES

From the Teacher's Resource Package, use:
■ Section Review 1.1 and Activity Recordsheet 1-1 from Unit 1 Review Module
■ Lab 1: "What's Alive?"
■ Consumer Applications 1-1

 TECHNOLOGY RESOURCES

Relevant technology resources include:
■ Spanish Student Edition CD-ROM
■ Teacher's Resource Planner CD-ROM
■ Biology Alive! Video Series

FIGURE 1.2

Spontaneous Generation or Biogenesis?

Scientists in the early 1600s thought life came from nonliving things and ethers. Redi conducted experiments to test this theory. What did his experiments demonstrate? ❶

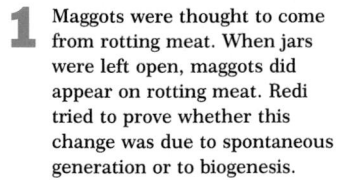

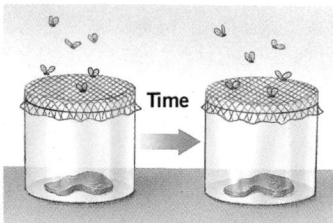

1 Maggots were thought to come from rotting meat. When jars were left open, maggots did appear on rotting meat. Redi tried to prove whether this change was due to spontaneous generation or to biogenesis.

2 According to the theory of spontaneous generation, maggots did not appear in sealed jars because ethers could not enter the jars. According to the theory of biogenesis, maggots did not appear because flies could not enter the jars.

3 When jars were covered with cloth, maggots did not appear. Although the theoretical ethers could enter the jars in this setup, flies could not. The absence of maggots supported biogenesis.

generation, maggots emerged when rotting meat was filled with ethers. Redi suspected that the maggots came from flies. As you can see in *Figure 1.2,* Redi demonstrated that flies did account for the appearance of maggots on rotting meat. You will learn more about the scientific method Redi used in his experiments later in this chapter.

The debate over whether spontaneous generation occurred lasted for hundreds of years. The theory that eventually replaced spontaneous generation in the late 1800s is called biogenesis. **Biogenesis** is the principle that life comes only from life. "Bio-" literally means "life" and *genesis* means "beginning." According to this theory, each type of living organism produces more of its own kind, or species.

Another theory, sparked by the work of Redi and others, is called mechanism. According to this principle, both living and nonliving organisms obey the same laws of physics and chemistry. Living things, however, have a special status because of their complexity. But as you will see later, sometimes it is not so easy to distinguish between organisms and nonliving things. Stay tuned!

Ideas about what distinguishes a living organism from a nonliving thing have changed dramatically over the past 500 years. During this time, the rise of science as a tool for answering questions and solving problems has increased our understanding of how the world works.

New tools, such as the telescope and the microscope, allowed scientists to see things that had never been seen before. New theories about the structure of the natural world emerged during this time as well. The English physician William Harvey, for example, demonstrated that the human heart was a mechanical pump

EVERYDAY BIOLOGY

Measurement Made Easy

The metric system of weights and measures made scientific communication much easier. The metric system is the international standard. Although we still use some English measurements, metric units are also common in the United States. Where have you seen metric units?

Chapter 1 The Study of Life **5**

MEETING DIVERSE NEEDS

LEP Encourage LEP students to preview the chapter looking for words in bold print and other key terms. Have students compile a glossary in which they define each term in English and in their native language. Suggest that students also include illustrations when appropriate.

Gifted Have students make a time line to show the events that led people to reject the idea of spontaneous generation and accept the principle of biogenesis. Have them describe the major experiments.

Use the Visual

Have students study Figure 1.2. Ask:

- **What idea was Francesco Redi testing?** (The idea of spontaneous generation, which suggested that living things could develop from nonliving matter and ethers)
- **How did the absence of maggots in the cloth-covered jar support the idea of biogenesis?** (Ethers could enter the jar and flies could not, suggesting that maggots did not come from ethers.)

Apply

Challenge students to identify situations that might lead people to accept the idea of spontaneous generation if all variables were not considered. For example, some people might believe that bees form when a can of soda is left outdoors and open on a hot summer day. Have students use the recipe for bees in Figure 1.1. as a model to devise a similar recipe for another type of organism. Have students explain why people might believe their recipe would work.

Everyday Biology

Bring to class some familiar items displaying metric measurements. Ask students how metric measurement is used in everyday life. (Speedometer markings, highway signs, and tools).

❶ The presence of "ethers" did not produce maggots.

FIGURE 1.3

Organization

The snowflake has a very complex and structured organization. The plant root also has a regular pattern of organization. What differences make the root a living thing? ❶

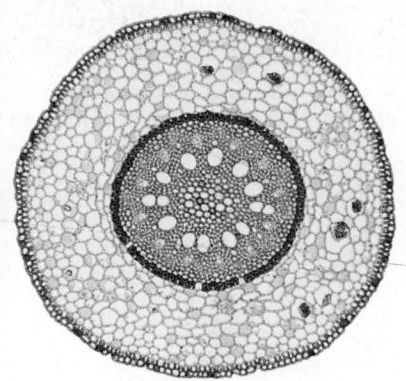

for blood and not the organ of emotion. Most important, the scientific revolution encouraged the study of the natural world and the development of new ideas.

PROPERTIES OF LIFE

To be or not to be

At this point, you may be wondering if there really is a difference between living and nonliving things. Would you be surprised to learn that at some physical level, the answer is actually no? Both living and nonliving objects are composed of the same materials. They are all made from the elements present on Earth, and they all obey the same laws of nature.

It is clear that organisms have characteristics that make them different from the nonliving world—characteristics that you can usually recognize. The characteristics of living things are organization, energy, growth and development, reproduction, and response and adaptation.

Many of these characteristics are not unique to living systems. Some can be found in nonliving objects as well. Clouds move across the sky; highly organized ice crystals appear to grow across a cold windowpane; fire uses and releases energy and can reproduce by starting other fires. But

clouds do not adapt, ice crystals cannot reproduce, fire is not made of cells, and it is not organized. So although some nonliving things have some of the characteristics of life, none show all of these characteristics.

Organization Living things are highly organized. Specialized structures perform specific functions at every level of organization, from a single bacterial cell to the multicellular human body. In most multicellular organisms, structures are organized according to repeating patterns.

The basic unit of organization in living things is the **cell.** All organisms are made of cells. Some organisms, such as protists and bacteria, are unicellular; they are made of only one cell. Others—multicellular organisms—are made of many cells. Multicellular organisms, such as plants and animals, can be composed of trillions of cells. Each cell of every organism displays the characteristics of life.

Energy Physicists—scientists who study the properties, changes, and interactions of matter and energy—have discovered that energy exists in many forms. Forms of energy include sound, light, and chemical energy. Each of these forms is important to living things. We use light energy, like that produced by the match shown

6   *Chapter 1 The Study of Life*

❶ The root is made of cells and can reproduce.

FIGURE 1.4
Energy

The match and the firefly both use energy. How do they differ? What characteristics make the firefly a living organism? ❸

Explain ✳

Point out that most living things use hydrocarbon compounds for energy. These compounds are made up of hydrogen, carbon, and sometimes other elements. When hydrocarbon compounds react with oxygen, they release energy. In living things, this process is called respiration.

Clarify Misconceptions

Discuss the concept of growth. Explain that while many nonliving things, such as an icicle or a ball of clay, can be made to increase in size, these things do not "grow" in the same way as living things. In living things, growth results as cells increase in size and then divide.

in *Figure 1.4,* to see. Living things also use energy for life processes. The firefly shown in *Figure 1.4* uses chemical energy to grow, fly, and produce its greenish glow.

Where does the energy needed for life processes come from? All organisms are able to take in energy from the environment and use it for their life processes. For example, light energy enables plants to make food from carbon dioxide and water. Some organisms take in chemical energy as food and use it for many daily activities.

Growth and development
Compare your body with the body of an infant. How have you changed? Humans, like all living things, grow and develop. Growth is an increase in size. Development is a change in shape or form. Look at the cloud and the butterfly shown in *Figure 1.5.* What makes one example living and the other nonliving?

❷ The magnitude, or amount, of growth varies among living things. Some organisms grow very little. A single ameba, for example, does not change much in size. There is great change in the size of some organisms, however. An elephant grows from a

single fertilized egg cell into an enormous adult animal.

The nature of development also varies from species to species. Do you think that your body has changed much as you've grown? Compare the changes you have gone through with the development of a caterpillar or a tadpole, and you will soon realize that other organisms undergo developmen-

FIGURE 1.5
Growth and Development

Have you ever compared cloud shapes to living things? Although changes in the size and shape of clouds are similar to growth and development, clouds are not organisms. How do these cloud changes differ from the changes a caterpillar undergoes when it becomes a butterfly? ❹

Teacher Demo

Obtain photographs showing the changes in form that are typical in the life cycles of frogs, butterflies, and humans. Tell students that the extensive developmental changes they observe in the frog and butterfly are known as a metamorphosis, which is a process of development in which a young organism undergoes changes in appearance and structure to become an adult. Ask:

■ **How do the developmental changes of a frog or butterfly compare with those of humans?** (The human baby is a "miniature" adult; the early stages of a frog or butterfly do not resemble adult traits.)

Chapter 1 The Study of Life **7**

MEETING DIVERSE NEEDS

Gifted Have gifted students conduct research to identify the different forms of energy. Have students create a visual device that shows each form of energy in use and explains how each works. Challenge students to identify which forms of energy are important to living things.

❷ A living thing carries on the processes necessary for life.

❸ The firefly is able to movc, cat, and reproduce.

❹ The clouds change in form, size, and shape; changes are random. The caterpillar develops new structures and different types of organization; changes are predictable.

FIGURE 1.6

Reproduction

Although a camera can copy images, it cannot reproduce living things. The bacterium can reproduce—making a new bacterium.

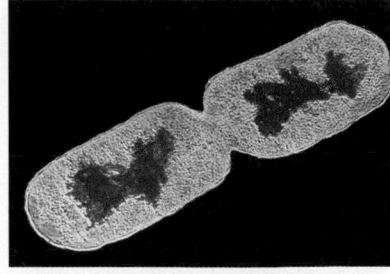

tal changes even more dramatic than those you have experienced.

Reproduction As you have learned, biogenesis explains that living things come from other living things. The process through which new living things are formed is called reproduction. Reproduction involves making new cells. A new cell can be part of an existing organism, part of a new organism, or an entirely new, independent unicellular organism.

Like growth and development, reproduction is part of the life cycle of many organisms. Without reproduc-

tion, there would be no living things to replace those that die. Although it is not necessary for each organism in a population to reproduce, reproduction is necessary for the survival of a species. Reproduction can result in an exact duplicate of the parent, or in duplication with variation.

Response and adaptation Have you ever blinked when your eye was irritated? Or sneezed in response to dust? Responding to stimuli is another characteristic shared by all living things.

Growth, migration, color changes, and movement are just a few of the many ways in which living things respond to environmental stimuli. Some seeds, for example, sprout in response to the presence of water. Some bird species respond to the change of seasons by migrating from place to place. What type of response is shown in *Figure 1.7*? How does the response of the plant differ from the response of the water wheel?

Adaptation is a way for an entire population of organisms to respond to long-term changes in their surroundings. Adaptations are passed on from generation to generation. You will

FIGURE 1.7

Response

A plant responds by growing toward a light source. How does this response compare with the response of the wheel to the water? ❶

❶ The plant has internal chemicals that make it respond; the wheel is forced to move by the action of water.

learn more about adaptations and the theory of evolution later in this chapter and in Unit 3.

Each species has unique adaptations that enable it to survive in its particular environment. As a result, life can exist under some very extraordinary conditions. For example, one type of bacterium can survive the subfreezing temperatures of the Arctic ice fields because it is able to produce a biological "antifreeze." Tube worms and giant clams live in the sulfur-rich vents of the ocean bottom where water temperatures reach the boiling point!

Wherever life is found, organisms must meet the challenges of survival. To varying degrees, all living things need water, temperatures within a certain range, and a source of energy. Most organisms also need oxygen. The more extreme the conditions, the more specialized organisms must be in order to survive.

THE ORGANIZATION OF LIFE

The architecture of the living world

As you now know, one of the characteristics of living systems is organization. The organization in the biosphere can be broken down to many different levels. You can see some of these levels illustrated in *Figure 1.8* on page 10. Biologists study life at each level of organization.

Some of these levels of organization are universal—present in all living things. For example, all organisms have cells and are part of a population, community, and ecosystem. Other levels of organization are present in some organisms but not in others. Humans and other animals have specialized tissues, organs, and systems. Bacteria, however, do not have these levels of organization.

The smallest level of organization

of all things, living or not, is the atom. Atoms often bond to one another to form molecules. Molecules can consist of as few as two atoms, but most biological molecules are made of hundreds, or even thousands, of atoms. Biochemists and molecular biologists study the molecules essential to living organisms.

Cells are the fundamental units of life that exhibit all of the characteristics of living things. Even the largest organisms begin life as a single cell. Thousands of unicellular organisms, which you cannot see with the unaided eye, inhabit Earth.

Inside the cell are specialized "compartments" in which life's functions take place. The cell can be thought of as a complex factory that manufactures the products of life. Biologists who study cells are called

Chapter 1 The Study of Life **9**

Use the Visual

Have students study Figure 1.8. Ask:

- **How are cells and tissues related?** (Tissues are made up of cells that work together to perform a specific function.)
- **At what level is a multicellular organism capable of independent life?** (The individual level)
- **What is an ecosystem?** (All the communities and the nonliving things in an area)
- **What is the relationship of an ecosystem to the biosphere?** (Each ecosystem is a part of the Earth's biosphere.)

Discuss

Discuss with students the organized relationships among cells, tissues, organs, and organ systems. Using human blood as an example, identify the individual types of cells (red blood cells, white blood cells) that work together to form the tissue called blood. Explain that the function of blood is to transport needed materials to the cells of the body and carry away wastes. Point out that in order to carry out this function, the blood travels through blood vessels (arteries, veins, and capillaries) that are part of the circulatory system. Explain that the heart is the main organ of the circulatory system.

FIGURE 1.8
Levels of Organization

Each living thing can be made of atoms, molecules, cells, tissues, organs, and organ systems. The biosphere is made of individuals, populations, communities, and ecosystems.

1 Atom, molecule
Atoms are the smallest units of organization. They bind together to make molecules.

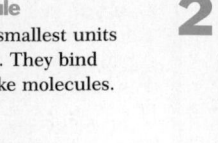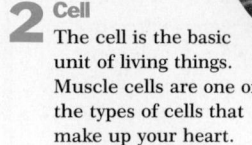

2 Cell
The cell is the basic unit of living things. Muscle cells are one of the types of cells that make up your heart.

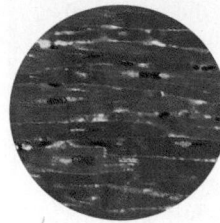

3 Tissue
Muscle tissue, like all tissue, is made of a group of cells that work together to perform a specific function.

8 Ecosystem
The ecosystem includes all of the communities in an area and all the nonliving things, such as snow, water, soil, and air.

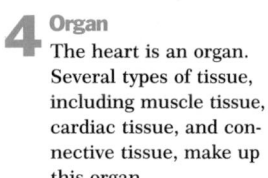

4 Organ
The heart is an organ. Several types of tissue, including muscle tissue, cardiac tissue, and connective tissue, make up this organ.

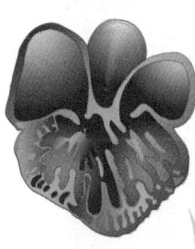

7 Population and community
A population is a group of similar organisms, such as turtles, living in the same place. The turtles and all the other populations in an area, including the reeds at the water's edge, make up a community.

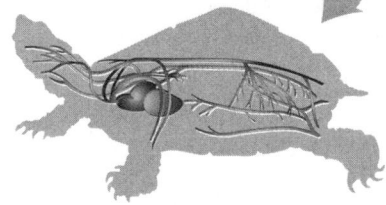

6 Individual
Large multicellular organisms, such as this turtle, are made of several organ systems.

5 Organ system
The circulatory system is one of several organ systems that enable a turtle to survive.

MEETING DIVERSE NEEDS

At Risk Encourage students to develop a mnemonic device to help them remember the levels of organization shared by all living things. Tell students to use both the text and Figure 1.8 as references.

❶ Answers may include lungs, kidneys, intestines, brain, and liver.

❷ The school's student body

❸ Living things in the surrounding city, county, and state

cellular biologists or cytologists ("cyt-" means "cell").

In many multicellular organisms, cells are organized into tissues. **Tissues** are made of cells working together to perform a specific function. In the turtle shown in *Figure 1.8*, muscle, bone, and blood are examples of different types of tissues.

In many multicellular living things, tissues are further organized to form organs. **Organs** are made of several different types of tissues that function together for a specific purpose. Roots and leaves are organs found in members of the plant kingdom. The heart is a common organ in animals. What human organs can you identify? ❶

In many organisms, organs are further organized into organ systems, made of several organs working together to perform a function. The circulatory, digestive, and reproductive systems are some of the organ systems in the human body. Together, the organ systems make up an individual organism. Doctors, zoologists, botanists, and other specialists study organ systems in different types of organisms.

The field of biology does not end with an understanding of individual organisms, however. After all, individual organisms interact with other living things. Population biologists study all the members of a particular type of organism living in an area. A population is a group of organisms of the same species that live together in a particular location. The turtles in a pond, the sugar maples in a forest, and the pigeons in a city are examples of populations. How would you describe your population? ❷

Scientists who study the interactions of populations within an area focus on communities. Communities include all of the organism populations in a particular location. A lawn is an example of a community. The lawn community includes populations of grasses, insects, worms, bacteria, and other organisms. What populations share your community? ❸

If you add all of the nonliving parts of a location to the community, you have an ecosystem. Ecosystems include all the living and nonliving elements in a location. Environmental biologists and conservation biologists study communities and ecosystems. Their studies confirm the long-held belief that there are no truly isolated areas on Earth. Events taking place in one part of the globe can have an effect on living organisms hundreds or even thousands of miles away! All forms of life are interconnected.

You are a new biologist. With this textbook, you will begin your study of biology by considering life at the smallest level of organization. You will discover how the basic characteristics of life are rearranged in an almost infinite number of ways to produce the diversity of life on Earth. When you have completed your study, you will increase your understanding and appreciation of the biosphere, which some scientists view as the largest living system of all.

EVERYDAY BIOLOGY

Get Organized

There are different levels of organization in many fields. Our government has federal, state, and local levels. You may by familiar with your school's organizational levels—for example, school committee, principal, teaching staff, and student body. What other kinds of organization can you identify? Consider areas such as work, school, sports, or extracurricular activities.

CHECKPOINT 1.1

1. Compare the principles of spontaneous generation and biogenesis.
2. List and describe the characteristics of living things.
3. Choose an organism and identify the levels of organization that characterize it and its environment.
4. **Critical Thinking** A copier machine displays many of the characteristics of a living thing, including the use of energy and the ability to reproduce. Explain why it is not alive.

Build on What You Know

5. Which levels of organization have you studied in previous science courses?

Chapter 1 The Study of Life **11**

Language Arts

Explain that the suffix *-logy* means "the study of," and the suffix *-ist* refers to "one who specializes in a specific art, science, or skill." Ask students to cite examples of how these suffixes are used in this section. (Biology/biologist; zoology/ zoologist)

❸ ASSESS

Evaluate Understanding

Assess students' understanding of the section by asking:

- **What parts of the Earth are included in the biosphere?** (All parts in which organisms live, including the air, land, and water)
- **What is the smallest functioning unit of life?** (The cell)
- **What characteristic of living things supports the idea of biogenesis?** (Reproduction)
- **What are the components of an ecosystem?** (All the organisms in a community, as well as nonliving things such as climate, soil, and water)

Reteach

Have volunteers list on the board the characteristics of living things. Discuss each characteristic. Then as a class develop a graphic that illustrates the levels of organization in living things. Discuss the relationships among the levels.

CHECKPOINT 1.1

1. Spontaneous generation theorizes that living things come from nonliving things and ethers; biogenesis theorizes that life comes from living things.
2. Organization, use of energy, growth and development, reproduction, response, and adaptation; descriptions will vary.
3. Answers should include all the levels shown in Figure 1.8.
4. **Making analogies** The copy machine does not grow and develop.
5. Answers may include levels of organization in matter and in Earth science.

1.2 Adaptation and Interdependence

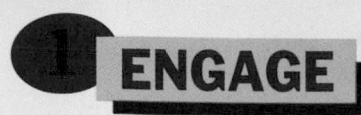

① ENGAGE

Use the Visual

Have students study the photograph and read the text that opens the section. Explain that the behavior described is an adaptation to climactic changes. Ask:

- **What other adaptations do you think the butterfly will have to make?** (It will have to find new sources of food and new places to live.)

Check Prior Knowledge

To assess students' knowledge about organisms, ask:

- **What are some traits shared by living things?** (All living things are organized, take energy from the environment and use it for life processes, grow and develop, reproduce, and adapt.)

Quick Activity

Display photographs or drawings of dinosaurs in natural environments. Have students infer how Earth and its life forms have changed over time. Record their responses on the board. Have students add to the list after they read the section.

What you'll learn

IDEAS
- To explain how organisms respond and adapt to their environment
- To compare the various interdependent relationships of organisms
- To summarize the role of humans in the ecosystem

WORDS
predator, prey

Heading for the north country
Edith's checkerspot butterflies, found along North America's Pacific coast, are homebodies. An entire population can live in a small area for many generations. Yet these butterflies have begun steadily moving north—perhaps in response to the gradual warming of the Earth's atmosphere. In the increasingly warm south, checkerspots are dying out.

ADAPTATION

The struggle to survive

Earth has a very long history—over [appears to be] four billion years! During that time, conditions on Earth have changed a great deal, and they will surely continue to change. The ability to respond and adapt to changes in the environment is one of the most important characteristics of living things. This ability includes adjustments for short-term changes, such as the temperature difference between day and night, and long-term changes, such as the warming or cooling of Earth over thousands of years. Living organisms must have characteristics that enable them to cope with these changes or they will die out.

FIGURE 1.9
Daily life for this Bengal tiger requires reacting to various changes in its environment, such as temperature fluctuations.

Responses to most short-term changes can often occur quickly and easily with a change in behavior. For example, the Bengal tiger shown in *Figure 1.9* may wake up cold at dawn and move into the direct rays of the rising sun to warm up. At midday, however, the tiger may escape the heat of the sun by seeking the shade of a tree.

But what about the long-term changes that tigers face? The Bengal tiger's natural environment has changed dramatically during the past century. Cities and towns have formed in what used to be the animals' hunting ground. How will the tigers adapt to changes in the supply of food, water, and living space? These adaptations require changes in the very nature of the entire species. In fact, the characteristics and behaviors of modern tigers are the result of adaptations that allowed the tigers to cope with changes in the past.

Until about two hundred years ago, the idea of a changing world was unacceptable. Throughout recorded human history, life seemed very stable. Tigers have looked and acted relatively the same for as long as anyone has been observing them and writing about them.

12 *Chapter 1 The Study of Life*

STUDENT RESOURCES

From the Teacher's Resource Package, use:
- Section Review 1.2, Activity Recordsheet 1-2, and Enrichment Topic 1-1 from Unit 1 Review Module
- Issues and Decision Making 1-1

TECHNOLOGY RESOURCES

Relevant technology resources include:
- Spanish Student Edition CD-ROM
- Teacher's Resource Planner CD-ROM
- Biology Alive! Video Series

FIGURE 1.10
Saber-toothed tiger skulls shown in *Figure 1.11* have been found in the San Fernando Valley in California. How do you think this area has changed over time? ❷

By the 1700s, however, geologists had uncovered evidence that Earth's history was full of change. Older layers of Earth's crust reveal organisms that flourished millions of years ago, and these organisms are different from those living today. For example, fossils reveal the existence of the saber-toothed tiger, a cat species quite different from the Bengal tiger. Compare the saber-toothed tiger skull shown in *Figure 1.11* with the Bengal tiger shown on page 12. How are these species similar? Different? ❶

Species that no longer exist are said to be extinct. The saber-toothed tiger is an example of an extinct species. You may be familiar with other extinct groups, or species, such as dinosaurs, woolly mammoths, and dodo birds. The extinction of a species is a concern for several reasons. Species are interdependent—they rely on one another. The loss of a species always affects other organisms.

Fossil evidence shows that many species have become extinct over Earth's history. The discovery of fossil evidence of an extinct species was clearly at odds with the traditional view that Earth and its inhabitants had remained unchanged since they came into being. By the middle of the nineteenth century, the evidence for a changing Earth was strong.

What was missing, however, was an explanation of how Earth's changes might lead to changes in organisms. Charles Darwin, the English naturalist, proposed a theory to answer this important question. While earlier scientists had used the term evolution, it was Darwin who first explained how evolution may be involved in changes in organisms over time.

Darwin viewed life as a competitive struggle for Earth's limited resources. Most often, more living things are born than can survive. Only those organisms that can successfully compete for Earth's resources can survive and reproduce. The traits that enable an organism to survive are passed to its offspring. The theory of evolution states that these traits can eventually become adaptations for the entire species.

EVERYDAY BIOLOGY

Fossil Walls

In New York City you can take a tour of fossils on display in an unusual place—on the surfaces of public buildings! Ancient stone used in construction often contains fossilized remains. Check stone buildings in your area for fossils.

FIGURE 1.11
This skull belongs to a large predator known as the saber-toothed tiger. Now extinct, this animal roamed North America during the late Pleistocene period.

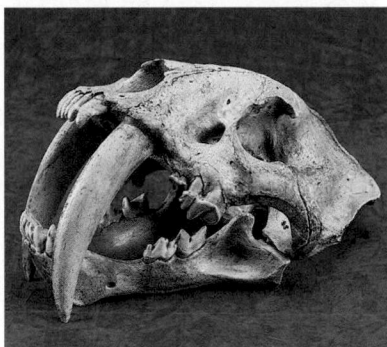

Use the Visual

Have students study Figure 1.10. Discuss how the development of the urban environment shown has changed the natural environment. Challenge students to identify ways in which each change may have effected the organisms that once made the area their home.

Class Activity

TEAM WORK

Have groups of students research a plant or animal species that is now extinct. Ask groups to prepare a chart or other visual that identifies the species, and depicts its appearance, habitat, and importance to other organisms. Visuals should also show when the organism became extinct and possible causes of its extinction. Give each group an opportunity to share its visual with the class.

Class Activity

Invite a speaker from the local chapter of the Audubon Society or an environmental or conservation group to speak to the class about species in danger of becoming extinct. Ask the speaker to discuss zoos, wildlife refuges, bird sanctuaries, and other efforts being made to protect species. Have students prepare questions to ask the speaker.

MEETING DIVERSE NEEDS

At Risk Have students list the section objectives in their notebooks, leaving space after each objective. Suggest that as they read the section, they list terms and phrases that will help them identify the information requested by each objective. Check their entries for accuracy.

❶ They have structures adapted for eating meat and similar body plans. Both are felines. Saber-toothed tiger's canines are much larger and shape of skull differs from Bengal tiger.

❷ In addition to major environmental change, humans moved into the area and adapted it for their use by constructing buildings and roads, and farming the land.

FIGURE 1.12
The lynx population is dependent on the hare population for survival.

FIGURE 1.13
The crab *Lybia tessellata* carries a pair of anemones on its claws. In this mutualistic relationship, the crab gets protection from the anemones' stinging tentacles, while the anemones benefit from the crab's release of small food particles when it feeds.

INTERDEPENDENCE

The web of life has many connections

Organisms have complex interactions with their environments. Each species requires a very precise combination of temperature, moisture, soil composition, and other environmental conditions in order to survive. Organisms are tightly connected to the nonliving world in which they live. Complex relationship webs also connect organisms to other organisms. As you read this textbook, you will learn about many of these relationships. Each chapter about a specific group of organisms includes a section that explains the roles that group plays in the biosphere.

Many of the roles that organisms play involve food—how they obtain food and how other organisms might use them for food. Many organisms depend upon a specific plant or animal for food. This relationship is called a predator-prey relationship. A **predator** is an organism that kills and eats another organism. The organism that is eaten is the **prey**. Consider the predator-prey relationship shown in *Figure 1.12*. Which animal in the photo is the predator? Which animal is the prey? ❶

In a predator-prey relationship, the need of one organism to respond and adapt to evolutionary changes drives the process of adaptation in both species. For example, if the predator population begins to use a new, more efficient way to catch prey, the prey population may have to develop new ways to avoid getting caught. If the

14 *Chapter 1 The Study of Life*

❶ The lynx is the predator and the hare is the prey.

prey species began to escape its predators, how would the predator population be affected?

The predator-prey relationship is one of the many types of interrelationships you will read about as you study living things. In other types of relationships, one organism depends on another living thing for shelter, for protection from predators, and for access to resources such as light or water. Relationships in which different species depend upon each other are known as symbiosis. Symbiosis is one of the characteristics of the interdependence among organisms. There are three types of symbiosis—mutualism, commensalism, and parasitism.

In mutualism, both partners in a symbiotic relationship benefit from their association. *Figure 1.13* shows one example of mutualism. The crabs benefit from the relationship with anemones because they are protected by the anemones' stinging tentacles. The anemones also benefit from their relationship with crabs. When crabs feed, some food particles are scattered into the surrounding water. The anemones take in this food with their tentacles.

Commensalism, a second kind of symbiosis, is a relationship in which one partner benefits and the other partner is unaffected. The bromeliads and tree shown in *Figure 1.14* are partners in a relationship that demonstrates commensalism. Bromeliads growing high on tree branches benefit by gaining greater exposure to sunlight. The tree, on the other hand, is neither helped nor harmed by the presence of the bromeliad. How does this relationship differ from mutualism?

In parasitism, the relationship between an organism and its partner is one-sided. One member of a partnership (the parasite) benefits from the relationship, and the other (the host) is harmed. How do the parasites shown in *Figure 1.15* affect their hosts?

Understanding the interdependence among organisms helps us to understand the fragile nature of the biosphere. The relationships may have evolved over millions of years and may be quite specialized.

Even a small change to one type of organism, such as a change in its population size, can have a major impact on all the other organisms in an environment. If long-term relationships change before all the organisms involved can adapt, some organisms will become extinct. It is often difficult, if not impossible, to predict how a change in one species or one aspect of the environment could affect the other organisms in the area. The connections among living things are like a spider's web. Each thread in the web of life is a species. If one thread is disturbed, the entire web can be threatened.

FIGURE 1.14
These bromeliads live on the trunk of a tree and benefit from the tree's height.

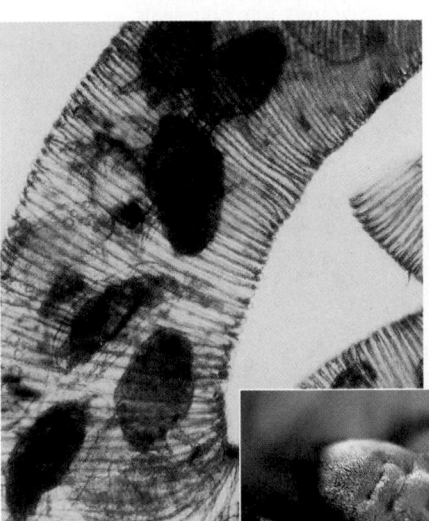

FIGURE 1.15
Many parasites can seriously injure or kill their hosts. The tracheal mite (left) lives and breeds in the tracheal tubes of honeybees, obstructing the flow of oxygen and killing the bee. The velvet mite (below) is a plant parasite that harms or kills its host.

Chapter 1 The Study of Life **15**

Use the Visual

Have students study Figure 1.14. Ask:

- **Why is the relationship between the orchids and the trees upon which they grow an example of commensalism?** (The orchids benefit from the relationship, while the tree is unaffected by the relationship.)
- **How do the orchids benefit from living on the tree trunk?** (They gain greater exposure to sunlight.)

Apply

Explain to students that bacteria called *E. coli* normally live in the human intestinal tract. Tell them that the bacteria are provided with a home and all the materials they need to survive, while their human host is usually neither helped nor harmed. Ask:

- **What kind of relationship exists between a healthy human and the *E. coli* that live in the intestines?** (Commensalism)

Teacher Demo

Invite a veterinarian to speak to the class about common parasites that infect animals kept as pets. Ask the veterinarian to bring in preserved specimens of some of the common worms that parasitize dogs and cats, if available, and allow students to examine the specimens. Work with students to compile a list of questions to ask the speaker.

MEETING DIVERSE NEEDS

Hearing Impaired Have hearing impaired students look up the pronunciations of unfamiliar terms used in this chapter. Suggest that they begin a glossary of scientific terms on index cards.

❷ It would be reduced for lack of food.
❸ In mutualism both partners benefit.
❹ Both harm or kill the host.

ENVIRONMENTAL
AWARENESS

Humans and the Web of Life

You are part of the web of life—the "structure" that represents the interconnectedness of living things. As part of that web, you affect and are affected by the living things around you. Without an understanding of biology, you will not be able to make wise decisions about many issues that affect you, your family, and your community.

Take a look around you. How many objects can you identify that are living, made from living things, or made from the products of living things? Did you include all the wood products? How ❶ about plastics, clothing, and paper? All these things and many more are made from or by organisms. Biology affects many aspects of everyday life, including food, clothing, shelter, and health.

Biotechnology is the use of organisms to produce things that people need. For example, using bacteria to turn milk into cheese or yogurt is a biotechnology technique people have practiced for centuries. Modern techniques, such as genetic engineering,

have greatly increased the applications of biotechnology. Biotechnology is essential for farming, livestock management, food processing and preservation, medicine, and many other human needs.

Food You cannot live more than three months without food, which gives you energy to carry out all your activities. All foods are made directly from living things or indirectly from the products of living things.

The science of biology has helped improve the quantity and quality of food available to people all over the world. As you may know, plants we use as food can grow in the wild. Some animal food sources are also wild. At one time in human history, people depended on wild, unmanaged resources for all food. Today most of the food supply for people comes from managed areas, such as the sheep farm shown in *Figure 1.16.* Farmers use biology to plan their farms and cultivate crops. Ranchers use biology to feed, breed, and care for their animals.

Medicine Living things provide many solutions to medical problems. The discovery and production of

FIGURE 1.16
Natural and Managed Ecosystems

Livestock
Domestic sheep (above) are raised on farms for their food, wool, and leather. Their relatives, the Dall sheep (right), roam freely in Alaska.

Fish
Many fish that are caught (below) can also be raised in fish hatcheries (right).

16 *Chapter 1 The Study of Life*

medicines has changed many diseases from fatal illnesses into minor inconveniences. The role of biology in health goes beyond the treatment of illnesses. Healthful community practices of water treatment, garbage disposal, and food handling can prevent many kinds of human suffering.

Clothing Most clothing is made from biological products. Wool, silk, and leather come from animal products. Cotton and linen are common plant materials used for clothing. Biotechnology has expanded the types of living things we can use as sources for clothing. Rayon, for example, is made using wood chips.

Additional resources Many fuels are made from the remains or the products of organisms. For example, wood comes from plants and coal comes from the fossilized remains of plants. Petroleum products, such as oil and gasoline, are made from the decayed remains of tiny marine organisms that lived millions of years ago. Together, petroleum and coal are referred to as fossil fuels.

We rely on living things for many other materials and products as well. As you can see in *Figure 1.16* below,

some trees are farmed and some flowers are cultivated. We use trees and other plants to build structures and make paper. We also rely on trees in managed and natural ecosystems to recycle oxygen and carbon dioxide and provide shade and shelter from the wind. What other living resources can you think of? ❷

PROTECTING LIFE'S WEB

Living things are priceless

Perhaps the most important reason to gain an understanding of biology is to help protect the diverse life of the biosphere. Biology reveals the interactions between organisms and their environments.

It is not always easy to predict the value of a species. Although some plants and animals may seem at a given time to have little impact on human survival, nothing could be further from the truth. For example, in the early 1990s the Pacific yew tree was found to contain a chemical that may be useful in treating certain types of human cancer. The yew tree tends to grow among valuable timber

be effective at our job as co-caretakers of God's creation

Wood Products
Tree farms, like this long-leaf pine plantation (below), can reduce the need to harvest from natural forests, like this evergreen forest in Washington (left).

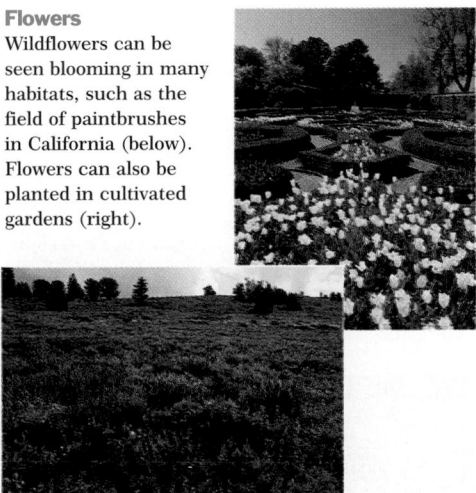

Flowers
Wildflowers can be seen blooming in many habitats, such as the field of paintbrushes in California (below). Flowers can also be planted in cultivated gardens (right).

MULTICULTURAL PERSPECTIVE

Wood has been used for the construction of shelters for many years. However, wood is not the only living thing from which shelters are made. Native Americans living in the plains regions of the United States used buffalo hides to construct their tepees. Native Americans living in the southwestern part of the United States, used thatch for the roofs of their shelters.

Explain that in many societies, both ancient and modern, people who treat the sick use herbs and other plants. Ask:

- **Should herbal treatments and cures be considered medicine? Why or why not?** (Responses will vary, but should indicate that many of today's medicines are created from plants and plant products. Also, one definition of medicine is "a substance or preparation used in treating disease.")

Explain

Point out that fuels formed from the remains of living things of millions of years ago are called fossil fuels. Explain that other fuels, such as wood and ethanol (a fuel made from corn), which are made from organisms still alive today are often referred to as biomass.

Class Activity

Have students working in small groups list the names of 200 different kinds of plants, animals, and other organisms on a sheet of paper, without duplicating any names. Circulate among the groups, providing help as needed. After students have completed this task, tell them to cross off the names of 100 organisms. Explain that this is the number of species that many scientists believe become extinct each day. Use the exercise to emphasize the need to protect Earth's biodiversity.

Do It! **TEAM WORK**

Observing Biodiversity

Encourage students to count both small and large organisms. Remind students not to mishandle any organisms.

Analyze Your Results

1 Answers will depend on the area and time of year.
2 If environmental conditions changed, different types of organisms might be observed.

❸ ASSESS

Evaluate Understanding

To assess students' understanding of life's web, ask:

- **Why is it important for organisms to adapt to changes in their environment?** (So they are better able to survive.)
- **How does commensalism differ from mutualism?** (In commensalism, only one partner benefits.)
- **In what ways does biology impact your life?** (Organisms provide humans with food, clothing, fuels, medicines, and many products.)

Reteach

Work with students to create a concept map that identifies the various types of symbiosis discussed in this section and the features of each relationship. Challenge students to explain how such relationships relate to an organism's survival.

 **Do It!**

Observing Biodiversity

The biodiversity of an ecosystem refers to the numbers of organisms that have adapted to live there. You can explore the biodiversity of your community when you . . .

Try This

1 Go to a park, woodland, or other unpaved outdoor location. With nails or pegs, measuring stick, and string, mark out an area one meter square.
2 Take a census of living organisms in the marked-off area (a hand lens will help). Count, as accurately as you can, the number of individual organisms you find. Sketch and describe the different types of plants and animals you observe. Record your observations.
3 When you are done, remove your materials and leave the location as you found it. Record the time, place, and weather conditions of your study.

Analyze Your Results

1 How many different types of organisms did you find? Which types were the most abundant? Was it easy or hard to count individual organisms? Why?
2 How different do you think your results would be if your study had taken place at a different time of year, a different time of day, or in a different location or climate?

FIGURE 1.17
The bark of the Pacific yew tree contains a chemical called taxol, effective in treating certain types of cancer.

environment? It is impossible to predict whether or how living things will adapt to future changes. But it is possible to understand, appreciate, and protect the intricate, delicate web of life.

CHECKPOINT 1.2

1. Choose an organism and describe a typical response. How is the species adapted to its environment?
2. Describe ways in which organisms depend on other organisms.
3. How do humans rely on other organisms?
4. **Critical Thinking** Give an example of a type of organism that humans depend upon for survival. How would life change if this organism became extinct?

Build on What You Know

5. List three examples of nonliving products developed from living things. Describe which properties of life they have, and which they do not have. *(Need to jog your memory? Revisit relevant concepts in Section 1.1.)*

trees and is considered by the lumber industry to be a weed. Before the discovery of its medicinal value, the yew tree was almost driven to extinction.

Without the knowledge that biology brings, it will be impossible for the growing human population to exist alongside the other species on Earth, and guarantee the continued survival of all of Earth's diverse species. Many people wonder about Earth's future. Will most organisms survive the rapid changes currently taking place in the

 What are the characteristics that living things share?

18 *Chapter 1 The Study of Life*

CHECKPOINT 1.2

1. Answers should distinguish between responses, which are short-term reactions of individuals, and adaptations, which are longer-term changes of an entire population.
2. Organisms depend on other organisms for food, shelter, and protection from predators.
3. Answers may include for food, medicine, fuel and energy, and other products.
4. **Predicting** Answers should describe the effect of the loss of the organism on its importance, for example, food production.
5. Answers should recognize the differences between living and nonliving things.

THE BIG IDEA! Scientists use careful observation and controlled experiments to study the natural world. 1.3

1.3 Doing the Science of Biology

Who is a scientist?

What does your mental image of a scientist look like? Someone in a white lab coat? A scientist is generally defined as a person having expert knowledge in science. But you can begin learning to do science right now, like the students in the photograph, who are collecting samples to test the water in their community.

What you'll learn

IDEAS
• To summarize the scientific method
• To explain the role of science in society

WORDS
scientific method, hypothesis, variable, control setup, theory

SCIENTIFIC METHOD

The "how to" of science

We all observe the world around us, in order to survive! We observe our surroundings so we can reach destinations without running into obstacles. We observe the weather so we can wear appropriate clothing. And so on. What makes the observations of a scientist different from those of the casual observer? The answer lies in understanding the process of doing science in general, and of doing biology in particular.

The work of science, and of any other discipline, involves the careful observation of events. Scientists make meaningful connections between their observations and past observations made by themselves and others. Mastering science is like mastering any other discipline, such as law, art, and philosophy. In science and in

FIGURE 1.18

Making Observations

Smell
The unpleasant odor of the giant carrion flower may give clues about interactions with its environment.

Sound
Observations made by sound, such as the trumpeting of an elephant, can be sensed by the ears or enhanced with technology. The scientist above is recording bird songs.

Sight
Observations made by sight can give clues about physical variance within a species. The male and female argus pheasants have a very different appearance.

Chapter 1 The Study of Life **19**

---

1 ENGAGE

Consider the Big Idea

Have students read The Big Idea! at the top of the page. Point out that observation and experimentation are essential components of the scientific method.

Use the Visual

Have students study the photograph that opens the section. Explain that curiosity is an important tool for someone who wants "to do science." Encourage students to share their experiences in learning about their environment.

Check Prior Knowledge

To assess students' knowledge about the science of biology, ask:

■ **What is biology?** (The study of life)
■ **How did Redi disprove the theory of spontaneous generation?** (By conducting an experiment)

Quick Activity   TEAM WORK

Provide students working in groups with flashlights in which the batteries have been inserted incorrectly. Challenge students to determine why the flashlights do not work and to explain how they could check the accuracy of their responses. Use the activity to introduce the idea of scientific method as a problem-solving approach in science.

2 TEACH

Teacher Demo

Display a metric ruler, a hand lens, a microscope, a graduated cylinder, and litmus paper. Explain to students that each of these objects is a tool used in biology. Discuss how each tool is used. Emphasize that tools of measurement, such as the metric ruler and the graduated cylinder, help make observations more accurate by quantifying data. Ask:

- **What other tools do biologists use?** (Computers, binoculars, and cameras.)

Discuss

Ask students to describe how a detective goes about solving a crime. Use student responses to point out that scientists work in much the same way. Both search for evidence, make observations, develop hypotheses, and try to prove their case.

Think Critically

Explain to students that the mythology of the ancient Greeks and Romans was an attempt to explain observations of nature and the workings of the universe, then Ask:

- **How does mythology differ from science?** (Science is based on observations and experiments.)

FIGURE 1.19
The development of the microscope allowed scientists to make observations on a cellular level. A light microscope was used to photograph fat cells (near right), and a scanning electron microscope was used to photograph fat in human skin cells (far right).

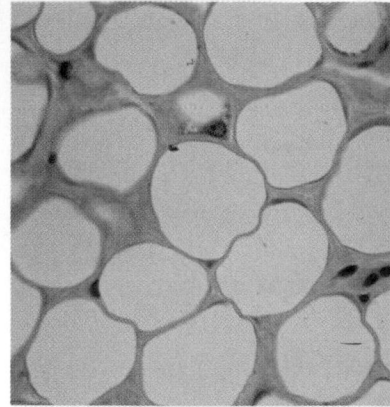
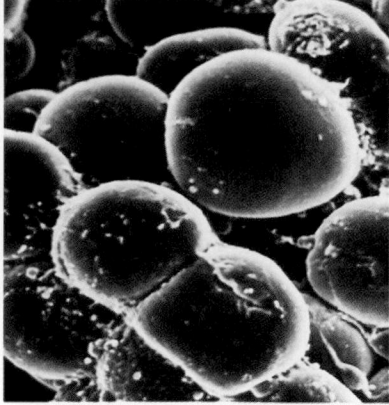

other disciplines, researchers build upon the historical record and follow logical paths to reach new conclusions about their field of expertise.

Science has some unique features that make it different from other fields of study, however. One of those features is a sequence of logical steps to generate new ideas, answer questions, and draw conclusions. Although the exact sequence of these steps can vary depending on the nature of a question, the characteristic steps in a scientific inquiry are commonly called the scientific method.

The **scientific method** involves making predictions, designing an experiment (or series of observations) to test those predictions, making careful observations of that experiment, and interpreting those observations. Often, the results of one experiment form the basis for predicting the results of the next experiment.

As you read earlier in this chapter, spontaneous generation was at one time an accepted scientific idea. Now the principle of biogenesis is used to explain life. But how did scientists first support biogenesis? They used the scientific method.

Observations The process of science begins with making careful observations. Sometimes, making observations requires little more than

carefully looking at an object. But there is much more to life than can be observed with the unaided human eye.

Many of the tools used by scientists enable them to observe things that cannot otherwise be seen. The progress of modern science is therefore tied directly to the invention of tools that help scientists observe. For example, the invention of the microscope hundreds of years ago enabled scientists to learn about the cellular nature of life. Medical equipment allows doctors to observe changes within a patient's body. A Geiger counter, which measures radiation, enables scientists to detect invisible radioactivity.

Observations are often confused with conclusions. Conclusions are assumptions that are based on observations. What would you think, for example, if you observed a pot of boiling water? Would you conclude that the water temperature was 100°C? Many people would probably draw this conclusion. However, you cannot know the temperature of the water, without measuring it. Factors such as air pressure and dissolved substances can result in water boiling at different temperatures. The water could, in fact, be 105°C or 95°C. How might you accurately determine the water temperature? **1**

20   *Chapter 1 The Study of Life*

MEETING DIVERSE NEEDS

LEP Have LEP students work with a partner to describe, act out, or illustrate in a drawing the different steps that make up the scientific method. Challenge students to identify how they have used each step to solve problems in the past. Suggest students record the steps in their notebooks in both English and their native language.

In science, it is very important to distinguish between observations and conclusions. As you conduct experiments, make sure you record your observations carefully. Consider your observations thoughtfully before drawing conclusions.

Hypotheses Observations inspire curiosity, which can then lead to a hypothesis. A **hypothesis** is a possible explanation for an event or set of observations. Hypotheses are sometimes confused with the observations themselves. Suppose, for example, that you observed a scene like the one shown in *Figure 1.20*. You might think that hyenas kill zebras. This explanation of an animal's behavior is a hypothesis. It proposes an explanation for your observations. Spontaneous generation, the explanation that living things come from nonliving things, was a hypothesis that was used to explain the birth of new organisms.

Often scientists formulate several hypotheses before designing an experiment. The zebra below, for example, may have been killed by other animals, such as lions. The hyenas may be scavengers. Before you begin any

experiment, consider many different possible hypotheses.

Although hypotheses are not facts, they are not simply wild guesses either. Scientific hypotheses are based on investigating scientists' observations, including the results of experiments. A hypothesis serves as a prediction about the outcome of an experiment.

Experiments To test a hypothesis, a scientist must design an experiment that focuses directly on the problem being investigated. The hypothesis must be clearly stated at the beginning of the experiment. The results of the experiment may or may not support the hypothesis.

All experiments have variables. A **variable** is a factor that can change in an experiment. Temperature, length of time, size, and chemical composition are possible variables with which you may be familiar. Scientific experiments are frequently designed so that only one variable is tested in each experiment. The variable being tested is called the experimental variable.

Most scientific experiments are designed to consider only one experimental variable. To add certainty to the cause-and-effect

FIGURE 1.20

How would you explain the scene shown here? What other information would you need to support any hypothesis you make? ❷

Clarify Misconceptions

Students often think that there is only one method for solving scientific problems. Emphasize that scientists do not always test the validity of a hypothesis by conducting a controlled experiment in the laboratory. To verify a hypothesis, a scientist may conduct field work to observe organisms in their natural environments, conduct a survey, or collect and analyze data from other experiments.

Class Activity

TEAM WORK

Have each student write down three topics related to biology that he or she would like to research. Review students' lists. Then have students with similar topics form groups to discuss how they would investigate the topic. Have groups pursue their topics, write a report, and share their research with the class. Point out to students that scientists often work in the same cooperative way.

❶ By measuring the water temperature with a thermometer.

❷ Hyenas kill zebras. To support this hypothesis, you would need to know if hyenas have body structures capable of killing a large animal, if they are predators or scavengers, and if they are carnivorous.

 Interactive Biological Simulations

Scientific Method After selecting one of three species of fishes, students use control and experimental tanks to determine the optimal tank conditions for that fish.

Use the Visual

Have students study Figure 1.21 which shows Pasteur's experiment on spontaneous generation. Ask:

- **What did Pasteur control in his experiment?** (Temperature, light, amount and type of broth)
- **What variable was tested in Pasteur's experiment?** (Exposure to dust from the air)
- **How did Pasteur control exposure of the broth to dust from the air?** (A curved neck prevented dust from reaching the broth; a straight neck allowed the dust to fall into the broth.)
- **Why is the flask with the curved neck called the control setup?** (The curved neck eliminates the dust.)

Build Writing Skills

Have students select a product teenagers use daily, such as shampoos, soap, juices, or snack bars. Ask them to explain in writing how they would use the scientific method to determine how to tell the difference among selected brands of the same product.

Everyday Biology

Pasteurization heats milk at temperatures high enough to kill bacteria but not high enough to harm the milk. Today, because fewer cows carry infectious diseases, the process is mainly used to make milk products less perishable. Ask students to compare the dates on various milk products. Have them report which products keep the longest and ask them to hypothesize why some milk products keep longer than others.

FIGURE 1.21

Pasteur's Scientific Experiment

How does Pasteur's experiment demonstrate the scientific method? **❶**

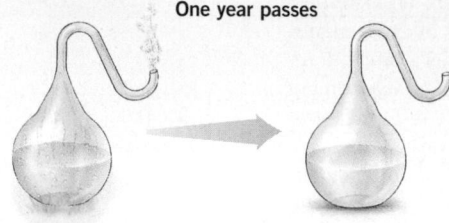

Control setup — One year passes

Experimental setup — One day passes

1 The broth is heated. The curved neck of the flask prevented dust from entering the broth.

2 After one year, Pasteur observed the broth again and there were still no bacteria!

1 The straight neck allowed dust from the air to settle in the broth. All other variables were kept constant.

2 After one day, the broth was cloudy. When Pasteur observed a sample under the microscope, he found bacteria.

EVERYDAY BIOLOGY

Pasteur's Process

You may have seen the word "pasteurized" on milk cartons. It means that the milk was heated to a high temperature to kill disease-causing microorganisms. This process is named for Louis Pasteur.

relationship between the experimental variable and the observed results, all other variables must be controlled. In a **control setup,** all factors remain the same during the experiment, except for the change in the experimental variable.

In 1862 the French chemist Louis Pasteur performed an experiment that helped to support biogenesis. Although Redi and others had disproved spontaneous generation in various ways, the scientific steps used by Pasteur finally convinced most of the remaining skeptics. The experiment still serves as an elegant model of scientific experimentation.

Louis Pasteur was one of many scientists who challenged the idea of spontaneous generation. Prior to Pasteur's discovery that microorganisms cause disease, doctors did not understand why surgical patients died of infection so often. His discovery of this relationship, called the germ theory, changed modern medicine forever.

Supporters of spontaneous generation observed that microorganisms could grow in broth where there had previously been no life. They claimed that life arose from an "active principle" that was present in the broth.

After repeated observations of microorganisms, Pasteur hypothesized that the bacteria that grew in broth were carried by dust particles falling from the air, and that the bacteria did not arise spontaneously from broth. To test his hypothesis, Pasteur designed a controlled experiment.

He set up two different flasks—one with a curved neck and the other with a straight neck. The variable Pasteur chose to isolate in this experiment was the exposure to dust from the air. He exposed each flask to dust in the air. However, dust that entered the flask with the curved neck remained in the neck and did not reach the broth.

In order to isolate this variable, Pasteur had to control the other variables, such as temperature, light, and the amount of broth. To ensure that both flasks were free of contaminants, Pasteur boiled the broth in both flasks. With the experimental variable isolated, Pasteur conducted

❶ He conducted a controlled experiment to test a hypothesis. In his experiment, both setups were exactly alike except dust could not reach the broth in the control setup.

his experiment. *Figure 1.21* shows Pasteur's results.

When Pasteur observed the results of his experiment, he found bacteria in the flask with a straight neck, but no bacteria in the flask with the curved neck. This observation supported the hypothesis that exposure to dust resulted in the appearance of bacteria.

Theory A hypothesis that is supported by many experiments done over a period of time is called a **theory**. Like hypotheses, theories can be confused with facts. Theories are not facts. Theories are probable explanations for events that are supported by a wide range of evidence.

There are many theories that explain the characteristics of living things. Biogenesis is a theory. It is supported by experiments performed by Redi, Pasteur, and other scientists. Other scientific theories you will learn about in this textbook include the cell theory, the theory of evolution, and the germ theory.

It might surprise you to learn that one of the main characteristics of science is uncertainty. Theories are constantly challenged and refined as new discoveries are made. Throughout this course, you will read about and participate in experiments that test theories. You will also learn more about current debates among scientists and about refinements or changes to theories. We encourage you to thoughtfully question theories, propose hypotheses, and analyze the information presented in this textbook. Questioning, hypothesizing, and analyzing are important scientific skills.

ISSUES IN BIOLOGY

Science and society

For a subject to be studied scientifically, one must be able to observe and test it. Questions about ethics and values cannot be tested scientifically. Scientists cannot construct experiments to answer such questions.

All people, including scientists, must carefully consider the way they use the products of science. The products of science can be of great benefit to humans and to the environment. However, science can also deliver products that have the potential to cause harm. Often, the question of what to do with scientific discoveries must be considered along with the ethics and values of society. The question of how a particular scientific breakthrough can be used is usually determined by scientists. How it is actually used depends, at least in part, on the values of society.

Science and scientists If experimental results, or data, support a hypothesis, scientists can use the results to make further hypotheses. Two very important features of science relate to experimental results.

First, experimental results must be made public along with the methods

LAB ZONE — Think About It! — bioSURF

Identifying Experimental Controls and Variables

While conducting his experiment on spontaneous generation, Redi was careful to have only one experimental variable and to control all other factors that might change during the course of the experiment. Learn how to evaluate variable and control conditions by analyzing Redi's experiment.

Analyzing the Experiment

1 Study the setups in Redi's experiment shown in Figure 1.2 on page 5. What is the variable in Redi's experiment? How are the conditions of the experiment altered using this variable?

2 What factors were the same in both the experimental setup and the control setup? That is, what were the controlled variables in the experiment?

3 How could the experiment be altered to test a new variable?

LAB ZONE — Think About It!

Identifying Experimental Controls and Variables

Analyzing the Experiment

1 The variable studied is the accessibility of flies to the meat. Jars were left open to flies or covered with a cloth.

2 Both jars were the same size, made of the same material, allowed the entry of ether, and contained the same type and portion of meat. The jars were exposed to the same conditions of light and temperature.

3 Substances other than meat could be used.

Discuss

Hold a class discussion about the relationship among facts, hypotheses, and theories. Help students recognize that facts are used to support hypotheses and theories. To help students understand the differences among the terms emphasize that facts do not change over time; a hypothesis or a theory may change as new information becomes available.

STS

Have students bring in newspaper or magazine articles relating to a controversial issue in science. Discuss the different issues and have students select one to explore further. Have students discuss both sides of this issue in small groups and debate the issue as a class.

New scientific discoveries happen frequently, and important research is going on all the time. Search your local newspaper and other area publications for stories about science. How is science affecting your community right now? What science stories are of interest nationally?

IN THE COMMUNITY
Science in the News

Consider how the scientific method is applied in the studies or experiments you read about. You may also want to check recent issues of science publications. For more information about finding science in your community, refer to http://basis_of_life.biosurf.com

FIGURE 1.22
A scientist points to some fur caught in the bark of a damaged tree—presumably from an Alaskan brown bear. How might such observations about the environment influence public policy? ❶

by which the experiments were conducted. This process is called peer review. Scientists provide all important experimental data to others working in their field so that others can analyze the results. After a panel of peers agrees that the experiments were sound, the work can be published and made available to other scientists and to the general public.

Science that is examined in this rigorous way is often published in scientific journals. Currently there are more than ten thousand peer-reviewed journals in the field of biology alone! The experiments that you will conduct as student-scientists will follow a similar path, as the data are reviewed by your teacher and fellow students.

The second important aspect of science is that the results of experiments must be repeatable. Once the experimental results are published, other labs will try the same experiments in order to get the same results. If the same results can be achieved by other scientists, the original work can be considered a legitimate contribution to the field of science.

Sometimes scientists must be patient. Experiments may take a long time to conduct, and experimental results may not reach a target audience for a long time. The most important factor is the honesty of the science and the validity of the results. But caution is necessary because the information will become part of the scientific foundation upon which new knowledge will be built. When he commented on the historical nature of experimental science, Sir Isaac Newton (1642–1727), the great English mathematician and inventor of calculus, stated eloquently, "We see farther because we can stand on the shoulders of giants."

Science and change Another feature of science is its changeable nature. Scientists do not consider their ideas to be absolute facts. One cannot accept scientific theory on faith. Scientists must always be ready to change or reject an idea if new evidence disproves it.

New techniques and tools often provide such evidence. Innovative technology may open up new branches of science. For example, the field of genetic engineering grew

24 *Chapter 1 The Study of Life*

❶ A picture of how damage to the environment actually affects an organism can cause people to change environmental policy.

FIGURE 1.23
You do not have to be a scientist to make an impact on the living world. The volunteers working to save these beached pilot whales come from many different professions.

from the development of techniques to alter the traits of bacteria.

Sometimes the needs of society change the direction that scientific progress takes. For example, many significant scientific breakthroughs resulted from our exploration of space. On the other hand, scientific developments can change the direction that society takes. Can you think of examples of scientific developments that have affected your life?

❷ **Science and public policy** Data collected by scientists are often used to make public policy. Many of the laws and regulations in our society are the direct result of scientific evidence collected in response to a problem. Laws about environmental issues, food and drug safety, and wildlife management are most often based on biological data collected by experimentation.

Most science is funded by grants from public agencies such as the National Science Foundation. These agencies are supported by tax dollars from citizens like your family members.

Therefore, all citizens have a voice and a contributing role in the progress of science.

Science cannot answer all of the questions of society or address all of the conditions of planet Earth, however. Remember that the scientific method requires a question that can be approached experimentally. The unknowns, or variables, must be clearly identifiable, and the results repeatable. Some of the important questions that stir the human soul may never be answered by science.

CHECKPOINT 1.3

1. Describe the scientific method. *→ flowchart*
2. How can scientific experiments affect society?
3. Critical Thinking Design and describe an experiment to test whether temperature alone can affect the growth rate of a plant. *→ Do Gizmo or Scientific Method*

Build on What You Know

4. How are politicians and other non-scientists involved in protecting fragile environments?

What is the scientific method?

Use the Visual

Refer students to Figure 1.23. Point out that this volunteer group is working to return the animal to its natural habitat. Some volunteer groups organize to preserve the habitats of species threatened with extinction.

❸ ASSESS

Evaluate Understanding

To assess students' understanding of doing biology, ask:

- **What are some unique features of the field of science?** (A sequence of logical steps that comprise the scientific method)
- **What is the difference between an observation and an inference?** (An observation can be made directly by the senses; an inference is an assumption.)
- **How many variables are tested during an experiment?** (An experiment must test only one variable.)

Reteach

As a class, create a diagram that shows some possible sequences of steps involved in solving a scientific problem. As the sequences are recorded and discussed, be sure to review the meanings of the following terms: *observation, hypothesis, theory, experiment, variable, control setup,* and *scientific method.*

❷ Answers may include easily available transportation, entertainment and communication links with the rest of the world, a healthy diet, and advances in health care.

CHECKPOINT 1.3

1. The scientific method is a process that involves making predictions, designing and conducting experiments, observing, and interpreting those observations.
2. Answers may include medical advances, increased environmental awareness, and changes in the law.
3. Designing an experiment Answers should include isolation of a single variable, temperature, and a description of how and when observations will be made.
4. Answers may include producing newspaper and television reports, enacting new laws, participating in recycling efforts, and creating of parks.

Designing a Scientific Experiment

SAFETY FIRST!

Require students to get approval for their experimental designs and make them aware of any potential hazard and precautions.

Lab Prep and Planning

Prepare a place for students to keep their plants for long-term observations. Students can work in groups to reduce the number of plants needed.

Lab Tips

Check to make sure that students have included a control in their experimental designs. Remind students to test only one variable at a time.

Hypothesis Help

Hypotheses will vary according to the variable students select. Guide students to develop a reasonable hypothesis.

Lab Extension

Directed

Have students design an experiment to find out if tomato seeds germinate best in acidic, neutral, or basic soil. Check to make sure students include a control in their experiment.

 **LAB ZONE Investigate It!**

Designing a Scientific Experiment

WHAT YOU WILL DO Design and carry out a scientific experiment

SKILLS YOU WILL USE Estimating, predicting, observing, recording data

WHAT YOU WILL NEED Living plants or seeds, other materials and measuring instruments

Propose a Hypothesis

You know that plants need water and light for healthy growth. What other factors or substances might affect a plant's growth? Soil conditions? Fertilizer or nutrients? Music or human conversation? Choose a variable, then propose a hypothesis about how the presence and absence of that factor affects the growth or survival of a plant.

Conduct Your Experiment

1 Outline the steps of your experiment. Identify the variable and the controls in your experiment. (Remember, there should be only one experimental variable—the presence or absence of the factor you are testing.)

2 Select a time period for your experiment.

3 Specify the data that you will observe in the experimental and control setups. Choose data that can be accurately measured and compared.

4 Conduct your experiment and record your observations.

Analyze Your Data

1 Compare the measured data from the experimental and control plants.

2 Organize your data into a table.

3 Make a graph to display your results.

Draw Conclusions

Did the presence of your experimental variable make a difference in the growth of the experimental and control plants? Was the effect more or less than you had proposed?

Design a Related Experiment

Design an experiment that would give information on another factor that might affect plant growth.

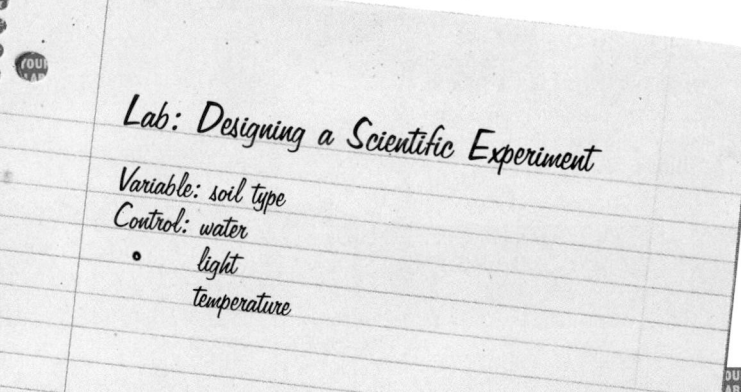

Lab: Designing a Scientific Experiment

Variable: soil type
Control: water
- light
  temperature

Analyze Your Data

1-3 Tables and graphs should show data from both experimental and control plants. Check tables and graphs for clarity and format.

Draw Conclusions

Answers will vary depending on the variable chosen and the experimental procedure.

Chapter 1 Review

 **THE BIG IDEA!**
1.1–1.2 Living things share many characteristics, including organization and adaptation.
1.3 Scientists use careful observation and controlled experiments to study the natural world.

Sum It Up
Use the following summary to review the main concepts in this chapter.

1.1 Similarities Among Living Things

- Redi's experiments in 1668 disproved spontaneous generation, showing that organisms arise only from other organisms.
- Although some nonliving things share some of the characteristics of living things, none displays the entire set of characteristics.
- The characteristics of living things are organization into cells; processes that are fueled by energy; growth and development; reproduction; response and adaptation.
- There are many levels of organization in the biosphere: Atoms make up molecules, which are the components of cells. Cells can be organized into tissues, and tissues into organs with specific functions. The organ systems make up an organism. Organisms form populations, and populations form communities within an ecosystem.

1.2 Adaptation and Interdependence

- Fossils of extinct species show that life has changed over time. Darwin explained how competition for resources could account for the evolution of species.
- Organisms are connected to one another and to the environment through complex webs of relationships. Relationships between organisms can be one-sided or beneficial to both partners.

- Symbiotic relationships include mutualism, where both partners benefit; commensalism, where one partner benefits without harming the other; and parasitism, where one partner benefits and the other is harmed.
- Humans are dependent on other organisms for food, medicine, clothing, fuel, and shelter.

1.3 Doing the Science of Biology

- Scientists make careful observations, develop hypotheses based on observations, and design experiments to test hypotheses.
- Scientists distinguish between observations and any conclusions that may be based on observations.
- To test hypotheses, scientists design experiments in which they control all variables except the one being tested.
- Scientific theories are challenged and refined as scientists submit their data for peer review. Scientific results must be repeatable.
- Results of scientific experiments are made public. Often public policy is based on scientific data. Scientific research is often funded by public agencies.

Use Terms and Concepts

Use each of the following words or terms in a complete sentence.
If you need to review a meaning, turn to the page indicated.

biosphere (p. 4)	cell (p. 6)	scientific method (p. 20)
organisms (p. 4)	tissues (p. 11)	hypothesis (p. 21)
spontaneous generation (p. 4)	organs (p. 11)	variable (p. 21)
	predator (p. 14)	control setup (p. 22)
biogenesis (p. 5)	prey (p. 14)	theory (p. 23)

Chapter 1 The Study of Life **27**

Review the Big Ideas

Before students begin the Chapter review, you may wish to discuss main concepts from the Big Ideas in Chapter 1. Point out that living things can be identified by their common characteristics, such as their organization and adaptations to their environments. In addition, scientists have discovered that living things share a common history. What is known about living things is the result of careful observations and controlled experiments, which scientists use to study the natural world.

Answers

1. cell
2. scientific method
3. organ
4. biosphere
5. prey
6. variable
7. organisms
8. False; biogenesis
9. False; hypothesis
10. True
11. False; all variables except the one being tested
12. True
13. True
14. Fossils showed that species could change over time and even become extinct.
15. An ecosystem includes non-living factors in addition to populations of organisms.
16. Darwin argued that competition among species for resources caused species to adapt.
17. Biotechnology is the use of organisms to produce things that people need. Traditionally, bacteria is used to turn milk into cheese. Modern techniques include genetic engineering.
18. Symbiosis is a collective term describing relationships in which different species of organisms depend on each other. Mutualism: both organisms benefit; commensalism: one benefits, one does not; parasitism: one benefits, one is harmed
19. People live in a biological environment in which they use animals for food, recreation and work, and many other organisms for food, shelter, and medicine.
20. A control setup ensures that the results of an experiment are due to the single variable being tested.
21. A theory is a hypothesis

Use Your Word Power

COMPLETION Write the word or phrase that best completes each statement.

1. The smallest unit of life that displays all the characteristics of life is the _____ .

2. The process that involves designing experiments to test hypotheses is called the _____ .

3. A(n) _____ contains several different types of tissues that function together.

4. The _____ is that part of Earth in which life exists.

5. The size of the _____ population can affect the size of a predator population.

6. Any factor that can change during an experiment is called a(n) _____ .

7. Bacteria, butterflies, grasses, and bears are all examples of living things, or _____ .

TRUE-FALSE Write true if the statement is true. If the statement is false, replace the underlined word(s) to make the statement true.

8. The process by which organisms arise from other organisms is called <u>spontaneous generation</u>.

9. A possible explanation for a set of observations is a <u>theory</u>.

10. All the cells in a <u>tissue</u> work together to perform a specific function.

11. In a control setup, <u>all</u> variables must be controlled.

12. In the relationship between lynxes and hares, the lynx is the <u>predator</u>.

13. Biogenesis is a <u>theory</u> about the origin of new organisms.

Show What You Know

14. How did the discovery of fossils change scientific thinking about species?

15. How do an ecosystem and a community differ?

16. What was Darwin's explanation for the evolution of species?

17. What is biotechnology? Give a traditional and a modern example of biotechnology.

18. What is symbiosis? Name and describe the three types of symbiosis.

19. Describe four ways in which your daily activities are affected by biology.

20. What is the advantage of using a control setup?

21. What is the relationship between a hypothesis and a theory?

22. **Make a Concept Map** Complete the concept map below by adding the following terms: adaptation, atom, cell, community, ecosystem, energy, development, growth, individual, molecule, organ, organization, organ system, population, reproduction, response, tissue.

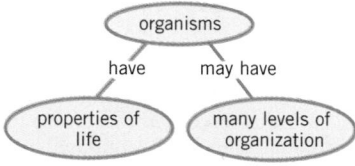

For help in making concept maps, see Appendix E.

Take It Further

23. **Applying Concepts** Pharmaceutical companies often test new medicines by giving pills with the medicine to one group and pills without the medicine to a second group. Neither the doctors nor the patients know which pills they are using. Identify the variables and controls in this procedure. What is the advantage of this procedure? Would the experiment work as well if the second group took no pills? Explain.

24. **Developing a Hypothesis** In 1847 doctors in Vienna ridiculed Ignaz Semmelweis when he urged them to wash their hands with germ-killing solution before examining patients. In 1865 Joseph Lister was successful in this regard. What might have made the difference?

supported by considerable evidence collected over a long period of study.

22. Concept maps should show the following: <u>organisms</u> have <u>properties of life</u>, which are <u>energy</u>, <u>growth and development</u>, <u>reproduction</u>, <u>response and adaptation</u>; <u>organisms</u> may have <u>many levels</u> of <u>organization</u>, beginning with <u>cells</u>, which are made of <u>atoms</u> and <u>molecules</u>, (<u>cells</u>) make up <u>tissues</u>, which make up <u>organs</u>, which make up <u>organ systems</u>, which make up <u>individuals</u>, which make up a <u>population</u>, <u>populations</u> make up a <u>community</u>, and <u>communities</u> make up an <u>ecosystem</u>.

23. The second group is a control group. Its members need to take pills so that all factors in the experiment except the

25. Designing an Experiment Plan an experiment to find out the effects of preservatives on bread. What variable will you be testing? What variables will you need to control? Make a hypothesis about your experimental results.

26. Interpreting a Graph The graph shows eight countries ranked by land area and population. What inferences can you make about their population densities? What information would enable you to calculate their population densities exactly?

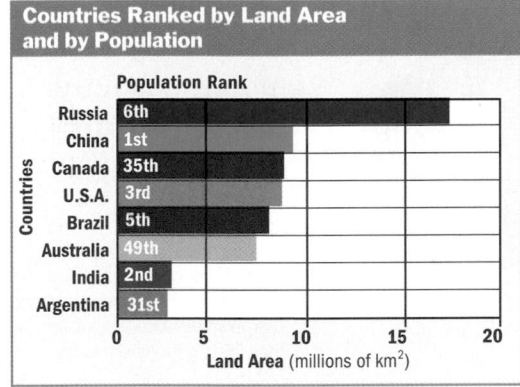

Countries Ranked by Land Area and by Population

Countries	Population Rank	Land Area (millions of km²)
Russia	6th	
China	1st	
Canada	35th	
U.S.A.	3rd	
Brazil	5th	
Australia	49th	
India	2nd	
Argentina	31st	

27. Analyzing Data In 1974 the federal government reduced speed limits on highways to 55 miles per hour (89 kilometers per hour) to conserve gasoline. Some people predicted that the lower speed limit would also save lives. Use the table to decide whether that prediction was accurate. What other variables might have affected fatality rates between 1960 and 1990?

Motor Vehicle Traffic Fatalities

Year	Registered Vehicles	Traffic Deaths	Fatality Rate*
1960	74,444,000	36,399	5.06
1965	91,673,000	47,089	5.30
1970	111,243,000	54,180	4.92
1975	137,915,000	44,525	3.36
1980	161,491,000	51,059	3.35
1985	177,098,000	43,825	2.47
1990	193,057,000	44,599	2.08

*Deaths per 100 million vehicle miles

Consider the Issues

28. Publish or Perish Sometimes the first person to make a scientific discovery does not get the credit for the discovery. Credit is usually given to the first person to publish the new findings. How does science benefit from this practice? What problems might arise if researchers rush to get their work into print?

Make New Connections

29. Biology and Art Recalling what you have learned about the properties of life and its levels of organization, draw or photograph some organisms living in your area. Make an exhibit of your work, adding captions to explain how each image represents a property or level.

30. Biology and History Research and report on what the world was like in the late 1600s and early 1700s, when Redi and Pasteur were conducting their experiments. What was medicine in Europe like? What was the United States like at that time in history?

31. Biology and Technology Many experiments require measurements of time and temperature. Trace the development of accurate devices for measuring these variables.

FAST-FORWARD TO CHAPTER 2

All life processes depend on interactions between molecules. In Chapter 2, you will learn about chemical reactions and the kinds of molecules that are essential for life.

experimental variable are identical. Since the doctors and patients do not know which patients are actually taking the drug, they are prevented from assessing the results based on their expectations.

24. Knowing about Pasteur's work done in 1862 and his discovery of the relationship between microorganisms and

disease probably encouraged the practice of more sterile medical procedures.

25. The presence of preservatives; students would need to use bread that had similar ingredients other than the preservatives. The bread samples would need to be exposed to the air at room temperature. In a warm room, the bread without preservatives will likely show signs

of mold within a few days.

26. Students can make some qualitative conclusions, such as: Population density in China is greater than in Russia. Population density in India is probably higher than in most countries. If students had the actual population counts and inhabitable area, they could calculate exact densities.

27. The prediction was correct. The number of highway deaths peaked in 1970 despite the continued increase in the number of registered vehicles. The use of seat belts, regulations requiring motorcycle helmets, and enforcement of drunk driving laws are also possible factors.

28. The practice encourages the timely dissemination of data for scrutiny by other scientists. Some researchers may rush their work and, on rare occasions, falsify data to beat a competitor into print.

29. Encourage students to recognize that many images of organisms may suggest more than one property of life or level of organization.

30. Students should focus on living conditions, hygiene, and medical practices, as well as techniques in scientific experimentation.

31. First thermometer: Galileo, 1592; first closed thermometer: Ferdinand II de Medici, 1654; mercury thermometer: Fahrenheit, 1714; Celsius scale, 1742. Timepieces trace back to the pendulum clock, which was accurate to the nearest minute (Huygens, 1656) to the first atomic clock based on molecular vibration (Harold Lyons, 1949).

Unit Overview

Living things differ in their structures and activities, but they all have certain features in common. The universal characteristics of the cell, including chemistry, physical structure, metabolism, and reproduction are explored in this unit. A clear understanding of the processes and challenges common to all living things form a strong foundation for the study of biology.

Unit Objectives

- Describe the categories of biochemicals common to all living things
- Explain the cell theory and describe several cellular functions
- Diagram the flow of energy through cells, organisms, and the biosphere

Connect the Units

This unit introduces basic concepts necessary for understanding universal life processes. If you choose to focus on environmental issues, you may precede this unit with Unit 9: *Organisms and the Environment*, and follow this unit with Unit 3: *Change and Diversity*. If you prefer a human-based curriculum, you may choose to proceed directly to Unit 8: *Human Biology* after completing this unit.

UNIT 1
The Basis of Life

Which of these statements about the world around us and inside us are fact, and which are fiction?

Hit *or* Myth?

If birds stored energy as **carbohydrates** instead of **fat,** they would weigh so much that they couldn't fly.

(Fact. Fat stores energy in a highly concentrated form that is also very light—it contains more than twice as much energy per gram as carbohydrates do.)

The hydra, an organism the size of a pencil point, has fewer **chromosomes** than an alligator.

(Fiction. Both organisms have 32 chromosomes, structures that contain genetic material. The size of an organism has no bearing on chromosome number. For example, one type of fern has 1010 chromosomes.)

Celery has **zero** calories.

(Fiction. Celery has 18 Calories per 100-gram serving. However, this is such a small number that you may burn more calories chewing the crunchy vegetable than it actually contains.)

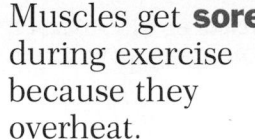

DAY 1

1

DAY 2

10,000,000,
000,000,000,
000,000,000,
000,000,000,
000,000,000

Bacteria reproduce so rapidly that the number of bacteria produced in just two days **surpasses** the number of humans that have ever lived.

(Fact. In the right environment some types of bacteria reproduce—by dividing—every 20 minutes.)

Muscles get **sore** during exercise because they overheat.

(Fiction. Lactic acid makes muscles sore. This waste product is created when your muscles generate energy during strenuous exercise, such as running a long distance.)

Spider silk is **stronger** than steel.

(Fact. A strand of a spider web, which is made of protein, is stronger than a piece of steel of the same thickness.)

There are more **cells in your body** than there are stars in the Milky Way.

(Fact. There are about 50 trillion cells in an adult human, which is at least 100 times more than the number of stars in our galaxy.)

Unit 1 The Basis of Life   **31**

Hit *or* Myth?

Use It

Review each of the statements with the class. Ask students to share their prior knowledge and misconceptions on each topic. Ask them to consider which sources of information on these topics are generally reliable and which may not be. Have students preview the Table of Contents for this unit and correlate text sections with information related to the concepts in the Hit or Myth statements.

Link It

Chapter 2 links the concepts of biochemicals and stored energy (spider web, pelican, celery, muscles) to living things. Further information can be found in Chapters 23, 29, and 30. Chapter 3 links the concept of cells (hand) to organisms. Further information can be found in Chapter 6. Chapter 5 links the concept of cellular reproduction (bacteria, hydra) to the growth and reproduction of organisms. Further information can be found in Chapters 14 and 22.

Expand It

Other adaptations that reduce the weight of modern birds include hollow bones and the lack of teeth. *Archaeopteryx*, perhaps the earliest known fossil that is clearly a bird, was too heavy to fly. Without modern weight-reducing adaptations, it could probably only glide down from trees.

Spider silk is not only strong, but also extremely elastic. It is able to expand to four times its length.

PLANNING GUIDE

Section	Student Activities/Features	Teacher's Resource Package
2.1 Chemicals in Organisms **Objectives** ■ Identify the four groups of substances that make up most living things ■ Compare the functions of each of those four groups	**Lab Zone Discover It!** *Observing a Chemical Reaction,* p. 33	**Unit 1 Review Module** ■ Section Review 2.1 ■ Enrichment Topic 2-1 **Consumer Applications** 2-1
2.2 Basics of Chemistry **Objectives** ■ Distinguish elements from compounds ■ Describe how atoms form different chemical bonds	**Lab Zone Think About It!** *Examining Isotopes,* p. 39 **Everyday Biology** *Tough Spots,* p. 40	**Unit 1 Review Module** ■ Section Review 2.2 ■ Interpreting Graphics 2 ■ Enrichment Topic 2-2 **Issues and Decision Making** 2-1 **Interpreting and Developing Graphics** 4, 5, 6
2.3 Chemicals at Work **Objectives** ■ Explain what happens during a chemical reaction ■ Show how an enzyme functions	**Lab Zone Do It!** *What Does a Chemical Reaction Look Like?* p. 43 **Everyday Biology** *Tender Wounds,* p. 44 **Lab Zone Investigate It!** *Analyzing a Chemical Reaction,* p. 45	**Unit 1 Review Module** ■ Section Review 2.3 ■ Activity Recordsheets 2-1 and 2-2 ■ Critical Thinking Exercise 2 **Laboratory Manual** ■ Lab 2: "Enzymes: Catalysts of Life" ■ Lab 3: "Enzymes: Reaction Rates"
2.4 Chemistry in Life Processes **Objectives** ■ Describe different life processes ■ Explain that life processes are based on chemical reactions		**Unit 1 Review Module** ■ Section Review 2.4
2.5 Water and Solutions **Objectives** ■ Identify the properties of water that support life ■ Distinguish between acids and bases	**In the Community** *Where Does Your Water Come From?* p. 50 **Lab Zone Do It!** *What Is the pH of Common Foods?* p. 51 **STS: Environmental Awareness,** *When It Rains Acid,* p. 52	**Unit 1 Review Module** ■ Section Review 2.5 ■ Activity Recordsheet 2-3 ■ Enrichment Topic 2-3 ■ Vocabulary Review 2 ■ Chapter 2 Tests **Laboratory Manual,** Lab 4: "Measuring pH" **Spanish Reviews** Chapter 2

Technology Resources

Internet Connections

Within this chapter, you will see the (**bioSURF**) logo. If you and your students have access to the Internet, the following URL address will provide various Internet connections that are related to topics and features presented in this chapter:

http://basis_of_life.biosurf.com

You can also find relevant chapter material at **The Biology Place** address:

http://www.biology.com

CD-ROMs

Biología: la telaraña de la vida,
   (Spanish Student Edition) Chapter 2
Teacher's Resource Planner, Chapter 2
   Supplements
TestWorks CD-ROM
- Chapter 2 Tests

Videodiscs

Animated Biological Concepts Videodiscs
- Enzymatic Reactions
- Atomic Structure
- Energy Levels and Ionic Bonding
- Covalent Bonding

Overhead Transparencies

- Periodic Table, #3
- Chemical Bonding, #4
- Enzyme Reactions, #5

Videotapes

Biology Alive! Video Series
Rewind: The Web of Life Reteach Videos

Planning for Activities

STUDENT EDITION
Lab Zone
Discover It! p. 33
- small plastic or glass container
- dark iced tea
- lemon

Lab Zone
Think About It! p. 39
- periodic table on pages 944–945

Lab Zone Do It! p. 43
- baking soda
- glass jars
- vinegar

Lab Zone
Investigate It! p. 45
- baby food jars with lids
- tape
- permanent marker
- metric balance
- meat tenderizer
- rotini pasta
- beef suet
- ham

Lab Zone Do It! p. 51
- oranges
- apples
- potatoes
- bananas
- milk
- paper towels
- pH paper
- knife

TEACHER'S EDITION
Quick Activity, p. 34
Sources of carbohydrates
- photos of foods rich in carbohydrates

Teacher Demo, p. 35
Butter
- cream
- bowl
- wooden spoon or paddle

Teacher Demo, p. 40
Electrical charges
- comb
- bits of paper

Teacher Demo, p. 46
Observing pond microorganisms
- microprojector
- slides
- pond water

Class Activity, p. 47
Homeostasis
- thermometer for humans

Teacher Demo, p. 50
Saltwater is a solution
- saltwater solution
- beaker
- hot plate

Class Activity, p. 52
pH of rainwater or snow
- pH paper
- rainwater or snow
- container for rainwater or snow

Chapter Objectives

Students will learn the main concepts of this chapter as they complete the following objectives.

- Identify the four groups of substances that make up most living things
- Compare the functions of each of those four groups
- Distinguish elements from compounds
- Describe how atoms form different chemical bonds
- Explain what happens during a chemical reaction
- Show how an enzyme functions
- Describe different life processes
- Explain that life processes are based on chemical reactions

Key Words

2.1 *carbohydrates, lipids, proteins, nucleic acids*

2.2 *element, compound, organic compounds, ion, isotopes, chemical bonds*

2.3 *chemical reaction, enzyme*

2.4 *metabolism, homeostasis*

The Opening Story

Have students discuss how they think the story relates to the content of the chapter. Point out that honeybees are simple organisms with amazingly complex behavior. They are used as models throughout the chapter to explain how chemicals are manufactured, changed, and utilized in every phase of an organism's life.

---

bioSURF

You can find out more about the chemical processes of living things by exploring the following Internet address:
http://basis_of_life.biosurf.com

In this chapter . . .

FEATURES

Everyday Biology
- Tough Spots
- Tender Wounds

In the Community
Where Does Your Water Come From?

 Environmental Awareness
When It Rains Acid

LAB ZONES

Discover It!
- Observing a Chemical Reaction

Do It!
- What Does a Chemical Reaction Look Like?
- What Is the pH of Common Foods?

Think About It!
- Examining Isotopes

Investigate It!
- Analyzing a Chemical Reaction

A Bee's Eye View of the World

A beehive shelters many thousands of bees. Bees can be divided into groups. There are worker bees, drones, a queen bee, and developing bee larvae, seen here about to emerge and join the life of the colony. Each individual bee is a complex organism of many parts. The architecture of the hive is also made of smaller units. Honeycomb, which is made from beeswax, is formed into thousands of hexagonal building blocks, and sheets of honeycomb form the "walls" inside the hive.

You can compare the structural units of a beehive—hexagons—with the units of matter—atoms. Just as the individual hexagons together form the honeycomb, atoms link to one another to form larger units.

In this chapter you will learn more about the units of matter in living and nonliving things. Although all matter consists of atoms, different chemicals make up living and nonliving things. The chemical substances that are vital for all living things are carbohydrates, lipids, proteins, and nucleic acids. The honeybee colony is a good example of how these essential chemical substances are integrated into living systems.

LAB ZONE Discover It!

Observing a Chemical Reaction

You need *a small plastic or glass container of dark iced tea and a lemon cut into quarters*

1. Squeeze the juice from one lemon quarter into the iced tea. Record the result in your lab notebook.
2. Repeat step 1 until all the lemon quarters are used up.

What happened to the appearance of the tea? The tart taste of lemon comes from a chemical called citric acid, and the change in the tea results from a reaction between citric acid and the chemicals that give tea its brown color.

WRITE ABOUT IT!

In your science journal, list examples of possible chemical reactions that occur around you at home, school, or work every day. If you need ideas, think about how the lemon juice affected the tea in the activity above. What substances that are used in the kitchen or in the laundry have a similar effect?

PORTFOLIO PREVIEW

Students should be encouraged to add to their portfolios as they work through this chapter. In addition to the *Write About It* opportunity, the following sections are excellent opportunities for portfolio entries:

■ Section 2: *Basics of Chemistry*
■ Section 5: *Water and Solutions*

Opening Activities

bioSURF If you have access to the Internet in your classroom or school, you may wish to have students connect to the address shown on page 32. You may also want to have students conduct new searches for information using key words related to this chapter. For example, they could search for entries under atomic particles, covalent bonds, or pH and foods.

LAB ZONE Discover It!

Observing a Chemical Reaction   TEAM WORK

You may want students to perform this activity in class with a partner or as homework. Ask:

■ **How do you think the citric acid in the lemon will affect the tea?** (Make it taste sour)

WRITE ABOUT IT

Call on volunteers to give examples of chemical reactions in everyday life such as rusting, burning, and bleaching. Tell students to list other examples in their journals and if possible, to identify the cause of the reaction.

REWIND to Chapter 1
Briefly review concepts learned in Chapter 1, *The Study of Life*. Ask:

■ **How will learning about important concepts in chemistry help you better understand the connections among living and nonliving things?**

1 ENGAGE

Consider the Big Idea

Have students read The Big Idea! at the top of the page. Explain that this statement summarizes the relationship between chemistry and living things.

Use the Visual

Have students study the photograph that opens the section and then explain the meaning of the statement "you are what you eat." Point out that the bat and the flower are both living things made up of the same basic substances.

Check Prior Knowledge

To assess students' prior knowledge about chemicals in organisms, ask them to name foods in each of the following groups: carbohydrates (Pasta, bread, milk products, vegetables, and fruits); proteins (Meat, milk, and some vegetables); fatty foods or lipids (Oil, butter, and fat on meats).

Quick Activity

Display pictures of foods rich in carbohydrates and have students tell what the foods have in common. Ask:

- **What is the source of sugar, starch, or cellulose in these foods?** (Energy from the sun.)
- **How are carbohydrates important to living things?** (They provide energy.)

❶ Carbon, hydrogen, oxygen

2.1 Chemicals in Organisms

What you'll learn

IDEAS
- To identify the four groups of substances that make up most living things
- To compare the functions of each of those four groups

WORDS
carbohydrates, lipids, proteins, nucleic acids

You are what you eat
Does that mean this bat is really a flower? Of course not. But the bat and the flower are both made of the same basic substances. Although there is an almost endless variety of living things on Earth, most living things are made of four kinds of chemicals—carbohydrates, lipids, proteins, and nucleic acids.

CARBOHYDRATES

How sweet it is

The night before a big event many athletes "carbo-load"—they eat foods rich in carbohydrates. Why? Many carbohydrates provide a usable energy source. Your body breaks down carbohydrates and uses the energy in their chemical bonds to fuel the activities of life. **Carbohydrates** are a group of chemicals that include sugars, starches, and cellulose. Carbohydrates store energy and provide shape to organisms.

Sugars, such as those that make up the honey in *Figure 2.1*, are relatively small, simple carbohydrates. Simple sugars are the easiest chemicals for your body to break down. Have you ever had a sudden burst of energy after eating something sweet? Sweet foods usually contain sugars. Sugars commonly come in two forms: monosaccharides ("single sugars") and disaccharides ("double sugars").

Many monosaccharides and disaccharides can be linked together into more complex carbohydrates called polysaccharides ("many sugars"). Organisms form various complex carbohydrates for energy storage. Most plants store energy in a polysaccharide called starch. When you eat a potato, you are taking in the potato plant's stored starch. Animals store energy in a polysaccharide called glycogen, formed in muscles and the liver.

When athletes carbo-load before an event, they eat foods high in starches, which their bodies break down to simple sugars. Their liver and muscles convert the simple sugars into stored glycogen. The glycogen can be broken down into simple sugars when energy is needed.

FIGURE 2.1

Chemicals in a Beehive

Making honey
Honeybees gather nectar from plants and change it into honey. Both nectar and honey are made of carbohydrates.

Beeswax, a mixture of lipids
Honeybees produce beeswax, which they use to build the honeycomb.

STUDENT RESOURCES

From the Teacher's Resource Package, use:
- Section Review 2.1 and Enrichment Topic 2-1 from Unit 1 Review Module
- Consumer Applications 2-1

TECHNOLOGY RESOURCES

Relevant technology resources include:
- Spanish Student Edition CD-ROM
- Teacher's Resource Planner CD-ROM

Plants and animals use different carbohydrates to store energy. Most plants store energy in the form of starch. When you eat a potato, you are taking in some of the plant's stored starch. Animals store energy in a carbohydrate called glycogen. Glycogen is formed in muscles and in the liver.

Simple sugars can also be joined together to make structural carbohydrates, such as cellulose. You may not be familiar with the word *cellulose*, but cellulose is all around you—in desks, pencils, paper, and any other plant material you see. In fact, cellulose is one of the most abundant biological molecules on Earth.

LIPIDS

Greasy molecules store energy for organisms

Carbohydrates are used for some energy storage. When energy is to be stored for an even longer period of time, carbohydrates are converted into a different chemical—fat, a kind of lipid. **Lipids** are a group of chemicals that include fats, oils, waxes, phospholipids, and steroids. Beeswax, shown in *Figure 2.1*, is a mixture of lipids.

Pollen contains proteins
The pollen covering this bee comes from a flower.

Fats, oils, and waxes are the most common lipids. Fats and oils provide long-term energy storage. Fats also act as insulation by helping to keep animals such as whales and penguins warm. Waxes provide a different kind of protection. They repel water. Fruits and leaves produce waxes to keep water in and thus prevent the plants from drying out. Ducks and other water fowl produce waxes that make feathers more waterproof.

Phospholipids are important structural chemicals in cells. These molecules form the membrane, or protective covering, that surrounds cells. Phospholipids help control the substances that enter and leave cells.

The last group of lipids, steroids, serve structural and control functions in your body. Some steroids, such as cholesterol, are components of the membranes that surround your cells. Although cholesterol is essential to life functions, too much of it can be harmful to your body. You will learn about the control functions of the steroid hormones in Chapter 33.

PROTEINS

An amazing variety

More than one half of the dry weight of your body is made up of a third kind of chemical—protein. **Proteins** are large, complex molecules composed of many smaller molecules called amino acids. The pollen shown in *Figure 2.1* is the most important source of protein for bees. The pollen eaten by bees may contain as much as 28 percent protein.

FIGURE 2.2
Molecules of Life

Below are representations of three molecules of life. The color key identifies the elements present in the molecular structures. Which elements are part of all three molecules?

Carbohydrate

Lipid

Protein

Molecular Model Color Key	
■	Carbon
■	Hydrogen
■	Nitrogen
■	Oxygen
■	Phosphorus

Chapter 2 Chemical Basis of Life **35**

2 TEACH

Explain

Point out that plants are the source of carbohydrates. Starch and sugars stored in plants are used as food by living things. Ask:

- **In what forms are carbohydrates stored in plants?** (As starch, sugar, or cellulose)

Language Arts

Discuss the meaning of the prefixes "mono," "di," and "poly." Have students use a dictionary to find five words that start with each prefix and explain how the prefix changes the meaning of each word.

Teacher Demo

Explain that butter is a lipid and and demonstrate how it is made from cream. Cream with a high fat content should be about 58° F. Pour the cream into a bowl and beat it quickly with a wooden spoon or paddle until the butter fat separates from the cream. Show students the butter and the thin watery whey that results. Ask:

- **What are the characteristics of the butter?** (Greasy, lighter than the whey, and insoluble in water)
- **What are some other lipids that you use as food?** (Vegetable oils, margarine and other hydrogenated oils, and animal fats)

MEETING DIVERSE NEEDS

LEP Have LEP students cut out examples from magazines and newspapers of carbohydrates, sugars, and lipids, and paste each picture on an index card. Suggest that as they read the section, they add words relating to each type of chemical on the back of the card.

MULTICULTURAL PERSPECTIVE

Have students select a dish that is popular in another culture. Have them list what foods are used to make the dish and identify each food as a carbohydrate, lipid, or protein. Have students make posters to display the information, the recipe, and a picture of the dish to show the class.

Use the Visual

Direct students to Figures 2.3 and 2.4. Have them explain how honeybees use the following.

- **Proteins** (For movement, regulation, defense)
- **Nucleic acids** (DNA to control cell activities and RNA to make proteins)

3 ASSESS

Evaluate Understanding

Write the terms *carbohydrate, lipid, protein,* and *nucleic acid* on the board. Have students define each term and then identify the chemical substance(s) described below.

- **Sweet substance used for quick energy** (Sugar, a carbohydrate)
- **Collected by bees from plants** (Pollen, a protein)
- **Long-term energy source from plants** (Polysaccharide, carbohydrate)
- **Stored as food in plants** (Starch, carbohydrate)
- **Used as long-term energy and as insulation by animals** (Fats, lipids)
- **Helps control chemical reactions** (Enzymes)
- **Uses DNA instructions to make proteins** (RNA, nucleic acid)

Reteach

Draw a chart on the board with the following heads: *Group, Examples, Characteristics, Function.* Work with students to fill in the chart for the following groups: carbohydrates, lipids, proteins, and nucleic acids.

FIGURE 2.3
Proteins have many functions. Which functions are most familiar to you? Which ones are surprising?

Functions of Proteins	
Function	**Example**
Movement	Actin and myosin are proteins necessary for contraction of muscle fibers.
Structure	Collagen, the most abundant protein in the human body, forms bones, tendons, ligaments, and cartilage.
Regulation	Proteins called enzymes help control chemical reactions in cells.
Transport	The protein hemoglobin in red blood cells carries oxygen through the bloodstream.
Nutrition	The protein casein in milk stores amino acids for use by some newborn animals.
Defense	Antibodies are proteins that help animals fight off invasion by viruses and bacteria.

FIGURE 2.4
Nucleic Acids
Nucleic acids, such as the spiral-shaped DNA molecule (left), contain the genetic information of organisms. A queen bee (right) lays eggs that contain copies of her DNA.

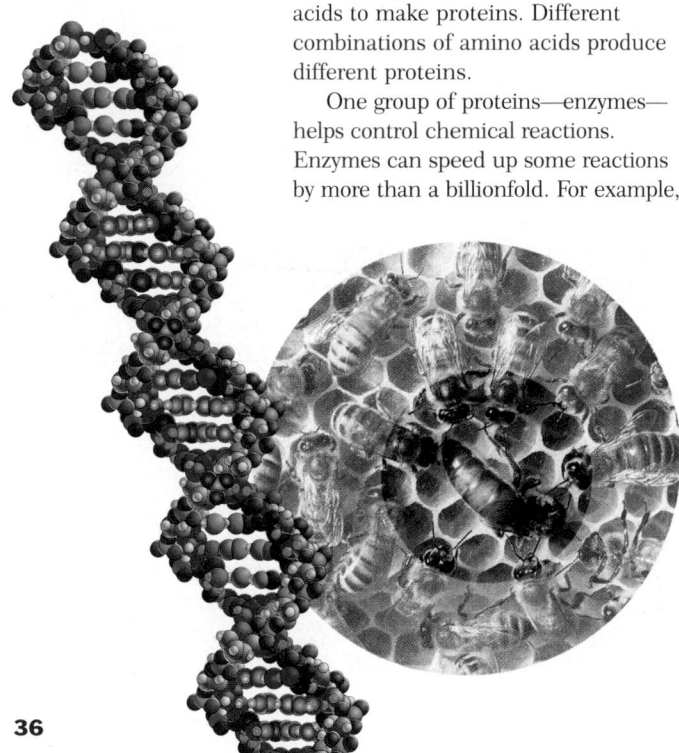

Proteins are important for many reasons. *Figure* 2.3 lists some of the various functions that proteins perform in living things.

Although their functions may differ, all proteins are similar in composition. Organisms use only 20 amino acids to make proteins. Different combinations of amino acids produce different proteins.

One group of proteins—enzymes—helps control chemical reactions. Enzymes can speed up some reactions by more than a billionfold. For example, enzymes are involved in digesting food, releasing energy during cellular respiration, and building up proteins.

NUCLEIC ACIDS
Molecules of heredity

Killer bees are more aggressive when threatened than other types of bees. What makes these bees behave differently? Some of their characteristics (and some of yours) are inherited. Inherited characteristics are controlled by molecules called nucleic acids. **Nucleic acids** are large, complex molecules that contain hereditary, or genetic, information.

There are two kinds of nucleic acids—deoxyribonucleic acid (DNA) and ribonucleic acid (RNA). DNA and RNA differ in their structures and functions. Similar to a blueprint for a builder, DNA carries instructions that control the activities of a cell. Similar to a builder, RNA uses those instructions to make proteins.

CHECKPOINT 2.1

1. What four groups of substances make up most living things?
2. Compare the functions of each of the four groups of substances.
3. **Critical Thinking** Wood is made mostly of cellulose. Using what you know about wood, describe the properties of cellulose.

Build on What You Know

4. Relate these four groups of chemicals to the properties of living things. *(Need to jog your memory? Revisit relevant concepts in Chapter 1, Section 1.1.)*

36

CHECKPOINT 2.1

1. Carbohydrates, lipids, proteins, nucleic acids
2. Carbohydrates provide energy and structure. Lipids provide long-term energy storage and insulation. Proteins function in movement, structure, biochemical control, transport, storage, regulation, and defense. Nucleic acids control inherited information.
3. **Making generalizations** Suggested properties may include strength, hardness, rigidity, insolubility in water.
4. Properties of living things—have structure, require energy, and reproduce

2.2 Basics of Chemistry

Worth your salt

Sodium is a metal that reacts explosively with air or water. Chlorine is a poisonous gas. When these two chemicals join together, they form . . . ordinary table salt. Today salt is inexpensive and plentiful, but in ancient times salt was so valuable that it was sometimes used as currency. Soldiers of the Roman Empire were paid in salt. Where do you think we got the word *salary*?

What you'll learn

IDEAS
- To distinguish elements from compounds
- To describe how atoms form different chemical bonds

WORDS
element, compound, organic compounds, ion, isotopes, chemical bonds

ELEMENTS AND COMPOUNDS

Countless combinations

Just as all the words in a dictionary are made from combinations of the 26 letters of the English alphabet, all the matter on Earth is made from about 100 elements. An **element** is a substance that cannot be broken down by chemical processes into simpler substances. Common elements include aluminum, gold, iron, and oxygen. The molten iron in the photo (right) in *Figure 2.5* is an example of an element. The table lists the elements that make up most of the human body.

Sometimes elements exist in nature in a pure form. Usually elements exist in combinations called compounds. A **compound** is a substance made of two or more elements chemically combined in definite proportions. In *Figure 2.5* the red blood cells in the small photo contain the compound hemoglobin. Hemoglobin contains the element iron.

All of the substances you read about in section 2.1—carbohydrates, lipids, proteins, and nucleic acids— are compounds, and all of these substances contain the element carbon. Almost all compounds that contain carbon are called **organic compounds**. Organic compounds are generally associated with living things.

Other compounds, for example, water and table salt, are inorganic compounds. Most inorganic compounds do not contain carbon.

Each element has its own distinct characteristics, or properties. But, as you read in the introductory story, when elements combine, their properties

Some Common Elements

Element	Symbol	Approximate % by Weight	
		Human Body	Earth's Crust
Oxygen	O	65	46.6
Carbon	C	18	0.03
Hydrogen	H	10	0.14
Nitrogen	N	3	Trace
Calcium	Ca	2	3.6
Phosphorus	P	1	0.07
Potassium	K	0.4	2.6
Silicon	Si	Trace	27.7
Aluminum	Al	Trace	8.1
Iron	Fe	Trace	5.0

FIGURE 2.5
Molten iron is an element. Iron also is part of the compound hemoglobin in red blood cells. Using the table (left), compare the percentages of elements found in the human body and in Earth's crust. Which elements show the greatest differences? ❶

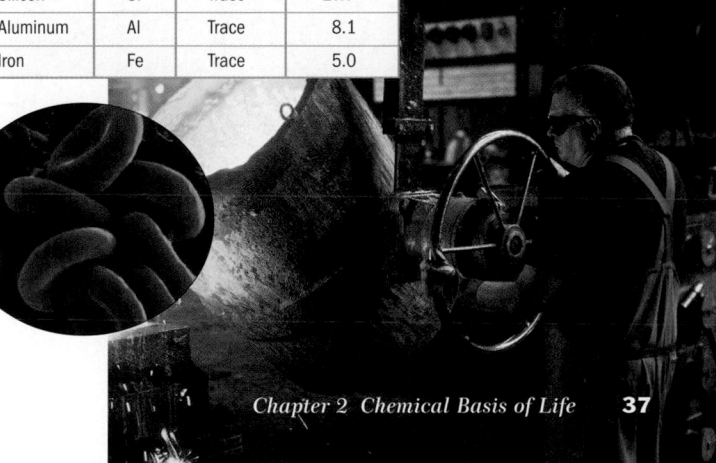

Chapter 2 Chemical Basis of Life **37**

---

❶ ENGAGE

Use the Visual

Have students study the photograph that opens the section. Explain that salt is a chemical compound because it is made of two chemicals (called elements)—sodium and chlorine. Ask students to name some other compounds.

Check Prior Knowledge

To check students' prior knowledge of chemicals, ask:
- **What are the simplest chemical parts of a living organism?** (Atoms and molecules)
- **What happens when a chemical compound breaks down?** (The bonds between the elements in the compound break. The elements can form other compounds, or they can remain as pure elements.)

Quick Activity

Display a variety of common items, for example, a glass of water, a spoon, aluminum foil, silver jewelry, iron nails. Ask students to identify the element(s) in each.

❶ The human body contains more carbon, hydrogen, and nitrogen. The Earth's crust contains more silicon, aluminum, iron, and potassium.

2 TEACH

Explain

Point out that the properties of a substance do not necessarily indicate the combination of atoms it contains. If all the atoms are the same, the substance is an element and has the properties of the element. However, if the atoms are combined chemically, the substance formed has properties that differ from those of its elements. For example, pure oxygen is a gas. Oxygen chemically combined with hydrogen is water. Oxygen chemically combined with iron forms iron oxide or rust.

Think Critically

Ask students what effect the charge of the atomic particles might have on each other. Guide students to reason that since opposite charges attract and like charges repel, an atomic particle would be affected in some way by the charge of another particle.

Animated Biological Concepts

Atomic Structure   Play

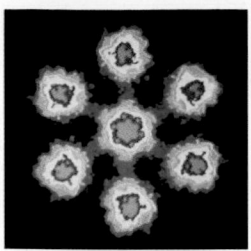

FIGURE 2.6
This artificially colored scanning electron micrograph shows the geometric arrangement of uranium atoms in a crystal.

change. How do the properties of table salt differ from the properties of ❶ sodium and chlorine?

Scientists use symbols to represent the elements. These symbols can be one or two letters. For example, the symbol for hydrogen is H; the symbol for oxygen is O. All of the elements and their symbols appear in the periodic table on pages 944–945.

ATOMS

Atomic particles take charge

An atom is the smallest particle of an element that has the properties of that element. Atoms are the building blocks of matter. All atoms are made of smaller particles—protons, neutrons, and electrons—arranged in a specific way.

Protons are positively charged (+) particles located in the center, or nucleus, of an atom. Neutrons, which have no electrical charge and are described as neutral, are also in the nucleus. Protons and neutrons account for about 99 percent of an atom's mass.

FIGURE 2.7

The Parts of an Atom

Electrons
Most of the volume of an atom is occupied by its moving electrons. Electrons have a negative charge.

Protons
Protons are located in the center, or nucleus, of an atom. Protons have a positive charge.

Neutrons
Neutrons have no charge. They are located in the nucleus of an atom.

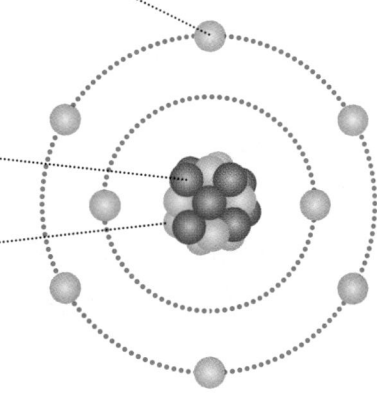

The atoms of each element have a distinctive number of protons. For example, all hydrogen atoms have 1 proton. All oxygen atoms have 8 protons. All gold atoms have 79 protons.

Electrons are negatively charged (–) particles that are much smaller than either protons or neutrons. Electrons are located outside the nucleus in regions called energy levels. Electrons are in constant motion, forming a "cloud" around the nucleus. Because it is difficult to represent the movement of an electron, electrons are sometimes drawn as dots in circular energy levels. See *Figure* 2.7. Because the number of positively charged protons is always equal to the number of negatively charged electrons, an atom is electrically balanced, or neutral.

Ions An atom is most stable, or unlikely to react, when its outermost energy level is completely filled. Each energy level has a set maximum number of electrons. Atoms can lose or gain one or more electrons and thereby achieve an outer energy level with the maximum number of electrons.

An atom that has lost or gained electrons is called an **ion.** Atoms that lose electrons become positive ions. Atoms that gain electrons become negative ions.

In *Figure* 2.8 you see an illustration of how a sodium atom becomes a sodium ion. How many electrons do the sodium atom and sodium ion have in their outermost energy levels? ❷

Isotopes All atoms of the same element have the same number of protons. And, as neutral atoms, they have the same number of electrons. However, individual atoms of the same element can have different numbers of neutrons. Atoms of the same element that have different numbers of neutrons are called **isotopes** of the element.

38   *Unit 1 The Basis of Life*

MEETING DIVERSE NEEDS

Sight Impaired Provide atomic models that sight impaired students can manipulate. If possible, have them discuss with peers the similarities and differences between the model atoms and real atoms.
Gifted Have students research the development of atomic models, beginning with John Dalton's model. Suggest that their written report highlight how the concept of the atom has changed through the years. Encourage students to include drawings, photos, or other illustrations with their reports.

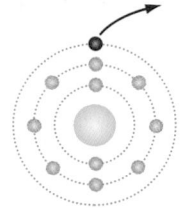 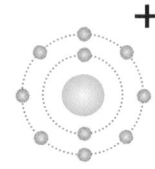

Sodium atom   Sodium ion

FIGURE 2.8
A sodium atom is neutral. It has the same number of protons and electrons. However, this atom can lose its outermost electron and become a positively charged ion.

About 50 naturally occurring isotopes are radioactive. A radioactive isotope has an unstable nucleus that breaks apart spontaneously, giving off energy in the form of radiation. Although radiation can harm living organisms, some radioactive isotopes are useful tools for biologists. Radiation from isotopes can be measured to determine the age of fossils, rocks, and artifacts. Radioactive isotopes can also act as tags or tracers. *Figure* 2.9 shows images of a brain formed by a positive emission tomography, or PET, scan. In a PET scan, radioactive isotopes show where chemical processes are occurring in body tissues. Radioactive isotopes are also used to preserve food and treat cancer.

CHEMICAL BONDS

Let's get together

As you have read, sodium chloride—salt—is a compound. But what holds the elements sodium and chlorine together in a compound? The answer is chemical bonds. **Chemical bonds** are the attractions that hold two or more atoms together to form a compound. Whenever a chemical bond is formed or broken, energy is either absorbed or released.

Examining Isotopes

In nature most elements occur as a mixture of two or more isotopes. The atomic mass given for each element in the periodic table is an average value based on the percentage of each of the isotopes found in a naturally occurring sample. Generally, the average atomic mass of an element will be closest to the actual mass of its most common, or most abundant, isotope.

Analyzing the Periodic Table

Consult the periodic table located on pages 944–945. Answer the following questions for each pair of isotopes:

- C-12 and C-14
- S-32 and S-33
- Si-28 and Si-29
- N-14 and N-15

1 What is the average atomic mass of each element?
2 How many neutrons are in each isotope?
3 For each pair of isotopes listed above, which isotope would you expect to be most abundant?

Ionic bonds Positive and negative ions attract each other because of opposite electrical charges. An **ionic bond** is the chemical bond formed from the attractive force between ions with opposite charges. The resulting compound has no electrical charge. In an ionic bond, electrons are lost by one element and gained by another

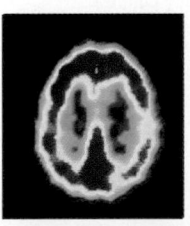 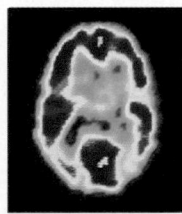
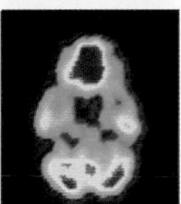

FIGURE 2.9
PET scans measure the amount of physiological activity in the brain, with red indicating the most active areas. These images show how, at any moment, the amount of activity varies in different parts of the brain.

Chapter 2 Chemical Basis of Life **39**

❶ Sodium is a metal, chlorine is a gas. Together they form a crystalline solid.
❷ The sodium atom has one electron in its outer level. The sodium ion has eight electrons in its outer level.

Use the Visual

Refer students to Figure 2.8. Have them count the number of electrons in the sodium atom and in the sodium ion. Ask:

- **How do the particles differ?** (The atom has 11 electrons, the ion has 10.)
- **How did the sodium atom become an ion?** (The sodium atom lost an electron.)
- **What did the electron movement accomplish?** (An ion with eight electrons in the outermost energy level is more stable than an atom with one.)

LAB ZONE **Think About It!**

Examining Isotopes

Analyzing the Periodic Table

- The atomic mass of C is 12.01115. C-12 has 6 neutrons, and C-14 has 8. C-12 is the most abundant isotope.
- The atomic mass of Si is 28.086. Si-28 has 14 neutrons, and Si-29 has 15. Si-28 is the most abundant isotope.
- The atomic mass of S is 32.06. S-32 has 16 neutrons, and S-33 has 17 neutrons. S-32 is the most abundant isotope.
- The atomic mass of N is 14.0067. N-14 has 7 neutrons, and N-15 has 8. N-14 is the most abundant isotope.

Use the Visual

Have students study Figure 2.10 and observe the differences between the sodium atom and the sodium ion, and the chlorine atom and the chlorine ion. Ask:

- **When are the atoms neutral?** (When they have an equal number of electrons and protons)
- **Why does the sodium ion have a + charge?** (It gave up one electron and now has more protons than electrons.)
- **Why does the chlorine ion have a − charge?** (It received one electron and now has more electrons than protons.)

Teacher Demo

Most students know that objects with opposite electrical charges attract. Demonstrate this by having a volunteer comb his or her hair and then place the comb near bits of paper. If the air is dry, the paper should be attracted to the comb. The act of combing took electrons off the hair and negatively charged the comb.

40

EVERYDAY BIOLOGY

Tough Spots

Protein-rich stains left by milk, egg, or blood are difficult to remove from fabric. Other types of stains tend to dissolve in water—but not protein stains! Some detergents contain enzymes that break the bonds in proteins so detergent and water can do their work.

---

element. You can see an illustration of the bonding process in *Figure 2.10*. Sodium has one electron in its outer energy level. As you have learned, an atom is most stable when its outermost energy level is filled. The sodium atom's lone outer electron represents an unstable arrangement. The chlorine atom's outermost energy level would be filled with the addition of one more electron.

When sodium reacts with chlorine, the sodium atom loses its outermost electron and becomes a positive ion. The chlorine atom gains that electron and becomes a negative ion. How many electrons are now in the outer energy level of each ion? **❶**

The attractive force between the positively charged sodium ion and the negatively charged chlorine ion is very strong. The two ions come together to form an ionic bond. The compound that forms is sodium chloride, or table salt.

Covalent bonds Some compounds have bonds in which electrons are not gained or lost, but are shared

by atoms. This type of bond is called a covalent bond. (Think of the "co-" in *cooperative* as a reminder that sharing takes place.) Water, carbohydrates, lipids, proteins, and nucleic acids all have covalent bonds.

In covalent bonds, atoms may share electrons in several different ways. If atoms share two electrons between them, a single bond is formed. If atoms share four electrons, a double bond is formed. If atoms share six electrons, a triple bond is formed. *Figure 2.11* illustrates the structure of each type of covalent bond.

The units that are formed by covalent bonds are called molecules. Most molecules are made of atoms from different elements. Some molecules, however, consist of atoms from the same element that are covalently bonded. Oxygen gas, O_2, and nitrogen gas, N_2, are two common examples. Each molecule exists as a pair of atoms bound by a covalent bond.

Polar molecules In some covalent bonds, atoms do not share electrons equally. As a result, some

FIGURE 2.10
Ionic Bonds

In this chemical reaction, an ionic bond has formed between a positive and a negative ion. The compound formed—sodium chloride—is shown at right in crystallized form, artificially colored.

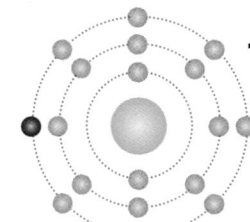
Salt crystal (artificially colored)

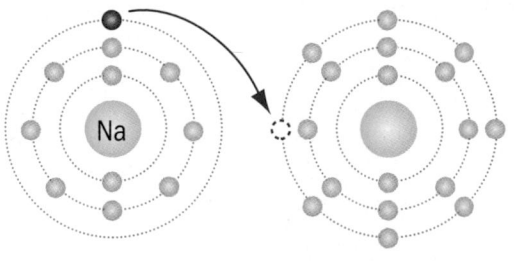

Sodium atom
This atom loses the lone electron from its outer energy level.

Chlorine atom
This atom gains an electron from the sodium atom, filling its outer energy level.

Sodium ion
The sodium atom is now an ion, and it carries a net positive charge.

Chlorine ion
The chlorine atom is now a negative ion. The sodium and chlorine ions form an ionic bond.

40 *Unit 1 The Basis of Life*

MEETING DIVERSE NEEDS

Sight Impaired Use foam ball models to illustrate the parts of an atom (Figure 2.7) and ionic and covalent bonding (Figures 2.10 and 2.11). You may wish to have students use the foam balls to illustrate ionic and covalent bonding .

❶ Sodium now has eight; chlorine now has eight.

CHECKPOINT 2.2

1. A compound is made up of two or more elements chemically combined in definite proportions. An element is a substance that cannot be chemically broken down into simpler substances.

FIGURE 2.11
Covalent Bonds

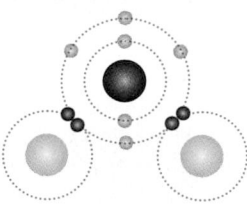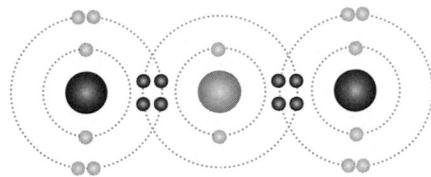

Single bond
In the water molecule, each of the two hydrogen atoms is sharing two electrons with the oxygen atom.

Double bond
In the carbon dioxide molecule, each oxygen atom is sharing four electrons with the central carbon atom.

Triple bond
In the atmospheric nitrogen molecule, two nitrogen atoms are sharing six electrons with each other.

atoms in the molecule have a slightly negative charge and other atoms have a slightly positive charge. Molecules with a slightly negative end and a slightly positive end are called polar molecules.

Water is a polar molecule. *Figure 2.12* shows a diagram of a water molecule. In a water molecule, shared electrons are attracted more to the single oxygen atom than to the two hydrogen atoms. As a result, the oxygen end of the water molecule has a slightly negative electrical charge, and the hydrogen end has a slightly positive charge. How do you think the polar water molecule affects the

❷ charged parts of ionic compounds?

Other chemical forces As you have read, ionic and covalent bonds hold atoms together. In addition, there are other forces of attraction between molecules. These forces are much weaker than either ionic or covalent bonds, but they have a significant effect on organic compounds.

One kind of relatively weak attraction between molecules is called the hydrogen bond. Hydrogen bonds hold together molecules that contain hydrogen, such as water molecules, and they also exist in some proteins and nucleic acids. Hydrogen bonds are important in determining both the properties of water and the chemistry of living things.

CHECKPOINT 2.2

1. Compare compounds and elements.
2. Explain how atoms form the following types of chemical bonds: ionic, covalent, and polar.
3. **Critical Thinking** How are polar molecules similar to ionic compounds? How are they different?

Build on What You Know

4. Compare the levels of organization in matter with the levels of organization in the biosphere. *(Need to jog your memory? Revisit relevant concepts in Chapter 1, Section 1.1.)*

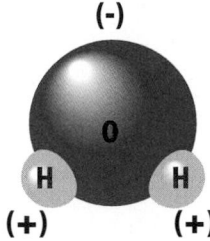

(-)

O

H **H**

(+) **(+)**

FIGURE 2.12
Unequal sharing of electrons causes the water molecule to be polar.

What kinds of chemicals are living things made of?

Chapter 2 Chemical Basis of Life **41**

CHECKPOINT 2.2 (cont.)

1. Ionic bonds: electrons are lost from the atoms of one element and gained by the atoms of another. Covalent bonds: electrons are shared among atoms. Polar molecules: atoms share electrons unequally.
2. **Making comparisons** Ionic compounds are made of ions, which are charged; polar molecules have slight charges. In ionic compounds, atoms have either gained or lost electrons; in polar molecules, electrons are shared unequally.
3. Levels of organization in both go from simple to complex. Elements join to form compounds; individuals join to form populations, communities, ecosystems, etc.

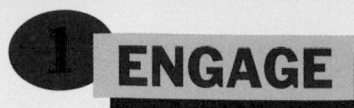

2.3 Chemicals at Work

ENGAGE

Consider the Big Idea!

Have students read The Big Idea! at the top of the page. Explain that chemical reactions are important in all life processes.

Use the Visual

Have the students study the photograph that opens the section. Discuss how the adaptation of the butterfly to cold weather helps to preserve its species.

Check Prior Knowledge

To assess the students' prior knowledge about how chemicals work, ask:

- **What are some common examples of chemical reactions?** (Rusting, bleaching, burning)
- **What are chemical bonds?** (Forces that hold two or more atoms together)

 **Previewing** To practice strategies for effective reading, use pages 27-28 in *Super Read!*

Use the Visual

Call students' attention to Figure 2.13. Explain that chemical equations are like sentences. They state what happens during a chemical reaction. Point out that the chemical symbol for each element is used by the scientific community everywhere. The arrow means "yields" and indicates the direction of the reaction.

What you'll learn

IDEAS
- To explain what happens during a chemical reaction
- To show how an enzyme functions

WORDS
chemical reaction, enzyme

SUPER READ!

Animal antifreeze
Not all organisms have a place to go when it gets cold. Some insects, such as the cabbage white butterfly shown here, produce chemicals that protect them against harsh winters by lowering the freezing point of the insects' body fluids. One of these substances, glycerol, is similar to the antifreeze used in cars.

CHEMICAL REACTIONS

Changing atomic partners

Your body obtains energy by breaking chemical bonds in compounds such as carbohydrates. Carbohydrates, like all compounds, result from chemical bond formation. Both of these processes require chemical reactions. In a **chemical reaction,** one or more substances is changed into a new substance by the breaking or forming of chemical bonds.

When a cracker dissolves in your mouth, the breakdown of starch that occurs is an example of a chemical reaction. As you may remember, starch is a polysaccharide—a complex molecule made of a long chain of sugars. As you chew the cracker and it mixes with enzymes in your saliva, a chemical reaction occurs and the bonds between the sugar molecules in the starch are broken. You begin to notice a sweet taste. The appearance of one or more new substances, in this case sugar, is a sign that a chemical reaction has taken place.

You will often see chemical reactions represented by an equation like the one in *Figure 2.13*. Chemical equations are a shorthand way of showing what happens during a reaction. The letters are symbols for elements, and they can also be combined in chemical formulas to represent compounds. A chemical formula indicates the elements and numbers of atoms in the smallest unit representing a substance.

Typically, equations are "balanced," meaning that the kind of elements and total number of atoms of each element on the left side of the arrow equal the kind and total number on the right

FIGURE 2.13

A Chemical Equation

This chemical equation represents the formation of water molecules (H_2O). H is the chemical symbol for hydrogen; O is the symbol for oxygen.

The original substances, called reactants, are located on the left side of the arrow.

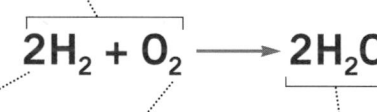

$$2H_2 + O_2 \longrightarrow 2H_2O$$

This represents the number of hydrogen molecules involved in the reaction.

This subscript represents the number of atoms in each molecule of oxygen.

Substances appearing on the right side of the arrow are the products of the reaction.

STUDENT RESOURCES

From the Teacher's Resource Package, use:
- Section Review 2.3, Activity Recordsheets 2-1 and 2-2, and Critical Thinking Exercise 2 from Unit 1 Review Module
- Lab 2: "Enzymes: Catalysts of Life"
- Lab 3: "Enzymes: Reaction Rates"

 TECHNOLOGY RESOURCES

Relevant technology resources include:
- Spanish Student Edition CD-ROM
- Teacher's Resource Planner CD-ROM
- Animated Biological Concepts Videodiscs: "Enzymatic Reactions"

TEACH

SUPER READ! **Previewing** To practice strategies for effective reading, use pages 27-28 in *Super Read!*

LAB ZONE Do It! TEAM WORK

What Does a Chemical Reaction Look Like?

Analyze Your Results

1 Mixing baking soda and vinegar, or baking soda and water plus vinegar and water resulted in chemical reactions.

2 When vinegar and water, or baking soda and water, were mixed, they did not change. When vinegar and baking soda were mixed, they foamed and fizzled, which means a gas was produced.

3 Water does not react with vinegar or with baking soda.

side of the arrow. How many molecules of water are formed in the reaction in ❶ *Figure 2.13*?

All chemical reactions involve energy. Energy can be either absorbed or released in a chemical reaction. When water is formed from hydrogen and oxygen gases, energy is released. When water is broken down, energy is absorbed. The energy that is given off when a substance is formed is equal to the energy needed to break it down.

REACTION SPEED

Faster than ever

Chemical reactions, such as the ones shown in *Figure 2.14*, take place around us every day. Some chemical reactions are involved in life processes, such as the growth of an eaglet or the chemical breakdown of fruit. Other chemical reactions occur in nonliving matter, such as a rusting car or exploding fireworks. All of these reactions take place at different rates of speed, however. Can the rate of a chemical reaction be altered?

It is possible to speed up a chemical reaction by increasing the temperature. The speed of the reaction increases

because the higher temperature makes the atoms or molecules move faster and collide with each other more often.

Another way to change the speed of a chemical reaction is with a catalyst. A catalyst is a substance that speeds up or slows down a reaction

FIGURE 2.14

Color change, heat, and light are typical evidence that chemical reactions are occurring. What evidence of reactions is shown in these photos? ❷

SUPER READ!

LAB ZONE Do It! **bioSURF**

What Does a Chemical Reaction Look Like?

Chemical reactions cause substances to change into new substances. You can observe a chemical reaction if you . . .

Try This

1 Mix 5 grams (g) of baking soda and 120 milliliters (mL) of water in a glass jar. Write your observations about the mixture.
2 Mix 5 mL of vinegar and 120 mL of water in another jar. Again, note the results.
3 Mix 5 mL of vinegar and 5 g of baking soda in another jar. What happens?
4 Combine the baking-soda-and-water mixture with the vinegar-and-water mixture.

Analyze Your Results

1 Which combinations resulted in chemical reactions?
2 What happened to the ingredients in the mixtures that reacted and in those that did not?
3 What do the results of this lab indicate about the reactivity of water with baking soda and with vinegar?

MEETING DIVERSE NEEDS

At Risk Ask students to work with a partner, taking turns using snap-together plastic blocks to form water molecules. Suggest that they use four red blocks to make two molecules of hydrogen (H_2) and

two white blocks to make one molecule of oxygen (O_2). Help them understand that when chemicals react with each other, bonds within the molecules break apart and new bonds and molecules are formed.

❶ Two molecules formed.
❷ Immediate evidence includes exploding fireworks; changed fruit breaking down.

44

Use the Visual

Have students study Figure 2.15. Ask:

- **What is the substrate in this reaction?** (Sucrose)
- **What products are released?** (Glucose and fructose)
- **What happens to the enzyme?** (It does not change.)

3 ASSESS

Evaluate Understanding

Ask students to give examples of chemical reactions. Then have them name the reactant, product, and number of molecules in the following equations.

- $H_2 + Cl_2 \rightarrow 2HCl$ (One molecule of hydrogen and one molecule of chlorine yield two molecules of hydrogen chloride, or hydrochloric acid.)
- $C + O_2 \rightarrow CO_2$ (One atom of carbon and one molecule of oxygen yield one molecule of carbon dioxide.)

Reteach

Demonstrate how chemical equations are balanced by using different coins to represent individual atoms. Show how the numbers of each are equal on both sides of a balanced equation.

Animated Biological Concepts

Enzymatic Reactions   Play

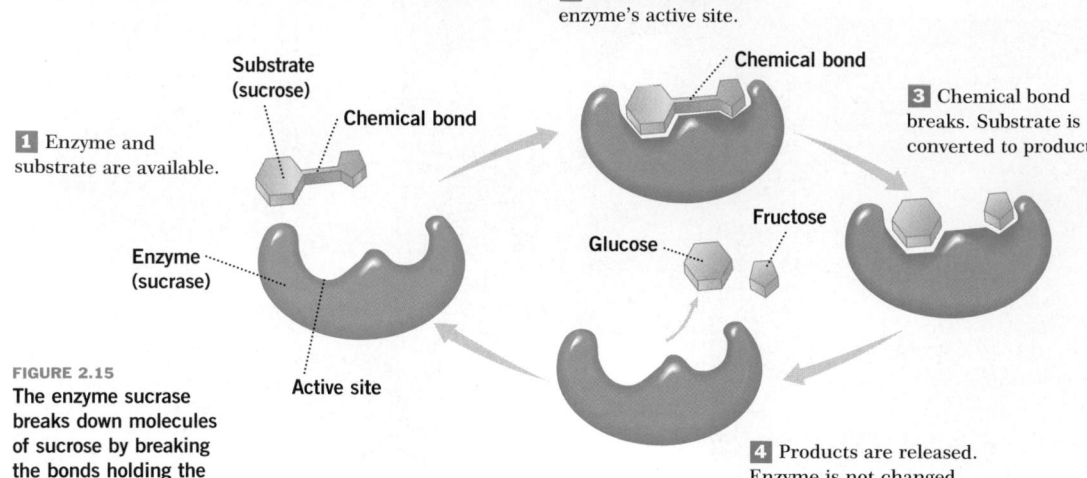

1 Enzyme and substrate are available.

Substrate (sucrose)

Chemical bond

2 Substrate binds to enzyme's active site.

Chemical bond

3 Chemical bond breaks. Substrate is converted to products.

Enzyme (sucrase)

Active site

Glucose

Fructose

4 Products are released. Enzyme is not changed.

FIGURE 2.15
The enzyme sucrase breaks down molecules of sucrose by breaking the bonds holding the glucose and fructose molecules together. How do the shapes of the substrate and the active site compare? ❶

EVERYDAY BIOLOGY

Tender Wounds

The pain of bee and jellyfish stings can be soothed with a paste made of meat tenderizer and water. An enzyme in meat tenderizer breaks down the proteins in the venom, making the area less painful.

without being changed or used up in the reaction. Because the catalyst does not change, it is highly effective in small amounts. All living organisms contain catalysts. These catalysts are called enzymes. As you may recall from Section 2.1, an **enzyme** is a protein catalyst that speeds up the chemical reactions within an organism. Enzymes work quickly, typically taking part in about a thousand reactions per second.

Consider one enzyme that is involved when you digest sucrose (table sugar). A molecule of sucrose is made up of two simple sugars. The enzyme sucrase binds to sucrose and breaks the bond between the two simple sugars, glucose and fructose.

Figure 2.15 illustrates how an enzyme works. The reactant, or substance to be changed (in this case, sucrose), is called the substrate. The region on the enzyme where the substrate attaches is called the enzyme's active site. At that site, the substrate is changed slightly by the enzyme so that a specific chemical bond is weakened. This weakened chemical bond allows sucrose to break apart quickly.

Specific enzymes catalyze specific chemical reactions, much as a key works with a specific lock. Some enzymes cause compounds to break apart. Others cause compounds to be formed. Enzymes provide a way to speed up life's essential functions without raising the temperature of an organism's body.

CHECKPOINT 2.3

1. Summarize what happens during a chemical reaction.
2. Make a labeled drawing that shows how an enzyme works.
3. **Critical Thinking** Suppose that when you mix two colorless liquids, they turn bright blue. You then observe a blue solid slowly settle on the bottom of the beaker. Has a chemical reaction taken place? Explain why or why not.

Build on What You Know

4. Do enzymes follow chemical or physical laws that are different from the laws governing nonliving substances? *(Need to jog your memory? Revisit relevant concepts in Chapter 1, Section 1.1.)*

44 *Unit 1 The Basis of Life*

CHECKPOINT 2.3

1. Answers should mention the reactants, energy absorbed or released, and the products released.
2. Drawings should include the enzyme, substrate, active site, and chemical reaction that takes place.
3. **Developing a hypothesis** The presence of the colored solid, a substance with new properties, indicates that a chemical reaction has taken place.
4. Enzymes follow the same chemical and physical laws that all substances follow.

❶ The shapes of the substrate and active site fit together like puzzle pieces.

Analyzing a Chemical Reaction

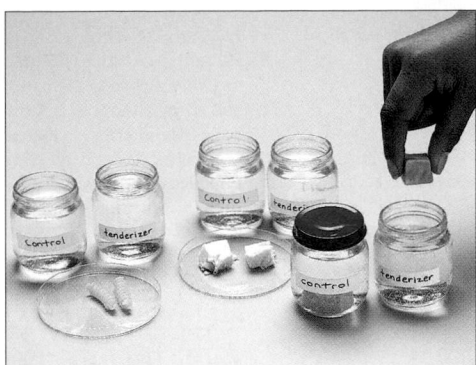

WHAT YOU WILL DO Observe the effects of meat tenderizer on starch, fat, and protein

SKILLS YOU WILL USE Observing, predicting, controlling variables, collecting and recording data

WHAT YOU WILL NEED 6 empty baby food jars with lids, tape, permanent marker, metric balance, meat tenderizer, 2 pieces of rotini pasta, 2 pieces of beef suet, 2 pieces of ham

Propose a Hypothesis

Meat tenderizer contains an enzyme that breaks down proteins. Propose a hypothesis about the effects of meat tenderizer on starch, fat, and protein. Record your hypothesis in your lab notebook.
Caution: Be careful when working with glassware to avoid breakage.

Conduct Your Experiment

DAY 1

1 Use the tape and the marker to put your name on each jar. Then label the six jars *Control Starch*, *Control Fat*, *Control Protein*, *Tenderizer Starch*, *Tenderizer Fat*, and *Tenderizer Protein*.
2 Fill each jar with water. Use the metric balance to measure 9 g of meat tenderizer. Add it to one of the *Tenderizer* jars and stir until completely dissolved. Repeat for the other two *Tenderizer* jars.

3 You have two samples each of starch (pasta), fat (suet), and protein (ham). Place the samples in their assigned *Control* and *Tenderizer* jars, as shown in the photograph. Put the lids on the jars.

DAY 2

4 Examine both pieces of pasta. How do they look? How do they feel? Squeeze the pasta between your fingers. Record the look and feel of both pieces.
5 Repeat step 4 for the suet and the ham.

Analyze Your Data

1 Were there any differences in look or feel of the two pieces of pasta on Day 2? If so, explain.
2 Were there any differences in look or feel of the two pieces of suet on Day 2? If so, explain.
3 Were there any differences in look or feel of the two pieces of ham on Day 2? If so, explain.

Draw Conclusions

1 Why do you need the control jars?
2 Was the hypothesis supported by your observations? Why or why not?

Design a Related Experiment

Design an experiment to compare the effects of substances used in marinades (for example, vinegar or lemon juice) on proteins.

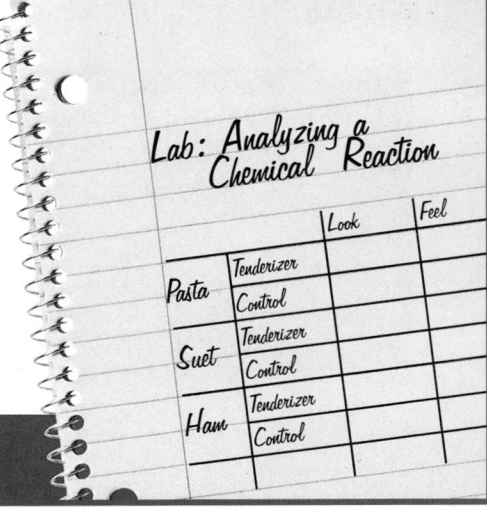

Lab: Analyzing a Chemical Reaction

		Look	Feel
Pasta	Tenderizer		
	Control		
Suet	Tenderizer		
	Control		
Ham	Tenderizer		
	Control		

Analyze Your Data

1 Both samples of pasta soften but keep their shape when squeezed.
2 Both samples of suet remain about the same.
3 The outer surface of the ham in meat tenderizer becomes soft and slimy, and the ham can be easily broken apart when squeezed. The ham in water remains solid.

Draw Conclusions

1 The controls were needed to ensure that the changes observed in the foods were not due to the water.
2 Answers depend on students' hypothesis.

TEAM WORK Analyzing a Chemical Reaction

SAFETY FIRST!

Remind students of the proper safety precautions to follow when using glassware and what to do if glassware is broken. Tell them never to taste any materials used in a laboratory activity.

Lab Tips

You may wish to review how to measure 9 g on the metric balance. Have students fill each jar with the same amount of water. Be sure students place the correct samples in the appropriately marked jars with the lids firmly in place.

Hypothesis Help

Because meat tenderizer contains enzymes for digesting meat, students will probably hypothesize that the meat in meat tenderizer will get softer. After students complete the Investigation, they should conclude that because meat tenderizer softened the protein and starch, but not the fat, it must contain enzymes that break down protein and starch, but not fat.

Lab Extension

Open Ended

Have students test substances such as egg white and gelatin to determine if they are made of starch, fat, or protein. Evidence to support that both egg white and gelatin are protein is that meat tenderizer causes a change in both substances.

Time Required

- 35 minutes on Day 1
- 15 minutes on Day 2

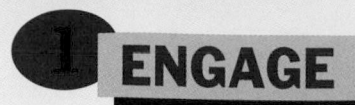

1 ENGAGE

Use the Visual

Direct students to study the photograph that opens the section. Have them identify the types of food that would give the mouse the most energy. (Carbohydrates, lipids)

Check Prior Knowledge

To assess the students' prior knowledge about how chemistry is involved in life processes, ask:

- **What are some important life processes in which chemical reactions occur?** (Answers may include digestion, respiration, transformation of energy, excretion, and the immune response)

SUPER READ! **Previewing** To practice strategies for effective reading, use pages 27-28 in *Super Read!*

Interpreting Visuals To practice strategies for effective reading, use pages 31-32 in *Super Read!*

Teacher Demo

Use a microprojector to display a slide of pond water containing microorganisms. Give students an opportunity to observe the organisms. Then have them explain how they can tell if the organisms are alive and using energy.

2.4 Chemistry in Life Processes

What you'll learn

IDEAS
- To describe different life processes
- To explain that life processes are based on chemical reactions

WORDS
metabolism, homeostasis

Mighty mouse
Rodents, like this yellow-necked mouse, are very active organisms. Their energy is stored in chemical bonds in the food they eat. This energy is released by chemical reactions. In fact, all of an organism's life processes, including reproduction, growth, and maintenance, depend on chemical reactions.

FIGURE 2.16
The slow metabolic rate of this python, combined with its ability to consume large prey, means that it eats much less often than birds or mammals. Many large snakes eat only eight to ten times a year.

METABOLISM AND ENERGY

Fuel for life

During your lifetime your body never stops functioning. Even when you are in a deep sleep, comfortable and motionless, your body is busy. It is producing chemicals that help you sleep, and it is regulating your heartbeat, blood flow, and body temperature. Twenty-four hours a day, your body works to keep you alive by carrying out a series of chemical changes. The combination of all the chemical changes that take place in an organism is called **metabolism.**

The chemical changes of each organism's metabolism are coordinated to allow the organism to obtain and use energy to perform its body functions. Organisms require energy for just about everything they do, including moving, growing, taking in food, and reproducing.

Organisms use compounds that contain energy in chemical bonds as sources of energy. As you learned earlier, when sugars and starches are broken down in your body, energy is released. Plants and some other organisms can use sunlight to make energy-rich compounds. You will learn more about the synthesis and breakdown of energy-rich compounds in Chapter 4.

In addition to supplying energy, food compounds also contain elements that your body needs as building blocks. Your body uses the elements in food compounds to make all of the materials your cells need to stay alive. These materials include proteins, lipids, and carbohydrates.

The products of the chemical reactions in your body include heat and

STUDENT RESOURCES

From the Teacher's Resource Package, use:
- Section Review 2.4 from Unit 1 Review Module

 ### TECHNOLOGY RESOURCES

Relevant technology resources include:
- Spanish Student Edition CD-ROM
- Teacher's Resource Planner CD-ROM
- Biology Alive! Videos: "Signs of Life" and "The Domain of Life"

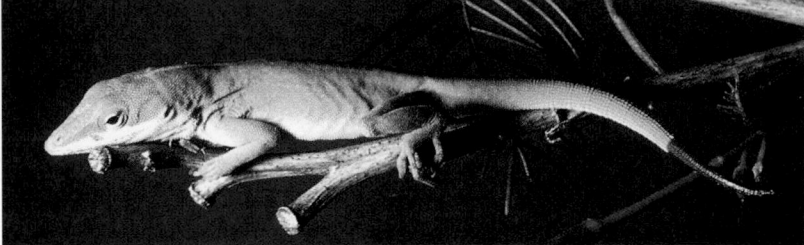

FIGURE 2.17
This anole is growing a new tail after losing the original one. The process of growing back a lost body part is called regeneration.

wastes. Humans and other organisms need heat to stay alive, but too much heat is harmful and must be removed. Carbon dioxide, food wastes, and salts are examples of body wastes. Such wastes are poisonous, so your body must eliminate them.

GROWTH AND REPAIR
A look at a lifetime

During their life span, some organisms undergo many, sometimes dramatic, changes. Think of how you have changed since you were an infant, and how you expect to change in the years to come. In some organisms very complex changes can occur, such as the metamorphosis of a tadpole into a frog. The changes that occur as organisms grow and develop are the result of many complex chemical reactions.

To grow and develop, the cells of organisms must make many new carbohydrates, proteins, and lipids. The nucleic acids in cells control the production of these materials. You will learn more about the chemical control of nucleic acids in Chapter 8.

In addition to growing, organisms must repair damage from injuries. For example, when an anole such as the one in *Figure 2.17* loses its tail, it can grow a new one. In the repair process, chemical reactions are needed to produce new cells to replace the injured cells. When you break a bone, the broken bone heals by producing new bone cells in a process that involves many chemical reactions.

HOMEOSTASIS AND CONTROL
Staying in balance

In section 2.3 you read that chemical changes are constantly occurring in living things. For an organism to stay alive, those changes must be controlled. The internal conditions of the organism must remain constant, or stable. The tendency of an organism to maintain stable internal conditions is called **homeostasis.** You might think of homeostasis as an internal balance system.

Just as it takes many tiny motions to steady a gymnast on a balance beam, it takes millions of chemical reactions to keep the internal conditions of living things stable. Consider the sagebrush in *Figure 2.18*. This plant may be immobile, but chemicals inside the sagebrush are in constant motion. Chemical reactions and physical processes help the plant maintain the proper water balance and temperature. They also help the plant absorb nutrients to keep the cells healthy and to make new cells.

Throughout this textbook you will learn about many kinds of controls that are involved in maintaining homeostasis. For example, many chemical reactions in cells are controlled by feedback loops. A feedback loop is a series of reactions in which the products of the last reaction cause the first reaction to start or stop. In multicellular organisms, some feedback loops are controlled by hormones, such as the protein insulin, that are sent from one organ to another.

FIGURE 2.18
Plants keep their internal conditions in balance through chemical and physical processes. This desert sagebrush draws water from the soil through a physical process. Water balance greatly affects the main chemical processes of the plant.

Chapter 2 Chemical Basis of Life **47**

Clarify Misconceptions

Students may think that growth is just an increase in size. Guide students to recognize that physical changes do not affect the chemistry of a substance. Point out that living things grow because their cells divide to create more cells. This kind of growth involves changes that affect the chemistry of the cell. Some animal cells, such as fat cells, can also increase in size. When a fat cell enlarges, both physical and chemical changes take place.

Explain

Tell students that all organisms have an average life span, which is the period of time the organism lives. During its life span, an organism goes through a cycle of change called growth, maturity, and old age. The life span of different organisms varies, from a few days for a mayfly to many years for humans.

Class Activity

Ask a volunteer to take his or her body temperature while sitting and relaxing. Then ask the same student to run in place or do jumping jacks for one or two minutes until he or she has "worked up a sweat." Have the volunteer take his or her temperature again. Explain to students that sweating is a mechanism of homeostasis because it helps the body cool itself to maintain a constant body temperature.

2.4

Math

Refer students to Figure 2.19. Have them calculate how many molecules of pheromone would be needed in a liter of air for the silk moth to detect the chemical. (100,000)

ASSESS

Evaluate Understanding

Assess the students' comprehension of the role of chemistry in life processes. Ask:

- **What occurs during metabolism?** (The chemical changes that occur in the organism are coordinated, allowing the cells of the organism to obtain and use energy.)
- **Why is maintaining stable internal conditions important to living things?** (To sustain life, internal conditions must remain constant and stable.)
- **Why are chemical reactions important to an organism's growth and repair?** (Chemical reactions take place to produce new cells for growth and to replace injured or diseased cells.)

Reteach

Have students write the five section subheads identifying the life processes, leaving five lines under each. For each life process, have them write one main idea statement and two supporting details. You may wish to model the first one for them.

48

FIGURE 2.19
This male silk moth is attracted to a potential mate by the female's pheromones. The male moth's large antennae can detect as few as 100 molecules of the female's pheromone combination in 1 mL of air.

COMMUNICATION AND RESPONSE

"Talking" without words

In the world of living things, communication takes place both within an organism and between organisms. In many animals, internal communication occurs in the nervous system. Chemicals called neurotransmitters carry impulses across the small spaces between nerve cells. You will learn more about this process in Chapter 34.

Communication between organisms can take place through sight, sound, touch, smell, and taste. For insects and many other animals, communication occurs through chemical signals called pheromones, which the animals smell or taste. Pheromones are produced by chemical reactions. In a beehive, for example, the queen produces a substance called queen mandibular pheromone, which worker bees lick from the queen's body. This pheromone stops worker bees from rearing new queens. What are some other examples of organisms using odors and tastes for communication?

REPRODUCTION

Making new life

One of life's most amazing processes is reproduction. During reproduction, parents create offspring by providing the necessary chemical information to begin and continue life. That information, as you learned in section 2.1, is carried in nucleic acids such as DNA.

The chemical characteristics of DNA enable it to carry the information needed for producing new cells. In a series of chemical reactions, enzymes duplicate DNA. Other enzymes translate the information in DNA into materials needed for new cells. Reproduction requires the doubling of almost all of the materials in a living cell. Doubling the materials in a cell involves countless chemical reactions. Ultimately, DNA's characteristics enable organisms to reproduce. You will learn more about the structure and function of DNA in Chapter 8.

CHECKPOINT 2.4

1. Name the major life processes discussed in this section.
2. Explain how each of those life processes is dependent on chemical reactions.
3. **Critical Thinking** An ant can move along a path that other ants can later follow. Propose a hypothesis to explain this phenomenon.

Build on What You Know

4. How are the processes discussed in this section related to the characteristics of life? *(Need to jog your memory? Revisit relevant concepts in Chapter 1, Section 1.1.)*

? Why are chemical reactions important for life?

48 *Unit 1 The Basis of Life*

CHECKPOINT 2.4

1. Metabolism, communication, reproduction, homeostasis, growth and repair
2. Answers may vary but should address each major life process. An example follows. Metabolism: dependent on reactions that produce and/or consume energy-rich molecules
3. **Developing a hypothesis** Answers should suggest the presence of chemical markers, or pheromones.
4. The processes discussed are all characteristics of living things.

❶ Some animals and many insects use chemicals as sex attractants; ants mark trails; dogs, deer, antelope, and other animals mark territory.

2.5 Water and Solutions

The blue planet

As this view from space shows, Earth seems to be more water than land. The overwhelming expanses of blue that cover three quarters of the planet's surface are testament to the crucial roles that water plays in life on Earth. What things in your life are not affected by water?

What you'll learn

IDEAS
- To identify the properties of water that support life
- To distinguish between acids and bases

WORDS
solution, acid, base, pH scale

SOLUTIONS

Molecules all wet

Water, though common, is an extraordinary substance. Its chemistry allows it to form solutions easily. A **solution** is a uniform mixture of two or more substances. Water solutions are important because all of life's chemical processes occur in solutions.

In a solution, two or more substances are mixed together so completely and evenly that they cannot be distinguished. Think of what happens when you pour sugar into a glass of water. Although visible at first, the sugar soon disappears. The sugar molecules become evenly distributed throughout the water to form a sugar solution. There is no chemical change in the sugar or water molecules.

Solutions have two components. The dissolved substance in a solution is called the solute. The dissolving substance is called the solvent. In the sugar and water solution, sugar is the solute and water is the solvent.

Most ionic compounds dissolve readily in water because of the polar nature of the water molecule. For example, as a crystal of common table salt, or sodium chloride (NaCl),

dissolves, the positive regions of the water molecules attract the negative ions of the NaCl crystal. The negative regions of the water molecules attract the positive ions of the NaCl crystal. These attractions separate the ions, and the salt dissolves into sodium ions (Na^+) and chloride ions (Cl^-).

Covalent compounds that are polar can dissolve in water. As you may recall, polar molecules have regions of slightly positive and slightly negative charge. Because water is also polar, water dissolves many polar molecules. The ability of water to form solutions so readily has earned it the title of "the universal solvent."

Most living things depend on water to survive. Most organisms can live without food for a longer time than

SUPER READ!

FIGURE 2.20
Solid crystals of copper sulfate are added to a solvent (water). What is happening in each picture?

Chapter 2 Chemical Basis of Life **49**

ENGAGE

Consider the Big Idea!

Have students read The Big Idea! at the top of the page. Explain that this statement points out how life's chemical reactions depend on water.

Use the Visual

Have students study the photograph that opens this section. Ask them to explain how water affects their life. Guide the discussion toward identifying water as the main ingredient in most solutions.

Check Prior Knowledge

To assess students' prior knowledge about the dependence of organisms on water, ask:

- **What happens if plants and animals are unable to get water for a long period?** (They die of dehydration.)
- **How do living organisms use water?** (Water is used to transport substances throughout the body and to control body temperature.)

SUPER READ! **Previewing** To practice strategies for effective reading, use pages 27-28 in *Super Read!*

Interpreting Visuals
To practice strategies for effective reading, use pages 31-32 in *Super Read!*

STUDENT RESOURCES

From the Teacher's Resource Package, use:
- Section Review 2.5, Activity Recordsheet 2-3, Enrichment Topic 2-3, Vocabulary Review 2 and Chapter 2 Tests from Unit 1 Review Module
- Lab 4: "Measuring pH"

TECHNOLOGY RESOURCES

Relevant technology resources include:
- Spanish Student Edition CD-ROM
- Teacher's Resource Planner CD-ROM
- TestWorks CD-ROM: Chapter 2 Tests

❷ Copper sulfate dissolves in the water to form a solution.

2 TEACH

Explain

Draw a water molecule on the board, identifying the poles. Point out that an unshared pair of electrons in oxygen bends the hydrogen atoms toward each other and causes the molecule to have a positive and negative pole. The surface molecules cling together to form a compact layer of water molecules. This layer, or film, of water is strong enough for the water strider to walk on.

Apply

Write the terms *solution, solute,* and *solvent* on the board. Emphasize that a solution is a uniform mixture of substances, a solute is the substance that is dissolved, and the solvent is the dissolving substance. Ask students to refer to the glass of saltwater and give an example of each term. (Salt/solute, water/solvent, salt water/solution) Then ask them to name other common solutions. (Tea, coffee, lemonade)

Teacher Demo

Boil a saltwater solution in front of the class. After the water evaporates, have students examine the beaker with a hand lens and describe what they see. Ask them how this experiment shows that saltwater is a solution and not a compound.

Most of us get our water from a public water supply or from a well. Water must meet safety standards set by the federal government. Find out if your water at home comes from a public supply or a well. Then contact local government officials and find out what would happen if your water supply became unsafe or if a natural disaster such as a hurricane or tornado damaged water delivery systems. Most communities have civil defense plans for distributing clean water in the event of an emergency. To learn more about water supplies, go to this Internet address: *http://basis_of_life.biosurf.com.*

IN THE COMMUNITY
Where Does Your Water Come From?

FIGURE 2.21

The Cohesion of Water Molecules

Water in plants
The cohesion of water molecules allows plants such as this tree to move water through a tissue called xylem from the ground up to its leaves.

Xylem

Water strider
The surface tension of water supports the weight of this water strider, allowing it to "skate" across the surface.

50 *Unit 1 The Basis of Life*

they can live without a fresh supply of water. The seeds of plants and the spores of certain plants, fungi, and bacteria can exist without water only if they are dormant. In order to become metabolically active, their water content must increase. In fact, the very presence of water prompts most seeds and spores to germinate.

TWO FEATURES OF WATER
How bugs water-ski

In addition to being the universal solvent, water has other important characteristics, many of which are related to hydrogen bonding. Hydrogen bonds, as you have learned, are weak chemical attractions between hydrogen and other atoms. Two characteristics related to hydrogen bonding in water are cohesion and expansion.

Cohesion means "sticking together." Hydrogen bonding causes water molecules to cling to each other. Cohesion produces surface tension, which causes a filmlike boundary to form on the surface of water. The water strider in *Figure 2.21* is supported by the surface tension of the water in the pond.

The cohesion characteristic of water also is important for the movement of water through the trunks of tall trees. Water molecules stick together and are literally pulled up narrow tubes called xylem in the trunk. You will learn more about this process in Chapter 18.

You have probably seen ice floating on top of water. This common phenomenon demonstrates another important characteristic of water—it expands as it freezes. (Most substances shrink as they freeze.) Because water expands as it freezes, ice has a lower density than liquid water. This lower density causes ice to float on water. Because ice floats on water, ponds freeze from the top down, enabling pond-dwelling organisms to survive in the cold liquid water beneath the ice.

ACIDS, BASES, AND SALTS
Keep that balance

When an ionic compound is placed in water, forming a solution, the compound breaks apart and releases ions. A compound that releases hydrogen ions (H^+) in water is called an **acid.** Hydrogen chloride (HCl), for example, produces hydrogen ions (H^+) and chloride ions (Cl^-) when dissolved in water. In solution with water, HCl is called hydrochloric acid. Hydrochloric acid is present in the digestive juices in your stomach. Other acidic substances include orange juice and vinegar.

A **base** is a compound that produces hydroxide ions (OH^-) when dissolved in water. Sodium hydroxide (NaOH) is a base. When dissolved in water, it produces sodium ions (Na^+) and hydroxide ions (OH^-). Examples of bases include soaps and egg whites. You can find examples of other acids and bases in *Figure* 2.22. Strong acids and bases that do not occur naturally in food can be extremely dangerous and should be handled with care.

Compounds that yield ions other than hydrogen or hydroxide ions when in solution are called salts. Sodium chloride and potassium chloride are examples of salts.

The degree or range of acidity is defined by the pH scale. The "p" can be thought of as standing for "power," and the "H" stands for the hydrogen ion. The **pH scale** is the standard measurement of the concentration of hydrogen ions (H^+) present in a solution. The pH scale ranges from 0 to 14.

Examine the pH scale in *Figure* 2.22. Notice that a pH value of 7 indicates a neutral solution, one that is

pH of Common Substances			
Property	Substance	pH	Color
Strong base	Lye	14	■
	Bleach	13	■
Weak base	Baking soda	9	■
	Egg white	8	■
	Blood	7.4	■
Neutral	Pure water	7	■
	Many soils	6	■
	Coffee	5	■
Weak acid	Tomatoes	4	■
	Vinegar	3	■
	Digestive juice	2	■
Strong acid	Battery acid	0.5	■

FIGURE 2.22
You can use the pH scale to measure the acidity of a substance. Standard pH paper indicates the pH of a substance by changing to the characteristic color shown in the table. What is the most acidic food substance on this chart? The most basic?

neither an acid nor a base. In a neutral solution the concentration of hydrogen ions equals that of hydroxide ions. A substance with a pH of less than 7 is an acid. The lower the pH number, the more acidic the substance is. Conversely, the higher the pH reading, the more basic that substance is.

LAB ZONE Do It!

What Is the pH of Common Foods?

Standard pH paper responds to a wide range of pH values. You can use pH paper to find the pH of common foods if you . . .

Try This

1 Assemble samples of a variety of foods. (Oranges, apples, potatoes, bananas, and milk are some good choices.)
2 On a paper towel, line up enough squares of pH paper to test each of your samples.
3 For each sample, apply the cut surface of the food or a drop of the liquid to a clean pH square. Avoid touching the pH paper because substances on your hands could affect your results.
4 Compare the color of each pH square to the chart on the pH paper dispenser. Record the pH of each sample.

Analyze Your Results

1 Make a class chart displaying the pH of some common foods.
2 Which substance is the most acidic? Which is most basic?
3 What characteristics do acidic foods share? Basic foods?

 ### Science History

The model for acids and bases described in the text was proposed by the Swedish chemist Svante Arrhenius. Although his model was greeted with some skepticism at first, he was later awarded the Nobel Prize in Chemistry for his theory (1903).

Build Writing Skills

Ask students to write one or two paragraphs explaining the practical use of the pH scale in common situations, such as in gardening, in medicine, and in pool maintenance.

LAB ZONE Do It! TEAM WORK

What is the pH of Common Foods?

Analyze Your Results

1-2 Common foods, from most acidic to most basic, have the following pH readings: lemons 2.3; vinegar 2.8; soft drinks 3.0; grapefruits 3.1; apples 3.1; oranges 3.5; bananas 4.6; milk 6.5; eggs 7.8.
3 All acidic foods have a pH under 7; all basic foods have a pH over 7.

---

❶ The most acidic food substance is vinegar; the most acidic food listed is tomatoes. The most basic food substance is baking soda. The most basic food is egg white.

Class Activity

Have students use universal pH paper to test the pH of the rainwater or snow in the area in which they live. Students should keep a record of the pH of precipitation that occurs during several weeks or months.

3 ASSESS

Evaluate Understanding

To assess students' understanding of the characteristics of solutions, ask:

- **Why is water referred to as a "universal solvent?"** (It forms solutions readily.)
- **What happens when water is added to acid?** (An acid in water releases hydrogen ions.)
- **What occurs when water is added to base?** (A base produces hydroxide ions when it dissolves in water.)

Reteach

Have students prepare a list of common solutions, such as foods, beverages, and medications, that are mostly water. Discuss why the water content is important in each solution.

❶ It killed them.

FIGURE 2.23
Acid rain can have very damaging effects on plant life. How did acid rain in the soil affect the Frasier firs? ❶

Almost all chemical reactions of living things take place at pH levels between 6 and 8. The pH of your blood is constant at about 7.4, which is slightly basic. If it were to become more acidic than 7, or more basic than 7.8, you would not survive more than a few minutes. However, in your stomach the presence of digestive gastric acids results in pH levels as low as 2. Because of the stomach's protective mucous coat, the acidic pH does not harm the stomach lining.

The chemical reactions that take place in your body are very sensitive to the presence of hydrogen ions. Even a small change in pH can cause some enzymes to stop functioning effectively. For this reason, your body has a control system to regulate the pH level of your blood and ensure homeostasis.

 Why is water important to life processes?

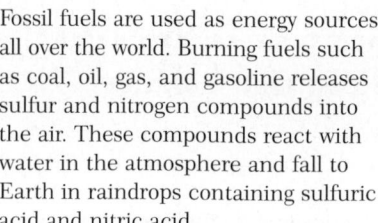

ENVIRONMENTAL AWARENESS

When it rains acid

Fossil fuels are used as energy sources all over the world. Burning fuels such as coal, oil, gas, and gasoline releases sulfur and nitrogen compounds into the air. These compounds react with water in the atmosphere and fall to Earth in raindrops containing sulfuric acid and nitric acid.

Rain water with a pH of less than 5.6 is called acid rain. Acid rain is a persistent threat to the environment. Acid rain (including acid snow, fog, and dew) washes away vital minerals from soil. The acids also release some metals, such as aluminum, from soil particles. High levels of some metals in soil can kill many plants.

Lakes are also vulnerable to acid rain, which kills aquatic organisms and throws off the balance of the ecosystem. The problems of acid rain can be resolved, in part, by reducing the amount of pollutants in the air.

CHECKPOINT 2.5

1. List and explain the properties of water that support life.
2. Compare acids and bases, and give an example of each.
3. **Critical Thinking** The cohesive properties of water allow it to absorb heat without indicating a large increase in temperature. How does this property help your body to maintain a constant temperature?

Build on What You Know

4. Use the scientific method to design an experiment testing the effects of pH on a plant species. *(Need to jog your memory? Revisit relevant concepts in Chapter 1, Section 1.3.)*

CHECKPOINT 2.5

1. Water forms solutions in which all life's processes occur; cohesion and expansion during freezing are important to life; and living organisms are sensitive to the acids, bases, and salts that are dissolved in water.
2. An acid is a substance that releases H^+ ions upon dissolution; a base is a substance that releases OH^- ions upon dissolution. Examples may include vinegar, citric acid, and HCl (acids) and lye, baking soda, and ammonia (bases).
3. **Drawing conclusions** Because the body contains so much water, it can absorb some heat as the air temperature rises without overheating.
4. Students' experiments will vary. Accept reasonable responses.

Chapter 2 Review

 **2.1–2.2** Living things are made of chemicals with characteristic structures and functions.
2.3–2.4 Life processes depend on breaking and forming chemical bonds in chemical reactions.
2.5 Life processes depend on the properties of water and the characteristics of solutions.

Sum It Up

Use the following summary to review the main concepts in this chapter.

2.1   Chemicals in Organisms

- Organisms use the energy stored in carbohydrates as fuel for life activities.
- Some lipids provide long-term energy storage and heat insulation. Other lipids serve structural and control functions.
- Twenty small molecules called amino acids make up the many complex proteins with their diverse functions.
- Large molecules called nucleic acids store genetic information.

2.2   Basics of Chemistry

- An atom is the smallest particle of an element. Uncombined atoms are neutral because they contain equal numbers of protons (+) and electrons (–).
- Atoms of different elements combine to form compounds, which are held together by chemical bonds. Ionic bonds form when atoms gain or lose electrons. Covalent bonds form when atoms share electrons.

2.3   Chemicals at Work

- Chemical equations represent chemical reactions. During a chemical reaction, bonds are broken and new bonds are formed. Energy is absorbed or released.
- Most enzymes are protein catalysts that speed up or slow down the chemical reactions in living organisms.

2.4   Chemistry in Life Processes

- The metabolism of an organism comprises all the chemical reactions that occur, including those involved in obtaining energy, producing new cells, maintaining homeostasis, communicating, and reproducing.

2.5   Water and Solutions

- Life's chemical reactions all occur in water solutions. Because water is a polar molecule, it can dissolve many kinds of compounds.
- For an organism to function properly, the degree of acidity, or pH, of internal fluids such as blood must be maintained within a narrow range.

Use Terms and Concepts

Use each of the following words or terms in a complete sentence. If you need to review a meaning, turn to the page indicated.

carbohydrates (p. 34)	ion (p. 38)	solution (p. 49)
lipids (p. 35)	isotopes (p. 38)	acid (p. 51)
proteins (p. 35)	chemical bonds (p. 39)	base (p. 51)
nucleic acids (p. 36)	chemical reaction (p. 42)	pH scale (p. 51)
element (p. 37)	enzyme (p. 44)	
compound (p. 37)	metabolism (p. 46)	
organic compounds (p. 37)	homeostasis (p. 47)	

Chapter 2 Chemical Basis of Life   **53**

Review the Big Ideas

Before your students begin the Chapter Review, you may wish to discuss the Big Ideas they have learned in this chapter. Explain that this chapter was important because they learned how and why chemistry is a basis for understanding the life processes that are discussed throughout the textbook. Point out that in Sections 2.1 and 2.2, they learned about the chemicals that make up living things—carbohydrates, lipids, proteins, and nucleic acids— and their functions. Under this Big Idea, the basics of chemistry were introduced and explained. Discuss how these sections built the foundation for understanding the Big Idea for Sections 2.3 and 2.4, in which they learned about the chemistry involved in life processes, including the breaking and forming of chemical bonds in chemical reactions and the chemical reactions involved in the metabolism of living things. Point out that Section 2.5 helped them understand the important role of water in the chemical reactions of living things.

Answers

1. metabolism
2. nucleic acids
3. homeostasis
4. pH scale
5. organic compounds
6. True
7. False. An acid is a substance that releases hydrogen ions in solution.
8. False. Proteins are composed of smaller molecules called amino acids.
9. True
10. True
11. Chemical reactions within organisms take place in water solution. Because water turns to ice when frozen, it becomes less dense and floats. This allows organisms to survive in the liquid water below the ice. Because water molecules cohere, water and nutrients can be transported upward in plants.
12. Acids release hydrogen ions in solution; bases release hydroxide ions. Acids have a pH below 7; bases have a pH above 7.
13. Isotopes are atoms of an element that contain different numbers of neutrons. Some have unstable nuclei. Biologists can use radioactive isotopes to trace processes inside an organism.
14. Protons are positively charged, electrons are negatively charged, and neutrons have no charge. Protons and neutrons are located in the nucleus of an atom; electrons are in motion outside the nucleus. Electrons form bonds between atoms that make up compounds.
15. A solution is a uniform mixture of two or more substances. When table salt and

Use Your Word Power

COMPLETION Write the word or phrase that best completes each statement.

1. The combination of all the chemical reactions that take place in an organism is _____ .

2. Large molecules that carry genetic information are called _____ .

3. The maintenance of a stable set of internal conditions is called _____ .

4. The _____ measures the concentration of hydrogen ions in a solution.

5. Carbon compounds that are associated with living things are called _____ .

TRUE-FALSE Write true if the statement is true. If the statement is false, replace the underlined word(s) to make the statement true.

6. A protein catalyst that speeds up chemical reactions in organisms is called an <u>enzyme</u>.

7. A <u>base</u> is a substance that releases hydrogen ions in solution.

8. <u>Lipids</u> are composed of smaller molecules called amino acids.

9. An atom that has lost or gained electrons is called an <u>ion</u>.

10. The forces that hold two or more atoms together are called <u>chemical bonds</u>.

Show What You Know

11. Why is the compound water considered essential for life on Earth?

12. Compare acids and bases. Include a discussion of the pH scale in your answer.

13. What are isotopes? How are some isotopes used in biological research?

14. Compare the properties of protons, neutrons, and electrons.

15. What is a solution? Describe what happens when table salt and water form a solution.

16. What occurs during a chemical reaction? Give an example of a chemical reaction.

17. Which type of organic compound contradicts water's reputation as a "universal solvent"? Give a specific example to support your answer.

18. How are elements and compounds similar? How do they differ?

19. **Make a Concept Map** Complete the concept map below by adding the following terms: carbon, carbohydrates, lipids, nucleic acids, proteins, and enzymes. For help with making a concept map, see page 952.

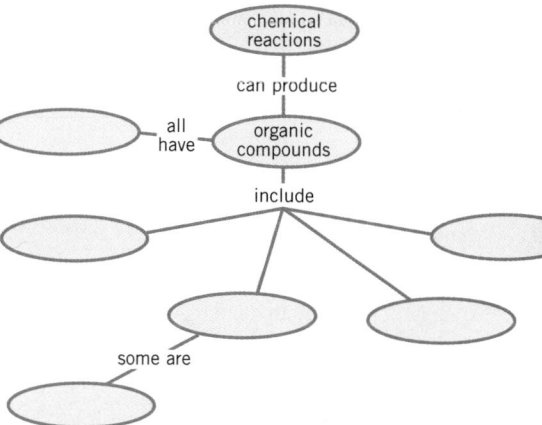

Take It Further

20. **Designing an Experiment** Design an experiment to compare the speed with which ionic, non-polar covalent, and polar covalent compounds dissolve in water. Ionic compounds include table salt and baking soda. Non-polar covalent compounds include vegetable oil and sugar. Polar covalent compounds include acetone and hydrogen chloride. Predict the results of your experiment.

21. **Applying Concepts** Explain why you should not put a sealed container that is completely filled with a water solution in a freezer.

water form a solution, the negative end of polar water molecules are attracted to positive ions, and the positive ends of the water molecules are attracted to negative ions. These attractions overcome the attractions between the positive and negative ions within the ionic compound, causing the compound to dissolve.

16. Chemical bonds are broken and formed, resulting in new substances. Examples will vary.

17. Lipids are not water soluble. Examples may vary. Students may refer to the separation of oil and water in salad dressing or to oil slicks floating on the surface of the ocean.

18. Elements and compounds are pure sub-

22. Designing an Experiment Suggest one or two simple experiments to determine whether a solid white substance is a lipid or a carbohydrate. What evidence would you need to support each hypothesis?

23. Interpreting a Graph The bar graph below shows the total amount of product formed from a chemical reaction that was performed at three different temperatures for the same time period. The same enzyme was involved each time in the chemical reaction. Describe the results at each temperature. Explain why you think these results were obtained.

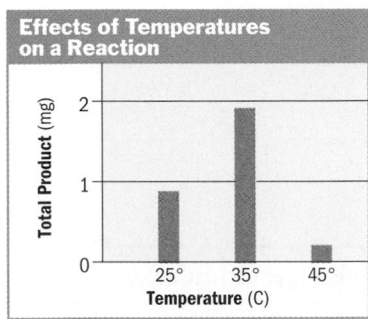

Effects of Temperatures on a Reaction

24. Analyzing Data The three boxes below are part of the periodic table. From the information in the boxes, answer the following questions: What is the name of each element? What is the chemical symbol for each element? What is the atomic number of each element? What is the average atomic mass of each element? How many protons and electrons are there in an atom of each element? How many neutrons are in the most common form of each element?

6	7	8
C	**N**	**O**
Carbon	Nitrogen	Oxygen
12.011	14.007	15.999

Consider the Issues

25. Conflicts About Foods Many organizations publish recommendations about the quantities of carbohydrates, fats, and proteins that people should eat. Sometimes the nutritional guidelines disagree. Describe the information that you would need to decide if the nutritional recommendation of a particular group was based on fact or opinion.

Make New Connections

26. Biology and Art Make three-dimensional models of organic compounds such as single sugars and amino acids. Refer to illustrations in this textbook or in other reference books.

27. Biology and Chemistry Research an element from the table in *Figure 2.5*. When was the element discovered, and how did it get its name? What is the key function of the element in the human body? What foods are sources of the element? What happens to the body if the element is missing? Prepare a poster or short written report to summarize your findings.

28. Biology and Community After discussing your plans and safety procedures with your teacher, collect precipitation (rain and snow) and water samples from local sources, such as puddles, ponds, lakes, or streams. Test the pH of your samples and present your findings to the class.

FAST-FORWARD TO CHAPTER 3

Atoms are the building blocks of cells. Cells are the building blocks of organisms. The next chapter describes the structure of a cell and how the cell functions as the unit of all living things.

stances with distinct sets of characteristic properties. Compounds can be broken down into their constituent elements. Elements cannot be broken down chemically into simpler substances.

19. Concept maps vary, but should show the following: <u>Chemical reactions</u> can produce <u>organic compounds</u>; <u>organic compounds</u> all have <u>carbon</u>; <u>organic compounds</u> include <u>carbohydrates</u>, <u>proteins</u>, <u>lipids</u>, <u>nucleic acids</u>; <u>proteins</u>, some are <u>enzymes</u>.

20. Experiments will vary but should include equivalent amounts of each compound and a method (such as dye) for observing the dissolution of a colorless compound in water. The ionic and polar covalent compounds should dis-

solve readily in water. Nonpolar covalent compounds should dissolve more slowly or not at all.

21. Water expands when frozen. If there is no room left in the container for expansion, the container will shatter.

22. Students may suggest seeing if the substance leaves a greasy mark when rubbed on brown paper, in which case the substance is probably a lipid. If the substance dissolves in water, it is probably a carbohydrate because lipids are not water soluble.

23. At 25° the enzyme catalyzes the chemical reaction. At 35° the increase in temperature doubles the activity of the catalyst and twice as much product is obtained. At 45°, the temperature is high enough to denature the enzyme so it is unable to catalyze the reaction.

24. C=Carbon, atomic #6, mass=12.011, 6 protons, 6 neutrons, 6 electrons
N=Nitrogen, atomic #7, mass=14.007, 7 protons, 7 neutrons, 7 electrons
O=oxygen, atomic #8, mass=15.999, 8 protons, 8 neutrons, 8 electrons

25. Answers will vary but should determine if the recommendation was based on scientific testing.

26. Students could borrow model kits from the chemistry class or use common items.

27. The CRC Handbook of Chemistry and Physics has descriptions of the elements.

28. Results will vary.

PLANNING GUIDE

Section	Student Activities/Features	Teacher's Resource Package
3.1 A Look at Cells **Objectives** ■ Explain the key ideas that make up the cell theory ■ Summarize the role of the microscope in the development of the cell theory	**Lab Zone Discover It!** *Using a Hand Lens,* p. 57 **STS: Frontiers in Biology,** *Seeing Smaller,* p. 60 **Lab Zone Do It!** *How Do You Use the Microscope?* p. 61	**Unit 1 Review Module** ■ Section Review 3.1 ■ Activity Recordsheet 3-1 **Laboratory Manual,** Lab 5: "Viewing the Hidden World"
3.2 Basic Cell Structures **Objectives** ■ Describe the structures and functions of the cell membrane, the cytoplasm, and the nucleus ■ Contrast the cell structures of prokaryotes and eukaryotes	**Everyday Biology** *No Room for a Nucleus,* p. 64	**Unit 1 Review Module** ■ Section Review 3.2
3.3 Cell Organelles **Objectives** ■ Describe the function of key organelles ■ Compare and contrast the characteristics of cilia and flagella		**Unit 1 Review Module** ■ Section Review 3.3 **Laboratory Manual,** Lab 6: "Cells: Living Machines"
3.4 Cell Diversity **Objectives** ■ Contrast the components of plant and animal cells ■ Describe some similarities and differences in the cells of unicellular and multicellular organisms	**Everyday Biology** *Cellulose—Yum!,* p. 70 **Lab Zone Investigate It!** *Comparing Plant and Animal Cells,* p. 71	**Unit 1 Review Module** ■ Section Review 3.4 ■ Activity Recordsheet 3-2 ■ Interpreting Graphics 3 ■ Critical Thinking Exercise 3 ■ Enrichment Topic 3-1 **Interpreting and Developing Graphics** 7, 8
3.5 Cells and Their Environment **Objectives** ■ Describe the process of osmosis in cells and explain its significance ■ Explain active transport and bulk movement	**In the Community** *Cellular Research,* p. 73 **Lab Zone Do It!** *Observing Osmosis and Semipermeability,* p. 74 **Lab Zone Think About It!** *Analyzing Ion Concentrations,* p. 75	**Unit 1 Review Module** ■ Section Review 3.5 ■ Activity Recordsheet 3-3 ■ Vocabulary Review 3 ■ Chapter 3 Tests **Laboratory Manual** ■ Lab 7: "Diffusion and Cell Size" ■ Lab 8: "Osmosis and the Incredible Egg" **Issues and Decision Making** 3-1 **Consumer Applications** 3-1 **Interpreting and Developing Graphics** 9 **Spanish Reviews** Chapter 3

Technology Resources

Internet Connections

Within this chapter, you will see the logo. If you and your students have access to the Internet, the following URL address will provide various Internet connections that are related to topics and features presented in this chapter:

http://basis_of_life.biosurf.com

You can also find relevant chapter material at **The Biology Place** address:

http://www.biology.com

CD-ROMs

Biología: la telaraña de la vida, (Spanish Student Edition), Chapter 3
Teacher's Resource Planner, Chapter 3 Supplements
Interactive Biological Simulations
- Cell Structure
- Transport Through Membranes
TestWorks CD-ROM
- Chapter 3 Tests

Videodiscs

Animated Biological Concepts Videodiscs
- Diffusion and Osmosis
- Passive and Active Transport
- Endocytosis and Exocytosis

Overhead Transparencies

- Fluid Mosaic Model, #6
- Organelles, #7
- Plant and Animal Cells, #8

Videotapes

Biology Alive! Video Series
- Signs of Life Video
- The Domain of Life Video
Rewind: The Web of Life Reteach Videos

Planning for Activities

STUDENT EDITION
Lab Zone
Discover It! p. 57
- hand lens
- black and white and/or color newspaper pictures, comics, or magazine

Lab Zone Do It! p. 61
- compound light microscope
- slide
- coverslip
- scissors
- strands of hair

Lab Zone
Investigate It! p. 71
- compound light microscope
- leaf from Elodea plant
- forceps
- medicine dropper
- slide
- coverslip
- prepared slide of human cheek cells

Lab Zone Do It! p. 74
- raw egg
- jar with lid
- white vinegar
- tape measure

TEACHER'S EDITION
Teacher Demo, p. 58
A look at different cells
- microprojector
- prepared slides of plant, animal, and unicellular organism cells

Teacher Demo, p. 59
Looking through a "microscope"
- dish
- pond water
- overhead projector
- hole punch
- cardboard
- medicine dropper

Teacher Demo, p. 60
Effects of staining specimens
- prepared slides of specimens

Quick Activity, p. 62
Mixing oil and water
- beaker
- salad oil
- glass container

Teacher Demo, p. 63
Modeling a cell membrane
- petri dish
- overhead projector
- vegetable oil
- ground chili powder

Teacher Demo, p. 64
Cell cytoskeleton model
- clay
- drinking straws

Teacher Demo, p. 68
Cilia and flagella movement
- microprojector
- Paramecium
- Euglena
- petri dishes

Teacher Demo, p. 72
Water through a cell membrane
- muslin cloth bag
- pan

Class Activity, p. 73
A model of osmosis
- food coloring
- sugar
- fine tea strainer
- glass beaker

Teacher Demo, p. 73
Testing a "plant membrane"
- medicine dropper
- food coloring
- test tube
- strip of cellophane
- rubber band
- jar

Chapter Objectives

Students will learn the main concepts of this chapter as they complete the following objectives.

- Explain the key ideas that make up the cell theory
- Describe the structure and function of the cell membrane, the cytoplasm, and the nucleus
- Contrast the cell structures of prokaryotes and eukaryotes
- Describe the functions of key organelles
- Contrast the components of plant and animal cells
- Describe the processes of osmosis, active transport, and bulk movement

Key Words

3.1 *cell theory*

3.2 *cell membrane, phospholipid, cytoplasm, cytoskeleton, nucleus, chromosomes, nucleolus, prokaryotes, eukaryotes*

3.3 *ribosomes, endoplasmic reticulum, Golgi apparatus, mitochondria, lysosomes, cilia, flagella*

3.4 *cell wall, chloroplasts, vacuole*

3.5 *semipermeable, passive transport, active transport, diffusion, osmosis, exocytosis, endocytosis*

The Opening Story

Have students explain how tasks on a factory assembly line might compare to the contribution specialized cell parts make to a living organism.

CHAPTER 3

Cell Structure and Function

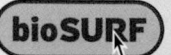

You can find out more about cell structure and function by exploring the following Internet address:
http://basis_of_life.biosurf.com

In this chapter . . .

FEATURES

Everyday Biology
- No Room for a Nucleus
- Cellulose—Yum!

In the Community
Cellular Research

 Frontiers in Biology
Seeing Smaller

LAB ZONES

Discover It!
- Using a Hand Lens

Do It!
- How Do You Use the Microscope?
- Observing Osmosis and Semipermeability

Think About It!
- Analyzing Ion Concentrations

Investigate It!
- Comparing Plant and Animal Cells

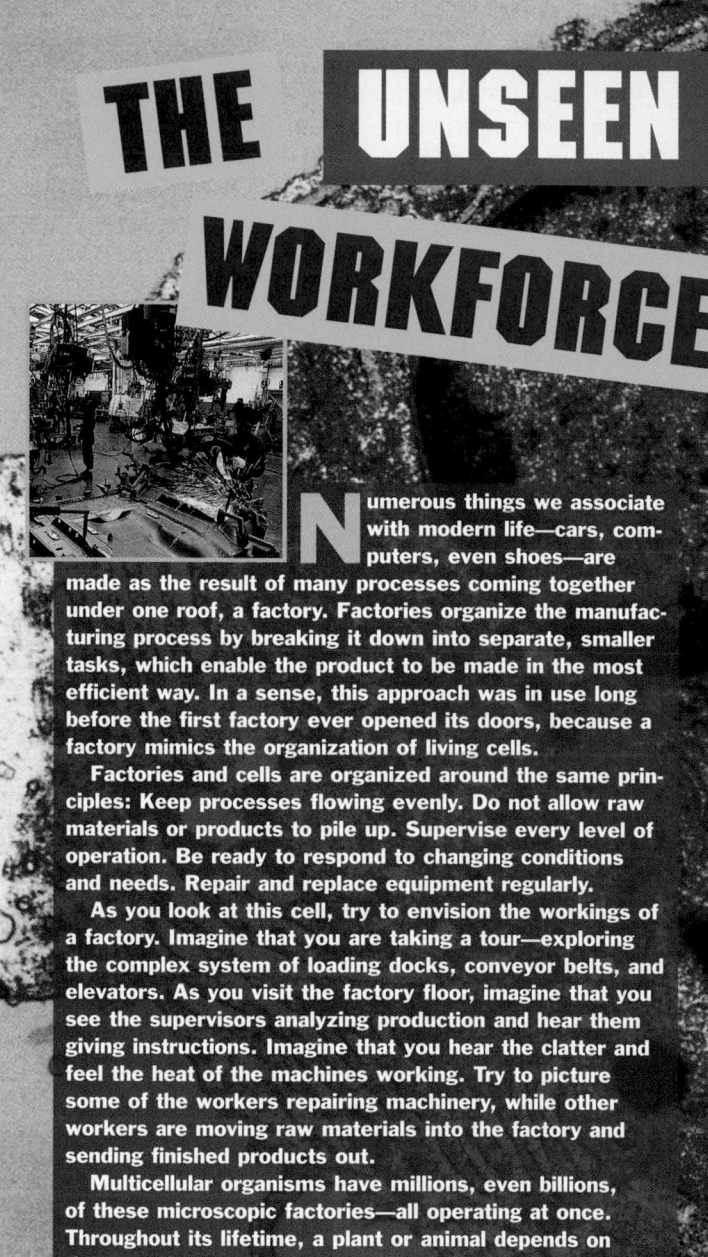

THE UNSEEN WORKFORCE

Numerous things we associate with modern life—cars, computers, even shoes—are made as the result of many processes coming together under one roof, a factory. Factories organize the manufacturing process by breaking it down into separate, smaller tasks, which enable the product to be made in the most efficient way. In a sense, this approach was in use long before the first factory ever opened its doors, because a factory mimics the organization of living cells.

Factories and cells are organized around the same principles: Keep processes flowing evenly. Do not allow raw materials or products to pile up. Supervise every level of operation. Be ready to respond to changing conditions and needs. Repair and replace equipment regularly.

As you look at this cell, try to envision the workings of a factory. Imagine that you are taking a tour—exploring the complex system of loading docks, conveyor belts, and elevators. As you visit the factory floor, imagine that you see the supervisors analyzing production and hear them giving instructions. Imagine that you hear the clatter and feel the heat of the machines working. Try to picture some of the workers repairing machinery, while other workers are moving raw materials into the factory and sending finished products out.

Multicellular organisms have millions, even billions, of these microscopic factories—all operating at once. Throughout its lifetime, a plant or animal depends on the smooth and effective operation of nature's unseen assembly lines.

 Discover It!

Using a Hand Lens

You need *a hand lens, black and white and/or color newspaper pictures, comics, or magazines*

1. Look at a picture from the newspaper without magnification. Then examine the same picture with the hand lens. What do you see now that you could not see before?
2. Go on a hunt. Try to find an object in the classroom that reveals something unexpected when you look at it under the hand lens. You may want to try looking at fabrics, school supplies, or plants.

Most hand lenses magnify objects only about 1.25 to 1.5 times. Biologists have more powerful tools—microscopes— for examining cells and their structures, which are invisible to the unaided eye. Light microscopes, such as the ones you will use later in this chapter, have the ability to magnify objects up to 1000 times.

WRITE ABOUT IT!

In your science journal, write an imaginative description of one or more things you examined under the hand lens. You might want to start by thinking of an analogy—a comparison between the object you saw and something it resembled.

PORTFOLIO PREVIEW

Students should be encouraged to add to their portfolios as they work through this chapter. In addition to the *Write About It* opportunity, the following sections are excellent opportunities for portfolio entries:

- Section 3.1: *A Look at Cells*
- Section 3.5: *Cells and Their Environment*

Opening Activities

 If you have access to the Internet in your classroom or school, you may wish to have students connect to the address shown on page 56. You may also want to have students conduct net searches for information using key words related to this chapter. For example, they could search for entries under cell organelles, eukaryotic and prokaryotic cells, and osmosis and diffusion.

Discover It!

Using a Hand Lens

TEAM WORK

Before students begin this chapter, have them do the suggested activity either with a partner or in small groups. Discuss their observations as a class.

WRITE ABOUT IT

To prepare students for the writing assignment, provide examples of an analogy, such as comparing the veins in a leaf to the lines on a road map.

REWIND to Chapter 2

Briefly review the concepts learned in Chapter 2, *Chemical Basis of Life*. Ask:

- **How will learning about living cells help you to understand how chemistry is important to living things?**

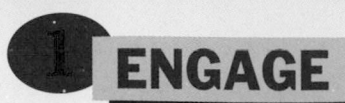

ENGAGE

Consider The Big Idea

Have students read The Big Idea! at the top of the page. Ask students to explain what life function cells must perform.

Use the Visual

Have students study the photographs that open the section. Point out that Marcello Malpighi is considered the founder of microscopic anatomy. Explain that cells are living matter, but they are not all alike. Ask:

■ **What are some characteristics of the red blood cells shown in the photo?** (Students should notice shape, color, and size.)

Check Prior Knowledge

To assess students' prior knowledge about cells and their environment, ask:

■ **What are some kinds of cells that make up your body?** (Skin, hair, bone, nerve, and organ cells are examples.)
■ **What is meant by solution concentration?** (The amount of soluble substance dissolved in a fluid)

Teacher Demo

Use a microprojector to show prepared slides of different cells. Include plant, animal, and unicellular organisms. List each type of cell on the board and ask students to identify the characteristics of the cells you display.

3.1 A Look at Cells

What you'll learn

IDEAS
• To explain the key ideas that make up the cell theory
• To summarize the role of the microscope in the development of the cell theory

WORD
cell theory

Seeing cells

Marcello Malpighi (1628–1694), a physician in Bologna, Italy, was one of the first to use microscopes in medicine. His discovery of capillaries, the smallest blood vessels, provided the missing link in the understanding of blood circulation. Malpighi was also the first to see and describe red blood cells, shown here moving through a capillary. Because he questioned long-held beliefs about living organisms, Malpighi struggled throughout his career against his colleagues' disbelief and resentment.

FIGURE 3.1
These cells are magnified 700 times their actual size. What differences do you observe? ❶

WHAT IS A CELL?

Where life happens

You read in Chapter 1 that a cell is the smallest unit of life that can carry out all the functions of a living thing. The size, shape, and structures of cells are very diverse, as you can see from the six kinds of cells in *Figure 3.1.*

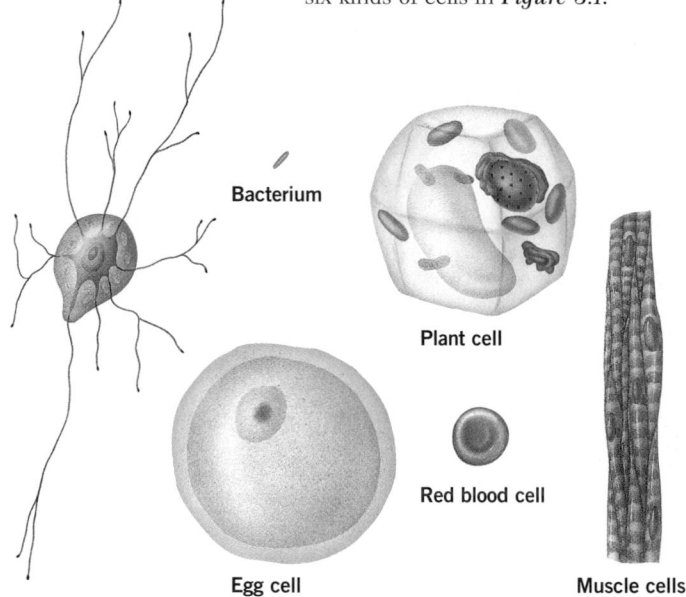

Bacterium

Plant cell

Egg cell

Red blood cell

Muscle cells

Living things may be either unicellular (consisting of one cell) or multicellular (many-celled). Bacteria are one type of unicellular organism. Most of the organisms you are familiar with—including yourself—are multicellular.

As you see in *Figure 3.1,* cells can also vary greatly in size. Notice that the smallest cell is a bacterium. About 8000 of the smallest bacteria could fit inside one of your red blood cells. The longest cells are the very thin nerve cells of large animals. These cells can be more than a meter long. The cell with the greatest volume is an unfertilized ostrich egg. It has about a liter's worth of contents, including stored food.

Notice also that the shape of cells can vary greatly. A cell's shape is related to its function. A long nerve cell, for example, can carry messages from your spine to your toes. Long, slender muscle cells that are grouped together form long, slender muscle tissues. The contraction and relaxation of muscle tissue is responsible for movement in animals.

58 *Unit 1 The Basis of Life*

STUDENT RESOURCES

From the Teacher's Resource Package, use:
■ Section Review 3.1, Activity Record-sheet 3-1 from Unit 1 Review Module
■ Laboratory Manual: Lab Skill 13: "Identifying Parts of a Microscope" and Lab 5: "Viewing the Hidden World"

TECHNOLOGY RESOURCES

Relevant technology resources include:
■ Spanish Student Edition CD-ROM
■ Teacher's Resource Planner CD-ROM

FIGURE 3.2
Robert Hooke's drawings of cork seen through a microscope show rows of empty spaces. What did he call these spaces? ❷

DISCOVERY OF CELLS

A small new world

You are living at a time when a great deal is known about microscopic life. However, in the beginning of the 1600s people knew only about organisms they could see with the unaided eye. They certainly had no knowledge of the existence of cells.

The invention of the microscope was one of the most important breakthroughs in biology. The microscope was invented by a trio of Dutch eyeglass makers in the late 1500s. It consisted of a tube with lenses ground from rock crystal, and it magnified objects up to nine times their actual size. Many other inventors produced variations of this simple model in the early 1600s.

In 1665 the British scientist Robert Hooke published a set of drawings illustrating what he had observed with a microscope. One of these drawings is shown in *Figure 3.2*. Hooke called the empty chambers he saw "cells" because they reminded him of the small rooms, or cells, in a monastery. Scientists later learned that the cells Hooke observed had once contained living matter.

In the early 1670s Anton van Leeuwenhoek (LAY-vun-hohk), a Dutch fabric-store owner, began to grind lenses as a hobby. Leeuwenhoek used his handheld microscopes to examine materials such as pond water and blood. To his amazement, he discovered a world of microscopic organisms and living cells.

CELL THEORY

Biologists build a theory

The invention of the microscope led to many advances in the study of science. By the 1830s many biologists were using the microscope as their chief investigative tool. Some of the key discoveries biologists made during the 1800s are included in *Figure* 3.3. Three of these advances were especially important in building one of the key theories in biology.

Matthias Schleiden was a botanist, a scientist who studies plants. He found that the plant parts he examined were made of cells. In 1838 Schleiden made the generalization that all plants are made of cells.

About the same time, Theodor Schwann was studying animals. His microscopic investigations of animal parts led him to generalize that all animals are made of cells. He further proposed that all organisms are made of cells.

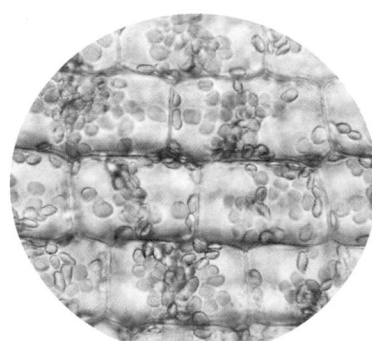

FIGURE 3.4
A micrograph of cells from an *Elodea* plant Is shown at left. Matthias Schleiden determined that all plants are made of cells, but he did not understand how new cells are formed.

Chapter 3 Cell Structure and Function **59**

FIGURE 3.3
Discoveries with the Light Microscope

1665 Robert Hooke (English) publishes *Micrographia*, which contains drawings of cork and other objects he has observed.

1674 Anton van Leeuwenhoek (Dutch) begins to make single-lens microscopes that magnify objects about 200 times.

1838 Matthias Schleiden (German) concludes that all plants are made of cells.

1839 Theodor Schwann (German) concludes that all living things are made of cells.

1855 Rudolf Virchow (German) infers that all new cells come from existing cells.

1862 Louis Pasteur (French) publishes his theory that microscopic organisms cause contagious diseases.

1879 Hermann Fol (Swiss) is the first person to see an egg cell being fertilized by a sperm.

1882 Walther Flemming (German) publishes his discovery of chromatin, a threadlike material in cell nuclei, and the steps of cell division, or mitosis.

TEACH

Use the Visual

Have students study Figure 3.2. Ask:

- **What do you see in the individual cells?** (They are empty.)
- **How did the development of better microscopes advance cell theory?** (Scientists could see more detail inside cells)

Clarify Misconceptions

Students may assume that the larger an organism is, the larger its cells are. Explain that while cells vary in shape and size, most are only about 0.0025 cm in diameter. Cell number, not size, determines an organism's total size.

Teacher Demo

Put a dish of pond water on the overhead. Construct a "microscope" similar to the first one van Leeuwenhoek used by punching a small hole in a piece of cardboard and putting a drop of water in the hole. Have volunteers look at the pond water through the "microscope." Ask:

- **How does the image change through the "microscope?"** (The image is larger.)

MULTICULTURAL PERSPECTIVE

Point out that the advancement of knowledge about cell theory involved scientists from western Europe. The keen interest in science that flourished in the universities in these countries during the 1800s was a major factor in advancing scientific knowledge.

❶ Answers may vary, but should include differences in size, shape, and grouping (either multi- or unicellular).
❷ Cells, because they reminded him of the cells in a monastery.

Build Writing Skills

Have students write an essay about a scientist discussed in the chapter who made a major contribution to one principle of cell theory. Have them identify the contribution the scientist made and explain why it is important. Volunteers can share their essays with the class.

Class Activity

Have students make a water lens by covering a page of newsprint with plastic wrap and then putting a drop of water on the plastic. The words on the newsprint will appear larger. Explain that light bends, or refracts, as it passes through the water. Tell students that the lens in a microscope also enlarges an image by refracting light.

Teacher Demo

Prepare several slides of the same kind of specimen stained with different staining solutions. Use a microprojector to illustrate the effect each type of stain has on the specimen. Point out that some parts of the specimen absorbed some stains more readily than other parts. Explain that the differences in absorption make staining a useful tool for studying various specimens.

❶ Phase contrast

FIGURE 3.5
These three photographs of paramecia were taken using different light microscopy techniques. Which technique provides the most contrast and detail? ❶

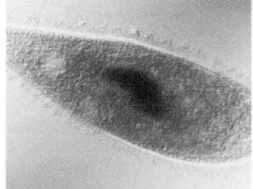 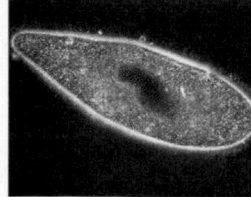 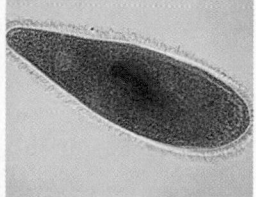

Bright-field micrograph　　Dark-field micrograph　　Phase contrast micrograph

FIGURE 3.6

Milestones in Microscopy

1931 Ernst Ruska builds the first electron microscope.

1950s Biologists begin to use electron microscopes to study living things.

1965 Electron microscope shows fossilized cells that are 3.5 billion years old.

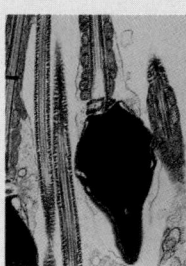

Transmission electron micrograph of sperm

Scanning electron micrograph of sperm

During the 1830s most people, including many scientists, thought that new living things could appear spontaneously from nonliving matter. You may recall from Chapter 1 that this idea was called spontaneous generation. In 1858, a German doctor named Rudolf Virchow disputed the idea of spontaneous generation. Virchow reasoned that new plant cells arise only from existing plant cells, and new animal cells arise only from existing animal cells.

The ideas of Schleiden, Schwann, and Virchow make up what is now called the cell theory. The **cell theory** consists of three principles:

- Cells are the basic units of all life.
- All organisms are made of one or more cells.
- All cells arise from existing cells.

The cell theory emphasizes that all organisms are composed of cells, the fundamental units of life. Historically the cell theory has provided direction for the work of many biologists and physicians as they study life processes, genetics, and diseases.

FRONTIERS IN BIOLOGY

Seeing smaller

The progress of biology often depends on the advances of technology. In fact, the study of life has paralleled the invention of tools that extend scientists' ability to observe and analyze information. One of the most important tools used by biologists is the microscope.

Until the 1950s all readily available microscopes were light microscopes—instruments that use either sunlight or artificial light to view objects. One of the main advantages of the light microscope is that it can magnify many microscopic organisms while they are alive. However, if the object being studied is too large, it has to be sliced thin to allow light to pass through it.

Light microscopes can magnify objects such as tiny organisms up to about 1000 times their actual size. If you try to obtain a larger magnification, the image begins to look blurry. Over the years, scientists have found ways to observe objects better by increasing the contrast between different parts of a specimen.

One way to increase the contrast is by using dyes to stain or color a specimen. Dyes improve contrast by selectively staining certain parts of the specimen. The stained areas then become more visible. One drawback to the staining method, however, is that the dyes usually kill the specimen. Another way to increase the contrast is by manipulating the light. Notice how contrast affects the three images in *Figure 3.5*. How do the three views compare? ❷

Since the 1950s biologists have been using microscopes that use electrons instead of light. Electron microscopes can magnify objects up to a million times their actual size. Before

At Risk Have students create a video storyboard about a character shrunk to a tiny size capable of exploring the inside of a cell. Suggest students keep a record of their ideas.

❷ Bright field; light passes directly through the specimen; requires staining. Dark-field; light passes through specimen at an angle and only light-reflecting particles are seen. Phase contrast; density variations within specimen are amplified. Image has more contrast.

❸ The SEM provides a three-dimensional view of surface features. The TEM shows the cell's internal structure.

FIGURE 3.7
This image was created using SIAM, a microscope that can resolve features as small as 1 nanometer (nm), which is about five times the size of an individual atom.

a specimen can be viewed, all parts of it must be fixed, or locked in position, and placed in a vacuum. Consequently, electron microscopes cannot be used to view organisms that are alive.

Electron microscopes work in two ways to produce images. Some microscopes pass, or transmit, electrons through a thin slice of an object. These microscopes are called transmission electron microscopes (TEM).

Scanning electron microscopes (SEM) examine, or scan, the outside of an object. Compare the images produced by two kinds of electron microscopes in *Figure 3.6*. How **3** does the TEM differ from the SEM?

A new microscopic technique has recently been developed. It uses some principles of the light microscope but has the potential to allow the imaging of single atoms. Called a scanning interferometric apertureless microscope (SIAM), it produces about 500 times better resolution than is possible with existing light microscopes.

For biologists the SIAM could be an important tool for studying DNA because it can be used to view and identify individual molecules.

LAB ZONE Do It!

How Do You Use the Microscope?

You will use a compound light microscope in many activities throughout this textbook. You can learn how when you . . .

Try This

1 Cut a 2-centimeter (cm) piece of one of your hairs. Without the microscope, examine the hair and record your observations about its color, thickness, shape, and texture.
2 Follow instructions in the Appendix under "Using a Microscope" (p. 947) and reexamine the piece of hair using low and high power. Add to your observations about the hair's characteristics.
3 Compare the cut end of the hair with the natural end. How are they different? Why?

4 Exchange samples with a classmate and compare his or her hair with your own. Record your observations.

Analyze Your Results

Compare the level of detail you saw without the microscope, with the microscope on low power, and with the microscope on high power. Give examples of the way the hair appeared in each case.

Currently, mapping genetic profiles of organisms takes years. In the future, with SIAM's help, DNA sequencing might be accomplished much faster.

CHECKPOINT 3.1

1. Explain the key ideas of the cell theory.
2. Summarize the role of the microscope in the development of the cell theory.
3. Critical Thinking Why do you think that most biologists were unimpressed when the microscope was first invented?

Build on What You Know

4. Compare the relationship between structure and function in chemicals and in cells. *(Need to jog your memory? Revisit relevant concepts in Chapter 2, Section 2.1.)*

Chapter 3 Cell Structure and Function **61**

LAB ZONE Do It! TEAM WORK

How Do You Use the Microscope?

Analyze Your Results

Without microscope: students may see color differences, thickness, and curliness of hair strand; may feel bulbous hair root. *Low power microscope:* students may see some scales on hair surface and pigment within, and difference between bulbous hair root and cut end of hair. *High power microscope:* students may see bulbous hair root and some hair follicle cells, scales on hair surface and details of pigment, and clear differences in hair strands.

3 ASSESS

Evaluate Understanding

To determine students' knowledge about cell theory, ask:

■ **How does cell theory contradict the idea of spontaneous generation?** (It shows that cells are the basic units of life, all organisms are made of one or more cells, and new cells generate from other living cells.)

Reteach

Work with students to develop a flowchart showing how cell theory explains the generation of a new organism. Have students explain their charts and check them for accuracy.

CHECKPOINT 3.1

1. Cells are the basic units of all life; all organisms are made of one or more cells; all cells arise from existing cells.
2. The invention of the microscope made possible the discovery that cells exist. This discovery led to the realization that all living things are made of cells.
3. **Developing a hypothesis** Answers may vary. Students may say that when the first microscope was invented it was regarded as a toy. No one believed in the existence of things that could not be seen with the naked eye, biologists did not realize the importance of the microscope.
4. The structures of both chemicals and cells are analogous to their function.

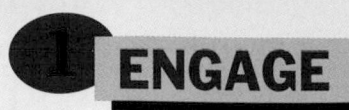

Use the Visual

Have students study the photo that opens the section. Point out that the stained structure in the cell is chromatin. Today, scientists know that chromatin carries hereditary information.

Check Prior Knowledge

To assess students' prior knowledge about the chemistry of life processes. Ask:

- **Why is water referred to as the universal solvent?** (Many substances will dissolve in water.)

Quick Activity

Display a beaker of salad oil to students, and have them identify it as a lipid. Pour the salad oil into a glass container of water. Have students observe what happens. Ask:

- **How do the oil and water react?** (They do not mix, the oil floats.)

Explain that the solubility of these substances in water is important in cell activity.

❶ These features are clearly visible in the micrograph.

 Interactive Biological Simulations
Cell Structure Students can choose to "construct" either a bacterial, plant, or animal cell. Once a cell has been properly constructed, students are quizzed on the cell's structure.

3.2 Basic Cell Structures

What you'll learn

IDEAS
- To describe the structure and function of the cell membrane, the cytoplasm, and the nucleus
- To contrast the cell structure of prokaryotes and eukaryotes

WORDS
cell membrane, phospholipid, cytoplasm, cytoskeleton, nucleus, chromosomes, nucleolus, prokaryotes, eukaryotes

When stains are good
In 1880 German biologist Walther Flemming was the first to describe a complex material located in the nuclei of cells. The new material was called "chromatin" because the tightly bundled fibers readily absorbed colored stains. "Chroma-" comes from the Greek word for color. You can see darkly stained nuclei in these cheek cells. Many structures in cells become visible when stained.

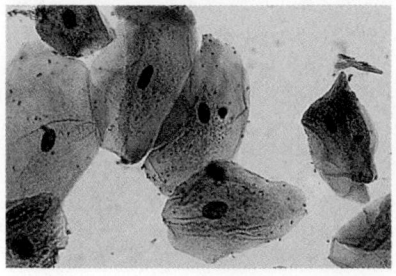

THE CELL MEMBRANE

Controlling the flow

As you now know, all living things consist of one or more cells. Although cell structure may vary from one organism to another, certain features are common to the cells of animals, plants, and many other living things. *Figure 3.8* shows a cross section of a cell and highlights three common features: the cell membrane, cytoplasm, and nucleus.

The cells of all organisms are surrounded by a cell membrane. The **cell membrane** is a thin layer of lipid and protein that separates the cell's contents from its environment. Cell membranes are 5 to 10 nm thick. A stack of 10,000 membranes is about equal to the thickness of this page.

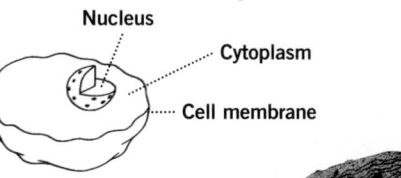
Nucleus — Cytoplasm — Cell membrane

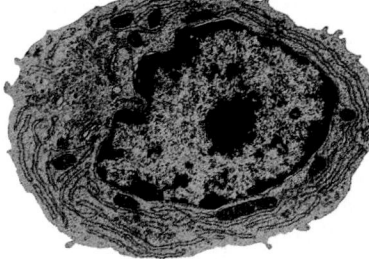

FIGURE 3.8
The cutaway diagram of a cell is shown above. Notice the cell's three principal features: cell membrane, cytoplasm, and nucleus. Can you locate these features in the micrograph on the right? ❶

The cell membrane functions like a fence with gates, controlling what enters and leaves the cell.

Membranes are made mostly of phospholipid (fos-foh-LIP-id) molecules. You can see a phospholipid molecule in *Figure 3.9*. A **phospholipid** is a type of lipid made from glycerol, two fatty acids, and a phosphate group.

The two ends of the phospholipid molecule have different properties in water. The phosphate head of a phospholipid is hydrophilic (hy-droh-FIL-ik), meaning "water-loving." The phosphate head dissolves easily in water. The lipid tails of the molecule are hydrophobic (hy-droh-FOH-bik), meaning "water-fearing." The lipid tails do not dissolve in water.

When dropped in water, phospholipids will form two layers, called a lipid bilayer. The phosphate heads on both sides of the bilayer face the water. The lipid tails of each layer face each other. You can see the structure of a lipid bilayer in *Figure 3.9*.

The structure of cell membranes is based on a lipid bilayer. The phosphate heads face the watery fluids inside the cell and outside the cell. Lipid tails are sandwiched inside the bilayer. The phospholipids in the cell membrane are constantly being formed and broken down by chemical reactions in living cells.

Protein molecules are embedded in the lipid bilayer. About 30 percent of the proteins are attached to one side of the membrane. The rest extend all the way through the bilayer. There are many kinds of proteins in membranes. For example, red blood cell membranes contain more than 50 different proteins. Some of these proteins help move materials in and out of the cell. Others serve as identification badges that enable cells to recognize each other.

Cell membranes are fluid and have the consistency of vegetable oil. The lipids and proteins are always in motion, like the surface of a soap bubble. The phospholipids drift across the membrane, changing places with one another. Cholesterol molecules interact with the phospholipids, helping to keep the membrane intact, yet fluid.

Proteins in and on the membrane form patterns, or mosaics, on the membrane, such as the one shown in *Figure 3.10*. These proteins move sideways across the membrane like slow-moving ships at sea. Because the membrane is fluid with a mosaic of proteins, scientists call the modern view of membrane structure the fluid mosaic model.

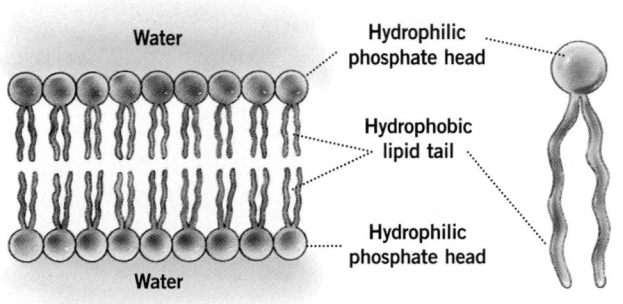

Water
Hydrophilic phosphate head
Hydrophobic lipid tail
Hydrophilic phosphate head
Water
Lipid bilayer
Phospholipid molecule

THE CYTOPLASM

Inside the great membrane

The material between the cell membrane and the nucleus is called the cytoplasm. The **cytoplasm** is a semifluid substance made primarily of water and organic compounds. Various structures called organelles, or "little organs," are suspended in the cytoplasm. Organelles are structures that work like miniature organs within the cell to perform specific functions. You will learn more about these important structures and their specific functions in section 3.3.

FIGURE 3.9
The phospholipid molecule consists of a phosphate head and two lipid tails. The cutaway view of a lipid bilayer shows the orientation of the lipid molecules. Why are the lipid tails located facing each other? ❷

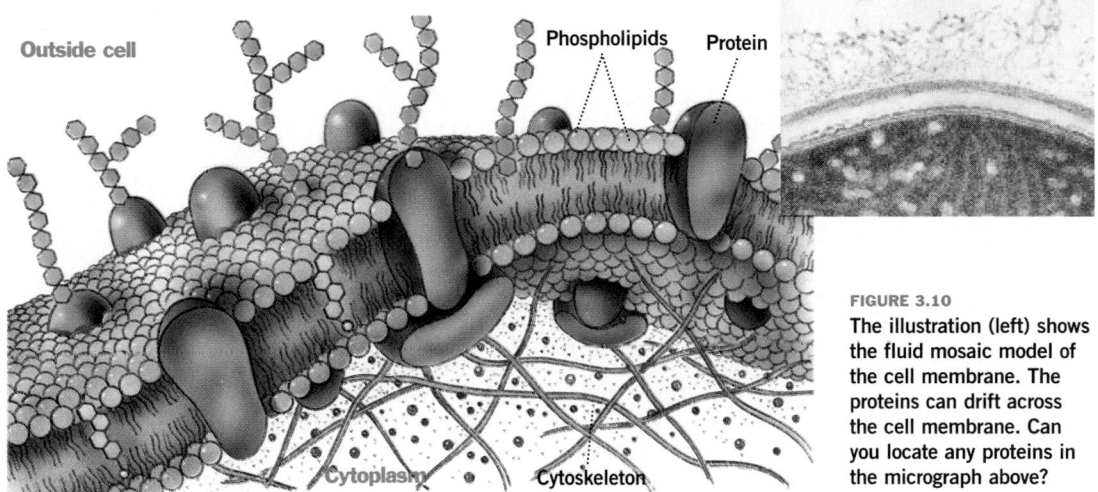

Outside cell
Phospholipids   Protein
Cytoplasm   Cytoskeleton

FIGURE 3.10
The illustration (left) shows the fluid mosaic model of the cell membrane. The proteins can drift across the cell membrane. Can you locate any proteins in the micrograph above?

Chapter 3 Cell Structure and Function **63**

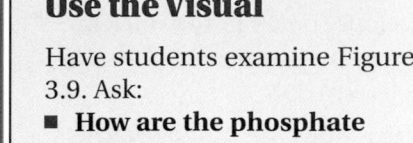

2 **TEACH**

Use the Visual

Have students examine Figure 3.9. Ask:

- **How are the phosphate heads oriented in the cell membrane?** (The heads are in contact with the fluid inside and outside the cell.)
- **Where are the lipid tails oriented?** (The tails are grouped together in the center of the bilayer away from the fluid.)

Think Critically

Point out the membrane bilayer is a lipid. Have students discuss what would happen to the cell membrane if water and oil mixed.

Teacher Demo

Place a petri dish filled with water on an overhead projector. Add a thin layer of vegetable oil to the water. Sprinkle ground chili powder on top of the oil. Refer students to Figure 3.10. Ask:

- **How does this model resemble a cell membrane?** (The cell membrane consistency is similar to vegetable oil. Chili powder floating on the oil represents the protein molecules embedded in the membrane. The water represents cytoplasm.)

❷ Because they are hydrophobic and the membrane is surrounded by water.

MEETING DIVERSE NEEDS

Sight Impaired Illustrate the fluid mosaic model with a tub of water, ping-pong balls, and several tennis balls. Float a layer of ping-pong balls on top of the water and put in the tennis balls. Explain that the water represents the cytoplasm of the cell, the ping-pong balls are the phospholipids, and the tennis balls are proteins. Have students discuss how the movement of the tennis balls through the ping-pong balls demonstrates the activity of the cell membrane.

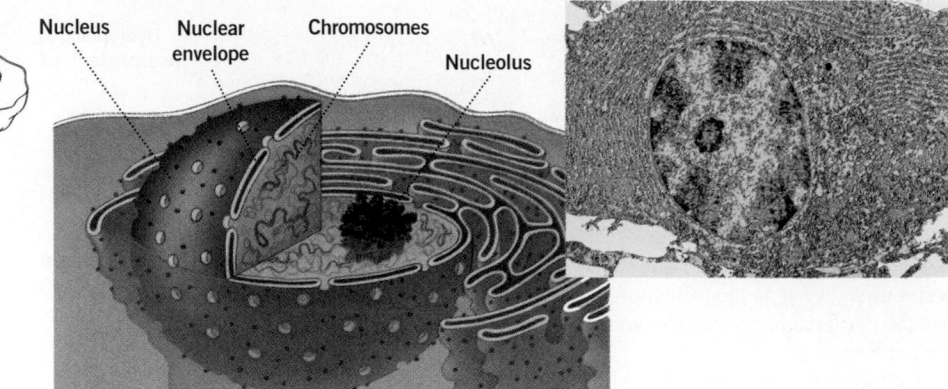

Nucleus   Nuclear   Chromosomes
           envelope   Nucleolus

Use the Visual

Have students study Figure 3.11. Ask them to identify the nuclear envelope, pores in the nuclear envelope, chromosomes, and nucleolus. Ask:

- **How does the nuclear envelope compare to the cell membrane?** (Both are made of lipid bilayers; the nuclear envelope separates the nucleus from the cytoplasm.)

FIGURE 3.11
The image above (left) shows a cutaway view of a nucleus. Why are the pores on the nucleus **①** important? The micrograph (right) shows the nucleus of a human cell.

No Room for a Nucleus

Upon reaching maturity, a human red blood cell actually spits out its nucleus. It uses the space for hemoglobin, the protein that enables red blood cells to carry oxygen from the lungs to the rest of the body.

Teacher Demo

Prepare a three-to-four layer disorganized structure with clay and straws. Show "pipes" going in different directions in each layer. Explain that the model illustrates the cytoskeleton of a cell. The fluid cytoplasm is able to flow through the cytoskeleton, which holds the mitochondria, endoplasmic reticulum, and other structures in place in the cytoplasm.

 Science History

American biologist Lynn Margulis proposed a hypothesis to explain how prokaryotic cells that lacked membrane-bound organelles evolved into eukaryotic cells. Known as the endosymbiotic theory, it suggests that ancient prokaryotes similar to mitochondria and chloroplasts began a symbiotic relationship in a host cell. Eventually these prokaryotes started to function as organelles in the host cells.

One of a cell's most intricate components is its cytoskeleton. The **cytoskeleton** is a network of protein fibers and tubes extending throughout the cytoplasm. The network gives the cell support and helps it to maintain or change its shape. The cell membrane and some organelles are anchored to the cytoskeleton. Materials are transported throughout the cell on the cytoskeleton. Also, the cytoskeleton enables the cell itself to move. For example, amebas move by a coordinated flow of cytoplasm caused by the elongation and contraction of their cytoskeleton.

THE NUCLEUS

Chromosome keeper

Within the cytoplasm lies the most prominent of a cell's organelles, the nucleus. Often called the control center of a cell, the **nucleus** contains most of the cell's genetic material. As you can see in *Figure 3.11,* the nucleus is surrounded by a double membrane called a nuclear envelope. Like the outer membrane of a cell, each membrane of the nuclear envelope is a lipid bilayer. Together the two membranes separate the nucleus from the cytoplasm. In a microscopic view, the nuclear envelope looks pitted. The surface is pierced by tiny pores

through which proteins and other compounds can pass.

Most of a cell's genetic information is kept in distinct structures called **chromosomes.** The nucleic acid in chromosomes carries the genetic information. All organisms have a definite number of chromosomes. Human body cells have 46 chromosomes. Chromosomes contain the genetic "blueprints" that control all cellular activity, such as growth and cell division. You will learn more about chromosomes in Chapter 7.

Another identifying structure of the nucleus is the nucleolus. Organelles called ribosomes are formed in the **nucleolus** (plural: *nucleoli*). Ribosomes help make proteins. Cells that are primarily involved in protein synthesis have rather large nucleoli and many ribosomes.

TWO KINDS OF CELLS

Nucleus or not?

Living things are classified into two large groups, based on the presence or absence of a nucleus in their cells. Organisms whose cells have no definite nucleus are called **prokaryotes.** Organisms whose cells have a nucleus surrounded by a nuclear membrane are called **eukaryotes.** Bacteria and

---

MEETING DIVERSE NEEDS

Gifted Have interested students research to find out when different cell parts were discovered and by whom. Students should present discoveries as entries on a time line. Encourage students to add to their time lines as they continue the chapter.

① Pores on nucleus allow proteins and other compounds to pass through.

Prokaryotic cell
Prokaryotic cells contain no nucleus or membrane-bound organelles. This micrograph shows a bacterium.

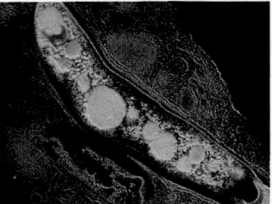

Eukaryotic cell
The eukaryotic cell contains a nucleus and membrane-bound organelles. This eukaryotic cell is a human pancreatic cell.

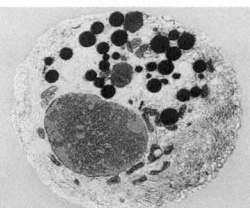

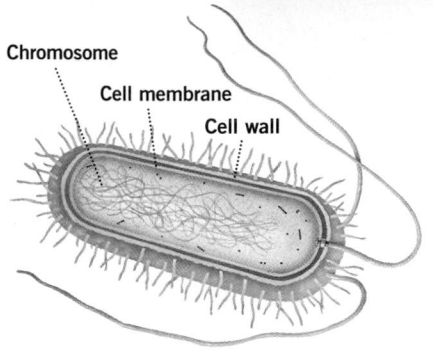

Chromosome
Cell membrane
Cell wall

⊢ 0.1 to 1.0 micrometer ⊣

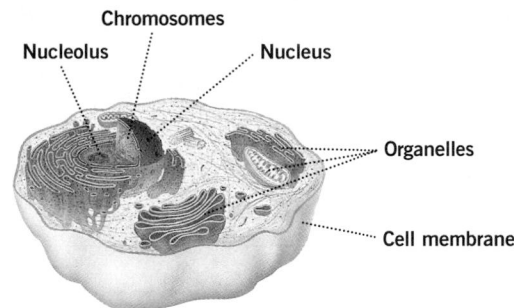

Chromosomes
Nucleolus
Nucleus
Organelles
Cell membrane

⊢ 1.0 to 10.0 micrometers ⊣

FIGURE 3.12
Compare the structure of the prokaryotic cell and the eukaryotic cell. Notice the size indicated on the scale below each cell.

their relatives are prokaryotes; all other organisms, including plants and animals, are eukaryotes.

The cells of prokaryotes are called prokaryotic cells. The cells of eukaryotes are called eukaryotic cells. Prokaryotic cells and eukaryotic cells are easily distinguished by their structural differences, as you can see in *Figure 3.12*. What similarities and differences do you see?

Prokaryotic cells are typically much smaller than eukaryotic cells. Most prokaryotic cells are tiny—about one-tenth the width and one-thousandth the volume of eukaryotic cells. The tiny size of prokaryotic cells is the reason scientists could not view their internal structures before the invention of the electron microscope.

Prokaryotic cells have a less complex internal structure than eukaryotic cells. Prokaryotic cells do not have a nuclear membrane and most lack organelles surrounded by membranes. Although prokaryotic cells contain

fewer internal structures, they can perform all of the activities of life, including reproduction and response to the environment. Because of their small size and comparatively simple structure, prokaryotic cells are considered the forerunners of eukaryotic cells.

CHECKPOINT 3.2

1. Describe the three main parts of a eukaryotic cell. What are the functions of each part?

2. How does a prokaryotic cell differ from a eukaryotic cell?

3. Critical Thinking What characteristic of eukaryotic cells gives them a greater capacity for specialization than prokaryotic cells have? Explain.

Build on What You Know

4. You have learned about the chemicals that make up living things. Match each chemical with the cell structure(s) for which it is a main component. *(Need to jog your memory? Revisit relevant concepts in Chapter 2, Section 2.1.)*

Use the Visual

Have students study the prokaryotic and eukaryotic cells in Figure 3.12. Ask:

■ **What are the main similarities of the two cells?** (Both have a cell membrane and chromosomes.)

■ **What is lacking in the prokaryotic cell?** (Organelles, nucleolus, and nucleus.)

3 ASSESS

Evaluate Understanding

On the board, draw a three-column chart. Across the top, write three heads: Structure, Function, and Description. Under Structure, write in a single column the terms *cell membrane, cytoplasm, cytoskeleton, nucleus, chromosomes,* and *nucleolus.* Call on volunteers to complete the chart. You may wish to keep the chart for use in the next section.

Reteach

Draw an outline of a eukaryotic cell on the board. Write the terms *cell membrane, cytoplasm, cytoskeleton, nucleus, chromosomes,* and *nucleolus* on the board. Have students reproduce the outline on paper and complete the drawing of the cell. Check students' drawings for accuracy.

CHECKPOINT 3.2

1. Cell membrane defines cell boundary. Cytoplasm contains a semifluid substance and organelles. Nucleus controls all cellular activity.

2. Prokaryotic cells are smaller than eukaryotic cells and lack a nucleus and membrane-bound organelles.

3. Developing a hypothesis The presence of membrane-bound organelles, each has a specialized function.

4. Carbohydrates—in cytoplasm and cell membrane; lipids—in cell membrane; proteins—in cytoplasm, cell membrane, and nucleus; nucleic acids—in nucleus

❷ Students should notice the similar internal structures and the difference in their sizes.

Use the Visual

Have students study the photograph that opens the section. Point out the cilia. Explain that tiny hairlike projections move dust-laden mucus along the bronchi much like a conveyor belt moves objects from one location to another.

Check Prior Knowledge

To assess students' prior knowledge about cell organization, ask:

- **What cell parts did you study in the previous section?** Write their responses on the board and ask students to describe the position of each cell part.

SUPER READ! **Using SQR3** To practice strategies for effective reading, use pages 29-30 in *Super Read!*

Quick Activity

Compare a functioning cell to a factory. Tell the class to consider the departments, people, and machines that work together to keep a factory operating efficiently. Brainstorm to generate a list of things a factory needs to operate, such as an energy supply, command center, production machinery, receiving and shipping, waste removal, packaging, storage, and cleanup. List each department on the board. Have students copy the list for reference as they study the section.

What you'll learn

IDEAS
- To describe the function of key organelles
- To compare and contrast the characteristics of cilia and flagella

WORDS
ribosomes, endoplasmic reticulum, Golgi apparatus, mitochondria, lysosomes, cilia, flagella

3.3 Cell Organelles

Many parts and functions
Cells have many different parts, each of which performs a specific task. The tiny hairs, called cilia, on human tracheal cells (right) are one type of specialized cell structure. The waving cilia move a coating of mucus through the airways to help remove dust, bacteria, and other foreign matter from the body. Cilia perform different functions in other types of cells.

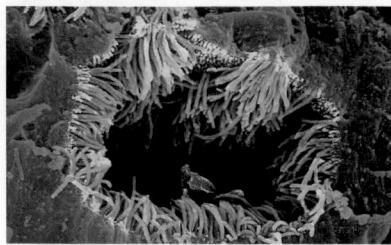

ORGANELLES IN CYTOPLASM

Little machines

Despite their small size, cells are by no means simple structures! Cells function like miniature factories, constructing new molecules from raw materials. At any moment, cells may be taking in nutrients; making new molecules; sorting, secreting, and storing chemicals; and breaking down foreign materials. Organelles are the cell structures that perform these specific functions. In many ways organelles are like machines in a factory, each with a specific role.

Organelles called **ribosomes** (RY-buh-sohmz) make the proteins needed by cells. Groups of ribosomes function like an assembly line, helping to make proteins from amino acids. Ribosomes are found suspended in the cytoplasm or bound to membranes.

Both prokaryotes and eukaryotes have ribosomes. Other organelles, all membrane-bound, are found only in eukaryotes. *Figure 3.13* illustrates some of the different organelles found in a eukaryotic cell.

The **endoplasmic reticulum** (en-do-PLAZ-mik ri-TIK-uh-lum) or ER, is an extensive network of membranes that produces materials for the cell. There are two types of ER: rough and smooth. Rough ER has ribosomes on its surface and functions in the synthesis of proteins that will be secreted by the cell. Rough ER also manufactures new cell membranes. Smooth ER makes lipids, processes carbohydrates, and modifies chemicals that are toxic to the cell.

Molecules that are produced in the ER are transported by the Golgi apparatus (GOHL-jee). The **Golgi apparatus** is a series of flat, membrane-bound sacs where molecules are sorted, often modified, packaged, and distributed to their destination. For example, the Golgi apparatus distributes some molecules to the cell membrane for secretion. The Golgi apparatus is the cell's conveyor belt, transporting materials.

Most of the energy necessary to power the cell's activities is generated in organelles called mitochondria (my-tuh-KAHN-dree-uh). **Mitochondria** (singular: mitochondrion) change the energy stored in food compounds into a form useful for the cell—the energy-storing molecule adenosine triphosphate (ATP). You will read more about ATP in Chapter 4. Mitochondria are similar to a factory generator that changes mechanical energy into electrical energy.

Inside many cells, large molecules are digested inside of saclike organelles called lysosomes (LY-suh-sohmz). **Lysosomes** contain digestive enzymes that help break down large molecules

---

FIGURE 3.13

Organelles—
Machines in the Cell Factory

Assembling proteins

Ribosomes are protein assemblers. Whether free-floating in the cytoplasm or attached to rough endoplasmic reticulum, they help assemble long chains of amino acids that are called proteins.

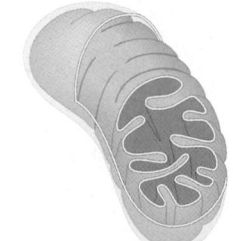

Generating energy

Mitochondria are energy-producing organelles. The folded inner membrane of a mitochondrion surrounds a space called the mitochondrial matrix, where ATP is produced. Most cells have hundreds or thousands of mitochondria.

Ribosomes   Mitochondrion

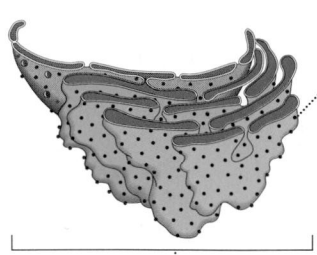

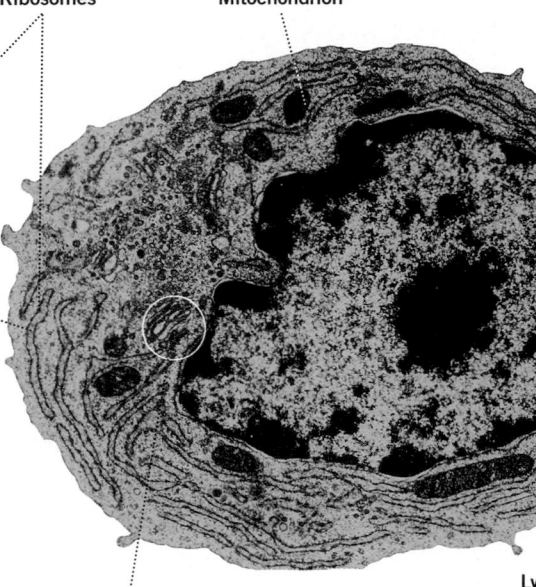

Endoplasmic reticulum

Processing materials

The endoplasmic reticulum is a complex network of tubules and sacs. It connects the nuclear membrane to the cell membrane. Rough ER, shown here, helps make protein secretions, such as hormones, and assists in membrane production. Smooth ER makes lipids and rids the cell of toxic waste. What makes rough ER rough? ❶

Lysosome   Nucleus

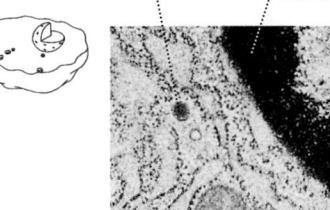

Golgi apparatus

Packaging and transporting

The Golgi apparatus sorts, packages, and transports substances in the cell. These substances may include products of the endoplasmic reticulum.

Preparing raw materials

Lysosomes are small sacs containing digestive enzymes. Large molecules are absorbed into the cell in membranous sacs. Lysosomes fuse with the sacs and release digestive enzymes into them. The enzymes break down the molecules for the cell's use.

Chapter 3 Cell Structure and Function   **67**

3.3

Use the Visual

Point out that the photo of the cell in Figure 3.13 identifies the location and characteristics of the organelles. Have students refer to their factory list and identify the organelle that performs a similar function. Ask:

- **What is the structure of a mitochondrion?** (An outer membrane and folded inner membranes called the mitochondrial matrix)
- **What do mitochondria do?** (Produce energy, ATP)
- **How does the endoplasmic reticulum perform in the cell?** (Connects nuclear and cell membranes, aids in making protein secretions and lipids, eliminates toxic waste)
- **What is the function of ribosomes?** (Assemble amino acids into proteins)
- **What are the functions of the Golgi apparatus?** (To sort, package, and transport substances in a cell)
- **Which organelles release powerful digestive enzymes?** (Lysosomes)

Think Critically

Ask students to explain why the mitochrondia are considered the cell's powerhouses. (They provide energy for cell function, and ultimately for life processes.)

MEETING DIVERSE NEEDS

LEP Have students draw a cell showing the organelles. Ask them to label each one and write a short description of its function.

FACTS AND FIGURES

The Golgi apparatus is named for its discoverer, Italian anatomist and pathologist Camillo Golgi. He also described nerve endings in tendons and muscles, identified the life cycle and structure of malarial parasites, and won a Nobel Prize for his study of the immune system.

❶ The presence of ribosomes attached to the endoplasmic reticulum.

FIGURE 3.14
Compare the micrograph of cilia (left) with the micrograph of a flagellum (right). How do the two different structures enable organisms to move? ❶

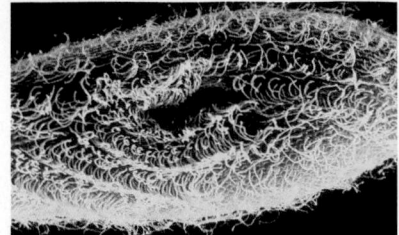
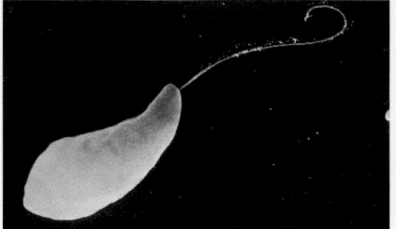

of carbohydrates, proteins, and lipids. Lysosomes also digest old organelles that are no longer useful to the cell. Because the digestive enzymes are isolated in lysosomes, the rest of the cell is protected. Lysosomes are like a factory furnace that melts down scrap metals into materials that can be used again. How might a cell use lysosomes ❷ for defense?

STRUCTURES FOR MOVEMENT

Getting around

You may recall reading about the cytoskeleton and its role in cellular mobility. Many cells have unique extensions of their cytoskeleton for movement. These specialized cellular appendages are called cilia and flagella. They are composed of bundles of cytoskeletal proteins wrapped in the outer cell membrane. Although both cilia and flagella are used for movement, they are different in structure and function. You can see cilia and flagella in *Figure 3.14*.

Cilia (singular: *cilium*) are short, hairlike projections that usually occur in large numbers on the surface of certain cells. Some unicellular eukaryotes, known as ciliates, eat and move using their cilia. Ciliates are found mostly in fresh water. The movement of cilia closely resembles that of oars,

with alternating strokes generating the force needed for locomotion. Cilia are also found in multicellular organisms. In fact, cilia on the cells lining the human trachea, or windpipe, aid in the removal of debris from this area.

Flagella (singular: *flagellum*) are long, tail-like projections. Unlike ciliates, flagellates usually have one flagellum. Prokaryotic flagella differ structurally from their eukaryotic counterparts. The movement of prokaryotic flagella also differs from that of eukaryotic flagella. Prokaryotic flagella spin like propellers, whereas eukaryotic flagella move with a whip-like motion.

CHECKPOINT 3.3

1. Describe the function of five key organelles.
2. How do cilia and flagella differ in structure and function?
3. **Critical Thinking** Would you expect skin cells to contain more or fewer mitochondria than muscle cells? Explain your reasoning.

Build on What You Know

4. What substances are affected by the digestive enzymes of the lysosomes? What is the general term for all materials that are acted upon by enzymes? *(Need to jog your memory? Revisit relevant concepts in Chapter 2, Section 2.3.)*

 What are some cell strucures, and what do they do?

THE BIG IDEA!

Cells of major groups of organisms can be distinguished by their structural differences. 3.4

3.4 Cell Diversity

How many cells in a termite?
There are probably more cells than you think. The termite is a relatively complex organism with many specialized cells, but it could not feast on wood without the help of the unicellular protists that live in its digestive tract. Each stowaway protist, (in turn), is home to bacteria, whose ability to digest cellulose enables both termite and protist to survive.

What you'll learn

IDEAS
• To contrast the components of plant and animal cells
• To describe some similarities and differences in the cells of unicellular and multicellular organisms

WORDS
cell wall, chloroplasts, vacuole

PLANT AND ANIMAL CELLS

The little things that keep us apart

You have just finished reading about the organelles and other cell parts that are common to many cells. But not all cells are identical. Among the eukaryotes, there are great differences between the cells of plants and animals. You can see some important structural differences between plant and animal cells in *Figure 3.15*.

One of the most significant differences is that plant cells have a cell wall. The **cell wall** is a tough, rigid outer covering that protects a plant cell and helps it maintain its shape. The cells of fungi, algae, and bacteria also have cell walls. Animal cells lack cell walls, but they have other structures, such as cytoskeletons, for support.

Another difference is that plant cells contain organelles called chloroplasts. **Chloroplasts** are structures that enable the plant to make sugars through photosynthesis. Animal cells do not have chloroplasts and cannot make their own food. Animals get

FIGURE 3.15

Plant and animal cells share many of the same features, but some specialized structures distinguish them. Which structures are present only in plant cells? ❸

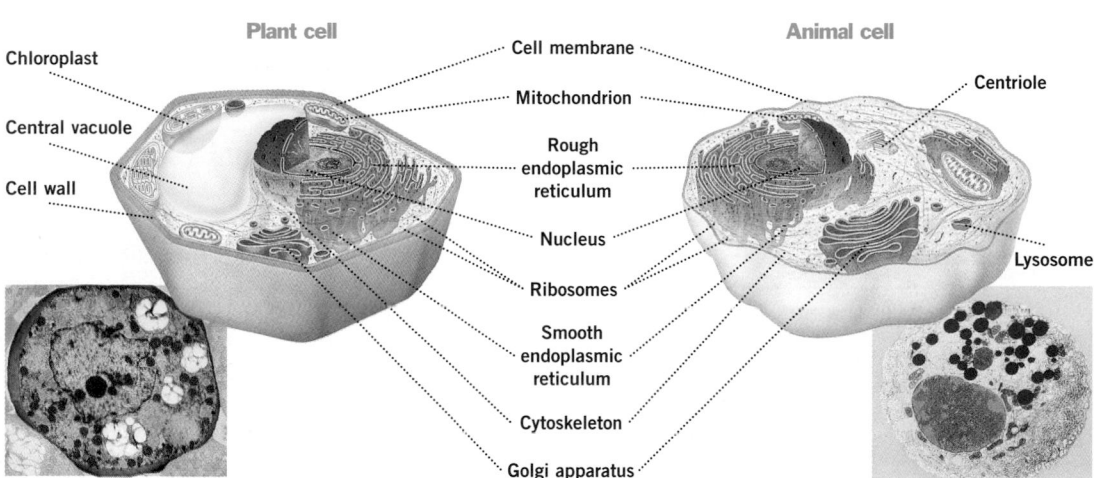

Plant cell — Chloroplast, Central vacuole, Cell wall — Cell membrane, Mitochondrion, Rough endoplasmic reticulum, Nucleus, Ribosomes, Smooth endoplasmic reticulum, Cytoskeleton, Golgi apparatus — Animal cell — Centriole, Lysosome

Chapter 3 Cell Structure and Function **69**

1 ENGAGE

Consider The Big Idea

Have students read The Big Idea! at the top of the page. Discuss how structural differences contribute to cell diversity.

Use the Visual

Have students study the photograph that opens the section. Point out that it illustrates a cooperative relationship between a multicellular organism, the termite, and unicellular organisms, the protists and bacteria. It also illustrates relationships between prokaryotes (bacteria) and eukaryotes (termites)

Quick Activity

Display the various parts of a large flower: stem, leaf, petal, and root. Have students describe differences in texture, color, and shape among the parts. Ask:

■ **What is the function of each flower part?** (Students should cite stem support, photosynthesis in leaf, protection of center by petal, and nutrient supply by roots.)
■ **What are three distinguishing characteristics of a plant cell?** (Cell wall, chloroplasts, and a central vacuole)

❷ Lysosomes inside of some human cells, like macrophages, help defend the body by digesting bacteria and other invaders.
❸ Cell wall, chloroplasts, and a central vacuole

TEACH

Everyday Biology

Cellulose in its cell wall provides rigidity to a plant. Have students identify fruits and vegetables high in cellulose and low in cellulose. (High: celery, broccoli, sweet potatoes; Low: artichokes, bananas)

ASSESS

Evaluate Understanding

To assess students' understanding of cell diversity, ask:

- **What are some functions performed by specialized cells?** (Movement, reproduction, digestion)
- **How are all cells alike?** (All cells have a cell membrane, chromosomes, and ribosomes.)
- **What is the main difference between prokaryotic and eukaryotic cells?** (Prokaryotic cells have no nuclear membrane and organelles are not enclosed in membranes.)

Reteach

Model how to draw a Venn diagram, showing the common and diverse cell parts in eukaryotes and prokaryotes. Then have students review the information in the section and draw a second diagram comparing animal cells and plant cells. Put a student diagram on the board for discussion.

❶ Cell membrane, chromosomes, and ribosomes

EVERYDAY BIOLOGY

Cellulose—Yum!

Even though we cannot digest the cellulose in the cell walls of plants, this fiber is still an important part of our diet. Fiber helps move material through the intestinal tract and encourages the efficient elimination of wastes.

FIGURE 3.16
This table shows structural similarities and differences between different kinds of cells. What structures do all of these cells have in common? ❶

their nourishment by eating other organisms or their products.

All plant cells also contain a large central **vacuole,** a membrane-bound compartment that serves many functions. Vacuoles may absorb water, or they may store proteins, ions, and the waste products of metabolism. Animal cells lack a large central vacuole but may contain smaller vacuoles.

COMPARING CELL DIVERSITY

Together or apart

There is great diversity among cells. As you have learned, there are differences between plant and animal cells, and between prokaryotic and eukaryotic cells. The diversity of cells can be explored in a number of ways.

As you have already done with plant and animal cells, the structures in cells can be compared. In contrast to eukaryotic cells, prokaryotic cells do not have a nucleus or membrane-bound organelles. In addition, some prokaryotic cells have cell walls, similar to plant cells.

Cells can also differ with respect to their associations with other cells. For example, some cells exist alone as unicellular organisms. Unicellular organisms perform almost all life functions as individuals. Some unicellular organisms do interact when they combine briefly for reproduction.

Conversely, some cells live together as multicellular organisms. Multicellular organisms depend on the interaction of many cells, which generally cannot survive as separate cells outside the organism.

The cells of multicellular organisms typically are specialized to perform different functions. For example, specialized cells in animals are adapted for reproduction, digestion, or movement. A unicellular organism must perform all of these functions. *Figure 3.16* summarizes the diversity of the cells that you have studied.

A Comparison of Cells			
Structure	**Prokaryotic Cells**	**Eukaryotic Cells**	
		Animal	*Plant*
Cell membrane	Yes	Yes	Yes
Cell wall	Yes	No	Yes
Nucleus	No	Yes	Yes
Chromosomes	Yes (one circular strand of DNA)	Yes (many)	Yes (many)
Ribosomes	Yes (small)	Yes (large)	Yes (large)
Endoplasmic reticulum	No	Yes	Yes
Golgi apparatus	No	Yes	Yes
Lysosomes	No	Yes	No
Vacuoles	No	Yes (small or none)	Yes
Mitochondria	No	Yes	Yes
Chloroplasts	No	No	Yes
Cytoskeleton	No	Yes	Yes

CHECKPOINT 3.4

1. Describe two differences between plant and animal cells.
2. Name the main differences and some of the similarities between unicellular and multicellular organisms.
3. **Critical Thinking** How do the cell walls, chloroplasts, and vacuoles of plant cells illustrate the idea that cell structure mirrors cell function?

Build on What You Know

4. How is the organization of the cells of the human body similar to the organization of a eukaryotic cell? *(Need to jog your memory? Revisit relevant concepts in Chapter 1, Section 1.2.)*

What is the relationship between cells and organisms?

CHECKPOINT 3.4

1. Any two of the following: cell walls, chloroplasts, and large central vacuoles.
2. Unicellular organisms perform all life processes in one cell; multicellular organisms have specialized cells that perform specific life processes. Both perform all life functions.
3. **Applying knowledge** Cell walls, chloroplasts, and vacuoles provide protection and structure, photosynthesis, and storage.
4. Human cells are organized into tissues; tissues into organs; organs comprise systems which are responsible for distinct life functions. Organs and systems are similar to organelles that carry out the life processes of eukaryotic cells.

 **Investigate It!**

Comparing Plant and Animal Cells

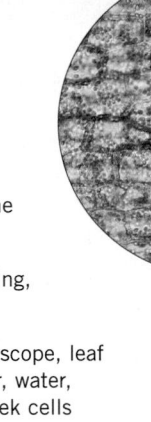

Elodea cell

Human cheek cell

WHAT YOU WILL DO Compare and contrast the structures of plant and animal cells

SKILLS YOU WILL USE Hypothesizing, observing, recording data

WHAT YOU WILL NEED Compound light microscope, leaf from *Elodea* plant, forceps, medicine dropper, water, slide, coverslip, prepared slide of human cheek cells

Propose a Hypothesis

Based on what you have read in the chapter, list the similarities and differences you expect to see in the cells of a plant and an animal. Propose a hypothesis about how the differences in structure of plant and animal cells are related to differences in function.

Conduct Your Experiment

1 Make a three-column chart in your notebook. Label the columns *Leaf Cells, Cheek Cells,* and *Both Types of Cells.*
2 Make a wet-mount slide of an *Elodea* leaf taken from the tip of the plant, where there is new growth. Use forceps and handle the leaf carefully.
3 Observe the specimen with the microscope on low power. This will show the outermost cell layer.
4 Draw several of the cells you see and label the cell structures that are visible. Record the cell structures on your chart.

5 Observe the specimen on high power. What other cell structures are now visible? Add them to your drawing and chart.
6 Using a prepared slide of human cheek cells, repeat steps 3–5.

Analyze Your Data

1 In the third column of your chart, list the structures you saw that are common to plant and animal cells.
2 Which organelles are unique to plant cells? To animal cells?
3 What makes a leaf green?
4 The cells in the lining of your cheek are organized in sheets. Did the cheek cells in your slide look different? If so, what might have affected their appearance?

5 As you viewed the cell structures in the plant leaf with the microscope, how could you make the structures more visible?

Draw Conclusions

Was your prediction supported by your observations? Were there any organelles that you expected to see, but did not? How do you explain this?

Design a Related Experiment

Imagine you are given a slide of unidentified cells. Explain the procedure you would use to determine if they are plant or animal cells.

Lab: Comparing Plant and Animal Cells

Leaf Cells	Cheek Cells	Both Types of Cells

Draw Conclusions

Students may have expected to see chromosomes, ribosomes, ER, Golgi apparatus, lysosomes, mitochondria, and a cytoskeleton. These structures cannot be viewed unless specimens are specially prepared.

Design a Related Experiment

Designs may vary, but procedures should include looking for the presence or absence of plant cell structures.

 Investigate It!

TEAM WORK **Comparing Plant and Animal Cells**

SAFETY FIRST!

Remind students to handle glassware carefully.

Lab Prep and Planning

Forty minutes is required. You may wish to have students work in pairs. Review the correct procedure for making a wet mount.

Hypothesis Help

Students should hypothesize how plant cells contrast to animal cells in structure and function.

Lab Extension

Open Ended
Provide a variety of prepared slides from both plants and animals. Encourage students to identify a cell by its characteristics.

Analyze Your Data

1 Nucleus, cell membrane, cytoplasm
2 The cell wall, large vacuoles, and chloroplasts are unique to plant cells. Mitochondria are visible in animal cells but not in plant cells.
3 Chloroplasts, containing chlorophyll make a leaf green.
4 Some of the cells will be in sheets. Some may be on edge or folded.
5 To make the cell structures in the plant more visible, add a stain, or change the contrast.

Time Required

■ 45 minutes

3.5

ENGAGE

Consider The Big Idea

Have students read The Big Idea! at the top of the page. Discuss the importance of the cell membrane.

Use the Visual

Have students study the photo that opens the section. Discuss the environmental impact on the resurrection plant. Ask:

- **What is the plant's response to a dry environment?** (It shrivels and becomes brown.)
- **What is the plant's response to rain?** (It becomes green. It "resurrects.")

Teacher Demo

Wet a muslin cloth bag, then fill it with water. Hold the bag over a pan and have students observe water drip from the bag. Explain that the bag is like a cell membrane. The force of gravity causes the water to pass through the bag just as it would through a membrane.

 Interactive Biological Simulations

Transport Through Membranes Students manipulate different molecules to see which can freely cross the cell membrane. Students are given a cell in either a hypertonic, hypotonic, or isotonic solution and asked to determine the net flow of water into or out of the cell.

72

THE BIG IDEA! Cells exchange materials with their environment by chemical and physical processes. 3.5

3.5 Cells and Their Environment

What you'll learn

IDEAS
- To describe the process of diffusion in cells and explain its significance
- To explain active transport and bulk movement

WORDS
semipermeable, passive transport, active transport, diffusion, osmosis, exocytosis, endocytosis

FIGURE 3.17

Diffusion

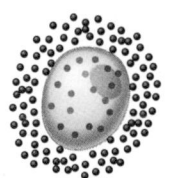

Initially, the concentration of a substance outside the cell is higher than inside.

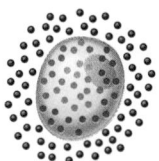

Later, the substance has diffused into the cell so that the concentration is the same on both sides of the membrane.

Waiting for water
How can a plant that appears brown and shriveled come back to life? The cells of several types of resurrection plants like this one are able to endure extreme dehydration. When rain falls, water diffuses from an area of abundance to an area of scarcity—from the outside to the inside of the leaves—and the plant becomes green again. This process is an example of one way that cells exchange materials with their environment.

INSIDE AND OUTSIDE

Be prepared to stop

All cells live at least partly in touch with a water solution. In order to live, all cells must take in nutrients and eliminate wastes. Somehow nutrients and waste materials must cross the cell membrane between the solution outside the cell and the solution inside the cell.

A **semipermeable** membrane lets certain molecules pass through and prevents other molecules from crossing. Cell membranes are semipermeable membranes. Small molecules, such as water, can enter and leave the cell freely. Large molecules, such as proteins and carbohydrates, cannot. And even though they are small, particles with strong electrical charges, such as ions, cannot pass easily through the membrane. The electrical charge prevents the ion from moving through the lipid bilayer.

Several processes are involved in moving materials across the cell membrane. These processes can be classified either as passive transport or

active transport. **Passive transport** is the movement of a substance across a cell membrane without the input of the cell's energy. **Active transport** uses cellular energy to move substances across a cell membrane.

DIFFUSION

Going with the flow

The most common form of passive transport is simple diffusion. **Diffusion** is the random movement of molecules from an area of higher concentration (more molecules) to an area of lower concentration (fewer molecules). Simple diffusion enables oxygen and carbon dioxide to cross cell membranes. *Figure 3.17* illustrates the process of diffusion.

The rate of diffusion depends on the temperature and the size of the molecules involved. Molecules diffuse faster at high temperatures than at low temperatures, and small molecules diffuse faster than large ones.

Diffusion always occurs down a concentration gradient. A concentration

72 *Unit 1 The Basis of Life*

STUDENT RESOURCES

From the Teacher's Resource Package, use:
- Section Review 3.5 and Activity Recordsheet 3-3 from Unit 1 Review Module
- Lab 7: "Diffusion and Cell Size"
- Lab 8: "Osmosis and the Incredible Egg"
- Issues and Decision Making 3-1
- Consumer Applications 3-1

 **TECHNOLOGY RESOURCES**

Relevant technology resources include:
- Spanish Student Edition CD-ROM
- Teacher's Resource Planner CD-ROM
- Animated Biological Concepts Videodiscs
- Interactive Biological Simulations CD-ROM: "Transport Through Membranes"

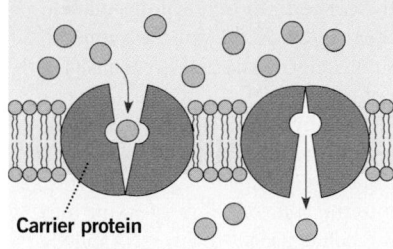

FIGURE 3.18
During facilitated diffusion, carrier proteins shuttle molecules across the lipid bilayer of the cell membrane.

gradient is the difference between the concentration of a particular molecule in one area and its concentration in an adjacent area. When the molecules have been dispersed evenly, there is no concentration gradient. A state of equilibrium has been reached, and diffusion stops.

Some molecules diffuse across cell membranes with the help of carrier proteins in the membrane, as shown in *Figure 3.18*. This form of passive transport is called facilitated diffusion. In facilitated diffusion, molecules always move down a concentration gradient, from higher concentration to lower concentration. Facilitated diffusion increases the rate that some molecules cross the cell membrane, such as large molecules or ions. For example, facilitated diffusion enables the transport of glucose from the blood into body cells.

OSMOSIS
Water's way

Water moves freely across cell membranes by diffusion. The diffusion of water across a semipermeable membrane is called **osmosis.** Osmosis like all diffusion, is a form of passive transport.

Osmosis occurs when the concentrations of solutes in the solutions on the two sides of a semipermeable membrane are different. Like other diffusing molecules, water moves down its concentration gradient. In other words, water moves from solutions with higher water (lower solute) concentration to solutions with lower water (higher solute) concentrations. *Figure 3.19* shows what happens during osmosis.

Cytoplasm is a solution of water and many dissolved solutes. The different concentrations of solutes in the cytoplasm and in the surrounding solution cause water to move in or out of a cell by osmosis.

The natural tendency of water to move from low solute concentrations to high solute concentrations has an effect on cells, as you can see in

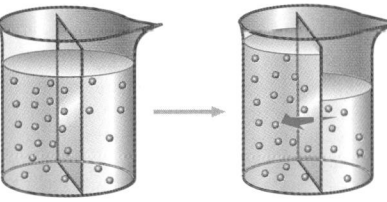

FIGURE 3.19
Water moves by osmosis across a semipermeable membrane. How has the concentration of the solute changed in the beaker on the right?

Chapter 3 Cell Structure and Function **73**

IN THE COMMUNITY
Cellular Research

Scientists have learned a great deal about the function of cells. For example, research in the 1980s led to the discovery that people with the genetic disease cystic fibrosis have a missing or defective protein in certain cells, which affects the movement of sodium ions across the cell membrane. In 1996 researchers then discovered how this problem causes the symptoms of cystic fibrosis: The buildup of salt outside cells in the lungs makes the lungs vulnerable to bacteria. This information raised hopes for the development of new cystic fibrosis treatments. Use the library or other resources to learn more about current research on cellular diseases. Give a brief presentation to your class, explaining the significance of the research. Log on to *http://basis_of_life.biosurf.com* for information on cell research.

❶ The concentration of solute is now in equilibrium though the volume of solvent has changed.

MULTICULTURAL PERSPECTIVE

Explain to students the custom of preserving food by drying or salting it. A high concentration of salt on food causes water to diffuse out of cells and dry the food, making it last longer. Have students research the use of dried or salted foods in other cultures.

3.5

TEACH

Class Activity

TEAM WORK

Make a saturated sugar solution with colored, warm water and sugar. Have students slowly pour the sugar solution into a fine tea strainer set over a glass beaker three-quarters full of cold water. Ask:

- **What happens to the sugar solution?** (It goes through the strainer and into the water.)
- **Explain how this model illustrates osmosis.** (A concentrated solution, sugar water, moves through a semipermeable membrane, the strainer, into a less concentrated fluid, water.)

Teacher Demo

Place several drops of food coloring in a test tube half-full of water. Secure a strip of cellophane (dialysis tubing) over the top with a rubber band. Explain that chemically the cellophane is like a plant membrane. Next place the tube upside down in a jar of water. Have students observe the jar the next day and discuss their observations.

Animated Biological Concepts

Diffusion and Osmosis

Play

LAB ZONE Do It! TEAM WORK

Observing Osmosis and Semipermeability

Analyze Your Results

1 The egg shell dissolved and the egg, contained by a membrane, swelled.
2 The circumference increased.
3 The membrane
4 The vinegar is a hypotonic solution. The egg's membrane is semi-permeable and allows water to seep in but does not allow the contents of the egg to seep out. Thus, the egg swells.

 Interpreting Visuals To practice strategies for effective reading, use pages 31-32 in *Super Read!*

Use the Visual

Have students study Figure 3.20. Ask:

- **Why did the cell in the hypertonic solution shrink?** (Water moved out the cell in order to dilute the outside solution.)
- **Why did the cell in the hypotonic solution increase in size?** (Water from the solution entered the cell to dilute the solution inside.)

Animated Biological Concepts

Passive and Active Transport   Play

LAB ZONE Do It! bioSURF

Observing Osmosis and Semipermeability

You can observe the results of osmosis through a cell membrane when you . . .

Try This

1 Record the appearance of a raw egg in its shell. Measure and record its circumference.
2 Gently place the egg in a jar and cover it with white vinegar. Put the lid on the jar. Record your observations.
3 After 72 hours record the egg's appearance after being in the vinegar. Then remove the egg from the jar and measure its circumference.

Analyze Your Results

1 Compare your recorded observations. How did the egg change?
2 What happened to the egg's circumference after 72 hours?
3 What kept the contents of the egg from seeping into the vinegar?
4 Propose an explanation for the changes you observed.

Figure 3.20. For example, in a hypertonic solution, the fluid outside the cell has a higher concentration of solutes than the cytoplasm inside the cell. Water diffuses out of the cell.

You can see the effect of hypertonic conditions by placing a small piece of lettuce in a bowl of salt water. As you will see after a few minutes, the lettuce wilts because its cells have lost their water to the salty, hypertonic environment. In an isotonic solution, the concentration of solutes outside the cell equals the concentration of solutes inside the cell, so osmosis does not occur.

In a hypotonic solution, the concentration of solutes is lower outside the cell than inside, and water moves into the cell. The flow of water into the cell causes it to swell. Distilled water is very hypotonic because it contains no solutes. Animal cells placed in distilled water will swell and often burst because of osmosis. Plant cells do not burst in distilled water. Can you explain why? A piece of lettuce in distilled water becomes firm and crisp because of the diffusion of water into its cells. Good cooks know that they must keep lettuce damp and chilled if they want to serve crisp salad.

ACTIVE TRANSPORT

Movin' on up

Passive transport allows molecules to cross a cell membrane without using the cell's energy. Molecules always move down a concentration gradient during passive transport. However, a cell must use energy to move molecules across the membrane against a concentration gradient, from areas of lower concentration to areas of higher concentration. This process is called active transport.

FIGURE 3.20

Effect of Solution Concentrations

The cells in this figure depict reactions to the osmotic effects of different solution concentrations. In what direction has the water moved in each of these examples? ❶

Normal cell

Hypertonic
The concentration of solutes outside is higher than it is inside the cell.

Isotonic
The concentration of solutes outside the cell is equal to that inside the cell.

Hypotonic
The concentration of solutes outside is lower than it is inside the cell.

Very Hypotonic
This cell has burst due to the large amount of water entering it.

FACTS AND FIGURES

The antibiotic penicillin uses osmotic pressure to destroy bacterial cells. Penicillin interferes with the ability of bacteria to produce a compound that strengthens its cell walls. The bacteria cell wall weakens and eventually buckles from the stress of osmotic pressure and bursts as water rushes in through its cell wall.

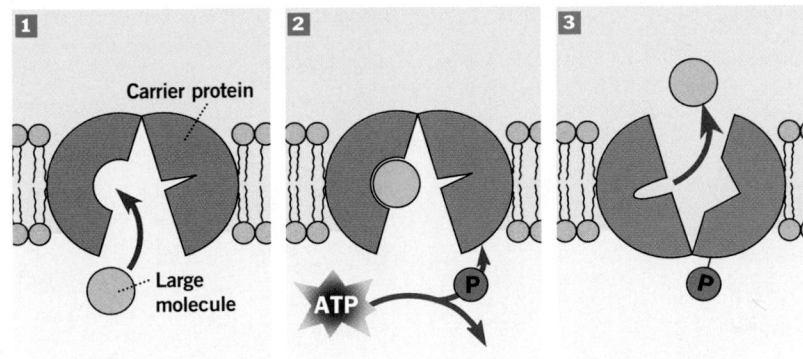

FIGURE 3.21
Active transport of molecules and ions against a concentration gradient requires membrane-bound carrier proteins and the energy of ATP. What happens in each of these three steps? ❸

Explain

Tell students that energy is required for the active transport of molecules in and out of a cell. Relate the movement of molecules through the cell membrane to the movement of people through a revolving door or turnstile. Just as energy is required to move the door, so is energy required to move molecules through the semipermeable cell membrane. People passing through an open door would be passive transport since no energy is required to move the door.

Like facilitated diffusion, active transport often involves carrier proteins. These carrier proteins use energy to pump ions and molecules across the membrane. The energy for active transport usually comes from ATP, as illustrated in *Figure 3.21.*

Active transport is especially important in maintaining proper ion concentrations inside cells. Animal cells, for example, pump sodium ions out of the cell and potassium ions into the cell. This sodium-potassium pump uses about one third of a cell's available energy. As a result of active transport, the concentration of potassium ions remains high inside the cell, while the accumulation of sodium ions remains high outside the cell. These gradients are important for the contraction of muscles, the transmission of nerve impulses, and the absorption of nutrients.

Active transport is vital to all organisms. In plants, active transport enables the roots to absorb nutrients from the soil. Plant nutrients are more concentrated inside the roots than in the surrounding soil. Without active transport, these nutrients would diffuse out of the roots. Overall, active transport is one of several ways that an organism maintains homeostasis.

BULK MOVEMENT

Package and handling

When a cell needs to transport large molecules such as polysaccharides or proteins across its membrane, it uses several processes, all of which are classified as bulk movement. During bulk movement large molecules move across the cell membrane by being packaged in membrane-bound sacs. Cells typically rely on two types of bulk movement, exocytosis and endocytosis.

LAB ZONE ? Think About It! bioSURF

Analyzing Ion Concentrations

The graph at the right shows the relative concentrations of different ions inside (red) and outside (yellow) an animal cell. Use this information and what you have read in the chapter to answer the following questions.

Analyzing the Graph

1 Which ions are transported into the cell by active transport?
2 Which ions are transported out of the cell by active transport?
3 Explain how you determined your answers.

LAB ZONE Think About It!

Analyzing Ion Concentrations

Analyzing the Graph

1 K^+ and Mg^{++} are transported inside the cell.
2 Na^+ and Cl^- are transported outside the cell.
3 If the ion concentration is greater outside than inside, the cell actively transported them out against the concentration gradient. If the ion concentration is greater inside than outside, the cell actively transported them into the cell.

❶ Hypertonic-water moved out of cell; isotonic-no net water movement; hypotonic and very hypotonic-water moved into cell.
❷ The rigid cell wall keeps the plant cell from bursting.
❸ Step 1—molecule moves into carrier protein. Step 2—energy is added to carrier. Step 3—carrier shifts and releases large molecule on opposite side membrane.

ASSESS

Evaluate Understanding

Write the terms *semipermeability, passive transport, energy, active transport, diffusion, osmosis, endocytosis,* and *exocytosis* on the board. Have students use the words to prepare a flowchart showing the movement of materials through a membrane.

Reteach

Discuss the differences between osmosis and diffusion and endocytosis and exocytosis. Have students work in pairs to draw four diagrams to show the activity that takes place during each process. The drawings should include arrows and explanatory terms.

❶ Exocytosis: The membrane around a sac of materials fuses with the cell membrane and expels the materials from the cell. Endocytosis: The cell membrane surrounds materials to be taken into the cell, then the membrane forms a sac. The sac can release its contents into the cell or fuse with another organelle.

❷ Endocytosis

❸ The phagocyte benefits by getting nutrients, and the body benefits by having the bacterium removed.

Animated Biological Concepts

Endocytosis and Exocytosis   Play

FIGURE 3.22
Exocytosis (left) and endocytosis (right) are both forms of bulk transport. What are the steps of exocytosis? Endocytosis? ❶

Exocytosis

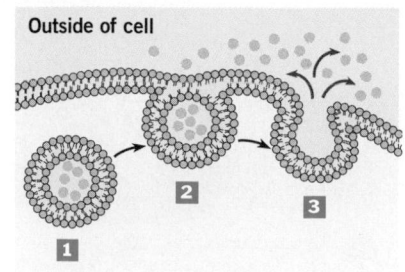

Endocytosis

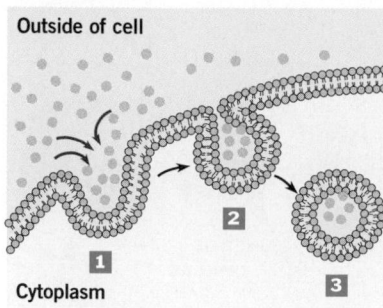

During **exocytosis,** wastes and cell products are packaged by the Golgi apparatus in sacs called Golgi vesicles. The Golgi vesicles then fuse with the cell membrane, and the materials in the vesicles are secreted out of the cell. When you cry, tear gland cells use exocytosis to excrete a salty solution containing proteins.

During **endocytosis,** a portion of the cell membrane surrounds desirable macromolecules that are outside the cell. The cell pinches off a saclike portion of its outer membrane to form a tiny new vesicle. The membranous vesicle moves into the cell, where it can fuse with other organelles or release its contents into the cytoplasm. You can see this process in *Figure* 3.22.

Pinocytosis and phagocytosis are forms of endocytosis. During pinocytosis (sometimes called cellular drinking), the cell membrane encloses a droplet of fluid and its solutes and brings the droplet into the cell.

Phagocytosis is similar to pinocytosis. However, in phagocytosis, the cell engulfs a food particle or

other solid substance, rather than a liquid. The vesicle containing food can then fuse with a lysosome carrying digestive enzymes. Many unicellular organisms, such as amebas, obtain food by phagocytosis. Human white blood cells, such as the one shown in *Figure* 3.23, are phagocytes that engulf and destroy bacteria. How is phagocytosis by white blood cells beneficial for both the white blood cells and the body? ❸

CHECKPOINT 3.5

1. Describe the process of osmosis, and explain its significance.
2. Explain how active transport and bulk movement differ.
3. **Critical Thinking** Meat can spoil if bacteria grow on it. One way to preserve meat is to soak it in a strong salt solution. Use what you have learned about cells in different solutions to explain how salt in meat would stop bacteria from growing.

Build on What You Know

4. How does active transport contribute to homeostasis? *(Need to jog your memory? Revisit relevant concepts in Chapter 2, Section 2.5.)*

FIGURE 3.23
In this picture three tumor cells are engulfed by a white blood cell. What form of bulk transport is this process? ❷

? How do cells and their environment interact?

CHECKPOINT 3.5

1. During osmosis, water diffuses across a semipermeable membrane down a concentration gradient. Osmosis maintains the water balance between a cell and its surroundings.
2. Active transport maintains ion concentrations within and among cells while bulk movement serves to move "raw materials" into the cell and finished

products and wastes out.
3. **Applying knowledge** The high concentration of salt outside the meat cells will cause them to lose water and prevent microorganisms from living in the cells.
4. Active transport maintains homeostasis on a cellular level, as well as in the organism, by balancing solute concentrations.

Chapter 3 Review

THE BIG IDEA!

3.1–3.3 Cell structures of living organisms perform life functions.

3.4 Cells of major groups of organisms can be distinguished by their structural differences.

3.5 Cells exchange materials with their environment by chemical and physical processes.

Sum It Up

Use the following summary to review the main content of this chapter.

3.1 A Look at Cells

- Cells may be complete organisms or components of multicellular organisms. Cells vary in size and shape.
- Cells were discovered after the invention of the microscope, an instrument that produces an enlarged image.
- According to the cell theory, cells are the basic units of life, all organisms are made of one or more cells, and all cells arise from existing cells.

3.2 Basic Cell Structures

- The cell membrane separates a cell's contents from its environment. The membrane consists of a bilayer of phospholipids with embedded proteins.
- The semifluid cytoplasm contains specialized organelles plus a cytoskeleton, which provides structure and allows for movement.
- The cell nucleus contains the chromosomes of the cell, which store genetic information, and the nucleolus, which makes ribosomes.
- Cells of prokaryotes do not have a definite nucleus. Cells of eukaryotes have a nucleus.

3.3 Cell Organelles

- Ribosomes assemble proteins from amino acids.
- The endoplasmic reticulum transports material.
- Mitochondria generate energy from food.
- The Golgi apparatus packages and transports proteins.
- Lysosomes contain digestive enzymes.
- Cilia and flagella move cells or substances.

3.4 Cell Diversity

- In plant cells, cell walls provide protection and shape; chloroplasts produce sugar; vacuoles store substances such as water and wastes.
- Cells can differ in their components, and their relationship to other cells.

3.5 Cells and Their Environment

- In diffusion and osmosis, substances move passively from areas of higher concentration to areas of lower concentration.
- In active transport, energy is used to move substances against the concentration gradient.
- During endocytosis and exocytosis, materials are packaged in sacs and moved in bulk.

Use Terms and Concepts

Use each of the following words or terms in a complete sentence. If you need to review a meaning, turn to the page indicated.

cell theory (p. 60)

cell membrane (p. 62)

phospholipid (p. 62)

cytoplasm (p. 63)

cytoskeleton (p. 64)

nucleus (p. 64)

chromosomes (p. 64)

nucleolus (p. 64)

prokaryotes (p. 64)

eukaryotes (p. 64)

ribosomes (p. 66)

endoplasmic reticulum (p. 66)

Golgi apparatus (p. 66)

mitochondria (p. 66)

lysosomes (p. 66)

cilia (p. 68)

flagella (p. 68)

cell wall (p. 69)

chloroplasts (p. 69)

vacuole (p. 70)

semipermeable (p. 72)

passive transport (p. 72)

active transport (p. 72)

diffusion (p. 72)

osmosis (p. 73)

endocytosis (p. 76)

exocytosis (p. 76)

Chapter 3 Cell Structure and Function **77**

Review the Big Ideas

Before your students begin the Chapter Review, you may wish to discuss the Big Ideas that they have learned in this chapter. Explain that in Sections 3.1 through 3.3, they learned the basic functions of cell structures in living organisms, the significance of microscope development and technology in studying cells, and how this technology led to the cell theory. In Section 3.4, they learned about cell diversity by comparing plant and animal cell structures and prokaryotic and eukaryotic cell structures. How cells exchange material with their environment was the basis of the last section of the chapter.

Answers

1. chloroplasts
2. osmosis
3. cytoplasm
4. cilia and flagella
5. endoplasmic reticulum
6. cell membrane
7. b
8. d
9. c
10. d
11. A light microscope can magnify objects to about 1000 × original size. Objects can be magnified intact, but must be thin enough for light to pass through. Electron microscopes can magnify up to a million times but cannot be used to view live organisms.
12. Schleiden made the generalization that all plants are made of cells; Schwan concluded that all animals are made of cells and, further, that all life is made of cells.
13. Nucleus: stores genetic material, directs cell activities; mitochondria: convert food into usable energy; ribosomes; assemble proteins; endosplasmic reticulum: transports materials through cell; Golgi apparatus: packages and exports proteins; lysome: digests molecules
14. The phospholipids that make up the two layers of membrane are constantly being formed and broken down. Both the lipids and the proteins embedded in the membrane move about. The moving proteins form patterns called mosaics.
15. A concentration gradient is the difference between the concentration of a given substance in one area and the concentration of that substance in an adjacent area.

Use Your Word Power

COMPLETION Write the word or phrase that best completes each statement.

1. _____ are organelles that enable plants to make sugars.

2. The diffusion of water across a semipermeable membrane is called _____ .

3. _____ is the material between the cell membrane and the nucleus.

4. Two structures that some cells use for movement are _____ and _____ .

5. The _____ is an extensive network of smooth or rough membranes that transport materials through cells.

6. A _____ is a thin layer of lipids and proteins that separates a cell's contents from its surroundings.

MULTIPLE CHOICE Choose the letter of the word or phrase that best completes each statement.

7. A structure that contains a cell's genetic information is called a (a) nucleolus; (b) chromosome; (c) ribosome; (d) lysosome.

8. Energy from ATP is needed for (a) diffusion; (b) osmosis; (c) facilitated diffusion; (d) active transport.

9. Animal cells contain (a) chlorophyll; (b) chloroplasts; (c) cell membranes; (d) cell walls.

10. Which of the following processes is NOT a form of bulk transport? (a) endocytosis (b) phagocytosis (c) exocytosis (d) osmosis.

Show What You Know

11. Compare the capabilities of a light microscope and an electron microscope.

12. Describe the contributions of Matthias Schleiden and Theodore Schwan to the cell theory.

13. List the organelles, and describe their functions.

14. Explain why the modern view of cell membrane structure is called the fluid mosaic model.

15. What is a concentration gradient?

16. What are differences between prokaryotes and eukaryotes?

17. What is a semipermeable membrane?

18. Name and describe two forms of passive transport.

19. Compare endocytosis and exocytosis.

20. **Make a Concept Map** Complete the concept map below by adding the following terms: Golgi apparatus, energy, chromosomes, organelles, proteins, ribosomes, endoplasmic reticulum, mitochondria, lysosome, genetic material.

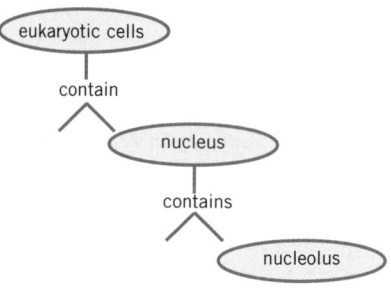

For help making a concept map, see Appendix E.

Take It Further

21. **Making a Generalization** Based on what you have learned, tell why you agree or disagree with the following statement: *Membranes are the most important structures in cells.* If you agree, provide specific evidence to support the statement. If you disagree, offer an alternative proposal and explain your reasoning.

22. **Making a Prediction** What would happen to your cells if a hypotonic solution were placed directly into your bloodstream? Explain your answer.

16. Eukaryotes are generally larger and their cells contain membrane bound organelles and a nucleus. Prokaryotes do not have these features.
17. A semipermeable membrane is one that lets certain molecules pass through while stopping other molecules from passing.
18. Diffusion—random movement of molecules from an area of higher concentration to one of lower concentration; osmosis—water molecules diffuse across a semipermeable membrane.
19. Both endocytosis and exocytosis involve the use of sacs to transport substances across the cell membrane. During endocytosis, large molecules from outside the cell are moved into the

23. Interpreting a Graph The graph shows the sizes of several molecules that can diffuse across a lipid bilayer. Which substances do you think will diffuse most quickly? Which substances will diffuse most slowly? Which substances will diffuse at about the same rate? Explain your answers for each group of substances.

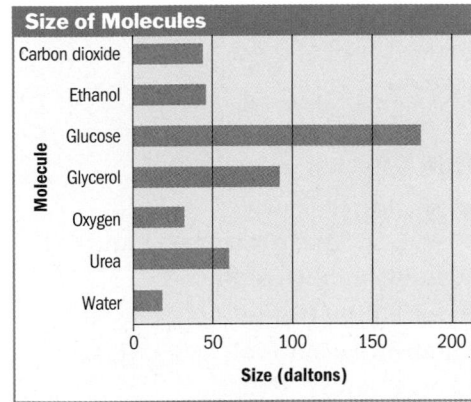

Size of Molecules

Molecule (y-axis): Carbon dioxide, Ethanol, Glucose, Glycerol, Oxygen, Urea, Water

Size (daltons) (x-axis): 0, 50, 100, 150, 200

24. Designing an Experiment Do you think that the rate of diffusion increases or decreases with temperature? Design an experiment to test your hypothesis.

25. Analyzing Data The table shows data for three different cells. Figure out whether each cell is prokaryotic or eukaryotic. If the cell is eukaryotic, is it from an animal or a plant? List the reasons for the decisions you made about each cell.

Structure	Cell A	Cell B	Cell C
Cell wall	Yes	Yes	No
Cell membrane	Yes	Yes	Yes
Chloroplasts	Yes	No	No
Mitochondria	Yes	No	Yes
Nucleus	Yes	No	Yes

Consider the Issues

26. What's the Solution? Different beverages have different concentrations of solutes. Some beverages have low solute concentrations and can be a source of water for body cells. Other beverages have high solute concentrations and can actually dehydrate your body cells. Should companies that market high-solute beverages be able to say these drinks quench your thirst? What information should consumers be given about the concentration of beverages?

Make New Connections

27. Biology and Art Choose either a plant or an animal cell. Prepare either a two-dimensional color poster with labels or a three-dimensional model.

28. Biology and Journalism Imagine that you are Rudolph Virchow. The year is 1858. You have just reached some exciting conclusions about the origins of plant cells, and you wish to share your conclusions with the general public. Write a short description of your theory for publication. Assume that your audience has not studied biology.

29. Biology and Medicine Interview a nurse or doctor about the use of intravenous (IV) solutions. Find out why patients might be placed on an IV drip. Who prepares the solutions? How does the concentration of solutes differ for different patients?

 FAST-FORWARD TO CHAPTER 4

Cells could not function without energy. The next chapter describes the two major processes involved in storing and releasing energy— photosynthesis and cellular respiration.

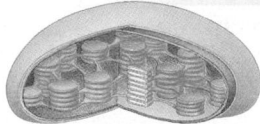

Chapter 3 Cell Structure and Function **79**

cytoplasm; during exocytosis, wastes and cell products are transferred out of the cell.

20. Eukaryotes cells contain organelles and a nucleolus and chromosomes which store genetic material. Organelles include Golgi apparatus, which package proteins; ER, which transports proteins; lysosomes, which digest proteins;

ribosomes, which assemble proteins; and mitochondria, which make energy.

21. Answers will vary. Some students might argue that homeostasis and cell specialization would not be possible without the membranes surrounding the cell, the nucleus, and the organelles, which isolate one cell process from another. Other students might argue that chloro-

plasts are more important because the sugar they produce provides the energy for all plants and many other organisms.

22. Your cells will swell.

23. Water diffuses most quickly, and glucose most slowly. Carbon dioxide and ethanol diffuse at about the same rate. The smaller substances diffuse the fastest.

24. Students could observe how long it takes food coloring to diffuse through a cup of water at cool, lukewarm, and hot temperatures. Diffusion should be noticeably faster at higher temperatures.

25. Cells A and C are eukaryotic; they have a nucleus; Cell B is prokaryotic; it does not have definite nucleus. Cell A is a plant cell with a cell wall and chloroplasts; Cell C is an animal cell without a cell wall or chloroplasts.

26. Answers will vary. Student may point out that beverage companies already list the sodium content of beverages, many beverages that contain electrolytes also claim to quench thirst. While they may seem to relieve thirsts they may not actually be hydrating your cells.

27. You might want to challenge students to construct a generic model with removable parts so that the same model can illustrate both plant and animal cells.

28. Descriptions will vary.

29. Students can either interview the nurse or doctor on site, or invite the expert to come and be interviewed by the entire class. An IV drip can be used to replace lost fluids, as an alternative to oral ingestion of nutrients, or to provide medications.

PLANNING GUIDE

Section	Student Activities/Features	Teacher's Resource Package
4.1 Energy and ATP **Objectives** ■ Explain how energy is stored and released during the ATP cycle ■ Contrast the ways autotrophs and heterotrophs obtain food	**Lab Zone Discover It!** *Seeing a Leaf "Breathe,"* p. 81 **Lab Zone Think About It!** *Examining Patterns of Food Consumption,* p. 84	**Unit 1 Review Module** ■ Section Review 4.1 ■ Enrichment Topic 4-1 **Interpreting and Developing Graphics** 10
4.2 Photosynthesis **Objectives** ■ Identify the substances and structures involved in photosynthesis ■ Compare the steps in photosynthesis that require light with those that do not	**Lab Zone Do It!** *How Does Light Affect Chlorophyll Development?* p. 87 **Lab Zone Do It!** *How Does Iodine React with Starch?* p. 90 **Everyday Biology** *The Foundation of a Healthful Diet,* p. 90	**Unit 1 Review Module** ■ Section Review 4.2 ■ Activity Recordsheets 4-1 and 4-2 ■ Interpreting Graphics 4 ■ Enrichment Topic 4-2 **Laboratory Manual,** Lab 9: "Energy Flow: Photosynthesis" **Issues and Decision Making** 4-1 **Consumer Applications** 4-1 **Interpreting and Developing Graphics** 11
4.3 Cellular Respiration **Objectives** ■ Explain how cellular respiration releases energy from food ■ Compare aerobic and anaerobic respiration	**Everyday Biology** *Warming Up,* p. 93 **Everyday Biology** *Future Fuel,* p. 94 **In the Community** *Breads Around Town,* p. 95 **Everyday Biology** *Feeling Dead?* p. 95 **Lab Zone Investigate It!** *Measuring CO_2 Produced by Yeast,* p. 96	**Unit 1 Review Module** ■ Section Review 4.3 ■ Activity Recordsheet 4-3 ■ Critical Thinking Exercise 4 **Laboratory Manual** ■ Lab 10: "Energy Flow: Digestion and Aerobic Respiration" ■ Lab 11: "Energy Flow: Anaerobic Respiration" **Interpreting and Developing Graphics** 12
4.4 Energy Flow in the Biosphere **Objectives** ■ Summarize the flow of food and energy in the biosphere ■ Infer the importance of photosynthesis and cellular respiration for living things	**STS: Frontiers in Biology** *Artificial Chloroplasts,* p. 98	**Unit 1 Review Module** ■ Section Review 4.4 ■ Vocabulary Review 4 ■ Chapter 4 Tests **Spanish Reviews** Chapter 4

Technology Resources

Internet Connections

Within this chapter, you will see the bioSURF logo. If you and your students have access to the Internet, the following URL address will provide various Internet connections that are related to topics and features presented in this chapter:

http://basis_of_life.biosurf.com

You can also find relevant chapter material at **The Biology Place** address:

http://www.biology.com

CD-ROMs

Biología: la telaraña de la vida,
  (Spanish Student Edition) Chapter 4
Teacher's Resource Planner, Chapter 4
  Supplements
Interactive Biological Simulations
- Photosynthesis
- Cellular Respiration
TestWorks CD-ROM
- Chapter 4 Tests

Videodiscs

Animated Biological Concepts Videodiscs
- ATP Formation
- Photosynthesis
- Light-Dependent Reactions
- Calvin Cycle
- Aerobic Respiration
- Glycolysis
- Krebs Cycle
- Electron Transport Chain

Overhead Transparencies

- Light-Dependent Reactions, #9
- Calvin Cycle, #10
- Glycolysis and the Krebs Cycle, #11

Videotapes

Biology Alive! Video Series
- The Domain of Life Video
Rewind: The Web of Life Reteach Videos

Planning for Activities

STUDENT EDITION
Lab Zone
  Discover It! p. 81
- freshly picked leaf
- bowl or other container
  large enough to hold the
  leaf

Lab Zone Do It! p. 87
- paper towels
- glass jars with lids
- bean seeds
- red, blue, green, yellow,
  and clear cellophane
- permanent marker

Lab Zone Do It! p. 90
- samples of carbohy-
  drates
- permanent marker
- medicine dropper
- iodine

Lab Zone
  Investigate It! p. 96
- yeast
- scale for weighing
- beakers
- various sweeteners
- funnel
- balloons
- permanent marker
- tape measure

TEACHER'S EDITION
Teacher Demo, p. 82
Testing electrical energy
- flashlight with batteries

Quick Activity, p. 85
*The effect of color on energy
absorption*

- thermometers
- black and white pieces
  of cloth
- watch or clock

Teacher Demo, p. 86
Separating "white light"
- prism

Class Activity, p. 87
Examining onion cells
- onion
- microscope
- microscope slides and
  slipcovers

Teacher Demo, p. 91
*Energy-releasing and
energy-absorbing reactions*
- matches
- candle

Teacher Demo, p. 94
Fermentation
- yeast
- beakers
- stirrer
- sugar

Class Activity, p. 95
Reading nutritional labels
- nutritional labels on
  food products

Quick Activity, p. 97
Photosynthesis in flowers
- white flowers
- jars
- medicine dropper
- red food coloring

Chapter Objectives

Students will learn the main concepts of this chapter as they complete the following objectives.

- Explain how energy is stored and released during the ATP cycle
- Contrast the ways autotrophs and heterotrophs obtain food
- Identify the substances and structures involved in photosynthesis
- Compare the steps of photosynthesis that require light to the steps that do not
- Explain how cellular respiration releases energy from food
- Compare aerobic and anaerobic respiration
- Summarize the flow of food and energy in the biosphere

Key Words

4.1 *ATP, autotroph, heterotroph*

4.2 *photosynthesis, pigment, chlorophyll, chloroplast, Calvin cycle*

4.3 *cellular respiration, glycolysis, Krebs cycle, electron transport, fermentation, calorie*

The Opening Story

Have students discuss how they think the story relates to the content of this chapter. Ask them to name foods they often eat, and if they cite animal products, foods the animals eat. Conclude by discussing the accuracy of the following statement: *Ultimately, all animals depend on plants for food.*

CHAPTER 4

Photosynthesis and Cellular Respiration

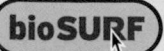

You can find out more about photosynthesis and cellular respiration by exploring the following Internet address:
http://basis_of_life.biosurf.com

In this chapter . . .

FEATURES

Everyday Biology
- The Foundation of a Healthful Diet
- Warming Up
- Future Fuel
- Feeling Dead?

In the Community
Breads Around Town

 Frontiers in Biology
Artificial Chloroplasts

LAB ZONES

Discover It!
- Seeing a Leaf "Breathe"

Do It!
- How Does Light Affect Chlorophyll Development?
- How Does Iodine React with Starch?

Think About It!
- Examining Patterns of Food Consumption

Investigate It!
- Measuring CO_2 Produced by Yeast

Picky Eaters

Partial to Poisonous Plants

Many animals, such as the koalas of Australia, depend directly on plants for their food. Koalas are small, slow-moving mammals that rear their young in pouches. Koalas take a diet of plants to the extreme—they satisfy all but a few of their nutritional requirements by dining on the leaves of eucalyptus trees, supplemented with an occasional helping of soil. Koalas may prefer the flavor of leaves from certain species of the eucalyptus, or even from a single tree—and their tastes can change frequently!

Koalas are food specialists, animals that subsist primarily on one food, which makes them difficult to raise in captivity. The San Francisco Zoo has been successful in keeping koalas, aided by the eucalyptus that thrives in California's moderate climate. Zoo workers traverse the city daily, gathering fresh eucalyptus leaves to tempt the animals.

All animals ultimately depend on plants for food, but few benefit from the eucalyptus—the oils in its leaves are poisonous to most animals. A specialized digestive system allows the koala to survive on this unusual food source.

LAB ZONE Discover It!

Seeing a Leaf "Breathe"

You need *a freshly picked leaf, a bowl or other container large enough to hold the leaf, water*

1. Fill the bowl with water and submerge the leaf in it.
2. Wait 30 minutes. Observe the surface of the leaf.

The bubbles that have formed on the surface of the leaf are oxygen. After the leaf is separated from the plant, for a time it continues to manufacture food from the sunlight it has absorbed. This process releases a waste product, oxygen, which must be eliminated by the leaf.

WRITE ABOUT IT!

Plants take sunlight and water and turn them into food and the waste product oxygen. In your science journal, describe a project that you have done—it might be cooking, carpentry, or homework. What materials did you use? What waste products did you create in the process?

81

Opening Activities

 bioSURF If you have access to the Internet in your classroom or in school, you may wish to have students connect to the address shown on page 80. You may also want to have students conduct net searches for information using key words related to this chapter. For example, they could search for entries under the Calvin cycle, light-dependent reactions, and cellular respiration.

LAB ZONE Discover It!

Seeing a Leaf "Breathe"

TEAM WORK

Before students begin the chapter, have them do the suggested activity for homework or at the beginning of class with a partner. Students should record and discuss their observations.

WRITE ABOUT IT!

Remind students that they may use any one of a variety of formats, including cartoon strips, to describe their projects.

REWIND to Chapter 3

Briefly review concepts learned in Chapter 3, *Cell Structure and Function*. Ask:

■ **How do you think the study of cell organelles will help you understand the processes of photosynthesis and respiration?**

PORTFOLIO PREVIEW

Students should be encouraged to add to their portfolios as they work through this chapter. In addition to the *Write About It* opportunity, the following sections are excellent opportunities for portfolio entries:

■ Section 3: *Cellular Respiration*

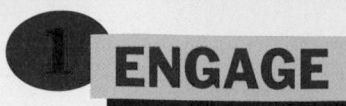

1 ENGAGE

Consider the Big Idea

Have students read The Big Idea! at the top of the page. Discuss the meaning of a closed cycle and ask students to cite examples from everyday life.

Use the Visual

Have students study the photograph that opens the section. Point out that the grizzly bear spends the entire summer gorging and storing body fat for its winter hibernation. Explain that the high oil content in salmon provides more energy than does the protein in animals or the starch in plants.

Check Prior Knowledge

To assess students' prior knowledge about chemistry, ask:

- **What is a molecule?** (A molecule is a particle made up of atoms chemically bonded to each other.)
- **What holds the elements together in a compound?** (Chemical bonds)

Teacher Demo

Display a flashlight and set of batteries. Discuss what is needed for the bulb to light up. Insert the batteries. Ask:

- **Why does the bulb light up?** (When the bonds in the battery's chemicals are broken, energy is released, converting it into electrical energy, and then into light energy.)

What you'll learn

IDEAS

- To explain how energy is stored and released during the ATP cycle
- To contrast the ways autotrophs and heterotrophs obtain food

WORDS

ATP, autotrophs, heterotrophs

THE BIG IDEA! All organisms get energy by breaking down the chemical compounds in food and making ATP and other molecules. 4.1–4.3

4.1 Energy and ATP

Stockpiling energy

All animals get the energy they need to perform life functions by eating other organisms. Energy that is not used immediately can be stored and released later. This grizzly bear obtains energy from a varied diet of salmon, deer, leaves, tubers, berries, and insects.

THE ATP CYCLE

Molecules recycled and reused

Life depends on energy. But where does this energy come from? Energy for life's activities is stored in the chemical bonds of energy-storing compounds. These compounds release energy when certain chemical bonds are broken.

Compounds that store energy include ATP, NADH, NADPH, and FADH$_2$. (These letters are abbreviations for the complex names of the compounds.) In this chapter you will see how energy-storing compounds take part in the chemical reactions that are vital for life processes.

One of the most important energy-storing compounds is shown in *Figure 4.1*. This molecule, called adenosine triphosphate (uh-DEN-uh-seen try-PHOS-fayt), or **ATP,** is the chief energy-storing molecule used by organisms. An ATP molecule consists of three parts: ribose (a 5 carbon sugar), adenine, and phosphates. Ribose and adenine are chemically bonded to form a molecule called adenosine. A chain of three phosphates—the triphosphate group ("tri-" means "three")—is bonded to adenosine.

An ATP molecule releases chemical energy whenever a bond holding a phosphate group to the molecule is broken. This chemical reaction—the release of the end phosphate from ATP—creates a new molecule: ADP, or adenosine diphosphate ("di-" means "two"). Compare ATP and ADP in *Figure 4.1*. How are they similar? How are they different? **2**

The chemical energy released by the breaking of a phosphate bond in ATP can be used by a cell to do work. ATP is involved in three main types of biological work. First, ATP provides energy for the mechanical functions of cells. For example, cells need energy for the movement of cilia and flagella. Muscle cells require energy to contract during movement. Second, ATP is used for the active transport of ions and molecules across cell membranes. Third, ATP is used during synthesis and breakdown of large molecules.

Because cells are constantly at work, they need a constant supply of ATP. Cells generate a continuous supply of ATP by attaching a phosphate to an ADP molecule. Forming this chemical bond requires energy. You may be wondering where the energy needed to make ATP

FIGURE 4.1
ATP and ADP are very similar. ADP is formed by breaking the bond holding the last phosphate on ATP. What is released when ADP is formed? **1**

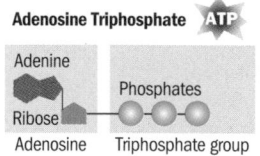
Adenosine Triphosphate ATP

Adenine
Phosphates
Ribose
Adenosine — Triphosphate group

Adenosine Diphosphate ADP

Adenine
Phosphates
Ribose
Adenosine — Diphosphate group

STUDENT RESOURCES

From the Teacher's Resource Package, use:
- Section Review 4.1 and Enrichment Topic 4-1 from Unit 1 Review Module

TECHNOLOGY RESOURCES

Relevant technology resources include:
- Spanish Student Edition CD-ROM
- Teacher's Resource Planner CD-ROM
- Animated Biological Concepts Videodiscs: "ATP Formation"

FIGURE 4.2

The ATP Cycle

1 Stored energy
Energy is stored in chemical bonds. The phosphate bonds in ATP are especially useful for storing energy.

2 Releasing energy
Energy that is released by breaking chemical bonds between phosphate groups in ATP is used to power cell activities.

4 Making ATP
Energy released by other chemical reactions and processes can be used to bond a phosphate group to ADP, making ATP.

3 Energy depleted
ADP has less chemical energy than ATP. ADP also has one less phosphate group than ATP.

ATP

Energy from food

Energy for cells

ADP +P

comes from. Stay tuned. The chemical reactions that make ATP will be described later in this chapter.

The cycle of making and breaking down ATP occurs continuously in cells. This cycle is summarized in *Figure 4.2.* The cycle turns very rapidly—10 million new ATP molecules are made in each cell every second.

SOURCES OF ENERGY

Choices from the menu of life

You may recall that all cells need energy to carry out the functions of life. This energy comes from food—substances containing organic compounds. Organisms break down organic compounds and use the energy stored in the chemical bonds. Organisms are classified into two groups, according to their method of obtaining food.

Autotrophs Organisms that can make food from carbon dioxide and an energy source such as sunlight are called **autotrophs** (AH-toh-trohfs). Plants, algae, and some bacteria are

autotrophs. The foods made by autotrophs are mainly carbohydrates such as glucose, a six-carbon sugar.

Because autotrophs can produce food for their own use as well as provide food for other organisms, they are known as producers. Producers are vitally important to all life on Earth. Without them, other life could not exist. But despite the huge role that producers play in sustaining life on this planet, they account for only about 17–20 percent of the 5 million species alive today.

In addition to making food for immediate use, autotrophs store food for future use—an autotroph's stored food is sometimes used by other organisms. Each year, autotrophs make enough sugar to fill a string of boxcars reaching to the moon and back 50 times! Much of the food stored by autotrophs is used by organisms that cannot make their own food.

Not all autotrophs depend on sunlight for energy to make food. In the 1970s, scientists discovered bacteria living near volcanic thermal vents in the deep sea. The thermal-vent bacteria

SUPER READ!

Chapter 4 Photosynthesis and Cellular Respiration **83**

2 TEACH

Use the Visual

Have students study Figure 4.2. Discuss the following key ideas:

■ Energy released by the breakdown of food is stored in the chemical bonds linking the phosphate groups to ATP molecules.

■ ADP is formed and energy is released when the bond holding the third phosphate group of ATP is broken.

■ ATP is formed and energy is stored when a phosphate group is added to a molecule of ADP.

SUPER READ! **Interpreting Visuals** To practice strategies for effective reading, use pages 31-32 in *Super Read!*

Clarify Misconceptions

Students may equate the breakdown of food with the burning, or rapid oxidation, of fuel and an accompanying release of considerable heat. Explain that most of the energy released during the breakdown of food is used to form chemical bonds. However, some heat is released and is used to maintain the body temperature of the organism.

MEETING DIVERSE NEEDS

LEP To help LEP students understand the importance of repeating the ATP cycle during the manufacture of food, use the analogy of a bicycle. A bicycle wheel turns constantly to move a person from one place to another. The ATP cycle makes energy constantly available to the organism.

❶ Chemical energy

❷ Both have adenosine attached to a phosphate group; ATP has 3 phosphate groups whereas ADP has 2.

Animated Biological Concepts

ATP Formation

Play

LAB ZONE **Think About It!**

Examining Patterns of Food Consumption

Analyzing the Table

1 Autotrophs include grain products, vegetables, potatoes, and fruit; Heterotrophs include meat, poultry, fish, beef, pork, milk, and eggs

2 The consumption of food from autotrophs increased and decreased for heterotrophs. Awareness of problems with cholesterol may contribute to the trend.

3 Answers will vary.

3 ASSESS

Evaluate Understanding

To assess students' understanding of the ATP cycle, ask:

- **How does ATP release its stored energy?** (By breaking a phosphate bond)

- **How do autotrophs and heterotrophs differ?** (Autotrophs produce food for their own use and and provide food for other organisms. Heterotrophs cannot make their own food and are consumers.)

Reteach

Review the basic concepts covered in the section. Then have students work with a partner or in a small group to create two graphics, one illustrating the ATP cycle, and the second, comparing autotrophs and heterotrophs.

LAB ZONE **Think About It!** **bioSURF**

Examining Patterns of Food Consumption

Most humans obtain energy by consuming autotrophs and other heterotrophs. Human patterns of consumption change over time. The table below shows the percentage change over a decade (late 1970s–late 1980s) in the consumption of some foods.

Analyzing the Table

1 Which food sources come from autotrophs? Which sources come from heterotrophs?

2 According to the chart, were humans eating more or less food from autotrophs at the end of the decade? More or less from heterotrophs? What factors might explain the trends?

3 How have your own eating habits changed over the past five years? To what do you attribute the changes?

Patterns of Food Consumption
(Percentage Change Over a Decade)

Type of Food	% Increase	% Decrease
Meat, poultry, fish	9	
Beef		45
Pork		37
Milk, milk products		7
Whole milk		32
Low-fat/skim milk	112	
Eggs		33
Grain products	20	
Vegetables		10
Potatoes		5
Fruit	6	

FIGURE 4.3
Some heterotrophs are such voracious consumers that they deplete other organisms' food sources. Grasshoppers, such as the ones shown here, can ravage crops.

use energy obtained from inorganic compounds to produce food. These bacteria are producers for vast communities of worms, clams, and other organisms that inhabit a deep-sea world without sunlight.

Heterotrophs Organisms that cannot make their own food are called **heterotrophs** (HET-uh-roh-trohfs). Heterotrophs, which include animals, fungi, and many unicellular organisms, depend on autotrophs or other heterotrophs for food. Because heterotrophs must consume other organisms to obtain food, they are also referred to as consumers.

Food may be passed from autotrophs to heterotrophs directly or indirectly. A heterotroph, such as a grasshopper

that eats corn, gets its food directly from autotrophs. Other heterotrophs, such as birds that eat grasshoppers, obtain food from autotrophs indirectly through other autotrophs.

When a heterotroph eats, what happens to food's stored energy? Some of the energy is lost with expelled waste. Cellular processes use some energy. The remaining energy is stored by the heterotroph for future use. This stored energy can also be passed on when the heterotroph is eaten.

CHECKPOINT 4.1

1. Summarize the steps of the ATP cycle by making a drawing with labels.
2. Contrast the food sources for autotrophs and heterotrophs.
3. **Critical Thinking** Compare ATP with a rechargeable battery. What are some other systems that store, transfer, and regain energy?

Build on What You Know

4. Write the conversion of ATP to ADP as a chemical equation. What are the reactants and products? *(Need to jog your memory? Revisit relevant concepts in Chapter 2, Section 2.3.)*

CHECKPOINT 4.1

1. Energy releases when a bond between phosphate group and adenosine molecule is broken releasing a molecule of ADP. Attachment of another phosphate group to ADP requires energy and produces a molecule of ATP, restarting the cycle.

2. Autotrophs use the energy of the sun to make their own food. Heterotrophs get energy by consuming other organisms.

3. **Making analogies** Students may cite solar cells and photosynthesis.

4. ATP → ADP + P + energy

4.2 Photosynthesis

From sun, life
Famine has been a threat to humans and other animals throughout history, but some organisms do not rely on others for food. About 3 billion years ago, organisms developed the ability to utilize an inexhaustible energy source: the sun. How do organisms use sunlight to form sugars?

ENERGY FROM SUNLIGHT

Plants find sun enlightening

Without the energy of sunlight, life as we know it could not exist. Perhaps you have experienced one of the painful effects of the sun's energy—sunburn. Sunburn happens, in part, because your cells cannot directly use the sun's abundant energy. As you have learned, most autotrophs can use the sun's energy. The process by which autotrophs convert sunlight to a usable form of energy is **photosynthesis** (FOH-toh-SIN-thuh-sis). Organisms capable of photosynthesis evolved about 3 billion years ago. Today, photosynthesis supports most of the life on Earth.

Only a small percentage of the sun's energy is in the form of visible light. Although visible light appears as white light, it is actually a combination of different colors. Each color has a different wavelength and different energy.

Autotrophs that perform photosynthesis contain chemicals called pigments. A **pigment** is a molecule that absorbs certain wavelengths of light and reflects others. The reflected wavelengths determine what color you perceive an object to be. For example, notice the apple in *Figure 4.4*. If the pigments of the apple absorb all wavelengths of light except red, the red

wavelength is reflected to your eye, and the apple appears to be red. The combination of pigments in an object determines the wavelengths that are absorbed and reflected—in other words, its color. What wavelengths are reflected by a carrot?

Certain pigments in autotrophs are essential for photosynthesis. The most common and important of these photosynthetic pigments is called **chlorophyll** (KLOR-uh-fil). Chlorophyll absorbs violet, blue, and red light—the wavelengths that provide energy for photosynthesis. Because chlorophyll does not absorb green light but rather reflects it, most plants look green. In *Figure 4.5* you can see a graph of the wavelengths of light that are absorbed by chlorophyll.

FIGURE 4.4
You see many colored objects because of their pigments. Why does this apple look red? ❷

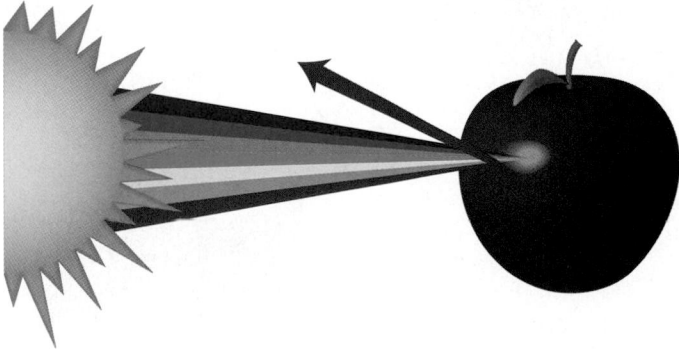

Chapter 4 Photosynthesis and Cellular Respiration **85**

What you'll learn

IDEAS
• To identify the substances and structures involved in photosynthesis
• To compare the steps in photosynthesis that require light with those that do not

WORDS
photosynthesis, pigment, chlorophyll, chloroplast, Calvin cycle

① ENGAGE

Use the Visual

Refer students to the photograph that opens the section. Point out that the food energy comes from sunlight. When an organism dies, the stored energy from the sun is released.

■ **What is the original source of all Earth's energy?** (The sun)

■ **How do farmers reuse the sun's energy in plant material?** (Farmers plow under old vegetation, which fertilizes a new food crop.)

Quick Activity

Determine the effect of color on energy absorption. Wrap the bulb of one thermometer in black cloth, another in white cloth, and place the two thermometers in direct sunlight. Ask a volunteer to record the temperature every minute for five to seven minutes. With the class, graph the data and discuss the results.

❶ Since carrots are orange, they must reflect red and yellow wavelengths.

❷ An apple looks red because it absorbs all wavelengths except red, which is reflected.

Animated Biological Concepts

Photosynthesis   Play

STUDENT RESOURCES

From the Teacher's Resource Package, use:
■ Section Review 4.2, Activity Record-sheets 4-1 and 4-2, Interpreting Graphics 4, and Enrichment Topic 4-1 from Unit 1 Review Module
■ Lab 9: "Energy Flow: Photosynthesis"
■ Issues and Decision Making 4-1

TECHNOLOGY RESOURCES

Relevant technology resources include:
■ Interactive Biological Simulations CD-ROM: "Photosynthesis"
■ Animated Biological Concepts Videodiscs: "Photosynthesis," "Light-Dependent Reactions," "Calvin Cycle"

Teacher Demo

Use a prism to separate white light into its individual colors. Point out that a rainbow forms when sunlight is separated into its colors as it passes through raindrops or suspended particles of water. Explain that visible light or "white light" is actually a combination of different colors of light. Each color has a characteristic wavelength and energy.

Use the Visual

Have students examine Figure 4.5. Explain that on the visible spectrum, the wavelength indicates the amount of energy in each color of light. The shorter the wavelength, the greater the amount of energy. The wavelength of red light is the longest, the wavelength of purple light, the shortest. Ask:

- **Where is green light on the visible spectrum?** (At the center, between blue and yellow light)

- **What light energy is absorbed during photosynthesis?** (Red, orange, yellow, blue, and indigo)

❶ Green and yellow

 Interactive Biological Simulations

Photosynthesis Students match the correct terms for compounds and processes within the chloroplast. Once completed, students can experiment with the wavelenght of light and its effect on the rate of photosynthesis.

86

FIGURE 4.5
This graph shows you the wavelengths of light that are absorbed by chlorophyll and two kinds of accessory pigments. What colors are not absorbed? ❶

Chlorophyll _a_ is the primary pigment for photosynthesis in all plants and algae. Other pigments, called accessory pigments, absorb some colors of light that are not absorbed by chlorophyll. These pigments release energy to chlorophyll molecules for photosynthesis.

CHLOROPLASTS

Sunbathing organelles

In many autotrophs, the chlorophyll and other pigments are located in specialized organelles called chloroplasts. A **chloroplast** is an organelle that performs photosynthesis. A photosynthetic cell contains anywhere from one to several thousand chloroplasts. Just one square millimeter of a castor bean leaf, for example, contains about 500,000 chloroplasts.

The structure of the chloroplast is shown in _Figure 4.6_. Notice the stacks of disc-shaped structures inside the chloroplast. These stacks are called grana, and they are surrounded by a material called stroma. The individual disc-shaped structures in the grana are called thylakoids. In the thylakoid space is chlorophyll and all of the other pigments necessary for photosynthesis.

Each chloroplast may contain a hundred or more grana. Inside the thylakoids, hundreds of chlorophyll molecules and other pigments are organized into units called photosystems. Photosystems are the light-collecting units of the chloroplast. Inside chloroplasts, the sun's energy is captured and converted into chemical energy.

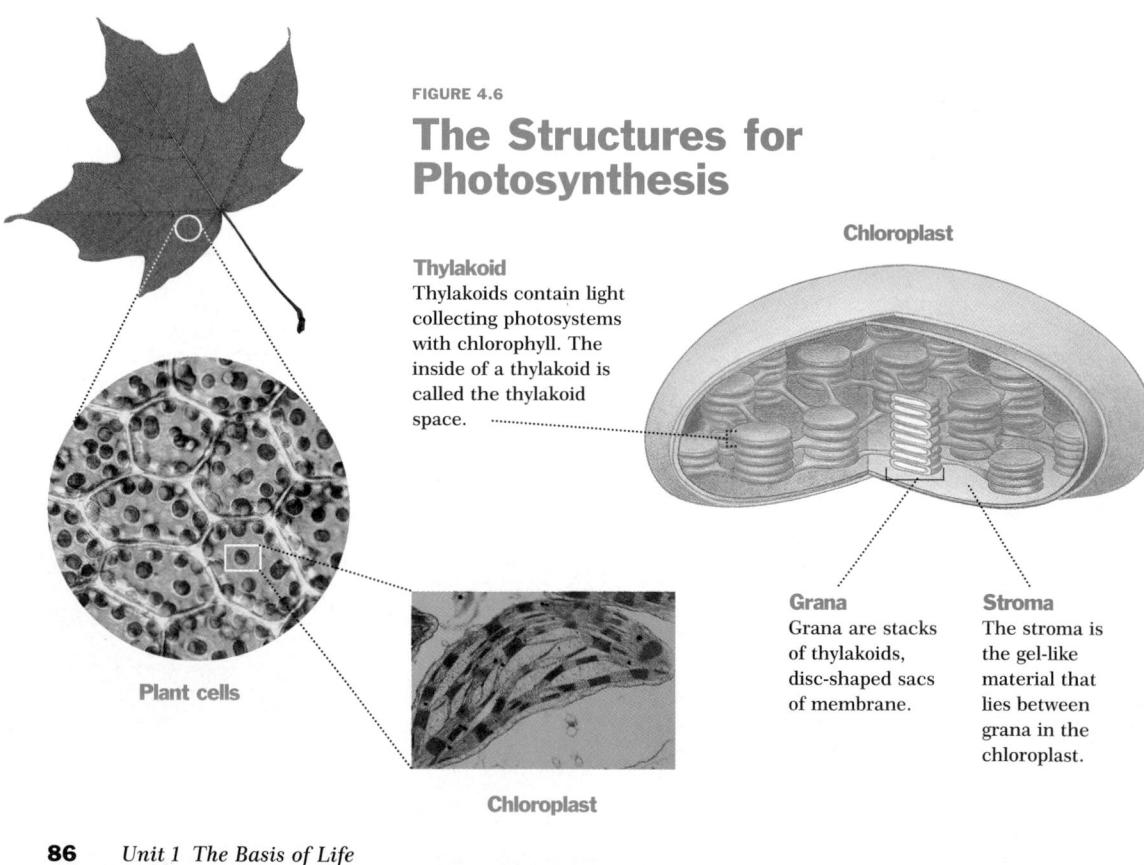

FIGURE 4.6

The Structures for Photosynthesis

Chloroplast

Thylakoid
Thylakoids contain light collecting photosystems with chlorophyll. The inside of a thylakoid is called the thylakoid space.

Plant cells

Chloroplast

Grana
Grana are stacks of thylakoids, disc-shaped sacs of membrane.

Stroma
The stroma is the gel-like material that lies between grana in the chloroplast.

MULTICULTURAL PERSPECTIVE

The discovery of the process of photosynthesis was the sequential effort of scientists from different countries. In 1804 a Swiss chemist, Nicolas de Saussure, discovered that plants placed in carbon dioxide-enriched air grew better than those in normal air. In the 1930s C. B. van Niel of Holland showed that light energy split water and released oxygen. In the 1950s the American R. Emerson determined that photosynthesis involves two photosystems.

OVERVIEW OF PHOTOSYNTHESIS

The big picture

During photosynthesis, autotrophs use the sun's energy to make carbohydrate molecules from water and carbon dioxide, releasing oxygen as a byproduct. The process of photosynthesis can be summed up in the following chemical equation:

Light energy

$$6CO_2 + 6H_2O \longrightarrow C_6H_{12}O_6 + 6O_2$$

In this chemical equation the six-carbon sugar glucose is a product. The energy stored in glucose and other carbohydrates can be used later to produce ATP.

The process of photosynthesis does not happen all at once; rather, it occurs in two stages. The reactions in these stages are summarized in *Figure* 4.7. Photosynthesis begins when light is absorbed in the grana of the chloroplast. This starts the first stage, called the light-dependent reactions (shown in the left part of *Figure* 4.7). During the light-dependent reactions, water is split into hydrogen ions, electrons, and oxygen (O_2). The O_2 diffuses out of the chloroplast and NADPH and ATP are produced.

The Calvin cycle (shown in the right part of *Figure* 4.7) follows the light-dependent reactions. The products of the light-dependent reactions, ATP and NADPH, are used in the Calvin cycle. The Calvin cycle also requires an input of carbon dioxide (CO_2) to produce sugars.

FIGURE 4.7
Photosynthesis has two stages: the light-dependent reactions and the Calvin cycle. Which stage releases oxygen? Which stage produces sugars? ❷

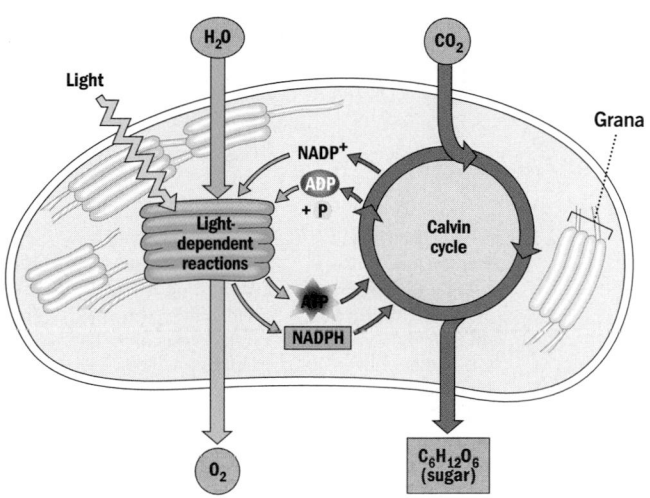

❷ The light-dependent reaction produces oxygen; Calvin cycle produces sugars.

 **Do It!**

How Does Light Affect Chlorophyll Development?

You can find out which wavelengths of light are needed for chlorophyll development in plants if you . . .

Try This

1 Place a damp paper towel in the bottom of each of five small glass jars and put two bean seeds on the towel in each jar. Cap the jars tightly.
2 Cover the five jars with red, blue, green, yellow, or clear cellophane. Label the lids with the color of the cellophane.
3 Place the jars in a sunny place for seven days.
4 After seven days, remove the cellophane from the jars and observe the color of the seedlings. Record your observations.

Analyze Your Results

1 Why is it important to wrap one jar in clear cellophane?
2 What color of light was reflected from each jar wrapped in cellophane? What colors passed through to the seedlings?
3 What substance is missing in the white seedlings and why?
4 What color of light is required for chlorophyll development?
5 What do you think would happen if you exposed the uncovered seedlings to the sun?

Chapter 4 Photosynthesis and Cellular Respiration **87**

Class Activity

Have students examine onion cells under a microscope and sketch a plant cell based on what they see. Students may use Figures 4.6 and 4.7 to help them illustrate the chloroplasts. Ask:

- **What is the shape of the chloroplasts?** (Round and disk-shaped)
- **How do your observations compare to those of other classmates?** (Students' observations should be similar.)

Do It! **TEAM WORK**

How Does Light Affect Chlorophyll Development?

Analyze Your Results

1 The jar with clear cellophane is the control.
2 Red light is reflected by the red cellophane; green light by the green cellophane; yellow light by the yellow cellophane. All colors of light except the one reflected passes through to the seedlings.
3 The white seedlings are missing chlorophyll because they were deprived of violet, blue, orange, and red light.
4 All colors except green.
5 The seedlings would become green(er) because they would develop chlorophyll in the presence of sunlight.

4.2

Explain

Point out that a concentration gradient refers to the rule of diffusion: "A substance will diffuse from an area of high concentration to an area of lower concentration." Explain that any substance will diffuse down its concentration gradient. Diffusion is a spontaneous process.

Clarify Misconceptions

Students may not fully grasp the idea that the light-dependent reactions and the Calvin cycle work in tandem during photosynthesis. Explain that the goal of photosynthesis is to make glucose. The light-dependent reactions make NADPH and ATP, which are required by the Calvin cycle to make a glucose molecule. The NADP+ and ADP released by the Calvin cycle are used during the light dependent reactions to generate more NADPH and ATP. You may wish to reiterate that ADP becomes ATP when a phosphate molecule is added.

 Earth Science

Tell students that the air they breathe is about 21 percent oxygen. The major contributors to Earth's oxygen are the alga and phytoplankton that live near the ocean's surface where light penetrates. These organisms release large amounts of oxygen into the atmosphere as well as into sea water.

 Animated Biological Concepts

Light-Dependent Reactions

Play

88

ATP and O₂ too

The first stage of photosynthesis consists of the light-dependent reactions, so named because they depend on sunlight. These reactions occur in different areas of the thylakoid, called Photosystem I and Photosystem II. Recall that a photosystem is a light-collecting unit of the chloroplast.

The light-dependent reactions require water and sunlight. In this first stage, a water molecule is split in Photosystem II. Splitting a water molecule releases O₂, hydrogen ions (H⁺) and energized electrons (e⁻). Most of the O₂ diffuses out of the plant to become part of the air you breathe.

Follow the pathway of the electrons in *Figure 4.8*. Energized electrons moving from Photosystem II to Photosystem I provide energy for the active transport of H⁺ ions from the stroma to the thylakoid space. What role does the resulting H⁺ ion concentration gradient play in ATP production? ❶

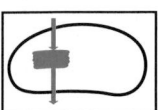

FIGURE 4.8

Light-dependent Reactions

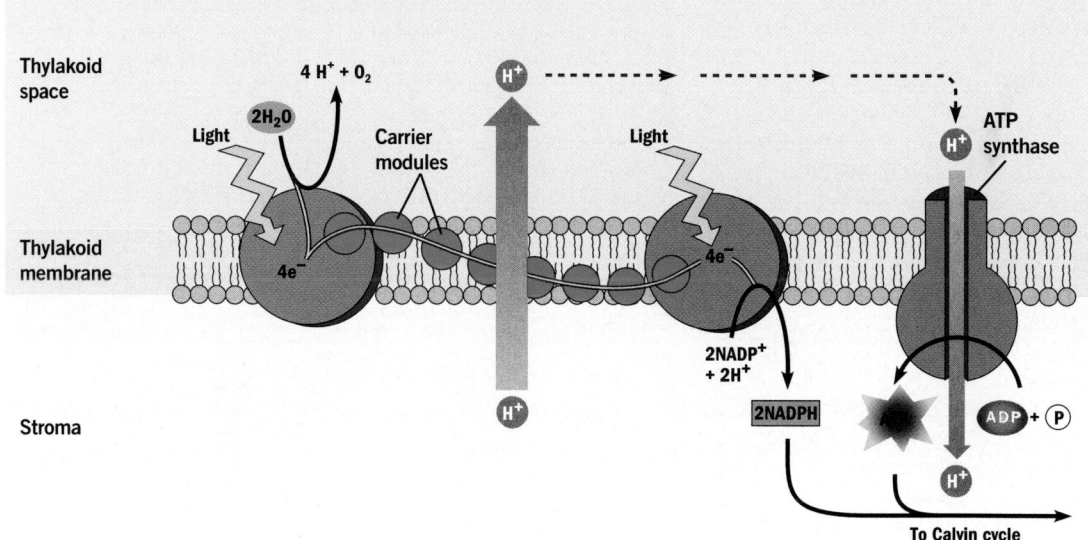

Photosystem II
Photosystem II uses sunlight to split water molecules into hydrogen ions (H⁺), oxygen (O₂) and energized electrons (e⁻). Most of the O₂ diffuses into the air. The electrons enter the electron transport chain.

Electron transport
Energized electrons are shuttled from Photosystem II across carrier molecules. The carrier molecules use the electrons' energy to actively transport H⁺ ions from the stroma into the thylakoid space.

Photosystem I
Using the sun's energy, energy-depleted electrons are reenergized in Photosystem I. The energized electrons are used to produce NADPH, a molecule that will later be used to make glucose.

ATP synthesis
The high H⁺ ion concentration in the thylakoid space creates a concentration gradient. H⁺ ions diffuse back into the stroma through a membrane protein, ATP synthase. The energy released by the flow of H⁺ ions converts ADP to ATP.

88   *Unit 1 The Basis of Life*

❶ When the concentration of H+ ions increases, they move with the concentration gradient into the stroma, causing the production of ATP.

The price of sugar

The next series of reactions require the products of the light-dependent reactions, as well as the input of carbon dioxide. The carbon dioxide is used to build carbohydrates. The process of constructing carbohydrates from carbon dioxide—the second stage of photosynthesis—occurs in the **Calvin cycle.** You can follow this cycle, named after its discoverer, Melvin Calvin, in *Figure 4.9*. The Calvin cycle takes place in the stroma, the gel-like material inside the chloroplast.

In the Calvin cycle, ATP and NADPH made in the light-dependent reactions are used for energy and hydrogen. By investing energy and hydrogen in several stages of synthesis, carbohydrates are built. Overall, one glucose molecule is produced for every six molecules of CO_2 that enter the cycle.

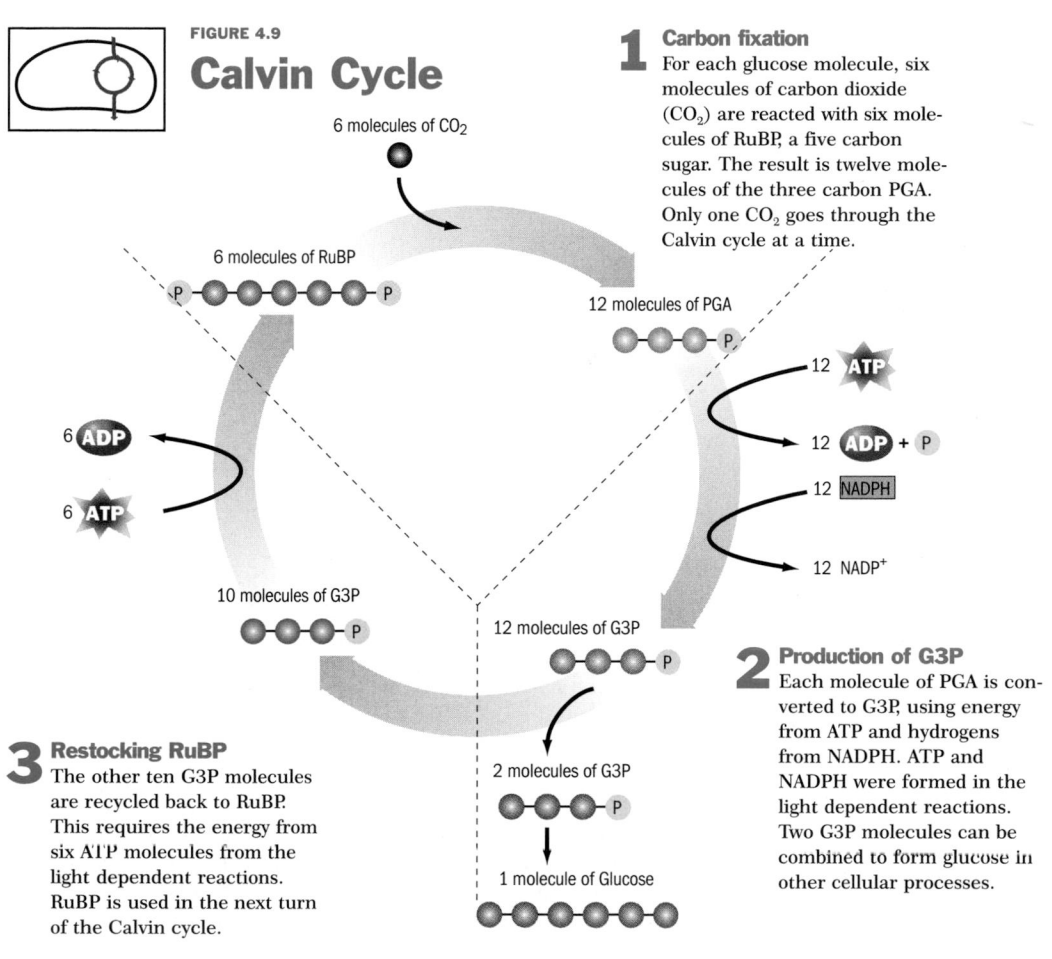

FIGURE 4.9

Calvin Cycle

6 molecules of CO_2

6 molecules of RuBP

P ⬤⬤⬤⬤⬤ P

6 **ADP**

6 **ATP**

10 molecules of G3P

⬤⬤⬤⬤ P

3 Restocking RuBP
The other ten G3P molecules are recycled back to RuBP. This requires the energy from six ATP molecules from the light dependent reactions. RuBP is used in the next turn of the Calvin cycle.

1 Carbon fixation
For each glucose molecule, six molecules of carbon dioxide (CO_2) are reacted with six molecules of RuBP, a five carbon sugar. The result is twelve molecules of the three carbon PGA. Only one CO_2 goes through the Calvin cycle at a time.

12 molecules of PGA

⬤⬤⬤ P

12 **ATP**

12 **ADP** + P

12 **NADPH**

12 NADP$^+$

12 molecules of G3P

⬤⬤⬤ P

2 molecules of G3P

⬤⬤⬤ P

1 molecule of Glucose

⬤⬤⬤⬤⬤⬤

2 Production of G3P
Each molecule of PGA is converted to G3P, using energy from ATP and hydrogens from NADPH. ATP and NADPH were formed in the light dependent reactions. Two G3P molecules can be combined to form glucose in other cellular processes.

Chapter 4 Photosynthesis and Cellular Respiration **89**

FACTS AND FIGURES

In 1950 Melvin Calvin, an American biochemist, successfully identified the products of the carbon-fixing reactions. He used paper chromatography to trace the movements of carbon dioxide containing radioactive isotopes of carbon. In recognition of his contribution, the pathway of the carbon-fixing reactions is called the Calvin cycle.

Use the Visual

Refer students to Figure 4.9 and explain the following formulas.

- RuBP is ribulose bisphosphate. RuBP carboxylase, called *rubisco,* is the most abundant protein on Earth.
- PGA is 3-phosphoglycerate.
- G3P is glyceraldehyde 3-phosphate
- NADPH is the reduced form of nicotinamide adenine dinucleotide phosphate

Explain

Point out that each turn of the Calvin cycle uses only one molecule of carbon, so the cycle must occur six times to make one molecule of glucose.

Animated Biological Concepts

Calvin Cycle   Play

Do It! **TEAM WORK**

How Does Iodine React with Starch?

Try This

1 Students should note differences in their samples.

Analyze Your Results

1 The iodine will turn purple in the presence of starch.

2 Samples could be sugar.

3 Most leaves contain sugars but not starches, thus they would not turn purple in the presence of iodine.

 ASSESS

Evaluate Understanding

Ask students to write out the meaning of the following formula.

$$6CO_2 - 6\,H_2O \xrightarrow[\text{chlorophyll}]{\text{Light energy}} C_6H_{12}O_6 + 6O_2$$

Carbon dioxide   Water   Glucose   Oxygen

Explain that this is the formula for the reactions of photosynthesis. Ask students to name the source of each molecule.

Reteach

Work with students to diagram the steps of photosynthesis as a flowchart. Begin by reviewing the steps in the first stage and then move on to the steps in the Calvin cycle.

LAB ZONE Do It! **bioSURF**

How Does Iodine React with Starch?

Chemists use iodine to test for the presence of starch. You can identify the chemical reaction between iodine and starch if you . . .

Try This

1 Obtain small samples of two unidentified carbohydrates from your instructor. Label them *1* and *2*. Are there any differences in the appearance of the two substances?

2 Apply one drop of iodine solution to each of your samples.

Caution: Iodine is poisonous. Clean up any spills promptly and wash your hands thoroughly at the end of the lab.

Analyze Your Results

1 Describe the reaction. Based on the results of the iodine test, which sample is a starch?

2 If the other substance is a carbohydrate but did not test positive for starch, what type of carbohydrate could it be?

3 Do you think a leaf would test positive for starch in the iodine test? Why or why not?

THE FATE OF SUGARS

Molecules of power

What happens to all the sugar molecules formed during photosynthesis? Autotrophs—as well as heterotrophs—need energy to carry out their own life processes, such as growth and reproduction. Autotrophs and heterotrophs convert glucose to ATP and use this energy to power all of their functions.

Having worked to make the sugar molecules, autotrophs are the first to use them. Large autotrophs such as plants need to make energy available to all of their cells. Large plants have fluid-carrying tissues that transport the energy-rich glucose molecules from the leaves to the other cells of the plant.

EVERYDAY BIOLOGY

The Foundation of a Healthful Diet

Complex carbohydrates, found in grains, are an important source of energy for humans. Rice, bread, and pasta are examples of foods rich in complex carbohydrates.

Plants use some glucose for growth. For example, plants form structural molecules such as cellulose by linking many glucose molecules into long chains. Cellulose is the most abundant substance produced by living things. It provides strength and rigidity to plant structures. Only a few organisms can use cellulose as an energy source. Bacteria that inhabit the digestive tracts of cows are one example of organisms that can utilize this substance.

Most plants store as starches the energy rich glucose that they do not immediately use for energy or structural use. Like cellulose, starches are made of chains of glucose molecules, but bonded together in a different way. Starches are found in plant foods such as corn, potatoes, and wheat.

Plants and other autotrophs are consumed by heterotrophs, providing them with starches. Heterotrophs break down starches to glucose and use the stored energy in glucose for their own energy and structural needs. Any energy-rich glucose that is not used can be stored again as starch by the heterotrophs.

CHECKPOINT 4.2

1. Identify three substances or structures involved in photosynthesis, and describe their roles.

2. Summarize the main steps of photosynthesis.

3. **Critical Thinking** The Calvin cycle is sometimes described as the light-independent reactions. Look at Figure 4.9 and give evidence to refute or support the idea that the Calvin cycle is independent of light.

Build on What You Know

4. Some autotrophs do not store excess energy in starch. What other chemical compounds might they use to store energy? Explain your answer. *(Need to jog your memory? Revisit relevant concepts in Chapter 2, Section 2.1.)*

CHECKPOINT 4.2

1. Accept all answers that identify and describe a substance or structure involved in photosynthesis.

2. In the light-dependent reactions, water molecules are split releasing electrons and hydrogen ions that are used in the production of NADPH and ATP. In the Calvin cycle, NADPH, ATP, and carbon dioxide react to produce glucose.

3. **Interpret a diagram** Without light energy, the Calvin cycle would not be supplied with NADPH or ATP, which are essential in the production of glucose.

4. Sugars, lipids, and proteins

4.3 Cellular Respiration

The universal hunger

Your body cells share one important feature with the cells of all other living things: the need for chemical energy. Whether a diatom, a pine tree, a monitor lizard, or a cat—all organisms rely on cellular respiration for the energy they need to carry out life functions. The cells of all organisms, with the exception of bacteria, generate energy in "factories" called mitochondria, shown at right.

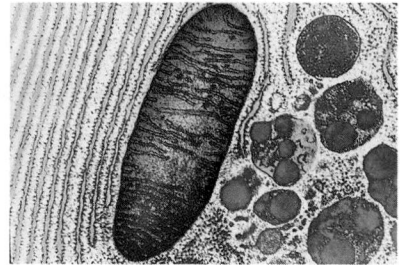

BREAKING DOWN FOOD

Chemical bonds are a mouthful

You have learned that both autotrophs and heterotrophs use the organic compounds in food for energy sources. Complex carbohydrates are a major source of energy for most organisms. Before the energy in complex carbohydrates can be used by cells, the carbohydrates are broken down into simple sugars such as glucose ($C_6H_{12}O_6$).

The process by which glucose molecules are broken down to release energy is cellular respiration. Cellular respiration is a series of chemical reactions which produces ATP. Most cellular processes use ATP for energy. There are two types of cellular respiration. One is aerobic meaning that it requires oxygen. The other is anaerobic, meaning it can take place without oxygen ("an-" means "without").

Aerobic respiration produces 36 ATP molecules from each glucose molecule, as illustrated in *Figure 4.10*. Anaerobic respiration produces only 2 ATP molecules. Some organisms are only capable of anaerobic respiration. Other organisms are capable of both types of cellular respiration. Which type of cellular respiration occurs most commonly in your body cells?

❶

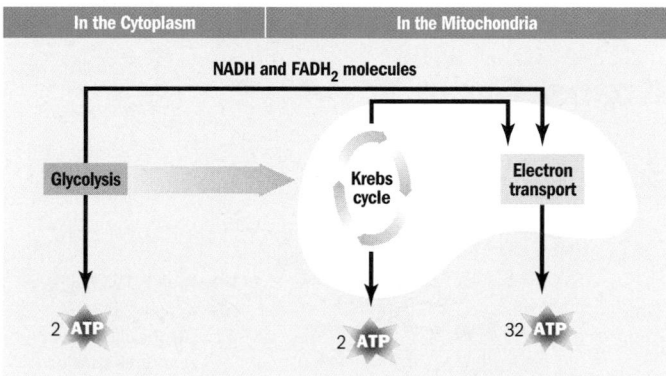

Compare the reactants and products of photosynthesis and cellular respiration in *Figure 4.11*. Cellular respiration appears to be the reverse of photosynthesis: The reactants of one process are the products of the other. However, the steps of cellular respiration are not simply the reverse of photosynthesis.

FIGURE 4.10

In most organisms, cellular respiration begins in the cytoplasm of the cell and continues in the mitochondria. ATP is produced in several steps. At which step is the most ATP produced? **❷**

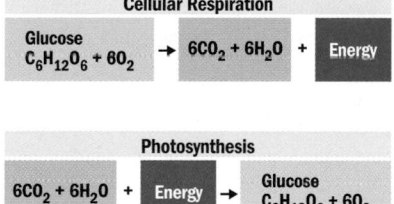

FIGURE 4.11

Compare the overall process of cellular respiration with photosynthesis. How are the reactants and the products of the two processes related? **❸**

Chapter 4 Photosynthesis and Cellular Respiration **91**

What you'll learn

IDEAS
- To explain how cellular respiration releases energy from food
- To compare aerobic and anaerobic respiration

WORDS

cellular respiration, glycolysis, Krebs cycle, electron transport, fermentation, calorie

---

STUDENT RESOURCES

From the Teacher's Resource Package, use:
- Section Review 4.3 and Activity Recordsheet 4-3 and Critical Thinking Exercise 4 from Unit 1 Review Module
- Lab 10: "Energy Flow: Digestion and Aerobic Respiration"
- Lab 11: "Anaerobic Respiration"

TECHNOLOGY RESOURCES

Relevant technology resources include:
- Interactive Biological Simulation CD-ROM: "Cellular Respiration"
- Animated Biological Concepts Videodiscs: "Aerobic Respiration," "Glycolysis," "Krebs Cycle," "Electron Transport Chain"

---

❶ ENGAGE

Use the Visual

Have students study the photograph that opens the section. Point out that the folds, *cristae*, of the inner layer project into the interior of the mitochrondrion. Tell students that some enzymes needed for cellular respiration are organized along these folds. Mitochrondia can be shaped like spheres, rods, sausages, or threads.

Teacher Demo

Demonstrate an energy-releasing reaction by striking a match. Demonstrate an energy-absorbing reaction by lighting a candle with the match. Write the chemical equation for photosynthesis and cellular respiration on the board. Ask:

- **Which process absorbs energy? How do you know?** (Photosynthesis; the formula shows energy absorption.)
- **Which process releases energy? How do you know?** (Respiration; the formula shows energy is given off.)

❶ Aerobic respiration
❷ Most of the ATP is produced in the electron transport chain.
❸ Cellular respiration: reactant is glucose; products are carbon dioxide, water, and energy. Photosynthesis; reactants are carbon dioxide, water, and energy; product is glucose.

4.3

Use the Visual

Have students study Figure 4.12, then check their understanding of glycolysis. Ask:

- **How many PGAL molecules are produced from each glucose molecule?** (Two)
- **What is added when NAD+ becomes NADH?** (Electrons)
- **What are the end products of glycolysis?** (Pyruvate and energy)

Use the Visual

Have students study Figure 4.13. Explain that the Krebs cycle is also referred to as the citric acid cycle because the first reaction forms the six-carbon compound, citric acid. Call on a volunteer to trace the path of carbon and the flow of energy from pyruvate to citric acid. (Pyruvate reacts to become acetyl CoA, releasing CO_2. Acetyl CoA goes through a series of reactions. Each turn of the cycle produces one ATP molecule and four electron transport molecules (3 NADH and 1 $FADH_2$.)

❶ The net yield is 2 ATP molecules.

Animated Biological Concepts

Aerobic Respiration   Play

Glycolysis   Play

FIGURE 4.12

Glycolysis

To split glucose into pyruvate, a cell must first use the energy of two ATP molecules. What is the net yield of energy-storing molecules from glycolysis? ❶

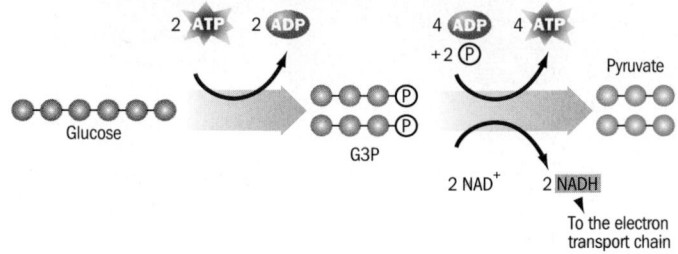

To the electron transport chain

FIGURE 4.13

Krebs Cycle

1 Pyruvate change
Pyruvate is transformed into acetyl-CoA, losing a carbon in the form of CO_2. Acetyl-CoA enters the cycle.

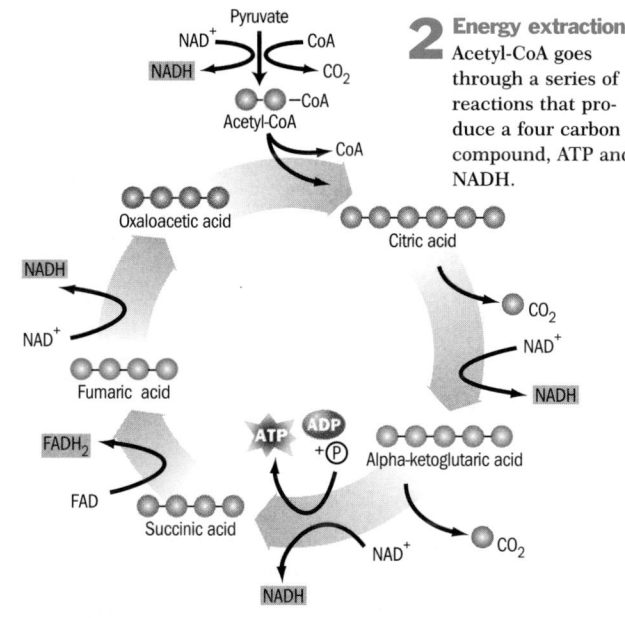

2 Energy extraction
Acetyl-CoA goes through a series of reactions that produce a four carbon compound, ATP and NADH.

3 Completing the cycle
A four-carbon compound is recycled into a compound that can react with acetyl-CoA. $FADH_2$ and NADH are formed.

THREE PHASES OF AEROBIC RESPIRATION

Oxygen for dinner

Aerobic respiration can be divided into three stages: glycolysis, the Krebs cycle, and electron transport.

Glycolysis Both aerobic and anaerobic respiration begin with a step called glycolysis. **Glycolysis** (gly-KOL-uh-sis) is the process by which glucose is converted to pyruvate and energy is released. Pyruvate is a three-carbon molecule that enters the Krebs cycle.

Glycolysis occurs in the cytoplasm of the cell. *Figure 4.12* shows only two steps of the process. Glycolysis is actually a ten-step process, with intermediate products made at each step.

A single glucose molecule that has undergone glycolysis will produce a net yield of two NADH, two ATP, and two pyruvate molecules. You may recall from section 4.1 that NADH is an energy-storing compound. Only about 2 percent of the chemical energy contained in each glucose molecule is released by glycolysis. Most of the remaining chemical energy is in the pyruvate molecules. This energy is released in the next stage, the Krebs cycle.

Krebs cycle The pyruvate molecules produced by glycolysis are transformed into acetyl-CoA, which enters the Krebs cycle. The **Krebs cycle**, named after its discoverer Hans Krebs, is a set of reactions that breaks down acetyl-CoA to form CO_2, ATP, NADH, and $FADH_2$. This cycle is also called the citric acid cycle because the first reaction forms citric acid. Notice in *Figure 4.13* that one ATP is formed from each pyruvate molecule. Because glycolysis forms two pyruvate molecules from every glucose molecule, the result of the Krebs cycle is two ATP for each glucose molecule. The energy in NADH and $FADH_2$ will be used to make more ATP.

MEETING DIVERSE NEEDS

LEP Some LEP students may have difficulty understanding the connection between the processes that lead up to respiration. Draw the different parts of a plant cell on the board or on a transparency. Ask students to identify the cytoplasm, chloroplasts, and mitochondria.

Next ask students to identify the location where photosynthesis, light-dependent reactions, Calvin cycle, glycolysis, Krebs cycle, and electron transport take place. Highlight each location and each process identified.

Electron transport So far you have seen that glycolysis yields two molecules of ATP per molecule of glucose. The Krebs cycle produces another two. However, there is still more energy from the glucose molecule available for use by the cell.

The rest of the energy is contained in electrons carried by NADH and $FADH_2$. Before it can be used by the cell, the electrons' energy must be converted to ATP. **Electron transport** is the process by which energy is transferred from NADH and $FADH_2$ to ATP. This phase of aerobic respiration requires oxygen.

The movement of electrons from NADH and $FADH_2$ occurs along an electron transport chain in the inner membrane of the mitochondrion. Follow the path of the electrons in

Figure 4.14. Where do the electrons end up? ❷

The electron transport chain generates 32 of the 36 ATP molecules produced from each glucose molecule. Due to some energy loss in the form of heat, aerobic respiration is relatively inefficient. The 36 ATP molecules represent less than half of the chemical energy in one glucose molecule. Yet enough energy is collected by this method for humans and all other aerobic organisms to live.

As cells release energy through cellular respiration, they produce waste products. These waste products are carbon dioxide, water, and heat. High levels of carbon dioxide can kill cells, and for this reason all organisms have specialized mechanisms for removing this waste product.

Cross section of a mitochondrion

- Outer membrane
- Intermembrane space
- Inner membrane
- Matrix

FIGURE 4.14

Electron Transport

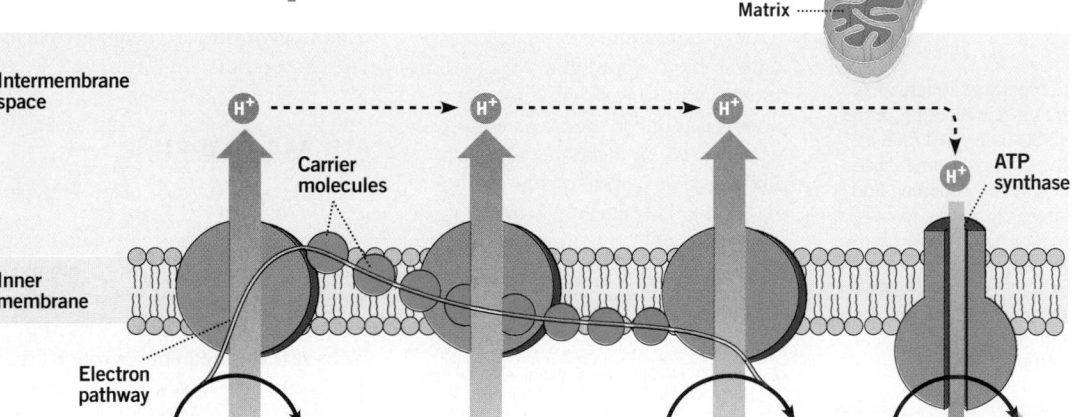

Intermembrane space

Carrier molecules

Inner membrane

ATP synthase

Electron pathway

Matrix

NADH → NAD+
FADH₂ → FAD

$4 H^+ + O_2$ → H_2O / H_2O

ADP + P → ATP

From the carriers . . .
Electrons (e⁻) are released from NADH and $FADH_2$ and start on the electron transport chain.

down the chain . . .
As the electrons pass across carrier molecules, their energy is used to pump H⁺ ions across the inner membrane, creating a concentration gradient.

and into water.
The final electron acceptor is oxygen, which then forms a water molecule with free H⁺ ions.

Go with the flow.
As in photosynthesis, ATP synthase uses the diffusion of H⁺ ions down the concentration gradient to form ATP molecules.

Chapter 4 Photosynthesis and Cellular Respiration **93**

❷ The electrons end up in water molecules.

Explain

Explain that during anaerobic respiration, no additional ATP is produced after glycolysis. In aerobic respiration, the Krebs cycle and the electron transport chain produce 34 additional ATP molecules. Thus, fermentation extracts much less energy from a glucose molecule than does aerobic respiration.

Apply

Most students are familiar with milk that has "gone sour." Point out that the sour taste is lactic acid produced by the fermenting action of bacteria on pyruvate in the milk.

Teacher Demo

Add a small package of yeast to about 75 mL of warm water (30°C) in a beaker. Set up a control beaker containing only water. Stir the contents until the yeast has dissolved and observe the mixture. Add a small amount of sugar to each beaker and observe for several minutes. Point out that a reaction between the yeast and the sugar is producing ethanol and CO_2. Ask:

- **What happened when the yeast dissolved in water?** (No observable reaction results.)
- **What happened when sugar was added to the yeast and water mixture?** (The mixture bubbled.)
- **What did the bubbling mixture smell like?** (Alcohol)

EVERYDAY BIOLOGY

Future Fuel

Some vehicles are powered by a mixture of gasoline and ethanol, a fuel produced through alcoholic fermentation of corn and other carbohydrates. These vehicles have been credited with reducing carbon monoxide pollution in Phoenix, Arizona, and Denver, Colorado.

FIGURE 4.15
Competitive athletes like these, participating in the 1500-meter (m) race at the Olympic Games, use aerobic conditioning and strength training to increase the blood supply to their muscles. Why do you think these types of training help minimize the effects of lactic acid buildup? ❶

ANAEROBIC RESPIRATION

No O_2 at the fermentation station

As you know, you cannot survive without oxygen. However, certain cells in your body—namely, your muscle cells—can produce energy without oxygen. Some unicellular organisms such as yeast can also break down carbohydrates without oxygen. Anaerobic respiration is the process that releases energy from food molecules in the absence of oxygen. Through fermentation, anaerobic organisms and cells can exist without oxygen by using the small amount of energy supplied by glycolysis.

Fermentation is the extraction of energy from pyruvate in the absence of oxygen. There are two types of fermentation: alcoholic fermentation and lactic acid fermentation. In both types of fermentation, only two ATP molecules are formed from each molecule of glucose.

Yeasts are unicellular fungi that use aerobic respiration when oxygen is present. But yeasts switch to anaerobic respiration when oxygen is absent. Yeasts carry out alcoholic fermentation, the type of anaerobic respiration that converts pyruvate to carbon dioxide and ethanol. The process, shown below, gets its name from the fact that one of its products, ethanol, is an alcohol.

$$Pyruvate + NADH \longrightarrow Ethanol + NAD^+ + CO_2$$

Alcoholic fermentation is an important economic resource. Bakers use the alcoholic fermentation of yeast to make breads. As yeasts break down the carbohydrates in dough, CO_2 is produced and trapped in the dough. The bubbles of trapped CO_2 cause the dough to rise and are visible as the small holes in baked bread. As the dough bakes, the yeasts die, and the alcohol evaporates. Alcoholic

94 *Unit 1 The Basis of Life*

fermentation is also used to make wine, beer, and the ethanol that is added to gasoline to make gasohol.

Animal cells cannot perform alcoholic fermentation. However, some cells, such as your muscle cells, can convert pyruvate to lactic acid. Anaerobic respiration in which pyruvate is converted to lactic acid is called lactic acid fermentation. During strenuous exercise, your breathing cannot provide you with all of the oxygen that your cells need. When muscle cells run out of oxygen, they switch from aerobic respiration to lactic acid fermentation. The process is shown below:

$$Pyruvate + NADH \longrightarrow Lactic\ acid + NAD^+$$

The athletes shown in *Figure 4.15* may soon experience the muscle fatigue and soreness caused by the buildup of lactic acid. Most of the lactic acid made in the muscles diffuses into the bloodstream and then into the liver, where it will be converted back to pyruvate. Have you ever felt muscle soreness after exercise?

ATP AND CALORIES

In the heat of the food

You share the process of cellular respiration with most other living organisms. Using this process, all organisms break down glucose molecules and convert the stored energy into ATP.

As you may recall, glucose that is not used immediately can be stored by organisms in different substances. Plants store excess glucose in starch molecules. Some animals store glucose in glycogen or fat. When the organism needs energy, these storage molecules can be broken down to yield ATP.

The energy contained in these substances can be measured and expressed in units called calories. A

MULTICULTURAL PERSPECTIVE

Fermentation is used to make many familiar food products, such as cheese, kim chee, soy sauce, and sauerkraut. These foods are a part of American culture contributed by diverse ethnic groups. Discuss which groups contributed these foods to American cuisine.

❶ Aerobic conditioning increases the amount of oxygen that can be absorbed, reducing lactic acid buildup.
❷ You will lose weight.

Bread comes in a great variety of shapes, sizes, and textures, from fluffy challah to the flat, stretchy Ethiopian bread, *injera*. Some breads are leavened (made to rise) with yeast, baking powder, or sourdough; breads such as tortillas have no leavening. Talk to relatives and neighbors about breads served in their homes now and when they were growing up. Did any of their bread recipes originate in other countries? What leavening, if any, is used in the breads? You may also want to speak with a cook or baker at a local ethnic restaurant. What breads are traditionally served in the culture featured at the restaurant? Are the breads leavened or unleavened? Make a class chart of types of bread and their leavening, if any.

IN THE COMMUNITY
Breads Around Town

calorie is the amount of heat energy needed to raise the temperature of 1 gram (g) of water 1 degree Celsius. Although a calorie is expressed as a unit of heat energy, the energy can be used for all of the countless functions of the cell.

You may be familiar with Calorie values on food items that you buy in the store. When Calorie is spelled with a capital "C," it actually represents a kilocalorie (kcal), or 1000 calories. To measure the energy value of food, a small sample of the food is burned. The amount of heat the burning food gives off is measured using an instrument called a calorimeter. This process is used to determine the number of Calories a particular kind of food contains.

Your body is constantly balancing the calories you take in with the calories you use. People "counting Calories" are actually keeping track of the amount of energy in the food they consume. If people consume food

containing more energy than they need, the excess energy is stored by the body. What do you think happens if the situation is reversed, and you do not consume enough energy for the cells' needs?

CHECKPOINT 4.3

1. Explain how cellular respiration releases energy from food.
2. Compare the processes of aerobic and anaerobic respiration. What are the reactants and products of each process? How much ATP does each process yield?
3. **Critical Thinking** Certain bacteria can remain alive in food canned in airtight but improperly prepared containers. What can you conclude about the bacteria's cellular respiration?

Build on What You Know

4. How is cellular respiration related to metabolism? *(Need to jog your memory? Revisit relevant concepts in Chapter 2, Section 2.4.)*

EVERYDAY BIOLOGY

Feeling Dead?

If you read mystery novels, you are probably aware of the use of arsenic as a poison. Arsenic accumulates in mitochondria, where it disables cellular respiration and paralyzes energy production. How would the action of arsenic in mitochondria harm an organism?

How do organisms get energy?

ASSESS

Evaluate Understanding

Write the following terms on the board: *alcoholic fermentation, ATP cycle, Calvin cycle, electron transport, glycolysis, Krebs cycle, lactic acid fermentation, light-dependent reactions.* Ask students to identify which of these process(es) take place during each of the following:

■ **Photosynthesis** (ATP cycle, Calvin cycle, electron transport, light dependent reactions)

■ **Anaerobic respiration** (alcoholic fermentation, lactic acid fermentation)

■ **Aerobic respiration** (ATP cycle, Krebs cycle, glycolysis, electron transport)

Reteach

Prepare transparencies showing the various reactants and products involved in aerobic respiration. Lead students through a step-by-step explanation of the process.

CHECKPOINT 4.3

1. Glycolysis converts glucose to pyruvate, the Krebs Cycle breaks down pyruvate and produces ATP, and electron transport converts the remaining energy from the electron carriers to ATP.
2. Both start with glycolysis, extract energy from pyruvate, and convert it to ATP. Reactants: cellular respiration—$C_6H_{12}O_6$, O_2; photosynthesis—CO_2, H_2O, energy.

Products: cellular respiration—CO_2, H_2O, energy; photosynthesis—$C_6H_{12}O_6$, O_2. Each glucose molecule in aerobic respiration produces 36 ATP molecules, anaerobic respiration produces 2.

3. **Applying knowledge** They must use anaerobic respiration.
4. Cell respiration releases the energy that fuels an organism's metabolism.

LAB ZONE Investigate It!

TEAM WORK Measuring CO₂ Produced by Yeast

Lab Tips

- Make sure the temperature of water added to the yeast is no greater than 110°F. Hot water will kill the yeast.
- For the most scientific results, use equal amounts (by weight) of each type of sweetener you select.
- Remove all the air from the balloon after the sweetened yeast solution is put into it.

Hypothesis Help

An acceptable student hypothesis for this activity could be which sweetener will produce the most CO₂.

Lab Extension

Directed

If you wish for the lab to be more directed than open-ended, have students choose a single variable, such as water temperature, to conduct the experiment. You may wish to also have students redo the lab and compare the results when air temperature is closely controlled. Put the balloons inside an insulated container with a thermometer inserted through a hole. Place the thermometer bulb inside the container, and leave the calibrated section on the outside. Seal the space around the hole with tape. Before removing the lid, record the air temperature each time an observation is made.

Time Required

- 35 minutes on Day 1
- 15 minutes on Day 2

Measuring CO₂ Produced by Yeast

WHAT YOU WILL DO Carry out an experiment to test a hypothesis about the effects of sweeteners on carbon dioxide production by yeast

SKILLS YOU WILL USE Measuring, calculating, observing, collecting and recording data

WHAT YOU WILL NEED Yeast, warm water, scale, beakers, various sweeteners, funnel, balloons, permanent marker, tape measure

Propose a Hypothesis

In this lab, you will test the rates of alcoholic fermentation by yeast when combined with different types and amounts of sweeteners, such as table sugar, corn syrup, molasses, honey, fruit juice concentrate (with no added sugar), saccharine, and aspartame. Propose a hypothesis about how different sweeteners will affect the amount of CO₂ production by yeast.

Conduct Your Experiment

1 Choose two sweeteners to use in your experiment. Label them *1* and *2*.
2 Mix the yeast and the warm water to make a yeast solution. How much yeast will you use? How much water will you use?
3 Decide on the amount of sweetener and yeast solution for all samples. You will also need a control with no sweetener added.
4 Label three balloons as follows: *Control*, *Sweetener 1*, and *Sweetener 2*. Also label each balloon with your name. Record the types of sweeteners you will place in two of the balloons.
5 Using a separate beaker for each sample, mix the sweeteners with the yeast solution in the amounts you determined in your plan.
6 Pour the mixtures and the control into the designated balloons and tie them. They should be as airtight as possible. Place the balloons in a warm area.
7 Observe the balloons 24 hours after completing step 6. Use a measuring tape to determine the diameter of each balloon, and record your measurements.

Analyze Your Data

1 What caused some of the balloons to inflate?
2 Which of the sweeteners that you used caused the yeast to produce more CO₂?
3 What characteristics of the sweeteners might be responsible for the difference in CO₂ production?

Draw Conclusions

1 Was your hypothesis supported by your results? Why or why not?
2 What can you conclude from your experiment about how different sweeteners affect alcoholic fermentation?

Design a Related Experiment

Design a lab to test the effects of other variables—such as the amount of sweetener, the amount of yeast, or the temperature—on the rate of CO₂ production by yeast.

Conduct Your Experiment

2 For the best results, add 2.5 mL of dry yeast to 125 mL of water, and add about 15 mL of sweetener for each treatment.

Analyze Your Data

1 The CO₂ gas given off by yeast production inflates the balloons.

2 The sweeteners with the highest sugar content and availability produce the most CO₂.

3 Students should conclude that yeast, in the presence of sweeteners and the absence of oxygen, ferments and produces CO₂ and alcohol. The reaction depends on the kind and amount of the sweetener.

4.4 Energy Flow in the Biosphere

The power of photosynthesis

The green layer floating on top of this pond is algae, millions of tiny photosynthetic organisms. In a typical pond ecosystem, algae provide food for other unicellular organisms, which provide food for fishes, which in turn feed birds and mammals. Photosynthesizers form the base of many food chains, and they supply nearly all the energy in the biosphere.

What you'll learn

IDEAS
- To summarize the flow of food and energy in the biosphere
- To infer the importance of photosynthesis and cellular respiration for living things

MAKING FOOD

"Cooking" for billions

By now you have probably gained a new respect for photosynthetic organisms. After all, it is no small task to provide food for the entire planet.

Plants, algae, and photosynthetic bacteria use energy from the sun to make sugars and other compounds. The sugars are used as food to fuel the reactions of cellular respiration. Through the chemical reactions of photosynthesis and cellular respiration, living organisms capture and harness energy. The flow of food and the flow of energy run parallel courses.

In the biosphere there is a continuous flow of energy from the sun, through a series of organisms, and back to the environment. Consider, for example, *Figure 4.16,* which shows chimpanzees eating bamboo. As an autotroph, the bamboo plant uses CO_2 and the energy from the sun to make sugars. This process, as you have learned, is photosynthesis. Cellular respiration enables the plant to utilize the energy in the sugars for growth and other cellular activities.

Most photosynthetic organisms, including bamboo plants, produce more sugars than they need. They often store the excess sugars by making larger molecules such as starches. The starches and other compounds made by autotrophs are important food sources for heterotrophs such as the chimpanzee.

When the chimp digests the bamboo, the plant's stored carbohydrates become available to the chimp's body cells. By the process of cellular respiration, the chimp's cells obtain energy from the carbohydrates. This energy powers all of the chimp's activities, including picking, eating, and digesting the bamboo plant. If the chimp consumes more carbohydrates than it

FIGURE 4.16
Chimpanzees get carbohydrates by eating bamboo and other plants, fruits, and seeds. What happens to the carbohydrates in the foods that you eat? ❶

Chapter 4 Photosynthesis and Cellular Respiration   **97**

STUDENT RESOURCES

From the Teacher's Resource Package, use:
- Section Review 4.4, Vocabulary Review 4, Chapter 4 Tests from Unit 1 Review Module

TECHNOLOGY RESOURCES

Relevant technology resources include:
- Spanish Student Edition CD-ROM
- Teacher's Resource Planner CD-ROM
- Biology Alive! Video: "The Domain of Life"
- TestWorks CD-ROM: Chapter 4 Tests

---

❶ ENGAGE

Consider the Big Idea

Have students read The Big Idea! at the top of the page. Discuss how energy flows through the biosphere.

Use the Visual

Direct students to the photograph that opens this section. Point out that living organisms and plants are major contributors to the recycling process that takes place in Earth's biosphere. Ask:

- **What substances produced by algae can be used by the fish?** (Glucose and oxygen)
- **What substances produced by the fish can be used by the algae?** (Carbon dioxide)

Quick Activity

Have students put three white flowers into a jar with clear water and three white flowers into a jar filled with water to which five drops of red food coloring have been added. Examine the flowers at the end of the lesson. Ask:

- **Why did the white petals turn pink?** (The red water is taken in by the cells and turns them pink.)
- **How were the leaves affected by the red water?** (Students should note some reddish discoloration.)

❶ The carbohydrates are converted to sugars, which are used for life processes or stored as fat in the body.

Answers

1. False (heterotrophs)
2. False (cellular respiration)
3. True
4. False (glucose)
5. True
6. anaerobic respiration
7. Krebs cycle
8. Calvin cycle
9. glycolysis
10. electron transport
11. ATP has one more phosphate group than ADP, and thus has more energy.
12. Choroplasts are organelles inside photosynthesizing plant cells. Choroplasts contain stacks of disk-shaped grana, which are surrounded by the gel-like stroma.
13. Autotrophs are organisms that can produce their own food. Heterotrophs are not able to produce their own food, and must acquire it from other sources. For this reason, autotrophs are called producers, and the heterotrophs that benefit from them are called consumers.
14. The light-dependent reaction and the Calvin cycle (dark reaction); the former uses water and produces oxygen, the latter produces glucose.
15. Photosystem II uses sunlight to split water into hydrogen ions and oxygen. Electrons from the water molecule undergo electron transport, and their energy is used to move hydrogen ions. Then Photosystem I re-energizes the electrons and uses them to change $NADP^+$ to NADPH. Hydrogen ions collect in the thylakoid spaces and their energy is used to produce ATP.

Use Your Word Power

TRUE-FALSE Write true if the statement is true. If the statement is false, replace the underlined word(s) to make the statement true.

1. <u>Autotrophs</u> are organisms that cannot make their own food.

2. During <u>photosynthesis</u>, food molecules are broken down to release energy.

3. A <u>calorie</u> is the amount of heat energy needed to raise the temperature of 1 gram of water 1 degree Celsius.

4. <u>Chlorophyll</u> is the chief energy-storing molecule used by organisms.

5. Many autotrophs contain <u>chloroplasts</u>, specialized organelles that contain chlorophyll and other pigments involved in photosynthesis.

COMPLETION Write the word or phrase that best completes each statement.

6. The process of getting energy from pyruvate in the absence of oxygen is called _____ .

7. _____ is the series of reactions that breaks down pyruvate during aerobic respiration.

8. The second stage of photosynthesis, the _____ , is the process of making carbohydrates from carbon dioxide.

9. The process by which glucose is converted to pyruvate and energy is released is called _____ .

10. Energy is transferred from NADH and $FADH_2$ to ATP during _____ .

Show What You Know

11. Which is the larger molecule, ATP or ADP? How are these two molecules different?

12. Explain the structure of chloroplasts.

13. Define autotrophs, heterotrophs, producers, and consumers in relation to each other.

14. What are the two main stages of photosynthesis? Which stage uses water and produces oxygen? Which stage produces glucose?

15. Summarize what happens during the light-dependent reactions of photosynthesis.

16. Which compounds are recycled during the Calvin cycle?

17. What are the main stages of aerobic respiration?

18. Contrast alcoholic fermentation and lactic acid fermentation.

19. **Make a Concept Map** Complete the concept map below by adding the following terms: pigments, Calvin cycle, chlorophyll, chloroplasts, heterotrophs, light-dependent reactions, food, ATP, ADP, light, water, carbon dioxide.

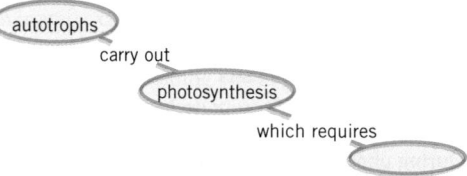

For help making concept maps, see Appendix E.

Take It Further

20. **Interpreting a Graph** The graph below shows the absorption of light by a particular pigment. What wavelengths of light does the pigment absorb? What color would you expect the pigment to be? Refer to Figure 4.5 on page 86.

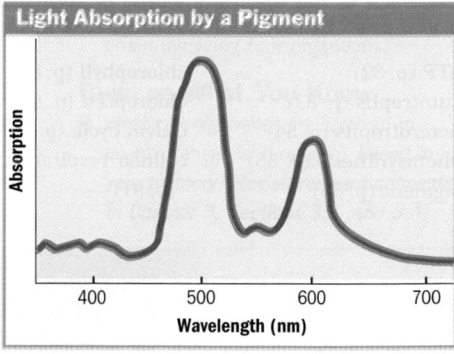

Light Absorption by a Pigment

16. RuBP is a carrier, formed from G3P, which carries carbon dioxide into the Calvin cycle. ADP cycles to become ATP, and ATP is used to form RuBP from G3P. NADPH from the light-dependent reactions forms $NADP^+$, which can be regenerated to NADPH using hydrogen ions from Photosystem I.

17. Glycolysis—glucose breaks down to pyruvate, producing ATP and electrons. The Krebs cycle further reduces pyruvate to yield ATP and more electrons. The electron transport chain which transforms the energy of electrons to produce more ATP.

21. Designing an Experiment How could you demonstrate the effects of different amounts of light on plant growth? Formulate a hypothesis, and then design an experiment to test your hypothesis.

22. Making an Analogy Suppose you and five friends represent the six carbons of a glucose molecule. Describe the events and changes that happen to you and your friends as the molecule of glucose is broken down by aerobic respiration.

23. Analyzing Data The table below shows the amount of energy released from chemical compounds by three different processes. How does the release of energy compare in the three processes? What happens to the energy that is "lost"?

Comparing Energy Efficiency

Fuel	Conditions of Fuel Use	New Form of Converted Energy	% Energy
glucose	burned during laboratory experiment	heat, light	100%
glucose	"burned" during cellular respiration	ATP	40%
gasoline	burned in auto engine	kinetic (motion)	25%

Consider the Issues

24. Plants for Fuel The world supply of fossil fuels such as oil and natural gas is being used up. Some scientists have proposed using plants to produce compounds such as ethanol that could be used as fuel. What questions should be considered in deciding whether the proposed use of plants is worth trying? How could some of these questions be answered?

Make New Connections

25. Biology and Art: A Local Field Trip Find an area near your school with several varieties of plants. Without disturbing any organisms, identify heterotrophic and autotrophic relationships between plants and other organisms. Create a poster showing some of the food chains present in your community.

26. Biology and Food Production Yeasts ferment sugars by anaerobic respiration. The byproducts of this process give many foods their unique qualities. Identify foods that are made with yeast, and find out how yeasts are used in various food-making processes.

27. Biology and Math Chemical equations are shown on pages 87 and 91. You can determine the number of atoms involved in a chemical equation by multiplying the number of atoms in each molecule by the number of molecules. For example, $4H_2O$ includes 8 hydrogen atoms (4 molecules × 2 atoms per molecule) and 4 oxygen atoms (4 molecules × 1 atom per molecule). Calculate the number of atoms involved in the chemical equations shown in this chapter.

FAST-FORWARD TO CHAPTER 5

Cells require energy for all their life processes, including making new cells. In the next chapter you will learn how cells reproduce, as well as the results of cellular reproduction.

f) <u>Light-dependent reactions</u> which require <u>light</u>.

g) <u>Light-dependent reactions</u> which require <u>water</u>.

h) <u>Light-dependent reactions</u> which convert <u>ADP</u> into <u>ATP</u>.

20. The peaks at 500 nm and 600 nm suggest that green and yellow light would be absorbed, while blue and red light would be reflected. The pigment should be purple in color.

21. Hypotheses about plants growing with different amounts of light may vary. Experimental variables could include different distances from a common source, different periods of illumination, and different numbers of source lights.

22. Answers will vary, but eventually each person will be separate from the others.

23. Glucose burned in the lab is totally converted to heat and light. During cellular respiration, some energy in glucose is converted into ATP; the rest, into heat. In an engine, some energy in gasoline is converted into mechanical energy; the rest, into heat.

24. Answers will vary, but should consider how quickly and easily the plants will grow and how much waste is created in making the fuels. Questions could be answered by research.

25. Check posters for scientific accuracy.

26. Yeast is used in making breads and some alcoholic beverages.

27. Photosynthesis and cellular respiration both have 6 carbon, 12 hydrogen, and 18 oxygen atoms are on each side of the equation.

18. Alcoholic fermentation produces carbon dioxide and ethanol as byproducts of fermentation; lactic acid fermentation produces lactic acid as a byproduct.

19. The following connections are some suggestions:

a) <u>Photosynthesis</u> which requires <u>pigments</u>, which may include <u>chlorophyll</u>.

b) <u>Photosynthesis</u> which is composed of <u>light-dependent reactions</u> which are followed by the <u>Calvin cycle</u>.

c) <u>Pigments</u> which are found in the <u>chloroplasts</u>.

d) <u>Calvin cycle</u> which produces <u>food</u> which is consumed by <u>heterotrophs</u>.

e) <u>Calvin cycle</u> which uses <u>carbon dioxide</u>.

PLANNING GUIDE

Section	Student Activities/Features	Teacher's Resource Package
5.1 When Do Cells Divide? **Objectives** ■ Analyze the limits on cell size ■ Identify the roles of cell division in reproduction, growth, and repair	**Lab Zone** Discover It! *Observing a Plant Cutting*, p. 103 **Lab Zone Think About It!** *Calculating Surface Area to Volume Ratio*, p. 105 **In the Community** *Healing Cuts*, p. 106 **STS: Frontiers in Biology** *Multiplying Division*, p. 106	**Unit 1 Review Module** ■ Section Review 5.1 ■ Enrichment Topic 5-1 **Consumer Applications** 5-1
5.2 How Do Cells Divide? **Objectives** ■ Explain the functions of a cell in interphase ■ Distinguish the steps of mitosis and cytokinesis	**Lab Zone Do It!** *Modeling the Phases of Mitosis*, p. 109 **Lab Zone Investigate It!** *Observing Mitosis*, p. 113	**Unit 1 Review Module** ■ Section Review 5.2 ■ Activity Recordsheets 5-1 and 5-2 **Biotechnology Manual,** Lab 3: "Mitosis in Onion Root Tips" **Interpreting and Developing Graphics** 13
5.3 What Is Meiosis? **Objectives** ■ Show how the reduction in numbers of chromosomes relates to the process of sexual reproduction ■ Summarize the phases of meiosis	**Everyday Biology** *The Chicken and the Egg*, p. 115 **Lab Zone Think About It!** *Calculating Haploid and Diploid Numbers*, p. 115	**Unit 1 Review Module** ■ Section Review 5.3 ■ Critical Thinking Exercise 5 **Laboratory Manual,** Lab 12: "Meiosis and Fertilization" **Biotechnology Manual,** Lab 7: "Sea Urchin Fertilization and Early Development" **Interpreting and Developing Graphics** 14
5.4 New Chromosome Combinations **Objectives** ■ Compare meiosis and mitosis ■ Explain the significance of genetic variation	**Lab Zone Do It!** *Modeling the Phases of Meiosis*, p. 120	**Unit 1 Review Module** ■ Section Review 5.4 ■ Activity Recordsheet 5-3 ■ Interpreting Graphics 5 ■ Vocabulary Review 5 ■ Chapter 5 Tests **Issues and Decision Making** 5-1 **Interpreting and Developing Graphics** 15 **Spanish Reviews** ■ Chapter 5 ■ Unit 1

Technology Resources

Internet Connections

Within this chapter, you will see the **bioSURF** logo. If you and your students have access to the Internet, the following URL address will provide various Internet connections that are related to topics and features presented in this chapter:

http://basis_of_life.biosurf.com

You can also find relevant chapter material at **The Biology Place** address:

http://www.biology.com

CD-ROMs

Biología: la telaraña de la vida,
  (Spanish Student Edition) Chapter 5
Teacher's Resource Planner, Chapter 5
  Supplements
Interactive Biological Simulations
- Mitosis and Cytokinesis
- Meiosis
TestWorks CD-ROM
- Chapter 5 Tests

Videodiscs

Animated Biological Concepts Videodiscs
- Animal Cell Mitosis and Cytokinesis
- Meiosis Overview
- Animal Cell Meiosis

Overhead Transparencies

The Phases of the Cell Cycle, #12 and #13

Videotapes

Biology Alive! Video Series
Rewind: The Web of Life Reteach Videos

Planning for Activities

STUDENT EDITION
Lab Zone
Discover It! p. 103
- plant
- scissors
- small clear glass or plastic container

Lab Zone Do It! p. 109
- pipe cleaners
- string
- glue
- paper clips
- modeling clay
- toothpicks

Lab Zone
Investigate It! p. 113
- microscope
- prepared slide of mitosis in onion root tip
- pencil
- paper

Lab Zone Do It! p. 120
- models made from **Lab Zone Do It!** p. 109
- pipe cleaners

- string
- glue
- paper clips
- modeling clay
- toothpicks

TEACHER'S EDITION
Quick Activity, p. 104
Modeling cell growth
- balloons

Quick Activity, p. 107
DNA replication
- variously colored chalk
- black construction paper

Class Activity, p. 110
Mitosis
- string

Quick Activity, p. 118
Moths in a specific environment
- scissors
- black paper
- white paper
- dark background

Chapter Objectives

Students will learn the main concepts of this chapter as they complete the following objectives.

- Analyze the limits on cell size
- Identify the roles of cell division in reproduction, growth, and repair
- Explain the functions of a cell in interphase
- Distinguish the steps of mitosis and cytokinesis
- Relate the reduction of chromosome number to the process of sexual reproduction
- Summarize the phases of meiosis
- Compare meiosis to mitosis
- Explain the significance of genetic variation

Key Words

5.1 *asexual reproduction, sexual reproduction*

5.2 *interphase, replication, chromatin, sister chromatids, centromere, mitosis, cytokinesis, prophase, metaphase, anaphase, telophase*

5.3 *diploid, haploid, meiosis, homologous pair*

5.4 *variation*

The Opening Story

Have students discuss how they think the story relates to the content of this chapter. Call on a volunteer to explain how cell division relates to the growth and development of the baby zebra.

102

You can find out more about the process of cell division by exploring the following Internet address: *http://basis_of_life.biosurf.com*

In this chapter . . .

FEATURES

Everyday Biology
The Chicken and the Egg

In the Community
Healing Cuts

 Frontiers in Biology
Multiplying Division

LAB ZONES

Discover It!
• Observing a Plant Cutting
Do It!
• Modeling the Phases of Mitosis
• Modeling the Phases of Meiosis
Think About It!
• Calculating Surface to Volume Ratio
• Calculating Haploid and Diploid Numbers
Investigate It!
• Observing Mitosis

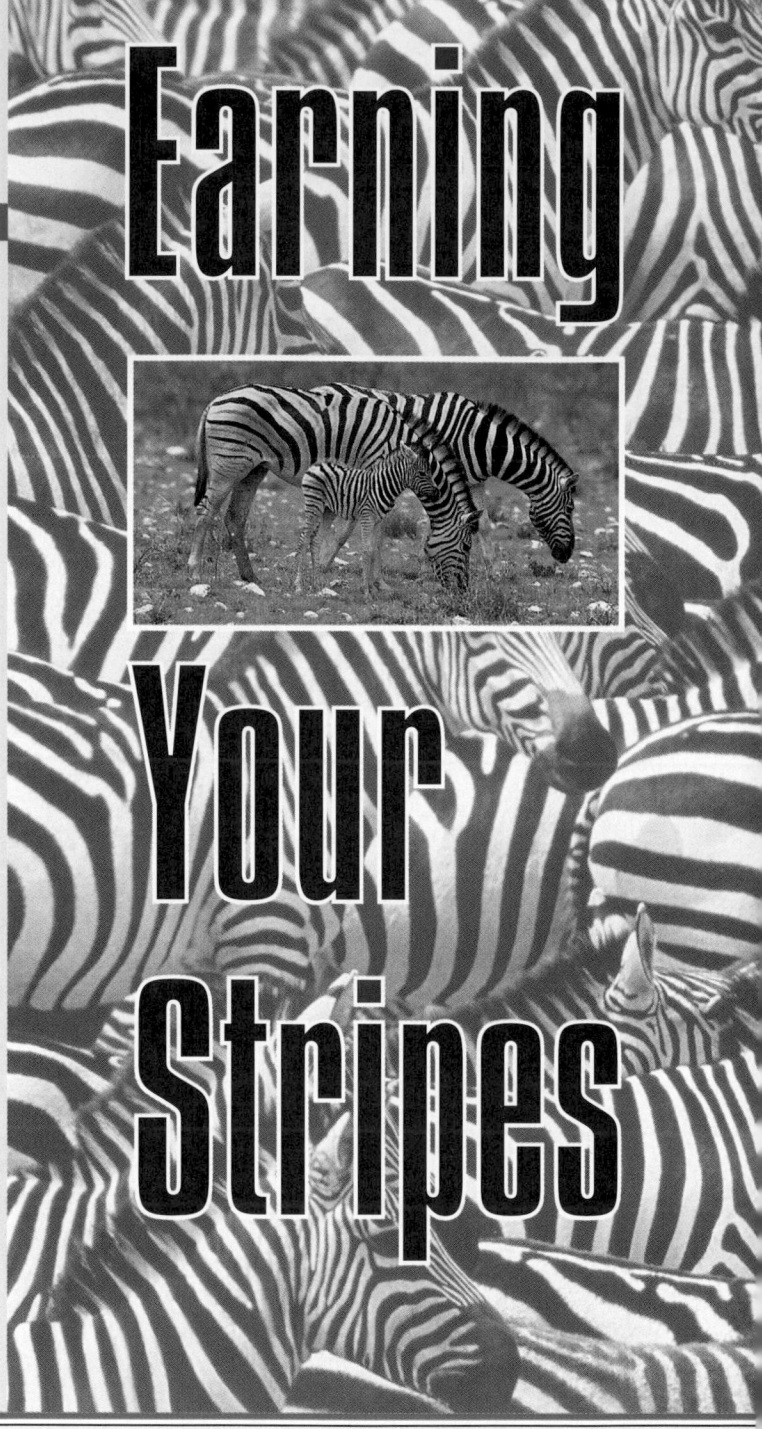

Earning Your Stripes

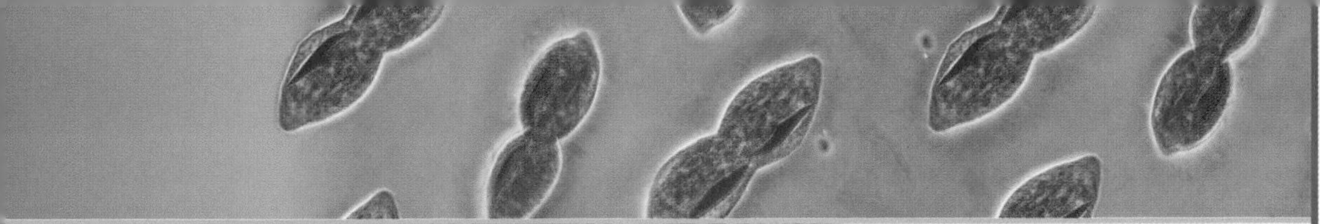

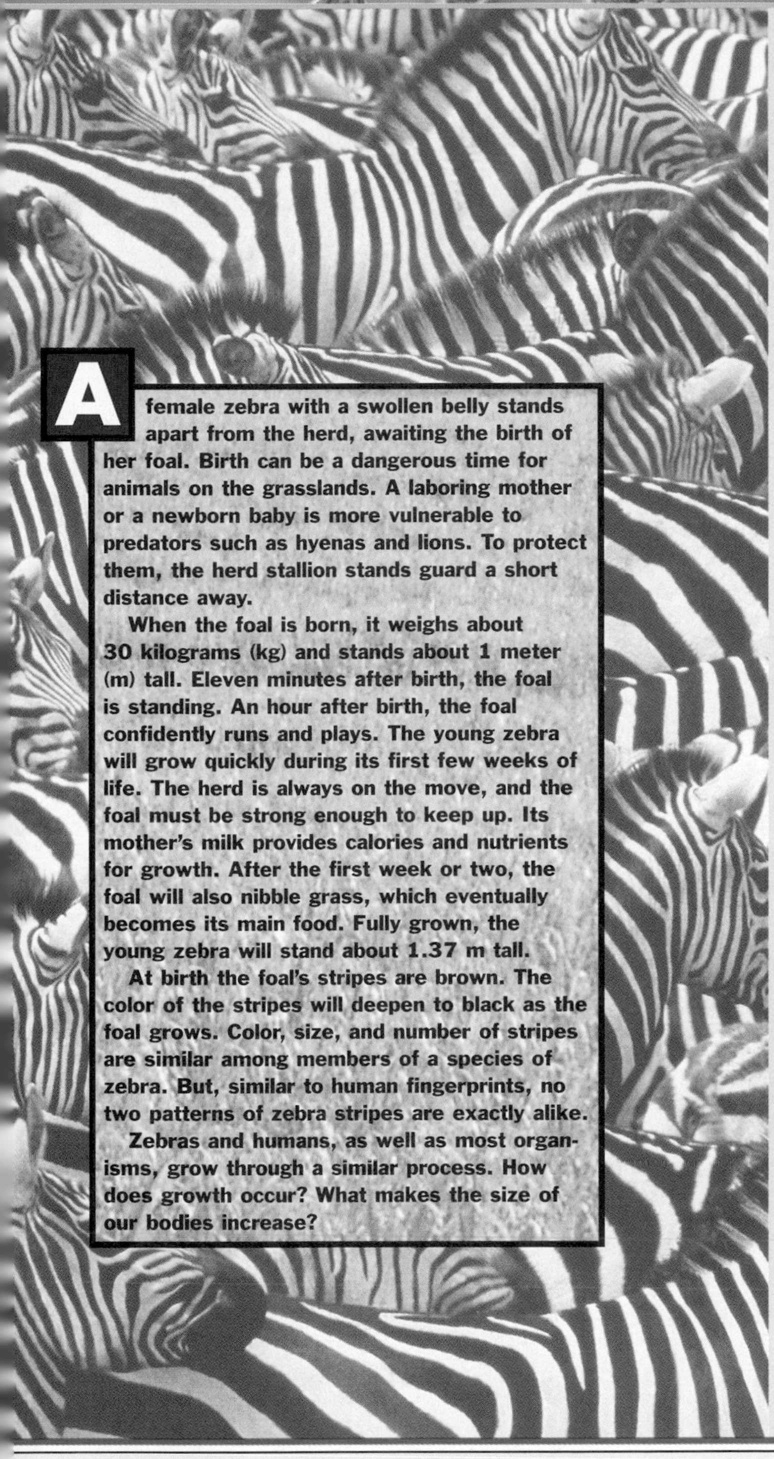

A female zebra with a swollen belly stands apart from the herd, awaiting the birth of her foal. Birth can be a dangerous time for animals on the grasslands. A laboring mother or a newborn baby is more vulnerable to predators such as hyenas and lions. To protect them, the herd stallion stands guard a short distance away.

When the foal is born, it weighs about 30 kilograms (kg) and stands about 1 meter (m) tall. Eleven minutes after birth, the foal is standing. An hour after birth, the foal confidently runs and plays. The young zebra will grow quickly during its first few weeks of life. The herd is always on the move, and the foal must be strong enough to keep up. Its mother's milk provides calories and nutrients for growth. After the first week or two, the foal will also nibble grass, which eventually becomes its main food. Fully grown, the young zebra will stand about 1.37 m tall.

At birth the foal's stripes are brown. The color of the stripes will deepen to black as the foal grows. Color, size, and number of stripes are similar among members of a species of zebra. But, similar to human fingerprints, no two patterns of zebra stripes are exactly alike.

Zebras and humans, as well as most organisms, grow through a similar process. How does growth occur? What makes the size of our bodies increase?

LAB ZONE Discover It!

Observing a Plant Cutting

You need a plant, scissors, a small clear glass or plastic container, water

1. What do you think will happen when you cut off part of a plant and place it in water? Propose a hypothesis.
2. Use scissors to cut a small piece, including leaves and stem, from the tip of the plant. Place the cut end into a container filled with water.
3. Observe the cutting for a week.

What happened to the cut end of the plant? Plant parts have the ability to grow from a piece into a whole organism, unlike most animals. Although plants and most animals differ in this respect, their growth processes at the cellular level are much the same. You will read about these processes in this chapter.

WRITE ABOUT IT!

Have you ever grown plants from seeds or cuttings, raised baby animals, or observed a younger sibling or cousin? Describe what it is like to watch plants, animals, or humans grow. What stages do they go through? How does their appearance change?

Opening Activities

bioSURF If you have access to the Internet in your classroom or school, you may wish to have students connect to the address shown on page 102. You may also want to have students conduct net searches for information using key words related to this chapter. For example, they could search for entries under asexual reproduction, cell growth and repair, and genetic variation.

LAB ZONE Discover It!

Observing a Plant Cutting
Before students begin this chapter, have them prepare the plant cutting. Students should observe the cuttings as they study this chapter. You may wish to have them log the progress in their portfolio.

WRITE ABOUT IT!

After students complete their journal entries, you may wish to have them write an essay on the importance of cell division to their health and life processes.

REWIND to Chapter 4

Briefly review with students concepts learned in Chapter 4, *Photosynthesis and Cellular Respiration.* Ask:

- **How do you think the energy needs of an organism relates to this chapter on cell division?**

PORTFOLIO PREVIEW

Students should be encouraged to add to their portfolios as they work through this chapter. In addition to the *Write About It* opportunity, the following sections are excellent opportunities for portfolio entries:
- Section 5.1: *When Do Cells Divide?*
- Section 5.4: *How Do Cells Divide?*

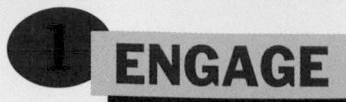

1 ENGAGE

Consider the Big Idea

Have students read The Big Idea! at the top of the page. Explain that this statement summarizes the importance of cell division to life.

Use the Visual

Have students study the photograph that opens the section. Point out that the newborn infant is a miniature of its parents. As the infant grows, its cells divide constantly, creating more cells.

Quick Activity

Have students blow up ten balloons to varying sizes. Hold the five largest balloons in one hand and the five smallest balloons in the other. Ask:

- **Which handful of balloons takes up the most space?** (The five largest balloons)
- **If each balloon is a cell, which handful of "cells" is likely to divide? Why?** (Just as balloons break as they get larger, the largest "cells" divide when they become too "big".)
- **Which handful of "cells" has the greater potential for growth?** (The smallest "cells," because each can become larger)

5.1 When Do Cells Divide?

What you'll learn

IDEAS
- To analyze the limits on cell size
- To identify the roles of cell division in reproduction, growth, and repair

WORDS
asexual reproduction, sexual reproduction

Divide and grow!
All living things are made of cells. Cells must divide in order to reproduce, grow, and repair themselves. The trillions of cells that make up an elephant come from just one original cell: a fertilized egg. Each time this cell reproduces, the new cells that are formed contain all the essential cytoplasm, organelles, and chromosomes needed for the elephant to develop, survive, and function.

CELL SIZE

Bigger is not better

FIGURE 5.1
With the exception of muscle and nerve cells, cell size is not determined by the overall size of an organism. Most cells of this giraffe and this mouse are about the same size.

If you compare cells from a giraffe with cells from a mouse, you might be surprised to find that the cells are structurally alike. Although the animals themselves are vastly different in size and shape, their cells are not. In fact, the diameter of most eukaryotic cells falls within the fairly narrow range of 10-100 micrometers (μm).

One of the most important factors affecting cell size is the size of the cell membrane. Cells obtain nutrients and eliminate wastes through the cell membrane.

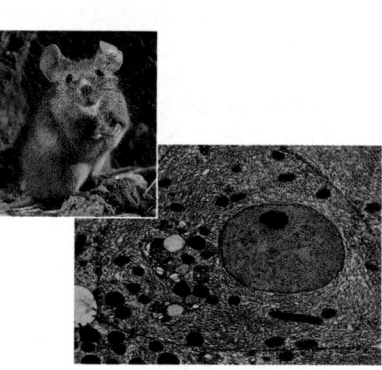

Eukaryotic cell

A cell must have a membrane surface large enough for all of the needed exchanges to take place with the environment. As cells increase in size, their need for nutrients increases, as does their production of wastes. Therefore, larger cells require a larger membrane surface area for survival.

Can cells continue to increase in size without limit? To answer this question, consider the models of cells in the activity on page 105. How do their surface areas compare? How do the volumes of the cells compare?

Smaller cells, similar to the model with 1-centimeter (cm) sides, have larger surface area to volume ratios. Larger cells, similar to the model with 4-cm sides, have smaller surface area to volume ratios. As cells increase in size, their volume increases more rapidly than their surface area does. It is more difficult for cells with a larger volume to transport needed nutrients in and harmful wastes out. Therefore, cells need to remain relatively small to survive.

The nucleus, as you have learned, controls many of the cell's activities. It also has an effect on cell size. Control is vital to cell functions, and the

nucleus can control only a limited amount of living, active cytoplasm. The scope of nuclear control, therefore, can limit the size of cells.

GROWTH, REPAIR, AND REPRODUCTION

The great divide

When a cell reaches its maximum size, the nucleus initiates cell divison. Cell division is the splitting of a single cell into two cells. This process accounts for three essential life processes: growth, repair, and reproduction.

Growth You know from experience that living things grow, or increase in size. Growth is a result of cells producing new cells through cell division. The number of cells making up the organism increases, and the organism grows.

When some cells divide and then enlarge, they also develop specialized shapes and functions. The changes that take place in cells as they develop are called differentiation. As an organism develops, new cells differentiate into particular forms for particular functions. A nerve cell, for example, differentiates into a form that can conduct electric impulses. An intestinal cell differentiates into a form that can aid in digestion. Can you name some other types of specialized cells in ❷ your body?

Repair Cell division is also crucial for repairing tissues. Organisms vary in their ability to repair tissues by cell division. For example, when a sea star loses one of its five arms (*Figure* 5.2), the cells surrounding the injury are stimulated to divide repeatedly until they form a new arm. This level of repair, which replaces a missing body part, is called regeneration.

Regeneration to the extent seen in sea stars is not possible in humans. However, cell division is responsible for repairs that your body requires—

LAB ZONE **Think About It!**

Calculating Surface Area to Volume Ratio

The limits to cell size are governed by the surface area to volume ratio. Learn how to calculate the surface area to volume ratio of a cube by using the diagram and the formulas below.

Analyzing the Diagram

1 The formula for surface area is 6 × height × width (because a cube has six sides). The formula for volume is height × width × depth.
2 Calculate the surface area and volume for the two single cubes below. (The measurements are shown in centimeters.)
3 Place your answers in a ratio, with the surface area first. Reduce the ratio to simplest terms, if necessary.
4 How does the surface area to volume ratio change for the large cube when it is divided into 64 small cubes?

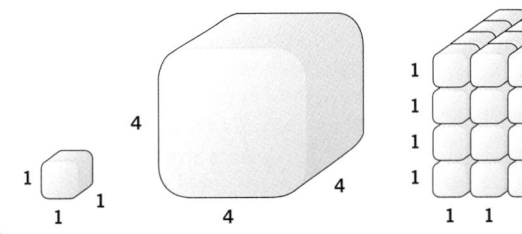

mending of skin, blood vessels, and bone, for example. Repairs are accomplished by cell regeneration at the site of an injury. Regeneration also replaces cells that die. Your skin cells are replaced by regeneration every 28 days!

Reproduction When the sea star loses its arm, it grows a new one. The lost arm's cells can also divide to form a whole new sea star. When an offspring is produced by only one parent, the process is called **asexual reproduction.** Asexual reproduction is a result of cell division.

Asexual reproduction is common among many

FIGURE 5.2
Cellular division has regenerated the lost arm of this sea star. What other organisms are capable of limb regeneration?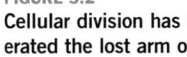

Chapter 5 Cell Division **105**

❶ The large "cube," or cell, has a larger surface area and more volume than the small cube. But when the large cube is divided, its surface area to volume ratio changes, becoming equal to the small cube.
❷ Answers may include muscle cells, bone cells, liver cells, skin cells.

❸ Animals capable of limb regeneration include some reptiles, worms, and echinoderms, and many crustaceans.

❷ **TEACH**

LAB ZONE

Calculating Surface Area to Volume Ratio

You may want to borrow cube models from the math teacher and use these manipulatives to demonstrate how to calculate surface area.

Analyzing the Diagram

2. Small cube: surface area = 1 × 1 × 6 = 6; volume = 1 × 1 × 1 = 1
   Large cube: surface area = 4 × 4 × 6 = 96; volume = 4 × 4 × 4 = 64
3. Small cube: surface area: volume = 6:1. Large cube: surface area: volume = 3:2
4. It changes from 3:2 to 6:1.

Think Critically

Ask students to explain why an organism, like an animal or a human, has many kinds of cells that perform different functions, even though the organism is the product of one fertilized cell. (All cells have the same DNA but different segments of DNA, genes, are active or "turned on" in different cells.)

5.1

In the Community

Students will probably identify antiseptics, salves, and bandages as healing remedies. Ask:

- **Do healing agents generate new cells?** (No, they prevent infection and promote healing.)

3 ASSESS

Evaluate Understanding

To determine students' comprehension of cell division, ask:

- **What two factors limit cell size?** (The ratio of cell membrane surface area to cell volume and nuclear control)
- **Identify the three life processes for which cell division is essential.** (Growth, repair, and reproduction)
- **In what type of reproduction are offspring genetically identical to the parents?** (Asexual)

Reteach

Draw a concept map on the board for the term *cell division*. As students reread the section have them complete the concept map with words and phrases that tell how cell division relates to growth, repair, and reproduction.

❶ In asexual reproduction, cell division involves exact replication of one parent cell's chromosomes. In sexual reproduction, a specialized form of cell division produces offspring that have a combination of genetic material from two parent organisms.

106

When we injure ourselves, our bodies generate new cells to replace the cells that were damaged or lost. We use many procedures and products to enhance the healing of injuries. Investigate products available at your pharmacy or grocery store that claim to promote healing of injuries. How do they claim to work? Do they affect cell division? Or prevent infection? Arrange to speak with a pharmacist, school nurse, or physician about the methods of treating a cut. What products and procedures do they recommend? How do the products and procedures work?

IN THE COMMUNITY
Healing Cuts

---

types of organisms, including bacteria, protists, fungi, plants, and some animals. During asexual reproduction cell division replicates the chromosomes of one parent cell. Asexual reproduction, therefore, produces offspring that are genetically identical to their parent.

Many plants and animals, including humans, are the result of a different kind of reproduction—sexual reproduction. **Sexual reproduction** produces offspring that have a combination of genetic material from two parent organisms. The recombination of chromosomes requires meiosis—a specialized form of cell division which you will learn about later in this chapter. After chromosomes combine in sexual reproduction, cell division results in growth of a new organism.

FIGURE 5.3
The unicellular eukaryote *Paramecium* can reproduce asexually. After replicating its genetic material, a *Paramecium* divides, producing two identical offspring. How does asexual reproduction differ from sexual reproduction? ❶

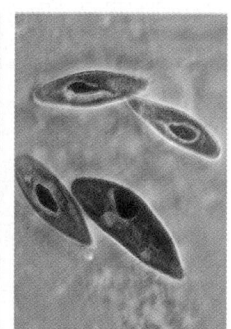

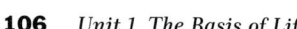

106　*Unit 1　The Basis of Life*

FRONTIERS IN BIOLOGY
Multiplying division

In humans, the rate of cell division, and therefore growth, is controlled by growth hormone, which is produced in the pituitary gland. During puberty, a large amount of growth hormone is produced, causing rapid gains in height and development. At the peak of their growth spurt, young adults increase in height by 8–9 cm a year.

When the pituitary gland malfunctions and does not produce enough growth hormone, dwarfism may result. Dwarfism is a condition in which a person never attains a height within the normal adult range. (Dwarfism can be caused by factors other than growth hormone deficiency.)

Researchers discovered that injections of human growth hormone could help stimulate growth. But the original method of obtaining growth hormone—from the pituitary glands of human cadavers—had several disadvantages. Only minute quantities could be obtained, and the hormone had the potential to transmit disease to the patients receiving it. In 1985 researchers discovered a way to use genetic engineering to produce a safe and plentiful supply of human growth hormone.

CHECKPOINT 5.1

1. Describe the factors that limit cell size.
2. Identify the roles of cell division in growth, repair, and reproduction.
3. **Critical Thinking** Which process do you think requires the greatest number of cell divisions in humans: growth, repair, or reproduction?

Build on What You Know

4. Choose two organelles and describe how their functions would be impaired in a cell that is too large. *(Need to jog your memory? Revisit relevant concepts in Chapter 3, Section 3.3.)*

CHECKPOINT 5.1

1. Small surface to volume ratio would make membrane unable to perform life functions. Cell size also limits control by the nucleus.
2. Growth: Cells divide, increasing total number. Repair: Cells divide and replace damaged or dead cells. Reproduction: asexual reproduction, cell division produces genetically identical offspring.

Sexual reproduction produces genetically different offspring.

3. **Developing a hypothesis** Asexual reproduction, growth, and repair take the same amount of energy. Sexual reproduction requires more energy.
4. Smooth endoplasmic reticulum could not rid cell of toxins and wastes. Lysosomes could not break down sufficient food.

5.2 How Do Cells Divide?

One nucleus is not enough
Cells divide in stages. In most cells the nucleus divides first, followed by division of the cytoplasm. A few types of cells do not undergo this final stage. For example, in the cells of skeletal muscles, which attach to bones and move them, the nucleus divides, but the cytoplasm does not. Skeletal muscle cells grow by enlarging, not dividing, and can end up with many nuclei.

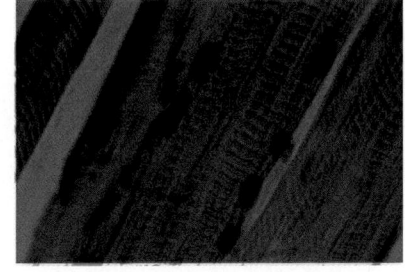

What you'll learn

IDEAS
• To describe the characteristics of a cell in interphase
• To distinguish the steps of mitosis and cytokinesis

WORDS
interphase, replication, chromatin, sister chromatids, centromere, mitosis, cytokinesis, prophase, metaphase, anaphase, telophase

INTERPHASE: PREPARATION FOR DIVISION

Getting ready to split

Has anyone ever told you that you were "going through a phase"? A phase is a defined period within a cycle of change. Cells go through phases, too. The sequence of phases in the life cycle of a cell is called the cell cycle. The cell cycle is the period from the beginning of one cell division to the beginning of the next cell division. The cell cycle has two parts: growth and preparation (interphase) and cell division. Cell division in turn is divided into two stages—mitosis (nuclear division) and cytokinesis (cytoplasm division).

Interphase is the part of the cell cycle that occurs between divisions. At one time, biologists thought that interphase was simply a resting period. When they looked through a light microscope, cells seemed to be relatively inactive and unchanging during interphase.

Biologists now know that cells are very active during interphase, producing all of the materials necessary for cell growth and preparing for cell division. As you can see in *Figure 5.4*, interphase is by far the longest part of the cell cycle—typically about 90 percent of the total time. Can you ❷ explain why?

Interphase can be divided into three stages based on the metabolic activity taking place in the cell. The first stage, G1, or gap 1, is a period of activity characterized by growth and development. The second stage, during which the cell becomes committed to cell division, is called synthesis, or the S stage. During the S stage the chromosomes in the nucleus replicate. **Replication** occurs when material makes copies of itself.

The third and final stage of interphase is G2, or gap 2. During G2, the cell synthesizes organelles and other materials, many of which will play

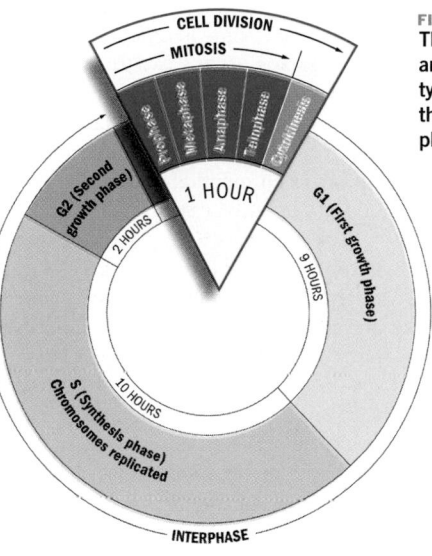

FIGURE 5.4
This figure shows the amount of time spent by a typical cell in each stage of the cell cycle. How do the phases compare? ❸

5.2

① ENGAGE

Use the Visual

Have students study the photo that opens the section. Ask students to describe how the muscle in their upper arm feels. Tell them to keep in mind that muscle cells can have many nuclei as they study the section.

Check Prior Knowledge

To assess students' prior knowledge about cell division, ask:
■ **What are the main functions of cell division?** (Growth, repair, and reproduction of an organism)

Quick Activity

Have students make a series of thick chalk marks of different colors on one half of a piece of black construction paper. Next, have them fold the other half over the chalk marks and press the two sides together. Ask:

■ **What do you see when you unfold the paper?** (An exact replica of the chalk marks)
■ **How are your chalk marks like DNA replication?** (An exact copy has been produced.)

STUDENT RESOURCES

From the Teacher's Resource Package, use:
■ Section Review 5.2 and Activity Recordsheets 5-1 and 5-2 from Unit 1 Review Module
■ Biotechnology Manual, Lab 3

TECHNOLOGY RESOURCES

Relevant technology resources include:
■ Spanish Student Edition CD-ROM
■ Teacher's Resource Planner CD-ROM
■ Interactive Biological Simulations CD-ROM: "Mitosis and Cytokinesis"
■ Animated Biological Concepts Videodiscs: "Animal Cell Mitosis and Cytokinesis"

❷ Interphase is long, because all material needed for growth is being produced.
❸ Synthesis phase takes 10 hours, G1 phase takes 9 hours, G2 takes 2 hours, and cell division takes 1 hour.

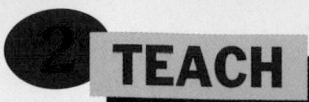

TEACH

Use the Visual

Direct students to Figures 5.5. and 5.6 and guide them to understand what happens during the *S* stage of interphase. Ask:

- **What are sister chromatids?** (Identical copies of DNA)
- **What are daughter nuclei?** (Identical nuclei formed when the cell nucleus divides)
- **When are daughter cells formed?** (When the cell's cytoplasm divides during cytokinesis)

 Art

Have students develop a flowchart to show chromosome activity during the cell cycle. The charts should illustrate the development and change of chromosomes during interphase and mitosis and include the labels chromatin, chromosomes, chromatids, and daughter cells.

 Interactive Biological Simulations

Mitosis and Cytokinesis Using either the names or pictures of the phases of mitosis and cytokinesis, students direct an animal cell through the phases of cell division.

 Animated Biological Concepts

Animal Cell Mitosis and Cytokinesis   Play

FIGURE 5.5

DNA in Cell Division

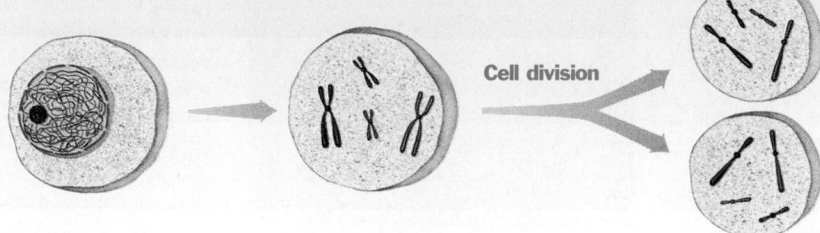

Cell division

Chromatin
During interphase, chromosomes are in the form of long, thin strands called chromatin. Chromosomes are replicated during the S stage of interphase.

Chromatids
Each replicated chromosome consists of two sister chromatids. During cell division, the DNA condenses into short, thick strands.

Chromosomes
After cell division, each daughter cell receives a full set of chromosomes—one chromatid from each pair.

Centromere   Chromatid

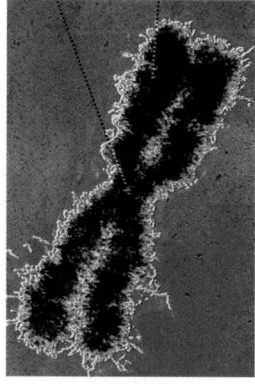

FIGURE 5.6
In a replicated chromosome, the chromatids—two identical strands of DNA—are joined at the centromere. How do chromatids compare with chromatin? ❶

specific roles in cell division. In animal cells, a pair of organelles called centrioles replicate to form two pairs.

If you used a microscope to observe a cell nucleus at the beginning of interphase, you would see what looked like a tangled bundle of threads, as illustrated in *Figure 5.5*. **Chromatin** is a thin, fibrous form of the DNA and proteins that make up a chromosome. A cell's chromosomes are in chromatin form throughout interphase.

During the S stage of interphase, each chromosome is replicated. **Sister chromatids** are the two identical structures that result from chromosome replication. As cell division begins, the chromosomes coil and condense and the sister chromatids are clearly visible under a light microscope.

You can see what condensed sister chromatids look like under an electron microscope in *Figure 5.6*. The coiled chromatin makes each chromatid look hairy. A **centromere** is the point where sister chromatids are joined together. Centromeres are located at different points on different chromosomes. Biologists use characteristics such as centromere location to identify particular chromosomes during mitosis.

108 *Unit 1 The Basis of Life*

CELL DIVISION

Nuclear fission

After interphase, chromosomes condense into a form visible under the light microscope, and changes occur in the nuclear envelope. These events signal the beginning of **mitosis**—the process during which a cell's nucleus divides into two identical nuclei.

In most cells, mitosis is followed by **cytokinesis,** the process in which a cell's cytoplasm divides to make two daughter cells. Each daughter cell forms around one of the two nuclei produced during mitosis. Daughter cells can continue the cell cycle by proceeding through interphase and another division, or they can differentiate structurally for specialized functions.

Both mitosis and cytokinesis proceed differently in plant and animal cells. These differences probably stem from the fact that plant cells—unlike animal cells—are surrounded by a rigid cell wall. In animals, formation of new cell membranes creates the two distinct daughter cells. In plants, both a new cell membrane and a new cell wall are needed to divide the parent cell into distinct daughter cells.

MEETING DIVERSE NEEDS

Sight Impaired Give students a football and have them feel the three-dimensional shape. Have them find the ends of the football and explain that they represent the centrioles in the cell. The spindle fibers then span the football from one end to the other.

❶ Chromatin looks like tangled threads. Chromotids are pairs of short, thick chromosome strands joined at the centromere.

PHASES OF MITOSIS AND CYTOKINESIS

When cells divide

Mitosis is a continuous process that replicates the chromosomes and forms two new nuclei. Mitosis begins after interphase and ends before cytokinesis. In the late 1800s biologists defined four phases of mitosis. You can follow interphase and the phases of mitosis in *Figure 5.7* on pages 110–111.

Prophase The first phase of mitosis is called **prophase.** During this stage, the chromosomes in the nucleus condense. The sister chromatids of the condensed chromosomes are visible under a light microscope. In the cytoplasm, a bridge of proteins begins to assemble into microtubules, forming a fibrous structure called the mitotic spindle.

By late prophase the mitotic spindle stretches out between the opposite poles of the cell. The nuclear envelope and nucleolus break into fragments and then disappear. A part of each chromosome's centromere attaches to a spindle fiber, and the spindle fibers begin to move the sister chromatids toward the center of the cell.

Metaphase During the next phase, **metaphase,** the chromosomes are pulled to the center of the cell, where they line up on an imaginary line called the metaphase plate. At the end of metaphase, each chromosome is lined up an equal distance from the ends of the cell.

Anaphase As metaphase ends, anaphase, the third phase of mitosis, begins. During **anaphase,** the centromeres divide, the spindle fibers pull one set of chromatids toward one pole and the other set toward the opposite pole. Once separated the chromatids are two identical sets of daughter chromosomes.

Anaphase ends when the two sets of daughter chromosomes are located

at opposite ends of the cell. The precise alignment of sister chromatids during metaphase is critical. When properly aligned, complete sets of daughter chromosomes move to opposite ends of the cell during anaphase. This ensures that each daughter nucleus receives a set of chromosomes identical to that of the parent cell.

Telophase In the last phase of mitosis, or **telophase,** two daughter nuclei are formed. The process is the reverse of what occurs during prophase. Nuclear envelopes form around each set of chromosomes. The chromosomes uncoil to form a loose mass of chromatin. By the end of telophase, the mitotic spindle has disassembled. In animal cells, each new nucleus has a pair of centrioles outside of its nuclear envelope. The centrioles remain in the cytoplasm of the new cells.

Cytokinesis, or cytoplasm division, begins during telophase as the daughter

 Do It!

Modeling the Phases of Mitosis

Building a model of a process may help you visualize and understand it better. You can find a way to represent the phases of mitosis if you . . .

Try This

1 Working in groups, assess the materials you have available. (Pipe cleaners, string, glue, paper clips, modeling clay, and toothpicks may be helpful.)
2 Make a sketch of each phase of mitosis and describe a plan for how you will construct a model of each phase.
3 Build the models.

Analyze Your Results

1 Test the accuracy of your group's models by asking other classmates to identify the stages represented. What responses did you get?
2 If any stages prove hard to identify from the models, how could you revise the models to make them clearer?

 Do It! **TEAM WORK**

Modeling the Phases of Mitosis

Try This
Suggest that group members find diagrams illustrating each phase of mitosis and use them as references.

Analyze Your Results

1. A good model should include: interphase-chromatin as long strands in nucleus; prophase-sister chromatids joined at centriole; metaphase-sister chromatids lined up at cell plate with spindle fiber formed; anaphase-spindles pulling chromatids to each end of cell; telophase-each set of chromosomes surrounded by new nuclear membrane.

2. Check students' responses.

Clarify Misconceptions

Students may not understand that cytokinesis is the final stage in cell division. Explain that mitosis is the process during which the nucleus divides. Cytokinesis is the process of cytoplasmic division during which the cell membrane divides to encompass each daughter cell.

Think Critically

Have students explain why division of the cell membrane occurs if the cell nucleus has already divided. (Cell division is not complete until two independent nuclei are surrounded by cytoplasm and a cell membrane.)

Class Activity

Work with students to act out the activity that takes place during mitosis, as shown in Figure 5.7. Assign students the following roles: two centrioles; four chromosomes (each with a partner chromatid); three groups who, when holding hands, form two circular nuclear envelopes and the cell membrane; and a moderator to explain what is happening in each step. Use string for mitotic spindles. Go through the movements several times to help students understand each phase.

- **1 Interphase:** Students form two circles to show the nuclear and the cellular membranes. The four chromosomes should imitate the chromatin initially. A partner then joins each chromosome to illustrate replication and sister chromatids.
- **2 Prophase:** Students acting as the cell membrane, the nuclear envelope, two centrioles, and four chromosomes with partner sister chromotids, perform the movements of their role during prophase, as stated in step 2.

nuclei form. In animal cells, the cell membrane at the center of the parent cell folds inward to form a cleavage furrow. As the furrow deepens, the cell is pinched in half until the membrane meets and forms a division in the middle. When this happens, two distinct cells with complete cell membranes are formed.

1 Interphase
The cell spends most of the cell cycle in interphase, the phase between cellular divisions. Initially, the cell is in a period of growth. DNA is replicated and structures for mitosis are produced during this phase.

2 Prophase
The cell's chromosomes condense. In animal cells, a pair of centrioles migrates to each pole of the cell. The mitotic spindle forms and attaches to the centromeres of the chromosomes. The nuclear membrane and the nucleolus disappear.

FIGURE 5.7

The Phases of the Cell Cycle

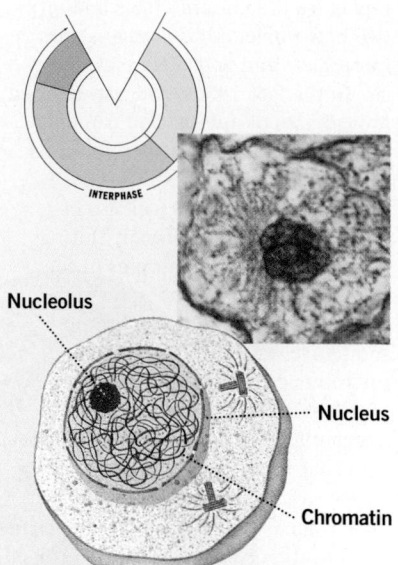

Nucleolus

Nucleus

Chromatin

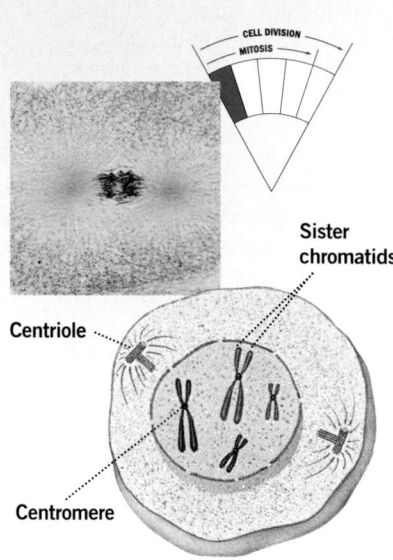

Sister chromatids

Centriole

Centromere

MEETING DIVERSE NEEDS

Sight Impaired Prepare tactile boards illustrating the five phases of mitosis. Use the following objects to represent each cell structure and glue them in position: cord string—membrane outline; yarn—chromatin; plastic disc—nucleolus; toothpicks—sister chromatids; fishing line—spindle fibers; tiny satin ribbon — centromere; macaroni—centriole. Break the toothpicks to illustrate the chromosomes being pulled by the spindle fibers. Have students follow the procedure on the tactile board as the narrator explains the phases of mitosis.

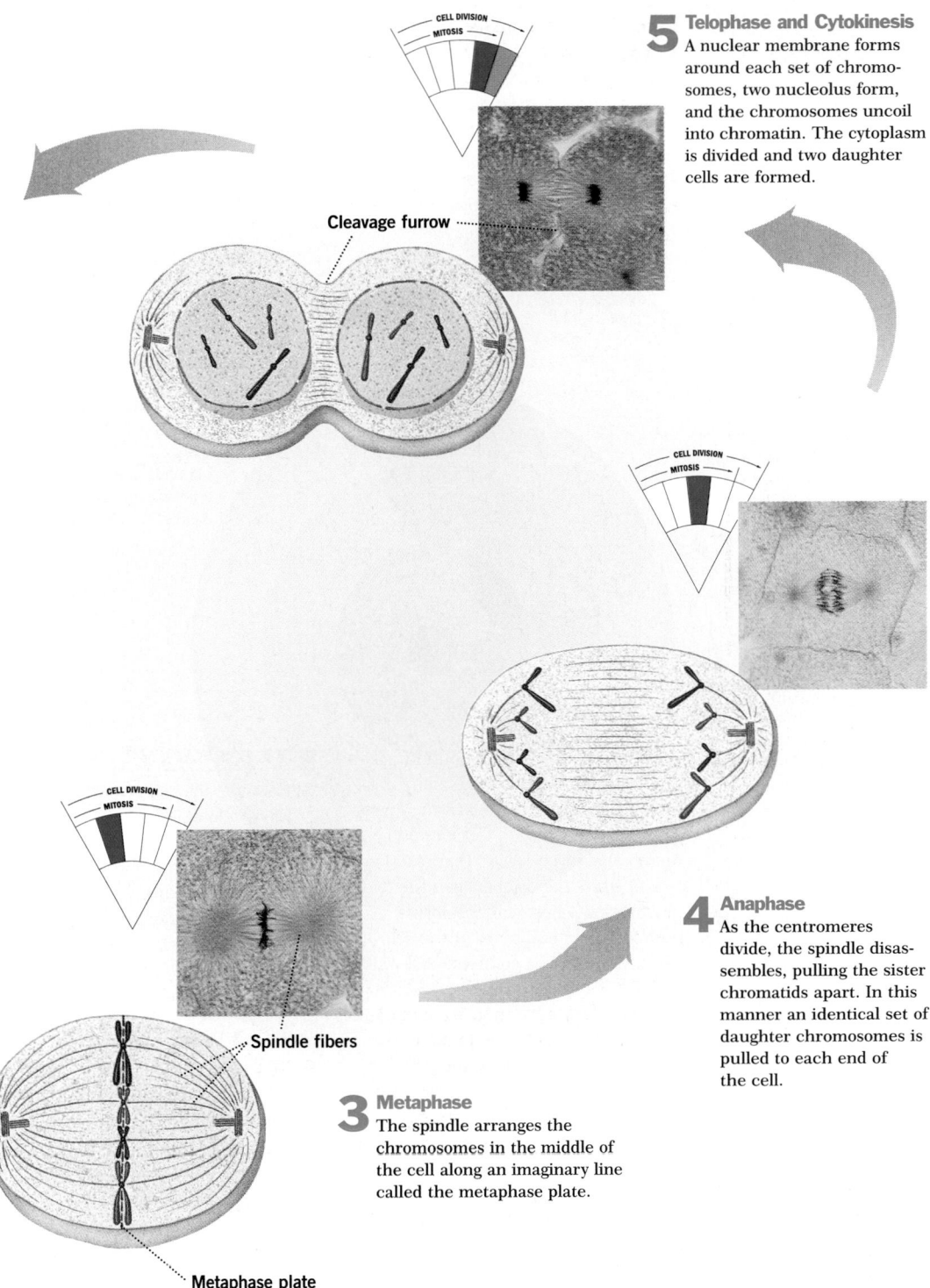

5 **Telophase and Cytokinesis**
A nuclear membrane forms around each set of chromosomes, two nucleolus form, and the chromosomes uncoil into chromatin. The cytoplasm is divided and two daughter cells are formed.

Cleavage furrow

4 **Anaphase**
As the centromeres divide, the spindle disassembles, pulling the sister chromatids apart. In this manner an identical set of daughter chromosomes is pulled to each end of the cell.

Spindle fibers

3 **Metaphase**
The spindle arranges the chromosomes in the middle of the cell along an imaginary line called the metaphase plate.

Metaphase plate

Chapter 5 Cell Division **111**

Class Activity (cont.)

Have students study Meiosis II before continuing the activity.

- **3 Metaphase:** Students acting as the nuclear envelope, chromatids, and chromosomes perform the movements of their role during metaphase, as stated in step 3. Use string to show the spindle fibers.
- **4 Anaphase:** Have students perform the movements for anaphase, as stated in step 4.
- **5 Telophase:** Students enter the cell membrane and form a nuclear envelope around each set of chromosomes, as shown in step 5. Develop some kind of movement to represent chromatin.

Use the Visual

Have students study Figure 5.8. Ask:

- **What will form between the plant's two daughter cells?** (A cell wall)
- **During what process is the cell wall formed?** (During cytokinesis)

ASSESS

Evaluate Understanding

To determine students' comprehension of what occurs during the cell cycle ask:

- **Name the three main processes in the cell cycle and tell what happens in each.** (Interphase, growth and preparation; mitosis, division of nucleus; and cytokinesis, division of cell membrane to complete cell division.)
- **What four phases occur during mitosis?** (Prophase, metaphase, anaphase, telophase)

Reteach

Reproduce Figure 5.4 on a transparency. Have students review the section and give one sentence to explain what happens during each stage labeled on the graphic. Add their responses in the correct place on the transparency.

❶ Cell wall forms between plant cells to complete the division. In animal cell, a membrane forms dividing the cytoplasm and separating the nuclei.

FIGURE 5.8

Cytokinesis in Plant and Animal Cells

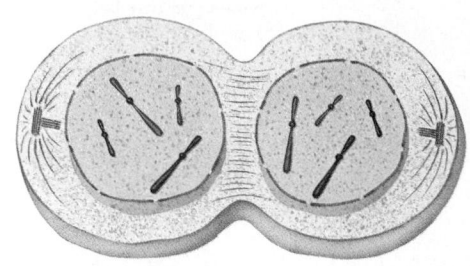

Animal cell
An animal cell completes cytokinesis by "pinching off" its membrane to form two new cells. The cleavage furrow is clearly visible in this human embryo (right), about 24 hours after fertilization.

Daughter cells

Cell plate

Plant cell
A cell wall is being formed between two plant cells. The cell plate forms a new cell membrane and cell wall between two daughter cells.

In plants, membrane-bound fragments begin to accumulate along the metaphase plate during late anaphase. The fragments fuse to form a double membrane, or cell plate, that extends the length of the cell between the two new nuclei. A new cell wall forms between the membranes of the cell plate. Eventually, a complete cell wall that divides the two daughter cells is formed. The double membrane remains and forms part of the cell membrane inside the wall. Compare the dividing plant cells with the animal cells in *Figure 5.8*. How do the differences in cytokinesis reflect the structural differences in plant and animal cells? ❶

CHECKPOINT 5.2

1. How does the cell prepare for mitosis while in interphase?
2. Briefly summarize the steps of mitosis and cytokinesis.
3. **Critical Thinking** The cancer drug colchicine interferes with mitosis by dissolving proteins that form the spindles in cells. What effect would this drug have on cell division? Why?

Build on What You Know

4. Describe the differences between plant and animal cells. How do these differences affect cell division? *(Need to jog your memory? Revisit relevant concepts in Chapter 3, Section 3.4.)*

? What process enables organisms to reproduce and develop?

CHECKPOINT 5.2

1. The cell grows, replicates genetic material, and forms mitotic structures, or centrioles.
2. In mitosis, chromosomes condense and cell nucleus divides into two identical daughter nuclei. In cytokinesis, cell cytoplasm divides forming two daughter cells.
3. **Cause and Effect** Spindle fibers would dissociate, sister chromatids would not separate, and cell would not divide.
4. Plants have cell wall, chloroplasts, and vacuole; animal cells do not.

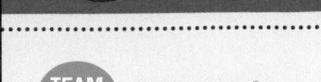

Observing Mitosis

WHAT YOU WILL DO Observe cell division in an onion root tip, identify the places in an onion root tip where mitosis is occurring, and estimate the percentage of dividing cells

SKILLS YOU WILL USE Hypothesizing, observing, recording data, calculating

WHAT YOU WILL NEED Microscope, prepared slide of mitosis in onion root tip

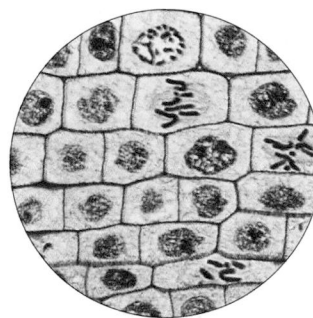

Propose a Hypothesis

Propose a hypothesis about which parts of onion root tips have the highest rate of cell division.

Conduct Your Experiment

1 Place the prepared slide on the stage of the microscope, and focus with low power.

2 Scan the onion root tip for a region in which cells are in various phases of cell division and switch to high power.

3 Find a cell that is in one of the phases of mitosis and draw it. Label visible parts and record which phase it is in.

4 Try to find examples of cells in all the phases of mitosis. Repeat steps 2 and 3 for each.

5 Switch to low power and choose one region of the root tip. Count the number of cells undergoing mitosis and the number of cells that are not undergoing mitosis. Record the numbers.

6 Repeat step 5 for three additional regions of the root tip. Draw a simple sketch of the root tip, and shade in the areas you observed.

Analyze Your Data

1 Are cells undergoing mitosis in every part of the onion root tip? If not, in which part(s) is mitosis occurring?

2 Are all the mitotic cells in the same phase of mitosis? If not, which phases of mitosis are occurring, and in which parts of the root tip?

3 Is the number of cells undergoing mitosis the same in every region of the onion root tip? If not, how do the regions differ?

4 For each of the four regions you observed, calculate the percentage of mitotic cells compared with the total number of cells.

5 Based on your samples of the four regions, estimate the percentage of mitotic cells in the entire root tip.

Draw Conclusions

Summarize the pattern of mitosis in onion root tips. Why would mitosis occur in such a pattern?

Design a Related Experiment

Design a lab to compare mitosis in the cells of different organisms.

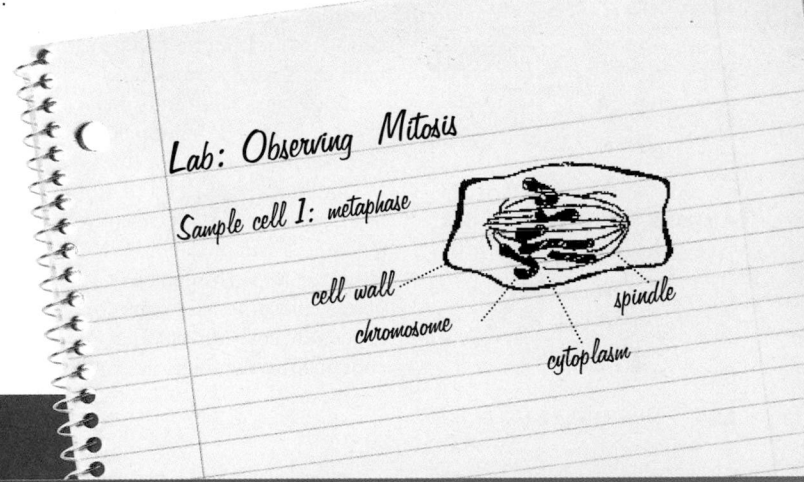

Lab: Observing Mitosis

Sample cell 1: metaphase

cell wall

chromosome

spindle

cytoplasm

TEAM WORK **Observing Mitosis**

Lab Prep and Planning

Sketch a root on the board and arbitrarily label four regions of the root with the numbers 1-4. If you plan to use fresh material for the open-ended lab, begin growing onion roots several days in advance. Have students work in groups and provide one set of materials for each group.

Hypothesis Help

Some students may think that cell division occurs everywhere in the onion root tip. Others may hypothesize that cell division occurs only in certain regions in the root tip.

Lab Extension

Open Ended

Use fresh onion roots and check for regions of cell division over a period of days. Tell students to record root length and where they observe the most mitotic activity. Add fertilizer to the water for one set of growing onion roots. Have students compare the root length and mitotic activity to the control.

Time Required

■ 50 minutes

Analyze Your Data

1. No, cell division takes place in the zone above the tip of the onion root.
2. No, cells are in all different stages of mitosis.
3. No, cells at the root tip are not dividing. Zone just above tip has most cell division. Cells above dividing zone are elongating.
4. In general, over 50% of cells in the zone above the root tip undergo mitosis.
5. Check students' calculations.

Draw Conclusions

Students should conclude that cell division occurs only in central zone above the root tip and below the elongating cells.

113

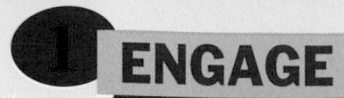

ENGAGE

Consider the Big Idea

Have students read The Big Idea! at the top of the page. Explain that the reduction of chromosome number is vital to sexual reproduction.

Use the Visual

Have students study the photograph that opens the section. Point out that the developing frogs are incubating inside the egg sac. Explain that the process of development began for the frogs when a reproductive cell from each parent combined. The incubation period varies from one organism to another.

Quick Activity

To help students understand the purpose of meiosis, trace five generations of a mouse family. Tell students that in the first generation, each mouse sperm and each mouse ovum has 20 chromosomes. Write the numbers 1-5 on the board and ask students to fill in the number of chromosomes in the cells of the offspring in each generation if only mitosis occurs. (40, 80, 160, 320, 640)

Interactive Biological Simulations

Meiosis Using either the names or pictures of the phases of meiosis, students direct an animal cell through meiosis. Animations show the genetic combinations resulting from crossing over and nondisjunction.

114

5.3 What Is Meiosis?

What you'll learn

IDEAS

• To show how the reduction in numbers of chromosomes relates to the process of sexual reproduction

• To summarize the phases of meiosis

WORDS

diploid, haploid, meiosis, homologous pair

Froggy went a-courting
In most eukaryotic species, offspring are produced by the union of two specialized cells that contain the genetic instructions for creating a new organism. In this section you will learn about the process through which those cells are produced. Here you see *Agalychnis* tree frogs in development—the result of the union of two of those specialized cells. What ❶ familiar features are already visible?

REDUCING CHROMOSOME NUMBERS

When less is more

Earlier in this chapter you learned that organisms can reproduce asexually (with DNA contributed by one parent) or sexually (with DNA contributed by two parents). Some organisms, such as the sea star, can reproduce either asexually or sexually. Other organisms, such as mammals, can produce offspring only through sexual reproduction. In sexual reproduction, the genetic information of one parent is combined with that of the other parent to produce a genetically distinct offspring.

The life cycles of organisms that reproduce sexually vary considerably. In most organisms, however, sexual reproduction includes a special form of cell division in which the number of chromosomes is reduced.

You may recall that the body cells of every species have a characteristic number of chromosomes. Humans have 46 chromosomes (23 pairs) in each body cell. Any cell that contains two complete sets of

chromosomes is called a **diploid** (DI-ployd) cell (2n). Almost all of the cells in your body are diploid cells. Human sex cells—the egg and sperm that combine to produce offspring—contain only 23 chromosomes, half the number of a diploid cell. A cell with only one complete set of chromosomes is called a **haploid** (HA-ployd) cell (n). Haploid reproductive cells are called gametes, or sex cells.

Why is it important that gametes be haploid cells? If human gametes, like human body cells, were produced through mitosis, each gamete would have 46 chromosomes (2n). When the gametes (sperm and egg) of two parents fused, the offspring's cells would have 92 chromosomes (4n)! If this offspring could survive and reproduce, it would produce gametes with 92 chromosomes. How many chromosomes would the third generation have? ❷

To keep the number of chromosomes stable from generation to generation, haploid cells are produced by a process called meiosis. **Meiosis** is a type of cellular reproduction in which the number of chromosomes is reduced by half, so that the daughter cells are haploid (n). Over generations, meiosis maintains a stable number of

FIGURE 5.9
In sexual reproduction, haploid cells are formed by the process of meiosis. Two haploid cells are then able to fuse to produce diploid cells.

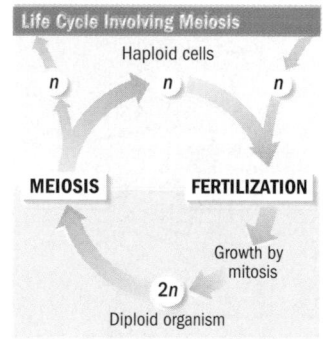

Life Cycle Involving Meiosis

Haploid cells

n — n — n

MEIOSIS — FERTILIZATION

Growth by mitosis

2n
Diploid organism

114 *Unit 1 The Basis of Life*

CHROMOSOME PAIRING

The buddy system

You already know that all human cells, except for sex cells, contain 46 chromosomes. These 46 chromosomes are arranged in 23 pairs. Each of the 23 pairs is called a **homologous pair.** With one exception, each pair (of the 23 pairs) contains chromosomes that are exactly alike in size, location of the centromere, and the dark-and-light banding pattern seen after staining with dyes. See *Figure 5.10.* Only one pair can differ. In females, this pair is alike and is called XX. In males, this pair is dissimilar in appearance and is called XY.

During meiosis, chromosomes in each homologous pair replicate and a single copy from each pair is distributed to each daughter nucleus. In humans, a cell with 46 chromosomes

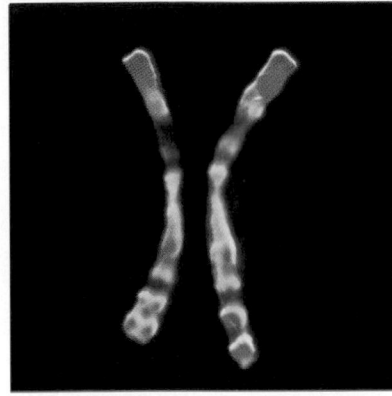

FIGURE 5.10
The pair of homologous chromosomes in the micrograph above look identical.

chromosomes by producing gametes that have one set of chromosomes instead of two sets.

In some organisms, such as plants, two kinds of haploid cells are formed by meiosis. Gametes are formed at one stage of a plant's life cycle and special haploid cells called spores are formed at another stage. Spores give rise to a haploid organism. In other organisms, such as animals, only gametes are formed by meiosis. In all organisms, meiosis keeps the number of chromosomes stable over generations.

As you can see in *Figure 5.9,* the fusion of haploid gametes ($n + n$) creates offspring with diploid cells ($2n$). As the offspring develops into an adult, diploid body cells are produced through repeated rounds of mitotic cell division. Mitotic cell division maintains the diploid chromosome number ($2n$). Eventually, a diploid reproductive cell undergoes meiosis to form the next generation of haploid gametes (n).

Organisms that reproduce sexually typically have both diploid and haploid cells during some stage of their life cycle. However, the timing of meiosis and mitosis can vary among different types of organisms.

EVERYDAY BIOLOGY

The Chicken and the Egg

Eggs, the gametes produced by hens and other fowl, are a common part of the human diet. Most eggs produced for human consumption are not fertilized and therefore cannot develop into offspring.

LAB ZONE Think About It! bioSURF

Calculating Haploid and Diploid Numbers

Haploid and diploid are designated by the algebraic notations *n* and *2n*, respectively. Either number can be calculated when the other number is known. For example, if the haploid number (*n*) is 3, the diploid number (*2n*) is 2×3, or 6. If the diploid number (*2n*) is 12, the haploid number (*n*) is 12÷2, or 6. The table below shows the haploid or diploid numbers of a variety of organisms. Copy the table onto a separate sheet of paper and complete it. Then use the table to answer the following questions.

Analyzing the Table

1 What are the haploid numbers for the two plants listed in the table?
2 In the table, which organisms' diploid numbers are closest to that of a human?
3 Explain why a diploid number is always even.
4 Which organism's haploid and diploid numbers do you find most surprising? Why?

Organism	Haploid Number	Diploid Number
ameba	25	
chimpanzee	24	
earthworm	18	
fern		1010
hamster	22	
honeybee		56
human		46
onion		16

2 TEACH

Everyday Biology

Display a chicken egg and discuss its parts. Explain that the yolk is the main food source for the embryo. The egg white is a source of water and other materials that are important for the developing embryo. The stringy bands visible in the egg white hold the yolk in place. Point out the small white sex cell in the yolk.

LAB ZONE Think About It!

Calculating Haploid and Diploid Numbers

Analyzing the Table

1 Haploid number for fern is 505, and haploid number for onion is 8.
2 Chimpanzee (48) and hamster (44)
3 Diploid are always even, because they are two times the haploid number.
4 Students may be surprised that an ameba has more chromosomes than a human and that a fern has almost 22 times more than a human.

Animated Biological Concepts

Meiosis Overview

Play

Animal Cell Meiosis

Play

❶ Answers may include eyes and tail.
❷ 184 chromosomes

Clarify Misconceptions

Students may confuse mitosis and meiosis. Explain that mitosis is the process of cell division during which living cells are duplicated. The cells that result are diploid. The function of mitosis is the repair and/or growth of an organism. In contrast, meiosis is the process of cell division that produces sex cells. Meiosis occurs in two divisions, meiosis I and meiosis II. The cells that result after meiosis is complete are haploid.

Use the Visual

Guide students through the process of meiosis I illustrated in Figure 5.11. Ask:

- **How does prophase I in meiosis I differ from prophase in mitosis?** (During prophase I in meiosis I, each homologous pair comes into intimate association with each other to form a tetrad. This does not occur during prophase in mitosis.)

- **What is the result of meiosis I?** (Two haploid cells result. Each daughter-cell nucleus contains one complete set of chromosomes, *n*, one chromosome from each homologous pair. Each chromosome consists of two sister chromatids joined at the centromere.)

- **What is the result of meiosis II?** (Four daughter-cell nuclei with one complete set of chromosomes, *n*.)

❶ Males produce more gametes because all male haploid cells become gametes, but only one in four female haploid cells become gametes.

FIGURE 5.11

The Phases of Meiosis

Meiosis I

Homologous pair of chromosomes

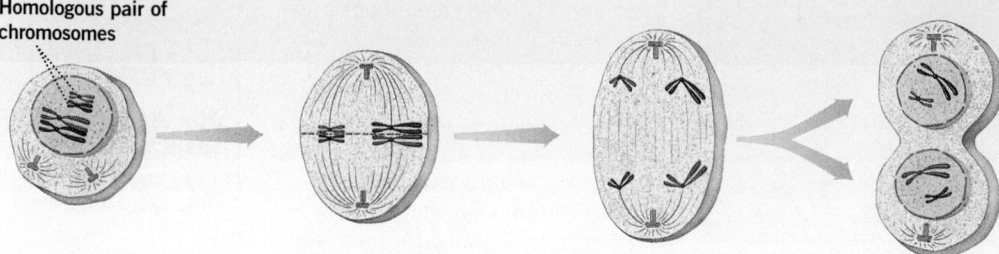

Prophase I
The replicated pairs of homologous chromosomes condense and attach to each other.

Metaphase I
The spindle fibers arrange the homologous chromosome pairs in the middle of the cell.

Anaphase I
The spindle fibers separate the homologous pairs and pull them to opposite poles of the cell.

Telophase I
Cytokinesis takes place, resulting in two haploid cells. Each chromosome in the haploid cells consists of two sister chromatids.

undergoes meiosis to yield four haploid cells with 23 chromosomes.

The process that determines which chromosomes of a homologous pair move to a specific daughter cell is random. For example, in the first cell shown in *Figure 5.11*, a given chromosome from the top homologous pair in prophase I could end up in a haploid cell with either of the homologous chromosomes from the bottom pair.

THE PHASES OF MEIOSIS

One becomes four

Before meiosis, a diploid cell replicates its chromosomes, so that each chromosome consists of two sister chromatids joined at a centromere. The cell is then ready to start meiosis. Meiosis consists of two stages: meiosis I and meiosis II. Each stage can be divided into four phases. You can follow the phases in the process of meiosis in *Figure 5.11*.

In the first phase of meiosis—prophase I—the chromosomes condense and each homologous pair becomes attached to one another. Each homologous pair of chromosomes contains four sister chromatids, two per replicated chromosome. This grouping is called a tetrad. The word *tetrad* means "four."

The tetrad formation of homologous chromosomes during prophase I ensures that each pair will separate during meiosis. Recall that tetrad formation does not occur during mitosis, where homologous pairs do not separate.

During metaphase I, anaphase I, and telophase I, movements of chromosomes similar to those in mitosis take place. The chromosomes move to the center of the cell and are then pulled along spindle fibers to the cell poles, where daughter nuclei form. After meiosis I, each daughter-cell

---

MEETING DIVERSE NEEDS

LEP Have students use manipulatives to explain the phases of meiosis. Give students string, large cardboard circles for nuclei, and dominoes or plastic disks to use as chromosomes. Challenge students to work in groups to simulate the processes of meiosis I and II. Suggest that they refer to Figure 5.11. Provide time for students to share their simulations.

Meiosis II

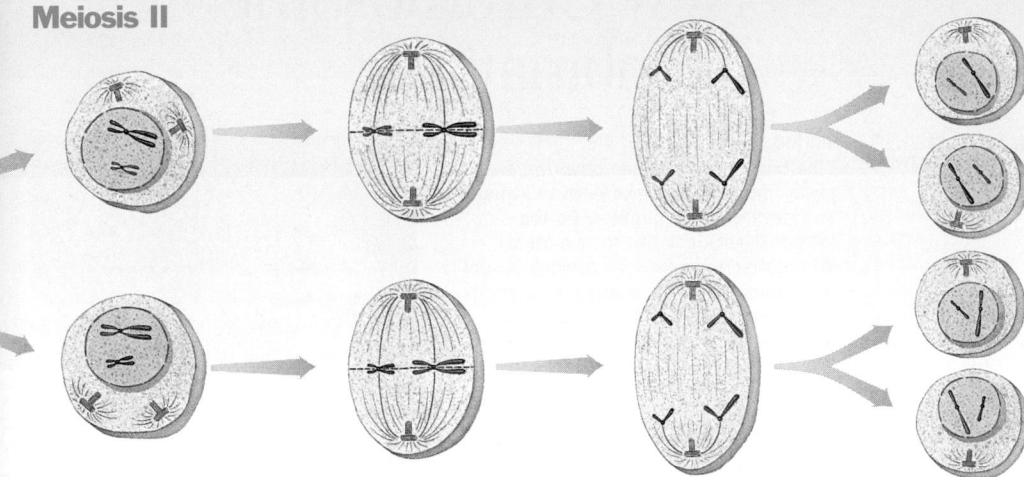

Prophase II
Spindle fibers form again, and chromosomes condense once more.

Metaphase II
Spindle fibers align chromosomes along the center of the cell.

Anaphase II
Sister chromatids are separated and pulled to opposite poles of the cell.

Haploid cells
Cytokinesis produces four haploid cells.

nucleus contains one member of each homologous pair (*n*). Each member still consists of two sister chromatids joined at the centromere.

The two haploid daughter cells from meiosis I then undergo a second division. In meiosis II, the sister chromatids move to the center of the cell. The centromeres split, separating the chromatids. The individual chromosomes are then pulled to the cell poles, where daughter nuclei form. As you can see in *Figure 5.11,* each of the four resulting daughter-cell nuclei contains one copy of one complete set of chromosomes (*n*).

Depending on the species and the sex of the individual, the cytokinesis that follows each meiotic division proceeds differently. In human males, all four haploid nuclei form sperm cells. In human females, only one of the four haploid nuclei forms an egg cell. The other three nuclei receive almost no cytoplasm and do not

form gametes. Do you think males or females produce the greater number of gametes? **❶**

CHECKPOINT 5.3

1. What is the importance of meiosis to sexual reproduction?
2. Explain the difference between a haploid cell and a diploid cell.
3. Write a summary of each phase of meiosis.
4. **Critical Thinking** Compare the chromosomes of a diploid cell to a collection of shoes in a closet. How are they similar? What would make the shoe collection comparable to the chromosomes of a haploid cell?

Build on What You Know

5. Cells are specialized in structure to match their function. Compare cell specialization in gametes with other examples of cell specialization. *(Need to jog your memory? Revisit relevant concepts in Chapter 3, Section 3.4.)*

Chapter 5 Cell Division **117**

Use the Visual

Have students study the stages of meiosis II shown in Figure 5.11. Ask:

- **How are meiosis I and meiosis II similar?** (The phases and chromosome movement are the same.)
- **How are meiosis I and meiosis II different?** (In anaphase I, homologous chromosomes separate. In anaphase II, sister chromatids separate.)

3 ASSESS

Evaluate Understanding

Have students develop a flowchart showing the process of meiosis I and meiosis II and explain the activity of each phase. Ask:

- **How is the number of chromosomes in a species maintained in the offspring?** (During meiosis homologous pairs are separated. Each gamete receives just one set of chromosomes. At fertilization each gamete contributes its one set of chromosomes, restoring the diploid chromosome number of the species.)

Reteach

Have students work in pairs to study Figure 5.11 phase by phase. Have one partner read the explanatory text aloud while the other points out what is happening on the diagram. Conclude by asking each partner to write a brief summary of the process of meiosis.

CHECKPOINT 5.3

1. Meiosis produces haploid gametes so that when two gametes join during sexual reproduction, the offspring will have the correct diploid number.
2. Haploid cell—one set of chromosomes; diploid cell—two sets of chromosomes
3. Answers should include: Mitotic cell separates homologous chromosome pairs and divides in two. These cells divide again, separating sister chromatids. Four cells with half the chromosomes of parent cell result.
4. **Making analogies** Students may respond that shoes are in pairs as are chromosomes in a diploid cell. A "haploid" shoe collection would have only one shoe.
5. Major difference is gametes have half the chromosomes.

ENGAGE

Use the Visual

Have student study the photograph that opens the section. Explain that the number of chromosomes in each cell depends on the species. Ask:

- **What are some advantages of offspring having different traits from the parents?** (Variation allows a species to adapt to and survive changes in its environment)

Check Prior Knowledge

Assess students' prior knowledge about cell division and meiosis by asking:

- **What is DNA?** (Deoxyribonucleic acid, the nucleic acid that comprises the chromosomes)
- **Why is it necessary for homologous chromosome to separate during meiosis?** (To ensure that only one set of chromosomes are contributed by each parent during fertilization)

Quick Activity

Cut out two moth figures, one from black paper, the other from white. Display the cutouts against a dark background. Ask students which moth has an advantage and why. If the environment were lighter, which moth would have the advantage.

5.4 New Chromosome Combinations

What you'll learn

IDEAS
- To compare meiosis and mitosis
- To explain the significance of genetic variation

WORD
variation

Variety is the spice of life

Like begets like: Human offspring are always human, cats give birth to kittens, and dogs produce puppies. Do the kittens (right) look like their mother? While offspring produced through sexual reproduction may resemble their parents, meiosis ensures that they will not be identical to them.

COMPARING MEIOSIS AND MITOSIS

Different ways to split

Mitosis and meiosis are similar in many ways. They are both forms of cell division. Both involve similar steps, including replication, the disappearance of the nucleus and nucleolus, and movement of chromosomes to opposite ends of the cell.

What other similarities do you see in *Figure 5.12*?

Notice that there are three main differences between mitosis and meiosis. First, meiosis produces daughter cells that have half the number of chromosomes found in the parent cell. This reduction in the amount of DNA produces haploid gametes. In sexual reproduction, haploid gametes fuse, genetic information is combined,

FIGURE 5.12

Two Types of Cell Division

Parent diploid cell (*2n*)

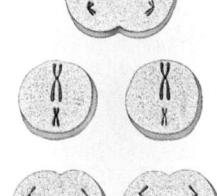

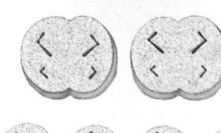

Meiosis I
The chromosomes replicate, and the cell divides once.

Mitosis
One cell division produces daughter cells that are genetically identical to the parent cell.

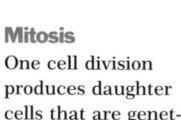
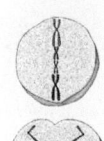
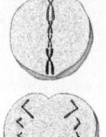

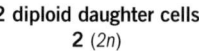

Meiosis II
Each new cell divides, producing daughter cells that are genetically different from the parent cell.

2 diploid daughter cells
2 (*2n*)

4 haploid daughter cells
4 (*n*)

118 *Unit 1 The Basis of Life*

STUDENT RESOURCES

From the Teacher's Resource Package, use:
- Section Review 5.4, Activity Recordsheet 5-3, Interpreting Graphics 5, Vocabulary Review 5, and Chapter 5 Tests from Unit 1 Review Module
- Issues and Decision Making 5-1

TECHNOLOGY RESOURCES

Relevant technology resources include:
- Spanish Student Edition CD-ROM
- Teacher's Resource Planner CD-ROM
- TestWorks CD-ROM: Chapter 5 Tests

and diploid offspring are produced. Mitosis, on the other hand, produces daughter cells with the same number of chromosomes as the parent cell. These daughter cells enable organisms to grow, repair damaged tissues, and replace dying cells.

A second difference between mitosis and meiosis is that the daughter cells produced by meiosis are not genetically identical to each other. The separation of homologous chromosomes during meiosis is random, so each daughter cell has a new mix of chromosomes. In contrast, the daughter cells produced by mitosis have exact copies of the parent cell's chromosomes.

The third difference is that in meiosis, cell division takes place twice, producing four daughter cells. How many daughter cells are produced by mitosis? How do the number of daughter cells and the number of chromosomes compare? ❷

THE VALUE OF VARIATION

Mixing it up

You may ask yourself, "Why do some organisms (such as the sea star discussed in Section 5.1) usually reproduce sexually if they can do so more easily through asexual reproduction?" Scientists do not know the complete answer to this question, but they do know that sexual reproduction has long-term advantages—it produces differences between organisms.

The differences between members of a population are collectively called **variation.** Variation results, in part, from the recombination of DNA that occurs during meiosis and fertilization. Compare the gametes in *Figure 5.13.* In this example, the species has a diploid number of four chromosomes ($2n=4$); the two red chromosomes were contributed by the mother, and the two blue

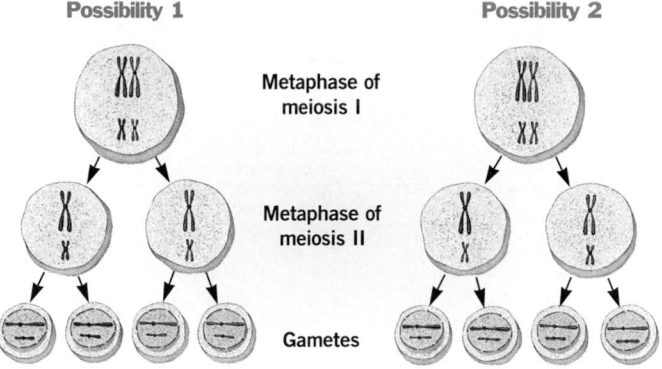

Possibility 1 Possibility 2

Metaphase of meiosis I

Metaphase of meiosis II

Gametes

Combination 1 Combination 2 Combination 3 Combination 4

chromosomes by the father. As you can see, the combination of red and blue chromosomes in each gamete is determined by the way the homologous pairs line up in the metaphase of meiosis I. Meiosis results in a random separation of chromosomes in the gametes.

Because each parent can produce a variety of gametes, two parents can produce a variety of offspring. Each kitten in the litter pictured at the beginning of this section was produced by the same two parents, yet each offspring is very different-looking. Such variation is possible because the gametes combine randomly during fertilization.

To appreciate the effects of the random combination of gametes, consider the fusion (joining) of gametes from two parents. When male and female gametes fuse during fertilization, the DNA from both gametes becomes the genetic material for the new diploid cell. Suppose that the four combinations of gametes shown in *Figure 5.13* were produced by a female cat. Assume that a male cat also produces the same gametes. How many different combinations of chromosomes would be possible in their offspring? ❸

Random separation of homologous pairs of chromosomes and random combination of haploid gametes are sources of variation associated with

FIGURE 5.13
The same parent cell can produce different combinations of chromosomes. How are the gametes different from one another? ❹

SUPER READ!

MULTICULTURAL PERSPECTIVE

The 1959 Nobel Prize in physiology and medicine was shared by Severo Ochoa (1905-1993), a Spanish-born American biochemist, and another American biochemist Arthur Kornberg (1918-). Ochoa, who moved to the United States in 1941 and became a citizen in 1956, discovered a bacterial enzyme that enabled him to synthesize RNA, the hereditary material of some viruses. In 1982 Kornberg and a team of scientists successfully reproduced DNA.

❷ TEACH

Think Critically

Have students discuss the reasoning behind the statement: *No two humans are exactly alike.*

✚ Language Arts

Write the terms *genetic* and *mitosis* on the board. Tell students that each word represents a chromosome and each of the seven letters represents one trait. Have students combine the "traits" to create a new "chromosome" combination for each of the four gametes resulting from one meiosis division. Students can share their "chromosomes" with the class.

SUPER READ! Interpreting Visuals
To practice strategies for effective reading, use pages 31-32 in *Super Read!*

❶ Division into daughter cells
❷ Mitosis; two diploid daughter cells with two sets of chromosomes. Meiosis; four daughter cells each with one set of chromosomes.
❸ Thirty-two different combinations.
❹ Genetically, they are identical with parents and each other.

Do It! TEAM WORK

Modeling the Phases of Meiosis

Analyze Your Results

1 Mitosis; cells divide once, chromosomes pairs line up and split, two daughter cells like parents. Meiosis; two divisions, half number of chromosomes in four resulting cells.

2 Line chromosomes in pairs so each daughter cell has half, add second division to produce four daughter cells with one-half number of chromosomes.

3 Meiosis model is more complex.

 **ASSESS**

Evaluate Understanding

To review the major concepts in this section, ask:

- **What is the major difference between mitosis and meiosis?** (Mitosis results in two identical diploid daughter cells. Meiosis results in four different haploid daughter cells.)

- **What causes variation in the members of a population?** (When the DNA, recombines during meiosis and fertilization, traits of both parents are shuffled randomly.)

Reteach

Draw a Venn diagram and label one circle *mitosis* and the other, *meiosis*. Have students use the diagram to compare the two processes.

120

 **Do It!** bioSURF

Modeling the Phases of Meiosis

Learn the phases of meiosis "inside-out" when you . . .

Try This

1 Reappraise the models you made to illustrate the stages of mitosis. Make a sketch of the phases of meiosis, and plan how you would change your models to represent meiosis.

2 Using the same materials (pipe cleaners, string, glue, paper clips, modeling clay, toothpicks, etc.), redesign the models to show meiosis.

Analyze Your Results

1 Compare and contrast the processes of mitosis and meiosis.

2 What did you need to change in order to convert the mitosis model to a representation of meiosis?

3 Which model had a more complex construction?

sexual reproduction. In the next unit you will learn about a related process that also produces recombination.

In a changing environment, variation resulting from new chromosome combinations can be key to a population's survival. If a significant environmental change occurs, a trait that was once beneficial can become a disadvantage, and a trait that was not helpful can become an advantage. As the degree of variation in a population increases, so does the likelihood that individuals will survive environmental changes. For example, a population of diverse sea stars produced by sexual reproduction has a better chance of surviving a new disease than a population with less variation. The population with greater

variation has more genetic resources, and it has a better chance of responding successfully to any changes in the environment.

How does the enormous variation in organisms that reproduce sexually compare with the variation in organisms that reproduce asexually? Offspring produced through asexual reproduction do not have a recombination of chromosomes. They have the same chromosomes and therefore the same traits as their parent. In such organisms, genetic variation rarely occurs from generation to generation. A change in the environment that destroys one individual, such as the arrival of a new disease, could destroy the entire population. Variation is thought to be the reason that sexual reproduction is the dominant form of reproduction for so many species.

CHECKPOINT 5.4

1. What are three differences between mitosis and meiosis? Explain.

2. What is the advantage of sexual reproduction to a population whose environment changes?

3. **Critical Thinking** Organisms such as certain plants, fungi, and algae have the ability to reproduce either sexually or asexually. What would be the advantage of having both abilities?

Build on What You Know

4. How are organisms that reproduce asexually similar to autotrophic organisms? How are organisms that reproduce sexually similar to heterotrophic organisms? *(Need to jog your memory? Revisit relevant concepts in Chapter 4, Section 4.1.)*

 What effect does meiosis have on chromosome number?

CHECKPOINT 5.4

1. Mitosis; one cell division, two daughter cells with same chromosome number as parent: meiosis; two cell divisions, four daughter cells with half chromosome number of parents. After mitosis, daughter cells are identical; after meiosis daughter, cells are not genetically identical.

2. New genetic combinations could result in traits helpful to survival.

3. **Developing a hypothesis** Organisms can remain same through asexual reproduction in stable environment, or benefit from variation by sexual reproduction in changing environment.

4. Asexual reproducers and autotrophs can live and reproduce independently. Sexual reproducers and heterotrophs need other organisms for food and reproduction.

Chapter 5 Review

 **THE BIG IDEA!**   5.1–5.2 Cell division is the basis of reproduction and development.
5.3–5.4 Chromosome number is reduced in meiosis.

Sum It Up

Use the following summary to review the main concepts in this chapter.

5.1 When Do Cells Divide?

- The ratio of cell membrane surface area to cell volume is a factor that limits cell size. When a cell reaches its optimum size, the nucleus initiates cell division.
- Cell division is the mechanism for growth and differentiation in multicellular organisms; for the replacement of old cells and the regeneration of injured cells; and for asexual reproduction and the growth that follows sexual reproduction.

5.2 How Do Cells Divide?

- The two parts of a cell's life cycle are interphase and cell division. Cell division involves mitosis and cytokinesis.
- During interphase, cells grow, chromosomes replicate, and cells prepare for cell division.
- During mitosis, the nucleus divides into daughter nuclei containing identical sets of chromosomes. For most cells, the final stage of cell division is the division of cytoplasm during cytokinesis.

5.3 What Is Meiosis?

- Almost all cells in an organism contain two complete sets of chromosomes. Reproductive cells contain only one set.
- Cells produced by mitosis are diploid; cells produced by meiosis are haploid.
- Meiosis keeps the number of chromosomes constant from generation to generation. During meiosis, homologous pairs of chromosomes separate to form four haploid daughter-cell nuclei.

5.4 New Chromosome Combinations

- Offspring produced asexually have DNA nearly identical to that of the parent cell.
- Offspring produced sexually differ genetically from their parent cells.
- The variation in offspring produced through meiosis can be the key factor in the survival of a population faced with environmental change.

Use Terms and Concepts

Use each of the following words or terms in a complete sentence. If you need to review a meaning, turn to the page indicated.

asexual reproduction
 (p. 105)
sexual reproduction
 (p. 106)
interphase (p. 107)
replication (p. 107)

chromatin (p. 108)
sister chromatids
 (p. 108)
centromere (p. 108)
mitosis (p. 108)
cytokinesis (p. 108)

prophase (p. 109)
metaphase (p. 109)
anaphase (p. 109)
telophase (p. 109)
diploid (p. 114)
haploid (p. 114)

meiosis (p. 114)
homologous pair
 (p. 115)
variation (p. 119)

Review the Big Ideas

Before students begin the Chapter Review, you may wish to discuss the Big Ideas that they have learned in the chapter. Explain that the growth, repair, and reproduction of all organisms depend on cell division. Cell division through mitosis produces identical diploid cells and results in the reproduction cells for repair and growth, as well as asexual reproduction. Cell division through meiosis produces genetically different haploid cells that combine to produce genetically different individuals. By reducing the chromosome number during meiosis, organisms that reproduce sexually retain the identify of and diversity in their species.

Answers

1. sexual
2. chromatin
3. metaphase
4. asexual
5. centromere
6. replication
7. variation
8. b
9. d
10. d
11. a
12. c
13. During G1 (gap1), the cell grows and develops; during S (synthesis) chromosomes replicate in the nucleus; during G2 (gap2), the cell synthesizes organelles—such as the centrioles—that have specific functions in cell division.
14. The size of an individual cell in multicelled organisms is limited by the surface area of the cell membrane. As a cell grows, it needs a larger membrane for exchange of nutrients and waste products with the environment. Cell size does not relate to the size of the organism.
15. The centrioles locate at opposite poles of the cell with the mitotic spindle stretched between them. Chromatids attach by their centromeres to the spindle. The spindle fibers move the chromatids to the center of the cell during prophase and move the separated chromosomes back to the poles during anaphase.
16. If gametes were diploid, the number of chromosomes would double with each generation, and the offspring would not survive.
17. Mitotic cell division occurs in asexual reproduction; the two daughter cells are

Use Your Word Power

COMPLETION Write the word or phrase that best completes each statement.

1. Variation in a population results from _____ reproduction.

2. During interphase, the DNA in the nucleus is present in the form of thin strands called _____ .

3. Chromatids line up at the center of the cell during _____ .

4. Growth, regeneration, and _____ reproduction use the same method of cell division.

5. The structure at which sister chromatids are joined together is called the _____ .

6. The process of copying chromosomes is called _____ .

7. Differences between members of a population are collectively referred to as _____ .

MULTIPLE CHOICE Choose the letter of the word or phrase that best completes each statement.

8. Copies of chromosomes are made during (a) anaphase; (b) interphase; (c) telophase; (d) prophase.

9. Cells with two complete sets of chromosomes are (a) haploid; (b) reproductive cells; (c) gametes; (d) diploid.

10. Two identical daughter nuclei are produced during (a) meiosis; (b) endocytosis; (c) interphase; (d) mitosis.

11. Two sets of chromosomes are located at opposite ends of a cell at the end of (a) anaphase; (b) cytokinesis; (c) endocytosis; (d) interphase.

12. The mitotic spindle first makes its appearance during (a) cell plate formation; (b) exocytosis; (c) prophase; (d) metaphase.

Show What You Know

13. Name and describe the three stages of interphase.

14. Explain why a large animal and a tiny animal have cells that are about the same size.

15. What are the functions of the mitotic spindle in mitosis?

16. Explain why it is necessary for gametes to be haploid rather than diploid.

17. What are the major differences between mitosis and meiosis?

18. How do the chromosomes of an offspring produced by sexual reproduction compare with the chromosomes of its parents?

19. How does cytokinesis in animal cells differ from cytokinesis in plant cells?

20. Is there any difference between sister chromatids and homologous pairs? Explain your answer.

21. Briefly describe what happens inside the cell during telophase.

22. **Make a Concept Map** Complete the concept map below by adding the following terms: meiosis, haploid cells, diploid cells, sexual reproduction, asexual reproduction.

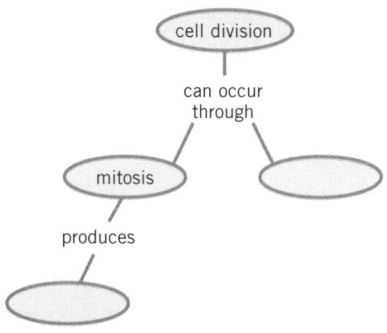

diploid. Meiosis produces haploid gametes that join during sexual reproduction. The four daughter nuclei are haploid.

18. Zygotes produced by sexual reproduction receive half of their DNA from one parent and half from the other. Thus the DNA of either parent and the DNA of an offspring cannot be identical.

19. During cytokinesis in animal cells, the cell membrane folds inward to form a division between the two halves of the cell. During cytokinesis in plant cells, membrane–bound fragments fuse to form a two–layer cell plate. A cell wall develops between the two layers of the cell plate.

20. The sister chromatids are identical. The

Take It Further

23. Developing a Hypothesis If sexual reproduction helps a population survive in a changing environment, what advantage(s) could a population that reproduces asexually have?

24. Designing an Experiment Design an experiment to test the hypothesis that mitosis in plants is affected by temperature.

25. Interpreting a Graph The graph below shows the typical time segments for mitosis in many mammal cells. Which stage of mitosis is the longest? Which is the shortest? What do you think is happening to the chromosomes when the cell is 55 minutes into mitosis?

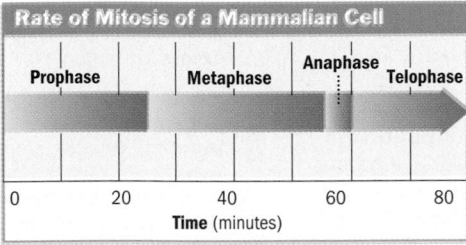

Rate of Mitosis of a Mammalian Cell

Prophase | Metaphase | Anaphase | Telophase

0   20   40   60   80
Time (minutes)

26. Analyzing Data Use the table below to answer the questions about mitosis.

Growth Rate of Rapidly Dividing Eukaryotic Cells	
Time (hours)	Number of Cells
0	1
10	2
20	4
30	8
40	16
50	32

A) Assuming that no cells die, how many cells will there be in one week?

B) Assuming that the original cell is diploid and divides mitotically, how many copies of each chromosome will there be in 60 hours?

Consider the Issues

27. Spinal Injury Research When the spinal cord is damaged, the nerve cells do not regenerate. Some recent studies with rodents suggest that nerve regeneration might be possible. What factors should society consider when allocating funds for spinal cord research or for educational programs on the prevention of spinal cord injuries?

Make New Connections

28. Biology and Art Mitosis is divided into phases for ease of discussion. To show how the action flows from one phase to the next, prepare a flip-book to show an animated version of mitosis. Focus on what happens to the chromosomes during each phase.

29. Biology and Community: A Project Find out what familiar food plants, such as apples or tomatoes, are grown in your community. Talk to gardeners, use the library, consult catalogs, or visit greenhouses to determine at what time of year cell growth from mitosis occurs most rapidly in these plants.

FAST-FORWARD TO CHAPTER 6

In Chapter 6 you will use your knowledge of meiosis to track the inheritance of chromosomes and traits in offspring.

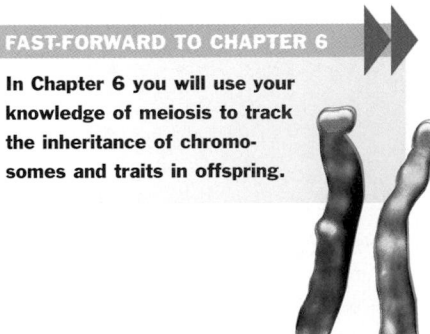

tors such as height. Given that direct sunlight can noticeably affect temperature in a room, students may want to reconsider growing the plants with artificial light.

25. Metaphase is the longest stage. Anaphase is the shortest phase. At 55 minutes, the sister chromatids are starting to be pulled apart towards opposite ends of the cell.

26. A) Approximately 131,072 cells.
B) 128 chromosomes, or 2 copies per cell.

27. Answers will vary. Students may consider the cost of the research against the probability of a cure. Students may suggest that education about wearing helmets, using seat belts, and driving properly is a cost-effective alternative.

28. A flip–book can emphasize the movement of the chromatids along the mitotic spindle.

29. Answers will vary. Students are likely to find considerable variation between plants that experience a significant growth spurt in the spring, and those that experience most of their growth—in the form of fruit or vegetable production—later in the growing season.

---

homologous pairs are not.
21. During telophase, nuclear envelopes form around the two new sets of chromosomes. The chromosomes then uncoil into a loose mass of chromatin. The mitotic spindle disassembles.
22. Mitosis or meiosis.
Mitosis produces diploids, which can result in asexual reproduction.

Meiosis produces haploid cells, which can result in sexual reproduction.
23. Asexual reproduction is a simpler process that requires less energy. Asexual reproduction is accomplished by a single isolated organism.
24. Answer will vary. Students may suggest growing a set of related seedlings at different temperature and measuring fac-

Connect the Chapters

1. Cells contain water. Water moves across cell membranes by osmosis. If a cell contains too much or too little water, it can die.
2. Active transport; energy for active transport is produced, stored, and released through chemical reactions.
3. Mitosis requires energy and molecules that can be assembled into new cell parts as mitosis proceeds. Animals get the energy and molecules from the food they eat, which comes directly or indirectly from photosynthetic organisms.
4. Phosophorus is in phospholipids, which help form cell membranes, and in ATP, the molecule that stores and releases energy, making phosphorus essential for life.
5. If the solutions were identical, there would be no diffusion across the membrane.
6. Tissue samples could be examined under a microscope to observe cell division and identify chromosomes.

Connect the Units

7. Check to make sure students have briefly described the processes of mitosis and meiosis to support the fact that cells can only arise from preexisting cells.
8. A large, adult multicellular organism develops from a single diploid cell and is made up of many cells specialized and grouped in tissues, which are composed of similar cells. Tissues, in turn, are assembled in organs, and organs form systems.

Unit 1 Review

THE BIG IDEA! Answering the following questions will help you to link ideas and grasp the core concepts.

Connect the Chapters

1. How do cell structures and processes demonstrate that life depends on water?
2. Which process is more likely to involve chemical reactions—passive transport or active transport? Explain.
3. Explain how mitosis in animal cells, as an energy-dependent cellular process, is dependent on photosynthesis in other organisms.
4. Phosphate groups contain phosphorous atoms. What role does phosphorous play in mitosis, photosynthesis, and cellular respiration?
5. How can you tell if the solutions on both sides of a semipermeable membrane are identical in concentration?
6. What scientific experiments might be done to determine if a newly discovered life-form has chromosomes and grows by cell division?

Connect the Units

7. Use what you have learned about cell division and chromosome number to argue against the idea of spontaneous generation.
8. What is the difference between a large, adult multicellular organism and the cell from which it developed?

Connect to Themes

9. **Unity and Diversity** How do the number and characteristics of organic compounds demonstrate the basic unity of all living things?
10. **Stability and Equilibrium** How do organelles contribute to homeostasis?
11. **Energy** Summarize the process of cellular respiration. What are the reactants and products? How is energy used by living things?

CRITIC'S CORNER

A CD-ROM REVIEW BY CARLOS CONTRERAS EDINBURG, TEXAS

SimEarth, a simulation game by Maxis, allows you to control nearly every aspect of Earth. You can create your own planet or use one of the existing planets to create a whole new civilization, based on your decisions alone. You also learn how civilizations develop and how Earth is affected by our decisions. I would recommend this game to anyone who likes to use his or her imagination, as well as to anyone who enjoys simulation games. You can have hours of fun creating worlds you never thought were possible.

1 Write a report on one of the scientists mentioned in this unit. When the scientist began doing research, what was already known about the topic? What contribution did the scientist make? What questions were left unanswered?

2 Pigments are important to art as well as photosynthesis. The availability of pigments in prepared paints is a relatively recent development. In the past, what materials have artists used to prepare pigments? How do art experts use their knowledge of pigments to expose art forgeries?

3 As a class, design a method of testing the pH of soil from different locations in your community. Note which plants thrive in which type of soil. If you test soil from landscaped yards, find out whether chemicals were added to the soil to change the pH. Plot the data on a map of your community.

Connect to Themes

9. All organisms use four types of compounds for the same chemical pathways.
10. Organelles provide a physical organization that isolates processes such as digestion and respiration from one another.
11. $C_6H_{12}O_6 + O_2 \rightarrow CO_2 + H_2O +$ energy. The reactants are glucose and oxygen. The products are carbon dioxide and water. Energy is used by all living things for all cellular reactions.

Project Plans

1. You may want to suggest other scientists.
2. Students might also want to learn about techniques for art restoration.
3. Students may also want to contact a local agricultural extension service.

SPOTLIGHT ON CAREERS

ANTHONY LAROSE
Cheese maker and team leader at Franklin County Cheese
EDUCATION: High school diploma and on-the-job training

❝Cream cheese is made of butterfat and other nonfat solids like gums and proteins. Making it is a matter of getting the right percentages of each and reaching the proper pH level. One way to make cheese is with cultures. We use another method, called direct set, which means we use natural chemicals and machinery. First, we measure the fat content of the cream. Then we add other solids according to a formula. We pasteurize and homogenize the mix and adjust the pH level. Then you have cream cheese, and you're ready to pack. You have to do a lot of tasting during the process. When you taste the mix for flavor and texture, you can tell if you're doing it right.❞

bioSURF You can visit the Internet address *http://basis_of_life.biosurf.com* to find out more about jobs that involve organic compounds and biochemical processes.

DR. CHARLES S. CRAIK
Professor of biochemistry, biophysics, and pharmacology at the University of California, San Francisco, School of Pharmacy
EDUCATION: Ph.D. in chemistry

❝I work with enzymes called proteases. One critical role enzymes play is in digesting food. . . . In the past, most proteases were thought of as digestive enzymes, but now we know they can also play a much more sophisticated role. . . . When a virus is replicating in the cell, it creates proteins that will eventually become part of the new virus. The protease enzyme serves as a pair of molecular scissors, trimming the viral proteins into the right shapes, like pieces of a jigsaw puzzle. Blocking that event can block viral assembly and replication of the virus. By designing molecules that can do this, we can help stop viral infections like AIDS that require a protease for survival.❞

bioSURF Look up the UCSF School of Pharmacy at *http://basis_of_life.biosurf.com* to learn more about Dr. Craik and other career-related information.

> **"It's risky to hope your research will actually lead to an application, but when you succeed, it is a very rewarding experience."**
> — DR. CHARLES S. CRAIK

SPOTLIGHT ON CAREERS

bioSURF Have students connect to the bioSurf Internet address to learn about schools, educational programs, and scholarships that would prepare them for a career or occupation in a field related to biochemistry or chemistry.

Consider These Careers

Many biotechnology companies have entry-level positions for people with an education in cell biology or biochemistry. Other careers related to the topics in this unit include biomedical researcher, public health microbiologist, and food chemist.

Plan for a Career

- **Researching local employment opportunities** Who is hiring biologists in your area? Have students obtain copies of the Sunday Classified Ads from your community or the nearest large city. Ask students to identify all the advertised positions that require an education in biology, and what type of experience is asked for. You may choose to follow this assignment with a discussion of the rewards and challenges of the careers that students identify.

Critic's Corner

Have students read the review of *SimEarth* on page 2. Ask if any students have played this game, and have them share opinions with the class. If possible, arrange to have the software available for interested students to try. Encourage students to point out limitations of the simulation and possible applications of the concepts involved.

Unit Overview

The mechanisms of heredity enable organisms to produce offspring like themselves. The modern understanding of genetics began with Gregor Mendel in the 1860s and continues today in research facilities around the world. With the understanding of DNA manipulation, scientists have the ability to alter the very nature of many types of organisms and search for cures for many diseases in new ways.

Unit Objectives

- Explain the basic mechanisms of heredity
- Describe the structure and function of DNA and RNA molecules
- Diagram the process by which proteins are synthesized from amino acids
- Give examples of practical applications for biotechnology

Connect the Units

This unit builds on the concepts of cellular reproduction introduced in Unit 1. The concepts of heredity presented in Unit 2 enhance the understanding of evolution and adaptation discussed in Unit 3: *Change and Diversity.* If you prefer to focus on the human body, you may follow this unit with Unit 8: *Human Biology.*

Which of these amazing statements about genetics are fact and which are fiction?

Hit *or* Myth?

You can grow a **square** watermelon.

(Fiction. However, biotechnology researchers are attempting to produce fruits and vegetables that are easier to stack.)

Taste is inherited.

(Fact. While your "taste" in clothing, art, and music is not inherited, your ability to taste certain flavors is inherited.)

mmm...

eww!

You may someday get **body parts** from a pig.

(Fact. Scientists are working to breed pigs with organs that can be safely transplanted into humans. These pig organs will not carry diseases—a stumbling block of today's experimental pig-to-human organ transplants.)

Clones exist only in science fiction stories.

(Fiction. These two sheep are clones produced through genetic engineering techniques. Their genes are exactly alike.)

Pete

Re-Pete

When you **lick a stamp,** you leave behind enough information to be identified.

(Fact. Like every cell in your body, cells in your saliva contain genetic information unique to you. If the genetic information on the back of a stamp matches yours, then you licked it!)

hobby: stamp collecting
best friend: "Buddy"
favorite pizza: Hawaiian
first job: grocery bagger
favorite tune: "Science Rocks"

In **all** organisms, sex is determined by genetics.

(Fiction. The sex of the map turtle is influenced by the eggs' incubation temperature. The hotter the temperature, the greater the percentage of female offspring.)

Unit 2 Genetics **127**

Hit *or* Myth?

Use It

Review each of the statements with the class. Ask students to share their prior knowledge and misconceptions on each topic. Ask them to consider which sources of information on these topics are generally reliable and which may not be. Have students preview the Table of Contents for this unit and correlate text sections with information related to the concepts in the Hit or Myth statements.

Link It

Chapter 6 links the concept of characteristics (taste) to inheritance of traits from parent to offspring. Further information about the mechanisms for taste can be found in Chapter 34. Chapter 7 links human DNA (genetic information in saliva) to the structure of chromosomes. More information on the contents of saliva can be found in Chapter 30. Chapter 8 explores the concepts of gene expression. Further information on reproduction in reptiles can be found in Chapter 26. Chapter 9 links the concepts of genetic engineering (watermelon, pig parts, clones) to practical applications. Applications for cloning plants can be found in Chapter 19.

Expand It

Certain types of coral-reef fishes have the ability to change sex midway through life in response to social interactions among other individuals. In some species, the fish begins life as a male but may change to become a female. In other species, they change from female to male.

PLANNING GUIDE

Section	Student Activities/Features	Teacher's Resource Package
6.1 Patterns of Inheritance **Objectives** ■ Distinguish between dominant traits and recessive traits ■ Analyze the results of Mendel's experiments with three generations of garden peas	**Lab Zone Discover It!** *Find Characteristics That Are Inherited,* p. 129 **Everyday Biology** *Bloodlines,* p. 130	**Unit 2 Review Module** ■ Section Review 6.1 ■ Enrichment Topics 6-1 and 6-2
6.2 Principles of Inheritance **Objectives** ■ Explain the chromosome theory of heredity ■ Summarize Mendel's laws	**Lab Zone Think About It!** *Predicting Parakeet Color,* p. 135 **Lab Zone Do It!** *Can You Illustrate the Law of Dominance?* p. 137	**Unit 2 Review Module** ■ Section Review 6.2 ■ Activity Recordsheet 6-1
6.3 Genetics and Predictions **Objectives** ■ Explain how probability is used in genetic predictions ■ Construct a Punnett square for monohybrid and dihybrid crosses ■ Infer genotype by using a test cross	**Lab Zone Do It!** *How Is Genetics Related to Probability?* p. 139	**Unit 2 Review Module** ■ Section Review 6.3 ■ Activity Recordsheet 6-2 ■ Interpreting Graphics 6 **Consumer Applications** 6-1 and 6-2 **Laboratory Manual,** Lab 13: "Genetics and Chance" **Interpreting and Developing Graphics** 16, 17, 18
6.4 Predictions and People **Objectives** ■ Interpret pedigrees and understand their purpose ■ Contrast dominant and recessive genetic disorders ■ Identify some methods used to determine the likelihood of a genetic disorder occurring in offspring	**STS: Frontiers in Biology** *Genetic Counseling,* p. 144 **Everyday Biology** *Ears to You!* p. 145 **Lab Zone Investigate It!** *Using a Pedigree,* p. 146	**Unit 2 Review Module** ■ Section Review 6.4 ■ Activity Recordsheet 6-3 ■ Critical Thinking Exercise 6 ■ Enrichment Topic 6-3 **Laboratory Manual,** Lab 14: "Pedigree Analysis" **Biotechnology Manual,** Lab 10: "Assessing Genetic Variation in Humans" **Issues and Decision Making** 6-1
6.5 Difficult Predictions **Objectives** ■ Compare and contrast patterns of inheritance that do not follow Mendel's laws ■ Explain how traits are influenced by the environment	**Everyday Biology** *Hold the Eggs,* p. 148 **In the Community** *Blood Drive,* p. 148 **STS: Issues in Biology** *The Genetics of Behavior,* p. 152	**Unit 2 Review Module** ■ Section Review 6.5 ■ Enrichment Topic 6-4 ■ Vocabulary Review 6 ■ Chapter 6 Tests **Issues and Decision Making** 6-2 **Spanish Reviews** Chapter 6

Technology Resources

Internet Connections

Within this chapter, you will see the **bioSURF** logo. If you and your students have access to the Internet, the following URL address will provide various Internet connections that are related to topics and features presented in this chapter:

http://genetics.biosurf.com

You can also find relevant chapter material at **The Biology Place** address:

http://www.biology.com

CD-ROMs

Biología: la telaraña de la vida, (Spanish Student Edition) Chapter 6
Teacher Resource Planner, Chapter 6 Supplements
Interactive Biological Simulations
■ Punnett Squares
TestWorks CD-ROM
■ Chapter 6 Tests

Videodiscs

Animated Biological Concepts Videodiscs
■ Segregation of Chromosomes

Overhead Transparencies

■ Punnett Square, #14
■ Dihybrid Cross, #15

Videotapes

Biology Alive! Video Series
Rewind: The Web of Life Reteach Videos

Planning for Activities

STUDENT EDITION
Lab Zone
Discover It! p. 129
- pencil
- paper
- graph paper

Lab Zone Do It! p. 137
- buttons: two different colors
- paper
- pencil

Lab Zone Do It! p. 139
- coins
- pencil
- paper

TEACHER'S EDITION
Class Activity, p. 131
Diagramming the parts of a flower
- variety of flowers

Teacher Demo, p. 134
Modeling chromosome pairs
- black and red plastic disks

Class Activity, p. 135
Dominant and recessive alleles
- permanent marker
- paper

Teacher Demo, p. 147
Testing for dominance
- bottle
- red beads
- white beads

Teacher Demo, p. 148
Expressing incomplete dominance
- plastic plates
- variously-colored beans

Chapter Objectives

Students will learn the main concepts of this chapter as they complete the following objectives.

- Distinguish between dominant traits and recessive traits
- Explain the chromosome theory of heredity
- Summarize Mendel's laws
- Explain how probability is used in genetic predictions
- Construct a Punnett square
- Infer genotype by using a test cross
- Interpret pedigrees
- Contrast dominant and recessive genetic disorders
- Compare and contrast patterns of inheritance that do not follow Mendel's laws
- Explain how traits are influenced by the environment

Key Words

6.1 *genetics, trait, purebred, hybrid, genes, allele, dominant allele, recessive allele*

6.2 *chromosome theory of heredity, genotype, phenotype, homozygous, heterozygous*

6.3 *Punnett square, test cross*

6.4 *pedigree, carrier*

6.5 *incomplete dominance, codominance, polygenic traits, multiple alleles, pleiotropy*

The Opening Story

Have students discuss how they think the story relates to the content of this chapter. Ask students how the members of each animal family resemble one another.

CHAPTER 6

Fundamentals of Genetics

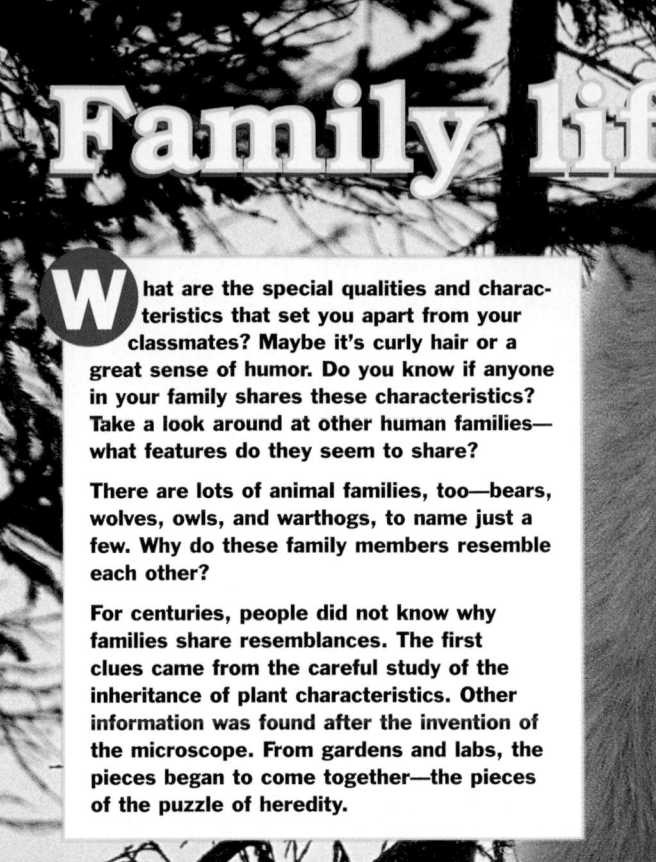

bioSURF

You can find out more about genetics by visiting the following Internet site:
http://genetics.biosurf.com

In this chapter . . .

FEATURES

Everyday Biology
- Bloodlines
- Ears to You!
- Hold the Eggs

In the Community
Blood Drive

 Frontiers in Biology
Genetic Counseling

Issues in Biology
The Genetics of Behavior

LAB ZONES

Discover It!
- Find Characteristics That Are Inherited

Do It!
- Can You Illustrate the Law of Dominance?
- How Is Genetics Related to Probability?

Think About It!
- Predicting Parakeet Color

Investigate It!
- Using a Pedigree

128 *Unit 2 Genetics*

Family life

What are the special qualities and characteristics that set you apart from your classmates? Maybe it's curly hair or a great sense of humor. Do you know if anyone in your family shares these characteristics? Take a look around at other human families—what features do they seem to share?

There are lots of animal families, too—bears, wolves, owls, and warthogs, to name just a few. Why do these family members resemble each other?

For centuries, people did not know why families share resemblances. The first clues came from the careful study of the inheritance of plant characteristics. Other information was found after the invention of the microscope. From gardens and labs, the pieces began to come together—the pieces of the puzzle of heredity.

 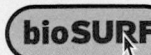

Find Characteristics That Are Inherited

You need pencil, paper, and graph paper

1. Make sure you can identify each characteristic. Make a chart to use in surveying your family or friends.
2. Survey as many people as you can for each characteristic. Tally your findings. Make a bar graph of your findings. Which is the most common characteristic?

Here are some questions to consider for your survey: Which human characteristics are easily observed? Can you roll your tongue into a U shape? Do you have attached ear lobes or free ear lobes? Do you have hair between your second and third knuckle? How about dimples?

WRITE ABOUT IT!

In your science journal, describe the results of your survey. For each characteristic, use fractions or percentages to describe how many surveyed people had the characteristic. If you add the fractions or percentages for those having dimples, for example, and for those who do not have dimples, what fraction or percent do you get? Explain why.

Chapter 6 Fundamentals of Genetics **129**

Opening Activities

bioSURF If you have access to the Internet, you may wish to have students connect to the address shown on page 128. You may also want to have students conduct net searches for information using key words related to this chapter. For example, they could search for entries under Gregor Mendel, sickle-cell anemia, or genetic counseling.

LAB ZONE Discover It!

Find Characteristics That are Inherited `TEAM WORK`

Prepare the class for the activity by drawing up some guidelines for students to follow when conducting their surveys. Consider modeling the correct way to ask survey questions as well as how to analyze survey results.

WRITE ABOUT IT!

Suggest that students explain the procedure they used for their research and identify the traits and group surveyed. Before writing, they should analyze the data presented in their graphs to draw conclusions about what they learned.

Rewind to Chapter 5

Briefly review concepts learned in Chapter 5, *Cell Division*. Ask:

- **How do you think your study of meiosis and sexual reproduction will help you understand how traits are inherited?**

PORTFOLIO PREVIEW

Students should be encouraged to add to their portfolios as they work through this chapter. In addition to the *Write About It* opportunity, the following sections are excellent opportunities for portfolio entries:

- Section 6.1: *Patterns on Inheritance*
- Section 6.2: *Principles of Inheritance*
- Section 6.4: *Predictions and People*

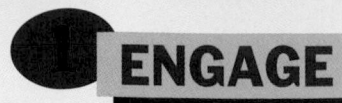

6.1

ENGAGE

Consider the Big Idea

Have students read The Big Idea! at the top of the page. Ask students to give examples of inherited traits.

Check Prior Knowledge

To assess students' prior knowledge about DNA and the function of chromosomes ask:

- **How many sets of chromosomes do most animals have?** (Two)
- **What do the two sets of chromosomes contribute to an offspring?** (A combination of genetic material necessary for life)

Use the Visual

Have students study the photo that opens the section. Point out that behavioral psychologists are able to determine how the trait for shyness is manifested in people by observing the behavior of infants and toddlers, and then studying their behavior as they develop into adults.

SUPER READ! **Comparing and Contrasting**

To practice strategies for effective reading, use pages 37-38 in *Super Read!*

❶ They consider the head of the pack as their master, thus they are loyal and obedient. A keen sense of smell and hearing makes them good watch dogs and helps them find prey.

130

THE BIG IDEA! Traits are inherited in a consistent pattern. 6.1–6.2

6.1 Patterns of Inheritance

What you'll learn

IDEAS
- To distinguish between dominant traits and recessive traits
- To analyze the results of Mendel's experiments with three generations of garden peas

WORDS
genetics, trait, purebred, hybrid, genes, allele, dominant allele, recessive allele

Bloodlines

A popular myth about inheritance is that traits are passed from parents to offspring through the blood. The term "bloodline," used by animal breeders, reflects this myth. In this term, "blood" refers to lineage, or inheritance of traits.

Can a wallflower grow?
Are you ever too shy to talk to someone you really want to meet or too bashful to deliver a speech? Most people are shy at times. Scientists have used genetics to predict shyness in toddlers. As you may know, many toddlers are shy. Just how shy they are is partially determined by genetics. This shyness generally diminishes as individuals reach adulthood.

THE HISTORY OF GENETICS

Prehistoric pooches

Some people call dogs our best friends, but when did this friendship start? Dogs and humans have been companions for thousands of years. The domestication of dogs may have been one of the earliest human experiences with genetics. **Genetics** is the scientific study of heredity.

Millions of years ago there were no dogs. Today's domestic dogs are descended from a wild, wolfish ancestor. How did the snarling, dangerous wolf of millions of years ago become the loyal lapdog of today? Although we have no record of dog domestication, it seems certain that ancient peoples selected certain wolves to mate and thereby affected the traits that were passed from the parents to the pups.

A **trait** is a characteristic that can be passed from parent to offspring. With each generation, the traits of the wolves living with humans became more distinct from the traits of the wild wolves. Eventually, this process led to a new breed—the domestic dog. What wolf traits might our ancestors have prized most when breeding the ❶ domestic dog?

We have known for centuries that traits are passed from parents to offspring. What has not always been understood is how traits are determined. One explanation that appealed to scientists for many centuries was that traits of parents were blended, or mixed, in offspring. The blending hypothesis accounted for many observable traits and was widely accepted for many years. However, the idea of blending could not account for the appearance of unexpected traits in some offspring. It was not until scientists discovered the cellular basis of life that the inheritance of traits was better understood.

FIGURE 6.1
This artwork from the year 510 B.C. shows a Greek teenager playing with a domesticated cat and dog.

130 *Unit 2 Genetics*

STUDENT RESOURCES

From the Teacher's Resource Package, use:
- Section Review 6.1 and Enrichment Topics 6-1 and 6-2 from Unit 2 Review Module

TECHNOLOGY RESOURCES

Relevant technology resources include:
- Spanish Student Edition CD-ROM
- Teacher's Resource Planner CD-ROM

In Chapter 5 you learned about chromosomes and cell division. During cell division, chromosomes are replicated and then distributed to daughter cells. Reproduction requires cell division and chromosome replication. We now know that traits are passed from parents to offspring in these chromosomes. But the relationship between chromosomes and traits was not always understood.

The first clues to understanding inheritance came from Gregor Mendel, one of the most outstanding scientists in the field of genetics. Mendel, an Austrian monk, began his work in the 1860s. He used garden pea plants to study how traits were passed from one generation to another.

Most biologists in the 1860s did not use mathematics in their studies. However, Mendel recognized the importance of statistics in experimentation. After gathering detailed information on more than 20,000 pea plants, Mendel applied mathematics to his observations and found that the statistics did not support the blending hypothesis. Instead, the statistics led him to suggest several new hypotheses to explain inheritance of traits.

MENDEL'S EXPERIMENTS

Like peas in a pod

Analyzing statistics was just one of the requirements of Mendel's work. Another was patience. Mendel worked for more than eight years on his pea plant experiments. Mendel chose the garden pea plant for three reasons: the structure of the pea flowers, the presence of distinctive traits, and the rapid reproduction cycle. These characteristics enabled Mendel to isolate and control variables and to produce observable results that he could duplicate.

The anthers are cut from the purple flower, which is then fertilized by pollen from the white flower.

FIGURE 6.2
How did the shape of pea plants allow Mendel to manipulate pollination and control his experiments? ❷

The structure of the pea flower enabled Mendel to isolate an important variable—fertilization. In fertilization, the male plant gamete, located in pollen produced by the anther, is transferred to the female plant gamete, located at the base of the pistil. The relatively closed structure of the pea flower petals makes it very easy for pollen from the anther to fertilize the pistil of the same flower. This process is called self-fertilization. If a plant or any organism receives the same genetic traits from both of its parents, it is called **purebred.** Self-fertilization produces purebred pea plants.

As you can see in *Figure 6.2*, Mendel also altered plants and transferred pollen by hand. By controlling pollination and preventing self-fertilization, Mendel crossbred plants, producing hybrids. A **hybrid** is an organism that receives different forms of a genetic trait from each parent.

Garden pea plants have some traits that are easy to see, which made it possible for Mendel to produce observable results. Mendel studied seven traits. Each of these traits is unusual in that it has only two distinct forms. For example, the pea pods are either yellow or green. There is no intermediate, or blended, color. The height of the plant is either tall or

FIGURE 6.3
Gregor Mendel (1822–1884) is known as the father of genetics.

Chapter 6 Fundamentals of Genetics **131**

short, never medium. Distinct traits like this are rare in nature, as you will see later in this unit. The distinct traits in pea plants allowed Mendel to see his results without guesswork.

Another important feature of pea plants is that most plants reproduce in about 90 days. The short reproductive cycle gave Mendel results relatively quickly and allowed him to repeat the experiments many times to test his results.

FIGURE 6.4
Mendel's Crosses

Mendel crossed pea plants and observed the traits that appeared in the offspring. This cross examines the trait of pea color. Which color is dominant, yellow or green? ❶

MENDEL'S OBSERVATIONS

Chartreuse pea soup?

Mendel began his experiments using two different groups of purebred plants, as you can see in *Figure 6.4.* He called this generation the parental,

or P, generation. He called the first generation of offspring the first filial generation, because "filial" refers to offspring. He gave this generation the notation F_1. Mendel allowed F_1 plants to self-fertilize, producing the second filial, or F_2 generation. *Figure 6.4* shows Mendel's pea plant crosses and results using pea plants with either yellow or green peas.

What results did Mendel expect? According to the blending hypothesis, the green and yellow peas of Mendel's plants in the P generation should have blended to produce chartreuse offspring. Instead, Mendel found that all of the F_1 hybrid plants had yellow peas. There were neither green nor chartreuse peas in the first generation of pea plants, even though one of the parent plants had green peas.

When Mendel let the F_1 hybrid plants self-fertilize, he found green peas in the F_2 generation. About 75 percent of the plants in the F_2 generation had yellow peas and 25 percent of the plants had green peas. In other words, there was a ratio of three pea plants with yellow peas to one with green peas, or 3:1. Again, there were no chartreuse peas.

Mendel repeated his experiments for the other six traits. For each trait, he observed the same results in the F_1 generation–all of the F_1 plants were only one form of the trait. Mendel defined each form of the trait as either dominant or recessive. A dominant form appeared in the F_1 generation. A recessive form did not appear in the F_1 generation. For pea color, yellow is the dominant form and green is the recessive. According to *Figure 6.5,* which other six forms are dominant? ❷

In the F_2 generation of his experiments, Mendel found that there were always two types of plants. About 75 percent of the F_2 plants showed the dominant form of the trait. About 25 percent of the F_2 plants showed the

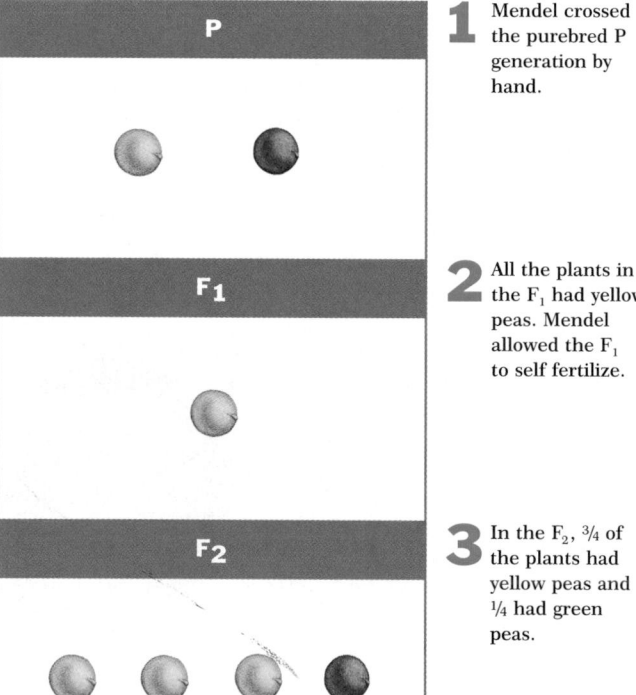

P

1 Mendel crossed the purebred P generation by hand.

F₁

2 All the plants in the F_1 had yellow peas. Mendel allowed the F_1 to self fertilize.

F₂

3 In the F_2, ¾ of the plants had yellow peas and ¼ had green peas.

FIGURE 6. 5

Mendel's Seven Traits

	Flower Color	Flower Position	Pea Color	Pea Shape	Pod Color	Pod Shape	Height
Dominant	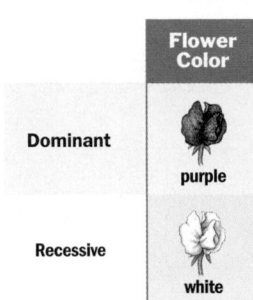 purple	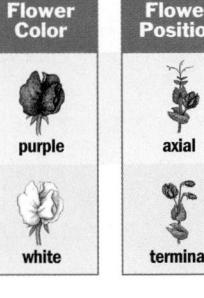 axial	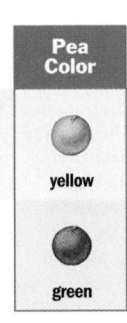 yellow	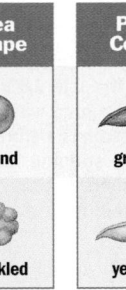 round	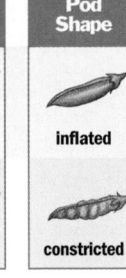 green	 inflated	tall
Recessive	white	terminal	green	wrinkled	yellow	constricted	short

recessive form of the trait. How did these results disprove the blending hypothesis?

MENDEL'S CONCLUSIONS

Factor in the evidence

Mendel's experiments showed that the blending hypothesis was wrong. He never observed pea plants with mixtures of two forms of a trait, such as chartreuse pea color. Mendel reasoned that forms of a trait must remain separate in offspring.

Mendel hypothesized that each trait is controlled by a distinct "factor." Since there were two forms of each trait, Mendel realized that there must be at least two forms of each factor.

Mendel was surprised that recessive forms of traits disappeared in the F_1 generation but reappeared in the F_2. He reasoned that, for every trait, a pea plant must carry a pair of factors which could affect each other. When a trait is inherited, Mendel concluded, the offspring receives one factor from each parent.

We now know that the Mendel's "factors" are genes. **Genes** are sections of a chromosome that code for a trait. Most organisms have two copies of every gene and chromosome, one from each parent.

We refer to the different forms of Mendel's factors as alleles. An **allele**

is a distinct form of a gene. If an organism has two different alleles for a trait, only one is expressed, or visible. A **dominant allele** is a form of a gene that is fully expressed when two different alleles are present. A **recessive allele** is a form of a gene that is not expressed when paired with a dominant allele.

Mendel published an account of his experiments in 1866. At that time, the scientific community was focused on the work of another scientist, Charles Darwin, whom you will read about in Chapter 10. Mendel's published work went unrecognized for 37 years. As you will learn in the next chapter, the rediscovery of Mendel's work led to the formulation of the basic principles of inheritance.

CHECKPOINT 6.1

1. Explain the difference between a dominant trait and a recessive trait.
2. What result would you predict for Mendel's cross of a short pea plant with a tall one in the P generation?
3. **Critical Thinking** If the blending hypothesis were true, how would Mendel's results have been different?

Build on What You Know

4. Compare self-fertilization with asexual reproduction. (**Need to jog your memory? Revisit relevant concepts in Chapter 5, Section 5.3.**)

Mendel studied seven distinct traits of pea plants. Which flower—purple or white—has the dominant trait? ❹

Chapter 6 Fundamentals of Genetics **133**

6.1

Explain

Have students study Figure 6.5. Explain that the dominant trait will be visible. The recessive trait is still present, even though it is not expressed.

Clarify Misconceptions

Students may not understand why the same letter is used for coding both the recessive color (green) of the pea and the dominant color (yellow). Point out that letter *y* was chosen to represent the dominant color. Capital *Y* indicates the dominant allele while lower case *y* indicates the recessive allele.

③ ASSESS

Evaluate Understanding

To assess students' understanding of Mendel's experiments, ask:

- **Why did Mendel choose garden peas for his experiments?** (Their distinctive traits and quick reproductive cycle enabled him to control variables and produce reproducible results.)
- **What did Mendel discover when his cross-bred plants did not show blended traits?** (Something specific inside the plant determined traits.)

Reteach

Work with students to fill in a chart outlining the information in the section. Label each column with a section subhead: Mendel's Experiments, Mendel's Observations, and Mendel's Conclusions.

CHECKPOINT 6.1

1. If a dominant trait and a recessive trait are both present, the dominant trait will mask the recessive trait.
2. The F_1 generation will be entirely made up of tall pea plants.
3. **Developing a hypothesis** Mendel would have observed an F_1 generation with traits that were a mix of parental traits.
4. In self-fertilization, two gametes from the same organism are joined to create offspring with some genetic variation. In asexual reproduction, all of the genetic information is copied and then the cell splits forming two identical daughter cells.

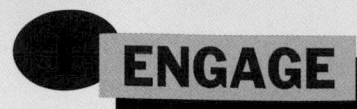

ENGAGE

Use the Visual

Have students study the photographs that open the section. Ask:

- **Why are staining techniques important in the study of cells?** (Stains enable scientists to distinguish parts of the cell.)

Check Prior Knowledge

To assess students' prior knowledge about cell division, draw four cell outlines on the board and label them prophase, metaphase, anaphase, and telophase. Ask:

- **What happens to the chromosomes during each phase of mitosis?**

Teacher Demo

Display two stacks of plastic disks, one black, the other red. Tell students that the stacks model a chromosome pair. Point out that the same information (same gene) is expressed in a slightly different manner in the two stacks (different alleles). Use this analogy to explain how chromosomes and their respective genes carry the same information but in slightly different ways.

What you'll learn

IDEAS
- To explain the chromosome theory of heredity
- To summarize Mendel's laws

WORDS
chromosome theory of heredity, genotype, phenotype, homozygous, heterozygous

Good stains

Most of the time stains are bad news. But in the late 1800s a new technique called staining was developed that made chromosomes visible for the first time. The new staining technique allowed researchers to observe the chromosome changes during stages of mitosis and meiosis.

THE CELLULAR BASIS OF INHERITANCE

Dominant alleles call the shots

Soon after the rediscovery of Mendel's work, the American biologist Walter S. Sutton was observing stained cells through a microscope. He noticed that chromosomes acted like Mendel's factors. By 1903 Sutton had outlined the **chromosome theory of heredity.** This theory states that the material of inheritance is carried by the genes in chromosomes. You can use *Figure 6.6* to compare Mendel's conclusions with Sutton's. As Sutton was formulating his theory, a German biologist named Theodor Boveri independently

reached the same conclusion—specific genes are located on specific chromosomes.

Representing alleles In order to explain the new chromosome theory of heredity, biologists came up with several terms and symbols. You are already familiar with some of these terms. Genes are sections of chromosomes that code for traits. Alleles are different forms of a gene. Pea color in pea plants is controlled by a single gene with two alleles—one for green, one for yellow.

As you work with traits and inheritance, you may use letters to represent alleles. The allele for yellow peas, the dominant trait, is represented by an uppercase letter Y. The allele for green peas, a recessive trait, can be represented by a lowercase y. We use the uppercase and lowercase forms of the same letter because the alleles for yellow and green peas are two versions of the same gene. As a rule, an uppercase letter represents a dominant allele. A lowercase letter represents a recessive allele.

Genes affect traits The genetic makeup of an organism is called its **genotype.** The genotype includes both genes in a homologous pair of chromosomes. The genotype of a pea plant that is purebred for yellow peas is written YY. A hybrid is written Yy. How would you write the genotype of

---

FIGURE 6.6

Mendel's Hypothesis

Mendel hypothesized the existence of chromosomes 37 years before Sutton observed them. Compare Mendel's factors with Sutton's chromosomes.

1866
Mendel used statistics to hypothesize the action of trait carriers, which he called factors.

1903
Sutton used a microscope and observed that chromosomes behaved like Mendel's factors.

Mendel's Factors	Chromosomes
Occur in pairs	Occur in pairs
Segregate in gamete production	Separate during meiosis
Pairs sort independently	Pairs sort independently

STUDENT RESOURCES

From the Teacher's Resource Package, use:
- Section Review 6.2 and Activity Recordsheet 6-1 from Unit 2 Review Module

TECHNOLOGY RESOURCES

Relevant technology resources include:
- Spanish Student Edition CD-ROM
- Teacher's Resource Planner CD-ROM
- Animated Biological Concepts Videodiscs: "Segregation of Chromosomes"

a purebred pea plant with green peas?

① The **phenotype** of an organism is the outward expression of the trait. For example, the phenotype of Mendel's F₁ hybrid is yellow peas. Because Y is the dominant allele, both the YY and the Yy genotypes produce yellow peas. The genotype yy produces the green pea phenotype.

Scientists use two terms—homozygous and heterozygous—to describe genotypes. An organism in which the two alleles in a gene pair are identical is called **homozygous** (HOH-moh-ZY-gus) for that trait. YY and yy are both homozygous genotypes. Mendel's P generation, the purebred plants, were also homozygous.

In contrast, an organism in which the two alleles for a particular trait are different is **heterozygous** (HET-er-oh-ZY-gus). Yy is an example of a heterozygous genotype. The plants in Mendel's F₁ generation were heterozygous for the alleles being studied. Using the letters P and p for the color of pea flowers, what is the genotype of a pea plant that is heterozygous for flower color? What is its phenotype?

②

MENDEL'S LAWS

Law-abiding genes

The basic rules of inheritance are referred to as Mendel's laws. Like many of the laws that govern scientific processes, Mendel's laws have exceptions. You will read about these exceptions later in this chapter. However, many traits do follow Mendel's laws and are called Mendelian traits. Keep in mind the steps of meiosis as you read about Mendelian inheritance.

The Law of Segregation Mendel hypothesized that gene pairs separate when gametes form. This idea is now known as the Law of Segregation. This law states that each

pair of genes segregates, or separates, during meiosis. Because of segregation, half of an organism's gametes contain one gene from a homologous pair, and half of the gametes contain the other gene.

The Law of Independent Assortment Mendel also studied the inheritance of two traits at the same time. In one study he crossed pea plants that had yellow, round peas (*YYRR*) with plants that had green, wrinkled peas (*yyrr*). In the F₁ generation, all the peas were yellow and round (*YyRr*). The F₁ plants were allowed to self-fertilize. All possible combinations of the pea colors and shapes appeared in the F₂ generation. The association of traits in a parent did not seem to matter. From this

 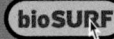

Predicting Parakeet Color

Parakeets are most often light green with a yellow head and black markings. One variation is blue with a white head and black markings. How are colors determined?

Analyzing the Diagram

1 A purebred green-and-yellow parakeet and a purebred blue-and-white parakeet are P generations in an experiment. All of the F₁ generation is green and yellow. Which trait is dominant?
2 Describe the genotypes and phenotypes in each generation.
3 Using your answers to the previous question, identify which genotypes are homozygous and which are heterozygous.

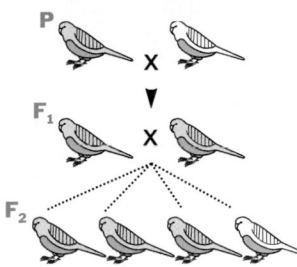

LAB ZONE **Think About It!**

Predicting Parakeet Color

Assume that the F₂ generation are all offspring of F₁ parents, which have the same parents in the P generation.

Analyzing the Diagram

1 Green and yellow is the dominant trait.
2 P generation: genotypes are homozygous, phenotypes are green and yellow and blue and white. F₁ generation: genotypes are heterozygous, phenotypes are green and yellow. F₂ generation: genotypes are homozygous and heterozygous, phenotypes are green and yellow and blue and white.
3 Genotypes in which both alleles are the same are homozygous; genotypes with different alleles are heterozygous.

❶ Purebred pea plant with green peas is *yy*.
❷ Genotype of pea plant heterozygous for flower color is *Pp*. Phenotype is purple.

Animated Biological Concepts

Segregation of Chromosomes

Play

Use the Visual

Help students understand how Mendel's laws apply to meiosis and fertilization as illustrated in Figure 6.7. Ask:

- **What occurs during Meiosis I?** (The homologous pairs of chromosomes separate and two cells result, each containing two copies of one chromosome from each homologous pair.)
- **What occurs during Meiosis II?** (The two new cells divide to produce four haploid cells, each genetically different from the parent cell. Daughter cells contain one copy of one chromosome from each homologous pair.)
- **How is meiosis related to the Law of Segregation?** (Meiosis explains how gene pairs separate when gametes are formed.)

Build Writing Skills

Tell students to imagine that they are assistants to Gregor Mendel. While crossing several generations of pea plants, all with purple flowers, they find one with a white flower. Ask them to describe this experience in a letter to a colleague and propose a hypothesis explaining the presence of the white flower.

FIGURE 6.7

Mendel's Laws at Work

Mendel's three laws correspond with events during meiosis and fertilization. What is the result of meiosis? ❶

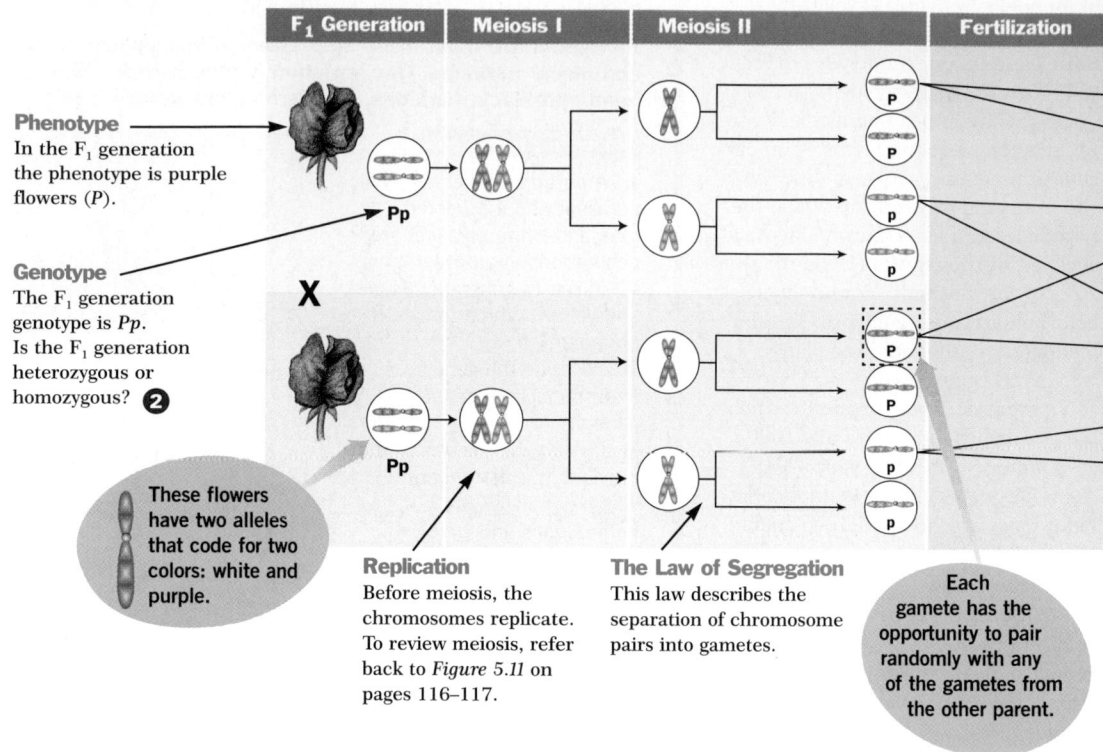

Phenotype
In the F₁ generation the phenotype is purple flowers (*P*).

Genotype
The F₁ generation genotype is *Pp*. Is the F₁ generation heterozygous or homozygous? ❷

These flowers have two alleles that code for two colors: white and purple.

Replication
Before meiosis, the chromosomes replicate. To review meiosis, refer back to *Figure 5.11* on pages 116–117.

The Law of Segregation
This law describes the separation of chromosome pairs into gametes.

Each gamete has the opportunity to pair randomly with any of the gametes from the other parent.

information, Mendel concluded that traits are inherited independently.

Geneticists now recognize Mendel's idea of independent assortment as a law, called the Law of Independent Assortment. This law states that gene pairs segregate into gametes randomly and independently of each other.

Compare the Law of Independent Assortment with the behavior of chromosomes during meiosis, as shown in *Figure 6.7*. The separation of chromosome pairs occurs randomly and produces all possible combinations of chromosomes in the gametes. If the chromosome pairs did not separate

randomly, offspring would have the same combination of traits as one of the parents. In other words, without the Law of Independent Assortment, you could not have your father's eyes and your mother's smile!

The Law of Dominance
According to the Law of Dominance, the dominant allele is expressed and the recessive allele can be hidden. Recall that the letter representing the dominant trait is capitalized to represent the dominant allele. The same letter in lowercase is used to represent the recessive allele. In pea plants heterozygous for flower color (*Pp*), the purple-flower allele (*P*) controls

136   *Unit 2 Genetics*

❶ The result of meiosis is that half the gametes contain one gene from each homologous pair and half contain the other gene from each homologous pair.

❷ Heterozygous

❸ The Law of Dominance is useful for describing heterozygous organisms because they have only one copy of dominant allele.

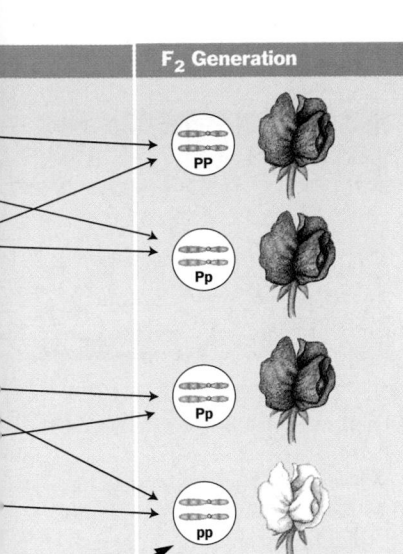

F₂ Generation

PP

Pp

Pp

pp

Recombination
In the offspring, the alleles can appear in three combinations: *PP, Pp,* and *pp.*

The Law of Dominance
If the dominant allele is in the genotype, then that trait is expressed.

the phenotype, and the flowers are purple. The other allele in the pair, the allele for white flowers (*p*), does not affect phenotype. A recessive allele is expressed only when the organism has no copy of the corresponding dominant allele. Is the Law of Dominance more useful when describing heterozygous organisms or ❸ homozygous organisms?

LAB ZONE Do It! **bioSURF**

Can You Illustrate the Law of Dominance?

Each offspring gets one gene from each parent. You can model the offspring if you . . .

Try This

1 Use four buttons, two of one color and two of another color, to represent two alleles. Select a color as the dominant trait; the other color is the recessive trait. Make a model to represent two parents, each of whom is heterozygous for the trait.
2 Each parent will give the offspring one allele for this trait. What are the possible combinations? Move the buttons to model each combination. Be sure to return the buttons to their original parent model. Record each of your offspring models.
3 Repeat until you have made all possible models.

Analyze Your Results

1 How many different arrangements of alleles can occur in the offspring of these parents?
2 How many ways can an offspring receive the same alleles (one of each color) as the parent?
3 How are two of Mendel's laws represented in this activity?

CHECKPOINT 6.2

1. What is the chromosome theory of heredity?
2. Describe and give examples of Mendel's laws.
3. Critical Thinking Using Mendel's laws, explain why his F₂ generation contained more pea plants with dominant traits than with recessive traits.

Build on What You Know

4. What phase of meiosis is described by Mendel's Law of Segregation? *(Need to jog your memory? Revisit relevant concepts in Chapter 5, Section 5.3.)*

What are traits, and how do scientists know they are inherited? **?**

LAB ZONE Do It! **TEAM WORK**

Can You Illustrate the Law of Dominance?

Analyze Your Results

1 Gametes (buttons) can combine in four ways, in three allele arrangements: *CC, Cc, cC,* and *cc.*
2 Offspring can receive the same alleles as parents in two ways. *C* from mother and *c* from father, or *C* from father and *c* from mother.
3 Law of Segregation: each offspring gets only one gamete from each parent. Law of Dominance: on average, three of four offspring will be dominant color (*CC, Cc,* or *cC*).

 **❸ ASSESS**

Evaluate Understanding

Using paper to represent the alleles of the gene for flower color (purple, *P,* dominant; white, *p,* recessive) and plant height (tall, *T,* dominant; short, *t,* recessive), have students represent all possible genotypes (*PP; pp; TT; tt;* Pp; Tt). Have students name which of Mendel's laws applies to the various combinations.

Reteach

Walk students through Figure 6.7. Have them work in pairs to create a flowchart showing how the process of meiosis works in inheritance.

CHECKPOINT 6.2

1. The theory states that specific genes are located on specific chromosomes.
2. Segregation: gene pairs separate when gametes are formed (during meiosis). Independent Assortment: traits are inherited independently from both parents. Dominance: dominant allele is expressed and the recessive allele can be hidden.

3. Analyzing Three possible allele combinations can result with a dominant allele in the genotype. Only one allele combination results with two recessive alleles.
4. Anaphase II is described by the Law of Segregation.

ENGAGE

Consider the Big Idea!

Have students read The Big Idea! at the top of the page. Ask students to identify some traits that are the same among their siblings.

Use the Visual

Have students study the photograph that opens the section. Discuss how the job of a meteorologist compares with that of a geneticist.

Quick Activity

Draw a Punnett square showing parents' height, *Tt* and *Tt*, on the board. (T: tall; t: short) Have students fill in the genotypes using the letters and the name of each phenotype. Ask:

- **How many tall off-spring?** (Three)
- **How many short off-spring?** (One)
- **What determines the kind of offspring the F₁ generation could have?** (The genotype of the other parent)

Interactive Biological Simulations

Punnett Squares Students select the type of trait, or traits, and genotype for each of the parents. After making these selections, they are able to fill in the Punnett squares with the gametes, genotypes, and phenotypes. The simulation concludes with a test cross.

6.3 Genetics and Predictions

What you'll learn

IDEAS
- To explain how probability is used in genetic predictions
- To construct a Punnett square for monohybrid and dihybrid crosses
- To infer genotype by using a test cross

WORDS
Punnett square, test cross

Sunny with a chance of clouds
What will the weather be tomorrow? Meteorologists use Doppler radar and other tools to predict the weather. But even if you know the forecast, you won't actually know the weather until tomorrow. Geneticists also have tools to predict probable offspring phenotypes. You will learn about one such tool in this section.

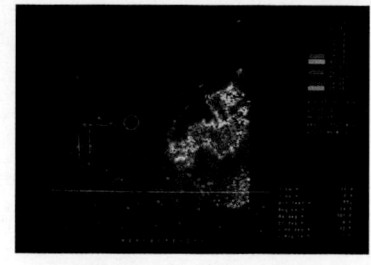

PREDICTIONS FOR ONE TRAIT

In all probability

What comes to mind when you hear "there's a fifty-fifty chance" or "chances are one in ten"? When you use fractions, percentages, or ratios to predict the likelihood of an event or outcome, you are measuring probability. Probability is symbolized by the letter P.

When you flip a coin, you can get either heads or tails. The probability of getting heads on any one flip is $P = \frac{1}{2}$. If you flipped the coin ten times, you would expect heads to appear about five times, or 50 percent of the time. Probability can be

---

FIGURE 6.8

How to Make a Punnett Square

Punnett squares allow geneticists to predict the possible genotypes and phenotypes of offspring.

In this example, both parents are heterozygous for yellow-pea allele (*Yy*).

1 Make the grid
Place the alleles of the gametes of one parent along the top of a grid and those of the other parent along the left-hand side.

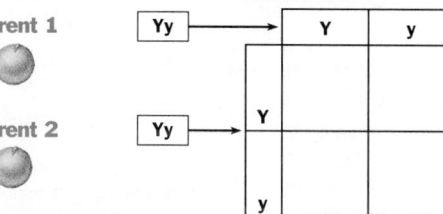

2 Fill in the grid
Combine the parent alleles inside the boxes. The letters show the genotypes of the offspring.

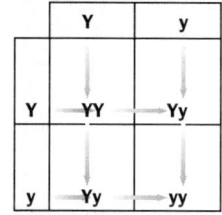

The genotype ratio is 1:2:1, meaning 1 YY, 2 Yy, 1 yy.

3 Fill in the offspring
Use the Law of Dominance to determine the phenotypes and phenotype ratio of the offspring.

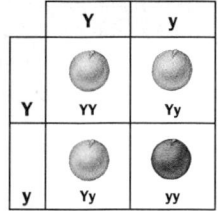

The phenotype ratio is 3:1, meaning 3 yellow peas to 1 green pea.

138 *Unit 2 Genetics*

STUDENT RESOURCES

From the Teacher's Resource Package, use:
- Section Review 6.3, Interpreting Graphics 6, and Activity Recordsheet 6-2 from Unit 2 Review Module
- Lab 13: "Genetics and Chance"
- Consumer Applications 6-1 and 6-2

TECHNOLOGY RESOURCES

Relevant technology resources include:
- Spanish Student Edition CD-ROM
- Teacher's Resource Planner CD-ROM
- Interactive Biological Simulations: "Punnett Squares"

represented as a fraction ($\frac{1}{2}$), a percentage (50%), or a ratio (1:1).

Probability is useful in biology. Scientists often use probability to predict the phenotypes and genotypes of offspring in breeding experiments. They can even predict the numbers of kinds of offspring before fertilization takes place.

Scientists use a tool to make predictions about genetics—a Punnett square. A **Punnett square,** like the one in *Figure 6.8,* is a grid for organizing genetic information. A Punnett square shows probabilities, not actual results.

You can use Punnett squares to predict the offspring of crosses between pea plants. Consider the inheritance of pea color in pea plants, ignoring all of the plant's other traits. When you study the inheritance of only one trait at a time, you are studying a monohybrid cross. (The prefix "mono-" means "one.")

A Punnett square can be used to make predictions about a cross between two organisms. Consider, for example, a cross between two pea plants. Both plants are heterozygous for the yellow-pea trait (*Yy*). The cross is written *Yy* × *Yy*. Each parent can contribute two types of gametes. Half of the gametes carry the Y allele, and half carry the *y* allele.

Follow *Figure 6.8* to see how to complete a Punnett square for this cross. To fill in the square, write the alleles that one parent can contribute along the top and the alleles that the other parent can contribute along the side of the Punnett square. Then combine the alleles from both parents inside each box.

The combinations of alleles inside the boxes are the possible genotypes of the offspring. As you can see in the figure, there are three different offspring genotypes that are possible as a result of the F₁ cross. They are YY, Yy,

LAB ZONE Do It!

How Is Genetics Related to Probability?

You can use a Punnett square and two coins to learn more about probability if you . . .

Try This

1 Toss a coin 20 times. Record your results, heads (*H*) and tails (*T*).
2 Draw a Punnett square like the one shown here.
3 With a partner, toss two coins at the same time. Repeat 49 times and record each toss (*HH, HT, TH, TT*). Make sure that you note when you get heads and your partner gets tails *separately* from when you get tails and your partner gets heads. Add up the number of times you get each combination and fill in your Punnett square.

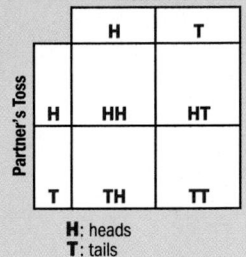

Your Toss

	H	T
H	HH	HT
T	TH	TT

Partner's Toss (vertical label)

H: heads
T: tails

Analyze Your Results

1 How does tossing one coin relate to gamete separation?
2 Based on your 50 tosses of two coins, what is the probability of one coin coming up heads and the other coming up tails?

and *yy.* What are the phenotypes of each of these genotypes? As you see from the Punnett square in *Figure 6.8,* the probable ratio of the offspring genotypes is 1:2:1. As you have learned, probability can also be shown as a percentage—25 percent YY, 50 percent *Yy,* and 25 percent *yy.* Again, keep in mind that a Punnett square tells you the probable proportion of offspring genotypes, not the guaranteed outcome. ❶

Now that you have seen how to predict the outcome of a monohybrid cross using a Punnett square, you can go back to section 6.1 and predict the outcomes of other monohybrid crosses using Mendel's pea plant crosses. What would be the results of a cross between a purebred tall pea plant (*TT*) and a hybrid tall pea plant (*Tt*)? ❷

Chapter 6 Fundamentals of Genetics **139**

❶ The phenotype of *YY* and *Yy* is yellow peas and the phenotype of *yy* is green peas.
❷ All of the offspring will be tall. 50% of the offspring will be homozygous and 50% will be heterozygous.

140

Use the Visual

Guide students through the process illustrated in Figure 6.9. Ask:

- **What is the ratio of yellow peas to green peas?** (3:1)
- **What is the ratio of round peas to wrinkled peas?** (3:1)
- **Explain how you determined your answers.** (12 and 4 are divisible by 3 and yield a 3:1 ratio.)

Apply

Have students prepare a Punnett square of a dihybrid cross for two parents heterozygous for purple flowers and tall plants. (*PpTt*). Ask them to list all the phenotypes that result and give the ratios of purple to white flowers and tall to short plants.

Clarify Misconceptions

Students may not understand the function of gametes. Explain that gametes are sex cells, which can be either male (sperm) or female (ova).

Two traits are better than one

You just learned how to predict the results of a monohybrid cross. But why stop there? Predicting two traits with Punnett squares is like tossing two coins at the same time. Because the coins are not attached in any way, the outcome of one flip does not influence the outcome of the other. What is the chance that both coins show heads? You can find out by multiplying their separate probabilities. The chance of one coming up heads is $P = \frac{1}{2}$. The probability that both coins will show heads is $\frac{1}{2} \times \frac{1}{2}$, or $P = \frac{1}{4}$.

To study the inheritance of two traits at a time, you apply the same rules of probability as you do when you flip two coins. You can predict two traits by making a dihybrid cross. As you might guess, "di-" means "two."

The steps in predicting the results of a dihybrid cross are shown in *Figure 6.9*. The example cross is written $RrYy \times RrYy$. As you have learned, Mendel's Law of Independent Assortment states that alleles will sort into all possible combinations. Thus, there are four possible combinations of alleles in the gametes of the parent plants: *RY*, *Ry*, *rY*, and *ry*.

To predict the results of the dihybrid cross, you set up a 4 × 4 Punnett square. List the alleles in the gametes of one parent along the top of the square and the alleles in the gametes of the other parent along the side. Combine the alleles inside the boxes.

The phenotypes in the Punnett square in *Figure 6.9* include 9 round

FIGURE 6.9

How to Predict the Results of a Dihybrid Cross

Dihybrid crosses allow geneticists to predict the possible genotypes and phenotypes for two traits.

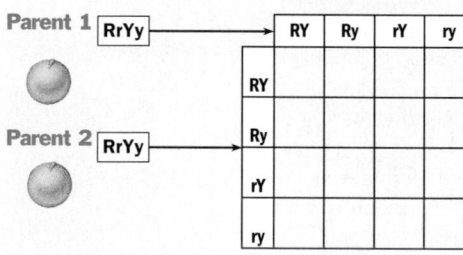

1 Make the grid Place all four combinations of alleles for one parent along the top of a grid and those of the other parent along the side.

In this example, both parents are heterozygous for round yellow-pea alleles (*RrYy*).

2 Fill in the grid Combine the parent alleles inside the boxes. The letters show possible genotypes of the offspring.

There are 9 different genotypes: *RRYY*, *RRYy*, *RrYY*, *RRyy*, *RrYy*, *Rryy*, *rrYY*, *rrYy*, and *rryy*. Which genotype is most numerous? ❶

3 Fill in the offspring Determine the offspring's phenotypes for both traits.

The phenotype ratio is 9:3:3:1, meaning 9 round yellow peas, 3 wrinkled yellow peas, 3 round green peas, and 1 wrinkled green pea.

MEETING DIVERSE NEEDS

Sight Impaired Prepare a Punnett-square board with a raised grid. Use different shaped objects to represent dominant and recessive alleles. Place the parent traits at the top of the board and have students complete the Punnett square and describe the resulting phenotypes.

❶ *RrYy*
❷ 3/16
❸ The unknown genotype is *YY*.

yellow peas, 3 wrinkled yellow peas, 3 round green peas, and 1 wrinkled green pea. The phenotype ratio is 9:3:3:1. Recall that this result can be written in many ways. For example, the probability of getting an offspring plant with wrinkled green peas is $P=\frac{1}{16}$. What is the probable percentage of offspring with round green peas? Notice that the offspring have combinations of traits that were not present in the parents. For example, neither parent had round green or wrinkled yellow peas. This outcome is a result of Mendel's Law of Independent Assortment and has some important implications that you will learn about in Chapter 7.

TEST CROSS

Seeing the invisible

As you just discovered, it is essential to know the genotypes of the parent generation of pea plants to make a Punnett square. How do geneticists know the genotype of a pea plant, or of any organism? The phenotype is often easy to determine by observation. But if an organism has the dominant phenotype, how can you tell if it is homozygous or heterozygous for this allele?

Scientists can distinguish between homozygous dominant and heterozygous organisms by doing test crosses. In a **test cross,** geneticists breed the organism whose genotype is unknown with a homozygous recessive organism. As you learned in section 6.2, the recessive allele is expressed only if the organism is homozygous for that allele. For this reason, the genotype of a recessive organism is always known. A test cross is the crossing of a known recessive genotype and an unknown dominant genotype, resulting in offspring with observable phenotypes.

If the unknown genotype is heterozygous, about half the offspring should show the recessive phenotype.

FIGURE 6.10

Using a Test Cross to Determine Genotype

A plant with yellow peas could be homozygous (*YY*) or heterozygous (*Yy*) for pea color. If a test cross results in 1 green pea: 1 yellow pea, what is the genotype? **4**

Test Cross

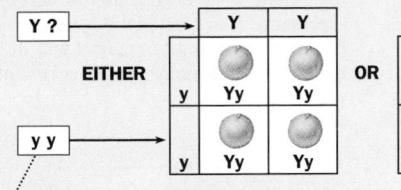

The genotype of the green pea plant (*yy*) is always known because it is recessive.

If the pea plant being tested is homozygous dominant (*YY*), then all offspring will be yellow (*Yy*).

If the pea plant is heterozygous (*Yy*), then half of the offspring will be yellow (*Yy*) and half will be green (*yy*).

If the unknown genotype is homozygous dominant, all the offspring will show the dominant phenotype.

To demonstrate how a test cross is done, consider pea color in the test cross in *Figure 6.10*. Both YY and Yy genotypes produce yellow peas, because yellow color is the dominant allele. In a test cross, the unknown plant (Y?) is crossed with a homozygous recessive (yy) plant. What would the unknown genotype be if all of the offspring had yellow peas? **3**

CHECKPOINT 6.3

1. How do geneticists use probability to predict genotype and phenotype?
2. Compare and contrast a monohybrid cross and a dihybrid cross.
3. **Critical Thinking** Use Punnett squares to show the results of the following crosses:
a) *Dd* × *dd* b) *QQ* × *qq* c) *MM* × *Mm*

Build on What You Know

4. In what step of the scientific method would you use a Punnett square? *(Need to jog your memory? Revisit relevant concepts in Chapter 1, Section 1.3.)*

Chapter 6 Fundamentals of Genetics **141**

CHECKPOINT 6.3

1. Scientists use Punnett squares to predict the probability of offspring genotypes and phenotypes.
2. Both monohybrid and dihybrid crosses are used to predict offspring traits. Monohybrid crosses predict the appearance of one trait; dihybrid crosses predict the appearance of two traits.

3. **Applying** a) Half are *Dd* and half are *dd*. b) All are *Qq*. c) Half are *MM* and half are *Mm*.
4. Punnett squares could be used to develop a hypothesis.
4 The genotype is *Yy*.

Apply

Have students explain how two brown-eyed parents can produce a blue-eyed offspring. Ask:

- **What do you know about the eye color of the four grandparents?** (At least one will have blue eyes.)
- **What do you know about the eye color of the eight great-grandparents?** (At least one on each side will probably have blue eyes.)

Evaluate Understanding

Have students do a test cross of four offspring with one blue-eyed and one brown-eyed parent. Ask:

- **What are the probable phenotypes if the brown-eyed parent is homozygous?** (brown eyes); **heterozygous?** (half will be brown-eyed and half blue-eyed.)
- **What are the genotypes if both parents are homozygous?** (Each will have one gene for blue eyes and one for brown eyes.)
- **Explain how a test cross can reveal a recessive gene.** (If two parents have the recessive gene, some offspring will have blue eyes because both parents have the recessive gene.)

Reteach

Have students study Figure 6.8. Then have them work in groups of three and use Figures 6.9 and 6.10 to show how to make and use Punnett squares to describe a dihybrid cross and a test cross.

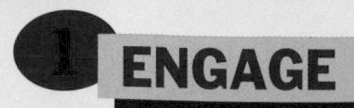

ENGAGE

Use the Visual

Have students study the photo that opens the section. Determine the percentage of students in the class who have dimples. Ask:

- **How many students who do not have dimples have siblings with dimples?** (Answers will vary.)
- **How many students with dimples also have siblings with dimples?** (Answers will vary.)

Teacher Demo

Select a common recessive trait, such as attached earlobes, and develop a pedigree for two matings. Show one mating of two parents with blue eyes. Show a second mating of one parent with attached earlobes and one parent with nonattached earlobes. Have the students help you complete the pedigree if each set of parents has four children.

SUPER READ! **Finding Supporting Details** To practice strategies for effective reading, use pages 35-36 in *Super Read!*

What you'll learn

IDEAS
- To interpret pedigrees and understand their purpose
- To contrast dominant and recessive genetic disorders
- To identify some methods used to determine the likelihood of a genetic disorder occurring in offspring

WORDS
pedigree, carrier

The dimple life
Do your cheeks dimple when you smile? Do you know a dimpled family? Dimples are controlled by a dominant allele. If the dominant allele is inherited, then it will be expressed. However, just because an allele is dominant does not mean it will be a common trait. How many people with dimples do you know?

PEDIGREE STUDIES

All in the family

Unlike Mendel's pea plants, which produced seeds every 90 days, patterns of human inheritance are not easy to study. Humans mature slowly, and many years pass between one generation and the next. Compared to other organisms, humans have few offspring. What we do have to aid the study of human inheritance are family trees and family histories.

Recently, researchers have developed techniques that enable them to study human genes directly. But most of our knowledge of human genetics still comes from studying the patterns of heredity in human populations and families.

Geneticists study family trees, or pedigrees, to learn about human inheritance patterns. A **pedigree** is a chart that shows how a trait and the genes that control it are inherited within a family. Pedigrees are used to

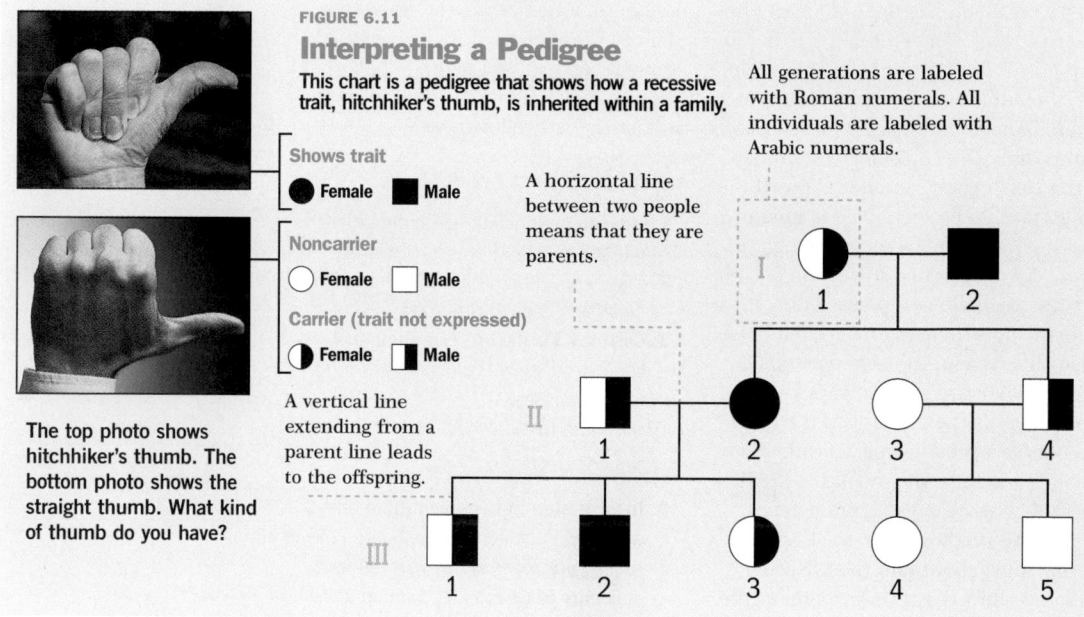

FIGURE 6.11
Interpreting a Pedigree
This chart is a pedigree that shows how a recessive trait, hitchhiker's thumb, is inherited within a family.

All generations are labeled with Roman numerals. All individuals are labeled with Arabic numerals.

Shows trait
● Female ■ Male

Noncarrier
○ Female □ Male

Carrier (trait not expressed)
◑ Female ◧ Male

A horizontal line between two people means that they are parents.

A vertical line extending from a parent line leads to the offspring.

The top photo shows hitchhiker's thumb. The bottom photo shows the straight thumb. What kind of thumb do you have?

From the Teacher's Resource Package, use:
- Section Review 6.4, Activity Recordsheet 6-3, Critical Thinking Exercise 6 and Enrichment Topic 6-3 from Unit 2 Review Module
- Lab 14: "Pedigree Analysis"
- Issues and Decision Making 6-1

Relevant technology resources include:
- Spanish Student Edition CD-ROM
- Teacher's Resource Planner CD-ROM

study all sorts of families, from human families to fruit fly families. To develop a human pedigree, geneticists interview family members and friends of the family to collect as much information as they can about a family's genetic history and traits.

The pedigree in *Figure 6.11* traces a trait called hitchhiker's thumb through three generations of a family. Hitchhiker's thumb is a recessive trait. Compare the two thumbs shown in *Figure 6.11*. Do you have this trait?

As you now know, recessive alleles are not expressed in the presence of the dominant allele. If a pedigree is tracking a recessive trait, there may be heterozygous individuals who have one allele for the trait but do not express the trait because the dominant allele is also present. An individual who carries a recessive trait that is not expressed is called a **carrier.** What are the symbols for a carrier according to *Figure 6.11*?

Pedigrees help to determine the inheritance of some alleles and predict them in offspring. You will now learn about two kinds of genetic traits: those caused by recessive alleles and those caused by dominant alleles.

RECESSIVE TRAITS

It takes two

You know that a trait caused by recessive alleles is not expressed in a heterozygous person. While a recessive allele that can produce a genetic disorder does not affect a carrier's health, a carrier can pass the recessive allele on to offspring. Passed from generation to generation, the allele remains in the population.

Tay-Sachs disease, a fatal genetic disorder, is caused by a recessive allele. A person who is homozygous for the Tay-Sachs allele is not able to metabolize (break down) a particular

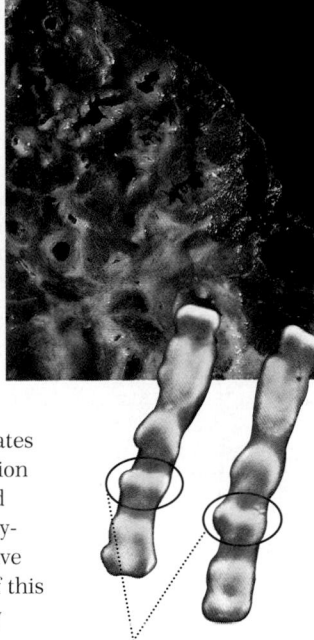

type of lipid, so the lipid accumulates in the brain. This lipid accumulation eventually results in blindness and brain damage. Individuals with Tay-Sachs disease do not usually survive more than a few years. Carriers of this disease, however, do not show any effects of Tay-Sachs, and thus the allele is preserved in the population.

Cystic fibrosis (SIS-tik fy-BROH-sis) is another disease caused by recessive alleles. The gene for cystic fibrosis is located on a region of chromosome 7, as shown in *Figure 6.12*. Cystic fibrosis is a genetic disorder that results in an excessive secretion of thick mucus. This secretion accumulates in the digestive tract and in the lungs. Left untreated, children with cystic fibrosis die at a very young age. However, current treatments are prolonging life into young adulthood and beyond.

Albinism is another example of a condition caused by a recessive allele. True albinos have no skin pigment. You may have seen albino rabbits, which have completely white fur and pink eyes. A person who is homozygous for the albino trait cannot produce the skin pigment melanin. People with albinism typically have very pale skin and whitish-blond hair, and can be of any racial background.

FIGURE 6.12

The gene for cystic fibrosis is located on this region of chromosome 7. The image at top left is of a normal lung. The top right image is of the lung of a person with cystic fibrosis.

❶ The symbol for a carrier is either a circle or a square half black and half white.

TEACH

Science History

Point out that the frequency of Tay-Sachs disease was observed to be high among Jews from northeastern Poland, southern Lithuania, and the area of White Russia adjoining Lithuania. Because of the decimation of the Jewish population during World War II, the incidence of Tay-Sachs increased in the Jews from these areas. Discuss why the rare incidence of Tay-Sachs in Asian Jews would be useful information to geneticists. (The rarity may indicate that Tay-Sachs is an inherited trait.)

Think Critically

Have students determine the accuracy of this statement: *If people who are carriers for a certain trait never mate with another carrier, the trait will eventually die out in the general population.* (The trait will not appear in an offspring, but some individuals will probably be carriers.)

Science History

Albinism in people has been noted as far back as the first century. European explorers spoke of white natives in Africa and in Indian groups in Central and North America. For years albinism was regarded as an inborn error of metabolism resulting from a lack of some end-product rather than the excess of some biochemical product. Today we know that albinism is a complex and inherited genetic disorder.

SUPER READ! **Finding Supporting Details** To practice strategies for effective reading, use pages 35-36 in *Super Read!*

FIGURE 6.13
Albinism is a recessive trait that affects humans of all races.

Like other recessive traits, a single copy of a gene for albinism results in the normal, pigmented phenotype. Without a pedigree or information on family history, a person would be unaware that he or she was a carrier of the trait. Unlike many recessive traits, however, albinism can be caused by several different alleles on different chromosomes. Two parents could have the albinism trait, but if the trait in each parent were caused by different alleles, the children of such parents would have the normal, pigmented phenotype.

DOMINANT TRAITS

Some alleles are more expressive than others

Dominant alleles control many human traits, including the inheritance of freckles, widow's peak, farsightedness, broad lips, and polydactyly—extra fingers and toes. You will recall that a dominant allele is always expressed in a person's phenotype. In many cases, a person who has inherited a dominant allele that produces a fatal disorder is likely to die before passing the allele on to offspring.

If a disorder caused by dominant alleles results in early death, then it cannot be passed on. For this reason,

disorders caused by dominant alleles are much less common than those caused by recessive alleles. A few dominant genetic disorders, however, do not show up until years after sexual maturity. In such cases the dominant allele may be passed on to offspring.

One example of a dominant allele disorder is Huntington disease. This disease is a fatal genetic disorder that results in deterioration of the nervous system, particularly the brain. Although a dominant allele causes Huntington disease, people typically do not develop symptoms until they are in their late thirties or early forties. By that time they may have already passed the allele on to their offspring. Huntington disease can now be identified before onset with a test that involves analysis of the genetic material.

FRONTIERS IN BIOLOGY

Genetic counseling

A couple aware of genetic disorders in their family histories and who are planning to have children may seek genetic counseling. A genetic counselor provides prospective parents with information about the probabilities of passing genetic disorders on to their offspring.

FIGURE 6.14
The gene for Huntington disease is located in this region on chromosome 4. The image on the left shows the brain of a Huntington patient. The image on the right shows the brain of a nonaffected person.

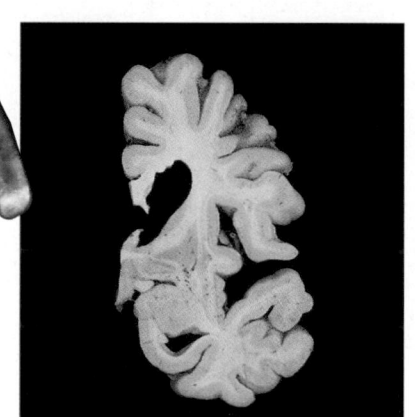

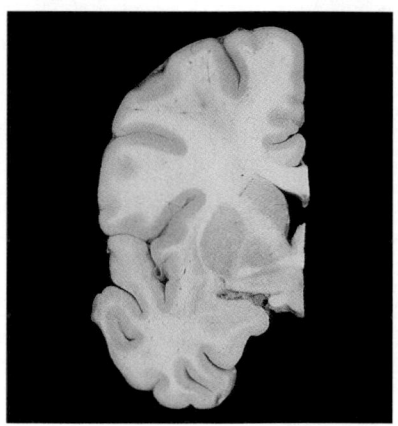

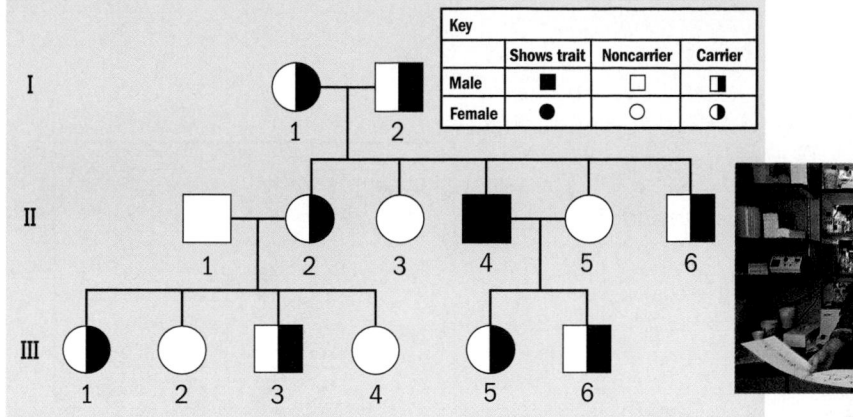

Physical Science

Ferric chloride is used to determine PKU in infants. Urine samples from infants with the disease turn olive green with the addition of ferric chloride.

Genetic counselors begin their work by tracing the histories of both families. They then look for inherited disorders. A pedigree is developed, showing the probability of one or both parents carrying certain alleles. The probability that certain disorders will occur in the offspring can then be determined. With this information, the couple can consider the risk of passing a particular allele on to their children.

In addition to pedigrees, molecular techniques are used to identify genetic problems including the presence of abnormal genes. For example, a test for the amount of a specific protein in the mother's body early in pregnancy can reveal if the fetus has an extra copy of a chromosome, a condition that can cause Down syndrome.

Another test, which is now conducted on almost all newborn babies, identifies a genetic disorder called phenylketonuria (FEN-il-KEE-toh-NYOO-ree-uh), or PKU. A person with PKU lacks the enzymes needed to break down the amino acid phenylalanine, which is found in milk and many other foods. Without these enzymes, the amino acid accumulates in the body and begins to damage nerve cells. Untreated, PKU can lead to severe developmental disabilities and death. Sometimes, giving birth to a child with PKU is the first indication to parents that they are carriers for the allele.

PKU can be treated when diagnosed early. A special diet lacking phenylalanine prevents damage to the nerve cells. The child can grow normally and adopt a normal diet during adulthood. Thanks to genetic counselors, PKU and other disorders can be detected and treated early in life.

CHECKPOINT 6.4

1. What does a pedigree show?
2. Describe recessive and dominant alleles in humans.
3. **Critical Thinking** What steps can parents take to determine the likelihood of passing certain genes on to their offspring? Cite specific examples.

Build on What You Know

4. Suppose two parents are both carriers for a recessive disorder. Make a diagram showing all the possible pairings of their gametes after meiosis. *(Need to jog your memory? Revisit relevant concepts in Chapter 5, Section 5.2.)*

FIGURE 6.15
The pedigree (left) is for PKU. Genetic counselors prepare pedigrees for prospective parents to assess the risk of passing on disease alleles. Which individual in the pedigree has PKU? ❶

Ears to You!

You have learned about traits in pea plants, but did you know that the laws of inheritance decide what kind of ear wax you have? There are two types of ear wax: sticky/wet (W) and dry (w). What kind do you have?

3 ASSESS

Evaluate Understanding

To determine the students' knowledge about pedigrees, ask:

- **How can a trait not expressed in parents or grandparents occur in offspring?** (A recessive trait can be carried for many generations and not be expressed until two carriers have offspring.)
- **Why are some dominant and fatal disorders passed on through offspring while others are not?** (Some disorders cause death in childhood; others do not develop until after maturity.)

Reteach

Have students list traits that their parents have but which are not present in any of the offspring. Use Figure 6.15 to help students understand how a pedigree can show how parents can have these traits even though none of the offspring do.

Chapter 6 Fundamentals of Genetics **145**

CHECKPOINT 6.4

1. It shows the history of traits in a family.
2. Dominant alleles are always expressed when they are present in the genotype. Recessive alleles are only expressed when both alleles are present in the genotype.
3. **Applying** Parents can work with a genetic counselor, who will construct a pedigree tracing a specific trait in the family's history. For example, counselors can trace PKU and Huntington disease through pedigrees.
4. Diagrams should show the following pairings: *AA, Aa, aA, aa*

❶ II-4 male

 **LAB ZONE** Investigate It!

TEAM WORK Using a Pedigree

Lab Tips

If students are having trouble interpreting the pedigree for deafness, suggest that they use the pedigree in Figure 6.15 as a model.

Have students answer the following questions as they work through the pedigree: Are the heterozygotes hearing or deaf? If they are deaf, then the gene for deafness is dominant, if they are hearing, then the gene is recessive.

Hypothesis Help

Tell the students that no one in the parent generation is deaf, but three or more carry the gene for deafness. In this particular pedigree, the allele for deafness is recessive.

Lab Extension

Have students extend the pedigree for deafness one more generation. Use two different sets of partners for the fourth generation. Each set of parents should have four offspring. Use Punnett squares to determine which offspring inherit the allele for deafness. For the first set, select partners who are all carriers. For the second set, select partners who do not carry the gene for deafness. Compare the offspring of each set of parents.

Open Ended

Have students make their own pedigree and exchange it with a partner, then follow the steps outlined in the activity.

Time Required
■ 30 minutes

Using a Pedigree

WHAT YOU WILL DO Use a pedigree chart to determine parents' genotypes

SKILLS YOU WILL USE Observing, recording data, predicting

Propose a Hypothesis
Based on the pedigree shown here, form a hypothesis concerning whether the allele for deafness is dominant or recessive.

Conduct Your Experiment
1 Copy the pedigree and the key onto a piece of paper and study it. Label each individual in the pedigree with their phenotype: hearing or deaf.
2 Analyze the pattern in the inheritance of the deafness trait. Does the trait skip generations or show up in every generation? Does it affect all the members of any generation?
3 Use your analysis and what you know about patterns of inheritance to infer the genotype of each individual. Write the genotypes on your pedigree. It is possible that you will not be able to infer the complete genotype of every individual.

Analyze Your Data
1 What is the genotype of an individual with deafness? Can a deaf family member have more than one genotype?
2 What is the genotype of a hearing individual? Can a hearing family member have more than one genotype? Are any hearing individuals carriers?
3 Is the allele for deafness dominant or recessive?

Draw Conclusions
Describe what you have concluded about the dominant or recessive inheritance of deafness in this family. Write a paragraph discussing what you learned in this activity. Support your conclusion with your observations.

Design a Related Experiment
Prepare a pedigree for three generations of an imaginary family that has another trait.

Key

	Deaf	Hearing
Male	■	□
Female	●	○

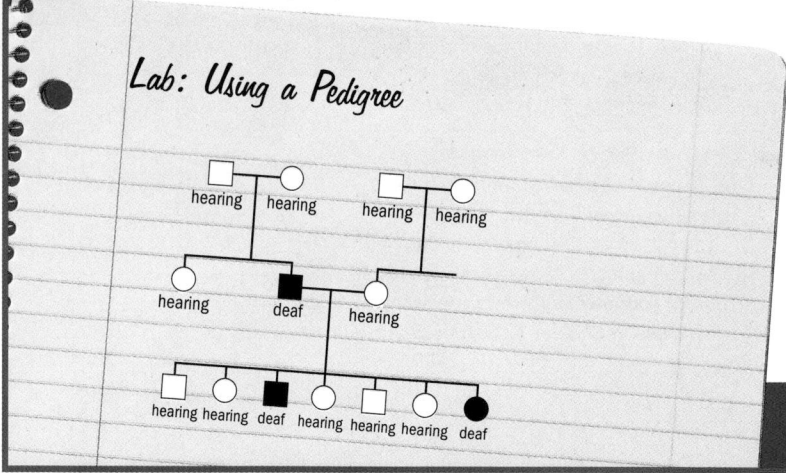

Lab: Using a Pedigree

Analyze Your Data

1 An individual with deafness can only have one genotype: *dd*.
2 A hearing individual can have the genotypes *DD* or *Dd*. In this pedigree, most of the hearing individuals are carriers with the genotype *Dd*.
3 The allele for deafness is recessive, since it did not show up in the first generation.

Design a Related Experiment

Possible human traits for recessive or dominant genes: attached or unattached (dominant) earlobes; ability to taste the chemical PTC (dominant).

6.5 Difficult Predictions

Caterpillar camouflage capers

Certain caterpillars may vary their appearance to resemble either a twig or a flower. The caterpillar's phenotype is determined by its diet. If the caterpillar eats oak twigs, then it appears as shown at the left. If it eats oak flowers, it appears as shown at the right. This relationship between diet and appearance is the basis for the caterpillar's camouflage.

What you'll learn

IDEAS
- To compare and contrast patterns of inheritance that do not follow Mendel's laws
- To explain how traits are influenced by the environment

WORDS
incomplete dominance, codominance, polygenic trait, multiple alleles, pleiotropy

INTERMEDIATE INHERITANCE
Genes in between

For the pea plant traits that Mendel studied, one allele was always dominant over the other. However, traits with two distinct forms are rare in nature. Many genes do not have purely dominant and recessive alleles. Instead, these genes show a form of intermediate inheritance.

In intermediate inheritance, the heterozygous offspring have a trait that is not exactly like the trait of either purebred parent. The phenotype of the heterozygous offspring shows the effects of more than one allele. You will now read about three forms of intermediate inheritance— incomplete dominance, codominance, and polygenic inheritance.

Incomplete dominance When two different alleles for the same trait combine, but neither allele "wins" expression over the other, the offspring have a form of intermediate

FIGURE 6.16
Incomplete Dominance in Snapdragons

Incomplete dominance occurs when the allele of neither parent is fully expressed and the offspring's phenotype is intermediate between that of the two parents. In this example, white and red flowers produce pink flowers.

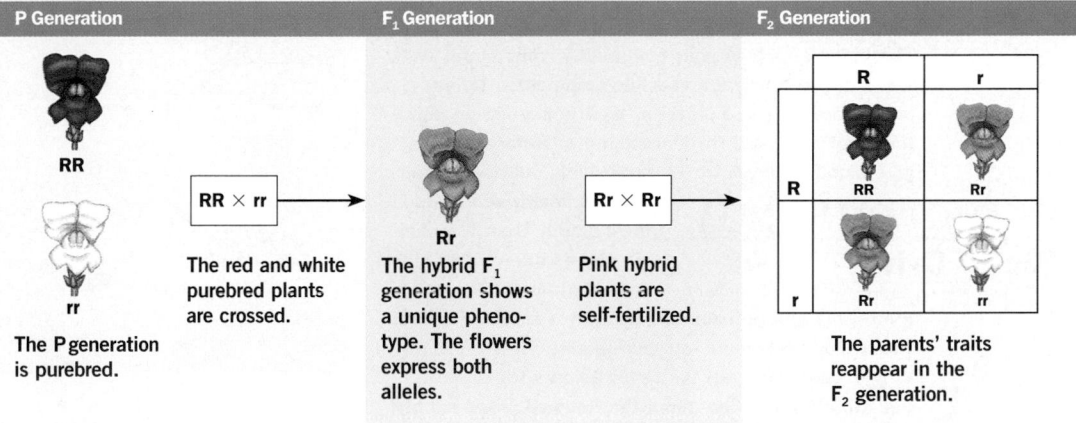

P Generation	F₁ Generation	F₂ Generation

RR

rr

The P generation is purebred.

RR × rr

The red and white purebred plants are crossed.

Rr

The hybrid F₁ generation shows a unique phenotype. The flowers express both alleles.

Rr × Rr

Pink hybrid plants are self-fertilized.

	R	r
R	RR	Rr
r	Rr	rr

The parents' traits reappear in the F₂ generation.

Chapter 6 Fundamentals of Genetics **147**

STUDENT RESOURCES

From the Teacher's Resource Package, use:
- Section Review 6.5, Enrichment Topic 6-4, Vocabulary Review 6, and Chapter 6 Tests from Unit 2 Review Module
- Issues and Decision Making 6-2

TECHNOLOGY RESOURCES

Relevant technology resources include:
- Spanish Student Edition CD-ROM
- Teacher's Resource Planner CD-ROM
- TestWorks CD-ROM: Chapter 6 Tests

1 ENGAGE

Use the Visual

Have students study the photos that open this section. Ask:

- **Why is it important for the caterpillar to be camouflaged?** (To avoid being eaten by predators)

Teacher Demo

Hold up a bottle of red beads and a bottle of white beads. Have students identify the colors. Then thoroughly mix half the red beads with half the white beads in another jar. Hold the jar up and have the students squint while looking at the jar. Ask:

- **Why do the beads appear pink?** (When neither color is clearly evident, neither is dominant.)

2 TEACH

Use The Visual

Guide students through Figure 6.16. Help them to understand the results of incomplete dominance in contrast to complete dominance. Ask:

- **If the R allele was completely dominant, what would be the phenotype of the F₁ generation?** (Red)
- **If the R allele was completely dominant, what would be the phenotypes of the F₂ generation?** (RR and Rr would be red, rr would be white.)

Everyday Biology

Ask students to cite examples of foods high in saturated fat and examples of foods high in unsaturated fats.

Teacher Demo

Show the class two plastic plates on which are two piles of different colored beans placed side by side. Explain that each plate represents an offspring and each color represents a genetic trait. In Plate 1, swirl the beans together in bands to show incomplete dominance. In Plate 2, mix the beans thoroughly in one pile to show codominance. Ask:

- **How are the "traits" expressed in "offspring 1"?** (Both traits are expressed, but not completely.)
- **How are the "traits" expressed in "offspring 2"?** (Both traits are expressed together in an even mix.)

In the Community

You may want to invite a speaker from the American Red Cross to talk to the class about blood drives, donor requirements, and screening procedures for donated blood. Donors must be in good health, between the ages of 17 and 75, and weigh 110 pounds or more. Before donating blood, donors must complete a questionnaire about their general health.

❶ Yes; eggs can increase cholesterol.

148

Hold the Eggs

Diet can affect your blood cholesterol level whether you are HH, Hh, or hh. Saturated fats in your diet increase blood cholesterol, whereas polyunsaturated or monounsaturated fatty acids lower blood cholesterol. Eggs are a food high in saturated fats. Do eggs increase your cholesterol level? ❶

---

inheritance called incomplete dominance. In **incomplete dominance,** heterozygous offspring show a phenotype that is in between the phenotypes of the two homozygous parents. Neither allele is fully expressed.

One example of incomplete dominance is flower color in snapdragons, such as those shown in *Figure 6.16* on page 147. If a snapdragon plant with red flowers is crossed with a white-flowered snapdragon plant, the offspring will have pink flowers. The alleles have not blended to make pink alleles. The red and white alleles remain separate in the snapdragon cells. Only the phenotype is intermediate, giving the appearance of pink flowers. Half the gametes of a pink snapdragon plant carry the allele for red flowers, and half carry the allele for white flowers.

Incomplete dominance is also responsible for the coat colors of many animals. Roan cows, whose coats are primarily red with white hairs, are offspring of red cows and white cows. A palomino—a creamy-golden horse with a pale mane and tail—is the offspring of a chestnut-colored horse and a white horse.

An example of a human trait that shows incomplete dominance is

hypercholesterolemia (HI-per-coh-LESS-ter-ruh-LEE-mee-ah). People with this disorder have too much ("hyper-") cholesterol in their blood. Cholesterol is a steroid produced by our bodies and used to make and repair cell membranes.

People with normal cholesterol levels have the homozygous dominant genotype (*HH*). People with this genotype generally can maintain healthy blood cholesterol levels with a low-fat diet and exercise. About one in 500 people are heterozygous (*Hh*) for the trait, and their cholesterol levels are twice as high as normal. Diet, exercise, and medical treatments can help to reduce their cholesterol levels. About one in a million people are homozygous recessive (*hh*) for the trait. Their cholesterol levels are about five times greater than normal. This rare homozygous recessive condition is very serious—it has even caused heart attacks in two-year-old children.

Codominance As you just learned, incomplete dominance occurs when two alleles are partially expressed and the offspring have a phenotype that is intermediate, or in-between, two parent phenotypes. In

---

IN THE COMMUNITY
Blood Drive

The blood supply in your community, your state, and the entire country is a valuable commodity. When people are hurt in a disaster, emergency aid organizations put out a call for blood donors. Before donors give blood, a physician or nurse finds out about their general health and tests their blood. Then a technician takes one pint of blood from the donor. The donor then rests and perhaps has juice or a snack. Find out about blood drives in your community. How often do they occur? What are the requirements for donors? For more information about the national blood supply, visit *http://genetics.biosurf.com.*

FACTS AND FIGURES

Atherosclerosis is a cardiovascular condition in which arteries are narrowed by plaque deposits. Cholesterol, which has a vital role in the development of atherosclerosis, is a lipid that is a normal part of cell membranes. One kind of cholesterol, called low-density lipoprotein, or LDL, increases the tendency of plaque to form in arteries. The other form of cholesterol, high-density lipoprotein, HDL, reduces the tendency to develop plaque. The higher the ratio of LDL is to HDL, the greater is the risk of developing atherosclerosis.

FIGURE 6.17

The Eyes Have It

Human eye color is a polygenic trait — many genes control the pigment melanin in the eye. What differences can you see between these two eyes?

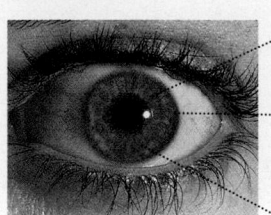
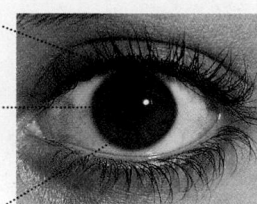

Tone of pigment
The tone, or color of the eye pigment differs for each eye.

Amount of pigment
Blue eyes have less pigment than brown eyes.

Position of pigment
Eye pigment is not distributed evenly, creating patterns.

codominance, both alleles in the heterozygote express themselves fully. Because both of the alleles are fully expressed, both alleles are equally emphasized in the notation.

An example of a codominant trait in humans is blood type. The letters *A* and *B* that identify blood types refer to the two different carbohydrates that coat the surface of red blood cells. If you have type A blood, you have type A carbohydrate on your red blood cells. If you have type B blood, you have type B carbohydrate on your red blood cells. And if you have blood type AB, you have both carbohydrate types. People who have neither carbohydrate on their red blood cells have type O.

These alleles are represented by an *I*, and a superscript *A* or *B* to indicate whether the allele codes for type A or type B blood. The two alleles are I^A and I^B. If you received the blood type A allele (I^A) from one parent and the blood type B allele (I^B) from the other, your genotype is $I^A I^B$, and your phenotype is AB blood. You will find out more about blood types later in this section.

Polygenic traits Most traits are affected by more than one gene. A trait controlled by two or more genes

is called a **polygenic trait** (the prefix "poly-" means "many"). Your eye color is an example of a polygenic trait. As you can see in *Figure 6.17*, the tone, amount, and distribution of the pigment melanin all play a role in determining eye color. These characteristics are determined by many different gene pairs. And, like Mendel's pea plant genes, each gene pair for eye color might be inherited independently. Human skin color is also a polygenic trait. Many genes control the amount of the melanin in the skin.

MULTIPLE ALLELES AND PLEIOTROPY

Many alleles and traits

Most genes have more than two alleles. If three or more alleles are found in the population, we say these genes have **multiple alleles**. Human blood type genes are an example of a codominant trait and of a trait with multiple alleles. Blood types are phenotypes that can be produced by three different alleles—I^A, I^B, and i. Each person has only two of these alleles, one from each parent.

As you already learned, the alleles for A and B blood types are codominant. If you have blood type O, then

FIGURE 6.18

This table shows the different blood genotypes and phenotypes. How do blood types show codominance? ❷

Blood Groups	
Phenotypes	**Genotypes**
A	$I^A I^A$ or $I^A i$
B	$I^B I^B$ or $I^B i$
AB	$I^A I^B$
O	ii

Chapter 6 Fundamentals of Genetics **149**

Use the Visual

Have students study the table in Figure 6.18. The genotype with type O blood is identified as *ii*. Draw three blank Punnett squares on the board and have students identify the phenotypes that would occur with an $I^A I^A$ and an *ii* parent, with an $I^A I^A$ and an $I^B I^B$ parent, and with an $I^B I^B$ and an *ii* parent. Ask:

- **Which offspring have type O blood?** (The ii genotype)
- **Which offspring have type A blood?** (The $I^A I^A$ or $I^A i$ genotype)
- **Which offspring have type B blood?** (The $I^B I^B$ or $I^B i$ genotype)
- **Which offspring have type AB blood?** (The $I^A I^B$ genotype)

Think Critically

Ask the students to discuss how the following statement can be true: *The eye color of offspring of parents who both have the brown-eye gene and the blue-eye gene can be green, hazel-brown, hazel-green, a variety of blue shades, a variety of brown shades, yellow, or one blue eye and one brown eye.*

❷ The alleles for A and B blood types are codominant so individuals who have both alleles are type AB rather than type A or type B.

Mathematics

List the percent distribution of blood types in the United States on the board. Type O-44%, type A-42%, type B-10%, type AB-4%. Ask students who know their blood type to stand and count the number of students with each blood type. Have students determine the percentage of each blood type represented in the class.

Use the Visual

Direct students to Figure 6.19. Point out that a normal red blood cell is donut-shaped and has a slight depression in the center. A sickled red blood cell has a distorted, elongated shape. After the hemoglobin in the red blood cell releases its oxygen in the capillaries, the sickled cell impedes the blood flow through the vessel, lengthening the time it takes for the sickled cell to return to the lung for oxygenation, and increasing the degree of sickling. The increasingly sickled cell slows the blood flow even further, creating irreversibly distorted cells. These sickled cells live only a few weeks compared to three months for a normal blood cell.

Explain

Persons who are heterozygous for the sickle-cell trait have some sickled cells, but they are less likely to contract malaria than persons with normal red blood cells. Should they do so, they usually have a very mild form of the disease. The reason for the immunity is that the malarial parasite, which spends its life inside the red blood cell, does not flourish well when the cells have some sickle-cell hemoglobin.

FIGURE 6.19
Sickled red blood cells stick together, jamming the circulatory system. What is the difference between the sickled cell (left) and the normal red blood cell (right)? ❶

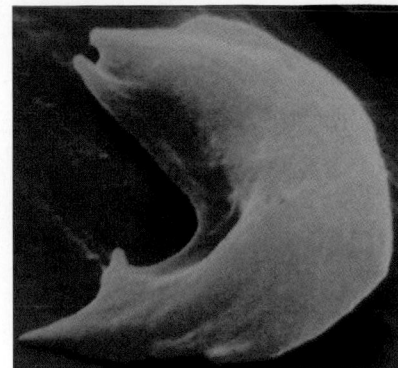

you have neither type A nor type B carbohydrates coating your red blood cells. O blood type is recessive, so the allele for O blood type is i. Thus, there are four blood types—A, B, AB, and O—and three blood type alleles—I^A, I^B, and i. *Figure 6.18* shows the phenotypes and genotypes for blood.

Another variation on the simple patterns of inheritance seen in Mendel's pea plants is called pleiotropy (plee-AH-troh-pee). **Pleiotropy** occurs when a single gene affects more than one trait.

Sickle-cell disease is an example of pleiotropy in humans. The allele that causes sickle-cell disease affects the shape of red blood cells. As you can see in *Figure 6.19,* blood cells in people with sickle-cell disease have a bent, or sickled, shape. The sickled cells do not flow well through the body and tend to clump together, blocking and damaging parts of the circulatory system. Damage to the circulatory system can have many phenotypic results. People with sickle-cell disease can experience weakness, anemia, brain damage, spleen damage and heart damage. Because of its numerous effects on the body, this allele is an example of pleiotropy.

ENVIRONMENTAL EFFECTS

Fair-weather genes

As you have discovered, many factors—including the activity of other genes—can influence the way a gene is expressed. Genes can also be affected by the environment—both the external environment and the environment inside an organism. In fact, phenotype is a combination of genetic and environmental influences.

Climate conditions are an outside environmental factor that can influence the expression of alleles. An

FIGURE 6.20
The Himalayan rabbit's fur color is affected by temperature. Why are the tips of the rabbit's ears darker than its body? ❷

MULTICULTURAL PERSPECTIVE

Anthropologic studies on the worldwide distribution of the blood-type B allele indicate that the greatest frequency (30%) appears in central Asia. The B allele is 5% in western Europeans and is absent among Native Americans. Ask:

- **Why would the United States have a different statistical trend than Asia or Europe?** (America is a melting pot of different nations. When the nationalities intermarry, the blood type distribution changes in the offspring.)

unusual effect of temperature is seen in the Himalayan rabbit, as you can see in *Figure 6.20*. This rabbit is normally covered with white fur, whereas its ears, nose, and feet are black. This pattern occurs because most of the rabbit's body is generally warmer than its extremities. Body temperature affects the expression of genes that code for fur color. When researchers remove a patch of hair from the body and cool the skin as new fur grows back, the new fur is black. When they shave hair from the feet or ears and keep those areas warm, the fur that grows back is white.

Environmental temperature also affects wing coloration patterns of the western white butterfly, found in the west of North America. These butterflies need their body temperature to be between 28°C and 40°C to take off in flight. Researchers have found that butterflies reaching adulthood in the spring exhibit darker wing coloration patterns than butterflies that mature in the summer. As you may know, dark colors absorb more heat. As a result of their darker wing patterns, the butterflies that live during the cooler spring weather will be able to reach a warm enough temperature to fly. In this case, the expression of the wing color genes is affected by day length, which varies from season to season.

Another example of environmental influence on gene expression is flower color in hydrangeas. Hydrangea flowers are either blue or pink, depending on soil acidity. If the soil is rather acidic, the hydrangeas have blue flowers. If the soil is neutral or somewhat basic, then the blooms are pink.

Changes in the social environment of an organism can also affect gene expression. The Japanese goby fish can change its sex back and forth in response to changes in its social environment. If a large male goby leaves a population, a female goby will become

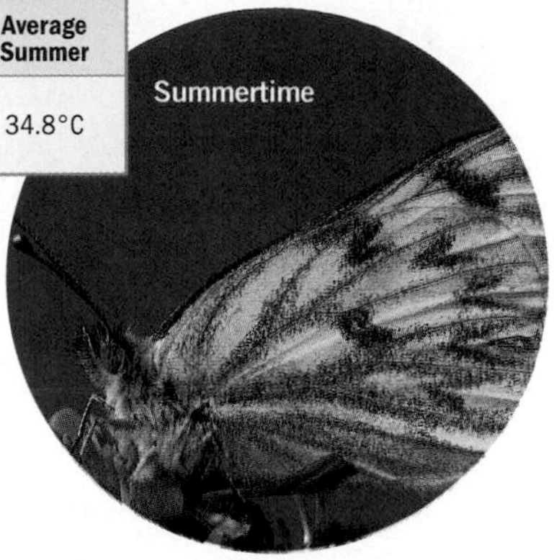

FIGURE 6.21

Western white butterflies have darker wing patterns if they hatch in the spring. The dark wing color regulates temperature, a vital adaptation because the butterflies need to reach a certain temperature to fly. What is the temperature difference between a flying springtime butterfly and the air? ❸

Springtime

Summertime

Temperature Table

Required for Takeoff	Average Spring	Average Summer
28–40°C	26.5°C	34.8°C

male. If another large male enters that goby population, this new male turns back into a female.

Gene expression can be influenced by the environment inside an organism's body. Although human height is determined by a form of polygenic inheritance, it is also affected by the nutrients in your diet. As you read earlier in this chapter, shyness can also be affected by genes. But, as individuals mature, the effect of genes on shyness diminishes, and the effect of the environment increases.

It is important to realize that the inheritance of shyness, height, and many other human traits is affected by genetics and also by the environment. In Chapter 8, you will learn more about effects of the environment on gene expression, particularly in the development of cancer.

Chapter 6 Fundamentals of Genetics **151**

Think Critically

Ask students to give examples that show how the following statement is true. *The reaction of an organism to its environment can protect the organism from its predators or cause its death.*

Build Writing Skills

Ask students to select two or three environmental factors and research how one organism is adversely affected and another is favorably affected by each factor. Have them write a brief prediction on the survival of each organism.

❶ The sickle cell is bent rather than round.
❷ The tips of the rabbit's ears are colder than the rest of its body.
❸ 1.5°C

STS

Explain that twins can be fraternal or identical. Fraternal twins have entirely different chromosomes. Identical twins, have identical chromosomes, because the fertilized egg splits into two.

3 ASSESS

Evaluate Understanding

To assess students' understanding of gene expression, ask:

- **What is the difference between incomplete dominance and codominance?** (In incomplete dominance, each allele is only partially expressed; in codominance, each allele is completely expressed.)
- **What is the main difference between polygenic traits and pleiotropy?** (Polygenic traits are the result of action by more than one gene pair. Pleiotropy refers to a single gene that has more than one genetic effect.)

Reteach

Have students reread the section and identify which term, *incomplete dominance, codominance, polygenic trait,* or *pleiotropy,* applies to each of the following:

- **Red and white streaked flowers** (Incomplete dominance)
- **Pink pea flowers** (Codominance)
- **Hazel-green eyes** (Polygenic trait)
- **Sickle cells** (Pleiotropy)

FIGURE 6.22
These teenage twins share a love for roller coasters. What other characteristics do they have in common? ❶

ISSUES IN BIOLOGY

The genetics of behavior

How can you determine if the inheritance of a trait is affected more by genetics or by the environment? This question—commonly expressed as "nature or nurture?"—is difficult to answer, especially for human traits. To find answers, some scientists study identical twins—people with the same genes—that have been separated at birth. Twins separated at birth or at a very young age and brought up by different families have different environments. These twins offer scientists an opportunity to study genetic and environmental influences.

Twin studies have shown some surprising results. For example, when one set of identical twin sisters met for the first time, each sister was wearing seven rings, three bracelets and a watch. Another set of identical twins were both named Jim by their adoptive parents. Both had dogs named Toy, married women named Linda, and named their sons James. Surveys of reunited twins found that, in addition to their shared habits, they also shared many opinions.

Although studies of identical twins separated at birth suggest some links between heredity and behavior, identical twins do not lead identical lives. Despite having similarities that could be explained by their identical genes, these separated twins also exhibited differences as a result of the different environments in which each grew up. This fascinating mix of similarities and differences gives researchers a unique opportunity to explore the effects of heredity and environment.

CHECKPOINT 6.5

1. Name and describe the forms of intermediate inheritance.
2. Describe a trait that is affected by the environment.
3. **Critical Thinking** When geneticist Lucien Cuénot attempted to produce a strain of mice homozygous for the dominant yellow-fur allele, all of the homozygous offspring died. This is an example of what kind of intermediate inheritance?

Build on What You Know

4. When scientists study identical twins, what variable is controlled?
(Need to jog your memory? Revisit relevant concepts in Chapter 1, Section 1.3.)

 What are some patterns of inheritance that make traits predictable?

CHECKPOINT 6.5

1. Incomplete dominance-both alleles expressed somewhat; codominance-both alleles fully expressed; polygenic inheritance-one trait controlled by many alleles
2. Answers will vary. Himalayan rabbit fur color is controlled by temperature. Hydrangea color is determined by soil acidity.
3. **Identifying cause and effect** Pleiotropy, in this case, the dominant allele that produced yellow fur in mice was also lethal when homozygous.
4. The identical twin's identical genetic information serves as the control variable.

❶ Answers will vary

Chapter 6 Review

 **THE BIG IDEA!**
6.1–6.2 Traits are inherited in a consistent pattern.
6.3–6.5 There are patterns of inheritance that make some traits predictable.

Sum It Up

Use the following summary to review the main concepts in this chapter.

6.1 Patterns of Inheritance

- Genetics is the study of heritable characteristics, or traits.
- Gregor Mendel used mathematics to study the inheritance of traits.
- Alleles are alternate forms of a gene. In a hybrid organism, the dominant allele is expressed.

6.2 Principles of Inheritance

- The chromosome theory of heredity states that the inheritance of traits is controlled by genes, which are located on chromosomes.
- The genotype of an organism is all the alleles for a trait; the phenotype is the trait.
- The Law of Segregation describes how chromosome pairs separate during meiosis.
- The Law of Independent Assortment states that gene pairs separate independently of each other.
- The Law of Dominance states that the dominant allele, if present, will be expressed.

6.3 Genetics and Predictions

- Scientists use probability to predict traits in offspring.
- A Punnett square organizes information in order to make genetic predictions.

6.4 Predictions and People

- Pedigrees are used to trace the history of traits among relatives.
- Genetic counselors help identify the likelihood of a trait being passed to offspring.

6.5 Difficult Predictions

- Incomplete dominance, codominance, and multiple alleles can result in intermediate phenotypes.
- Genes can have more than two alleles.
- Alleles can have many phenotypic effects.

Use Terms and Concepts

**Use each of the following words or terms in a complete sentence.
If you need to review a meaning, turn to the page indicated.**

genetics (p. 130)
trait (p. 130)
purebred (p. 131)
hybrid (p. 131)
genes (p. 133)
allele (p. 133)

dominant allele (p. 133)
recessive allele (p. 133)
chromosome theory of
  heredity (p. 134)
genotype (p. 134)
phenotype (p. 135)
homozygous (p. 135)

heterozygous (p. 135)
Punnett square (p. 139)
test cross (p. 141)
pedigree (p. 142)
carrier (p. 143)
incomplete dominance
  (p. 148)

codominance (p. 149)
polygenic trait (p. 149)
multiple alleles (p. 149)
pleiotropy (p. 150)

Review the Big Ideas

Before your students begin the Chapter Review, you may wish to discuss the Big Ideas that were covered in this chapter. Explain that traits are inherited in certain patterns that enable geneticists to predict whether or not traits will be expressed in offspring. Mendel's laws, Punnett squares, and pedigrees are examples of tools that geneticists use to predict how and if genetic material will be inherited.

Answers

1. phenotype
2. codominance
3. genetics
4. chromosome theory of heredity
5. Law of Dominance
6. T
7. F: In Mendel's experiments, the F_1 generation was always heterozygous for the studied trait.
8. T
9. T
10. F: A Punnett square can be used to show all possible outcomes for genetic crosses.
11. Incomplete dominance, codominance, pleiotropy, polygenic traits, and multiple alleles.
12. A purebred organism is homozygous for a trait. A hybrid organism is heterozgous for a trait.
13. When a purebred dominant organism is crossed with homozygous recessive organism, all of the offspring have the dominant phenotype. When a heterozygous organism is crossed with a homozygous recessive organism, half of the offspring have the dominant phenotype, and half have the recessive phenotype.
14. Microscopic observation of stained chromosomes revealed that they behave like Mendel's factors: they separate during meiosis, occur in pairs, and sort independently.
15. The pea traits that Mendel studied had two distinct alleles. In addition, peas reproduce quickly and have a structure that enables control of pollination.

154

Use Your Word Power

COMPLETION **Write the word or phrase that best completes each statement.**

1. The _____ of an organism is the trait that is observed.

2. In _____ , both alleles are fully expressed in the heterozygous condition.

3. The study of the inheritance of traits is called _____ .

4. Similarities between Mendel's factors and the behavior of chromosomes led Sutton to propose the _____ .

5. The _____ describes how a dominant trait is expressed if the allele is present.

TRUE-FALSE **Write true if the statement is true. If the statement is false, replace the underlined word(s) to make the statement true.**

6. A <u>carrier</u> of a trait does not express the allele for that trait.

7. In Mendel's experiments, the F_1 generation was always <u>homozygous</u> for the studied trait.

8. The hidden <u>recessive trait</u> of the F_1 generation always appears in the F_2 generation.

9. Both of the alleles of a gene pair make up an organism's <u>genotype</u>.

10. A <u>test cross</u> can be used to show all possible outcomes for genetic crosses.

Show What You Know

11. What patterns of inheritance do not follow Mendel's laws?

12. What is the difference between a purebred organism and a hybrid organism?

13. How is a test cross used to distinguish the homozygous dominant genotype from the heterozygous phenotype?

14. Summarize the evidence that led to the chromosome theory of heredity.

15. What qualities of pea plants made them a good choice for Mendel's experiments?

16. How do genetic counselors use pedigrees?

17. What is the difference between incomplete dominance and codominance?

18. Why are twin studies performed in genetics?

19. **Make a Concept Map** Complete the concept map below by adding the following terms: alleles, genes, chromosomes, dominant.

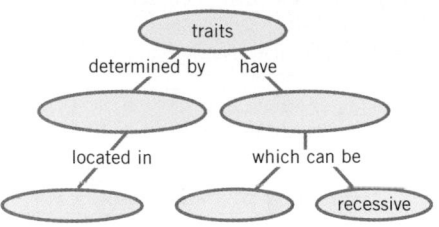

Take It Further

20. **Applying Concepts** In pea plants, round seed shape is dominant over wrinkled seed shape. Gray seed coat color is dominant over white seed coat color. Use a Punnett square to show a cross between a purebred plant with round seeds and gray seed coats and a purebred plant with wrinkled seeds and white coats. What traits are seen in the F_1 generation?

21. **Making a Prediction** Suppose Mendel had studied the inheritance of flower color in snapdragons instead of pea plants. How might his results have affected the laws that he developed?

22. **Analyzing Data** A man with blood type AB marries a woman with blood type O. Is it possible for them to have children with the same blood type as either of the parents? Use a Punnett square to explain your answer.

23. **Designing an Experiment** Petunias come in many different colors. Design an experiment to determine if purple or pink flower color is a dominant trait, or if there is an intermediate mode of inheritance.

16. They use pedigrees to study the history of a trait in the families of potential parents and to determine the probability of that trait being passed to offspring.

17. Incomplete dominance occurs when neither allele is fully expressed, whereas codominance occurs when both alleles are fully expressed.

18. Twin studies, especially of twins separated at birth, evaluate the effects of both environment and heredity on human traits.

19. Concept map: <u>traits</u> determined by <u>genes</u> located in <u>chromosomes</u> have <u>alleles</u> which can be <u>dominant</u> or <u>recessive</u>

20. All offspring would have round seeds with gray seed coats.

21. Because Mendel would have been

24. Interpreting a Graph This graph shows the traits of 1355 butterflies. Which traits are dominant? Which are recessive? Explain your answer.

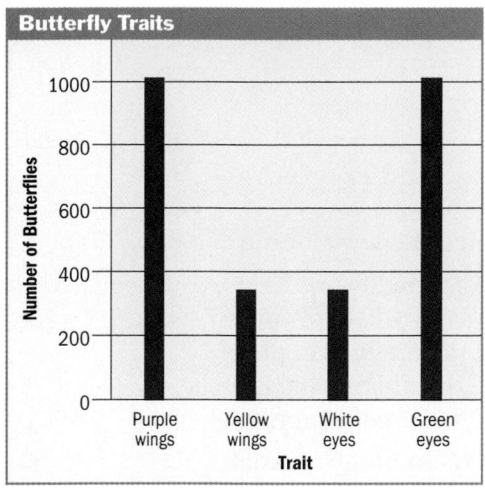

Butterfly Traits

25. Analyzing Data What form or forms of inheritance are indicated by the table below? Use the data to create a graph.

Average Height for Italian Males	
Year	Average Height (meters)
1938	1.66
1958	1.68
1970	1.70
1976	1.72
1982	1.73

Consider the Issues

26. Separated at Birth Twin studies are most reliable when comparing twins separated since birth. Sometimes the participants are not told that they are participating in a twin study nor that they have a twin. What are the pros and cons of this process?

Make New Connections

27. Biology and Art Many artists, such as Charles Neal, have painted landscapes and gardens. What traits could Mendel have studied in this painting? What traits can scientists study in portraits of people? Make your own drawing or painting of a garden. Identify traits that can be determined by genetics.

28. Biology and Community Go to a local greenhouse or flower store and investigate the inheritance of traits in different plants. Find out about new hybrids. What traits in the parent plants were crossed? What traits appear in the offspring?

29. Biology and History: A Project Mendel's work went unnoticed for 35 years. Investigate some other scientific discoveries that took place in the middle to late 1800s. Why was Mendel's work ignored? Make a time line, using the results of your investigation.

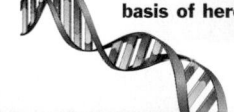

FAST-FORWARD TO CHAPTER 7

Mendel put together the first pieces of the heredity puzzle. In the next chapter, you will read about experiments that established the molecular basis of heredity.

Chapter 6 Fundamentals of Genetics **155**

dominant color. If there is a blended color or the offspring are both colors, then it is a form of intermediate inheritance.

24. Purple wings and green eyes are both dominant traits because they appear most often. Yellow wings and white eyes are both recessive traits because they appear less often.

25. The table indicates a form of inheritance that is influenced by environment.

26. Answers will vary. Students may determine that researchers would not want this knowledge to affect their subjects' responses to the study.

27. Answers will vary. Mendel could have studied flower color or plant height. Portraits of people can provide information about eye color, ear lobes, hair color, and other physical traits.

28. Students should describe F_1 plants.

29. Answers will vary. Mendel's work was primarily mathematical, and biologists might not have understood its significance. Also, a most biology at that time was descriptive, and Mendel's contemporaries may not have been qualified to accept experimental data.

studying a form of incomplete dominance, he would not have developed his laws. Instead, his results may have confirmed the blending hypothesis.

22. No, the children will have either blood type A or type B blood. None will have type AB like their father, or O like their mother.

23. Materials needed: Purebred purple and purebred magenta petunias, and

a notebook and pencil for recording observations

Procedure: Cross the purple and magenta petunias.

Observations to be made: Observe the color of the offspring.

Method of recording results: Write down observations in notebook.

Analysis of results: If all of the offspring are one color, then that color is the

Section	Student Activities/Features	Teacher's Resource Package
7.1 Molecule of Heredity **Objectives** ■ Describe the experiments that led to the discovery of DNA as the genetic material in cells ■ Appraise the use of the scientific method in these experiments	**Lab Zone Discover It!** *Making a Model of Genetic Material*, p. 157	**Unit 2 Review Module** ■ Section Review 7.1
7.2 DNA Structure and Replication **Objectives** ■ Describe the structure of DNA ■ Explain the process of DNA replication	**Lab Zone Do It!** *What Is a Twisted Ladder?* p. 163 **Everyday Biology** *DNA Duplicates,* p. 163 **Lab Zone Investigate It!** *Extracting DNA,* p. 164	**Unit 2 Review Module** ■ Section Review 7.2 ■ Activity Recordsheets 7-1 and 7-2 ■ Interpreting Graphics 7 ■ Critical Thinking Exercise 7 ■ Enrichment Topic 7-1 **Biotechnology Manual** ■ Lab 4: "Modeling DNA" ■ Lab 5: "Extracting DNA from Halobacterium Cells" ■ Lab 6: "Extracting DNA from Onions" **Interpreting and Developing Graphics** 19, 20
7.3 Linked Genes **Objectives** ■ Relate genes, traits, chromosomes, and DNA ■ Contrast gene linkage with Mendelian inheritance ■ Define recombination and mapping	**Lab Zone Think About It!** *Gene Linkage in Imaginary Aliens,* p. 167 **Lab Zone Do It!** *What Does Recombination Look Like?* p. 168	**Unit 2 Review Module** ■ Section Review 7.3 ■ Activity Recordsheet 7-3 **Laboratory Manual,** Lab 15: "Genes in Action: Drosophila Mating" **Biotechnology Manual,** Lab 2: "Modeling the Process of Gene Mapping"
7.4 Sex Linkage **Objectives** ■ Distinguish between autosomes and sex chromosomes ■ Compare and contrast sex-linked, sex-limited, and sex-influenced traits		**Unit 2 Review Module** ■ Section Review 7.4 **Consumer Applications** 7-1 **Interpreting and Developing Graphics** 21
7.5 The Human Gene Map **Objectives** ■ Explain genomes and current genome research ■ Compare monosomy and trisomy and their effects	**STS: Issues in Biology** *The Human Genome Project,* p. 174 **In the Community** *On-Ramp to Biology,* p. 176 **Everyday Biology** *A Cat Called Calico Carl,* p. 176	**Unit 2 Review Module** ■ Section Review 7.5 ■ Vocabulary Review 7 ■ Chapter 7 Tests **Laboratory Manual,** Lab 16: "Clues from the Karyotype" **Issues and Decision Making** 7-1 **Spanish Reviews** Chapter 7

Technology Resources

Internet Connections

Within this chapter, you will see the bioSURF logo. If you and your students have access to the Internet, the following URL address will provide various Internet connections that are related to topics and features presented in this chapter:

http://genetics.biosurf.com

You can also find relevant chapter material at **The Biology Place** address:

http://www.biology.com

CD-ROMs

Biología: la telaraña de la vida,
   (Spanish Student Edition) Chapter 7
Teacher's Resource Planner, Chapter 7
   Supplements
Interactive Biological Simulations
■ DNA Structure and Replication
TestWorks CD-ROM
■ Chapter 7 Tests

Videodiscs

Animated Biological Concepts Videodiscs
■ Griffith's Experiments
■ DNA Replication
■ Crossing Over
■ Human Sex Determination
■ Nondisjunction

Overhead Transparencies

■ DNA Replication, #16
■ Refining Mendel's Laws, #17

Videotapes

Biology Alive! Video Series
Rewind: The Web of Life Reteach Videos

Planning for Activities

STUDENT EDITION

Lab Zone
Discover It! p. 157
- one piece of yarn about 6 centimeters (cm) long
- scissors
- tweezers

Lab Zone Do It! p. 163
- one meter (m) of thick string
- 20 toothpicks
- clothing hanger
- metric ruler

Lab Zone
Investigate It! p. 164
- fresh beef or pork liver
- scalpel or dissecting scissors
- blender
- 25-mL graduated cylinder
- saline solution (0.9% NaCl)
- cheesecloth
- 250-mL beaker
- eyedropper
- liquid soap
- 95% ethanol
- glass stirring rod

Lab Zone Do It! p. 168
- two colors of modeling clay

TEACHER'S EDITION

Quick Activity, p. 158
Examining sandpapers
- small pieces of fine-grained, wet-or-dry sandpaper, coarse-grained sandpaper
- hand lenses

Teacher Demo, p. 160
Identifying objects using shadows
- overhead projector
- various objects

Teacher Demo, p. 165
Chromosomes and genes
- different colors of chalk

Teacher Demo, p. 167
Modeling homologous chromsomes
- pop-beads or snap-together beads of various colors

Teacher Demo, p. 170
Chromosomes in fruit flies
- colored chalk

Teacher Demo, p. 175
Different types of chromosomes
- overhead projector
- pieces of yarn

Chapter Objectives

Students will learn the main concepts of this chapter as they complete the following objectives.

- Describe experiments that led to the discovery of DNA as genetic material
- Describe the structure of DNA
- Explain the process of DNA replication
- Relate genes, traits, chromosomes, and DNA
- Contrast gene linkage with Mendelian genetics
- Define recombination and mapping
- Distinguish between autosomes and sex chromosomes
- Compare and contrast sex-linked, sex-limited, and sex-influenced traits
- Explain genomes and current genome research
- Compare monosomy and trisomy and their effects

Key Words

7.2 *adenine, guanine, cytosine, thymine, double helix, replication*

7.3 *linked genes, crossing over*

7.4 *sex chromosomes, autosomes, sex-linked genes, sex-limited traits, sex-influenced traits*

7.5 *karyotype, genome, nondisjunction, monosomy, trisomy, polyploidy*

The Opening Story

Have students discuss how the "Tyrolean Ice Man" might relate to this chapter. Ask what an analysis of genetic material might reveal about a person's identity.

156

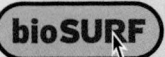

You can find out more about DNA, genes, and chromosomes by exploring the following Internet address:
http://genetics.biosurf.com

In this chapter . . .

FEATURES

Everyday Biology
- DNA Duplicates
- A Cat Called Calico Carl

In the Community
On-ramp to Biology

 Issues in Biology
The Human Genome Project

LAB ZONES

Discover It!
- Making a Model of Genetic Material

Do It!
- What Is a Twisted Ladder?
- What Does Recombination Look Like?

Think About It!
- Gene Linkage in Imaginary Aliens

Investigate It!
- Extracting DNA

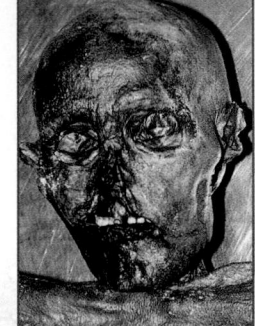

TYROLEAN ICE MAN LOOKS GREAT FOR HIS AGE

The glacier that had entombed him for 5000 years had preserved him almost perfectly. A little *too* perfectly, thought some scientists. Had hikers in the Swiss Alps found a Stone Age resident of the area, or was he a South American mummy that had been placed there as a hoax?

To resolve these questions about the "Tyrolean Ice Man," researchers analyzed his genetic material. Analyses of genetic material are often used to solve mysteries such as this one. As it turned out, the Tyrolean Ice Man's genetic material matched the genetic material of modern inhabitants of the Swiss Alps. This finding indicates that he did, indeed, live in the Alps 5000 years ago. But what is the genetic material, and how can it be used to identify relationships?

 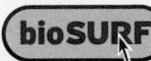 **Discover It!**

Making a Model of Genetic Material

You need one piece of yarn about 6 centimeters (cm) long, scissors, tweezers

1. Use the piece of yarn to represent a chromosome. Cut the yarn into segments. Each segment represents a gene. Caution: Use care when handling scissors.
2. Describe the relationship between the segments of yarn and your original piece of yarn.
3. Use the tweezers to pull apart the strings that make up the yarn. These strings represent molecules of DNA.
4. Describe the relationship between the strings and the "genes," and the relationship between the strings and the "chromosome."

The units of chromosomes have a great effect on how traits are inherited and expressed.

WRITE ABOUT IT!

In your science journal write about the genetic material and what you think its importance might be. Use your knowledge about the inheritance of traits.

Chapter 7 DNA, Genes, and Chromosomes **157**

PORTFOLIO PREVIEW

Students should be encouraged to add to their portfolios as they work through this chapter. In addition to the *Write About It* opportunity, the following section is an opportunity for portfolio entries:

■ Section 7.5: *The Human Gene Map*

Opening Activities

bioSURF If you have access to the Internet in your classroom or school, you may wish to have students connect to the address shown on page 156. You may also want to have students conduct net searches for information using key words related to this chapter. For example, they could search for entries under DNA, the Human Genome Project, or Down syndrome.

LAB ZONE **Discover It!** **TEAM WORK**

Make a Model of Genetic Material

Have students work with a partner or in a small group to construct genetic materials and discuss the relationships between the different units. You may wish to model step 1 for the class.

WRITE ABOUT IT!

Have students discuss their journal entries in small groups. Encourage the groups to make any necessary corrections and then discuss the entries as a class.

◄••••••••••••••••••••••

REWIND to Chapter 6

Briefly review concepts learned in Chapter 6, *Patterns of Inheritance*. Ask:

■ **How do you think the study of inheritance patterns might relate to DNA, genes, and chromosomes in Chapter 7?**

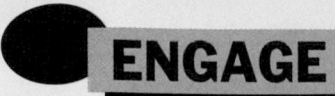

ENGAGE

Consider The Big Idea

Have students read the Big Idea! at the top of the page. Remind them that the inheritance of traits is controlled by DNA.

Use the Visual

Have students study the photograph and read the text that opens the section. Point out that Miescher recognized the importance of phosphorus in living organisms.

Quick Activity

Provide students with small pieces of different kinds of sandpaper. Allow students time to observe differences in texture and appearance. Point out that these differences can be used to distinguish one piece of sandpaper from another. Tell students that in this section they will learn how a scientist used observable differences in the coats of two varieties of bacteria to determine whether DNA was the hereditary material of organisms.

Animated Biological Concepts

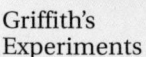

Griffith's   Play
Experiments

THE BIG IDEA! The structure of DNA, the molecule of heredity, enables the molecule to copy itself. 7.1–7.2

7.1 Molecule of Heredity

What you'll learn

IDEAS
- To describe the experiments that led to the discovery of DNA as the genetic material in cells
- To appraise the use of the scientific method in these experiments

Pus proves a valuable research tool!
In 1874 Friedrich Miescher discovered acid molecules in the nuclei of pus cells. Miescher's discovery became known as deoxyribonucleic acid, or DNA. Once the DNA molecule was discovered, it took more than 50 years to determine its role in cell function.

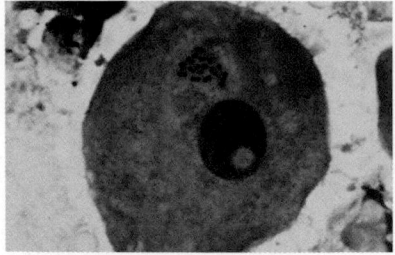

GENETIC MATERIAL TRANSFORMS CELLS

"Living dead" bacteria?

Discoveries in the late 1800s and early 1900s helped put together many pieces of the heredity puzzle. As you learned in Chapter 6, Sutton and Boveri formulated the chromosome theory of heredity in 1903. But many questions remained, including, what are genes made of?

In 1928 British researcher Frederick Griffith took the first steps toward determining whether genes are composed of DNA or protein. You can follow his experiments in *Figure 7.1*. Griffith worked with bacteria called *Streptococcus pneumoniae*. One variety, strain S, looks smooth and causes pneumonia in mice. Another variety, called strain R because of its rough appearance, does not cause pneumonia in mice.

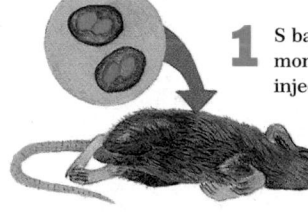

1 S bacteria caused pneumonia and death when injected into mice.

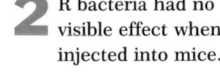
2 R bacteria had no visible effect when injected into mice.

FIGURE 7.1

Griffith's Experiments

Griffith injected bacteria into mice and observed the effects in four separate experiments. How did his research help answer the "DNA or protein" question? **❶**

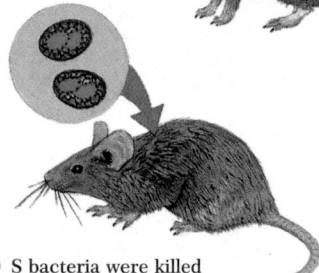

3 S bacteria were killed by heating. Heat-killed S bacteria did not harm mice.

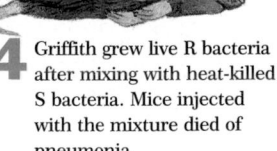
4 Griffith grew live R bacteria after mixing with heat-killed S bacteria. Mice injected with the mixture died of pneumonia.

158 *Unit 2 Genetics*

STUDENT RESOURCES

From the Teacher's Resource Package, use:
- Section Review 7.1 from Unit 2 Review Module

TECHNOLOGY RESOURCES

Relevant technology resources include:
- Spanish Student Edition CD-ROM
- Teacher's Resource Planner CD-ROM
- Animated Biological Concepts Videodiscs: "Griffith's Experiments"

Griffith found that strain S bacteria were coated with mucus but strain R bacteria were not. He also found that heating strain S bacteria killed them and that injections of the heat-killed S bacteria did not harm mice.

Griffith then injected a mixture of heat-killed S bacteria and living R bacteria into mice. Griffith hypothesized that the mice would not be affected by the mixture. To his surprise, however, the mice died of pneumonia. To find out what killed the mice, Griffith allowed bacteria from the dead mice to reproduce. The offspring bacteria had the mucous coats characteristic of S bacteria.

Griffith reasoned that somehow a transforming material had passed from heat-killed S bacteria to living R bacteria changing R bacteria into S bacteria. He concluded that the transforming material was genetic material, since new inherited traits were observed in the offspring. Other scientists observed that many proteins are harmed by heat, and proposed that DNA, not protein, was the genetic material.

In 1944 American biologist Oswald Avery and his colleagues discovered that only DNA from strain S bacteria was necessary to transform strain R bacteria into the S strain. These findings supported the theory that DNA is the molecule of heredity. This additional evidence still did not convince everyone. More information was needed.

DNA OR PROTEIN?

Phage factor

In 1952 American geneticists Martha Chase and Alfred Hershey found the final missing piece of the "DNA or protein?" puzzle. Their experiments used viruses called bacteriophages (bak-TEER-ee-oh-FAY-juz), or phages

for short. You will learn how phages infect bacterial cells in Chapter 14.

A phage has only two components: DNA and protein. You can see in *Figure* 7.2 that when phages infect bacteria, they attach to the bacterium's surface and inject material into the bacterium. The rest of the phage remains outside the bacterium. The injected material controls the metabolism and characteristics of the bacterial cell, as genes do. Hershey and Chase reasoned that the injected substance must be the genetic material, but they still had to determine whether the substance was DNA or protein.

To find out, they mixed phages containing radioactive DNA with bacterial cells. They also mixed phages containing radioactive protein with other bacterial cells. The phages attached themselves to bacteria and injected their genetic material. After the material was injected, the bacteria began producing new phage viruses.

As you can see in *Figure* 7.2, only the radioactive DNA entered the bacteria, indicating that the phages had injected their DNA into the bacteria. The scientists concluded that DNA, and not protein, must be the genetic material.

CHECKPOINT 7.1

1. How did Griffith, Hershey, and Chase establish DNA as the genetic material in cells?

2. Critical Thinking Identify the steps of the scientific method in an experiment described in this section.

Build on What You Know

3. What nucleic acid, in addition to DNA, was responsible for the transformation of R bacteria into S bacteria in Griffith's experiments? *(Need to jog your memory? Revisit relevant concepts in Chapter 2, Section 2.1.)*

FIGURE 7.2
Hershey and Chase's Experiments

Is DNA or protein the genetic material?

Cell culture 1
When phages with radioactive (green) DNA infected bacteria, the bacteria became radioactive. The DNA, therefore, was the material that entered the bacteria.

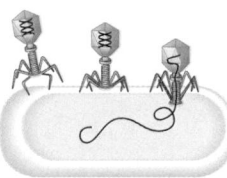
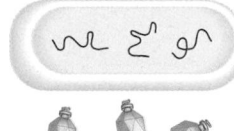

Cell culture 2
When phages with radioactive (green) protein infected bacteria, the bacteria did not become radioactive. Protein, therefore, did not enter the bacteria.

Chapter 7 DNA, Genes, and Chromosomes **159**

Explain

The ability of S bacteria to cause infection is related to the mucus coat, which makes the bacteria resistant to the defenses of the immune system. Explain that the R bacteria did not acquire mucus coats directly. Instead they absorbed hereditary material for producing their mucous coats. Emphasize that at the conclusion of his experiment, Griffith did not know which part of the bacteria was carrying the information.

Evaluate Understanding

Draw a time line on the board with the dates 1868, 1873, 1903, 1928, 1944, and 1952. Have volunteers write why each date is significant in the discovery of DNA as the hereditary material of organisms. Have other volunteers write the steps in each of the experiments. Encourage students to copy the completed time line into their notebooks.

Reteach

Work with students to diagram or sketch the steps in the experiments of Griffith and of Hershey and Chase. Then ask them to add captions and labels to the visual to describe how the experiments led to the identification of DNA as the genetic material.

CHECKPOINT 7.1

1. Griffith concluded that genetic material had to enter the bacteria in order to control the bacterial cells. Chase and Hershey found that radioactive DNA—and not radioactive protein—entered the bacteria. The genetic material must be DNA.

2. Applying Hypothesis: Are genes DNA or protein? Experimentation on reproduction of R bacteria and S bacteria and

behavior of phages. Conclusion: genes are DNA.

3. RNA is the nucleic acid responsible for constructing the proteins coded by DNA.

❶ The experiments shows that something in the heat-killed S bacteria, either DNA or protein, combined with the live R bacteria and changed them into S cells.

ENGAGE

Use the Visual

Have students study the photograph that opens the section. Explain that X-ray photos were one tool scientists used to determine the unique structure of DNA. Ask:

- **Why did scientists have to use a tool other than a microscope to study DNA?** (Detailed DNA structures are too small to be seen with a microscope.)

SUPER READ! **Interpreting Visuals** To practice strategies for effective reading, use pages 31-32 in *Super Read!*

Teacher Demo

Use an overhead projector to project shadows of several different items, without showing the actual objects. Challenge students to identify the objects. Explain that an X-ray also shows objects as shadows and that scientists are able to use these shadows to determine the structure and identity of an object.

Use the Visual

Ask students to examine the structure of DNA shown in Figure 7.3. Ask:

- **What chemical substances make up the backbone of the helix?** (Sugars and phosphates)
- **What chemical substances make up the rungs of the DNA ladder?** (Nitrogenous-base pairs)

7.2 DNA Structure and Replication

What you'll learn

IDEAS
- To describe the structure of DNA
- To explain the process of DNA replication

WORDS
adenine, guanine, cytosine, thymine, double helix, replication

FIGURE 7.3

The DNA Double Helix

The shape of DNA, which looks like a twisted ladder, is commonly referred to as a double helix.

Where is DNA?
In eukaryotes, chromosomes contain DNA and are located in the cell nucleus.

What is it?

The top picture at right is of an everyday object photographed to show features that you cannot ordinarily see. What is it? When scientists were modeling the structure of DNA, they produced images by bouncing X rays off the DNA molecule. X-ray photos, such as the bottom one shown at right, helped scientists discover the structure of DNA.

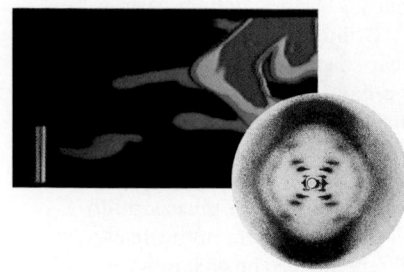

NUCLEOTIDES AND BASES

Bases go hand in hand

After researchers had pinpointed DNA as the genetic material, they needed to solve the next part of the heredity puzzle: the structure of the DNA molecule. Like many great achievements, the modeling of DNA resulted from the work of many researchers.

You may be wondering why knowing the structure of DNA is so important. The structure of a molecule is related to its function, so knowing what a molecule looks like gives researchers insight into how the molecule works.

Before DNA was modeled, scientists already knew that it was made up of nucleotides. A DNA nucleotide has three components: a five-carbon sugar called deoxyribose; a

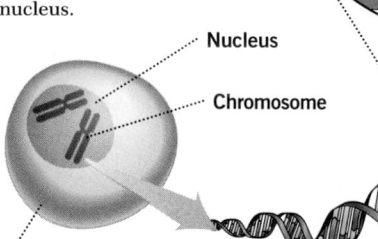

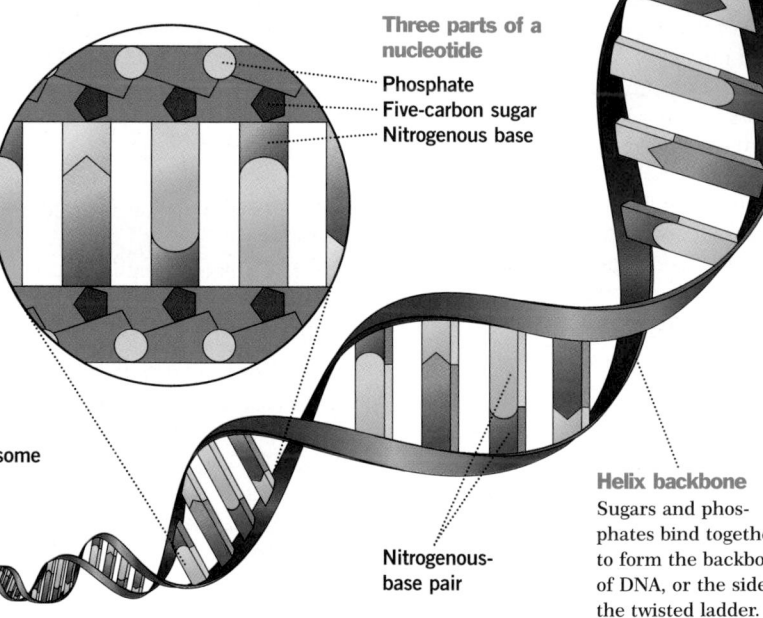

Three parts of a nucleotide
- Phosphate
- Five-carbon sugar
- Nitrogenous base

Nucleus

Chromosome

Cell

Nitrogenous-base pair

Helix backbone
Sugars and phosphates bind together to form the backbone of DNA, or the sides of the twisted ladder.

160 *Unit 2 Genetics*

STUDENT RESOURCES

From the Teacher's Resource Package, use:
- Section Review 7.2, Activity Record-sheets 7-1 and 7-2, Interpreting Graphics 7, Critical Thinking Exercise 7, and Enrichment Topic 7-1 from Unit 2 Review Module
- Biotechnology Manual: Labs 4, 5, and 6

TECHNOLOGY RESOURCES

Relevant technology resources include:
- Spanish Student Edition CD-ROM
- Teacher's Resource Planner CD-ROM
- Interactive Biological Simulations CD-ROM: "DNA Structure and Replication"
- Animated Biological Concepts Videodiscs: "DNA Replication"

Purines	Pyrimidines
Guanine (G)	Cytosine (C)
Adenine (A)	Thymine (T)

FIGURE 7.4

The four nitrogenous bases pair up to form the rungs of the DNA twisted ladder.

phosphate group; and one of four nitrogenous bases.

The four nitrogenous bases in DNA are **adenine** (A), **guanine** (G), **cytosine** (C), and **thymine** (T). Two of these four nitrogenous bases—adenine and guanine—are purines (PYOOR-eenz). The other two bases—thymine and cytosine—are pyrimidines (pi-RIM-ih-DEENZ). One difference between purines and pyrimidines is that purine molecules are larger than pyrimidine molecules.

In the early 1950s American scientist Edwin Chargaff made an important discovery about the four nitrogenous bases. When he analyzed the amounts of the four bases in different species, Chargaff discovered that the amount of adenine is always equal to the amount of thymine, and that the amount of cytosine is always equal to the amount of guanine. These findings, called Chargaff's rules, proved to be an important clue in later investigations into the structure of DNA.

DOUBLE HELIX

The twisted ladder

Soon after Chargaff reported his findings, a new piece was placed in the DNA puzzle. Maurice Wilkins and Rosalind Franklin photographed DNA using X rays. Their images showed a wide, tightly coiled molecule with a spiral shape.

Rosalind Franklin showed one of her DNA images to the American scientist James Watson. Watson and his partner, Francis Crick, realized that the DNA molecule was too thick to be a single strand. After trying several models, they made one in which two strands were wrapped around each other. According to this model, which is now accepted as the correct structure for DNA, the DNA molecule is shaped like a twisted ladder. This shape is called a **double helix.** As shown in *Figure* 7.3, the DNA double helix is formed by two strands of nucleotides.

Watson and Crick found that two components of nucleotides, the sugar and the phosphate, bind to each other with a strong chemical bond to form a "backbone." The backbone forms the sides of the twisted ladder. The third component of nucleotides, the nitrogenous base, attaches to the sugar. Two bases bind together with weak chemical bonds to form the "rungs" of the ladder. In this way, the nucleotides form the DNA double helix.

Each rung, or base pair, of DNA consists of a purine and a pyrimidine. *Figure* 7.4 shows that adenine pairs with thymine, and cytosine pairs with guanine. Because they always pair with each other, scientists say that adenine is complementary to thymine, and cytosine is complementary to guanine. How do Chargaff's rules support this part of Watson and Crick's model?

FIGURE 7.5

A Short History of Genetics

1866 Gregor Mendel experiments with pea plants.

1868 Friedrich Miescher extracts DNA from pus cell nuclei.

1900 Mendel's work is rediscovered.

1903 Walter Sutton and Theodor Boveri develop the chromosome theory of inheritance.

1910 Thomas Morgan (right) verifies Sutton's theory with fruit fly experiments.

1928 Frederick Griffith explores genetic material with mouse experiments.

1944 Oswald Avery's work indicates that DNA is most likely the genetic material.

1952 Edwin Chargaff determines rules that govern the proportion of DNA bases.

 1952 Maurice Wilkins and Rosalind Franklin (left) photograph DNA using X-ray crystallography.

1952 Alfred Hershey and Martha Chase confirm that DNA is the genetic material.

1953 James Watson (below left) and Francis Crick (below right) model DNA.

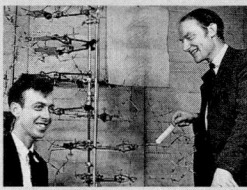

Chapter 7 DNA, Genes, and Chromosomes **161**

Use the Visual

Have students study Figure 7.4. Ask:

- **Which nitrogen base always pairs with cytosine?** (Guanine)
- **Which nitrogen base always pairs with adenine?** (Thymine)
- **What base must always pair with a pyrimidine?** (Purine)

Think Critically

Remind students that prokaryotes do not have a nucleus and membrane-bound organelles, but they do contain DNA. Ask:

- **How does the location of the DNA of a prokaryote compare to that of a eukaryote?** (In both, DNA is located in the chromosomes; in prokaryotes, chromosomes are scattered throughout the cytoplasm, not within a membrane-bound nucleus.)

Mathematics

Watson and Crick's original model was based on mathematical measurements. Knowing the physical dimensions of the helix enabled Watson and Crick to determine the molecule's structure.

Interactive Biological Simulations

DNA Structure and Replication Students are introduced to the parts of a nucleotide and the bonding of complementary bases, and then use DNA polymerase and free DNA nucleotides to replicate a strand of DNA.

MEETING DIVERSE NEEDS

LEP Encourage LEP students to make a sketch of the structure of the DNA molecule. Have them label the key features of the molecule in their native language as well as in English. Tell students to add a key to their diagram that identifies base pairing.

❶ Infrared photo of feet and footprints
❷ Watson and Crick found that bases fit together in a specific way, which explained why Chargaff found specific proportions of bases.

Use the Visual

Review the series of events shown in Figure 7.6. Ask:

- **What causes the base pairs in the DNA molecule to break apart and unwind?** (Enzymes)
- **What determines where free nucleotides will attach to the new strands?** (Free nucleotides find and attach to their complementary bases, always A-T or C-G, along the new strands.)
- **What is the last step in the replication process?** (The new backbone is assembled.)

 Language Arts

Have students use a dictionary to define the homophones *complimentary* and *complementary*. Challenge them to think of a mnemonic to help them choose the right spelling.

Literature

James Watson's account of the discovery of the structure of DNA, *The Double Helix*, provides a glimpse into the nature of scientific investigation. Tell students to be sure to read the introduction, in which Watson discusses the role of Rosalind Franklin and how she was originally portrayed.

Animated Biological Concepts

DNA Replication

Play

FIGURE 7.6

DNA Replication

This diagram represents a snapshot of replication. At the moment pictured, the top of the strand is in the first step of replication, unzipping; the middle of the strand is building new rungs and a new backbone; and the bottom is already copied. How does the DNA strand serve as a template, or pattern, for its replication? ❶

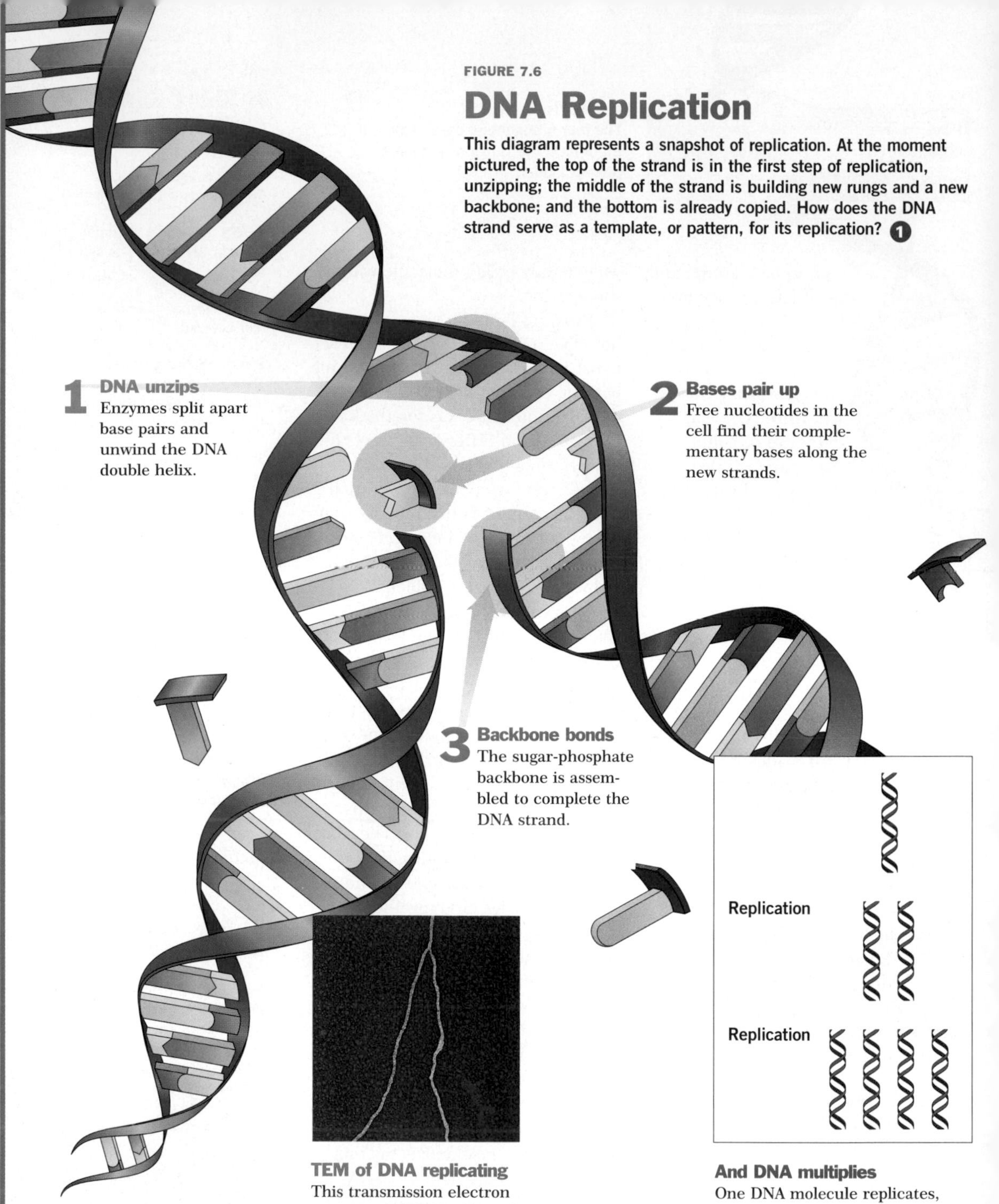

1 DNA unzips
Enzymes split apart base pairs and unwind the DNA double helix.

2 Bases pair up
Free nucleotides in the cell find their complementary bases along the new strands.

3 Backbone bonds
The sugar-phosphate backbone is assembled to complete the DNA strand.

TEM of DNA replicating
This transmission electron micrograph (TEM) shows the "replication fork" of DNA.

Replication

Replication

And DNA multiplies
One DNA molecule replicates, producing two DNA molecules. Each replicated molecule has a strand of parent DNA and a strand of new DNA.

MEETING DIVERSE NEEDS

At Risk Encourage students to outline the steps of DNA replication in pictures. Have them label each part of the DNA molecule and use different colors for each base.

❶ Once unzipped, the bases always pair up in the same way (cytosine with guanine and thymine with adenine). One strand of DNA replicates to become two strands of new, identical DNA.

❷ They are structurally identical to the parent DNA.

Because the bases are complementary, each base has a tight and unique fit with only one other base. This description can be applied to the entire DNA strand. If you know the bases on one strand, you can determine the bases on the other strand through complementary-base pairing.

DNA REPLICATION

Unzip the blueprints

With one discovery, Watson and Crick revealed the structure of DNA and gained insight into its function. One of the important functions of genetic material is the ability to copy itself. The process by which DNA is copied is called **replication.** As you may recall from Chapter 5, DNA replicates prior to cell division. You can follow the steps of replication in *Figure 7.6.*

At the beginning of replication, the DNA double helix unwinds, or unzips. An enzyme breaks the weak bonds between the base pairs, separating the two strands of the DNA molecule. Each parent strand of DNA serves as a pattern, or template, for a new complementary strand.

The new strands are assembled from lone nucleotides in the nucleus, called free nucleotides. An enzyme called DNA polymerase (POL-ih-meh-RAYZ) matches the bases on the parent strand one by one with new bases of free nucleotides. Strong sugar-phosphate bonds form between nucleotides that are next to one another, creating a new backbone. Eventually, two new double helixes are formed. How do the new molecules compare with the parent DNA?

 **LAB ZONE Do It!** **bioSURF**

What Is a Twisted Ladder?

DNA is described as a twisted ladder. You can build a model of a double helix if you . . .

Try This

1 Get one meter (m) of thick string and 20 toothpicks.
2 Loop the string over a hanger. The string represents the sugar-phosphate backbone of a DNA molecule.
3 Insert the ends of the toothpicks into the two sides of the string. Space them about 4 cm apart. The toothpicks represent the complementary-base pairs.
4 Tie the two ends of the string together. Twist the knot a few times, and watch the shape of a double helix form.

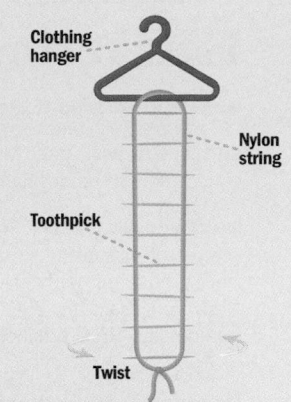

Clothing hanger

Nylon string

Toothpick

Twist

Analyze Your Results

1 Why is DNA described as a twisted ladder?
2 How could this twisted-ladder model more accurately represent DNA?

 **CHECKPOINT 7.2**

1. Describe the discoveries that led to the modeling of DNA.
2. What are the components of a nucleotide?
3. Why are the base pairs in DNA considered complementary?
4. Critical Thinking How is the structure of DNA related to its function?

Build on What You Know

5. How does mitosis result in two daughter cells that contain the same genetic information? *(Need to jog your memory? Revisit relevant concepts in Chapter 5, Section 5.4.)*

EVERYDAY BIOLOGY

DNA Duplicates

As you may know, a photocopier makes exact copies of documents. In what way is DNA replication similar to this duplicating process? How is DNA replication different from the duplicating process used by copying machines?

How does the structure of DNA allow the molecule to copy itself?

Chapter 7 DNA, Genes, and Chromosomes **163**

 **LAB ZONE Do It!** **TEAM WORK**

What Is a Twisted Ladder?

Have students work in small groups. You may wish to have students use glue to hold the toothpicks.

Analyze Your Results

1 The molecules double helix shape resembles a twisted ladder.
2 Using colored toothpicks to show which base pairs form each rung.

Everyday Biology

Each new molecule contains half the original molecule. A machine duplicated copy is a new image and original is intact.

3 ASSESS

Evaluate Understanding

Ask students to sketch the structure of DNA and the stages of DNA replication. Also, label the helix backbone and its components, the nitrogenous-base pairs and their components, the two sides of the helix after it has been broken apart, and the free nucleotides finding base pairs.

Reteach

On the board, use colored chalk to draw a strand of DNA, with the bases identified. Have a student sketch and label the complementary base until the complementary strand is complete. Briefly review DNA structure and the steps involved in replication.

CHECKPOINT 7.2

1. Chargaff determined the proportions of DNA bases, A=T and G=C. Franklin's and Wilkins' X-ray photographs of DNA, revealed a wide, spiral structure. These facts helped Watson and Crick model the double helix structure with complementary base-pairing.

2. A five-carbon sugar, a phosphate, and a nitrogenous base
3. They fit together uniquely.
4. Analyzing The complementary structure of DNA explains how DNA replicates.
5. DNA is replicated and identical copies passed to daughter cells.

TEAM WORK **Extracting DNA**

SAFETY FIRST!

This investigation should be carried out in a well-ventilated area. Students should wear safety goggles and a lab coat or apron.

Lab Prep and Planning

Have students work in pairs. Allow at least 45–50 minutes to complete the lab.

Lab Tips

Purchase fresh or frozen liver directly from a butcher rather than in packages in the meat section of the supermarket. To prepare the 0.9% saline solution, dissolve 9 g of noniodized or Kosher salt in 91 mL of warm water.

Hypothesis Help

You may want to review the effect of dissolved salt on osmosis across the cell membrane and the fact that ethanol is a solvent.

Lab Extension

Open Ended

Divide the class into small groups and assign each group a different reagent. Try various alcohols such as methanol, ethanol, and isopropyl alcohol, or use different detergents. Have students blot dry their DNA sample and weigh it. Draw a data table on the board and have students enter their data. Discuss the results and determine which materials are best for extracting DNA.

 **Investigate It!**

Extracting DNA

WHAT YOU WILL DO Extract DNA from liver

SKILLS YOU WILL USE Measuring, predicting, collecting and recording data, observing

WHAT YOU WILL NEED Fresh beef or pork liver, scalpel or dissecting scissors, blender, 25-milliliter (mL) graduated cylinder, saline solution (0.9% NaCl), cheesecloth, 250-mL beaker, eyedropper, liquid soap, 95% ethanol, glass stirring rod

Propose a Hypothesis

You know that DNA is located in the cell nucleus. Propose a hypothesis about why the materials for this lab can extract the DNA in the liver cells.

Conduct Your Experiment

1 Cut a piece of liver about 2 cm long. Put 10 mL of saline solution and the liver into the blender. Blend until the mixture is uniform. **Caution:** Use care when handling scissors and using the blender.

2 Fold two pieces of cheese-cloth in half. Use the cheese-cloth to strain the liver mixture into a beaker.

3 Use an eyedropper to add approximately 10 mL of liquid soap to the mixture. Mix thoroughly with the glass stirring rod.

4 Measure and record the volume of the soap-liver mixture in the beaker. Multiply this number by 2 and record your result. Add this volume of ethanol to the mixture.

5 Slowly stir the mixture with the glass stirring rod. A white substance will form where the ethanol and liver mixture meet.

6 Watch as the DNA precipitates up through the ethanol. The DNA will appear to be fibrous strands. Small bubbles will attach to these strands as they move up through the ethanol. Twirl the glass rod slowly in the mixture. Precipitated DNA strands will accumulate and clump together on the rod, forming a visible mass. Record your results.

Draw Conclusions

1 What does the DNA that you have extracted look like?
2 Now that you have performed this lab, how do you think Miescher first discovered DNA?

Design a Related Experiment

Design a lab to extract DNA from another substance, such as onions, dried peas, or yeast.

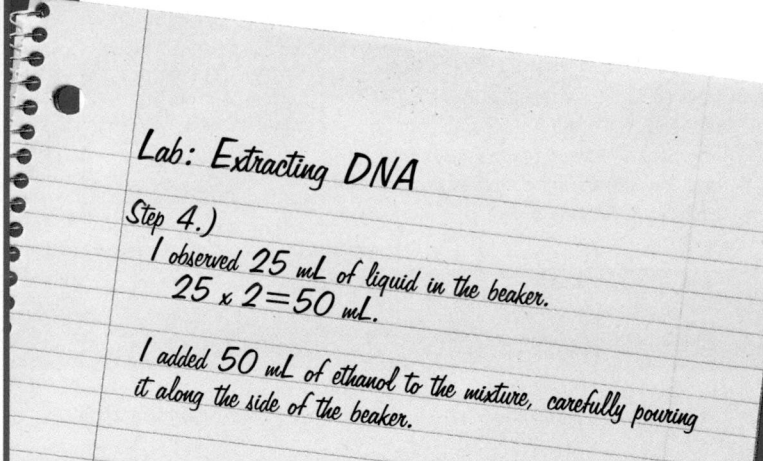

Lab: Extracting DNA

Step 4.)
I observed 25 mL of liquid in the beaker.
25 x 2 = 50 mL.

I added 50 mL of ethanol to the mixture, carefully pouring it along the side of the beaker.

Draw Conclusions

1 The DNA looks like white, opalescent goop that can be spooled up.
2 Miescher was trying to find out what types of compounds were found in the nucleus. He treated cells with different chemicals, just as students treated liver tissue with different chemicals. What he learned was that the nuclear material behaved very differently from protein, and it contained phosphorus, which is not found in proteins.

Design a Related Experiment

Students' designs will vary, but should include a way to break up the cells, and a way to precipitate out the DNA from the nuclei.

THE BIG IDEA!

Genes, sections of DNA that code for a specific trait, are linked together on chromosomes. 7.3 – 7.5

7.3 Linked Genes

The stickleback mystery

To study inheritance among stickleback fishes, scientists crossbred a short, slender, small-mouthed stickleback with a long, fat, wide-mouthed stickleback. They found that the offspring were either all short, slender, and small-mouthed, or long, fat, and wide-mouthed. These particular traits were inherited together because of a special mode of inheritance.

LINKAGE

Trait show

How can organisms have hundreds of traits, yet not have hundreds of chromosomes? To answer this question, biologists hypothesized that a single chromosome must contain many different genes that control many different traits.

DNA, genes, and chromosomes are related to each other in much the same way as the parts of a city. Nucleotides, which are the components of DNA, can be thought of as individual people who all work together in a building. Each section of a DNA molecule is comparable to one building where people work. Each section of DNA is a gene, so a gene, too, is comparable to a building, each with its own function. Each chromosome with thousands of genes is like a city, with many different functions in many different buildings.

As you learned in Chapter 6, Walter Sutton developed the chromosome theory of heredity. The principle

What you'll learn

IDEAS
• To relate genes, traits, chromosomes, and DNA
• To contrast gene linkage with Mendelian inheritance
• To define recombination and mapping

WORDS
linked genes, crossing over

FIGURE 7.7

Chromosome Structure

What is the relationship between chromosomes and DNA? ❶

A chromosome contains very tightly wound DNA.

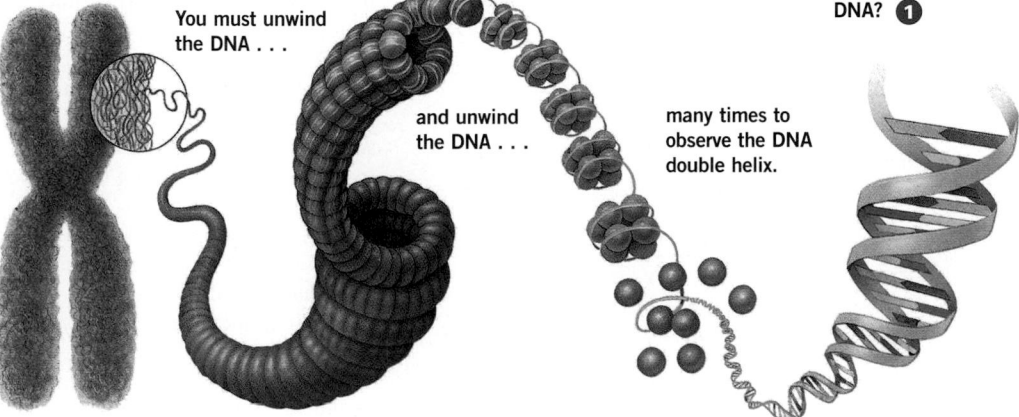

You must unwind the DNA . . .

and unwind the DNA . . .

many times to observe the DNA double helix.

Chapter 7 DNA, Genes, and Chromosomes **165**

STUDENT RESOURCES

From the Teacher's Resource Package, use:
■ Section Review 7.3, and Activity Recordsheet 7-3, from Unit 2 Review Module
■ Lab 15: "Genes in Action: Drosophila Mating"
■ Biotechnology Manual, Lab 2

TECHNOLOGY RESOURCES

Relevant technology resources include:
■ Spanish Student Edition CD-ROM
■ Teacher's Resource Planner CD-ROM
■ Animated Biological Concepts Videodiscs: "Crossing Over"

❶ ENGAGE

Consider The Big Idea

Have students read The Big Idea! at the top of the page. Explain that inheritance through gene linkage differs from inheritance described by Mendel's laws.

Use the Visual

Have students study the photograph that opens the section. Explain that in some organisms certain traits pass from parent to offspring in combination with other traits.

Check Prior Knowledge

To assess students' knowledge about genes, ask:

■ **How are genes and chromosomes related?** (Genes are found in chromosomes.)

SUPER READ! **Interpreting Visuals** To practice strategies for effective reading, use pages 31-32 in *Super Read!*

Teacher Demo

Draw an elongated oval on the board to represent the shape of a chromosome. Using two or three different colors of chalk, draw bands along the chromosome to represent genes. Each location is referred to as a locus. Explain that genes are sections of paired bases of DNA that code for specific traits. Explain to students that they will learn how genes can be linked together.

❶ Chromosomes contain DNA.

Use the Visual

As you discuss Bateson and Punnett's work, have students study Figure 7.8. Ask:

- **Is the cross an example of a monohybrid cross or a dihybrid cross? Explain.** (Dihybrid, because two traits are examined at the same time)
- **Why do all flowers in the F₁ generation have purple flowers and long pollen?** (They inherited dominant alleles for flower color and pollen shape. Those traits are expressed.)
- **How did the results obtained by Bateson and Punnett in the F₂ generation differ from the expected results?** (The four phenotypes did not appear in the expected ratio of 9:3:3:1. Instead, the parental phenotype appeared more often than expected and some of the offspring had a new and unexpected combination of traits.)
- **What do the results suggest about Mendel's Law of Independent Assortment?** (Some alleles do not sort independently as suggested by Mendel's law.)

FIGURE 7.8

Refining Mendel's Laws

Bateson and Punnett studied two traits in sweet pea plants: flower color and pollen shape. What was their hypothesis? ❶

1 In the P generation, purebred plants with purple flowers and long pollen (*PPLL*) were crossed with purebred plants with red flowers and round pollen (*ppll*).

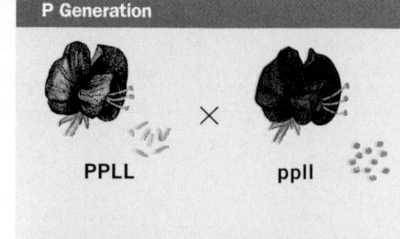

P Generation

PPLL × ppll

2 All of the F₁ generation had purple flowers and long pollen, as predicted by Mendel's laws. Which traits are dominant? ❷

F₁ Generation

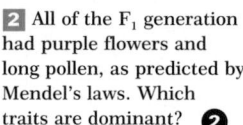

PpLl × PpLl

3 When the F₁ generation self-fertilized, the offspring did not have a 9:3:3:1 ratio. A greater number than expected had the same phenotype as the P generation.

Phenotypes	Observed Offspring	Prediction with Independent Assortment
Purple, long	284	216
Purple, round	21	72
Red, long	21	72
Red, round	55	24

4 Thomas Morgan hypothesized that the traits for flower color and pollen shape were linked on the same chromosome. Notice that this Punnett square does not account for the "Purple, round" or "Red, long" phenotypes from the table.

F₂ Generation

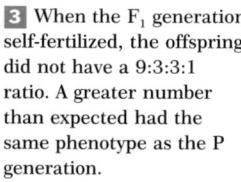

Punnett square for linked genes

	PL	pl
PL	Purple, long **PPLL**	Purple, long **PpLl**
pl	Purple, long **PpLl**	Red, rounded **ppll**

---

behind this theory is that specific genes controlling specific traits are located on specific chromosomes.

Sutton's theory helped to explain the results of an experiment conducted by geneticists William Bateson and R. C. Punnett (the man who developed the Punnett square). You can better understand their dilemma by following their experiment, shown in *Figure* 7.8.

These two researchers bred sweet pea plants. In sweet pea plants, purple flower color (*P*) is dominant over red flower color (*p*), and long pollen shape (*L*) is dominant over round pollen shape (*l*). Bateson and Punnett crossed purebred plants in their parent generation—*PPLL* × *ppll*. As expected, the F₁ generation was heterozygous for purple flowers and long pollen (*PpLl*).

Bateson and Punnett allowed the F₁ plants to self-fertilize. They expected flower color and pollen shape to sort independently. According to Mendel's Law of Independent Assortment, which you also learned about in Chapter 6, there are four different phenotypes possible as a result of a dihybrid cross. These four phenotypes should occur in a ratio of 9:3:3:1.

Bateson and Punnett's results differed from the expected ratio. The two parental phenotypes (purple flowers with long pollen, red flowers with short pollen) showed up more often than expected. It appeared that the traits of flower color and pollen shape did not sort independently. Did these results mean that Mendel's Law of Independent Assortment was incorrect? ❸

The scientists suspected that the genes for the two traits were somehow connected and did not sort independently. Without independent assortment, the offspring should have the same combination of traits as the parents.

MEETING DIVERSE NEEDS

At Risk Have students work in pairs to draw Punnett squares to show the results Bateson and Punnett expected in the F₁ and F₂ generations. Have them explain how the actual results differed from expected results.

❶ They hypothesized that the two traits would follow Mendel's laws.

❷ Purple flowers, long pollen

❸ If the genes are located on the same chromosome, they stay together during meiosis. They do not sort independently.

In 1910, the American geneticist Thomas Morgan conducted a similar experiment. Instead of sweet peas, Morgan used the fruit fly *Drosophila* (droh-SOF-ih-luh) in his experiment.

When Morgan bred fruit flies, he found that the traits of body color and wing shape did not sort independently. Aware of Sutton's chromosome theory of heredity, Morgan hypothesized that the genes for these traits were located on the same chromosome. During meiosis and gamete formation, the two traits would stay together.

The work of Sutton, Bateson and Punnett, and Morgan expanded Mendel's laws of inheritance. The chromosome theory of inheritance hypothesizes that each chromosome has many genes. When genes for two traits are located on the same chromosome, the two genes travel together into the same gamete. The two traits are inherited together, instead of sorting independently. **Linked genes** are genes that are located on the same chromosome.

Are Bateson and Punnett's results explained by the concept of linked genes? If the genes for flower color and pollen size are linked, the F_1 generation produces two kinds of gametes (PL and pl), instead of the four that would be predicted by the Law of Independent Assortment (PL, Pl, pL, pl). The Punnett square in *Figure 7.8* predicts that the F_2 generation will only have the same phenotypes as the P generation–plants with purple flowers and long pollen or red flowers and short pollen.

Remember that Bateson and Punnett also got two other phenotypes in the F_2: purple flowers with short pollen and red flowers with long pollen. Since the genes are linked, the Law of Independent Assortment cannot explain these combinations of traits. Thomas Morgan hypothesized

that there must be another reason to account for the new phenotypes.

RECOMBINATION

Do the gene shuffle

When Morgan performed his experiments with fruit flies, he concluded that the genes for body color and wing shape were linked and did not sort independently. However, like Bateson and Punnett, Morgan would get some offspring with a combination of traits that differed from the parental phenotypes. Since the genes for body color and wing shape were linked, the Law of Independent Assortment could not explain this result. Morgan decided that there must be a different explanation.

Chapter 7 DNA, Genes, and Chromosomes **167**

Think Critically

To assess students' understanding of the results of crossing over, ask:

- **How might crossing over help a species survive?** (The resulting diversity or variation increases the chance that some individuals will survive environmental changes.)

 Do It!

LAB ZONE — TEAM WORK

What Does Recombination Look Like?

Review Figure 5.11 on page 116 with students. Their models of meiosis should be similar, except that the two chromosomes that line up during the first division should be two different colors of clay. To show crossing over, homologous chromosome segments should be broken off and switched, as shown in Figure 7.9.

Analyze Your Results

1 Because crossing over occurred during meiosis

2 If traits are linked, the frequency of crossing over is related to the distance between the genes which is greater with recombination.

Animated Biological Concepts

Crossing Over

Play

FIGURE 7.9

Crossing Over

Neighboring segments of these tetrads crossed over, or switched with each other. How does this process cause recombination? ❶

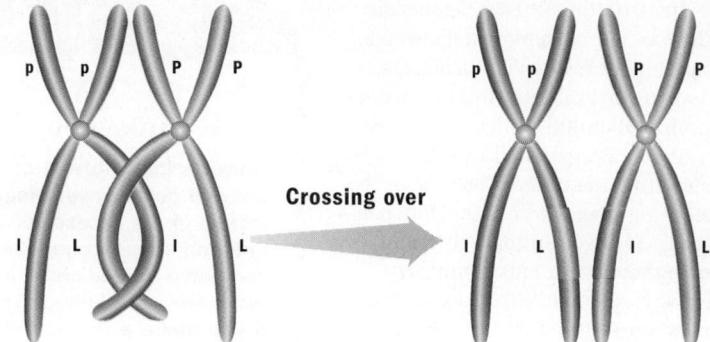

Crossing over

The new combination of traits was the result of a change in the position of alleles. When there are new combinations of alleles in offspring, the process is called recombination, and the offspring are referred to as recombinant.

Recombination can occur during meiosis, as you can see in *Figure 7.9*. As you learned in Chapter 5, homologous replicated chromosomes pair up in a set of four chromatids, or tetrads, during prophase I. Recombination occurs when the DNA strands in a tetrad cross over during prophase I.

Do It!

LAB ZONE

What Does Recombination Look Like?

You can model recombination if you . . .

Try This

1 Obtain two different colors of modeling clay.
2 Make one chromosome out of each color of clay. The chromosome should look like duplicated chromosomes at the beginning of meiosis.
3 Using your two clay chromosomes, model the steps of meiosis as shown in Figure 5.11, pages 116–117.
4 Repeat step 3, including crossing over in prophase I.

Analyze Your Results

1 Why did Bateson and Punnett see recombined traits in sweet pea plants?
2 How could recombination help geneticists locate genes on chromosomes?

168 *Unit 2 Genetics*

Crossing over refers to the recombining of alleles that occurs when neighboring segments of tetrads break off where they meet and exchange genetic material.

In Bateson and Punnett's experiment, crossing over sometimes occurred during meiosis in the F_1 generation. The alleles for pollen shape switched, producing the gametes Pl and pL in addition to PL and pl. When the F_1 self-fertilized, the F_2 included recombinant offspring: purple flowers with round pollen and red flowers with long pollen.

Crossing over is only one type of recombination. In Chapter 9, you will learn about recombinant DNA technology, where scientists insert the genes of one organism into a second organism. The recombinant organism has a combination of genes that is different from its parents.

MAPPING

Go two blocks on chromosome 16 . . .

Scientists use data on recombination to determine the location of certain genes. Knowing the location of genes and whether they are linked can help genetic counselors. As you learned in Chapter 6, genetic counselors help people to determine if they will pass a

---

MEETING DIVERSE NEEDS

Sight Impaired For the Lab Zone activity, have sight-impaired students work with sighted students, using yarn and twine with observably different textures. For steps 3 and 4, the sighted student should explain the steps of meiosis as the sight-impaired student models the process.

❶ Genes change position or are shuffled between homologous chromosomes during recombination.

harmful gene to their children. Linked genes can serve as guideposts for identifying genes associated with diseases.

To prepare gene maps, which show where genes are located on chromosomes, geneticists work with two traits (from two genes) at a time. For simplicity, we will assume that both genes have only two alleles. Alleles are the options available for a certain trait.

Once geneticists have identified two traits to study, they collect statistics on the inheritance of these two traits. If these traits are inherited independently, the geneticists can assume they are not located on the same chromosome. If the traits are not inherited independently, the traits are linked on the same chromosome.

After determining whether traits are linked, geneticists can pinpoint the location of genes by counting the number of recombinant offspring. The number of recombinant offspring indicates the number of times crossing over has occurred between two genes. Since crossing over can occur at any point between two genes, the amount of crossing over is related to the distance between two genes.

If two genes recombine often, they are located far apart. If you locate *s* and *n* in *Figure 7.10,* you can see how easily these two genes might be separated by crossing over.

If traits do not recombine often, they are more likely to be located close together on a chromosome. As genes get closer on the same chromosome, they recombine less frequently because there is less opportunity for crossing over. Do you see *b* and *r* in *Figure 7.10*? The *b* and *r* genes are not very likely to separate during crossing over. In this situation, very few offspring are recombinant. When fewer than one percent of offspring have a trait combination that differs from both parents, researchers assume that the two genes responsible for

Drosophila
(actual size 2.5–4.5 mm)

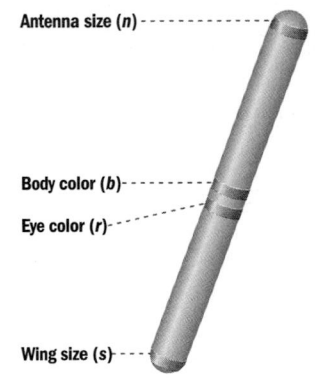

Antenna size (*n*)
Body color (*b*)
Eye color (*r*)
Wing size (*s*)

Chromosome 2
(actual size 0.5 μm)

those traits are located next to each other on the same chromosome.

Geneticists can approximate the distance between two genes on a chromosome by calculating the fraction of offspring that recombine two traits from their parents. Keep in mind, however, that this method of gene mapping does not give the exact location of a gene on a chromosome; it only indicates the relative distance between the two genes being studied. To locate genes, geneticists use molecular mapping techniques, which you will learn about in Chapter 8.

FIGURE 7.10
In this illustration, the labeled genes are all located on chromosome 2 of the fruit fly *Drosophila*. Which genes are likely to recombine? ❷

CHECKPOINT 7.3

1. How are DNA, genes, and chromosomes related?
2. How does recombination enable scientists to map genes on chromosomes?
3. **Critical Thinking** How did Bateson and Punnett's experiment with sweet pea plants support the chromosome theory of heredity?

Build on What You Know

4. Rewrite the Law of Independent Assortment to include your knowledge of linked genes. *(Need to jog your memory? Revisit relevant concepts in Chapter 6, Section 6.2.)*

Chapter 7 DNA, Genes, and Chromosomes **169**

ASSESS

Evaluate Understanding

To assess students' understanding of recombination, ask:

- **How does gene linkage explain how traits can be inherited together?** (Genes located near each other on the same chromosome tend to travel together to the same gamete.)
- **How do genes undergo recombination?** (DNA strands in one chromosome cross over to the homologous chromosome.)
- **How do geneticists map genes?** (By studying two traits and the data on recombination, they calculate the fraction of offspring that recombine the two traits. This knowledge enables them to approximate the distance between the two genes.)

Reteach

On the board, list the following terms: *genes, traits, chromosomes, DNA, gene linkage, Law of Independent Assortment, crossing over, recombination,* and *gene map.* Begin a concept map with two or more of the words. Have students work in small groups to complete the map. Have each group present its map and discuss the accuracy of each.

CHECKPOINT 7.3

1. Genes are made up of DNA and are located on chromosomes.
2. The relative frequency of recombined traits in offspring allows them to determine how close together genes are on the same chromosome, or if they are located on different chromosomes.
3. **Developing a hypothesis** They showed that genes could somehow change position on the same chromosome.
4. Genes for traits sort independently as long as they are not located on the same chromosome.

❷ The genes for wing size and antenna size are more likely to recombine, because they are far apart on the chromosome.

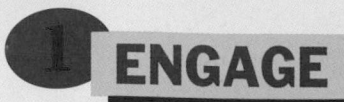

ENGAGE

Use the Visual

Have students study the photograph that opens the section. Explain that this test is commonly used to determine red-green colorblindness in people. People with this form of colorblindness see the dots making up the picture as brown. Ask:

- **If this disorder is most often observed in men, what can you infer about its pattern of inheritance?** (It must be related to gender.)

Teacher Demo

On the board, draw the four pairs of chromosomes present in male and female fruit flies, using the same colors to represent pairs of homologous chromosomes. Explain that the three similar pairs are autosomes. The nonmatching set are sex chromosomes which determine gender. Tell students that they will explore the role of sex chromosomes in determining gender and learn about other traits associated with these chromosomes.

Animated Biological Concepts

Human Sex Determination

Play

170

7.4 Sex Linkage

What you'll learn

IDEAS
- To distinguish between autosomes and sex chromosomes
- To compare and contrast sex-linked, sex-limited, and sex-influenced traits

WORDS
sex chromosomes, autosomes, sex-linked genes, sex-limited traits, sex-influenced traits

Color my world

If you can distinguish between the colored dots in this image, you may be able to make out a number. People who do not see the number may have a form of red-green color blindness. This common trait, as well as others that you will learn about in this section, has a unique pattern of inheritance.

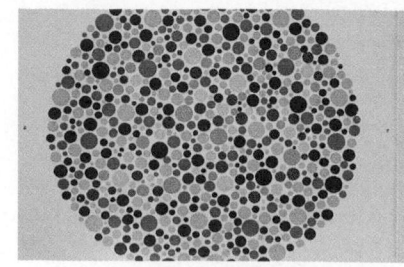

SEX CHROMOSOMES

Y they're X-cellent

You have learned that chromosomes come in homologous pairs. As is often the case in science, there are exceptions to the rule. In this instance, the exceptions are the sex chromosomes.

In some species, it is the **sex chromosomes** that determine whether the offspring are male or female. Some plants and animals have sex chromosomes; others do not. All of the non-sex chromosomes are called **autosomes.** Humans and other mammals have two sex chromosomes—X and Y. Females have two X chromosomes (XX), and males have an X and a Y chromosome (XY).

During meiosis, sex chromosomes behave like other chromosome pairs. In humans, for example, sex chromo-

somes segregate with the autosome pairs during meiosis. Because females have two X chromosomes (XX), all eggs have a single X chromosome. In males (XY), half of the sperm carry a Y chromosome and half carry an X chromosome. Which gamete—egg or sperm—determines the sex of the offspring? Study *Figure 7.11* to find the answer. ❷

SEX-LINKED TRAITS

The flies have it

As you have just read, X and Y chromosomes are not homologous—they do not contain matching genes. Genes found only in the X chromosome are X-linked, and genes found only in the Y chromosome are Y-linked. Together, the X-linked and Y-linked genes are **sex-linked genes.**

Morgan's experiments The first scientist to study sex-linked genes was Thomas Morgan. Morgan, you may recall, worked with the fruit fly *Drosophila. Drosophila* is used in many genetics experiments. Fruit flies are easy to feed and maintain, they reproduce quickly, and each generation has huge numbers of offspring, enabling researchers to gather large quantities of data in a short time. In addition, *Drosophila* has only four pairs of chromosomes.

FIGURE 7.11
The sex of humans is determined by X and Y chromosomes (below). What percentage of the offspring will be female? ❶

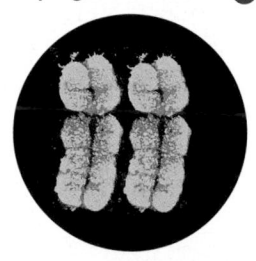

Mother's chromosomes

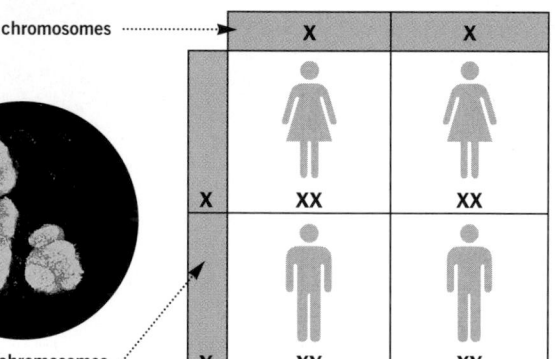

Father's chromosomes

	X	X
X	XX	XX
Y	XY	XY

170 *Unit 2 Genetics*

In 1910 Morgan noticed a mutation in one of his fruit flies—a male fly was born with white eyes instead of the usual red eyes. Morgan crossed a red-eyed female with the white-eyed male. The F₁ offspring all had red eyes. Next, Morgan bred males and females of the F₁ generation to produce an F₂ generation. He expected to find a 3:1 ratio of red-eyed to white-eyed flies. As expected, Morgan got a 3:1 ratio of red-eyed to white-eyed flies. But the white-eyed flies were all males! The surprising result of this experiment is shown in *Figure 7.12*. Nothing in Mendel's hypotheses could explain a trait that was somehow tied to the sex of the organism.

Morgan hypothesized that the white-eye allele was recessive and the red-eye allele was dominant. Furthermore, he reasoned, the eye-color gene in *Drosophila* must be located only in the X chromosome. In other words, there was no eye-color gene in the Y chromosome. If this hypothesis were true, a male fly (XY) would have white eyes if his X chromosome contained that allele. Females (XX), which carry eye-color genes in both X chromosomes, would not express a single white-eye gene because that allele is recessive. Morgan tested his hypothesis by crossing white-eyed males with red-eyed females from the F₁ generation. About half of the female offspring had white eyes.

Morgan's results confirmed his hypothesis. His fruit fly experiments were the first to locate a specific gene in a specific chromosome. His results supported the chromosome theory of heredity.

Sex-linked traits in humans
Many more sex-linked genes were discovered in the years following Morgan's breakthrough experiments. Color blindness is a sex-linked trait in humans. Red-green color blindness is caused by an X-linked recessive allele,

X^c. The allele for normal color vision, X^C, is dominant. A color-blind male has the genotype X^cY. A female who is color-blind has the genotype X^cX^c. What can you infer about the genotype of the mother of a color-blind boy? ❹

Hemophilia is another example of an X-linked disorder in humans. This disorder results in excessive bleeding after even a minor injury. The heavy bleeding is due to the absence of a blood chemical needed for normal clotting. Hemophilia is treated with concentrated doses of this chemical extracted from normal blood.

Because males receive their X chromosome from their mother, they inherit color blindness and other X-linked traits only from their mothers. Females expressing X-linked traits inherit them from both parents, because they receive an X chromosome from each parent.

P Generation

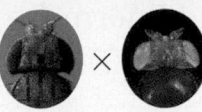

Red-eyed female × White-eyed male

F₁ Generation

Males and females all red-eyed

F₂ Generation

About ½ red-eyed females | About ¼ red-eyed males | About ¼ white-eyed males

FIGURE 7.12
Morgan was surprised when only the males had white eyes. Why did he expect a 3:1 ratio of red eyes to white eyes in the F₂ generation? ❸

Chapter 7 DNA, Genes, and Chromosomes **171**

2 TEACH

Clarify Misconceptions

Explain that the *X* and *Y* chromosomes were not named for their shape. The *X* chromosomes were called *X* only to give them a name. Later, the *Y* chromosome was so named because the letter *Y* followed *X*.

Use the Visual

Have students study Figure 7.12. Ask:

■ **In the F₂ generation, what is surprising about flies with white eyes?** (They are all male.)

■ **What do the results of the F₂ generation suggest about the trait for white eyes?** (It is on the X chromosome.)

Class Activity

Have students construct Punnett squares to show the results Morgan expected from his experiments. In the P₁ cross, have students cross female flies X^RX^R and male flies X^rY. In the F₁ cross, have students use a red-eyed female X^RX^r and a red-eyed male X^RY. Discuss the results of both crosses as a class.

Explain

Morgan ended up with fewer white-eyed flies than expected. These results were explained in later experiments that showed white-eyed flies are more likely to die before hatching than are red-eyed flies.

FACTS AND FIGURES

The X and Y chromosomes do not indicate gender in all organisms in the same way. In some birds, butterflies, and amphibians, XX indicates a male, and the female has only one X chromosome. In grasshoppers, males have only one chromosome, an X.

❶ 50%
❷ The male gamete
❸ The allele for red eye color is dominant and the allele for white eye color is recessive.
❹ She has an X-linked recessive allele, X^c.

ASSESS

Evaluate Understanding

List the following terms on the board: *chromosomes, sex chromosomes, autosomes, sex-influenced traits, sex-limited traits, gender,* and *sex-linked traits.* Have students construct a concept map that explains the relationships among the terms. Review the maps as a class.

Reteach

Work with students to create a table or other type of graphic that compares and contrasts sex-linked, sex-influenced, and sex-limited traits and provides examples of each. Then have students use the table to write a paragraph that explains the role of gender and sex chromosomes in the appearance of each type of trait.

❶ The male's colorful plumage
❷ The female can blend with the environment during nesting. The male can ward off predators.
❸ Dominant

Animated Biological Concepts

Nondisjunction   Play

SEX-LIMITED AND SEX-INFLUENCED TRAITS

Just add hormones

In addition to sex-linked traits, there are sex-limited traits. **Sex-limited traits** are only expressed in the presence of sex hormones and are only observed in one sex or the other. Like most phenotypes, sex-limited traits are controlled by genes located in autosomes, not in the sex chromosomes. Although both males and females carry these genes, they are only expressed by one sex.

In order for the sex-limited trait to be expressed, the appropriate sex hormone must be present. Because sex hormones are not produced in large amounts until a person reaches puberty, most human sex-limited traits are not expressed in children. You will learn more about hormones in Chapter 33.

Sex-limited traits explain many of the differences between the sexes. For example, male birds often have more colorful plumage than female birds. How does this sex-limited trait enable some bird populations to survive? Human traits that are sex-limited include beard growth in men and milk production in women.

FIGURE 7.13
Sex-limited traits are observed in only one sex. In the photos below, the male cardinal is on the left, and the female is on the right. What sex-limited trait ❷ can you spot in these cardinals?
❶

FIGURE 7.14
Sex-influenced traits, such as baldness, are expressed differently in each sex. Is the allele for baldness dominant or recessive in these people? ❸

Traits controlled by other autosomal genes are sex-influenced. **Sex-influenced traits** are expressed in both sexes, but they are expressed differently. For example, the allele for baldness is sex-influenced. In the presence of male sex hormones, this allele is dominant. Female sex hormones, however, cause the allele to be recessive. Thus, a woman may lose hair if she has two alleles for baldness.

CHECKPOINT 7.4

1. What is the difference between autosomes and sex chromosomes?
2. What is the difference between sex-linked traits, sex-limited traits, and sex-influenced traits?
3. **Critical Thinking** What results would you expect from a cross between a white-eyed female and a white-eyed male *Drosophila*? Use a Punnett square.

Build on What You Know

4. How would you revise the Law of Dominance to accommodate sex-linked traits? *(Need to jog your memory? Revisit relevant concepts in Chapter 6, Section 6.2.)*

CHECKPOINT 7.4

1. Sex chromosomes determine the gender of an organism, autosomes do not.
2. Sex-linked traits are present on either sex chromosome; sex-limited and sex-influenced traits are found on autosomes and require sex hormones to be expressed or to determine if the gene is dominant or recessive.

3. **Developing a hypothesis** Half the offspring will be white-eyed females, half white-eyed males.
4. Recessive alleles are not expressed in the presence of dominant alleles, unless there is no homologous chromosome.

7.5 The Human Gene Map

What you and bread have in common
Did you know that you share about one quarter of your genes with baker's yeast, the microorganism that makes bread rise? These genetic similarities have given scientists insight into several human diseases, including cancer. Scientists discovered these similarities by studying the bases that make up the 16 chromosomes of the yeast cell.

What you'll learn

IDEAS
• To explain genomes and current genome research
• To compare monosomy and trisomy and their effects

WORDS
karyotype, genome, nondisjunction, monosomy, trisomy, polyploidy

GENOMES

No place like genome

Scientists have developed several different tools and techniques for studying chromosomes, genes, and base pairs in humans and other organisms. These techniques help doctors diagnose and treat genetic disorders. They have also provided great insight into the characteristics of all living things.

Figure 7.15 shows a karyotype, one tool scientists use to learn more about chromosomes. A **karyotype** is a photograph of all of an organism's chromosomes. To make a karyotype, scientists use chemicals to freeze cells at the metaphase stage of cell division. At this stage, chromosomes are easy to isolate and stain. Karyotypes allow researchers to study differences in chromosome shape, structure, and size. The chromosomes in the karyotype shown in *Figure 7.15* are arranged so that homologous pairs are grouped together. Can you find the sex chromosomes in this karyotype? Remember, sex chromosomes are not always homologous.

Using modern molecular techniques, scientists can also study genes and base pair sequences directly. These types of analyses are called genome studies. A **genome** (JEE-nohm) is the base sequence of all of

the DNA in an organism. Nitrogenous bases, as you may recall, include adenine, guanine, cytosine, and thymine.

Genome size varies greatly from organism to organism. For example, the yeast genome includes 12.5 million bases, whereas the human genome includes 3 billion bases. However, many genes are similar in all organisms, such as the genes that control the production of common substances in eukaryotic cells.

FIGURE 7.15
Karyotypes, like the human karyotype below, are photographs of chromosomes.

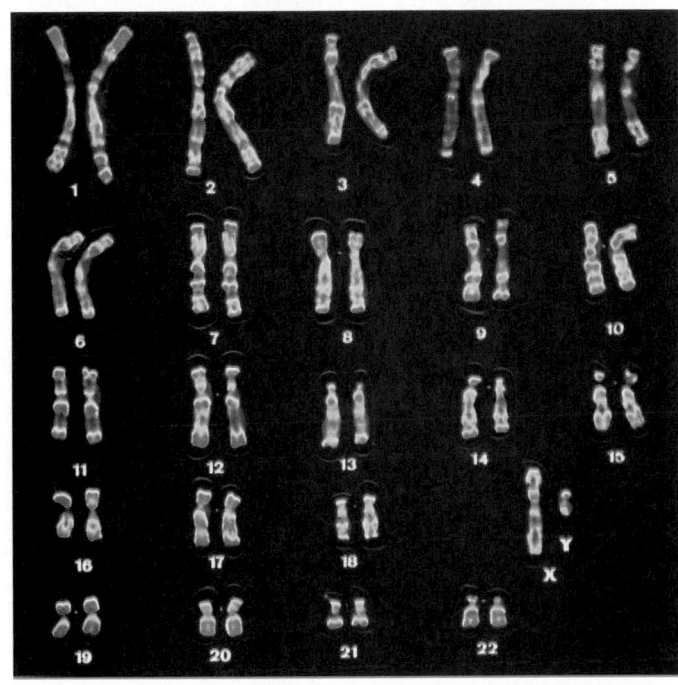

Chapter 7 DNA, Genes, and Chromosomes **173**

---

① ENGAGE

Use the Visual

Have students study the photograph that opens the section. Explain that students will learn about some methods and techniques scientists use to study genetic relationships among organisms.

Check Prior Knowledge

To assess students' knowledge about the importance of genetic research, ask:

■ **Why is identifying the genes that carry a specific trait important?** (Locating the gene responsible for a specific genetic disorder may help prevent or control the disorder.)

SUPER READ! **Finding Supporting Details** To practice strategies for effective reading, use pages 35-36 in *Super Read!*

Teacher Demo

Use a microprojector to display cells in various stages of cell division. Identify the location of the chromosomes in a cell that is in the metaphase stage. If possible, enlarge this stage. Explain that scientists developed a way to arrest cells in metaphase in order to isolate and stain the cell's chromosomes for study. Point out that one result of such studies is the karyotype shown in Figure 7.15.

❹ The X and Y chromosomes are the sex chromosomes.

2 TEACH

You may wish to have students research the progress of the Human Genome Project during the last five years in the library or at http://genetics.biosurf.com on the Internet. Students can work as a class to develop a time line showing the project's progress.

Explain

Emphasize to students that because of the large numbers of genes and the even larger number of DNA bases in the human body, it is almost impossible for two people to be genetically identical, with the exception of identical twins.

Think Critically

Students may be familiar with the use of fingerprints and DNA analysis in the field of criminology. Ask:

- **How is the DNA of a person like a fingerprint?** (The DNA of a person is as unique to that person as is his or her fingerprint. With the exception of identical twins, no two people have exactly the same genetic makeup.)

Build Writing Skills

Have students write a newspaper account that details an important discovery that has resulted from the Human Genome Project. Have them include the potential importance of these discoveries and the issues raised by people who are opposed to the project.

ISSUES IN BIOLOGY

The Human Genome Project

Researchers are very interested in sequencing all of the DNA in the human body. A worldwide effort—the Human Genome Project—is working toward this goal. The project was officially established in 1988 by scientists from thirteen nations. The Human Genome Project will not be completed until at least 2005 because the human genome is so large. To complete the project, scientists will have to sequence the 23 human chromosome pairs, which contain approximately 90,000 genes with more than 3 billion bases! As new information regarding the human genome is discovered, disease-causing genes—as well as genes for other traits—are being identified. For example, the genes responsible for cystic fibrosis, Duchenne muscular dystrophy, and Huntington disease have already been identified.

Supporters of the Human Genome Project expect that it will provide a wealth of information about human genes and how they might be manipulated. While the potential for new information is exciting, the project also raises some concerns.

FIGURE 7.16
These two high school students are researching genes for the Human Genome Project. According to the graph (below), how has the Human Genome Project progressed? ❶

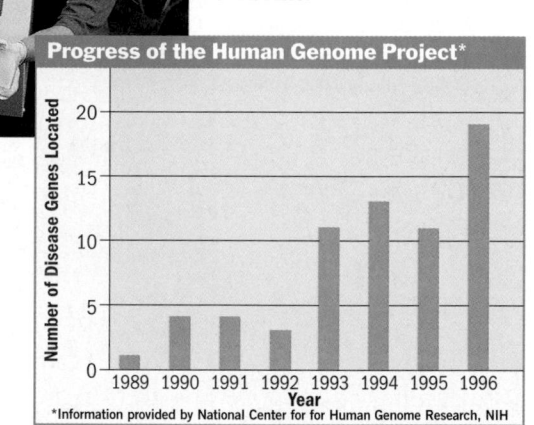

Progress of the Human Genome Project*

[Bar graph: Number of Disease Genes Located (y-axis, 0 to 20) vs. Year (x-axis, 1989–1996). 1989: 1; 1990: 4; 1991: 4; 1992: 3; 1993: 11; 1994: 13; 1995: 11; 1996: 19]

*Information provided by National Center for for Human Genome Research, NIH

Those who oppose the Human Genome Project question how useful the information will actually be. Eukaryotes have long stretches of DNA with no apparent function. In contrast, prokaryotes "use" all of their DNA sequence. Because so much of the DNA of humans and other eukaryotes appears to be unused, many people question whether the time and money spent on the project will be worthwhile.

Despite objections, the Human Genome Project continues. Other endeavors are underway as well, including projects to sequence the entire genomes of mice, cats, dogs, and the fruit fly *Drosophila*. In addition to the yeast genome, researchers have sequenced the genomes of the common bacterium *Escherichia coli,* the ulcer-causing bacterium *Helicobacter pylori,* and some viruses.

CHANGES IN THE GENOME

Two's company

Karyotypes and genome studies can reveal many characteristics of an organism. Because genome studies are difficult and take so much time, they are not used for genetic counseling. Genetic counselors do use karyotypes, however.

A karyotype can be used to find certain types of chromosomal abnormalities. For example, a karyotype may show too many or too few chromosomes. Changes in chromosome number occur when pairs of chromosomes fail to separate correctly during mitosis or meiosis. The failure of chromosomes to separate during cell division is called **nondisjunction,** which means "not separating." When nondisjunction occurs in mitosis, the individual cell may die, but the organism as a whole is not usually harmed. In contrast, nondisjunction during

---

MULTICULTURAL PERSPECTIVE

Scientists hope that research from the Human Genome Project will help them find a prevention or cure for genetic disorders that affect people from specific regions of the world. These diseases include thalassemia which is widespread in Mediterranean countries, Africa, India, and the Middle East; Tay-Sachs which affects Eastern Europeans of Jewish descent; and sickle-cell anemia common among people of African descent.

Nondisjunction in Meiosis

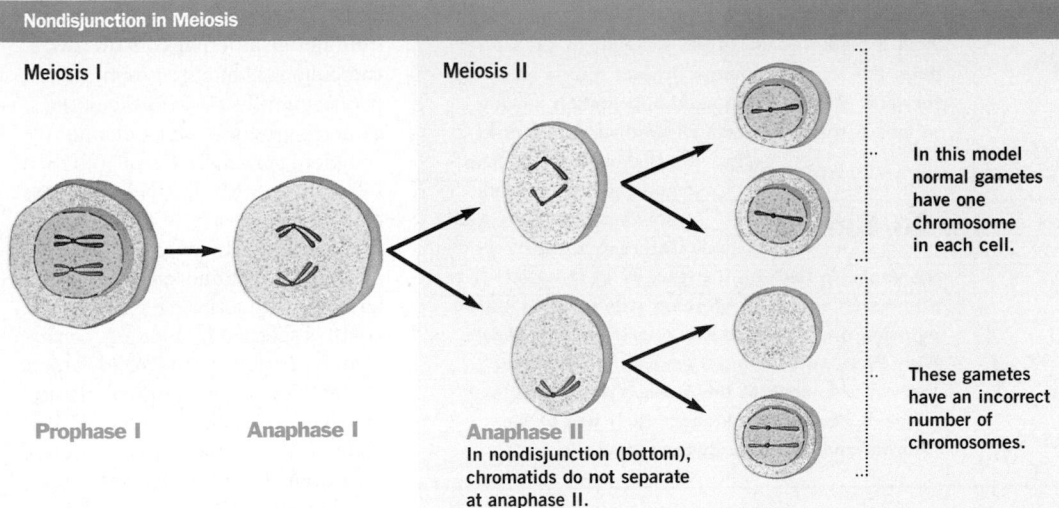

Meiosis I

Prophase I · Anaphase I

Meiosis II

Anaphase II
In nondisjunction (bottom), chromatids do not separate at anaphase II.

In this model normal gametes have one chromosome in each cell.

These gametes have an incorrect number of chromosomes.

---

anaphase I or II of meiosis causes a pair of chromosomes to remain together. Because both chromosomes are located in one daughter cell, the other daughter cell does not receive a copy of the chromosome. As a result, abnormal gametes—which can produce abnormal offspring—are formed.

As you can see in *Figure 7.17*, one gamete has too many chromosomes, while another has too few. If an abnormal gamete joins with a normal gamete, the zygote will have an abnormal number of chromosomes. In **monosomy** (MON-oh-SOH-mee), the zygote has only one copy of a particular chromosome. In **trisomy** (try-SOH-mee), the zygote has three copies of a chromosome. Which gamete in *Figure 7.17* would produce ❷ a zygote with monosomy? Trisomy?

In humans, monosomy or trisomy of most chromosomes is so disruptive that it kills the embryo. When it occurs in certain chromosomes, however, the embryo survives but has developmental difficulties. Nondisjunction can involve both autosomes and sex chromosomes. Such specific

changes in the genome cause specific, recognizable disorders.

Down syndrome is a disorder caused by trisomy of chromosome 21 (trisomy 21). How would the karyotype in *Figure 7.15* on page 173 differ for individuals with this disorder? People ❸ with Down syndrome can be mildly or severely developmentally challenged.

Abnormalities in the number of sex chromosomes can also occur. These disorders include trisomy of the sex chromosomes, resulting in XXX or XXY. Monosomy of the sex chromosomes, XO, also occurs.

FIGURE 7.17
This diagram shows nondisjunction during meiosis II, resulting in abnormal gametes. How would the diagram look if nondisjunction occurred in meiosis I? ❹

FIGURE 7.18
The child in the center has Down syndrome, a condition arising from trisomy of chromosome 21.

Chapter 7 DNA, Genes, and Chromosomes **175**

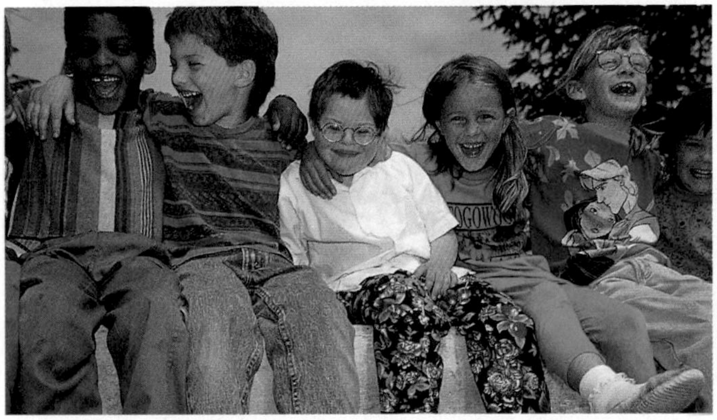

❶ The number of diseased genes located each year has increased.

❷ The gamete with no chromosomes, if fertilized, would result in monosomy in the zygote. The gamete with two chromosomes rather than one, if fertilized, would result in trisomy in the zygote.

❸ Instead of two number 21 chromosomes, they would have three.

❹ The chromosomes in Anaphase I would not separate. Half the gametes would have two chromosomes, half would have none.

In the Community

Encourage students who locate relevant areas on the Internet to share the addresses with their classmates. Suggest that students use e-mail to conduct an on-line interview with a person involved in genetics research. Have the students ask about the work, educational requirements needed for the job, and Internet sites helpful in the research.

3 ASSESS

Evaluate Understanding

On an overhead transparency, create a human karyotype that shows examples of each genetic disorder discussed in this section. Ask volunteers to identify the type of disorder shown at various points in the karyotype and explain how the disorder occurs. After all disorders have been identified and discussed, ask students why karyotypes are important and what information may be revealed through the Human Genome Project.

Reteach

Write the following main idea statements on the board: (1) Scientists have developed different tools and techniques to study and treat genetic disorders. (2) The goal of the Human Genome Project is to sequence all of the DNA in the body. (3) Karyotypes and genomes can reveal many characteristics of an organism. Tell students to look for two or more details to support each main idea as they review the section.

IN THE COMMUNITY
On-ramp to Biology

With the emergence of the Internet to exchange data, the Human Genome Project took a leap forward. The ability to send information quickly to labs across the world allowed researchers to collaborate more than ever before. Find out how scientists use the Internet in their research. To find the homepages of scientists in a research area that interests you, you can start by using one of the search engines on the World Wide Web, such as *http://genetics.biosurf.com.* You can also contact the science departments at a local college and ask about their use of the Internet and other computer resources.

EVERYDAY BIOLOGY

A Cat Called Calico Carl

Chances are you have never seen a male calico cat. Male calicoes are very rare because calico-patterned fur requires two X chromosomes. A male calico cat has trisomy of the sex chromosomes: XXY.

In **polyploidy** (POL-ee-PLOY-dee), nondisjunction occurs in all chromosome pairs. In many cases of polyploidy, nondisjunction occurs during the process of gamete production. Some of the resulting gametes will have more than one set of chromosomes. These gametes may then fuse with normal gametes or other polyploid gametes. For this reason, a polyploid organism has more than two entire sets of chromosomes. If polyploidy occurred in parent organisms with two chromosomes, for example, the resulting offspring would have four chromosomes.

In animals, polyploidy almost always results in death. However, in plants, polyploidy can actually produce a more robust plant. Because they often combine the hardiest characteristics of their parent species, polyploid plants are frequently healthier with larger flowers or fruit than plants with normal genomes.

Polyploidy in plants results when nondisjunction occurs during meiosis.

Some of the gametes produced from nondisjunction contain two complete sets of chromosomes. (Consequently, some of the other gametes produced do not contain a complete genome.) The plants then self-fertilize with diploid gametes or haploid gametes.

Polyploidy also occurs when a polyploid gamete of one species cross-fertilizes with a normal gamete from another species. In addition, because plants produced by polyploid gametes are often larger and hardier, plant breeders artificially produce polyploid plants with chemicals that prevent the separation of chromosomes.

About 25 to 50 percent of all plant varieties are polyploids, including many of the plants you eat. The wheat used to make bread is a polyploid that has 42 chromosomes. This wheat plant was an accidental hybrid of a cultivated wheat that had 28 chromosomes, and a wild grass that had 14 chromosomes. Potatoes, oats, bananas, peanuts, barley, plums, apples, sugarcane, coffee, and cotton also are polyploid plants.

CHECKPOINT 7.5

1. What is a genome?
2. Explain the difference between monosomy and trisomy.
3. **Critical Thinking** Make a sketch that shows how the chromosomal abnormality leading to Down syndrome is produced.

Build on What You Know

4. How does polyploidy emphasize the difference between mitosis and meiosis? *(Need to jog your memory? Revisit relevant concepts in Chapter 5, Section 5.4.)*

 Where are genes located?

CHECKPOINT 7.5

1. All the nucleotide bases in all the genes in all the chromosomes of an organism
2. In monosomy, zygote has one copy of a particular chromosome instead of two; in trisomy, zygote has three copies instead of two.
3. **Applying** Sketches should focus on nondisjunction in Anaphase II.
4. Polyploidy in meiosis results in polyploid cells throughout the surviving offspring; polyploidy in mitosis results in fewer polyploid cells.

Chapter 7 Review

 **THE BIG IDEA!**

7.1–7.2 The structure of DNA, the molecule of heredity, enables the molecule to copy itself.

7.3–7.5 Genes, sections of DNA that code for a specific trait, are linked together on chromosomes.

Sum It Up

Use the following summary to review the main concepts in this chapter.

7.1 Molecule of Heredity

- Frederick Griffith's experiments showed that genetic material transformed cells.
- Martha Chase and Alfred Hershey proved that DNA is the genetic material of cells.

7.2 DNA Structure and Replication

- DNA is composed of nucleotides and is shaped like a double helix.
- A nucleotide has three parts: a sugar, a phosphate, and a nitrogenous base.
- Bases always form complementary base pairs: adenine binds with thymine, and cytosine binds with guanine.
- Complementary base pairing enables DNA to replicate, or copy itself.

7.3 Linked Genes

- Linked genes are located in the same chromosome and do not sort independently.
- Chromosomes sometimes cross over during meiosis, resulting in recombination of alleles.

7.4 Sex Linkage

- Sex chromosomes determine the sex of offspring. All other chromosomes are autosomes.
- The human sex chromosomes are the X chromosome and the Y chromosome.
- Genes located on sex chromosomes are sex-linked genes.
- Sex-limited and sex-influenced traits are controlled by genes located on autosomes, but these traits are affected by sex hormones.

7.5 The Human Gene Map

- A karyotype is an image showing all of an organism's chromosomes.
- A genome is the base sequence of all of the DNA in an organism.
- The Human Genome Project is the effort to sequence the entire human genome.
- Nondisjunction occurs when chromosomes fail to separate during cell division.

Use Terms and Concepts

Use each of the following words or terms in a complete sentence. If you need to review a meaning, turn to the page indicated.

adenine (p. 161)
guanine (p. 161)
cytosine (p. 161)
thymine (p. 161)
double helix (p. 161)
replication (p. 163)

linked genes (p. 167)
crossing over (p. 168)
autosomes (p. 170)
sex chromosomes (p. 170)
sex-linked genes (p. 170)

sex-limited traits (p. 172)
sex-influenced traits (p. 172)
karyotype (p. 173)
genome (p. 173)

nondisjunction (p. 174)
monosomy (p. 175)
trisomy (p. 175)
polyploidy (p. 176)

Chapter 7 DNA, Genes, and Chromosomes **177**

Review the Big Ideas

Before students begin the Chapter Review, you may wish to discuss main concepts from the Big Ideas in Chapter 7. Point out that DNA, the molecule of heredity, is carried in the chromosomes of an organism. Shaped like a double helix, DNA copies itself during a process called replication. Genes are the sections of DNA that code for a specific trait. Linked genes can be shuffled by crossing over.

Answers

1. Monosomy, trisomy
2. Adenine
3. double helix
4. genome
5. crossing over
6. Chromosomes
7. False; Autosomes
8. True
9. True
10. False; karyotype
11. True
12. By observing the frequency with which traits recombine, researchers can determine if genes are located on the same chromosome, and if so, the relative distance between them.
13. The DNA double helix unzips. Free, complementary nucleotides pair up with bases on both strands of DNA. At the same time, sugars and phosphates on the forming chains bind to each other.
14. They expected a 9:3:3:1 ratio of PL, pL, pL, and pl phenotypes. They did not get these results because the genes for these two traits are linked or located on the same chromosome.
15. Linked genes on a chromosome are separated when segments of homologous chromosomes cross over during meiosis.
16. The resulting gametes have an incorrect number of chromosomes. Because chromosomes contain all of the genetic information, offspring produced by these gametes have an incorrect genome.
17. Males receive one X chromosome and exhibit the traits on that chromosome, whether the alleles are recessive or dominant.

Use Your Word Power

COMPLETION Write the word or phrase that best completes each statement.

1. _____ or _____ can result from nondisjunction during meiosis.

2. _____ and thymine are complementary bases.

3. The shape of DNA is described as a twisted ladder, or a(n) _____ .

4. A(n) _____ is the base pair sequence of all of the DNA of an organism.

5. Recombination can occur during _____ of chromosomes.

6. _____ do not follow Mendel's Law of Independent Assortment.

TRUE-FALSE Write true if the statement is true. If the statement is false, replace the underlined word(s) to make the statement true.

7. <u>Sex chromosomes</u> are responsible for sex-influenced traits.

8. Sex-limited traits are controlled by genes on <u>autosomes</u>.

9. <u>Nondisjunction</u> occurs when chromatids fail to separate.

10. An image of all of an organism's chromosomes is called a <u>genome</u>.

11. The process by which DNA copies itself is called <u>replication</u>.

Show What You Know

12. How can researchers map genes?

13. Using words or drawings, describe how DNA replicates.

14. How did the results of Bateson and Punnett's experiments differ from their hypothesis? How did they explain the difference?

15. How does recombination of linked genes occur? Explain.

16. Why can nondisjunction be harmful when it occurs during meiosis?

17. Why do human males always exhibit recessive traits located in X chromosomes?

18. What is polyploidy? What are two ways that polyploidy can occur in plants?

19. What two major concepts did Morgan discover when working with the fruit fly *Drosophila*?

20. What is the Human Genome Project?

21. **Make a Concept Map** Complete the concept map below by adding the following terms: adenine, thymine, cytosine, guanine, sugar, phosphates, chromosomes, autosome, sex chromosome.

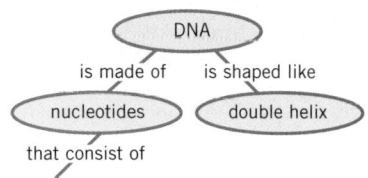

Take It Further

22. **Applying Concepts** Use sketches to show that the farther apart linked genes are, the more likely they are to be separated during crossing over.

23. **Identifying Cause and Effect** Suppose a man with hemophilia marries a woman who is a carrier of the disorder. Determine the probability that any son or daughter will have the disorder.

24. **Making a Prediction** How would survival be affected if everyone had the same genome?

25. **Analyzing Data** Chargaff measured the distance between DNA's sugar-phosphate backbones. Using your knowledge of purines and pyrimidines, describe how this knowledge helped Watson and Crick model DNA.

18. A polyploid organism has three or more sets of chromosomes. Polyploidy occurs in plants by self-fertilization with diploid gametes or cross-fertilization with a polyploid gamete.

19. He discovered a sex-linked gene and provided evidence that chromosomes were the location of Mendel's heritable factors.

20. The Human Genome Project is the effort to identity all the bases on all the DNA on all chromosomes in the human body.

21. Concept maps should include these terms and ideas.
DNA is made of <u>nucleotides</u> that consist of <u>sugar</u>, <u>phosphate</u>, and nitrogenous bases. The bases include <u>adenine, thymine, cytosine,</u> and <u>guanine</u>. <u>DNA</u> is

26. Interpreting a Graph An imaginary kind of beetle has two alleles each for color and pattern: maroon or ochre, spotted or solid. Two beetles heterozygous for both traits are crossed. This graph shows the observed phenotypes of the offspring. Are these traits linked? Which traits are dominant?

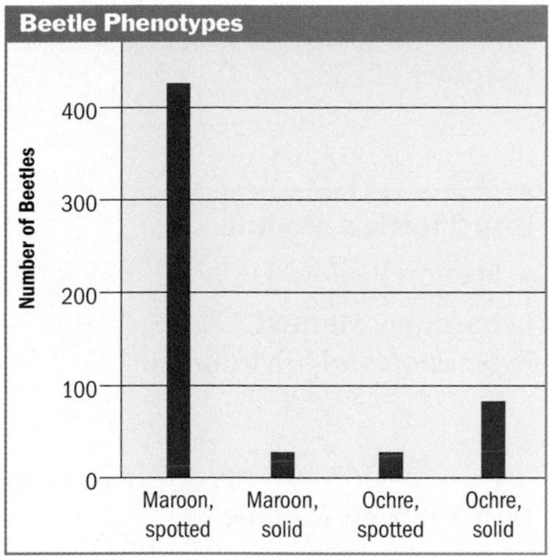

27. Analyzing Data Which strands are complementary pairs? Which strand doesn't have a pair? Graph the data to determine the answer.

Some Common Elements

	Base Percentages			
	A	*T*	*C*	*G*
DNA Strand #1	23.6	24.8	29.2	22.4
DNA Strand #2	23.2	19.4	29.8	27.6
DNA Strand #3	19.6	26.8	26.3	27.3
DNA Strand #4	27.1	19.2	26.9	26.8
DNA Strand #5	25.2	23.1	22.7	29.0

28. Designing an Experiment Researchers suspect that a certain disease is caused by a recessive allele in a gene located in the X chromosome in fruit flies. Design an experiment to test this hypothesis.

Consider the Issues

29. Genome Money Matters The United States Congress contributed $53 million to begin the Human Genome Project. The final cost of the project is expected to be in the billions of dollars, with much of the money coming from government and private grants. Write a speech to deliver to Congress defending or opposing funding for the project. Support your argument.

Make New Connections

30. Biology and Physics Research and report on the characteristics of X rays. Describe how X rays produced the images used to research DNA structure.

31. Biology and Community Investigate the production of polyploid plants in your state. What methods and chemicals are used to produce the polyploid plants?

32. Biology and Design Use different materials than those in the Do It! activity to plan and construct a model of DNA. Use your model to show how DNA replicates.

FAST-FORWARD TO CHAPTER 8

DNA was established as the genetic material in cells because it transfers information from parents to offspring. The next chapter explains how DNA affects traits.

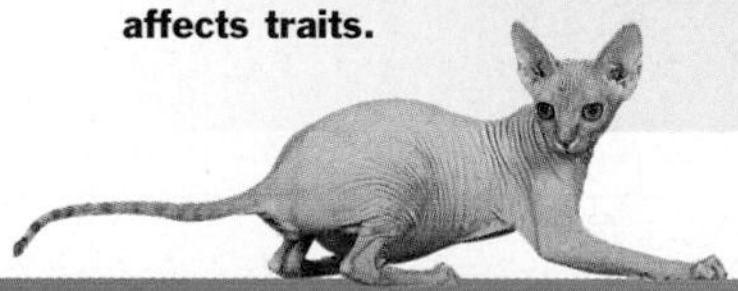

shaped like a double helix and is the main component in chromosomes which include autosomes and sex chromosomes.

22. Drawings will vary, Students can use Figure 7.10 as a starting point.

23. Half the sons and half the daughters are likely to be affected.

24. If everyone had an identical DNA sequence for all genes, there would still be some variation as the environment also influences the behavior of organisms.

25. Chargaff's data led Watson and Crick to the idea of complementary base pairing.

26. The traits are linked; maroon color and a spotted pattern are dominant.

27. DNA strands #1 and #5 are complementary, as are strands #3 and #4. DNA strand #2 does not have a complementary strand.

28. Answers may vary but should include a cross between a carrier female (offspring of a "diseased" male) and a normal male. If the gene is sex-linked, the disease will appear only in male offspring; if the gene is on an autosome, the disease will occur in both sexes.

29. Accept all logical responses.

30. The X-ray image of the DNA indicated showed a tightly coiled molecule with a spiral shape, indicating that the DNA molecule was not a single strand, but rather a double helix.

31. Varieties will vary. Polypoid plants can be produced by cross breeding a polypoid gamete with a normal gamete from another species, or by using chemicals that prevent the separation of chromosomes.

32. Students' designs should show the double helix, different base pairs, and a mechanism by which the double helix can unwind and rewind. Encourage students to use their imagination in developing a model.

PLANNING GUIDE

Section	Student Activities/Features	Teacher's Resource Package
8.1 From Genotype to Phenotype **Objectives** ■ Describe the process of transcription of DNA to mRNA ■ Demonstrate the process of translation of mRNA to build proteins	**Lab Zone Discover It!** *Identifying Ways to Prevent Skin Cancer,* p. 181 **Lab Zone Do It!** *What Is Your Codon Count?* p. 186 **Lab Zone Investigate It!** *Modeling Protein Synthesis,* p. 187	**Unit 2 Review Module** ■ Section Review 8.1 ■ Activity Recordsheets 8-1 and 8-2 ■ Enrichment Topic 8-1 **Interpreting and Developing Graphics** 22, 23
8.2 Protein and Phenotype **Objectives** ■ Describe the control of gene expression in prokaryotes ■ Appraise the effects of gene control in eukaryotic cells	**Everyday Biology** *Tidy Proteins,* p. 188	**Unit 2 Review Module** ■ Section Review 8.2 **Laboratory Manual,** Lab 17: "Gene Expression and Environment"
8.3 Changes in Chromosomes **Objectives** ■ Explain how mutations can affect proteins and protein synthesis ■ Distinguish between chromosomal mutations and gene mutations	**Lab Zone Think About It!** *From Milk to Wasp: Modeling Mutations,* p. 195	**Unit 2 Review Module** ■ Section Review 8.3 ■ Interpreting Graphics 8 **Interpreting and Developing Graphics** 24
8.4 Genes and Cancer **Objectives** ■ Summarize the role of oncogenes in the development of cancer ■ Identify environmental causes of mutation	**In the Community** *Where There's Smoke . . .* p. 199 **STS: Frontiers in Biology** *Eat Your Vegetables,* p. 199 **Everyday Biology** *Feeling the Burn?* p. 199	**Unit 2 Review Module** ■ Section Review 8.4 ■ Critical Thinking Exercise 8 ■ Vocabulary Review 8 ■ Chapter 8 Tests **Consumer Applications** 8-1 **Issues and Decision Making** 8-1 **Biotechnology Manual,** Lab 13: "A Simulation of DNA Mutations and Cancer" **Spanish Reviews** Chapter 8

Technology Resources

Internet Connections

Within this chapter, you will see the **bioSURF** logo. If you and your students have access to the Internet, the following URL address will provide various Internet connections that are related to topics and features presented in this chapter:

http://genetics.biosurf.com

You can also find relevant chapter material at **The Biology Place** address:

http://www.biology.com

CD-ROMs

Biología: la telaraña de la vida, (Spanish Student Edition) Chapter 8
Teacher's Resource Planner, Chapter 8 Supplements
Interactive Biological Simulations
- Protein Synthesis Overview
- Transcription
- Translation
TestWorks CD-ROM
- Chapter 8 Tests

Videodiscs

Animated Biological Concepts Videodiscs
- DNA Transcription
- Protein Synthesis
- Duplication and Deletion
- Translocation and Inversion
- Point Mutations

Overhead Transparencies

- Transcription, #18
- Translation, #19
- Prokaryotic Control Mechanisms, #20

Videotapes

Biology Alive! Video Series
Rewind: The Web of Life Reteach Videos

Planning for Activities

STUDENT EDITION
Lab Zone
Discover It! p. 181
- old photograph or painting showing people participating in outdoor activities

Lab Zone Do It! p. 186
- four sheets of paper of four different colors
- scissors
- table or floor

Lab Zone
Investigate It! p. 187
- 36 pushpins (5 different colors)
- metric ruler
- 3 strips of corrugated cardboard (18 cm × 3 cm)
- marker

TEACHER'S EDITION
Quick Activity, p. 182
Deciphering a DNA code
- copies of code sheet

Teacher Demo, p. 184
A eukaryote cell
- transparency or wall chart of an eukaryote cell

Quick Activity, p. 188
Gene—on or off?
- flashlight

Teacher Demo, p. 196
Cancer cells and non-cancerous cells
- microprojector
- slides of cancer cells and noncancerous cells

Chapter Objectives

Students will learn the main concepts of this chapter as they complete the following objectives.

- Describe the process of transcription of DNA to mRNA
- Demonstrate the process of translation of mRNA to build proteins
- Describe the control of gene expression in prokaryotes
- Appraise the effects of gene control in eukaryotic cells
- Explain how mutations can affect proteins and protein synthesis
- Distinguish between chromosomal mutations and gene mutations
- Summarize the role of oncogenes in the development of cancer
- Identify environmental causes of mutation

Key Words

8.1 *protein synthesis, RNA, transcription, translation, introns, exons, codon, anticodon*

8.2 *repressor, promoter*

8.3 *mutation, deletion, duplication, translocation, inversion, frameshift mutation, point mutation*

8.4 *oncogene, mutagen, carcinogen*

The Opening Story

Explain that DNA can be changed, or mutated, by factors in the environment such as ultraviolet light. Ask students to think of other factors that might change DNA. Tell students that in this chapter they will explore the causes and effects of mutations.

180

CHAPTER 8
Protein Synthesis

You can find out more about protein synthesis by exploring the following Internet address:
http://genetics.biosurf.com

In this chapter . . .

FEATURES

Everyday Biology
- Tidy Proteins
- Feeling the Burn?

In the Community
Where There's Smoke . . .

 Frontiers in Biology
Eat Your Vegetables

LAB ZONES

Discover It!
- Identifying Ways to Prevent Skin Cancer

Do It!
- What Is Your Codon Count?

Think About It!
- From Milk to Wasp: Modeling Mutations

Investigate It!
- Modeling Protein Synthesis

Older than your years

Do you sometimes wish you looked a little older? The ultraviolet rays of the sun can grant that wish. Scientists have found that exposure to sunlight without protection—either from clothing or a sunscreen lotion—damages the skin, causing wrinkles and skin cancer.

You may think that skin cancer and wrinkles do not occur until old age. But the ultraviolet rays of the sun may already be changing the genetic material in your skin cells, so that new cells are not as healthy as their parent cells. By combining magnification and lighting to view a person's skin, doctors are able to detect skin damage, as shown in the photo.

But exactly what cellular changes are initiated by ultraviolet radiation? In this chapter, you will learn about how cellular processes work and what causes some of those processes to go awry—leading to the development of skin cancer and wrinkles. But you have the power right now to help prevent skin cancer—put on some sunscreen and a hat!

 **Discover It!**

Identifying Ways to Prevent Skin Cancer

You need an old photograph or painting showing people participating in outdoor activities

1. Look at the people in the image and observe any precautions they have taken to avoid the sun.
2. Write down your observations.

Fashion in many sunny climates has often included head coverings, long sleeves, and umbrellas to block the sun, even though the dangers of skin cancer may have been unknown at the time. How do you protect yourself from the sun? How do others around you protect themselves? How can you improve your sun-safety habits?

WRITE ABOUT IT!

In your science journal, write about a sunny day you spent outdoors. Did you and your companions wear sunscreen or protective clothing? If not, rewrite the story of your sunny day and include details of the preventive measures you could have taken.

Chapter 8 Protein Synthesis **181**

PORTFOLIO PREVIEW

Students should be encouraged to add to their portfolios as they work through this chapter. In addition to the *Write About It* opportunity, the following section is an excellent opportunity for portfolio entries:

- Section 8.2: *Protein and Phenotype*

Opening Activities

bioSURF If you have access to the Internet in your classroom or school, you may wish to have students connect to the address shown on page 180. You may also want to have students conduct net searches for information using key words related to this chapter. For example, they could search entries under proteins, mutagens, and cancer.

Discover It!

Identifying Ways to Prevent Skin Cancer  TEAM WORK

You may want to assign this activity as homework and then discuss the responses in class or use the lab as a class activity. Divide the class into small groups and provide each group with a photograph of people from different countries. Ask:

- **What observations did you make?**

WRITE ABOUT IT!

After students write their journal entries, have volunteers read their stories aloud and discuss what they changed in the rewrite.

REWIND to Chapter 7

Briefly review concepts learned in Chapter 7, *DNA, Genes, and Chromosomes.* Ask:

- **How do you think DNA, genes, and chromosomes relate to the process of protein synthesis?**

ENGAGE

Consider The Big Idea

Have students read The Big Idea! at the top of the page. Explain that DNA directs protein synthesis in the cell.

Use the Visual

Have students study the photograph that opens the section. Explain that hormones are compounds made in one part of the body that affect activities in another part of the body. Introduce the idea that DNA and the expression of DNA can be altered by environmental factors.

Check Prior Knowledge

To assess students' knowledge about RNA, ask:

- **What two nucleic acids are present in living things?**
  (DNA and RNA)
- **What is the function of RNA?**
  (To make proteins using the instructions in DNA)

Quick Activity

Make and distribute a simple code sheet with numbers representing the letters of the alphabet. Write on the board, in code, this message: *DNA codes for the manufacture of proteins.* Have students decode the message. Explain that the genetic message in DNA is in a code that RNA uses to assemble proteins.

THE BIG IDEA! Genes are sequences of DNA bases that can be translated into proteins or parts of proteins when they are activated. 8.1–8.2

8.1 From Genotype to Phenotype

What you'll learn

IDEAS
- To describe the process of transcription of DNA to mRNA
- To demonstrate the process of translation of mRNA to build proteins

WORDS
protein synthesis, RNA, transcription, translation, introns, exons, codon, anticodon

Special diet creates super ants!
Most larvae of the ant species *Pheidole pallidula* develop into docile worker ants. But during times of danger the ants produce many more larvae that develop into large, aggressive soldier ants. Research indicates that the ants change their food supply when under threat. The change in diet alters their hormonal balance which, in turn, affects their genes. If genes are inherited, how do you think their effects **1** can be changed?

GENE EXPRESSION

Protein rules

Protein has a role in virtually every activity of every organism, from the respiration of a bacterium to the blink of an elephant's eye. Organisms make the proteins they need through a process called protein synthesis. **Protein synthesis** is the process by which an organism's genotype (the genetic makeup) is translated into its phenotype (the traits). An organism's phenotype depends on the formation of specific structural proteins based on its genotype.

Genes code for the sequence of amino acids that make up proteins. A gene is made of DNA. The sequence of DNA bases in a gene determines the composition of one or more proteins. You can think of DNA as a template, or pattern, for making proteins.

Some genes code for proteins that regulate the expression of other genes; that is, they determine which genes are expressed at a given moment and which are not expressed. A gene is "expressed" when the protein that it codes for is synthesized.

DNA works with another nucleic acid—ribonucleic (RY-boh-noo-KLAY-ik) acid, or RNA. The structural differences between DNA and RNA are shown in *Figure 8.1*. **RNA** is a single-stranded nucleic acid that is involved in protein synthesis. There are three types of RNA—messenger RNA (mRNA), transfer RNA (tRNA), and ribosomal RNA (rRNA). Each type has a specific function.

Protein synthesis occurs in two stages. During the first stage—called **transcription**—the genetic information from a strand of DNA is copied into a strand of mRNA. The word "transcribe" means "to copy." You can see the steps of transcription in *Figure 8.2*.

FIGURE 8.1
Both DNA and RNA are nucleic acids, but they differ in structure. What are the differences? **2**

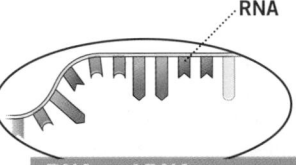
—RNA

RNA and DNA: Structural Differences	
RNA	**DNA**
Single-stranded	Double-stranded
Base pairs: C–G, A–U	Base pairs: C–G, A-T
(Cytosine–Guanine Adenine–Uracil)	(Cytosine–Guanine Adenine–Thymine)
Ribose sugar group	Deoxyribose sugar group

DNA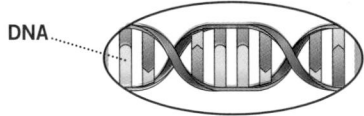

STUDENT RESOURCES

From the Teacher's Resource Package, use:
- Section Review 8.1, Activity Record-sheets 8-1 and 8-2, and Enrichment Topic 8-1 from Unit 2 Review Module

 **TECHNOLOGY RESOURCES**

Relevant technology resources include:
- Interactive Biological Simulations CD-ROM: "Protein Synthesis Overview", "Transcription" and "Translation"
- Animated Biological Concepts Videodiscs: "DNA Transcription" and "Protein Synthesis"

FIGURE 8.2

Transcription

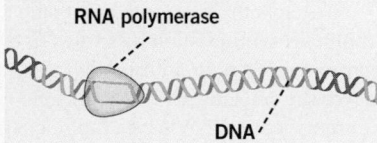

RNA polymerase

DNA

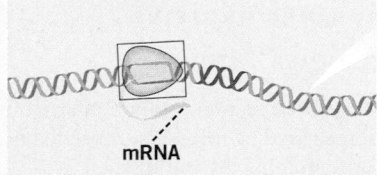

mRNA

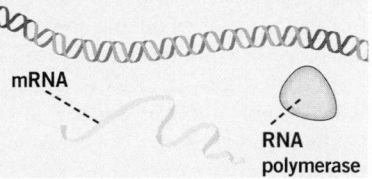

mRNA

RNA polymerase

1 **Transcription begins**
The enzyme RNA polymerase separates, or "unzips," a section of DNA.

2 **mRNA synthesis begins**
RNA polymerase binds unattached RNA bases to their complementary bases on the DNA strand and link the RNA nucleotides to form a molecule of mRNA.

3 **Transcription ends**
After a section of DNA is transcribed, the next section is exposed. The process repeats until DNA signals mRNA synthesis to end.

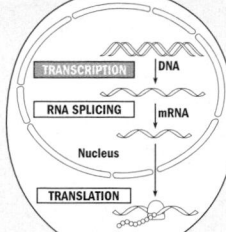

Use this locator diagram of a eukaryotic cell to identify where the stages of protein synthesis take place.

TRANSCRIPTION — DNA
RNA SPLICING — mRNA
Nucleus
TRANSLATION
Cytoplasm

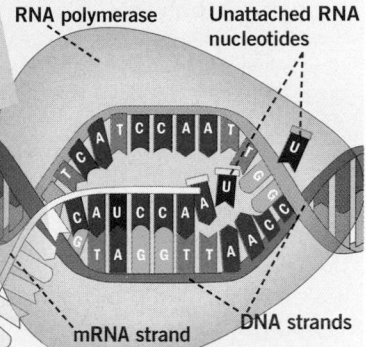

RNA polymerase

Unattached RNA nucleotides

mRNA strand

DNA strands

Direction of transcription ⟶

The second stage of protein synthesis is called translation. You may be familiar with this word. Translation in cells is similar to translation in speech or writing. In cells, **translation** is a process by which the "language" of nucleic acids (bases) is changed into the "language" of proteins (amino acids).

In order for genes to be expressed, the DNA in chromosomes has to be made accessible. Recall from *Figure 7.7* that DNA is coiled and wound in chromosomes. Inactive DNA is tightly coiled, whereas active DNA is loosely coiled. The coiling and uncoiling of DNA is one way of controlling gene expression. Scientists hypothesize that chemicals such as growth factors and hormones cause chromosomes to tighten or loosen their coils.

BUILDING RNA

Making the messenger

Transcription is the process of transferring genetic information from a strand of DNA to a strand of mRNA. Once the chromosome coils loosen, transcription can begin with RNA polymerase (POL-ih-meh-rayz). This enzyme separates the two strands of a DNA double helix, exposing the base pairs of a gene. Unattached RNA bases are present in the nucleus. RNA polymerase matches RNA bases with the complementary bases on one strand of the DNA template. As you see in *Figure 8.2,* RNA bases (U, A, G, and C) bind with complementary DNA bases (A, T, C, and G). Note that in RNA it is uracil, not thymine, that binds with adenine. Because of these specific binding

Chapter 8 Protein Synthesis **183**

Class Activity

On the board, draw a two-column chart with the heads *Base* and *Complementary Base*. Divide the *Complementary Base* column in half and label with subheads *DNA* and *RNA*. Under the *Base* head list: A, T, G, C. Have students list the complementary bases for DNA and RNA in the proper column. (DNA: T, A, C, G. RNA: U, A, C, G.). Ask:

■ **How do the bases for DNA and RNA differ?** (In DNA, adenine binds with thymine; in RNA adenine binds with uracil.)

Interactive Biological Simulations
Protein Synthesis Overview
Students first view an animation describing the process of protein synthesis, and then label a diagram that outlines the steps of protein synthesis.
Transcription Students use RNA polymerase and free RNA nucleotides to transcribe a strand of DNA.

Animated Biological Concepts

DNA Transcription

Play

MEETING DIVERSE NEEDS

LEP Encourage LEP students to work with a partner to enhance their understanding of Figure 8.2. Suggest that they take turns explaining the process to each other. Students may also want to rewrite the captions in their native language. Suggest that partners also work together on Figure 8.4.

❶ Students can look for the answer as they read the chapter.

❷ The table in Figure 8.1 lists the three differences.

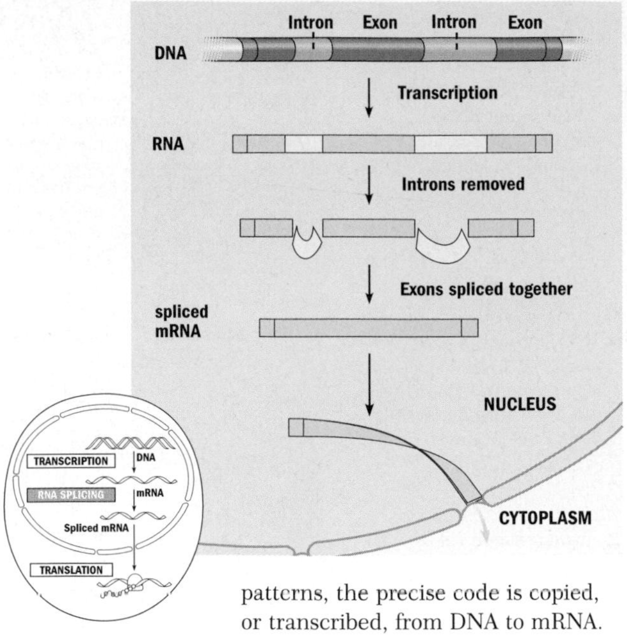

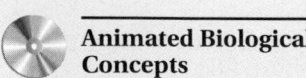

FIGURE 8.3

Before mRNA leaves the nucleus of a eukaryotic cell, it undergoes RNA splicing. What happens to exons during mRNA splicing? **1**

patterns, the precise code is copied, or transcribed, from DNA to mRNA.

In prokaryotic cells, which have no nuclei, mRNA travels directly to a ribosome. In fact, both transcription and translation can proceed simultaneously in prokaryotes. Because proteins are made quickly, prokaryotes can multiply rapidly. This rapid reproduction is one reason you get sick so quickly when infected by some disease-causing prokaryotes, such as the bacterium that causes strep throat.

In eukaryotic cells, or cells with nuclei, mRNA must go through an additional step before it reaches a ribosome. This additional step, shown in *Figure 8.3*, is called RNA splicing. DNA in eukaryotic cells contains regions that do not code for proteins. These noncoding regions of DNA or RNA are called **introns.** The sections of DNA or RNA that do contain codes for proteins are called **exons.**

DNA introns and exons are both transcribed into mRNA. Before the mRNA leaves the nucleus, enzymes remove the introns and join the exons to one another. In this way, mRNA is

spliced, or cut and rejoined, and the mRNA that leaves the nucleus includes only exons.

RNA splicing is an important step in protein synthesis in eukaryotes. It controls the genetic information that leaves the nucleus. Once the introns are removed, mRNA leaves the nucleus and moves to a ribosome in the cytoplasm, where translation occurs.

BUILDING PROTEINS

A new "language"

During translation, genetic information carried by mRNA is translated to form proteins. As you learned in Chapter 2, proteins are made of specific sequences of amino acids. Translation involves linking amino acids together into these sequences.

In the cytoplasm, mRNA attaches to a ribosome, a tiny organelle that can be found either floating freely in the cytoplasm or attached to endoplasmic reticulum. The ribosome, with its attached mRNA, is now ready to synthesize a protein. *Figure 8.4* shows the interactions of mRNA and ribosomes during the second stage of protein synthesis, translation.

During translation, a tRNA molecule transfers an amino acid to the ribosome. The tRNA's main function is to transport amino acids. As shown in *Figure 8.4* each new amino acid links with the previous amino acid, forming an amino acid chain. As more and more tRNAs arrive, each with an amino acid, the chain grows longer. The lengthening of the amino acid chain is called elongation.

You might wonder how tRNA delivers the amino acids in the correct order. This sequencing is done through a system of complementary codons and anticodons. A **codon** is a three-base section of mRNA. Most codons carry a code for a specific amino acid. For example, the codon

FIGURE 8.4

Translation

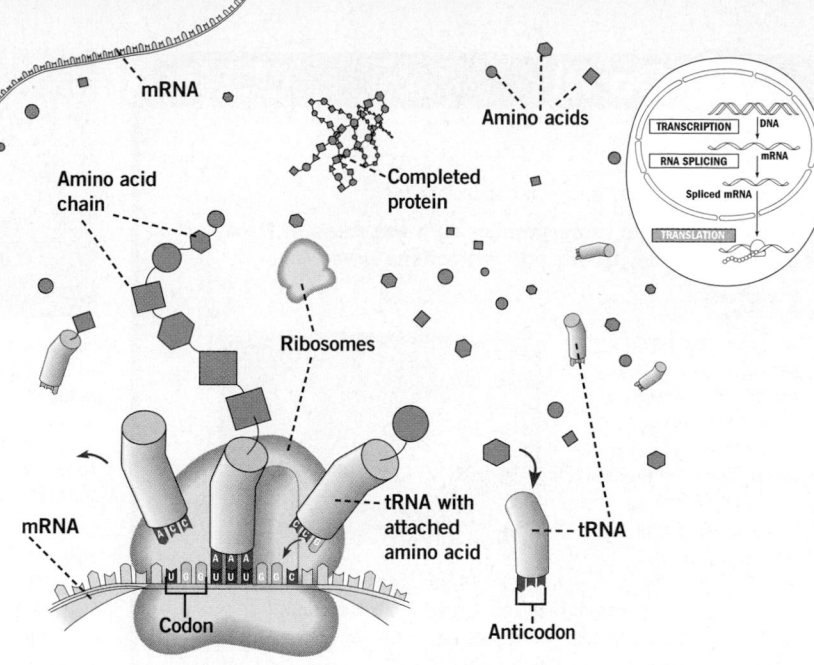

mRNA

Amino acids

Amino acid chain

Completed protein

Making proteins

In the cytoplasm, one kind of amino acid is attached to each tRNA. An mRNA is attached to a ribosome. During elongation, tRNAs bring amino acids to the ribosome. Amino acids are added one at a time to the growing amino acid chain. Each tRNA anticodon pairs with a complementary mRNA codon, making sure that amino acids are added in the coded sequence.

Ribosomes

tRNA with attached amino acid

tRNA

mRNA

Codon

Anticodon

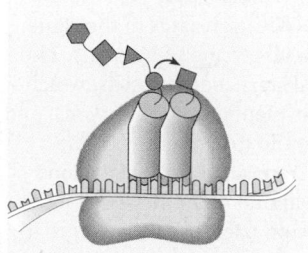

Elongation cycle: step 1
During elongation, the ribosome has two tRNAs bound to the mRNA. One tRNA (left) is attached to the growing amino acid chain. A new tRNA (right) brings a new amino acid.

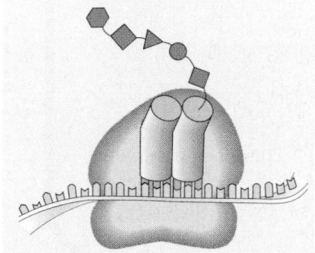

Elongation cycle: step 2
The growing amino acid chain is bonded to the new amino acid on the new tRNA. The chain is now one amino acid longer.

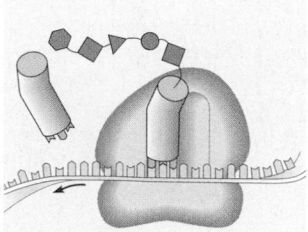

Elongation cycle: step 3
The tRNA that released the growing chain leaves the ribosome. The mRNA moves down the ribosome, and the elongation cycle begins again.

GCU (guanine, cytosine, uracil) codes for the amino acid known as alanine (AL-uh-neen).

An **anticodon** is a sequence of three bases found on tRNA. Each tRNA carries only one anticodon, in contrast to the many codons in an mRNA molecule. Each tRNA anti-codon complements a specific mRNA codon. For example, the mRNA codon AGU is complemented by the tRNA anticodon UCA. Based on what you know about complementary base pairs, what is the tRNA anticodon for the mRNA codon GCU? For the mRNA codon GCA?

Chapter 8 Protein Synthesis **185**

Discuss

Emphasize that codons and anticodons are complementary and that each is carried by a different type of RNA. Ask:

- **What structure carries the anticodon?** (tRNA)
- **How many anticodons does each tRNA carry?** (One)
- **How many codons are carried by each mRNA?** (Many)
- **What is the function of anticodons and codons?** (To ensure that the amino acids are linked in the proper order.)

Use the Visual

Review the steps in translation illustrated in Figure 8.4 and then have students act out the process. Divide the class into three groups: mRNA, tRNA, and amino acids. Randomly assign a different codon to each mRNA student, and a corresponding tRNA anticodon and amino acid name to the remaining students. Ask the mRNA students to line up and "anchor" them to a desk, representing the ribosome. Have the students act out steps 2-4 until the mRNA is fully translated.

❶ The exons are joined together.
❷ CGA; CGU

 Interactive Biological Simulations

Translation Students use a ribosome, tRNA, and amino acid molecules to translate a strand of messenger RNA.

What Is Your Codon Count?

Analyze Your Results

1 Answers will vary.
2 Answers will vary. Note that the tRNA base sequence and the DNA base sequence are the same, except for T in DNA is U in tRNA.
3 Answers will vary, but students are likely to have stop or start codons.

3 ASSESS

Evaluate Understanding

Have students use Figures 8.2 and 8.4 to describe the events of protein synthesis in their own words.

Reteach

Help students use the information presented in Figures 8.2, 8.3, and 8.4 to develop a flow-chart tracing the steps involved in protein synthesis in a eukaryotic cell. Once all details have been recorded, have students work in small groups to create their own graphic outlining the stages of transcription and translation.

❶ Ribosomes stop translating when they read stop codons.

186

LAB ZONE **Do It!**   **bioSURF**

What Is Your Codon Count?

You can become more familiar with the roles of DNA, mRNA, codons, tRNA, and anticodons if you . . .

Try This

1 Take four sheets of paper of four different colors, and assign a DNA base (adenine, thymine, cytosine, guanine) to each color. Cut the sheets into squares about 3 × 3 cm. Mix all the squares.

2 On a table or the floor, place 30 squares in a left-to-right line. Group the squares by threes to represent DNA codons.
3 In your notebook, list the base sequences for these DNA codons, recording from left to right.

Analyze Your Results

1 What are the base sequences for the complementary mRNA codons? List them in your notebook.
2 What would the base sequences be for tRNA anticodons? List them.
3 The universal mRNA start codon is AUG. The three possible mRNA stop codons are UAA, UAG, and UGA. Are there any start or stop sequences among your codons? If so, record them.

Anticodons and codons fit together in much the same way as plugs fit into sockets. The codons and anti-codons ensure that the amino acids are linked in the proper order. Because a specific amino acid attaches only to a tRNA with a specific anticodon, the tRNA carries the appropriate amino acid when it plugs into its complementary mRNA codon.

Several codons on mRNA have a different purpose. These codons do not code for an amino acid; they are the "start" and "stop" codons. The start and stop codons do exactly what their names suggest. They signal a ribosome to either start or stop translation. As

186 *Unit 2 Genetics*

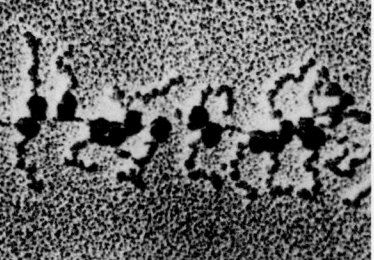

FIGURE 8.5
In this SEM photograph, you can see that many ribosomes have translated a single strand of mRNA, and the amino acid chains have begun forming at each ribosome. When do the ribosomes stop translating? ❶

you would expect, these codons are located at the beginning and end of a mRNA code for a particular protein.

The codes for amino acids, as well as the start and stop codons, are universal. In humans, mice, bacteria, or viruses, GGG translates to the same amino acid: glycine (GLY-seen). The universal start codon is AUG, which codes for methionine. UAA, UAG, and UGA are the three universal stop codons. You can see all the codons and the amino acids they code for in the table on page 187. The fact that all viruses and organisms share the same codons demonstrates the basic unity of life on Earth.

CHECKPOINT 8.1

1. During transcription, what is the relationship of mRNA to DNA ?
2. Explain the role of tRNA in protein synthesis.
3. **Critical Thinking** Translating the mRNA message into a protein can be compared to translating a language. Create an analogy for gene splicing.

Build On What You Know

4. Compare and contrast DNA replication and protein synthesis. *(Need to jog your memory? Revisit relevant concepts in Chapter 7, Section 7.2.)*

CHECKPOINT 8.1

1. Information in the form of a DNA base sequence is transferred to mRNA in the form of a complementary sequence.
2. A tRNA transfers an amino acid to a growing amino acid chain. Anticodons on tRNA complement codons on mRNA, ensuring a specific sequence of amino acids.

3. **Making analogies** Accept all logical responses.
4. DNA replication generates an identical copy of the DNA molecule; no RNA is involved. Protein synthesis is the interpretation of the DNA code, resulting in a protein product. RNA is needed.

Modeling Protein Synthesis

WHAT YOU WILL DO Make a model to show the two processes of protein synthesis

SKILLS YOU WILL USE Modeling, collecting and recording data, analyzing, classifying

WHAT YOU WILL NEED 36 push-pins (5 different colors), metric ruler, 3 strips of corrugated cardboard (18 cm × 3 cm), marker

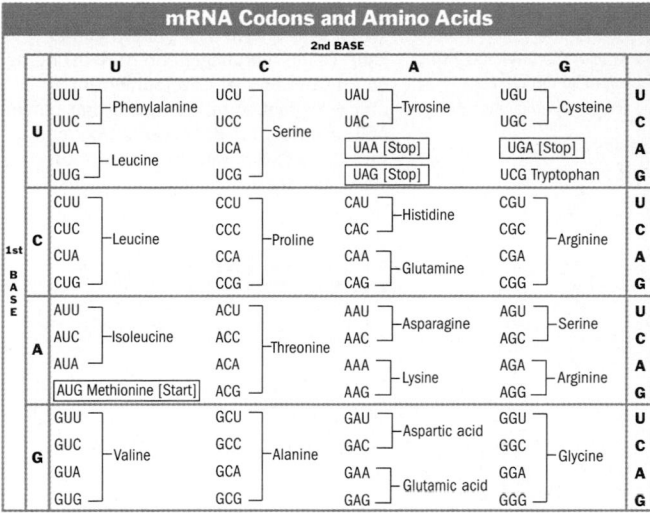

mRNA Codons and Amino Acids

1st BASE		2nd BASE: U	2nd BASE: C	2nd BASE: A	2nd BASE: G	3rd BASE
U		UUU, UUC Phenylalanine; UUA, UUG Leucine	UCU, UCC, UCA, UCG Serine	UAU, UAC Tyrosine; UAA [Stop]; UAG [Stop]	UGU, UGC Cysteine; UGA [Stop]; UCG Tryptophan	U C A G
C		CUU, CUC, CUA, CUG Leucine	CCU, CCC, CCA, CCG Proline	CAU, CAC Histidine; CAA, CAG Glutamine	CGU, CGC, CGA, CGG Arginine	U C A G
A		AUU, AUC Isoleucine; AUA; AUG Methionine [Start]	ACU, ACC, ACA, ACG Threonine	AAU, AAC Asparagine; AAA, AAG Lysine	AGU, AGC Serine; AGA, AGG Arginine	U C A G
G		GUU, GUC, GUA, GUG Valine	GCU, GCC, GCA, GCG Alanine	GAU, GAC Aspartic acid; GAA, GAG Glutamic acid	GGU, GGC, GGA, GGG Glycine	U C A G

Propose a Hypothesis

Propose a hypothesis about the relationship between bases in nucleic acids and amino acids in a model of protein synthesis.

Conduct Your Experiment

1 Group the pushpins by color to represent the five bases in DNA and RNA. Use the ruler and marker to divide each cardboard strip into six equal sections. Label the strips "DNA," "mRNA," and "tRNA." **Caution:** Pushpins are sharp.

2 Using the color pushpin you have chosen for each base, create the base sequence CCGAGTTAACCGACGTAA on the DNA cardboard strip. Put one codon in each section. Record your results.

3 Align the mRNA strip and the DNA strip. Use pushpins to model the complementary base sequence on the mRNA strip. Record the sequences.

4 Align the tRNA strip and the mRNA strip. Use pushpins to model the anticodons on the tRNA strip. Record these base sequences.

5 Use the table above to determine the names of the amino acids coded for by the mRNA base sequences. Record this information.

Analyze Your Data

1 Which parts of the activity represented transcription?
2 Which parts represented translation? Explain.
3 How would you change your model to show RNA splicing?

Draw Conclusions

How was your model similar to protein synthesis? How is the sequence of bases in nucleic acids related to the sequence of amino acids in proteins?

Design a Related Experiment

Design an experiment to show how a small change to a DNA or RNA base sequence can change the amino acids synthesized. Consider at least two different types of changes.

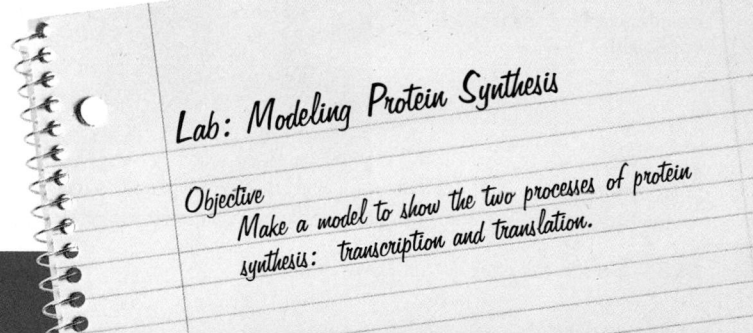

Lab: Modeling Protein Synthesis

Objective
Make a model to show the two processes of protein synthesis: transcription and translation.

 TEAM WORK | **Modeling Protein Synthesis**

SAFETY FIRST!

Caution students to be careful when working with the push-pins. Instruct students to pick up any pins that fall to the floor.

Lab Tips

To reduce the amount of materials needed, have students work in pairs. Tell students to create a key that identifies the base represented by each color. If necessary, review the four DNA bases, the four RNA bases, and complementary base pairing.

Hypothesis Help

Likely hypotheses will state that sequence of bases in DNA specifies the sequence of bases in RNA through transcription; the RNA base sequence specifies the animo acids in proteins through translation.

Lab Extension

Open Ended
To alter the lab so that students work with different models, have students randomly select 18 pushpins to represent the DNA base sequence they begin with in step 1.

Time Required

■ 30 minutes

Analyze Your Data

1 Step 3 represented transcription.
2 Steps 4 and 5 represented translation.
3 In the DNA sequence, a base sequence is inserted which does not code for any amino acid, stop or start signal. In step 3 this sequence is spliced out during transcription.

Draw Conclusions

The model included both transcription of DNA and translation of mRNA. The sequence of bases in nucleic acids code for the sequence of amino acids in proteins.

Design a Related Experiment

Designs may vary. Students may exchange one base pair for another, delete or add a base pair, or change a sequence so that it creates a premature stop signal.

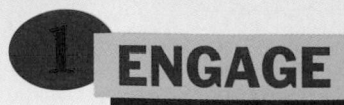

ENGAGE

Use the Visual

Have students study the photograph that opens the section. Explain that webbed chicken feet resulted from the activities of a protein. Tell students they will discover how proteins can affect an organism's traits.

Check Prior Knowledge

To assess students' knowledge about proteins, ask:

- **What are some of the functions of proteins?** (Movement, structure, transport, defense, storage, and regulation through the action of enzymes)

Quick Activity

Stand before the class with a flashlight. Tell students to stand up, one after the other, when the light is on. When the light is off, everyone should sit down. When the light goes back on, students should again stand, beginning with the student who would have been the next to stand had the light not been turned off. Turn the light on and off several times. Ask:

- **What is the role of the light?** (The light directs the actions of the students.) Explain to students that proteins also determine whether genes are turned on or off.

---

❶ The foot is webbed.

8.2 Protein and Phenotype

What you'll learn

IDEAS
- To describe the control of gene expression in prokaryotes
- To appraise the effects of gene control in eukaryotic cells

WORDS
repressor, promoter

A chicken with duck feet?
Ducks have webbed feet. Chickens do not. Why? In part, because a molecular signal in the form of a protein called BMP (bone morphogenetic protein) helps control the normal development of a chicken's foot. A mutant gene that blocks cell receptors for BMP was introduced into this chicken embryo's right foot. What was the result? ❶

PROTEINS AND CELL FUNCTIONS

What's your function?

Your body contains more than 50,000 different proteins. In fact, each individual cell can contain hundreds of different proteins. Proteins are the products of genes. When genes are changed, the proteins they code for may change. Changed proteins can affect cell structure and function and can result in an altered phenotype, as you can see in *Figure 8.6*.

As you know, all of your cells contain the same genes. But not all of your cells produce the same proteins. What, then, happens inside each cell to cause the same genes to produce different proteins? The answer is that genes in each of your cells—and in the cells of all living things—have control

mechanisms. These control mechanisms "turn on" or "turn off" genes, depending on specific environmental factors.

When a gene is "turned on," it is activated. Gene activation means that its product, a specific protein, is being synthesized by the cell. Protein synthesis indicates that a gene is being expressed. When a gene is "turned off," it is deactivated, and no protein synthesis (or gene expression) takes place.

The control of gene expression—that is, protein synthesis—differs in prokaryotes and eukaryotes. In prokaryotes, genes turn on and off primarily in response to changes in environmental factors. In multicellular eukaryotes, gene regulation often involves several rather complex systems.

EVERYDAY BIOLOGY

Tidy Proteins

Do you like your laundry folded just so? The chains of amino acids that form proteins need to be folded just so, too. Scientists think that the way proteins are folded may be a key to understanding many traits.

FIGURE 8.6
A change in this person's DNA caused a change in protein synthesis in the cells of his fingers. The result is a phenotype that includes webbing and extra digits.

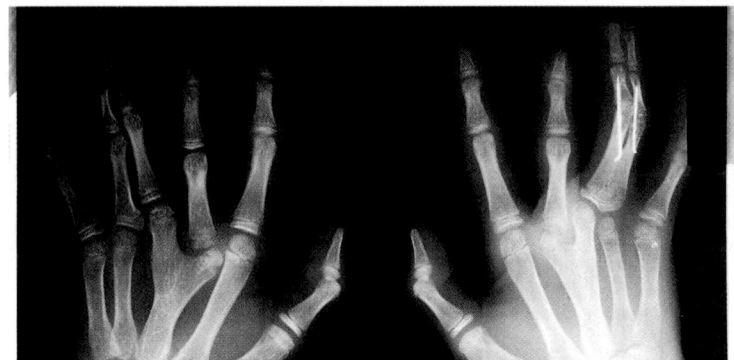

188 *Unit 2 Genetics*

FIGURE 8.7

A Prokaryotic Control Mechanism

1 **The genes are off**
The regulatory gene codes for the production of the repressor. The repressor binds to DNA, preventing RNA polymerase from binding to the promoter. Protein synthesis of the digestive enzymes cannot occur.

2 **The repressor is inactivated**
Lactose binds to the repressor, changing its shape, so that the repressor cannot bind to the DNA. RNA polymerase is free to bind to the promoter. Production of the enzymes can begin.

3 **The genes are on**
As RNA polymerase moves along DNA, mRNA is translated to produce the digestive enzymes. When all the lactose is digested, the repressors take their original shape and bind to DNA again.

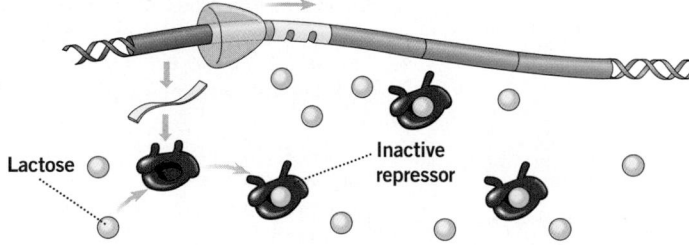

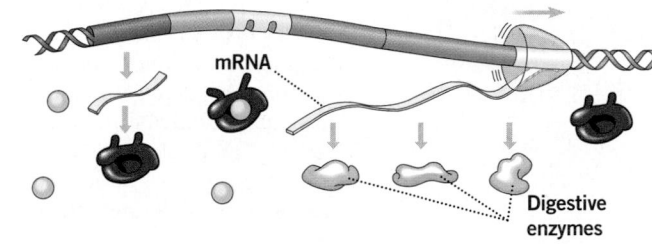

CONTROL IN PROKARYOTES

On again, off again

In a bacterial cell, some proteins are needed all the time, whereas other proteins are needed only under certain environmental conditions. Bacteria have mechanisms that turn the genes for such proteins on and off as needed. In 1961, French biochemists François Jacob and Jacques Monod proposed a hypothesis to explain this control of gene expression in bacteria. Their hypothesis describes how some proteins, once produced, turn off genes.

One example of the mechanism Jacob and Monod proposed is shown in *Figure 8*.7. The bacterium *E. coli* needs three enzymes to digest the sugar lactose. These enzymes are needed only when lactose is present. The genes that code for these enzymes are grouped on the *E. coli* chromosome. The relative amounts of lactose and enzymes in the cell are part of the mechanism that turns the genes for the digestive enzymes on and off.

Study *Figure 8*.7 to see how the mechanism works: Inside an *E. coli* cell, a regulatory gene codes for the production of a specific protein called a repressor. A **repressor** is a protein that binds to DNA, turning off the genes that code for the digestive enzymes (step 1). The regulatory gene is continuously transcribed to make

Chapter 8 Protein Synthesis **189**

TEACH

Use the Visual

After discussing the steps outlined in Figure 8.7, ask:

■ **What is the advantage of the control mechanism?** (The bacterium does not waste energy making a digestive enzyme when no lactose is present to digest.)

Discuss

Help students draw an analogy to emphasize changes in the repressor. Have them imagine a bicycle tire rolling over sharp objects like shards of glass or nails. Ask:

■ **What happens when the tire makes contact with the sharp objects?** (It goes flat.)
■ **How does the function of the tire change?** (It no longer rolls.)
■ **How are the tire and sharp objects analogous to the repressor and lactose?** (The sharp objects and lactose cause a change in shape that results in a change of function in the tire and repressor.)

Science History

Jacob and Monod were awarded the 1965 Nobel Prize in medicine and physiology for their operon model of gene expression. Monod, a molecular biologist, was particularly interested in the philosophical implications of discoveries in genetics and evolution. He proposed that the universe and all life are the result of random events.

MEETING DIVERSE NEEDS

At Risk Have students work with a partner. As one partner reads the captions in Figure 8.7, the other traces what is happening on the diagram. Encourage students to describe what factors are involved in each step of the process.

Explain

Have students study Figure 8.8. Explain that both the thermostat and genes are controlled by a system called feedback control. Feedback control uses the last step in a process to regulate the rate of the process.

Build Writing Skills

Many familiar processes are regulated by control systems. Have students select processes that are regulated by bar-coding systems. Have them research how these systems operate and describe their findings in a brief written summary. Then ask students to compare the control function of the bar-coding system to the way control systems operate on genes.

FIGURE 8.8

Gene Control: An Analogy

You can compare the way lactose turns genes on and off to the way cold air signals a furnace to turn on.

1 Furnace "gene" on
In the presence of cold air, the thermostat signals the furnace to produce heat.

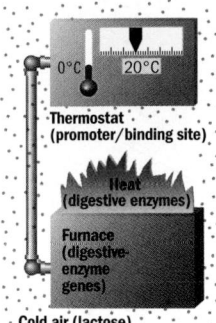

Thermostat (promoter/binding site)

Heat (digestive enzymes)

Furnace (digestive-enzyme genes)

Cold air (lactose)

2 Furnace "gene" off
Once the cold air is warmed, the furnace is signaled to shut off.

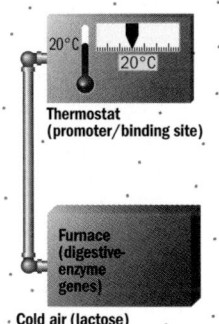

Thermostat (promoter/binding site)

Furnace (digestive-enzyme genes)

Cold air (lactose)

190 *Unit 2 Genetics*

---

mRNA, which is translated to make the repressor.

Near the digestive enzyme genes is the **promoter,** a section of DNA that serves as the binding site for the enzyme RNA polymerase. RNA polymerase is the enzyme that transcribes the DNA. The repressor blocks RNA polymerase from binding to the promoter. Because RNA polymerase is essential for transcription, the repressor prevents protein synthesis of the digestive enzymes. As you can see in step 1 of *Figure 8.7,* on page 189, no digestive enzymes are being produced.

So what turns the genes on? This is where lactose comes into the picture. When *E. coli* enters an environment high in lactose (step 2), lactose binds to the repressor, changing its shape. The changed repressor is inactivated and can no longer bind to DNA. Now RNA polymerase can bind to the promoter and move along the DNA, transcribing the genes that code for the digestive enzymes (step 3). The mRNA is translated and the digestive enzymes are synthesized— the genes that code for digestive enzymes are on.

Now look at *Figure 8.8.* Compare the concentration of lactose with the cold air (step 1). The furnace represents the digestive-enzyme genes, and the heat produced by the furnace represents the digestive enzymes coded by those genes. A high concentration of lactose turns on the digestive-enzyme genes, and the level of digestive enzymes increases.

A high temperature (less cold air) shuts the furnace off (step 2). Similarly, a high concentration of digestive enzymes causes lactose levels to fall, shutting off the genes.

The digestive enzymes are produced until all lactose is removed. In the absence of lactose, repressors are once again active, free to bind to

DNA, and the digestive-enzyme genes are switched off.

You have just read how the presence or absence of an environmental factor—lactose—determines whether certain genes are on or off. This is only one model of control. Sometimes the amount of the protein produced by a gene controls that gene's expression. How does this happen? The repressors are normally inactive (not bound to DNA), so the genes are on (producing their protein product). But high levels of the protein product activate the repressors, causing them to bind to the DNA. The repressor then prevents protein synthesis, and the genes are off. Once levels of the protein drop to normal, the repressors are inactivated and the genes are again on.

CONTROL IN EUKARYOTES

New cell, new control

Almost all types of cells in your body have the same set of chromosomes. Yet each type of cell has a different structure and function. You can see a few of these specialized cells in *Figure 8.9.* Specialized cells result from differences in the control of gene expression.

In humans and other eukaryotes, the control of gene expression is more complex than in prokaryotes such as bacteria. Most prokaryotes are unicellular. Eukaryotes are often multicellular. The development of specialized cells and tissues in eukaryotes requires complex systems of gene control.

One way the specialization of eukaryotic cells can be controlled is through selective gene expression. In other words, only some of the genes on a eukaryote's chromosomes actually function; the rest are turned off permanently. The genes that do function may be turned on or off, depending on the organism's stage of development or on environmental factors.

MEETING DIVERSE NEEDS

Gifted Challenge gifted students to make a model of a gene in eukaryotes that includes introns and exons. Have them display and explain their models to the class.

In *Figure* 8.7 you saw how an environmental factor can turn genes on or off in prokaryotes. Research indicates that genes in eukaryotes also have regulatory proteins to turn the genes on or off. However, unlike the digestive enzyme genes in *E. coli*, the eukaryotic genes for related proteins are not linked together. Related genes can be far apart or on different chromosomes. Therefore, a single promoter or repressor cannot always control protein synthesis.

Another method for controlling eukaryotic gene expression is by controlling RNA splicing. Recall that mRNA in the cytoplasm contains only exons. In some cases, the splicing of RNA from a single gene varies according to cell type. The result is that each cell type produces a mRNA with a different combination of exons. Regulation of RNA splicing means that one gene produces different proteins in different cell types.

Sometimes the control mechanisms fail. A change in the expression of a gene can result in proteins being made at the wrong time. This can alter the development, structure and function of a cell. Sometimes this can cause a cell to become cancerous. A cancer cell lacks the genetic controls that normally limit its ability to grow and divide.

Nerve cells found in the brain

Skin cells and shaved hairs

Lung tissue

Colon tissue in the digestive system

Muscle cells like those found in the arms and legs

FIGURE 8.9
This athlete's body contains about 300 different cells with different functions. Almost all of these cells contain exactly the same DNA. The genes that are activated in specific cells determine their specialized functions.

CHECKPOINT 8.2

1. How is gene expression controlled in prokaryotes?

2. What is meant by the term *cell specialization?* How is cell specialization controlled?

3. Critical Thinking Suppose the first intron in a gene was not removed but was treated as an exon. How might mRNA's protein product be affected?

Build on What You Know

4. Using your knowledge of cell organelles and their functions, describe an imaginary defect in a cell's DNA and its effect on one organelle. *(Need to jog your memory? Revisit relevant concepts in Chapter 3, Section 3.3, and Chapter 7, Section 7.2.)*

What is a gene? What is the result of gene translation?

ASSESS

Evaluate Understanding

Have students make sketches to show how gene expression is regulated in prokaryotes. Encourage students to write captions that explain what is depicted in their sketches.

Reteach

Have students work in groups to review how gene expression is regulated in prokaryotes and eukaryotes. Then have them create a graphic showing how gene regulation in eukaryotes compares to that in prokaryotes. Provide assistance as needed. Review the graphics for accuracy.

CHECKPOINT 8.2

1. Gene expression is controlled through the action of repressors and promotors.

2. Specialization refers to certain cells having specific structures and functions. It is controlled through selective gene expression and RNA splicing.

3. Applying If the intron is read as an exon, additional amino acids are added to the protein chain. This may change the shape of the protein and alter its normal function.

4. Answers should recognize that changes in DNA can alter protein synthesis and in turn affect organelle structure and function.

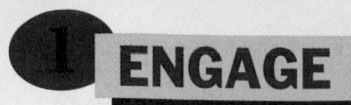

① ENGAGE

Consider The Big Idea

Have students read The Big Idea! Explain that changes in DNA are called mutations, and that mutations are caused by a variety of factors.

Use the Visual

Have students study the photograph that opens the section. Initiate a discussion about traits people intentionally breed into animals that are kept as pets. Have students debate the issues raised in the caption and explain their views on the subject.

Check Prior Knowledge

To assess students' knowledge about chromosomes, ask:

- **What are chromosomes?**
  (Condensed bundles of chromatin that contain DNA)

Quick Activity

Write this sentence on the board: *The entrance to the park was closed.* Have students read the sentence. Erase the "d" from "closed." Have students again read the sentence. Discuss how the change affected the meaning of the sentence. Explain that in a similar way, a small change in genetic messages can have a great impact on an organism or its offspring.

SUPER READ! **Comparing and Contrasting** To practice strategies for effective reading, use pages 37-38 in *Super Read!*

192

8.3 Changes in Chromosomes

What you'll learn

IDEAS
- To explain how mutations can affect proteins and protein synthesis
- To distinguish between chromosomal mutations and gene mutations

WORDS
mutation, deletion, duplication, translocation, inversion, frameshift mutation, point mutation

FIGURE 8.10
Deletion

The notched wing on this fruit fly (bottom) results from a deletion mutation.

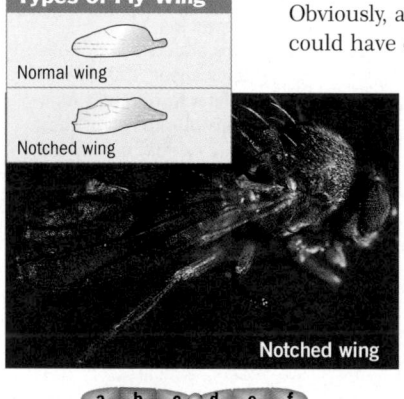

Types of Fly Wing

Normal wing

Notched wing

Notched wing

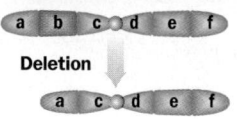

Deletion

192   *Unit 2 Genetics*

Bald cats have mutant gene
The hairless Sphinx is a rare breed of cat. Its hairlessness results from a change in a chromosome—a recessive mutation of a gene. Some people think these cats are good pets for people who suffer from allergies. Others think that breeding cats for this trait is cruel because it leaves the cats unprotected from the cold.

PROTEINS AND MUTATIONS

Small changes, big results

You know that proteins are an important part of an organism's structure and ability to function. Some proteins carry out functions within the cells of an organism. Others are exported from cells for other purposes. Still other proteins act as activators or repressors, turning genes on or off. Obviously, a change in a cell's proteins could have dramatic effects on the cell's structure or function. How can the composition of a cell's proteins change?

Changes in DNA can change the proteins that a cell synthesizes. A random change in the sequence of nucleotides in DNA is called a **mutation.** Many factors can cause mutations. You will learn about some of these factors in the next section. Some mutations have little or no effect on

an organism, others are harmful or fatal, and a very few are beneficial. There are two categories of mutations: chromosomal mutations and gene mutations. Chromosomal mutations involve entire chromosomes. Gene mutations involve individual genes.

CHROMOSOMAL MUTATIONS

Chaotic rearrangements

Chromosomal mutations are changes in the structure of a chromosome. There are four types of chromosomal mutations: deletion, duplication, translocation, and inversion.

A **deletion** occurs when a chromosome breaks and a piece of the chromosome is lost. If you use a computer, you probably know that the delete key can be used to remove letters or words from a document. Deleting words or letters changes the document. As you can see in the diagram in *Figure 8.10*, gene *b* has been deleted from the chromosome. How do you think this change affects the original chromosome?

Compare the two types of fruit fly wings shown in *Figure 8.10*. The

---

STUDENT RESOURCES

From the Teacher's Resource Package, use:
- Section Review 8.3 from Unit 2 Review Module

TECHNOLOGY RESOURCES

Relevant technology resources include:
- Spanish Student Edition CD-ROM
- Teacher's Resource Planner CD-ROM
- Animated Biological Concepts Videodiscs: "Duplication and Deletion," "Translocation and Inversion," and "Point Mutations"

FIGURE 8.11
Duplication

In fruit flies, the bar eye mutation (bottom) is the result of a duplication. Which gene in the diagram was duplicated? ❷

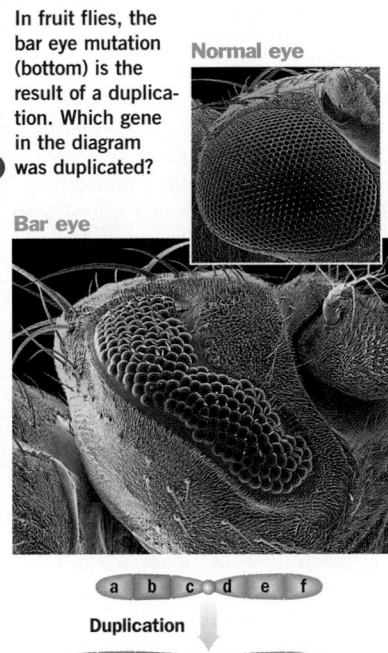

Normal eye

Bar eye

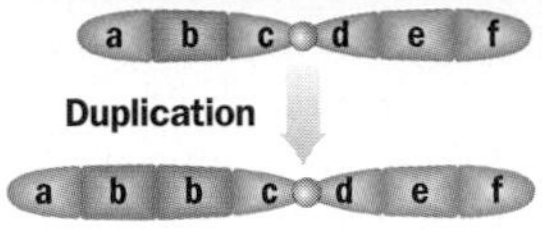

 ...

a b c d e f

Duplication

a b b c d e f

notched-wing phenotype results from a deletion. This mutation is not especially harmful to the fly. Most deletions, however, are lethal, killing the organism.

A **duplication** occurs when part of a chromosome breaks off and is incorporated into its homologous chromosome. The homologous chromosome then has an extra copy of one of its parts. In Chapter 7 you learned about crossing over during meiosis. Duplication can result from an unequal crossover of chromosomes. Look at the diagrams of the chromosome in *Figure 8.11.* How did duplication change the chromosome? Now take a ❸ look at the photographs in *Figure 8.11.* The fly's bar eyes are the result of a duplication in the X chromosome.

In **translocation,** a chromosome part breaks off and attaches to a different, nonhomologous chromosome.

Translocation is illustrated in *Figure 8.12.* Translocation may result in too many or too few genes in a chromosome and can affect organisms in several ways. As in deletion and duplication, a change in the number of genes can harm or kill an organism. Changing the order of genes can also affect the control of gene expression.

An unusual series of translocations can occur in all seven chromosomes of a flower called the evening primrose. Although the results of the translocations are not visible, the mutation limits the plant's fertility, or ability to reproduce.

Invert means to "turn upside down" or "reverse the order of." When part of a chromosome breaks off, turns around, and reattaches in the reverse order, it has undergone **inversion.** *Figure 8.13* illustrates inversion. Inversions generally cause less harm than deletions or duplications, primarily because an inversion changes the order of genes in a chromosome but not the number of genes it contains.

GENE MUTATIONS
A little off base

Gene mutations are errors that occur within individual genes in a chromosome. Gene mutations can involve a single nucleotide or they can affect sections of DNA that include many nucleotides.

Frameshift mutations The deletion or addition of nucleotides that disrupts codons is called a **frameshift mutation.** Because mRNA is read in codons (three-base sections) during translation, an addition or deletion of nucleotides can alter the sequence of bases, or reading frame, of the genetic message.

Compare a frameshift mutation to a sentence composed of three-letter

FIGURE 8.12
Translocation

One type of evening primrose commonly undergoes translocation. Note that the original chromosomes are nonhomologous—they have different types and arrangements of genes. How are ❹ the chromosomes changed?

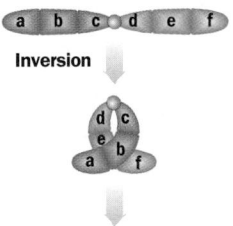

a b c d e f
g h i j k l

Translocation

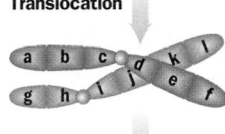
a b c d k l
g h i j e f

a b c k l
g h i j d e f

FIGURE 8.13
Inversion

In an inversion, part of a chromosome is broken off and reattached in reverse order, but no genes are lost. How have the genes changed? ❺

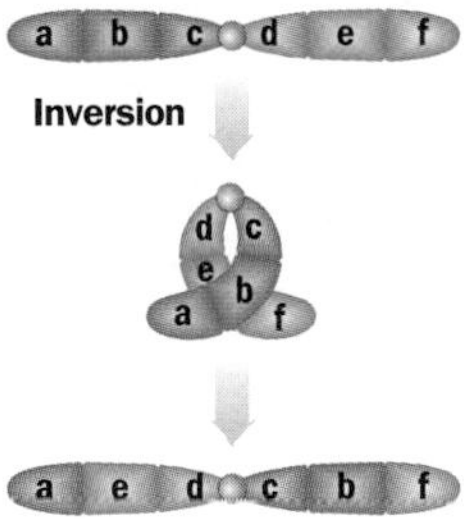

a b c d e f

Inversion

d c
e
a b f

a e d c b f

Chapter 8 Protein Synthesis **193**

8.3

② TEACH

Explain

Give students time to study Figure 8.11. Explain that duplication occurs when part of a chromosome breaks off during replication and is incorporated into its homologous chromosome, resulting in a gene that appears twice on a chromosome.

Class Activity

Select five to seven students to form a line and join hands. Tell the class that the order of the first names of the students is the genetic code for an important cellular protein. Alter the line by reversing the position of two students. Ask:

■ **How did the movement of the students affect the code?** (The sequence in the code changed.)

■ **Which type of mutation was modeled?** (Inversion) Suggest that students use this activity idea to model other types of mutation.

Animated Biological Concepts

Duplication and Deletion

Play

Translocation and Inversion

Play

Clarify Misconceptions

Many students believe that all mutations are harmful. Emphasize that most mutations have no effect at all and that some are even advantageous to organisms.

Think Critically

Explain to students that gene mutations can occur during replication and during translation. Ask:

- **Which mutations do you think are more likely to have extensive effects on an organism, those occurring during replication, or those occurring during translation? Explain**. (Gene mutations occurring during replication will cause more damage because all future replications will be affected.)

words: *Pat the bad cat.* Each word in this sentence can be compared to a codon in a DNA sequence. If a letter is deleted, for example *a* in *pat*, the sentence changes into *Ptt heb adc at.* As you can see, the sentence becomes nonsense. Analyze the frameshift mutation in *Figure 8.14.* What are the codons in the original reading frame? What are the codons in the shifted **①** reading frame?

Recall what happens when a strand of mRNA is transcribed from DNA. Using that information, predict what might happen if one base is deleted from the DNA. You are right if you said the transcribed mRNA would also be affected. Unlike the sentence analogy, however, a frameshift mutation does not create nonsense. It can still be translated. Because each codon corresponds to an amino acid, altering the codons may alter the amino acid sequence. As you can see in *Figure 8.14,* the end result may be an entirely different protein product.

The amount of genetic material that is lost or gained during frameshift mutations is much smaller than

the amount lost or gained in chromosomal mutations. However, because frameshift mutations affect the sequence of amino acids, they can have an enormous impact on an organism's structure and function.

Point mutations A change that occurs in only one nucleotide is a **point mutation.** A point mutation can result from a base-pair substitution in which just one pair of bases is replaced in a gene.

Because a point mutation affects a single codon, it tends to be far less disruptive than a frameshift mutation. Some amino acids are coded for by more than one codon, and substitution may simply change one codon to another codon for the same amino acid. For example, look at the table of codons on page 187. You can see that any substitution of the third base of a codon for arginine will still result in arginine. About 30 percent of all substitution mutations produce no changes in proteins.

In the remaining 70 percent of substitutions, changed nucleotides cause a different amino acid to be incorporated into a protein. The resulting protein may function normally or may be defective. *Figure 8.15* shows how the substitution of a single base in the gene for hemoglobin can produce the gene for sickle-cell hemoglobin, which in turn causes sickle-cell disease. When oxygen is low, sickle-cell hemoglobin causes the blood cells to change into the sickle shape that characterizes the disease.

A third and very common point mutation occurs when a codon in the middle of a gene is

FIGURE 8.14
A frameshift mutation begins when DNA is changed and then transcribed. The resulting mRNA is missing a uracil base. Compare the amino acids normally coded for by mRNA with those it codes for after the mutation. **②**

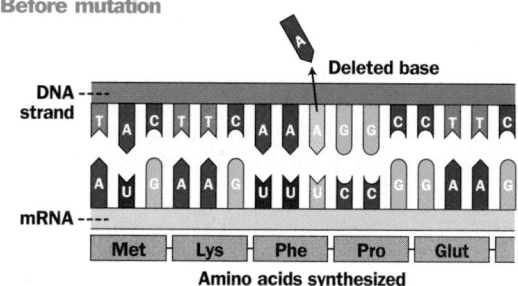

Before mutation

Amino acids synthesized

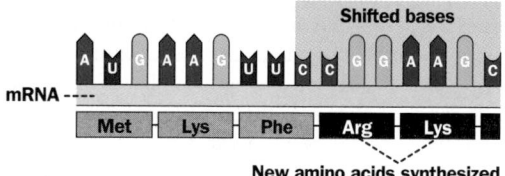

After mutation

New amino acids synthesized

Normal hemoglobin

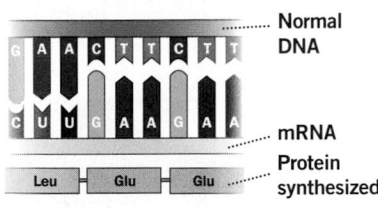

Normal DNA

mRNA

Protein synthesized

Leu — Glu — Glu

Sickle-cell hemoglobin

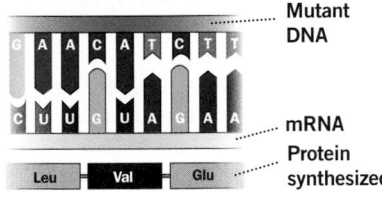

Mutant DNA

mRNA

Protein synthesized

Leu — Val — Glu

FIGURE 8.15
Sickle-cell disease is a result of abnormal hemoglobin production caused by a point mutation. How does the DNA sequence change? The mRNA sequence? The amino acid sequence? ❸

LAB ZONE — Think About It! — bioSURF

From Milk to Wasp: Modeling Mutations

Small mutations in DNA can cause huge changes in the protein synthesized. Similarly, small changes in a word can drastically alter its meaning. Look at the following sequence of words:

milk mile wile wise wisp wasp

Note that each word differs from the previous word by only one letter and none of the words is meaningless. Consider these changes as "point mutations" affecting word meaning.

Try This

1 Think of a word. Then change the word letter by letter as modeled above. Make sure each word you create is an actual word. What word did you end up with?

2 Think of a way to use words to model frameshift mutations. Hint: You might take one sentence and make only one change in one word.

3 Model jumping gene mutation by inserting one sentence into another. Does the new sentence make sense?

---

changed to a stop codon. When genes with this mutation go through protein synthesis, translation is halted before the amino acid chain is completed.

Jumping genes A gene mutation can also occur when large stretches of DNA are inserted into the gene. American geneticist Barbara McClintock studied kernel color in maize (corn). Her research revealed that some genes "jump" from one location to another–they are called jumping genes. A jumping gene sometimes inserts itself into another gene, disrupting the DNA sequence of that gene.

McClintock proposed her theory in 1947, but her ideas were not acknowledged for years. In 1983, almost three decades after her first publication on

the subject, McClintock won the Nobel prize for her discovery.

CHECKPOINT 8.3

1. How do DNA mutations affect proteins?
2. Compare and contrast chromosomal mutations and gene mutations.
3. **Critical Thinking** The effects of a mutation are not always visible. How might a researcher determine whether a mutation has occurred and, if so, what type of mutation it is?

Build on What You Know

4. In Chapter 7 you learned about some changes in the human genome. Compare and contrast those types of genetic changes with chromosomal and gene mutations. *(Need to jog your memory? Revisit relevant concepts in Chapter 7, Section 7.5.)*

Chapter 8 Protein Synthesis **195**

LAB ZONE — Think About It!

From Milk to Wasp: Modeling Mutations

Try This

Have students work in groups or as a class to do the activity.

1 Answers will vary. Example: four, foul, fool, food, mood.
2 Answers will vary. Example for The dog and cat ran: The dog ndc atr an
3 Answers will vary. Most sentences will not make sense.

ASSESS

Evaluate Understanding

Have students record a sequence of five to seven DNA bases. Have students create two illustrations that show how a point mutation and a frameshift mutation affect the chain.

Reteach

Use strips of different colored construction paper to model genes along a chromosome. Illustrate varied types of chromosome mutations by moving the "genes" as appropriate. Then use the strips of paper to represent the bases along a strand of DNA. Manipulate these pieces of paper to model a gene mutation. Challenge students to use this concept to make their own models of mutations.

CHECKPOINT 8.3

1. DNA mutations may have no affect on proteins or they may alter a protein's amino acid sequence and affect a cell's structure or function.
2. Chromosomal mutations are changes in the structure of a chromosome. Gene mutations are changes in the base sequence of individual genes.
3. **Applying knowledge** Compare the DNA fingerprint of the "normal" DNA to the "mutated" DNA. The base sequence should reveal the type of mutation.
4. Nondisjunction is similar to a duplication or deletion. However, nondisjunction results in extra chromosomes or the absence of a chromosome; a duplication or deletion involves only a segment of the chromosome.

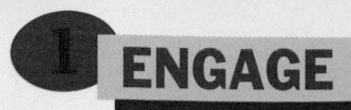

ENGAGE

Use the Visual

Have students study the photograph that opens the section. Explain that precautions must be taken to prevent patients and medical personnel from unnecessary exposure to radiation during X-ray procedures.

Check Prior Knowledge

To assess students' knowledge about genes and cancer, ask:

- **What are the different types of mutations?** (Deletion, duplication, translocation, inversion, frameshift and point mutations)
- **How can a change in a gene harm an organism?** (By changing the protein produced or by preventing its production)

Teacher Demo

Use a microprojector to show students cells that are normal and cells that show evidence of cancer. Discuss the differences in the appearance of the two types of cells.

8.4 Genes and Cancer

What you'll learn

IDEAS
- To summarize the role of oncogenes in the development of cancer
- To identify environmental causes of mutation

WORDS
oncogene, mutagen, carcinogen

Handle with care
Wilhelm Roentgen discovered X rays in 1895. One of his first photographs was of his wife's hand. Almost overnight doctors put X rays to widespread use, but later experiments showed that X rays trigger mutations that can cause cancer. Today, the careful use of X rays can help diagnose and treat cancer, reveal living bones and teeth, and aid in medical research.

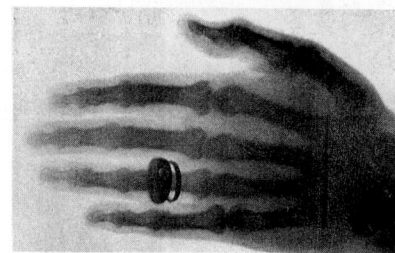

MUTATIONS AND CONTROL

Mutant genes let cells grow out of control

As you learned in section 8.3, mutations are random events with unpredictable results. Most mutations have little or no effect on an organism's function. Such mutations are a source of genetic variation. Genetic variations in a population can contribute to the adaptation of a species to a changing environment.

Some mutations, however, are harmful or even lethal. When mutations change the genes that control cell growth and specialization, cancer may result. In Chapter 5 you learned that cancer is uncontrolled, abnormal cell division. There are many different types of cancer, because any of the hundreds of types of cells in the human body can become cancerous.

FIGURE 8.16
These MRI (magnetic resonance imaging) photographs show cross sections of two skulls; the patients' eyes are at the top of each image. Compare the healthy patient's eyes (right) with those of the patient with the eye cancer retinoblastoma (left). Retinoblastoma results from the mutation of a gene that normally prevents tumor growth.

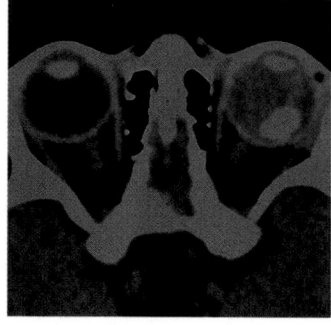

Cancer cells can also migrate from one part of an organism to another part.

The causes of cancer vary. Some cancers, such as the one causing the eye tumors shown in *Figure 8.16*, can be inherited. Other cancers result from environmental factors. Still others are a result of combination of genetic and environmental factors. Regardless of their cause, all cancers share one feature: The genes that control production of new cells do not shut off as they should.

A gene that causes a cell to become cancerous is called an **oncogene** (ON-koh-jeen). Researchers have found that some oncogenes in viruses have been linked to certain types of cancer. Other oncogenes in human chromosomes appear to be mutated forms of genes that code for proteins called growth factors. These growth factors help control cell division and differentiation.

As you can see in *Figure 8.17*, there are three basic ways a gene can become an oncogene. First, a mutation may occur in a growth-factor gene. The mutation can result in production of normal amounts of growth factor, but the protein may be altered to a "super" growth factor, causing rapid and uncontrolled cell division.

Second, an error in DNA replication can result in multiple copies of a

196 *Unit 2 Genetics*

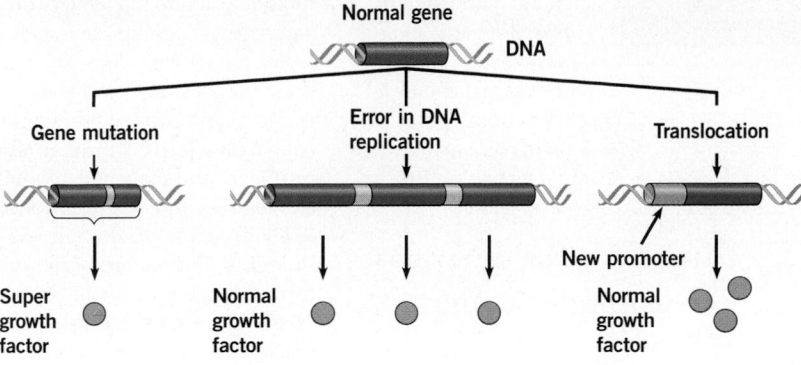

Normal gene

Gene mutation

Error in DNA replication

Translocation

New promoter

Super growth factor

Normal growth factor

Normal growth factor

single growth-factor gene. Where one gene would normally be transcribed to produce growth factor, now several are transcribed, and the amount of growth factor in the cell increases. In this case, the replicated genes are acting together as oncogenes.

Third, a change in a gene's location can create an oncogene. As you learned in section 8.3, translocation can change a gene's position in a chromosome. In some cases, the translocated gene comes under the control of a new promoter that permits more frequent transcription of the gene. As a result, the growth factor is produced much more often.

Cancers may also arise because of changes in genes responsible for preventing uncontrolled cell growth, called tumor-suppressor genes. You can think of tumor suppressors as "anti-oncogenes" because they help prevent the growth of tumors. A gene mutation can make a tumor suppressor non-functional. If a tumor-suppressor gene is mutated or deleted, the result can be uncontrolled cell reproduction.

The rare, life-threatening cancer retinoblastoma (REH-tin-oh-blas-TOH-muh) was one of the first heritable cancers to be identified. Retinoblastoma results in tumors of the eyes. One form of the disorder was traced to changes in a tumor-suppressor gene on chromosome 13.

The inherited form of this cancer is caused by a recessive mutation in the tumor-suppressor gene. Recall that a recessive mutation is expressed only when both chromosomes in a homologous pair have the mutation. Patients with the recessive mutation in only one chromosome are said to be predisposed to the cancer. Tumors are almost certain to appear when there is a second, noninherited change on the homologous chromosome.

Another form of retinoblastoma is not inherited. Scientists have determined that the noninherited form is caused by deletions in both copies of chromosome 13, within immature cells of the eye. You can see the site of the tumor-suppressor gene and the deletions that affect the gene in *Figure 8.18*.

By identifying the sites of genes linked to cancers, geneticists can predict whether someone is predisposed to or almost certain to develop a cancer. This knowledge enables doctors to treat the disease more effectively. Work on the Human Genome Project, as well as research on organisms such as yeast and the *Drosophila* fruit fly, has helped identify heritable cancers

FIGURE 8.17
Here are three ways oncogenes may arise from a normal gene. The effects of the mutations are similar. How do the types of mutations differ? ❶

FIGURE 8.18
A tumor-suppressor gene in chromosome 13 normally prevents the growth of retinoblastoma tumors. Any deletion of a tumor-suppressor gene can result in cancer.

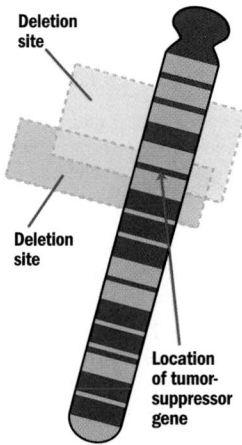

Deletion site

Deletion site

Location of tumor-suppressor gene

Chapter 8 Protein Synthesis **197**

Use the Visual

Have students study Figure 8.17. To assess their understanding of the diagram, ask:

■ **What are three ways that oncogenes can arise from a normal gene?** (From a gene mutation, an error in DNA replication, or translocation)

Discuss

Direct students to Figure 8.18. Explain that the chromosome shown has a tumor-suppressor gene. Ask:

■ **What other kinds of mutations could prevent the normal functioning of the tumor-suppressor gene?** (An inversion that interrupts the gene, a point mutation that creates a premature stop signal, a frameshift mutation that alters the amino acid sequence and function)

❶ The site of each mutation is different.

Use the Visual

Direct students' attention to Figure 8.19. Have students interpret the table by asking:

- **Which chromosome plays a role in the development of both breast and colon cancer?** (17)
- **In addition to its role in the development of eye cancer, what other role does chromosome 13 play with respect to cancer?** (It carries genes that suppress tumor growth.)

 Science History

Marie Curie and her daughter Irene Joliot-Curie are well known for their early work with radiation. Both women won separate Nobel Prizes for their discoveries of radioactive substances. Unfortunately, the work that won both women international fame also brought about their demise. Both women died from forms of cancer caused by exposure to radiation.

Cancers Linked to Deletion Mutations	
Site of Cancer	Chromosome Affected
Breast	17
Colon	5, 17
Eye (retinoblastoma)	13
Kidney (Wilms tumor)	11

FIGURE 8.19
Some cancers at the sites listed above have been linked to deletions in specific chromosomes. Other cancers, however, have not been linked to genetic factors. To what other factors have cancers been linked? ❶

FIGURE 8.20
In 1986, an accident at the Chernobyl nuclear power plant in Ukraine (then part of the Soviet Union) released a large amount of radiation. Since then, scientists have observed an extremely high mutation rate in the mitochondria of Siberian voles living in the area. What environmental factor probably caused the mutations? ❷

such as those listed in *Figure 8.19.* It is important to keep in mind, however, that the development of cancer depends on environmental factors as well as genetic factors.

CAUSES OF GENE MUTATIONS

Environment comes into play

Environmental factors can play a major role in the development of cancer. A person with only a predisposition to a type of cancer will, under certain environmental conditions, almost certainly develop the disease. The same person can reduce his or her risk of developing cancer by controlling environmental conditions, because environmental factors can contribute to the formation of unfavorable gene mutations.

A factor in the environment that can cause mutations in DNA is called a **mutagen** (MYOO-tuh-jen). Well-known mutagens include some forms of radiation—such as the type released from nuclear accidents—and a variety of chemicals, including many found in tobacco products.

Some—but not all—mutagens cause cancer. An agent that causes or tends to cause cancer is called a **carcinogen** (kar-SIN-oh-jen). Examples include the tars in cigarette smoke, some drugs, certain chemicals in smoked meats, coal tars in some hair dyes, viruses that have been linked to cancers, and some types of radiation.

Ultraviolet (UV) radiation is a mutagen and a carcinogen—UV rays cause DNA in cells to mutate, and exposure to UV radiation has been linked to skin cancer. Like other mutagens, UV rays cause changes in the DNA message that can be passed on to daughter cells when a cell divides.

A layer of ozone in the upper atmosphere normally protects us from some UV rays. However, the ozone layer has been damaged in recent decades, most likely by chemical pollutants called chlorofluorocarbons. These chemicals were once widely used in aerosol sprays and refrigerants. Many countries have passed laws to limit the use of chlorofluorocarbons.

How do carcinogens change DNA? The answer varies with the type of mutagen. Carcinogens can cause cancer by either replacing or changing DNA bases. Some carcinogens are chemically similar to the bases of DNA. These carcinogens are called base analogs (*analog* means "parallel"). Base analogs can be incorporated into a DNA molecule. Because they are not exactly the same as DNA

❶ Environmental factors
❷ Radiation

MULTICULTURAL PERSPECTIVE

The incidence of some types of cancer varies along racial and ethnic lines. For example, Asian women generally have a much lower incidence of breast cancer than do European women. Similarly, men of African descent have a higher incidence of prostate cancer than do European men. Scientists do not know if these differences result from variations in lifestyle, such as diet and exercise, or genetic variations.

In the Community

IN THE COMMUNITY
Where There's Smoke...

Research has shown that tobacco smoke can cause cancer. To protect the public health, many communities have regulated smoking in public places. For example, some communities do not allow smoking in restaurants; others require that restaurants have separate smoking and nonsmoking areas. Find out about the regulations that are in effect in your community and how they are enforced. Then survey community members to find out their opinion of local regulations. What do residents, business owners, and local officials think of the regulations? Compile your results and write a summary of your conclusions. Are the smoking regulations in your community appropriate? Should they be stricter or more lenient?

In the Community

Many regulations will be the same for all communities surveyed due to federal laws, such as one prohibiting the sale of tobacco products to persons under age 18. Other regulations will vary from one community to another. Have students include the fines or penalties that apply to these regulations.

Everyday Biology

This would be a good time to have students repeat the chapter opening activity. Discuss all responses as a class, paying particular attention to responses that have changed and the reasons cited for the changes.

bases, these analogs form abnormal base pairs and confuse the genetic message. Other carcinogens react with the DNA bases, changing them. Then, when the cell divides, the changed DNA messages are passed on to daughter cells.

The ability of chemicals to cause cancer is linked to their ability to cause mutations. Scientists have devised a test for possible carcinogens called the Ames test. In the Ames test, bacteria are treated with the chemical that is a suspected carcinogen. If mutations are detected in the bacteria, it is assumed that the chemical may produce cancer-causing mutations in humans. Researchers then perform different tests to see if the substance poses a substantial risk to humans. If it does, measures may be taken to control or ban its use.

FRONTIERS IN BIOLOGY
Eat your vegetables

The information scientists have gathered about cancer, genes, and the environment may seem pretty grim. But there is good news—as scientists

learn more about cancer, they also learn more about how to prevent it and how best to treat it.

Scientists are using the ever-growing body of knowledge about the genetics of cancer to develop new approaches to treatment. Gene therapy—replacing mutated genes with normal ones—has already been attempted for some cancers and may become commonplace. Through genetic engineering, scientists are using viruses to help treat cancers. More conventional cancer treatments, such as radiation and chemotherapy, as well as methods of early detection, continue to be developed and refined.

As you have just read, environmental factors can increase a person's risk of developing cancer. But by controlling certain environmental factors, an individual can reduce his or her risk.

Screening to detect early-stage cancers is also an important preventive measure. The best times for screenings depend on a person's age, sex, and family history. Preventive screenings include tests for testicular and prostate cancer in men and the Pap test for cervical cancer in women.

Feeling the Burn?

Why is skin cancer on the rise? For one reason, a lot of people think a tan looks good. Another reason may be the damaged ozone layer, which allows more UV rays to reach Earth's surface. The longer your exposure to UV rays, the greater your risk of developing skin cancer.

Chapter 8 Protein Synthesis **199**

MULTICULTURAL PERSPECTIVE

Some types of cancer seem to be related to mutagens found in food. Conversely, some foods appear to contain chemicals that reduce the risk of cancer. Have students do library research on the connection between cancer, particularly those of the digestive tract, and diet. Students can report their findings to the class.

Evaluate Understanding

To assess students' understanding, ask:

- **How does a gene become an oncogene?** (Through mutation, an error in DNA replication, or a change in chromosomal location)
- **How do carcinogens cause cancer?** (By either replacing or changing DNA bases)
- **What role do mutagens play in the development of cancer?** (Mutugens cause mutations; some mutations can cause cancer.)
- **What can you do to reduce your chances of developing cancer?** (Eat a high-fiber, low-fat diet, avoid smoking, wear sunscreen)

Reteach

Work with students to turn each section head into a question. For example: How do mutant genes let cells grow out of control? What environmental factors tend to cause cancer? What can you do to reduce your risk of developing cancer? Then have students find answers to each question as they reread the section.

200

FIGURE 8.21
Because of the work of researchers, more and more people are surviving cancer. Angus Bradshaw survived Hodgkin disease and is now a healthy teenager leading an active life.

FIGURE 8.22
Healthy behaviors, such as wearing sunscreen, can help you reduce your risk of developing certain types of cancer.

Some doctors, as well as the American Cancer Society, recommend that beginning at age 40 women have regular mammograms to screen for breast cancer. Some experts urge that women with a family history of breast cancer begin having mammograms at an earlier age and have them more often than women without such a family history. Self-examinations for breast, skin, or testicular cancers are also helpful when combined with regularly scheduled screenings.

Because tobacco is a carcinogen, avoiding it is a healthy behavior that can lower your risk of developing lung and mouth cancers. About a third of all cases of cancer in the United States can be linked to cigarette smoking. As you will learn in Chapter 31, smoking can also lead to heart disease and lung disorders.

There are other healthy behaviors you can follow. Eat a diet low in fat and high in fiber and the vitamin source called beta-carotene. Such a diet includes lots of whole-grain breads, fruits, and vegetables (especially carrots, broccoli, cauliflower, and spinach),

all of which can reduce your risk of developing certain digestive cancers. A diet rich in certain vitamins (A, C, and E) is also thought to reduce the risk of cancer in general. You can reduce your risk of developing skin cancer by using a sunscreen with a high sun-protection factor (SPF) and by wearing clothing and a hat that blocks the sun.

New discoveries in cancer research are being made all the time, and scientists are continually reviewing and refining their viewpoints as new data are collected. Advances in science, combined with the preventive steps people can take themselves, increase the chances for winning the fight against cancer.

CHECKPOINT 8.4

1. Describe the role of oncogenes in the development of cancer.
2. Name three environmental factors that can cause cancer and three factors that reduce the risk of developing it.
3. **Critical Thinking** Why would a recessive mutation—a mutation in only one of the chromosomes of a homologous pair—not necessarily result in cancer?

Build on What You Know

4. Describe the relationship between cell division and cancer. *(Need to jog your memory? Revisit relevant concepts in Chapter 5, Section 5.1.)*

? What types of changes can occur in DNA? What are some results caused by changes in DNA?

CHECKPOINT 8.4

1. Oncogenes are genes that cause a normal cell to become cancerous.
2. Environmental carcinogens include: tars in cigarette smoke, ultraviolet radiation, and certain chemicals in smoked meat. Factors that reduce cancer risk include: a low-fat, high-fiber diet; avoiding tobacco and exposure to UV rays.
3. **Developing a hypothesis** The gene on the homologous chromosome would function normally.
4. A mutation can change the DNA that controls cell division, resulting in uncontrolled cell division or cancer.

Chapter 8 Review

THE BIG IDEA! 8.1–8.2 Genes are sequences of DNA bases that can be translated into proteins or parts of proteins when they are activated.

8.3–8.4 Changes in DNA can cause changes in phenotype.

Sum It Up

Use the following summary to review the main concepts in this chapter.

8.1 From Genotype to Phenotype

- Protein synthesis occurs in two stages: transcription and translation.
- Transcription is the process by which information is copied from DNA into a strand of messenger RNA (mRNA).
- Translation is the process by which the information from nucleic acids is coded for amino acids.
- mRNA splicing occurs between transcription and translation in eukaryotes.

8.2 Protein and Phenotype

- The function and structure of a cell is determined by the kinds of protein it makes.
- The control of gene expression is different in prokaryotic and eukaryotic cells.
- Repressor proteins can block transcription when they bind to promotor regions of DNA.

8.3 Changes in Chromosomes

- A change in an organism's DNA is a mutation. A mutation can be beneficial, but it is usually harmful to or has no effect on the organism.
- Four types of chromosomal mutation are deletion, duplication, translocation, and inversion.
- Two kinds of gene mutation, or change in base sequence, are frameshift mutation and point mutation.

8.4 Genes and Cancer

- Oncogenes change a normal cell into a cancerous cell—one that reproduces abnormally.
- Mutagens are environmental factors that cause DNA mutations. Mutagens that cause cancer are carcinogens.

Use Terms and Concepts

**Use each of the following words or terms in a complete sentence.
If you need to review a meaning, turn to the page indicated.**

protein synthesis (p. 182)
RNA (p. 182)
transcription (p. 182)
translation (p. 183)
introns (p. 184)
exons (p. 184)
codon (p. 184)

anticodon (p. 185)
repressor (p. 189)
promoter (p. 190)
mutation (p. 192)
deletion (p. 192)
duplication (p. 193)
translocation (p. 193)

inversion (p. 193)
frameshift mutation (p. 193)
point mutation (p. 194)
oncogene (p. 196)
mutagen (p. 198)
carcinogen (p. 198)

Chapter 8 Protein Synthesis **201**

Review the Big Ideas

Before students begin the Chapter Review, you may wish to discuss main concepts from the Big Ideas in Chapter 8. Explain that genes are sequences of DNA bases that can be translated to form proteins or parts of proteins in the process of protein synthesis. The structure and function of a cell is determined by gene expression. Changes in genes, called mutations, can cause changes in the phenotype, or traits, of an organism. Cancer is an example of a change caused by gene mutations.

Answers

1. Promoters
2. mRNA
3. point mutation
4. codon
5. translation
6. transcription
7. d
8. f
9. a
10. e
11. h
12. g
13. b
14. c
15. A codon is a three-base section of mRNA. Each mRNA has many codons. An anticodon is a three-base section of tRNA. Each tRNA molecule carries only one anticodon.
16. Repressors block promoters, so transcription cannot occur; without mRNA from transcription, translation cannot occur and protein synthesis stops.
17. RNA polymerase binds DNA at the start of transcription, and a section of DNA opens. RNA polymerase matches complementary RNA bases to the open DNA strand. Enzymes link the RNA bases, forming a strand of mRNA.
18. During translation tRNA helps to translate the message of mRNA into a sequence of amino acids, or protein. This process occurs on the ribosomes, outside the cell nucleus.
19. Exons are regions of genes that code for a protein, introns are regions that do not code for a protein. Only exons are involved in protein synthesis.
20. Addition, in which a base is added to DNA, and deletion in which a base is removed

Use Your Word Power

COMPLETION Write the word or phrase that best completes each statement.

1. _____ are located in DNA and signal RNA polymerase to begin transcribing.

2. During transcription, DNA serves as a template for producing _____, which then leaves the nucleus to begin translation.

3. A(n) _____ involves the replacement of a single base in a codon.

4. A(n) _____ is a three-base section of mRNA.

5. The assembly of proteins is called _____ .

6. During protein synthesis in prokaryotes and eukaryotes, the process of _____ occurs before translation.

MATCHING Write the letter corresponding to the definition of each word.

7. Frameshift mutation ____

8. Deletion ____

9. Duplication ____

10. Translocation ____

11. Inversion ____

12. Oncogene ____

13. Carcinogen ____

14. Mutagen ____

a. When part of a chromosome breaks off and joins with its homologous chromosome

b. A mutagen that causes cancer

c. A mutation-causing agent

d. A gene mutation that affects the series of codons

e. When part of a chromosome breaks off and joins with a nonhomologous chromosome

f. A mutation in which part of the chromosome breaks off and is lost to the genome

g. A gene that changes a normal cell into a cancerous cell

h. When part of a chromosome breaks off, reverses order, and rejoins the chromosome

Show What You Know

15. What are codons and anticodons? How are they similar? How are they different?

16. How do repressors affect promoters? How do repressors affect protein synthesis?

17. Explain the process of transcription.

18. What is translation, and where in a eukaryotic cell does it occur?

19. Distinguish between introns and exons. Why is mRNA splicing necessary?

20. Name and describe the two types of gene mutations.

21. What role do mutagens play in cancer?

22. **Make a Concept Map** Complete the concept map below by adding the following terms: protein synthesis, mRNA, tRNA, translation, codon, elongation, anticodon.

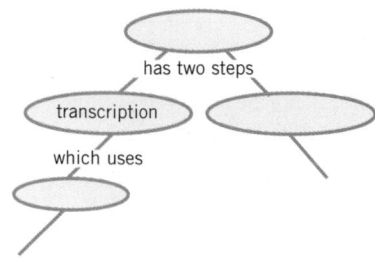

Take It Further

23. **Identifying Cause and Effect** To determine the codons for specific amino acids, scientists add mRNA molecules of one base (i.e. UUUUUU) to a test tube mixture capable of synthesizing proteins. What result will researchers then look for?

24. **Applying Concepts** About 30 percent of substitution mutations result in no change in the genetic code. Use the table on page 187 to explain why.

25. **Developing a Hypothesis** Many hormones are proteins. How might the production of a hormone affect the activation of genes in eukaryotic cells? (Hint: Use promoters in your hypothesis.)

---

from DNA, are frameshift mutations.
21. Mutagens can mutate genes that control cell reproduction and differentiation, possibly triggering cancer.
22. Concept maps should show the following: <u>Protein synthesis</u> has two stages, <u>transcription</u> which produces <u>mRNA</u> which contains <u>codons</u>, and <u>translation</u> which uses <u>tRNA</u> which contain <u>anti-</u>

codons. Translation has an <u>elongation</u> step.
23. Scientists would analyze the amino acid sequence of the synthesized protein and compare this to the codon sequence of the mRNA.
24. You are substituting a code that spells out the same amino acid.
25. Since the hormone is a protein, it might

26. Designing an Experiment You suspect that a certain substance is a mutagen. Design an experiment to test your hypothesis.

27. Interpreting a Graph The Ames test determines mutation rates by measuring the effects of substances on bacterial cell growth under special conditions. According to the graph, which of these imaginary substances are likely to be mutagens?

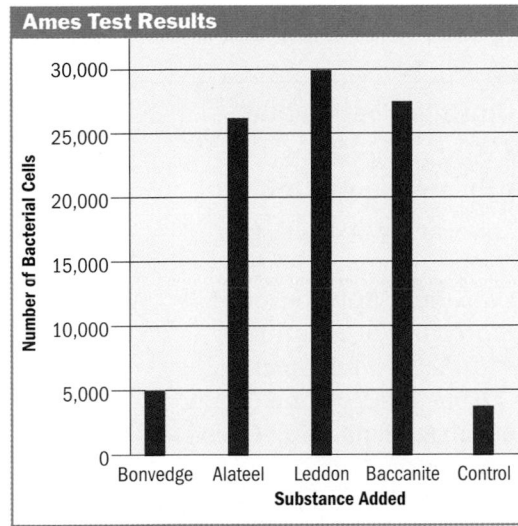

Ames Test Results

Number of Bacterial Cells (y-axis: 0 to 30,000)

Substances (x-axis): Bonvedge, Alateel, Leddon, Baccanite, Control

Substance Added

28. Analyzing Data The table below shows the percentage of bases in both strands of DNA and in the mRNA of an imaginary citizen from Atlantis, the lost city. Which DNA strand is the mRNA template? Explain your answer.

Base Percentages

	A	G	C	T	U
DNA Strand 1	28.2	22.3	22.6	27.9	0
DNA Strand 2	27.9	22.6	22.3	28.2	0
mRNA	28.2	22.3	22.6	0	27.9

29. Making Analogies Working with a two-letter alphabet (*A* and *B*), devise a coding system using only *A*'s and *B*'s to give names to the colors *red, blue, yellow,* and *green*. Now write this sequence, using your code: *red, yellow, blue, red, red, green, yellow, blue.* How is your system similar to protein synthesis?

Consider the Issues

30. Regulating Cancer You have read about healthy behaviors that can help people reduce the risk of getting cancer. How do you think local and federal governments should regulate the production of carcinogenic substances?

Make New Connections

31. Biology and Music Some composers have created music based on gene sequences. Research the sequence of the gene that codes for a specific protein, such as insulin. Assign four notes to the four nitrogenous bases and play or sing your piece.

32. Biology and Community Contact a local chapter of the American Cancer Society or a local hospital. Volunteer to help at a cancer-awareness program or a fund-raiser for cancer research. Report your activities by telling what you have learned to the class.

33. Biology and Literature Write a skit about protein synthesis. Include characters such as ribosomes, amino acids, proteins, DNA, and RNA.

FAST-FORWARD TO CHAPTER 9

Using information discovered by geneticists, genetic engineers can now manipulate genes. In the next chapter, you will learn about genetic engineering and consider some of its applications.

substance is mutagenic. If the bacterial growth is the same as in the control dish, then the substance is not likely a mutagen.

27. Alateel, leddon, and baccanite

28. The chart indicates that DNA strand 1 is the mRNA template. Both the mRNA and the non-template strand are complementary to the template strand, and both would have the same base composition. The mRNA and strand 2 have similar base composition, so strand 1 must be the template.

29. Answers for the codes will vary. Students may suggest that this process resembles codons coding for an amino acid.

30. Answers will vary. Students may wish to use Internet resources to find out current information about this topic.

31. You may wish to assign this project to volunteers. Check to make sure that gene sequences are correct before students "write" their songs.

32. This project may also be completed by volunteers. Students may wish to pair up for this activity. Tell students to take notes that describe their activities so they can share their experiences with the class.

33. This project may be especially useful for those students who may be struggling with the complex concepts presented in this chapter.

bind to the operator, turning it on or off.

26. Materials Needed: sample of suspected mutagen, culture of *Salmonella* bacteria, 2 petri dishes with bacterial medium, microscope
Procedure: Put the bacteria and the suspected mutagen in one petri dish. Put only the bacteria in the other petri

dish (the control).
Observations to be Made: Observe if the suspected mutagen affects bacterial growth.
Method of Recording Results: Write down observations in notebook.
Analysis of Results: If there is more bacterial growth in the dish with the suspected mutagen, it is likely the

PLANNING GUIDE

Section	Student Activities/Features	Teacher's Resource Package
9.1 Breeding **Objectives** ■ Compare inbreeding and out-breeding ■ Distinguish between the benefits and dangers of selective breeding	**Lab Zone Discover It!** *Discovering What Makes Fingerprints Unique*, p. 205 **STS: Environmental Awareness** *Seed Banks*, p. 208 **Everyday Biology** *The Ugliest Fruit*, p. 208	**Unit 2 Review Module** ■ Section Review 9.1
9.2 Genetic Engineering **Objectives** ■ Analyze the process of gel electrophoresis ■ Explain the process of gene cloning	**Lab Zone Think About It!** *Analyzing Gel Electrophoresis Results*, p. 211	**Unit 2 Review Module** ■ Section Review 9.2 ■ Interpreting Graphics 9 **Laboratory Manual,** Lab 18: "Extraction of DNA" **Consumer Applications** 9-1 **Biotechnology Manual** ■ Concepts of Biotechnology: Concepts 2, 3, and 5 ■ Lab 8: "Separating Dyes by Electrophoresis ■ Lab 9: "Vegetable Electrophoresis" ■ Lab 11: "Analyzing DNA Fingerprints" ■ Lab 14: "Modeling Gene Transfer with a Plasmid" ■ Lab 15: "Bacterial Transformation with pBLU®Plasmid" **Interpreting and Developing Graphics** 25, 26, 27
9.3 Applications of Genetic Engineering **Objectives** ■ Describe applications of genetic engineering ■ Compare the techniques used in these applications	**Lab Zone Do It!** *How Big Is the Human Genome?* p. 215 **In the Community** *Biotech Bulletin*, p. 216 **Everyday Biology** *Little Clues of You*, p. 217 **Lab Zone Investigate It!** *Modeling DNA Probes*, p. 218	**Unit 2 Review Module** ■ Section Review 9.3 ■ Activity Recordsheets 9-1 and 9-2 ■ Critical Thinking Exercise 9 ■ Enrichment Topic 9-1 **Biotechnology Manual,** Concepts of Biotechnology 4
9.4 Safety and Ethics in Biotechnology **Objectives** ■ Appraise the safety issues and precautions taken in biotechnology ■ Contrast the benefits and concerns associated with genetic engineering	**Lab Zone Do It!** *How Can Ethical Questions Be Answered?* p. 220 **STS: Issues in Biology** *Ethical Questions*, p. 220	**Unit 2 Review Module** ■ Section Review 9.4 ■ Activity Recordsheet 9-3 ■ Vocabulary Review 9 ■ Chapter 9 Tests **Issues and Decision Making** 9-1 and 9-2 **Biotechnology Manual,** Issues and Decisions 2 and 3 **Spanish Reviews** ■ Chapter 9 ■ Unit 2

Technology Resources

Internet Connections

Within this chapter, you will see the **bioSURF** logo. If you and your students have access to the Internet, the following URL address will provide various Internet connections that are related to topics and features presented in this chapter:

http://genetics.biosurf.com

You can also find relevant chapter material at **The Biology Place** address:

http://www.biology.com

CD-ROMs

Biología: la telaraña de la vida,
   (Spanish Student Edition) Chapter 9
Teacher's Resource Planner, Chapter 9
   Supplements
Interactive Biological Simulations
■ Genetic Engineering: Gel Electrophoresis
■ Genetic Engineering: Cutting DNA
■ Genetic Engineering: Recombinant DNA
TestWorks CD-ROM
■ Chapter 9 Tests

Videodiscs

Animated Biological Concepts Videodiscs
■ Gene Transfer and Cloning
■ Transformation

Overhead Transparencies

■ Gene Cloning, #21

Videotapes

Biology Alive! Video Series
Rewind: The Web of Life Reteach Videos

Planning for Activities

STUDENT EDITION
Lab Zone
Discover It! p. 205
■ ink pad
■ plain paper
■ tracing paper
■ thin black marker

Lab Zone
Do It! p. 215
■ calculators

Lab Zone
Investigate It p. 218
■ graph paper
■ pencil
■ scissors
■ a partner

TEACHER'S EDITION
Quick Activity, p. 206
Traits of breeds
■ poster showing dog breeds

Teacher Demo, p. 212
Model of a bacterium in genetic engineering
■ metric ruler
■ two-three meters one-color yarn
■ small circles of yarn of other colors

Teacher Demo, p. 213
A transgenic tomato
■ transgenic tomato

Quick Activity, p. 219
Favorable traits
■ paper
■ pencil

Chapter Objectives

Students will learn the main concepts of this chapter as they complete the following objectives.

- Compare inbreeding and out-breeding
- Identify the benefits and dangers of selective breeding
- Analyze the process of gel electrophoresis
- Explain the process of gene cloning
- Describe applications of genetic engineering
- Compare the techniques used in these applications
- Appraise the safety issues and precautions taken in biotechnology
- Contrast the benefits and concerns associated with genetic engineering

Key Words

9.1 *selective breeding, inbreeding, outbreeding*

9.2 *genetic engineering, restriction enzymes, DNA fingerprint, recombinant DNA, vector, plasmids*

9.3 *transgenic organisms*

The Opening Story

Have students discuss how they think the story relates to the content of this chapter. Explain that the DNA fingerprinting used to identify the DNA in the skeletons is an example of biotechnology. Have students infer what biotechnology is and how it is used.

204

CHAPTER 9
The Biotechnology Revolution

You can find out more about genetic engineering by exploring the following Internet address:
http://genetics.biosurf.com

In this chapter . . .

FEATURES

Everyday Biology
- The Ugliest Fruit
- Little Clues of You

In the Community
Biotech Bulletin

 Environmental Awareness
Seed Banks

Issues in Biology
Ethical Questions

LAB ZONES

Discover It!
- Discovering What Makes Fingerprints Unique

Do It!
- How Big Is the Human Genome?
- How Can Ethical Questions Be Answered?

Think About It!
- Analyzing Gel Electrophoresis Results

Investigate It!
- Modeling DNA Probes

ROYALTY WAS IN THEIR BONES

T he location of the skeletons was known for almost 15 years before political changes permitted the remains to be examined. But in 1991 the time was right to uncover the 73-year-old bones and confirm their identity. The bones were scattered (as shown above) in a shallow pit. Were the skeletons the remains of Russia's last royal family, the Romanovs?

Although the bones' shapes and sizes seemed to match descriptions of the Romanovs, scientists needed more conclusive evidence. So they studied the DNA contained in the bones. Genetics researchers used a technique called DNA fingerprinting to confirm familial relationships among the skeletons. They also compared the DNA fingerprints with those of living relatives of the Romanov family—including Prince Philip of Great Britain—to prove that they had indeed found the skeletons of the royal family. By examining the sequence of bases in DNA, genetic engineers had solved one of Russia's great mysteries: the location of the final resting place of the royal Romanovs. But what is DNA fingerprinting, and how can it be used for identification?

  **Discover It!**

Discovering What Makes Fingerprints Unique

You need *an ink pad, plain paper, tracing paper, and a thin black marker*

1. Use the ink pad and paper to obtain the prints of all the fingers on one of your hands.
2. Place the tracing paper over your fingerprints. Trace the major patterns in your fingerprints with the black marker.

Fingerprints have been used for identification purposes for many years. Compare your traced fingerprints with those of your classmates. How are they unique?

Fingerprints have their shortcomings as an identification tool, however. Based on this exercise, what might the shortcomings be? Recently, scientists have used DNA fingerprints for identification purposes. Compared to your real fingerprints, your DNA fingerprint is more reliable.

WRITE ABOUT IT!

In your science journal, write about the similarities and differences you have seen between fingerprints. Then use what you know about DNA structure to hypothesize what might be unique about DNA to "fingerprint."

205

Opening Activities

bioSURF If you have access to the Internet in your classroom or school, you may wish to have students connect to the address shown on page 204. You may also want to have students conduct Internet searches for information using key words related to this chapter. For example, they could search for entries under gene therapy, cloning, DNA fingerprinting, or genetic engineering.

Discover It!

Discovering What Makes Fingerprints Unique

TEAM WORK

Have plenty of paper towels and soap for students to wash ink from their hands. Likely shortcomings include: smudging when taken or after the print was made, unclear or inaccurate tracings.

WRITE ABOUT IT

After students write their journal entries, you may wish to have them discuss what they wrote as a class. Have volunteers share their hypotheses.

REWIND to Chapter 8

Briefly review concepts learned in Chapter 8, *Protein Synthesis*. Ask:

- **How does protein synthesis and the control of gene expression relate to genetic engineering?**

ENGAGE

Consider the Big Idea

Have students read The Big Idea! at the top of the page. Explain that changing genotype is one goal of biotechnology, the application of biological science.

Use the Visual

Have students study the photograph that opens the section. Explain that this labrador retriever is a field dog trained to retrieve animals killed by the hunter.

Check Prior Knowledge

To assess students' knowledge about breeding, ask:

- **How are traits passed from parent to offspring?** (Chromosomes from each parent carry DNA that encodes various traits.)
- **Explain the difference between dominant and recessive traits.** (If a trait is dominant, it is expressed; recessive traits are expressed when the dominant trait is not present.)

Quick Activity

Display pictures of dogs of various breeds, grouping them by function—hunting, sporting, toy, etc. Remind students that all dogs belong to the same species and can mate to produce healthy, fertile offspring. Discuss traits of breeds with students and ask students to speculate how such traits are maintained in the breeds.

THE BIG IDEA! Genotypes can be changed through selective breeding and genetic engineering. 9.1–9.2

9.1 Breeding

What you'll learn

IDEAS
- To compare inbreeding and outbreeding
- To identify the benefits and dangers of selective breeding

WORDS
selective breeding, inbreeding, outbreeding

Basic instincts
Not only do different dog breeds look different, they also exhibit different behaviors. For what unique traits do you think ❶ retrievers like this one were bred? Of course, it took many generations to establish these traits. In this chapter you will learn about faster ways to establish traits within a breed.

SELECTIVE BREEDING

The first biotechnology

The breeding of organisms to produce certain desired traits in their offspring is called **selective breeding.** Our ancestors were actually using laws of genetics when they selectively bred dogs and other animals. Selective breeding is one example of biotechnology. Biotechnology is the use of living organisms to make products, such as medicines and improved crops, or to benefit humans.

Humans used basic principles of genetics long before they understood those principles very well. For example, ancient peoples native to North and South America used selective breeding to develop corn and potatoes from wild plants. How does the wild grass teosinte, shown in *Figure 9.1,* differ from modern domestic corn? ❷ Today, farmers still use selective breeding to develop new crops.

In order for a new breed with a desired trait to be established, only the offspring that inherit the desired trait are selected to reproduce. This selection process is then repeated for subsequent generations until the trait has been successfully established in the population.

To maintain a desirable set of traits, breeders use a type of selection called inbreeding. **Inbreeding** is the crossing of organisms that have a similar genotype. For example, an animal breeder may mate two closely related animals that possess desirable traits.

FIGURE 9.1

Teosinte (left) was selectively bred to produce many varieties of corn, including modern domestic corn (right). The center photograph shows how a small teosinte cob compares to a modern corn kernel. What traits do teosinte and modern domestic corn share? ❸

206 *Unit 2 Genetics*

STUDENT RESOURCES

From the Teacher's Resource Package, use:
- Section Review 9.1 from Unit 2 Review Module

TECHNOLOGY RESOURCES

Relevant technology resources include:
- Spanish Student Edition CD-ROM
- Teacher's Resource Planner CD-ROM

FIGURE 9.2

Inbreeding and Animal Health

Inbreeding can result in health problems. These problems are sometimes due to harmful recessive alleles.

A Persian cat's flat face is a trait often associated with breathing problems.

The shar-pei was bred for its huge rolls of skin—a trait that can lead to skin diseases.

A basset hound's characteristic droopy, baggy eyes are prone to infection.

As its population has diminished, the Florida panther has been forced to inbreed, resulting in heart defects and fertility problems.

After several generations, the offspring are probably purebred, or homozygous, for most of the desired traits. Certain crops and breeds of dogs, horses, and other animals are maintained by inbreeding.

Although inbreeding can produce and maintain desirable traits, it can also result in problems. Inbred organisms can carry recessive alleles that produce harmful traits when homozygous. As long as the recessive alleles for undesirable traits are paired with normal, dominant alleles, they cause little or no harm. However, close relatives are more likely to carry the same harmful recessive allele than are distant relatives. Therefore, the offspring of closely related parents are more likely than offspring of unrelated parents to be homozygous for undesirable traits. Review the information given in *Figure 9.2*. What types of health problems can arise through inbreeding?

HYBRIDIZATION

Mixing it up

Another type of selective breeding is called outbreeding, or hybridization. **Outbreeding** is the crossing of distantly related organisms. Such

organisms may come from different species and be very different genetically from each other. More often, outbreeding involves individuals from two breeds of the same species—for example, a shar-pei and a basset hound. Animal and plant breeders often use outbreeding to combine the desirable qualities from two different parents.

Outbreeding is an important tool in efforts to conserve endangered species. For example, the Florida panther is one of the most endangered land animals in the world, with fewer than 100 members of this species left. Inbreeding among Florida panthers has led to health problems such as heart disease. In an effort to save the Florida panthers from total extinction and to bolster the panthers' genetic variation, Florida state officials have introduced Texas cougars into the panther population.

In some cases, outbreeding produces larger, healthier offspring—an effect called hybrid vigor. A mule, the result of crossing a male donkey and a female horse, is hardier than a horse but more docile than a donkey. Another example of a hybrid is shown in *Figure 9.3* on page 208. The "liger" is a large, strong hybrid produced by crossing a

Chapter 9 The Biotechnology Revolution **207**

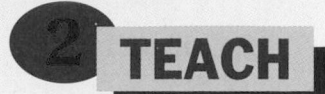
Use the Visual

After reviewing Figure 9.2 and the supporting text, ask:

- **What is the goal of inbreeding?** (To produce a desirable set of traits)
- **Why does inbreeding sometimes produce health problems?** (Close relatives are more likely to carry recessive alleles for undesirable or harmful traits that can appear in offspring.)

Science History

Many archaeologists think that wheat and corn crops became more productive as a result of selective breeding. With increased yields, fewer farmers were needed to meet the food needs of a given population. Surpluses could be stored and traded, and some people began performing tasks other than farming. This division of labor among the members of a community is the foundation of a diverse society.

Think Critically

Point out that in some cases hybrids have restrictions. A female mule, a jenny, is sterile and unable to bear young. Have students discuss the possible traits of the F_2 generation.

MEETING DIVERSE NEEDS

Gifted In 1956, scientists tried to cross African bees with European bees. Have students research the goals and results of this attempt at hybridization. Then have them use their findings to debate if this experiment should have been conducted.

❶ Traits might include a thick, water-resistant coat, a "soft mouth," and good swimming skills.
❷ The cob of teosinte is much smaller; the kernels are shaped differently and overlap more.
❸ Both have tassels and provide food.
❹ Possible problems are skin disorders, sight problems, and disorders of the respiratory and immune systems.

Evaluate Understanding

Write the terms *Selective Breeding, Hybridization,* and *Seed Banks* on the board. Have students describe each method, identify desirable and undesirable traits produced by each, and cite examples to support their answers.

Reteach

On the board or on an overhead transparency, create a Venn diagram. Label one circle *Inbreeding* and the second circle *Outbreeding.* Work with students to fill in the diagram. The *Inbreeding* circle should include: *similar parents, purebred, homozygous,* and *possible health problems.* The *Outbreeding* circle should include: *distantly related parents, hybrid vigor,* and *possible sterility.* Ask students to explain why both are examples of selective breeding.

FIGURE 9.3
A liger is the offspring of a male lion and female tiger. Why is the liger an example of hybrid vigor?

The Ugliest Fruit

The Uglifruit is a type of tangelo that comes from the West Indies. Tangelos are hybrids produced by crossing tangerine trees with grapefruit trees. The name tangelo comes from TANGerine and pomELO, another name for grapefruit.

male lion with a female tiger. Hybrids that have parents from different species, such as mules and ligers, are usually sterile. Because the chromosomes of parents from different species do not usually match up in homologous pairs, they cannot undergo meiosis, and the hybrid offspring cannot produce normal gametes.

ENVIRONMENTAL AWARENESS

Seed banks

One of the most important banks in the world does not store gold, money, or jewels. This bank has the awesome task of preserving life as we know it. The bank contains seeds.

The National Seed Storage Laboratory (NSSL) is located in Colorado and has hundreds of thousands of seed samples. The majority of these samples are seeds for food crops from all over the world. Perhaps you are wondering why this facility exists. The answer to this question lies in our discussion of selective breeding. The NSSL is a storehouse of genetic material that allows breeders access to all kinds of plant varieties.

Suppose you wanted to grow corn that could be easily dried and made into cornmeal. You could acquire seeds that would produce that kind of corn. But what if you then discovered that the corn would not grow well in your field's dry soil? Thanks to the NSSL, you might be able to solve the problem by obtaining seeds for corn that would grow well in dry soils. Using outbreeding, you could then produce a hybrid of the two corn varieties. Eventually you could grow corn that was easily dried for cornmeal and that grew well in dry soil. Without the seed bank, producing such a hybrid would be difficult, if not impossible, in one person's lifetime.

Today the role of the NSSL is more important than ever. Farmers tend to grow large fields of crops using only one variety of a plant. Many other varieties of the same plant are therefore in danger of dying out. Should a blight ever strike the present-day crops, the NSSL could provide genetic material with which to start new, blight-resistant crop varieties. The NSSL also is a valuable source of plant genes for genetic engineers.

CHECKPOINT 9.1

1. Compare and contrast inbreeding and outbreeding.
2. What are the benefits of selective breeding?
3. **Critical Thinking** Suppose you are trying to develop a new food crop. A desirable trait and an undesirable trait are both determined by recessive alleles. Develop a pedigree to determine the advantages and disadvantages of selective breeding.

Build on What You Know

4. How did Mendel use inbreeding and outbreeding in his experiment? *(Need to jog your memory? Revisit relevant concepts in Chapter 6, Section 6.1.)*

CHECKPOINT 9.1

1. Inbreeding is mating two close relatives; outbreeding is crossing distantly related breeds of closely related species.
2. Inbreeding—maintaining desired traits; outbreeding—robustness of outbred offspring
3. **Applying** Pedigrees should show the inheritance pattern of recessive alleles. Students should point out the difficulties in establishing and maintaining a desirable recessive trait and in eliminating an undesirable one.
4. Mendel inbred pea plants to produce purebred plants with desired traits and then outbred these plants to determine dominant and recessive traits.

9.2 Genetic Engineering

Pests from the past
Could researchers remove the DNA from a prehistoric mosquito trapped in amber and re-create this ancient organism in a laboratory? Although DNA from these organisms can be extracted, the organisms themselves cannot be re-created. For that to happen, the DNA would have to be in a dormant state, like that of a seed.

What you'll learn

IDEAS
• To analyze the process of gel electrophoresis
• To explain the process of gene cloning

WORDS
genetic engineering, restriction enzymes, DNA fingerprint, recombinant DNA, vector, plasmids

---

IDENTIFYING GENES

The little DNA that could

Countless science fiction stories have been written about genetics experiments gone awry, or about human clones taking over the planet. In more positive stories, people dream of an era when gene manipulation rids the world of disease. What is genetic engineering? And what possible effects might it have on our lives?

Genetic engineering refers to any technique used to identify or change genes at the molecular level. When genes are manipulated, an organism's characteristics are changed. In selective breeding, a genome is changed slowly and deliberately, over many generations. In contrast, genetic engineering can change genes in a shorter period of time. These techniques also enable scientists to identify a person from a strand of hair, to find out if a person carries the gene for a particular disorder, and to determine the basepair sequences of an organism's DNA.

One technique of genetic engineering is called gel electrophoresis. Gel electrophoresis is a process used by researchers to sort large molecules by size. DNA is usually cut into fragments before gel electrophoresis.

To do this, laboratory scientists mix the DNA sample with a restriction enzyme. **Restriction enzymes** are proteins that break DNA bonds in specific ways at precise base pairs sequences.

There are many different restriction enzymes, and each one recognizes a different short sequence of a DNA molecule, usually four, six, or eight bases in length. When a restriction enzyme is added to a DNA sample, it breaks the DNA bonds wherever the specific base pair sequence is located. In this way, the DNA sample is digested into fragments, as shown in *Figure 9.4*. The ends of the "cut" DNA include several unpaired nucleotides. These

FIGURE 9.4
In the example shown here, a restriction enzyme recognizes the six-base sequence GAATTC. Where does it "cut" the sequence? ❷

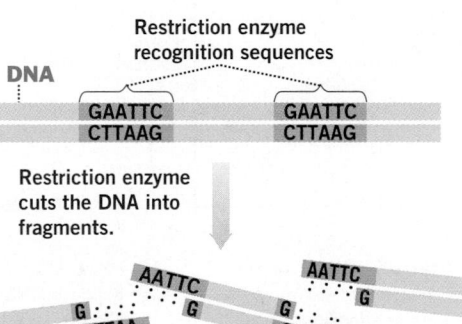

Restriction enzyme recognition sequences

DNA

GAATTC / CTTAAG   GAATTC / CTTAAG

Restriction enzyme cuts the DNA into fragments.

AATTC
G
CTTAA
Sticky end

Chapter 9 The Biotechnology Revolution **209**

Build Writing Skills

DNA fingerprinting has been used in many criminal cases, particularly those involving assaults. Have students check newspapers for accounts of the use of DNA fingerprinting as evidence in criminal trials. Ask them to assume the role of a defense attorney, prosecutor, police detective, or forensic expert and prepare a written statement citing reasons why DNA fingerprinting should or should not be introduced as evidence.

Use the Visual

Have students study Figure 9.5. Help them interpret the diagram by asking:

- **What does a restrictive enzyme do?** (It cuts DNA at specific base sequences.)
- **Why does DNA in a gel track move toward the positive end of the track?** (DNA is negatively charged.)
- **How is the speed at which DNA segments travel along the track determined?** (Short segments move fastest, long segments move slowest.)

Think Critically

Ask students to discuss why separating the base pairs is important. (Students should recognize that separating and spreading the DNA base pairs allows their identification.)

❶ DNA is negatively charged, so the fragments move toward the positive end of the gel at speeds proportional to their size.

---

ends are called sticky ends because they are open to new bonds.

During gel electrophoresis the DNA fragments are dropped into thin slits that have been cut in a track of gel. The gel tracks have a positive charge at one end and a negative charge at the other end. Because DNA has a negative charge, the DNA fragments move toward the positive end of the gel tracks. The smallest fragments move farthest along the tracks, whereas the larger DNA fragments do not travel as far.

Next, the fragments are dyed so they are visible as bands in the gel. You can see a gel electrophoresis photograph in step 4 of *Figure 9.5*. Why ❶ do the different fragments spread out?

The results of gel electrophoresis can yield a wealth of important information. For example, a strand of hair can be identified as from a person if restriction enzyme digestion and gel electrophoresis is performed on the DNA from the hair sample and DNA from that person's cells. If DNA fragments from both samples are the same, then it is likely that the samples came from the same person. For this reason, the pattern of bands obtained from gel electrophoresis is called a **DNA fingerprint.** Every person's DNA has a unique pattern that can be used for identification.

Gel electrophoresis can also be used to determine if a person carries a gene associated with a genetic disorder. The person's pattern of DNA bands is compared with the pattern known to be associated with the disease. If the two patterns match, that person may someday develop the disorder.

Another application of gel electrophoresis is finding the base-pair sequence of DNA strands. As you may recall from Chapter 7, the Human Genome Project is the effort to identify the nitrogenous base sequence of all of the DNA in every human chromosome. In one DNA sequencing method, scientists use four different special chemicals to recognize and

FIGURE 9.5

Gel Electrophoresis

Gel electrophoresis allows researchers to separate DNA fragments according to size.

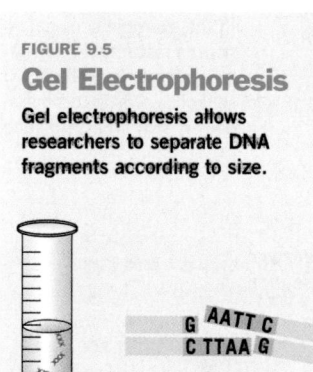
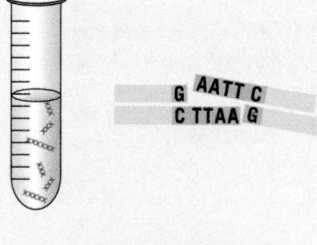
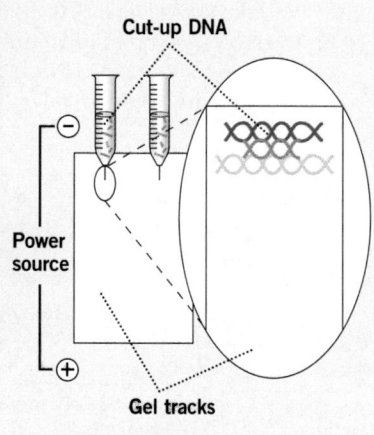
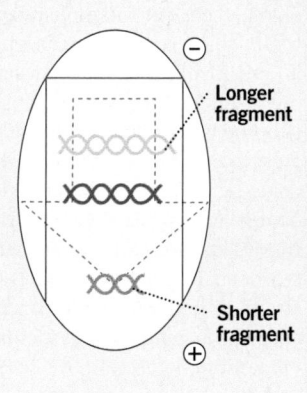

1 **Make DNA fragments**
A restriction enzyme cuts DNA at specific base sequences.

2 **Place DNA in gel tracks**
Because DNA is negatively charged, the DNA fragments move toward the positive end of the gel tracks.

3 **Allow DNA to travel**
As DNA fragments travel along the tracks, the shortest fragments travel the fastest and farthest.

210 *Unit 2 Genetics*

---

cut four samples of the same DNA at each of the four bases of DNA. The samples are then poured into four gel electrophoresis tracks. Computers can "read" the order of the bases by analyzing the bands in the tracks.

CHANGING GENOMES

Wheel of DNA fortune

Genetic engineers do more than identify genes. Using modern techniques, scientists alter genomes by combining DNA from the genes of different organisms. DNA with components from different organisms is called **recombinant DNA** (ree-KAHM-bih-nuhnt).

With recombinant DNA technology, scientists can transfer genes from one organism into the cells of another organism. For example, genetic engineers have transferred specific human genes into bacteria or yeast. The yeast or bacteria can use the human gene to mass-produce human proteins. When genes are transferred into

such organisms, the genes are copied by the organism's cells along with the organism's chromosomes. Exact copies are called clones. Gene cloning is the process of using genetic engineering to make copies of genes.

To transfer DNA into a cell, genetic engineers use a carrier of genetic material called a **vector.** Bacteria contain vectors called plasmids. **Plasmids** are small circular pieces of DNA separate from the bacterial chromosome. Scientists also use viruses as vectors to transfer DNA into cells.

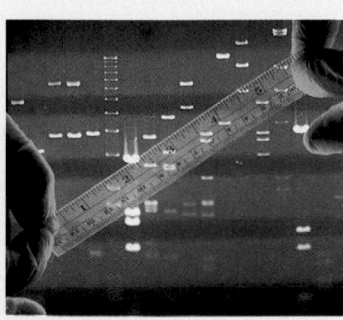

4 Look at the results
A dye is added to the gel. DNA fragments are visible as bands. The gel can be photographed.

LAB ZONE Think About It! bioSURF

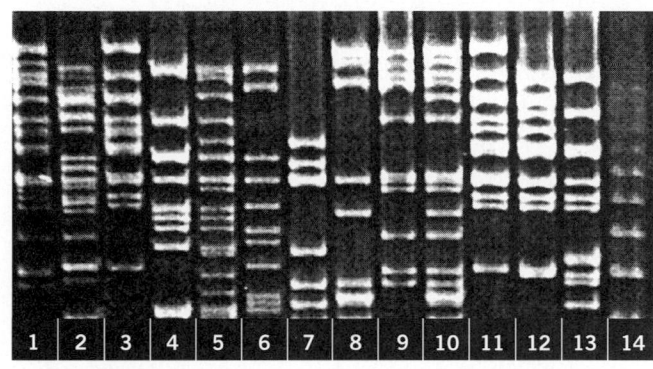

1 2 3 4 5 6 7 8 9 10 11 12 13 14

Analyzing Gel Electrophoresis Results

Researchers can compare DNA samples using restriction enzymes and gel electrophoresis to produce band patterns like those shown above. Similar band patterns indicate similar base sequences. The above results were obtained by cutting twelve DNA samples into fragments with a restriction enzyme. Each sample was put into a separate track of a gel, where the fragments separated according to size. The fragments were visualized as bands using a dye. Tracks 2–13 contain the twelve samples.

Analyze the Results

1. Study and compare the gel electrophoresis results. Which tracks contain matching band patterns? What conclusion can you draw about the DNA samples in these tracks?
2. Which track does not contain any matching bands? What conclusion can you draw about the DNA sample in this track?

LAB ZONE Think About It!

Analyzing Gel Electrophoresis Results

Analyze the Results

1 The tracks that match have the same base sequence.
2 The base sequences differ.

Discuss

Before students study the process of gene cloning to produce human insulin, discuss the disorder diabetes mellitus and the function of insulin in the body. Be sure students understand that individuals with diabetes mellitus must take daily injections of insulin to control their blood glucose levels. Guide students to see that genetic engineering has made large quantities of human insulin available to those who need it.

 Interactive Biological Simulations
Genetic Engineering: Recombinant DNA Students use restriction enzymes to isolate a gene from a strand of DNA. This gene is inserted into a plasmid, forming recombinant DNA.

Genetic Engineering: Gel Electrophoresis In this animation, students pour a gel, load markers and an unknown sample into the wells, and run the gel.

 Animated Biological Concepts

Gene Transfer and Cloning

Play

MEETING DIVERSE NEEDS

LEP Encourage LEP students to record the steps involved in gel electrophoresis and gene cloning (Figure 9.6) in their notebooks in English as well as their native language.

MULTICULTURAL PERSPECTIVE

The importance of cloning is evident in the work of Asian American molecular biologist Flossie Wong-Staal. Wong-Staal developed a technique for cloning genes from HIV, making it possible to produce the virus in sufficient quantities to study.

212

Teacher Demo

Model the steps involved in gene cloning illustrated in Figure 9.6. Form a circle with a Velcro strip to represent the plasmid. Then cut the circle open. Take a Velcro strip of another color to represent the insulin gene. Insert the insulin gene into the plasmid to produce a recombined plasmid. Insert the recombined plasmid into a paper tube to model step 4. Ask:

■ **How can this recombinant cell be used to produce insulin?** (The bacterial cell uses the insulin gene to produce the protein insulin.)

ASSESS

Evaluate Understanding

Have students create two flowcharts, one illustrating how a gene is transferred from one organism to another and the second outlining the steps involved in gel electrophoresis. Check that the information presented is accurate and complete.

Reteach

Write the heads *Gel Electrophoresis* and *Gene Transfer* on the board. Have volunteers list the steps of each process beneath the appropriate heading. Review the completed lists to delete inaccurate information and add missing information.

❶ Students should name the five steps shown in Figure 9.6.

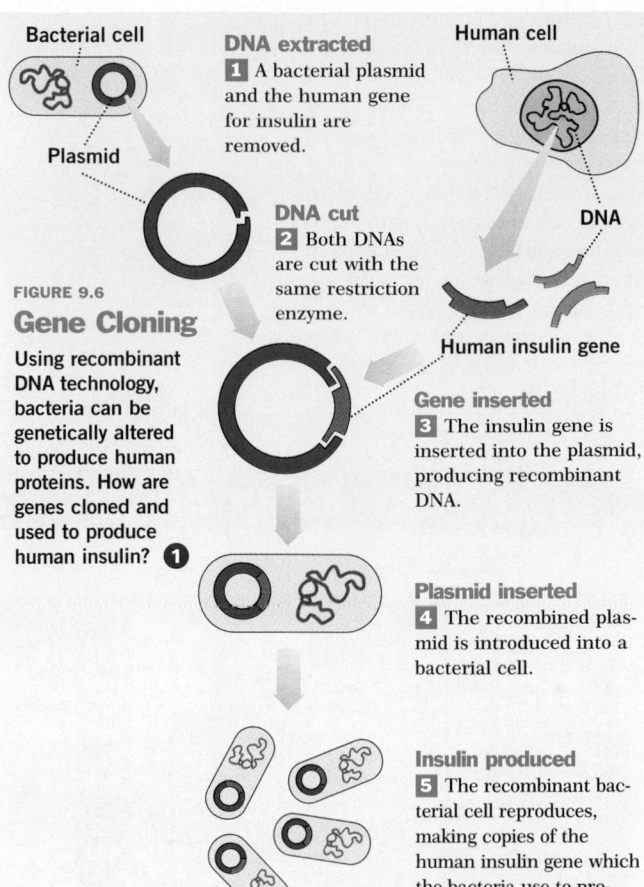

FIGURE 9.6

Gene Cloning

Using recombinant DNA technology, bacteria can be genetically altered to produce human proteins. How are genes cloned and used to produce human insulin? ❶

Bacterial cell

Plasmid

DNA extracted
1 A bacterial plasmid and the human gene for insulin are removed.

DNA cut
2 Both DNAs are cut with the same restriction enzyme.

Human cell

DNA

Human insulin gene

Gene inserted
3 The insulin gene is inserted into the plasmid, producing recombinant DNA.

Plasmid inserted
4 The recombined plasmid is introduced into a bacterial cell.

Insulin produced
5 The recombinant bacterial cell reproduces, making copies of the human insulin gene which the bacteria use to produce the protein insulin.

growing bacterial population produces insulin, which can then be harvested from the bacterial cells.

Before genes can be transferred from humans to bacteria, however, restriction enzymes must cut the DNA of the human insulin gene and the DNA of the plasmid. Recall that restriction enzymes cut DNA at specific locations. As you can see in step 2 of *Figure 9.6*, the DNA fragments have unmatched bases at each end.

The sticky ends of the human DNA fragment and plasmid DNA fragment are complementary. In other words, the sequence of bases at the ends of the piece of human DNA will bond with the sticky ends of the plasmid DNA fragment. Through this bonding process, the human DNA fragments combine with the plasmid.

Once the genes have recombined, the plasmid is inserted into a bacterial cell. As the bacterium reproduces, the resulting bacterial colony produces clones of the protein human insulin.

CHECKPOINT 9.2

1. What is gel electrophoresis and how is it performed?
2. What is gene cloning? What are the steps involved in gene cloning?
3. **Critical Thinking** Bacteria and humans are very different organisms. How is it possible to combine their DNA to make a human protein?

Build on What You Know

4. How might a person find out if he or she carries the gene for Huntington's disease? *(Need to jog your memory? Revisit relevant concepts in Chapter 6, Section 6.4.)*

Let us follow an example of recombinant DNA technology used to clone genes: the process of adding a human insulin gene to a bacterium. Insulin, a hormone that is normally produced by the pancreas, regulates the amount of glucose (a type of sugar) in the blood. Insulin is used to treat people with diabetes. The human insulin gene can be inserted into a bacterial plasmid. As the bacterium reproduces, the

? How can genotypes be changed?

CHECKPOINT 9.2

1. Gel electrophoresis separates molecule fragments by size. Restriction enzymes cut DNA molecules into fragments, which are placed in charged gel tracks. Size and charge affect movement; gel is dyed to visualize DNA.
2. Gene cloning, the process of using genetic engineering to make copies of genes, is performed by inserting a gene into a vector, which reproduces the recombinant DNA.
3. **Analyzing** Even though they are very different, the human and bacterial DNA are made of the same bases and use the same codons.
4. Genetic counselors could create family pedigrees and perform molecular analysis.

THE BIG IDEA! Technology enables us to find out about genotype and use this knowledge to affect phenotype. 9.3–9.4

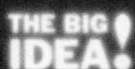

9.3 Applications of Genetic Engineering

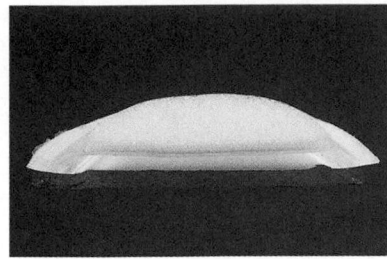

A little DNA to make it better

How about some genetic engineering for that boo-boo? The Genetically Engineered Biological Bandage (GEBB) may someday heal cuts. The GEBB contains genetically engineered human skin cells that produce a protein that stimulates growth. Using genetically engineered products can be as easy as putting on a bandage.

SUPER READ!

What you'll learn

IDEAS

- To describe applications of genetic engineering
- To compare the techniques used in these applications

WORDS

transgenic organisms

AGRICULTURE AND INDUSTRY

Bumper crop

You are now living in the midst of a revolution—the application of genetic engineering to almost every aspect of life. One goal of genetic engineers is to improve the quantity and quality of food. Genetic engineering can improve crops in many ways, as you can see in *Figure 9.7*. New genetic engineering techniques can make plants resistant to pests and weed killers and produce fruits and vegetables that are better suited for shipping and storage. Plants or other organisms that have been altered by adding a gene from a different species are called **transgenic organisms.**

One transgenic vegetable has already arrived in supermarkets—a tomato genetically engineered to ripen more slowly, thus preventing spoilage. Genetic engineers have changed and cloned the gene that codes for ripening in tomatoes. To date, the genetically engineered tomato has received mixed reviews from the public because it is rather expensive and has a slightly different taste. However, the

FIGURE 9.7

Engineering a Tomato

Tomatoes and other crops are the targets of many genetic engineering innovations.

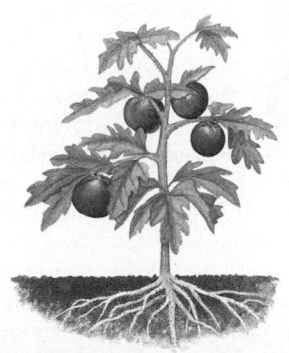

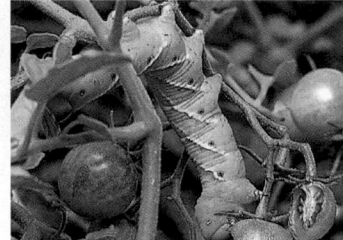

Crops may be engineered to resist destructive pests.

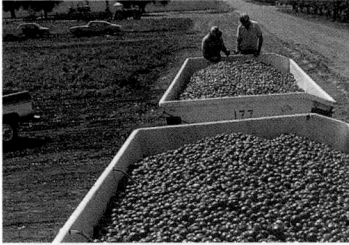

Genetic engineers may make produce easier to ship.

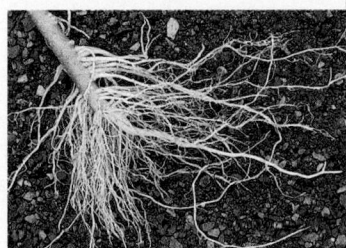

Biotechnology may produce roots that resist drying.

STUDENT RESOURCES

From the Teacher's Resource Package, use:

- Section Review 9.3, Activity Recordsheets 9-1 and 9-2, Critical Thinking Exercise 9, and Enrichment Topic 9-1 from Unit 2 Review Module
- Biotechnology Manual, Concepts of Biotechnology 4

TECHNOLOGY RESOURCES

Relevant technology resources include:

- Spanish Student Edition CD-ROM
- Teacher's Resource Planner CD-ROM

1 ENGAGE

Consider the Big idea

Have students read The Big Idea! at the top of the page. Explain that students are about to learn how biotechnology is used to alter the traits of organisms.

Use the Visual

Have students study the photograph and read the text that opens the section. Explain that GEBB is one of the many products produced by genetic engineering. Ask:

- **When would genetically altered skin cells be used?** (To replace severely burned or disease-damaged skin.)

Check Prior Knowledge

To assess students' knowledge about genetic engineering, ask:

- **What are some techniques of genetic engineering?** (Gel electrophoresis, and gene cloning)

Teacher Demo

If possible, obtain and display a transgenic tomato (or other genetically altered food) and briefly describe the process used in its development. Elicit from students what concerns they might have about eating foods created in this way. Discuss the reasons for their concerns.

SUPER READ! **Comparing and Contrasting**

To practice strategies for effective reading, use pages 37-38 in ***Super Read!***

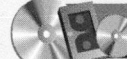

2 TEACH

Discuss

Point out to students that it is fairly common for cows to be given a growth hormone obtained from genetically engineered bacteria. Dairy cows treated with this hormone produce more milk, while beef cattle yield leaner meat. Ask:

- **Should cows be treated with growth hormones? Why or why not?** (Discuss students' ideas.)

Class Activity

TEAM WORK

Have groups of students research the annual medical costs of the following diseases: cystic fibrosis, hemophilia, diabetes, and hepatitis B. Have the groups present their research and compare costs.

Build Writing Skills

Ask students to write a recipe for the creation of a specific trait that involves the gene transfer process. Tell students to include detailed instructions in their recipes. Review some of the recipes to reinforce how the gene transfer process occurs.

214

tomato is just one example of the genetic engineering revolution in produce farming.

Genetic engineers are also studying ways to improve livestock. Transgenic animals can be produced by inserting DNA strands directly into an animal's egg, as shown in *Figure 9.8*. Genes for animals that produce more meat or are resistant to disease may someday be inserted into the reproductive cells of livestock to create these desirable characteristics in their offspring.

Research has revealed how to genetically engineer bacteria that can produce a milk-stimulating hormone for cattle. If you eat cheese, chances are you have already consumed a genetically engineered food. Most of the cheese produced in the United States has a genetically engineered component, called chymosin. Chymosin can replace rennin, a substance obtained from the stomach lining of slaughtered cattle. Both rennin and chymosin coagulate (clot) milk to make cheese.

Chymosin is made by transferring the cow genes that code for rennin into bacteria. The bacterial cells are then cloned to make chymosin. Genetically engineered chymosin makes smoother cheese, and it also has been marketed by some companies as "vegetarian." Do you think genetically engineered cheese is vegetarian? Why or why not?

In addition to these examples, transgenic organisms are used to process sewage, change cellulose in plant cell walls into fuel oil, and clean up oil spills and toxic waste dumps. Bacteria are the most common organisms used for genetic engineering. You

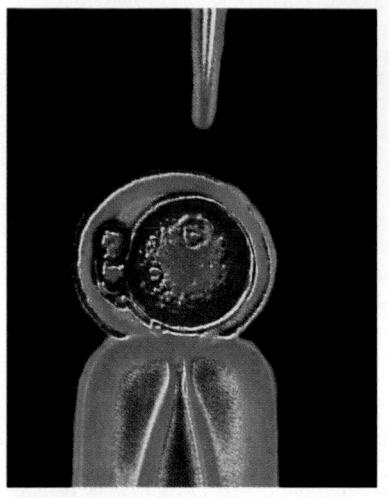

FIGURE 9.8
Scientists produce transgenic animals by using a microneedle (top) to inject DNA into an animal egg. How does this process differ from the development of transgenic bacteria? ❶

will read more about how bacteria are used in biotechnology in Chapter 14.

MEDICINE
Cures found in DNA codes

The area in which genetic engineering has had the greatest effect on our lives is medicine. Genetic engineering techniques have been used to develop gene therapy, to improve and develop vaccines and medicines, and to diagnose disorders.

Gene therapy Gene therapy is one of the fastest-growing areas in genetic engineering. Gene therapy differs from vaccines and medicines in that the treatment involves actually changing the genes that cause a genetic disorder.

Another form of gene therapy, designed to control the symptoms of cystic fibrosis, has already met with some success. One of the symptoms of cystic fibrosis is secretion of excess mucus, which can accumulate in the lungs and other organs. The excess mucus secretion is caused by a malfunctioning gene. In gene therapy, healthy genes that have recombined with certain viruses or carrier cells can be delivered to lung cells via a nasal spray. The healthy genes can then replace the malfunctioning genes, correcting the genetic defect.

Gene therapy provides researchers with a new tool to treat some human disorders, many of which had previously been untreatable or incurable. Such research may lead to a cure for hemophilia, a disease characterized by the inability of blood to clot. People who have hemophilia lack a protein that is necessary for blood clotting.

The search for a cure highlights one of the major stumbling blocks in gene therapy: How much is enough? The first step in developing a cure for

214 *Unit 2 Genetics*

MEETING DIVERSE NEEDS

LEP Pair students and have them create captioned drawings illustrating the applications of genetic engineering discussed in the section (agriculture, medicine, forensics). Have them exchange drawings with a second pair and discuss the applications.

❶ Bacteria incorporate the introduced DNA on a plasmid; animal cells must incorporate the injected DNA in a chromosome or it will be lost during cell division.

❷ Yes, because the gene that codes for chymosine still originates from a cow. No, because bacteria produce the chymosine and bacteria are not members of the Animal Kingdom.

FIGURE 9.9
Cleaning Out Clots

This SEM shows a large blood clot obstructing blood flow in an artery. How can genetically engineered bacteria clear the artery? **3**

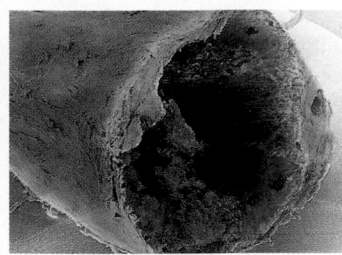

1 The blood clot in this artery restricts blood flow. When arteries that supply the heart muscle are blocked, heart tissue can be damaged, and a heart attack can result.

2 Protein from genetically engineered bacteria can dissolve blood clots, restoring blood flow to heart tissue.

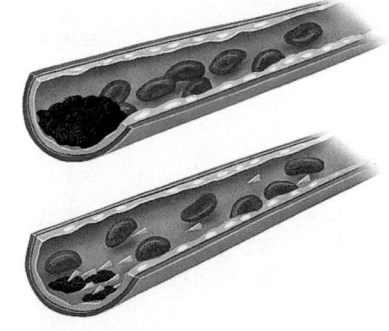

■ Blood clot
■ Red blood cells
◄ Genetically engineered protein

hemophilia is finding a way to make the protein needed for clotting. The next and hardest step is controlling production of the protein. Too much protein could harm the patient just as much as the disease itself.

Vaccines and medicines

Researchers have used genetic engineering to produce vaccines and medicines. Products now available include veterinary vaccines; a vaccine for hepatitis B, a serious liver infection; human growth hormone; and a cell growth factor for patients with low blood-cell counts. Recombinant DNA technology is now being used to slow the progression of multiple sclerosis. In addition, genetically engineered bacteria can help dissolve blood clots in arteries of heart attack patients, as shown in *Figure 9.9*. A protein produced by the bacteria can clear the clogged arteries, allowing blood to flow freely again.

Scientists have used genetic engineering to design a protein that binds to a specific type of cell. The protein carries a radioactive tracer or a small amount of medicine. Because the protein binds to specific cells, abnormal cells can be targeted and treated while normal cells are unaffected. This technique may prove useful for cancer treatment.

LAB ZONE Do It! bioSURF

How Big Is the Human Genome?

The Human Genome Project is possible only through cooperative efforts of many scientists worldwide. You can find out just how much information researchers need to complete the project if you . . .

Try This

1 Choose a page from one of your textbooks that has only text, no illustrations.
2 Count the number of characters (all letters, numbers, punctuation, and spaces) in five lines of text. Divide this number by 5; your result is the average number of characters per line.
3 Count the number of lines on the page. Multiply the number of lines by the average number of characters per line. Your result is the average number of characters on a page.
4 Each character represents a DNA base. Divide the average number of characters per page by 2 in order to represent the number of "base pairs" per page.
5 Determine the number of pages in your textbook, and multiply that number by the number of base pairs per page. How many base pairs are in the textbook?
6 The human genome has about 3 million base pairs. How many books would you need to store all of that information?

Analyze Your Results

1 If you stacked all the textbooks you would need to "store" the Human Genome Project, how tall would the stack be?
2 Research the number of stars in the Milky Way. How does this number compare with the number of base pairs in the human genome?

Health

Huntington disease was named for the American physician George Huntington, who first identified the disease in the early 1870s. Symptoms of the disease include involuntary movements, irritability, and a decrease in intellect and memory. It is common for people who have this disease to be misdiagnosed as suffering from schizophrenia or other forms of mental illness.

Build Writing Skills

Have students research retinoblastoma to answer one of the following questions:

- In what age group does retinoblastoma occur?
- What chromosome carries retinoblastoma?
- What is the present treatment for retinoblastoma?

After students research and write short reports have volunteers discuss their findings.

In the Community

Magazines that may help students with their research include *Cell,* the *Journal of the American Medical Association* (JAMA), *Scientific American, Science,* and *Science News.* Suggest that students with access to the Internet conduct net searches using key words such as gene therapy, cloning, DNA fingerprinting, and genetic engineering. For their displays, students may wish to include a pictorial explanation of recombinant DNA technology.

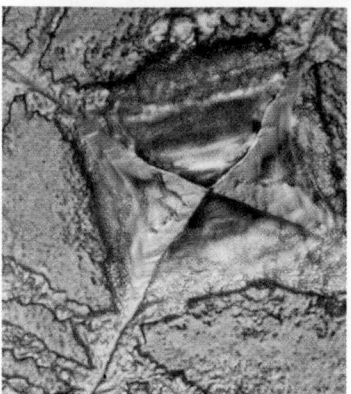

FIGURE 9.10

Human insulin, like the magnified sample above, is produced by recombinant DNA technology. What are the steps in the insulin production process? ❶

As you read in the previous section, insulin was one of the first medicines to be manufactured using genetic engineering. From 1921 until the early 1990s, diabetes was treated with insulin extracted from pigs or cows.

This insulin, however, caused allergic reactions in some patients. Today, genetic engineers mass-produce insulin by inserting the human insulin gene into bacteria. The transgenic bacteria make insulin that is identical to human insulin but does not cause allergic reactions. A sample of this insulin is shown in *Figure 9.10.*

Diagnosing disorders

Genetic engineering has enabled doctors to diagnose hundreds of disorders. Recently, genetic researchers developed a test that detects the gene for Huntington's disease. As you may recall from Chapter 6, Huntington disease is a fatal genetic disorder that involves the deterioration of the brain and nervous system. Huntington disease is caused by a dominant gene. The test for the gene is a search for a section of DNA called a marker. The DNA marker is on the same chromosome as the Huntington gene and is present only if the Huntington gene is on that chromosome. If the test detects the marker, then the person being tested probably carries the gene for Huntington disease.

Another test detects the gene that causes retinoblastoma, an eye cancer. If the gene causing retinoblastoma is detected, doctors can begin treatment to eradicate the cancer early, potentially saving a person's eyesight.

Research Scientists use bacteria and other types of cells to clone and study defective human genes. In this way, scientists can better understand genetic disorders. Do you recall learning about the Human Genome Project in Chapter 7? Using genetic engineering, researchers aim to sequence all of the DNA in the 46 human chromosomes. With that knowledge, they hope to discover the function of every human gene, from the genes that determine eye color to those that cause disorders. This enormous project has already enhanced our understanding of human genetics and will do so in the years ahead.

Misconception and mystery surround genetic engineering. Now that you have learned about this topic, inform your community about it as well. Ask your teacher or local librarian for a bulletin board where you and your classmates can create a genetic engineering informa-

IN THE COMMUNITY

Biotech Bulletin

tion center. To gather information, you can find articles in magazines and newspapers, ask for literature from biotech companies, and check out genetic engineering homepages. Visit *http://genetics.biosurf.com* for links to these homepages. You also may want to survey your friends and neighbors about their hopes and fears regarding genetic engineering and make an effort to address these concerns in your information center.

---

❶ The human insulin gene is inserted into a bacterium using a plasmid vector. The insulin is harvested as the bacteria produce it.

❷ Every band in the two children's lanes is also in either the mother's or father's lane.

❸ Each child inherits genetic information from each parent.

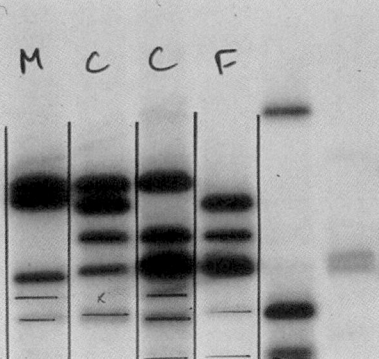

FIGURE 9.11
After years of separation, this family (left) was reunited through DNA fingerprinting. The DNA fingerprints (right) show the patterns of a mother (M), father (F), and two children (C). What similarities among the parental and offspring DNA fingerprints can you see? ②

FORENSICS
Crime still doesn't pay

Sherlock Holmes had his magnifying glass. Today's detectives use more sophisticated tools as they search for courtroom evidence. Like Sherlock Holmes, modern detectives practice forensics, the use of the scientific method to solve crimes.

As always, someone's guilt or innocence can hang on analyzing the precise sequence of events occurring on the day of a crime. Today, with the advances of DNA fingerprinting, guilt or innocence can also hinge on determining the precise sequence of bases in a microscopic fragment of DNA. With the exception of identical twins, no two people have identical DNA. Because DNA fingerprints are unique, they can help solve crimes.

DNA fingerprints can even help unravel mysteries that have remained unsolved for decades. In 1991, a grave site that was thought to contain the remains of Butch Cassidy and the Sundance Kid was examined. A comparison of DNA fingerprints from the skeletons with DNA fingerprints from known relatives of the famous outlaws proved conclusively that neither Butch Cassidy nor the Sundance Kid was buried at the site.

DNA fingerprints can also be used to establish family relationships and reunite relatives. Parts of the patterns of both the mother and the father will be present in the DNA fingerprints of their offspring. The family in *Figure 9.11* was reunited through DNA fingerprints. Why do the offspring's DNA fingerprints have parts of their parents' patterns? ③

The applications you have just read about are only a few of many possible uses of genetic engineering principles. As researchers learn more about the exact mechanisms of genes, genetic engineering will become an even more significant part of everyday life.

CHECKPOINT 9.3

1. Name and describe three applications of genetic engineering.
2. How is recombinant DNA technology used in medicine?
3. **Critical Thinking** Would you want to find out if you carried a gene for an incurable disease? Why or why not?

Build on What You Know

4. How did investigators establish that the Tyrolean Ice Man was an inhabitant of the Swiss Alps? *(Need to jog your memory? Revisit relevant concepts in Chapter 7, page 156.)*

Chapter 9 The Biotechnology Revolution **217**

Little Clues of You

Have you brushed your hair, bathed with a washcloth, or trimmed your nails today? If so, you've left behind all the evidence forensics experts would need to obtain a DNA fingerprint.

CHECKPOINT 9.3

1. Students should cite specific examples in agriculture, medicine, and forensics.
2. Recombinant DNA technology is used to produce human insulin for diabetes, human growth hormone, and a vaccine for hepatitis B. Accept all logical responses.
3. **Making decisions** Check that students give reasons to support their responses.
4. They obtained DNA samples from Tyrolean Ice Man's bones and compared his DNA fingerprint with those of modern Swiss inhabitants.

Modeling DNA Probes

TEAM WORK

Modeling DNA Probes

Lab Prep and Planning

The procedure and analysis should take a full class period.

Hypothesis Help

Remind students how the traits of individuals are determined. Ask them to explain why their set of traits is unique from that of any other person. You may also want to discuss the unique sequence of DNA bases before students propose their hypotheses.

Lab Extension

Open Ended

Have half the students in the class conduct the activity using a different DNA probe, such as GAGCTC. Have students who use the different probe compare their results to those of students using the probe provided in the text to determine whether changing the probe alters the results.

WHAT YOU WILL DO Use DNA sequences to identify individuals

SKILLS YOU WILL USE Making models, classifying, organizing

WHAT YOU WILL NEED Graph paper, scissors, a partner

Individual 1	ATCTCGAGACTGATTGGCCATAAGCTCGAG
Individual 2	ATTGGCCACTCGAGACGTTGGCCAAGTCCG
Individual 3	ATGACCATGGCCAGGCTCGAGCTGATGACG
Individual 4	ATATGGCCATTGCTCGAGTGGCCAGATCCG
Individual 5	ACTCGAGGTCCCTCGAGTGATGGCCATACG

Background

Scientists often use a probe to identify DNA. A probe is a short, single stranded DNA molecule that is labeled. Because the probe is single stranded, it can bind to other DNA that has a complementary sequence. For example, a probe with the sequence AGCT can bind to DNA containing the sequence TCGA. Scientists mix a probe with an unknown DNA sample. The probe will only bind to a DNA sample that has a complementary sequence.

Propose a Hypothesis

Propose a hypothesis regarding the uniqueness of DNA sequences in individuals.

Conduct Your Experiment

1 The DNA sequences for five individuals are shown in the figure. Copy the DNA sequences onto graph paper, putting one letter from the DNA sequence into each square.

2 Look for DNA sequences in each individual that are complementary to this six-base DNA probe: TCCGAG.

3 Circle any DNA sequence in each individual that is complementary to the sequence of the DNA probe.

4 Record the numbers of the individuals who were identified by the DNA probe.

5 Choose one of the five individuals, and construct a new DNA probe that will identify only that individual. Write out the DNA sequence of the probe, and exchange it with a new sequence written by your partner.

6 Repeat steps 2 and 3 to identify the unknown individual, using the DNA probe that your partner constructed.

Analyze Your Data

1 What DNA sequence is the complement of the DNA probe shown in step 2?

2 Which individual(s) was identified by the DNA probe given in step 2?

3 What is the complementary DNA sequence of the DNA probe from your partner (step 5)?

4 Which individual was identified by the DNA probe from your partner?

Draw Conclusions

Explain how a person can be identified by DNA probes. Is it possible for more than one individual to be identified by a DNA probe? Would DNA probes with longer or shorter sequences be more likely to identify only one individual? Write a paragraph discussing the answers to these questions.

Design a Related Experiment

Design an experiment to model how restriction enzymes could be used to create DNA fingerprints for the five individuals shown. Before writing your experiment, consider the fact that restriction enzymes cut DNA at specific base sequences.

Analyze Your Data

1 The complementary DNA sequence is: AGGCTC.
2 Only individual 3 is identified.
3 Check students' responses.
4 Check students' responses.

Draw Conclusions

Students should relate that if a tiny segment of DNA is unique to an individual, then the person can be identified by it. Some DNA segments are found in more than one individual, and others are found in only one. Longer DNA segments are more likely to identify one individual.

9.4 Safety and Ethics in Biotechnology

If you make it, you own it
How would you like to patent your own virus? These mice (left) are patented. According to the United States Supreme Court, if you create a new virus or organism through genetic engineering, then you can get a patent for it. The ethics of an individual owning an entire genome is one of many concerns raised by biotechnological advances.

What you'll learn

IDEAS
• To appraise the safety issues and precautions taken in biotechnology
• To contrast the benefits and concerns associated with genetic engineering

SAFETY ISSUES

A new challenge

Life has existed on Earth for billions of years, but only recently have scientists acquired the knowledge to change the genes of living things. Biotechnology has already proven to be a method of creating products of great benefit to humans. But biotechnology also has a dark side—potential abuse and accidents.

Some people worry that genetic engineers might accidentally create deadly bacteria or viruses. What would happen if a modified bacterium or virus spread from a laboratory into the environment? How can you guard against the release of a dangerous bacterium?

In response to these fears, scientists adhere to strict laboratory regulations, as shown in *Figure 9.12*. Although no procedure is foolproof, precautions such as protective gear help guard genetic researchers from infection by a newly engineered organism. As another safety measure, genetically engineered organisms can be altered so that they cannot survive outside the laboratory.

Some organisms, however, are specifically designed for release into the environment. Bacteria that protect

crops from frost damage are one example. Although these bacteria are helpful, will their release have any harmful, long-term effects? Could such organisms change natural cycles or enter food chains and ultimately affect other organisms? These questions deserve careful consideration.

FIGURE 9.12
Safety Precautions

Scientists always use safety precautions. Procedures vary with the type of organism used and the potential health risks it may pose.

Protective clothing
A face mask, gloves, and lab coat protect the eyes and skin from contact with potentially harmful organisms.

Contamination precautions
Strict procedures help workers avoid touching, breathing, or ingesting experimental materials.

Safe disposal
The disposal of contaminated wastes is federally regulated by OSHA, the Occupational Safety and Health Administration.

Chapter 9 The Biotechnology Revolution **219**

9.4

2 TEACH

 Do It! TEAM WORK

How Can Ethical Questions Be Answered?

Try This

Recommend that students survey people of varying ages and backgrounds to obtain results that reflect the values of diverse groups in society.

 STS

Have students prepare a mock court or debate to justify releasing genetic information.

3 ASSESS

Evaluate Understanding

Divide the class into groups to simulate a press conference on ethics in biotechnology. Assign one student in each group the role of moderator, four the roles of genetic researchers and four the roles of reporters. Begin by having each scientist read a prepared statement.

Reteach

On the board, write *Safety Issues* and *Ethical Issues*. Guide students to identify and list concerns people have about biotechnology. Discuss the lists and identify measures taken to address these concerns.

220

LAB ZONE Do It!

How Can Ethical Questions Be Answered?

The ethical questions raised by biotechnology have no "right" or "wrong" answers but are decided by society as a whole. You can model the information-gathering process of government officials if you . . .

Try This

1 Choose three safety or ethical issues related to genetic engineering. Design a survey to ask people their opinions on the issues. Your questions may have a format similar to the sample question (right).
2 Find 15 people who will complete your survey. Collect the surveys and tabulate the answers.

I support keeping personal genome information private. (check one)

☐ *Strongly agree*

☐ *Agree somewhat*

☐ *Disagree somewhat*

☐ *Strongly disagree*

Analyze Your Results

1 Was there total agreement on any issue? If more people were surveyed, would there be more or less agreement in the responses?
2 How informed about biotechnology issues were the people you surveyed? If you were a politician or government official, how would you act upon the results of this survey?

ISSUES IN BIOLOGY

Ethical questions

Because of its potential for modifying human genes, biotechnology also raises some ethical issues. For example, it may soon be possible to treat or correct genetic disorders before they are passed on to offspring. It follows that human genes for traits other than genetic disorders could also be altered. Parents might engineer their children's physical and intellectual traits. What would be the result? Who

---

should be able to judge whether a trait is desirable or not?

Another ethical issue concerns the Human Genome Project. If this project is completed, it might be possible to screen people for their genetic predisposition to many diseases. Some insurance companies already use genetic screening and have denied insurance on the basis of test results. For this reason, many people feel that personal genome information should be kept private. What are the benefits of genetic screening? Would you feel safer knowing, for example, that an airplane pilot or firefighter had no genetic predisposition to heart disease?

At this time many questions remain unanswered. Perhaps you will be one of the scientists who helps resolve these difficult ethical issues. If not, you will definitely be a voter. By being informed, you can make wise decisions about the biotechnology issues that will arise.

CHECKPOINT 9.4

1. What are some safety precautions scientists use when working with genetically engineered organisms?
2. Identify a benefit and a concern in connection with the alteration of human genes.
3. **Critical Thinking** What are the possible harmful, long-term effects of engineering a crop to resist weed killers?

Build on What You Know

4. How could the scientific method help resolve safety and ethical issues related to biotechnology? *(Need to jog your memory? Revisit relevant concepts in Chapter 1, Section 1.3.)*

? **How can technology be used to affect phenotype?**

220 *Unit 2 Genetics*

CHECKPOINT 9.4

1. They wear protective clothing and follow strict laboratory procedures.
2. Benefit: Prevention or cure of many genetic diseases. Concern: Technology may be used to affect frivolous traits in offspring.
3. **Developing a hypothesis** In the following year a different crop may be planted. If leftover seeds from the resistant crop

germinate, weed killer will not destroy the engineered plant.
4. Peer review, controlled experimentation, and careful examination of cause and effect may be important in deciding ethical and safety issues.

❶-❷ Accept all reasonable statements.

Chapter 9 Review

 **THE BIG IDEA!** 9.1–9.2 Genotypes can be changed through selective breeding and genetic engineering.
9.3–9.4 Technology enables us to find out about genotype and use this knowledge to affect phenotype.

Sum It Up

Use the following summary to review the main concepts in this chapter.

9.1 Breeding

- Humans have practiced selective breeding of plants and animals for centuries.
- Outbreeding is the crossing of two different breeds and can result in hybrid vigor.
- Biotechnology is the use of living organisms to make products.

9.2 Genetic Engineering

- Genetic engineering rcfcrs to any technique used to identify or change DNA sequences.
- Scientists use gel electrophoresis to determine the sequence of DNA bases and to obtain DNA fingerprints.
- Recombinant DNA is a combination of the genetic material of two different breeds.
- Genes can be cloned using recombinant technology.

9.3 Applications of Genetic Engineering

- Genetic engineering has current and potential applications in agriculture, industry, medicine, and forensics.
- Genetic engineering enables scientists to perform gene therapy, develop medicines, diagnose disorders, and study genomes.

9.4 Safety and Ethics in Biotechnology

- Scientists are addressing concerns about the safety of creating and releasing genetically engineered organisms.
- Potential applications of genetic engineering, such as the alteration of human genes, raise ethical questions for members of society to consider.

Use Terms and Concepts

Use each of the following words or terms in a complete sentence. If you need to review a meaning, turn to the page indicated.

selective breeding (p. 206)

inbreeding (p. 206)

outbreeding (p. 207)

genetic engineering (p. 209)

restriction enzymes (p. 209)

DNA fingerprint (p. 210)

recombinant DNA (p. 211)

vector (p. 211)

plasmids (p. 211)

transgenic organisms (p. 213)

Review the Big Ideas

Before students begin the Chapter Review, you may wish to discuss main concepts from the Big Ideas in Chapter 9. Point out that by using technology such as gel electrophoresis and DNA fingerprinting, scientists are able to determine genotypes. Through selective breeding and genetic engineering, they can use this knowledge to alter phenotypes. This practice has current and potential applications in agriculture, industry, medicine, and forensics, but raises ethical questions for society.

Answers

1. outbreeding
2. restriction enzymes
3. Plasmids
4. DNA fingerprint
5. selective breeding
6. Transgenic organisms
7. False. A plasmid is a type of vector.
8. True
9. True
10. False. Outbreeding produces hybrid organisms.
11. True (Except identical twins)
12. Selective breeding is the manipulation of traits through controlled reproduction. It is used to promote desired traits in plants and animals.
13. 1) Cut DNA into fragments with restriction enzymes. 2) Put DNA samples into gel tracks. 3) Apply charge to gel tracks and allow DNA to travel. 4) Examine results.
14. The human gene responsible for insulin production is isolated. The gene is then inserted into a plasmid. The recombinant plasmid is inserted into a bacterial cell, which will produce human insulin.
15. Close relatives are more likely to have the same recessive allele than are two randomly mated organisms.
16. Answers may include genetic engineering of crops, medicine such as human insulin, chymosin in cheese, and DNA fingerprinting.
17. Scientists wear special clothes and follow strict safety precautions. Transgenic microorganisms are crippled so they cannot survive outside the laboratory.
18. A transgenic organism is an organism with recombinant DNA.

Use Your Word Power

COMPLETION Write the word or phrase that best completes each statement.

1. Hybrid vigor can result from _____ .

2. To perform gel electrophoresis, scientists use _____ to "cut" DNA into fragments.

3. _____ are bacterial vectors.

4. A _____, obtained through gel electrophoresis, can be used for identification.

5. For centuries, humans have used _____ to produce crops and livestock.

6. _____ are genetically engineered life-forms with the DNA of two different breeds.

TRUE-FALSE Write true if the statement is true. If the statement is false, replace the underlined word(s) to make the statement true.

7. A plasmid is a type of <u>vector</u>.

8. <u>Genetic engineering</u> has many potential benefits.

9. Transgenic organisms contain <u>recombinant DNA</u>.

10. <u>Inbreeding</u> produces hybrid organisms.

11. Everyone has a unique <u>DNA fingerprint</u>.

Show What You Know

12. What is selective breeding, and what are the applications of selective breeding?

13. What are the steps in gel electrophoresis?

14. How is recombinant DNA technology used to produce human insulin?

15. Why are recessive alleles more likely to be expressed in the offspring of close relatives?

16. Name and describe two applications of genetic engineering.

17. What are some safety precautions used by scientists involved in genetic engineering?

18. What is a transgenic organism?

19. What is forensics, and how can genetic engineering be used in forensics studies?

20. How are vectors and plasmids related?

21. **Make a Concept Map** Complete the concept map below by adding the following terms: recombinant DNA technology, vector, plasmid, gene cloning, biotechnology, restriction enzymes, DNA fragments, DNA fingerprint.

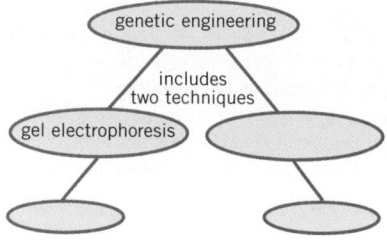

Take It Further

22. **Applying Concepts** What advantages does genetic engineering have over selective breeding?

23. **Making a Prediction** What might be a negative result of growing a crop that is genetically engineered to resist weed killer?

24. **Developing a Hypothesis** A genetically engineered medicine for heart attack patients, tPA, is being used on some stroke victims. A stroke is caused by a blood clot in the brain. Why might tPA effectively treat strokes?

25. **Designing an Experiment** The use of DNA fingerprints as legal evidence is sometimes contested. Design an experiment to test the accuracy of DNA fingerprints.

26. **Interpreting a Graph** The following graph shows death rates for infectious diseases (influenza, pneumonia, and tuberculosis) and noninfectious diseases (heart disease and cancer). How have antibiotics and vaccines affected death rates? How might further applications of genetic engineering to cancer and heart disease treatment change death rates in the future?

---

19. Forensics uses the scientific method to solve crimes. DNA fingerprints are used for identification in forensics.
20. Plasmids are bacterial vectors.
21. Concept maps should show the following: <u>Biotechnology</u> uses <u>genetic engineering</u> which includes two techniques, <u>gel electrophoresis</u> and <u>recombinant DNA technology</u>. In gel electrophoresis, <u>restriction enzymes</u> cut <u>DNA fragments</u> to obtain <u>DNA fingerprints</u>. Recombinant DNA technology uses <u>vectors</u> for <u>gene cloning</u>, or vectors which can be <u>plasmids</u>.
22. Genetic engineering is faster and more precisely controlled than selective breeding.
23. In the following year a different crop

U.S. Death Rates from Diseases

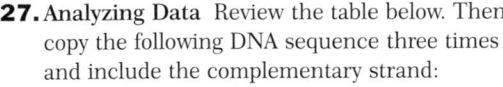

Deaths per 100,000 People (y-axis)
Year (x-axis): 1910, 1930, 1950, 1970, 1990

- ■ Infectious diseases
- ■ Noninfectious diseases

27. Analyzing Data Review the table below. Then copy the following DNA sequence three times and include the complementary strand:

ATGACATCTACGGAATTCTCAAGTTCGAATCG

Identify where each restriction enzyme will cut the strand.

DNA Restriction Enzymes

Enzyme	Recognition Sequence
BglII	A ▼ GATCT TCTAG ▲ A
EcoRI	G ▼ AATTC CTTAA ▲ G
HindIII	A ▼ AGCTT TTCGA ▲ A

Consider the Issues

28. Make a New Organism If you could use genetic engineering to create a new organism or to mass-produce a product, what would it be? How would it affect the world? What safety precautions might you take? You may illustrate or create a model to accompany your answer.

Make New Connections

29. Biology and Cartoons What is the joke in the following cartoon? How is the cartoon

"Looks like we grafted a few too many human genes into the kohlrabi."

inaccurate? Critique the cartoon using your knowledge of genetic engineering.

30. Biology and Economics Find a genetically engineered product at the grocery store or pharmacy. Examples include engineered produce, cheese containing chymosine, or human insulin. Compare the price of the engineered product with that of the traditionally produced product. Is there a difference? Why or why not?

31. Biology and Community: A Project Interview someone who has been affected by genetic engineering—an employee in the field, a farmer, or a person treated with genetically engineered medicine. Ask about his or her experiences, both positive and negative, and inquire about any misconceptions he or she may have had or encountered.

FAST-FORWARD TO CHAPTER 10

People can change genomes through biotechnology. Other environmental influences can also affect genomes. In the next unit you will learn about theories that explain how traits of organisms have changed over time.

Chapter 9 The Biotechnology Revolution **223**

or skin sample from the same person.

26. Antibiotics and vaccines have decreased death by infections diseases. Genetic engineering could decrease death from noninfectious disease.

27. Bgl II will cut after the second A; Eco RI will cut after the fourth G; Hind III will cut after the ninth A.

28. Accept all answers that include consideration of ethics.

29. The joke is that the scientists used genetic engineering to create "human plants." Humans and plants do not have similar enough genomes to create transgeric hybrids.

30. A genetically engineered product could be more expensive because of the price of the research and development, or less expensive because it is easier to produce.

31. Accept all logical answers.

may be planted. If leftover seeds from the resistant crop germinate, weed killer will not destroy the unwanted plant.

24. The tPA could break up brain clots in the same manner that it dissolves clots in coronary arteries.

25. To test the accuracy of DNA fingerprints several different samples should

be tested. A blood sample from several volunteers could be collected and coded. The same volunteers would then provide a hair or skin sample, coded differently. The DNA fingerprint pattern would then be generated through the process of gel electrophoresis. If the method is accurate each blood sample should be correctly matched to a hair

Connect the Chapters

1. Recombination involves a change in position of existing genes. To produce insulin by recombination, the human gene for insulin production is inserted into bacterial DNA.
2. The gene therapy affects the genetic makeup of lung cells, not reproductive cells.
3. Mendel's experiments with peas were a type of selective breeding. Biotechnology can require work at a cellular level and sometimes involves the manipulation of genes.
4. Test crosses show whether a dominant trait is an expression of a homozygous or a heterozygous genotype, which would carry the recessive gene. Sections of DNA called genetic markers can be used to identify carriers of recessive genes.
5. Genes are sections of chromosomes. Genes control the synthesis of proteins. Codons are three-base sequences that code for the specific amino acids in proteins.
6. Griffith changed genes at the molecular level when DNA from the S strain combined with DNA from the R strain.

Connect the Units

7. Enzymes are not used up in chemical reactions, and they are produced in very small quantities.
8. Active transport is required when spliced mRNA crosses the nuclear membrane from the nucleus to the cytoplasm.
9. DNA polymerase connects nucleotides to parent strands of DNA to produce sister chromatids.

Unit 2 Review

 **THE BIG IDEA!** Answering the following questions will help you to link ideas and grasp the core concepts.

Connect the Chapters

1. Compare recombination as it occurs in crossing over with the recombinant DNA technology used to produce insulin.
2. Explain why gene therapy for cystic fibrosis does not prevent the malfunctioning gene from being passed on to offspring.
3. Compare Mendel's breeding experiments with pea plants to biotechnology.
4. Contrast the use of test crosses and DNA markers to identify carriers of recessive genes.
5. How are chromosomes, genes, codons, anticondons, and proteins related?
6. Explain how Griffith's 1928 experiment with bacterial strains was an early example of genetic engineering.

Connect the Units

7. Cells do not need as much energy to produce RNA polymerase as they need to produce other proteins. Why?
8. Identify one event in the process of gene expression in a eukaryotic cell for which active transport is essential.
9. Explain the function of DNA polymerase during the interphase portion of the cell cycle.

Connect to Themes

10. **Unity and Diversity** How does eukaryotic gene expression show unity and diversity?
11. **Patterns and Changes** How do linked genes affect the Law of Independent Assortment?
12. **Systems and Interactions** How does the concentration of lactose control lactose digestion in *E.coli*?

1 In the past, marriages in European royal families were arranged to strengthen political alliances. The bride and groom were often related to some degree. Such inbreeding was widespread among the descendants of England's Queen Victoria. Unfortunately, strong political alliances did not lead to equally robust genomes. One problem was the incidence of the genetic disorder hemophilia. Make a poster displaying a pedigree of Queen Victoria's lineage. Identify the descendants who carried the hemophilia gene, and those who expressed the gene.

2 As a class, research and experiment with varieties of a flower or vegetable. For example, find out how many varieties of tomatoes can be grown in your area. Then design an experiment to find the variety best suited for local soil and weather conditions.

CRITIC'S CORNER

A BOOK REVIEW BY STACIE SIMMONS OF KANSAS CITY, MISSOURI

The Double Helix, by Nobel Prize winner James D. Watson, tells the story of scientists and their determination to discover the structure of DNA. The book describes a scientific team working together to decipher a mystery (with a little help from x-rayed molecules). Each scientist had his or her own job to do; each had a unique way of helping out. The unity of these scientists, and their often humorous relationships with each other, make this book a page-turner for students of all interests and backgrounds.

The Double Helix
James D. Watson

Connect to Themes

10. All eukaryotic cells carry the same genetic information; the expression of the genes varies with cell specialization.
11. Because linked genes remain coupled during sorting, they do not produce the ratios predicted by the Law of Independent Assortment.
12. Lactose binds with repressors, freeing up DNA to transcribe the genes that code for digestive enzymes in *E.coli.*

Project Plans

1. Students might also want to look at the history of these alliances.
2. Results will vary. Remind students to set up a control for their experiment.

SPOTLIGHT ON CAREERS

DR. KEITH BLACK
Neurosurgeon, UCLA Medical Center;
professor of neurosurgery at UCLA

EDUCATION: Neurological surgery residency;
general surgery internship; M.D.; B.S.

"I specialize in brain tumors. Most of these tumors are very complex, and about half of them are malignant. One part of my work is surgery, because malignant tumors cannot be cured without it. I also do research—I try to find ways of curing or improving the treatment of brain tumors. One of the newer treatments is gene therapy. We aim to develop a brain-tumor vaccine. We've learned that tumors release proteins that turn off the ability of immune cells to fight disease. We genetically modify tumor cells so that they no longer release these proteins, then we can take the modified cells and inject them back into the patient. That way, the person's immune system can recognize the tumor's cells and fight them."

bioSURF Learn more about Dr. Black's cancer research at UCLA Johnson Cancer Center by visiting *http://genetics.biosurf.com* for more information.

ANAMARIA CRAICI
College intern at the National Cancer Institute,
National Institutes of Health

EDUCATION: College junior majoring in biochemistry and molecular biology; high school diploma

"Science is a lot of fun. It's like solving a mystery, and you have to choose the way to find the answers."
—ANAMARIA CRAICI

"I have always known that science was where I wanted to go. You work with an unknown, a question. I study the systems plants have to defend themselves against all kinds of pathogens. A pathogen is an organism that can cause a disease—a bacterium, or a virus, for example. My professor, Dr. Craig Tepper, is looking for the genes that 'turn on' when a plant is attacked. My job is to do nonradioactive DNA sequencing. By studying how plants defend themselves, we hope to learn how to induce plants to grow in places where they normally wouldn't, or cure plants that are dying."

bioSURF Find out about internships at the National Cancer Institute at the National Institutes of Health by visiting the site *http://genetics.biosurf.com*.

Unit 2 Genetics **225**

SPOTLIGHT ON CAREERS

bioSURF Have students connect to the bioSurf Internet address to learn about schools, educational programs, and scholarships that would prepare them for careers or occupations in fields related to genetics and biotechnology.

Consider These Careers

Technicians with various levels of education can find employment creating the products of genetic engineering, from human growth hormones to agricultural products. Other careers related to the field of genetics include genetic counselor, virologist, botanist, and forensic scientist.

Plan for a Career

- **Informational Interviewing** Job interviews usually focus on the employer finding out information about the prospective employee. However, many organizations will also agree to informational interviews in which the job seeker learns about the needs, structure, and hiring practices of the company. Have students develop a list of questions they might ask in an informational interview. If possible, arrange for a human resource representative from a local company to come to class and discuss what employers look for in a candidate.

Critic's Corner

Have students read the review of *The Andromeda Strain* on page 126. Ask if any other students have read this book, and have them share opinions with the class. If possible, arrange to have the book available for interested students to read. Encourage students to consider why the story could or could not happen in real life.

Discuss some new techniques that enable scientists to fight such a virus today. Point out that these techniques were not available when the book was written.

Unit Overview

When did life on Earth begin? No one really knows the answer to that question. Scientists do know that life a million years ago was very different from life today. Fossils, biochemistry, and modern structures provide evidence that help researchers link the past to the present. By determining evolutionary links, scientists can sort out the relationships among today's diverse organisms.

Unit Objectives

- Discuss scientific theories of how life began.
- Explain the theory of evolution developed by Darwin and Wallace.
- Describe the evidence supporting current theories of human evolution.
- Outline the five kingdom system of classification

Connect the Units

This unit explores modern scientific theories that explain current biodiversity on Earth. Although Units 1 and 2 provide a useful foundation for these concepts, the critical precedent for this unit is found in Chapter 1, in which students are introduced to the methods of doing science. Unit 3 can be followed by Units 4, 5, or 6 in any order, depending on whether you prefer to focus on microbiology, plants, or animals.

UNIT 3
Change and Diversity

Which of these amazing statements about change and diversity are fact, and which are fiction?

Hit *or* Myth?

Life on Earth came from **Mars.**

(Fiction. No one knows how life on Earth began, but scientists are debating whether some meteorites from Mars contain bacterial fossils.)

Poodle puppies are born with **fancy haircuts.**

(Fiction. Poodle haircuts are not inherited. Poodles are groomed to achieve that look, and their offspring must also be groomed.)

Scientists **date** dinosaurs.

(Fact. Scientists can determine the age of dinosaur bones by measuring radioactivity.)

226

Lizards are more closely related to birds than to crocodiles.

(Fact. Researchers have found that looks are deceiving—a lizard is genetically more similar to a bird than to a crocodile.)

Tweet Tweet ♪ ♪ ♪

In a healthy population, everyone has the **same** genes.

(Fiction. Genetic variety is a source of beneficial mutations, which can be key to a population's survival.)

Panda bears are **not** bears.

(Fact and fiction. Most scientists classify the giant panda as a bear, but they consider the red panda to be a type of raccoon.)

FLAP
FLAP

Dragonflies were once as **large as pigeons.**

(Fact. Fossil evidence indicates that giant dragonflies cruised Earth 290 million years ago.)

Hit _or_ Myth?

Use It

Review each of the statements with the class. Ask students to share their prior knowledge and misconceptions on each topic. Ask them to consider which sources of information on these topics are generally reliable, and which may not be.

Link It

Chapter 10 links the theory of evolution to modern biodiversity (poodle, flamingos). Further information on adaptation can be found in Unit 9. Chapter 11 links fossil and biochemical evidence of change through time to modern evolutionary theory (Mars, dinosaur, dragonfly). More information on biochemistry was presented in Chapters 2 and 7. Chapter 13 explores the modern system of classification (panda, lizard).

Expand It

The theory that life on Earth actually came from Mars was sparked by the discovery of shapes similar to ancient fossils, in a meteorite found in Australia in 1979. It was not until August 1996 that the theory was presented publicly at a NASA conference. Since then, the significance of the shapes has been hotly debated.

The connection between dinosaurs and birds was strengthened in 1996 with the discovery of a fossil in China that appears to be a 140 million year old dinosaur with feathers. This one meter long fossil is about 10 million years older than _Archaeopteryx_, the first known bird.

227

Section	Student Activities/Features	Teacher's Resource Package
10.1 Variation and Adaptation **Objectives** ■ Distinguish between variation and adaptation ■ Explain how fossils are used to study ancient life forms	**Lab Zone Discover It!** *Observing the Variety of Life*, p. 229 **Everyday Biology** *New Species with Many Niches*, p. 231	**Unit 3 Review Module** ■ Section Review 10.1 **Laboratory Manual,** Lab 19: "The Same, but Different"
10.2 Darwin and His Theory **Objectives** ■ Explain the theories that led to the theory of evolution ■ Analyze Darwin's theory of evolution by natural selection	**Everyday Biology** *The Bright Side of Motion Sickness*, p. 235	**Unit 3 Review Module** ■ Section Review 10.2 ■ Interpreting Graphics 10 ■ Critical Thinking Exercise 10 ■ Enrichment Topic 10-1 **Interpreting and Developing Graphics,** 28
10.3 Tracking Changes **Objectives** ■ Explain how scientists reconstruct history through fossils ■ Describe how scientists reconstruct evolutionary history through present-day organisms	**Lab Zone Think About It!** *Recording Observations*, p. 240	**Unit 3 Review Module** ■ Section Review 10.3 **Issues and Decision Making** 10-1 **Interpreting and Developing Graphics,** 29
10.4 Origin of Species **Objectives** ■ Identify the characteristics that define a species ■ Compare the different modes of speciation	**Lab Zone Do It!** *How Are Inventions Like Evolution?* p. 243 **Lab Zone Investigate It!** *Modeling Coevolution*, p. 245	**Unit 3 Review Module** ■ Section Review 10.4 ■ Activity Recordsheets 10-1 and 10-2 **Consumer Applications** 10-1
10.5 Population Genetics **Objectives** ■ Describe the principles of population genetics ■ Analyze the effects of changes in the environment on populations	**Lab Zone Do It!** *How Quickly Do Populations Decrease?* p. 248 **In the Community** *The World in Their Eyes*, p. 249 **STS: Environmental Awareness** *The Story of the English Peppered Moth*, p. 250	**Unit 3 Review Module** ■ Section Review 10.5 ■ Activity Recordsheet 10-3 **Laboratory Manual,** Lab 20: "Population Model of Genes" **Interpreting and Developing Graphics,** 30 **Spanish Reviews** Chapter 10

Technology Resources

Internet Connections

Within this chapter, you will see the **bioSURF** logo. If you and your students have access to the Internet, the following URL address will provide various Internet connections that are related to topics and features presented in this chapter:

http://evolution.biosurf.com

You can also find relevant chapter material at **The Biology Place** address:

http://www.biology.com

CD-ROMs

Biología: la telaraña de la vida,
   (Spanish Student Edition) Chapter 10
Teacher's Resource Planner, Chapter 10
   Supplements
TestWorks CD-ROM
■ Chapter 10 Tests

Overhead Transparencies

■ Gradualism and Punctuated Equilibrium, #22
■ Homology, #23

Videotapes

Biology Alive! Video Series
■ The Continuity of Life Video
Rewind: The Web of Life Reteach Videos

Planning for Activities

STUDENT EDITION
Lab Zone
Discover It! p. 229
   ■ this textbook
   ■ paper
   ■ pencil

Lab Zone
Investigate It p. 245
   ■ long tweezers
   ■ teaspoons
   ■ dried peas or beans
   ■ 25-milliliter (mL) gradu-
     ated cylinders
   ■ 100-mL beakers
   ■ watch or clock

TEACHER'S EDITION
Quick Activity, p. 230
Survival traits
   ■ pictures of organisms in
     their natural environ-
     ments

Quick Activity, p. 233
Fish features
   ■ fish in a bowl

Quick Activity, p. 241
Comparing species
   ■ pictures of two related
     yet obviously different
     organisms

Chapter Objectives

Students will learn the main concepts of this chapter as they complete the following objectives.

- Relate variation and adaptation
- Describe how fossils are used to study ancient life-forms
- Explain the theories that led to the theory of evolution and analyze Darwin's theory of evolution
- Explain how scientists reconstruct history through fossils and present-day organisms
- Identify characteristics defining a species
- Describe the principles of population genetics
- Explain the effect of environmental change on populations

Key Words

10.1 *species, variation, adaptation, niche, fossil*

10.2 *evolution, natural selection, gradualism, punctuated equilibrium*

10.3 *homologous characteristics, vestigial structures, analogous structures*

10.4 *speciation, divergent evolution, convergent evolution, coevolution, adaptive radiation*

10.5 *gene pool, genetic equilibrium, genetic drift*

The Opening Story

Have students discuss how they think the story relates to the content of this chapter. Ask students what conditions are needed to support the diversity of life-forms that Darwin observed.

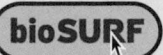

You can find out more about diversity and change in biology by exploring the following Internet address: *http://evolution.biosurf.com*

In this chapter . . .

FEATURES

Everyday Biology
- New Species with Many Niches
- The Bright Side of Motion Sickness

In the Community
The World in Their Eyes

 Environmental Awareness
The Story of the English Peppered Moth

LAB ZONES

Discover It!
- Observing the Variety of Life

Do It!
- How are Inventions Like Evolution?
- How Quickly Do Populations Decrease?

Think About It!
- Recording Observations

Investigate It!
- Modeling Coevolution

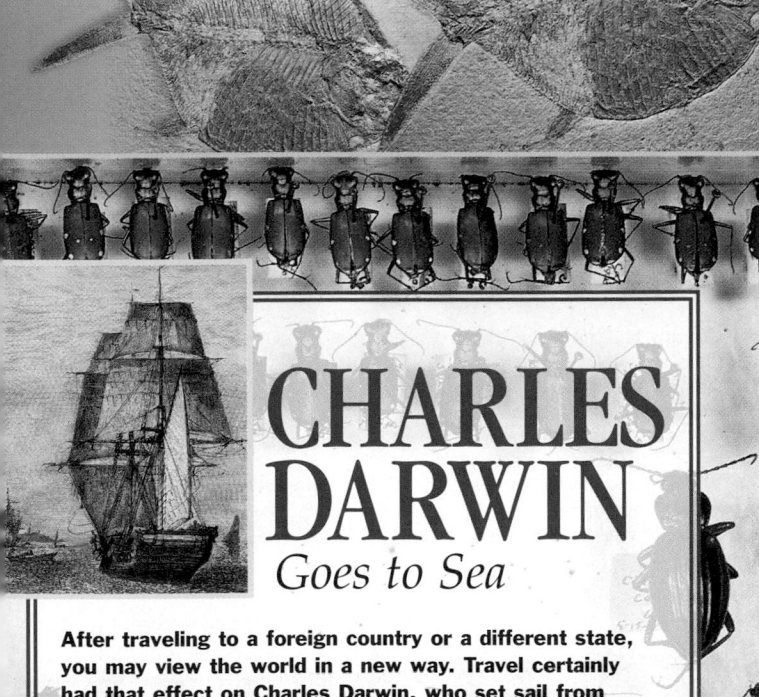

CHARLES DARWIN
Goes to Sea

After traveling to a foreign country or a different state, you may view the world in a new way. Travel certainly had that effect on Charles Darwin, who set sail from England in 1831 bound for the Galapagos Islands, located off the western coast of South America. During his five-year voyage aboard HMS *Beagle*, Darwin pursued his interest in the wildlife that inhabited the islands. Fascinated by the diversity of life-forms he observed, Darwin made copious notes in his diary and collected vast numbers of plant and animal specimens. He was most intrigued by the thirteen varieties of finches and countless types of beetles he observed.

Not content to merely observe, Darwin speculated about the variety of life-forms he saw. Why were there thirteen kinds of finches on the Galapagos? Did just one kind of finch inhabit the islands at one time? What advantages did a brightly colored beetle have? And why were some beetles tiny, compared with others? In answering these questions, Darwin developed one of the most revolutionary theories in the history of science: the theory of evolution.

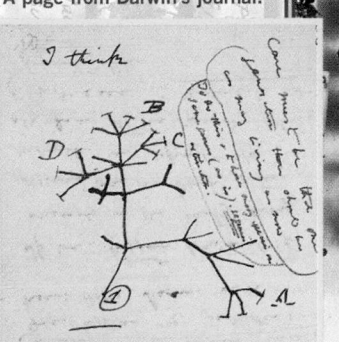

A page from Darwin's journal.

Discover It!

Observing the Variety of Life

1. Carefully observe the beetle collection shown on this page. Select five beetles.
2. Record all of the characteristics—similarities and differences—that you observe among the five beetles.
3. Based on your observations, predict the conditions in which each beetle lived. For example, a small, dull-colored beetle probably lived in a similarly colored environment, avoiding predators by blending with its surroundings.

Charles Darwin made observations similar to these when he sailed to the Galapagos Islands. Darwin developed his theory of natural selection to explain why beetles that live in different environments look different.

WRITE ABOUT IT!

In your science journal, write about the observations you made when you traveled to a different part of your town, state, or country. In what ways did you gain a different perspective about your surroundings?

229

Opening Activities

bioSURF If you have access to the Internet in your classroom or school you may wish to have students connect to the address shown on page 228. You may also want to have students conduct net searches for information using key words related to this chapter. For example, they could search for entries under natural selection, mutations, or gene pool.

Discover It!

Observing the Variety of Life

TEAM WORK

Before students begin this chapter, have them do the suggested activity. Call on volunteers to share their observations and predictions with the class.

WRITE ABOUT IT!

Suggest students write about different habits, behaviors, and dress of their peers in another locale.

REWIND to Chapter 9

Briefly review concepts learned in Chapter 9, *The Biotechnology Revolution*. Ask:

■ **How does selective breeding and genetic engineering relate to variation and biodiversity?**

PORTFOLIO PREVIEW

Students should be encouraged to add to their portfolios as they work through this chapter. In addition to the *Write About It* opportunity, the following sections are excellent opportunities for portfolio entries:

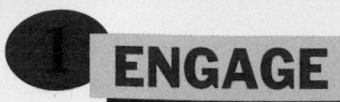
ENGAGE

Consider The Big Idea

Have students read The Big Idea! at the top of the page. Explain that natural selection affects the survival and extinction of different species.

Use the Visual

Have students study the photograph that opens the section. Elicit through a show of hands how many students did not see a sea horse when they first looked at the photo. Ask:

- **How might blending in with its environment help the sea horse survive?** (It may help escape predators.)

Check Prior Knowledge

To assess students' knowledge about variation and adaptations, ask:

- **Why are organisms produced through sexual reproduction not identical to either parent?** (They inherit traits from both parents, so as an individual they are different than both parents)

Quick Activity

TEAM WORK

Divide the class into small groups. Distribute pictures showing several organisms of the same species in their natural environments. Have students list traits and adaptations that might help each species survive in its environment.

❶ Students should cite coat color, size and shape of features.

10.1 Variation and Adaptation

Come into my parlor . . .
The organism in this photo may look like seaweed, but it is actually a sea horse. Through its camouflage, the sea horse remains hidden until its prey approaches close enough to be captured and eaten. Camouflage also hides the sea horse from its enemies. While all organisms do not show such amazing camouflage, they do fit into their environment in some way.

What you'll learn

IDEAS
- To distinguish between variation and adaptation
- To explain how fossils are used to study ancient life forms

WORDS
species, variation, adaptation, niche, fossils

FIGURE 10.1
Members of a species can vary greatly. Red foxes can be red (top) or silver (bottom). What other differences can you see between the two foxes? ❶

VARIATION

The spice of life

We often talk about an individual's unique characteristics and easily recognize the uniqueness of many species. A **species** consists of interbreeding populations of organisms that can produce healthy, fertile offspring. Within any species, an amazing amount of variation exists. **Variation** is defined as the differences between individual members of a population. The unique attributes of each animal—for example, the way it hunts and communicates, the color of its fur, and the shape of its teeth—distinguish it from its peers.

Variation can be dramatic, or it can be subtle. As you can see, the two foxes in *Figure 10.1* are very different in color. The foxes can also vary greatly in size. There are subtle differences, too. A fox may have many or few offspring. The size of a fox's territory can vary, and different foxes might have slightly different diets.

Not all variations in organisms can be observed. Some differences are biochemical. Look again at the foxes in *Figure 10.1*. These two members of the same species may have different blood types or hormone levels. They certainly have slightly different genomes.

Many, though not all, variations are genetically determined. Inherited variation is the result of two random processes: mutation and recombination. As you may recall from Chapter 8, new alleles, or forms of a trait, can arise by random mutation. A mutation is a change in the sequence of a gene.

Most mutations are either neutral or harmful. Occasionally, a mutation will increase the chances of an organism's survival. When this happens, the mutation is beneficial. A mutation is more likely to be beneficial when the environment is in a state of change. Under changing conditions, mutations that were once neutral or harmful to the organism may become advantageous. For example, the mutation that produced the silver-colored red fox

230 *Unit 3 Change and Diversity*

STUDENT RESOURCES

From the Teacher's Resource Package, use:
- Section Review 10.1 from Unit 4 Review Module
- Lab 19: "The Same, but Different"

TECHNOLOGY RESOURCES

Relevant technology resources include:
- Spanish Student Edition CD-ROM
- Teacher's Resource Planner CD-ROM

would have been harmful in the temperate habitat of the red-colored red fox. But in a snowy environment, the silver color is a beneficial mutation, as silver foxes have better camouflage.

Although mutation is important, most variation results from the recombination of existing alleles. During sexual reproduction, alleles recombine by three different mechanisms: independent assortment of chromosomes, crossing over during meiosis, and combination of genes from egg and sperm during fertilization.

ADAPTATION

To niche its own

Variation creates a population with diverse traits. The particular traits inherited by each individual organism determine whether or not an organism will survive in a particular environment. An **adaptation** is an inherited trait that increases a population's chances of survival and reproduction in a particular environment.

Adaptations are an advantage to a population, although sometimes that advantage is hard to measure. Notice the adaptations of the anteater shown in *Figure 10.2*. What advantages do these adaptations provide the species? ❷

Through adaptations, populations often become suited to a specific niche. Broadly speaking, a **niche** (NICH) is a habitat and the role a population plays in that habitat. A niche includes where organisms live, what and how they eat, how they raise their offspring, and what their predators are. Conditions such as space, light, moisture, and temperature also define a population's niche.

Niches include all the environmental factors to which populations are adapted. The anteater and termite niches shown in *Figure 10.2* are examples. As you can see, the termites occupy a smaller area and have a

New Species with Many Niches

A previously unknown animal, the Panay cloudrunner, was discovered in the Philippines in 1992. The cloudrunner resembles a squirrel and occupies niches in many habitats, including grasslands and forests.

② TEACH

Use the Visual

Remind students that an adaptation is an inherited trait that increases an organism's chances for survival in a particular environment. Ask students to study Figure 10.2 to determine what adaptations help termites and anteaters survive in their environment. Ask:

- **How are the anteater's snout and tongue suited to eating termites?** (The long, narrow snout enables the anteater to explore the termite mound; the long, sticky tongue enables the anteater to scoop up termites.)
- **How does the shape of the termite mound help protect the termites living inside?** (The shape of the mound prevents most animals from exploring the mound.)

✛ Language Arts

Have students look up different meanings for the word *niche* in the dictionary. Discuss how the meanings are related and ask students to cite examples of how they might use the word in everyday language.

Everyday Biology

Locate Panay, one of the Philippine islands, on a globe or on a world map. Ask students to describe the habitat of the Panay cloudrunner based on what they know about the geography of the Philippines or the niches of squirrels.

❷ Its long snout, sticky tongue, and long tail help the anteater get food. The nest's structure and soldier termites protect the nest.

FIGURE 10.2

The Anteater and Termite Niches

Anteaters and termites have adaptations that make them well suited for their roles in their habitat.

Snout
The anteater uses its long snout to explore the termite mound for food.

Tongue
Its long, sticky tongue can grab termites from deep within their nest.

Tail
The anteater uses its long tail for balance.

Termite nest
The structure of the termites' nest makes it difficult for most animals to attack them.

Termite defense
Thousands of soldier termites rush to the walls of the mound to defend their home.

MEETING DIVERSE NEEDS

LEP Encourage LEP students to scan the section for terms in bold print as well as other key terms. Have them create a section glossary, recording a definition for each term in both English and their native language.

Hearing Impaired Have students use a dictionary to find the phonetic pronunciation for words in boldface and the following terms: *camouflage, mechanism,* and *soldier.* Have them make flashcards to use for study.

FIGURE 10.3
Fossils can be formed and later discovered in very different environments.

1 An animal lived in an ocean environment millions of years ago.

2 When the animal died, its remains became embedded in sediments on the ocean floor.

3 Millions of years pass. Humans discover fossilized remains high above sea level. Over time, the ocean floor had become part of a mountain chain!

larger population than does the anteater. The size and nature of a niche can be quite different for different populations. When two populations attempt to occupy the same niche, fierce competition arises. Eventually, one population proves better adapted to the niche and drives out the competition.

BIODIVERSITY

Global village

You do not have to go far to appreciate the abundance and variety of life. A walk through the woods or along a city street is a walk through a biological community where many populations of organisms live together, interact, and often compete for natural resources. Such a community includes a collection of niches to which its members have adapted. The variety and abundance of species that make up a biological community are called its biodiversity.

In any community, change creates advantages for some species and disadvantages for others. Natural disasters, such as fires or floods, destroy some habitats and create others. During times of drastic change, populations whose members are better able to adapt to the new environment will fare better than those whose members are highly specialized. Populations with a broad variety of traits are better able to compete for natural resources in a changing environment.

Scientists estimate that Earth is currently home to between 5 million and 30 million different species. But today's biodiversity is a fraction of what has existed during Earth's history: 99 percent of all types of organisms that ever lived are now extinct. Earth's environments and the species that populate those environments have changed many times over the 4-billion-year history of life.

232 *Unit 3 Change and Diversity*

Much of Earth's history can be studied using **fossils,** the preserved remains or imprints of ancient organisms. When scientists speak of the fossil record, they are referring to the information that is stored in fossilized remains. Scientists who study ancient life through fossils are called paleontologists (PAY-lee-uhn-TAL-uh-jists).

Most fossils are found in the sedimentary rock formed when sand and silt settled to the bottom of a body of water. As *Figure 10.3* illustrates, organisms die, then settle into the sediment. The dead organisms and the sediment are compressed into rock. As Earth's surface shifts, layers of rock that were once at the bottom of a body of water become dry land.

Paleontologists do not have a complete fossil record of ancient life. By their very nature, fossils are hard to find and are vulnerable to weathering and erosion. In addition, the soft bodies of some animals do not fossilize well. Most living things do not leave any trace of their existence, as the conditions necessary for fossil formation are rarely present when an organism dies. However, a great deal of our knowledge about the history of life comes from fossils.

CHECKPOINT 10.1

1. How are adaptation and variation related?
2. How do paleontologists study ancient species?
3. **Critical Thinking** If a zebra was born with very thick fur, under what circumstances would that mutation lead to an adaptation?

Build on What You Know

4. Compare and contrast how variation arises in organisms that reproduce sexually and organisms that reproduce asexually. *(Need to jog your memory? Revisit relevant concepts in Chapter 5, Section 5.4.)*

CHECKPOINT 10.1

1. Adaptations are the result of beneficial variations.
2. Paleontologists use fossils to study ancient life forms.
3. **Predicting** If the climate became colder or the zebra was forced to migrate to a colder climate, its thicker fur would be beneficial.
4. Variation in sexually reproducing organisms occurs because the traits of parents can be recombined. Variation occurs in asexually reproducing organisms due to mutation.

10.2 Darwin and His Theory

Follow your dreams and write a theory
Charles Darwin had a love of nature from boyhood, but his father encouraged him to become a doctor. When Darwin lost interest in studying medicine, his father urged him to go into the clergy. Eventually Darwin found his career interest. He pursued his love of nature when he sailed to the Galapagos Islands. His observations there led to a theory that revolutionized biology.

What you'll learn

IDEAS
- To explain the theories that led to the theory of evolution
- To analyze Darwin's theory of evolution by natural selection

WORDS
evolution, natural selection, gradualism, punctuated equilibrium

SUPER READ!

THEORIES CHANGE OVER TIME
Evolution revolution

Many people have tried to explain Earth's biodiversity. Where do you think the diverse species of today came from? Explanations of the origin and diversity of life are not new. More than 2000 years ago, the topic of biodiversity was discussed by Greek philosophers. They had many ideas, including the idea that the form, or shape, of an organism is related to its function.

In the mid-1700s, Swiss naturalist Charles Bonnet published a theory to explain biodiversity. He noticed that many fossilized remains bore no resemblance to modern organisms. He theorized that periodic catastrophes had affected the entire planet, and that after each catastrophe, life began anew. According to Bonnet, the fossils that remained represented the organisms that lived prior to these catastrophes. He first used the word *evolution* to describe the development of diverse life-forms. **Evolution** means change over time.

Bonnet's views were later challenged by Jean-Baptiste Lamarck, a French naturalist who reasoned that the fossils of extinct animals were the ancestors of those living today. Lamarck's hypothesis included three main ideas.

FIGURE 10.4
Time Line of Theories

People debated for thousands of years about how different life-forms developed.

1809
Lamarck hypothesizes that "simple" organisms emerge spontaneously and evolve to greater "complexity."

1844
Darwin writes his theory on the origin of the species.

1858
Wallace and Darwin publish their theories of evolution.

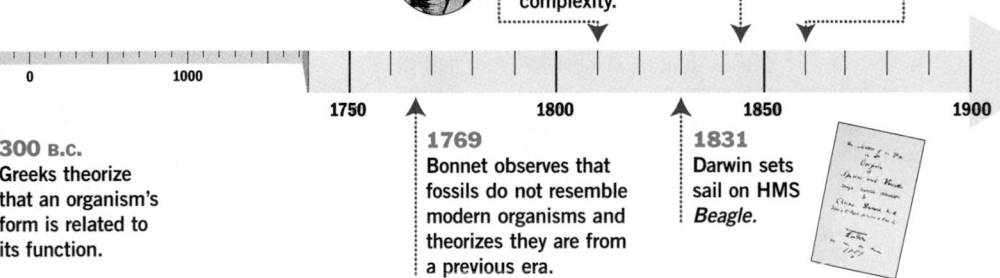

| 0 | 1000 | 1750 | 1800 | 1850 | 1900 |

300 B.C.
Greeks theorize that an organism's form is related to its function.

1769
Bonnet observes that fossils do not resemble modern organisms and theorizes they are from a previous era.

1831
Darwin sets sail on HMS *Beagle.*

Chapter 10 The Theory of Evolution **233**

2 TEACH

Use the Visual

Have students study Figures 10.4 and 10.5. Point out that Lamarck's evolution theories were based on observations and information available to him at the time. Although initially accepted by many scientists, Lamarck's hypothesis was displaced by Darwin's theory 80 years later. Ask:

■ **How did Charles Bonnet's view of evolution disagree with Lamark's view?** (Bonnet thought that after each catastrophe, life began again. Lamark reasoned that extinct animals were the ancestors of the living animals.)

■ **How did Lamarck view the development of organisms from simple to complex?** (Simple organisms evolve to greater complexity by striving constantly to improve themselves.)

Explain

Tell students that Darwin was unaware of Mendel's 1865 report on genetics experiments and did not recognize that the genetic cause of variation was important to his theory of evolution. Explain that Darwin's hypothesis of the survival of the fittest is directly related to the traits an organism inherits.

FIGURE 10.5
According to Lamarck, when short-necked giraffes stretched their necks to reach leaves high on a tree, their necks became longer. The longer neck was then passed on to the offspring. What principles of Lamarck's hypothesis are represented here? ❶

First, Lamarck thought that organisms constantly strive to improve themselves. Second, he believed that the most-used body structures develop, whereas unused structures waste away. This idea was called the principle of use and disuse. Third, Lamarck thought that once a structure is modified by use or disuse, the modification is inherited by the organism's offspring. This third principle is called the inheritance of acquired characteristics. Study *Figure 10.5* to see how Lamarck's hypothesis explains the evolution of the giraffe's long neck.

Lamarck published some of his ideas on evolution in 1809, the same year Charles Darwin was born. His work had a strong influence on Darwin. Lamarck's hypothesis about the inheritance of acquired characteristics was later disproved by German biologist August Weismann. Through experiments with mice, Weismann concluded that changes in an individual during its lifetime do not affect its reproductive cells or its offspring.

INFLUENCES ON DARWIN

Interdisciplinary studies

In 1831 Charles Darwin joined an around-the-world trip on a ship called the HMS *Beagle*. As you read at the beginning of this chapter, Darwin used the trip as an opportunity to collect plant samples and study animal species from the shore.

Darwin was especially intrigued by the finches he observed, such as those shown in *Figure 10.6*. Darwin observed that each different group of finches had its own niche. This led Darwin to wonder whether each group of finches was a different species.

Darwin later learned that the 13 different finches he had studied were indeed separate species. Each species was suited to the environment of its niche. Darwin hypothesized that

the adaptations of animals to their environment and the emergence of new species were closely related processes.

Geology After Darwin returned home, he spent a great deal of time studying his notes, reading, and conversing with colleagues. From the books of his friend Charles Lyell, Darwin learned that geological change is an extremely slow, uniform process. Lyell reasoned that Earth must be very old. Using Lyell's hypothesis, Darwin concluded that gradual geological changes over long periods of time influence plant and animal life.

Artificial selection Darwin also studied the selective breeding of domestic animals and crops. By selecting a parental generation with the

FIGURE 10.6
Darwin studied finches as he sailed to the Galapagos Islands. What similarities and differences do you think Darwin might have observed in the finches below? ❷

GALAPAGOS ISLANDS

Isabela Island

Fernandina Island

San Salvador Island

Santa Cruz Island

San Cristóbal Island

---

❶ The principle of use and disuse and the inheritance of acquired characteristics

❷ Habitat, shape of beak, coloring

most desirable characteristics, farmers and animal breeders can raise more desirable offspring, such as cows that give more milk, or hardier horses. Any domesticated plant or animal bred to accentuate desirable characteristics is the result of artificial selection.

Because of artificial selection, domesticated organisms often bear little resemblance to their ancestors. For example, careful artificial selection for certain traits of the wild mustard plant resulted in the vegetables shown in *Figure 10.7*. Darwin suspected that a selection process also occurred in nature.

Population control Darwin was also influenced by the economist Thomas Malthus, who stated that the human population was growing so fast that the supply of resources could not keep up with demand. According to Malthus, when a population exceeds its resources, disasters such as war, starvation, or widespread disease limit the population's growth.

Darwin recognized that Malthus's principles applied not only to humans, but to all species. If all the offspring of a population survive, the population quickly outgrows its supply of resources. Therefore, not all offspring can survive. Darwin reasoned that there is always competition for food, water, and space in the environment. The individuals that survive the competition can then reproduce. Darwin proposed that the ability to reproduce and pass on traits that aid survival is as important as survival itself.

THE THEORY OF EVOLUTION

It's only natural

In 1844 Darwin wrote a paper explaining his theory of evolution. He based his theory on the observations and studies he had made over the previous 15 years. Because he knew his ideas would challenge popular beliefs,

FIGURE 10.7
Artificial Selection

Artificial selection led to the development of many vegetables from the wild mustard plant.

Cauliflower and broccoli were the result of selectively breeding mustard plants to accentuate the flowers.

Selective breeding for side buds resulted in brussels sprouts.

Mustard plants were selectively bred to produce plants with large, broad leaves—cabbage.

Darwin did not publish his work for more than ten years.

Meanwhile, another young English biologist named Alfred Wallace made a sea voyage to the West Indies. Wallace also observed and collected many plant and animal specimens from which he developed a theory similar to Darwin's. Eager to publish his conclusions, Wallace wrote to Darwin, explaining his theory.

In 1858 both men agreed to send their papers together to the same scientific organization. Wallace graciously gave Darwin credit for having

EVERYDAY BIOLOGY

The Bright Side of Motion Sickness

Have you ever had motion sickness? Darwin was very prone to seasickness. For that reason, he spent a lot of time ashore during his five-year voyage and obtained important data for his research.

Chapter 10 The Theory of Evolution **235**

MEETING DIVERSE NEEDS

Gifted Ask students to conduct research in the library or on the Internet to determine the role of selective breeding in the production of other plants and animals used for food or other purposes. Encourage students to create a visual similar to Figure 10.7 to present their findings.

MULTICULTURAL PERSPECTIVE

Indians of South America who predated the Incas of 6000 years ago cultivated the white potato as a food crop. These peoples made use of selective breeding to create a potato that improved in quality from generation to generation.

Use the Visual

Direct students' attention to Figure 10.7. Have them discuss the role of selective breeding and artificial selection in producing a variety of vegetables from the mustard plant. Ask:

- **What traits of these vegetables suggest that they had a common ancestor?** (Students may mention similar shapes, taste, and scent.)

Discuss

Stress that in developing his theory of evolution, Darwin synthesized information from many sources. Discuss the ideas of Charles Lyell and Thomas Malthus and their impact on Darwin's ideas.

Think Critically

To focus students' attention on the role played by competition in evolution, ask:

- **Why is there a limit to the number of fish that can be kept in an aquarium?** (Students may indicate that fish in an aquarium are in competition for food, dissolved oxygen, and living space. When the population becomes too large, fishes that cannot meet their needs die, and the more aggressive and hardier ones survive.)

Build Writing Skills

Have students research world population growth between 1850 and 1990. Then have them research the production of food during the same period. Have students write a report discussing the role selective breeding and artificial selection played in population growth.

10.2

Clarify Misconceptions

Students often think examples of evolution include changes that occur in an individual organism during its lifetime. Emphasize that evolution refers to the adaptive changes that occur in a species over many generations. A temporary change made by an individual to survive, such as the color change of a chameleon, is not evolution. However, the ability of a chameleon to change color is an adaptation that is part of the evolutionary process.

Discuss

After students read the four points comprising Darwin's idea of natural selection, restate and review the key ideas of each point. In this discussion, stress the role of genetics in passing favorable traits from parent to offspring. Explain that the phrase "survival of the fittest," is often applied to one of the points in Darwin's idea of natural selection. Ask:

■ **Which of the four points in Darwin's idea of natural selection would most likely be referred to as "survival of the fittest?" Why?** (The last point because the organisms most "fit" for survival are those with the most favorable variations. These organisms are the most likely to reproduce and pass their "survival" variations to their offspring.)

FIGURE 10.8
The fastest ostrich in a population has a favorable variation. How might this variation lead to natural selection? ❶

developed the theory first. The theory was presented more fully in the book *On the Origin of Species by Means of Natural Selection*, which Darwin published a year later.

Natural selection Darwin observed an amazing variety of plants and animals on the Galapagos Islands. But what was the process that shaped their adaptations? Darwin called the process **natural selection,** a theory that consists of four main points.

There is variation within populations. Many variations are inherited, and such traits are passed from parent to offspring. Though little was known of genetics in Darwin's time, variation among species was well documented. Darwin's own work on the *Beagle* provided evidence of inherited variations.

Some variations are favorable. Darwin observed many examples of favorable variations on the Galapagos

FIGURE 10.9
This lion is about to eat an ostrich egg. Which point of natural selection does this photograph illustrate? ❷

236 *Unit 3 Change and Diversity*

Islands. A favorable variation is one that improves an organism's ability to function and reproduce in its own particular environment. For example, some ostriches can run faster than the others. This favorable variation enables faster ostriches to escape predators more easily, making them more likely to live and reproduce.

Not all young produced in each generation can survive. Many die as a result of disease or starvation. As you can see in *Figure 10.9*, some off-spring are killed by predators. Consequently, only a few live long enough to reproduce.

Individuals that survive and reproduce are those with favorable variations. The offspring of the survivors will inherit the favorable variations. Therefore, with each new generation, a progressively larger proportion of offspring will have these variations. This idea is the main concept of natural selection.

Ostriches are probably a result of natural selection. They are the fastest birds on land, achieving running speeds of up to 65 kilometers per hour. Their speed is due to favorable traits such as long, powerful legs. Only the fastest ostriches have lived long enough to reproduce, and they have passed on the traits that enable them to run so quickly.

THE NATURE OF CHANGE

Stop and go

Evidence indicates that natural selection is the mechanism of evolution, or change over time. Natural selection can result in the evolution of new species. But at what rate does evolution take place?

According to some scientists, small genetic changes occur slowly within a population. This theory, known as **gradualism,** proposes that new species evolve as the genomes of two

❶ The fastest ostriches escape from predators and survive long enough to reproduce and pass on this favorable trait.
❷ Not all the young produced in each generation can survive.

❸ In gradualism small genetic changes occur over a long period of time; in punctuated equilibrium abrupt genetic change interrupts long periods of genetic stability.

236

populations differentiate over enormous spans of time. Darwin originally proposed that evolution occurred at a slow, gradual rate.

In 1972 scientists Stephen Jay Gould and Niles Eldridge advanced another explanation about the rate of evolution. Their theory, known as **punctuated equilibrium,** suggests that populations remain genetically stable for long periods of time, interrupted by brief periods of rapid genetic change. This abrupt genetic change can be caused by sudden changes in the environment or by an increased mutation rate. Rapid genetic changes in a population can result in the evolution of new species.

What evidence supports or contradicts these theories? If gradualism is correct, the fossil record should show steady, gradual changes from ancient organisms to modern ancestors.

However, the fossil record lacks many of the intermediate life-forms Darwin and proponents of gradualism would expect to see. These scientists point out that many changes cannot be preserved in fossils. Darwin's explanation for the lack of intermediate life forms was that the fossil record was not yet complete. However, Gould and Eldridge suggest that the gaps in the fossil record support punctuated equilibrium. Scientists on both sides of the debate continue to search for and find evidence supporting their theories. As in many areas of science, conflicting theories help drive scientific research about evolution.

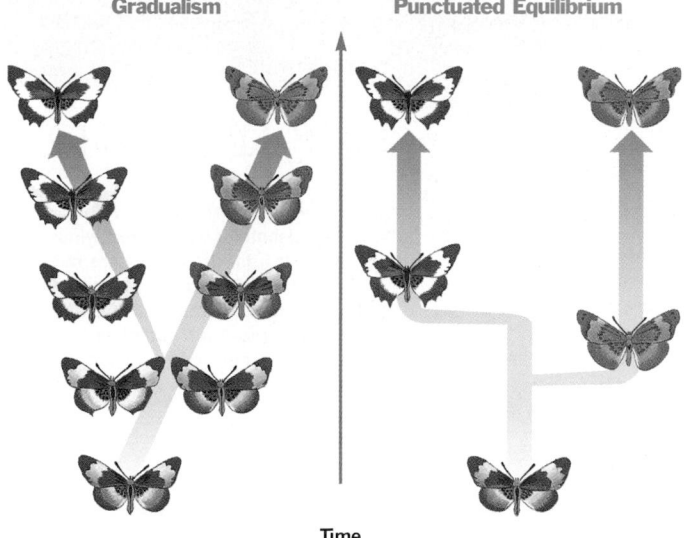

Gradualism   Punctuated Equilibrium

Time

CHECKPOINT 10.2

1. Compare and contrast the three main points of Lamarck's theory with the four points of Darwin's theory of natural selection.
2. Describe two sources of information that Darwin used to formulate his theory of natural selection.
3. **Critical Thinking** Why do you think rapid evolution might occur when a small population becomes isolated from the main population?

Build on What You Know

4. How might Mendel have helped Darwin develop his theory? Write a letter from Mendel to Darwin. **(Need to jog your memory? Revisit relevant concepts in Chapter 6, Section 6.1.)**

FIGURE 10.10
Compare the theory of gradualism with that of punctuated equilibrium.

How do populations change over time? **?**

Chapter 10 The Theory of Evolution **237**

CHECKPOINT 10.2

1. Lamarck theory: organisms strive to improve and body structure changes could be passed to offspring. Darwin: variations within a population were favorable adaptations for survival; body structure changes that occurred during an organism's lifetime could not pass to offspring.
2. Data collected on Galapagos Islands, Lyell's work on slow nature of geological change, and Malthus' principles of population control.
3. **Predicting** Students should note that isolation from main population may mean new niches are available.
4. Students should link Mendel's discovery of inheritance mode to changes resulting in speciation.

Use the Visual

Direct students' attention to Figure 10.10. Emphasize that advocates of the theory of gradualism as well as those of punctuated equilibrium agree that large gaps exist in the fossil record. Explain that the point upon which these groups differ is whether organisms of intermediate forms actually existed, as suggested in the diagram explaining gradualism.

3 ASSESS

Evaluate Understanding

Ask students to create a graphic to compare and contrast the theories of evolution presented by Lamarck and Darwin. Check graphics for accuracy and then ask students to explain why one theory has been rejected and the other accepted by most scientists.

Reteach

On the chalkboard, list the following: *evolution, Lamarck, Darwin, natural selection, principle of use and disuse, punctuated equilibrium,* and *gradualism.* As a class, develop a concept map that defines each term and shows how the terms are related. Have volunteers supply the information and fill in as needed. Encourage students to copy the completed map into their notebooks.

1 ENGAGE

Consider the Big Idea

Have students read The Big Idea! at the top of the page. Point out that fossils can explain how the ancestors of modern organisms adapted to environmental changes.

Use the Visual

Have students study the photograph that opens the section. Explain that only the hard parts of organisms, such as teeth, bones, and shells, break down slowly enough to remain as fossils.

Check Prior Knowledge

To assess students' knowledge about how scientists track evolutionary changes, ask:

- **What might scientists learn about evolution by studying present-day organisms?** (How the organisms are related to those of the past and how they have changed as a result of evolutionary processes.)

SUPER READ! Finding the Unstated Main Idea

To practice strategies for effective reading, use pages 39-40 in *Super Read!*

❶ Trend is toward larger animal, fewer toes, and larger teeth.

238

10.3 Tracking Changes

What you'll learn

IDEAS
- To explain how scientists reconstruct history through fossils
- To describe how scientists reconstruct evolutionary history through present-day organisms

WORDS
homologous structures, vestigial structures, analogous structures

SUPER READ!

FIGURE 10.11
The fossil record of the evolution of the horse is incomplete but informative. Compare the modern horse species (below, far right) with the older species to its left. How would you describe the apparent evolutionary trend shown here? ❶

Fossil firms up family history

Why are paleontologists excited when they discover a fossil? Fossils are rare, and finding a well-preserved fossil, such as the fish shown here, can be thrilling. Fossils can capture a moment in time—a moment so far removed that no human record exists of what life was like then.

CHANGES IN THE PAST

Fossils make history

According to evolutionary theory, all life originated from a common unicellular ancestor through natural selection. The fossil record reveals changes in populations over time, and supports the theory of evolution.

Using radiometric dating, scientists can often calculate a fossil's age. The oldest fossils are of ancient prokaryotes. By pinpointing the age of fossils, scientists can reconstruct an evolutionary time line.

Figure 10.11 shows fossils of different horselike species. The oldest fossils (far left) are the leg and tooth of the small animal. How do the older fossils compare with the more recent fossils? This fossil record provides information about the evolutionary history of today's horse. If you study only the fossils below, there appears to be a straight-line progression from the first horse ancestor to the modern horse species. Such a progression implies an evolutionary "goal," since there is a trend toward larger body size, fewer toes, and flat teeth.

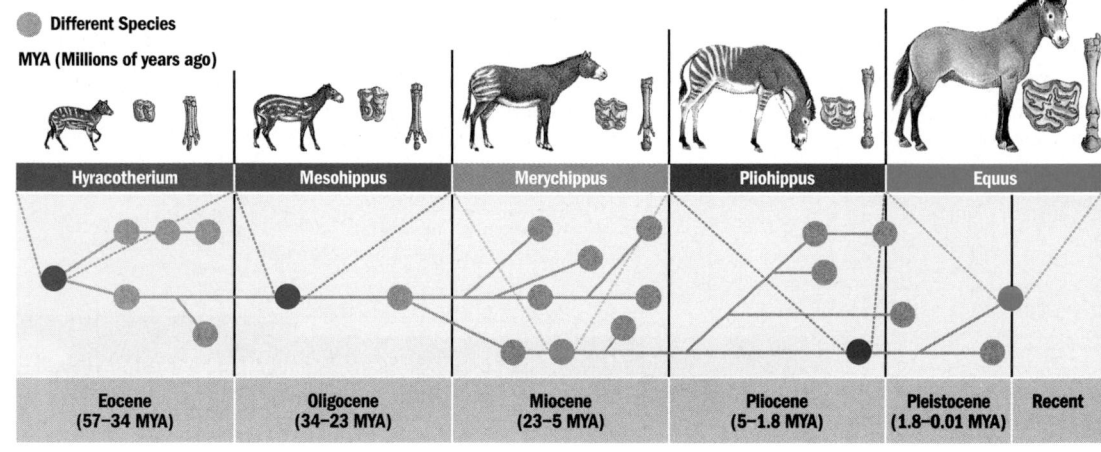

Hyracotherium	**Mesohippus**	**Merychippus**	**Pliohippus**	**Equus**
Eocene (57–34 MYA)	Oligocene (34–23 MYA)	Miocene (23–5 MYA)	Pliocene (5–1.8 MYA)	Pleistocene (1.8–0.01 MYA) · Recent

● Different Species
MYA (Millions of years ago)

STUDENT RESOURCES

From the Teacher's Resource Package, use:
- Section Review 10.3 from Unit 4 Review Module
- Issues and Decision Making 10-1

TECHNOLOGY RESOURCES

Relevant technology resources include:
- Spanish Student Edition CD-ROM
- Teacher's Resource Planner CD-ROM

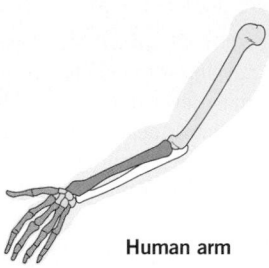
Human arm

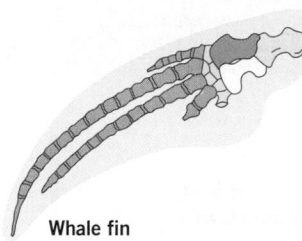
Whale fin

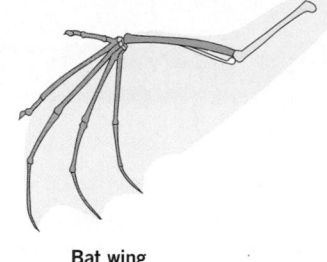
Bat wing

However, evolution rarely follows a straight line to a goal. Scientists are careful to consider all known horse-related fossils—representing more than 20 species—when drawing conclusions about the evolution of the modern horse. Not all of the horselike species evolved with fewer toes or flatter teeth. There are no goals in evolution.

Reconstructing the evolutionary history of a species can be difficult. As you have learned, the fossil record can be incomplete. Despite these uncertainties, the fossil record reveals relationships between species and how their structures have changed over time.

STRUCTURES

Whale claws, snake legs

The degree of relatedness between two different species depends on how long ago they shared a common ancestor. In addition to using the fossil record, scientists compare the anatomy of living species to establish relatedness.

Homologous structures Traits that are similar in different species because the species share a common ancestor are referred to as **homologous** (hoh-MOL-uh-gus) **structures.** Compare the homologous structures in *Figure 10.12*. The arm, fin, and wing may have evolved from the forelimb of a common vertebrate ancestor. Their appearance differs

because these species are adapted to different niches.

Vestigial structures Pythons have leg and hip bones, as shown in *Figure 10.13*. **Vestigial structures** (veh-STIH-juhl) are inherited, but reduced in size and often unused. They suggest structures of the ancestors of modern organisms.

Although vestigial structures like the python's leg and hip bones are no longer used in locomotion, they are remnants of functional structures inherited from an ancestor. A python's vestigial structures are homologous to the leg and hip bones of other reptiles, evidence that pythons are related to legged reptiles. Humans have a vestigial structure—the appendix, a tiny, dead-end pouch on the intestine that may play a minor role in the immune system.

Analogous structures Distantly related organisms sometimes have characteristics that are similar in function but different in structure. For example, insect wings are quite unlike bird wings, even though they serve the same function—flight. Their structural differences indicate that insects and birds evolved independently. **Analogous** (an-AL-uh-guhs) **structures** are those

FIGURE 10.12
The homologous bones illustrated here are shown in the same color. How are the human arm, whale fin, and bat wing similar? ❸

FIGURE 10.13
Pythons have vestigial hip and leg bones, evidence of a legged ancestor.

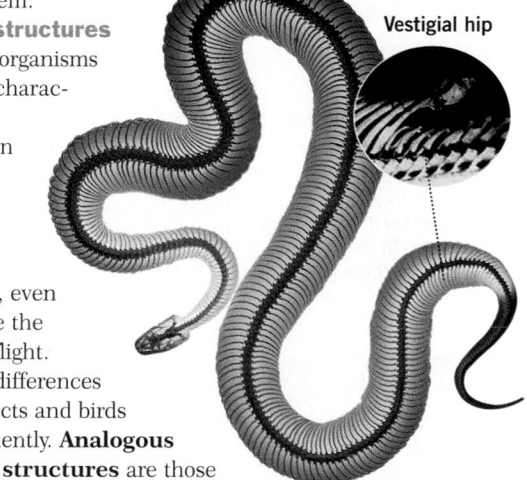

Vestigial hip

Chapter 10 The Theory of Evolution **239**

MULTICULTURAL PERSPECTIVE

The horse evolved in North America but became extinct during the late Pleistocene. Horses returned to North America with the Spanish conquistadors in the 1500s. The many breeds of domestic horses evolved from wild horse forms that crossed the Bering land bridge.

❷ The older fossils show a leg with four toes and a smaller, less complex tooth.
❸ All three organisms have bones for the forearm and digits.

2 TEACH

Literature

Many examples of homology and analogy are discussed in Stephen J. Gould's *The Panda's Thumb*. This book and others by Gould provide fascinating reading for the student who is interested in the curiosities of life.

Apply

After discussing the three types of structures, cite the following examples and have students identify each as homologous, analogous, or vestigial.

- **The coccyx or tail vertebrae in humans** (Vestigial)
- **Bones in the human ear that were transformed from supports for gills to props for the braincase, and articulation for the jaw** (Homologous)
- **The wing of a bat and the wing of a butterfly** (Analogous)
- **The femur of a whale** (Vestigial)

Build Writing Skills

Tell students to imagine themselves as paleontologists who have just discovered a well-preserved fossil of a fish, ancient horse, or other organism. Ask them to record their impressions in their scientific journal or in a letter to a professional colleague.

LAB ZONE **Think About It!**

Recording Observations

Analyzing Your Results

1 Students will probably choose the second set for accuracy because data were recorded at the time observations were made, rather than based on memory.

2 A journal of daily observations maintained over a long period would provide the soundest basis for an accurate hypothesis.

3 ASSESS

Evaluate Understanding

Divide the class into three groups. Assign each group one of these subtopics: comparative anatomy, comparative embryology, and comparative biochemistry. Ask each group to answer the following question from their professional perspective.

■ **How do you as scientists go about tracking evolutionary changes?**

Encourage groups to create visuals to support their topics, and to share them with the class.

Reteach

Write the terms *homologous, vestigial,* and *analogous* on the chalkboard. Have students define each term and review the section for examples of structures that illustrate the terms.

LAB ZONE **Think About It!**   **bioSURF**

Recording Observations

Darwin carefully recorded his observations in journals. Recording accurate observations is an important part of the scientific method. How can you ensure that you record accurate observations?

Observe the weather over a five-day period. On the last day, record from memory each day's weather in as much detail as possible. Repeat the process for another five days, but record your observations at least once a day.

Analyze Your Results

1 Compare your records. How do they differ? Which record is more accurate?

2 If you were to propose a hypothesis about weather patterns in your area, what type of journal would help you form an accurate hypothesis? Why?

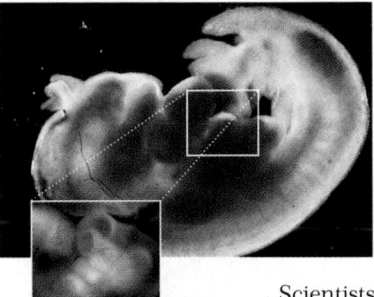

Gill pouch

FIGURE 10.14
Like the embryos of all animals with backbones, this human embryo has gill pouches. In humans, these pouches develop into inner ear tubes. In fishes, gill pouches become gill slits.

that are similar in function, but are not inherited from a common ancestor.

ADDITIONAL DATA

Living history

Scientists also rely on embryology and biochemistry to understand evolution. Embryology is the study of the early stages of an organism's development. Biochemists study and compare chemicals found in living things.

Embryos of related organisms develop in similar ways. For example, all vertebrate embryos have folds of tissue in the neck region called gill pouches. An example of gill pouches

What evidence supports the theory of evolution?

---

is shown in *Figure 10.14*. These folds develop into gill slits in fishes. Mammals never develop gills, but the gill pouches appear in mammalian embryos. The gill pouches are thought to be inherited from a common ancestor.

In addition to embryo structures, living things share biochemical characteristics, such as a dependence on ATP. Perhaps the clearest biochemical evidence of the common origin of living things is the genetic code. The same four nitrogenous bases—adenine, thymine, guanine, and cytosine—exist in every form of life. In addition, the genetic code itself—the codons for the amino acids—is almost universal.

The exact sequence of nitrogenous bases is unique to each species. Closely related species share more base sequences than do distantly related species. In the 1990s, genes from fossils have been sequenced using new DNA technology. Molecular biologists use similar gene sequences to reconstruct evolutionary history and to identify closely related species.

CHECKPOINT 10.3

1. How do scientists learn about life's history through fossils?
2. What can scientists learn from the DNA of present-day organisms?
3. **Critical Thinking** A whale fin and a human hand are thought to be homologous. Do you think a whale would have vestigial hip and leg bones?

Build on What You Know

4. Why do you think all living things depend on water? *(Need to jog your memory? Revisit relevant concepts in Chapter 2, Section 2.5.)*

CHECKPOINT 10.3

1. Fossils provide evidence of the ancestral origins of modern organisms.
2. The more similar the DNA base sequence is between two organisms, the more recent the evolutionary branch.
3. **Making generalizations** Homologous characteristics between the human arm and the whale limb indicate a common

ancestor. It is possible that whales have vestigial leg and hip bones if the common ancestor had them.
4. Because of its properties as a solvent, water promotes the circulation and excretion of essential substances throughout an organism.

10.4 Origin of Species

New niches

In 1883 the Krakatoa volcano blast destroyed most of the island and buried the rest under meters of hot ash, leaving the area lifeless. Separated from the nearest land life-forms by more than 40 km, Krakatoa today teems with new plants and animals. Destroyed niches are eventually replaced.

What you'll learn

IDEAS
• To identify the characteristics that define a species
• To compare the different modes of speciation

WORDS
speciation, divergent evolution, convergent evolution, coevolution, adaptive radiation

SPECIATION

My, how you've changed

Evolution is the process by which populations change in response to their environments. Sometimes these changes result in striking variation within populations of a species. In some cases, the changes are so great that members of the original population can no longer successfully breed with members of the changed population. In such circumstances, the changed population has become a new species. As you have learned, a species is interbreeding populations of organisms that can produce healthy, fertile offspring. **Speciation** is the evolution of one or more species from a single ancestor species.

Species can originate when members of a population become isolated from their original population. Such isolation often happens as a result of geographic change. For example, a mountain range or body of water may separate a group from its original population.

With the geographic barrier in place, the separated group may respond differently to the unique selection pressures of its new environment. If two populations stay apart long enough, they become reproductively isolated. In other words, the populations cannot or will not interbreed. Once two populations are reproductively isolated, the populations are considered to be separate species, and speciation will have occurred.

FIGURE 10.15

Speciation

Although these squirrels look very much alike, they cannot interbreed and are thus two different species. How were the two species isolated? ❶

White-tailed antelope squirrel

Harris's antelope squirrel

Chapter 10 The Theory of Evolution **241**

ENGAGE

Consider the Big Idea

Have students read The Big Idea! at the top of the page. Describe how natural selection and genetic changes can explain the Earth's variety of species.

Use the Visual

Have students study the photograph that opens the section. Explain that no life was left after the volcano blast. Ask:

■ **How did life-forms begin to repopulate the island?**
(Accept logical responses. Species could be carried in by birds, sea mammals, or humans.)

Quick Activity

Display pictures of two related yet obviously different organisms, such as an arctic hare and a jackrabbit, in their natural environments. Have students write down the similarities between the two species. Ask:

■ **Do you think the organisms shown are of the same species? Explain.**
(Students should note that both are rabbits, and that the many variances exist in their physical features.)

❶ By a body of water

10.4

② TEACH

Explain

Discuss how a polar bear survives the extreme cold of the Arctic regions. Tell students that the hairs of the polar bear are actually transparent optical fibers that trap ultraviolet light. The rough inner surface of the hollow hair reflects light, so that the fur appears white. The sun's radiant energy transfers down the hair and is absorbed by the bear's skin which is black.

Use the Visual

Direct students to study Figure 10.17. Briefly review the shared traits shown by the cat and dog and explain how the traits provide examples of convergent evolution. Ask:

- **Are these animals close relatives? Explain.** (No, they evolved separately on widely separated continents.)
- **Why do these animals have similar traits?** (They adapted to similar environments and filled similar niches.)

Apply

Show pictures illustrating other examples of convergent evolution, such as a seal and a penguin. Point out that the seal is classified as a mammal and the penguin as a bird. Ask students to note differences as well as analogous structures such as the fishlike shape of their bodies and webbed appendages.

❶ The species adapted to different environments.

242

FIGURE 10.16

Divergent Evolution

Fur color in polar bears is an adaptation to their environments. How could divergent evolution have resulted in these two bear species? ❶

FIGURE 10.17

Convergent Evolution

Although this serval cat (left) and maned wolf (right) have similar traits, they have different ancestors from different continents. The two species are the result of convergent evolution.

MECHANISMS OF EVOLUTION

Constantly changing

As new species originate, they may go through different processes of evolution. Some of the different evolutionary processes are divergent evolution, convergent evolution, and coevolution. Convergent evolution differs from the other processes in that it occurs independently among members of different species.

Divergent evolution When isolated populations of a species evolve independently, the process is called **divergent evolution.** Divergent evolution often occurs when geographic barriers separate members of a population. But it may also occur when a small group leaves an original population to colonize a new area.

The ancestors of the polar bears, for example, migrated from land onto Arctic ice and became isolated from the ancestors of the brown bear. Because the two bear populations lived in different environments, different traits were advantageous. How would white fur in the polar bear ancestors help them to survive?

According to the theory of natural selection, individuals with the advantageous traits survived, reproduced, and passed on these traits to their offspring. As generations passed, the genomes of the two populations became so different that the new population of polar bears could no

Serval cat

Both serval cats and maned wolves have very long ears, an adaptation that enables them to hear their prey move in tall grasslands.

Serval cats and maned wolves both eat rodents and lizards.

Serval cats and maned wolves both have long legs, useful characteristics for chasing their prey.

Maned wolf

242 *Unit 3 Change and Diversity*

MEETING DIVERSE NEEDS

At Risk and LEP Have students write the terms *Divergent Evolution* and *Convergent Evolution* at the top of a sheet of paper. Suggest that, below each term, students list key terms and phrases associated with the process it names. Encourage students to add drawings or pictures as well. Tell students to use the terms, phrases, and/or graphics to write a prepare a written or visual summary of the similarities and differences in the two evolutionary processes.

longer breed with the original population of brown bears.

Convergent evolution Sometimes, different species with different ancestors develop similar characteristics. When unrelated species display similar features, they may owe these likenesses to convergent evolution. **Convergent evolution** occurs when natural selection has produced analogous (similar) adaptations in response to similar environments. Darwin compared convergent evolution to two people coming up with the same invention independently.

Convergent evolution can sometimes mislead scientists into concluding that organisms are more closely related than they actually are. In these instances, scientists must rely on other methods of analysis, such as embryology or biochemistry.

You can see an example of convergent evolution—the African serval cat and the South American maned wolf—in *Figure 10.17*. In addition to their physical similarities, these two animals have similar niches. They both hunt rodents and lizards, live in tall, grassy areas, and count on their extraordinary hearing ability to catch their prey. Yet they are very different, unrelated species.

Coevolution A population's physical environment is not the only factor that shapes the adaptations that will be favored by natural selection. Sometimes, interactions with other plants or animals affect evolution. Over millions of years, species that interact closely often adapt to one another in a process called **coevolution.**

Many species of plants depend on a coevolutionary relationship to reproduce. The shape, smell, and color of their flowers have been naturally selected to attract certain pollinating insects, birds, or bats. These species of pollinators, in turn, have evolved specialized structures to reach the flowers'

nectar. Such an exclusive relationship benefits both the plant and the pollinator. Many flowers and hummingbirds, such as those shown in *Figure 10.18*, have coevolved in this manner.

ADAPTIVE RADIATION
Filling the vacuum

Populations cannot evolve and new species cannot survive unless there are resources to support them. You may remember from section 10.1 that a niche includes all the factors to which a population must adapt, including habitat, food supply, and temperature. An empty habitat does not stay empty very long, as populations will invariably evolve to fill it. As a result, many different species may evolve from one ancestral species. Each species will have a different niche.

Adaptive radiation is the evolution of many diversely adapted species from one common ancestor. Darwin observed the effects of

FIGURE 10.18
The hummingbird's long, thin beak enables it to harvest nectar from these flowers. How have hummingbirds and these flowers coevolved? ❸

LAB ZONE Do It!

How Are Inventions Like Evolution?

Darwin compared convergent evolution to the independent invention of the same product by two different people. You can see how his analogy holds up if you. . .

Try This

1 With your class, select an aspect of life that you would like to change. One idea might be the classroom.
2 For 15 minutes, everyone in your class (alone or in small groups) should brainstorm inventions that would change that aspect of life. Be creative as you brainstorm.
3 Compare ideas with your classmates.

Analyze Your Results

1 Were any of your ideas the same as those of your classmates? How many ideas were similar, and in what ways?
2 How does this activity illustrate convergent evolution? How might you improve Darwin's analogy?

Clarify Misconceptions

Students may believe adaptations and evolution result from the conscious actions of organisms. Emphasize that variations exist in populations and become beneficial as new environmental conditions arise. Organisms with variations that help them adapt to their environment survive and produce offspring. Those lacking such variations die before reproducing.

Class Activity

Take students to a zoo or natural history museum; or you may wish to use photographs or magazines. Have them locate 20 adaptive features on at least 10 species of plants and animals. Challenge them to explain how each feature might contribute to the survival of the organism. Have students prepare a report on their research.

LAB ZONE Do It! TEAM WORK

How Are Inventions Like Evolution?

Analyze Your Results

1 The activity shows that different organisms (individual students) sharing the same niche (classroom) may respond to their environment in similar ways.
2 Check that suggestions to improve Darwin's analogy are logical and can be supported by students.

MEETING DIVERSE NEEDS

Gifted Have students research the Panda bear and discuss the problem taxonomists have in classifying it.

❷ The white fur provides camouflage in the polar bear's snowy environment.

❸ The hummingbird's beak allows it to reach nectar deep in the flower and to transport pollen. Thus, the flower and the hummingbird support each other's evolution.

10.4

Use the Visual

Allow students time to study Figure 10.19. Ask:

- **How are the beak shapes adapted to each finch's food source?** (Cactus eater—beak helps finch peck into the cactus plant and protects from spines. Seed eater—curved beak helps finch pick seeds from the ground.)

Evaluate Understanding

Ask students to identify the characteristics that define a species. Then have them compare the different processes of evolution. Ask:

- **Give examples of each of the four kinds of evolution.** (Divergent evolution—polar and brown bears; convergent evolution—African serval cat and South African maned wolf; coevolution—hummingbirds and flowers; adaptive radiation—finch populations in the Galapagos)
- **How does convergent evolution and coevolution differ from the other two types of evolution?** (Members of different species are involved.)

Reteach

Work with students to create a graphic comparing and contrasting convergent evolution, divergent evolution, coevolution, and adaptive radiation. Include examples or organisms that exemplify each evolutionary process.

244

FIGURE 10.19
Adaptive Radiation

As populations of finches migrated to the different Galapagos Islands, they adapted to the different environments.

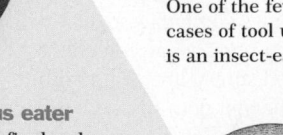

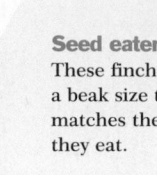

Insect eater
One of the few known cases of tool use by birds is an insect-eating finch.

Cactus eater
These finches have large, crushing beaks for eating cactus.

Seed eater
These finches have a beak size that matches the seeds they eat.

Common ancestor

adaptive radiation in the Galapagos Islands. Each of the thirteen different finches he collected belonged to a separate species. They were similar in many ways, but differed in beak size and feeding habits.

Evidence shows that the original species of Galapagos finch, an immigrant from South America, lived on one island. Then a few individuals migrated to neighboring islands, where they were exposed to new environments and isolated from the original population. Over time, the migrant finch populations adapted to their new environments and so became separate species.

While the unique demands of life on each island left each population of finches specifically adapted, they still retained enough common features to link them to the original species population. Adaptive radiation describes how a chain of islands like the

Galapagos becomes populated by diverse forms of life. Species migrate to these islands in unusual circumstances and then evolve in isolation.

CHECKPOINT 10.4

1. What is the difference between two different species and a single species in which there is a lot of variation?
2. Name and describe three processes of evolution.
3. **Critical Thinking** Scientists are not sure whether the American red wolf is a hybrid of a coyote and a grey wolf, or if it is a separate species. How might this question be resolved?

Build on What You Know

4. Compare and contrast selective breeding (artificial selection) and coevolution. *(Need to jog your memory? To revisit relevant concepts, see Chapter 9, Section 9.1.)*

244   *Unit 3 Change and Diversity*

CHECKPOINT 10.4

1. Members of a single species can interbreed.
2. Divergent evolution: Populations are separated by geography and evolve into different species. Adaptive radiation: One species scatters and evolves into different species. Convergent evolution: Two species in different locations are similar. Coevolution: Two species evolve to become more dependent on each other.
3. **Identifying cause and effect** Determine whether the red wolf can interbreed with either the coyote or grey wolf.
4. Selective breeding is determined by human judgment of desired traits; coevolution is driven by natural selection.

Modeling Coevolution

WHAT YOU WILL DO Model coevolution

SKILLS YOU WILL USE Modeling, collecting and recording data, predicting

WHAT YOU WILL NEED Long tweezers, teaspoons, dried peas or beans, 25-milliliter (mL) graduated cylinders, 100-mL beakers, watch or clock

Propose a Hypothesis

Write a hypothesis about how using differently shaped objects to retrieve seeds from differently shaped containers models adaptations in species that have undergone coevolution.

Conduct Your Experiment

1 Divide your class into three teams—A, B, and C. Each team represents a bird species; each team member a single bird. For the experiment, "species" A will use tweezers, B will use their fingers, and C will use spoons. The tweezers, fingers, and spoons represent the different birds' beaks.

2 Fill the containers half full with dried peas or beans. The beakers and graduated cylinders represent two different species of flowers. The seeds represent the birds' food.

3 For one minute, each team member removes seeds, one at a time, from his or her own beaker. The beaker must remain stationary. Do not tip the beaker.

4 After one minute, count the number of seeds each team has "eaten." Record this data.

5 Assume that a flower was successfully pollinated each time a seed was successfully eaten. Record the number of successful pollinations for each one-minute trial.

6 Repeat steps 2 through 5, using the graduated cylinders.

Analyze Your Data

1 Which team retrieved the most seeds from the beakers? From the graduated cylinders?

2 From what type of flower was each team the most successful at obtaining food?

Draw Conclusions

1 From which flower would species A feed most effectively? From which flower would each species feed most often?

2 Which type of bird is the most likely pollinator of each flower?

3 For each bird and flower species, describe what would happen to the other populations if one species became extinct.

4 How does this activity model coevolution? (Hint: Use the terms *variation, competition,* and *natural selection* in your answer.)

5 How could you improve this model?

Design a Related Experiment

Design an experiment that models coevolution between flowers of different colors and pollinating insects attracted to specific colors.

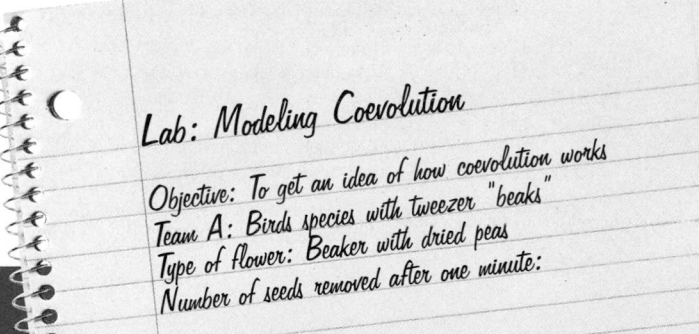

Lab: Modeling Coevolution

Objective: To get an idea of how coevolution works
Team A: Birds species with tweezer "beaks"
Type of flower: Beaker with dried peas
Number of seeds removed after one minute:

TEAM WORK Modeling Coevolution

SAFETY FIRST!

Instruct students to pick up any peas or beans that fall on the floor to prevent slips and falls.

Lab Prep and Planning

If available, use plastic beakers and cylinders. You may need to review the concept of coevolution with students before they begin the lab.

Hypothesis Help

You may wish to discuss examples of coevolution.

Lab Extension

Open Ended

Divide the class into small groups and direct each group to design a laboratory procedure to model coevolution. Encourage students to use concepts other than flower pollination, such as beetle color and camouflage. Have the groups exchange procedures to test the models.

Time Required

■ 50 minutes

Analyze Your Data

1 A species should retrieve the most from cylinders; B and C species from beakers.

2 "Beaker" flowers

Draw Conclusions

1 "Cylinder" flower; "beaker" flower

2 A species for "cylinder" flower, B and C species for "beaker" flower

3 A species and "cylinder" flower are totally dependent; B and C species and "beaker" flowers would not survive without each other.

4 This activity models coevolution because it shows how certain characteristics have been naturally selected in organisms so that reproduction can occur. The activity models how organisms interact, compete, and adapt to one another, forming exclusive relationships that enable them to survive.

5 Accept all logical responses.

Design a Related Experiment

You may wish to suggest the bee orchid for students' experiment.

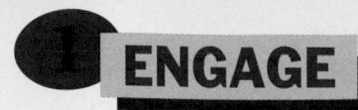

1 ENGAGE

Use the Visual

Have students study the photograph that opens the section. Call on volunteers to describe the population density of the area in which they live.

Check Prior Knowledge

To assess students' knowledge about genetics, ask:

- **What is the relationship between a genotype and a phenotype?** (Genotype identifies the alleles an organism has for a trait; the phenotype is the visible expression of the trait.)
- **What are multiple alleles? Give an example.** (Three or more alleles found in a population, for example, human blood types)

Quick Activity

Have students recall what they know about the dominant and recessive alleles for human eye color. Determine the dominant eye color of the class. Assess whether the data from the class population supports what they learned about how eye color is determined. If the data is not consistent, discuss possible reasons for the variation.

10.5 Population Genetics

What you'll learn

IDEAS

- To describe the principles of population genetics
- To analyze the effects of changes in the environment on populations

WORDS

gene pool, allele frequency, genetic equilibrium, genetic drift, directional selection, disruptive selection

Night lights in the USA

This photo shows the United States at night. The light areas indicate where many people live, or where the population is the most dense. Can you identify the area where you live? How would you describe the population in that area? Researchers study populations of many different kinds of organisms and observe how the populations are evolving.

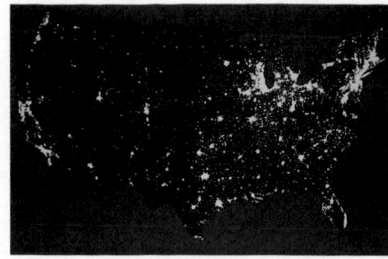

GENE POOL

Hardy populations

As you continue to study the diversity of life, remember that populations are the smallest unit in which evolution takes place. Each individual member of a population exhibits unique characteristics, but the effect of natural selection—evolution—can only be measured in terms of an entire population. The study of genetic traits and changes in populations is called population genetics.

You have read about some ways in which species may evolve. All mechanisms of evolution involve changes in the gene pool. A **gene pool** is the combined genetic material of all the members of a given population. The gene pool includes all the genes for every trait on every chromosome of every reproductive individual within that population.

In Chapter 6 you learned that genes often have two or more different forms, called alleles. In any gene pool, the number of each allele is a fraction of all the genes for a particular trait. These fractions are known as **allele frequencies.** In *Figure 10.20,* you can see an example of how a population's allele frequencies are determined. Evolution often begins with a change in allele frequencies over time within a population.

In 1908, two researchers studying population genetics independently came to the same conclusion: if a population is not evolving, the allele frequencies in the population remain stable. This idea is called the Hardy-Weinberg principle, named after the two researchers who developed it. This constant state of allele frequencies is called **genetic equilibrium** (ee-kwih-LIH-bree-um).

FIGURE 10.20

Allele Frequency

Given a population of 500 wildflowers that are either
pink or white
AA or Aa
aa
There are 1000 flower-color genes. The pink allele (A) is dominant over the white allele (a).
80% pink alleles
20% white alleles
In this given population
20 are
because they are homozygous (aa) for the recessive allele.
480 are
because 320 are homozygous dominant (AA) and 160 are heterozygous (Aa).
There are 640 + 160 = 800 dominant (A) alleles.
There are 160 + 40 = 200 recessive (a) alleles.
800 alleles are dominant (A) and the allele frequency is 800/1000 = 80%.
200 alleles are recessive (a) and the allele frequency is 200/1000 = 20%.

STUDENT RESOURCES

From the Teacher's Resource Package, use:

- Section Review 10.5 and Activity Recordsheet 10-3 from Unit 4 Review Module
- Lab 20: "Population Model of Genes"

TECHNOLOGY RESOURCES

Relevant technology resources include:

- Spanish Student Edition CD-ROM
- Teacher's Resource Planner CD-ROM
- TestWorks CD-ROM: Chapter 10 Tests

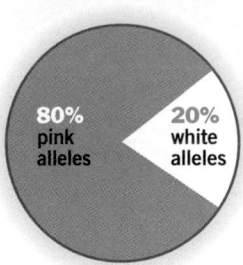

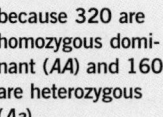

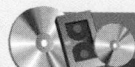

FIGURE 10.21
Genetic Equilibrium

How well do these puffins meet the requirements for genetic equilibrium?

Puffins with brighter bills may have better mating success.

Assume that there is no net change in alleles.

Migration is unlikely due to the specific habitat and poor mobility of puffins.

Natural selection favors birds that can catch more fish.

Large puffin colonies may contain hundreds of thousands of puffins.

The Hardy-Weinberg principle states that, under specific conditions, allele frequencies in a population remain constant from generation to generation. If specific conditions are not met, the genetic equilibrium is disrupted, and the population may evolve. Five conditions are required to maintain equilibrium: no natural selection, random mating, no migration, no mutation, and a very large population size. Review *Figure 10.21* to learn whether or not a puffin population meets the conditions of the Hardy-Weinberg principle.

For a population to remain in equilibrium, all alleles in the population must be equally favored. There must be no reason for one allele to have a selective advantage over another—in other words, no natural selection.

In most animal populations, mating is not completely random. In fact, many animal species put effort into selecting a specific mate. However, for a population to remain in genetic equilibrium, there must be no trait that makes some individuals more attractive as mates than others.

Because migrating individuals may bring new alleles into a population and change gene frequencies, there must be no migration into or out of a population for genetic equilibrium to be maintained. In other words, the population must be isolated from other populations of the same species. The mixing of genes as a result of migration is called gene flow.

Like migration, mutation can introduce new alleles into the population. But if the number of existing alleles mutating to new alleles equals the number of new alleles mutating back to old alleles, there is no net change in alleles. Genetic equilibrium is maintained.

In some populations, all four conditions may be met or nearly met for long periods of time. However, genetic equilibrium is often disrupted. Evolution is the result of a disruption in genetic equilibrium.

Population size is also an important factor in the Hardy-Weinberg principle. The larger the population, the smaller the effect of migration or mutation.

Chapter 10 The Theory of Evolution **247**

TEACH

Use the Visual

Call attention to Figure 10.21. Ask:

- **Why is migration among puffins uncommon?** (Puffins have a specific habitat and poor mobility.)
- **What four conditions must be met to maintain genetic equilibrium in a population?** (Random mating, no natural selection, no migration, and no significant mutations)

Mathematics

Point out that if the four conditions of genetic equilibrium are met, the frequency of alleles in a population can be determined using the Hardy-Weinberg mathematical equation: $p^2 + 2pq + q^2 = 1$ or $p + q = 1$. In this equation, *p* is the frequency of one allele for a trait and *q* is the frequency of the other allele. The frequency of homozygous dominant individuals is p^2; the frequency of heterozygous individuals or "carriers" is *2pq*, and that of homozygous recessive individuals is q^2. Have students use calculators to solve the following problem.

- **A certain recessive disease (q^2) has a frequency of 1 in 2500 people or .0004. What is the frequency of each allele and the frequency of carriers?** (q=.02, p=.98, 2pq=.04 or 1 in 25)

❶ Very well: the only exception is the mating advantage of a brighter bill.

MULTICULTURAL PERSPECTIVE

Display a world map. Explain that the gene pool in some countries is essentially restricted to one ethnic group living in a confined geographic area. This is especially true for isolated parts of developing countries and islands in the South Pacific. Discuss how the gene pool has changed in North America over the past 400 years and why the United States is often called a melting pot.

Do It!

FIGURE 10.22
Genetic drift occurs when natural disasters, such as forest fires, kill large numbers of a population.

GENETIC DRIFT

A sea of changes

Even when all the Hardy-Weinberg conditions are met, genetic equilibrium can be affected by chance changes in allele frequencies. **Genetic drift** is the random change in allele frequencies in a population due to chance events.

 **Do It!** **bioSURF**

How Quickly Do Populations Decrease?

You can calculate how long it takes for a population to decline to the size that it will be affected by genetic drift if you . . .

Try This

1 Imagine that a certain population in a South American rain forest currently numbers 200. The population is decreasing by 10 percent each year.
2 Calculate the projected population size for each of the next 10 years.
3 Graph your results. Place population numbers on the y-axis (vertically) and time on the x-axis (horizontally).

Analyze Your Results

1 How many years does it take the population to fall below 100?
2 Describe your graph. How would you describe the decline of the population?
3 How might the genetic variation in the original population of 200 compare to the genetic variation in the population of 100?
4 How could bottlenecking affect the population?

Chance events, such as migrations or natural disasters, can cause dramatic reductions in population size and create a new, small population from a larger one. Through chance the gene pool of the new population will often have a different allele frequency from the original gene pool. Genetic drift has a greater impact on smaller populations, groups with fewer than 100 individuals.

The term "bottlenecking" refers specifically to the genetic drift occurring after a random population-reducing event. The Florida panther is an example of a species that has undergone bottlenecking. Early Florida settlers hunted the panthers to protect their homes and livestock. Then, as homes and cities were built in panther habitats, the panther population was reduced further. Today, the Florida panthers number fewer than 100.

The resulting genetic drift means that today's Florida panther population has much less genetic variation than the original population. Populations with little genetic variation are vulnerable because they cannot easily adapt to environmental changes. Due to their lack of genetic variation, Florida panthers are more susceptible to genetic disorders, and the population is less likely to survive than more genetically diverse populations of panthers.

Recently, Texas cougars have been introduced into Florida to crossbreed with the Florida panther and increase the genetic variation. How do you think this action will affect the future of the Florida panther population?

DISTRIBUTION AND SELECTION

For whom the bell tolls

Populations are not static. Variation and adaptation allow populations to respond to the unique challenges of their environment. Scientists often study the effect of natural selection on the phenotypes of populations.

By graphing the number of individuals in a population with specific phenotypes, scientists can measure how much variation exists in a population. And by studying changes over time in the distribution of variations, scientists can evaluate evolutionary change.

Suppose a scientist determines the colors and numbers of all rabbits in a test area. A graph of these data might show a bell-shaped curve like the one in *Figure 10.23*. This pattern indicates that the largest number of individuals are a medium shade, and fewer individuals are very light or very dark. This bell-shaped curve is called a normal distribution.

Now suppose the environment changes and becomes more barren, exposing more dark soil. Rabbits with dark coats would be less visible against the darker background and would be more able to avoid predators. Light-colored rabbits would be more visible. In this darker environment, darker

individuals would survive to reproduce more often than lighter ones, and more offspring would tend to be dark.

After several generations, the distribution might shift in the direction of darker coat color. Such a shift in frequency to an extreme phenotype is called **directional selection.** A typical graph of directional selection is shown in *Figure 10.23* (center).

Selection can also act against the middle of a distribution pattern. A

Humans have a definite effect on the population genetics of many organisms. Take a stroll through your community and look for habitats that have been affected by humans. One example might be an area where a new road or housing development has displaced plants and animals. Another might be a wildlife preserve or sanctuary. The Biosurf web site *http://evolution.biosurf.com* includes other examples. List the examples you find.

IN THE COMMUNITY
The World in Their Eyes

FIGURE 10.23
Distribution Curves

Environmental changes can affect the frequencies of the phenotypes that occur within a population.

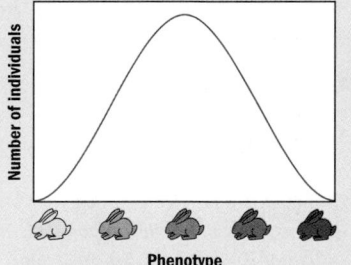

Phenotype

Normal distribution
This curve is called a normal distribution because it is so common in nature. What color are most of the rabbits? ❷

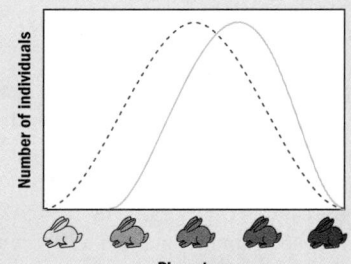

Phenotype

Directional selection
Directional selection occurs when a change in the environment favors an extreme phenotype. Which phenotype is favored now? ❸

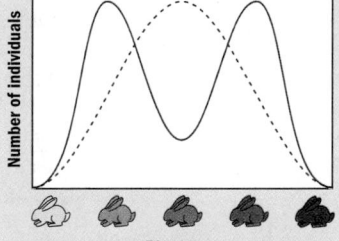

Phenotype

Disruptive selection
Disruptive selection occurs when an environmental change makes it unfavorable to have the medium phenotype. Describe the favored phenotype(s). ❹

Chapter 10 The Theory of Evolution **249**

---

❷ Medium shade
❸ Darker shades
❹ Both lighter and darker shades

10.5

Use the Visual

Have students study the three distribution curves in Figure 10.22. Explain that the curve at the left shows a normal distribution. Then ask:

- **How does the curve for disruptive selection differ from the normal distribution curve?** (The curve indicates that the most favorable trait is now the least favorable.)
- **How does the curve for directional selection differ from the normal distribution curve?** (Curve shifts from organisms with medium phenotype toward organisms with extreme phenotype.)

In the Community

Encourage students to sketch, photograph, or videotape their observations of human effects on local habitats. Examples of habitat disruption include: new roads, housing developments, shopping centers, entertainment facilities, or public-works projects such as dams. Strategies for correction might include "green" areas left in a natural state, or relocation of species.

Build Writing Skills

Encourage students to find out what local officials are doing to remedy harmful effects of humans on natural habitats in their community. Then have students summarize their findings in the form of an editorial to be submitted to a local newspaper. You may wish to have students compose a letter or e-mail to their local representative suggesting what should be done to improve or protect a specific community habitat.

STS

After reviewing the text, ask:

- **Is the peppered moth population in genetic equilibrium? Why?** (No, the alleles for wing color are not equally favored.)
- **If a virus was introduced that killed the moth-eating birds, how might this change the moth population?** (Assuming no other predators, moth population would increase. There would be no selective advantage to color.)

3 ASSESS

Evaluate Understanding

To check students' understanding of the basic principles of population genetics, ask:

- **State the Hardy-Weinberg principle in your own words.** (All alleles remain constant in a population in genetic equilibrium.)
- **What kind of events can disrupt genetic equilibrium?** (Migration of a few individuals away from the original population, natural disasters, human activities.)

Reteach

On an overhead transparency, create an outline with section heads as main heads. Have volunteers provide the information that should be listed under each head, including definitions for key terms.

FIGURE 10.24
On dark tree trunks light moths are not a favored phenotype. Which of the moths shown above would best survive on dark tree trunks?

selection that does not favor the most common variation within a population is called **disruptive selection.** For example, if the environment changed to dark ground with light-colored sage brush, only very dark or very light rabbits would be safe from predators. A medium-colored coat would not be advantageous.

ENVIRONMENTAL AWARENESS

The story of the English peppered moth

Actions of humans can have a dramatic impact on other organisms' lives. Consider the English peppered moths, which inhabit forested areas. Before the Industrial Revolution, most peppered moths were a light color. Tree trunks in rural England were covered with light gray lichens, allowing light-colored moths to blend perfectly with the tree trunks. Darker moths were seen occasionally, probably due to mutations. But darker moths were easy for predators to spot, and they were quickly eaten by birds. Natural selection maintained a low number of dark moths.

When England became industrialized, soot and smoke from factories killed the lichen on trees, exposing darker bark. Within a few years, people noticed a change in the peppered moth population: most moths were now dark-colored. Industrial pollution had changed the background against which the moths rested; the light-colored trait had become a disadvantage. Natural selection now favored the darker moths. In only a few generations, directional selection caused a change in the color of the majority of peppered moths from light to dark.

In recent years, air pollution has decreased. Less soot is now released into the air. As a result, the lichen population has revived and some tree trunks are light-colored once again. How do you think the change in the lichen population has affected the peppered moths? **❶**

CHECKPOINT 10.5

1. Describe the following principles of population genetics: genetic equilibrium, genetic drift, directional selection, disruptive selection.
2. How do changes in the environment affect populations?
3. **Critical Thinking** Draw a normal distribution curve for dog size, assuming that medium-size dogs are most common and very small and very large dogs are least common.

Build on What You Know

4. How would a complex pattern of inheritance (such as codominance or multiple alleles) affect a population genetics study? *(Need to jog your memory? Revisit relevant concepts in Chapter 6, Section 6.5.)*

? What factors can contribute to the formation of a new species?

CHECKPOINT 10.5

1. Genetic equilibrium: allele frequencies remain constant if specific conditions are met. Genetic drift: accidental changes in the environment can upset genetic equilibrium. Directional selection: changes in the environment favor one phenotype and shift the distribution toward that phenotype. Disruptive selection: changes in the environment favor the phenotypic extremes.
2. Adaptations that were once favorable may no longer be favorable.
3. **Interpreting** Graphs should resemble a typical bell-shaped curve.
4. Allele frequencies would still follow the Hardy-Weinberg principle if the population is in genetic equilibrium.
❶ Reduced population

Chapter 10 Review

 **THE BIG IDEA!** 10.1–10.2 Populations change over time through natural selection.
10.3 Scientific analysis of fossils and modern organisms supports the theory of evolution.
10.4–10.5 New species can originate through natural selection and other changes in a population's gene pool.

Sum It Up

Use the following summary to review the main concepts in this chapter.

10.1 Variation and Adaptation

- Most variation in a population results from mutation and recombination of existing alleles.
- Some variations are adaptations that increase a population's chances for survival and reproduction.
- Each species in an environment has its own niche. Niches are created and destroyed by environmental changes.

10.2 Darwin and His Theory

- Based on observations made during his voyage, Darwin concluded that adaptation and the evolution of species were related.
- Darwin drew analogies between biological change and geological change, and between artificial selection and natural selection.
- When organisms compete for limited resources, those with favorable traits survive and pass those traits along to the next generation.
- Some scientists, including Darwin, propose that evolution occurs gradually. Other scientists infer from gaps in the fossil record that evolution occurs in short periods of rapid change.

10.3 Tracking Changes

- To reconstruct evolutionary history, scientists examine fossils, compare structures of living and extinct species, study embryonic development, and analyze DNA.

10.4 Origin of Species

- New species can develop when populations become separated and isolated.
- Similar traits can develop in unrelated species occupying comparable niches.
- Interactions with other organisms affect evolution.
- Many diverse species can evolve from one ancestral species.

10.5 Population Genetics

- Evolution results from disruptions in genetic equilibrium.
- The normal distribution of variations in a population can be changed by natural selection.

Use Terms and Concepts

**Use each of the following words or terms in a complete sentence.
If you need to review a meaning, turn to the page indicated.**

species (p. 230)
variation (p. 230)
adaptation (p. 231)
niche (p. 231)
fossils (p. 232)
evolution (p. 233)
natural selection (p. 236)
gradualism (p. 236)

punctuated equilibrium (p. 237)
homologous structures (p. 239)
vestigial structures (p. 239)
analogous structures (p. 239)
speciation (p. 241)

divergent evolution (p. 242)
convergent evolution (p. 243)
coevolution (p. 243)
adaptive radiation (p. 243)
gene pool (p. 246)

allele frequencies (p. 246)
genetic equilibrium (p. 246)
genetic drift (p. 248)
directional selection (p. 249)
disruptive selection (p. 250)

Review the Big Ideas

Before students begin the Chapter Review, you may wish to discuss the main concepts from the Big Ideas in Chapter 10. Point out that by studying fossils and present-day organisms, scientists have been able to reconstruct an evolutionary history of plant and animal life. The principle of evolution, proposed by Charles Darwin in the 1850s, states that populations change over time through natural selection. Favorable adaptations are passed from generation to generation through reproduction. New species can originate through natural selection or other changes in a population's gene pool, such as migration or geographic isolation.

Answers

1. gene pool
2. coevolution
3. fossils
4. niche
5. evolution
6. species
7. natural selection
8. b
9. a
10. c
11. b
12. d
13. Migration changes allele frequencies.
14. Adaptive radiation is a type of speciation in which many diverse species evolve from a common ancestor.
15. Darwin learned that the supply of resources limits the growth of a population.
16. Two populations could temporarily share a single niche. Eventually the better adapted population will drive out the competition.
17. Widespread extinction of species opens up niches that can be filled through adaptive radiation of surviving species.
18. Genetics does not provide a mechanism for inheritance of acquired characteristics.
19. A gene pool with constant <u>allele frequencies</u> is in <u>genetic equilibrium</u>, that is disrupted by <u>natural selection</u>, <u>mutation</u>, and <u>migration</u>.
20. Because sea horses and kangaroos are not closely related, the pouches are an example of analogous structures.
21. Darwin's and Wallace's theories—similar ideas developed independently— are best represented by convergent evolution.

Use Your Word Power

COMPLETION Write the word or phrase that best completes each statement.

1. A(n) _____ is the combined genetic material of all individuals in a population.

2. Over millions of years, two interacting species may adapt to one another's needs through _____ .

3. The preserved remains or imprints of organisms are known as _____ .

4. A(n) _____ is a population's habitat and the role the population plays in the habitat.

5. Change over time is another description of _____ .

6. A(n) _____ is an interbreeding population that produces healthy, fertile offspring.

7. Darwin proposed that the adaptation of a species to its environment occurs through _____ .

MULTIPLE CHOICE Choose the letter of the word or phrase that best completes each statement.

8. Camouflage is an example of (a) variation; (b) adaptation; (c) speciation; (d) mutation.

9. Structures that are inherited but have no current function are (a) vestigial; (b) analogous; (c) divergent; (d) homologous.

10. A process that explains gaps in the fossil record is (a) genetic equilibrium; (b) gradualism; (c) punctuated equilibrium; (d) genetic drift.

11. The selection that favors an extreme phenotype is (a) natural selection; (b) directional selection; (c) artificial selection; (d) disruptive selection.

12. Species that have descended from different ancestors but have similar traits evolved through (a) divergent evolution; (b) adaptive radiation; (c) coevolution; (d) convergent evolution.

Show What You Know

13. How does migration affect the genetic equilibrium of a population?

14. What is the relationship between speciation and adaptive radiation?

15. What did Darwin learn from Malthus?

16. Is there a one-to-one relationship between species and niches? Explain your answer.

17. How does extinction affect adaptive radiation?

18. What aspect(s) of Lamarck's hypothesis contradicts what you have learned about genetics?

19. **Make a Concept Map** Complete the concept map below by adding the following terms: allele frequencies, genetic equilibrium, natural selection, migration, and mutation.

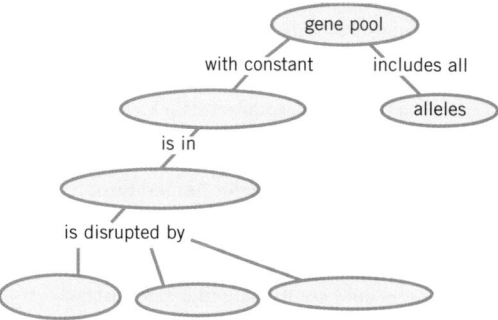

Take It Further

20. **Applying Concepts** The sea horse is a fish of the genus *Hippocampus*. Male sea horses carry developing eggs in a short, broad pouch. Kangaroos belong to the genus *Macropus*. Female kangaroos have a pouch for carrying newborns. Do you think the two pouches are homologous or analogous structures? Explain your answer.

21. **Making an Analogy** Was the development of Darwin's and Wallace's theories most like divergent evolution, convergent evolution, or coevolution? Give reasons for your answer.

---

22. Trout are favored by sport fishermen. Fishing competitions is one source of data. However, the data might produce distribution curves skewed toward the high end due to size limits mandated by state of federal agencies.

23. As the area of an island increases, so does the number of species. The reverse is also true: as island size decreases, the number of species decreases. Species are similarly threatened when the area of tropical rain forests is reduced by deforestation.

24. Accept logical responses.

25. Answers will vary. By definition, wolves and dogs should not breed, but can and sometimes do. St. Bernards and chihuahuas can breed, but do not.

22. Designing an Experiment If you want to graph distribution curves for length of adult trout, how would you collect the data? What drawback might there be to using data that has already been collected?

23. Interpreting a Graph Suppose you determined the number of species on seven islands of various sizes. The graph below summarizes your data. What can you conclude from the graph? How might this conclusion be applied to the reduction in size of tropical rain forests?

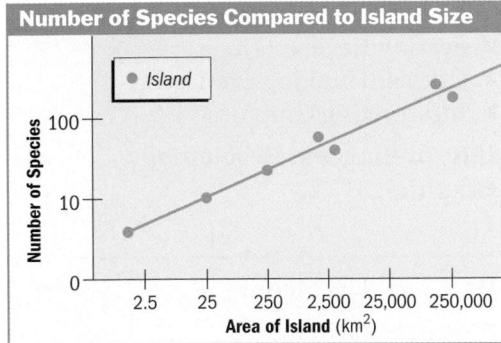

Number of Species Compared to Island Size

● Island

Number of Species

Area of Island (km^2)

Consider the Issues

24. Society and Evolution As medical technology has advanced through the centuries, some people believe natural selection for humans has been replaced by "Social Darwinism." Explain what is meant by Social Darwinism. Decide whether or not you believe Social Darwinism is a factor in human evolution.

25. Fine-tuning the Definition Wolves and dogs are classified as different species, but they interbreed and their offspring are fertile. However, a Saint Bernard weighing about 85,000 grams (g) and a Chihuahua weighing less than 435 g are both dogs, *Canis familiaris,* but are unlikely to mate. Should organisms be classified as separate species if they *cannot* interbreed, or when they *do not* interbreed?

Make New Connections

26. Biology and Art Some fossils are the original remains of an organism—a fly trapped in amber, for example. Other fossils form when an organism's remains are buried and decompose, leaving a hollow in the rock that serves as a mold. When a material similar to plaster of Paris fills the hole, a cast of the original organism forms. Ask your art instructor to help you create a mold and cast some "fossils" of your own.

27. Biology and History Darwin's theory was not well received when it was first proposed. The year after Darwin published his theory, a famous confrontation occurred between Bishop Samuel Wilberforce and Thomas Henry Huxley at a meeting of the British Association for the Advancement of Science. Work with a partner to present a reenactment of the debate.

28. Biology and Geography In developing a theory of natural selection, Darwin was strongly influenced by data he collected on the Galapagos Islands. The islands still provide valuable scientific data. Research and report on the islands. Where are they located? What political background do the islands have?

FAST-FORWARD TO CHAPTER 11

Chapter 10 has focused on how natural selection could have produced Earth's diverse species. In Chapter 11, you will learn how scientists have applied the theory of evolution to theories about the origin of life on Earth.

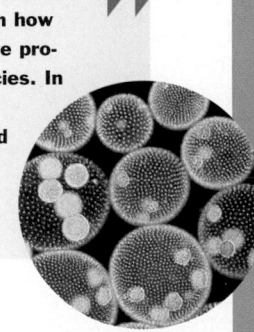

Chapter 10 The Theory of Evolution **253**

26. Results will vary. Students may cast footprints or handprints, or encase a flower in resin.

27. Students may also want to explore the encounter between William Jennings Bryan and Clarence Darrow immortalized in *Inherit the Wind.*

28. Answers will vary. Encourage students to research the topic in depth.

PLANNING GUIDE

Section	Student Activities/Features	Teacher's Resource Package
11.1 Earth's Early History **Objectives** ■ Explain how the scientific method is used in studying Earth's early history ■ Compare and contrast two hypotheses about how life began on Earth	**Lab Zone Discover It!** *Describing Basic Requirements,* p. 255 **Everyday Biology** *Shooting Stars,* p. 260 **Lab Zone Investigate It!** *Constructing Microspheres,* p. 262	**Unit 3 Review Module** ■ Section Review 11.1 ■ Activity Recordsheet 11-1 ■ Enrichment Topic 11-1 **Laboratory Manual,** Lab 21: "Pasteur's Experiment" **Consumer Applications** 11-1
11.2 The First Organisms **Objectives** ■ Describe how the age of fossils is determined ■ Summarize the development of the first prokaryotic and eukaryotic cells	**Lab Zone Think About It!** *Determining the Age of a Fossil,* p. 265 **Everyday Biology** *Mighty Mitochondria,* p. 267	**Unit 3 Review Module** ■ Section Review 11.2 ■ Critical Thinking Exercise 11 ■ Interpreting Graphics 11 **Interpreting and Developing Graphics,** 31, 32
11.3 History of Living Things **Objectives** ■ Explain the emergence of multicellular organisms ■ Evaluate the effect of plate tectonics and mass extinctions on speciation	**In the Community** *Hometown History,* p. 270 **Everyday Biology** *Strolling Across the Ocean,* p. 272 **STS: Issues in Biology** *Mass Extinctions,* p. 272 **Lab Zone Do It!** *How Did Plate Tectonics Result in Speciation?* p. 273	**Unit 3 Review Module** ■ Section Review 11.3 ■ Activity Recordsheet 11-2 ■ Enrichment Topic 11-2 ■ Vocabulary Review 11 ■ Chapter 11 Tests **Issues and Decision Making** 11-1 **Interpreting and Developing Graphics,** 33 **Spanish Reviews** Chapter 11

CHAPTER 11   The History of Life

Technology Resources

Internet Connections

Within this chapter, you will see the logo. If you and your students have access to the Internet, the following URL address will provide various Internet connections that are related to topics and features presented in this chapter:

http://evolution.biosurf.com

You can also find relevant chapter material at **The Biology Place** address:

http://www.biology.com

CD-ROMs

Biología: la telaraña de la vida,
   (Spanish Student Edition) Chapter 11
Teacher's Resource Planner, Chapter 11
   Supplements
TestWorks CD-ROM
■ Chapter 11 Tests

Overhead Transparencies

■ Radiocarbon Dating, #24

Videotapes

Biology Alive! Video Series
Rewind: The Web of Life Reteach Videos

Planning for Activities

STUDENT EDITION
Lab Zone
Discover It! p. 255
- paper
- pencil

Lab Zone
Investigate It! p. 262
- safety goggles
- 500-mL beaker
- hot plate
- 0.5 g aspartic acid
- 0.5 g glutamic acid
- 0.5 g glycine
- 2 250-mL Erlenmeyer flasks
- stirring rod
- ring stand
- graduated cylinder
- 1% NaCl solution
- oven mitts
- tongs
- dropper
- microscope slide
- coverslip
- microscope

TEACHER'S EDITION
Teacher Demo, p. 256
Living or nonliving?
- solution of gum arabic and gelatin
- petri dish
- overhead projector

Teacher Demo, p. 259
Chemical reactions
- matches

Teacher Demo, p. 263
"Fossil" impressions
- clay
- keys, shells, pencils, or paper clips

Teacher Demo, p. 264
Identifying radioactive substances
- Geiger counter
- alpha emitter from a smoke alarm or a gas-lamp mantle

Class Activity, p. 271
Forming Pangaea
- scissors
- outline maps of the continents

Chapter Objectives

Students will learn the main concepts of this chapter as they complete the following objectives.

- Explain how the scientific method is used in studying Earth's early history
- Compare and contrast two hypotheses about how life began on Earth
- Describe how the age of fossils is determined
- Summarize the development of the first prokaryotic and eukaryotic cells
- Explain the emergence of multicellular organisms
- Evaluate the effect of plate tectonics and mass extinctions on speciation

Key Words

11.1 *microspheres*

11.2 *half-life, stromatolites, endosymbiosis*

11.3 *eras, periods, epochs, plate tectonics*

The Opening Story

After students read the opening story, have them discuss how they think the story relates to the content in this chapter. Ask students to infer what the conditions were like as Surtsey Island developed and how conditions changed to support the first plant life.

254

CHAPTER 11

The History of Life

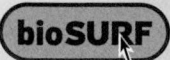

You can find out more about the history of life by exploring the following Internet address:
http://evolution.biosurf.com

In this chapter . . .

FEATURES

Everyday Biology
- Shooting Stars
- Mighty Mitochondria
- Strolling Across the Ocean

In the Community
Hometown History

 Issues in Biology
Mass Extinctions

LAB ZONES

Discover It!
- Describing Basic Requirements

Do It!
- How Did Plate Tectonics Result in Speciation?

Think About It!
- Determining the Age of a Fossil

Investigate It!
- Constructing Microspheres

AN ISLAND IS BORN

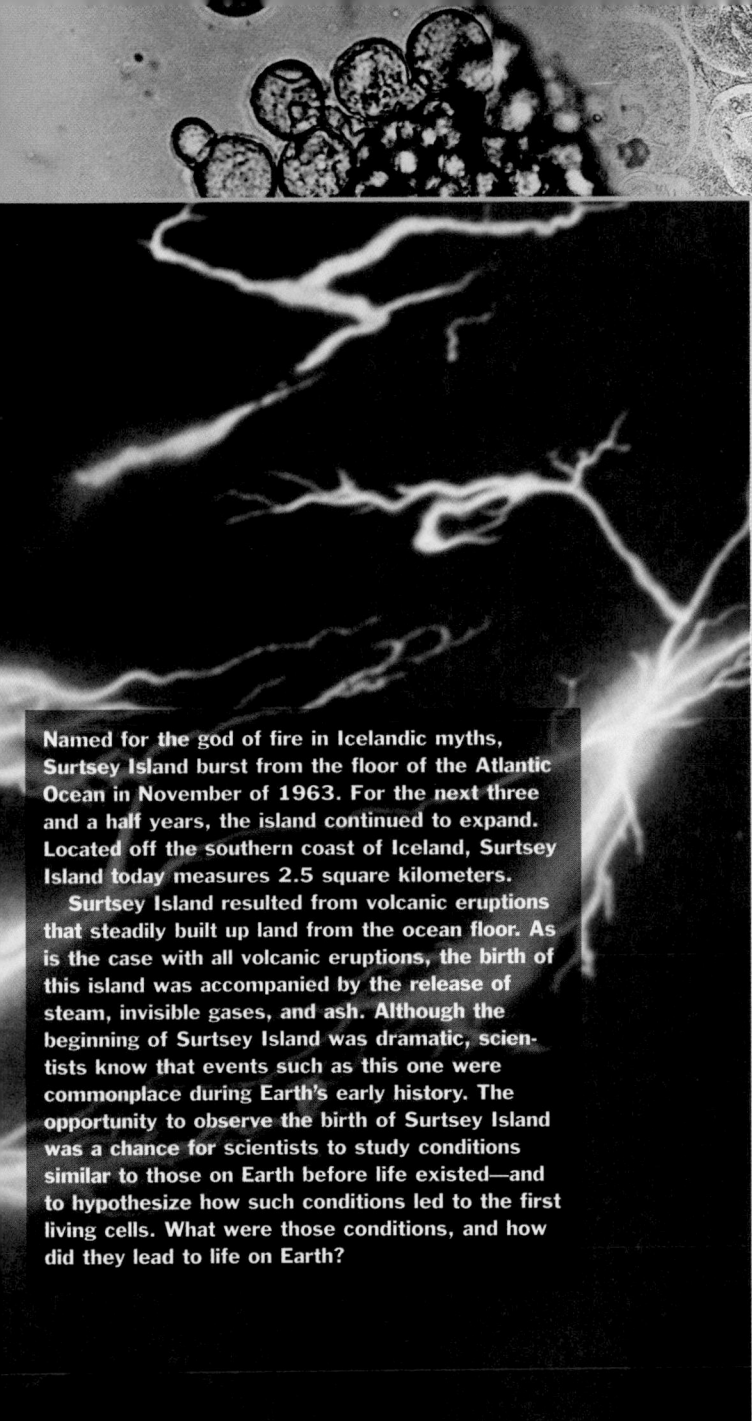

Named for the god of fire in Icelandic myths, Surtsey Island burst from the floor of the Atlantic Ocean in November of 1963. For the next three and a half years, the island continued to expand. Located off the southern coast of Iceland, Surtsey Island today measures 2.5 square kilometers.

Surtsey Island resulted from volcanic eruptions that steadily built up land from the ocean floor. As is the case with all volcanic eruptions, the birth of this island was accompanied by the release of steam, invisible gases, and ash. Although the beginning of Surtsey Island was dramatic, scientists know that events such as this one were commonplace during Earth's early history. The opportunity to observe the birth of Surtsey Island was a chance for scientists to study conditions similar to those on Earth before life existed—and to hypothesize how such conditions led to the first living cells. What were those conditions, and how did they lead to life on Earth?

 Discover It!

Describing Basic Requirements

You need paper and pencil

1. Record as many as possible of the basic requirements for human life. One example is water.
2. Speculate on which of these requirements may not have been present when Earth first formed.

Earth was very different when it first formed. Frequent volcanic eruptions, intense lightning storms, and the absence of life were just some of the existing conditions. By using the scientific method, scientists from many fields have developed theories that explain the history of life.

WRITE ABOUT IT!

Imagine you could observe the formation and early history of Earth. In your science journal, describe the conditions you would see and the difficulty you would have living on Earth at that time.

255

PORTFOLIO PREVIEW

Students should be encouraged to add to their portfolios as they work through this chapter. In addition to the *Write About It* opportunity, the following section is an opportunity for portfolio entries:

■ Section 11.3: *History of Living Things*

Opening Activities

 If you have access to the Internet in your classroom or school, you may wish to have students connect to the address shown on page 254. You may also want to have students conduct a net search for information using key words related to this chapter.

Discover It!

Describing Basic Requirements

TEAM WORK

Have students do the activity in small groups. Ask students to explain why each requirement is important. Provide time for students to compare their ideas with other groups.

WRITE ABOUT IT

Encourage students to illustrate their journal entries. Ask for volunteers willing to share their entries with the class. Have students review what they wrote when they finish the chapter.

SUPER READ! **Finding the Unstated Main Idea** To practice strategies for effective reading, use pages 39-40 in *Super Read!*

REWIND to Chapter 10

Briefly review concepts learned in Chapter 10, *Variation and Adaptation.* Ask:

■ **How do you think Darwin's theory of evolution will help you understand how life began on Earth as you study Chapter 11?**

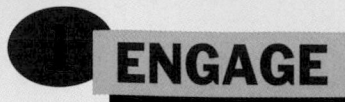

ENGAGE

Consider The Big Idea

Have students read The Big Idea! at the top of the page. Explain that organic molecules make life possible.

Use the Visual

Have students study the photograph and text that opens the section. Explain that meteorites are solid masses that reach Earth's surface from outer space.

SUPER READ! | **Finding the Unstated Main Idea** To practice strategies for effective reading, use pages 39-40 in *Super Read!*

Teacher Demo

Mix a solution of gum arabic and gelatin in a petri dish on an overhead projector. Identify the two substances. Have students observe the activity of the resulting aggregate. Ask:

- **Do you think the substance that formed is living or nonliving? Explain.** (Likely responses include that the substance is nonliving, since it was formed from nonliving matter.)
- **What characteristics of living things are shown by the substance that formed?** (Responses may include movement, growth, ameba-like fission, and ingestion.)

THE BIG IDEA! Evidence indicates that organic molecules and cells may have formed spontaneously on ancient Earth. 11.1

11.1 Earth's Early History

What you'll learn

IDEAS
- To explain how the scientific method is used in studying Earth's early history
- To compare and contrast two hypotheses about how life began on Earth

WORD
microspheres

It's a bird! It's a plane! It's molecules! In 1984 scientists found pieces of a meteorite that had slammed into Antarctica about 13,000 years ago. Analysis showed that the meteorite contained complex organic molecules, leading scientists to wonder: Was life started by molecules from outer space? This idea is the basis for one of two hypotheses about the beginning of life on Earth.

STUDYING LIFE'S ORIGINS

Detecting life

Until a few hundred years ago, most people believed that life could arise from nonliving matter. This belief could explain how life originated on Earth. According to this belief, called spontaneous generation, living things can spring from nonliving materials when invisible "active principles" are present.

As you read in Chapter 1, living things do not come from nonliving material. According to the theory of biogenesis, life arises from living things. Even if life comes only from life, the question remains: Where did the first life-form come from? Many different answers to this question have been proposed.

Scientists have approached this question the same way they approach other questions—through the scientific method. The scientific method involves several steps, including formulating a hypothesis or possible explanation, gathering evidence through observation and experimentation, and drawing conclusions that support or refute the hypothesis.

A scientist studying the origin of life works like a detective. Detectives do not witness events. Instead, they must search for clues, try to reconstruct events, and formulate theories to explain the evidence. Like detectives, scientists cannot witness how life started on our planet. But scientists can use evidence and models to make and test hypotheses about the origin of life on Earth.

FIGURE 11.1
Astronomers study the universe to learn more about the origin of Earth. What other scientists study Earth's origin? ❶

FIGURE 11.2
Geologists study rock samples to uncover Earth's early history.

256

STUDENT RESOURCES

From the Teacher's Resource Package, use:
- Section Review 11.1, Activity Recordsheet 11-1, Interpreting Graphics 11, and Enrichment Topic 11-1 from Unit 3 Review Module
- Lab 21: "Pasteur's Experiment"

 **TECHNOLOGY RESOURCES**

Relevant technology resources include:
- Spanish Student Edition CD-ROM
- Teacher's Resource Planner CD-ROM

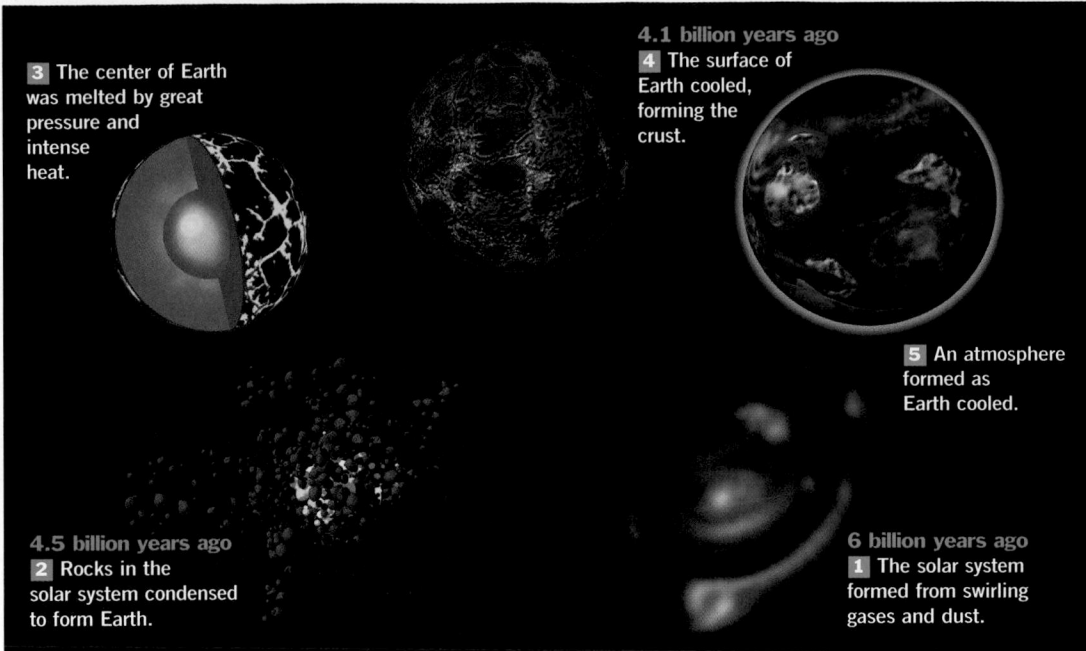

3 The center of Earth was melted by great pressure and intense heat.

4.1 billion years ago
4 The surface of Earth cooled, forming the crust.

5 An atmosphere formed as Earth cooled.

4.5 billion years ago
2 Rocks in the solar system condensed to form Earth.

6 billion years ago
1 The solar system formed from swirling gases and dust.

Scientists have strong evidence indicating that the conditions on Earth today are very different from those that existed during Earth's formation and early history. Many scientists think that life could have arisen spontaneously under the conditions that existed on early Earth. To formulate theories about past conditions and life's origin on Earth, scientists have gathered information from many different scientific disciplines, including astronomy, geology, chemistry, and biology.

FORMATION OF EARTH

Hot dust collides

Scientists have hypothesized about conditions on Earth when life began. These conditions were the result of the planet's formation. According to most current theories, the solar system formed about 6 billion years ago from a swirling cloud of gas and dust. The process is summarized in *Figure 11.3.*

Scientists infer that most of this gas and dust condensed at the center of the solar system, producing the sun. Held by the gravity of the sun, pockets of dust and rocks around the cloud's edges then condensed to become planets, such as Earth; comets; and asteroids.

Gravity compressed Earth's basic materials, producing intense pressure. This pressure, along with radiation from certain elements, generated heat that melted the core material of the young planet. The heavier elements— such as nickel and iron—settled to the center and formed the planet's core. The lighter materials—such as hydrogen, helium, and other gases—rose to the surface and cooled to a solid crust about 4.1 billion years ago. Hydrogen gas, the lightest of materials, probably formed the outermost layer—Earth's first atmosphere.

After the planet's formation, frequent and violent volcanic eruptions shaped many landforms and emitted gases into the changing

FIGURE 11.3
Formation of Earth

SUPER READ!

Chapter 11 The History of Life **257**

MEETING DIVERSE NEEDS

At Risk Encourage students to work with a partner to recreate the sequence of events shown in Figure 11.3 as a flowchart. Have students include information about the timing of each change and their causes or effects. Encourage students to illustrate their charts.

❶ Paleontologists, geologists, astrophysists, geneticists

---

2 TEACH

Use the Visual

Have students study Figure 11.3. Point out that the figure summarizes the current theory about how Earth formed. Ask:

- **About how long ago did Earth form?** (About 4.5 billion years ago)
- **How has the temperature of Earth changed over time?** (It has cooled.)
- **What happened when the Earth cooled?** (The crust and the atmosphere formed.)

Class Activity

TEAM WORK

Before students read about the formation of the Earth, divide the class into small groups. Provide each group with equal-size samples of iron, nickel, aluminum, and carbon and gloves. Have students arrange the elements in order of weight from lightest to heaviest. Ask:

- **Which elements would be found at the center of the Earth? Why?** (Iron and nickel because they are the most dense)

SUPER READ! **Distinguishing Facts from Hypotheses** To practice strategies for effective reading, use pages 41-42 in *Super Read!*

Understanding Sequence To practice strategies for effective reading, use pages 43-44 in *Super Read!*

Use the Visual

Use the Visual

Ask students to study Figure 11.4. To help students recognize the change in Earth's atmosphere over time, ask:

- **What gases present in the atmosphere of Earth today were not present in Earth's ancient atmosphere?** (Oxygen and argon)
- **In the ancient atmosphere, what three gases were the most abundant?** (Carbon dioxide, nitrogen, and sulfur dioxide)
- **In the atmosphere today, what three gases are most abundant?** (Nitrogen, oxygen, and argon)

Think Critically

Explain that carbon dioxide in the atmosphere lets solar radiation reach Earth's surface but stops heat from radiating into space. Have students compare the carbon dioxide in the air of ancient and modern Earth. Ask:

- **Based on the amount of carbon dioxide in the air, how would you expect temperatures on ancient Earth to differ from Earth's temperatures today?** (Ancient Earth's temperatures would be higher.)

Class Activity

TEAM WORK

Divide the class into four groups. Have each group research the effect of one of the following on the Earth's atmosphere: volcanic eruptions; nitrogen; carbon dioxide; and an ozone layer. Have students present their findings in a visual or oral report.

258

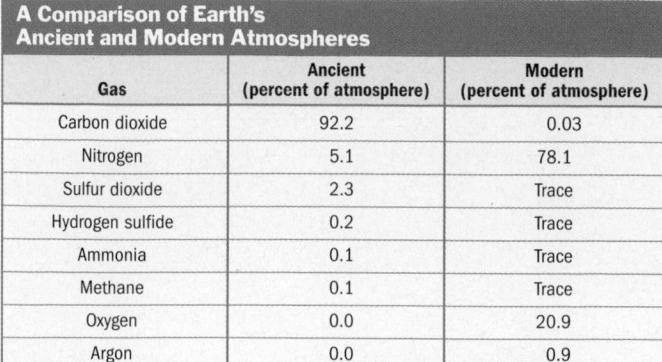

A Comparison of Earth's Ancient and Modern Atmospheres

Gas	Ancient (percent of atmosphere)	Modern (percent of atmosphere)
Carbon dioxide	92.2	0.03
Nitrogen	5.1	78.1
Sulfur dioxide	2.3	Trace
Hydrogen sulfide	0.2	Trace
Ammonia	0.1	Trace
Methane	0.1	Trace
Oxygen	0.0	20.9
Argon	0.0	0.9

FIGURE 11.4

How is today's atmosphere different from the atmosphere that probably existed about the time life appeared? ❶

Inorganic matter

Simple organic molecules 1

Polymers 2

Protocells 3

Cells 4

FIGURE 11.5

Most scientists agree that the formation of life had to follow these four steps.

258 *Unit 3 Change and Diversity*

atmosphere. Today, volcanoes still pour gases into the atmosphere. Geologists and astronomers study these gases and the atmospheres of other planets to identify gases that might have been present in Earth's ancient atmosphere. Their studies suggest that Earth's atmosphere 4 billion years ago probably consisted of gases such as ammonia (NH_3), methane (CH_4), carbon dioxide (CO_2), and nitrogen (N_2).

Evidence indicates that there was little or no oxygen (O_2) in the atmosphere when life appeared. Today, oxygen in the atmosphere is produced by photosynthetic organisms. The absence of oxygen, as you will see, was a key factor in the beginning of life on Earth. Using *Figure 11.4,* you can compare the composition of the ancient and modern atmospheres.

Scientists hypothesize that there was also water vapor in Earth's ancient atmosphere. The water vapor condensed to produce torrential rainstorms. Rainwater flowed from the land into basins in Earth's crust, forming seas. The rainwater carried dissolved gases and dissolved minerals such as phosphorus from rocks. These dissolved compounds formed a rich mixture in the seas.

Some energy sources present on the surface of early Earth are absent or reduced today. For example, the atmosphere lacked an ozone layer

such as the one that now surrounds Earth and shields us from the sun's harmful ultraviolet radiation. Without an ozone layer, enormous amounts of energy in the form of ultraviolet radiation reached Earth's surface. In addition, intense lightning storms may have contributed great amounts of electrical energy.

THE FIRST ORGANIC COMPOUNDS

Sparking to life

Evidence indicates that Earth was lifeless for as long as a half-billion years after it formed. Scientists may never know exactly when and how life originated, but they have formed several hypotheses based on what they know of life today. This information indicates that certain events had to occur before life could begin. Taking these events into account, scientists infer that life originated in four steps, as summarized in *Figure 11.5*.

In the first step, nonliving, or inorganic, matter was transformed into simple organic molecules. Organic molecules were then bonded to form chains of molecules, or polymers. Polymers began to develop characteristics of living cells, becoming "protocells." Finally, protocells evolved into true living cells, with the ability to replicate and pass on traits. With this overview, you can now review in more detail the steps leading to the formation of life.

Organic molecules The first step toward life may have been the formation of organic molecules. One of the theories that explains how these molecules formed was proposed by Russian biochemist Alexander Oparin in 1924. Oparin hypothesized that energy in ultraviolet radiation and lightning stimulated chemical reactions in the ancient atmosphere. These random chemical reactions, occurring over

---

MEETING DIVERSE NEEDS

LEP and At Risk Some students may have difficulty interpreting information presented in tables. To help them see how Earth's atmosphere has changed in 4 billion years, ask them to present the data in Figure 11.4 as either a bar graph or a line graph. Provide assistance as needed.

❶ The ancient atmosphere consisted mostly of carbon dioxide and had no oxygen. Today's atmosphere is 78 percent nitrogen and about 21 percent oxygen.

❷ Energy is needed to produce organic molecules. New organic molecules form from water vapor, methane, ammonia, hydrogen gases, and energy.

millions of years, produced organic molecules. This hypothesis is called chemical evolution.

American scientists Stanley Miller and Harold Urey performed a test of Oparin's hypothesis in 1953. Using the apparatus depicted in *Figure 11.6*, Miller and Urey modeled the ancient atmosphere by mixing water vapor, methane, ammonia, and hydrogen gases in a reacting chamber. Electrodes produced sparks to simulate lightning. After one week, Miller analyzed the liquid produced by the experiment and found that it contained amino acids and other organic molecules.

In keeping with the scientific method, Miller performed control experiments to verify his results. The first control experiment was a repeat of the experiment without the use of electrodes. Since no organic molecules were formed, this experiment confirmed the requirement of an energy source.

In another control experiment, Miller checked for contaminants. He sterilized the apparatus by heating it to 130°C for 18 hours, insuring that no organic molecules remained in the apparatus. The experiment still produced many organic molecules. What questions were answered by the two control experiments?

Miller and Urey's results demonstrated that chemical evolution could have occurred under the conditions modeled by their experiments. Other scientists have tested the chemical evolution hypothesis using different mixtures of gases that might model the atmosphere of early Earth. These scientists have also tried using different energy sources, including ultraviolet light, to stimulate the chemical reactions. Their experiments have produced not only amino acids, but also ATP and the nitrogenous bases of DNA and RNA.

FIGURE 11.6

Miller-Urey Apparatus

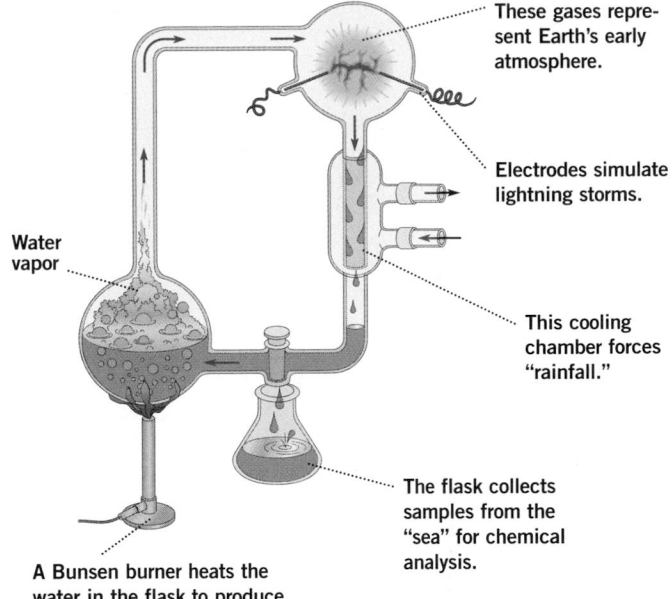

These gases represent Earth's early atmosphere.

Electrodes simulate lightning storms.

Water vapor

This cooling chamber forces "rainfall."

The flask collects samples from the "sea" for chemical analysis.

A Bunsen burner heats the water in the flask to produce water vapor.

A second hypothesis about the origin of organic molecules was proposed by Francis Crick, one of the scientists who discovered the structure of DNA. His hypothesis stated that organic molecules came from outer space. Geologists have found traces of amino acids and other compounds in meteorites, such as the one shown in *Figure 11.7*. Crick hypothesized that meteorites might have been the source of organic molecules in ancient seas.

Polymers In the second step in the formation of living cells, the newly formed organic molecules may have undergone a chemical change that led to the formation of polymers, which are chains of monomers. Each monomer is a small organic molecule, such as an amino acid, that acts as a building block for a larger molecule. For example, protein molecules are

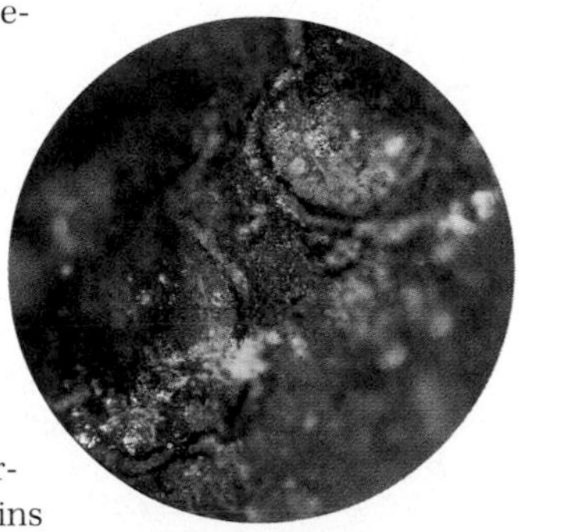

FIGURE 11.7

Some scientists hypothesize that life originated from complex molecules found in meteorites.

Chapter 11 The History of Life **259**

Teacher Demo

Have students observe as you light a match by running it across its striker. Challenge students to explain what factors are involved in lighting the match. (Energy and a chemical reaction) Use the demonstration to reinforce the concept of energy as a prerequisite for chemical reactions. As students learn about the work done by Oparin, Miller, and Urey, relate this concept to the role ultraviolet radiation and lightning played in stimulating the chemical reactions that led to the development of early organic molecules.

Use the Visual

After students read the description of the experiment performed by Urey and Miller, have them examine Figure 11.6. Ask:

- **What gases simulated the early atmosphere?** (Water vapor, hydrogen, ammonia, and methane)
- **What is added to the "atmosphere" by the "ancient seas"?** (Water vapor)
- **Where in the apparatus did Miller and Urey find organic molecules?** (In the collection flask)
- **What was the hypothesis being tested?** (Oparin's hypothesis that energy in ultraviolet radiation and lighting simulated chemical reactions in the ancient atmosphere)

FACTS AND FIGURES

The organic molecules in the Murchison meteorite included lipids and all five nitrogen bases that are present in DNA and RNA.

MEETING DIVERSE NEEDS

Hearing Impaired Have students make flashcards showing the pronunciation of the following names and terms: *Oparin, Urey, amino acid, meteorite, meteor, microsphere, deoxyribonucleic,* and *ribonucleic.*

Language Arts

Tell students to use the prefixes in the terms *monomer* and *polymer* to help them remember the meanings of the terms. For example, the prefix "mono" means "one", and the prefix "poly" means "many."

Chemistry

Review the chemical process by which monomers join to form polymers. Explain that monomers form polymers through dehydration synthesis during which a covalent bond forms between two monomers. In the process, a molecule of water is produced as a hydrogen atom given up by one monomer combines with a hydroxyl group of a second monomer. The reverse process, hydrolysis, occurs when polymers break apart to form monomers.

 Distinguishing Facts from Opinions To practice strategies for effective reading, use pages 41-42 in *Super Read!*

Everyday Biology

Students may confuse the terms *meteor, meteoroid,* and *meteorite.* Explain that a *meteoroid* is an object, such as a chunk of rock or metal, that enters Earth's atmosphere from space. A *meteor* is the light given off by a meteoroid as it burns up when moving through Earth's atmosphere. A *meteorite,* as students observed in the section opening photograph, is a meteoroid that does not burn up completely as it passes through Earth's atmosphere and lands on its surface.

Shooting Stars

About 200 million meteors, commonly known as shooting stars, enter the atmosphere every day. Visible meteors, as well as those too small to be seen, add over 900 metric tons to Earth's mass on a daily basis—and most meteors are the size of a grain of sand when they form.

polymers composed of chains of amino acids.

Two events must occur for monomers to form polymers. First, the monomers must come close enough to react with each other. Second, the monomers must chemically bond. In modern cells, enzymes initiate and speed up these two reactions. There were no enzymes when the first polymers formed, so the conditions under which the reactions occurred must have initiated polymer formation. There are several theories as to what those conditions were, most of which focus on where the organic molecules accumulated.

Some scientists propose that, in Earth's early seas, chance encounters of monomers occurred frequently enough to enable polymer formation. Other scientists hypothesize that polymers formed in evaporating puddles of sea water. Ocean waves may have splashed water onto rocks, forming puddles. Heat from the prehistoric sun or the volcanic rock could have heated the water. As the puddles dried, the solution left behind would become very concentrated; therefore, organic molecules could be close enough to react with each other. Over time, the material deposited on the rocks may have formed long polymers.

A third hypothesis about polymer formation involves common clay. Many organic molecules are attracted to the surface of particles found in clay. On early Earth, amino acids and other monomers may have collected on clay particles. There the monomers could have become concentrated, and polymer formation could have occurred.

THE FIRST CELLS

Shape of things to come

The formation of a cell membrane was probably the third step in the origin of life. Because of its membrane, a cell's

internal environment is separate and different from its surroundings. This separation allows the chemical reactions of life to occur inside the cell.

Protocells The first cell membranes probably formed when polymers, large organic molecules, chemically interacted with their surroundings. Researchers have discovered that if certain protein molecules are mixed with water, tiny bubble-like structures will form. These protein and water bubbles, called **microspheres,** look and behave somewhat like cell membranes.

While microspheres are not cells, they may resemble early protocells that probably formed in the ancient seas. Early protocells may have absorbed nutrient molecules from their surroundings, enlarged, and then divided. When the protocells divided, however, they could not pass on traits to their offspring. This situation would not change until the evolution of the nucleic acids RNA and DNA.

Cells At some point in Earth's history, protocells absorbed nucleic acids from the environment. Once

FIGURE 11.8
What does lava flow do to ocean water? How might this have affected polymer formation on early Earth? ❶

❶ Heat from volcanic rock raised the temperature of the water in which the reactions could occur, which speeded up the reactions. The higher temperature caused the water to evaporate which made the chemicals in the water more concentrated.

FIGURE 11.9

Origin of Living Cells

Some scientists theorize that living cells evolved in a multistep process.

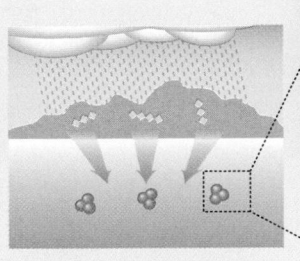

Microspheres

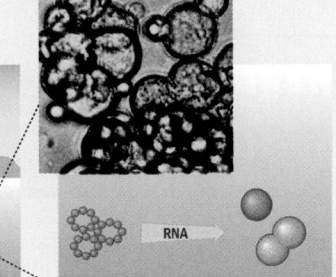

RNA

1 Organic monomers formed from inorganic molecules, concentrated on hot rocks or clay, and then formed polymers.

2 Polymers washed off the rocks and surrounded water droplets, forming protocells similar to microspheres. The polymers acted as a membrane.

3 Protocells absorbed RNA and evolved into cells that could reproduce.

they contained DNA or RNA, the early cells could reproduce and transfer genetic information to offspring. Which nucleic acid was first present in early cells? The answer to this question lies in the replication process.

As you may recall from Chapter 7, replication of DNA and RNA in cells requires enzymes. However, RNA replication can occur in a test tube without the help of enzymes. When free RNA is mixed with RNA nucleotides, new segments of complementary RNA are formed. Therefore, scientists theorize that RNA was the first molecule to evolve with the ability to self-replicate, and that early cells probably contained RNA.

Once RNA was enclosed in a protocell membrane, the membrane would allow organic compounds to concentrate in the protocell. The increased concentration of organic compounds would enable essential

chemical reactions and energy production similar to cellular metabolism. If this newly formed structure were capable of reproduction and metabolism, it could truly be called a living thing—the first cell.

CHECKPOINT 11.1

1. How do researchers use the scientific method to discover the origins of life on Earth?

2. Describe a theory that explains the origin of cells.

3. Critical Thinking Compare and contrast the environment of early Earth with that of modern Earth.

Build on What You Know

4. Why were protocells unable to inherit traits until DNA or RNA evolved? *(Need to jog your memory? Revisit relevant concepts in Chapter 7, Section 7.2, and Chapter 8, Section 8.1.)*

How did the first organic molecules and cells probably form on Earth?

Chapter 11 The History of Life **261**

CHECKPOINT 11.1

1. They propose a hypothesis, develop a procedure to test it, conduct the experiment, and use the data to draw conclusions.

2. Organic monomers formed polymers as they collected in tidal pools, on rocks, or on clay. The polymers surrounded water droplets, forming microspheres. RNA was

absorbed, forming cells capable of reproduction.

3. Comparing and contrasting Early Earth's atmosphere had little O_2 and N_2 and a high percentage of CO_2. Modern Earth has more O_2 and N_2, and far less CO_2.

4. DNA and RNA pass genetic information to offspring.

TEAM WORK — Constructing Microspheres

SAFETY FIRST!

Have students wear goggles and lab aprons during the experiment. Tell them to be cautious around the hot plate, boiling water, steam, and hot glassware. Remind them to run cold water immediately over any burns.

Lab Prep and Planning

Have students work with a partner or in small groups. Allow about 50 minutes for the lab activity.

Lab Tips

Show students how to assemble the flask and ring stand, and how to lower the flask into the water.

Hypothesis Help

Have students review the definition of *microspheres* and how they are similar to and different from cells.

Lab Extension

Open Ended

Divide the class into small groups and assign each group a different amount of amino acids. Determine if a critical concentration is needed to form the microspheres.

 **Investigate It!**

Constructing Microspheres

WHAT YOU WILL DO Construct microspheres and identify their parts

SKILLS YOU WILL USE Measuring, observing, collecting and recording data, predicting

WHAT YOU WILL NEED Safety goggles, 500-mL beaker, hot plate, 0.5 g aspartic acid, 0.5 g glutamic acid, 0.5 g glycine, two 250-mL Erlenmeyer flasks, stirring rod, ring stand, graduated cylinder, 1% NaCl solution, oven mitts, tongs, dropper, microscope slide, coverslip, microscope

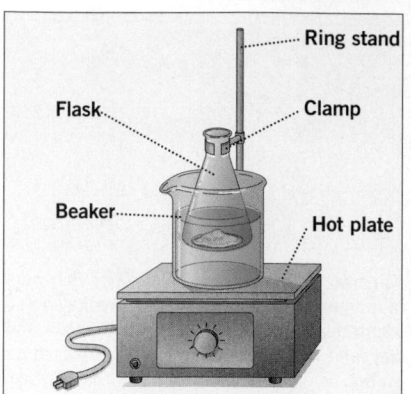

Propose a Hypothesis

Propose a hypothesis about the composition and appearance of microspheres.

Conduct Your Experiment

Caution: Wear your lab coat and safety goggles for protection.

1 Fill a 500-milliliter (mL) beaker half full of water. Place the beaker on a hot plate and bring the water to a boil.
Caution: Be careful of the hot plate and boiling H_2O.

2 Add 0.5 gram (g) each of aspartic acid, glutamic acid, and glycine to a 250-mL flask. Use a stirring rod to mix the amino acids well.

3 Clamp the flask to a ring stand and lower it into the beaker of boiling water, as shown above. Heat the amino acids for 20 minutes. Remove from heat.
Caution: The steam and the beaker will be hot.

4 Measure 5 mL of a 1% NaCl solution, and pour it into a clean flask. Place the flask on a hot plate, and heat the solution to boiling.

5 Put on a pair of oven mitts, and use tongs to pick up the flask of boiling NaCl solution. Slowly pour the solution into the flask of amino acids.

6 Loosen the clamp holding the flask of amino acids, and lift it out of the boiling water. Turn off the hot plate, and allow the flask to cool on the ring stand for 10 minutes.

7 Use a dropper to transfer a drop of the amino acid mixture to a microscope slide. Cover with a coverslip.

8 Examine the slide with a microscope under low and high power. Draw diagrams of what you observe.

Analyze Your Data

1 What did you observe with the microscope?
2 What does your model represent?
3 How are microspheres similar to cells? How are they different?

Draw Conclusions

Did your findings support your hypothesis? Revise your original hypothesis to reflect your observations and analysis.

Design a Related Experiment

Would you get the same results using the DNA bases cytosine, guanine, adenine, and thymine? Design an experiment to find out.

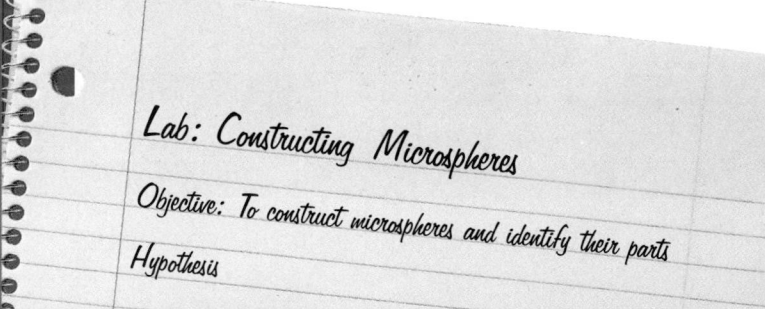

Lab: Constructing Microspheres

Objective: To construct microspheres and identify their parts

Hypothesis

Analyze Your Data

1. Check student diagrams for accuracy.
2. The model represents a possible explanation for the evolution of protocells.
3. Microspheres are small spheres that seem to grow and divide like cells. Microspheres show some activities of cells, but are not alive.

Draw Conclusions

Depending on the hypothesis, the findings may or may not have supported it.

11.2 The First Organisms

How old are you now?
You have read that Earth is about 4.5 billion years old and that the solar system is about 6 billion years old. Scientists discovered this information by studying rocks on Earth, moon rocks, and meteorites. By measuring the amount of radioactive elements such as uranium in the rocks, scientists could estimate the age of Earth and the solar system.

What you'll learn

IDEAS
• To describe how the age of fossils is determined
• To summarize the development of the first prokaryotic and eukaryotic cells

WORDS
half-life, stromatolites, endosymbiosis

READING THE FOSSIL RECORD
Dating isotopes

As you read in Chapter 10, biologists have developed a theory of evolution that explains the changes in living things over time. The appearance of cells marked the beginning of the amazing biodiversity that exists today.

Of the many methods scientists use to study life's history, the most well-known is analyzing fossil evidence. Scientists can estimate the relative age of fossils from their location in rock. The oldest fossils are found in lower rock layers. As time passes, layers of rock are deposited on top of the previous layer. The oldest rock layers are on the bottom, and the most recently formed layers are on the top. The comparison of rock layers does not provide the actual age of a fossil, but it can indicate that one fossil is older than another.

A fossil's real age can be estimated by analyzing the isotopes in the rock surrounding the fossil. Isotopes are single atoms of the same element that have different numbers of neutrons.

Some isotopes are radioactive and undergo a change called radioactive decay. During radioactive decay, the isotope gives off particles and energy, changing its identity to a different element. For example, radioactive potassium (^{40}K) decays to produce a gas called argon. Radioactive decay occurs at a constant rate, called a half-life. The **half-life** of an element is the time it takes for half of the atoms in a sample to undergo radioactive decay. The half-life of ^{40}K is 1.3 billion years.

By studying radioactive isotopes in rocks and fossils, paleontologists can use radioactive dating methods to determine the fossil's age. Two of the most frequently used methods are potassium-argon dating and radiocarbon dating.

Potassium-argon dating is used for rocks that are suspected to be billions of years old. Once certain types of rocks form, the ^{40}K in the rocks decays to form argon, which is trapped in the rock crystals. The amount of argon in the rock can be compared to the amount of ^{40}K in the

FIGURE 11.10
Scientists can infer the relative age of fossils from their location in rock. Which of the rock layers shown here is probably the oldest? ❶

Chapter 11 The History of Life **263**

STUDENT RESOURCES

From the Teacher's Resource Package, use:
■ Section Review 11.2 and Critical Thinking Exercise 11 from Unit 3 Review Module

TECHNOLOGY RESOURCES

Relevant technology resources include:
■ Spanish Student Edition CD-ROM
■ Teacher's Resource Planner CD-ROM

❶ ENGAGE

Consider The Big Idea

Have students read The Big Idea! at the top of the page. Explain that life on Earth changed from simple cells to the complex forms we see today.

Use the Visual

Have students study the photograph and text that opens the section. Explain that astronauts collected rocks and soil samples beginning in 1969. Ask:

■ **What information can scientists gain by analyzing rocks and meteorites?** (Likely responses include: What elements and compounds are present in space; whether life is likely to be found on extraterrestrial bodies; and when the rocks and meteorites were formed.)

Teacher Demo

Display pieces of clay in which you have made identifiable impressions using objects such as keys, shells, pencils, or paper clips. Ask students to examine the "fossils" to identify the object that left each impression. Tell students that the impression in clay is a model of a type of fossil called a *mold*. Explain that by studying fossils, scientists can learn about organisms from the past.

❶ The bottom layer of rock.

TEACH

Teacher Demo

Obtain a Geiger counter and several samples of substances, including an alpha emitter from a smoke alarm or a mantle from a gas lantern. Show students how to identify radioactive substances using a radiation detector. As you begin, explain the slow, random clicks signal background radiation that is always in the environment. When you get a count from a radioactive sample, ask:

- **What do you think the count for the sample would be after one half-life?** (Half the value of the present reading)

✳ Mathematics

Direct students' attention to Figure 11.11. Have students look at the graph portion of the diagram. Ask:

- **If the carbon-14 in the mollusk has undergone two half-lives, how old is the mollusk?** (2 x 5600 or 11,200 years)
- **If the mollusk contained 1000 grams of carbon-14 at the time of its death, how much carbon-14 should still be present in the mollusk after 3 half-lives?** (Approximately 125 grams: 1000 to 500 to 250 to 125)
- **How long will it take for over 90 percent of the carbon-14 in the mollusk to decay?** (About 20,000 years based on data presented in the bar graph)

FIGURE 11.11

Radiocarbon Dating

Paleontologists use radiocarbon dating to determine the age of rocks and fossils.

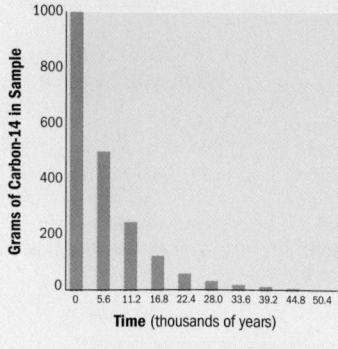

This graph shows how the amount of radioactive carbon-14 (^{14}C) in an organism decreases over time.

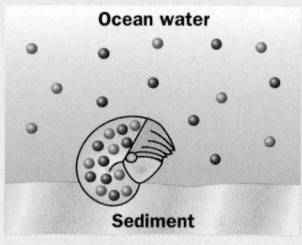
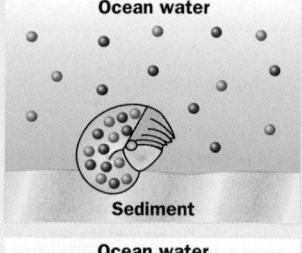

Living organism

1 Like all living organisms, this mollusk is absorbing ^{12}C and ^{14}C from the environment. The ratio of ^{14}C to ^{12}C is constant.

Dead organism

2 Once the mollusk dies, it no longer absorbs carbon. The radioactive ^{14}C begins to decay and the amount of ^{14}C in the mollusk shell decreases, while the amount of ^{12}C remains the same.

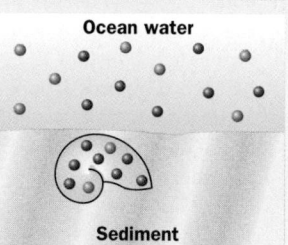

History

3 Because half of the ^{14}C decays every 5600 years, the mollusk fossil's age can be determined by finding the ratio of ^{14}C to ^{12}C in the fossil and comparing it with the ratio in living organisms.

● ^{14}C (Carbon-14)
● ^{12}C (Carbon-12)

rock. From this ratio, scientists can calculate how long ago the rock formed. In older rocks, the ratio of argon to ^{40}K will be higher than in younger rocks. Fossils found in or very near the rocks are assumed to be the same age as the rock.

Scientists use another method of dating, radiocarbon dating, on younger fossils. There are two isotopes of carbon: the radioactive isotope carbon-14 (^{14}C) and the more common, non-radioactive isotope carbon-12 (^{12}C). In the atmosphere, the two isotopes are found in a constant ratio. Since living organisms are continually taking in carbon compounds from the

atmosphere, the ratio of ^{14}C to ^{12}C (^{14}C:^{12}C) in living cells also remains constant.

After an organism dies, no new carbon compounds are taken in. The amount of ^{12}C does not change, but the amount of radioactive ^{14}C decreases as it decays to other compounds. As the amount of ^{14}C decreases, the ^{14}C:^{12}C ratio changes over time. The age of a fossil can be determined by measuring the ratio of ^{14}C to ^{12}C and comparing the ratio with that of a living organism.

Since the half-life of ^{14}C is 5600 years, every 5600 years one half of the ^{14}C in a fossil will decay. For example,

264 *Unit 3 Change and Diversity*

❶ 11,200 years
❷ 8.93 half lives

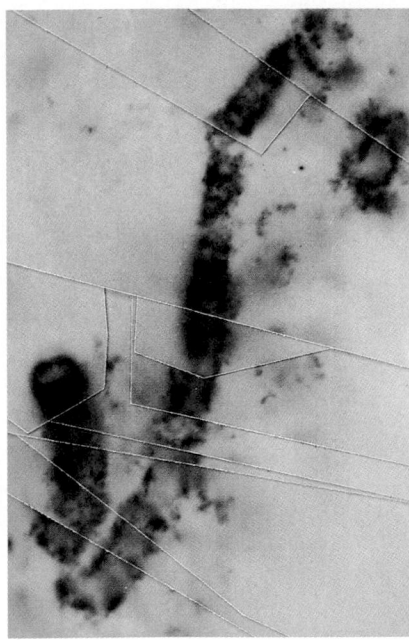

FIGURE 11.12
Finding the First Fossils

The fossilized prokaryote (left) is about 3.5 billion years old.

Fossilized remains of bacterial mats (above) are some of the oldest known fossils. Modern colonies of bacteria form similar mats (below).

suppose there are 8 g of ^{14}C in a fossilized snail shell and 16 g of ^{14}C in a living snail shell. The amount of ^{12}C in both shells is the same. Since the ^{14}C:^{12}C ratio in the fossil is one-half the ^{14}C:^{12}C ratio in the living snail shell, the fossil is approximately 5600 years old. How old is a fossilized snail shell containing 4 g of ^{14}C?

The radiocarbon dating method is accurate only for fossils younger than 50,000 years. About how many ^{14}C half-lives is that? Radiocarbon dating is useful for dating fossils of prehistoric humans, because such remains are less than 50,000 years old.

EARLY PROKARYOTES
How long has life lived?

The oldest fossil evidence of cells that scientists have found so far is 3.5 billion years old. Therefore, scientists know that life is at least that old, and probably older. These fossils, shown in *Figure 11.12*, are called stromatolites.

LAB ZONE Think About It! bioSURF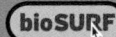

Determining the Age of a Fossil

Scientists use radiocarbon dating to determine the age of fossils. You can find out how they arrive at their conclusions if you . . .

Try This

1 Imagine you found a fossil, such as the one shown here.
2 You are given the following data: The leaf originally contained 12 g of ^{14}C. The fossil contains 3 g of ^{14}C.
3 Find out how many half-lives the fossil has had. Knowing that the half-life of ^{14}C is 5600 years, calculate the age of the fossil.

Analyze Your Results

1 How old is your fossil?
2 How has the amount of ^{12}C changed since the fossil was formed?
3 How do scientists determine how much ^{14}C was originally in the fossil?

Think Critically

To determine if students understand the concept of half-life, present them with the following problem:

- **About how old is a mollusk fossil containing 1/16 the amount of C-14 of living organisms? Explain your reasoning.** (The fossil would be approximately 44,800 years old. 1/2 = 5600 years; 1/4 = 11,200 years; 1/8 = 22,400 years; 1/16 = 44,800 years.)

LAB ZONE Think About It!
Determining the Age of a Fossil

Analyze Your Results

1 11,200 years (2 half-lives)
2 It has not changed.
3 By comparing the amount of ^{14}C in the fossil to the amount of ^{12}C it contains

Clarify Misconceptions

Students often think that the first organisms were autotrophs. To correct this misconception, emphasize that the earliest known fossils support the idea that heterotrophs appeared before autotrophs. Point out that autotrophs are chemically more complex than heterotrophs. Since organisms have generally become more complex over time, it is unlikely that the chemically complex autotrophs arose before the chemically simpler heterotrophs.

MEETING DIVERSE NEEDS

At Risk Some students may have difficulty understanding what isotopes are. To ensure that these students understand the concept of isotopes, challenge them to draw an atomic model that shows how carbon-12 differs from carbon-14. Model as necessary. Check student models and correct any inaccuracies.

After students read about the conditions leading to the evolution of autotrophs from heterotrophs, have them study Figure 11.13. Ask:

- **How do heterotrophs affect the atmosphere?** (Heterotrophs release carbon dioxide into the atmosphere.)
- **Why did autotrophs evolve from heterotrophs?** (Competition for nutrients and increased carbon dioxide levels in the atmosphere led to fewer organic molecules. Variations resulted in cells that could make food from inorganic molecules and sunlight.)

Discuss

Tell students that according to the Big Bang hypothesis, the universe is between 10 billion and 20 billion years old. To help students develop a sense of when life first appeared on Earth and when early heterotropic cells evolved into autotrophic cells, ask:

- **About how long after Earth formed did the first eukaryotic cells appear?** (Slightly more than 3 billion years)
- **About how long after Earth formed did the first cells capable of carrying out photosynthesis appear?** (Slightly more than 2 billion years)

 Distinguishing Facts from Opinions To practice strategies for effective reading, use pages 41-42 in *Super Read!*

FIGURE 11.13
Changing Atmosphere

Heterotrophs consumed many organic molecules and released carbon dioxide.

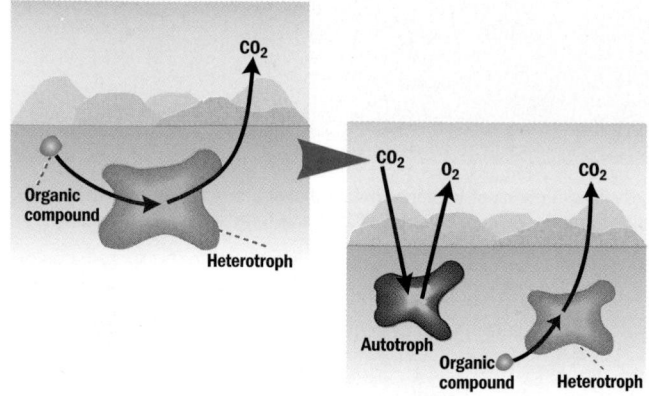

Stromatolites are the fossilized remains of layered mats of prokaryotic cells and sediment. The prokaryotic cells are similar to modern bacteria.

Most scientists agree that the first living cells were heterotrophs, organisms that cannot make their own food. Autotrophs can make their own food. The first heterotrophs absorbed organic compounds from their environment and produced carbon dioxide. As these early cells reproduced and their numbers increased, they began to use up the available supply of organic compounds. Strong competition developed among the heterotrophs for the available nutrients. Which cells would survive?

Many genetic variations occurred in the first billion years of life. Some of these variations resulted in the emergence of autotrophs. Because Earth's first autotrophs did not need organic compounds for food, they were freed from competition with heterotrophs for nutrients.

In order to use solar energy to make food, the first autotrophs evolved with a system resembling photosynthesis. But these earliest autotrophs did

---

not produce oxygen. You read in Chapter 4 that photosynthesis is the process in which plants use the energy in sunlight, carbon dioxide, and water to make food and produce oxygen. It was not until about 2.5 billion years ago that autotrophs evolved with a photosynthetic process similar to that of modern plants. It was then that oxygen was first released into the water, and eventually into the atmosphere, as diagrammed in *Figure 11.13*. The evolution of autotrophs had a dramatic effect on Earth's atmosphere.

Most modern cells, called aerobes, require oxygen for survival. Other modern cells, called anaerobes, cannot survive in the presence of oxygen. The earliest cells on Earth were probably anaerobes, and most were killed by the new, oxygen-containing atmosphere. However, some early anaerobes survived because they lived buried in places without oxygen, as some anaerobes do today. Other cells survived because they developed the ability to tolerate oxygen. Eventually, these cells also developed the ability to use oxygen to obtain energy from food. Thus the first aerobes—cells needing oxygen for survival—evolved.

THE FIRST EUKARYOTES
Organellegenesis

Evidence indicates that the first eukaryotic cells evolved about 1.5 billion years ago. How did eukaryotic cells evolve to have inner membranes, such as a nuclear membrane and membrane-bound organelles? Two widely accepted hypotheses explain this phase of evolution. You can compare these hypotheses in *Figure 11.14*.

Some scientists hypothesize that inner membranes originated from infolding of the outer cell membrane, in a process similar to modern endocytosis. As you may recall from

---

FIGURE 11.14

Two Hypotheses of Eukaryotic Origins

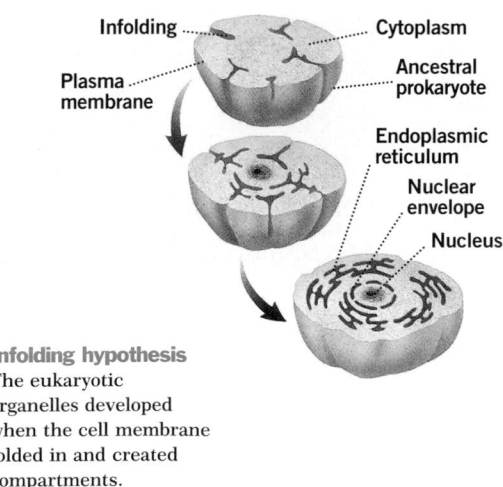

Infolding hypothesis
The eukaryotic organelles developed when the cell membrane folded in and created compartments.

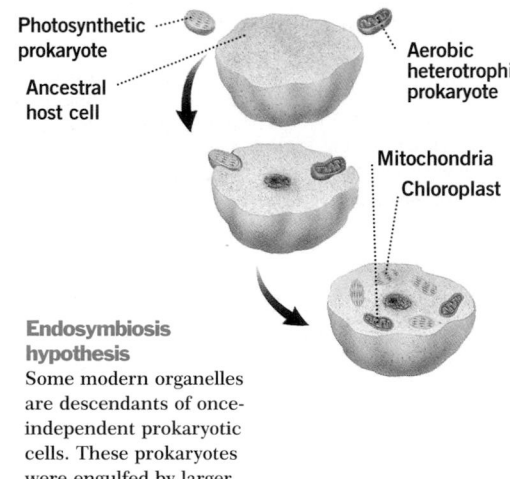

Endosymbiosis hypothesis
Some modern organelles are descendants of once-independent prokaryotic cells. These prokaryotes were engulfed by larger cells that became eukaryotic cells.

Chapter 3, endocytosis occurs when the cell membrane folds into a pouch that encloses particles. According to the infolding hypothesis, organelles developed when cell membranes folded in, creating compartments where specialized functions were carried out. These compartments probably resembled the endoplasmic reticulum, Golgi apparatus, and vacuoles of modern cells.

American scientist Lynn Margulis developed a second hypothesis called **endosymbiosis.** According to this hypothesis, the ancestors of mitochondria and chloroplasts were independent aerobic prokaryotes that were engulfed by larger cells. The larger cells eventually depended on the engulfed prokaryotes, which took on the specialized roles of cellular organelles.

Some organelles contain their own DNA and ribosomes. These organelles make their own proteins and reproduce—an indication that they may have once been capable of an independent existence.

Regardless of the method by which organelles evolved in eukaryotic cells, a permanent partnership was established. With their specialized organelles, these early eukaryotic cells were ideally suited for the development and specialization of multicellular organisms.

CHECKPOINT 11.2

1. How do scientists establish the approximate age of fossils?

2. Explain one of the hypotheses about the formation of eukaryotic cells.

3. Critical Thinking Write a paragraph describing the cause-and-effect relationship between the atmospheric changes on early Earth and evolution of life forms.

Build on What You Know

4. Why were autotrophs so important in the evolution of life? *(Need to jog your memory? Revisit relevant concepts in Chapter 4, Section 4.1.)*

Mighty Mitochondria

The evolution of organelles resulted in a valuable material for research: mitochondrial DNA, or mtDNA, which mutates more frequently than nuclear DNA.

Chapter 11 The History of Life **267**

Everyday Biology

To review the role of mitochondria, DNA, and mitochondrial DNA, have students refer back to Chapter 3, Section 3.

3 ASSESS

Evaluate Understanding

On the board, draw a horizontal line divided into seven segments. Label the first segment 6 million years ago. List the following events: *Earth forms, first eukaryotic cells, solar system forms, stromatolites, first heterotrophs, first autotrophs,* and *first prokaryotic cells.* Have students place each event in its correct location on the time line. Then ask them to write a paragraph to explain the relationship among the events.

Reteach

Draw four ovals joined by arrows on the board. In the first three ovals write: *Solar System Forms (6 billion years ago), Earth Forms (4.5 billion years ago no oxygen present), First Cells (3.5 billion years ago).* Next to the third oval list: *stromatolites, prokaryotes,* and *heterotrophs.* Discuss how each term applies to the first cells. In the last oval, write: *First eukaryotes (1.5 billion year ago).* Next to it, list the terms *autotrophs, organelles,* and *oxygen.* Discuss how each term relates to the last oval. Write the phrases *infolding hypothesis* and *endosymbiosis hypothesis* beside the arrow between the last two ovals. Conclude the discussion by reviewing the main points.

CHECKPOINT 11.2

1. They use radioactive dating.
2. Infolding or endosymbiosis as explained in Figure 11.14.
3. **Identifying cause and effect** Heterotrophs consumed organic molecules and released CO_2. Competition led to the emergence of autotrophs and the production of oxygen, which killed many heterotrophs.
4. Because autotrophs produce their own nutrients, they did not compete with heterotrophs. Also, autotrophs produce O_2; as a result of directional selection, heterotrophs using oxygen survived.

11.3 History of Living Things

Use the Visual

Have students study the photograph that opens the section. Explain that the lemur shown is one of many species unique to the island of Madagascar. Ask:

■ **How might an island become populated by species not found elsewhere?** (Likely responses include: Organisms evolved in isolation and adapted to an island's specific environment.)

Explain that in this section, students will learn how changes in Earth's features led to the development of new species in different parts of the Earth.

Quick Activity

Have the class make a time line on the board showing the important events described in the previous two sections. Have volunteers date the approximate time of each event and tell why each event was important in the development of life. Events should include the formation of the solar system, origin of the Earth, the first prokaryotic cells, the first autotrophs, and the first eukaryotic cells. Keep the time line on the board and refer to it as you study this section.

What you'll learn

IDEAS
• To explain the emergence of multicellular organisms
• To evaluate the effect of plate tectonics and of mass extinctions on speciation

WORDS
eras, periods, epochs, plate tectonics

FIGURE 11.15
Earth's Geological Clock

A clock can be used as a model of the geological time scale. The spiral represents the increasing number of species.

Earthdancing

Madagascar, a large island off the eastern coast of Africa, is home to many unique species, such as the black-and-white lemur (right). Like other land masses, Madagascar has drifted around Earth throughout geological history, hosting new species and isolating its existing ones. This land movement also explains why each continent has different species.

MEASURING TIME

From another era

Do you agree with the expression "Time flies when you're having fun"? No matter how much fun you are having, 250,000 years is a long time—unless you compare it with 4 billion years. As you can see in *Figure 11.15*, the time period that humans have been on Earth—just 250,000 years—is comparable to just seconds, when compared with the length of time that life has been on Earth.

In order to catalog the 4 billion years of life on Earth, scientists have created a geological time scale. This scale divides the history of life into large time spans called **eras.** Eras are subdivided into **periods,** and periods into **epochs.** You may be familiar with the names of many of these divisions, such as Mesozoic era, Jurassic period, and Pleistocene epoch.

The beginning and end of each time span is marked by the extinction of many life-forms and the appearance of new ones. *Figure 11.17* shows living things that characterize the different periods, as well as major changes that mark each period.

Scientists date the beginning and end of epochs, periods, and eras by studying the fossil record. They use radioactive dating of fossils to identify the time when a life-form became extinct or a new organism appeared. These milestones are integrated with evolutionary theory to create a geological time line tracing the history of life.

One of the most important milestones in this time line follows the end of the Precambrian era. Fossil evidence shows that the beginning of the Cambrian period was marked by an explosive increase in the number and diversity of living things. The lack of

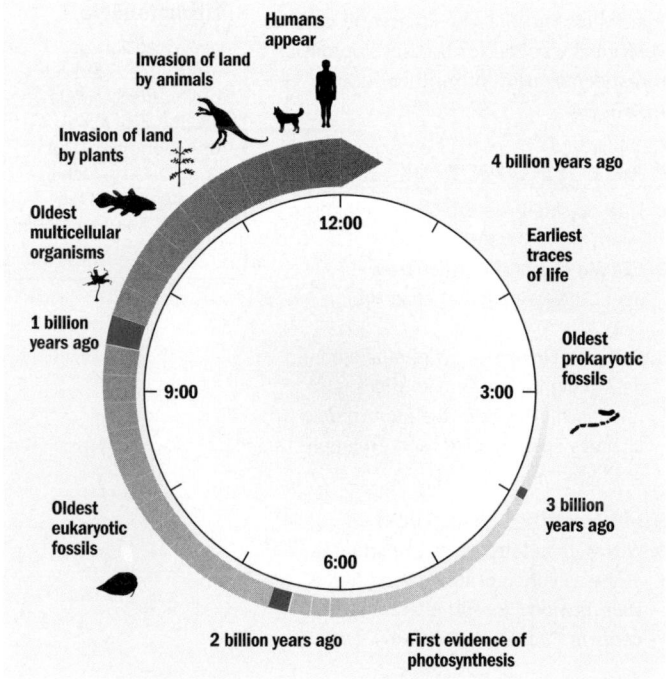

Humans appear
Invasion of land by animals
Invasion of land by plants
Oldest multicellular organisms
1 billion years ago
9:00
12:00
4 billion years ago
Earliest traces of life
3:00
Oldest prokaryotic fossils
3 billion years ago
Oldest eukaryotic fossils
6:00
2 billion years ago
First evidence of photosynthesis

268 *Unit 3 Change and Diversity*

FIGURE 11.16
This table shows the different eras, periods, and epochs of Earth's history.

Geological Time Scale			
Age*	Era	Period	Epoch
0.01	CENOZOIC	Quaternary	Recent
1.8			Pleistocene
5		Tertiary	Pliocene
24			Miocene
38			Oligocene
54			Eocene
65			Paleocene
144	MESOZOIC	Cretaceous	
213		Jurassic	
248		Triassic	
286	PALEOZOIC	Permian	
360		Carboniferous	
408		Devonian	
438		Silurian	
505		Ordovician	
590		Cambrian	
	PRECAMBRIAN		

*Millions of years ago

fossils in the Precambrian era was once seen as evidence against Darwin's theory of evolution. However, in this century, microscopic fossils of prokaryotes have been found, filling in some holes in the Precambrian fossil record. After the appearance of the first living cells and the first eukaryotes in the Precambrian era, the next major event in the history of life was the appearance of multicellular organisms.

MULTICELLULAR ORGANISMS
A whole new dimension

As eukaryotic cells evolved, a variety of cells arose with different shapes and different combinations of organelles and membranes. The population of eukaryotic cells was more diverse than the population of prokaryotic cells. This variety of eukaryotes gave rise to a very important kind of life-form: the multicellular organism.

Eukaryotic cells did not automatically form multicellular organisms. Most scientists theorize that there was an intermediate, colony-forming stage. Colonies are formed when daughter cells remain attached to each other after cell division. Some modern green algae, such as the *Volvox* shown in *Figure 11.18*, exist as colonies that probably resemble early eukaryotic colonies.

Scientists propose that all of the cells in early colonies were identical and could move independently. Gradually the colonies became organized and some cells began to perform specialized functions. Groups of cells in the colonies became more specialized and formed tissues—cells that worked together to perform a function for the whole colony. As some cells became dependent on others for specialized functions, they lost their ability to

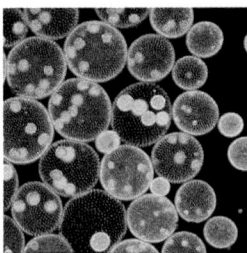

FIGURE 11.18
Some modern protists, such as these green algae, resemble the first colonial organisms.

FIGURE 11.17
Geological Time Line

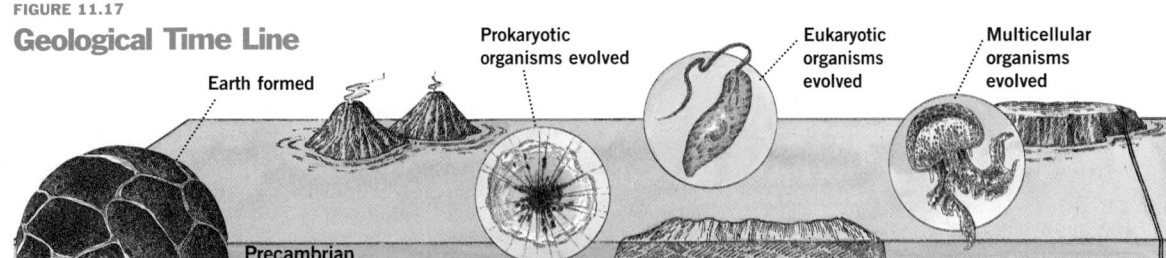

Earth formed · Prokaryotic organisms evolved · Eukaryotic organisms evolved · Multicellular organisms evolved

Precambrian

Chapter 11 The History of Life **269**

FACTS AND FIGURES
Some scientists divide the Precambrian Era into two parts, the Archean Eon and the Proterozoic Eon. The Precambrian Era comprises about 87 percent of the geologic time scale.

TEACH

Use the Visual

Ask students to study Figure 11.16. Point out that the figure shows the major divisions of geologic time. Explain that the beginning and end of each time span shown on the diagram is marked by the extinction of many life-forms and the appearance of other life-forms. To make sure students understand the table, ask:

- **What is the name of the earliest period in geologic time?** (Precambrian)
- **From oldest to most recent, what are the names of the six periods that make up the Paleozoic Era?** (Cambrian, Ordovician, Silurian, Devonian, Carboniferous, and Permian)
- **What is the name of the era and period in which you are living?** (Cenozoic and Quaternary)

Language Arts

Encourage students to look up the meanings of prefixes that appear in the names of epochs, periods, and eras. The following prefixes come from the Greek: "pale" or "paleo" (ancient); "meso" (middle); "cen" (recent); and "zo" (animals).

 Understanding Sequence To practice strategies for effective reading, use pages 43-44 in *Super Read!*

11.3

In the Community

If there is no natural history museum in your area, students may be able to obtain information by interviewing a geology professor from a local college or university.

Use the Visual

Direct students' attention to the time line at the bottom of the page. Explain that the diagram identifies when various types of life-forms evolved. Ask:

■ **During which period did amphibians evolve?** (The Devonian)
■ **How do the plants that existed during the Ordovician period differ from those of the Silurian period?** (Plants living during the Ordovician period were mostly water plants; those of the Silurian evolved adaptations to live on land.)
■ **Did land animals evolve before or after the Devonian period? Explain.** (After, the time line shows land plants appearing, but not land animals—only amphibians.)

IN THE COMMUNITY
Hometown History

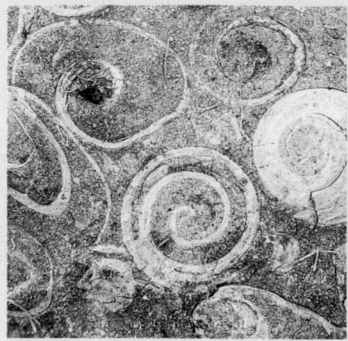

move. This evolution of colonies gave rise to multicellular organisms with specialized, interdependent cells.

These early multicellular organisms probably inhabited the ancient seas, like their unicellular predecessors. The emergence of terrestrial organisms did not occur until 430 million years ago.

INVASIONS OF THE LAND
How life stayed wet

Clearly, the biggest difference between life in the ocean and life on land is that organisms on land are not surrounded by water. This difference was also the biggest challenge that the first land organisms faced.

Organisms living in water depend on their surroundings for many essential functions, including reproduction, respiration, excretion, and mobility. For example, the swimming sperm of aquatic organisms require water to

reach the egg and support development of offspring. This type of reproduction is not possible on dry land. In order to survive on land, organisms had to adapt to new, waterless surroundings. How could early land organisms conserve and replenish water?

As multicellular organisms adapted, some species gained the ability to overcome these obstacles. Plants were the first organisms to make the transition from water to land. Waxy coverings on most plant parts prevented excessive water loss. An internal transport system brought water and nutrients from the soil to all parts of the plant. Fossil evidence shows the earliest land plants to be about 450 million years old.

Fungi became land dwellers shortly after plants, followed by the arthropods, invertebrate animals such as insects. Insects and other arthropods evolved with hard body coverings, which prevented water loss. The oldest insect

FIGURE 11.17
(continued)

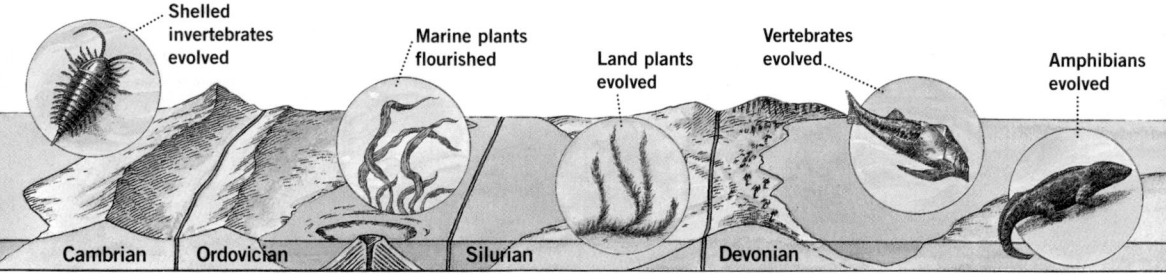

Shelled invertebrates evolved — Marine plants flourished — Land plants evolved — Vertebrates evolved — Amphibians evolved

Cambrian | Ordovician | Silurian | Devonian

270 *Unit 3 Change and Diversity*

MEETING DIVERSE NEEDS

At Risk Encourage students to make a table that combines the information presented in the time line on pages 270-273. Suggest the following heads for their tables: *Geologic Period and Life-Forms*

Which Evolved. You may way want to model one or more entries for them. Encourage students to add illustrations and use their table as a study tool for this section.

fossils are 400 million years old. Amphibians were the last group to make the transition from sea to land. However, most groups of prehistoric amphibians eventually became extinct.

PLATE TECTONICS
Continental crash course

Paleontologists have found fossils of subtropical plants and animals in Alaska, a place known for its cold, harsh climate. You may be wondering how warm-weather organisms could have lived there.

According to geological evidence, at one time Alaska was connected to Asia by a land bridge. This entire region was much closer to the equator—and was therefore much warmer than it is today. But Alaska is not the only area that has moved during Earth's history.

The fossil evidence indicates that all modern continents have moved—together and apart as well as closer to and farther from the equator. Why do the continents move?

Earth consists of a molten core and a hard crust. The crust is broken into plates, which float on the molten core like rafts on water. Continents and other land masses move as the plates move. **Plate tectonics** is the movement of Earth's crustal plates over its molten core. Plate tectonics affect land, climate, and organisms.

Land changes There have been many different continent configurations in the past. Continents stay together if they are located on the same plate, and move apart if they are located on different plates. For example, most of Asia and Europe always remain together because these two continents are located on the same plate. In contrast, the distance between North America and Europe increases about 2 centimeters (cm) every year. North America and Europe are located on different plates.

If you look closely at a map, you may notice that some of the continents could fit together. The eastern coast of South America, for instance, looks as if it could fit together with the western coast of Africa. In fact, all the world's major continents once formed a supercontinent called Pangaea (pan-GEE-uh). *Figure 11.19* shows how the continents have moved over time. How do you think the movement of continents affected evolution? ❷

Climate changes In addition to changes in land, there have been many climate changes during Earth's history. Some of these changes resulted from the movement of land masses. Other climate changes had different causes. Both global cooling and global warming, for example, can be explained by increased volcanic activity. Plate tectonics is responsible for volcanic activity, as you see in *Figure 11.20* on page 272.

Amphibian and reptile fossils on the barren antarctic desert indicate that there have been at least two

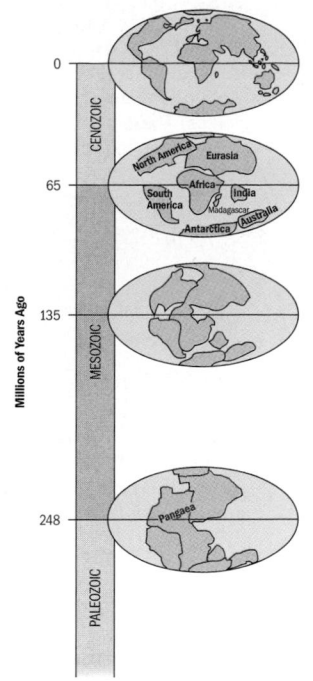

FIGURE 11.19
The continents are parts of floating pieces of Earth's crust called plates.

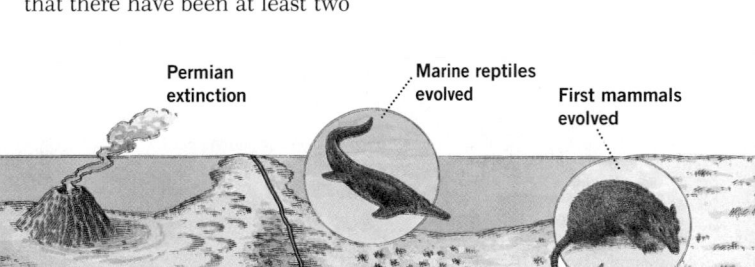

Carboniferous — Reptiles evolved

Permian — Permian extinction

Triassic — Marine reptiles evolved — First mammals evolved

Chapter 11 The History of Life **271**

❶ With leaves and taproots
❷ As the environment changed, so would the species. Those organisms that could not adapt would become extinct, those that could adapt would flourish.

Use the Visual

Have students study the time line at the bottom of pages 270-273. Have them note the unique environmental changes that take place each period. Discuss students' observations and challenge them to explain how different types of organisms evolved by adapting to changes in the environment.

Class Activity

Provide students with scissors and outline maps of the world that clearly show the shapes of the continents. Challenge students to cut out the continents and reassemble them to form Pangaea. Students should include the continental shelf as part of the continent. Suggest that students use Figure 11.19 as a model.

Clarify Misconceptions

Students may believe that only Earth's continents are located on tectonic plates and that continents and plates have the same shape. Explain that Earth's entire crust, including that making up the ocean floor, is divided into plates. Both continents and oceans change in size and shape as a result of plate movement.

Use the Visual

Direct students to Figure 11.20. To assess students' understanding of changes that result from plate movement, ask:

- **What can you assume about an area in which earthquakes are common?** (It is located on or near a plate boundary.)
- **How is plate movement involved in the formation of mountains?** (Mountains may form when two plates collide or when tectonic activity creates volcanoes.)

Teacher Demo

Display two blocks of clay and tell students the clay blocks represent tectonic plates. Place the clay blocks a few centimeters apart. Ask two students to push the blocks of clay slowly toward each other with some force as the class observes what happens. Explain to students that this type of plate movement can result in the formation of mountains.

 Geography

Locate the Himalayas on a world map. Explain that the Himalayas, Earth's tallest mountains, were formed by a violent collision of the plates of the land masses we now call India and Asia.

 STS

You may wish to have student teams develop a series of drawings to illustrate the theories discussed.

FIGURE 11.20

Plate Tectonics

Volcanic eruptions, earthquakes, and mountain formations are caused by plate tectonics. These geological processes occur at plate boundaries.

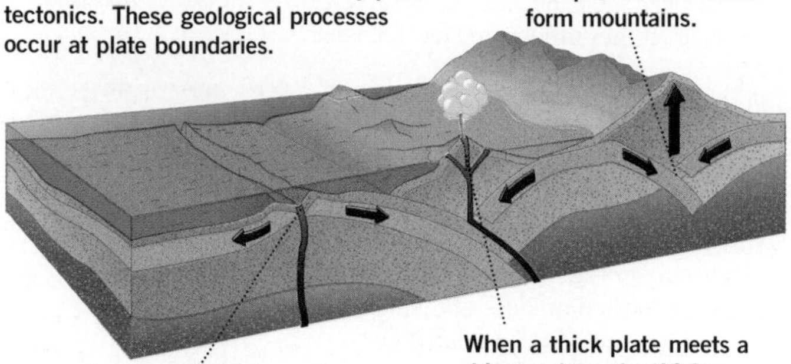

Two plates collide and form mountains.

As two plates spread apart on the ocean floor, molten material surfaces, solidifies, and becomes new land.

When a thick plate meets a thinner plate, the thicker plate falls beneath, resulting in earthquakes and volcanoes.

EVERYDAY BIOLOGY

Strolling Across the Ocean

The land bridge that formed between Asia and Alaska was probably the route followed by the first human settlers of North and South America. Scientists think this crossing took place 50,000 years ago.

FIGURE 11.17 (continued)

---

instances of significant global warming in history. These changes made Antarctica subtropical in the past. In extreme contrast, Earth was much colder during an ice age just 15,000 years ago. At that time, glaciers containing an enormous amount of water covered much of the land. As a result, the seas were shallower and the coastlines around continents extended farther out than they do today.

Life changes Plate tectonics is one factor affecting the pattern of Earth's speciation—the evolution of one species into many separate species. The movement of continents would have isolated some species from others. For example, Australia has some of the most unique life-forms on the planet. It probably comes as no surprise that Australia is also the continent that has been isolated the

---

longest from other land masses on Earth.

The isolation of species was only one factor that affected evolution. Migration can also significantly affect a population's gene pool. Land bridges between Alaska and Asia and between North and South America allowed species to migrate. The camel is an example of a species that migrated across land bridges. The fossil record indicates that camels' ancestors first lived in North America and then spread to South America and Asia. In South America, the population evolved into the present-day llama. The camel's ancestors in Asia evolved into today's camel. In North America, the camel's ancestors eventually became extinct.

Climate changes and land movements are responsible for much of the speciation on Earth. Without the fossil record, however, this information would be difficult to obtain.

ISSUES IN BIOLOGY

Mass extinctions

The fossil record reveals the existence of many life-forms that are no longer with us. The dinosaurs are the most famous example, but many species have become extinct over time. Scientists have identified five mass extinctions, periods when a majority of species were eliminated.

These mass extinctions could have had different causes. One of the earliest—the Permian extinction at the

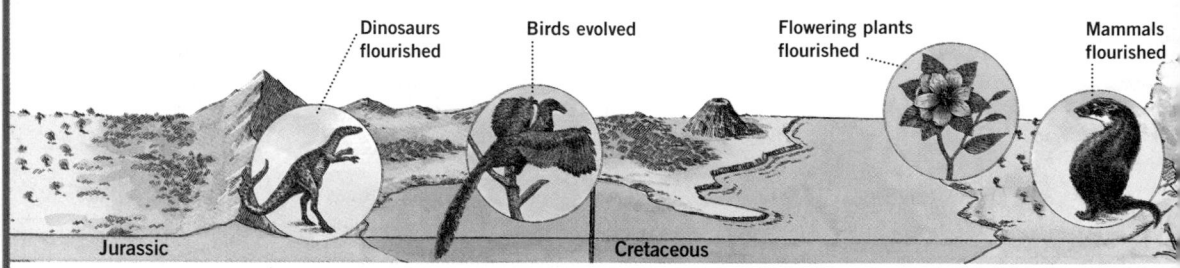

Dinosaurs flourished   Birds evolved   Flowering plants flourished   Mammals flourished

Jurassic   Cretaceous

272   *Unit 3 Change and Diversity*

Gifted Tectonic plates form different types of boundaries when they meet. Have gifted students research the differences between divergent boundaries, transform boundaries, and the various types of convergent boundaries. Ask students to construct clay models to show the different formations that can result at each type of plate boundary. You may wish to have them include photographs of landforms that illustrate each boundary type.

end of the Permian period—occurred 250 million years ago. More than 90 percent of the ocean animal species were eliminated. Many land insects also perished. What could have caused this massive destruction?

One theory is based on the fact that the Permian extinction occurred at about the same time that the continents came together to form Pangaea. The combining of the continents eliminated many water habitats, accounting for the extinction of much of the sea life. At the same time, volcanoes were unusually active. The resulting changes in the atmosphere, such as cooling due to ash in the air, may have resulted in the extinction of many land organisms.

The Cretaceous mass extinction, 65 million years ago, is best known for the elimination of the dinosaurs. Many other species in the sea and on land also disappeared at this time.

An intriguing explanation for the Cretaceous mass extinction is that it was caused by a large comet or asteroid striking Earth. This hypothesis is supported by the existence of a layer of material in Earth's crust that is common in extraterrestrial debris but uncommon elsewhere. This layer is located at the same place in the fossil record as the Cretaceous extinction. In addition, an exceedingly large crater, possibly caused by the impact of a comet or asteroid, has been found that dates back to this time.

Many scientists hypothesize that the amount of dust released into the

air from the impact of a comet or asteroid would be enough to darken the sky for years, drastically affecting photosynthetic organisms. As a result, the entire food chain would be disrupted, causing the extinction of many species, including dinosaurs.

Not all theories account for the dinosaurs' dying out so suddenly. Changes in the environment from increased volcanic activity and

LAB ZONE Do It! bioSURF

How Did Plate Tectonics Result in Speciation?

Because the continents move around on plates, many populations separated and evolved into different species. You can better understand how this occurred if you . . .

Try This

1 Review the relationship between Earth's plates and its molten core.
2 Design a model of the movement of plates on Earth's core. Your model should show how mountains form when plates collide.
3 Model a population located on two plates that are together. Then make the plates separate.

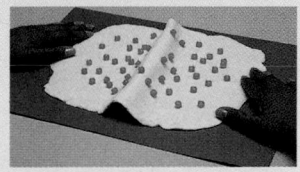

Analyze Your Results

1 How do colliding plates result in mountains? Based on your model, why do earthquakes occur at the boundary between plates?
2 Why does speciation occur when plates move, causing continents to move together or apart?

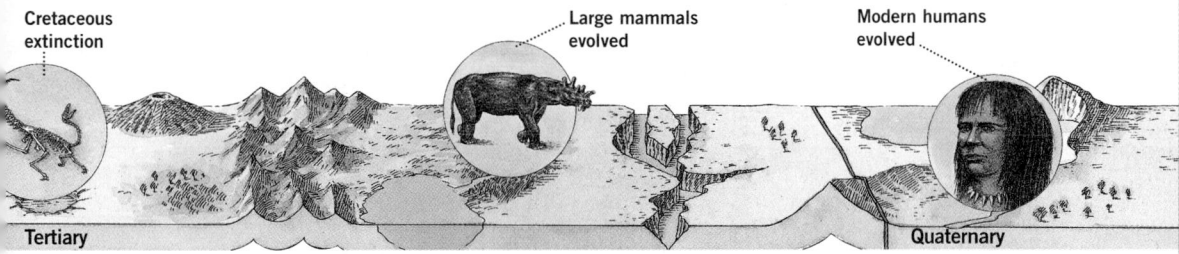

Cretaceous extinction

Large mammals evolved

Modern humans evolved

Tertiary

Quaternary

Chapter 11 The History of Life **273**

LAB ZONE Do It! TEAM WORK

How Did Plate Tectonics Result in Speciation?

You may wish to provide students with papier mâché or clay for their models. Challenge them to determine how changing the rigidity or thickness of part of the model affects the results.

Analyze Your Results

1 The plates compress and buckle at the point of impact, creating mountains. If the plates do not buckle upward, the collision or rubbing of the plates can cause an earthquake.
2 Species become isolated from each other. They may adapt to their new environments in different ways. Over time, such adaptations may result in new species.

Think Critically

To relate geologic changes and a change in the life-forms that exist on Earth, ask:

■ **Why do geologic changes often accompany mass extinctions?** (Geologic changes can cause major environmental changes in temperature and rainfall. Because organisms are adapted to specific environments, they may not survive the altered environment.)

MULTICULTURAL PERSPECTIVE

In 1975, Nobel Prize-winning geochemist Harold C. Urey first suggested that the impact of a comet caused the Cretaceous mass extinction. Hispanic planetary geologist, Adriana Ocampo, agrees with his hypothesis. To find supporting data, she has conducted field research in the Yucatan peninsula of Mexico, the area on Earth where she believes the impact occurred. At the Jet Propulsion Laboratory of NASA where she works, Ocampo also has been involved in projects designed to gather data about features of planets in the solar system and why the features exist.

ASSESS

Evaluate Understanding

List the names of selected geologic periods on the board from oldest to most recent. Have students copy this information on a clean sheet of paper. Next to each period, ask students to identify and describe one significant event that took place during that period. Review responses as a class.

Reteach

Together with students create a concept map or time line that identifies and shows the relationships among the major eras, periods, and epochs of geologic time from the most recent to the most distant. Ask volunteers to list significant changes in the history of life that are associated with each segment of geologic time. Record their responses and add to the list as necessary. Have students copy this information in their notebooks.

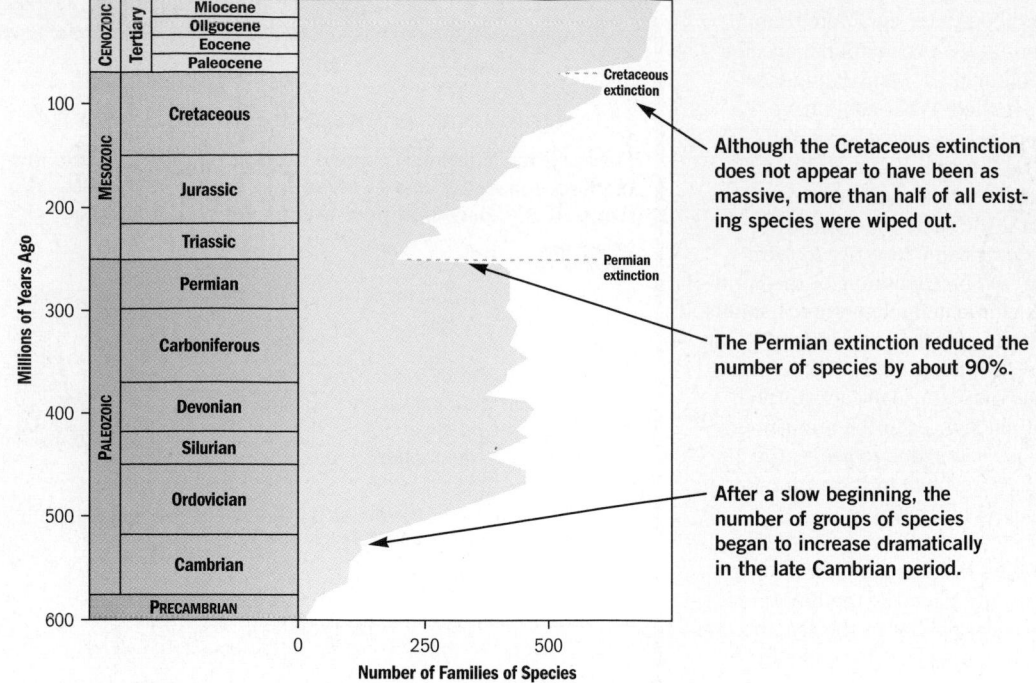

FIGURE 11.21
Over time, the number of species on Earth has changed and many species have become extinct. Which two mass exinctions are labeled? ❶

continental movement could have radically changed the dinosaurs' ability to survive. Evidence to support one of these theories needs to come from a careful examination of the fossil record. If the dinosaurs disappeared quickly from the fossil record, then it is likely that a single catastrophic event, such as an asteroid crash, was responsible. If the fossil record indicates a slow decline of the dinosaurs, then climate changes were more likely the cause of extinction.

Whatever the cause, all mass extinctions resulted in the adaptive radiation of the species that survived. The species that survived a mass extinction faced much less competition. The availability of new niches

after mass extinctions probably sparked the evolution of many species, including primates.

CHECKPOINT 11.3

1. Explain how multicellular organisms emerged from unicellular life.
2. How did plate tectonics and mass extinctions result in speciation?
3. **Critical Thinking** Why was there increased volcanic activity during the Permian extinction?

Build on What You Know

4. Why can adaptive radiation occur after mass extinctions? *(Need to jog your memory? Revisit relevant concepts in Chapter 10, Section 10.4.)*

How have our planet and the organisms that inhabit it changed over time?

274 *Unit 3 Change and Diversity*

CHECKPOINT 11.3

1. Unicellular, eukaryotic cells assembled into colonies. As the colonies became more organized and interdependent, they became multicellular organisms.
2. Plate tectonics separated populations which then evolved into separate species. Mass extinctions created new niches for new species to fill.
3. **Developing a hypothesis** The increased movements of the continental plates caused increased volcanic activity.
4. Mass extinctions create niches that can be populated by other species.

❶ Permian extinction and Cretaceous extinction

Chapter 11 Review

 **11.1** Evidence indicates that organic molecules and cells may have formed spontaneously on ancient Earth.
11.2–11.3 Our planet and the organisms that inhabit it have changed greatly over time.

Sum It Up

Use the following summary to review the main concepts in this chapter.

11.1 Earth's Early History

- Between 5 and 4.5 billion years ago, Earth formed when dust and rocks in the solar system condensed.
- Earth's early atmosphere differed from today's in many ways, such as the absence of both oxygen and a protective ozone layer.
- The seas that formed from condensed water vapor contained dissolved minerals and gases.
- Most scientists agree that the origin of life required the completion of four steps: simple organic molecules, polymers, protocells and cells.

11.2 The First Organisms

- Radioactive isotopes are used to determine the age of fossils.
- The oldest-known fossils are from bacteria that lived 3.5 billion years ago.
- As heterotrophs multiplied, they competed for a decreasing supply of organic nutrients. Around 2.5 billion years ago, autotrophs evolved that produced oxygen.

- Cells that could tolerate oxygen evolved into the first aerobes.
- The first eukaryotes evolved about 1.5 billion years ago.

11.3 History of Living Things

- Scientists theorize that multicellular organisms evolved from colonies of eukaryotic cells.
- Terrestrial organisms evolved about 450 million years ago. Adaptations for life on land included internal transport systems and methods to conserve water.
- The locations of Earth's continents have changed over time. Land movements and climate changes are major causes of speciation on Earth.
- Mass extinctions resulted in the adaptive radiation of surviving species.

Use Terms and Concepts

Use each of the following words or terms in a complete sentence. If you need to review a meaning, turn to the page indicated.

microspheres (p. 260)   eras (p. 268)
half-life (p. 263)   periods (p. 268)
stromatolites (p. 266)   epochs (p. 268)
endosymbiosis (p. 267)   plate tectonics (p. 271)

Review the Big Ideas

Before students begin the Chapter Review, you may wish to discuss main concepts from The Big Ideas in Chapter 11. Point out that paleontologists have found evidence that indicates organic molecules and cells may have formed spontaneously on Earth. Fossil studies and the study of the composition of early rock indicate that Earth and its organisms changed greatly over geologic time and that Earth's first organisms were prokaryotes. Many scientists believe that over millions of years some early prokaryotes evolved into eukaryotic cells capable of independent life.

Answers

1. stromatolites
2. epochs
3. microspheres
4. plate tectonics
5. eras
6. half–life
7. endosymbiosis
8. False; Stromatolites
9. False; half–life
10. True
11. False; microspheres
12. True
13. True
14. Concentrations of monomers could have used the crystal structure as a template.
15. An ozone layer would have absorbed ultraviolet radiation, one of the energy sources needed for chemical evolution of organic molecules.
16. Volcanic eruptions, earthquakes, and mountain formations.
17. Energy from lightning and ultraviolet radiation might have sparked random reactions of chemicals in water, which would have eventually produced organic molecules; meteorites might have brought organic chemicals to Earth.
18. Unicellular organisms living in colonies could have begun to specialize and to lose their ability to survive independently.
19. Oxygen would have reacted with and destroyed the newly–formed anaerobes.
20. Era is divided into <u>periods</u> which are divided into <u>epochs</u>. Era includes Precambrian which is distinguished by <u>stromatolites</u> and <u>prokaryotes</u> formed from <u>protocells</u> formed from <u>polymers</u> formed from

---

Use Your Word Power

COMPLETION **Write the word or phrase that best completes each statement.**

1. When colonies of bacteria fossilize, they can form _____ .

2. On the geological time scale, periods are divided into _____ .

3. When certain protein molecules are mixed with water, they form _____ .

4. The movement of the Earth's continents over time is caused by _____ .

5. The longest time spans in the geologic time scale are called _____ .

6. The time it takes for half the isotopes in a sample to decay is called its _____ .

7. According to the _____ hypothesis, organelles were once independent prokaryotes.

TRUE-FALSE **Write true if the statement is true. If the statement is false, replace the underlined word(s) to make the statement true.**

8. <u>Microspheres</u> contain remains of the earliest known prokaryotes.

9. The <u>epoch</u> of potassium-40 is 1.3 billion years.

10. <u>Plate tectonics</u> causes earthquakes and volcanic eruptions.

11. <u>Stromatolites</u> provide a model for the evolution of a cell membrane.

12. The presence of DNA in some organelles supports the <u>endosymbiosis</u> hypothesis.

13. An explosive increase in biodiversity separates the Precambrian and Cambrian <u>periods</u>.

Show What You Know

14. Explain how clay crystals might have contributed to the formation of polymers.

15. How could the absence of an ozone layer have affected conditions on Earth billions of years ago?

16. What are some of the changes caused by plate tectonics?

17. Summarize the two scientific theories that explain the origin of Earth's organic molecules.

18. What role might colonies have played in the evolution of multicellular organisms?

19. How did atmospheric oxygen alter the evolution of primitive life?

20. **Make a Concept Map** Complete the concept map below by adding the following terms: periods, epochs, stromatolites, microspheres, monomers, polymers, protocells, prokaryotes.

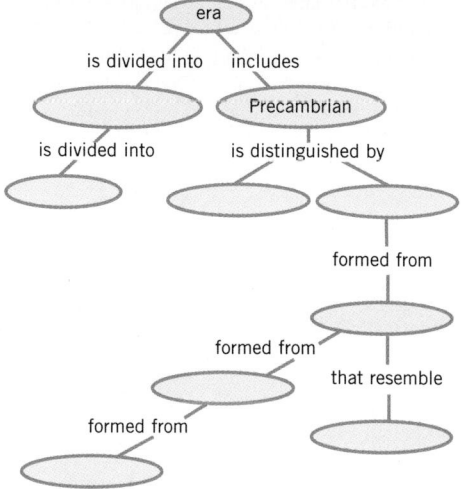

Take It Further

21. **Developing a Hypothesis** When Earth's atmosphere first began to form, hydrogen (H_2) was the most abundant element in the solar system. However, there is very little H_2 in the atmosphere today, and the element makes up less than 1 percent of Earth's mass. What might have happened to the H_2? **Hint:** Review Figure 11.4, and research the uses of H_2 and the chemical compounds in which H_2 can occur.

---

monomers. Protocells resemble <u>microspheres</u>.

21. Answers will vary. Hydrogen might have reacted with sulfur to form hydrogen sulfide; carbon to form methane; or oxygen to form water vapor. Hydrogen might have escaped Earth's gravitational field because it is so light.

22. The Burgess Shale contains vast numbers of previously unknown Cambrian fossils. The marine invertebrates were deposited in layers of sediment on the ocean floor, which were lifted up during the formation of the Rockies. The Canadian Shield uplift occurred as a result of plate tectonics.

23. The meteorite's age matches the age of life on Earth. Life might have been car-

22. Analyzing Data In 1909 Charles Walcott found fossils on the Burgess Shale of the Canadian Rockies. Explain how fossils of bottom-dwelling sea creatures half a billion years old were found 2 kilometers above sea level.

23. Analyzing Data A meteorite contains evidence that life may have begun about 3.5 billion years ago. Explain how this data could support Crick's hypothesis about the origin of life. Suggest an alternate interpretation of the data that could support Oparin's hypothesis about the chemical origin of life.

24. Identifying Cause and Effect Could the first aerobes have evolved before the first autotrophs? Explain your answer.

25. Applying Concepts Could radiocarbon dating be used to accurately determine the age of dinosaur fossils? Explain your answer.

26. Designing an Experiment Describe an experiment to test one of the hypotheses explaining how polymers formed. What differences between modern and ancient Earth environments would you need to address?

27. Interpreting a Graph The graph below summarizes changes in the amount of atmospheric oxygen since life first appeared on Earth. What evolutionary events occurred at the arrows? Explain your answer.

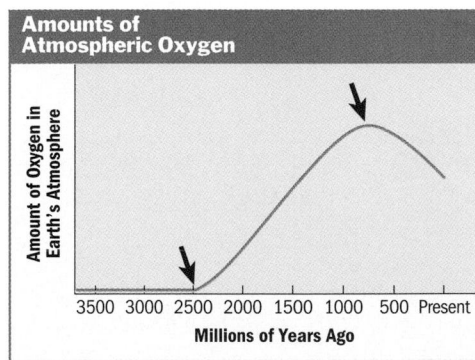

Amounts of Atmospheric Oxygen

Amount of Oxygen in Earth's Atmosphere

3500 3000 2500 2000 1500 1000 500 Present

Millions of Years Ago

Consider the Issues

28. New Model Resisted In 1915 the German meteorologist Alfred Wegener proposed a theory of continental drift. He concluded that fossils of certain reptiles found only in South Africa and Brazil (see below) supported his theory. His idea was rejected until the 1960s, when evidence of sea-floor spreading was found. Consult Figure 11.22. Why was Wegener's model rejected? Research Wegener's work and decide whether or not his theory was criticized fairly. Present your decision in the form of a "news report."

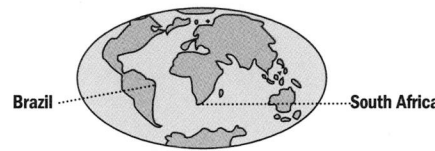

Brazil · South Africa

Make New Connections

29. Biology and Art Refer to Figure 11.17 and make a large geological time line for your classroom. As you study Units 3–7, add evolutionary events to the time line.

30. Biology and Creative Writing Imagine the world as it might be if autotrophs had not evolved. What would Earth be like? What types of organisms would exist? Would humans have evolved?

FAST-FORWARD TO CHAPTER 12

In Chapter 11, you learned about the history of life on Earth. In Chapter 12, you will focus on the evolution of the primates, including monkeys, apes, and humans.

Chapter 11 The History of Life **277**

autotrophs, which begin to produce oxygen as a by-product of photosynthesis. The autotrophs produce more oxygen than they use. The second arrow marks the evolution of aerobes, which use up some of the excess oxygen.

28. Answers will vary. Scientists may have thought that the fossils in two such separated environments were not enough to support his theory. No logical explanation for the distance between the continents was developed. You may want to discuss Thomas Kuhn's landmark book, *The Structure of Scientific Revolutions,* first published in 1962.

29. Have groups of students select specific geologic periods to illustrate and then assemble the sections into one class time line.

30. Answers will vary, but students should note that Earth's atmosphere would probably not contain significant amounts of oxygen, and that organisms would probably be heterotrophic.

ried to Earth from another body in outer space. To support Oparin, life might have evolved independently on Earth and on another planet.

24. The first aerobes needed the oxygen produced by the first autotrophs.

25. No, dinosaurs became extinct around 65 million years ago. Radiocarbon dating only works for fossils less than 50,000 years old.

26. Answers will vary. Solutions of simple organic molecules could be evaporated slowly under an atmosphere that replicated the atmosphere of early Earth. Students should address the gases present in the atmosphere and the energy sources available on ancient Earth.

27. The first arrow marks the evolution of

PLANNING GUIDE

Section	Student Activities/Features	Teacher's Resource Package
12.1 Primates **Objectives** ■ Summarize the evolutionary history of primates ■ Compare the characteristic traits of the different types of primates	**Lab Zone Discover It!** *Analyzing Adaptations,* p. 279 **Everyday Biology** *Big Ape!* p. 284 **Lab Zone Investigate It!** *Comparing Genetic Relationships,* p. 285	**Unit 3 Review Module** ■ Section Review 12.1 ■ Activity Recordsheet 12-1 **Laboratory Manual,** Lab 22: "Comparison of Primates"
12.2 Hominids **Objectives** ■ Identify various hominid species and the time periods in which they existed ■ Compare the characteristics of major hominid groups	**Lab Zone Think About It!** *Hominid Origins,* p. 288	**Unit 3 Review Module** ■ Section Review 12.2 ■ Interpreting Graphics 12 ■ Critical Thinking Exercise 12 **Interpreting and Developing Graphics,** 34, 35, 36
12.3 Homo sapiens **Objectives** ■ Compare and contrast Neanderthals, Cro-Magnons, and modern *Homo sapiens* ■ Evaluate hypotheses about the origin and distribution of modern *Homo sapiens*	**Lab Zone Do It!** *Modeling Archaeological Activity,* p. 291 **Everyday Biology** *What is Race?* p. 292 **STS: Issues in Biology** *Difficulties in Interpretation,* p. 294 **In the Community** *The Big Dig,* p. 294	**Unit 3 Review Module** ■ Section Review 12.3 ■ Activity Recordsheet 12-2 ■ Enrichment Topic 12-1 ■ Vocabulary Review 12 ■ Chapter 12 Tests **Consumer Applications** 12-1 **Issues and Decision Making** 12-1 **Spanish Reviews** Chapter 12

Technology Resources

Internet Connections

Within this chapter, you will see the bioSURF logo. If you and your students have access to the Internet, the following URL address will provide various Internet connections that are related to topics and features presented in this chapter:

http://evolution.biosurf.com

You can also find relevant chapter material at **The Biology Place** address:

http://www.biology.com

CD-ROMs

Biología: la telaraña de la vida,
   (Spanish Student Edition) Chapter 12
Teacher's Resource Planner, Chapter 12
   Supplements
TestWorks CD-ROM
■ Chapter 12 Tests

Overhead Transparencies

■ Hominid Species, #25

Videotapes

Biology Alive! Video Series
Rewind: The Web of Life Reteach Videos

Planning for Activities

STUDENT EDITION
Lab Zone
Discover It! p. 279
■ pennies
■ pencil
■ paper

Lab Zone
Investigate It! p. 285
■ graph paper

Lab Zone Do It! p. 291
■ 25 pieces from a 250-
   piece jigsaw puzzle

TEACHER'S EDITION
Quick Activity, p. 280
Dextrous hands
■ small objects: paper
   clips, pens, or coins

Teacher Demo, p. 281
Opposable thumb
■ horizontal bar or a
   broom handle

Class Activity, p. 282
Binocular vision
■ any small object

Teacher Demo, p. 283
*Distinguishing between
monkeys and apes*
■ pictures of monkeys and
   apes

Quick Activity, p. 286
Digging for buried objects
■ small containers
■ sand
■ keys, coins, and pottery

Teacher Demo, p. 290
*Neanderthals or Cro-
Magnons*
■ drawings or cartoons
   that depict ancestors of
   modern humans

Chapter Objectives

Students will learn the main concepts of this chapter as they complete the following objectives.

- Summarize the evolutionary history of primates
- Compare the characteristic traits of the different types of primates
- Identify various hominid species and the time period in which they existed
- Compare the characteristics of major hominid groups
- Compare and contrast Neanderthals, Cro-Magnons, and modern *Homo sapiens*
- Evaluate hypotheses about the origin and distribution of modern *Homo sapiens*

Key Words

12.1 *primates, prosimian, anthropoids, opposable thumb, binocular vision, prehensile tail*

12.2 *hominids, bipedal*

The Opening Story

Have students discuss how they think the story relates to the content of this chapter. Ask students to share what they know about the fossil remains discovered in the East African digs of British archaeologists Louis and Mary Leakey. Mary Leakey, one of the world's foremost paleoarchaelogists, died in 1996 at the age of 83.

CHAPTER 12

Human History

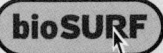

You can find out more about human evolution by exploring the following Internet address:
http://evolution.biosurf.com

In this chapter . . .

FEATURES

Everyday Biology
- Big Ape!
- What Is Race?

In the Community
The Big Dig

 Issues in Biology
Difficulties in Interpretation

LAB ZONES

Discover It!
- Analyzing Adaptations

Do It!
- Modeling Archaeological Activity

Think About It!
- Hominid Origins

Investigate It!
- Comparing Genetic Relationships

First steps

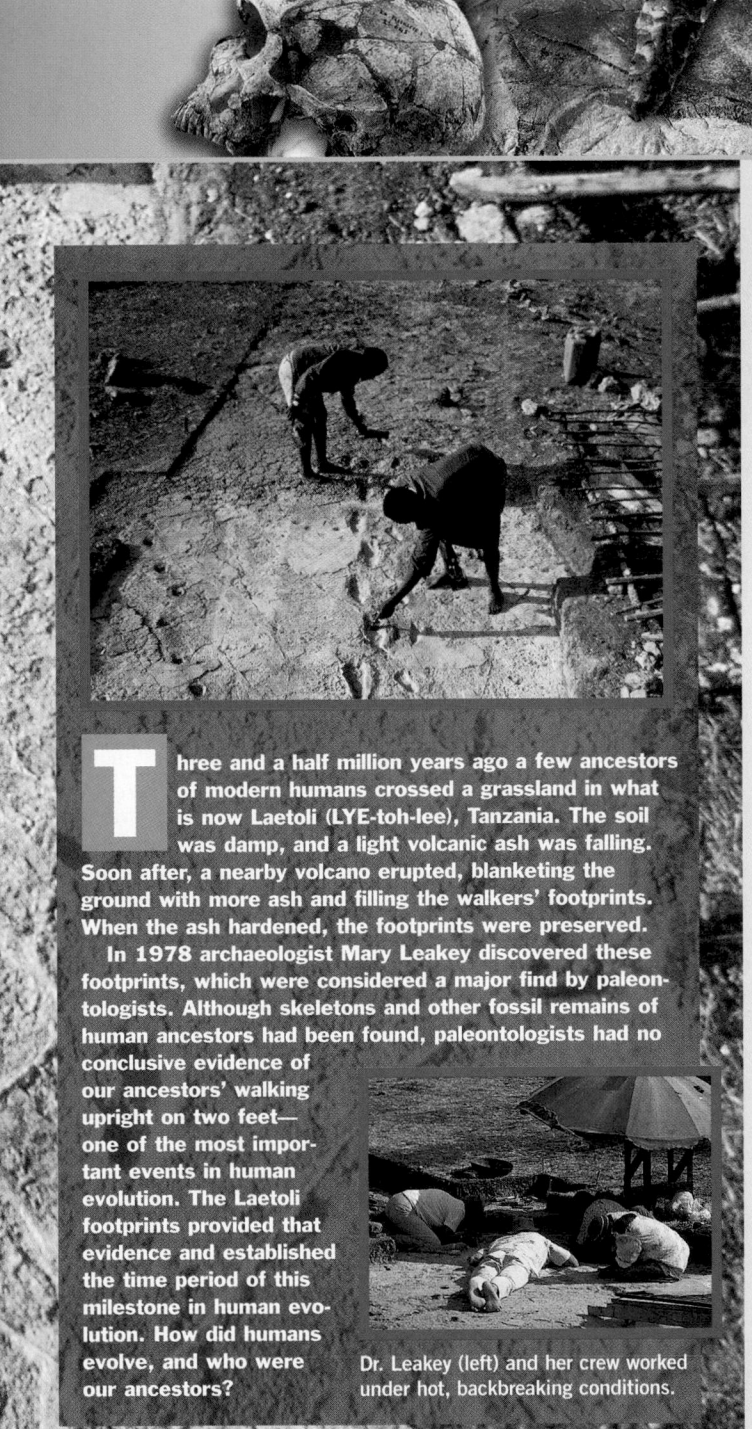

LAB ZONE Discover It!

Analyzing Adaptations

You need pennies

1. Place a few pennies on your desk. Try to pick up the pennies with your hand closed into a fist.
2. Pick up the pennies as you usually would. Observe how you use your thumb when picking up the pennies. Record your observations.

Walking on two legs freed the ancestors of humans to use their hands and eventually to fashion and use tools. In what other ways might the use of hands have affected human evolution? What other animals have thumbs that are similar to those of humans? What can these animals do that cannot be done by animals lacking this type of thumb?

T hree and a half million years ago a few ancestors of modern humans crossed a grassland in what is now Laetoli (LYE-toh-lee), Tanzania. The soil was damp, and a light volcanic ash was falling. Soon after, a nearby volcano erupted, blanketing the ground with more ash and filling the walkers' footprints. When the ash hardened, the footprints were preserved.

In 1978 archaeologist Mary Leakey discovered these footprints, which were considered a major find by paleontologists. Although skeletons and other fossil remains of human ancestors had been found, paleontologists had no conclusive evidence of our ancestors' walking upright on two feet— one of the most important events in human evolution. The Laetoli footprints provided that evidence and established the time period of this milestone in human evolution. How did humans evolve, and who were our ancestors?

Dr. Leakey (left) and her crew worked under hot, backbreaking conditions.

WRITE ABOUT IT!

Imagine that your footprints are discovered 3.5 million years from now. In your science journal, describe the conclusions that archaeologists might draw, based on your footprints. What additional information would enable future archaeologists to reconstruct accurately a typical day of your life?

Opening Activities

bioSURF If you have access to the Internet in your classroom or school, you may wish to have students connect to the address shown on page 278. You may also want to have students conduct net searches using key words related to this chapter. For example, they could search for entries under *Homo erectus*, Neanderthals, or Louis and Mary Leakey.

LAB ZONE Discover It!

Analyzing Adaptations   **TEAM WORK**

Before students begin the chapter, have them do the activity with a partner. Suggest the partners watch each other pick up the pennies and record their observations. As a class, discuss the questions in the activity.

WRITE ABOUT IT!

Suggest that students record their conclusions from the perspective of an archaeologist. Students should base their observations on the footprints they would leave.

REWIND to Chapter 11

Briefly review with students concepts they learned in Chapter 11, *The History of Life.* Ask:

- **What evidence indicates to scientists that living things changed over time?**

PORTFOLIO PREVIEW

Students should be encouraged to add to their portfolios as they work through this chapter. In addition to the *Write About It* opportunity, the following sections are excellent opportunities for portfolio entries.

- Section 12.1: *Primates*
- Section 12.2: *Hominids*
- Section 12.3: *Homo sapiens*

ENGAGE

Consider The Big Idea

Have students read The Big Idea! at the top of the page. Discuss how the ability to use tools identifies humans as primates.

Use the Visual

Have students study the photograph that opens the section. Explain that tree shrews are the smallest of all mammals. Ask:

- **What primate characteristics can you observe in the tree shrew?** (Eyes in the front of its head and dexterous hands)

Check Prior Knowledge

To assess students' knowledge about primates, ask:

- **What factors could affect the evolution of one species into separate species?** (Plate tectonics, migration, climate, and environmental changes)

Quick Activity

Have students scatter small objects such as paper clips, pens, or coins. Challenge them to pick up the objects without using their fingers or thumbs. Explain that animals with dexterous hands can use their fingers and thumbs to manipulate objects. Ask:

- **How might hand dexterity help an animal obtain food?** (Allows animal to gather food and carry it to a safe place for eating or storage)

THE BIG IDEA! Primates are mammals with binocular vision and dexterous hands and arms. 12.1

12.1 Primates

What you'll learn

IDEAS
- To summarize the evolutionary history of primates
- To compare the characteristic traits of the different types of primates

WORDS
primates, prosimian, anthropoids, opposable thumb, binocular vision, prehensile tail

Small mammal makes good
While dinosaurs roamed Earth, small mammals were creeping around the dinosaurs. The first primates may have resembled the small, insect-eating tree shrew (right) currently found in Southeast Asia and India. Weighing less than half a kilogram, the primate's small size and nocturnal habits help keep it out of harm's way.

THE EVOLUTION OF PRIMATES

A chip off the old block

The oldest mammal fossils date back to the Triassic period (220 million years ago). Mammals are thought to have evolved from small, active, meat-eating reptiles. Fossil evidence linking the reptiles to mammals includes similarities in their skulls, jaws, and teeth.

The mass extinctions at the end of the Cretaceous period mark the beginning of a surge of adaptive radiation in many species. About 65 million years ago, following the dinosaur extinctions, the number of mammal species increased greatly. The oldest primate fossils date from about this time. The **primates** (PRY-mayts) are a group of mammals that includes all monkeys, apes, and humans.

According to the fossil evidence, the earliest primates were similar to the tree shrew shown above. Although

FIGURE 12.1

All modern primates evolved from a common ancestor between 65 and 55 million years ago. Which primates are prosimians? Which are anthropoids? ❶

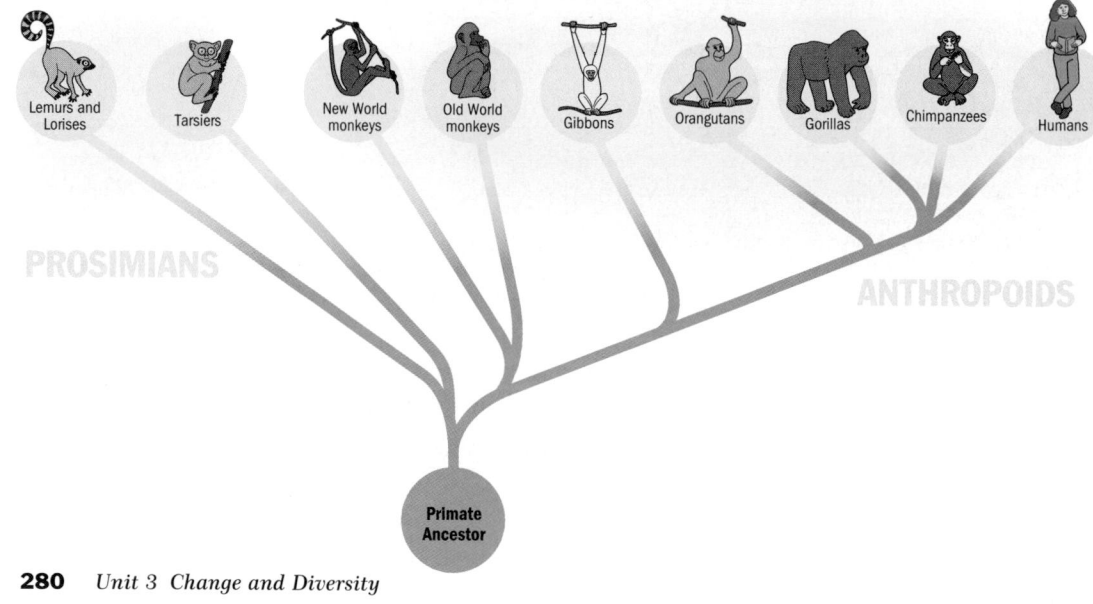

PROSIMIANS

Lemurs and Lorises | Tarsiers | New World monkeys | Old World monkeys | Gibbons | Orangutans | Gorillas | Chimpanzees | Humans

ANTHROPOIDS

Primate Ancestor

STUDENT RESOURCES

From the Teacher's Resource Package, use:
- Section Review 12.1 and Activity Recordsheet 12-1 from Unit 3 Review Module
- Lab 22: "Comparison of Primates"

TECHNOLOGY RESOURCES

Relevant technology resources include:
- Spanish Student Edition CD-ROM
- Teacher's Resource Planner CD-ROM

the early primates' overall anatomy resembles that of a shrew, fossil evidence also shows some characteristics common to later primates.

Early primates are thought to have evolved into two groups, the prosimians and the anthropoids. A **prosimian** (proh-SIM-ee-un) is a small, monkey-like primate with large, forward-facing eyes. Prosimian means "pre-monkey." Modern prosimians probably resemble the primates' earliest ancestors. **Anthropoids** (AN-thruh-poydz) are humanlike primates, and include monkeys, apes, and humans. Anthropoid means "humanlike." Scientists use these terms to describe both modern and extinct primates.

There are nine groups of primates living today, as you can see in *Figure 12.1*. Evidence indicates that the two types of prosimians first evolved about 55 million years ago. The ancestral anthropoids, however, evolved into many different groups. Most scientists agree that the earliest anthropoids evolved from a common prosimian ancestor some 50 million years ago. However, which prosimians evolved into the anthropoids is still under debate.

Adaptive radiation may have resulted in the formation of separate anthropoid groups. One group, the New World monkeys, evolved on the American continents. The other groups, including the Old World monkeys and the apes, evolved on the African, Asian, and European continents. Because large bodies of water isolated these populations, these two primate groups evolved separately.

Chimpanzees, gorillas, orangutans, and gibbons are modern examples of apes. Evidence indicates that the gibbons have been on Earth the longest, around 35 million years. The most recent primates—orangutans, gorillas, chimpanzees, and humans—are thought to have evolved from a

common ancestor between 8 and 5 million years ago. Because of their shared evolutionary histories, all primates share some common traits.

Most of our knowledge about primate evolution comes from the fossil record. But the fossil record is incomplete, leaving gaps in our knowledge. One reason for the incomplete fossil record of primates is that many primate ancestors lived in tropical forests, and fossils are not readily preserved in acidic tropical soils.

Genetic research has helped fill in some gaps. As you read in Chapter 10, scientists can analyze genetic material to clarify relationships between species. Scientists can compare differences between specific base sequences to infer how long ago two organisms split from a common ancestor. For example, through genetic similarities, scientists know much about the evolutionary relationship between humans and chimpanzees. As more is learned about the genes of primates, the picture of their evolution becomes more complete.

FIGURE 12.2
What adaptation to primate environments is visible here? ❷

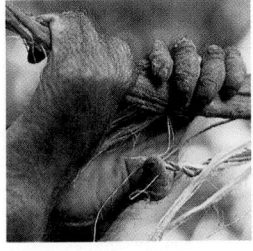

FIGURE 12.3
With an opposable thumb and long flexible fingers, primates have a strong, secure grip. Why might this be important? ❸

CHARACTERISTICS OF PRIMATES

Mammals swing!

Scientists agree that the first primates lived in trees, because most modern primates have adaptations to such an environment. *Figures 12.2* through *12.5* show several of these adaptations. Although humans do not spend their lives in trees, we have many features associated with a tree-dwelling life.

Make a fist and observe the directions your fingers point. Like other primates, you have an **opposable thumb,** a digit that can be placed in the opposite direction from the other

Chapter 12 Human History **281**

❶ Prosimians: lemurs and lorises, tarsiers; Anthropoids: monkeys, apes, humans
❷ Opposable thumbs that enable primates to grip trees and free arm movement around the shoulder joint, which enables hand-to-hand swinging
❸ The grip enables them to grasp branches firmly and live in trees.

Class Activity

Work with students to develop a Venn diagram showing the relationship among primates, prosimian groups, anthropoids, Old World monkeys, apes, New World monkeys, shrews, and humans. Have students add more information to the diagram as they complete this section.

Discuss

On a world map, identify the regions in the Old World and New World where groups of monkeys evolved after the landmasses separated. Ask:

■ **What factors contributed to separate evolution of the two groups of monkeys?** (They were separated geographically by large bodies of water, the gene pool narrowed, and each group adapted to its environment.)

Teacher Demo

Bring a baseball bat, hockey stick, or similar item to class. Ask students to compare the way they grip the bat or stick with the way some primates grip tree limbs. Emphasize the role of the opposable thumb in enabling them to grasp objects. Have students suggest other activities that demonstrate the use of an opposable thumb.

Class Activity

Have students focus on a small object at a distance. Tell them to view the object first with one eye, then with the other. Have them repeat several times, alternating eyes. Tell them to look at the object with both eyes. Ask:

- **What do you observe about the position of the object when you switch from one eye to the other?** (It seems to move slightly to the right or left.)
- **What is the position of the object when viewed with both eyes at the same time?** (Appears to be at midpoint between that seen with either eye)
- **What advantage does binocular vision provide?** (Better depth perception and judgment of distance)

Explain

Have students discuss how birds, dogs, and cats care for their young. Explain that the amount of time most animals spend raising offspring is relatively brief—a few weeks or months. Contrast this with the prolonged care primates give their offspring—three to five years for most. Explain that prolonged nurturing of offspring is a trait shared by most primates.

Build Writing Skills

Have students research the development and care needed by infant apes as they progress to full independence with that needed by human infants.

FIGURE 12.4
Primates like this slender loris have binocular vision, an adaptation that allows for accurate judging of distance and depth.

FIGURE 12.5
Prolonged and close care of offspring is a primate trait exhibited by orangutans. Young primates other than humans may spend as long as three to five years with their mothers before living on their own.

FIGURE 12.6
Like many species of New World monkeys, this capuchin monkey has a prehensile tail. What other primate characteristics does this animal have? ❶

four fingers. Look at the ends of your fingers. Like many primates, you have sensitive finger pads and protective nails, not claws. These structures enable primates to grip objects firmly, and to move and manipulate tiny objects. Like other primates, your arms move freely around the shoulder joint, an adaptation that allows swinging from hand-to-hand. All of these adaptations enable primates to move easily and securely in trees.

Most primates have excellent hand-eye coordination, which is enhanced by their binocular vision. With **binocular vision,** both eyes are used at once in overlapping fields, so that objects appear to have depth. Through the course of evolution, the long snout of the early primates flat-tened and the eyes migrated to the front of the face. The resulting binocular vision increased depth perception and allowed primates to judge distances accurately, an important adaptation when moving high above ground.

Primates share other traits as well. They have relatively large brains when compared to other mammals. Like humans, a few other species of primates have been observed making and using simple tools. For example, some chimpanzees know how to fashion a probe from a twig and use it to "fish" for termites. Others have been seen using a crumpled leaf as a simple sponge to retrieve drinking water from a deep hollow in a tree.

Many primates have complex social behaviors and strong family relationships. Typically primates attentively care for their young for a long time after birth. Extended parental care is important for life in the trees. Without the constant attention of a family member, a newborn that cannot swing or climb well would not survive long in the treetops.

DIVERSITY OF PRIMATES
More than a barrelful

Despite their common origin and similar traits, the primates are quite different from one another. The two primate groups—prosimian and anthropoid—are divided further according to physical traits and evolutionary relationships. Each type of primate, whether living or extinct, is characterized by specific traits.

Prosimians Like the loris shown in *Figure 12.4,* many prosimians are nocturnal, or active mostly at night. Their large eyes are an adaptation to their nighttime activities. Because fossils of the earliest primate ancestors also have large eye sockets, scientists suspect that they, too, were nocturnal.

Some prosimians are insect-eaters, as the first primates probably were. Other modern prosimians eat plants or fruit. Most prosimians are agile tree-climbers.

Today there are about 35 species of prosimians, including lemurs, lorises, and tarsiers. These primates live in the tropical forests of southeast Asia, India, Africa, and Madagascar. Of all modern prosimians, the lemurs of Madagascar most closely resemble the common primate ancestor, possibly because of their isolation from other primates on their island home. Habitat destruction threatens prosimians.

Anthropoids There are about 113 different species of anthropoids, including New World monkeys, Old World monkeys such as the Celebes macaques shown in *Figure 12.7,* and the apes. The terms Old World and New World were used by the first Europeans who came to the Americas. To them, the American continents were new. The terms are still used to describe these groups of primates, which show distinct differences.

The New World monkeys of Central and South America have broad, flat noses. A common trait of most New World monkeys is a long, prehensile tail. A **prehensile tail** (pree-HEN-sil) is composed of many muscles and can be used to grip branches while climbing. The tail acts as an extra hand as the animals move through the trees. Almost all New World monkeys are tree-dwelling and are active during the day. They are social animals, usually living in family groups of various sizes.

Old World monkeys can be found in Africa, southeast Asia, and the Philippines. They usually have long, prominent noses and short tails. Many Old World monkeys have brightly patterned fur, or brightly colored patches of skin on their face or rump. Although members of this

group typically spend most of their time on the ground, many are good climbers. Most are active during the day and live in groups. Compare the features of the Old World monkey shown in *Figure 12.7* to those of the New World monkey in *Figure 12.6.* How are they alike? How are they different?

Species of apes live in tropical forests of Africa, southeast Asia, Java, and Borneo. Almost all apes move about on the ground, although they are good tree climbers. Apes are different from other primates. Most apes are larger and more powerful than monkeys, with larger brains and no visible tails. Apes can spend more time upright than other primates, but like many primates, tend to move on four limbs when on the ground. Apes are typically vegetarians, although chimpanzees sometimes eat insects and small mammals.

Of all the anthropoids, the apes are most similar to humans. As you can see in *Figure 12.8,* some proteins in humans and chimpanzees are very similar. Biochemical analysis indicates that chimpanzees and gorillas are more closely related to us than they are to the other apes, the orangutans and the gibbons. In fact, the DNA of humans and chimpanzees differs by less than 3 percent, compelling evidence of an evolutionary connection.

② FIGURE 12.7
Old World monkeys include baboons, langurs, and macaques like these Celebes macaques of Indonesia. Macaques are social animals that live in family troops of various sizes.

Comparison of Human and Chimpanzee Proteins

Protein	Number of Amino Acids	Amino Acid Differences
Hemoglobin	579	1
Myoglobin	153	1
Cytochrome *c*	104	0
Serum albumin	580	7

FIGURE 12.8
Biochemically, there are very few differences between chimpanzees and humans, indicating a close evolutionary relationship.

Chapter 12 Human History **283**

Evaluate Understanding

Have students make a concept map that shows the evolution of the two main groups of primates from a common ancestor and the subgroups that make up each group. Beneath each subgroup, ask students to list the major characteristics of each group, including habitat, physical characteristics, and behavioral traits. Review the completed concept maps as a class.

Reteach

On an overhead transparency, redraw Figure 12.1, placing the common ancestor at the top and the group names below the lines showing divergences. Work with students to list the traits of each group. As you move along the evolutionary time line, emphasize the key differences used to distinguish groups. Have students copy the completed diagram into their notebooks for use as a study tool.

Everyday Biology

Discuss other ways in which humans compare with apes. Point out that with their large brains, apes are capable of learning a variety of behaviors. Also, the DNA sequences of humans resemble those of chimpanzees.

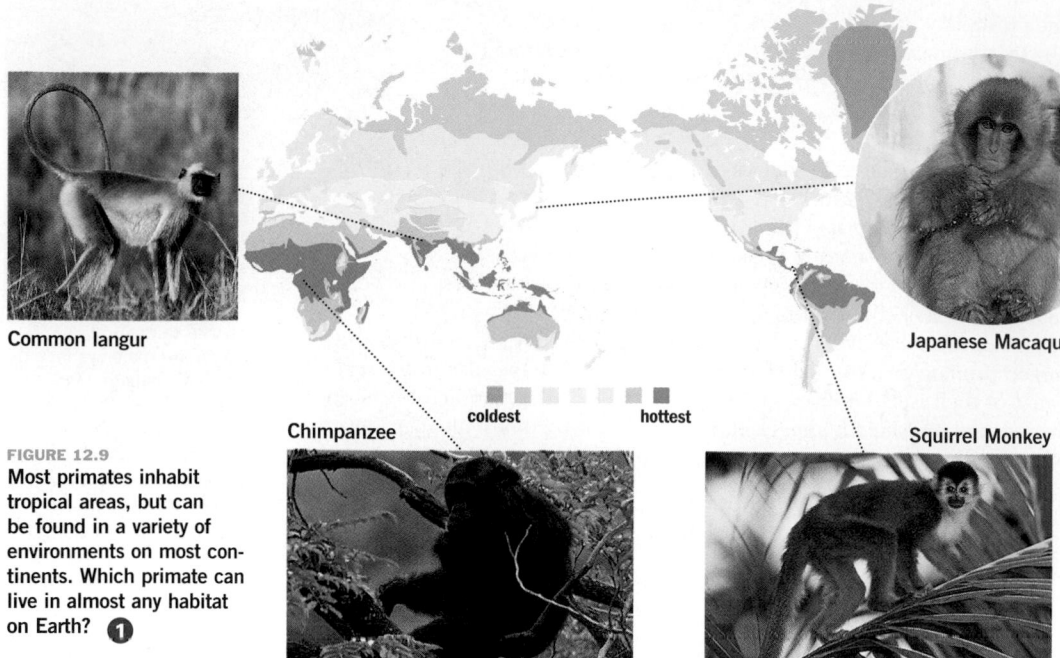

Common langur

Japanese Macaque

FIGURE 12.9
Most primates inhabit tropical areas, but can be found in a variety of environments on most continents. Which primate can live in almost any habitat on Earth? ❶

coldest ▪ ▪ ▪ ▪ ▪ ▪ hottest

Chimpanzee

Squirrel Monkey

EVERYDAY BIOLOGY

Big Ape!

The smallest ape, the gibbon, weighs about 5 kg. In contrast, the largest gorilla weighs about 270 kg. How do humans compare? The high end of the normal range for an adult male is about 125 kg.

Primates are a diverse group—physical appearance, behaviors, and habitats vary among species. Some of this diversity is shown in *Figure 12.9*. Most primates live in tropical areas of the world, although some species of Old World monkeys can tolerate mild winters. One primate—humans—can live in just about any region of the world. This is because of our ability to adjust to different environments and to change environments to fit our needs. Humans are the most adaptable of the primates. Despite these differences, all primates share some common characteristics which indicate common evolutionary origin.

CHECKPOINT 12.1

1. List the nine primate groups and the approximate time of their evolution.
2. What do most primates have in common?
3. **Critical Thinking** The gibbon least resembles the other apes. It is smaller and lives mostly in trees. What factors account for these differences? Why are gibbons still considered apes?

Build on What You Know

4. Humans have 46 chromosomes and chimpanzees have 48. Do these numbers indicate a close genetic relationship? Why or why not? *(Need to jog your memory? Revisit relevant concepts in Chapter 5, Section 5.3 and in Chapter 7, Section 7.5.)*

What traits do all primates have in common? Why is a human considered a primate?

CHECKPOINT 12.1

1. Lemurs and lorises, tarsiers, 55 million years ago; New World and Old World monkeys, 40 million years; gibbons, 35 million years; orangutans, gorillas, chimpanzees, humans, 8 to 5 million years
2. Opposable thumb, binocular vision, extended parental care

3. **Making generalizations** Students may identify factors that affect gene pools and infer that gibbons are genetically, biochemically, and physically similar to apes.
4. No, distantly related organisms can have the same number of chromosomes.

❶ Humans

Comparing Genetic Relationships

WHAT YOU WILL DO You will model how gene sequences can be used to determine evolutionary relationships.

SKILLS YOU WILL USE Predicting, observing, collecting and recording data

WHAT YOU WILL NEED Graph paper

Human
GCAGAGGAACCGCTACAAGAGCATACGCAAGAGCGGGT AGTAAAACCATACCTTAAATGGGGGGGCCACCTTCGGCG GATACTCTTTCAA

Gorilla
GAGGAGGAACCGCTACAAGAGCATACGCAAGAACGCG TAGTAAAACCATACCTTAAATGGGGGGGCCACCTTCGG CGGATACTCTTTCAA

Horse
GCAGAGGAACCGCTACAAGAGCGGGAGCAAGAACGCG CAGTAAAACCTTACCTAAAATGCGGGCTTGACCTTCGAAG TATACTCTTTCAT

Propose a Hypothesis

Write a hypothesis comparing the genetic relationships of a horse, a gorilla, and a human. Which two do you think are more closely related?

Conduct Your Experiment

1 Answer the following questions before you begin. What are the base pairs in DNA? In RNA? By what processes are proteins produced in a cell? What is a codon? An anticodon?

2 The illustration shows partial DNA sequences of the hemoglobin gene in a human, a horse, and a gorilla. "Transcribe" the DNA into mRNA. Record each mRNA sequence on graph paper.

3 Refer to the chart on page 185 and "translate" the mRNA sequences into amino acid sequences. Record each amino acid beneath its mRNA codon.

4 Circle and count the number of bases in the horse mRNA sequence that differ from bases in the same location in the human mRNA sequence. Record your data.

5 Circle and count the number of amino acids in the horse amino acid sequence that differ from the human amino acid sequence. Record your findings.

6 Count and record the number of bases in the horse mRNA sequence that differ from the human mRNA sequence but do not code for a different amino acid.

7 Repeat steps 3, 4, and 5, but compare the gorilla and human sequences.

Analyze Your Data

1 Which mRNA sequence— the horse's or the gorilla's—is most similar to the human mRNA sequence?

2 Which amino acid sequence—the horse's or the gorilla's—is more similar to the human amino acid sequence?

Draw Conclusions

Based on your results, which two organisms are more closely related? Write a paragraph in which you support your conclusion with your observations. Was your hypothesis supported or disproved?

Design a Related Experiment

Plan an experiment in which you determine evolutionary relationships based on a physical characteristic. For example, choose several different plants and compare their flowers. Based on this trait, how would you describe their evolutionary relationships? How accurate is this method?

Lab: Comparing Genetic Relationships

1. Objective
Model how gene sequences can determine
evolutionary relationships: DNA: GGG AAA
RNA: CCC UUU   Protein: Pro Phe.

Lab Prep and Planning

To reduce class time, you may wish to have students do the *Getting Ready* portion of the lab as a homework assignment.

Hypothesis Help

Before students write their hypotheses, you may wish to have them review the information in Section 12.1 on the genetic similarities among humans, chimpanzees, and gorillas.

Lab Extension

Open Ended

Direct students to examine, compare, and contrast the DNA sequences in the three animals. Ask them to report on their observations, as well as their conclusions about the relative degrees of relationships among the animals.

Time Required

■ 50 minutes

Analyze Your Data

1 Gorilla's
2 Gorilla's

Draw Conclusions

Students should conclude that gorillas and humans are more closely related, and support this conclusion with their data from the comparison of mRNA and amino acid sequences. Check students' graphs for accuracy.

Design a Related Experiment

Encourage students to select a physical characteristic that varies among flower species, such as petal color, size, or shape.

1 ENGAGE

Consider the Big Idea

Have students read The Big Idea! at the top of the page. Point out that anthropoids evolved to form different species of hominids.

Use the Visual

Have students study the photograph that opens the section. Explain that archaeologists found less than half of the skeleton, but an analysis revealed that it lived between 3 and 3.6 million years ago and walked upright.

Quick Activity

TEAM WORK

Provide groups of students with small containers of sand with buried objects such as keys, coins, and pottery. Have them sift though the sand and imagine that an earlier archaeological team discovered bones that appeared to be human from this site. Ask:

■ **What can you infer about the bones in light of the objects you just recovered?** (The bones are probably recent because the objects suggest fairly advanced humans.) Explain that this activity is like an archaeological dig. Once archaeologists remove objects, they try to determine the time relationship among them, using direct observation and technology, such as radioactive dating.

THE BIG IDEA! There have been many different hominid species over time, each species with its own unique characteristics. 12.2–12.3

12.2 Hominids

What you'll learn

IDEAS
• To identify various hominid species and the time periods in which they existed
• To compare the characteristics of major hominid groups

WORDS
hominids, bipedal

Primates in the sky?
In 1974 a team led by Donald Johanson found a skeleton of what appeared to be a small female hominid. The skeleton was nicknamed "Lucy" because the Beatles' song "Lucy in the Sky with Diamonds" was playing in the camp as the crew celebrated the discovery. Ironically, recent studies of Lucy's pelvis indicate "she" might have been male—"*Luke* in the Sky with Diamonds"?

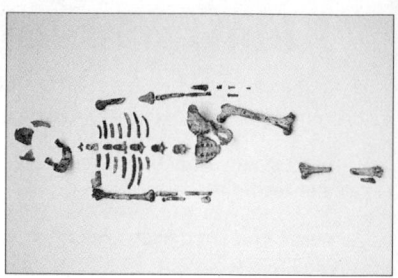

COMPARISON OF HOMINIDS

Stand by your hominid

As you read in the last section, apes and humans evolved between 8 and 5 million years ago. The anthropoids that evolved to become the human family are called **hominids** (HAH-mih-nidz). Hominids are the human-like anthropoids.

Evidence of the hominids' appearance and way of life is provided by the hominid fossil record. For example, a comparison of modern and fossil teeth can yield information about the ancient hominid diet. By comparing fossil bones with those of modern primates, scientists can infer whether an ancient hominid was bipedal or walked in an apelike manner, using its hands. **Bipedal** refers to the ability to walk on two legs. Since humans are bipedal, an early bipedal hominid may be more closely related to humans than to the early, apelike hominids. In *Figure 12.10* you can see some examples of the skeletal structures that scientists compare.

According to the fossil record, several hominid species coexisted at various times during the past 5 million years. Today, modern humans, known scientifically as *Homo sapiens*, are the only surviving hominid species. Why the ancient hominids became extinct is still a matter of scientific debate. One theory is that competition among hominid species may have led to their extinction.

It is not known which of the hominids shown in *Figure 12.11* are our distant relatives and which, if any, are our direct ancestors. Scientists have not yet identified the very first hominid ancestor, nor have they identified a direct line of descent from the earliest known hominid to modern humans. Some of the older species may be evolutionary

FIGURE 12.10
A bipedal hominid walks on two legs. What skeletal features promote this type of movement?

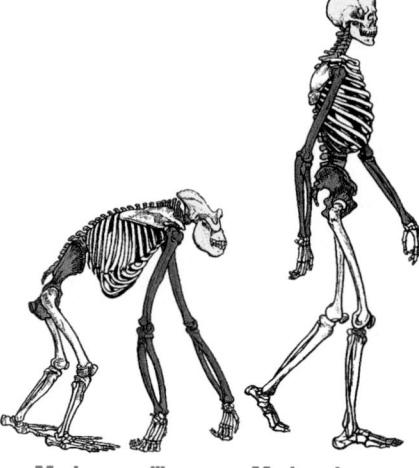

Modern gorilla **Modern human**

Comparison of Gorilla and Human Skeletons	
Modern Gorilla	**Modern Human**
C-shaped spine	S-shaped spine
Spinal cord exits near back of skull	Spinal cord exits at bottom of skull
Arms are longer than legs, used when walking	Arms are shorter than legs, not used when walking
Pelvis is long and narrow	Pelvis is bowl-shaped

STUDENT RESOURCES

From the Teacher's Resource Package, use:
■ Section Review 12.2, Interpreting Graphics 12, and Critical Thinking Exercise 12 from Unit 3 Review Module

 **TECHNOLOGY RESOURCES**

Relevant technology resources include:
■ Spanish Student Edition CD-ROM
■ Teacher's Resource Planner CD-ROM

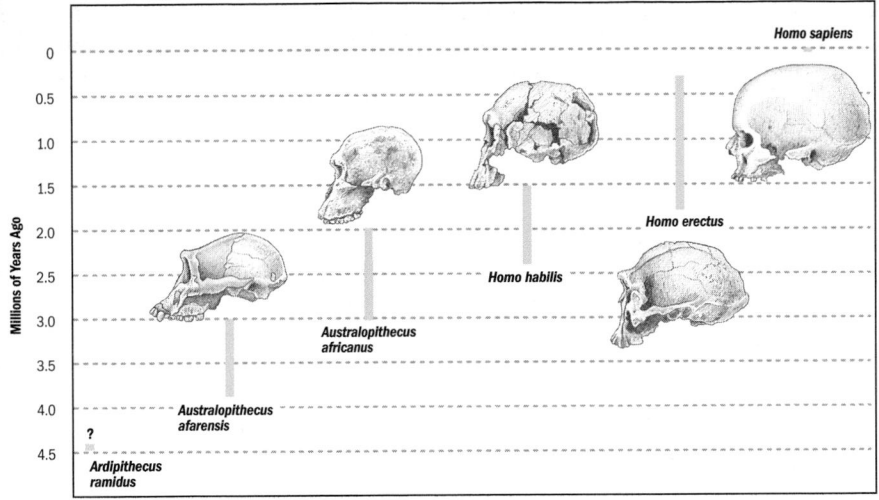

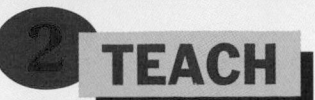

FIGURE 12.11
This illustration identifies some important hominid species. Each vertical bar indicates the time period in which a particular hominid group existed. How does the modern human skull (far right) compare with the other hominid skulls? ❷

2 TEACH

Use the Visual

Have students study Figure 12.11. To help students interpret the information shown, ask:

- **Of the hominids shown, which existed on Earth between 1.5 and 2 million years ago?** (*Homo habilis* and *Homo erectus*)
- **How does the size and shape of the hominid skulls differ among the earliest and the most recent hominids?** (The most recent skulls are larger and more rounded.)

Think Critically

Ask students what the existence of *Homo sapiens, Homo habilis,* and *Australopithecus robustus* indicates about homonid ancestry. (They branched from a common ancestor.)

Discuss

Explain that a major adaptation distinguishing hominids from other primates and mammals is bipedal locomotion. After hominids began walking upright, large brains evolved. Ask:

- **What are other uniquely human adaptations?** (Highly specialized hands, ability to reason and to communicate using speech)

✚ Literature

Lucy, a book by Donald Johanson, describes the discovery of the first fossil of *Australopithecus afarensis.* Johanson offers his views on the evolutionary relationships among early hominids.

---

branches became extinct and did not lead to a modern species. However, many scientists conclude that at least some of these hominids are part of the evolutionary line that led to humans.

THE EARLY HOMINIDS

Can you dig it?

Fossils of the oldest known hominid date from about 4.4 million years ago. This hominid, *Ardipithecus ramidus* (ahr-deh-PITH-uh-kus RAM-eh-dus), was discovered in 1994 in Ethiopia by Dr. Gen Suwa. In the language of that area, *ramid* means "root." The hominid's name implies that it is a "root species," one from which other species may have evolved.

Ardipithecus ramidus (abbreviated *A. ramidus*) is the most apelike fossil hominid. The fossil evidence of *A. ramidus* is not complete. Scientists have not found fossils of the pelvis, knee, and foot bones, which would reveal whether or not *A. ramidus* was bipedal. However, some fossil evidence indicates that *A. ramidus* could carry an infant in its arms, and so might have been bipedal. From fossilized wood and seeds found at the site, we

know that *A. ramidus* probably lived in forests.

The next four species of hominids share the same first name—*Australopithecus* (ah-stray-loh-PITH-uh-kus). *Australopithecus* means "southern ape," referring to the sites south of the equator where most of the fossils of these hominids were found. The oldest species, *Australopithecus anamensis* (ah-nah-MEN-sis), is between 4.2 and 3.9 million years old. *A. anamensis* weighed about 55 kg (121 lb) and lived in lakeside forests. In some ways this hominid was apelike—it had large teeth and small ear openings. Its leg bones, however, resemble human leg bones—strong evidence that *A. anamensis* was bipedal.

The next oldest hominid is *Australopithecus afarensis* (ah-far-EHN-sis). "Lucy," the hominid described at the beginning of this section, belongs to this group. Because of Lucy's remarkably complete skeleton, we know a great deal about *A. afarensis. Figure 12.12* shows what Lucy might have looked like.

Lucy lived between 4 and 3 million years ago. She had a low forehead, a flat nose, and no chin. Lucy's skull is

FIGURE 12.12
Hypotheses about the physical appearance and lifestyle of *Australopithecus* are based on fossil evidence. How does "Lucy" differ from modern humans? ❸

Chapter 12 Human History **287**

MEETING DIVERSE NEEDS

ESL and At Risk Encourage students to create a graphic that lists the name of each hominid discussed in this section, when it lived, and its traits. ESL students may wish to record this information in both English and their native language.

❶ An S-shaped spine, spinal cord that exits at the bottom of the skull, long legs, and a bowl-shaped pelvis

❷ The human skull has flatter facial features, is larger, and lacks a protruding brow ridge.

❸ She has a low forehead, a very flat nose, and no chin.

Clarify Misconceptions

Students may think all extinct hominids are direct ancestors of modern humans. Create a family tree to illustrate relationships in an extended family. Help students recognize that aunts, uncles, and cousins are not ancestors. Point out that individuals in a family and in hominid species can be indirectly related.

LAB ZONE Think About It!

Hominid Origins

You may want to point out the different sites on a more detailed wall map of the world.

Analyzing the Map

1. Concentrated on the eastern coast of Africa and in scattered sites in southern Europe and southeastern Asia
2. Older fossils are found exclusively on the eastern coast of Africa; more recent fossils in Europe, Asia, and Africa.
3. After the evolution of *H. erectus,* hominids began to migrate to Asia and Europe.
4. More *H. erectus* fossils showing a migratory route from Africa

❶ *Australopithecus* was bipedal and had teeth that closely resemble human teeth.

---

like that of a chimpanzee, but her teeth are more like those of a human. From her pelvis and leg bones we know that Lucy was bipedal. She stood only about 130 centimeters (cm) tall (a little over 4 feet), but was quite strong.

The jaw of *A. afarensis* protruded and had large back teeth. These hominids probably ate whatever they could find—seeds, fruits, and any small animals they could catch or scavenge. *A. afarensis* probably spent most of the time on the ground, but its long fingers and toes may have helped it climb trees.

In 1924, Raymond Dart discovered the first member of the hominid group known as *Australopithecus africanus* (ah-freh-KAHN-us), or *A. africanus.* *A. africanus* lived between 3 and 2 million years ago. Like *A. afarensis,* *A. africanus* was bipedal and had some apelike features. However, *A. africanus* had a slightly larger body and brain. The teeth of *A. africanus*

LAB ZONE Think About It! **bioSURF**

Hominid Origins

About nine different hominid species have been described. Where did these different hominids first evolve? What might account for the existence of different hominid species and their distribution?

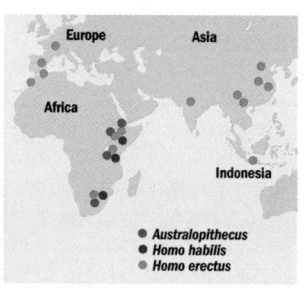

- ● *Australopithecus*
- ● *Homo habilis*
- ● *Homo erectus*

Analyzing the Map

1 The map above shows where various hominid fossils have been found. How would you describe the distribution and location of the sites?
2 Note where the oldest fossils have been discovered. How does their distribution and

location compare with that of the more recent fossils?
3 Develop a hypothesis explaining the difference in distribution between the oldest and the most recent fossils.
4 What additional information would you need to support your hypothesis?

---

more closely resemble human teeth than those of apes. Because *A. africanus* lived later than *A. afarensis,* and because the two species had similar features, many scientists hypothesize that *A. africanus* evolved from *A. afarensis.*

About 2 million years ago, *Australopithecus boisei* (BOY-see-eye) and *Australopithecus robustus* (roh-BUS-tus) evolved. Many scientists agree that *A. boisei* and *A. robustus* are not our direct ancestors. This conclusion is based on the thick, heavy bones and other differences between these two species and modern humans. Some scientists call them *Paranthropus* (PAR-uhn-throh-pus) instead of *Australopithecus.* These species are thought to represent branches of the human family tree that became extinct more than 1 million years ago.

HOMO HABILIS AND HOMO ERECTUS

Handy hominids take a stand

In 1964, the famous archaeology team of Louis and Mary Leakey announced the discovery of what appeared to be the first hominids to make and use tools and weapons. Because of this unique ability, the new species was named *Homo habilis* (HO-mo HAH-beh-lus), or "handy man." *H. habilis* probably existed between 2.4 and 1.5 million years ago.

Scientists generally agree that *Homo habilis* is a direct ancestor of our modern human species, *Homo sapiens.* The name *Homo* indicates that a fossil is more like *Homo sapiens* than any earlier hominid. As you can see in *Figure 12.13,* *H. habilis* was bipedal. The *H. habilis* brain was much larger than that of any species of *Australopithecus,* but it was still only about half the size of a modern human brain. *H. habilis* may also

---

MULTICULTURAL PERSPECTIVE

Many discoveries of hominid fossils have been made by African members of research groups in eastern and southern Africa. For example, an *Australopithecine* jawbone was discovered by Kamoya Kimeu at Lake Nation, near the Olduvai Gorge. The oldest known *Homo habilis* specimen was discovered by Bernard Ngeneo, an associate of Richard Leakey.

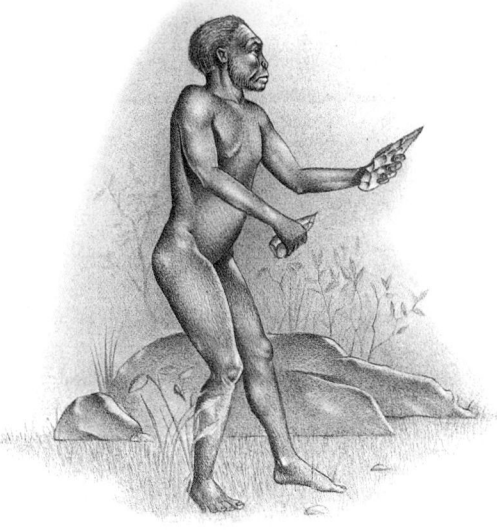

 Science History

In the 1800s, many scientists thought the earliest hominids appeared in Asia. Reinforcing the idea was a partial skeleton discovered in Java by Eugene Dubois, and named *Pithecanthropus erectus,* or "the ape man who walked erect." More recently, the specimen, often called "Java Man," has been reclassified as the first fossil specimen of *Homo erectus.*

have had some form of simple speech and probably hunted and collected seeds, fruits, and vegetables.

For almost 1 million years, *H. habilis* coexisted in Africa with various species of *Australopithecus*. The evolutionary relationship between *Australopithecus* and *H. habilis* is unclear, but they do have some common characteristics. What are some of the similarities

❶ between these two hominid groups? At some point, *H. habilis* may have evolved into a new species with an even larger brain—*Homo erectus* (uh-REK-tus), or "upright man."

H. erectus was probably the first hominid to migrate out of Africa, into Asia and Europe. Compared to earlier hominids, *H. erectus* most closely resembles modern humans. In general, *H. erectus* was taller and had a larger brain than *H. habilis. H. erectus* built fires, wore animal skin clothing, lived in caves, and made relatively refined stone tools.

The oldest *H. erectus* fossil is about 1.8 million years old. The *H. erectus* fossil known as Java Man was found in 1891 in Java, Indonesia. *H. erectus* remains found in China became

known as Peking Man.

Most *H. erectus* populations probably died out 300,000 years ago. In 1996, scientists dated some *H. erectus* fossils as only 50,000 years old. Did *H. erectus* live at the same time as *H. sapiens*? New discoveries, techniques, and debates are needed to answer this question.

CHECKPOINT 12.2

1. What is the earliest hominid? What is the next-oldest fossil hominid?

2. Compare and contrast the groups *Homo* and *Australopithecus*. How are they similar? How do they differ?

3. Critical Thinking Suppose you find a 1 million-year-old hominid fossil with humanlike traits. Which hominid species might it be? Which hominids can you eliminate? Why?

Build on What You Know

4. At least three types of hominids could have lived at the same time, in the same area. What does this coexistence mean in terms of available niches? *(Need to jog your memory? Revisit relevant concepts in Chapter 10, Section 10.1.)*

FIGURE 12.13
Evidence indicates that *H. erectus* (above right) had a larger body and brain than *H. habilis* (above left), used a wider variety of tools, and knew how to make fire. In what other ways do these two hominids differ? **❷**

FIGURE 12.14
Homo erectus used tools to make tools. The hand ax (left) and cleaver (right) were formed using specially selected stones as shaping tools.

Chapter 12 Human History **289**

 **ASSESS**

Evaluate Understanding

Draw a line on the board labeled in 0.5 million year increments from 4.5 million years ago to the present. Next to the line list the following: *H. habilis, A. afarensis, Ardipithecus ramidus, H. erectus, H. sapiens,* and *A. africanus*. Have students place the name of each hominid correctly along the time line and list a major feature of the hominid named. Review the completed time line.

Reteach

On an overhead transparency or on the board, create a table with seven columns and five rows. Label the first column *Feature* and the remaining columns with the names of each hominid group. Beneath the *Feature* head, use the following labels for rows: *When Hominid Lived, Where Remains Found, Approximate Size and Weight,* and *Other Key Features*. Complete the table as a class. Suggest students copy the completed tables into their notebooks for use as a study tool.

CHECKPOINT 12.2

1. Earliest is *Ardipithecus ramidus;* the next oldest is *Australopithecus afarensis.*

2. Members of *Australopithecus* were more apelike, but some may have been bipedal. Members of *Homo* were taller and heavier, had a larger brain, and made and used tools.

3. Developing a hypothesis *Homo habilis* or

Homo sapiens; Homo erectus, because it lived earlier than 1 million years ago

4. Each hominid was adapted to the environment of a specific niche.

❷ The tools, clothing, and shelters of *H. erectus* were more refined; also, their living habits more closely resembled those of modern humans.

1 ENGAGE

Use the Visual

Have students study the photograph that opens the section. Explain that the Cro-Magnons, dating back about 40,000 years, are ancestors of modern humans. Point out that many scientists think that the art may have been used in ceremonies or other rituals.

Check Prior Knowledge

To assess students' understanding of the evolution of modern humans, ask:

- **About how long ago do you think *Homo sapiens* first appeared on Earth?** (About 300,000 years ago)
- **What can scientists learn about evolution by studying the DNA of different species?** (They can use gene structures to reconstruct evolutionary history and identify closely related species.)

Teacher Demo

Display drawings or cartoons that depict ancestors of modern humans. Discuss which visual details students think are accurate and which details are fictional. Ask them to support their responses. After students read the section, repeat the activity to determine how students may have changed their views. Challenge them to determine if the people in each drawing more closely resemble Neanderthals or Cro-Magnons.

12.3 *Homo sapiens*

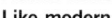

What you'll learn

IDEAS
- To compare and contrast Neanderthals, Cro-Magnons, and modern *Homo sapiens*
- To evaluate hypotheses about the origin and distribution of modern *Homo sapiens*

Cave men had culture
Popular myth is that the "cave men," the first modern *Homo sapiens*, were primitive brutes. However, archaeological evidence, such as paintings from France's Cro-Magnon cave and Spain's Altamira cave (right), suggests that these humans thought about matters beyond their next meal, or who had the biggest and best shelter.

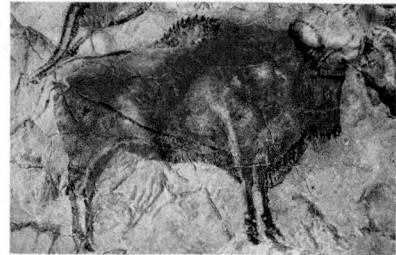

THE NEANDERTHALS

Something old

The earliest *Homo sapiens* may have evolved from *H. erectus* between 300,000 and 200,000 years ago. Two of the best known groups of *H. sapiens* in the fossil record are the older Neanderthals (nee-AN-der-tholz) and the more recent Cro-Magnons (kro-MAG-nuhnz).

In 1856, three years before the publication of Darwin's *On the Origin of Species by Means of Natural Selection,* the first Neanderthal fossils were found in the Neander Valley of Germany. Some scientists refer to the Neanderthals as *Homo neanderthalensis*, a dead-end branch of our family tree. Other scientists consider the Neanderthals early humans—*H. sapiens*—and possible direct ancestors of modern humans.

In this textbook we group the Neanderthals with *H. sapiens*. We know that the Neanderthals lived throughout Europe, Asia, and the Middle East between 230,000 and 30,000 years ago. Although they are related to modern humans, the Neanderthals have some unique characteristics.

Physical characteristics As you can see in *Figure 12.15*, Neanderthals were short and solid, with short arms and legs. Their thick, heavy bones indicate that they were quite strong.

FIGURE 12.15
Like modern humans, the Neanderthals are classified as *Homo sapiens*. However, they are distinguished by their short, solid build and distinctive facial features.

Based on reconstructions, the Neanderthal face was similar to ours, but with a heavier brow, larger nose, and smaller chin.

Neanderthal brains were slightly larger than those of modern humans, perhaps because of their overall larger and heavier body size. The Neanderthal skull was longer than that of both modern humans and Cro-Magnons, and it had a bulge at the back. Compare the three skulls in *Figure 12.16*. What other differences can you see?

Tools and culture The entrances of Neanderthal caves often had a fire at the center. The ground around the hearth was cleared of debris, and animal bones were typically thrown to the back of the cave. Flint chips found around the hearths are evidence that Neanderthals fashioned stone tools while sitting around a fire. Such evidence has led scientists to conclude that Neanderthals had a simple but organized social structure.

Although the number of animal bones at campsites indicates that Neanderthals were good hunters, they also probably made plants an important part of their diet. A specific pattern of wear on Neanderthal teeth and some of their stone tools indicates that Neanderthals used to scrape hides for clothing or shelter.

Scientists have found many Neanderthal tools made of bone and stone.

290 *Unit 3 Change and Diversity*

STUDENT RESOURCES

From the Teacher's Resource Package, use:
- Section Review 12.3, Activity Recordsheet 12-2, Enrichment Topic 12-1, Vocabulary Review 12, and Chapter 12 Tests from Unit 3 Review Module
- Consumer Applications 12-1
- Issues and Decision Making 12-1

TECHNOLOGY RESOURCES

Relevant technology resources include:
- Spanish Student Edition CD-ROM
- Teacher's Resource Planner CD-ROM
- TestWorks CD-ROM: Chapter 12 Tests

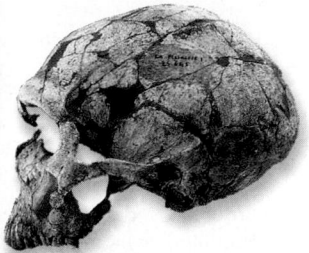

Neanderthal

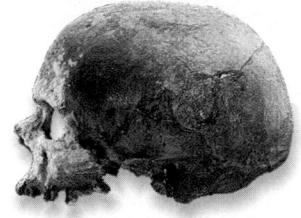

Cro-Magnon

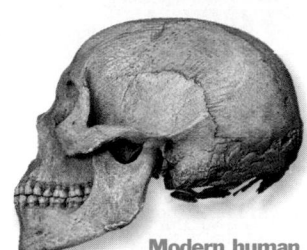

Modern human

FIGURE 12.16
Note the differences and similarities between these human skulls.

One researcher claims to have identified over 60 different types of stone flake tools and 20 types of hand axes. Only a few examples of decorated tools and jewelry (ivory rings and pierced animal teeth) have been discovered in Neanderthal cave sites.

Neanderthal skeletons have been found in arranged positions and with food, weapons, and even flowers. This evidence suggests that Neanderthals were the first hominids to participate in ritual burials.

Neanderthals apparently lived at the same time as modern hominids for at least 10,000 years. Scientists do not know why the Neanderthals disappeared. Some think modern hominids may have driven the Neanderthals to extinction through competition. The Neanderthals may have relied on foods that were harder to find and eat. If modern hominids were more efficient at finding and eating food, they may have been able to specialize—some remaining with their children in a protected area, while others collected food. Such advantages may have given modern hominids an evolutionary edge.

THE CRO-MAGNONS

Something new

The first fossils of a fully modern *H. sapiens*, found in Africa, appear to be about 120,000 years old. However, the Cro-Magnons, dating back about 40,000 years, are the best known example of modern *H. sapiens*.

Physical characteristics

Physically the Cro-Magnons were nearly identical to modern humans. Cro-Magnon skulls, like those of modern humans, have a vertical rather than a sloping forehead. Unlike Neanderthals, Cro-Magnons have small or no eyebrow ridges, and their lighter jaw has a prominent chin and smaller molars. Overall, Cro-Magnons were taller and lighter than Neanderthals; their build is typical of many modern humans. In fact, if you were to pass a Cro-Magnon on the street, you would probably never know it!

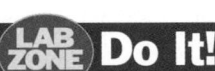

LAB ZONE Do It! bioSURF

Modeling Archaeological Activity

Although fossils are scarce, archaeologists can infer much information from such evidence. You, too, can get the big picture, if you . . .

Try This

1 Obtain 25 pieces from a 250-piece jigsaw puzzle. (Do not assemble the puzzle or look at the puzzle box.)
2 Study the pieces carefully. Record your observations.
3 Based on your observations, infer how the whole picture looks. Try to infer the size and shape of the puzzle as well.
4 Confirm your inference by completing the puzzle or by looking at the box.

Analyze Your Results

1 How accurate was your inference?
2 What is your estimate of the smallest percentage of the puzzle needed to make an accurate inference?
3 Which inference would be more accurate: one based on 10 percent of a 1000-piece puzzle or one based on 10 percent of a 250-piece puzzle?

2 TEACH

Use the Visual

Have students trace the skulls shown in Figure 12.16 on thin tracing paper. Then have them lay one tracing over the other. Ask:

- **How does the brow of the Neanderthal skull differ from that of the Cro-Magnon or modern human?** (It appears heavier and protrudes more than the others.)
- **Which Cro–Magon skull features are similar to those of modern humans?** (Smooth, oval head, vertical brow, eye socket size, nose bridge, jaw, and chin)

LAB ZONE Do It! TEAM WORK

Modeling Archaeological Activity

Analyze Your Results

1 Students may say their accuracy depends upon the relationship of the puzzle pieces chosen, rather than the percentage of pieces.
2 Answers will vary, but students should choose a number between 10 and 15 percent.
3 Ten percent of a 1000-piece puzzle would be more accurate because there are more pieces to study.

❶ The Neanderthal skull had a slightly more pronounced brow ridge and smaller chin than Cro-Magnon or modern human skulls.

MULTICULTURAL PERSPECTIVE

Although hominid fossils are studied by scientists all over the world, the fossils are usually displayed in museums of the nations where they were discovered. Kenya, for example, has a rich collection of early hominid fossils.

MEETING DIVERSE NEEDS

Sight Impaired Enlarge Figure 12.16 and trace the skulls into soft clay with a stylus. Fill the grooves with liquid plastic and mount the models on a board when dry. Identify each skull in Braille. Have sight–impaired students use the models to compare the skulls.

Build Writing Skills

Ask students to write a short story to compare their lives with the lives of early *Homo sapiens,* either Neanderthal or Cro-Magnon. The person they choose should suddenly face a situation in the modern world, while the student travels back in time to live in a Neanderthal or Cro-Magnon culture. Encourage students to include scientifically accurate details about their characters.

 Literature

The cultures of the Neanderthals and Cro-Magnons provide the background for a novel about a Cro-Magnon girl raised by Neanderthals in *The Clan of the Cave Bear* by Jean Auel. This best-selling novel has also been made into a motion picture.

Class Activity

TEAM WORK

Organize the class into two teams to debate the question "Where is the flaw in the 'Out of Africa' theory?" You may wish to have students do some outside research.

Everyday Biology

Point out that scientists also hold conflicting views on how and when different racial groups evolved. One group contends that racial differences represent the descent of each racial group from a different population of *Homo erectus.* Another contends that the unique traits of different races reflect adaptations to local conditions that occurred after *Homo sapiens* migrated out of Africa.

EVERYDAY BIOLOGY

What is Race?

Race is a biological term that describes genetic groupings of animals, including humans. For example, a race of sparrows may have different feather patterns than others of its species. People have misused the term race for political, religious, and economic reasons. All humans belong to the species *Homo sapiens*.

Tools and culture The Cro-Magnon culture appears to have been more complex than that of Neanderthals. Archaeological evidence reveals that 30,000 years ago, these humans had well-designed dwellings, language, art, trade, and even class distinctions. In some ways, their culture was similar to today's cultures.

Cro-Magnon sites provide evidence of an organized social structure. Their settlements show separate areas for butchering, for cooking, and for dumping garbage. Areas were also set aside for tool and blade making. Tools were finely crafted from materials including bone, antler, wood, and various types of stone. Cro-Magnon artwork includes decorated tools, ivory carvings, clay figures, musical instruments, and extensive cave paintings.

Cro-Magnon burials suggest complicated rituals and perhaps a developed spiritual life. Elaborate items were placed with the bodies, which were often richly decorated.

DISTRIBUTION OF HOMO SAPIENS

Where is home, sweet home?

Scientists are currently debating the origin and subsequent distribution of *H. sapiens.* Two main hypotheses are the multiregional hypothesis and the

FIGURE 12.17
Compare the Neanderthal stone tools (below left) to the Cro-Magnon tool and sewing needle (below right).

Sewing needle

292 *Unit 3 Change and Diversity*

"Out of Africa" hypothesis, both illustrated in *Figure 12.18.*

According to the multiregional hypothesis, various *H. sapiens* populations evolved from different *H. erectus* populations in different parts of the world. If this is true, modern *H. sapiens* date back 1 to 2 million years, when groups of *H. erectus* first left Africa and became established elsewhere. Interbreeding of these groups would account for the genetic similarity found in all humans.

The "Out of Africa" hypothesis states that modern *H. sapiens* evolved in Africa from ancient populations of *H. erectus* before spreading to other continents. In this scenario, humans left Africa as fully modern *H. sapiens,* and later replaced older *H. sapiens* populations, such as the Neanderthals. If this hypothesis is correct, such a migration from Africa would have occurred relatively recently, and modern human diversity would date back only 100,000 years. Scientists point out that Africa is the only continent where human fossils chronicle a relatively uninterrupted evolutionary path.

Do other types of data support the "Out of Africa" hypothesis? Geneticists Rebecca Cann and Alan Wilson, from the University of California at Berkeley, analyzed the mitochondrial DNA of a broad range of people. They found that mitochondrial DNA in

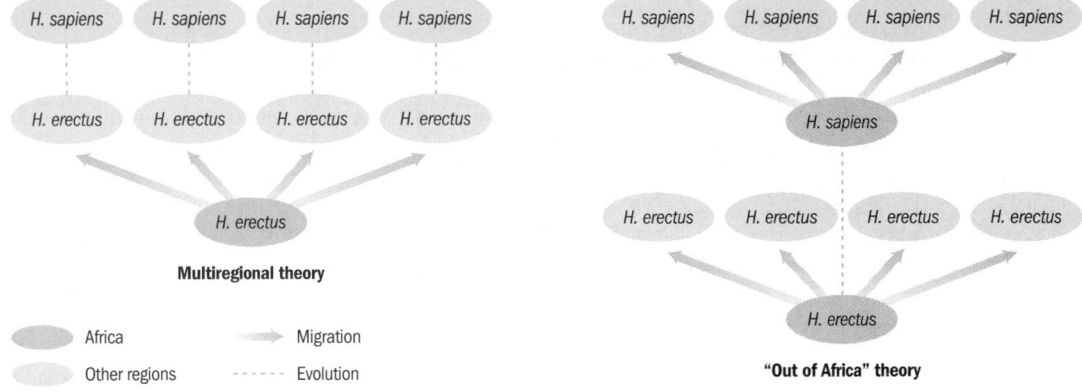

Multiregional theory

"Out of Africa" theory

Africa
Other regions
→ Migration
----- Evolution

today's population is nearly uniform. As you know, the greater the difference between two individual's DNA, the longer ago they diverged from a common ancestor.

From their results, Cann and Wilson concluded that the various modern human populations split from a common source relatively recently. They also traced the modern DNA to an African source. Many scientists propose that these data support the "Out of Africa" hypothesis.

However, other scientists interpret the evidence differently. According to these scientists, the data support the multiregional hypothesis because small populations—like those first established by *H. erectus*—lose genetic diversity over time due to genetic drift. When these different populations interbreed, mitochondrial DNA among them becomes more uniform. Scientists propose that even 2 million years is not enough time for *H. sapiens* to have evolved significant genetic differences.

Meanwhile, researchers are trying to recover DNA from Neanderthal and other extinct human fossils. They hope to identify the similarities in DNA between ancient humans and modern humans and then compare those to the similarities in DNA among different populations of modern humans. The results could help to resolve this question.

FIGURE 12.18
The two models of the origin and distribution of *Homo sapiens* are the multiregional hypothesis and the "Out of Africa" hypothesis. Scientists have data to support both hypotheses.

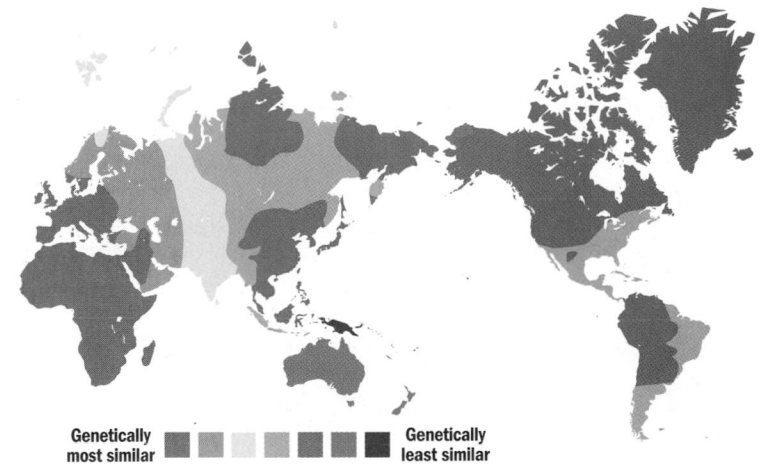

Genetically most similar ■■■■■■■ Genetically least similar

FIGURE 12.19
This map shows the degree of relatedness among populations of modern humans, based on analysis of mitochondrial DNA. Which hypothesis do these data support? ❶

Chapter 12 Human History   **293**

❶ These data support the "Out of Africa" hypothesis because humans who are genetically similar live in Africa. When fossil remains of humans living farther from Africa are analyzed, they show less genetic similarity.

Use the Visual

Ask students to study Figure 12.18 which illustrates the two models of the origin and distribution of *Homo sapiens*. Remind students that scientists are not yet certain about the details of human evolution, but two hypotheses seem most likely. Ask:

■ **In which model did populations of *H. erectus* interbreed before giving rise to populations of *H. sapiens*?** (Multiregional)

■ **In which model did *H. sapiens* evolve directly from *H. erectus* before giving rise to other populations of *H. sapiens*?** (Out of Africa)

Explain

Tell students that fossil reconstruction, a procedure involving a knowledge of anatomy and math as well as a creative mind, is often used to depict the appearance of an organism had its soft tissues been preserved. The first step in reconstruction is visualizing how an organism probably looked from observing just a few of its skeletal parts. The actual sculpture, painting, and cosmetic design of the reconstructed figure requires the talents of highly skilled artists. Refer students to the reconstruction of dinosaurs and the Burgess Shales. You may wish to have them make a collage of photos of reconstructed fossils.

In the Community

You may want to introduce this feature by displaying in class a wide range of everyday artifacts, such as a paper clip, a manual can opener, a computer disk, a stapler, a pocket knife, and a pager. Tell students to imagine themselves as archaeologists on a dig in the year 10,000 A.D. and propose hypotheses explaining how these items might have been used in the past. Challenge them to piece together a picture of life around 2000 A.D. by analyzing the structure and function of these items.

3 ASSESS

Evaluate Understanding

Have students summarize the evolution of Neanderthals, Cro-Magnons, and modern humans on a time line extending from the present back to about 150,000 years ago. The range for each group should indicate when each group appeared and how long it existed. Beneath the time line, have students provide a few details about the physical features, tools, and art or customs of each group.

Reteach

Have students work in small groups to create a graphic organizer of their choice comparing and contrasting Neanderthals, Cro-Magnons, and modern humans. Suggest that students begin by reviewing the section to identify the physical traits, tools, and culture of each.

294

Archaeologists of the future might draw conclusions about today's society by looking at our trash. Consider the items in your trash can, or in your community garbage dump. How would an archaeologist use these items to form hypotheses

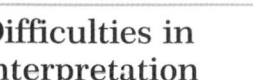

IN THE COMMUNITY
The Big Dig

about today's society? Archaeologists use remnants of items used by ancient hominids, such as tools, cooking utensils, or jewelry. The ancient trash gives archaeologists a picture of the lives of ancient hominids and helps them answer questions about human evolution. You can visit *http://evolution.biosurf.com* to find more information about this work.

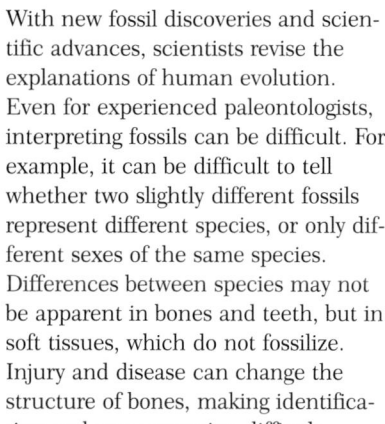

FIGURE 12.20
The Piltdown skull was a hoax, consisting of a modern human skull cap and an orangutan jaw. Scientists debated the bones for more than 40 years, until new dating techniques proved the "fossil" was modern.

ISSUES IN BIOLOGY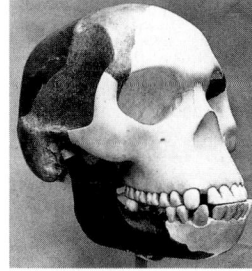

Difficulties in interpretation

With new fossil discoveries and scientific advances, scientists revise the explanations of human evolution. Even for experienced paleontologists, interpreting fossils can be difficult. For example, it can be difficult to tell whether two slightly different fossils represent different species, or only different sexes of the same species. Differences between species may not be apparent in bones and teeth, but in soft tissues, which do not fossilize. Injury and disease can change the structure of bones, making identification and reconstruction difficult.

Because of conflicting interpretations of fossils and the need to revise hypotheses with each new discovery, the public can misinterpret archeological findings. The debate among scientists has also led to misconceptions about human evolution. For

example, some people assume that humans evolved from modern apes. Instead our close genetic relationship implies that apes and humans evolved from a common ancestor; humans did not evolve from apes. Likewise, human evolution did not occur in a linear fashion, with less advanced hominids evolving directly to modern *Homo sapiens*. Instead, there have been many hominid groups in the family tree, with several human species co-existing during various times.

Keep in mind that archaeologists make interpretations by comparing their fossil findings with known data. Like all scientific hypotheses, archeological hypotheses are based on reason and supported by data. When the data are wrong or are interpreted incorrectly, an incorrect hypothesis can be formed. Continuous research and debate are needed to yield the most accurate picture of human evolution.

CHECKPOINT 12.3

1. Name three members of the group *Homo sapiens*. What traits characterize each group?
2. Compare and contrast the "Out of Africa" and the multiregional hypotheses. What evidence supports each?
3. **Critical Thinking** Review Figure 12.19. How might you use arrows on a map to draw migration routes based on the information shown?

Build on What You Know
4. Geneticists have used mitochondrial DNA to infer migration patterns of *H. sapiens*. Where could they obtain other forms of DNA? *(Need to jog your memory? Revisit relevant concepts in Chapter 3, Section 3.2.)*

What different hominid species have been identified?

CHECKPOINT 12.3

1. Neanderthals: short and solid, long skull with bulge at the back, simple culture; Cro-Magnons: vertical forehead, small or no eyebrow ridges, more complex culture; Modern humans: physically similar to Cro-Magnons, advanced culture
2. Modern humans evolved in ancient Africa from populations of *H. erectus* as evidenced by tracing modern DNA to African source. Multi-regional, *H. sapiens* evolved from different *H. erectus* populations in different parts of the world as evidenced by genetic similarities.
3. **Applying** Migratory paths should originate in Africa.
4. From DNA in the nucleus

Chapter 12 Review

**THE BIG IDEA!**
12.1 Primates are mammals with binocular vision and dexterous hands and arms.
12.2–12.3 There have been many different hominid species over time, each species with its own unique characteristics.

Sum It Up

Use the following summary to review the main concepts in this chapter.

12.1 Primates

- After the Cretaceous extinction, the number of mammal species increased dramatically.
- Modern primates evolved from a common ancestor between 65 and 55 million years ago.
- The earliest primates were tree-dwellers with grasping hands, swinging arms, and enhanced depth perception. They evolved into two groups, the prosimians and the anthropoids.
- Many primates have relatively large brains and complex social behaviors and relationships.
- The main groups of modern primates are the prosimians, New World monkeys, Old World monkeys, and apes.
- DNA analysis shows that chimpanzees and humans are closely related.

12.2 Hominids

- The oldest hominid fossil is about 4.4 million years old. About nine different hominid species have been identified. *Homo sapiens* is the only surviving hominid species.
- Archaeologists use fossils of primates' teeth and leg and pelvic bones to infer their diet and mode of locomotion.

- *Homo habilis* coexisted with *Australopithecus* species. *Australopithecus* died out, but *Homo habilis* gave rise to *Homo erectus*—a direct ancestor of modern humans.
- *Homo erectus* migrated from Africa to Europe and Asia.

12.3 *Homo sapiens*

- Neanderthals lived in Europe, Asia, and the Middle East as recently as 30,000 years ago.
- Neanderthals were shorter than modern humans, with heavier bones and larger brains. They made tools from stone and bone.
- Some scientists think that competition with Cro-Magnons caused the extinction of Neanderthals.
- Cro-Magnons are physically identical to modern humans. They had a complex culture with an organized social structure.
- Explanations for the origin of *Homo sapiens* include the multiregional and "Out of Africa" hypotheses.

Use Terms and Concepts

Use each of the following words or terms in a complete sentence. If you need to review a meaning, turn to the page indicated.

primates (p. 280)
prosimian (p. 281)
anthropoids (p. 281)
opposable thumb (p. 281)
binocular vision (p. 282)
prehensile tail (p. 283)
hominids (p. 286)
bipedal (p. 286)

Review the Big Idea

Before students begin the Chapter Review, you may wish to discuss main concepts from the Big Ideas in Chapter 12. Point out that primates are a group of mammals that include all monkeys, apes, and humans. Primates have binocular vision, dexterous hands and arms, and relatively large brains. Many exhibit complex social relationships. Anthropoids that evolved to become the human family are called hominids. The only surviving hominid species is *Homo sapiens*, three members of which are the Neanderthals, Cro-Magnons, and modern humans.

Answers

1. Binocular vision
2. prosimian
3. Anthropoids
4. prehensile tale
5. opposable thumb
6. Bipedal
7. True
8. False. Most prosimians living in tropical forests eat insects.
9. False. Anthropoids probably evolved from a common prosimian ancestor.
10. True
11. True
12. True
13. False. New World monkeys, Old World monkeys, and apes are all anthropoids.
14. They are excluded as an ancestor based mainly on their thick, heavy bones.
15. The acid soils of tropical forests where many primates evolved destroy the calcium carbonate bones.
16. Binocular vision increases depth perception and enhances eye-hand coordination.
17. The fossils of the earliest primates have large eye sockets like nocturnal prosimians.
18. They were named for their ability to make tools and for their upright posture, respectively.
19. New World monkeys have prehensile tails.
20. Neanderthals' bone and stone tools were relatively crude. Cro-Magnons' tools were finely crafted from a variety of materials and often decorated. Cro-Magnons set aside special areas for toolmaking.
21. Concept maps should show that <u>primates</u> include <u>prosimians</u> and <u>anthropoids</u>; <u>anthropoids</u> include

---

Use Your Word Power

COMPLETION Write the word or phrase that best completes each statement.

1. _____ is an adaptation that results in increased depth perception.

2. A monkeylike creature with large, forward-facing eyes is a(n) _____ .

3. _____ include lemurs, gibbons, and humans.

4. The muscular _____ acts as an extra hand for some primates.

5. The _____ allows humans to grip objects firmly.

6. _____ is the term used to describe the ability to walk on two legs.

TRUE-FALSE Write true if the statement is true. If the statement is false, replace the underlined word(s) to make the statement true.

7. <u>Binocular vision</u> produces overlapping fields of vision.

8. Most <u>primates</u> living in tropical forests eat insects.

9. Anthropoids probably evolved from a common <u>hominid</u> ancestor.

10. Pelvic, knee, and foot bones can reveal whether a fossil is <u>bipedal</u>.

11. <u>Primates</u> evolved from a small tree-dwelling ancestor.

12. A <u>prehensile tail</u> is a common trait of New World monkeys.

13. New World monkeys, Old World monkeys, and apes are all <u>prosimians</u>.

Show What You Know

14. Why do scientists think that *Australopithecus robustus* and *A. boisei* are not ancestors of *Homo sapiens*?

15. Explain why the fossil record of primates is relatively incomplete.

---

16. What are the advantages of binocular vision?

17. Explain why scientists think that the earliest primate ancestors were nocturnal.

18. For which traits were *Homo habilis* and *H. erectus* named?

19. What is the major difference between Old World and New World monkeys?

20. Compare the tools of Neanderthals and Cro-Magnons.

21. **Make a Concept Map** Complete the concept map below by adding the following terms: monkeys, apes, hominids, chimpanzees, prosimians, anthropoids, gorillas.

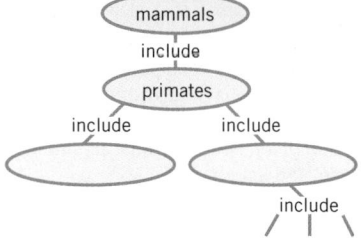

Take It Further

22. **Developing a Hypothesis** Neanderthals often camped at the entrances of caves, in which evidence of fires has been preserved. Suggest at least three reasons why Neanderthals might have built fires at their campsites.

23. **Making an Analogy** Primates are adapted to a tree-dwelling environment. What events in gymnastic competitions remind you of this adaptation?

24. **Making an Analogy** Genealogists specialize in researching and constructing family trees. How is the work of genealogists and archaeologists similar? How do they differ?

25. **Developing a Hypothesis** What might have happened differently in the evolution of anthropoids had North America and Eurasia been connected?

---

monkeys, apes, chimpanzees, gorillas, and hominoids.

22. For warmth, for cooking, for light, to ward off predators

23. High bars provide the most obvious comparison, but pommel horses, low bars, and rings all allow athletes to demonstrate flexibility in the upper limbs as well as the ability to grasp.

24. Both genealogists and archaeologists establish relationships over time. However, genealogists work with much shorter time periods and fewer, if any, gaps in the record. They connect individuals, not species. Genealogists use oral histories, written records, and grave markers as evidence—not fossilized remains.

26. Analyzing Data Compare the skulls in this sketch. Which skull might belong to an *Australopithecus* species? Which to another hominid species? Explain your answer.

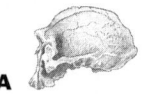

A   B

27. Interpreting a Graph Suppose the graph below shows the average difference between the DNA of humans and other anthropoids. Based on this analysis, which group is most closely related to humans? Which large group is missing? Explain your answer.

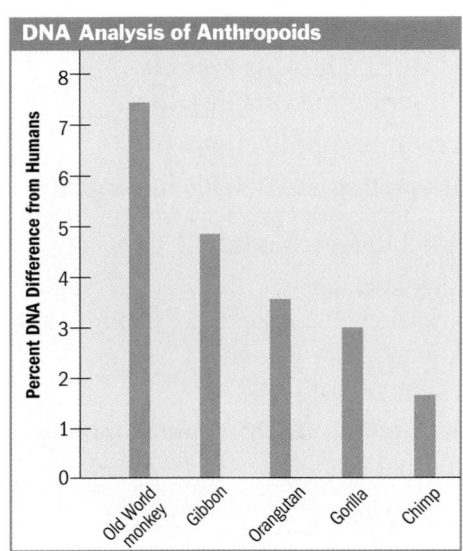

DNA Analysis of Anthropoids

Percent DNA Difference from Humans

Old World monkey, Gibbon, Orangutan, Gorilla, Chimp

28. Designing an Experiment Suppose you found a site containing hominid bones. Propose at least one method (other than studying teeth) for determining the hominids' diet.

Consider the Issues

29. Burying the Bones In 1996, hikers found a skeleton on Federal land in Washington State. Radiocarbon dating indicated an age of 9400 years, among the oldest human remains found in North America. The Oregon Umatilla tribe claimed the skeleton. According to law, Native American remains found on federal lands must be returned to the appropriate tribe for reburial. According to scientists, the evidence is insufficient to support the Umatilla claim, and the skeleton requires further study to determine its ancestry. If you were the judge, what would you decide? Why?

Make New Connections

30. Biology and Language One of the defining characteristics of *Homo sapiens* is the use of language. Linguistics, from the Latin *lingua*, meaning "tongue," is the study of languages. Like species, languages are classified and studied to determine if and how they are related. How are relationships between languages determined? How many languages do you and your classmates know? Create a linguistic family tree including those languages.

31. Biology and Art Learn more about the prehistoric cave paintings in Europe. When and how were they discovered? What tools and supplies did the artists use? What explanations have been proposed for why the paintings were made?

FAST-FORWARD TO CHAPTER 13

In Chapter 13, you will learn about the system for grouping species. You will also learn how species are named and how they can be identified.

words, sentence structure, phonetics, and vocabulary to classify and compare languages.

31. The first drawings were discovered in the mid-1800s. Because the drawings were located where they could not be routinely viewed, many scientists have inferred that the drawings were part of hunting rituals. The artists used tools such as flint burins and feather brushes, and pigments such as charcoal and red ochre.

Chapter 12 Human History **297**

---

25. Most likely, the two separate groups, Old World monkeys and New World monkeys, would not have occurred.

26. Skull A is hominid; B is Australopithecine. The hominid skull is more vertical in aspect and has a larger cranial capacity.

27. Chimpanzees are most closely related to humans. New World monkeys are not

included. The data help determine how close the other anthropoid "branches" will be to the human "branch."

28. Possible answers: They could look for animal bones discarded at the site. Scientists also analyze fossilized fecal remains, looking for seeds.

29. Answers will vary.

30. Linguistics uses evidence such as root

PLANNING GUIDE

Section	Student Activities/Features	Teacher's Resource Package
13.1 Classification **Objectives** ■ Describe the system for classifying organisms ■ Distinguish between different classification systems	**Lab Zone Discover It!** *Discovering a Reason for Classification*, p. 299 **Lab Zone Do It!** *How Do Taxonomists Classify Organisms?* p. 301 **Everyday Biology** *Who Is K.P. Cofgs?* p. 301 **STS: Issues in Biology** *Kingdom Battles*, p. 303	**Unit 3 Review Module** ■ Section Review 13.1 ■ Activity Recordsheet 13-1 ■ Enrichment Topic 13-1 **Laboratory Manual,** Lab 23: "Classifying: Constructing Keys" **Issues and Decision Making** 13-1 **Interpreting and Developing Graphics,** 37
13.2 Basis for Classification **Objectives** ■ Relate phylogenetic trees and evolutionary relationships ■ Explain the basis for classification and some problems in classifying organisms	**Lab Zone Think About It!** *Constructing a Phylogenetic Tree,* p. 309 **Lab Zone Do It!** *Why Is Classification Difficult?* p. 312	**Unit 3 Review Module** ■ Section Review 13.2 ■ Activity Recordsheet 13-2 ■ Critical Thinking Exercise 13 ■ Interpreting Graphics 13 **Consumer Applications** 13-1 **Interpreting and Developing Graphics,** 38
13.3 Identifying Organisms **Objectives** ■ Demonstrate the applications of a dichotomous key ■ Explain the relationship of classification to biodiversity	**STS: Environmental Awareness** *Using Classification,* p. 314 **Lab Zone Do It!** *How Do I Use a Field Guide?* p. 314 **In the Community** *Looking for Diversity,* p. 315 **Everyday Biology** *Guiding Life,* p. 315 **Lab Zone Investigate It!** *Designing a Key,* p. 316	**Unit 3 Review Module** ■ Section Review 13.3 ■ Activity Recordsheets 13-3 and 13-4 ■ Vocabulary Review 13 ■ Chapter 13 Tests **Interpreting and Developing Graphics,** 39 **Spanish Reviews** ■ Chapter 13 ■ Unit 3

Technology Resources

Internet Connections

Within this chapter, you will see the **bioSURF** logo. If you and your students have access to the Internet, the following URL address will provide various Internet connections that are related to topics and features presented in this chapter:

http://evolution.biosurf.com

You can also find relevant chapter material at **The Biology Place** address:

http://www.biology.com

CD-ROMs

Biología: la telaraña de la vida,
   (Spanish Student Edition) Chapter 13
Teacher's Resource Planner, Chapter 13
   Supplements
Interactive Biological Simulations
■ Classification of Organisms
TestWorks CD-ROM
■ Chapter 13 Tests

Overhead Transparencies

■ Phylogenetic Tree, #26 and #27

Videotapes

Biology Alive! Video Series
Rewind: The Web of Life Reteach Videos

Planning for Activities

STUDENT EDITION

Lab Zone
Discover It! p. 299
 ■ photograph of an organism that is unfamiliar

Lab Zone Do It! p. 301
 ■ place that contains a variety of objects, such as a closet, a locker, or the space under a bed

Lab Zone
Think About It! p. 309
 ■ table on page 309
 ■ paper
 ■ pencil

Lab Zone Do It! p. 312
 ■ rocks, preserved specimens, leaves, and classroom objects

Lab Zone Do It! p. 314
 ■ field guides

Lab Zone
Investigate It! p. 316
 ■ 6–10 different types of leaves
 ■ ruler
 ■ hand lens

TEACHER'S EDITION

Quick Activity, p. 300
Taxonomy
 ■ pictures of living things

Teacher Demo, p. 303
Classifying by cell characteristics and structures
 ■ microprojector
 ■ a variety of cells

Teacher Demo, p. 305
Generations from a common ancestor
 ■ a family tree

Teacher Demo, p. 307
Phylogenetic tree and kingdoms
 ■ overhead transparency
 ■ different color marking pens

Class Activity, p. 309
Classification of animal hearts
 ■ models, preserved specimens, or pictures of hearts from an amphibian, a reptile, a bird, and a mammal

Quick Activity, p. 313
Dichotomous key
 ■ photos of three similar organisms

Chapter Objectives

Students will learn the main concepts of this chapter as they complete the following objectives.

- Describe the system for classifying organisms
- Distinguish among different classification systems
- Relate phylogenetic trees and evolutionary relationships
- Explain the basis for classification and some problems in classifying organisms
- Demonstrate the applications of a dichotomous key
- Explain the relationship of classification to biodiversity

Key Words

13.1 taxonomy, kingdom, phylum, class, order, family, genus, division, binomial nomenclature

13.2 phylogenetic tree

13.3 dichotomous key

The Opening Story

Have students discuss how they think the story relates to the content of this chapter. Explain that the process of classifying organisms depends on knowing the similarities and differences between like species.

298

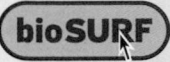

You can find out more about classification by exploring the following Internet address:
http://evolution.biosurf.com

In this chapter . . .

FEATURES

Everyday Biology
- Who Is K. P. Cofgs?
- Guiding Life

In the Community
Looking for Diversity

 Issues in Biology
Kingdom Battles

Environmental Awareness
Using Classification

LAB ZONES

Discover It!
- Discovering a Reason for Classification

Do It!
- How Do Taxonomists Classify Organisms?
- Why Is Classification Difficult?
- How Do I Use a Field Guide?

Think About It!
- Constructing a Phylogenetic Tree

Investigate It!
- Designing a Key

WHERE IS THE GIANT SQUID?

If you ever see a giant squid in its natural environment, be sure to take plenty of notes, for you might be the first person to observe such a sight! In the words of one researcher, more is known about extinct dinosaurs than about giant squids. Of the many giant squids that have washed ashore (top left), the longest was more than 18 meters. These ocean dwellers have appeared in countless legends and stories. Yet researchers have little data about the habitat, eating habits, and mechanisms of movement of these enormous animals and other organisms that live in the open ocean.

Researchers can hypothesize about how giant squids live, but they cannot identify the closest relatives of these mysterious marine animals. Are giant squids more closely related to the *Idiosepius* squid, just 2.5 centimeters long, or to the 3.5-meter-long Humboldt squid? Researchers need direct observation of the giant squids in their environment in order to discover how squids are related to each other. What types of information could researchers use to classify the giant squid? And what other strange living things inhabit the ocean? Why is the classification of organisms vital to the study of life on Earth?

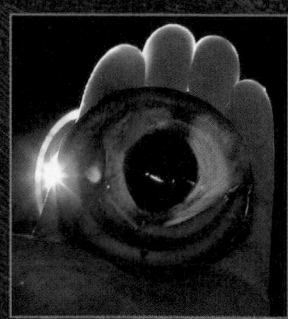

This eye of a Humboldt squid is much smaller than the average giant squid eye.

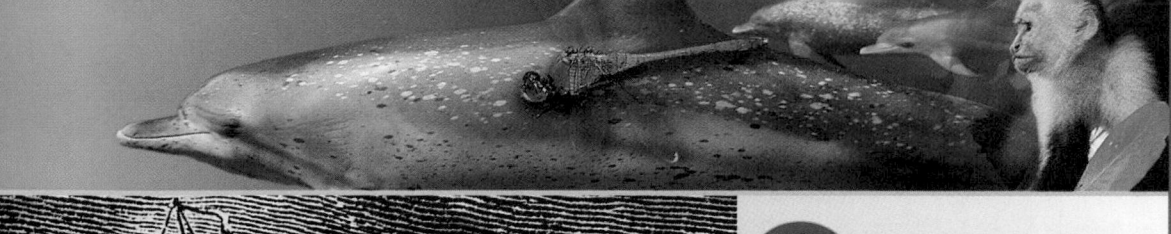

 Discover It!

Discovering a Reason for Classification

You need a photograph of an organism that is unfamiliar to you

1. Your teacher will display the photograph to your class.
2. Everyone in your class should write down one name they would assign to the organism. What other species might this organism be related to? Why?
3. Compare the different names that you and your classmates gave the unfamiliar organism. What criteria were used in naming the organism?

Although classification may be difficult under certain circumstances, it serves an important purpose. Classification eliminates confusion caused by name differences, organizes vast amounts of information into manageable levels, and reveals evolutionary relationships among organisms.

WRITE ABOUT IT!

In your science journal, write about how your name identifies you. Do you have a common name that leads to confusion, or a name that is difficult to spell? Write about any nicknames you may have and explain how you got them.

Chapter 13 Classification **299**

PORTFOLIO PREVIEW

Students should be encouraged to add to their portfolios as they work through this chapter. In addition to the *Write About It* opportunity, the following section is an excellent opportunity for portfolio entries:

■ Section 13.2: *Basis for Classification*

Opening Activities

bioSURF If you have access to the Internet in your classroom or school, you may wish to have students connect to the address shown on page 298. You may also want to have students conduct net searches for information using key words related to this chapter. For example, they could search for entries under taxonomy, classification, and binomial nomenclature.

Discover It!

Discovering a Reason for Classification

TEAM WORK

You may wish to choose a relatively uncommon animal, such as a marmot, lemming, warthog, llama, zebra, or Gila monster. Students should identify adaptations, physical characteristics, or behavior similar to more common animals as a basis for their answers.

WRITE ABOUT IT

Call on volunteers to share their journal entries. Have students relate their experiences to identifying organisms in a classification system.

REWIND to Chapter 12

Briefly review concepts learned in Chapter 12, *Human Evolution.* Ask:

■ **What are some genus and species names used to identify the human family?**

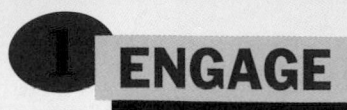

13.1

① ENGAGE

Consider The Big Idea

Have students read The Big Idea! at the top of the page. Point out that classification systems change as information about a species increases.

Use the Visual

Ask students to study the photograph that opens the section. Explain that a classification system organizes things according to similar characteristics. Ask:

- **What are some advantages of classifying organisms?** (Classification makes it easier to find and study data, to identify relationships, and to trace evolutionary progress and extinction of organisms.)

Quick Activity

Display pictures of 15 to 20 living things and ask students to suggest ways to arrange them so that organisms with similar characteristics are grouped together. Explain that this type of task is one concern of taxonomy, which is the branch of biology that deals with the classification of living things.

Interactive Biological Simulations

Classification of Organisms
Students are introduced to the five-kingdom classification system and the taxa that make up each kingdom. Students use a dichotomous key to identify a number of conifers.

13.1 Classification

What you'll learn

IDEAS
- To describe the system for classifying organisms
- To distinguish between different classification systems

WORDS
taxonomy, kingdom, phylum, classes, orders, family, genus, divisions, binomial nomenclature

Classified information

Can you imagine shopping in a store that did not organize its stock? It would be chaos! Most hardware stores first sort items into general categories, such as electrical and plumbing supplies. Then they create smaller categories—for example, metal and plastic pipes in the plumbing section. Scientists have a similar method for categorizing organisms.

GROUPING ORGANISMS

Sorting life is a taxing business

FIGURE 13.1

Classifying Life

Trace the taxonomy of house cats, from kingdom to species. Which of the animals shown is most closely related to the house cat? ❶

Biologists study an enormous variety of organisms. Imagine trying to identify relationships between whales, bacteria, sponges, and redwood trees. Just sorting out species of ants can be challenging. Biologists organize living things into categories. The field of biology that identifies and classifies organisms is called **taxonomy** (taks-ON-oh-mee). Taxonomists analyze shared characteristics to determine evolutionary relationships between species. These organisms are then grouped, or classified. The biological classification system groups the most closely related organisms together.

	Kingdom	Phylum	Class	Order	Family	Genus	Species
	Animalia	Chordata	Mammalia	Carnivora	Felidae	Felis	Sylvestris
House cat							
Mountain lion							
African lion							
Horse							
Giant squid							

House cats are members of the kingdom Animalia. Their skeletal structure places them in the phylum Chordata.

Members of the class Mammalia have hair and nurse their offspring. Most members of the order Carnivora have sharp teeth and eat meat.

Members of the family Felidae have long, lithe bodies and are excellent hunters. The small, domesticated cat belongs to the genus *Felis* and the species *sylvestris*.

300 *Unit 3 Change and Diversity*

STUDENT RESOURCES

From the Teacher's Resource Package, use:
- Section Review 13.1, Activity Recordsheet 13-1, and Enrichment Topic 13-1 from Unit 3 Review Module
- Lab 23: "Classifying: Constructing Keys"
- Issues and Decision Making 16-1

TECHNOLOGY RESOURCES

Relevant technology resources include:
- Spanish Student Edition CD-ROM
- Teacher's Resource Planner CD-ROM
- Interactive Biological Simulations CD-ROM: "Classification of Organisms"

The classification system that biologists use today is based on a system developed by Carl von Linné, a Swedish biologist of the mid-1700s. Linné established a system of groups called taxa (singular: *taxon*). Each taxon is a category into which related organisms are placed. The system of classification Linné developed is a hierarchy of taxa. Linné ranked taxa from the broadest, most general groups to the smallest, most specific groups.

Linné's classification system originally included five levels; modern scientists have added two more. The broadest, most general group into which all organisms are divided is called a **kingdom.** Organisms that have similar characteristics such as cell structure, level of cell specialization, and method of obtaining nutrients are grouped together in a kingdom. Kingdoms are divided into phyla (singular: **phylum**). Within each phylum there are groups called **classes.** Classes are further divided into **orders.** The next level is **family,** which is divided into genera (singular: **genus**). A genus is further divided into species.

At each classification level, organisms that share the most characteristics are grouped together. Compare the organisms shown at each level in *Figure 13.1.* What characteristics do all of the organisms shown in the class Mammalia share? Species is the most specific level of the classification system because members of one species can interbreed and produce offspring. Typically, members of a genus and the taxa above cannot interbreed or produce offspring.

The seven categories apply to many, but not all, organisms. The plant kingdom is divided into categories called **divisions** instead of phyla. Bacterial species are often divided into groups called strains.

See Khan Academy

See DE World of Living Things

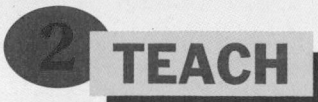

How Do Taxonomists Classify Organisms?

Taxonomists categorize organisms based on their evolutionary relationships. You can model this process and assign objects to taxonomic categories if you . . .

Try This

1 Pick a place that contains a variety of objects, such as a closet, a locker, or the space underneath your bed.
2 Make a list of all of the objects in that place. Be sure to include any dust, crumbs, and scrap papers you find.
3 Divide the objects into several kingdoms. Continue to divide the objects into the other taxa: phyla, classes, orders, families, genera, and species. Record your results.

Analyze Your Results

1 What characteristics did you use to organize the objects? Could you have used other criteria?
2 Was there an object that had a kingdom of its own? What distinguished it from the objects in other kingdoms?

shoes @ lab

THE KINGDOMS

Kingdom borders

Linné classified all organisms into two kingdoms, Plantae and Animalia. A third kingdom, Protista, was added to the classification system in the 1800s. The kingdom Monera was added later. In 1969 a fifth kingdom, Fungi, was added. Although the number of kingdoms used by taxonomists is still a subject of debate, a five-kingdom system is commonly used today.

Monera All bacteria belong to the kingdom Monera. These unicellular prokaryotes do not have a nuclear membrane or any membrane-bound organelles. Most bacteria are heterotrophs, but some are autotrophs.

Protista The kingdom Protista includes unicellular and multicellular eukaryotes. Eukaryotic cells have nuclei and organelles that are surrounded by membranes. The cells of

EVERYDAY BIOLOGY

Who Is K.P. Cofgs?

A mnemonic device helps you to remember something. You can memorize the seven taxa if you come up with a sentence in which the first letter of each word represents a taxon. Here is one example: Kings Play Chess On Fuzzy Green Stools.

Chapter 13 Classification **301**

Explain

Point out to students that in moving from the kingdom to the species level, the taxa narrow and organisms become more closely related. For example, organisms classified in the same family—wolf and domestic dog—are more closely related than are organisms that share only the kingdom, phylum, class, and order—mountain lion and domestic dog.

Clarify Misconceptions

Students may think that breeds of dogs and cats are also of different species. The term *breed* refers to a domesticated variety of animal and is a subgroup of species. Animals of the same species but different breeds can mate to produce fertile, healthy offspring. Dogs of different breeds all belong to the species *Canis familiars.*

 Do It!

How Do Taxonomists Classify Organisms?

Analyze Your Results

1 Classification criteria will vary. Likely responses will indicate that other criteria could have been used.
2 An object that does not share traits with the other objects can be classified in its own kingdom.

❶ The mountain lion
❷ They have hair and nurse their offspring.

Handwritten note: ✱ More specifically, they can produce offspring that are able to produce offspring (not sterile)

MULTICULTURAL PERSPECTIVE

During the Age of Exploration, European explorers discovered new lands and many organisms unfamiliar to European scientists. It became necessary to establish standard names so that scientists from different countries could understand each other.

Using long, Latin names that described the shape, color, and other traits of the organisms, was complex and not very useful. In the mid-1700s, Carl von Linné established a simple system for classifying and naming organisms.

Use the Visual

Ask students to study Figure 13.2. Point out that the lines connecting the circles indicate evolutionary relationships. Ask:

- **How do organisms in the Kingdom Monera differ from organisms in the other four kingdoms?** (Monerans are the only prokaryotes.)
- **Lines connect the kingdoms Fungi, Plantae, and Animalia to the Protists. What does this suggest?** (Organisms in these kingdoms evolved from protists.)

 Science History

Tell students that until the seventeenth century, most scientists classified organisms according to a system developed by the Greek scholars Aristotle and Theophrastus in the fourth century B.C. In this system, organisms were classified as either plants or animals. Animals were placed into three subgroups based on where they lived—air, water, or land. Plants were classified by size: tall plants as trees; medium plants as shrubs; and small plants as herbs.

Think Critically

After students read the descriptions of the five kingdoms in the text and in Figure 13.2, ask:

- **Why are mushrooms not in the same kingdom as other "vegetables"?** (Mushrooms are heterotrophs. Foods classified as "vegetables" come from plants, which are autotrophs. They obtain food through photosynthesis.)

302

FIGURE 13.2
The Five Kingdoms

The five kingdoms are arranged according to their evolutionary relationships (right). In the diagram below, the size of the circle indicates the number of species. Which kingdom has the most species? ❶

Plantae
Plants are multicellular, autotrophic eukaryotes. Their cells have cell walls.

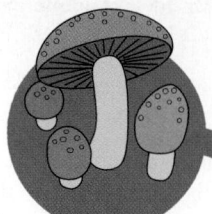

Fungi
Members of the kingdom Fungi are heterotrophic eukaryotes whose cells have cell walls.

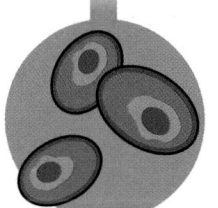

Animalia
An animal is a multicellular heterotroph whose eukaryotic cells lack cell walls.

Protista
Protists are eukaryotes. Most are unicellular, but some are multicellular with little cell specialization.

Monera
Monerans are unicellular prokaryotes; there are both heterotrophic and autotrophic monerans.

most multicellular protists are not specialized. Some protists are autotrophs, but others are heterotrophs. Protists include amebas, as well as algae such as kelp.

Fungi Fungi are eukaryotes. Most are multicellular, with cells that have cell walls. Fungi are also heterotrophs. They obtain nutrition by releasing digestive enzymes into a food source and absorbing the digested nutrients. Fungi include molds, mildews, mushrooms, and yeasts.

Plantae Plants are multicellular eukaryotes. The cells of plants have cell walls and are specialized to form tissues, which are organized into distinct organs. Most plants are autotrophs. They carry out photosynthesis to obtain nutrition for life processes. The kingdom Plantae includes mosses, ferns, cone-bearing plants, and flowering plants.

Animalia Animals are multicellular, eukaryotic, and heterotrophic. Animal cells do not have cell walls,

302 *Unit 3 Change and Diversity*

302

but they do have cell membranes. Most members of the animal kingdom can move from place to place at some stage in their life cycle. In addition to the many familiar representatives, this kingdom includes sponges, jellyfish, worms, sea stars, and insects.

ISSUES IN BIOLOGY
Kingdom battles

As in most scientific fields, technological advances have provided equipment and techniques—for example, the electron microscope and molecular analysis—that reveal new information about evolutionary relationships. As more is learned about different organisms, scientists debate and revise the way they classify them. In fact, there are several classification systems.

Bacteria are one example of organisms that are difficult to classify. Their evolutionary relationships are unclear. One reason is that bacteria do not fossilize easily, so their fossil record is incomplete. For many years, the classification of living bacteria was based on traits that can be easily observed.

Today, thanks to advances in molecular biology, scientists are able to compare RNA in bacterial ribosomes. The biochemical data are used to infer evolutionary relationships between bacteria. As a result, many scientists argue that the kingdom Monera should be divided into two separate kingdoms, for a total of six kingdoms.

→ not observable fact

As you can see in *Figure 13.3*, the six-kingdom system splits monerans into the kingdoms Eubacteria and Archaebacteria. Scientists base this distinction on the argument that these two groups are as different as prokaryotes and eukaryotes. Other scientists interpret recent biochemical findings differently and use an eight-kingdom system. As more information is discovered, the trend toward more kingdoms may continue.

archaebacteria—live in extremely harsh environments (ie Yellowstone springs)

In contrast, some taxonomists favor using an even more general category than kingdoms, which they call domains. According to this system, there are three domains: Bacteria, Archaea, and Eukarya. Domains are further divided into kingdoms. Which classification system do you support? ❷

FIGURE 13.3
Some scientists prefer classification systems other than the five-kingdom system. How do these systems differ? How are they similar? ❸

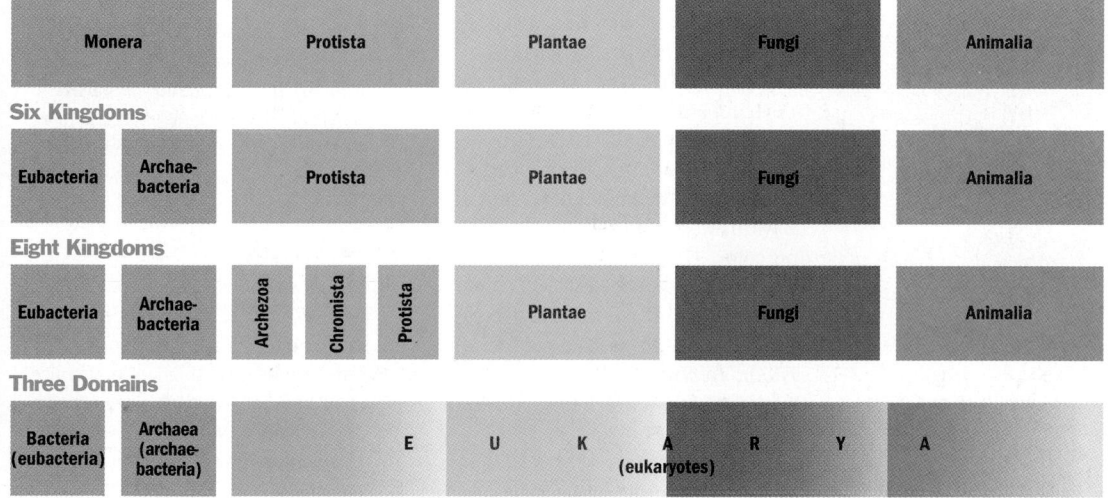

Chapter 13 Classification **303**

Teacher Demo

Use a microprojector to display a variety of cells. Point out the cell characteristics that are used to classify organisms. Since both plants and fungi have cell walls, emphasize the chloroplasts in plant cells that help distinguish them from other organisms.

 STS

Initiate a class discussion on the changing nature of taxonomy. Point out that with the invention of the microscope, scientists discovered new organisms and began to rethink the two-kingdom system. Ask:

- **Why do scientists continue to revise the way they classify organisms?** (Advanced technologies and gene analysis lead to new discoveries about organisms and their evolutionary relationships.)

Use the Visual

To help students understand differences in the proposed kingdoms in Figure 13.3, ask:

- **What is the difference between the proposed six-kingdom and the five-kingdom classification systems?** (Monera is divided into two kingdoms.)
- **What does the third bar in the diagram represent?** (A system with another hierarchy level of domains, which are divided into kingdoms.)
- **How do the eight-kingdom system and the six-kingdom systems differ?** (Protists are divided into three kingdoms.)

Language Arts

During the Middle Ages and the Renaissance, scholars reintroduced Latin as a language in the sciences, philosophy, literature, and law. Latin words entered the English language as religious vocabulary and as the vocabulary of science, scholarship, government, and law. Ask:

- **What Latin words or phrases are often used today?**
(*Etcetera*—and so forth; *habeas corpus*—you should have the body; *Carpe diem*—seize the day; *E pluribus unum*—from many one)

3 ASSESS

Evaluate Understanding

Have each student develop a graphic organizer showing Linné's classification system and the five kingdoms recognized by most scientists. Ask students to add the characteristics of the organisms in each kingdom. Have them add side branches of other classification systems being considered. Review the graphics as a class.

Reteach

Work with students to develop an outline of the information presented in the section. Use the five-kingdom classification as heads. Then ask students to review the section to find two or more characteristics of each kingdom to add as subheads. After the outline is filled in, ask students to explain why there are several systems of classifying organisms.

NAMING ORGANISMS

A rose is a rose is a rose

What do a crawdad, crayfish, and mudbug have in common? The answer is everything—these are all common names for the same species of freshwater crustacean. Within a language, there are often several different words for the same object. And because there are hundreds of languages, hundreds of words can be used to describe the same thing.

Clear communication among scientists around the world requires an international system for naming organisms. Linné and the scientists of his time used Latin for the names of taxa. Because Latin was no longer a spoken language, the meanings of the words were not likely to change, as the meanings of words in modern language do. In English, for example, the word *cool* was once used only to describe a temperature. Today, *cool* can also mean "excellent." Linné was so enthusiastic about his new system that he changed his own name to a Latin version—Carolus Linnaeus (lih-NAY-us).

Before Linnaeus developed his system, scientists used very long Latin names to describe organisms. This system was not useful because the names became too long and complex. The scientific name for the common European honeybee, for example, consisted of 12 words describing the bee's shape and color.

Linnaeus proposed using a system called **binomial nomenclature,** meaning "two-name naming." In that system, an organism's scientific name consists of the genus name and the species name. For example, the crayfish shown in *Figure 13.4* is *Cambarus bartoni*. The genus name is first and

Why Latin?

mudbug

crawdaddy

crayfish

ha! text that!

FIGURE 13.4

Its scientific name is *Cambarus bartoni*, but you may know this crayfish by any of its three nicknames.

304 *Unit 3 Change and Diversity*

Genus + species = name (in Latin)

Linnaeus = Linné

FIGURE 13.5

Binomial nomenclature ensures that biologists are referring to the same organism. What is the scientific name of this plant? ❶

is capitalized; the species name is second and is not capitalized. Both words are printed in italics or underlined. The genus name can be abbreviated to a single letter, as in *C. bartoni*. Using binomial nomenclature, the honeybee's name is reduced from 12 words to 2: *Apis mellifera*. What other scientific names do you know? ❷

CHECKPOINT 13.1

1. How are organisms classified? Describe the modern classification system.
2. What characteristics distinguish the five-kingdom classification system from other classification systems?
3. **Critical Thinking** What items are commonly found in a grocery store? Use Linnaeus' system to classify these items into groups.

Build on What You Know

4. The classification system organizes huge amounts of information into a usable form. What other ranking systems are used in science to organize large amounts of data? *(Need to jog your memory? Revisit relevant concepts in Chapter 1, Section 1.1, and Chapter 2, Section 2.2.)*

CHECKPOINT 13.1

1. Organisms are classified according to characteristics. The modern classification system includes kingdom, phylum, class, order, family, genus, species.
2. Bacteria are included in Monera; other systems divide this kingdom into two. Also, the five-kingdom system does not recognize domains.

3. **Organizing and classifying** Students' classification systems should progress from broad to narrow groups.
4. Organizing cells into tissues, organs, and systems; the periodic table.

❶ *Primula auricula*
❷ Answers will vary.

13.2 Basis for Classification

Not just for the birds
When is a Baltimore Oriole not a Baltimore Oriole? When it is a Northern Oriole! Bird specialists once considered the Baltimore Oriole (left) and Bullock's Oriole variations of a single species—the Northern Oriole. However, it has been discovered that the birds rarely interbreed, so now both birds are called by their original names. New data often lead researchers to reclassify organisms.

What you'll learn

IDEAS
• To relate phylogenetic trees and evolutionary relationships
• To explain the basis for classification and some problems in classifying organisms

WORDS
phylogenetic tree

EVOLUTIONARY RELATIONSHIPS

Taxa are branching out

A family tree illustrates relationships among individuals and includes ancestors as far back as records allow. The more distant ancestors appear at the base or on the trunk of the tree. Recent relatives make up the branches or the branch ends. Taxonomists use a diagram similar to a family tree. The diagram, called a **phylogenetic** (fy-loh-juh-NEH-tik) **tree,** shows the evolutionary relationships among organisms.

Family historians use family records and photographs to create a family tree. Scientists use the fossil record and structural and molecular comparisons to construct phylogenetic trees similar to the one in *Figure 13.6*. Like a family tree, a phylogenetic tree has a trunk and branches, but a phylogenetic tree illustrates relationships among species—not individuals.

According to the theory of evolution, all organisms are descendants of a common ancestor—the first cell. Therefore, all organisms, living or extinct, are related to some degree.

FIGURE 13.6

A Phylogenetic Tree
You can use a phylogenetic tree to compare evolutionary relationships among organisms. The number of branches indicates the degree to which two organisms are related. For example, a domestic cat is more closely related to a lion than it is to a horse. The boxes show milestones, or distinguishing characteristics of each branch.

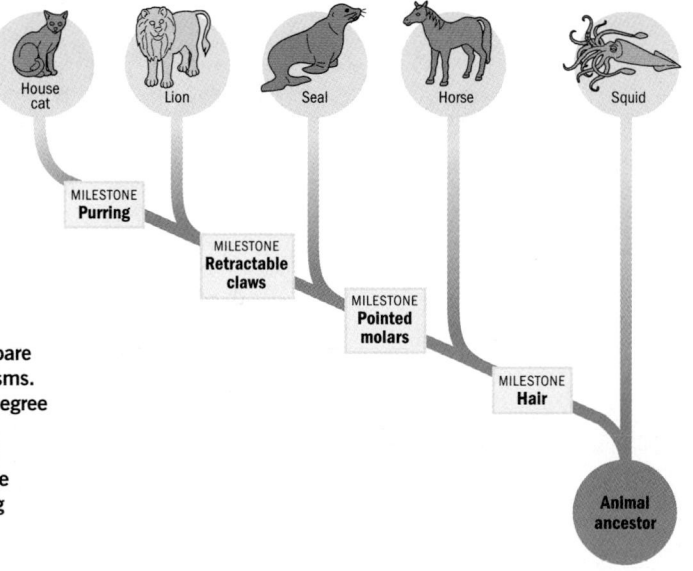

Chapter 13 Classification **305**

STUDENT RESOURCES

From the Teacher's Resource Package, use:
■ Section Review 13.2, Activity Record-sheet 13-2, and Critical Thinking Exercise 13 from Unit 3 Review Module
■ Consumer Applications 13-1

TECHNOLOGY RESOURCES

Relevant technology resources include:
■ Spanish Student Edition CD-ROM
■ Teacher's Resource Planner CD-ROM

① ENGAGE

Use the Visual

Have students study the photograph that opens the section. Explain that organisms often are identified by a variety of common names. Ask:

■ **Why is a consistent identification system important in taxonomy?** (It helps scientists study and clarify evolutionary links among organisms.)

Check Prior Knowledge

To assess students' knowledge about classification, ask:

■ **What types of evidence do scientists use to help determine evolutionary relationships?** (Microscopic analyses, fossilized and contemporary physical characteristics, cell structure, level of cell specialization, DNA analysis, and behavior)
■ **What is DNA?** (Deoxyribonucleic acid; a double helix of nucleotides located in a cell's nucleus; DNA contains hereditary information and carries instructions that control cellular activity.)

Teacher Demo

Display a family tree. Explain that it shows relationships among several generations of descendants from a common ancestor. Show split branches for each generation. Compare it to the phylogenetic tree in Figure 13.6.

TEACH

Use the Visual

Direct students' attention to Figure 13.7, which shows a phylogenetic tree of the major taxa. Explain that the tree illustrates the evolutionary history of organisms from oldest (at the base) to most recent (at the tips). Emphasize that organisms located along the same branch are closely related, while those appearing on different branches are not. Help students interpret the diagram by asking:

- **Which type of organisms evolved first from the prokaryotes?** (Monera)
- **Which group of organisms evolved last?** (Mammals)
- **How is the first milestone passed by plants similar to the first milestone passed by animals?** (Both mark the formation of tissues.)
- **Into what groups are organisms in the plant kingdom classified?** (Mosses, ferns, conifers, and flowering plants)
- **What is common to all the organisms that appear on the longest branch?** (They are all animals.)

FIGURE 13.7

A Phylogenetic Tree of Major Groups

This phylogenetic tree illustrates the evolutionary relationships among major groups of modern organisms. The branch points of the tree represent common ancestors. Each time a branch divides into a smaller branch, it shows the emergence of a new group of organisms.

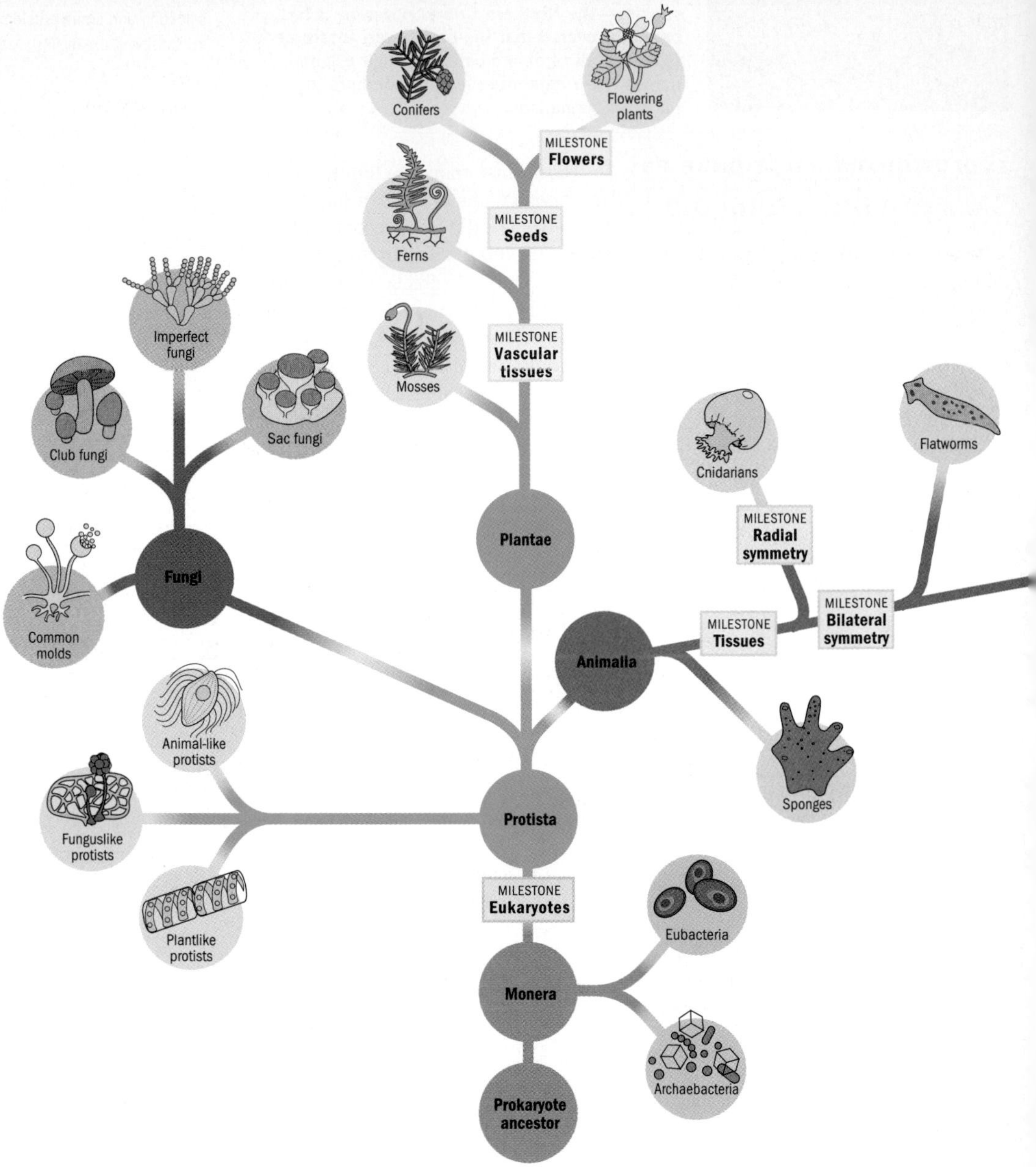

MEETING DIVERSE NEEDS

LEP Suggest that students draw the phylogenetic tree in their notebooks and copy the labels as they appear in Figure 13.7. Tell students to add the word(s) from their native language, when possible, next to each label on the diagram. Students may find it helpful to illustrate their completed trees.

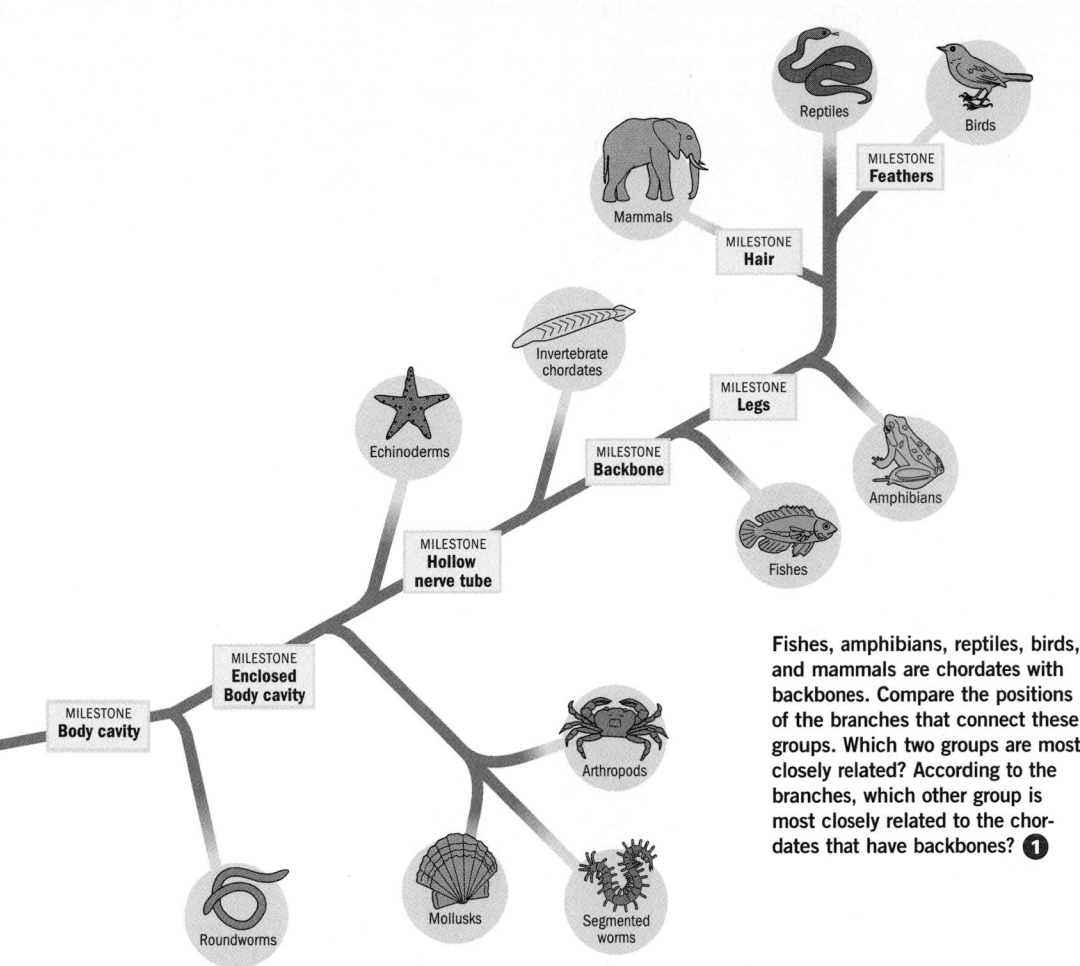

Fishes, amphibians, reptiles, birds, and mammals are chordates with backbones. Compare the positions of the branches that connect these groups. Which two groups are most closely related? According to the branches, which other group is most closely related to the chordates that have backbones? ❶

 Math

Explain that mathematicians often use Venn diagrams to classify information about numbers into sets and subsets. Venn diagrams are an effective way to show relationships among different things, and they have applications in many disciplines. Model how to develop a Venn diagram. Then have students create a Venn diagram comparing two organisms described in this chapter.

Teacher Demo

On an overhead transparency, draw the phylogenetic tree shown. Use different colors to add one kingdom at a time to the tree. As the branches representing each kingdom are added, review the traits of the organisms in that kingdom. Emphasize that the place at which the drawing changes color identifies the evolutionary beginning of that kingdom.

Build Writing Skills

Have students write an essay, poem, or song lyrics to summarize the evolutionary relationships shown in Figure 13.7. Have students emphasize the evolution of organisms from one kingdom to the next and the traits that distinguish the groups.

Chapter 13 Classification **307**

MEETING DIVERSE NEEDS

At Risk Have students create their own schematic to show how different groups of organisms are related. Encourage students to illustrate their schematics using pictures they draw or cut from magazines.

❶ Reptiles and birds are the most closely related groups of those listed. Invertebrate chordates are most closely related to vertebrate chordates.

Apply

Explain that the evolutionary basis of classification indicates that closely related species have a recent common ancestor. Ask:

- **Who is more closely related to you, your first cousins, your nieces and nephews, or your aunts and uncles? Explain.** (Students should recognize that nieces and nephews are closer relatives as they go back only one generation to share two common ancestors.) Point out that students' parents are the grandparents of their nieces and nephews. Grandparents are the most common ancestors shared by cousins, aunts, and uncles.

Physical Science

Show students a periodic table of the elements. Point out that the elements are classified within the table according to the structure of their atoms and their chemical properties. Explain that taxonomists study chemical similarities among organisms to find evolutionary patterns. This information is used to classify organisms.

Evolutionary relationships can be compared to relationships between family members. Brothers and sisters are very closely related. They share very recent common ancestors—their parents. Cousins are less closely related than brothers and sisters because they share less recent common ancestors, grandparents.

In a similar manner, species are closely related if they share a recent ancestor, and are classifed to share more specific taxa such as Family or Order. For example, lions and domestic cats are both classified as belonging to the family Felidae.

Species whose shared ancestor is very distant are less closely related and are classified to share more general taxa such as Phylum or Kingdom. House cats and the giant squid only share the kingdom Animalia. How does the phylogenetic tree in *Figure 13.7* show these relationships? ❷

FIGURE 13.8
The shark (top) and the dolphin (bottom) have fins that look similar. However, internal examination reveals that the shark fin contains cartilage and the dolphin fin contains bone. How does this difference indicate a distant evolutionary relationship? ❶

PHYSICAL STRUCTURE
Books and their covers

Linnaeus based his classification system on features that he could observe. Scientists still observe physical features of modern organisms to determine evolutionary relationships. As you now know, structures that are similar because they were inherited from a common ancestor are homologous structures. For example, lions and other big cats of the family Felidae share many obvious similarities, such as long, lithe bodies, powerful claws, and rounded ears.

Physical similarities do not always indicate a close evolutionary relationship. As you may recall, structures that look similar but evolved from different ancestors are called analogous structures. The fins on the dolphin and shark shown in *Figure 13.8* are analogous structures. By comparing the fins, scientists have concluded

MEETING DIVERSE NEEDS

Sight Impaired Dictate the labels on Figure 13.7 to a student with a Braillewriter. Have sight-impaired students work with sighted students to prepare a phylogentic tree by gluing string to a mat board. The sight-impaired student should place the labels in the correct location on the board.

❶ The difference in composition of the fins indicates that the structures evolved from different, not common, ancestors.

❷ A branch point represents a common ancestor. The more closely related organisms are, the fewer are the branch points between them.

❸ Students are not likely to recognize that the two animals are related.

FIGURE 13.9
The hyrax (above) is about the size of a rabbit. The inset (left) gives you an idea of the hyrax's size relative to the largest land mammal, the African elephant (far left). Yet the fossil record suggests that the elephant and the hyrax share a common ancestor.

that the two types of fins evolved separately. Therefore, they cannot be used as evidence of relatedness. To pinpoint true homologous structures that indicate common ancestry, scientists often study internal structures, such as cells and organs or developing embryos.

Like analogous structures, physical differences do not always prove that two organisms are not related. Do you think the elephant and hyrax, shown in *Figure 13.9*, are related? Structural comparisons from the fossil record show that these species evolved from a common ancestor.

BIOCHEMISTRY
Looks aren't everything

In addition to studying fossil evidence and comparing physical structures, scientists use other tools to classify organisms. Biochemical analyses of DNA, RNA, and proteins can provide evidence of evolutionary relationships.

In analyzing DNA, scientists infer that, after speciation, the mutations that occur in one new species will be different from those in the other new species. The more differences there are between the DNA sequences of

LAB ZONE ? Think About It! bioSURF

Constructing a Phylogenetic Tree

Scientists compare the amino acid sequences of the same protein in different species. These data reveal degrees of relatedness between organisms, and can be used to create a phylogenetic tree. You, too, can use biochemical data to construct a phylogenetic tree if you . . .

Sequence of Amino Acids in Cytochrome *c* Protein	
Organism	**Sequence of First 25 Amino Acids**
Dog	G D V E K G K K I F V Q K C A Q C H T V E K G G K
Tuna	G D V A K G K K T F V Q K C A Q C H T V E N G G K
Moth	G N A D V G K K I F V Q R C A Q C H T V E A G G K
Wheat	G N P D A G A K I F K T K C A Q C H T V D A G A G

Try This

1 Letter by letter, compare the amino acid sequences for cytochrome *c* (a mitochondrial protein) in dogs and tuna. Record the number of amino acids that differ.
2 Repeat this process until you have compared each of the four sequences with the other three. You will have six numbers.
3 Use your results to sketch a phylogenetic tree.

Analyze Your Results

1 How does your tree indicate the relationships among the organisms? Which two organisms are most closely related? Which organisms are least closely related?
2 If you determined relationships based on external features, how would your phylogenetic tree look? Would it match the tree you created based on the amino acid sequences? Why or why not?

Class Activity

Show models, or pictures of hearts of an amphibian, reptile, bird, and mammal. Name the class and animal from which each heart came. Allow students to examine the display and note the differences. Emphasize that such differences are used as a criterion for classification.

LAB ZONE Think About It!

Constructing a Phylogenetic Tree

Try This

1 Three
2 Tuna and moth: 7; moth and wheat: 9; tuna and wheat: 12; dog and wheat: 11; dog and moth: 6
3 The tree should show wheat as an ancestor, splitting to moth, which splits to dog and tuna.

Analyze Your Results

1 Cytochrome *c* should be the determining factor. Closely related, fewest differences in cytochrome *c* sequence; distantly related, most variation: Most closely related, dog and tuna; least closely related, tuna and wheat.
2 Answers may suggest dog and moth are more closely related than the dog and tuna.

FACTS AND FIGURES

In one DNA biochemical analysis used to determine the relatedness of organisms, a strand of DNA is taken from two organisms. One strand is made radioactive and each double helix is made into single-stranded DNA. A single strand from each is combined and observed for bonding sites. Since bonding occurs only where base-pairs are complementary, the greater the number of bonds, the more closely related the organisms are.

Use the Visual

Direct students' attention to Figure 13.10 which compares two classification schemes. Ask:

- **How does the classification of birds in the top diagram differ from that shown in the bottom diagram?** (The top diagram shows birds evolving separately from reptiles. The bottom diagram shows birds evolving after some reptile groups. It also indicates a close relationship between birds and crocodiles.)
- **About how long after the branch that gave rise to turtles and snakes did birds evolve?** (About 100 million years)
- **In what class are birds classified?** (Aves)

Explain

Point out that guinea pigs once were classified together with hamsters, gerbils, mice, and rats in a group of mammals called rodents. Scientists recently compared proteins in the DNA of guinea pigs with the DNA of other rodents and discovered that guinea pig proteins were very different from those of other rodents. As a result, guinea pigs now are classified in their own group.

Scientific thought is always changing based on discovery of new evidence (invention of new tools)

two organisms, the more distant the common ancestor, and the less closely the organisms are related.

Biochemists also study the proteins coded for by DNA. For example, cytochrome *c* is a protein in the mitochondria of almost all eukaryotes. Scientists use differences in the amino acid sequences of cytochrome *c* to determine relationships among species. The cytochrome *c* amino acid sequence in humans differs from the sequence in chickens by 14 amino acids. The human sequence differs from the sequence in fruit flies by 25 amino acids. Based on this data, with which species—chickens or fruit flies—do humans share a more recent common ancestor?

FIGURE 13.10

How Should Birds Be Classified?

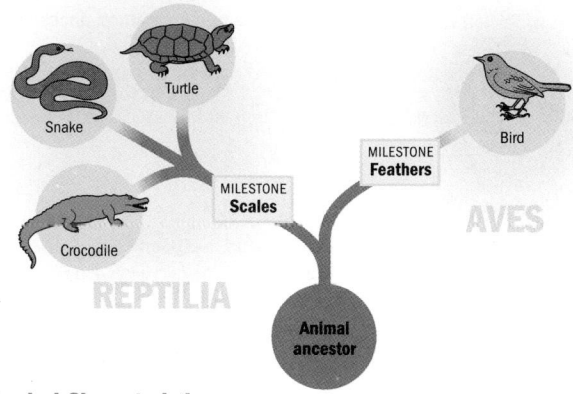

Physical Characteristics
Based on physical characteristics, crocodiles, snakes, and turtles are all classified as Reptilia. Birds are classified as Aves.

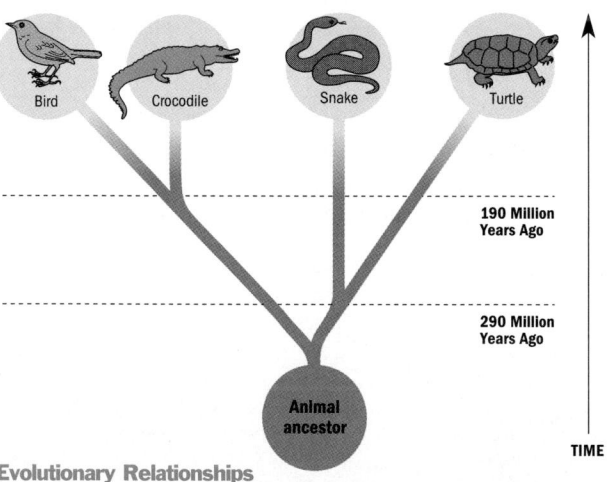

Evolutionary Relationships
Based on fossil evidence, crocodiles are more closely related to birds.

PROBLEMS IN CLASSIFICATION

Identity crisis

Despite the methods scientists have developed, it is still often difficult to classify organisms. Like every scientific field, taxonomy constantly changes as researchers discover new information and refine theories. As you have read, all taxonomists do not use the five-kingdom system. At each taxon below kingdom, the difficulty in classification tends to increase.

One example of a difficulty in classification involves the members of the class Reptilia. Older taxonomy methods placed snakes, turtles, and crocodiles together in the same class, based on shared traits such as scales and skull structure. Birds were assigned to their own class, Aves.

According to the most recent evidence, however, crocodiles and birds share a common dinosaur ancestor that lived about 190 million years ago. Snakes and turtles have a more distant common ancestor that lived almost 100 million years earlier. The fossil evidence indicates that crocodiles are actually more closely related to birds than they are to snakes or turtles.

Such evidence leads some taxonomists to conclude that birds should be reclassified as a type of reptile. Based on the information in *Figure 13.10*, how do you think birds should be classified? Additional information, such as the breeding habits of the

---

MEETING DIVERSE NEEDS

Gifted Many scientists classify the panda with bears. Others contend that the panda is more closely related to the raccoon. Have gifted students research the classification of the giant panda to find out what evidence supports each hypothesis and which classification is currently accepted by the greatest number of scientists.

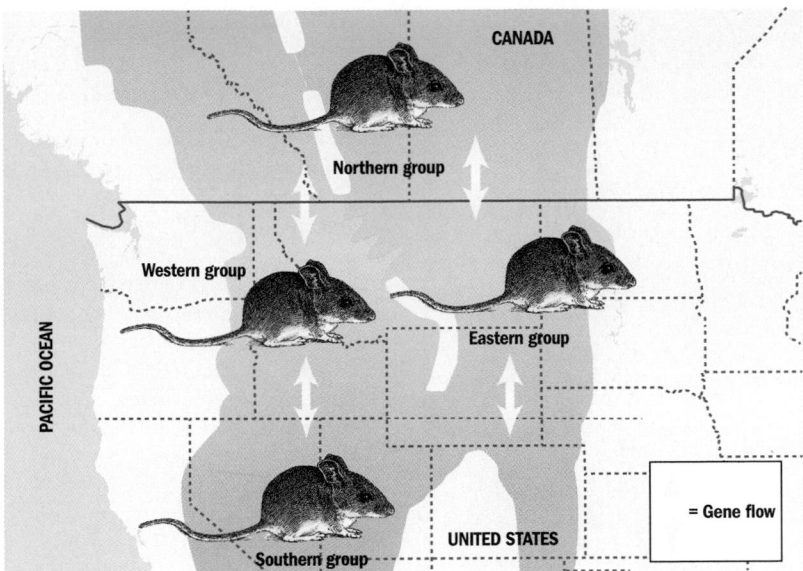

FIGURE 13.11

Two Species or Not Two Species?

This figure shows the range of four populations of the deer mouse *Peromyscus maniculatus.* What factors prevent the eastern and western populations from becoming genetically separate species? ❸

extinct ancestors of birds and reptiles, would further clarify the relationships among members of the class Reptilia and the class Aves. Unfortunately, fossils contain few clues about organisms' breeding habits.

Species definitions can also be problematic. You may recall that a species is populations that can interbreed and produce fertile offspring. But this definition is difficult to apply to organisms that reproduce asexually. These organisms are classified based on their cell shape, organelles, and DNA.

It is also difficult to classify organisms that can reproduce sexually but do not live in the same area. An example of populations that are difficult to classify is four groups of deer mice in the Rocky Mountains, shown in *Figure 13.11.* The groups are physically similar but live in different regions. Interbreeding takes place where ranges overlap, except between the eastern and western groups. Yet, these two groups are considered the same species because gene flow occurs via the northern and southern groups.

Interbreeding among overlapping groups allows gene flow — the transfer of genetic information among all four mouse populations, even the two groups that never breed. However, some scientists speculate that all four mouse populations are evolving into different species. Someday perhaps none of the groups will interbreed.

Sometimes, classification proves so difficult that taxonomists need to propose new taxa. In 1995 the discovery of organisms living on the mouthparts of lobsters excited researchers worldwide. *Figure 13.12* shows one of these new organisms. The organism, *Symbion pandora*, has reproductive and structural characteristics that placed it in a newly proposed phylum—the Cycliophora.

The study of evolutionary relationships is an evolving field, as taxonomists attempt to construct more accurate phylogenetic trees. Perhaps you will be among the scientists who collect new data and debate their meaning.

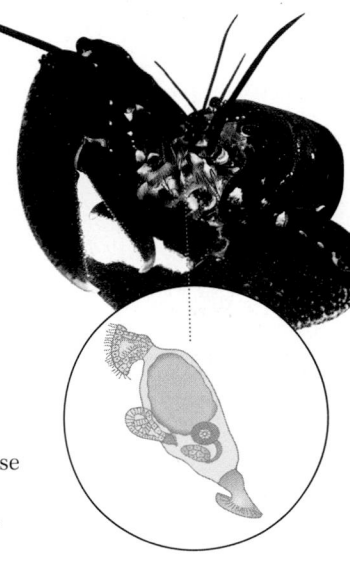

FIGURE 13.12

Imagine researchers' surprise when they discovered members of a new phylum, Cycliophora, living on the mouthparts of lobsters.

Chapter 13 Classification **311**

Use the Visual

Ask students to study Figure 13.11 and read the caption. Ask:

- **Why might the eastern and western mouse groups evolve into separate species if the groups of mice between them become extinct?** (Genes from the two farthest groups intermix because of breeding with the mouse populations between them. If the groups of mice separating the eastern and western populations are extinct, genes no longer mix.)

Think Critically

Challenge students to think about how new species might evolve. Ask:

- **How might interbreeding among different mouse groups change the genetic makeup of the groups enough to result in a new species?** (With interbreeding, new genes are introduced into each population. With time, the new traits may make one group better suited to its environment than its predecessors. Competition may result in the survival of one group at the expense of the other, and allow a new species to evolve.)

❶ Chickens, based on the amino acid sequence data

❷ In the same class as crocodiles; Snakes and turtles belong to another class.

❸ Even though the western and eastern populations never interbreed, there is some gene flow because both interbreed with the northern and southern groups. Because some gene flow is occurring, the eastern and western groups are capable of interbreeding, even if they usually do not.

Why Is Classification Difficult?

Analyze Your Results

1 Responses will vary.

2 The new object might require a new category. Students should note that science is not absolute and theories may change as new information becomes available.

3 ASSESS

Evaluate Understanding

Ask students to summarize the main ideas of this section by writing a brief essay that completes each of the following phrases.

- **Taxonomists use trees to show**
- **Scientists determine an organism's classification by**
- **Some problems in classifying organisms are**

Reteach

Draw the bottom part of Figure 13.10 on the board. Explain that the diagram shows evolutionary relationships among organisms, in this case, reptiles and birds. Guide students to recognize that the branch including snakes and turtles indicates that these animals began to evolve from a common ancestor about 290 million years ago. Discuss what information the tree provides about the evolution of birds and crocodiles.

 Do It!

Why Is Classification Difficult?

Phylogenetic trees grow and change. You can discover why if you . . .

Try This

1 Your teacher will give you an assortment of objects, such as rocks, preserved specimens, leaves, and classroom objects.
2 Classify the objects. Record your classifications, as well as the criteria for classification. Criteria may include shape, color, function, or size.
3 Your teacher will then give you a new object. Classify the new object according to your system.
4 Now swap your objects for those of a classmate. Devise a classification system for your classmate's objects.

Analyze Your Results

1 How do your systems compare with your classmate's? Using the practice of peer review in the scientific method, analyze both systems.
2 How did the new objects affect the classification system? Compare this activity to the process of scientific classification.

FIGURE 13.13
In the phylogenetic trees in this textbook, each of the five kingdoms has been assigned a different color.

STUDYING BIODIVERSITY

Kingdoms up close

In this textbook you will learn about many phyla and classes of the five kingdoms. As you have read, members of a kingdom also share evolutionary relationships. The phylogenetic tree shown in *Figure 13.13* will appear in many of the following chapters to remind you of the relationships between kingdoms.

Monerans are prokaryotes with few structures to study and compare. Until scientists could study their DNA, RNA, and proteins, monerans were difficult to classify. There are about 10,000 species in the kingdom Monera.

The approximately 100,000 species of the kingdom Protista are grouped together because they lack characteristics that would classify them in any of the other four kingdoms. All protists are eukaryotes, and most protists are unicellular.

Taxonomists classify fungi by the structures used in sexual reproduction. Because fungi were once classified as plants, the second taxon of the kingdom Fungi is called a division, not a phylum. About 100,000 species of fungi have been classified to date.

There are more than 260,000 plant species. Members of the kingdom Plantae can be divided into two broad categories: nonvascular plants and vascular plants. Most plants are vascular and differ widely in their physical characteristics.

Taxonomists estimate that there are at least 800,000, and perhaps as many as 12 million, species in the kingdom Animalia. Scientists have proposed more than 30 animal phyla. In this textbook, you will study 10 of the most abundant animal phyla.

CHECKPOINT 13.2

1. How do phylogenetic trees show evolutionary relationships among organisms?
2. What methods do scientists use to obtain data for phylogenetic trees?
3. **Critical Thinking** How is it possible for two different species to have similar physical characteristics yet be only distantly related?

Build on What You Know

4. How might taxonomists use the presence of vestigial structures to classify animals? *(Need to jog your memory? Review relevant concepts in Chapter 10, Section 10.3.)*

 How do scientists organize the vast numbers of Earth's organisms?

add relevant info to concept maps created from p. 302

CHECKPOINT 13.2

1. The closer two organisms are on the phylogenetic tree, the more recent their common ancestor is.
2. Fossil record, biochemical evidence, and homologous structures
3. **Developing a hypothesis** They may have a common ancestor. In addition, similar adaptations may evolve in species that are distantly related, but which inhabit similar niches.
4. Vestigial structures may reveal a relationship to a very different species, placing these two species closer together on a phylogenetic tree than might be assumed from physical appearance.

13.3 Identifying Organisms

Lemur tricks

A German college student, Jutta Schmid, thought she had discovered a new species of primate when she saw this tiny lemur. However, records revealed that this species was discovered in the 1840s, but became confused later on with another species of lemur. Such events show the need for effective classification systems to catalog biodiversity.

What you'll learn

IDEAS
• To demonstrate the applications of a dichotomous key
• To explain the relationship of classification to biodiversity

WORDS
dichotomous key

DICHOTOMOUS KEYS

Your key to nature

Identifying organisms is not limited to the science of taxonomy. Many people are curious about organisms. Some people identify birds, trees, or other organisms as a hobby. Others use this information to plan gardens or to learn more about their surroundings. Have you ever seen a bird or a flower that you wanted to identify?

Have you ever wondered what type of bug just bit you? If so, then you would probably find a dichotomous (dy-KAH-toh-mus) key helpful. A **dichotomous key** is a tool used for identifying organisms. You can use a dichotomous key, such as the one in *Figure 13.14*, to identify insects.

A dichotomous key lists specific observable traits of many organisms. For each trait, the key lists two contrasting options. By picking the options that match an organism's features, you can identify the organism. Dichotomous keys are often found in field guides—books that identify many species of a certain phylum or class.

Most often, people who use field guides will notice an organism in their environment and want to identify it.

Show examples of examples of our fieldguides

FIGURE 13.14

How to Use a Dichotomous Key

Suppose you want to identify the topmost insect shown here. Follow the steps starting at number 1 to learn the insect's name.

1
 a. Insect has wings .... go to 2.
 b. Insect has no wings .... go to 9.

Because the insect has wings, go to the choices numbered 2a and 2b. If your insect had no wings, you would go to the choices numbered 9a and 9b. The next set of choices reads:

2
 a. Insect has two wings .... go to 3.
 b. Insect has four wings .... go to 12.

Your insect has four wings, so you skip ahead to number 12, which gives the following choices:

12
 a. Wings are of equal size .... go to 13.
 b. Wings are of unequal size .... go to 18.

The insect has wings of unequal size, leading you to number 18 with the following choices:

18
 a. No projections in rear .... go to 21.
 b. Long thin projections in rear .... go to 25.

Eventually, you reach a choice that does not direct you to another set of choices. Instead, the key states the identity of the organism. In this case, number 25 identifies the insect as a mayfly.

Chapter 13 Classification **313**

ENGAGE

Consider the Big Idea

Have students read The Big Idea! at the top of the page. Point out that identification of species is only one application of classification.

Use the Visual

Have students study the photograph that opens the section. Discuss how people might confuse two species.

Check Prior Knowledge

To assess the students' knowledge about classifying organisms, ask:

■ **What does it mean when an organism is extinct?** (Members of its species no longer exist.)
■ **Can an extinct organism be classified? Explain.** (Yes, if enough physical evidence exists)

Quick Activity **TEAM WORK**

Display pictures of three similar organisms, such as fishes or birds. Have students list the similarities and differences among the organisms. Then have students form groups to develop a dichotomous key. You may wish to let students present their keys to the class.

STUDENT RESOURCES

From the Teacher's Resource Package, use:
■ Section Review 13.3, Activity Recordsheet 13-3 and 13-4, Vocabulary Review 13, and Chapter 13 Tests from Unit 3 Review Module

TECHNOLOGY RESOURCES

Relevant technology resources include:
■ Spanish Student Edition CD-ROM
■ Teacher's Resource Planner CD-ROM
■ TestWorks CD-ROM: Chapter 13 Tests

2 TEACH

STS

Explain to students that although extinction is a natural process, many organisms are in danger of becoming extinct because of human activities. Discuss how habitat destruction, pollution, and introducing new species to an area may lead to the extinction of a native species. You may also wish to discuss efforts being made to protect species such as the Javan rhinoceros that have been identified as endangered.

LAB ZONE Do It! TEAM WORK

How Do I Use a Field Guide?

If weather permits, you may want to take students outdoors. Caution students to treat all organisms humanely, and not to disturb natural habitats. Also, instruct students to obtain permission from property owners when necessary.

Analyze Your Results

1 Students should recognize that a dichotomous key makes identifying the organism easier.

2 Students could confirm their identification by using other field guides, consulting an "expert," having a "peer" identify the same organism, or examining biochemistry of the organism's tissues.

Rather than looking through the entire field guide for a photograph of that organism, a person can use the field guide's dichotomous key to make an identification.

In order to use a dichotomous key, you need to have some information about the organism you are trying to identify. For example, you may need to know that the organism is a tree, not a bush. With this information, you can select the appropriate key in the field guide. The key will then present you with a series of options focused on the organism's distinguishing features. These options are not always based on evolutionary relationships; distantly related organisms with analogous structures may be in the same key. By choosing the options that match the features of an unknown organism, you can identify it.

LAB ZONE Do It!

How Do I Use a Field Guide?

Field guides often have taxonomy information and dichotomous keys to help users identify insects, flowers, birds, shells, fishes, mammals, and more. You too can learn to use a field guide if you . . .

Try This

1 Choose an organism common to your environment. Observe it closely or frequently. Record your observations.
2 Obtain a copy of an appropriate field guide from your local library.
3 Refer to your notes and follow the directions in the field guide to identify the organism you have observed. Then use the field guide while observing the organism in its environment.

Analyze Your Results

1 If your field guide included a dichotomous key, how did it help you identify the organism? What is the organism's name?
2 How do you know that you correctly identified your chosen organism? What could you do to confirm your identification?

ENVIRONMENTAL AWARENESS

Using classification

Taxonomists estimate that there are 1.5 to 12 million different species living on Earth today. The variety in living things is called biodiversity.

Thousands of researchers work in nearly every type of Earth's environment studying many different species. Their work can reveal unknown facts about a species, or show that a group of organisms should be considered two species, not one.

Researchers are also constantly searching for organisms that have not yet been classified. In 1994 researchers discovered a mammal—a type of Vietnamese ox—which they named *Pseudoryx nghetinhensis*. That same year a new species of tree kangaroo was discovered in New Guinea. And recently scientists found a previously unknown form of fungi, which will allow them to classify the form that produces the drug cyclosporin. Cyclosporin is used to prevent the rejection of transplanted organs in humans.

Without doubt, identifying and classifying the millions of species on Earth will be a difficult task for taxonomists. These researchers are constantly constructing and reconstructing phylogenetic trees. However, the biodiversity of life is not limitless.

Human existence has taken a huge toll on many other organisms. Habitat destruction and pollution have resulted in the extinction of thousands of species. In addition, scientists estimate that nearly 25,000 species are endangered, which means that they may face extinction if circumstances do not change. Extinction is a natural by-product of evolution. However, the rate of extinction has been higher in recent times than at almost any other time in Earth's history.

we infer

FACTS AND FIGURES

Of the species that have been identified and classified, approximately 72 percent are invertebrate animals; 55 percent are insects, 8 percent are noninsect arthropods, and 8 percent make up the other invertebrates. The next largest group of organisms are the flowering plants, which make up approximately 14 percent of the species on Earth. Although, vertebrates are some of the more familiar organisms to people, they make up only about 3 percent of Earth's organisms.

Even a small community is biologically diverse. Observation will reveal representatives of most, if not all, of the five kingdoms. Walk through your community or the area around your school. Observe and record the organisms you see. Keep in mind that monerans and protists are not readily visible. How many different types of organisms can you find in your community?

IN THE COMMUNITY
Looking for Diversity

Use a field guide or a dichotomous key to identify the different organisms. Check a local library to see if local organisms have been cataloged. A resource such as *http://evolution.biosurf.com* may also help you to classify the different organisms. Present your "biodiversity catalog" to your school or local library.

Biodiversity—the result of billions of years of evolutionary history—is the safeguard of natural selection and a nonrenewable resource. As you may recall from Chapter 10, the more variation there is within a population, the better that population can adapt to a changing environment. Biodiversity describes the variation among all species and is the reason why life has been able to adapt to changing environments on Earth for 3.5 billion years.

As classification efforts reveal more information about Earth's biodiversity, the importance of protecting all varieties of species is confirmed. In recent years, we have learned much about the importance of diversity and the interdependence of organisms. This knowledge has helped scientists and legislators formulate policies to preserve our biodiversity.

Skip & do Gizmo instead

CHECKPOINT 13.3

1. What is a dichotomous key, and how is it used?
2. How does classification of organisms lead to a better understanding of biodiversity?
3. **Critical Thinking** Dichotomy is defined as a division into two parts. How does the word *dichotomy* relate to a dichotomous key?

Build on What You Know

4. How do mutations contribute to biodiversity? *(Need to jog your memory? Revisit relevant concepts in Chapter 8, Section 8.3.)*

Guiding Life

If there is life, then there is a field guide for it. Guides about birds, trees, insects, and even nonliving stars and rocks are available to help you identify the natural wonders around you.

FIGURE 13.15
The *Pseudoryx*, a Vietnamese ox, was unclassified until 1994.

How is the classification of organisms useful?

Chapter 13 Classification **315**

CHECKPOINT 13.3

1. A dichotomous key is a series of questions with two answers that is used to identify organisms.
2. In order to classify an organism, much information about it must be obtained. This information will provide clues to the differences and similarities of this organism to similar organisms.
3. **Making analogies** Dichomotous keys have two answers to a question about an organism.
4. Mutations lead to variation within species, which leads to biodiversity, which can lead to evolution and speciation, which contributes to biodiversity.

In the Community

Encourage students to look for evidence of members of the Monera, Protista, and Fungi kingdoms. Suggest students use a hand lens to make accurate observations of small organisms. Caution them to avoid touching potentially harmful plants and not to eat wild berries or mushrooms. Encourage students to make drawings of the organisms, and remind them that small shaded or sunny areas are also communities.

Everyday Biology

Invite students to bring to class any field guides they use and find helpful in identifying specific items they may collect, such as rocks, shells, or coins.

③ ASSESS

Evaluate Understanding

Ask students to write an essay that explains the relationship of classification to biodiversity. Be sure they discuss how information sources, such as field guides and dichotomous keys, can help identify and classify organisms.

Reteach

Display pictures of two or three wild mammals common to your area. Help students use a dichotomous key from a field guide to identify them. Ask the questions in the dichotomous key in sequence. Have volunteers provide answers to each question. Review the relationship of classification to biodiversity.

SAFETY FIRST!

If students collect their own specimens, review some safety tips which include: wear appropriate clothing; do not trespass; and avoid disrupting or damaging natural habitats.

Lab Prep and Planning

Have students work in groups and provide one set of materials for each group. The lab should take about 45 minutes.

Hypothesis Help

Students should base their hypotheses on the characteristics they observe.

Lab Extension

Open Ended

Have students develop a dichotomous key to classify the ads in a magazine. Students should cut out all the ads and group them according to their key. Allow students a choice of magazines. You may wish to have them work in groups of two or three.

LAB ZONE **Investigate It!** Gizmo Dichotomus Key

Designing a Key

WHAT YOU WILL DO Classify a group of leaves and design a dichotomous key that can be used to identify the leaves

SKILLS YOU WILL USE Observing, organizing, and classifying

WHAT YOU WILL NEED 6–10 different types of leaves, a ruler, hand lens

Make Some General Observations

1 Gather the leaves to be classified. If you wish to collect your own leaves, get permission from your teacher before you begin collecting. **Caution:** Avoid plants that are dangerous or harmful, such as poison ivy.

2 Count the number of different leaves.

3 Use the ruler and hand lens to examine each leaf carefully. What traits characterize each type of leaf? Record your observations.

Propose a Hypothesis

Propose a hypothesis about which characteristics can be used for classifying the leaves.

Plan Your Procedure and Conduct Your Experiment

1 Identify the characteristics you will use to classify your leaves. Will you use size, color, shape, or a combination of traits? Keep in mind that you will divide specimens based on two contrasting, or dichotomous, characteristics.

2 Design your dichotomous key and test it by using it to identify each specimen.

3 Revise your key as needed. Review a field guide or dichotomous key for ideas on how to make your key easier to use.

Analyze Your Data

1 How did you organize the specimens into groups?

2 How many different characteristics did you use to divide the groups?

3 Are there other ways in which you could have grouped the specimens? Describe the alternate ways.

Draw Conclusions

Was your hypothesis supported by the results of the experiment? Which characteristics were most useful when differentiating between two different leaves? Explain.

Design a Related Experiment

Suppose you wanted to design a dichotomous key for birds. What characteristics might you use to differentiate groups of birds? Propose a hypothesis and design an experiment to test it.

Lab: Designing a Key

Objective
Classify a group of leaves and design a dichotomous key.

General Observations
10 leaves total
Leaf 1: heart-shaped, dull green on top, lighter underneath, fuzzy, about 8 centimeters long, edges smooth
Leaf 2: many indentations along edge, very smooth both sides, bright green on top, whitish underneath

---

Analyze Your Data

Answers will vary. Accept all reasonable responses.

Draw Conclusions

Answers will vary. Students are likely to conclude that unique characteristics, such as shape, were more useful when differentiating between two different leaves.

Design a Related Experiment

Students might suggest differences in coloring, size, shape, beak shape, flight patterns, and habitats. Hypotheses might focus on habitat differences.

Chapter 13 Review

 **13.1–13.2** Scientists classify organisms into a hierarchy of groups based on evolutionary relationships.

13.3 Classification has numerous applications, including identifying species.

Sum It Up

Use the following summary to review the main concepts in this chapter.

13.1 Classification

- Biological classification systems group organisms into categories based on shared characteristics.
- The modern classification system has seven taxa and is modeled after the system developed by Linnaeus in the 18th century.
- Modern classification systems group organisms into kingdoms based on such characteristics as cell structure, level of cell specialization, and method of obtaining nutrients.
- Based on recent biochemical data, some scientists use classification systems with additional kingdoms; others use three overarching categories called domains.
- Linnaeus introduced the system of binomial nomenclature, in which an organism is identified by its genus and species.

13.2 Basis for Classification

- Taxonomists use phylogenetic trees to show degrees of relatedness among biological groups.
- When classifying organisms, Linnaeus was limited to features that he could observe. Today's scientists also use organisms' fossil record and biochemistry to clarify relationships.
- Scientists may change classifications or create new taxa as more data becomes available.

13.3 Identifying Organisms

- Naturalists can use dichotomous keys to identify organisms. A dichotomous key lists the observable traits of an organism.
- Some of the estimated 1.5 to 12 million species living on Earth have not been discovered and classified. The diversity of living things, or biodiversity, is a nonrenewable resource; nearly 25,000 species are endangered.

Use Terms and Concepts

Use each of the following words or terms in a complete sentence. If you need to review a meaning, turn to the page indicated.

taxonomy (p. 300)

kingdom (p. 301)

phylum (p. 301)

classes (p. 301)

orders (p. 301)

family (p. 301)

genus (p. 301)

divisions (p. 301)

binomial nomenclature (p. 304)

phylogenetic tree (p. 305)

dichotomous key (p. 313)

Review the Big Idea

Before students begin the Chapter Review, you may wish to discuss main concepts from the Big Ideas in Chapter 13. In taxonomy, scientists organize organisms into a hierarchy of groups based on evolutionary relationships. The hierarchy includes five kingdoms of organisms: monerans, protists, fungi, plants, and animals. Within each kingdom, organisms are further classified into a phylum or division, class, order, family, genus, and species.

Answers

1. binomial nomenclature
2. taxonomy
3. genus
4. dichotomous key
5. class
6. phylogenetic tree
7. kingdom
8. b
9. c
10. c
11. d
12. Binomial nomenclature avoids confusion by providing a single, unique name in a language shared by scientists worldwide.
13. Monerans; animals
14. Kingdoms are the broadest category, species are the narrowest.
15. Linnaeus used only two kingdoms.
16. Microscopic studies of fossil bones indicate that crocodiles and birds evolved from a common dinosaur ancestor.
17. Analyses of DNA sequences are often better indicators of degree of relatedness than are observable traits.
18. Fungi are heterotrophs; plants are autotrophs.
19. If organisms are grouped together based on analogous structures, the classification will not reflect degree of relatedness and evolutionary history. Dolphins and sharks have similar fin structures, but the different composition of the fins indicates a distant evolutionary relationship.
20. Concept maps should show the following: <u>Kingdoms</u> are divided into <u>phyla</u> or <u>divisions</u>; phyla are divided into <u>classes</u>, are divided into <u>orders</u>, are divided into <u>genera</u>, are divided into <u>species</u>. Kingdoms include <u>Monera</u>,

Use Your Word Power

COMPLETION Write the word or phrase that best completes each statement.

1. The two-word term that comprises the scientific name *Homo sapiens* is an example of _____ .

2. The field of biology that deals with classifying organisms is _____ .

3. Scientific names are made of a(n) _____ and a species.

4. A(n) _____ guides users to the identification of an organism.

5. Members of the _____ Aves are birds.

6. A(n) _____ is a diagram used by taxonomists to show relationships among organisms.

7. In most classification systems, _____ is the broadest taxon.

MULTIPLE CHOICE Choose the letter of the word or phrase that best completes each statement.

8. In a scientific name, the genus is never (a) italicized; (b) lowercase; (c) abbreviated; (d) capitalized.

9. The category in animals that is equivalent to a division in plants is a(n) (a) class; (b) order; (c) phylum; (d) family.

10. Phylogenetic trees (a) map relationships among individuals; (b) are used in field guides; (c) show evolutionary relationships; (d) are based on analogous structures.

11. Giant squids and cats belong to the same (a) order; (b) class; (c) phylum; (d) kingdom.

Show What You Know

12. What is an advantage of binomial nomenclature? Explain your answer.

13. In terms of number of species, which kingdom is the smallest? Which is the largest?

14. How do kingdoms and species differ?

15. Identify a difference between Linnaeus's taxonomic system and the one used in this textbook.

16. What evidence has caused some taxonomists to reconsider the classification of birds?

17. How have technological advances affected scientific classification?

18. What characteristic differentiates the kingdom Fungi from the kingdom Plantae?

19. Explain how using physical characteristics to classify organisms can be misleading. Give an example.

20. **Make a Concept Map** Complete the concept map below by adding the following terms: divisions, classes, orders, genera, species, Protista, Fungi, Plantae, Animalia, eukaryotes, prokaryotes, heterotrophs.

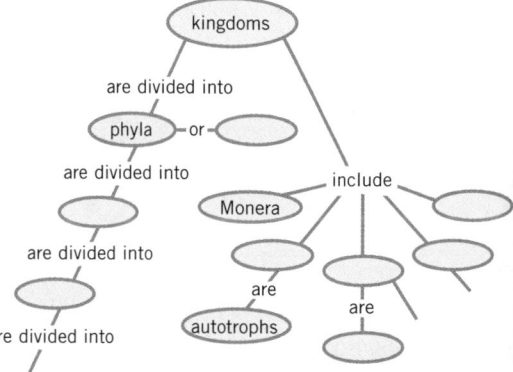

Take It Further

21. **Making an Analogy** What do first and last names have in common with binomial nomenclature?

22. **Organizing and Classifying** Imagine that you have discovered a new multicellular organism that has cells with nuclear membranes and cell walls. How could you classify this organism? What else would you need to know before placing it in an appropriate kingdom? Explain.

Plantae (which are <u>auto-trophs</u>), <u>Animalia</u> (which are <u>heterotrophs</u> and <u>eukaryotes</u>), Protista (which are <u>prokaryotes</u>), and <u>Fungi</u>.

21. The last name is like the genus; it includes a group of related family members. The first name added to the last name refers to a specific family member. (Unlike binomial nomencla-

ture, human names are often not unique.)

22. Eukaryote. You would need to know whether it was a heterotroph or an autotroph to decide between fungi and plant kingdoms.

23. The classification system for instruments is based exclusively on how the sound is produced. Behavior is rarely

23. Making an Analogy The classification system for instruments in a symphony orchestra includes strings, woodwinds, brass, and percussion. What characteristics distinguish one category from another? How are the classification systems for instruments and species different?

24. Designing an Experiment Scientists are debating the classification of spotted skunks. Some taxonomists think that all spotted skunks belong to a single species. Other taxonomists would rather split the species into two groups, eastern spotted skunks and western spotted skunks. Design an experiment to determine how to classify these skunks.

25. Analyzing Data The table below shows the approximate number of species in each kingdom. Graph these data, indicating the number ranges as appropriate. Why are these numbers approximate? Research and graph the number of phyla in two kingdoms of your choice.

Species Number per Kingdom	
Kingdom	**Approximate Number of Species**
Monerans	10,000
Protists	65,000–200,000
Fungi	100,000
Plants	260,000
Animals	800,000–12,000,000

Consider the Issues

26. Politics and Classification The Endangered Species Act protects species in danger of extinction. The classification of a population as a separate species, therefore, can be an important decision politically. The red wolf, for example, is currently considered an endangered species. Some people argue that the red wolf is a hybrid between a coyote and a gray wolf. How could scientists determine whether or not the red wolf is a separate species? If it is a hybrid, should the dwindling red wolf population still be protected?

27. Computers Used for Classification Many organisms have not yet been classified. Even if a trained professional could classify 10 species per year—including time for field trips, analysis, and publication—it would take about one million years to classify an estimated 10 million species worldwide. With Statistical Analysis System (SAS) computer programs, researchers can integrate new data and compare large numbers of traits quickly. Why is classification important? What are some drawbacks of computerized classification?

Make New Connections

28. Biology and Art Imagine that you have to prepare a page in a field guide. Choose several related organisms. Pick an appropriate format, using field guides in the library as models. Then decide on the traits that would best identify the organisms you chose. Create the illustrations for your guide.

29. Biology and Library Science A library would be of little use if its collection was not catalogued. Most libraries use one of two systems—either the Dewey decimal system or a system devised by the Library of Congress. Investigate these two systems. What are the differences between them? Which system does your school library use? Your public library?

30. Biology and History Columbus and other early explorers collected many species of plants and animals. Research one of the early explorers. Find out what geographic and scientific discoveries the explorer made.

FAST-FORWARD TO CHAPTER 14

In Chapter 13 you learned about five kingdoms. In Chapter 14 you will study bacteria—members of the kingdom Monera—and viruses, which do not belong to any of the five kingdoms.

Chapter 13 Classification **319**

species remain unrecognized. In addition, it can provide evidence of changes in biodiversity that might indicate detrimental environmental changes. Computerized classification might be vulnerable to loss of data and data might be difficult to verify.

28. Students should choose organisms that have both diverse and common characteristics. Students' illustrations should show each characteristic clearly.

29. The Dewey Decimal System allows the librarian more choice in classifying a book. Local anomalies are more common. Libraries using the Library of Congress system use identical call numbers for a given book.

30. Student research should focus on a relatively narrow time frame. Also, students may include the relationship of scientific discoveries contributed by explorers to modern or extinct organisms.

the most important factor in the classification of species.

24. Students could suggest observing mating between skunks, comparing cell structure, and performing biochemical analyses.

25. Scientists have not had the time or resources to classify all types of living things. In addition, scientists continue to debate the classification of known species. Populations of organisms that some scientists identify as a single species, other scientists identify as two separate species.

26. Answers will vary.

27. Answers will vary. Classification is vital for a variety of reasons. It is difficult to measure trends in biodiversity if

Connect the Chapters

1. The grasping ability of opposable thumbs and prehensile tails, depth perception provided by binocular vision, and their free-swinging arms and legs indicate that primates evolved in arboreal niches.

2. Binomial nomenclature indicates the relationship of these fossils to each other and to other hominids. The common names Java man and Peking man do not reveal evolutionary relationships or classification information.

3. Adaptive radiation is reflected by a concentration of branches diverging from one common ancestor.

4. There was genetic variation in the existing heterotroph populations. Increased competition for organic resources favored cells that could use the energy of sunlight. Those cells survived and reproduced. Populations of these cells evolved to become autotrophs.

5. Their gene pools are similar in that all three species are primates and evolved from a common ancestor. However, students should infer that biochemical and structural analysis show more similarities between baboons and gibbons than between either species and lemurs, as they share a more recent common ancestor.

6. The breakup of Pangaea allowed for greater adaptive radiation. New World monkeys developed noticeable differences, particularly prehensile tails, as they evolved to fill different niches on the different land masses; geologic forces of plate movements affected the separation.

Unit 3 Review

THE BIG IDEA! Answering the following questions will help you to link ideas and grasp the core concepts

Connect the Chapters

1. Explain how the key adaptations of primates provide clues about the niches in which they evolved.
2. What classification information is provided by the designation *Homo erectus* but not by the names Java Man or Peking Man?
3. Explain how adaptive radiation is reflected on a phylogenetic tree.
4. Use the emergence of the first autotrophs to illustrate the four main points of Darwin's theory of evolution.
5. What relationships would you expect between the gene pools of baboons, gibbons, and lemurs?
6. How was anthropoid evolution affected by the separation of North America from Eurasia? What geologic forces affected this separation?

Connect the Units

7. What are the key differences between carbon-12 and carbon-14?
8. Why are few of the mutations that occur in a parent passed along to offspring?
9. Could a normal distribution curve describe the offspring of red and white snapdragons? Why or why not?

Connect to Themes

10. **Unity and Diversity** Does the increase in taxa since the mid-1700s necessarily reflect an increase in biodiversity? Explain your answer.
11. **Patterns of Change/Cycles** Study the timeline and the graph in *Figure 11.21* that shows when mass extinctions occurred. Can you infer any patterns or cycles? Why or why not?
12. **Stability and Equilibrium** How might the concept of genetic drift support the theory of punctuated equilibrium?

CRITIC'S CORNER

A FILM REVIEW BY DANA DENSON, MARVELL, ARKANSAS

Filled with entertainment and suspense, *Inherit the Wind* is a film based on the true story of the John Scopes trial in Dayton, Tennessee. It focuses on the inability of a community to "hear about" anything that appears to contradict its religious beliefs. Henry Drummond, an energetic high-school teacher, believes that education is a growing process cultivated through open-mindedness. Drummond presents, explains, and discusses Darwin's Theory of Evolution to his science class. As a result, he is forced to defend himself and his convictions in court.

320

Connect the Units

7. The carbon-14 isotope has two additional neutrons.
8. Although mutations can occur in any cell in the body, only those that occur in reproductive cells can be inherited.
9. No, the data could not be graphed because all the offspring would be pink as a result of incomplete dominance.

Connect to Themes

10. No; it probably reflects increased data and advances in technology.
11. There is a pattern of an increasing number of families of species through time and a cycle of a rebound in the number of families after each mass extinction.
12. Genetic drift could speed up natural selection and evolution.

SPOTLIGHT ON CAREERS

DR. WILLIAM NIERING
Professor of botany at Connecticut College,
Director of research at Connecticut College Arboretum
EDUCATION: B.A. and M.S.; Ph.D. in ecology

"Plant taxonomy is critical to the study of biodiversity, because most plant species haven't been identified yet. To study plants, you have to be able to identify what you are looking at, especially if you need to collect more of it. As a field ecologist, I determine how much of a species is in an ecosystem—a difficult task because different plants are found in different elevations within an area. To make matters worse, the difference between plants can be small, but critical. So, taxonomy helps me make sense out of chaos.

Taxonomy is also important to businesses. Some industries today are testing plants to see if they are medicinally useful. Somewhere there may be an unidentified plant that could cure a deadly disease."

bioSURF Visit the Internet site *http://evolution.biosurf.com* to explore taxonomy.

> Somewhere there may be an unidentified plant that could cure a deadly disease.
> — DR. WILLIAM NIERING

VERONICA ARREOLA
Intern and project leader,
Field Museum of Natural History
EDUCATION: College senior studying to become a science teacher

"My main project is about the locomotion of burrfish. We're trying to figure out exactly how burrfish move. Our work could help scientists compare burrfish to other fish in the same family, as well as to their ancestors. This comparison could help us classify burrfish more accurately, since it sheds light on the differences between fish.

We put burrfish into a flow tank, vary the water flow to different speeds, and videotape the fish to see which fins they use. Burrfish look something like puffer fish—they have hard spines all over their bodies, so they really can't move much. Most fish move only one or two fins at once, or just undulate. Burrfish use all of their fins at once."

bioSURF Search *http://evolution.biosurf.com* for more information about classification.

Unit 3 Change and Diversity **321**

SPOTLIGHT ON CAREERS

bioSURF Have students connect to the bioSurf Internet address to learn more about schools, educational programs, and scholarships that would help prepare them for a career related to the studies of evolution and classification.

Consider These Careers
Unraveling the history of life on Earth draws from a variety of scientific disciplines. Paleontologists, biochemists, geologists, and anthropologists all participate in these debates. Naturalists, zoologists, wildlife managers, zoo curators, and entomologists are all involved in the work of identifying and classifying modern organisms.

Plan for a Career
- **Arranging an Internship**
Hands-on experience is one of the most valuable qualifications when it comes to careers in biology and other sciences. A part-time internship is an excellent way to obtain such experience. Many local organizations, such as animal shelters, zoos, aquariums, and environmental protection groups offer internships for high school students. Contact local organizations and make a list of those that have internship opportunities.

Project Plans
1. Each group could research a species from one of the nine genera of modern primates.
2. For each "fossil" have students list conclusions that can be inferred about their lifestyle. Compare this list with the "findings" of the "archaeologists."
3. Students should note that some species thrive while others do not sprout or die.

Critic's Corner
Have students read the review of *Inherit the Wind*. Ask if any other students have seen the film, and have them share opinions with the class. Encourage students to consider times when they tried to suggest ideas that were unpopular or tried to accept the ideas of others with which they did not agree.

Unit Overview

This unit explores the biology of microbes and their multicellular relatives. Monerans are prokaryotes that are often classified by their metabolic activities. The protists include single and multicellular organisms that do not fit into the other kingdoms. Fungi are important as decomposers and parasites. Viruses display some, but not all, of the characteristics of life. There are many pathogens within the kingdoms of viruses, Monera, Protista, and Fungi.

Unit Objectives

- Discuss the discovery and characteristics of viruses.
- Describe different types of monerans and explain their importance to other organisms.
- Describe the various protists and explain the criteria for their classification.
- Discuss the characteristics and ecological importance of fungi.

Connect the Units

This unit explores the biology of some of the less familiar, but extremely important kingdoms of living things. The pathological nature of these organisms, and their role in human health is further developed in Chapter 32: *Immune System*. Their role as decomposers in the ecosystem is developed in Chapter 37: *Ecosystem Dynamics*. Unit 4 is closely linked to the discussion of the evolution of prokaryotes and eukaryotes presented in Unit 3.

Monerans, Protists, and Fungi

Which of these amazing statements about monerans (bacteria), protists, and fungi are fact, and which are fiction?

Hit or Myth?

Some termites are **gardeners.**

(Fact. Some types of termites prepare and tend underground fungus gardens. They eat the fungi, which enable their bodies to digest woody materials.)

Cows contribute to **global warming.**

(Fact. A type of bacterium in the digestive tracts of cows produces methane gas in the cows' intestines. When the methane is released by cows, it contributes to global warming.)

Bacteria **make gold.**

(Fiction, but close to fact. Bacteria are used as "miners" to leach minerals, including gold and copper, from ores.)

AH CHOO

Bacteria can **"catch" a virus.**

(Fact. There are specific viruses that infect and kill bacteria.)

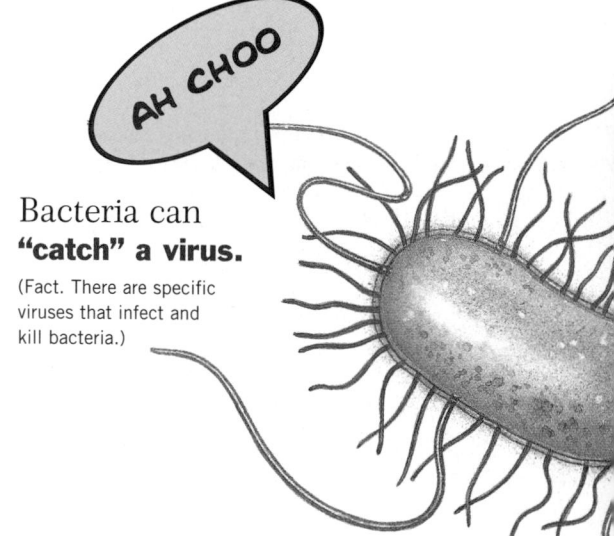

There are **protists** in your pudding.

(Fact. A substance extracted from seaweed, a type of protist, is used as a thickener in pudding, ice cream, and many other foods.)

Bacteria-produced **headphones** can make music sound better.

(Fact. Headphones made of bacteria-produced cellulose have great acoustic qualities.)

Blue whales are the largest organisms.

(Fiction. Would you believe that a fungus growing in Michigan is one of the world's largest organisms, much larger than any whale?)

Your **jeans** are made with fungus.

(Fact. A type of fungus in soil is used to treat jeans to give them a "stone-washed" look.)

Unit 4 Monerans, Protists, and Fungi   **323**

Hit _or_ Myth?

Use It

Review each of the statements with the class. Ask students to share their prior knowledge and misconceptions on each topic. Ask them to consider which sources of information on these topics are generally reliable, and which may not be. Have students preview the Table of Contents for this unit and correlate text sections with information related to the concepts in the Hit or Myth statements.

Link It

Chapter 14 links the biology of bacteria (headphones) and viruses (sneeze) to their roles in the biosphere (gold, cows, headphones). More information on the use of bacteria in bioremediation, and the mechanisms of global warming are discussed in Chapter 38: *People and the Environment.* Chapter 15 links the properties of algae and other protists to human applications (pudding). Chapter 16 links the properties of fungi to their uses by humans (jeans) as well as their roles in the biosphere (termites, whale).

Expand It

In addition to mining for minerals, bacteria are also being used for environmental clean-up. When nitrogen and phosphorus are sprayed on oil spills, they act as fertilizers which increase the population of oil-eating bacteria. These bacteria then feed on the spilled oil, providing a low-cost way to clean oil-fouled beaches.

PLANNING GUIDE

Section	Student Activities/Features	Teacher's Resource Package
14.1 Characteristics of Viruses **Objectives** ■ Identify the structural characteristics of viruses ■ Compare forms of viral replication	**Lab Zone Discover It!** *Imitating the Spread of a Virus*, p. 325 **Everyday Biology** *Sick Computers?* p. 329	**Unit 4 Review Module** ■ Section Review 14.1 ■ Interpreting Graphics 14 **Laboratory Manual,** Lab 24: "Tobacco Mosaic Virus" **Interpreting and Developing Graphics** 40
14.2 Origin and Diversity of Viruses **Objectives** ■ Explain one hypothesis about the origin of viruses ■ Compare and contrast methods for classifying viruses	**Lab Zone Do It!** *Model a Bacteriophage*, p. 332 **Everyday Biology** *The All-Too-Common Cold*, p. 333	**Unit 4 Review Module** ■ Section Review 14.2 ■ Activity Recordsheet 14-1
14.3 Viruses in the Biosphere **Objectives** ■ Describe the role of viruses in the environment ■ Explain viral diseases and uses of viruses	**Lab Zone Think About It!** *Analyzing Disease Occurrence*, p. 334 **STS: Frontiers in Biology** *Human Uses*, p. 335	**Unit 4 Review Module** ■ Section Review 14.3 ■ Enrichment Topic 14-1 ■ Critical Thinking Exercise 14 **Issues and Decision Making** 14-1 **Consumer Applications** 14-1
14.4 Characteristics of Monerans **Objectives** ■ Identify the structural characteristics of monerans ■ Compare how monerans grow, reproduce, and survive	**Lab Zone Investigate It!** *Does Temperature Affect Bacterial Growth?* p. 339	**Unit 4 Review Module** ■ Section Review 14.4 ■ Activity Recordsheet 14-2 **Interpreting and Developing Graphics** 41
14.5 Origin and Diversity of Monerans **Objectives** ■ Analyze the evolution and classification of monerans ■ Compare and contrast methods of classifying monerans	**Lab Zone Do It!** *Identify Shapes of Bacteria*, p. 343	**Unit 4 Review Module** ■ Section Review 14.5 ■ Activity Recordsheet 14-3 **Laboratory Manual**, Lab 25: "Gram Stain: Positive Identification"
14.6 Monerans in the Biosphere **Objectives** ■ Describe the ecological role of bacteria in the environment ■ Explain how monerans affect humans	**Everyday Biology** *In the Bacteria Cafeteria*, p. 344 **In the Community** *Beefing Up Inspections*, p. 345 **STS: Frontiers in Biology** *Employing Bacteria*, p.345	**Unit 4 Review Module** ■ Section Review 14.6 ■ Enrichment Topic 14-2 ■ Vocabulary Review 14 ■ Chapter 14 Tests **Laboratory Manual,** Lab 26: "Familiar Bactericides and Bacteriostatic Agents" **Consumer Applications** 14-2 **Issues and Decision Making** 14-2 **Interpreting and Developing Graphics** 42 **Spanish Reviews** Chapter 14

Technology Resources

Internet Connections

Within this chapter, you will see the (bioSURF) logo. If you and your students have access to the Internet, the following URL address will provide various Internet connections that are related to topics and features presented in this chapter:

http://microorganisms.biosurf.com

You can also find relevant chapter material at **The Biology Place** address:

http://www.biology.com

CD-ROMs

Biología: la telaraña de la vida,
    (Spanish Student Edition) Chapter 14
Teacher's Resource Planner, Chapter 14
    Supplements
TestWorks CD-ROM
■ Chapter 14 Tests

Videodiscs

Animated Biological Concepts Videodiscs
■ Lytic and Lysogenic Cycles

Overhead Transparencies

■ An Influenza Virus, #28
■ Viral Replication, #29 and 30
■ A Typical Moneran, #31

Videotapes

Biology Alive! Video Series
Rewind: The Web of Life Reteach Videos

Planning for Activities

STUDENT EDITION
Lab Zone Do It! p. 332
- toothpicks
- pipe cleaners
- string
- clear plastic food wrap

Lab Zone
Investigate It! p. 339
- three sterile agar plates
  (per group of 3 students)
- clock
- hand lens
- paper and pencil

Lab Zone Do It! p. 343
- microscope
- three numbered slides
  of bacteria (cocci,
  bacilli, and spirilla)

TEACHER'S EDITION
Teacher Demo, p. 330
Wilting leaves of a plant
- wilting, discolored leaf
  from a plant

Quick Activity, p. 336
Identifying moneran cells
- pictures of a plant cell,
  an animal cell, a fungal
  cell, a protist cell, and
  two or three moneran
  cells

Quick Activity, p. 340
Classifying monerans
- pictures of different
  kinds of monerans

Teacher Demo, p. 342
Shapes of bacteria
- marble
- piece of rice
- piece of rotini
- overhead projector

Teacher Demo, p. 344
Products made by bacteria
- yogurt container
- can of sauerkraut
- package of Swiss cheese
- jar of vinegar

Chapter Objectives

Students will learn the main concepts of this chapter as they complete the following objectives.

- Identify the structural characteristics of viruses
- Compare forms of viral replication
- Explain one hypothesis about the origin of viruses
- Compare and contrast methods for classifying viruses
- Understand the role of viruses in the environment
- Identify the structural characteristics of monerans
- Compare how monerans grow, reproduce, and survive
- Analyze the evolution and classification of monerans
- Describe the ecological role of bacteria in the environment

Key Words

14.1 *virus, capsid, envelope, host, lytic cycle, lysogenic cycle, prophage*

14.2 *retrovirus, viroid, prion*

14.3 *vaccination*

14.4 *plasmid, endospore, binary fission, conjugation*

14.5 *archaebacteria, eubacteria, aerobe, anaerobe*

14.6 *decomposer, symbiosis*

The Opening Story

Have students discuss how they think the story relates to the content of this chapter. Ask if the smallpox virus should be retained or destroyed. Students should support their viewpoint.

Viruses and Monerans

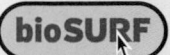

You can find out more about viruses and monerans by exploring the following Internet address:
http://microorganisms.biosurf.com

In this chapter . . .

FEATURES

Everyday Biology
- Sick Computers?
- The All-Too-Common Cold
- In the Bacteria Cafeteria

In the Community
Beefing Up Inspections

 Frontiers in Biology
- Human Uses
- Employing Bacteria

LAB ZONES

Discover It!
- Imitating the Spread of a Virus

Do It!
- Model a Bacteriophage
- Identify Shapes of Bacteria

Think About It!
- Analyzing Disease Occurrence

Investigate It!
- Does Temperature Affect Bacterial Growth?

Should we destroy a deadly virus?

In 1989, while renovating a church in London, workers opened a century-old crypt. To their horror they found themselves viewing the mummified remains of smallpox victims. Could the deadly virus escape the grave to infect the living? Scientists confirmed that the poxvirus that causes smallpox could survive about 100 years in mummified bodies buried in ground that was frozen year-round. London's temperate climate eliminated this possibility.

Fears and facts like these fuel a raging debate about whether or not humans should destroy the poxvirus. This virus killed about 20 percent of the people it infected in the centuries before immunization stopped its spread. The photo above shows the skin lesions of smallpox. Today it exists only in high-security laboratory containment. Many people want the contents of the containers destroyed because they fear the virus may escape. Others argue that the risk of the virus's escape is far outweighed by the wealth of scientific information the virus can provide.

 Discover It!

Imitating the Spread of a Virus

1. Your teacher whispers a statement about viruses to one student at the front of the classroom. That student whispers what he or she has heard to another student. Each student in turn passes on what he or she has heard until the statement has been whispered to everyone in the class.

2. The last student to hear the statement writes what he or she has heard on the chalkboard. Then the teacher writes the original statement on the chalkboard.

How different are the two statements? By comparing them, you can get an idea of how a virus can change as it spreads from one organism to another over time.

WRITE ABOUT IT!

In your science journal, write about any memorable experiences you have had with flu viruses that infected people in your family or school. How long did it take for the virus to spread from person to person? Describe your symptoms and how you felt while you were sick.

325

Opening Activities

bioSURF If you have access to the Internet in your classroom or school, you may wish to have students connect to the address shown on page 324. You may also want to have students conduct net searches for information using key words related to this chapter. For example, they could search for entries under viruses, genetic engineering, and bacteria.

LAB ZONE Discover It!

Imitating the Spread of a Virus TEAM WORK

The final statement will probably be quite different from the original one. In the same way that the statement changed as it passed from one person to another, a virus changes as it is copied and passed from one person to another.

WRITE ABOUT IT

After students finish their journal entries describing their bouts with the flu, call on volunteers to read their entries aloud. Have students discuss any similarities in symptoms.

◀ • • • • • • • • • • • • • • • • • •

REWIND to Chapter 13

Briefly review concepts learned in Chapter 13, *Classification*. Ask:

■ **What characteristics are used to classify living things?**

Students should be encouraged to add to their portfolios as they work through this chapter. In addition to the *Write About It* opportunity, the following sections are excellent opportunities for portfolio entries:

■ Section 14.1: *Characteristics of Viruses*
■ Section 14.6: *Monerans in the Biosphere*

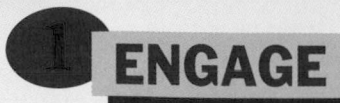

❶ ENGAGE

Consider the Big Idea

Have students read The Big Idea! at the top of the page. Explain to students that they will learn that replicating is different from reproducing.

Use the Visual

Have students study the photograph that opens the section. Explain that scientists wear special clothing to protect themselves from any viruses in the lab. Ask:

- **Why do you think scientists at the CDC are interested in studying viruses?** (To prevent and/or cure viral diseases.)

Check Prior Knowledge

To assess students' knowledge of the chemical basis of organisms, ask:

- **What four groups of chemicals make up most living things?** (Carbohydrates, lipids, proteins, and nucleic acids)
- **What are two types of nucleic acids?** (RNA, DNA)

Quick Activity *TEAM WORK*

Ask students to name movies or books about viral outbreaks. Have them tell what they learned about viruses. Record student responses on the board. Correct any inaccuracies and misconceptions as they read the chapter.

SUPER READ! **Comparing and Contrasting** To practice strategies for effective reading, use pages 37-38 in *Super Read!*

14.1 Characteristics of Viruses

What you'll learn

IDEAS
- To identify the structural characteristics of viruses
- To compare forms of viral replication

WORDS
virus, capsid, envelope, host, lytic cycle, lysogenic cycle, prophage

SUPER READ!

Avoiding an outbreak
Protective clothing and high-tech gear are a daily reality for scientists who work in a Level 4 laboratory at the Centers for Disease Control (CDC) in Atlanta, Georgia. There, biologists work in a science-fiction-like environment to control the potentially deadly viruses they are studying.

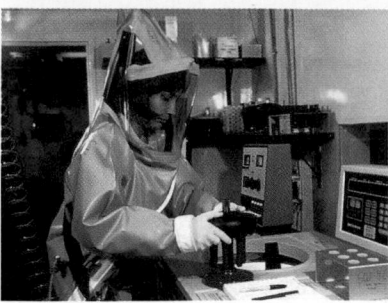

THE STRUCTURE OF VIRUSES

Trouble in a small package

If you ever had a cold or the flu, you probably hosted viruses. How well do you know these guests? A **virus** is an infectious agent made up of a core of nucleic acid and a protein coat.

Viruses are not cells. Unlike plant and animal cells, a virus particle does not have a nucleus, a membrane, or cellular organelles such as ribosomes, mitochondria, or chloroplasts. Although viruses are not cells, they do have organized structural parts.

Compared to even the smallest cell, a virus is tiny. The virus that causes polio, for example, measures only 20 nanometers (nm) in diameter. One

nanometer is one billionth (10^{-9}) of a meter. At that size, 3000 polioviruses could line up across the period at the end of this sentence. In *Figure 14.1* you can see the difference in size between a cell and a virus.

All viruses have at least two parts—a protective protein coat and a core of nucleic acid. The protein coat around the core of nucleic acid is called a **capsid.** Depending on the virus, the capsid may consist of one or several kinds of protein. The capsid protects the viral nucleic acid core from its environment.

As you learned in Chapter 2, nucleic acids include DNA and RNA. In cells, DNA is the hereditary material. Some viruses also contain DNA, while other viruses only contain RNA. In viruses containing RNA, the RNA functions as the hereditary material.

Compared to a cell, a virus has a relatively "simple" existence. Viruses do not eat, respire, or respond to environmental changes as cells do. It should not surprise you, therefore, to learn that viruses have fewer genes than cells have. While a human cell

FIGURE 14.1
Appearing as tiny blue dots in this photo, AIDS viruses attack a human immune system cell (T-cell).

326 *Unit 4 Monerans, Protists, and Fungi*

STUDENT RESOURCES	**TECHNOLOGY RESOURCES**
From the Teacher's Resource Package, use: ■ Section Review 14.1 and Interpreting Graphics 14-1 from Unit 4 Review Module ■ Lab 24: "Tobacco Mosaic Virus"	Relevant technology resources include: ■ Spanish Student Edition CD-ROM ■ Teacher's Resource Planner CD-ROM ■ Animated Biological Concepts Videodiscs: "Lytic and Lysogenic Cycles"

may contain about 100,000 genes and a bacterial cell about 1000, a virus may contain only 5 genes.

In *Figure 14.2* you can see the parts of an influenza (flu) virus: a core of RNA, a surrounding capsid, and an outer covering called an envelope. An **envelope** is an additional protective coating usually made of lipids, proteins, and carbohydrates. Envelopes are found only in some viruses that infect animal cells. An envelope has spikelike projections that recognize and bind to complementary sites on the membrane of the infected cell. Think about how a prickly burr sticks to objects. The small illustration below shows how the projections on a viral envelope help a virus cling to an animal cell in a similar manner.

VIRAL REPLICATION

Ticking time bombs

Viruses do not reproduce; they replicate. Reproduction, which is a characteristic of living things, involves cell division. Replication does not involve cell division.

Viruses cannot replicate on their own. In order to replicate, viruses require a host. A **host** is an organism that shelters and nourishes something.

FIGURE 14.2

An Influenza Virus

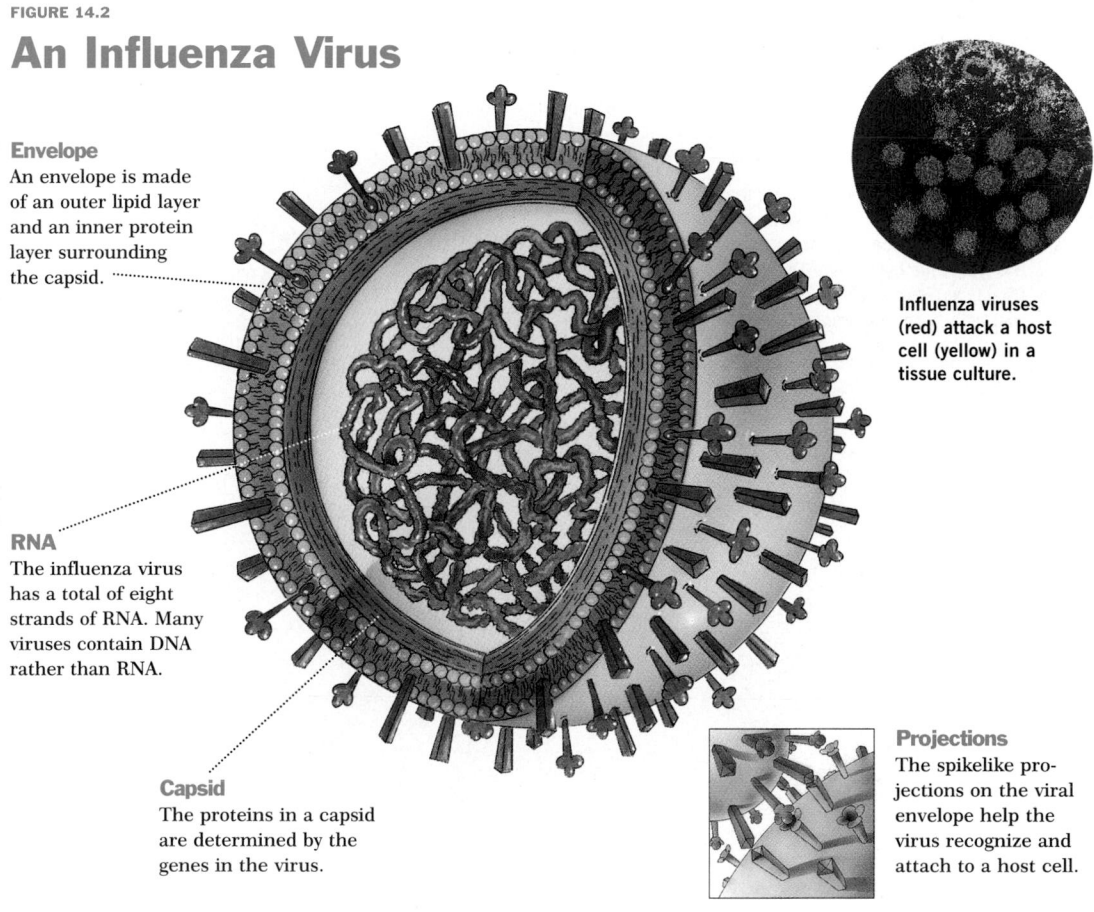

Envelope
An envelope is made of an outer lipid layer and an inner protein layer surrounding the capsid.

RNA
The influenza virus has a total of eight strands of RNA. Many viruses contain DNA rather than RNA.

Capsid
The proteins in a capsid are determined by the genes in the virus.

Influenza viruses (red) attack a host cell (yellow) in a tissue culture.

Projections
The spikelike projections on the viral envelope help the virus recognize and attach to a host cell.

Chapter 14 Viruses and Monerans **327**

2 TEACH

Use the Visual

Give students time to study the influenza virus shown in Figure 14.2. Ask:

- **What is the relationship between the envelope and the capsid?** (The envelope surrounds the capsid.)
- **What kinds of viruses are surrounded by an envelope?** (Viruses that infect animal cells)
- **What analogy can you make to describe how the projections attach to a host cell?** (Answers will vary; they mesh like two gears.)

Class Activity

Have students work in groups to compare the structure of a virus to the structure of a plant cell and an animal cell. Tell them to arrange their data in two lists. Then have groups share their lists with the class.

Use the Visual

Direct students' attention to Figure 14.3. Ask:

- **How soon after a virus enters a host cell does the lytic cycle begin?** (Immediately; as soon as the virus enters the host cell)

- **What is the main difference between the lytic cycle and the lysogenic cycle?** (Replication in the lytic cycle immediately destroys the host cell. During the lysogenic cycle, the virus remains inside the host cell without harming it.)

- **What is a prophage?** (A viral DNA segment that is attached to a bacterial cell's chromosome)

- **What happens when a cell containing virus particles lyses?** (The cell bursts open, releasing the virus particles)

❶ Only the viral DNA enters the bacterial cell.

❷ In both cycles the virus attaches to a host cell and injects its DNA.

❸ The cell may replicate the viral DNA along with its own when the cell divides, or it may be killed.

❹ Both contain a nucleic acid, DNA or RNA, and protein. Viruses are not made of cells; they require a host to replicate.

Animated Biological Concepts

Lytic and Lysogenic Cycles   Play

Living cells host viruses. These host cells provide all the materials that viruses need to copy themselves.

When it enters a host cell, a virus may immediately begin to replicate, or it may remain relatively inactive. The viral replication process that rapidly kills a host cell is called the **lytic** (LIT-ik) **cycle.** You can follow the lytic cycle in *Figure 14.3*. The lytic cycle begins when a virus invades a host cell and begins to replicate immediately, producing many new viruses. Eventually the host cell lyses, or breaks apart, releasing the newly made viruses. The new viruses may then enter other cells and repeat the cycle.

As a child you may have had chicken pox, which is caused by a virus. While you were ill, most of the viruses were in the lytic cycle.

Because your cells were being destroyed by the chicken pox virus, you showed symptoms of the disease.

Sometimes a virus does not start the lytic cycle immediately. Instead, the virus enters the lysogenic cycle. The **lysogenic** (ly-soh-JEN-ik) **cycle** is a type of replication in which a virus does not immediately kill a host cell. The lysogenic cycle in a bacterial cell is shown on the right side of *Figure 14.3*. Which steps do the lytic and lysogenic cycles share?

During the lysogenic cycle, viral DNA inserts itself into a host cell's chromosome. A viral DNA segment that is inserted in a bacterial cell's chromosome is called a **prophage** (PROH-fayj). A host cell carrying a prophage may divide many times. The prophage is replicated every

FIGURE 14.3

Lytic and Lysogenic Cycles

Follow the replication cycles of a virus that has invaded a bacterium. In the lytic cycle, a virus immediately replicates after entering a cell. In the lysogenic cycle, viral DNA attaches itself to a host's chromosome, where it may exist as a harmless prophage for years. What part or parts of the virus enter the bacterial cell? ❶

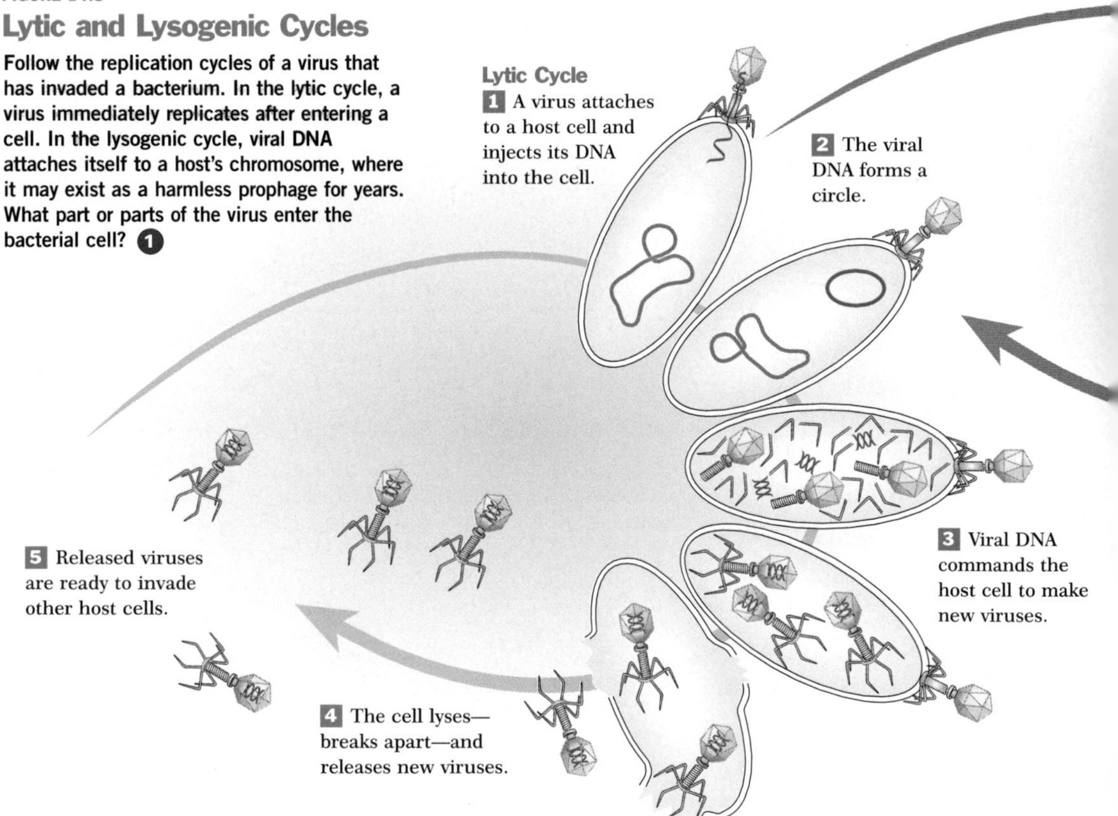

Lytic Cycle

1 A virus attaches to a host cell and injects its DNA into the cell.

2 The viral DNA forms a circle.

3 Viral DNA commands the host cell to make new viruses.

4 The cell lyses—breaks apart—and releases new viruses.

5 Released viruses are ready to invade other host cells.

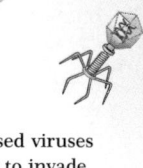

328   *Unit 4 Monerans, Protists, and Fungi*

MEETING DIVERSE NEEDS

At Risk Encourage students to create flow-charts that show the series of events in the lytic and lysogenic cycles. Suggest that students highlight the stages that differ in the two cycles.

LEP The terms *prophage* and *prophase* sound and look similar. Review the definitions of both words and explain that the term *prophage* will be used in this chapter.

time the host cell's chromosome replicates.

Some prophages remain in the lysogenic cycle indefinitely. Usually, however, some type of environmental stimulus eventually results in the separation of a prophage from the chromosome of its host cell. The viral DNA then enters the lytic cycle. The virus that causes cold sores in humans can go through the lysogenic cycle, for example. Cold sores erupt when these viruses enter the lytic cycle.

Lysogenic Cycle

1 After a virus injects its DNA into a bacterial cell, the viral DNA inserts itself into a host's chromosome.

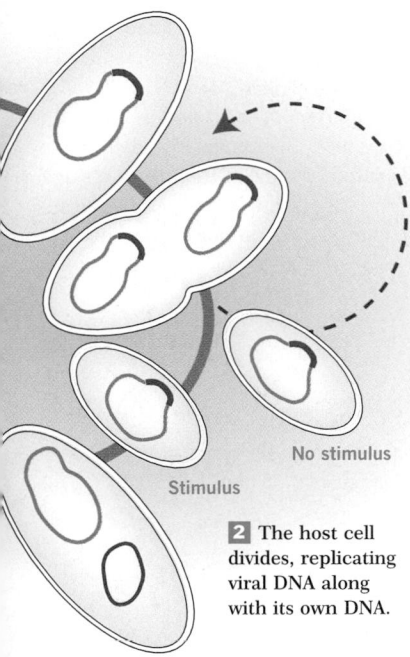

No stimulus

Stimulus

2 The host cell divides, replicating viral DNA along with its own DNA.

3 A stimulus allows the viral DNA to separate from the cell's chromosome and enter the lytic cycle. Without a stimulus, the viral DNA stays in the cell's chromosome.

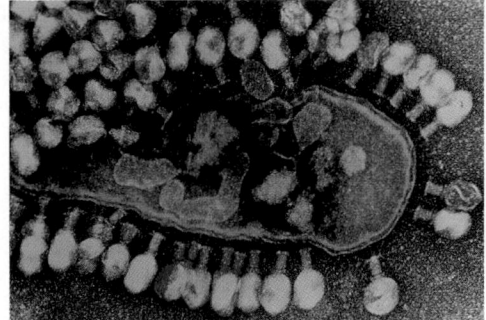

FIGURE 14.4
Many viruses are attacking this *E. coli* bacterial cell, which is defenseless against their onslaught. What happens once the cell is infected? **3**

ALIVE OR NOT?

To be or not to be . . .

Do you think viruses are alive? To answer this question, ask yourself two additional questions. Which characteristics of living things do viruses share? Which do they not share? **4**

When viruses are inside host cells, they share some of the characteristics of life with host cells. Viruses contain nucleic acid and protein. Viruses also change over time as a result of mutations in their DNA or RNA that affect the composition of their proteins.

Outside living cells, viruses are inactive; that is, they cannot grow or replicate. Viruses must be inside living cells to be active. After entering host cells, viruses act like parasites, organisms that harm or destroy the host as they use it for their own benefit.

CHECKPOINT 14.1

1. What are the structural characteristics of viruses?
2. Compare the lytic and lysogenic cycles.
3. **Critical Thinking** Make a diagram to show the lytic and lysogenic cycles in a eukaryotic host cell.

Build on What You Know

4. Make a chart to compare viruses with prokaryotes and eukaryotes. *(Need to jog your memory? Revisit relevant concepts in Chapter 3 Section 3.2.)*

Chapter 14 Viruses and Monerans **329**

EVERYDAY BIOLOGY

Sick Computers?

Computer viruses behave much like biological viruses. They attach themselves to files, then spread and multiply as the files move between disks, computers, and networks. They may cause odd system behavior or may damage data.

CHECKPOINT 14.1

1. A core of nucleic acid surrounded by a protein capsid. Some viruses also have an outer envelope.
2. In the lytic cycle, the host cell is killed immediately; in the lysogenic cycle the viral DNA inserts itself into the host chromosome and causes no harm until the virus re-enters the lytic cycle.
3. **Organizing** The diagram should basically be a version of Figure 14.3 on pages 328-329.
4. Viruses, prokaryotes, and eukaryotes all have nucleic acids and proteins. Prokaryotes and eukaryotes have a cell membrane, and eukaryotes have organelles

Build Writing Skills

Have students write an essay discussing whether viruses are alive or not. Students should use scientific fact and creative reasoning to support their conclusions.

Everyday Biology

Ask students to share their experiences with computer viruses and the precautions that they take to prevent the spread of computer viruses.

3 ASSESS

Evaluate Understanding

Have students make a sketch of a virus and label its capsid, nucleic acid, envelope, and the projections it would use to attach to a cell. Then ask them to summarize in a chart the processes by which the virus could replicate. Review volunteers' charts and emphasize the differences between the two cycles.

Reteach

Write the terms *Lytic Cycle* and *Lysogenic Cycle* on the board. Tell students the class is going to summarize the methods of viral replication via flowcharts. Have volunteers write the information for each step in a flowchart on the board and summarize what happens. Conclude the review by emphasizing that during the lytic cycle, the host is immediately killed; during the lysogenic cycle, the host cell is not killed immediately.

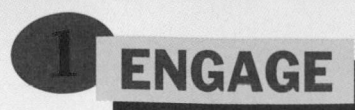

① ENGAGE

Use the Visual

Have students study the photograph that opens the section. Explain that warts are caused by one type of virus that infects humans. One way viruses are classified is according to the type of host they infect.

Check Prior Knowledge

To assess students' prior knowledge about viruses, ask:
- **How do viruses that infect animal cells differ from viruses that infect other types of cells?** (Some viruses that infect animal cells are enclosed within an envelope.)

Teacher Demo

Show students a wilting, discolored leaf that has been removed from a plant. Tell them that all the leaves of the plant from which this leaf was removed have the same appearance. Ask:

- **What may have caused the leaves of the plant to take on this appearance?** (Responses may include a lack of water or infection by some type of parasite.)

SUPER READ! **Skimming and Scanning** To practice strategies for effective reading, use pages 45–46 in *Super Read!*

14.2 Origin and Diversity of Viruses

What you'll learn

IDEAS
- To explain one hypothesis about the origin of viruses
- To compare and contrast methods for classifying viruses

WORDS
retrovirus, viroid, prion

Where do warts come from?
Contrary to superstitious belief, warts—rough growths that most commonly appear on the skin of our hands and feet—are not caused by touching a toad or a frog. Viral infection is the real culprit. Although they are only slightly contagious, warts are more likely to spread if they are scratched open.

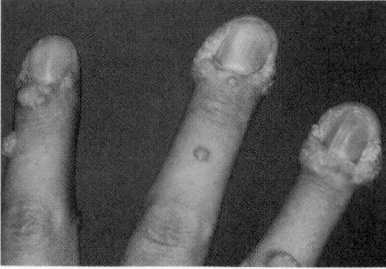

DISCOVERY AND ORIGIN OF VIRUSES

Finally found

Have you ever made a surprising discovery while searching for an ordinary object such as keys or a missing book? If so, was your surprise so great that you stopped your original search and turned your attention to your new discovery?

Like your discovery, the discovery of viruses was a scientific surprise. It happened while biologists were looking for something else—the cause of tobacco mosaic disease. Tobacco mosaic disease stunts the growth of tobacco plants and discolors their leaves. You can see the disease's effect on tobacco leaves in *Figure 14.5*.

The Russian biologist Dmitri Ivanovsky was one of the first scientists to look for the cause of tobacco mosaic disease. After a series of experiments in 1892, Ivanovsky concluded that unusually small bacteria or poisons from bacteria must cause tobacco mosaic disease.

Five years later the Dutch biologist Martinus Beijerinck discovered that the agent causing

FIGURE 14.5
Compare the healthy tobacco leaf on the left with the diseased leaf on the right. How do they differ? ❶

tobacco mosaic disease replicated in tobacco cells. Beijerinck hypothesized that tobacco mosaic disease was caused by something smaller than any known bacterium. He called the infectious agent a *virus*, a Latin word meaning "poison."

Nearly 40 years later, in 1935, the American biochemist Wendell Stanley isolated crystals of the infectious agent from diseased tobacco plants. Because bacterial cells do not form crystals,

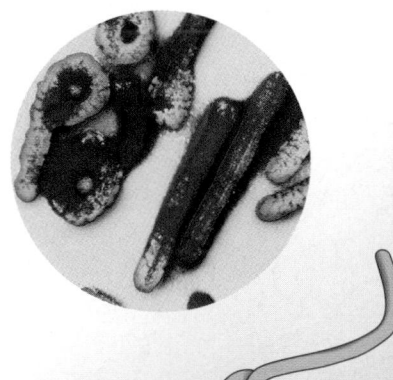

Filovirus
Filoviruses do not have a distinct, uniform shape. Some of these Ebola viruses are threadlike, and some are looped at one end.

STUDENT RESOURCES

From the Teacher's Resource Package, use:
- Section Review 14.2 and Activity Recordsheet 14-1 from Unit 4 Review Module

TECHNOLOGY RESOURCES

Relevant technology resources include:
- Spanish Student Edition CD-ROM
- Teacher's Resource Planner CD-ROM

Stanley confirmed Beijerinck's conclusion: The infectious agent could not be a bacterium. Biologists suddenly had a new type of infectious agent, a virus, to study.

Although biologists have learned much about viruses since 1935, they still can only hypothesize about how viruses originated. One hypothesis is that viruses evolved from their host cells. At first, viruses may only have been short fragments of chromosomes in host cells. These fragments replicated along with host chromosomes as the host cell divided (just as they do in the lysogenic cycle). In time, these pieces evolved the ability to produce capsid proteins. You may notice that this hypothesis implies that a host cell is the closest relative of a virus. Is this hypothesis a good explanation of the origin of viruses? Why or why not?

DIVERSITY OF VIRUSES

An unending supply

Classifying viruses is difficult because they are so diverse. As a result, biologists have developed several different ways of organizing viruses. Sometimes they are organized by shape, sometimes by the host they infect. Viruses may also be classified according to the way they function inside a cell.

Shape You can see the four shapes of viruses in *Figure 14.6*. The arrangement of proteins in capsids determines the shape of the viruses.

Host Viruses can be organized according to the type of host they

FIGURE 14.6

Viral Shapes

Viruses have many different shapes. What characteristics do all the viruses you see here share? ❸

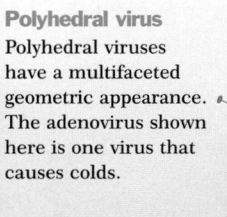
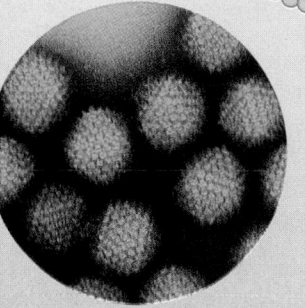

Polyhedral virus
Polyhedral viruses have a multifaceted geometric appearance. The adenovirus shown here is one virus that causes colds.

DNA

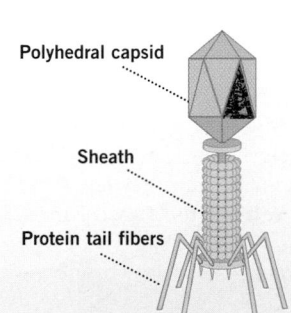

Polyhedral capsid

Sheath

Protein tail fibers

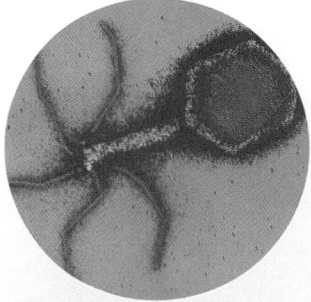

Binal virus
A binal virus consists of two distinct parts: a polyhedral capsid and a helical tail. Compare this virus with the one shown below. ❹

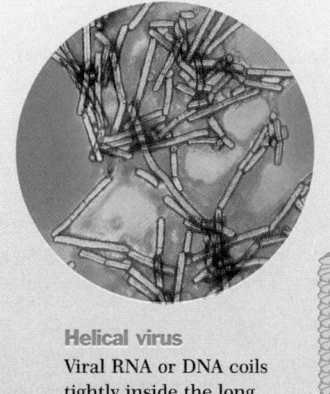

Helical virus
Viral RNA or DNA coils tightly inside the long, narrow capsid of a helical virus.

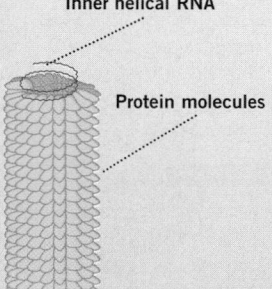

Inner helical RNA

Protein molecules

Chapter 14 Viruses and Monerans **331**

② TEACH

✦ Physical Science

In the branch of chemistry called crystallography, crystal forms and structures are studied. Many substances always form crystals with the same shape and with the same angles between their faces. As a result, crystal structure can be used to help identify structures such as viruses.

Use the Visual

Have students study Figure 14.6. Ask:

- **How does the name of each virus relate to its structure?** (Polyhedral virus has many faces and a binal virus has two parts.)
- **What relationship do you observe between the shapes of the parts of the binal virus and the shape of the other two viruses shown?** (The capsid has the shape of the polyhedral virus, while the tail has the shape of the helical virus.)

❶ The diseased leaf is discolored and wilted.
❷ It depends on the similarity between the viral nucleic acid and the host cell's DNA.
❸ In each, DNA or RNA is surrounded by a protein capsid.
❹ The binal virus resembles the helical virus with a polyhedral capsule on top and tail fibers on the bottom.

Language Arts

Viruses that attack bacteria are called *bacteriophages*. The suffix "phage" comes from the Greek word *phagein*, which means "to eat." *Bacteriophage* literally means "bacteria eater." Explain to students that the shortened term *phage* is often used to refer to bacteriophages.

Use the Visual

Have students study Figure 14.7. To help students understand how retroviruses differ from other viruses, ask:

- **How does the replication of a retrovirus differ from that of the viruses you studied earlier?** (The RNA in the core of the virus replicates by transcribing RNA to form DNA. Most viruses and all other organisms make RNA by transcribing DNA.

 Do It! **TEAM WORK**

Model a Bacteriophage

Other useful materials include acorn nuts (for the polyhedral head), washers, a bolt that fits inside a spring (for the helical nucleic acid core), and wire (for the projections or tail fibers.)

Analyze Your Results

Student models should include representation of a polyhedral capsid containing DNA, a helical tail, and protein tail fibers. To change the model to that of another virus, students would have to change the shape to resemble the shapes shown on page 331.

332

infect. There are animal viruses, plant viruses, and bacterial viruses. Viruses that infect only bacterial cells are referred to as bacteriophages (bak-TEER-ee-oh-FAY-juhz).

Many but not all viruses invade only a specific type of organism. For example, the virus that causes polio replicates only inside human host cells. The virus that causes rabies infects only the cells of particular animal species, such as dogs and humans.

You may wonder how viruses can be so specific. In section 14.1 you learned that capsids and envelopes contain specific proteins. Receptor sites on host cells also contain specific proteins. If the outer proteins in a virus do not fit with the outer proteins of a cell, the virus will not attach to the cell. Without attachment, the viral nucleic acid cannot enter the host cell to replicate.

Function Some viruses, such as retroviruses, can also be classified based on how they function in a host. A **retrovirus** is a virus that contains

 **LAB ZONE Do It!** **bioSURF**

Model a Bacteriophage

Building a model gives you an idea of structure. You can model a bacteriophage, which is a binal virus, if you . . .

Try This

1 Study the illustration of the binal virus on page 331.
2 Gather any materials that will help you to build your model. These might include toothpicks, pipe cleaners, string, and clear plastic food wrap.
3 Build your model, trying to keep the sizes of the parts in relative proportion.

Analyze Your Results

1 Name the bacteriophage parts on your model.
2 How is your model similar to or different from the models that other students have made? How could you improve yours?
3 What would you change to make a model of a different virus?

FIGURE 14.7

The Retrovirus

Notice how the enzyme reverse transcriptase is packaged in the core of the HIV shown below. If the enzyme did not enter the host along with the viral RNA, what step in replication could not occur? ❶

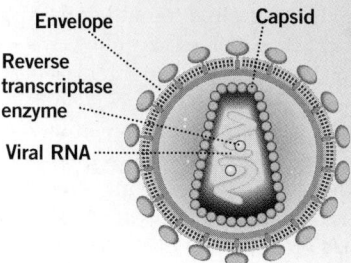

Envelope
Capsid
Reverse transcriptase enzyme
Viral RNA

an RNA core that replicates by first transcribing its RNA into DNA. The prefix "retro-" means "reverse." What do you think might work in reverse in this group of viruses?

Most viruses and all organisms make RNA from DNA in the process of transcription. Retroviruses are able to make nucleic acids in reverse order from the usual process. In retroviruses DNA is made from RNA.

As you can see in *Figure 14.7*, retroviruses have an enzyme called reverse transcriptase, which transcribes viral RNA into viral DNA inside the host cell. You can study this figure to better understand the replication of a human immunodeficiency virus (HIV). This retrovirus causes acquired immunodeficiency syndrome (AIDS).

Retroviruses include tumor-producing viruses as well as HIV. Tumor-producing retroviruses and HIV follow a similar invasion pattern. Many tumor-producing viruses, however, enter the lysogenic cycle after step 3 in *Figure 14.7*. Tumors do not immediately appear, but the virus DNA replicates along with the host

---

Gifted Ask students to research when different viruses were discovered and what impact each virus had on society. Ask students to pool their data to display a time line on the class bulletin board. Students may want to work cooperatively with the rest of the class to illustrate the display.

❶ The viral RNA would not be transcribed to viral DNA.
❷ Transcription, RNA is transcribed to DNA.
❸ The viral DNA will separate from the host's DNA and the virus will enter the lytic phase.

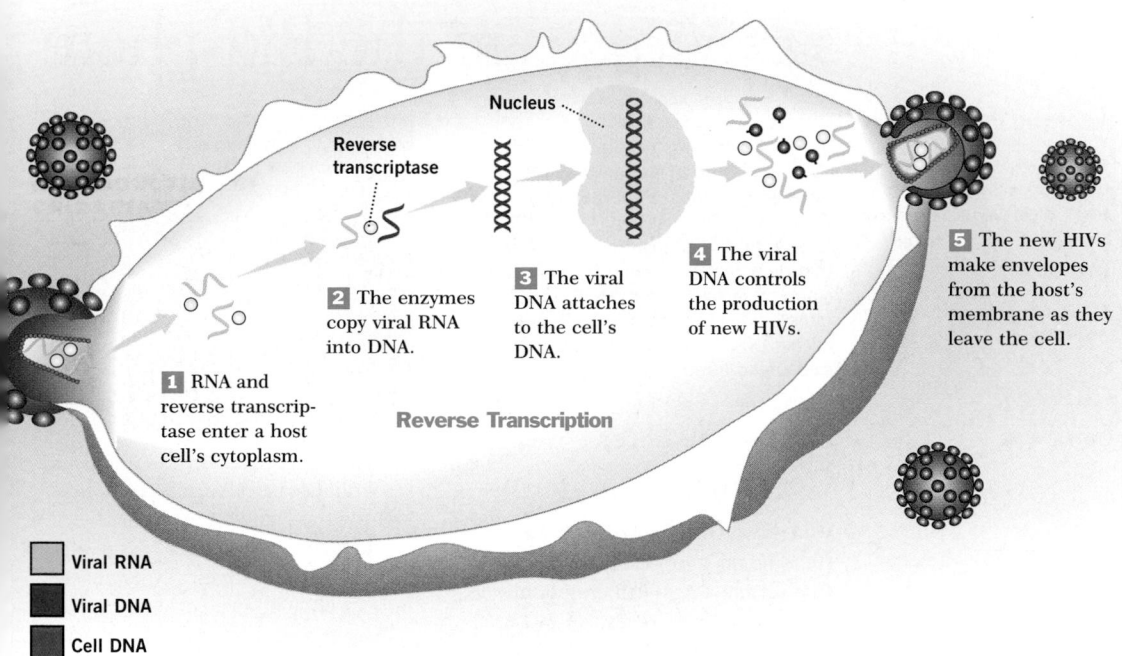

Nucleus

Reverse transcriptase

1 RNA and reverse transcriptase enter a host cell's cytoplasm.

2 The enzymes copy viral RNA into DNA.

3 The viral DNA attaches to the cell's DNA.

4 The viral DNA controls the production of new HIVs.

5 The new HIVs make envelopes from the host's membrane as they leave the cell.

Reverse Transcription

Viral RNA

Viral DNA

Cell DNA

Everyday Biology

Have students discuss precautions they think help to prevent colds and reduce cold symptoms, such as taking vitamin C and zinc tablets, or frequently washing their hands to curb the spread of the virus.

3 **ASSESS**

Evaluate Understanding

Draw a two-column chart on the board. Label each column with the section objectives. Ask volunteers to come to the board one at a time to list information from the section that provides the details requested by each objective. When all details have been listed, review them as a class, deleting those details that do not belong and adding information that may be missing. Have students copy the completed lists in their notebooks for use as a study tool.

Reteach

Let students work in groups to create a sentence outline of the main points in this section using the section objectives, headings, and subheadings as a guide. Review the completed outlines as a class to make sure all significant information has been included.

cell DNA. Eventually, many host cells will contain tumor-producing viral DNA. Using what you have learned about the lysogenic cycle, predict what will happen next.

Nonviral particles Scientists have discovered two infectious agents that have simpler structures than viruses: viroids and prions. A **viroid** is a single strand of pure RNA. Viroids cause plant diseases. For example, viroids have killed many coconut palm trees in the Philippines. Other viroids affect the health of crops such as potatoes and tomatoes. Unlike viruses, viroids do not have capsids protecting their nucleic acids.

A **prion** is a protein molecule that can cause disease in animals. Prions are the only known infectious agents that do not contain DNA or RNA but can, nonetheless, spread throughout an organism.

A prion causes a fatal disease called scrapie in sheep. Prions have

also been found in the brains of cows that died from the so-called mad cow disease. Other prions are found in humans who suffer from kuru or Creutzfeldt-Jakob disease. Both of these diseases affect the central nervous system. A cure has not yet been found for diseases caused by viroids or prions.

CHECKPOINT 14.2

1. What hypothesis did scientists develop to explain the origin of viruses?
2. In what ways are viruses diverse?
3. **Critical Thinking** Make a table to show the similarities and differences between viruses, viroids, and prions.

Build on What You Know

4. How were viruses used to answer the "DNA or protein" question? Why was this finding important? *(Need to jog your memory? Revisit relevant concepts in Chapter 7, Section 7.1.)*

EVERYDAY
BIOLOGY

The All-Too-Common Cold

Studies have shown that frigid weather and wet feet do not cause colds. Hundreds of different viruses and viral strains are the true culprits.

Chapter 14 Viruses and Monerans **333**

CHECKPOINT 14.2

1. Viruses evolved from their host cells as short fragments of chromosomes that replicated with every cell division.
2. Viruses differ in shape, in the type of host they infect, and in how they function in a host.
3. **Organizing** All are infectious agents and none can replicate outside their hosts.

Viruses are made up of RNA or DNA coils surrounded by a capsid. Viroids are single strands of RNA, without a capsid. Prions contain only a carbohydrate-protein molecule.

4. Experiments showed that radioactive DNA—not radioactive protein—entered bacteria, proving that genetic material must be DNA.

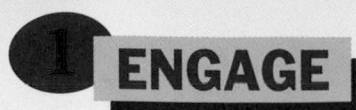

ENGAGE

Use the Visual

Have students study the photograph that opens the section. Explain that inoculations prevent spreading disease. Certain inoculations are mandated by law. Ask:

- **What are some diseases against which pets must be vaccinated?** (Rabies, Lyme disease, distemper, feline leukemia, parvo)

SUPER READ! **Skimming and Scanning** To practice strategies for effective reading, use pages 45-46 in *Super Read!*

LAB ZONE Think About It!

Analyzing Disease Occurrence

Provide graph paper and instruct students to create a bar graph or a line graph with three curves for information given. Have students analyze graphs.

Analyzing the Table

1 Rubeola
2 Not all are vaccinated.
3 Check students' graphs.

What you'll learn

IDEAS
- To describe the role of viruses in the environment
- To explain viral disease and uses of viruses

WORD
vaccination

Dog virus kills big cats

In 1994 scientists were puzzled when about one third of the lions in the Serengeti National Park died of a mutant strain of canine distemper virus (CDV). After extensive study, they concluded that dogs that had died of CDV had been eaten by jackals and hyenas. The infected jackals and hyenas then transmitted CDV to the lions through mucus exchanged during fights.

ECOLOGICAL ROLES

Hosting bad company

When you visit someone's home, you try to be on your best behavior. Viruses that invade a host cell are not always so polite. Some viruses can live in cells without harming them. Other viruses, however, cause specific diseases that develop as the viruses destroy host cells.

LAB ZONE Think About It! bioSURF

Analyzing Disease Occurrence

The numbers of reported cases of some vaccine-preventable viral diseases appear in the table below.

Analyzing the Table

1 Which disease had the most dramatic decrease in number of cases between 1990 and 1994?
2 Why do you think these diseases continue to occur?
3 Make a graph that displays the information in the table.

Reported Cases of Viral Diseases in the United States, 1990–1994					
Viral Disease	**1990**	**1991**	**1992**	**1993**	**1994**
Rubeola (Measles)	27,786	9,643	2,237	312	963
Pertussis (Whooping cough)	4,570	2,719	4,083	6,586	4,617
Rubella (German measles)	1,125	1,401	160	192	227

Source: U.S. Dept. of Health and Human Services

Viral diseases that infect humans include the common cold, measles, chicken pox, and mumps. Some viral diseases have dramatically decreased human populations. For example, an influenza virus outbreak after World War I killed more people than the war itself. Before the development of a polio vaccine in the 1950s, thousands of people died from or were permanently disabled by the poliovirus. More recently, the spread of HIV has resulted in a worldwide AIDS epidemic. Millions of humans have already been infected, and thousands more become infected with HIV each day.

Animals and plants are also susceptible to viruses. Viral diseases that can infect animals include distemper, rabies, and pneumonia. Viral diseases that affect plants may discolor leaves, stunt growth, or eventually kill a plant. These plant viruses are often spread from plant to plant by insects and air currents.

Viral diseases cannot be cured by antibiotics, which are effective only against bacterial cells. Although antiviral drug research continues, treatment of many viral diseases is often limited to relieving symptoms while the body's immune system battles the disease.

STUDENT RESOURCES

From the Teacher's Resource Package, use:
- Section Review 14.3, Critical Thinking Exercise 14-1, and Enrichment Topic 14-1 from Unit 4 Review Module
- Issues and Decision Making 14-1
- Consumer Applications 14-1

TECHNOLOGY RESOURCES

Relevant technology resources include:
- Spanish Student Edition CD-ROM
- Teacher's Resource Planner CD-ROM

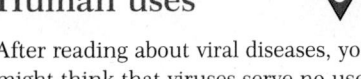

FRONTIERS IN BIOLOGY

Human uses

After reading about viral diseases, you might think that viruses serve no useful purposes. That is not true.

Vaccines Viruses can be used against themselves in the production of life-saving vaccines. **Vaccination** is the process of injecting a person with a harmless—weakened or dead—form of a virus. The vaccine stimulates the immune system to produce cells and proteins that will destroy that type of virus if it enters the body. The vaccination of large numbers of people helped to end epidemics of diseases such as smallpox, polio, and measles.

Genetic engineering Through ongoing research using viruses, virologists—scientists who study viruses—have learned more about basic cell processes and structures. Concentrating on the behavior of viral DNA in the host cell, virologists have applied their findings to the field of genetic engineering. You read about genetic engineering in Chapter 9.

Viruses sometimes pick up pieces of host cell genes and carry them into other cells. Under controlled conditions, genetic engineers can correct genetic defects by using viruses to carry desirable genes from one cell to another. For example, some children are born with a defect in the gene that produces an enzyme needed by a healthy immune system. These children can survive only in a germ-free "bubble" environment. Through genetic engineering, a virus can be used to insert a corrected gene into their body cells. This inserted gene makes the immune system function properly.

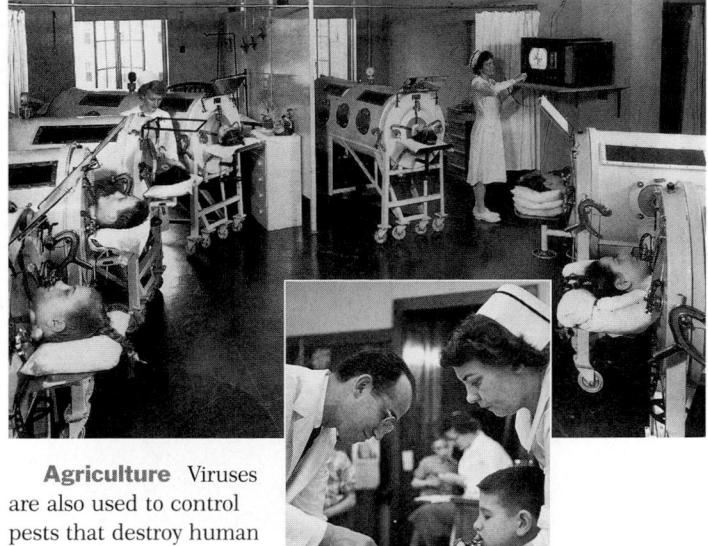

Agriculture Viruses are also used to control pests that destroy human food crops. The benefit of viral treatments for crops is that they eliminate harmful insects without creating pollution.

You may be surprised to learn that viruses can create natural beauty. For example, viral infections produce the stripes and bright color combinations in the petals of gladiolas and tulips.

FIGURE 14.8
Polio patients unable to breathe were placed in iron lungs, which "breathed" for them. Jonas Salk (above) developed a preventative vaccine from three strains of dead polioviruses.

CHECKPOINT 14.3

1. What populations can be altered by viruses in the environment?
2. Name three viral diseases that may infect humans.
3. **Critical Thinking** What factors would have to be considered before using a virus to kill insects?

Build on What You Know

4. What characteristics of viruses make them useful to genetic engineers? *(Need to jog your memory? Revisit relevant concepts in Chapter 9, Section 9.2.)*

What are viruses and how do they replicate? **?**

Chapter 14 Viruses and Monerans **335**

CHECKPOINT 14.3

1. Human, animal, bacterial, and most plant populations
2. Diseases include colds, measles, influenza, chicken pox, mumps, poliomyelitis, and AIDS.
3. **Identifying cause and effect** Scientists must consider possible harmful effects on an environment, such as whether the virus would infect other organisms, or if the insects control other organisms that might multiply if the insects were killed.
4. Viruses can pick up pieces of host DNA and carry them into other cells. Genetic engineers can use viruses to insert desirable genes into cells.

2 TEACH

Clarify Misconceptions

Students often believe that all viruses are harmful. Review the human uses of viruses, such as producing new medicines.

3 ASSESS

Evaluate Understanding

Ask students to write a brief essay titled *Viruses in the Biosphere*. In their essays, have students answer the following questions:

- **What roles do viruses play in the environment?** (Likely responses; viruses often cause disease and some alter the appearance of plants they infect.)
- **How are viruses both helpful and harmful?** (Likely responses will indicate that viruses are harmful when they cause disease. Viruses are helpful when they are used to produce vaccines, medicines, or are used to control agricultural pests.)

Reteach

On an overhead transparency, make a table with two columns: *Helpful* and *Harmful*. Initiate a class discussion about viruses in the biosphere can be helpful or harmful to people, plants, and animals. List students' responses beneath the appropriate head. Then review the information. Remove any wrong information and add missing information.

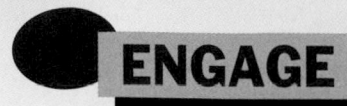

ENGAGE

Consider the Big Idea

Have students read The Big Idea! at the top of the page. Explain that monerans are the simplest life forms that perform all the life functions.

Use the Visual

Have students study the photographs that open the section. Ask:

- **What is the more common name for monerans?** (Bacteria. Explain that bacteria can live in hot springs, the deep ocean, and inside organisms.)

Check Prior Knowledge

To assess students' prior knowledge about monerans, ask:

- **How does the kingdom Monera compare with other animal kingdoms?** (It is the simplest and least developed.)
- **Are monerans prokaryotes or eukaryotes?** (Prokaryotes)

Quick Activity

Display pictures of a plant cell, animal cell, fungal cell, protist cell, and two or three moneran cells. Have students use the information in The Big Idea! to identify the monerans. Have volunteers defend their choices. Be sure students recognize that all of the moneran cells lack nuclei and membrane-bound organelles.

THE BIG IDEA! Monerans are microscopic organisms that lack a membrane-bound nucleus and membrane-bound organelles. 14.4–14.6

14.4 Characteristics of Monerans

What you'll learn

IDEAS
- To identify the structural characteristics of monerans
- To compare how monerans grow, reproduce, and survive

WORDS
plasmids, endospores, binary fission, conjugation

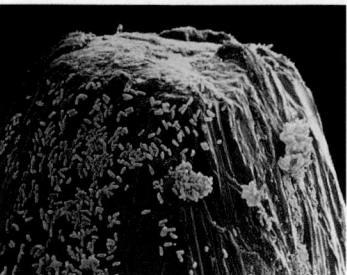

A universe of monerans
This photo shows the point of a pin magnified many times. Those microscopic organisms dotting the pin's surface are monerans. An amazing array of monerans can be found everywhere on Earth. In fact, they exist on most objects you touch every day, and there are trillions of them on and in your body. What exactly are monerans?

MONERAN STRUCTURE

Just the basics

The word *monera* (moh-NAYR-uh) may be unfamiliar, but you have probably heard the word *bacteria.* Most organisms in the kingdom Monera are bacteria (singular: *bacterium*). One characteristic that classifies an organism as a moneran is the lack of a membrane-bound nucleus. As you learned in Chapter 3, cells that lack a membrane-bound nucleus are called prokaryotic cells. Organisms that consist of prokaryotic cells are called prokaryotes. All of the 5000 known species of monerans are prokaryotes.

FIGURE 14.9
Monerans share five characteristics. How do their characteristics compare with those of viruses? ❶

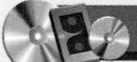

Characteristics of Monerans
Monerans lack a membrane-bound nucleus.
Monerans have a cell membrane but do not have membrane-bound organelles such as mitochondria and chloroplasts.
Ribosomes in monerans are slightly different from the ribosomes in other organisms.
Monerans are smaller than almost all other organisms.
Most monerans are unicellular organisms.

Monerans share other characteristics, as you can see in *Figure 14.9.* Most bacterial DNA is in a single, double-stranded, circular chromosome that attaches itself to the cell membrane. Some kinds of bacteria also contain smaller pieces of circular DNA called **plasmids.** As many as 80 plasmids may be found in a cell. You can compare chromosomes and plasmids in *Figure 14.10.*

LIFE CYCLE

Millions of multiplying monerans

When it has enough food and an efficient waste disposal system, some bacteria can reproduce every 20 minutes. At that rate, from 1 bacterium about 500 bacteria would be produced in three hours and about 16,000,000 in eight hours. Can you imagine how heavily populated Earth would be if every animal multiplied that quickly? Fortunately such unlimited growth does not occur. Lack of food and a buildup of waste keep populations of bacteria in check. Although their

STUDENT RESOURCES

From the Teacher's Resource Package, use:
- Section Review 14.4 and Activity Recordsheet 14-2 from Unit 4 Review Module

TECHNOLOGY RESOURCES

Relevant technology resources include:
- Spanish Student Edition CD-ROM
- Teacher's Resource Planner CD-ROM

FIGURE 14.10

A Typical Moneran

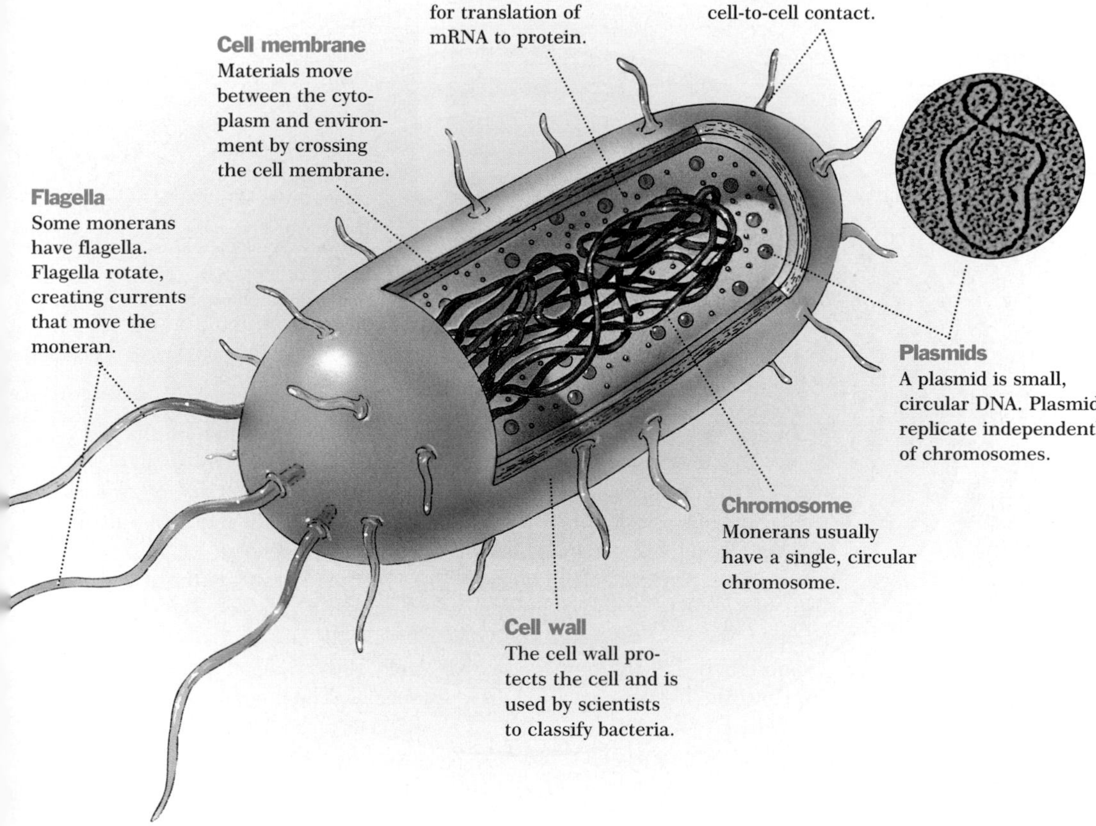

Ribosome
The ribosomes in monerans are used for translation of mRNA to protein.

Pili
These short, hairlike structures are involved in reproduction and cell-to-cell contact.

Cell membrane
Materials move between the cytoplasm and environment by crossing the cell membrane.

Flagella
Some monerans have flagella. Flagella rotate, creating currents that move the moneran.

Plasmids
A plasmid is small, circular DNA. Plasmids replicate independently of chromosomes.

Chromosome
Monerans usually have a single, circular chromosome.

Cell wall
The cell wall protects the cell and is used by scientists to classify bacteria.

growth may be limited by environmental factors, bacteria can adjust in order to survive harsh conditions.

Survival When living conditions become unfavorable, some monerans can form dehydrated cells known as **endospores.** You can see an illustration of an endospore in *Figure 14.11*. Endospores have thick walls and can resist heat, drought, and radiation.

Monerans that form endospores have an advantage for survival. Endospores can be alive but inactive for many years, possibly even for centuries. Then, when conditions are right, the endospores can break open and produce new bacterial

cells. Endospore formation allows some species of monerans to survive harsh conditions and to reproduce when conditions improve.

Reproduction Most monerans can reproduce either asexually or sexually. However, most monerans

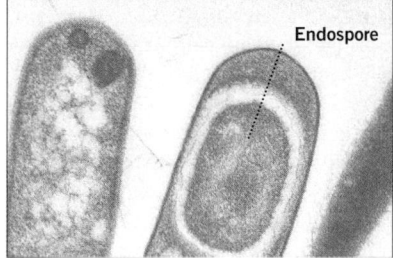

Endospore

FIGURE 14.11

This cell has replicated its chromosome and surrounded it with a strong wall, forming an endospore. Why might it be an advantage for a bacterium to form an endospore? ❷

Chapter 14 Viruses and Monerans **337**

❶ Monerans reproduce on their own, viruses do not.
❷ An endospore increases the chances of bacterial survival because it can resist extreme conditions.

Use the Visual

Have students examine Figure 14.12. Ask:

- **How is binary fission different from conjugation?** (Binary fission is a form of asexual reproduction in which the cell simply splits in two. Conjugation is a form of sexual reproduction in which two bacteria exchange genetic material.)
- **What structure is needed for conjugation to occur?** (Sex pili)

ASSESS

Evaluate Understanding

Have students make sketches showing reproduction of a bacterium through binary fission and reproduction through conjugation. Have them label their drawings and include captions that explain each reproductive process and how the genetic makeup of the offspring compares to that of the parents.

Reteach

On the board, write the terms *conjugation* and *binary fission*. Have students provide one- or two-word phrases that describe each process. List each word or phrase beneath its heading. Review the word lists, crossing out any words that are listed under the wrong heading and adding words that are missing. Have students use the revised lists to write a summary of each process.

FIGURE 14.12

Moneran Reproduction

Binary fission (left) is a form of asexual reproduction. Conjugation (right) is a form of sexual reproduction. What might be an advantage of conjugation over binary fission? **❶**

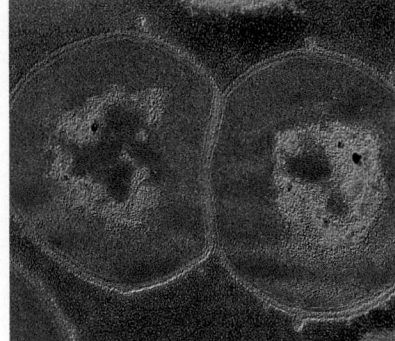

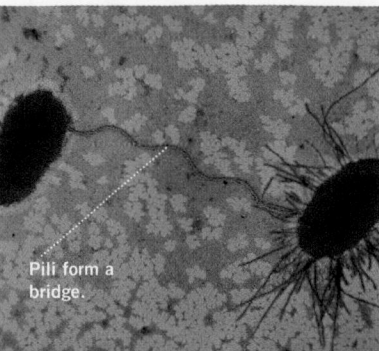
Pili form a bridge.

Binary fission
Binary fission means literally "division in half."

Conjugation
DNA from a plasmid or chromosome moves through the sex pili.

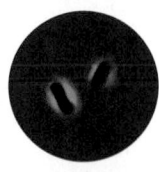

FIGURE 14.13
Binary fission can occur as rapidly as every 20 minutes. The photos above show bacterial reproduction over 5 hours.

reproduce asexually through binary fission. **Binary fission** is a process in which the chromosome of a unicellular organism is continually replicated, after which the cell divides forming two identical cells. *Figure 14.12* shows bacteria during binary fission.

Bacteria usually reproduce asexually. However, bacteria occasionally do exchange genetic information through a form of sexual reproduction called conjugation. **Conjugation** is the process of exchanging genetic material through cell-to-cell contact. During conjugation, some chromosomal DNA and plasmids may move from one bacterial cell to another.

You can see bacteria during conjugation in *Figure 14.12*. As conjugation begins, bacteria are attached together by special hairlike structures called pili (singular: *pilus*). During the later stages of conjugation, a bridge of cytoplasm forms between two bacterial cells, and the DNA passes from one cell to another.

Conjugation increases the genetic diversity of bacteria. Greater genetic diversity increases the chance that some bacteria will survive environmental change, such as the change

that takes place when antibiotics are introduced. Scientists have observed that bacterial DNA is occasionally altered by mutation, further increasing diversity.

Bacteria have additional methods of exchanging genes. Sometimes bacterial cells take up DNA from dead cells of the same or a closely related species. The process by which bacterial cells pick up and incorporate DNA from dead bacterial cells is called transformation. As you read in Chapter 7, this process helped Griffith discover some properties of DNA.

CHECKPOINT 14.4

1. What are the structural characteristics of monerans?
2. What adaptations enable monerans to survive and reproduce?
3. **Critical Thinking** How does the outcome of endospore formation differ from that of binary fission and conjugation?

Build on What You Know

4. What structures might you find in a eukaryotic cell but not in a prokaryotic cell? *(Need to jog your memory? Revisit relevant concepts in Chapter 3, Section 3.2.)*

338 *Unit 4 Monerans, Protists, and Fungi*

CHECKPOINT 14.4

1. Monerans have a cell wall, cell membrane, cytoplasm, ribosomes, DNA, RNA, and sometimes flagella.
2. Monerans reproduce by means of binary fission and conjugation. When conditions are unfavorable, they survive by forming endospores.
3. **Comparing** Binary fission and conjugation result in reproduction, whereas endospore formation is a survival method.
4. Membrane-bound organelles and a membrane-bound nucleus

❶ Conjugation increases genetic diversity, thus increasing the bacterium's biological fitness.

 **Investigate It!**

Does Temperature Affect Bacterial Growth?

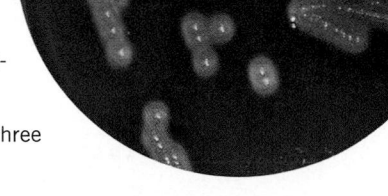

WHAT YOU WILL DO Observe and graph the growth of bacterial colonies at three different temperatures

SKILLS YOU WILL USE Observing, controlling variables, collecting and recording data

WHAT YOU WILL NEED Three sterile agar plates (per group of three students), a clock, a hand lens

Propose a Hypothesis

Propose a hypothesis about the effects of temperature on the growth of bacteria.

Conduct Your Experiment

1 Look at the sterile agar plates through the hand lens. They should appear clean with no bacterial growth. Number the plates from 1 to 3.
Caution: Wash your hands with warm water and soap before and after handling the agar plates.
2 Remove the covers from the three plates and expose them all to the air for 20 minutes. Replace the covers.
3 Refrigerate plate 1. Leave plate 2 at room temperature. Incubate plate 3 at 37°C. Make a table listing the plate numbers with their temperature conditions and intervals for observation.
4 After 24 hours examine each plate with a hand lens. Record the numbers of bacterial colonies at 24 hours for each plate number. Return the plates to the locations described in step 3.
5 Repeat step 4.

Analyze Your Data

1 Use the data on your table to create a bar graph of your results. Look at your graph. Which agar plate had the most bacteria after 24 hours?
2 Did the same plate have more bacteria after 48 hours?
3 Describe the growth rates on the three plates.

Draw Conclusions

Did your results support your hypothesis? Explain how and why temperature affected the growth of bacteria.

Design a Related Experiment

Think of another single variable, such as exposure to light, that might affect the growth of bacteria. Propose a hypothesis about the effects of that variable on the growth of bacteria. Design an experiment to test your hypothesis.

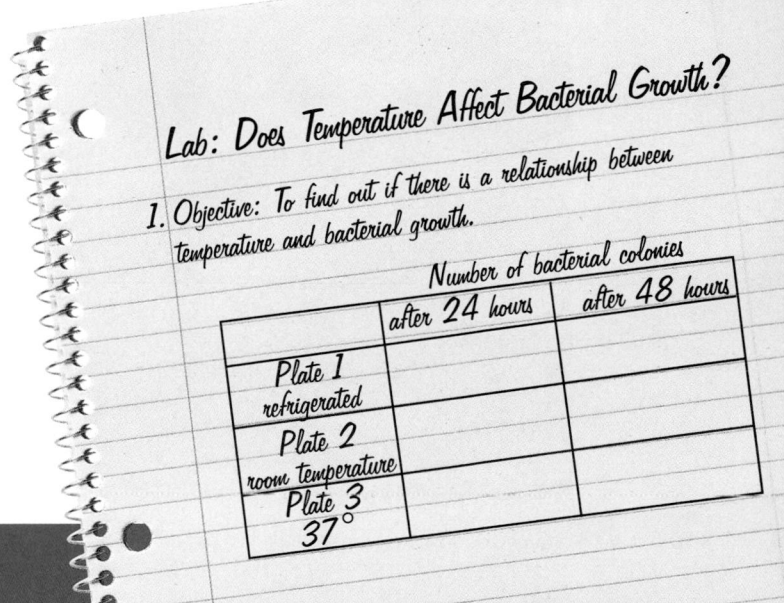

Lab: Does Temperature Affect Bacterial Growth?

1. Objective: To find out if there is a relationship between temperature and bacterial growth.

	Number of bacterial colonies	
	after 24 hours	after 48 hours
Plate 1 refrigerated		
Plate 2 room temperature		
Plate 3 37°		

Analyze Your Data

1 The agar plate at 37° C has the most bacteria after 24 hours.
2 Yes, the same plate has the most bacteria after 48 hours.
3 Answers may vary.

Design a Related Experiment

Student designs will vary, but should be controlled so that only one variable is being tested at a time.

 Investigate It!

TEAM WORK **Does Temperature Affect Bacterial Growth?**

SAFETY FIRST!

Caution students to wash their hands with warm, soapy water before and after they handle the agar plates. Review with students the proper techniques to follow when handling bacterial cultures. If a bacterial culture is spilled, cover the area with a disinfectant for about 30 minutes. Use gloves when wiping away the spills with paper towels. Bacterial cultures should be autoclaved before they are disposed.

Lab Tips

Agar plates can be purchased through biological supply houses. Tell students not to open the agar plates in steps 4 and 5.

Hypothesis Help

Before students write their hypotheses, suggest that they review the information regarding the needs of living things, which they studied in Chapter 1.

Lab Extension

Open Ended
To make the lab more open-ended, you may wish to have students select their own area for placement of the agar plates and keep track of the temperature in those areas. At the conclusion of the lab, students can pool their data to determine the temperature range at which most bacterial growth occurred.

Time Required
■ Two lab periods

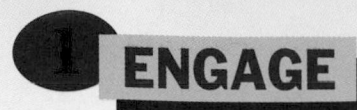

Use the Visual

Have students study the photograph and read the text that opens the section. Explain that the bacteria living in the eye pouches of the fish provide a benefit to the fish. At the same time, the bacteria benefit because they live in a habitat that meets all their needs. Ask:

- **What name is used to describe a close association between two organisms in which both organisms benefit?** (Accept symbiosis, a symbiotic relationship, or mutualism.)

Check Prior Knowledge

To assess students' knowledge about monerans, ask:

- **What distinguishes the cells of prokaryotes?** (They do not have a nuclear membrane or any membrane-bound organelles.)
- **In what kinds of environments do monerans live?** (Monerans live in all kinds of environments, even extreme, harsh ones.)

Quick Activity

Display pictures of different kinds of monerans. Ask students how they would classify the samples. Write their suggestions on the board and retain them to discuss during the section.

14.5 Origin and Diversity of Monerans

What you'll learn

IDEAS
- To analyze the evolution and classification of monerans
- To compare and contrast methods of classifying monerans

WORDS
archaebacteria, eubacteria, aerobes, anaerobes

Bacteria blinkers
The flashlight fish produces bright blue-green light with the aid of bacteria in the pouches below its eyes. To confuse its predators, the flashlight fish can swim one way with its lights on and then swim the other way with its lights off. This bright bacterium is only one of the millions of monerans that inhabit Earth.

CLASSIFICATION OF MONERANS

Ancient and true

Until recently it has been difficult to study the evolution of monerans because their fossils yield minimal information. The techniques of molecular biology, however, have helped scientists discover a lot about the evolution of monerans. Scientists have studied the DNA, RNA, and proteins of living monerans to infer their evolutionary relationships. Based on these studies, most microbiologists divide the kingdom Monera into two groups: archaebacteria (AR-kee-bak-TEER-ee-uh) and eubacteria (YOO-bak-TEER-ee-uh). These groups are so different that some scientists consider them to be separate kingdoms.

Archaebacteria The group of monerans that are often found living in harsh environments are the **archaebacteria.** Archaebacteria can live where no other organisms can survive—in acidic hot springs, near undersea volcanic vents, and in highly salty water.

Archaebacteria are considered ancient ("archae-" means "ancient") because they probably resemble the first forms of life on Earth. Scientists think that the harsh environments in which archaebacteria now live resemble conditions that existed on Earth when life appeared.

FIGURE 14.14
Archaebacteria thrive in the extremely hot environment of Morning Glory Pool in Yellowstone National Park, Wyoming.

STUDENT RESOURCES

From the Teacher's Resource Package, use:
- Section Review 14.5, Activity Record-sheet 14-3, Interpreting Graphics 14-2, Critical Thinking Exercise 14-2 from Unit 4 Review Module
- Lab 25: "Gram Stain: Positive Identification"

TECHNOLOGY RESOURCES

Relevant technology resources include:
- Spanish Student Edition CD-ROM
- Teacher's Resource Planner CD-ROM

Archaebacteria can be divided into three groups, based on the environments in which they live: methanogens, thermophiles, and halophiles. Archaebacteria that live in oxygen-free environments and produce methane (CH$_4$) are called methanogens (METH-an-oh-jenz). Methanogens live in the digestive tracts of cows and other mammals, in swampy areas, and in sewage.

A second group of archaebacteria live in extremely hot water (60°C to 250°C). This group is called the thermophiles (THER-moh-fylz; "therm-" means "heat"). You can see one of the hot environments inhabited by thermophiles in the photo in *Figure 14.14.*

Archaebacteria that live in extremely salty conditions are called halophiles ("salt-lovers"). Halophiles have been found growing in the Great Salt Lake in Utah and in the Dead Sea—places where the water is up to ten times saltier than sea water!

Eubacteria The so-called true bacteria, **eubacteria,** include all other bacteria (the prefix "eu-" means "true"). Eubacteria live in environments much less harsh than those of archaebacteria. This group contains many types of organisms—so many, in fact, that they are difficult to classify. Using molecular biology comparisons taxonomists divide eubacteria into several subgroups, as shown in *Figure 14.16.*

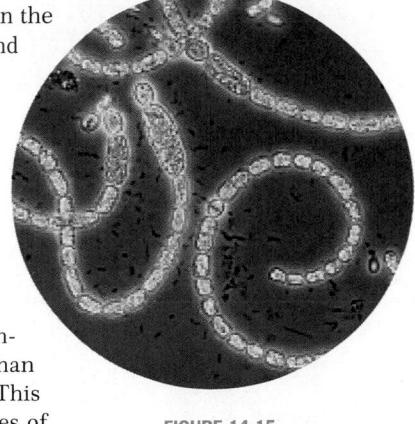

FIGURE 14.15
Eubacteria are an extremely diverse group of monerans. Most Eubacteria are unicellular. *Nostoc,* a freshwater cyanobacterium, forms filaments.

FIGURE 14.16
Kingdom Monera

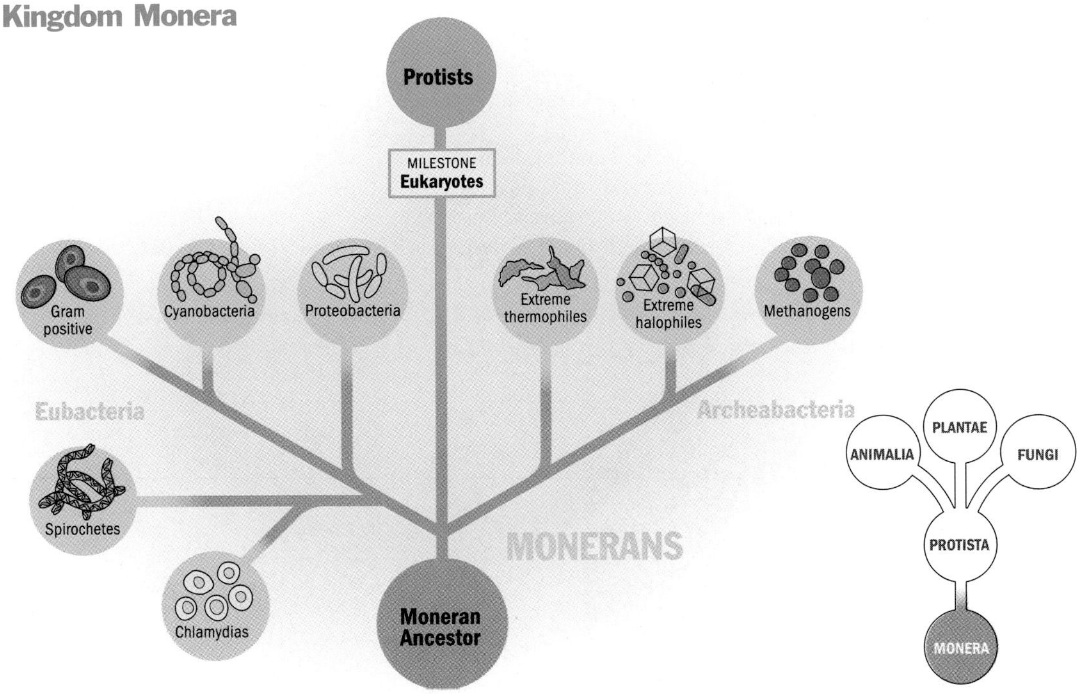

Protists

MILESTONE
Eukaryotes

Gram positive
Cyanobacteria
Proteobacteria
Extreme thermophiles
Extreme halophiles
Methanogens

Eubacteria

Archeabacteria

Spirochetes

Chlamydias

Moneran Ancestor

MONERANS

ANIMALIA
PLANTAE
FUNGI
PROTISTA
MONERA

Chapter 14 Viruses and Monerans **341**

MEETING DIVERSE NEEDS

At Risk Have students use a dictionary to define the prefixes "methano," "thermo," and "halo." and record the definitions in their notebooks. Then have them describe the traits of methanogens, thermophiles, and halophiles and circle the part that relates to the prefix meaning.

FACTS AND FIGURES

Scientists have named more than 4000 species of bacteria. Almost every time they look among bacteria in soil or water, they discover unknown species. Scientists now estimate the number of unknown species to be in the millions.

2 TEACH

Chemistry

Tell students that methane (CH$_4$) is a natural gas that comes from the ground in areas where oil deposits are common. Explain that this gas is commonly used as a heating fuel. Ask students to write an article suggesting how methanogens might be used as an energy source in the future.

Use the Visual

Have students study Figure 14.16. Explain that the diagram shows the classification groups into which monerans are placed as well as their evolutionary history. Ask:

- **What groups shown are classified as archaebacteria?** (Thermophiles, halophiles, methanogens)
- **What groups of eubacteria are shown?** (Gram-positive bacteria, cyanobacteria, proteobacteria, spirochetes, and chlamydias)
- **What group of organisms evolved from the monerans?** (Protista)
- **What is the main difference between the monerans and protists?** (The Protista are eukaryotic.)

Science History

The Gram-staining method was developed to distinguish pneumonia bacteria from the nuclei of the cells they infected. Ironically, the trait of Gram's stain that made it useful to microbiologists (Gram's stain is not retained by all bacteria in the same way) was a disappointment to the stain's creator.

Explain

Tell students that the bacterium that produces the kind of food poisoning known as botulism is an anaerobe. (It grows without oxygen.) Explain that as these bacteria grow, they give off a gas, which can cause the food to swell up and bulge. Advise student never to eat food from such cans. Eating even a very small amount of food contaminated with botulism bacteria toxins can be life-threatening.

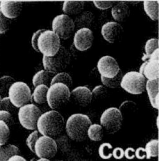

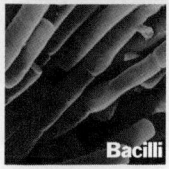

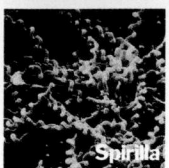

FIGURE 14.17

Examples of bacterial shapes: cocci are spherical, bacilli are rod-shaped, and spirilla are spirals.

OTHER WAYS TO IDENTIFY AND CLASSIFY MONERANS

Many fingerprints

Before the development of techniques in molecular biology, classification by molecular comparison was not possible. Instead, scientists classified and identified bacteria using different criteria. Among these criteria are cell shape, cell wall composition, nutrition, and respiration.

Cell shape Bacteria have various shapes. *Figure 14.17* illustrates three of the most common bacterial shapes: spheres (cocci), rods (bacilli), and spirals (spirilla). Bacteria may exist in chains (for example, streptococci) or clusters (staphylococci).

Cell wall composition The presence of a cell wall is a characteristic common to most monerans. However, the structure of that cell wall can differ. Scientists have developed a technique for identifying eubacteria based on cell wall differences. This technique, called Gram staining, was developed in 1884 by Hans Christian Gram, a Danish microbiologist. *Figure 14.18* shows how this technique reveals cell wall structure.

Gram staining identifies distinct groups of eubacteria: gram-positive and gram-negative eubacteria. Both of these groups include organisms that cause human diseases such as scarlet fever and toxic-shock syndrome. An extra lipid bilayer in gram-negative eubacteria prevents many antibiotics from entering the cell, thereby making the antibiotic ineffective. Therefore, Gram staining is important in both the identification and the treatment of infection.

Nutrition Another common method of moneran identification is based on how bacteria obtain nutrition. Organisms that cannot make their own food are known as heterotrophs. Most monerans are heterotrophs: they get energy by consuming organic molecules made by other organisms.

Organisms that can make their own food are known as autotrophs. Autotrophs that make food by using sunlight and carbon dioxide are called photoautotrophs. Many photoautotrophs, such as the cyanobacteria, contain chlorophyll, which gives them a green color. Autotrophs that make their own food by using chemicals such as ammonia or sulfur are called chemoautotrophs. The archaebacteria that inhabit the hot spring in *Figure 14.14* are chemoautotrophs.

Respiration Still another method of identifying bacteria is based on cellular respiration. Organisms that use oxygen during respiration are called

FIGURE 14.18

Gram Staining

In Gram staining, eubacteria are stained first with a purple dye, rinsed, and then stained with a red dye. Depending on the structure of their cell walls, eubacteria appear purple or red. What color are Gram-positive ❶ eubacteria after staining? Gram-negative?

Gram-positive eubacteria

Gram-negative eubacteria

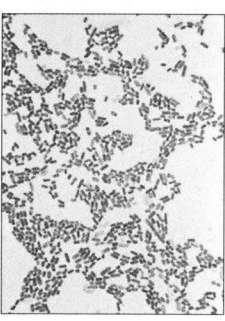

❶ Gram-positive eubacteria absorb purple dye, and gram-negative eubacteria absorb red dye.

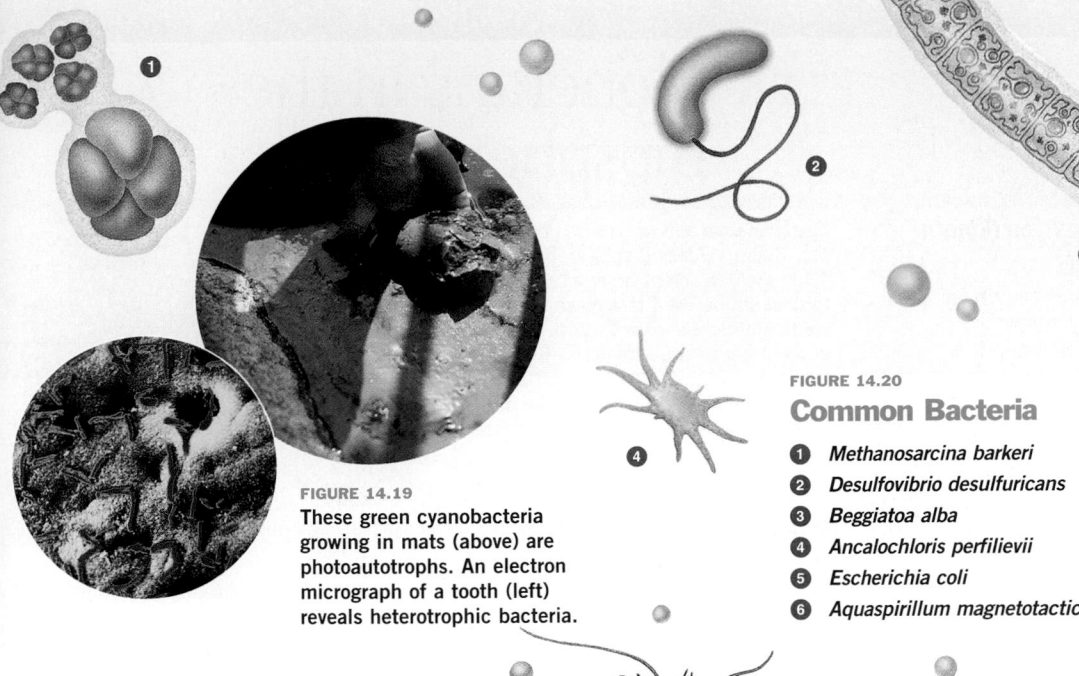

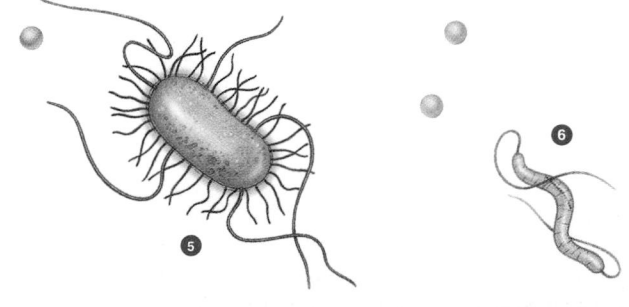

FIGURE 14.19

These green cyanobacteria growing in mats (above) are photoautotrophs. An electron micrograph of a tooth (left) reveals heterotrophic bacteria.

FIGURE 14.20

Common Bacteria

1. *Methanosarcina barkeri*
2. *Desulfovibrio desulfuricans*
3. *Beggiatoa alba*
4. *Ancalochloris perfilievii*
5. *Escherichia coli*
6. *Aquaspirillum magnetotacticum*

aerobes. The bacterium that causes tuberculosis is an aerobe that lives in human lungs, where it is bathed in the oxygen it needs for respiration.

Anaerobes are organisms that do not use oxygen during respiration. Anaerobes typically get energy through the process of fermentation, which you read about in Chapter 4. The anaerobic tetanus bacterium may grow in deep puncture wounds where oxygen is nearly absent.

CHECKPOINT 14.5

1. How are archaebacteria and eubacteria related?
2. Describe the different methods for identifying and classifying monerans.
3. **Critical Thinking** Where in your home would you most likely find archaebacteria?

Build on What You Know

4. According to the theory of evolution, what role did monerans play in the origin of life? *(Need to jog your memory? Revisit relevant concepts in Chapter 11, Section 11.2.)*

LAB ZONE Do It!

Identify Shapes of Bacteria

You will identify the shapes of bacteria when you . . .

Try This

1 Examine under the microscope each of the three numbered slides your teacher has given you.
2 Make a rough sketch of each bacterium, and classify it as either cocci, bacilli, or spirilla.

Analyze Your Results

1 Uncover the slide labels and check to see that you identified the shapes correctly.
2 How did the appearance of the bacteria under the microscope differ? Did they vary much from the photos of cocci, bacilli, and spirilla in Figure 14.17?

LAB ZONE Do It! TEAM WORK

Identify Shapes of Bacteria

Extend the lab by providing students with slides of bacteria that have been treated with Gram's stain. In addition to having students identify the bacteria by shape, have them state whether the bacteria are Gram-positive or Gram-negative.

Analyze Your Results

The bacteria should appear very similar to those in the textbook photograph.

3 ASSESS

Evaluate Understanding

Direct students to construct a graphic organizer entitled *Classification of Bacteria*. Have students use the following section headings: *Cell Shape, Cell Wall Composition, Nutrition,* and *Respiration*. The graphic organizer should include a brief explanation of each heading and examples of bacteria. Allow time for students to share their completed graphic with the class.

Reteach

On the chalkboard or on an overhead transparency, list the different ways to identify and classify monerans. After students have reviewed the section, have them cite specific examples for each classification.

CHECKPOINT 14.5

1. They are both classified as monerans, and have cells lacking a nucleus and membrane-bound organelles.
2. Monerans are classified into two groups: archaebacteria and eubacteria. They are also classified according to cell wall composition, cell shape, nutrition, and how they respire.
3. **Making generalizations** Archaebacteria that exist in a home would most likely be in the digestive tracts of animals, or in the septic system.
4. The ancestral cells of monerans gave rise to the protists, which in turn gave rise to all the other kingdoms.

Use the Visual

Have students study the photograph and read the text that opens the section. Explain that bacteria evolved to make use of natural oil seeps on land and underwater. Today, these bacteria are abundant around oil wells and gas stations.

Check Prior Knowledge

To assess students' prior knowledge about the roles monerans play in the biosphere, ask:

- **How are bacteria able to survive in so many different environments?** (They can adapt, reproduce sexually or asexually, and some can form endospores.)
- **How are bacteria helpful to people?** (Bacteria are used to make foods and medicines; they play an important role as decomposers in the environment.)

Teacher Demo

Display as many of the following items as possible: yogurt container, can of sauerkraut, package of Swiss cheese, jar of vinegar. Explain that all of these products were made possible by bacteria.

SUPER READ! **Skimming and Scanning** To practice strategies for effective reading, use pages 45-46 in **Super Read!**

14.6 Monerans in the Biosphere

What you'll learn

IDEAS
- To describe the ecological role of bacteria in the environment
- To explain how monerans affect humans

WORDS
decomposers, symbiosis

SUPER READ!

In the Bacteria Cafeteria

High-quality strains of fermenting bacteria are used to make Swiss cheese. The carbon dioxide emitted by the bacteria during fermentation forms the cheese's characteristic holes.

Bacteria's oil-eating debut
The Exxon *Valdez* oil spill in Alaska in 1989 yielded scientific proof that bacteria could be used to remove oil from contaminated beaches. Test plots of oil-covered beach were treated with liquid fertilizer containing bacteria; others were left untreated. Results: Oil in the treated areas degraded two to four times faster.

ECOLOGICAL ROLES

No life without bacteria

Although they are tiny, monerans are the most numerous individual organisms on Earth. This large kingdom has a significant impact on the biosphere. Imagine that dead organic material littered the Earth's surface and never decayed. This is just one example of what would occur without bacteria. In fact scientists say that, without bacteria, life as we know it would cease to exist in just a few weeks. Bacteria are vital to the well-being of all organisms because they recycle important chemicals in the environment.

Monerans and other organisms that break down dead organic materials are called **decomposers.** Monerans in soil and water help recycle carbon, nitrogen, and sulfur along with other chemicals needed by living things. Some species of bacteria live in the roots of plants and convert gaseous nitrogen from the

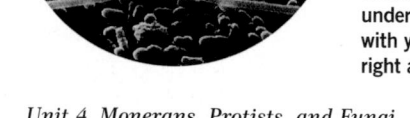

FIGURE 14.21
This scanning electron micrograph shows underarm bacteria. It is with you always, even right after a shower!

air into useful nitrogen compounds. Plants and animals then use these compounds to make other nitrogen-containing compounds such as proteins. The recycling of organic materials is essential for the continuation of life on Earth.

In addition to recycling chemicals in the environment, bacteria interact closely with other organisms. Many bacteria live with organisms of other species in a type of relationship called symbiosis (SIM-bee-OH-sis). **Symbiosis** is a relationship involving direct contact between two organisms in which at least one of the partners benefits. The other partner may be helped, harmed, or remain unaffected. You share a symbiotic relationship with the bacteria in your mouth. The bacteria benefit from the environment of the mouth, but they may harm you by causing plaque and tooth decay.

The bacteria living in the rumen of a cow are also symbiotic monerans. These bacteria benefit from being provided with nutrients in a warm, protective environment. The cow also benefits because the bacteria in its digestive tract break down the cellulose in plants the cow has eaten. This process aids digestion and makes nutrients available to the cow.

STUDENT RESOURCES

From the Teacher's Resource Package, use:
- Section Review 14.6, Enrichment Topic 14-2, Vocabulary Review 14, and Chapter 14 Tests from Unit 4 Review Module
- Lab 26: "Familiar Bactericides"
- Consumer Applications 14-2
- Issues and Decision Making 14-2

 **TECHNOLOGY RESOURCES**

Relevant technology resources include:
- Spanish Student Edition CD-ROM
- Teacher's Resource Planner CD-ROM

DISEASES CAUSED BY MONERANS

Bacteria can kill

Although bacteria play an important role in recycling chemicals, not all species of bacteria are helpful. Disease-causing bacteria do exist and can be deadly to humans and other organisms. Harmful bacteria may enter our bodies from the air, food, and water. They may also invade through body openings such as the nose or through breaks in the skin. Other bacteria live in our bodies and only cause illness when the body's defenses have been weakened.

Scientists began to understand the connection between bacteria and disease in the 1800s. Robert Koch, a German physician, was the first to connect diseases with specific bacteria when he identified two species of bacteria: one responsible for tuberculosis and one responsible for anthrax. Tuberculosis is a disease that usually affects humans; anthrax is a disease that usually affects livestock. The table in *Figure 14.22* provides facts about some other bacterial diseases. The symptoms of bacterial infection range from fevers and sore throats to stomach cramps and rashes.

Antibiotics that kill harmful bacteria can cure many bacterial diseases when the drugs are used as prescribed. Application of antibiotic ointment to any cuts in the skin is a good precaution against possible bacterial infection.

IN THE COMMUNITY

Beefing Up Inspections

Although beef and poultry are inspected for bacterial contamination, sometimes these foods are stored or cooked improperly at home or in restaurants. As a result, people can become sick after ingesting contaminated beef and poultry. Contact your local or state board of health to request information on safe food-handling techniques you can use at home. Ask specifically for information about Hazard Analysis Critical Control Point, or HACCP. Many restaurants use this system to monitor how they receive, prepare, and store foods. To learn about national inspection regulations for beef and poultry before they reach your home or a restaurant, contact the U.S. Department of Agriculture (USDA) or log on to *http://microorganisms.biosurf.com.* Ask about the newest methods being used to detect contamination—methods that do not rely on only surface inspection of meat.

FRONTIERS IN BIOLOGY S T S

Employing bacteria

Scientists have found many ways in which to harness nature's microscopic army of bacteria. Bacteria serve several useful purposes, including helping us rid the environment of harmful substances. Bioremediation is the process of using microorganisms to help restore natural environmental conditions. For example, bacteria can be put to work at hazardous waste sites to break down harsh chemicals such as creosote and coal tar. In modern sewage treatment plants, such as the one shown in *Figure 14.23*, bacteria decompose solid and liquid waste

Some Bacterial Diseases

Disease	Mode of Transmission	Major Symptoms
Lyme disease	through the bite of infected deer ticks	rash at bite site, headache, chills, and fatigue
Toxic strep	through mouth or skin lesions	sore throat, fever, sudden rash, or slow-healing wound
Cholera	by ingesting water contaminated by human feces	acute diarrhea, stomach cramps, and dehydration
Tetanus	through deep puncture wounds that close to air	neurological disturbances resulting in spastic paralysis

FIGURE 14.22
Lyme disease and toxic strep are readily treated with antibiotics such as penicillin and erythromycin. Both cholera and tetanus can be prevented by vaccination.

MULTICULTURAL PERSPECTIVE

While teaching at Tuskegee Institute, George Washington Carver had his students use leaves, weeds, and potato peelings to make fertilizer. When the fertilizer was added to soil, bacteria in the soil decomposed these materials and returned to the soil vital nutrients for plant growth.

FACTS AND FIGURES

Human babies are born with no bacteria. Within hours, a baby will be host to billions of bacterial cells, weighing about a quarter of a pound.

TEACH

In the Community

Safe handling instructions include: thaw meat and poultry in the refrigerator or in the microwave; keep raw meat and poultry separate from other foods, wash working surfaces, utensils, and hands after touching raw meat or poultry. To find out about HACCP, and to get answers to other food safety questions, students can call the Meat and Poultry Hotline of the U.S. Department of Agriculture toll-free at (800) 535-4555.

Think Critically

After discussing the role of monerans as decomposers, ask:

- **Why can prokaryotes live without eukaryotes, but eukaryotes cannot live without prokaryotes?** (Prokaryotes that are decomposers break down organic substances from dead organisms. They recycle essential nutrients for eukaryotes back into the environment.)

Explain

Direct students' attention to Figure 14.22. Explain that the table shows just a few of the many diseases caused by bacteria. Point out that some diseases affect animals as well as people. For example, Lyme disease which is transmitted through the bite of a tick has become an epidemic among dogs kept as pets. Many states now encourage pet owners to vaccinate their dogs against this disease.

ASSESS

Evaluate Understanding

Write the heads *Helpful Bacteria* and *Harmful Bacteria* on the board. Summarize the section by having volunteers list one example of how bacteria are helpful or harmful under the appropriate heading. Review the completed list, deleting any inaccurate information and adding new information as appropriate.

Reteach

Review the section with students and write key words and concepts on the board. Then have students work in pairs to classify the words and concepts as relating to "helpful bacteria" or "harmful bacteria."

into harmless and sometimes helpful materials.

In addition to helping restore the environment, bacteria are used in the production of many foods. Bacteria ferment sugar in the making of cheese, yogurt, some beverages, and vinegar.

Bacteria can also be used in manufacturing products that we use. They can help extract minerals from mined ores, including gold and copper. Other bacteria are involved in making products such as flushless toilets, biodegradable plastics, and pharmaceuticals.

Bacteria also have many applications in medicine. Molecular biologists insert human genes into bacteria and use the altered bacteria to make important medical products. For example, a strain of *E. coli* bacteria has been genetically engineered to produce human insulin, which must be taken by people with some forms of diabetes. Scientists have genetically

FIGURE 14.24
Proteins extracted from *Pseudomonas syringae* bacteria are mixed with water, causing the water molecules to crystallize at higher temperatures, and aiding in snowmaking.

engineered bacteria to produce human proteins that can be used to treat growth defects, heart attacks, burns, ulcers, and possibly cancer.

CHECKPOINT 14.6

1. What roles do monerans play in the environment?
2. Describe five ways in which humans are affected by monerans.
3. **Critical Thinking** Compare the roles and effects of viruses and monerans in the environment.

Build on What You Know

4. Most monerans are decomposers, helping to recycle materials, including organic molecules. How are chemical reactions involved in the formation of organic molecules? *(Need to jog your memory? Revisit relevant concepts in Chapter 2, Section 2.3.)*

FIGURE 14.23
At water-treatement plants, such as the one in Oakland, California, (below, right) water being purified is sprayed over a rock bed coated with aerobic bacteria and fungi. As the water seeps through the treated rock bed, the bacteria help to cleanse it of harmful pollutants.

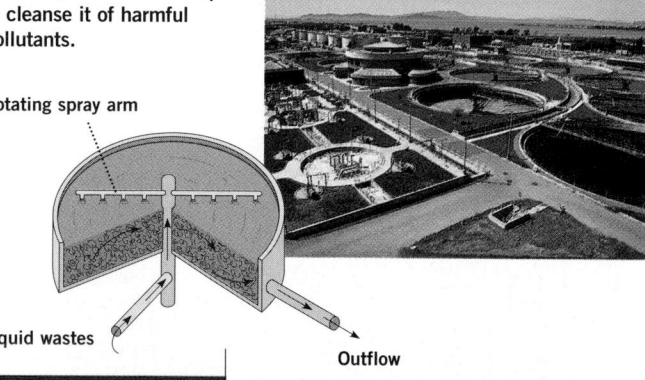

Rotating spray arm

Liquid wastes

Outflow

? What are monerans?

346 *Unit 4 Monerans, Protists, and Fungi*

CHECKPOINT 14.6

1. Bacteria break down the material in dead organisms and recycle organic nutrients.
2. Monerans can cause disease and are used in bioremediation, sewage treatment, food fermentation processes, and in medical biotechnology.
3. **Comparing** Both organisms can cause disease and are used in medical biotechnology and bioremediation. Monerans, unlike viruses, are decomposers.
4. Bacteria break down carbon so it can be used to make all four types of organic molecules.

Chapter 14 Review

 **THE BIG IDEA!** 14.1–14.3 Viruses are particles that depend on living things to replicate.
14.4–14.6 Monerans are microscopic organisms that lack a membrane-bound nucleus and membrane-bound organelles.

Sum It Up

Use the following summary to review the main concepts in this chapter.

14.1 Characteristics of Viruses

• A virus has a core of nucleic acid—either DNA or RNA (never both)—and a protective capsid.
• A virus can be active and replicate only inside a host cell.
• Viruses can replicate immediately (lytic cycle) or after a period of time (lysogenic cycle).

14.2 Origin and Diversity of Viruses

• Viruses probably appeared after cells evolved.
• Viruses can be divided into groups based on the type of nucleic acid they contain, their shape, and the type of host they infect.
• Retroviruses, unlike any other organisms, make DNA from RNA.

14.3 Viruses in the Biosphere

• Viruses can affect plants and animals, including humans.
• Viruses may invade and destroy host cells.
• Viruses are used in making vaccines, in genetic engineering, and in pest control.

14.4 Characteristics of Monerans

• Monerans are usually unicellular prokaryotes.
• Monerans reproduce by binary fission or conjugation.
• Monerans can survive harsh conditions by forming endospores.

14.5 Origin and Diversity of Monerans

• Monerans probably resemble the first life forms on Earth.
• The kingdom Monera is composed of archaebacteria and eubacteria.
• Monerans can be identified by cell wall structure, shape, metabolism, or respiration.

14.6 Monerans in the Biosphere

• Monerans are vital as decomposers.
• Many monerans live in symbiotic relationships.
• Some monerans cause disease.
• Humans use bacteria in many ways.

Use Terms and Concepts

Use each of the following words or terms in a complete sentence.
If you need to review a meaning, turn to the page indicated.

virus (p. 326)
capsid (p. 326)
envelope (p. 327)
host (p. 327)
lytic cycle (p. 328)
lysogenic cycle (p. 328)
prophage (p. 328)

retrovirus (p. 332)
viroid (p. 333)
prion (p. 333)
vaccination (p. 335)
plasmids (p. 336)
endospores (p. 337)
binary fission (p. 338)

conjugation (p. 338)
archaebacteria (p. 340)
eubacteria (p. 341)
aerobes (p. 343)
anaerobes (p. 343)
decomposers (p. 344)
symbiosis (p. 344)

Review the Big Ideas

Before students begin the Chapter Review, you may wish to discuss main concepts from the big ideas in Chapter 14. Point out that viruses are particles that have organized structural parts, but they are not cells. Viruses do not reproduce. They copy themselves, or replicate, inside host cells. Viruses affect plants, animals, and humans. Explain that monerans are classified as prokaryotes because their cells lack membrane-bound nuclei. Monerans are unique living things because they have cell membranes, but do not have membrane-bound organelles such as chloroplasts and mitochondria. Monerans reproduce by binary fission or conjugation.

Answers

1. envelope
2. host
3. lysogenic cycle
4. viroid
5. binary fission
6. plasmids
7. endospores
8. archaebacteria
9. aerobes
10. anaerobes
11. decomposers
12. symbiosis
13. true
14. true
15. false: retrovirus
16. true
17. false: lytic
18. true
19. false: replicate
20. false: conjugation
21. false: archaebacteria
22. Although cells vary greatly in size, viruses are much smaller than even the smallest of cells. Viruses have only a core of nucleic acid and a protective capsid. Plant and animal cells have a nucleus and organelles.
23. Viruses depend on cells for survival; they are unable to replicate on their own. One hypothesis is that chromosomal viral fragments, which were stored and replicated in host cells, evolved the ability to form capsids, which allowed viruses to survive the journey between host cells.
24. Vaccination with a weakened or dead virus stimulates the immune system to produce cells and proteins that can attack a specific disease–causing virus.
25. Strep, lyme disease and food poisoning are bacterial; AIDS, measles and mumps are viral.
26. Infectious agents include viruses which have an

Use Your Word Power

COMPLETION Write the word or phrase that completes each statement.

1. A(n) _____ is the viral cover of animal viruses.

2. A(n) _____ is an organism whose organelles are used by a virus to replicate.

3. The _____ begins with the virus inserting its DNA into the host cell DNA.

4. A(n) _____ is a single strand of pure RNA.

5. Bacteria most commonly reproduce by _____ .

6. Small circular DNA molecules in bacteria are called _____ .

7. The dehydrated cells that enable bacteria to resist unfavorable conditions are called _____ .

8. _____ are monerans that usually live in harsh environments.

9. Organisms that need oxygen to respire are called _____ .

10. Organisms that do not use oxygen to respire are called _____ .

11. _____ are bacteria and other organisms that break down dead organic material.

12. A relationship called _____ may help, harm, or have no affect on an organism.

TRUE-FALSE Write true if the statement is true. If the statement is false, replace the underlined word(s) to make the statement true.

13. A prion is an infectious particle that is associated with mad cow disease.

14. A bacteriophage is a virus that infects bacteria.

15. A plasmid produces nucleic acid in the reverse of the usual process.

16. The protein coat around the core of a virus is a capsid.

17. During the lysogenic cycle of a viral infection, a host cell is destroyed.

18. A prophage is a segment of viral DNA that is inserted in the DNA of a bacterium.

19. Viruses reproduce.

20. Binary fission is a means for some bacteria to exchange genetic material.

21. Eubacteria are monerans that live in conditions that most closely resemble ancient Earth.

Show What You Know

22. Compare the relative size and structure of a virus and a cell.

23. Why do biologists hypothesize that cells evolved before viruses?

24. Explain how vaccines prevent diseases.

25. Name and describe three disorders caused by a virus and three caused by a bacterium.

26. **Make a Concept Map** Complete the concept map by adding the following terms: viruses, bacteria, cell walls, replication, binary fission, conjugation.

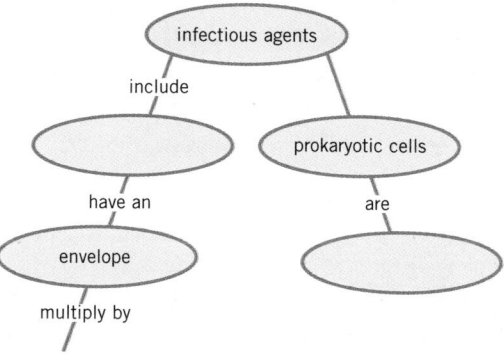

---

envelope and undergo replication. Infectious agents can be prokaryotic cells which are bacteria protected by cell walls and reproduce by binary fission and conjugation.

27. Answers will vary. Students are likely to argue that viruses lack key attributes of life such as metabolism and response to stimuli. However, some students may argue that viruses are a very simple life form with an ingenious mechanism for reproduction; students may not accept the distinction made between reproduction and replication.

28. Digestive juices could potentially destroy viruses that have only a protein coat. However, some proteins are not easily destroyed.

Take It Further

27. Making a Generalization If you were asked your view on whether or not viruses are alive, what would you reply, and how would you support your conclusion?

28. Analyzing Data Proteins in food are digested by enzymes and secretions in the stomach and small intestine. If you swallow a virus, which has a protein coat, what effect do you think the enzymes and secretions will have on the virus?

29. Designing an Experiment Develop an experiment to test the hypothesis that contact of an agar plate with a finger results in more bacterial growth than the exposure of the plate to classroom air.

30. Interpreting a Graph The graph below shows the result of an experiment with bacterial cells. At the start of the experiment, one group of bacterial cells was infected by a virus and the other group was not. The two curves on the graph indicate the number of living cells in each group. What effect did the virus have on the bacterial cells? Explain your answer.

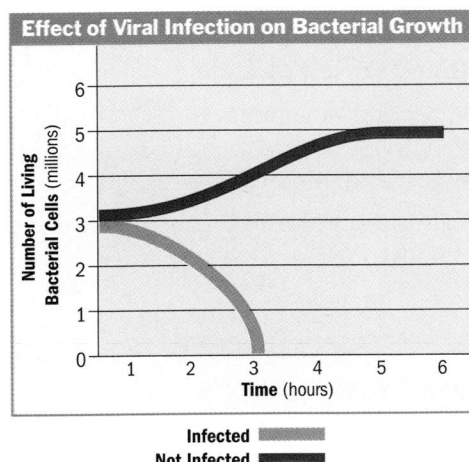

Effect of Viral Infection on Bacterial Growth

Number of Living Bacterial Cells (millions) vs *Time (hours)*

Infected
Not Infected

Consider the Issues

31. Who Gets the First Shot? How do you think new experimental vaccines should be tested? In some cases, people at high risk for contracting a certain disease, such as the flu, volunteer to be vaccinated with newly developed vaccines. Explain your ideas.

32. Releasing Altered Genes A bacterium that lives in the corn ear worm—a destructive crop pest—has been genetically altered to kill the worm. Many people think that altered bacteria should be sprayed on crops that are infested with the worm. Others argue that the altered organism should not be released into the environment. What reasons might they give?

Make New Connections

33. Biology and Art Assume that there has been a recent outbreak of rabies, which infects squirrels, skunks, and raccoons in your community. Create a poster to alert people to this virus and to show commonsense steps people can take to avoid infection.

34. Biology and the Community Investigate local resources for ensuring that people and pets receive adequate vaccinations. Find out what the medical guidelines are for vaccination.

FAST-FORWARD TO CHAPTER 15

Monerans are prokaryotes. Protists, which you will read about in Chapter 15, are eukaryotes. Abundant and diverse, they range from microscopic amebas to giant kelps.

---

29. Students would need two labeled agar plates. Touch one plate with a finger. Leave both plates uncovered for 20 minutes. Then cover the plates and store them together in a protected corner of the classroom. Use a hand lens and count the bacterial colonies after 24 hours and 48 hours.

30. The bacterial cells that were not infected continue to multiply over time. The infected cells are reduced in number over time because replication of the virus is killing the cells.

31. Answers will vary. Some possible issues are: Who is drawn to these experimental vaccines and why? (For example, some people may be drawn to experimental studies because they cannot

afford more conventional treatments.) What constitutes informed consent, that is, can the patient understand the potential benefits and risks? If early results are favorable, should individuals in the control group be switched to the new drug even though the switch diminishes the scientific value of the study?

32. Answers will vary. A major objection of some environmentalists is that we cannot know the full implications of introducing a genetically altered organism into the environment. What other organisms might it affect, directly or indirectly (including birds or insects that feed on the corn ear worms)?

33. Student posters will vary. The steps students suggest will also vary, but should express an awareness of how the viruses might be transmitted.

34. Although local resources usually recommend that everyone receive a flu shot each fall, the resources aggressively target the elderly, those with chronic respiratory ailments, and those with damaged immune systems. Rabies and distemper shots are urged for dogs and cats, and often there are free or very inexpensive clinics offered several times a year by veterinarians. Horses and dairy cows also receive regular vaccinations.

PLANNING GUIDE

Section	Student Activities/Features	Teacher's Resource Package
15.1 Characteristics of Protists **Objectives** ■ Compare prokaryotic and eukaryotic cells ■ Explain how protists are classified	**Lab Zone Discover It!** *The Protist Search*, p. 351 **Everyday Biology** *Don't Drink the Water!* p. 353 **Lab Zone Do It!** *Can You Find Protists in Pond Water?* p. 354	**Unit 4 Review Module** ■ Section Review 15.1 ■ Activity Recordsheet 15-1
15.2 Animal-like Protists—Protozoans **Objectives** ■ Describe common characteristics of protozoans ■ Compare diverse protozoans	**Lab Zone Think About It!** *Protozoan Excretion*, p. 356	**Unit 4 Review Module** ■ Section Review 15.2 ■ Interpreting Graphics 15 **Laboratory Manual,** Lab 27: "Protozoans: Animal-like Microbes" **Interpreting and Developing Graphics** 43, 44
15.3 Plantlike Protists—Algae **Objectives** ■ Describe the characteristics of plantlike protists ■ Compare unicellular and multicellular algae		**Unit 4 Review Module** ■ Section Review 15.3 **Consumer Applications** 15.1
15.4 Funguslike Protists—Molds **Objectives** ■ Describe the structural and functional characteristics of funguslike protists ■ Distinguish between the three groups of funguslike protists	**Lab Zone Investigate It!** *Observing Protist Responses to Light*, p. 364	**Unit 4 Review Module** ■ Section Review 15.4 ■ Activity Recordsheet 15-2 ■ Critical Thinking Exercise 15 **Laboratory Manual,** Lab 28: "Algal Blooms"
15.5 Protists in the Biosphere **Objectives** ■ Describe the ecological roles of protists ■ Explain diseases caused by protists and the importance of protists to humans	**In the Community** *A Protist Investigation*, p. 366 **STS: Frontiers in Biology** *Medicines vs. Malaria*, p. 367 **Everyday Biology** *Is There Algae in Your Sundae?* p. 368	**Unit 4 Review Module** ■ Section Review 15.5 ■ Enrichment Topic 15-1 ■ Vocabulary Review 15 ■ Chapter 15 Tests **Issues and Decision Making** 15-1 **Interpreting and Developing Graphics** 45 **Spanish Reviews** Chapter 15

Technology Resources

Internet Connections

Within this chapter, you will see the logo. If you and your students have access to the Internet, the following URL address will provide various Internet connections that are related to topics and features presented in this chapter:

http://microorganisms.biosurf.com

You can also find relevant chapter material at **The Biology Place** address:

http://www.biology.com

CD-ROMs

Biología: la telaraña de la vida,
  (Spanish Student Edition) Chapter 15
Teacher's Resource Planner, Chapter 15
  Supplements
TestWorks CD-ROM
■ Chapter 15 Tests

Overhead Transparencies

Life Cycle of a Plasmodium, #32

Videotapes

Biology Alive! Video Series
■ Signs of Life Video
■ The Domain of Life Video
Rewind: The Web of Life Reteach Videos

Planning for Activities

STUDENT EDITION
Lab Zone
Discover It! p. 351
- abrasive household cleaning product
- toothpaste carton
- empty ice cream container
- dictionary

Lab Zone Do It! p. 354
- small, fresh sample of pond water
- toothpick
- methyl cellulose
- microscope slide
- medicine dropper
- microscope

Lab Zone
Investigate It! p. 364
- microscope
- microscope slides
- toothpick
- methyl cellulose
- *Paramecium* and *Euglena* cultures
- forceps
- metric ruler
- index card

TEACHER'S EDITION
Quick Activity, p. 352
Prokaryotic and eukaryotic cells
- overhead projector
- prepared slides or photomicrographs of protists and eukaryotic cells

Teacher Demo, p. 355
Movement of Paramecia and Ameba
- methyl cellulose

- culture of *Paramecia* and ameba
- microprojector

Teacher Demo, p. 357
Movement of a sporozoan
- small styrofoam ball

Teacher Demo, p. 358
Uses of diatoms
- tube of toothpaste
- car polish
- diatomaceous earth used in pool filters

Teacher Demo, p. 362
Funguslike protist on a dead fish.
- dead tropical fish
- jar
- water

Class Activity, p. 363
Growing mold
- starch
- water
- fresh garden soil

Quick Activity, p. 365
Simulating a baleen whale and phytoplankton
- fine-tooth comb (nit comb)
- infant's hair brush
- wheat germ

Class Activity, p. 368
Examining diatomaceous earth samples
- sample of diatomaceous earth
- water
- slide and coverslip
- microscope

Chapter Objectives

Students will learn the main concepts of this chapter as they complete the following objectives.

- Compare prokaryotic and eukaryotic cells
- Explain how protists are classified
- Describe common characteristics of protozoans
- Compare diverse protozoans
- Describe the characteristics of plantlike protists
- Compare unicellular and multicellular algae
- Describe the structural and functional characteristics of funguslike protists
- Distinguish between the three groups of funguslike protists
- Describe the ecological roles of protists
- Explain diseases caused by protists and the importance of protists to humans

Key Words

15.2 *protozoan, pseudopods, flagella, cilia*

15.3 *algae, alternation of generations*

15.4 *mold, plasmodium*

15.5 *plankton*

The Opening Story

Have students read the story and discuss how the environment can affect the growth of natural molds. Have students relate their observations of molds and fungi they encounter every day. Conclude by discussing how protists might be beneficial to the environment.

CHAPTER 15
Protists

bioSURF

You can find out more about protists by exploring the following Internet address:
http://microorganisms.biosurf.com

In this chapter . . .

FEATURES

Everyday Biology
- Don't Drink the Water!
- Is There Algae in Your Sundae?

In the Community
A Protist Investigation

 Frontiers in Biology
Medicine vs. Malaria

LAB ZONES

Discover It!
- The Protist Search

Do It!
- Can You Find Protists in Pond Water?

Think About It!
- Protozoan Excretion

Investigate It!
- Observing Protist Responses to Light

YELLOW
BLOBS
OOZE OVER
SUBURBS

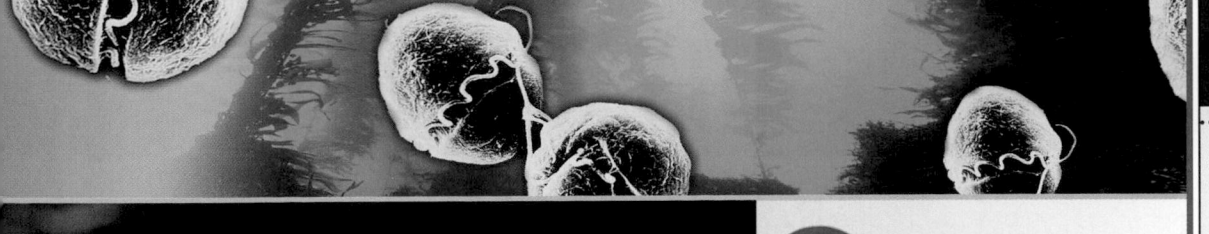

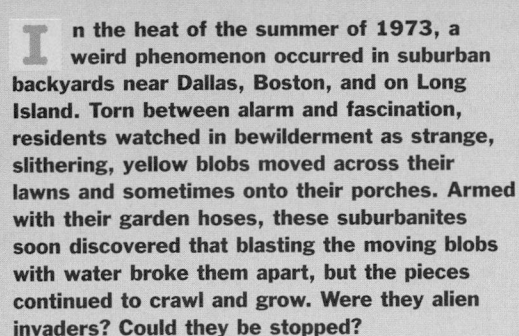

In the heat of the summer of 1973, a weird phenomenon occurred in suburban backyards near Dallas, Boston, and on Long Island. Torn between alarm and fascination, residents watched in bewilderment as strange, slithering, yellow blobs moved across their lawns and sometimes onto their porches. Armed with their garden hoses, these suburbanites soon discovered that blasting the moving blobs with water broke them apart, but the pieces continued to crawl and grow. Were they alien invaders? Could they be stopped?

Scientists soon assured the panicked public that the mysterious yellow blobs were harmless plasmodia—slime molds in the crawling stage of their life cycle. Environmental conditions that included a rainy spring had created prime conditions for the slime molds to grow, and now they were moving in search of food. Slime molds are just one of the amazingly diverse types of living organisms called protists.

LAB ZONE Discover It!

The Protist Search

You need an abrasive household cleaning product, a toothpaste carton, an empty ice cream container, and a dictionary

1. Examine the list of ingredients on each household product, carton, or container.
2. List the ingredients that contain any form of the words *diatom, silica, carrageenan, algin,* or *agar.* Look up the names of these ingredients in the dictionary. All of these words indicate the presence of a protist.

Protists exist nearly everywhere on Earth where there is moisture. As you read this chapter, you will find out more about slime molds such as the type in the story on this page. You will also learn about the sources of the protists that you discovered in household products.

WRITE ABOUT IT!

In your science journal, describe an experience you have had that involved a seaweed or a mold. How did the seaweed or mold look and feel? Where did you find it— in a fish tank? In the bathroom? In a pool? At the beach? Use as many adjectives as you can to describe the seaweed or mold.

Chapter 15 Protists **351**

Opening Activities

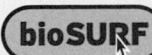 If you have access to the Internet in your classroom or school, you may wish to have students connect to the address shown on page 350. You may wish to have students conduct a search of key words related to protists studied in this chapter. For example, students could search under protozoans and algae.

LAB ZONE Discover It!

The Protist Search

Encourage students to use a dictionary to identify ingredients unfamiliar to them. You may also wish to have them review Chapter 2, *Chemical Basis of Life*, to help them identify chemical ingredients.

WRITE ABOUT IT

Suggest that students use a hand lens to obtain a good description of the molds they discuss in their journal. Point out that seaweed is used in different ethnic dishes and is available in dry form in markets.

REWIND to Chapter 14

Briefly review the concepts studied in Chapter 14, *Viruses and Monerans*. Ask:

- **How do you think protists might be like viruses and monerans?**

PORTFOLIO PREVIEW

Students should be encouraged to add to their portfolios as they work through the chapter. In addition to the *Write About it* opportunity, the following sections provide an opportunity for portfolio entries.

- Section 15.2: *Animal-like Protists—Protozoans*
- Section 15.3: *Plantlike Protists—Algae*

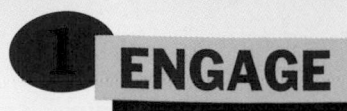

15.1

1 ENGAGE

Consider The Big Idea

Have students read The Big Idea! at the top of the page. Ask students to restate it in their own words.

Use the Visual

Have students study the photograph that opens the section. Point out that the kelp shown are one type of multicellular algae—plantlike protists that carry out photosynthesis.

Check Prior Knowledge

To assess students' knowledge about protists and how they differ from monerans, ask:

- **How do prokaryotes differ from eukaryotes?** (Eukaryotes cells contain a nucleus and membrane-bound organelles; prokaryote cells contain neither.)

SUPER READ! **Skimming and Scanning** To practice strategies for effective reading, use pages 45-46 in ***Super Read!***

Quick Activity

Display on an overhead projector prepared slides or photomicrographs of protists, such as *Paramecium, Euglena,* and *Ameba* and eukaryotic cells, such as onion skin cells and human cheek cells. Ask students to identify any cell structures they recognize. Have them point out similarities and differences among the cells, and identify each cell as prokaryotic or eukaryotic.

THE BIG IDEA! **Protists are a diverse group of eukaryotes that include unicellular and multicellular organisms. 15.1**

15.1 Characteristics of Protists

What you'll learn

IDEAS

- To compare prokaryotic and eukaryotic cells
- To explain how protists are classified

SUPER READ!

An undersea forest of protists

Like trees in a forest, giant kelp are large plantlike protists that form a fertile ecosystem in cold coastal waters. Kelp beds, which sometimes stretch from the seafloor to the water's surface, provide food and shelter for many marine plant and animal species.

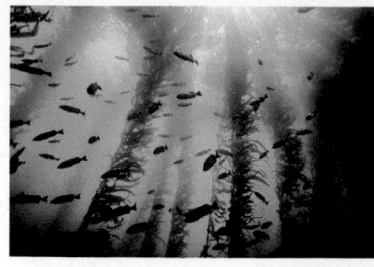

THE STRUCTURE OF PROTISTS

Leftovers share few characteristics

Protists live wherever there is water—in oceans, ponds, mud puddles, on the surface of snow, and even inside other organisms. The variety of protists is amazing. Some are plantlike organisms, others are animal-like. Still others are decomposers. A few are even parasites. Protists range in size from microscopic algae to giant seaweeds. The shapes of protists include bells, stars, snowflakes, and pincushions.

The only characteristic common to protists is that they are all eukaryotic organisms. As you may recall from Chapter 3, eukaryotic cells have membrane-bound nuclei and membrane-bound organelles. *Figure 15.1* illustrates the main differences between a typical eukaryotic and prokaryotic cell.

FIGURE 15.1

Comparison of Prokaryotic and Eukaryotic Cells

How do the structure and size of this prokaryotic cell and eukaryotic cell compare? 1

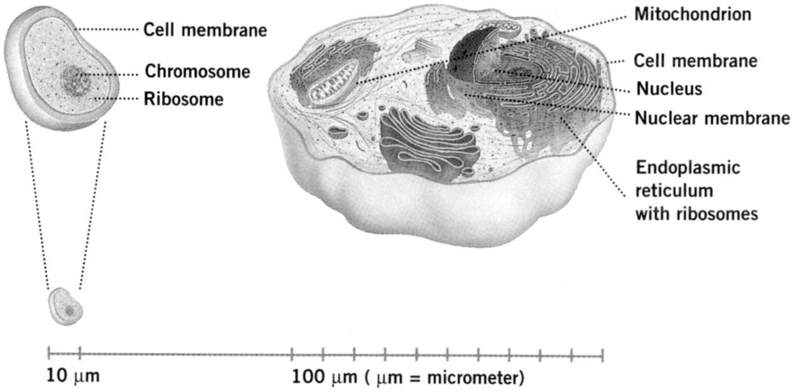

Prokaryote (Moneran)
Eukaryote (Includes Protists)
Cell membrane
Chromosome
Ribosome
Mitochondrion
Cell membrane
Nucleus
Nuclear membrane
Endoplasmic reticulum with ribosomes
10 µm
100 µm (µm = micrometer)

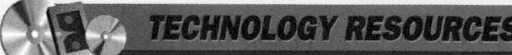

STUDENT RESOURCES

From the Teacher's Resource Package, use:

- Section Review 15.1 and Activity Recordsheet 15-1 from Unit 4 Review Module

TECHNOLOGY RESOURCES

Relevant technology resources include:

- Spanish Student Edition CD-ROM
- Teacher's Resource Planner CD-ROM

FIGURE 15.2

Kingdom Protista

Protists can be organized into three groups based on their nutritional requirements: animal-like, plantlike, and funguslike.

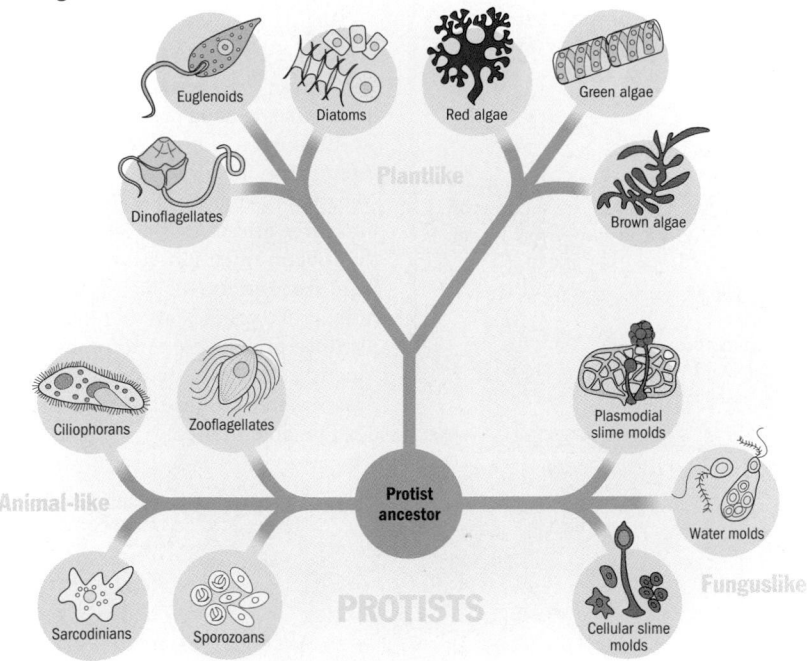

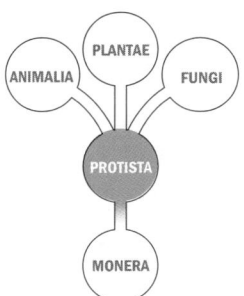

ORIGIN AND DIVERSITY OF PROTISTS

Very old and varied

The first eukaryotes are thought to have evolved about 1.5 billion years ago. As you learned in Chapter 11, eukaryotes may have formed from a symbiotic relationship among prokaryotes. The membrane-bound organelles in eukaryotic cells may have once been prokaryotic cells. Can you visualize how the organelles of the eukaryotic cell in *Figure 15.1* may have resulted from small prokaryotic cells living inside a larger prokaryotic cell? The early eukaryotes may be ancestors of the first unicellular protists.

Protists can also be multicellular. How, then, did multicellular protists arise? Scientists hypothesize that as the first eukaryotic cells increased in number, the cells may have assembled to form colonies. (A colony is a group of similar organisms living and growing together.) Over time, the cells of organisms in colonies may have developed specialized functions that increased the success of that colony. For example, some of the cells may have become specialized for reproduction, while others may have been useful in anchoring the colony at a single location. These specialized colonies may represent the ancestors of multicellular protists such as kelp.

EVERYDAY
BIOLOGY

Don't Drink the Water!

When you are hiking, be sure not to quench your thirst in streams, ponds, or lakes—even if they look clear and clean. Unseen protists in the water can cause serious illness in humans.

Chapter 15 Protists **353**

② TEACH

Use the Visual

Have students study Figure 15.2. Ask:

- **What are the names of the three groups of protists?** (Animal-like, plantlike, and funguslike)
- **How do algae differ from other protists in their method of securing food?** (Algae are plantlike and can make their own food.)
- **What groups of organisms are classified as funguslike protists?** (Plasmodial slime molds, water molds, and cellular slime molds)

Science History

The first protozoans were observed by Anton van Leeuwenhoek in 1674 with a hand-held microscope he built. At the time of the discovery, van Leeuwenhoek called the organisms *animalcules,* or "tiny animals." Today, these organisms are classified as protozoans, the animal-like protists, and van Leeuwenhoek is known as the Father of Protozoology.

Clarify Misconceptions

Students may think that the cell of a single-celled organism is simpler in structure and function than the cells of a multicellular organism. In fact, the cells of some single-celled protists are able to perform most of the processes carried out by an entire multicellular organism. Explain that a single-celled organism's many complex organelles perform the necessary life functions.

MEETING DIVERSE NEEDS

LEP Encourage students to use the information in Figure 15.2 to create a graphic organizer that identifies the major groups of protists, their characteristics, and subgroups. Instruct students to leave space to add information as they study protists.

❶ Eukaryotic cell is larger, more complex, has a nucleus and membrane-bound organelles.

15.1

 **Do It!**

Can You Find Protists in Pond Water?

Analyze Your Results

1 Responses will vary depending on where samples were obtained.

2 Most students are likely to indicate that most of the organisms are unicellular like the protists shown in Figure 15.3. Depending on individual samples, some students may identify few organisms in their sample as different from those shown in Figure 15.3.

Evaluate Understanding

List the following terms on the board: *protists, eukaryotes, unicellular, multicellular, plantlike, animal-like, funguslike, autotrophs, heterotrophs,* and *decomposers*. Ask students to use each term in a one or two-paragraph summary of this section. Check paragraphs for accuracy.

Reteach

On the board, begin a concept map with the terms *monerans* and *protists*. Identify each organism as prokaryote or eukaryote and have a volunteer add these terms to the concept map. Tell students to copy the concept map in their notebooks and add the characteristics of each type of cell and other relevant information to their maps.

 **Do It!**

Can You Find Protists in Pond Water?

Observing protists first-hand gives you a better idea of how they move and how plentiful and varied they are. You can do this when you . . .

Try This

1 Bring a small, fresh sample of pond water to class.
2 Use a toothpick to spread a circle of methyl cellulose on a slide, then place a drop of pond water on the slide. Use a coverslip.
3 Use a microscope to examine the pond water under low power. Sketch the organisms you see, and record how they move.

Analyze Your Results

1 How many different organisms did you observe?
2 Compare the organisms you observed with those in Figure 15.3. Are any of them similar? Are any of them different?

FIGURE 15.3
Note the variety of sizes and shapes among these protists found in drops of pond water.

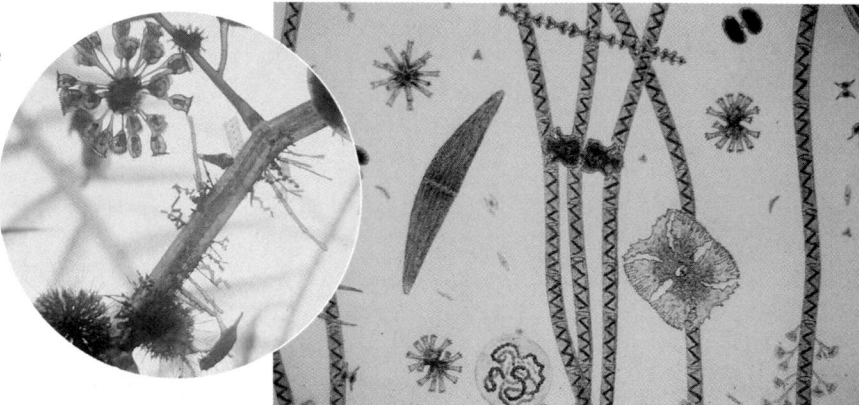

CHECKPOINT 15.1

1. What are the differences between a prokaryotic and eukaryotic cell?
2. Explain the classification of protists.
3. **Critical Thinking** Why is it difficult to develop a system of classification for protists?

Build on What You Know

4. What is the difference between an autotroph and a heterotroph? *(Need to jog your memory? Revisit relevant concepts in Chapter 4, Section 4.1.)*

 What are protists?

The diversity of protists reflects several significant evolutionary developments. As you can see in *Figure 15.3*, these developments include variety in the size, shape, and color of protists. This diversity has made it difficult for scientists to classify protists. Some biologists suggest that 20 new kingdoms would need to be created to account for the diversity among protists.

Although it is not based on evolutionary history, one popular classification system divides the protists into three groups based on the way they obtain nutrition—animal-like, plantlike, and funguslike protists. Animal-like protists are heterotrophs; plantlike protists are autotrophs; and funguslike protists are mostly decomposers, heterotrophs that feed on dead organic matter.

CHECKPOINT 15.1

1. A eukaryotic cell has a nucleus and membrane-bound organelles; a prokaryotic cell does not. Eukaryotic cells are on average ten times larger than prokaryotic cells.
2. Protists are often classified into three groups, according to how they obtain nutrition. [—heterotrophs, autotrophs, and decomposers—]

3. **Making generalizations** Protists are very diverse.
4. Autotrophs can use sunlight to make their own food and heterotrophs need to get their food from other organisms.

15.2 Animal-like Protists— Protozoans

Cliff-building protists?
It may be difficult to believe, but the enormous White Cliffs of Dover on the southeastern coast of England were made from animal-like protists. The deposits of limestone that form the cliffs are the hard outer shells of dead protists that have accumulated over many centuries.

What you'll learn

IDEAS
• To describe common characteristics of protozoans
• To compare diverse protozoans

WORDS
protozoan, pseudopods, flagella, cilia

SUPER READ!

CHARACTERISTICS AND DIVERSITY OF PROTOZOANS

Hop, skip, or jump

When you think about the characteristics that are common to animals, you may recognize that all animals are heterotrophs—they consume other organisms for food. A protist with the animal-like characteristic of heterotrophy is called a **protozoan.** Protozoans differ from animals in that they are unicellular and do not have specialized tissues, organs, or organ systems that carry out life functions.

Protozoans are a very diverse group of organisms. They are classified into four groups according to how they move. These groups are the sarcodinians, zooflagellates, ciliophorans, and sporozoans.

Sarcodinians You may have seen science fiction films in which an oozing blob engulfs everything in its path. Some protozoans move in a similar flowing manner and are called sarcodinians—organisms that move by extending lobes of cytoplasm.

Some sarcodinians are surrounded by hard shells. These sarcodinians move by extending lobes of cytoplasm through

holes in their shells. Two types of shelled sarcodinians are foraminiferans and radiolarians. These are shown in *Figure 15.4*. The shells of foraminiferans are part of White Cliffs of Dover, which you read about above.

FIGURE 15.4
The radiolarians (below) and the foraminiferan (right) are sarcodinians with hard shells made of calcium carbonate and silica.

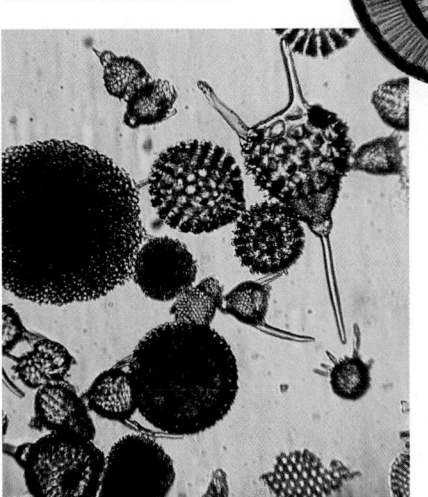

Chapter 15 Protists **355**

15.2

ENGAGE

Consider The Big Idea

Have students read The Big Idea! at the top of the page. Explain that protozoans meet their nutritional needs the same way animals, plants, and fungi do.

Use the Visual

Ask students to study the photograph that opens the section. Explain that the composition of the Dover Cliffs is calcium carbonate, the substance that makes up the shells of foraminiferan, which were deposited on the ocean floor when the tiny marine animals died. These protozoans, illustrated in Figure 15.4, are one type of sarcodinian, a protist that moves by extending lobes of cytoplasm.

Teacher Demo

Add some methyl cellulose to a culture of *paramecia* and ameba to slow their movement. Use a microprojector to show the organisms on a monitor. Identify each type of organism and the structures it uses for locomotion. If movement of the contractile vacuoles of the paramecia is noticeable, point this out to students.

STUDENT RESOURCES

From the Teacher's Resource Package, use:
■ Section Review 15.2 and Interpreting Graphics 15 from Unit 4 Review Module
■ Lab 27: "Protozoans: Animal-like Microbes"

TECHNOLOGY RESOURCES

Relevant technology resources include:
■ Spanish Student Edition CD-ROM
■ Teacher's Resource Planner CD-ROM
■ Biology Alive! Videotape: "The Domain of Life"

SUPER READ! **Comparing and Contrasting** To practice strategies for effective reading, use pages 37-38 in *Super Read!*

2 TEACH

Use the Visual

Direct students' attention to Figure 15.5. Explain that the diagram shows representative organisms from each protozoan group and identifies their means of locomotion. Ask:

- **What structures are used by amebas, *Trichonympha,* and *Paramecium* for movement?** (Ameba–extensions of cytoplasm called pseudopods; *Trichonympha*–flagella; *Paramecium*–cilia)

- **How do sporozoans differ from other protozoans?** (Sporozoans have no structures for locomotion.)

Think Critically

Have students compare the *Trichonympha* to an organ in the human body and explain their choice. (It is comparable to the stomach, because it digests what the termite eats and releases nutrients the termite can use.)

LAB ZONE Think About It!

Protozoan Excretion

Analyze the Information

1 The saltwater in marine environments would dehydrate protozoans. Because there is no excess water, protozoans would not need a contractile vacuole.
2 It would burst.

❶ 6

❷ Some move in a straight path, others spin.

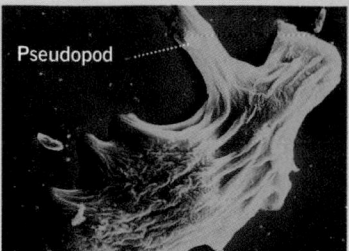
Pseudopod

FIGURE 15.5

The Movement of Protozoans

Sarcodinians
An ameba stretches its cell membrane into a lobe of cytoplasm and anchors the lobe at its tip. Cytoplasm then flows into the pseudopod, and the ameba "creeps forward."

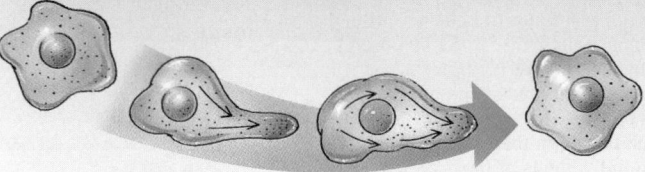
Ameba

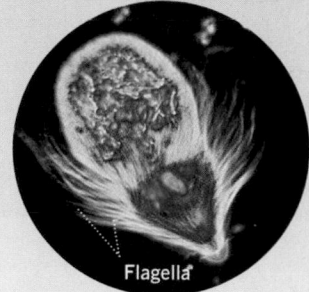
Flagella

Trichonympha

Other sarcodinians, like the ameba, do not have shells. An ameba extends lobes of cytoplasm called **pseudopods** (SOO-doh-pahdz) to move and obtain food. "Pseudo-" means "false," and "-pod" means "foot." Because it constantly extends and retracts its pseudopods, an ameba has no definite shape. How many pseudopods do you see ❶ in the ameba shown in *Figure 15.5?*

An ameba, like many protists, has an adaptation that enables it to survive harsh conditions. When the environment is unfavorable, an

Zooflagellates
Zooflagellates move by means of flagella. How would the motion of these flagella affect the way the protozoan moves?

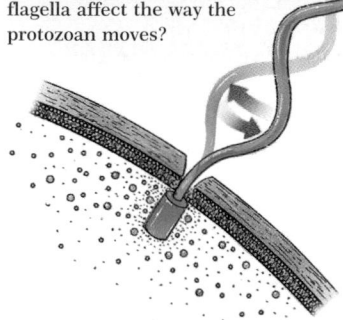

ameba becomes a hard cyst. In the cyst state, an ameba can withstand drought, heat, famine, or ingestion by other organisms. When people ingest food or water that contains amebic cysts, they may become infected with parasitic amebas. For example, amebic dysentery is a parasitic infection transmitted by contaminated water.

Zooflagellates Some protozoans use **flagella**—whiplike structures that aid in movement. Protozoans that use flagella are called zooflagellates.

Zooflagellates use flagella in a variety of ways. Some whip their flagella to move in a relatively straight path. Others use their flagella to create currents that spin them through the water.

LAB ZONE Think About It! bioSURF

Protozoan Excretion

Water constantly enters many protozoan cells by osmosis. These protozoans have contractile vacuoles to get rid of excess water. Water is collected in the vacuole. When the vacuole reaches a certain size, it moves to the cell surface and contracts, expelling the water through a temporary opening in the cell membrane.

Analyze the Information

1 Most marine protozoans have no contractile vacuoles. Can you propose a hypothesis to explain why this is?
2 What would happen to a protozoan that was unable to expel excess water?

MEETING DIVERSE NEEDS

Gifted Have students find out about sporozoans that cause human disease. Ask them to make drawings showing the life cycle of these organisms and explain how the sporozoans are transmitted. Students can share their research when this topic is studied in Section 15.5.

FACTS AND FIGURES

The cytoplasm of *Paramecium* has a concentration of about 92 percent water. The *Paramecium's* contractile vacuoles pump water out of the cell about 15 times per minute to maintain homeostasis.

Ciliophorans
Ciliophorans are covered with short, hairlike projections called cilia. How do cilia differ from flagella?

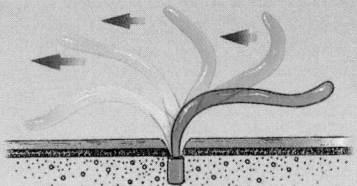

Power stroke: forward movement

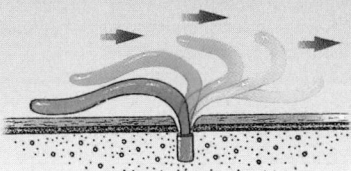

Recovery stroke: no forward movement

Paramecium

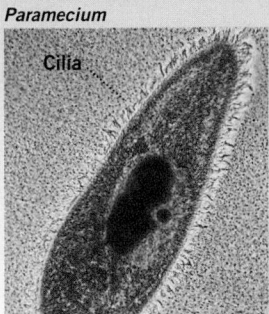
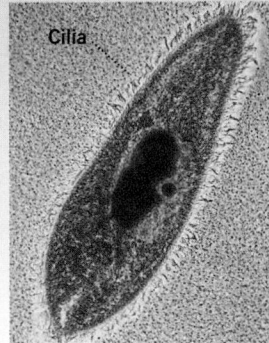

Cilia

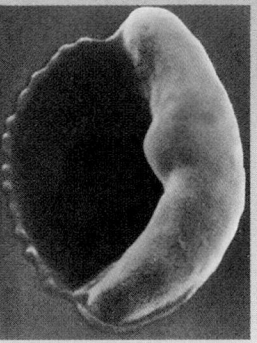

Plasmodium in a blood cell

Sporozoans
The red blood cell above has been invaded by a sporozoan parasite.

Some zooflagellates inhabit other organisms in long-term, symbiotic relationships. In *Figure 15.5* you see *Trichonympha*, a zooflagellate that lives in the gut of a termite. *Trichonympha* digests the cellulose in the wood that the termite eats. In return, *Trichonympha* releases nutrients that the termite can use, allowing the termite to benefit from the relationship.

Ciliophorans The ciliophorans (sil-ee-oh-FOR-unz), or ciliates, are the most numerous and diverse group of protozoans. Ciliates are protozoans that are covered with cilia. **Cilia** are short, hairlike projections used for movement. Look carefully at *Figure 15.5* and notice the cilia of a *Paramecium*. A paramecium's cilia move in unison like boat oars as they propel the cell through water. In some other ciliates, the cilia may be shaped like teeth, paddles, or feet.

Most ciliates live in freshwater habitats and, like the majority of protozoans, can form cysts to survive unfavorable environments. Most

ciliates are also harmless, but a few are parasitic and can harm their host.

Sporozoans Some parasitic protozoans are called sporozoans. Despite their name, sporozoans do not form true spores the way bacteria and some other protists do. Sporozoans are characterized by the absence of structures used for movement.

The life cycles of sporozoans are complex and include both sexual and asexual phases. Sporozoan life cycles often involve more than one host. For example, in section 15.5 you will see how the sporozoan *Plasmodium* infects both mosquitos and humans, causing human malaria.

CHECKPOINT 15.2

1. What characteristics are common to protozoans?
2. Describe the four groups of protozoans.
3. **Critical Thinking** How can parasitic sporozoans move from one host to another if they do not have structures for movement?

Build on What You Know

4. Compare endospores in monerans with cysts and spores in protists. *(Need to jog your memory? Revisit relevant concepts in Chapter 14, Section 14.4.)*

Kingdom: Protista
Category: Protozoa
Phyla:
Sarcodina
Zooflagellata
Ciliophora
Sporozoa

Chapter 15 Protists **357**

CHECKPOINT 15.2

1. All protozoans are unicellular, eukaryotic, and heterotrophic.
2. Sarcodinians, move by extending lobes of cytoplasm; zooflagellates, use flagella to move; sporozoans, parasitic and spore-forming; ciliaphorans, use cilia to move
3. **Making generalizations** They need a vector or carrier, such as a mosquito.
4. The spores and cysts of protists are resistant to heat, drought, and harsh conditions. When conditions improve, they break open and produce new cells, very much like moneran endospores.
❸ Cilia are short and cover the cell; flagella are long and a cell has only one or two.

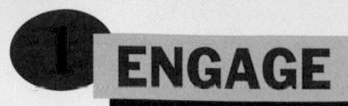

1 ENGAGE

Use the Visual

Direct students to look at the photograph that opens the section. The "huge green snake" seen by sailors in the Pacific Ocean and shown in the photograph is formed by organisms known as diatoms. Explain that diatoms are a type of unicellular, plantlike protist that are classified as algae. Remind students that the kelp shown in the photograph on page 352 are also a type of algae. Ask:

■ **How are the diatoms shown here different from the kelp?** (The kelp are multicellular and grow to be quite large, the diatoms are very tiny and unicellular.)

■ **How are the two organisms alike?** (Both are plantlike protists classified as algae.)

Teacher Demo

Display a tube of toothpaste, car polish, and diatomaceous earth used in pool filters. Explain that each of these products uses the abrasive quality of diatom shells. Allow students to feel the grittiness of the diatamaceous earth. Explain that this is only one way these protists are useful.

What you'll learn

IDEAS
• To describe the characteristics of plantlike protists
• To compare unicellular and multicellular algae

WORDS
algae, alternation of generations

A long dark snake in the Pacific
When sailors reported seeing something that looked like a dark snake about 150 kilometers (km) north of the equator, people thought they had been at sea too long. But images taken from the space shuttle also showed it. In the photo at the right, the dark line under the shuttle's wing is dense algae growth along the boundary between two ocean currents.

CHARACTERISTICS OF ALGAE

Is it easy being green?

Did you see any green organisms when you looked at pond water through the microscope? Most of those green organisms were probably plantlike protists. Some protists are considered plantlike because they perform photosynthesis.

Protists that perform photosynthesis are called **algae** (singular: *alga*). Like most plants, algae contain chlorophyll and produce food and oxygen as a result of photosynthesis. Unlike plants, most algae do not contain specialized tissues or organs.

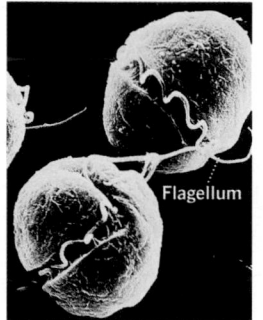

Flagellum

Gonyaulax

FIGURE 15.6
Dinoflagellates
Gonyaulax (left) can form toxic "red tide." The eight organisms (below) are *Ceratium*, a colonial chain-forming dinoflagellate.

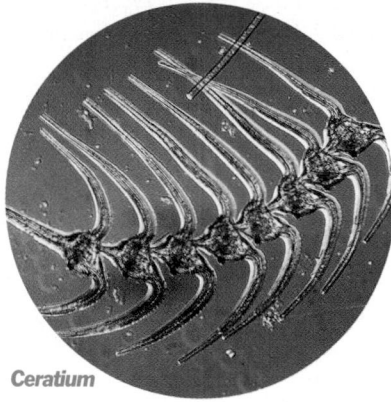

Ceratium

As with other protists, the evolutionary origins of algae are not very well documented in the fossil record. Consequently, algae have been classified based on differences in their structures. One way to organize algae for study is to divide them into two groups: unicellular and multicellular.

UNICELLULAR ALGAE

Making it on their own

Unicellular, or single-celled, algae include dinoflagellates, diatoms, and euglenoids. Important differences between these organisms include their outer covering and means of movement. Dinoflagellates are covered with cellulose plates, diatoms are covered with silica (glass) shells, and euglenoids have no rigid cell wall. Euglenoids and dinoflagellates use flagella for movement, while diatoms secrete substances for movement. Dinoflagellates and diatoms are among the most numerous algae in the oceans, whereas euglenoids are common in fresh water.

Dinoflagellates Algae with two flagella that beat to spin their cell in corkscrew fashion through the water are called dinoflagellates. With the exception of some that live with coral on reefs, all dinoflagellates have flagella. Cellulose plates that cover each dinoflagellate give the organism its unique shape.

358 *Unit 4 Monerans, Protists, and Fungi*

STUDENT RESOURCES

From the Teacher's Resource Package, use:
■ Section Review 15.3 from Unit 4 Review Module
■ Consumer Applications 15-1

TECHNOLOGY RESOURCES

Relevant technology resources include:
■ Spanish Student Edition CD-ROM
■ Teacher's Resource Planner CD-ROM
■ Biology Alive! Videotape: "The Domain of Life"

FIGURE 15.7
Diatoms

A bucket of water scooped from an ocean may contain millions of these microscopic algae. How does a diatom move material into and out of its cell? ❶

Kingdom: Protista
Category: Algae
Phyla:
Dinoflagellata
Bacillariophyta
Euglenophyta
Chlorophyta
Rhodophyta
Phaeophyta

The majority of dinoflagellates grow in saltwater habitats. While most dinoflagellates are free-living, some have symbiotic relationships with jellyfish, sea anemones, coral, and other organisms that live near coral reefs. Symbiotic dinoflagellates, which lack flagella, supply nutrients to the animals in which they live.

Diatoms The snowflakelike organisms in *Figure 15.7* are unicellular algae called diatoms. Diatoms have glasslike cell walls containing silica. The walls have two parts that fit together like a box and lid. Pores in the cell walls allow material to pass into and out of the diatom. Diatoms have thousands of different shapes and patterns. Many diatoms float in water—probably because they contain oil, which is less dense than water. Diatoms are among the most abundant organisms in the oceans.

Euglenoids Organisms similar to the euglena shown in *Figure 15.8* are called euglenoids. Euglenoids are difficult to classify because they resemble both algae and protozoans. Some biologists classify organisms such as euglena as protozoans because they lack rigid cell walls and they move using

flagella. However, taxonomists have traditionally classified euglenoids as algae because they have chloroplasts and perform photosynthesis.

MULTICELLULAR ALGAE

A cooperative venture

Multicellular algae have specialized structures that resemble the parts of plants. Once considered plants because they have chloroplasts, multicellular algae are now classified as protists

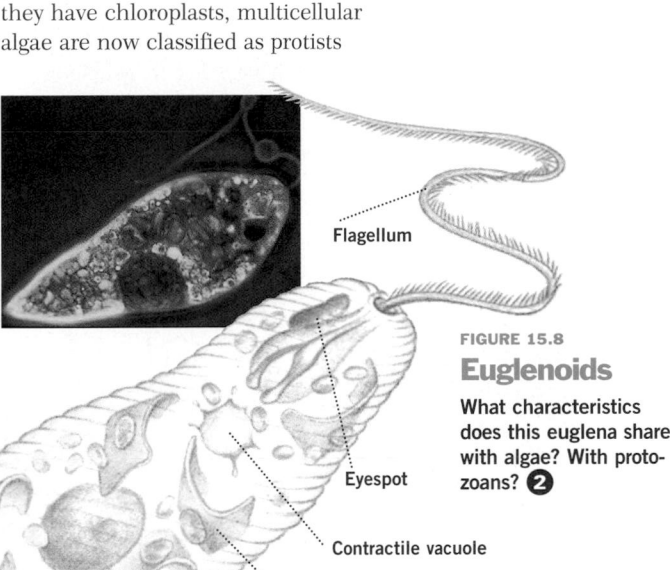

Flagellum

FIGURE 15.8
Euglenoids

What characteristics does this euglena share with algae? With protozoans? ❷

Eyespot

Contractile vacuole

Chloroplast

Chapter 15 Protists **359**

2 **TEACH**

Apply

Tell students that diatoms are used to make the reflective paint used to mark lines on highways. Diatoms are useful in such paints because the glassy substance called *silica* in their shells reflects light and their shells do not break down. You may wish to have students look up the term *silica* in the dictionary to learn more about it.

Use the Visual

Have students examine the euglena shown in Figure 15.8. Ask:

- **What traits of the euglena are similar to those of protozoans?** (They lack a rigid cell wall and have flagella that enable them to move.)
- **What traits of the euglena are used to classify them as algae?** (They have chloroplasts and can carry out photosynthesis.)

Explain

Point out to students that although the *Euglena* can carry out photosynthesis, it does not need to do so in order to meet its nutritional needs. If light is scarce, the *Euglena* can obtain nutrients by feeding on other organisms. In this way, the *Euglena* is more similar to protozoans than to algae.

❶ They have pores in their cell wall which allow materials to move in and out.
❷ It photosynthesizes like algae; like protozoans, it moves with a flagella and has no rigid cell wall.

15.3

Physics

Initiate a class discussion on how light penetration in seawater decreases with water depth. Point out that blue light penetrates the ocean water to a depth of about 200 meters (660 feet), green and violet light penetrate to 100 meters (330 feet), and yellow light penetrates to about 50 meters (165 feet) Red and orange light reach only about 20 to 30 meters (65 to 100 feet.) No light reaches the floor of the deep ocean. Explain that the ocean floor is pitch black because the suspended particles in seawater scatter the light waves so they do not reach the deep seafloor.

Think Critically

Have students think about light penetration of the ocean water and explain why green algae does not grow in the deep ocean. (Photosynthesis requires light, which is absent in the deep ocean.)

Apply

Insulators are materials that do not allow heat, electricity, or sound to pass through them easily. Wood and styrofoam are examples of insulators. Currently, balsa wood is used as a sound insulator in train cars and aircraft; however, a new, lighter-than-air foam made from the kelp extract, agarose, may soon be used in place of balsa and is being considered for use in refrigerators and oil tankers.

360

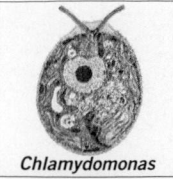

FIGURE 15.9
Green algae: unicellular (top), colonial (center), and multicellular (bottom)

because few of them have true tissues, and their reproductive methods are more like those of protists than of plants. Multicellular algae are classified by color, which is determined by the type of pigment in their cells.

Green algae Organisms classified as green algae, the Chlorophyta, are protists that have the pigment called chlorophyll *b* as a major component in their cells. The composition of the cell wall of green algae and the structure of their chloroplasts most closely resemble those of plants.

In *Figure 15.9* you can see some diverse representatives of green algae. Some green algae are unicellular. One example is *Chlamydomonas*, which grows abundantly in ponds and moist soil. Other green algae, such as *Volvox*, live in colonies that may include several thousand cells. Some multicellular green algae, such as *Ulva*, are made of flat, leaflike sheets of cells. Other multicellular algae grow as filaments with cells linked end to end.

Most green algae live in fresh water or in moist soil. Some types of green algae, such as *Ulva*, live in the oceans. Many green algae live in symbiotic

relationships with other organisms. For example, lichens result from symbiotic relationships between green algae and fungi.

Red algae Most red algae, called Rhodophyta, grow in warm, saltwater habitats. Although some red algae live near the ocean surface, others dwell as deep as 260 meters (m), nearly 26 stories beneath the surface. At these depths, few wavelengths of light are available for photosynthesis. However, red algae contain accessory pigments that enable them to use the available wavelengths of light to perform photosynthesis.

Red algae respond to reduced light by adjusting the ratio of the accessory pigments they produce. An accessory pigment that produces a reddish color gives members of this group their name. Depending on the presence of other pigments, red algae can also appear green, orange, or almost black.

Brown algae The Phaeophyta, or brown algae, are multicellular and grow mostly in cool saltwater habitats. This group includes the largest organisms in the kingdom Protista, the giant kelps. Giant kelps can grow up to

FIGURE 15.10

Diversity of Algae

Green algae
Which of these two types of green algae might have the common name "vinegar cup"? ❶

360   *Unit 4 Monerans, Protists, and Fungi*

FIGURE 15.11

Alternation of Generations

Some algae exhibit a complex life cycle, such as that of *Ulva*. Compare the gametophyte and sporophyte stages. How does the cycle alternate between haploid and diploid? ❷

Spores

Male gametophyte

Gametes

Female gametophyte

MEIOSIS

FUSION OF GAMETES

Zygote

Sporophyte

Haploid

Diploid

100 m long and are found in deep water beyond the intertidal zone. Like land plants, brown algae have some specialized parts. For example, the giant kelp has specialized air bladders, which act as life jackets and cause the leaflike portion of the kelp to float near the surface, where it can absorb sunlight for photosynthesis.

Some multicellular algae have complex life cycles that alternate between a spore-producing stage called the sporophyte generation and a gamete-producing stage called the gametophyte generation. This type of life cycle is called **alternation of generations.** You can see the steps in the life cycle of algae called *Ulva* in *Figure 15.11*. In *Ulva*, both the sporophyte and gametophyte generations look the same. In other algal life cycles, the sporophyte and gametophyte generations may look different.

CHECKPOINT 15.3

1. What are the characteristics of algae?

2. What are the differences and similarities between unicellular and multicellular algae?

3. Critical Thinking Make a chart to compare the characteristics of members of the algae phyla.

Build on What You Know

4. What are the reactants and products of photosynthesis? Where might algae get photosynthetic reactants? *(Need to jog your memory? Revisit relevant concepts, in Chapter 4, Section 4.2.)*

Red algae
This red alga is a frequent inhabitant of cool-water reef communities.

Brown algae
This common brown alga is *Macrocystis pyrifera*. Does its name seem to fit its appearance?

Chapter 15 Protists **361**

CHECKPOINT 15.1

1. All algae contain chlorophyll and carry on photosynthesis.

2. Unicellular algae have one cell. Multicellular algae have many cells organized into specialized structures. Both contain chlorophyll and perform photosynthesis.

3. Classifying Charts should note differences and similarities in structures, means of locomotion, and habitats.

4. Reactants: CO_2, H_2O. Products: O_2, glucose. Algae get the reactants from the water in which they live.

❶ The photo at the top has the common name "vinegar cup," describing its cup shape.

❷ The life cycle goes from the diploid sporophyte generation to the haploid gametophyte generation.

ENGAGE

Use the Visual

Have students study the photograph that opens the section. Ask them to imagine that they discovered this mass while walking through the woods. Ask:

- **How would you determine if this mass is a living thing?** (By poking it to see if it moves, by watching it to see if it grows)
- **What role does it play in the environment?** (It is a decomposer.)

Discuss student responses. Explain that the unusual organism shown is a funguslike protist known as a slime mold that grows in moist areas where it feeds on dead organisms.

Teacher Demo

Saprolegnia is a water mold that feeds on dead aquatic life, including tropical fishes raised in aquariums. Several days before beginning this section, obtain a dead tropical fish from a local pet store. Place the dead fish in a jar filled with water until it becomes covered with a white fuzz. Display the jar and point out the fuzzy growth on the fish. Explain that the "fuzz" is a funguslike protist that uses the dead fish as its food source. Discuss with students the important role such organisms play in the environment.

❶ Although both are unicellular, this plasmodium is much larger than a protozoan.

15.4 Funguslike Protists— Molds

What you'll learn

IDEAS
- To describe the structural and functional characteristics of funguslike protists
- To distinguish between the three groups of funguslike protists

WORDS
mold, plasmodium

Mold or movie star?
The oozing mass grows larger as it moves ever so silently and slowly along the ground, devouring every microorganism in its path. This may sound like a scene from a science fiction movie, but it is really a description of one of the most intriguing of the funguslike protists—the slime mold.

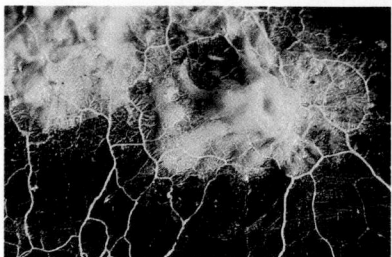

CHARACTERISTICS OF MOLDS

Nature's dustbusters

Kingdom: Protista
Category: Molds
Phyla:
Myxomycota
Acrasiomycota
Oomycota

Most funguslike protists are small and live in damp or watery places, helping to break down dead organic matter. A protist that acts as a decomposer is known as a **mold.**

Most taxonomists divide the molds into three groups: plasmodial slime molds, cellular slime molds, and water molds. Slime molds are named for their most obvious characteristics—a shiny, wet appearance and a texture like gelatin. Water molds are funguslike protists that live mostly in the water.

Plasmodial slime molds The organism in *Figure 15.12* is a plasmodial slime mold. In the feeding stage of its life cycle it is called a **plasmodium.** A plasmodium can weigh as much as 50 grams (g) and grow as large as the palm of a human hand. However, regardless of its size, a plasmodium is a single cell with many nuclei.

When environmental conditions become unfavorable a plasmodium either creeps somewhere else, or it enters a different stage of its life cycle. The plasmodium does this by forming a structure called a fruiting body. The fruiting body produces spores, which are then distributed by wind and animals. Spores can remain dormant for many years. When conditions are favorable, the spore releases haploid gametes that fuse to form a diploid zygote. This diploid zygote then develops into a new plasmodium.

FIGURE 15.12
This plasmodium is unicellular but has many nuclei. It feeds on bacteria and other microorganisms as it creeps along a surface. How does this protist differ from protozoans? ❶

362   *Unit 4 Monerans, Protists, and Fungi*

STUDENT RESOURCES

From the Teacher's Resource Package, use:
- Section Review 15.4, Activity Recordsheet 15-2, and Critical Thinking Exercise 15 from Unit 4 Review Module
- Lab 28: "Algal Blooms"

TECHNOLOGY RESOURCES

Relevant technology resources include:
- Spanish Student Edition CD-ROM
- Teacher's Resource Planner CD-ROM

Cellular slime molds Like the plasmodial slime mold, a cellular slime mold alternates between a spore-producing, fruiting body form and an amebalike feeding form. In *Figure 15.13* you can see the different forms of a cellular slime mold. The feeding stage of a cellular slime mold consists of small, single cells that move, engulf, and ingest food much as amebas do. These cells live in fresh water, in damp soil, or on decaying plant matter.

When food runs low or water becomes scarce, the cells secrete a chemical attractant that causes nearby mold cells to clump together to form a pseudoplasmodium. A pseudoplasmodium is a clump of cells that produces fruiting bodies. The fruiting bodies then produce spores. Unlike a true plasmodium, however, the cells of a pseudoplasmodium are independent entities. Also, the cells of a pseudoplasmodium are haploid; a true plasmodial cell is diploid.

Water molds You may have observed a scene like that shown in *Figure 15.14* in real life. The cottonlike fluff is actually an organism called a water mold. Water molds are decomposers in freshwater ecosystems. Some water molds are parasitic and attack the injured skin or gill tissues of fishes. A few water molds, such as white rusts and downy mildews, are parasites of certain land plants.

White rusts and downy mildews used to be classified as fungi but are now considered to be protists for several reasons. One reason is that true fungi have cell walls that contain chitin, whereas the water molds have cell walls that are mostly cellulose. Moreover, asexual reproduction in the water molds produces spores with flagella. True fungi produce spores without flagella.

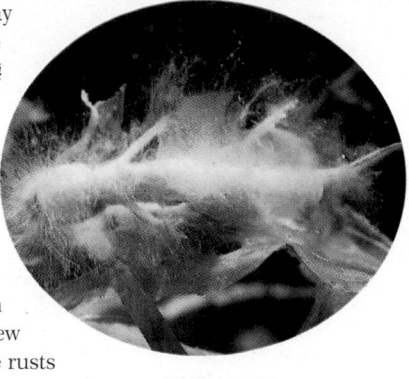
FIGURE 15.14
This water mold is decomposing a salamander.

CHECKPOINT 15.4

1. How are funguslike protists structurally and functionally alike?
2. What are the differences between the three groups of funguslike protists?
3. **Critical Thinking** What advantages do slime molds gain by producing fruiting bodies when food is scarce?

Build on What You Know

4. Compare the roles of protists and monerans as decomposers. How do the two groups differ? *(Need to jog your memory? Revisit relevant concepts, in Chapter 14, Section 14.6.)*

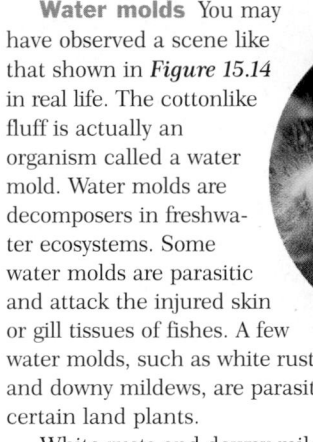
FIGURE 15.13
What three life stages of a cellular slime mold are shown in these images of the slime mold *Dictyostelium*?

How are protists classified? **?**

Chapter 15 Protists **363**

CHECKPOINT 15.4

1. All funguslike protists act as decomposers and alternate between spore-producing and feeding forms.
2. Plasmodial slime molds look like creeping formless masses in their feeding stage and have fruiting bodies in their spore-producing stage. The feeding stage of cellular slime molds consists of small single cells that come together to form a pseudoplasmodium that produces fruiting bodies. Water molds are decomposers in freshwater ecosystems; however, some are parasitic.
3. **Developing a hypothesis** Fruiting bodies produce spores that become dormant until conditions improve.
4. Both break down organic matter into nutrients for reuse by other organisms.

Class Activity

Place a mixture of starch and water and some garden soil in warm water in a warm area for one week. Have students check the mixture daily to be sure it is moist. Have students examine the soil surface closely with a hand lens for the presence of mold growth. Students should record their observations in their portfolios. (They should observe slime molds on the soil surface.)

Evaluate Understanding

Have students make Venn diagrams for *Plasmodial Slime Molds, Cellular Slime Molds,* and *Water Molds* using the terms: *pseudoplasmodium, fruiting body, zygote, plasmodium, diploid, spores, decomposer, cellulose cell walls, haploid, spore-producing, amoeboid cells,* and *spores with flagella*. Check the diagrams for accuracy.

Reteach

Have small groups of students make posters to "advertise" the characteristics of each type of mold. Encourage them to use cartoons and bright colors and to be accurate.

❷ Feeding stage, pseudoplasmodium, and fruiting pseudoplasmodium

 **LAB ZONE** Investigate It!

Observing Protist Responses to Light

WHAT YOU WILL DO Observe and compare the responses of two different protists to light

SKILLS YOU WILL USE Predicting, observing, collecting and recording data

WHAT YOU WILL NEED Microscope, microscope slides, toothpick, methyl cellulose, *Paramecium* and *Euglena* cultures, forceps, metric ruler, index card

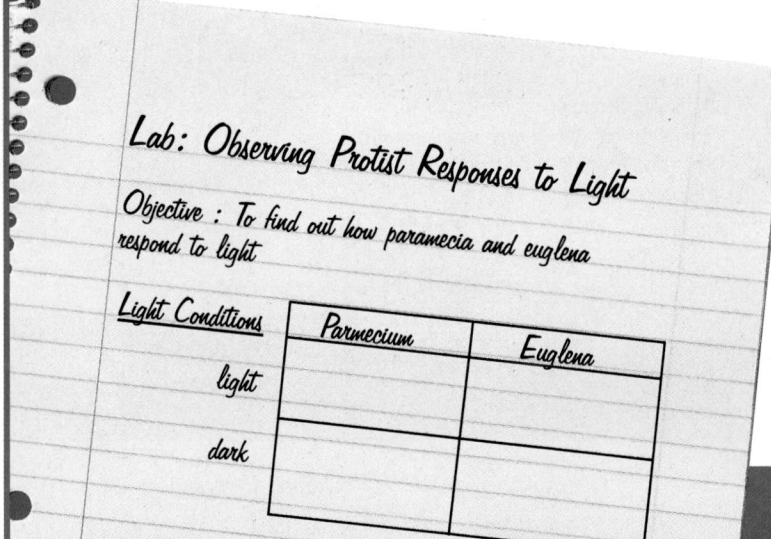

Propose a Hypothesis

Formulate a hypothesis about what you think will happen when two different protists—paramecia and euglena—are exposed to light.

Conduct Your Experiment

1 Use a toothpick to spread a small circle of methyl cellulose on the center of a slide. Place a drop of paramecium culture in the ring of methyl cellulose.

Using forceps, gently lower a coverslip over the culture.

2 Use the low power lens of a microscope to locate several paramecia. Focus on one paramecium with the high power lens. Examine its characteristics under high power. Record your observations and draw a paramecium.

3 Cut an index card to the same size as a microscope slide. In the center of this strip, cut a slit that is 1.5 centimeters (cm) long and 0.2 cm wide. Slip the strip under the slide on the microscope.

4 After 5 minutes, carefully remove the strip and locate the paramecia. Record your observations in your notebook.

5 Repeat steps 1–4 using the euglena.

Analyze Your Data

1 Describe the characteristics of the two types of protists you observed.

2 Compare the characteristics of both protists.

3 Compare the response of each type of protist to light.

Draw Conclusions

Was your hypothesis correct? If not, why not? If it was incorrect, rephrase it to reflect the results of your experiment.

Design a Related Experiment

Design an experiment to test how paramecia and euglenoids respond to the concentration of salt in a solution. Begin by proposing a hypothesis. Then write out the procedure you would follow to test your hypothesis.

TEAM WORK **Observing Protist Responses to Light**

SAFETY FIRST!

Remind students to use care when using and moving the microscope.

Lap Prep and Planning

If you do not have access to a bird bath or pond, prepare a source of paramecia and euglena by placing a garden rock in a jar of water for several days. Use a drinking straw to draw out the water close to the rock.

Lab Tips

You may want to demonstrate how to use the index card to block out light.

Hypothesis Help

Some may hypothesize that *Euglena* will move toward light because it needs light for photosynthesis, whereas the *Paramecium* will move away from light because it does not need light for photosynthesis.

Lab Extension

Open Ended

Suggest that students look for a dividing paramecium and make a drawing of their observations.

Time Required

■ 50 minutes

Analyze Your Data

1. *Paramecium* is slipper-shaped and uses cilia for movement. *Euglena* is generally oval in shape, uses flagella for movement, and has a greenish coloring.
2. Both protists have nuclei, vacuoles, and structures to help them move. Only the *Euglena* has chloroplasts. Only the *Paramecium* has an oral groove.
3. The *Paramecium* moved out of the slit away from the light, but the *Euglena* moved into the slit toward the light.

Design a Related Experiment

One possible experiment would be to observe both organisms under the microscope, add saltwater to one side of the coverslip, and observe their movements.

15.5 Protists in the Biosphere

Algae in your tank?
Imagine pulling up to a gas pump and saying, "Fill it up with algae." Well, it could happen. Scientists have considered algae as a supplement to biodiesel fuels—those made from plant oils. In addition to being plentiful, algae would be cleaner than existing fuels. So someday, you may be pumping protists like the ones these swans are swimming through.

What you'll learn

IDEAS
• To describe the ecological roles of protists
• To explain diseases caused by protists and the importance of protists to humans

WORD
plankton

SUPER READ!

ECOLOGICAL ROLES

Can't live without you

Algae and protozoans are two of the most numerous types of organisms in the oceans. These two groups of protists play an essential role in the lives of other aquatic organisms.

As you know, all organisms need a source of energy. As the major component of plankton, protists provide an essential food base in aquatic food chains. **Plankton** are mostly microscopic organisms that float near the surface of oceans and lakes. In *Figure 15.15* you can see a whale, which is a water-dwelling heterotroph that obtains energy directly by eating plankton. Other heterotrophs obtain energy indirectly by eating organisms that may have eaten plankton.

The algal component of plankton is called phytoplankton because the algae perform photosynthesis. Green algae, dinoflagellates, and diatoms are phytoplankton found in the oceans and freshwater lakes.

In addition to serving as a food source in aquatic environments, phytoplankton carry out more than 70 percent of Earth's photosynthesis. Recall from Chapter 4 that photosynthesis results in the production of oxygen. Algae help to maintain Earth's oxygen and carbon dioxide levels.

Protozoans, too, play an important ecological role. Many protozoans are predators of bacteria and other organisms. In many environments, protozoans help keep the numbers of bacteria in balance with other organisms. Other protozoans and molds feed on dead organisms and thereby play an important role in recycling chemicals in the environment.

FIGURE 15.15
Some large mammals, such as baleen whales, feed on plankton. Imagine the tremendous amount of plankton it takes to feed one humpback whale.

Chapter 15 Protists **365**

1 ENGAGE

Consider The Big Idea

Have students read The Big Idea! at the top of the page. Discuss how protists might affect the environment, provide food, and be infectious.

Use the Visual

Direct students' attention to the photograph that opens the section. Using algae as a fuel supplement is only one way scientists have found to make products using protists. Point out that protists are used in everyday products such as car waxes and car polishes.

Quick Activity

Explain that baleen whales have triangular plates of rough, horny material, called baleen, in the roof of their mouth, that are used to remove plankton from the water. Display a fine-tooth comb like one used to remove lice nits and an infant's hair brush that has wheat germ spread evenly through it. Explain that the wheat germ represents phytoplankton, the hair brush represents the sea water, and the comb represents the whale baleen. Use the nit comb to remove the wheat germ from the hair brush.

SUPER READ! **Comparing and Contrasting** To practice strategies for effective reading, use pages 37-38 in *Super Read!*

TEACH

In the Community

Suggest that students use the telephone directory and library resources to locate environmental and health agencies in their area. The response from these organizations will vary, however. Likely problems associated with protists may include infections of *Giardia*, a protist which lives in lakes and streams. Students living in or near ocean communities may cite food poisoning associated with toxins released by red tides and contaminated shellfish.

Clarify Misconceptions

Students may confuse protists, molds, and fungi. Remind students that only plasmodial slime molds, cellular slime molds, and water molds are classified as protists. Other organisms known as molds are generally classified as fungi. As students gather information about molds that affect people, food crops, and other vegetation, they will need to find out if the mold is classified as a protist or a fungus.

 ### Social Studies

Have students research the immigration of Irish people into the United States during the Great Potato Famine from 1845 to 1849. Students may wish to focus on the contribution of Irish-Americans to the railroad industry or to the settling of major cities in the East. Ask some students to share their research with the class.

366

DISEASES CAUSED BY PROTISTS

Not so nice

Not all protists are beneficial. Some protozoans, algae, and molds cause disease. Protists may cause disease either directly or indirectly.

A protozoan called *Trypanosoma* causes the fatal disease African sleeping sickness if it infects the central nervous system cells of humans or some other animals. Another protozoan called *Giardia* causes disease when humans ingest water containing giardia cysts. Each cyst releases giardia organisms that attach to a host's intestinal lining, causing diarrhea, nausea, and fatigue.

Figure 15.16 illustrates slicks of an alga called *Gonyaulax*, which produces a toxin (poison) that can paralyze and sometimes kill humans and other animals. A gonyaulax toxin can concentrate in the shellfish that live in the same waters. Humans or other consumers who eat the contaminated

FIGURE 15.16
Red tide results from periods of rapid reproduction among protists called *Gonyaulax*.

FIGURE 15.17
Phytophthora infestans is the organism you see destroying this potato plant.

shellfish may become ill from exposure to the toxin.

The funguslike protist *Phytophthora infestans* causes a potato disease called late blight, which makes potatoes inedible. Currently, the disease threatens potato crops around the world. Because the potato is a food staple in many countries, an outbreak of this disease can seriously affect a country's social, political, and economic stability. In Ireland in the mid 1800s, the disease devastated the potato crop and eventually forced more than one million Irish people to emigrate to other countries, including the United States.

Contact your state health officials to find out about illnesses in your state caused by protozoans, algae, or molds. Ask what steps, including water testing and purification, are taken by health officials to prevent the illnesses. Also contact state agricultural officials to determine if blights threaten food crops or other vegetation in your state. Find out if there are environmentally safe products that can prevent these plant diseases. Log on to *http://microorganisms.biosurf.com* to gather additional information. Design a presentation to share your investigation results with classmates.

IN THE COMMUNITY
A Protist Investigation

MULTICULTURAL PERSPECTIVE

Another kind of *Trypanosoma* called *T. rhodesiense* is a parasite that infects wild and domesticated animals in some parts of Africa. In humans, *T. rhodesiense* is thought to be the cause of East African sleeping sickness. In the Western Hemisphere, Chagas' disease, sometimes called *Trypanosomiasis Americana*, is caused by *T. cruzi*. The disease is characterized by prolonged high fever, an excess accumulation of foods, and enlargement of the spleen, liver, and lymph nodes.

FIGURE 15.18
The Life Cycle of *Plasmodium*

The life cycle of the protozoan *Plasmodium* includes stages in both mosquitos and humans. *Plasmodium* protists cause malaria in humans.

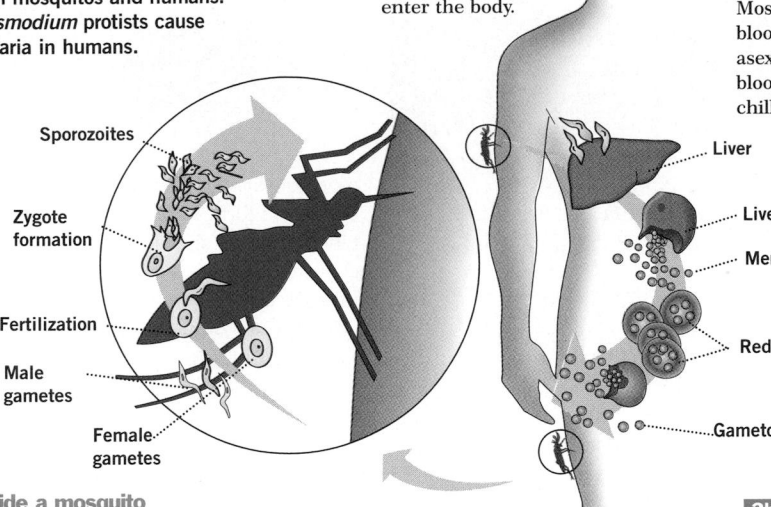

Life cycle begins

1 An infected mosquito bites a healthy human. The protozoans, in the form of sporozoites, enter the body.

Inside the human

2a Inside liver cells, the sporozoites develop into cells called merozoites. Most merozoites enter red blood cells and reproduce asexually, rupturing the blood cells and causing chills and high fever.

Sporozoites

Zygote formation

Fertilization

Male gametes

Female gametes

Liver

Liver cell

Merozoite

Red blood cells

Gametocyte

Inside a mosquito

4 In the digestive tract, gametocytes develop into gametes, which fuse to form a zygote. The zygote develops many sporozoites that travel to the mosquito's salivary glands.

Life cycle continues

3 A mosquito bites an infected human and picks up some gametocytes along with other blood components.

2b Some merozoites do not enter the blood cells, but remain in the blood as gametocytes.

FRONTIERS IN BIOLOGY
Medicine vs. malaria

Malaria is a disease that kills several million people every year. It is spread by *Anopheles* mosquitoes. The organism that causes malaria is a parasitic protozoan called *Plasmodium*. One stage of a *Plasmodium*'s life cycle occurs in the digestive tract of a mosquito. Another stage of its life cycle occurs in the liver and red blood cells of humans who have been bitten by an infected mosquito. *Figure 15.18* shows how both humans and mosquitoes host the *Plasmodium* parasite and thus spread malaria.

In spite of decades of scientific efforts to control it, malaria remains the leading cause of death worldwide for children under five. Why is it difficult to control? Part of the reason lies in the short reproductive cycle of *Anopheles*. In addition, this mosquito has acquired immunity to pesticides that were previously effective. Similarly, the *Plasmodium* protozoan multiplies rapidly in the human body and has developed a resistance to drugs. For example, the drug chloroquine is no longer effective in treating malaria. As the incidence of this disease increases, efforts to create a vaccine and new malaria-fighting drugs continue.

❶

Chapter 15 Protists **367**

FACTS AND FIGURES

Only mosquitoes of the genus *Anopheles* transmit the *Plasmodium* that causes malaria. The four species of *Plasmodium* capable of causing malaria are *P. vivax, P. falciparum, P. ovale,* and *P. malariae.*

❶ Control is difficult due to anopheles mosquito's short reproduction cycle and resistance to pesticides, plus rapid reproduction of plasmodium protozoan and its resistance to drugs.

FIGURE 15.19
Seaweed salad (below) is just one of the foods that seaweed supplies humans. It is also harvested as a food source for animals, as well as for use in fertilizer, cosmetics, and pharmaceuticals.

HUMAN USES

Delicious protists!

How would you like a dish of seaweed for dessert? Perhaps you would prefer to drink a glass of seaweed with your meal. No? Actually you have been eating some form of algae all your life.

Three complex carbohydrates used in food products—carrageenan, agar, and algin—are extracted from seaweed. Carrageenan, a thickener and flavor-enhancer for foods, is added to many dairy products, such as milk shakes and chocolate milk. The agar taken from red algae is sometimes used to thicken soups, puddings, and cake frostings.

Some people eat seaweed for its mineral components, especially iodine. In Japan, sheets of a red algae called nori are used to wrap sushi. In *Figure 15.19* you can see farmers harvesting seaweed for use as livestock feed and crop fertilizer.

In addition to their role as a food source, protists are useful in other ways. When diatoms die, for example, their shells sink to the bottom of the sea. Over millions of years, geological processes have thrust these deposits upward to form new land. Land containing diatom shells—called diatomaceous earth—is mined and used in the manufacture of everyday products. The gritty texture of diatomaceous earth makes it useful in products such as insulation, filters, detergents and cleansers, abrasives, and polishing agents in toothpaste.

Protists are also useful as bioindicators. Their presence or absence gives some indication of the health of an ecosystem. For example, marine biologists—scientists who study ocean life—collect plankton. The kinds and numbers of protists present in the plankton are indicators of the general health of an ocean region.

EVERYDAY BIOLOGY

Is There Algae in Your Sundae?

Algin, a product extracted from brown algae, is often added to ice cream and frozen whipped toppings to make them smoother.

CHECKPOINT 15.5

1. What is the ecological importance of protists?
2. Describe negative and positive ways in which protists affect humans.
3. **Critical Thinking** Do you think malaria could be transmitted by blood transfusion? Explain your answer.

Build on What You Know

4. How do parasitic protists display coevolution? *(Need to jog your memory? Revisit relevant concepts in Chapter 10, Section 10.4.)*

 What impact do protists have on other organisms in their environment?

368 *Unit 4 Monerans, Protists, and Fungi*

CHECKPOINT 15.5

1. Protists provide an essential food base in aquatic chains. Phytoplankton carry out over 70 percent of photosynthesis. Molds are decomposers.
2. Many protists and their products are used by humans for food or in pharmaceuticals. Some protists cause infections that can be fatal.
3. **Drawing conclusions** Yes, if not tested, because the blood could contain merozoites.
4. They must change as their host changes, or they will die.

Chapter 15 Review

 **THE BIG IDEA!**

15.1 Protists are a diverse group of eukaryotes that include unicellular and multicellular organisms.

15.2 – 15.4 Protists can be classified into three groups—protozoans, algae, and molds.

15.5 Protists have a major ecological impact as food sources, decomposers, and infectious agents.

Sum It Up

Use the following summary to review the main concepts in this chapter.

15.1 Characteristics of Protists

- Protists have eukaryotic cells.
- Protists are diverse; they differ in size, shape, and manner of movement.

15.2 Animal-like Protists—Protozoans

- Animal-like protists are called protozoans.
- Protozoans are classified by how they move: sarcodinians move by extending lobes of cyto-plasm; zooflagellates use flagella to move; ciliophorans live mostly in fresh water and use cilia to move; and sporozoans cannot move themselves.

15.3 Plantlike Protists—Algae

- Plantlike protists are called algae.
- Unicellular algae include dinoflagellates, diatoms, and euglenoids and some green algae.
- Multicellular algae include green algae, red algae, and brown algae.

15.4 Funguslike Protists—Molds

- Funguslike protists are classified as either plasmodial slime molds, cellular slime molds, or water molds.
- Plasmodial slime molds have single cells with multiple nuclei that can form spore-producing fruiting bodies.
- Cellular slime molds have single ameboid cells that can come together to form fruiting bodies and produce spores.
- Water molds include different freshwater and land protists that act as decomposers and some-times as parasites.

15.5 Protists in the Biosphere

- Protists in plankton are important in the food chain and in oxygen production.
- Protists cause disease directly and indirectly.
- Protists have many commercial uses including food additives and other household products.

Use Terms and Concepts

Use each of the following words or terms in a complete sentence.
If you need to review a meaning, turn to the page indicated.

protozoan (p. 355)
pseudopods (p. 356)
flagella (p. 356)
cilia (p. 357)
algae (p. 358)

alternation of
  generations (p. 361)
mold (p. 362)
plasmodium (p. 362)
plankton (p. 365)

Review the Big Ideas

Before students begin the Chapter Review, you may wish to discuss the Big Ideas they have learned in this chapter. Point out that protists are a diverse group of organisms that are an essential part of the bio-sphere. They provide food, cause disease, and help to recy-cle dead organisms. Explain that protists are like other organisms in the biosphere. Some protists have characteristics that are plantlike, such as the ability to perform photosynthesis. Other protists have animal-like char-acteristics, such as the ability to move. Tell students they will understand more about the relationship of protists to other organisms as they complete the unit.

Answers

1. protozoan
2. alternation of generations
3. flagella
4. algae
5. cilia
6. plasmodium
7. pseudopods
8. plankton
9. mold
10. b
11. a
12. d
13. b
14. b
15. a
16. d
17. b
18. Eukaryotic cells have membrane-bound nuclei and organelles.
19. Protozoans are unicellular and do not have specialized tissues or organs.
20. Amebas change shape as they move by extending and retracting pseudopods. Amebas do not have hard shells.
21. Algae are often multicellular, have chloroplasts, and carry out photosynthesis.
22. Three complex carbohydrates used in many food products come from seaweed.
23. Euglenoids lack rigid cell walls and have flagella.
24. Pigments in red algae can use the few wavelengths of light that penetrate to the ocean depths for photosynthesis.
25. Concept maps should show that <u>protists</u> include <u>unicellular</u> <u>protozoans</u> which are <u>animal-like</u>; and <u>multicellular</u> <u>protists</u> include <u>algae</u> which are <u>plantlike</u> and <u>molds</u> which are <u>funguslike</u>.

Use Your Word Power

MATCHING Look at the list of terms on the previous page and write the word or phrase that best matches each of the following phrases.

1. The general name for an animal-like protist

2. A reproductive life cycle with both haploid and diploid stages

3. Whiplike structures that allow some animal-like protists to move

4. The general name for plantlike protists

5. Short, hairlike projections that some animal-like protists use to move

6. The feeding stage of a plasmodial slime mold

7. The "false feet" that sarcodinians use for movement

8. A collection of mostly microscopic organisms that float near the surface of oceans and lakes

9. The general name for a funguslike protist

MULTIPLE CHOICE Choose the letter of the word or phrase that best completes each statement.

10. Funguslike protists include (a) algae; (b) slime molds; (c) sporozoans; (d) sarcodinians.

11. All protists are (a) eukaryotes; (b) prokaryotes; (c) unicellular; (d) multicellular.

12. Among the five kingdoms, protists have (a) the fewest varieties; (b) the least diversity; (c) the most features in common; (d) the fewest features in common.

13. Amebas survive harsh environments by (a) extending pseudopods; (b) forming cysts; (c) ingesting other organisms; (d) releasing toxins.

14. Protists that lack structures for movement are (a) zooflagellates; (b) sporozoans; (c) sarcodinians; (d) ciliophorans.

15. The organisms that could NOT be classified as phytoplankton are (a) fungi; (b) green algae; (c) diatoms; (d) dinoflagellates.

16. A plasmodium is (a) multicellular; (b) dormant; (c) stationary; (d) multinucleated.

17. The type of organisms LEAST closely related to euglenoids are (a) dinoflagellates; (b) foraminiferans; (c) diatoms; (d) green algae.

Show What You Know

18. What is the major difference between prokaryotic and eukaryotic cells?

19. How do protozoans differ from animals?

20. Why does an ameba have no definite shape?

21. What characteristics distinguish algae from other protists?

22. Describe how protists are used indirectly in food products.

23. How do euglenoids differ from other algae?

24. How is it possible for red algae to grow at ocean depths of more than 250 meters?

25. **Make a Concept Map** Complete the concept map below by adding the following terms: molds, algae, plantlike, animal-like, funguslike, unicellular, multicellular.

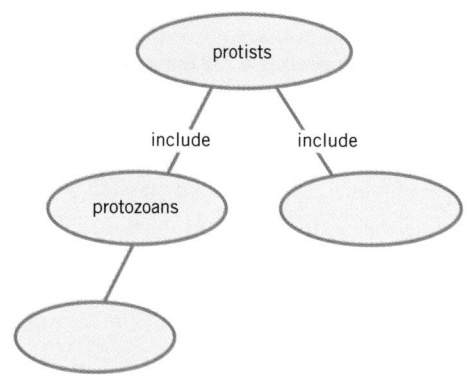

26. The ability to reproduce sexually can extend the life span of *Paramecia*.
27. Southeast Asia and the Americas show a stable number of reported cases from 1985 to 1993. Africa shows a sharp increase from 1985 until 1989, then a decrease until 1993. There may have been 210,000,000 cases of malaria in Africa in 1987.

28. It is difficult to determine what happened to the incidence of malaria in Africa after 1989 without more information. The actual incidence could have decreased rapidly had more medication and treatment reached a very large number of people. It is more likely that fewer cases were reported. This could be due to civil unrest, war, famine, or

Take It Further

26. Developing a Hypothesis A paramecium can reproduce asexually about 700 times, after which it dies. However, it can reproduce many more times if it conjugates in addition to reproducing asexually. How might the ability for sexual reproduction affect the life span of *Paramecia*?

27. Interpreting a Graph The graph below shows reported cases of malaria in three regions of the world in selected years. Describe the trend exhibited by each of the three regions. Officials estimate that there are at least ten actual cases for each one reported. Based on this estimate, about how many actual cases of malaria were there in Africa in 1987?

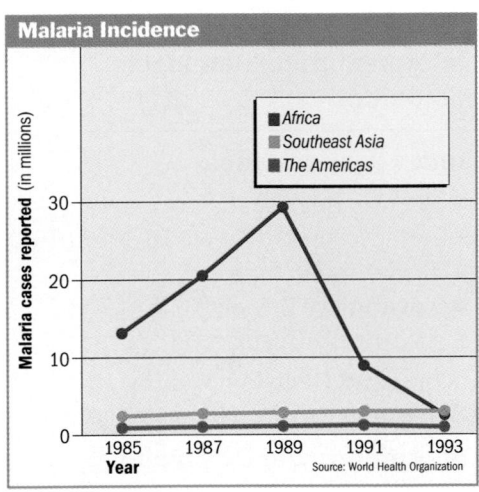

Malaria Incidence

Malaria cases reported (in millions)
■ Africa
■ Southeast Asia
■ The Americas

Year
Source: World Health Organization

28. Analyzing Data In the graph above, notice the dramatic drop in reported cases of malaria in Africa after 1989. Is it likely that the actual incidence of malaria would have decreased so rapidly? What other factors could affect the number of cases reported? Explain your answer.

Consider the Issues

29. Toxic Plankton on the Rise Blooms of toxic plankton are increasing around the world, with serious consequences. For example, fish kills,—deaths of millions of fishes—have been linked to toxic plankton, and the dangers to humans are quite real as well. A major factor is increased coastal development and the resulting pollution. What should be done to decrease toxic plankton blooms? Should coastal development be stopped or should the scientific community come up with other options? What are your thoughts on this issue?

Make New Connections

30. Biology and History Research the causes and effects of the potato famine that began in 1845 in Ireland. As you research, answer these questions: How is the protist that causes late blight transmitted? To prevent the spread of late blight, what strategies do governments use today that were not available in 1845? Present your answers, along with any illustrations you find, on a class bulletin board.

31. Biology in the Community In this chapter you have read about various protists and their uses by humans. Go to a local food store, supermarket, or restaurant. Try to find some samples of protists. Describe the type of organisms you found and where you found them. If they were in a food or food product, describe how you were able to detect their presence.

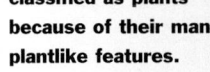
FAST FORWARD TO CHAPTER 16

Protists are eukaryotes. Fungi, which you will read about in Chapter 16, are also eukaryotes. Like protists, fungi are diverse and abundant. They were once classified as plants because of their many plantlike features.

Chapter 15 Protists **371**

31. Students should mention dairy products, soups, puddings, and cake frostings. Students can detect the presence of protists in food by reading the label.

other emergencies that would have disrupted normal reporting procedures.
29. Answers will vary, but should discuss the role of pollution and how pollution can be controlled and how pollutants themselves can be treated.
30. Potato blight is caused by the fungus-like protist *Phytophthora infestans,* which is transmitted by pests. Scientists

have developed blight-resistant strains of potato. Scientists also discourage the growing of single crops over large expanses of land. A mixed-planting strategy minimizes the target and the impact of any given agricultural pest.

PLANNING GUIDE

Section	Student Activities/Features	Teacher's Resource Package
16.1 Characteristics of Fungi **Objectives** ■ Identify the common characteristics of fungi ■ Describe the structure, nutrition, and growth of typical fungi	**Lab Zone Discover It!** *Grouping Mushrooms,* p. 373 **Lab Zone Think About It!** *Modeling Fungi Growth,* p. 376	**Unit 4 Review Module** ■ Section Review 16.1 **Laboratory Manual,** Lab 29: "Fungi Have Needs, Too" **Interpreting and Developing Graphics** 46
16.2 Origin and Diversity of Fungi **Objectives** ■ Compare and contrast the group of fungi ■ Describe the reproduction of fungi	**Everyday Biology** *A Shower Smorgasbord,* p. 379 **In the Community** *Pharmacies and Fungi,* p. 383	**Unit 4 Review Module** ■ Section Review 16.2 ■ Interpreting Graphics 16 ■ Critical Thinking Exercise 16 ■ Enrichment Topic 16-1 **Interpreting and Developing Graphics** 47
16.3 Fungi in the Biosphere **Objectives** ■ Describe the role of fungi in the environment and their relationships with other organisms ■ Compare and contrast fungal diseases and appraise the importance of fungi to humans	**Lab Zone Do It!** *Does Moisture Affect Bread Mold Growth?* p. 386 **STS: Frontiers in Biology** *Fungi in Medicine,* p. 387 **Everyday Biology** *A Fungus for a Headache?* p. 387 **Lab Zone Investigate It!** *Comparing Spores of Fungi and Green Plants* p. 388	**Unit 4 Review Module** ■ Section Review 16.3 ■ Activity Recordsheets 16-1 and 16-2 ■ Enrichment Topics 16-2 ■ Vocabulary Review 16 ■ Chapter 16 Tests **Issues and Decision Making** 16-1 **Consumer Applications** 16-1 and 16-2 **Interpreting and Developing Graphics** 48 **Spanish Reviews** ■ Chapter 16 ■ Unit 4

Technology Resources

Internet Connections

Within this chapter, you will see the (bioSURF) logo. If you and your students have access to the Internet, the following URL address will provide various Internet connections that are related to topics and features presented in this chapter:

http://microorganisms.biosurf.com

You can also find relevant chapter material at **The Biology Place** address:

http://www.biology.com

CD-ROMs

Biología: la telaraña de la vida, (Spanish Student Edition) Chapter 16
Teacher's Resource Planner, Chapter 16 Supplements
TestWorks CD-ROM
■ Chapter 16 Tests

Overhead Transparencies

■ Life Cycle of a Common Mold, #33
■ Life Cycle of a Club Fungi, #34

Videotapes

Biology Alive! Video Series
Rewind: The Web of Life Reteach Videos

Planning for Activities

STUDENT EDITION
Lab Zone
Discover It! p. 373
■ several different varieties of fresh mushrooms

Lab Zone Do It! p. 386
■ sliced bread
■ water
■ plastic bags
■ plain, rounded toothpicks

Lab Zone
Investigate It! p. 388
■ mushroom
■ fern frond with spore cases
■ single-edged razor blade
■ 2 pairs of forceps
■ microscope
■ microscope slides

TEACHER'S EDITION
Class Activity, p. 376
Modeling absorption of digested food molecules
■ thin strips of paper towels
■ Petri dishes
■ colored water

Teacher Demo, p. 378
Identifying the four fungal divisions

■ molded bread
■ mushroom
■ package of Brewer's yeast
■ empty prescription bottle labeled *Penicillin*

Teacher Demo, p. 382
Dissecting a mushroom
■ large mushroom
■ knife
■ hand lens

Class Activity, p. 380
Mushroom spore prints
■ mushrooms
■ scissors
■ small jar
■ paper
■ jar
■ microscope

Teacher Demo, p. 384
Molds in cheese
■ Brie cheese

Class Activity, p. 386
Preservatives in food preparation
■ water
■ commerically prepared bread
■ fresh baked bread
■ plastic bags
■ plain, rounded toothpicks

Chapter Objectives

Students will learn the main concepts of this chapter as they complete the following objectives.

- Identify the common characteristics of fungi
- Describe the structure, nutrition, and growth of typical fungi
- Compare and contrast the groups of fungi
- Describe the reproduction of fungi
- Describe the role of fungi in the environment and their relationships with other organisms
- Compare and contrast fungal diseases and the importance of fungi to humans

Key Words

16.1 *hyphae, septa, mycelium*

16.2 *spores, rhizoids, stolons, zygospore, asci, basidia*

16.3 *lichen, mycorrhizae*

The Opening Story

Have students read the chapter opener and identify the "black gold" described in the story. Point out that fungi have many uses; some, like these truffles, are edible, but others are harmful. Fungi are usually found in dark, moist areas, such as the woods pictured in the opener.

372

CHAPTER 16

Fungi

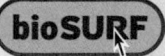 **bioSURF**

You can find out more about fungi by exploring the following Internet address:
http://microorganisms.biosurf.com

In this chapter . . .

FEATURES

Everyday Biology
- A Shower Smorgasbord
- A Fungus for a Headache?

In the Community
Pharmacies and Fungi

 Frontiers in Biology
Fungi in Medicine

LAB ZONES

Discover It!
- Grouping Mushrooms

Do It!
- Does Moisture Affect Bread-Mold Growth?

Think About It!
- Modeling Fungal Growth

Investigate It!
- Comparing Spores of Fungi and Green Plants

Pigs and dogs smell black gold

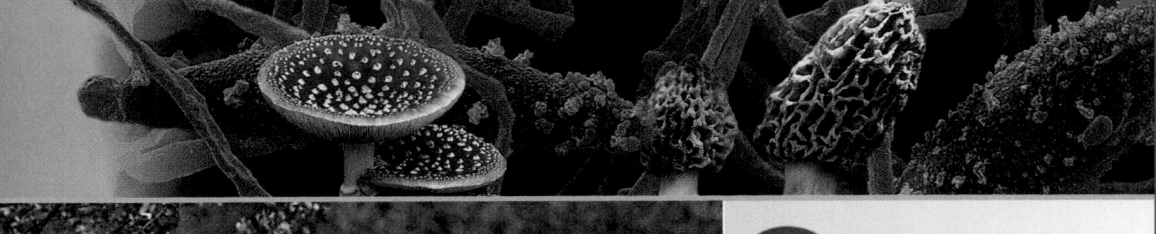

F rance, midwinter: An air of secrecy surrounds the small hunting party as a pig and his owner slip quietly into a grove of oak trees. The pig sniffs the ground as his owner looks anxiously behind him to be sure he is not being followed. Their quest: to find the valuable fungi called the black Perigord truffle—*Tuber melanosporum.* Why would a landowner guard the location of a bed of fungi so carefully? The answer lies in value: The wholesale price for a kilogram (kg) of Perigord truffles in the United States ranges from $550 to $750, and may increase depending on scarcity.

Pigs and dogs have been used as truffle hunters for centuries because those mammals are strongly attracted to the odor that truffles emit. In fact, pigs and dogs have detected the presence of truffles growing underground in the soil around tree roots from distances of more than 46 meters (m).

How do fungi such as the Perigord truffle grow? What exactly is a fungus anyway?

LAB ZONE Discover It!

Grouping Mushrooms

You will need *several different varieties of fresh mushrooms*

1. Examine the mushrooms. Look for similarities and differences. Slice the mushrooms in half lengthwise and note their structures.
2. Devise your own system for classifying the mushrooms. Explain your reasons for grouping specific items together or separately.

WRITE ABOUT IT!

Go on a "mold patrol" and write about your findings in your journal. Look for any places outside or inside your home where mold is growing. As you write, describe the molds, their specific locations, and any physical characteristics that appear to be common to all of the locations.

Chapter 16 Fungi **373**

PORTFOLIO PREVIEW

Students should be encouraged to add to their portfolios as they work through this chapter. In addition to the *Write About It* opportunity, the following sections provide an opportunity for portfolio entries:

■ Section 16.1: *Characteristics of Fungi*
■ Section 16.2: *Origin and Diversity of Fungi*

Opening Activities

bioSURF If you have access to the Internet, you may wish to have students connect to the address shown on page 372. Students may conduct a search of key words related to fungi studied in this chapter. Students could search under mold and mushroom.

LAB ZONE Discover It!

Grouping Mushrooms

TEAM WORK

You may wish to provide some students with hand lenses, some with compound microscopes, clean slides, and coverslips, and others with no tools for magnification. Have students use the tools to examine the mushrooms. Then discuss how different types of tools affected their observations and classification schemes.

WRITE ABOUT IT

Encourage students to use vivid language in their descriptions so that someone reading their entries can visualize the mold and pinpoint its location.

REWIND to Chapter 15

Briefly review concepts learned in Chapter 15, *Protists*. Ask:

■ **How will the study of Kingdom Protista help you understand the next kingdom, Fungi?**

ENGAGE

Consider the Big Idea

Have students read The Big Idea! at the top of the page. Explain that fungi are similar to and different from organisms classified as plants and animals. Like animals, fungi are heterotrophs; like plants, fungi cannot move from place to place.

Use the Visual

Have students look at the photograph that opens the section. Point out that the stinkhorn, like the mushroom, is one of the many diverse members of the kingdom Fungi.

Check Prior Knowledge

To assess students' prior knowledge of fungi, ask:

- **What role do fungi play in the natural world?** (Answers will vary, but may include recycling dead organisms.)

 **Comparing and Contrasting** To practice strategies for effective reading, use pages 37-38 in *Super Read!*

What you'll learn

IDEAS
- To identify the common characteristics of fungi
- To describe the structure, nutrition, and growth of typical fungi

WORDS
hyphae, septa, mycelium

SUPER READ!

16.1 Characteristics of Fungi

A fungus to offend everyone

What attracts flies, makes your yard smell like rotting flesh, and appears almost overnight? The answer is the stinkhorn—one of the thousands of members of the kingdom Fungi. The characteristics of this smelly fungus definitely make it an unwelcome guest at picnics and outdoor parties. Other fungi, such as button mushrooms and yeasts, are important ingredients for food at those same picnics and parties.

STRUCTURE OF FUNGI

Tangled webs

Imagine a pizza without crust and mushrooms, or a doctor without antibiotics. If you can imagine those things, then you are imagining a world without fungi. Fungi contribute to food, to medicine, and to the recycling process that returns nutrients from dead organisms to the environment.

Fungi come in many forms; two are shown in *Figure 16.1*. The kingdom Fungi includes microscopic yeast as

well as the giant puffball, which can grow to the size of a basketball.

The cell walls of most fungi are made of chitin—a tough, flexible carbohydrate that also makes up the hard outer skeleton of insects. What advantage do cell walls made of chitin provide for fungi?

Yeasts are typical unicellular fungi. Yeast cells have a cell wall, a cell membrane, a nucleus, a large vacuole, and membrane-bound organelles. Like other eukaryotic organisms, yeasts undergo cell division.

There are no typical multicellular fungi. The mushrooms in *Figure 16.2* contain structures common to most multicellular fungi, however. For example, the mushrooms display above-ground reproductive structures—a stipe, an annulus, and a cap.

In contrast to the unicellular fungi, multicellular fungi are composed of a mass of tiny, individual filaments, barely visible to the unaided eye. The individual filaments, called **hyphae** (HY-fee), are tubules filled with cytoplasm and nuclei. Some hyphae may be divided into segments by walls

FIGURE 16.1
Brightly colored pink-capped mushrooms (right), photographed in the rain forest of Costa Rica, and filamentous coral fungus (below) give some indication of the wide variety of fungi.

STUDENT RESOURCES

From the Teacher's Resource Package, use:
- Section Review 16.1 from Unit 4 Review Module
- Lab 29: "Fungi Have Needs, Too"

 ## TECHNOLOGY RESOURCES

Relevant technology resources include:
- Spanish Student Edition CD-ROM
- Teacher's Resource Planner CD-ROM

FIGURE 16.2
Structure of a Mushroom

A mushroom displays characteristics common to all fungi. Its cells are eukaryotic, with cell walls made of chitin. Why do you think the reproductive structures of these mushrooms are above ground? ❷

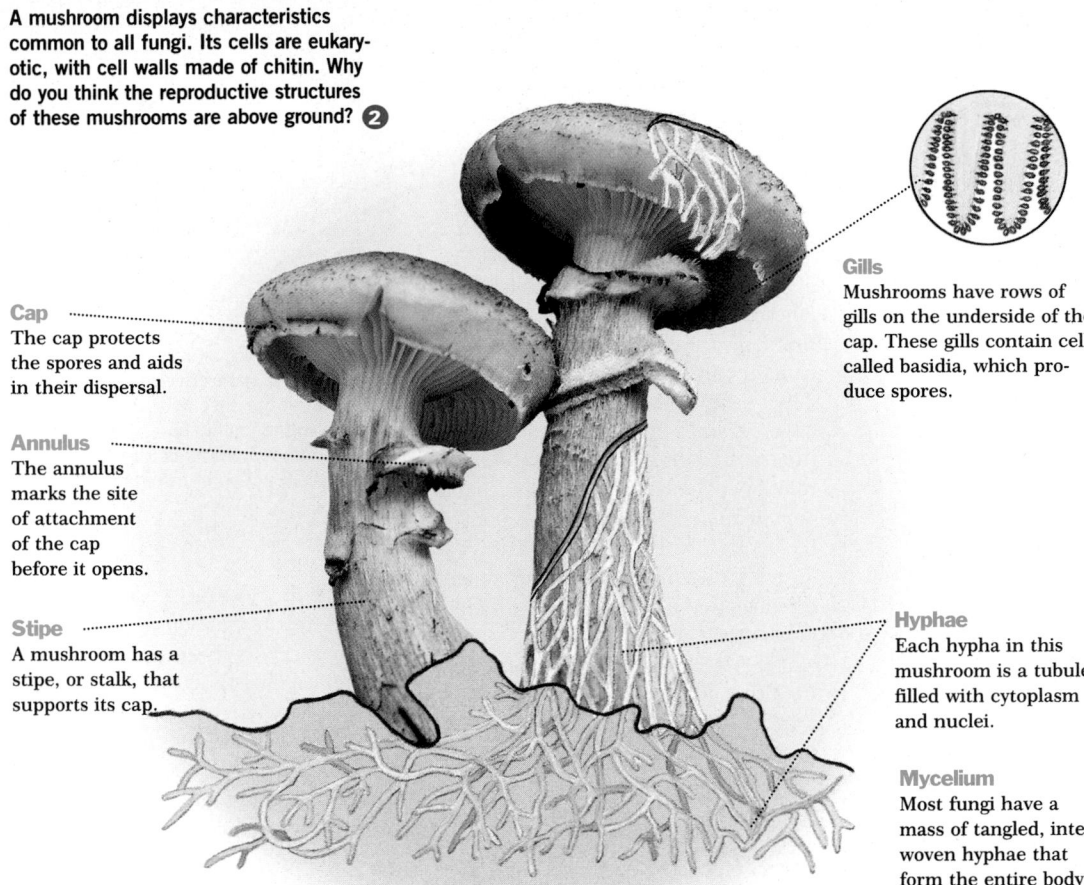

Gills
Mushrooms have rows of gills on the underside of the cap. These gills contain cells called basidia, which produce spores.

Cap
The cap protects the spores and aids in their dispersal.

Annulus
The annulus marks the site of attachment of the cap before it opens.

Stipe
A mushroom has a stipe, or stalk, that supports its cap.

Hyphae
Each hypha in this mushroom is a tubule filled with cytoplasm and nuclei.

Mycelium
Most fungi have a mass of tangled, interwoven hyphae that form the entire body of the fungus.

called **septa** (singular: *septum*), as shown in *Figure 16.3*. Septa have holes through which cytoplasm and organelles move. Some fungi do not have septa in their hyphae, and each hypha is one continuous filament containing cytoplasm and nuclei.

Hyphae are the living, growing parts of fungi. Hyphae can weave together in a variety of ways, thereby producing many different forms of fungi. Hyphae can grow quite quickly; certain fungi produce about 35 to 40 m of hyphae in only one hour!

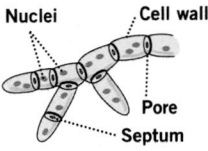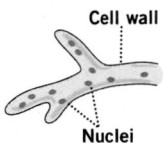

Nuclei   Cell wall   Cell wall

Pore

Septum   Nuclei

FIGURE 16.3
Most groups of fungi have hyphae with septa (left). Some fungi have no septa (right). Their cytoplasm is continuous within hyphae.

The mass of tangled, interwoven hyphae that forms the body of a fungus is called a **mycelium** (my-SEE-lee-um) (plural: *mycelia*). In *Figure 16.2* you can see how hyphae interweave to form the mycelium of a mushroom.

Chapter 16 Fungi   **375**

---

❷ TEACH

Use the Visual

Have students study Figure 16.2. Explain that a mushroom displays characteristics that are common to all fungi, including eukaryotic cells, an inability to move from place to place, and nutrient intake through decomposition. Ask:

■ **What is a mycelium?** (A mass of tangled, interwoven hyphae that form the body of a fungus)

■ **Which parts of the fungus shown are composed of hyphae that have formed a mycelium?** (All of them: the cap, gills, annulus, and stipe)

Explain

Review the relationship among hyphae, septa, and mycelia. Emphasize that some hyphae have septa; others do not. Point out that hyphae do not join as mycelia in all fungi. For example, yeast cells are unicellular and are not composed of hyphae.

Language Arts

Explain the rule for the formation of plurals of Latin words ending in "-um," such as *mycelium*. On the board, list the following terms: *data, flagellum, cilia,* and *septa.* Have students copy each term, indicate if it is singular or plural, write its alternate form, and use each form in a sentence.

MEETING DIVERSE NEEDS

LEP Have students preview the chapter by looking for unfamiliar terms. Encourage students to write the terms, their phonetic respellings, and their definitions in their notebooks. For terms with unusual plurals, suggest to students that they copy both the singular and plural forms.

❶ It would help keep them hydrated and provide structure.

❷ The reproductive structures are basidia, each of which produce spores. They are above ground so that the spores can be dispersed by wind, water, and animals.

Class Activity

Give groups of students thin strips of paper towels and petri dishes containing colored water. Tell them that the strips represent the hyphae of a fungus and the colored water represents organic matter that has been broken down through the action of the digestive enzymes released by the fungus. Have students place the "hyphae" into the "digested food matter" and observe what happens. Explain that the movement of the solution into the paper strip models the absorption of digested food molecules by hyphae. Students can also manipulate other strips of various sizes, or warm the water to see what effect these variables have on the rate at which the "food matter" is taken in.

LAB ZONE **Think About It!**

Modeling Fungal Growth

Analyze Your Results

1 On average, each hypha grows 0.00001 km, or 1 cm, in one day.
2 The amount and type of nutrition, temperature, and location of the fungus may affect growth rate.

---

❶ Reproduction and dispersal of spores outside the ant
❷ From the ant; it's not a saprophyte because it feeds on living tissue.

NUTRITION AND GROWTH OF FUNGI

Feeding a fungus

All fungi are heterotrophs; they obtain their nutrition from other organisms. However, nutrients must first be transported from the environment into the fungi. How do fungi accomplish this task?

Nutrition Fungi obtain food by absorbing it—that is, they take food in by the diffusion of small organic molecules from the environment. The environments that fungi inhabit usually contain only large organic molecules. Fungi have evolved an ability to produce enzymes in their hyphae, which they secrete directly into their environment. The enzymes break the large organic molecules into small organic molecules that the fungi can easily absorb. Fungi are capable of producing enzymes that break down large, complex organic molecules such as lignin, which is a major component of wood.

Although fungi are similar in the way they absorb nutrients from the environment, they differ in the types of organisms that they use as a source

of nutrition. Most fungi are saprophytes—organisms that digest and absorb nutrients from dead organisms. Where does the fungus in *Figure 16.4* get its nutrients? Is it a saprophyte? ❷

Other fungi depend on living hosts for food. Fungi that obtain nutrients from living things can be parasites, mutualistic partners, or predators. Parasitic fungi absorb nutrients from living hosts, a process that often causes disease in, and sometimes the death of, the host. Still other fungi live in a mutualistic relationship with their host. Fungi in mutualistic relationships absorb nutrients from the host, but they reciprocate by providing the host with needed materials, such as minerals from the soil. A few fungi are predators—organisms that trap and kill their prey. What types of specialized structures would you expect to find in predatory fungi? ❸

Growth Fungi use the nutrients they absorb primarily for growth. Fungi usually grow very rapidly, as nutrient transport to the actively growing areas of hyphae is extremely

FIGURE 16.4
When ants ingest spores of a certain tropical fungus, the spores develop a mycelium that feeds on the ant's body tissue until the ant dies. In the photo above, fungal fruiting bodies protrude from a dead ant's head. What is the function of the fruiting bodies? ❶

LAB ZONE **Think About It!** **bioSURF**

Modeling Fungal Growth

You can model one day's growth of one hypha when you . . .

Try This

1 Draw a circle 2 centimeters in diameter to represent the size of a fungus.
2 If the 100,000 hyphae of a fungus grow a total of 1 kilometer a day, calculate the average growth of 1 hypha in one day.
3 Draw a second circle outside the first to represent the size of the fungus after one day's growth.

Analyze Your Results

1 How much did each hypha grow in one day?
2 What factors might affect this rate of growth?

MEETING DIVERSE NEEDS

At Risk and LEP These students may have difficulty distinguishing among the variety of ways fungi meet their nutritional needs. List the following terms on the board: *heterotrophs, saprophytes, mutualistic partners, predators, parasites,* and *host.* Have students work with a partner to develop concept maps illustrating the relationships among the terms as they relate to fungi. Review the maps with students to help them correct any misinformation. Suggest that they use their maps for review.

FIGURE 16.5
Growth of Fungus

The photo (left) shows a *Penicillium* mycelium growing on an orange. If you used a microscope, you could see the hyphae of *Penicillium* penetrating orange cells, as shown in the drawing (right). What is the function of these penetrating hyphae? **4**

efficient. Materials move quickly through a fungal mycelium because the hyphae of the mycelium share the same cytoplasm. So materials from the entire mycelium are available to all hyphae. The Think About It! activity on page 376 will help you understand just how quickly the mycelium of a fungus can grow.

FIGURE 16.6

A ring of mushrooms, popularly called a fairy ring, feeds on dead plant material. As the expanding mycelium consumes nutrients, what do you think happens to the grass under the mushrooms? **5**

Growth in the hyphae occurs at the tips. The hyphae grow longer, but they remain very narrow. As a result of this growth pattern, the mycelium spreads outward quickly, occupying an increasingly large area. The many mushrooms you see in *Figure 16.6* may look like individual organisms, but they are all part of a single fungus. The visible mushrooms of a single, underground mycelium can spread to cover more than 1000 acres.

CHECKPOINT 16.1

1. What are the characteristics common to all fungi?
2. How do typical fungi grow?
3. How do fungi obtain nutrients?
4. **Critical Thinking** What characteristics would you expect to find in environments where saprophytes flourish? Explain your answer.

Build on What You Know

5. Make a chart to compare fungal cells with prokaryotes, animal cells, and plant cells. *(Need to jog your memory? Revisit relevant concepts in Chapter 3, Section 3.2 and Section 3.4.)*

Chapter 16 Fungi **377**

Discuss

The growth of fungi at the tops of the hyphae is another similarity between fungi and plants. Explain to students that in plants, root growth occurs at the root tips.

3 ASSESS

Evaluate Understanding

Draw an outline figure of a mushroom on the board. Ask the following questions and then have volunteers label each structure on the drawing:

- **What are the names of the three reproductive structures of a mushroom?** (Cap, annulus, and stipe)
- **What are the living, growing parts of fungi?** (Hyphae)
- **Where does the mushroom produce spores?** (In the gills)
- **Through what part of the mushroom do nutrients move?** (Mycelium)

Reteach

Write the following headings on the board: *Structure of Fungi, Nutrition of Fungi, Growth of Fungi.* For each heading, have students revisit the section to find one main idea and two supporting details. Record student responses under the appropriate heading and then help them to apply the information listed to mushrooms.

CHECKPOINT 16.1

1. Fungi have a cell membrane, a nucleus, large vacuoles, membrane-bound organelles and cell walls that contain chitin. Multicellular fungi are made up of masses of hyphae.
2. Fungi grow when hyphae grow longer at their tips. They reproduce by producing spores.
3. They absorb nutrients through hyphae.

4. **Predicting** Warm, damp environments with dead organic matter. Saprophytes absorb nutrients from dead organisms.
5. Both fungi and prokaryotes have cell membranes, fungi also have nuclei and membrane-bound organelles. Fungal cell walls contain chitin; plant cell walls contain cellulose. Animal cells do not have cell walls.

3 Structures that trap prey
4 To exchange materials such as enzymes that break apart molecules in the orange
5 It dies because no nutrients are available.

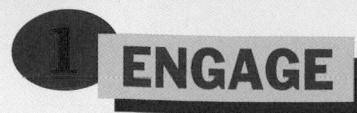

ENGAGE

Use the Visual

Direct students to the opening photograph of the giant puff-ball, paying particular attention to its size. Have students compare the size of the puffball with other fungi, such as mushrooms in supermarkets. After students read the text, use the photograph and students' observations to discuss the diversity of fungi and their traits.

Check Prior Knowledge

To assess students' prior knowledge about the traits of fungi, ask:

- **What are the common characteristics of fungi?** (All are eukaryotic and depend on other organisms for food; most are multicellular and cannot move by themselves.)

Teacher Demo

Display a piece of molded bread, a mushroom, a package of Brewer's yeast, and an empty prescription bottle labeled penicillin. Explain to students that these four items represent organisms from each of the four fungal divisions. Tell students that fungi are grouped into divisions based upon their method of reproduction. As you hold each item up, identify the division name and common name for the fungal group represented and write this information on the board.

What you'll learn

IDEAS
- To compare and contrast the groups of fungi
- To describe the reproduction of fungi

WORDS
spores, rhizoids, stolons, zygospore, asci, basidia

Kingdom: Fungi
Four divisions:
Zygomycota
Ascomycota
Basidiomycota
Deuteromycota

How large is the fungus among us?
Looking more like a mutant marshmallow than a fungus, *Lypcoperdon giganteum*, or the giant puffball, is certainly an armful. It is tiny, however, compared to the fungus *Armillaria bulbosa*. The mycelium of a single one of these fungi spreads out under many acres of forest floor in Michigan and is estimated to weigh at least 100 tons.

ORIGIN OF FUNGI

Fungus among us

You may wonder how fungi evolved. Well, so do mycologists—biologists who study fungi. The fossil record does not provide much information about fungi origins. Many mycologists hypothesize, however, that fungi evolved at least 400 million years ago from a protist ancestor.

Fungi were long classified as members of the plant kingdom because they appeared to be similar to plants. However, fungi differ from plants in several distinct ways. Compare what you have learned about cell wall composition in fungi and plants. The cell walls of plants are composed of cellulose, whereas the cell walls of almost all fungi contain chitin. In addition, plants are autotrophs, whereas fungi are heterotrophs—they cannot make their own food. Because of these and other differences, fungi are now classified in their own kingdom. However, because fungi were once classified as plants, the main groups of the kingdom Fungi are called divisions rather than phyla.

Fungi are grouped in one of four divisions based primarily on their method of reproduction. Three of these divisions—common molds, sac fungi, and club fungi—are classifications based on the structures used in sexual reproduction. The fourth division—the imperfect fungi—includes fungi that have been observed to reproduce only asexually.

Fungi in all four divisions are known to reproduce asexually. Asexual

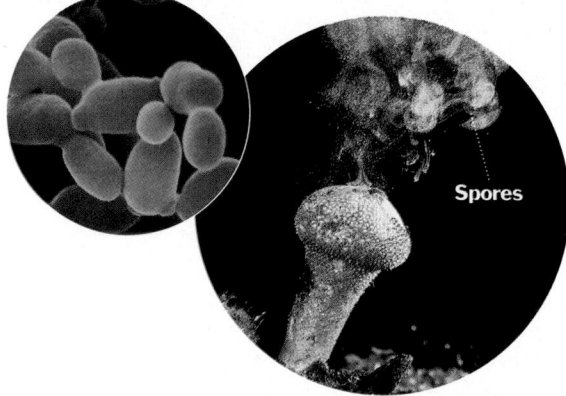

Spores

FIGURE 16.7
The yeast cell (far left) is budding—a form of asexual reproduction in which a small budlike cell grows from a larger cell. Another form of asexual reproduction occurs as a puffball (near left) disperses its spores. Why are so many spores released at once? ❶

STUDENT RESOURCES

From the Teacher's Resource Package, use:
- Section Review 16.2, Interpreting Graphics 16, Enrichment Topic 16.1, and Critical Thinking Exercise 16 from Unit 4 Review Module

TECHNOLOGY RESOURCES

Relevant technology resources include:
- Spanish Student Edition CD-ROM
- Teacher's Resource Planner CD-ROM

reproduction can occur in three ways: budding, regeneration, and spore production. During budding, a parent cell divides and produces offspring by forming a small bud, which separates from the parent. Regeneration occurs when a piece of mycelium breaks off from a fungus and grows on its own. *Figure 16.7* illustrates two asexual reproductive forms.

Most fungi reproduce asexually by producing spores in a structure called a fruiting body. **Spores** are reproductive cells that can remain dormant or develop into a new organism. Fungi produce many spores. A typical mushroom, for example, makes 16 billion spores. Fruiting bodies are above-ground stalks that support the structures in which spores are made. You can see different types of fruiting bodies in *Figure 16.9*.

Common molds, sac fungi, and club fungi are the divisions of fungi that can reproduce sexually. As you learned in Chapter 5, sexual reproduction generally involves combining the genes from two different parents. In fungi there are no males or females.

FIGURE 16.8
Kingdom Fungi

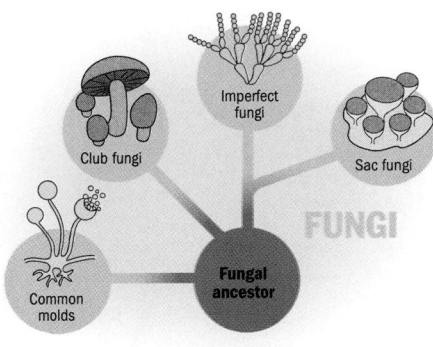
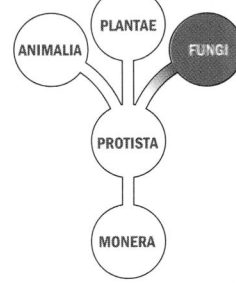

Instead, fungi have two different mating types of hyphae: plus (+) and minus (−). Sexual reproduction in fungi occurs by the fusion of two hyphae with different mating types and the resulting production of spores.

As you just learned, spore production occurs in both asexual and sexual reproduction. Although the spores produced by both methods of reproduction look the same, spores that are produced sexually contain a new combination of genetic information.

FIGURE 16.9
All fruiting bodies produce spores. How are these bodies adapted for dispersing spores? How could animals, wind, and water help to disperse spores? ❷

A Shower Smorgasbord

What feeds a bathroom fungal mold? Traces of soap and shampoo, which contain fatty acids, and your dead skin cells provide nourishment for the fungal mold growing on your shower curtain.

Chapter 16 Fungi **379**

2 TEACH

Explain

Direct students to look at Figure 16.9. Explain that the photographs show the different types of fruiting bodies of fungi. Emphasize that spores are formed within the fruiting body and are then released into the environment, where they are dispersed by wind, water, and animals.

Health

Spores released by fungi, especially molds, cause allergic reactions in some people, similar to "hay fever" caused by pollen. Such allergies are most common in the early autumn months, after deciduous trees shed their leaves. Challenge students to explain why mold spores might be more prevalent at this time of year.

Everyday Biology

You can extend this feature by having students collect and observe samples of bathroom fungal mold. Provide students with petri dishes and sterile swabs and tell them to remove mold from one or more bathroom items (tile, grout, shower curtain) with the swab, place the mold in the dish, and check what happens over a given period of time.

MEETING DIVERSE NEEDS

At Risk and LEP The differences in traits used to classify plants and fungi into separate kingdoms is an important concept in this chapter. Help these students to create a Venn diagram or other graphic that compares the traits of plants and fungi.

❶ Increase the chances of survival because only a small percentage of them will land in places where conditions are favorable for growth.

❷ They have a large surface area; animals come in contact with spores and disperse them as they move. Wind and water carry the spores along to new locations.

380

Build Writing Skills

Have students observe a fungus in nature or in a photograph. Then ask them to write a poem to describe what they see.

Explain

Emphasize that spore production in fungi can happen sexually or asexually. The spores produced in each way look the same; however, their genetic characteristics differ. Ask:

- **If a fungus produced spores both sexually and asexually, which spores would result in offspring most similar to the original fungus? Why?** (The spores produced asexually because they would be genetically identical)

Use the Visual

Help students understand the life cycle illustrated in Figure 16.10. Ask:

- **Why is step 1 part of sexual reproduction?** (Hyphae from two different parents join to form a 2n zygote.)
- **Why is step 3 part of asexual reproduction?** (The nucleus undergoes mitosis to form new, identical cells called spores.)
- **Why is step 3 also part of sexual reproduction?** (The sporangium in step 3 produces the hyphae used in sexual reproduction shown in step 1.)

❶ In sexual reproduction, two hyphae fuse to form a zygote. Two haploid hyphae fuse and undergo meiosis. In asexual reproduction, haploid hyphae do not fuse and instead undergo mitosis.

❷ To facilitate spore dispersal

FIGURE 16.10

The Life Cycle of a Common Mold

Compare sexual and asexual reproduction in the common bread mold called *Rhizopus*. How do they differ? ❶

Haploid (*n*)
Diploid (*2n*)

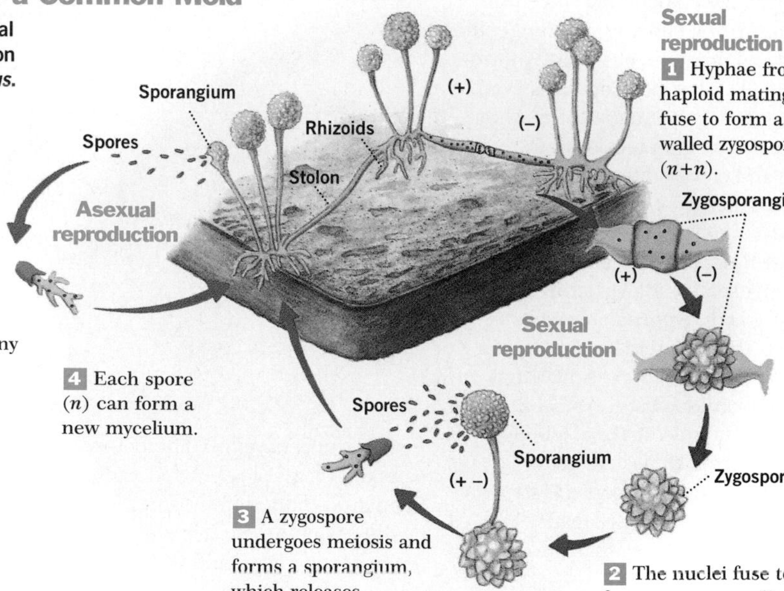

Asexual reproduction
Upright hyphae develop sporangia, from which many spores (*n*) are dispersed.

Sporangium

Spores

Rhizoids

Stolon

Asexual reproduction

(+) (−)

Sexual reproduction
❶ Hyphae from two haploid mating types fuse to form a thick-walled zygosporangium (*n+n*).

Zygosporangium

(+) (−)

Sexual reproduction

Zygospore

❷ The nuclei fuse to form a zygospore (*2n*).

Spores

Sporangium

(+ −)

❸ A zygospore undergoes meiosis and forms a sporangium, which releases spores (*n*).

❹ Each spore (*n*) can form a new mycelium.

COMMON MOLDS

A spore at the door

You have probably seen mold on bread or mildew on a shower curtain. These organisms are common molds. Scientists call this division of fungi Zygomycota (ZY-goh-my-KOH-tuh). Zygomycetes, as fungi in this group are called, are frequently found in soil or on dead animals or plants.

Common molds are structurally unique. Their hyphae lack septa, the walls that divide a hypha into segments. The hyphae of common molds also have some specialized functions.

There are three kinds of specialized hyphae in common molds—rhizoids, stolons, and sporangia. **Rhizoids** absorb nutrients and hold common molds to their food source like roots anchor plants to soil. **Stolons** connect groups of rhizoids to one another. Stolons transport cytoplasm containing nutrients and other materials through the body of the fungus. Sporangia (singular: *sporangium*) produce spores during reproduction. As you can see in *Figure 16.10*, sporangia

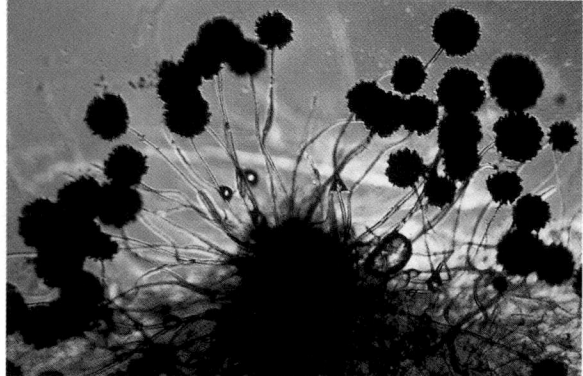

FIGURE 16.11

The mycelium of the bread mold *Rhizopus* has hyphae that produce sporangia. Why do sporangia grow upward? ❷

MULTICULTURAL PERSPECTIVE

In ancient times, Egyptians believed that the tombs of the pharaohs were protected by spirits who placed a "curse" on anyone trying to steal the contents. Some scientists have recently suggested that the "curse" of the ancient tombs was actually extremely high levels of spores, released by molds growing in the dark tombs. High levels of mold spores can cause sickness.

produce haploid spores (*n*) during asexual reproduction. These spores bear genetically identical offspring.

During other stages in the life cycles of common molds, genetic material from two different mating types, a (+) mating type (*n*) and a (−) mating type (*n*), merge. Nuclei from the two mating types fuse to form a diploid (2*n*) structure called a **zygospore**. Division Zygomycota gets its name from these tough spores. Zygospores can survive for many years in harsh conditions. When conditions are right, the hard shell of the zygospore cracks open to produce a new sporangium. After the nuclei undergo meiosis, the sporangium bursts and thousands of new haploid (*n*) spores are released into the environment.

FIGURE 16.13

The Life Cycle of a Sac Fungus

Sac fungi usually reproduce asexually. Under what environmental conditions might they reproduce sexually? ❸

SAC FUNGI

A mixed bag

The sac fungi are a diverse division that includes unicellular yeasts, powdery mildews, the fungi in most lichens, and the flavorful morels. In fact, there are more than 60,000 species of sac fungi.

The characteristic that links the members of this group together is the production of saclike structures called **asci** (singular: *ascus*) during sexual reproduction. This characteristic gives the division its name—Ascomycota (AS-koh-my-KOH-tuh).

As you can see in *Figure 16.13*, the sexual reproduction cycle includes two mating types fusing to form a cell called an ascogonium. This structure produces hyphae that grow upward. Asci—the saclike reproductive structures—form at the tips of the ascogonium. The nuclei in asci go through several changes that eventually result in the formation of spores with

FIGURE 16.12
Morels (above) and bird's nest fungi (below) are both sac fungi. Morels, prized by gourmet cooks for their flavor, can be more expensive than caviar.

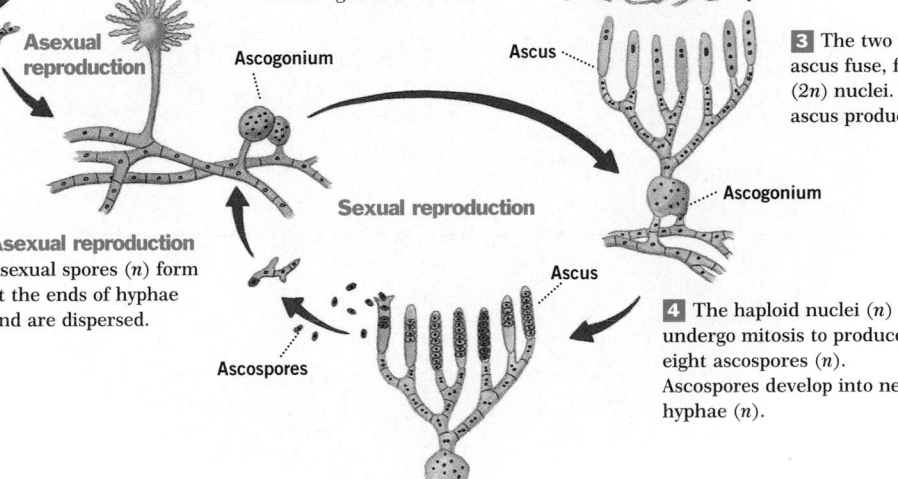

Spores

Asexual reproduction

Sexual reproduction
1 Hyphae (*n*) of two mating types fuse, forming an ascogonium.

Ascogonium

Ascus

Sexual reproduction

Asexual reproduction
Asexual spores (*n*) form at the ends of hyphae and are dispersed.

Ascospores

Ascus

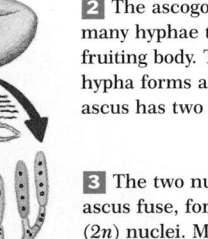

2 The ascogonium produces many hyphae that become the fruiting body. The end of each hypha forms an ascus. Each ascus has two nuclei (*n*+*n*).

3 The two nuclei in each ascus fuse, forming diploid (2*n*) nuclei. Meiosis in each ascus produces haploid nuclei.

Ascogonium

4 The haploid nuclei (*n*) undergo mitosis to produce eight ascospores (*n*). Ascospores develop into new hyphae (*n*).

Chapter 16 Fungi **381**

16.2

Use the Visual

Have students study Figure 16.13 which shows the life cycle of a sac fungus. To help students trace the sequence of events, ask:

- **Where are the asexual spores of sac fungi formed?** (At the ends of the hyphae)
- **Are the asexual spores of sac fungi haploid or diploid?** (Haploid)
- **What forms when hyphae of opposite mating types fuse in a sac fungus?** (A cell called an ascogonium results.)
- **Into what structure does an ascogonium develop?** (The ascus, the cup-shaped fruiting body of a sac fungus)
- **What forms when the two nuclei in the ascus fuse?** (A diploid nucleus)
- **How does the diploid nucleus formed in the ascus become haploid nuclei?** (By undergoing meiosis)

Discuss

Point out how the names of the fungal divisions are related to their sexual reproductive structures. For example, sexual reproduction in zygomycetes results in the production of zygospores and ascomycetes produce ascospores in a structure called an ascus. Have students infer what the name for spores produced by basidiomycetes might be and what the name for the fruiting body in which spore formation takes place might be. (Basidiospores, basidium)

❸ When conditions are unfavorable and genetic diversity increases chances of survival

FIGURE 16.14
This green-headed jelly fungus is just one example of a species of club fungi.

new genetic combinations. In favorable environmental conditions, these spores grow into new fungal organisms.

Sexual reproduction in sac fungi is rare. In most cases, sac fungi reproduce asexually by producing haploid spores and releasing them into the environment. Unicellular sac fungi most often reproduce by cell division and budding, which you read about earlier.

CLUB FUNGI

Welcome to the club

When you think of fungi, you probably think of mushrooms. Mushrooms are club fungi. Club fungi are members of the division Basidiomycota (bay-SID-ee-oh-my-KOH-tuh).

One of the most distinguishing characteristics of club fungi is their tendency to reproduce sexually. Asexual reproduction is possible in club fungi but very rare. You can follow the most common life cycle of a club fungus in *Figure 16.15*, which shows a mushroom as a representative example.

The visible parts of the mushroom—stalk, cap, and gills—are made of tightly packed mycelia. These reproductive structures form a fruiting body that houses the tiny spore-producing **basidia** (singular: *basidium*).

Spores that are produced in basidia are released, and if environmental

FIGURE 16.15

The Life Cycle of a Club Fungus

Mushrooms usually reproduce sexually. Their spores develop in basidia on their gills.

Haploid (n)
Diploid ($2n$)

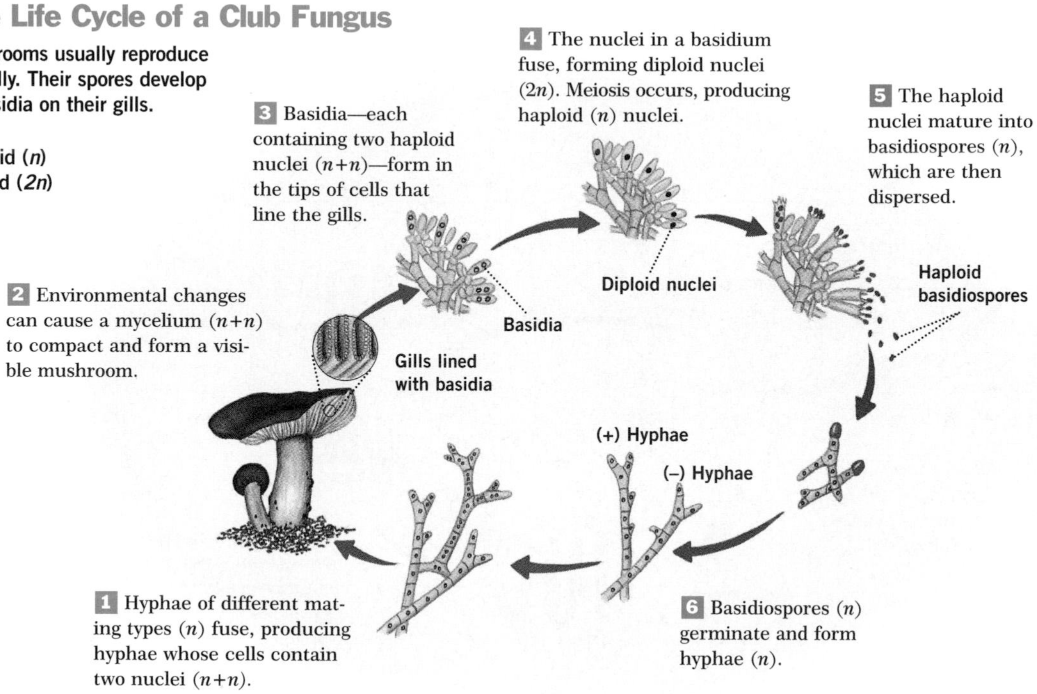

3 Basidia—each containing two haploid nuclei ($n+n$)—form in the tips of cells that line the gills.

4 The nuclei in a basidium fuse, forming diploid nuclei ($2n$). Meiosis occurs, producing haploid (n) nuclei.

5 The haploid nuclei mature into basidiospores (n), which are then dispersed.

2 Environmental changes can cause a mycelium ($n+n$) to compact and form a visible mushroom.

Diploid nuclei

Basidia

Haploid basidiospores

Gills lined with basidia

(+) Hyphae

(−) Hyphae

1 Hyphae of different mating types (n) fuse, producing hyphae whose cells contain two nuclei ($n+n$).

6 Basidiospores (n) germinate and form hyphae (n).

382   *Unit 4 Monerans, Protists, and Fungi*

CHECKPOINT 16.2

1. Common molds have specialized hyphae called rhizoids, stolons, and sporangia; club fungi have basidia; imperfect fungi have conidiophores.
2. Molds, sac fungi, and club fungi reproduce sexually by the fusion of two hyphae and the production of spores. Common molds have sporangia that produce

conditions are favorable, new mushrooms grow. As a result of the genetic recombination that occurred during the process of sexual reproduction, there is variation among these offspring fungi.

IMPERFECT FUNGI
Can't have it all

Some fungi apparently reproduce only asexually. These fungi are commonly called imperfect fungi and are grouped in the division Deuteromycota (DOO-ter-oh-my-KOH-tuh).

If you have ever had athlete's foot or ringworm, you have been a host for an imperfect fungus. Not all imperfect fungi are harmful, however. The imperfect fungus *Penicillium* produces the antibiotic penicillin, which you may have taken to help fight a bacterial infection.

Imperfect fungi reproduce asexually by producing spores called conidia in specialized hyphae called conidiophores. These asexually produced spores are released into the environment. If they land in a suitable place, they start growing. Most imperfect fungi are moldlike in appearance.

IN THE COMMUNITY
Pharmacies and Fungi

Visit a pharmacy in your community and locate the aisle containing antifungal medications. Look at the list of ingredients on the packages of these over-the-counter medications. Make a list of the ingredients used in each brand of medication. Be careful to note the "active ingredient" in each product. The active ingredient is the chemical that acts to prevent the growth of the particular fungus. Does the active ingredient vary from product to product? Carefully read the information on the product to see if it treats only certain types of fungi. Also note the indications or symptoms that are connected with certain fungal infections. Log on to *http://microorganisms.biosurf.com* to gather more information about fungi. Share your observations with the class.

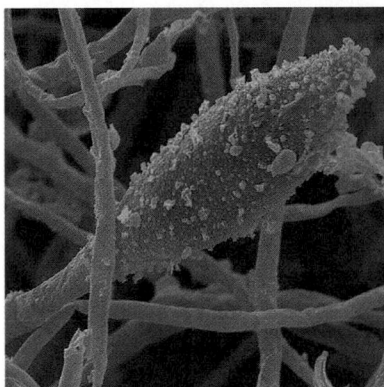

FIGURE 16.16
The imperfect fungus you see here causes athlete's foot, a condition easily transferred between humans in the humid environment of a locker room.

CHECKPOINT 16.2

1. What are some of the diverse characteristics of fungi?
2. How do the different groups of fungi reproduce?
3. Critical Thinking Why do you think most fungi have evolved the ability to produce spores through both sexual and asexual reproduction?

Build on What You Know
4. Compare the reproductive cycles of fungi with those of funguslike protists. How are they similar? Different? *(Need to jog your memory? Revisit relevant concepts in Chapter 15, Section 15.4)*

What are the major characteristics of fungi?

Chapter 16 Fungi **383**

16.2

In the Community

To aid students in their search, tell them that many pharmacies arrange over-the-counter medications according to the illnesses, symptoms, or part of the body they are designed to treat. Antifungal medications would most likely be found with topical anti-infectives and first-aid products. You may want to review some of the uses of antifungal medications, such as in the treatment of ringworm, athlete's foot, and yeast infections.

③ ASSESS

Evaluate Understanding

List the names of the four divisions of fungi on the board. Ask:

■ **How did each division get its name?** (Zygomycota form zygotes; Ascomycota form asci; Basidiomycota form basidia; Deuteromycota are imperfect fungi.)

Then have volunteers list structures that are important in the reproductive cycles of the first three divisions under the appropriate heading. Ask students to describe each structure.

Reteach

Have students work in groups of three and provide each group with index cards. Tell students to choose one of the life cycles pictured in the section and draw each step on a separate card. Then have students mix their cards and exchange them with a group member who puts the set in the proper order.

CHECKPOINT 16.2 (cont.)

spores in asexual and sexual reproduction; sac fungi produce asci, but usually reproduce asexually by producing haploid spores; unicellular sac fungi reproduce by cell division and budding; imperfect fungi reproduce asexually.
3. Making generalizations Fungi have evolved the ability to produce sexual

spores so they can survive in unfavorable environmental conditions.
4. Both have alternation of generations and produce spores. Fungi do not have a mobile stage like funguslike protists do and protists cannot produce spores sexually.

① ENGAGE

Consider the Big Idea

Read aloud The Big Idea! which summarizes the main concept in this section. Tell students that this section will discuss some of the roles fungi play in the biosphere, including how fungi cause diseases and act as cures.

Use the Visual

Have students study the opening photograph. Explain that the matsutake mushrooms are somewhat rare and very expensive. Ask:

- **What other fungi are highly valued as foods?** (Truffles, discussed in the chapter opening story, and morels, shown in Figure 16.12 on page 381.)

Emphasize that although many fungi are used by humans as food, most fungi are extremely poisonous. Gathering wild fungi for use as food should be left to experts.

Teacher Demo

Display a piece of Brie cheese and ask students if they have ever eaten this type of cheese. Identify the layer of mold that covers the cheese. Explain that molds are a key ingredient in many cheeses and in other food products. Then tell students that some molds and other fungi also have unwanted effects such as spoiling food.

What you'll learn

IDEAS
- To describe the role of fungi in the environment and their relationships with other organisms
- To compare and contrast fungal diseases and appraise the importance of fungi to humans

WORDS
lichen, mycorrhizae

A good day's work

"It's a great harvest!" was the enthusiastic cry of the hunters who pull the treasured mushrooms from the pine and fir forests of central Oregon. One recent autumn, prized matsutake mushrooms gathered from these woods in only four hours sold for $1500.

16.3 Fungi in the Biosphere

ECOLOGICAL ROLES

Close associations

Fungi are key members of stable ecosystems. To feed, fungi break down organic materials, converting them into a form that can be used by the fungi and other living things. In this way fungi recycle the nutrients needed to keep communities alive.

In addition to their role in maintaining ecosystems, fungi often participate in symbiotic relationships with members of other species. Recall that symbiosis is a relationship between organisms of different species that live together in direct contact.

Lichens When a fungus and a photosynthetic organism "join forces," the entity that results from the symbiotic partnership is called a **lichen** (LY-ken). Among the lichens, the most common partnership is between a sac fungus and a green alga, or a cyanobacterium. The alga, or the cyanobacterium, provides food for the fungus through the process of photosynthesis. In this partnership, the photosynthetic organism provides the food, whereas the fungus provides the physical environment that contains the food producer. What kind of symbiosis would you call this relationship? ①

FIGURE 16.17
Below is a cross section of a lichen. Lichens like those shown in the photograph (left) can grow almost anywhere, including in caves and on rocks. What characteristics allow them to grow in such barren places? ②

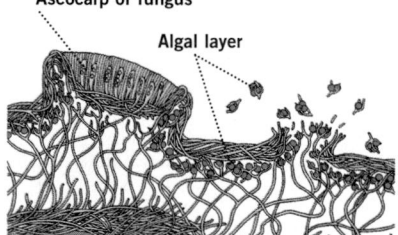

Ascocarp of fungus

Algal layer

384 *Unit 4 Monerans, Protists, and Fungi*

STUDENT RESOURCES

From the Teacher's Resource Package, use:
- Section Review 16-3, Activity Record-sheets 16-1 and 16-2, Enrichment Topics 16-2 and 16-3, and Vocabulary Review 16 from Unit 4 Review Module
- Issues and Decision Making 16-1
- Consumer Applications 16-1 and 16-2

TECHNOLOGY RESOURCES

Relevant technology resources include:
- Spanish Student Edition CD-ROM
- Teacher's Resource Planner CD-ROM
- TestWorks CD-ROM: Chapter 16 Tests

FIGURE 16.18
Which plant probably has
mycorrhizae associated with
③ its roots? The inset photo
shows mycorrhizae growing
densely around plant roots.

The ability to perform photosynthesis and absorb nutrients dissolved in rainwater and dew enables lichens to survive in extremely harsh environments. *Figure 16.17* shows one of the varied locations lichens inhabit. When lichens grow on bare rock they help break down the rock into soil particles. The large size of many lichens indicates that they are thousands of years old. In fact, lichens are some of the oldest individual organisms on Earth.

Mycorrhizae Fungi are not always "freeloaders" in symbiotic relationships. **Mycorrhizae** (my-kuh-RY-zee) result from mutually beneficial relationships between plants and fungi. Mycorrhizae form when the tiny hyphae of a fungus grow on and in the roots of a host plant. Over time, the mycorrhizae can account for as much as 15 percent of the total mass of the roots.

The fungus in mycorrhizae benefits from the relationship because it can absorb nutrients made by the plant— a photosynthetic organism. The plant also benefits. The hyphae of the fungus act as root extensions for the plant, increasing the ability of the roots to absorb water and nutrients from the soil. In addition, the fungus secretes digestive enzymes that help break down organic matter in the soil. The plant can then absorb the decomposed material as nutrients and minerals.

In their symbiotic relationship, the plant and the fungus can survive harsher conditions than either could individually. Plants with mycorrhizae also grow faster and are more disease resistant than those without mycorrhizae. Which plant in *Figure 16.18* might benefit from a mycorrhizal association?

Many biologists hypothesize that mycorrhizae were instrumental in the evolution of land plants. Today, more than 90 percent of tree species and 80 percent of all other plant species have mycorrhizae. Many trees and plants could not survive without their fungal partners.

DISEASES CAUSED BY FUNGI

Living rusts

As you have just read, fungi can be extremely beneficial to some plants. However, not all fungi have mutualistic relationships with plants. Some fungi act as parasites that cause disease. Fungal diseases can occur in both plants and humans, although their effect on plants is generally more deadly.

Plant disease In some parts of the world, disease-causing fungi destroy large amounts of harvested food crops each year. Parasitic fungi that attack grain crops include smuts and rusts, both of which are types of club fungi.

Dutch elm disease has killed millions of American elm trees. The fungus that causes Dutch elm disease was accidentally imported to the United States from Europe after World War I. The fungus, which is spread from tree to tree by bark beetles, is both a parasite and a decomposer. As a parasite,

FIGURE 16.19
Corn smut is a food delicacy in some cultures. In other cultures, however, farmers fear corn smut and wheat rust, because these fungi devastate crops.

Chapter 16 Fungi **385**

FACTS AND FIGURES

Puccinia graminis is a rust that destroys the stems of wheat plants. During part of its life cycle, this rust requires the European barberry as a host. To protect the wheat crop, the U.S. Department of Agriculture began a program in 1917 to eradicate the European barberry.

MULTICULTURAL PERSPECTIVE

Many fungi make already harvested food inedible. Food would often spoil as it was transported from the farm to market. In 1930, the problem was solved when African American truck mechanic Frederick McKinley Jones invented the first practical refrigerated trucking unit.

② TEACH

Discuss

Tell students that lichens are unique in their ability to grow and develop in regions that are too cold and barren to support of plant life. Lichens have become not only a pioneer species responsible for soil development, but also a primary food source of many large mammals, such as moose and reindeer, that inhabit these cold regions.

✳ Environmental Science

Scientists sometimes use lichens to study air pollution levels. Some species are extremely sensitive to air pollution and can be used as air pollution indicators.

Build Writing Skills

Ask students to write an essay about how symbiotic relationships can be beneficial or harmful from the point of view of a plant or fungus.

❶ Parasitism, since the fungi benefit at the expense of the host
❷ They can photosynthesize and absorb nutrients from rainwater or dew.
❸ The larger one
❹ The smaller one

LAB ZONE Do It! TEAM WORK

Does Moisture Affect Bread-Mold Growth?

For this activity, you may wish to provide students with freshly baked bread, which does not have preservatives and will show mold growth more quickly and in greater amounts than commercially prepared breads.

Analyze Your Results

1. Students should observe more mold on the moistened bread.
2. This observation should lead to the conclusion that moisture increases bread mold growth.

Class Activity

After students have conducted the Do It! activity, they can repeat the activity to compare how the use of preservatives in commercially prepared foods affects mold growth. Have students add equal amounts of water to a slice of commercially prepared bread and a slice of freshly baked bread. Use the results to discuss how different types of food preparation techniques are used to prevent food spoilage by fungi and other organisms.

LAB ZONE Do It! bioSURF

Does Moisture Affect Bread-Mold Growth?

You can compare conditions for growing bread mold when you . . .

Try This

1 You need two slices of bread. Moisten the surface of one slice with water, and leave both slices exposed to the classroom air for a few hours.
2 Put a little more water on the moistened slice and place the slices of bread in separate plastic bags. To keep the bags from touching the bread, insert plain, rounded toothpicks in the bread as needed. Seal the bags.
3 After four or five days, look for mold growing on the bread.

Analyze Your Results

1 Do you see mold? Is there more mold on one slice than on the other?
2 What conclusions can you draw about the effect of moisture on bread-mold growth?

the fungus feeds on and kills the elm tree. Then, as a decomposer, it digests the dead tree.

Human diseases Fungi also cause disease in humans. Like all fungi, fungal parasites obtain nutrition in order to live. Fungi that infect humans obtain nutrients from body tissues. As you now know, fungi secrete digestive enzymes into the environment and then absorb the nutrients the enzymes break down. When fungi release these enzymes into human tissues, the tissues often become irritated and inflamed. Irritation and inflammation are symptoms of infection.

Some of the more common fungal diseases in humans are athlete's foot, ringworm, and thrush, a painful mouth infection in infants. Scientists have not always known that these diseases are caused by fungi. What organisms might the scientists have ❶ originally suspected?

386   *Unit 4 Monerans, Protists, and Fungi*

HUMAN USES

From cooking to cures

Versatile might not be the first word you would choose to describe fungi, but it is an appropriate adjective. The beneficial uses of fungi are so varied that one type might appear on your dinner plate and another type might save your life.

Want a treat? Many edible fungi, including the matsutake mushroom you read about at the beginning of this section, are considered delicacies. The common button mushroom, *Agaricus campestris*, is popular for making sauces and salads. You may see other mushrooms, both wild and cultured, for sale in your local supermarket.

Although some wild mushrooms are edible, many are poisonous, such as the one shown in *Figure 16.20*. If eaten, such mushrooms can cause severe illness and even death. For this reason, gathering and eating wild mushrooms should be left to experts who can distinguish the poisonous mushrooms from those that are harmless.

FIGURE 16.20
This *Amanita muscaria*, also known as the death cap mushroom, is very common—and deadly.

❶ Answers may include bacteria and viruses.

Fungi provide many of the distinct aromas and tastes in our foods. The flavor of many cheeses results from the presence of fungal molds. An imperfect fungus, *Aspergillus*, is used in making citric acid and soy sauce. Perhaps the most widely used food-related fungi are yeasts. Yeast has been used around the world for centuries to make bread rise and to ferment beverages.

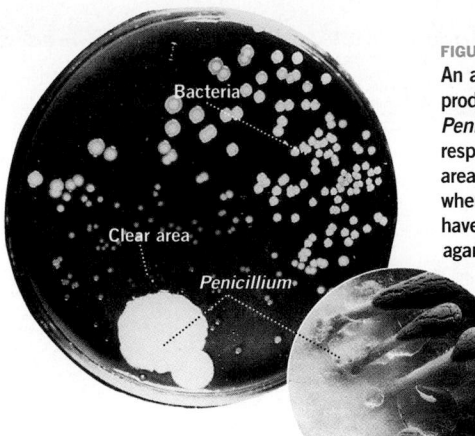

FIGURE 16.21
An antibiotic (penicillin) produced by the *Penicillium* mold is responsible for the clear area around the mold where bacterial colonies have been killed on this agar plate.

FRONTIERS IN BIOLOGY
Fungi in medicine

In 1928 an unexpected discovery involving *Penicillium*, a fungal mold that rots fruit, changed medical history. Scottish scientist Alexander Fleming was studying *Staphylococcus*, a type of bacteria that causes skin infections. He grew the bacteria in culture dishes containing agar and nutrients. One day he noticed that a *Penicillium* mold was growing in some of the culture dishes. In the area around the fungal mold there was a clear zone with no *Staphylococcus*.

Hypothesizing that the fungus had killed the bacteria, Fleming conducted more tests. His hypothesis proved correct. He had discovered a chemical that destroyed disease-causing bacteria. Fleming named his discovery penicillin, after the fungus that produces it. This important antibiotic has saved millions of lives. Penicillin prevents bacterial infection in wounds and promotes healing in burns.

Many other discoveries of antibiotics followed Fleming's discovery of penicillin. Today, most antibiotics are synthesized chemically in laboratories rather than isolated from living fungi and bacteria. The chemical structure of synthetic antibiotics is usually based on a natural chemical made by fungi or bacteria.

As you will recall from Chapter 9, yeasts are important tools in genetic engineering. Like their moneran counterparts, genetically altered yeasts are used to synthesize many important proteins. Moreover, yeasts are eukaryotes, so the proteins produced by genetically engineered yeasts may provide a better match for other eukaryotes—including you!

CHECKPOINT 16.3

1. What is the role of fungi in the environment?

2. Compare the general effects of fungal diseases on plants and humans.

3. Critical Thinking How do you think the discovery of penicillin affected those who fought in World War II? Explain your answer.

Build on What You Know

4. What characteristics do bacteria and fungi share as decomposers? *(Need to jog your memory? Revisit relevant concepts in Chapter 14, Section 14.6.)*

EVERYDAY BIOLOGY

A Fungus for a Headache?

Believe it or not, a parasitic rye fungus, called ergot, is the source of a drug called ergotamine, which can relieve migraine headache symptoms.

How do fungi act as decomposers and symbiotic partners of other organisms?

Explain

Explain to students that penicillin works by interfering with the formation of new bacterial cell walls as the bacteria reproduce. The new cell walls are weak and unable to withstand the pressure of the growing cell. As a result, the cells rupture, killing the bacterium.

STS

You may wish to have students conduct research on the work of Elizabeth Lee Hazen and Rachel Fuller Brown. Working together, they developed the antibiotic known as Nystatin, which is used as an antifungal agent. For their work, Hazen and Fuller became the first women to receive the Chemical Pioneer Award from the American Institute of Chemists. They were also inducted into the National Women's Hall of Fame in Ohio.

3 ASSESS

Evaluate Understanding

Divide the board into two columns, one labeled *Harmful*, the other, *Beneficial*. Call on students to cite the beneficial and harmful roles of fungi in the biosphere and record their responses in the correct column.

Reteach

Work with students to fill in an outline on an overhead transparency. Record the section headings and subheadings and have students volunteer key points that should be listed beneath each head.

CHECKPOINT 16.3

1. Fungi recycle nutrients by breaking down organic materials and converting them into a form that can be used by other living things.
2. When fungi secrete digestive enzymes onto human tissues, the tissues become irritated and inflamed. When fungi attacks a plant, it acts as a decomposer as it digests the dead plant.
3. **Identifying cause and effect** Penicillin saved many lives because it could fight bacterial infection in wounds.
4. Both bacteria and fungi act as recyclers by feeding on organic materials and converting them into a form that can be used by other living things.

TEAM WORK

Comparing Spores of Fungi and Green Plants

SAFETY FIRST!

Have students wear a laboratory coat or apron while performing this activity. Use only single-edged razor blades and caution students to handle the razor blades carefully. Have first aid available in case of cuts. Remind students not to eat anything used in the lab.

Lab Tips

It is imperative that the gill sections be as thin as possible. You may wish to demonstrate the procedure for obtaining the thin section from the mushroom gill before students begin step 1. Encourage students to make their diagrams as accurate as possible since the diagrams will be used to develop their conclusions.

Hypothesis Help

Have students review the life-cycle figures in Section 16.2, jotting some generalizations about spores in fungi. Then have them review what they know about spores in plants, also recording their ideas. Students can compare their notes before proposing their hypotheses.

Lab Extension

Open Ended

If you choose to have students conduct this as an open-ended lab, you may want to have them make slides to compare other structures of the mushroom and fern.

Time Required
■ 50 minutes

 **LAB ZONE** Investigate It!

Comparing Spores of Fungi and Green Plants

WHAT YOU WILL DO Examine and compare the external reproductive structures and spores of the mushroom and fern and design a related experiment

SKILLS YOU WILL USE Observing, collecting and recording data, predicting, experimenting

WHAT YOU WILL NEED A mushroom, a fern frond with spore cases, a single-edged razor blade, 2 pairs of forceps, a microscope, 2 microscope slides

Propose a Hypothesis

How do you think spores from plants compare with spores from fungi? Propose a hypothesis.

Conduct Your Experiment

1 Use a razor blade and forceps to cut a paper-thin section of a gill from the underside of a mushroom cap, as shown in the photograph above. **Caution:** Handle the razor blade with care.

2 Prepare a wet mount of the gill section. Examine the slide under a microscope set at low power.

3 Take notes on your observations of the mushroom gill and diagram what you see.

4 Remove a spore case from the fern frond and transfer it to a microscope slide. Examine it at low power.

5 Take notes on your observations of the fern spore case and record what you see.

6 Remove the slide. Using the other pair of forceps, gently pull open the fern's spore case.

7 Examine the slide again, and record your observations of the inside of the fern spore case.

Analyze Your Data

1 Describe any similarities you observed in the mushroom and fern spores.

2 Describe any differences you observed in the mushroom and fern spores.

Draw Conclusions

What characteristics were you able to compare in this experiment? From this experiment, what conclusions can you draw about the similarities and differences between the reproductive structures of fungi and ferns?

Design a Related Experiment

Suppose your teacher gives you another spore case and asks you to identify its source as either a mushroom or a fern. Propose a hypothesis, then design an experiment that will test your hypothesis.

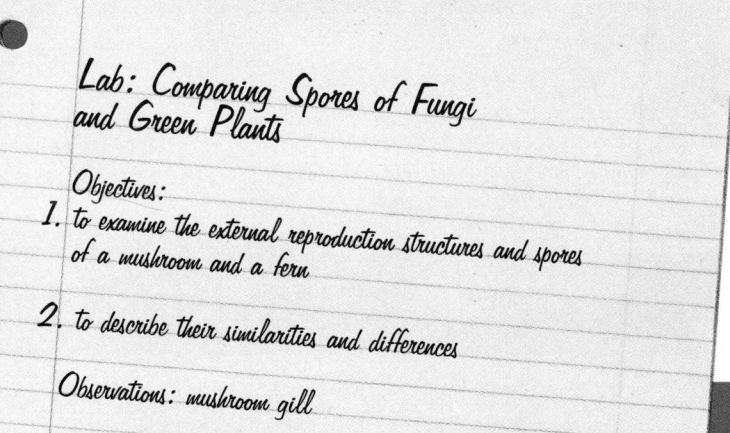

Lab: Comparing Spores of Fungi and Green Plants

Objectives:
1. to examine the external reproduction structures and spores of a mushroom and a fern
2. to describe their similarities and differences

Observations: mushroom gill

Analyze Your Data

1. Responses will vary and may include the size of spores and their location in gills or in a spore case. Also, many fern spores have a thick netlike outer coating and an outer marking shaped like a triangle.
2. Responses will vary and may include similarities in appearance and structure.

Draw Conclusions

Students are likely to find that the spores are similar in observable structrure, but may vary in size and appearance.

Design a Related Experiment

If the spore is enclosed in a sporangium, it is from a fern; if it is hanging from a basidium, it is from a mushroom.

Chapter 16 Review

 **16.1–16.2** Fungi are stationary organisms that live as heterotrophs.
16.3 Fungi act as decomposers and symbiotic partners of humans and many other organisms.

Sum It Up

Use the following summary to review the main concepts in this chapter.

16.1 Characteristics of Fungi

- Most fungi are multicellular organisms composed of individual filaments called hyphae.
- The bodies of most fungi are composed of interwoven hyphae called mycelia.
- Most fungi obtain nutrition by absorbing nutrients from dead organisms.
- Growth in fungi is usually very rapid because absorbed nutrients are efficiently transported to growing areas of hyphae; the hyphae of the mycelium share the same cytoplasm.

16.2 Origin and Diversity of Fungi

- Mycologists hypothesize that fungi evolved at least 400 million years ago from an ancestral protist.
- The four divisions of fungi are: Zygomycota (common molds); Ascomycota (sac fungi); Basidiomycota (club fungi); Deuteromycota (imperfect fungi).

- Some fungi are classified on the basis of structures used in reproduction: zygospore, ascus, and basidium.

16.3 Fungi in the Biosphere

- Many fungi are decomposers.
- Symbiotic relationships between certain fungi and algae result in lichens.
- Symbiotic relationships between fungi and plants can result in mycorrhizae.
- Fungal diseases in plants include smuts, rusts, and Dutch elm disease; fungal diseases in humans include athlete's foot, ringworm, and thrush.
- Some fungi are important to humans as a source of food, medicines, and eukaryotic cells for genetic engineering applications.

Use Terms and Concepts

Use each of the following words or terms in a complete sentence. If you need to review a meaning, turn to the page indicated.

hyphae (p. 374)   rhizoids (p. 380)   basidia (p. 382)
septa (p. 375)   stolons (p. 380)   lichen (p. 384)
mycelium (p. 375)   zygospore (p. 381)   mycorrhizae (p. 385)
spores (p. 379)   asci (p. 381)

Review the Big Ideas

Before students begin Chapter 16 Review, you may wish to review the Big Ideas with them. Explain that fungi are heterotrophs and have developed structures to help them feed on other organisms and move food quickly through their mycelia for rapid growth. Because of their ability to act as decomposers and partners with other organisms, fungi play important roles in the biosphere. Fungi are harmful to some organisms and beneficial to others.

Answers

1. hyphae
2. zygospore
3. rhizoids
4. stolons
5. mycelium
6. hyphae
7. mycorrhizae
8. lichen
9. spores
10. basidium
11. septae
12. True
13. False; enzymes
14. False; eukaryotic
15. True
16. False; yeast
17. A septum is a wall that subdivides a hypha. Some fungi do not have septa; each hypha is one continuous filament. Other fungi have septae with holes through which cytoplasm and organelles move.
18. Through the tips of the hyphae, fungi secrete digestive enzymes that help break down large nutrient molecules. They easily absorb these molecules to use for energy.
19. Growth takes place only at the tips of a hypha. Hyphae grow long but remain narrow.
20. Fungi appear similar to plants and they have cell walls.
21. Sexual reproduction in fungi involves the production of spores after the fusion of (+) and (−) hyphae.
22. During asexual reproduction of fungi, fruiting bodies produce spores. Each fruiting body has evolved efficient methods for spore dispersal by wind, water, and animals.
23. The parent cell divides and

390

Use Your Word Power

COMPLETION Write the word or phrase that best completes each statement.

1. Sac fungi reproduce sexually by means of a(n) _____ .

2. A(n) _____ is the diploid structure with strong walls produced during a common mold's sexual reproductive cycle.

3. The _____ are the parts of hyphae that anchor a fungus to its source of nutrients.

4. The hyphae that connect groups of rhizoids are called _____ .

5. The _____ is the body of a fungus.

6. The filaments of multicellular fungi are _____ .

7. Symbiotic relationships between plant roots and fungi result in _____ .

8. A(n) _____ is the result of a symbiotic relationship between a fungus and a green alga or cyanobacterium.

9. The reproductive cells produced in fruiting bodies are _____ .

10. Club fungi reproduce sexually by forming spores in a(n) _____ .

11. Some hyphae are divided into segments by _____ .

TRUE-FALSE Write true if the statement is true. If the statement is false, replace the underlined word to make the statement true.

12. The mycelium of a fungus consists of many <u>hyphae.</u>

13. Fungi digest their food by secreting <u>nutrients</u> into the food.

14. A mushroom's cells are <u>prokaryotic.</u>

15. A mushroom is <u>heterotrophic</u> because it depends on other organisms for its nutrition.

16. <u>Molds</u> are unicellular sac fungi that reproduce either sexually or asexually.

Show What You Know

17. Explain what septa are and how they differ among groups of fungi.

18. How do fungi obtain nutrition?

19. Explain how the process of hyphae growth makes fungi grow rapidly.

20. Why did scientists originally classify fungi as plants?

21. What is a common characteristic of sexual reproduction in fungi?

22. How do fruiting bodies function in fungal reproduction?

23. Describe the budding process in yeasts.

24. Why are the activities of fungi important in maintaining ecosystems?

25. Why might drought, cold, or lack of food trigger sexual reproduction in fungi?

26. **Make a Concept Map** Complete the concept map by adding the following terms: common molds, sac fungi, imperfect fungi, zygospore, basidia, asci, sexual reproduction, mycelium, septa, hyphae.

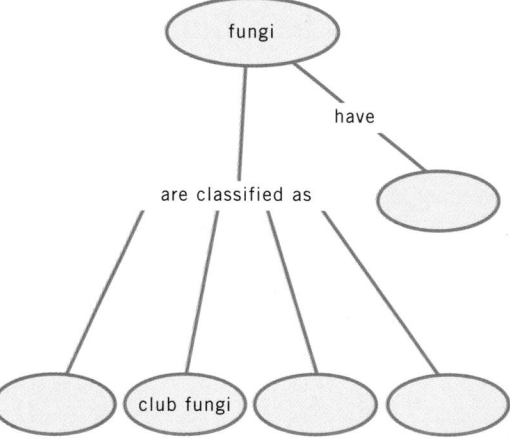

produces offspring by forming a small bud which separates from the parent.

24. Fungi break down organic materials, recycle nutrients, and participate in symbiotic relationships with other organisms.

25. Sexual reproduction in fungi may involve the dispersal of spores to a more hospitable environment.

26. Concept maps should show that <u>fungi</u> are classified as <u>common molds</u>, which produce <u>zygospores</u> during <u>sexual reproduction</u>; <u>club fungi</u>, which produce <u>basidia</u> during <u>sexual reproduction</u>; <u>imperfect fungi</u>; and <u>sac fungi</u> which produce <u>asci during sexual reproduction</u>. Fungi have <u>mycelia,</u>

Take It Further

27. Applying Concepts In which of the four divisions of fungi would you classify the fungus in the photograph below? Give reasons for your answer. What would you examine to verify your answer?

28. Interpreting a Graph The graph below illustrates the growth rates of four species of trees—two individuals of each. One tree of each species grew with mycorrhizae and one grew without mycorrhizae. For each species, how does the growth of the two plants compare? Make a generalization about the growth rate of plants with mycorrhizae.

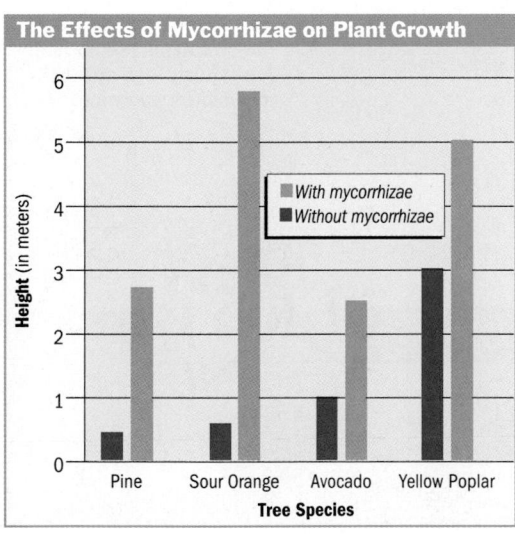

The Effects of Mycorrhizae on Plant Growth

Legend:
- With mycorrhizae
- Without mycorrhizae

Y-axis: Height (in meters), 0 to 6

X-axis: Tree Species — Pine, Sour Orange, Avocado, Yellow Poplar

29. Designing an Experiment Design an experiment to test the effect of mycorrhizae on plant growth. What variables would you control?

Consider the Issues

30. Mushroom Dilemma Suppose mushrooms of a poisonous species resemble mushrooms of a harmless, edible species. When people pick and eat the poisonous mushrooms, they become ill. Mycologists know of a chemical that kills the poisonous mushrooms, but its effect on plants and wildlife is unknown. Do you think the chemical should be used to eliminate the poisonous mushrooms? Explain your answer. Suggest some alternative solutions.

Make New Connections

31. Biology and History Ergotism is a disease caused by a fungus. Some historians have suggested that the Salem witchcraft trials in 1692 may have involved people with ergotism. Research and write a short story or skit about ergotism and the Salem witchcraft trials.

32. Biology and the Community What forms of fungi exist where you live? Find out if there is a mushroom farm in your community. Investigate fungi that harm crops grown in your state, and find out if the crops can be treated to prevent fungal diseases.

> **FAST-FORWARD TO CHAPTER 17**
>
> **Fungi are heterotrophs assigned to their own kingdom. In the next unit you will learn about plants—autotrophs that form the base of many food chains.**

poison is not a good choice because it is unlikely that the chemical would be harmful to just one organism. Mushroom gatherers could avoid picking both the safe and poisonous mushrooms. Perhaps a hand lens could be used to recognize a subtle but distinguishing visual characteristic.
31. Stories will vary.
32. Some possible sources of information other than the library are agricultural extension services, 4-H clubs, vocational schools, granges, and local produce markets.

---

which have <u>hyphae</u>, which have <u>septa</u>.
27. Club fungi; examine the gills on the underside of the cap for spore producing basidia.
28. The trees with mycorrhizae grew taller. Plants with mycorrhizae have a faster rate of growth than plants without mycorrhizae.
29. Answers will vary. Students would need

to control all variables except the presence or absence of mycorrhizae. Some possible factors are amount of water and nutrients; amount of sunlight; temperature; exposure to wind; same pH of soil. Ideally, the plant should be the same size and equally healthy at the start of the experiment.
30. Answers will vary. Indiscriminate use of

Connect the Chapters

1. Cysts and endospores are structures that remain alive but dormant until harsh conditions improve. Fungal spores are reproductive structures.
2. Like most fungi, most slime molds and water molds are decomposers of dead organisms. Both funguslike protists and true fungi can produce spores.
3. The fungus is dependent on the alga for its survival, as is the virus on its host. Viruses are capable of destroying host cells; lichens can survive for thousands of years.
4. Both cyanobacteria and diatoms are capable of photosynthesis. Fungi are heterotrophs. They get their food by decomposing other organisms.

Connect the Units

5. Both conjugation and meiosis increase genetic diversity in populations. During conjugation, genetic material is exchanged directly between existing cells. Meiosis produces gametes that may later combine with other gametes to produce a zygote.
6. The insertion of viral nucleic acids into the DNA of a host is similar to the process used by genetic engineers to recombine DNA from two different organisms. Monerans and yeasts are used for cloning genes.
7. Most archaebacteria live in harsh environments where other species cannot survive. Thus, they have no competition for resources (and little pressure to evolve).

Unit 4 Review

 **THE BIG IDEA!** Answering the following questions will help you to link ideas and grasp the core concepts.

Connect the Chapters

1. Some protozoans produce cysts. Some bacteria produce endospores. What do both structures have in common? How do these structures compare to the spores produced by fungi?
2. Which characteristics of slime molds or water molds characterize them as funguslike?
3. Compare the relationship between a virus and its host to that between a sac fungus and green alga in a lichen.
4. What characteristic do cyanobacteria and diatoms share? Would you expect any fungi to have this characteristic? Explain.

Connect the Units

5. What do meiosis and conjugation have in common? How do they differ?

6. Explain how the characteristics of viruses, monerans, and fungi enable them to be used in genetic engineering.
7. How might the niches that archaebacteria occupy have helped them to survive?

Connect to Themes

8. **Unity and Diversity** The kingdom Fungi is a highly diverse collection of species. What general traits unify this kingdom?
9. **Systems and Interactions** How does the addition of an enzyme change transcription in retroviruses?
10. **Evolution** What evidence supports the hypothesis that mycorrhizae evolved with plants?
11. **Systems and Interactions** How do bacterial, protist, and fungal decomposers affect ecosystems?

CRITIC'S CORNER

A BOOK REVIEW BY NORA CANNICK HILTON HEAD, SOUTH CAROLINA

The Hot Zone, written by Richard Preston, is a work of serious nonfiction. It tells the horrifying tale of people infected with two sister viruses, Ebola and Marburg, and of the doctors who treat them. The deadliest of the two viruses is Ebola. Ebola attacks every organ and tissue in the human body except skeletal muscle and bone. I enjoyed reading this book and finding out about two dangerous viruses that I didn't know much about.

THE HOT ZONE
A TERRIFYING TRUE STORY
RICHARD PRESTON

392

Connect to Themes

8. All fungi are heterotrophs whose cell walls are made of chitin. Fungi secrete digestive enzymes. All fungi are capable of asexual reproduction. Fungi maintain ecosystems by recycling nutrients.
9. Cells ordinarily transcribe DNA into RNA. Retroviruses contain RNA and the enzyme reverse transcriptase, which transcribes the viral RNA into DNA, which can then combine with DNA in the host cell.
10. Many disease-resistant plants that have mychorrhizae could not survive without their fungi, which increase absorption of water and nutrients from soil.
11. All decomposers are important to the ecosystem in that they break down and recycle nutrients from dead organisms.

SPOTLIGHT ON CAREERS

DR. KIMBERLY HOLDING
Epidemic Intelligence Service Fellow,
Centers for Disease Control and Prevention
EDUCATION: M.D., B.A. in biology

"I travel all around the country and the world studying epidemics. Working in the field is exhilarating. I feel like I'm doing something that will help other people. When I'm not traveling on a case, I'm assigned to the Division of HIV/AIDS Patient Surveillance here in Atlanta. We look at the numbers of AIDS patients nationwide by category, in order to target people for prevention programs.

My first job after college was as a secretary at a lab, and I gradually started doing some lab work, too. I guess I went from the typewriter to the lab to medical school!

Biology is great because it is a never-ending field—as long as there are cells in the world, there will always be biology to study. In science, everyone benefits from everyone else's knowledge, and you're always learning."

bioSURF Log on to *http://microorganisms.biosurf.com* where you can connect to the Internet site for the Centers for Disease Control and Prevention in Atlanta, Georgia, to find out more about epidemiologists.

KAREN BROWN
Scuba diver, educator, and photographer;
owner, Ocean Adventure
EDUCATION: B.A. in sociology; self-taught in underwater biology, photography, and education

"We try to show the students what it would be like to go scuba diving with us. . . . We don't hammer them on the head about ecology. We feel it's more effective to educate people about what the underwater world is like and show them that it's very beautiful. Conservation comes naturally from there. . . . As a diver, I would like to have something to say about the way sewage is treated. Pollution from sewage makes sea urchins thrive. And sea urchins eat kelp. Usually, they just eat dead kelp, but if there are too many sea urchins, they will cut the living kelp off right at the roots."

bioSURF To find out more about careers in ecology, log on to the Internet site *http://microorganisms.biosurf.com.*

"If people can try to learn as much as they can about something as small as the kelp forest, they can't help but appreciate it." — KAREN BROWN

Unit 4 Monerans, Protists, and Fungi **393**

SPOTLIGHT ON CAREERS

bioSURF Have students connect to the bioSurf Internet address to learn more about schools, educational programs, and scholarships that will help them prepare for a career or vocation related to viruses and/or monerans.

Consider These Careers

There is a wide variety of careers in the field of health care, almost all of which deal with pathogenic viruses, bacteria, protists, or fungi. Many of these positions, like medical records administrators, insurance examiners and medical assistants do not require a degree in medicine. People with special training in areas such as nursing and public health administration are in great demand. Health and safety inspectors work for public departments of health.

Plan for a Career

■ **Choosing a Field**
Have students consider the following questions: How do you think you would like to spend your professional time? Do you prefer fast-paced changes, or more a steady, predictable workday? Do you prefer to work indoors or outdoors? Do you like to travel, or would you prefer to stay close to home? All of these factors, and many more, should be considered before investing in career training. Suggest that students use a career guide, such as *What Color is Your Parachute?* to identify careers that would appeal to them.

Project Plans

1. Students would need to refer to the appropriate field guides for your region.
2. Students might want to compare their findings with data collected by your local health department or by the Center for Disease Control. You might also want to collect data on outbreaks of the common cold.

Critic's Corner

Have students read the review of *The Hot Zone.* Ask if any other students have read this book, and have them share opinions with the class. Encourage students to consider how the environment described in the book compares to environments with which they are familiar.

UNIT 5
Plants

Unit Overview

Plants are an essential part of the biosphere, providing food, oxygen and shelter for most other organisms. Plants exhibit all the characteristics of living things, including the ability to use energy, grow, respond, and reproduce. Vascular tissues enable plants to grow tall on land. Seeds aid in the dispersal of plants. Angiosperms, the flowering plants, are the most abundant plants and like all plants, evolved from nonvascular, seedless ancestors.

Unit Objectives

- Describe the main characteristics of the plant kingdom
- Discuss how plants use the energy from sunlight to grow and respond to changes in the environment
- Describe the structures of vascular plants
- Explain how reproduction is used to classify plants

Connect the Units

This unit discusses the structure, function, and ecological role of the members of the plant kingdom. A prior understanding of basic cell functions and energy conversions as presented in Unit 1 is essential to fully appreciate the concepts in this unit. If you choose to focus on environmental issues, you may follow this unit with Unit 9: *Organisms and the Environment,* or with Unit 3: *Change and Diversity.* If you prefer to focus on animal biology, you may choose to cover Units 6 and 7 before you begin this unit.

Which of these amazing statements about the world of plants are fact, and which are fiction?

Hit *or* Myth?

All flowers smell **sweet.**

(Fiction. When the titan arum at England's Royal Botanical Gardens bloomed in 1996, gardeners had to plan exits so that visitors could quickly escape from the flower's strong odor.)

Plants can get **sunburned.**

(Fact. During hot, dry, windy weather, plants can develop a condition called leaf scorch. The symptoms include withered, discolored leaves.)

You may find ferns on the menu at some **restaurants.**

(Fact. The tops of young fiddlehead ferns are considered a delicacy in some parts of the United States. If you see them on a menu and feel adventurous . . . *bon appétit!*)

Flowers never get bigger than about the size of a **dinner plate.**

(Fiction. The flowers of the rafflesia plant, which grows in Indonesia, can reach sizes of up to 1 meter across.)

A plant cannot control its **temperature.**

(Fact and fiction. Some plants can maintain a constant temperature while flowering. For example, the lotus flower keeps its temperature between 30° and 35° Celsius. Forty lotus blossoms produce about as much heat as one lightbulb.)

A **weed** inspired the invention of Velcro.

(Fact. Swiss engineer George de Mestral used a microscope to examine a cocklebur he removed from his dog. The pesky weed led to the idea for a fastener that uses tiny hooks and loops.)

Clothing can be made from trees.

(Fact. Viscose rayon is made of processed wood pulp, often from spruce or hemlock trees.)

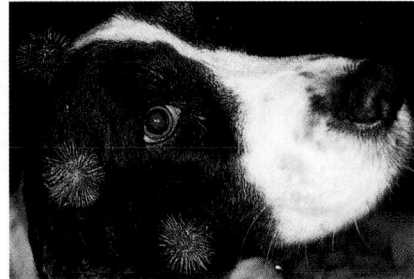

Unit 5 Plants **395**

Use It

Review each of the statements with the class. Ask students to share their prior knowledge and misconceptions on each topic. Ask them to consider which sources of information on these topics are generally reliable, and which may not be.

Link It

Chapter 17 links the components of plant cells and their cell walls (rayon) to their ecological niche. The structure of wood and the role of xylem in plant transport is also discussed in Chapter 18. Chapter 19 links the reproductive process of plants to the structures and characteristics of flowers (titan arum, rafflesia plant, Velcro) to their roles in the ecosystem, as well as their importance to humans. Chapter 20 links the structure of plants (fern) to their classification.

Expand It

There is no formal scientific definition of the word "weed," but it is generally used to describe rapidly growing, unwanted plants in lawns and other cultivated areas. Weeds are usually dicots, which are more sensitive to auxins than are monocots. Weed killers often contain auxins because they target the dicots rather than the lawn grasses, which are monocots.

Not only does the rafflesia plant have huge flowers, it has no stems or leaves. It is a parasite that buries fine filaments into the roots and stems of grape plants.

PLANNING GUIDE

Section	Student Activities/Features	Teacher's Resource Package
17.1 The Structure of Plants **Objectives** ■ Identify the main characteristics of and structures in leaves, stems, and roots ■ Compare the key functions of leaves, stems, roots, and flowers	**Lab Zone Discover It!** *Observing a Flowering Plant*, p. 397 **Everyday Biology** *Leaves Fall in Autumn*, p. 399 **In the Community** *Leaves, Stems, Roots*, p. 401 **Everyday Biology** *What's a Weed?* p. 402 **STS: Environmental Awareness** *Part-time Farmers*, p. 403 **Lab Zone Investigate It!** *Examining the Parts of a Plant*, p. 404	**Unit 5 Review Module** ■ Section Review 17.1 ■ Activity Recordsheet 17-1 ■ Interpreting Graphics 17 **Interpreting and Developing Graphics,** 49, 50
17.2 Plants in the Biosphere **Objectives** ■ Explain the role of plants in food chains ■ Summarize the variety of ways that people use plants	**Everyday Biology** *You Say To-MAY-to, I Say To-MAH-to*, p. 406 **Lab Zone Think About It!** *What Parts of Plants Do We Eat?* p. 407	**Unit 5 Review Module** ■ Section Review 17.2 ■ Enrichment Topics 17-1, 17-2, and 17-3 **Issues and Decision Making** 17-1 **Consumer Applications** 17-1 **Project Biology:** Project 14 **Biotechnology Manual,** Concept 7: "Flavr Savr™ Tomatoes: Genetically Engineered for Better Storage, Taste"
17.3 Characteristics of Plants **Objectives** ■ Describe the stationary existence of a plant ■ Compare the three types of plant tissues ■ Summarize the alternation of generations that occurs in plants	**Lab Zone Do It!** *Observing the Effects of Light on Plants*, p. 411	**Unit 5 Review Module** ■ Section Review 17.3 ■ Activity Recordsheet 17-2 **Laboratory Manual**, Lab 30: "Fruits and Seeds" **Interpreting and Developing Graphics,** 51
17.4 Overview of Plant Diversity **Objectives** ■ Discuss the diversity of plant size, woodiness, reproduction, and life spans ■ Identify some features used to classify plants	**Lab Zone Do It!** *Categorizing Plants*, p. 414 **Everyday Biology** *That Bread Is Really Stale!* p. 416	**Unit 5 Review Module** ■ Section Review 17.4 ■ Activity Recordsheet 17-3 ■ Vocabulary Review 17 ■ Chapter 17 Tests **Spanish Reviews** Chapter 17

Chapter 17 Introduction to Plants

Technology Resources

Internet Connections

Within this chapter, you will see the **bioSURF** logo. If you and your students have access to the Internet, the following URL address will provide various Internet connections that are related to topics and features presented in this chapter:

http://plants.biosurf.com

You can also find relevant chapter material at **The Biology Place** address:

http://www.biology.com

CD-ROMs

Biología: la telaraña de la vida, (Spanish Student Edition) Chapter 17
Teacher's Resource Planner, Chapter 17 Supplements
TestWorks CD-ROM
■ Chapter 17 Tests

Overhead Transparencies

■ Important Agricultural Plants, #35

Videotapes

Biology Alive! Video Series
Rewind: The Web of Life Reteach Videos

Planning for Activities

STUDENT EDITION
Lab Zone
Discover It! p. 397
■ whole plant with flower
■ hand lens
■ black paper

Lab Zone
Investigate It! p. 404
■ whole tomato plant
■ sharp knife
■ hand lens
■ small brush

Lab Zone Do It! p. 411
■ 6 plants of same species and age
■ 3 pots
■ marking pen
■ water
■ potting soil

Lab Zone Do It! p. 414
■ samples of wood and wood products
■ photographs or illustrations of plants

TEACHER'S EDITION
Teacher Demo, p. 400
Woody and herbaceous stems
■ variety of woody and herbaceous stems: potato or yam tubers, and iris, fern, or bamboo rhizomes

Teacher Demo, p. 402
Similarities and differences among seeds
■ seeds: include peach, apple, watermelon, various unshelled nuts, tomatoes, squash, and avocado
■ knife

Teacher Demo, p. 402
A fruit and its seed
■ variety of fruits with seeds: include tomatoes, squash, and cucumbers
■ knife

Class Activity, p. 407
Cereals in a diet
■ colored chalk

Teacher Demo, p. 409
Characteristics that make an organism a plant
■ flowering plant

Teacher Demo, p. 410
Plant cells structures
■ photograph, drawing, or model of a plant cell and an animal cell

Quick Activity, p. 413
Classifying by similarities and differences
■ screws, nails, and bolts

Teacher Demo, p. 414
How a flowering plant develops its seeds
■ flowering plant that has seed pods, flowers in full bloom, and buds
■ overhead projector

Class Activity, p. 413
Comparing fruit seeds
■ nuts
■ dry fruits
■ fleshy fruits

Class Activity, p. 415
Locating annuals, biennials, and perennials
■ illustrated seed and/or gardening catalogs

Chapter Objectives

Students will learn the main concepts of this chapter as they complete the following objectives.

- Identify the main characteristics of and structures in leaves, stems, and roots
- Compare the key functions of leaves, stems, roots, and flowers
- Explain the role of plants in food chains
- Summarize the variety of ways that people use plants
- Describe the stationary existence of a plant
- Compare the three types of tissues
- Summarize the alternation of generations in plants
- Discuss the diversity of plant size, woodiness, reproduction, and life spans
- Identify some features used to classify plants

Key Words

17.1 *blade, veins, petiole, taproot, fibrous root, flower, pollination, seed, fruit*

17.2 *cereals, cellulose*

17.3 *xylem, phloem, alternation of generations*

17.4 *vascular plant, nonvascular plant, gymnosperm, angiosperm, annuals, biennials, perennials*

The Opening Story

Have students discuss how the story might relate to the content of this chapter. Have them consider the structures and functions necessary to support such a large tree. Ask students to discuss how the giant sequoia compares with other plants.

396

You can find out more about plants by exploring the following Internet address:
http://plants.biosurf.com

In this chapter . . .

FEATURES

Everyday Biology
- Leaves Fall in Autumn
- What's a Weed?
- You Say To-MAY-to, I Say To-MAH-to
- That Bread Is Really Stale!

In the Community
Leaves, Stems, Roots

 Environmental Awareness
Part-time Farmers

LAB ZONES

Discover It!
- Observing a Flowering Plant

Do It!
- Observing the Effects of Light on Plants
- Categorizing Plants

Think About It!
- What Parts of Plants Do We Eat?

Investigate It!
- Examining the Parts of a Plant

History Written in World's Largest Plants

T
housands of tourists who visit California's Richardson Grove State Park each year peer into history inside the world's largest plant: the coastal redwood. These immense redwoods, called *Sequoia sempervirens*, or "evergreen" sequoias, are among the world's oldest trees.

Professor Emanuel Fritz of the University of California made an extensive study of a redwood. He had the trunk cut open to reveal the rings—a living record of the tree's history. In redwoods, each spring's growing season produces a ring of light-colored wood. Each summer adds a narrower band of dark wood. The number of light-dark rings provides an accurate record of the life of trees that may be as much as 3500 years old. Fritz found that the tree he studied had started to grow in about A.D. 730. Before falling to the ground in 1933, it stood 95 meters high and weighed almost half a million kilograms.

Scars inside a tree trunk can pinpoint the year a fire ravaged the forest or a disease struck the tree. By studying the scars, Fritz discovered the cause of his tree's death. Exactly 113 years earlier, a fire had so damaged the tree's trunk and roots that eventually the tree could no longer support its own weight.

Botanists learn about plants by carefully examining them . . . inside and out. What can botanists tell us about a plant's growth?

 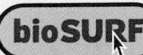 Discover It!

Observing a Flowering Plant

You need a whole plant with a flower, a hand lens, black paper

1. Observe the plant closely, and make a drawing of it. Label as many parts as you can.
2. Use the hand lens to observe the plant parts more closely. Make notes about their appearance and texture.
3. Tap the flower against the black paper. What happens? Observe the substance with the hand lens.

The substance that is released by the flower is pollen—small grains of protein that contain the male gametes for reproduction. All seed plants—including the giant redwoods shown here—produce pollen to reproduce sexually.

WRITE ABOUT IT!

In your science journal, write about how plants affect your life. Name the kinds of plants that are common in your neighborhood or community.

397

Opening Activities

 bioSURF If you have access to the Internet in your classroom or school, you may wish to have students connect to the address shown on page 396. You may also want to have students conduct net searches for information using key words related to the chapter. For example, they could search for entries under Garden Clubs, agriculture, and photosynthesis.

LAB ZONE **Discover It!**

Observing a Flowering Plant

TEAM WORK

Before students begin this chapter, have them do the suggested activity. You may wish to have students work in pairs. Have students share their observations about the plant's appearance, texture, and flower.

WRITE ABOUT IT

Before students begin writing, suggest that they discuss common indoor and outdoor plants with an interested family member or neighbor.

REWIND to Chapter 16

Briefly review concepts learned in Chapter 16, *Fungi*. Ask:

■ **In what ways might fungi be both beneficial and harmful to plants?**

397

Use the Visual

Have students study the stems of each plant shown in Figure 17.3. Ask:

- **What is the function of all the stems in this figure?** (Support leaves and flowers)
- **How is the tree stem different from the vine stem?** (Tree stem is woody, bigger, stronger, more protective.)

Teacher Demo

Bring to class a variety of woody and herbaceous stems. Include some modified stems such as tubers (potatoes or yams) and rhizomes (iris, fern, or bamboo.) Point out the nodes, internodes, and buds on each stem. Allow students to examine each stem.

Think Critically

Encourage students to think about the differences in flexibility between an herbaceous stem and a woody stem. Ask:

- **How is the flexible stem of an herbaceous plant a beneficial adaptation?** (Its flexibility keeps it from breaking in the wind, rain, or snow.)

Explain

Tell students that leaf arrangement on a stem is one way to identify plants. *Alternate* leaves are arranged in a spiral along the stem length. *Opposite* leaves oppose each other on either side of a node. Two or more leaves at each node form a *whorled* leaf arrangement. Show a variety of stems with leaves and have students identify them.

STEMS

Holding up the plant

Leaves do not function alone in a typical plant but are attached to structures called stems. Stems have two main functions: supporting leaves and flowers, and transporting water and nutrients within the plant.

Transport in stems is accomplished by some tubelike cells that carry sugars from leaves to other parts of the plant. Other tubelike cells transport water and minerals up from the soil into the veins of leaves and flowers. In a few plants, the stems also function as food storage places. A potato is an underground stem that stores a large amount of starch.

The arrangement of a plant's stems and leaves determines its overall shape. The size of a typical plant depends on the size of its stems. Based on their shape, size, and kind of stem, plants are traditionally grouped in one of four categories: herbaceous plant, shrub, vine, or tree. In *Figure 17.3* you can see examples of these.

Stems vary in strength. Herbaceous (her-BAY-shus) stems are nonwoody, composed of relatively soft tissue covered with a thin protective layer. The woody and strong stems of a tree or bush include its trunk, branches, and twigs. You can identify many trees and bushes by their stems even during seasons when the leaves have fallen. Vines have slender, woody stems that are usually supported by trees, posts, or other objects.

Leaves attach to stems at locations called nodes. The sections of stem between the nodes are called internodes ("inter-" means "between"). Compare the shapes and functions of the stems in *Figure 17.3*. How do they vary?

In most stems, growth begins in structures called buds, which may grow into leaves, branches, or flowers. Buds usually develop in regular patterns. For example, buds develop on opposite sides of a mint stem. On a sunflower stem, buds grow in a staggered pattern along the stem. The pattern of bud growth is an adaptation that provides a plant's leaves with the greatest exposure to light.

FIGURE 17.3

A Variety of Stems

Stem

Stem

Herbaceous plants

Stems

Vines

Trees and shrubs

MEETING DIVERSE NEEDS

Gifted Provide gifted students with illustrated field guides or taxonomic keys and illustrated guides to houseplants. Encourage them to identify the leaves collected by the class with both their common and scientific names.

❶ Answers may include length, width, and overall size.

Fibrous root   **Tap root**

FIGURE 17.4
Contrast these two types of roots. Describe their shapes. Which type grows more deeply into the soil? ❷

ROOTS

Stuck in the mud

In a typical plant, the root is the portion of the plant that grows below the surface of the soil. The two main functions of roots are to absorb water and minerals and to anchor the plant firmly. Some roots also store food.

Roots absorb water and minerals from the soil, an essential activity for a plant. Most of the absorption of water and minerals takes place at the root tips, which are covered with root hairs. Root hairs are tiny narrow tubes growing from the cell membranes of some root cells. Root hairs greatly increase the surface area that is available for water absorption.

There are two common types of roots, as you can see in *Figure 17.4*. One type, a **taproot,** is a single large central root with much smaller side roots branching out from it. Taproots can grow deep below the ground and "tap" the groundwater. If you have ever tried to pull up a dandelion plant, you know that taproots make strong anchors. You can see an example of taproot strength in *Figure 17.5*. Some plants with taproots, such as

Do field research near your home or school and find three or four examples of stems, leaves, and visible roots. Do not damage or remove the plants—record your findings with sketches and written descriptions. Record the names of the plants you know. In addition to houseplants and plants found outdoors, these basic plant structures may be no farther away than the pantry. Many of the foods that we eat are plants, and other kitchen staples such as spices are made from plants.

IN THE COMMUNITY
Leaves, Stems, Roots

carrot and beet plants, store large amounts of food, which they use to produce flowers and fruits. Gardeners and farmers usually harvest these roots before flowering occurs.

Another type of root, a **fibrous root,** is in the form of a clump of short, threadlike divisions. Fibrous roots often grow only in the upper few centimeters of the soil. They collect water and minerals from a shallow but wide area. Because the numerous roots wrap tightly around soil particles, fibrous roots are efficient at preventing soil erosion. Grasses are typical plants with fibrous roots.

FIGURE 17.5
Despite the prevailing winds that have made these branches grow sideways, this tree's deep roots anchor it firmly in place.

Chapter 17 Introduction to Plants **401**

In the Community

Suggest that students work with a partner when doing field research. Remind students to include illustrations and/or samples with their written descriptions. Students may wish to photograph the plants they research.

 Math

Most tree roots grow outward as well as downward. The roots of a tree 50 meters (164 feet) tall typically grow no more than about 2.5 meters (8.2 feet) into the soil. However, a tree this size may have roots that spread horizontally to a distance equal to the tree's height. Provide graph paper. Have students draw such a tree and its root system to scale.

 Health

Explain that the roots of many plants are good sources of vitamins and minerals that help prevent or fight disease. Root vegetables such as carrots, radishes, and turnips, and tuberous vegetables, such as yams, and potatoes are rich in beta-carotene, vitamin C, and potassium, all of which help the body fight cancer and heart disease.

SUPER READ! **Identifying Cause and Effect** To practice strategies for effective reading, use pages 55-56 in *Super Read!*

MULTICULTURAL PERSPECTIVE

Ask students to name a prepared food or dish that is popular in their culture or ethnic group. Have them identify the plant, its structure, and/or spices used as ingredients in the dish.

❷ The fibrous root is shallower and composed of many threadlike roots. The taproot is a single, deep root with some small hair-like roots.

Categorizing Plants

Analyze Your Results

3 Students may need guidance in estimating the size of illustrated plants.

 Language Arts

Have students define the terms *lignin*, *polysaccharides*, and *pectin* using a dictionary. Have students research the connection between *pectin* and *polysaccharides*. Ask:

■ **How is pectin used in food preparation?** (It is used to gel fruit jelly and jam)

■ **Where is lignin located in woody plants?** (It forms the woody cell wall, along with cellulose.)

Teacher Demo

Display a flowering plant that has seed pods, flowers in bloom, and buds. Use an overhead projector to show how the flowering plant develops its seeds.

Build Writing Skills

Have students write a short story in which a severe winter storm kills all the outside plants in their community. Encourage them to describe what their community would look like and what their life would be like without the plants. You may wish to have students share their stories.

414

 **Do It!**

Categorizing Plants

In order to categorize plants, botanists examine and compare plants. You can categorize types of plants when you . . .

Try This

1 Collect samples of wood and wood products—for example, sticks, children's blocks, or kitchen spoons. Collect photographs or illustrations of plants.

2 For each wood sample or wood product, decide if it came from a tree, shrub, or vine. Record your categorizations.

3 Estimate the actual size of the plants shown in each photograph or illustration. Record your estimates.

4 If the plants have stems, note their appearance and diameter. Record your observations about the stems of all specimens, leaving room under each entry for further data.

Analyze Your Results

1 Sort all the photos and illustrations into two groups: woody and nonwoody plants.

2 Test this hypothesis: Woody shrubs and trees tend to be bigger than nonwoody plants.

3 Use the categories you devised in step 2 to compare the sizes of plants to their kinds of wood products. Explain your findings.

WOODINESS

Some plants are harder than others

Vascular plants can be subdivided into various groups according to the characteristics of their stems. One of the most important and noticeable stem characteristics is woodiness. Wood is a substance composed primarily of layers of xylem cells. The cellulose in the cell walls of vascular tissue provides structure for the plant. However, cellulose is just one of the many structural components of wood. Other wood components include lignin and polysaccharides called pectic substances.

Woody plants are often described as trees, shrubs, or vines. Shrubs are typically smaller than trees, and vines have stems that are relatively flimsy. Examples of woody vines are grapes, blackberries, and climbing roses. Examples of shrubs include blueberry, rhododendron, dwarf spruce, boxwood, and roses.

Plant stems that are smooth and nonwoody are characteristic of the second group of vascular plants. Plants with nonwoody stems are called herbaceous plants. Herbaceous plants do not produce wood as they grow. Examples of herbaceous plants are ferns, zinnias, tomatoes, petunias, daisies, and birds-of-paradise.

REPRODUCTION

Flowers are just one way to reproduce

A plant's reproductive system is another characteristic used for classification. Based on their mechanism for sexual reproduction, there are two main groups of plants. One group, the seed plants, form seeds for protection and nourishment of the plant embryo. This group can be further divided according to whether the seeds are formed in a cone or fruit. A second group, the seedless plants, do not form seeds.

Mosses and ferns are examples of seedless plants. Plants of their haploid generation form gametes. Fertilization occurs in specialized structures in a haploid parent. The fused gametes develop immediately into growing embryos. The moss or fern embryo develops into a diploid offspring within the structure of a parent plant. For this reason, the embryo does not need to await favorable conditions before developing. What are some of the advantages and disadvantages of plant reproduction without seeds? ❶

---

❶ Disadvantage: offspring are not dispersed and therefore compete for nutrients; advantage: the plant expends less energy with no seed production.

As you just read, there are two categories of seed plants. A vascular plant that produces seeds enclosed in cones is a **gymnosperm.** Gymnosperms include pines, firs, spruces, cypresses, and redwoods. After fertilization occurs, the seeds of gymnosperms develop within cones and are released when the cones open. You will learn more about the life cycle of gymnosperms in Chapter 20.

A vascular plant that produces seeds enclosed in fruit is called an **angiosperm.** A fruit is a structure that provides a means for protecting and spreading seeds. Seeds usually do not sprout and grow until the fruit that encloses them has been removed from the parent plant.

Fruit exists as two types: fleshy and dry. Fleshy fruits, including apples, cherries, grapes, strawberries, tomatoes, and cucumbers, have a high moisture content. (Some of the foods we think of as vegetables are considered to be fruits by scientists.) Dry fruits include walnuts, acorns, wheat kernels, and the tiny parachute structures of dandelions.

You may wonder about reproduction in grasses, which are common herbaceous plants. Grasses are flowering plants that produce seeds. To maintain their lawns, most people cut the grass before it can "go to seed." Actually, mowing prevents the grass plants from developing any seed producing flowers.

FIGURE 17.18

Shopping for Plants

In nurseries across the country, people select plants to grow as houseplants or in home gardens. What traits might be important in determining the types of plants to purchase? ❷

Chapter 17 Introduction to Plants **415**

Class Activity

TEAM WORK

Divide the class into three groups: annuals, biennials, and perennials. Provide each group with illustrated seed and/or gardening catalogs. Have each group locate examples of annuals, biennials, or perennials. Students can cut out the plants they identified and create a poster or flyer suitable for advertising plants.

3 ASSESS

Evaluate Understanding

To assess students' knowledge of key features, ask:

- **How are vascular plants classified according to their stems?** (Woody or herbaceous)
- **How does reproduction differ among plants?** (Seed plants form seeds. Offspring of seedless plants grow directly from the parent plant.)
- **What specific feature is used to classify annuals, biennials, and perennials?** (Life span)

Reteach

Work with students to draw a Venn diagram comparing and contrasting vascular and nonvascular plants. Check that the key words used in the section are included in the diagram.

❶ Severe winters, floods, fires

416

LIFE SPAN

A day or a century . . .

The fourth feature used to classify plants is the length of time they live—their life span. Plants vary greatly in life spans. Some plants live for a matter of days, whereas others live for centuries. There are three general categories of plant life spans.

An **annual** is a plant that lives, reproduces, and dies in one year or in one growing season. Most vegetables and garden flowers are annuals. Most annuals are herbaceous plants.

A **biennial,** less common than an annual, is a plant that completes its life cycle in two years. Biennials usually do not flower until their second year. Biennials include garden flowers such as pansies and foxglove. Two other familiar biennials, carrots and beets, are usually harvested for their stems and roots during the first growing season.

A **perennial** is a plant that lives, reproduces, and continues to grow year after year. Perennials may be either herbaceous or woody. Some of the most familiar woody plants—trees—are perennials.

The life span of plants is determined by a combination of genetic and environmental factors. Many long-lived plants continue growing despite yearly environmental fluctuations. However, harsh environmental conditions can shorten the life of other plants. What kinds of weather conditions do you think adversely affect plant life? Have you had any experience with situations in which environmental conditions caused the ❶ early death of plants?

EVERYDAY BIOLOGY

That Bread Is Really Stale!

4000-year-old loaves of bread were found in ancient Egyptian tombs. Analysis of the bread shows that the Egyptians baked with emmer, a tough-hulled type of wheat. When the grain was allowed to sprout before it was dried and ground, it produced a more nutritious flour.

FIGURE 17.19
Bristlecone pines have one of the longest known life spans. Some of them are more than 5000 years old.

CHECKPOINT 17.4

1. Summarize the diversity found in plants' size, woodiness, reproduction, and life span.
2. Give examples of the way plants are classified, based on specific features.
3. **Critical Thinking** Propose a hypothesis to explain why angiosperms have become the dominant type of plant.

Build on What You Know

4. Annual, biennial, and perennial plants all have different lifespans. What types of niches do each of the three groups of plants occupy? Would the niches be different in different environments? Explain your answers. *(Need to jog your memory? Revisit relevant concepts in Chapter 10, Section 10.1.)*

What are four key features used to classify plants?

CHECKPOINT 17.4

1. Height varies from tiny mosses to tall trees, plant may be woody or herbaceous, reproduction may occur with or without seeds, flowers, or fruits, life span can range from days to centuries.
2. Based on woodiness, plants may be classified as shrubs, trees, or herbaceous plants.
3. **Developing a hypothesis** Their seeds are adapted for dispersal, and their vascular systems allow them to live in dry environments.
4. Niches are based on plant's longevity and productivity. Annuals provide food and shelter for other organism for one season; biennals for two seasons; perenniels year after year. Niches for all three are likely similar.

Chapter 17 Review

17.1–17.3 Most plants have structures that enable them to survive on land and produce food.
17.4 Key features can be used to classify plants.

Sum It Up

Use the following summary to review the main concepts in this chapter.

17.1 The Structure of Plants

- The basic structures of a leaf—blades, veins, and petioles—enable the leaf to function as an organ of photosynthesis.
- Leaves can be classified as simple or compound. Compound leaves can be further classified as pinnate or palmate.
- Stems support leaves and flowers. Stems also transport water and nutrients within the plant.
- Roots absorb water and minerals and anchor plants. Plants can have either a single large, taproot or numerous small, diffuse roots.
- Flowering plants reproduce by means of flowers, seeds, and fruits.

17.2 Plants in the Biosphere

- Carbohydrates produced by plants begin most food chains on land. Plants are also a source of oxygen for cellular respiration.
- Humans obtain 90 percent of their food directly or indirectly from 20 kinds of cultivated plants.
- Many plant extracts are used as medicines.
- Wood and cellulose are used for fuel, construction, and fabrics.

17.3 Characteristics of Plants

- Most plants have dermal tissues for protection, vascular tissues for transport, and ground tissues for all other functions.
- Plants are stationary; they depend on gases in the air and nutrients from the soil dissolved in water to survive.
- Plant life cycles alternate between haploid and diploid generations.

17.4 Overview of Plant Diversity

- The size of a plant is related to the presence or absence of vascular tissue.
- Trees and shrubs have woody stems. Herbaceous plants such as ferns and many flowering plants have nonwoody stems.
- Plants can be classified by whether or not they have seeds and whether or not they have flowers.
- Plants can be classified by whether they live one year, two years, or many years.

Use Terms and Concepts

Use each of the following words or terms in a complete sentence. If you need to review a meaning, turn to the page indicated.

blade (p. 398)	pollination (p. 402)	phloem (p. 410)	gymnosperm (p. 415)
veins (p. 399)	seed (p. 402)	alternation of generations (p. 412)	angiosperm (p. 415)
petiole (p. 399)	fruit (p. 403)		annual (p. 416)
taproot (p. 401)	cereals (p. 407)	vascular plant (p. 413)	biennial (p. 416)
fibrous root (p. 401)	cellulose (p. 407)	nonvascular plant (p. 413)	perennial (p. 416)
flower (p. 402)	xylem (p. 410)		

Review the Big Ideas

Before students begin the Chapter Review, you may wish to discuss main concepts from the Big Ideas in Chapter 17. Point out that special structures and characteristics enable plants to survive on land. Successful adaptation to a dry environment required plant structures to absorb and transport water, manufacture food, and reproduce the next generation. Plants can be classified by these specialized structures. Point out that understanding plant structures and characteristics, as well as the diversity and environmental role of plants will help students in their study of Unit 5.

Answers

1. alternation of generations
2. blade
3. Cellulose
4. Cereals
5. vascular
6. pollination
7. c
8. d
9. b
10. b
11. a
12. Veins in monocot leaves are usually parallel; veins in dicot leaves are usually branched.
13. Xylem is vascular tissue as is phloem. Xylem carries water and dissolved minerals; phloem carries dissolved sugar.
14. Fruits house and protect seeds and may also help disperse seeds to new locations.
15. Annuals live, reproduce, and die in one growing season. Biennials complete their life cycle in two growing seasons. Perennials continue to grow and reproduce for many years.
16. Taproots can reach water that is far below the surface; they provide a strong anchor for a plant. Fibrous roots can collect water over a greater but shallower area; they prevent soil erosion.
17. They have seeds, which allow the offspring of angiosperms and gymnosperms to remain dormant until conditions are suitable for survival. A species with seeds can be disseminated widely.
18. Both the haploid and diploid generations grow by mitosis. Only the diploid generation undergoes meiosis, to produce spores.

Use Your Word Power

COMPLETION **Write the word or phrase that best completes each statement below.**

1. The life cycle of plants is called _____ .

2. The _____ is the flat part of the leaf that contains the cells for photosynthesis.

3. _____ is a compound in cell walls that is made of long chains of glucose molecules.

4. _____ are the edible fruits or seeds of grasses.

5. Plants that have an extensive transport system are called _____ .

6. During _____ , pollen from male flower parts is transported to female flower parts.

MULTIPLE CHOICE **Choose the letter of the word or phrase that best completes each statement.**

7. Veins transport fluids between leaves and stems through (a) fibrous roots; (b) blades; (c) petioles; (d) taproots.

8. The plant reproductive structure that consists of an embryo and its food is a (a) flower; (b) cereal; (c) gamete; (d) seed.

9. The tubelike vessels in leaves that carry water, minerals, and sugar are (a) taproots; (b) veins; (c) vascular plants; (d) blades.

10. Plants that lack transport tissues are (a) vascular plants; (b) nonvascular plants; (c) perennials; (d) flowering plants.

11. The reproductive organs of flowering plants are (a) flowers; (b) cones; (c) fruits; (d) petioles.

Show What You Know

12. How do the patterns of veins differ in monocot and dicot leaves? Draw examples.

13. What kind of tissue is xylem? How does it differ from phloem?

14. Describe the structure and function of fruit.

15. Compare annuals, biennials, and perennials.

16. What are the relative advantages of taproots and fibrous roots?

17. What reproductive structure do angiosperms and gymnosperms have that mosses and ferns lack? What advantage is there to having such a structure?

18. What are the similarities and differences between the two stages of a plant's life cycle?

19. **Make a Concept Map** Complete the concept map below by adding the following terms: flower, xylem, phloem, gymnosperms, angiosperms, cones.

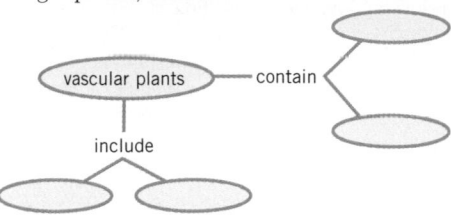

Take It Further

20. **Making an Analogy** What do short-distance runners, middle-distance runners, and long-distance runners have in common with annuals, biennials, and perennials?

21. **Organizing and Classifying** Imagine that you are serving on a committee for economic development in your area. Research some businesses and industries related to plants that the committee might want to bring into the area to promote economic growth. Take into account the area's climate, soil type, and available resources when making your recommendations.

22. **Designing an Experiment** Suppose you find some flower seeds in an envelope that has no identifying label. Design an experiment to show whether or not the seeds are those of an annual plant.

19. Vascular plants contain <u>xylem</u> and <u>phloem</u>. Vascular plants include <u>gymnosperms</u> which produce <u>cones</u> and <u>angiosperms</u> which produce <u>flowers</u>.
20. The increasing durations of the running events parallel the life span of the plants. An annual expends its energy in a single season before dying; a sprinter expends maximum energy for a few moments. By contrast, long–distance runners pace themselves to run over an extended period of time.
21. Plants could produce food, fibers, wood, medicine, or other materials.
22. The experimental designs will vary but should involve germinating the seeds to see whether flowers are produced during the first growing season.

23. Interpreting a Graph Many gardeners spread a layer of mulch—pine bark, wood chips, straw, or other organic matter—on the soil around plants. This graph shows one effect that mulch has on soil. Describe that effect. What conditions might have produced the changes shown in the graph?

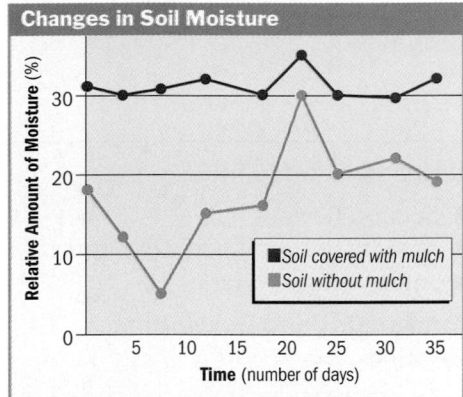

Changes in Soil Moisture

y-axis: Relative Amount of Moisture (%)

- ■ Soil covered with mulch
- ■ Soil without mulch

x-axis: **Time** (number of days)

24. Analyzing Data Examine these leaves and write a description of each. Classify each leaf according to its structure.

a   b

Consider the Issues

25. Production Versus Population Scientists are trying to develop new varieties of food crops that will increase the amount of food produced on a given plot of land. At the same time, the world population keeps increasing. Do you think it is possible to solve the problem of world hunger by increasing agricultural production? Explain your answer.

Make New Connections

26. Biology and Art Notice how one sixteenth-century artist used plant forms in a portrait. Consult art history books to find other works that use plants in fanciful ways, and then create your own "plant art."

Emperor Rudolph II (1590), painted by Guiseppi Arcimboldo

27. Biology and Economics Research how much wheat, rice, and corn are produced by the world's four leading nations for each crop. Why are there different production patterns?

28. Biology and Community: A Project Find out about the most important kinds of plants grown in your county or state, and investigate the ways these plants are used. Report your findings.

FAST-FORWARD TO CHAPTER 18

Chapter 18 will explore three topics that were introduced in this chapter: how plants obtain energy, how plants transport water and other nutrients, and how plants grow.

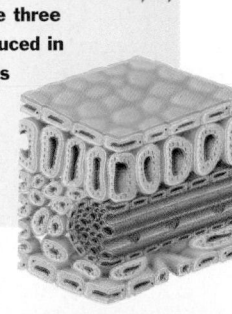

Chapter 17 Introduction to Plants **419**

of living, which usually correlates to a decrease in the birthrate.
26. Students' art work will vary.
27. Wheat– former Soviet Union, China, United States, India; rice–China, India, Indonesia, Thailand; corn–United States, China, Brazil, former Soviet Union: different climates and uses probably account for the pattern.
28. Students' work will vary.

23. The relatively steady moisture level in the upper graph reflects the ability of mulch to retain moisture in the soil. The changes in the graphs may be due to the presence and absence of rainfall or watering. Plants growing in the soil without mulch may die if the moisture in the soil drops too low.
24. In leaf *a,* the leaflets radiate from a central point. It is classified as a palmately compound leaf. In leaf *b,* the leaf veins are branched. It is classified as a dicot leaf.
25. Answers will vary. Students may argue that increasing production is a losing battle if population growth is uncontrolled. However, an increase in food production might raise the standard

PLANNING GUIDE

Section	Student Activities/Features	Teacher's Resource Package
18.1 Photosynthesis in Plants **Objectives** ■ Describe the structure of a leaf and identify where photosynthesis occurs ■ Explain the roles of sunlight, water, and carbon dioxide in photosynthesis	**Lab Zone Discover It!** *Experimenting with Leaves,* p. 421 **Lab Zone Do It!** *Observing Stomata and Guard Cells,* p. 423 **STS: Environmental Awareness** *Too much CO$_2$?* p. 426	**Unit 5 Review Module** ■ Section Review 18.1 ■ Activity Recordsheet 18-1 ■ Critical Thinking Exercise 18 **Interpreting and Developing Graphics,** 52, 53
18.2 Transport in Plants **Objectives** ■ Describe the structure and function of vascular tissue in plants ■ Explain the mechanisms of water and sugar transport in plants	**Everyday Biology** *Drowning Plants,* p. 429 **Lab Zone Do It!** *Observing Plant Transport,* p. 431 **Everyday Biology** *Where Does Maple Syrup Come From?* p. 432 **Lab Zone Investigate It!** *Observing Leaves, Stems, and Roots,* p. 434	**Unit 5 Review Module** ■ Section Review 18.2 ■ Activity Recordsheets 18-2 and 18-3 ■ Interpreting Graphics 18 **Interpreting and Developing Graphics,** 54 **Laboratory Manual** Lab 31: "Transpiration Rates"
18.3 Plant Growth **Objectives** ■ Explain where cells and tissues develop in plants ■ Compare two patterns of plant growth	**Lab Zone Do It!** *Measuring Root and Stem Growth,* p. 437 **In the Community** *Trimming Trees,* p. 438 **Lab Zone Think About It!** *Analyzing Tree Rings,* p. 439 **Everyday Biology** *Steady as a . . . Hammock?* p. 439	**Unit 5 Review Module** ■ Section 18.3 ■ Activity Recordsheet 18-4 ■ Enrichment Topic 18-1 ■ Vocabulary Review 18 ■ Chapter 18 Tests **Consumer Applications** 18-1 **Issues and Decision Making** 18-1 **Spanish Reviews** Chapter 18

CHAPTER 18   Energy, Transport, and Growth in Plants

Technology Resources

Internet Connections

Within this chapter, you will see the **bioSURF** logo. If you and your students have access to the Internet, the following URL address will provide various Internet connections that are related to topics and features presented in this chapter:

http://plants.biosurf.com

You can also find relevant chapter material at **The Biology Place** address:

http://www.biology.com

CD-ROMs

Biología: la telaraña de la vida, (Spanish Student Edition) Chapter 18
Teacher's Resource Planner, Chapter 18 Supplements
TestWorks CD-ROM
■ Chapter 18 Tests

Videodiscs

Animated Biological Concepts Videodiscs
■ Water Transport in Plants
■ Sugar Movement in Plants

Overhead Transparencies

■ Leaf Structure, #36
■ Root Structure and Vascular Tissue, #37
■ Secondary Growth of a Woody Stem, #38

Videotapes

Biology Alive! Video Series
Rewind: The Web of Life Reteach Videos

Planning for Activities

STUDENT EDITION
Lab Zone
Discover It! p. 421
■ potted plant
■ petroleum jelly

Lab Zone Do It! p. 423
■ small plant leaf
■ microscope slide
■ microscope

Lab Zone Do It! p. 431
■ two colors of food coloring
■ two containers
■ plastic wrap
■ white carnation
■ scalpel

Lab Zone
Investigate It! p. 434
■ live bean plant
■ microscope slides
■ scalpel
■ dropper
■ coverslips
■ microscope
■ safranine stain
■ paper towel

Lab Zone Do It! p. 437
■ seeds: radishes, corn, or peas
■ clear plastic or glass container
■ paper towels
■ ruler
■ permanent marker

TEACHER'S EDITION
Teacher Demo, p. 422
Plant adaptations
■ plants or photographs of plants with specialized structures

Teacher Demo, p. 426
Guard cell action
■ two long balloons
■ tape

Teacher Demo, p. 428
Crisp and wilted celery
■ crisp and wilted celery stalk
■ container

Class Activity, p. 429
Functions of roots
■ several plants
■ hand lens

Class Activity, p. 430
Monocot and dicot stems
■ samples of a variety of stems: celery, geraniums, lilies, and other plants or weeds
■ scalpel

Teacher Demo, p. 431
Water transport
■ turkey baster

Quick Activity, p. 435
Examining plants for growth
■ variety of plants showing new growth
■ hand lens

Class Activity, p. 436
Three zones of primary growth
■ prepared slides of a root tip exhibiting the three zones of primary growth

Class Activity, p. 437
Plant growth patterns
■ seedling plants
■ scissors

Teacher Demo, p. 438
Examining bark samples
■ bark samples

Chapter Objectives

Students will learn the main concepts of this chapter as they complete the following objectives.

- Describe the structure of the leaf and identify where photosynthesis occurs
- Explain the roles of sunlight, water, and carbon dioxide in photosynthesis
- Describe the structure and function of vascular tissues in plants
- Explain the mechanisms of water and sugar transport in plants
- Explain where cells and tissues develop in plants
- Compare two patterns of plant growth

Key Words

18.1 cuticle, stomata, mesophyll, compensation point

18.2 turgor, transpiration, pressure-flow hypothesis

18.3 meristems, primary growth, secondary growth, cambium

The Opening Story

Have students discuss how they think the story relates to the content of the chapter. Discuss plants that were once useful and became a problem in their area.

 Restating and Summarizing
To practice strategies for effective reading, use pages 51-52 in *Super Read!*

Identifying Cause and Effect
To practice strategies for effective reading, use pages 55-56 in *Super Read!*

You can find out more about life processes in plants by exploring the following Internet address:
http://plants.biosurf.com

In this chapter . . .

FEATURES

Everyday Biology
- Drowning Plants
- Where Does Maple Syrup Come From?
- Steady as a . . . Hammock?

In the Community
Trimming Trees

 Environmental Awareness
Too Much CO_2?

LAB ZONES

Discover It!
- Experimenting with Leaves

Do It!
- Observing Stomata and Guard Cells
- Observing Plant Transport
- Measuring Root and Stem Growth

Think About It!
- Analyzing Tree Rings

Investigate It!
- Observing Leaves, Stems, and Roots

The vine that ate the South

Experimenting with Leaves

You need a potted plant and petro-leum jelly

1. Coat the top of several leaves with a heavy layer of petro-leum jelly.
2. Coat the underside of several different leaves with a heavy layer of petroleum jelly.
3. Observe the leaves daily for one week. Record your observations.

In Chapters 4 and 17 you read about photosynthesis. What changes, if any, did you observe in the two sets of leaves you used in your experiment? How do you think coating the leaves with petroleum jelly affected the plant's ability to perform photosynthesis?

WRITE ABOUT IT!

In your science journal, write what you know about plant growth and reproduction. If possible, include examples from your own observations of your yard or community. Or, ask gardeners or people who grow houseplants about their experience with plants. Record what you learn.

421

The "mile-a-minute vine"—that's what people from the southern United States sometimes call kudzu (KUHD-zoo). Kudzu can grow about one foot per day; it is one of the fastest-growing plants that we know.

Native to parts of Asia, kudzu arrived in 1876, when it was displayed in the Japanese pavilion at the United States Centennial Exhibition. Americans liked its attractive, fragrant flowers and began planting the vine. During the Great Depression of the 1930s, farmers controlled soil erosion by cul-tivating acres of kudzu. In the warm, damp climate of the South, removed from its natural insect enemies, kudzu flourished—too well. It covered fences and buildings, choked trees, and toppled utility poles. In just a few years, kudzu came to be regarded as an annoying, destructive weed. Kudzu is difficult to kill, and one herbicide even increases its growth! Kudzu now covers more than 7 million acres of the South.

In Japan, where kudzu does not grow as well, it is used for a variety of products, including a cornstarchlike substance, herbal remedies, baskets, fabrics, and paper. The demand for these products in Japan could make kudzu a cash crop for southern farmers in the United States. It seems that the weed's new uses may gain it some respect again.

Although kudzu's growth rate is unusual, its life processes are the same as those of other plants. What are the life processes of plants?

PORTFOLIO PREVIEW

Students should be encouraged to add to their portfolios as they work through this chapter. In addition to the *Write About It* opportunity, the following sections are excellent opportunities for portfolio entries:

- Section 18.1: *Photosynthesis in Plants*
- Section 18.3: *Plant Growth*

Opening Activities

bioSURF If you have access to the Internet in your classroom or school, you may wish to have students connect to the address shown on page 420. You may also want to have students con-duct net searches for informa-tion using key words related to the chapter. For example, they could search for entries under forestry, plant propagation, or greenhouse effect.

LAB ZONE Discover It!

Experimenting with Leaves

TEAM WORK

Before students begin this chapter, have them do the suggested activity in small groups. Have each group predict what they think will happen over the next week. (The petroleum jelly will inter-fere with the function of stomata affecting transpi-ration and the exchange of gases. Without carbon dioxide, photosynthesis cannot occur.)

WRITE ABOUT IT

Students can record informa-tion in any format they choose; essay, outline, or graphic orga-nizer.

REWIND to Chapter 17

Briefly review concepts learned in Chapter 17, *Introduction to Plants*. Ask:

- **What are the main functions of leaves, stems, and roots?**

THE BIG IDEA!

① ENGAGE

Consider the Big Idea

Have students read The Big Idea! at the top of the page. Explain that plants need specialized cells, tissues, and structures to perform essential life functions.

Use the Visual

Have students study the photograph that opens the section. Explain that some plants have modified structures to maximize photosynthesis. Ask:

■ **Why is it advantageous for plants to increase photosynthesis?** (It increases food supply which the plant may need to survive unfavorable environmental conditions.)

Check Prior Knowledge

To assess students' knowledge about photosynthesis, ask:

■ **What part of a plant absorbs light?** (Chlorophyll)
■ **What occurs during photosynthesis?** (The energy from sunlight is used to convert water and carbon dioxide to oxygen and glucose.)

Teacher Demo

Display plants or photographs of plants with specialized structures—vines with tendrils, cacti with thorns, a Venus's fly trap, or a pitcher plant. Point out the plant modification and ask students to suggest an advantage of each type of adaptation.

18.1 Photosynthesis in Plants

What you'll learn

IDEAS
• To describe the structure of a leaf and identify where photosynthesis occurs
• To explain the roles of sunlight, water, and carbon dioxide in photosynthesis

WORDS
cuticle, stomata, mesophyll, compensation point

Making the best of it
Several adaptations for maximizing photosynthesis have evolved in plants. For example, in some plants, such as the one shown here, the undersides of the leaves have pigments that reflect escaping light back into the leaves for a second harvest. In other plants, transparent patches on each leaf's surface act as lenses to concentrate the light on the chlorophyll inside the leaf.

LEAVES: SITES OF PHOTOSYNTHESIS

Secrets of leaves

As you learned in Chapter 17, plants can make their own food from molecules of carbon dioxide and water, provided they have the right source of energy—light. During photosynthesis, plants transform light energy into the chemical bonds in glucose and other compounds.

Photosynthesis occurs primarily inside the green leaves of plants. (In mosses, photosynthesis occurs in the green leaflike structures.) Although photosynthesis is the main function of leaves, it is not their only function. In some plants, leaves also store food.

Figure 18.1 includes a micrograph and a drawing that show a typical leaf. Recall that a leaf consists of a flat, broad blade and a stemlike petiole that

FIGURE 18.1

Leaf Structure

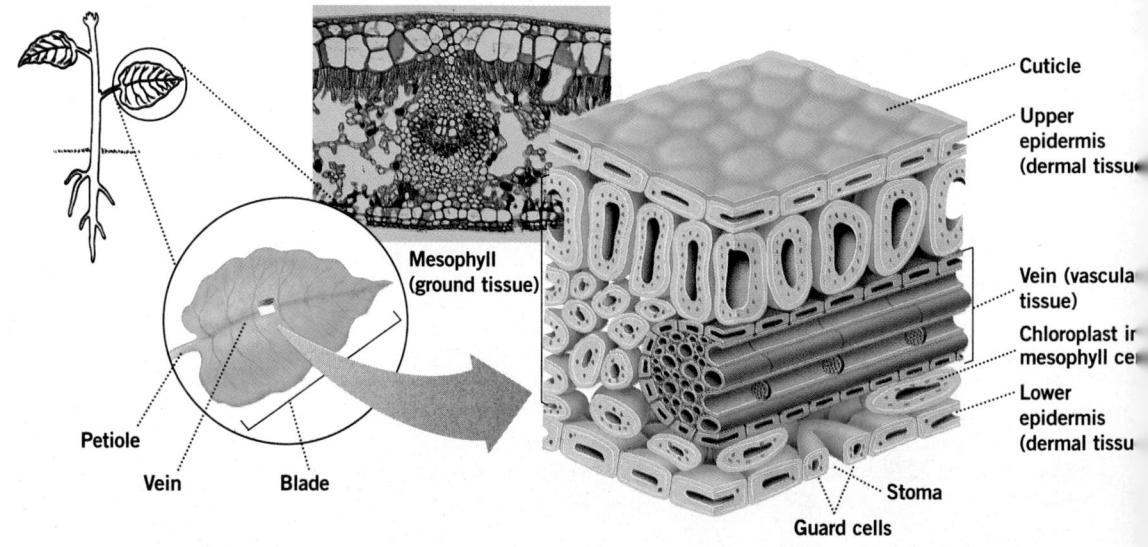

Petiole

Vein   Blade

Mesophyll (ground tissue)

Cuticle

Upper epidermis (dermal tissue)

Vein (vascular tissue)

Chloroplast in mesophyll cell

Lower epidermis (dermal tissue)

Stoma

Guard cells

attaches the blade to the stem. Internally, leaves contain the same three types of tissue—dermal, ground, and vascular—as stems and roots.

A leaf epidermis has two specialized structures that are adaptations for photosynthesis on land: the waxy cuticle and the stomata (stoh-MAH-tuh). The **cuticle** is a waterproof layer that coats the parts of the plant exposed to the air. This waxy covering helps conserve water by slowing evaporation. You can use your fingernail to scrape off the thick cuticle of some plants, such as the wax palm. The cuticle from the wax palm is called carnauba wax and is used to make polishes, candles, and lipstick.

The **stomata** (singular: *stoma*) are pores, or holes, in the epidermis that allow gas exchange. In the leaf shown in *Figure 18.1,* the stomata are on the underside. Stomata allow carbon dioxide to enter a leaf, and water vapor and oxygen to diffuse out. Guard cells like those shown in *Figure 18.2* surround each stoma. The guard cells open or close the stomata, depending on environmental conditions and the needs of the plant. In general, stomata are open during the day and closed at night.

FIGURE 18.2

When a pair of guard cells open to form a pore, or stoma, water vapor and oxygen diffuse from the leaf. What substance enters the leaf through the stoma? ❶

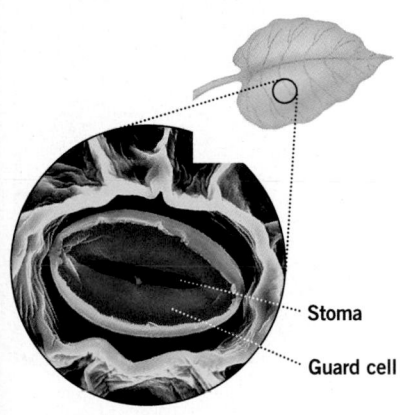

Stoma

Guard cell

LAB ZONE Do It! bioSURF

Observing Stomata and Guard Cells

Some of the raw materials and products of photosynthesis enter and exit through stomata in leaves. Guard cells open or close the stomata depending on environmental conditions. Watch how guard cells work when you . . .

Try This

1 Cut a small leaf from a plant. (Plants with smooth leaves work best.) Place it on a slide. Examine the underside of the leaf with the microscope on low and high power.
2 Identify and sketch a stoma and its guard cells.
3 What conditions could you manipulate to change the size of the stoma? Design an experiment that involves changing one environmental condition.
4 Record the appearance of the stoma and guard cells again. Then implement your idea for altering the leaf's environmental conditions. Record any changes you observe.

Analyze Your Results

1 What happened when you changed the leaf's environmental conditions? Why?
2 If the guard cells did not react, how might you change your procedure to produce a response?

If you look more closely at the cutaway section in *Figure 18.1,* you will see that there is a region of ground tissue between the two layers of epidermis. This region, called the **mesophyll,** is a tissue made of parenchyma cells (pah-REN-kih-muh). Parenchyma cells are the most abundant and least specialized type of plant cells. Air spaces make up 20 to 70 percent of the volume of the mesophyll. The air spaces allow carbon dioxide and oxygen gases to be exchanged inside the leaf.

The mesophyll is the part of the leaf where most photosynthesis takes place. Cells in the mesophyll contain hundreds of tiny green structures called chloroplasts. Inside each chloroplast are thousands of chlorophyll molecules that capture the sun's energy.

Chapter 18 Energy, Transport, and Growth in Plants **423**

---

2 TEACH

Use the Visual

Have students study Figures 18.1 and 18.2. Explain that most photosynthesis occurs in the leaves, so leaf structure is important. Ask:

- **What makes up the surface layer of the leaf?** (The cuticle and epidermis)
- **Where are the stomata located?** (Underside of the leaf)
- **What is the relationship between the guard cells and the stomata?** (Guard cells open or close stomata.)
- **In what layer do you think most of the photosynthesis takes place? Why?** (The mesophyll because many chloroplasts are located here)

LAB ZONE Do It! TEAM WORK

Observing Stomata and Guard Cells

Try This

Use leaves with large, easily visible stomata for this activity. A second option is to have students use a strong hand lens to observe the stomata.

Analyze Your Results

1 Leaves separated from plant may not respond to environmental changes.
2 Keep leaves on plant and change conditions for whole plant.

MEETING DIVERSE NEEDS

LEP In discussing key terms used throughout the chapter, encourage students whose first language is a Romance language to share words in their language that use the same roots. For example, in Spanish: *vascular*/vascular; *cutis*/skin, complexion; and *dermatologia*/dermatology.

Sight Impaired Provide leaves from a variety of plants. Have students work together to describe where plant structures are located.

❶ Carbon dioxide

Discuss

Write out the chemical reaction for photosynthesis on the board: Water + carbon dioxide + sunlight yields oxygen + simple sugars. Discuss with students how the different structures in the leaf play a role in photosynthesis. If necessary, have students review the main steps of photosynthesis described on pages 85-89.

Clarify Misconceptions

Students may think that photosynthesis takes place only in plant cells and that respiration takes place only in animal cells. Stress that both animal cells and plant cells use the process of respiration to release energy.

Use the Visual

Discuss the plants shown in Figure 18.3. Ask students to suggest other plants that require different amounts of sunlight. Encourage them to draw on personal observations of houseplants, gardens, or plants in wilderness areas. Ask:

- **Which of these plants do you think require direct sunlight?** (Answers will depend on students' observations.)
- **Which plants do you think require the least amount of sunlight?** (Answers will depend on students' observations.)

As you learned in Chapter 17, leaves have a network of tubelike structures called veins. Veins are made of vascular tissue arranged in bundles. Like other vascular tissue, veins in leaves transport water and food. Water moves from the veins to the mesophyll cells, which transport sugar to back to the veins. Veins have an outer layer of cells called the bundle sheath. In some plants, photosynthesis occurs in the bundle sheath as well as in the mesophyll.

FACTORS AFFECTING PHOTOSYNTHESIS

A simple threesome

As you learned in Chapter 4, in nature photosynthesis requires three key factors: energy from the sun, water, and carbon dioxide.

Light Photosynthesis takes place in two stages. It begins with a light-trapping stage that occurs only when the sun or artificial light shines on the plant. Chlorophyll and other photosynthetic pigments in the plant act as "light antennas," absorbing light energy and transforming it into chemical energy. Oxygen is given off during the light-trapping stage.

The second stage, called the Calvin cycle, does not need light to proceed. The Calvin cycle uses stored energy and certain compounds made during the light reactions to convert carbon dioxide into simple sugars such as glucose.

In addition to carrying out photosynthesis, plants also respire. Cellular respiration is the breakdown of molecules such as glucose into simpler molecules such as carbon dioxide and water. Cellular respiration provides energy for plants. Plants use the energy released from breaking down glucose to grow, reproduce, and synthesize essential compounds. The waste products of cellular respiration in plants are the same as those in animals—carbon dioxide and water.

As you may have guessed, plants perform both processes simultaneously: they make glucose by photosynthesis and utilize the glucose for energy at the same time. The net amount of sugar made by a plant depends on several factors, including the plant's rate of

FIGURE 18.3

Sugar cane (left), a tropical grass, requires lots of sunlight. How would the light requirements of the plants that grow under redwood trees compare to the light requirements of sugar cane? ❶

FACTS AND FIGURES

The rate of photosynthesis is reduced greatly at very low or very high temperatures. The intensity of light, however, is not usually a limiting factor in photosynthesis. In most plants, the maximum amount of photosynthesis takes place in 20 to 25 percent of full sunlight.

❶ Sugar cane requires full sunlight most of the day. Plants under redwoods can grow in filtered sunlight or shade.

❷ The plant will not flourish, will reproduce poorly or not at all, and may die.

cellular respiration. One factor that affects the production of sugar is the amount of available light. The **compensation point** is the amount of light energy, captured through photosynthesis, that will just keep a plant alive.

You can think of the compensation point as the amount of light energy needed by a plant to balance its energy needs. If the sugar made by photosynthesis just balances the sugar used by the plant to stay alive, there is no net energy gain or loss. If a plant makes more sugar than it uses, the plant gains energy. Plants can store this excess energy or use it for growth. If a plant uses more sugar than it makes, there is a net energy loss for the plant. What do you think happens if a plant receives less sunlight than its compensation point over a long period of time?

The amount of sunlight required for specific plants to reach their compensation point varies. Some plants, such as sugar cane and other tropical grasses, need a great deal of light and grow best in full sunlight. Other plants, such as ivy and azaleas, need only a moderate amount of sunlight. They can grow in the shade. Some garden plants are designated shade-loving plants.

Many shade plants grow beneath the larger trees of a mature forest, along with younger trees. Shade plants and young trees grow relatively slowly when light is scarce. However, after old trees fall or are cut down, more light can reach the forest floor. Smaller shade plants may then grow more quickly, reaching their full height and width. Young trees may also begin to approach their full potential size.

Water As mentioned previously, water is a key ingredient for photosynthesis. Plants need water to complete the first stage of photosynthesis—the light-trapping reactions.

FIGURE 18.4
Van Helmont's Experiment

Year one
Van Helmont planted a 2-kg willow tree in about 90 kg of soil.

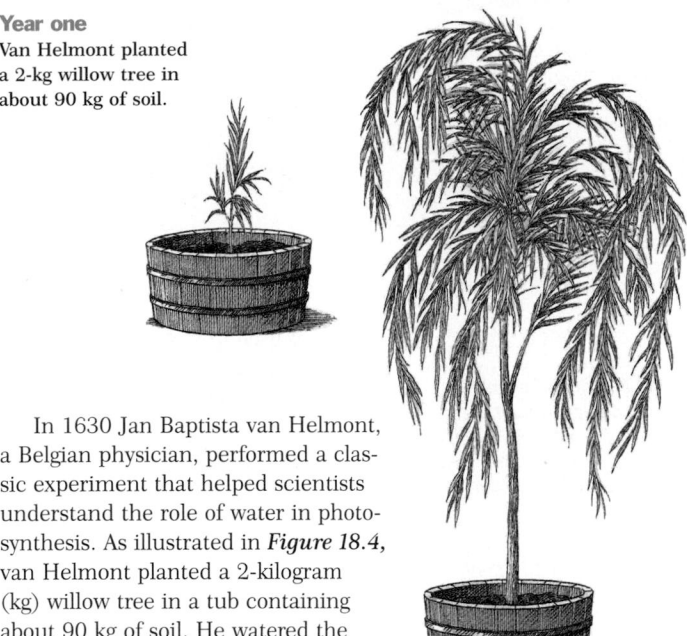

Year five
After five years, the tree gained 75 kg, and the soil lost about 55 g.

In 1630 Jan Baptista van Helmont, a Belgian physician, performed a classic experiment that helped scientists understand the role of water in photosynthesis. As illustrated in *Figure 18.4*, van Helmont planted a 2-kilogram (kg) willow tree in a tub containing about 90 kg of soil. He watered the tree with rainwater for five years, and then he weighed the tree and the dried-out soil. The tree had gained about 75 kg, whereas the soil had lost only about 55 grams (g). (Recall that 1000 g make up 1 kg, so the loss in the soil's weight was extremely small.)

Van Helmont concluded that the tree's growth was due almost exclusively to the water that had been added to the soil. But he was only partly right. Van Helmont had neglected to consider that a substance from the air (carbon dioxide) might also affect the plant's weight. However, van Helmont did show that soil does not contribute very much to the new material of a growing plant.

Van Helmont's experiment illustrates the way scientific knowledge is sometimes gained. When researchers investigate an unknown event, they may discover the explanation a step at a time. Today, scientists know that about 90 percent of the water taken in

Chapter 18 Energy, Transport, and Growth in Plants **425**

Explain

Before reviewing the text on van Helmont's experiment, ask:

■ **How does a plant obtain the energy needed for growth?** (The products of photosynthesis are used in respiration. The energy released in respiration is used for growth.)

Tell students that today van Helmont's experiment may seem simple and obvious. Help students appreciate its importance by putting van Helmont's work in perspective. Explain that in 1630 carbon dioxide had not yet been identified and would not be discovered until the next century (1756). The light and dark reactions of photosynthesis were not identified until the discovery of the Calvin cycle in 1950.

Use the Visual

Direct students to Figure 18.4 and discuss van Helmont's experiment and results. Ask:

■ **What do you think van Helmont was trying to learn?** (The roles soil and water played in plant growth)
■ **What did van Helmont's experiment show?** (The soil contributed very little to the tree's gain in mass.)

Think Critically

Ask students why van Helmont did not consider air as a contributor of mass to a growing plant. (Students may suggest that van Helmont was focused on water and soil and did not consider that air has mass which might contribute to the change in the tree's mass.)

Gifted Have students compare the growth of plants over a period of time in a closed environment. Grow one set of plants in soil, the other hydroponically. Control the amount of nutrients and water given to each plant. Encase all the plants in a plastic sack. Have students prepare a log and a brief oral report describing the results of the experiment.

FIGURE 18.5
When water (H_2O) enters the guard cells of a leaf, they swell, opening the stoma, or pore. When guard cells lose water, they become limp, closing the stoma. What is the role of the stoma? ❶

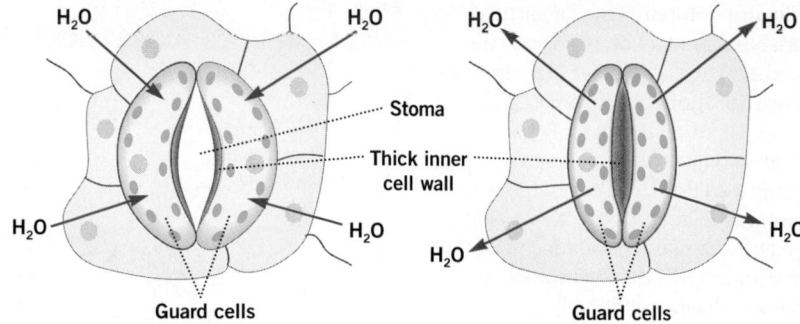

FIGURE 18.6
In 1782 Jean Senebier used an experiment like the one illustrated here to show that photosynthesis requires carbon dioxide (CO_2).

Without CO_2
Leaves placed in water that does not contain CO_2 give off no O_2 when exposed to sunlight.

With CO_2
Leaves placed in water that contains CO_2 give off O_2 when exposed to sunlight.

by plants is lost through evaporation and is not used in photosynthesis. Consequently, most of the water absorbed by the plant does not add to the plant's mass.

Scientists also now know that the amount of water in a plant is controlled by the opening and closing of the stomata through the action of guard cells. Exactly how does this occur?

Look at the pair of guard cells surrounding each stoma, or pore, shown in *Figure 18.5*. As you can see, the cell walls nearest the pore are thicker than the cell walls on the opposite side. When water is abundant in a plant, the two guard cells expand and their thin outer walls are forced into a curved shape. This action causes the thick inner walls to be pulled away from each other, and the stoma opens wider. When water is scarce in the plant, the guard cells shrink. The thick inner walls are not pulled away from each other, and the stoma becomes smaller or closes.

Overall, the availability of water affects photosynthesis in two ways. First, water is needed as a raw material for the reactions that trap light energy. Second, enough water must be available to keep the guard cells full so the stomata in the leaves will stay open. When the stomata close, carbon dioxide cannot enter the leaves, and the plant is rapidly depleted of

another key ingredient for photosynthesis: carbon dioxide.

Carbon dioxide Carbon dioxide (CO_2) is the third key factor for photosynthesis. As you may recall, CO_2 is used to make simple sugars during the Calvin cycle.

Although many scientists have studied the role of CO_2 in photosynthesis, French scientist Jean Senebier performed a crucial experiment in 1782. As shown in *Figure 18.6*, he placed cut leaves in a solution of carbonated water (water mixed with CO_2). When the leaves were exposed to sunlight, they produced what Senebier called "pure air." We now know that Senebier observed oxygen (O_2). However, when Senebier put cut leaves into water without CO_2 and exposed those leaves to sunlight, they did not produce O_2. From this experiment and others he performed, Senebier concluded that leaves use CO_2 in a process that requires sunlight and produces O_2.

ENVIRONMENTAL AWARENESS

Too much CO_2?

There is more carbon dioxide (CO_2) in the air today than there was in the late 1800s. In 1870, CO_2 concentration in the air was about 270 parts per million (ppm); now the concentration is about 360 ppm. Much of the additional CO_2 is from the burning of wood and fossil fuels. We use the energy in these fuels for nearly all of our present-day activities.

The CO_2 in the atmosphere traps heat in almost the same way that the glass roof and sides of a greenhouse do. The heat-trapping action of CO_2 in the atmosphere is called the greenhouse effect. The greenhouse effect is natural. Without it the temperature of the surface of Earth would average only –18°C. But if the level of CO_2 in the atmosphere increases, the greenhouse effect intensifies.

An intensified greenhouse effect may lead to global warming. Global warming is an increase in Earth's temperature from the rapid buildup of CO_2 and other greenhouse gases. What do you think might result from ❷ global warming? Although all scientists do not agree that the problem is serious, many are concerned. Some researchers are asking whether we should try to restore the balance of oxygen and CO_2 in the atmosphere, and if so, how.

To more fully understand the impact of the greenhouse effect, some scientists are investigating the capacity of plants to take in more CO_2 than is currently in the air. If plants can take in more CO_2 than the current amounts and remain healthy, then these plants may be able to reduce the amount of CO_2 in the atmosphere.

Researchers have already discovered that some plants, including certain crops, do appear to grow larger and produce more leaves and fruit when they are exposed to higher levels of CO_2 than are now present in the air. During tests performed in Arizona with sour orange trees and cotton plants, high CO_2 levels increased the crop yields 10 to 15 percent. Some researchers think that exposure to higher CO_2 levels will cause major

crops such as wheat and rice to produce more grain.

The question of whether plants in natural ecosystems will benefit from higher CO_2 levels has not yet been resolved. Scientists are testing an area of trees and shrubs in North Carolina by exposing the area to additional amounts of CO_2. Although the scientists expect the trees and shrubs to grow more, they have not yet determined how the rest of the ecosystem will be affected. In the long term, it is uncertain whether natural ecosystems will benefit from higher levels of CO_2 in the air.

FIGURE 18.7
Researchers use pipes to pump extra CO_2 into an area of forest, where they can study the effects of CO_2 on the ecosystem. The concentration of CO_2 in the experimental plot is 550 ppm, a level that will be reached in Earth's atmosphere sometime in the next century.

CHECKPOINT 18.1

1. Describe the structure of a leaf.
2. Explain the roles of light, carbon dioxide, and water in photosynthesis.
3. **Critical Thinking** Design an experiment to measure a plant's rate of photosynthesis. Keep in mind the reactants and products of photosynthesis.

Build on What You Know

4. During photosynthesis, carbon dioxide and water move by diffusion and osmosis. Under what circumstances would each process occur? *(Need to jog your memory? Revisit relevant concepts in Chapter 3, Section 3.5.)*

Chapter 18 Energy, Transport, and Growth in Plants   **427**

 STS

Scientists constantly monitor the amount of carbon dioxide in the atmosphere. Many countries go to great lengths to control the industries that generate large amounts of carbon dioxide.

❸ ASSESS

Evaluate Understanding

Have students trace the path of a CO_2 molecule from the atmosphere, into the leaf, through its conversion in photosynthesis. In their explanation, students should use these terms: *stoma, mesophyll, chloroplast, Calvin cycle, vein, vascular tissue.*

Reteach

Draw the basic parts of a leaf structure similar to the one in Figure 18.1 on the board or a transparency. Then record the following terms and functions: *petiole, cuticle and upper epidermis* (protection), *mesophyll* (primary location for photosynthesis), *chloroplast* (contain chlorophyll, the pigment needed for photosynthesis), *vascular tissue* (transport water and food), *bundle sheath, and stomata* and *guard cells* (openings that allow gas exchange). Guide students to match the name and function with the correct part of the leaf. Encourage students to copy the structure and fill in the details.

CHECKPOINT 18.1

1. Leaf contains, in order from top surface, cuticle, upper epidermis, mesophyll, vein, mesophyll, lower epidermis, and stomata.
2. Students should explain how these three factors are essential for photosynthesis.
3. **Applying knowledge** The most practical method is to measure the rate of O_2 production by collecting the oxygen gas produced by an aquatic plant.

4. CO_2, which is more concentrated in the atmosphere than in a leaf, diffuses through the stomata into the leaf. Water passes into the mesophyll cells by osmosis and out through the stomata by diffusion.

❶ To allow carbon dioxide to enter and water vapor and oxygen to diffuse out

❷ Environment changes that could adversely affect organisms

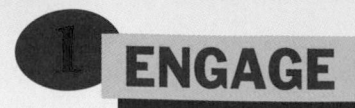

ENGAGE

Use the Visual

Have students study the photograph that opens the section. Explain that many plants react quickly to stimuli. Tell students that the *Mimosa pudica* leaf can respond to touch in 0.1 seconds. This response can spread throughout the plant at a rate of 50 cm a second.

Check Prior Knowledge

To assess students' knowledge about plant structure, ask:

- **What is the function of a root?** (To absorb water and nutrients, and in some plants, to store food)
- **What tissue is responsible for transport?** (Vascular tissue)

Teacher Demo

Display a crisp and a very wilted celery stalk. Invite speculation about why they look different. Place the wilted celery in a container of cold water and have students observe the celery at the end of the period. Explain how the celery regained its rigidity.

Use the Visual

Have students study Figure 18.8 and ask:

- **What two types of vascular tissue are shown?** (Xylem and phloem)
- **Where do you think water first enters the root?** (The root hair)

428

18.2 Transport in Plants

What you'll learn

IDEAS
- To describe the structure and function of vascular tissue in plants
- To explain the mechanisms of water and sugar transport in plants

WORDS
turgor, transpiration, pressure-flow hypothesis

Some plants play possum
You brush against a plant. Within a few seconds, the plant's leaves fold and become limp. The sensitive mimosa plant, shown here, responds to touch by imitating the appearance of a wilted plant. This response may make the plant less likely to be an herbivore's next meal.

TRANSPORT IN ROOTS

Roots absorb their surroundings

Have you ever left celery out of water until it wilted? Next time that happens, try putting the celery in a container of water for a few hours and observe how it regains its rigidity. The celery wilted because it lost water to the air. The cells in the celery are said to have lost their turgor. **Turgor** is the rigidity of a cell caused by osmotic pressure of the cell's membrane on the cell's wall.

Turgor depends on water. When the central vacuoles in plant cells are full of water, they exert pressure on the cell walls in the same way that air keeps a balloon inflated. When the central vacuoles are not full, plant cells deflate like a balloon without air.

How does a plant obtain the water necessary to maintain turgor? Vascular plants absorb water through their roots. Once water is absorbed, plants transport water and nutrients through vascular tissue, which extends from the roots to the stems and the leaves.

There are two types of vascular tissue: xylem and phloem, shown in *Figure 18.8*. Both contain specialized conducting cells. Xylem is the vascular tissue that carries water and minerals upward in a plant. Water always moves through xylem in one direction: from roots to stems to leaves. Water finally evaporates into the surrounding air through the stomata.

Phloem is the vascular tissue that transports sugar dissolved in a solution called sap. Unlike water in the xylem, sap can flow in two directions in a plant. Sap flows from the places where sugars are made (usually the leaves) to the areas where sugars are used or stored (usually stems and roots). Sap also flows from the places where

FIGURE 18.8

Root Structure

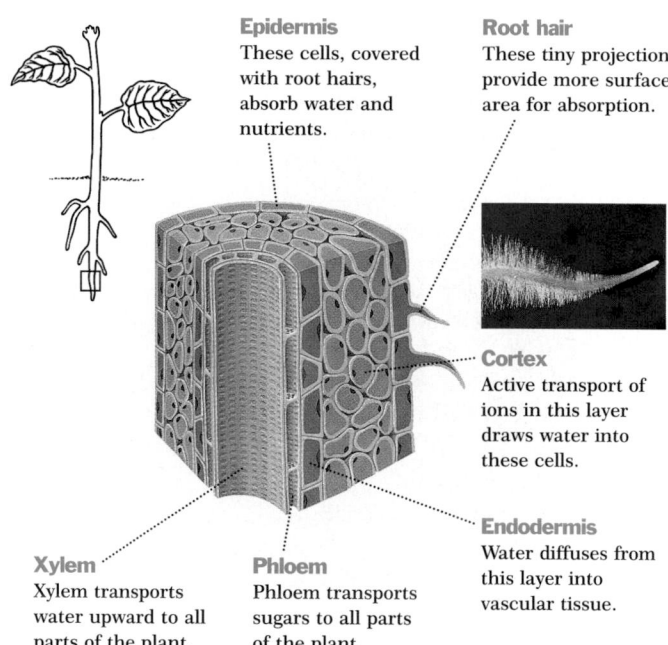

Epidermis
These cells, covered with root hairs, absorb water and nutrients.

Root hair
These tiny projections provide more surface area for absorption.

Cortex
Active transport of ions in this layer draws water into these cells.

Endodermis
Water diffuses from this layer into vascular tissue.

Xylem
Xylem transports water upward to all parts of the plant.

Phloem
Phloem transports sugars to all parts of the plant.

428 *Unit 5 Plants*

STUDENT RESOURCES

From the Teacher's Resource Package, use:
- Section Review 18.2, Activity Recordsheets 18-2 and 18-3 and Interpreting Graphics 18 from Unit 5 Review Module
- Lab 31: "Transpiration Rates"

TECHNOLOGY RESOURCES

Relevant technology resources include:
- Spanish Student Edition CD-ROM
- Teacher's Resource Planner CD-ROM
- Animated Biological Concepts Videodiscs: "Water Transport in Plants," "Sugar Movement in Plants"

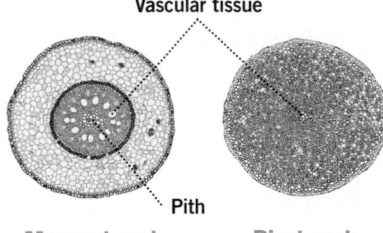

FIGURE 18.9
Vascular tissue in monocot and dicot roots is arranged differently.

Monocot root   Dicot root

Vascular tissue

Pith

sugars are stored to the places where the sugars are being used.

Xylem and phloem are both located in the center of a root. Notice in *Figure 18.9* that the arrangement of the vascular tissue differs in monocots and dicots. In dicots, the vascular tissue forms a solid core at the center of the root. In monocots, the vascular tissue forms a ring that surrounds a central region of cells called the pith. Despite the difference in arrangement, the vascular tissue in monocots and dicots transports materials in the same way to and from the stem and the rest of the plant.

Water Plants use their roots to absorb water from the soil. The water enters the roots primarily through osmosis. You can see the root structures that absorb water in *Figure 18.8*. Water enters the outer layer of the

root, or epidermis, through root hairs. Next, water moves by osmosis into cells in the cortex, because these cells have high concentrations of mineral ions. Then, water moves through the endodermis into the xylem.

The amount of water absorbed by a root depends on the moisture content of the soil. When soil contains a large amount of water, more water can be taken up by the roots. During a drought or in an ecosystem with low rainfall, the soil is drier, and less water is absorbed.

Minerals Plants also need minerals from the soil to carry out life processes. These minerals are water-soluble (can dissolve in water). Some minerals diffuse into the roots in solution along a concentration gradient. Others are carried into the roots by active transport.

Two important factors affect a plant's ability to obtain minerals. These factors are the amount of water in the soil and the amount of oxygen available to the roots. Most roots need oxygen to provide energy for active transport and other activities.

To obtain minerals from the soil, plants get help from other organisms. Decomposers such as fungi are important to plants because they release organic compounds and minerals from the bodies of dead organisms, making these substances available for absorption by plants. Mycorrhizae are special fungi that live in symbiotic relationships with the roots of some plants. The mycorrhizae secrete digestive enzymes that help break down organic material in the soil and release minerals, which plants can then absorb.

FIGURE 18.11
If a plant does not receive adequate minerals, such as nitrogen-containing nitrates, its growth will be stunted and its leaves discolored (bottom photo).

EVERYDAY BIOLOGY

Drowning Plants

Overwatering can be just as bad for plants as not giving them enough water. When soil is filled with water, oxygen may not reach the roots. If root cells do not have enough oxygen for cellular respiration, they cannot produce the energy needed for cell activities.

FIGURE 18.10
The red mangrove survives in salty ocean water that would kill most other plants. The mangrove's network of roots supports the leafy branches above the water and silt.

Chapter 18 Energy, Transport, and Growth in Plants **429**

2 TEACH

Use the Visual

Have students study Figure 18.9 and ask:

- **How are monocot and dicot roots similar?** (Vascular tissue is at the root center of both.)
- **How is the vascular tissue in monocot and dicot roots different?** (A dicot root has a solid core of vascular tissue; a monocot has a ring of vascular tissue around a pith.)

Class Activity

Display several types of uprooted plants. Have students examine the roots and root hairs with a hand lens. Explain that the continuous vascular tissue stretches from the leaves to the roots. Have students make a flowchart to explain how water, oxygen, and minerals move through a plant.

Everyday Biology

Ask students which situation is easier to correct, overwatering a plant or under watering. Students may conclude that it is easier to add water than to dry out the soil. Discuss what can occur when a wooded area is flooded for a long period.

Health

Compare the vascular tissue of plants to the blood vessels of humans and other animals. Ask:

- **What is the function of blood vessels in the body?** (Blood vessels transport blood cells, oxygen, water, and nutrients to cells and waste products away from cells.)
- **What vascular tissues perform a similar function in plants?** (Xylem and phloem)

Use the Visual

Have students study Figure 18.12 illustrating vascular tissue in stems. Ask:

- **What characteristics make it possible for tracheid cells to transport water easily?** (The cells are shaped like hollow, thick-walled, cylinders.)
- **Why are vessel elements able to transport more water than tracheids?** (Vessel elements are wider and have no separations between them.)

Class Activity

Use an overhead projector to familiarize students with the xylem and phloem in a variety of stems. Provide plant material and a hand lens to groups of students. As you dissect the stems and examine the tracheids and vessel elements, have students do the same with their specimens. Students may use Figure 18.12 as a guide. Have students make a drawing of each type of vascular tissue, identify the cells, and record their observations. Suggest they keep the work in their portfolio.

TRANSPORT IN STEMS

A plant's nutrition superhighway

Stems typically have two main functions: supporting leaves and flowers, and transporting water and food between roots and leaves. In a few plants, stems have additional functions, such as food storage. White potatoes, for example, are underground stems that store large amounts of food as starch.

Xylem After water and minerals are absorbed by the roots of a plant, these substances are transported up to the plant's stems and leaves. As you probably recall, xylem is the tissue that carries water and dissolved minerals from roots to other parts of a plant. Two kinds of conducting cells are present in xylem: tracheids (TRAY-kee-idz) and vessel elements. These cells do not conduct water until they are dead and empty of cytoplasm. Because these cells have thick walls, they form hollow cylinders through which water flows easily.

As you can see in *Figure 18.12*, tracheids are long, narrow xylem cells with thin separations between them. Vessel elements are short, wide xylem cells with no end walls, and thus no separations between them. Vessel elements are arranged end to end like barrels stacked on top of one another. Because of their width, vessel elements allow greater water flow than tracheids, just as more water flows through a wide pipe than through a narrow pipe.

Flowering plants, or angiosperms, contain tracheids and vessel elements. Cone-bearing seed plants, however, contain only tracheids. Because vessel elements move water more efficiently than tracheids, vessel elements enable flowering plants to transport water more easily than cone-bearing plants. This difference may help to explain why angiosperms dominate many landscapes.

Phloem Sugars made in the leaves of a plant by photosynthesis must be transported throughout the plant. You have learned that phloem carries sap upward and downward in a plant.

Phloem has two types of cells: sieve tube elements and companion cells. Can you locate these cells in

FIGURE 18.12

Vascular Tissue

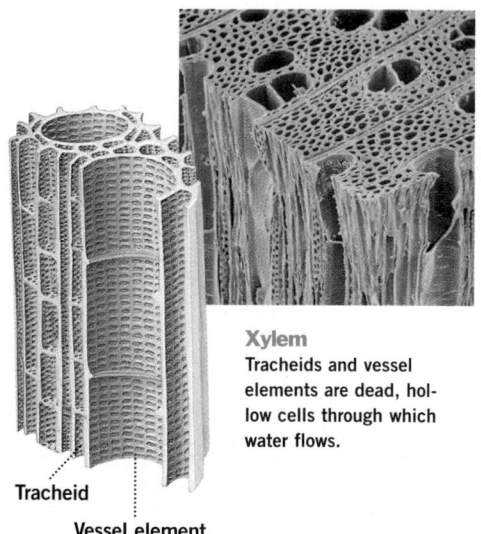

Xylem
Tracheids and vessel elements are dead, hollow cells through which water flows.

Tracheid

Vessel element

Phloem
The movement of sugars through sieve tube elements is controlled by companion cells.

Sieve tube element

Companion cell

MEETING DIVERSE NEEDS

At Risk Have students work in groups to demonstrate the amount of water that will move through a wide tube and a narrow tube in one minute. Supply wide and narrow funnels and two sizes of plastic tubing, one wide and one narrow, and large containers to catch the water. Have students pour water through each apparatus for one minute, measure the volume of water collected, and compare the results. Have students discuss which transport system would be most useful in plant growth.

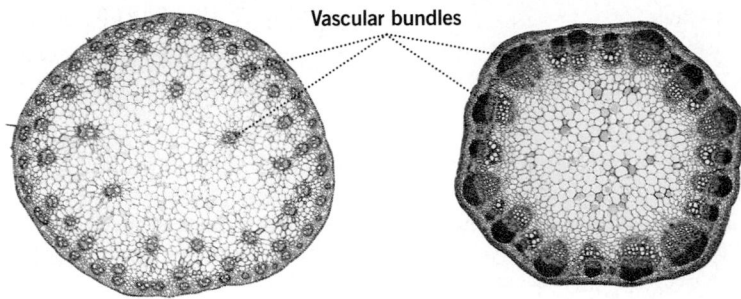

Vascular bundles

Monocot stem

Dicot stem

FIGURE 18.13
The vascular bundles in monocot and dicot stems are organized differently. Which kind of stem has scattered vascular bundles? **①**

Figure 18.12? Unlike the cells in xylem, phloem cells are alive when they transport materials. Sieve tube elements are stacked end to end to form long tubes called sieve tubes. Like a sieve or strainer, their end walls have holes through which the sap moves. Sieve tube elements do not have ribosomes and nuclei, and they depend on companion cells for their basic needs. Companion cells enable the sieve tube elements to function, thereby controlling the movement of substances through the sieve tubes.

Although vascular tissue is found throughout the plant, its arrangement is different in stems and roots. In roots, the vascular tissue forms a central cylinder. In stems, it is arranged in vascular bundles. The arrangement of these vascular bundles differs in monocots and dicots, as shown in *Figure 18.13*. In dicots, the vascular bundles form a ring that divides the ground tissue into cortex and pith. In monocots, the bundles are scattered throughout the ground tissue.

Water transport The theory that best explains water movement in plants was proposed more than a century ago and is known today as the transpiration-cohesion theory. According to this theory, water movement in plants is driven by **transpiration,** the evaporation of water from the parts of a plant exposed to air. This evaporation takes place through open stomata.

How does transpiration cause water to move up a plant? Substances tend to move from areas of higher pressure to areas of lower pressure. As water evaporates from a leaf stomata, the pressure lowers in the xylem of the leaf. To equalize the pressure, water in the xylem moves upward from the stem to the leaf. This in turn causes lower pressure in the stem xylem, and water moves there from

LAB ZONE Do It!

Observing Plant Transport

Stems transport water to the leaves and flowers of a plant. What happens when the water is mixed with food coloring? You can find out if you . . .

Try This

1 Use two different shades of food coloring to dye water in two containers. Use the same amounts of food coloring and water in each container. Cover the containers with plastic wrap, and poke a small hole in the center.
2 Without cutting off the flower, split the stem of a white flower (carnations work well) lengthwise in two.
3 Insert one of the stem halves into each cup through the hole in the plastic wrap.
4 Let the flower sit undisturbed for 1 to 24 hours.

Analyze Your Results

1 Record the results of the experiment in a sketch.
2 Did the two colors affect all parts of the flower equally? If the colored parts are unequal, how do you account for this? What does this effect tell you about the relationship between the stem and the flower?

❶ The monocot stem

Everyday Biology

Explain that the sap in the xylem of the sugar maple, *Acer saccharum,* is about two to three percent sugar in the springtime. Alternate freezing and thawing in the xylem causes sugars to move from the phloem into the xylem which is tapped. The maple sap is con-centrated by boiling. It takes about 40 liters of sap to produce 1 liter of maple syrup.

Use the Visual

Direct students to Figure 18.14. Have students make a flowchart to show the movement of sugar from the source cell to xylem or sink. Ask:

- **What type of cell is the source cell and where is it located?** (A photosynthetic cell in the leaf)
- **Which type of vascular tissue transports sugar?** (The sugar travels through the phloem.)

Think Critically

After discussing the flow and storage of sugars, ask:

- **What are other kinds of sinks a plant might use for sugar storage?** (Fruit, seed, corm, bulb, taproot, or rhizome)

 Animated Biological Concepts

Water Transportation in Plants

 Play

Sugar Movement in Plants

 Play

432

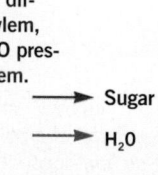

EVERYDAY BIOLOGY

Where Does Maple Syrup Come From?

In early spring, temperature fluctua-tions cause maple trees to convert stored starch to sugar. By puncturing the vascular bundles of the trees, humans harvest the sweet sap, which they make into maple syrup.

---

the root xylem.

Transpiration in plants creates a strong force, or pull. In order for water to be pulled up a plant, this force must move through a continuous chain of water molecules in the xylem, from the leaves to the roots. The water molecules in the xylem are linked together by another force called cohesion. As you learned in Chapter 2, cohesion is an attractive force between water molecules that causes water molecules to stick together. You can compare the results of the forces of transpiration and cohesion to mov-ing while holding hands with some-one. When you move, you pull the person with you.

Water movement through plants is very rapid because of the large amounts of water lost through transpi-ration. A maple tree can lose as much as 200 liters of water per hour. In fact, water can travel up a plant as fast as 75 centimeters per minute.

FIGURE 18.14
Pressure Flow

❶ Sugars are actively transported from source cells into sieve tube elements.

❷ Because of the high sugar concentration in the phloem, H_2O diffuses into the sieve tube elements, raising the H_2O pressure.

❸ Pressure causes the sap–sugar water–to flow through the phloem.

❹ Sugars are transported out of the phloem into sink cells; water dif-fuses into the xylem, reducing the H_2O pres-sure in the phloem.

→ Sugar

→ H_2O

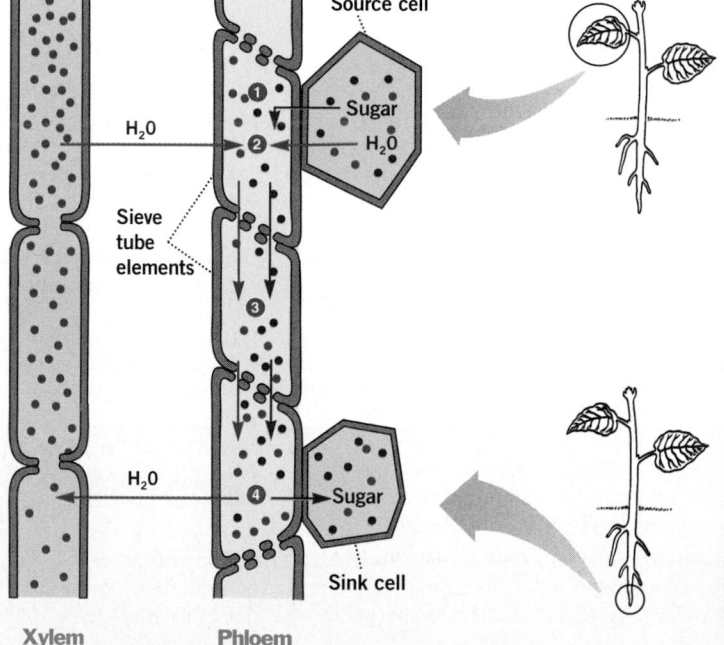

Xylem   Phloem

432   *Unit 5 Plants*

Sugars are forced to "leave" their source

As you know, leaves also have vascular tissue for transport of materials. The vascular bundles in leaves are called veins. Veins contain xylem and phloem for transportation of water and food.

The structure of leaves is very important for water transport in plants. Water is transported from the roots to the leaves through the xylem. You have just learned that water is pulled upward in a plant by transpira-tion and cohesion. Most transpiration occurs through the stomata cells in leaves, releasing enormous amounts of water to the atmosphere.

The movement of sugars is best explained by the **pressure-flow hypothesis.** You can follow the steps described by this hypothesis in *Figure 18.14.* Sugars are transported from a

---

MEETING DIVERSE NEEDS

At Risk Have students make a collage of food products that are sinks. The collage should show the plant on which the fruit or seed grows. Have students classify the sink according to its sugar and starch content.

❶ The potato that forms on the under-ground stem

❷ Approximately 15 hours

region of the plant called a source to a region called a sink. A source is any part of the plant where sugars are produced by photosynthesis or the breakdown of starch. A sink is part of the plant where sugars are utilized or stored. Leaves are typical sources, and roots are typical sinks. However, roots in which sugars have been stored can also function as sources. Where are the sinks in a potato plant?

At the start of the process, sugars are pumped by active transport from the source into sieve tubes. Then, water enters the sieve tube elements from the xylem by osmosis, raising the water pressure. Both water and sugar move down a pressure gradient. Finally, at the sink, the sugars are removed from the sieve tubes by active transport and water leaves by osmosis.

Energy is required to pump sugars into sieve tubes and sometimes to pump sugars out of the sieve tubes. Sieve tube elements in phloem must be alive to function, because only living cells can provide the energy needed for active transport.

Sugars move through plants more slowly than water does. The fastest rate of phloem transport is a little more than 2 meters per hour. At that speed, how long would it take for sugars to travel down a 30-meter tree trunk?

FIGURE 18.15

Plant Transport System

Leaves
Source cells in the leaves move sugars into the phloem for transport to the rest of the plant, while receiving water and nutrients from the xylem. Water evaporates through stoma in the leaf.

Stems
Water, minerals, and sugars move through vascular tissue in the stems to all parts of the plant.

Roots
Xylem in the roots absorbs water for the plant. Roots use and often store sugars delivered by the phloem.

CHECKPOINT 18.2

1. Identify the two types of vascular tissue in plants. Briefly discuss their structure and how they work.
2. Describe the mechanisms plants use to obtain water and nutrients and to transport sugars.
3. **Critical Thinking** Why is the transport of water fastest at midday and slowest at night? What environmental factors might be involved?

Build on What You Know

4. How do concentration gradients affect osmosis? *(Need to jog your memory? Revisit relevant concepts in Chapter 3, Section 3.5.)*

 What are the main structures of plants? What is the function of each?

Chapter 18 Energy, Transport, and Growth in Plants **433**

CHECKPOINT 18.2

1. Xylem cells, tracheids and vessel elements transport water through the plant. Phloem cells, sieve tube elements, and companion cells form long tubes that transport sugar.
2. Water loss through leaf transpiration creates negative pressure in root xylem, forcing water and dissolved nutrients upward through the hollow xylem cells. Sugar manufactured in leaves is actively transported through the phloem to a point of use or a storage sink.
3. **Making generalizations** Photosynthesis requires sunlight and water. Light and temperature
4. Fluids move from an area of high solute concentration to one of low solute concentration.

Math
Have students work in pairs and write word problems about the maximum movement of sugar in trees and plants of varying sizes. Then have them exchange papers and solve the problems.

ASSESS

Evaluate Understanding

To assess students' understanding of transport in plants, ask:

- **Name the types of vascular tissue and describe their functions.** (Xylem transports water and minerals from roots to leaves. Phloem transports sugars from where they are made to where they are used or stored.)
- **In what plant parts is vascular tissue located?** (Roots, stems, leaves)
- **What are two types of xylem cells and how do they differ?** (Tracheids are long, narrow tubes with thin separations between them. Vessel elements are short, wide tubes with no separations.)
- **How does transpiration aid transport in plants?** (It creates negative pressure in the xylem, which pulls water upward through the plant.)

Reteach

Review the functions of the following structures: *source cell, phloem, sieve tube, companion cell, sink cell.* Then have students work in small groups to construct a concept map to show the movement of sugar from the source to the sink.

TEAM WORK Observing Leaves, Stems, and Roots

SAFETY FIRST!

Have a first-aid kit available should any student sustain an injury using the scalpel. Remind students not to get the stain on their clothing.

Lab Prep and Planning

Purchase bean plants from a nursery or have students grow them from seed. Have students work in groups. Allow at least 50 minutes to complete the lab.

Lab Tips

Demonstrate the proper technique for preparing a wet mount.

Hypothesis Help

Suggest that students consider the types of cells they expect to observe in all three plant structures and which types of cells are unique to each structure.

Lab Extension

Open Ended

You may want students to choose only one characteristic to compare and contrast in their samples.

LAB ZONE Investigate It!

Observing Leaves, Stems, and Roots

WHAT YOU WILL DO Observe cross sections of a bean leaf, stem, and root; identify the parts of each section

SKILLS YOU WILL USE Observing, recording data, comparing and contrasting

WHAT YOU WILL NEED Live bean plant, microscope slides, scalpel, dropper, coverslips, microscope, safranine stain, paper towel

Propose a Hypothesis

Based on what you know about plant structures, propose a hypothesis about the similarities and differences in the organization of leaf, stem, and root tissue.

Conduct Your Experiment

1 Remove a leaf from the bean plant. Place it on a slide. Holding the scalpel at a slight angle, slice thin cross sections from the leaf. **Caution:** Be careful when using a scalpel.
2 Prepare a wet mount of a cross section.

3 Focus the microscope on low power. Switch to high. Draw what you see, and label epidermis, vascular bundle, guard cells, and stomata.
4 Add a drop of safranine stain to one edge of the coverslip. Place a paper towel on the other edge to draw the stain under the coverslip.
5 Repeat step 3.
6 Cut a piece from the stem below the first leaves. Repeat steps 2–5, labeling pith, vascular bundle, and cortex.
7 Cut a piece from the largest root. Repeat steps 2–5, labeling xylem, phloem, endodermis, cortex, and epidermis.

Analyze Your Data

1 Describe the internal structure you observed in the leaf stem and root, before the stain was added.
2 Where is the xylem located in the leaf? In the root? In the stem?
3 What structure is in the stem and root but not in the leaf? Suggest a function for this structure based on its location.

Draw Conclusions

Did you hypothesize correctly? If not, write a paragraph summarizing the similarities and differences among the tissues in leaves, stems, and roots.

Design a Related Experiment

Write a procedure for comparing and contrasting the leaves, stems, and roots of a monocot and a dicot.

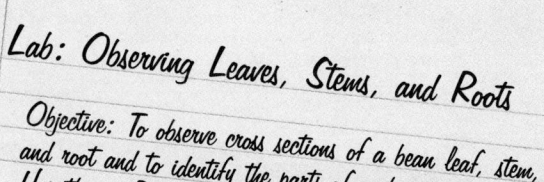

Lab: Observing Leaves, Stems, and Roots

Objective: To observe cross sections of a bean leaf, stem, and root and to identify the parts of each section.
Hypothesis: Roots, stems, and leaves are made of three types of tissue: dermal, ground, and vascular. The arrangement of the tissues is different in the different plant structures.

Analyze Your Data

1 Students should observe the layered epidermis of the leaf and may describe the mesophyll.
2 In bundles to the inside of the phloem
3 The xylem is concentrated toward the center of the root

Draw Conclusions

Students should be aware of the functional differences of plant tissue.

Design a Related Experiment

Students' procedures may include dissection of monocot and dicot leaves, stems and root. A visual analysis can also be used.

18.3 Plant Growth

Little gems

In the Japanese art of bonsai, people create miniature potted trees by training the tree limbs into graceful shapes with wire and by pruning. Bonsai trees are not dwarf species. Gardeners control the size by planting trees in small, shallow pots (which limit root growth) and by pruning the roots and shoots regularly.

What you'll learn

IDEAS

• To explain where cells and tissues develop in plants
• To compare two patterns of plant growth

WORDS

meristems, primary growth, secondary growth, cambium

MERISTEMS: SITES OF GROWTH

Take it from the top

Do you know how humans grow in height? As the length of certain bones, primarily the leg and spinal bones, increases, we grow taller. Plants grow taller by increasing in length at the tips of roots and stems. If humans grew taller in the same way as plants, they would grow at the tips of their toes and at the top of their heads.

The growing tissues of plants are called **meristems.** Meristems are located at the tips of stems and branches, at the tips of roots, and in buds in the joints where leaves attach to stems. In woody plants, meristems are also located between the xylem and phloem of the vascular system and near stem surfaces.

The function of meristems is to produce new cells by mitosis. As is common in mitosis, the new cells that are produced are all alike at first. However, the cells eventually specialize, or differentiate, to form one of three types of tissues—vascular tissue, dermal tissue, or ground tissue. As you have learned, these three tissues make up a plant.

The growing tissues at the tips of roots and stems are called apical

meristems. (*Apex* means "tip," and *apical* means "at the tip.") Apical meristems cause the tips of roots and stems to grow longer. Because of the activity of apical meristems, plants grow taller and their roots grow deeper into the soil.

Axillary meristems occur in buds that arise in the the joints, called axils, between leaves and stems. Axillary meristems cause side branches to grow on stems. You can see where apical and axillary meristems are located in *Figure 18.16.*

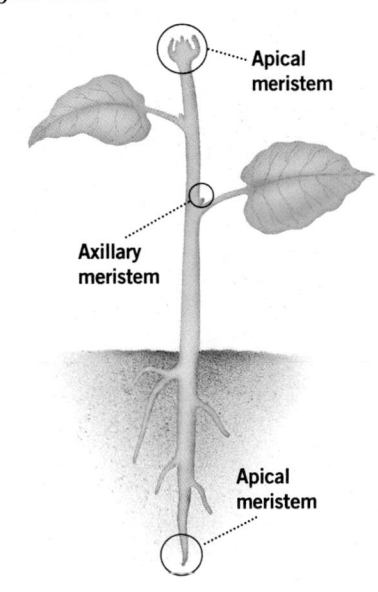

Apical meristem

Axillary meristem

Apical meristem

FIGURE 18.16

Meristems are regions of fast-growing areas, such as the tips of the roots and the stems.

① ENGAGE

Consider the Big Idea

Have students read the Big Idea! Explain that growth occurs at specific sites and in various kinds of plant tissues.

Use the Visual

Have students study the photograph that opens the section. Emphasize that the bonsai reflects controlled growth in the plant. Ask:

■ **How would limiting root growth limit the plant's growth?** (The roots control the amount of water and nutrients in the plant.) You may wish to remind students that van Helmont's experiment proved that most of a plant's mass comes from water.

Quick Activity

Display a variety of plants on which new growth is visible. Allow students time to examine the plant and point out where growth occurred. Then have them look for areas of budding growth. You may wish to have students use a hand lens to examine the plants.

STUDENT RESOURCES

sFrom the Teacher's Resource Package, use:

■ Section Review 18.3, Activity Record-sheet 18-4, Enrichment Topic 18-1, Critical Thinking Exercise 18-2, Vocabulary Review 18, and Chapter 18 Tests from Unit 5 Review Module

TECHNOLOGY RESOURCES

Relevant technology resources include:
■ Spanish Student Edition CD-ROM
■ Teacher's Resource Planner CD-ROM
■ TestWorks CD-ROM: Chapter 18 Tests.

Class Activity

Let students observe pre-pared slides of a root tip exhibiting the three zones of primary growth. Have students sketch what they observe and label each zone. Remind students that they may also observe a root cap at the very tip of the root. Ask:

- **What activity helps to identify the zone of cell division?** (Many cells are in mitosis.)
- **How does the cell shape help to identify the zone of elongation?** (The cells are long and all look similar.)
- **Which step or zone of primary root growth is responsible for pushing the root through the soil?** (Elongation)

Use the Visual

Have students study Figure 18.17. Call attention to the three zones labeled on the illustration and ask:

- **Which zone is responsible for pushing the root through the soil?** (Zone of elongation)
- **Which zone is responsible for producing new cells?** (Zone of cell division)
- **What type of cells might develop in the zone of differentiation?** (Dermal cells, ground tissue cells, or vascular cells)
- **Identify the location of the apical meristem.** (At the bottom of the zone of cell division)

PRIMARY GROWTH

Growing up

There are two patterns of growth in seed plants. During one kind of growth, all plants grow taller and deeper; in the other type, woody plants grow thicker. The first process—the elongation of stems and roots—is called **primary growth.** All plants exhibit primary growth. Primary growth occurs when a plant's stem gets longer and its roots grow deeper. You will learn more about the second growth pattern, which makes woody plants thicker, later in this section.

The first stem that emerges from a seed is called the primary shoot. The primary shoot forms the stems and leaves. Primary shoots have two types of meristems: apical meristems and axillary buds. Can you locate both types of meristems in *Figure 18.17*? Apical meristems, which are located at the tips of all stems, have cells that form the stem and leaves. Axillary buds form at the base of each leaf. Axillary buds can form either a branch or a flower. Because they can form side branches from the stem, axillary buds are also called lateral buds. (*Lateral* means "sideways.")

In most plants, the axillary buds are kept inactive by hormones produced in the meristem at the tip of the shoot. If this tip is damaged or removed, hormone production will stop and the axillary bud will begin to grow. You may have seen gardeners take advantage of this phenomenon.

FIGURE 18.17

Primary Growth

All plants exhibit primary growth, in which the stems grow longer and the roots grow deeper.

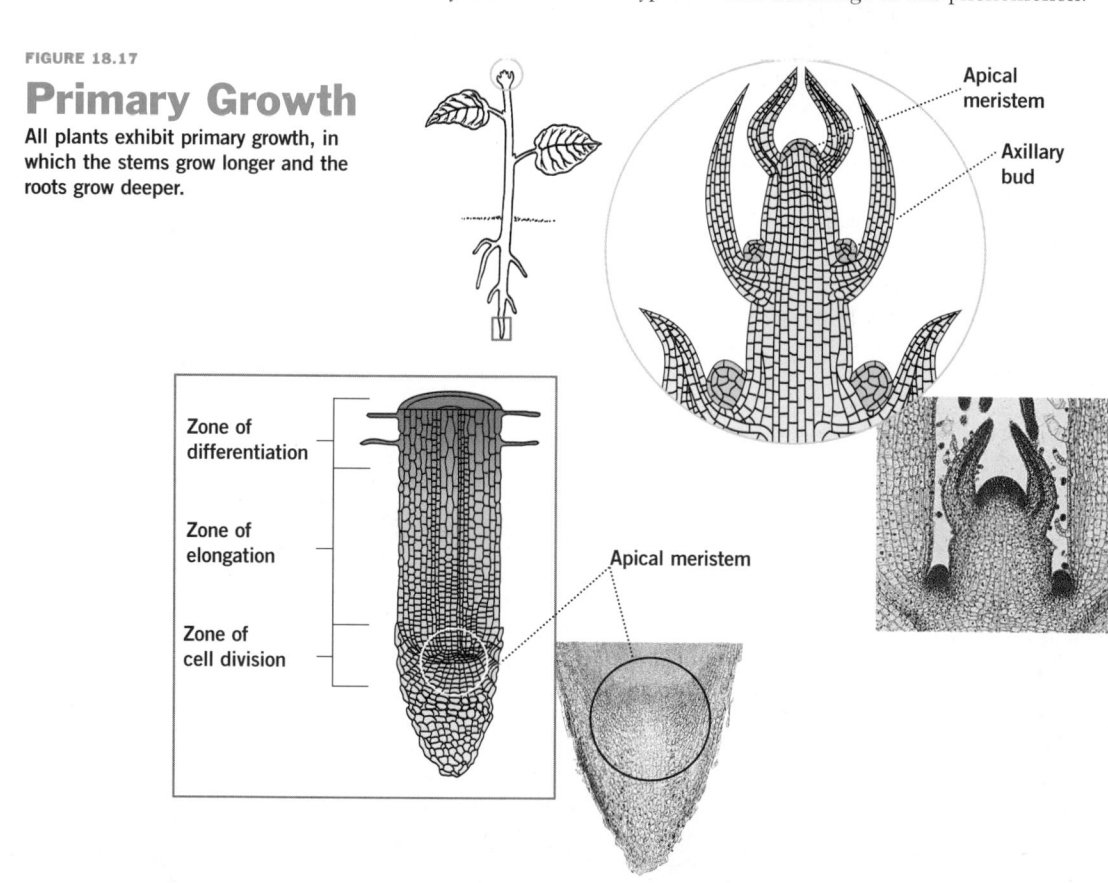

Apical meristem

Axillary bud

Zone of differentiation

Zone of elongation

Zone of cell division

Apical meristem

MEETING DIVERSE NEEDS

Hearing Impaired Have students use a dictionary to look up and write down the pronunciation of the following terms: *apex, apical, axillary, bonsai, meristem, parenchyma,* and *vascular.* You may wish to record the correct pronunciations for use by students with partial-hearing.

❶ Apical meristem is at top; axillary buds are along stem at base of each leaf.

In order to make plants grow bushier, gardeners often clip off the tops. This technique is used to create hedges. Cutting off the tops removes the hormonal inactivation and the axillary buds start to sprout side branches.

The primary growth of roots and stems involves three steps: cell division, elongation, and differentiation. In the first step, cell division in the apical meristem forms new cells. In the second step, cells grow longer in a region of the root called the zone of elongation. The elongation of cells pushes the root through the soil.

In the third step, cells become specialized in the zone of differentiation. In this zone, cells undergo changes to become part of the vascular tissue (xylem or phloem), dermal tissue, or ground tissue (parenchyma and supporting cells). In *Figure 18.17*, where are the cells in each of the three steps located in a root?

SECONDARY GROWTH
Putting on width

If you observe the growth of a tree over a long period of time, you will probably notice that the tree grows wider as it grows taller. During **secondary growth,** the roots, stems, and branches of certain seed plants grow wider. The widening of a tree trunk is an example of secondary growth.

Secondary growth does not occur in all plants. Most herbaceous plants have only primary growth. Secondary growth is usually only seen in woody vines, shrubs, and trees. For example, most gymnosperms show secondary growth. Secondary growth creates the layers of dead cell tissue called wood.

Secondary growth is an adaptation that enables some woody plants to survive in certain environments. As a plant's stem grows thicker, it becomes

stronger. A stronger stem allows a plant to grow taller. Plants that grow taller have an increased chance of reaching light. Because plants compete for light, tall plants are more likely to obtain vital sunlight and to reproduce successfully. Secondary growth is an adaptation that has contributed to the dominance of woody plants in many ecosystems.

Lateral meristems Secondary growth is caused by cell division in structures called lateral meristems. Unlike apical meristems, which are located at the tips of roots and stems, lateral meristems are located within and parallel to the sides of roots and stems. Generally, lateral meristems are shaped like a hollow cylinder inside a root or stem.

Chapter 18 Energy, Transport, and Growth in Plants   **437**

 **Do It!**

Measuring Root and Stem Growth

You can observe and measure the rate of root and stem growth when you . . .

Try This

1 For this activity, choose seeds for plants such as radishes, corn, or peas.
2 Fill a clear plastic or glass container loosely with crumpled paper towels. Dampen the towels with water.
3 Place a seed between the towels and the wall of the container so that the seed is easy to view and the roots have room to grow.
4 Keep the paper towels damp and make observations at the same time each day for one week. Record the date and your observations of the roots.
5 Once growth appears, remove the seedling from the container during each observation, and use a ruler and permanent marker to mark 1-centimeter increments on a root and the stem. Record the length of the root and the stem at each observation.

Analyze Your Results

1 Describe the rate of root growth in your seed. Did growth occur at a steady rate or did it occur at varying rates?
2 From your observations of the marks on the root and stem, where did growth occur in the seedling? Explain.

 **Do It!** TEAM WORK

Measuring Root and Stem Growth

Try This
Display a seed set-up to aid the students.

Analyze Your Results

1 Student graphs should show two curves, one for root and one for stem. Growth rates will vary.
2 Students should observe growth in the stem and root tissue and leaf formation.

Class Activity   TEAM WORK

Provide seedling plants and have groups of students experiment with plant growth by trimming the tops of some plants. Have students observe and compare growth patterns of trimmed plants with a control group. You may wish to have students record their observations in their portfolios.

Build Writing Skills

Have students research and write about everyday uses of monocots and dicots such as in holiday celebrations, preparation of medicines and food products, and in the manufacture of clothing and furniture. Encourage students to include captioned illustrations or photos with their reports.

 In the root meristem

MEETING DIVERSE NEEDS

Gifted Have students research why roots grow downward instead of upward like a stem. (Biologists do not know exactly why, but research suggests that auxins accumulate on the lower side of a root growing horizontally. The cells on the upper surface elongate more rapidly than those on the lower surface and so the root bends downward. It has been suggested that abscissic acid and gravity are also contributing factors.)

FIGURE 18.18

Secondary Growth of a Woody Stem

After year 1
The young tree's vascular cambium lies between primary xylem and phloem. The epidermis forms the outer layer.

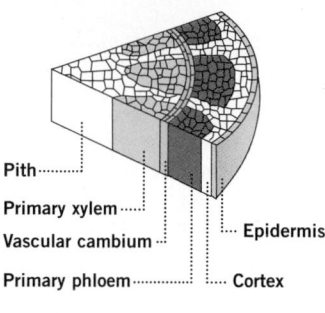

Pith
Primary xylem
Vascular cambium
Primary phloem
Epidermis
Cortex

After year 2
The vascular cambium produces new layers of secondary xylem and phloem, and the cork cambium produces cork.

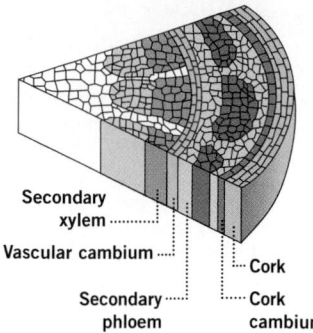

Secondary xylem
Vascular cambium
Secondary phloem
Cork
Cork cambium

After year 3
Old layers of xylem become heartwood, while old layers of phloem and accumulated cork thicken the bark.

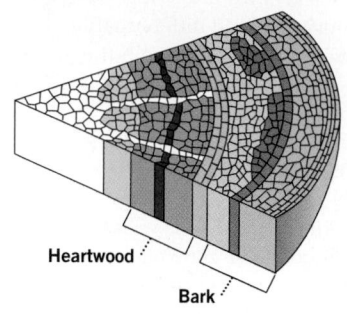

Heartwood
Bark

Lateral meristems are also called cambium. **Cambium** is the meristem in woody plants that produces new cells for lateral growth. There are two common types of cambium: vascular cambium and cork cambium. Find each type in the cross section of a tree trunk shown in *Figure 18.18*. Which cambium is part of the bark ❶ of the tree?

Vascular cambium One type of cambium, vascular cambium, is located between the xylem and phloem. Cell divisions in the vascular cambium produce new xylem toward the inside of the cambium, and new phloem toward the outside of the cambium. The growth of new xylem and phloem occurs in a cycle. Each year the vascular cambium produces new xylem and new phloem during a plant's growing season.

Starting in a woody plant's second year of growth, the new xylem that the vascular cambium produces each year is called secondary xylem. Secondary xylem is familiar to you as wood. Similarly, the new phloem formed by the vascular cambium each year is called secondary phloem. Secondary phloem has no common name. As the stems and roots grow thicker year by year, secondary xylem carries water and secondary phloem carries sugars through the plant.

Cork cambium The other type of cambium, cork cambium, is the lateral meristem between the phloem and the epidermis. Cell divisions in the cork cambium replace the cortex layer and the epidermis, or skin of the plant, with cork, which protects the tree. You are probably familiar with natural cork—the material used for some types of bulletin boards. The secondary phloem, cork cambium, and cork combine to form the bark that surrounds the trunk of a tree.

Many trees have several layers of cork that are dead and cannot expand. As a result, continued expansion of the tree trunk splits the outer layers. As the layers of cork split, they cause the bark to split. Trees such as oaks have split bark because of the growth of the cork cambium.

Certain trees are grown and maintained so that their cork can be harvested. Cork oak trees in Portugal produce about 60 percent of the world's supply of natural cork. Cork can be removed from cork oaks every 7 to 10 years, starting when the trees are about 25 years old. Trees up to 200 years old can still produce usable cork. Cork harvesters must be careful not to damage the vascular cambium layer when they remove cork from a tree. If this layer is damaged, the tree will die.

The structure of wood Xylem accumulates yearly, but only the newer outer layers continue to transport water. The outer light-colored layers of secondary xylem are sapwood.

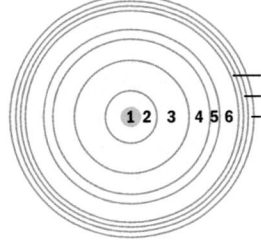

LAB ZONE Think About It! bioSURF

Analyzing Tree Rings

Growth rings contain a great deal of information about a tree's growth. Use this simple illustration of a cross section of a tree to answer the following questions.

Analyzing the Diagram

1 Look at ring 4. What does it tell you about the tree's growth that year? What environmental factors could have affected the tree's growth?
2 What pattern of growth do you see in rings 6–8?
3 If the tree from which this cross section was obtained died in 1990, in what year did it begin to grow?
4 In what part of a tree would you expect the rings to be widest? Why?
5 In which layers would you expect to find sapwood? Heartwood?

Eventually, older xylem cells get clogged and can no longer carry water. The clogged dark-colored layers of xylem at the center of the tree are heartwood. Heartwood typically contains substances such as oils, gums, resins, and tannins that are not present in sapwood. These substances can be extracted from lumber and used to produce valuable products such as acetone, lacquer, photographic film, and turpentine. Heartwood is stronger and more resistant to decay than sapwood.

You see the structure of wood in *Figure 18.19*. Notice the series of concentric rings, which are called growth rings. How do growth rings form? Xylem that grows in the spring is called

EVERYDAY BIOLOGY

Steady as a . . . Hammock?

You may never need to move your hammock. Because trees grow taller at their branch tips, a hammock attached to two trees will remain at about the same height for the life of the trees.

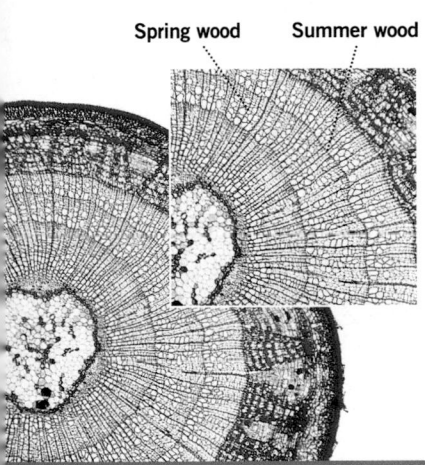

Spring wood   Summer wood

FIGURE 18.19
Compare the spring wood and the summer wood in this stained stem (left). Why is the spring wood wider?

❷ Growth is faster in the spring when water is plentiful and the xylem cells are wider.

LAB ZONE Think About It!

Analyzing Tree Rings

TEAM WORK

You may wish to provide a magnifying glass for some students.

Analyzing the Diagram

1 Much growth occurred. Long season, warm weather, abundance of rain
2 Year 6 was a best growing year.
3 1982
4 In a young tree, because a small tree would get more nutrients.
5 Soft layers are sapwood, small hard layers are heartwood.

Everyday Biology

Trees are planted close together to make windbreaks for gardens, roads, and buildings. Discuss other advantages of closely-placed trees.

Music

Rosin is a dark, solid substance obtained as a resin from the heartwood of a pine tree. Rosin is used on the bows of stringed instruments to increase friction between the bow and the strings thus causing greater string vibration.

Use the Visual

Have students study Figure 18.19. Before discussing the structure of wood, ask:

■ **Why do you think the summer cells are smaller than the spring cells?** (Summers are hotter and drier, and growth is slower.)

Think Critically

After students consider the history of the redwood tree in Figure 18.20, have them discuss the following question.

- **How can you explain the continued growth after being subjected to nine fires?** (Cell division in the vascular and cork cambiums supply new cells to replace those dead or damaged.)

ASSESS

Evaluate Understanding

On the board draw a chart with two columns labeled *Primary Growth* and *Secondary Growth*. Ask students to identify the processes and tissues involved in each type of growth. Ask:

- **What three zones of primary growth exist in the root apical meristem?** (Cell division, elongation, and differentiation)
- **Where are lateral meristem tissues found?** (Within and parallel to the sides of roots and stems)

Reteach

After reviewing the basics of plant growth, have students work in pairs to construct a flowchart in conjunction with an outline of a plant that includes the following terms: *apical meristem, cell division, primary tissues, differentiation, lateral meristem, secondary tissue, herbaceous plant, woody plant.* In addition, have students identify the primary and secondary tissues.

440

FIGURE 18.20

A Tale of a Tree

This redwood lived for 1204 years, from 729 to 1933. One scientist identified some of the major events that occurred during the tree's life.

1932 Last growth ring. The tree fell the following year.

1776 Declaration of Independence signed

1492 Europeans discover America

1215 Magna Carta signed

1066 Norman conquest of England

729 Seedling sprouts

Open ring shake
Open ring shake
Fire scar of 1820
Ring shake follows fire scar of 1147
Fire crack
Fire scars
Open ring shake
Ring shake & Fire scar 1595
Ring shake
Fire scar 1595
Fire scar 1595
Fire scar 1595
Fire scar 1595
Buttress
Charcoal-covered fire scar 13 feet long

Buttress
Before the 1820 fire, this tree had begun to grow a buttress, or support column, which grew even more rapidly after the fire. The buttress kept the tree standing for more than one hundred years.

Fire scars
This tree cross section shows evidence of at least nine fires, including a blaze in 1820 that burned through almost half of its bark, cambium, and heartwood.

spring wood. Spring wood consists of large, wide xylem cells that can transport large amounts of water.

During the summer, when conditions are often drier, the vascular cambium produces thick-walled, narrow xylem cells. This summer wood carries less water than spring wood. The alternating production of spring wood and summer wood produces growth rings in tree trunks.

Growth rings also form in roots. In both stems and roots, each ring represents one year's growth. Growth rings vary in width. When environmental conditions such as rainfall and temperature are favorable, more growth occurs, resulting in wider growth rings. There is less growth during a drought. Growth rings are narrower when conditions are unfavorable for growth. Why can you determine the age of a tree by counting its growth rings? **❶**

Sometimes a tree trunk tells an even more dramatic story, as you can see in *Figure 18.20*. This ancient tree was burned extensively in a fire in 1820, but it did not fall until more than 100 years later.

CHECKPOINT 18.3

1. Where do new cells and tissues develop in plants?
2. Describe two common patterns of plant growth. What kinds of plants exhibit each pattern of growth?
3. **Critical Thinking** Would you expect most monocots to produce cork? Explain your answer.

Build on What You Know

4. How does mitosis enable a growing plant to preserve the genetic message encoded in most of its cells? (*Need to jog your memory? Revisit relevant concepts in Chapter 5, Section 5.1.*)

  What specialized tissues enable plants to grow?

CHECKPOINT 18.3

1. In the meristems, which are: apical–at the tips of stems, branches, and roots; axillary–in the joints where leaves attach to stems; and lateral–in and around the sides of roots and stems.
2. Primary growth; taller stems and deeper roots: secondary growth; wider stems and roots: All vascular plants have primary

growth, woody plants have secondary growth.
3. **Predicting** No, cork is produced by cork cambium, which is not in monocots.
4. Mitosis produces daughter cells genetically identical to the parent cell.

❶ Each set of summer/spring rings represent one year.

Chapter 18 Review

 **THE BIG IDEA!**
18.1–18.2 Plants perform life processes using specialized structures.
18.3 The parts of most plants grow from specialized tissues.

Sum It Up

Use the following summary to review the main concepts in this chapter.

18.1 Photosynthesis in Plants

- In the layer of mesophyll cells between the upper and lower epidermis of a leaf, chloroplasts capture light energy.
- The epidermis of a leaf has a waterproof covering called a cuticle.
- Plants exchange oxygen and carbon dioxide and lose water through pores called stomata. Guard cells affect the size of stomata.
- For a plant to store energy or grow, it must produce more glucose than it needs for cellular respiration.
- Most of the water taken up by plants is lost through evaporation.

18.2 Transport in Plants

- Water in plant vacuoles maintains the rigidity, or turgor, of plant cells.
- Water enters roots from soil mainly by osmosis.
- Some minerals enter roots by diffusion; others, through active transport. All roots need oxygen to provide energy for active transport.

- In vascular plants, xylem transports water and dissolved minerals; phloem transports sap containing dissolved sugars.
- Xylem cells that transport water and minerals are dead and hollow. As water evaporates through leaves, replacement water is pulled up through the hollow tubes by cohesion.
- Living phloem cells use energy to actively transport sugars from source cells into sieve tubes, and from sieve tubes into sink cells.

18.3 Plant Growth

- Primary growth occurs only in apical meristems —at the tips of stems, branches, and roots, and in the joints where leaves attach to stems.
- All plants have primary growth. Woody plants can also grow thicker through secondary growth.
- Wood is layers of secondary xylem. Bark is formed from layers of cork, cork cambium, and phloem.
- The thickness of spring and summer xylem layers provides clues about climatic change.

Use Terms and Concepts

Use each of the following words or terms in a complete sentence. If you need to review a meaning, turn to the page indicated.

cuticle (p. 423)
stomata (p. 423)
mesophyll (p. 423)
compensation point (p. 425)

turgor (p. 428)
transpiration (p. 431)
pressure-flow hypothesis (p. 432)
meristems (p. 435)

primary growth (p. 436)
secondary growth (p. 437)
cambium (p. 438)

Review the Big Ideas

Before students begin the Chapter Review, you may wish to discuss main concepts from the big ideas in Chapter 18. Point out some examples of specialized structures that plants use to perform life processes. These include the guard cells which regulate the size of stomata and thus influence photosynthesis, and the xylem and phloem cells responsible for the transport of water and nutrients. Plant growth occurs in specific regions called meristems.

Answers

1. mesophyll
2. turgor
3. stomata
4. meristems
5. secondary
6. False. The amount of light required for a plant to reach its compensation point varies from plant to plant.
7. True
8. False. Absorption moves water from the soil into roots.
9. False. Primary growth increases the length of a plant's stem and roots.
10. True
11. Xylem cells are dead; phloem cells are alive. Xylem carries water and minerals; phloem carries sap. Water travels in one direction through xylem; dissolved sugars travel in many directions. Transport in xylem depends on transpiration and cohesion. Active transport and osmosis move sugars through phloem.
12. The air spaces in mesophyll allow for the exchange of gases involved in photosynthesis.
13. Apical meristems, which produce primary growth are located at the tips of stems and roots; lateral meristems, which produce secondary growth, are located within and parallel to the sides of roots and stems.
14. Vascular cambium produces the secondary growth of xylem and phloem.
15. Guard cells open when they are swelled with water and close when water is scarce. When closed there is little exchange of oxygen or carbon dioxide.
16. When gardeners cut off the tops of shrubs, the normally

Use Your Word Power

COMPLETION Write the word or phrase that best completes each statement.

1. The _____ is the region of the leaf in which photosynthesis takes place.

2. When vacuoles in plant cells are filled with water, the plant has _____ .

3. Pores in the epidermis that allow for gas exchange are called _____ .

4. Tissues of plants that provide new growth are called _____ .

5. The widening of a tree trunk is an example of _____ growth.

TRUE-FALSE Write true if the statement is true. If the statement is false, replace the underlined word(s) to make the statement true.

6. The amount of light required for a plant to reach its compensation point is <u>constant</u> from plant to plant.

7. The <u>pressure-flow hypothesis</u> explains the movement of sugars through phloem.

8. <u>Transpiration</u> provides the initial force that moves water from the roots to the leaves.

9. <u>Secondary growth</u> causes the elongation of stems and roots.

10. <u>Cambium</u> is a meristem that produces new cells for growth in woody plants.

Show What You Know

11. Describe the key differences between the structure of xylem and phloem tissue.

12. Explain why it is advantageous for plants to have 20 to 70 percent of the mesophyll volume composed of air spaces.

13. Use a diagram to compare the location and function of apical and lateral meristems.

14. What role does vascular cambium play in the growth of a woody stem?

15. How do guard cells control the exchange of oxygen, carbon dioxide, and water through stomata?

16. Explain how gardeners use axillary buds to control the growth of shrubs.

17. What is the cuticle? What is the cuticle's function?

18. What plant substances are responsible for converting light energy into chemical energy?

19. Describe what happens when a plant wilts. What causes wilting?

20. **Make a Concept Map** Complete the concept map below by adding the following terms: xylem, phloem, source cell, sieve tube, living, nonliving, sink cell, vessel element, transpiration, cohesion, tracheid.

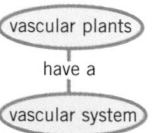

vascular plants
have a
vascular system

Take It Further

21. **Developing a Hypothesis** Many plants have stomata only on the underside of their leaves. The leaves of water lilies float on the surface of the water. Where would you expect their stomata to be? Explain your answer.

22. **Applying Concepts** Calculate the time it would take for water to travel to the top of the trunk of a 105-meter redwood tree. Assume that the water is traveling at its maximum rate.

23. **Designing an Experiment** Plan an experiment to determine whether the rate of transpiration is affected by wind. Hint: Include a method to measure the water that each plant absorbs.

24. **Applying Concepts** Sap for maple syrup is "tapped" from sugar maples in autumn.

dormant axillary buds produce side branches, which fill out the sections of the shrub that are closer to the ground.

17. The cuticle is a waxy waterproof layer that coats parts of the plant exposed to air. The cuticle conserves water by slowing evaporation.

18. Chlorophyll and other photosynthetic pigments.

19. A wilting plant loses its turgor and becomes less rigid. Wilting occurs when a plant loses water.

20. <u>Vascular system</u> consists of <u>xylem</u> and <u>phloem</u>. Phloem is <u>living</u>, xylem is <u>dead</u>. Phloem consists of <u>sieve tubes</u>. Xylem consists of <u>tracheids</u> and vessel <u>elements</u>. Phloem transports sugars from a <u>source cell</u> to a <u>sink cell</u>. Water moves

Propose a hypothesis to explain why sap rises in the spring rather than in autumn.

25. Designing an Experiment What relationship would you expect between the length of a plant's life and its ability to undergo secondary growth? What data could you collect and compare to test your hypothesis? Describe an experiment to collect this data.

26. Interpreting a Graph The graph below shows the result of an investigation about the percentage of dividing cells in a root tip. What do the data indicate about cell division in roots?

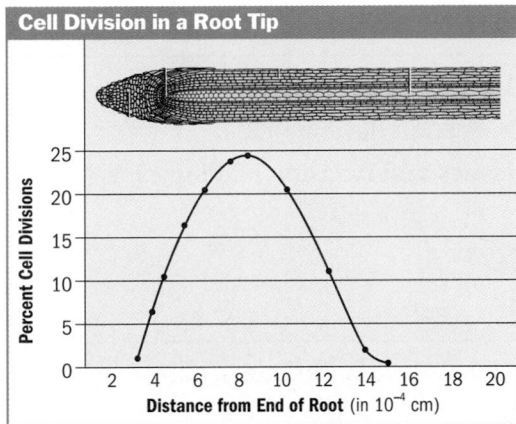

Cell Division in a Root Tip

Percent Cell Divisions (y-axis: 0, 5, 10, 15, 20, 25)
Distance from End of Root (in 10^{-4} cm) (x-axis: 2, 4, 6, 8, 10, 12, 14, 16, 18, 20)

27. Analyzing Data Examine this cross section of a root and determine whether the plant is a monocot or a dicot. Explain your answer.

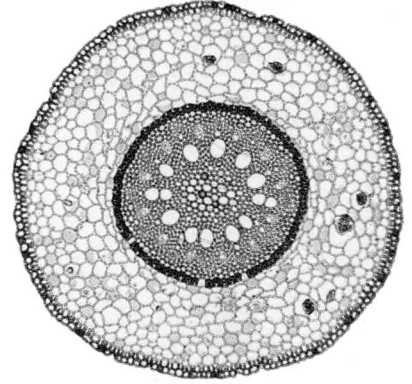

Consider the Issues

28. Urban-dwelling Plants It can be difficult for trees to survive in a city. Urban trees are exposed to air pollution from vehicles. Salt from icy roads and oil from poorly maintained engines are washed into the trees' water supply. Their roots are often buried under cement. What benefits do trees provide to a community? What actions can you take to increase the number of trees in your community and to increase their chances of survival?

Make New Connections

29. Biology and Art Make a three-dimensional model of one of the following: the layers in a plant leaf; the structure of a plant root; the structure of a woody plant stem with secondary growth.

30. Biology and Physics Find out about experiments NASA has done to investigate how plants grow in zero gravity. What is the long-term purpose of these experiments?

31. Biology and Community What kinds of plant-growing conditions are characteristic of your county or state? Consider the length of the growing season, the typical temperature range, the type of soil, and the usual amount of rainfall. How do these conditions support the crops that grow best in your area? What kind of outdoor ornamental plants thrive there? Consider using images and maps in the report of your findings.

FAST-FORWARD TO CHAPTER 19

In Chapter 19 you will study two important aspects of plant survival: how plants respond to and change their environments, and the strategies plants use for reproduction.

Chapter 18 Energy, Transport, and Growth in Plants **443**

the soil through the plants.

24. Sap rising in the spring carries sugar upward through the tree, supporting the spring growth of leaves from buds. The demands of the new growth serves as a sink.

25. Students should expect a positive correlation between the length of a plant's life and its ability to undergo secondary growth. They could collect data comparing the width of plants to their life–spans.

26. The graph shows that cell division is concentrated primarily in one region just above the root cap.

27. The plant is a monocot, with vascular tissue in a circle around a central pith.

28. Answers will vary. Trees provide shade and protection from wind and provide shelter for birds. Because many people like the look of a tree-lined street, trees affect property values. Students can ask their elected representatives to budget for money for trees. In some communities, citizens can help plant and water trees.

29. Students can use the diagrams in the text and in other resources as data for their models.

30. NASA has grown plants in zero gravity in anticipation of life on a space station. Some experiments that have been carried out on space shuttles were designed by students. Students can interact with NASA through the Internet.

31. Students may be able to obtain information about agriculture, forestry, and so on. They may also interview people such as landscape gardeners who are involved in growing outdoor plants.

through the xylem by <u>transpiration</u> and <u>cohesion</u>.

21. The stomata are located on the upper surface, which is exposed to the air containing the carbon dioxide the plants need for photosynthesis.

22. 140 minutes, or 2 hours and 20 minutes; multiply 105 m by 100 cm/m to get 10,500 cm, then divide this number

by the maximum rate of flow, which is 75 cm per minute.

23. Designs will vary. Students can expose some potted plants to a "wind" created by a fan and keep other plants protected. They can water each plant until the water drains from the pots, then measure the mass of the pots at regular times to determine how fast water passes from

Section	Student Activities/Features	Teacher's Resource Package
19.1 Plants Respond to the Environment **Objectives** ■ Give examples of environmental stimuli and plant responses ■ Explain what hormones are and give an example of a plant hormone	**Lab Zone Discover It!** *Ripening Green Bananas,* p. 445 **Lab Zone Do It!** *How Do Plants Respond to Light?* p. 447 **Everyday Biology** *Flowers for All Seasons,* p. 447 **Everyday Biology** *Apple a Day, Every Day,* p. 449 **Lab Zone Think About It!** *Analyzing Germination Conditions,* p. 451	**Unit 5 Review Module** ■ Section Review 19.1 ■ Activity Recordsheet 19-1 **Laboratory Manual,** Lab 32: "Auxins: Turning Toward the Light" **Interpreting and Developing Graphics,** 55, 56
19.2 Plants Change the Environment **Objectives** ■ Describe how plants change the environment ■ Explain how plants are essential for animal survival	**In the Community** *Irritating Plants,* p. 453 **STS: Environmental Awareness** *Computers on Farms,* p. 454	**Unit Review Module** ■ Section Review 19.2 **Issues and Decision Making** 19-1
19.3 Asexual Reproduction in Plants **Objectives** ■ Explain the benefit and process of asexual reproduction in plants ■ Identify the methods and uses of artificial propagation in plants	**Lab Zone Do It!** *Observing Asexual Reproduction in Plants,* p. 457	**Unit 5 Review Module** ■ Section Review 19.3 ■ Activity Recordsheet 19-2 ■ Enrichment Topic 19-1 ■ Critical Thinking Exercise 19 **Issues and Decision Making** 19-2 **Consumer Applications** 19-1
19.4 Sexual Reproduction in Plants **Objectives** ■ Identify the plant forms and the stages of alternation of generations ■ Explain the characteristics of seeds and the process of germination	**Lab Zone Investigate It!** *Observing Seedlings,* p. 462	**Unit 5 Review Module** ■ Section Review 19.4 ■ Activity Recordsheet 19-3 ■ Enrichment Topic 19-2
19.5 Focus on Flowers **Objectives** ■ Identify the male, female, and sterile parts of a flower ■ Explain the process of pollination		**Unit 5 Review Module** ■ Section Review 19.5 ■ Interpreting Graphics 19 ■ Vocabulary Review 19 ■ Chapter 19 Tests **Interpreting and Developing Graphics,** 57 **Spanish Reviews** Chapter 19

Technology Resources

Internet Connections

Within this chapter, you will see the bioSURF logo. If you and your students have access to the Internet, the following URL address will provide various Internet connections that are related to topics and features presented in this chapter:

http://plants.biosurf.com

You can also find relevant chapter material at **The Biology Place** address:

http://www.biology.com

CD-ROMs

Biología: la telaraña de la vida,
   (Spanish Student Edition) Chapter 19
Teacher's Resource Planner, Chapter 19
   Supplements
TestWorks CD-ROM
- Chapter 19 Tests

Videodiscs

Animated Biological Concepts Videodiscs
- Angiosperm Reproduction

Overhead Transparencies

- A Typical Flower, #39
- Seed Development, #40

Videotapes

Biology Alive! Video Series
Rewind: The Web of Life Reteach Videos

Planning for Activities

STUDENT EDITION
Lab Zone
Discover It! p. 445
- 3 green bananas and
  1 apple
- 2 resealable plastic bags

Lab Zone Do It! p. 447
- scissors
- cardboard carton with
  dividers
- 4 bean seeds
- small flower pot
- potting soil

Lab Zone Do It! p. 457
- runner from a spider
  plant
- scissors
- 2 containers
- potting soil

Lab Zone
Investigate It! p. 462
- 2 resealable plastic bags
- 2 paper towels
- metric ruler
- stapler
- corn seeds and beans
  seeds
- permanent marker

TEACHER'S EDITION
Teacher Demo, p. 446
Plant movements
- film/video with time-
  lapse photography of
  plant movement

Teacher Demo, p. 447
Venus's flytrap
- Venus's flytrap
- light

Teacher Demo, p. 449
Earth's seasons
- 1 orange
- knife
- pencil
- penlight

Teacher Demo, p. 450
Seed germination
- 3 petri dishes
- blotter paper
- seeds
- freezer or refrigerator

Teacher Demo, p. 455
Two kinds of oranges
- oranges—one with
  seeds and one seedless
- knife

Teacher Demo, p. 456
Asexual reproduction
- strawberry or crabgrass
  plants with runners,
  bulbs, potatoes with
  eyes, and other tubers

Class Activity, p. 456
Artificial propagation
- cuttings from three different kinds of plants
- vermiculite

Teacher Demo, p. 456
Demonstrating grafting
- tree branch
- knife
- wax

Teacher Demo, p. 458
Seed dispersal
- apples, berries, burrs
  from grasses, dandelion
  head

Class Activity, p. 460
Monocot and a dicot
- bean seed, corn seed
- hand lenses

Teacher Demo, p. 461
Parts of a germinating seed
- germinating seed

Teacher Demo, p. 463
Reproductive flower parts
- flowers in various stages
  of anthesis

Chapter Objectives

Students will learn the main concepts of this chapter as they complete the following objectives.

- Give examples of environmental stimuli and plant responses
- Explain what hormones are and give an example
- Describe how plants change the environment and how they are essential for animal survival
- Explain the benefit and means of asexual reproduction in plants and identify methods and uses of artificial propagation
- Identify the plant forms and stages of alternation of generations
- Explain seed characteristics and the germination process
- Identify the male, female, and sterile flower parts and explain the pollination process

Key Words

19.1 *stimulus, tropism, hormone, auxin, photoperiodism, dormancy*

19.2 *colonizers*

19.3 *vegetative reproduction, artificial propagation*

19.4 *gametophyte, sporophyte, seed, cotyledon, monocot, dicot*

19.5 *flower, ovary, ovule, pollen, pollination*

The Opening Story

Have students discuss how the story might relate to the chapter. Ask how plants respond to changes in sunlight or seasonal temperatures.

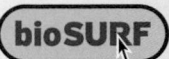

You can find out more about response and reproduction in plants by exploring the following Internet address: *http://plants.biosurf.com*

In this chapter . . .

FEATURES

Everyday Biology
- Flowers for All Seasons
- Apple a Day, Every Day

In the Community
Irritating Plants

 Environmental Awareness
Computers on Farms

LAB ZONES

Discover It!
- Ripening Green Bananas

Do It!
- How Do Plants Respond to Light?
- Observing Asexual Reproduction in Plants

Think About It!
- Analyzing Germination Conditions

Investigate It!
- Observing Seedlings

Alpine Adventurers Brave the Cold

nowbells blossom in the high mountain air of the Alps, below snow-covered peaks. Far to the north, in the heart of Alaska, a woolly lousewort pokes through the early summer snow on the permanently frozen earth. How do these plants survive in polar regions that are often dark, usually racked by wind, and nearly always cold? How do they reproduce in the thin air and frigid temperatures of a mountaintop? The answers to these questions are often astounding.

Some plants secrete alcohol, which acts as an antifreeze. Others, like the pasqueflower, have highly reflective petals that cup to catch the sun's rays. Inside the blossom it may be up to 10 degrees Celsius warmer than the surrounding air. These cold-weather, seed-bearing plants will slow down reproduction, taking two or three years to accomplish what a warm-air plant does in one growing season. Their buds form in one summer, lie dormant over the long winter, and flower with the first warm days of the next growing season. Many arctic plants reproduce underground, sending out rhizomes, or underground stems, in the protected earth to start new plants.

In the cold, some plants conserve heat and energy, protecting their internal fluids from freezing. But in severe cold, plants become dormant. What are other ways that plants respond to their surroundings as they grow and reproduce?

PORTFOLIO PREVIEW

Students should be encouraged to add to their portfolios as they work through this chapter. In addition to the *Write About It* opportunity, the following section is an excellent opportunity for portfolio entries:

■ Section 19.1: *Plants Respond to the Environment*

 **Discover It!**

Ripening Green Bananas

You need *3 green bananas, 1 apple, 2 resealable plastic bags*

1. Place 1 banana with an apple in a tightly sealed plastic bag. Place 1 banana by itself in a tightly sealed plastic bag. Place 1 banana in the open air, away from any other fruit.
2. For each of the next 3–5 days, take notes on the changes, if any, in the three bananas.

Plants, like many other living things, produce hormones. A hormone called ethylene controls the rate of ripening in fruit. The banana sealed in the bag with the apple tends to ripen fastest because it is exposed to the ethylene produced by the apple.

WRITE ABOUT IT!

In your science journal, write a brief description of a visit to a garden, orchard, or greenhouse where fruits or vegetables are growing. Base your account on personal experience, or use your imagination. What sights, sounds, and smells would you encounter?

445

Opening Activities

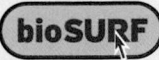 If you have access to the Internet in your classroom or school, you may wish to have students connect to the address shown on page 444. You may also want to have students conduct net searches for information using key words related to this chapter.

 Discover It!

Ripening Green Bananas   TEAM WORK

Before students begin this chapter, have them do the suggested activity in small groups. Have each group predict which banana will ripen first and why.

WRITE ABOUT IT

Encourage students to talk with the produce manager in their neighborhood supermarket. They could ask for tips for determining ripeness in various fruits or vegetables or discuss the shelf life of fresh produce.

SUPER READ! **Monitoring Understanding**

To practice strategies for effective reading, use pages 53-54 in *Super Read!*

◀••••••••••••••••••••••

REWIND to Chapter 18

Briefly review concepts learned in Chapter 18, *Energy, Transport, and Growth in Plants*. Ask:

■ **What specialized structures do you think plants use to respond to changes in their environment and to reproduce?**

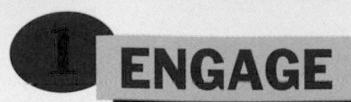

ENGAGE

Consider the Big Idea!

Have students read The Big Idea! at the top of the page. Explain that plants respond to such factors as light, water, touch, and temperature.

Use the Visual

Have students study the photograph that opens the section. Explain that plants must be able to respond to environmental conditions in order to survive. Ask:

- **How might the toadflax affect its environment?** (Seed germination, growth, and root pressure may crumble the surrounding rock.)

Check Prior Knowledge

To assess students' knowledge about plant functions, ask:

- **What do plants require to survive?** (Light, water, carbon dioxide, and minerals; most require soil.)
- **How do plants use light in photosynthesis?** (They use light energy to make food.)
- **How do plants respond to abundance or scarcity of water?** (Moisture levels affect turgor, which controls the opening and closing of stomata.)

Teacher Demo

Show a film or video with time-lapse photography of plant movements such as phototropism or the opening and closing of flowers.

19.1 Plants Respond to the Environment

What you'll learn

IDEAS
- To give examples of environmental stimuli and plant responses
- To explain what hormones are and to give an example of a plant hormone

WORDS
stimulus, tropism, hormone, auxin, photoperiodism, dormancy

The shady side of the street
Plants can respond to many different stimuli in their environments. Can you imagine why a plant would grow away from the light? The ivy-leaved toadflax grows on walls and rock faces. Its seeds need darkness to germinate. The stems carrying the seeds grow toward the shadowy cracks where new seeds can sprout.

TYPICAL PLANT RESPONSES

Fitting into the scene

Plants, like all other living organisms, respond to conditions in their environment. In most cases, they respond to specific environmental changes. Any environmental condition or change that causes a response by a plant or other organism is called a **stimulus** (plural: *stimuli*). External conditions such as gravity, day length, temperature, light, moisture, and physical contact can act as stimuli. Plants also respond to changes in their internal, or cellular, environment.

Plants respond to stimuli in various ways. For example, plants can change the direction of their growth, move individual parts, and undergo seasonal cycles of growth, flowering, and dormancy.

Tropisms The growth of a plant in a certain direction in response to a stimulus is called a **tropism** (TROH-piz-uhm). A tropism may be positive, with growth toward a stimulus, or it may be negative, with growth away from a stimulus. What type of tropism do you see in *Figure 19.1*? ❷

Phototropism is the response of plants to light. Positive phototropism, growth toward light, enables many growing embryos and new growth of mature plants to absorb the sunlight they need for photosynthesis.

A second type of tropism, gravitropism, is growth in response to gravity. Roots are positively gravitropic, meaning that root tips grow downward. Gravitropism is adaptive because roots

FIGURE 19.1

What stimulus is causing this plant to grow in one direction? What is the name for this type of growth? ❶

STUDENT RESOURCES

From the Teacher's Resource Package, use:
- Section Review 19.1, and Activity Recordsheet 19-1, from Unit 5 Review Module
- Lab 32: "Auxins: Turning Toward the Light"

TECHNOLOGY RESOURCES

Relevant technology resources include:
- Spanish Student Edition CD-ROM
- Teacher's Resource Planner CD-ROM

grow where they are more likely to get water and nutrients. New growth on plant stems is negatively gravitropic, meaning that the tips grow upward toward a light source.

A third type of growth response is called thigmotropism, or response to touch. An example of thigmotropism is the coiling of the stems of a plant such as the morning glory. Thigmotropism enables a plant to grow on a surface that can support it. Wherever the stem touches the support, the cells on the opposite side of the stem grow longer, causing the stem to coil around, or grasp hold of, the support.

Nastic movements Sometimes parts of plants will move slightly in response to any stimulus. Nastic movements are responses that occur in the same way, regardless of the stimulus. Nastic movements are usually short-term, reversible changes.

One of the most fascinating nastic movements is the opening and closing of the carnivorous Venus's flytrap leaves. When an insect brushes against their trigger hairs, the leaves close and capture it. What do you **❸** think happens to the insect?

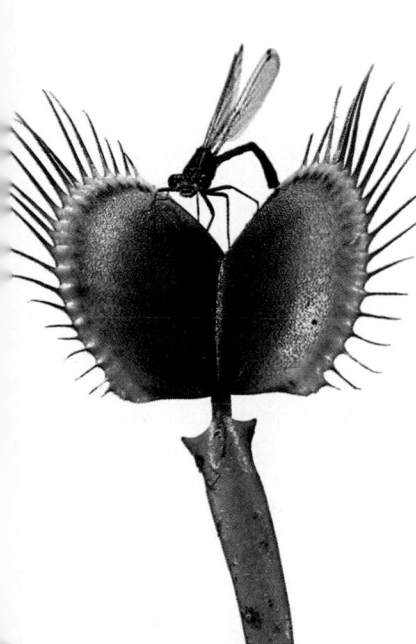

LAB ZONE Do It! bioSURF

How Do Plants Respond to Light?

Can plants find their way through a maze? Find out when you . . .

Try This

1 Set up a maze by cutting a hole in a cardboard carton with dividers, as shown in the photograph. **Caution:** Use care when handling scissors.
2 Plant four bean seeds in a small flower pot. Place the pot in a corner of the carton as far away from the outside hole as possible. Close the sides of the carton so that the only light in the box comes from the hole that you cut.

3 Over the next two weeks, open the carton every two to three days to water the seeds and observe the seedlings.

Analyze Your Results

1 Summarize what happened to the bean seeds.
2 What caused the bean plants to grow the way they did?

PLANT HORMONES

Chemicals in control

Nervous systems enable humans and other animals to respond to stimuli in their environment. Plants, however, do not have nervous systems. How, then, do they respond to changing environmental conditions? Plants respond by producing chemicals called hormones, which control plant growth and responses.

A **hormone** is an organic compound that is produced in small amounts and released by one part of an organism to affect another part. Sometimes, plant hormones also affect the tissues that produce them.

Each plant hormone can have several effects, depending on the nature

EVERYDAY BIOLOGY

Flowers for All Seasons

Growers force plants to bloom out of season by altering the light stimulus. Growers use artificial light to control day lengths in greenhouses. With this technique, we can have flowering chrysanthemums and poinsettias throughout the year.

FIGURE 19.2
When this Venus's flytrap leaf quickly closes its two lobes, it can capture an insect, a source of nitrogen for the plant.

Chapter 19 Response and Reproduction in Plants **447**

❶ Light; tropism
❷ Phototropism
❸ It is captured and digested by the plant.

LAB ZONE Do It! TEAM WORK

How Do Plants Respond to Light?

Analyze Your Results

Bean seeds will sprout. Plant will move toward light.

Teacher Demo

Obtain a Venus's flytrap or a mimosa, which also responds to touch. Touch the plant at the end of its leaves so that students can observe the plant move as it curls up away from your fingers. Allow students an opportunity to cause the same response.

Think Critically

Discuss geotropism. Ask:

- **Why is it unnecessary to plant a seed right-side up?** (The shoots are negatively geotropic and the roots are positively geotropic.)

Build Writing Skills

Assign students to research thigmotropic plants such as ivy, and hydrotropic plants such as weeping willow trees. Have them report on how these plants respond to stimuli and problems they may cause.

Everyday Biology

Forcing is also used with bulbs. Commercial nurseries refrigerate tulip bulbs to force early blooms.

Use the Visual

Give students time to read through Figure 19.3. Ask:

- **Which two hormones would be needed first by a newly planted seed?** (Gibberellin and cytokinin)
- **Which hormone would be used after fruit has formed?** (Ethylene)

Apply

Tell students that tomatoes that have ripened naturally show gradations of red color, while tomatoes that have ripened with the aid of hormones are even in color. Challenge students to find out how to distinguish between other fruits that have ripened naturally or with the aid of plant hormones.

 Language Arts

Tell students that the origin of the term *auxin* is the Greek word *auxein* which means "to increase." Ask students how the meaning of the term relates to how the hormone affects plants.

Use The Visual

Have students study Figure 19.4. Ask:

- **Why did the Darwins include a coleoptile with a collar in their experiment?** (It supported the conclusion that the tip of the plant, not another region, was sensitive to light.)

448

The Effects of Plant Hormones on Plants

Auxin

stimulates cell elongation

stimulates root growth, differentiation, and branching

stimulates development of fruit

controls branching of stems

controls phototropism and gravitropism

Gibberellin

promotes seed and bud germination

promotes stem elongation

promotes leaf growth

stimulates flowering and development of fruit

affects root growth and differentiation

Ethylene

promotes fruit ripening

opposes some auxin effects

inhibits stem elongation

simulates development of roots, leaves, or flowers, depending on the species

Cytokinin

affects root growth and differentiation

stimulates cell division and growth

stimulates germination

stimulates flowering

delays aging

Abscisic Acid

inhibits growth

closes stomata during excessive water loss

promotes seed and bud dormancy

FIGURE 19.3

Some of the effects of five plant hormones are listed here. Which one promotes the ripening of fruit? Which ones stimulate flowering? ❶

FIGURE 19.4

The Darwins' Experiments

Charles and Francis Darwin demonstrated that coleoptile tips will grow toward light, unless they are shielded from it.

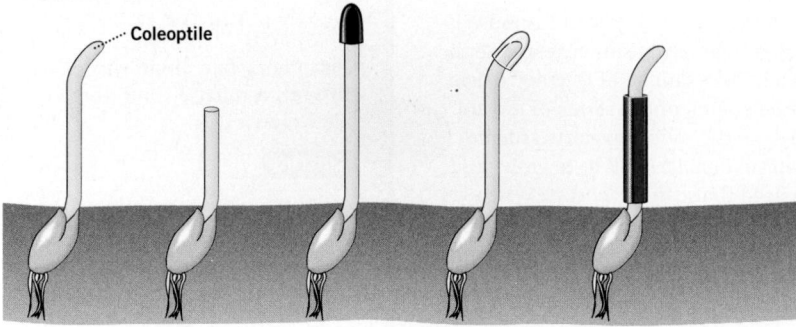

Coleoptile

Control | Tip removed | Tip covered by opaque cap | Tip covered by transparent cap | Base covered by opaque shield

of the hormone, the sensitivity of its target cells, and the amount of hormone present. Hormones in plants affect their growth and their ability to respond to changes in the environment. Some plant hormones and their various effects are listed in the table in *Figure 19.3*.

If you have ever grown a plant on a windowsill, you have probably observed an example of phototropism—the tendency of plant stems to grow toward sunlight. In the 1880s Charles Darwin and his son Francis studied the growth of plants toward light. *Figure 19.4* summarizes the results of their experiments. The Darwins studied the coleoptiles (KOH-lee-AWP-tulz) of oat seedlings. A coleoptile is a sheath covering the first leaves that emerge from the seeds of grasses.

The Darwins observed that the coleoptiles would curve toward the light only if the tip of the coleoptile remained intact. If the tip was cut off, the coleoptile did not curve toward the light.

The Darwins also discovered that if the coleoptile tip was covered with an opaque cap, which did not transmit

light, the coleoptile did not curve as it grew. However, if the cap was transparent, the coleoptile curved toward the light as it grew. The coleoptile also turned to the light when its base was covered with an opaque shield.

From these experiments, the Darwins concluded that the tip of the coleoptile, rather than the curving region, was sensitive to light. The coleoptile response did not occur in the tip where the light was sensed, but in a different place. In some way, the tip was transmitting a signal to the rest of the plant.

In 1926 Dutch botanist Fritz Went continued the experiments of the Darwins. His experiments are summarized in *Figure 19.5*. Went cut off the tips of oat coleoptiles and placed the tips upright on blocks of agar. (Agar is a gelatinlike substance made from seaweed.) After an hour, Went put the same agar blocks onto coleoptiles with cut-off tips that were growing in the dark. Went placed the agar blocks so that they covered only part of the tip of the coleoptile. Much to Went's surprise, the coleoptiles curved away from the agar.

448 *Unit 5 Plants*

MEETING DIVERSE NEEDS

Gifted Like plants, humans have hormones that regulate bodily functions. Have interested students research some human hormones and the functions they regulate. Ask them to compare human hormones to their plant counterparts in a written report.

At Risk and LEP Have students draw a tree or other plant and label the hormones that affect each part.

Went concluded that the agar blocks had absorbed from the coleoptile tips a substance that caused cells to grow longer. When this substance was applied to one side of a coleoptile, it stimulated the growth of cells on that side, causing the coleoptile to curve.

Went observed that the substance causing the growth was made in the tip of the coleoptile but caused growth below the tip. He concluded that the substance causing the growth was a hormone, because a hormone is produced in one part of an organism but affects another. Went named the hormone auxin, from the Greek word meaning "to grow." **Auxin** is a plant hormone that causes plant cells to grow longer, which results in plant growth.

Other scientists showed that light influences the diffusion of auxin through a plant. When a plant is exposed to light, the auxin diffuses from cells on the lighted side of the plant to cells on the shaded side of the plant. The auxin causes

FIGURE 19.5
Went's Experiment
Fritz Went showed that a substance from a coleoptile tip could diffuse into an agar block and then into another coleoptile, causing growth. He concluded that the substance was a hormone.

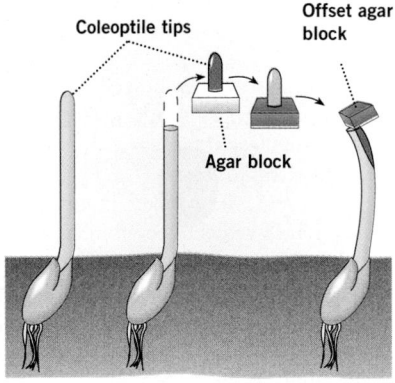

Coleoptile tips

Offset agar block

Agar block

| Control | Auxin from the coleoptile tip diffused into the agar block. | Auxin in the agar block caused the coleoptile to bend. |

the cells on the shaded side of the plant to grow longer. The result is that the plant curves toward light as it grows.

Auxin has other effects on plants. It promotes the new root growth in cuttings and causes fruit to develop. You can study the table in *Figure 19.3* to learn about other plant hormones. What are some of the different effects of other plant hormones? ❷

DAY-LENGTH RESPONSES
Plants take measure

Many plant species respond to changes in light. The flowers of some plants, such as daylilies and morning glories, close during the night and open again each morning. Many plants also respond to the seasons, forming flowers and growing buds only during a particular time of the year.

One way plants respond to seasonal conditons is by detecting changes in the length of daylight—shorter daylight in winter, longer in summer. In many plants, flowering time is linked to the lengths of daylight and darkness. Any response of a plant to daylight length is called **photoperiodism.**

Botanists divide plants into three groups, based on their response to specific photoperiods: long-day plants, short-day plants, and day-neutral plants. Long-day plants tend to bloom in late spring or early summer, when days are long and nights are short. Long-day plants include some irises, wheat, lettuce, radishes, and corn. Short-day plants bloom in late summer, autumn, or winter, when days grow short. Short-day plants include ragweed, soybeans, asters, and chrysanthemums. Day-neutral plants do not respond to changes in day length. Day-neutral plants include roses, snapdragons, sunflowers, and tomatoes.

You may be surprised to learn that long-day and short-day plants do

EVERYDAY BIOLOGY
Apple a Day, Every Day

In nature, apples ripen during the fall. To provide ripe apples in other seasons, growers store apples in refrigerated warehouses with high levels of carbon dioxide. Carbon dioxide postpones the production of ethylene that causes ripening until the fruit is sent to the market.

Everyday Biology

To prevent fruit from falling prematurely, some growers spray their orchards with a carefully controlled amount of 2-4-D, a synthetic auxin. The auxin apparently retards the formation of an abscission layer between the fruit and the stem.

Teacher Demo

Explain how number of daylight hours depends on the angle at which the sun strikes the Earth. Score the peel of an orange through the center, then score it again 1/4 the way between the center and the top. Make another score line between the center and the bottom. Tell students the score lines represent the Tropic of Cancer and the Tropic of Capricorn. Drive a pencil through the orange at a 23.5° angle to the floor. Use a penlight to represent the sun's rays, and show students how the sun strikes Earth's surface on the first day of summer, the fall equinox, the first day of winter, and the spring equinox by having the student move in a circle around you, while you keep the penlight trained on the orange. Discuss how the daylight and nighttime hours at the poles are affected. You may wish to have students research the size of vegetables grown in Alaska during the summer.

❶ Ethylene promotes fruit ripening. Gibberellin, ethylene, and cytokinin promote flowering.

❷ Gibberellin promotes seed and bud germination, stem elongation and leaf growth. Ethylene promotes fruit ripening and opposes some auxin effects. Cytokinin stimulates cell division and growth and delays aging. Abscisic acid inhibits growth and causes stomata to close.

not actually respond to the hours of sunlight, but rather to the hours of continuous darkness. So these plants could also be called short-night and long-night plants! *Figure 19.6* illustrates how short-day and long-day plants differ. Look for the presence or absence of flowers to see how night length affects each type of plant.

A brief flash of light during the night is enough to disrupt the flowering cycle of short-day (long-night) plants. In one practical application of the plant response to day length, growers use flashes of light in greenhouses to control flowering. How did a flash of light affect the plants illustrated in *Figure 19.6*? ❶

There is much about photoperiodism that scientists do not yet understand. However, they do know that photoperiodism and some other plant responses to light are controlled by a blue pigment called phytochrome (FY-toh-krohm). Phytochrome changes its structure in response to different light colors. It controls plant responses such as flowering, seed germination, and seasonal inactivity. Scientists actively continue to investigate phytochrome to learn more about how it functions.

FIGURE 19.6
Short-day plants flower only when the nights are long enough—longer than the critical night length. If the critical night length is interrupted by a flash of light, no flowering occurs.

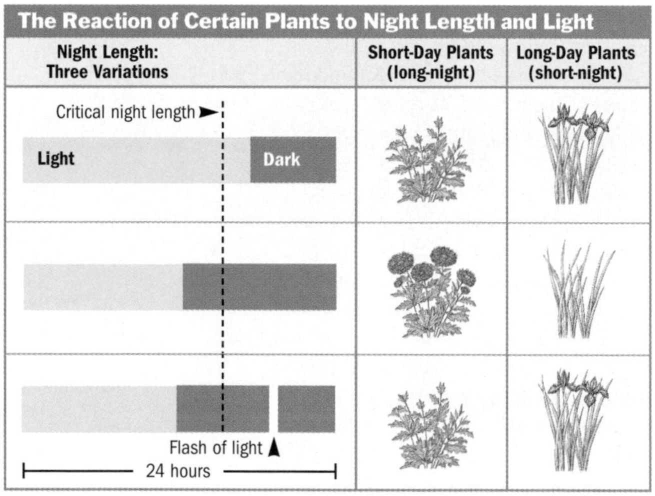

The Reaction of Certain Plants to Night Length and Light

Night Length: Three Variations	Short-Day Plants (long-night)	Long-Day Plants (short-night)
Critical night length ▶ Light / Dark		
Flash of light ▲ / 24 hours		

450 *Unit 5 Plants*

DORMANCY
Plants nod off, too

Some plants respond to the changing seasons by becoming dormant. **Dormancy** is a period of decreased activity that results from structural and chemical changes in a plant. Plants may undergo dormancy in climates that are extremely cold or very hot and dry. A dormant period may be needed before some seeds and bulbs will start to grow.

You can probably name some trees that lose their leaves and become dormant in the fall. Dormancy is common among deciduous plants that live in cold winter climates. It reduces the chance that plants will be damaged by freezing temperatures.

During autumn, longer nights stimulate the leaves of deciduous plants to loosen and drop. A leaf scar forms on the stem after a leaf drops. The remaining cells secrete wax, which seals the stem from pathogens, organisms that cause disease. Deciduous plants also respond to longer autumn nights by forming bud scales. Bud scales protect developing buds from cold and infection. You can usually see leaf scars and bud scales if you look at a dormant stem during winter.

Seasonal dry periods can also stimulate plant dormancy. The dormancy responses resulting from lack of water are similar to those resulting from cold. Plants lose their leaves and form drought-resistant buds.

Have you ever wondered how seeds that have been stored in a package for a long time can start to grow when planted in a garden? Many varieties of seeds and bulbs have a dormant period before they sprout. When mature seeds are released from the parent plant, they remain dormant until the right growth conditions exist. Packaged seeds remain dormant until they are planted because in a package

FIGURE 19.7

Crocus bulbs require a period of cold before they begin to grow. How can you use that information to force crocuses to bloom ahead of schedule? ❷

LAB ZONE ? Think About It!

Analyzing Germination Conditions

The table at right lists types of plants and the conditions required for their seeds to germinate.

Analyzing the Table

1 How do the conditions listed help each type of seed to germinate?
2 Using what you have read about plant responses, suggest another possible condition that could stimulate a seed to germinate. How would the signal and the timing of germination benefit the plant?

Plant	Condition or Mechanism
Apple	Exposure to temperatures below 10°C
Guanacaste	Seedpod weakened by the digestive acids in an animal's stomach
Hakea	Exposure to fire, which breaks the seed coat
Shadscale	Exposure to heavy rain that washes salt from the seed
White sweet clover	Agitation, such as shaking by wind, that causes a pluglike structure to fall from the seed

the seeds do not have the right conditions for growth.

Sometimes the period of dormancy is caused by growth inhibitors—chemicals that stop growth. Growth inhibitors must be removed before any new growth can occur. The seeds of many plants that are planted in autumn will not sprout until spring, after the moisture in the soil has washed growth inhibitors from the seeds.

A cold period is sometimes necessary to destroy the growth inhibitors in bulbs. If you wish to force a crocus or paper-white narcissus to flower before spring arrives, refrigerate the bulbs for about a month. You can then plant the bulbs in containers, and they will bloom indoors.

The dormancy of a few types of seeds is broken by intense heat. The loblolly-pine is the best-known example; its cones fly open during forest fires, and its seedlings are the first to grow when the scorched land begins to recover. Other examples of seeds that require heat to sprout include

Australian bush plants that have woody fruits with seeds inside. These fruits may stay attached to the trees for years until a fire causes the seeds to burst from the fruit. In this way, the land can be reseeded quickly as the new seeds begin to sprout.

CHECKPOINT 19.1

1. Name three types of stimuli that affect the growth of plants.
2. Explain what a hormone is, and give an example of a plant hormone and its effects.
3. Critical Thinking Why is it important that the flowers of a particular species open at the same time?

Build on What You Know

4. How might dormancy help a plant maintain homeostasis during dry, hot weather? *(Need to jog your memory? Revisit relevant concepts in Chapter 2, Section 2.4.)*

Chapter 19 Response and Reproduction in Plants **451**

① ENGAGE

Use The Visual

Have students study the photograph and read the text that opens the section. Explain that as plants interact with their environment they change it in some way. Have students give examples of ways in which plants have changed the environment.

Check Prior Knowledge

To assess students' knowledge about environmental change, ask:

- **How does photosynthesis affect the atmosphere?** (It absorbs carbon dioxide and gives off oxygen into the atmosphere.)
- **What happens to a garden if it is not weeded regularly?** (The growing weeds may compete with the cultivated plants for space, water, and nutrients.)

Quick Activity

Ask students to cite their personal observations of plant interaction. For example, are any students allergic to pollen? What plants provide shelter or food for animals? List student responses on the board and encourage students to add to the list as they complete the section.

19.2 Plants Change the Environment

What you'll learn

IDEAS
- To describe how plants change the environment
- To explain how plants are essential for animal survival

WORDS
colonizers

Seafaring seeds

Earth is always changing. New land appears in the form of volcanic islands and coral reefs. Gradually, these empty lots in the ocean acquire plant life. How do plants cross the water? Some seeds, like those of the coconut, float. Other seeds travel on and in animals, including humans. Wherever plants spring up, they cause many changes in the soil, the animal population, and even the climate.

PLANT COLONIZERS

Plants take turns

You have seen that plants interact with the environment in several ways. Plants also change the environment. If you observe a vacant lot or a natural meadow over a period of time, you will notice many changes. Some changes happen within one growing season; others occur over many years.

Plants appear soon after a tract of land is cleared. Although the land may seem to be composed of only dirt, plant seeds are often buried in soil or carried on wind or water currents, or by animals passing through the area. For plants, essential factors for growth are adequate moisture, nutrients in the soil, and sunlight. If the essential factors are present, some seeds will grow.

The first organisms to dwell in an uninhabited area are called **colonizers.** Plant colonizers often include mosses, which can grow even in rocky and barren areas. As mosses die and decay, they provide soil for other plants. Other colonizers, often called weeds, are hardy plants that can grow in harsh conditions. Most colonizers are short plants with dense, fibrous root systems. These plants are followed by small flowering plants and shrubs whose seeds soon spread through the area and germinate.

As colonizers inhabit an area for several years, there is a gradual change in the type of plants living in that area. The small pioneer plants

FIGURE 19.8
Plant Succession

1 Valley glaciers sometimes shrink, revealing large areas of barren earth.

2 Only hardy plants can live in the soil exposed by a retreating glacier.

3 Over the years, the soil becomes richer and new plants take root.

452   Unit 5 Plants

IN THE COMMUNITY
Irritating Plants

Plants such as ragweed and poison ivy often cause allergic reactions in humans. Investigate the types of pollen-bearing and poisonous plants that grow in your neighborhood. Do some research in the library or speak with a local botanist or allergist (a physician who specializes in treating allergies). Some newspapers report daily pollen levels and may provide further information. Share your findings by making a calendar that describes the types of plants that cause allergies and shows the times of the year and conditions under which their pollen production is at its peak. You can log on to the Internet at *http://plants.biosurf.com* to learn more about the plants that irritate humans.

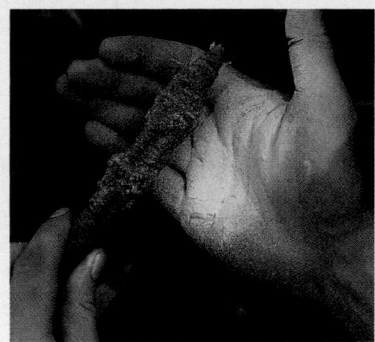

present at the beginning would decrease in number, while the larger plants would become more abundant. With time, the dominant plant species in the ecosystem—grasses, shrubs, or trees—would replace the pioneer species. This progression of different plant species over time is called succession. You will learn more about succession in Chapter 37.

As plants live and eventually die in an area, they cause changes in the soil. Plants' roots give off carbon dioxide that forms carbonic acid in the soil. This acid helps break down rocks. As roots grow, they exert pressure, which cracks pebbles and rocks around them.

Some plants enrich the soil through the symbiotic relationships they form with certain bacteria. Legumes, which are members of the pea family, form root sacs in which nitrogen-fixing bacteria live. The bacteria convert nitrogen gas into compounds the plants can use. When the legumes die, some of the nitrogen compounds released into the soil from the roots of legumes are used by other plants.

When leaves drop from plants and when plants die, the dead plant material starts to decay, forming a substance in the soil called humus.

Humus provides nutrients for plants, helps the soil hold water, and helps keep the soil open to air. All of these effects of humus help plants to grow.

Plants can also modify the local climate and landforms in many ways. For example, plants can act as windbreaks and prevent erosion; they can change the air temperature and raise the humidity. When plants are removed from an area, the local climate and soil also may be dramatically changed. The loss of plants through intentional deforestation or natural disaster can lead to increased erosion from water and wind and can alter the temperature and humidity.

A remarkable example of the effect of plants on the environment began in the 1950s in China when the government planted 300 million trees along its famous Great Wall. One goal of the planting was to slow the winds that blew from the desert regions of China, causing terrible dust storms. Chinese weather data showed that between 1950 and 1960 there were 10 to 20 dust storms per year. By the 1980s and 1990s, there were only 2 to 3 dust storms per year. Other factors may have affected the weather pattern, but it seems that as the trees matured, they helped change the environment.

Chapter 19 Response and Reproduction in Plants **453**

TEACH

In The Community

Have students examine different types of pollen under the microscope. Have them make drawings of the different kinds of pollen.

Apply

After discussing how plants cause changes in the soil, ask:

■ **How might farmers use plants to improve crop yield?** (Students may cite crop rotation and using plants as manure, ground cover, windbreaks, and insecticides.)

Explain

Point out that invading plant species can completely wipe out biodiversity in an area. Melaleuca trees, for example, are native to Australia and Malaysia, where more than 400 species of insect feast on them. In 1936, the U.S. Army Corps of Engineers planted the trees to stabilize levees on the southern shore of Lake Okeechobee. Because they had no natural enemies, the trees had invaded more than 400,000 acres of the Everglades by the 1990s. In one patch, they had crowded out all other plant species, as well as the animals that fed on them.

19.2

Think Critically

After students complete this section, ask:

■ **How is recycling done by fungi similar to recycling done by people?** (Fungi are heterotrophs that digest and decompose plant material, recycling the nutrients to the ecosystem. People who recycle metal, plastics, and glass return these materials to industries that reuse them in similar or different products.)

 STS

Ask students to research the kind of satellites that would be useful to farmers.

 Monitoring Understanding

To practice strategies for effective reading, use pages 53-54 in *Super Read!*

 **3 ASSESS**

Evaluate Understanding

Ask students to write a paragraph describing the sequence of plant and animal life that would be observed after a wooded area is cleared and crops are planted. Their descriptions should cover a period of five years.

Reteach

On the chalkboard or on a transparency, work with students to create a flowchart showing the plant succession in an area over time. Begin with colonizers and end with a mature forest. Discuss reasons for the changes in plant life.

454

FIGURE 19.9
Ants living in the thorns of acacia trees protect the trees from insects that would eat the leaves and branches. The trees provide a home for the ants and a sugar solution that nourishes them.

INTERACTION WITH ANIMALS
Consumers on scene

As you have learned, plants are necessary for the survival of land-dwelling animals. Plants provide food, protection, and shelter for animals. One or another species of animals eats the fruits, stems, or seeds of almost every plant. Animals that do not themselves eat plants consume animals that do. Trees and shrubs provide shelter from storms and sunlight. Their boughs or larger stems offer nesting sites for birds and other small animals, homes for insects, and dense shelter for larger animals such as deer.

As the types of plants change during the process of succession, so do the animals living in that area. For example, suppose an untended field undergoes succession to become a forest. When small plants start to grow in an open field, many insects can obtain food and shelter. Soon, grasses fill in the field and more insects, lizards, and burrowing rodents may arrive. Woody shrubs may eventually replace the grasses, allowing birds and larger mammals to inhabit the area. As trees replace the woody shrubs, many birds and other animals find food and shelter among the plants.

 What are some ways that plants respond to the environment and some ways that they influence the environment?

454 *Unit 5 Plants*

ENVIRONMENTAL AWARENESS
Computers on farms

You might be surprised to see a farmer on a tractor or a combine working with a laptop computer. But high-tech farming, also called precision or site-specific farming, could be the wave of the future. In an effort to reduce costs and increase crop yields, high-tech farmers use computer and satellite technology.

This technology enables farmers to analyze variations in soil type and quality in each of their fields. The farmers are then able to customize the amount of fertilizers and pesticides they need to apply to different fields or even to different areas of one field. Using this technology, farmers often reduce the total amount of fertilizers and pesticides they use. Precision farming helps farmers grow better crops and save money, and it also is good for the environment.

CHECKPOINT 19.2

1. Describe several ways in which plants can change the environment.
2. List three ways in which plants sustain animal life.
3. Critical Thinking Choose one of these environments: a plowed field, the mossy slope of a mountain, a vacant lot. What succession of plants would you anticipate finding there?

Build on What You Know

4. Roots give off substances into the soil that become acids. What kind of ions do acids release? What happens to the pH of the soil? *(Need to jog your memory? Revisit relevant concepts in Chapter 2, Section 2.5.)*

CHECKPOINT 19.2

1. Plants change the environment by colonizing uninhabited areas, enriching the soil with nutrients, and modifying humidity.
2. Plants provide food and shelter, and they harbor nitrogen-fixing bacteria.
3. Predicting Plowed field or vacant lot: seeds of weeds and small nonwoody plants land and sprout, shrubs and small flowering plants follow; mossy slope of a mountain: mosses take hold, grow and die, forming humus where shrubs, flowering plants, conifers can grow.
4. Acids release hydrogen ions. The pH of the soil decreases as the soil becomes more acidic.

19.3 Asexual Reproduction in Plants

How to clone a plant

When meristems are cut from a plant, placed in nutrient solution and shaken, the cells in the meristem tissue divide and the tissue grows. Then the tissue samples can be cut apart and grown again in fresh nutrient solutions. If grown in separate containers they will develop into whole plants. The plants shown here were cloned using this method of asexual reproduction.

What you'll learn

IDEAS
• To explain the process of asexual reproduction in plants
• To identify the methods and uses of artificial propagation in plants

WORDS
vegetative reproduction, artificial propagation

VEGETATIVE REPRODUCTION

Send in the clones

Sexual reproduction in plants, as in all organisms, combines genes from two individuals, thereby producing genetic variation. By contrast, asexual reproduction does not involve fertilization and therefore produces offspring that are genetically identical to the parent. As you may recall, genetically identical offspring are referred to as clones.

You can see examples of plant clones in *Figure 19.10*. Most clumps of cattails are clones of a single plant, as are many groves of aspen trees. Probably the oldest plant clones on Earth are the creosote bushes that grow in the Mojave Desert. These plants are about 12,000 years old. One of the largest clones of plants consists of aspen trees in the Rocky Mountains, which cover 43 hectares and weigh 5447 metric tons.

Although most plants reproduce asexually only at certain times during their lives, others use this means most often. Being able to reproduce both sexually and asexually has definite advantages. In a stable environment with abundant resources, asexual reproduction is faster than sexual reproduction and produces offspring that are well adapted to the existing

FIGURE 19.10
Naturally occurring plant clones include clumps of cattails (left) and groves of aspens (right). All of the plants in a group of clones are genetically identical and developed from one original plant.

455

STUDENT RESOURCES

From the Teacher's Resource Package, use:
■ Section Review 19.3, Activity Record-sheet 19-2, and Enrichment Topic 19-1 from Unit 5 Review Module
■ Issues and Decision Making 19-2
■ Consumer Applications 19-1

TECHNOLOGY RESOURCES

Relevant technology resources include:
■ Spanish Student Edition CD-ROM
■ Teacher's Resource Planner CD-ROM

19.3

① ENGAGE

Consider the Big Idea!

Have students read The Big Idea! at the top of the page. Explain that both types of reproduction produce the fruit and vegetables that we eat.

Use The Visual

Have students study the photograph and read the text that opens the section. Explain that many commercial growers use asexual reproductive techniques such as cloning. Ask:

■ **What do you think are some advantages of using asexual reproductive techniques?** (Asexual reproduction can be fast and will usually maintain the favorable traits of the plant.)

Check Prior Knowledge

To assess students' knowledge about asexual reproduction, ask:

■ **How do offspring produced asexually compare to the parents?** (Parent and offspring are genetically identical.)

Teacher Demo

Bring two oranges to class, one with seeds and one without seeds. Cut both oranges open and ask students to explain how they differ. Challenge students to explain how offspring would be produced from each type of orange. (Seeded varieties can be grown from seed. Seedless varieties are propagated by grafting.)

TEACH

Teacher Demo

Bring to class plants or plant parts that show the results of asexual reproduction. Consider, for example, strawberry or crabgrass plants with runners, bulbs, potatoes with eyes, and other tubers. Display them in the classroom and give students an opportunity to examine them.

Class Activity

Have volunteers bring in cuttings from different parts of three or more kinds of plants. Use the cuttings to try to grow new plants in water or in vermiculite. Tell students to observe the cuttings over a given period of time and describe (in writing or with pictures) the results of the class experiment with artificial propagation.

Teacher Demo

Obtain a section of branch from a tree and cut it into two sections. Use the sections to demonstrate the procedure for grafting as described on page 457. After the two pieces of branch have been joined, seal the joint with wax. Ask students why the joint is sealed. (For support)

Bulb

Tuber

Corms

Stolons

FIGURE 19.11
Stolons, tubers, corms, and bulbs are structures that can produce new plants by asexual reproduction. How do these structures differ? ❶

environment. In a changing environment, sexual reproduction can produce plants with new combinations of traits that may increase their chances of survival.

Asexual reproduction that takes place naturally in plants is called **vegetative reproduction.** Plants that reproduce by vegetative reproduction can duplicate themselves very rapidly, often crowding out other plants. Vegetative reproduction can occur in several ways.

The aspen trees you just read about are clones produced by stolons, also called runners. Stolons are stems that grow along the surface of the ground and produce several buds. Each bud grows into a new plant. The water hyacinth, an aquatic weed that clogs the canals and rivers in Florida, also uses stolons for vegetative reproduction. Reproduction in water hyacinths is so rapid that in one year, just ten plants can produce as many

456 *Unit 5 Plants*

as 600,000 offspring. Strawberries and crabgrass also spread by growing stolons.

Vegetative reproduction can also result from rhizomes, specialized stems that grow underground. A stand of bamboo trees may actually spring from the rhizomes of a single bamboo plant. Some plants, such as potatoes, form tubers—swollen tips of rhizomes—which are specialized for storing food. Tubers can also give rise to new plants.

Corms and bulbs are two more types of modified underground stems. Like tubers, corms are modified for food storage, but unlike tubers corms grow upright. Crocuses and gladioli produce corms. Bulbs are underground stems bearing modified fleshy leaves that store food. Onion plants and lilies form bulbs. You can compare several of the structures involved in vegetative reproduction in *Figure 19.11.*

ARTIFICIAL PROPAGATION

Trees get cultured

If you have ever eaten seedless grapes or navel oranges, you have tasted the products of artificial propagation. **Artificial propagation** occurs when

---

❶ Stolons (runners, often underground stems) and tubers (thickened underground stems) produce new plants from buds. Corms (thickened vertical underground stems) are offshoots. Bulbs are underground buds.

people use vegetative reproduction to produce new plants. The methods of artificial propagation include cutting, grafting, and growing tissue cultures. People frequently grow plants by artificial propagation because it is often faster than growing plants from seeds, and it produces a genetically identical crop. Bananas, apples, grapefruits, grapes, potatoes, and pears are crops often grown using artificial propagation.

Artificial propagation is the by-product of a plant's ability to regenerate lost parts. After a plant is injured, its parenchyma cells begin to divide, covering the wound with new tissue. Eventually, a plant can produce a bud in the new tissue. The bud may then develop into a whole new plant.

Plants such as grapes, ivy, raspberries, apples, blackberries, and potatoes are easily propagated by using cuttings. To make a cutting, gardeners or farmers remove a piece of the stem or leaf from a plant and place it in soil. Cuttings are so easy to establish that when farmers in tropical regions cut branches of some plants to make fences, the cut pieces often begin to grow. Soon, there is not just a fence but a living, growing hedge!

Grafting is a way to make two different plants grow as one. Grafting is done by inserting a piece of one plant into a slit made in a second plant. Many types of fruit trees are grown by grafting. For example, navel orange trees are propagated only by grafting or by cuttings. In fact, with this method, several kinds of fruit can be grown on one trunk.

Many plants are produced by growing tissue cultures. This method involves growing an entire plant from individual cells or from small pieces of leaf, stem, or root. This technique was developed in 1958 by American plant physiologist F. C. Steward. Steward grew entire carrot plants

from tiny pieces of carrot roots. Today, plant breeders use tissue cultures to reproduce plants that possess rare or desirable traits. For example, orchids and African violets are propagated by growing tissue cultures.

CHECKPOINT 19.3

1. Explain how asexual reproduction benefits plants.
2. List three structures that plants use for vegetative reproduction.
3. Describe three ways in which plants can be artificially propagated.
4. **Critical Thinking** How are artificial propagation and vegetative reproduction similar? How are they different?

Build on What You Know

5. What events might cause a new trait to appear in a cattail plant produced through cloning? *(Need to jog your memory? Revisit relevant concepts in Chapter 8, Section 8.4.)*

Chapter 19 Response and Reproduction in Plants **457**

 **Do It!**

Observing Asexual Reproduction in Plants
You can grow a new plant from a runner when you . . .

Try This

1 Select a healthy runner from a spider plant. Make a sketch of the parts of the runner.
2 Cut the runner from the plant. Place the cut end in a container of water, and drape the rest of the runner over a container of lightly dampened potting soil. Carefully press it into the soil.
3 Water the soil and observe changes in the runner every two days for a period of two weeks. Record changes by making additional sketches.

Analyze Your Results

1 Describe the changes in the runner.
2 From what structure on the runner did a new plant originate?
3 What would happen to the new plant if it were separated from the runner before acquiring roots? After?

 Do It! TEAM WORK

Observing Asexual Reproduction in Plants

Guide students to understand the types of observations they should make in step 3.

Analyze Your Results

1 A new plant develops on the runner.
2 From the offshoot at a joint
3 It would not survive without roots. After rooting, the plant will continue to grow.

 **ASSESS**

Evaluate Understanding

Ask students to explain in writing or with diagrams each of the following:

- **Advantages of both sexual and asexual reproduction**
- **Types of structures that can produce new plants by asexual reproduction**
- **Types of artificial propagation**

Give students an opportunity to discuss their explanations and diagrams.

Reteach

Draw a two-column chart on a transparency. Label one column *Vegetative Reproduction,* and the second, *Artificial Propagation.* Model several entries. Tell students to fill in additional words and ideas related to each type of reproduction as they reread the section.

CHECKPOINT 19.3

1. Under the right conditions, asexual reproduction produces new offspring fast that will be well adapted to the existing environment.
2. Adaptations include: stolons, tubers, rhizomes, bulbs, and corms.
3. Plants may be propagated artificially with cuttings, grafts, and tissue cultures.
4. **Comparing** Answers may vary. Both processes produce offspring that are genetically identical to the parent plant. Vegetative reproduction occurs naturally, artificial propagation is accomplished through human intervention.
5. A new trait could arise through a genetic mutation.

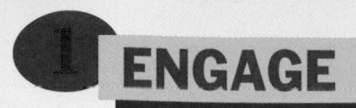

Use The Visual

Have students study the photograph that opens the section. Remind students that seeds are the products of sexual reproduction. Ask:

■ **How might projecting seeds away from the parent plant be beneficial for plant propagation?** (More offspring will be able to develop areas with less competition for sunlight and nutrients.)

Check Prior Knowledge

To assess students' knowledge about sexual reproduction in plants, ask:

■ **What term is used to describe the life cycle of a plant?** (Alternation of generations)

■ **What are haploid sex cells called?** (Gametes)

Teacher Demo

Display a wide range of fruits, burrs from plants, and a dandelion head. Point out that seeds are dispersed over long distances in a variety of ways. Ask:

■ **How the seeds in each fruit might be dispersed.** (Apples and berries transport by animals and/or humans; burrs cling to animal fur, dandelion seeds by wind)

■ **Why might seed dispersal be beneficial to plants?** (Reduces competition because seeds land in different areas)

19.4 Sexual Reproduction in Plants

What you'll learn

IDEAS
• To identify the plant forms and the stages of alternation of generations
• To explain the characteristics of seeds and the process of germination

WORDS
gametophyte, sporophyte, seed, cotyledons, monocots, dicots

Explosive seeds
If you take a walk in the woods in late autumn, you might hear sounds of tiny projectiles hitting objects. The seeds of the witch hazel shrub are forcefully expelled by the natural constriction of the seed pod. The seeds can be thrown as far as 14 meters (m). Seeds are the products of sexual reproduction in seed plants.

SEXUAL REPRODUCTION

Tossing the salad

Almost all plants have a phase of sexual reproduction at some time during their life cycle. Thus, the ability to make genetic hybrids must be advantageous to almost all plant species.

As you have learned, genetic variation is beneficial to a population. Genetic variation can enhance organisms' ability to resist disease, predation, or changes in the environment. Survival is enhanced because genetic recombination leads to new hybrids with somewhat different characteristics from the parent plants. *Figure 19.12* shows a hybrid rose.

Although flowers may be the most common and recognizable reproductive plant structures, not all plants have them. Mosses, ferns, and conifers, for example, reproduce without flowers. These plants have specialized structures to house the egg and the sperm—the gametes of plant cells. Botanists, scientists who study plants, use the details of plants' reproductive structures and cells as key characteristics to classify plants into divisions or families. You will study the full life cycles and classification of various plant types in Chapter 20.

The process of sexual reproduction in plants is more complex than in most animals. As you have learned, the plant life cycle involves two distinct stages. Because of the differences between these two stages, the life cycle of plants is defined as the alternation of generations.

FIGURE 19.12
This hybrid tea rose was produced by transferring pollen from one variety of rose to another. Growers often use this type of sexual reproduction to produce flowers with new scents, colors, and shapes.

ALTERNATION OF GENERATIONS

Spores and more

What does alternation of generations mean? Plants' life cycles alternate, or switch, from a diploid ($2n$) generation to a haploid (n) generation. You can see a diagram of the alternation of

---

generations in *Figure 19.13*. What events occur between the diploid phase and the haploid phase?

Alternation of generations includes two phases, the gametophyte phase and the sporophyte phase. The two phases are named for their products: gametes and spores. As you have learned, gametes are haploid cells that unite during fertilization to form a diploid zygote. The haploid (n), gamete-producing phase of a plant's life cycle is the **gametophyte.**

A **sporophyte** is the diploid ($2n$) phase of a plant life cycle that produces spores. Spores are haploid reproductive structures of plants that produce the gametophyte phase. The cells of the sporophyte each contain two sets of chromosomes ($2n$). Spores are produced when certain cells of the sporophyte phase undergo meiosis.

The cycle continues as spores undergo cell division to produce the haploid (n) gametophyte phase. Notice the position of the gametophyte phase in the life cycle of plants shown in *Figure 19.13*. The gametophytes may be independent plants, as in the mosses, or groups of cells dependent on the sporophyte cells, as in flowering plants.

The life cycle of plants differs from the typical life cycle of animals in two ways. First, the body cells of animals are diploid. In different kinds of plants, either the sporophyte (diploid) or the gametophyte (haploid) phase may be the more visible stage of the life cycle. In most plants, the sporophyte is the dominant phase. In mosses, the gametophyte is dominant.

Second, meiosis in animals leads directly to the formation of gametes. Meiosis in plants leads to the formation of spores. In some plants, spores can become independent gamete-producing plants. In other plants, spores develop into gamete-producing structures dependent on the sporophyte.

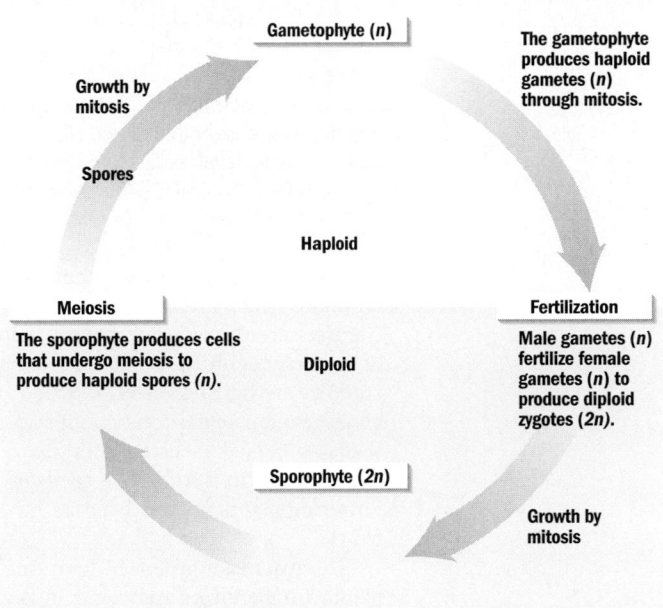

Alternation of Generations in Plants

Gametophyte (n)

Growth by mitosis

Spores

Haploid

The gametophyte produces haploid gametes (n) through mitosis.

Meiosis

The sporophyte produces cells that undergo meiosis to produce haploid spores (n).

Diploid

Fertilization

Male gametes (n) fertilize female gametes (n) to produce diploid zygotes ($2n$).

Sporophyte ($2n$)

Growth by mitosis

As in animals, fertilization in plants involves two gametes and yields a new diploid ($2n$) zygote. In some plants, such as mosses and ferns, fertilization takes place in water. In conifers and flowering plants, fertilization does not require water.

FIGURE 19.13
The figure above represents the alternation of generations in plants. How are gametes produced? ❷

REPRODUCTION BY SEEDS
Packed and ready to travel

Many plants produce seeds during sexual reproduction. A **seed** is a protective structure that contains a diploid plant embryo and stored food, mainly in the form of starch. Most seeds have a tough, protective seed coat. Carried by wind, water, or animals, seeds can travel far away from the parent plants, just as spores can.

It takes a lot energy for a plant to produce seeds. What advantages could

Chapter 19 Response and Reproduction in Plants **459**

❷ TEACH

✳ Language Arts

Check that students understand that the suffix "phyte" comes from a Greek word meaning "plant." The generation of a plant that bears spores is called "sporophyte" while the generation bearing gametes is called "gametophyte."

Use The Visual

Have students trace the sequence of events illustrated in Figure 19.13. Check that students understand the two stages in the life cycle of plants. Ask:

- **Which processes are shown on this figure?** (Meiosis, mitosis, fertilization)
- **Which process produces zygotes?** (Fertilization)
- **Which process produces spores?** (Meiosis)
- **Which process produces both the gametophyte and the sporophyte?** (Mitosis)

❶ Meiosis occurs between the diploid phase and the haploid phase. Fertilization occurs between the hapliod phase and the diploid phase.

❷ The gametophyte produces gametes by mitosis.

seeds provide for plants? In non-seed plants, such as mosses and ferns, the newly formed embryo must immediately develop into a sporophyte. In contrast, a seed can remain dormant for long periods of time. The seed coat provides protection for the embryo until the growing conditions are favorable. Once the embryo starts developing again, the seed's stored food provides nourishment.

Kinds of seed plants Two groups of plants produce seeds: cone-bearing plants (gymnosperms) and flowering plants (angiosperms). Conifers are the oldest surviving type of seed plants on Earth. The seeds of conifers are housed within female cones. Botanists describe conifer seeds as "naked" because they are not enclosed in a fruit. The seeds of flowering plants are enclosed in fruits.

The two major groups of flowering plants are monocots and dicots. A key difference between monocots and dicots is the number of seed leaves, or **cotyledons** (KOT-ih-LEE-dunz), in the plant's embryo. Although cotyledons look like leaves, they are different from the leaves you see on an adult plant. You may recall that "mono-" means "one," and "di-" means "two." **Monocots** are flowering plants with seeds that have one cotyledon. Monocots include bamboo, lilies, wheat, and corn. **Dicots** are flowering plants with seeds that have two cotyledons. Dicots include peas, tomatoes, grapes, and apples. You will learn about other distinguishing characteristics of monocots and dicots when you read Chapter 20.

Seed dispersal Seeds can be dispersed long distances or carried away from the parent plants. This adaptation has allowed seed plants to successfully colonize a wide variety of land habitats. Various adaptations

FIGURE 19.14

Germination

Seed
The embryo inside its seed casing becomes metabolically active after water activates enzymes that convert starch to sugar.

Primary root
The first sprout, the primary root, forces its way out of the seed casing.

Root growth
The primary root responds to gravity. It grows downward by cell divisions in the apical meristem (the growing tissue at the tip of the root).

Primary shoot
The primary shoot grows upward toward the sun, shedding its seed casing.

enable seeds to be dispersed. Some seeds are light enough to be carried on wind currents. Some seed coats have hooks that attach easily to a passing animal. A few seed packets have the ability to burst open and propel seeds through the air. Still other seeds remain inside a fruit. After the fruit is eaten by an animal, the undigestible seed is dispersed in animal wastes.

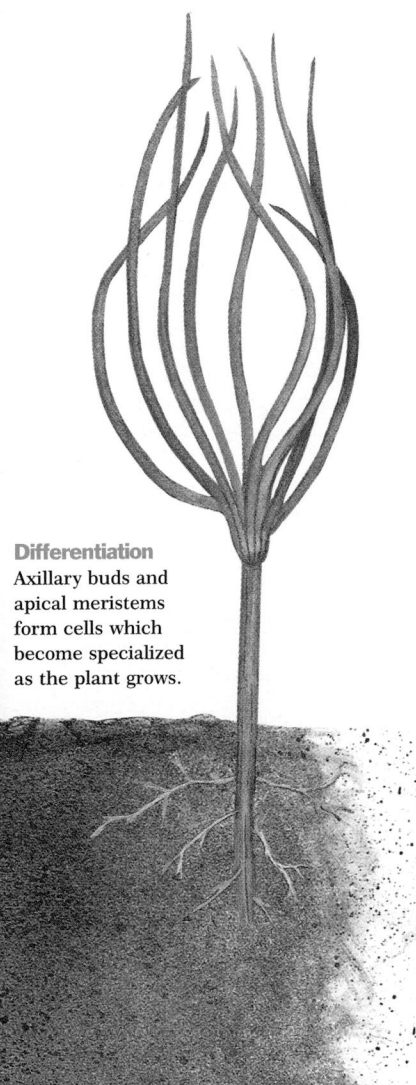

Differentiation
Axillary buds and apical meristems form cells which become specialized as the plant grows.

Germination When conditions are favorable for growth, seeds sprout and grow in a process called germination. You can follow this process in *Figure 19.14*. During germination, the embryo uses energy from the food stored in the seed. The embryo grows, splits the seed coat, and forms a root and a shoot. The root and shoot enlarge as the seedling develops.

Two environmental conditions affect germination: water availability and temperature. During the first stage of germination, water activates many enzymes, including the enzymes that convert starch into sugar. Sugar supplies energy for the growth of the embryo.

Temperature also affects germination. Many seeds need moderate to warm temperatures to germinate. Why do you think there is an abundance of plant growth in spring? When temperatures begin to get warmer, many dormant seeds sprout. Because seeds of different plants germinate at different temperatures and under different moisture conditions, plants are adapted to a wide range of niches.

CHECKPOINT 19.4

1. Describe the life cycle of alternation of generations in plants.
2. Compare the seeds of monocots and dicots. Explain the process of seed germination.
3. **Critical Thinking** At which stage of the plant's sexual reproduction cycle does genetic recombination occur? Which phase—gametophyte or sporophyte—is the first to inherit such variations?

Build on What You Know

4. Compare meiosis and mitosis with respect to plant and animal gametes. *(Need to jog your memory? Revisit relevant concepts in Chapter 5, Section 5.3.)*

Chapter 19 Response and Reproduction in Plants **461**

Teacher Demo

Show students a seed that has started to germinate. Have students point out the root and the shoot.

3 ASSESS

Evaluate Understanding

To assess the students' knowledge of sexual reproduction in plants, ask:

- **What is the difference between a gametophyte and a sporophyte?** (A gametophyte is haploid and produces haploid gametes through mitosis. A sporophyte is diploid and produces haploid spores through meiosis.)
- **What two environmental conditions can activate germination in dormant seeds?** (Water and warm temperatures)
- **What are some differences between seeds and spores?** (Spores are haploid, seeds are diploid. Spores do not have food stores, seeds do.)

Reteach

Make an unlabeled transparency of Figure 19.13. Provide a similar worksheet for the students. Work with students to label each part of the diagram as you review the cycle with them. If necessary, use a similar activity to review germination.

CHECKPOINT 19.4

1. Diploid sporophyte undergoes meiosis to produce haploid spores, mitosis to form a haploid gametophyte, mitosis to produce gametes, fertilization to form a diploid zygote, mitosis to form a diploid sporophyte.
2. Monocots have one seed leaf, dicots have two. Germination involves the seed responding to water and temperature, water activating starch-converting enzymes and embryo growth.
3. **Predicting** Fertilization; The sporophyte.
4. In animals, meiosis results in haploid gametes that form a zygote. In plants, meiosis results in haploid spores, which produce an entirely haploid organism.

 **TEAM WORK** Observing Seedlings

Lab Tips

Have students work in groups and provide one set of material per group.

Hypothesis Help

Explain that in this lab, a hypothesis might be a prediction about which seeds will germinate first. They might make predictions about which will sprout first, or in which type the root and the stem will grow longest in the time allowed.

Lab Extension

Directed

Encourage students to compare growth rates between bean and corn seeds. Provide a set of criteria for comparison and a format for presenting the observations of each group.

Time Required

- 20 minutes on first day
- 10 minutes for observations on Days 2-12
- 20 minutes for final graphing

 Investigate It!

Observing Seedlings

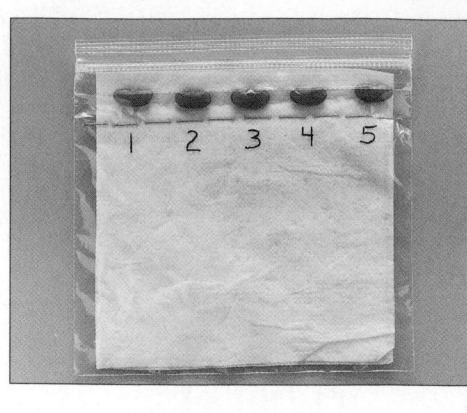

WHAT YOU WILL DO Design an experiment to test the effect of a variable on the growth of corn grains or bean seeds, observe their growth over a 14-day period, and graph the number of seeds that sprout

SKILLS YOU WILL USE Observing, measuring, collecting and recording data

WHAT YOU WILL NEED Two resealable plastic bags, paper towels, metric ruler, stapler, corn grains or bean seeds, marker

Propose a Hypothesis

Choose a variable that you think will affect the germination and growth of corn grains or bean seeds, such as temperature, amount of light, or water. Design an experiment to test if and how the variable affects seedling germination and growth. Propose a hypothesis about how the variable will affect the seedlings' growth.

Conduct Your Experiment

DAY 1

1 Line two plastic bags with paper towels. Place a line of staples through the bags 3 centimeters (cm) below the reclosable seal on each bag. Add enough water to soak the towels.

2 Place five corn grains or bean seeds in each bag so they rest on the staple line, as shown in the photo. Using the marker, number the seeds 1–5 and 6–10.

3 Close the bags and set them up to test the variable you chose. Record the date and time.

DAYS 2–14

4 Check the seeds at the same time each day. Draw the seeds and record the number that have germinated. Measure and record the length of each root and the height of each shoot.

5 Once the seeds germinate, leave the bags open.

6 Repeat step 4 for 12 days.

Analyze Your Data

1 Graph the number of seeds sprouted as compared to the number of days passed.

2 Calculate the average root length each day and graph the results.

3 Calculate the average shoot height each day and graph the results.

4 Add your data to a class data table. Compare the growth rates of the two bags of seeds.

Draw Conclusions

Was your hypothesis supported? Summarize the effects of the variable you chose on the seedlings' growth rates.

Design a Related Experiment

Design an experiment to compare the germination rates of two species of plants.

Lab: Observing Seedlings

Objective: To germinate corn or bean seeds, observe their growth over a 14-day period, and graph the number of seeds that sprout.

Day 1: February 8, 10:00 a.m.

Day 2: Number of seeds germinating = 0

Analyze Your Data

1-3 Students' graphs should show two curves, one for root growth and one for stem growth.

4 Class data table should show similar results.

Draw Conclusions

The average growth rate of the bean was faster than that of the corn.

Design a Related Experiment

Remind students that germination is the point at which the seed begins to sprout.

19.5 Focus on Flowers

Flowers that set sail
Pollination of water celery plants occurs when the free-floating male flower encounters a slight trough, or depression, in the water caused by the female flower, which is anchored by an underwater stem. The male flower slides into the trough and collides with the female. In the process, the female is dusted with pollen. While flowers are pollinated in a variety of ways, they all contain the structures that enable reproduction to take place.

What you'll learn

IDEAS
• To identify the male, female, and sterile parts of a flower
• To explain the process of fertilization

WORDS
flower, ovary, ovule, pollen, pollination

CHARACTERISTICS OF FLOWERS

The gender of a flower

Roses, tulips, lilacs, orchids—how dull the world would be without flowers! However, the importance of a flower is not in the way it looks or smells to humans, but in what it does. A **flower** is the reproductive structure of a flowering plant, or angiosperm.

Flowers are modified stems with specialized leaves and other structures for reproduction. Most flowers have three kinds of parts: male, female, and sterile. Male and female parts produce gametes. A flower may contain both male and female parts (a "perfect" flower), or just one of the two (an "imperfect" flower). Sterile parts attract pollinators and protect developing flowers or embryos.

The male structures of flowers produce sperm. **Pollen** grains are structures that contain sperm cells. The male part of a flower is called the stamen. Stamens usually have two parts: anther and filament. The anther produces pollen. The filament supports the anther.

The female structures of flowers produce eggs. All of the female parts form the pistil. Pistils are often located at the center of a flower and usually have three parts: stigma, style,

and ovary. You can locate these parts in *Figure 19.15*.

Each part of a pistil has a different function. The stigma is the structure on which pollen lands and germinates. The stigma is often sticky so the pollen grains will cling to it. The style connects the stigma to the ovary. The **ovary** is the structure that develops into a fruit. Each ovary contains one or more ovules. An **ovule** is a structure in which an egg develops. Ovules eventually become seeds.

FIGURE 19.15

A Typical Flower

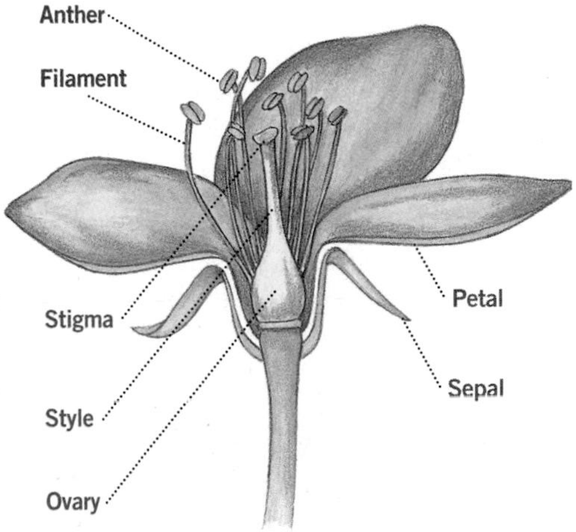

Anther
Filament
Stigma
Style
Ovary
Petal
Sepal

Male parts
These structures produce pollen that contain sperm.

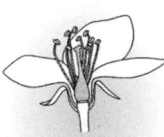

Female parts
These structures produce ovules that contain eggs.

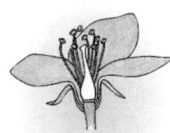

Sterile parts
These structures provide protection and attract pollinators to the flower.

Chapter 19 Response and Reproduction in Plants **463**

STUDENT RESOURCES

From the Teacher's Resource Package, use:
■ Section Review 19.5, Interpreting Graphics 19, Vocabulary Review 19, and Chapter 19 Tests from Unit 5 Review Module

TECHNOLOGY RESOURCES

Relevant technology resources include:
■ Spanish Student Edition CD-ROM
■ Teacher's Resource Planner CD-ROM
■ Animated Biological Concepts Videodiscs: "Angiosperm Reproduction"
■ TestWorks CD-ROM: Chapter 19 Tests

① ENGAGE

Use the Visual

Have students study the photograph that opens the section. Explain that pollination is an essential process because plants cannot travel to find a mate. Ask:

■ **What are some methods of pollination?** (Wind, rain, animals such as insects, birds, bats)

Check Prior Knowledge

To assess students' knowledge about plant reproduction, ask:

■ **What is a seed?** (A protective structure that contains an embryo and stored food)
■ **How are the seeds of flowering plants dispersed?** (By wind, water, or animals.)

Teacher Demo

Display a variety of flowers in different stages of anthesis. If possible, show students some flowers that have begun to form fruit. Include flowers such as a dandelion and point out that each "petal" is really a separate flower with a stamen and pistil. Encourage students to examine the flowers and point out the parts involved in reproduction. Ask:

■ **How might the petals attract pollinators?** (They are visible, often colorful, and frequently give off odors that attract pollinators.)

463

19.5

 TEACH

Health

Allergies to pollen are actually reactions to the proteins in the coat of the pollen grain. People are allergic to different pollens because each type has a different protein coat. Students may be interested in making wet-mount slides of pollen samples to observe the intricate pollen coats.

 **ASSESS**

Evaluate Understanding

Tell students to imagine themselves as seeds of a flowering plant and write a brief essay titled "How I Became a Seed." Tell them to name the parts of the parent plants used in the process and the steps involved in their development.

Reteach

Work with students to develop a concept map illustrating the different parts of a flower and the function of each part. Include the role of each flower part in the process of pollination.

 Animated Biological Concepts

Angiosperm Reproduction   Play

464

FIGURE 19.16

Seed Development

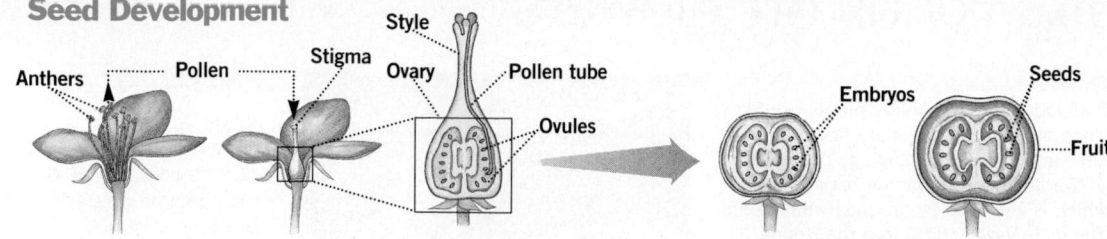

Pollination and fertilization
Pollen lands on a stigma; the pollen tube grows into the style. Two sperm are produced in the pollen by mitosis and travel to the ovary. One sperm fertilizes the egg in an ovule, forming a zygote. The other combines with two polar nuclei.

Seed development
The zygotes become embryos, the ovules develop into seeds, and a fruit forms around the seeds.

The sterile parts of a flower include the petals and sepals. Petals are the usually colorful, leaflike appendages on a flower. Petals often attract pollinators. The protective leaves at the base of a flower are sepals. Sepals, which are often green, cover the bud of a flower and protect the developing flower parts as they grow.

POLLINATION AND FERTILIZATION

Traveling gametes

During **pollination**, pollen is transferred from an anther to a stigma. When a pollen grain lands on a stigma, it sends out a pollen tube that grows through the style to the ovary. Sperm nuclei are carried along in the pollen tube as it grows. When the pollen tube reaches the ovary, it enters the ovule, which contains an egg.

Fertilization occurs when a sperm nucleus from a pollen tube fuses with the egg and forms a zygote. While one sperm fertilizes an egg, a second sperm nucleus from the pollen tube fertilizes two polar nuclei. The second

FIGURE 19.17
Some beetles become pollinators as they move from flower to flower in search of pollen.

fertilization forms a food-storing tissue in the seed called endosperm tissue. Endosperm tissue is triploid ($3n$). The process in plants that involves two fertilizations is called double fertilization; it happens only in angiosperms.

After fertilization, several processes occur. The zygote develops into an embryo, and the ovule becomes a seed. At the same time, the other parts of the ovary and surrounding tissues form a fruit that encases the developing seeds.

CHECKPOINT 19.5

1. Identify the male, female, and sterile parts of a flower.
2. Briefly explain the process of fertilization, including the roles of the male and female parts of flowers.
3. **Critical Thinking** Would you expect pollen grains of wind-pollinated flowers to be sticky? Why or why not? How can you test the accuracy of your answer?

Build on What You Know

4. How are plant adaptations related to pollinator adaptations? **(Need to jog your memory? Revisit relevant concepts in Chapter 10, Section 10.4.)**

? What are some ways that plants reproduce asexually? Sexually?

464   *Unit 5 Plants*

CHECKPOINT 19.5

1. Male: stamen-anther, filament; female: pistil-stigma, style, ovary; sterile: petal, sepal
2. Transfer of pollen from anther to stigma, growth of a pollen tube into the ovary, fusion of sperm nuclei with egg and polar nuclei, and development of embryo, endosperm and seed
3. **Predicting** Possibly, to aid fusion with stigma, but the stigma itself is sticky.
4. The smell, shape, and color of many flowers are adapted to attract certain pollinating insects birds, or bats. These pollinators have evolved specialized structures to reach the flower's nectar.

Chapter 19 Review

 **THE BIG IDEA!**

19.1–19.2 Plants respond to and affect the environment.
19.3–19.5 Plants reproduce both asexually and sexually.

Sum It Up

Use the following summary to review the main concepts in this chapter.

19.1 Plants Respond to the Environment

- Plants respond to conditions in their internal and external environments. A plant may respond to light, gravity, or touch.
- Plants produce small quantities of chemicals that control growth and response.
- Seasonal changes determine the timing of bud and flower production.
- Plants usually become inactive during periods of extreme cold or in dry conditions, and many seeds and bulbs are inactive for a time before they sprout.

19.2 Plants Change the Environment

- Colonizer plants usually arrive first in open land.
- Over time, a succession of plant species inhabit a given area. Small nonwoody plants are often replaced by larger woody plants. As the plant species change, so do the animal species that live in the area.
- As plants die and decay, the soil is enriched with nutrients. Plants also protect soil from erosion.

19.3 Asexual Reproduction in Plants

- Asexual reproduction produces offspring that are well suited to an existing stable environment.
- Farmers use cutting and grafting techniques on seed-bearing plants to produce genetically identical offspring.
- Plant asexual reproduction can involve structures such as runners, tubers, corms, and bulbs.

19.4 Sexual Reproduction in Plants

- Sexual reproduction involves the alternation of diploid and haploid generations.
- Many plants produce seeds during sexual reproduction.
- Temperature and the availability of water affect seed germination.

19.5 Focus on Flowers

- Most flowers have male, female, and sterile structures.
- Fertilization in angiosperms requires pollination, growth of pollen tube, and fusion of the egg and sperm nuclei. In angiosperms, fertilization leads to the development of seeds and fruit.

Use Terms and Concepts

Use each of the following words or terms in a complete sentence. If you need to review a meaning, turn to the page indicated.

stimulus (p. 446)
tropism (p. 446)
hormone (p. 447)
auxin (p. 449)
photoperiodism (p. 449)
dormancy (p. 450)

colonizers (p. 452)
vegetative reproduction (p. 456)
artificial propagation (p. 456)
gametophyte (p. 459)

sporophyte (p. 459)
seed (p. 459)
cotyledons (p. 460)
monocots (p. 460)
dicots (p. 460)
flower (p. 463)

ovary (p. 463)
ovule (p. 463)
pollen (p. 463)
pollination (p. 464)

Review the Big Ideas

Before students begin the Chapter Review, you may wish to discuss main concepts from the Big Ideas in Chapter 19. Point out that plants respond to light, gravity, touch, hormones, and seasonal changes in their environment. Plants also change an environment through colonization, succession, and decay. Explain that plants reproduce both sexually and asexually. Asexual reproduction produces identical offspring that are well suited for an existing, stable environment. Sexual reproduction involves an alternation of generations and introduces variety. In flowering plants, seeds are produced on a cone or in a fruit.

Answers

1. hormones
2. dormancy
3. auxin
4. artificial propagation
5. colonizers
6. pollination
7. photoperiodism
8. tropism
9. a
10. c
11. b
12. b
13. d
14. The roots of a plant respond positively to gravity—they grow downwards into the soil; the shoots respond negatively—they grow upward.
15. Monocot seeds have one cotyledon (seed leaf), while dicots have two cotyledons.
16. Temperature and amount of moisture affect germination.
17. Hormones control plant growth and the response of plants to stimuli.
18. In plants either the diploid or haploid phase may be more prominent in the cycle; in animals, the diploid phase is almost always more prominent. In animals, meiosis leads directly to gametes; in plants, spores form during meiosis. Depending on the species, the spores form either gametes or gamete–producing plants.
19. The terms *long–day* and *short–day* are misleading because the plants are actually responding to the continuous hours of darkness.
20. Plants remove nitrogen from the soil (to produce compounds such as amino acids). The nitrogen–fixing bacteria that live in sacs on legume roots convert atmospheric nitrogen gas into nitrogen compounds that plants can

---

Use Your Word Power

COMPLETION Write the word or phrase that best completes each statement.

1. A plant produces _____ , which are released in one part of the plant and affect another part of the plant.

2. Many seeds and bulbs need a period of _____ before they sprout.

3. The hormone _____ promotes the growth of roots, buds, and stems.

4. In a process called _____ , people use vegetative reproduction and other methods to produce new plants.

5. The first species to invade an uninhabited tract of land are _____ .

6. The process of transferring pollen from an anther to a stigma is called _____ .

7. A plant response that is linked to the hours of light and darkness is called _____ .

8. The growth of a plant in a certain direction in response to a stimulus is a(n) _____ .

MULTIPLE CHOICE Choose the letter of the word or phrase that best completes each statement.

9. During the alternation of generations, plants form a diploid (a) sporophyte; (b) gametophyte; (c) spore; (d) gamete.

10. The growth of plants from stolons and tubers are examples of (a) artificial propagation; (b) pollination; (c) vegetative reproduction; (d) colonization.

11. The seed leaves of flowering plants are called (a) monocots; (b) cotyledons; (c) dicots; (d) flowers.

12. In flowering plants, the structures that contain sperm cells are (a) spores; (b) pollen grains; (c) ovaries; (d) cotyledons.

13. The structure of a plant that develops into a fruit is a(n) (a) cotyledon; (b) seed; (c) spore; (d) ovary.

Show What You Know

14. Use the example of gravity to explain how a tropism can be positive or negative.

15. Contrast the seeds of monocots and dicots.

16. What are two environmental conditions that affect seed germination?

17. What are some effects of hormones in plants?

18. How do the typical life cycles of plants and animals differ?

19. Are the terms "long-day" and "short-day" really accurate? Explain why or why not.

20. What benefits do legumes provide to soil?

21. **Make a Concept Map** Complete the concept map below by adding the following terms: eggs, gamete, ovary, ovule, pollen, pollination, seed, sperm.

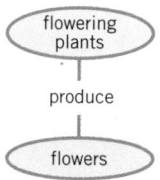

Take It Further

22. **Applying Concepts** Arctic lupines are plants whose seeds have evolved the ability to remain dormant for thousands of years. Explain why that characteristic could be an advantage in an arctic environment.

23. **Identifying Cause and Effect** Explain why it is advantageous for seed germination to begin with the emergence of a root rather than a shoot.

24. **Organizing and Classifying** Consider the methods of artificial propagation described in this chapter. Which method(s) would you use to produce an apple tree that bears two different kinds of apples?

---

absorb. When legumes die, these compounds are released into the soil.

21. Flowers produce gametes called sperm and eggs. Sperm is carried in pollen. Pollen is transferred during pollination. Eggs form in ovules in an ovary. Ovules develop into seeds.

22. For much of the year, the arctic is extremely cold and dark. A lupine seed

might have to wait many years until a suitable combination of soil, moisture, light, and temperature allowed for a successful germination.

23. The water and nutrients that the shoot needs to grow must first be absorbed by the root from the soil.

24. A branch from one apple tree could be grafted onto another to produce two

25. Designing an Experiment Design an experiment to show how different colors of light affect seed germination and plant growth.

26. Analyzing Data Suppose you are a gardener with a shady yard and moist soil. Use the table below to find a short flower that would bloom in your garden during the summer. What other flower(s) could grow in your garden?

Planning Your Garden

Plant	Flowering Period	Height	Light	Soil
Canada phlox	Late spring	30 cm	Light shade	Moist
Gentian	Mid- to late summer	20–30 cm	Light shade	Moist
Himalayan blue poppy	Early to mid-summer	0.6–1.8 m	Light shade	Well-drained
Mountain bluet	Early summer to early fall	60 cm	Full sun	Well-drained
Sea pink	Late spring to mid-summer	30–45 cm	Full sun	Well-drained

27. Interpreting a Graph The graph below shows how the mass of Texas bluebonnet seedlings, after one month's growth, compared to the mass of the seeds from which they sprouted. What is the relationship between the mass of the seedlings and the mass of the seeds? What hypothesis could you state that would explain these results?

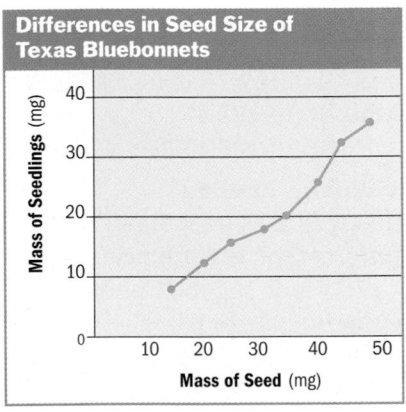

Differences in Seed Size of Texas Bluebonnets

Consider the Issues

28. Going Wild In many states, laws prevent people from picking native species of wildflowers. What is your opinion about these laws? Should the laws apply only to certain plants? Should people be allowed to pick wildflowers on their own property? Should people be allowed to collect seeds from wildflowers to plant in their own gardens? Present a logical argument for or against picking wildflowers.

Make New Connections

29. Biology and Art Many artists are known for their paintings of plants. Use museums or art books to find examples. Compare the paintings with illustrations and photographs in field guides and other references.

Striped Camellias,
1927
by Beatrice Bland

30. Biology and the Community Investigate how dominant types of plants in your area reproduce. Report your findings with drawings or photographs.

FAST-FORWARD TO CHAPTER 20

In Chapter 20, what you have read about transport and reproduction in plants will help you understand how plants are classified.

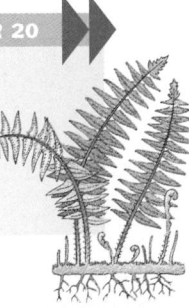

portionately to the mass of seeds.

28. Have students consider all sides of the issue as they form their opinions. You may wish to have two groups of students present a debate on the wildflower issue. Before they begin, have each group prepare by writing all valid statements that relate to the viewpoint they are presenting.

29. Answers will vary.

30. Answers will vary.

different fruits on the same tree. Cuttings and tissue cultures can only regenerate the single species from which they were taken.

25. Students might recommend growing seeds from the same species under identical conditions except for the available wavelengths of light. The variable could be controlled through filters

that absorb specific ranges of visible light. These filters would be placed between each group of seeds and the light source.

26. Students should recommend planting gentians for a summer flower. Canada phlox should also grow well in the spring.

27. The mass of seedlings increases pro-

PLANNING GUIDE

Section	Student Activities/Features	Teacher's Resource Package
20.1 Natural History of Plants **Objectives** ■ Compare and contrast the characteristics of modern plants and algae ■ Discuss the characteristics that are used in classifying plants	**Lab Zone Discover It!** *Observing Plant Diversity,* p. 469 **In the Community** *Classifying Plants,* p. 474	**Unit 5 Review Module** ■ Section Review 20.1 **Interpreting and Developing Graphics,** 58
20.2 Mosses **Objectives** ■ Identify the common characteristics of mosses ■ Compare and contrast the haploid and diploid phases of mosses	**Everyday Biology** *Absorbent Cells,* p. 477	**Unit 5 Review Module** ■ Section Review 20.2 ■ Enrichment Topic 20-1 **Laboratory Manual:** Lab 33: "Terrestrial Pioneers: Mosses, Liverworts" **Issues and Decision Making** 20-1
20.3 Ferns **Objectives** ■ Identify the common characteristics of ferns ■ Compare the haploid and diploid phases of the fern life cycle	**Lab Zone Do It!** *Examining Fern Leaves and Sori,* p. 480	**Unit 5 Review Module** ■ Section Review 20.3 ■ Activity Recordsheet 20-1 ■ Interpreting Graphics 20 ■ Critical Thinking Exercise 20 **Interpreting and Developing Graphics,** 59
20.4 Conifers **Objectives** ■ Identify common characteristics of conifers ■ Describe the life cycle of a conifer	**Lab Zone Do It!** *Examining the Structure of a Pine Cone,* p. 483	**Unit 5 Review Module** ■ Section Review 20.4 ■ Activity Recordsheet 20-2 **Biotechnology Manual** ■ Concept 8: "Designer Trees: A Way to Counteract the Greenhouse Effect" ■ Lab 17: "Modeling the Genetic Engineering of Trees" ■ Issue 4: "Should Trees Be Genetically Engineered to Use More Carbon Dioxide?"
20.5 Flowering Plants **Objectives** ■ Identify the common characteristics of flowering plants ■ Describe the life cycle of a flowering plant	**Everyday Biology** *Weeds in the Mail,* p. 486 **Everyday Biology** *Orchid Seeds in Your Ice Cream?* p. 487 **Lab Zone Think About It!** *Analyzing Changes in a Flower,* p. 488 **STS: Environmental Awareness** *What Bugs Bees,* p. 489 **Lab Zone Investigate It!** *Observing Plant Reproduction,* p. 490	**Unit 5 Review Module** ■ Section Review 20.5 ■ Activity Recordsheet 20-3 ■ Vocabulary Review 20 ■ Chapter 20 Tests **Consumer Applications** 20-1 **Interpreting and Developing Graphics,** 60 **Spanish Reviews** ■ Chapter 20 ■ Unit 5

Technology Resources

Internet Connections

Within this chapter, you will see the **bioSURF** logo. If you and your students have access to the Internet, the following URL address will provide various Internet connections that are related to topics and features presented in this chapter:

http://plants.biosurf.com

You can also find relevant chapter material at **The Biology Place** address:

http://www.biology.com

CD-ROMs

Biología: la telaraña de la vida,
　(Spanish Student Edition) Chapter 20
Teacher's Resource Planner, Chapter 20
　Supplements
TestWorks CD-ROM
■ Chapter 20 Tests

Overhead Transparencies

■ The Plant Kingdom, #41
■ Life Cycle of a Moss, #42
■ Life Cycle of a Fern, #43
■ Life Cycle of a Conifer, #44
■ Life Cycle of an Angiosperm, #45

Videotapes

Biology Alive! Video Series
Rewind: The Web of Life Reteach Videos

Planning for Activities

STUDENT EDITION
Lab Zone
Discover It! p. 469
■ several types of plants
■ hand lens

Lab Zone Do It! p. 480
■ fern frond with sori
■ microscope slide and coverslip
■ microscope
■ scalpel

Lab Zone Do It! p. 483
■ two female pine cones, open and closed scales
■ scalpel

Lab Zone
Investigate It! p. 490
■ *Brassica rapa* seeds
■ metric ruler
■ peat pots
■ soil
■ small wooden stakes
■ toothpicks
■ growth lights

TEACHER'S EDITION
Quick Activity, p. 470
Algae and vascular plants
■ hand lenses
■ samples of green algae, living mosses, and vascular plants

Teacher Demo, p. 473
Observing vascular plants
■ samples of mosses and leafy vascular plants
■ scalpel
■ hand lens

Class Activity, p. 474
Identifying plants
■ 10 common plants
■ field guides
■ posterboard
■ glue or tape

Teacher Demo, p. 475
Water absorption of sphagnum moss
■ sphagnum moss
■ water
■ beaker

Quick Activity, p. 478
Observing ferns
■ photographs or living specimens of ferns

Class Activity, p. 478
Comparing fern spores to various fruit leaves
■ hand lenses
■ fern leaves
■ apple, orange, and strawberry seeds

Quick Activity, p. 481
Identifying pine cones
■ pictures or specimens of a variety of pine cones

Quick Activity, p. 485
Why plants produce seeds
■ pumpkin and sunflower seeds
■ peanuts

Class Activity, p. 486
Identifying monocots and dicots
■ specimens of flowers and leaves

Chapter Objectives

Students will learn the main concepts of this chapter as they complete the following objectives:

- Compare and contrast the characteristics of modern plants and algae
- Discuss the characteristics that are used in classifying plants
- Identify the common characteristics of mosses
- Compare and contrast the haploid and diploid states of mosses
- Identify the common characteristics of ferns
- Compare the haploid and diploid stages of the fern life cycle
- Identify common characteristics of conifers
- Describe the life cycle of a conifer
- Identify the common characteristics of flowering plants
- Describe the life cycle of a flowering plant

Key Words

20.1 *division*

20.2 *archegonium, antheridium, capsule, peat bog*

20.3 *rhizome, sorus*

20.5 *double fertilization, pollinator*

The Opening Story

Have students discuss how the story might relate to this chapter. Ask students why they think saving the world's rain forests has become such a popular environmental issue in recent years.

CHAPTER 20
Origin and Diversity of Plants

You can find out more about plant diversity by exploring the following Internet address:
http://plants.biosurf.com

In this chapter . . .

FEATURES

Everyday Biology
- Absorbent Cells
- Weeds in the Mail
- Orchid Seeds in Your Ice Cream?

In the Community
Classifying Plants

 Environmental Awareness
What Bugs Bees

LAB ZONES

Discover It!
- Observing Plant Diversity

Do It!
- Examining Fern Leaves and Sori
- Examining the Structure of a Pine Cone

Think About It!
- Analyzing Changes in a Flower

Investigate It!
- Observing Plant Reproduction

THE RICHEST PLACE ON EARTH

If you were to measure wealth as biodiversity, the world's rain forests would be the richest places on Earth. The sheer weight of vegetation in one hectare of rain forest is greater than in the same size area in any other habitat on the planet.

No one knows how many undiscovered plant species wait in the rain forests, but it is estimated that a typical patch of rain forest measuring 6 square kilometers contains about 1500 species of flowering plants and about 750 species of trees. In comparison, there are only about 400 tree species in all of temperate North America.

Using the red inflatable raft as a home base, these scientists identify and study plants in the canopy, or uppermost level, of a rain forest in South America. Why are scientists interested in identifying all these plants? One reason came from a rain forest in Cameroon, in Africa, in 1992. A previously unknown species of *Ancistrocladus* vine was collected, studied, and found to contain a substance that may prove effective as a treatment for HIV, the virus that causes AIDS. Many other potential sources of useful materials and medicines may be waiting to be discovered in the rain forests.

 Discover It!

Observing Plant Diversity

You need several types of plants and a hand lens

1. Work in a small group. Discuss with other students what types of plants you may be able to bring to class. Try to include mosses, ferns, conifers, and flowering plants. Have your teacher approve your choices.
2. Examine your group's plant specimens with a hand lens and compare them.

What structures are common to all the plants? What structures appear only on certain types of plants?

WRITE ABOUT IT!

Think of a habitat and the type of plant life it contains. It could be a place you have visited or one you have read about, such as a rain forest. Write a poem or a story that takes place in the habitat, and include descriptions of the local flora.

469

PORTFOLIO PREVIEW

Students should be encouraged to add to their portfolios as they work through this chapter. In addition to the *Write About It* opportunity, the following sections are

excellent opportunities for portfolio entries:

- Section 20.1: *Natural History of Plants*
- Section 20.4: *Conifers*

Opening Activities

 If you have access to the Internet in your classroom or school, you may wish to have students connect to the address shown on page 468. You may also want to have students conduct net searches for information using key words related to this chapter.

Discover It!

Observing Plant Diversity

TEAM WORK

Before students begin this chapter, have them do the suggested activity. Students can use pictures of different types of plants if live specimens are not available. Students will probably observe leaflike and rootlike plant structures.

WRITE ABOUT IT!

Encourage students to share their work with the class. After students complete the chapter, have them reread their work to correct inaccuracies or add details.

SUPER READ! **Monitoring Understanding**

To practice strategies for effective reading, use pages 53-54 in *Super Read!*

REWIND to Chapter 19

Briefly review concepts learned in Chapter 19, *Response and Reproduction in Plants.* Ask:

- **How might the study of plant responses and reproduction help you understand plant classification?**

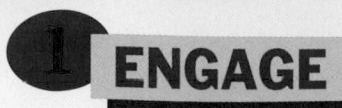

ENGAGE

Consider the Big Idea

Have students read The Big Idea! at the top of the page. Explain that the statement highlights the origins and characteristics of land plants.

Use the Visual

Have students study the photograph opening the section. Ask:

- **How are these plants similar to modern plants?** (Both are multicellular, green, and capable of photosynthesis.)

Check Prior Knowledge

To assess students' knowledge about plants, ask:

- **What three kinds of tissues do most plants have?** (Dermal, vascular, ground)
- **What are some reproductive structures in plants?** (Flowers, seeds, fruits, spores)

Quick Activity

Provide hand lenses and samples of green algae, living mosses, and vascular plants. Have students create a list of key characteristics for each. Ask:

- **How do the three types of organisms differ?** (Students should note that algae is not a plant and only vascular plants have vascular tissue.)
- **How are they similar?** (They are green and multicellular)

❶ Angiosperms

THE BIG IDEA! Plants are multicellular organisms with adaptations for life on land. 20.1–20.2

20.1 Natural History of Plants

What you'll learn

IDEAS
- To compare and contrast the characteristics of modern plants and algae
- To discuss the characteristics that are used in classifying plants

WORDS
division

Pioneering plants

The plants that first took hold on land (in the late Silurian and early Devonian periods, 421 to 387 million years ago) were small photosynthetic herbs. By the time dinosaurs first appeared (at the end of the Triassic period, about 208 million years ago) there were pockets of lush vegetation and taller plants, which probably resembled this modern-day swamp, near coasts and waterways.

PLANTS AND GREEN ALGAE

A search for ancestors

Despite the significant differences between today's plants and green algae, biologists have established that plants evolved from ancient multicellular green algae. They base their conclusions on fossil evidence and the biochemical and structural similarities of plants and green algae. These similarities include

- similar chloroplasts
- the same photosynthetic pigments
- cell walls that contain cellulose
- a cell plate that develops during cell division

Although plants and green algae share the characteristics just described, the differences between them are so numerous and significant that they are classified in different kingdoms. Many of the differences arise because plants are adapted to live on land, whereas green algae are adapted to live in water.

To survive on land, plants have to be able to transport materials, prevent water evaporation, support themselves, and reproduce. Based on the fossils that have been found in coal, scientists hypothesize that the earliest plants were probably similar to mosses—short structures without leaves, stems, or roots. Because the ancient plants were only a few cells thick, transporting materials was not a challenge.

The first land plants had to prevent the loss of water by evaporation in dry conditions. One adaptation that enabled plants to conserve water was the cuticle. As you have learned, the cuticle is a waxy, waterproof layer that coats plants and prevents water loss from evaporation.

Because they were small, the first land plants did not need much support. Early adaptations for support may have included specialized cells and compounds such as lignin. Lignin

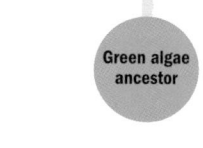

Angiosperms

Gymnosperms

MILESTONE
Flowers

Ferns

MILESTONE
Seeds

Mosses

MILESTONE
Vascular tissue

Green algae ancestor

FIGURE 20.1
Today's plants probably evolved from green algae. As they evolved, plant groups with new adaptations to life on land appeared. Each successive evolutionary step in the phylogenetic tree represents a new adaptation. What was the last group of plants to evolve? ❶

STUDENT RESOURCES

From the Teacher's Resource Package, use:
- Section Review 20.1 from Unit 5 Review Module

TECHNOLOGY RESOURCES

Relevant technology resources include:
- Spanish Student Edition CD-ROM
- Teacher's Resource Planner CD-ROM

is a hard substance that strengthens cell walls, enabling cells to support additional weight.

Evidence indicates that the first land plants had a life cycle that involved alternation of generations. Recall that the process of fertilization is part of the alternation of generations. Like their ancestors, the early plants were probably dependent on water for reproduction. Water was the medium through which sperm swam in order to fertilize an egg.

Because ancient plants needed water for fertilization, they probably grew only in moist areas, such as marshes and estuaries, where water was plentiful. Such environments also would have provided ancient land plants with a means of obtaining the minerals necessary for their survival.

TODAY'S PLANTS

Great variety from a lowly beginning

Most modern plants can now survive on land because they have specialized structures that green algae lack. These structures include leaves, stems, and roots. They perform the vital functions of transport and support.

Many different kinds of plants have evolved. The kingdom Plantae comprises 12 divisions of living plants. A **division** is a major taxonomic group used in classifying plants and fungi. For animals, the comparable taxonomic group is a phylum. With the exception of phyla, botanists use all the taxonomic levels you learned about in Chapter 13: class, order, family, genus, and species.

Nonvascular plants The first land plants were short nonvascular plants that lived in moist habitats. The modern descendants of these plants are classified in three divisions: mosses, liverworts, and hornworts.

Although the three divisions of nonvascular plants look different, they share many characteristics. For example, nonvascular plants lack true leaves and roots, and absorb most of their water through the plant body. Nonvascular plants reproduce without seeds and are therefore classified as seedless plants. Because their sperm must swim through water in order to reach the eggs, nonvascular plants need a readily available source of water for fertilization.

Mosses are members of the division Bryophyta (BRY-oh-FY-teh). In all mosses the gametophyte phase is the most prominent phase of the life cycle. The short, soft mats you see growing on rocks, trees, and other places are the moss gametophytes.

The liverworts comprise the division Hepatophyta. The name "liverwort" refers to the body of the plant, which resembles the lobes of a liver. Like the mosses, the most prominent phase of the liverwort life cycle is the gametophyte phase.

Hornwort gametophytes resemble liverwort gametophytes, but hornwort sporophytes can perform photosynthesis, unlike the sporophytes of other nonvascular plants. Botanists use this unique characteristic to classify the

FIGURE 20.2
These fossilized leaves came from a 360-million-year-old ancestor of today's cone-bearing plants. The fernlike leaves topped a large woody trunk.

Chapter 20 Origin and Diversity of Plants **471**

Use the Visual

Have students study Figure 20.3.
Ask:

- **Which plants on the diagram represent nonvascular plants? Where do they grow?** (Mosses; damp places)
- **What three kinds of plants are related to club mosses?** (Whisk ferns, horsetails, ferns)
- **What are two examples of vascular plants with seeds but no flowers?** (Gnetae, cycads, conifers, gingkoes)
- **Which division of plants is the most dominant type of plant on Earth?** (Flowering plants)

 Science History

One of the earliest plant classification systems was developed by Theophrastus (c.372–c. 287 B.C.), a Greek philosopher and scientist. He classified plants into three groups—herbs, shrubs, and trees—based on size and stem structure. Have students research other early classification systems.

Discuss

Explain that the first plants to live successfully on land were short nonvascular plants in moist habitats. Ask:

- **To what division do mosses belong?** (Bryophyta)
- **What characteristics do all bryophytes share?** (They lack true leaves and roots, have no vascular tissue, reproduce without seeds, and require water for fertilization. In their life cycle, the gametophyte phase is most prominent.)

hornworts in a separate plant division, the Anthocerophyta.

With the evolution of vascular systems, ancient plants no longer needed to live in very moist environments. Vascular plants have internal transport systems that allow them to move water and dissolved nutrients from their roots to other parts of the plant. As vascular systems became more specialized, vascular plants were able to populate drier regions of Earth.

Vascular plants Nine divisions of plants are vascular, either with or without seeds. As shown in *Figure 20.4*, there are four divisions of vascular seedless plants and five divisions of vascular seed plants.

All vascular plants have leaves, stems, and roots which all contain vascular tissue. Like all plants, vascular plants have both haploid (gametophyte) and diploid (sporophyte) generations.

FIGURE 20.3

The Plant Kingdom

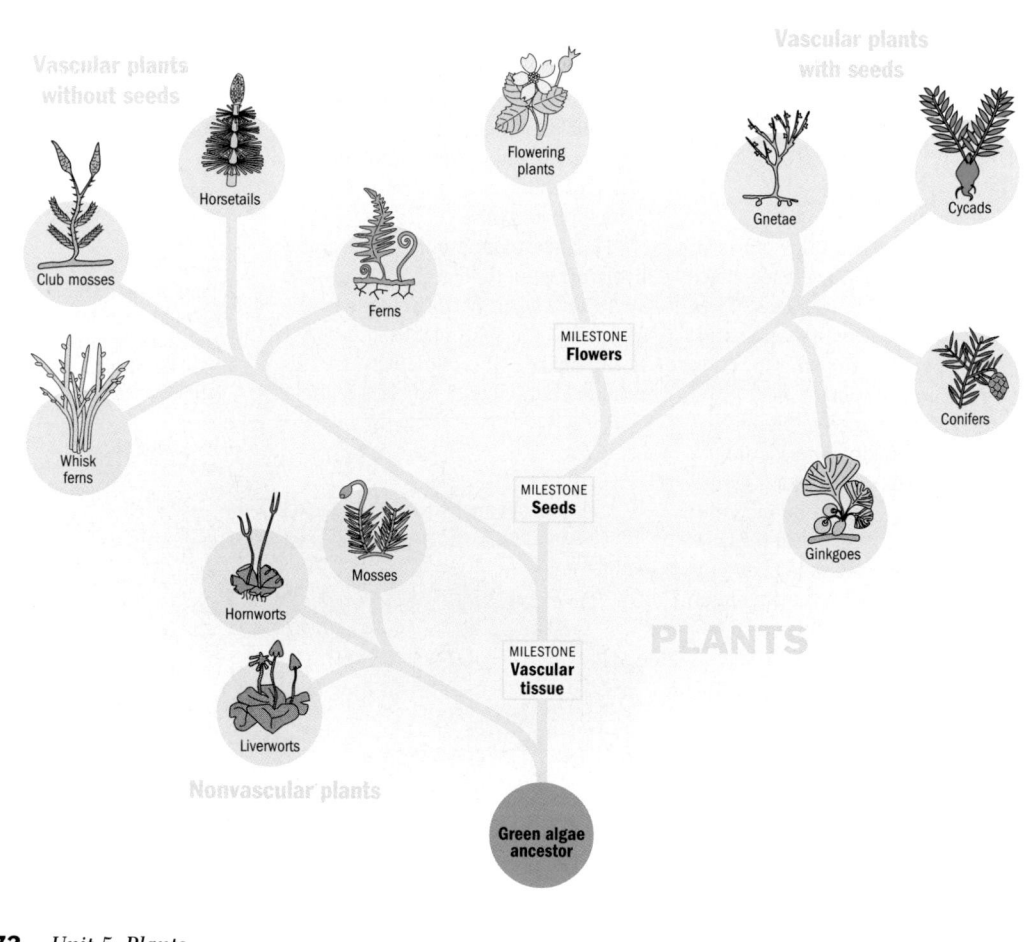

MEETING DIVERSE NEEDS

Gifted Have students expand upon the information presented in Figure 20.3 and create their own diagram of the plant kingdom. They should include photos or sketches and captions for each plant shown in their diagram.

In a seedless plant, the sporophyte releases spores. A spore grows into a small, separate gametophyte which produces gametes. Fertilization and new sporophyte formation occurs on the gametophyte. Seeds are not made.

A seed plant does not release spores. A gametophyte structure develops in flowers or cones of the sporophyte, where gametes are produced, and fertilization occurs. After fertilization, the new embryo is in a seed. After release, the seed can grow into a new sporophyte.

The largest and most familiar of the seedless vascular plants are ferns, members of the division Pterophyta (TER-eh-FY-teh). Although ferns can survive without constant contact with water, they do need water for fertilization. Most ferns have feathery leaves that collect light efficiently in shaded areas. Their stems are structurally simple and generally reach a maximum height of about 2 meters.

The club mosses (division Lycophyta), the horsetails (division Sphenophyta), and the whisk ferns (division Psilophyta) are other groups of seedless vascular plants. Although the ancestors of these plants were abundant during the Carboniferous period (340–280 million years ago), their modern descendants are comparatively scarce. All of the plants in these three divisions have vascular tissue, but not all have leaves.

The evolution and specialization of vascular systems allowed plants to colonize drier areas. However, embryos of seedless plants will dry out and die if they are not kept moist. The evolution of seeds was another factor that helped plants survive in dry areas.

The five divisions of seed plants are subdivided into two general categories according to the ways they produce seeds. The two categories are gymnosperms and angiosperms. Gymnosperms (JIM-noh-spermz) are vascular plants that produce seeds within cones. Angiosperms (AN-jee-oh–spermz) produce

Plant Classification

Botanical Name	Common Name	Living Species
NONVASCULAR PLANTS		
Division Bryophyta	Mosses	10,000
Division Hepatophyta	Liverworts	6500
Division Anthocerophyta	Hornworts	100
VASCULAR PLANTS		
Seedless Plants		
Division Pterophyta	Ferns	12,000
Division Lycophyta	Club mosses	1000
Division Sphenophyta	Horsetails	15
Division Psilophyta	Whisk ferns	13
Seed Plants		
Gymnosperms		
Division Coniferophyta	Conifers	550
Division Cycadophyta	Cycads	100
Division Gnetophyta	Gnetae	70
Division Ginkgophyta	Ginkgoes	1
Angiosperms		
Division Anthophyta	Flowering plants	235,000

FIGURE 20.4
The number of species in each of the major classifications of plants varies. Which division has the most species? The fewest? 1

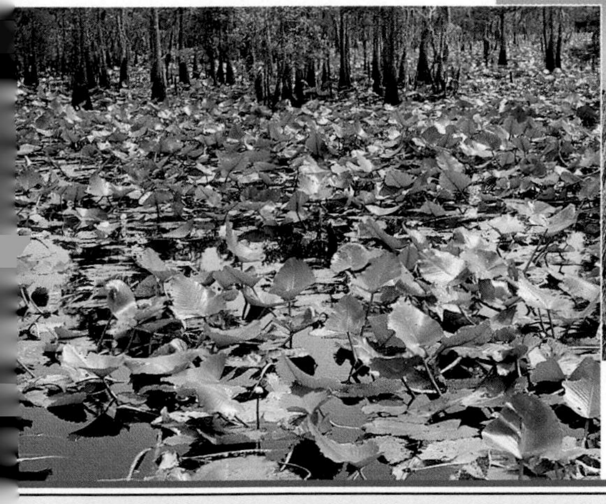

FIGURE 20.5
Plants have adaptations that enable them to live in a wide variety of environmental conditions. The spatterdock (left) is a flowering plant that thrives in swamps. The bloodwood tree of Australia (right) survives where water is scarce.

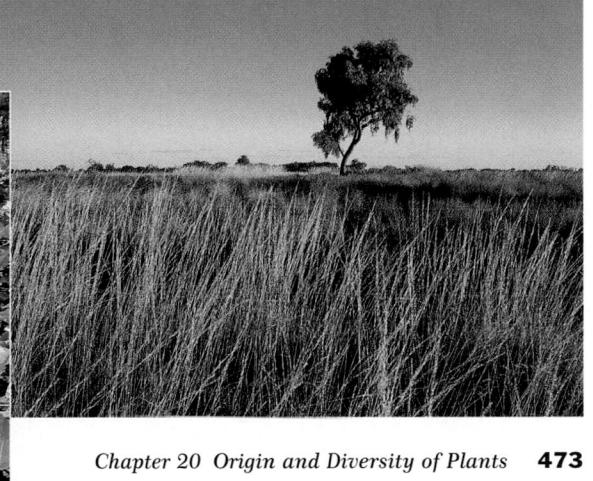

Ecology

TEAM WORK

Discuss how the plants shown in Figure 20.5 have adapted to their environment. Divide the class into groups and ask each group to research other examples of plant adaptations in different ecosystems such as the rain forest and the desert. Suggest students use the Internet or *Readers' Guide to Periodical Literature* to find articles in *National Geographic, Smithsonian* and similar magazines. Encourage groups to include illustrations with their reports.

Teacher Demo

Obtain samples of mosses and leafy vascular plants. Cut a stem of a vascular plant in cross section. Point out that the stem is a stiff structure made up of different tissues. Show a vascular plant's roots and compare it to the base of a moss. Draw students' attention to the veins in a vascular plant's leaves and the absence of veins in mosses. Allow students to observe these structures with a hand lens.

MULTICULTURAL PERSPECTIVE

In the early 1920s, at the age of 50, Ynez Mexia began studying botany at the University of California at Berkeley. As her interest in plants grew, she eventually embarked on a worldwide search of new plant species. Some of her discoveries, such as the *Mexianthus mexicanus*, were named after her. Have interested students find out more about Mexia's adventures collecting plant specimens in the Amazon River Basin and Alaska.

1 Division Anthophyta; Division Ginkgophyta

20.1

Class Activity

Challenge students to identify ten plants common to your area. Have students use field guides to identify the plants by both their common and scientific names. Suggest that they use their findings to assemble a class plant display on poster board.

3 ASSESS

Evaluate Understanding

On the board, draw a simple unlabeled phylogenetic tree of plant evolution similar to that in Figure 20.1. Have students label the tree with the following terms: *green algae ancestor, bryophytes, ferns, gymnosperms, angiosperms.* Then have students write the milestones in plant evolution that enable botanists to classify plants into the groups shown. (Students should record vascular tissue, seeds, and flowering plants in appropriate places on the tree.)

Reteach

On the board write the headings: *Nonvascular Plants, Vascular Plants Without Seeds, Vascular Plants With Seeds, Flowering Plants.* Beneath each, write the common name(s) for plants that belong to each general division. Together with students, list the key characteristics of plants in each category.

474

Do some research on the classification schemes of the plant kingdom. Then visit a nursery or garden store. How does the classification of plants in the nursery or garden store compare with botanical classifications?

IN THE COMMUNITY
Classifying Plants

Does the store use its own classification system? What kinds of plants are displayed together? Write down several examples of plants sold at the nursery and the method used to classify them. Is this method different from the way the same plants are classified in the formal system? What groups of plants are rare in nurseries or garden stores? Why? Visit *http://plants.biosurf.com* to learn more about the taxonomy of plants.

seeds that are encased in fruits.

The largest and most familiar division of gymnosperms is Coniferophyta, the conifers. Conifers include cone-bearing evergreens such as pines, firs, spruces, redwoods, and cypresses. A cone is a specialized reproductive structure that produces seeds without fruit. Most conifers have needlelike leaves.

The cycads (division Cycadophyta), ginkgoes (division Ginkgophyta), and the gnetae (division Gnetophyta) are other gymnosperms. All of these plants have vascular tissues and produce seeds. Cycads look like small palm trees and typically grow in tropical climates. Unlike palms (which are angiosperms), cycads produce seeds in cones. Ginkgoes, trees that lose their leaves in winter, are the sole survivors of a small division of plants. The gnetae are a group of three orders of unusual plants.

Angiosperms are characterized by the evolution of two important features: flowers and fruits. Flowers, which produce sperm, egg cells, or both, are important to plant reproduction because they attract pollinating organisms. These pollinating organisms, in search of food or mates, help to disperse the pollen that produces

the sperm cells of the plant.

Fruits, the other key angiosperm characteristic, are important to plant reproduction in two ways. Fruits protect seeds and can help disperse them.

The majority of the trees, bushes, and houseplants you are familiar with belong to the angiosperms. In fact, there are about a quarter of a million different species of angiosperms—more than 300 times the number of species of gymnosperms.

CHECKPOINT 20.1

1. Compare and contrast the physical characteristics of modern plants and algae.
2. Identify and discuss the major evolutionary adaptations that biologists use to classify plants.
3. **Critical Thinking** Suppose a friend gives you a plant and challenges you to classify it. How would you do this? Explain your answer.

Build on What You Know

4. Using what you know about natural selection, explain how the first nonvascular land plants might have evolved into vascular plants. *(Need to jog your memory? Revisit relevant concepts in Chapter 10, Section 10.2.)*

474 *Unit 5 Plants*

CHECKPOINT 20.1

1. They have similar pigments and chloroplasts; form a cell plate; have cellulose in cell walls; and store food as starch. Plants have specialized structures.
2. Adaptations include vascular tissue, which allows plants to live in dry regions, and seeds, fruits, or flowers that make plant reproduction more efficient.
3. **Applying knowledge** Examine the leaves, roots; check for flowers or cones; use reference materials
4. Plants with roots could get water and nutrients from soil. Vascular plants could grow taller to compete for sunlight.

20.2 Mosses

Mountain moss

Mosses growing on Mount Kenya in Africa lead very unstable lives. During the hot, damp day, the mosses flourish. At night, however, temperatures drop, the soil freezes, and the mosses lose their grip on the mountain. Turning into dry balls, they are blown by the wind to new locations. How does this adaptation help the moss species survive? ❶

CHARACTERISTICS OF MOSSES

Masses of mosses gather on wet stones

Many kinds of plants are called mosses—reindeer moss, Spanish moss, and Irish moss are just a few. Are they really entitled to that name? Actually, no! None of these is a true moss. Reindeer moss is a lichen, Spanish moss is a flowering plant related to pineapple, and Irish moss is a red alga, a type of seaweed. What, then, is a moss?

A moss is the most common type of nonvascular plant—a plant that has no vascular system. As you just read, the nonvascular plants also include liverworts and hornworts. This section, however, discusses only the mosses.

If you look carefully, you will probably find mosses growing in many familiar places. Mosses grow on damp brick walls, in sidewalk cracks, as thick mats on forest floors, and on the shaded sides of trees. Some mosses are even adapted to life in deserts. Mosses need water for reproduction. All of these places—even deserts— have enough water for mosses to complete their life cycle.

Mosses have a relatively uncomplicated system for transporting water. Water can pass from moss cell to moss cell by osmosis because most

mosses are only a few cells thick. As you may recall from Chapter 3, osmosis is the diffusion of water from an area of high concentration to an area of low concentration. Osmosis does not use a cell's energy.

Mosses do not have roots. Instead, they are anchored by slender projections called rhizoids. Mosses also lack true leaves, although they do have leaflike structures. These structures are often only one cell thick.

Mosses are small land plants, but they vary in appearance and habitat. Compare the three types of mosses shown in *Figure 20.6*.

What you'll learn

IDEAS
- To identify the common characteristics of mosses
- To compare and contrast the haploid and diploid phases of mosses

WORDS
archegonium, antheridium, capsule, peat bog

FIGURE 20.6

Seen from a distance, mosses look like lush green carpets. Up close, their thin green leaflike structures become visible. How does water move through these structures? ❷

STUDENT RESOURCES

From the Teacher's Resource Package, use:
- Section Review 20.2 and Enrichment Topic 20-1 from Unit 5 Review Module
- Lab 33: "Terrestrial Pioneers: Mosses and Liverworts"
- Issues and Decision Making 20-1

TECHNOLOGY RESOURCES

Relevant technology resources include:
- Spanish Student Edition CD-ROM
- Teacher's Resource Planner CD-ROM

❶ ENGAGE

Use the Visual

Have students study the photograph that opens the section. Ask:

- **Do you think this environment is a good place for mosses to grow? Why?** (Students should note that the extreme temperature changes on the mountain affect the mosses.)

Check Prior Knowledge

To assess students' knowledge about plant reproduction, ask:

- **How does the number of chromosomes change during meiosis?** (Reduced by half, from diploid to haploid)

SUPER READ! Monitoring Understanding
To practice strategies for effective reading, use pages 53-54 in *Super Read!*

Teacher Demo

Obtain a small quantity of sphagnum moss from a nursery. Have students touch the dry moss and describe its texture and appearance. Soak the sphagnum in warm water. After a few minutes, squeeze the water into a beaker and discuss the amount of water absorbed by the sphagnum. Conclude by having students touch the wet moss and comparing it to the dry moss.

❶ This keeps the moss from freezing and aids in seed dispersal
❷ From cell to cell by osmosis

Examining Fern Leaves and Sori

Analyze Your Results

1 Spores are released when the sporangia split open.

2 The spores develop into gametophytes through mitosis. Egg and sperm form a zygote. Zygote grows into sporophyte that produces spores.

 **ASSESS**

Evaluate Understanding

To assess students' understanding of the material in this section, ask:

- **What kinds of plants are ferns?** (Vascular, seedless)
- **What is a sorus?** (Spore-containing structure on the underside of a leaf)
- **What is the archegonium?** (Egg-producing organ)
- **How do ferns reproduce?** (Ferns alternate between a haploid gametophyte and a diploid sporophyte. Ferns do not produce seeds.)

Reteach

Help small groups of students create models or draw diagrams of ferns. Point out each feature and discuss its function. Be sure students correctly label fronds, blades, petioles, rhizomes, spores, and sori.

480

LAB ZONE Do It!

Examining Fern Leaves and Sori

You can observe the reproductive structures of a fern sporophyte when you . . .

Try This

1 Obtain a small piece of a fern frond that has sori on its underside. Sketch the leaf and sori as they appear without magnification.

2 Place the leaf on a slide. View the sori under a dissecting microscope using low and high power. Draw a magnified sorus.

3 Using a scalpel, make a thin cross section of the leaf, cutting through a sorus. **Caution:** Use care when handling the scalpel. Place the cross section on a slide. Examine and draw the interior of a sorus as it appears under low power.

4 View the cross section under high power and examine an individual spore. Draw and label the parts.

Analyze Your Results

1 Based on your examination of the structures inside a sorus, how do you think the fern distributes its spores? Explain.

2 Summarize the steps in the life cycle of the fern after the sporophyte releases spores.

two gametes occurs, a zygote is formed. For a time, the zygote remains inside the archegonium, relying on the gametophyte for nutrition. The zygote grows into a sporophyte, eventually growing larger than the gametophyte and becomes nutritionally independent. The gametophyte eventually dies. As the sporophyte grows, it produces leaves with sori, and the fern's life cycle is repeated.

? What are the main characteristics of ferns?

FERNS IN THE BIOSPHERE

The roles ferns play

Ferns often play a role in ecological succession. Some types of ferns can grow in the crevices of rocks. Others can grow in wetlands before the area is taken over by larger plants. Still others grow abundantly in fields that are no longer cultivated.

Several fern species, including the ostrich fern, are used for food. In the spring, the newly forming leaves of one species—called fiddleheads because of their shape—serve as a source of food.

The mosquito fern is important in Southeast Asia for the cultivation of rice. The leaves of this fern are home to nitrogen-fixing cyanobacteria. Cyanobacteria convert nitrogen gas into a form the plants can use, greatly enhancing the growth of plants and the productivity of rice paddies.

Ferns are also valuable economically because of their use in horticulture. Each year millions of ferns are bought for home decoration or for outdoor landscaping. What types of ferns have you seen used as indoor decoration?

CHECKPOINT 20.3

1. Describe the common characteristics of ferns.

2. Compare the haploid and diploid phases of the fern's life cycle.

3. Critical Thinking Why do ferns flourish in damp areas?

Build on What You Know

4. Identify the similarities and differences between ferns and algae. *(Need to jog your memory? Revisit relevant concepts in Chapter 15, Section 15.3.)*

CHECKPOINT 20.3

1. Ferns have leaves consisting of blades and petioles; stems and roots.

2. The prominent, diploid sporophyte stage has fronds and produces spores that develop haploid gametophytes. They produce sperm in antheridia and eggs in archegonia. Sperm and eggs fuse to form 2n zygotes, which develop into sporophytes.

3. **Making inferences** Water enables sperm cells to swim to eggs during the gametophyte stage.

4. Both ferns and algae carry out photosynthesis. But ferns are adapted to live on land, while algae live in water.

❶ Staghorn fern, maidenhair fern, shield fern, and bird's-nest fern

THE BIG IDEA!

Seed plants do not require water for fertilization and have therefore colonized extensive areas of land. 20.4–20.5

20.4 Conifers

Sitting pretty
This pine siskin nests in coniferous forests, finding shelter amid the thick, tough leaves, called needles. The needle shape is an adaptation that protects the tree from drought. Unlike the leaves of deciduous trees, needles are shed and regrown throughout the growing season. Conifers are vascular seed plants.

What you'll learn

IDEAS
• To identify common characteristics of conifers
• To describe the life cycle of a conifer

CHARACTERISTICS OF CONIFERS

Standing tall

Conifers include some of the largest and oldest organisms on Earth. The giant redwood tree, which can be taller than a 30-story building, is one of Earth's largest organisms. The bristlecone pine is among the oldest living individual organisms. Some bristlecone pines are more than 5000 years old.

Conifers are vascular plants that bear cones. Although some conifers lose their leaves in the winter, most conifers are trees that possess needle-like leaves throughout the year, which is why they are commonly called "evergreens." The needles are hard structures covered with a waterproof cuticle. Needles give off much less water during transpiration than do the flat leaves of deciduous trees. This adaptation enables many conifers to thrive in harsh conditions.

Conifers are a division of the gymnosperms. Like other gymnosperms, conifers produce their seeds in cones—specialized reproductive structures with many compartments. Like some other gymnosperms, conifers carry out fertilization without water by means of male and female cones.

Compare the male and female cones of the loblolly pine in *Figure 20.11*.

When the seeds of gymnosperms are released from their cones, the seeds are not encased in any protective covering. Botanists call the seeds of gymnosperms "naked seeds" because they are not enclosed in fruit. Remember that the seeds of angiosperms are typically encased in fruit.

Very recently, scientists in Australia found a grove of living conifers that were previously thought to be extinct. These trees, called Wollemi pines, are descendants of plants that lived during the time of the dinosaurs. This

FIGURE 20.11
Conifers bear male cones (above) and female cones (near right). The male cones produce cells that develop into pollen grains. Wind carries the pollen to female cones, where pollination occurs.

STUDENT RESOURCES

From the Teacher's Resource Package, use:
■ Section Review 20.4 and Activity Recordsheet 20-2 from Unit 5 Review Module
■ Biotechnology Manual: Concept 8, Lab 17, and Issue 4

TECHNOLOGY RESOURCES

Relevant technology resources include:
■ Spanish Student Edition CD-ROM
■ Teacher's Resource Planner CD-ROM

1 ENGAGE

Consider the Big Idea

Have students read The Big Idea! at the top of the page. Have students discuss why the seed plant has been able to thrive in so many places.

Use the Visual

Have students study the photograph that opens the section. Point out that a conifer is a seed plant. Ask:

■ **What characteristic makes this tree different from other kinds of trees?** (The tree has needlelike leaves.)

Check Prior Knowledge

To assess students' knowledge about seed plants and conifers, ask:

■ **What is a seed?** (Protective structure that contains a plant embryo and stored food)
■ **What are gymnosperms?** (Vascular plants that produce seeds lacking a protective covering)

Quick Activity

Display pictures or specimens of a variety of pine cones, or ask students to bring in samples. Challenge students to identify the male and female cones and tell how they differ. Discuss where the seeds are formed and ask:

■ **Why are there no seeds in the samples?** (The cone has matured and shed its seeds.)

Clarify Misconceptions

Students may believe that ever-green conifers retain their leaves throughout the year. Explain that although conifers retain some leaves year-round, they are constantly dropping their needles. Some conifers lose most of their old leaves at a particular time and retain their newer leaves.

Use the Visual

Have students study the life cycle of a conifer illustrated in Figure 20.12. Emphasize that the female and male gameto-phytes are very small and that the female gametophyte remains in the cone where it produces eggs. Ask:

- **What is the male gameto-phyte?** (The pollen grain)
- **How does the pollen reach the cone?** (It is carried by the wind.)
- **When does pollination occur?** (When the pollen grains reach a cone where there is a female gameto-phyte)
- **How does the male gameto-phyte reach the female gametophyte to fertilize it?** (It grows a pollen tube through which sperm travel to the egg.)

discovery has given scientists a chance to study a plant that thrived many millions of years ago.

As you read in section 20.1, conifers and three other divisions of gymnosperms still survive today. One of these divisions, the gnetae, are cone-bearing desert plants. Another division, the cycads, have palmlike leaves and produce seeds or seed cones. The third division, the ginkgoes, have fan-shaped leaves that turn yellow and fall from the trees in autumn. Ginkgoes were saved from extinction by surviving in few gardens in China.

FIGURE 20.12

The Life Cycle of a Conifer

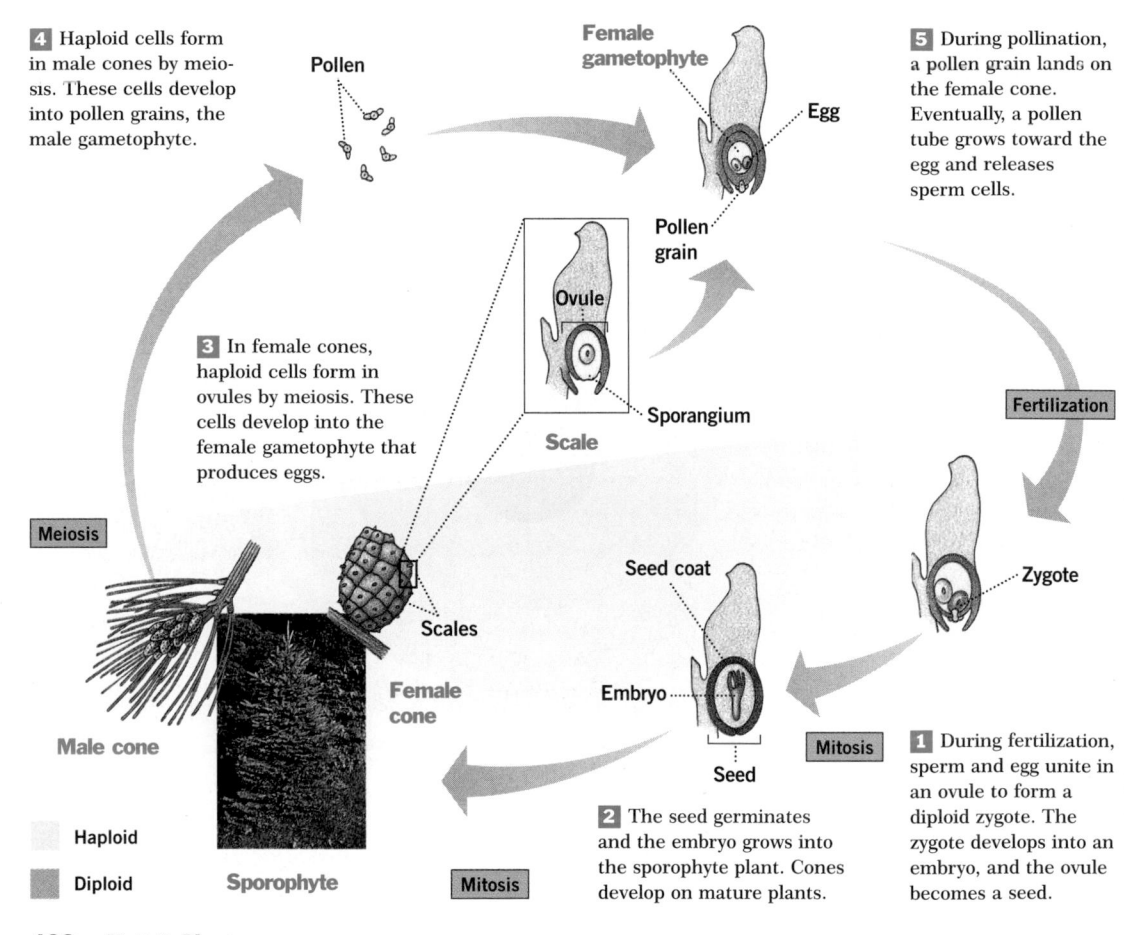

4 Haploid cells form in male cones by meio-sis. These cells develop into pollen grains, the male gametophyte.

3 In female cones, haploid cells form in ovules by meiosis. These cells develop into the female gametophyte that produces eggs.

5 During pollination, a pollen grain lands on the female cone. Eventually, a pollen tube grows toward the egg and releases sperm cells.

1 During fertilization, sperm and egg unite in an ovule to form a diploid zygote. The zygote develops into an embryo, and the ovule becomes a seed.

2 The seed germinates and the embryo grows into the sporophyte plant. Cones develop on mature plants.

Haploid
Diploid

482 *Unit 5 Plants*

PINE LIFE CYCLE
Blowing in the wind

The pine tree is a typical conifer. Like other vascular plants, it undergoes alternation of generations in which the sporophyte stage is dominant. The gametophyte stage consists of only the pollen and part of the female pinecone.

Perhaps you have used pinecones as decorations or as part of an art project. You probably used the large, familiar cones that are actually the female cones of a pine tree. Pine trees also have male cones, which are smaller than the female cones.

FACTS AND FIGURES

The ginkgo is the only surviving species in a division of gymnosperms that once was widespread. Many botanists presume the ginkgo to be extinct in the wild. The trees, native to temperate regions of China, Korea, and Japan gained popularity during the eighteenth century when Westerners brought seeds to Europe and the United States. Today, ginkgoes are popular shade trees in many parts of the world.

The female cones consist of spirally arranged scales that secrete a sticky resin. At the base of each scale are two ovules. As you have learned, an ovule is a structure that develops into a seed. An ovule consists of a female gametophyte with an egg.

Each male cone produces huge amounts of pollen grains that are released in the spring. The pollen grains have winglike structures that keep them aloft in the wind. Because of these structures, pollen grains can be carried long distances, which increases the opportunities for pollination. As you may recall, pollination is the transfer of pollen from the male to the female part of a plant.

When a pollen grain reaches a female cone, it sticks to the cone's resin. As the resin dries, the pollen grain begins to grow a structure called a pollen tube, which extends to an ovule near the base of a scale. Eventually a sperm cell is released from the pollen tube. The sperm fertilizes an egg in the ovule. A zygote forms and grows into an embryo surrounded by a seed coat.

As the embryo matures, the female cone grows larger and the scales separate. The seed is then released from the female cone. If the seed lands in an environment with the proper conditions for growth, it will germinate. The complete pine life cycle takes two to three years from the time the cones form until the seeds are released.

GYMNOSPERMS IN THE BIOSPHERE

Comfortable in the cold

Gymnosperms flourished and diversified about 250 million years ago, during the cold, dry Permian period. As a result, the plants that evolved in that environment were adapted to live in cold climates, where many of their descendants thrive today. If you have the chance to climb a mountain, you will find conifers growing at altitudes that would be too cold for deciduous flowering trees.

Some gymnosperms, including conifers such as cypresses and giant redwoods, do thrive in mild climates. The bald cypress can even thrive in a swamp. Swampy conditions are inhospitable to most trees, because the waterlogged soil is low in oxygen. But the cypress has specialized roots called breathing roots that grow above the water surface and enable the tree to collect oxygen.

Conifers often grow together in stands and may shade the forest floor throughout the year. The needles and scales that they drop decompose more slowly than deciduous leaves, and produce an acidic humus. The shady,

Chapter 20 Origin and Diversity of Plants **483**

Examining the Structure of a Pine Cone

Review the life cycle of the conifer as you . . .

Try This

1 Select two female pine cones, one with scales closed and one with scales open. Sketch the two cones.
2 Remove a single scale from each pine cone. Use a scalpel if necessary. **Caution:** Use care when handling the scalpel. Compare the appearance of the two scales and sketch.
3 Cross-section each scale by slicing it into thirds. Draw one of the cross sections from each pine cone. Identify and label the structures you see.

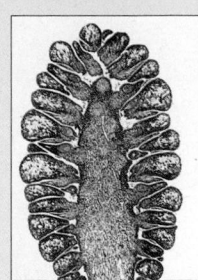

Analyze Your Results

1 Do you think your pine cone was pollinated? Why or why not?
2 Summarize the differences you observed between the two pine cones.

Clarify Misconceptions

Students often think that pollination and fertilization are the same. Explain that pollination is the process in which pollen is transferred from the male part to the female part of a plant. Fertilization is the actual union of male and female gametes. Explain that pollination does not guarantee fertilization.

Think Critically

Point out to students that conifers produce very large numbers of pollen grains in the spring. Ask:

■ **Why is it beneficial for a conifer to produce so many pollen grains?** (It increases the odds that some pollen grains will reach female gametophytes.)

Discuss

Discuss the adaptations that enable conifers to survive in cold, dry climates. For example, point out that conifers have needlelike leaves with waxy coatings that help prevent water loss.

LAB ZONE Do It! TEAM WORK

Examining the Structure of a Pine Cone

Analyze Your Results

2 The pine cone with closed scales has an open micropyle where pollen grains can enter. The pine cone with open scales has a closed micropyle, and if fertilized, an embryo and food reserve.

MEETING DIVERSE NEEDS

LEP Have students redraw the conifer life cycle as a flowchart. Encourage students to label each stage of the flowchart in both English and their native language. Instruct students to include labels indicating when mitosis and meiosis occur.

Build Writing Skills

Have students investigate and prepare a written or visual report about products available from conifers. Encourage students to identify as many uses as they can for conifer woods such as pine, cedar, and redwood. Possible responses include lumber for building, paper, boxes, turpentine, and pitch.

3 ASSESS

Evaluate Understanding

To assess students' understanding of the life cycle of a conifer, ask:

- **What is the dominant stage in a conifer life cycle?** (Sporophyte stage)
- **What structures make up the gametophyte stage?** (The gametophytes are produced by cones and consist of pollen grains or eggs inside the ovules.)
- **How are pollen grains transported to the female cone?** (Carried by the wind)
- **When does fertilization occur?** (When the sperm travels down the pollen tube and reaches the egg)

Reteach

Review the conifer life cycle by listing the steps on the board. Number each step. Help students understand that the last step is the same as the first step in the cycle.

484

FIGURE 20.13
Residing in coniferous forests are longhorn beetles that live on wood and owls that prey on small mammals. Red squirrels collect and store pinecones by the hundreds.

acidic environment is inhospitable to many other types of plants. However, some types of mosses and ferns thrive in the conifers' leaf litter, as do toadstools and other fungi.

In their communities, conifers are key producers and providers of shelter. Animals that live on or near conifers include adult and larval insects as well as mammals and birds. Some moths and fly larvae eat pine needles, while some wasps and flies eat the wood. Squirrels and birds such as nutcrackers and crossbills eat conifer seeds.

Other residents of conifer forests may include moose, reindeer, foxes, and wolves. Woodpeckers, warblers, hawks, owls, and various other birds use conifers for shelter. However, vertebrates that do not maintain a constant body temperature, such as frogs and snakes, are uncommon in the colder regions where many types of conifers thrive.

People have made use of conifers in many different ways. Many conifers are harvested for building lumber. Some humans eat the nuts of pines. For many years pine nuts were part

of a system of trade among Native Americans in the western United States.

Conifers and other gymnosperms are also used as ornamental plants in gardens, parks, and other landscaped areas. Conifers such as yews make excellent ground cover while especially tall evergreens are used as windbreaks. Ginkgoes are so hardy that they can be grown in cities where air pollution is high. Conifers are used for the art of bonsai, in which trees are grown in a dwarflike condition in containers, producing plants such as those shown on page 435.

CHECKPOINT 20.4

1. What are the main characteristics of conifers?
2. Describe the life cycle of a conifer.
3. **Critical Thinking** What adaptations do conifers have that enable certain species to live for thousands of years?

Build on What You Know

4. What advantage is gained by evergreens that retain green needles throughout the winter? *(Need to jog your memory? Revisit relevant concepts in Chapter 4, Section 4.2.)*

CHECKPOINT 20.4

1. Needlelike leaves and naked seeds; fertilization is not dependent on water.
2. Male cones on the sporophyte produce gametophytes or pollen grains through meiosis. The female gametophyte is located in the ovule of a female cone. Through pollination and fertilization, the zygote and seed form on the female cone. The seed germinates into a sporophyte.
3. **Applying knowledge** Strong, woody structures; needles can photosynthesize all year and retain water.
4. Some can photosynthesize in the winter, lengthening their growing seasons.

20.5 Flowering Plants

Why flowers?
Most of the plants that you are familiar with, including most trees, are flowering plants—about 235,000 species in all. How do plants benefit from flowers? Flowers contain the reproductive structures of plants. Because of their color and scent, flowers attract a variety of pollinators. These pollinators are vital to the process of reproduction, which ensures the continuation of the species.

What you'll learn

IDEAS
• To identify the common characteristics of flowering plants
• To describe the life cycle of a flowering plant

WORDS
double fertilization, pollinators

CHARACTERISTICS OF FLOWERING PLANTS

Flower power

In the previous chapter you read about the importance of flowers—they are the reproductive organs of flowering plants. Flowers may be large and conspicuous, or they may be tiny and hidden. Whatever their size, shape, or color, flowers are an essential part of life on this planet. Flowers not only enable certain plants to reproduce, but flowers also produce the pollen, nectar, fruit, and seeds that sustain many other types of organisms.

You now know that flowering plants are the most abundant types of plants. Flowering plants have certain characteristics that identify them as members of the division called angiosperms. These include the following:

• flowers
• leaves, stems, and roots that contain vascular tissue
• stems, branches, and roots that may be woody or nonwoody
• gametophytes that grow within the sporophyte plant
• sexual reproduction that depends on air currents or pollinating organisms, not water
• seeds
• double fertilization
• fruit

Angiosperms can be further classified according to differences in their seeds, flowers, stems, leaves, or roots. For example, all flowering plants are either monocots or dicots, depending on the characteristics of their seeds. As you have learned, monocot seeds have one cotyledon, or seed leaf, that nourishes the young seedling. Dicot seeds have two cotyledons. Monocots and dicots also differ in their leaf and flower structures, the arrangement of their vascular tissue, and their overall root shapes.

Monocots have parallel leaf veins. In their stems, the xylem and phloem bundles are scattered in a complex pattern. The flower parts of monocots come in multiples of three. And, monocots have fibrous root systems. Some examples of monocots are lilies, orchids, corn, and grasses.

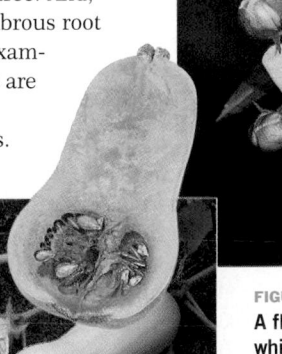

FIGURE 20.14
A flower produces seeds, which can produce new plants. You can see seeds in many familiar foods, including apples and squash.

Chapter 20 Origin and Diversity of Plants **485**

① ENGAGE

Use the Visual

Have students study the photograph and read the text that opens the section. Ask:

■ **What characteristics of flowers might attract pollinators?** (Color of petals, scent, shape, nectar, time of day when open)

Check Prior Knowledge

To assess students' knowledge about flowering plants, Ask:

■ **What are some examples of flowering plants?** (Names of garden flowers, wild flowers, vegetables, or weeds are acceptable.)
■ **What are the key features of plants that belong to the division of angiosperms?** (Flowers; true stems, leaves, roots; seeds; fruit; woody or nonwoody stems.)

Quick Activity

Display seeds familiar to students such as pumpkin and sunflower seeds and peanuts. Ask students whether they have ever eaten any of these types of seeds and initiate a discussion on why plants produce seeds. Tell students that in this section they will learn how seeds are formed and their role in plant reproduction.

STUDENT RESOURCES

From the Teacher's Resource Package, use:
■ Section Review 20.5, Activity Record-sheet 20-3, Vocabulary Review 20, and Chapter 20 Tests from Unit 5 Review Module
■ Consumer Applications 20-1

TECHNOLOGY RESOURCES

Relevant technology resources include:
■ Spanish Student Edition CD-ROM
■ Teacher's Resource Planner CD-ROM
■ TestWorks CD-ROM: Chapter 20 Tests

Use the Visual

Give students time to study Figure 20.15. Ask:

- **What are cotyledons?** (Leaflike parts of the seed that nourishes the plant.)
- **How do monocot leaves differ in appearance from dicot leaves?** (Monocots—narrow with parallel veins; dicots—broad with veins that form branching pattern)
- **How do the stems of monocots differ from the stems of dicots?** (Monocots—vascular bundles in a scattered arrangement; dicots—vascular bundles arranged in a ring)
- **How do the flowers of monocots and dicots differ?** (Monocots have flower parts in multiples of three; dicots have flower parts in multiples of four or five.)

Class Activity

TEAM WORK

Divide the class into small groups. Provide each group with several specimens of flowers and leaves. Have students identify each specimen as a monocot or dicot, then share their findings as a class.

Comparison of Two Major Groups of Angiosperms

Group	Seed leaves	Leaf veins	Stems	Flowers	Roots
Monocot	One cotyledon	Veins usually parallel	Vascular bundles in complex arrangement	Floral parts usually in multiples of three	Fibrous root system
Dicot	Two cotyledons	Veins usually branched	Vascular bundles arranged in ring	Floral parts usually in multiples of four or five	Taproot usually present

FIGURE 20.15

This table shows the major structural differences between monocots and dicots. Based on their different root structures, which group do you think tends to have the larger plants? ❶

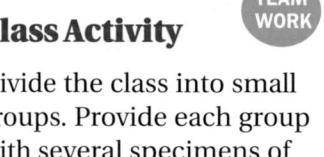

Weeds in the Mail

Seed catalogs, which many gardeners enjoy reading, became popular in the 19th century. Seeds from these catalogs led to the cultivation of many nonnative plant species, such as common barberry and jointed goat grass, which threatened native species.

In contrast, the leaf veins of dicots usually have a branching, netlike arrangement. In the stems, the xylem and phloem bundles are arranged in a circle. The flower parts of dicots come in multiples of four or five. And dicots usually have taproots. Roses, beans, clovers, and most trees are examples of dicots. *Figure 20.15* illustrates the major differences between monocots and dicots.

FLOWERING PLANT LIFE CYCLE

Nature's beautiful seed machines

In some ways, the life cycle of an angiosperm is similar to the life cycle of a gymnosperm or even a fern. As you can see in *Figure 20.16,* an angiosperm undergoes alternation of generations. Certain cells in the sporophyte undergo meiosis to form spores. The spores divide mitotically to form male and female gametophytes. The gametophytes form the gametes—the eggs and sperm.

For many years the next steps of the life cycle—the gametophyte stage and the processes of pollination and fertilization—were not well understood. Today botanists know that the gametophytes are quite tiny and always develop in the flower of the sporophyte plant.

Eggs form in ovules. Ovules are structures located inside the ovary. An ovary is an organ located where the petals connect to the plant. Inside the ovule, meiosis produces haploid (n) cells of which only one–the megaspore–survives. The megaspore undergoes three rounds of mitosis to form a haploid, multicellular female gametophyte. The female gametophyte contains a haploid egg and a large cell with two nuclei called polar nuclei.

Sperm form in pollen, which develop in anthers. Meiosis in anthers forms haploid cells called microspores. Each microspore undergoes mitosis to become a two-celled male gametophyte, the pollen grain.

In the next step—pollination—pollen is transferred from an anther to a stigma. A stigma is the sticky part at

❶ The dicots

FACTS AND FIGURES

Angiosperms are the most abundant of modern plants. There are an estimated 275,000 species, compared with 50,000 of all other plant species. Angiosperms appeared relatively late in the fossil record—in the Cretaceous period after the gymnosperms.

the top of the pistil. When a pollen grain lands on a stigma, the pollen grain produces a pollen tube that grows through the style to the ovary. Once in the ovary, the pollen tube enters an ovule. At this point, one cell in the pollen grain divides by mitosis to become two haploid sperm.

Fertilization occurs when a sperm nucleus from the pollen tube fuses with the egg in the ovule. The egg and sperm are both haploid, and the resulting zygote is diploid. The zygote develops into a diploid embryo within the ovule. The embryo soon stops developing and becomes dormant.

In angiosperms, a unique process occurs during fertilization, called double fertilization. In **double fertilization,** the second sperm nucleus from the pollen tube fuses with the two polar nuclei in the ovule. The result is a triploid (3*n*) cell, which divides to become triploid tissue called endosperm.

A tough seed coat forms from ovule tissue. The seed coat surrounds and protects the dormant embryo and endosperm. The endosperm will nourish the seed embryo when it sprouts. The seed coat, embryo, and endosperm form the seed. This structure is a fruit—the

Orchid Seeds in Your Ice Cream?

Those brown specks you see in real vanilla ice cream are chopped vanilla beans, the fruit of a type of orchid. The orchid is a flowering plant found mainly in the tropics.

FIGURE 20.16

The Life Cycle of an Angiosperm

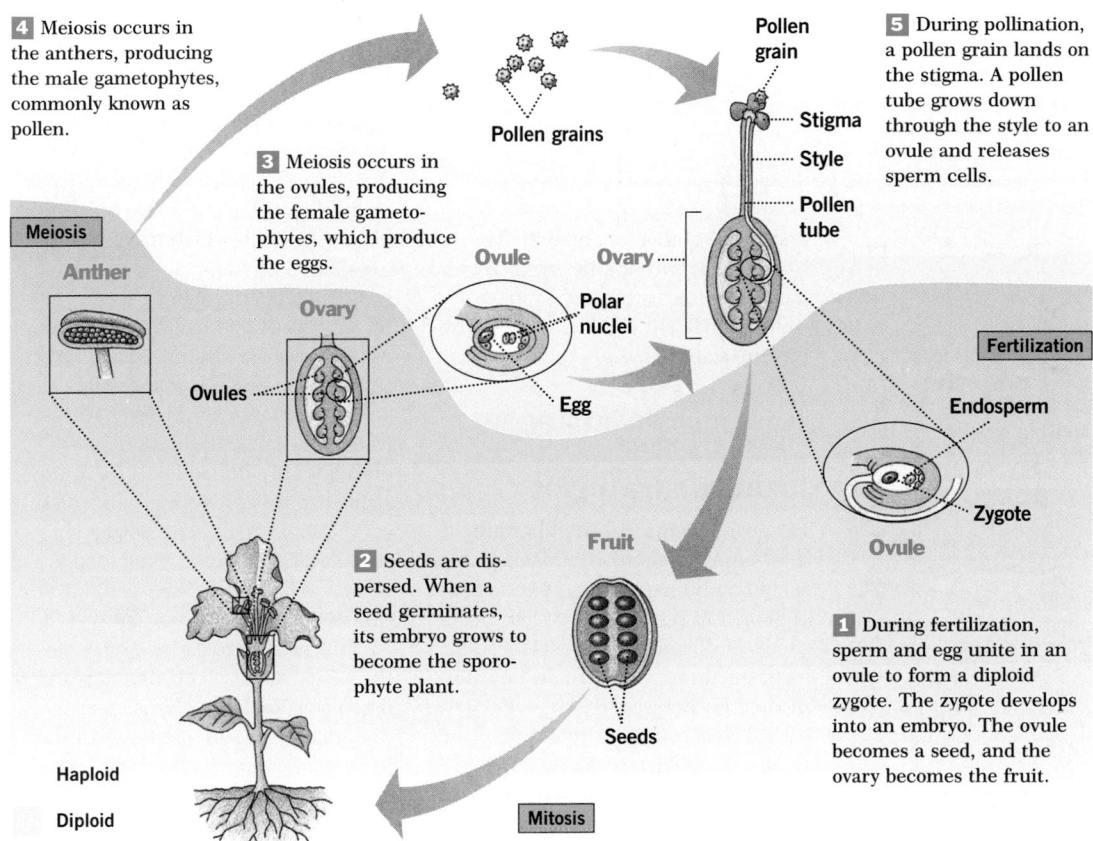

4 Meiosis occurs in the anthers, producing the male gametophytes, commonly known as pollen.

3 Meiosis occurs in the ovules, producing the female gametophytes, which produce the eggs.

Pollen grains

5 During pollination, a pollen grain lands on the stigma. A pollen tube grows down through the style to an ovule and releases sperm cells.

Pollen grain
Stigma
Style
Pollen tube

Meiosis

Anther

Ovary

Ovules

Ovule

Ovary

Polar nuclei

Egg

Fertilization

Endosperm

Zygote

Ovule

Fruit

2 Seeds are dispersed. When a seed germinates, its embryo grows to become the sporophyte plant.

Seeds

1 During fertilization, sperm and egg unite in an ovule to form a diploid zygote. The zygote develops into an embryo. The ovule becomes a seed, and the ovary becomes the fruit.

Haploid

Diploid

Mitosis

Chapter 20 Origin and Diversity of Plants **487**

Everyday Biology

You may wish to bring a whole vanilla bean to class. With a sharp knife, carefully cut the bean lengthwise. Using the tip of the knife, splay open the bean pod and gently scrape out the seeds. Allow students to use a hand lens to examine the seeds. Point out the aroma of the beans and pod.

Use the Visual

Have students study Figure 20.16. Ask:

- **Where is the female gametophyte located?** (The gametophyte or ovule is located within the ovary of the flower)
- **Where are microspores produced?** (In the anthers)
- **What are the haploid and diploid structures in the life cycle?** (Haploid—pollen grains, the egg, and polar bodies; diploid—the zygote, embryo, and seed)
- **Why are male flowers unable to produce fruit?** (Fruit develops from the ovary which is not part of a male flower)

Apply

Point out that the life cycle of different types of plants have many similarities. Ask:

- **How is the life cycle of an angiosperm similar to that of a gymnosperm?** (Both are characterized by alternation of generations, seeds, and a dominant sporophyte generation.)

MEETING DIVERSE NEEDS

LEP Ask LEP students to draw the angiosperm life cycle as a flowchart, labeling the events at each stage in both English and their native language. Next, have students draw the angiosperm life cycle as a flowchart, if possible, on the same sheet of paper.

LAB ZONE Think About It!

Analyzing Changes in a Flower

Analyzing the Graph

1 Temperature spiked during first four hours, then slowly declined.

2 CO_2 production took longer to reach its max, but declined at a rate parallel to temperature decline.

3 CO_2 production, which occurs during metabolism, occurs at its highest rate during blooming.

4 Odor release occurs during temperature increase and high metabolism. Odor attracts pollinators.

Clarify Misconceptions

Students may think that a self-pollinating plant is carrying out asexual reproduction. Although a self-pollinating plant produces offspring from only one parent plant, the offspring result from the union of two gametes, both of which the plant has. Because two gametes are involved, self-pollination is sexual reproduction.

❶ The endosperm, the food supply for the sprouting seed, is high in starch and also contains some protein and vitamins.

❷ Parasitic mites threaten bee populations.

LAB ZONE Think About It! bioSURF

Analyzing Changes in a Flower

The graph below shows the changing temperature (left axis) in a *Sauromatum* flower as it begins to bloom. The graph also shows how much CO_2 is produced (right axis) during the same period. While the flower was blooming, the air temperature stayed at about 27°C.

Analyzing the Graph

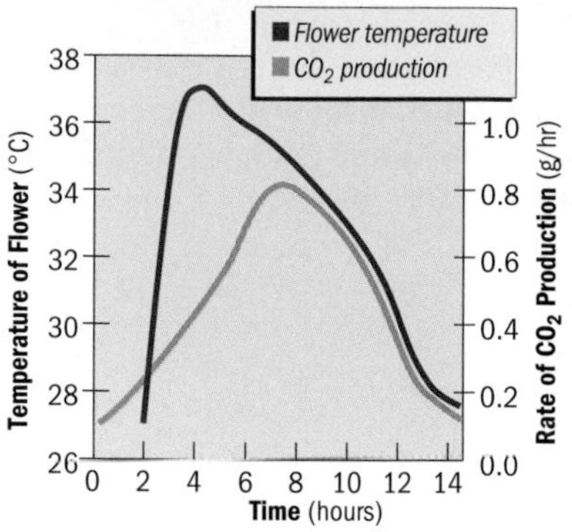

1 How would you describe the change in the flower temperature?
2 What is the relationship between the flower temperature and the plant's production of CO_2?
3 What evidence suggests that metabolism is involved in the blooming process?
4 When it blooms, the flower releases an odor of rotting meat that attracts pollinating insects. What can you infer about the process of odor release? How might the release of odor be beneficial to the plant?

FIGURE 20.17
This cardinal is feasting on wild grapes. Animals that eat fruits may deposit the seeds in locations far from the parent plant.

end result of this fertilization. The fruit may be soft and fleshy or dry and hard. The tomatoes, corn, apples, and walnuts that you enjoy are formed by this intricate process.

FLOWERING PLANTS IN THE BIOSPHERE

Fruitful strategies

Flowering plants are an important food supply to many organisms, including humans. Angiosperms provide food in the form of pollen, nectar, seeds, and fruit. Some flowers, such as nasturtiums, can actually be eaten in their entirety.

Pollen is usually carried from plant to plant by **pollinators.** The most common pollinators are wind and various animals. Animal pollinators and flowering plants live in mutually beneficial relationships. For example, the bee in *Figure 20.18* obtains nectar and pollen from the plant. At the same time, the bee provides a means of pollen dispersal for the plant. This process of transferring pollen enables angiosperms to reproduce without water. Pollen grains are a nutrition source for insects, including honeybees. Some insects consume pollen as adults, and some insect larvae are raised on a diet consisting only of pollen.

Pollinators also include organisms that obtain nectar produced by flowers. Nectar is a sweet, sugary liquid that attracts pollinators. Nectar-consuming pollinators include bats, hummingbirds, moths, and butterflies. As they obtain nectar, these organisms transport pollen from flower to flower.

Flowers attract pollinators in a variety of ways. The pleasant fragrances of flowers attract pollinating organisms. Many flowers also attract pollinators visually as a result of their colorful patterns. Some of these colorful patterns are visible only under ultraviolet light, which makes them invisible to humans but visible to some insects and spiders.

The seeds and fruits of many flowering plants are also important sources of energy. Seeds are consumed by mammals, birds, and insects. Because they can remain dormant for extended periods of time, seeds can be stored. Squirrels, mice, and other animals store dormant seeds over the winter when food is scarce. What part of the seed do you think is most nutritious? ❶

Fruits, the structures that enclose the seeds, are also consumed by many organisms, including birds, insects, mammals, and some reptiles. In the process of eating fruits, larger animals often ingest the seeds. You, too, ingest seeds when you eat fruits such as

MULTICULTURAL PERSPECTIVE

Cacao trees had been cultivated in Central America for centuries before Spanish explorers arrived in the 1400s. The explorers, impressed with the drink that Native Americans made from cacao seeds, took the beans and the recipe back to Spain. By the seventeenth century, small restaurants called chocolate houses were popular throughout Europe. Eventually, the word *cacao* became *cocoa.*

blueberries, strawberries, and blackberries. The protective coat of the seed keeps the seed intact as it passes through an animal's digestive tract. The seed may then be deposited some distance from the parent plant. In some cases, migrating birds enable plants to colonize previously inaccessible environments.

ENVIRONMENTAL AWARENESS

What bugs bees

What would happen if bees died out? Albert Einstein said the result would be the disappearance of plant life on Earth. That might seem like an exaggerated prediction, but consider that bees are the primary pollinators of many thousands of species of flowering plants. While bees are not yet endangered species, bee populations in the United States and several other countries have been decreasing as a result of two types of parasitic mites. In New York State alone, 60–70 percent of the bee population already has been destroyed.

One culprit is the voroa mite, which attaches itself to a bee's body and uses the bee's blood for nourishment. The other—the tracheal mite—invades a bee's windpipe, where it breeds and eventually cuts off the flow of oxygen. To complicate matters, both parasites can carry a virus. So bees may die directly from the effect of the mite or be so weakened that they cannot survive the winter.

Research into treatments to rid bees of mites is ongoing. To date, two synthetic chemical treatments have been found effective against one or

both types of mites. Botanical preparations such as oil of peppermint have some curative effect, although more study is underway. One of the most promising solutions under investigation is the breeding of bees that are resistant to the mites.

These treatments pose no known health risks to the bees or to humans who eat honey from treated hives. But some beekeepers are using pesticides that have not been approved for use on bees. Of course, none of these treatments helps wild bee populations, which are also at risk.

In the United States, bees pollinate about 200 different types of agricultural crops. These crops—which include citrus and orchard fruits, almonds, cranberries, and cucumbers—are worth approximately 15 billion dollars a year! With fewer bees available, the price of honey and certain foods is likely to increase as harvests decrease.

FIGURE 20.18
Lured by the nectar and pollen in flowers, bees visit one flower after another, transferring pollen as they travel. How are bee populations being threatened? ❷

CHECKPOINT 20.5

1. Describe the main characteristics of flowering plants.
2. Compare the two phases of an angiosperm's life cycle, and show how they fit the general pattern called alternation of generations.
3. **Critical Thinking** What are some adaptations that a flower pollinated by the wind might have? Explain.

Build on What You Know

4. Describe the coevolution of flowering plants and pollinators. *(Need to jog your memory? Revisit relevant concepts in Chapter 10, Section 10.4.)*

Why have seed plants been able to colonize large areas of land?

Chapter 20 Origin and Diversity of Plants **489**

CHECKPOINT 20.5

1. Flowers, vascular tissue, gametophytes that grow within the sporophyte, reproduction involving pollination, seeds
2. The sporophyte is the visible plant. The female gametophyte is the ovule at the base of the pistil. Male gametophytes are pollen grains. The structures correspond to fern structures in the pattern of alternation of generations.
3. **Making inferences** Small petals and sepals that do not block wind and pollen from reproductive parts; tall anthers that are exposed to wind and pollen
4. Flower color, shape, and scent attract pollinators that have developed specialized structures to reach nectar. In the process of feeding, flowers are pollinated and genetic material is passed on.

STS

Have students research the health and vitality of bees in their community. Suggest that they contact a county agent to find out if local bees are affected by mites or viruses.

SUPER READ! **Identifying Cause and Effect** To practice strategies for effective reading, use pages 55-56 in *Super Read!*

③ ASSESS

Evaluate Understanding

Make an overhead transparency of Figure 20.16 without labels. Ask students to identify the following: *egg, ovule, pollen grain, stigma, pollen tube, sperm, pollen, zygote, seed, embryo, seed coat, endosperm, fruit, ovary, ovule, anther.* Ask:

- **What is the dominant stage in the life cycle of an angiosperm?** (Sporophyte)
- **What are the major reproductive structures of an angiosperm?** (Flower, fruit, seed)
- **When does fertilization occur?** (When a sperm nucleus fuses with the egg to form a zygote.)

Reteach

Work with students to outline the information presented in the section. Begin by writing the following heads on the board: *Characteristics of Flowering Plants, Life Cycle of an Angiosperm,* and *Flowering Plants in the Biosphere.* Then have students add supporting details under each head as they reread the section.

Class Activity

Refer students to Figure 21.4. Have them use three colors of modeling clay to model embryo development. Then have them show how the three cell layers (endoderm, ectoderm, and mesoderm) arise during gastrula formation. They can identify each cell layer by using straight pins to attach labels.

Use the Visual

Encourage students to use the terms and information in Figure 21.4 to create a concept map that traces the steps in the tissue development of animals. Have them identify the types of tissues that result from the various cell layers.

Clarify Misconceptions

Students may think that all animals reproduce sexually, or that only animals that reproduce sexually form tissues. To clarify this misconception, direct students' attention to Figure 21.4 and ask the following questions:

- **Does the zygote in step 1 form as a result of sexual reproduction or asexual reproduction?** (Sexual)
- **How does the single-celled zygote in step 1 become a multicellular blastula in step 3?** (It undergoes cleavage or a series of rapid cell divisions.)
- **How do cell layers develop in the gastrula?** (Cells move into the interior of the blastula and differentiate, according to the type of animal that is developing.)

FIGURE 21.4

Embryo Development

A series of orderly, precise steps transform a zygote into a multicellular embryo. The embryo is organized into discrete layers of cells from which tissues and organs will develop.

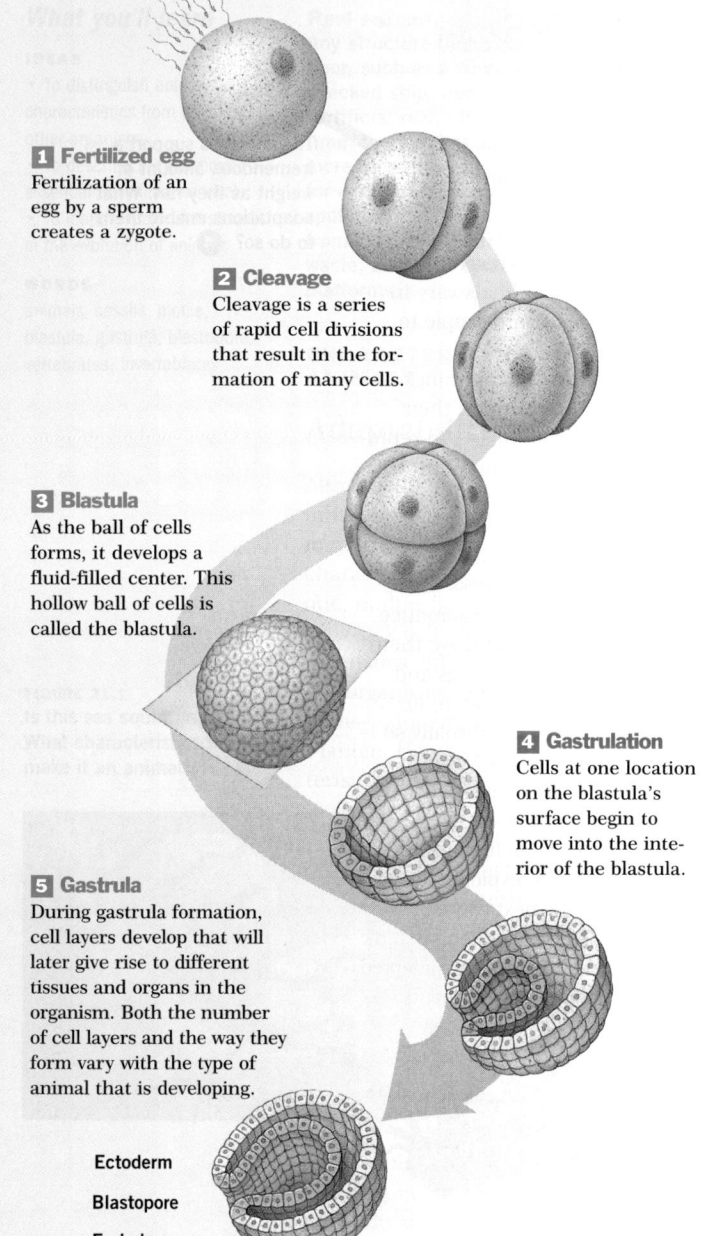

1 Fertilized egg
Fertilization of an egg by a sperm creates a zygote.

2 Cleavage
Cleavage is a series of rapid cell divisions that result in the formation of many cells.

3 Blastula
As the ball of cells forms, it develops a fluid-filled center. This hollow ball of cells is called the blastula.

4 Gastrulation
Cells at one location on the blastula's surface begin to move into the interior of the blastula.

5 Gastrula
During gastrula formation, cell layers develop that will later give rise to different tissues and organs in the organism. Both the number of cell layers and the way they form vary with the type of animal that is developing.

Ectoderm

Blastopore

Endoderm

502 *Unit 6 Invertebrate Animals*

DIVERSITY OF ANIMALS

What a zoo!

The fossil record of the Cambrian period, about 600 million years ago, has a large number of fossils of the earliest known animals. By then animals had evolved hard body parts that could be preserved or recorded as fossils. But the fossil record is incomplete, and it is difficult to understand relationships based only on fossils. As you may recall from Chapter 13, living things are classified by evolutionary relationships. These relationships can be determined by analyzing shared structural, developmental, and molecular characteristics.

Development of animal embryos provides some of the most critical insight into evolutionary relationships. Embryological development begins when a zygote is formed at fertilization, as shown in *Figure 21.4*. After many cell divisions, a zygote forms a hollow ball of cells called a **blastula**. Some cells begin to move inward from the surface of the blastula, resulting in a two-layered cuplike ball of cells called a **gastrula**. The inner layer of cells is called endoderm, and the outer cell layer is called ectoderm. The digestive tract and respiratory system develop from endoderm; the skin, sense organs, and nerves develop from ectoderm.

In most animal embryos, three cell layers—not two—result from the formation of a gastrula. A middle layer of cells, the mesoderm, forms between the ectoderm and endoderm in all but the most primitive animals. Mesoderm gives rise to muscles and to the circulatory, reproductive, and excretory systems.

Animals exibit similarities and differences in their embryological development. By studying these similarities and differences, taxonomists have recognized four major milestones

---

MEETING DIVERSE NEEDS

LEP Have LEP students use a dictionary to find the meanings of the prefixes "endo-," "ecto-," and "meso-." Then have them write definitions for the terms *endoderm, ectoderm,* and *mesoderm* in their own words. Tell them to circle the parts of the definitions that relate to the meaning of each prefix.

in the evolution of animals—evolution of tissues, of body symmetry, of internal body cavities, and of a new pattern of embryo development. You can trace these milestones in *Figure 21.5*.

Early in animal evolution, the first of these milestones occurred when animals developed tissues from ectoderm and endoderm—and later from mesoderm. As a result of tissue development, parts of animals could become specialized for different functions.

A second milestone was reached when some animals with true tissues developed body symmetry. Body symmetry refers to the arrangement of body parts around a central point or plane.

A third milestone occurred when some animals evolved body cavities that were at least partially lined with tissue. These body cavities formed from embryonic mesoderm.

The fourth major milestone occurred relatively recently in the evolution of animals. This milestone involves differences in the embryonic development of the **blastopore**—an opening that develops at the point where cells of the blastula move inward to form the cell layers of the gastrula.

Biologists also tend to group animals by whether or not they have a backbone. Animals with a backbone are called **vertebrates;** those without a backbone are called **invertebrates**.

CHECKPOINT 21.1

1. Identify the characteristics that distinguish animals from other organisms.
2. What are the functions essential for animal survival?
3. List the four major milestones in the evolution of animals.
4. **Critical Thinking** How does the ability to move enhance survival?

Build on What You Know

5. How is the process of mitosis important in the development of a blastula? *(Need to jog your memory? Revisit relevant concepts in Chapter 5, Sections 5.1 and 5.2.)*

FIGURE 21.5
Kingdom Animalia

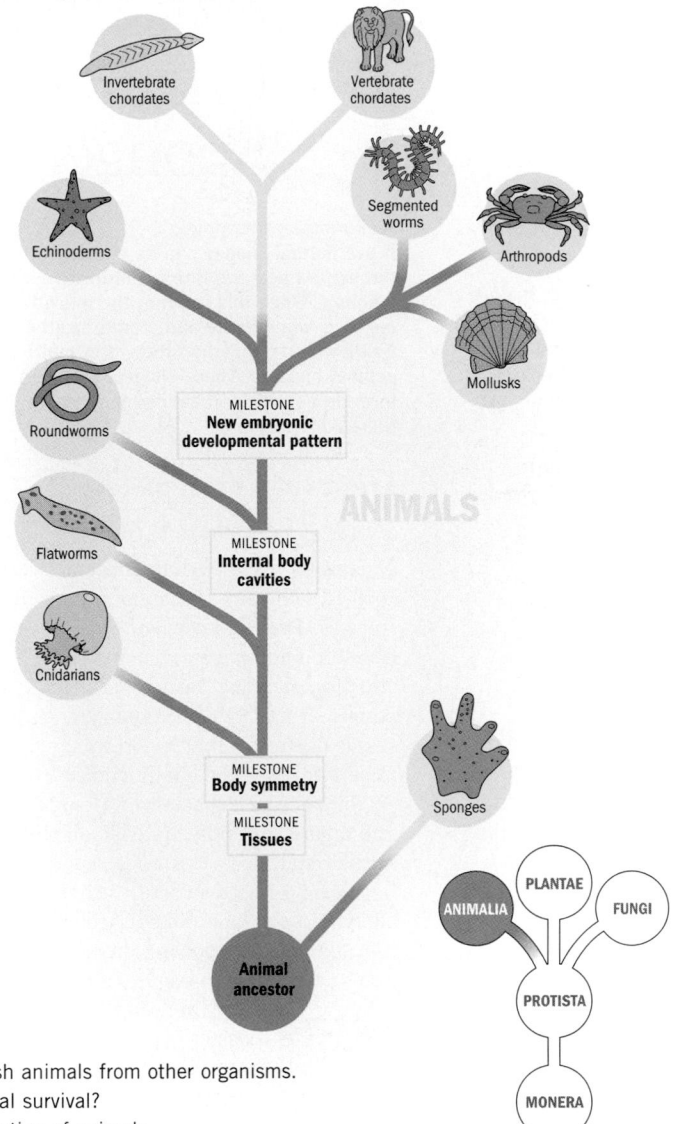

MILESTONE
New embryonic developmental pattern

ANIMALS

MILESTONE
Internal body cavities

MILESTONE
Body symmetry

MILESTONE
Tissues

What adaptations have evolved in animals that enable them to perform essential functions of life? **?**

Explain

Explain to students that in Figure 21.5 all vertebrates fall in the phylum Chordata, shown at the top of the diagram. All phyla of animals listed below chordates lack a backbone and are classified as invertebrates.

3 **ASSESS**

Evaluate Understanding

Work with students to arrange the terms *gastrula, cleavage, mesoderm, zygote, endoderm, ectoderm,* and *blastula* in a flowchart that shows the stages of tissue development in animals. Have them extend the flowchart by identifying what organ systems developed from each cell layer.

Reteach

Have students refer to Figure 21.5. Explain that organisms shown below each *Milestone* label lack the structure or evolutionary development, while those shown above the label have that structure or development. To make sure students understand the diagram, ask:

- **How do sponges differ from all other animals?** (They lack symmetry.)
- **What evolutionary developments do cnidarians, flatworms, and roundworms share?** (Body symmetry)
- **What phyla of animals have tissues, symmetry, body cavities, and show similarities in their evolutionary development?** (Mollusks, segmented worms, arthropods, echinoderms, and chordates)

CHECKPOINT 21.1

1. Animals are eukaryotic, multicellular, heterotrophic, and their cells lack cell walls.
2. Animals must maintain a basic shape, be able to move, find and digest food, egest and excrete wastes, respire, respond to stimuli, and reproduce.
3. development of tissues, development of body symmetry, evolved internal body cavities, different embryonic development pattern
4. **Identifying cause and effect** Being able to move enables an animal to find food and new habitats, protect itself, and find a mate.
5. Mitosis makes animals multicellular.

503

504

1 ENGAGE

Consider the Big Idea

Have students read The Big Idea! at the top of the page. Explain that sponges are simple animals that lack specialized tissues and organs.

Use the Visual

Have students study the photograph and read the text that opens the section. Explain that like all animals, sponges are a multicellular colony. However, sponges differ from all other animals in that they lack specialized tissues. Point out that although a sponge lacks specialized tissues, its cells are specialized to carry out a variety of life functions. Ask students what life process is described in the caption. (Reproduction) Point out that the ability of sponges to form new sponges from smaller parts is one way sponges reproduce asexually.

Quick Activity

Provide groups of students with pieces of natural and synthetic sponges. Have them compare the materials and then discuss the characteristics of sponges. Point out that synthetic sponges are usually made of cellulose or rubber and natural sponges are the remnants of living organisms.

21.2 Characteristics of Sponges

What you'll learn

IDEAS
- To describe the structure of typical sponges
- To compare and contrast the methods of reproduction in sponges

WORDS
osculum, amebocytes, spongin, spicules, gemmule, hermaphrodite

A multitude of sponges
A live natural sponge can be pressed through a fine sieve into a culture medium. When this is done, the individual cells will migrate and clump together. As they clump together, they form multicellular clusters. These clusters will then form new sponges, creating many where there once was one.

STRUCTURE OF SPONGES

Water in, water out

Organisms of the phylum Porifera (poh-RIF-eh-ruh) are commonly called sponges. The word *porifera* comes from the Latin *porus*, meaning "pore," and *fera*, meaning "bearers." Their porous structure enables sponges—sessile organisms that live in water—to perform essential life functions.

Sponges lack specialized tissues and organs, but they are well adapted to their stationary existence. Sponges have evolved with structures that allow water to be pumped through their bodies. The flowing water helps the sponge to respire, obtain food, and excrete wastes. The water-pumping ability of sponges is impressive. A 1-gram (g) sponge can pump as much as 1 liter (L) of water through its body per hour. How much water can this sponge pump in a day?

Many sponges have a body plan similar to the one shown in

FIGURE 21.6
This vase sponge displays the typical porous structure of a sponge, which enables water to flow through it freely.

Figure 21.7. The body forms a vaselike wall around a hollow cylinder, or sac. The sac is closed at the bottom and open at the top. The opening at the top of the sac is called the **osculum** (OS-kyoo-lum). The interior of a sponge is lined with flagellated cells called collar cells. The beating flagella of many collar cells create a current that moves water into the central cavity through pores in the sac, and out through the osculum. As water flows through a sponge, the collar cells trap particles of organic matter and microscopic organisms, which sponges use as food. This method of obtaining food is called filter-feeding or suspension-feeding.

Food may be digested in the collar cells or passed on to **amebocytes** (uh-MEE-boh-syts)—cells that move through the sponge's body, supplying nutrients to other cells and removing wastes. Wastes are later released into the water flowing through the sponge and carried out through the osculum.

In addition to cells that pump water and process food, sponges have structures that provide support. These structures are made of spongin, spicules, or both. **Spongin** is a network of

504 *Unit 6 Invertebrate Animals*

FIGURE 21.7

Structure of a Sponge

Sponges have very simple organization with no true tissues. They vary in shape, but all have the basic structure shown here. Can you explain how this structure would be well adapted to a sessile marine existence? ❷

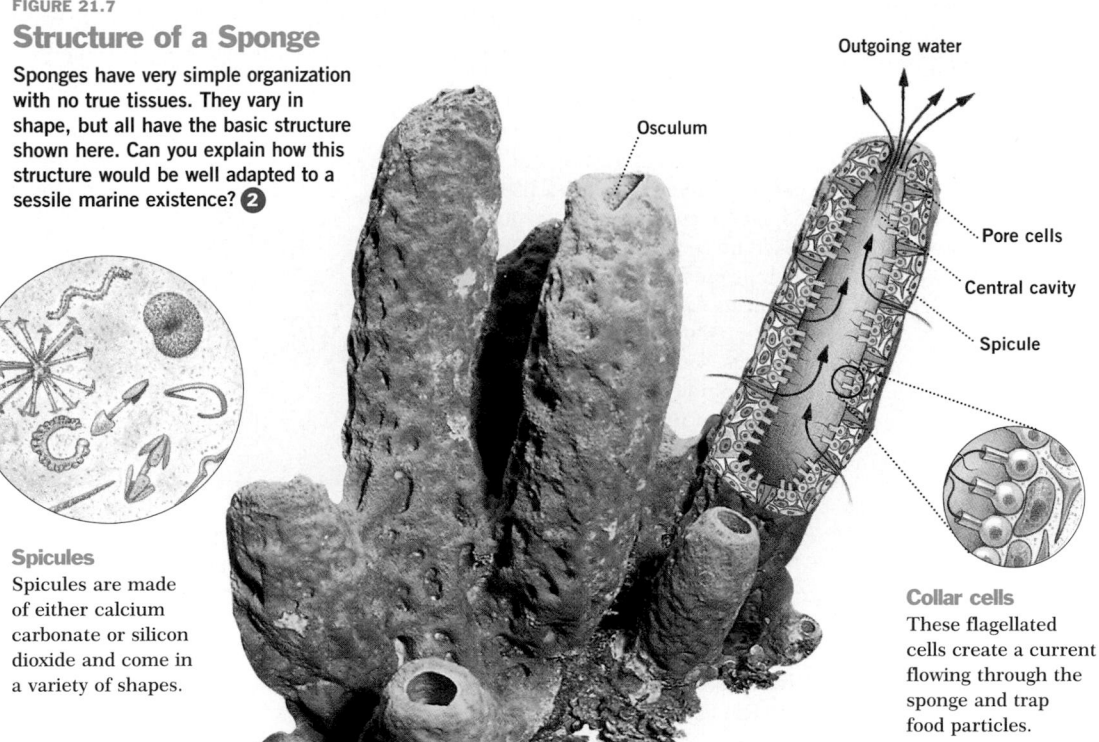

Outgoing water

Osculum

Pore cells

Central cavity

Spicule

Spicules
Spicules are made of either calcium carbonate or silicon dioxide and come in a variety of shapes.

Collar cells
These flagellated cells create a current flowing through the sponge and trap food particles.

protein fibers. What you see in a natural bath sponge, for example, is mostly spongin. **Spicules** are tiny needlelike structures made of silicon dioxide (glass) or calcium carbonate.

REPRODUCTION OF SPONGES

A fragmented relationship

The ability to find mates and reproduce can be a problem for sessile organisms. Sponges, however, have adapted—they are capable of both sexual and asexual reproduction.

Asexual reproduction Sponges reproduce asexually by budding, by regeneration, or by forming structures called gemmules. When sponges bud, the buds either detach and form new

LAB ZONE ▶ Do It!

bioSURF

Calculating the Pumping Capacity of a Natural Sponge

A typical natural sponge measuring 10 centimeters (cm) high and 1 cm in diameter can pump about 23 L of water in a day. How long would it take for this sponge to empty all the water in an aquarium holding 38 L of water? You can answer this problem when you . . .

Try This

1 Write an equation that includes the facts you know and the unknown factor, as follows: 24 hours ÷ 23 L = (x) hours ÷ 38 L.
2 Perform the mathematical calculations.

Analyze Your Results

How long would it take for the sponge to empty the aquarium?

FACTS AND FIGURES

The four classes of sponges are based on the composition of their support structures: *Calcarea,* shallow marine-water sponges, calcium carbonate spicules; *Hyalospongiae,* deepwater sponges, silicon dioxide spicules; *Demospongiae,* marine and freshwater sponges, silicon dioxide spicules or spongin support structures *Sclerospongiae,* tropical reef sponges, coral-like spicules of calcium carbonate and silicon dioxide, also spongin support structures.

Explain

Point out that when sperm are transferred from one sponge to another, they follow the same one-way path water takes in and out of the sponge.

3 ASSESS

Evaluate Understanding

Draw the outline of a sponge on the board. Beside the drawing, list these terms: *spicules, choanocytes, osculum, amebocytes,* and *central cavity*. Have students copy the drawing onto a clean sheet of paper, use the terms to label the parts of their sponge, and identify the function or functions of the labeled structures. Ask students to add arrows to their drawings to indicate the direction that water moves through the sponge. Review the drawings as a class, correcting any inaccurate information.

Reteach

Have students work with a partner to make a flowchart showing how water flows through the sponge. Tell them to include the function of each part of the sponge on the chart. To aid students, write the key terms from Figure 21.7 on the board.

❶ In most other sponges, fertilization occurs inside the sponge.

506

Just a Skeleton Crew

When you purchase a dull-colored, irregularly shaped natural "sponge," you are buying only the skeletal remains of the once-living sponge.

FIGURE 21.8
A female tube sponge releases thousands of golden eggs held together by sticky strands of mucus. The eggs of this sponge, *Agelas,* are fertilized externally when spawning male sponges release sperm. How does this differ from fertilization in most other sponges? ❶

sponges, or remain attached to the parent, forming a colony of sponges.

Sponges also have a remarkable ability to reproduce by regeneration. Fragments broken off a sponge can settle and grow into complete, new sponges. Regeneration is a useful adaptation, as sponges are frequently broken up by pounding surf or partially eaten by predators.

During extreme conditions such as droughts or periods of freezing temperatures, some freshwater sponges form gemmules. A **gemmule** (JEM-yool) is a dormant mass of sponge amebocytes surrounded by protective layers of spicules. When favorable conditions return, the amebocytes emerge and grow into new sponges.

Sexual reproduction Sexual reproduction begins with the formation of gametes—eggs and sperm. Many species of sponges are hermaphrodites. A **hermaphrodite** is an individual organism capable of producing both eggs and sperm. A hermaphroditic sponge can mate with any other sponge of its species.

Fertilization in sponges can be external, as shown in *Figure 21.8,* or internal. Most sponges have internal fertilization, a process that begins when sperm are released into the water flowing out through the osculum. If the

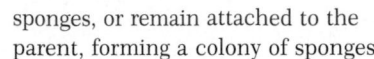

Bud

FIGURE 21.9
Notice the many buds forming on the parent colony. The members in a colony such as this can be genetically identical because they were formed by asexual reproduction.

sperm reach another sponge, they flow in through its pores. Amebocytes transport the sperm to an egg, enabling fertilization to occur. The resulting zygote develops into a flagellated larva that swims away from the parent sponge and settles on a new surface. The flagellated cells of the larva then reorganize and develop into a new sponge.

CHECKPOINT 21.2

1. Describe the structure of a typical sponge.
2. Compare and contrast the methods of reproduction in sponges.
3. **Critical Thinking** How would hermaphroditism be an advantage for sessile animals?

Build on What You Know

4. Which aspects of a sponge's structure and function are most like those of protists? *(Need to jog your memory? Revisit relevant concepts in Chapter 15, Section 15.2.)*

506   *Unit 6 Invertebrate Animals*

CHECKPOINT 21.2

1. It has a vaselike wall around a hollow sac, which is closed at the bottom and open at the top.
2. Asexual reproduction requires no mate and occurs when sponge fragments break off and relocate. Sexual reproduction requires a mate but enables the motile offspring to adapt to new environments.
3. **Making generalizations** Since sessile animals cannot move, they increase their reproductive chances by producing both eggs and sperm.
4. Flagella on the collar cells in sponges are like the flagella on protists; amebocytes in sponges are like the protist ameba.

21.3 Origin and Diversity of Sponges

Could you fit inside a sponge?
You bet you could! If you were diving in the ocean and came across a huge basket sponge—possibly 100 years old—you might even be tempted to slip inside it. Divers should avoid doing so, however, because the sponge is much more delicate than it appears and could be damaged by human contact.

What you'll learn

IDEAS
- To explain one hypothesis about the origin of sponges
- To compare different habitats of sponges

ORIGIN OF SPONGES
Uncommonly old

Scientists think sponges evolved from protists very early in the Cambrian period. In fact, the flagellated collar cells in sponges bear a striking resemblance to the cells in a group of colonial protists. This similarity has led scientists to hypothesize that sponges evolved from such colonial protists. Sponges living today have not changed much from their fossilized ancestors.

Sponges have very little in common with other animals. They lack specialized tissues or organ systems and have only some specialized cells. Most sponges have no body symmetry. Scientists have concluded that sponges probably evolved separately from all other animals.

DIVERSITY OF SPONGES
Colorful creatures

Most of the approximately 8000 known species of sponges live in the oceans, although about 3 percent live in freshwater lakes and streams. Marine sponges are found at many depths and display a remarkable variety of sizes,

FIGURE 21.10
Phylum Porifera

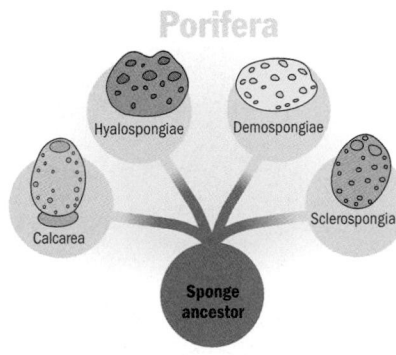

Porifera

Hyalospongiae
Demospongiae
Calcarea
Sclerospongiae
Sponge ancestor

shapes, and colors; they are often brilliant shades of red, orange, yellow, or blue. Freshwater sponges are more likely to be a dull brown or green. The smallest sponges can live on tiny mollusk shells, whereas the largest can exceed humans in size.

Sponges are organized into classes based on whether they have spongin, spicules, or both. As you have learned, spongin is a strong organic fiber, and spicules are calcareous or glasslike skeletal components that take on a variety of forms. The size, shape, and composition of spicules are used to classify sponges further. *Figure 21.11* illustrates sponge diversity.

Kingdom: Animalia
Phylum: Porifera
Four classes:
Calcarea
Hyalospongiae
Demospongiae
Sclerospongiae

Chapter 21 Sponges and Cnidarians **507**

ENGAGE

Use the Visual

Have students study the photograph and read the text that opens the section. Explain that human contact over the years has damaged coral reefs. Ask:

- **What characteristics of sponges are apparent in the photograph?** (Responses may indicate that the sponge is sessile, attached to the sea bottom, and has a large opening called an osculum at the top.)

Check Prior Knowledge

To assess students' knowledge about sponges, ask:

- **How do sponges obtain food?** (By filter-feeding)
- **How do sponges reproduce?** (Asexually by budding and regeneration and sexually by forming gametes)

Teacher Demo

Explain that people often buy natural sponges because of their ability to hold large amounts of water. To demonstrate this water-holding capacity, use a balance to weigh a dry natural sponge and a dry synthetic sponge. Record both masses on the board. Soak each sponge with water and weigh them again. Record the masses of the wet sponges on the board. Show students how to calculate how many grams of water were absorbed by each gram of sponge.

Explain

Point out that natural sponges have skeletons made of spongin, which is composed of a network of protein fibers. Before a harvested sponge is sold for use in cleaning, the living spongin cells forming the skeletal framework are removed.

Evaluate Understanding

Assess students' knowledge by asking:

- **When do scientists think sponges evolved?** (They may have evolved from protists early in the Cambrian era and represent the earliest animal group.)
- **What are three habitats in which sponges are likely to be found?** (Oceans, freshwater lakes, and streams)
- **How are sponges classified?** (Based on whether they have spongin, spicules, or both)

Reteach

Work with students to create a graphic classifying the likenesses and differences among sponges in terms of where they live, how they eat, and their structure and appearance.

Although many species of sponges have already been identified, scientists think that many have yet to be discovered. One recently discovered deep-sea sponge has no collar cells, and it does not filter water. This sponge obtains its food somewhat differently than most sponges. Its Velcro-like surface is covered with spicule-studded filaments that move. Tiny crustaceans get caught on the sharp spicules and, within the space of a day, can be covered by new filaments. By this process the sponge ingests and gradually digests its prey. Researchers hypothesize that, because of its environment, this deep-sea sponge has developed a different system for obtaining food.

CHECKPOINT 21.3

1. Explain one hypothesis about the origin of sponges.
2. Describe some of the diverse habitats occupied by sponges.
3. **Critical Thinking** What characteristics of sponges enable them to live in diverse habitats?

Build on What You Know

4. Compare and contrast the characteristics of sponges and plants. *(Need to jog your memory? Revisit relevant concepts in Chapter 17, Section 17.1.)*

FIGURE 21.11

The Diversity of Sponges

Some sponges assume the shape of the object on which they grow; others have their own distinctive shape. Colors may vary even among sponges of the same species.

1. Orange sponge
2. Azure vase sponge
3. Tube sponges
4. Vase sponge
5. Pacific coast sponge
6. Brittle stars on rope sponges

? How can sponges survive without specialized tissues and organs?

CHECKPOINT 21.3

1. They may have evolved from protists very early in the Cambrian era, since they have very little in common with other primitive animals.
2. Sponges inhabit oceans at many different depths, fresh water lakes, and streams.
3. **Making generalizations** Sponges require little energy for feeding and reproduction.

Because they have no specialized tissues, they can tolerate greater extremes in temperature and salinity than most marine animals.

4. Unlike plants, sponges are heterotrophs and have no cell walls.

THE BIG IDEA! Cnidarians are radially symmetrical animals with specialized tissues and stinging tentacles. 21.4–21.5

21.4 Characteristics of Cnidarians

So aptly named
Medusa, a character in Greek mythology, had hair made of serpents. In their adult medusa stage, jellyfish have waving, serpentlike tentacles trailing from their bell-shaped bodies. Although they can not turn humans to stone as Medusa did, jellyfish use stinging barbs on their tentacles to immobilize or kill their prey.

STRUCTURE OF CNIDARIANS

Harpoon carriers

Have you ever seen a stinging jelly-fish? Sometimes beaches are closed to swimmers when jellyfish are abundant. The sting of a jellyfish can be painful, or even fatal in some cases.

Jellyfish are a type of cnidarian (ny–DAYR–ee–uhn). Cnidarians have **radial symmetry,** which means their body parts radiate from a central point. This type of symmetry might remind you of the spokes of a wheel radiating from its center, or hub. Radially symmetrical objects do not have a front or a back side. Most sponges, as you just learned, exhibit **asymmetry;** that is, they lack body symmetry.

Along with corals, hydra, and sea anemones, jellyfish belong to the phylum Cnidaria. Cnidarians are named for their unique cells called cnidocytes (NY-doh-syts). Cnidocytes contain stinging, poisonous barbs that cnidarians use to capture their prey.

Cnidarians are soft-bodied animals with a hollow central cavity. This single opening is surrounded by tentacles. Cnidarians have two basic body types.

What you'll learn

IDEAS
• To describe the structure and symmetry of cnidarians
• To compare and contrast sexual and asexual reproduction in cnidarians

WORDS
radial symmetry, asymmetry, polyp, medusa, nematocyst, planula

The cylinder-shaped or vase-shaped **polyp** (PAH-lip) has its opening on the dorsal surface and tentacles that point upward. The umbrella-shaped or bell-shaped **medusa** (meh-DOO-suh) has its mouth on the ventral surface and tentacles that point downward. Which body form does the sea anemone in *Figure 21.12* have? Some ❶ cnidarians, such as the freshwater

FIGURE 21.12
Animal Body Symmetry

Most sponges (below left) lack body symmetry. Like most animals, cnidarians, such as the sea anemone (below right), have body symmetry.

A sponge is asymmetrical.   A cnidarian has radial symmetry.

Chapter 21 Sponges and Cnidarians **509**

STUDENT RESOURCES

From the Teacher's Resource Package, use:
■ Section Review 21.4, Activity Record-sheet 21.1, Interpreting Graphics 21, and Enrichment Topic 21.2 from Unit 6 Review Module
■ Lab 35: "Life of a *Hydra*"

TECHNOLOGY RESOURCES

Relevant technology resources include:
■ Spanish Student Edition CD-ROM
■ Teacher's Resource Planner CD-ROM
■ Biology Alive! Videotape: "Signs of Life"

❶ ENGAGE

Consider the Big Idea

Have students read The Big Idea! at the top of the page. Explain that cnidarians are animals with specialized tissues and appendages.

Use the Visual

Have students study the photograph that opens the section. Point out that the tentacles of jellyfishes have cells that can deliver a painful and sometimes poisonous sting.

SUPER READ! **Using Word Parts** To practice strategies for effective reading, use pages 59-60 in *Super Read!*

Quick Activity

Have students draw a circle on a sheet of paper and determine how many ways they can fold the paper through the center of the circle to make two similar halves. (Many times) Next, have students cut out a random shape, like that of an ameba. Ask them how many times they can fold this shape through the center to form two similar halves. (Students will probably not form any similar halves.) Explain asymmetrical things, like sponges and amebas, do not have a plane that can be divided into similar halves.

❶ Polyp

② TEACH

Use the Visual

Have students use Figure 21.13 to answer the following question:

- **What structures are common to both kinds of cnidarians?** (Mouth, tentacles, jellylike layer, epidermis, gastrovascular cavity, gastrodermis)

Teacher Demo

To demonstrate the difference between the medusa and the polyp, tape a colored plastic cup inside a colorless plastic cup. Tell students that each cup represents the cell layer of an organism that has a hollow body and only one body opening, such as a cnidarian. Demonstrate that when the mouth points downward and the cnidarian floats freely, it is called a medusa. When the mouth faces upward and its base is attached to a surface, the cnidarian is called a polyp.

LAB ZONE Think About It!

Finding Examples of Symmetry

Examples of radial symmetry include a bowl, a flower pot, a petri dish, a fan, and a doorknob. Examples of asymmetry include a plant, most pictures, a pile of books or clothes, and an American flag.

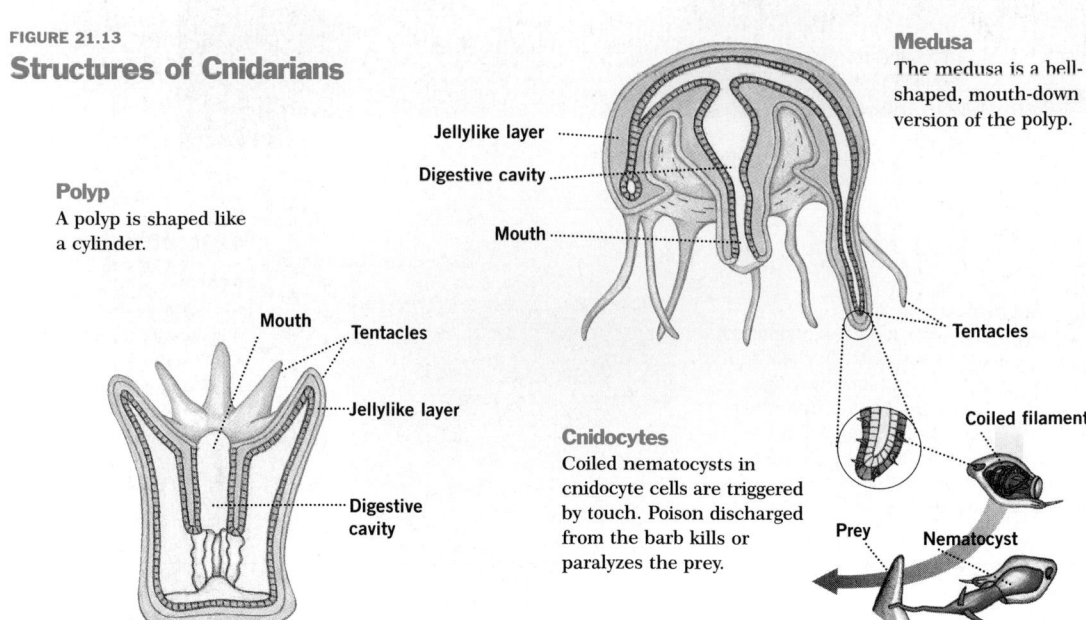

FIGURE 21.13
Structures of Cnidarians

Polyp
A polyp is shaped like a cylinder.

Mouth
Tentacles
Jellylike layer
Digestive cavity

Medusa
The medusa is a bell-shaped, mouth-down version of the polyp.

Jellylike layer
Digestive cavity
Mouth
Tentacles
Coiled filament

Cnidocytes
Coiled nematocysts in cnidocyte cells are triggered by touch. Poison discharged from the barb kills or paralyzes the prey.

Prey
Nematocyst
Barb

hydra and the sea anemone, exist only as polyps. Other cnidarians have both polyp and medusa life stages.

You may recall that sponges are filter-feeders, trapping food particles that flow into their bodies. Cnidarians, on the other hand, are carnivores that capture prey. Several types of specialized tissues and structures have evolved in cnidarians that enable them to capture food. You may remember that the development of

such tissues represents the first major milestone in the evolution of animals.

In cnidarians, tissues lining the digestive cavity and on the outer surface are made up of musclelike contractile cells. These cells contain proteins that can contract, or shorten in length, causing the cnidarian to change its shape. This change of shape enables some cnidarians to swim.

Another specialized tissue in cnidarians is made of cells called cnidocytes. Cnidocytes are armed with stinging organelles called nematocysts, which you can see in *Figure 21.13*. A **nematocyst** (nuh-MAT-uh-sist) is a coiled filament with a tiny harpoonlike barb on the end. When a cnidocyte touches an object or animal, it launches its nematocyst barb like a tiny harpoon. The poison in the barb kills or paralyzes the prey, which becomes tangled in various filaments. The cnidarian can then use its tentacles to draw the prey into its mouth.

For the cnidocytes and tentacles to function effectively, cnidarians must

LAB ZONE Think About It! bioSURF

Finding Examples of Symmetry

You can check your understanding of asymmetry and radial symmetry when you . . .

Try This

1 Look around your classroom to find living or nonliving examples of both asymmetry and radial symmetry.

2 List as many examples of each as you can find.

3 Sketch one item you have listed as asymmetrical and one you have listed as symmetrical. Explain why you think each item belongs in the category you selected.

FACTS AND FIGURES

Cnidarians were formerly classified as coelenterates. The phylum name Coelenterata means "hollow-bodied," and was based on the presence of the sac-shaped body cavity, called a coelenteron. Because the coelenteron is also characteristic of sponges, the phylum name was changed to Cnidarian. The term *cnidarian* reflects the presence of the stinging cells, called cnidocytes, which are unique to the organisms in this group.

have a nervous system. A diffuse, decentralized nerve net carries signals through the body of a cnidarian, coordinating the cnidocytes and tentacles.

REPRODUCTION OF CNIDARIANS

A bud off the old polyp

Like sponges, most cnidarians can reproduce either asexually or sexually. However, sexual reproduction in some cnidarians may require complex cycles that involve both the medusa and polyp forms.

For example, in the life cycle of the common jellyfish, the medusa is the dominant form. The medusa is also the form that produces gametes by meiosis. A medusa may produce either sperm or eggs and release them into the water, where fertilization takes place. The resulting zygote develops into a **planula,** or free-swimming larva. A planula uses cilia to move to a

new place. When a planula eventually settles and attaches to a firm surface, it develops into a sessile polyp. As it grows, the polyp develops a stack of medusae that bud off asexually and become the free-swimming jellyfish.

Other cnidarians, such as the common freshwater hydra, often reproduce asexually by budding. However, low water temperatures can stimulate the hydra to reproduce sexually. Fertilization occurs when sperm and egg unite. After an egg is fertilized, it grows into a ball of cells with a hardened coat. This structure can survive low temperatures, whereas the softbodied adult hydra cannot. When environmental conditions improve, a new polyp grows.

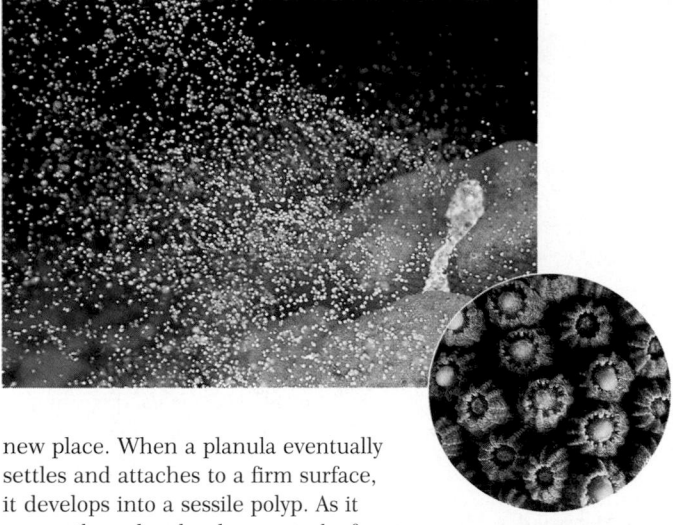

FIGURE 21.15
Coral polyps in coastal Florida waters release egg and sperm bundles (above) during sexual reproduction.

FIGURE 21.14

Reproduction in the *Aurelia* Jellyfish

Reproduction in the jellyfish involves both the medusa and polyp stages. The larva, called a planula, develops into a polyp. The polyp buds, asexually producing many new medusa.

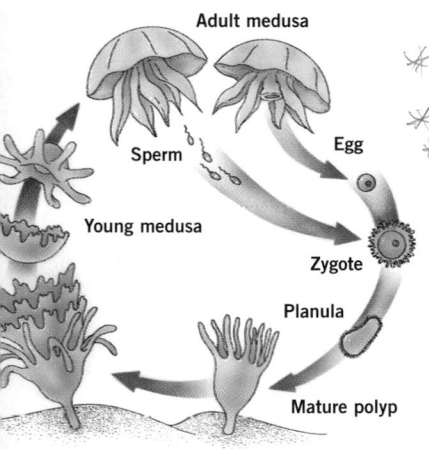

Adult medusa
Sperm
Egg
Young medusa
Zygote
Planula
Mature polyp

CHECKPOINT 21.4

1. Describe the structure and symmetry of cnidarians.
2. How do cnidarians reproduce?
3. **Critical Thinking** In the polyp and medusa stages of cnidarians, how is the position of the mouth adapted to its function?

Build on What You Know

4. How do the structures that cnidarians use for movement compare with the flagella and cilia of other organisms? *(Need to jog your memory? Revisit relevant concepts in Chapter 3, Section 3.3.)*

Chapter 21 Sponges and Cnidarians **511**

CHECKPOINT 21.4

1. Cnidarians have radial symmetry, a hollow central cavity surrounded by tentacles, and a central opening with body parts.
2. Either asexually or sexually.
3. **Making generalizations** Its mouth is located at the center of the tentacles that

disable prey. This position makes it easy to get the prey to the mouth.
4. Contractile cells shorten in length to make the cnidarian move. Cilia and flagella also use contractionlike movements, but create a very different motion.

TEAM WORK **Observing Hydra**

SAFETY FIRST!

Remind students to use care when handling the microscope. Also caution students to handle the *Hydra* and *Daphnia* gently.

Lab Prep and Planning

Obtain cultures of *Hydra* and *Daphnia* from a biological supply house. *Daphnia* should be protected from sunlight. If the *Daphnia* culture is kept for more than a week, the *Daphnia* will need to be fed algae. Do not feed *Hydra* for three days prior to the activity to ensure that the *Hydra* are hungry at the time of the activity.

Hypothesis Help

Have students review the sections of text that describe *Hydra* and their methods of locomotion and feeding to help them formulate a hypothesis.

Lab Extension

Open Ended

Have students estimate the number of *Daphnia* and *Hydra* in a water sample. Then have them count the number of *Hydra* each day to determine how many are consumed and any other changes that take place in the water sample. Students should prepare a hypothesis and report on the results.

Analyze Your Data

1 At first the *Hydra* appears round and tiny with small tentacles. If left undisturbed for awhile, it stretches out its body and tentacles.

Observing Hydra

WHAT YOU WILL DO Observe the structure and activity of hydra, including feeding behavior

SKILLS YOU WILL USE Observing, collecting and recording data, predicting, experimenting

WHAT YOU WILL NEED Dissection probe, two droppers, two depression slides, cultures of *Hydra* and *Daphnia*, dissecting microscope, toothpick

Propose a Hypothesis

Formulate a hypothesis about the process by which a hydra captures prey.

Conduct Your Experiment

1 Using the dissection probe, gently dislodge a *Hydra* from the culture container.
2 Draw the *Hydra* into the dropper and quickly transfer it to the depression slide. (The *Hydra* may attach itself to the inside of the dropper.)
3 Examine the slide of the *Hydra* for several minutes under low and high power. Note its shape, its size, and any movement of its tentacles. Record your observations, using words and diagrams.

4 Using the first dropper, transfer a drop of the *Hydra* culture to another depression slide. Using the second dropper, transfer a drop of the *Daphnia* culture to the same slide. If necessary, gently use a toothpick to connect the two drops.
5 Observe the slide under the microscope. Record your observations of the *Hydra's* feeding behavior, and make a drawing of a *Hydra* ingesting a *Daphnia*. (Note: If your *Hydra* does not exhibit feeding behavior, transfer another organism from the *Hydra* culture.)

Analyze Your Data

1 What were your observations of the *Hydra's* shape and the movement of its tentacles before you added the *Daphnia*?

2 Describe any changes in the *Hydra's* shape and the movement of its tentacles when in the presence of food.

Draw Conclusions

1 Do your results support your hypothesis?
2 Is a hydra a sessile organism? Is a daphnia a sessile organism? On what do you base these conclusions?
3 Based on your observations of the feeding behavior of a hydra, can you infer anything about the feeding behavior of other sessile organisms? Explain.

Design a Related Experiment

Suppose you wanted to find out if the hydra prefers one type of food over another. Propose a hypothesis and design an experiment to test your hypothesis.

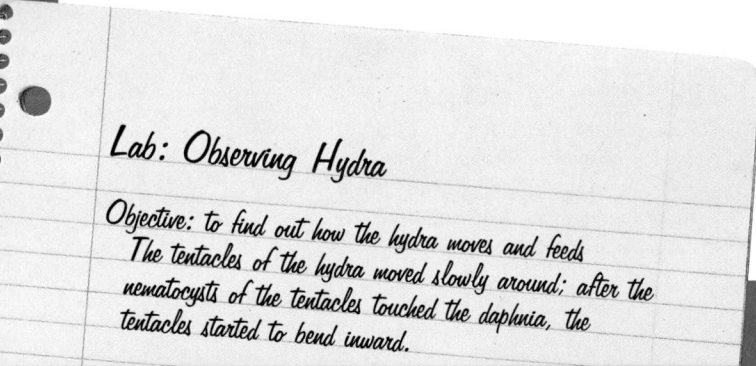

Tentacles
Mouth
Digestive cavity
Bud
Nerve net

Lab: Observing Hydra

Objective: to find out how the hydra moves and feeds
The tentacles of the hydra moved slowly around; after the nematocysts of the tentacles touched the daphnia, the tentacles started to bend inward.

2 Students may observe *Hydra* manipulating food into its mouth with its tentacles.

Draw Conclusions

1 Answers will vary.
2 *Hydra* stayed in one spot and is sessile. *Daphnia* swam around. It is not sessile.

3 Other sessile organisms must also have tentacles or some other mechanism to capture food as it drifts or swims nearby.

Design a Related Experiment

Designs will vary, but should include observations of *Hydra* in the presence of several types of food.

21.5 Origin and Diversity of Cnidarians

Quite a sting

If you ever see this animal, watch out! This is a sea wasp, or box jellyfish. Although sea wasps are about 25 cm in length, their toxin is more lethal than any snake venom, and they can kill a human in minutes. In fact, in Australian waters sea wasps kill more people than sharks do.

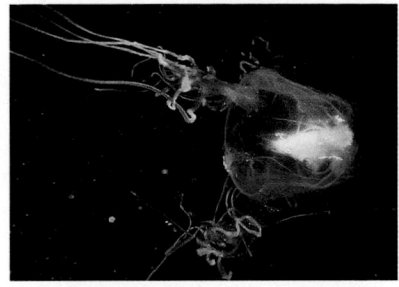

What you'll learn

IDEAS
- To explain two important milestones in the evolution of cnidarians
- To compare the three classes of cnidarians

ORIGIN OF CNIDARIANS

Soft as jelly

Cnidarians are soft-bodied and do not preserve well as either impressions in sediments or actual fossils. So scientists have not been able to learn much about the origin of cnidarians from fossils.

Instead, scientists have relied on information obtained from studying cnidarians' embryological development. From this information, scientists have identified two important milestones in the evolution of cnidarians—the development of true tissues and of radial symmetry.

True tissues enable cnidarians to use different body parts for different functions. For example, when stimulated, the tentacles of cnidarians move to capture prey. Without nerve and muscle tissues, cnidarians would not be able to obtain food.

Because cnidarians have radial symmetry, their sense organs are located in a radial pattern around their bodies. This form of body symmetry enables an organism to sense its environment from all sides. How would this sensory adaptation benefit an organism?

Scientists study embryological development and compare anatomy to determine cnidarians' evolutionary origin. In their larval form, cnidarians resemble animal-like, ciliated protists such as paramecia. You learned about paramecia and other protists in Chapter 15. The structural similarities between cnidarian larvae and ciliated protists suggest that the organisms have a common ancestor.

Kingdom: Animalia
Phylum: Cnidaria
Three classes:
Hydrozoa
Scyphozoa
Anthozoa

FIGURE 21.16

Phylum Cnidaria

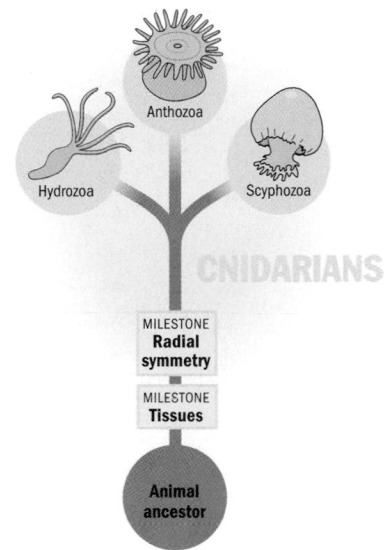

Anthozoa

Hydrozoa

Scyphozoa

CNIDARIANS

MILESTONE
Radial symmetry

MILESTONE
Tissues

Animal ancestor

Chapter 21 Sponges and Cnidarians **513**

514

TEACH

Clarify Misconceptions

Students may think the alternation of body forms between polyp and medusa in cnidarians is the same as the alternation of generations in the life cycles of plants and some fungi. Remind students that an alternation of generations occurs whenever an organism has two or more distinct forms in its life cycle that differ in appearance, habit, or method of reproduction. In some cnidarians, the life cycle is spent partly as a polyp and partly as a medusa. The change between the polyp and the medusa forms is an example of alternation of generations in cnidarians.

Use the Visual

Refer to Figures 21.17 and 21.18. Point out that the Portuguese man-of war, unlike the hydra, is composed of both medusa and polyp forms that live together in a colony. Ask:

- **What is another difference between the man-of-war and the hydra?** (The tentacles of the man-of-war are longer and poisonous to prey.)

 Geography

On a world map locate Guam, Nauru, and Fiji. Explain that these and many other islands in the South Pacific were formed from coral. Identify at least one atoll and discuss how it was formed. Point out that most of the islands in the region not formed by coral, such as the Hawaiian Islands, are the result of volcanic activity.

FIGURE 21.17
The hydra is a freshwater hydrozoan that spends most of its life in the polyp form. It usually reproduces by budding.

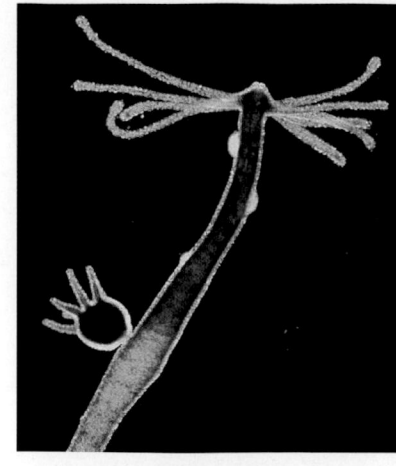

DIVERSITY OF CNIDARIANS

Very touchy creatures

Cnidarians are a highly diverse group of organisms. Most live the greater part of their lives in one of two distinct forms. While most cnidarians live as individual animals, others such as the corals live in colonies. To classify cnidarians more accurately, scientists have recently begun using molecular technology to sequence and compare DNA, RNA, and proteins. In the future, this technology should reveal more information about cnidarians' evolutionary relationships. Presently,

FIGURE 21.18
The Portuguese man-of-war's tentacles may be as long as 9 meters. Although the poison discharged from this cnidarian's tentacles can kill its prey, its sting is rarely fatal to humans.

cnidarians are grouped in three classes—Hydrozoa, Scyphozoa (sy-foh-ZOH-uh), and Anthozoa.

Hydrozoa Most hydrozoans alternate between the polyp and medusa forms, which are illustrated in *Figure 21.13* on page 510. For hydrozoans, the polyp stage is generally the more conspicuous form.

The Portuguese man-of-war is an example of a colonial hydrozoan. It consists of many highly specialized medusae and polyps living together. This colonial hydrozoan, which you can see in *Figure 21.18*, has a life cycle similar to that of a jellyfish. The tentacles, which hang from an inflated bladderlike structure, can be meters long and contain many toxin-injecting nematocysts.

Scyphozoa Like the hydrozoans, most scyphozoans alternate between polyp and medusa forms. However, the primary body form of scyphozoans is the medusa.

If you have ever been swimming in warm ocean water, you may have seen a scyphozoan. This class of cnidarians comprises the animals we call jellyfish. There are more than 200 species of jellyfish, and they all are marine organisms.

Like the Portuguese man-of-war, jellyfish float near the surface of the ocean. Their tentacles hang in the water and trap prey. The medusae of some scyphozoan species can attain great size—several meters in diameter—if they can avoid being broken apart by waves.

Anthozoa Anthozoans, meaning "flower animals," make up the largest class of cnidarians and occur only in the polyp form. All anthozoans have a plantlike body, which is topped with a tuft of hollow tentacles. There are more than 6000 species of anthozoans, and they are all marine animals. Members of this class include the sea anemones and corals.

MEETING DIVERSE NEEDS

At Risk Encourage students to work in small groups to find out how fringing reefs, barrier reefs, and atolls differ from each other. Suggest that students make models, labeled drawings, or picture collages illustrating the differences among the three types of coral reefs.

FIGURE 21.19
Jellyfish are prominent members of the class Scyphozoa. In which body form is this mangrove jellyfish? ❶

Most sea anemones live independently, and they exhibit a wide variety of sizes and colors. The tentacles of sea anemones are particularly noticeable when they are feeding. A sea anemone "harpoons" a small fish or crustacean, folds its tentacles over it, draws it in, and digests it. Although

FIGURE 21.20
Named for their resemblance to anemone flowers, sea anemones usually attach to a hard surface such as coral.

Polyp

The living polyps are connected by a thin sheet of tissue.

Exoskeleton

FIGURE 21.21
Live coral polyps are found only on the top surface of a reef. The carbonate skeletons that form the coral reef are below.

sea anemones may actively hunt their prey, some species obtain nutrients from symbiosis with their photosynthetic partners.

Probably the best-known of the anthozoans are the corals. Corals are tiny, sessile, colonial polyps—many of which secrete an exoskeleton. Individual corals, or polyps, live on the surface of these exoskeletons, building on those of previous generations. As calcium carbonate is deposited in the exoskeletons of corals, old and new skeletons fuse to form a reef. Reef-building corals are found in clear, shallow, warm ocean waters.

CHECKPOINT 21.5

1. Explain the significance of the development of true tissues and radial symmetry in cnidarians.

2. Compare and contrast the three classes of cnidarians.

3. Critical Thinking Why do jellyfish sting their prey before folding their tentacles around them?

Build on What You Know

4. Using diagrams, compare the structure and function of specialized cnidocytes with those of a typical cell. *(Need to jog your memory? Revisit relevant concepts in Chapter 3, Section 3.2.)*

Coral Cautions
To prevent killing fragile, living coral polyps, snorkelers and scuba divers need to avoid stepping on, grabbing, or breaking off any coral. Even touching coral polyps with oily hands can cause them to die.

What are the characteristics of cnidarians? **?**

Chapter 21 Sponges and Cnidarians **515**

ENGAGE

Consider the Big Idea

Have students read The Big Idea! at the top of the page. Explain that sponges and cnidarians are important members in the web of life.

Use the Visual

Have students study the photograph that opens the section. Point out that the shrimp benefits from the sponge as it gets shelter and protection from predators. Other animals have similar relationships, for example, dinoflagellates living on organisms near coral reefs.

Teacher Demo

Obtain a sample of coral from a local aquarium store or a biological supply house. Display the coral and ask students to identify it. Use the coral sample to begin a discussion about some of the threats to coral reefs as a result of human activities. Ask students to speculate how destroying a coral reef may impact other organisms living along the reef.

21.6 Sponges and Cnidarians in the Biosphere

What you'll learn

IDEAS
• To identify the varied roles of cnidarians and sponges in their natural environments
• To describe how these organisms can affect humans

A sponge hotel?
Would you guess that many different organisms actually make their homes inside sponges? For example, the snapping shrimp, *Synalpheus regalis,* inhabits sponges in the Caribbean Sea. How do these organisms benefit from their sponge homes? The sponge is used by its residents as a shelter and a place to hide from their predators.

ECOLOGICAL ROLES

Living together for profit

Because of their great diversity, sponges and cnidarians are a form of food, camouflage, and protected habitats for many organisms. Sponges and cnidarians often benefit from the organisms that use them. As you have learned, relationships in which one organism benefits from another is known as symbiosis.

Corals and sponges are the two most abundant kinds of animals on many reefs, and are at the base of many aquatic food chains. Sponges are not eaten by many animals because their sharp spicules discourage most predators. Cnidarians, however, are consumed by small fish, crustaceans, and other animals. For example, sea stars, certain fish, and other reef dwellers graze on living coral.

FIGURE 21.22

Corals of the Great Barrier Reef

① Fan coral
② Soft tree coral
③ Staghorn coral
④ Lilypad coral

STUDENT RESOURCES

From the Teacher's Resource Package, use:
■ Section Review 21.6, Vocabulary Review 21, and Chapter 21 Tests from Unit 6 Review Module
■ Issues and Decision Making 21-2

TECHNOLOGY RESOURCES

Relevant technology resources include:
■ Spanish Student Edition CD-ROM
■ Teacher's Resource Planner CD-ROM
■ TestWorks CD-ROM: Chapter 21 Test

Sponges and cnidarians have many colors and shapes that provide other animals with a highly camouflaged environment. Certain sponges attach themselves to the back of a crab. One species of crab actually places sponges on its back. This strategy camouflages the crab and provides a sponge with the crab's leftover food. Both the sponge and the crab benefit from this symbiotic relationship.

Some cnidarians also form symbiotic relationships with other organisms. Reef-building corals have dinoflagellates—plantlike protists—living inside their cells. Although corals can grow without these protists, they form reefs only when they live symbiotically with them. This phenomenon is not yet fully understood.

Several species of fishes use the poisonous tentacles of sea anemones for protection. When a fish coats itself with a sea anemone's mucus, the sea anemone does not sense the fish as prey and cannot discharge its nematocysts. The fish can then live among the sea anemone's tentacles. The tentacles protect the fish from predators, and the fish, in turn, may help the sea anemone by removing parasites and debris.

Sponges and cnidarians provide habitats for a great variety of creatures. Small invertebrates, such as shrimps, can live in the pores and central cavities of sponges. Even small fish can live in the cavities of some sponges. A single sponge can house an astonishing number and variety of organisms.

Coral reefs also provide shelter for many organisms, and nooks and crannies for hiding. Coral reefs are, in fact, second only to tropical rain forests in the diversity of life they support.

HUMAN USES

Environmental snitches

Sponges and cnidarians are important indicators of changes in their environments. Living things that provide information about environmental conditions are called bioindicators. When a sponge filters water through its body, it tends to concentrate pollutants from the water in its cells. Eventually, the concentration of pollutants poisons and kills the sponge. An area that contains dead and dying sponges is a possible indication of environmental pollution.

FIGURE 21.23
Part of the Great Barrier Reef, which extends along the northeast coast of Australia, is shown in the aerial view below. The largest group of coral reefs in the world, most of the Great Barrier Reef lies within a national park and is protected by the regulations of a government agency.

② TEACH

Use the Visual

Have students study Figure 21.22. Tell students this reef, which is estimated to be composed of more than 350 species of coral, is more than 80 km (49.7 miles) wide and 200 km (124 miles) long. Ask:

■ **What are some ways the Great Barrier Reef would benefit other organisms living near the reef?** (The reef provides food and shelter to a variety of organisms such as fishes, algae, and sponges.)

Explain

The buildup of sediment along a coral reef and the ocean floor is known as siltation. Siltation can harm reef organisms by allowing the tiny particles making up the sediments to enter and clog the respiratory structures of organisms living along the reef. Point out that not all siltation results from the activities of humans. For example, many coral reefs in the South Pacific are damaged by siltation from volcanic eruptions.

✦ Art

Many artists use sponges to create unique effects in their paintings. One of the most common artistic uses of sponges is to create leaves on trees. Unlike brushes, which often leave evidence of individual strokes, sponges provide a texture that more closely resembles the natural texture of leaves. Encourage students to use sponges to create their own work of art.

MULTICULTURAL PERSPECTIVE

Native Americans living in the Amazon region often use sponge spicules to make clay pottery. Adding spicules to the clay makes the ceramic in the finished pottery stronger. Other unusual uses for sponges existed more than 3000 years ago among the inhabitants of Crete, a Greek island. The Cretans used sponges to make masks to filter out particles in foul air to prevent disease. The Cretans also burned sponges as a way to fumigate and sterilize the air in closed rooms.

STS

Neurology is one area of biomedical research that is using cnidarians. Scientists working in this field study the toxins released by the sea wasp and other types of jellyfish to observe how these toxins affect the nervous system.

3 ASSESS

Evaluate Understanding

To assess students' understanding of the roles of sponges and cnidarians in the biosphere, ask:

- **How do other organisms benefit from sponges and cnidarians?** (Sponges and cnidarians provide camouflage and habitats for other organisms.)
- **How do cnidarians and sponges indicate change in the environment?** (Coral reefs are possible bioindicators of global warming; dead and dying sponges indicate pollution.)

Reteach

Draw a concept map on the board or on a transparency. Label the center *Sponges and Cnidarians in the Biosphere,* and label three lines coming out of the center, *Ecological Roles, Human Uses,* and *Rx.* Work with students to add information as they consider how sponges and cnidarians are important in the biosphere.

518

IN THE COMMUNITY
The Business of Sponges

Check at home and visit local stores to see how many different sponge products you can find. What is the composition of artificial sponges? Look in department stores and bath shops to find natural sponges too. Conduct library research into the business of harvesting sponges from the Caribbean Sea and the Mediterranean Sea. How large is the sponge industry? How many sponges are harvested in a year? Does the harvesting of sponges threaten their ecosystems? Write a brief report explaining your findings.

FIGURE 21.24
These are the skeletal remains of spongin-containing sponges. Such natural sponges are prized for washing cars.

Like sponges, corals are sensitive to water pollution, changes in water temperature or oxygen concentrations, and water clarity, or the amount of sediment. Some scientists are studying coral reefs as possible bioindicators of global warming. Offshore reefs help protect shorelines from erosion. By decreasing the force of incoming waves, the reefs create an area of calm, peaceful waters at the shore. Reefs also protect marine life that humans use for food.

In addition to protecting the shoreline and marine life, sponges are used as consumer products. It is only in the twentieth century that artificial sponges—made of rubber, nylon, or cellulose—have become commonplace. For centuries, humans have harvested natural sponges—dull colored and irregularly shaped—for bathing and cleaning. These natural sponges contain only spongin. Spicule-containing sponges would be too abrasive for household use.

? How are sponges and cnidarians important in their ecosystems?

Sponge spicules are not without their consumer uses, however. Members of a South American tribe that inhabits the Amazon region add sponge spicules to the clay they use for making pottery. The spicules greatly strengthen their ceramic pots.

FRONTIERS IN BIOLOGY STS
Rx . . . sponges and jellyfish

A more recent use for sponges and cnidarians, especially jellyfish, is in the biomedical and pharmaceutical industries. Researchers have found promising new antibiotic and anticancer compounds in the small percentage of sponge species they have studied. Researchers are also investigating possible medical uses for the paralyzing toxins that some jellyfish use to capture prey. This branch of biotechnology is quite new, but very exciting. Research will probably result in the development of new medicines.

CHECKPOINT 21.6

1. Describe the roles of sponges and cnidarians in marine environments.
2. Explain how sponges and corals can be used for environmental monitoring.
3. **Critical Thinking** How would the death of a coral reef affect the island it surrounds and the inhabitants of that island?

Build on What You Know
4. What benefits might the dinoflagellates living in reef-building corals derive from their symbiotic relationship? How would the coral benefit? *(Need to jog your memory? Revisit relevant concepts in Chapter 15, Section 15.3.)*

CHECKPOINT 21.6

1. Both provide food, camouflage, and protected habitats for many organisms, some of which provide services in return.
2. Pollutants in water concentrate in sponges. An area with dead and dying sponges is probably polluted. Corals are sensitive to water pollution, temperature variations, decreased oxygen concentrations, and churning sediment.
3. **Predicting** The coastline will begin to erode, bringing about decline in the fishing and tourism industries.
4. The dinoflagellates might benefit from the carbon dioxide given off by the coral, or from a protected habitat. The coral may benefit from the oxygen given off by the dinoflagellates.

Chapter 21 Review

21.1 Animals have evolved a number of adaptations enabling them to perform essential functions of life.
21.2–21.3 Sponges are sessile animals without specialized tissues and organs.
21.4–21.5 Cnidarians are radially symmetrical animals with specialized tissues and stinging tentacles.
21.6 Sponges and cnidarians provide food and protection for a large number of organisms.

Sum It Up

Use the following summary to review the main concepts in this chapter.

21.1 Introduction to Animals

- Animals are eukaryotic and multicellular.
- Animals are heterotrophic organisms, and their cells lack cell walls.
- The evolution of animals is highlighted by four major developmental milestones.
- Animals perform certain functions for survival: movement, respiration, reproduction, digestion, excretion, and sensing their environment.

21.2 Characteristics of Sponges

- Sponges are sessile filter-feeders.
- Sponges have a simple, asymmetrical body organization supported by spongin and/or spicules.
- Sponges can reproduce sexually and often are hermaphrodites. They can also reproduce asexually by regeneration.

21.3 Origin and Diversity of Sponges

- Sponges most likely evolved from flagellated colonial protists.
- Sponges do not have specialized tissues and most are asymmetrical.
- Sponges are numerous and vary in size, shape, and color.

21.4 Characteristics of Cnidarians

- Cnidarians are soft-bodied and have radial symmetry. They have two basic body plans: polyp and medusa.
- Cnidarians have stinging cells armed with nematocysts.
- Some cnidarians have ciliated planula larvae.

21.5 Origin and Diversity of Cnidarians

- Cnidarians probably evolved from ciliated colonial protists.
- Most hydrozoans have both a polyp and medusa stage.
- Scyphozoans, the common jellyfish, have a prominent medusa stage.
- Anthozoans are colonial polyps that include corals and sea anemones.

21.6 Sponges and Cnidarians in the Biosphere

- Sponges and cnidarians form symbiotic relationships with other organisms. Some are the principle organisms of reefs.
- Sponges and cnidarians are indicators of pollution and have biopharmaceutical applications.

Use Terms and Concepts

Use each of the following words in a sentence. If you need to review a meaning, turn to the page indicated.

animals (p. 500)
sessile (p. 500)
motile (p. 500)
blastula (p. 502)
gastrula (p. 502)
blastopore (p. 503)

vertebrates (p. 503)
invertebrates (p. 503)
osculum (p. 504)
amebocytes (p. 504)
spongin (p. 504)

spicules (p. 505)
gemmule (p. 506)
hermaphrodite (p. 506)
radial symmetry (p. 509)

asymmetry (p. 509)
polyp (p. 509)
medusa (p. 509)
nematocyst (p. 510)
planula (p. 511)

Chapter 21 Sponges and Cnidarians **519**

Review the Big Ideas

Before students begin the Chapter Review, you may wish to discuss the Big Ideas they have learned in this chapter. Explain that sponges and cnidarians are the simplest animals in the process of evolution. Sponges have no specialized tissues, but cnidarians have both specialized tissues and radial symmetry. Both animals are important to other living organisms in the biosphere.

Answers

1. False; planula
2. True
3. False; A spongin is a network of protein fibers.
4. False; osculum
5. False; hermaphrodites
6. True
7. False; polyp
8. True
9. Invertebrates
10. Spicules
11. gemmule
12. Nematocysts
13. vertebrates
14. Amebocytes
15. medusa
16. Animals
17. Scientists determine evolutionary relationships by analyzing shared structural, developmental, and molecular characteristics.
18. Taxonomists recognize four major milestones in the evolution of animals—evolution of tissues, body symmetry, internal body cavities, and a new pattern of embryo development.
19. Depending on the animal, the cell layers are ectoderm, mesoderm, and endoderm. From endoderm, digestive tract, respiratory system; from ectoderm, skin, sense organs, and nerves; from mesoderm, circulatory, reproductive, and excretory systems
20. Collar cells trap particles of organic matter and microscopic organisms from the water flowing through the sponge.
21. Cnidocytes are specialized cells that release stinging organelles when the cnidarian touches an object or animal. The poison in the barb kills or paralyzes prey.
22. When sponges bud, the buds either detach and form

Use Your Word Power

TRUE-FALSE Write true if the statement is true. If the statement is false, change the underlined word to make it true.

1. A(n) <u>gemmule</u> is a free-swimming ciliated larva.

2. A(n) <u>sessile</u> organism is attached to one location.

3. The network of protein fibers that makes up a sponge skeleton is made of <u>spicules</u>.

4. The opening at the top of a sponge through which water flows is the <u>polyp</u>.

5. Animals capable of producing both eggs and sperm in one body are called <u>nematocysts</u>.

6. <u>Radial symmetry</u> is exhibited by organisms that have a central body axis from which other body parts extend.

7. A(n) <u>planula</u> is the vase-shaped body plan of a cnidarian.

8. Free-moving animals are <u>motile</u>.

COMPLETION Write the word or phrase that best completes each statement.

9. _____ have no backbones.

10. Needlelike structures in sponges that are made of silicon dioxide or calcium carbonate are called _____.

11. A(n) _____ is a dormant mass of sponge amebocytes surrounded by layers of spicules.

12. _____ are the stinging barbs of a cnidarian.

13. Animals with backbones are _____ .

14. _____ are migrating cells in a sponge that carry food and wastes.

15. The jellyfish _____ is umbrella shaped.

16. _____ are eukaryotic, multicellular heterotrophs whose cells lack cell walls.

Show What You Know

17. What criteria do scientists use to classify organisms and to identify evolutionary relationships?

18. List and describe the four major milestones in the evolution of animals.

19. What animal tissues are formed by the embryonic cell layers?

20. Explain how sponges obtain food.

21. What are cnidocytes? What is their function?

22. Describe the difference between fragmentation, budding, and regeneration as methods of reproduction.

23. Give some examples of symbiotic relationships formed between sponges, cnidarians, and other organisms.

24. **Make a Concept Map** Use the following terms to make a concept map that shows the classification and characteristics of sponges and cnidarians: cnidaria, animalia, radial symmetry, porifera, sessile, asymmetry, motile, cnidocytes, porous, polyp, medusa.

Take It Further

25. **Applying Concepts** Some of the animals you studied in this chapter are sessile their entire lives, and others are motile. Still others have both motile and sessile stages. What are the advantages and disadvantages of each lifestyle?

26. **Applying Concepts** Why is it important for a motile animal to be able to sense its environment?

27. **Making a Prediction** Predict what would happen to a coral reef ecosystem if all of the sponges were eliminated.

28. **Analyzing Data** Draw a diagram to illustrate the four main evolutionary branches of sponges that are recognized by scientists.

new sponges or remain attached and form a colony. Fragments broken off a sponge can settle and regenerate new sponges.

23. Sponges and cnidarians provide highly camouflaged habitats for other organisms; reef-building corals need dinoflagellates living within them in order to build reefs; a single sponge houses many other organisms

24. Concept maps should show that sponges and cnidaria are <u>animilia</u> and regenerate from <u>polyps</u>. <u>Cnidaria</u> have <u>radial symmetry</u>, are <u>motile</u>, and have a <u>medusa</u>, a mouth-down version of a <u>polyp</u>, and use <u>cnidocytes</u> to kill prey. Sponges are in the phylum <u>porifera</u>, are <u>sessile</u>, and show <u>asymmetry</u>.

29. Interpreting a Graph Coral growth is affected by sea level. If the sea level rises too rapidly, reefs are "drowned" and die. Using the graph, explain how much the rate of coral growth must increase to reach its maximum annual growth. One projected rise in sea level over the next century is 15 millimeters per year. How will that increase affect coral reefs?

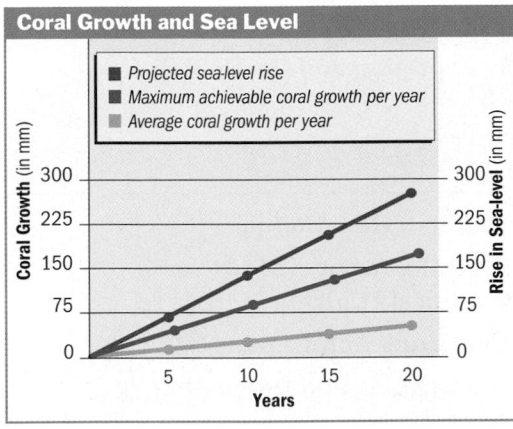

Coral Growth and Sea Level

- ■ Projected sea-level rise
- ■ Maximum achievable coral growth per year
- ■ Average coral growth per year

Coral Growth (in mm) / Rise in Sea-level (in mm)

300, 225, 150, 75, 0

Years: 5, 10, 15, 20

Consider the Issues

30. Protecting the Reefs Many coral reefs are experiencing significant long-term damage. Collectors remove organisms and coral skeletons, and tourists walk on the fragile reefs. Simple warnings and prohibitions have not been effective. What else could be done to alleviate the problem? Should people be prohibited from collecting the coral?

31. Protecting the Animals Marine invertebrates have become prime targets of pharmaceutical research because of the medically important chemicals they produce. How might the discovery of new chemicals affect the populations of these marine invertebrates? What could be done to ensure that these chemicals could be manufactured, without threatening the species that produced the chemicals?

Make New Connections

32. Biology and Geology Corals produce calcium carbonate ($CaCO_3$). Limestone, a type of rock, is formed from compacted $CaCO_3$. Research the properties of limestone. How is limestone involved in cave formation? Report your findings.

33. Biology and Physics The movement of a hydra's nematocyst is one of the fastest known cell activities. A hydra nematocyst travels at two meters per second. The formula used to calculate speed is: Speed = Distance/Time. Calculate the time that it would take for a nematocyst to travel 0.02 mm (the typical distance between a hydra and its prey).

34. Biology and the Community The widespread use of plastic bags and balloons, which are released at parades, games, and other special events, has caused problems when these items make their way into the ocean. Floating plastic bags and balloons can look like jellyfish. Find out the jellyfish predators that are most affected by this problem. Find out what happens to plastic bags in your community. Are they recycled? Where?

FAST-FORWARD TO CHAPTER 22

Sponges are asymmetrical and cnidarians have radial symmetry. The four phyla you will learn about in the next chapter exhibit bilateral symmetry. They include flatworms, roundworms, mollusks, and segmented worms.

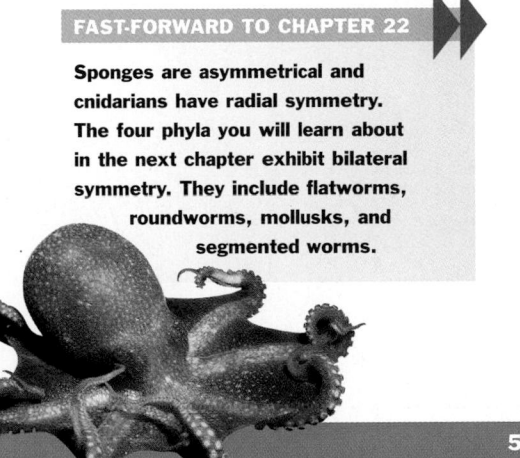

521

tion, and camouflage.

28. Diagrams should show classes *Calcarea, Hyalospongiae, Demospongiae,* and *Sclerospongoae*

29. Rate must increase from 3.5 mm/yr to 8.5 mm/yr for total increase of 5 mm/yr. The 15 mm/yr rise in sea level will drown the coral.

30. Tours could be supervised so that tourists were kept at a safe distance from the reef. If natives were trained to supervise tours, a ban on collection of coral might be feasible.

31. Answers will vary. Researchers might harvest large quantities of marine invertebrates, which could disrupt the ecology of the marine environments.

32. Answers will vary.

33. 0.00001 seconds

34. Animals that prey on jellyfish include sea turtles, ocean sunfish, and blue rockfish.

---

25. Motile animals can move around to find food and can change environments. This motion, however, requires energy. Sessile animals require less energy, but are restricted to a passive role in obtaining food and they cannot move to a new habitat. Animals who are sessile and motile during different life stages use less energy when sessile, but their larva can be dispersed into new environments.

26. A motile animal changes its position in its environment and must be able to determine what prey and predator might be there.

27. The ecosystem would be disrupted because other animals and plants depend on sponges for food, protec-

PLANNING GUIDE

Section	Student Activities/Features	Teacher's Resource Package
22.1 Flatworms and Roundworms **Objectives** ■ Explain the concept of bilateral symmetry ■ Compare and contrast the characteristics of flatworms and roundworms	**Lab Zone Discover It!** *Examining Mollusks,* p. 523 **Lab Zone Do It!** *Observing Roundworms,* p. 525 **Lab Zone Think About It!** *Solving a Reproduction Puzzle,* p. 527 **Everyday Biology** *Protect Your Pet,* p. 529	**Unit 6 Review Module** ■ Section Review 22.1 ■ Interpreting Graphics 22 ■ Activity Recordsheet 22-1 **Consumer Applications** 22-1 **Laboratory Manual,** Lab 36: "Senses in Planarians" **Interpreting and Developing Graphics** 64
22.2 Mollusks **Objectives** ■ Describe the characteristics of mollusks ■ Distinguish among the four classes of mollusks	**Everyday Biology** *Planting Pearls,* p. 531 **STS: Environmental Awareness** *Mussels on the Move,* p. 535	**Unit 6 Review Module** ■ Section Review 22.2 ■ Critical Thinking Exercise 22 **Consumer Applications** 22-2 **Interpreting and Developing Graphics** 65
22.3 Segmented Worms **Objectives** ■ Identify the characteristics of segmented worms ■ Compare and contrast the three classes of segmented worms	**In the Community** *Worms for Profit,* p. 539 **Lab Zone Investigate It!** *Observing Earthworms,* p. 540	**Unit 6 Review Module** ■ Section Review 22.3 ■ Enrichment Topic 22-1 ■ Activity Recordsheet 22-2 ■ Vocabulary Review 22 ■ Chapter 22 Tests **Laboratory Manual** ■ Lab 37: "Earthworm Anatomy" ■ Lab 38: "Earthworm: Alternative Anatomy Investigation" **Issues and Decision Making** 22-1 **Interpreting and Developing Graphics** 66 **Spanish Reviews** Chapter 22

Technology Resources

Internet Connections

Within this chapter, you will see the **bioSURF** logo. If you and your students have access to the Internet, the following URL address will provide various Internet connections that are related to topics and features presented in this chapter:

http://invertebrates.biosurf.com

You can also find relevant chapter material at **The Biology Place** address:

http://www.biology.com

CD-ROMs

Biología: la telaraña de la vida,
  (Spanish Student Edition) Chapter 22
Teacher's Resource Planner, Chapter 22
  Supplements
TestWorks CD-ROM
- Chapter 22 Tests

Videodiscs

Animated Biological Concepts Videodiscs
- Earthworm Anatomy

Overhead Transparencies

- Structure of a Mollusk, #48
- System of an Annelid, #49

Videotapes

Biology Alive! Video Series
- Signs of Life Video
- The Domain of Life Video
Rewind: The Web of Life Reteach Videos

Planning for Activities

STUDENT EDITION
Lab Zone
Discover It! p. 523
- several fresh or canned clams or mussels

Lab Zone Do It! p. 525
- water
- teaspoon
- soil from underneath decaying leaves or near a compost pile
- gloves
- microscope
- roundworm
- pencil
- paper

Lab Zone
Investigate It! p. 540
- live earthworms
- moist soil
- microscope
- glass pan
- flashlight

TEACHER'S EDITION
Class Activity, p. 525
Body structure and movement of planaria
- petri dish with planaria
- hand lens
- flashlight
- paper

Quick Activity, p. 530
Examining aquatic snails
- freshwater fish tank containing aquatic snails
- hand lenses

Class Activity, p. 532
Identifying shells
- collection of different kinds of shells
- reference books

Teacher Demo, p. 533
How a radula works
- rasp file
- piece of scrap wood

Class Activity, p. 533
Determining the age of a clam
- clam shells
- picture of a cross section of a tree

Teacher Demo, p. 533
Comparing a pill box to bivalve shells
- hinged pill box or face powder compact
- two bivalve shells
- tape

Teacher Demo, p. 534
Observing a cuttlebone
- cuttlebone

Teacher Demo, p. 536
Illustrating the diffusion of gas across a worm's skin
- large square of cotton cloth
- water

Teacher Demo, p. 538
Demonstrating filtering in tube dwelling polychetes
- spoon
- fine lint from a clothes dryer filter
- beaker
- fine sieve

Chapter Objectives

Students will learn the main concepts of this chapter as they complete the following objectives.

- Explain the concept of bilateral symmetry
- Compare and contrast the characteristics of flatworms and roundworms
- Differentiate between the classes of flatworms and roundworms
- Describe the characteristics of mollusks
- Distinguish among the four classes of mollusks and compare their environmental adaptations
- Identify the characteristics of segmented worms
- Compare and contrast the three classes of segmented worms

Key Words

22.1 *bilateral symmetry, pharynx, hydrostatic skeleton*

22.2 *mantle, coelom, closed circulatory system*

22.3 *annelids, setae, nephridia, parapodia*

The Opening Story

Discuss with students how the environment around the ocean floor vents can support life. Explain that eyeless organisms can function well in an environment without light.

CHAPTER 22

Worms and Mollusks

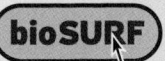

You can find out more about worms and mollusks by exploring the following Internet address:
http://invertebrates.biosurf.com

In this chapter . . .

FEATURES

Everyday Biology
- Protect Your Pet
- Planting Pearls

In the Community
Worms for Profit

 Environmental Awareness
Mussels on the Move

LAB ZONES

Discover It!
- Examining Mollusks

Do It!
- Observing Roundworms

Think About It!
- Solving a Reproduction Puzzle

Investigate It!
- Observing Earthworms

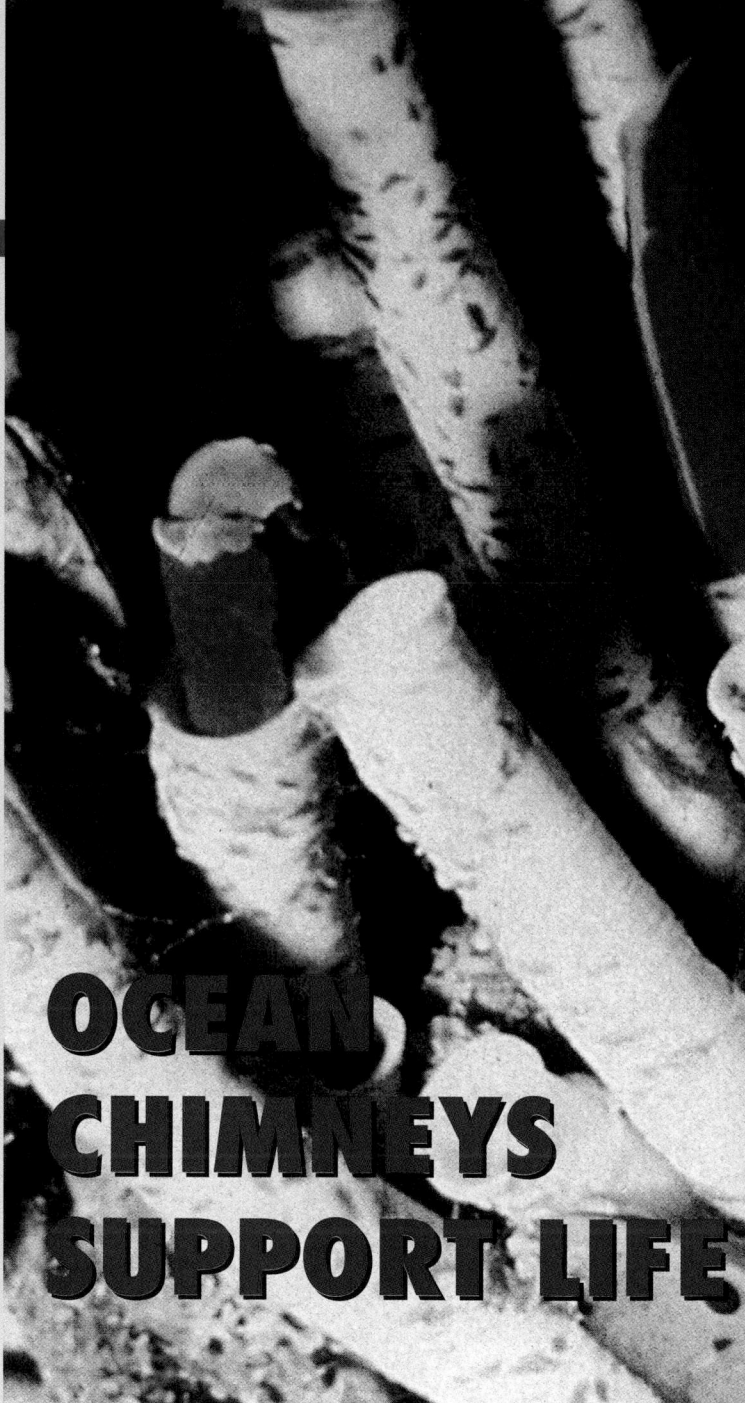

OCEAN CHIMNEYS SUPPORT LIFE

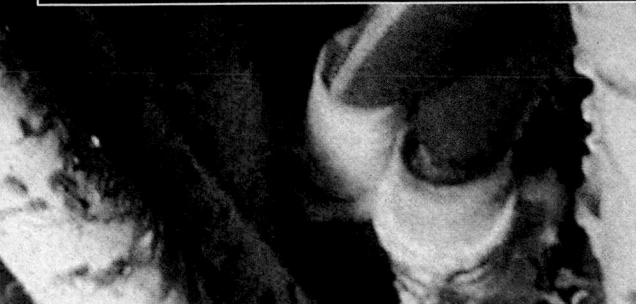

Many stretches of ocean floor are barren and bleak with few signs of marine life, but there are exceptions. One occurs where the gigantic plates that comprise Earth's crust are moving apart, allowing lava—hot, molten rock—to emerge. As the lava cools, it adds new ocean floor between the crustal plates. Cold seawater sinks deep into vents, or cracks, created in the ocean floor. When the seawater, heated to temperatures as high as 400°C (750°F), spews back out of the vents, it contains dissolved minerals. These minerals are deposited around the vents, forming hollow, cylindrical "chimneys," some of which reach heights of more than 10 meters (m).

The hot water exiting these chimneys encourages the growth of bacteria, which in turn feed and support an amazing array of animals. Picture, for example, the thriving life in a vent community in the eastern Pacific Ocean: tall, smoking chimneys surrounded by clusters of tube worms and clams and mussels, all feeding on the abundant clouds and mats of bacteria. These giant worms, a sensation when they were first discovered, live in tubes they build from seafloor debris cemented with mucus. Using submersible vehicles, scientists can observe the teeming life in these unusual ecosystems thousands of meters below the ocean's surface.

LAB ZONE Discover It!

Examining Mollusks

You need *a hand lens and several fresh or canned clams or mussels*

1. If you can obtain fresh clams or mussels, do so.
   Caution: As you open them, be careful not to cut yourself on the shells.
   If you are using canned clams or mussels, open the can and lay the mollusks on a clean surface.
2. Examine the mollusks, and draw what you see.
   Caution: Wash your hands thoroughly after touching the clams or mussels.

Worms and mollusks share many features, including the soft, muscular body you just observed. Save your drawings, and use them to write labels or notes about common parts of these mollusks as you read this chapter.

WRITE ABOUT IT!

Suppose you were invited on an underwater research voyage to the depths of the vent communities. Describe what you might see, and write a journal entry for the activities of one day in your imaginary deep-sea adventure.

523

  If you have access to the Internet in your classroom or school, you may wish to have students connect to the address shown on page 522. You may want to have students conduct a net search for information using the key words in this chapter. For example, students could search for entries under roundworms, flukes, leeches, or squid.

LAB ZONE Discover It!

Examining Mollusks **TEAM WORK**

Caution students to prod the mollusk carefully so as not to damage the delicate tissue. Have students identify as many parts of the animal as possible.

WRITE ABOUT IT!

Suggest to students that they use drawings to describe the vent community. Encourage students to include information about the environment of the ocean bottom community.

REWIND to Chapter 21

Briefly review concepts learned in Chapter 21, *Introduction to the Animal Kingdom.* Ask:

■ **How will your study of the behavior of sponges and cnidarians help you understand the important characteristics of worms and mollusks?**

PORTFOLIO PREVIEW

Students should be encouraged to add to their portfolios as they work through this chapter. In addition to the *Write About It* opportunity, the following sections are

excellent opportunities for portfolio entries:
■ Section 22.1: *Flatworms and Roundworms*
■ Section 22.2: *Mollusks*

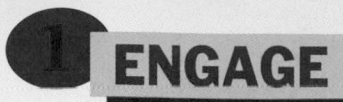

ENGAGE

Consider The Big Idea

Have students read The Big Idea! stated at the top of the page. Tell students to observe the pattern of specialized body systems as they study invertebrates.

Use the Visual

Have students study the photograph that opens the section. Ask:

■ **What does the discovery of flatworm eggs in mummified humans tell scientists?** (Flatworms have existed in parasitic relationships with humans for thousands of years.)

Check Prior Knowledge

Have students renew their knowledge about parasites and asexual reproduction. Ask:

■ **Why are some organisms considered parasites?** (They depend completely on a host organism for food.)

■ **How do asexual and sexual reproduction differ?** (In asexual reproduction, the organism regenerates itself; in sexual reproduction, two organisms are necessary.)

Quick Activity

Ask students to list examples of bilateral symmetry that occur in the classroom.

SUPER READ! **Using Word Parts** To practice strategies for effective reading, use pages 59–60 in *Super Read!*

524

THE BIG IDEA! Flatworms and roundworms have bilateral symmetry and specialized tissues. 22.1

22.1 Flatworms and Roundworms

What you'll learn

IDEAS
• To explain the concept of bilateral symmetry
• To compare the characteristics of flatworms and roundworms

WORDS
bilateral symmetry, pharynx, hydrostatic skeleton

A time-honored relationship
Many flatworms and roundworms are parasites that have coevolved with their specific animal hosts, including humans. The eggs of parasitic flatworms have actually been found in mummified humans from ancient Egypt and other places.

STRUCTURE AND CHARACTERISTICS

A head for symmetry

Flatworms and roundworms are classified in separate phyla. However, the organisms that comprise both phyla share characteristics related to their body plans and nervous systems.

Flatworms and roundworms are bilaterally symmetrical. As you can see in the diagram in *Figure 22.1*, when animals with **bilateral symmetry** are cut longitudinally (lengthwise), the result is right and left mirror images. The word *bilateral* is formed from "bi-," meaning "two," and "lateral," meaning "sides." Animals with bilateral symmetry have an anterior (front) end, a posterior (rear, or tail) end, a ventral (lower, or front) side, and a dorsal (upper, or back) side.

Most organisms with bilateral symmetry, including flatworms and roundworms, have nervous systems that consist of sensory receptors and nerve cells. Ganglia are clusters of nerve tissues. Sensory receptors and ganglia are concentrated at the anterior end of the body. How would the location of these structures benefit an organism?

FIGURE 22.1

Structures of a Planarian

Name some ways that a flatworm's body shape affects its ability to survive. ❶

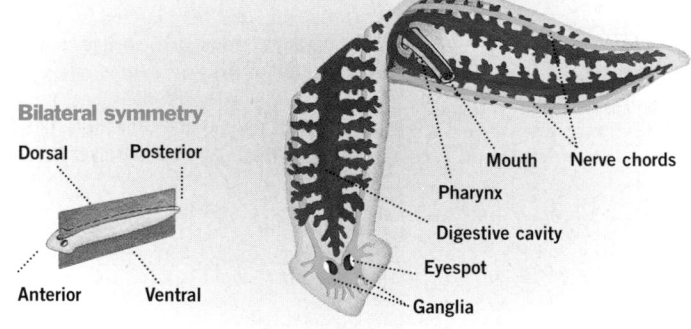

Bilateral symmetry

Dorsal   Posterior

Anterior   Ventral

Mouth   Nerve chords
Pharynx
Digestive cavity
Eyespot
Ganglia

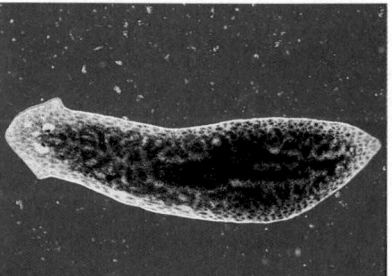

524 *Unit 6 Invertebrate Animals*

STUDENT RESOURCES

From the Teacher's Resource Package, use:
■ Section Review 22.1, Activity Recordsheet 22.1, and Interpreting Graphics 22 from Unit 6 Review Module
■ Consumer Applications 22-1
■ Lab 36: "Senses in Planarians"

TECHNOLOGY RESOURCES

Relevant technology resources include:
■ Spanish Student Edition CD-ROM
■ Teacher's Resource Planner CD-ROM
■ Biology Alive! Video: "Signs of Life"

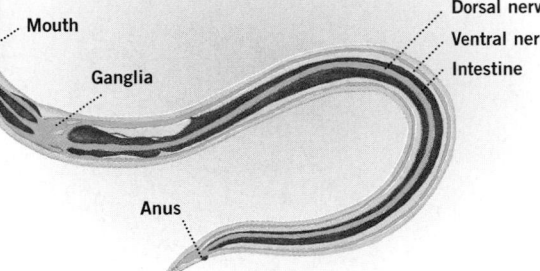

FIGURE 22.2
Structures of a Roundworm

A roundworm's tubelike digestive system is efficient because food moves in one direction, and foods at different stages of digestion do not mix.

Mouth

Ganglia

Dorsal nerve

Ventral nerve

Intestine

Anus

Flatworms Flatworms are unsegmented and appear flat. They are classified in the phylum Platyhelminthes (plat-ih-HEL-min-theez).

In *Figure 22.1* you can see a typical flatworm—a planarian. Cilia on a planarian's ventral surface push the animal along on slimelike material that it secretes. A planarian moves to escape predators and to obtain food. Chemical receptors, light-sensitive eyespots, and touch receptors help a planarian navigate through its environment.

A planarian's digestive system includes a single ventral opening in the middle of its body—the mouth—through which food enters and undigested wastes leave. To feed, a planarian extends a muscular tube called the **pharynx** (FAR-inks) through the mouth. The pharynx sucks in food, which then passes into the digestive cavity, where it is broken down and absorbed.

Planarians have an excretory system that consists of small, bulblike structures called flame cells. Flame cells excrete water and chemical wastes. Planarians do not have a circulatory or respiratory system; their flat body structure enables gases to diffuse directly across the skin and to their internal tissues.

Planarians reproduce asexually by regeneration, but they can also reproduce sexually. Planarians are hermaphrodites. As you may recall, hermaphrodites are organisms capable

of producing both eggs and sperm. However, individual planarians cannot fertilize their own eggs. Instead, they exchange sperm with other planarians.

Roundworms Roundworms are members of the phylum Nematoda (NEE-muh-tohd-uh). As you can see in *Figure 22.2*, a very important difference between roundworms and

---

LAB ZONE Do It! **bioSURF**

Observing Roundworms

Many roundworms live in soil. You can observe and examine roundworms when you . . .

Try This

1 Moisten a few teaspoons of soil that you have collected from underneath decaying leaves or near a compost pile. **Caution:** Wear gloves and use care when collecting soil, and wash your hands thoroughly when you are done.
2 Examine a small amount of the soil under a microscope, using low and then high power.
3 Examine the external anatomy of a roundworm. Draw and label what you see.

Analyze Your Results

1 How many roundworms did you observe?
2 Describe the surface of a roundworm.
3 How does the anterior end of the roundworm differ from the posterior end?

---

2 TEACH

Class Activity   TEAM WORK

Provide small groups of students with a petri dish with planaria, a hand lens, and a flashlight. Have students record their observations of each organism's body structure and movement. Then have them cover half the petri dish with a piece of paper and shine a light over the dish. Ask:

- **What did the planaria do?** (They moved away from the light.)
- **What can you conclude about where planaria live?** (They tend to live in moist, dark places.)

LAB ZONE Do It! **TEAM WORK**

Observing Roundworms

Try This

3 Drawings should include any external features shown in Figure 22.2.

Analyze Your Results

1 Answers will vary.
2 Students should observe the roundworms as slender, cyclindrical, and pointed at each end with a smooth, simple surface.
3 The anterior end has a mouth and the posterior end has an anus.

Clarify Misconceptions

Because a parasite harms its host, some students may think that it eventually kills the host. Although this sometimes happens, it is not in the parasite's best interest to kill the host because it would lose its food supply. Most adult parasitic organisms would not be able to find another host.

 Physical Science

Show students how hydrostatic pressure works by pumping colored water through a thin, clear plastic hose with a siphon pump. Explain that the roundworm is able to use hydrostatic pressure for both motility and circulation.

 Art

Have students use different colors of clay to make a three-dimensional model showing the cross section of a flatworm and a roundworm. Suggest that they label each layer with a flag attached to a toothpick.

FIGURE 22.3

Flatworms and Roundworms

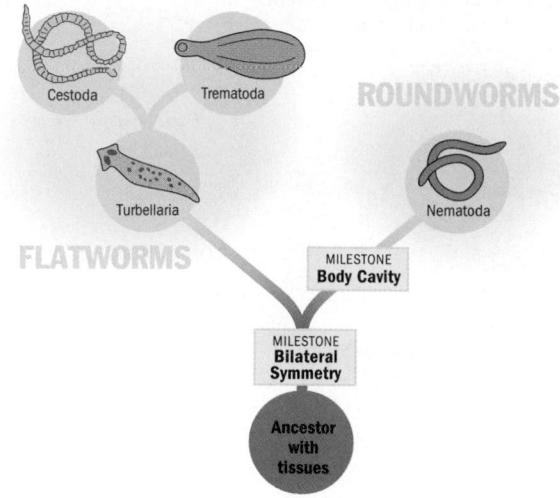

Cestoda
Trematoda
ROUNDWORMS
Turbellaria
Nematoda
FLATWORMS
MILESTONE
Body Cavity
MILESTONE
Bilateral Symmetry
Ancestor with tissues

flatworms is the presence of a tubelike digestive system with two openings. Food enters a roundworm through its mouth, and wastes leave its body through an anus. How does a digestive system with two openings function differently from a digestive system **①** with one opening?

Another difference between roundworms and flatworms is that roundworms have a hydrostatic skeleton. A **hydrostatic skeleton** includes muscles that surround, and are supported by, a water-filled cavity. Water pressure in the cavity keeps the body firm, like air pressure in a tire. Muscles push against the water-filled cavity to cause movement. The cavity also serves as a circulatory system, carrying materials throughout a roundworm's body.

Unlike flatworms, roundworms only reproduce sexually. Most species of nematodes have separate sexes, and fertilization occurs inside a female's body. Many flatworms and roundworms are parasites with life cycles that require two or more different hosts.

526 *Unit 6 Invertebrate Animals*

ORIGIN AND DIVERSITY

The good host

As embryos, flatworms and roundworms have three layers of tissue—ectoderm, endoderm, and mesoderm. Embryos of cnidarians have only ectoderm and endoderm. These layers develop into various body tissues and organs. For example, the lining of an animal's digestive tract comes from endoderm and an animal's outer body covering comes from ectoderm. The evolution of mesoderm resulted in muscles in flatworms and roundworms.

You may recall from Chapter 21 that a major milestone in animal evolution was the appearance of a body cavity. A body cavity is a fluid-filled space between the digestive tract and the outer body wall. As you can see in *Figure* 22.4, flatworms (and sponges and cnidarians) do not have a body cavity. Roundworms (and most other

FIGURE 22.4

Cross Sections of an Acoelomate and a Pseudocoelomate

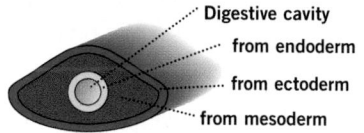

Digestive cavity
from endoderm
from ectoderm
from mesoderm

Acoelomate (flatworm)
Why are flatworms classified as acoelomates? ②

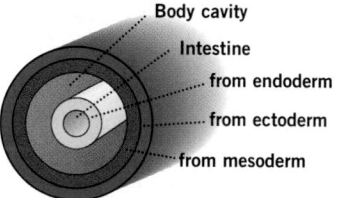

Body cavity
Intestine
from endoderm
from ectoderm
from mesoderm

Pseudocoelomate (roundworm)
Why is the body cavity of a roundworm described as false? ③

---

❶ More food can be processed faster. With a one-opening digestive system, there are times when an organism cannot eat because it is excreting waste.
❷ Flatworms lack a body cavity.
❸ It is not lined with mesoderm.

animals) have a body cavity.

A "true" body cavity is called a coelom and is completely lined with mesoderm. Organisms without a body cavity, such as flatworms, are called acoelomates. ("A-" means "no.") Organisms with a body cavity that is not completely lined with mesoderm tissue are called pseudo-coelomates. ("Pseudo-" means "false.") Roundworms are pseudocoelomates.

The many thousands of known flatworm species belong to three classes: Turbellaria, Trematoda, and Cestoda. All free-living flatworms belong to the class Turbellaria. Organisms that are free-living can feed and reproduce independently of living hosts. You may remember from Chapter 14 that parasites need living host cells to reproduce. Flatworms that belong to the classes Trematoda and Cestoda are parasitic.

Members of the class Turbellaria live in oceans, lakes, ponds, and moist places on land. A planarian is a typical turbellarian. Most turbellarians range in length from 0.5 to 50 centimeters. Turbellarians are either scavengers that eat dead organic matter or carnivores that prey on small organisms.

Parasitic flatworms called flukes belong to the class Trematoda. Several

FIGURE 22.5
This colorful marine flatworm (*Pseudoceros zebra*) is a free-living member of the class Turbellaria. How can you identify its anterior end? ❹

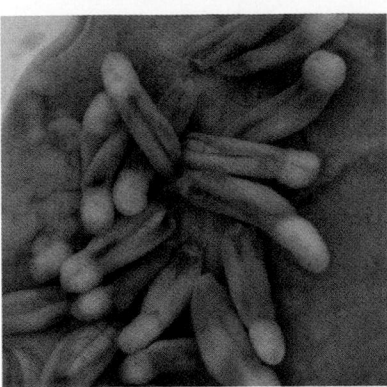

FIGURE 22.6
This photograph shows living flukes (class Trematoda, genus *Alariz*) attached to the interior of a dog's intestine.

structures enable flukes to survive in animal hosts. For example, some flukes have tough, protective body coverings that prevent hosts from digesting them. Other flukes have hooks that help them attach to their hosts. Still other flukes have suckers, which they use to attach to a host or to ingest a host's cells and body fluids.

Most flukes have life cycles that involve two to four different hosts. Blood flukes belong to the genus *Schistosoma*. In humans a blood fluke can cause a serious disease called schistosomiasis (shis-toh-soh-MY-uh-sis), which is characterized by allergic responses, swelling, ulcers, and liver damage.

Parasitic flatworms are widespread in human populations living with substandard or nonexistent sewage

Kingdom: Animalia
Phylum: Platyhelminthes
Three classes:
Turbellaria
Trematoda
Cestoda

LAB ZONE **Think About It!** **bioSURF**

Solving a Reproduction Puzzle

A common New Zealand freshwater snail is host to a parasitic flatworm belonging to the class Trematoda. In lakes where this flatworm is rare, snails commonly reproduce asexually. In lakes with large populations of this trematode, however, snails most often reproduce sexually.

Analyzing the Data

1 Propose a hypothesis to explain these findings.
2 How would you go about testing your hypothesis?

---

❹ There are eyespots at the anterior flat end.

Explain

Tell students that 6000 species of parasitic flukes make up Class Trematoda. Three species of blood flukes in the genus *Schistosoma* infect more than 200 million people in Africa, South America, and Asia. Ask:

■ **What precautions can humans take to avoid infection by a blood fluke?** (Improving sanitation and not walking barefoot in places where larvae are found, such as free standing water.)

Build Writing Skills

Have students research actions taken by the Department of Agriculture and/or by veterinarians to control fluke infection in this country. Suggest that students write up their data as an article to be published in a consumer health magazine.

LAB ZONE **Think About It!**

Solving a Reproduction Puzzle

Analyzing the Data

1 A possible hypothesis might be that the sexually reproduced forms of the mollusk are not parasitized by the flatworm, whereas the asexually reproduced forms are.
2 The hypothesis could be tested by observing several generations of snails that reproduced sexually and asexually.

MEETING DIVERSE NEEDS

Gifted Have students research the latest figures on blood fluke infections in different regions of the world. Ask students to design a brochure to educate people about how to eradicate the problem.

Math

A tapeworm can shed up to ten proglottids daily. Each proglottid can contain up to 10,000 fertilized eggs. Ask:

- **How many fertilized eggs can a tapeworm produce in one day? One week? One year?** (100,000; 700,000; 36,500,000 respectively)

Use the Visual

Have students study the tapeworm and the hookworm in Figures 22.7 and 22.8. Ask:

- **How do the hookworm and tapeworm attach themselves to a host?** (A hookworm uses hooks in its mouth and a tapeworm uses hooks and suckers to attach to a host.)

Geography

Have students use an atlas to identify the different climate regions of the world. Ask them to discuss how nematodes would have to adapt to survive in the various climates.

❶ The worm is identified by the mechanism in its mouth with which it hooks its prey.

528

Kingdom: Animalia
Phylum: Nematoda
Two classes:
Adenophorea
Secernentea

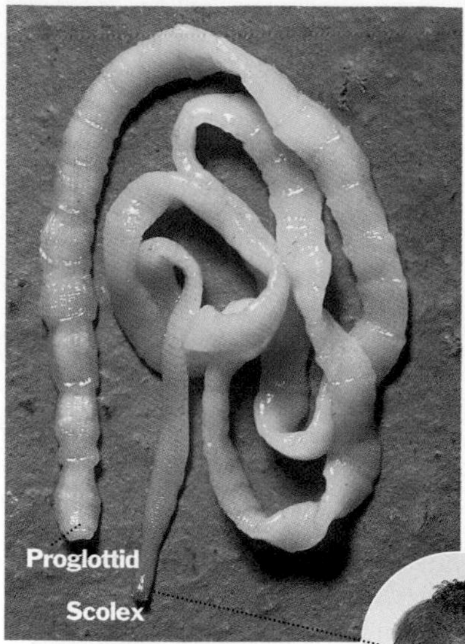

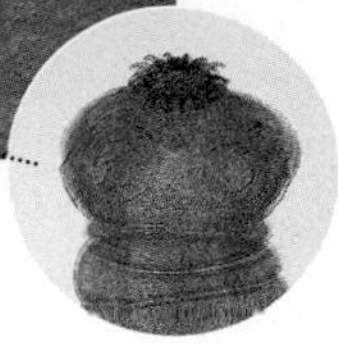

FIGURE 22.7
Notice the scolex of this tapeworm. The scolex is a specialized attachment structure equipped with hooks and suckers.

Proglottid
Scolex

FIGURE 22.8
Hookworms are parasitic roundworms (phylum Nematoda) that infect humans and other animals. Notice the highly adapted mouth on the hookworm in this photograph. How do you suppose these parasites came to be called hookworms? ❶

systems. Human feces contaminate water supplies, and poor sanitary practices may allow worm larvae on unwashed hands to contaminate food.

Tapeworms are members of the class Cestoda. Like many trematodes, tapeworms live in the digestive tracts of their hosts. They have neither a mouth nor a digestive system. To obtain food, they absorb nutrients through their body walls. Tapeworms do have an excretory and a nervous system, as well as a highly developed reproductive system.

The life cycles of tapeworms include at least two different hosts, such as cattle and humans. Tapeworm eggs are consumed by beef cattle if the eggs are on the grass the cattle eat. Inside the cattle's digestive system, the eggs hatch into larvae that bore into intestinal blood vessels. The larvae travel in the blood to the muscles of the cattle, where they form cysts. Thorough cooking of beef kills

---

tapeworm cysts. However, when a human eats undercooked, infected beef, the larvae are released in the person's intestine. There they develop and grow into tapeworms like the one shown in *Figure* 22.7. Tapeworms shed proglottids—body segments containing a complete reproductive system—full of eggs. The proglottids pass out of the human host with feces, continuing the life cycle.

Roundworms, or nematodes, live in all of Earth's climate regions. In a single shovelful of topsoil, you might find a million nematodes. The round-ended, unsegmented bodies of nematodes clearly distinguish them from other worms. They range in length from 1 millimeter to about 1 meter. Some scientists estimate that more than one million species of nematodes exist. Most are free-living and harmless, but some are parasitic.

A roundworm called *Ascaris* is a common human parasite. Humans become infected with *Ascaris* if they eat food or drink water that is contaminated with *Ascaris* eggs. The roundworms that develop from these eggs grow in the small intestine, where they may cause intestinal blockage.

IN THE BIOSPHERE

Just a fluke of nature

Flatworm and roundworm parasites significantly impact human populations. Blood and liver flukes, in particular, infect millions of people around the world. Although fluke infections in humans are rarely fatal, they can be debilitating. Flukes are often resistant to drugs, so instead of working on new drugs, scientists are trying to control these parasites by interrupting their life cycle in the alternate host or in the free-swimming larval stages. In some cases, the

---

FACTS AND FIGURES

Some tapeworms can grow up to 3 meters, (9.8 feet) long, and if undetected, can survive for up to 15 years.

MULTICULTURAL PERSPECTIVE

Sushi describes a variety of Japanese foods made with raw fish. If the fish is contaminated with cysts, consumers risk tapeworm infection. Students may be interested in finding out what steps and precautions fish suppliers and restaurants take to prevent contamination.

alternate host can be eliminated from certain bodies of water. In other cases, a body of water can be treated to kill the free-swimming larvae.

Mosquitoes can spread some parasitic roundworms called filariae. Filariae can invade the human lymphatic system, which is part of the circulatory system. Filariae may become so numerous that they block lymph vessels, causing swelling. *Figure 22.9* shows the swollen leg of a person with elephantiasis, a disease caused by filariae.

Some roundworms cause serious diseases in livestock, pets, and crops. Agricultural losses from parasitic nematodes can amount to billions of dollars each year.

Certain situations increase the chance of infection by parasitic flatworms and roundworms. For example, eating undercooked beef, pork, or fish that is infected with tapeworm cysts can cause infections in humans. Inadequate sanitation conditions and unhealthy drinking water allow many parasites to spread among human hosts. It is estimated that roundworm parasites alone infect more than one billion humans worldwide. In addition to *Ascaris,* roundworm parasites that commonly infect humans include hookworms and pinworms, which are both spread by fecal contamination.

In contrast to parasitic worms, free-living flatworms and roundworms tend to be beneficial. They decompose organic matter and help recycle nutrients. Some free-living nematodes prey on tiny organisms that cause plant diseases. Scientists are exploring one species of roundworm that may control mosquito populations.

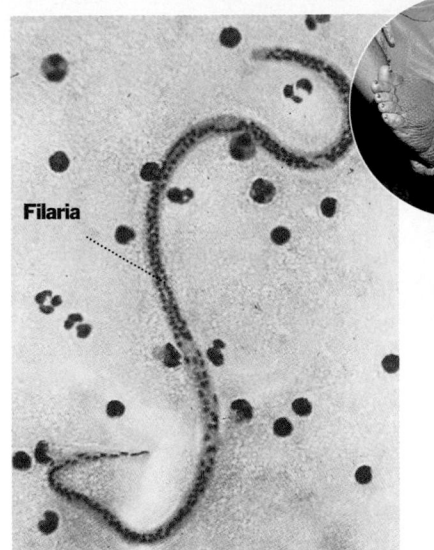

Filaria

FIGURE 22.9
When filariae clog lymph vessels, severe swelling can occur, as in the patient pictured above. At left you can see a filaria found in a blood sample.

Medical and pharmaceutical researchers are interested in enzymes and other types of proteins secreted by some roundworms. For example, hookworms secrete a protein that prevents blood from clotting. After further testing, this protein may be used to treat dangerous blood clots.

CHECKPOINT 22.1

1. Explain the concept of bilateral symmetry, and give one example of an object or organism with bilateral symmetry.
2. Compare and contrast the characteristics of flatworms and roundworms.
3. **Critical Thinking** Why would it be a disadvantage for parasitic worms to kill their hosts?

Build on What You Know

4. List some fundamental differences between flatworms and cnidarians. *(Need to jog your memory? Revisit relevant concepts in Chapter 21, Section 21.4.)*

EVERYDAY BIOLOGY

Protect Your Pet

Did you know that pets can get worms from fleas? Fleas carry tapeworm larvae. When a cat or dog swallows a flea, the tapeworm larvae begin to grow in the animal's intestine. To protect your pet from tapeworms, keep it free of fleas.

What characteristics do flatworms and roundworms share?

Everyday Biology

Signs of tapeworm infection include loss of appetite and listlessness. Evidence of shedded worm body segments, which resemble rice, are seen in the animal's stool and under its tail. Evidence of heartworm infection includes panting and coughing, listlessness, weight loss, and a poor coat. A pet suspected of being infected should be examined by a veterinarian.

 **ASSESS**

Evaluate Understanding

Have students create a two-column chart comparing the physical characteristics, digestive system, and reproduction method(s) of flatworms and roundworms. Check the charts for accuracy.

Reteach

Draw a Venn diagram on the board or on a transparency. Label one circle *Flatworms,* and the second circle *Roundworms.* Work with students to fill in the graphic to show how the worms are similar and how they differ.

CHECKPOINT 22.1

1. If an organism with bilateral symmetry, such as a flatworm or a roundworm, is cut longitudinally, it will form right and left mirror images.
2. Both are bilaterally symmetrical, have sensory receptors, and are unsegmented. Flatworms have one digestive opening and reproduce sexually and asexually; roundworms have one digestive and one excretory opening and reproduce sexually.
3. **Identifying cause and effect** The parasite would no longer have a food supply.
4. Cnidarians have radial symmetry and a simple sac body. Flatworms have bilateral symmetry and a more complex body organization with definite organs.

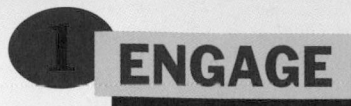

ENGAGE

Consider the Big Idea

Have students read The Big Idea! at the top of the page. Point out that mollusks share some characteristics with nematoda, but are more developed.

Use the Visual

After students have studied the photograph that opens the section and read the accompanying text, ask:

- **Describe the slug in the photograph.** (It is long, fat, slimy, and yellow.)

Check Prior Knowledge

To assess students' prior knowledge about mollusks ask:

- **Describe the method of locomotion used by snails.** (They move slowly on a wet, slimy trail.)

SUPER READ! **Distinguishing Fact From Opinion** To practice strategies for effective reading, use pages 57-58 in *Super Read!*

Using Word Parts To practice strategies for effective reading, use pages 59-60 in *Super Read!*

Quick Activity

Allow students to observe a freshwater fish tank containing aquatic snails attached to the sides of the tank. Point out the foot. Provide hand lenses and help students locate a snail's mouth and radula. Often the radula can be seen scraping algae from the glass walls of the tank.

530

 Mollusks share a common body plan that includes a muscular foot, a visceral mass, and a mantle. 22.2

22.2 Mollusks

What you'll learn

IDEAS
- To describe the characteristics of mollusks
- To distinguish among four classes of mollusks

WORDS
mantle, coelom, closed circulatory system

Have you ever seen a slug race? In Elma, Washington, where banana slugs are abundant, slug races are a highlight of the Elma Slug Festival. Training for the big race may include a special vegetarian diet and trial workouts. A "fast" winner takes about 43 seconds to go 0.003 furlongs at 0.055 kilometers per hour (0.034 miles per hour)—not too sluggish for a slug.

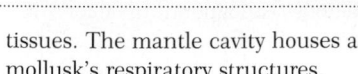

CHARACTERISTICS OF MOLLUSKS

Soft and squishy?

What do snails, slugs, scallops, and squids have in common? They are all mollusks. Although mollusks differ in appearance, they share important structural characteristics. Mollusks have a soft body that may be protected by a hard shell. Some mollusks, such as snails, have a single shell. Other mollusks, such as clams, have a two-piece shell. Squids and slugs have a light internal shell, and octopuses have no shell at all.

With or without a shell, all mollusks have a structure called a mantle—one of their three common characteristics. The **mantle** is the soft outer tissue layer on mollusks. In most mollusk species, the mantle produces a protective shell. An internal chamber—the mantle cavity—forms between the mantle and underlying tissues. The mantle cavity houses a mollusk's respiratory structures.

A second characteristic common to all mollusks is a muscular foot that is used for locomotion or attachment. In *Figure 22.10*, you can see two types of muscular foot.

Between the mollusk's foot and mantle is the visceral mass—the third structural characteristic of all mollusks. The visceral mass contains most of the mollusk's internal organs, such as the heart, gonads, and stomach.

Most—but not all—mollusks share a fourth characteristic: an open circulatory system. In this type of system, blood is enclosed in vessels in some places, but flows freely over body tissues in other places. A heart pumps blood into vessels that are open-ended. The blood flows out of the vessels and bathes the body organs. It then drains into small vessels, which carry it to the respiratory structures. These structures include the gills in the mantle cavity of aquatic mollusks and the lunglike mantle cavity of terrestrial mollusks. Gas exchange occurs in the respiratory structures as water or air moves over them. From the respiratory structures, blood moves back into the heart.

Clam foot

Squid foot

FIGURE 22.10
A clam's spade-like foot digs the clam into mud. A squid's modified foot is in the form of tentacles used to capture prey.

530 *Unit 6 Invertebrate Animals*

STUDENT RESOURCES

From the Teacher's Resource Package, use:
- Section Review 22.2 and Critical Thinking Exercise 22 from Unit 6 Review Module
- Consumer Applications 22-2

TECHNOLOGY RESOURCES

Relevant technology resources include:
- Spanish Student Edition CD-ROM
- Teacher's Resource Planner CD-ROM
- Biology Alive Video: "The Domain of Life"

Mollusks can move in a variety of ways. For example, clams burrow by using their foot as a shovel and a wedge. Snails "slide" on the mucus secreted by their foot. Squids and octopuses move by taking in water and then forcefully expelling it. A few mollusks, such as oysters and mussels, are sessile as adults.

Like roundworms, all mollusks have a digestive tract with two openings and specialized regions. In some mollusks, the digestive tract is a straight tube. In other mollusks, the digestive tract is coiled. A coiled intestine increases the length of the digestive tract and enables the animal to digest and absorb more nutrients.

Mollusks have evolved many methods of obtaining food. Most sessile and slow-moving mollusks are filter feeders. Filter feeders draw water into their mantle cavity, filtering bits of food from the water. Some mollusks, such as snails, are herbivores with special mouthparts adapted to gather vegetation or algae. Predatory mollusks, such as squids and octopuses, use their beaklike jaws to capture prey.

Some mollusks have simple nervous systems and lack true sense organs. Octopuses, however, have a complex nervous system, which includes a brain, eyes, and other sense organs.

Most mollusks have separate sexes, and all mollusks reproduce sexually. Reproduction in mollusks can involve external fertilization, as in clams, or internal fertilization, as in squids and some snails. External fertilization can

Planting Pearls

In aquatic mollusks, sand or grit often becomes trapped in the mantle. Some mollusks cover the sand or grit with the same material they use to make shells. When several layers of this shell material accumulate, the result is a pearl.

2 TEACH

Everyday Biology

Oyster farmers who own oyster beds can ensure a pearl is formed by implanting a grain of sand in each oyster in their oyster beds. This process, called seeding, also increases the chances of the oyster producing a high-quality pearl.

Use the Visual

Direct students to Figure 22.11 and discuss the function of each structure pictured. Point out that aquatic snails breathe with gills located in the mantle cavity, while land snails have a modified mantle cavity that acts like a lung. Snails are active in a moist environment. In a dry environment, they retreat into their shells, secreting a mucus plug that seals the opening to the shell and keeps them from drying out.

Think Critically

Explain that a visible difference between snails and slugs is the snail's shell. Ask:

- **What advantage do mollusks with shells have over those without shells?** (A shell protects soft body parts from predators and the environment. The shell captures and retains moisture, allowing some species to live on land.)

FIGURE 22.11

Structures of a Mollusk

No single organism is truly representative of mollusks because this phylum is so diverse. The snail pictured here illustrates some characteristics common to all mollusks.

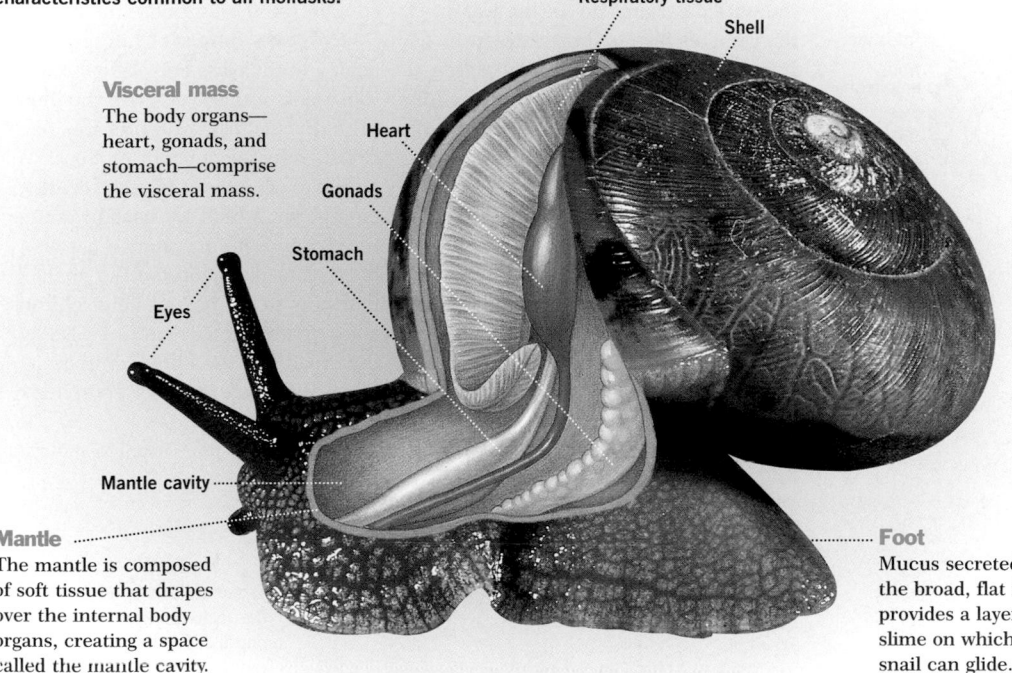

Visceral mass
The body organs—heart, gonads, and stomach—comprise the visceral mass.

Respiratory tissue

Shell

Heart

Gonads

Stomach

Eyes

Mantle cavity

Mantle
The mantle is composed of soft tissue that drapes over the internal body organs, creating a space called the mantle cavity.

Foot
Mucus secreted from the broad, flat foot provides a layer of slime on which the snail can glide.

Chapter 22 Worms and Mollusks **531**

MEETING DIVERSE NEEDS

Sight Impaired Provide students with examples of mollusks, either live specimens, models, or shells. Have them describe the structures. Help them to identify each mollusk. Students may wish to make models out of clay and other materials.

FACTS AND FIGURES

A clam anchors itself in mud or in sand with its foot. Once dug into the surface, its end swells with blood, causing the foot to enlarge and form a type of anchor. The muscles contract and pull the animals into the sand.

Use the Visual

Have students copy Figure 22.12 in their notebooks. Have them use resource materials to identify two animals that belong to each class.

Class Activity

Display a collection of different kinds of shells in class. Allow students to handle and observe the shells. Then have them use reference books to identify and label each different type of shell. You may wish to have students write a caption describing each shell and create a classroom display.

Use the Visual

Have students study Figure 22.13. Explain how an animal benefits from having a true coelom. Point out that the coelom allows food to move through the body because it separates the gut from the body and provides a space for a circulatory system to function without interference from other organs. The coelom also creates a hydrostatic skeleton. Ask:

■ **What is an important function of the coelom?** (It protects body organs.)

Kingdom: Animalia
Phylum: Mollusca
Four classes:
Polyplacophora
Gastropoda
Bivalvia
Cephalopoda

FIGURE 22.12
Phylum Mollusca

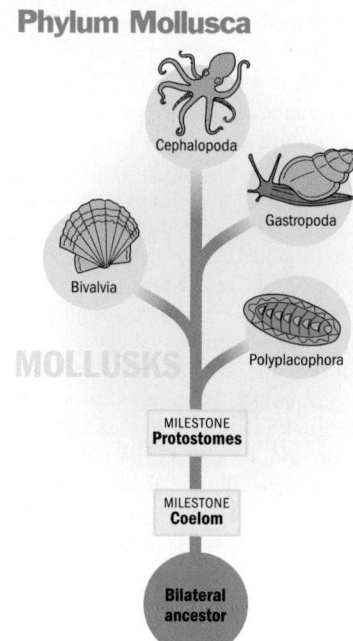

MOLLUSKS

MILESTONE
Protostomes

MILESTONE
Coelom

Bilateral ancestor

FIGURE 22.13
Cross Section of a Coelomate

A true coelom is a body cavity that is completely lined with mesoderm.

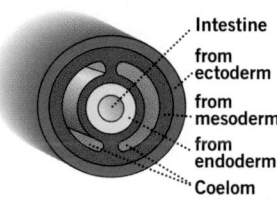

Intestine
from ectoderm
from mesoderm
from endoderm
Coelom

occur when two organisms simultaneously release sperm and eggs into the water, as clams do. In the water, the gametes fuse to form a zygote. Internal fertilization can occur when a male mollusk transfers sperm from his mantle cavity into the mantle cavity of a female mollusk. After fertilization, the female deposits the fertilized eggs in a protected place, where they continue their development.

Radula

ORIGIN AND DIVERSITY OF MOLLUSKS

From sea to desert

Mollusks are an ancient group of organisms that have adapted to almost every environment on Earth. With more than 100,000 species, mollusks are the second largest animal phylum.

Mollusks are descendants of the first animals to evolve with a coelom. A **coelom** (SEE-lum) is a body cavity completely lined with mesoderm. Animals with a coelom are called coelomates. A cross section of a coelomate is illustrated in *Figure 22.13*.

Recall from Chapter 21 that a major milestone in animal evolution involves different embryonic development patterns. Different patterns produce protostomes and deuterostomes. You will learn about these development patterns in Chapter 24. Mollusks are protostomes.

Scientists classify mollusks by their shell type, foot structure, and internal body arrangement. Of the seven mollusk classes currently recognized, four contain the most familiar mollusks.

Polyplacophora Chitons, which belong to the class Polyplacophora (poly-plak-oh-FOR-uh), are the most primitive mollusks and probably most closely resemble ancient mollusks. All chiton shells consist of eight overlapping plates, which are used to protect the chiton from predators. Chitons have a broad suction foot. In shallow marine waters, the foot helps chitons cling tightly to rocky surfaces. Using the broad foot for a hold, chitons move slowly across rocks, scraping

FIGURE 22.14
These chitons cling tightly to the rock, using their suction-cup-like foot to move and their radula to feed.

FIGURE 22.15
Some gastropods (left) have shells and others do not. Marine nudibranchs (below) have no shells, but their startling shapes and colors warn predators that they may be poisonous.

algae from the rocks with a tonguelike organ called a radula. A chiton's radula can have as many as 250,000 sharp, tiny, teethlike projections. You can see a close-up of radula in *Figure 22.14*.

Gastropoda This large class includes mollusks with shells, such as snails and conches. Gastropods also include slugs, which lack an external shell. Gastropods have a radula that either scrapes algae, shreds leaves, or captures prey. Their nervous system is more complex than that of chitons, as is their respiratory system. Most aquatic gastropods have gills. Terrestrial gastropods have a mantle cavity lining that is modified for gas exchange.

Bivalvia Have you ever eaten a bivalve—a clam, mussel, scallop, or oyster? The word *bivalve* comes from

"bi-," meaning "two," and "valvia," meaning "shells." A hinge attaches the two shells of a bivalve. Strong muscles control the opening and closing of the hinged shells, allowing a bivalve to control the flow of water over its body.

Most bivalves are filter feeders. As water containing plankton flows over their gills, mucus produced by the gills traps the plankton. Cilia on the gill cells move the plankton from the gills into the bivalve's mouth. In mollusks and other filter feeders, gills can function in both feeding and respiration.

Although some bivalves live in fresh water, most inhabit marine environments. Bivalves such as clams are slow-moving; others, such as mussels, are sessile.

Eyespots

FIGURE 22.16
Scallops can rapidly open and close their shells, allowing them to move through the water. Their eyespots enable them to see predators.

Chapter 22 Worms and Mollusks **533**

FACTS AND FIGURES

One species of clam is known as the giant clam. It lives in the South Pacific Ocean and can grow to 1.5 meters (4.9 feet) across and weigh more than 250 kilograms (550 pounds).

As gastropod larvae develop, the visceral mass twists 180 degrees. This brings the mantle cavity to the front and allows the animal to pull its head into the mantle cavity when in danger.

Teacher Demo

Display a rasp file and allow students to touch its surface. Use the file on a piece of scrap wood. Explain that a radula works in much the same manner as the file as it scrapes algae from surfaces in the animal's habitat.

Class Activity

TEAM WORK

Provide small groups of students with several clam shells and show a picture of a cross section of a tree. Explain that just as the rings in the wood indicate the age of the tree, so do the rings on a clam shell indicate age. Have students determine the age of each shell.

Clarify Misconceptions

Mussels, clams, shrimp, and oysters often are referred to as "shellfish." Explain that these animals are not true fishes. They belong to the Phylum Mollusca or Phylum Arthropoda. True fishes are vertebrates.

Teacher Demo

Show students a hinged pill box or face powder compact and two bivalve shells. Explain that the shells of a bivalve, such as a clam or oyster, operate in the same way as the pill box does. Point out that the animal's muscle acts as a hinge to open and close the shells.

Explain

The chambered nautilus got its name because its shell is divided into chambers. The animal lives in the outer chamber. It releases gas into another chamber to regulate the depths at which it swims. Ask:

- **How do you think the gas chamber would help the nautilus to change its depth?** (When the chamber is filled with gas, the animal rises in the water. Releasing the gas from the chamber would cause the animal to sink.)

Think Critically

Have students discuss what advantage well-developed eyes would be to an octopus.

Teacher Demo

Show students a cuttlebone used in bird cages. Explain that the cuttlebone is the internal shell of the cuttlefish. Canaries and budgies use the cuttlebone to sharpen their beaks. You may wish to allow students to handle the bone and observe its color, weight, and porosity.

 Literature

Read aloud to the class "The Chambered Nautilus," a popular poem written by Oliver Wendell Holmes and first published in 1858. Point out that the "ship of pearl" described in the poem is found in the Indian Ocean and the South Pacific Ocean. Encourage students to share their impressions of the poem.

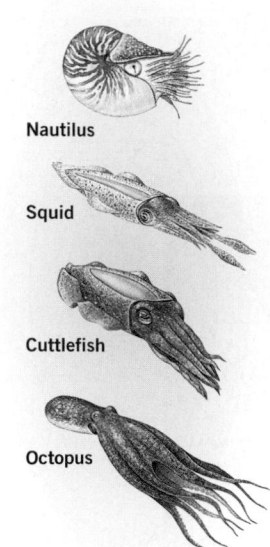

Nautilus

Squid

Cuttlefish

Octopus

FIGURE 22.17

Shell Evolution in Cephalopods

Beginning with the nautilus, the cephalopods' shells have gradually reduced over time. Squid and cuttlefish have only small, internal shells, and octopuses have entirely lost their shells.

Cephalopoda Cephalopods (SEF-uh-loh-pahdz) include nautiluses, cuttlefishes, squids, and octopuses. Scientists think this group is the most recently evolved class of mollusks. There are four cephalopods shown in *Figure 22.17*. Cephalopods first appeared in the fossil record of about 500 million years ago. The modern cephalopods, such as the octopus, differ little from its ancient ancestor.

Cephalopods have a highly developed nervous system. A large brain and an extensive network of nerves enable cephalopods to respond quickly and control their body motions efficiently. Octopuses are considered to be among the most intelligent invertebrates.

Unlike other mollusks, cephalopods have a **closed circulatory system.**

In a closed circulatory system, blood travels inside a continuous network of vessels. A closed circulatory system provides tissues with a more controlled supply of oxygen and nutrients than does an open circulatory system. The closed circulatory system has probably contributed to the success of cephalopods as fast-moving predators. In a closed circulatory system, the supply of blood to different body parts can be controlled. This system supports the active, predatory lifestyle of cephalopods by more rapidly supplying their muscles with oxygen and nutrient-rich blood.

Some species of squids and octopuses grow very large. The giant squid *Architeuthis* is the world's largest living invertebrate. The largest one measured was longer than 18 meters! Giant squids live in deep waters of the North Atlantic, where their only predators are thought to be sperm whales.

FIGURE 22.18

The cuttlefish (left) has remarkable color-changing abilities, blending with the background or contrasting with it when excited or threatened. The octopus (below) has a large brain and versatile tentacles that make it a fearsome predator.

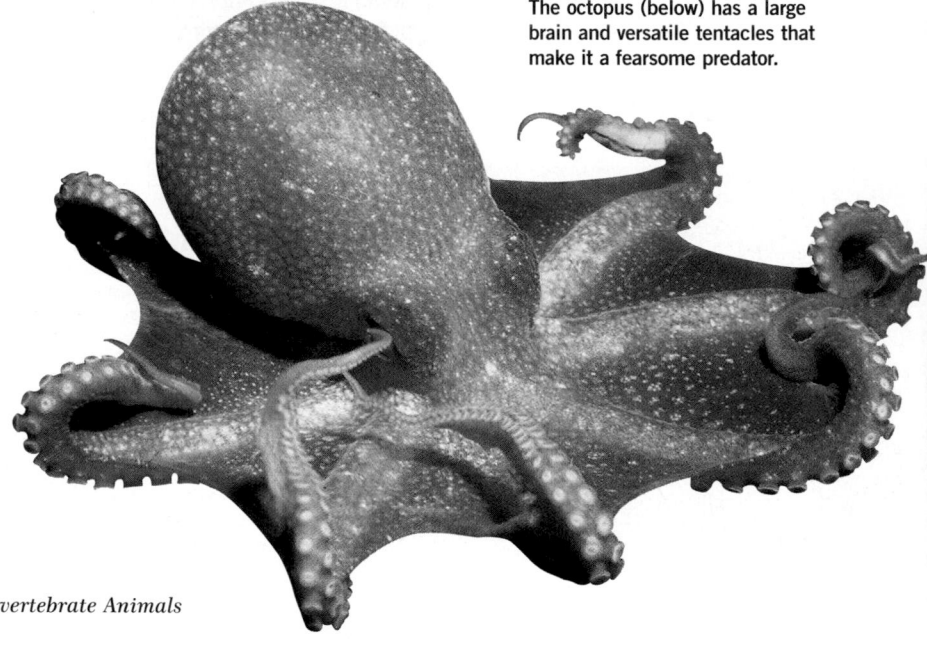

534 *Unit 6 Invertebrate Animals*

MULTICULTURAL PERSPECTIVE

Mollusks have been part of the folklore of many cultures. A mythological giant squid is the "kraken" in Jules Verne's novel. Aphrodite, the Greek goddess of love and beauty, sat on a silver throne shaped like a scallop shell and traveled on a giant scallop shell.

FACTS AND FIGURES

Shipworms are not really worms, but filter-feeding mollusks that ingest wood. Symbiotic protozoa living in the shipworms' intestines break down the cellulose in the wood.

MOLLUSKS IN THE BIOSPHERE

Put a foot in your mouth

Many mollusks—such as clams, oysters, mussels, scallops, snails, squids, and octopuses—are valued as food in many cultures. Humans even eat chitons and sea slugs. Mollusks also have a role in other food chains—either as predators or prey.

In addition to being a food source, mollusks are used to monitor environmental conditions. Filter-feeding mollusks concentrate pollutants in their tissues, which scientists can analyze to determine water purity. Some mollusks, including sea slugs, are also being investigated as potential sources of medicines.

Mollusks are not always beneficial, however. Snails and slugs consume crops, costing farmers millions of dollars annually. Marine mollusks called shipworms destroy boats and docks constructed of wood.

ENVIRONMENTAL AWARENESS

Mussels on the move

In 1988 a small freshwater species of zebra mussel was accidentally introduced into Lake Erie from Europe. Less than ten years later the mollusks had spread into all the Great Lakes and their tributaries. These rapidly reproducing mussels compete with other species for food. They also clog water-intake pipes, causing major problems for water-treatment and power plants. They have even clogged farm-irrigation pipes miles inland.

In order to stop the spread of zebra mussels into other lakes and streams, county extension services distribute information to people who use mussel-infested waters for industry or recreation. Boaters and anglers are reminded not to carry water from one lake or stream to another. The larval stage of the mussel is microscopic and can live undetected for days in bilges and bait buckets. Although natural predators of zebra mussels exist in Europe, none has been identified in North America. Most states east of the Mississippi River are gearing up for an "invasion" of these pests, and researchers are feverishly investigating ways to control them.

The spread of zebra mussels has had one benefit, however. Where zebra mussels have heavily colonized cloudy Great Lakes waters, their filter-feeding action has made the water clearer.

FIGURE 22.19
Zebra mussels reproduce rapidly, settling on any available hard surface, including one another. Treatments to kill the mussels that have settled in pipes do not necessarily remove them. What are some ways engineers might deal with this problem? ❶

CHECKPOINT 22.2

1. Describe the main structures of mollusks. How can they vary?
2. Compare four classes of mollusks.
3. **Critical Thinking** In addition to being transported by boaters and anglers, how might zebra mussels spread to new environments?

Build on What You Know

4. How is filter feeding in mollusks similar to the way sponges gather food? *(Need to jog your memory? Revisit relevant concepts in Chapter 21, Section 21.2.)*

What characteristics are common to all mollusks? **?**

Chapter 22 Worms and Mollusks **535**

Chapter Objectives

Students will learn the main concepts of this chapter as they complete the following objectives.

- Describe the characteristics and diversity of arthropods
- Compare the three main groups of arthropods
- Describe the characteristics of crustaceans
- Compare the four types of crustaceans
- Describe the characteristics of chelicerates
- Compare chelicerate diversity and explain functions of chelicerate adaptations
- Describe the characteristics of the uniramians
- Compare and contrast the diversity of insects
- Describe various insect adaptations
- Identify many of the varied roles arthropods play in the biosphere

Key Words

23.1 *exoskeleton, endoskeleton, compound eyes*

23.2 *cephalothorax, mandibles*

23.3 *chelicerae, Malpighian tubules, pedipalps*

23.4 *spiracles, metamorphosis, pheromones, social insects, mimicry*

The Opening Story

Have students read the story and discuss the amazing migration of these monarch butterflies. Have students infer how the butterflies find their way to and from Mexico each year. Ask if students can name other animals that migrate.

---

bioSURF

You can find out more about arthropods by exploring the following Internet address:
http://invertebrates.biosurf.com

In this chapter . . .

FEATURES

Everyday Biology
- Silk Stops Bullet
- No Stinger, Less Pain

In the Community
Insect Control?

Frontiers in Biology
Pesticide Alternatives

LAB ZONES

Discover It!
- Looking Under a Rock

Do It!
- Look at Those Sensors!

Think About It!
- Identifying Insect Camouflage and Mimicry

Investigate It!
- Observing the Mealworm Life Cycle

MONARCHS
FLY MORE THAN 2000 MILES

One of the most spectacular animal migrations occurs each fall, when vast swarms of monarch butterflies leave the United States for the winter. For years no one knew where the monarchs actually went, but in the mid-1970s their winter hiding place was discovered in a stretch of highlands just west of Mexico City. There, in warmer temperatures, the butterflies roost—as many as 4 million per acre—covering the trees with brilliant blankets of color.

During this amazing odyssey, several generations of the monarchs are born, breed, and die before a generation reaches the Mexican mountains—as far as 2200 miles from the departure point. The same is true during the monarchs' return migration from Mexico in the spring, when some of the butterflies travel as far north as Canada.

How do monarch butterflies that have never been to the roosting sites in Mexico find their way there each year? This is one of many mysteries that scientists seek to unlock as they study arthropods.

 Discover It!

Looking Under a Rock

You need some small boxes or jars in which to collect your specimens

1. Find at least three large flat rocks or decaying logs. Turn them over and collect a representative sample of the organisms living there. Identify as many as you can. Then return the specimens where you found them, and replace the logs or stones. Caution: Some organisms bite and may be poisonous.
2. Repeat step 1 in a different environment. Environments to sample may include a stream, the woods, a field or pasture, a stone wall, a woodpile, desert areas, or city parks.
3. Compare your results with those of your classmates. How many different environments did you and your classmates sample? How many different organisms did you all find?

Arthropods are present in just about every environment. If you chose two sufficiently different environments to investigate, you should have found a different group of organisms in each.

WRITE ABOUT IT!

In your journal, write a story from the perspective of one of the insects you collected.

Chapter 23 Arthropods **545**

Opening Activities

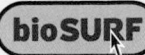 If you have access to the Internet in your classroom or school, you may wish to have students connect to the address shown on page 544. You may also want to have students conduct net searches for information using key words related to this chapter. For example, they could search for entries under crustaceans, Lyme disease, and insects.

Discover It!
Looking Under a Rock TEAM WORK

Before assigning the activity, discuss safety tips and guidelines for field research with the class. Suggest students work with a partner or in a small group to explore different environments.

WRITE ABOUT IT

Have volunteers read their stories to the class. Have students compare their findings, then write some of the similarities and differences on the board. You may want to return to this activity later in the chapter.

REWIND to Chapter 22

Briefly review concepts learned in Chapter 22, *Worms and Mollusks.* Ask:

■ **How do you think the study of worms and mollusks will help you when you study crustaceans, spiders, and insects in Chapter 23?**

PORTFOLIO PREVIEW

Students should be encouraged to add to their portfolios as they work through this chapter. In addition to the *Write About It* opportunity, the following sections are excellent opportunities for portfolio entries:

■ Section 23.1: *Arthropods*
■ Section 23.4: *Insects and Their Relatives*

ENGAGE

Consider The Big Idea!

Have students read The Big Idea! at the top of the page. Point out that arthropods have more specialized structures than mollusks and annelids.

Use the Visual

Have students look at the photograph and read the text that opens the section. Explain that the key to the beetle's strength is in its specialized structures. Ask:

- **How many pounds could you carry if you were as strong as the rhinoceros beetle?** (Answers will vary.)

Teacher Demo

Show students photographs, preserved specimens, or jointed models of arthropods. Point out their structural characteristics and list the traits on the board. Ask:

- **What do you find most interesting about arthropods?** (Answers will vary.)
- **How do arthropods differ from the worms and mollusks you studied in Chapter 22?** (Arthropods have an exoskeleton and jointed appendages.)

❶ They have claws for catching prey.

❷ No, the images are seen as a mosaic and they are out of focus.

546

THE BIG IDEA! Arthropods are segmented invertebrates with jointed appendages and an exoskeleton. 23.1

23.1 Arthropods

What you'll learn

IDEAS
- To describe the characteristics of arthropods
- To compare the three arthropod subphyla

WORDS
exoskeleton, endoskeleton, compound eyes

World-class weight lifter
The rhinoceros beetle—able to carry up to 100 times its own weight—is a model of biomechanical efficiency. Because it can tote over 200 grams on its 2-gram frame, it is, gram for gram, the world's strongest animal. Researchers are studying the beetle's muscles and skeleton to try to explain its mighty strength.

CHARACTERISTICS OF ARTHROPODS

Bend a leg

The phylum Arthropoda is the largest and most diverse animal phylum. Arthropods inhabit every region of Earth—from ocean bottoms to mountain tops. Spiders, crabs, scorpions, and lobsters; bees, beetles, caterpillars, and fleas; ticks, mites, and lice are all arthropods. Why are such different organisms classified together?

All arthropods share certain structural characteristics. Like annelids, arthropods have segmented bodies. But in most arthropods, the segments are fused into larger body regions.

FIGURE 23.1
Arthropods have specialized jointed appendages. Notice the differences between the three pairs of legs on this praying mantis. How is the first pair of legs adapted to a predatory lifestyle? ❶

Unlike annelids, arthropods have jointed appendages. (In fact, the word *arthropoda* means "jointed feet.") The jointed appendages of arthropods are specialized for sensing, eating, reproducing, defending, or moving.

In addition to a segmented body with jointed appendages, arthropods have an exoskeleton made of chitin. An **exoskeleton** is a hard covering on the outside of the body, which provides both support and protection. The muscles that move the appendages of arthropods are attached to the inside of the exoskeleton. In contrast, humans and other vertebrates have an endoskeleton. An **endoskeleton** is a framework of bones and cartilage on the inside of the body. Exoskeletons provide greater protection for the body than do endoskeletons.

Although an exoskeleton provides protection, it limits the size of the organism. To grow, arthropods must shed their exoskeletons periodically in a process called molting. When an arthropod molts, it grows a new layer of chitin beneath its exoskeleton. Then it forces fluid between the new layer of chitin and its old exoskeleton. The pressure from the fluid splits the old exoskeleton, and the arthropod crawls

546 *Unit 6 Invertebrate Animals*

STUDENT RESOURCES

From the Teacher's Resource Package, use:
- Section Review 23.1 from Unit 6 Review Module

 **TECHNOLOGY RESOURCES**

Relevant technology resources include:
- Spanish Student Edition CD-ROM
- Teacher's Resource Planner CD-ROM

out. In *Figure* 23.2, you can see an arthropod that has just molted. At first, its new exoskeleton is tough, but soft and flexible. Eventually it hardens. The hardening process can take from minutes to days, depending on the species. During and immediately after molting, arthropods are highly vulnerable to injury and predation.

Along with specialized jointed appendages, arthropods have evolved a complex muscular system. This system is more extensive than the circular and longitudinal muscles that are common to the invertebrates discussed earlier. This extensive muscular system enables the arthropod to perform a great variety of movements.

The arthropod nervous system consists of a ventral nerve cord and brain. In each body segment, the nerve cord swells into additional ganglia (nerve cell clusters). Nerve impulses are transmitted to and from the body parts through these ganglia.

You may recall that most mollusks have an open circulatory system, in which blood flows through open-ended vessels and bathes the body tissues directly. Arthropods also have an open circulatory system.

Aquatic arthropods, such as crabs, have external gills for respiration. Terrestrial arthropods, such as insects, have tracheal tubes—chitin-lined channels—where the exchange of oxygen and carbon dioxide occurs.

Many arthropods have **compound eyes**—multifaceted eyes with many separate lenses that work together to form a single, mosaic image. In a compound eye, such as that of the horsefly shown in *Figure* 23.3, each lens sees a slightly different part of an object. It is possible that the image of the object is not in focus, but its motion and color are clearly sensed. Not all arthropods have compound eyes. Many, such as spiders, have single-lens eyes. Some arthropods, such as horseshoe crabs, have both types of eyes.

ORIGIN AND DIVERSITY

From trilobites to insect bites

Trilobites are an extinct group of arthropods that scientists think were among the first arthropods to evolve. This group of organisms thrived on Earth about 600 million years ago. More than 4000 species of trilobites have been identified from the fossil record. Like all arthropods, trilobites had segmented bodies. Each trilobite body segment had an identical pair of jointed legs. But unlike modern arthropods, none of the trilobite species had legs modified for a special function.

Modern, more recently evolved arthropods tend to have fewer body

FIGURE 23.3

The compound eye—a structure that evolved only in arthropods—has many separate lenses. Do compound eyes detect images as we see them?

FIGURE 23.2

This cicada has just molted, leaving behind its old exoskeleton. A newly molted arthropod has difficulty moving until its new exoskeleton hardens.

Chapter 23 Arthropods **547**

TEACH

Use the Visual

Have students study Figures 23.1 and 23.2. Point out how the arthropod's body is divided into regions. Explain that arthropods and segmented worms are similar because they both have segmented bodies. Ask:

- **How is segmentation in the body of an arthropod different from segmentation in a worm?** (The arthropod does not have as many repeated segments; the segments are fused into larger body regions.)

Earth Science

Some paleontologists use trilobites in dating rock layers. Trilobites evolved during the Cambrian period (about 570 million years ago) and became extinct in the Permian period (280 million years ago). Trilobites evolved rapidly, but no one species existed for a long time. As a result, each geologic period is marked by specific species of trilobites.

Use the Visual

Have students study the arthropods pictured in Figure 23.2 Ask:

- **How does an exoskeleton protect arthropods?** (It helps protect them from dehydration, predators, external parasites, and injury.)
- **What would happen to an arthropod if it could not molt?** (It would not grow larger because an exoskeleton does not grow or stretch as skin does.)

MEETING DIVERSE NEEDS

LEP Have LEP students compile a picture dictionary illustrating the meaning of key words used in each section. Suggest that they begin by looking up the meanings of the prefixes "exo-" and "endo-" in the dictionary.

FACTS AND FIGURES

Students may be interested to know that humans have found some practical uses for arthropods. For example, because of its strength and transparency, chitin from discarded exoskeletons is used in making surgical sutures and dressings, contact lenses, artificial skin, and varnish.

Explain

Point out to students that some biologists consider the *Peripatus* shown in Figure 23.5 to be a true arthropod, not just a "missing link" between annelids and arthropods. These biologists contend that annelids and arthropods may not be closely related. They hypothesize that segmentation evolved independently in annelids and arthropods and that their last common ancestor may have been an unsegmented animal such as an early mollusk.

Build Writing Skills

Have students write a short paragraph or poem describing their last encounter with an arthropod. Ask them to describe what they saw, felt, heard, thought, and possibly even tasted!

3 ASSESS

Evaluate Understanding

List the following traits on the board: *segmented body, jointed appendages, antennae, exoskeleton, molting, open circulatory system, and compound eyes.* Ask students to use these traits to compare arthropods with mollusks and annelids.

Reteach

Have students work in pairs and take turns describing the characteristics and systems of arthropods to each other. Remind them to use the illustrations as well as the text as reference.

| Kingdom: Animalia |
| Phylum: Arthropoda |
| **Four subphyla:** |
| Crustacea |
| Chelicerata |
| Uniramia |
| Trilobita |

segments than trilobites had. Many have highly specialized appendages adapted for very specific functions.

It is not clear whether arthropods and annelids both evolved from a common ancestor, or whether arthropods evolved from annelids. The wormlike *Peripatus*, shown in *Figure 23.5*, has some characteristics of annelids and others of arthropods. Some biologists think that ancestors of *Peripatus* may represent an evolutionary link between annelids and arthropods. For this reason, they classify *Peripatus* in a separate phylum.

One possible theory of arthropod evolution is shown in the phylogenetic tree in *Figure 23.4*. The three living subphyla of arthropods are distinguished by differences in their appendages. Crustaceans (krus-TAY-shunz) have legs with claws, chewing mouthparts, and two pairs of antennae. Chelicerates (kee-LIS-er-uhts)

FIGURE 23.5

Peripatus is segmented and has paired appendages, as well as antennae and claws typical of arthropods. However, its appendages are not jointed, and it lacks a hard exoskeleton. Is *Peripatus* more like an annelid or an arthropod? ❶

FIGURE 23.4

Phylum Arthropoda

The evolutionary history of arthropods is not well established. This depiction is only one theory of arthropod evolution.

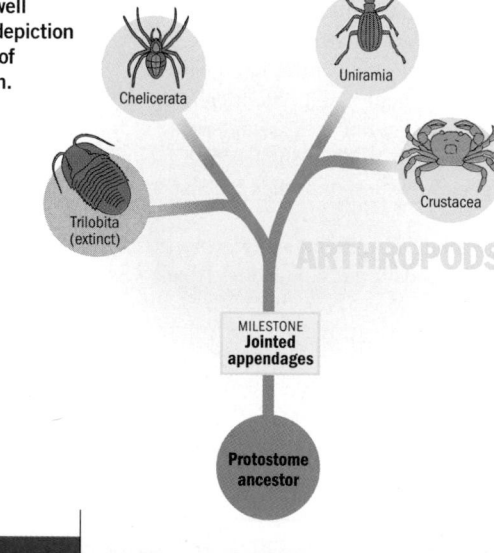

Chelicerata

Uniramia

Trilobita (extinct)

Crustacea

ARTHROPODS

MILESTONE
Jointed appendages

Protostome ancestor

? **What characteristics are common to all arthropods?**

548 *Unit 6 Invertebrate Animals*

have pincerlike mouthparts and no antennae. Uniramians (yoo-nih-RAY-mee-unz) have chewing mouthparts, one pair of antennae, and no claws. You will learn about each of these groups as you continue reading this chapter.

CHECKPOINT 23.1

1. Describe the main characteristics of all arthropods.
2. What are the distinguishing features of the three living subphyla of arthropods?
3. **Critical Thinking** Why might arthropods that have just molted be more at risk from predators?

Build on What You Know

4. What characteristics do arthropods and mollusks share? *(Need to jog your memory? Revisit relevant concepts in Chapter 22, Section 22.2.)*

CHECKPOINT 23.1

1. Segmented body, jointed appendages, and chitin exoskeletons
2. Crustaceans—legs with claws, chewing mouthparts, two pairs of antennae; chelicerates—pincerlike mouthparts, no antennae; uniramians—chewing mouthparts, one pair of antennae

3. **Developing a hypothesis** Their bodies are softer.
4. Open circulatory systems, gills (marine only), and some organs

❶ *Peripatus* seems more like an annelid; both are segmented, have paired appendages, and lack a hard exoskeleton.

23.2 Crustaceans

Spiny lobsters, single file

When fall arrives and the Atlantic waters off the Florida coast get cold, spiny lobsters migrate toward warmer waters. As many as 100,000 lobsters travel day and night in chains of 50 or 60. They move single file in a crustacean "conga line," using their antennae to keep in touch.

What you'll learn

IDEAS
- To describe the characteristics of crustaceans
- To compare four groups of crustaceans

WORDS
cephalothorax, mandibles

CHARACTERISTICS OF CRUSTACEANS

Moving swimmingly

Crustaceans, like all arthropods, are so diverse that no single species is truly representative of the entire group. However, the lobster shown in *Figure 23.6* and the crayfish in *Figure 23.7* show some typical crustacean characteristics.

Most crustaceans have two body regions: a cephalothorax and an abdomen. The **cephalothorax** (sef-uh-loh-THOR-aks) is the fused head and thorax, or chest region, to which legs and other appendages are attached. The cephalothorax is covered by a hard shield of chitin called the carapace, which protects the body organs. The abdomen in lobsters and crayfish is the long narrow tail region that ends with the central telson and paired uropods.

As you study *Figure 23.6*, observe the appendages on the anterior end. The first two pairs of appendages are antennae. The first pair of antennae is short, but the second pair is usually as long as the crustacean's body. All crustaceans also have one pair of jaw-like appendages called **mandibles** that chew and crush food. Behind the mandibles are two other pairs of

mouthparts, called maxillae, that hold food and pass it to the mouth. The lobster has three pairs of jaw feet, called maxillipeds, that touch, taste, and handle food. Large claws are used for catching food and for defense. The last four segments of the cephalothorax have one pair of walking legs each.

FIGURE 23.6

The Appendages of a Crustacean (lobster)

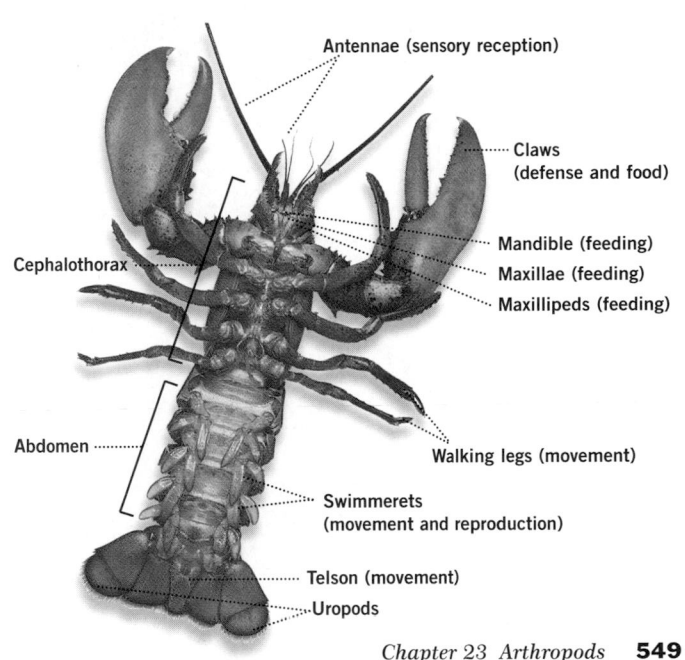

- Antennae (sensory reception)
- Claws (defense and food)
- Mandible (feeding)
- Maxillae (feeding)
- Maxillipeds (feeding)
- Cephalothorax
- Abdomen
- Walking legs (movement)
- Swimmerets (movement and reproduction)
- Telson (movement)
- Uropods

Chapter 23 Arthropods **549**

1 ENGAGE

Consider The Big Idea

Have students read The Big Idea! at the top of the page. Point out that crustaceans, although divided into four groups, share similar characteristics.

Use the Visual

Have students study the photograph that opens the section. Explain that antennae are appendages that crustaceans use for sensory reception. Discuss the fact that the responses of crustaceans, like those of all arthropods, depend solely on the various stimuli received by their nerves. Ask:

- **Why do you think lobsters use their antennae to "keep in touch" during their migration?** (The antennae help facilitate movement in low light.)

Teacher Demo

Display a preserved crayfish or a model. Point out the features shown in Figure 23.6. Let students touch the crayfish or model and have them compare the physical characteristics of the crayfish with those of arthropods.

STUDENT RESOURCES

From the Teacher's Resource Package, use:
- Section Review 23.2 from Unit 6 Review Module

TECHNOLOGY RESOURCES

Relevant technology resources include:
- Spanish Student Edition CD-ROM
- Teacher's Resource Planner CD-ROM
- Animated Biological Concepts Videodiscs: "Crayfish Anatomy"
- Biology Alive! Videotape: "Signs of Life"

2 **TEACH**

Class Activity

Divide the class into small groups. Provide each with a sample of living brine shrimp, hand lenses or stereoscopes, petri dishes, and eyedroppers. Have students study the shrimp and record their observations. Discuss observations as a class. Ask:

- **What characteristics of crustaceans could you see in your samples?** (Answers should include exoskeletons, jointed appendages, and two body segments.)

 Chemistry

Students may be interested to know that some crustaceans have calcium carbonate in their exoskeletons. Explain that calcium carbonate is the same chemical compound from which limestone rocks on land are made. Explain that $CaCO_3$ is dissolved in sea water and diffuses into the crustaceans' blood through gills.

 Animated Biological Concepts

Crayfish Anatomy   Play

Kingdom: Animalia
Phylum: Arthropoda
Subphylum: Crustacea
Classes:
Copepoda
Cirripedia
Orders:
Decapoda
Isopoda

The abdomen has pairs of appendages called swimmerets that are used for swimming. In female crabs, crayfish, and lobsters, developing eggs are attached to the swimmerets. At the end of the abdomen is the telson and uropods which are used for rapid backward locomotion.

Crustaceans, like all arthropods, have a ventral nerve cord. In each body segment, the nerve cord swells into a pair of ganglia. Nerve impulses are transmitted to and from other body parts through the ganglia. The brain, located at the front end of the nerve cord, consists of fused ganglia.

Like most crustaceans, the crayfish has a pair of compound eyes. The eyes are located above the sensory antennae, at the ends of movable eyestalks. The eyestalks allow the animal to look in any direction, and even in two different directions at once.

The crayfish begins feeding by crushing and chewing food with its mandibles. In the stomach, teeth made of chitin located on the stomach wall grind the crushed food into smaller particles. The food particles are moved to a structure called the digestive gland, where food is mixed with digestive enzymes and nutrients are absorbed into the body. Undigested material is passed through the intestines and out the anus.

At the base of the antennae is an excretory organ called the green gland, which regulates the amount of salt

FIGURE 23.7

The Structures of a Crustacean (crayfish)

Some of the internal structures of a typical crayfish are schematically represented.

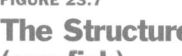 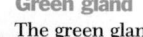

Green gland The green gland enables aquatic crustaceans to maintain proper salt and water concentrations in the blood.

Antennae Crustaceans have two pairs of antennae, used in sensing taste, touch, water chemistry, and balance.

Intestine · Digestive gland · Heart · Stomach · Brain · Eye

Gills The gills are located under the carapace. A pair of appendages called gill bailers located on the second maxillae beat back and forth, creating a current that draws water over the gills towards the head.

Nerve cord

MEETING DIVERSE NEEDS

Sight Impaired Have these students work with sighted students to create raised-letter labels for the preserved crayfish or model. Have them use Figures 23.6 and 23.7 as guides.

and liquid in the blood. In freshwater crustaceans, the green gland is especially important because it retains salt and removes excess water.

CRUSTACEAN DIVERSITY

A crabby bunch

Lift a rock or a log, and you will probably see small, gray bugs scurrying away. In the supermarket, you have probably seen tanks of live lobsters or crabs. These animals, along with shrimps, barnacles, and hermit crabs, are all crustaceans. Most of the tens of thousands of crustaceans are adapted to a marine environment. But some, like the crayfish, live in fresh water. Pill bugs and a few species of tropical crabs are some of the only crustaceans that live in terrestrial environments.

Crustaceans vary in size. Among the smallest crustaceans are copepods, which are less than 0.25 millimeter (mm) across. Copepods are a main component of plankton; they feed on microscopic algae. They have five pairs of appendages on the thorax, but do not have gills or abdominal appendages.

Crustaceans with 10 walking legs are decapods. ("Deca-" means "ten.") Crayfish, crabs, lobsters, and shrimp are all decapods. Decapods are the largest crustaceans; the king crab can grow as large as 5 meters (m) across. Most decapods are carnivores and scavengers that live on the ocean bottom.

Pill bugs, sow bugs, and wood lice are all isopods. These isopods are well adapted to moist, dark, terrestrial environments, feeding on decayed organic matter. Their swimmerets are modified to obtain oxygen from the air. When threatened, pill bugs roll up into a tight ball for protection, as shown in *Figure 23.8*. How might this behavior protect them from predators?

FIGURE 23.8
Commonly called pill bugs, these isopods can be found in almost any dark, terrestrial environment—even in houses. Have you ever seen them in or around your house?

Cerripeds, which include the barnacles shown in *Figure 23.9*, are shelled, sessile crustaceans. They are often found attached to coastal rocks, boat hulls, and even whales and sea turtles. Adult barnacles secrete a pyramid-shaped exoskeleton with an opening at the top. They extend specialized appendages— featherlike legs—through this opening to sweep food from the water into their mouths.

Unlike most crustaceans, adult barnacles have no eyes, gills, heart, or blood vessels. However, the free-swimming larvae of barnacles closely resemble the larvae of other crustaceans. Until scientists studied their motile larval stage, barnacles were not classified as crustaceans.

FIGURE 23.9
Large numbers of barnacle larvae attach themselves to an underwater object, where they remain for the rest of their lives. These adult barnacles have their feeding appendages extended.

CHECKPOINT 23.2

1. Describe the main characteristics of crustaceans.
2. What are the differences between the four groups of crustaceans discussed?
3. **Critical Thinking** Nearly all crustaceans are aquatic. What challenges do terrestrial crustaceans face, and what adaptations help them overcome these challenges?

Build on What You Know

4. How do marine crustaceans differ from cnidarians that live in the ocean? *(Need to jog your memory? Revisit relevant concepts in Chapter 21, Section 21.4.)*

Chapter 23 Arthropods **551**

Language Arts

Have students look up the words *copepod, isopod, decapod,* and *cirripedia* in the dictionary. Tell them to write definitions and the origins of each word.

3 **ASSESS**

Evaluate Understanding

To assess students' understanding of crustaceans, ask:

- **What are the four groups of crustaceans? Give an example from each group.** (Copepoda, copepods; Decapoda, crayfish, crabs, lobsters, shrimp; Isopoda; pill bugs, sow bugs, wool lice; Cirripedia, barnacles)
- **What are the major characteristics shared by all crustaceans?** (Most are aquatic and have two body regions, mandibles and maxillae, a ventral nerve cord, two pairs of antennae, and clawed and other specialized appendages.)

Reteach

Work with students to fill in a chart with the headings *Function* and *Structure*. In the first column list these functions: *movement digestion, sensory reception, respiration, excretion,* and *reproduction*. Then have students list the crayfish structures associated with each function.

CHECKPOINT 23.2

1. Two body regions, two pairs of antennae, mandibles, compound eyes
2. Copepods—no gills or abdominal appendages; decapods—five pairs of walking legs; isopods—modified swimmerettes; barnacles—sessile, no eyes, gills, heart, or blood vessels

3. **Applying** They must get oxygen from air using modified swimmerettes; they need to retain water by living in moist areas or by rolling into a ball.
4. Marine crustaceans have exoskeletons and more highly developed body systems and sense organs than cnidarians.

❶ They are smaller and harder to grab; none of the smaller, softer body parts are accessible.

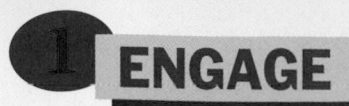

Use the Visual

Have students study the photograph and read the text that opens the section. Ask:

- **What observations can you make about the eyes of this wolf spider?** (Student should observe that the spider has eight, or four pairs, of simple eyes.)
- **How would you describe the vision of this spider species?** (Acute enough to differentiate other spiders of its species in a video)

Teacher Demo

Bring a toy rubber spider to class or display pictures of different types of spiders. Ask students why they think so many people are afraid of spiders. Point out that spiders typically do not bother humans, but are actually beneficial because they eat insects and help to control the insect population.

Everyday Biology

Explain to students that spider silk is produced as a liquid in glands in the spider's abdomen. It later solidifies into extremely strong threads that form the radial framework of the web.

23.3 Spiders and Their Relatives

What you'll learn

IDEAS

- To describe the characteristics of chelicerates
- To compare types of chelicerates
- To describe structures and adaptations of chelicerates

WORDS

chelicerae, Malpighian tubules, pedipalps

EVERYDAY BIOLOGY

Silk Stops Bullet

In 1881 a physician noted that the fatal bullet in a man's chest had not penetrated his silk pocket handkerchief, which protruded from the wound. Some spider silk is even stronger. In many ways it is superior to the material used in bulletproof vests.

A spider video-dating service?
Male wolf spiders have hairy legs; males of a related species do not. Researchers altered images of both species of males, adding hair to hairless legs and removing it from hairy legs. When female wolf spiders viewed videos of the males, they reacted positively to those with hairy legs, regardless of the species.

CHARACTERISTICS OF CHELICERATES

Good reception without antennae

Like the bodies of crustaceans, those of most chelicerates are divided into two segments: a cephalothorax and an abdomen. Chelicerates—spiders and their relatives—share three broad characteristics. First, unlike other arthropod groups, chelicerates do not have sensory antennae. Second, most chelicerates have simple eyes, not compound eyes. Third, all chelicerates have a pair of appendages called chelicerae. **Chelicerae** (kih-LIS-uh-ray) are the anterior-most appendages, modified into pincers or fangs for killing prey. The chelicerae of some species can inject poison. *Figure 23.10* shows the chelicerae of a tarantula.

Most chelicerates live in terrestrial environments. To live successfully on land, the organisms had to evolve with ways to retain water in their bodies. Terrestrial chelicerates, such as spiders, have three structures that aid in water retention: Malpighian tubules, an exoskeleton, and book lungs. **Malpighian** (mal-PIG-ee-uhn) **tubules** are excretory structures that remove metabolic wastes from blood and return water to the cells. The hard exoskeleton of chelicerates prevents excessive water evaporation. The book lungs provide efficient gas exchange without excessive water loss. These respiratory structures are called book lungs because they look like the inverted pages of a book. The location of the Malpighian tubules and book lungs is shown in *Figure 23.11*.

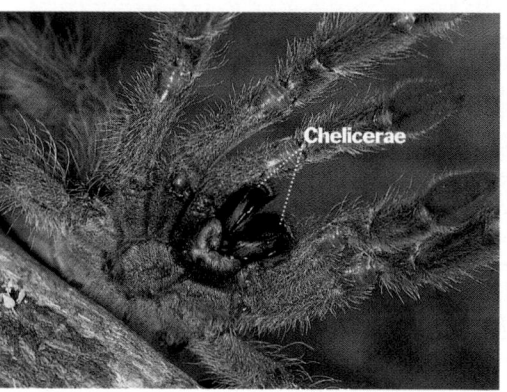

Chelicerae

FIGURE 23.10

Chelicerates have a pair of anterior appendages, called chelicerae, which are often modified into fangs.

ORIGIN AND DIVERSITY OF CHELICERATES

Legs, legs, legs…

There are two classes of chelicerates. Horseshoe crabs are marine animals that belong to the small class Meristomata. There are only four living species of horseshoe crabs. Three of these species live off the coast of Southeast Asia, and one species of horseshoe crab lives in the coastal regions of the western North Atlantic and the Gulf of Mexico.

Arachnids (uh-RAK-nidz) are terrestrial chelicerates that make up the much larger class Arachnida. There are three familiar orders of arachnids: spiders, scorpions, and mites and ticks. All arachnids have a cephalothorax with six pairs of appendages: one pair of chelicerae, one pair of specialized appendages called **pedipalps,** and four pairs of walking legs.

FIGURE 23.11

The Structures of a Spider

Like all chelicerates, spiders have pedipalps, chelicerae, and a two-part body. This spider also has Malpighian tubules, book lungs, and spinnerets.

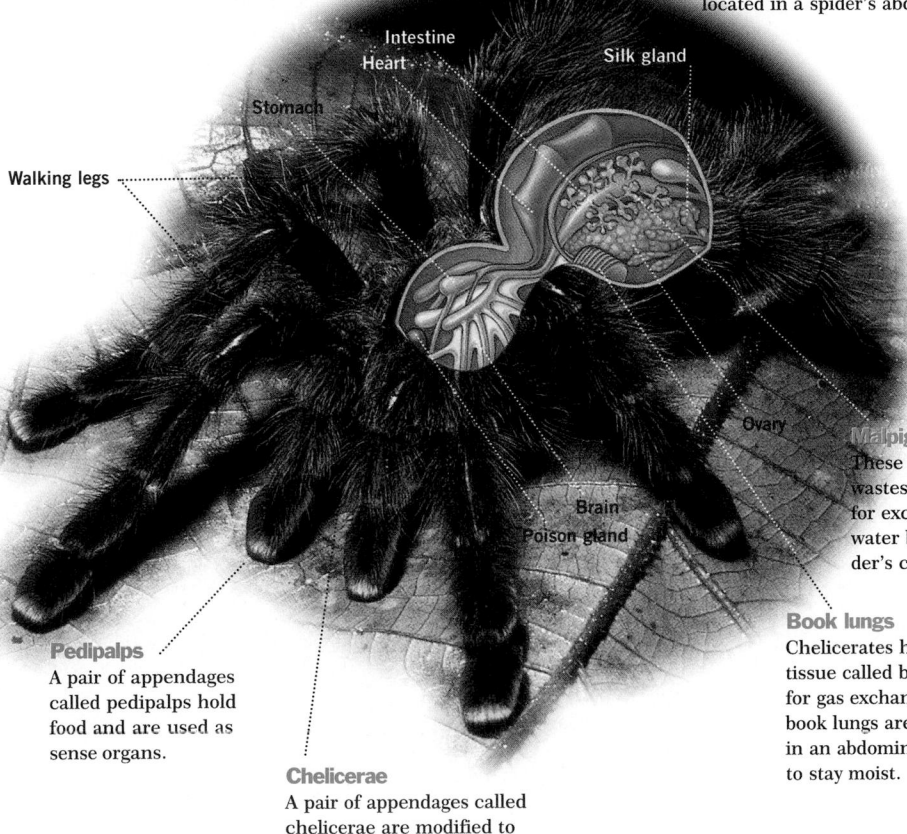

Spinnerets
Paired spinnerets release silk strands that are used for web building, movement, and shelter. The silk is produced in silk glands located in a spider's abdomen.

Intestine
Heart
Stomach
Silk gland
Walking legs

Ovary

Malpighian tubules
These structures secrete wastes into the intestine for excretion and return water back into the spider's circulatory system.

Brain
Poison gland

Book lungs
Chelicerates have folds of tissue called book lungs for gas exchange. The book lungs are enclosed in an abdominal pouch to stay moist.

Pedipalps
A pair of appendages called pedipalps hold food and are used as sense organs.

Chelicerae
A pair of appendages called chelicerae are modified to seize food and inject poison.

Chapter 23 Arthropods **553**

MULTICULTURAL PERSPECTIVE

Malpighian tubules are named for the Italian physiologist Marcello Malpighi (1628-1694). Recognized as the founder of microscopic anatomy, he demonstrated how blood reaches the tissues through capillaries that are too small to be seen with the naked eye.

FACTS AND FIGURES

The world's largest spider is the Goliath bird-eating spider (*Theraphosa leblondi*). It has a leg span of 0.25 meters (about 10 inches).

② TEACH

Use the Visual

Point out the abdomen and cephalothorax of the spider in Figure 23.11. Ask:

- **What structures are located on the cephalothorax?** (Pedipalps, eyes, chelicerae, four pairs of walking legs)
- **What structures are located on the abdomen?** (Spinnerets, Malpighian tubules, book lungs)
- **What is the purpose of a spinneret?** (It releases the silk strands needed for web–building, movement, and shelter.)

Explain

Explain that air enters a spider's body through thin slits in the exoskeleton. Some spiders have book lungs that give them a large area for gas exchange. In other spiders, oxygen from the air diffuses directly into body cells.

✛ Literature

The word *arachnid* comes from the Greek "arachne," meaning "spider." In Greek mythology, Athena, the goddess of wisdom, skills, and warfare, turns the girl Arachne into a spider for challenging the goddess to a weaving contest.

✛ Art

Constructing a spider web is a complex architectural feat. Ask students to research and describe the steps involved in spinning a spider web. Encourage students to include pictures or drawings of different webs.

Clarify Misconceptions

Many types of spider webs are made up of sticky strands of silk. Students may assume that spiders' legs somehow keep them from getting stuck in their own webs. Explain to students that spiders weave some strands that are not sticky. They walk along these "safe pathways" to build and repair their webs and to paralyze and wrap prey. But if a spider does step onto a sticky strand, it usually has the ability to become unstuck.

Think Critically

Explain that horseshoe crabs are ancient invertebrates. Fossils of different types date back 220 million years to the Triassic Period, and some date back 400 million years. Some horseshoe crabs can grow 30 to 60 centimeters in length (12 to 24 inches), and can live up to 19 years. Ask:

- **Why do you think horseshoe crabs have survived so many millions of years?** (The protection of a large and strong exoskeleton has most likely contributed to the success of the species.)

STS

Spider venom is a threat to any potential prey and can leave behind a painful reminder of an arachnid encounter. However, researchers are studying spider venom as a potential natural insecticide and as a source of drugs to treat cardiac and nervous disorders.

Kingdom: **Animalia**
Phylum: **Arthropoda**
Subphylum: **Chelicerata**
Two classes:
Meristomata
Arachnida

Horseshoe crabs
How many pairs of walking legs can you find on this horseshoe crab (above)? What other chelicerate characteristics do you see? **②**

Horseshoe crabs Horseshoe crabs are not really crabs. They belong to an ancient class of marine arthropods that evolved about 400 million years ago. Scientists often refer to the four surviving species of horseshoe crabs as "living fossils" because they closely resemble their fossil ancestors.

Horseshoe crabs have both compound and simple eyes. They do not have Malpighian tubules. Horseshoe crabs exchange gases in five pairs of book gills. Book gills are similar to book lungs and may have evolved into the book lungs found in terrestrial arachnids. Horseshoe crabs are among the few chelicerates that eat solid food. They feed on clam worms, soft-shelled clams, and other animals.

Spiders Most scientists divide spiders into two groups, based on how they gather food. One group includes spiders that actively hunt and capture prey. The other group includes spiders that weave webs to catch prey. Hunting spiders usually have strong legs and excellent eyesight. In some species, two pairs of eyes swivel together or independently, while two other pairs provide peripheral vision. Web weavers generally have long, slender legs and relatively poor eyesight.

Although not all spiders weave webs, they all produce silk. Some spiders use silk for movement—as droplines or parachutes, for example. Other spiders use silk for protection—as a covering for their burrows or a canopy under which they sleep. Still other spiders use silk to wrap their food for storage.

Spiders paralyze or kill their prey with chelicerae modified into fangs. While holding their prey with their pedipalps, spiders secrete enzymes that digest and liquefy the prey. They then suck the liquefied food into their stomach.

Scorpions The second order of arachnids includes scorpions. Unlike other arachnids, scorpions have a long segmented abdomen that ends in a poisonous stinger. A scorpion's pedipalps are modified into large claws for

FIGURE 23.12
Diversity of Chelicerates

The chelicerates include two classes: horseshoe crabs and arachnids. How do these classes compare? **①**

Hunting spider
This hunting spider has caught a frog. Hunting spiders are strong, agile predators with keen eyesight. How can a spider subdue a frog? **③**

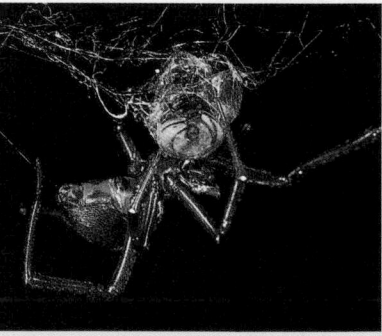

Web-weaving spider
A web-weaving spider is born knowing how to weave the unique web of its ancestors. How would you explain this phenomenon? **④**

MULTICULTURAL PERSPECTIVE

In China, farmers use spiders as a natural pesticide to protect rice crops. Before a rice field is flooded, farmers set out stacks of rice straw. Spiders crawl into the stacks and the straw is moved to infested areas. Spiders come out of the stacks and eat the insects.

① Horseshoe crabs are marine; arachnids are terrestrial.

② Five pairs of legs, exoskeleton

③ It uses strong legs and quick acting digestive enzymes.

④ Information is contained in DNA.

⑤ Dust

⑥ Both have a single body section and piercing, sucking mouthparts; ticks are parasites, mites are not.

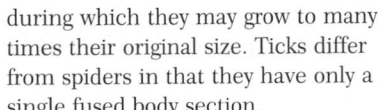

capturing and holding prey. As it curls its abdomen over trapped prey, the scorpion stings and paralyzes it, then crushes it and sucks its internal liquids. Despite their reputation, only a few species of scorpions are harmful to humans.

Mites Mites are classified in a third order of arachnids. Unlike spiders, mites have only one body segment. Some mites use their piercing and sucking mouthparts to drain the contents of plant cells. Other mite species eat bacteria that live in animal hair follicles. Some mites even feed on the dead skin cells of humans. Millions of dust mites live in our houses. They are usually harmless but can cause problems for people with allergies. What do you think dust mites feed on?

Ticks The third order of arachnids also includes ticks. Most ticks are parasites that require meals of blood before they molt. Ticks attach to their hosts with specially adapted mouthparts. Their feeding process can take several days,

during which they may grow to many times their original size. Ticks differ from spiders in that they have only a single fused body section.

You may have seen ticks feeding on dogs, cats, or humans. Ticks can be dangerous because they can act as hosts to parasites that cause diseases such as Rocky Mountain spotted fever. A common dog tick is easy to see because it is as large as a sesame seed. However, the deer tick, which carries the parasite that causes Lyme disease, is very small and difficult to see.

CHECKPOINT 23.3

1. Describe the main characteristics of chelicerates.
2. Discuss the variations among members of the chelicerate classes.
3. **Critical Thinking** Why are Malpighian tubules absent in aquatic arthropods?

Build on What You Know

4. Chitin is made of protein and polysaccharides. What are these two substances? *(Need to jog your memory? Revisit relevant concepts in Chapter 2, Section 2.1.)*

Stinger

Tick
Ticks may tranmit disease-causing organisms when they feed. What can you conclude about the tick in this photograph? ❼

Scorpion
A scorpion captures insects and spiders with its claws. This female scorpion carries her young on her back.

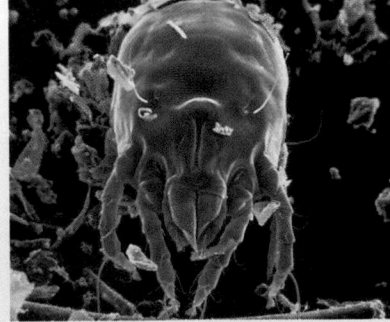

Dust mite
If you looked at a dust mite under a powerful microscope, this is what you would see. What are the similarities and differences between dust mites (above) and ticks (above right)? ❻

Chapter 23 Arthropods **555**

Point out to students that even astronomers like arthropods. One summer constellation of the Southern Hemisphere is called *Scorpius*. A constellation in the Northern Hemisphere is called Cancer, or the crab, and is located near Leo and Gemini. Have interested students find out if there are other constellation names associated with arthropods.

**ASSESS**

Evaluate Understanding

To assess students' understanding of chelicerates, ask:

- **What structures enable archnids to live in a dry environment?** (An exoskeleton that inhibits water vaporization, Malpighian tubules that filter wastes from water, and book lungs that enable gas exchange)
- **What are some similarities and differences among spiders?** (All produce silk and paralyze or kill their prey with chelicerae; however, some spiders weave webs, others hunt.)

Reteach

Draw a concept map on the board or on a transparency and label the center *Arachnids*. Draw and label four lines coming out of the center: *spiders, scorpions, mites,* and *ticks*. Work with students to complete the map by filling in the characteristics of each group.

CHECKPOINT 23.3

1. Two body regions, simple eyes, appendages called chelicerae, and no sensory antennae
2. Horseshoe crabs are marine, have compound eyes, book gills, and no Malphigian tubules. Arachnids are mostly terrestrial and have Malphigian tubules and book lungs.
3. **Applying** Malphigian tubules enable arachnids to conserve water. Aquatic arthropods live in water and do not need them.
4. Both are organic molecules. Protein is composed of amino acids, polysaccharides are composed of simple sugars.

❼ The tick was feeding and is engorged with blood.

Use the Visual

Have students look at the photograph that opens the section. Explain that diets vary from culture to culture. Ask:

■ **Why would insects be part of a balanced diet?** (They are a source of protein.)

Check Prior Knowledge

To assess students' prior knowledge about insects, ask:

■ **Why are insects classified as arthropods?** (They share the same basic characteristics as other arthropods—exoskeleton, body segments, and jointed appendages.)

Quick Activity

List on the board as many insects as students can name, then count the entries. Tell students that this is but a tiny fraction of all insects. More than 800,000 species have been identified; many more are thought to exist.

Think Critically

Give students time to examine the photos in Figure 23.13. Ask:

■ **What can you conclude about the type of food an insect eats by examining its mouthparts?** (Possible answers include: chewing— solid foods; piercing—liquids from animals or plants; sponging—liquids; long and coiled—sucking liquids such as nectar from flowers.)

What you'll learn

IDEAS

• To describe the characteristics of uniramians
• To compare and contrast the diversity of uniramians
• To explain several adaptations of insects

WORDS

spiracles, metamorphosis, pheromone, social insects, mimicry

Gourmet insects

Have you ever had leaf-footed bugs on your pizza? Many people choose to eat those insects and others for their protein and their taste. For example, grasshoppers boiled in soy sauce are a popular snack in Japan, toasted stinkbugs flavor salsa in Mexico, and mopane caterpillars are tasty treats in Africa.

CHARACTERISTICS OF UNIRAMIANS

A buggy bunch

Although picnics vary in location, participants, and menu, most picnics have one thing in common—insects! Insects, along with centipedes and millipedes, are classified in the subphylum Uniramia. As you can see in *Figure 23.13*, mouthparts in uniramians are varied and specialized. Although their mouthparts may be different, most uniramians share two characteristics: a single pair of antennae and unbranched appendages. You can locate these structures in the grasshopper shown in *Figure 23.14*.

The uniramians, and particularly the insects, are the most numerous and diverse group of organisms on Earth. One reason for their successful survival is that uniramians have a wide range of senses. Uniramian antennae are very sensitive to odors. In addition, some insects have thin, flexible tympanic membranes that detect sound. Although the insects'

compound eyes might not form sharp images, they easily detect movement. If you have ever tried to swat a fly, you know how well its quick response to your slightest motion helps it escape danger.

Uniramians also have a complex digestive system with specialized organs. In a grasshopper, for example, food passes through an esophagus to a crop, where it is moistened. From the crop, food moves to a gizzard, which is lined with hard, toothlike structures that grind the food into small pieces. The small food pieces then move to the midgut, where digestive enzymes break them down. Nutrients are then absorbed and transported to cells. Undigested wastes move into the hindgut and leave the body through the anus. Like arachnids, uniramians have Malpighian tubules that remove nitrogen wastes from body fluids.

The uniramians' respiratory system enables them to obtain oxygen from the air without losing too much moisture. Their respiratory system is composed of a branched system of internal air tubules. Air enters a uniramian's respiratory system through **spiracles**— small openings in the exoskeleton. It then passes directly into tracheal tubes that wind through the body tissues and carry oxygen directly to body cells.

Mosquito

Housefly

Butterfly

FIGURE 23.13

The close-up photos of these insects show mouthparts that are piercing (top), sponging (center), and sucking (bottom).

STUDENT RESOURCES

From the Teacher's Resource Package, use:
■ Section Review 23.4, Activity Record- sheets 23-1 and 23-2, Interpreting Graphics 23, Critical Thinking Exercise 23, and Enrichment Topics 23-1 and 23-2 from Unit 6 Review Module
■ Lab 39: "Insect Metamorphosis"

TECHNOLOGY RESOURCES

Relevant technology resources include:
■ Spanish Student Edition CD-ROM
■ Teacher's Resource Planner CD-ROM
■ Biology Alive! Video Series

ORIGIN AND DIVERSITY OF UNIRAMIANS

Legs and segments bug taxonomists

With their exoskeletons and specialized appendages, the arthropods were among the first animals that could survive on land. Of the arthropods, it was the uniramians—especially the insects—that prospered during the Carboniferous and Permian periods (about 300–250 million years ago). A second evolutionary explosion in the number of uniramian species occurred at the end of the Cretaceous period (about 65 million years ago). This explosion coincided with the evolution of flowering plants. Today, insect populations continue to grow. Approximately one million insect species have already been described. Millions more are known to exist, and new ones are discovered every day.

Centipedes Uniramians are divided into three classes. The first class, Chilopoda, contains the centipedes. Centipedes are carnivores with one pair of fanglike claws. You can see a photograph of a centipede in

| Phylum: Arthropoda |
| Subphylum: Uniramia |
| **Three classes:** |
| Chilopoda |
| Diplopoda |
| Insecta |

FIGURE 23.14

Structures of a Grasshopper

Like all uniramians, grasshoppers have one pair of antennae and unbranched appendages. Grasshoppers also have compound eyes and specialized mouthparts.

Wings
Heart
Nerve cord
Brain
Antennae
Spiracles
Malpighian tubules
Crop
Esophagus
Gizzard
Tracheal tubes

Mouth
A grasshopper has biting and chewing mouthparts. It has an upper lip with two mandibles and maxillae on each side, and a lower lip with two maxillae attached. The lower parts of the maxillae bear many sensory receptors.

Digestive system
Food passes through the grasshopper's esophagus, crop, and gizzard before it is digested and absorbed in the midgut.

Respiratory system
Spiracles open to let air in, and then they close. Air travels through small tracheal tubes that branch into a fine network over individual cells.

Chapter 23 Arthropods **557**

2 **TEACH**

Explain

Point out that insect wings are not appendages but are thin outgrowths of the exoskeleton, evolved for flight. Most of the power for flapping the wings comes from large vertical and horizontal muscles in the thorax. As the muscles alternately contract, the upper and lower surfaces of the thorax are pulled close together, then pushed apart, causing the wings to move up and down. At the base of the wings, other muscles adjust the angle of each stroke, determining the direction of flight.

Class Activity

TEAM WORK

Provide small groups of students with live or preserved grasshoppers and hand lenses. Have students identify and locate the external structures shown in Figure 23.14. Ask:

■ **How did the grasshopper specimen compare to the one in Figure 23.14? How similar are they? What differences did you notice?** (Students should be able to identify the eye, antennae, mouth, and wings; they may note differences in coloration and relative size of structures.)

FACTS AND FIGURES

Students may be interested to learn that some aquatic insects, such as the water beetle, have extra tracheal air stores or "gills" under their wings to use underwater. When oxygen in the stored air is depleted by respiration, the water beetle forms an air bubble at the end of its abdomen. The air is renewed as carbon dioxide goes into the water and oxygen from the water enters the bubble. As a result, the beetle can stay submerged in the water.

23.4

Clarify Misconceptions

Although all bugs are insects, all insects are not bugs. Bugs belong to the order *Hemiptera*, and have flattened, oval bodies, two pairs of wings, and piercing and sucking mouthparts. Aphids, mealy bugs, and water boatmen are true bugs.

LAB ZONE Do It! **TEAM WORK**

Look at Those Sensors!

Suggest that students place their insect specimens in a box padded with soft tissue or cotton. They may wish to pick up their specimens with tweezers or forceps, or scoop them up with a piece of clean paper.

Analyze Your Results

1. Answers may include the size, shape, and texture of the antennae.

2. Answers should discuss the use of antennae to detect movement, sound, and chemicals.

Figure 23.15. They have 15 or more pairs of walking legs, one pair per segment. Centipedes hide during the day and feed on earthworms, insects, and snails at night.

Millipedes The members of the class Diplopoda are the millipedes, which are often confused with centipedes. Although millipedes have two pairs of walking legs per segment, they move slowly. When alarmed, they roll up into a ball. Millipedes are herbivores and vary in size. Small millipedes are common in houses and gardens, but some tropical species can reach almost half a meter in length.

Insects Insects belong to the class Insecta. More than three

FIGURE 23.15
Many people confuse centipedes (right) and millipedes (above). What differences are there between these two uniramians? ❶

LAB ZONE Do It! **bioSURF**

Look at Those Sensors!

Insect antennae are incredibly varied in form and function. You can observe just a few of the possible variations if you . . .

Try This

1 Collect as many different intact, dead insects as you can. **Caution:** Dead bees and wasps still have stingers.
2 Group them roughly by type (moths, beetles, and so on).
3 Using a microscope, examine their antennae carefully, and sketch the different types.

Analyze Your Results

1 What basic differences did you observe?
2 Based on what you know about the types of insects you collected, how does the form of the antennae match their function?

FIGURE 23.16

Insect Diversity

Uniramians vary enormously in size, form, and habitat. How many different insects can you name? ❷

quarters of all known animal species are insects. Scientists classify insects by structural differences, such as the type of mouthparts they have or the number and structure of their wings.

The diversity of insects is truly amazing. There are aphids, bees, crickets, dragonflies, earwigs, fireflies, gnats, horseflies, inchworm moths, Japanese beetles, katydids, ladybugs, mosquitoes, nectar-sucking blister beetles, orchid bees, potato bugs, queen bees, roaches, scale, termites, unlined giant chafers, velvet mites, wasps, *Xylocopa*, yellow jackets, and zebra butterflies—and thousands more, covering every letter of the alphabet.

Unlike crustaceans and chelicerates, insects have three distinct body regions: a head, a thorax, and an abdomen. All insects have compound eyes, and some also have simple eyes.

FIGURE 23.17
The three body regions of insects are shown below.

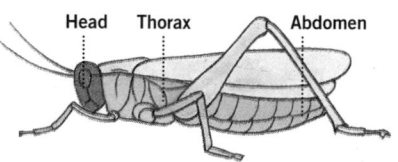

Head   Thorax   Abdomen

FACTS AND FIGURES

The largest insect is the Goliath beetle, with a length of 0.11 meters (about 4.5 inches). The largest butterfly, Queen Alexandra's birdwing, has a wingspan of 0.28 meters (about 11 inches).

❶ Millipedes have two pairs of walking legs per segment and are slow moving. Centipedes are nocturnal.
❷ Answers will vary.

1. *Diptera*, mosquito
2. *Hymenoptera*, wasp
3. *Orthoptera*, katydid
4. *Lepidoptera*, butterfly
5. *Odonata*, dragonfly
6. *Coleoptera*, glorious beetle
7. *Coleoptera*, water beetle

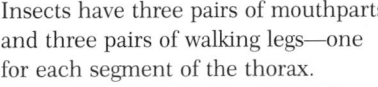

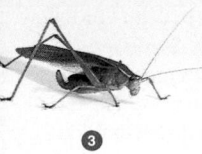

Egg

Larva

Pupa

Adult

Insects have three pairs of mouthparts and three pairs of walking legs—one for each segment of the thorax.

Some insects have two pairs of wings, some have one pair, and others have no wings at all. Insect wings are not appendages; they are folded extensions of the exoskeleton. With their ability to fly, insects could inhabit new environments and were better able to escape from predators, obtain food, and migrate.

Insects often display a developmental pattern called metamorphosis. **Metamorphosis** is a series of changes young organisms undergo as they develop into adults.

Insects such as grasshoppers, termites, cicadas, and aphids undergo incomplete metamorphosis. This type of metamorphosis includes two stages: the nymph and the adult. Nymphs are insects that resemble an adult but are very small and lack wings and reproductive organs. After hatching from the eggs laid by an adult female,

nymphs go through a series of molts. Each molt results in an insect that more closely resembles the adult.

Many other insects, such as butterflies, beetles, and flies, undergo complete metamorphosis. *Figure 23.18* shows the stages of complete metamorphosis. Larvae—often called caterpillars, grubs, or maggots—hatch from eggs laid by an adult. The larvae are greedy eaters. They munch their way through leaves, plants, and decaying organic matter, molting as they grow. Once the larvae reach a certain size, they find a sheltered place and surround themselves with a protective case, or cocoon. In this stage of metamorphosis, the organism is referred to as a pupa. While in the cocoon, the larval tissues break down. Adult tissues

FIGURE 23.18
During complete metamorphosis of a butterfly (shown top to bottom), the insect develops from an egg into an adult.

Chapter 23 Arthropods **559**

Explain

Point out to students that pupae are referred to by different names, depending on the animal. Fly pupae are called grubs or maggots. A butterfly or moth pupa is called a chrysalis.

Use the Visual

Guide students to understand the stages of complete metamorphosis illustrated in Figure 23.18. Ask:

- **How does metamorphosis contribute to the success and survival of insect species?** (Answers may include that there is no competition between larvae and adults for food, and insects can survive harsh and cold weather while protected as pupae.)

Literature

Franz Kafka (1883-1924), an existential writer born in Prague, Czechoslovakia, wrote *The Metamorphosis* in 1916. It is a story about the life of a man who wakes up one day to find that he has turned into a giant cockroach. Invite students who have read the book to share their impressions with the class.

Everyday Biology

Tell students that because a bee's stinger continues to pump venom even when separated from the bee's body, it is important not to remove the stinger with tweezers. The squeezing action can force more venom into the skin. Advise students to scratch lightly at the stinger with a fingernail to remove it.

Use the Visual

Have students classify each form of communication shown in Figure 23.19 as either chemical, touch, sound, or visual. (Crickets—sound; ants—chemical, touch; moth antennae—sense chemicals)

 ## Chemistry

Point out that insects are found in every biome, except in the deep ocean. Some insect species can survive in biomes with extremely cold climates because they have a natural antifreeze, called glycerol, in their body fluids. Their cells do not freeze until the temperature drops to 20°C. These protected cells excrete fluids so that ice forms outside the cells.

Build Writing Skills

Suggest that students write a report on bees, ants, or termites. Have them research the insect's social system and compare the different duties performed by the insects to the roles people might play in a group or organization.

560

---

develop from a few specialized cells. After development is complete, an adult emerges from the cocoon.

EVERYDAY BIOLOGY

No Stinger, Less Pain

When a honeybee stings you, the stinger and its poison gland remain in your body, and the gland continues to pump its toxin. The sooner you pull out the stinger, the less pain, swelling, and itching you will experience.

INSECT ADAPTATIONS

Networking in the insect world

Insects have evolved many adaptations to the different environments they inhabit. Some of these adaptations are behavioral, and some are structural.

Behavioral adaptations Insects display many different kinds of behaviors, ranging from the simple to the complex. Have you ever watched fireflies signal each other at dusk? Have you seen ants carry food back to their nests? These behaviors are not learned. They are instincts—automatic behaviors coded for by genes.

Insects behave in predictable patterns based on the stimuli they sense. Some stimuli that insects sense come from other members of their species. Many species of insects communicate with one another. Male and female fireflies use flashes of light to find each other. Crickets and grasshoppers rub their wings together to produce sounds that attract mates or mark their territories.

A chemical signal used by insects for communication is called a **pheromone** (FAIR-uh-mohn). When pheromones are smelled or tasted, they affect the behavior of other insects. For example, ants leave a trail of pheromones for other ants to follow to a new food source. Some female moths secrete pheromones to attract mates. By sensing pheromones, a male moth can find a female several kilometers away.

Some insect species have a complex social system. These species are often called social insects. **Social insects** live in colonies where individual insects perform specific jobs in the colony and are usually adapted structurally to do so.

Many species of bees, ants, and termites are social insects. An individual social insect, such as a honeybee, cannot survive on its own. A beehive has

FIGURE 23.19
These photos illustrate several insect adaptations. Moths' feathery antennae (left) are highly sensitive to airborne pheromones. Crickets (top right) rub their forewings together to produce the familiar chirping noise and attract a mate. Leafcutter ants (bottom right) clasp each other's head to assure that they are from the same colony.

FACTS AND FIGURES

In one summer, a male grasshopper seeking a mate may make sounds as often as 50 million times! Sounds are also used to ward off enemies. For example, the long-horned beetle makes a loud threatening sound with a sound organ between the thorax and abdomen. The male cicada has a sound organ on his abdomen and a hollow resonating chamber that amplifies the sound.

FIGURE 23.20
The patterns of the round and waggle dances of bees (far right) communicate information about the location of food. Why is the queen bee (near right) so much larger than the others? ❶

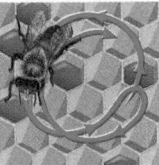

Round dance

Waggle dance

three types of individuals: a queen, drones, and workers. Workers—female bees that cannot reproduce—are the most numerous members of a hive. Their job in the colony is to build and maintain the hive, collect food, feed the queen and larvae, and defend the hive.

One type of worker bee is a food scout. The scout uses complicated dances to communicate the location of a food source to other workers. If the food source is closer than 50 m from the hive, the scout performs a round dance. When the food source is more than 50 m away, the scout performs a waggle dance. Food-gathering workers follow the scout's dance and touch antennae to communicate the scout's information. Then they fly off to find and gather the food.

Another type of worker cares for larvae. The larvae, which will become the hive's new bees, will develop into various types of bees depending on the food they receive from workers. Workers feed an enriched diet—called "royal jelly"—only to larvae that are destined to become queens.

The sole function of the one queen bee and the many male drones in a hive is reproduction. The queen lays all the eggs from which new bees first hatch into larvae. She produces a pheromone that tells worker bees not to feed "royal jelly" to growing larvae. When

the queen dies or leaves the hive, the absence of her pheromone signals the workers to feed "royal jelly" to some of the larvae. The new queens that emerge fight to the death, and the survivor becomes the new queen of the hive.

A hive limits the number of its drones because their sole function is reproduction, and a queen mates only once in her life. The inhabitants of a hive behave as if drones are their most expendable members.

LAB ZONE Think About It! bioSURF

Identifying Insect Camouflage and Mimicry

Insects use both form and color to protect themselves or hide in their environment. You can study how insects use camouflage and mimicry to avoid detection by predators and prey when you . . .

Try This

1 Look at the pictures in this chapter. How many examples of camouflage can you find? How many examples of mimicry?
2 Can you identify examples of camouflage or mimicry that you have seen among insects in the environment?

Analysis

1 Look at Figure 23.18. Why might the larval stage of an insect, such as a caterpillar, be more highly camouflaged than the adult stage?
2 How do camouflage and mimicry help an insect to increase its food supply?

Apply

Discuss how movement can be used for communicating, such as in honeybees. Ask:

- **What types of human movement are a form of communication?** (Dance, mimes, sign language, body language) Challenge students to develop a new form of physical communication. Encourage them to be as creative as possible. Have them take turns demonstrating a simple message to the class.

LAB ZONE Think About It!

Identifying Insect Camouflage and Mimicry

Many crustaceans are drab-colored and blend in with the marine environment. Figure 23.21 shows examples of mimicry and camouflage.

Analysis

1. Larvae are soft-bodied and slower moving than adults and more susceptible to predators.
2. They can sneak up on unsuspecting prey.

❶ She gets an enriched diet.

Evaluate Understanding

Have students review the different arthropods they have studied. Ask:

- **In what major ways are arthropods similar?** (Exoskeleton, segments, jointed legs)
- **In what major ways are arthropods different?** (Answers should include ways they move, size, mouthparts, and number of appendages.)
- **What special uniramian characteristics enable them to survive so successfully in their environments?** (Answers should include wide range of senses, highly evolved appendages, and complex digestive and respiratory systems.)

Reteach

Help students list the major structures of uniramians. Tell them to record the function next to each structure as they reread the section. Then have them use their notes to cite reasons why uniramians are so successful.

FIGURE 23.21
The giant walking stick (far right) blends in perfectly with twigs and underbrush. The green coloration and shape of the katydid (near right) disguises it among the leaves.

Structural adaptations One of the most remarkable ways that insects have adapted to their environment is by evolving with structures that enable them to blend in with their surroundings. Some insects blend in with the textures, shapes, and colors of their environment. This adaptation is called camouflage. Other insects resemble plants or other animals. This adaptation is called **mimicry**. Using camouflage or mimicry, insects often avoid detection by predators and prey. Although other animals use camouflage and mimicry, these adaptations are most diverse and visible in insects.

The adaptations of camouflage and mimicry can occur at any stage of an insect's life. For example, insects that undergo complete metamorphosis are vulnerable during the pupal stage. So the pupae are often disguised as something else—a dead leaf or a twig perhaps. This disguise decreases the chance that the pupae will be eaten. You can see some remarkable examples of insect camouflage and mimicry in *Figure 23.21* and *Figure 23.22*.

CHECKPOINT 23.4

1. Describe the common characteristics of uniramians.
2. Compare and contrast insects, millipedes, and centipedes.
3. List two types of insect adaptations and give examples of each.
4. **Critical Thinking** What characteristics have helped insects to diversify so successfully?

Build on What You Know

5. Compare the individual members of an insect colony with the individual cells in an organism. *(Need to jog your memory? Revisit relevant concepts in Chapter 3, Section 3.1.)*

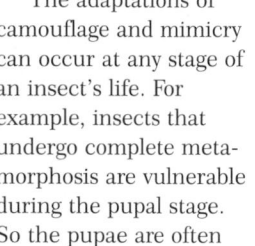

FIGURE 23.22
This caterpillar (left) flattens and twists its abdomen, which is patterned like the head of a snake, to scare away predators. The sphinx moth (right) closely resembles its wooden resting place.

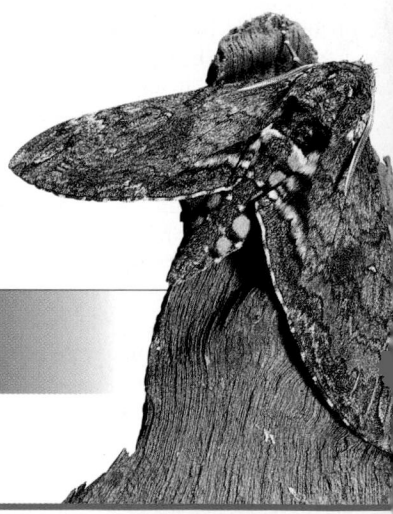

? **How are arthropods classified?**

CHECKPOINT 23.4

1. Two antennae, unbranched appendages, specialized mouthparts, complex body systems, wide range of senses
2. Answers should include that all insects have three body parts, compound eyes, three pairs of mouthparts, and three pairs of walking legs; millipedes and centipedes have many segments; centipedes have one pair of legs per segment, millipedes have two pairs.
3. Behavioral—communication, social living; structural—camouflage and mimicry
4. **Analyzing** Insects have a wide range of senses and can adapt to environmental stimuli; they can fly to a variety of habitats and communicate with each other.
5. They function in similar ways, working together to benefit the whole organism or colony with specific roles.

LAB ZONE Investigate It!

Observing the Mealworm Life Cycle

WHAT YOU WILL DO Observe the stages in the life cycle of a mealworm

SKILLS YOU WILL USE Observing, measuring, collecting and recording data, hypothesizing

WHAT YOU WILL NEED Spoon, specimen dish, container, marker, mealworm larvae, hand lens, metric ruler, cornmeal, cheesecloth

Propose a Hypothesis

Propose a hypothesis about the size of the mealworm at each stage in its life cycle and the amount of time it spends in each stage.

Conduct Your Experiment

1 Using a spoon, carefully place a mealworm larva into a specimen dish. Use a hand lens to observe the larva. Draw and label the parts of the larva, then measure and record its length.
Caution: Always handle living organisms carefully.
2 Label a container and place the larva in it. Add two spoonfuls of cornmeal and cover the container with cheesecloth. Set the container aside.
3 Observe and measure the mealworm daily until it reaches its adult stage. Be sure to record your observations and measurements.

Analyze Your Data

1 Make a line graph from your data on the length of the mealworm.
2 In which stage was the mealworm the longest? Was there a period of rapid growth, or was its growth gradual?
3 Make a bar graph to show the number of days the mealworm spent in each stage of its life cycle.
4 In which stage did the individual spend the most time? How long?
5 What body parts are common to all stages?

Draw Conclusions

Was your hypothesis supported by the results of the experiment? What conclusions can you draw from the results? Explain.

Design a Related Experiment

Suppose you wanted to study the effects of a variable, such as amount of food, light, or temperature, on the development of a mealworm. Propose a hypothesis and design an experiment to test it.

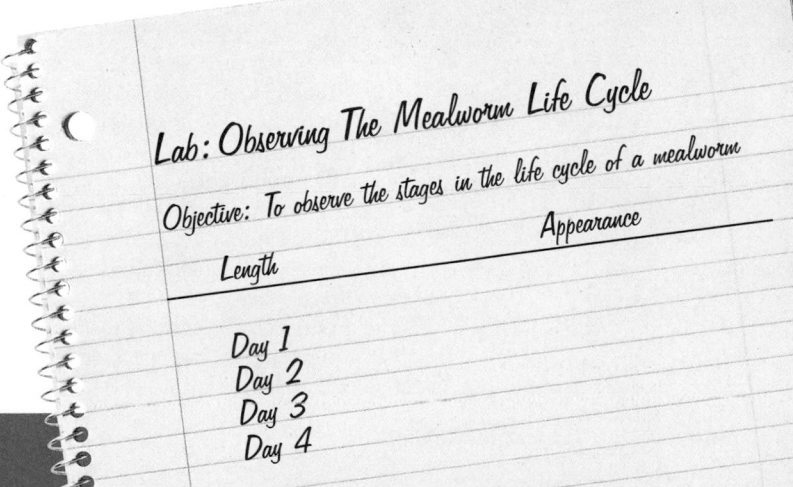

Lab: Observing The Mealworm Life Cycle

Objective: To observe the stages in the life cycle of a mealworm

Length	Appearance
Day 1	
Day 2	
Day 3	
Day 4	

Analyze Your Data

1 Answers will vary
2 Larval stage; growth is gradual
3 Answers will vary
4 Larval stage; answers will vary depending on temperature
5 Exoskeleton, compound eyes

Draw Conclusions

Answers will vary. Accept all logical responses.

SUPER READ! **Following Written Directions** To practice strategies for effective reading, use pages 61-62 in **Super Read!**

TEAM WORK **Observing the Mealworm Life Cycle**

SAFETY FIRST!

Tell students to be gentle when handling live animals.

Lab Tips

Remind students to return the mealworms and larvae to the containers. Tell them to be sure to replace the lids to prevent the mealworms from escaping.

Hypothesis Help

Tell students to apply what they have learned about insect metamorphosis to predict what might happen during each stage of the mealworm's life cycle.

Lab Extension

Open Ended
Have students follow the life cycle of mealworms by examining them daily. Students should place some in a ventilated (not opened) container, along with some oatmeal and a slice of apple or potato. Have students observe and record the development of the mealworms for the next month.

Time Required

- 20 minutes on first day
- 10 minutes on each observation day

23.5 Arthropods in the Biosphere

What you'll learn

IDEAS
- To identify several key roles arthropods play in the biosphere
- To describe the effects of arthropods on humans

Bugs become plant food

The sundew plant (near right) traps a bug in its sticky nectar, then the plant closes over the insect (far right) and digests it. Another predatory plant, the pitcher plant, entices insects to its opening. Spiky hairs point downward, trapping the insects, which the plant then digests in its pool of enzymes. Insects and other arthropods supply nutrients to many organisms.

FIGURE 23.23
This bumblebee is gathering pollen from apple blossoms. Notice the heavily laden pollen baskets on its hind legs.

ECOLOGICAL ROLES

Arthropods can really bug you

Arthropods—by far the largest phylum—play important roles in the biosphere. Many other animals and plants, including food crops, depend upon arthropods for their existence.

On land and in water, arthropods are an important food source for other animals. Many crustaceans and insects, for example, are near the base of the food chain in their respective environments. Krill, crustaceans in some plankton, provide food for much of the Antarctic ecosystem. Fishes, seabirds, seals, and penguins all consume vast quantities of krill, and a single blue whale may eat up to four tons of krill a day! Insects are the main dietary component for a great many animals, including birds, reptiles, amphibians, and many small mammals.

Some arthropods also serve as food for other arthropods. One web-spinning spider, for example, is capable of catching about 100 insects a day. Some wasps sting caterpillars or spiders and carry the paralyzed prey to their nests. The wasps then lay eggs on the immobilized prey, and when the larvae hatch, the prey provides a ready supply of fresh food.

Insects eat many plants, but they help to increase the numbers of others through pollination. In fact, many plants have coevolved with the insects that pollinate them. Coevolution is a process in which species adapt to each other after closely interacting for millions of years. In many cases, only a single insect species can pollinate a particular plant species. How would an insect's extinction affect the plant species that depends on it?

Some insects can cause great damage to crops. For example, boll weevils devastate cotton plants, hornworms destroy tomatoes, and borers ruin corn crops. Termites can also be destructive, causing so much damage to wooden structures that the structures have to be torn down.

Arthropods are host to many dangerous parasites. They can transmit a

❶

number of serious, even fatal, diseases. For example, mosquitoes can carry parasites that cause malaria, yellow fever, and encephalitis. Malaria is one of the largest public-health problems in some parts of the world today. Some ticks transmit parasites that cause Lyme disease, and others carry the organisms that cause Rocky Mountain spotted fever. Rats, and the fleas that live on them, carry the bacteria that cause bubonic plague—a deadly disease that drastically reduced Europe's population during the Middle Ages. Today, because of improved living conditions and public-health measures, only isolated cases of bubonic plague occur.

Certain biting flies native to tropical regions also carry disease-causing organisms. For example, the tsetse fly of East Africa transmits a parasite that causes trypanosomiasis (tri–PAN-uh-soh–MY–uh–sis), or sleeping sickness, which afflicts cattle and humans. Another fly carries the agent of river blindness.

Blood-sucking arthropods transmit disease in many other animals, too. The flea is a host for the dog tapeworm. Mosquitoes transmit heartworm between dogs and other animals. In a few tropical regions, insect-borne diseases are so common and dangerous that neither humans nor their livestock inhabit those areas.

FIGURE 23.24
This beekeeper is inspecting a section of honeycomb that he has pulled out of a hive. The comb's cells are filled with honey and capped at the end with beeswax.

What county do you live in? Did you know that each county in the United States has an agricultural extension service? Extension service agents ("county agents") will answer questions about crops, gardens, and arthropod pests. Call your county extension service to find out about the mosquito or tick diseases that are prevalent in your area. Find out if a control program is in place for your community, and determine the precautions you should take against arthropod pests. Log on to http://invertebrates.biosurf.com to find out more about insect-born diseases.

IN THE COMMUNITY
Insect Control?

IMPORTANCE OF ARTHROPODS TO HUMAN USES

Feast and famine

In addition to transmitting diseases, arthropods can affect the human food supply. We depend on insects, such as honeybees, to pollinate a huge variety of flowering plants and crops. A bad year for honeybees is a bad year for farmers, because the decrease in pollination results in fewer successful crops. In addition to their role as pollinators, bees are valued for honey and beeswax, which are used in products ranging from candles to skin moisturizers.

Other arthropods of importance to humans include silkworms and crabs. Silkworms spin the threads to make silk fabric. Crab shells yield chitin, used to make surgical thread and dressings for wounds. Horseshoe crab blood is used for testing the purity of pharmaceuticals and lab equipment.

Finally, arthropods are an important source of food for humans. In

FIGURE 23.25
This tomato hornworm caterpillar, a member of the sphinx moth family, can quickly destroy tomato plants as it eats its way to maturity.

2 TEACH

In the Community

Have students prepare a list of questions before they contact the county agent. They can also contact the State Agricultural Department for more information. Suggest that they look up the addresses and phone numbers in the government section of their directory.

Science History

Rat fleas infected with the bacteria *Yersinia pestis* spread bubonic plague. During the sixth century, it killed about 100 million people in the Middle East, Europe, and Asia. Another outbreak of the bubonic plague, called the Black Death, occurred during the fourteenth century. It is estimated that between one-third and one-half of Europe's population perished in this epidemic. Have interested students find out more about the Black Death and report their findings to the class.

Health

Tse-tse flies have piercing mouthparts. As they suck blood, they transmit a parasite that damages the central nervous system. Symptoms include fever, headache, swollen glands, sleepiness, and motor problems. If untreated, victims may eventually die.

MULTICULTURAL PERSPECTIVE

Silk is reputed to have originated in China as early as 2000 B.C. However, it was not available in the West until the sixth century A.D. The reputed inventor of silk was Xilingji (Hsi-ling-chi) who was the 14-year-old wife of Emperor Huangdi (Huang-ti).

MEETING DIVERSE NEEDS

At Risk Some students may find arthropods fascinating and want information on related careers. Suggest that they research different types of careers in the field of entomology to identify what skills and education are needed and what the jobs entail.

Think Critically

Many insects are food sources for other animals. Have students infer how a forest biome would be affected if all the insects suddenly disappeared.

STS

After students read the STS on pesticide alternatives, have them form teams for a debate on pesticide use. Tell them to consider the following questions before they begin their debates:

- **Will natural pesticide methods truly be as useful and effective as chemical methods?**
- **What are the benefits of both methods? What are the drawbacks of both?**

Following Written Directions To practice strategies for effective reading, use pages 61-62 in *Super Read!*

3 ASSESS

Evaluate Understanding

To assess students' understanding of the role of arthropods in the biosphere, ask:

- **What types of diseases are transmitted by arthropods?** (Answers may include malaria, yellow fever, encephalitis, Lyme disease, plague, and tapeworm.)

Reteach

Have students restate the subheads in the section as main idea statements. Then ask them to review the section to find two or more details to support each main idea.

FIGURE 23.26
The success of an organic garden (right) depends, in part, on insects. In the photos below, a ladybug beetle (top) is making a meal of aphids, while a praying mantis (bottom) dispatches a tomato hornworm.

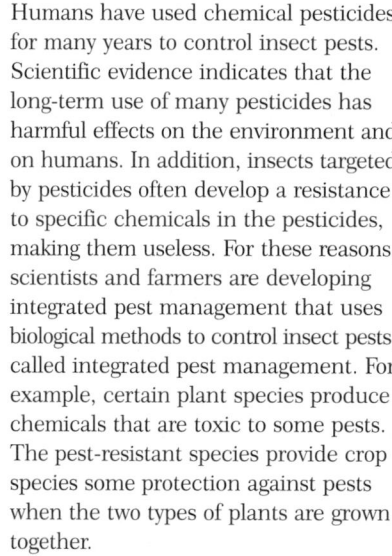

many cultures, people consume large amounts of shrimp, lobster, crabs, and crayfish. In some parts of the world, people consume many insects, including grasshoppers, termites, and caterpillars.

FRONTIERS IN BIOLOGY
Pesticide alternatives

Humans have used chemical pesticides for many years to control insect pests. Scientific evidence indicates that the long-term use of many pesticides has harmful effects on the environment and on humans. In addition, insects targeted by pesticides often develop a resistance to specific chemicals in the pesticides, making them useless. For these reasons, scientists and farmers are developing integrated pest management that uses biological methods to control insect pests, called integrated pest management. For example, certain plant species produce chemicals that are toxic to some pests. The pest-resistant species provide crop species some protection against pests when the two types of plants are grown together.

In other attempts to control insects,

researchers are studying the reproductive cycles of insects and trying to develop sterile adults of certain species. The adults can mate but cannot reproduce, thereby reducing their populations. Another technique is to infect targeted insects with a parasite, bacteria, or viruses. A common control method is to expose pests to natural predators. For example, home gardeners often purchase ladybug beetles and praying mantises to help control other insects.

CHECKPOINT 23.5

1. Describe at least five roles arthropods have in the biosphere.
2. List three ways in which arthropods are important to humans. List three ways in which they can be harmful to humans.
3. **Critical Thinking** If all insects were suddenly eliminated, what would be some immediate consequences?

Build on What You Know

4. What other organisms make up plankton? What is plankton's role in the biosphere? *(Need to jog your memory? Revisit relevant concepts in Chapter 15, Section 15.5.)*

 What role do arthropods play in the biosphere?

566 *Unit 6 Invertebrate Animals*

CHECKPOINT 23.5

1. Answers should include providing food for other animals and materials for human use, pollinating and eating plants, and transmitting parasites.
2. Bees pollinate crops and give humans honey and beeswax; silkworms give us silk, and crabs give us surgical thread. Arthropods also destroy crops, transmit disease, and destroy wooden structures.
3. **Predicting** Many plants would not be able to reproduce; animals that depend on insects for food would die.
4. Small arthropods, small worms, eggs and larvae of larger animals, and small algae make up plankton. Plankton is an important food source.

Chapter 23 Review

**THE BIG IDEA!**
23.1 Arthropods are segmented invertebrates with jointed appendages and an exoskeleton.
23.2–23.4 In general, arthropods are classified by the number of body segments they have and the structure of their appendages.
23.5 Arthropods, as members of the largest phylum, have many important roles in the biosphere.

Sum It Up

Use the following summary to review the main concepts in this chapter.

23.1 Arthropods

- Arthropods comprise the largest and most diverse phylum. The segmented bodies of arthropods have jointed appendages.
- Arthropods have a chitinous exoskeleton which must be molted and shed for growth to continue.
- Many arthropod appendages have specialized functions.

23.2 Crustaceans

- Most crustaceans have two main body parts: a cephalothorax and an abdomen.
- Most crustaceans have two pairs of antennae, a pair of jawlike mandibles, and at least four pairs of walking legs. They have eyestalks with compound eyes.

23.3 Spiders and Their Relatives

- Chelicerates have a cephalothorax and an abdomen. They have no sensory antennae or mandibles, but they have chelicerae and pedipalps.
- Chelicerates are divided into two classes: Meristomata (horseshoe crabs) and Arachnida (arachnids).

- Arachnids have four pairs of walking legs, book lungs, Malpighian tubules, and simple eyes. They include spiders, scorpions, mites, and ticks.

23.4 Insects and Their Relatives

- Uniramians have one pair of antennae, compound eyes, varied mouthparts, spiracles, and tracheae. They have highly developed nervous systems and sensory organs, as well as complex digestive systems.
- Centipedes, millipedes, and insects are three groups of uniramians.
- Metamorphosis, ability to communicate, complex social systems, camouflage, and mimicry are adaptations of insects.

23.5 Arthropods in the Biosphere

- Arthropods play a key role in food chains and in plant pollination. They supply products such as honey and silk.
- Arthropods transmit diseases to humans and other animals. Some arthropods can cause great damage to crops; others can be used to control pests.

Use Terms and Concepts

Use each of the following words or terms in a complete sentence. If you need to review a meaning, turn to the page indicated.

exoskeleton (p. 546)
endoskeleton (p. 546)
compound eyes (p. 547)
cephalothorax (p. 549)
mandibles (p. 549)

chelicerac (p. 552)
Malpighian
  tubules (p. 552)
pedipalps (p. 553)
spiracles (p. 556)

metamorphosis (p. 559)
pheromone (p. 560)
social insects (p. 560)
mimicry (p. 562)

Review the Big Ideas

Before students begin the Chapter Review, you may wish to discuss Chapter 23 Big Ideas. Point out that arthropods represent the largest and most diverse animal phylum. Explain that much of their evolutionary success can be attributed to certain characteristics, such as jointed appendages with specialized functions and protective exoskeletons. Discuss that biologists mainly classify arthropods by observing how many body segments they have and their appendage structures. Emphasize that although many arthropods can be harmful to other organisms, they play a very important role in maintaining a balance in the Earth's biosphere. Arthropods are a major source of food for many animals and the largest group of arthropods, the insects, increase plant growth through pollination.

Answers

1. mandibles
2. metamorphosis
3. exoskeleton
4. pedipalps
5. social insects
6. Malpighian tubules
7. pheromone
8. book lungs
9. a
10. b
11. c or d
12. b
13. b
14. Stationary pupating insects are especially vulnerable; they use camouflage and mimicry to make themselves less conspicuous.
15. The arthropod grows a new layer of chitin beneath its exoskeleton; it forces fluid between the layers; pressure from the fluid splits the exoskeleton and the arthropod crawls out.
16. Alternatives include mixing plantings with some species that secrete natural toxins; importing natural predators; and introducing sterile adults to inhibit reproduction.
17. The queen bee secretes a pheromone that prevents premature feeding of "royal jelly" to larva. When the pheromone is no longer detected, workers feed "royal jelly" to some larvae, producing queens that battle for dominance.
18. Trilobites did not evolve specialized appendages.
19. Adult barnacles are sessile marine organisms without eyes, gills, or blood vessels.
20. Web-building spiders have relatively poor eyesight and long slender legs. Hunting spiders have excellent eyesight and heavy legs.
21. Concepts maps should

Use Your Word Power

COMPLETION Write the word or phrase that best completes each statement.

1. Arthropod jawlike appendages that crush food are called _____ .

2. During _____ caterpillars develop into butterflies.

3. The muscles in an arthropod are attached to the inside of its _____ .

4. Spiders have _____ that secrete poisons and digestive enzymes.

5. Insects that live in cooperative groups are called _____ .

6. In spiders' excretory systems, _____ filter wastes from water.

7. A chemical called _____ is secreted by some insects to communicate and to attract mates.

8. Terrestrial chelicerates have respiratory structures called _____ .

MULTIPLE CHOICE Choose the letter of the word or phrase that best completes each statement.

9. All uniramians have (a) compound eyes; (b) one pair of walking legs per segment; (c) wings; (d) fanglike claws.

10. Arthropods do NOT have (a) jointed appendages; (b) an endoskeleton; (c) a complex system of muscles; (d) an open circulatory system.

11. Chelicerae (a) digest food; (b) chew food; (c) crush food; (d) paralyze food.

12. Arthropods are the only organisms that have (a) segmented bodies; (b) compound eyes; (c) mimicry; (d) an open circulatory system.

13. Openings in an exoskeleton that let in air are (a) gills; (b) spiracles; (c) spicules; (d) book lungs.

Show What You Know

14. When are insects especially vulnerable to predators? How do insects minimize the danger?

15. Describe the sequence of events that take place during molting.

16. What alternatives are there to pesticides for controlling insect pests?

17. What role do pheromones play in the life cycles that occur in a beehive?

18. How do the extinct trilobites differ from modern arthropods?

19. Explain why scientists observing only adult barnacles would be unlikely to classify them as crustaceans.

20. How do web-building spiders differ from hunting spiders?

21. **Make a Concept Map** Use the following terms to create a concept map: adult, cocoon, exoskeleton, incomplete metamorphosis, larva, molt, nymph, pupa, and wings.

22. Is this arthropod a chelicerate or a uniramian? Give at least 3 reasons for your answer.

Take It Further

23. **Developing a Hypothesis** Many characteristics of organisms have drawbacks as well as benefits. Compound eyes in some insects are one example. What advantages could compound eyes provide that would compensate for the possibly blurry images they produce?

24. **Making an Analogy** Suppose you decided to attend a sports rally at a rival school. What could you do to blend in? Compare your behavior to adaptations in insects.

show: <u>metamorphosis</u> can be <u>complete</u> or <u>incomplete</u>; incomplete → <u>eggs</u> which hatch to <u>nymphs</u>, which lack <u>wings</u>; <u>nymphs</u> molt to <u>adults</u>, who have <u>exoskeletons</u>; <u>complete</u> → <u>eggs</u> which hatch to <u>larvae</u> which will be sheltered in a <u>cocoon</u>, during which the <u>larva</u> is called a <u>pupa</u>, then becomes an <u>adult</u> with an <u>exoskeleton</u>

22. It is a chelicerate: pincer-like mouthparts, no antennae, and pedipalps.
23. Compound eyes allow insects to detect the slightest movement of a predator. Compound eyes in crustaceans are mounted on stalks to allow vision in any direction or in two directions at once, which is advantageous for detecting food and potential predators.

25. Interpreting a Graph The type of population increase shown in the graph below is called exponential growth because each population increases by an exponent of 10 with each generation. If insect B loses 90 percent of offspring in each generation, what will its actual growth be? How many individuals could theoretically be produced in generation 3 by insects A, B, and C? In generation 4? Could this happen in nature? Explain your answer.

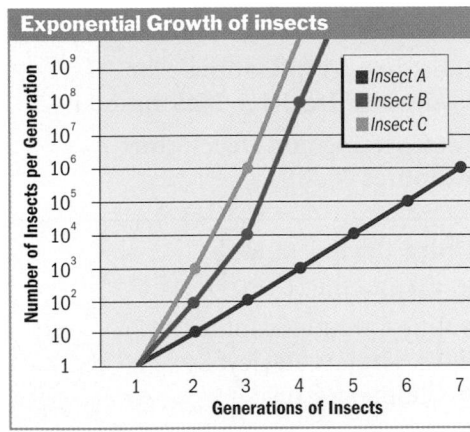

Exponential Growth of insects

Number of Insects per Generation vs. Generations of Insects

- ■ Insect A
- ■ Insect B
- ■ Insect C

26. Analyzing Data The eastern cicada has a 17-year life cycle, most of it spent underground in the juvenile stage. These cicadas last emerged in great numbers in Connecticut in 1996. The southwestern cicada has a 13-year life cycle. Its last great emergence was in Arkansas in 1985. When will both groups emerge in the same year? How many generations will have passed for each type of cicada?

Consider the Issues

27. Collecting Specimens In the late nineteenth century, it was popular for amateur naturalists to have large collections of mounted insects or birds' eggs. Today collections are usually centralized at natural history museums. For example, the Smithsonian Institution in Washington, D.C., has over 31 million preserved specimens of chelicerates and insects. The public can visit the museum and qualified researchers can borrow specimens from the collection for two years or more. What are the benefits and drawbacks of private and public collections? What advances in technology have improved access to public collections?

28. Using Pesticides Make a list of pros and cons for the use of insecticides in a home garden. Using this list, make a recommendation for insect control in your area.

Make New Connections

29. Biology and Literature The title character in E. B. White's *Charlotte's Web* is a grey web-building spider whose species is *Araneus cavaticus*. Other than the fact that Charlotte can talk, how accurate is White's description of the spider's anatomy and behavior?

30. Biology and Mythology Arachnids share their name with the mythological Lydian princess Arachne, who was a skilled weaver. Find out what happened when the goddess Athena (also known as Minerva), another weaver, challenged Arachne to a contest.

FAST FORWARD TO CHAPTER 24

Most crustaceans are marine invertebrates. So are horseshoe crabs. In Chapter 24 you will study a phylum that contains many other species of marine invertebrates. You will also be introduced to some invertebrates that share a phylum with vertebrates.

through 11 generations (1985 is generation 1).

27. Answers will vary. Students may argue that private collectors have instant access to all specimens. However, private collections have gaps and are costly to maintain. Depletion of the environment was often a concern, especially with birds' eggs and rarer species of insects. Centralized collections are usually larger, better documented, and available to more scholars. The Internet promises to increase access to data.

28. Students should be able to support their decisions with scientific facts.

29. Answers will vary. You might also want to suggest a more challenging classic, Franz Kafka's short story "Metamorphosis."

30. Athena heard of Arachne's boast that she was a better weaver than the goddess, who then challenged Arachne to a contest. When Athena saw Arachne's excellent work, she destroyed it and attacked the princess. After Arachne hanged herself, Athena repented and changed the princess into a spider so that she could continue to weave. The myth, which was reported by Ovid, reflects his fascination with metamorphosis.

24. Students might suggest wearing clothes that display the colors or logo of the rival school. This behavior is analogous to mimicry in insects.

25. If insect B loses 90% of it's population with each generation, its growth rate will resemble that of insect A. In generation 3, insect A, B, and C could produce 10^2, 10^4, and 10^6 individuals respectively. In generation 4, insects A, B, and C could produce 10^3, 10^8, and 10^{12} individuals respectively. This probably could not happen in nature due to competition.

26. In the year 2115, the eastern cicada will have passed through 8 generations (1996 is generation 1) and the southwestern cicada will have passed

PLANNING GUIDE

Section	Student Activities/Features	Teacher's Resource Package
24.1 Echinoderms **Objectives** ■ Describe the common characteristics of echinoderms ■ Explain the origin and diversity of echinoderms	**Lab Zone Discover It!** *Modeling Suction,* p. 571 **Everyday Biology** *A Writing Urchin?* p. 572 **Lab Zone Do It!** *Modeling Symmetry,* p. 574 **Everyday Biology** *Echinoderm Drillers,* p. 577 **In the Community** *Looking for Echinoderm Specimens,* p. 578 **STS: Environmental Awareness** *Coral Attack!* p. 578 **Lab Zone Investigate It!** *Exploring Echinoderm Diversity,* p. 579	**Unit 6 Review Module** ■ Section Review 24.1 ■ Activity Recordsheets 24-1 and 24-2 ■ Critical Thinking Exercise 24 ■ Enrichment Topic 24-1 **Laboratory Manual** ■ Lab 40: "Sea Star Anatomy" ■ Lab 41: "Sea Star: Alternative Anatomy Investigation" **Consumer Applications** 24-1 **Issues and Decision Making** 24-1 **Interpreting and Developing Graphics** 70, 71
24.2 Invertebrate Chordates **Objectives** ■ Describe the four characteristics of chordates ■ Distinguish between the two subphyla of invertebrate chordates	**Lab Zone Think About It!** *Comparing Structures and Systems of an Echinoderm and a Chordate,* p. 581	**Unit 6 Review Module** ■ Section Review 24.2 ■ Interpreting Graphics 24 ■ Vocabulary Review 24 ■ Chapter 24 Tests **Interpreting and Developing Graphics** 72 **Spanish Reviews** ■ Chapter 24 ■ Unit 6

Technology Resources

Internet Connections

Within this chapter, you will see the bioSURF logo. If you and your students have access to the Internet, the following URL address will provide various Internet connections that are related to topics and features presented in this chapter:

http://invertebrates.biosurf.com

You can also find relevant chapter material at **The Biology Place** address:

http://www.biology.com

CD-ROMs

Biología: la telaraña de la vida, (Spanish Student Edition) Chapter 24
Teacher's Resource Planner, Chapter 24 Supplements
TestWorks CD-ROM
■ Chapter 24 Tests

Overhead Transparencies

■ Sea Star Structures, #52
■ Structures of a Tunicate, #53

Videotapes

Biology Alive! Video Series
■ Signs of Life Video
Rewind: The Web of Life Reteach Videos

Planning for Activities

STUDENT EDITION

Lab Zone
Discover It! p. 571
■ medicine dropper
■ beaker
■ water

Lab Zone Do It! p. 574
■ pencil
■ tissue paper
■ scissors

Lab Zone
Investigate It! p. 579
■ preserved echinoderm specimens or photographs of echinoderms

Lab Zone
Think About It! p. 581
■ diagrams on pages 573 and 580

TEACHER'S EDITION

Teacher Demo, p. 573
Surfaces
■ stuffed animal
■ sea star

Teacher Demo, p. 574
Suction cups of a sea star
■ suction darts
■ small metal box

Teacher Demo, p. 580
Notochord
■ heavy-duty garden hose

Teacher Demo, p. 581
Vertebral column
■ model or wall chart of a human skeleton

Chapter Objectives

Students will learn the main concepts of this chapter as they complete the following objectives.

- Describe the common characteristics of echinoderms
- Explain the origin and diversity of echinoderms
- Describe the four characteristics of chordates
- Distinguish between the two subphyla of invertebrate chordates

Key Words

24.1 *echinoderm, water vascular system, ampulla, tube foot, protostome, deuterostome*

24.2 *dorsal hollow nerve cord, notochord, gill slits, post-anal tail*

The Opening Story

Have students discuss how they think the story relates to the content of this chapter. Point out that all echinoderms live in marine environments. Ask students to infer what traits enabled echinoderms to survive in their shipwreck habitat.

You can find out more about echinoderms and invertebrate chordates by exploring the following Internet address: *http://invertebrates.biosurf.com*

In this chapter . . .

FEATURES

Everyday Biology
- A Writing Urchin?
- Echinoderm Drillers

In the Community
Looking for Echinoderm Specimens

 Environmental Awareness
Coral Attack!

LAB ZONES

Discover It!
- Modeling Suction

Do It!
- Modeling Symmetry

Think About It!
- Comparing Structures and Systems of an Echinoderm and a Chordate

Investigate It!
- Exploring Echinoderm Diversity

ECHINODERMS

Life on sunken treasure

I n 1988, almost 130 years after it sank in a hurricane en route from Panama to New York, the steamer SS *Central America* was found about 270 kilometers (km) off the coast of Cape Fear, North Carolina. Of the more than 550 people aboard, 425 perished, and several tons of gold from the California gold fields were lost. Today the ship and its treasure rest under 2200 meters (m) of water, on a dark, silent deep-sea ridge.

In the environment that surrounds the shipwreck, almost no marine life exists, but a research submersible discovered that the wreck itself was teeming with life. Like an artificial reef, the wreck housed a diverse community of animals. A wide variety of echinoderms—including sea lilies, sea stars, feather stars, and brittle stars—were attached to or crawling on the ship and among stacks of gold coins and bullion.

How do the echinoderms and other animals survive? The shipwreck provides an ecosystem for the deep-sea animals. The organic materials at the site, including decaying food and wood, attract various species. The ship's framework provides shelter and a place for these species to reproduce. Over time, a large, self-sustaining community has been established. The site has provided an unusual opportunity for marine biologists to study echinoderms in an artificial-reef habitat.

LAB ZONE Discover It!

Modeling Suction

You need a medicine dropper and a beaker.

1. Fill the medicine dropper with water. Empty it. How does this tool work?
2. With the dropper empty, squeeze the bulb, place the tip firmly against one of your fingers, and reduce the pressure on the bulb. Can you feel the "suction" on your finger? What causes this phenomenon?

Many echinoderms use a similar method to the one you just demonstrated to move themselves around and to pry open the shells of prey.

WRITE ABOUT IT!

Imagine that you are a writer invited to descend in a submarine to observe the shipwrecked SS *Central America*. Write a paragraph, short story, or poem that conveys your first impressions of the ship.

571

Opening Activities

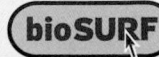 If you have access to the Internet in your classroom or school, you may wish to have students connect to the address shown on page 570. You may also want to have students conduct net searches for information using key words related to this chapter. For example, they could search for entries under starfish, sea urchins, or sand dollar.

LAB ZONE Discover It!

Modeling Suction   TEAM WORK

Introduce the chapter by having students do the activity at the beginning of class or as a homework assignment. If medicine droppers are not available, have students use turkey basters.

WRITE ABOUT IT!

Encourage students to use vivid language in their descriptions to help the reader visualize the shipwreck site.

REWIND to Chapter 23

Briefly review concepts learned in Chapter 23, *Arthropods*. Ask:

- **How do you think your knowledge of arthropods will help you recognize the evolutionary advances of echinoderms and invertebrate chordates described in Chapter 24?**

PORTFOLIO PREVIEW

Students should be encouraged to add to their portfolios as they work through this chapter. In addition to the *Write About It* opportunity, the following sections are excellent opportunities for another portfolio entry:

- Section 24.1: *Echinoderms*
- Section 24.2: *Invertebrate Chordates*

ENGAGE

Consider the Big Idea

Have students read The Big Idea! at the top of the page. Point out that these are the three characteristics of echinoderms and that the name itself means "spiny skin."

Use the Visual

Have students study the photograph that opens the section. Ask them to describe what they think is happening to the sea star. Ask:

- **What other animals have the ability to regenerate body parts?** (Planarians)

Check Prior Knowledge

To assess students' knowledge about animals in general, ask:

- **What kinds of body symmetry occur in animals?** (Bilateral and radial)
- **What functions are essential for animal survival?** (Reproduction, growth, respiration, digestion, excretion)

Teacher Demo

Illustrate radial symmetry by drawing the outline of a sea star on the board. Mark the center and draw a line into each arm. Next draw a dot and many lines radiating from the dot. Create a bicycle wheel from the dot and lines to show that the wheel has radial symmetry. Have students suggest other common items with radial symmetry. (Ferris wheel, racing track, dart board)

24.1 Echinoderms

What you'll learn

IDEAS
- To describe the common characteristics of echinoderms
- To explain the origin and diversity of echinoderms

WORDS
echinoderm, water vascular system, ampulla, tube foot, protostome, deuterostome

Multiplication, not subtraction

In the past, when people who harvested shellfish for a living caught sea stars, they chopped them up and threw them back into the sea. Why? Because the sea stars ate large numbers of shellfish. What the harvesters didn't know was that the pieces of sea stars could grow into new sea stars! So, instead of being eliminated, the sea star population increased.

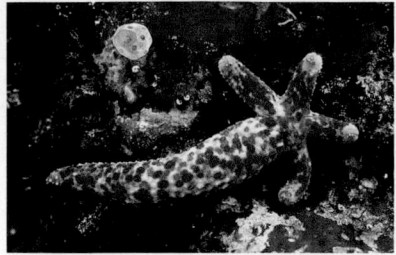

CHARACTERISTICS OF ECHINODERMS

Prickly packages

If you have ever visited the seashore, you have probably seen the remains of sand dollars and sea urchins washed onto the beach. Perhaps you have seen live sea stars in a saltwater aquarium. These animals are echinoderms. An **echinoderm** (eh-KY-noh-derm) is a marine animal characterized by spiny skin, an endoskeleton, radial symmetry, and a water vascular system.

The word *echinoderm* comes from "echin-," which means "spiny," and "-derma," which means "skin." Spines can be long, as in the sea urchin, or short, as in the sea star. In addition to having spiny skin, echinoderms have an endoskeleton made of calcium that supports the echinoderm's body.

Echinoderms are radially symmetrical. The body parts of radial animals are arranged around a central point, or axis. The body of most echinoderms consists of five parts in an arrangement known as penta-radial symmetry. For example, the sea star in *Figure* 24.2 has five arms that radiate from the center of its body.

Another characteristic of echinoderms is a water vascular system, which allows them to move, obtain food, and exchange gases. An echinoderm's

EVERYDAY BIOLOGY

A Writing Urchin?

One urchin got its common name, the slate-pencil urchin, because its spines were used to write on slate boards. Now its spines are often used as wind chimes.

FIGURE 24.1
A sea star pries open its prey's shell. The sea star pushes part of its stomach through its mouth and into the opened shell. The sea star then digests its prey.

STUDENT RESOURCES

From the Teacher's Resource Package, use:
- Section Review 24.1, Activity Record-sheets 24-1 and 24-2, Critical Thinking Exercise 24, and Enrichment Topic 24-1 from Unit 6 Review Module
- Lab 40: "Sea Star Anatomy," Lab 41: "Sea Star: Alternate Anatomy"

TECHNOLOGY RESOURCES

Relevant technology resources include:
- Spanish Student Edition CD-ROM
- Teacher's Resource Planner CD-ROM
- Biology Alive! Video: "Signs of Life"

water vascular system is a network of fluid-filled tubes. This system consists of a number of important structures: the ring canal, radial canals, ampullae, and tube feet. These structures are shown in *Figure 24.3*.

The water vascular system has one opening through which water enters and leaves. This opening—located on the dorsal surface of the sea star—is called the sieve plate. Water flows through the sieve plate, into the ring canal, and down the radial canal in each arm of the sea star. Ampullae extend from both sides of the radial canal. An **ampulla** (AM-pyoo-luh) is a muscular sac that helps force water into a tube foot. A **tube foot** is a hollow tube which may have a suction-cup-like end. A tube foot is located beneath each ampulla.

An echinoderm moves by pumping water into its tube feet. By contracting the muscles in each ampulla, the sea star forces water into the tube feet, causing them to extend.

FIGURE 24.3
Water Vascular System
The water vascular system functions in movement, obtaining food, and respiration. Gases diffuse across the membranes of the tube feet.

Sieve plate   Ring canal

Tube foot   Radial canal   Ampulla

FIGURE 24.2
Structures and Systems of a Sea Star

In a sea star, the digestive, reproductive, and nervous systems are stacked within the central disk and radiate outward into each arm. How does the fact that each arm contains all of the systems benefit the sea star? ❶

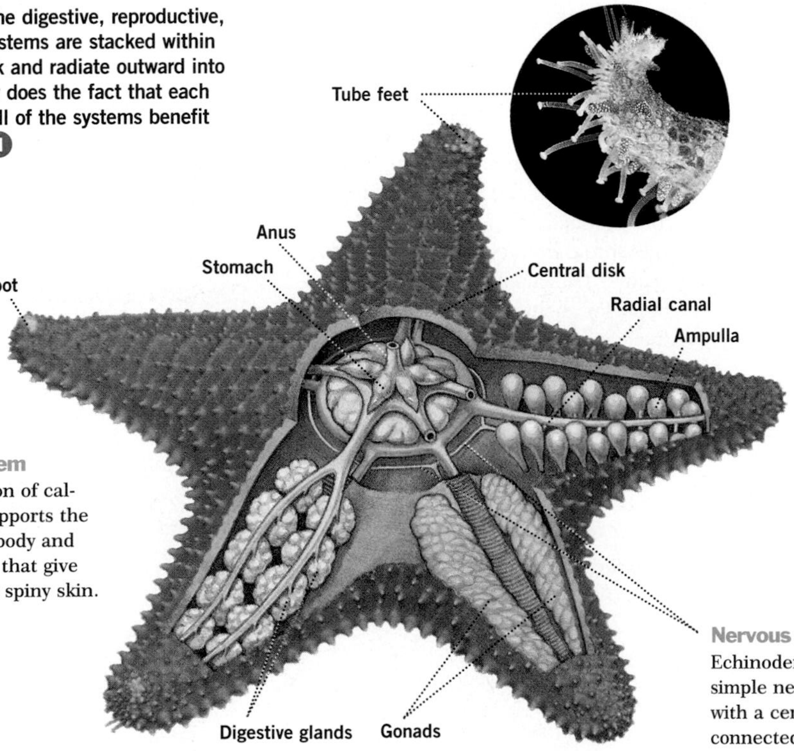

Tube feet

Anus

Stomach

Eyespot

Central disk

Radial canal

Ampulla

Skeletal system
An endoskeleton of calcium plates supports the echinoderm's body and has the spines that give the sea star its spiny skin.

Nervous system
Echinoderms have a simple nervous system with a central nerve ring connected to nerves in each arm.

Digestive glands   Gonads

Digestive system
Nutrients from food pass from the digestive organs to the coelom. Then the nutrients spread through the body. Digestive wastes leave the body through the anus.

Reproductive system
Each sea star has gonads—a pair of either testes or ovaries—in each arm.

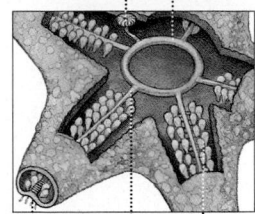

Chapter 24 Echinoderms and Invertebrate Chordates **573**

MEETING DIVERSE NEEDS

Sight Impaired For impaired students, you may want to provide a plastic sea star model with textured anatomy. Prepare identification tags with raised letters or Braille identifying the names and locations of the structures shown in Figure 24.2.

LEP Encourage LEP students to compile a picture dictionary illustrating the meaning of unfamiliar terms used throughout the chapter. Suggest that they write each term on an index card and keep their cards in alphabetical order.

---

② **TEACH**

Explain

To ensure that students recognize the difference between radial and bilateral symmetry, draw a rectangle and five-pointed star on the board. Ask:

■ **What kind of symmetry is shown in the rectangle? In the star?** (Bilateral, radial)

Teacher Demo

Hold up a stuffed animal and a sea star. Point out that the stuffed animal has anterior and posterior ends, ventral and dorsal surfaces, and right and left sides. Point out that the sea star has only ventral and dorsal surfaces.

Use the Visual

Obtain a sea star model or a mounted, preserved sea star from a biological supply house. Review the structures of the sea star shown in Figure 24.2. As each structure is discussed, point out its location on the specimen. Ask:

■ **What roles do tube feet play?** (Locomotion, food capture)
■ **What body systems are contained in the arms?** (Digestive, reproductive, nervous)
■ **How can you tell that sea stars reproduce sexually?** (Existence of gonads)

❶ If it loses an arm, it can still function.

The suction-cup-like ends of the extended tube feet then attach to a hard surface, such as a rock. When muscles in the tube feet contract, water flows out of the tube feet and back into the ampullae. The tube feet shorten, pulling the sea star forward. Sea stars can also use their water vascular system to secure food. By attaching their tube feet to the two shells of a mollusk, for example, they can pull open its shell.

Like the water vascular system, the digestive, reproductive, and nervous systems in a sea star are stacked within the central disk and radiate into each arm. You can see the location of these systems in *Figure 24.2* on page 573.

Although many echinoderms can reproduce asexually by regeneration, all echinoderms reproduce sexually. Sea stars gather at certain times of the year to reproduce. Most release sperm and eggs into the water, where fertilization occurs. The larvae produced swim freely for about two years, then settle to the ocean floor and mature into adults.

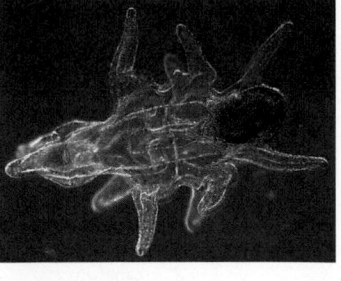

FIGURE 24.4
These starfish larvae have bilateral symmetry. They live as larvae for about two years. How does bilateral symmetry compare with radial symmetry? ❶

SUPER READ!

Echinoderm larvae interest biologists because, unlike the adults, they have bilateral symmetry. Scientists speculate that the first adult echinoderms probably had bilateral symmetry, and that their radial symmetry evolved later.

ORIGIN AND DIVERSITY OF ECHINODERMS

It's all in the tissues

You learned in Chapter 21 that taxonomists can classify animals based on similarities in the development of their embryos. These similarities can be an indicator of evolutionary relationships between animals. Animal embryos develop from a fertilized egg into a blastula, as shown in *Figure 24.6*. The cells of the blastula then move inward to form the gastrula. The place where the cells move inward becomes an opening into a cavity of the gastrula. This opening is

FIGURE 24.5
Phylum Echinodermata

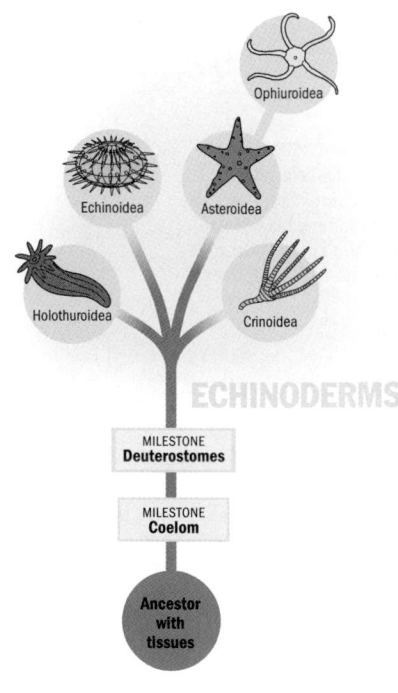

Ophiuroidea

Echinoidea

Asteroidea

Holothuroidea

Crinoidea

ECHINODERMS

MILESTONE
Deuterostomes

MILESTONE
Coelom

Ancestor with tissues

LAB ZONE Do It!   **bioSURF**

Modeling Symmetry

You can model asymmetry, radial symmetry, and bilateral symmetry when you . . .

Try This

1 Experiment with pieces of paper to create models of each form.
2 Select three organisms that you have read about—each of which displays a different type of symmetry.
3 Trace the shape of each organism on tissue paper, cut them out, and fold them.

Analyze Your Results

Were your selections of organisms correctly matched to their type of symmetry?

---

❶ In radial symmetry, the body parts are arranged around a central point. In bilateral symmetry, the body parts are arranged around a midline.

called the blastopore. The blastopore will become either the mouth or the anus of the developing organism.

In many animals, such as mollusks, worms, and arthropods, the blastopore develops into a mouth. An animal in which a blastopore develops into a mouth is called a **protostome** (PRO-toh-stome), which means "first mouth." Later in the protostome's development, a second digestive tube opening forms at the opposite end of the digestive tract. This becomes the anus.

In echinoderms, the blastopore develops into an anus, and a mouth forms later at the opposite end of the digestive tube. An animal in which a blastopore develops into an anus is called a **deuterostome** (DOO-ter-oh-stome), which means "second mouth." The evolution of deuterostomes and protostomes represents a major milestone in the evolutionary development of animals.

In addition to echinoderms, animals called chordates are also deuterstomes. You will read about chordates in the next section. Taxonomists have concluded that echinoderms and chordates are closely related. The two groups may have shared a common ancestor.

Echinoderms are divided into five classes based on their structural differences. These classes are Asteroidea (ah-stur-OID-ee-uh), Ophiuroidea (ahf-ee-yur-OID-ee-uh), Echinoidea (eck-ih-NOID-ee-uh), Holothuroidea (hahl-oh-thur-OID-ee-uh), and Crinoidea (krih-NOID-ee-uh). Although these names may sound strange to you, you are probably familiar with some members of the classes.

Sea stars Sea stars, or starfish, make up the class Asteroidea. Although most sea stars have five arms, some species may have 20 or more! Look again at *Figure 24.2* to review the basic structure of sea stars.

FIGURE 24.6

Protostome and Deuterostome Development

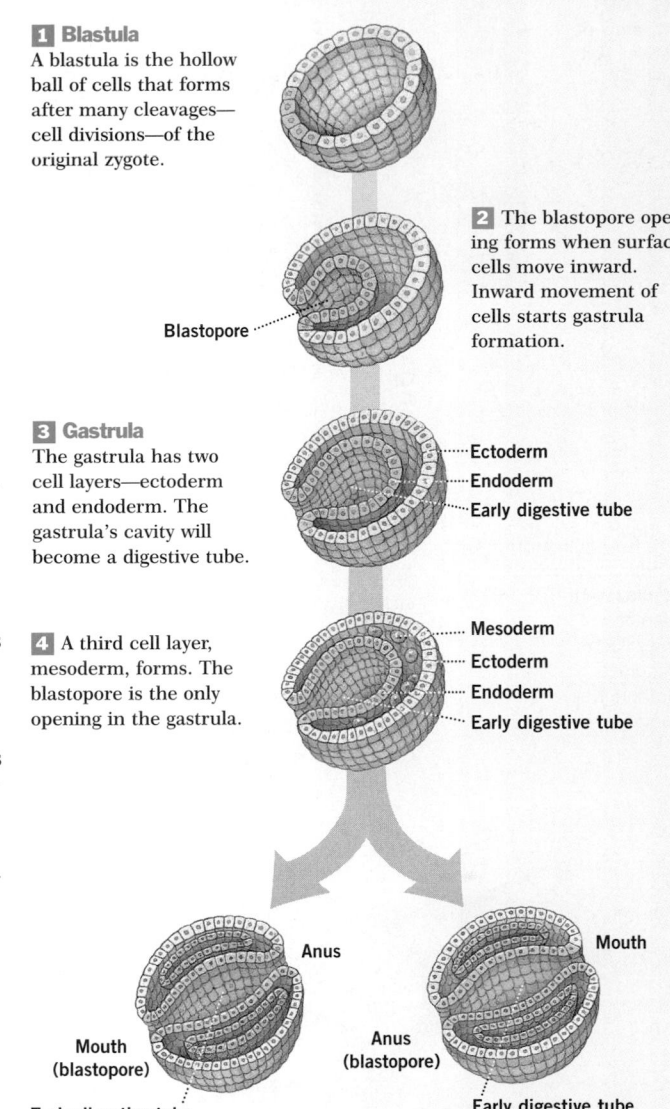

1 Blastula
A blastula is the hollow ball of cells that forms after many cleavages—cell divisions—of the original zygote.

2 The blastopore opening forms when surface cells move inward. Inward movement of cells starts gastrula formation.

Blastopore

3 Gastrula
The gastrula has two cell layers—ectoderm and endoderm. The gastrula's cavity will become a digestive tube.

— Ectoderm
— Endoderm
— Early digestive tube

4 A third cell layer, mesoderm, forms. The blastopore is the only opening in the gastrula.

— Mesoderm
— Ectoderm
— Endoderm
— Early digestive tube

Anus

Mouth

Mouth
(blastopore)

Anus
(blastopore)

Early digestive tube

Early digestive tube

5a Protostome
In a protostome, the blastopore becomes the mouth. Later in development, an anus forms where the digestive tube makes another opening.

5b Deuterostome
In a deuterostome, the blastopore becomes the anus. Later in development, a mouth forms where the digestive tube makes a second opening.

Chapter 24 Echinoderms and Invertebrate Chordates **575**

Build Writing Skills

Have students write an article for a nature magazine explaining why scientists think echinoderms and chordates may be related. Review the articles as a class. Then use the definition of echinoderms given in the text to make sure students can describe the main characteristics of the group.

Use the Visual

Direct students to Figure 24.6. To enhance their understanding of protostome and deuterostome development, you may want them to review the steps involved in embryological development illustrated in Figure 21.4 on page 502, then ask:

- **What is the blastopore?** (The opening formed when cells on the blastula's surface move inward)
- **What happens during gastrula formation?** (Cell layers develop that will give rise to different tissues and organs.)
- **How does the development of a protostome differ from that of a deuterostome?** (In a protostome, the blastopore becomes the mouth; in a deuterostome the blastopore becomes the anus.)

FIGURE 24.7
Some sea stars, like this one, have many arms. How many arms do most sea stars have? **❶**

Most asteroids are scavengers and carnivores. They locate food sources by sensing them chemically. Asteroids feed primarily on gastropods, bivalves, crustaceans, polychaetes, and other echinoderms.

Kingdom: Animalia
Phylum: Echinodermata

Five classes:
Asteroidea
Ophiuroidea
Echinoidea
Holothuroidea
Crinoidea

Brittle stars and basket stars
The brittle stars and basket stars comprise the class Ophiuroidea. Like most of the sea stars, these animals have five arms. Their arms, however, are longer, thinner, and more mobile than those of sea stars. Their tube feet lack suction-cup-like ends, and they do not have ampullae. Basket stars capture

plankton with highly branched arms, which they then roll in toward the mouth.

The brittle stars and basket stars move more quickly than any other echinoderm. Brittle stars move by extending an arm in the direction they are headed. They trail two other arms behind and use the remaining two arms as oars. Like sea stars, ophiuroids tend to be scavengers and carnivores, although some obtain nutrition by filter feeding.

Sea urchins and sand dollars
The sea urchins and sand dollars are members of the class Echinoidea. The echinoids have bodies shaped like spheres or discs and have no arms. Their bodies are covered with movable spines. In some sea urchin species, the spines are very long and sharp and sometimes contain poisons. Methods of locomotion and feeding differ among echinoid species. Sea urchins use both their tube feet and their spines to move. Sand dollars burrow, using their spines to dig into the sand. Most sea urchins are grazers—although deep-sea species tend to be sediment feeders and scavengers.

FIGURE 24.8
In what direction do you think the brittle star on the left is moving? **❷**

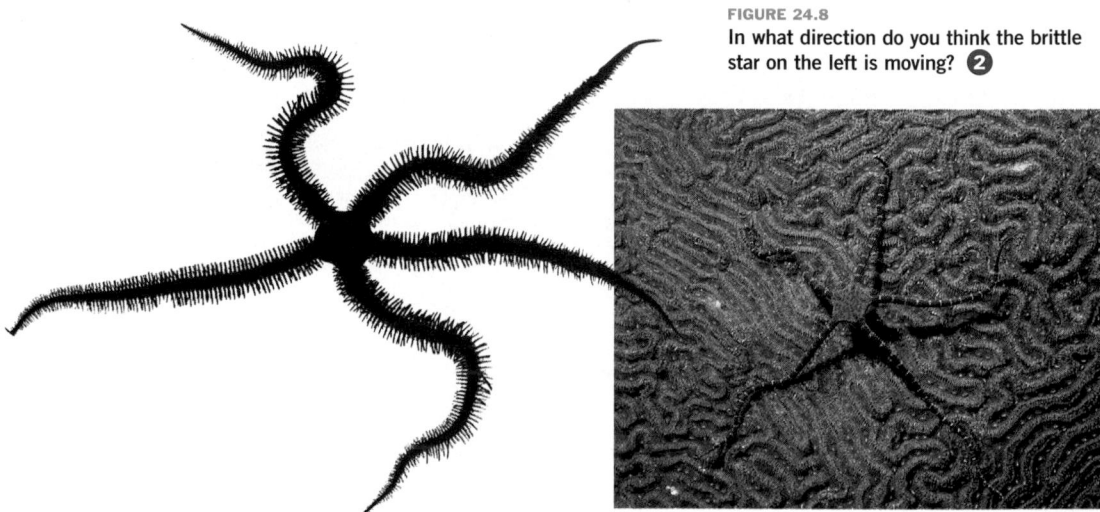

576   *Unit 6 Invertebrate Animals*

❶ Five

❷ To the left

❸ The mouths are on the dorsal surface in the center of the arms.

FIGURE 24.9
Protective, movable spines are characteristic of sea urchins. Note the radial symmetry in the view of the mouth (below).

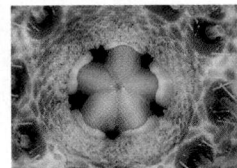

Sand dollars are sediment feeders, selecting food particles from the sediments in which they burrow.

Sea cucumbers Sea cucumbers belong to the class Holothuroidea. Sea cucumbers lack the characteristics of many echinoderms, particularly the arms and a five-part body. The only obvious signs of a five-part body plan in sea cucumbers are the five rows of tube feet running the length of the body. Like sea stars and sea urchins, sea cucumbers use their tube feet for movement.

Some sea cucumbers have sticky tentacle-like tube feet surrounding the mouth, which collect plankton. When disturbed by a predator, a sea cucumber protects itself by shooting long thin tubules out of its anus. By doing so, a sea cucumber sometimes ejects its entire digestive system. However, because of its regenerative abilities, it can grow a new digestive tube in a matter of days.

Sea lilies and feather stars Sea lilies and feather stars comprise the class Crinoidea, the most ancient looking of echinoderms. Only a few species of this class remain today, but crinoids are quite common in the fossil record. Sea lilies have stalks and are sessile. Feather stars can creep and even swim. Unlike all other echinoderms, crinoids have their mouth on the dorsal surface. Five or more arms reach up, swaying around the mouth. Their tube feet, which are covered with sticky mucus, capture plankton and move it to their mouth.

EVERYDAY BIOLOGY

Echinoderm Drillers

Sea urchins usually use their spines and teeth to burrow into sand and rocks. One sea urchin in California, however, drilled 10 millimeters (mm) into a solid steel girder—a feat that took 20 years!

FIGURE 24.10
Compare the sea cucumber (left) with the sea lily (right). Where are the mouths located in these two species? ❸

Chapter 24 Echinoderms and Invertebrate Chordates **577**

Explain

Not all echinoderms have arms. However, in echinoderms with arms, the number is always five or a multiple of five, unless arms have been lost. The largest number of arms observed in an echinoderm species is 50.

Earth Science

Many ancient echinoderms, such as crinoids, blastoids, and cystoids, became extinct at the end of the Permian period. A number of factors caused the extinction, including climate changes and the formation of Pangaea. Have students research the changes that were taking place at the end of the Permian period and share the information in a class discussion.

Build Writing Skills

Have students write a poem, a song, or a rap about an echinoderm. Encourage them to be descriptive as well as scientifically accurate in their writing.

In the Community

In place of a field trip, invite a zoologist or biologist from a nearby university, zoo, or aquarium to speak to the class. As an alternative to preparing an illustrated notebook, some students may prefer to sculpt one or more models of echinoderms.

 STS

Point out the location of the Great Barrier Reef on a world map. Have students write an essay describing the water depths, water temperatures, plant life, and echinoderms that live on the reef. Encourage students to include pictures of the reef and its life.

 **ASSESS**

Evaluate Understanding

Write the following class names on the board: *Asteroidea, Ophiuroidea, Crinoidea, Echinoidea, Holothuroidea.* Ask students to describe and give the common names for animals in each of these classes. Ask:

■ **What characteristics do all echinoderms have in common?** (Radial symmetry, body parts in fives or multiples of five, water vascular system, bilateral larvae)

Reteach

Using the sea star model from earlier in this section, describe each system. Guide students to locate the organs for each body system and explain their functions.

578

Investigate local sources, such as aquariums, where you may be able to examine live or skeletal echinoderms. You could also arrange to visit the zoology department of a nearby college or university to observe its echinoderm specimens. In addition, museums usually have skeletal echinoderms that you can view. Sketch the echinoderms you find, and gather facts about them to create an illustrated notebook to share with the class. Log on to *http://invertebrates.biosurf.com* to learn more about echinoderms.

IN THE COMMUNITY
Looking for Echinoderm Specimens

ECHINODERMS IN THE BIOSPHERE
Food for thought

Sea cucumbers and sea urchin eggs are considered food delicacies in many cultures. Researchers also use sea urchin eggs for biological research. And like members of nearly all other marine invertebrate phyla, echinoderms are a potential source of new pharmaceuticals.

When sea urchins overpopulate, however, they prevent kelp and other seaweeds from attaching to the ocean floor. Their overpopulation can affect an entire ecosystem. In California, predation of abalone by sea otters led abalone harvesters to hunt sea otters. Sea otters are also a predator of sea urchins. What do you think happened to the marine ecosystem when otters were hunted to near extinction? **❶**

FIGURE 24.11
It might take several hundred years to grow the coral that this crown-of-thorns (*A. planci*) sea star can eat in one year.

? What characteristics do echinoderms share?

Coral attack!

In 1969 the crown-of-thorns sea star, *Acanthaster planci*, destroyed 90 percent of the coral off the northwest coast of Guam. During the past 20 years, this sea star has also attacked more than 25 percent of the 2000-km-long Great Barrier Reef of Australia. In fact, just one sea star can consume the polyps from up to 13 square meters (m^2) of coral each year.

The effect of *A. planci* on the ecosystem is like that of a forest fire. In one reproductive season, one crown-of-thorns sea star can produce 65 million eggs. Normally, most of the freshly hatched larvae are eaten by fish and other animals. However, there are periodic population explosions, and a huge number of *A. planci* larvae mature into a hoard of hungry, coral-eating adults. Because the coral and the algae housed by coral are at the lowest level of the food chain, an outbreak of *A. planci* can destroy the ecosystem for many years.

CHECKPOINT 24.1

1. What are the common characteristics of echinoderms?
2. How does the embryonic development of echinoderms and chordates differentiate them from other animals?
3. **Critical Thinking** Compare tube feet—their structure and function—among the classes of echinoderms.

Build on What You Know

4. List ways in which echinoderms are structurally different from arthropods. *(Need to jog your memory? Revisit relevant concepts in Chapter 23, Section 23.1.)*

CHECKPOINT 24.1

1. Spiny skin, endoskeleton, radial symmetry, water vascular system, and tube feet
2. Their blastopore becomes an anus; in other animals, the blastopore becomes the mouth.
3. **Making analogies** Asteroidea: suction cuplike ends; Ophiuroidea: lack suction cups: Echinoidea: use feet to move; Holothuroidea: use five rows of feet to move; Crinoidea: feet covered with mucus capture food.
4. Echinoderms have an endoskeleton, rather than an exoskeleton, and more primitive nervous and circulatory systems.

❶ The number of sea urchins increased, resulting in less kelp and other seaweeds.

LAB ZONE Investigate It!

Exploring Echinoderm Diversity

SUPER READ!

WHAT YOU WILL DO Observe specimens or photographs of a variety of echinoderms and note differences and similarities

SKILLS YOU WILL USE Observing, hypothesizing, collecting and recording data, classifying

WHAT YOU WILL NEED Preserved echinoderm specimens or photographs of echinoderms

Propose a Hypothesis

Can you classify echinoderms by observing their external anatomy? Propose a hypothesis that suggests your opinion on this question.

Conduct Your Experiment

1 Briefly examine each of the echinoderm specimens or photographs of echinoderms.
2 Make a chart entitled "Echinoderm Features." Along the top of the chart, list the observable physical characteristics of echinoderms, including structures for feeding and movement. Along the side of the chart, list the names of the specimens or photographs.
3 Examine each of the echinoderms more closely. Fill in the relevant information about each echinoderm on your chart.
4 Draw each of the echinoderms and label its distinguishing features.

Analyze Your Data

1 Do any of the echinoderms on your chart share the same major features? If so, which animals share which features?
2 Which feature allows echinoderms to adapt to a slow-moving or sessile existence? Are any of the specimens you observed truly sessile?

Draw Conclusions

1 Are the echinoderms you examined more different than they are alike, or more alike than they are different? Explain.
2 Based on your observations, classify the echinoderms.

Design a Related Experiment

Suppose you were given an unidentified echinoderm and asked to classify it. What criteria would you use to determine the class to which it belongs? Design an experiment to test your procedure.

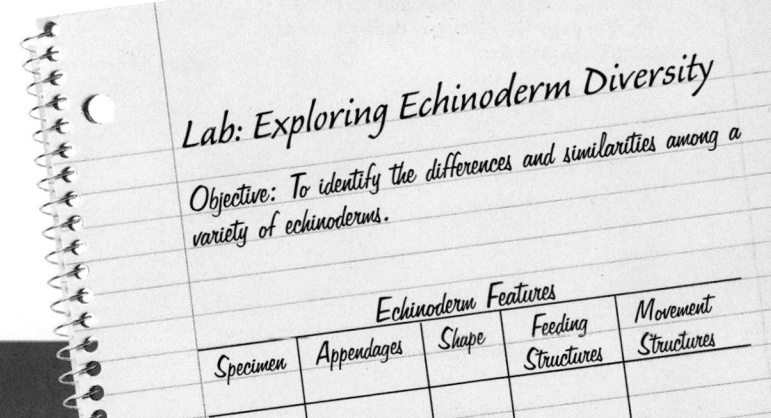

Lab: Exploring Echinoderm Diversity

Objective: To identify the differences and similarities among a variety of echinoderms.

Echinoderm Features

Specimen	Appendages	Shape	Feeding Structures	Movement Structures

Analyze Your Data

1 All have radial symmetry and tube feet. Sea stars, basket stars, brittle stars, feather stars, and sea lilies have at least five arms.
2 Most echinoderms have tube feet and a water vascular system that allow them to move. Sea lilies are sessile.

Draw Conclusions

1 They are all similar in that they have a five-part radial symmetry and spiny skin (except for sea cucumbers), and they all live in the sea. However, they come in many different shapes.
2 Check students' classifications.

ENGAGE

Consider the Big Idea

Have students read The Big Idea! at the top of the page. Point out that there are only two invertebrate chordate subphyla.

Use the Visual

Have students study the photograph that opens the section. Ask them to observe the characteristics of the organisms. Point out that these microscopic salps are tunicates, animals that show chordate characteristics during their larval stage.

Teacher Demo

Lightly bend a piece of heavy-duty garden hose to demonstrate its flexibility. Tell students that chordates have a firm, flexible tube, called a notochord, at some stage of development. Explain that in vertebrates this structure is replaced by another structure. Ask:

- **What structure probably replaces the notochord in vertebrates?** (The backbone)

Use the Visual

Ask students to identify the structures in Figure 24.12 that characterize the organism pictured as a chordate. (Dorsal hollow nerve cord, notochord, gill slits, post-anal tail)

580

THE BIG IDEA! Invertebrate chordates represent possible evolutionary links between invertebrates and vertebrates. 24.2

24.2 Invertebrate Chordates

What you'll learn

IDEAS
- To describe the four characteristics of chordates
- To distinguish between the two subphyla of invertebrate chordates

WORDS
dorsal hollow nerve cord, notochord, gill slits, post-anal tail

A food chain surprise
Scientists have made a recent discovery about the food chain in the Antarctic Ocean. Krill, which are small, shrimplike crustaceans, have always been considered the main food supply there. But in some years, planktonic tunicates called salps (right) are so numerous that they replace krill as the base of the food chain.

CHARACTERISTICS OF CHORDATES

Missing links?

As you may recall from Chapter 21, scientists commonly divide animals into two main groups: vertebrates—animals with a backbone—and invertebrates—animals without a backbone. The phylum Chordata contains both types of animals and can therefore be subdivided into the invertebrate chordates and the vertebrate chordates.

The vertebrates—fishes, amphibians, reptiles, birds, and mammals—are the most familiar members of the phylum Chordata. The invertebrate chordates, which do not have a backbone, are less familiar. You will

learn about the invertebrate chordates—tunicates and lancelets—in this section.

All chordates share four structural characteristics at some point in their life cycle: a dorsal hollow nerve cord, a notochord, gill slits, and a post-anal tail. In most chordates, including humans, these characteristics are present only during early stages of embryonic development. You can locate the four characteristic chordate structures in the lancelet shown in *Figure 24.12*.

Most invertebrates that are not chordates have a nerve cord that is solid and located on the ventral side

FIGURE 24.12

Structure of a Lancelet

The lancelet is an invertebrate chordate. Why might scientists think that an ancestor of today's lancelets may have given rise to the primitive fish? **1**

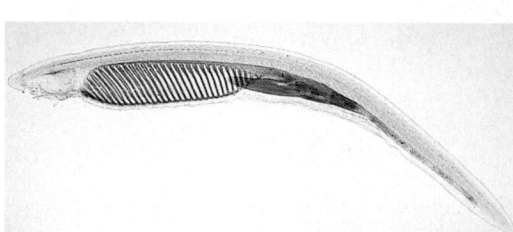

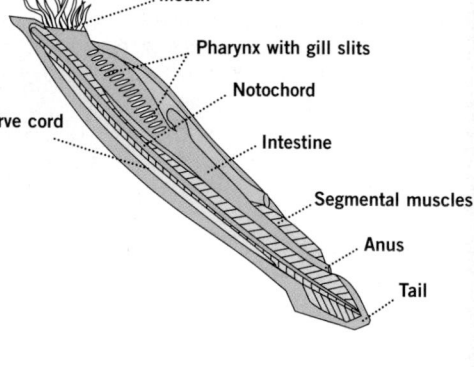

Mouth
Pharynx with gill slits
Notochord
Intestine
Segmental muscles
Anus
Tail
Dorsal hollow nerve cord

580 *Unit 6 Invertebrate Animals*

---

of the animal's body. Chordates, however, have a **dorsal hollow nerve cord**—a nerve cord that is located along the back of the animal. In most chordates, the anterior (front) end of the nerve cord develops into a brain.

A **notochord** is a firm but flexible supporting rod located just below the nerve cord. The notochord gives the phylum Chordata its name. Chordates are the only animals that have a notochord at some point in their lives. In nearly all vertebrate chordates, a backbone replaces the notochord during embryonic development. In invertebrate chordates, the notochord may or may not remain in the adults.

Gill slits are paired openings along the pharynx. Invertebrate chordates use the gill slits for filter-feeding. In most vertebrate chordates, the gill slits have become modified for gas exchange or other purposes.

At some point in development, all chordates, including humans, have a tail that extends beyond the anus. This tail is called a **post-anal tail**. In most invertebrates that are not chordates, both the body and digestive tract end at the anus.

ORIGIN AND DIVERSITY OF INVERTEBRATE CHORDATES

Relatively speaking

What might a starfish and a lancelet have in common? The question is not easily answered by looking at the adult organisms. But by comparing larval stages of echinoderms, invertebrate chordates, and vertebrate chordates, biologists have concluded that the three types of organisms may share a common ancestor. All three may have evolved from an organism that was a sessile, filter-feeding adult with a motile larval form.

There are two subphyla of invertebrate chordates: Urochordata and Cephalochordata. The urochordates

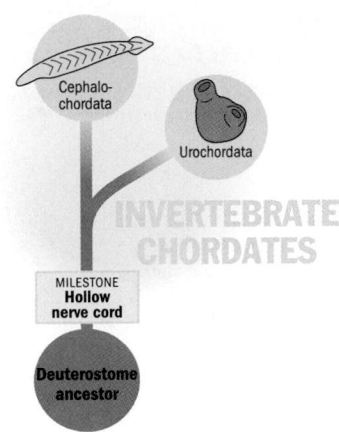

FIGURE 24.13

Phylum Chordata

There are two chordate subphyla that contain invertebrates: Urochordata (tunicates) and Cephalochordata (lancelets).

Kingdom: Animalia

Phylum: Chordata

Subphyla:
Urochordata
Cephalochordata

are the tunicates, and the cephalochordates are the lancelets.

Tunicates Tunicates, or sea squirts, are named for their leathery outer covering—a tunic—and for their tendency to squirt sea water when they are disturbed. Most adult tunicates are sessile, but the larvae are free-swimming. Larval tunicates have the four chordate characteristics. As *Figure 24.14* shows, adult tunicates retain only gill slits—they have lost all

LAB ZONE ? Think About It! — bioSURF

Comparing Structures and Systems of an Echinoderm and a Chordate

You have already read about the external structures and internal systems of several invertebrates. You can compare animals from two phyla when you . . .

Try This

1 The diagram on page 573 shows a sea star. Note the animal's structures and systems.
2 Review the lancelet diagram on page 580, noting its structures and systems.

Analyze Your Results

1 Do the the sea star and lancelet share any similar external structures? If so, which?
2 What characteristics does the lancelet have that the sea star, as an echinoderm, does not have?

MEETING DIVERSE NEEDS

Gifted Have students conduct research to identify the stage of human development at which each chordate characteristic is lost. Provide an opportunity for students to present their research to the class.

❶ There is a physical resemblance.

---

② TEACH

Explain

Point out that at some point in their development, all chordates have: a dorsal hollow nerve cord; a notochord; gill slits or pouches; and a post-anal tail. Lancelets and tunicates are the two invertebrate subphyla of the phylum Chordata.

Build Writing Skills

Have students observe the embryo of a fish. Then show them photos of the early development of a human embryo. Have students write a descriptive paragraph comparing the two embryos. Encourage them to include their own drawings.

Teacher Demo

Use a model or wall chart of a human skeleton to show the vertebral column. Remind students that in all vertebrates, the vertebral column develops from the notochord. Note that the coccyx (tailbone) is a vestigial tail.

LAB ZONE Think About It!

Comparing Structures and Systems of an Echinoderm and a Chordate

Analyze Your Results

1 Anus, digestive tract.
2 Sea stars do not have segmental muscles, gill slits, dorsal hollow nerve cord, or notochord.

582

Use the Visual

Have students study Figure 24.14. Ask:

■ **How does the adult tunicate differ from the larval tunicate?** (Larval tunicates have the four chordate characteristics. Having lost the other chordate characteristics, adults retain only gill slits.)

ASSESS

Evaluate Understanding

Show students unlabeled illustrations of a lancelet and a larval tunicate. Ask students to point out four structures that identify these organisms as chordates. Also ask students to describe the function of each structure.

Reteach

Write the four characteristics of chordates on the board. Review the structure, function, and location of each feature. Have students draw an outline of a lancelet or a tunicate in their notebooks and label the four characteristic chordate structures on their drawings. Check students' drawings for accuracy.

582

FIGURE 24.14

Structure of a Tunicate

What similarities do you see in the larval and adult characteristics? ❶

Larval tunicate

- Dorsal hollow nerve cord
- Notochord
- Tail
- Atriopore (excurrent siphon)
- Mouth (incurrent siphon)
- Intestine
- Stomach
- Pharynx with gill slits

Adult tunicate

- Incurrent siphon to mouth
- Pharynx with gill slits
- Tunic
- Excurrent siphon
- Anus
- Intestine
- Stomach

signs of a notochord, dorsal hollow nerve cord, and post-anal tail.

Lancelets The other invertebrate chordate subphylum includes the lancelets. Many biologists think that an ancestor of today's lancelets evolved into a primitive, fishlike vertebrate.

FIGURE 24.15
What differences do you see between this tunicate and the sponges you saw in Chapter 21? ❷

Lancelets retain the four chordate characteristics as adults. Although they can swim, they are usually buried in sand with just their heads exposed. Like tunicates, they feed by filtering particles from water through their mucus-lined gill slits.

CHECKPOINT 24.2

1. What are the four characteristics of chordates?
2. How do urochordates and cephalochordates differ?
3. **Critical Thinking** Why would a free-swimming larval stage be an advantage for tunicates?

Build on What You Know

4. Compare how the following two sessile organisms obtain food: a sponge and a tunicate. **(Need to jog your memory? Revisit relevant concepts in Chapter 21, Section 21.2.)**

? What is the evolutionary relationship between invertebrate chordates and vertebrates?

CHECKPOINT 24.2

1. Dorsal hollow nerve cord, notochord, gill slits, post-anal tail
2. Adult cephalochordates retain all the chordate characteristics; urochordates retain only the gill slits.
3. **Making generalizations** Most adult tunicates are sessile, having free-swimming larvae helps disperse their young.
4. Adult tunicates' gill slits filter food particles from the water. Sponges' collar cells bring water and food particles through pores into a central cavity.

❶ Both have a mouth, stomach, intestine, and pharynx with slits.
❷ Tunicates have two siphons; sponges have pores rather than an incurrent siphon.

Chapter 24 Review

24.1 Echinoderms are marine animals with spiny skin, an endoskeleton, and a water vascular system.

24.2 Invertebrate chordates represent possible evolutionary links between invertebrates and vertebrates.

Sum It Up

Use the following summary to review the main concepts in this chapter.

24.1 Echinoderms

- Echinoderms are marine invertebrates. They have external or internal spines, an endoskeleton made of calcium, and radial symmetry.
- Echinoderms have a water vascular system—a network of fluid-filled tubes that allows them to move, obtain food, and exchange gases.
- A sea star's digestive, nervous, and reproductive systems extend from a central disk into each of the organism's arms.
- Although many echinoderms reproduce asexually by regeneration, all can reproduce sexually.
- Echinoderms are divided into five classes: Asteroidea, Ophiuroidea, Echinoidea, Holothuroidea, and Crinoidea.
- Echinoderms are a source of food and new pharmaceuticals for humans. Echinoderms can cause problems in the environment through overpopulation or predation.

24.2 Invertebrate Chordates

- Most members of the phylum Chordata are vertebrates. There are, however, two subphyla of invertebrate chordates: tunicates and lancelets.
- Invertebrate and vertebrate chordates share certain embryonic-stage characteristics: a dorsal hollow nerve cord, notochord, post-anal tail, and gill slits. Some adult chordates retain these features, but most lose them by the end of embryonic development.
- Tunicates have a leathery outer covering and are sessile as adults. Most chordate characteristics are seen in tunicate larvae only.
- Lancelets are filter-feeding, fishlike organisms.

Use Terms and Concepts

Use each of the following words or terms in a complete sentence. If you need to review a meaning, turn to the page indicated.

echinoderm (p. 572)

water vascular system (p. 573)

ampulla (p. 573)

tube foot (p. 573)

protostome (p. 575)

deuterostome (p. 575)

dorsal hollow nerve cord (p. 581)

notochord (p. 581)

gill slits (p. 581)

post-anal tail (p. 581)

Review the Big Ideas

Before students begin the Chapter Review, you may wish to discuss main concepts from The Big Ideas! in this chapter. Explain that echinoderms are bilaterally symmetrical as larvae, but as adults, they have five-part radial symmetry and an endoskeleton. Echinoderms move by means of a water vascular system. Echinoderms and chordates are closely related and may have shared a common ancestor. A branch of the phylum Chordata includes invertebrates such as tunicates and lancelets.

Answers

1. A protostome
2. water vascular system
3. gill slits
4. ampulla
5. notochord
6. tube foot
7. deuterostome
8. False. A sea star's digestive system stores waste in the body.
9. True
10. False. Adult sea stars have tube feet.
11. False. In vertebrate chordates, the notochord is replaced by a backbone.
12. False. All chordates have a post–anal tail at some point in their development.
13. True
14. True
15. False. Sea stars and crinoids are examples of deuterostomes.
16. False. It has no ampulla. It uses branched arms to capture and move plankton to its mouth.
17. Sea cucumbers shoot spines; sea squirts squirt water.
18. Fishermen who hunted abalone killed otters that competed with them for the abalone. Otters are the primary predator of sea urchins.
19. A sea star attaches its tube feet to both sides of a bivalve shell; it uses its vascular system to contract the tentacles and force open the shell.
20. Gonads on each arm of the sea star release either sperm or eggs into the water where fertilization occurs. The resulting larvae swim freely for about two years until settling on the ocean floor and maturing into adults.
21. Brittle stars extend an arm in the direction they are headed, leave two arms

584

Use Your Word Power

COMPLETION Write the word or phrase that best completes each statement.

1. _____ is an animal in which a blastopore develops into a mouth.

2. The _____ is a network of fluid-filled tubes.

3. Tunicates have _____ , paired openings along the pharynx that are used for filter feeding.

4. A muscular sac in echinoderms that helps pump water is called a(n) _____ .

5. A firm but flexible supporting rod present in lancelets is the _____ .

6. A(n) _____ is hollow, with an end that functions like a suction cup.

7. The _____ is an animal in which a blastopore develops into an anus.

TRUE-FALSE Write true if the statement is true. If the statement is false, replace the underlined word(s) to make the statement true.

8. A sea star's <u>water vascular system</u> stores wastes in the body.

9. An echinoderm larva has <u>bilateral</u> symmetry.

10. Adult <u>sea squirts</u> have a dorsal hollow nerve cord.

11. In vertebrate chordates, the <u>dorsal hollow nerve cord</u> is usually replaced by a backbone.

12. All chordates have a <u>post-anal tail.</u>

13. In a <u>protostome</u>, a mouth forms from a blastopore.

14. Invertebrate chordates use <u>gill slits</u> for filter feeding.

15. Sea stars and crinoids are examples of <u>vertebrates</u>.

16. When feeding, a sea star uses its <u>ampulla</u> to pry open the shells of clams.

Show What You Know

17. Compare the reactions of sea cucumbers and sea squirts to predators.

18. Explain how a decrease in abalone off the coast of California led to an increase in sea urchins.

19. How do sea stars use their vascular and digestive structures to feed on mollusks?

20. Briefly describe the process of sexual reproduction in sea stars.

21. Describe the process brittle stars use to move. How does this method of movement differ from that used by sea stars?

22. **Make a Concept Map** Make a concept map that shows how the relationships between invertebrate and vertebrate chordates are revealed through embryology. Use the following terms: gill slits, notochord, post-anal tail, lungs, backbone, dorsal hollow nerve cord, embryo, gills, protostome, deuterostome, anus, mouth, and blastopore.

Take It Further

23. **Developing a Hypothesis** Some scientists suggest that the common ancestor of chordates was sessile and looked something like a tunicate. They hypothesize that lancelets and vertebrates developed from the motile larvae of these sessile chordates. Evaluate this hypothesis and give reasons why you agree or disagree.

24. **Making a Generalization** What is the general pattern in the distribution of digestive, vascular, nervous, and reproductive systems in sea stars? Relate this pattern to a sea star's ability to reproduce by regeneration.

25. **Making an Analogy** *Urchin* comes from the Latin *ericius*, meaning "hedgehog." What do sea urchins and hedgehogs have in common?

---

trailing behind, and use the two remaining arms as oars. Sea stars force water into the tube feet, causing them to extend. The suction-cup-like ends of the tube feet then attach to a hard surface. When muscles in the tube feet contract, water flows back to the ampullae, the tube feet shorten, and the sea star is pulled forward.

22. The concept map should show the following: <u>Blastopore</u> develops into <u>mouth</u> in <u>protostomes</u> and into <u>anus</u> in <u>deuterostomes</u>. Chordate <u>embryos</u> have <u>dorsal hollow nerve cords</u>; <u>notochords</u>, which develop into <u>backbones</u> in vertebrates; <u>gill slits</u>, which can develop into <u>gills</u> or <u>lungs</u>; and <u>post-anal tails</u>.

26. Analyzing Data Organisms A and B have five arms. Organism C has internal spines. C and D have no arms, but D has movable spines. A and C feed on plankton and have sticky tentacles. B feeds on bivalves. Using these data, decide which class the organisms belong to: Asteroidea, Ophiuroidea, Echinoidea, Holothuroidea, and Crinoidea.

27. Interpreting a Graph An adult crown-of-thorns starfish can consume 13 square meters (m^2) of coral a year. This graph shows how many starfish were present on a hectare of reef at selected locations. (A hectare is equal to 10,000 m^2.) How much coral could be consumed in a year at location C? At location D? What is the maximum number of starfish that could theoretically be supported in one hectare? What do you think will happen at location E?

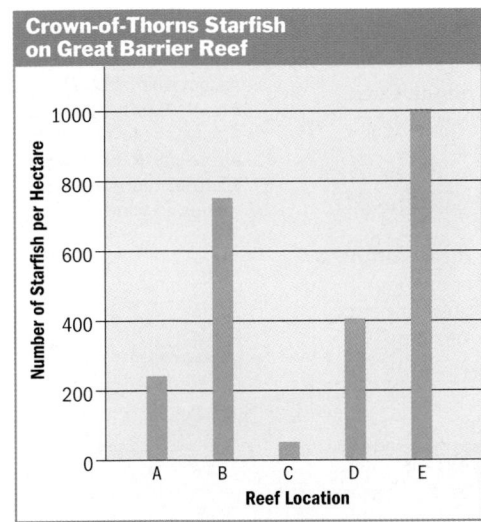

Crown-of-Thorns Starfish on Great Barrier Reef

Number of Starfish per Hectare (y-axis: 0, 200, 400, 600, 800, 1000)

Reef Location (x-axis: A, B, C, D, E)

28. Designing an Experiment Sea stars have receptor cells that are sensitive to the concentration of chemicals in sea water. Predict how sea stars would respond to a sharp increase or decrease in the concentration of salt in the water. Design an experiment to test your prediction.

Consider the Issues

29. Coral Carnivores Suppose you were assigned to protect a coral reef that is under attack from sea stars. Local inhabitants have suggested the following solutions: (a) Chop up adult sea stars and return them to the ocean to provide food for other species. (b) Import predators to feed on the sea star larvae. (c) Disperse chemicals around the reef that are poisonous to sea star larvae. (d) Remove the sea star eggs before they can hatch. (e) Wait until there are no longer enough coral polyps to sustain the population of sea stars. Offer arguments for and against each proposed solution.

Make New Connections

30. Biology and Physics The ends of an echinoderm's tube feet act as suction cups. The ability of those structures to cling tightly to an object can be explained using principles of physics. Look up *fluid pressure* in a physical science book, and explain how these suction cups work.

31. Biology and Language Research the connection between common terms and biological terms. Find out what a Roman ampulla and a biological ampulla have in common. Compare a radial canal to the Erie Canal. What do a kitchen sieve and a sieve plate have in common? What traits do a basket and a basket star share? Compare a sea lily to a calla lily. What might a tunic and a tunicate have in common?

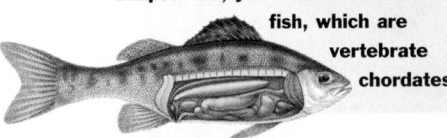

FAST-FORWARD TO CHAPTER 25

Biologists hypothesize that lancelets with their gill slits and fish with their gills share a common ancestor. In Chapter 25, you will learn about fish, which are vertebrate chordates.

23. Students could argue that both tunicate larvae and chordates have bilateral symmetry. Tunicate larvae also have other chordate characteristics. Adult lancelets retain chordate characteristics. The embryos of vertebrate chordates display similar characteristics to both organisms.

24. The general pattern is the duplication of digestive, vascular, nervous, and reproductive structures in each arm of the sea star. This duplication makes regeneration from only a small portion of the organism more likely.

25. Both have spines.

26. A: Crinoidea; B: Asteroidea; C: Holothuroidea; D: Echinoidea

27. At location C, 650 square meters would be consumed; 5200 square meters would be consumed at location D. The theoretical maximum is 769 starfish. At location E, the reef will be wiped out.

28. An increase or decrease in the concentration of salt in water could upset the homeostasis of the sea star (or interfere with its ability to detect food). The researcher would need to increase or decrease the concentration of salt gradually to determine the limits of the range of acceptable concentrations.

29. Solution *a* would not work because of regeneration. Solution *b* might work, but the fish would have to be native to the reef. Solution *c* would endanger other organisms in the ecosystem, especially corals, which are sensitive to pollutants. Solution *d* sounds ideal except for the number of eggs that would need to be removed. Solution *e* is depressing but may be the only practical solution.

30. As fluid volume inside the tube foot decreases, fluid pressure increases and holds the animal's foot fast to an object.

31. A Roman ampulla is a two–handled flask; both ampullae are globular containers for fluids. A radial canal and the Erie Canal are internal transport ducts for water. A kitchen sieve and a sieve plate are both filtering devices. Both a basket and a basket star are designed to encircle objects—in the case of the basket star, plankton. A sea lily and a calla lily are both sessile objects with stalks. Early tunics might have been made from leather.

Connect the Chapters

1. Arthropods and annelids have segmented bodies. In most arthropods, the segments are fused together into one or more larger structures.

2. Jellyfish use their tentacles to draw in prey they have killed or paralyzed with the barbed, poisonous nematocysts located on the tips of the tentacles. Squid use their tentacles and their jaws to immobilize prey.

3. A sponge has flagellated collar cells to move water in and out of its central cavity. Cilia on a mussel's gills move trapped food toward its mouth. Barnacles use featherlike legs to sweep food toward their mouths. As sessile feeders, sponges, mussels, and barnacles are attached to one location and feed by capturing food from the surrounding environment.

4. Earthworms have tubes called nephridia through which cellular wastes are excreted. Malpighian tubules in spiders filter cellular wastes into the intestine for excretion.

5. Most ticks and leeches are external, blood-sucking parasites that attach to a host until they have absorbed sufficient blood.

6. Sea anemones are sessile marine cnidarians. Scorpions are mobile terrestrial arachnids. Both species sting and paralyze prey.

7. Sea stars have specialized tissues for functions such as digestion and reproduction; they have radial body symmetry; they have internal body cavities formed from mesoderm; their blastopores develop into anuses.

Unit 6 Review

THE BIG IDEA! Answering the following questions will help you to link ideas and grasp the core concepts.

Connect the Chapters

1. What characteristics do the bodies of annelids and arthropods have in common? How do their body structures differ?

2. Both jellyfish and squid have tentacles surrounding their mouths. Compare how the tentacles function to capture their prey.

3. Describe the adaptations that sponges, mussels, and barnacles use to obtain food. What common obstacle do these adaptations address?

4. Compare the excretory structures of earthworms and spiders.

5. What characteristics do most ticks and leeches have in common?

6. Compare the habitats, locomotion, and food-gathering strategies of sea anemones and scorpions.

7. Using a sea star as an example, illustrate the four major milestones in the evolution of animals.

Connect the Units

8. Compare how sponges and some monerans respond to harsh conditions.

9. Zebra mussels eat green algae. How could removing zebra mussels from Lake Erie affect the amount of dissolved oxygen in the lake?

10. How does the absence of a complex transport system affect the structure of mosses and flatworms?

Connect to Themes

11. **Unity and Diversity** What features are common in the digestive systems of earthworms and grasshoppers? What features vary?

12. **Patterns of Change/Cycle** Compare the life cycle of jellyfish and butterflies.

13. **Evolution** What do trilobite fossils reveal about arthropod evolution?

14. **Systems and Interactions** How does the interaction of muscles with water influence the locomotion of roundworms and echinoderms?

project plans

1 Choose an insect that is a threat to either an agricultural crop or an ornamental plant that grows in your region of the country. Find out what farmers or gardeners have done in the past to limit damage from the insect. Are there any drawbacks to the traditional methods? Describe alternative control methods that have been, or are being, developed.

2 Amateur naturalists in North America take part in a butterfly census each July. Scientists who study butterflies can analyze the data collected over a number of years. Find out more about the annual butterfly count by writing to the North American Butterfly Association, 909 Birch Street, Baraboo, WI 53913. Ask what the requirements are to participate, and whether there are local groups in your area.

CRITIC'S CORNER

A BOOK REVIEW BY ABBY GREENBAUM GLOUCESTER, MA

The Sea of Cortez, by novelist John Steinbeck and marine biologist Ed Ricketts, chronicles the authors' six-week voyage in the Gulf of California. The book describes the marine wildlife of the Gulf and the people who participated in the expedition, and it includes several humorous anecdotes. The combination of scientific information and poetic description keeps the book moving and provides a rare insight into the wonders of the marine world.

Sea of Cortez
John Steinbeck & E. F. Ricketts

586

Connect the Units

8. Sponges can form gemmules; some monerans form endospores.

9. Green algae produce oxygen during photosynthesis. If populations of green algae increased due to the removal of a predator, the concentration of dissolved oxygen would increase.

10. Mosses are only a few cells thick because water must pass from cell to cell by osmosis. Flatworms are thin because gases are exchanged directly by diffusion across the skin.

SUPER READ! **Distinguishing Fact From Opinion** To practice strategies for effective reading, use pages 57-58 in *Super Read!*

SPOTLIGHT ON CAREERS

JUNE KANTZ
Lobster fisher off Peaks Island, Maine
EDUCATION: B.A. in sociology; Kantz's father is a lobster fisher, and she always wanted to work on the water.

"I fish alone and I like it that way. It's peaceful. I've always liked being on the water. Once you pull the lobster traps in, you always end up throwing some back. If you have a female with eggs you have to notch its tail and throw it back, so that she can release her eggs. In Maine, there are minimum and maximum size limits for lobsters. They have to be at least $3\frac{1}{4}$ inches from the eyeball socket to the end of the carapace, where the tail starts. The reason for the limits is to allow them to spawn at least once before you trap them. . . . Lobsters need to shed their shells to grow. Just after they shed, they hide in the rocks because they are vulnerable to predators. Lobsters are cannibals; if a lobster finds a smaller one with a soft shell, it will eat it."

bioSURF Explore the Internet site *http://invertebrates.biosurf.com* to find out more about lobsters and lobster fishing.

DR. JOSHUA FEINGOLD
Visiting Professor of marine biology, Nova Southeastern University
EDUCATION: Ph.D. in marine biology, M.S. in biological oceanography, B.S. in biology and philosophy.

SUPER READ!

"What I like best about my work is the challenge of complex problem solving. I have new experiences every time I go back to the field. I'm discovering things about the natural world that nobody else knows, and I'm contributing to a better understanding of how coral ecosystems function. This work requires scuba diving, computer expertise, and the ability to maintain and repair scientific equipment. . . . In one project, I worked in the Galapagos Islands. . . . One of the great benefits of this job is the ability to work in the natural world and to see a lot of beautiful things. But when the water is cold and the equipment malfunctions, you still have to do the work! It is a glamorous-sounding job, but you need dedication and perseverance."

bioSURF Explore the Internet address *http://invertebrates.biosurf.com* to find out more about marine biology and coral reefs.

"My findings can make it easier for wildlife managers to protect and conserve natural resources."
— DR. JOSHUA FEINGOLD

Unit 6 Invertebrate Animals **587**

Connect to Themes

11. Similar feature is gizzard function; varying features are the crop functions and location of digestion.

12. The mobile larvae of jellyfish and butterflies develop from fertilized eggs. The next stage for both species is sessile—polyps or pupae. Polyps bud off medusae, which develop into adult jellyfish. Inside cocoons, pupae are transformed into adult butterflies.

13. Trilobite fossils reveal two key evolutionary trends: a decrease in body segments and an increase in the specialization of jointed appendages.

14. Roundworms move when muscles push against a water-filled cavity. Echinoderms move as muscles in ampullae force water into tube feet and muscles force water back into the ampullae.

Unit Overview

Vertebrate animals display an amazing diversity in form, size, and niche. They have many different adaptations that allow them to survive in Earth's diverse environments, yet all vertebrates share several important characteristics. Among these characteristics is the column of skeletal units called vertebrae, which enclose the spinal cord.

Unit Objectives

- Identify the characteristics that distinguish the vertebrates from other groups of animals
- Compare the characteristics of the major classes and orders of vertebrates
- Explain how various groups of vertebrate animals are uniquely adapted to survive in their environments
- Describe various types of animals behaviors

Connect the Units

This unit builds on the survey of animal diversity introduced in Unit 6. The discussion of mammalian physiology in Chapter 35 provides a strong foundation for the study of the human body that follows in Unit 8: *Human Biology.* Because the vertebrates are the most familiar animals in the environment, this unit also provides a meaningful introduction to a study of the environment. You may therefore chose to follow this Unit with Unit 9: *Organisms in the Environment.*

Which of these amazing statements about vertebrates are fact, and which are fiction?

Hit *or* Myth?

There are **no penguins** at the North Pole.

(Fact. There are no penguins anywhere in the Northern Hemisphere. All 17 varieties of penguins are found below the equator, primarily in Antarctica.)

Rattlesnakes can **hear** sounds.

(Fiction and Fact. Snakes cannot hear sounds in the air as people can, but they have an extraordinary ability to detect vibrations in the surfaces on which they lie. A rattlesnake, therefore, could sense a mouse walking nearby even though it could not hear a person talking softly.)

Woodpeckers get **headaches** from all their hammering.

(Fiction. Pockets of air in the woodpecker's head cushion its head bones as it bores or drills.)

Nose prints are used to identify dogs the way fingerprints are used to identify people.

(Fact. Breeders and trainers even keep nose prints on file, and insurance companies require them if a dog is being bonded.)

588

SUPER READ!

The chameleon's tongue is **longer than its body.**

(Fact. With a tongue several centimeters longer than its body, the chameleon can catch an insect some 25 centimeters away.)

The archerfish uses **spitballs** to catch prey.

(Fact. Adult archerfishes can shoot down insects by spitting water droplets up to 1.5 meters into the air.)

Birds keep their eggs **warm** by sitting on them.

(Fact and fiction. Although this is true in cool climates, in desert environments birds insulate their eggs from the heat by sitting on them.)

This amphibian is enjoying a tasty **meal.**

(Fiction. This frog has swallowed a poisonous insect and is eliminating the noxious food by ejecting its stomach.)

Unit 7 Vertebrate Animals **589**

Hit *or* Myth?

Use It

Review each of the statements with the class. Ask students to share their prior knowledge and misconceptions on each topic. Ask them to consider which sources of information on these topics are generally reliable and which may not be.

Link It

Chapter 25 links the role of fishes and amphibians as predators and prey (archerfish, frog) with the concepts of food chains and food webs. More information about predator/prey relationships can be found in Chapter 37: *Ecosystem Dynamics.* Chapter 26 explores how the structures and niches of reptiles and birds (chameleon, woodpecker, snake) relate to their behaviors. The adaptive nature of animal behavior is further discussed in this unit in Chapter 28: *Animal Behavior.*

Expand It

Although penguins account for more than 80 percent of the birds in Antarctica, only two species, the Emperor and Adelie penguins, actually breed there. The rest migrate to the Galapagos Islands near the equator to lay their eggs.

Archerfish shoot their spitballs by rapidly compressing their gill covers.

 Interpreting Visuals To practice strategies for effective reading, use pages 67-68 in *Super Read!*

PLANNING GUIDE

Section	Student Activities/Features	Teacher's Resource Package
25.1 Vertebrates **Objectives** ■ Describe the characteristics of chordates and vertebrates	**Lab Zone Discover It!** *Observing Vertebrate Jaws*, p. 591	**Unit 7 Review Module** ■ Section Review 25.1
25.2 Characteristics of Fishes **Objectives** ■ Explain the adaptations of fishes to their environment ■ Describe the life cycle of fishes	**Everyday Biology** *Greasing the Way to Health*, p. 594 **Lab Zone Do It!** *How Does a Fish's Swim Bladder Work?* p. 596 **Lab Zone Investigate It!** *Analyzing the Respiration of a Fish*, p. 598	**Unit 7 Review Module** ■ Section Review 25.2 ■ Activity Recordsheets 25-1 and 25-2 ■ Critical Thinking Exercise 25 **Laboratory Manual** ■ Labs 42 through 44 **Interpreting and Developing Graphics** 73, 74
25.3 Origin and Diversity of Fishes **Objectives** ■ Explain the evolutionary steps that led to modern fishes ■ Contrast the classes of fish		**Unit 7 Review Module** ■ Section Review 25.3 ■ Enrichment Topics 25-1 and 25-2
25.4 Fishes in the Biosphere **Objectives** ■ Compare the roles of different fishes in aquatic food webs ■ Explain the importance of fish as a food source	**In the Community** *Fish-Smart Markets*, p. 604	**Unit 7 Review Module** ■ Section Review 25.4 **Consumer Applications** 25-1 **Issues and Decision Making** 25-1 and 25-2
25.5 Characteristics of Amphibians **Objectives** ■ Explain adaptations of amphibians to their environment ■ Summarize the life cycle of amphibians	**Lab Zone Think About It!** *Comparing Amphibian and Fish Circulatory Systems*, p. 607	**Unit 7 Review Module** ■ Section Review 25.5 ■ Interpreting Graphics 25 **Laboratory Manual** ■ Labs 45 and 46 **Issues and Decision Making** 25-3 **Interpreting and Developing Graphics** 75
25.6 Origin and Diversity of Amphibians **Objectives** ■ Explain the evolutionary steps that led to modern amphibians ■ Compare and contrast the different orders of amphibians		**Unit 7 Review Module** ■ Section Review 25.6
25.7 Amphibians in the Biosphere **Objectives** • Explain the ecological roles of amphibians • Summarize the importance of amphibians to humans	**Lab Zone Do It!** *How Is Tadpole Development Affected by Temperature?* p. 613 **STS: Environmental Awareness** *Amphibian Alarm*, p. 614 **Everyday Biology** *Frog Skin Cream*, p. 614	**Unit 7 Review Module** ■ Section Review 25.7 ■ Activity Recordsheet 25-3 ■ Enrichment Topic 25-3 ■ Vocabulary Review 25 ■ Chapter 25 Tests **Consumer Applications** 25-2 **Spanish Reviews** Chapter 25

Technology Resources

Internet Connections

Within this chapter, you will see the **bioSURF** logo. If you and your students have access to the Internet, the following URL address will provide various Internet connections that are related to topics and features presented in this chapter:

http://vertebrates.biosurf.com

You can also find relevant chapter material at **The Biology Place** address:

http://www.biology.com

CD-ROMs

Biología: la telaraña de la vida,
 (Spanish Student Edition) Chapter 25
Teacher's Resource Planner, Chapter 25
 Supplements
TestWorks CD-ROM
■ Chapter 25 Tests

Videodiscs

Animated Biological Concepts Videodiscs
■ Frog Anatomy

Overhead Transparencies

■ Structure of a Fish, #54
■ Structure of a Frog, #55

Videotapes

Biology Alive! Video Series
■ Signs of Life Video
■ Continuity of Life Video
■ Conflict and Cooperation Video
■ Life's Fragile Balance Video
Rewind: The Web of Life Reteach Videos

Planning for Activities

STUDENT EDITION
Lab Zone
Discover It! p. 591
 ■ magazines and books
   that contain pho-
   tographs of fishes,
   amphibians, and other
   vertebrates

Lab Zone Do It! p. 596
 ■ tank or large basin
 ■ water
 ■ small balloon
 ■ small clamp
 ■ string
 ■ 8–10 keys
 ■ paper clip

Lab Zone
Investigate It! p. 598
 ■ tap water exposed to
   room temperature air
   for 24 hours
 ■ 500-mL and 1000-mL
   beakers
 ■ fish net
 ■ 1 goldfish
 ■ thermometer
 ■ timer
 ■ ice
 ■ hot water (about 80°C)

Lab Zone Do It! p. 613
 ■ tadpoles
 ■ 2 water-filled glass
   aquariums or a large
   bowl

TEACHER'S EDITION
Quick Activity, p. 592
Chordates and vertebrates
 ■ overhead transparency

Quick Activity, p. 594
*Similarities and differences
among fish species*

 ■ established aquarium
   containing a variety of
   fish species or pictures
   of different fish species

Teacher Demo, p. 595
Fish scales
 ■ microscopic slides of
   ganoid, cycloid, ctenoid,
   and placoid scale types

Quick Activity, p. 599
Traits used to classify fishes
 ■ pictures of fishes representative of the three
   fish classes

Teacher Demo, p. 601
A shark's skeleton
 ■ gelatinous tip from the
   breastbone of a chicken

Teacher Demo, p. 607
Frog dissection
 ■ frog or videodisc or
   computer simulation of
   frog dissection
 ■ dissecting tray and pins
 ■ scalpel
 ■ scissors
 ■ forceps
 ■ disposable gloves
 ■ opaque projector

Quick Activity, p. 609
*Frogs, toads, newts, and
salamanders*
 ■ photographs or slides of
   frogs, toads, newts, and
   salamanders

Quick Activity, p. 612
Uses for frogs and toads
 ■ pictures of toad shelters
   for gardens

Chapter Objectives

Students will learn the main concepts of this chapter as they complete the following objectives.

- Explain why vertebrates belong to the same phylum as invertebrate chordates
- Describe the characteristics of chordates and vertebrates
- Explain the adaptations of fishes to their environment
- Describe a fish's life cycle
- Explain the evolutionary steps that led to modern fishes
- Contrast the different classes of fishes
- Compare the roles of fishes in aquatic food webs
- Explain amphibian adaptations to the environment
- Summarize the life cycle of amphibians
- Explain the evolutionary steps that led to modern amphibians
- Compare and contrast the different orders of amphibians
- Explain the ecological roles of amphibians
- Summarize the importance of amphibians to humans

Key Words

25.1 *vertebrates, ectotherms, endotherms*

25.2 *swim bladder, lateral line system*

25.3 *lungfish*

25.5 *amphibian, cloaca*

The Opening Story

Have students discuss how they think the story relates to the content of this chapter. Point out that the characteristics of sharks are useful in the study of fishes.

590

CHAPTER 25
Fishes and Amphibians

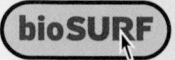

You can find out more about fishes and amphibians at the following Internet address: *http://vertebrates.biosurf.com*

In this chapter . . .

FEATURES

Everyday Biology
- Greasing the Way to Health
- Frog Skin Cream

In the Community
Fish-Smart Markets

 Environmental Awareness
Amphibian Alarm

LAB ZONES

Discover It!
- Observing Vertebrate Jaws

Do It!
- How Does a Fish's Swim Bladder Work?
- How Is Tadpole Development Affected by Temperature?

Think About It!
- Comparing Amphibian and Fish Circulatory Systems

Investigate It!
- Analyzing the Respiration of a Fish

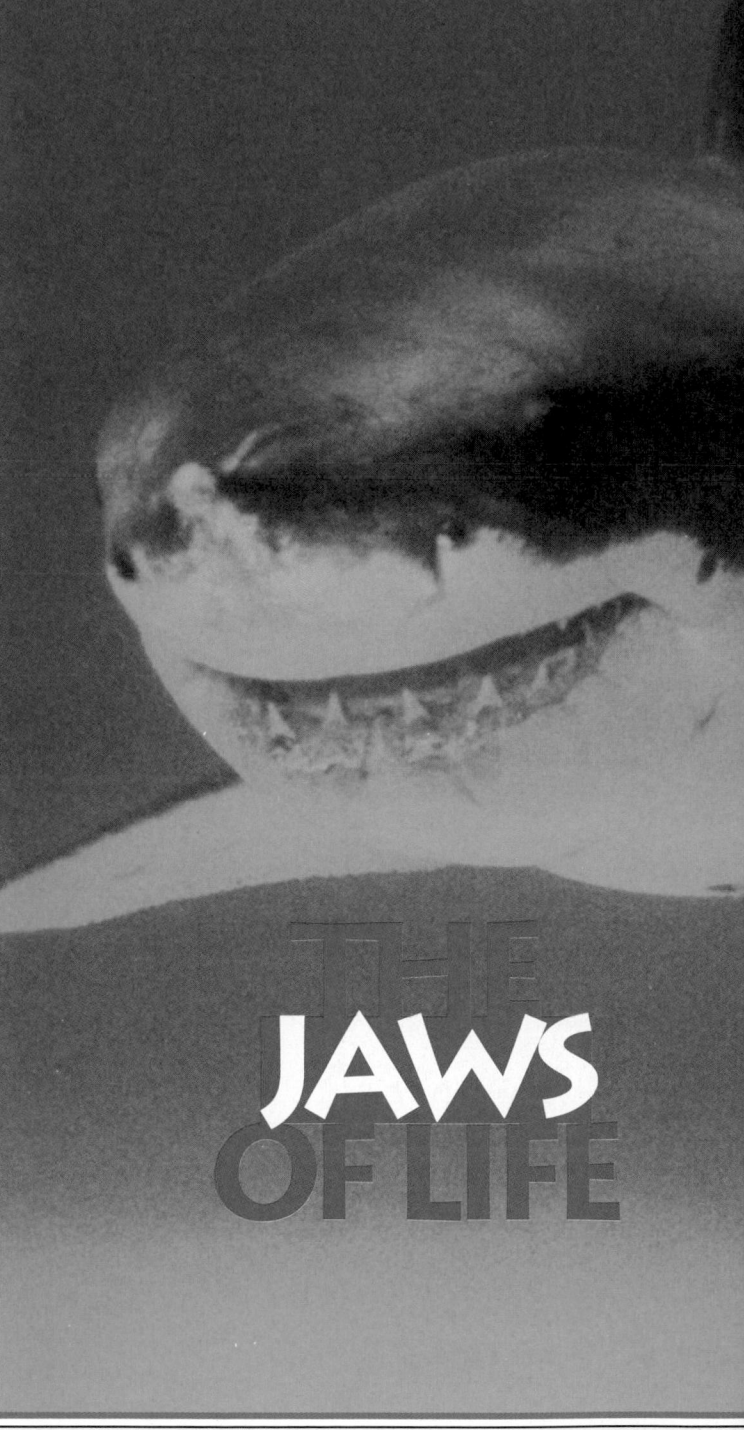

THE JAWS OF LIFE

More than 400 million years ago, long before any animal walked on land, the first sharks swam the seas. Compared with many other animals, sharks have changed relatively little since then. They have not had to change, because their basic structure has been so successful. Sharks share a feature with nearly all other vertebrates that later evolved: powerful, hinged jaws—an astounding collaboration of muscle, cartilage, and bone working together.

The tiger shark and the great white shark use their strong, flexible jaws, along with rows of razor-sharp teeth, to bite large chunks of meat from their prey. But the largest living shark, the whale shark, uses its immense jaws to swallow huge mouthfuls of sea water and then filter out the plankton and small crustaceans on which it feeds. Even the smallest sharks, which are only 10–15 centimeters (cm) long, have similar jaws that are capable of bearing down hard on prey.

Jaws that can snap shut are one of the adaptations that evolved in animals with backbones over millions of years, as they spread through the ocean, land, and air. What other adaptations do humans share with fishes and amphibians, the two oldest groups of vertebrates?

The tooth on the right came from a great white shark. On the left is a fossilized tooth from a shark that lived at least 5 million years ago. The megalodon shark could grow to 18 meters (m)—about the length of two school buses! The largest shark alive today is the whale shark, which grows to lengths of over 12m.

 **Discover It!**

Observing Vertebrate Jaws

You need magazines and books that contain photographs of fishes, amphibians, and other vertebrates

1. Find at least three photographs of each type of vertebrate. Make a simple drawing of the jaw of each animal, including any specialized structures such as teeth.
2. Arrange your drawings in groups based on similarities and differences.

The structure of an animal's jaw can provide you with evidence about the type of food an animal eats and the way it obtains that food. Write one or more inferences about the feeding habits of the three vertebrate groups you examined. If your observations inspired any questions, write them down for later investigation.

WRITE ABOUT IT!

You have probably seen movies and read stories about sharks and other carnivores that attack their prey with powerful jaws. Outline your own story about such a predator, or write a summary of a story or scene that impressed you. Include a vivid description of the animal's appearance.

591

 **bioSURF** If you have access to the Internet in your classroom or school, you may wish to have students connect to the address shown on page 590. You may also want to have students conduct a net search for information using key words related to this chapter. For example, they could search for entries under marine life, salamanders, or fish farms.

LAB ZONE **Discover It!**

Observing Vertebrate Jaws

Encourage students to consider how the animal uses its jaws to capture, kill, and masticate its prey.

WRITE ABOUT IT!

In addition to writing their journal entries, you may wish to suggest that students include photos, diagrams, or sketches to illustrate their story.

Rewind to Chapter 24

Briefly review concepts learned in Chapter 24, *Echinoderms and Invertebrate Chordates*. Ask:

- **How do you think the study of echinoderms and invertebrate chordates will help you understand the structure and evolution of fishes and amphibians described in Chapter 25?**

PORTFOLIO PREVIEW

Students should be encouraged to add to their portfolios as they work through this chapter. In addition to the *Write About It* opportunity, the following sections are excellent opportunities for portfolio entries:

- Section 25.2: *Characteristics of Fishes*
- Section 25.5: *Characteristics of Amphibians*
- Section 25.6: *Origin and Diversity of Amphibians*
- Section 25.7: *Amphibians in the Biosphere*

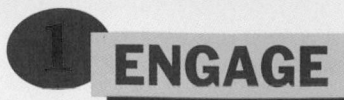

ENGAGE

Consider the Big Idea

Have students read The Big Idea! at the top of the page. Explain that backbones are the distinguishing trait of vertebrates. All the animals studied in this unit are vertebrates.

Use the Visual

Have students study the photograph that opens the section. Explain that the ferret is a vertebrate that feeds on small rodents. Ask:

■ **What trait must the ferret have to be classified as a vertebrate?** (A backbone)

Check Prior Knowledge

To assess students' knowledge about vertebrates, ask:

■ **To what phylum do vertebrates belong?** (Chordata)

Quick Activity

On an overhead transparency, draw a chart with two columns: *Chordates* and *Vertebrates*. As a class, list several traits of chordates. Then have students copy the chart and complete it with vertebrate traits and adaptations as they read this section. Have them include adaptations for both water and land environments.

---

❶ The backbone or spinal column.

25.1 Vertebrates

What you'll learn

IDEAS
• To explain why vertebrates belong to the same phylum as invertebrate chordates
• To describe the characteristics of chordates and vertebrates

WORDS
vertebrates, ectotherms, endotherms

FIGURE 25.1
Which parts of this lizard skeleton contain the greatest number of movable joints? ❶

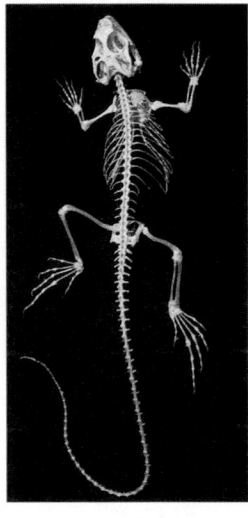

The flexible ferret
The basic vertebrate skeleton includes a flexible but sturdy backbone. The ferret has a streamlined head, short legs, and an extraordinarily twistable spine. It is well adapted for crawling into the narrow holes of its prey—small rodents who live in underground burrows. Ferrets, which are sometimes also called polecats, are often kept as pets.

CHARACTERISTICS OF VERTEBRATES

No longer spineless

What do an elephant, a guppy, a turtle, and a parakeet have in common? Each has a backbone. Animals with a backbone are called **vertebrates.** Of all the animals, you are probably most familiar with vertebrates, for the simple reason that you are a vertebrate. Fishes, amphibians, reptiles, birds, and mammals are all vertebrates.

Recall from Chapter 24 that vertebrates belong to the phylum Chordata, which also includes the invertebrate chordates. At some stage in their development, all chordates share four main characteristics: a dorsal hollow nerve cord, a notochord, gill slits or pouches, and a post-anal tail. As you may recall, these characteristics change as most vertebrates develop. For example, the dorsal nerve cord becomes a spinal cord and brain. The notochord is replaced by a backbone. In aquatic vertebrates, the gill slits or pouches become gills. In terrestrial vertebrates, the gill slits or pouches develop into other structures. The post-anal tail is the only characteristic of chordates that most vertebrates keep throughout their lives.

In addition to these four chordate characteristics, all vertebrates have an endoskeleton, which can support a larger body than an exoskeleton can. Also, an endoskeleton grows as the animal grows, so the animal does not have to molt.

As you can see in *Figure 25.1,* the vertebrate skeleton includes a backbone. The backbone is actually a series of bones called vertebrae (VER-tuh-bray; singular: *vertebra*). The vertebrae surround the spinal cord and provide a hard yet flexible structure that protects this vital organ while providing support.

Attached to the anterior end of the backbone is another vertebrate characteristic, a distinct skull. A well-developed brain and sensory organs are located in the skull, a characteristic known as cephalization.

In addition to a rigid endoskeleton and a distinct skull, all vertebrates have a closed circulatory system with a multichambered heart. A closed system means that all the blood that flows through the body is contained within blood vessels. The vertebrate circulatory system allows for the rapid circulation of blood and the efficient delivery of oxygen and nutrients to all the muscles and organs of the body.

592 *Unit 7 Vertebrate Animals*

DIVERSITY OF VERTEBRATES

Vertebrate evolution runs cold and hot

Vertebrates first appeared in the fossil record about 500 million years ago. The earliest known vertebrates were fishlike animals called ostracoderms (as-TRAK-uh-durmz), which had neither jaws nor appendages. About 400 million years ago, some descendants of the ostracoderms evolved jaws and paired fins. Subsequent adaptations led to the evolution of other groups of vertebrates, such as amphibians, reptiles, birds, and mammals. You can see the groups of vertebrates in *Figure* 25.2. Notice that the appearance of each new group of vertebrates corresponds to an evolutionary milestone. You will learn about these milestones later in this unit.

One important difference among vertebrates is the ability to regulate body temperature. All animals produce some heat as a result of breaking down the food they eat. But some animals, such as fishes, amphibians, and reptiles, lose heat almost as fast as they produce it. Fishes, amphibians, and reptiles are **ectotherms,** which means their temperature is regulated mainly by their external environment ("ecto-" means "outside," and "-therm" means "heat").

Unlike the ectotherms, birds and mammals can maintain a constant body temperature. Animals that control their temperature with internal processes are **endotherms** ("endo-" means "inside"). Endotherms maintain their body temperature by converting food energy to heat and by controlling heat loss.

FIGURE 25.2

Phylum Chordata
Subphylum Vertebrata

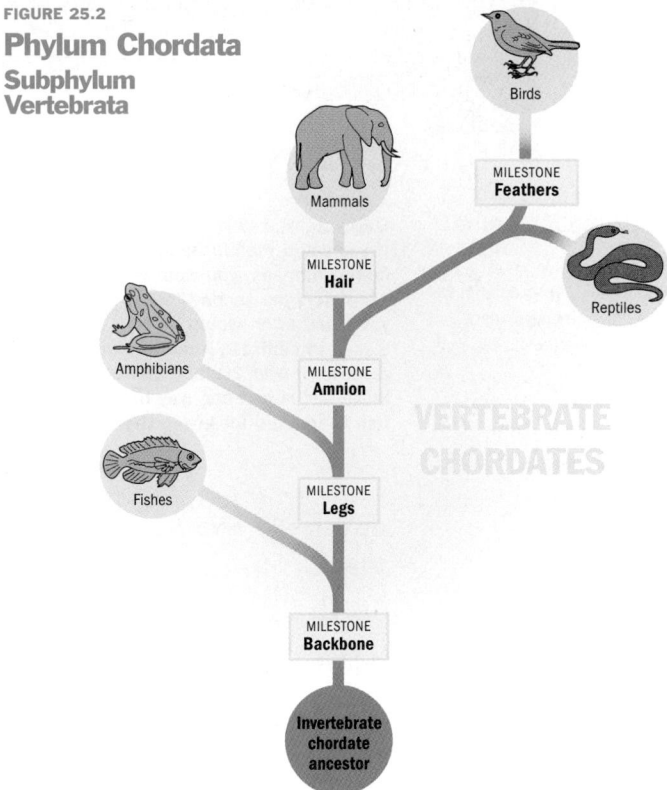

VERTEBRATE CHORDATES

- MILESTONE **Feathers**
- MILESTONE **Hair**
- MILESTONE **Amnion**
- MILESTONE **Legs**
- MILESTONE **Backbone**

Birds · Mammals · Reptiles · Amphibians · Fishes

Invertebrate chordate ancestor

CHECKPOINT 25.1

1. Why are vertebrates classified as members of the phylum Chordata?
2. What are the characteristics common to all vertebrates?
3. **Critical Thinking** Describe how the evolutionary milestone characteristics enabled some vertebrates to live on land.

Build on What You Know

4. By what process is food converted to energy within animal cells? How would endothermy affect an animal's need for food? *(Need to jog your memory? Revisit relevant concepts in Chapter 4, Section 4.3.)*

What is the main characteristic of a vertebrate? **?**

Chapter 25 Fishes and Amphibians **593**

Use the Visual

Have students study Figure 25.2. Ask:

- **What animal groups are classified as vertebrates?** (Fishes, amphibians, reptiles, birds, and mammals)
- **How are reptiles and birds similar?** (They both have amnions.)
- **What milestone separates birds and reptiles?** (Birds have feathers.)

Evaluate Understanding

Have students write a summary that compares and contrasts chordates and vertebrates. As a class, review the traits of each group. Then discuss with students the evolutionary adaptations that allowed most kinds of vertebrates to live on land.

Reteach

Take out the chart outline used in the *Quick Activity.* Review students' completed charts, correcting inaccurate data and adding any missing data. Then direct students' attention to Figure 25.2. Use the diagram to review the evolutionary milestones that have enabled some vertebrates to adapt to life on land.

SUPER READ! **Interpreting Visuals** To practice strategies for effective reading, use pages 67-68 in *Super Read!*

CHECKPOINT 25.1

1. They share the four characteristics of chordates: a dorsal nerve cord, a notochord, gill slits, and a post-anal tail during some stage of development.
2. The four chordate characteristics plus an endoskeleton, a distinct skull, and a closed circulatory system with a multichambered heart.
3. **Identifying cause and effect** A backbone provided necessary support; legs provided a means of movement on land.
4. Cellular respiration; an endotherm would have to consume large amounts of food frequently to convert food energy to heat.

593

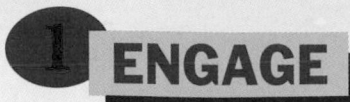

1 ENGAGE

Consider the Big Idea

Have students read The Big Idea! at the top of the page. Explain that fishes have specialized structures that enable them to live in water.

Use the Visual

Have students study the photograph that opens the section. Explain that because marlins swim fast, they are able to pursue quick moving prey.

- **What features of the marlin make it well adapted to swimming?** (Gills, streamlined body, powerful tail)
- **How does the marlin's large gill area enable it to swim rapidly?** (It enables the marlin to take in sufficient oxygen.)

Check Prior Knowledge

To assess students' knowledge about fishes, ask:

- **What milestone separates fishes from lower chordates?** (A backbone)
- **Why are fishes classified as ectotherms?** (Their body temperature is regulated by external conditions.)

Quick Activity

Display an aquarium or show pictures of different fish species. Have students observe the fishes and list the similarities and differences among them. Discuss students' lists, emphasizing those features that they think are adaptations to life in water.

THE BIG IDEA! Fishes are a diverse group of vertebrates that are adapted for life in the water. 25.2–25.4

25.2 Characteristics of Fishes

What you'll learn

IDEAS
- To explain the adaptations of fishes to their environment
- To describe the life cycle of fishes

WORDS
swim bladder,
lateral line system

Can you race that fish?
If you could match the speed of the fastest humans, you would run about 10 meters per second (m/s). The fastest you could swim would be only about 2 m/s. In contrast, a marlin can swim at a speed of over 20 m/s. The ability to move fast is just one way in which this fish is adapted for life in the water.

MOVEMENT AND RESPONSE

Sleek, slippery, and on the go

Fishes are well adapted for living in water. Look at *Figure* 25.3. Most fishes have overlapping scales that cover the skin. The scales are coated with slippery mucus. This mucus, in addition to smooth scales and narrow shape of a fish, reduce friction as the fish swims through the water.

Most fishes have a **swim bladder** that helps them move up and down in the water or remain at a given depth. The swim bladder is a thin-walled sac that can inflate or deflate when gases from the blood pass into or out of it. You can see the swim bladder in *Figure* 25.3. As the swim bladder fills with gas, the fish becomes more buoyant and rises in the water. When the swim bladder deflates, the fish becomes less buoyant and sinks.

Sharks do not have a swim bladder, but they do have a large, oily liver. Because oil is less dense than water, the liver provides some buoyancy. Constant swimming also helps prevent some sharks from sinking. The flow of the water over the lateral fins provides lift, similar to the movement of air

over an airplane wing. Fishes depend on their fins to steer and provide stability in the water.

Some fishes have well-developed sense organs that help them locate prey. A shark's keen sense of smell allows it to detect blood that is one-half a kilometer away. Salmon use their sense of

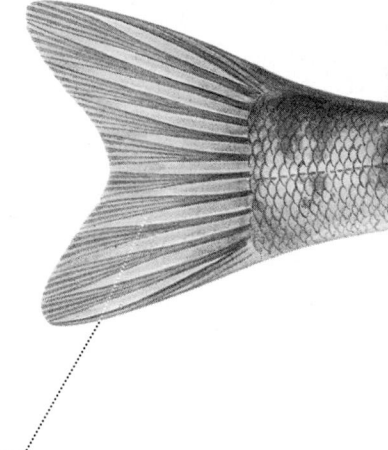

Fin
Notice the fins. Fins are adaptations for movement. Fishes use their fins to thrust, steer, brake, move up and down, and even swim backwards. Fins are attached to the fish's internal skeleton and are moved by muscle.

EVERYDAY BIOLOGY

Greasing the Way to Health

A diet high in fats is not healthy, but one type of fat from fish—omega-3—may be different. There is evidence that fish oil in the diet reduces the risk of heart disease, and may also protect the digestive system against autoimmune disorders.

594 *Unit 7 Vertebrate Animals*

STUDENT RESOURCES

From the Teacher's Resource Package, use:
- Section Review 25.2, Activity Recordsheets 25-1 and 25-2, and Critical Thinking Exercise 25 from Unit 7 Review Module
- Lab 42: "Fish Anatomy"; Lab 43: "Fish Alternative Anatomy Investigation"

TECHNOLOGY RESOURCES

Relevant technology resources include:
- Spanish Student Edition CD-ROM
- Teacher's Resource Planner CD-ROM

smell to identify and return to the stream in which they hatched. Some fishes also have specialized receptors on their head that enable them to sense weak electrical charges produced by the muscle contractions of predators and prey. These specialized receptors may also help fishes use Earth's magnetic field to navigate in the ocean.

Most fishes have a set of sensory organs called the **lateral line system** for detecting vibrations and changes in water pressure. The lateral line looks like a groove that runs from head to tail. This adaptation alerts fishes to the movement of other organisms in the water around them.

ENERGY AND WASTES

Fish gills are a gas

Most adult fishes are carnivores with sharp teeth and jaws. The bones and muscles of the jaw enable the mouth to open wide and clamp down on prey. Fishes do not chew their food. Each bite passes to the stomach whole, where it is stored and later digested in the intestine. The digested food is then carried in the blood to all cells of the body. The cells use the food to release energy and build tissues.

To release energy from food, a fish's body cells need oxygen. Fishes use their gills to obtain oxygen. Water

FIGURE 25.3

Structure of a Fish

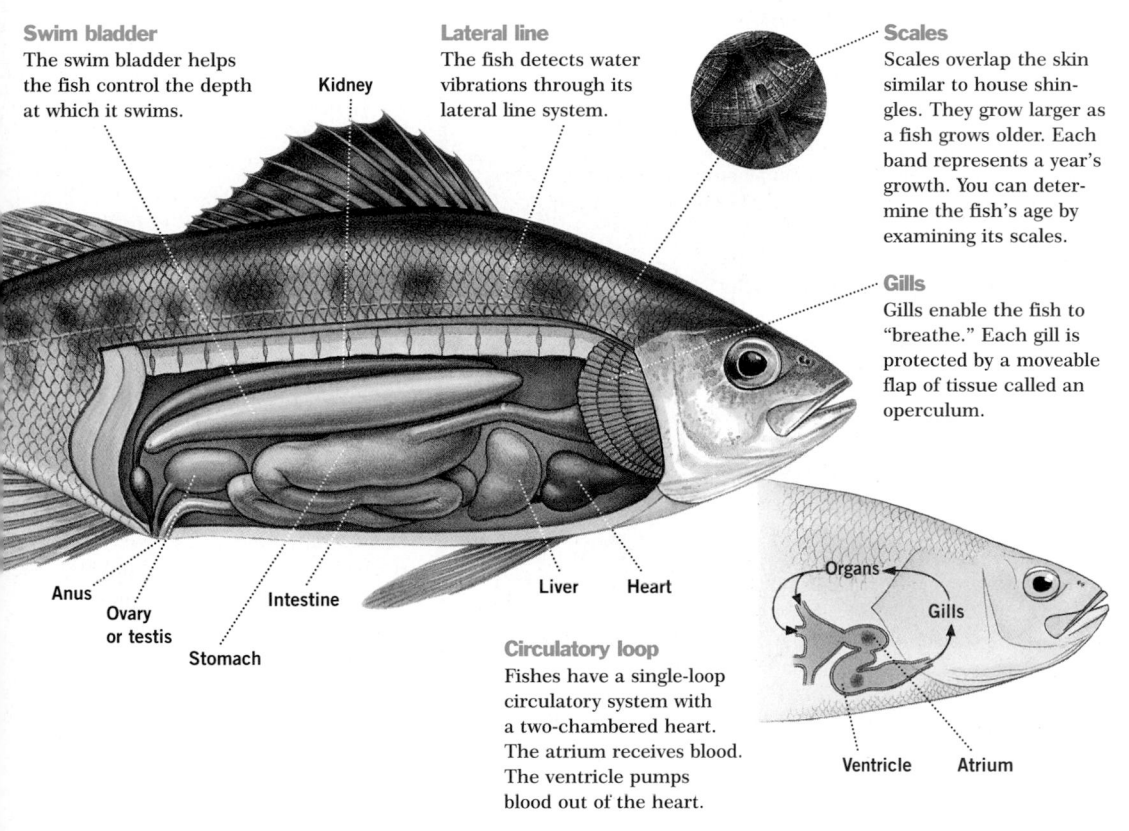

Swim bladder
The swim bladder helps the fish control the depth at which it swims.

Kidney

Lateral line
The fish detects water vibrations through its lateral line system.

Scales
Scales overlap the skin similar to house shingles. They grow larger as a fish grows older. Each band represents a year's growth. You can determine the fish's age by examining its scales.

Gills
Gills enable the fish to "breathe." Each gill is protected by a moveable flap of tissue called an operculum.

Anus
Ovary or testis
Stomach
Intestine
Liver
Heart

Circulatory loop
Fishes have a single-loop circulatory system with a two-chambered heart. The atrium receives blood. The ventricle pumps blood out of the heart.

Organs
Gills
Ventricle
Atrium

Chapter 25 Fishes and Amphibians **595**

MEETING DIVERSE NEEDS

LEP Suggest students duplicate Figure 25.3 in their notebooks and label the names and functions of the structures shown in both English and their native language. Encourage students to use their visuals as study tools.

2 TEACH

Use the Visual

Direct students' attention to Figure 25.3. As a class, review the function of each labeled structure. Ask:

- **What is the operculum?** (A bony flap of tissue that protects the gills)
- **How does the fish move its fins?** (With muscle)
- **How can you tell how old a fish is?** (By examining its scales; each band represents one year)

Teacher Demo

Show microscopic slides of ganoid, cycloid, ctenoid, and placoid scales and have students discuss similarities and differences. Explain to students that the age of a fish can be determined by counting the annual rings on its scales.

Build Writing Skills

As a group, fishes have a wide variety of unusual adaptations. Assign students a fish with an unusual adaptation and have them research the animal. Ask them to write a report that describes the fish's habitat and unusual traits.

Literature

Read aloud some poems about fishes, such as "The Fish" by Elizabeth Bishop, and "The Red Mullet" by Robert Penn Warren. Ask students to find other poems about fishes to share with the class.

25.2

Explain

Tell students that not all fishes have an operculum. However, in fishes with this structure, gas exchange takes place as the operculum pumps water in through the mouth and over the gills. Folds of tissue called gill rakers and gill filaments increase the surface area of the gills. Ask:

- **Why is surface area of the gills important?** (A large surface area increases the oxygen intake.)

Think Critically

To assess students' understanding of how fishes relate to their environments, ask:

- **What do you think would happen to a freshwater fish that was suddenly placed in sea water? Why?** (It would die because the natural flow of water and ions between the fish and its environment would be disrupted.)

Do It! **TEAM WORK**

How Does a Fish's Swim Bladder Work?

Try This

Suggest students attach a small flexible plastic tube to the neck of the balloon to add air. Allow students to experiment with other types of weights.

Analyze Your Results

1 The fish's swim bladder
2 It adjusts the air in the swim bladder to maintain the buoyancy level.

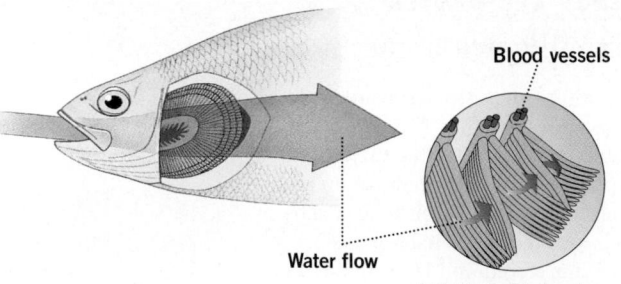

FIGURE 25.4
The gills enable a fish to obtain oxygen and give off carbon dioxide. These projections contain blood vessels so thin that red blood cells pass through in a single file.

Blood vessels

Water flow

Detail of gill structure

passes through the mouth of a fish into two cavities behind the mouth, where the gills are located. Blood vessels in the gills pick up oxygen and release carbon dioxide into the water. Water flows over the gills from front to back, but the blood flows through the

LAB ZONE **Do It!** **bioSURF**

How Does a Fish's Swim Bladder Work?

The swim bladder of a bony fish enables the fish to remain at the same spot easily at any depth in the water. You can observe how the swim bladder works if you . . .

Try This

1 Fill a tank or a large basin with water and inflate a small balloon. Use a small clamp to tie off the balloon.
2 Try to submerge the balloon in the water. What happens?
3 Tie 8–10 keys together and drop them into the water. What happens?
4 Attach a paper clip to the clamp on the balloon. Hang the keys on the paper clip as close as possible to the balloon. Drop the objects into the water.
5 Using the clamp, add or release air until the balloon floats just under the surface of the water as shown in the diagram on the right.

Analyze Your Results

1 Think of the balloon-and-keys combination as a fish. What does the balloon represent?
2 How does this demonstration explain how a fish can remain at the same spot just below the surface of the water?

blood vessels of the gills in the opposite direction. The blood passing through the gills is constantly in contact with water that is high in oxygen and low in carbon dioxide. Gills are efficient organs for taking dissolved oxygen from water. Efficiency is important because there is less available oxygen in the water than in air. You can see the path that water takes through the gills in *Figure* 25.4.

The process of respiration is helped by the opening and closing of the movable flaps over the gills, called the opercula (singular: *operculum*). When the mouth opens, the opercula close. The mouth cavity expands and causes water to rush in. When the mouth closes, the opercula open, and water is forced over the gills to the outside. Sharks do not have opercula. Their constant movement keeps water flowing over the gills.

In fishes and other vertebrates, the kidney is an organ that excretes waste. It also plays a role in maintaining the proper amount of water and ions in body fluids. Also, glands in the gills regulate salt. Maintaining water balance is necessary because if there is too little or too much water in the body, the fish will die.

In freshwater fishes the concentration of ions is greater inside the body than in the surrounding water. So water tends to enter the body by osmosis. Freshwater fishes keep the proper water balance by excreting large amounts of water in their urine.

In fishes that live in salt water, the concentration of ions is lower inside the body than in the surrounding water. Without an organ to prevent water loss, saltwater fishes would dry up inside, even though they live in water! The kidneys of these fishes function to prevent water loss. Kidneys allow some fishes to live in both saltwater and freshwater environments.

FACTS AND FIGURES

Fishes, such as salmon, that are born in freshwater, live and grow in the sea, and return to freshwater to spawn are described as *andodromous*. Some fishes, such as the American eel, are *catadromous*. Born in the sea, they grow in freshwater and return to the sea to spawn.

MEETING DIVERSE NEEDS

Sight Impaired Provide a large whole fish from a market. Allow students to touch and hold the fish while you point out its external characteristics. You may wish to let students use a clay or plastic model to study the fish's internal organs.

FIGURE 25.5
Life Cycle of the Salmon

Hatching
1 These salmon eggs hatch within four months of being fertilized. The hatchlings, called fry, will remain in the gravel for a few weeks, feeding from their yolk sac.

Juvenile
2 When they reach a length of about 15 cm, Pacific salmon will begin their journey to the sea, where they will live for months or years.

Adults
3 Adult salmon return to spawn in the river in which they were born. This trip can take several months, covering as much as 3200 kilometers.

Spawning
4 Upon reaching the spawning ground, the female scoops a nest out of gravel on the stream bed and lays her eggs. The male fertilizes the eggs, and the female covers them with more gravel.

LIFE CYCLE OF FISHES
Not a parent in sight

In most fishes, the individuals have a distinct sex. The reproductive habits of fishes are varied. Fertilization may be internal or external. In sharks, fertilization is internal. The eggs are fertilized inside the female's body, where they undergo development. The young sharks, called pups, are born alive.

The life cycle of salmon is an interesting example of external fertilization. You can follow the salmon life cycle in *Figure 25.5*. The female salmon, like all fishes who undergo external fertilization, releases her eggs into the environment. The male swims over the eggs and fertilizes them.

Female fishes typically lay hundreds, thousands, or even millions of eggs, many of which never become fertilized. With few exceptions, parents generally do not care for the eggs or the young, and most eggs are eaten or die before they hatch. Only a very few individuals survive to become adults.

Reproduction in fishes is a good example of the process of natural selection. Fishes produce many more offspring than their environment can support. Only the fastest, strongest, best-adapted young survive to produce offspring and continue the species.

CHECKPOINT 25.2

1. List the key characteristics of fishes, and explain how each one is an adaptation.
2. Describe the stages in the life cycle of a typical fish.
3. Critical Thinking How do each of a fish's sense organs help it to locate prey or escape predators?

Build on What You Know
4. What does the life cycle of fishes illustrate about Darwin's evolutionary theories? *(Need to jog your memory? Revisit relevant concepts in Chapter 10, Section 10.2.)*

FIGURE 25.6
Playing an unusual reproductive role, this male *tilapia* protects the fertilized eggs by carrying them in his mouth. He does not eat until they hatch, about five days later.

Chapter 25 Fishes and Amphibians **597**

CHECKPOINT 25.2
1. A swim bladder provides buoyancy that enables a fish to maintain its depth in the water; the lateral line helps the fish to detect water vibrations.
2. Fertilization is usually external. When fish hatch they are often called fry. There is no parental care so many young die before adulthood.
3. Lateral line—detects vibrations; smell—fish can smell blood of prey; receptors on head detect electrical charge of muscle contractions.
4. Fishes able to survive until reproduction exhibit favorable variations.

Use the Visual

Have students study the life cycle of the salmon shown in Figure 25.5. Explain that while they share the same stages in their life cycle, most fishes do not migrate back and forth from freshwater to marine environments at various stages in their life cycles.

3 ASSESS

Evaluate Understanding

Ask students to sketch a fish on a sheet of paper. Then have them draw and label the following structures: *fins, swim bladder, lateral line, kidney, gills, operculum,* and *scales.* Have students write captions for their sketch that explain how each adaptation makes life in water possible. Review the sketches as a class.

Reteach

List the following life processes on the board: *Movement and Support, Energy Production, Waste Removal, Digestion,* and *Response.* Guide students to identify the structures shown in Figure 25.3 that relate to each process. Have volunteers write the names of each structure under the appropriate head. Review responses as a class.

SUPER READ! Drawing Conclusions To practice strategies for effective reading, use pages 63-64 in *Super Read!*

LAB ZONE Investigate It!

TEAM WORK
Analyzing the Respiration of a Fish

SAFETY FIRST!

Remind students to treat all living things humanely. Caution students to keep the water temperature of the fish at or below 30°C. If at any point during the lab the fish appears to be in distress, advise students to discontinue the lab.

Lab Tips

Demonstrate to students how to scoop up the goldfish in their nets. Point out that respiration rates will be inaccurate if students do not allow the fish to acclimate to the temperature changes.

Hypothesis Help

Likely hypotheses will state: As water temperature rises, the respiratory rate of the fish increases.

Lab Extension

Open Ended
Have different lab groups use other types of fishes in place of the goldfish. Have these students compare their data to that of students who used the goldfish. Ask students to use the combined data to determine how the effects of temperature on respiratory rate vary among different fish species.

Time Required
■ 50 minutes

Analyzing the Respiration of a Fish

WHAT YOU WILL DO Observe the respiration rate of a goldfish, and develop a hypothesis about the effect of a change in water temperature on fish respiration

SKILLS YOU WILL USE Observing, collecting and recording data, predicting

WHAT YOU WILL NEED Tap water exposed to room temperature air for 24 hours, 500-mL and 1000-mL beakers, fish net, one goldfish, thermometer, timer, ice, hot water (about 80°C)

Propose a Hypothesis

The amount of oxygen that can dissolve in water depends on the temperature of the water. The higher the temperature of the water, the lower the amount of oxygen that can be dissolved. Propose a hypothesis about the effect of water temperature on the rate of fish respiration.

Conduct Your Experiment

1 Pour 250 milliliters (mL) of the room-temperature water into the 500-mL beaker. Using the fish net, place the goldfish in this beaker. Place the thermometer in the beaker.

2 Allow the fish to adjust to its new surroundings for a few minutes. Observe its respiration rate by counting the number of times its opercula open during one minute. Record this rate, along with the temperature of the water.

3 Fill the 1000-mL beaker one-quarter full with crushed ice (as shown in the photo). Place the beaker containing the goldfish inside the large beaker. Allow time for the water temperature of the small beaker to drop to about 15°C.

4 Repeat step 2.

5 Remove the small beaker and empty the large beaker. Pour a small amount of 80°C water in the large beaker and replace the small beaker inside of it. **Caution:** Use care when handling the hot water. You may need an oven mitt.

6 Repeat step 2.

7 Add a small amount of hot water to the large beaker until the temperature of the water in the small beaker reaches 20°C. Record the temperature and the respiration rate of the fish.

8 Repeat Step 7 twice, increasing the temperature to 25°C and 30°C, taking measurements at each step. (**Caution:** Temperatures over 30°C may be harmful to the fish.) Return the fish to its aquarium after the water in the small beaker has reached room temperature.

Analyze Your Data

1 Make a graph to record the respiration rate versus temperature. Plot temperature on the x-axis.

2 What happens to the respiration rate as the temperature increases? Decreases?

Draw Conclusions

Did the results support your hypothesis? What can you conclude from this experiment?

Design a Related Experiment

Suppose you wanted to find out how fish movement is affected by water temperature. Propose a hypothesis and design an experiment to test it.

Lab: Analyzing the Respiration of a Fish

Temperature	Respiration Rate

Analyze Your Data

1 Plotted points should form a line with a positive slope.

2 As the temperature rises, the respiration rate increases. As temperature decreases, the respiration rate decreases.

Draw Conclusions

Students should conclude that respiration rates increase with a rise in temperature and decrease with a drop in temperature.

25.3 Origin and Diversity of Fishes

Incredible fish story

How would you feel if you discovered a fish thought to be extinct for more than 70 million years? That is what museum curator Marjorie Courtenay-Latimer did when she recognized a coelacanth (SEE-luh-kanth). South Africans had been catching coelacanths regularly, unaware that they knew something that scientists did not. Today's coelacanths descended from ancestors that lived 400 million years ago.

What you'll learn

IDEAS
• To explain the evolutionary steps that led to modern fishes
• To contrast the different classes of fish

WORDS
lungfish

ORIGIN OF FISHES

Something's fishy in vertebrate evolution

Fishes may have evolved from invertebrate chordates similar to the lancelet shown in *Figure* 25.7. The lancelet shares many characteristics of the first fishes. It has a closed circulatory system similar to that of the early fishes, but it does not have a heart. Its blood is pumped by contractions of the blood vessels. The lancelet also has segmented muscles, which are characteristic of vertebrates, but its brain is as small as a blister at the anterior end of its nerve cord.

Although lancelets resemble fishes, they are invertebrates. The earliest known vertebrate fossils are of fishlike animals called ostracoderms. They were covered with body plates, inspiring their name which comes from *ostrakon*, meaning "shell," and "-derm," meaning "skin." These animals had no jaws or teeth, so their food was limited to small particles that could be strained from the water. Ostracoderms, such as the *Drepanaspis* in *Figure* 25.7, are the ancestors of the modern fishes.

Modern fishes have several adaptations that ostracoderms did not share. One important adaptation was the

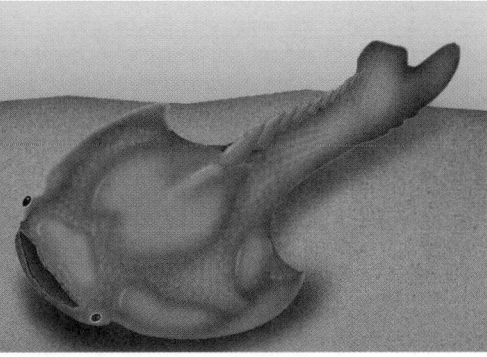

FIGURE 25.7
The lancelet (left) closely resembles fossil organisms that are thought to be the ancestors of fishes. The heavily armored, jawless *Drepanaspis* (right) is an extinct ancestor of modern fishes.

Chapter 25 Fishes and Amphibians **599**

STUDENT RESOURCES

From the Teacher's Resource Package, use:
■ Section Review 25.3 and Enrichment Topics 25-1 and 25-2 from Unit 7 Review Module

TECHNOLOGY RESOURCES

Relevant technology resources include:
■ Spanish Student Edition CD-ROM
■ Teacher's Resource Planner CD-ROM
■ Biology Alive! Video: "Signs of Life" and "The Continuity of Life"

---

① ENGAGE

Use the Visual

Have students study the photograph that opens the section. Explain that the coelacanth recognized by the curator closely resembled those that lived 70 million years ago. Ask:

■ **Why did scientists think coelacanths were extinct?** (Responses might suggest the absence of recorded information on coelacanth sightings.)

Quick Activity

Display pictures of fishes representative of the three fish classes. Have students examine the pictures noting any similarities and differences. Review student responses. Explain that in this section students will explore the traits used to classify fishes.

Use the Visual

Have students study the photos in Figure 25.7. Ask:

■ **How do the characteristics of the lancelet and *Drepanaspis* differ?** (Lancelet has a segmented body, *Drepanaspis* has heavy body plates and no jaw.)

 **Drawing Conclusions** To practice strategies for effective reading, use pages 63-64 in *Super Read!*

2 TEACH

Use the Visual

Have students study Figure 25.8. Point out that the evolutionary milestones of jaws and bony skeletons have led to the grouping of modern fishes in three classes: agnathans, chondrichthyes, and osteichthyes.

Use the Visual

Have students study Figure 25.9. Ask:

- **What is the key characteristic of agnathans?** (They lack jaws.)
- **What are the surviving types of agnathans?** (Lampreys, hagfish)

Art

Have students prepare a visual presentation on a poster board, transparency, or drawing paper illustrating the common internal and external characteristics of agnathans, chondrichthyes, or osteichthyes. Tell students that they may use any specimen within a group to show common traits. You may wish to have students work in pairs.

FIGURE 25.8

Classes of Fishes

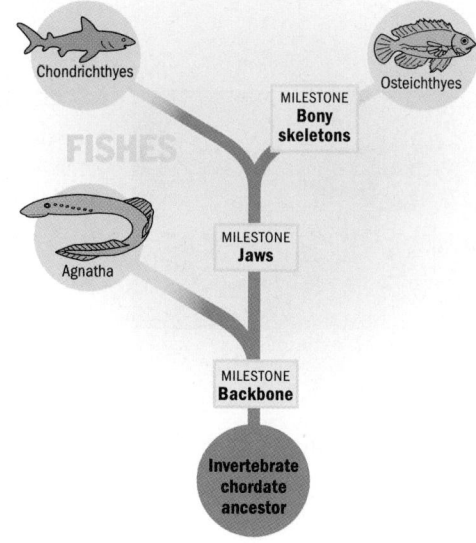

FISHES

- Chondrichthyes
- Osteichthyes
- MILESTONE **Bony skeletons**
- Agnatha
- MILESTONE **Jaws**
- MILESTONE **Backbone**
- **Invertebrate chordate ancestor**

formation of jaws. Another adaptation was paired fins, which gave the fishes more control over their movements in water. Later, fishes developed strong internal skeletons that could withstand the pulling force of powerful muscles.

| Kingdom: Animalia |
| Phylum: Chordata |
| Subphylum: Vertebrata |
| Classes: |

Agnatha
Chondrichthyes
Osteichthyes

FIGURE 25.9

Notice the lamprey's sharp teeth (right). It also has a strong rasplike tongue. Lampreys attach themselves to other fishes (left), living on their body fluids.

FISH DIVERSITY

"And the survivors are. . ."

About 70 percent of Earth's surface is covered with water. Since most of this water is in the ocean, that is where most of the world's fishes live. Today's fishes are classified into three groups. These groups are represented in *Figure 25.8*.

Agnathans These jawless fishes most closely resemble the earliest fishes from which all other vertebrates may have evolved. The agnathans are the only vertebrates that retain a notochord throughout life. The agnathans that survive today belong to two groups: the lampreys and the hagfishes.

Both groups have snakelike bodies without paired fins. Lacking paired fins, which help in balance and steering, agnathans are not good swimmers. Lampreys attach themselves to other fishes by means of a round mouth with rasping parts. As parasites, they feed on their host's body fluids. Hagfishes are scavengers. They move slowly through cold water, using sensory tentacles to locate dead and dying fishes.

Chondrichthyes The members of this class—sharks, rays, and skates—all have skeletons made almost entirely of flexible cartilage rather than rigid bone. You may think that these fishes are primitive because of the cartilage skeleton. Actually, it has been shown that the cartilage skeleton of these fishes may have evolved from an earlier bony skeleton. The cartilage skeleton may be an adaptation to deep-sea life.

FACTS AND FIGURES

Students may be interested to know that hagfish are blind. Surrounding the mouth of hagfish are six fleshy tentacles which serve as sensory organs and are used primarily to locate food.

MEETING DIVERSE NEEDS

At Risk Have students work with a partner to develop a graphic that compares and contrasts the three classes of fishes. Encourage students to include information presented in the text as well as in the graphics.

FIGURE 25.10
Many sharks have streamlined bodies with fins and a powerful tail. These features allow the shark to move gracefully through the water.

Sharks have torpedo-shaped bodies, which are propelled through the water by the thrashing motion of their forceful tails. In *Figure 25.10*, you can see the pectoral, pelvic, and dorsal fins of the shark. While the tail provides downward thrust, the stiff pectoral fins counteract by producing upward lift. Pelvic and dorsal fins balance the swimming shark.

Osteichthyes While early cartilaginous fishes are thought to have evolved in deep oceans, evidence indicates that the bony fishes, or Osteichthyes, evolved in fresh water. The bony fishes are a more diverse group, compared with the sharks and their relatives. This is to be expected because bodies of fresh water are smaller than oceans. Changes in climate affect a lake more than an ocean and tend to divide it into smaller ponds during droughts. When this happens, freshwater animals can become isolated from the rest of their species. Changes in the environment and the isolation of populations are important factors in evolution. Many types of bony fishes are also adapted to live in the ocean.

The three surviving groups of bony fishes are lobe-finned fishes, lungfishes, and ray-finned fishes. The fins of lobe-finned fishes are similar to the legs of early terrestrial vertebrates. This similarity is considered evidence that amphibians may have evolved from ancestral lobe-finned fishes. These fishes were thought to be extinct for at least 60 million years. But in 1938 a group of South African fishers caught an unusual fish. As you read at the beginning of this section, it was identified as a coelacanth, a type of lobe-finned fish. Modern coelacanths

FIGURE 25.11
The lungfish is able to breathe air due to its unique swim bladder, which also functions as a lung.

Chapter 25 Fishes and Amphibians **601**

 Earth Science

Scientists searching for new places to mine minerals have discovered that manganese nodules can be removed from the ocean floor. These nodules develop when manganese oxide in ocean water forms around sharks' teeth and other debris that collect on the ocean bottom. The shark's tooth which provides a core around which the mineral deposit builds is also useful for determining the age of shark species.

Teacher Demo

Show the class the gelatinous tip from the breastbone of a chicken. Allow the students to handle it to experience its flexibility. Explain that sharks have skeletons made of the same kind of material rather than hard bone.

Use the Visual

Ask students to use Figure 25.11 to answer the following:

- **What is the key characteristic of osteichthyes?** (Bony skeleton)
- **Why do you think this fish is called a lungfish?** (It has a lung as well as gills.)

MULTICULTURAL PERSPECTIVE

Fish is a mainstay in the diets of many Native American Inuits, who live in the Arctic. Although they eat many fatty meats, they rarely develop heart disease. Researchers theorize that their good health may be due to fish oils in their diet which seem to reverse the effects of cholesterol.

FACTS AND FIGURES

The most diverse group of bony fishes is the ray-finned fishes, which have fanlike fins made of thin membranes supported by bony rays. They are the only fishes with a swim bladder, a structure that evolved from the lungs of lobe-finned fishes.

Use the Visual

Have students study the fishes in Figure 25.12. Ask students to explain in writing what physical characteristics influenced the name given to each fish. You may wish to have students write their explanations in their portfolios.

3 ASSESS

Evaluate Understanding

Ask students to make a table that compares and contrasts the three classes of fishes. Have them include information about the key characteristics, diversity, and appearance of each class as well as any other notable characteristics. Review the tables as a class.

Reteach

On an overhead transparency, create a phylogenetic tree that traces the evolutionary development of fishes. As you add each fish class to the tree, discuss the traits of that class. Conclude the review by pointing out the key similarities and differences of fishes in each class.

FIGURE 25.12

Ray-finned Fishes

Bluefin tuna
Most of the muscle tissue in a tuna is "red"—very vascular and well oxygenated. This tissue helps the tuna retain heat better than most fishes.

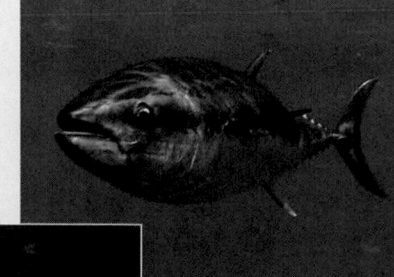

Clown trigger fish
When threatened, the triggerfish will wedge itself in a crevice and erect a long spine on its back, which is locked in place by a second spine, or "trigger."

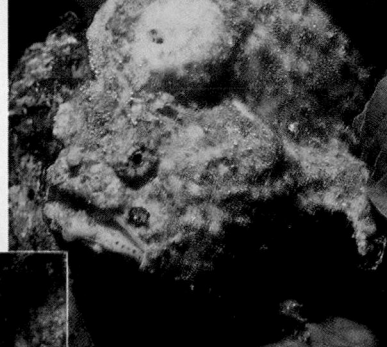

Frog fish
The frog fish, a close relative of the angler fish, uses a modified fin as a lure to capture smaller fish.

Seahorse
The upright-swimming seahorse shows a great amount of parental care. The male of the species carries the eggs in a pouch until they hatch.

live in deep ocean water and do not have lungs. Fossil evidence shows that ancient coelacanths did have lungs. Scientists think that the lobe-finned fishes were the first vertebrates to live on land.

The **lungfish,** a close relative of the coelacanth, has lungs as well as gills. There are only a few living species of lungfishes. They live in shallow, tropical rivers. South American and African lungfishes regularly use their lungs to supplement the oxygen taken in by their gills. The Australian lungfishes use their lungs only during part of the year, when rivers dry up or have low levels of oxygen. These lungfishes also have lobed fins.

The ray-finned fishes are the largest group of bony fishes. They have fanlike fins made of thin membranes supported by bony rays. Salmon, guppies, and tuna are familiar examples. Ray-finned fishes vary greatly in shape, behavior, and habitat. They are successful because they have adapted to every kind of aquatic environment and have evolved into thousands of species. Compare the different species of ray-finned fishes shown in *Figure 25.12.*

CHECKPOINT 25.3

1. Name and describe the ancient groups of fishes. Compare them to modern fishes.
2. What are the key differences between the three classes of fishes living today?
3. **Critical Thinking** Besides breathing and movement, what other challenges would be faced by a fish trying to live on land?

Build on What You Know

4. What fish structure is similar to the mandible of an arthropod? How are the two kinds of structures different? *(Need to jog your memory? Revisit relevant concepts in Chapter 23, Section 23.2.)*

CHECKPOINT 25.3

1. The ostracoderms were covered with thick plates of armor, had no teeth or jaws, and filtered their food from the water.
2. Agnathans: no jaws; chondrichthyes: cartilage skeletons; osteichthyes: bony skeletons
3. **Developing a hypothesis** Possible answers include not drying out, escaping from predators, finding food, and finding mates.
4. The jaws of chondrichthyes and osteichthyes are similar. In arthropods, the mandibles are used more for chewing food; in many fishes, the jaws are used to capture and chew food.

25.4 Fishes in the Biosphere

Floating fish food factories
Many fishes depend on algae for survival. Algae capture the energy of sunlight and store it in food molecules. These tiny photosynthesizers are at the base of aquatic food chains. Propelled by currents, they drift along near the surface of the ocean. Traveling with and living on the algae are protozoans and tiny animals. This floating mass of life supports many organisms in the food chain.

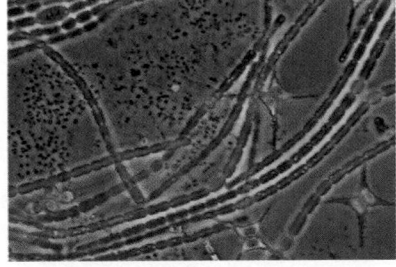

What you'll learn

IDEAS
- To compare the roles of different fishes in aquatic food webs
- To explain the importance of fish as a food source

SUPER READ!

ECOLOGICAL ROLES

A "fish eat fish" world

As you know, life on land involves food chains and food webs. The same relationships exist in water. In both freshwater and saltwater bodies, fishes play an important role in aquatic food chains.

Some fishes eat plants and plankton, which are the first links in an aquatic food chain. Others are bottom dwellers that live on dead and decaying organisms. A few other types of fishes are parasites. Most fishes, though, are carnivores, or meat eaters. The carnivorous fishes help maintain balanced ecosystems by limiting the number of organisms that survive long enough to reproduce.

All these fishes, in turn, are preyed on by other animals, including larger fishes, birds, aquatic mammals such as seals, and humans. They are also affected by disease-causing organisms such as bacteria and fungi.

HUMAN USES

And on his farm he had some . . . fishes?

You probably know that fish is eaten by people all over the world. Fish is nourishing because it contains about as much protein as red meat but much less fat and cholesterol. In fact, in some places around the world, fish

is the primary protein source. As more people in the United States become health conscious, fish is becoming a staple in the Amerian diet.

Fishing is one of the world's major industries. Most of the fishes are taken from naturally occurring ecosystems. However, so much fishing is being done that the numbers of available fishes are dwindling. Still, as the human population increases, so does the demand for fish. To help meet these needs, fish farmers cultivate fishes in a controlled environment and harvest them when they reach the desired size. Currently, fish farms provide about 10 percent of the world's annual commercial fish supply.

Fish ranching is another way to increase fish numbers. It involves raising species in captivity for the first few years of their lives and then releasing them into the wild. In this way, greater numbers of fishes return to spawn and can be harvested at that time.

In addition to providing an important food source, fishes give people a lot of enjoyment. You may raise fishes in an aquarium because of the satisfaction you get from caring for these interesting animals and learning about their habits. Scuba divers also enjoy watching fishes in their natural environments.

FIGURE 25.13
Fish caught from lakes and streams are an important part of the bald eagle's diet. The eagle also scavenges dead or dying fish, such as salmon that have spawned.

Chapter 25 Fishes and Amphibians **603**

ENGAGE

Use the Visual

Have students study the photograph that opens the section. Explain that algae in the oceans provide most of the oxygen released through photosynthesis and also serve as the base of aquatic food chains.

Check Prior Knowledge

To assess students' knowledge about the role of fishes in the environment, ask:

- **What adaptations have enabled fishes to live in different aquatic environments?** (Fishes' kidneys are adapted to enable them to live in environments with various salt content; different forms of reproduction produce more offspring than the environment can support, ensuring continuation of the species and food for others species.)

Quick Activity

On the board, create a simple ocean food chain using algae as the producer. Explain to students what a food chain represents. Challenge them to identify the producers and consumers in the food chain you have drawn. Then have them identify which consumers are herbivores and which are carnivores.

SUPER READ! **Drawing Conclusions** To practice strategies for effective reading, use pages 63-64 in *Super Read!*

STUDENT RESOURCES

From the Teacher's Resource Package, use:
- Section Review 25.4 from Unit 7 Review Module
- Consumer Applications 25-1
- Issues and Decision Making 25-1 and 25-2

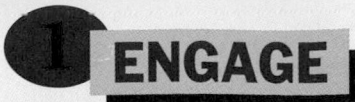
TECHNOLOGY RESOURCES

Relevant technology resources include:
- Spanish Student Edition CD-ROM
- Teacher's Resource Planner CD-ROM
- Biology Alive! Video: "Life's Fragile Balance"

25.4

In the Community

Encourage students to survey workers from several fish markets, including fish stands at a nearby wharf or fishing pier. Remind students that fish availability varies by season. Availability and shipping distance affect the variety, quantity, and price of fishes. Procedures for ensuring freshness will likely include: icing the fishes when they are caught, transported, and stored; changing the ice frequently; and limiting the sell date for fresh fishes.

ASSESS

Evaluate Understanding

Have students write a summary explaining the importance of fish as a food source for people as well as for other organisms. Encourage students to illustrate their summaries with a food chain. Review the summaries as a class.

Reteach

Work with students to use the information in the section to develop an ocean food chain. You may want to draw a food chain on an overhead transparency for them to use as a model. Discuss individual food chains and what the food chains and food web show. Challenge students to identify where in the web humans should be added and have them defend their choice.

604

Survey a local food market to find out what varieties of fishes are available there. Arrange to talk to someone in the fish department who can tell you how fish availability changes during the year and how availability affects prices. Ask where the fishes are caught and how far they are shipped to the store. Also research the proce-

IN THE COMMUNITY
Fish-Smart Markets

dures that are followed to insure the freshness of fish and any federal government regulations that may apply.

To do this you may want to investigate the U.S. Food and Drug Administration (FDA) site on the Internet at *http://vertebrates.biosurf.com*. There you will find specific information relating to the regulation of seafood, including checking for dangerous levels of mercury in fish.

FIGURE 25.14
Asthma sufferers can be helped by medicine made from the puffer fish. These fish are named for their ability to inflate their bodies with air or water.

Some people like to fish. They may view it as an opportunity to enjoy the outdoors, or they may enjoy the challenge of catching a game fish that puts up a powerful fight. Many people who enjoy fishing release the fishes they catch to avoid depleting natural populations.

Fishes are also at the cutting edge of medical research. For example, a recent study of native people in Greenland shed new light on the role that fish plays in reducing heart disease. On average, the adult Eskimos in the study ate about 1453.6 grams of fish per day. They also ate huge strips of fat from whales. You might think all this fat consumption would lead to heart disease. But researchers found that the oil in the fish seemed to counteract the effects of animal fat in the subjects' blood vessels. They rarely had heart dis-

ease. This finding led to a study of Japanese people, who also eat large amounts of fish. The Japanese studied also had a lower incidence of heart disease than people who ate less fish.

Fishes are also used in other ways. Other products that are made from fishes include medicine, glue, livestock feed, and pet food.

CHECKPOINT 25.4

1. How do carnivorous fishes help to maintain a balanced ecosystem?
2. Why are fishes so important as a food source?
3. **Critical Thinking** Why is eating fish considered to be healthful? Explain your answer.

Build on What You Know

4. What effects do you think the extinction of a plantlike protist would have on fishes? *(Need to jog your memory? Revisit relevant concepts in Chapter 15, Section 15.5.)*

? **What characteristics make fishes adapted to life in the water?**

604 *Unit 7 Vertebrate Animals*

CHECKPOINT 25.4

1. They prey on planktonic feeding fishes that would otherwise reproduce in large numbers. In turn, they are preyed upon by larger carnivorous fishes.
2. Many countries, particularly those where geography and climate prevent the raising of land animals, depend on fishes and other marine animals for protein.
3. **Making generalizations** Fish is high in protein, yet contains much less fat and cholesterol than other meats.
4. Extinction of a plantlike protist would be detrimental to any fish that prey on it and fish preying on those fish, on up the food chain.

THE BIG IDEA! Although amphibians share some fish traits, they are adapted to life on land. 25.5–25.7

25.5 Characteristics of Amphibians

Frog "love songs"

Frogs usually live alone. When the time comes to mate, males and females need a way to find one another. In many species of frogs, the male makes sounds to attract mates. Females hear the male's call and move toward the sound. Each species has a distinctive sound. Some people can more easily tell frog species apart by their songs than by their looks.

What you'll learn

IDEAS
• To explain the adaptations of amphibians to their environment
• To summarize the life cycle of a typical amphibian

WORDS
amphibian, cloaca

MOVEMENT AND RESPONSE

Legs give amphibians a lift

An **amphibian** is a vertebrate that is well adapted to life both in water and on land. Most amphibians start life as aquatic larvae but live their adult lives on land. One of the challenges of life on land for amphibians is being able to support their own bodies, because air provides less support than water. An additional challenge is the response of the organisms to their environment. Light and sound waves travel differently through air, requiring different sense organs.

With strong limb bones and muscles to lift their bodies off the ground, amphibians are well adapted to life on land. Amphibians have four strong limbs—two forelimbs and two hind limbs—the basic structure of a tetrapod. The strong bones, girdles, and muscles of amphibian limbs help them to support their bodies. Some fully aquatic amphibians have lost their legs and returned to fishlike locomotion. Others, like frogs, leap by rapidly straightening their long,

powerful hind limbs. Toads have shorter hind limbs than frogs and move by small hops rather than leaps.

Like all vertebrates, amphibians have a nervous system made up of a brain, spinal cord, and nerves. Many also have sensory organs that function well in both aquatic and terrestrial environments. For example, a frog's eyes see well in both water and air. They are covered by a transparent eyelid called a nictitating (NIK-tih-tay-ting) membrane. This membrane keeps the eye moist in air and protects it in water.

FIGURE 25.15

Tympanic membranes enable the frog to detect sound waves.

Chapter 25 Fishes and Amphibians **605**

STUDENT RESOURCES

From the Teacher's Resource Package, use:
■ Section Review 25.5 and Interpreting Graphics 25 from Unit 7 Review Module
■ Lab 44: "Development in Frogs"; Lab 45: "Frog Anatomy"; Lab 46: "Frog: Alternative Anatomy Investigation"
■ Issues and Decision Making 25-3

TECHNOLOGY RESOURCES

Relevant technology resources include:
■ Spanish Student Edition CD-ROM
■ Teacher's Resource Planner CD-ROM
■ Animated Biological Concepts Videodiscs: "Frog Anatomy"
■ Biology Alive! Video: "Conflict and Cooperation"

---

1 ENGAGE

Consider the Big Idea

Have students read The Big Idea! at the top of the page. Explain that amphibians differ from fishes because amphibians have legs and can live on land.

Use the Visual

Have students study the photograph that opens the section. Explain that frogs reproduce sexually and must be able to locate mates. Ask:

■ **How might frogs that do not use mating calls locate suitable mates?** (By sight, by smell, through the use of courtship rituals)

Check Prior Knowledge

To assess students' knowledge about amphibians, ask:

■ **What are two important traits shared by fishes and amphibians?** (Both have backbones and are ectotherms.)

Quick Activity

Elicit, through a show of hands, if students ever played leapfrog as children. Ask volunteers to come to the front of the class to demonstrate the stance assumed for this game. Discuss with students how this stance compares to that used by frogs. Ask:

■ **Why would amphibians need to evolve legs?** (Legs are needed to move about on land.)

TEACH

Health

As you discuss the mucous covering of the frog's skin, explain that biologists have discovered that some frogs secrete chemical substances. Medical researchers are studying the effects of these substances on humans to find possible uses of frog secretions in treating disease.

Explain

As students examine the frog's digestive system, explain that the tongue of the frog is very sticky, much like flypaper. Point out that the tongue's stickiness enhances the ability of the frog to catch flying insects.

Use the Visual

Have students study Figure 25.16. As a class, discuss each labeled structure and its function. Have students use information from the discussion and their own observations to answer the following questions.

- **What structures does a frog use for respiration?** (Lungs and skin)
- **What structures does a frog use for jumping?** (Its hind legs)
- **What structure indicates that the frog is a vertebrate?** (Its backbone)

Animated Biological Concepts

Frog Anatomy   Play

Frogs hear through two circular structures behind the eyes called tympanic (tim-PAN-ik) membranes. Find the tympanic membrane in *Figure 25.15* on page 605. These structures detect sound waves in air or water.

ENERGY AND WASTES

The skin that breathes

One key to the success of amphibians on land is their skin. Many amphibians have skin that enables the exchange of gases with the environment. Because oxygen and carbon dioxide must first dissolve in water before they can diffuse into or out of living tissues, an amphibian's skin must stay moist enough to allow the diffusion of gases and to prevent the animal from drying out. Many amphibians have mucous glands that keep the skin moist.

Although most amphibian larvae breathe through gills, the majority of adult amphibians breathe with lungs. The lungs of these amphibians contain internal air sacs that stay moist even if the outside environment is dry, allowing a constant exchange of gases.

The adult frog's digestive tract is similar to a human's. It consists of a mouth, esophagus, stomach, small intestine, and large intestine. Undigested food passes into a structure common to most vertebrates called the cloaca. The **cloaca** is a common chamber into which products of the digestive, reproductive, and excretory systems empty. Mammals, except for monotremes, do not have a cloaca.

You will recall that fishes have a single-loop circulatory system and a two-chambered heart. Amphibians have a double-loop circulatory system and a three-chambered heart. This adaptation distributes oxygen efficiently to all the cells and removes carbon dioxide and other wastes.

FIGURE 25.16

Structure of a Frog

Powerful legs
The hind legs of a frog are so strong that it can jump a distance of more than ten times its own body length.

A three-chambered heart partially separates oxygen-rich from oxygen-poor blood.

Like fishes, amphibians have kidneys that excrete wastes from the bloodstream and regulate the amount of water in the body. In an aquatic environment, the kidneys form large amounts of dilute urine to rid the body of excess water. On land, the kidneys function to conserve water by forming small amounts of concentrated urine. Wastes from the kidneys remain in the bladder until they are released from the body.

MEETING DIVERSE NEEDS

Sight Impaired If available, use a model, specimen, or fossil of a frog to help students locate and identify the function of different structures of amphibians.

Respiration

The frog has lungs that enable it to breathe air on land, but not enough air to keep the frog alive. It must also take in oxygen through its skin.

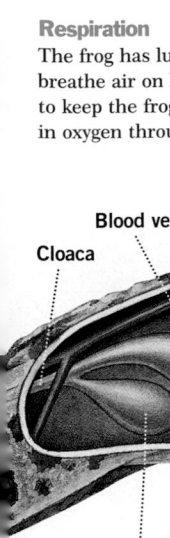

Liver

Gall bladder

Lung

Kidney

Blood vessel

Cloaca

Heart

Pancreas

Intestines   Stomach

Bladder

Digestion

The frog's digestive system resembles that of a fish. Enzymes break down food into tiny particles that enter the bloodstream.

Circulation

The frog's blood carries oxygen and digested food to the body's cells. It carries carbon dioxide and other wastes away from the body cells.

LIFE CYCLE

Going through stages

Some amphibian eggs look like a mass of clear tapioca pudding floating in the water. An amphibian's eggs are covered with a jellylike coating that protects them from injury, disease, and changes in temperature. The coating also provides nourishment for the developing embryos. Amphibians lay their eggs in water or in moist places on land so that the eggs will not dry out. Even though amphibians were the first land animals, water still plays an important role in their reproduction.

Frogs fertilize their eggs outside the body. In temperate climates, they migrate in large numbers to ponds or streams during the early, warm days of

LAB ZONE   Think About It!   bioSURF

Comparing Amphibian and Fish Circulatory Systems

These diagrams show the circulatory systems of fishes and amphibians. As you have learned, fishes possess a single-loop circulatory system. Most amphibians, on the other hand, possess a double-loop circulatory system.

Analyzing the Diagram

1 Look at the diagrams. What is the most prominent difference between the two systems? Describe that difference.
2 What new adaptation is present in the amphibian's heart?
3 How did this adaptation help the amphibian function on land?

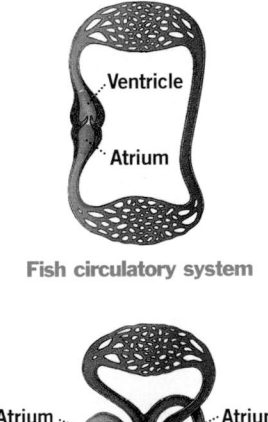

Ventricle

Atrium

Fish circulatory system

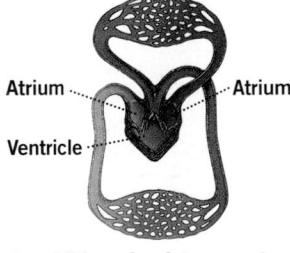

Atrium   Atrium

Ventricle

Amphibian circulatory system

Teacher Demo

Perform a frog dissection on the stage of an opaque projector. Point out organs and organ systems as the dissection proceeds. As an alternative, you may wish to obtain a videodisc that shows a frog dissection or a computer simulation of the procedure.

LAB ZONE   Think About It!

Comparing Amphibian and Fish Circulatory Systems   **TEAM WORK**

Analyzing the Diagram

1 The number of circulatory loops; the amphibian system has two, the fish only one.
2 An additional atrium
3 It separates oxygen-rich blood from oxygen-poor blood, increasing the oxygen delivered to the tissues.

Build Writing Skills

Tell students that the North American bullfrog *Rana catesbeiana* is able to jump nine times its own length. Every year, frog-jumping competitions are held in Calaveras County, California. Have interested students research one competition and write an account to be published in a local newspaper.

MEETING DIVERSE NEEDS

At Risk Encourage students to create a concept map or visual showing how food and water circulate in the frog. Suggest that students use their graphics as study tools.

FACTS AND FIGURES

In tropical regions, many species of tree frogs breed in trees by depositing their eggs in water trapped in the crotch between a tree trunk and a large limb. The eggs are fertilized and metamorphosis takes place in these pockets of water.

Literature

Mark Twain gained nationwide attention as a writer with a story about a frog. "The Celebrated Jumping Frog of Calaveras County," written by Twain while he lived in California, appeared in the *New York Saturday Press* in November 1865. You may wish to suggest that students read the story.

Explain

Have students recall the process of metamorphosis from their study of insects. Point out that frogs, like butterflies, undergo complete metamorphosis.

Evaluate Understanding

Ask students to make a flow-chart that explains the stages in the life cycle of a frog. Have volunteers describe the appearance of the frog at each stage and explain how it is adapted to its environment.

Reteach

Work with students to outline the information presented in the section. Write the three main heads on the board: *Movement and Response, Energy and Wastes,* and *Life Cycle.* Then have students review the section to find two or more details about amphibians to add under each head.

FIGURE 25.17

Frog Life Cycle

Mating frogs
1 Mating occurs with the male frog clasping the female tightly. The male fertilizes the eggs as they are laid.

Eggs
2 As many as 20,000 eggs may be laid at once. Tadpoles hatch about six days after fertilization.

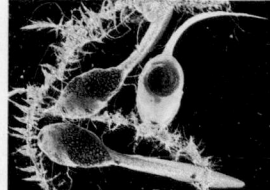

Developing tadpole
4 As the tadpole matures, internal gills develop, legs emerge, and the tail is absorbed.

Young tadpole
3 After exhausting the food supply that it was born with, each young tadpole begins to feed on algae.

Adult frog
5 Upon reaching adulthood, the frog can leave the water and breathe air, and pursue terrestrial prey.

spring. Males of some species call out loudly to attract females of their species. When a female approaches a calling male, the male climbs onto her back, grasps her tightly under the forelimbs, and the life cycle shown in *Figure* 25.17 begins.

As is true for fishes, a great many eggs and tadpoles are eaten by aquatic predators. In most species, few of the fertilized eggs survive to grow and reproduce. However, some species of frogs have developed ways of providing parental care, including carrying young on their backs.

Amphibians are the only vertebrates that have a life cycle that includes metamorphosis. Metamorphosis in frogs is accompanied by many external and internal changes. It is triggered by a hormone called thyroxine, which circulates in the bloodstream. The major stages of metamorphosis are shown in *Figure* 25.17. What are some of the external changes that occur as the tadpole develops into an adult?

At the same time that external changes are taking place, internal

changes are also occurring. The frog develops adult teeth and a jaw, as well as the shorter digestive tract typical of a carnivore. A double-loop circulatory system with a three-chambered heart replaces the single-loop, two-chambered heart system. The gills disappear, and lungs develop from saclike structures in the throat. Development can be completed in as few as eight days in desert-dwelling toads, or it can take as long as two to three years in bullfrogs.

CHECKPOINT 25.5

1. How do the characteristics of amphibians differ from those of fishes?
2. What changes occur during the life cycle of a typical amphibian?
3. Critical Thinking Would you expect to find a nictitating membrane on animals other than amphibians? Why or why not?

Build on What You Know

4. Compare metamorphosis in amphibians and insects. *(Need to jog your memory? Revisit relevant concepts in Chapter 23, Section 23.4.)*

608 *Unit 7 Vertebrate Animals*

CHECKPOINT 25.5

1. Fishes are adapted for life in water; amphibians are adapted for an aquatic larval stage and for life on land as an adult.
2. Most begin life in water. Metamorphosis enables them to develop legs, lungs, and other structures for living on land.

3. **Making generalizations** Any animal that spends time in both the air and water could benefit from such an adaptation.
4. The main difference is the state in which the changes take place. Insect pupa are in a relatively dormant stage in the cocoon. Amphibians are relatively active during metamorphosis.

25.6 Origin and Diversity of Amphibians

Frogs from the sky?
There is an old myth that it sometimes rains frogs. Why would people believe that? Well, in places where conditions get too dry or too cold, frogs may find a patch of mud or leaf litter and bury themselves. When a warm rain signals the return of more favorable conditions, the frogs suddenly reappear.

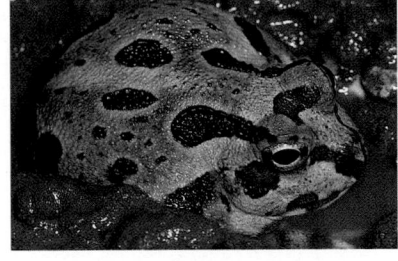

What you'll learn

IDEAS
• To explain the evolutionary steps that led to modern amphibians
• To compare and contrast the different orders of amphibians

ORIGIN OF AMPHIBIANS

Legs and lungs invade land

If you could travel back in time to about 400 million years ago, you would probably find vascular plants growing abundantly in warm, swampy places. You would see only a few types of animals, however, most of which would be insects and arachnids.

Fast-forward to about 370 million years ago. There are still swampy areas, but some places are drier now. A few million years later, you might witness periodic droughts that shrink the size of lakes and streams. Among the vertebrates living at that time are lobe-finned fishes with primitive lungs. They also have a pair of muscular fins that function like legs. Some

of these fishes may have evolved into the first amphibians. *Figure 25.18* shows the structural features of the muscular fins of lobe-finned fishes and early amphibians. What similarities and differences can you see? **❶**

For the first vertebrates that left the water, land offered escape from both predation by other fishes and competition for food. Evidence indicates that there were no predators on land, and food in the form of insects and arthropods was plentiful. From about 345 million to 285 million years ago, the early amphibians thrived. Early amphibians thrived so abundantly that this period is often called the Age of Amphibians.

Fossils show that the early amphibians were similar to fishes. They lived mostly in water and fed on fishes and

FIGURE 25.18
Compare the muscular fin structure of the lobe-finned fish (left) with the leg of an early amphibian (right).

Lobe-finned fish

Early amphibian

Chapter 25 Fishes and Amphibians **609**

STUDENT RESOURCES

From the Teacher's Resource Package, use:
■ Section Review 25.6 and Enrichment Topic 25-3 from Unit 7 Review Module

TECHNOLOGY RESOURCES

Relevant technology resources include:
■ Spanish Student Edition CD-ROM
■ Teacher's Resource Planner CD-ROM

❶ ENGAGE

Use the Visual

Have students study the photograph that opens the section. Explain that the myth that it sometimes rains frogs arose in regions with great variations in weather.

SUPER READ! Drawing Conclusions To practice strategies for effective reading, use pages 63-64 in *Super Read!*

Check Prior Knowledge

To assess students' knowledge about amphibians, ask:

■ **What are some major differences between fishes and amphibians?** (Amphibians have legs, live on land near water, and have skin. Fish have fins, live in water, and have scales.)

Quick Activity

Display photographs or slides of frogs and toads. Call on volunteers to share what they know about these amphibians and discuss their responses. Then show students pictures or slides of newts and salamanders. Explain that these animals are also amphibians. Have students discuss how these animals are similar to frogs and toads.

❶ Students should note the similar body shapes and the differences in bone structures.

2 TEACH

Use the Visual

Have students compare the skin of frogs and toads shown in Figure 25.20. Ask:

- **Why is the skin of a frog moist?** (Frogs secrete mucus that keeps their skin moist.)
- **How has the skin of toads adapted to living on land?** (Its greater thickness is resistant to drying.)

Clarify Misconceptions

Many students believe they can get warts from touching the rough skin of a toad. Explain that this idea is a myth that probably arose because many toads have bumpy, wartlike protuberances on their skin that resemble warts. Remind students that they learned in Chapter 14 that warts are caused by viruses.

Discuss

As you discuss the differences among the various groups of amphibians, remind students that one characteristic shared by all amphibians is that they are ectotherms. Ask:

- **How is the body temperature of an ectotherm determined?** (By the temperature of its environment)

❶ Frogs live in or near water and have moist skin. Toads live in drier environments and have dry, bumpy skin.

FIGURE 25.19

Class Amphibia

AMPHIBIANS

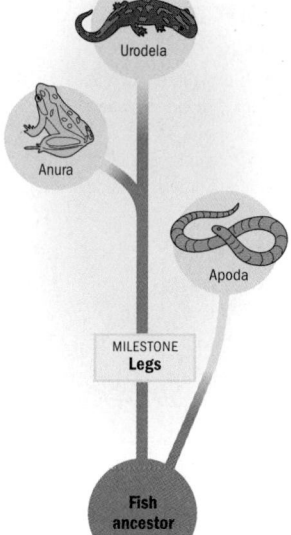

Urodela

Anura

Apoda

MILESTONE
Legs

Fish ancestor

Kingdom: **Animalia**
Phylum: **Chordata**
Subphylum: **Vertebrata**
Class: **Amphibia**
Orders:
Anura
Urodela
Apoda

aquatic invertebrates. These early amphibians were covered with scales, had fishlike teeth, and had a lateral line system. Except for some caecilians (sih-SIH-lee-uhnz), present-day amphibians do not have scales and have only modified teeth. They may have a lateral line system in the larval stage, but most amphibians lose this feature as they develop.

DIVERSITY OF AMPHIBIANS

Variations on a theme

By about 245 million years ago, most amphibians had become extinct. A few, however, survived to become the ancestors of modern amphibians. The evolution of modern amphibians is summarized in the phylogenetic tree in *Figure 25.19*. Modern amphibians belong to three orders: Anura (frogs and toads), Urodela (salamanders), and Apoda (caecilians).

Anura Frogs and toads are similar in many ways, but there are noticeable differences. Compare the frog and toad shown in *Figure 25.20*. One important difference is their skin. Frogs have smooth, moist skin, while toads have dry, bumpy skin. Frogs also tend to have longer legs and more

tapered bodies than toads. Adult frogs live in or near water. Adult toads can live in drier environments than frogs can because their thicker skin is more resistant to drying. Toads typically return to water only to reproduce.

Anurans have adapted to a greater variety of environments than have other amphibians. They live in deserts, savannas, mountains, and tropical rain forests, as well as in temperate regions. Many anurans have adaptations that enable them to survive in a specific environment. The spadefoot toad, for example, has hind feet adapted for digging. It survives in hot, dry climates by burrowing into the ground and absorbing water from the soil.

Urodela Salamanders belong to the order Urodela. As you can see in *Figure 25.21*, salamanders typically have a long tail, a long body, and two pairs of legs. Like most amphibians, salamanders are covered by a smooth, moist skin. They retain their tail throughout life.

Salamanders vary in size and color. Most are from 5 to 15 cm long. However, the giant salamander *Andrias japonicus* grows to about 1.5 m long. Some salamanders are dull in color, which helps them blend with their

FIGURE 25.20
The pickerel frog (left) lives in streams, swamps, and meadows. The American toad (above) can be found in grassy areas and heavily forested mountains. How is the skin of each amphibian suited to its habitat? ❶

610 *Unit 7 Vertebrate Animals*

FIGURE 25.21
The axolotl (left) becomes sexually mature while in a larval state and remains in water its entire life. The Kentucky salamander (right) has no lungs and must breathe through its moist skin.

environments. Many, however, are brightly colored, with stripes or spots that often secrete poisons. The bright colors are a warning to potential predators.

The larvae of most salamanders live in rivers, lakes, streams, or ponds. Aquatic larvae have gills for respiration. In most adult salamanders, the gills are replaced with lungs. Some species do not have gills or lungs. Instead, they respire by exchanging gases directly through their skin, just as earthworms and many other invertebrates do. Some urodelans, such as sirens, axolotls, and hellbenders, live in water most or all of their lives. They retain gills and other larval structures as adults.

Apoda Do you think the animal in *Figure 25.22* is an earthworm? Many people have been fooled by this organism. The long, wormlike caecilians have scales that make them look like segmented worms. However, unlike earthworms, caecilians have the skeleton of a vertebrate.

Caecilians are adapted to a life of burrowing through soil. Although they have tiny eyes, caecilians are blind or nearly blind. They feed on worms and insects as they burrow through the

moist soil of tropical forests in South America, Africa, and Southeast Asia. A few species live in water. They average about 30 cm in length. Caecilians are rarely seen by humans, because they remain hidden in their burrows.

Caecilians reproduce by internal fertilization and have a larval stage. Some females guard their eggs until they hatch. Others produce live young and the embryos of some obtain nourishment from the tissues of the mother's reproductive system.

FIGURE 25.22
Caecilians may look like earthworms, but these burrowing carnivores have jaws and vertebrae. One species of caecilian can grow up to 1.5 m long!

CHECKPOINT 25.6

1. Explain the environmental conditions that led to the evolution of modern amphibians.
2. Contrast the three orders of amphibians.
3. **Critical Thinking** Caecilians do not have the varied color patterns found in the other two groups of amphibians. Why might this be so?

Build on What You Know

4. What vestigial structures would you expect to find in a caecilian? *(Need to jog your memory? Revisit relevant concepts in Chapter 10, Section 10.3.)*

Chapter 25 Fishes and Amphibians **611**

CHECKPOINT 25.6

1. swampy areas as well as drier areas
2. Anurans: adapted to a wide variety of environments; urodelans: tailed amphibians that spend most or all of their lives in water; apodans: look like worms and burrow through the soil
3. **Developing a hypothesis** Since they spend most of their lives underground,

bright coloration would be ineffective in deterring predators that could not see them anyway.

4. Based on the physical structures of most amphibians, one might expect to find vestigial legs, which may have become less useful as the caecilians adapted to life underground.

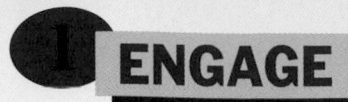

ENGAGE

Use the Visual

Have students study the photograph that opens the section. Explain that camouflage and bright colors are two adaptations frogs use to escape predators. Ask:

- **Why would bright colors help frogs escape predators?** (Humans and other animals identify these frogs as undesirable by their bright colors.)

Check Prior Knowledge

To assess students' knowledge about amphibians in the biosphere, ask:

- **In what environments are you likely to find amphibians?** (On land, near water or a moist environment, and in water)

Quick Activity

Display pictures of toad shelters for gardens. Ask students if they know why gardeners want toads to live nearby. (For pest control) Then ask students to cite other ways humans use frogs and toads. List student responses on the board and tell students to copy the list and add to it as they read the section.

 **Drawing Conclusions** To practice strategies for effective reading, use pages 63-64 in *Super Read!*

25.7 Amphibians in the Biosphere

What you'll learn

IDEAS
- To explain the ecological roles of amphibians
- To summarize the importance of amphibians to humans

SUPER READ!

The shy ones versus the show-offs
If you visit a typical frog habitat in your area, you are not likely to see many frogs. Most frogs blend in with their surroundings. This camouflage helps them capture prey and escape predators. In contrast, the brilliant colors of other frogs advertise their presence. Many of these colorful frogs are poisonous, and predators have learned to leave them alone.

ECOLOGICAL ROLES

Keeping bugs in check

You might think amphibians are not very important to humans. After all, they are a major food source in only a few human societies. Although they may become medically useful in the future, applications to date are few.

Ecologically there is a different story. You now know that amphibians spend a portion of their lives in water and a portion on land. They are part of different but related food chains.

On land, amphibians of all types frequently prey on insects, both larvae and adults. They help to control the size of insect populations that could otherwise destroy important food crops and transmit diseases. Adult amphibians also eat worms and other animals such as birds, snakes, and small mammals, as you can see in *Figure* 25.23.

The food of young amphibians varies according to their species. In the water, most tadpoles feed on algae,

FIGURE 25.23
Yes, that is a half-grown rat being eaten by this large African bullfrog. Notice the frog's bleeding foot, bitten by the rat as it was caught.

612 *Unit 7 Vertebrate Animals*

STUDENT RESOURCES

From the Teacher's Resource Package, use:
- Section Review 25.7, Activity Recordsheet 25-3, Vocabulary Review 25, and Chapter 25 Tests from Unit 7 Review Module
- Consumer Applications 25-2

TECHNOLOGY RESOURCES

Relevant technology resources include:
- Spanish Student Edition CD-ROM
- Teacher's Resource Planner CD-ROM
- TestWorks CD-ROM: Chapter 25 Tests
- Biology Alive! Video: "Life's Fragile Balance"

FIGURE 25.24
Some species of bats found in tropical environments have developed the ability to pinpoint frogs' mating calls.

small plants, and decaying animal matter. Newly hatched salamanders and caecilians are carnivores, with diets similar to those of their parents.

Amphibians, in turn, are eaten by other animals. Some animals that consume adult amphibians include fishes, snakes, turtles, birds, and some mammals. Recall, however, that poisons in their skins help protect many species from predators.

HUMAN USES

Pass the frog legs, please!

In section 25.3, you read that fishes are a major human food source. Amphibians are not. Some frog species are edible, and the flesh has a high protein content, but most frogs contain little meat. One large South American species is roasted whole, but most people tend to limit their frog meals to the legs.

Perhaps the most economically important role of amphibians is their ability to control insect pests that might otherwise threaten crops or spread disease. Home gardeners sometimes place toad shelters in their

---

LAB ZONE **Do It!**

How Is Tadpole Development Affected by Temperature?

Tadpole eggs hatch more quickly in warm water than in cool. You can find out if tadpoles develop more quickly into frogs in warm water when you . . .

Try This

1 Put several tadpoles in a water-filled glass aquarium or a large glass bowl and place it in a shaded area in your classroom. Leave it at room temperature. (Be sure to use water from the tadpoles' natural habitat and add some of the algae they feed on.)

2 Put several more tadpoles in a similar water-filled glass aquarium or bowl and place it in a spot that is warmer than the first one. The water can be warmed by the sun or artificial light, or heated by an aquarium heater if you have one.

3 For a minute or two each day, observe, compare, and record physical development of each group of tadpoles.

Analyze Your Results

1 Did the development of the tadpoles in the two tanks differ? If so, how did it differ?

2 Would there be a difference in tadpole development during a cold, rainy, spring season as opposed to a sunny one? Explain.

---

2 TEACH

Discuss

Hold a class discussion about some of the problems associated with the use of chemical pesticides. Ask:

- **How might pesticides targeting insects affect amphibians?** (They could be harmed or killed by the chemical or from eating poisoned insects.)
- **How are natural predators useful for controlling pests?** (They reduce the pest numbers without harming other animals.)

Build Writing Skills

Have students conduct research in the library or on the Internet to learn how natural predators are used to control unwanted pest populations. Ask students to prepare a written report of their findings, including the success of the programs they studied.

LAB ZONE **Do It!** **TEAM WORK**

How Is Tadpole Development Affected by Temperature?

Caution students to monitor water temperature to be sure it does not rise above 30°C.

Analyze Your Results

1 Yes, the tadpoles in the warmer tank should have developed faster.

2 You would expect tadpoles to develop more quickly in a warmer environment in which algae, a major food source, would flourish.

MULTICULTURAL PERSPECTIVE

In the South American rain forest some cultures live as their ancestors did centuries ago, using their understanding of a seemingly hostile environment to their advantage. For example, they use poisons secreted by the glands of certain frog species for a variety of purposes. Chief among these uses is making poison-tipped arrows and darts that stun or kill animals hunted for food and clothing.

STS

3 ASSESS

Evaluate Understanding

Ask students to compile a brief list of the important roles amphibians play in the environment and how they are used by humans. Review the lists as a class and ask students to explain their choices.

Reteach

Write the following statements on the board: *Amphibians are important to the environment* and *Amphibians are important to humans.* Have volunteers add information from this section that illustrates each concept and record it under the appropriate statement. Review the lists, making sure to correct inaccurate information or add information.

614

FIGURE 25.25
A hunter from the Embará Chocó people of Colombia holds down a poisonous frog as he rubs a dart against the frog's skin. The dart will remain poisonous for more than a year.

EVERYDAY BIOLOGY

Frog Skin Cream

Researchers have discovered a compound in the skin of an African frog that may be useful as an antibiotic in curing human skin infections.

yards to encourage amphibians to take up residence. Toads help control pests naturally.

Traditionally, frogs have assisted humans in other ways. They help to increase human knowledge about vertebrates. You probably already know that frogs are widely used in biology classes.

Even amphibian poisons have proved useful to humans. In certain cultures, poisoned arrows have been used for generations to hunt game. The arrows are carefully coated with poisons that are secreted by amphibians such as the poison arrow frog, shown in *Figure* 25.25. Usually, a leaf or some other object is used to avoid touching the amphibian.

ENVIRONMENTAL AWARENESS

STS

Amphibian alarm

The life processes of amphibians are closely tied to their environments throughout their lives. As you have learned, amphibians live both on land and in the water and depend on the quality of these natural resources for

their survival. Their small ectothermic bodies, porous skins, and unshelled eggs make them very vulnerable to changes in the environment. For this reason, some scientists consider amphibians to be useful as bioindicators. A bioindicator is an organism or species whose health serves as an indicator of the health of the environment or ecosystem.

In recent years, researchers have noticed a worldwide drop in both the number and diversity of amphibians. Some people find this alarming, but no one has been able to determine the exact cause of the decline. Because the jellylike eggs of amphibians are not well protected, some scientists have hypothesized that the decline may be due to an increase in solar radiation—a result of the thinning of the ozone layer. Others have suggested air or water pollution as possible explanations. Still others have suggested global warming. Researchers are struggling to find the cause of the problem before it is too late for the populations to recover, or before other populations begin to decline as well.

CHECKPOINT 25.7

1. What is one important ecological role of amphibians?
2. List three ways that amphibians are important to humans.
3. **Critical Thinking** What might be the consequences of a global extinction of amphibians?

Build on What You Know

4. How would the pH of water affect amphibians? *(Need to jog your memory? Revisit relevant concepts in Chapter 2, Section 2.5.)*

What characteristics make amphibians well adapted to life both in water and on land?

CHECKPOINT 25.7

1. They control insect populations.
2. They control pest populations, provide poisons for poison arrows, and are useful for learning about vertebrate structure.
3. **Predicting** Students should mention that amphibians play an important role in many food chains. Their extinction could cause overabundance of their prey and extinction of their predators.
4. Because amphibians develop and grow in water, any changes to the quality of the water (including its pH) may pose problems for the development and success of those amphibians.

Chapter 25 Review

THE BIG IDEA!

25.1 Vertebrates are animals with backbones.
25.2–25.4 Fishes are a diverse group of vertebrates that are adapted for life in the water.
25.5–25.7 Although amphibians share some fish traits, they are adapted to life on land.

Sum It Up

Use the following summary to review the main concepts in this chapter.

25.1 Vertebrates

- The vertebrate skeleton contains a skull and a protective backbone that surrounds the spinal cord.
- Vertebrates have a closed circulatory system.
- The temperature of fishes, amphibians, and reptiles varies with the external environment. Birds and mammals have internal temperature controls.

25.2 Characteristics of Fishes

- A typical fish has scales for protection and insulation, fins for directional movement, a swim bladder to control buoyancy, a two-chambered heart, sense organs for locating prey and for navigation, kidneys to maintain water balance, and gills for respiration.
- Fertilization in fishes is usually external.

25.3 Origin and Diversity of Fishes

- The earliest fishes were filter feeders that resembled lancelets. With the evolution of paired fins and jaws, fishes could pursue prey.
- Agnathans are jawless parasites or scavengers. They lack scales and paired fins. Chondrichthyes have skeletons made of cartilage. Osteichthyes have bony skeletons.

25.4 Fishes in the Biosphere

- Most fishes are carnivores.
- Fishes provide food, a source of income, recreation, and medicine for humans.

25.5 Characteristics of Amphibians

- Amphibians live both on land and in water.
- The typical amphibian has moist skin and lungs for gas exchange, powerful limbs, and a three-chambered heart.
- Amphibians reproduce through external fertilization, and they undergo metamorphosis.

25.6 Origin and Diversity of Amphibians

- Amphibians evolved from lobe-finned fishes with primitive lungs.
- Frogs and toads have no tail; salamanders have visible tails; caecilians have no legs.

25.7 Amphibians in the Biosphere

- Amphibians help to control insect populations.
- Amphibians are useful as bioindicators.
- Amphibian populations are declining.
- In certain cultures, amphibians are a source of food.

Use Terms and Concepts

Use each of the following words or terms in a complete sentence. If you need to review a meaning, turn to the page indicated.

vertebrates (p. 592)
ectotherms (p. 593)
endotherms (p. 593)

swim bladder (p. 594)
lateral line system (p. 595)

lungfish (p. 602)
amphibian (p. 605)
cloaca (p. 606)

Review the Big Ideas

Before students begin the Chapter Review, you may wish to discuss main concepts from the Big Ideas in Chapter 25. Point out that all animals with a backbone are called vertebrates. Fishes, the most diverse of all vertebrates, have a swim bladder, gills, scales, a lateral line system, and other structures that enable them to live in every kind of aquatic environment. Amphibians are vertebrates that have adapted to life both in water and on land. They are the only vertebrates with a life cycle that includes metamorphosis. The most important role of vertebrates in the biosphere is controlling insect populations that destroy crops and transmit diseases.

Answers

1. lateral line system
2. amphibian
3. swim bladder
4. cloaca
5. endotherms
6. False; lungfish
7. False; vertebrate
8. True
9. True
10. False; Amphibians
11. The frog develops lungs to breathe air and legs to move about on land.
12. Jaws enabled fishes to extend their diet beyond small particles that could be strained from the water. Jaws are used to capture and chew prey.
13. Adult amphibians exchange gases through their lungs and their skin. Mucous glands keep the lungs and skin moist.
14. Sharks' constant movement keeps water flowing over the gills, eliminating the need for an operculum. Their oily livers provide some buoyancy. Sharks never stop swimming and so keep from sinking without the help of a swim bladder.
15. Amphibian kidneys release excess fluid in water, and conserve water on land by controlling the concentration of urine. On land, amphibian kidneys act like the kidneys of saltwater fishes. Because of differences in ion concentrations in saltwater, water would flow from inside the fish to its surroundings if the kidneys did not conserve water.
16. Adult fishes have a spinal cord that developed from a dorsal nerve cord, a backbone that developed from a notochord, gills that devel-

616

Use Your Word Power

COMPLETION **Write the word or phrase that best completes each statement.**

1. The _____ is a group of sense organs that many fishes use to detect vibrations.

2. A(n) _____ is a vertebrate that is adapted to both aquatic and terrestrial habitats.

3. The _____ is an internal organ that helps some fishes adjust their depth in the water.

4. A structure in amphibians that excretes undigested food is called a(n) _____ .

5. Organisms that can maintain constant body temperature are _____ .

TRUE-FALSE **Write true if the statement is true. If the statement is false, replace the underlined word(s) to make the statement true.**

6. Both fossil coelacanths and <u>modern coelacanths</u> have lungs as well as gills.

7. As <u>invertebrate</u> chordates develop, the notochord is replaced by a backbone.

8. An <u>ectotherm</u> is an organism in which body temperature is regulated by its surroundings.

9. Fishes in the class <u>Chondrichthyes</u> do not have swim bladders or opercula.

10. <u>Mammals</u> have a cloaca, which releases products of the digestive, reproductive, and excretory systems.

Show What You Know

11. How do the changes that accompany the metamorphosis from tadpole to adult frog enable the frog to adapt to a terrestrial environment?

12. How are jaws an important adaptation for fishes? How does their function in feeding compare to the feeding habits of jawless fishes?

13. What adaptations do most adult amphibians have that make the exchange of gases such as oxygen and carbon dioxide possible?

14. How do sharks adjust to the lack of a swim bladder or operculum?

15. How do the kidneys of amphibians adjust to life on land and in the water? In which of these environments are their kidneys acting like the kidneys of saltwater fishes? Explain.

16. How are the typical characteristics of members of the phylum Chordata displayed in adult bony fishes?

17. What adaptation does a double-loop circulatory system with a three-chambered heart provide that a single-loop system with a two-chambered heart does not?

18. **Make a Concept Map** Create a concept map that relates the following terms: Agnatha, amphibians, Anura, Apoda, caecilians, Chondrichthyes, fishes, frogs, lampreys, Osteichthyes, ray-finned fishes, salamanders, sharks, toads, Urodela, and vertebrates.

Take It Further

19. **Applying Concepts** Why is it important to control the temperature of an aquarium within narrow limits?

20. **Making a Generalization** How would the number of offspring produced by a species that uses internal fertilization compare with the number produced by a species that uses external fertilization? Explain your answer.

21. **Organizing and Classifying** Suppose you were visiting South America and you discovered an organism that reproduces by laying eggs. The organism has a backbone, lungs, kidneys, and a two-chambered heart. Is the organism a fish or an amphibian? Explain your reasoning.

22. **Making an Analogy** How is the use of a lateral line system to detect prey similar to the use of a seismograph to detect earthquakes?

oped from gill slits, and a post-anal tail.
17. The double-loop system partially separates oxygen-rich from oxygen-poor blood.
18. Concept maps should show the following: <u>Vertebrates</u> split to <u>fishes</u> and <u>amphibians</u>; fishes split to <u>Agnatha</u> (<u>lampreys</u>), <u>Chondrichthyes</u> (<u>sharks</u>), and <u>Osteichthyes</u> (<u>rayfinned fishes</u>);

amphibians split to <u>Anura</u> (<u>frogs</u>, <u>toads</u>), <u>Urodela</u> (<u>salamanders</u>), and <u>Apoda</u> (<u>caecilians</u>).
19. Because fish are ectotherms, their internal body temperature reflects the temperature of their surroundings.
20. In general, there should be fewer offspring in species that use internal fertilization because the eggs are protected

23. Designing an Experiment Design an experiment to determine the effect of diet on tadpole development. What information would you need before you could begin? What variables would you need to control? How could you compare the development of individual tadpoles?

24. Interpreting Graphs The graph below shows the total number of fishes caught worldwide between 1970 and 1993. What conclusions can you draw from the graph? Can you draw any conclusions about future catches from the data shown? Explain your answer.

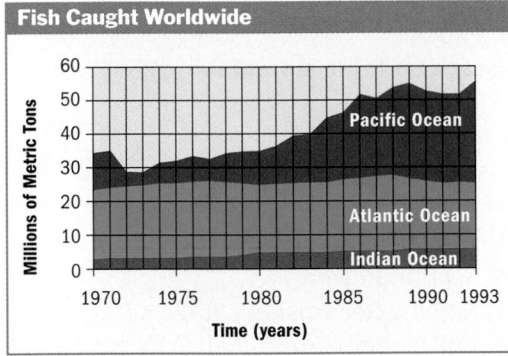

Fish Caught Worldwide

25. Analyzing Data Use the chart below to answer the following questions: In which country do people eat the least amount of fish? In which country the greatest amount? In which country is twice as much fish consumed as in the United States? Does that country have a population twice that of the United States? Explain your responses.

Human Consumption of Fish		
Country	Total Fish Consumed Yearly (millions of metric tons)	Fish Eaten per Person (kg per year)
China	18	12.2
Japan	13	66.6
Russia	5	25.2
United States	7	20.4

Consider the Issues

26. Fish Supplies Sink Modern fishing technology includes remote sensing devices for locating schools of fishes; huge nets; and factory ships that can process fishes as they are caught. Because of overfishing, populations of fishes have been dramatically reduced. In many areas, fishing has been banned entirely or restricted to a few weeks a year. Should there be restrictions on the types of technology that can be used? How can fishing be regulated in international waters?

27. Absent Amphibians Some people argue that amphibians should be allowed to survive or disappear without any human interference. What is your opinion?

Make New Connections

28. Biology and Physics Some biologists study deep-sea fishes. When they bring these fishes to the surface rapidly, they often find that the fishes look distorted, as though they have exploded. Look up *fluid pressure* in a physics textbook, and use this information and your knowledge of fish anatomy to propose an explanation for the distortion of these fishes.

29. Biology, Photography, and Writing Create a field guide about the amphibians that are native to your community. Use a page for each species that you can observe. Include photographs or drawings. Describe the habitat for each species.

FAST-FORWARD TO CHAPTER 26

The amphibian life cycle involves periods on land and in the water. In Chapter 26, you will study reptiles—vertebrates that spend their entire life on land. You will also study the evolution of birds.

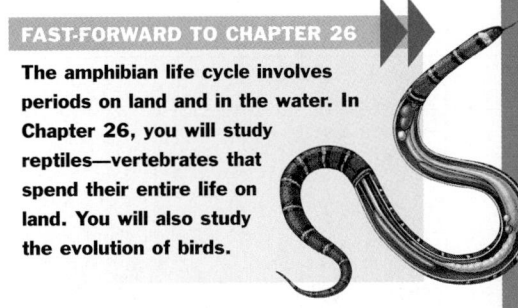

Chapter 25 Fishes and Amphibians **617**

ment cycles. They would have to decide whether to use increases in mass or length, or total time required for metamorphosis as the measure of development.

24. Fish catches in the Indian and Atlantic oceans have held steady. Increases in total catch reflect an increased harvest in the Pacific Ocean. The graph does not indicate how many fish are not caught, which would be critical data for predicting future harvests.

25. People eat the least amount of fish in China. Japan consumes twice as much fish as the United States. However, there are not twice as many people living in Japan. On average, individuals in Japan consume three times as much fish as individuals in the United States.

26. Students may want to consider the relative success of marketing campaigns aimed at getting consumers to buy previously unfamiliar species that have not yet been overfished.

27. Students may want to consider whether the decline of amphibian populations can be traced back to human actions.

28. Gases trapped in the fish's body will expand as the water pressure on the fish's body decreases.

29. Students could work in small groups or contribute individual pages to a single booklet.

internally during development and have a greater chance of survival. Species that use external fertilization produce a great number of eggs; many are not fertilized and most are eaten or die before they hatch.

21. The key clue is the combination of lungs and a two-chambered heart, which would indicate a type of lungfish rather than an amphibian.

22. Both systems are designed to detect and pinpoint the source of vibrations.

23. Students would need to find out what foods tadpoles normally eat. They would need to control the temperature, the pH, and the oxygen content of the water. Students should avoid species such as bullfrogs with lengthy develop-

PLANNING GUIDE

Section	Student Activities/Features	Teacher's Resource Package
26.1 Characteristics of Reptiles **Objectives** ■ Explain key reptile adaptations ■ Describe the structures and functions of the amniotic egg	**Lab Zone Discover It!** *Examining an Egg,* p. 619 **Lab Zone Investigate It!** *Comparing Reptiles and Amphibians,* p. 624	**Unit 7 Review Module** ■ Section Review 26.1 ■ Activity Recordsheet 26-1 **Interpreting and Developing Graphics** 76
26.2 Origin and Diversity of Reptiles **Objectives** ■ Explain two hypotheses about the origin and evolution of reptiles ■ Compare the different orders of reptiles		**Unit 7 Review Module** ■ Section Review 26.2 **Laboratory Manual:** Lab 47: "Turtle Behavior" **Issues and Decision Making** 26-1
26.3 Reptiles in the Biosphere **Objectives** ■ Explain the ecological roles of reptiles ■ Compare reptile behaviors	**Lab Zone Do It!** *How Does Egg-burying Behavior in Reptiles Benefit Reproduction?* p. 630 **STS: Frontiers in Biology** *Poisons or Promises?* p. 631 **Everyday Biology** *Heat Sensing Snakes,* p. 631	**Unit 7 Review Module** ■ Section Review 26.3 ■ Activity Recordsheet 26-2 ■ Enrichment Topic 26-1 **Consumer Applications** 26-1
26.4 Characteristics of Birds **Objectives** ■ Explain the structural adaptations that allow birds to fly ■ Summarize the life cycle of a typical bird	**Lab Zone Do It!** *How Do Contour Feathers Compare with Down Feathers?* p. 634 **In the Community** *Look! Up in the Sky!* p. 636	**Unit 7 Review Module** ■ Section Review 26.4 ■ Activity Recordsheet 26-3 ■ Critical Thinking Exercise 26 **Interpreting and Developing Graphics** 77
26.5 Origin and Diversity of Birds **Objectives** ■ Summarize the differences between birds and other vertebrates ■ Analyze evidence for the evolutionary origin of birds		**Unit 7 Review Module** ■ Section Review 26.5 ■ Interpreting Graphics 26 **Laboratory Manual,** Lab 48: "Bird Adaptations" **Interpreting and Developing Graphics** 78
26.6 Birds in the Biosphere **Objectives** ■ Explain the roles that birds play in ecosystems ■ Compare courtship behavior in birds	**Everyday Biology** *Birds Re-tern,* p. 641 **Lab Zone Think About It!** *Analyzing Bird Migratory Routes,* p. 642	**Unit 7 Review Module** ■ Section Review 26.6 ■ Enrichment Topics 26-2 and 26-3 ■ Vocabulary Review 26 ■ Chapter 26 Tests **Issues and Decision Making** 26-2 **Consumer Applications** 26-2 **Spanish Reviews** Chapter 26

Technology Resources

Internet Connections

Within this chapter, you will see the bioSURF logo. If you and your students have access to the Internet, the following URL address will provide various Internet connections that are related to topics and features presented in this chapter:

http://vertebrates.biosurf.com

You can also find relevant chapter material at **The Biology Place** address:

http://www.biology.com

CD-ROMs

Biología: la telaraña de la vida,
  (Spanish Student Edition) Chapter 26
Teacher's Resource Planner, Chapter 26
  Supplements
TestWorks CD-ROM
■ Chapter 26 Tests

Overhead Transparencies

■ Structures of a Snake, #56
■ Structures of the Amniotic Egg, #57
■ Structures for Flight, #58

Videotapes

Biology Alive! Video Series
■ Continuity of Life Video
■ Conflict and Cooperation Video
■ Life's Fragile Balance Video
Rewind: The Web of Life Reteach Videos

Planning for Activities

STUDENT EDITION
Lab Zone
Discover It! p. 619
  ■ raw egg
  ■ container
  ■ tweezers

Lab Zone
Investigate It! p. 624
  ■ aquarium with live
    lizard
  ■ aquarium with live frog

Lab Zone **Do It!** p. 630
  ■ layers of dirt and dead
    plant material
  ■ long thermometer

Lab Zone **Do It!** p. 634
  ■ contour feather
  ■ downy feather
  ■ microscope

TEACHER'S EDITION
Teacher Demo, p. 620
Snakes
  ■ snake

Class Activity, p. 621
*Muscular contractions in
snakes*
  ■ plastic straws
  ■ soft clay

Class Activity, p. 622
Comparing eggs
  ■ chicken eggs
  ■ containers
  ■ knife

Teacher Demo, p. 625
Classifying amphibians
  ■ aquariums
  ■ lizard and a salamander
    or newt (or colored
    photos)

Teacher Demo, p. 629
*Objects made from hides
and shells*
  ■ items or pictures of
    items made from skins
    of snakes, alligators, and
    crocodiles, and the
    shells of tortoises

Teacher Demo, p. 632
Uses of bird feathers
  ■ variety of bird feathers

Teacher Demo, p. 633
Observing chicken bones
  ■ several clean chicken
    bones

Quick Activity, p. 638
Pterosaurs
  ■ drawings of pterosaurs:
    *Dimorphodon,
    Pterodanstro,* and
    Archaeoteryx

Teacher Demo, p. 640
Male and female birds
  ■ pictures of male and
    female birds of the same
    species that show vast
    differences in coloring

Teacher Demo, p. 641
Courtship rituals of birds
  ■ movie or videotape on
    the various courtship
    rituals of birds

Chapter Objectives

Students will learn the main concepts of this chapter as they complete the following objectives.

- Explain the reptile adaptations that suit their environment
- Describe the structures and functions of the amniotic egg
- Explain two hypotheses about the origin and evolution of reptiles
- Compare the different orders of reptiles
- Explain the ecological roles of reptiles
- Compare reptile behaviors
- Explain the structural adaptations that allow birds to fly
- Summarize the life cycle of a typical bird
- Summarize the differences between birds and other vertebrates
- Analyze evidence for the evolutionary origin of birds
- Explain the roles that birds play in ecosystems
- Compare and contrast the different aspects of bird reproductive behavior

Key Words

26.1 *amniotic egg, yolk, chorion*

26.4 *crop, gizzard, chalaza*

The Opening Story

Have students discuss how they think the story relates to the content of this chapter. Have students consider how sea turtles have survived as a species, given the number of their natural enemies.

You can find out more about reptiles and birds by exploring the following Internet address:
http://vertebrates.biosurf.com

In this chapter . . .

FEATURES

Everyday Biology
- Heat-sensing Snakes
- Birds Re-tern

In the Community
Look! Up in the Sky!

 Frontiers in Biology
Poisons or Promises?

LAB ZONES

Discover It!
- Examining an Egg

Do It!
- How Does Egg-burying Behavior in Reptiles Benefit Reproduction?
- How Do Contour Feathers Compare with Down Feathers?

Think About It!
- Analyzing Bird Migratory Routes

Investigate It!
- Comparing Reptiles and Amphibians

Making a Run for It

S̲ea turtles live their lives coursing through the open ocean. But every two or three years, the females return—on a journey that may be thousands of kilometers—to the beach where they were born. There they lay their eggs, bury them in the sand to keep them warm and moist, and then return to the ocean. From 60 to 90 days pass before hatchlings break through the shells. On their own, baby turtles must make a perilous journey across open sand to the relative safety of the ocean. The dangers are many.

Sea turtles, compared to other turtles, have small shells that leave their head and limbs exposed. They are slow and awkward on land. Crabs threaten them on the beach and they are easily visible prey from the air, where gulls and terns fly in wait. If hatchlings make it to the ocean's edge, they will swim for 24 hours straight, into safer open water. The odds are against them. From a nest of 200 eggs, only one or two turtles may live to adulthood.

Turtles are reptiles, land animals, that thrive in the water. According to some scientists, birds may have descended from reptile-like ancestors that took to the air. What can we learn about evolution by studying these animals?

LAB ZONE Discover It!

Examining an Egg

You need one raw egg, a container, tweezers

1. Crack the raw egg into a container. Examine the shell. How thick is it? What do the inside and outside surfaces look like? What do they feel like?
2. Examine the egg's contents. Use the tweezers to probe the egg. Can you recognize distinct parts of the egg? Can you identify the part of the egg that would develop into a chicken?
   Caution: Wash your hands with soap and warm water after this activity.

Birds and reptiles have amniotic eggs that protect a developing embryo. How do the structures of the amniotic egg serve this function?

WRITE ABOUT IT!

In your journal, write a description of what it might be like to be a bird or reptile developing inside an egg. What sounds or movement might you feel? What would it be like getting out of the shell when hatching?

619

Opening Activities

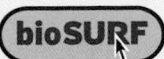 **bioSURF** If you have access to the Internet in your classroom or school, you may wish to have students connect to the address shown on page 618. You may also want to have students conduct a net search for information using key words related to this chapter. For example, they could search for entries under lizards, iguanas, or migratory birds.

LAB ZONE Discover It!

Examining an Egg **TEAM WORK**

Point out the small white dot on the egg yolk and identify it as the sex cell that contains the genetic material. Have students discuss the embryo's use of the yolk and white.

WRITE ABOUT IT

Suggest that students also consider the developing animal's need for warmth and oxygen. Tell students that they can use any format, from a descriptive essay to a cartoon strip, to record their observations.

REWIND to Chapter 25

Briefly review concepts learned in Chapter 25, *Fishes and Amphibians*. Ask:

- **How do you think the study of fishes and amphibians will help you understand the structures and adaptations of reptiles and birds described in Chapter 26?**

PORTFOLIO PREVIEW

Students should be encouraged to add to their portfolios as they work through this chapter. In addition to the *Write About It* opportunity, the following sections are excellent opportunities for portfolio entries:

ENGAGE

Consider the Big Idea

Have students read The Big Idea! at the top of the page. Explain that reptiles do not depend on a water environment for any part of their life cycle, although some reptiles live in water.

Use the Visual

Have students study the photograph and read the text that opens the section. Explain that most snakes do not chew their food, but swallow it whole. Ask:

- **How does the small snake eat the large egg?** (Its jaws unhinge)

Check Prior Knowledge

To assess students' knowledge about reptiles, ask:

- **What animals can you identify as reptiles?** (Students should identify alligators, crocodiles, lizards, Gila monsters, chameleons.)
- **Are reptiles ectotherms or endotherms?** (Ectotherms)

Teacher Demo

Ask a student who has a pet snake or a representative from a local pet store to bring a snake to class. Allow students to touch the snake's skin and observe the snake as it feeds. Be aware of students in class who may be afraid of snakes and help allay their fears.

26.1 Characteristics of Reptiles

What you'll learn

IDEAS
- To explain key reptile adaptations
- To describe the structures and functions of the amniotic egg

WORDS
amniotic egg, yolk, chorion

Egg-eating snakes
Although only as wide as your thumb, an African egg-eating snake eats nothing but eggs. It can even eat hard-shelled bird eggs that are twice as wide as its body. The snake's double-hinged jaws allow it to swallow the egg. Sharp bones in the throat cut the egg open. The contents of the egg slide down the snake's throat into its digestive system. The compacted shell is forced up the throat and back out the snake's mouth.

MOVEMENT AND RESPONSE
Life in a dry world

If you ever held a snake or lizard in your hand you may have been surprised to find that the animal's skin was smooth and dry, not wet and slimy. Did you notice the tight-fitting scales that covered the animal's body? A reptile's dry, scaly skin helps prevent the evaporation of water from its body. Conserving water is just one of many challenges reptiles face living on land.

Reptiles were the first vertebrates with adaptations that enabled them to survive completely independent of a water environment. A reptile's skin is one of its most important characteristics for surviving on land. The skin is covered with hard, dry scales made of a water-resistant protein called keratin. Human hair and fingernails, and bird feathers, are also made of keratin. Because keratin is water resistant, it helps prevent the escape of water from skin cells.

Another important structural adaptation that enables many types of reptiles to move on land is the position

FIGURE 26.1

For reptiles, claws are an adaptation that enable them to live on land. Reptiles, such as these Komodo dragons, use their claws to dig burrows and nests. Reptiles also use their claws for traction when running and climbing.

of their legs. You can see in *Figure 26.1* that reptilian legs are close to the body, compared to the legs of frogs and other amphibians you read about in Chapter 25. This leg position enables reptiles to run more quickly on land. As you read this chapter, you will see that modern reptiles have many adaptations—including the absence of legs—that result in efficient movement.

Many groups of reptiles have unique structures that enable them to sense and respond to their environments. Study the snake structures shown in *Figure 26.2*. How does the snake smell? ❶

ENERGY AND WASTES
Awesome jaws

Structural adaptations in reptiles reflect their need to find and capture prey, exchange gases with the environment, transport nutrients and wastes, and maintain water balance—all in the absence of water. Some of these adaptations have also been

620   *Unit 7 Vertebrate Animals*

STUDENT RESOURCES

From the Teacher's Resource Package, use:
- Section Review 26.1 and Activity Recordsheet 26-1 from Unit 7 Review Module

TECHNOLOGY RESOURCES

Relevant technology resources include:
- Spanish Student Edition CD-ROM
- Teacher's Resource Planner CD-ROM

FIGURE 26.2

The Structure of a Snake

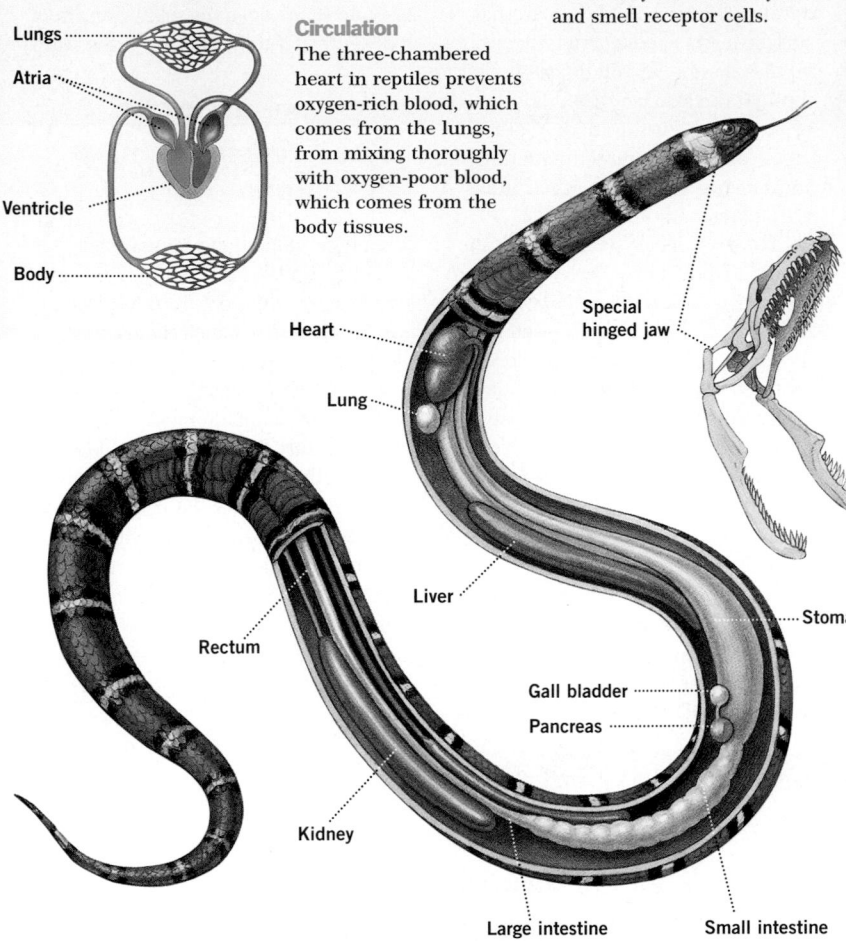

Circulation
The three-chambered heart in reptiles prevents oxygen-rich blood, which comes from the lungs, from mixing thoroughly with oxygen-poor blood, which comes from the body tissues.

Lungs
Atria
Ventricle
Body

Heart
Lung
Rectum
Liver
Kidney
Large intestine

Special hinged jaw
Gall bladder
Pancreas
Small intestine

Stomach

Sense and response
As a snake darts its tongue in and out of its mouth, chemicals are carried into the mouth where they are sensed by taste and smell receptor cells.

Flexible jaws
Snakes have flexible jaws that enable them to engulf prey several times larger than their own bodies.

Shedding skin
A snake's scaly skin protects it from drying out, but it does not increase in size as the animal grows. Instead, most snakes and other reptiles periodically shed their skin when it becomes worn out or too small.

inherited by birds and mammals. Other structural adaptations remain unique to reptiles.

Most reptiles are carnivores. They eat insects when they are young and other animals as they mature. Most reptiles do not chew food into small pieces. They simply bite or tear the food into pieces they can swallow. The food is digested mainly by enzymes in the stomach. In reptiles, digestion is a long, slow process.

Reptiles have a circulatory system that is more efficient for an animal that breathes only air. All reptiles, except crocodilians, have a partially divided, three-chambered heart. A reptile's heart is more distinctly divided than that of an amphibian. A reptile therefore achieves a greater separation of oxygen-rich and oxygen-poor blood. *Figure 26.2* shows a diagram of a three-chambered heart. In crocodilians, the partition between

Chapter 26 Reptiles and Birds **621**

② TEACH

Use the Visual

Have students study Figure 26.2. Ask:

- **How does the snake heart compare to an amphibian heart?** (A snake has a three-chambered heart; amphibians have a two-chambered heart.)
- **How is a snake's skin similar to an insect's exoskeleton?** (The skin does not grow. The snake must molt in order to grow, just as an insect must shed its exoskeleton.)

Clarify Misconceptions

Students may think the skin of reptiles is slimy and slippery. Explain that reptiles have dry skin that is covered with scales.

Class Activity

TEAM WORK

Distribute plastic straws and soft clay to students. Challenge students to find a way to move the clay through the straw to the center. (The clay can be moved through the straw by pinching the sides of the straw.) Explain that snakes use a similar pinching action—muscular contractions—to swallow and ingest food.

❶ The snake's tongue transfers scent chemicals to smell receptor cells in the snake's mouth.

MEETING DIVERSE NEEDS

LEP Encourage LEP students to compile a glossary that includes all terms in bold print and technical terms. Have students write definitions in both English and their native language and illustrate their glossaries. Encourage them to add to their glossaries as they study the chapter.

Hearing Impaired Have students make flash cards showing the phonetic pronunciations and definitions for the following terms: *keratin, amniotic, chorion, embryo,* and *allantois.*

Build Writing Skills

Have students write an essay explaining how they think their life would be different if they were ectothermic instead of endothermic.

Class Activity

TEAM WORK

Distribute one hard-boiled chicken egg to each lab group. Invite students to cut the eggs in half and identify structures. Have them compare the chicken egg to the reptile egg shown in Figure 26.4. Ask them to compare their observations with those they made in the Discover It! activity. What parts can they identify now that they did not know about before?

Health

Tell students that chicken eggs are rich in protein and nutrients. Have them research the vitamins and minerals in eggs. You may also want to discuss the pros and cons of eating eggs, given the amount of cholesterol in them.

❶ Move to a shady location
❷ Lowers internal temperature

---

the ventricles is complete, forming a four-chambered heart.

In addition to a more efficient circulatory system, reptiles have well-developed lungs with large internal surface areas. Unlike amphibians, reptiles do not depend on gas exchange through the skin, so they do not need to stay moist. Furthermore, reptiles inhale and exhale more frequently than amphibians, while filling their lungs with a larger volume of air.

The excretory system of most reptiles is adapted to conserve water from body wastes. Notice the snake's kidneys in *Figure* 26.2. Most of the water that the kidneys remove from the blood is returned to the tissues. Reptiles living in dry climates excrete thick, pasty urine containing very little water. Like fishes, aquatic reptiles excrete waste as a liquid.

Although reptiles require large amounts of energy to move quickly and easily on land, they do not require energy to maintain their body temperature. Reptiles are ectotherms. Recall from Chapter 25 that ectotherms control their body temperature by their

FIGURE 26.3
The lizard below is raising its body temperature by lying in the sun's rays. What would the lizard do if it was too hot? ❶

---

behavior. If its body temperature is too low, for example, the lizard lies in the sun's rays. If its body temperature is too high, the lizard usually seeks shade. How does this behavior affect the internal temperature of the lizard? ❷

REPTILIAN LIFE CYCLE

The "eggciting" new development

Another adaptation necessary for reproduction on land is internal fertilization. How is this different from fertilization in amphibians? Male reptiles have specialized organs to introduce sperm directly into the female's reproductive tract. This adaptation makes water unnecessary for sperm and egg to unite.

Another advantage of internal fertilization is that the fragile sperm are protected from the environment, ensuring a higher rate of fertilization. As a result, reptiles do not need to lay as many eggs as aquatic animals do to produce enough offspring to maintain the species. On average, reptiles lay between 8 and 100 eggs at a time, instead of the thousands laid by amphibians.

You have probably heard the question "Which came first, the chicken or the egg?" In terms of the theory of evolution, there is no doubt. The amniotic egg probably developed long before birds evolved. An **amniotic egg** is one that provides nourishment to the embryo and protects the embryo while it develops in a terrestrial environment.

Look at the illustration of the egg in *Figure* 26.4. The embryo is connected to the yolk by a stalk. The **yolk** is the food source for the developing embryo. The embryo is completely surrounded by a membrane called the amnion. The amnion is a fluid-filled envelope that cushions the embryo. The allantois (uh-LAN-toh-is) is a membrane-bound sac that stores wastes and is the site for

---

MULTICULTURAL PERSPECTIVE

Throughout history, snakes have held a certain fascination for people of many cultures. In ancient Egypt, for example, the poisonous asp was held in high esteem and its symbol is found in many writings and artifacts. In colonial America, Benjamin Franklin published a cartoon depicting the separate colonies as parts of a disjointed snake and captioned it "Join or die." Invite students to share how snakes are used as symbols in art or in celebrations in different cultures.

FIGURE 26.4

The Structure of the Amniotic Egg

Embryo
The embryo is connected to the yolk by a stalk. The yolk is the food source for the developing embryo.

Amnion
The amnion is a fluid-filled sac that surrounds and cushions the embryo.

Allantois
The allantois is a membrane-bound sac that stores wastes and is the site of gas exchange.

Chorion
The chorion surrounds the embryo, yolk, and allantois. It helps regulate gas exchange. In turtles and crocodilians, the chorion contains albumin, commonly called egg white.

Yolk

Shell
The waterproof eggshell may be soft and leathery, or strengthened with calcium. The shell is porous, allowing oxygen and carbon dioxide to pass through it.

gas exchange. The allantois becomes larger as the embryo grows, while the yolk shrinks. The outermost membrane, called the **chorion** (KOR-ee-ahn), envelopes the embryo, yolk, and allantois. The chorion provides another layer of protection and helps regulate gas exchange.

The developing egg represents the most defenseless stage in a reptile's life. Environmental conditions, such as temperature and humidity, affect the developing embryo. Many eggs are lost to predators. Reptilian young, like the one shown in *Figure 26.5*, look like miniature adults when hatching from the eggs. Although the young are at risk from predators, they are much better equipped than fish or amphibian larvae to survive their first few months of life.

Not all reptiles lay eggs. Some lizards and snakes give birth to live young. Reptiles that produce live young carry the eggs inside their bodies until the young hatch. Other reptiles have a specialized sac that connects the developing embryo to the mother. These embryos still have a yolk for nourishment.

CHECKPOINT 26.1

1. Name three adaptations that enable reptiles to live in their environments.
2. What are the functions of the yolk, amnion, allantois, and chorion in the amniotic egg?
3. **Critical Thinking** Most reptiles produce fewer, larger eggs than amphibians and fishes. How is this adaptation an advantage?

Build on What You Know

4. How do the life cycles of reptiles differ from those of amphibians? *(Need to jog your memory? Revisit relevant concepts in Chapter 25, Section 25.5.)*

FIGURE 26.5
This Northern Diamondback terrapin is freeing itself from its egg. The young terrapin will search out food—marine snails and worms—without the help of a parent.

Chapter 26 Reptiles and Birds **623**

TEACH

Think Critically

Explain that fossil evidence indicates that early reptiles had teeth adapted for eating insects, not plants. Ask:

- **Why was it advantageous for early reptiles to eat insects?** (Plant tissues contain less energy than do animal tissues. Reptiles would have to eat more plants than insects to obtain the same amount of energy.)

Earth Science

In 1980, American physicist Luis Alvarez discovered an unusual amount of the element iridium in rock layers in Italy deposited about 65 million years ago. Because iridium is rare in rocks formed on Earth, Dr. Alvarez hypothesized that the rock layers were formed from materials produced by a collision between Earth and an asteroid. He hypothesized that the catastrophic event may have led to the mass extinction of dinosaurs at the end of the Cretaceous period.

Build Writing Skills

Have students create a comic strip to illustrate one of the hypotheses explaining the extinction of the dinosaurs. Challenge them to make the comic strip as scientifically accurate as possible.

Clarify Misconceptions

Point out that dinosaurs and humans did not inhabit the Earth at the same time. You may wish to refer students to the geologic time scale.

FIGURE 26.7
Land dinosaurs flourished during the Jurassic period. The largest animals ever to walk on Earth, the brachiosaurs, existed at this time.

FIGURE 26.8
During the Cretaceous period, dinosaurs continued to diversify until the extinctions began. Some of the reptile species that survived the extinctions are still alive today.

reptiles also died out. Only a handful of species survived.

After the decline of the amphibians, the remaining species of reptiles probably flourished and soon became the most abundant animals on Earth. Through adaptive radiation, the ancestral species could have rapidly evolved. You may recall from Chapter 10 that adaptive radiation is the evolution of many different species from one common ancestor. The resulting reptiles are adapted to many different niches.

EXTINCT REPTILES

Terrible lizards that roamed Earth

Dinosaurs were the most abundant reptiles during the Mesozoic era, which lasted from about 245 million to 65 million years ago. Although the word *dinosaur* means "terrible lizard," the first dinosaur species were two-legged animals no larger than a chicken. Over time, dinosaur populations increased in size. One of the largest dinosaur species was an herbivore called *Apatosaurus*. This

reptile was 24 meters (m) long and may have weighed as much as 50,000 kilograms (kg). Some species, such as *Tyrannosaurus rex* stood 6 m tall. *Figure 26.7* illustrates what some of these dinosaurs may have looked like. Some scientists think the larger body was an adaptation that enabled dinosaurs to maintain a constant body temperature. As the body mass increased, the relative amount of body surface decreased, reducing the amount of heat lost through the skin.

Dinosaurs and other reptile populations began to decline toward the end of the Cretaceous period, the last period of the Mesozoic era. Many scientists think the period between the end of the Cretaceous and the beginning of the Tertiary, called the K-T boundary, lasted 5 to 10 million years. These scientists think the mass extinction occurred gradually, due to climatic changes caused by the land masses drifting north. *Figure 26.8* shows what the environment may have looked like during the Cretaceous period.

Some recent evidence indicates that a catastrophic event, such as a huge meteor crashing into Earth, or

MEETING DIVERSE NEEDS

At Risk Have students work with a partner to create an illustrated flowchart tracing the evolutionary history of the reptiles through geologic time as presented in the text.

Horny shield layer

Bony layer

Skull

Neck vertebrae

Think Critically

Explain that some species of turtles are adapted to life in aquatic environments. Ask:

- **How do you think sea turtles get the oxygen needed for respiration?** (Because they are reptiles, turtles use lungs for gas exchange. They must come to the water's surface to obtain oxygen.)

the release of large amounts of carbon dioxide gas from volcanoes, may have caused a more abrupt extinction of dinosaurs. Such a catastrophic event might have shortened the K-T boundary to as few as 100,000 years. (Yes, in terms of Earth's history, 100,000 years are considered a few!)

There is still much debate over the length of the K-T boundary and the cause of the mass extinction at the end of the Mesozoic era. The only reptilian survivors were turtles, crocodilians, and the ancestors of other modern reptiles.

MODERN DIVERSITY OF REPTILES

Scales, tails, and shells

Today only three major orders of reptiles exist: Squamata, including snakes and lizards, Chelonia (keh-LOH-nee-uh), including turtles and tortoises, and Crocodilia. A fourth order, Rhynchocephalia (ring-koh-seh-FAY-lee-uh) has only one remaining species: the tuatara. Tuataras, the reptiles you read about at the beginning of this section, look much the same as they did more than 200 million years ago.

Tuataras Today, tuataras are found only on two small groups of islands off the coast of New Zealand. A few hundred years ago, they also

lived on mainland New Zealand. The introduction of sheep and goats to the mainland destroyed the tuatara habitat. Tuataras survive today in part because the New Zealand government has passed strict laws to protect them in their isolated island homes. On some islands, however, the number of tuataras has recently declined because of the introduction of Polynesian rats, which prey on young tuataras.

Turtles and tortoises Another one of the oldest living orders of reptiles is Chelonia. Chelonians are divided into three groups: tortoises, sea turtles, and freshwater turtles. Tortoises live entirely on land; sea turtles live in oceans. Male sea turtles rarely come to shore, and female sea turtles do so only to lay eggs. Freshwater turtles have webbed feet and live an amphibious life, sunning themselves on shore but feeding in the water.

A unique characteristic of chelonians is their shells. Turtles generally have flatter shells than tortoises. *Figure 26.9* shows the structure of a tortoise's shell. A streamlined body enables the turtle to move efficiently through water. Freshwater turtles and tortoises have shells that consist of a series of bony plates covered with hornlike scales. Sea turtles, by comparison, have lightweight, leathery shells.

FIGURE 26.9

The ribs and vertebrae of the tortoise are fused to the shell, but the neck and limbs are not fused and are retractable. The shell of a tortoise is composed of two layers. How do these layers compare? ❶

Explain

Point out that tuataras live only where they have little competition with other animals. Explain that attempts to provide secure habitats for tuataras have met with mixed success. You may wish to locate New Zealand on a world map and point out its isolation.

Use the Visual

Have students study Figure 26.9. Discuss the labeled structures of the tortoise and their functions. Point out how the features of the tortoise differ from those of turtles. Ask:

- **How does the shape of a sea turtle's shell differ from that of a tortoise?** (The sea turtle has a less rounded, more streamlined shell that is adapted for movement through water.)
- **What is an advantage for the tortoise of having the backbone and ribs fused to its shell?** (It reinforces the shell, giving the tortoise added protection against predators.)

Chapter 26 Reptiles and Birds **627**

❶ The outer layer is made of hornlike scales. The inner layer is made of bony plates.

FIGURE 26.10
Microscopic, hairlike structures on the pads of the gecko's toes enable it to climb on almost any surface. Geckos can scale walls and even walk on ceilings!

Although the shell reduces a turtle's mobility, it protects the turtle from predators. Most turtles can pull their head into their shell. Some can also pull their legs inside the shell. Because they are so well protected, individual turtles and tortoises can live a very long time. Some giant tortoises of the Galapagos Islands, for example, live as long as 150 years.

Snakes and lizards Although most lizards have four legs and snakes have none, both groups are classified in the order Squamata. Snakes and lizards live in most habitats on land and in water, with the exception of cold polar regions.

Although the absence of legs may seem like an evolutionary step backward, it actually increases a snake's mobility. By pushing its body against the ground, a snake can move quickly and fit into small spaces.

Lizards have many specialized adaptations that enable them to live in different habitats. The gecko shown in *Figure 26.10* has pads on its toes that help it to cling to trees. In what other ❶ ways are the gecko's toes an advantage?

Some lizards have unique adaptations to help them escape from predators. Chameleons and anoles can blend into their environment by changing the color of their skin. Skinks and geckos can cast off their tails when grabbed by predators. In skinks, the discarded tail will continue to wiggle after it has broken off, confusing the would-be predator. The lizard's tail will regenerate quickly.

Crocodilians Reptiles in the order Crocodilia include crocodiles, alligators, caimans, and gavials. Crocodilians have changed little in the past 150 million years. They differ from other reptiles by having a four chambered heart and by the care they give their young. These characteristics make crocodilians more similar to dinosaurs and birds than to other modern reptiles.

Compare the crocodile and alligator shown in *Figure 26.11*. Notice that the crocodile has a narrower head and a longer snout. Crocodiles live in the tropical regions of Africa, Asia, Australia, and North and South America. Both alligators and caimans have short, broad snouts. Alligators are found in tropical regions of China and in the southern United States. Caimans are native to Central and South America. Gavials have long, slender snouts that broaden slightly at the end. Gavials spend most of their lives in the water and are found only in India and Burma.

CHECKPOINT 26.2

1. Explain two hypotheses about the origin and evolution of reptiles.
2. Compare the different orders of reptiles.
3. **Critical Thinking** How might a huge meteor crashing into Earth have caused the extinction of dinosaurs?

Build on What You Know

4. How does reptilian evolution compare to amphibian evolution? *(Need to jog your memory? Revisit relevant con-*

FIGURE 26.11
Alligators and crocodiles are the largest reptiles. Both species can grow to lengths of over 6 m. What similarities and differences can you see in the head structure of the alligator (right) and the crocodile (far right)? ❷

26.3 Reptiles in the Biosphere

The deadly look is in
The poisonous eastern coral snake (top right) and the nonpoisonous scarlet king snake (bottom right) both have brightly colored bands of red, yellow, and black along their bodies. Predators such as birds avoid these brightly colored snakes—poisonous or not. How is this pattern of coloration beneficial to both snakes? ❸

What you'll learn

IDEAS
• To explain the ecological roles of reptiles
• To compare reptile behaviors

ECOLOGICAL ROLES

The hunter and the hunted

Although the section opener describes snakes as prey to birds, reptiles are not always prey. Many snakes and lizards are predators. Snakes and other reptiles are important predators in grasslands, prairies, and rain forests. On farms, snakes play a major role in controlling rat and mice populations that feed on crops. In many tropical countries, it is not uncommon to see small lizards crawling along sidewalks or even climbing on walls inside a house. Lizards are welcome guests because they consume large numbers of unwanted insects.

Reptiles have roles in all levels of a food chain. Some lizards, such as large iguanas and skinks, eat a variety of leafy green plants. Most reptiles, however, will eat whatever animal prey is available: insects, worms, snails, and mammals.

Some reptiles are preyed upon by birds such as eagles and owls, mammals such as pigs and cats, and even other larger, more aggressive reptiles. The unprotected young of many reptiles, including sea turtles and alligators, are easy prey after they hatch from their eggs.

REPTILE BEHAVIOR

Staying alive

Most reptiles spend their time quietly searching for food, adjusting their body temperature, and avoiding danger. When threatened, they run away or hide. Other reptiles, however, exhibit a wide variety of behaviors to keep their predators away.

The Australian frilled lizard, shown in *Figure 26.12*, employs one of the most spectacular methods of scaring

FIGURE 26.12
The South American armadillo lizard (far left) rolls itself into a tight ball when it spots a predator. The Australian frilled lizard (near left), on the other hand, takes a different approach. How might these behaviors help the lizards survive? ❹

Chapter 26 Reptiles and Birds **629**

STUDENT RESOURCES

From the Teacher's Resource Package, use:
■ Section Review 26.3, Activity Record-sheet 26-2, and Enrichment Topic 26-1 from Unit 7 Review Module
■ Consumer Applications 26-1

TECHNOLOGY RESOURCES

Relevant technology resources include:
■ Spanish Student Edition CD-ROM
■ Teacher's Resource Planner CD-ROM
■ Biology Alive! Video: "The Continuity of Life"

ENGAGE

Use the Visual

Have students study the photograph that opens the section. Explain that the similar coloring of the two snakes is an adaptation called *mimicry.* Ask:

■ **How would birds benefit from the pattern of coloration among snakes?** (Birds would avoid eating a snake that might be poisonous.)

Check Prior Knowledge

To assess students' knowledge about reptiles in the biosphere, ask:

■ **What do reptiles eat?** (Small rodents, eggs, insects)
■ **What animals eat reptiles?** (Cats, birds)

Teacher Demo

Display items or pictures of items made from the skins of snakes, alligators, and crocodiles, and the shells of tortoises. Explain that the objects were made from hides and shells of reptiles. Tell students they are about to discover how reptiles are important to the biosphere and how people sometimes threaten their survival.

❸ The coloration wards off certain predators, giving the snakes a better chance of survival.
❹ Rolling into a tight ball protects soft ventral tissue and many internal organs; the frills may scare away unsuspecting predators.

TEACH

Explain

Tell students that many newly hatched sea turtles use moonlight reflected off the ocean as a guide to find the sea. In populated areas, baby turtles are often drawn to artificial lighting of homes, streets, or cars instead of the moonlight. As a result, many baby sea turtles migrate in the wrong direction and die from injury by cars or from starvation.

 Do It! TEAM WORK

How Does Egg-burying Behavior in Reptiles Benefit Reproduction?

Try This

Suggest that students take three temperature measurements each time and average their results.

Analyze Your Results

1 Students should see a more stable temperature curve for the test period inside the compost heap.

2 The warmth inside a decaying compost heap provides a more stable environment for the eggs to develop in because it is independent of surrounding air temperature fluctuations. Also, burying the eggs offers more protection from predators and other environmental disturbances, such as storms.

FIGURE 26.13
The male anole lizard inflates its fanlike throat sac to display aggression towards another anole. Though these displays can last for hours, violence is usually avoided when the weaker of the two lizards flees.

off predators. Most of the time the lizard avoids predators by lying very still, camouflaged against its environment. But when a predator comes too close, the lizard raises a frilled, colorful collar of skin around its neck, hisses loudly, puffs up its body with air, rises up on its clawed feet, and waves its tail back and forth. If all this fails, it turns around and runs.

Like other vertebrates, reptiles need to find and mate with a member of the opposite sex in order to reproduce. Many male lizards display colorful frills or flaps of skin to attract females. The male anole lizard, shown in *Figure 26.13,* inflates a brightly colored fanlike throat sac to attract its mate. Male anole lizards also display this throat sac to defend their territories and chase away other males.

After mating, many reptiles lay their eggs in sand, soil, or rotting logs.

 Do It! **bioSURF**

How Does Egg-burying Behavior in Reptiles Benefit Reproduction?

Some reptiles bury their eggs under heaps of plant material and dirt. The eggs remain under this mixture until they hatch. You can find out how this behavior benefits the eggs if you . . .

Try This

1 Construct a compost heap outside of your school by alternating layers of dirt and dead plant material. Build up the heap until it is 0.5 m high.
2 Using a long thermometer, determine and record the air temperature and the temperature at the center of the compost heap. Take these measurements twice weekly for four weeks.

Analyze Your Results

1 Graph the changes in air temperature over the four weeks. Do the same for the temperature inside the compost heap. How do they differ?
2 How do you think the temperature in the heap would benefit developing eggs? What other advantages would burying eggs in this way provide?

Some reptiles bury their eggs in nests dug deep in the soil. Other reptiles lay their eggs in small depressions in the ground. The eggs are usually laid where they will stay warm, to ensure proper development. After they lay their eggs, most reptiles leave them. The young hatch on their own and receive no parental care.

The behavior of the American alligator does not follow the typical pattern. Female alligators provide care for their eggs and young. They lay their eggs in a hole, then cover the eggs with rotting plants and soil. After the eggs are laid, the female maintains the nest and protects it from predators. After the eggs hatch, the mother will often carry the young in her mouth, three or four at a time, and take them to water. The young follow their mother around for several weeks before going off on their own.

Some reptiles migrate during different stages of their life cycles. Giant sea turtles have roamed the world's oceans for millions of years. Using radio and satellite equipment, scientists have recently learned about the behavior of these mysterious animals. Sea turtles travel along regular migration routes, sometimes for thousands of kilometers (km). Every two or three years the turtles return to the same beaches where they hatched from eggs. Green turtles, for example, travel 3,340 km from the coast of Brazil to a small island in the middle of the Atlantic Ocean. Once there, females go ashore and lay their eggs.

HUMAN USES

Products are skin-deep

Humans use reptiles in many different ways. Sea turtles are eaten as food, as are turtle eggs. Some turtles, such as the hawksbill turtle, are hunted for their beautiful black and yellow shells. The shells are made into tortoiseshell

---

MEETING DIVERSE NEEDS

Gifted Have students research the impact hunting American alligators for their skins and meat had on the species earlier in this century. Ask them to find out what efforts were made to restore populations of these animals to their normal ranges and the success of these efforts. Have students also investigate if alligator hunting has resumed in some areas. Provide time for students to share their findings with the class.

hair combs and barrettes, jewelry, and decorations for the home. At one time, these turtles were hunted to near extinction because of the popularity of tortoiseshell ornaments.

Reptiles are raised or hunted for their colorful and strong skins, which are made into boots, belts, purses, and luggage. Some reptiles, including snakes, lizards, and turtles, are also raised as pets.

Today, many reptiles are endangered. Their numbers are decreasing rapidly due to hunting and loss of habitat. Fortunately, many endangered reptiles are now protected by international law. These laws prevent the sale and purchase of products made from the skins, bones, hides, or shells of endangered reptiles.

FRONTIERS IN BIOLOGY

Poisons or promises?

Zap! The snake's poison glands compress. Deadly venom enters the body of the bitten animal through razor-sharp fangs. Blood pressure drops, lungs burst, and the animal soon dies. The snake *Bothrops jararaca* of southern Brazil has claimed another victim.

Something in the snake's venom causes the blood pressure to drop in the bitten animal. Scientists hypothesized that the same substance could reduce blood pressure in humans. High blood pressure, or hypertension, is a leading cause of death in humans. To study the effects of the venom of the *Bothrops*, Brazilian scientist Dr. J. Ferreira collected snakes from the grasslands of Brazil. He then "milked" the snakes of their venom and tested it on lab

animals. His work produced some very valuable results. The venom reduced the blood pressure in the lab animals.

Researchers have identified more than 25 active substances in the venom of reptiles. Most of these substances are large proteins that act as enzymes. The effect of the *Bothrops* venom is to widen the victim's blood vessels, causing the blood pressure to drop fatally.

Using Ferreira's information about the poison, researchers began to develop an artificial venom. The result of the research was a blood pressure drug called captopril, which has saved many lives since the 1970s.

CHECKPOINT 26.3

1. Name two reptiles and the role each plays in the environment.
2. List three behaviors of reptiles and explain their evolutionary significance.
3. **Critical Thinking** Why do you think it is important to protect reptiles from unnecessary hunting and collecting?

Build on What You Know

4. Compare one example of reptile behavior to one example of insect behavior. **(Need to jog your memory? Revisit relevant concepts in Chapter 23, Section 23.4.)**

EVERYDAY BIOLOGY

Heat-sensing Snakes

The rattlesnake belongs to a group of snakes known as pit vipers. These snakes have a shallow, heat-sensing pit located between their nostrils and eyes that allows them to sense changes in temperature, to a fraction of a degree. This organ helps the snake locate and strike the warm bodies of prey, even in total darkness!

What characteristics enable reptiles to live their entire lives out of water?

Chapter 26 Reptiles and Birds **631**

Explain

Point out that of some 2700 known species of snakes, only about 200 are poisonous. In North America, the only venomous snakes are pit vipers and coral snakes. Pit vipers include rattlesnakes, water moccasins, and copperheads. Coral snakes are easily recognized by their bright colors.

Everyday Biology

Ask students if they have ever seen infrared photos. These specialized images record heat that comes from objects or living things. Invite them to study the infrared photo in Section 7.2 on page 158.

 ASSESS

Evaluate Understanding

Have students write a one-paragraph summary explaining the importance of reptiles in the biosphere. Have them share their summaries in small groups. Discuss sample paragraphs as a class and make any necessary corrections and additions.

Reteach

Guide students to create an outline that summarizes the main concepts of this section. Using the section headings as a guide, have students supply the information to be included in the outline. Review the completed outlines as a class.

CHECKPOINT 26.3

1. Answers should include the role of reptiles in all levels of the food chain.
2. Rolling up in a ball, producing offensive smells, and performing elaborate displays to deter predators; colorful displays to attract mates; burying eggs to maintain proper temperature
3. **Identifying cause and effect** Reptiles are important predators and are needed at many levels in the food chain.
4. Both reptiles and insects attract mates, defend territories, protect themselves from predators, and generally act to increase survival and reproductive success.

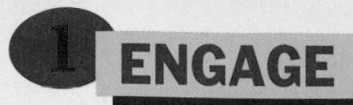

1 ENGAGE

Consider the Big Idea

Have students read The Big Idea! at the top of the page. Explain that feathers distinguish birds from reptiles. Feathers enabled birds to be the first endotherms.

Use the Visual

Have students study the photograph and read the text that opens the section. Point out that the peregrine falcon is classified as a bird of prey. Ask:

- **How are the claws and beak of the peregrine falcon adapted for obtaining food?** (The claws are long and sharp for grasping and tearing food. The beak is strong with a sharp, curved tip for tearing apart prey.)

Check Prior Knowledge

To assess students' knowledge about birds, ask:

- **What evolutionary milestone is common to both birds and reptiles?** (The amnion)
- **What evolutionary milestone separates birds from reptiles?** (Feathers)

Teacher Demo

Display a variety of bird feathers. Tell students that throughout history people have made use of bird feathers. Ask:

- **What are some ways people use feathers?** (For adornment, as insulation material, in pillows, and as pens)

26.4 Characteristics of Birds

What you'll learn

IDEAS
- To explain the structural adaptations that allow birds to fly
- To summarize the life cycle of a typical bird

WORDS
crop, gizzard, chalaza

Which bird flies the fastest?
The fastest bird in the world is the peregrine falcon, which hunts other birds in the air. When chasing its prey, the falcon dives at speeds of up to 280 km/h. As it dives, the falcon slashes at its victim with sharp claws, interrupting its flight. The falcon, extremely agile, then wheels back to catch its victim as it falls.

MOVEMENT AND SUPPORT

Fly, fly away

Have you ever wondered how birds fly? A bird's entire body is adapted to enable flight. In fact, many differences between a bird's body and a reptile's body are the result of structural adaptations for flight. These adaptations do one of two things: reduce a bird's body weight, or make the body more compact. Some of the structural adaptations for flight are in a bird's feathers, skeleton, muscles, and skin.

The shape of a bird's wings is similar to the shape of an airplane wing. Its wings are slightly curved from front to back and are thicker in the front, as shown in *Figure 26.15*. The curved surface of the top of the wing causes air above the wing to travel faster than air beneath the wing. This difference in air speed decreases the relative air pressure above the wing, providing the lift needed for flight.

Birds have thin skin covered with feathers. The only gland that birds have in their skin is the oil gland at the base of the tail. The oil from this gland is used for smoothing and waterproofing feathers. The one reptilian characteristic of a bird's skin is the presence of scales covering the legs and feet. Feathers are modified from reptilian scales; they are larger and fringed along the edges. Like reptilian scales, feathers are made of keratin. Feathers insulate a bird's body, protect the bird against weather, and form a smooth, low-friction surface. But feathers wear out and must be shed, or molted, once or twice a year. The two main types of bird feathers are described in *Figure 26.16*.

A bird, or avian, skeleton is also an important adaptation that enables flight. Compared with a reptile's skeleton, a bird's skeleton is light in weight. As you can see in *Figure 26.16*, avian bones are hollow. The air inside the bone reduces the bone's density, greatly reducing the weight of the body. Hollow bones are not brittle and

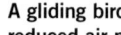
FIGURE 26.15
A gliding bird uses the reduced air pressure above its wings to stay aloft, much like an airplane.

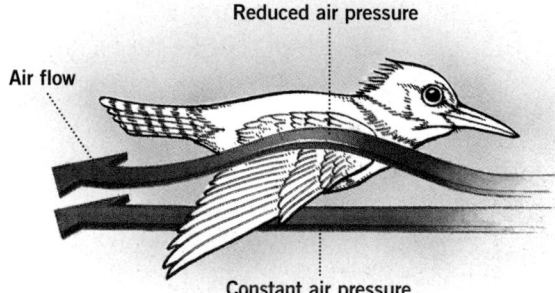

Reduced air pressure

Air flow

Constant air pressure

FIGURE 26.16

Structures for Flight

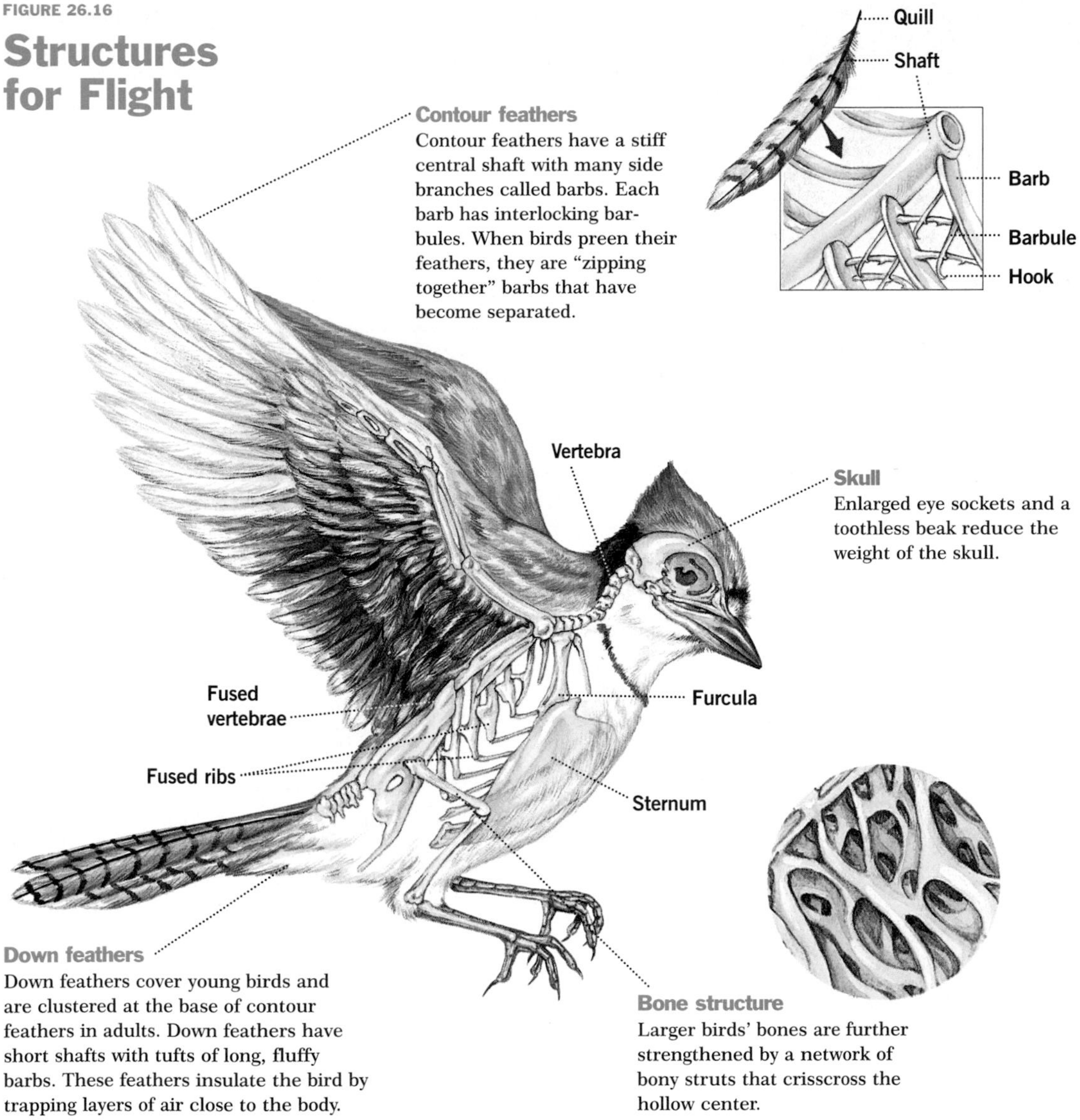

Contour feathers
Contour feathers have a stiff central shaft with many side branches called barbs. Each barb has interlocking barbules. When birds preen their feathers, they are "zipping together" barbs that have become separated.

Quill
Shaft
Barb
Barbule
Hook

Vertebra

Skull
Enlarged eye sockets and a toothless beak reduce the weight of the skull.

Fused vertebrae

Fused ribs

Furcula

Sternum

Down feathers
Down feathers cover young birds and are clustered at the base of contour feathers in adults. Down feathers have short shafts with tufts of long, fluffy barbs. These feathers insulate the bird by trapping layers of air close to the body.

Bone structure
Larger birds' bones are further strengthened by a network of bony struts that crisscross the hollow center.

weak; they are very strong, due to the network of cross braces, or struts within the bone.

Some of the bones that make up joints in reptiles and mammals are fused in birds. Fused bones make the skeleton more rigid and provide extra stability for flight. Fused bones also reduce the need for heavy ligaments.

As you can see in *Figure 26.16,* the ribs are attached to one another, and some of the vertebrae and the collarbone, or furcula, are also fused. The furcula is the bone commonly called the wishbone in poultry.

Although a bird's skeletal system is adapted to reduce body weight, its muscles are large and relatively heavy.

Chapter 26 Reptiles and Birds **633**

26.4

② TEACH

Use the Visual

Have students study Figure 26.16. Review the labeled structures and their functions as a class. Ask:

- **Why do birds lack teeth?** (Their absence makes the skull much lighter.)
- **How is the structure of the furcula an adaptation for flight?** (The furcula is fused with some of the vertebrae, making the skeleton more rigid, reducing the need for heavy ligaments, and providing extra stability for flight.)

Teacher Demo

Bring several clean chicken bones to class. Pass out the bones so students can observe their low mass. Break the bones in half and pass them around so students can observe their hollow structure.

✛ Physics

Show students the cross section of an airplane wing. Point out the similarity of the shape of the bird wing to the airplane wing. Explain that the laws of physics apply to flight. Encourage interested students to research Daniel Bernoulli (1700-1782), a Swiss mathematician and scientist, and his findings on hydrodynamics.

MEETING DIVERSE NEEDS

LEP Encourage LEP students to draw a diagram of the skeletal structure of the bird. Have them label important structures and their functions in both English and their native language. Then have them find pictures of birds from their native country or another country that illustrate each feature.

How Do Contour Feathers Compare with Down Feathers?

Try This

Encourage students to create their drawings to scale and to note the scale used.

Analyze Your Results

1 The barbs of a contour feather are attached to each other by small hooks which allow the barbs to interlock. This interlocking system allows the contour feather to retain its stiff shape when the bird is flying.

2 Interlocking barbs of down feathers would cause these feathers to be stiff like contour feathers, and thus would not be as effective as insulators.

3 The stiff, interlocking structure of the contour feather is necessary for diverting air currents during gliding and flying. The soft, fluffy down feathers are used to trap insulating layers of air close to the bird's body.

LAB ZONE Do It!

How Do Contour Feathers Compare with Down Feathers?

You can examine the structural differences between two types of feathers if you . . .

Try This

1 Obtain a contour feather, a downy feather, and a microscope.
2 Study the contour feather. Record your observations on paper. Is the feather curved or straight? Is it symmetrical? Now examine the feather under the low-power setting of the microscope. Note the individual barbs that are attached to one another. Draw what you see.
3 Repeat step 2 using the down feather.

Analyze Your Results

1 How are the barbs of a contour feather attached to one another? How do these attachments make the feather strong?
2 Explain why the barbs of a down feather do not fit together like the barbs of a contour feather.
3 How are the structures of the feathers related to their functions?

The chest, or pectoral, muscles make up almost 25 percent of a bird's body weight. The pectoral muscles are located on the sternum and are used to move the bird's wings.

FIGURE 26.17
Because the snowy owl is an endotherm, it can exist in very cold climates. This owl lives in the Arctic.

ENERGY AND WASTES

Eating like a bird

Birds generate and maintain a constant internal body temperature. As you may recall from Chapter 25, animals that maintain a constant internal body temperature are called endotherms. Because birds are endothermic, they can live in very cold climates where reptiles cannot survive. Birds' overlapping feathers trap layers of air and minimize the loss of body heat. Birds prevent water from soaking into their feathers by preening with oil secreted by the oil gland at the base of the tail.

Generating heat to maintain a constant body temperature requires a lot of energy. As is true for all aerobic organisms, energy is released in cells when food combines with oxygen. Cellular wastes, such as carbon dioxide and nitrogenous wastes, must be removed efficiently, too. Birds have more efficient respiratory, circulatory, and digestive systems than reptiles.

Birds have a rapid heartbeat and high blood pressure, making circulation fast and efficient. Birds also have a four-chambered heart that completely separates oxygen-rich blood from oxygen-poor blood. Because the blood is completely separated, the body tissues receive a high concentration of oxygen. As you may recall from section 26.2, crocodilians also have a four-chambered heart, which suggests that crocodiles and birds are closely related.

A bird's respiratory system can obtain large amounts of oxygen. Avian lungs are attached to a system of air sacs that extend into all parts of the body. Some air sacs even open into the hollow spaces inside bones. The respiratory system is unique in that air flows through the lungs in only one direction. Use *Figure 26.18* to trace the path of air during respiration.

Birds must eat and digest large amounts of food to provide enough energy for flight and for generating body heat. When birds eat, the unchewed food passes from the mouth to the esophagus. Notice in *Figure 26.18* that the lower end of the esophagus enlarges to form the **crop.** The crop is a storage area of the digestive tract where food is softened. Many birds store food in the crop to eat later or to feed their young in the nest.

From the crop, the food mixes with enzymes and is ground to a pulp in the gizzard. The **gizzard** is a digestive organ with muscular walls that often contains small stones swallowed by

634 *Unit 7 Vertebrate Animals*

Respiratory and Digestive Structures

FIGURE 26.18

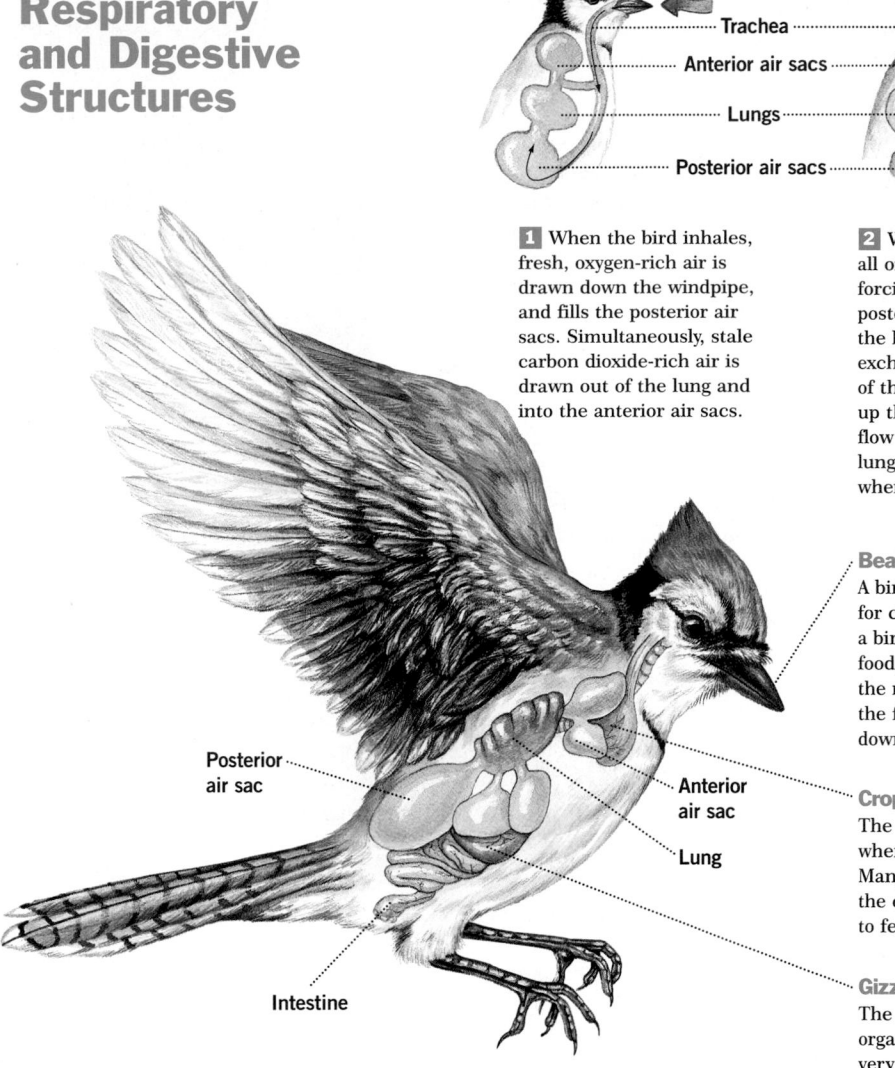

Trachea

Anterior air sacs

Lungs

Posterior air sacs

1 When the bird inhales, fresh, oxygen-rich air is drawn down the windpipe, and fills the posterior air sacs. Simultaneously, stale carbon dioxide-rich air is drawn out of the lung and into the anterior air sacs.

2 When the bird exhales, all of the air sacs collapse forcing fresh air from the posterior air sacs into the lung for more gas exchange, and stale air out of the anterior air sacs and up the windpipe. Thus, the flow of air through the lungs is continuous, even when the bird is exhaling.

Posterior air sac

Anterior air sac

Lung

Intestine

Beak
A bird's beak has no teeth for chewing food. So when a bird eats, the unchewed food mixes with saliva in the mouth, which helps the food pass smoothly down the esophagus.

Crop
The crop is a storage area where food is softened. Many birds store food in the crop to digest later or to feed their young.

Gizzard
The gizzard is a digestive organ that breaks food into very small pieces.

the bird. The gizzard breaks the food into very small pieces, which travel to the intestines, where nutrients are absorbed.

The excretory system of birds is adapted to conserve water from body wastes. Urine is excreted in a pasty form, similar to the urine excreted by reptiles. Unlike reptiles and most other types of land vertebrates, however, birds do not have a urinary

bladder in which to store liquid wastes. This modification lowers body weight by reducing the amounts of water and waste in the body.

Shore birds have a special adaptation to eliminate excess salt obtained from drinking sea water and eating marine animals. Small salt-excreting glands above the eyes remove excess salt, which leaves the body through the nostrils. The sparkling crystals that

Chapter 26 Reptiles and Birds **635**

Think Critically

The meat of chicken and turkey eaten by some people is muscle tissue. Muscle tissue with few blood vessels appears light. Muscles with many blood vessels appears dark. Ask:

- **Why is the leg and thigh meat of chickens and turkeys dark, while the breast meat is light in color?** (Chickens and turkeys do not use their wings for movement. The wings, therefore, do not have as many blood vessels as the legs and thighs.

Use the Visual

Have students study Figure 26.18. As a class, review the labeled structures and their functions. Ask:

- **What is the crop and where is it located? What is its function?** (The crop is a storage area for food located at the lower end of the esophagus. Food is softened in the crop.)
- **What is unique about the respiratory system of birds?** (Air flow is continuous, even while the bird is exhaling; air flows through the lungs in one direction.)

Explain

Point out to students that air sacs contained in the bones of birds are an adaptation for flight.

Build Writing Skills

Ask students to choose a format and describe in writing all the anatomical features of a bird that are adaptations for flight. Encourage students to be scientifically accurate.

FACTS AND FIGURES

The bodies of birds in the subclass Ratitae do not contain air sacs. This group of flightless birds includes ostriches, kiwis, and emus, all of which have muscular legs suited to movement on land.

MEETING DIVERSE NEEDS

At Risk Have students work with a partner to diagram the path of food through the bird digestive system as a flowchart. Tell students to include all of the digestive structures shown in Figure 26.18 as well as a description of the function of each structure.

In the Community

Tell students that people who watch birds as a hobby are called *birders.* Encourage students to observe birds living in their area. Suggest they photograph or videotape local birds and record their observations in writing as well. You may want to invite guests from a local birding group to speak to the class about their hobby. The Audubon Society provides beginning birders with information about species common to their area, bird migration routes, and organized outings.

 Literature

The Audubon Society is named for John James Audubon (1785-1851), an American ornithologist and artist born in Santo Domingo (now Haiti) to a French mercantile agent and a Creole mother. In 1827, after traveling extensively observing and painting birds, Audubon published the first part of *Birds of America,* which was reprinted four times during his lifetime.

Build Writing Skills

Have groups of students prepare a presentation illustrating the types of nests built by different birds, or the differences in shape, size, and color of eggs wild birds lay. Provide time for students to share their presentations with the class.

can be seen on the bill of a sea gull are actually dried salt excretions from the bird's nostrils.

As you have learned, birds are endothermic animals that fly and, therefore, require a great deal of energy. To meet their energy needs, birds must spend a lot of their time getting food. Birds eat almost everything, from seeds and insects to fishes and small land animals.

Because their forelimbs are adapted for flight, birds must use their feet to grasp food. Many birds use their beaks to break or tear food into pieces small enough to swallow. Special adaptations enable bird species to obtain food from a variety of sources. How do you think the adaptations shown in *Figure 26.18* enable a bird to live successfully in its ❶ environment and to get food?

FIGURE 26.19
This raven is using its strong beak and sharp claws to tear apart food, which may be fed to its young later.

636 *Unit 7 Vertebrate Animals*

LIFE CYCLE
Bird families are egg-cellent

Birds spend a lot of time and energy attracting mates, building nests, and caring for their young. Like reptiles, birds reproduce by internal fertilization. They also produce amniotic eggs. However, similar to birds' respiratory and digestive systems, their reproductive system is adapted to enable flight.

During most of the year, the reproductive organs in both male and female birds are greatly reduced in size. As nesting season approaches, hormones stimulate the reproductive organs to enlarge and begin functioning. Unlike reptiles and mammals, most male birds do not have external reproductive structures. Sperm are produced in internal testes, which are surrounded by air sacs that decrease the body temperature around the testes. The females of most bird species have only one ovary and oviduct, rather than two, as reptiles and mammals do.

Internal fertilization occurs through the cloaca, an opening near the base of a bird's tail. The cloaca also serves as the opening through

❶ The raven's strong beak and sharp claws enables it to tear apart food. Its ability to fly and perch enable the crow to escape predators and travel great distances in search of food.

which body wastes are excreted. After an egg is fertilized, it travels through a passage called the oviduct, where it is coated with albumin and a hard shell of calcium carbonate. The shelled egg leaves the female through the cloaca.

The amniotic egg of birds is similar in structure to that of reptiles. The yolk in the bird egg, however, is much larger. All bird eggs contain albumin, or egg white, which provides additional nutrients to the embryo. In birds, the yolk is supported by a ropelike strand of albumin, called the **chalaza** (kuh-LAH-zuh), which connects to the chorion. You can examine the structure of the avian egg in *Figure 26.20.*

Bird eggs vary greatly in size. The smallest eggs are laid by hummingbirds. The tiniest hummingbird egg is smaller than a pea and weighs only 0.35 gram (g), about one fifth the weight of an adult. The largest egg, from an ostrich, is about the same size as a grapefruit. Weighing in at about 1.5 kg, an ostrich egg weighs about one hundredth of what an adult bird weighs. An ostrich egg is almost 4500 times heavier than a hummingbird egg.

Because birds are endothermic, their eggs must be incubated—kept at a constant, warm temperature—while an embryo develops. Birds incubate their eggs in a variety of ways. Some birds sit on nests to keep eggs warm. A male emperor penguin holds an egg on its feet and tucks it under a fold of skin on its belly. The male and female penguins take turns incubating the egg in this way for about 52 days.

Many baby birds are helpless and depend entirely on their parents for food. Some parents feed their nestlings every few minutes, making 500 trips a day in search of food. The young birds gain weight rapidly and begin to grow feathers in three or four days.

Some birds, such as robins, hatch poorly developed young. They have a well-developed digestive system, but

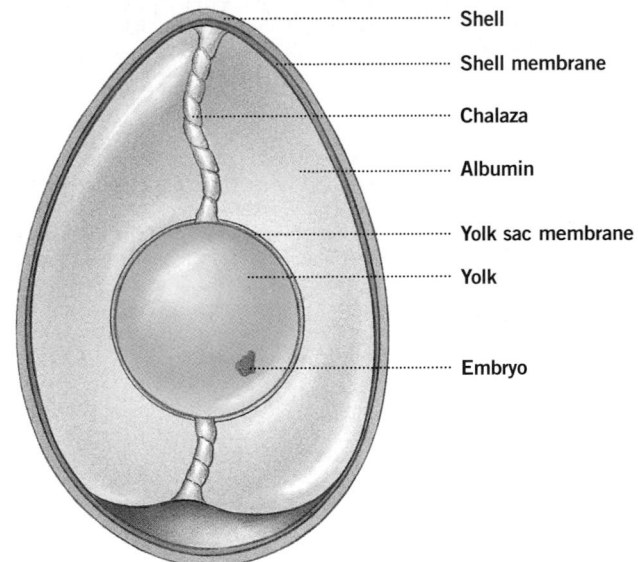

everything else is less well developed. Their eyes are still closed, and they have no feathers. In about two weeks, baby robins are fully developed and ready to leave the nest. Other birds, such as chickens, hatch well developed and covered with feathers. They can soon feed themselves and survive on their own.

FIGURE 26.20
As you can see, the structure of the avian egg is very similar to that of the reptilian egg. However, the chalaza, which anchors the yolk, is a structure not found in the reptilian egg.

CHECKPOINT 26.4

1. What are two main ways in which structural adaptations assist birds in flight?
2. Summarize the life cycle of a typical bird.
3. **Critical Thinking** Air sacs remove the excess body heat that is produced during flight. Propose a hypothesis to explain how this function is accomplished.

Build on What You Know

4. What information do bird characteristics reveal about the evolutionary relationship of crocodilians and birds? *(Need to jog your memory? Revisit relevant concepts in Chapter 26, Section 26.2.)*

Chapter 26 Reptiles and Birds **637**

Teacher Demo

Review the structure of the amniotic egg shown in Figure 26.20. Remind students of the functions of the parts of the egg. If possible, obtain photographs showing the embryonic development of a chick and discuss the changes shown in the photographs.

3 ASSESS

Evaluate Understanding

List the section objectives on the board. For each objective have students write a paragraph or create a graphic that addresses the objective. Then have students share their work with each other in small groups. Tell the groups to determine which points are common in each paragraph or graphic.

Reteach

Use the illustrations and photographs in this section to point out features of birds that suggest an evolutionary relationship to reptiles. Then have students use Figures 26.16 and 26.18 to write a summary of the structures of birds and their functions. Ask volunteers to share their summaries.

CHECKPOINT 26.4

1. They either reduce weight or increase energy efficiency.
2. The internally fertilized egg is laid and incubated at a constant, warm temperature. After hatching, the baby bird is cared for by its parents until it can survive on its own.
3. **Developing a hypothesis** Energy in the form of body heat is exchanged with cool air when the bird inhales. The heat is removed when the warmed air is exhaled.
4. Crocodilians have a four-chambered heart and care for their young, as do birds. These characteristics make crocodilians more similar to birds than to modern reptiles.

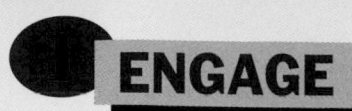

ENGAGE

Use the Visual

Have students study the photograph that opens the section. Explain that although puffins and penguins are adapted to life in cold waters, they are not the only birds adapted to life in watery environments. Ask:

- **What other birds are adapted to life in watery environments?** (Likely responses will include ducks, geese, seagulls, and possibly egrets and terns.)
- **What adaptations do these birds have to life in watery environments?** (Webbed feet for swimming; wide, flattened bills or long beaks suited to capturing water organisms)

Check Prior Knowledge

To assess students' knowledge about bird diversity, ask:

- **What different kinds of birds are common in your area?** (Students might name sea gulls, starlings, hummingbirds, robins, sparrows, and chickens.)
- **How do these birds vary?** (In size, habitat, and nest building)

Quick Activity

Obtain and display drawings of the following pterosaurs: *Dimorphodon, Pterodanstro,* and *Archaeopteryx.* Ask students to list the traits that birds share with the pterosaurs. Discuss their responses.

❶ Reptilian features include teeth and scaly skin.

26.5 Origin and Diversity of Birds

What you'll learn

IDEAS
- To summarize the differences between birds and other vertebrates
- To analyze evidence for the evolutionary origin of birds

Penguins are not the only ones
Although penguins are the polar birds most familiar to humans, they are not the only birds adapted to the intense cold of polar seas. Another seabird able to brave the polar cold is the colorful puffin. Unlike penguins, puffins can fly. But like the penguin, the puffin swims and fishes in icy water.

ORIGIN OF BIRDS

Taking to the sky

Birds probably evolved from reptiles about 225 million years ago during the Triassic period. Fossils show evolutionary links between reptiles and birds. However, the fossil record of birds is fragmented and incomplete because their feathers and fragile bones do not fossilize well.

Several species of flying reptiles known as pterosaurs lived during the Mesozoic era. Although these reptiles resembled birds in their flight and environmental niche, they were distinctly different from birds.

In 1986 a fossil of a birdlike vertebrate was found in west Texas. The chicken-sized animal was named *Protoavis,* and it lived about 225 million years ago. It had some reptilian features but also had some characteristics of birds.

The earliest fossil known to have feathers is *Archaeopteryx,* which dates back 150 million years to the Jurassic period. Because feathers are a distinguishing feature of birds, scientists usually consider *Archaeopteryx* to be the first known bird.

FIGURE 26.21
Scientists think that *Archaeopteryx* used its wings to pursue large, slow-flying insects.

However, recently discovered fossils of a small bird called *Liaoningornis,* which lived at about the same time, suggest that *Archaeopteryx* probably represents a smaller branch on the bird family tree and was not a direct ancestor of modern birds. In *Figure 26.21,* you can see that *Archaeopteryx* had reptilian as well as avian features. What reptilian features can you identify in the illustration of *Archaeopteryx?* ❶

In addition to *Archaeopteryx,* the fossil record contains several birdlike animals with various combinations of reptilian and avian features. These animals were abundant 100 million years ago during the Cretaceous period.

After the extinction of dinosaurs, birds probably evolved rapidly. They filled many habitats on land and in water and air that once were occupied by dinosaurs and flying reptiles. Some scientists hypothesize that birds evolved from reptiles that ran very fast and fed upon flying insects. Those that could leap the highest and longest had an advantage in catching the insects. Feathers probably served as an adaptation for retaining body heat. Eventually, the feathered forelimbs enabled the animals to glide and, ultimately, to fly.

638 *Unit 7 Vertebrate Animals*

STUDENT RESOURCES

From the Teacher's Resource Package, use:
- Section Review 26.5 and Interpreting Graphics 26 from Unit 7 Review Module
- Lab 48: "Bird Adaptations"

TECHNOLOGY RESOURCES

Relevant technology resources include:
- Spanish Student Edition CD-ROM
- Teacher's Resource Planner CD-ROM

FIGURE 26.22
Diversity of Birds

Falconiformes
This order includes harpy eagles (above), hawks, and vultures.

Passeriformes
This large order contains the perching birds, including cardinals (left), sparrows, swallows, and ravens.

Casuariiformes
This order includes emus (above) and cassowaries.

Podicipediformes
This order contains only grebes. A horned grebe is shown above.

Piciformes
This order includes keel-billed toucans (left), woodpeckers, barbets, and jacamars.

Ciconiiformes
This order includes great blue herons (above), storks, ibis, flamingos, and spoonbills.

DIVERSITY OF BIRDS

A bird in every bush

Birds share so many characteristics with reptiles that some scientists think birds should be classified as an order of reptiles. Birds, however, are distinctly different from reptiles and other vertebrates in many ways. Birds are the only animals that have feathers. They are also the only vertebrates, except for bats, that can fly.

Birds make up a very diverse class of vertebrates called Aves. They range in size from the 6-cm Cuban bee hummingbird weighing 2 g to the 2.5-m ostrich weighing 136 kg. Among the largest flying birds are the Andean and California condors. They weigh about 11 kg and have a wingspan of 3 m.

At least 9000 different species of birds are alive today. They live high in trees, on the ground, and even on buildings. Birds eat seeds, insects, fruit, and small animals. Because of their number and diversity, it is difficult for taxonomists to classify birds. By using differences in body structure, beak structure, foot structure, behavior, and song, taxonomists have divided birds into 27 different orders. Some taxonomists divide birds into even more orders.

Some representative bird orders are listed and shown in *Figure* 26.22. Perching songbirds have the greatest range of adaptations and live in nearly every environment. Perching songbirds account for 60 percent of all avian species. Grebes are classified in their own order. These highly specialized diving birds use their streamlined bodies and lobed toes to swim underwater in search of prey.

CHECKPOINT 26.5

1. Name two characteristics that distinguish birds from other kinds of vertebrates.
2. Explain one hypothesis for the evolutionary origin of birds.
3. **Critical Thinking** Use Figure 26.22 to compare the orders Passeriformes and Ciconiiformes.

Build on What You Know

4. Why do feathers and fragile bones not fossilize well? *(Need to jog your memory? Revisit relevant concepts in Chapter 10, Section 10.1.)*

Chapter 26 Reptiles and Birds **639**

2 TEACH

Use the Visual
Have students study Figure 26.22. Discuss with students how the features of the birds, especially the shape of their beak and feet, are adaptations for their lifestyle.

3 ASSESS

Evaluate Understanding
Have students create a time line showing the evolutionary steps that may have led to modern birds. Check students' work for accuracy.

Reteach
Work with students to list the evolutionary steps that led to modern birds. Then have students work with partners to create a visual showing how birds are similar to and different from other vertebrates. Have pairs of students exchange graphics and check each other's work for accuracy.

CHECKPOINT 26.5
1. Birds have feathers and, except for bats, are the only vertebrates that can truly fly.
2. One hypothesis is that birds evolved from reptiles that ran very fast and fed upon flying insects. Those reptiles with adaptations enabling them to stay in the air longer would have a selective advantage over others.
3. **Comparing** Passeriformes contains the small to medium-sized perching birds. Ciconiiformes includes the wading birds, which are characterized by long, slender legs.
4. They often decompose or are broken before they have a chance to become preserved as fossils.

1 ENGAGE

Use the Visual

Have students study the photograph and read the text that opens the section. Explain that vultures are considered decomposers because they feed on dead animals. Ask:

- **What other organisms perform a similar ecological role as vultures?** (Likely responses will include bacteria and fungi.)

Check Prior Knowledge

To assess students' knowledge about birds and the biosphere, ask:

- **What are some contributions birds make to the environment?** (They are scavengers and provide food, spread seeds and pollen, eat pests, and are sometimes used as couriers.)

Teacher Demo

Obtain and display pictures of male and female birds of the same species that exhibit vast differences in coloring. Identify the males and females in each picture. Ask:

- **What feature most distinguishes the male from the female bird?** (Likely responses will indicate that the males are more brightly colored.)

❶ The sharp spines of the cacti and the thorns on the bushes help keep predators away from the nests.

640

26.6 Birds in the Biosphere

What you'll learn

IDEAS
- To explain the roles that birds play in ecosystems
- To compare courtship behavior in birds

What do vultures eat?
Vultures feed only on dead animals. They sometimes spend a great amount of time searching for a meal. They circle at heights up to 3500 m and locate food with their incredibly sharp eyesight. Some vultures can spot a dead animal from more than 1.6 km away. Vultures play an important role in many different food chains.

ECOLOGICAL ROLES

The appetite of a bird

Birds play many important roles in the environment. Some birds, such as hummingbirds, are important pollinators of plants. Birds are also important in the dispersal of seeds. Many birds eat ripe fruits from trees and bushes. The seeds from the fruit pass undamaged through the birds' digestive systems. As the birds fly, they disperse the seeds from place to place.

Birds also have roles in all levels of a food chain. Many live entirely off the seeds and fruits of plants. Birds also eat large numbers of insects—sometimes thousands in a single night! This helps to control the populations of insect pests, such as mosquitoes and

FIGURE 26.23
The cactus wren builds its nest on the side of cacti or thorny bushes. How might this location help protect the young shown here? ❶

grasshoppers. As you have read, birds such as vultures feed on dead animals.

Eagles, owls, and hawks are predators, birds of prey, feeding on fishes, reptiles, amphibians, small mammals, and even other birds. Birds in turn are preyed upon by many different animals, including snakes, lizards, and mammals.

BIRD BEHAVIOR

Public displays of attraction

Compared with reptiles, birds have large brains in relation to their body size. Areas of the brain that control flight and flight-related activities are highly developed. Also well developed are the areas of the brain that control complex reproductive behaviors, such as nest building, mating, singing, and caring for young. These complex behaviors are not learned. They are instinctive, or inborn, behaviors. Some of these instincts, however, may be modified by experience.

Have you ever been awakened in the morning by singing birds? Bird songs play a very important role in mating. When mating season begins, males establish a territory and defend it from other males. Perching birds, such as robins and red-winged blackbirds, use song to establish and defend their territories. When females arrive

640 *Unit 7 Vertebrate Animals*

STUDENT RESOURCES

From the Teacher's Resource Package, use:
- Section Review 26.6, Enrichment Topics 26-3 and 26-4, Vocabulary Review 26, and Chapter 26 Tests from Unit 7 Review Module
- Issues and Decision Making 26-2
- Consumer Applications 26-2

TECHNOLOGY RESOURCES

Relevant technology resources include:
- Spanish Student Edition CD-ROM
- Teacher's Resource Planner CD-ROM
- Biology Alive! Videos: "The Continuity of Life," "Conflict and Cooperation," and "Life's Fragile Balance"
- TestWorks CD-ROM: Chapter 26 Tests

in the area, they are attracted to the males of their species by song.

Most courtship behaviors have evolved to help a female find and select mature males of her own species. To attract a female, male peacocks and turkeys spread their brightly colored tail feathers and parade around the females. Male bower birds build elaborate nests of many different sizes and shapes, then decorate them with flowers and fruit or even coins, ribbons, and jewelry that they find. The male frigate bird attracts a female by inflating a large, red throat pouch to the size of a soccer ball. It then throws back its head, lets out a piercing cry, and shakes its wings.

In most species of birds, once a male and female are attracted to each other and mate, they stay together as a pair for the rest of the breeding season. Some species remain a pair for a much longer period of time. The eagle, for example, mates for life.

Birds build nests in which they lay their eggs and protect their young. They build their nests from just about anything they can find, including mud, leaves, animal hair, moss, string, and paper. Some birds even decorate their nests with brightly colored buttons and bits of aluminum foil. Others make their nests in almost any available shelter, even an empty tin can or abandoned flowerpot.

Nesting behavior differs from species to species. Eagles return to the same nests year after year. The twig nests they build can grow to an enormous size, sometimes measuring 3 m wide and 7 m high, and weighing 275 kg. Baltimore orioles have distinctive baglike nests that hang from branches. Weaverbirds are able to tie knots using their beaks and feet. They use this skill to build elaborate tunnel-like or bell-shaped nests.

Many birds remain in the same location year-round. Other birds make

FIGURE 26.24
Courtship, nest building, and migration are examples of complex, instinctive behavior. These photographs all show birds displaying inborn behavior (clockwise from right): the masked weaverbird building a nest, geese migrating in formation, and the courtship display of the male frigate bird.

yearly migrations in the spring and fall. In the Northern Hemisphere, birds generally fly north in the spring to their breeding grounds. In the winter, they fly south to warmer weather and their winter feeding grounds. The rufous hummingbird, for example, travels nearly 4000 km (2500 miles) from Alaska to Central America every fall and returns in the spring by the same route.

Scientists are still studying the perplexing question of how birds find their way over such long distances. Research shows that birds navigate in a number of ways. Some birds use landmarks such as rivers, mountains, and coastlines, or monitor Earth's magnetic field. Others navigate by the position of stars, while those that migrate in flocks follow their neighbors.

HUMAN USES

Pass the poultry

Humans use birds in many different ways. Birds have been an important food source for humans for thousands of years. Their meat is high in protein and usually low in fat. Around the world, people hunt or raise chickens, turkeys, ducks, geese, pheasants, and guinea

EVERYDAY BIOLOGY

Birds Re-tern

Arctic terns migrate farther than any other bird. A few weeks after it hatches in June, a tern chick leaves its nest in Greenland on its yearly migration. It flies 18,000 km to the South Pole where it spends the summer. It returns to Greenland the following spring—a round trip of 36,000 km!

2 TEACH

Teacher Demo

If possible, show students a movie or videotape on the various courtship rituals that have been observed in birds. At the conclusion of the film, discuss the importance of courtship rituals.

Think Critically

Male birds will establish and defend a territory before they begin attracting a mate. Ask:

- **What is the adaptive advantage of this behavior?** (Food for the young must be collected from the territory. By claiming and defending a territory before seeking a mate, the male ensures that the young will have a supply of food.)

Everyday Biology

Trace the route of arctic terns on a globe or world map. Have students convert the number of kilometers to miles.

Literature

The albatross was an important bird in the novel *Moby Dick* by Herman Melville. You may wish to have students research the habits of the albatross and the folklore presented in the novel.

MULTICULTURAL PERSPECTIVE

Their beauty, bright colors, and ability to imitate human sounds make parrots attractive pets. Most parrots captured for sale in the pet trade come from tropical rain forest regions of South America and Africa. In some cases, so many birds have been removed from their native lands that their species are in danger of extinction. Many countries now forbid importing parrots as pets. Instead, birds to be kept as pets must be bred by people and hand raised.

LAB ZONE **Think About It!**

Analyzing Bird Migratory Routes

Analyzing the Map

1 Not all raptors migrate the same distance each year.
2 Factors may include: availability of food and roots; environmental disturbances such as urban development; and natural geographical features, such as mountains and rivers.
3 Recognizable geographic features that may help a raptor recognize its migration route include: mountains, valleys, rivers, and oceans.

Evaluate Understanding

To assess students' understanding of the section, ask:

■ **What role do birds play in the food chain?** (Students should note that birds play roles in all levels of the food chain.)

Reteach

On the board, draw a large "T" with the head *Ecological Roles* on one side and *Importance to Humans* on the other. Have volunteers suggest what information should be listed below each head to explain the roles of birds in the biosphere.

LAB ZONE **Think About It!**   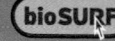 **bioSURF**

Analyzing Bird Migratory Routes

Many species of migratory birds use the same routes, or flyways, to travel to new habitats in the winter and the spring. The map below shows migration flyways used by some North American raptors, such as sharp-shinned hawks and Cooper's hawks.

Analyzing the Map

1 Judging from the flyways represented on the map, do all raptors in North America migrate the same distance each year?
2 What are some of the environmental factors that might determine the paths of such flyways?
3 What are some of the geographical features that may assist a young raptor in recognizing its migration route?
4 Choose one of the routes shown below. Using an atlas, estimate the number of miles in that route.

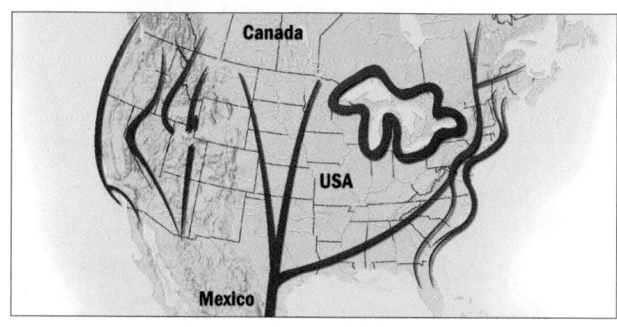

---

fowl for meat. They also raise ducks, chickens, and geese for their eggs.

Humans also use other products of some birds that live in the wild. Certain families in Iceland, for example, have tended flocks of wild geese called eiders for thousands of years. The families collect the birds' down feathers for use in pillows, comforters, and clothing. These soft feathers provide excellent insulation. When the eiders come to nest on a group of

small, rocky islands, the Icelanders remove the down with which the birds line their nests. The female geese simply replace the down lining and raise their young without further interference.

Humans also wear jewelry and clothing decorated with colorful bird feathers. Many people enjoy birds as pets. They are attracted by the birds' brightly colored feathers, by their songs, and in some cases by their ability to imitate the sound of a human voice. Many tropical birds, such as parrots, are illegally trapped and sold as pets. The collection, export, and sale of these birds are regulated by law, but these laws are often difficult to enforce. When purchasing a parrot or other tropical bird for a pet, make sure it was bred in captivity for that purpose.

Over many years humans have come to appreciate birds for their beauty, flight, and song. Many bird-watchers use bird feeders to attract birds so they can watch them up close.

CHECKPOINT 26.6

1. What roles do birds play in ecosystems around the world?
2. Compare the courtship behaviors of two bird species.
3. Critical Thinking In bird species in which the males and females look exactly alike, each sex usually has very distinct and unique courtship rituals. How are these rituals advantageous to each sex?

Build on What You Know

4. How do the behaviors of birds compare with the corresponding behaviors of insects? *(Need to jog your memory? Revisit relevant concepts in Chapter 23, Section 23.4.)*

? **How was the evolution of feathers a favorable adaptation for birds?**

CHECKPOINT 26.6

1. Birds pollinate flowers, disperse seeds, and act as predators and prey.
2. Answers may include a peacock displaying tail feathers, a frigate bird inflating the throat pouch, or a grebe offering a fish and dancing
3. Developing a hypothesis They help individuals distinguish between members of the same and opposite sex. Early recognition of the sex of a potential mate saves time and energy, which can be used searching for a useful mate.
4. Both birds and insects exhibit behaviors that attract mates, defend territories, protect themselves, and increase their survival and reproductive success.

Chapter 26 Review

 **THE BIG IDEA!** 26.1–26.3 Reptiles represent the first vertebrates with adaptations that enable them to live their entire lives out of water.

26.4–26.6 With the development of feathers, birds were the first vertebrates able to maintain a constant body temperature.

Sum It Up

Use the following summary to review the main concepts in this chapter.

26.1 Characteristics of Reptiles

- Water-resistant skin helps reptiles conserve water. Reptile body structure allows quick movement on land.
- Reptiles have efficient lungs and water-conserving urinary bladders, and most have hearts with three chambers.
- Amniotic eggs, which are fertilized internally, provide nourishment and protection for embryos.

26.2 Origin and Diversity of Reptiles

- Reptiles may have evolved from amphibians or from lobe-finned fishes. Extinct reptiles include the dinosaurs, which were dominant during the Mesozoic era.
- Chelonians—turtles and tortoises—have protective shells.
- Snakes and lizards live in most land and water habitats.
- Crocodilians are more like dinosaurs or birds than they are like modern reptiles.

26.3 Reptiles in the Biosphere

- Reptiles are both predators and prey.
- Reptiles have a range of adaptations for combating predators and finding mates.
- Many reptiles are endangered because their flesh, shells, and skins are considered valuable.

26.4 Characteristics of Birds

- Adaptations for flight either reduce body weight or make the body more aerodynamic.
- Birds have four-chambered hearts, and lungs through which air flows in one direction.
- Birds eat large amounts of food to fuel flight and maintain a constant body temperature.
- Birds expend energy on mating, building nests, incubating eggs, and caring for young.

26.5 Origin and Diversity of Birds

- Birds evolved from a reptilian ancestor.
- Feathers and flight distinguish the diverse avian species from other vertebrates.

26.6 Birds in the Biosphere

- Birds pollinate flowers, disperse seeds, control insect pests, and serve as predators and prey.
- Many male birds attract mates with songs, displays, or by building physical structures.
- Many birds make seasonal migrations.
- Humans use birds as food and for their feathers.

Use Terms and Concepts

Use each of the following words or terms in a complete sentence. If you need to review a meaning, turn to the page indicated.

amniotic egg (p. 622)
yolk (p. 622)
chorion (p. 623)
crop (p. 634)
gizzard (p. 634)
chalaza (p. 637)

Chapter 26 Reptiles and Birds **643**

Review the Big Ideas

Before students begin the Chapter Review, you may wish to discuss main concepts from the Big Ideas in Chapter 26. Point out that reptiles were the first animals able to live their entire lives on land. With the adaptation of feathers that insulate the body, birds became endothermic, generating and maintaining a constant internal body temperature. Reproduction on land for both reptiles and birds became possible with the adaptation of an amniotic egg, which provides a protective environment for developing offspring.

Answers

1. gizzard
2. yolk
3. crop
4. chorion
5. chalaza
6. amniotic egg
7. False; crop
8. True
9. True
10. False; reptiles
11. True
12. True
13. A drier climate favored niches for reptiles over niches for amphibians.
14. They both contain waterproof keratin; both snakes and birds molt.
15. Hollow bones are lighter; fused bones are more stable and require fewer heavy ligaments; larger bones have cross struts for support.
16. Gases used and produced during cellular respiration must be exchanged through pores in the shell.
17. The chorions of birds, turtles, and crocodiles all contain albumin.
18. Oxygen-rich air continues to flow into a bird's lungs as it exhales oxygen-poor air. This system is more efficient than a two-way respiratory system.
19. Sense organs on the tongue help detect prey; a hinged jaw helps with ingestion of large prey; the three-chambered heart and well-developed lungs support efficient cellular respiration; an absence of legs increases mobility.
20. Anoles change color as camouflage against predators; male anoles display colorful frills to attract mates.
21. Contour feathers are used on apparel as decoration;

Use Your Word Power

COMPLETION Write the word or phrase that best completes each statement.

1. A(n) _____ has muscular walls for grinding food.
2. The food source for the developing reptile embryo is the _____ .
3. In the digestive system of birds, food is stored in the _____ .
4. The membrane that surrounds the embryo, yolk, and allantois is called the _____ .
5. The _____ is a strand of tissue that supports the egg yolk in a bird's egg.
6. The two functions of the _____ are nourishment and protection of the embryo.

TRUE-FALSE Write true if the statement is true. If the statement is false, replace the underlined word(s) to make the statement true.

7. Some birds can regurgitate food stored in the gizzard to feed their young.
8. The yolks of bird eggs are, on average, larger than those of reptile eggs.
9. Food is mixed with digestive enzymes and ground to a pulp in the gizzard.
10. The evolution of an amniotic egg occurred first in birds.
11. In bird eggs, the chalaza is a ropelike strand of tissue that supports the yolk.
12. The chorion is the outermost membrane in an amniotic egg.

Show What You Know

13. How was the evolution of reptiles affected by a decrease in precipitation?
14. What do snake skins and bird feathers have in common?
15. What characteristics of a bird's skeleton are adaptation for flight?

16. Why must an eggshell be porous?
17. What do the eggs of turtles, crocodiles, and birds have in common?
18. What is the advantage of a one-way flow of air through a bird's respiratory system?
19. Which adaptations of snakes make them efficient carnivores? Explain the contribution made by each adaptation.
20. Describe two situations in which anole lizards use coloration to their advantage.
21. What use have humans made of contour feathers? What use have they made of down feathers?
22. **Make a Concept Map** Construct a concept map that compares reptiles and birds using the following terms: amnion, bird, chorion, ectotherm, egg, endotherm, feathers, reptile, scales, yolk.

Take It Further

23. **Developing a Hypothesis** A hummingbird flaps its wings about 80 times per minute, on average. Why is it advantageous for a hummingbird to eat foods such as nectar and fruit, which contain simple sugars?
24. **Applying Concepts** Some birds rarely fly. But most birds spend a lot of time in the air. List at least four situations in which a bird might take to the air.
25. **Making an Analogy** Migrating birds often fly in a formation that saves energy. Explain how this strategy works by comparing it to similar strategies used by long-distance runners or bicycle racers.
26. **Designing an Experiment** In New Zealand, black-billed gulls raise their young in crowded, often noisy colonies on dry stream beds. Design an experiment to find out whether young gulls can recognize the calls of their parents when the parents return to the colony with food.

down feathers are used as insulation in clothing and quilts.

22. Concept maps should show the following: Amniotic egg has a chorion that surrounds amnion and yolk; amniotic egg is characteristic of reptiles (which are ectotherms and have scales) and birds (which are endotherms and have feathers).

23. Simple sugars can be converted to energy more readily than most other kinds of food.
24. To escape predators; to find food for itself or offspring; to migrate; to collect materials for a nest; to court a mate; to establish a territory
25. Drafting, or moving behind someone else, is a common technique in racing.

27. Interpreting Graphs The graph below compares the body temperature of a lizard to the air and burrow temperatures during the daytime. Describe what happens to the temperature of the burrow, the air temperature, and the lizard's body temperature between sunrise and sunset. When is the lizard likely to be in its burrow? In the sun? In the shade?

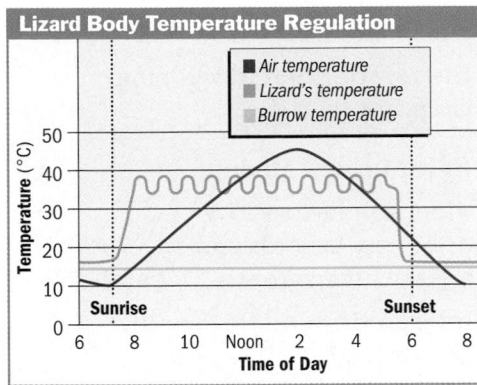

Lizard Body Temperature Regulation

- ■ Air temperature
- ■ Lizard's temperature
- ■ Burrow temperature

Temperature (°C) / Time of Day — Sunrise / Sunset

28. Analyzing Data The table below shows Nile crocodiles and the animals that were found in their stomachs. The crocodiles are grouped by size. What is the most common food source for each group? What is the relationship between size of crocodile and size of prey?

Percentage of Crocodiles Eating Food Sources

Animals	Group A 0.3–0.5 m	Group B 2.5–3.0 m	Group C 4.5–5.0 m
Mammals	0%	18%	65%
Reptiles	0%	17%	48%
Fish	0%	62%	38%
Birds	0%	17%	0%
Snails	0%	25%	0%
Shellfish	0%	5%	0%
Spiders	20%	0%	0%
Frogs	35%	0%	0%
Insects	100%	2%	0%

Consider the Issues

29. No Admittance Sometimes human activities are restricted to protect other species. For example, some beaches where plovers nest are closed to the public during breeding season. Off-road vehicles are a common target of regulation. Do you support restrictions on the use of dune buggies, motorbikes, or skimobiles? What other alternatives exist? Explain your position.

Make New Connections

30. Biology and Art Many governments have issued postage or commemorative stamps that feature birds. Design a stamp that highlights a native bird from your region.

31. Biology and History A bird's ability to fly has often stirred the human imagination. Starting about 500 years ago with Leonardo da Vinci, inventors have made detailed observations of birds in order to understand the mechanics of flight. Report on one of the following people: Leonardo da Vinci, Sir George Cayley, Otto Lilienthal, Louis-Pierre Mouillard, or Etienne-Jules Marey. How did observations of birds contribute to each inventor's undestanding of flight?

32. Biology and Social Studies Reptiles or reptile-like figures have played a prominent role in the traditions of many cultures for many years. Investigate one example and decide which physical or behavioral traits of reptiles might have inspired the tradition.

FAST-FORWARD TO CHAPTER 27

Birds are not the only endotherms. In the next chapter, you will find out how mammals are similar to and different from other kinds of vertebrates.

35° C all day. The lizard is likely to be in its burrow before sunrise and after sunset; in the sun in the early morning and late afternoon; in the shade at midday.

28. Insects for A, fish for B, and mammals for C; the larger the crocodile the larger the prey

29. Students may want to find out what local restrictions, if any, exist.

30. Students may want to survey existing bird stamps to see how artists have responded to the artistic challenges of the assignment.

31. Answers will vary, depending on the person chosen.

32. Possible choices include: St. George and the dragon; Sobek, the crocodile-headed Egyptian deity, or Buto, the cobra goddess of Lower Egypt; Chinese dragons; the Aztec image of a reptile carrying the world on its back; Mayan rain and earth deities, which blended features of snakes and crocodiles; rattlesnakes in Native American folklore and dance; the serpent deities of aboriginal India.

Chapter 26 Reptiles and Birds **645**

The strategy lessens the exposure of the one behind to the force of wind resistance. The one in the lead runs into the wind and must overcome the resistance. Teammates may alternate being the front-runner just as birds do when flying in formation.

26. Students could record the parents' voices and play them back through a loudspeaker. Within a few days after birth, the young gulls should be able to recognize their parents' voices and get the food.

27. The burrow temperature remains constant at about 25°C. Air temperature rises gradually to about 45°C at 2 P.M. and then drops gradually. The lizard maintains a body temperature of about

Section	Student Activities/Features	Teacher's Resource Package
27.1 Characteristics of Mammals **Objectives** ■ Identify characteristics of mammals ■ Compare monotremes, marsupials, and placental mammals	**Lab Zone Discover It!** *Mammalian Preschool,* p. 647 **Everyday Biology** *Whole or Skim,* p. 651 **Lab Zone Do It!** *How Does Mammal Hair Vary?* p. 652 **Lab Zone Investigate It!** *Comparing Skeletons,* p. 653	**Unit 7 Review Module** ■ Section Review 27.1 ■ Activity Recordsheets 27-1 and 27-2 ■ Interpreting Graphics 27 ■ Critical Thinking Exercise 27 **Laboratory Manual,** Lab 49: "Mammalian Brains" **Interpreting and Developing Graphics** 79, 80
27.2 Origin and Diversity of Mammals **Objectives** ■ Describe the evolution of mammals ■ Compare the three orders of mammals	**Lab Zone Do It!** *Is Whale Blubber an Effective Insulator?* p. 658	**Unit 7 Review Module** ■ Section Review 27.2 ■ Activity Recordsheet 27-3 ■ Enrichment Topics 27-1 and 27-2 **Interpreting and Developing Graphics** 81
27.3 Mammals in the Biosphere **Objectives** ■ Identify the roles of mammals in the biosphere ■ Explain the interactions of humans and other mammals	**Lab Zone Think About It!** *Comparing the Gestation Periods of Various Mammals,* p. 661 **In the Community** *Cataloging Mammals,* p. 662 **STS: Frontiers in Biology** *Living in a Mammalian World,* p. 662 **Everyday Biology** *Monkey Help,* p. 662	**Unit 7 Review Module** ■ Section Review 27.3 ■ Vocabulary Review 27 ■ Chapter 27 Tests **Issues and Decision Making** 27-1 **Consumer Applications** 27-1 **Spanish Reviews** Chapter 27

Technology Resources

Internet Connections

Within this chapter, you will see the **bioSURF** logo. If you and your students have access to the Internet, the following URL address will provide various Internet connections that are related to topics and features presented in this chapter:

http://vertebrates.biosurf.com

You can also find relevant chapter material at **The Biology Place** address:

http://www.biology.com

CD-ROMs

Biología: la telaraña de la vida,
   (Spanish Student Edition) Chapter 27
Teacher's Resource Planner, Chapter 27
   Supplements
TestWorks CD-ROM
■ Chapter 27 Tests

Overhead Transparencies

■ Mammalian Teeth, #59

Videotapes

Biology Alive! Video Series
■ Signs of Life Video
■ Conflict and Cooperation Video
■ Life's Fragile Balance Video
Rewind: The Web of Life Reteach Videos

Planning for Activities

STUDENT EDITION
Lab Zone
Discover It! p. 647
  ■ litter of kittens, puppies, or other mammals (or a videotape)

Lab Zone Do It! p. 652
  ■ mammals with hair

Lab Zone
Investigate It! p. 653
  ■ three skeletons, or diagrams of skeletons, labeled *A, B,* and *C*

Lab Zone Do It! p. 658
  ■ test tubes
  ■ thermometers
  ■ warm water
  ■ vegetable shortening or animal lard
  ■ small plastic bags
  ■ larger beaker filled with ice water
  ■ timer

TEACHER'S EDITION
Quick Activity, p. 648
Identifying mammals
  ■ pictures of vertebrate animals labeled with their names

Quick Activity, p. 654
Comparing a shrew to an eozostrodon
  ■ photographs of a shrew

Class Activity, p. 657
Observing placental mammals
  ■ trip to a zoo
  ■ maps of the world

Chapter Objectives

Students will learn the main concepts of this chapter as they complete the following objectives.

- Identify characteristics of mammals
- Compare monotremes, marsupials, and placental mammals
- Describe the evolution of mammals
- Compare the three orders of mammals
- Identify the roles of mammals in the biosphere
- Explain the interactions of humans and other mammals

Key Words

27.1: *mammal, mammary glands, diaphragm, monotreme, marsupials, placental mammals, gestation period*

The Opening Story

Have students read the opening story and discuss how they think the story relates to the content in this chapter. Ask students to identify other types of mammals that are similar in behavior to the cheetahs.

CHAPTER 27
Mammals

You can find out more about mammals by exploring the following Internet address: *http://vertebrates.biosurf.com*

In this chapter . . .

FEATURES

Everyday Biology
- Whole or Skim
- Monkey Help

In the Community
Cataloging Mammals

 Frontiers in Biology
Living in a Mammalian World

LAB ZONES

Discover It!
- Mammalian Preschool

Do It!
- How Does Mammal Hair Vary?
- Is Whale Blubber an Effective Insulator?

Think About It!
- Comparing the Gestation Periods of Various Mammals

Investigate It!
- Comparing Skeletons

646   *Unit 7 Vertebrate Animals*

Fast Food

A streak of furred lightning crosses the African savanna at more than 100 kilometers (km) per hour. A clawed limb slashes at a gazelle's hindquarters and the unlucky animal is grabbed by the throat. A cheetah, the fastest land animal in the world, has just caught a family meal.

Although cheetahs have a number of unique adaptations, they share mammalian characteristics such as the prolonged nurturing behavior that accompanies the development of mammary glands and milk. A cheetah mother lives with her cubs and helps feed them for nearly two years, teaching them hunting skills and licking their faces clean after meals. Cheetah mothers are extremely protective, moving their cubs frequently to keep them safe.

Mammals thrive in many different environments and may have many diverse adaptations, such as the cheetah's speedy hunting. What other characteristics unite—and separate—different types of mammals?

 **Discover It!**

Mammalian Preschool

You need to observe an active litter of kittens, puppies, or other mammals (a videotape will do).

1. Observe and list the interactions taking place among these youngsters. How would you distinguish between play and interactions that are not play? Are some clearly play and others not?

2. See if you can determine whether one youngster is clearly dominant and another clearly at the bottom of the "pecking order."

The play of young animals such as kittens and puppies often reflects behaviors that they would need to survive in the wild. Kittens will stalk toys or other kittens before pouncing on them as they would on prey. Puppies spend a lot of time mock fighting, an activity that would prepare them for their place in the pack hierarchy. And all young animals learn appeasement gestures—cringing, lowered posture—to ward off attack by other members of their species.

WRITE ABOUT IT!

Write a story or poem from the perspective of one of the young animals you observed.

Chapter 27 Mammals **647**

Opening Activities

 If you have access to the Internet in your classroom or school, you may wish to have students connect to the address shown on page 646. You may also want to have students conduct net searches for information using key words related to this chapter. For example, they could search for entries under cheetahs, primates, manatees, or zoology.

 Discover It!

Mammalian Preschool

TEAM WORK

If possible, arrange a class trip to a nearby pet store or a zoo so that students can observe mammalian behavior firsthand. Also ask students who have kittens or puppies as pets to share their observations.

WRITE ABOUT IT!

Suggest that students focus on the observations the animal might make about the humans visiting a zoo, or a pet's view of its typical day. Have volunteers read their stories aloud.

REWIND to Chapter 26

Briefly review concepts learned in Chapter 26, *Reptiles and Birds.* Ask:

■ **What characteristics and adaptations of reptiles and birds do you think are also present in mammals? What characteristics are unique to mammals?**

PORTFOLIO PREVIEW

Students should be encouraged to add to their portfolios as they work through this chapter. In addition to the *Write About It* opportunity, the following section offers an opportunity for portfolio entries:

■ Section 27.2: *Origin and Diversity of Mammals*

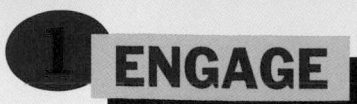

ENGAGE

Consider the Big Idea

Have students read The Big Idea! at the top of the page. Ask students to use the characteristics cited to give examples of animals that are mammals.

Use the Visual

Have students study the photograph and read the text that opens the section. Explain that humans differ from most mammals because they do not move their outer ears in the direction of a sound. Ask:

- **Do you think a dog or a human is more likely to have acute hearing? Why?** (A dog, because of its ability to help direct sound to the inner ear)

- **How is your ability to hear affected when you cup your hand behind your ear?** (Hearing improves; sounds are louder.)

Quick Activity

Display pictures of vertebrate animals, such as reptiles, birds, and mammals. Label each picture with the name of the animal. Have students study the pictures and identify the animals they think are mammals. Ask:

- **What traits do the animals you identified as mammals have in common?** (Presence of hair and possibly mammary glands) Review students' responses and correct any inaccurate information.

THE BIG IDEA! Although different species have unique adaptations, all mammals are endothermic vertebrates with hair and mammary glands. 27.1–27.2

27.1 Characteristics of Mammals

What you'll learn

IDEAS
- To identify characteristics of mammals
- To compare monotremes, marsupials, and placental mammals

WORDS
mammal, mammary glands, diaphragm, monotreme, marsupials, placental mammals, gestation period

FIGURE 27.1
Shrews such as the pygmy shrew (below) must eat continually throughout the day to satisfy their high energy requirements. Without food, a shrew can starve to death in as little as three hours.

The better to hear you
Many mammals, such as the kit fox (right), have large, well-developed outer ears that help direct sound to the inner ear. You have probably seen dogs perk up their ears when they hear something. Dogs and many other mammals can also move their ears in the direction of the sound. The ability to move the outer ear helps mammals locate the source of a sound with greater accuracy.

WHAT IS A MAMMAL?

Hairy animals drink milk

Mammals belong to the class Mammalia. A **mammal** is an endothermic vertebrate with hair. Female mammals have specialized glands called mammary glands, from which mammals get their name. The **mammary glands** secrete milk that nourishes the young.

Scientists have identified and described approximately 4500 species of mammals living on Earth. Familiar mammals include cats, dogs, horses, cows, and humans. The smallest mammal is the pygmy shrew, shown in *Figure 27.1*. It is about 8 centimeters (cm) long and weighs less than a dime. The largest mammal is the blue whale. It can reach 30 meters (m) in length and weigh 100,000 kilograms (kg)—as much as 32 adult elephants!

Mammals live in almost every environment on Earth, from cold arctic regions to hot, dry deserts. Many mammalian adaptations are associated with maintaining body temperature. Hair and body size, for example, affect heat loss. Mammals that live in warm climates are generally smaller than their cold-climate relatives. Their smaller size enables them to lose heat quickly. Also, mammals that live in warm climates usually have thinner coats of hair and layers of fat than mammals that live in cold climates.

MOVEMENT AND RESPONSE

Run, swim, and fly

Land mammals move at different speeds, from very slow to very fast. The slowest mammal is the South American two-toed sloth. Active for only about four hours each day, the sloth moves through trees at the speed of about 1 m every 15 seconds. In contrast, the cheetah, shown on pages 646 and 647, and in *Figure 27.2*, can cover 400 m in the same amount of time. The cheetah is the fastest land animal. The fastest humans run about 150 m in about 15 seconds.

The basic structure of the mammalian skeleton enables high-speed running. The long legs and flexible hip and shoulder joints of most mammals have a wider range of motion than

648 *Unit 7 Vertebrate Animals*

STUDENT RESOURCES

From the Teacher's Resource Package, use:
- Section Review 27.1, Activity Recordsheets 27-1 and 27-2, Interpreting Graphics 27, and Critical Thinking Exercise 27 from Unit 7 Module
- Lab 49: "Mammalian Brains"

 **TECHNOLOGY RESOURCES**

Relevant technology resources include:
- Spanish Student Edition CD-ROM
- Teacher's Resource Planner CD-ROM
- Biology Alive! Video: "Signs of Life"

FIGURE 27.2

The cheetah's long, stream-lined body structure allows it to achieve speeds of more than 100 km per hour. But the cheetah can maintain this level of exertion for only a few hundred meters. How are the cheetah's limbs adapted for running? **❶**

TEACH

Clarify Misconceptions

Students often classify whales as fishes. Explain that although whales live in aquatic environments, they lack gills and scales. Instead, whales have lungs and a body covering of hair. Females give birth to and nurse their young. These traits are used to classify whales as mammals. Point out that dolphins and porpoises are types of whales and also are mammals.

those of other vertebrates. This enables mammals to take long, rapid strides. Similarly, other modifications allow many types of mammals to move quickly in different environments. For example, the skeleton of a whale is modified for swimming, and the skeleton of a bat is modified for flying.

As a group, mammals have the largest and most well-developed brains in the animal kingdom. The largest part of the brain, called the cerebrum, processes information that makes thinking and learning possible. You will learn more about the brain's functions in Chapter 34.

In many mammals the organs of taste, smell, sight, and hearing are structurally similar to those of humans. The sensitivity of these organs, however, varies between mammalian orders. The sense of smell is more

developed in meat eaters such as cheetahs and dogs. The sense of hearing also varies. Many mammals, including dogs and bats, can detect higher-frequency sound waves than humans can.

Most mammals have good eyesight but do not see colors well. Underground mammals, such as moles, have poor vision. They sense their environment through smell and touch.

ENERGY AND WASTES

What big teeth you have

As you may recall from Chapter 26, endotherms require large amounts of food to generate the energy they need to maintain a constant body temperature. Specialized teeth, such as those shown in *Figure 27.3*, are an adaptation that helps mammals meet their

Use the Visual

Have students study Figure 27.3. As a class, review the types of teeth shown and their functions. Ask:

- **Dogs and cats have large, well-developed canines. What does this suggest about their diet?** (They are able to tear apart meat; they are carnivores.)
- **Cows and horses have small canines and well-developed premolars and molars. What does this suggest about their diet?** (They chew on plants; they are herbivores.)

FIGURE 27.3

The size, shape, and type of teeth are modified according to a mammal's diet. What adaptations can be seen in the herbivore's skull that reflect its diet? **❷**

Carnivore

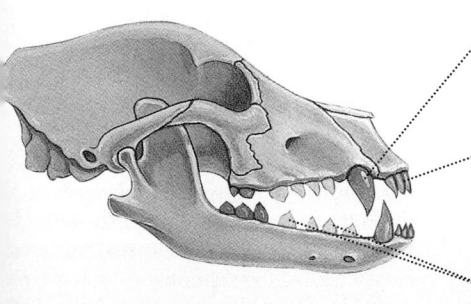

Herbivore

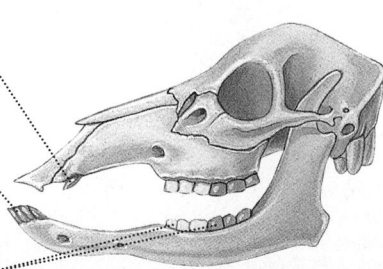

Canines are long, pointed teeth used for piercing and tearing.

Incisors are conelike teeth specialized for stripping and cutting.

Premolars and molars are the broad, flattened teeth adapted for grinding and crushing.

Chapter 27 Mammals **649**

---

❶ Flexible joints allow a wide range of motion; muscular legs supply power.

❷ Herbivore has small canines and incisors. Molars are less pointed and better suited for grinding and chewing plants.

Discuss

Elicit from students whether they remember losing their baby teeth. Explain that most mammals have two sets of teeth during their lifetime. The first set, called deciduous or milk teeth, eventually fall out and are replaced with permanent teeth. In humans, tooth replacement begins around five years of age; in dogs, at about five months of age. Ask:

- **What are some reasons for having two sets of teeth?** (Jaw size changes, permanent teeth are deeply rooted and larger.)

Use the Visual

Have students study Figure 27.4. Review the labeled structures and their functions. Ask:

- **Which structures are used in digestion?** (Teeth, stomach, and intestines)
- **Which organs are involved in respiration?** (Lungs and diaphragm)
- **What is the function of the diaphragm?** (It regulates the pressure in the chest cavity, which signals the lungs to either inflate or deflate.)

FIGURE 27.4
Internal Structure of an Elephant

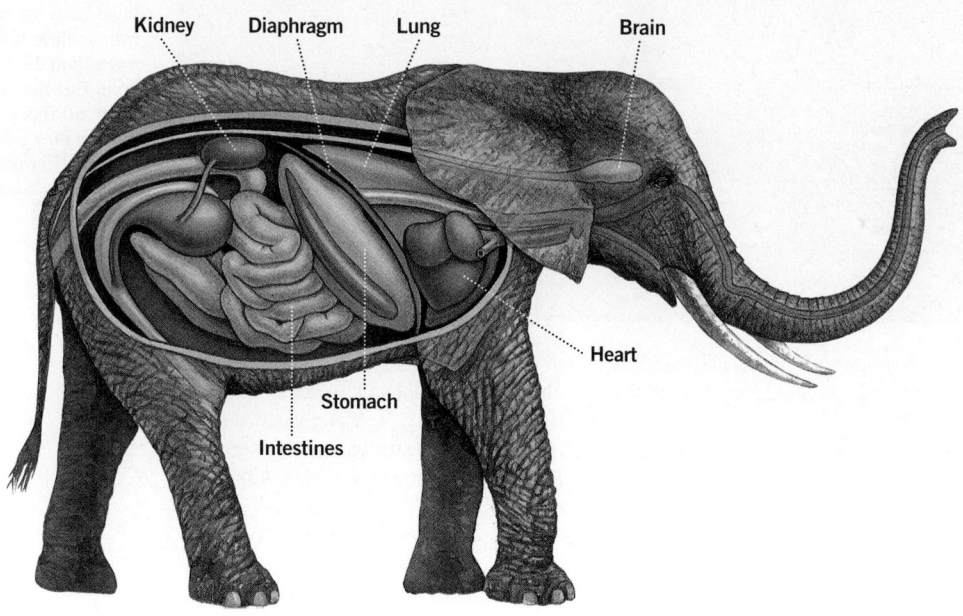

Kidney Diaphragm Lung Brain Heart Stomach Intestines

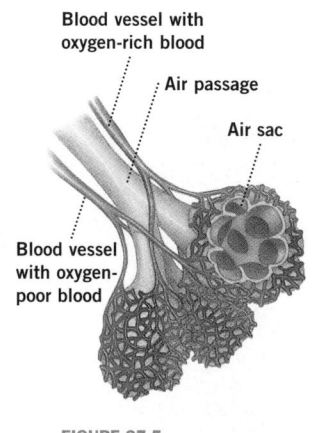

Blood vessel with oxygen-rich blood

Air passage

Air sac

Blood vessel with oxygen-poor blood

FIGURE 27.5
How do air sacs enable animals to exchange oxygen efficiently? ❶

energy needs. Compare the structures of these teeth with their functions.

Varied teeth enable various mammals to eat a wide range of food. Which types of teeth do humans have? How ❷ are they adapted to the human diet?

Figure 27.4 shows an elephant's digestive tract. The length and structure of the elephant's and other mammals' digestive tracts also reflects their diets. In general, mammals that eat only plants have longer digestive tracts than mammals that eat only meat. The trip through the digestive tract of an herbivore must be long and slow because plants contain tough fibers that take time to break down.

In addition to large amounts of food, endotherms require a rich supply of oxygen for cellular respiration. Mammals have two adaptations that increase the efficiency of the lungs: the diaphragm and air sacs. The **diaphragm,** shown in

Figure 27.4, is a dome-shaped sheet of muscle that separates the chest cavity and the abdomen. When the diaphragm contracts, the pressure in the chest cavity decreases, causing air to be forced into the lungs. When the diaphragm relaxes, the opposite happens; pressure in the chest cavity increases, and air is forced out of the lungs.

Oxygen enters the blood through vessels in the air sacs, which are shown in *Figure* 27.5. These tiny air sacs are located at the ends of breathing passages in mammalian lungs. The exchange of gases between the air and the blood occurs in the air sacs. The air sacs increase the surface area across which gas exchange takes place.

The circulatory system of mammals efficiently supplies oxygen to the cells of the body and collects wastes. Like birds, which are also endothermic, mammals have a double-loop circulatory system

650 *Unit 7 Vertebrate Animals*

MEETING DIVERSE NEEDS

LEP Have LEP students look up and record the meanings of the words *carnivore, herbivore,* and *omnivore* in their notebooks. Suggest that as they read the chapter, they list each mammal in the appropriate group.

At Risk Encourage students to develop flowcharts that trace the path of food through the mammalian digestive system and the path of air through the respiratory system. Have students use their flowcharts as study tools.

with a four-chambered heart. The four-chambered heart separates oxygen-rich blood coming from the lungs and oxygen-poor blood that has circulated through the body.

You can see in *Figure 27.4* that elephants, like other vertebrates, have kidneys. Mammalian kidneys remove cellular wastes and regulate the water balance in the body by producing urine. Mammalian urine is a dilute fluid composed of wastes and excess water.

LIFE CYCLE
Taking care of baby

All mammals have internal fertilization. All female mammals have mammary glands that secrete milk to nourish their young. These two characteristics are the only reproductive similarities shared by the three groups of mammals discussed below: monotremes (MON-oh-treemz), marsupials (mar-SOO-pee-ulz), and placental (pluh-SEN-tul) mammals.

Monotremes A **monotreme** is a mammal that reproduces by laying eggs. Shortly after fertilization, the female monotreme lays two or three eggs, which are incubated by the heat from her body. Like birds and reptiles, the developing monotreme embryos are nourished by nutrients inside the egg. After the eggs hatch, young monotremes feed on milk that flows from pores on the mother's belly. Newly hatched monotremes are very immature and must develop further under parental care before they can survive on their own.

Marsupials Mammals that give birth to small, immature young that further develop inside the mother's external pouch are called **marsupials.** After fertilization, a marsupial embryo is nourished inside its mother by a yolk sac similar to that in an amniotic egg. The yolk sac is not large enough to nourish the embryo through its

complete development, however. About 30 days after fertilization, a female red kangaroo gives birth to a tiny, underdeveloped baby. The blind, hairless baby weighs about 28 grams (g) and is only about 2.5 cm long. It could fit easily inside a teaspoon!

After it is born, the baby kangaroo, like most marsupials, crawls into its mother's pouch. It remains in the pouch, as in *Figure 27.6,* until it is large enough and strong enough to survive on its own.

Marsupial reproduction has several differences from monotreme reproduction. Newborn marsupials are protected and kept warm in the mother's pouch. Also, marsupial mothers can move around to look for food or escape from predators even while their young are nursing. Monotreme mothers, on the other hand, must stay in one place while incubating their eggs or nursing their young.

Whole or Skim

When baby kangaroos (called joeys) are born, they drink low-fat, high-protein milk. After they leave the pouch, joeys drink high-fat, low-protein milk from a different nipple. But, do not confuse this with the whole and skim milk you may drink. To create the low-percent milk or skim milk you find in stores, fat is removed from cow's milk.

FIGURE 27.6
The female duck-billed platypus (above) lays her eggs in a nesting burrow. Inside the pouch, the baby kangaroo (left) attaches to the nipple of a mammary gland and remains there, drinking its mother's milk, until it is fully developed. Which animal is a monotreme? A marsupial? ❸

Chapter 27 Mammals **651**

Everyday Biology

Pour skim (nonfat) milk into a glass and have a volunteer describe its color and taste. Then pour whole milk into a glass and have a volunteer describe its color and taste. Pour whipping cream into a glass and have a student describe its color and taste. Explain that skim milk has the cream "skimmed" from it. Read the nutritional facts on the cartons and discuss how the content of each product differs.

Build Writing Skills

Have students research the marsupials that live in Australia. Ask them to write a report discussing what marsupials have in common. Students should focus on the physical characteristics, habits, and habitats of several different marsupials.

Explain

Like the duck-billed platypus, the echidna (pictured on page 655) is classified as a monotreme because it lays eggs. Echidnas differ from platypuses because they have a pouch on the mother's body like marsupials. When an echidna lays its eggs, it puts them into its pouch to incubate for about ten days, until the eggs hatch.

❶ Air sacs increase surface area available for the exchange of gases with the blood.
❷ Humans have flat incisors for biting, short canines, and molars with grinding surfaces for chewing meat and plant material.
❸ The duck-billed platypus is a monotreme; the kangaroo is a marsupial.

 **Do It!** TEAM WORK

How Does Mammal Hair Vary?

If possible, provide magnifying glasses or microscopes so students can examine the hairs in detail.

Analyze Your Results

1 Answers will vary, but students should focus on the length and amount of hair and the size of the animal and its natural habitat if they cite domesticated animals.
2 Hair color would provide camouflage; shape, length, and texture of the hair would determine warmth and ability of hair to hold oil that would repel water.

 **ASSESS**

Evaluate Understanding

List the objectives for this section on the board. Have students write paragraph summaries or create graphics for each objective. Review several of the summaries and graphics as a class, correcting any inaccurate information.

Reteach

On the board, develop a flowchart that explains the classification of mammals as monotremes, marsupials, or placental mammals. Have students reread the section to identify key features that distinguish each group and add them to the chart. Discuss the traits all groups share.

652

LAB ZONE Do It! bioSURF

How Does Mammal Hair Vary?

All mammals have hair, but not all mammal hair is the same. You can examine different kinds of hair when you . . .

Try This

1 Observe mammals with hair (pets, humans, livestock, and so on). Collect single hairs from a variety of mammals.
2 Observe the length, thickness, color, and shape of each type of hair. Record your observations.

Analyze Your Results

1 Which animal had the longest hair? The thickest? Considering the habits of these animals, how would these traits help the animals survive in their environment?
2 How might the color and shape of hair affect the survival of an animal?

FIGURE 27.7
Many placental mammals are born well developed. This calf will be able to walk within hours of its birth.

Placental mammals Mammals whose young develop inside the mother's body and are nourished by the mother's body until birth are called **placental mammals.** Compared with the young of marsupials, the embryo of a placental mammal develops more fully before birth. Almost 95 percent of all mammals are placental mammals.

Placental mammals get their name from the placenta, an organ through which nutrients, oxygen, carbon dioxide, and wastes are exchanged between the mother and the embryo. The placenta is a spongy tissue that completely surrounds the embryo. Blood vessels of the mother and the embryo intertwine in the placenta, enabling the exchange of materials to take place.

652 *Unit 7 Vertebrate Animals*

The time that the embryo stays inside the mother's body is called the **gestation period.** This period varies greatly among placental mammals. In general, the gestation period increases with the size of the adult and the degree to which the newborns are developed. Mice, for example, have a gestation period of 21 days, while elephants have a gestation period of 22 months. The gestation period of humans is approximately nine months.

Although some animals, such as birds and alligators, care for their young, mammals provide more care and protection for their young than most animals do. Nursing alone keeps mother and offspring together for a long time. The length of time that adults spend with their young, combined with the advantage of a well-developed cerebrum, enables the young to learn a great deal about survival. Many scientists think that the long period of parental care has contributed to the evolutionary success of mammals.

CHECKPOINT 27.1

1. Identify the key characteristics of mammals.
2. Compare the reproductive processes of monotremes, marsupials, and placental mammals.
3. **Critical Thinking** Many humans have their wisdom teeth extracted because their jaws are too small to accommodate them. What might this suggest about the evolution of the human jaw?

Build on What You Know

4. Compared with many fishes, mammals produce few offspring. How is the amount of time spent caring for offspring related to the number of offspring produced? Propose an explanation for this. *(Need to jog your memory? Revisit relevant concepts in Chapter 25, Section 25.2.)*

CHECKPOINT 27.1

1. Mammals are endothermic vertebrates with hair and mammary glands.
2. Monotremes lay eggs. Marsupials give birth to tiny underdeveloped young, which crawl into their mother's pouch where they develop further. Placental mammals grow and develop inside the mother's body.

3. **Developing a hypothesis** The smaller jaw may be due to increased use of incisor and canine teeth and reduced use of wisdom teeth, which are molars.
4. More time caring for fewer offspring helps to ensure that genes are passed on.

 **Investigate It!**

Comparing Skeletons

WHAT YOU WILL DO Compare the skeletons of different animals

WHAT SKILLS YOU WILL USE Collecting and recording data, observing, analyzing, classifying

WHAT YOU WILL NEED Three skeletons, or diagrams of skeletons, labeled *A*, *B*, and *C*

Propose a Hypothesis

The structure of an animal's skeleton can be used for classification. Hypothesize which skeletal structures are most useful in determining an animal's identity.

Conduct Your Experiment

1 Examine each skeleton.
2 Set up a chart using *Skeleton A, B, and C* as headings for three columns.
3 Count the number of vertebrae in each skeleton, and record the data in the chart.
4 The vertebrae that make up a tail are called caudal vertebrae. Do any of the skeletons have caudal vertebrae? Record these data in the chart.
5 Which skeleton or skeletons have limbs? Do the limbs point outward from the vertebrae or downward, underneath the vertebrae? Record these data.
6 For the skeletons with limbs, count the number of digits on each limb and record this number.
7 In the chart, describe the shape of each skeleton's skull.

8 Do any of the skulls have teeth in their jaws? What kind of teeth are they? Record this information in the chart.

Analyze Your Data

1 Do any of the skeletons lack limbs? If so, which one(s)? What kinds of vertebrate animals lack limbs? Based on this information, can you infer the identity of the limbless skeleton(s)? What other clues might help in your identification?
2 Of the skeletons that have limbs, which limbs have an outward orientation? Based on this information and the relative sizes of the limbs, can you infer what type of animal this skeleton belongs to?

3 Of the skeletons that have limbs, which limbs are oriented under the body? Can you infer what type of animal this skeleton belongs to?

Draw Conclusions

1 Write a paragraph discussing how you inferred the identity of each skeleton.
2 What features of the skeleton can be used to distinguish one type of organism from another?

Design a Related Experiment

Design a related experiment in which you infer the skeletal structure of an animal, based on a photograph of the animal.

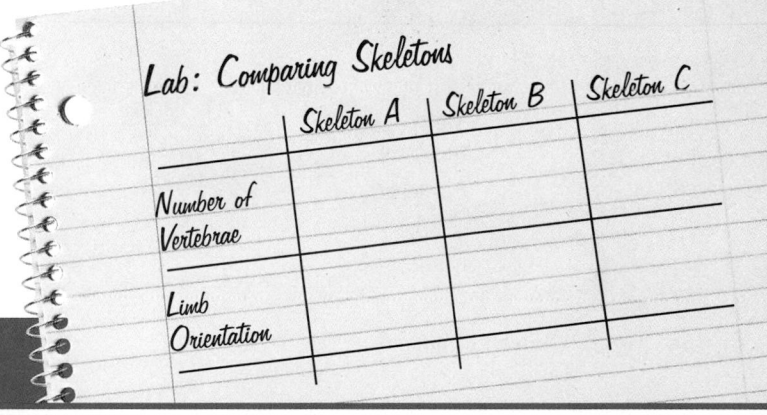

Lab: Comparing Skeletons

	Skeleton A	Skeleton B	Skeleton C
Number of Vertebrae			
Limb Orientation			

Analyze Your Data

1 Students should focus on the size and shape of the skull, and the length of the vertebra of limbless animals for identification.
2 Students should take into consideration the size and location of the limbs, as well as their orientation.
3 Answers will vary.

Draw Conclusions

1 Students should focus on their observations that led them to identify each animal.
2 Students should cite the size and shape of bones as an indication of the eating habits, survival techniques, and environment of different animals, as well as their identity.

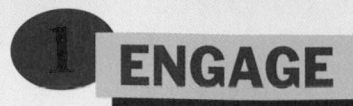

1 ENGAGE

Use the Visual

Have students study the photograph that opens the section. Explain that true lemurs have a long, pointed muzzle, a rounded head, large eyes and ears, and a long tail. Ask:

■ **How do true lemurs compare with flying lemurs?** (Flying lemurs have added folds of skin between their front and back legs.)

Check Prior Knowledge

To assess students' knowledge about mammal diversity, ask:

■ **Into what three groups are mammals classified?** (Monotremes, marsupials, and placental mammals)

 **Interpreting Visuals** To practice strategies for effective reading, use pages 67-68 in *Super Read!*

Quick Activity

Obtain and display photographs of a shrew. Ask students to compare the shrew with the eozostrodon shown in Figure 27.8. Point out that the eozostrodon lived during the Mesozoic era. Have students list the similarities and differences they observe between the eozostrodon and the modern shrew. Record responses on the board and discuss.

27.2 Origin and Diversity of Mammals

What you'll learn

IDEAS
• To describe the evolution of mammals
• To compare the three orders of mammals

 **SUPER READ!**

A daring young lemur
Flying lemurs live in the rain forests of Southeast Asia. They do not really fly, but with large, thin folds of skin that connect the neck, legs, and tail, they certainly can glide. With these "wings" of skin outspread, a flying lemur—roughly the size of a cat—looks like a kite with legs. It can glide up to 91 m from tree to tree in search of the tropical flowers, fruits, and leaves to eat.

ORIGIN OF MAMMALS

Creatures of the night

As you learned in Chapter 12, the first mammals probably evolved about 245 to 195 million years ago, during the Triassic period, from a group of small mammal-like reptiles called therapsids. Fossil evidence indicates that the first mammals were small insect-eating animals similar to the one shown in *Figure* 27.8. These animals resembled modern shrews or mice and lived among the dinosaurs and other reptiles during the Mesozoic era.

Recall from Chapter 26 that Earth's climate was relatively warm during the Mesozoic era. The ectothermic reptiles of the time easily warmed their bodies by basking in the sun during the day. But at night their body temperatures dropped as the air cooled, and they became inactive. Unlike reptiles, ancient mammals were endothermic. They generated their own body heat and could remain active during the cold prehistoric nights.

Being endothermic had its disadvantages, however. To generate and maintain a warm body temperature, an endothermic mammal required about ten times more food than did an ectothermic reptile of the same size. Approximately 90 percent of a mammal's food is used to generate body heat. Therefore, mammals require more time, energy, and space than other animals seeking food. This huge demand for food and space limited the size of mammal populations for millions of years.

Fossil evidence indicates that many changes occurred at the end of the Mesozoic era (about 65 million years ago). The climate cooled, and angiosperms began replacing the gymnosperms that had previously dominated the land.

As dinosaurs died out at the end of the Mesozoic era, many habitats and resources became available to mammals. The mammals had little competition for food and space. As a result, a period of enormous adaptive

FIGURE 27.8
The first mammals, such as the *Eozostrodon* shown here, may have evolved from mammal-like reptiles. The early mammals probably occupied small niches not filled by dinosaurs.

654 *Unit 7 Vertebrate Animals*

STUDENT RESOURCES

From the Teacher's Resource Package, use:
■ Section Review 27.2, Activity Recordsheets 27-3 and Enrichment Topics 27-1 and 27-2 from Unit 7 Review Module

 **TECHNOLOGY RESOURCES**

Relevant technology resources include:
■ Spanish Student Edition CD-ROM
■ Teacher's Resource Planner CD-ROM

radiation probably occurred during this time span. Many new species of mammals may have evolved as different mammal populations spread out and adapted to new habitats.

Mammals became the dominant class of vertebrates during the Cenozoic era, which is known as the Age of Mammals. During this time, Earth's climate became cooler, and endothermy became a distinct advantage. An animal with a constant body temperature could remain active in cold temperatures. Because its muscles were kept warm, an endothermic mammal could escape from a predator or pursue prey quickly at all times. Hair was also an advantage. The layer of hair common to all mammals provided insulation against the loss of body heat.

MONOTREMES AND MARSUPIALS

Eggs and pouches

Scientists theorize that, by the early Cenozoic era, mammals had split into the three groups that survive today: monotremes, marsupials, and placental mammals. As you have just learned, scientists classify these mammals according to the development of their embryo. In the descriptions that follow, consider how each group's adaptations enable the species to survive.

The monotremes were the first mammals to evolve from the therapsids. These primitive mammals retain some of the characteristics of their reptilian ancestors, such as laying eggs. Monotremes cannot control their body temperature as well as other mammals can and usually have a lower body temperature.

There are only three species of monotremes, and all are are native to Australia. The duck-billed platypus lives in a burrow. Its flat, beaverlike tail and webbed feet are adaptations to an aquatic lifestyle. The rubbery,

duck-bill-like muzzle probes for shellfish, insects, and worms in the muddy bottoms of lakes and streams.

The other two species of monotremes are echidnas, or spiny anteaters. They live in the forests, mountains, and plains of Australia and New Guinea. As you can see in *Figure 27.10,* the echidna has a long snout and is covered with a thick coat of hair and spines. The echidna's long snout searches for insects and earthworms in logs or soil. When an echidna is threatened, it burrows into the ground so that only its spiny back shows.

Most of the nearly 250 living species of marsupials live in Australia or on nearby islands. One exception are the opossums, which are abundant in parts of North and South America. At one time, marsupials lived throughout

FIGURE 27.9

Class Mammalia

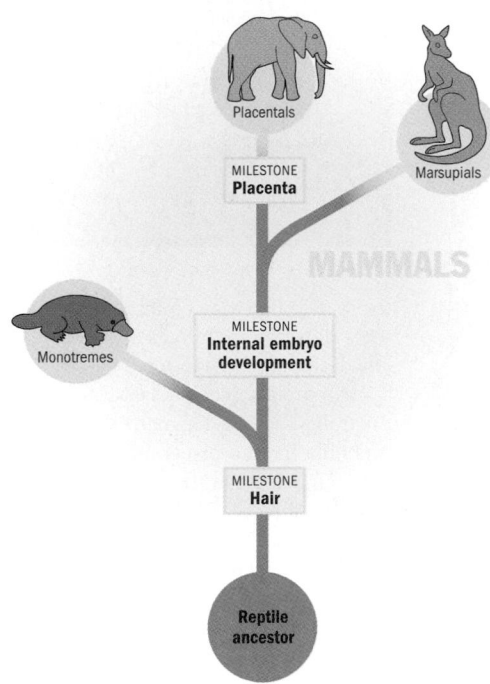

FIGURE 27.10
Echidnas are toothless monotremes. They use their long, rough tongue to crush insects against the roof of their mouth.

Chapter 27 Mammals **655**

Explain

The wallaby is a marsupial of Australia that closely resembles the kangaroo. These animals are often hunted for their skins, which, when tanned, resemble leather. The tanned hide is used to make footwear, clothing, and accessories.

Class Activity

Students are probably most familiar with the placental mammals. As students read about the various orders of placental mammals, have them create a table with the heads: *Order, Traits,* and *Local Examples.* In the *Local Examples* column, have students identify mammals that are native to the area belonging to each order. If students cannot think of examples, have them leave the space blank to fill in during class discussion. Review the completed tables at the conclusion of the section.

Art

Have students make a collage of lagomorphs. Have them add to their collage a hand-drawn diagram showing the structural differences among the different lagomorphs. You may wish to display students' collages.

FIGURE 27.11
The koala is a marsupial. How would this koala care for its offspring? ❶

FIGURE 27.12
Though they look very different from each other, both chipmunks and porcupines are rodents. How are all rodents similar? ❷

FIGURE 27.13
This black-tailed jackrabbit is a desert- and prairie-dwelling lagomorph. How does it differ from rodents? ❸

the world. But they could not compete with placental mammals and eventually disappeared from most places.

Marsupials lived successfully in Australia because for many years Australia had no placental mammals. Scientists theorize that Australia broke away from other land masses before the Cretaceous period and before placental mammals had evolved. In this isolation, marsupials underwent adaptive radiation, filling niches that placental mammals occupied elsewhere. There are placental mammals in Australia today, however—many brought there by humans.

Two of the most familiar marsupials are the kangaroo and the koala. Most kangaroos are herbivores, and they can travel about 8 m in one hop. Koalas, like the one shown in *Figure 27.11,* live in the forests of Australia and eat only the leaves and shoots of the eucalyptus tree.

PLACENTAL MAMMALS

Lions, and tigers, and bears—oh my!

Ninety-five percent of all mammals are placental mammals. They are a very diverse group that make their homes in water, on land, and in the air. These mammals have specialized

---

adaptations for movement and obtaining food that fit the environments in which they live.

Rodents The largest order of mammals is Rodentia, which includes more than 1700 species. Beavers, chipmunks, guinea pigs, mice, porcupines, rats, and squirrels are all rodents. Rodents are herbivores, with a pair of very long, sharp teeth in each jaw. Unlike the teeth of most mammals, these long teeth continue to grow. They enable rodents to gnaw on tough stems and roots, in addition to leaves and seeds.

Lagomorphs Hares, pikas, and rabbits are members of the order Lagomorpha (lay-go-MOR-fuh), which consists of about 65 species. Rabbits and hares have long ears, long and powerful hind legs, clawed toes, and a stubby tail. Pikas have rounded ears and legs of equal length. Although similar in appearance to rodents, lagomorphs differ from rodents in the structure of their teeth. A lagomorph's diet is also somewhat different from that of a rodent, consisting mostly of leaves, grasses, and bark.

Bats The order Chiroptera (key-ROP-ter-uh) is the second-largest order of mammals. All of the 925 species of chiropterans are commonly known as bats. Bats are small nocturnal (active at night) animals, the only mammals that can fly. Powerful muscles move the bat's wings, resulting in flight at speeds of up to 65 km per hour. Bats live wherever the climate is warm enough to support trees. In colder climates, bats migrate to warmer areas in the winter. The smallest bats weigh only about 4 g, and the largest bats weigh as much as 1.5 kg.

The diversity of bat diets is reflected in the variations in bats' teeth. Insect-eating bats have curved teeth that mash insects into a paste. Bats that eat fruit and other plant materials have flattened teeth that

---

FACTS AND FIGURES

The term *altricial* is sometimes used to describe animals born blind and helpless, such as mice. Animals born with their eyes open, such as horses and deer, have less need of parental care and are described as *precocial.*

❶ Develop and nurture its young in its pouch
❷ All are herbivores with a pair of long, sharp teeth in each jaw.
❸ Tooth structure differs

FIGURE 27.14
Like most bats, the greater horseshoe bat uses ultrasonic echolocation to find prey. However, unlike most bats, it emits sounds through its nostrils, not its mouth.

grind the plants. Perhaps the most notorious adaptation of bats is the razor-sharp teeth of vampire bats. These bats feed on large mammals by cutting the skin and lapping up the blood. Vampire bats do not, however, suck the blood out of the prey's body.

Carnivores Most of the 240 species of the order Carnivora are strictly meat-eating mammals. But there are many exceptions, such as the panda which feeds primarily on bamboo shoots, and bears which eat roots, nuts, and berries in addition to meat. All carnivores evolved from ancestors adapted to a diet of meat. Carnivores have a pair of long, sharp teeth, strong jaws, and clawed toes, and are considered one of the strongest and most intelligent groups of animals. Lions, tigers, wolves, coyotes, weasels, skunks, and raccoons are all carnivores.

The order Carnivora includes a suborder of animals adapted to a somewhat aquatic lifestyle. These carnivores, called pinnipeds, include walruses, sea lions, otters, and seals. Pinnipeds have limbs modified for swimming, a streamlined body, and a thick layer of fat that insulates them in icy waters. These carnivores return to land to reproduce.

Cetaceans Dolphins, porpoises, and whales are members of the order Cetacea (seh-TAY-shuh). Cetaceans have a torpedo-shaped body with a long, pointed head and no neck. Cetaceans do not have hind limbs but they have a broad, flat, horizontal tail and flipperlike forelimbs for swimming. The cetacean body closely resembles that of a fish. As mammals, however, cetaceans have no gills and must come to the surface for air. Unlike sea lions, cetaceans are completely aquatic. They cannot move on land, and they reproduce entirely in the water.

Sirenians The order Sirenia (sy-REEN-ee-uh) is a small group of aquatic mammals that includes manatees and dugongs. Sirenians have a large, slow-moving, barrel-shaped body with flipperlike forelimbs, no hind limbs, and a flat, horizontal tail. Like all mammals, sirenians must come to the surface for air. Manatees are common off the coast of Florida. In fact, manatees seen from distant ships inspired legends about mermaids.

FIGURE 27.15
The black panther, a carnivore, is actually a species of leopard with dark fur, which makes its spots either hard to see or completely invisible. How does this carnivore differ from the carnivores shown below? **4**

FIGURE 27.16
Though both are aquatic, carnivorous mammals, sea lions (above) and killer whales (left) are members of different orders. What are some of their physical similarities and differences? **5**

Chapter 27 *Mammals* **657**

4 The panther lives on land.
5 Large barrel-shaped bodies with flipperlike forelimbs and a flat, horizontal tail; unlike killer whales, sea lions can remain on land for long periods of time.

Explain

Point out that whales are divided into two large groups: the toothed whales, which include the dolphins and porpoises, and the baleen whales, which include the humpback whales and blue whales. Explain that toothed whales have teeth to grasp their prey. In contrast, baleen whales, which feed largely on plankton, krill, and small fishes, use plates of modified mucous membrane called *baleens,* to strain food from water. Although they feed on small organisms, baleen whales grow to be quite large. On average, baleen whales tend to be larger than their toothed counterparts.

 Literature

Ask students who have read Herman Melville's *Moby Dick* to describe how the great white whale is portrayed in the story. Elicit from students other books or stories they have read in which aquatic mammals play significant roles.

Do It! **TEAM WORK**

Is Whale Blubber an Effective Insulator?

Before students begin the lab, review the function of insulation and the ocean's water temperatures at different latitudes. Suggest using a plastic bag filled with air as the control.

Analyze Your Results

1 Temperature change in the center of insulating fat: Read thermometers every 5-10 minutes until both have the same reading.

2 The air-filled plastic bag is the control.

3 Fat layer represents whale's blubber layer.

4 Results will vary, but should show that the fat layer increased the time required for temperatures to equalize.

5 Blubber layer helps whale retain its body heat in very cold ocean.

 Science History

The classification system developed by Aristotle in the fourth century B.C. grouped pinnipeds, cetaceans, and sirenians together. Because the basis for Aristotle's system was habitat rather than evolutionary history, these mammals were classified with fishes.

LAB ZONE **Do It!**

Is Whale Blubber an Effective Insulator?

Unlike the skin of most land mammals, a whale's skin is smooth and almost hairless. Under its skin, the whale has a thick layer of fat, or blubber, which serves to insulate the whale from cold ocean water. You can test the effectiveness of blubber as an insulator when you . . .

Try This

Design your own experiment in which you demonstrate the insulating qualities of fat, using the following materials: test tubes, thermometers, warm water, vegetable shortening or animal lard, small plastic bags, large beaker filled with ice water, timer.

Analyze Your Results

1 What type of data are you collecting? How often do you plan to collect data?
2 What is your control?
3 How does your experiment model a whale's blubber?
4 What did your results show? Is blubber an effective insulator?
5 Given what you know about endotherms, how does blubber affect the whale's ability to live in a variety of environments?

FIGURE 27.17
The manatee spends much of its time sleeping and consuming aquatic plants. It can grow up to 4.5 m in length and weigh 500 kg.

FIGURE 27.18
Though its vision is poor, the hedgehog's sense of smell is excellent. It uses this skill to sniff out insects, as well as worms, snails, and even small vertebrates.

Insectivores As their name suggests, members of the order Insectivora are insect-eating mammals. Moles, shrews, and hedgehogs are insectivores. They have a high metabolic rate and sharp claws for digging insects from the ground.

Ungulates Ungulates, or hoofed mammals, are divided into two orders: Artiodactyla (ART-ee-oh-DAK-til-uh) and Perissodactyla (peh-riss-oh-DAK-til-

FIGURE 27.19
All species of rhinoceroses are now threatened with extinction due to poaching. Perhaps the biggest reason they are hunted is for their horns, which are actually formed of compacted hair fibers.

uh). Members of the order Artiodactyla have an even number of toes. Pigs, hippopotamuses, camels, deer, antelopes, cows, goats, sheep, giraffes, elk, and bison are artiodactyls. Members of the order Perissodactyla have an odd number of toes. Horses, zebras, rhinoceroses, and tapirs are perissodactyls. Both groups of ungulates are herbivorous grazing mammals. They have flat teeth for grinding plant material, and in some species the digestive tract has a specialized chamber in which cellulose is broken down.

FIGURE 27.20
Warthogs are herbivores, dining mainly on grasses and herbs, while avoiding humans and their crops. The warthog's even number of toes puts it in a different order than the rhinoceroses.

MEETING DIVERSE NEEDS

Gifted Encourage students to conduct research and prepare a class presentation that includes visuals on one of the following topics: five endangered mammals and efforts to prevent their extinction; or placental mammals that are kept as pets and how to care for them.

❶ African elephant is larger, taller, and has larger ears than does the Indian elephant.

FIGURE 27.21
Elephants are the largest living terrestrial mammals; the African elephant (left) can grow to be larger than the Indian elephant (right). They are social animals and travel in groups of relatives that are most often led by an elderly female.

Elephants The order Proboscidea (pro-BOSS-id-ee-uh) has only two species: African elephants and Indian elephants. Elephants have a massive body, a large head, broad flat ears, a short neck, and thick skin with little hair. Their muscular, boneless trunk transfers food and water to the mouth and makes loud, trumpetlike noises. Elephants also have long, modified teeth called tusks that dig up plant roots or pry bark from trees. Elephants are herbivores, and it is not uncommon for them to eat plants for as many as 18 hours a day to obtain enough food to survive. What are some of the differences between the two species of **❶** elephants shown in *Figure 27.21*?

Primates The 175 species of the order Primates include humans, apes, monkeys, and prosimians. Primates have an opposable thumb on each hand and usually each foot as well. The position of the thumb enables primates to grasp branches and other objects. Primates also have large eyes that face forward. Primates are omnivores and will eat whatever food is available. They

have large brains and live in organized social groups. With the exception of humans, most primates live in tropical and subtropical parts of the world.

Other placental mammals
The remaining orders of placental mammals are small groups, many containing only one species. Aardvarks are the only species in the order Tubulidentata. Hyraxes, small shrewlike animals, are the only members of the order Hyracoidea. The order Pholidota contains one genus of animals, called scaly anteaters. The classification of some placental mammals may change in coming years as more is learned about their evolutionary history.

FIGURE 27.22
Though extremely different physically, the tarsier (top) and the gorilla (bottom) are members of the same order. The tarsier is a small nocturnal primate that spends its days in the trees. The gorilla, which weighs about 2000 times more than the tarsier, lives mainly on the ground.

CHECKPOINT 27.2

1. Explain the role of adaptive radiation in the evolution of animals.
2. Compare the many orders of mammals. What are some general characteristics that differentiate species?
3. **Critical Thinking** Which are more fully adapted to an aquatic lifestyle—cetaceans or pinnipeds? Explain your answer.

Build on What You Know
4. Both birds and mammals are thought to have evolved independently from reptilian ancestors. Compare the adaptations of birds to those of mammals. Discuss how birds and mammals are adapted to their different niches. *(Need to jog your memory? Revisit relevant concepts in Chapter 26, Section 26.4.)*

What are the characteristics of all mammals? **?**

Chapter 27 Mammals **659**

Music

At one time, the white keys of pianos were made from ivory, the material that composes the tusks of elephants. The black keys were carved from ebony. In an effort to save elephants from extinction, it is no longer legal to hunt and kill these animals for their ivory tusks. Today, most piano manufacturers have replaced ivory and ebony keys with plastic keys.

Build Writing Skills

Have students conduct research in the library or on the Internet and write a report on the work of one of the following primatologists: Dian Fossey, Biruté Galdikas, or Jane Goodall. Collectively, these women are sometimes called Leakey's "trimates" because Louis Leakey arranged for the original sponsorship of their research on one group of primates.

3 ASSESS

Evaluate Understanding

Have students write a summary that explains the classification of mammals. Students should identify features of monotremes, marsupials, and placental mammals as well as the features of the main orders of placental mammals.

Reteach

Use the section heads and subheads to help students create an outline of this section. After the outline is completed, have students compare and contrast the three mammal groups as well as the orders of placental mammals.

CHECKPOINT 27.2

1. With the extinction of the dinosaurs, many niches became available. With little competition for food and space, mammals probably went through a period of diverse adaptations.
2. The orders of mammals are diverse. Species are differentiated by adaptations to their environments, diets, and means of reproduction.
3. **Applying** Cetaceans because they reproduce in water
4. Both are endothermic animals and have bodies that can inhabit the air, land, and water; birds have feathers that provide insulation and bodies adapted for flight. Mammals have hair that insulates.

Chapter Objectives

Students will learn the main concepts of this chapter as they complete the following objectives.

- Explain the relationship between a stimulus and a response
- Distinguish between innate and learned behavior
- Explain innate behavior
- Distinguish between a reflex and an instinct
- Explain how and why behaviors can be learned
- Compare and contrast the types of learned behavior
- Explain what functions are served by communication between animals
- Compare different means and forms of communication

Key Words

28.1 *behavior, response, stimulus, innate behavior, learned behavior*

28.2 *reflex, instinct, fixed-action pattern*

28.3 *habituation, imprinting, classical conditioning, operant conditioning*

28.4 *circadian rhythm*

The Opening Story

Have students discuss how they think the story relates to the content of this chapter. Ask students with different pets to discuss complex patterns of behavior they have observed.

CHAPTER 28
Animal Behavior

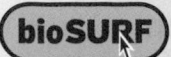

You can find out more about animal behavior by exploring the following Internet address:
http://vertebrates.biosurf.com

In this chapter . . .

FEATURES

Everyday Biology
- Born to Run
- The Nose Knows

In the Community
Learning to Help

 Frontiers in Biology
Insect Robots

LAB ZONES

Discover It!
- Observing the Pupil Reflex

Do It!
- How Quickly Do Birds Become Habituated to Disturbances?
- How Do People's Sleep Needs Differ?

Think About It!
- Analyzing Firefly Behavior

Investigate It!
- Observing Sow Bugs' Behavior

INTERIOR DECORATION
. . . for the Birds

The bowerbirds of New Guinea are no ordinary nest builders. Male bowerbirds build stagelike structures called bowers, in which they dance and display themselves to attract mates.

Each of the nearly 20 species of bowerbird has its own particular building style. When a male orange-crested gardener bowerbird wants to attract a mate, he pads a tree trunk with moss and builds a soft-roofed cabin one meter (m) in diameter around it. The male decorates his bower with berries, feathers, and bits of shell. This resourceful bird also uses pieces of cloth, colored glass, or tinsel taken from human communities. Each

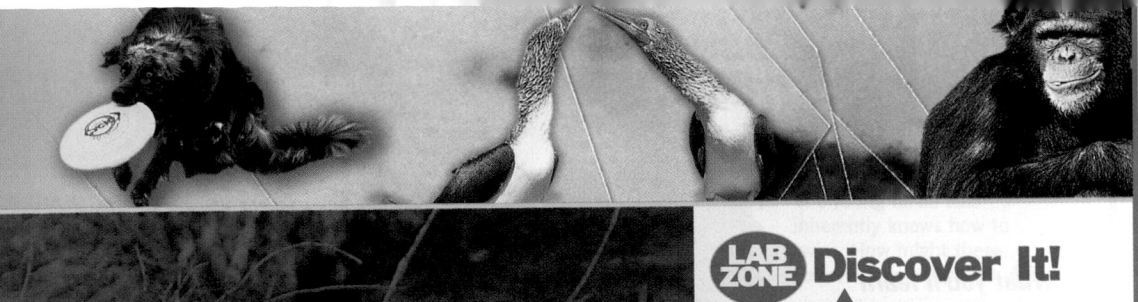

bower is usually decorated in a single color, often matching the coloration of the male or female of the species.

If a female visits the bower, the male will bow, dance, sing, and pick up the decorative berries or bits of glass in his beak to display them. If the female approves of the decorations, the birds mate inside the bower. The female then flies off to build her nest, and the male redecorates his bower to attract another female.

Each species of bowerbird displays a similar complex pattern of mating behavior, generation after generation. What patterns of behavior do other animals have?

 **Discover It!**

Observing the Pupil Reflex

You need a flashlight

1. Have your lab partner shield his or her eyes from the light while keeping the eyes open. Look at your partner's eyes and note the size of the pupil (the dark opening in the center of the eye).

2. Shine the flashlight on just one of your partner's eyes. What happens to the pupil? Caution: You may experience temporary loss of vision from the bright flashlight. Wait a few moments before walking.

The automatic response of the eye's pupil to light and dark is a simple reflex action—you cannot control the opening (dilating) or contracting of your pupil. The pupil regulates the amount of light entering your eye in an effort to provide you, the viewer, with the optimum conditions for sight.

WRITE ABOUT IT!

Write a scene for a film in which the quantity or quality of light is very important. Describe for the director exactly the effect you want to achieve with lighting.

667

Opening Activities

 If you have access to the Internet in your classroom or school, you may wish to have students connect to the address shown on page 666. You may also want to have students conduct net searches for information using key words related to this chapter. For example, they could search for entries under imprinting behaviors, ethology, animal communication, or bird migration.

LAB ZONE Discover It!

Observing the Pupil Reflex

TEAM WORK

Before students begin this chapter, have them choose a partner and do the suggested activities. You may want to let students use mirrors so that they can see their own pupils contract.

WRITE ABOUT IT!

Tell students that they can create their own scene or describe one they saw in a movie or on a TV show. After students write their journal entries, invite volunteers to read their scenes aloud or to act them out, if possible.

REWIND to Chapter 27

Briefly review concepts learned in Chapter 27, *Mammals*. Ask:

■ **What behaviors in mammals do you think are innate behaviors? What behaviors are learned?**

667

PORTFOLIO PREVIEW

Students should be encouraged to add to their portfolios as they work through this chapter. In addition to the *Write About It* opportunity, the following sections offer opportunities for portfolio entries:

■ Section 28.1: *Animal Behaviors*
■ Section 28.3: *Learned Behavior*
■ Section 28.4: *Behavior in the Life of Animals*

Unit Overview

The human body is often described as one of the world's most efficient machines, made up of many parts and systems that work together to maintain life. Virtually all activities require the cooperation of each body system. Like any complex machine, the human body works best when it is carefully maintained by its owner.

Unit Objectives

- Introduce the study of human biology
- Explain the structure and function of the major body systems
- Discuss some of the basic requirements of maintaining a healthy body
- Describe some of the dangers of substance abuse

Connect the Units

This unit builds on the biology of mammals discussed in Unit 7. An understanding of basic cellular activities and life functions as discussed in Unit 1: *The Basis of Life* is essential for full comprehension of the concepts in this unit. Human biology can be studied before the units on microbes and plants, if you prefer to focus on a human curriculum.

Which of these amazing statements about human biology are fact, and which are fiction?

Hit <u>or</u> Myth?

There is **fat** on the bottom of your feet.

(Fact. There is fat there. It helps protect the skin on the bottom of your feet when you walk.)

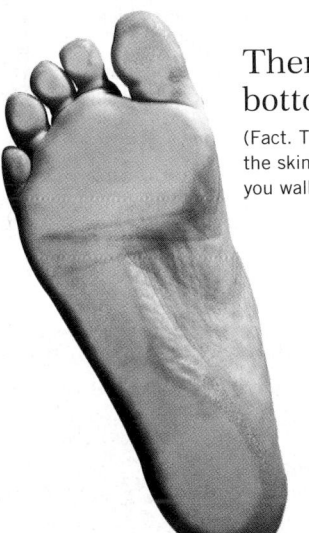

Your **jaws** move.

(Fiction. Only one jaw— your lower jaw—moves. Your upper jaw is fused into position and does not move at all.)

You "see" the world **upside down.**

(Fact. Light entering the lens of the eye is bent so that images appear upside down on the retina. The brain interprets these images right side up.)

If all the **blood vessels** in your body were laid end to end, they would wrap around Earth's equator four times.

(Fact—or they would reach halfway to the moon!)

688

Newborns are protected from disease.

(Fact. Before birth, the fetus receives the mother's antibodies, and newborns have natural immunity to most infections—at least for the first few months. Breast-fed babies have longer-lasting resistance to specific infections.)

A bird can **swallow upside down,** but a human cannot.

(Fiction. The reverse is true. A human can swallow in that position, but a bird cannot.)

Goosebumps help keep you warm.

(Fiction. Goosebumps help furry and downy animals stay warm by trapping an insulating layer of air next to the skin—a technique that does not work on our furless, featherless bodies.)

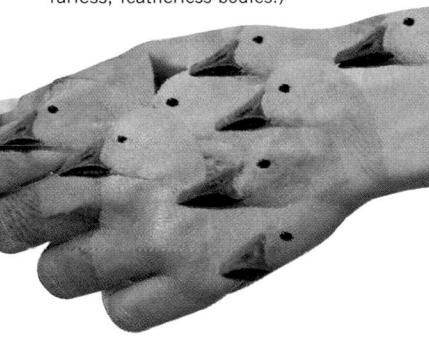

Unit 8 Human Biology **689**

Answers

1. marrow
2. melanin
3. cephalization
4. integumentary system
5. arthritis
6. cardiac muscle
7. tendons
8. osteoblasts
9. appendicular skeleton
10. smooth muscle
11. b
12. d
13. b
14. d
15. b
16. b
17. c
18. When the body overheats, sweat glands produce sweat. The excess body heat is used to evaporate the sweat, which passes through pores in the epidermis.
19. Hair and nails are both made from dead epidermal cells.
20. Sweat glands can be part of the excretory system; nerve endings, the nervous system.
21. If a muscle does not get enough oxygen during exercise, the mitochondria switch from aerobic to anaerobic respiration. A buildup of lactic acid causes the cramping.
22. Haversian canals provide passage for nerve cells and blood vessels. They also decrease the mass of compact bones.
23. In both processes, cartilage is the precursor to bone.
24. Striated muscles are thicker when contracted because the thin and thick filaments overlap, which causes the shortening, or contraction.
25. Skeleton → bones and joints and connective tissue; connective tissue → ligaments

Use Your Word Power

MATCHING **Write the term from the list of key terms that best matches each of the phrases below.**

1. A tissue located in spongy bone that produces blood cells.

2. A pigment that protects skin from ultraviolet radiation.

3. The tendency for sense organs to be located in the anterior portion of a body.

4. The system that provides a protective barrier between the body and its environment.

5. A disease that involves inflammation of the joints.

6. A striated, involuntary type of muscle that is found only in the heart.

7. Tissue that attaches muscles to bones.

8. Cells that produce new bone cells.

9. The set of bones that are formed by the arms, legs, pelvis, and shoulders.

10. An involuntary muscle found in blood vessels and internal organs.

MULTIPLE CHOICE **Choose the letter of the word or phrase that best completes each statement.**

11. Your vital organs are protected by your (a) appendicular skeleton; (b) axial skeleton; (c) endoskeleton; (d) epidermis.

12. An internal hard skeleton is (a) an exoskeleton; (b) a hydrostatic skeleton; (c) a cardiac muscle; (d) an endoskeleton.

13. The type of skeleton that must be shed as an organism grows is an (a) endoskeleton; (b) exoskeleton; (c) axial skeleton; (d) appendicular skeleton.

14. Sweat glands are located in the (a) epidermis; (b) mesoderm; (c) endoderm; (d) dermis.

15. Which of the following are part of a human skeleton? (a) skeletal muscles; (b) joints; (c) ligaments; (d) tendons.

16. A diet rich in calcium and vitamin D can help prevent (a) periostitis; (b) osteoporosis; (c) bursitis; (d) arthritis.

17. Cnidarians have (a) skeletal muscles; (b) smooth muscles; (c) a hydrostatic skeleton; (d) an endoskeleton.

Show What You Know

18. How do sweat glands help regulate body temperature?

19. What do hair and nails have in common?

20. Which parts of the integumentary system perform functions in other body systems? Explain your answer.

21. Explain what causes muscle cramps.

22. What is the function of Haversian canals in compact bone?

23. How is the healing of a broken bone similar to the development of the skeleton in a fetus?

24. Are striated muscles thicker when relaxed or when contracted? Explain your answer.

25. **Make a Concept Map** Make a concept map that relates the human skeletal system and muscular system.

Take It Further

26. **Developing a Hypothesis** Suppose you heard that someone had a bone marrow transplant. For what type of problem would such an operation be needed?

27. **Applying Concepts** One symptom of the childhood disease called rickets is bowed legs. The bones are not strong enough to support the body's weight. What treatment would you recommend for rickets? Explain your answer.

28. **Analyzing Data** In a boxing match there are rules against "hitting below the belt." Based on what you know about the human skeleton, explain why this rule makes sense.

and tendons; bones (meet at) joints; bones (form from) cartilage; cartilage (cushions) joints; ligaments (join) bones; tendons (attach muscles to) bones.
26. There likely was a problem with blood cell production.
27. The approved treatment is a diet rich in calcium and vitamin D.

28. There are no bones to protect digestive and excretory organs located below the rib cage.
29. The muscles take about two minutes to warm up from a resting temperature of about 24 °C. They must be around 38°C before flight.
30. According to the table, slow twitch fibers are Type Y because athletes who

29. Interpreting a Graph A sphinx moth has powerful flight muscles located in its thorax region. Pairs of muscles alternate contractions to produce wing beats. As a preflight warmup, the moth contracts both sets of muscles at the same time. According to the graph, how long does it take the moth to warm up its flight muscles? What temperature must those muscles be before the moth can fly?

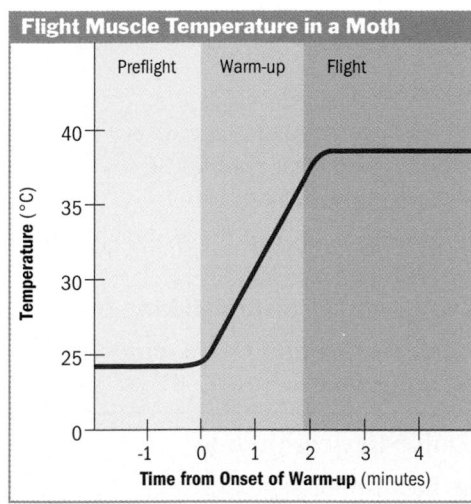

Flight Muscle Temperature in a Moth

Preflight Warm-up Flight

Temperature (°C) — vertical axis with values 0, 25, 30, 35, 40

Time from Onset of Warm-up (minutes) — horizontal axis with values -1, 0, 1, 2, 3, 4

30. Analyzing Data There are two types of skeletal muscle fibers—slow-twitch and fast-twitch. People are born with different amounts of each type. Type X is best for short bursts of activity that require maximum strength. Type Y is better for aerobic activities that require a lot of endurance. Based on the following table, are slow-twitch fibers Type X or Type Y?

Physical Activity and Slow-twitch Muscle Fibers	
Activity	**Proportion of Slow-twitch Muscle Fibers**
Cross-country skier	80%
Long-distance runner	65%
Swimmer	58%
Weight lifter	55%
Sprinter	50%

31. Designing an Experiment Flexibility is the ability to bend joints and stretch muscles. Design an experiment to measure the effects of exercise on flexibility. How could you measure flexibility? What exercises could you do to increase flexibility? Caution: Do not perform any tests or exercises without the help of a trained adult supervisor.

Consider the Issues

32. The Steroid Quick Fix Some athletes take a synthetic version of the male hormone testosterone to increase muscle fibers. The potential side effects of steroid use include increased blood pressure, higher cholesterol levels, infertility, severe depression, and violent behavior. Should athletes who take steroids be allowed to compete with those who do not?

Make New Connections

33. Biology and Literature Locate the Achilles tendon in the body. How did it get its name? What is the relationship between the Achilles tendon and the phrase "Achilles' heel"?

34. Biology and Physical Education People with varying physical abilities participate in a variety of strenuous activities. For example, some wheelchair athletes compete in marathons. Research other examples. Find out the different methods athletes use to meet their goals.

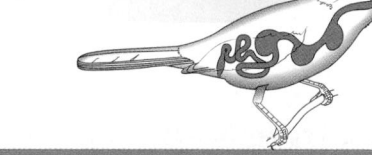

FAST-FORWARD TO CHAPTER 30

Muscles get the energy they need from cellular respiration. In Chapter 30 you will study the digestive system, which supplies the fuel for cellular respiration, and the excretory system, which removes waste products from the body.

side of the ankle. Thetis, the mother of Achilles, a hero of Greek myth, dipped him in the river Styx after birth to make him invulnerable. She held him by the heel, which didn't get wet. With Apollo's help, Paris killed him during the Trojan War with an arrow to his ankle. To have an "Achilles heel" is to have a weakness.

34. Students may want to investigate the history of the Special Olympics.

Chapter 29 Skin, Skeletal, and Muscular Systems **717**

compete in endurance activities such as cross-country skiing and long-distance running have a higher proportion of that type of fiber.

31. The flexibility of lower back and leg muscles can be tested with a sit-and-reach activity. Disciplines such as yoga focus on stretching activities. Perhaps a physical education instructor could

demonstrate some recommended warmup exercises.

32. You may want to ask students why someone might pursue risky behavior even when they are aware of the consequences. Students may also want to discuss whether drug testing is an effective deterrent.

33. The Achilles tendon is on the dorsal

PLANNING GUIDE

Section	Student Activities/Features	Teacher's Resource Package
30.1 Digestion **Objectives** ■ Define the activities of digestive systems ■ Compare the digestive systems of different organisms	**Lab Zone Discover It!** *Modeling the Function of Bile,* p. 719 **Everyday Biology** *Thin Fat,* p. 722 **Lab Zone Do It!** *How Do You Read a Food Label?* p. 724	**Unit 8 Review Module** ■ Section Review 30.1 ■ Activity Recordsheet 30-1 **Consumer Applications** 30-1 **Interpreting and Developing Graphics** 88
30.2 Human Digestive System **Objectives** ■ Describe the organs and structures of the human digestive tract ■ Explain the processes of digestion and absorption in humans	**Lab Zone Do It!** *How Does Peristalsis Work?* p. 727	**Unit 8 Review Module** ■ Section Review 30.2 ■ Activity Recordsheet 30-2 ■ Interpreting Graphics 30 ■ Enrichment Topic 30-1 **Laboratory Manual,** Lab 53: "Protein Digestion" **Issues and Decision Making** 30-1 **Interpreting and Developing Graphics** 89
30.3 Health of the Digestive System **Objectives** ■ Analyze the overall balance between eating food and using energy ■ Identify injuries and disorders of the digestive system ■ Evaluate ways to maintain a healthy digestive system	**Everyday Biology** *Outside Help, Inside,* p. 729 **In the Community** *A Helping Hand with the Groceries,* p. 730 **Lab Zone Think About It!** *Determining How Many of Your Calories Come from Fat,* p. 731 **Lab Zone Investigate It!** *Digesting Lactose,* p. 732	**Unit 8 Review Module** ■ Section Review 30.3 ■ Activity Recordsheet 30-3 ■ Critical Thinking Exercise 30 ■ Enrichment Topic 30-2
30.4 Excretion **Objectives** ■ Explain the functions of the excretory system ■ Contrast the excretory systems of various organisms		**Unit 8 Review Module** ■ Section Review 30.4
30.5 Human Excretory System **Objectives** ■ Describe the structure and function of the human excretory system ■ Judge the importance of the kidneys to blood chemistry and human health	**Everyday Biology** *Why Does Urine Change Color?* p. 738 **STS: Frontiers in Biology** *Kidney Help,* p. 738	**Unit 8 Review Module** ■ Section Review 30.5 ■ Vocabulary Review 30 ■ Chapter 30 Tests **Laboratory Manual,** Lab 54: "Simulated Urinalysis" **Issues and Decision Making** 30-2 **Interpreting and Developing Graphics** 90 **Spanish Reviews** Chapter 30

CHAPTER 30　Digestive and Excretory Systems

Technology Resources

Internet Connections

Within this chapter, you will see the **bioSURF** logo. If you and your students have access to the Internet, the following URL address will provide various Internet connections that are related to topics and features presented in this chapter:

http://body_systems.biosurf.com

You can also find relevant chapter material at **The Biology Place** address:

http://www.biology.com

CD-ROMs

Biología: la telaraña de la vida,
  (Spanish Student Edition) Chapter 30
Teacher's Resource Planner, Chapter 30
  Supplements
TestWorks CD-ROM
■ Chapter 30 Tests
How Your Body Works CD-ROM

Videodiscs

Animated Biological Concepts Videodiscs
■ Human Digestion
■ Kidney Function

Overhead Transparencies

■ Food Pyramid, #67
■ Human Digestive System, #68
■ Human Excretory System, #69
■ Nephron Function, #70

Videotapes

Biology Alive! Video Series
■ Domain of Life Video
Rewind: The Web of Life Reteach Videos

Planning for Activities

STUDENT EDITION
Lab Zone
Discover It! p. 719
■ bowl
■ water
■ vegetable oil
■ dishwashing liquid
■ medicine dropper

Lab Zone　Do It! p. 724
■ nutrition label

Lab Zone　Do It! p. 727
■ marbles
■ 25- to 30-cm length of
  flexible plastic or rubber
  tubing

Lab Zone
Investigate It! p. 732
■ liquid milk treatment
  product
■ microscope slides
■ eyedroppers
■ whole and skim milk
■ glucose solution
■ glucose test strips

TEACHER'S EDITION
Class Activity, p. 723
Examining vitamin labels
■ labels from various
  vitamin containers, to
  include multivitamins

Quick Activity, p. 725
Taste testing
■ 2 pieces of bread per
  student

Teacher Demo, p. 726
*Demonstrating chemical
digestion*
■ small pieces of lean
  meat
■ 3 test tubes
■ pepsin
■ water
■ dilute HCl
■ test tube rack

Teacher Demo, p. 727
The Heimlich Maneuver
■ poster of the Heimlich
  maneuver

Teacher Demo, p. 729
*Demonstrating a calori-
meter*
■ calorimeter
■ foods rich in different
  chemical nutrients

Teacher Demo, p. 733
Waste elimination
■ balloon
■ sink spigot

Quick Activity, p. 735
Kidney function
■ container
■ sand
■ clay
■ filter paper
■ funnel
■ 2-L bottle

Chapter Objectives

Students will learn the main concepts of this chapter as they complete the following objectives.

- Define the activities of digestive systems and compare those of different organisms
- Describe the organs and structures of the human digestive tract and explain the processes of digestion and absorption in humans
- Analyze the overall balance between eating food and using energy
- Identify injuries to and disorders of the digestive system
- Evaluate ways to maintain a healthy digestive system
- Explain the functions of the excretory system
- Contrast the excretory systems of various organisms
- Describe the structure and function of the human excretory system and judge the importance of the kidneys to blood chemistry and health

Key Words

30.1 digestive system, nutrient

30.2 salivary glands, esophagus, peristalsis, stomach, small intestine, villi, large intestine, liver, gallbladder, pancreas

30.3 metabolism, calorie, anorexia, bulimia

30.5 kidneys, nephrons

The Opening Story

Have students discuss how the story relates to the content of this chapter. Ask students how they think St. Martin felt about being the subject of ongoing medical experiments.

CHAPTER 30

Digestive and Excretory Systems

You can find out more about digestive and excretory systems at the following Internet address:
http://body_systems.biosurf.com

In this chapter . . .

FEATURES

Everyday Biology
- Thin Fat
- Outside Help, Inside
- Why Does Urine Change Color?

In the Community
A Helping Hand with the Groceries

 Frontiers in Biology
Kidney Help

LAB ZONES

Discover It!
- Modeling the Function of Bile

Do It!
- How Do You Read a Food Label?
- How Does Peristalsis Work?

Think About It!
- Determining How Many of Your Calories Come from Fat

Investigate It!
- Digesting Lactose

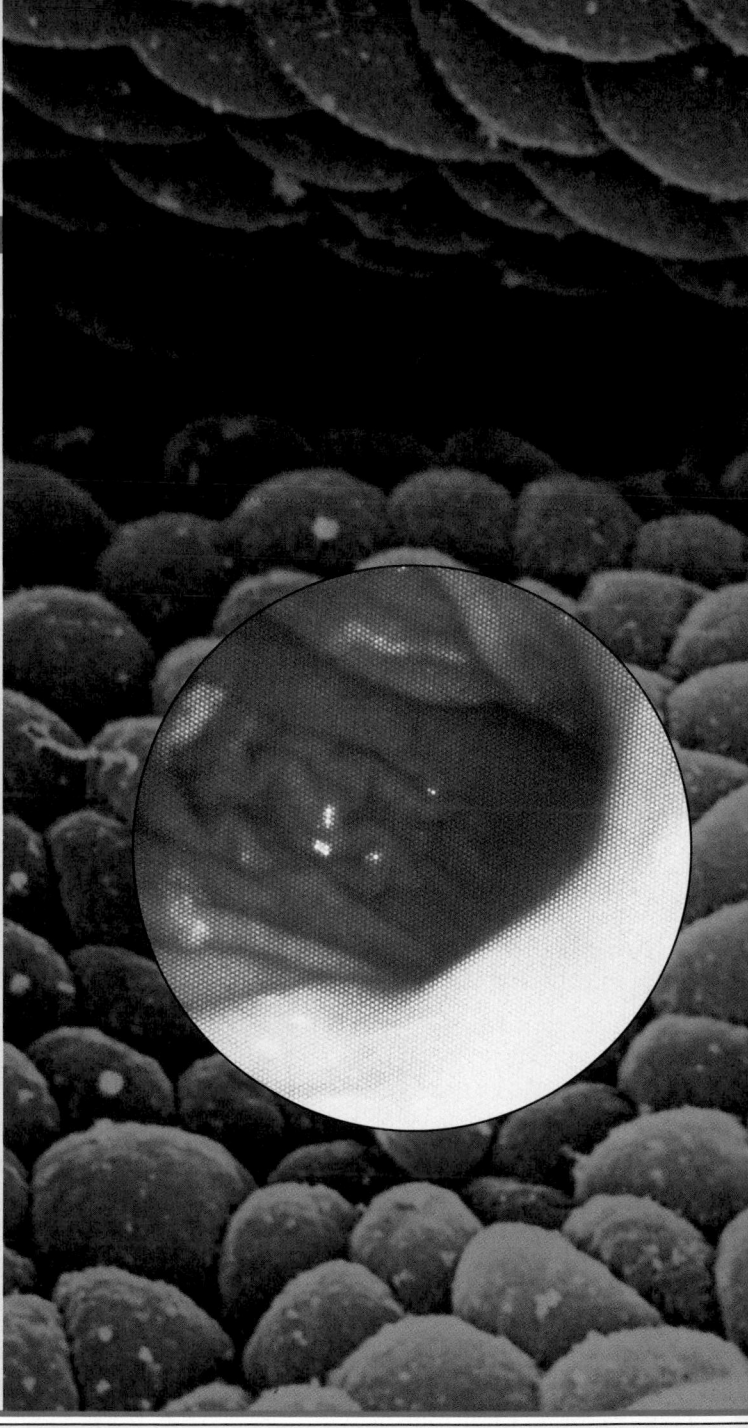

The man with a hole in his stomach

In 1822 Dr. William Beaumont, a young army surgeon at Fort Mackinac on the northwestern frontier, met the most important patient of his career. A 19-year-old French Canadian, Alexis St. Martin, received a shotgun blast to his chest and stomach at close range. It left a hole larger than the palm of his hand. No one, least of all the surgeon, expected him to live. But Beaumont treated St. Martin, who gradually improved over the next two years. At first St. Martin could not eat and had to be fed with a tube. Eventually, Beaumont was able to patch the hole with daily compresses.

Although the opening was partially healed, it would not close, despite Beaumont's best efforts. Fascinated by his "window" on St. Martin's digestive system, Beaumont began to experiment on his patient (with St. Martin's permission). Beaumont was able to look directly into St. Martin's stomach and observe the process of digestion. For example, food such as oysters or meat could be tied to string, inserted, and reexamined at specific intervals. In 1833 Beaumont published the results of more than 200 experiments on St. Martin.

St. Martin eventually recovered and lived to the age of 86. Beaumont and St. Martin's unusual doctor-patient relationship greatly contributed to our knowledge of the human digestive system. Today, sophisticated medical devices provide us with internal views of the stomach, like those shown on these pages.

 **Discover It!**

Modeling the Function of Bile

You need *a bowl, water, vegetable oil, dishwashing liquid, a medicine dropper*

1. Using the dropper, add about ten drops of vegetable oil to a bowl of water. Observe and record what happens.
2. Add five or six drops of dishwashing liquid to the middle of the bowl. Observe and record what happens.

The detergent breaks up the large drops of oil into smaller droplets. In a similar manner, bile in your digestive system breaks fat globules into smaller droplets of fat.

WRITE ABOUT IT!

Imagine that you are the young surgeon. Write a letter to a friend describing your experience treating St. Martin.

719

30.1

ENGAGE

Consider the Big Idea

Have students read The Big Idea! at the top of the page. Explain that animals have developed specialized structures that enable them to break food down for nutrition.

Use the Visual

Have students study the photograph and read the text that opens the section. Explain that digestion provides the body with materials needed for energy. Ask:

- **What is the source of energy used by blue whales?** (Plankton)
- **What process makes the energy in plankton available to the blue whale?** (Digestion)

Quick Activity

Have students select a popular fast-food restaurant and name the different kinds of foods served there. Record the foods on the board. Then have students use the foods listed to plan a nutritious and balanced meal for themselves. Have students support their choices. Tell students that in this section they will learn about the nutritional value of foods.

30.1 Digestion

What you'll learn

IDEAS
- To define the activities of digestive systems
- To compare the digestive systems of different organisms

WORDS
digestive system, nutrient

Big (and small) appetites
During the four months each year that blue whales eat, they consume about 4000 kilograms (kg) of plankton a day. To eat that amount, a whale takes 79 immense gulps of ocean water daily. A rat eats only 12 to 15 grams (g) of food a day. Both animals replace 4 to 5 percent of their body weight each day, regardless of the food quantity they eat.

THE DIGESTIVE PROCESS
Chew, chew, chew...

How much food do you eat in a day? What foods do you eat every day to stay healthy? Humans and other animals have a **digestive system** to process food. The processing begins when an animal ingests food by taking it into the body. The animal moves the food through its digestive system, breaking down the food to extract nutrients. A **nutrient** is a substance needed by the body for growth, repair, and maintenance. Finally, the animal eliminates the remaining material as solid waste.

During this process, three activities take place to extract nutrients from foods: mechanical digestion, chemical digestion, and absorption. Mechanical digestion breaks food into tiny pieces without changing its chemical structure. Chemical digestion breaks food down into smaller, simpler molecules—nutrients. Absorption

occurs when these nutrients are taken into the body's cells.

Heterotrophic organisms have various ways of digesting food. *Figure 30.1* shows a unicellular protist called *Paramecium*. Paramecia ingest food particles and digest them in specialized food vacuoles. This type of digestion, called intracellular digestion ("intra-" means "inside"), is relatively slow and can process only small amounts of food at a time. You may remember from Chapter 16 that fungi secrete chemicals into their foods and then absorb the food's nutrients. This process is called extracellular digestion, ("extra-" means "outside"). Simple multicellular organisms, such as sponges, also depend on intracellular digestion to obtain their nutrients.

Most types of animals need a faster way to digest food. They have specialized digestive systems for ingesting and processing larger amounts of food. Nutrients from the processed food are transported to body cells. In complex multicellular animals, nutrients are transported to body cells by another specialized organ system, the circulatory system. The digestive system eliminates any undigested material from the body.

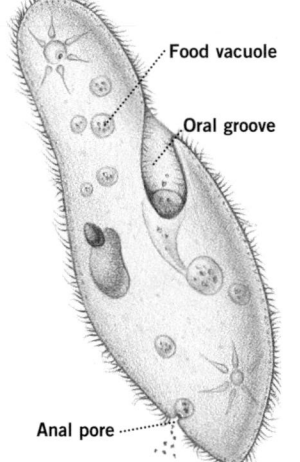

Food vacuole

Oral groove

Anal pore

FIGURE 30.1

Why is the digestive process of this paramecium described as intracellular?

720 *Unit 8 Human Biology*

STUDENT RESOURCES

From the Teacher's Resource Package, use:
- Section Review 30.1 and Activity Recordsheet 30-1 from Unit 8 Review Module
- Consumer Applications 30-1

TECHNOLOGY RESOURCES

Relevant technology resources include:
- Spanish Student Edition CD-ROM
- Teacher's Resource Planner CD-ROM
- How Your Body Works CD-ROM

Some animals, such as cnidarians and certain flatworms, have a saclike digestive system with one opening to the outside of the body. This opening serves both to ingest food and expel wastes. For example, the sea anemone in *Figure 30.2* uses a ring of tentacles to capture prey. The tentacles push food into the body opening of the sea anemone. The food is partly digested in the animal's digestive cavity. Fragments of partly digested food are ingested by cells lining the digestive cavity, and digestion is completed intracellularly. After the food is digested, any wastes exit out of the same opening through which they entered.

Other animals, such as worms, mollusks, echinoderms, arthropods, and vertebrates, have a tubelike digestive system with two openings to the outside of the body. You can see two examples of this type of digestive system in *Figure 30.3*. Food enters through a mouth opening and moves in one direction through the body as it is processed. Undigested material moves out of the body through an opening called an anus.

Along the way through the body, different parts of the digestive system perform different jobs. There may be areas for cutting and grinding, storing, and mixing food, and for its chemical

breakdown. There are also areas for the absorption of nutrients and storage of waste.

For example, mechanical digestion begins in the mouth of a mammal, as teeth cut and chew the food. Glands in the mouth produce saliva to mix with the food and start the process of chemical digestion. After being swallowed, the food travels to the stomach, where muscular action softens it to a pulpy mass and digestive fluids break it down chemically. Glands in the liver and pancreas secrete fluids into the digestive system that break the food down further as it travels through the small intestine. There, nutrients from food are absorbed into the bloodstream to be transported all over the body.

FIGURE 30.2
What type of digestion occurs in this sea anemone? ❷

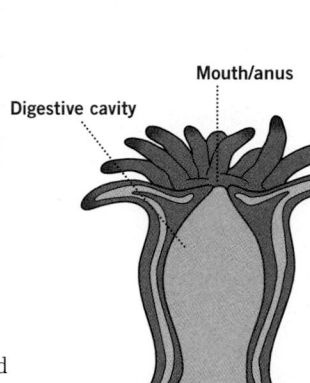

Mouth/anus

Digestive cavity

FIGURE 30.3
What must happen to food as it moves between the mouth and anus of a grasshopper or a bird? ❸

Mouth

Anus

Anus

Mouth

■ Digestive tract

Chapter 30 Digestive and Excretory Systems **721**

---

❶ The whole process takes place within a single cell.
❷ One opening in a saclike digestive system ingests food and expels wastes.
❸ Both mechanical and chemical digestion must take place.

30.1

TEACH

Use the Visual

Direct students' attention to Figure 30.2. Review how cnidarians obtain and digest food. Have students trace the path of digestion in the cnidarian shown. Ask:

- **How would you describe the digestive system of a cnidarian?** (It is a simple system in which food enters through an opening, is digested in the body cavity. Wastes then exit through the same opening.)

Use the Visual

After students read about the digestive process, have them study Figure 30.3. Ask:

- **How are the digestive systems of the bird and grasshopper similar?** (Both consist of a mouth, a digestive tract, and an anus.)
- **What is the function of the anus?** (The anus is an opening through which undigested food and wastes exit the body.)
- **What other animals have digestive systems similar to those of grasshoppers and birds?** (Complex animals such as vertebrates, arthropods, and echinoderms)

Class Activity

TEAM WORK

Have students work in pairs to prepare a flow chart, concept map, or other graphic to show the mechanical and chemical processes that occur as food progresses through the digestion process. Check students' work.

Everyday Biology

Encourage interested students to use the *Readers' Guide to Periodical Literature* or the Internet to locate current articles about olestra. Have them use their research to write a position paper on whether or not olestra should be marketed.

Use the Visual

Before students read about the chemistry of foods, have them study Figure 30.4. Ask:

- **What types of food make up the pyramid base?** (Bread, cereal, rice, and pasta)
- **How do the recommended daily servings of milk, cheese, and yogurt compare to the daily servings of meat?** (They are the same.)
- **What types of foods should be eaten sparingly?** (Foods rich in fats, oils, and sweets.)

Class Activity

Have students list all the foods they eat each day for one week. Tell them to compare their diet to the food pyramid. Then have students list the changes needed to make their diet match the recommended diet in the food pyramid.

 Art

Have students make a three-dimensional model of a food pyramid with pictures of foods from magazines to illustrate their model.

Undigested material moves into the large intestine and leaves the body through the anus.

EVERYDAY BIOLOGY

Thin Fat

Food chemists have invented olestra, a fat that passes through the digestive system without being absorbed. To some people, olestra is a guilt-free fat. Others dislike olestra's taste and question whether it is healthful.

CHEMISTRY OF FOODS

Little things count

Foods contain five types of chemical nutrients: carbohydrates, fats, proteins, vitamins, and minerals. Each nutrient has a role in keeping a body healthy. Although it is not a nutrient, water is another substance that is vital to life.

The food pyramid in *Figure 30.4* represents the relative amounts of each type of food a person should eat daily to obtain all the necessary nutrients. How does your own daily diet compare to the food pyramid ❶ recommendations?

Carbohydrates Human body cells obtain most of their energy from carbohydrates. Carbohydrates (KAR-boh-HY-drayts) are compounds made

of carbon, hydrogen, and oxygen in a 1:2:1 ratio. Sugars and starches are examples of carbohydrates.

There are three types of carbohydrates. Single sugars, such as glucose, are monosaccharides (MON-oh-SAK-uh-rydz). Disaccharides (DY-sak-uh-rydz), such as sucrose or table sugar, consist of two single sugars linked together. Starches, like those in potatoes and bread, are polysaccharides (POL-ee-SAK-uh-rydz). Polysaccharides are carbohydrates made of long chains of simple sugars.

Fats Fats and oils belong to a group of compounds called lipids. As you may recall from Chapter 2, lipids are important for energy storage, and for the formation of cell membranes, hormones, and the oils on skin and hair. Most of the lipids your body needs come from the fats you eat. If your diet is very low in fat, your body will make lipids from other nutrients.

FIGURE 30.4

Food Pyramid

According to this food pyramid, what food group should form the largest part of your diet? ❷

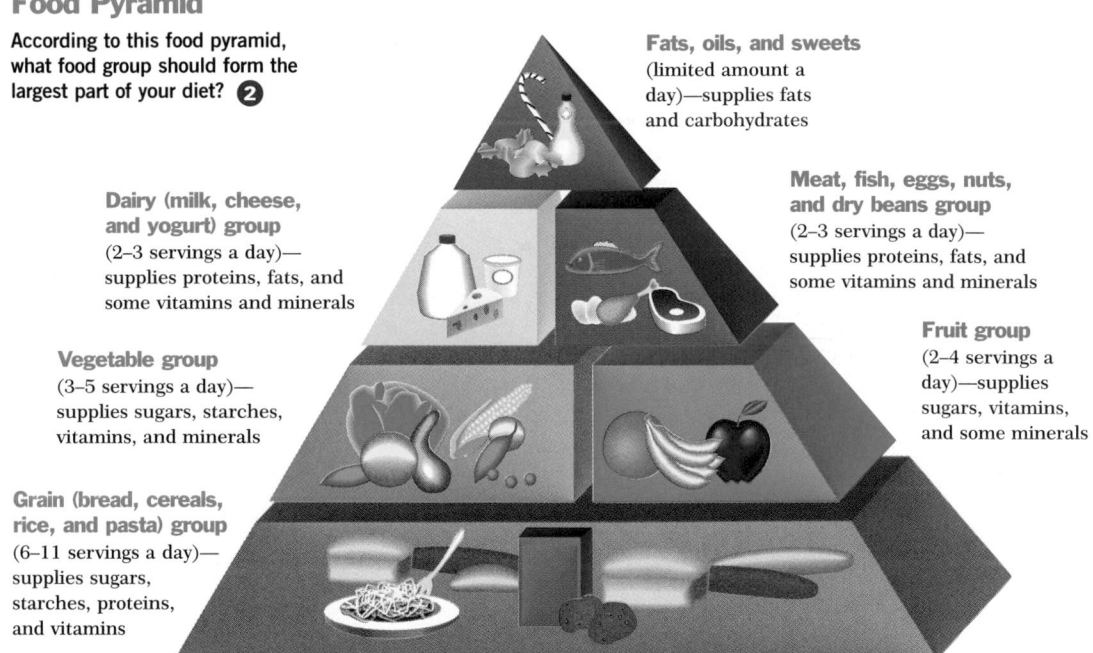

Fats, oils, and sweets (limited amount a day)—supplies fats and carbohydrates

Meat, fish, eggs, nuts, and dry beans group (2–3 servings a day)—supplies proteins, fats, and some vitamins and minerals

Fruit group (2–4 servings a day)—supplies sugars, vitamins, and some minerals

Dairy (milk, cheese, and yogurt) group (2–3 servings a day)—supplies proteins, fats, and some vitamins and minerals

Vegetable group (3–5 servings a day)—supplies sugars, starches, vitamins, and minerals

Grain (bread, cereals, rice, and pasta) group (6–11 servings a day)—supplies sugars, starches, proteins, and vitamins

722 *Unit 8 Human Biology*

MULTICULTURAL PERSPECTIVE

Several African Americans have gained recognition for their work with sugars. In the 1800s, Norbert Rillieux invented the triple-evaporator, a vacuum process used in the refining of sugar. He established scientific principles that made possible the process now used to make condensed milk, soap, and glue. In 1989, the Alexander von Humbolt Foundation named Bertram D. Frasier-Reid Sr. Distinguished U.S. Scientist for his work involving the synthesis of sugars from nonsugars.

A fat is made of three fatty acids joined to a glycerol molecule. Fatty acids are chains of carbon and hydrogen atoms with a weak acid attached to one end. When you eat foods containing fats, your body breaks the fats down into glycerol and fatty acids. Your body can use these raw materials to make the lipids it needs.

Fats are classified as either saturated or unsaturated, depending on the type of chemical bonds between the carbons in the fat molecule. Fats with one or more double bonds are unsaturated fats. A fat with one double bond is a monounsaturated fat, while a fat with many double bonds is a polyunsaturated fat. Most unsaturated fats, such as vegetable oil and olive oil, are liquids at room temperature. Saturated fats have no double bonds and are usually solid at room temperature. Butter and lard are common examples of saturated fats.

Proteins Your body contains hundreds of different proteins. Proteins are materials used to construct body parts such as muscle, skin, and blood. All these proteins are formed from 20 different amino acids. Twelve of these amino acids can be made by your body. Amino acids that cannot be made by the body are called essential amino acids. Humans must obtain the eight essential amino acids from proteins in food.

In order for your body to use the proteins in foods, the proteins must be broken down into their component amino acids. Cells then use the amino acids to make new proteins. These proteins are used for growth, repair, and as enzymes in cellular metabolism. During severe dieting or starvation, the body will break down the protein in its own muscles to obtain the energy it needs.

Vitamins Vitamins are complex organic molecules that are needed by the body in very small amounts. Unlike other nutrients, vitamins do

Some Important Vitamins

	Vitamin	Major Sources	RDA
Water Soluble	Thiamin (B1)	Beans, peanuts, meat (especially pork), whole grains, eggs	1.1–1.5 mg
	Riboflavin (B2)	Dairy products, eggs, green leafy vegetables, yeast	1.3–1.7 mg
	Niacin	Meat, poultry, fish, peanuts	20 mg
	B6	Meat, poultry, fish, potatoes, sweet potatoes	2.0–2.2 mg
	B12	Meat, poultry, fish, eggs, dairy products	3–6 mg
	C	Fruits and vegetables, especially citrus fruits, cantaloupe, strawberries, tomatoes, green leafy vegetables	60 mg
Fat Soluble	A	Dark yellow vegetables (such as carrots), green leafy vegetables, liver, eggs	4000–5000 IU*
	D	Sunlight, fish liver oil, fortified milk	400 IU
	E	Vegetable oils, seeds, whole grains	30 IU
	K	Green leafy vegetables, cabbage, pork liver, intestinal bacteria	55–70 mg

*IU = international unit

FIGURE 30.5
What vitamins did you ingest with your breakfast this morning? ❸

not contain energy. Most vitamins play a role in cellular reactions by acting in conjunction with enzymes. With the exception of vitamin D, vitamins are not made by the body and must be obtained from food.

Water-soluble vitamins cannot be stored in the body and must be obtained from the daily diet. Fat-soluble vitamins, on the other hand, can be stored in the liver or body fat for future use.

The United States government has established guidelines for the recommended daily allowance (RDA) of each vitamin. These numbers are updated periodically to reflect current research. *Figure 30.5* lists some important vitamins and their sources. What foods are major sources of vitamin B6? Vitamin C? ❹

Minerals Minerals are inorganic molecules that perform vital functions in the body. For example, calcium is a major component of bones and teeth. Iron is essential for transporting oxygen in the blood. Nerves and muscles need potassium, sodium, calcium, and

Chapter 30 Digestive and Excretory Systems **723**

 Health

Unsaturated fats are generally considered more healthful than saturated fats. Most saturated fats are in animal products, including dairy products. Some oils, such as palm oil, coconut oil, and other "tropical oils," also contain saturated fats. Unsaturated fats are extracted from vegetable products, such as soy beans, cotton seed, and peanuts.

Use the Visual

Have students study Figure 30.5. Ask students which foods they should eat daily to ensure that they are getting recommended daily allowances of water soluble vitamins.

Build Writing Skills

Have students choose a specific vitamin and write a report on what diseases or health problems may result from a deficiency or an excess of the vitamin. Have students share their reports with the class.

Class Activity

Bring in, or ask students to bring in, labels from varied vitamin containers. Make sure that different brands of multivitamins are included. Give students an opportunity to examine the labels and discuss the kinds of information presented. To extend the lesson, you may want to have students compare prices of selected vitamins in a local pharmacy, supermarket, and health food store.

MEETING DIVERSE NEEDS

At Risk Have students work with a partner to create a graphic that identifies essential nutrients, their functions, and the foods in which they are found. Students can make cartoons, collages, or concept maps.

❶ Answers will vary.
❷ Grain group
❸ Answers will vary.
❹ Meat, poultry, fish, potatoes; fruits and vegetables, especially citrus fruits and green leafy vegetables

How Do You Read a Food Label?

Encourage students who choose food labels from similar products to compare the labels.

Analyze Your Results

1 They are based on a 2000-calorie diet.
2 Answers will vary.
3 Check that students support their choices.

ASSESS

Evaluate Understanding

Have students sketch a food pyramid that identifies the daily number of servings recommended for each food group. Have students list the most abundant nutrients in each food group and identify the nutrients' function in the body.

Reteach

Draw an unlabeled food pyramid on the board or a transparency. Work with students to fill in the names (or paste pictures) of foods making up each food group in the correct place on the pyramid. Then have students review the section to identify which foods on the pyramid are good sources of selected vitamins and minerals.

FIGURE 30.6
A balanced diet usually provides all the minerals the body needs each day.

Some Important Minerals

Mineral	Major Sources	RDA
Calcium	Dairy products, shellfish, green leafy vegetables	800–1200 mg
Phosphorus	Milk, eggs, meat, poultry, fish, beans, whole grains	800 mg
Magnesium	Dairy products, whole grains, beans	300–350 mg
Iron	Meat, liver, shellfish, dried fruit, molasses	10–15 mg
Iodine	Shellfish, fish liver oil, iodized salt	0.15 mg

magnesium to function properly. Some important minerals are listed in *Figure 30.6.*

Your body cannot store most minerals. Therefore, minerals must be included regularly in your diet. Some minerals come from plants, which absorb the minerals from the soil. Other minerals can be obtained by eating animal products.

Water Although it is not a nutrient, water is necessary for life. Water in body tissues accounts for at least half of your total body mass. About 90 percent of plasma, the liquid part of the blood, is water. Every day your body loses 3–5 liters (L) of water through sweat, urine, and exhaled air. The water is replaced when you drink and eat. Water is also produced in the body as a by-product of cellular respiration.

Water serves many functions in the body. It transports nutrients and wastes and is necessary for many chemical reactions. Water also helps cool the body through perspiration.

How Do You Read a Food Label?

A food label contains important information about the nutritional value of a food. You can determine a food's nutritional value if you . . .

Try This

1 Locate the nutrition label on a packaged food product. Find the serving size on the label.
2 Locate the total amount of calories, fat, cholesterol, sodium, carbohydrates, and protein in a serving.
3 Record the percentages of the total daily requirements for all nutrients, minerals, and vitamins in a serving of the product.

Analyze Your Results

1 How are the percentages of nutrients, minerals, and vitamins calculated?
2 Is the listed serving size the amount of that food that you would normally eat? If necessary, recalculate all data to reflect your usual serving size.
3 What nutrients, vitamins, and minerals might we have too little of in our diet? Why? Too much? Why?

2% REDUCED FAT MILK

Nutrition Facts
Serving Size: 1 cup (240 mL)
Servings Per Container: 8

Amount per serving

Calories 130 Calories from fat 45

	%Daily Value*
Total Fat 5g	8%
Saturated Fat 3g	15%
Cholesterol 20g	7%
Sodium 130g	5%
Total Carbohydrate 12g	4%
Dietary Fiber 0g	0%
Sugars 12g	
Protein 8g	

Vitamin A	15%	Vitamin C	4%
Calcium	30%	Iron	0%
Vitamin D	4%		

*Percent Daily Values are based on a 2000 calorie diet. Your daily values may be higher or lower depending on your calorie needs.

CHECKPOINT 30.1

1. What are the three activities of the digestive system?
2. Compare and contrast the digestive systems of a paramecium and an arthropod.
3. Critical Thinking Imagine you have a friend who is trying to lose weight by eating only eggs and grapefruit. Explain to this friend what nutrients are missing from the diet, and suggest foods that might balance the diet.

Build on What You Know

4. How are enzymes involved in an animal's digestive process? *(Need to jog your memory? Review relevant concepts in Chapter 2, Section 2.3.)*

CHECKPOINT 30.1

1. Digestive systems carry out mechanical digestion, chemical digestion, and absorption.
2. Digestion in paramecia is slow and takes place inside cellular vacuoles. In arthropods, digestion takes place in a tubelike tract.
3. **Analyzing** This diet is lacking vitamins such as E, niacin, B6, and K, and in minerals such as calcium, magnesium, and iron. Adding whole grains, green leafy vegetables, and fish, meat, or poultry, would improve the diet.
4. Enzymes are catalysts that speed up the reactions involved in chemical digestion to a biologically useful rate.

30.2 Human Digestive System

A round and skinny diet?
What if you decided to eat only spaghetti? In order to get enough calories, a 56-kg teenage girl would need to eat nearly 3.8 kg of pasta a day, about 36 large servings. A 61-kg boy would need to eat nearly 5 kg, about 44 servings each day. And that is without the sauce.

What you'll learn

IDEAS
• To describe the organs and structures of the human digestive tract
• To explain the processes of digestion and absorption in humans

WORDS
salivary glands, esophagus, peristalsis, stomach, small intestine, villi, large intestine, liver, gallbladder, pancreas

FROM DIGESTIVE TRACT TO BODY CELLS

Digestion is absorbing

Could you create a list of foods that contain all the nutrients your body needs in a day? Your body cannot use the nutrients in foods you eat until the food is chemically broken down into small molecules. As you learned in the previous section, digestion is the process by which foods are broken down into usable nutrients. Digestion in humans occurs in the organs of the digestive tract. The process is assisted by other organs of the human digestive system. Is digestion in humans **❶** intracellular or extracellular?

The human digestive tract (shown on page 726) consists of the mouth, pharynx, esophagus, stomach, small intestine, and large intestine. All three activities of the digestive process—mechanical digestion, chemical digestion, and absorption—occur in the human digestive tract. As you read about these organs, try to identify which activities occur at each step in the digestive process.

Mouth The first step in the human digestive process is to begin chewing food. Chewing starts the process of mechanical digestion. You may remember from Chapter 27 that

different types of chewing are performed by different teeth: incisors, canines, molars, and so on. At the same time, the **salivary glands** produce saliva to begin the process of chemical digestion. Study *Figure 30.7*. Where are the salivary glands located in your mouth? The watery saliva mixes with **❷** the chewed food. Enzymes in saliva kill bacteria and begin the breakdown of starches into sugars. The food is pushed to the back of the mouth by the tongue and then swallowed.

FIGURE 30.7
What is the digestive function of each structure in the mouth? ❸

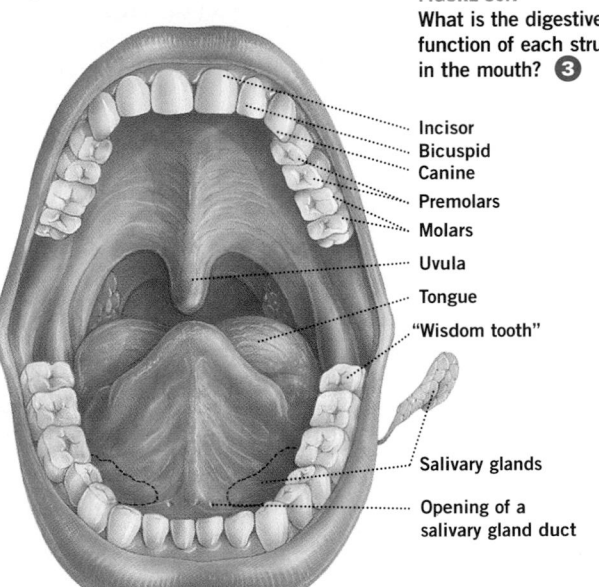

- Incisor
- Bicuspid
- Canine
- Premolars
- Molars
- Uvula
- Tongue
- "Wisdom tooth"
- Salivary glands
- Opening of a salivary gland duct

Chapter 30 Digestive and Excretory Systems **725**

❶ ENGAGE

Use the Visual

Have students study the photograph that opens the section. Remind students that a person should eat 6 to 11 servings of grain products daily, but that a balanced diet should also include servings from other food groups.

Quick Activity

Distribute two pieces of bread to each student. Have students chew the first piece quickly and describe how it tastes. Then have them chew the second piece slowly until it breaks down and describe how it tastes. Challenge them to explain why the second piece had a sweet taste and the first piece did not. (Saliva had time to break down complex carbohydrates into simple sugars in the second piece.)

❶ Extracellular
❷ On either side of the mouth
❸ Teeth chew the food; salivary glands begin chemical digestion; the tongue pushes the food to the back of the mouth.

 Animated Biological Concepts

 Human Digestion

 Play

② TEACH

Use the Visual

After students read about the digestive process, refer them to Figure 30.8. Use the visual to trace the pathway food takes as it moves through the body. Ask:

- **Into what organ does food pass after it is swallowed?** (Esophagus)
- **What action moves food through the esophagus?** (Peristalsis)
- **Where is chyme and mucus produced?** (In the stomach)
- **Where would you find villi?** (In the small intestine)
- **What organ processes undigested wastes and water from digestion?** (The large intestine)

Teacher Demo

To demonstrate chemical digestion, place small pieces of lean meat into three test tubes. Add pepsin to the first and second test tubes until they are one quarter full. Next, add water to the first test tube and dilute HCl to the second until the tubes are half full. Fill the third tube halfway with water. Place all test tubes in a rack and let them remain undisturbed for 24 hours. Have students observe how the liquids affect the meat. (Test tube 2 containing pepsin and HCl will digest the most meat, test tube 1 containing pepsin will digest some of the meat, test tube 3 containing water will not digest the meat.)

726

FIGURE 30.8

The Human Digestive System

What structures shown in this diagram produce chemicals that aid in digestion? ❶

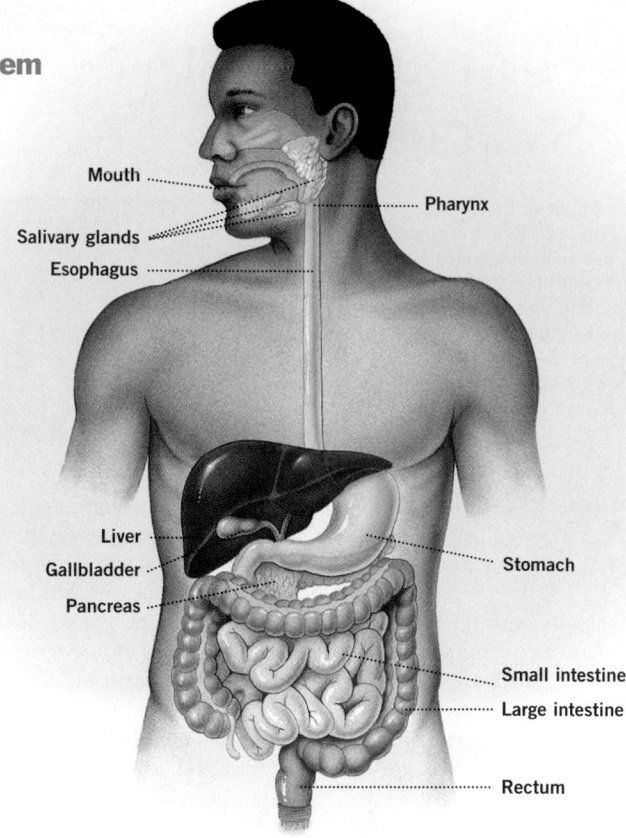

Pharynx and esophagus As you swallow food, it moves through the region in the back of the throat called the pharynx (FAIR-inks). When you swallow, a small flap of tissue called the epiglottis closes the trachea at the entrance to your respiratory tract. This ensures that food enters a long muscular tube called the **esophagus** (eh-SOF-uh-gus). Food moves toward the stomach by **peristalsis,** a successive wave of smooth muscle contractions in the esophagus wall. A circular muscle at the bottom of the esophagus acts as a valve. When the muscle relaxes, the valve opens, and food enters the stomach.

Stomach Your **stomach** is a muscular sac with thick, expandable walls. Mechanical digestion occurs as the stomach walls contract strongly,

mixing and churning the food you have swallowed. Chemical digestion continues as hydrochloric acid and an enzyme called pepsin are secreted by glands in your stomach. Pepsin breaks down protein. Glands in the stomach also produce mucus. Mucus lubricates the digestive tract and coats the stomach lining to protect it from digestive fluids.

After about three hours in the stomach, food is reduced to a soft pulp called chyme (kym). Chyme is made of acids, partially digested proteins and carbohydrates, and undigested fats. A valve at the bottom of the stomach opens, allowing small amounts of chyme to pass into the small intestine.

Small intestine In the **small intestine,** digestion of carbohydrates and proteins is completed, fats are

726 *Unit 8 Human Biology*

---

❶ Salivary glands, liver, gallbladder, pancreas, stomach, and small intestine digested, and nutrients are absorbed. Your small intestine is about 2.5 centimeters (cm) wide and 7 meters (m) long. You can see fingerlike projections called villi in *Figure 30.9*. **Villi** line the internal surface of the small intestine, increasing its surface area and making absorption more efficient.

Nutrients are absorbed in the cells of the villi and passed into blood vessels and lymph vessels called lacteals. Blood vessels absorb carbohydrates and proteins. Lacteals absorb fats and fatty acids. Absorbed nutrients are carried to your body's cells by your circulatory system. Undigested material passes through a valve at the end of the small intestine to enter the large intestine.

Large intestine Your colon, or **large intestine,** is about 6 cm wide and 1.5 m long. In the large intestine, water and water-soluble vitamins are absorbed from undigested material. The water is redistributed to the rest of your body.

When most of the water has been removed, a solid waste matter, called feces (FEE-seez), remains. The feces move through the large intestine and into the rectum. Feces move out of the body through the anus.

The complete journey through the digestive tract is a long one. From mouth to anus, a bite of food must travel a distance of about 9 m. Typically 8 to 48 hours pass from the time food first enters your mouth until what remains of that food leaves your body.

 **Do It!**

How Does Peristalsis Work?

You can duplicate the way muscles move pieces of food through the esophagus to the stomach if you . . .

Try This

1 Place a marble inside one end of a 25- to 30-cm length of flexible plastic or rubber tubing.
2 With a squeezing motion of your hands, try to move the marble down and out the other end of the tube.
3 Repeat the process with two or three marbles in the tube.
4 Try it with one hand held tightly around the bottom end of the tube.

Analyze Your Results

1 What pattern of squeezing did you use to move the marble in the right direction?
2 Did including more marbles make a difference?
3 Which part of the esophagus did your closed hand at the bottom of the tube act like?

FIGURE 30.9

Villi are fingerlike projections that line the small intestine. What nutrients are absorbed by lacteals in the villi? ❷

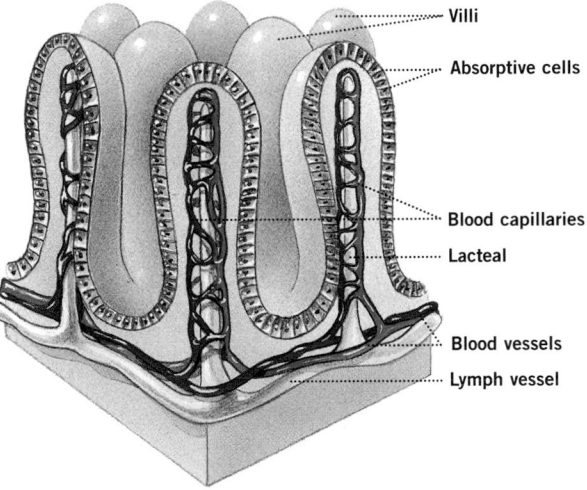

- Villi
- Absorptive cells
- Blood capillaries
- Lacteal
- Blood vessels
- Lymph vessel

Villi

Chapter 30 Digestive and Excretory Systems **727**

MEETING DIVERSE NEEDS

Gifted Have students research different enzymes that act in the digestive system to break down foods. Suggest that students present their research as a chart that can be displayed in class.

❷ Fats and fatty acids

Do It! **TEAM WORK**

How Does Peristalsis Work?

Try This

Check that the marbles fit properly in the tubing before students carry out the activity. You may need to model the squeezing motion for students.

Analyze Your Results

1 Successive, smooth squeezing
2 No, as long as the squeezing continued
3 The circular muscle at the bottom

Teacher Demo

Obtain a poster that shows how the Heimlich maneuver is performed. Tell students that the Heimlich maneuver is an emergency procedure performed on people who are choking. Ask:

- **What causes a person to choke?** (Swallowed food enters the pathway to the lungs instead of the pathway to the stomach.) If possible, invite an EMT or Red Cross worker to demonstrate the Heimlich maneuver to students.

Explain

Emphasize that when food is ready to pass from the small intestine to the large intestine, most digestion is complete.

Use the Visual

Have students study Figure 30.10. Point out on Figure 30.8 or another diagram of the human body where the organs in the figure are located. Ask:

- **Which organ stores bile?** (The gallbladder)
- **Where does the bile go after it is produced?** (To the small intestine)
- **What gland secretes a fluid into the small intestine?** (The pancreas)

ASSESS

Evaluate Understanding

To assess students' understanding of the human digestive system, reproduce Figure 30.8 on an overhead transparency. Replace the labels on the diagram with numbers. On a sheet of paper, have students identify each numbered structure and its function. Review their responses as a class.

Reteach

On the board, create a flowchart that traces the movement of food through the digestive system. Then have volunteers describe the role of each organ in digestion.

❶ Bile digests fats; pancreatic insulin controls uptake of glucose by cells.

FIGURE 30.10
The liver secretes bile and the pancreas secretes pancreatic fluid. How do these secretions aid in digestion? ❶

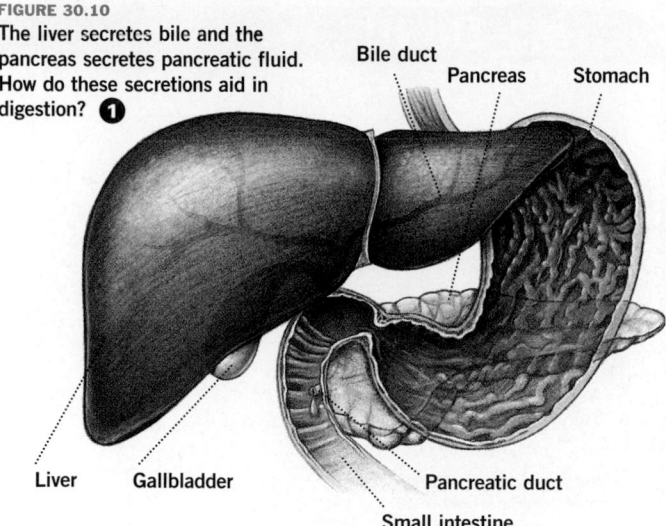

Bile duct · Pancreas · Stomach · Liver · Gallbladder · Pancreatic duct · Small intestine

ACCESSORY DIGESTIVE ORGANS

Digestive fluids and more

Although food does not pass through the liver, gallbladder, and pancreas, these organs play a key role in digestion. Each of these organs produces digestive fluids that are delivered to the digestive tract through ducts. In addition to aiding the digestive process, these organs perform many other vital body functions.

The **liver** is one of the largest organs of your body. In *Figures 30.8* and *30.10,* you can see the liver's size relative to other organs. This vital organ produces bile, which is a digestive fluid, and carries out more than 500 other functions. The liver is the body's main chemical factory. It processes nutrients, such as carbohydrates, fats, and proteins, into substances needed by the body.

Nutrients are also stored in the liver. For example, the liver converts glucose to glycogen for storage. The liver also stores iron and fat-soluble vitamins. Detoxification is another

important function of the liver. The liver breaks down alcohol, drugs, or toxic chemicals that enter the body.

As you can see in *Figure 30.10,* the **gallbladder** is a small saclike organ connected to the liver. The gallbladder's main function is to concentrate and store the bile produced by the liver. Bile is a yellow-green liquid containing cholesterol, pigments, bile salts, and other compounds. Bile emulsifies fats, breaking up large fat globules into many tiny droplets to make them easier to digest. The bile is released as needed through a duct to the small intestine.

The pancreas is located near the gallbladder. The **pancreas** is a gland that secretes pancreatic fluid into the small intestine. Pancreatic fluid is a mixture of digestive enzymes and sodium bicarbonate. Some cells of the pancreas also secrete hormones, chemical messengers of the endocrine system, into the blood. The pancreatic hormone called insulin controls the uptake of glucose by the cells of the body. You will learn more about the endocrine function of the pancreas in Chapter 33.

CHECKPOINT 30.2

1. Name the parts of the human digestive system, and explain what each part does.
2. Compare and contrast digestion and absorption.
3. **Critical Thinking** How would standing on your head while you ate a meal affect your digestive process?

Build on What You Know

4. Indigestion can occur when the stomach's contents become too acidic. Baking soda, also known as sodium bicarbonate, can be dissolved in water and taken as a remedy for indigestion. Why? *(Need to jog your memory? Revisit relevant concepts in Chapter 2, Section 2.5.)*

728 *Unit 8 Human Biology*

CHECKPOINT 30.2

1. Mouth: chewing, chemical digestion begins; pharynx and esophagus: moves food to stomach where mechanical and chemical digestion continues; small intestine: completes digestion of proteins and carbohydrates; and large intestine: processes wastes
2. Digestion breaks down food into small parts; absorption moves nutrients from the digestive tract into the blood.
3. **Developing a hypothesis** Swallowing might be more difficult, but peristalsis would continue to allow digestion to progress.
4. Baking soda forms a basic solution in water which neutralizes the low pH of stomach acid.

30.3 Health of the Digestive System

Lying down on the job
When you exercise, your metabolism speeds up. Running burns up more than ten times as much fuel as resting. Those who exercise regularly also increase their resting metabolism. In general, people who exercise often need to consume more calories than those who do not exercise regularly.

ENERGY BALANCE

A balancing act

Have you ever heard someone being told that they have a high metabolism? This usually means that their bodies use the energy in food almost as fast as they eat it. Recall from Chapter 2 that **metabolism** is the combination of all the chemical processes that take place within an organism. Metabolic processes control and manage the organism's energy resources.

Metabolism is a two-way street. Some metabolic pathways store energy, and others release energy. Pathways that release energy by breaking down complex compounds into simpler ones are called catabolic pathways. Pathways that use energy to build complex molecules from simpler ones are called anabolic pathways. Together, catabolic pathways and anabolic pathways make up metabolism.

Measuring energy One unit used to measure energy is the calorie. A **calorie** is the amount of heat energy needed to raise the temperature of 1g of water by 1°C. A calorie represents a very small amount of energy, so nutritionists use a unit called the kilocalorie (kcal) to measure energy. A kilocalorie is 1000 calories and is usually written as *Calorie* with a capital *C*. The calories you see listed on food labels are actually Calories, or kilocalories.

To measure the energy value of a food, a small sample of the food is burned, and the amount of heat it gives off is measured with an instrument called a calorimeter. Using a calorimeter, scientists have determined the approximate energy value of fats, proteins, and carbohydrates. As you can see in the table in *Figure 30.11*, fats have more than twice the energy per unit of mass than do carbohydrates or proteins.

Many doctors and nutritionists recommend that people obtain no more than 30 percent of their energy from fats. To determine the percentage of kilocalories derived from fat in a commercial food product, check the nutritional information label. If the percentage is not shown, multiply the number of fat grams by 9. Then divide this number by the total number of

Approximate Energy Values	
Compound	**Energy Value (kcal/g)**
Fats	9
Carbohydrates	4
Proteins	4

What you'll learn

IDEAS
- To analyze the overall balance between eating food and using energy
- To identify injuries and disorders of the digestive system
- To evaluate ways to maintain a healthy digestive system

WORDS
metabolism, calorie, anorexia, bulimia

Outside Help, Inside

Bacteria—nearly enough to fill a soup can—live inside the human intestines. These bacteria aid in the process of digestion and secrete useful vitamins, including thiamine and vitamin K. The antibiotics taken to kill disease-causing germs can also kill these helpful organisms and upset the digestive system.

FIGURE 30.11
Scientists measure the approximate energy value of compounds in food in kilocalories per gram (kcal/g).

Chapter 30 Digestive and Excretory Systems **729**

2 TEACH

Explain

Explain to students that the glycogen stored in the liver and muscles, and the fat stored in other body tissues provide their bodies with an energy reserve. This reserve is used when fewer Calories are taken into the body than are used. A person who diets to lose weight must use these reserves, especially the fat reserves, before weight is lost.

Math

Suggest students estimate their BMR in kilocalories for a day. Females should add a zero to their weight and then add their weight to that figure. (For a 110-pound female: 1100 + 110 = 1210 kilocalories/day) Males should add a zero to their weight, then add 2 times their weight to that figure. (For a 150-pound male: 1500 + 300 = 1800 kilocalories/day)

In the Community

Some students may have worked in community food banks. Invite them to share their experiences with the class. Suggest that students locate the names and addresses of local food banks in their telephone directory.

FIGURE 30.12
The scale below shows the average number of kilocalories used per hour during various activities.

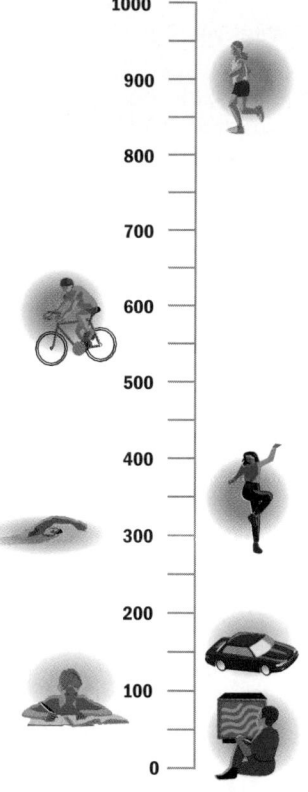

kilocalories in the food product, and multiply by 100.

Metabolic rate If a laboratory technician measured your metabolism while you were at rest, the result would be a number called the basal metabolic rate (BMR). Your BMR is equal to the number of kilocalories you use in a set amount of time just to stay alive. The BMR of a human female is about 1300 to 1500 kcal per day. A human male has a BMR of about 1600 to 1800 kcal per day. Your actual BMR depends on factors such as your age and level of fitness. Your overall metabolic rate is your BMR plus the number of kilocalories you use during your activities. If you participate in more strenuous activities, your overall metabolic rate rises.

Storing energy Your body is constantly balancing the calories you consume with the calories you use. This balance can be upset, however, by changing either the number of calories you eat or the number of calories you use for activities. The body stores extra calories first as glycogen in the liver and muscles, and then as fat. A healthy body stores enough glycogen to last approximately one day, and enough fat to last several days.

If you regularly take in more calories than you use, you will gain weight. On the other hand, if you take in fewer calories than your body uses every day, you will gradually lose weight. Deprived of food, the body starts using stored glycogen. Then the body uses stored fat. Finally, the body uses protein stored in muscles and other organs. Burning calories as you exercise can also help you lose weight. Which activities in *Figure 30.12* use the most calories? The fewest calories? **❶**

DIGESTIVE SYSTEM DISORDERS

It must be something you ate

Your digestive system constantly processes food from the environment. As a result, it is susceptible to attack by infectious organisms. Bacteria such as *Salmonella*, which grow in contaminated food, produce a poison or toxin that irritates the digestive tract. The body tries to eliminate the toxin by means of vomiting and diarrhea. Many ulcers, once thought to be caused by stress, are actually caused by a type of bacteria. Meats and fish that are eaten rare or raw may transmit parasites,

IN THE COMMUNITY
A Helping Hand with the Groceries

Find a food bank that operates in or near your community. Learn how it works and make a diagram of its operational structure. What people does it serve? Where does it obtain food, and how does it distribute its supplies? Does it distribute the food at specific times and locations? Does the organization offer any cooked meals or training and advice on how to buy and cook meals that are inexpensive yet nutritious? To learn more about hunger and malnutrition in America, look at the Contact Center Network's page on U.S. Hunger and Poverty Resources at *http://body_systems.biosurf.com* on the Internet.

❶ Running, dancing, biking, swimming; reading and writing, watching TV

❷ The saying pertains to a person's health and well-being. A healthy person eats healthful foods.

such as worms or flukes. Undercooked pork can sometimes transmit a parasitic disease called trichinosis.

Hepatitis is a viral infection of the liver that can result in scarring of the liver—a condition called cirrhosis. The scar tissue prevents the liver from functioning properly. Excessive alcohol consumption can also cause cirrhosis. Severe cirrhosis can result in death.

Eating disorders are a serious health problem in the United States. A person with **anorexia** refuses to eat and may overexercise. Without treatment, a person with anorexia can literally starve to death. A person with **bulimia** eats huge amounts of food, and then vomits or takes laxatives to get rid of the food. Bulimia can result in many health problems including swollen salivary glands; kidney, liver, and pancreas problems; stomach and esophagus irritations; and tooth decay from stomach acids. Both psychological and physical treatments are needed for these disorders. If left untreated they can be life-threatening.

CARE OF YOUR DIGESTIVE SYSTEM

Watch what you put in your mouth!

You can keep your digestive system healthy by paying attention to what you put into it. There are several ways to avoid infecting your digestive tract with viruses, bacteria, and parasites. Always wash your hands before eating or preparing food. Make sure that the water you drink is from an uncontaminated source. Avoid eating spoiled or improperly cooked food. "When in doubt, throw it out."

Avoid ingesting foods or beverages that damage or irritate your digestive system. For example, people who lack the enzyme to digest lactose (milk sugar) can prevent painful cramps by avoiding milk and other dairy products. By avoiding alcohol you can prevent digestive irritation and serious liver damage.

CHECKPOINT 30.3

1. Why does a person who is physically active need to take in more Calories than a person who is inactive?
2. What are some digestive problems? What can you do to avoid them?
3. **Critical Thinking** A meal of a large hamburger, french fries, and a milkshake can provide about 900 Calories. How many hours would you have to swim to burn the energy?

Build on What You Know

4. How is energy obtained from food? *(Need to jog your memory? Revisit relevant concepts in Chapter 4, Section 4.3.)*

FIGURE 30.13
Your body functions better when you eat healthful foods. What is the meaning of the saying "You are what you eat"? ❷

What is the function of the digestive system? **?**

CHECKPOINT 30.3

1. Physical activity is fueled by food Calories, thereby increasing the body's energy need.
2. Problems include food poisoning, which can be prevented with careful handling, and eating disorders which require physical and psychological treatment.
3. **Applying** Swimming uses approximately 250 kcal per hour. You would have to swim for about 3.6 hours to burn the energy in the meal described.
4. Energy is obtained from food by the process of cellular respiration, which converts blood sugar to ATP.

LAB ZONE **Think About It!**

Determining How Many of Your Calories Come from Fat

You may want to work through a calculation as an example.

Analyzing the Diagram

1 One serving is 240 ml, fat content varies for whole milk and skim milk.
2 Answer depends on type of milk.
3 Recommended daily fat intake should be less than 30% of total calories and not exceed 65 g.

③ ASSESS

Evaluate Understanding

List the section objectives on the board. Have students write a paragraph about each objective. Then have volunteers read their paragraphs. As a class, discuss the paragraphs, correcting inaccurate information and adding any necessary information.

Reteach

List the following words on the board: *Salmonella infection, ulcers, hepatitis, anorexia,* and *bulimia.* Ask:

■ **What do these terms have in common?** (All problems associated with the digestive system.) Discuss the cause and symptoms of each problem.

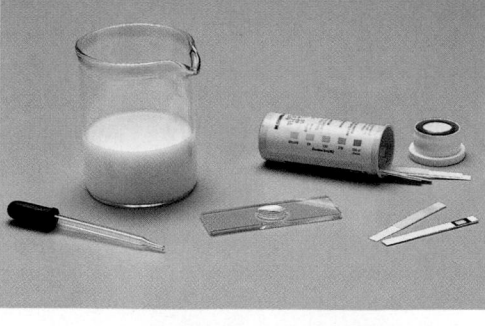

Digesting Lactose

Digesting Lactose

SAFETY FIRST!

Caution students not to drink the milk.

Lab Prep and Planning

Have students work in groups and provide one set of materials for each group.

Lab Tips

Review with students the instructions for using the glucose test strips before they carry out step 1 of the procedure. Instruct students on the proper disposal of materials when they have completed the lab.

Hypothesis Help

Adults are often intolerant of lactose products because their bodies stop secreting lactase. Such people can eat products that have lactose removed.

Lab Extension

Directed

Have different groups of students conduct tests on different types of milk products, such as low-fat milk, reduced fat milk, skim milk, lactose-free milk, half and half, and cream. Have groups compare their results.

Time Required

■ 50 minutes

Digesting Lactose

WHAT YOU WILL DO Test a product that is used to treat milk

SKILLS YOU WILL USE Analyzing, hypothesizing, observing, recording data

WHAT YOU WILL NEED Liquid milk treatment product, slides, eyedropper, whole and skim milk, water, glucose solution, glucose test strips

Background Information

All infant mammals drink milk, but adult mammals, except for humans, do not. The ability to digest lactose, or milk sugar, depends on the ability to secrete lactase, the enzyme that digests lactose. Many adults experience cramps after drinking milk. This condition is known as lactose intolerance.

Propose a Hypothesis

Propose a hypothesis to explain why adults tend to become less tolerant of lactose as they become older, and how lactose intolerance might be alleviated.

Conduct Your Experiment

1 Place several drops of the glucose solution on a microscope slide. Follow the instructions on the glucose test strip container to test the glucose content of the solution. Record your observations.
2 Design an experiment to test the other liquid—whole milk, skim milk, and water—both before and after treating them with the milk-treatment product. Do not forget to include an experimental control. In your notebook, write your predictions for the outcome of each test.

Analyze Your Data

1 What happened when you tested the untreated liquids for glucose? What happened when you tested the treated liquids?
2 What are the ingredients of the milk-treatment product? How did it change the milk? How would it help a person who is lactose intolerant?

Draw Conclusions

1 In some countries and cultures, nearly all adults are lactose intolerant. In others, such as Sweden, for instance, nearly all adults can digest lactose. Identify possible reasons for this difference and explain your reasoning.
2 Why might lactose intolerance increase with age?
3 How can lactose intolerance be alleviated?

Design a Related Experiment

Does the use of a milk treatment product change the taste of milk? Propose a hypothesis and carry out an experiment to test it, using materials from this lab.

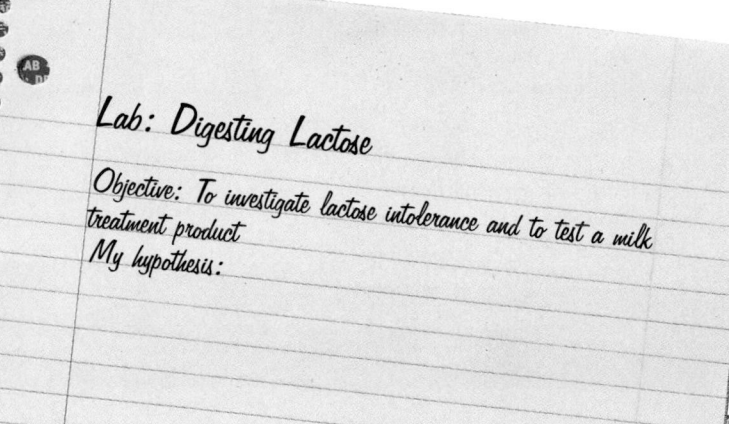

Lab: Digesting Lactose

Objective: To investigate lactose intolerance and to test a milk treatment product
My hypothesis:

Analyze Your Data

1 Untreated liquids indicate little or no glucose is present. Product with lactose indicates some glucose is present.
2 Lactase: It digested the lactose. Lactose would be predigested and would not be present.

Draw Conclusions

1 Lactose intolerance is an inherited trait, since it appears in one population and not in another.
2 The ability to make lactase decreases with maturity.
3 By using lactase to predigest the lactose before drinking milk

The excretory system eliminates nitrogen-containing wastes and helps maintain homeostasis. 30.4–30.5

30.4 Excretion

Who drinks like a fish?
Freshwater fishes never drink water. They need to maintain an osmotic balance of salt and water roughly like that of the ocean—while living in a nearly salt-free home. Unlike the kidneys of most other vertebrates, the kidneys of freshwater fishes do not excrete salt. The fishes do not drink water but actively transport salt into their bodies through their gills.

What you'll learn

IDEAS
- To explain the functions of the excretory system
- To contrast the excretory systems of various organisms

FUNCTIONS OF EXCRETORY SYSTEMS

Get rid of it

Animals produce waste materials that must be removed. The skin and digestive system help to remove some wastes. Most animals have a specialized system to deal with nitrogen-containing wastes, which form when animals break down proteins and nucleic acids. These wastes are removed by the excretory system.

During metabolism, proteins and nucleic acids break down to form ammonia—a toxic nitrogen-containing waste. Ammonia must be quickly eliminated from the body. The process of removing nitrogen-containing wastes is called excretion.

In addition to removing wastes, the excretory system helps control homeostasis. It maintains osmotic balance and pH by either excreting or conserving salts and water.

EXCRETION IN ANIMALS

Gotta have a plan!

Excretory systems in animals have a variety of designs. Many animals that live in water, such as cnidarians,

echinoderms, and some fishes and planarians, have a simple strategy for getting rid of nitrogen-containing wastes. Since ammonia dissolves easily in water, most aquatic animals simply excrete ammonia by diffusion through gills or other body surfaces into the environment. For these aquatic animals, the main function of the excretory system is aiding homeostasis.

As shown in *Figure 30.14*, flatworms have a system made of closed tubules with bulblike ends called

FIGURE 30.14
The main function of this planarian's excretory system is to maintain osmotic balance. How does this aquatic organism excrete ammonia? ❶

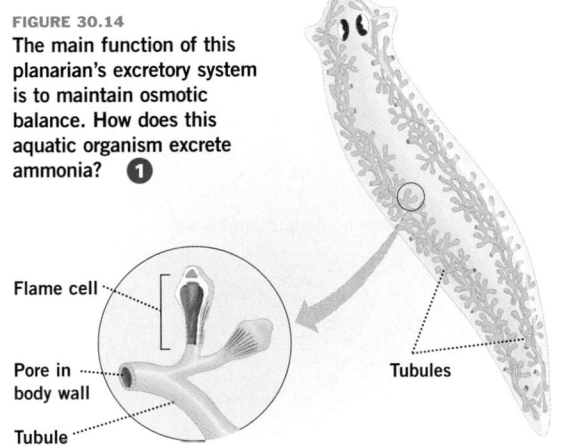

Flame cell

Pore in body wall

Tubule

Tubules

Chapter 30 Digestive and Excretory Systems **733**

STUDENT RESOURCES

From the Teacher's Resource Package, use:
- Section Review 30.4 from Unit 8 Review Module

TECHNOLOGY RESOURCES

Relevant technology resources include:
- Spanish Student Edition CD-ROM
- Teacher's Resource Planner CD-ROM

① ENGAGE

Consider the Big Idea

Have students read The Big Idea! at the top of the page. Point out that the excretory system eliminates the wastes produced during the digestive process.

Use the Visual

Have students study the photograph and read the text that opens the section. Explain that excretion is the process by which organisms remove wastes from their bodies. Ask:

- **What wastes does a freshwater fish excrete from its body?** (Metabolic wastes such as nitrogen and food wastes)

Teacher Demo

Attach a balloon to a spigot of the sink and slowly begin filling the balloon with water. Ask:

- **What will happen to the balloon if water continues to be added and no water is removed?** (It will burst.) Explain to students that in the same way, the cells of organisms would burst if they could not eliminate waste products. This role is carried out by an excretory system.

❶ Flame cells filter body fluids and excrete them through the tubules.

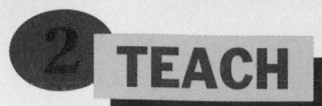

TEACH

Use the Visual

Have students study Figure 30.15. Review the structures an earthworm has for excretion and how these structures function. Ask:

- **What is the role of the external pore?** (To excrete wastes to the outside)
- **What other animal excretes waste through pores?** (Flatworms)

Use the Visual

Have students study Figure 30.16. Review with students how a grasshopper carries out its excretory functions. Ask:

- **What structure in the grasshopper performs the same function as the external pore in the earthworm?** (The anus)
- **What grasshopper structure is comparable to nephridium in the earthworm?** (The Malpighian tubule)

ASSESS

Evaluate Understanding

Have students explain how each organism discussed in this section carries out excretion.

Reteach

On the board, list the name of each organism discussed in this section. Have students review the text and list the excretory structures of each organism. As a class, compare the systems.

FIGURE 30.15
Earthworms have long, twisted nephridia for excretion.

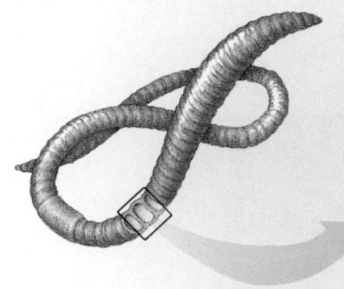
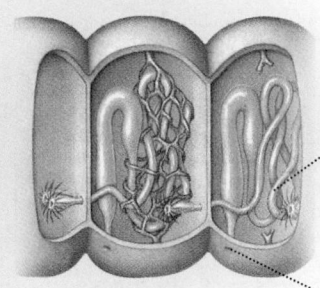

Opening in body cavity

Nephridium

External pore

flame cells. Flame cells filter body fluids, which enter the system of tubules and are excreted through pores in the body.

Animals that live on land cannot simply excrete ammonia by diffusion into the environment. Instead, they must convert ammonia to a less toxic substance that can be stored safely in the body until the waste can be excreted with minimal water loss. Why is **❶** this strategy important in land animals?

Birds, reptiles, land snails, and many types of insects convert ammonia to uric acid, which they excrete in semisolid or liquid form. Mammals, amphibians, and some fishes convert ammonia to urea which, along with other wastes, passes out of the body dissolved in water.

Annelids such as earthworms have excretory tubules called nephridia (singular: *nephridium*). Body fluids in

a segment enter the open end of the nephridium. As fluids move through the nephridium, salts and nutrients are reabsorbed, while wastes and excess water leave through a pore in the body wall.

Arthropods that live on land, such as the grasshopper shown in *Figure 30.16,* have an excretory system composed of Malpighian tubules. Uric acid collects in the tubules and is excreted into the stomach. It leaves the body through the anus.

Vertebrates such as humans have kidneys—excretory organs that filter urea and other wastes from the blood. In the next section, you will learn more about the function of the kidneys.

CHECKPOINT 30.4

1. What are the functions of an excretory system?
2. Compare the excretory systems of three types of organisms. How are they alike? How are they different?
3. **Critical Thinking** Why do different groups of animals excrete different forms of nitrogen-containing wastes?

Build on What You Know

4. What is osmosis? How does it affect excretory systems? *(Need to jog your memory? Revisit relevant concepts in Chapter 3, Section 3.5.)*

FIGURE 30.16
The excretory system of this grasshopper handles both osmotic balance and excretion of nitrogenous waste. What type of nitrogenous waste does it excrete? **❷**

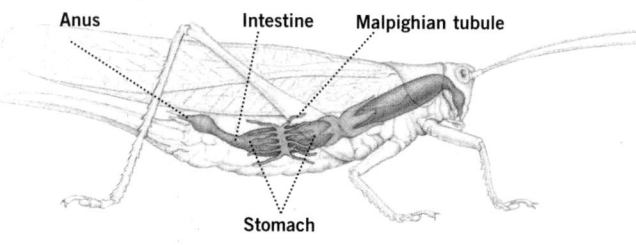

Anus   Intestine   Malpighian tubule

Stomach

734   *Unit 8 Human Biology*

CHECKPOINT 30.4

1. To remove metabolic wastes and control osmotic balance
2. Answers will vary by organism. Responses should address differences in structure as well as the type of wastes produced.
3. **Identifying cause and effect** The type of waste produced varies according to the animals' environments.

4. Osmosis is the movement of water from areas of low solute concentration to areas of high solute concentration. This process moves water in the excretory system.

❶ To conserve water
❷ Uric acid

30.5 Human Excretory System

A giant thirst

Would you be able to drink 170 L (about 45 gallons) of water a day? You would need that much water if your kidneys excreted all the water that they filter in a day. Fortunately, the kidneys retain 99 percent of the water that they filter. So, humans need to replace only the 1–2 L of water excreted daily as urine.

What you'll learn

IDEAS
- To describe the structure and function of the human excretory system
- To judge the importance of the kidneys to blood chemistry and human health

WORDS

kidneys, nephrons

EXCRETION IN HUMANS

Parts make a whole

Like all organisms, you must eliminate a variety of different waste materials in order to function properly. Different organ systems help in this process. Part of the digestive system moves undigested matter out of the body as solid waste. Wastes are also excreted through the skin in sweat. The human excretory system is specialized for removing most of the body's nitrogen-containing waste. The nitrogen-containing waste produced by the human body is urea. The excretory system also plays a crucial role in maintaining the homeostasis of body fluids. As you may recall from Chapter 2, homeostasis is the maintenance of a stable set of internal conditions within an organism.

The main organs of the excretory system are the **kidneys**, located at the bottom of the rib cage near the back, or dorsal, side of the body. Blood enters the kidneys from vessels that branch from the aorta, the body's largest artery. The kidneys remove wastes from the blood and process them into a yellow-colored liquid called urine. The kidneys also help control the amount of salts, water,

minerals, and vitamins in the blood, and they regulate the pH and volume of the blood. At any given time, up to 25 percent of the body's blood may be in the kidneys.

Urine produced by each kidney flows into a long thin tube called a ureter. There are two ureters, one for each kidney. Each ureter carries the urine a distance of 25 to 30 cm to a muscular bag called the urinary bladder. You can see how the ureters connect to the bladder in *Figure 30.17*.

The bladder, located in the lower pelvis, has a tube that opens to the outside of the body. This tube is called the urethra (yoo-REE-thruh). Rings of

FIGURE 30.17

The human urinary system, part of the excretory system, removes nitrogen-containing waste and helps maintain osmotic balance.

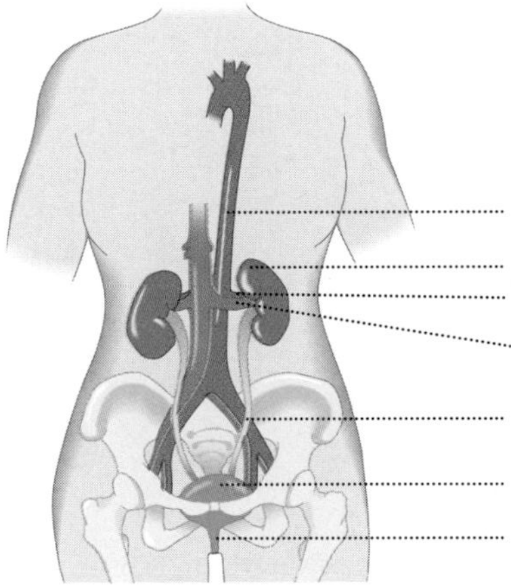

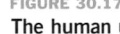

- Aorta
- Kidney
- Renal artery
- Renal vein
- Ureter
- Urinary bladder
- Urethra

Chapter 30 Digestive and Excretory Systems **735**

2 TEACH

Use the Visual

Have students study the structure of the kidney shown in Figure 30.18. Explain that the diagram shows both the location of the kidneys in the body as well as the functional structures located inside the kidney. Ask:

- **What is the name for the outer part of the kidney?** (The cortex)
- **What is the name for the inner portion of the kidney?** (The medulla)
- **What structures make up a nephron?** (A renal tubule and artery, the glomerulus, Bowman's capsule, and a collecting tubule) Briefly trace the path of liquid wastes into the kidney and through the nephron.

 Science History

Bowman's capsule is named for the British surgeon Sir William Bowman (1816-1892). In addition to discovering the capsules in the kidney, he determined the mechanism of urine production by filtration.

Explain

To help students understand the filtration process in the kidney, compare it to dumping out the entire contents of a drawer, then returning to the drawer only those objects you need to keep, and disposing of the unnecessary and useless ones. The kidney is able to rid the body of wastes and nonessential fluids to maintain homeostasis.

muscle around the junction of the bladder and urethra keep the urine in the bladder. When the bladder is full, its smooth muscles send signals to the brain. The brain then signals muscle contractions which expel urine from the bladder and out of the body through the urethra.

KIDNEY FUNCTIONS

Three for the price of one

Each kidney is a bean-shaped organ about 10 cm long. Notice the two regions of the kidney shown in *Figure 30.18*: the cortex and the medulla. A complex network of veins, arteries, and capillaries runs through the medulla and cortex. The blood vessels transport blood to the kidneys for filtration and back to the body after filtration.

Each kidney has approximately one million functional units called nephrons (NEF-rahnz). **Nephrons** are the kidney's filters; they remove wastes from the blood. Find the parts of the nephron shown in *Figure 30.18*. Each nephron consists of a long renal tubule surrounded by capillaries. The cup-shaped end of the renal tubule, called Bowman's capsule, surrounds a clump of capillaries called the glomerulus

(glom-AYR-yoo-lus) (plural: *glomeruli*). Blood pressure forces fluids and wastes out of the blood in the glomerulus. The fluids and wastes move into Bowman's capsule and accumulate in the renal tubule, where urine forms. Urine consists mostly of water, but it also contains urea, uric acid, and salts.

The renal tubules of a kidney's nephrons empty into a system of collecting tubules. As urine passes through the collecting tubules, water is removed, making urine more concentrated. Eventually, the system of collecting tubules empties into the ureter. From the ureter, the urine can move into the bladder and out of the body through the urethra.

Each day about 180 L of fluid from your blood passes through your kidneys. This amount is enough to fill a bathtub! Not all this fluid becomes urine. Most of it is returned to the bloodstream, along with glucose, salts, vitamins, and other substances needed by your body. Your kidneys form urine and control the homeostasis of your blood by three different processes: filtration, reabsorption, and secretion.

Figure 30.19 shows a model of these three processes and where they occur in the nephron. In each nephron, the glomerulus acts as a filter. The resulting filtered solution (filtrate) passes out of the capillary membranes through Bowman's capsule and into the renal tubules. During reabsorption in the renal tubules, water and other useful substances in the filtrate are returned to the blood in the capillaries.

Some wastes move from the blood directly to the renal tubules in a process called secretion. What are some of the substances that are secreted? Secretion is an important kidney function because it maintains the pH of your blood. **❶**

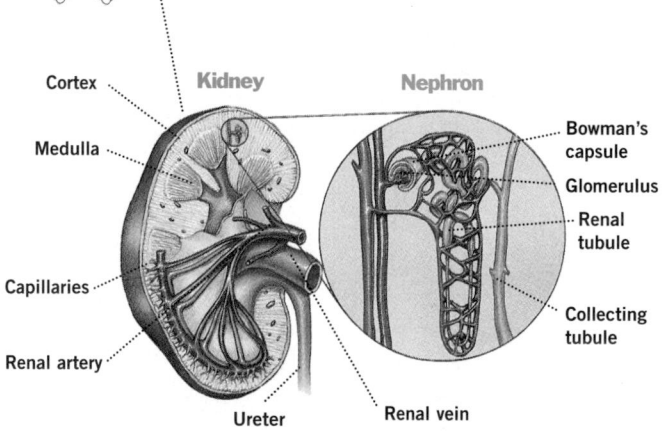

FIGURE 30.18
In the kidneys, the nephrons filter the blood.

Cortex — Kidney — Nephron
Medulla
Capillaries
Renal artery
Ureter — Renal vein
Bowman's capsule
Glomerulus
Renal tubule
Collecting tubule

736 *Unit 8 Human Biology*

At Risk Have students work with a partner and use varied food products such as kidney beans and pasta to make a model of the human excretory system. Suggest students label the organs in their model and use arrows to trace the flow of urine through the system.

❶ Salts, urea, and uric acid

FIGURE 30.19
Nephron Function

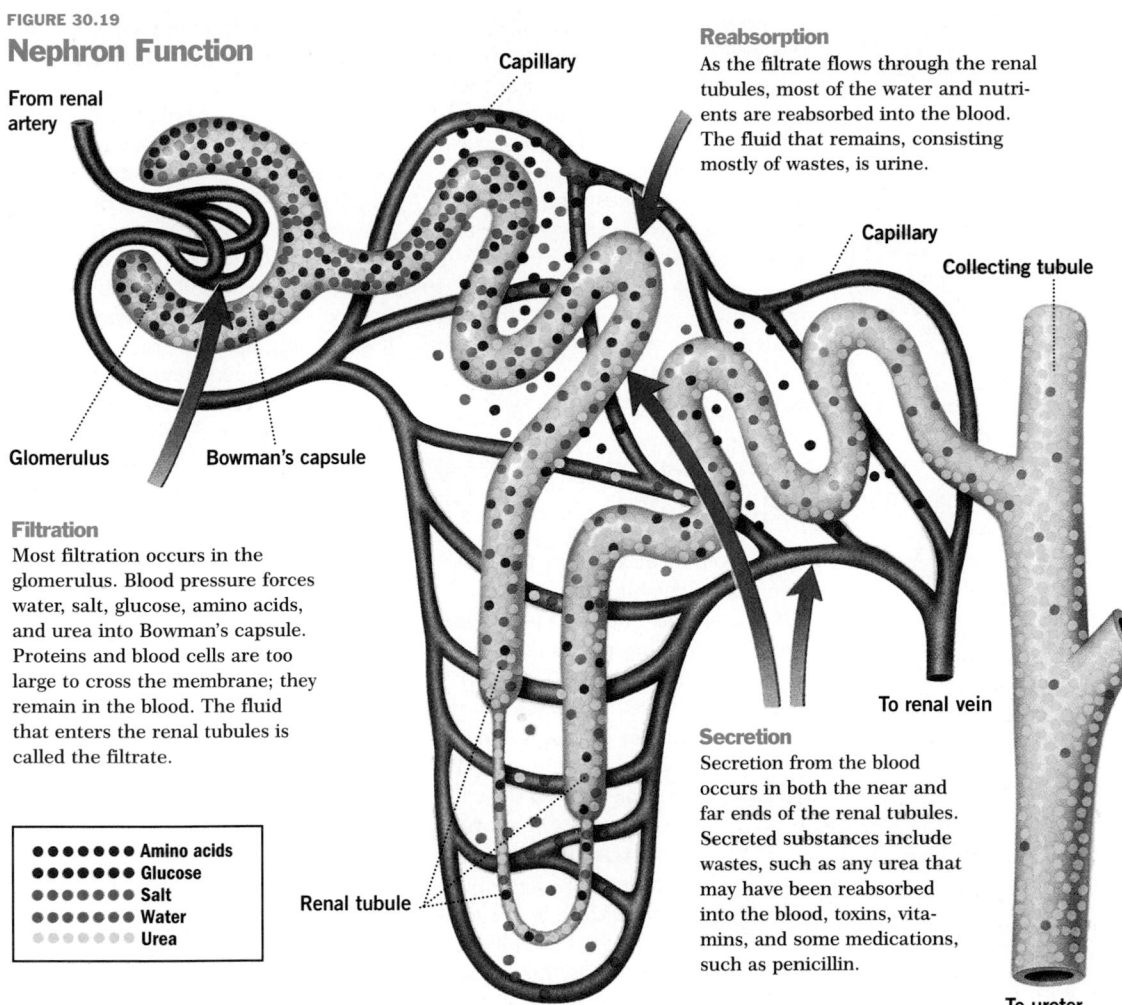

Reabsorption
As the filtrate flows through the renal tubules, most of the water and nutrients are reabsorbed into the blood. The fluid that remains, consisting mostly of wastes, is urine.

From renal artery

Capillary

Capillary

Collecting tubule

Glomerulus

Bowman's capsule

Filtration
Most filtration occurs in the glomerulus. Blood pressure forces water, salt, glucose, amino acids, and urea into Bowman's capsule. Proteins and blood cells are too large to cross the membrane; they remain in the blood. The fluid that enters the renal tubules is called the filtrate.

● ● ● ● ● ● ● Amino acids
● ● ● ● ● ● ● Glucose
● ● ● ● ● ● ● Salt
● ● ● ● ● ● ● Water
○ ○ ○ ○ ○ ○ ○ Urea

Renal tubule

To renal vein

Secretion
Secretion from the blood occurs in both the near and far ends of the renal tubules. Secreted substances include wastes, such as any urea that may have been reabsorbed into the blood, toxins, vitamins, and some medications, such as penicillin.

To ureter

HEALTH OF THE EXCRETORY SYSTEM

Water, water, water

Like all body systems that are connected to the outside of the body, your excretory system is susceptible to infection. The urethra is located in the genital area. The anus is a source of *E. coli* bacteria, a normal component of the feces. These bacteria can enter the urethra and infect the urinary bladder. From the bladder, the bacteria can move up the ureter and infect the kidneys. If a kidney infection is not treated promptly, the kidneys can be seriously damaged. Symptoms of problems of the excretory system include loss of bladder control, blood in the urine, excessive urination, and pain near the kidneys, conditions that require prompt medical attention.

The most important thing you can do to take care of your excretory system is to drink enough water. The whole system depends on water to carry wastes out of the body. Try to drink eight to ten glasses of water every day in addition to other

Chapter 30 Digestive and Excretory Systems **737**

● **Language Arts**

Have students look up and write down the meanings of the terms *filtration, reabsorption,* and *secretion.* Encourage students to keep these terms in mind as they study the function of a nephron.

Use the Visual

Direct students' attention to Figure 30.19. Discuss the three processes carried out in a nephron and where each occurs. Ask:

■ **Which process–filtration, reabsorption, or secretion–occurs first in a nephron?** (Filtration)
■ **Where in a kidney does filtration occur?** (In the glomerulus)
■ **Where does reabsorption take place?** (In the renal tubules)
■ **What fluid remains after reabsorption?** (Urine)

Think Critically

Explain to students that diuretics are substances that stimulate the kidneys to remove more fluid from the body. Ask:

■ **Why might diuretics be prescribed in the treatment of high blood pressure?** (Diuretics cause the kidneys to remove more water from the blood. A reduction in fluid can help lower blood pressure.)

MEETING DIVERSE NEEDS

LEP Have students work with native English speakers to review the three processes illustrated in Figure 30.19. Suggest that LEP students rewrite the captions in their notebooks in both English and their native language and use them as study tools.

STS

Explain that the newest technology includes portable kidney-dialysis machines, which allow the patient to undergo dialysis at home. This advance in technology relieves impacted hospital schedules and helps patients lead a normal life.

ASSESS

Evaluate Understanding

To assess students' understanding of the excretory system, ask:

- **What is the role of the kidneys in the excretory system?** (Remove wastes from the blood and help control amount of salts, water, minerals, and vitamins in the blood
- **What three processes occur in the nephron and what happens during each process?** (Filtration, filtrate is formed and enters the renal tubules; reabsorption, water and nutrients are returned to the bloodstream; secretion, waste and other substances move from the blood to the renal tubules.)

Reteach

On an overhead transparency, develop a flowchart that traces the path of waste products into the kidney, describes the removal of wastes within the kidney, and traces the path urine must follow to be eliminated from the body.

❶ Removing wastes from the blood, helping control the concentrations of salts, water, minerals and vitamins in the blood.

738

Why Does Urine Change Color?

Drinking large amounts of water lightens the color of urine. After exercising or after some time without drinking water, urine will have a heavier, amber color.

FIGURE 30.20

Figure 30.20 For people with damaged kidneys, dialysis machines perform the functions of the kidneys. What are those functions? ❶

beverages. Urinate frequently, as often as needed. It is also important to avoid drugs and toxic substances, as these substances can damage the kidneys.

Personal hygiene plays an important role in preventing bladder and kidney infections. Keep the area around the urethra clean with regular baths or showers. Be aware of the symptoms of a bladder infection so that you can seek prompt treatment if needed. These symptoms include pain or itching of the urethra, fever, and a frequent, intense need to urinate.

FRONTIERS IN BIOLOGY

Kidney help

Advances in medical technology have been a great benefit to people with kidney problems—for example, those who develop kidney stones. Kidney stones form from the crystallization of mineral salts and uric acid salts in the urine. These stones can block the passage of urine, causing extreme pain in the kidneys and urinary tract. Until recently, the only treatment was surgery. Today ultrasound waves are used to crush kidney stones while they are in the kidneys. The fragments then flush out in the urine.

A more serious condition exists when the kidneys fail to function. The most common causes of kidney failure are long-term diabetes, infections, physical injuries, and chemical

poisoning. Kidney failure causes toxic materials in the body to build up to lethal levels.

One solution for kidney failure is dialysis. During dialysis, the patient is connected to a dialysis machine, which removes wastes from the patient's blood in a manner similar to the way that the kidneys remove wastes from the blood. The development of the dialysis machine was possible only after extensive research showed how the kidneys function.

People with kidney failure must undergo dialysis every week for the rest of their lives unless they receive a kidney transplant. Because a human can live a normal life with one kidney, it is possible for a person to donate a kidney to someone with kidney failure. Kidneys were the first organs to be successfully transplanted, in 1954 by Nobel Prize winner Dr. Joseph Murray.

CHECKPOINT 30.5

1. Compare the structures and functions of each part of the excretory system.
2. Describe how the kidneys form urine and control the blood's volume.
3. **Critical Thinking** Thousands of people need kidney transplants, but there are never enough donor kidneys available. What criteria should be used to decide who gets a kidney transplant? Explain your reasoning.

Build on What You Know

4. What kind of transport must be involved between a nephron tubule and its environment? Explain your answer. *(Need to jog your memory? Revisit relevant concepts in Chapter 3, Section 3.5.)*

What does the excretory system do?

CHECKPOINT 30.5

1. The kidneys remove wastes from the blood and produce urine; the ureter carries urine to the bladder which stores it until the urine can be expelled through the urethra.
2. Urine is the fluid that remains after water and nutrients are reabsorbed into the blood. Blood volume is maintained by reabsorption; pH is controlled by secretion.
3. **Making decisions** Accept all responses supported with logical arguments.
4. Active transport must be involved when solutes or water move from areas of low concentration to high concentration.

Chapter 30 Review

 **THE BIG IDEA!**

30.1–30.3 The digestive system breaks down food into usable compounds.
30.4–30.5 The excretory system eliminates nitrogen-containing wastes and helps maintain homeostasis.

Sum It Up

Use the following summary to review the main concepts in this chapter.

30.1 Digestion

- During digestion, nutrients are extracted from food and absorbed by cells. Complex multicellular animals have a tubelike digestive tract with two openings—one for food and one for waste.
- A healthy diet includes appropriate amounts of different nutrients.

30.2 Human Digestive System

- In humans, mechanical digestion occurs in the mouth and stomach. Chemical digestion occurs in the mouth, stomach, and small intestine. Nutrients are absorbed into the circulatory system from the small intestine.
- In the large intestine, water and water-soluble vitamins are reabsorbed; solid undigested waste matter is expelled through the anus.

30.3 Health of the Digestive System

- The energy available in food is measured in calories. Per gram, fats contain twice the calories of proteins or carbohydrates.
- Exercise increases the body's metabolic rate and helps burn excess calories.

- The digestive tract is subject to attack by infectious organisms.
- Eating disorders can be life-threatening.

30.4 Excretion

- Excretion removes nitrogen-containing wastes and maintains osmotic balance.
- Many aquatic animals excrete water-soluble ammonia through gills or pores in the body wall. Terrestrial animals convert toxic ammonia into uric acid or urea before excretion.
- Annelids, arthropods, and vertebrates have tubular structures for filtering body fluids.

30.5 Human Excretory System

- The kidneys filter wastes from blood and produce urine, which flows through ureters to the urinary bladder. Contractions of the bladder expel urine through the urethra.
- Nephrons perform three functions—filtration of wastes from blood, reabsorption of water and nutrients back into the blood, and secretion of wastes from blood into the urine.

Use Terms and Concepts

Use each of the following words or terms in a complete sentence. If you need to review a meaning, turn to the page indicated.

digestive system (p. 720)
nutrient (p. 720)
salivary glands (p. 725)
esophagus (p. 726)
peristalsis (p. 726)
stomach (p. 726)

small intestine (p. 726)
villi (p. 727)
large intestine (p. 727)
liver (p. 728)
gallbladder (p. 728)
pancreas (p. 728)

metabolism (p. 729)
calorie (p.729)
anorexia (p. 731)
bulimia (p. 731)
kidneys (p. 735)
nephrons (p. 736)

Review the Big Ideas

Before students begin the Chapter Review, you may wish to discuss main concepts from the Big Ideas in Chapter 30. Point out that the digestive system breaks down the food needed by the body for energy. Maintaining health is an important function of the digestive system. The excretory system eliminates the wastes produced by the digestive process. Maintaining homeostasis is an important function of the excretory system.

Answers

1. villi
2. metabolism
3. nutrients
4. liver
5. peristalsis
6. pancreas
7. nephrons
8. Calorie
9. anorexia
10. d
11. b
12. c
13. a
14. d
15. Water can be reabsorbed in the large intestine and in the kidneys.
16. Vitamins work in conjunction with enzymes. Minerals are needed for building essential compounds and for the functioning of the nervous system.
17. Scientists use a calorimeter to determine the energy content of a small quantity of milk.
18. The person burns up stored glycogen, then stored fat, and eventually stored protein.
19. Extracellular digestion is more efficient because specialized cells can extract nutrients, which can then be transported to all cells in the organism.
20. Absorption of nutrients and reabsorption of water take place in the intestines. These processes need the maximum surface area possible.
21. The nitrogen comes from the breakdown of proteins and nucleic acids.
22. Blood pressure forces fluids and wastes from the glomerulus into the Bowman's capsule, which transports the fluids to the renal tubule.
23. Students should include the

Use Your Word Power

MATCHING Write the term from the list of key terms that best matches each of the phrases below.

1. Fingerlike projections in the small intestine that increase the surface area for absorption.

2. All the chemical reactions that take place in an organism.

3. Substances released from food during digestion, which are needed by the body for growth, repair, and maintenance.

4. The organ that produces bile, converts glucose into glycogen, and breaks down toxic chemicals.

5. A wave of smooth muscle contractions in the esophagus.

6. The organ that secretes digestive enzymes and hormones such as insulin.

7. The structures in kidneys that remove wastes from blood.

8. A unit of measurement of heat energy.

9. A type of eating disorder that is characterized by a refusal to eat and a tendency to over-exercise.

Multiple Choice Choose the letter of the word or phrase that best completes each statement.

10. Bulimia can cause (a) kidney stones; (b) incontinence; (c) ulcers; (d) tooth decay.

11. Fats are digested in the (a) stomach; (b) small intestine; (c) large intestine; (d) gallbladder.

12. Nitrogen-containing wastes are excreted in the (a) urinary bladder; (b) gallbladder; (c) kidneys; (d) large intestine.

13. Bile is stored in the (a) gallbladder; (b) liver; (c) pancreas; (d) small intestine.

14. Salivary glands produce enzymes that digest (a) sugar; (b) protein; (c) fat; (d) starch.

Show What You Know

15. How do organs in the digestive and excretory systems maintain a balance of water?

16. What role do vitamins and minerals play in metabolism?

17. How do scientists know that low-fat milk contains 130 Calories per cup?

18. What happens over time if a person consumes fewer Calories than he or she expends on a daily basis?

19. What is the advantage of extracellular digestion for a multicellular organism?

20. Your digestive tract is about 9 m long. Why is it advantageous that most of that length, 8.5 m, is occupied by intestines?

21. What is the source of the nitrogenous wastes that the kidneys excrete?

22. How do the glomerulus and Bowman's capsule in a nephron work together?

23. **Make a Concept Map** Create a concept map that shows the role digestive enzymes play in the digestive system.

Take It Further

24. **Developing a Hypothesis** How would prolonged chewing affect the digestion of carbohydrates and proteins?

25. **Applying Concepts** Some people consume quantities of vitamins that far exceed the recommended daily allowances. Explain why consuming large amounts of vitamin A on a daily basis would be riskier than consuming large quantities of vitamin C.

26. **Developing a Hypothesis** Explain why cirrhosis of the liver can be life-threatening.

27. **Applying Concepts** Are stomach muscles smooth or striated? Explain your answer.

salivary glands, stomach, liver, gallbladder, pancreas, and small intestine.

24. Prolonged chewing would speed up the digestion of carbohydrates through increased exposure to salivary enzymes. Breaking food into smaller pieces would provide greater surface area, which should theoretically speed up digestion of proteins in the stomach.

25. Excess vitamin C would be excreted in urine; excess vitamin A would be stored in the liver or body fat. Very large doses of fat-soluble vitamins can be toxic.

26. Cirrhosis causes scar tissue, which interferes with the liver's many vital functions.

27. Stomach muscles are not voluntary; like those in the esophagus, they are smooth.

28. Analyzing Data Over-the-counter products for indigestion often contain carbonate salts. What function does sodium bicarbonate perform in pancreatic fluid, which is emptied into the small intestine just below the stomach?

29. Making an Analogy In what ways is an automatic car wash similar to a digestive tract?

30. Designing an Experiment During carbohydrate digestion, water breaks some bonds between the glucose units in starch. Design an experiment to determine if digestive enzymes are necessary for the reaction between water and starch. What materials would you need?

31. Interpreting a Graph A vampire bat feeds at night on the blood of large mammals as they sleep. The graph below shows how the bat's excretory system adjusts to the sudden intake of a protein-rich liquid. What happens to the concentration and flow of urine when the bat begins to eat? Describe the concentration and flow of urine three hours after eating.

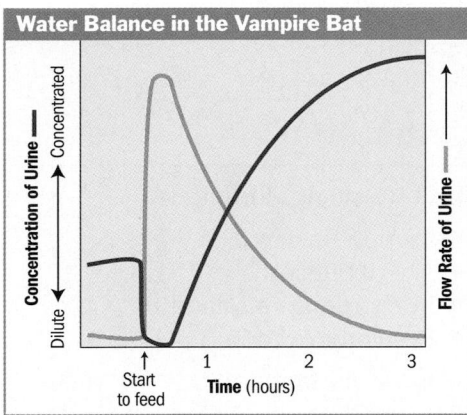

Water Balance in the Vampire Bat

32. Analyzing Data The following table shows the number of Calories in certain foods and the amount of time it would take to burn off those Calories while resting, walking, or jogging. How does walking compare to resting in terms of burning Calories? How does walking compare to jogging?

Time Needed to Burn Calories			
Food (kcal)	Resting	Walking	Jogging
Glass of orange juice (110)	85 min	22 min	11 min
Pizza slice (185)	142 min	37 min	18.5 min
Small steak (330)	254 min	66 min	33 min
Cup of shelled peanuts (840)	646 min	168 min	84 min

Consider the Issues

33. Organic Foods Because all foods contain carbon-based compounds, all foods are organic, strictly speaking. However, in the marketplace the label "organic" is often used for foods grown without pesticides and processed without preservatives. Have you purchased foods that were labeled organic? Did they taste or look different from other fruits and vegetables? Did you have to pay more?

Make New Connections

34. Biology and Art Design your own version of the USDA food pyramid, shown on page 722. Use the nutrients that your body needs—carbohydrates, proteins, fats, vitamins, minerals—as categories for your illustration.

35. Biology and Mathematics Design a menu for a family of four for three days that provides a balanced diet. Make a list of all the menu items and estimate their costs. Compare your estimates against supermarket prices.

> **FAST-FORWARD TO CHAPTER 31**
>
> The circulatory system transports the nutrients extracted from the digestive system to all the cells in the body. The respiratory system supplies the oxygen needed for metabolism. You will learn more about these systems in Chapter 31.

Chapter 30 Digestive and Excretory Systems **741**

32. Walking burns up Calories about four times faster than resting; jogging burns up Calories about twice as fast as walking.

33. Organically grown foods often cost more; they may have more blemishes. The taste is usually the same.

34. Students may even want to include the recommended amount of water.

35. As a variation, start with a given amount of money. Students would have to figure out how to serve three days worth of meals that would not exceed the given budget.

28. The sodium bicarbonate neutralizes the stomach acid in the chyme.

29. The car enters at one end and is automatically moved along until it exits at the other end. At different points on the route, different functions occur—washing, rinsing, drying.

30. Students would need an indicator that would change color in the presence of glucose. They would need to compare the reactions of starch in distilled water and in saliva.

31. When the bat starts to eat, the urine becomes diluted and the flow increases (bat gets rid of excess fluid). Three hours later, the urine is very concentrated and flow is minimal (bat conserves water until next meal).

PLANNING GUIDE

Section	Student Activities/Features	Teacher's Resource Package
31.1 Respiratory Systems **Objectives** ■ Compare respiratory systems in animals ■ Identify the parts of the human respiratory system	**Lab Zone Discover It!** *Measuring Your Breathing*, p. 743 **Everyday Biology** *Something He Swallowed?* p. 746 **Lab Zone Do It!** *What Happens When You Exhale?* p. 746	**Unit 8 Review Module** ■ Section Review 31.1 ■ Activity Recordsheet 31-1 **Interpreting and Developing Graphics** 91
31.2 Every Breath You Take **Objectives** ■ Explain the mechanisms that control breathing ■ Describe the process of gas exchange in the human body	**Lab Zone Investigate It!** *Measuring Lung Capacity*, p. 750	**Unit 8 Review Module** ■ Section Review 31.2 ■ Activity Recordsheet 31-2 **Consumer Applications** 31-1
31.3 Health of the Respiratory System **Objectives** ■ Explain how viruses, bacteria, and fungi can affect the respiratory system ■ Show ways to protect the respiratory system	**Everyday Biology** *Ah-choo!* p. 751 **STS: Issues in Biology** *Effects of Smoking*, p. 752 **In the Community** *Breaths of Life*, p. 752	**Unit 8 Review Module** ■ Section Review 31.3 ■ Enrichment Topic 31-1 **Issues and Decison Making** 31-1
31.4 Circulatory Systems **Objectives** ■ Compare open and closed circulatory systems ■ Describe the structure and function of the human circulatory system	**Lab Zone Do It!** *Examining the Effect of Exercise on Heart Rate*, p. 758	**Unit 8 Review Module** ■ Section Review 31.4 ■ Activity Recordsheet 31-3 ■ Interpreting Graphics 31 ■ Enrichment Topic 31-2 **Laboratory Manual:** Lab 55: "Heart Rate in *Daphnia*" **Interpreting and Developing Graphics** 92
31.5 Blood **Objectives** ■ Compare the components of blood ■ Explain the role of antigens in blood typing		**Unit 8 Review Module** ■ Section Review 31.5 ■ Enrichment Topic 31-3
31.6 Health of the Circulatory System **Objectives** ■ Describe illnesses of the cardiovascular system ■ Explain ways to care for the cardiovascular system	**Lab Zone Think About It!** *Relating Blood Pressure to Health*, p. 764	**Unit 8 Review Module** ■ Section Review 31.6 ■ Critical Thinking Exercise 31 ■ Enrichment Topic 31-4 ■ Vocabulary Review 31 ■ Chapter 31 Tests **Consumer Applications** 31-2 **Interpreting and Developing Graphics** 93 **Spanish Reviews** Chapter 31

Technology Resources

Internet Connections

Within this chapter, you will see the **bioSURF** logo. If you and your students have access to the Internet, the following URL address will provide various Internet connections that are related to topics and features presented in this chapter:

http://body_systems.biosurf.com

You can also find relevant chapter material at **The Biology Place** address:

http://www.biology.com

CD-ROMs

Biología: la telaraña de la vida,
   (Spanish Student Edition) Chapter 31
Teacher's Resource Planner, Chapter 31
   Supplements
TestWorks CD-ROM
- Chapter 31 Tests
How Your Body Works CD-ROM

Videodiscs

Animated Biological Concepts Videodiscs
- Human Respiration
- Circulatory Systems
- Human Circulation

Overhead Transparencies

- Human Respiratory System, #71
- Blood Circuits, #72
- Human Heart, #73

Videotapes

Biology Alive! Video Series
- Domain of Life Video
Rewind: The Web of Life Reteach Videos

Planning for Activities

STUDENT EDITION
Lab Zone
Discover It! p. 743
- watch or clock with a second hand

Lab Zone *Do It!* p. 746
- limewater
- clear glass container
- straw

Lab Zone
Investigate It! p. 750
- round balloon
- metric tape measure

Lab Zone Do It! p. 758
- watch or clock with a second hand

TEACHER'S EDITION
Quick Activity, p. 744
Plants and the environment
- established aquarium community that includes plants and animals

Teacher Demo, p. 748
Inhalation and exhalation
- X-rays of lungs filled with air and lungs without air

Teacher Demo, p. 752
Common respiratory problems
- school nurse

Quick Activity, p. 754
Counting heartbeats
- clock, watch, or timer

Teacher Demo, p. 756
Blood flow through the heart
- model of the heart or a computer simulation of the movement of blood through the heart

Teacher Demo, p. 759
Observing blood components
- microprojector
- prepared slides of red blood cells, white blood cells, and platelets

Teacher Demo, p. 762
Demonstrating atherosclerosis
- bicycle pump
- piece of rubber tubing

Teacher Demo, p. 763
Taking blood pressure
- school nurse
- stethoscope
- sphygmomanometer

Chapter Objectives

Students will learn the main concepts of this chapter as they complete the following objectives.

- Compare respiratory systems in animals
- Identify the parts of the human respiratory system
- Explain the mechanisms that control breathing
- Describe the process of gas exchange in the human body
- Explain how viruses, bacteria, and fungi can affect the respiratory system
- Show ways to protect the respiratory system
- Compare open and closed circulatory systems
- Describe the structure and function of the human circulatory system
- Compare the components of blood and explain the role of antigens in blood typing
- Describe illnesses of the cardiovascular system
- Explain ways to care for the cardiovascular system

Key Words

31.1 respiration, alveoli

31.2 diaphragm

31.4 heart, blood, blood vessels

31.5 plasma, red blood cells, white blood cells, platelets

The Opening Story

Have students discuss how they think the story relates to the content of this chapter. Invite students to share their experiences on learning how to swim underwater. Point out that swimming is an excellent way to develop cardiorespiratory fitness.

742

CHAPTER 31
Respiratory and Circulatory Systems

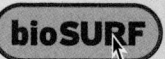

You can find out more about the respiratory and circulatory systems by exploring the following Internet address:
http://body_systems.biosurf.com

In this chapter . . .

FEATURES

Everyday Biology
- Something He Swallowed?
- Ah-choo!

In the Community
Breaths of Life

 Issues in Biology
Effects of Smoking

LAB ZONES

Discover It!
- Measuring Your Breathing

Do It!
- What Happens When You Exhale?
- Examining the Effect of Exercise on Heart Rate

Think About It!
- Relating Blood Pressure to Health

Investigate It!
- Measuring Lung Capacity

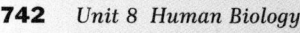

taking feat

a t the 1996 Summer Olympics in Atlanta, Georgia, swimmer Amy Van Dyken of the United States won four gold medals—an accomplishment that no other female athlete has ever achieved at a single Olympics. Amy's accomplishments are particularly remarkable because she has suffered from a severe case of asthma since childhood.

The strenuous training that athletes endure usually requires optimal respiratory and circulatory capacity. For Amy, however, maximum respiratory capacity is far less than average. As she says, "On a good day, my large airways are only 65 percent of normal. On a bad day, I'm at about 30 percent."

Amy Van Dyken's determination and hard work have helped her to excel in spite of all the obstacles. In high school, for example, her teammates did not want to include her on their relay swim team because they thought she was not capable. But Amy persevered. As she phrases it, "For all the kids out there who are struggling, . . . I hope I am an inspiration. If they love it and just keep plugging away at it, something good will come out of it." It certainly did for Amy. She left everyone breathless.

  **Discover It!**

Measuring Your Breathing

You need *a watch or clock with a second hand*

1. On three separate occasions, hold your breath for as long as you comfortably can and measure your time.
2. Calculate your average time and record it on a chart with the average times of your classmates. Organize and graph your data. Find the class average.

Most people can hold their breath for just under a minute. How long could you hold your breath? Your time gives you an idea of how long you could stay underwater without breathing equipment.

WRITE ABOUT IT!

Write a fictional story about the experiences of a character who can stay underwater indefinitely.

743

ENGAGE

Consider the Big Idea

Have students read The Big Idea! at the top of the page. Explain that gas exchange occurs by diffusion through lungs, gills, or skin.

Use the Visual

Have students study the photograph that opens the section. Explain that animals such as the tree frog have developed different ways of exchanging gases with their environment. Ask:

■ **Why does an adult tree frog not need gills for respiration?** (Gills are an adaptation to an aquatic environment and the tree frog lives on land.)

Quick Activity

Write the formula for respiration ($C_6H_{12}O_6 + O_2 \rightarrow CO_2 + H_2O + energy$) on the board. Then have students observe an established aquarium community that includes both plants and animals. Ask:

■ **Why is it important for the aquarium to contain both plants and animals?** (Plants provide oxygen to the environment as they carry out photosynthesis; plants and animals provide carbon dioxide as they carry out respiration.) Use students' responses to remind them that plants, as well as all other organisms, must respire to survive.

THE BIG IDEA! The vital exchange of oxygen and carbon dioxide occurs in the respiratory systems of animals. 31.1–31.3

31.1 Respiratory Systems

What you'll learn

IDEAS
• To compare respiratory systems in animals
• To identify the parts of the human respiratory system

WORDS
respiration, alveoli

Amphibians do it all!
Some animals exchange gases through skin, and others through gills or lungs. Some adult amphibians exchange gases using all three organs—skin, gills, and lungs. Others, like this red-eyed tree frog, breathe through gills as young aquatic animals, through lungs as adults, and through skin during both youth and adulthood.

GAS EXCHANGE IN ANIMALS

As they live and breathe

All living organisms depend on cellular respiration for the energy to survive. You may recall from Chapter 4 that during cellular respiration food molecules are broken down to make ATP. The most efficient form of cellular respiration uses oxygen (O_2). Animals must obtain O_2 from the environment. Cellular respiration produces carbon dioxide (CO_2), which is expelled into the environment. The gas exchange of O_2 and CO_2 between animals and their environment is vital for cellular respiration.

Gas exchange takes place in the respiratory system of an animal. The respiratory system provides surfaces where O_2 and CO_2 diffuse across cell membranes. Respiratory system tissues are moist, because O_2 and CO_2 must be dissolved in water before they can efficiently diffuse across cell membranes.

Different types of respiratory systems are adaptations that allow animals to live in different habitats. Terrestrial animals must obtain O_2 from air. Many aquatic animals must use the O_2 dissolved in water. The size of an animal can influence the size of its respiratory sytem. In general, larger organisms require more gas exchange to support a greater amount of cellular respiration. Therefore, the respiratory systems of larger animals have greater surface areas.

Some animals that are relatively small obtain O_2 by direct diffusion through the skin. This method provides enough O_2 for all life processes. For example, O_2 can dissolve directly into the moist secretions on an earthworm's skin. In order for its skin to stay moist, an earthworm must live in a damp habitat.

Fishes and some amphibians have gills to absorb O_2 from water. Gills are specialized extensions of folded skin.

FIGURE 31.1
How does the recycling of oxygen and carbon dioxide in the environment relate to cellular respiration? **❶**

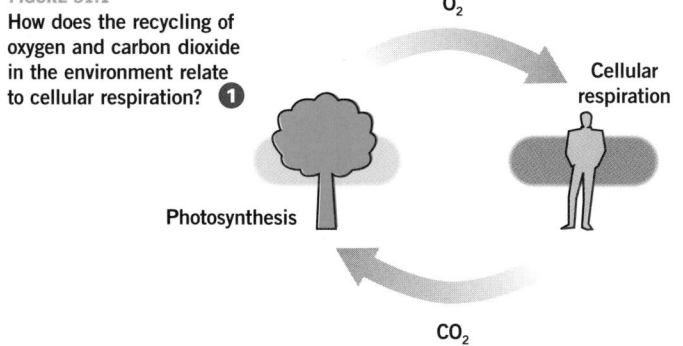

O₂

Cellular respiration

Photosynthesis

CO₂

744 *Unit 8 Human Biology*

The greater surface area of gills can provide enough O_2 for larger animals. Maintaining a moist surface is not a problem for aquatic animals.

Animals that live in dry environments do not absorb O_2 directly through their skin. These animals have internal respiratory systems. Insects have a system of tubes called tracheae through which air passes. The O_2 dissolves in the moist lining of these respiratory tubes and then diffuses into the insect's cells.

Most terrestrial vertebrates have respiratory systems that include lungs. Lungs are spongelike organs where gas exchange takes place. Mammals have millions of moist air sacs in lungs. In an adult male human, the surface area for gas exchange is about 70 to 80 square meters (m^2)—about one third the area of a tennis court! How do you think this increased surface ❷ area affects O_2 diffusion?

THE HUMAN RESPIRATORY SYSTEM

Full of hot air

Take a deep breath and let it out. When you breathe, you exchange gases with the environment. When you breathe in, or inhale, you absorb oxygen-rich air. When you breathe out, or exhale, the air you release into the environment contains CO_2. Your respiratory system brings O_2 from the air to the blood and releases CO_2 from the blood to the air.

Take another breath and let it out. Sometimes you can control your breathing. However, you probably cannot hold a breath for very long. In a short time, CO_2 begins to build up in your blood, and your body's control mechanisms cause you to start breathing again.

Respiration is the process by which a body obtains and uses O_2 and eliminates CO_2. Breathing is the

FIGURE 31.2

Gas Exchange Between Animals and the Environment

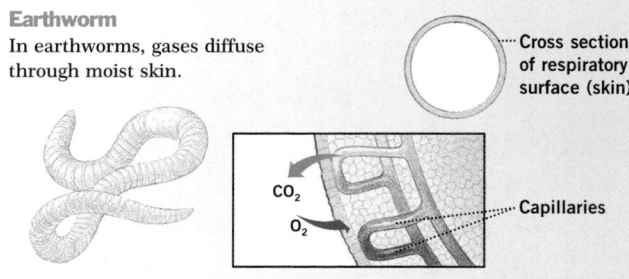

Earthworm
In earthworms, gases diffuse through moist skin.

Cross section of respiratory surface (skin)

CO_2
O_2

Capillaries

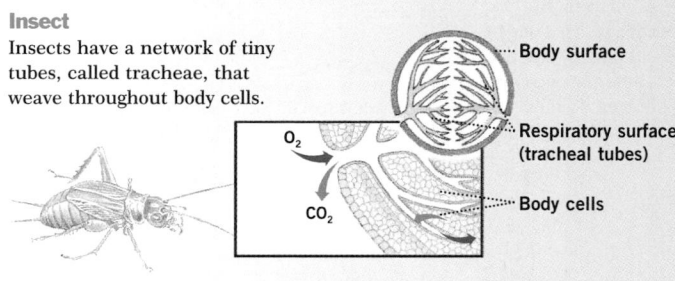

Insect
Insects have a network of tiny tubes, called tracheae, that weave throughout body cells.

Body surface

Respiratory surface (tracheal tubes)

O_2

CO_2

Body cells

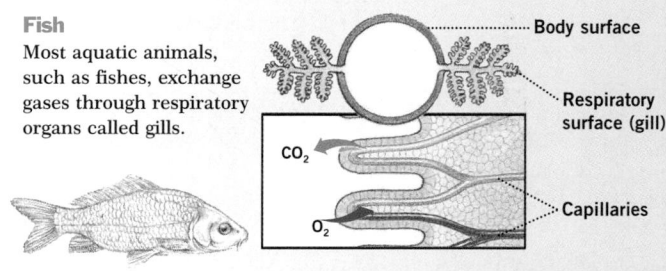

Fish
Most aquatic animals, such as fishes, exchange gases through respiratory organs called gills.

Body surface

Respiratory surface (gill)

CO_2

O_2

Capillaries

Mammal
The internal lungs of mammals contain millions of air sacs where gases are exchanged.

Body surface

Respiratory surface (lung)

CO_2

O_2

Capillary

❷ TEACH

Use the Visual

Have students study Figure 31.2. Ask:

- **What mechanism of gas exchange do earthworms and tree frogs have in common?** (Both exchange gases through their skin.)
- **How would you describe the skin of animals that use this organ for gas exchange?** (Their skin is moist.)
- **Which organism in the diagram has a respiratory system most like that of a human? Explain.** (The raccoon, because it has internal lungs)
- **Which of these animals must live in water or a moist environment?** (The earthworm and the fish)

Think Critically

Point out that hyperventilation is a result of abnormally rapid, deep breathing. Hyperventilation causes an abnormal loss of carbon dioxide in the blood. The carbon dioxide balance can be restored by breathing into a paper bag for a brief period. Ask students to discuss why rapid, deep breathing during strenuous exercise does not cause hyperventilation.

MEETING DIVERSE NEEDS

At Risk Encourage students to work with a partner to make a table in which they identify the respiratory organs for the organisms shown in Figure 31.2. Challenge students to identify other groups of animals that make use of the same organs in their respiratory processes. For example, like mammals, birds also have lungs. They can find this information by reviewing the chapters devoted to animal classification.

❶ Photosynthesis in plants releases the O_2 required for cellular respiration; CO_2 is produced in cellular respiration and used in photosynthesis.

❷ It increases diffusion.

Everyday Biology

Explain that the voice box consists of two elastic ligaments called the vocal cords. Air from the lungs causes the vocal cords to vibrate and make sounds. Have students put two fingers along their Adam's apple and hum. Ask what they feel with their fingers.

Discuss

Discuss the three levels of respiration. Emphasize the following: *Internal respiration* takes place *inside* the body between capillaries and cells; *External respiration* is the gas exchange with the *outside* of the body; *Cellular respiration* takes place in the *cells*. Ask:

- **What is the relationship between breathing and respiration?** (Breathing is the mechanics of respiration.)

 Do It! TEAM WORK

What Happens When You Exhale?

Caution students not to suck any of the solution into their mouths. To prepare limewater, make a saturated solution (0.02 M) of calcium hydroxide. Filter out any remaining solids. If bromthymol blue is used, color change will be from blue to greenish yellow.

Analyze Your Results

1 It turns cloudy.
2 Exhaled carbon dioxide
3 Carbon dioxide reacts with the limewater.
4 In both cases, carbon dioxide is mixing with other compounds.

FIGURE 31.3
The left lung is slightly smaller and has fewer sections, or lobes, than the right lung.

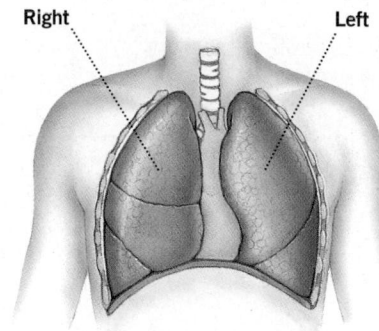

Right   Left

EVERYDAY BIOLOGY

Something He Swallowed?

Exhaled air rushes through the voice box to produce sound. The voice box is supported by cartilage that meets in a ridge in the throat. This ridge, called the Adam's apple, is usually larger in men than in women.

mechanical part of respiration. Respiration is both a chemical and a mechanical process.

The complete process of respiration occurs on three levels: cellular, internal, and external. Cellular respiration is the process by which cells get energy from the oxidation of glucose. Internal respiration is the exchange of O_2 and CO_2 between the blood in your

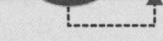 **Do It!** bioSURF

What Happens When You Exhale?

You can observe what happens when you exhale if you . . .

Try This

1 Pour some limewater into a clear glass container.
2 Exhale through a straw into the limewater.
3 Observe and record what happens.

Analyze Your Results

1 What happened to the limewater?
2 What gas is causing this change in the limewater?
3 Why do you think this is happening?
4 Compare what is happening to the limewater with what happens when you exhale into the surrounding air.

MEETING DIVERSE NEEDS

LEP As the path of air through the respiratory system is discussed, encourage students to list the organs through which air passes as a flowchart. Then have students identify the function of each organ listed, recording the information in both English and their native language.

capillaries and your body cells. The circulatory system carries out internal respiration. External respiration exchanges O_2 and CO_2 between the blood in the capillaries and the air. External respiration is made possible by the respiratory system. The human respiratory system consists of the lungs and the passageways that enable air to reach the lungs.

Your nose is the primary passageway by which air enters your body. Air can also enter and exit through your mouth. The air you breathe is filtered, cleaned, warmed, and moistened as it moves through the air passages that lead to your lungs. If air entering your body was not processed in these ways, the air could damage or carry diseases to lung tissue.

Air then passes through a series of tubes. The tubes of the respiratory system have similar structures and linings. Most respiratory tubes are surrounded by C-shaped cartilage structures that keep the tubes firm and open. Cilia and a moist tissue called the mucous membrane line the nasal cavity and other respiratory tubes. Mucus traps small particles of dust and bacteria. Cilia move the mucus and its trapped particles to the throat to be swallowed. Mucus-coated particles are destroyed by digestive juices in the stomach.

The first tube that air enters is the pharynx (FAH-rinks). The pharynx branches into the esophagus, a tube that leads to the stomach, and the larynx (LAYR–inks). A flap of tissue called the epiglottis covers and protects the larynx when you swallow. This prevents food from entering your respiratory system.

The larynx leads to the trachea (TRAY-kee-uh), the main passageway to the lungs. The trachea divides into two branches, the bronchi. Bronchi (singular: *bronchus*) are respiratory tubes that lead to the lungs. As you

FIGURE 31.4

The Human Respiratory System

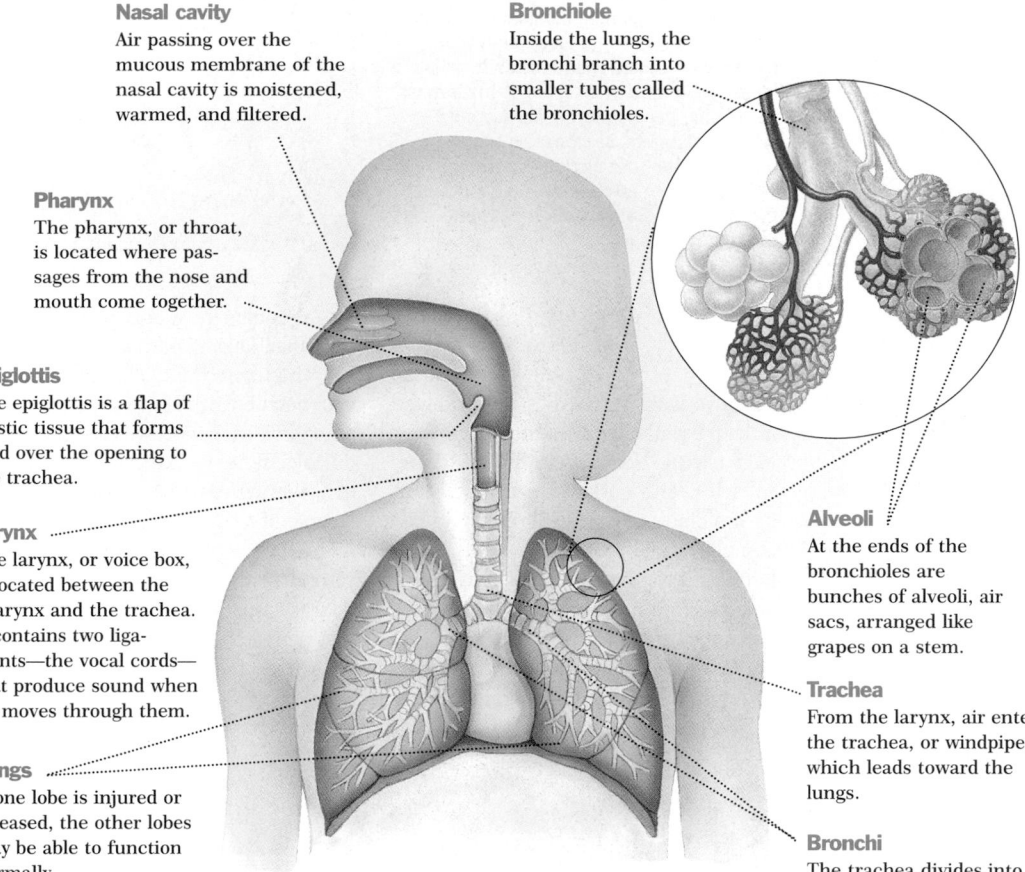

Nasal cavity
Air passing over the mucous membrane of the nasal cavity is moistened, warmed, and filtered.

Pharynx
The pharynx, or throat, is located where passages from the nose and mouth come together.

Epiglottis
The epiglottis is a flap of elastic tissue that forms a lid over the opening to the trachea.

Larynx
The larynx, or voice box, is located between the pharynx and the trachea. It contains two ligaments—the vocal cords—that produce sound when air moves through them.

Lungs
If one lobe is injured or diseased, the other lobes may be able to function normally.

Bronchiole
Inside the lungs, the bronchi branch into smaller tubes called the bronchioles.

Alveoli
At the ends of the bronchioles are bunches of alveoli, air sacs, arranged like grapes on a stem.

Trachea
From the larynx, air enters the trachea, or windpipe, which leads toward the lungs.

Bronchi
The trachea divides into two tubes called bronchi.

can see in *Figure 31.3*, the lungs surround the heart and fill most of the chest cavity within the rib cage. The lungs are divided into sections called lobes.

In the lungs, bronchi branch into smaller and smaller tubes called bronchioles. The bronchioles end in tiny air sacs called **alveoli** (al-VEE-oh-lie) (singular: *alveolus*). Most of the gas exchange occurring between the circulatory and respiratory systems takes place in the alveoli.

CHECKPOINT 31.1

1. What gases are exchanged in animal respiratory and circulatory systems?

2. What are the structures of the human respiratory system?

3. **Critical Thinking** Compare three systems for gas exchange in animals.

Build on What You Know

4. Compare gas exchange in animals and in plants. *(Need to jog your memory? Revisit relevant concepts in Chapter 18, Section 18.1.)*

Chapter 31 Respiratory and Circulatory Systems **747**

CHECKPOINT 31.1

1. O_2 from the environment is exchanged with CO_2 produced by metabolism.

2. Human respiratory structures include the lungs, larynx, epiglottis, pharynx, nasal cavity, bronchioles, alveoli, trachea, and bronchi.

3. **Analyzing** Earthworms diffuse gases through the skin; insects use tracheae; fish have gills; mammals have lungs.

4. Both plants and animals exchange O_2 for CO_2 during respiration. Plants reverse the process during photosynthesis.

Use the Visual

Have students study Figure 31.4. As a class, trace the path of air into the respiratory system. Ask:

- **Where in the lungs does gas exchange actually occur?** (In the alveoli)
- **Where does air enter the body?** (Through the nose or mouth)
- **Why is this epiglottis important?** (Prevents solid materials from entering the lung)

3 ASSESS

Evaluate Understanding

To assess students' understanding of the section, ask:

- **What is the function of a respiratory system?** (To supply oxygen to the body and remove carbon dioxide)
- **What are the main organs of the human respiratory system?** (The lungs)
- **What happens to the air that enters your body?** (It is filtered, cleaned, warmed, and moistened as it moves through air passages to the lungs.)

Reteach

Make an overhead transparency of Figure 31.4 with no labels. Challenge students to identify the structures shown and their functions.

 Animated Biological Concepts

Human Respiration   Play

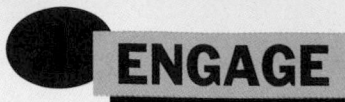

ENGAGE

Use the Visual

Have students study the photograph that opens the section. Explain that the way in which musicians breathe when playing a wind instrument is actually the correct method of breathing. Ask:

- **How does the way you inhale and exhale air compare to the technique used by the musician?** (Responses should indicate it is sometimes the same. At other times, humans exhale through the nose. Discuss all responses.)

Teacher Demo

Obtain and display X-rays that show how lungs filled with air differ in appearance from lungs without air. If visible, challenge students to identify the ribs on the X-rays. Point out how the position of the ribs change during inhalation and exhalation. You may want to suggest that students put their hands on their ribs and breathe.

❶ The diaphragm and intercostal muscles relax and the size of the chest cavity shrinks. The smaller size increases the air pressure in the lungs so that it is higher than the atmospheric pressure and air is forced out.

748

31.2 Every Breath You Take

What you'll learn

IDEAS
- To explain the mechanisms that control breathing
- To describe the process of gas exchange in the human body

WORDS
diaphragm

Blowing up a storm

Like a person inflating a balloon, a musician who plays a wind instrument that makes a sustained sound needs to exhale a large steady flow of air into the instrument. To do this, people playing instruments such as clarinets, saxophones, tubas, or trumpets often use circular breathing. This technique involves inhaling air through the nose while blowing it out through the mouth.

PROCESS OF BREATHING

Good air in, bad air out

Place your hands on your ribs and take a deep breath. Can you feel your rib cage expand? Your lungs do not have muscles. The work of breathing is done by the diaphragm (DY-uh-fram) and the intercostal muscles, the muscles between the ribs. The **diaphragm** is a sheet of muscle below the lungs that separates the chest cavity from the abdomen. *Figure 31.5* illustrates how the position of the diaphragm changes as you breathe.

An adult's lungs can hold up to 6 L of air. During normal, quiet breathing, only about 0.5 L of air is exchanged with each breath. However, up to 5 L of air can be exchanged with one breath during strenuous exercise. At least 1 L of air always remains in the lungs. This reserve of air keeps the lungs partially inflated at all times. The amount of air you normally inhale and exhale is called tidal volume. The largest volume of air that can be inhaled and exhaled is called the vital capacity of the lungs. Trained athletes, such as long-distance runners, have a large vital capacity.

FIGURE 31.5

You breathe by changing the air pressure in your lungs in relation to the atmospheric pressure. With inhalation, your diaphragm and intercostal muscles contract, expanding the chest cavity. The larger chest cavity decreases the air pressure in your lungs so that it is lower than the atmospheric pressure. Air then rushes into the lungs. What must happen with exhalation? ❶

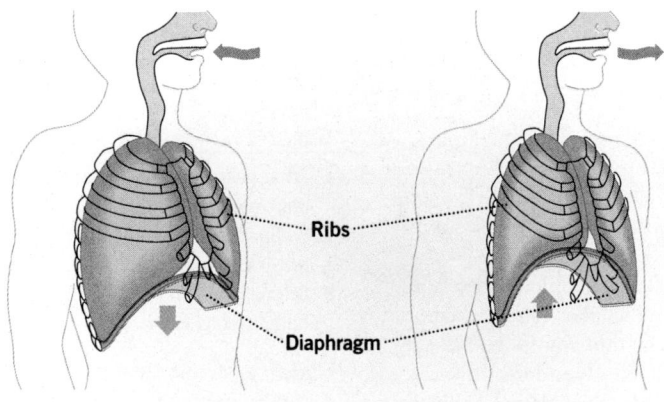

Ribs

Diaphragm

Inhalation
The diaphragm contracts and moves down.

Exhalation
The diaphragm relaxes and moves up.

748 *Unit 8 Human Biology*

STUDENT RESOURCES

From the Teacher's Resource Package, use:
- Section Review 31.2 and Activity Recordsheet 31-2 from Unit 8 Review Module
- Consumer Applications 31-1

TECHNOLOGY RESOURCES

Relevant technology resources include:
- Spanish Student Edition CD-ROM
- Teacher's Resource Planner CD-ROM
- How Your Body Works CD-ROM

Most people take 12 to 15 breaths per minute when they are at rest. You can consciously accelerate or slow your breathing for a short period. Most of the time, however, breathing is controlled automatically. The depth and rate of breathing are affected by several factors including exercise and stress. The nervous system basically adjusts breathing rate according to CO_2 levels. Only when O_2 levels are severely depressed do a few specialized sensors pick up O_2 deficiency.

Normally your breathing rate is regulated by the amount of CO_2 in your blood. The CO_2 dissolves in the blood, forming carbonic acid (H_2CO_3). Carbonic acid then breaks down into bicarbonate (HCO_3^-) and hydrogen ions (H^+). As you learned in Chapter 2, when the concentration of hydrogen ions in a solution increases, the pH drops. Blood that is high in CO_2 has a lower pH than blood that is low in CO_2.

Body sensors monitor blood pH. If the sensors detect a drop in the blood pH, they send nerve signals to the breathing center in the brain. The breathing center sends signals to the diaphragm and intercostal muscles, triggering deeper breathing. As more CO_2 is exhaled, CO_2 in the blood decreases, and the pH returns to normal.

GAS EXCHANGE IN THE LUNGS

A little give and take

As occurs in all other animals, gases are exchanged within the human body by diffusion. In Chapter 3 you learned that, when diffusing, substances move down a concentration gradient from an area of high concentration to an area of low concentration.

In the alveoli, O_2 is more concentrated than in the surrounding capillaries. The O_2 diffuses from the air across the cell membranes of the

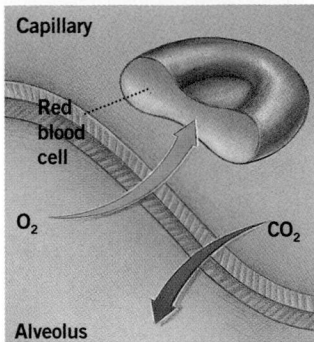
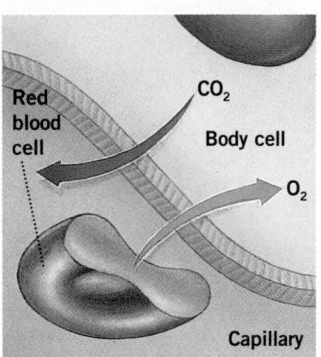

alveoli to the blood in the capillaries, as shown in *Figure 31.6*. In contrast, CO_2 is more concentrated in the capillaries of the lungs than it is in the alveoli. Therefore, CO_2 diffuses out of the capillaries into the alveoli, where it can be exhaled by the lungs. Body cells use O_2 and produce CO_2 during respiration. O_2 diffuses from the capillaries into body cells, and CO_2 diffuses out of body cells into the capillaries.

Most of the O_2 needed by the body is bound to a protein in red blood cells called hemoglobin. Hemoglobin is found in most animals and in some protists. You will learn more about hemoglobin later in this chapter.

FIGURE 31.6

In the lungs (left), gas exchange occurs by diffusion across the membrane of an alveolus and a capillary. What is happening to the oxygen and carbon dioxide in the body cell (right)? ❷

CHECKPOINT 31.2

1. Describe the mechanisms that control breathing.

2. Compare the diffusion of oxygen and carbon dioxide in alveoli and in body cells.

3. Critical Thinking A person who takes many deep, rapid breaths may feel dizzy. What has happened to the balance of oxygen and carbon dioxide in this person's blood?

Build on What You Know

4. What is a concentration gradient? How do concentration gradients affect diffusion? *(Need to jog your memory? Revisit relevant concepts in Chapter 3, Section 3.5.)*

Chapter 31 Respiratory and Circulatory Systems **749**

CHECKPOINT 31.2

1. An increased concentration of CO_2 lowers blood pH, which is detected by the breathing center in the brain. Nerve signals from the brain regulate breathing rate.

2. O_2 diffuses from air through alveoli cells to the blood to body cells. CO_2 diffuses in a reverse manner.

3. Identifying cause and effect With rapid, deep breaths carbon dioxide is not completely exhaled and its concentration increases.

4. Concentration gradient refers to an area with differing concentrations of a given molecule. Diffusion occurs down a concentration gradient.

❷ CO_2 diffuses out of the body cell and O_2 diffuses into the body cell.

TEAM WORK Measuring Lung Capacity

SAFETY FIRST!

Before conducting the experiment, make sure that no students have health conditions such as asthma or allergies that could be aggravated by doing the activity. Students with asthma should not blow up the balloons because the powder in some balloons can cause irritation in asthmatics. Also, caution students not to share balloons.

Lab Tips

It may be necessary to run through one or two sample calculations with students. Remind them that the quantity for π (pi) is 3.14. Allow students to use calculators and encourage them to double check all calculations.

Hypothesis Help

Likely hypotheses will state that lung capacity can be measured using simple tools.

Lab Extension

Open Ended

Have students design an experiment to determine if exercise affects lung capacity. After students get approval for their experiments, have them carry out the experiment.

Time Required

■ 50 minutes

 **LAB ZONE** Investigate It!

Measuring Lung Capacity

WHAT YOU WILL DO Measure your tidal volume, vital capacity, and total lung capacity

SKILLS YOU WILL USE Observing, recording data, measuring, calculating, designing an experiment

WHAT YOU WILL NEED Round balloon, metric tape measure

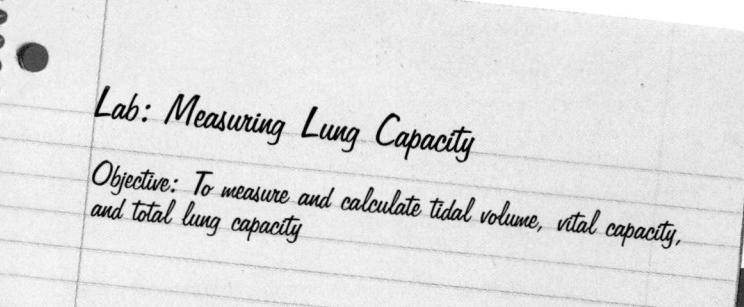

Propose a Hypothesis

Can lung capacity be measured using simple tools? Propose a hypothesis stating your position on this question.

Conduct Your Experiment

Caution: Do not share balloons. You should have your own balloon for this activity.

1 Stretch the balloon by blowing it up several times.

2 Inhale normally through your nose, then exhale normally through your mouth into the deflated balloon. The air you just exhaled is called your tidal volume. Hold the balloon closed with your index finger and thumb.

3 Have a partner fit the tape measure around the widest part of the balloon, as shown in the photograph above. Record the circumference of the balloon in centimeters (cm).

4 Repeat steps 2 and 3 four times. Calculate the average circumference of the balloon. Calculate the average volume of the balloon using the following formula: Volume = $\frac{1}{6} \times \frac{1}{\pi^2} \times C^3$ (C = average circumference). The volume is in cubic centimeters, or cm^3. (One cm^3 is equal to one mL.) Record the volume. This is your tidal volume.

5 Repeat steps 2–4, this time inhaling as deeply as you can through your nose and exhaling the air into the balloon. Record the volume. This is your vital capacity.

Analyze Your Data

1 What percentage of your vital capacity is your tidal volume?

2 Even after you exhale deeply, some air remains in your lungs. This air is called the residual volume. The average residual volume for females is 1000 mL and for males is 1200 mL. Calculate your total lung capacity by adding the residual volume to your vital capacity. What is your total lung capacity?

Draw Conclusions

1 Why is your vital capacity much larger than your tidal volume?

2 Would an animal that had no residual volume have an evolutionary advantage?

Design a Related Experiment

Propose a hypothesis about a smoker's vital capacity compared with that of a non-smoker. Design an experiment to test your hypothesis.

Lab: Measuring Lung Capacity

Objective: To measure and calculate tidal volume, vital capacity, and total lung capacity

---

Analyze Your Data

1 Answers will vary. The average tidal volume for a 15-year-old is 375 mL; the average vital capacity is 4000 mL.

2 Answers will vary, but total lung capacity would be greater than vital capacity.

Draw Conclusions

1 Tidal volume is the amount of air exhaled during normal breathing; vital volume is the amount exhaled under stress or when heavier breathing is necessary.

2 Accept all logical responses.

31.3 Health of the Respiratory System

Morgan's lifesaving mask

In 1914, African American inventor Garrett Morgan patented a gas mask. In 1916, this safety mask became a life-saver. Morgan and his brother, wearing the new devices, rescued more than 20 workers trapped by an explosion inside a tunnel filled with poisonous gases near Cleveland, Ohio.

What you'll learn

IDEAS
- To explain how viruses, bacteria, and fungi can affect the respiratory system
- To show ways to protect the respiratory system

RESPIRATORY DISORDERS
Trouble in the airways

Your respiratory system is constantly exposed to substances and organisms in air. Four disorders that affect the respiratory system are the cold, pneumonia, bronchitis, and asthma.

Colds Chances are you have had at least one cold. A cold is a disease caused by a virus. There are many different viruses that can cause a cold.

Viruses that cause colds can affect any part of your respiratory system, but most often they first attack nasal mucous membranes. When this happens, white blood cells respond by producing a chemical called histamine. Histamine causes blood vessels to expand, resulting in swollen respiratory tissues that make breathing difficult. Histamine also causes eyes to tear and nasal passages to secrete more mucus. Medications can relieve cold symptoms, but they cannot destroy cold-causing viruses.

Pneumonia Pneumonia is a disease that causes inflammation of the alveoli. Like a cold, pneumonia can be caused by viruses, but it can also be caused by bacteria, fungi, and chemical agents. The body responds to these agents and organisms by accumulating fluid and debris in the alveoli. The fluid interferes with gas exchange, resulting in less oxygen entering the blood. As a result, a person with pneumonia feels weak and tired. To help reduce symptoms, people with pneumonia are often given oxygen. If the pneumonia is caused by bacteria or fungi, the patient may be treated with antibiotics.

Bronchitis Bronchitis is an inflammation of the membranes of the bronchial tubes. People may develop bronchitis from bacteria or from the viruses that cause colds or flu. Like a cold, bronchitis results in an increased production of mucus that blocks the airways, making breathing difficult. As a result, a person with bronchitis feels very tired and weak. In addition, a

Ah-choo!

A single sneeze shoots out a million droplets of particle-laden fluid at more than 161 kilometers per hour. In less than a second, most of the water evaporates; the tiny packets of viruses and bacteria can float in the air for weeks.

FIGURE 31.7

By sneezing, a person with a cold clears excess mucus from the nasal passages.

Chapter 31 Respiratory and Circulatory Systems **751**

STUDENT RESOURCES

From the Teacher's Resource Package, use:
- Section Review 31.3 and Enrichment Topic 31-1 from Unit 8 Review Module
- Issues and Decision Making 31-1

TECHNOLOGY RESOURCES

Relevant technology resources include:
- Spanish Student Edition CD-ROM
- Teacher's Resource Planner CD-ROM
- Biology Alive! Video: "Domain of Life"
- How Your Body Works CD-ROM

31.3

1 ENGAGE

Use the Visual

Have students study the photograph that opens the section. Explain that rescue workers and firefighters wear gas masks to prevent inhalation of smoke and debris. Ask:

- **Why do you think some people wear surgical masks when outdoors?** (To filter out pollen, air pollutants, or germs that might aggravate a respiratory condition)

Check Prior Knowledge

To assess students' knowledge about respiratory illnesses, ask:

- **What diseases, disorders, or illnesses affect the respiratory system?** (Answers may include colds, allergies, asthma, bronchitis, pneumonia, lung cancer, emphysema.)

Quick Activity

Draw a two-column chart on the board. Label one column *Harmful* and the other *Healthful.* Have students brainstorm things people do that affect their respiratory system. Record the activities in the appropriate column. Tell students to copy the lists in their notebooks and add or delete information as they read the section.

2 TEACH

Teacher Demo

Invite the school nurse to speak to the class about common respiratory problems that require emergency medical treatment such as asthma attacks. Ask the speaker to demonstrate first-aid procedures.

 **STS**

Divide the class into groups and assign each group a tobacco product to research. Include varied products such as filtered and unfiltered cigarettes, low-tar/low-nicotine cigarettes, clove/herbal cigarettes, pipe tobacco, cigars, and smokeless tobacco. Students should look for the amount of tars, nicotine, and other carcinogens in their assigned product as well as warning labels. Provide time for each group to share their research.

In the Community

You may wish to have an emergency medical technician come to class to teach CPR. CPR is an emergency procedure that is used when the heart stops. The procedure involves artificial (mouth-to-mouth) respiration along with applying pressure to the heart muscle at regular intervals to help the heart reestablish a beat.

FIGURE 31.8
To quickly open the bronchial tubes of a person with an asthma attack, medication can be delivered directly to the bronchi by inhalation.

person with bronchitis coughs frequently to clear the bronchial tubes of mucus. The symptoms of bronchitis can be treated with cough syrup and cold medications. Antibiotics may be used to treat bacterial bronchitis.

Asthma A person with an asthma attack has difficulty breathing because their bronchial tubes are narrowed. Asthma results from a sudden spasm of the bronchial tubes or from swelling of their mucous membranes. People with asthma may wheeze, trying to move air through the narrowed bronchial tubes. Treatment for an asthma attack involves using drugs that relax the bronchial tubes, increasing their openings.

Doctors do not know what causes asthma. However, many doctors think asthma is a type of allergic reaction. Attacks often seem associated with emotional and physical stress, with fatigue, and with hormonal factors.

Many harmful substances and organisms are present in the air.

Measures that can help to keep your respiratory system healthy are illustrated in *Figure 31.9*.

ISSUES IN BIOLOGY
Effects of smoking

Health researchers estimate that as many as 30 percent of Americans smoke. These people place themselves and others at risk for diseases associated with smoking.

Tobacco smoke contains harmful substances, such as cyanide, cancer-causing tar, and carbon monoxide (CO). When CO is inhaled, it binds with hemoglobin, preventing the hemoglobin from carrying oxygen. Tobacco also contains nicotine, an addictive drug that stimulates the nervous system, resulting in such effects as increased heart rate and narrowed blood vessels.

Several types of cancer are associated with tobacco use. Among the most common is lung cancer. People who smoke, as well as people who use smokeless tobaccos, such as snuff and chewing tobacco, increase the likelihood of developing cancers of the mouth and throat. These cancers have

Cardiopulmonary resuscitation (CPR) is a procedure that might restore the natural functioning of a person's lungs and heart. It requires no equipment and is relatively simple to learn. Explore how CPR is taught in your community, then sign up to learn the procedure. A local hospital, American Red Cross office, fire department, or rescue squad is a good place to start. You can learn which professionals use CPR regularly and who teaches the procedure to the public. Find out if there are special methods of CPR for infants and for pets. You can learn more about CPR and the American Red Cross on the Internet at *http://body_systems.biosurf.com.*

IN THE COMMUNITY
Breaths of Life

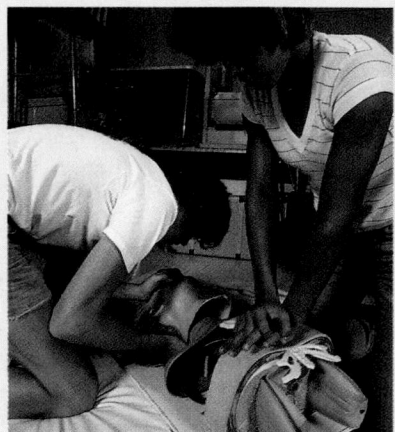

MEETING DIVERSE NEEDS

Gifted Encourage students to find out how an artificial respirator works. Have students share their findings with the class and explain why the machine might be more accurately referred to as an artificial breathing machine.

even been detected in new tobacco users and people who have not used tobacco products for a while.

Smoking is associated with a number of respiratory problems. Chronic "smoker's cough" can develop because smoking paralyzes the cilia that line the respiratory system, making them unable to move mucus. A person must cough to clear mucus from the respiratory system. Eventually, smoking destroys the cilia, increasing the smoker's risk of respiratory infections.

Another respiratory ailment associated with smoking is emphysema. Emphysema is a lung disease that is often linked to smoking, although long-term exposure to specific air pollutants can also cause emphysema. In this disease, the walls of the alveoli lose their elasticity and stay filled with air when the person exhales. A person with emphysema must work very hard to exhale. Eventually, damaged alveoli are replaced by connective tissue, and the area for gas exchange is reduced.

Breathing smoke from another person's cigarette can result in many of the health problems described above. For this reason, smoking has been banned in many public areas.

CHECKPOINT 31.3

1. How can viruses, bacteria, and fungi affect your respiratory system?
2. How can you protect your respiratory system from harmful substances?
3. **Critical Thinking** Do smoking bans limit smokers' rights? Explain.

Build on What You Know

4. Compare and contrast carbon monoxide and carbon dioxide. *(Need to jog your memory? Revisit relevant concepts in Chapter 2, Section 2.2.)*

FIGURE 31.9
Caring for Your Breath

You can help to keep your respiratory system healthy by doing the following:

Limit your exposure to air particulates by using air purifiers. Wear a face mask when working on projects that release dust or other irritating particulates.

Do not smoke and, when possible, avoid environments in which people are smoking.

Avoid direct or close contact with people who have a cold, the flu, pneumonia, or some other infectious disease of the respiratory system.

Exercise regularly. This will increase your lung capacity, allowing your lungs to work more efficiently.

What vital processes occur in the respiratory system? **?**

Chapter 31 Respiratory and Circulatory Systems **753**

CHECKPOINT 31.3

1. They can cause pneumonia and other infections, resulting in inflammation, increased mucus production, and difficulty breathing.
2. Limiting exposure to particulates, smoke, and people with infectious respiratory diseases can help protect the respiratory system.
3. **Identifying cause and effect** Answers will vary. Smoking has been banned in many public areas because of the harmful effects of second-hand smoke.
4. A carbon monoxide molecule contains one oxygen atom and a carbon dioxide molecule has two oxygen atoms.

Use the Visual

Have students study Figure 31.9. As a class, review the information in the illustration and discuss how each activity helps keep the respiratory system healthy.

3 ASSESS

Evaluate Understanding

To assess students' understanding of the key concepts of the section, ask:

- **Why is breathing difficult for a person with a cold or bronchitis?** (Organisms attack nasal and mucous membranes. Increased production of mucus blocks the airways.)
- **What can you do to keep your respiratory system healthy?** (Use air masks when exposed to particles in air, avoid contact with people with an infectious disease, get plenty of exercise, and do not smoke.)

Reteach

On the board, write the following terms: *pneumonia, colds, bronchitis,* and *asthma.* Have volunteers explain what each condition is and its cause. Discuss all responses. Then review ways that people can protect themselves from developing such illnesses.

1 ENGAGE

Consider the Big Idea

Have students read The Big Idea! at the top of the page. Explain that another function of the circulatory system is to remove potentially toxic wastes from cells.

Use the Visual

Have students study the photograph that opens the section. Explain that while the heart pumps about 24 tons of blood in a day, the heart itself weighs only about 2.2 kg.

Quick Activity

Have students place a thumb on the main neck artery to find their pulse. Have them count how many times the heart beats as you time one minute. Then have students calculate how many times their hearts beat in one day by multiplying their heart rate by 1,440 minutes. Remind them that the heart must pump some 43,000 L of blood each day. (The heart may beat as many as 100,000 times a day.)

 Animated Biological Concepts

Circulatory Systems   Play

754

31.4 Circulatory Systems

What you'll learn

IDEAS
• To compare open and closed circulatory systems
• To describe the structure and function of the human circulatory system

WORDS
heart, blood, blood vessels

Can you trust your heart?
In one day, your heart can pump as much as 43,000 L of blood. That much blood has a total weight of 21,844 kg—nearly seven times the weight of a bull elephant. Quite a feat for an organ the size of a fist! When diseased, the heart may not be able to handle this workload—and, in serious cases, open-heart surgery (right) may be the only answer.

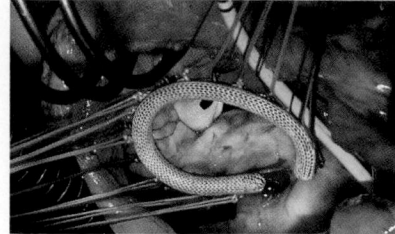

INTERNAL TRANSPORT IN ANIMALS

System on the move

You now know that an animal obtains nutrients through the digestive system, and oxygen (O_2) through the respiratory system. Most animals have a circulatory system for transporting O_2, nutrients, and other essential compounds to all cells. At the same time, a circulatory system transports carbon dioxide (CO_2) and other wastes away from cells for elimination from the body. The circulatory system also helps to maintain homeostasis of body cells.

The circulatory system has three main parts. The **heart** is the main

pump of the circulatory system. **Blood** is a liquid tissue containing blood cells in suspension. **Blood vessels** are the tubes through which blood flows to and from different parts of an animal.

In some animals such as cnidarians, a specialized circulatory system is not necessary. The exchange of essential materials and wastes occurs by diffusion between the main body cavity and the other cells of the animal. In many animals, diffusion would not be an efficient method for exchange of essential materials and wastes. These animals have open or closed circulatory systems.

In an open circulatory system, the heart pumps blood into open-ended blood vessels. The heart pumps blood out of the vessels to the body tissues.

FIGURE 31.10
What are the differences between the open circulatory system of a grasshopper and the closed system of a fish? ➊

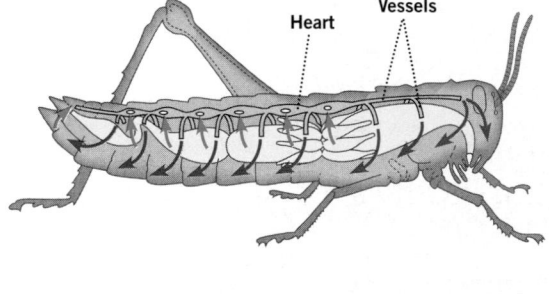
Heart   Vessels

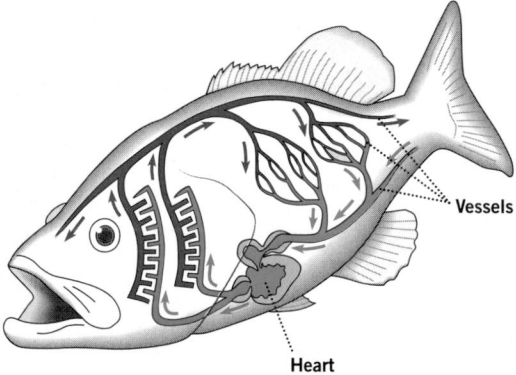
Vessels
Heart

754   *Unit 8 Human Biology*

STUDENT RESOURCES

From the Teacher's Resource Package, use:
■ Section Review 31.4, Activity Recordsheet 31-3, Interpreting Graphics 31-2, and Enrichment Topic 31-2 from Unit 8 Review Module
■ Lab 55: "Heart Rate in *Daphnia*"

TECHNOLOGY RESOURCES

Relevant technology resources include:
■ Spanish Student Edition CD-ROM
■ Teacher's Resource Planner CD-ROM
■ Animated Biological Videodiscs: "Circulatory Systems" and "Human Circulation"
■ How Your Body Works CD-ROM

The motion of skeletal muscles moves blood through the body. When the heart relaxes, blood returns through pores in the heart. Most arthropods and mollusks have an open circulatory system.

In a closed circulatory system, the heart pumps blood only through blood vessels, which have extensive branches that carry blood to all body tissues and return blood to the heart. Earthworms, squids, and vertebrates have a closed circulatory system. You can compare the open and closed circulatory systems shown in *Figure 31.10.*

What kind of circulatory system do you have? Humans, like all vertebrates, have a closed circulatory system. Within the human body, blood travels in two paths or circuits: the pulmonary circuit and the systemic circuit.

The pulmonary circuit is a short loop that carries blood between your heart and lungs. In the lungs, the blood absorbs O_2 and releases CO_2. The oxygenated blood returns to the heart and is pumped to the systemic circuit, which carries the oxygenated blood to all other body cells. The blood releases O_2 to the cells and picks up CO_2 and other wastes. The deoxygenated blood is returned to the heart, where it again enters the pulmonary circuit to be oxygenated. The path of blood in each pulmonary circuit is shown in *Figure 31.11.*

In addition to the circulatory system, you have a transport sytem called the lymphatic system. The lymphatic system consists of vessels and nodes and some associated organs that collect and clean the fluid around your cells. Chapter 32 provides information about this system.

FIGURE 31.11
The arrows show the path of blood through the pulmonary and systemic circuits.

- Oxygenated blood
- Deoxygenated blood
- Pulmonary circuit
- Systemic circuit

Upper body vessels

Right lung vessels

Left lung vessels

Lower body vessels

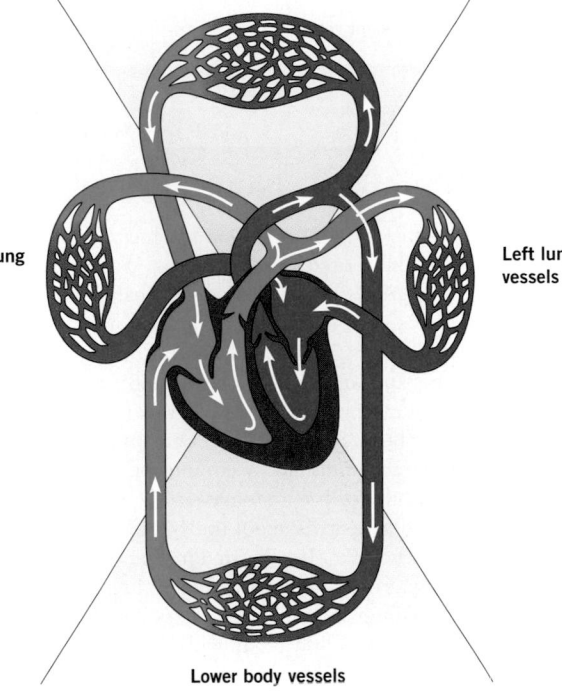
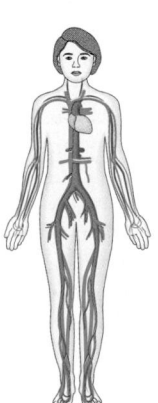

2 TEACH

Use the Visual

Have students study Figure 31.11. As a class, trace the path of blood through the pulmonary and systemic circuits. Ask:

- **What is the pulmonary circuit?** (The short loop of the circulatory system that moves blood between the heart and lungs)
- **What is the systemic circuit?** (The loop of the circulatory system that moves blood between the heart and the rest of the body)
- **How does the blood carried from the heart to the lungs differ from the blood carried from the lungs to the heart?** (Blood carried from the heart to the lungs is low in oxygen; blood carried from the lungs to the heart is rich in oxygen.)
- **How is the blood carried from the heart to the body different from the blood carried from the body to the heart?** (Blood carried from the heart to the body is rich in oxygen; blood carried from the body to the heart is low in oxygen.)

Language Arts

Explain to students that the word *pulmonary* means "referring to the lungs." Students can use this definition to remember the role of the pulmonary circuit.

 Animated Biological Concepts

Human Circulation   Play

MEETING DIVERSE NEEDS

LEP Have students look up the term *circuit* in a dictionary. Then have them work with a partner and use Figure 31.11 to trace and explain how blood travels in two circuits.

❶ In an open circulatory system, the blood bathes the body tissues directly. In a closed system blood stays in vessels and materials diffuse into and out of the walls of the vessels.

Use the Visual

Have students study Figure 31.12. To determine students' understanding of the diagram, ask:

- **After blood leaves the atria, where does it go?** (Into the ventricles)
- **What structure separates the right side of the heart from the left side?** (The septum)
- **Where does the blood go when it leaves the right ventricle? The left ventricle?** (Right ventricle, to the lungs; Left ventricle, to the body)

Teacher Demo

Obtain a model of the heart that can be taken apart to show the inside of the atria and ventricles. Use the model to trace the path of blood through the heart and to show the one-way action of valves in the heart. As an alternative, show a computer simulation of the movement of blood through the heart.

Think Critically

Have students think about the the movement of the front door to their homes. Ask:

- **How is the door's movement similar to the movement of heart valves?** (The door opens in only one direction, as do the heart valves.)

Build Writing Skills

Have students imagine that they are microscopic in size and able to travel in the bloodstream as it moves through the human heart. Ask them to select a format and describe their journey.

756

FIGURE 31.12

Blood Flow Through the Heart

The heart is a pump that moves blood through a circulatory system. What differences do you see between the left and right sides of the heart? Trace the flow of blood through the heart. ❶

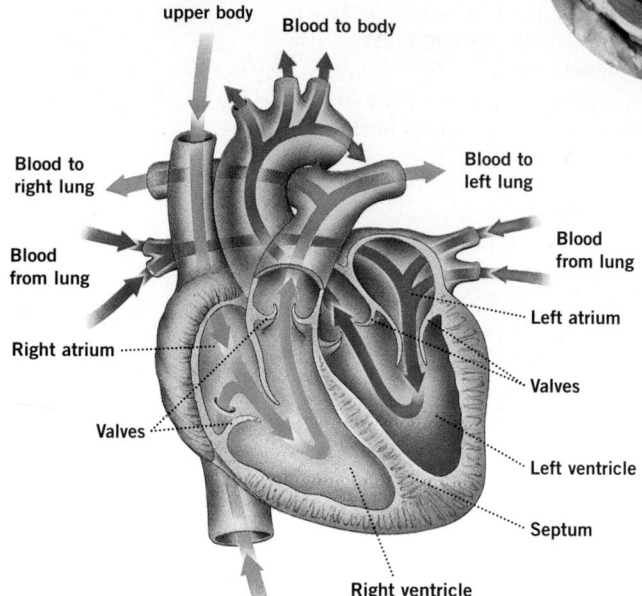

Valves
Valves, such as the one in the photo (left), channel blood into, through, and out of the heart. Closed valves keep blood from moving backward.

Blood from upper body

Blood to body

Blood to right lung

Blood to left lung

Blood from lung

Blood from lung

Left atrium

Right atrium

Valves

Valves

Left ventricle

Septum

Right ventricle

Blood from lower body

THE HUMAN HEART

Pumping chambers

People once thought that the heart was the source of all emotions. We now know that the brain is primarily responsible for feelings. Then what is the heart's function? The heart is a muscular organ that forces blood through the body. You can think of your heart as two pumps. One pump drives the pulmonary circuit; the other drives the systemic circuit.

Your heart is about the size of your clenched fist. It is located just beneath the sternum, or breastbone, and near the center of your chest cavity. The heart is a hollow organ with thick walls made of cardiac muscle. It is surrounded by a loose-fitting, double-walled sac called the pericardium. In addition to covering and protecting the heart, the pericardium anchors the heart by connecting it to structures such as the diaphragm and the breastbone.

The heart has two sides, separated by a thick wall of muscle called the septum. The heart has a total of four chambers, two on each side. The upper chambers of the heart are called atria (singular: *atrium*). Atria receive blood coming into the heart from the lungs or the body. They pump blood into the two lower chambers called ventricles. Ventricles pump blood out of the heart to the lungs or the body. You can follow the flow of blood through the heart in *Figure 31.12*.

Atria are small and have relatively thin walls. Ventricles are larger than the atria and have thicker, more muscular walls. The muscular walls are important because ventricles work harder than atria, pumping blood to the entire body.

The heart has valves that keep blood moving in one direction. Valves located between the atria and the ventricles prevent blood from flowing back into the atria. Other valves are located between each ventricle and the major blood vessels leading to the lungs and the rest of the body.

MEETING DIVERSE NEEDS

Sight Impaired Obtain a three-dimensional model of the heart that can be taken apart. Allow students to manipulate the model as a sighted student identifies each structure and traces the path of blood through the heart.

❶ On the right side of the heart, blood is low in oxygen; on the left side of the heart, blood is rich in oxygen.

HUMAN BLOOD VESSELS

Life's plumbing

The human body has three types of blood vessels: arteries, veins, and capillaries. Each type of vessel has a different job in the circulatory system. The size and structure of each type vary according to the vessel's function. The inner layer of all three vessels, composed of epithelial tissue, is a barrier between blood and the rest of the body. Capillaries consist of only epithelial tissue. Arteries and veins also have smooth muscle and connective tissue layers. Smooth muscle allows vessels to contract. Connective tissue gives vessels elasticity.

Arteries Vessels that carry blood away from the heart are called arteries. You can feel the pulsing pressure of blood in an artery at several places on your body where arteries are near the skin. These places are called pulse points.

Arteries branch throughout the body into smaller arteries. The smallest arteries are called arterioles. The arterioles eventually become capillaries. By the time blood enters capillaries, its pressure has dropped significantly.

Capillaries Thin-walled blood vessels are called capillaries. Many capillaries are so small that blood cells flow through them in single file. Most of the exchange of gases, nutrients, and wastes takes place by diffusion through the thin capillary walls.

Some capillaries directly connect arteries and veins. Others form branching networks. These networks provide a greater surface area for diffusion, enabling large amounts of material to be exchanged rapidly.

Veins Capillaries merge to form vessels called venules, which in turn merge to become veins. Blood returns to the heart in veins. Blood in veins is under very low pressure and often

FIGURE 31.13

The Structure of Blood Vessels

The photo (right) shows a vein next to a thicker walled artery. What are the differences between the structure and function of an artery, a vein, and a capillary? ❷

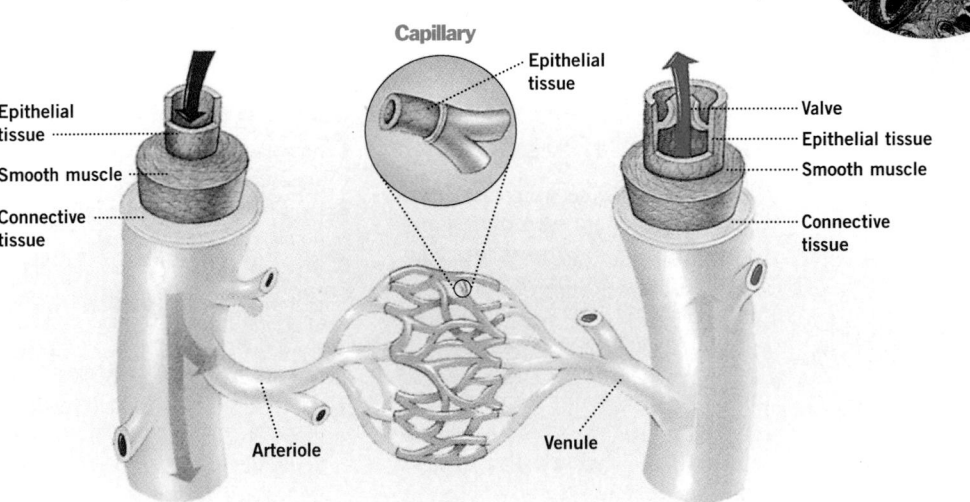

❷ Arteries contain a thicker layer of muscle than do veins; capillary walls consist only of epithelium. Arteries carry blood from the heart; veins carry blood to the heart; capillaries join arteries and veins or branch out from them.

LAB ZONE Do It! · TEAM WORK

Examining the Effect of Exercise on Heart Rate

Pair students with a condition that would prevent them from doing step 3 with another student.

Analyze Your Results

1–3 Answers will vary. Heart rate will probably be in the 60-80 range at rest and in the 120-175 range after exercise.

3 ASSESS

Evaluate Understanding

To assess students' understanding of the section, ask:

- **How does the human circulatory system work?** (It is a closed circulatory system in which blood travels through pulmonary and systemic circuits)
- **What are the three types of blood vessels and the function of each?** (Arteries, carry blood away from the heart; capillaries, through which gases, nutrients, and wastes are diffused; veins, return blood to the heart)

Reteach

List the following terms on the board: *atria, ventricles, septum, heart valves, arteries, veins, capillaries, vessel valves.* Have students work in pairs to create graphic organizers identifying each structure and its function.

LAB ZONE Do It!

Examining the Effect of Exercise on Heart Rate

You can demonstrate the relationship between heart rate and exercise when you . . .

Try This

1 Sit quietly and press your middle and ring fingers firmly, but not hard, on the carotid artery in your neck, as shown in the photo.
2 Count the pulses for 15 seconds and multiply this number by 4 to calculate beats per minute. Record this number as *Heart Rate at Rest.*
3 Run in place for 2 minutes. Repeat step 2—but this time record the number as *Heart Rate after Exercise.*

Analyze Your Results

1 What is the difference between your heart rate at rest and your heart rate after exercise?
2 Create a graph that shows the heart rates of each student at rest (in blue) and after exercise (in red).
3 What are the highest and lowest rates at rest? After exercise?

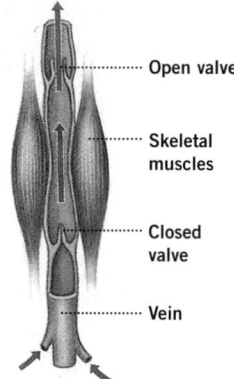

Open valve

Skeletal muscles

Closed valve

Vein

FIGURE 31.14
The squeezing of skeletal muscles surrounding a vein helps move the blood against gravity, toward the heart.

flows against gravity. To keep the blood flowing in one direction, veins have valves that prevent backflow. The squeezing action of skeletal muscles around the veins also helps move blood toward the heart.

HEART RATE

You've got rhythm!

The number of times your heart beats each minute is your heart rate. Each heartbeat has two parts, the diastole and the systole. During diastole (dy-AS-tuh-lee) the ventricular muscles relax and blood flows into the atria and ventricles. During systole (SIS-tuh-lee) the ventricles contract, pumping the blood out to the body.

If you use a stethoscope to listen to a heart, you can hear a "lub-dup" sound caused by the closing of heart

valves. The "lub" sound is made as valves between the atria and ventricles close. The shorter "dup" sound is made when the valves close between the ventricles and the blood vessels.

Two masses of nerve and muscle cells called nodes send out electrical signals that control your heart beat. The sinoatrial (SY-noh-AT-re-uhl) node, or SA node, located in the wall of the right atrium, signals the atria to contract. The SA node's signal also travels to the atrioventricular (AT-ree-oh-ven-TRIK-yoo-ler) node, or AV node, which is located in the septum between the atria. The AV node signals the ventricles to contract. The SA node controls the rate of the heartbeat and is called the pacemaker. Electrical signals through the heart can be detected by a machine called an electrocardiograph (ee-LEK-troh-KAR-dee-oh-graf). This device draws the heart's electrical activity, which is called an electrocardiogram (EKG or ECG).

Your heart beats faster when you are angry or afraid, or after you exercise. In times of stress, body cells send messages to the brain, demanding more O_2 and nutrients. The brain relays the messages to the SA node, which speeds up the rate at which the heart pumps the needed O_2 and nutrients to body cells.

CHECKPOINT 31.4

1. Compare the circulatory systems of a grasshopper and a fish.
2. Diagram the flow of blood through the human circulatory system.
3. **Critical Thinking** How does the structure of capillaries compare to that of arteries and veins?

Build on What You Know

4. Compare the heart structures of humans, amphibians, and fish. *(Need to jog your memory? Revisit relevant concepts in Chapter 25, Section 25.2 and Section 25.5.)*

CHECKPOINT 31.4

1. Blood vessels in the grasshopper are open-ended; fish have a closed system in which blood is contained within vessels.
2. Diagrams should show a flow from the body to the right atrium, right ventricle, lungs, left atrium, left ventricle, and back to the body.
3. **Analyzing** Capillaries are much smaller

and do not contain the layers of muscle and connective tissues found in arteries and veins.
4. The human heart has four chambers, fish and aquatic amphibians have two chambers, terrestrial amphibians have three chambers.

31.5 Blood

An ocean of cells
One drop of blood from a finger prick contains 250,000–500,000 white cells and 15–20 million platelets. Most blood cells, however, are red cells. There are approximately 200 million red blood cells in a drop of a woman's blood and over 250 million in a man's blood. But don't worry about pricking your finger. In one second, the body produces 2 million new red blood cells to replace those that are lost.

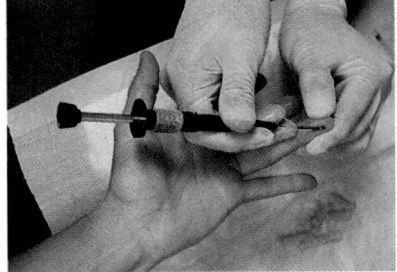

What you'll learn

IDEAS
• To compare the components of blood
• To explain the role of antigens in blood typing

WORDS
plasma, red blood cells, white blood cells, platelets

PLASMA AND BLOOD CELLS

Red, white, and . . .

Your body contains about 5 L of blood. Blood is a type of connective tissue in which specialized cells are suspended in a liquid. The yellowish liquid in which blood cells are suspended is called **plasma.** Plasma is 90 percent water, but it also contains dissolved salts, proteins, nutrients, wastes, and other chemicals.

Almost half of the blood's volume consists of blood cells. Blood cells begin as unspecialized cells called stem cells, which are formed in the red marrow of bones. Stem cells differentiate and mature into blood cells as your body needs more blood cells. When stem cells mature, they enter the bloodstream as red blood cells, white blood cells, or platelets.

Red blood cells Red blood cells are the most numerous cells in your blood—you have about 25 trillion of them in your body! **Red blood cells,** or erythrocytes (eh-RITH-roh-syts), carry oxygen (O_2) to all cells of the body.

As you read in section 31.2, red blood cells contain a large, complex protein called hemoglobin. Each red blood cell contains about 250 million hemoglobin molecules. Each hemoglobin molecule can bind four molecules

of O_2. Thus, a single red blood cell can contain about one billion O_2 molecules. Red blood cells that contain O_2 bound to hemoglobin molecules cause blood to be red.

Hemoglobin binds or releases O_2 depending on the O_2 concentration in the environment. In the alveoli of the lungs, the concentration of O_2 is high. The O_2 diffuses into the blood of the lungs' capillaries and is bound by hemoglobin in the red blood cells. In muscle and other organ cells, the O_2 concentration is low. In these body areas, O_2 is released by the hemoglobin in red blood cells passing through nearby capillaries. The released O_2 diffuses into the body cells.

Hemoglobin can also bind carbon dioxide (CO_2). It releases or binds CO_2 depending upon the concentration of the gas in the area surrounding the hemoglobin. However, most of the CO_2 in blood is carried in the blood plasma, not in the red blood cells.

Red blood cells are disk-shaped, giving them

FIGURE 31.15
Normal red blood cells are disk-shaped. How does this shape aid in gas diffusion? ❶

STUDENT RESOURCES

From the Teacher's Resource Package, use:
■ Section Review 31.5 and Enrichment Topic 31-3 from Unit 8 Review Module

TECHNOLOGY RESOURCES

Relevant technology resources include:
■ Spanish Student Edition CD-ROM
■ Teacher's Resource Planner CD-ROM
■ How Your Body Works CD-ROM

① ENGAGE

Use the Visual

Have students study the photograph that opens the section. Explain that in addition to red blood cells and white blood cells, a drop of blood also contains cell fragments called platelets and a liquid called plasma. Ask:

■ **Why is it important that the body produce so many new blood cells?** (To replace those which are lost or damaged)

Check Prior Knowledge

To assess students' knowledge about cell function, ask:

■ **What organelle in eukaryotic cells is essential for cell division?** (The nucleus)

Teacher Demo

Use a microprojector to display prepared slides of red blood cells, white blood cells, and platelets. Identify each cell and ask students to sketch their appearance. Discuss with students differences they observe in number, size, shape, and general appearance of the blood components.

❶ The disk shape gives the red blood cell a large surface area for gas diffusion.

31.5

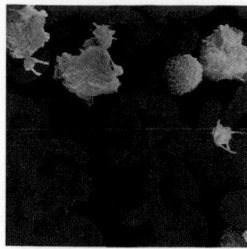

Explain

Point out to students that blood consists of about 55 percent plasma, 43 percent red blood cells, and 2 percent white blood cells and platelets.

Use the Visual

Have students study Figure 31.17. Ask:

- **What are some of the functions of white blood cells?** (Some white blood cells destroy bacteria, some release histamines that cause inflammation, and others produce antibodies to fight disease.)

Discuss

Ask students to think about the last time they sustained a minor cut. Discuss how long the cut bled and what, if anything, they did to stop the bleeding, and if the blood clotted. Direct students to Figure 31.18. Point out that platelets are not true cells, but cell fragments that bud off from large cells in the bone marrow. Ask:

- **How do clotting factors help to mend damaged blood vessels?** (They react with fibrinogen, a blood protein, that is converted into fibrin, which prevents blood cells from leaving the blood vessel.)

❶ There are fewer white blood cells and white blood cells have nuclei and organelles.

❷ All have organelles; some kill harmful cells by phagocytosis, others manufacture antibodies to combat specific diseases.

FIGURE 31.16
White blood cells are larger than red blood cells. What other differences can you see between white blood cells and red blood cells in the photo above? ❶

a large surface area for efficient gas diffusion. Red blood cells lack a nucleus as well as any organelles. Therefore, red blood cells cannot reproduce or repair themselves. A red blood cell lives for three to four months before being broken down in the spleen. New red blood cells form continuously in red bone marrow. Iron, a component of hemoglobin, is recycled into newly-produced hemoglobin molecules.

White blood cells Leukocytes (LOO-koh-syts), or **white blood cells,** help the body fight disease. There are fewer leukocytes than red blood cells in blood, as you can see in *Figure 31.16*. In contrast to red blood cells, white blood cells have nuclei and organelles, and they can move out of blood vessels and into tissue where they may be needed. White blood cells are larger than red blood cells. Lymphoid tissues, such as the spleen, tonsils, and thymus, store white blood cells.

White blood cells can fight disease in different ways. One way is to engulf and digest dead or harmful cells such as bacteria. This method is called phagocytosis, and these white blood cells are phagocytes. In *Figure 31.17*

Types of White Blood Cells

Cell Type	Appearance	Function
Neutrophils		Kill bacteria by phagocytosis
Eosinophils		Kill parasitic worms Inactivate allergic reactions
Basophils		Release histamines that cause inflammation and allergies
Lymphocytes		Produce antibodies that fight disease and destroy cancerous and virus-infected body cells
Monocytes		Destroy bacteria, infected cells, and old red blood cells by phagocytosis

FIGURE 31.18
Strands of insoluble fibrin trap blood cells, forming a mesh that prevents blood from leaving a damaged blood vessel.

you can see five types of white blood cells and the role each plays in fighting disease. You will learn more about how some types of white blood cells function when you study the immune system in Chapter 32.

Platelets Platelets are involved in the formation of blood clots. **Platelets** are formed from pieces of cytoplasm that break off of large cells in the bone marrow. A cell membrane forms around the cytoplasmic pieces. However, no nuclei form, even as platelets mature.

When you cut or injure yourself, platelets move to the damaged blood vessel in large numbers. The resulting plug of platelets prevents excessive loss of blood during the time it takes for a blood clot to form. The platelets secrete chemicals called clotting factors into the blood. Clotting factors react with fibrinogen, a protein in blood. The fibrinogen is converted into an insoluble threadlike substance

FIGURE 31.17
Compare the appearance and function of white blood cells. ❷

MULTICULTURAL PERSPECTIVE

In 1940, African American Charles Drew earned a Doctor of Science degree for his dissertation, "Banked Blood." The blood bank program devised by Dr. Drew involved methods for adequate storage of blood for transfusions. The development of blood banks saved the lives of many soldiers fighting in World War II. Following the war, Dr. Drew became the first director of the American Red Cross Blood Bank and a professor at Howard University.

Blood Donor Table		
Blood Type	**Can Donate To**	**Can Receive From**
A	A, AB	A, O
B	B, AB	B, O
AB	AB	A, B, O
O	A, B, AB, O	O

FIGURE 31.19

Using information in the table, what blood types might have been mixed together in the sample shown in the photo? ❸

Clumped blood cells

called fibrin. Strands of fibrin entwine, making a mesh that traps blood cells and prevents them from passing through the damaged blood vessel. You can see these strands in *Figure 31.18*. The resulting clot of fibrin, platelets, and blood cells forms a scab that seals the wound until it can be replaced with new tissue.

BLOOD TYPES

All in the family

You have just learned about the components of blood—plasma, red blood cells, white blood cells, and platelets. These components are present in everyone's blood. Yet everyone's blood is different. Why? Because human blood types differ.

As you learned in Chapter 6, your blood type is determined by your genes. Humans have four different, familiar blood types: type A, type B, type AB, and type O. The type of blood you have is determined by the presence or absence of molecules called antigens on the surfaces of your red blood cells. For example, people with type B blood have a molecule called the B antigen on their red blood cells. The red blood cells of people with type A blood have the A antigen. People with type AB blood have both A and B antigens. Those with type O blood have neither A nor B antigens.

Everyone's blood type is identified not only by letter, but also as being positive or negative. The identification of a blood type as positive or negative refers to the presence or absence of an anti-

gen called the Rh group or Rh factor. When the Rh group antigen is present, a person is identified as being Rh positive, or Rh$^+$. A person who does not carry the Rh factor on their red blood cells is described as being Rh negative, or Rh$^-$.

As long as you remain healthy, the types of antigens present on your red blood cells is of little concern. However, should you require a blood transfusion, this information is vital. For a blood transfusion to be successful, the blood from a donor must have the same antigens as the patient's blood. When the antigens are different, the patient's lymphocytes will usually produce antibodies that bind the antigens on red blood cells of the transfused blood. This will cause the red blood cells to clump together, which can be fatal to the recipient. Study the table in *Figure 31.19*. What type of blood can be given to all patients? ❹

CHECKPOINT 31.5

1. Name and describe the components of blood.
2. Explain the role of antigens in blood typing.
3. **Critical Thinking** If you had an infection, would the number of leukocytes in your blood be higher or lower than normal? Why?

Build on What You Know

4. Describe the patterns of inheritance of blood types. *(Need to jog your memory? Revisit relevant concepts in Chapter 6, Section 6.5.)*

Chapter 31 Respiratory and Circulatory Systems **761**

① ENGAGE

Use the Visual

Have students study the photograph that opens the section. Explain that being able to pump more blood with fewer beats helps prevent heart muscle from tiring when overworked. Ask:

- **What other steps do you think athletes take to develop cardiovascular fitness?** (Eating balanced meals low in cholesterol and salt and not smoking.)

Check Prior Knowledge

To assess students' knowledge about blood cells, ask:

- **What is the normal shape of a red blood cell?** (Disk-shaped)

Teacher Demo

Obtain a bicycle pump and a piece of rubber tubing that fits over the air nozzle. Have a volunteer use the pump to push air through the tube. Then pinch the tubing closed and have the volunteer pump air through the tube again. Have the student describe the difference in the amount of work required in each trial. Explain that in a condition called atherosclerosis, the arteries narrow, causing the heart to work harder, just as a person must work harder to pump air through a restricted tube. Tell students that they will learn how to care for the circulatory system in this section.

31.6 Health of the Circulatory System

What you'll learn

IDEAS
- To describe illnesses of the cardiovascular system
- To explain ways to care for the cardiovascular system

The heart of an athlete
Athletic training can increase the size and power of heart muscle. A swimmer's heart pumps one-third more blood than does the heart of an unfit person. Also, an athlete's resting pulse is slower, because the heart pumps more blood per beat. It is literally true that athletes put a lot of heart into their sport.

CARDIOVASCULAR DISEASES

A "broken heart"

Cardiovascular diseases—diseases of the heart and blood vessels—are the number-one cause of death among people in the United States today. About 63 million people, or about one out of four people in the United States, have a cardiovascular disease. Two common cardiovascular diseases are atherosclerosis and hypertension.

Atherosclerosis The disease atherosclerosis (ATH-er-oh-skler-OH-sis) is a cardiovascular condition in which arteries have narrowed. A narrowed artery is shown in *Figure 31.20.*

The arteries of a person suffering from atherosclerosis narrow because fatty deposits called plaques form inside blood vessel

FIGURE 31.20
Blood flows freely through a healthy artery (right). In atherosclerosis, plaques reduce the flow of blood (left).

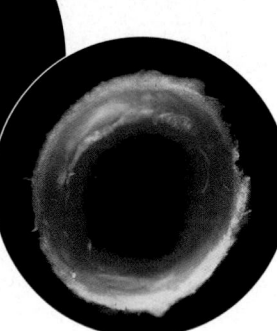

walls. If the disease progresses, the plaques may become hardened by deposits of calcium. The result is a related condition called arteriosclerosis, commonly known as hardening of the arteries.

Atherosclerosis creates two problems. First, a narrowed blood vessel reduces the flow of blood through the vessel. Second, the plaques roughen the smooth endothelial lining. The rough surface seems to stimulate platelets to form clots. If the clot breaks free, it can get stuck in a narrow artery and block the flow of blood. As a result, any organ or tissue served by the artery is deprived of its oxygen supply. If a clot blocks the blood flow in a coronary artery—an artery that carries blood to the heart—a heart attack can result. If a clot blocks the blood flow in an artery of the brain, a stroke can result.

Although many unanswered questions about the cause of atherosclerosis remain, scientists have gathered a lot of data about the disease. A person's tendency to develop atherosclerosis is related to the ratio of two kinds of cholesterol in the blood. One kind of cholesterol, called low-density lipoprotein (LDL), increases the tendency of

762   *Unit 8 Human Biology*

STUDENT RESOURCES

From the Teacher's Resource Package, use:
- Section Review 31.6, Critical Thinking Excercise 31, Enrichment Topic 31-3, Vocabulary Review 31, and Chapter 31 Tests from Unit 8 Review Module
- Consumer Applications 31-2

TECHNOLOGY RESOURCES

Relevant technology resources include:
- Spanish Student Edition CD-ROM
- Teacher's Resource Planner CD-ROM
- How Your Body Works CD-ROM
- TestWorks CD-ROM: Chapter 31 Tests

plaques to form in arteries. The other form of cholesterol, high-density lipoprotein (HDL), reduces the tendency of plaques to form. The higher the ratio of LDL to HDL in the blood, the greater the risk of atherosclerosis.

Hypertension High blood pressure, or hypertension, occurs when the force of blood pumping through blood vessels is too great. Your blood pressure normally increases temporarily from exercise, fever, or stress, but usually returns to normal relatively quickly. When blood pressure remains high for a longer period, however, it eventually overworks the heart and damages the arteries. Hypertension often increases the risk of heart attack and stroke. Atherosclerosis often causes high blood pressure, but heredity also plays a role.

Have you ever had your blood pressure measured? Blood pressure is recorded in millimeters of mercury (mm Hg). The device used to measure blood pressure is shown in *Figure 31.21.* A person's blood pressure is recorded in two parts. The first number is systolic pressure, the force of the blood in the arteries when the ventricles contract. The second number is diastolic pressure, the force of the blood in the arteries when the ventricles relax. An average adult's blood pressure is 120/80, or "120 over 80." A high diastolic pressure is usually more indicative of hypertension than a high systolic pressure.

BLOOD DISEASES

Blood can be sick and tired, too

When a person has a condition called anemia, the blood transports too little oxygen. A person with anemia feels tired and weak. Anemia can result from too little iron in the diet, bleeding due to injury or menstruation, or other causes.

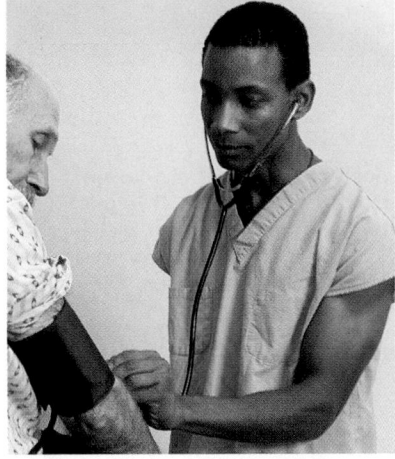

FIGURE 31.21
Because there are usually no symptoms of hypertension, people should have their blood pressure checked regularly.

Sickle-cell disease, characterized by the misshapened red blood cells you see in *Figure 31.22,* can cause anemia. The sickle shape of the blood cells also causes them to clog blood vessels. Unlike most other types of anemia, sickle-cell disease is hereditary. The hereditary factors of the disease were discussed in Chapter 6.

Blood can also be affected by a form of cancer called leukemia. In a person with leukemia, the bone marrow produces immature stem cells in great numbers and releases them into the bloodstream. Because these stem cells are not fully mature, they cannot fight infection as normal white blood cells do. At the same time, fewer red blood cells and platelets may be formed, making the body prone to anemia and abnormal bleeding.

Although doctors are uncertain what causes a person to develop leukemia, they have found ways to treat some forms of the disease. One of the most recent developments in this area involves the use of bone marrow transplants. In this procedure, healthy bone marrow from a matched donor is used to replace cancerous marrow from a leukemia sufferer. Stem cells from umbilical cords have also been used to treat leukemia.

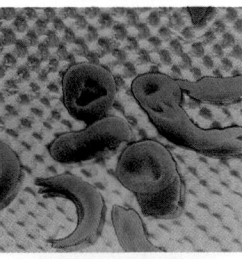

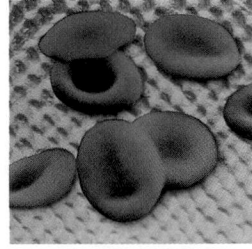

FIGURE 31.22
The sickled red blood cells (top) are caused by a mutation in the hemoglobin gene. Normal blood cells (bottom) have normal hemoglobin.

Chapter 31 Respiratory and Circulatory Systems **763**

2 TEACH

Language Arts

Explain to students that the prefix *cardio-* means "referring to the heart," and the term *vascular* means "of or relating to vessels." Have students relate these definitions to the term cardiovascular and the types of conditions classified as *cardiovascular* disorders.

Teacher Demo

Invite the school nurse to class to demonstrate to students how blood pressure is taken. Have the nurse explain how the stethoscope and a sphygmomanometer are used in this process.

Use the Visual

Have students study Figure 31.22. Ask:

- **Why are sickle cells harmful to the body?** (The sickle cells clog blood vessels and prevent blood flow.)

Build Writing Skills

Divide the class into groups and assign each group a cardiovascular disease to research. Have students identify the causes, people who are at risk, treatment, and preventive measures. Have each group decide on a format for its presentation. You may wish to ask students to share the results of their research.

MEETING DIVERSE NEEDS

Gifted Have students research famous "firsts" relating to the heart. Such information may include the first heart transplant, the development of an artificial heart, and the first implant of an animal heart in a human. Suggest that students present their research as an illustrated time line.

Relating Blood Pressure to Health

Analyzing the Graph

1 Risk increases with high blood pressure.
2 After the "optimal" blood pressure range
3 Ideal blood pressure, less than 110 over 80, can be reached by not smoking, a low-fat diet, and regular exercise.

ASSESS

Evaluate Understanding

To assess students' understanding of the key concepts of this section, ask:

■ **How do cardiovascular and blood diseases vary?**
(Cardiovascular, diseases of heart and blood vessels; blood, problems with blood cells.)

■ **What can you do to reduce the risk of developing cardiovascular disease?**
(Exercise, do not smoke, reduce cholesterol and saturated fat intake.)

Reteach

Work with students to create a concept map describing cardiovascular diseases and disorders. Then discuss ways to prevent them.

 Using Prior Knowledge To practice strategies for effective reading, use pages 69-70 in *Super Read!*

LAB ZONE **Think About It!** 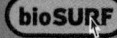 **bioSURF**

Relating Blood Pressure to Health

High blood pressure, or hypertension, generally causes no symptoms but is dangerous to your health. It is one of the three major risk factors for cardiovascular disease. Smoking and high LDL/HDL blood cholesterol ratios are the other two risk factors. Study the graph below and then answer the questions that follow.

Analyzing the Graph

1 What is the relationship indicated in the graph between blood pressure and the risk of dying from heart attack or stroke?
2 When does the risk of dying from heart attack or stroke start to increase noticeably?
3 Write a paragraph describing what your ideal blood pressure would be based on the graph's data. Include a plan for reaching that blood pressure.

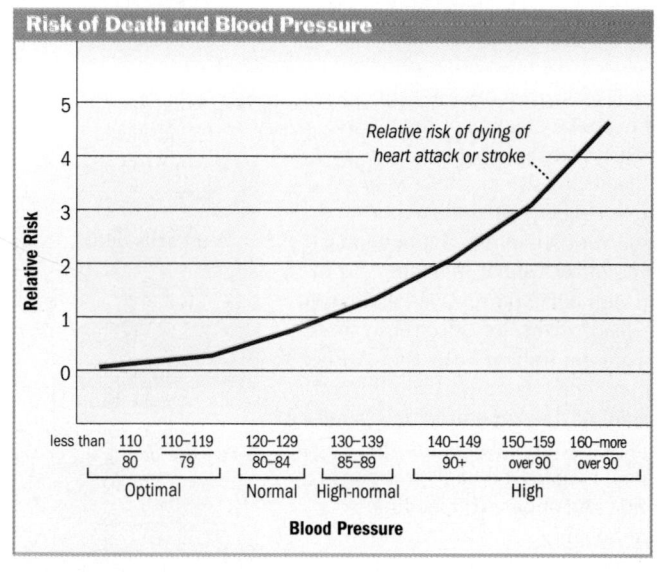

Risk of Death and Blood Pressure

Relative risk of dying of heart attack or stroke

Blood Pressure

SUPER READ!

 How are materials transported throughout the body?

CARE OF YOUR CIRCULATORY SYSTEM

The heart of health

Can a person reduce the risk of developing cardiovascular disease? The tendency to develop atherosclerosis and hypertension is inherited. However, a healthy lifestyle is the most important preventive factor.

Smoking increases the risk of cardiovascular disease. Nicotine in tobacco raises the heart rate and narrows arteries. Smoking also lowers the efficiency of respiratory organs. Consequently, the heart must pump faster to deliver oxygen to the body's cells.

Diet and exercise also affect the cardiovascular system. Exercise increases the lungs' vital capacity, influences the body's weight, and reduces stress. It also strengthens muscles, including heart muscle.

A high dietary intake of cholesterol and saturated fats can lead to high levels of LDL cholesterol. A diet low in saturated fats can help reduce your risk of cardiovascular disease.

CHECKPOINT 31.6

1. Name and describe two cardiovascular disorders.
2. List three factors that can increase a person's risk of cardiovascular disease.
3. **Critical Thinking** HDL is sometimes referred to as good cholesterol, and LDL has been called bad cholesterol. Explain.

Build on What You Know

4. What are the dietary recommendations regarding foods high in fats? *(Need to jog your memory? Revisit relevant concepts in Chapter 30, Section 30.1.)*

CHECKPOINT 31.6

1. Atherosclerosis is the narrowing of blood vessels. Hypertension is a chronic increase in blood pressure. Both conditions can cause a heart attack or stroke.
2. Smoking, a diet high in cholesterol and saturated fat, and lack of exercise are risk factors.

3. **Comparing** HDL cholesterol is "good" because it reduces the risk of developing atherosclerosis. LDL cholesterol increases the risk.
4. Foods high in fat should be consumed sparingly. Although unsaturated fats are less harmful than saturated fats, too much of either can raise LDL levels.

Chapter 31 Review

 **THE BIG IDEA!** 31.1–31.3 The vital exchange of oxygen and carbon dioxide occurs in the respiratory systems of animals.
31.4–31.6 Circulatory systems transport materials necessary for life.

Sum It Up

Use the following summary to review the main concepts in this chapter.

31.1 Respiratory Systems

- Oxygen and carbon dioxide are exchanged in respiratory systems.
- Gases may be exchanged through skin, gills, tracheal tubes, or lungs.
- In humans, dissolved gases are carried to and from the lungs by the blood.
- As air travels to air sacs in the lungs, it is cleaned, moistened, and warmed.

31.2 Every Breath You Take

- The diaphragm and intercostal muscles control breathing. The carbon dioxide concentration in blood regulates the breathing rate.
- Carbon dioxide and oxygen are exchanged by diffusion during respiration.

31.3 Health of the Respiratory System

- The symptoms of respiratory ailments are excess mucus, inflamed membranes, and narrowed passages—which make breathing difficult.
- In addition to causing lung cancer, smoking increases the risk of respiratory infections and of emphysema.

31.4 Circulatory Systems

- Circulatory systems can be open, as in arthropods, or closed, as in vertebrates.
- The heart pumps oxygen-poor blood through the pulmonary circuit and oxygen-rich blood through the systemic circuit. Valves keep blood flowing in one direction.
- Thick-walled arteries carry blood away from the heart; diffusion occurs in thin-walled capillaries; blood returns to the heart in veins.

31.5 Blood

- The blood cells are suspended in a liquid called plasma. Red blood cells carry oxygen, white blood cells fight infection, and platelets secrete clotting factors.
- Antigens on the surface of red blood cells determine blood type.

31.6 Health of the Circulatory System

- In atherosclerosis, the arteries are narrowed by plaque deposits, which can lead to heart attacks or strokes. Hypertension can also increase the risk of heart attack and stroke.
- Anemia limits oxygen transport by the blood; leukemia limits the normal functioning of white blood cells.

Use Terms and Concepts

Use each of the following words or terms in a complete sentence. If you need to review a meaning, turn to the page indicated.

respiration (p. 745)
alveoli (p. 747)
diaphragm (p. 748)
heart (p. 754)
blood (p. 754)
blood vessels (p. 754)

plasma (p. 759)
red blood cells (p. 759)
white blood cells
 (p. 760)
platelets (p. 760)

Review the Big Ideas

Before students begin the Chapter Review, you may wish to discuss main concepts from the Big Ideas in Chapter 31. Point out that the respiratory system provides animals with a way to exchange carbon dioxide and oxygen with their environment. The exchange of gases occurs in the lung alveoli. The human circulatory system consists of the heart, which pumps blood through the pulmonary and systemic circuits, and a network of blood vessels, which transport materials necessary for life.

Answers

1. plasma
2. diaphragm
3. platelets
4. alveoli
5. white blood cells
6. heart
7. blood vessels
8. False; plasma
9. True
10. True
11. True
12. False; red blood cells
13. False; contracts
14. There are no antigens on Type O red blood cells to bind with a recipient's antibodies.
15. The atria, which pump blood to the ventricles, have thinner, less muscular walls than the ventricles, which must pump blood to the body.
16. Stem cells produced in the marrow mature into red blood cells, white blood cells, and platelets as needed.
17. A larger surface area provides more opportunity for gas exchange through diffusion. Both systems branch into smaller and smaller vessels, culminating in the alveoli and the capillaries.
18. Blood in arteries is moved along by high pressure from the contracting ventricle. Blood in veins is traveling at low pressure and often against gravity. Veins need valves to prevent back flow.
19. The membranes produce mucus, which traps small particles. Cilia moves mucus and its trapped particles from the respiratory passageways to the throat to be swallowed.
20. An increase in carbon dioxide in the blood; emotions such as anxiety or anger; exercise; drugs such as nicotine.

Use Your Word Power

COMPLETION **Write the word or phrase that best completes each statement.**

1. Blood cells are suspended in a watery liquid called _____ .

2. The muscle that separates the chest cavity from the abdomen is the _____ .

3. The blood cells that secrete clotting factors are called _____ .

4. In the lungs, gases diffuse between air in the _____ and blood in capillaries.

5. Leukocytes is another name for the _____ that fight disease.

6. The _____ is the organ that is the main pump of the circulatory system.

7. In arthropods and mollusks _____ are open-ended.

TRUE-FALSE **Write true if the statement is true. If the statement is false, replace the underlined word(s) to make the statement true.**

8. Most of the carbon dioxide transported in blood is carried by red blood cells.

9. White blood cells have nuclei and organelles.

10. The exchange of gases between blood and body cells is called internal respiration.

11. The blood that travels from the heart to the lungs is oxygen-poor.

12. The antigens on the surface of white blood cells determine blood type.

13. When the diaphragm relaxes, air rushes into the lungs.

Show What You Know

14. Explain why people with Type O blood are called universal donors.

15. Relate the structure of atria and ventricles to their functions.

16. What is the role of stem cells in the circulatory system?

17. What is the importance of surface area to respiration? How do the structures of the respiratory and circulatory systems provide the maximum surface area possible?

18. Explain why valves are needed in veins but not in arteries.

19. What roles do cilia and mucous membranes play in respiration?

20. Name at least three conditions that can cause heart rate to increase.

21. **Make a Concept Map** Make a concept map that relates the respiratory and circulatory systems.

Take It Further

22. **Developing a Hypothesis** Before birth, a fetus produces a form of hemoglobin that can bind more oxygen at lower concentrations than can the hemoglobin produced after birth. Why would fetal hemoglobin need to be different from adult hemoglobin? (Hint: A fetus gets oxygen from its mother's blood, not from the air.)

23. **Applying Concepts** One possible cause for shock—a sudden lowering of blood pressure—is massive internal or external bleeding. Replacing blood volume quickly is critical. If there is no time to find a matching blood type, doctors use blood plasma to restore blood volume. Why is blood plasma an effective alternative to whole blood in an emergency?

24. **Making an Analogy** Compare the role of a piston in an automobile engine to that of the diaphragm in the respiratory system.

25. **Developing a Hypothesis** What symptoms might lead a doctor to consider installing an artificial pacemaker in a patient?

21. Concept maps should show the following: Oxygen and carbon dioxide are exchanged by the respiratory system through diffusion in the lung alveoli. Oxygen and carbon dioxide are transported by the circulatory system.

22. The concentration of oxygen in blood is lower than the concentration of oxygen in air.

23. Once the blood cells are removed, there are no antigens in the plasma to cause clotting and the plasma quickly restores blood volume.

24. The movement of a piston changes the volume of air in a cylinder just as the movement of the diaphragm changes the volume of air in the chest cavity.

25. The patient might have an irregular

26. Designing an Experiment Suppose you had four vials of blood, one each of Type A, Type B, Type AB, and Type O. You want to confirm that the labels are accurate. Design an experiment to verify the contents of the vials. Would you be able to tell all the types apart without any additional blood samples?

27. Interpreting a Graph The graph shows how the concentration of inhaled gases affects the breathing rate. How does the breathing rate change as the percent of carbon dioxide (CO_2) in inhaled air increases? What is the effect on the breathing rate of a decrease in the oxygen (O_2) content of inhaled air? Based on the graph, is the breathing rate more sensitive to the O_2 content or the CO_2 content of inhaled air?

Effect of Inhaled CO_2 and O_2 on Breathing Rate

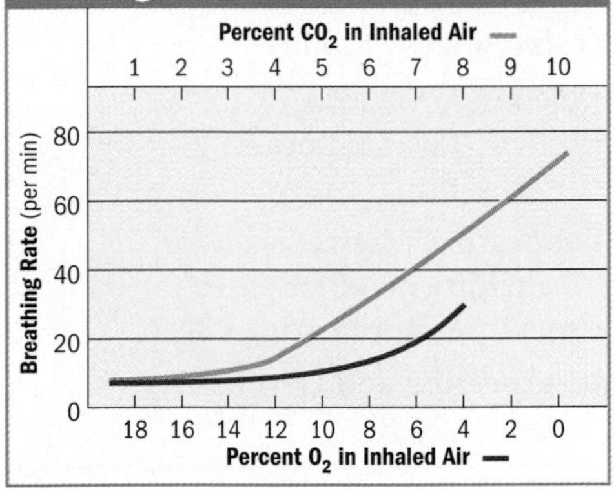
Percent CO2 in Inhaled Air
1 2 3 4 5 6 7 8 9 10
Breathing Rate (per min)
0 20 40 60 80
18 16 14 12 10 8 6 4 2 0
Percent O2 in Inhaled Air

28. Analyzing Data The following table shows the relative blood flow through various organs in the human body—that is, the fraction of blood that flows through a given human organ. Through which organ(s) does all of the blood flow? Describe and explain the change in blood flow to skeletal muscles during exercise. The kidneys consume only 6 percent of the oxygen used in the body. Why would 22 percent of blood flow through the kidneys?

Blood Flow Through Human Organs

Organ	Percentage of Total Flow
Brain	14%
Heart muscle	5%
Kidneys	22%
Liver	13%
Lungs	100%
Skeletal muscles	18%
Skeletal muscles during exercise	75%
Skin*	4%

*Maximum dilation of blood vessels

Consider the Issues

29. Air Quality When the level of pollutants in the air is high, communities warn their citizens, especially those with respiratory problems, to stay indoors. What are the major sources of air pollution? What local or federal regulations have been enacted to alleviate the problem? Describe their effectiveness.

Make New Connections

30. Biology and Mathematics Large animals usually live longer and have a slower heart rate than do smaller animals. Collect data on the average lifespans and heart rates for different mammals. Compute and compare the number of heartbeats per lifetime.

31. Biology and History Learning about human anatomy by dissecting human remains, or cadavers, was initially very controversial. Research the history of anatomical studies beginning in Great Britain during the 1600s.

FAST-FORWARD TO CHAPTER 32

The lymphatic system, which you will study in Chapter 32, also circulates materials through the body. The lymphatic system helps to defend the body against foreign substances.

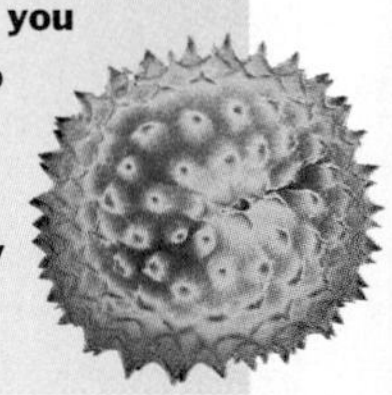

heartbeat or a very rapid or very slow heartbeat.

26. All four samples can be verified by noting the absence or presence of a clumping reaction which indicates an antigen-antibody reaction.

27. The breathing rate increases sharply with an increase in carbon dioxide; only a large drop in oxygen concentration affects the breathing rate; the breathing rate is more sensitive to carbon dioxide.

28. All the blood flows through the lungs. Blood flow quadruples as the muscles need additional oxygen for cellular respiration. The kidneys filter wastes from the blood.

29. Automobiles and factories have been major contributors to air pollution. Regulations on emissions have helped. Effectiveness will vary from locale to locale.

30. For most mammals, the result is about one million heartbeats. Humans are an exception. If humans followed the trend, their lifespan would be about 30 years.

31. Students may also want to research how the controversy surrounding dissection was reflected in popular fiction. A comparison could be made with modern best sellers that focus on the potential evils of organ transplants.

Section	Student Activities/Features	Teacher's Resource Package
32.1 Protecting the Organism **Objectives** ■ Explain the characteristics of a pathogen ■ Compare specific and nonspecific defenses	**Lab Zone Discover It!** *Graphing Vaccinations,* p. 769 **Lab Zone Think About It!** *Calculating Bacterial Growth,* p. 773	**Unit 8 Review Module** ■ Section Review 32.1
32.2 Overview of the Immune System **Objectives** ■ Describe the components of the immune system ■ Compare the lymph system to the circulatory system	**Lab Zone Investigate It!** *Modeling Disease Transmission,* p. 776	**Unit 8 Review Module** ■ Section Review 32.2 ■ Activity Recordsheet 32-1
32.3 Activities of the Immune System **Objectives** ■ Explain the functions of non-specific defenses ■ Identify the components and functions of specific defenses	**Lab Zone Do It!** *How Does Skin Protect Humans?* p. 779 **Everyday Biology** *End Run Around the Defense,* p. 780 **Everyday Biology** *Coming Back to Haunt Us,* p. 782	**Unit 8 Review Module** •Section Review 32.3 •Activity Recordsheet 32-2 •Interpreting Graphics 32 **Laboratory Manual,** Lab 56: "Transmission of Diseases" **Consumer Applications** 32-1 **Interpreting and Developing Graphics** 94, 95
32.4 Health of the Immune System **Objectives** ■ Identify causes of allergies ■ Explain the effect of HIV on the immune system ■ Analyze the effects of different lifestyles on the immune system	**STS: Frontiers in Biology** *Shutting Down Immunity,* p. 784 **Everyday Biology** *Hope for a One-Two Punch,* p. 786 **Lab Zone Do It!** *Creating a Personal Health Journal,* p. 787 **In the Community** *Shots for Everyone,* p. 788	**Unit 8 Review Module** •Section Review 32.4 •Activity Recordsheet 32-3 •Critical Thinking Exercise 32 •Enrichment Topic 32-1 •Vocabulary Review 32 •Chapter 32 Tests **Issues and Decision Making** 32-1 **Interpreting and Developing Graphics** 96 **Spanish Reviews** Chapter 32

Technology Resources

Internet Connections

Within this chapter, you will see the bioSURF logo. If you and your students have access to the Internet, the following URL address will provide various Internet connections that are related to topics and features presented in this chapter:

http://body_systems.biosurf.com

You can also find relevant chapter material at **The Biology Place** address:

http://www.biology.com

CD-ROMs

Biología: la telaraña de la vida,
   (Spanish Student Edition) Chapter 32
Teacher's Resource Planner, Chapter 32
   Supplements
Interactive Biological Simulations
■ The Immune System
TestWorks CD-ROM
■ Chapter 32 Tests
How Your Body Works CD-ROM

Videodiscs

Animated Biological Concepts Videodiscs
■ Inflammatory Response
■ Humoral Immunity
■ Cell-Mediated Immunity

Overhead Transparencies

■ Koch's Postulates, #74
■ Human Lymphatic System, #75
■ Inflammatory Response, #76
■ Cell-Mediated Immune Response, #77

Videotapes

Biology Alive! Video Series
Rewind: The Web of Life Reteach Videos

Planning for Activities

STUDENT EDITION
Lab Zone
Investigate It! p. 776
- grease pencil
- clean, empty baby-food jar
- safety goggles
- rubber gloves
- dropper
- stock solution
- phenol red indicator

Lab Zone Do It! p. 779
- apple
- knife
- plastic food wrap
- dropper
- food coloring

TEACHER'S EDITION
Quick Activity, p. 770
Transmitting diseases to humans
- pictures of disease-causing viruses, bacteria, and invertebrates

Teacher Demo, p. 771
Sterilizing techniques
- culture of bacteria
- wire loop

- 2 sterile petri dishes containing nutrient agar
- Bunsen burner
- marking pen
- incubator

Class Activity, p. 772
- talcum powder

Teacher Demo, p. 774
Feeding amebas
- microprojector
- amebas that are feeding

Quick Activity, p. 777
Antigens and antibodies
- large jigsaw puzzle pieces

Teacher Demo, p. 783
Antihistamines and histamines
- over-the-counter allergy medications, one with an antihistamine and the other with a histamine

Teacher Demo, p. 784
Common allergy problems
- allergist or related health care professional

Chapter Objectives

Students will learn the main concepts of this chapter as they complete the following objectives.

- Explain the characteristics of a pathogen
- Compare specific and non-specific defenses
- Describe the components of the immune system
- Compare the lymph system to the circulatory system
- Explain the functions of non-specific defenses
- Identify the components and functions of specific defenses
- Identify causes of allergies
- Explain the effect of HIV on the immune system
- Analyze the effects of lifestyle on the immune system

Key Words

32.1 *pathogen, nonspecific defenses, specific defenses*

32.2 *lymph, lymph nodes, phagocytes, macrophages, lymphocytes*

32.3 *inflammatory response, histamine, antigen, humoral immunity, antibody, B lymphocytes, cellmediated immunity, T lymphocytes*

32.4 *allergy, autoimmune disease, HIV, vaccine*

The Opening Story

Have students discuss how they think the story relates to the content of this chapter. Point out that sections of the quilt have been displayed in varied locations nationwide. Invite students who have seen the quilt to share their impressions with the class.

768

CHAPTER 32

Immune System

You can find out more about the immune system by exploring the following Internet address:
http://body_systems.biosurf.com

In this chapter . . .

FEATURES

Everyday Biology
- End Run Around the Defense
- Coming Back to Haunt Us
- Hope for a One-Two Punch

In the Community
Shots for Everyone

 Frontiers in Biology
Shutting Down Immunity

LAB ZONES

Discover It!
- Graphing Vaccinations

Do It!
- How Does Skin Protect Humans?
- Creating a Personal Health Journal

Think About It!
- Calculating Bacterial Growth

Investigate It!
- Modeling Disease Transmission

768 *Unit 8 Human Biology*

A CHILLING AMERICAN QUILT

In October 1996, when the AIDS Quilt was unfurled in Washington, D.C., it stretched eleven blocks along the Mall, from the Washington Monument to the Capitol. The names of the deceased were read aloud, and parents and other family members, friends, and observers moved reverently and silently around the panels. Begun in 1987, the AIDS Quilt now contains about 45,000 individual panels—each one lovingly crafted by family members and friends to commemorate a life lost to AIDS. Each panel bears the name of a victim and attached memorabilia that relate to the person's life, ranging from baseball caps and other favorite clothing items to stuffed animals and car keys.

As yet, no cure has been found for AIDS—a viral disease that attacks the human immune system and leaves the body unable to fight infection. Although education about the causes of this disease is helping to slow its spread, AIDS has killed more than 300,000 Americans—people of all ethnic groups and ages, including teenagers and children. The worldwide death toll is estimated at 4 million to 6 million. In this chapter you will learn how your immune system works and how to keep it healthy and strong.

Discover It!

Graphing Vaccinations

1. Survey the class to find out which diseases your classmates have been vaccinated against.
2. Record the total number of classmates that were vaccinated for each disease.
3. Make a graph to show your findings.

Each vaccination you have received has helped to stimulate your immune system in a way that creates resistance to a specific disease. What vaccinations are the most common among your classmates?

WRITE ABOUT IT!

Talk to several persons of different generations and ask them whether they think a cure will be found for AIDS. Record their ideas and responses in your journal.

Opening Activities

bioSURF If you have access to the Internet in your classroom or school, you may wish to have students connect to the address shown on page 768. You may also want to have students conduct a net search for information using key words such as viral infections, HIV, AIDS, food poisoning, or immunization.

Discover It!

Graphing Vaccinations

TEAM WORK

Encourage students to discuss diseases they have been vaccinated against with a parent to prepare themselves for the activity.

WRITE ABOUT IT

Allow students time to compare their findings and draw conclusions.

Rewind to Chapter 31

Briefly review with students concepts they learned in Chapter 31, *The Respiratory and Circulatory Systems.* Ask students:

- **How do you think the circulatory and respiratory systems relate to the immune system?**

SUPER READ! **Using Prior Knowledge** To practice strategies for effective reading, use pages 69-70 in **Super Read!**

PORTFOLIO PREVIEW

Students should be encouraged to add to their portfolios as they work through this chapter. In addition to the *Write About It* opportunity, the following sections are excellent opportunities for portfolio entries:

- Section 32.1: *Protecting the Organism*
- Section 32.3: *Activities of the Immune System*

① ENGAGE

Consider the Big idea

Have students read The Big Idea! at the top of the page. Explain that the immune system has a variety of mechanisms for responding to harmful organisms.

Use the Visual

Have students study the photograph that opens the section. Explain that by studying the immune system of sharks scientists hope to learn information that may be used to help humans fight diseases such as cancer. Ask:

■ **How are the immune systems of sharks and humans similar?** (Both produce antibodies to fight bacteria and viruses.)

Check Prior Knowledge

To assess students' knowledge about pathogens, ask:

■ **What groups of organisms cause disease or illness?** (Likely responses will include viruses, bacteria, fungi, some worms.)

Quick Activity

Display pictures of disease-causing viruses, bacteria, and invertebrates with which students are familiar. Ask students to identify the organisms and explain how they transmit disease in humans. Record responses on the board, correcting any misconceptions students may have.

32.1 Protecting the Organism

What you'll learn

IDEAS
• To explain the characteristics of a pathogen
• To compare specific and nonspecific defenses

WORDS
pathogen, nonspecific defenses, specific defenses

Shark attacks germs
Sharks—like humans but unlike some other chordates—have complex immune systems. Like us, they produce antibodies and other chemical protectors to fight bacteria and viruses. Because sharks are extraordinarily resistant to cancer, scientists are eager to learn more about how the immune system evolved.

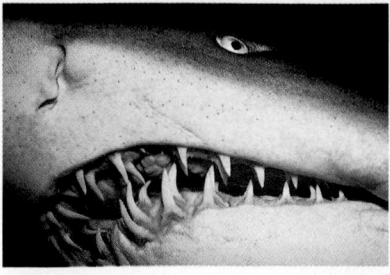

PATHOGENS AND DISEASE

The enemy within

Your body is constantly exposed to harmful organisms and substances in the environment. The immune system is the body's defense system against attack. A main function of the immune system is to fight infectious diseases. An infectious disease is any illness caused by organisms or viruses that enter and reproduce inside a host. The common cold, pneumonia, and influenza (the flu) are a few of the many infectious diseases that affect humans.

Not all illnesses are infectious diseases. For example, an illness caused by the bite of a poisonous snake is not an infectious disease. Illness from a snake bite is caused by snake poisons, not organisms or viruses that enter the body.

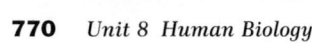

FIGURE 32.1

Entamoeba histolytica (top) is a protist that causes a type of dysentery. A tapeworm (bottom) attaches itself to the digestive wall of a host, sustaining itself on the host's nutrients.

770   *Unit 8 Human Biology*

Pathogens A virus or organism that causes an infectious disease is a **pathogen** (PATH-oh-jen). Viruses, bacteria, protists, fungi, and some invertebrate animals such as roundworms and flatworms can be pathogenic to humans.

Pathogens cause disease in different ways. Some pathogens produce poisons called toxins that disrupt the normal functioning of cells. For example, the bacterium that causes tetanus produces a toxin that affects nerve cells involved in muscle contraction.

As you learned in Chapter 14, viruses use the body's cells to replicate. In the process, the viruses destroy healthy cells. Chicken pox and the common cold are caused by viruses.

Protists and roundworms that cause disease destroy body tissues by feeding on and burrowing into the tissue. For example, one type of dysentery is caused by an ameba that eats colon cells, causing the host to suffer from internal sores and diarrhea. The roundworm that causes trichinosis burrows into muscle cells, forming cysts within the tissue.

Germ theory Before the 1800s it was not known that microscopic

---

STUDENT RESOURCES

From the Teacher's Resource Package, use:
■ Section Review 32.1 from Unit 8 Review Module

TECHNOLOGY RESOURCES

Relevant technology resources include:
■ Spanish Student Edition CD-ROM
■ Teacher's Resource Planner CD-ROM
■ How Your Body Works CD-ROM

pathogens caused disease. Three nineteenth-century scientists—Louis Pasteur, Joseph Lister, and Robert Koch—pioneered the study of infectious disease. Their discoveries formed the basis of the germ theory of disease. The germ theory proposes that there is a relationship between a microorganism and a specific disease.

In 1876 Robert Koch used four experimental steps to demonstrate that anthrax, a deadly disease of cattle and sheep, is caused by a specific bacterium. Called Koch's postulates, these steps are still used to study and identify the causes of infectious diseases. Koch's postulates are shown in *Figure 32.2*.

THE TRANSMISSION OF DISEASE

Germ warfare

Although they are caused by different pathogens, most infectious diseases are spread in one of four ways: through direct contact with an infected person, through indirect contact with an infected person, through the ingestion of contaminated food or water, or through the bite of an infected animal.

Direct contact Infectious diseases that spread from one person to another are called contagious diseases. Contagious diseases are often spread through direct contact. A healthy person contracts the disease by touching an infected person. For example, the viruses that cause colds can be transmitted by direct contact, especially by shaking hands.

Certain pathogens are transmitted through sexual contact with an infected person. Syphilis, gonorrhea, and AIDS are transmitted this way and are called sexually transmitted diseases.

Indirect contact Most contagious diseases are spread by indirect contact with an infected person.

FIGURE 32.2
Koch's Postulates

Koch's postulates are used to identify the pathogens that cause certain diseases. How do the four steps relate to the scientific method? **❶**

1 The suspected pathogen must be found in the bodies of sick organisms but not in the bodies of healthy organisms.

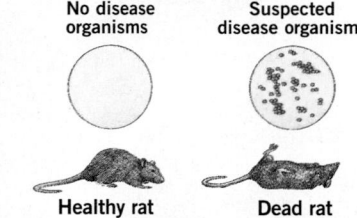

2 The pathogen must be removed from the infected host and grown in a pure culture in the laboratory.

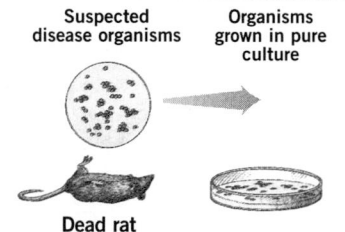

3 When the laboratory-grown pathogen is placed in a healthy organism, the pathogen must cause the same disease in the new host that was observed in the original host.

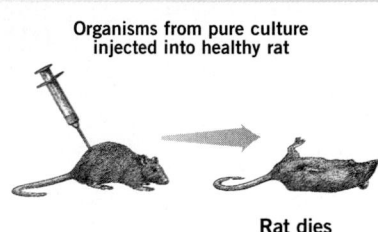

4 Once the new host has developed the disease, the pathogen must be recovered from the newly infected host.

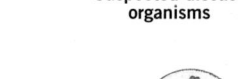
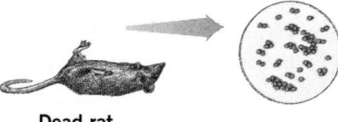

Chapter 32 Immune System **771**

❶ Observation is made, hypothesis is developed, experimentation occurs, and results are evaluated.

Language Arts

Point out that the term *pathogen* is from the Greek *pathos* meaning "suffering" and *genes* meaning "born." Have students look up other words relating to disease that begin with *patho.*

Build Writing Skills

Have students write about an infectious illness they have had. In their writing, ask students to speculate about the likely means of transmission.

Class Activity

Divide the class into groups of ten or more to model the spread of a pathogen by direct contact. Have one student in each group cover the palm of his or her hand with talcum powder and shake hands with a group member. Repeat the process until all group members have shaken hands. Have students examine their hands for signs of powder, which is evidence of transmission. Ask:

- **How many people transmitted the pathogen?** (Responses depend on how much talcum powder was used.)

Health

One indication that a canned food is contaminated with *Clostridium botulinum* bacteria is that the can bulges. Caution students to look for this indicator when they purchase canned foods.

772

FIGURE 32.3
Contagious diseases can be spread in many ways. What three ways of transmitting disease are depicted in the photos above? ❶

Indirect contact requires a carrier, or vector, for the pathogen. Air can be a vector for pathogens. When you sneeze, your respiratory system releases droplets into the air. Cold viruses in droplets can be transmitted to a person as far away as 5 meters. Cold viruses can also contaminate objects on which they settle. If you touch a contaminated object and then touch your nose, eyes, or mouth, you can become infected.

Water and food Some diseases are spread by contaminated water or food. Disease transmission through water is a serious problem in parts of the world with poorly designed sanitation systems and untreated sewage. Amebic dysentery is a disease spread by contaminated water.

Food poisoning can be caused by eating food that contains pathogens.

772 *Unit 8 Human Biology*

The bacteria *Salmonella* grow in foods such as eggs, chicken, turkey, sausage, and ground meat. Eating raw or undercooked foods containing *Salmonella* can cause vomiting, stomach cramps, and fever.

Botulism is a form of food poisoning caused by a bacterium that cannot live in the presence of oxygen. The bacterium can grow and produce a toxin in improperly canned foods. When ingested, the toxin attacks the nervous system. Serious cases of botulism can cause death from heart or respiratory failure.

Animal bites Animals, often insects, are vectors for many infectious diseases. For example, the bubonic plague, which killed 40 percent of Europe's population during the Middle Ages, is caused by a pathogen spread by fleas. The pathogen that causes malaria is transmitted through the bite of infected mosquitoes. Lyme disease is spread through the bite of an infected tick.

Rabies is a disease caused by a virus. The saliva of infected mammals, such as dogs or squirrels, contains the rabies virus. If an infected animal bites a human, the virus can be transmitted to the human.

FUNCTIONS OF THE IMMUNE SYSTEM

Recognizing the enemy

In many ways, your body is like a fort under constant attack. Pathogens try to enter your body so they can loot its nutrients. Fortunately, your defense system, the immune system, is usually successful in fighting off the attackers.

Like other body systems, the immune system is made of many specialized cells and tissues. Some prevent pathogens from entering the body. If pathogens do enter the body, other cells and tissues identify, seek out, and destroy the pathogens.

❶ Indirect contact with an infected person, contaminated food, and an insect bite

The immune system recognizes harmful organisms and substances that can cause disease. To do this, the body distinguishes "self" cells, which belong to the body, from "nonself" cells, which do not. The cellular components of the immune system recognize specific molecules on the surface of the body's self cells and do not attack those cells.

Little is known about the immune mechanisms of invertebrates. These animals do not seem to have a complex response to invading pathogens or substances. However, many invertebrates seem to be able to distinguish self cells from nonself cells.

Most vertebrates have three lines of defense against pathogens and foreign substances. Each line of defense has a different responsibility. The first and second lines of defense are effective against many different kinds of pathogens. These mechanisms are called **nonspecific defenses.** In contrast, the third line of defense protects an organism from specific pathogens. Defenses to specific pathogens are called **specific defenses.** These defenses are collectively known as the immune response.

CHECKPOINT 32.1

1. What is a pathogen? Give four examples of pathogens.
2. Explain the difference between specific defenses and nonspecific defenses.
3. **Critical Thinking** Hereditary diseases are not classified as contagious diseases. Why?

Build on What You Know

4. An important step in investigating an outbreak of food poisoning is to identify the bacteria present. How might scientists make this determination? *(Need to jog your memory? Revisit relevant concepts in Chapter 14, Section 14.5.)*

What does the immune system do?

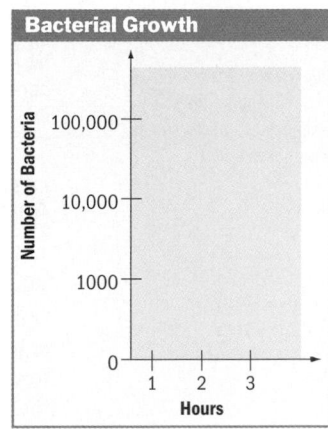

LAB ZONE Think About It! bioSURF

Calculating Bacterial Growth

A single bacterium that manages to enter the body can multiply exponentially for a long time if not attacked by the body's defense system. Bacteria undergo binary fission. Many bacteria can reproduce every 20 minutes. In one hour a single bacterium can become eight bacteria. Answer the following questions, assuming that there is one bacterium at time zero and the body's immune system is nonfunctional (unless instructed otherwise).

Analyzing the Graph

1 How many bacteria would be present after four hours? After five hours? After six hours?
2 Plot the values you calculate on a semi-log graph. Describe the line that appears when you connect the points.
3 Suppose a single bacterium has entered a body with a healthy immune system. How would the graph line be different?

Bacterial Growth

LAB ZONE Think About It!

Calculating Bacterial Growth

Provide students with graph paper and explain how to determine and plot values.

Analyzing the Graph

1 4096; 32,768; 262,144
2 It rises sharply.
3 The graph line would rise a little or not at all.

3 ASSESS

Evaluate Understanding

To assess students' understanding of the key section ideas, ask:

- **What did the germ theory propose?** (There is a relationship between a microorganism and a specific disease.)
- **What are four ways diseases are transmitted?** (Direct contact, indirect contact, through animal bites, in contaminated food or water)
- **What role does the immune system play in the body?** (It is the defense system.)

Reteach

Have students work in groups to prepare summaries of the steps of Koch's postulates or the methods of disease transmission. Have groups develop a creative way, such as a skit, to present their summary to the class. Review the key points of each summary after it is presented.

CHECKPOINT 32.1

1. A pathogen is an organism that causes an infectious disease such as a virus, bacterium, protist, fungus, or roundworm.
2. A nonspecific defense is effective against different pathogens; a specific defense is effective against one specific pathogen.
3. **Comparing** A contagious disease is spread by contact with an infected person. A hereditary disease is passed through genes.
4. Scientists can identify bacteria by: DNA, RNA, and protein analysis; cell shape; cell wall composition; nutrition and respiration.

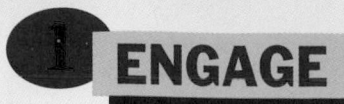

32.2

ENGAGE

Consider the Big Idea

Have students read The Big Idea! at the top of the page. Explain that in addition to specialized cells, the immune system includes the lymphatic system.

Use the Visual

Have students study the photograph that opens the section. Point out that there are many kinds of white blood cells, all with specialized functions. Ask:

- **How does the phagocyte know to attack the invader?** (It recognizes it as a "nonself" cell.)

Check Prior Knowledge

To assess students' knowledge about blood, ask:

- **What are the three main types of blood vessels?** (Arteries, veins, and capillaries)
- **What is plasma?** (Thick liquid in which blood cells are suspended)

Teacher Demo

Use a microprojector to show students amebas that are feeding. Point out the way the ameba engulfs its prey. Explain that the white blood cells, called phagocytes, attack and engulf bacteria and other pathogens in a similar way.

THE BIG IDEA! The immune system consists of specialized cells, organs, and organ systems that respond to the presence of a pathogen. 32.2–32.3

32.2 Overview of the Immune System

What you'll learn

IDEAS
- To describe the components of the immune system
- To compare the lymph system to the circulatory system

WORDS
lymph, lymph nodes, phagocytes, macrophages, lymphocytes

The amazing blobs
Phagocytes are white blood cells that surround and digest unwanted body visitors. They squeeze out of gaps in the walls of capillaries, then plump up and move toward an invader, oozing around the foreign matter. Dead phagocytes are the major components of the white material called pus.

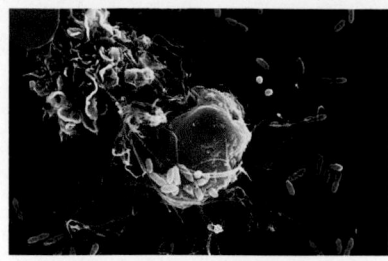

LYMPHATIC SYSTEM AND ORGANS

Defense department

The immune system of the human body comprises a variety of cells, organs, and organ systems, ranging from individual white blood cells to the lymphatic system. White blood cells are specialized cells that help fight disease. Both the circulatory system and the lymphatic system transport white blood cells through the body.

The lymphatic system plays a critical role in the immune system by producing, storing, and circulating white blood cells. As you can see in *Figure 32.4,* the lymphatic system is a network of vessels and associated organs. Lymph capillaries intertwine with blood capillaries, absorb the intercellular fluid that leaks from blood capillaries, and move the fluid into larger lymph vessels. The fluid in the lymph vessels is called **lymph.**

As lymph travels through lymph vessels, it is filtered through densely packed areas of tissue called **lymph nodes.** White blood cells are stored in lymph nodes and can attack pathogens

in the lymph. When the body is fighting an infection, white blood cells are produced in great numbers, and the lymph nodes can become swollen and sore. You may notice the swollen lymph nodes in your neck when you are sick.

The tonsils, thymus, and spleen are all composed of lymphoid tissues. Located in the back of the mouth, the tonsils filter and destroy bacteria. The thymus gland produces hormones that play a role in the maturation of white blood cells. The spleen removes worn-out red blood cells, platelets, bacteria, and other particles from the blood. The spleen stores lymphocytes which attack pathogens.

In addition to its role as part of the immune system, the lymphatic system returns fluid to the circulatory system. Intercellular fluid keeps the body's cells moist. The main component of intercellular fluid is plasma, which leaks from blood capillaries into surrounding tissues. Up to 3 liters of plasma a day may leak from the capillaries and must be replaced to maintain the blood's fluid volume.

774 *Unit 8 Human Biology*

STUDENT RESOURCES

From the Teacher's Resource Package, use:
- Section Review 32.2 and Activity Recordsheet 32-1 from Unit 8 Review Module

TECHNOLOGY RESOURCES

Relevant technology resources include:
- Spanish Student Edition CD-ROM
- Teacher's Resource Planner CD-ROM

774

The lymphatic system collects the intercellular fluid, cleans it, and returns it to the circulatory system. As lymph travels through the body, it moves into increasingly larger lymph vessels. In the neck region, lymph is returned to the circulatory system through two ducts that connect the lymphatic vessels with large veins underneath the collarbone. Unlike the circulatory system, the lymphatic system has no pump. Lymph is moved by the contraction of surrounding skeletal muscles. Lymph vessels have one-way valves, which direct fluid flow. Exercise also helps fluids move through the lymphatic system.

CELLS OF THE IMMUNE SYSTEM

The troops

White blood cells, the specialized cells of the immune system, are also called leukocytes (LOO-koh-syts). They are the main cellular components of the immune system. All leukocytes originate in the red bone marrow. Some leukocytes develop in the red bone marrow, while others migrate and develop in the thymus. Leukocytes reside in the lymph nodes, organs of the lymphatic system, and bloodstream. When an invasion of the body is detected, leukocytes gather at the infection site in great numbers.

Different kinds of white blood cells are involved in the nonspecific and specific defense systems. **Phagocytes** are leucocytes that engulf and digest unwanted cells and pathogens in a nonspecific manner. For example, phagocytes in the spleen engulf old red blood cells. **Macrophages** are the largest phagocytes. Each macrophage can engulf hundreds of bacterial cells.

Lymphocytes are leukocytes involved in the body's specific defense system. Some lymphocytes secrete antibodies specific to different invading pathogens. Other lymphocytes

FIGURE 32.4

The Human Lymphatic System

Fighting infection and returning fluid to the circulatory system are the two functions of the lymph vessels and organs.

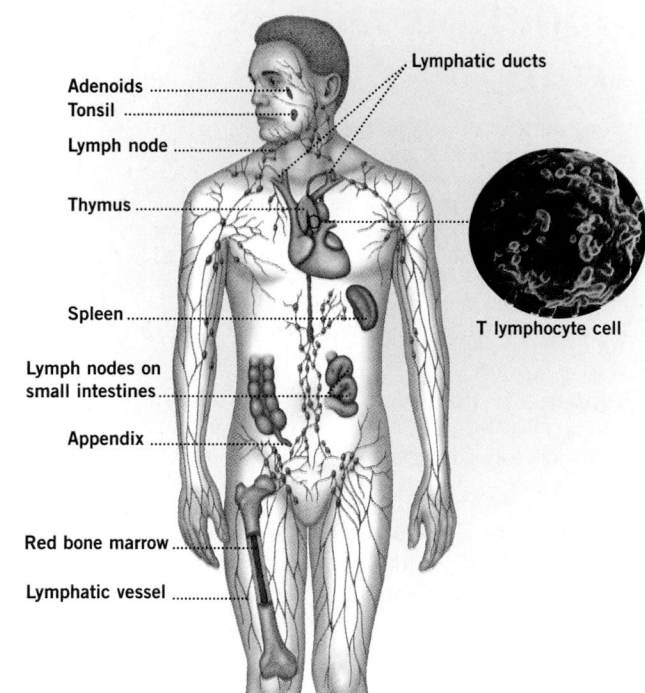

- Lymphatic ducts
- Adenoids
- Tonsil
- Lymph node
- Thymus
- Spleen
- T lymphocyte cell
- Lymph nodes on small intestines
- Appendix
- Red bone marrow
- Lymphatic vessel

recognize and destroy body cells that have been infected by specific pathogens. You will learn more about lymphocytes in the next section.

CHECKPOINT 32.2

1. What are the components of the immune system?
2. Describe the path of lymph through the lymphatic and circulatory systems.
3. **Critical Thinking** Compare the roles of phagocytes and lymphocytes in combating pathogens.

Build on What You Know

4. Compare the structure and function of the lymphatic system with those of the circulatory system. *(Need to jog your memory? Revisit relevant concepts in Chapter 31, Section 31.4.)*

Chapter 32 Immune System **775**

Use the Visual

Have students study Figure 32.4. Ask:

- **What role does the thymus gland play in the immune system?** (Produces hormones that play a role in the development of white blood cells)
- **What is the function of the spleen?** (To remove worn red blood cells, platelets, and bacteria, from the blood)

ASSESS

Evaluate Understanding

To assess students' understanding of the key concepts in this section, ask:

- **What is the function of the lymphatic system?** (To produce and circulate white blood cells.)
- **How are the roles of the immune system and circulatory system similar?** (Both transport substances throughout the body and help protect the organism from disease.)

Reteach

Make an overhead transparency of Figure 32.4 without labels. Have students identify the components of the immune system and their functions. Ask what cells or other structures are also part of the immune system. Discuss similarities and differences between the lymphatic and circulatory systems.

CHECKPOINT 32.2

1. White blood cells and the lymphatic system (lymph vessels, lymph nodes, tonsil, thymus, spleen, red bone marrow)
2. Lymph capillaries intertwine with blood capillaries, absorb intercellular fluid, move the fluid into lymph vessels to be filtered in lymph nodes and returned to the circulatory system.

3. **Comparing** Phagocytes are nonspecific and engulf pathogens. Lymphocytes are specific and secrete antibodies or destroy cells infected by pathogens.
4. Both systems move a fluid through a system of vessels. Lymph is moved by contractions of skeletal muscles. Blood is moved by the pumping of the heart.

Modeling Disease Transmission

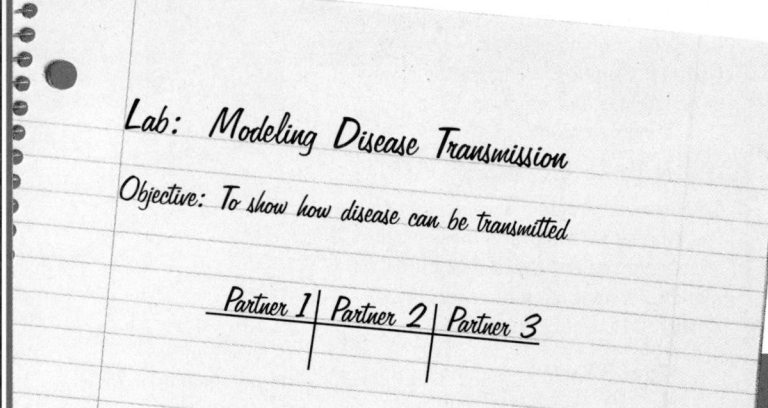

TEAM WORK Modeling Disease Transmission

Modeling Disease Transmission

SAFETY FIRST!

If available, have students wear lab aprons. Remind students not to allow the solution to come in contact with their hands. Have students immediately clean up any spills.

Lab Prep and Planning

This investigation requires approximately 45 minutes. Prepare three stock solutions: 1% (m/vol) phenol red, distilled water at pH 7.0, and 0.01M sodium hydroxide. Make the phenol red solution by dissolving 1 g phenol red in 99 mL of distilled water at pH 7.0. Give the basic solution, 0.01M sodium hydroxide, to one person in the class and give the neutral distilled water solution to the rest. Do not tell students if their solution is neutral or basic.

Hypothesis Help

Likely hypotheses will state that disease can be transmitted quickly from person to person.

Lab Extension

Open Ended

Explain to students that food poisoning may take several days to cause illness. Have students develop a method for determining where a number of sick people came in contact with the contaminated food.

Time Required

■ 50 minutes

WHAT YOU WILL DO Model the transmission of a disease as it spreads through your classroom

SKILLS YOU WILL USE Modeling, observing, recording and analyzing data

WHAT YOU WILL NEED grease pencil; clean, empty baby-food jar; safety goggles; rubber gloves; dropper; stock solution; phenol red indicator

Propose a Hypothesis
Propose a hypothesis stating how many people a single pathogen carrier might infect.

Conduct Your Experiment
1 Use a grease pencil to write your name on an empty baby-food jar.
2 Using a dropper, transfer three dropperfuls of the stock solution provided by your teacher into your jar.
Caution: Wear goggles and gloves while handling solutions. Do not allow solutions to come in contact with skin or clothing.
3 Choose a classmate as a partner. Exchange one dropperful of solution with your partner. Add the dropperful of your partner's solution to your jar. Gently swirl the solution in the jar.
4 Record the name of your partner on a piece of paper.
5 Find two different partners and repeat steps 3 and 4 with each of them.
6 Add one dropperful of phenol red indicator to the solution in your jar. Record the color of the solution.
7 If the solution turned red, you were infected; if it turned yellow, you were not infected. Your teacher will write the names of the infected persons and their partners on the board.
8 As a class, try to deduce the original source of the infection—there was only one—and the route of transmission.

Analyze Your Data
1 Diagram the route of transmission of the infection.
2 If you were infected, who infected you? Did you in turn infect anyone else?
3 How many of you were infected after each round of transfers?
4 What represented the infectious agent? (Phenol red is yellow in acidic solutions and red in basic solutions.)

Draw Conclusions
Write a paragraph about the way diseases are spread and how difficult it might be to track their sources.

Design a Related Experiment
Design an experiment to model the transmission of disease by using talcum powder on the hands.

Lab: Modeling Disease Transmission

Objective: To show how disease can be transmitted

Partner 1	Partner 2	Partner 3

Analyze Your Data

1 Diagrams should reflect the correct class deduction of the route of transmission.

2 Answers will vary.

3 Answers will vary, but if only one person was originally infected, the maximum possible number of infected persons after round two would be four.

4 The basic solution of sodium hydroxide represented the infectious agent. The indicator, phenol red, detected the infectious agent.

Draw Conclusions

Check students' responses for logic and accuracy.

32.3 Activities of the Immune System

It helps to cry

Tears do more than express emotion. Tears also defend the body against some pathogens. Your eyes tear all the time. Tears contain enzymes that kill bacteria. An eye produces an overload of tears if a particularly irritating piece of dust or dirt enters it. The extra tears help wash foreign substances from the eye.

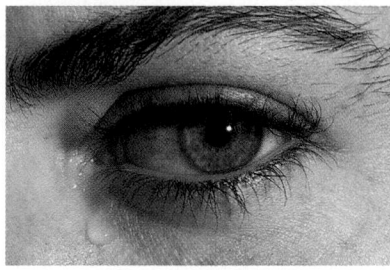

What you'll learn

IDEAS
- To explain the functions of nonspecific defenses
- To identify the components and functions of specific defenses

WORDS

inflammatory response, histamine, antigen, humoral immunity, antibody, B lymphocytes, cell-mediated immunity, T lymphocytes

NONSPECIFIC DEFENSES

The front lines

Each day you come in contact with many potential pathogens. Despite constant exposure to pathogens, you probably have only a few minor illnesses each year. With so many pathogens in the world, how does your body manage to stay healthy?

As mentioned in section 32.1, your body has three lines of defense against pathogens. *Figure 32.5* summarizes the role of each line of defense. First your immune system works to prevent disease-causing agents from entering your body. However, if pathogens do enter your body, your immune system has ways to fight them. Some of the weapons your immune system uses to fight disease are nonspecific—they are effective against many pathogens. Both the first and second lines of defense are nonspecific components of the immune system.

First line of defense Pathogens must enter the body in order to cause disease. The job of the body's first line of defense is to keep pathogens out. This role is carried out by the skin, mucus, tears, and sweat.

As you may recall from Chapter 29, skin covers all the external parts of your body, as well as your internal organs. Unbroken skin acts as a wall that blocks out most pathogens. Glands in the skin secrete sweat. The salinity and acidity of sweat helps prevent the growth of harmful bacteria. Sweat also contains an enzyme that destroys some bacteria. In addition, the many types of harmless bacteria that normally live on the skin help prevent pathogens from growing there.

Some parts of the body, such as your mouth and nose, provide openings through which pathogens can enter. These openings are lined with cells that secrete a sticky substance called mucus. Mucus coats the openings

Defenses of the Human Immune System

Type of Defense	Line	Characteristic
Nonspecific	First line	Principle barriers such as skin
	Second line	Inflammatory response
Specific	Third line	Immune responses—humoral and cell-mediated

FIGURE 32.5

The defenses of a human immune system include both specific and nonspecific defenses. What are the differences between the two?

Chapter 32 Immune System **777**

STUDENT RESOURCES

From the Teacher's Resource Package, use:
- Section Review 32.3, Activity Record-sheet 32-2, and Interpreting Graphics 32 from Unit 8 Review Module
- Lab 56: "Transmission of Diseases"
- Consumer Applications 32-1

TECHNOLOGY RESOURCES

Relevant technology resources include:
- Interactive Biological Simulations CD-ROM: "The Immune System"
- Animated Biological Concepts Video-discs: "Inflammatory Response," "Humoral Immunity," and "Cell-mediated Immunity"

ENGAGE

Use the Visual

Have students study the photograph that opens the section. Explain that excessive tearing of the eyes is common in people who suffer from allergies. Ask:

- **How do tears help the allergy sufferer?** (The tears wash particles from the eyes.)

Quick Activity

Provide each student with a large jigsaw puzzle piece, to which only one piece fits. Ask students to move around the classroom until they find the fit. When the match occurs stop the activity and explain this is similar to an antigen matching an antibody; it is a very specific fit. Now have several students exchange their puzzle pieces for new ones which have several matches. Have the students proceed until there is a match. Stop the activity and discuss how it differed from the first trial. Students should note that it took less time for a match to occur. Explain that the second time the body is infected by the same pathogen the response is much more rapid.

❶ Nonspecific defenses are effective against many types of pathogens, while specific defenses protect against one, specific pathogen.

TEACH

Use the Visual

Have students study Figure 32.6. Ask:

- **What chemical initiates the immune response?** (Histamine)
- **How does the release of histamine cause the body to respond?** (Histamine causes blood flow in the area to increase and capillaries to leak and release phagocytes and blood clotting factor into the wound.)
- **How do phagocytes work?** (They engulf and kill pathogens, dead cells, and cellular debris.)

Explain

Point out that when the skin is cut, the area around the cut often becomes warm. The warmth is actually a localized fever which increases the activity of phagocytes and decreases pathogen growth.

Build Writing Skills

Have students write a short essay to explain how their body would react to a paper cut on the finger. Encourage creativity by suggesting that the essay be written from the perspective of a bacterium or phagocyte.

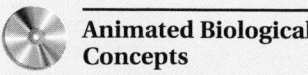

Animated Biological Concepts

Inflammatory Response | Play

and traps pathogens so they can be eliminated or destroyed. For example, bacteria entering your nose can become trapped by mucus. The beating of the cilia that line your nasal passages moves the mucus toward your throat, where it is swallowed. Bacteria that are trapped in the mucus are destroyed by strong acid in the stomach.

Second line of defense Pathogens sometimes evade the first-line defenses and invade body tissues. This activates the inflammatory response. The **inflammatory response** is a nonspecific defense reaction to tissue damage caused by injury or infection.

Imagine that you have cut your finger. The cut injures some cells and provides an opening for pathogens to enter your body. The injured cells release a chemical called **histamine,** which triggers the inflammatory response. You can follow the activities of the inflammatory response in *Figure 32.6.*

During the inflammatory response, capillaries in an injured or infected area expand. This increases blood flow to the injured site and increases the amount of plasma leaking into the intercellular fluid. The increase of intercellular fluid causes the area to

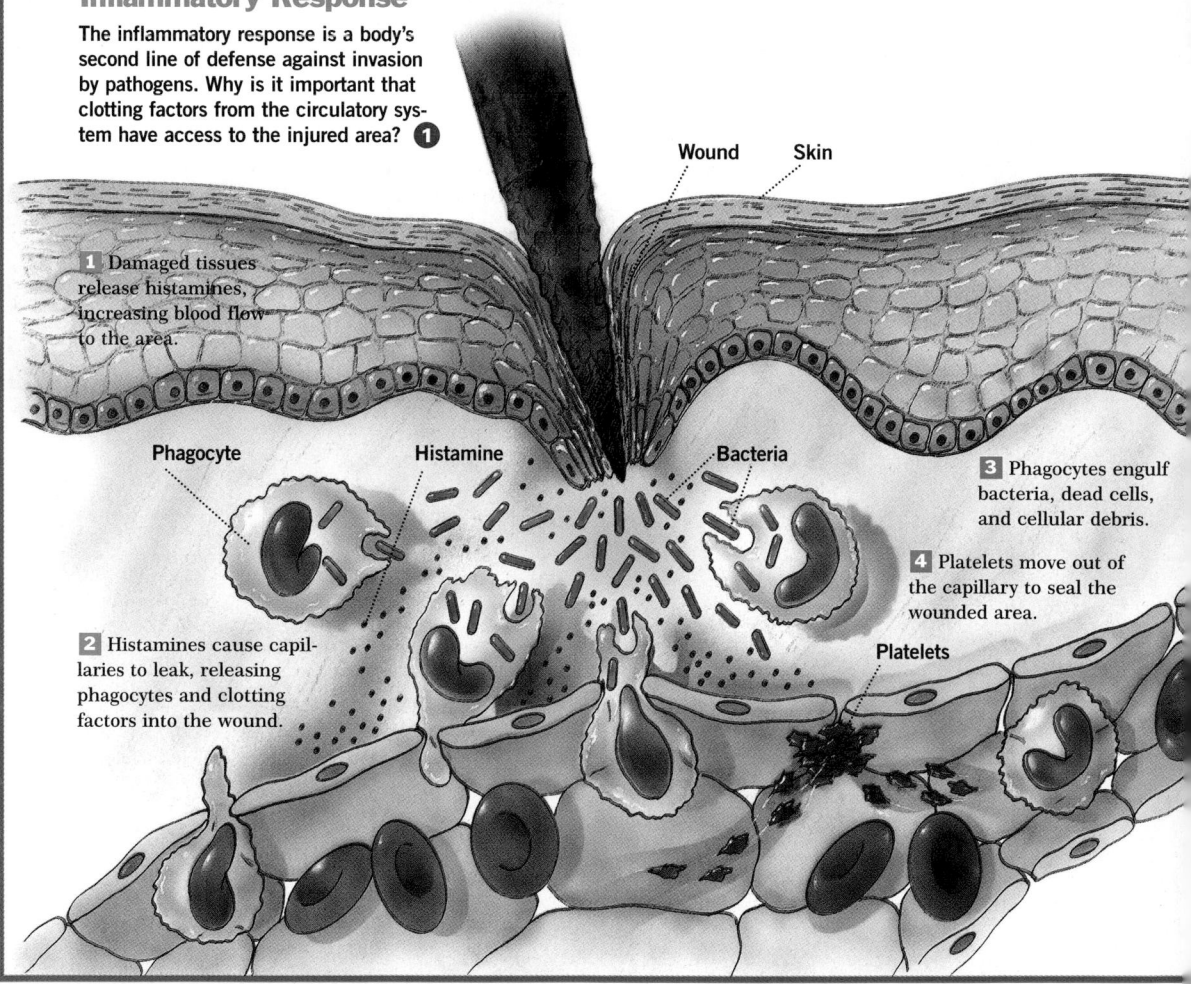

FIGURE 32.6

Steps of the Inflammatory Response

The inflammatory response is a body's second line of defense against invasion by pathogens. Why is it important that clotting factors from the circulatory system have access to the injured area? ❶

Wound   Skin

1 Damaged tissues release histamines, increasing blood flow to the area.

Phagocyte   **Histamine**   **Bacteria**

3 Phagocytes engulf bacteria, dead cells, and cellular debris.

4 Platelets move out of the capillary to seal the wounded area.

2 Histamines cause capillaries to leak, releasing phagocytes and clotting factors into the wound.

Platelets

MEETING DIVERSE NEEDS

At Risk Have students present the steps of the inflammatory response as a battle. Tell students to identify the invaders and defenders with technical terms. Allow students to use cartoons, graphics, or prose.

❶ The clotting factors help seal the wounded area.

become red and swollen. The plasma that leaks into the injured tissue contains platelets, the clotting factors in blood, which help seal the wounded area. Plasma also contains phagocytes—the white blood cells that engulf pathogens and other unwanted materials. These phagocytes engulf and kill bacterial cells that enter the body.

Sometimes a person with an infection develops a fever. Fever results when macrophages release chemical substances called pyrogens. Pyrogens stimulate the brain to raise body temperature. Fever causes phagocytes to be more active and makes it more difficult for pathogens to grow and reproduce.

Two other components of the second line of defense are interferon and natural killer cells. Interferon and natural killer cells attack many types of viruses, as well as cancer cells. Interferon (in-ter-FEER-ahn) is a protein that interferes with the replication of viruses. It is released by cells that have been invaded by viruses. Interferon cannot save an infected cell, but it can help protect nearby healthy cells.

Blood and lymph both contain natural killer cells. Unlike phagocytes, which attack invading cells, natural killer cells attack body cells that have been infected by viruses. Natural killer cells attack the cell membranes of virus-infected body cells and cause them to burst. Viruses can replicate only inside a host cell, so destroying the host cell also destroys the virus.

SPECIFIC DEFENSES
Knowing the enemy

In addition to nonspecific protection, the immune system has defenses against specific toxins and pathogens. Each specific defense affects only one kind of pathogen. The specific defenses

of the body are collectively known as the immune response. The immune response is the body's third line of defense against disease.

Bacteriologists E. A. von Behring and Shibasaburo Kitasato began to unravel the mystery of the immune response in the 1890s, using parts of blood serum. Serum is the liquid part of the blood that does not contain red blood cells or clotting proteins. Von Behring and Kitasato discovered that part of the blood serum from an animal that had survived tetanus could protect the animal from getting tetanus again. They also discovered that injecting the blood serum from an animal that had survived tetanus into a healthy animal protected the healthy animal from getting the disease.

In their research, von Behring and Kitasato discovered three characteristics of the immune response. First, the immune response is specific. Each defense of the immune response targets a specific pathogen. Second, the

LAB ZONE Do It! bioSURF

How Does Skin Protect Humans?

You can model how the skin helps protect the human body from disease-causing pathogens when you . . .

Try This

1 Cut an apple in half.
2 Cover one half of the apple with plastic food wrap and leave the other half uncovered.
3 Using a dropper, release several drops of food coloring on each half of the apple.

Analyze Your Results

1 What happened to the uncovered half of the apple? To the covered half?
2 How does the plastic wrap provide a model of the human skin?
3 What are a few traits of human skin that are not represented by the plastic wrap?

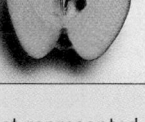

779

Think Critically

After discussing interferon, ask:

■ **Based on what you know about viruses and cells, how might interferon disrupt viral replication?** (Possible responses: Interferon may disrupt the replication of viral nucleic acids or the production of viral proteins.)

Clarify Misconceptions

Students may think of antigens as any foreign matter in the body. Explain that the definition is much more specific. Antigens are substances, usually proteins, that stimulate the body to produce antibodies. Compare the general response of the body to a foreign object (inflammation and phagocytes) with that caused by a virus (antibody protection).

LAB ZONE Do It! TEAM WORK

How Does Skin Protect Humans?

Some food wraps are perforated with tiny holes to allow food to "breathe." Be sure students work with nonperforated food wrap for this activity.

Analyze Your Results

1 Uncovered half dried out; covered half stayed the same.
2 Like skin, it protects the apple from drying out and keeps unwanted substances from entering.
3 Human skin also regulates internal temperature and serves as a sense organ.

32.3

Explain

As students begin their study of the body's specific defenses against disease, emphasize that in humoral immunity, the body produces antibodies, while in cell-mediated immunity, T cells destroy infected body cells.

Use the Visual

Have students study Figure 32.7. As students examine the illustration, point out that the shape of the antigen binding sites differ from location to location along the antigen. This difference in shape explains why different antibodies may bind to a single antigen molecule.

Everyday Biology

Poll the class to see how many colds each student has had during the school year. Ask:

- **When the cold virus changes, why are the "old" antibodies no longer effective?** (When the virus changes, it changes the shape of the antigen and the "old" antibody no longer recognizes it, just as an old key will not work in a new lock.)

 Interactive Biological Simulations
The Immune System: Humoral Immunity After observing the humoral response to a bacterial infection, students are asked to place the steps of the humoral response in the correct order.

 Animated Biological Concepts

Humoral Immunity   Play

780

immune response is most effective against a pathogen that an organism has previously encountered. Third, the immune response works throughout the entire body of an organism.

Other scientists later discovered that lymphocytes are the key players in the immune response. How do lymphocytes know when to act? Lymphocytes respond to antigens. An **antigen** is a molecule that elicits the immune response. Most antigens are molecules on the surfaces of pathogens. Certain toxins are also antigens. The immune response recognizes that an antigen is foreign to the body.

Macrophages play an important role in the immune response by bringing antigens to the lymphocytes. When a macrophage engulfs an invading cell, proteins on the outer surface of the macrophage interact with proteins on the outer surface of the invading cells to form a hybrid protein. The hybrid proteins on the surface of macrophages are recognized by lymphocytes as antigens, and the immune response is generated. The body can mount two different immune responses to antigens: humoral immunity and cell-mediated immunity.

Humoral immunity Blood and lymph were once known as humors. For this reason, immunity against pathogens in the body fluids is called **humoral** (HYOO-muh-rul) **immunity** Antibodies in body fluids are the agents of humoral immunity. An **antibody** is a disease-fighting protein produced in response to a specific antigen.

Antibodies are produced by white blood cells called **B lymphocytes,** or B cells. B cells originate and then mature in the red marrow of bones. After they mature, B cells move to the lymph nodes where they secrete antibodies into the lymph and blood.

The antibodies made by each B cell are produced in response to a specific antigen. Antibodies are Y-shaped proteins with binding sites at the tips of the Y, as shown in *Figure* 32.7. The antibodies bind to an antigen like a key fits into a lock. Each antibody can bind to only one site on one antigen molecule. Antibodies do not destroy antigens— they mark them for destruction. For example, antibodies bound to antigens on the surface of bacteria clump the bacteria together. Clumped bacteria are engulfed by macrophages.

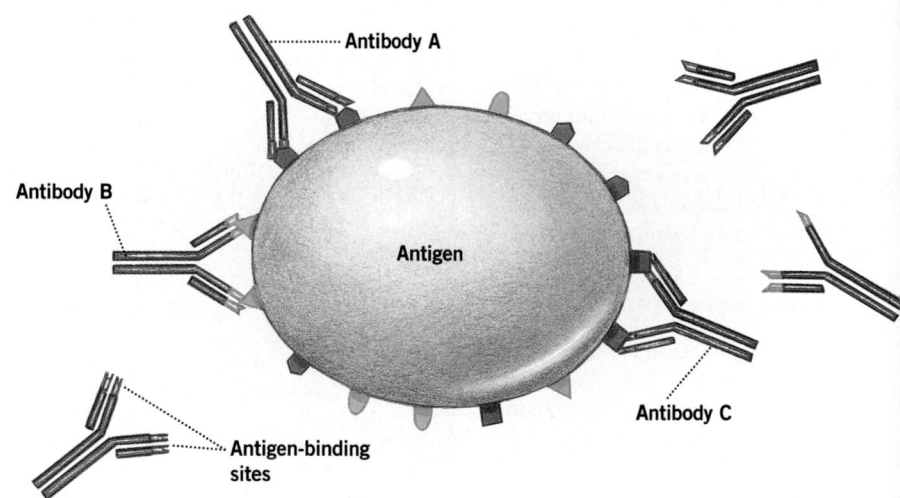

FIGURE 32.7
Antibodies attach to specific regions on antigens. Several types of antibodies may attach to one antigen. Each antibody is made of four proteins.

780   *Unit 8 Human Biology*

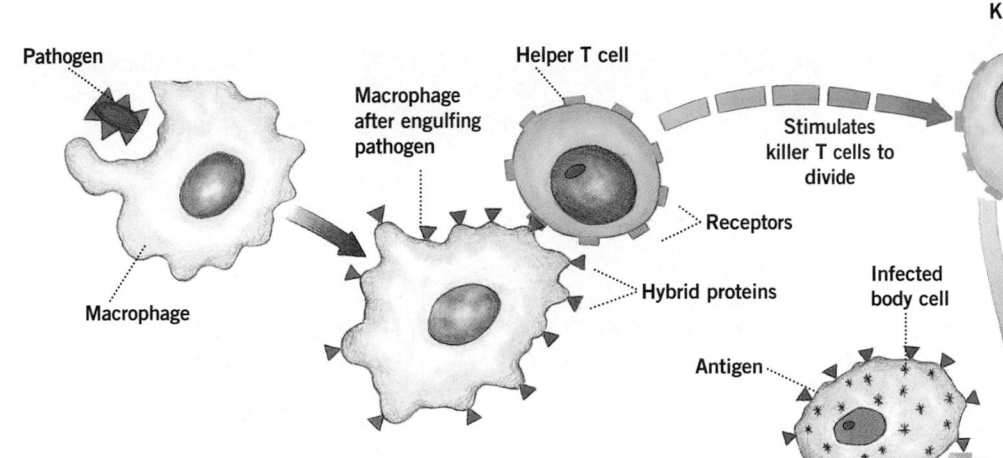

Pathogen

Macrophage

Macrophage after engulfing pathogen

Helper T cell

Receptors

Hybrid proteins

Stimulates killer T cells to divide

Killer T cell

Infected body cell

Antigen

Killer T cell

Ruptured body cell

Scientists estimate that your body has millions of different B cells, each ready to respond to a different antigen. When your body is exposed to a pathogen, B cells that recognize the antigens on the pathogen's surface respond by dividing many times. The result is a large army of B cells secreting antibodies against the pathogen.

Cell-mediated immunity A second immune response relies on lymphocytes themselves instead of antibodies produced by lymphocytes. In **cell-mediated immunity,** special lymphocytes directly attack cells that are harmful to the body. These harmful cells include cancerous cells, infected body cells, or cells of another person that enter the body during a transfusion or transplant. Because of cell-mediated immunity, organ transplants and skin grafts may be rejected. You can follow the process of cell-mediated immunity in *Figure 32.8.*

The specialized lymphocytes of cell-mediated immunity are T lymphocytes. **T lymphocytes,** or T cells, are white blood cells that recognize and destroy cells dangerous to a body. The T cells originate in the bone marrow, but they mature in the thymus gland. Unlike B cells, T cells do not produce antibodies. Each T cell has molecules on its surface that recognize a specific antigen on one type of dangerous cell.

There are several kinds of T cells. A cytotoxic T cell, or killer T cell, attacks a dangerous cell by producing a protein that ruptures the cell membrane. Killer T cells function in a manner similar to that of natural killer cells. However, unlike natural killer cells, killer T cells are specific — each killer T cell attacks only one specific type of dangerous cell.

Two other kinds of T cells, helper T cells and suppressor T cells, control the activity of killer T cells. Helper T cells stimulate killer T cells to divide, forming a large army of active killer T cells. Suppressor T cells inhibit the activity of other T cells when they are no longer needed. Helper T cells also play a role in humoral immunity and antibody production by stimulating B cells.

Because of specific proteins on their surface, helper T cells are also called T4 cells. T4 cells have recently received much attention because of their role in AIDS. You will learn about the role of T4 cells in AIDS later in this chapter.

Acquired immunity You probably know that if you have had certain diseases such as chicken pox or mumps you are immune to these diseases. Acquired immunity is the body's resistance to previously encountered pathogens. What happens when you acquire immunity?

FIGURE 32.8

During the cell-mediated immune response, macrophages with surface hybrid proteins bind and activate helper T cells with matching receptors. The helper T cells then stimulate killer T cells which also have matching receptors. The killer T cells divide, forming an army that recognizes and attacks infected body cells.

Chapter 32 Immune System **781**

Explain that the *varicella zoster* virus causes a rash that spreads along a section of the skin supplied by one of the infected nerves. Therefore, people with shingles have a painful, red, blistery band across their chest, arm, leg, or face.

Evaluate Understanding

Ask students the following:

- **What nonspecific and specific defenses does the body have against viruses?** (Nonspecific: interferon and natural killer cells; Specific: humoral and cell-mediated immunity)
- **What happens during a humoral immunity response?** (White blood cells produce antibodies or B cells that attach to specific sites on antigens.)
- **How does the function of B lymphocytes and T cells differ?** (B lymphocytes secrete antibodies; T cells work in groups to destroy cells.)

Reteach

As a class, create a table that identifies the body's nonspecific and specific defenses against disease. Include in the table the names of the processes involved in each type of response, a description of each process, and the types of cells involved. Review the table and use flowcharts to summarize the humoral and cell-mediated responses.

FIGURE 32.9
A killer T cell (right) recognizes an antigen on a cancer cell (left). The killer T cell will secrete a protein that destroys the cancer cell.

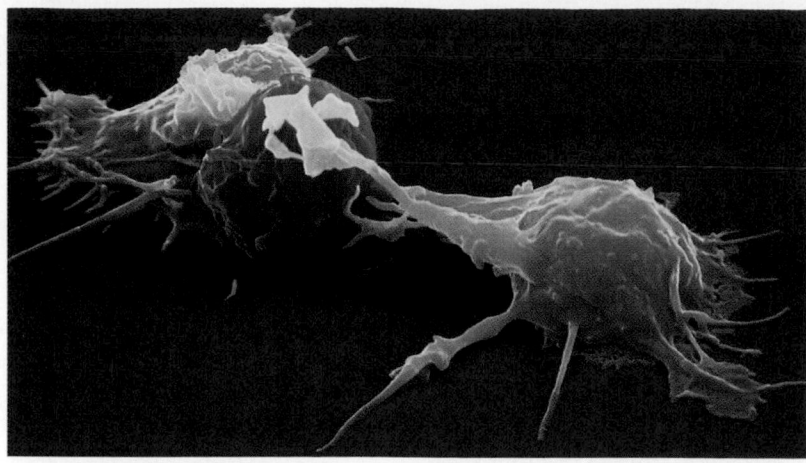

EVERYDAY BIOLOGY

Coming Back to Haunt Us

The virus that causes chicken pox does not leave the body after the pox markings fade. In rare cases, the virus hides in the nerve cells of its host. It can emerge again in its host's adult body as a disease called shingles.

The first step toward acquired immunity is called the primary immune response which was just described. This response begins when the immune system encounters a new pathogen. Time is required for the antigen-specific B cells and T cells to be found, and for them to multiply. The primary response can take five to ten days to reach its maximum production of B and T cells. During this time, an infection can become widespread and cause serious illness.

The second time the body is infected by the same pathogen, the immune response is faster. The rapid response of the immune system to a pathogen it has previously encountered is called the secondary immune response. The secondary response is so fast that the pathogen is often destroyed before an illness occurs.

Specialized cells called memory cells are responsible for the secondary immune response. These cells store information about the antigens they have encountered in the past. Your body has both memory B cells and memory T cells. Both types of cells are made during the primary immune response. Whereas other B cells and T cells live only a few days, memory cells can live for decades or even for your entire life. During a second encounter with a pathogen, the memory cells respond at once to a particular antigen and begin to divide rapidly. The actions of memory cells result in the production of many antibodies and active T cells in a day or two.

CHECKPOINT 32.3

1. How do humoral immunity and cell-mediated immunity differ?
2. Describe the roles of three types of T lymphocytes.
3. **Critical Thinking** Develop a flowchart that traces the series of events involved in cell-mediated immunity.

Build on What You Know

4. Describe the structure of a virus. Why can killer T cells not destroy viruses directly? *(Need to jog your memory? Revisit relevant concepts in Chapter 14, Section 14.1.)*

 How do the different parts of the immune system respond to pathogens?

CHECKPOINT 32.3

1. During humoral immunity, B cells secrete antibodies that bind to antigens. During cell-mediated immunity, killer T cells rupture infected body cells.
2. Killer T cells recognize and attack infected body cells. Helper T cells recognize macrophage-engulfed pathogens, and stimulate production of T cells and B cells. Suppressor T cells suppress production of T cells and B cells.
3. **Organizing** Flowchart should trace the events shown in Figure 32.8.
4. A virus is a nucleic acid core with a protein coat. A virus does not have a cell membrane that can be ruptured by killer T cells.

32.4 Health of the Immune System

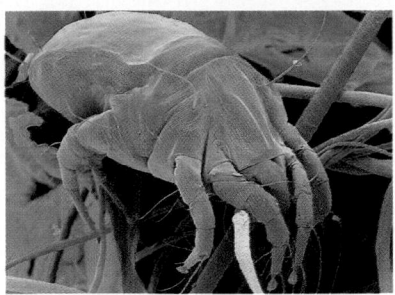

Dragons in your mattress
It may be too late to keep this creature out of your home. This is a dust mite that eats skin flakes and lives in mattresses, pillows, and carpets. In an average double bed there may be as many as 2 million dust mites. Each mite produces about 20 fecal pellets which, along with the bodies of dead mites, float up and provoke allergic sneezes in many people.

What you'll learn

IDEAS
- To identify causes of allergies
- To explain the effect of HIV on the immune system
- To analyze the effects of different lifestyles on the immune system

WORDS
allergy, autoimmune disease, HIV, vaccine

IMMUNE SYSTEM DISORDERS

A weakened army

The function of the immune system is to keep the body free of disease. But the activities of the immune system itself can sometimes cause unpleasant or even life-threatening problems. For example, fever is one way your immune system fights disease, but a very high fever can cause brain damage and other serious problems. Certain disorders can occur when the immune system overreacts or underreacts. If the immune system itself is attacked by pathogens, as in the case of AIDS, its normal functioning can be disrupted.

Allergies The immune system can usually distinguish pathogens from harmless chemicals and particles in the environment. However, the immune system occasionally reacts to a harmless substance as if it were an antigen, producing antibodies. This kind of response is called an **allergy.** For example, the symptoms of hay fever result from an allergy.

Earlier in this chapter you learned about the role of histamine in the inflammatory response. During an allergy attack, antibodies stimulate macrophages to release histamine. Histamine causes the blood vessels to expand, the eyes to produce tears, and the nasal passages to secrete mucus. Drugs called antihistamines decrease these actions of histamine.

Common causes of allergies include flower pollen, dust, mold spores, and some foods. You can see these kinds of particles in *Figure 32.10.* Chemical

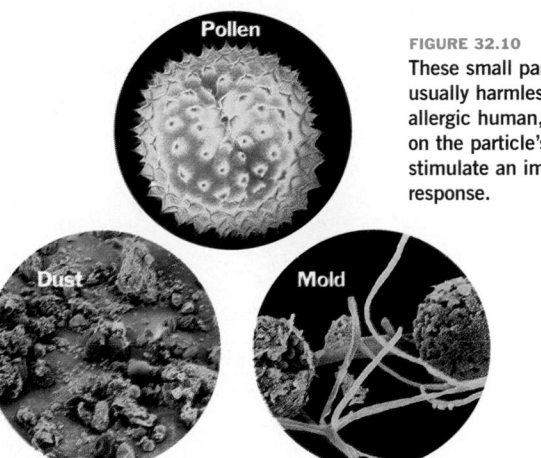

FIGURE 32.10
These small particles are usually harmless. In an allergic human, molecules on the particle's surface stimulate an immune response.

Chapter 32 Immune System **783**

TEACH

Teacher Demo

Invite an allergist or related health care professional to speak with the class about common allergy problems and their treatments. Ask the speaker to discuss symptoms of a severe allergic reaction and how a person suspected of having such a reaction should be treated.

 Language Arts

Write the term *autoimmune* on the board. Explain to students that the prefix *auto-* means "self." The base word *immune* means "resistant to disease" or "not affected by or responsive to." Use these definitions to reinforce the idea that in a person with an autoimmune disease, the body does not recognize its own cells and the immune system attacks the cells.

 STS

Point out that some people indicate in advance that they wish to donate parts of their body after death. In some areas, this decision can be noted on a person's driver's license. Encourage interested students to learn more about organ-donor programs and what issues need to be addressed before making a decision.

FIGURE 32.11
Humans have allergic reactions to the chemicals of plants like these. What characteristics of these plants would help you identify them? **1**

Poison ivy

Poison oak

Poison sumac

substances in some plants—such as poison ivy, poison oak, and poison sumac—can also cause allergic reactions, including skin rashes and itching.

In a severe allergy attack, the blood vessels expand so much that blood pressure drops dangerously low and breathing may become difficult. Such an attack is called anaphylactic (a-nuh-fuh-LAK-tik) shock, and it can be life-threatening. Treatment with epinephrine, a chemical of the nervous system, reverses the effects of anaphylactic shock.

Autoimmune disorders

Sometimes the immune system mistakes its own cells for pathogens. When this happens, the immune system attacks the tissues of the body, causing an **autoimmune disease.** Multiple sclerosis is an autoimmune disease. In multiple sclerosis, T cells destroy the myelin sheath that surrounds the nerve cells in the central nervous system. As the myelin sheath is destroyed, nerve cell function is disrupted. Some scientists think that Type I diabetes may result from an immune system attack on the insulin-producing cells of the pancreas. Scientists do not fully understand how and why the immune system sometimes turns against the body.

FRONTIERS IN BIOLOGY

Shutting down immunity

The immune system is the body's best natural defense against infectious diseases. However, some medical procedures are more successful when a person's immune system is inactive. Organ or tissue transplants are examples. After an organ transplant, the recipient's immune system identifies the new tissue as "nonself." Killer T cells rapidly multiply and attack the new tissue. A physician can stop a patient's body from rejecting a transplanted organ by administering drugs that suppress the patient's immune system.

FIGURE 32.12
A sting from a bee stimulates an allergic reaction in some humans. What occurs during an allergy attack? **2**

MEETING DIVERSE NEEDS

Gifted Have students research genetic disorders which affect the immune system, such as Severe Combined Immunodeficiency (SCID) and DiGeorge's syndrome. Have students state the immune system activity which is affected and common infections that result. Some students may prefer to research autoimmune disorders such as rheumatoid arthritis, type I diabetes mellitus, Grave's disease, systemic lupus erythematosis, or scleroderma. Have students share their research with the class.

Drugs that suppress the immune system act by interrupting mitosis. With mitosis interrupted, immune cells cannot multiply in response to the presence of foreign tissue. Some cancer medications are also designed to interrupt mitosis, but in this case the goal is to stop the cancer cells from reproducing. Unfortunately, a side effect is to suppress the immune system, as well. As a result, cancer patients sometimes have weakened immune systems as a complication of their treatment.

AIDS

Living without defenses

AIDS stands for Acquired Immune Deficiency Syndrome. AIDS is not a specific disease; it is a condition in which the body's immune system cannot protect itself against pathogens. This condition is caused by the human immunodeficiency virus, or HIV. **HIV** is a virus that attacks the human immune system, destroying the body's ability to fight infection.

HIV replicates inside helper T cells, or T4 cells, eventually destroying them. As you have learned, T4 cells stimulate the production and activity of B cells and killer T cells. By attacking T4 cells, HIV interferes with both humoral and cell-mediated immunity and destroys the body's ability to defend itself.

HIV can be spread from one person to another only through direct contact of certain body fluids, such as blood, semen, or breast milk. HIV is not spread by casual contact, such as shaking hands or using dishes previously used by a person with HIV. It is also not transmitted by insects. Most often, HIV is transmitted through sexual intercourse, through the sharing of needles among intravenous (IV) drug users, or by the transfusion of contaminated blood products. HIV can

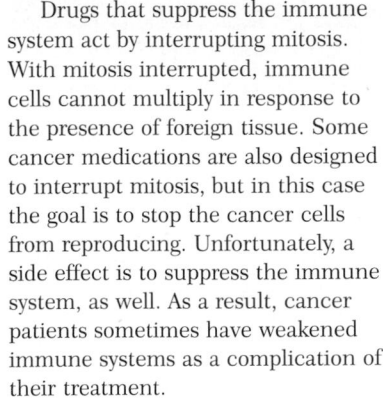
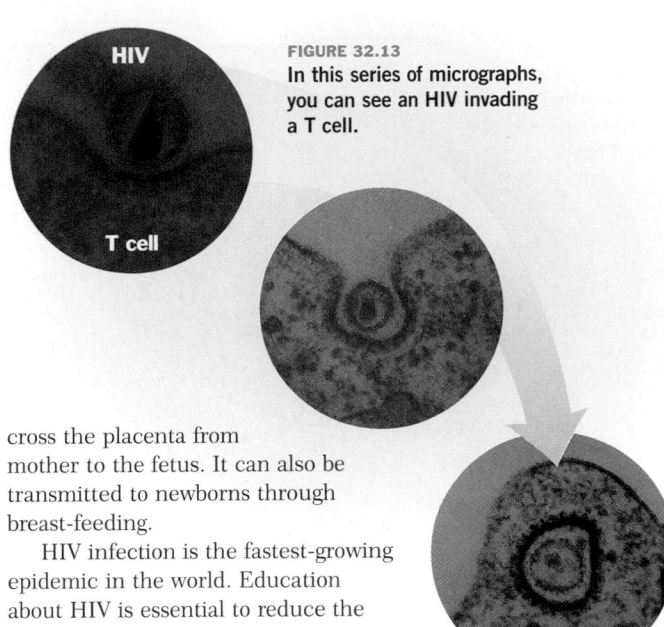

cross the placenta from mother to the fetus. It can also be transmitted to newborns through breast-feeding.

HIV infection is the fastest-growing epidemic in the world. Education about HIV is essential to reduce the incidence of the disease, as well as to improve people's attitudes toward those who have HIV.

At present, there is no known cure for HIV infection. Researchers worldwide are looking for effective treatments and cures, and trying to develop vaccines to prevent the disease. Even after years of research, there is much to be discovered about HIV. For now, the best way to prevent HIV infection is to learn as much as you can about HIV transmission and to avoid behaviors that place you at risk of contracting the virus.

Facts About HIV Transmission

Condoms reduce the risk of transmitting HIV from one person to another during sexual intercourse.

Using IV drugs and sharing needles with others who use IV drugs is one of the main ways HIV is transmitted from person to person. Having sexual intercourse with a person using IV drugs increases the risk of contracting HIV.

There is no risk of getting HIV while donating blood. HIV testing has almost eliminated the risk of getting HIV from receiving a blood transfusion.

FIGURE 32.14
HIV cannot be transmitted through casual contact. What other facts do you know about HIV transmission?

Chapter 32 Immune System **785**

 Language Arts

Point out to students that the terms *AIDS* and *HIV* are acronyms, words created using the first letters of the terms they represent. Challenge students to identify other familiar acronyms.

 Science History

In 1981, the U.S. Centers for Disease Control (CDC) published a report of five cases of a rare type of pneumonia, *Pneumocystis carinii*. Faced with a growing number of cases in which the immune system collapses for no apparent reason, public health officials coined the term AIDS a year later. By the end of 1996, according to the United Nations' AIDS program, about 6.4 million people worldwide had died from AIDS, and 22.6 million were infected with the virus. Recent reports of newly infected patients suggest that multidrug therapy may be able to keep the virus in check.

Apply

Discuss with students how the presence of antibodies in the blood is used to diagnose HIV infection. Explain to students that the presence of these antibodies makes it possible to screen donated blood and prevent transmission of the disease by blood transfusions.

❶ Number and shape of leaves and how they are arranged

❷ Antibodies stimulate macrophages to release histamine.

❸ Responses will vary. Correct any misinformation students may have about HIV transmission.

Use the Visual

Have students study Figure 32.15. To help students trace the events shown in the diagram, ask:

- **How does the number of T4 cells at the beginning of an HIV infection compare to those of a person who has AIDS?** (A person infected with HIV has many T4 cells, while a person with AIDS has few T4 cells.)

- **Why is a person who has been infected with HIV not likely to test HIV positive immediately?** (The body requires time to make antibodies to the HIV. Until the antibodies are present, the person will test negative.)

Everyday Biology

If you have access to the Internet in your classroom or school, students can connect to the Clearinghouse for AIDS Information, run by the Center for Disease Control. This website, www.cdcnac.org/, offers the latest HIV research and treatment information. For more generalized information on allergies and infectious diseases, students can connect to the National Institute for Allergy and Infectious Disease at: www.niaid.nih.gov/

Clarify Misconceptions

Students may think that AIDS is not transmitted during sexual intercourse among heterosexuals. Explain that AIDS can be transmitted through sexual contact with an infected person and that currently, the fastest growing population of HIV-infected people is the heterosexual population.

FIGURE 32.15
During the course of an HIV infection, the immune system becomes progressively weaker.

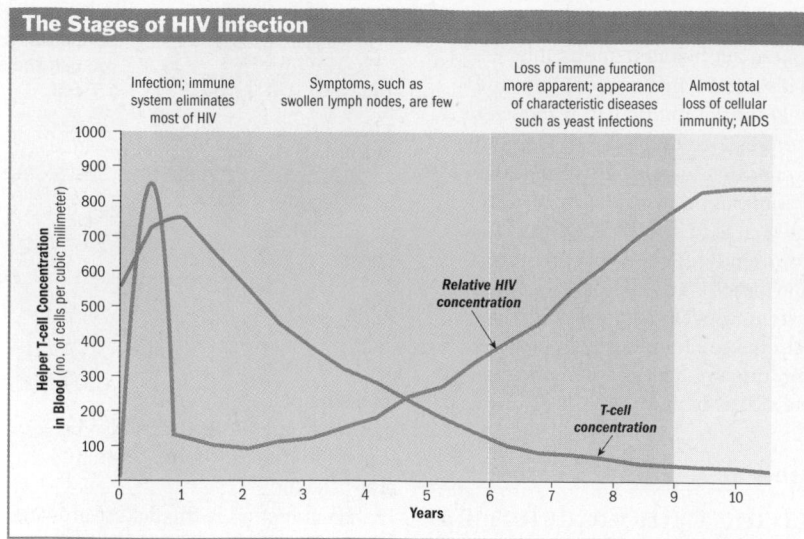

The Stages of HIV Infection

EVERYDAY BIOLOGY

Hope for a One–Two Punch

A recent development in the drug treatment of AIDS is to use more than one drug simultaneously, because different drugs affect HIV in different ways. This approach drastically reduces the number of HIV virus particles in the blood of some patients.

An HIV infection progresses along a fairly predictable course. Each stage of the infection is associated with certain symptoms, but the timing of the stages varies widely with different people.

When first infected by the virus, a person may have flulike symptoms or no symptoms at all. Within a few weeks to several months, antibodies to HIV begin to appear in the blood. The presence of antibodies in the blood is used to diagnose the disease and to screen donated blood. A person is said to be HIV-positive when HIV antibodies are present in the blood. However, even when a person is diagnosed as HIV-positive, other symptoms of the syndrome may not appear for months or years.

At first, an HIV-positive person may experience a phase of mild symptoms, including fever, weight loss, and swollen lymph nodes. As the HIV concentration increases, the T4 cell concentration decreases, and the immune response becomes less effective against disease. When the number of T4 cells in the body becomes so low that the immune system cannot fight disease,

an HIV infection has developed into AIDS. The length of time it takes for an HIV infection to become AIDS varies from person to person, but it may take an average of 10 years. *Figure 32.15* shows the change over time of T4 cell concentrations in blood.

People with AIDS may have a variety of diseases, including a kind of cancer called Kaposi's sarcoma. It was the outbreak of this rare cancer that led to the discovery of AIDS in 1981. Typically people with AIDS become sick when they are infected by pathogens that do not normally cause disease in people with healthy immune systems. These are called "opportunistic" infections because the pathogens have the opportunity to infect only people with unhealthy immune systems. For example, a kind of pneumonia caused by the protozoan *Pneumocystis carinii* is common among AIDS patients but rare among healthy people.

An HIV infection is generally considered fatal. However, not everyone who has been diagnosed as HIV-positive has developed AIDS. People with AIDS die when their body's

---

MEETING DIVERSE NEEDS

At Risk Encourage students to develop a time line that shows the stages of HIV infection and the development of AIDS. Encourage students to use the information in Figure 32.15 to develop their diagrams.

weakened immune system cannot fight off an infection caused by a pathogen.

CARE OF YOUR IMMUNE SYSTEM

An ounce of prevention

Throughout this chapter, you have learned about how your immune system works to keep your body healthy. For your immune system to work at its best, however, it is essential that you practice behaviors that reduce your exposure to pathogens and help keep your body in good health. These behaviors are summarized in *Figure 32.16*.

Diet, exercise, and rest You know that food provides your body with the nutrients and energy your cells need to function properly. These functions include producing white blood cells and repairing cells that are damaged through injury or disease. To help all your other body systems work at their best, it is important that you eat a balanced diet that provides your body with the nutrients it needs.

In section 32.2, you learned that the squeezing action of skeletal muscles helps move lymph throughout the body. Exercise provides much of this action and therefore aids in this movement. Adequate rest is also important for keeping your body functioning at its best. For most people, adequate rest means getting about eight hours of sleep each night.

Personal hygiene Keeping your body clean is an important way to reduce your exposure to pathogens. Bathing or showering removes dirt and pathogens that may be present on the skin. Brushing your teeth several times each day reduces the number of bacteria that can enter your body through the mouth. Brushing your teeth also keeps your teeth healthy so you can digest your food properly.

Taking Care of Your Immune System

- Eat a well-balanced and healthful diet.
- Get plenty of exercise and rest.
- Brush your teeth and bathe or shower regularly.
- Keep your home clean.
- Avoid tobacco, drugs, and alcohol.
- Abstain from sexual activities.
- Get vaccinations that prevent diseases.

FIGURE 32.16
There are many things a person can do to maintain the health of the immune system. In which ways do you maintain your immune system? ❶

A clean environment You can help reduce the number of pathogens you come in contact with by keeping your home—particularly the kitchen and bathroom—clean. For example, you have learned that food contaminated with bacteria can cause food poisoning. By regularly cleaning surfaces where food is prepared, you can reduce your risk of picking up pathogens.

Avoiding drugs Drugs, alcohol, and tobacco products can have harmful effects on the body. Many types of drugs, including alcohol, can slow or suppress the immune system. And as you just learned, sharing needles

LAB ZONE Do It!

Creating a Personal Health Journal

You can check on the status of your health habits by creating a personal health journal for your own use.

Try This

1 Look at the list of behaviors in Figure 32.16.
2 Write each of the behaviors at the top of a separate piece of paper.
3 Jot down your habits related to each behavior during a typical week.

Analyze Your Results

1 Do you think that your weekly habits are healthy?
2 Clip the pages together and place them in your journal. Continue to record your health behaviors in your journal.

32.4

Discuss

Direct students to the health tips listed in Figure 32.16. Ask students to suggest effective ways to target this type of information to a teenage audience.

LAB ZONE Do It! TEAM WORK

Creating a Personal Health Journal

In addition to the behaviors listed in Figure 32.16, tell students to include personal hygiene habits in their lists.

Analyze Your Results

Check that students continue to update their journals.

Class Activity TEAM WORK

Have students debate the following statement: *People with AIDS or HIV should be confined to hospitals or specific geographic locations.* Allow students to work in teams of debaters, judges, and time keepers.

 Using Prior Knowledge To practice strategies for effective reading, use pages 69-70 in *Super Read!*

MEETING DIVERSE NEEDS

Gifted Many cleaning products claim that their use helps prevent the spread of disease. Encourage gifted students to identify several such products and to devise an experiment to test these claims. Have students who gain approval for their experiments carry them out and report their findings to the class.

❶ Student answers will vary, but may include details on diet or hours of sleep.

32.4

In the Community

Vaccinations that are recommended or required will vary by school district or state. Recommended vaccinations may include those for measles, pertussis, German measles, polio, and diphtheria.

Evaluate Understanding

To assess students' understanding of diseases of the immune system, ask:

- **How does a person who is infected with HIV differ from a person who is HIV-positive?** (A person who is HIV-positive has antibodies to HIV in his or her blood. An infected person has the virus but may not have developed antibodies against the virus.)
- **When does an HIV infection become AIDS?** (When the number of T4 cells becomes so low the body cannot defend itself from disease)
- **What are some ways you can keep your immune system healthy?** (Accept all responses reflecting the information in Figure 32.16 along with personal hygiene habits.)

Reteach

Have small groups of students develop a quiz for the section. Have groups exchange quizzes, answer the questions, and check responses. As a class, discuss any questions students had trouble answering.

788

Vaccination does not protect only one individual against disease—it prevents the spread of disease between populations. Find out from a town or city public-health agency, or from your school nurse, what vaccinations are recommended. What age groups are targeted for each vaccination? Are vaccinations required by law? Also determine how vaccinations are delivered. Are they given in public locations, such as schools or workplaces? Or are they administered only in doctors' offices? Are the programs paid for publicly or individually? You can learn more about vaccinations and public health at *http://body_systems.biosurf.com.*

IN THE COMMUNITY
Shots for Everyone

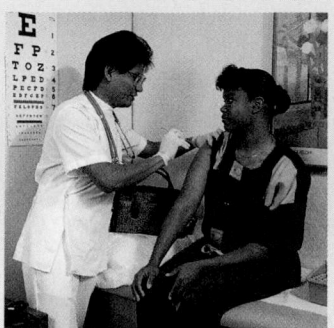

among IV drug users is one of the main ways HIV is transmitted. This practice also provides a means by which other pathogens, including the viruses that cause the various types of hepatitis, can be transmitted.

Sexual responsibility In this chapter, you learned that HIV, syphilis, gonorrhea, and some other diseases can be spread through sexual contact with an infected person. The only way to absolutely prevent exposure to sexually transmitted diseases is to abstain from all sexual activity. For sexually active people, the use of condoms can reduce the risk of exposure. You will learn more about sexually transmitted diseases in Chapter 33.

Vaccinations Many serious diseases can be prevented through the use of vaccines. A **vaccine** is a preparation containing dead or weakened pathogens that is designed to increase the body's immunity. The pathogens in a vaccine are too weak to cause illness, but their presence stimulates the immune system to make antibodies

that resist the disease. Vaccinations have almost eliminated diseases, such as polio, that were once widespread.

CHECKPOINT 32.4

1. What is an allergy? Identify three common causes of allergies.
2. Explain the roles of diet, exercise, good hygiene, and vaccination in keeping the immune system healthy.
3. **Critical Thinking** Bone marrow transplants are a method of treatment being considered for some AIDS patients. How might a bone marrow transplant benefit some AIDS patients? What might be some problems with this treatment?

Build on What You Know

4. In this chapter, you learned about the lock-and-key binding of antibodies to an antigen. What other biological example with a similar type of system have you learned about? *(Need to jog your memory? Revisit relevant concepts in Chapter 14, Section 14.1.)*

? How do you care for your immune system?

CHECKPOINT 32.4

1. The immune system reacts to a harmless substance as if it were an antigen. Causes include small particles, chemical substances in plants, and food.
2. A healthy diet provides nutrients important for cell functions; exercise aids the movement of through lymph vessels; good hygiene reduces exposure to pathogens; vaccinations prevent diseases.
3. **Making generalizations** It could increase the number of T cells since T cells are made in the bone marrow. The new T cells could be rejected.
4. Before an enzyme can catalyze a reaction, the substrate must fit into an enzyme's active site much like a key fits into a lock.

Chapter 32 Review

THE BIG IDEA!
32.1 The immune system protects the body from harmful organisms and substances.
32.2–32.3 The immune system consists of specialized cells, organs, and organ systems that respond to the presence of a pathogen.
32.4 A healthy immune system requires a healthy lifestyle.

Sum It Up

Use the following summary to review the main concepts in this chapter.

32.1 Protecting the Organism

- The immune system fights infections.
- Koch's postulates provide a method for identifying the cause of an infectious disease.
- Diseases can be spread by direct contact with an infected person, by indirect contact through the air, through contaminated food or water, and by animal bites.
- Most vertebrates have both nonspecific and specific defenses against disease. Nonspecific defenses are effective against many different types of pathogens. Specific defenses, or the immune response, protect an organism against specific pathogens.

32.2 Overview of the Immune System

- The lymphatic system is a network of organs and vessels. The lymphatic and circulatory systems are intertwined.
- White blood cells stored in lymph nodes attack pathogens in lymph fluid.
- The lymphatic system collects, filters, and returns plasma that leaks from the bloodstream.
- Some leukocytes engulf unwanted cells and pathogens in a nonspecific manner. Others recognize and attack specific pathogens.

32.3 Activities of the Immune System

- The body's first line of defense—skin, mucus, tears, and sweat—acts as a barrier to pathogens.
- Histamine, released by injured cells, increases blood flow—bringing phagocytes and platelets to the injured area.
- Interferon and natural killer cells are nonspecific defenses against viruses.
- B cells attack specific pathogens by producing antibodies that bind to antigens on the pathogens' surface. T cells can directly attack cells recognized as dangerous to the body. The body can acquire immunity to pathogens.

32.4 Health of the Immune System

- Sometimes the immune system responds to harmless substances, or even to the body's own cells, as though they were pathogens. Organ transplants require suppression of the body's immune system.
- By attacking helper T cells, or T4 cells, HIV interferes with humoral and cell-mediated immunity.
- A well-balanced diet, exercise, rest, and vaccinations contribute to a healthy immune system. Maintaining personal hygiene and avoiding drugs and unsafe sexual activities limit exposure to pathogens.

Use Terms and Concepts

Use each of the following words or terms in a complete sentence. If you need to review a meaning, turn to the page indicated.

pathogen (p. 770)
nonspecific defenses (p. 773)
specific defenses (p. 773)
lymph (p. 774)
lymph nodes (p. 774)

phagocytes (p. 775)
macrophages (p. 775)
lymphocytes (p. 775)
inflammatory response (p. 778)
histamine (p. 778)
antigen (p. 780)

humoral immunity (p. 780)
antibody (p. 780)
B lymphocytes (p.780)
cell-mediated immunity (p. 781)
T lymphocytes (p. 781)

allergy (p. 783)
autoimmune disease (p. 784)
HIV (p. 785)
vaccine (p. 788)

Chapter 32 Immune System **789**

Review the Big Ideas

Before students begin the Chapter Review, you may wish to review the Big Ideas presented in the chapter. Point out that the immune system is the body's defense against harmful substances, pathogens, and organisms and viruses that cause infectious diseases. The immune system is made up of the specialized white blood cells which are produced and circulated by the lymphatic system. Some leukocytes digest unwanted cells and pathogens; others attack specific pathogens. The immune system is best able to fight infection when people practice healthy behaviors and avoid drugs and tobacco and activities that place one at risk of developing sexually transmitted diseases.

Answers

1. specific defense
2. antigens
3. HIV
4. lymph nodes
5. allergy
6. pathogen
7. B lymphocytes
8. c
9. b
10. a
11. c
12. b
13. Phagocytes attack invading cells; natural killer cells attack infected body cells.
14. It is an example of direct contact because HIV is transmitted through sexual intercourse, the sharing of needles, or through a transfusion of contaminated blood.
15. A person can contract the disease or receive a vaccine against the disease.
16. Swollen, painful nodes are a sign of increased leukocyte production, usually in response to an infection.
17. B cells secrete antibodies into lymph and blood.
18. White blood cells are produced in the bone marrow.
19. Because HIV destroys T4 cells, a low T4 count indicates the onset of full–blown AIDS.
20. Expanded blood vessels stimulate blood flow, which increases the amount of platelets and white blood cells in the intercellular fluid.
21. Concept maps should show the following: Sulfites (detected by) → antibodies (stimulate) → macrophages (produce) → histamine (triggers) → allergic reaction.
22. Contaminated food and water are less common in

Use Your Word Power

MATCHING Write the term from the list of key terms that best matches each of the phrases below.

1. A response designed to protect against a specific toxin or pathogen.

2. Molecules that trigger an immune response.

3. A virus that destroys helper T cells.

4. Densely-packed areas of tissue in which white cells are stored.

5. The response of the immune system to a normally harmless chemical such as a food protein.

6. An organism or virus that causes an infectious disease.

7. The white blood cells that produce antibodies.

MULTIPLE CHOICE Choose the letter of the word or phrase that best completes each statement.

8. An inflammatory response is triggered by (a) an antigen; (b) an antibody; (c) histamine; (d) pyrogens.

9. An example of a nonspecific defense is a(n) (a) antibody; (b) macrophage; (c) T lymphocyte; (d) vaccine.

10. The attack of cancer cells by lymphocytes is an example of (a) cell-mediated immunity; (b) an autoimmune response; (c) humoral immunity; (d) an inflammatory response.

11. The major component of pus is (a) lymph; (b) mucus; (c) phagocytes; (d) lymphocytes.

12. Vaccines stimulate the production of (a) antigens; (b) antibodies; (c) T lymphocytes; (d) histamine.

Show What You Know

13. Compare the roles of phagocytes and natural killer cells.

14. Is the transmission of HIV an example of direct or indirect contact? Explain.

15. Describe two ways that a person can acquire immunity to a specific disease.

16. What information could doctors obtain by examining lymph nodes?

17. What is the role of B cells in the immune system?

18. Why is bone marrow considered part of the immune system?

19. What can a T4 cell count indicate?

20. How do expanded blood vessels help heal injured tissues?

21. **Make a Concept Map** Some people are allergic to sulfur-containing compounds called sulfites, which are used as food preservatives. Create a concept map that describes the immune system's response to sulfites.

Take It Further

22. **Developing a Hypothesis** Cardiovascular diseases are the major cause of death in the United States. Infectious diseases are the primary cause of death worldwide. Suggest possible reasons for the difference.

23. **Applying Concepts** If a doctor wants to know whether a patient has an infection, the doctor may draw blood and ask for a test called a white blood cell count. Explain the reasons for the doctor's action.

24. **Applying Concepts** What does it mean to describe a pathogen as waterborne or airborne?

25. **Applying Concepts** Why is a second bee sting more dangerous than the first for a person who is allergic to bee stings?

26. **Designing an Experiment** Suppose a student needs to provide proof of immunity to certain diseases before entering college, but the student is unable to locate any record of his or her vaccinations. Design an experiment that would show which vaccines the student had received.

the United States. Access to medical services is not consistent across the world. Americans often eat diets that put them at risk of heart disease.

23. The number of white blood cells should be high if the body is fighting off an infection.

24. The descriptions refer to methods of transmission.

25. The second inflammatory response will be faster due to the presence of memory cells.

26. With a sample of the student's blood, you could test for specific antibodies.

27. 1985; 1995. Although only 23 percent of reported cases were fatalities in 1995, the number of deaths was highest because the total number of cases reported that

27. Interpreting a Graph The graph below shows the fatality rates for reported cases of AIDS in adults and adolescents in the United States for specific years. Which year had the highest percentage of deaths among reported cases of AIDS? Which year had the highest number of deaths? Explain how the year with the lowest percentage of fatalities could have the highest number of deaths.

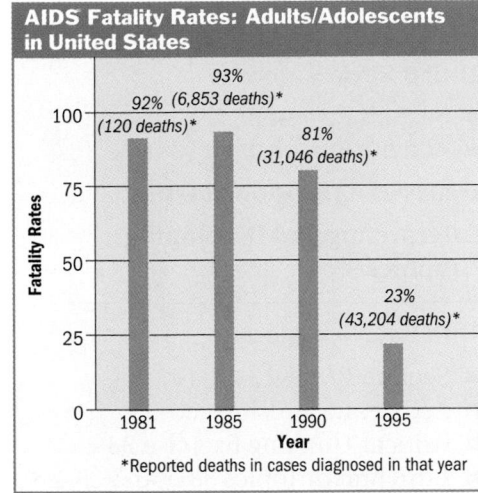

AIDS Fatality Rates: Adults/Adolescents in United States

Reported deaths in cases diagnosed in that year

28. Analyzing Data A person with red, itchy, swollen skin might have contact dermatitis. The culprit might be clothing, metal jewelry, or a cosmetic product. The following statistics show how different categories of cosmetic products contribute to the overall incidence of dermatitis caused by cosmetics. Skin products, 28% of cases; hair products, 24%; facial makeup, 11%; nail products, 8%; fragrances, 7%; personal hygiene products, 6%; shaving products, 4%; eye makeup, 4%; sunscreens and suntan lotions, 3%; other cosmetic products, 5%. What percent of cases result from makeup? The fragrance category includes items such as colognes. In what other cosmetics might colognes be used? What do you think it means when a product is labeled "hypoallergenic"?

Consider the Issues

29. Allergies on the menu Food allergies are common in humans. Examples include allergies to peanuts, garlic, or citrus fruits. While some food allergy reactions are minor, others can be severe, or even lethal. Do you think school or office cafeterias should avoid foods commonly associated with allergies in the dishes they prepare? Should they post ingredients to all dishes? What other solutions can you think of to help people with food allergies?

Make New Connections

30. Biology and First Aid Call your local Poison Control Center. Find out what to do if a person ingests a poison. Prepare a poster to educate others.

31. Biology and Consumer Education Make a survey of over-the-counter (OTC) medications. Ask a local pharmacist what OTC products are best-sellers. Which of these products contain antihistamines? How would antihistamines help an allergy victim's runny nose?

32. Biology and Medicine Non-Hodgkin lymphoma, a cancer of the immune system, is the sixth most common cancer in the United States. Research the theories that have been proposed to explain this cancer's rapid increase in recent decades. Evaluate the evidence for each theory.

FAST-FORWARD TO CHAPTER 33

The thymus gland is one of the glands in the endocrine system. The hormones produced in the endocrine system help regulate body functions. You will learn about the endocrine and reproductive systems in Chapter 33.

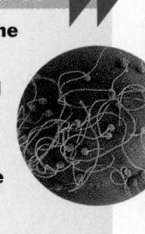

Chapter 32 Immune System **791**

decreases the action of the histamine in causing the nasal passages to secrete mucus.

32. The theories already proposed are improved diagnosis, pesticides, hair dyes, AIDS, and immune–suppressing therapies—for organ transplants and diseases such as arthritis.

year must have been very high.

28. Fifteen percent result from facial and eye makeup. Colognes may also be contained in skin products, hair products, hygiene products, shaving products, and suntan lotions. The manufacturer is claiming that potentially irritating ingredients have been eliminated.

29. Responses will vary.

30. The general rule is to call the local control center and/or 911 before doing anything. A normal instinct is to induce vomiting, which might cause further damage.

31. In a survey of 300,000 OTC medications in 1990, excluding pain-killers, 6 of the top 10 best–selling products contained antihistamines. An antihistamine

PLANNING GUIDE

Section	Student Activities/Features	Teacher's Resource Package
33.1 Endocrine Control **Objectives** ■ Explain the functions of endocrine systems ■ Describe how endocrine systems function in different animals	**Lab Zone Discover It!** *Observing Newborns,* p. 793	**Unit 8 Review Module** ■ Section Review 33.1
33.2 Human Endocrine System **Objectives** ■ Identify and describe the human endocrine glands ■ Analyze how hormones function	**Everyday Biology** *Instant Sleep?* p. 796 **Lab Zone Investigate It!** *Identifying a Negative Feedback System,* p. 800	**Unit 8 Review Module** ■ Section Review 33.2 ■ Activity Recordsheet 33-1 **Issues and Decision Making** 33-1 **Interpreting and Developing Graphics** 97
33.3 Health of the Endocrine System **Objectives** ■ Distinguish between disorders of the endocrine system ■ Assess the dangers of steroid use	**Lab Zone Do It!** *Can You Raise Your Pulse Rate?* p. 802 **STS: Issues in Biology** *Dangers of Steroids,* p. 802	**Unit 8 Review Module** ■ Section Review 33.3 ■ Activity Recordsheet 33-2 ■ Critical Thinking Exercise 33 ■ Enrichment Topics 33-1 and 33-2 **Consumer Applications** 33-1
33.4 Reproduction **Objectives** ■ Distinguish between the human male and female reproductive systems ■ Explain the human female reproductive cycle		**Unit 8 Review Module** ■ Section Review 33.4 ■ Interpreting Graphics 33 **Interpreting and Developing Graphics** 98, 99
33.5 Human Development **Objectives** ■ Describe the steps in the development of a human embryo ■ Explain the birth process ■ Describe the life stages of a human	**Everyday Biology** *Funny, You Don't Look Like Twins,* p. 809 **STS: Frontiers in Biology** *Health of the Fetus,* p. 812 **Lab Zone Do It!** *What Is the Average Human Growth Rate?* p. 813 **In the Community** *Making the Most of Long Life,* p. 814	**Unit 8 Review Module** ■ Section Review 33.5 ■ Activity Recordsheet 33-3 **Laboratory Manual,** Lab 57: "Fetal Growth Rates"
33.6 Health of the Reproductive System **Objectives** ■ Describe disorders of the reproductive system ■ Distinguish between sexually transmitted diseases	**Lab Zone Think About It!** *Comparing STD Occurrence,* p. 816	**Unit 8 Review Module** ■ Section Review 33.6 ■ Enrichment Topic 33-3 ■ Vocabulary Review 33 ■ Chapter 33 Tests **Spanish Reviews** Chapter 33

Technology Resources

Internet Connections

Within this chapter, you will see the (bioSURF) logo. If you and your students have access to the Internet, the following URL address will provide various Internet connections that are related to topics and features presented in this chapter:

http://body_systems.biosurf.com

You can also find relevant chapter material at **The Biology Place** address:

http://www.biology.com

CD-ROMs

Biología: la telaraña de la vida,
   (Spanish Student Edition) Chapter 33
Teacher's Resource Planner, Chapter 33
   Supplements
TestWorks CD-ROM
■ Chapter 33 Tests
How Your Body Works CD-ROM

Videodiscs

Animated Biological Concepts Videodiscs
■ Regulation of Blood Sugar

Overhead Transparencies

■ Human Endocrine Systems, #78
■ Human Reproductive Systems, #79
■ Fetal Development, #80

Videotapes

Biology Alive! Video Series
Rewind: The Web of Life Reteach Videos

Planning for Activities

STUDENT EDITION
Lab Zone
Discover It! p. 793
■ photographs of new-born humans

Lab Zone
Investigate It! p. 800
■ sketching paper
■ pencil

Lab Zone Do It! p. 802
■ watch or clock with second hand

TEACHER'S EDITION
Quick Activity, p. 794
Endocrine systems
■ pictures of a football coach, orchestra conductor, movie director, and traffic police

Quick Activity, p. 796
Hormones and organ cells
■ lock and several keys

Quick Activity, p. 801
Testing for glucose
■ glucose test strips
■ containers with mixture of sugar, water, and yellow food coloring

Teacher Demo, p. 803
Binary fission
■ microprojector
■ slide of ameba or other protozoan reproducing by binary fission

Teacher Demo, p. 805
Sperm cells
■ microprojector
■ prepared slides of a sperm cell
■ slides of cellular organisms such as *Euglena*

Quick Activity, p. 809
Human embryonic development
■ photographs of several stages of human embryonic development

Teacher Demo, p. 815
Warning labels and pregnancy
■ warning labels from cigarette packages and alcoholic beverages that are directed at pregnant women

Chapter Objectives

Students will learn the main concepts of this chapter as they complete the following objectives.

- Explain the functions of endocrine systems and describe how these systems function in different animals
- Identify and describe the human endocrine glands and analyze hormone function
- Describe endocrine system disorders and assess dangers of steroid use
- Distinguish between the human reproductive systems and explain the female reproductive cycle
- Describe the steps in the development of a human embryo, the birth process, and the life stages of a human
- Describe disorders of the reproductive system and sexually transmitted diseases

Key Words

33.1 *hormones, endocrine glands*

33.2 *hypothalamus, pituitary gland, feedback control, insulin, glucagon*

33.3 *diabetes mellitus*

33.4 *eggs, sperm, testes, penis, ovary, uterus, ovarian cycle, menstruation, menstrual cycle, ovum, ovulation*

33.5 *implantation, placenta, fetus, puberty*

The Opening Story

Have students discuss how the story relates to the chapter. Ask students if they know families with multiple-birth children.

CHAPTER 33

Endocrine and Reproductive Systems

You can find out more about the endocrine and reproductive systems at the following Internet address: *http://body_systems.biosurf.com*

In this chapter . . .

FEATURES

Everyday Biology
- Instant Sleep?
- Funny, You Don't Look Like Twins

In the Community
Making the Most of Long Life

 Issues in Biology
Dangers of Steroids

Frontiers in Biology
Health of the Fetus

LAB ZONES

Discover It!
- Observing Newborns

Do It!
- Can You Raise Your Pulse Rate?
- What Is the Average Human Growth Rate?

Think About It!
- Comparing STD Occurrence

Investigate It!
- Identifying a Negative Feedback System

THE MULTIPLE–BIRTH **BOOM**

The Shier Quints

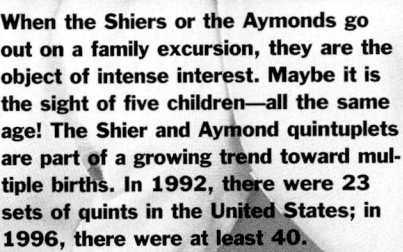

When the Shiers or the Aymonds go out on a family excursion, they are the object of intense interest. Maybe it is the sight of five children—all the same age! The Shier and Aymond quintuplets are part of a growing trend toward multiple births. In 1992, there were 23 sets of quints in the United States; in 1996, there were at least 40.

How do multiple-birth families cope? Faced with lack of sleep, mounds of daily diapers, and countless other challenges, many families like these two manage their situation with a lot of help from family and friends.

The Aymond Quints

Whether it leads to a single birth or to multiple births, reproduction is a complex process that relies on hormones. How are hormones involved? How are eggs fertilized, and how do they develop? What other body systems are affected by hormones? You will find the answers to these questions as you learn more about the endocrine and reproductive systems.

 **Discover It!**

Observing Newborns

You need photographs of newborn humans

1. Examine photographs of newborn humans.
2. Record your observations of several newborns. Do they all seem to share certain characteristics? If so, what are they?

The development of a newborn human from a fertilized egg is truly dramatic. In this chapter, you will learn about reproduction, including the growth and development of the fetus prior to birth.

WRITE ABOUT IT!

Write a paragraph or a poem from the point of view of a human newborn. In your writing, express the sensory changes you think a baby may be experiencing as it is born.

793

Opening Activities

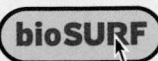 If you have access to the Internet in your classroom or school, you may wish to have students connect to the address shown on page 792. You may also want to have students conduct net searches for information using key words related to this chapter. For example, they could search for entries under growth hormones, steroids, puberty, or amniocentesis.

LAB ZONE **Discover It!**

Observing Newborns

 TEAM WORK

Before students begin the chapter, have them do the suggested activity in small groups. Provide time for groups to share their descriptions with the class. Record common characteristics on the board.

WRITE ABOUT IT

Encourage students to use all five senses in their paragraphs or poems.

REWIND to Chapter 32

Briefly review concepts learned in Chapter 32, *Immune System*. Ask:

■ **How do you think your knowledge of the immune system will help you understand the endocrine system and reproduction?**

PORTFOLIO PREVIEW

Students should be encouraged to add to their portfolios as they work through this chapter. In addition to the *Write About It* opportunity, the following sections offer opportunities for portfolio entries:

■ Section 33.2: *Human Endocrine System*
■ Section 33.5: *Human Development*
■ Section 33.6: *Health of the Reproductive System*

793

ENGAGE

Consider the Big Idea

Have students read The Big Idea! at the top of the page. Explain that the endocrine system produces chemicals that act as agents of change.

Use the Visual

Have students study the photograph that opens the section. Explain that prolactin is one example of a chemical called a hormone.

Check Prior Knowledge

To assess students' knowledge about endocrine control, ask:

■ **What are the functions of plant hormones?** (To control plant growth and responses)

■ **What animal life processes are controlled by hormones?** (Growth, development, reproduction, digestion)

Quick Activity

Display pictures of or write these names on the board: *football coach, orchestra conductor, movie director,* and *traffic police officer.* Ask:

■ **What is the main function of all these people?** (They direct others to do what needs to be done.)

Tell students that the endocrine systems functions in a similar way to regulate body functions.

33.1 Endocrine Control

What you'll learn

IDEAS
• To explain the functions of endocrine systems
• To describe how endocrine systems function in different animals

WORDS
hormones, endocrine glands

The caregiving hormone
A chemical may not be warm and cuddly, but a chemical messenger called prolactin induces protective, nurturing behavior in many animals. In mammalian mothers, prolactin stimulates milk production. In birds, this hormone can make even nonparents care for eggs and bring food to baby birds.

FIGURE 33.1
Hormones control whether this hydra will reproduce sexually or asexually.

FUNCTIONS OF ENDOCRINE SYSTEMS

Controlling slow changes

An animal's cells, tissues, and organs need control systems to coordinate and regulate their many activities. In most animals two control systems work to regulate these activities—the nervous system and the endocrine system. These two systems monitor all other body systems in order to respond to changes and maintain homeostasis.

Although both the nervous system and the endocrine system act to control the body, they do so in different ways. The nervous system controls the body through high-speed nerve impulses. It can quickly respond to immediate changes either inside or outside the body. In contrast, the endocrine system controls the body by means of chemical messengers. The endocrine system brings about slower, longer-lasting responses and changes that may occur over hours or years. For example, an animal's changes as it develops into an adult are controlled by the endocrine system.

Hormones are the chemical messengers of the endocrine system.

Specialized endocrine cells secrete hormones. In vertebrates, including humans, endocrine cells are located in organs called **endocrine glands.** Hormones are produced in one part of an animal's body, but usually affect another part of the body. Hormones control a wide range of activities that include growth, development, metabolism, behavior, and reproduction.

ENDOCRINE SYSTEMS IN ANIMALS

Hormones in control

The best understood feature of invertebrate endocrine systems is hormonal control of reproduction. For example, the cnidarian *Hydra* uses one hormone to stimulate growth and asexual reproduction by budding. The same hormone suppresses sexual reproduction. The mollusk *Aplysia*, also known as the sea hare, produces a hormone that stimulates egg laying. This hormone also suppresses feeding and movement, behaviors that could prevent the animal from laying eggs.

Arthropods have diverse and complex endocrine systems. Crustaceans, such as crabs and lobsters, produce a variety of hormones. These hormones

794 *Unit 8 Human Biology*

STUDENT RESOURCES

From the Teacher's Resource Package, use:
■ Section Review 33.1 from Unit 8 Review Module

TECHNOLOGY RESOURCES

Relevant technology resources include:
■ Spanish Student Edition CD-ROM
■ Teacher's Resource Planner CD-ROM

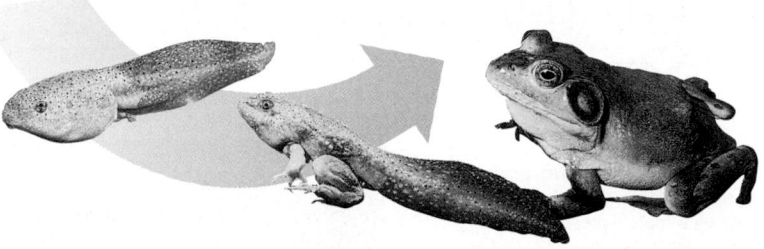

control processes such as growth, reproduction, homeostasis, metabolism, and coloration. The hormonal control of insect molting is the most well understood. During molting, an insect sheds its old exoskeleton and secretes a new one. Molting also involves changes and growth in the insect's body. All of these processes are controlled by three different hormones secreted by the insect.

The endocrine systems of vertebrates, such as amphibians, reptiles, birds, and mammals, produce more than 20 different hormones. These hormones control a range of activities including growth, development, and reproduction. For example, hormones in amphibians trigger the metamorphosis that changes a tadpole into a frog. In mammals, specific hormones support pregnancy, trigger the birth of young, and make the mother's mammary glands produce milk.

Hormones are not exclusive to the animal kingdom. As you may recall from Chapter 19, plant hormones trigger growth and reproduction. Stem growth and the production of flowers and fruits are two examples of hormone action. What are the names of the main plant hormones? ❶

CHECKPOINT 33.1

1. What are the functions of the endocrine system?

2. Give examples of endocrine control in three groups of animals.

3. Critical Thinking Why is it advantageous for an animal to have both a nervous and an endocrine system?

Build on What You Know

4. How does the circulatory system carry hormones to body parts? *(Need to jog your memory? Revisit relevant concepts in Chapter 31, Section 31.4.)*

FIGURE 33.2
What structural changes occur as an amphibian undergoes metamorphosis? ❷

FIGURE 33.3
Three hormones that interact with the nervous system and each other monitor molting in arthropods. Why does an arthropod have to molt? ❸

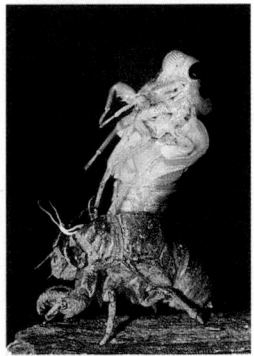

FIGURE 33.4
Hormones control many activities in mammals, including reproduction, birth, and milk production.

Chapter 33 Endocrine and Reproductive Systems **795**

CHECKPOINT 33.1

1. Monitor body systems, respond to changes, monitor homeostasis
2. Insect molting, milk production in mammals, amphibian metamorphosis
3. **Analyzing** Two systems enable appropriate responses to short-term stimuli and longer-term changes.
4. Blood transports dissolved hormones from the glands where they are made to the body part that produces the response.

❶ Auxins, gibberellins, cytokinins, ethylene, and abscisic acid are the main plant hormones.
❷ The frog develops lungs and legs.
❸ Its exoskeleton does not grow.

33.2

① ENGAGE

Use the Visual

Have students study the photograph that opens the section. Explain that many of the changes that take place in human males and females during adolescence are controlled by hormones. Ask:

- **What changes during adolescence do you think are controlled by hormones?** (Possible responses include development of breasts and onset of menstruation in females, increase in facial hair of males.)

Check Prior Knowledge

To assess students' knowledge about the endocrine system, ask:

- **What is the function of the endocrine system?** (To control body activities by means of chemical messengers)
- **What are glands?** (Structures that release chemicals)
- **Name two glands in the digestive system.** (Salivary glands and pancreas)

Quick Activity

Provide groups of students with a lock and several keys. Have them attempt to open the lock. Explain that each hormone is able to act on only one organ, because the hormone fits the cells of the organ much as a key fits a lock.

33.2 Human Endocrine System

What you'll learn

IDEAS
- To identify and describe the human endocrine glands
- To analyze how hormones function

WORDS
hypothalamus, pituitary gland, feedback control, insulin, glucagon

Instant Sleep?

As we age, the pineal gland makes less melatonin, a hormone that helps regulate our sleep cycle. Scientists are investigating whether taking melatonin capsules might be a safe way to promote sleep.

Do, re, mi . . .

Why do a female's vocal cords produce sounds with a higher pitch than the sounds produced by a male's vocal cords? This occurs because the surge of hormones produced in the body of an adolescent male causes the vocal cords—a pair of muscles inside the larynx—to thicken. Thinner vocal cords vibrate more rapidly than thicker ones, which is why females can reach those high soprano notes.

THE ENDOCRINE GLANDS

Ductless control

As you now know, the organs of the human endocrine system are the endocrine glands. Located throughout the body, these ductless glands secrete hormones directly into the bloodstream. You can see some of the human endocrine glands and read about the hormones they produce in *Figure 33.5*. What types of activities are controlled by hormones?

Humans produce over 20 different hormones, each with a different function. Because the blood carries the hormones to all parts of the body, each hormone reaches many organs. Some hormones affect many organs, while others affect only one or a few organs. In the organs, the cells that are affected by hormones are called target cells.

Some endocrine glands are also a part of other body systems. For example, the pancreas is part of both the endocrine system and the digestive system. As an endocrine gland, the pancreatic endocrine cells called islets of Langerhans release hormones directly into the blood.

The pancreas also releases sodium bicarbonate and enzymes directly into the digestive tract, as you may

remember from Chapter 30. As a digestive organ, the pancreas acts as an exocrine gland. Unlike a ductless endocrine gland, an exocrine gland has tubelike ducts that carry secretions directly to a specific location.

There are also exocrine glands in your stomach that secrete digestive acids. Other exocrine glands in the human body are sweat glands and salivary glands. What substances are produced by sweat glands and salivary glands? ❶

The endocrine system and the nervous system are both functionally and structurally connected. As you have learned, both of these systems regulate the activities of the body.

One important link between the endocrine system and the nervous system is the hypothalamus. A part of the nervous system, the **hypothalamus** is the region of the brain that controls blood pressure, body temperature, and emotions. The hypothalamus is also an endocrine gland that makes and secretes hormones. The hypothalamus is physically connected to the pituitary gland and controls the release of pituitary hormones. You will learn more about the functions of the pituitary gland and the hypothalamus and their interactions later in this chapter.

STUDENT RESOURCES

From the Teacher's Resource Package, use:
- Section Review 33.2 and Activity Recordsheet 33-1 from Unit 8 Review Module
- Issues and Decision Making 33-1

TECHNOLOGY RESOURCES

Relevant technology resources include:
- Spanish Student Edition CD-ROM
- Teacher's Resource Planner CD-ROM
- How Your Body Works CD-ROM
- Animated Biological Concepts Videodiscs: "Regulation of Blood Sugar"

FIGURE 33.5

Human Endocrine System

Endocrine glands produce hormones that control many body functions.

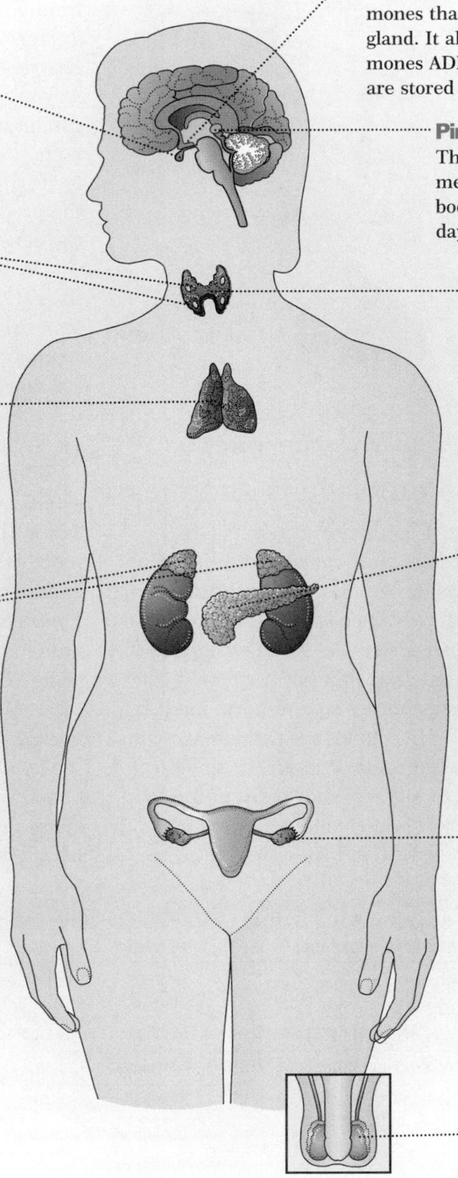

Pituitary gland
Responding to signals from the hypothalamus, the pituitary gland releases hormones some of which control other endocrine glands.

Parathyroid gland
These four patches of tissue on the thyroid gland release the parathyroid hormone, which regulates the blood calcium level.

Thymus
Thymosin, which stimulates the development of T cells for the immune system, is secreted by the thymus.

Adrenal glands
The adrenal glands make epinephrine and norepinephrine, two hormones which cause the "fight or flight" response. They also secrete aldosterone, which affects the body's osmotic balance, and cortisol, which promotes glucose synthesis.

Hypothalamus
The hypothalamus makes hormones that control the pituitary gland. It also makes the hormones ADH and oxytocin, which are stored in the pituitary gland.

Pineal gland
The pineal gland secretes melatonin, which controls body functions in response to daylight and seasonal changes.

Thyroid gland
The hormone thyroxine, which speeds up metabolism and helps manage growth and development, is secreted by the thyroid gland.

Pancreas
The pancreas has patches of tissue called the islets of Langerhans, which have cells that make the hormones insulin and glucagon. Insulin and glucagon control the blood sugar level.

Ovaries
The hormones estrogen and progesterone are made in the ovaries. They maintain the female reproductive system and secondary sex characteristics. Progesterone maintains the uterus during pregnancy.

Testes
The testes make testosterone, a hormone that maintains the male reproductive system and secondary sex characteristics.

Chapter 33 Endocrine and Reproductive Systems **797**

② TEACH

Use the Visual

Have students study Figure 33.5. Review each organ of the endocrine system and its role in the body. Ask:

- **What does testosterone do?** (It maintains the male reproductive system and produces secondary sex characteristics.)
- **Which of the endocrine glands shown are present only in females?** (Ovaries)
- **Which organ secretes a hormone that affects the level of sugar in the blood?** (Pancreas)
- **What does the pituitary gland do?** (Releases hormones that control other endocrine glands)
- **What structure controls the pituitary gland?** (Hypothalmus)

Build Writing Skills

Have students write a poem, song, or rap about the glands of the endocrine system and their functions. Encourage students to retain scientific accuracy in their writing.

✹ Science History

The islets of Langerhans, which are responsible for the secretion of insulin, are named for the German pathologist Paul Langerhans (1847-1888), the first scientist to study these structures.

❶ Perspiration and saliva

FACTS AND FIGURES

The study of hormones and their effects on the body is called *endocrinology*. Endocrinologists generally classify hormones into three groups according to their chemical structures: steroid hormones, amino acid derivatives, and peptide hormones.

Use the Visual

Have students study Figure 33.7. Ask:

- **What are the primary functions of the pituitary hormones?** (To control growth and development, reproduction, metabolism)
- **Which hormones produced by the pituitary affect the reproductive system?** (Follicle-stimulating hormone, luteinizing hormone, and oxytocin)

Science History

The pituitary gland used to be called the "master gland" because scientists thought that the pituitary controlled the other glands. Now scientists know that the hypothalamus controls the pituitary.

Explain

Point out that steroid hormones include the corticosteroid hormones produced by the adrenal glands and the sex hormones. Corticosteroids have antiflammatory and immunosuppressive effects and are used to treat rheumatoid arthritis, asthma, some skin diseases, and some cancers. Anabolic steroids are testosterone-like chemicals. In medicine, they are used to treat growth problems, some anemias, and breast cancers.

Animated Biological Concepts

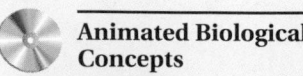

Regulation of Blood sugar   Play

FIGURE 33.6
Both lobes of the pituitary gland are controlled by the hypothalamus but release different hormones.

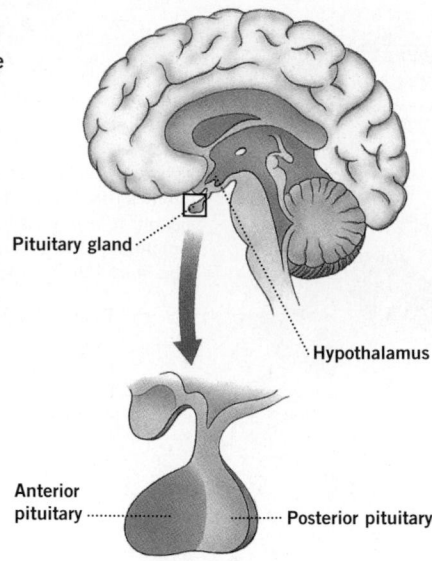

Pituitary gland

Hypothalamus

Anterior pituitary

Posterior pituitary

CONTROL BY HORMONES

The message is chemical

When a hormone reaches its target organ, the hormone binds with specific molecules in target cells. Just as a specific key opens a specific lock, a hormone binds only to specific target cells.

The effect of a hormone on a cell depends on the type of hormone it is. Protein hormones are peptides—chains of amino acids. Protein hormones bind to receptor molecules on the outside of a target cell membrane and cause a protein inside the cell to be activated. This protein then activates enzymes that change the cell's activity.

Steroid hormones are made of lipids. A steroid hormone can enter a cell easily because lipids pass easily through cell membranes. Once inside a target cell, steroid hormones cause changes in a cell by gene regulation. As you have learned, gene regulation can alter a cell's activity. A steroid hormone causes a specific section of DNA to "turn on" or "turn off." This affects the production of proteins coded by the genes near that section of DNA.

Different hormones can control the activities of a target organ through opposing effects. Usually, one hormone will stimulate an organ while another will inhibit it. The balance of the two opposing hormones affects the organ's functions.

Many organs, including endocrine glands, are controlled by hormones. The **pituitary gland** releases hormones that control several other endocrine glands. As you can see in *Figure 33.6,* the hypothalamus is located directly above the pituitary gland. The pituitary and hypothalamus are connected by blood vessels and nerves. Nerve impulses allow the hypothalamus to control the pituitary directly. The pituitary gland has two lobes—an anterior lobe and a posterior lobe. These lobes secrete different

FIGURE 33.7
What other endocrine glands are controlled by the pituitary gland? ❶

Pituitary Hormones	
Anterior Lobe Hormones	**Functions**
Growth hormone (GH)	Stimulates the division and growth of bone, muscle, and other body cells
Thyroid-stimulating hormone (TSH)	Stimulates the development and activity of the thyroid gland
Adrenocorticotropic hormone (ACTH)	Stimulates the adrenal glands to secrete other hormones
Follicle-stimulating hormone (FSH)	Stimulates the gonads to produce eggs and sperm
Luteinizing hormone (LH)	Stimulates the gonads to produce sex hormones
Posterior Lobe Hormones	**Functions**
Antidiuretic hormone (ADH)	Controls water absorption by the kidney
Oxytocin	Stimulates uterine contractions during childbirth and the flow of milk while nursing

MEETING DIVERSE NEEDS

Gifted Have gifted students research how a thermostat in a home controls temperature. Ask students to develop a visual device that relates the feedback system used by a thermostat to the control mechanism that regulates hormones in the body.

❶ Parathyroid, thymus, pineal, and pancreas

❷ The blood sugar level

hormones with different functions. The table in *Figure 33.7* summarizes these functions.

One function of the hypothalamus and the pituitary gland is to regulate the reproductive system by stimulating the sex organs to secrete sex hormones. The main sex hormone produced in males is testosterone. In females, the main sex hormones produced are estrogen and progesterone.

At puberty, usually between the ages of 10 and 16 for human males and females, the hypothalamus stimulates the pituitary gland to release two hormones—luteinizing (LOO-tuh-ny-zing) hormone (LH) and follicle-stimulating hormone (FSH). LH stimulates the gonads—testes or ovaries—to produce sex hormones. LH also stimulates the release of an egg from an ovary. FSH stimulates the testes to produce sperm and the ovaries to produce eggs.

Large amounts of sex hormones released by the testes or ovaries cause the development of secondary sex characteristics. In males, these characteristics include the growth of facial and body hair and a deepening of the voice. In females, secondary sex characteristics include the growth of the breasts and the widening of the hips.

One way in which pituitary and other hormones regulate the body is through feedback control. In **feedback control,** the rate of a process is controlled by a substance made in the process. There are two types of feedback control—negative and positive. In negative feedback control, the product of the process inhibits, or stops, the process. In positive feedback control, the product of the process accelerates the process.

Figure 33.8 shows how the pancreas regulates the blood sugar level with negative feedback control. When blood sugar is high, cells called beta (β) cells in the pancreas produce insulin. **Insulin** is a hormone that stimulates

FIGURE 33.8

Negative feedback control manages the relationship between insulin and glucagon. What factor affects the release of both hormones from the pancreas? ❷

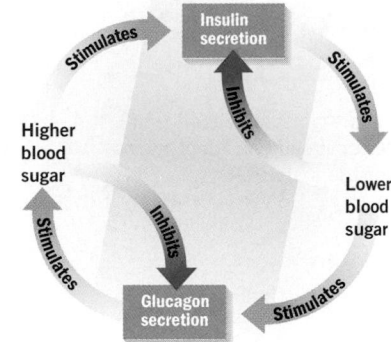

cells to absorb sugar from the blood and causes the liver to convert blood sugar, or glucose, to glycogen. The end result of insulin secretion—lower blood sugar—inhibits insulin secretion.

When blood sugar is low, alpha (α) cells in the pancreas produce glucagon. **Glucagon** is a hormone that stimulates the liver and muscles to convert stored glycogen into glucose, raising the amount of glucose in the blood. High blood sugar, in turn, inhibits glucagon secretion.

CHECKPOINT 33.2

1. Name four major endocrine glands and list their functions.
2. What are insulin and glucagon, and how are their functions related?
3. **Critical Thinking** Make an analogy between a thermostat and the control of the blood sugar level by hormones.

Build on What You Know

4. How do the functions of human hormones compare with the functions of plant hormones? *(Need to jog your memory? Revisit relevant concepts in Chapter 19, Section 19.1.)*

Chapter 33 Endocrine and Reproductive Systems **799**

CHECKPOINT 33.2

1. Responses can include any four of the ten glands named and described in Figure 33.5.
2. Both are hormones. Insulin lowers the concentration of sugar in the blood; glucagon increases the level of blood sugar.
3. **Making analogies** Both use a negative feedback system.
4. Both are transported by a vascular system to their target organs where they produce a response. Some plant hormones affect the area in which they are produced.

Use the Visual

Have students study Figure 33.8. Review why the production of insulin and glucagon is considered a negative feedback system. Ask:

- **What organ produces both insulin and glucagon?** (The pancreas)
- **What product regulates the negative feedback control?** (Glucose)
- **What process is inhibited by negative feedback control?** (The production of insulin)

③ ASSESS

Evaluate Understanding

Have students organize the information presented in Figures 33.5, 33.6, and 33.7 in a table. Ask:

- **What are the differences between steroid hormones and protein hormones?** (Steroid hormones are made of lipids and cause changes in a cell by gene regulation. Protein hormones are made of peptides and cause the release of substances that activate enzymes, which change cell activity.)

Reteach

Make an overhead transparency of Figure 33.5 with the labels removed. Challenge students to identify each endocrine gland shown and the hormone(s) it secretes. Then review the function of each hormone. Once all glands have been identified, guide students to distinguish between steroid hormones and protein hormones.

TEAM WORK

Identifying a Negative Feedback System

Lab Prep and Planning

Display a thermostat in class. Point out the different metals and the switch.

Lab Tips

Let students work in groups to brainstorm ideas for their experiment. Encourage them to draw pictures and diagrams as they propose and discuss their models.

Hypothesis Help

Review how a negative feedback system differs from a positive feedback system. Hypotheses should include the process, the product, and how the product of the process inhibits the process.

Lab Extension

Directed

Suggest a negative feedback system to the students and challenge them to describe its parts and how it works. Examples may include the mechanism in a toilet tank, population growth, and supply and cost of a popular item.

Time Required

■ 30–50 minutes

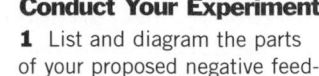

Identifying a Negative Feedback System

WHAT YOU WILL DO Locate a negative feedback system in your everyday environment. Identify and analyze the elements of the system.

SKILLS YOU WILL USE Predicting, observing and recording data, organizing

WHAT YOU WILL NEED Sketching paper

Background Information

A home heating system is an example of a system controlled by negative feedback. The flow of heat through a house is controlled to keep room temperatures at a steady level. The mechanism of control is a thermostat—a thin coil made of two different metals fastened together. Because the different metals expand and contract at different rates, the coil bends and unbends with changes in air temperature. The moving coil pushes on an electric switch that turns the heat source on or off.

The four elements of a negative feedback system are 1) the process that is controlled (in this case the flow of heat); 2) the feedback signal (here the measured air temperature); 3) the feedback mechanism (in this case the thermostat and switch); and 4) the outcome (here a steady level of desired heat measured as a constant room temperature).

Propose a Hypothesis

Find a system in your everyday life that you think is controlled by negative feedback. Propose a hypothesis about how accurately this model represents a negative feedback system in your body.

Conduct Your Experiment

1 List and diagram the parts of your proposed negative feedback system.
2 Identify the process that is controlled.
3 Identify the feedback signal.
4 Identify the feedback mechanism.
5 Identify the outcome of the system.

Analyze Your Data

How do the parts of your negative feedback system interact?

Draw Conclusions

Analyze a human body system that involves negative feedback. Are the same elements present in the body mechanism that were present in the heating system example? Diagram them in the same way.

Design a Related Experiment

Design a model of a negative feedback system that you could build yourself.

Lab: Identifying a Negative Feedback System

Objective: To select a negative feedback system in everyday life and analyze how it works

My hypothesis:

Analyze Your Data

Answers will vary but should show the product of the process inhibiting or stopping the process.

Draw Conclusions

Diagrams should show elements in the body system that function in the same way as elements in the heating system.

33.3 Health of the Endocrine System

Mom's milk, Mom's touch

Mother's milk protects a baby against disease. Immune factors made by a mother's body are passed to her child with each drop of milk. Besides the content of her milk, the touch of a mother or any other caring human also helps to keep a baby healthy. Stroking a baby starts a chain of hormonal messages that help the baby's cells absorb more food.

What you'll learn

IDEAS
- To distinguish between disorders of the endocrine system
- To assess the dangers of steroid use

WORDS
diabetes mellitus

ENDOCRINE SYSTEM DISORDERS

Out of control

When the messages carried by the endocrine system are not sent or received, the body cannot function properly. One of the most serious endocrine disorders is diabetes mellitus (dy-uh-BEE-teez ME-luh-tus). **Diabetes mellitus** is a disorder in which the body is unable to control blood sugar levels. Diabetes may lead to a dangerously high level of glucose in the blood, which can result in a coma or even death. The kidneys of a person who suffers from diabetes release large amounts of glucose in the urine. Sugar in the urine is one of the main warning signs of diabetes mellitus.

There are two main types of diabetes mellitus. The more serious type, Type I diabetes, is also called juvenile diabetes because it usually develops during childhood. In Type I diabetes, the beta cells of the islets of Langerhans do not produce insulin. The treatment for Type I diabetes requires regular injections of insulin and a carefully controlled diet. In the past, insulin was obtained from animal sources. Today, human insulin can be made in bacteria through genetic engineering.

Type II diabetes usually develops in people over the age of 40. In Type II diabetes, the beta cells may produce insulin, but body cells do not respond to the hormone properly. As a result, not enough glucose is removed from the blood. Type II diabetes is treated with exercise, medication, and a carefully controlled diet. People with either type of diabetes are advised to control the intake of sugary foods in their diets.

Disorders of other endocrine glands can cause problems in development or metabolism. For example, when the thyroid gland does not produce enough thyroid hormone—a condition called hypothyroidism—the body's metabolism slows down. A person feels sluggish and cold and may gain weight easily. In hyperthyroidism, the opposite condition, a person feels irritable and has high body temperature, sweating, weight loss, and high blood pressure.

Long-term stress can be harmful to your body because of the effects on the endocrine system. Short-term stress causes the adrenal glands to secrete epinephrine and norepinephrine. These two protein hormones are involved in what is called the "fight or flight" response. This response helps the body in an emergency by increasing alertness and providing a

FIGURE 33.9
Human insulin made by genetically engineered bacteria, is being packaged. What is the advantage of using human insulin to treat diabetes, as opposed to using insulin from other animals? ❶

Chapter 33 Endocrine and Reproductive Systems **801**

❶ ENGAGE

Use the Visual

Have students study the photograph that opens the section. Explain that babies respond to hormones that are stimulated by touch. Ask:

- **How do you think the babies of other mammals are likely to be affected by their mother's touch?** (The response will be similar.)

Quick Activity

Provide students with glucose test strips and small containers containing a mixture of sugar, water, and yellow food coloring. Tell students the solution models urine. Explain that diabetes is often diagnosed by testing urine for the presence of glucose. Explain how the test strips indicate the presence of glucose. Then have students use their test strips to find out if glucose is present in their samples.

STUDENT RESOURCES

From the Teacher's Resource Package, use:
- Section Review 33.3, Activity Recordsheet 33-2, Critical Thinking Exercise 33, and Enrichment Topic 33-1 from Unit Review Module
- Consumer Applications 33-1

TECHNOLOGY RESOURCES

Relevant technology resources include:
- Spanish Student Edition CD-ROM
- Teacher's Resource Planner CD-ROM
- How Your Body Works CD-ROM

❶ The insulin will be distributed to humans.

TEACH

 Do It! **TEAM WORK**

Can You Raise Your Pulse Rate?

Analyze Your Results

1 The pulse rate should increase under stress.
2 An increase in pulse rate means more blood is being oxygenated, which provides a burst of energy for the "fight or flight" response.

 STS

Because of health risks posed by prolonged use of steroids, the use of anabolic steroids is banned in most sporting events.

 Using Prior Knowledge To practice strategies for effective reading, use pages 69-70 in *Super Read!*

ASSESS

Evaluate Understanding

Have students create a written or visual summary of this section that identifies disorders of the endocrine system and their effects on the body.

Reteach

List the following on the board: *Type I diabetes, stress, Type II diabetes, hypothyroidism, steroid use,* and *hyperthyroidism.* Ask volunteers to explain how each condition affects the body.

802

 **Do It!** **bioSURF**

Can You Raise Your Pulse Rate?

Stress can affect your circulatory system. Your pulse can give you an indication of how your heart is doing. You can monitor your heart rate if you . . .

Try This

1 Follow your teacher's directions to find, measure and record your pulse rate.
2 To check your results, take your neighbor's pulse rate.
3 Visualize an upsetting situation such as a surprise quiz. Take your pulse again.

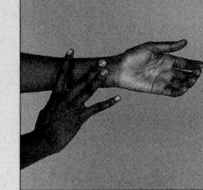

Analyze Your Results

1 How did your pulse rate change?
2 How can you explain the change in your pulse rate?

 **SUPER READ!**

burst of energy. Epinephrine and norepinephrine do this by raising the blood pressure and the blood glucose levels. When stress occurs over a long period of time, the adrenal glands secrete steroid hormones instead of the two protein hormones. Long-term exposure to steroid hormones can cause increased blood pressure and a suppressed immune system.

To maintain the health of your endocrine system, your body needs proper diet, exercise, and rest. Your diet needs to contain adequate protein and lipids to make all the various protein and steroid hormones. Exercise and rest help you manage stress and prevent overproduction of the adrenal hormones. You can also help your endocrine system by being aware of the symptoms of a disorder, such as diabetes or hypothyroidism, and seeking prompt treatment if necessary.

 What are the functions of the endocrine system?

802 *Unit 8 Human Biology*

ISSUES IN BIOLOGY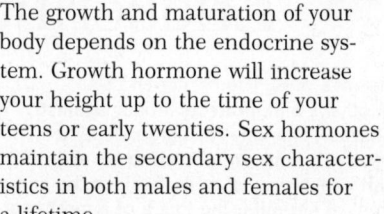

Dangers of steroids

The growth and maturation of your body depends on the endocrine system. Growth hormone will increase your height up to the time of your teens or early twenties. Sex hormones maintain the secondary sex characteristics in both males and females for a lifetime.

Sometimes young people are tempted to "boost" their development by abusing drugs that affect the endocrine system. Anabolic steroids are hormones that athletes and bodybuilders sometimes use illegally to stimulate the growth of muscles and increase strength and performance.

Steroid use can disrupt many body systems and eventually cause liver and heart disease. In males it can cause testes to shrink and female sex characteristics to develop. Females who take steroids may stop menstruating and develop male sex characteristics, such as increased body hair and a deep voice. Young people who take steroids can develop serious health problems that can lead to an early death.

CHECKPOINT 33.3

1. Name and describe two disorders of the endocrine system.
2. How can steroids affect human health?
3. Critical Thinking A friend of yours is thinking about using steroids to build bigger muscles. What could you say to discourage this person?

Build on What You Know
4. How is genetic engineering used to produce insulin? *(Need to jog your memory? Revisit relevant concepts in Chapter 9, Section 9.2.)*

CHECKPOINT 33.3

1. Type I diabetes mellitus: insulin is not produced and regular insulin injections are necessary; Type II diabetes mellitus: insulin is produced but cells do not respond, and a carefully controlled diet is required
2. Steroid use can cause liver and heart disease, change sex characteristics in both males and females, and cause serious health problems that can lead to early death.
3. Making decisions Discourage steroid use by pointing out the health risks and the reduction of sex characteristics.
4. Genes that control insulin production in humans are inserted into bacteria, which can then produce the hormone.

33.4 Reproduction

Many are called—one is chosen
A drop of human semen may contain five million sperm cells. Most of the sperm cells die as they race toward an egg. Many sperm cells live to lock onto the egg's surface, as shown in this photomicrograph. As soon as one sperm breaks through the egg's coating, the egg secretes a substance that prevents other sperm cells from entering.

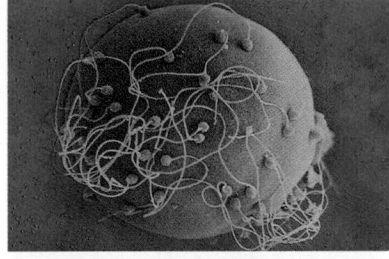

What you'll learn

IDEAS
• To distinguish between the human male and female reproductive systems
• To describe the human female reproductive cycle

WORDS
eggs, sperm, testes, penis, ovary, uterus, ovarian cycle, menstrual cycle, ovum, ovulation, menstruation

REPRODUCTION IN ANIMALS

And so on . . .

If a species is to survive, individual members of the species must reproduce, or make offspring. In humans and other multicellular animals, the body system that accomplishes this task is the reproductive system. The reproductive system uses hormones to trigger sexual maturity so that an organism is physically able to reproduce. The reproductive system also produces the cells that develop into the new individual. In some organisms, the reproductive system provides a place for the new individual to grow and develop.

Some animals, such as sponges and cnidarians, can reproduce asexually. Each individual can grow a new individual from body cells. Only one parent is required. The result is an offspring that is genetically identical to the parent.

In animals that reproduce sexually, the reproductive system produces sex cells called gametes (GAM-eets). Recall from Chapter 5 that gametes are haploid sex cells that contain only half of the normal number of chromosomes. Females produce large gametes called **eggs.** Males produce much smaller gametes called **sperm.**

Sexual reproductive systems can vary widely from one type of animal to another. For example, some annelids have separate sexes but do not have specialized organs to produce gametes. The gametes are made by cells in the body cavity and leave the body through excretory pores. In insects, males have organs that produce sperm, and a system of ducts and storage vesicles that release the sperm during mating. Female insects have organs that produce eggs, and ducts that carry the eggs to a body opening where fertilization can occur.

Vertebrates, such as birds and mammals, also have complex reproductive systems. Males have sex organs that produce sperm and a system of ducts

FIGURE 33.10
How does this sea anemone, a cnidarian, reproduce? ❶

Chapter 33 Endocrine and Reproductive Systems **803**

STUDENT RESOURCES

From the Teacher's Resource Package, use:
■ Section Review 33.4 from Unit 8 Review Module

TECHNOLOGY RESOURCES

Relevant technology resources include:
■ Spanish Student Edition CD-ROM
■ Teacher's Resource Planner CD-ROM
■ How Your Body Works CD-ROM

❶ ENGAGE

Consider the Big Idea

Have students read The Big Idea! at the top of the page. Explain that the reproductive system is controlled by hormones from the endocrine system.

Use the Visual

Have students study the photograph that opens the section. Explain that although millions of sperm are produced by a male's body, only one can fertilize the egg. Ask:

■ **What is the advantage of releasing millions of sperm instead of just one?** (A greater number of sperm increases the chance that one will fertilize an egg.)

Check Prior Knowledge

To assess students' knowledge about animal reproduction, ask:

■ **What happens during the process of fertilization?** (The egg cell and sperm cell of an organism join to form a zygote.)

Teacher Demo

Use a microprojector to display a slide of an ameba or other protozoan reproducing by binary fission. Ask:

■ **What type of reproduction is being shown?** (Asexual reproduction by binary fission)
■ **What kinds of animals reproduce this way?** (One-celled animals)

❶ Asexually

Use the Visual

Have students study Figure 33.11. Relate the release of millions of eggs by the fishes to the release of millions of sperm by the human male discussed in the section opening text. Explain that releasing large numbers of gametes helps increase an organism's chances of successful reproduction. Ask:

■ **What happens to most of the eggs released by the fish?** (They will die or be eaten by predators.)

Discuss

Review with students the concepts of internal and external fertilization. Ask:

■ **Which organisms shown in the photographs in this section use external fertilization?** (Fishes)

■ **Which organisms use internal fertilization?** (Penguin, kangaroo)

 Language Arts

Have students look up the origins of the terms *testes, testicle,* and *testosterone* and explain how the terms are related.

FIGURE 33.11
Why might the fishes shown above release large numbers of eggs at one time when they reproduce? ❶

FIGURE 33.12
A penguin's egg is fertilized internally but develops externally. What do you think the male penguin in the photo above is doing with the developing egg? ❷

FIGURE 33.13
In some mammals, such as the kangaroo, development of the young takes place both internally and externally. Where are the kangaroo's eggs fertilized? ❸

that carry the sperm out of the body when needed. Females have sex organs that produce and transport eggs. Both male and female sex organs produce hormones to control sexual function. As you can see above in *Figure 33.11,* some vertebrates, such as fishes, reproduce externally. The female lays eggs to be fertilized outside of her body. Other vertebrates, such as those in *Figures 33.12* and *33.13,* fertilize eggs internally. The female either lays the fertilized eggs, or the young develop inside her body.

REPRODUCTION IN HUMANS

Dynamic duos

Humans, like other mammals, reproduce sexually. Each individual has a reproductive system made up of either male or female reproductive organs. Production of eggs, fertilization, and development all take place inside structures of the female reproductive

system. The function of the male reproductive system is to produce sperm cells and deliver them to the female reproductive system.

Male reproductive organs
Figure 33.14 shows the human male reproductive system. The **testes** (singular: *testis*) are the male organs that produce sperm cells and the hormone testosterone. Each male has two testes. At puberty the testes begin to produce large amounts of testosterone, starting sperm cell production and the development of secondary sex characteristics.

The testes are inside a sac called the scrotum. Before birth, a male's testes are inside the pelvic cavity. The testes move down into the scrotum just before birth. Located outside the body cavity, the scrotum protects the testes and keeps them slightly cooler than body temperature. The cooler temperature is important for sperm cell development and survival.

804 *Unit 8 Human Biology*

❶ Because the eggs are fertilized externally, many will die or be eaten before they develop.
❷ He is protecting the egg and keeping it warm.
❸ Eggs are fertilized inside the mother.
❹ Penis and testes

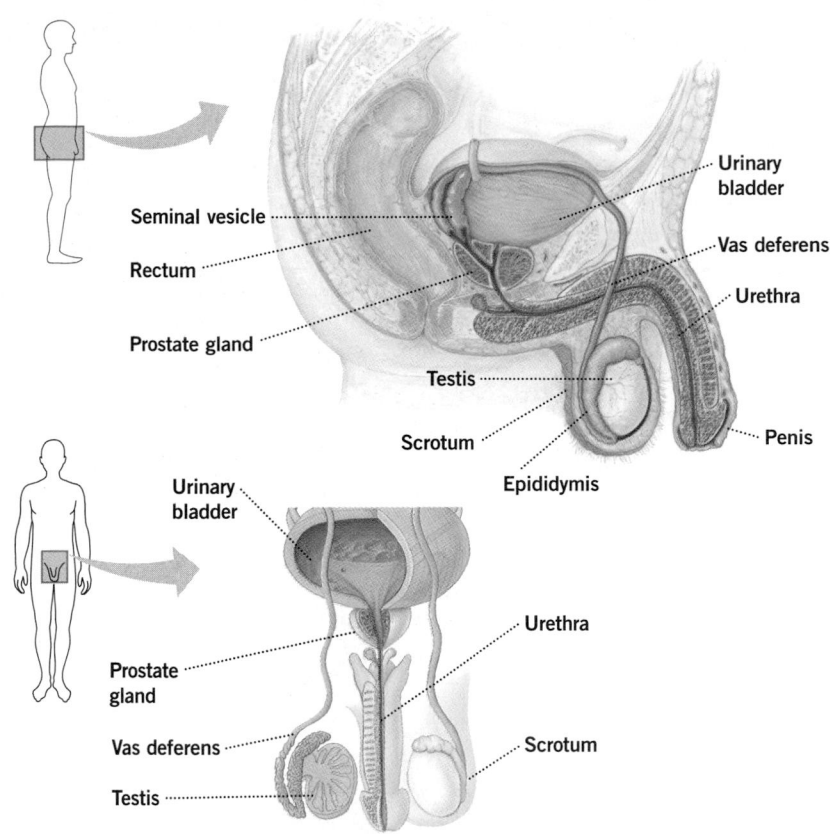

FIGURE 33.14
Male Reproductive Structures

What are the major organs of the male reproductive system? **4**

Seminal vesicle

Rectum

Prostate gland

Urinary bladder

Vas deferens

Urethra

Testis

Scrotum

Penis

Epididymis

Urinary bladder

Prostate gland

Vas deferens

Testis

Urethra

Scrotum

Each testis is made of tightly coiled structures called seminiferous tubules. Among the tubules are cells that produce testosterone. In the tubules, specialized diploid cells undergo meiosis to produce haploid sperm cells. As a result of meiosis, each specialized diploid cell forms four equal-sized sperm cells.

After meiosis, a developing sperm cell undergoes many changes. It first forms a long flagellum, or tail. Soon after the flagellum forms, the haploid nucleus condenses and becomes longer, forming the head. A tightly packed area of mitochondria forms between the head and tail. During its development, the sperm cell loses most of its cytoplasm. In *Figure 33.15* you can see the mature sperm cells that result from all of these changes.

Mature sperm are stored for a time in a coiled tube called the epididymis. The epididymis lies alongside each testis inside the scrotum.

For an egg to be fertilized, a sperm cell must leave the male and enter the reproductive system of the female. This occurs during sexual intercourse. The **penis** is the male organ that delivers sperm cells during intercourse.

Sperm cells from a male's testes travel from the epididymis through the vas deferens to the urethra in the penis. Strong contractions of the smooth muscles lining the vas deferens force semen through the urethra and out of the penis. Semen consists of sperm cells, fluids made by several glands such as the prostate gland, and fructose, which is an energy source for sperm cells.

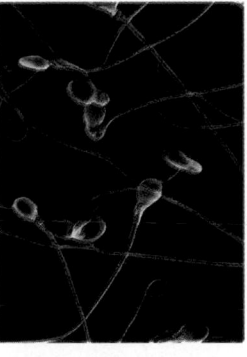

FIGURE 33.15
What parts of these mature sperm can you identify? **5**

MULTICULTURAL PERSPECTIVE

Dr. Percy Julian (1899-1975), an African American chemist, used a type of steroid to synthesize testosterone and estrogen. These synthetic hormones are now used to treat diseases and some forms of cancer. Using synthetic sex hormones as models,

Dr. Julian synthesized cortisone which is used as a treatment for allergies, rheumatoid arthritis, and certain cancers. Before Dr. Julian's work, only the wealthy could afford cortisone.

Use the Visual

Have students study Figure 33.14. Review each structure and its function. Then trace the path of sperm from the testes to the outside of the body. Ask:

■ **Which part of the male reproductive system is located outside the body? Why?** (The scrotum; to keep the testes and sperm cool)

Explain

Point out that the prostate gland secretes a thin, slightly alkaline fluid. This fluid, along with the fluid secreted by the seminal vesicles and Cowper's gland, is called seminal fluid. Seminal fluid is the liquid in which sperm swim.

Teacher Demo

Use a microprojector to show students prepared slides of a sperm cell. Identify the parts of the sperm cell and have students make a labeled sketch of the cell. Also show slides of cellular organisms such as *Euglena* that use flagella to move. Have students compare these organisms with the sperm cell. (The sperm cell is much smaller.)

Use the Visual

Have students study Figure 33.15. Explain that the sperm's nucleus, which is located in the head, contains genes. Just below the head is a packet containing mitochondria, which provide energy, and the tail, which propels sperm toward the egg.

❺ The head and the tail (flagellum)

33.4

Use the Visual

Have students study Figure 33.16. Explain that oviducts are also called Fallopian tubes. Explain that the fingerlike projections at the ends of the Fallopian tubes move in a wavelike motion that creates a current, which helps draw the egg into the tube. Ask:

- **What is the prime function of the fallopian tubes?** (To provide a path for the egg to travel between the ovary and the uterus)

 Language Arts

Explain to students that the term *ovary* comes from the Latin *ovarium*, which means "egg," and that *oviduct* comes from the Latin word for "egg" and the word *ductus,* which means "to lead."

Explain

Ask students to locate the urethra in Figure 33.16. Remind students that in males the urethra carries both sperm and urine to the outside of the body. However, in females, the urethra carries only urine. Thus, the urethra has no reproductive function in females.

 Science History

In the second century A.D., the Greek physician Galen proposed that a very small preformed baby existed within a woman's body. This theory was largely accepted until the seventeenth century, when scientists began to speculate that the preformed baby was carried in sperm cells.

❶ Ovaries, Fallopian tube, uterus, vagina and cervix

806

FIGURE 33.16

Female Reproductive Structures

What are the major organs of the female reproductive system? ❶

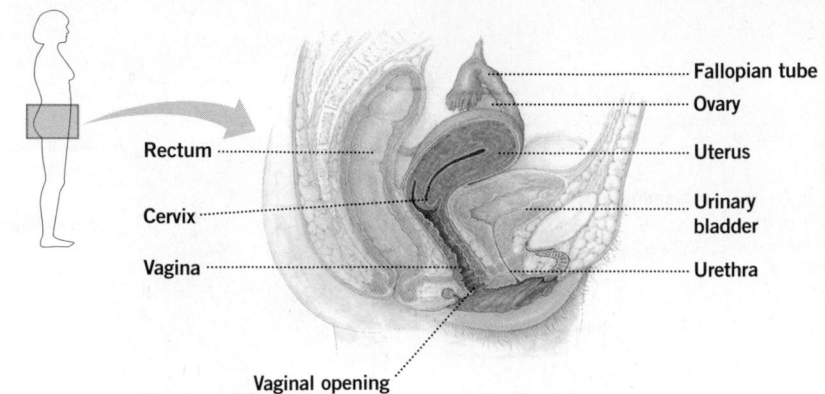

Rectum · Cervix · Vagina · Vaginal opening · Fallopian tube · Ovary · Uterus · Urinary bladder · Urethra

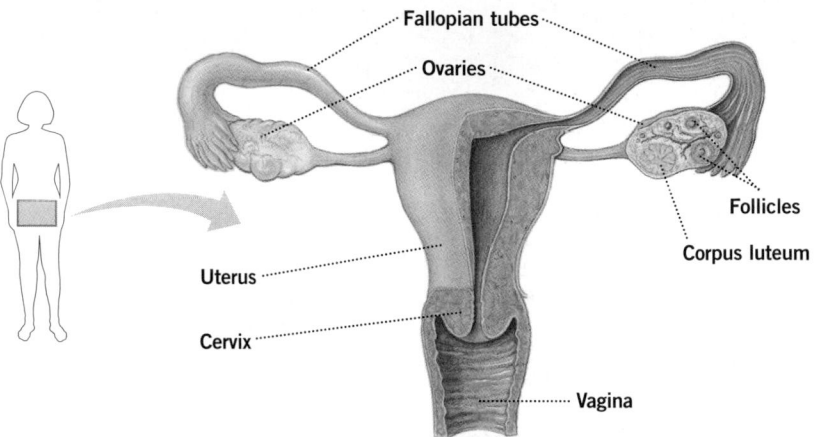

Fallopian tubes · Ovaries · Follicles · Corpus luteum · Uterus · Cervix · Vagina

Female reproductive organs
Two diagrams of the female reproductive system are shown in *Figure 33.16*. The **ovary** is the female organ that releases eggs and produces the hormones estrogen and progesterone. A female has two ovaries. The hormones produced by the ovaries control the female reproductive cycle and the development of secondary sex characteristics. Located close to each ovary is a structure called the fallopian tube, or oviduct. The fallopian tube is an organ that acts as a pathway through which an egg, released from an ovary, travels to the uterus.

The **uterus** is an organ with strong, muscular walls in which a fetus develops into an individual capable of surviving outside the mother's body. A structure called the cervix, located at the base of the uterus, connects the uterus with the vagina. The vagina is a muscular, tube-shaped organ that opens to the outside of the body. The vagina is sometimes called the birth canal because this is the opening in a female's body through which a baby is born. The vagina also provides the opening through which sperm can enter a female's body.

806   *Unit 8 Human Biology*

MEETING DIVERSE NEEDS

LEP Encourage LEP students to create a graphic that summarizes the functions of the structures in the male and female reproductive systems. Students may wish to record their information in both English and their native language.

Hearing Impaired Encourage students to look up the pronunciation and definitions of terms relating to human reproduction and compile a glossary.

THE FEMALE REPRODUCTIVE CYCLE

An egg a month?

A major function of the female reproductive system is to develop and release eggs. These events occur during the female reproductive cycle. The cycle is regulated by hormones secreted by the hypothalamus, the pituitary gland, and the ovaries.

Two sets of changes occur at the same time during the female reproductive cycle. The changes that take place in the ovary, including the development and release of an egg, are called the **ovarian cycle.** The ovarian cycle has two phases: the follicle phase and the luteal phase.

The changes that prepare the lining of the uterus to receive a fertilized egg are called the **menstrual cycle.** The lining of the uterus is called the endometrium. The menstrual cycle begins with the discharge of the uterine lining and an unfertilized egg.

The female reproductive cycle takes about 28 days, although the length of time can vary from 20 to 40 days. As you read about the cycle, you can use *Figure 33.18* on page 808 to follow the changes that occur in hormonal levels of the blood, in the ovaries, and in the endometrium.

The follicle phase of the ovarian cycle usually occurs during days 1 through 14 of a 28-day cycle. This phase begins when the hypothalamus stimulates the pituitary gland to release two hormones, FSH and LH. FSH stimulates a follicle to develop. Located in ovaries, follicles are structures where individual eggs develop.

Every female is born with a set number of potential eggs. In contrast, males produce sperm continuously. The ovaries contain 10,000 to 400,000 immature eggs at puberty. Immature eggs are diploid cells called oocytes. As an oocyte develops, it completes the first division of meiosis to form a mature egg, called an **ovum,** and a nonfunctional cell, called a polar body. The polar body later disintegrates. The ovum has a large amount of cytoplasm that contains stored food.

An oocyte matures into an ovum in a follicle. As the ovum matures, other cells of the follicle release estrogen, stimulating the endometrium to grow new tissue and blood vessels. This process prepares the uterus for receiving a fertilized egg.

As the follicle develops, it releases increasing amounts of estrogen. When the estrogen in the body reaches a critical level, the hypothalamus triggers the pituitary gland to release an increased amount of LH and FSH. This event usually occurs around days 12 to 14 of a 28-day cycle.

The high amount of LH stimulates the follicle to release an ovum. You can see an ovum being released from a follicle in *Figure 33.17*. This process is called **ovulation.** After ovulation, the ruptured follicle develops into a structure called the corpus luteum.

The formation of the corpus luteum begins the luteal phase of the ovarian cycle, which usually lasts from about day 15 until the end of the cycle. The corpus luteum releases large amounts of progesterone and estrogen. High levels of progesterone and estrogen have a negative feedback effect. The high levels stop the hypothalamus from signaling the pituitary gland to release LH and FSH. The increasing levels of progesterone and estrogen also cause the endometrium to grow even thicker.

The ovum released at ovulation moves through a fallopian tube to the uterus. The ovum is in the fallopian tube for approximately three days. During this time, fertilization may occur. If the ovum is fertilized, it completes a second meiotic division. The fertilized ovum becomes embedded in the

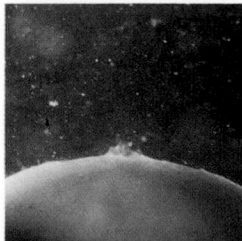
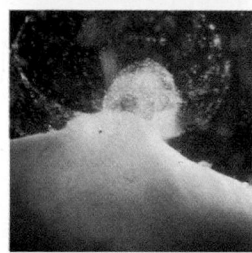
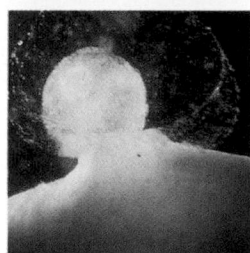

FIGURE 33.17
As shown in these photos, an ovum is released from an ovary during ovulation. What hormonal changes take place during these events? ❷

At Risk Have students work with a partner to make two flowcharts: one tracing the path of an egg through the female reproductive system assuming implantation occurs and a second tracing the stages involved in the female reproductive cycle.

❷ The high amount of LH stimulates the follicle to release the egg; then the corpus luteum develops and releases hormones to signal the pituitary to stop producing LH and FSH.

Explain

Point out that a human egg is about 0.14 mm in diameter; however, an ovum has almost 200,000 times the volume of a sperm. This larger size is necessary because the egg contains food needed by the developing zygote until it can implant itself in the uterus. The sperm must simply supply the genetic material to the egg.

✚ Language Arts

Have students look up the meaning of the prefix "men" or "meno" and relate its meaning to the terms *menstruation*, *menarche,* and *menopause.*

Think Critically

After students review the stages of the menstrual cycle, ask:

■ **Why is the menstrual cycle constantly repeated?** (Possible student responses: to provide many opportunities to renew the species; to constantly refurbish the endrometrium. Accept all reasonable answers.)

Clarify Misconceptions

Some students may believe that a disruption in the menstrual cycle is always an indication of pregnancy. Explain that while pregnancy does disrupt the menstrual cycle, other factors such as stress or illness can also disrupt the cycle. If the menstrual cycle is disrupted for more than a week, it may be a sign of illness and a doctor should be consulted.

Use the Visual

Have students study Figure 33.18. Ask:

- **What two hormones are present at the highest levels just before ovulation?** (LH, FSH)
- **When does the amount of progesterone peak?** (During the luteal phase)

Clarify Misconceptions

Explain that even though the average menstrual cycle is 28 days, the cycle length can vary. A cycle length anywhere from 21 to 30 days can be consistent and normal for some women. Also, the cycle length can vary for an individual, with some cycles being 21 days and others being 28 or 30 days.

ASSESS

Evaluate Understanding

Make overhead transparencies of the male and female reproductive systems with numbers in place of the labels. Have students identify each numbered structure and its function. Then ask them to make a flowchart that traces the path of the sperm and egg through the respective systems.

Reteach

List the following terms on the board: *menstrual-flow phase, follicle phase,* and *luteal phase.* Have students contribute to a list of the major changes that occur during each phase. Then review the functions of the organs of the male and female reproductive systems.

FIGURE 33.18
The hormones LH, FSH, progesterone, and estrogen control the female reproductive cycle. On what day does each hormone peak? ❶

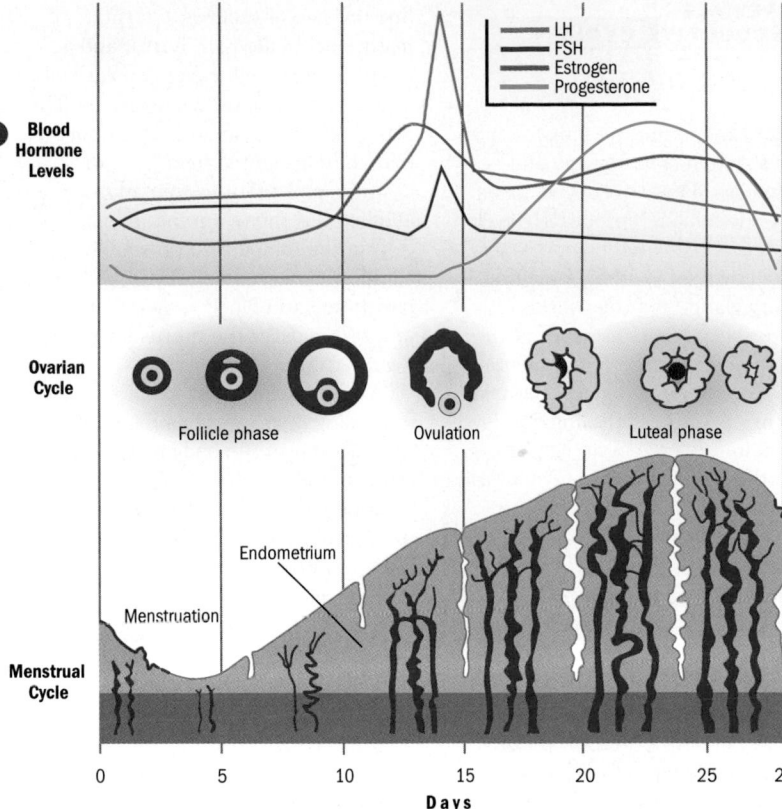

endometrium, resulting in pregnancy. The female reproductive cycle is interrupted.

If the ovum is not fertilized, the corpus luteum disintegrates, which results in decreasing levels of estrogen and progesterone. The drop in these two hormonal levels decreases the blood supply to the endometrium. This results in the breakdown of excess endometrial tissue.

The disintegrating endometrial tissue and the unfertilized ovum leave the body in a process called **menstruation** (men-stroo-AY-shun). Menstruation generally lasts from three to seven days. The first day of menstruation is the first day of the female reproductive cycle.

The cycle begins when a female reaches puberty, usually between ages 10 and 16. It continues until menopause—the hormonal changes that lead gradually to the cessation of the female reproductive cycle.

CHECKPOINT 33.4

1. Contrast the structures of the human male and female reproductive systems.
2. Describe the physical and hormonal changes that take place during the female reproductive cycle.
3. **Critical Thinking** What are some of the evolutionary advantages and disadvantages of internal fertilization and development?

Build on What You Know

4. Why do sperm cells contain many mitochondria? *(Need to jog your memory? Revisit relevant concepts in Chapter 4, Section 4.3.)*

808 *Unit 8 Human Biology*

CHECKPOINT 33.4

1. Male: vas deferens carries sperm produced in testes to urethra in penis. Female: Fallopian tubes carry eggs produced in ovaries to uterus, with cervix leading to vagina
2. Ovary: FSH stimulates egg development, LH stimulates release to oviduct; Uterus: hormones stimulate development of lining to receive egg

3. **Analyzing** Advantage: protection of sperm and developing fetus; Disadvantage: fewer offspring produced
4. To produce the ATP required to move the flagellum during travel to the Fallopian tubes

❶ LH and FSH, 14 days; progesterone, 23 days; estrogen 13 days

33.5 Human Development

Talking baby talk

Goo-gooing to a baby may make you feel a little foolish. But go ahead; babies pay attention to the slowed-down pace, big gestures, facial expressions, and simple words of baby talk. Even hearing-impaired infants are more responsive to the exaggerated motion of baby talk in sign language.

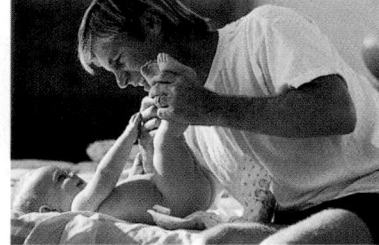

What you'll learn

IDEAS
- To describe the steps in the development of a human embryo
- To explain the birth process
- To describe the life stages of a human

WORDS
implantation, placenta, fetus, puberty

FERTILIZATION, DEVELOPMENT, BIRTH

1 + 1 = 1

The development of a human begins with fertilization, or the joining of an egg and a sperm. Fertilization occurs in the fallopian tubes, and it requires ovulation and sexual intercourse to have taken place. During ovulation, an egg is released from an ovary. The egg then moves into one of the two fallopian tubes. The egg stays in the tube for up to three days after ovulation.

During sexual intercourse, sperm-laden semen is deposited in the vagina. Millions of sperm swim rapidly from the vagina through the cervix, into the uterus, and on into the fallopian tubes. Although many sperm die along the way, some sperm live for up to three days in the fallopian tubes.

When a single sperm breaks through the outer membrane of an ovum, fertilization occurs. The sperm's nucleus enters the egg's cytoplasm and fuses with the egg's nucleus. The new cell formed as a result of fertilization is called a zygote.

As the zygote moves through the fallopian tube and undergoes a series of mitotic divisions called cleavage. During cleavage, the zygote divides again and again. By the fourth day, the zygote has become a solid ball of cells called a morula (MOR-yoo-luh). The morula continues to divide, forming a hollow ball of cells called a blastocyst (BLAS-toh-sist).

Within a week after fertilization, the blastocyst embeds itself in the uterine wall in a process called **implantation.** You can see the stages of fertilization, leading up to implantation, in *Figure 33.20* on page 810. If implantation is unsuccessful, the blastocyst will be discharged during the next menstrual flow. A pregnancy will not occur.

If implantation is successful, the blastocyst continues to develop into a structure called the gastrula. Three layers of cells form in the gastrula—the ectoderm, the mesoderm, and the endoderm. These layers are called germ layers because they later develop into all of the body's tissues and organs. The ectoderm, the outer germ layer, develops into the nervous system, skin, and sweat

EVERYDAY BIOLOGY

Funny, You Don't Look Like Twins

There are two types of human twins. Identical twins grow from one fertilized egg and share identical genes. Fraternal twins grow from two different fertilized eggs that develop at the same time, each with a unique set of genetic characteristics.

FIGURE 33.19

During the gastrula stage of embryo development (shown here in cross section), three distinct cell layers are formed.

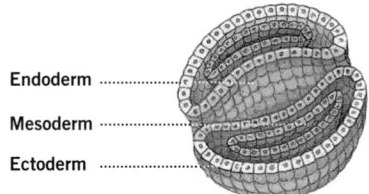

Endoderm ....

Mesoderm ....

Ectoderm ....

Chapter 33 Endocrine and Reproductive Systems **809**

① ENGAGE

Use the Visual

Have students study the photograph that opens the section. Explain that some changes babies experience as they develop are affected by environmental and social factors. Ask:

- **What other factor might affect a baby's development?** (Genetics)

Check Prior Knowledge

To assess students' knowledge about animal development, ask:

- **How does a zygote develop into an embryo?** (Zygote forms a blastula which develops into a gastrula. During gastrula stage, cell layers develop that give rise to different tissues and organs.)

Quick Activity

Obtain photographs of several stages of human embryonic development. Challenge students to sequence the photographs from the earliest stage to the latest stage. Tell students to check the accuracy of their sequence as they complete the section.

STUDENT RESOURCES

From the Teacher's Resource Package, use:
- Section Review 33.5, Activity Record-sheet 33-3, and Interpreting Graphics 33 from Unit 8 Review Module
- Lab 57: "Fetal Growth Rates"

TECHNOLOGY RESOURCES

Relevant technology resources include:
- Spanish Student Edition CD-ROM
- Teacher's Resource Planner CD-ROM
- How Your Body Works CD-ROM

Use the Visual

Have students study Figure 33.20. Ask:

- **Where does fertilization occur?** (In a Fallopian tube)
- **What does the zygote do before it reaches the uterus?** (Divide many times)
- **At what stage does implantation occur?** (Blastocyst)

Apply

Explain that *in vitro* fertilization may be used when couples are unable to produce a child. In this process, eggs are surgically removed from the mother's ovaries and placed in a container to which sperm is added. If fertilization occurs, the eggs are then placed in the woman's uterus to develop.

Discuss

Tell students that scientists learned that identical twins raised separately have many similarities in their personalities. Ask:

- **What factors might account for these similarities?** (The twins have the same genes and therefore many of the same traits.)

Explain

The protective function of the fluid that fills the amnion can be compared to the function of a hydraulic shock absorber on a car. When pressure is exerted on the shock absorber, the fluid inside absorbs the pressure. Similarly, fluid in the amnion absorbs pressure to protect the developing embryo.

FIGURE 33.20
Embryonic Implantation

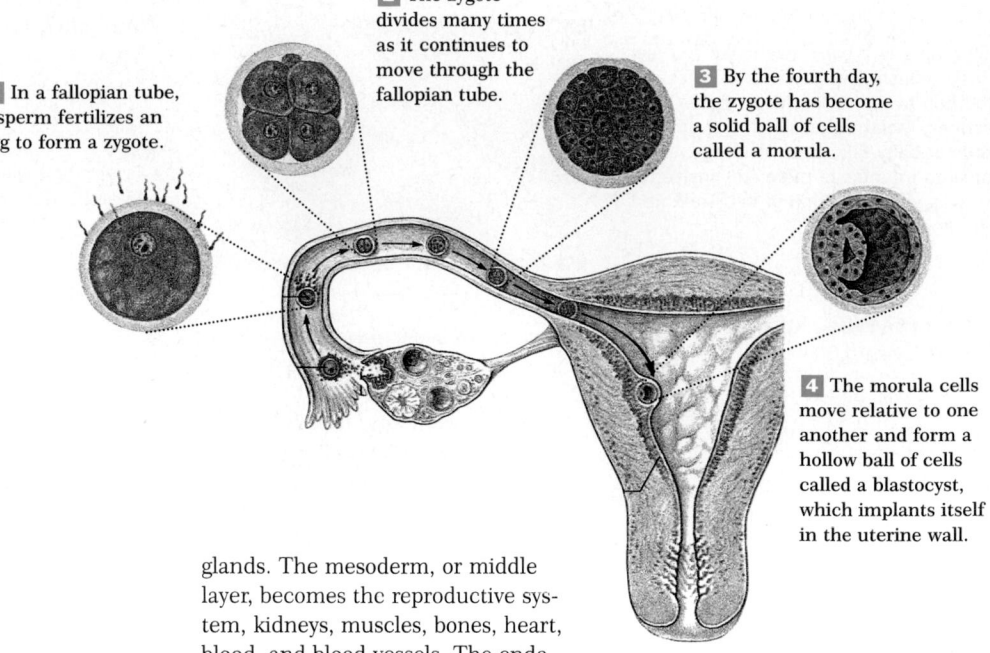

1 In a fallopian tube, a sperm fertilizes an egg to form a zygote.

2 The zygote divides many times as it continues to move through the fallopian tube.

3 By the fourth day, the zygote has become a solid ball of cells called a morula.

4 The morula cells move relative to one another and form a hollow ball of cells called a blastocyst, which implants itself in the uterine wall.

glands. The mesoderm, or middle layer, becomes the reproductive system, kidneys, muscles, bones, heart, blood, and blood vessels. The endoderm, or inner layer, forms the lungs, liver, linings of the digestive organs, and some endocrine glands.

After the development of the germ layers, the embryo is formed. The embryo has two outer supporting membranes, the amnion and the chorion. Along with some of the mother's endometrial cells, the chorion forms the placenta. The **placenta** (pluh-SEN-tuh) is an organ through which nutrients, oxygen, and wastes are exchanged between the mother and the developing embryo. The embryo is connected to the placenta by the umbilical cord, a tube containing blood vessels from the embryo. The amnion eventually fills with a fluid that forms a protective cushion around the embryo.

From the ninth week until birth, the developing embryo is called a **fetus.** Some stages of fetal development are shown in *Figure 33.21.* By

about three months, the fetus has started to develop most of the features of a human. What are the major developments at 5 weeks? At 22 weeks? ❶ Rapid growth of the fetus continues from the fourth month until birth.

After nine months of development, a surge in the amount of the pituitary hormone oxytocin in the mother starts the birth process, or labor. During labor, the uterus contracts strongly and rhythmically. The amniotic sac breaks, releasing its fluid. The cervix widens, allowing the fetus to pass through. The contractions become stronger and more frequent until the baby is delivered through the vagina. The baby begins to breathe on its own, and the umbilical cord is cut. After the baby is born, the uterus continues to contract for about 15 minutes to expel the placenta, now called the afterbirth.

MEETING DIVERSE NEEDS

At Risk Encourage students to create a visual that shows the sequence of development from the time an egg is fertilized until it implants on the uterine wall. Have students write a caption explaining how the egg changes from one stage to the next.

❶ At 5 weeks, heart is beating and hands and feet are developing; at 22 weeks, body is covered with downy hair and a waxy substance, infant has eyebrows.

FIGURE 33.21

Human Development

It takes 40 weeks for a fertilized egg to develop into a human infant. This amazing process involves millions of events that occur in a precisely timed and orderly sequence.

1 Most organs have begun to form in this embryo, which is about 5 weeks old and 1 centimeter (cm) long. The embryo's heart—the dark, rounded structure in the photo—is beating. Notice that both the arms and legs are developing.

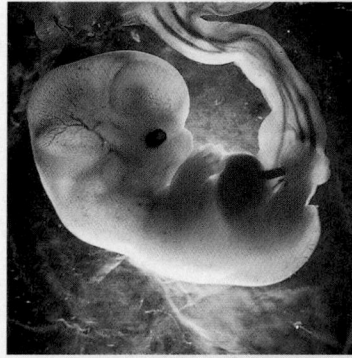

2 After 8 weeks, all body systems are present, and the embryo is called a fetus. Muscles move, the nervous system develops, and blood cell formation starts. This fetus is about 10 weeks old and weighs as much as an ordinary letter.

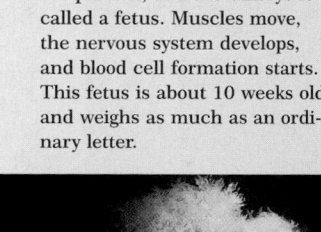

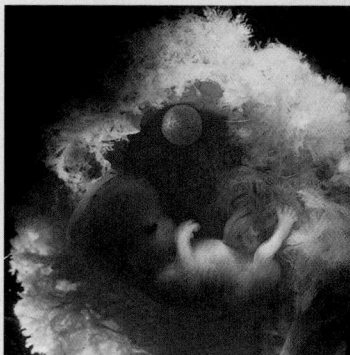

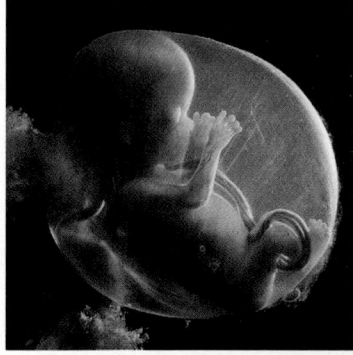

3 By 14 weeks, a fetus's hands, arms, legs, and feet have reached their birth proportions. Notice the well-developed eyes, nose, and ears. This fetus is about 6 cm long.

4 By 22 weeks, a fine downy hair—including eyebrows—and a waxy substance covers the body. The fetus is about 30 cm long and has regular sleep patterns. When awake, the fetus is active, and the mother can feel the movement.

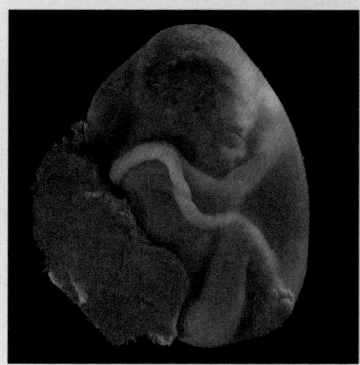

5 By 32 weeks, the fetus is fully developed. The bones have hardened, and the lungs and heart are ready for breathing air. As the fetus grows and runs out of space, it becomes less active. At birth, after 40 weeks, the average baby weighs 3.4 kilograms (kg).

Chapter 33 Endocrine and Reproductive Systems **811**

Use the Visual

Have students study Figure 33.21. Ask:

- **How long after fertilization does the embryo develop a heartbeat?** (5 weeks)
- **Which develops first, the nervous system or digestive system?** (Digestive system)
- **What structure enables nutrients and blood to pass from the mother to the fetus?** (The umbilical cord)

Apply

Explain that a developing embryo releases a hormone called human chorionic gonadotropin (HCG) which stops the menstrual cycle. The presence of this hormone in a female's urine can be used to indicate pregnancy.

 Math

Draw a very small dot on the board. Point out to students that the dot is much larger than a fertilized egg, which is about 0.14 mm in diameter. Then show them a doll that resembles a newborn baby. Tell them that the average length of a newborn baby is about 50 cm. Have them calculate the average rate of growth during the nine months of gestation. (About 55.5 mm per month) Ask them to calculate the average height of a 15-year-old if growth continued at the same rate. (Almost 10 meters or 33 feet) Point out that the fetus develops at a very fast rate.

33.5

Use the Visual

Have students study Figure 33.22. Explain to students that sometimes the baby is not in the correct position when birth is about to take place. For example, a birth in which the baby is delivered buttocks first is called a breech birth.

Build Writing Skills

Have students write a poem, rap, or descriptive essay that traces their embryonic development from implantation through birth. Encourage students to retain scientific accuracy in their writing.

Apply

Explain to students that the United States continues to have a relatively high infant death rate, given our medical technology. Many of these deaths are due to low birth weight. Have students find out how poor diet, smoking, alcohol, and the age of the mother affect the development of the fetus.

STS

Point out that amniocentesis helps doctors detect both chromosomal disorders such as Down syndrome and developmental problems. By diagnosing problems during pregnancy, doctors can prepare parents in advance for any special care or surgical procedures their baby may need.

Health of the fetus

Recent scientific and technological advances have enabled doctors to use a variety of diagnostic tools to monitor developing fetuses. For example, ultrasound waves directed at a pregnant woman's uterus can be used to make an image of a fetus. This technique allows doctors to check the growth and development of the fetus.

A method of checking for serious genetic diseases is called amniocentesis. In amniocentesis, a long needle is inserted into the amnion, and a sample of amniotic fluid is withdrawn. Fetal cells in the fluid are grown in a lab for two to four weeks. These cells can then be analyzed to determine if the fetus has any chromosomal abnormalities or genetic disorders. This test is usually performed around the sixteenth week of pregnancy.

Chorionic villi sampling is a technique that has been developed more recently for the same purpose. In this test, a small sample of chorionic tissue is removed from the placenta. The tissue is analyzed for genetic abnormalities. Chorionic villi sampling can be performed earlier in the pregnancy than amniocentesis, and the results can be obtained in a few hours. Both amniocentesis and chorionic villi sampling pose some risk to the fetus. With the help of genetic counselors, parents must weigh these risks against the chance of severe genetic abnormalities in the fetus.

FIGURE 33.22

Human Birth

During a normal birth, a baby is delivered headfirst through the vagina. The muscles of the uterus contract to push the baby out.

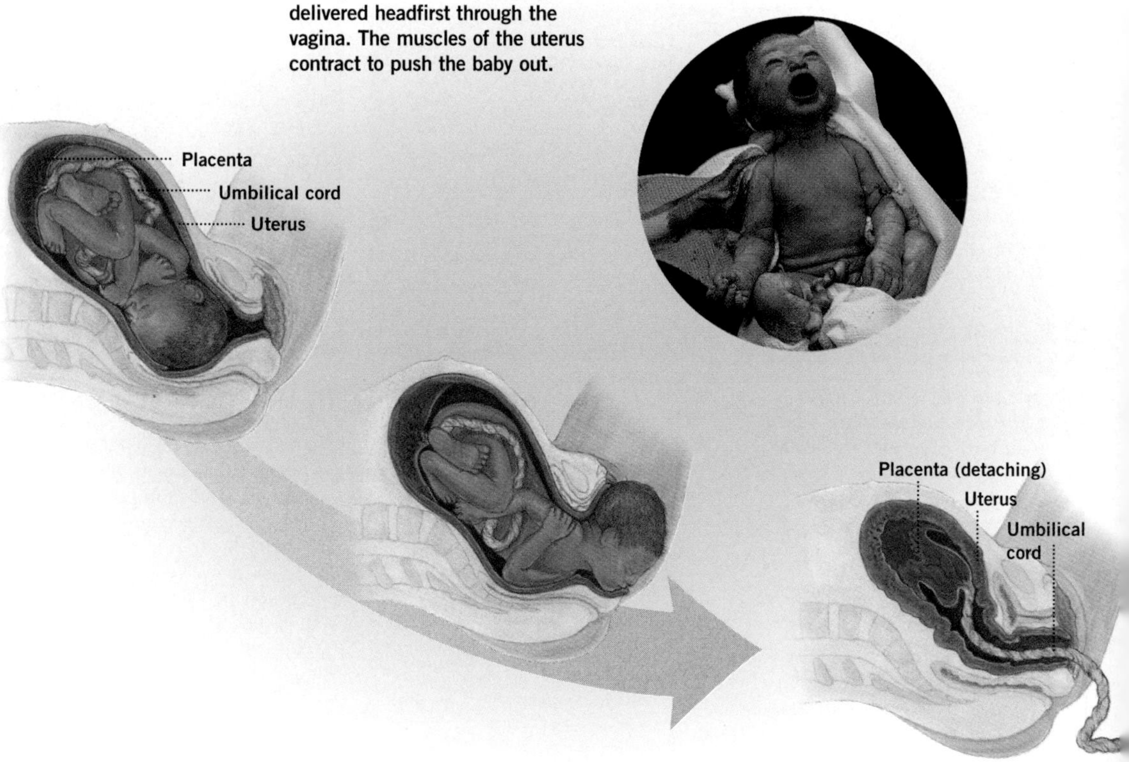

Placenta

Umbilical cord

Uterus

Placenta (detaching)

Uterus

Umbilical cord

812 *Unit 8 Human Biology*

MULTICULTURAL PERSPECTIVE

During the 1300s, the University of Sankore at Timbuktu was a major center of medical training. At about the same time, the Banjaro doctors of East Africa were performing Cesarean sections with the aid of anesthesia on a regular basis.

MEETING INDIVIDUAL NEEDS

Gifted Have students conduct research to find out how ultrasound waves are used to monitor the development of a fetus. Have them present their research as an oral report to the class.

STAGES OF LIFE

Not ageless

Birth is the end of fetal development, but humans continue to grow and change throughout life. Having developed from an infant into a child, and from a child into a young adult, you have experienced many of these changes already.

For the first two years after birth, an infant develops rapidly. During this time, the infant learns to sit up, stand, walk, eat solid foods, babble, perform simple reasoning, speak a few words, and imitate the actions of others. Height increases by about 20 cm per year. The brain grows to 75 percent of adult size by the age of 30 months.

From age 2 to age 5, a child learns to use the toilet and to master motor skills including the fine use of the hands as well as larger body movements. Language skills develop, and the child learns problem-solving and social skills. Do you remember how much you grew between the ages of 5 and 12? During this stage, a child grows to about 70 percent of his or her eventual adult height and weight. Vocabulary and reasoning skills increase, as do physical coordination and higher-level thinking skills.

Sometime between the ages of 10 and 16, puberty begins. **Puberty** is the human life stage during which the sexual organs mature and secondary sexual characteristics develop. You may recall that the hypothalamus secretes a hormone that triggers the release of two other hormones, LH and FSH. These hormones "tell" the testes to release testosterone or the ovaries to release estrogen and progesterone. Both sexes experience hair growth in the pubic area and under the arms. Females begin menstruating, and the breasts grow and the hips broaden. In males, facial hair develops, the voice deepens, and the muscles and genitals grow

FIGURE 33.23
What are some of the developmental changes occurring in each of the life stages shown here?

SUPER READ!

What Is the Average Human Growth Rate?

Humans grow and develop throughout life—but at different rates. You can compare the growth rates of human males and females when you . . .

Try This

1 Use the data in the table below to plot two graphs: *Mass by Age* and *Height by Age*. Use different colors for males and females.

Analyze Your Results

1 When is the increase in female mass the greatest? In male mass? When is the increase in female height the greatest? In male height?
2 Calculate the average growth rate in mass for males and for females between ages 8 and 18. Using the same age group, calculate the average growth rate in height for males and for females.
3 Explain the difference between the average male and female growth rates.

Average Human Mass and Height				
Age	Mass (kg)		Height (cm)	
	Female	Male	Female	Male
8	25	25	123	124
10	31	31	135	135
12	40	38	147	145
14	50	50	159	161
16	57	62	163	172
18	58	68	163	178

Build Writing Skills

Have students do library research or interview mothers with young children on the care of newborns. Have students present their reports to the class.

 Finding the Main Idea and Supporting Details
To practice strategies for effective reading, use pages 73-74 in *Super Read!*

 Do It!

What Is the Average Human Growth Rate?

Review with students how to graph data.

Analyze Your Results

1 Females; greatest mass increase is 12-14 years, greatest height increases are 8-10, 10-12, and 12-14 years: Males, greatest mass increases are 12-14 and 14-16 years, greatest height increase is 12-14 years.
2 Males; average mass increase is 11% per year, average height increase is 4% per year: Females; average mass increase is 9% per year, average height increase is 3% per year.
3 The average adult male is taller and heavier than is the average adult female and males start to grow rapidly later than females.

33.5

In the Community

Suggest that students use a local telephone directory to find out what services and centers are available for seniors in their area. Likely services will include recreational activities, meals, and in some cases nursing care. Accept all logical responses. Suggest that some students might wish to volunteer at a senior center.

ASSESS

Evaluate Understanding

List the section objectives on the board. Have students write a one-paragraph summary for each objective. Review the summaries as a class.

Reteach

On an overhead transparency, create a flowchart of the human life cycle beginning with fertilization and ending at about age 60. Be sure to include the stages leading to implantation, major points of development in the fetus, and stages following birth. Have volunteers suggest what details should be included at each stage.

814

Does your community have senior-citizen housing, an elderly day-care or drop-in center, or some other kind of facility especially for seniors? Most facilities for the elderly welcome visitors for volunteer work or just for conversation. What programs are offered by the facilities in your community? How do they accommodate the different needs of their patrons? Chart a typical day of a senior citizen served by one of these facilities. You can learn about issues of concern to senior citizens from the American Association of Retired Persons and the National Institute of Aging. Explore *http://body_systems.biosurf.com* to find out more about these organizations.

IN THE COMMUNITY
Making the Most of Long Life

larger. After puberty is complete, the body reaches its adult stage. In early adulthood, the body works at its peak efficiency. After about the age of 30, the body's functioning begins to decline slowly and gradually. Over time, the skin becomes less elastic, and the muscular, circulatory, and respiratory systems become less efficient. Reproductive functions also decline. Bodily changes leading to menopause in females usually begin between the ages of 45 and 50. After the age of 60, the decline in body functioning becomes more rapid. Eventually, important organs, such as the kidneys and the heart, begin to wear out. When the body can no longer function, natural death occurs.

FIGURE 33.24
Maintaining a healthy lifestyle can pay dividends in later life.

CHECKPOINT 33.5

1. Describe the events that occur from fertilization to development of an embryo.
2. Describe the human birth process.
3. List the developmental changes that occur during three life stages.
4. **Critical Thinking** Occasionally a zygote does not move into the uterus but instead attaches to the wall of a fallopian tube. Why might this be a dangerous situation for the mother?

Build on What You Know
5. Compare the development of a human fetus to that of a marsupial fetus. *(Need to jog your memory? Revisit relevant concepts in Chapter 27, Section 27.1.)*

814   *Unit 8 Human Biology*

CHECKPOINT 33.5

1. Zygote forms, divides many times to become a morula, which forms a blastocyst that implants into the uterine wall. Blastocyst develops germ layers after which embryo forms.
2. The baby is normally delivered headfirst through the vagina, as a result of uterine contractions.
3. Infancy: baby develops rapidly; ages 2-5, basic skills develop; puberty: sexual organs mature; adult to old age, body function declines.
4. **Analyzing** The Fallopian tube does not have adequate room for the baby to develop, causing the tube to rupture.
5. The human fetus is much more mature at birth.

33.6 Health of the Reproductive System

An answer to infertility
With in vitro fertilization, healthy eggs and sperm cells are removed from infertile couples and united in a laboratory. Four-celled embryos that result from the laboratory fertilization are implanted in the woman's uterus. The process succeeds in about one of five attempts.

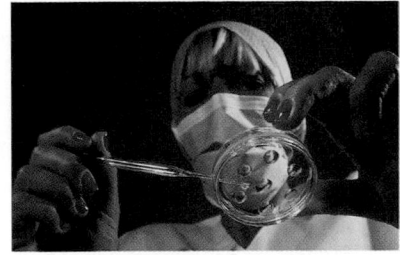

What you'll learn

IDEAS
• To describe disorders of the reproductive system
• To distinguish between sexually transmitted diseases

REPRODUCTIVE SYSTEM DISORDERS

Much can go wrong

In order to function correctly, a human reproductive system must be healthy. Unfortunately, a variety of disorders are possible. Some disorders result in infertility, or the inability to produce offspring. Other disorders result in pregnancy problems, illness, or even death.

In men, infertility can result from the production of too few sperm cells or the production of defective sperm cells that are unable to travel the distance to the fallopian tubes. Infertility in women can have many causes. Hormonal imbalances may prevent ovulation. Scarring of the fallopian tubes can physically block an egg from entering the uterus. This scarring can be caused by a pelvic infection or by a disease called endometriosis.

In endometriosis, parts of the uterine lining, the endometrium, migrate outside the uterus. This tissue thickens and bleeds each month as does the uterine lining, but it has no way to leave the body. Blood-filled cysts may appear in the abdomen. The cysts expand and contract each month, causing intense abdominal pain.

If a fertilized egg implants in a fallopian tube instead of in the uterus, an ectopic pregnancy occurs. A woman with an ectopic pregnancy will experience the physical changes of a normal pregnancy accompanied by severe abdominal pain. As the egg grows, the tube will rupture and massive internal bleeding will occur. Ectopic pregnancy is a medical emergency requiring immediate surgery.

The prostate gland is a gland near the base of the penis. The prostate often becomes enlarged as a man ages. An enlarged prostate may constrict the urethra so that a man is not able to pass urine. Prostate cancer is also a serious problem that can be deadly if not diagnosed and treated promptly. Regular prostate examinations can detect any problems.

Cancer may affect women's reproductive organs as well. Women should undergo a test called a Pap smear every year to check for cervical cancer. They should also perform a monthly breast self-examination to help spot any lumps that may be cancerous tumors. Any bleeding between periods, unusual abdominal pain, or masses in the abdomen should be reported to a physician, particularly if there is a family history of ovarian cancer.

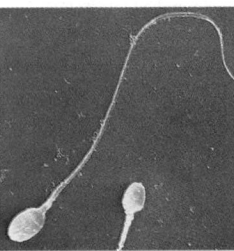

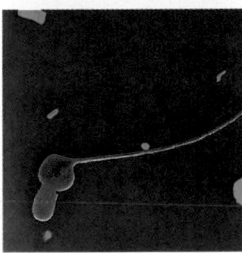

FIGURE 33.25
What differences can you see between the healthy sperm cell (top) and the defective sperm cell (bottom)? ❶

Chapter 33 Endocrine and Reproductive Systems **815**

TEACH

Science History

Syphilis is caused by the bacterium *Treponema pallidum*. In the late 1800s, Dr. William Hinton, an African American hematologist, developed a test for identifying syphilis before symptoms develop.

Build Writing Skills

TEAM WORK

Have small groups of students develop a poster on STDs. Each group should focus on a different disease. Posters should address the cause, symptoms, treatment, and prevalence.

LAB ZONE Think About It!

Comparing STD Occurrence

Analyzing the Table

2 Gonorrhea
3 A great increase until 1993, then a decrease.

ASSESS

Evaluate Understanding

Have students write each section head as a main idea. Have them write three details to support each statement.

Reteach

List on the board: *syphilis, AIDS, gonorrhea, chlamydia.* Have volunteers describe the cause of each STD. Have students also discuss the causes of reproductive disorders, such as endometriosis.

816

 LAB ZONE Think About It! **bioSURF**

Comparing STD Occurrence

The table below shows a summary of reported cases of STDs in the United States. Use the data in the table as you answer the following questions.

Analyzing the Table

1 Create a bar graph that shows the data in the table.
2 Which STD has a steady decline in reported cases in the time period shown?
3 How would you describe the trend in reported AIDS cases for the years shown?

Reported Cases of Selected STDs in the United States				
Disease	1985	1990	1993	1994
AIDS	8,249	41,595	103,533	78,279
Syphilis	27,131	50,223	26,498	20,627
Gonorrhea	911,419	690,169	439,673	418,068

FIGURE 33.26
A red ribbon has become a symbol of support for people living with AIDS.

SEXUALLY TRANSMITTED DISEASES

S-T-O-P STDs

Many diseases that affect the reproductive system are infections acquired through sexual contact. The infections are known as sexually transmitted diseases (STDs). Bacteria and viruses cause the most common STDs.

The STDs gonorrhea, chlamydia, and syphilis are caused by bacteria. They all can cause severe damage to the reproductive system and may lead to infertility. Women with untreated chlamydia or gonorrhea may develop an infection called pelvic inflammatory disease (PID). Prompt treatment with antibiotics is important to stop the spread of any of these STDs.

The most deadly STD is acquired immune deficiency syndrome (AIDS). Recall from Chapter 32 that AIDS is caused by HIV (human immunodeficiency virus), which can be transmitted through human body fluids. A variety of drugs can slow the course of AIDS, but a cure has not yet been found.

Viruses other than HIV can infect the reproductive system. The herpes virus causes painful genital sores that can last a week or two. The herpes virus remains in the body, leading to repeated outbreaks. Flat or cauliflower-shaped growths called genital warts are caused by the human papilloma virus. Removal of the warts by a physician is the only treatment.

The risk of contracting an STD can be greatly reduced by avoiding direct contact with the genitals and body fluids of an infected person. The use of condoms and spermicides during intercourse can reduce, but not eliminate, the risk. Abstinence, choosing not to have sexual intercourse, is the most effective way to avoid sexually transmitted diseases.

CHECKPOINT 33.6

1. Describe three disorders that affect the human reproductive system.
2. Which sexually transmitted diseases are caused by bacteria? By viruses?
3. **Critical Thinking** Why is it important to maintain the health of your reproductive system?

Build on What You Know

4. How does a virus reproduce in the human body? **(Need to jog your memory? Revisit relevant concepts in Chapter 14, Section 14.1.)**

? What do reproductive systems do?

816 *Unit 8 Human Biology*

CHECKPOINT 33.6

1. Endometriosis, in which uterine lining exists outside the uterus, can cause painful cysts. Prostate enlargement can interfere with urination. Cancer can affect the reproductive organs of both men and women.
2. Bacteria: gonorrhea, syphilis, and chlamydia; viruses: AIDS, herpes, and genital warts

3. **Making decisions** Maintaining a healthy reproductive system can reduce the risk of sexually transmitted diseases that can lead to infertility or death.
4. A virus invades and takes control of a host cell, replicates itself many times, and kills its host, releasing more viruses that invade other hosts.

Chapter 33 Review

 **THE BIG IDEA!** 33.1–33.3 The endocrine system controls long-lasting internal changes.
33.4–33.6 Reproductive systems make possible the continuation of life.

Sum It Up

Use the following summary to review the main concepts in this chapter.

33.1 Endocrine Control

- Fast-acting nerve impulses and slower-acting hormones control an animal's activities.
- Hormones control activities such as molting, metamorphosis, and milk production.

33.2 Human Endocrine System

- Hormones released from endocrine glands into the bloodstream are carried to target cells.
- The hormones produced by the pituitary gland control other endocrine glands.
- The hypothalamus and the pituitary gland trigger the release of sex hormones at puberty.
- Processes can be controlled by feedback from the products they produce. Insulin and glucagon control the level of glucose in the blood through negative feedback.

33.3 Health of the Endocrine System

- Diabetes is a disorder in which body cells do not produce or use insulin properly.
- Thyroid disorders affect metabolic rates.
- Adrenal glands produce hormones in response to short-term or long-term stress.

33.4 Reproduction

- Testes produce sperm, which are stored in the epididymis and released through the urethra.
- Ovaries produce estrogen and progesterone.
- During the ovarian cycle, an oocyte forms a mature egg, the lining of the uterus thickens, and an egg passes into the fallopian tubes.
- An unfertilized egg and extra uterine tissue are shed during menstruation.

33.5 Human Development

- A fertilized egg implanted in the uterus develops into three germ layers, plus an amnion and a chorion. The germ layers develop into the embryo; the amnion fills with fluid; the placenta exchanges materials between the embryo and the mother.
- The health of the developing fetus can be tested with ultrasound and amniocentesis.

33.6 Health of the Reproductive System

- Reproductive disorders can cause infertility.
- Sexually transmitted diseases (STDs) can damage the reproductive system and may lead to infertility. AIDS is an STD caused by the human immunodeficiency virus (HIV).

Use Terms and Concepts

Use each of the following words or terms in a complete sentence.
If you need to review a meaning, turn to the page indicated.

hormones (p. 794)
endocrine glands (p. 794)
hypothalamus (p. 796)
pituitary gland (p. 798)
feedback control (p. 799)

insulin (p. 799)
glucagon (p. 799)
diabetes mellitus (p. 801)
eggs (p. 803)
sperm (p. 803)
testes (p. 804)

penis (p. 805)
ovary (p. 806)
uterus (p. 806)
ovarian cycle (p. 807)
menstrual cycle (p. 807)
ovum (p. 807)

ovulation (p. 807)
menstruation (p. 808)
implantation (p. 809)
placenta (p. 810)
fetus (p. 810)
puberty (p. 813)

Review the Big Ideas

Before students begin the Chapter Review, you may wish to discuss main concepts from the Big Ideas in Chapter 33. Point out that the endocrine system controls many body functions, including reproduction. Hormones are produced in one part of the body and act on another part to control long-lasting internal changes. Sex hormones produced by the endocrine system control the reproductive system. The reproductive system enables parents to produce offspring that continue the species. Human males produce sperm to fertilize the eggs produced by females. Females carry the offspring in the uterus until birth.

Answers

1. sperm; penis
2. puberty
3. ovary; uterus
4. testes
5. egg; ovum
6. endocrine gland; hormone
7. placenta
8. False; implantation
9. True
10. False; ovarian cycle
11. True
12. True
13. False; hypothalamus
14. False; Insulin
15. True
16. Ductless endocrine glands release hormones into the blood stream; exocrine glands have ducts to direct secretions to a specific location.
17. When a protein hormone binds to receptors on target cells, it activates enzymes within the cells; steroid hormones enter the cells and act on specific sections of DNA, which affect protein production.
18. An egg travels through the Fallopian tube to the uterus. If the egg is fertilized, it attaches to the uterine lining; if it is not, it is shed during menstruation.
19. The amnion fills with a liquid that cushions the embryo. The chorion develops into the placenta, which exchanges materials between the mother and the embryo.
20. Insulin produced in beta cells lowers the glucose level in the blood; alpha cells produce glucagon, which stimulates the liver to convert stored glycogen into glucose; a rise in the glucose level triggers production of insulin.
21. Because sperm must travel

Use Your Word Power

COMPLETION **Write the word or phrase that best completes each statement.**

1. The epididymis stores _____ until they are expelled by muscle contractions of the _____ .

2. The development of secondary sex characteristics begins at _____ .

3. The fallopian tube carries gametes that are released by the _____ and move into the _____ .

4. At birth, the _____ move from the pelvic cavity to the scrotum.

5. The mature _____ that develops from an oocyte is called a(n) _____ .

6. The thymus is the ductless _____ that secretes the _____ thymosin.

7. The umbilical cord attaches the _____ to the embryo.

TRUE-FALSE **Write true if the statement is true. If the statement is false, replace the underlined word(s) to make the statement true.**

8. A zygote embeds itself in the uterine wall during <u>ovulation</u>.

9. <u>Type II diabetes mellitus</u> is usually controlled with diet, medication, and exercise.

10. There are two phases of the <u>menstrual cycle—</u> the follicle phase and the luteal phase.

11. The control of progesterone and estrogen production by the corpus luteum is an example of <u>negative feedback control</u>.

12. <u>Menstruation</u> occurs if an egg is not fertilized.

13. The <u>pituitary gland</u> controls the release of pituitary hormones.

14. <u>Glucagon</u> lowers the amount of blood sugar.

15. From the ninth week until birth, the developing embryo is called a <u>fetus</u>.

Show What You Know

16. What is the difference between endocrine and exocrine glands?

17. Compare the ways that protein hormones and steroid hormones control the activity of target organs.

18. Describe what happens to an egg during the luteal phase of the ovarian cycle.

19. What is the role of the amnion and chorion in the young embryo?

20. Explain how negative feedback controls the production of pancreatic hormones in the islet of Langerhans.

21. How does the structure of mature sperm cells support their function?

22. How do the adrenal glands respond differently to short-term and long-term stress?

23. How can doctors check for genetic disorders of a fetus?

24. **Make a Concept Map** Make a concept map that relates the endocrine system to the male and female reproductive systems.

Take It Further

25. **Applying Concepts** Diabetics avoid foods that are high in sugar. Why might a Type 1 diabetic keep a candy bar or orange juice nearby?

26. **Making an Analogy** In urban areas during rush hour, radio stations broadcast traffic reports. How are traffic reports similar to hormones? How do the reports act as a feedback control mechanism for the flow of traffic?

27. **Designing an Experiment** Women who live or work closely together may experience menstrual synchrony—menstruating at the same time. Suggest two experimental designs that could test the existence of menstrual synchrony.

---

to an egg, they are lightweight structures with a flagellum for locomotion and mitochondria to supply energy for the journey.

22. Hormones produced in response to short-term stress raise blood pressure and blood glucose, increasing alertness and energy. Steroid hormones produced in response to long-term stress can cause elevated blood pressure and suppression of the immune system.

23. Doctors can produce images with ultrasound waves; culture cells removed from the amniotic fluid; analyze tissue removed from the fetal portion of the placenta.

24. Concept maps should show the following: Hypothalamus → pituitary → FSH

28. Interpreting a Graph The dietary needs of women change when they are pregnant. The graph shows the increases in recommended dietary allowances for women who are pregnant. For which mineral is the increase most dramatic? How much extra calcium does a pregnant woman need? How much extra vitamin B-6 is recommended?

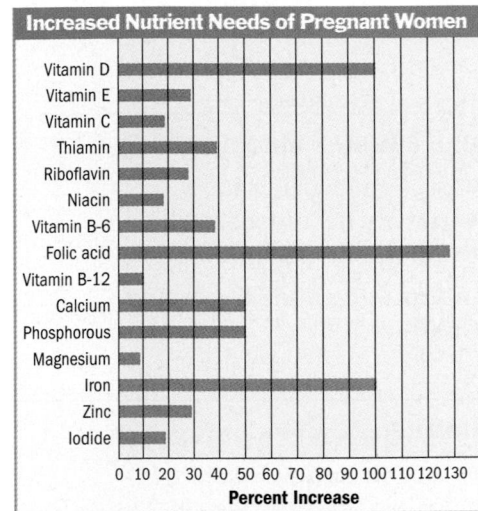

Increased Nutrient Needs of Pregnant Women

Vitamin D, Vitamin E, Vitamin C, Thiamin, Riboflavin, Niacin, Vitamin B-6, Folic acid, Vitamin B-12, Calcium, Phosphorous, Magnesium, Iron, Zinc, Iodide

0 10 20 30 40 50 60 70 80 90 100 110 120 130
Percent Increase

29. Analyzing Data The table shows what factors are involved in the regulation of some human endocrine glands. Which glands are regulated by external factors? internal factors? Using Figure 33.4, relate the functions of the glands to their source of regulation.

Endocrine Gland Regulation

Gland	Regulated by
Pineal gland	Light/dark cycles
Ovaries	FSH and LH
Testes	FSH and LH
Pancreas	Glucose in blood
Parathyroid	Calcium in blood
Posterior Pituitary (ADH)	Osmotic balance
Posterior Pituitary (Oxytocin)	Nervous system

Consider the Issues

30. Infertility Every year, people who are having trouble conceiving a child visit fertility clinics. The procedures they undergo can be time-consuming, expensive, and stressful. Despite the effort, some women do not conceive. Those who do conceive have an increased rate of multiple births. Are fertility clinics an effective use of health-care dollars? Should more effort be given to the prevention of infertility or to alternatives such as adoption?

Make New Connections

31. Biology and Art Draw two different human characters. A viewer should be able to tell which character has hypothyroidism and which has hyperthyroidism from observing your drawing.

32. Biology and Mathematics Young infants sleep almost continually. By late childhood, children need only about eight or nine hours of sleep each night. After puberty, the need for sleep temporarily increases. Are you getting enough sleep? Keep track of your sleep patterns for two weeks. On average, how many hours of sleep do you get each night? Compare your sleep patterns to those of other family members.

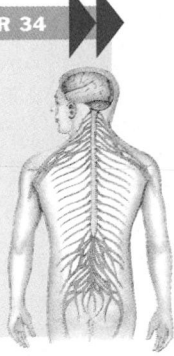

FAST-FORWARD TO CHAPTER 34

In Chapter 34, you will learn about the endocrine system's partner in controlling cellular activities—the nervous system. The nervous system allows you to respond quickly to signals from your external and internal environments.

to a closed community such as a monastery or a prison. (Menstrual synchrony may be linked to pheromones.)
28. Folic acid (125 percent, increase); 50 percent; 38 percent.
29. The pineal gland is regulated by external factors; all of the others are regulated by internal factors. Using the gland functions listed in Figure 33.4, students should note how feedback control is part of hormone regulation.
30. Have students state what costs would be reasonable. Students might consider the means of preventing diseases that cause infertility, and/or the problems associated with adoptions.
31. One character might be thin and active; the other might be fat and slow.
32. It is unlikely that most adolescents are getting sufficient sleep. You might want to pool data to produce a class average.

Chapter 33 Endocrine and Reproductive Systems   **819**

and LH and oxytocin; FSH → gonads → sperm and eggs; LH → sex hormones → secondary sex characteristics; LH → ovulation; oxytocin → uterine contractions and milk flow.
25. If glucose levels get too low, the person can experience symptoms of insulin shock, which are alleviated by ingestion of the candy bar or juice.

26. Drivers act on the information provided by traffic reports. When drivers respond to the reports by avoiding clogged routes, traffic on those routes can begin to flow again.
27. Compare menstrual cycles of women at random to those of women living in barracks or dorms; note what happens to the menstrual cycles of newcomers

PLANNING GUIDE

Section	Student Activities/Features	Teacher's Resource Package
34.1 Sensing and Control **Objectives** ■ Identify the functions of the nervous system ■ Compare the nervous systems of different animals ■ Describe the parts of the human nervous system	**Lab Zone Discover It!** *Testing Your Memory,* p. 821	**Unit 8 Review Module** ■ Section Review 34.1
34.2 Nerves at Work **Objectives** ■ Describe a nerve impulse ■ Define the different types of neurons ■ Explain how a reflex arc functions	**Lab Zone Do It!** *Can One of Your Reflex Arcs Be Stimulated?* p. 826	**Unit 8 Review Module** ■ Section Review 34.2 ■ Activity Recordsheet 34-1 ■ Interpreting Graphics 34 **Interpreting and Developing Graphics** 100
34.3 Central and Peripheral Nervous Systems **Objectives** ■ Identify brain structures ■ Analyze brain functions ■ Describe the role of the peripheral nervous system	**STS: Frontiers in Biology** *Watching a Movie?* p. 831 **Everyday Biology** *Bigger Is Not Wiser,* p. 831 **Lab Zone Investigate It!** *Analyzing Response Time,* p. 833	**Unit 8 Review Module** ■ Section Review 34.3 ■ Activity Recordsheet 34-2 ■ Critical Thinking Exercise 34 **Issues and Decision Making** 34-1 **Interpreting and Developing Graphics** 101
34.4 The Senses **Objectives** ■ Compare the structures and functions of the eye and ear ■ Explain the relationship between taste and smell ■ Describe the skin's sensitivity to pressure, temperature, and pain	**Everyday Biology** *Protective Pain,* p. 836 **Lab Zone Do It!** *Where Are Your Temperature Receptors?* p. 837	**Unit 8 Review Module** ■ Section Review 34.4 ■ Activity Recordsheet 34-3 ■ Enrichment Topic 34-1 **Laboratory Manual,** Lab 58: "Perceptions and Illusions" **Consumer Applications** 34-1 **Interpreting and Developing Graphics** 102
34.5 Nervous System Health and Substance Abuse **Objectives** ■ Identify various nervous-system disorders ■ Compare the effects of alcohol and tobacco	**Lab Zone Think About It!** *Analyzing Pain Pills and Their Cost,* p. 839 **Everyday Biology** *Wrong!* p. 841 **STS: Issues in Biology** *Fetal Alcohol Syndrome,* p. 842 **In the Community** *Drug Abuse Prevention,* p. 844	**Unit 8 Review Module** ■ Section Review 34.5 ■ Enrichment Topics 34-2 ■ Vocabulary Review 34 ■ Chapter 34 Tests **Issues and Decision Making** 34-2 **Consumer Applications** 34-2 **Spanish Reviews** ■ Chapter 34 ■ Unit 8

Technology Resources

Internet Connections

Within this chapter, you will see the bioSURF logo. If you and your students have access to the Internet, the following URL address will provide various Internet connections that are related to topics and features presented in this chapter:

http://body_systems.biosurf.com

You can also find relevant chapter material at **The Biology Place** address:

http://www.biology.com

CD-ROMs

Biología: la telaraña de la vida,
  (Spanish Student Edition) Chapter 34
Teacher's Resource Planner, Chapter 34
  Supplements
TestWorks CD-ROM
■ Chapter 34 Tests
How Your Body Works CD-ROM

Videodiscs

Animated Biological Concepts Videodiscs
■ Action Potential
■ Synaptic Transmission

Overhead Transparencies

■ Cells of the Nervous System, #81
■ A Reflex Arc, #82
■ Eye Structure and Vision, #83
■ Ear Structure and Hearing, #84
■ Taste and Smell, #85

Videotapes

Biology Alive! Video Series
Rewind: The Web of Life Reteach Videos

Planning for Activities

STUDENT EDITION
Lab Zone
Discover It! p. 821
  ■ watch or clock with a
    second hand

Lab Zone Do It! p. 826
  ■ table or high stool

Lab Zone
Investigate It! p. 833
  ■ metric ruler

Lab Zone Do It! p. 837
  ■ different color marking
    pens
  ■ cold nail
  ■ heated nail

TEACHER'S EDITION
Teacher Demo, p. 822
Paramecia reactions
  ■ microprojector
  ■ paramecia culture
  ■ dropper
  ■ vinegar

Teacher Demo, p. 825
*Electric charges move
through the nervous system*
  ■ series circuit with a
    power source, knife
    switch, and bulb

Teacher Demo, p. 826
Transmission impulses
  ■ simple circuit setup
  ■ electrolyte solution,
    such as sodium chloride
    in distilled water

Quick Activity, p. 828
Reactions
  ■ ruler
  ■ book

Class Activity, p. 829
Model of the brain
  ■ 3 colors of clay
  ■ straight pins
  ■ paper

Quick Activity, p. 834
Eye responses
  ■ flashlights

Class Activity, p. 836
*Testing salivary glands
responses*
  ■ cotton balls
  ■ vinegar
  ■ lemon juice
  ■ water

Class Activity, p. 842
Analyzing smoking
  ■ empty cigarette
    packages

Teacher Demo, p. 843
*Observing the color of
smoke*
  ■ cigarette
  ■ transparent rubber
    tubing
  ■ piece of cloth
  ■ tape
  ■ match or lighter

Chapter Objectives

Students will learn the main concepts of this chapter as they complete the following objectives.

- Identify the functions of the nervous system
- Describe the parts of the human nervous system
- Describe a nerve impulse
- Define different types of neurons and explain how a reflex arc functions
- Analyze brain functions
- Describe the human sense organs
- Identify various nervous system disorders

Key Words

34.1 *ganglia, central nervous system, peripheral nervous system, neurons, glial cells*

34.2 *resting potential, action potential, synapses, sensory neurons, motor neurons, interneurons, reflex arc*

34.3 *brain stem, cerebellum, cerebrum, somatic nervous system, autonomic nervous system, sympathetic nervous system, parasympathetic nervous system*

34.4 *retina, cochlea*

34.5 *concussion, Alzheimer disease, stimulants, depressants, hallucinogens, narcotics*

The Opening Story

Have students discuss how they think the story relates to the content of this chapter. Ask students to identify factors other than color that affect how they perceive their surroundings.

820

CHAPTER 34
Nervous Systems

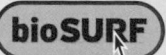
bioSURF

You can find out more about nervous systems by exploring the following Internet address:
http://body_systems.biosurf.com

In this chapter . . .

FEATURES

Everyday Biology
- Bigger Is Not Wiser
- Protective Pain
- Wrong!

In the Community
Drug Abuse Prevention

Frontiers in Biology
Watching a Movie?

Issues in Biology
Fetal Alcohol Syndrome

LAB ZONES

Discover It!
- Testing Your Memory

Do It!
- Can One of Your Reflex Arcs Be Stimulated?
- Where Are Your Temperature Receptors?

Think About It!
- Analyzing Pain Pills and Their Cost

Investigate It!
- Analyzing Response Time

One morning, a successful 65-year-old artist sustained a concussion in a traffic accident. Within days, the color drained from his vision. Traffic lights and color television became meaningless. Apples appeared black; oranges, bananas, and grapes a dull gray. He looked at a rainbow and saw only a colorless semicircle in the sky. How could an artist whose entire life had been based on seeing and creating color deal with a world in black and white?

In his book *An Anthropologist on Mars,* Dr. Oliver Sacks tells his patient's story. The concussion gave the artist a rare condition called achromatopsia—total color blindness caused by damage to one small part of the brain that processes color. Slowly the artist began to adjust to his new world. He came to prefer the nighttime—when his vision sharpened so that he could read license plates four blocks away—to the confusing grays of the day. He even ate in black and white, favoring foods like black olives and white rice. He continued painting, but only in black and white. His art flowered again, but without color.

We perceive our surroundings through an amazing—and sometimes fragile—chain of sensory organs, nerves, and brain cells. What can biology tell us about how our senses make sense of the world?

A WORLD IN BLACK AND WHITE

 **Discover It!**

Testing Your Memory

You need *a watch or clock with a second hand*

1. Look at the two-column list below for one minute, and attempt to memorize it.

734	sst
LJX	9248
OOG	bDJk
116	lz62

2. After one minute, cover the list and try to re-create it on a piece of paper.
3. Check your list against the original. Were you able to remember it all?

Memorizing and re-creating this list involves many signals that are transmitted by your nervous system. In this chapter, you will learn how those signals work.

WRITE ABOUT IT!

Have you noticed how certain sensations can trigger vivid memories? In your science journal, make a list of sensations—a song you hear, a scent you smell, a picture you see. List the memories you recall when you experience each sensation.

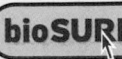 If you have access to the Internet in your classroom or school, you may wish to have students connect to the address shown on page 820. You may also want to have students conduct net searches for information using key words related to this chapter.

Discover It!

Testing Your Memory

TEAM WORK

Let students work in pairs to do the suggested activity. Then have them repeat the activity with eight three- and four-letter words. Ask them which list was easier to memorize and why.

WRITE ABOUT IT!

As students write their journal entries, encourage them to use vivid language to describe their sensations. Have them note which sense triggers the most vivid memories.

SUPER READ! **Finding the Main Idea and Supporting Details**
To practice strategies for effective reading, use pages 73-74 in **Super Read!**

REWIND to Chapter 33

Briefly review concepts learned in Chapter 33, *The Endocrine and Reproductive Systems*. Ask:

■ **What parts of the endocrine and reproductive systems are related to the nervous system?**

PORTFOLIO PREVIEW

Students should be encouraged to add to their portfolios as they work through this chapter. In addition to the *Write About It* opportunity, the following sections offer opportunities for portfolio entries:

■ Section 34. 4: *The Senses*
■ Section 34.5: *Health and Substance Abuse*

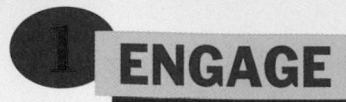

1 ENGAGE

Consider the Big Idea

Have students read The Big Idea! at the top of the page. Explain that animals and humans need nervous systems to perceive and react to their environments.

Use the Visual

Have students study the photograph that opens the section. Explain that the actions described are controlled by the nervous system. Ask:

■ **What do you usually do when your fingers or toes are numb? Why?** (Move fingers and toes to increase the flow of blood)

Check Prior Knowledge

To assess students' knowledge about animal nervous systems, ask:

■ **What different structures do animals use to sense their environment?** (Eyespots, nerve nets, ganglia, brains, spinal cords, and sensory organs)

Teacher Demo

Use a microprojector to show paramecia moving through water. Then, use a dropper to add a few drops of vinegar to the culture. Have students observe how the paramecia react. Explain that all organisms are able to respond to changes in their environment.

---

❶ There is no central processing area such as a brain.

822

What you'll learn

IDEAS
• To identify the functions of the nervous system
• To compare the nervous systems of different animals
• To describe the parts of the human nervous system

WORDS
ganglia, central nervous system, peripheral nervous system, neurons, glial cells

FIGURE 34.1

The nervous system of a hydra consists of a nerve net. Why might the hydra's nervous system be described as simple? ❶

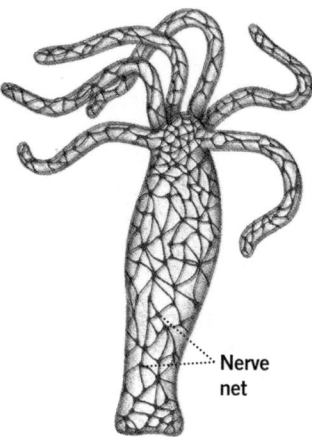

Nerve net

822 *Unit 8 Human Biology*

THE BIG IDEA! Nervous systems control our detection of and response to the environment. 34.1

34.1 Sensing and Control

A numbing cold
It is cold and you left your gloves at home. Nerve messages cause the blood vessels in your hands to narrow, preventing warm blood from reaching them. Instead, more blood flows to your internal organs. Nervous systems help regulate temperature and many other body functions. Animals have different methods of controlling their responses to environmental stimuli.

SENSING AND CONTROL IN ANIMALS

Information networks

To survive, all organisms need to be able to sense changes in the environment and control their responses. Single-celled organisms, such as bacteria and protists, can react directly to chemical or tactile clues and light. Most animals have two systems that control and coordinate their body systems. The endocrine system, as you may recall from Chapter 33, produces slower, longer-lasting responses. The nervous system enables the body to gather information and respond quickly to changes inside or outside the body.

A nervous system performs four functions that enable an animal to respond quickly. First, the nervous system uses sensors to gather information from inside and outside the body. Then the nervous system transmits the information over a network of specialized nerve cells to processing areas, such as the brain. Frequently animals have a nerve cord that transmits information between the network of nerve cells and the brain. The information is processed into possible responses.

Finally information to direct the best response is sent back through the network of nerve cells to the muscles, glands, and other parts of the animal.

All animals except sponges have nerve cells, but the organization of the nervous system varies depending on the animal. Cnidarians, such as the hydra in *Figure 34.1,* have nerve cells organized into a simple nerve net. The nerve net surrounds the body with simple sense receptors that the animal can use to detect and respond to changes all around it. Unlike most animals, the hydra does not have a central processing area such as a brain.

Figure 34.2 shows that annelids such as a leech have a small brain made of two ganglia (GANG-lee-uh). **Ganglia** are clusters of nerve cells. A ventral nerve cord that runs along the length of the animal is connected to the ganglia in each body segment.

In *Figure 34.2* you can see that insects such as grasshoppers have a brain made of several ganglia fused together. Insects have highly developed eyes, antennae, and other sense organs. A ventral nerve cord connects the brain with the rest of the body. Branched ganglia connect each body segment to the nerve cord.

STUDENT RESOURCES

From the Teacher's Resource Package, use:
■ Section Review 34.1 from Unit 8 Review Module

TECHNOLOGY RESOURCES

Relevant technology resources include:
■ Spanish Student Edition CD-ROM
■ Teacher's Resource Planner CD-ROM
■ How Your Body Works CD-ROM

FIGURE 34.2

How are the nervous systems of the leech (left) and the grasshopper (right) similar?

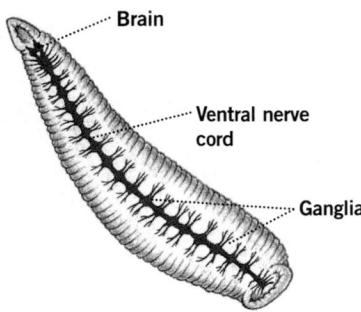

- Brain
- Ventral nerve cord
- Ganglia

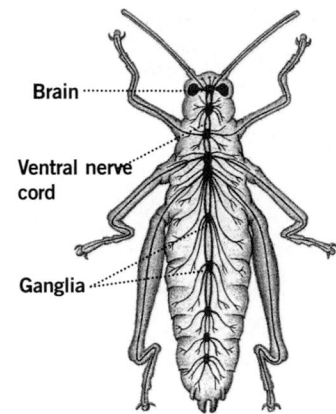

- Brain
- Ventral nerve cord
- Ganglia

HUMAN NERVOUS SYSTEM

Central command

The human nervous system is typical of the vertebrates. It includes a large, well-developed brain. A thick spinal cord connects the brain with a system of nerves that reaches all parts of the body. Specialized sense receptors in the eyes, ears, nose, and skin pick up sensory input from the environment and send it to the brain. The brain processes this input and sends messages back through the system of nerves to control all body parts.

The human nervous system has two main parts, as shown in *Figure 34.3*. The **central nervous system** (CNS) is the body's main control center and consists of the brain and the spinal cord. This part of the nervous system processes information and sends instructions to other parts of the body. The **peripheral nervous system** (PNS) is made of a network of nerves that extend throughout the body. The PNS gathers information and delivers it to and from the CNS. The CNS and PNS work together as a team to monitor, coordinate, and control the activities of the entire body.

The nervous system consists of two types of cells. **Neurons** (NYOOR-ahns)

are the functional cells of the nervous system. Neurons transmit signals through the body. The cell body is the part of a neuron that contains the nucleus, cytoplasm, and organelles.

FIGURE 34.3

How does the nervous system of the human (below) differ from that of the grasshopper? ❸

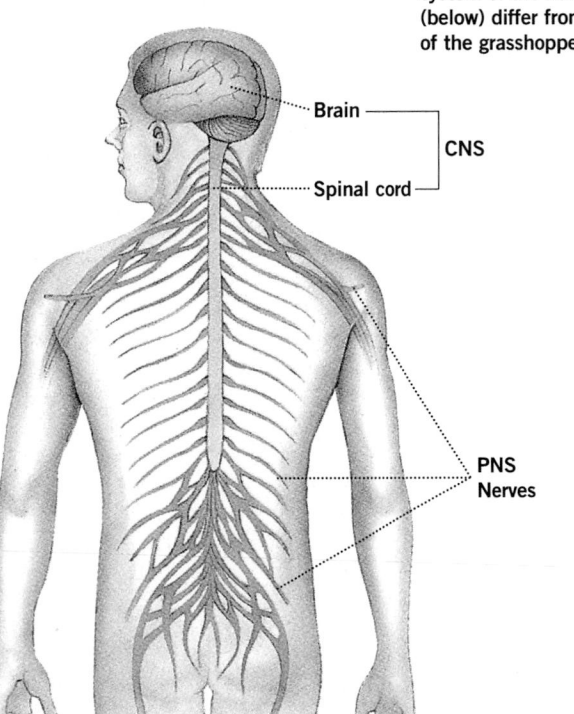

- Brain
- Spinal cord
- CNS
- PNS Nerves

Chapter 34 Nervous Systems **823**

---

❷ Both have a brain and ganglia.
❸ The human nervous system is more complex, and a human has a highly developed brain.

TEACH

Use the Visual

Have students study Figure 34.2. Point out the locations of the brain, nerve cord, and ganglia in each organism. Remind students that the leech has a definite head and tail end. Ask:

- **Where in the leech is the brain located?** (In the head)
- **How does the location of the nerve cord of the grasshopper differ from that of the leech?** (The grasshopper has a dorsal nerve cord; the leech has a ventral nerve cord.)

Explain

Have students study Figure 34.3. Point out that the nerve cord of humans has evolved into a spinal cord that runs down the dorsal side of the body. Remind students that this trait is shared by all vertebrates.

Science History

In the 1880s, Argentinean scientist Santiago Ramón y Cajal discovered that all neurons have the same basic function. In 1889, Cajal proposed the neuron doctrine which states that the cells of the nervous system carry impulses in only one direction and had tiny gaps between them. For his discovery, Cajal shared the 1906 Nobel Prize with Camillo Golgi, the discoverer of the Golgi apparatus.

Evaluate Understanding

Have students compare and contrast the nervous systems of hydra, annelids, insects, and humans in a table. Ask:

- **How are the nervous systems similar? How do they differ?** (All systems are composed of nerve cells and perform functions that enable an organism to gather information and respond. Systems differ in organization and complexity.)

Reteach

Work with students to develop a concept map illustrating the organization of the human nervous system and the functions of different structures. Have students review the section to describe how this system compares with that of other organisms.

❶ Schwann cells form the myelin sheath of the PNS and allow signals to be sent over long distances. Astrocytes are in the CNS and supply neurons with oxygen and nutrients from blood vessels.
❷ They look like stars.

824

FIGURE 34.4

Cells of the Nervous System

A neuron, shown in the photo below, transmits nerve signals. How do Schwann cells and astrocytes assist neurons? ❶

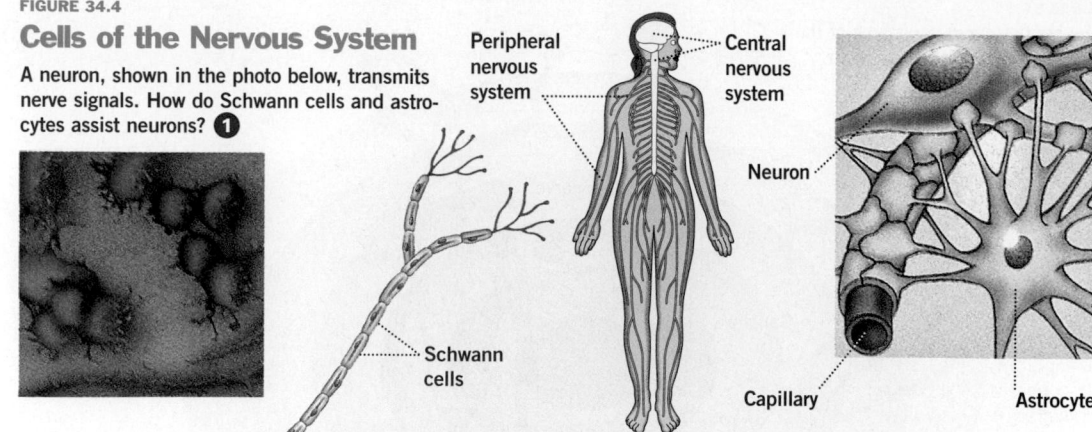

Unlike most cells, neurons have fiberlike extensions called axons and dendrites. In the PNS, these fibers are bundled into ropelike structures called nerves. In the CNS, the fibers are bundled into structures called tracts. You will learn more about neurons in the next section.

About 90 percent of the cells that make up the nervous system are not neurons. Instead, they are connective-tissue cells called glial (GLEE-ul) cells. The **glial cells** protect, support, and assist the neurons. There are several kinds of glial cells in the nervous system, including Schwann cells and astrocytes. Schwann cells and astrocytes have different functions.

In the PNS, Schwann cells are the most numerous glial cells. Schwann cells wrap around nerve fibers as they grow. The membranes of Schwann cells contain a fatty substance called myelin (MY-uh-lin), which forms a sheath that insulates and holds the nerve fibers together. Neurons with myelin sheaths can transmit signals faster than neurons without myelin sheaths.

Astrocytes are the most numerous glial cells in the CNS. Astrocytes help maintain a stable chemical environment near neurons, and they supply neurons with oxygen and nutrients from nearby blood vessels. Research indicates that astrocytes may play a role in the transmission of nervous system signals. Look at the illustration of an astrocyte in *Figure 34.4*. How do you think astrocytes got their name? ❷

CHECKPOINT 34.1

1. List the four functions of the nervous system.
2. Compare and contrast the nervous systems of humans and hydras.
3. What are the differences between the central and peripheral nervous systems?
4. **Critical Thinking** Why are most glial cells in the CNS different from the glial cells in the PNS?

Build on What You Know

5. How does it benefit animals such as jellyfish to have sense receptors all around the body? *(Need to jog your memory? Revisit relevant concepts in Chapter 21, Section 21.4.)*

 How do nervous systems function?

CHECKPOINT 34.1

1. Gather, transmit, and process information and direct the best response
2. Both have nerve cells. The hydra has a nerve net with no brain or central processing.
3. CNS processes information; PNS gathers and transmits it.
4. **Organizing and classifying** Function is different. PNS glial cells help neurons transmit information over long distances. CNS glial cells support neurons in processing information.
5. Animals with radial symmetry can encounter stimuli from all directions.

34.2 Nerves at Work

Endorphins, the natural painkillers
How does acupuncture work? The needles, which are inserted into the skin at specific points, may stimulate nerves that send messages to the brain to release endorphins. Endorphins lessen the feeling of pain and, by acting on special receptors in brain neurons, give a sense of well-being. Although scientists do not know for certain how or if acupuncture works, many people do feel relief after treatments.

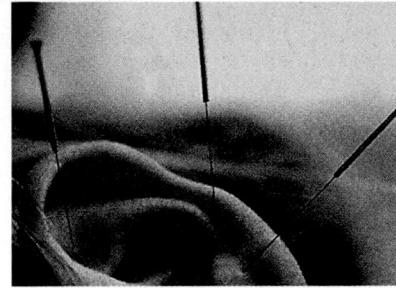

What you'll learn

IDEAS
- To describe a nerve impulse
- To define the different types of neurons
- To explain how a reflex arc functions

WORDS
resting potential, action potential, synapses, sensory neurons, motor neurons, interneurons, reflex arc

NEURONS IN ACTION

Go with the flow

Your nervous system carries thousands of signals through your body every moment in the form of nerve impulses. A nerve impulse is a wave of chemical and electrical change that moves along the membrane of a neuron. When a neuron is stimulated to conduct a nerve impulse, the electrical and chemical states are changed and restored in a few thousandths of a second.

A neuron, like all cells, has a membrane potential—an electrical charge difference across the cell membrane.

The inside of most cells has a negative charge relative to the outside of those cells. This is also true for a neuron in the resting state, before a nerve impulse. The membrane potential of a neuron in the resting state is called the **resting potential.**

When a neuron is stimulated, the electrical charge across the cell membrane reverses. The reversal and restoration of charges across the cell membrane of a neuron is called the **action potential.** Action potential is another name for a nerve impulse. Use *Figure 34.5* to follow the steps involved in the transmission of a nerve impulse.

FIGURE 34.5

Nerve Impulse Transmission

The transmission of a nerve impulse involves the movement of ions across a neural membrane.

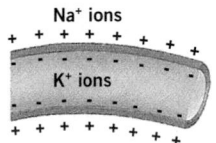

Na+ ions
K+ ions

1 A region of a neuron at resting state.

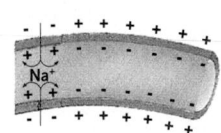

2 Upon stimulation, channels in the membrane of the first region open, and sodium ions (Na+) flow into the cell.

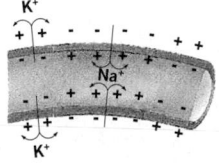

3 After Na+ enters the first region, potassium ions (K+) flow out of the cell, restoring the first region to its resting potential. The reversal of charge opens the channels in the next region of the neuron.

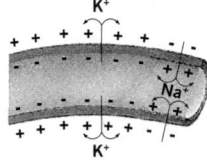

4 A charge reversal in the second region starts a charge reversal in the third region, and so on, as the nerve impulse is transmitted along the neuron.

Chapter 34 Nervous Systems **825**

ENGAGE

Consider the Big Idea

Have students read The Big Idea! at the top of the page. Explain that these structures are common to the nervous systems of many organisms.

Use the Visual

Have students study the photograph that opens the section. Explain that people may use acupuncture in place of medication to relieve pain. Ask:

- **Why might people use acupuncture instead of drug therapies for pain?** (Answers may include drug allergies, fear of addiction or other adverse side effects.)

Teacher Demo

Set up a series circuit with a power source, knife switch, and bulb. Close the switch and have students observe what happens. (The bulb lights.) Ask:

- **What will happen if the switch is opened?** (The bulb will go out.) Open the switch to show what happens. Tell students that electric charges move through the nervous system much as they do through the circuit.

STUDENT RESOURCES

From the Teacher's Resource Package, use:
- Section Review 34.2, Activity Recordsheet 34-1, and Interpreting Graphics 34 from Unit 8 Review Module

TECHNOLOGY RESOURCES

Relevant technology resources include:
- Spanish Student Edition CD-ROM
- Teacher's Resource Planner CD-ROM
- Animated Biological Concepts Videodiscs: "Action Potential" and "Synaptic Transmission"
- How Your Body Works CD-ROM

Animated Biological Concepts

Action Potential   Play

2 TEACH

 Do It! TEAM WORK

Can One of Your Reflex Arcs Be Stimulated?

Tell students that to obtain the best result, it is important that they do not tense their legs as they sit on the table or stool.

Analyze Your Results

1 The area sensitive to stimuli is limited.

2 Diagram should show the point of pressure on the tendon that releases a signal through the neurons to the lower part of the leg, and the resulting jerk of the foot upward.

Teacher Demo

To model the transmission of impulses across a synapse, set up a simple circuit that includes an electrolyte solution, such as sodium chloride in distilled water. Ask:

- **What parts of the nervous system are represented by the sodium chloride solution and cathodes?** (Sodium chloride solution: neurotransmitter moving across synapse; cathode and anode: neurons)

- **What would happen if the solution were changed to distilled water?** (The electrical impulse will not travel through the distilled water.)

 LAB ZONE **Do It!** bioSURF

Can One of Your Reflex Arcs Be Stimulated?

Reflex arcs are nerve pathways carrying automatic, involuntary responses to a stimulus before the stimulus is interpreted by the brain. You can see a reflex arc in action when you . . .

Try This

1 Sit on a table or high stool so that your lower legs dangle from the edge.
2 Have your partner strike the tendon just below your kneecap with the outer edge of his or her hand.
3 Repeat the procedure on your partner.

Analyze Your Results

1 Explain why the leg does not jerk upward unless you apply pressure to a very limited area.
2 Diagram what must be happening in the nervous system when sudden pressure is applied to the tendon just below the kneecap.

A nerve impulse moves through a cell in one direction. A dendrite receives and carries the impulse to the cell body. The axon carries the impulse away from the cell body. Each neuron has one axon, but it can have many dendrites.

FIGURE 34.6
Chemicals called neurotransmitters cross a gap in the synapse and continue the nerve impulse.

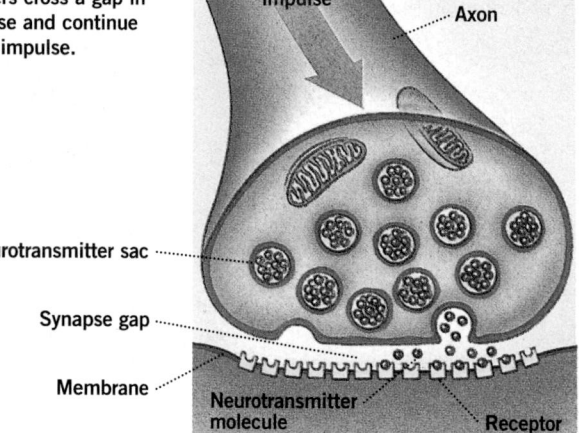

Nerve impulse

Axon

Neurotransmitter sac

Synapse gap

Membrane

Neurotransmitter molecule

Receptor

826 *Unit 8 Human Biology*

Most neurons do not actually touch one another, nor do they touch the organs to which they send messages. Nerve impulses move from neurons across synapses. **Synapses** (SIN-ap-sez) are junctions with tiny gaps between adjacent neurons and between neurons and the organs to which they send messages.

When a nerve impulse reaches the end of an axon, it sends information across the synapse. The information stimulates the next neuron or the organ that is to receive the message. Information crosses synapses in the form of chemical messengers called neurotransmitters.

Figure 34.6 shows a diagram of a synapse. Notice the end of the axon, where neurotransmitters are stored in small sacs. When a nerve impulse reaches the end of an axon, the impulse causes some of the sacs to fuse with the axon's membrane. Each fused sac releases its neurotransmitter into the synapse gap. The neurotransmitter diffuses across the gap and binds to receptors on the next neuron or on a cell of the organ that is receiving the message. The binding of the neurotransmitter causes a change in the membrane potential of the receiving cell. This change in membrane potential eventually leads to a new nerve impulse, or a response.

As you know, all neurons have the same basic structures. However, neurons vary greatly in appearance and function. There are three types of neurons, each with a different function.

Sensory neurons conduct nerve impulses toward the central nervous system. Sensory neurons transmit information from cells and organs that gather information about conditions inside and outside the body. Specialized sensory neurons called sensory receptors respond to an environmental stimulus, producing

---

MULTICULTURAL PERSPECTIVE

The Jendrassik's maneuver is one test for the knee-jerk response. The test, named for Hungarian physician Ernst Jendrassik (1858—1921), is used to diagnose problems such as poliomyelitis and nerve damage. The maneuver tests the response of the patellar tendon or Achilles tendon.

MEETING DIVERSE NEEDS

LEP Encourage LEP students to make a picture glossary of unfamiliar vocabulary words in the chapter. Glossaries may be prepared in both English and the student's native language.

FIGURE 34.7
A Reflex Arc

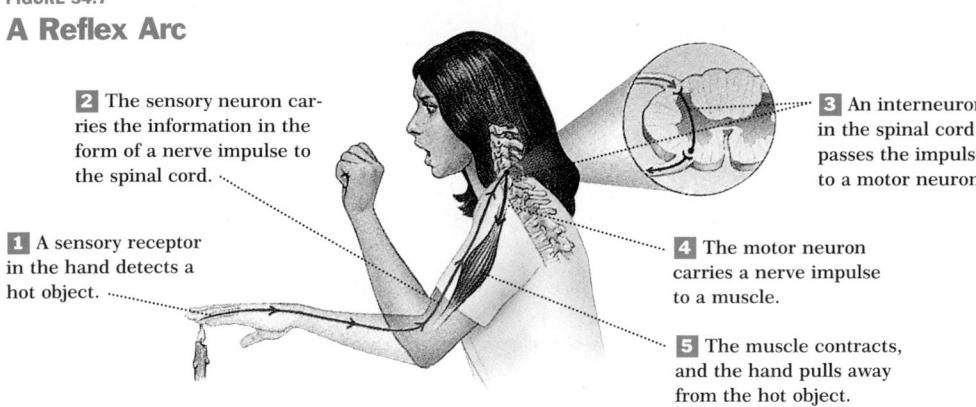

 2 The sensory neuron carries the information in the form of a nerve impulse to the spinal cord.

1 A sensory receptor in the hand detects a hot object.

 **3** An interneuron in the spinal cord passes the impulse to a motor neuron.

4 The motor neuron carries a nerve impulse to a muscle.

5 The muscle contracts, and the hand pulls away from the hot object.

signals. The signals become nerve impulses in sensory neurons.

Motor neurons conduct impulses away from the central nervous system. Impulses that motor neurons transmit cause muscles, organs, and glands to respond.

Interneurons conduct impulses within the central nervous system. Interneurons connect with sensory neurons, motor neurons, or other interneurons. There are about 100 billion interneurons in the brain alone. Interneurons in the central nervous system process and coordinate the nerve impulses coming from and going to the peripheral nervous system.

REFLEX ARCS

Ouch! That's hot!

One of the simplest responses of the nervous system is called a reflex. You may remember from Chapter 28 that a reflex is an automatic response to a change in the environment. For example, your eyes blink if they suddenly see an object coming toward them. Blinking is a reflex. Can you think of **❶** other reflexes that you have?

A **reflex arc** is the pathway of neurons that carries the nerve impulses for an automatic, involuntary

response to a stimulus. *Figure 34.7* shows how different types of neurons can work together in a reflex arc. The reflex shown is one that involves pulling your hand away from a hot object.

Notice that the interneuron in the spinal cord passes an impulse directly to a motor neuron that leads back to the arm muscles. This impulse does not travel through the brain. A reflex that does not involve the brain is called a spinal reflex. However, the brain does receive information that is interpreted as pain.

CHECKPOINT 34.2

1. How does a nerve impulse occur?
2. Contrast the functions of sensory neurons, motor neurons, and interneurons.
3. List the parts in a reflex arc.
4. **Critical Thinking** Figure 34.5 shows a neuron section at four consecutive movements during the transmission of a nerve impulse. Diagram what would happen in a Step 5.

Build on What You Know

5. What is exocytosis? When does exocytosis occur during the transmission of a nerve impulse? *(Need to jog your memory? Revisit relevant concepts in Chapter 3, Section 3.5.)*

Chapter 34 Nervous Systems **827**

Use the Visual

Have students study the photograph that opens the section. Explain that food supplies sugar from which the body obtains energy during respiration. Research suggests that the brain appears to function best right after a person eats. Ask:

■ **How does this research support the idea that breakfast is the most important meal of the day?** (Energy from food appears to help the brain function better. Eating breakfast may help people get a more productive start to their day.)

Check Prior Knowledge

To assess students' knowledge about the human nervous system, ask:

■ **What structures make up the central nervous system?** (The brain and spinal cord)
■ **What structures make up the peripheral nervous system?** (Networks of nerves that extend throughout the body)

Quick Activity

Without warning, slam a ruler or a book down on a desk. Ask students to describe how their body reacted and what emotions they experienced. Explain that in this section students will learn why their bodies responded in this way.

34.3 Central and Peripheral Nervous Systems

What you'll learn

IDEAS
• To identify brain structures
• To analyze brain functions
• To describe the role of the peripheral nervous system

WORDS
brain stem, cerebellum, cerebrum, somatic nervous system, autonomic nervous system, sympathetic nervous system, parasympathetic nervous system

Food for thought
Eating just before a test may help you get a higher score. Doctors have found that students who have recently eaten perform better on tests of verbal learning and memory. Scientists think that the temporary increase in sugar in the blood right after eating may help the brain work a little better and faster.

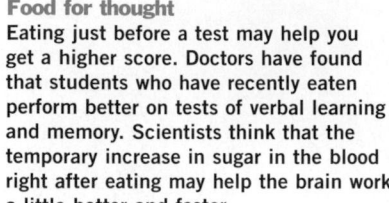

CENTRAL NERVOUS SYSTEM

The hub

The central nervous system (CNS), comprising the brain and spinal cord, is the command center of the body. Each part of the CNS has different functions. The spinal cord links the peripheral nerves with the brain, which is the body's main information processing center.

Spinal cord The spinal cord is a tubelike organ consisting of neurons, glial cells, and blood vessels. Located inside the backbone, or spine, the spinal cord is protected by the bones of the spine, three membranes called the meninges (meh-NIN-jeez), and a cushion of fluid.

Figure 34.8 shows part of a spinal cord in cross section. Notice that the spinal cord has two distinct regions. The outer region is called the white matter and the inner region is called the gray matter.

Neurons in CNS white matter are protected by glial cells called oligodendrocytes. As you may recall, Schwann cells form a myelin sheath that surrounds neurons in the PNS. The oligodendrocytes form a myelin sheath that surrounds neurons in the outer layer of the spinal cord, so this layer appears white. Neurons in the inner layer of the spinal cord do not have myelin sheaths, so this layer appears gray.

The spinal cord relays nerve impulses to and from the brain. Impulses from the peripheral nervous system (PNS) travel by sensory neurons to the spinal cord, then move through the spinal cord to the brain. The brain, in turn, sends impulses down the spinal cord to the motor nerves of the PNS. The spinal cord also controls spinal reflexes such as the reflex arc described in the previous section.

Brain The human brain is a complex organ. An average brain weighs about 1500 grams (g) and contains approximately 100 billion neurons and 900 billion glial cells. Like the spinal cord, the brain is protected by bone,

FIGURE 34.8
The spinal cord is the major nerve pathway to the brain. What is the structural difference between white and gray matter?

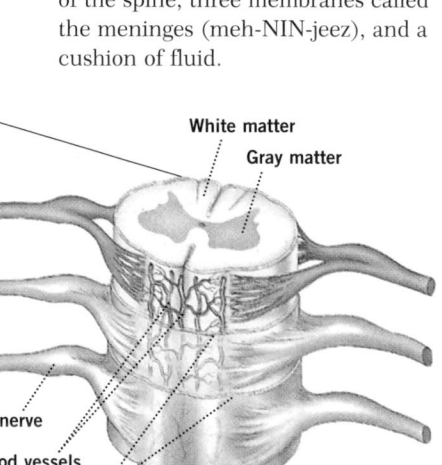

White matter
Gray matter
Spinal nerve
Blood vessels
Membranes

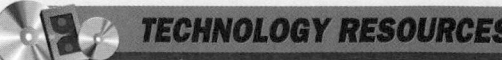

STUDENT RESOURCES

From the Teacher's Resource Package, use:
■ Section Review 34.3, Activity Recordsheet 34-2, and Critical Thinking Exercise 34 from Unit 8 Review Module
■ Issues and Decision Making 34-1

TECHNOLOGY RESOURCES

Relevant technology resources include:
■ Spanish Student Edition CD-ROM
■ Teacher's Resource Planner CD-ROM
■ How Your Body Works CD-ROM

meninges, and a cushion of fluid. The brain also has layers of white matter and gray matter. Unlike the spinal cord, however, the brain has an inner region of white matter and an outer region of gray matter. The brain has three main structural parts: the brain stem, the cerebellum, and the cerebrum. You can find these three parts in *Figure 34.9.*

The **brain stem,** which connects the spinal cord to the rest of the brain, coordinates many of the body's survival functions, such as breathing, heart rate, sleep, and wakefulness. Three distinct regions make up the brain stem: the midbrain, the pons, and the medulla oblongata.

Just above the brain stem are two important structures called the thalamus and the hypothalamus. The thalamus serves as a relay station. It directs incoming messages from the spinal cord to the appropriate parts of the brain. The hypothalamus monitors homeostasis of the body, such as water content and temperature. As you learned in Chapter 33, the hypothalamus is a link between the endocrine and nervous systems.

Located behind the brain stem, the cerebellum (sayr-uh-BEL-uhm) is the second largest part of the brain. The **cerebellum** coordinates muscle activities, enabling the body to move in a smooth, steady, and efficient manner. The cerebellum also controls balance, equilibrium, and posture.

The cerebrum (seh-REE-bruhm) constitues about 85 percent of the human brain. The **cerebrum** is responsible for all voluntary, or conscious, activity in the brain. Its surface, called the cerebral cortex, is covered with folds and creases. These folds give the brain a very large surface area. The cerebrum is divided into right and left halves, or hemispheres. For both hemispheres, the surface of the cerebral cortex is divided into four lobes, as shown

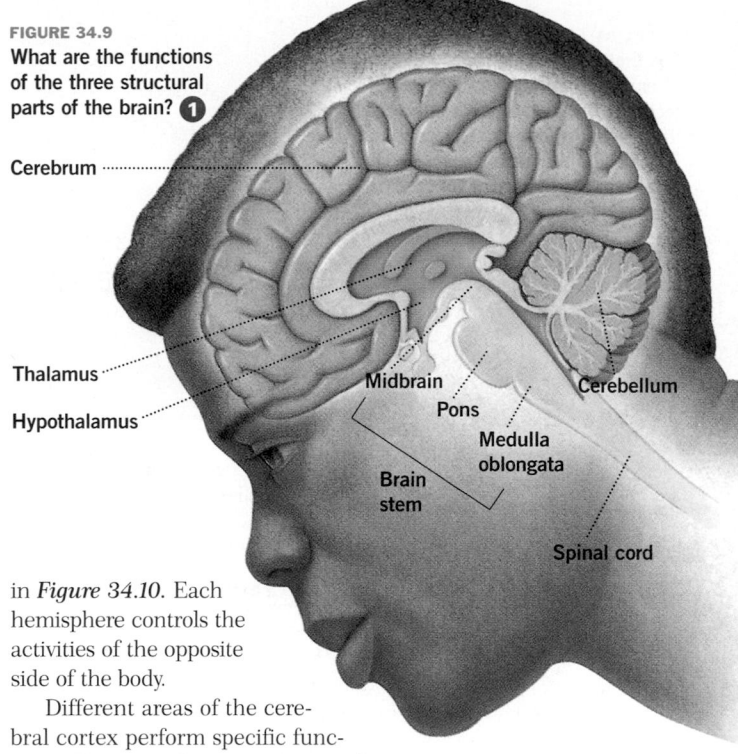

FIGURE 34.9
What are the functions of the three structural parts of the brain? ❶

Cerebrum

Thalamus

Hypothalamus

Midbrain

Pons

Brain stem

Medulla oblongata

Cerebellum

Spinal cord

in *Figure 34.10.* Each hemisphere controls the activities of the opposite side of the body.

Different areas of the cerebral cortex perform specific functions. For example, sensory areas of the cortex receive incoming information from sensory neurons. Motor areas control voluntary muscle movements. Association areas coordinate complex activities, such as speech, language, and memory.

FIGURE 34.10
Each hemisphere of the cerebral cortex is divided into four lobes. Different functions of the body are controlled by different association areas of the cerebral cortex.

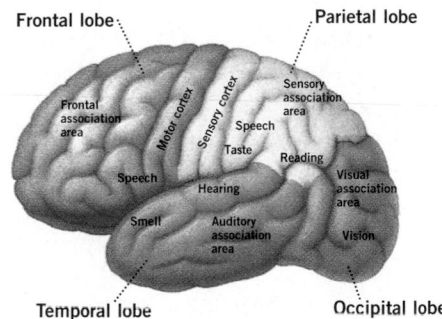

Frontal lobe

Parietal lobe

Frontal association area

Motor cortex

Sensory cortex

Sensory association area

Speech

Taste

Reading

Speech

Hearing

Visual association area

Smell

Auditory association area

Vision

Temporal lobe

Occipital lobe

Chapter 34 Nervous Systems **829**

❶ Brain stem connects the spinal cord to the rest of the brain and coordinates survival functions. Cerebellum coordinates muscle activity, and controls balance, equilibrium, and posture. Cerebrum controls all voluntary activity.

2 TEACH

Use the Visual

Have students study Figure 34.9. Ask:

- **What is the largest part of the brain?** (Cerebrum)
- **Where in the brain are the endocrine glands located?** (Just above the brain stem)

Class Activity

Provide students with three colors of clay, straight pins, and paper. Have students use Figure 34.9 to make a three-dimensional model of the brain that shows the brain stem, cerebrum, and cerebellum. Have students use straight pins to attach labels to the parts of their models.

Use the Visual

As students study Figure 34.10, remind them that they are looking at only the surface of the cerebrum. Ask:

- **What part of your brain allows you to raise your hand at will?** (Motor cortex)
- **What parts of your brain process information when you read?** (Association areas in the cerebral cortex.)

 Language Arts

Have students look up the origin and meaning of the prefix "cere" in the dictionary. Have them jot down five words with this prefix that relate to the nervous system.

Use the Visual

Have students study Figure 34.11 which shows the parts of the brain's limbic system. Ask:

- **What parts of the brain make up the limbic system?** (Thalamus, hypothalamus, amygdala, and hippocampus)
- **What is the function of the limbic system?** (The limbic system functions in emotional reactions, memory formation and storage, and complex reasoning.)

Social Sciences

Psychobiology combines psychology, the study of human behavior, with biology. Psychobiologists use information about anatomy, physiology, and pathology of the nervous system to study factors involved in mental growth and development.

Explain

Point out that most scientists agree that there are three distinct types of memory: momentary memory which is stored for just a few seconds or minutes, short-term memory which is lost after a few hours or days; and long-term memory which can last for many years. Researchers are just beginning to identify the biochemical and electrical bases of human memory.

FIGURE 34.11
The limbic system is the working center of human emotions and memory. It includes the thalamus, the hypothalamus, the amygdala, and the hippocampus. The Broca's and Wernicke's areas on the cerebrum are important for speech.

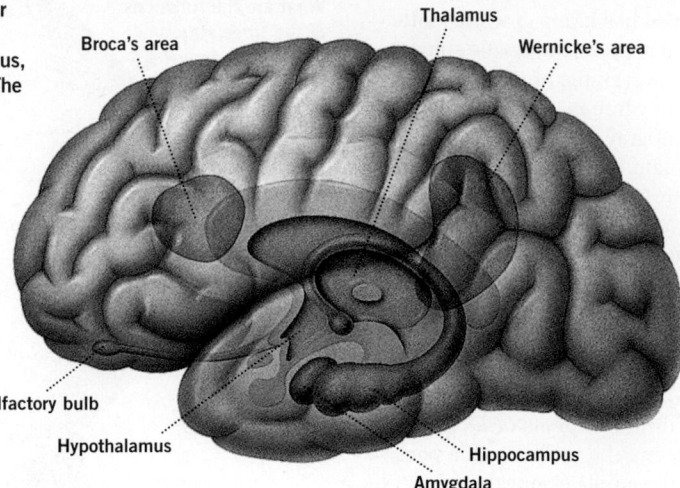

MEMORY, EMOTIONS, SPEECH

Integrated circuits

What processes are involved in feeling emotions? What parts of your brain are involved in memory and speech? Scientists have been trying to answer these questions for a long time. By using animal models, studying brain-damaged humans, and analyzing the effects on human brains of various stimulations, researchers have been able to create some partial maps of the human brain.

Human emotions, such as anger, love, and joy, involve the brain's limbic

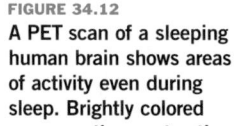

FIGURE 34.12
A PET scan of a sleeping human brain shows areas of activity even during sleep. Brightly colored areas are the most active.

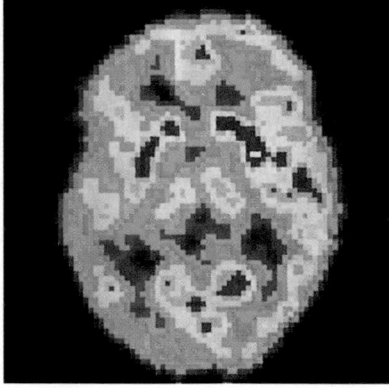

system. The parts of the limbic system are shown in *Figure 34.11*. The limbic system connects directly to the area of the brain used for complex reasoning, called the prefrontal cortex.

The limbic system is also involved in the formation of memories. The amygdala can connect incoming information with an emotion or an event. The hippocampus functions in memory storage and learning.

Where are memories stored? In the 1920s Canadian neurosurgeon Wilder Penfield found that his patients recalled specific memories when he stimulated different parts of the cerebral cortex. Further research has shown that memories are distributed throughout the cerebral cortex.

The process of speech involves several areas of the cerebrum. Two important regions are Broca's area and Wernicke's area. These regions are located on the left side of the cerebral cortex. Broca's area translates thoughts into speech and coordinates the muscles used for speaking. A person with an injury to Broca's area can understand language but cannot speak. Wernicke's area stores the information needed to understand

---

MEETING DIVERSE NEEDS

Hearing Impaired Encourage students to look up and record the pronunciations and meanings of key words and terms relating to the human nervous system.

language. A person with damage to Wernicke's area can speak, but the words make little or no sense.

FRONTIERS IN BIOLOGY
Watching a movie?

Scientists can observe the processes of the conscious brain in action. Using a technique called positron-emission tomography (PET), researchers can see which parts of the brain are used for different activities. PET scanning involves labeling a blood component such as sugar or oxygen with a radioactive element that emits tiny particles called positrons. When the positrons of a labeled blood component collide with electrons in body molecules, gamma rays are released. The gamma rays can be detected by a sensor. The information detected by the sensor is fed to a computer and converted to an image on a screen.

In the brain, the blood flow to a particular area greatly increases when the area is used. Therefore, every time an area of the brain is used during a PET scan, the area releases a burst of gamma rays and the computer produces an image of the area being used. Researchers instruct the patient to perform such activities as speaking, reading, or abstract thinking, and then watch the active areas of the brain light up on-screen. In *Figure 34.12,* you can see the results of a PET scan used to map areas of the brain that are active during sleep.

Since its introduction in 1988, PET scanning has provided a great deal of information about the normal function of the brain. This technique can be used to diagnose and treat brain disorders such as Alzheimer's disease, strokes, and cancer. In addition, PET scanning can be used to monitor and diagnose other parts of the body, including the heart.

PERIPHERAL NERVOUS SYSTEM
Outreach

Imagine you are trying on a new pair of shoes. Sensory nerves enable you to see and sense the texture of the shoes and to feel pressure in your toes. Motor nerves enable you to hold the shoes and slip them on. You may recall that sensory and motor nerves are part of the peripheral nervous system (PNS). Sensory nerves carry impulses from sensory receptors to the CNS. Motor nerves deliver impulses from the CNS to the rest of the body. The body's response to the impulses can be voluntary or involuntary. In general, the nerve impulses for voluntary and involuntary responses are carried by motor nerves in different areas of the PNS. *Figure 34.13* shows the organization of the PNS.

The **somatic nervous system** is part of the PNS and includes the motor nerves that control voluntary responses. For example, skeletal muscles respond to impulses from the somatic nervous system. However, some involuntary reflexes involving skeletal muscles also occur through the nerves of the somatic nervous system.

EVERYDAY BIOLOGY
Bigger Is Not Wiser

The brain of a 20-year-old person might weigh about 1400 grams. That same brain, in extreme old age, may weigh 115 to 120 grams less. However, there will be little or no decline in the brain's ability to reason, except in cases of disease.

FIGURE 34.13
An organizational chart of the nervous systems.

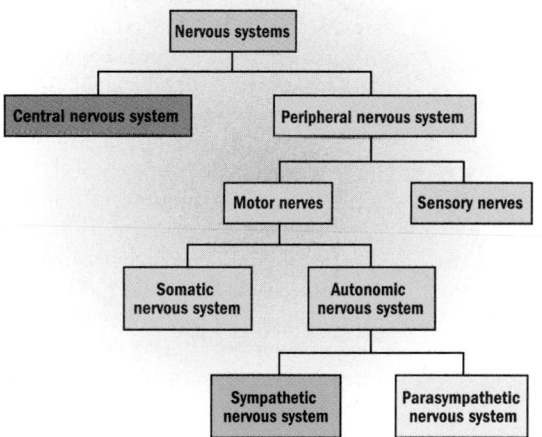

Chapter 34 Nervous Systems **831**

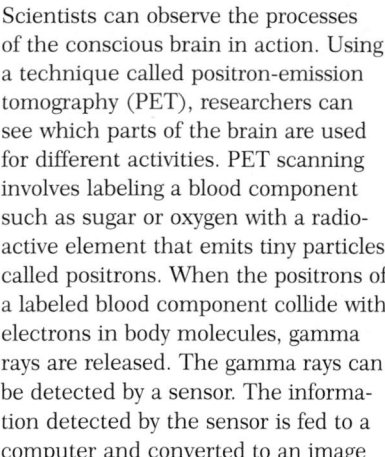

STS

Explain that a positron is an electron with a positive charge. In other words, electrons are matter and positrons are anti-matter. When matter and anti-matter collide, a burst of gamma radiation is released. Unlike X-rays, a PET scan shows the areas of the brain that are most active during a particular process.

Explain

Point out to students that radioactive labeling of a compound is accomplished by using radioactive elements to synthesize compounds. For example, radioactive carbon (carbon-14) can be used to synthesize and label glucose.

Discuss

Remind students that the peripheral nervous system is made up of the nerves that lie outside the central nervous system. Ask:

- **What happens to your heart rate when you are frightened?** (It increases.) Explain to students that this response is controlled by the part of the peripheral nervous system called the autonomic nervous system.

MEETING DIVERSE NEEDS

Gifted Have students research other tools used to study the function of the brain and nervous system. Have them find information about EEGs, EMGs, MRIs, and CAT scans. For each tool, have students report on when it is used, how it works, and what it may reveal. Have students share their research with the class.

831

Science History

German physiologist Otto Loewi discovered that the body releases specific chemical substances when either branch of the autonomic nervous system is stimulated. English physiologist Henry Dale identified the substance as acetylcholine, now recognized as one of the most vital neurotransmitters. For their work, Loewi and Dale received the 1936 Nobel Prize.

Think Critically

The sympathetic nervous system increases the heart rate and the force of heart contractions. Ask:

- **How would a person's ability to exercise strenuously be affected if the sympathetic nerves to the heart were not working?** (Strenuous exercise would not be possible, because the heart would not beat fast enough to supply the cells with adequate energy.)

Evaluate Understanding

Have students combine Figures 34.10 and 34.11 into one visual. Review a few sample visuals and ask students to describe the functions of each structure.

Reteach

Make a copy of Figures 34.10 and 34.14 on an overhead transparency. Review the main parts of the brain and their functions. Discuss the functions of each part of the PNS.

FIGURE 34.14
Two sets of motor nerves in the autonomic nervous system—the sympathetic and parasympathetic—work in balance to control the functioning of the body's organs and glands.

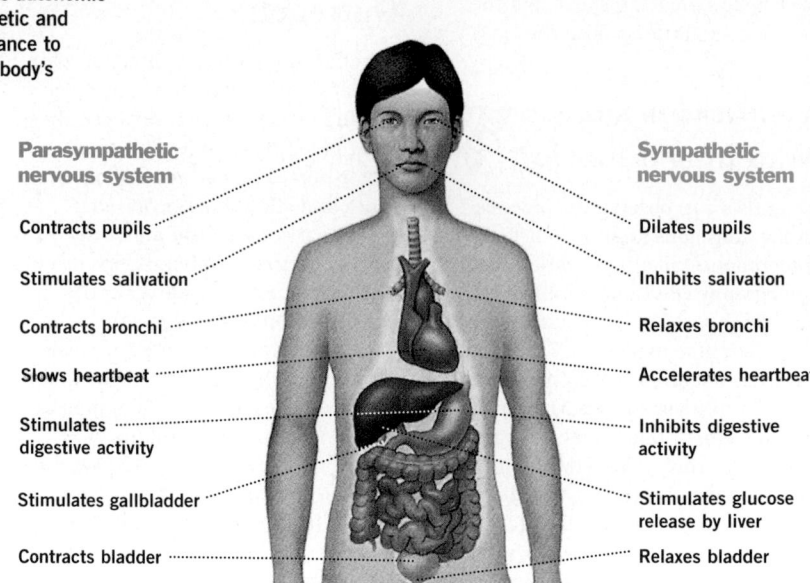

Parasympathetic nervous system
Contracts pupils
Stimulates salivation
Contracts bronchi
Slows heartbeat
Stimulates digestive activity
Stimulates gallbladder
Contracts bladder

Sympathetic nervous system
Dilates pupils
Inhibits salivation
Relaxes bronchi
Accelerates heartbeat
Inhibits digestive activity
Stimulates glucose release by liver
Relaxes bladder

The part of the PNS called the **autonomic nervous system** controls many involuntary responses. For example, smooth muscles, organs, and glands respond automatically to changes inside and outside the body.

The autonomic nervous system is divided into two parts. The **sympathetic nervous system** controls the responses of the body to stressful situations. It consists of motor nerves originating in the central section of the spine. The **parasympathetic nervous system** controls body functions associated with rest and digestion. It consists of motor nerves originating in the brain stem and in the base of the spine.

Nerves from these two systems have opposite effects on organs and glands. Stimulating a sympathetic nerve speeds heart rate; stimulating a parasympathetic nerve slows the heart down. The opposing effects of these two systems help the body maintain homeostasis despite constant changes in internal and external environments. *Figure 34.14* compares the effects of sympathetic and parasympathetic nerve stimulation on some organs.

CHECKPOINT 34.3

1. What part or parts of the brain coordinate breathing and heartbeat? Balance and posture? Speech and emotions?
2. The limbic system plays a role in what two functions?
3. **Critical Thinking** Based on the information in Figure 34.14, how do you think stress and relaxation are handled by your sympathetic and/or parasympathetic nervous systems? Explain.

Build on What You Know

4. Compare the ways the nervous systems and the endocrine system help the body maintain homeostasis. *(Need to jog your memory? Revisit relevant concepts in Chapter 33, Section 33.2.)*

832 *Unit 8 Human Biology*

CHECKPOINT 34.3

1. Breathing and heartbeat: brainstem; balance and posture: cerebellum; speech and emotions: cerebrum
2. Memories and emotions
3. **Making generalizations** Symptoms of stress, such as increased heartbeat, are handled by the sympathetic nervous system. Relaxation activities, such as digestion and slow breathing, are stimulated by the parasympathetic.
4. The endocrine system uses negative feedback to maintain homeostasis. The nervous system responds to the stimulation of receptors.

 **Investigate It!**

Analyzing Response Time

WHAT YOU WILL DO Measure and analyze your response times by catching a falling object when you are distracted and when you are focused

SKILLS YOU WILL USE Observing, measuring, collecting and recording data, calculating

WHAT YOU WILL NEED Metric ruler

Propose a Hypothesis

Can your response time vary depending on external distractions? How? Propose a hypothesis.

Conduct Your Experiment

1 Face your partner while he or she holds a metric ruler at the end with the highest measurement. Place your thumb and index finger at the opposite end of the ruler, but do not touch the ruler, as shown in the photo above.
2 Tell your partner when you are ready. Keep your eyes on your partner's hand and try to catch the ruler with your thumb and index finger as soon as your partner releases it. Record the centimeter mark at which you caught the ruler.
3 Repeat step 2 four times. Find and record the average of the five trial runs.
4 Repeat steps 1–3 while your partner creates environmental distractions. Your partner could ask you questions about homework, sing a song, whistle, or do some other distracting activity.

Analyze Your Data

1 How did your average distance with no distractions compare with your average distance with distractions?
2 How did your average distances compare with your classmates' averages?
3 Create a graph that shows the average distances for everyone in your class under both conditions.

Draw Conclusions

1 Was your hypothesis supported by the data? Why or why not?

2 Based on your findings, what would you recommend to a person doing something that requires quick response time, such as driving a car?

Design a Related Experiment

Internal distractions might affect your response time differently than external distractions. Propose a hypothesis and explain how you would test this in an experiment.

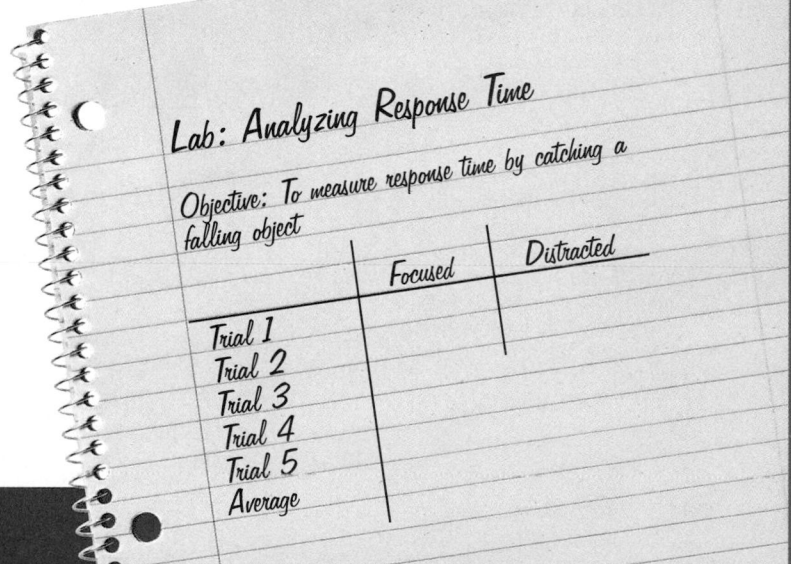

Lab: Analyzing Response Time

Objective: To measure response time by catching a falling object

	Focused	Distracted
Trial 1		
Trial 2		
Trial 3		
Trial 4		
Trial 5		
Average		

 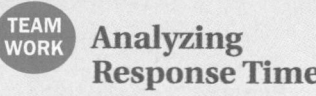 **Investigate It!**

TEAM WORK **Analyzing Response Time**

Lab Prep and Planning

Provide one metric ruler for each group of students.

Lab Tips

You may wish to have students work in groups of three. In this arrangement, the third student could provide the distractions.

Hypothesis Help

Likely hypotheses will indicate that response time is slowed when external distractions are present.

Lab Extension

Open Ended

Have students determine how changing the stimulus to one that is anticipated affects response time. Suggest they alter the experiment by blowing a whistle three seconds before the ruler is dropped. Have students determine how knowing when the ruler will be dropped affects their response time.

Time Required
- 30–50 minutes

Analyze Your Data

1 Answers will vary, but reaction time will probably increase with distractions.
2 Answers will vary, but most averages will be similar.
3 Analyze the graph for a norm.

Draw Conclusions

1 Suggest students revise hypotheses not supported by the data.
2 A person driving a car should focus on driving and avoid distractions such as, loud music, talking on a car phone, tuning the radio, or arguing.

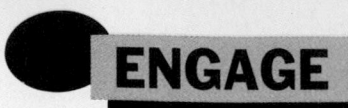

ENGAGE

Use the Visual

Have students study the photograph that opens the section. Explain that blinking is not the only way that people keep the eye's surface clean. Ask:

- **Besides blinking, what mechanism do the eyes have for keeping the eye surface clean?** (Tearing)

Check Prior Knowledge

To assess students' knowledge about human senses, ask:

- **What are the sense organs of the body?** (Eyes, ears, tongue, skin, and nose)

Quick Activity

Darken the room and provide pairs of students with flashlights. Have one student sit in a chair while the partner observes his or her eyes. Tell the observer to shine the flashlight briefly into the partner's eyes and observe any changes in the eyes' appearance. Have students switch roles and repeat the activity.

Use the Visual

After students study Figure 34.15 have them trace the path of the light as it passed through their partner's eyes when the acitivty above was performed.

834

34.4 The Senses

What you'll learn

IDEAS

- To compare the structures and functions of the eye and ear
- To explain the relationship between taste and smell
- To describe the skin's sensitivity to pressure, temperature, and pain

WORDS

retina, cochlea

A blink in time

Blinking does more work than you may think. Humans blink to keep the eye's surface clean, moist, and comfortable. In one year, we blink about 8 million times. Since the average blink closes our eyes for one sixth of a second, blinking closes our eyes for more than 170 hours a year.

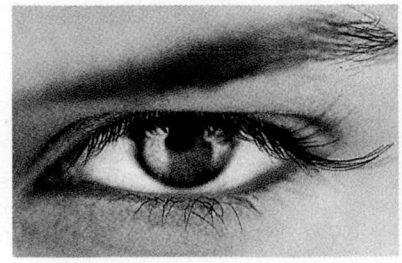

VISION

To see . . . to believe

How do you see? Your body has structures to sense and interpret patterns of light. Structures that make vision possible include the eye, the optic nerve, and a part of the brain's cerebral cortex called the visual cortex. Follow the steps in *Figure 34.15* to trace the path of light as it passes through the eye. The eye's structures help to produce a sharp image on the retina.

The **retina** (REH-tin-uh) contains receptor cells that respond to light energy. These receptors are called photoreceptors. The retina contains two types of photoreceptors: rods and cones. Rods can function with very little light but cannot detect color. Cones, on the other hand, can distinguish colors but require bright light. What do you think happens when you try to identify colors at dusk or in pale moonlight? ❶

FIGURE 34.15

An Eye and Vision

Cornea
1 Light from an object passes through a transparent cornea.

● ● ● ● ● Ⓛ Ⓘ Ⓖ Ⓗ Ⓣ ● ● ●

Iris
2 Light passes through an opening in the iris, a ring of muscle that can vary the amount of light that passes through it. The pupil is the opening in the center of the iris.

Lens
3 The lens focuses the light onto the retina.

Optic nerve
5 The optic nerve contains sensory neurons that carry nerve impulses to the brain's visual cortex. The brain interprets the impulses as an image of the object.

Retina
4 Photoreceptors in the retina respond to light energy, producing signals that become nerve impulses.

834 *Unit 8 Human Biology*

STUDENT RESOURCES

From the Teacher's Resource Package, use:

- Section Review 34.4, Activity Recordsheet 34-3, and Enrichment Topic 34-1 from Unit 8 Review Module
- Lab 58: "Perceptions and Illusions"
- Consumer Applications 34-1

TECHNOLOGY RESOURCES

Relevant technology resources include:

- Spanish Student Edition CD-ROM
- Teacher's Resource Planner CD-ROM
- How Your Body Works CD-ROM

FIGURE 34.16
An Ear and Hearing

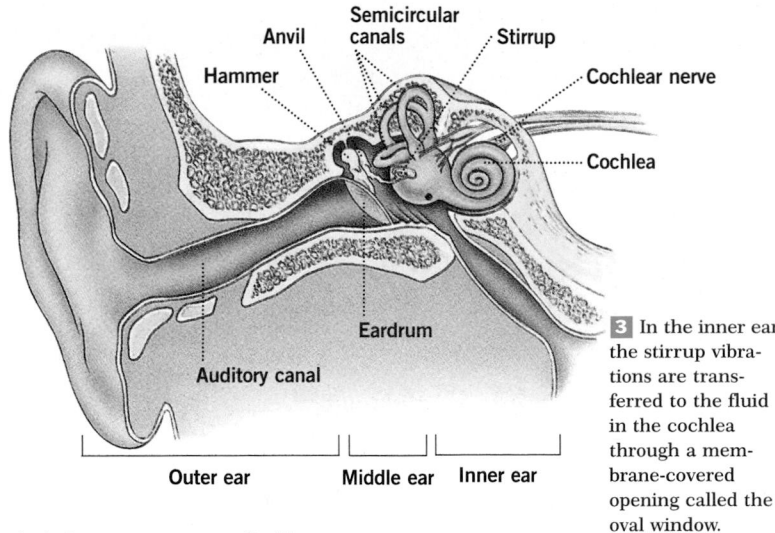

1 The outer ear collects sound waves, which travel through the auditory canal and vibrate the eardrum.

2 Eardrum vibrations move three bones in the middle ear: the hammer, anvil, and stirrup.

3 In the inner ear, the stirrup vibrations are transferred to the fluid in the cochlea through a membrane-covered opening called the oval window.

Anvil · Semicircular canals · Stirrup · Cochlear nerve · Hammer · Cochlea · Eardrum · Auditory canal · Outer ear · Middle ear · Inner ear

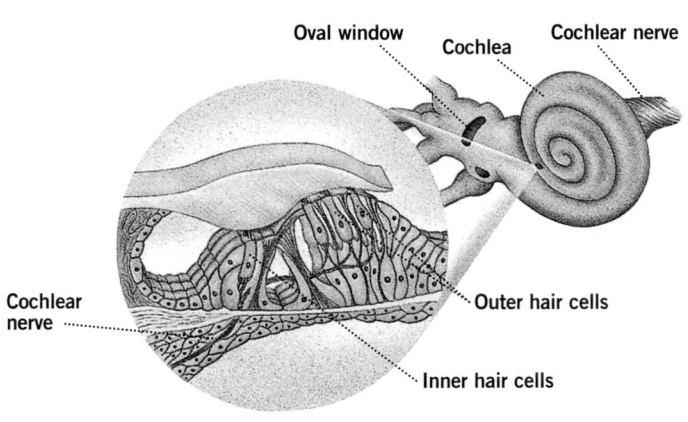

Oval window · Cochlea · Cochlear nerve · Cochlear nerve · Outer hair cells · Inner hair cells

4 The fluid vibrations in the cochlea bend hair cells, which transmit nerve impulses to the cochlear nerve. The brain interprets the impulses as sounds.

HEARING AND BALANCE
Did you hear that!

Your ear is a complex organ that enables you to hear sound and maintain balance. The receptor cells for both hearing and balance are called mechanoreceptors. Mechanoreceptors detect movement and are stimulated to transmit nerve impulses.

The **cochlea** (KOH-klee-uh) is the organ of the inner ear that contains the mechanoreceptors for hearing. This structure is filled with fluid. Sound waves cause vibrations in the fluid. The vibrations cause mechanoreceptors called hair cells to

bend, sending impulses to the cochlear nerve. The cochlear nerve transmits the impulses to the brain. Follow the steps in *Figure 34.16* to see how the ear collects sound waves and converts them to nerve impulses.

The semicircular canals of the ear contain mechanoreceptors that help maintain balance. Like the cochlea, the semicircular canals are filled with fluid. The three canals are oriented at right angles (90°) to each other. Whenever your body moves, mechanoreceptors in the canals detect the direction in which the fluid is moving. The brain uses this information to help you maintain balance.

Chapter 34 Nervous Systems **835**

MEETING DIVERSE NEEDS

At Risk Encourage students to create flowcharts that trace the path of light through the eye and the path of sound through the ear.

❶ It becomes more difficult to make out the colors because the cones do not function well in dim light.

---

2 TEACH

Use the Visual
Have students study Figure 34.16. Ask:
- **What is the function of the outer ear?** (To collect sound waves)
- **What three bones are located in the middle ear?** (The hammer, anvil, and stirrup)

Language Arts
Explain to students that the word cochlea comes from the Greek word *kochlias,* which means "snail shell." The name reflects the snail-like shape of the cochlea of the ear.

Think Critically
Discuss the function of the fluid in the inner ear. Ask:
- **What role does the fluid in the inner ear have to do with the "pop" that occurs during a rapid change in altitude?** (Students should deduce that the pressure between the inner ear and the outer environment is being equalized.)

Apply
Deafness, the significant loss of hearing, has various causes. It may be due to an impairment of the cochlea or the auditory nerve or from improper conduction by the bones of the middle ear. Hearing aids amplify sound and are often used to correct hearing loss. The artificial cochlea, a device that translates sound into electronic signals, may be surgically implanted in the ear to overcome deafness.

Use the Visual

Have students study Figure 34.17. Ask:

- **Where are the taste buds that recognize bitter substances located?** (At the back of the tongue)
- **What nerve carries information about smell from the nose to the brain?** (The olfactory nerve)

Class Activity
TEAM WORK

Provide students working in pairs with cotton balls, vinegar, lemon juice, and water. Blindfold one partner while the other saturates one cotton ball in one liquid and holds it under the blindfolded person's nose. Then have the person relate whether the odor of the cotton ball initiated a response from his or her salivary glands. Have students switch roles and repeat the activity until all the solutions are tested.

Build Writing Skills

Have students imagine themselves as food critics. Have them write a magazine article describing how their sensory organs enable them to enjoy the tastes and smells of a favorite holiday meal.

❶ Sour and salty; salty and sweet

836

FIGURE 34.17
Taste and Smell

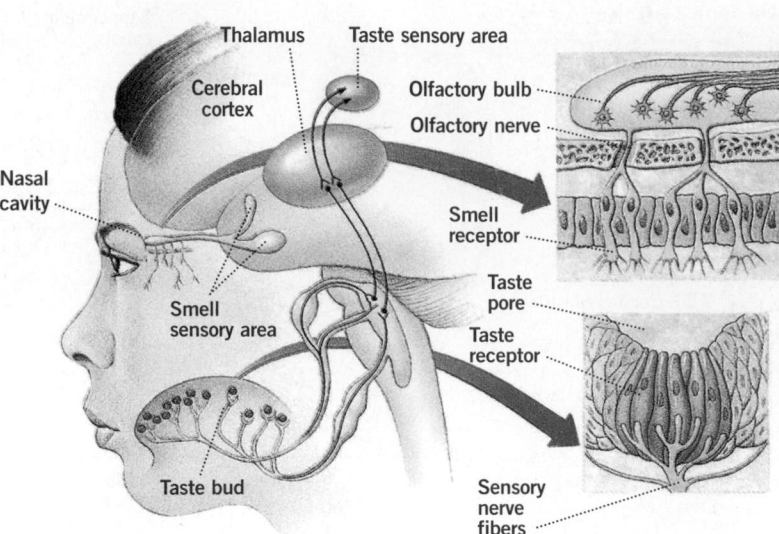

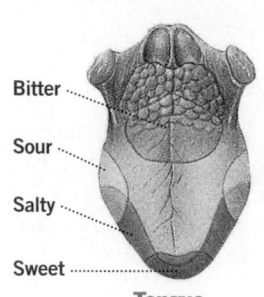

Labels: Thalamus, Taste sensory area, Cerebral cortex, Olfactory bulb, Olfactory nerve, Nasal cavity, Smell receptor, Bitter, Sour, Salty, Sweet, Tongue, Smell sensory area, Taste pore, Taste receptor, Taste bud, Sensory nerve fibers

---

TASTE AND SMELL

A little goes a long way

Taste and smell are closely related senses that often work together. Both senses rely on receptor cells called chemoreceptors. A chemoreceptor responds to a specific kind of chemical and sends impulses to the brain through sensory nerves. The brain interprets the impulses from taste and smell chemoreceptors and decides whether foods are safe to eat. You can use *Figure 34.17* to trace the pathways from taste and smell receptors to the corresponding areas of the brain.

The chemoreceptors that detect taste are located in structures called taste buds. Most taste buds are on the tongue. Each taste bud has about 50 taste receptors surrounded by supporting cells. To reach these taste receptors, a chemical must be dissolved in liquid. Three pairs of salivary glands in the mouth secrete a liquid called saliva when you are about to eat. You experience taste when molecules dissolved in saliva are detected by the receptors in the taste buds.

There are four primary tastes: sour, salty, bitter, and sweet. Other tastes are combinations of the primary tastes. Different taste receptors that detect each primary taste are located in different areas of the tongue. Look again at *Figure 34.17*. Which taste areas overlap? ❶

Smell, or olfactory, receptors are chemoreceptors located on mucous membranes in the upper cavity of the nose. Smell receptors respond to odor molecules that dissolve in the mucus. Sniffing increases the airflow into the nose and enhances the sense of smell. Smell receptors can detect tiny amounts of some molecules. For example, the molecule that gives garlic its odor can be detected at a concentration of 1/25,000,000,000 milligrams (mg) per milliliter of air.

Your sense of smell plays a role in your ability to taste. Think about what happens when you have a cold and your smell receptors are blocked. Food has little flavor. The characteristic flavors of foods result from a complex combination of smells and the four primary tastes.

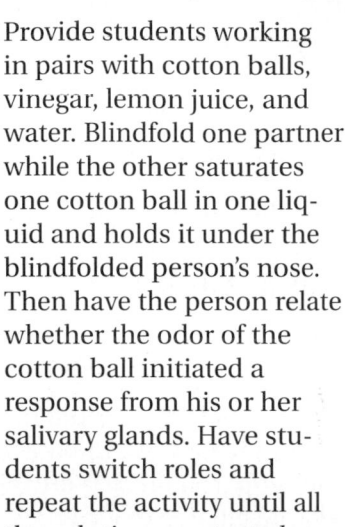

EVERYDAY BIOLOGY

Protective Pain

Feeling pain is essential to our self-protection. One of the effects of Hansen's disease, or leprosy, is an inability to feel pain. People with leprosy can cut or burn their fingers, toes, or even limbs and feel no pain.

FACTS AND FIGURES

Unlike humans, fishes have taste buds covering their entire bodies. The taste buds of fishes provide information about the surrounding water.

MULTICULTURAL PERSPECTIVE

In many countries, herbs and spices are used to achieve various flavors. For example, Indian curry contains turmeric, fenugreek, coriander, cumin, mace, and ginger. Have students research the herbs and spices of their ethnic heritage. Encourage students to bring samples to class.

OTHER SENSES

Hot, heavy, and hurtful

Various types of receptor cells sense changes inside and outside the body. Your skin is a sensory organ for touch, temperature, and pain. Each type of sensation involves a different type of receptor cell. The figure at right illustrates types of receptor cells in the skin.

Heat and cold are detected by thermoreceptors. Touch and pressure are detected by mechanoreceptors. Pain receptor cells, called nociceptors (NOH-sih-sep-terz), are located in most tissues in the body. Pain alerts the body to damage being done and helps prevent further damage. Nociceptors can respond to many kinds of strong stimuli.

Chemoreceptors in the brain can detect changes in the concentration of substances dissolved in the blood. When the blood is too concentrated, chemoreceptors send impulses that trigger thirst. Chemoreceptors are also present in arteries, where they detect the buildup of carbon dioxide in the blood. These chemoreceptors send impulses that trigger rapid breathing to release the carbon dioxide and bring in oxygen.

LAB ZONE Do It!

Where Are Your Temperature Receptors?

Your skin has receptor cells for both hot and cold temperatures. You can map the site of the receptors when you . . .

Try This

1 Use a marker to draw a 2-centimeter square box on the back of your hand.
2 Use a cold nail to touch different spots in the boxed area on your hand. Mark the spots that feel cold with the marker. **Caution:** Nails are sharp.
3 Repeat the process, using the same boxed area on your hand and a heated nail. Mark spots that feel hot with a different colored marker.

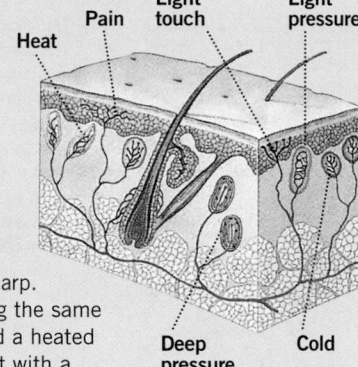

Analyze Your Results

1 Do you see a pattern to the location of your skin's temperature receptors?
2 Did you find more heat-sensitive spots or cold-sensitive spots? Explain your results.
3 Design an experiment that would allow you to map the pressure-sensitive areas of your skin.

CHECKPOINT 34.4

1. Describe the location and function of the two kinds of photoreceptors in the eye.
2. What is the cochlea? Briefly describe its shape and explain its function.
3. How can you stimulate the thermoreceptors, chemoreceptors, and nociceptors in your skin?
4. Critical Thinking A friend has stated that smell is a more valuable sense than taste. Do you agree? Explain your answer.

Build on What You Know

5. What groups of molecules are detected by the four kinds of taste receptors? *(Need to jog your memory? Revisit relevant concepts in Chapter 2, Sections 2.1 and 2.2.)*

What makes up the nervous system?

Chapter 34 Nervous Systems **837**

LAB ZONE Do It! TEAM WORK

Where Are Your Temperature Receptors?

Make sure students use water-soluble markers. To cool the nail, have students place it on an ice cube for a few minutes. To heat the nail, have students place the nail in a beaker of hot tap water.

Analyze Your Results

1 Students should be able to identify areas where sensations occurred.
2 Students may use a diagram to identify different sensitive areas.
3 Experiment should designate an experimentation area that cannot be observed by the subject.

 **3 ASSESS**

Evaluate Understanding

Divide the class into groups of four. Have each student write a summary for one of the subsections of Section 34.4. Then have the students in each group use the summaries to prepare a final summary of the entire section. Have each group present its combined summary to the class. Correct any misinformation.

Reteach

Work with students to create an outline of the section. Turn each head into a main idea statement. Then have students provide details that support each statement.

CHECKPOINT 34.4

1. Cones detect color in bright light. Rods detect low levels of light. Both are located in the retina.
2. The cochlea is a fluid filled, coiled organ in the ear that detects sounds.
3. Thermoreceptors—stimulated by hot or cold; chemoreceptors—stimulated by changes in concentration of blood chemicals; nociceptors—stimulated by damage to the body.
4. **Analyzing** Responses may suggest that humans can smell without taste, but cannot taste without smell.
5. Sweet receptors detect sugars; sour receptors detect acids; bitter receptors detect bases; and salt receptors detect sodium and chloride ions.

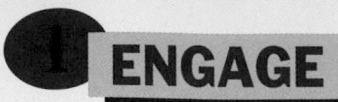

ENGAGE

Consider the Big Idea

Have students read The Big Idea! at the top of the page. Tell students that they will learn about three abuse factors: drugs, alcohol, and tobacco.

Use the Visual

Have students study the photograph that opens the section. Explain that caffeine is an example of a drug because it can change the way the body functions. Ask:

- **What changes can caffeine cause in the body?** (Likely responses: speeds heart rate, increases blood pressure, causes jitters)

Quick Activity

Ask students what words come to mind when they hear the word *drug*. List responses on the board. Tell students that a drug is any chemical substance that can affect the way the body functions. Ask students if they would now add or remove any words. Make the changes and have students copy the list and revisit it when they conclude this section.

THE BIG IDEA! The health of the nervous system can be affected by injury, disease, and substance abuse. 34.5

34.5 Nervous System Health and Substance Abuse

What you'll learn

IDEAS
- To identify various nervous system disorders
- To compare the effects of alcohol and tobacco

WORDS
concussion, Alzheimer's disease, stimulants, depressants, hallucinogens, narcotics

The most common addiction?
The caffeine in cola drinks, coffee, tea, and chocolate has mild effects. The most noticeable effect is a feeling of being awake. A surprisingly small amount of regular caffeine use can lead to a dependency. People who drink only two cups of coffee or three colas a day can get headaches if they suddenly give up the habit.

NERVOUS SYSTEM DISORDERS

System down!

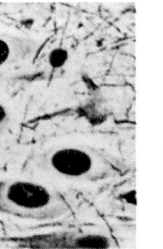

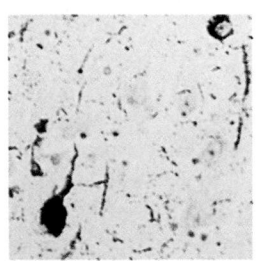

FIGURE 34.18
These electron micrographs show normal brain tissue (top) and diseased tissue from a patient with Alzheimer's disease (bottom). What differences do you see between the two tissues? ❶

Although well protected, your nervous system is still susceptible to injuries and diseases. Injuries and diseases that strike the nervous system are particularly serious because the parts of the nervous system cannot heal as other parts of the body can.

Most mature neurons cannot undergo mitotic cell division, so these cells cannot replace themselves if they are damaged or destroyed. If a neuron's cell body is damaged, the neuron will die. However, if a neuron's axon is damaged, the cell may survive. Under proper conditions, damaged axons that make up peripheral nerves can regenerate. If the axon's connections are not too far away, and if the axon's path is not blocked by other tissue, neurons can re-establish axon-dendrite connections. Axons that make up tracts in the central nervous system, however, do not regenerate under normal conditions.

Neurons and nerve tissue can be damaged either by injury or by disease. A blow to the head, such as a fall, can cause a brain injury called a

concussion. The blow knocks the brain against the inside of the skull, causing a bruise to the brain. The person may feel dizzy, see "stars," or become unconscious. Minor concussions usually do not result in permanent brain damage, but more serious injuries can cause permanent paralysis and coma. Injuries to sense organs, such as the eyes and ears, can also have permanent results, including blindness and deafness.

Damage to the brain's circulatory vessels can also result in neuron death. A blockage in one of the brain's blood vessels can lead to a stroke. The blockage may be the result of a blood clot or of narrowing of the blood vessels due to atherosclerosis. Because blood flow is interrupted, vital brain tissue dies from lack of oxygen. Symptoms of a stroke include paralysis, slurred speech, numbness, and blurred vision.

Another problem related to blood circulation is shock. In shock, significant blood loss or other serious injury suddenly reduces the amount of blood reaching the body's vital organs—including the brain. Symptoms of

838 *Unit 8 Human Biology*

STUDENT RESOURCES	TECHNOLOGY RESOURCES
From the Teacher's Resource Package, use: ■ Section Review 34.5, Enrichment Topics 34-2, Vocabulary Review 34, and Chapter 34 Tests from Unit 8 Review Module ■ Issues and Decision Making 34-2 ■ Consumer Applications 34-2	Relevant technology resources include: ■ Spanish Student Edition CD-ROM ■ Teacher's Resource Planner CD-ROM ■ How Your Body Works CD-ROM ■ TestWorks CD-ROM: Chapter 34 Tests

shock include weakness, dizziness, and loss of consciousness. A person in shock has pale, clammy skin; shallow, rapid breathing; and a weak, rapid pulse.

There are additional diseases that affect the brain. As you can see in *Figure 34.18*, in **Alzheimer's disease** the brain tissue deteriorates. Abnormal protein deposits build up in brain tissue, and parts of the brain waste away. People with Alzheimer's disease lose their memory, become disoriented, and may undergo a complete personality change.

Other diseases attack the nerves and spinal cord. A disease called multiple sclerosis affects the myelin sheaths that protect neurons and assist in transmitting nerve impulses. Damage to the myelin sheaths can slow or stop nerve impulses. A person with multiple sclerosis may experience impaired vision and speech, muscle weakness, tremors, and paralysis. Polio, a disease that can be prevented by vaccination, is caused by a virus that affects the gray matter of the spinal cord, damaging motor neurons and eventually causing paralysis.

AN OVERVIEW OF DRUGS

Aspirin to Xanax

A drug is a nonfood chemical substance that changes the way the body functions. Many drugs are used to treat illnesses. Other drugs have no medicinal use, and though many of these are illegal, some are legally available. Caffeine is the drug in coffee, tea, cola drinks, and even chocolate. Beer, wine, and liquor contain the drug alcohol. And cigarettes contain the powerful drug nicotine.

Of course, all drugs—from caffeine to street drugs such as crack and heroin—can be misused or abused. But any use of a medicinal drug other than for its intended purpose and in

the recommended amount is a misuse. Drugs taken without a prescription or for a nonmedical purpose are illegal, and use of them constitutes drug abuse.

Many drugs, legal and illegal, cause drug dependency. People with a drug dependency crave the drug and may endanger themselves or others in order to get more of the drug. Drug dependency can be psychological, physical, or both. Physical dependency on a drug is called addiction.

Many of the drugs for sale at pharmacies are over-the-counter drugs. These drugs are safe and effective when used according to the label instructions. Even then, some over-the-counter drugs have dangerous side effects. For example, over-the-counter diet aids may cause an abnormal heartbeat.

Chapter 34   Nervous Systems   **839**

LAB ZONE Think About It!   bioSURF

Analyzing Pain Pills and Their Cost

Do you know what the active ingredient is in the last pill you took for a headache or a sore muscle? The vast majority of popular over-the-counter pain medications contain one of just three drugs: aspirin, acetaminophen, or ibuprofen. Check pain medication labels the next time you are in a drugstore.

For example, Brand A is a widely advertised name brand. Each tablet contains 200 mg of ibuprofen. Brand A costs $4.99 for a 100-tablet bottle. Brand B is generic; it is just called ibuprofen. Each tablet contains 200 mg of ibuprofen; the bottle contains 200 tablets; and it costs $1.99.

Analyze Your Results

1 If a dose is one tablet, calculate the cost per dose for each brand.
2 If you take six pain pills per week for the next 30 years, how much money would you save by using a generic brand instead of Brand A?

---

❶ The brain cells are destroyed and disorganized in the Alzheimers patient.

---

② TEACH

Clarify Misconceptions

Many students may think that a brain tumor involves abnormal growth and division of the neurons of the brain. Remind students that unlike other cells, neurons do not undergo mitosis to produce new cells. A brain tumor involves abnormal growth and reproduction of the glial cells of the brain.

LAB ZONE Think About It!

Analyzing Pain Pills and Their Cost

Have students repeat the activity using the actual prices of these products.

Analyze Your Results

1 Brand A, 5¢; Brand B, 1¢
2 $374.40

Discuss

Point out that the Food and Drug Administration (FDA) defines the term *drug abuse* as "deliberately taking a substance for other than its intended purpose, and in a manner that can result in damage to the person's health or his ability to function." Ask:

■ **How does drug abuse differ from drug misuse?** (Drug misuse is taking a substance for its intended use but not in the recommended amount, frequency, or manner.)

Apply

Seizures may be caused by epilepsy as well as by drug abuse. Electroencephalography is a method used to diagnose convulsive disorders such as epilepsy. This procedure amplifies, records, and analyzes the electrical activity of the brain. In electroencephalography, electrodes are attached to the scalp to measure differences in the electrical potential of different sites of the cerebrum. The results are recorded as an electroencephalograph (EEG). Point out that epilepsy can be controlled with medication.

STS

Point out to students that fetal alcohol syndrome affects one in every 750 newborns in the United States. Women who drink three ounces (88 milliliters) or more of alcohol per day while pregnant have a one in three chance of delivering a baby with FAS.

Class Activity

Before beginning the section on tobacco, provide groups of students empty cigarette packages. Instruct each group to read the Surgeon General's Warnings printed on the packages. Ask:

- **What harmful chemical is contained in cigarette smoke?** (Carbon monoxide)
- **What are some health problems associated with smoking?** (Lung cancer, emphysema, complications during pregnancy)

FIGURE 34.24
What differences do you see in the three livers in the photo above? The liver on the left is normal; the liver in the center has fatty deposits from alcohol abuse; and the liver on the right is cirrhotic. ❶

functioning. This condition of the liver is called cirrhosis. Many people who seriously abuse alcohol die from cirrhosis. Compare the healthy liver tissue to the liver tissue with cirrhosis in *Figure 34.24*.

Many other health risks are associated with alcohol abuse. Alcohol is an addictive drug that produces both psychological and physical dependency. Alcohol dependency is called alcoholism. Symptoms of alcoholism may include a "need" for a drink to feel normal, drinking all day, and memory blackouts. Research suggests that a tendency to develop alcoholism is inherited. However, no one can become dependent on alcohol unless they drink it.

When alcoholics and heavy drinkers stop drinking, they experience a withdrawal period. Symptoms of alcohol withdrawal can be severe, especially if the drinker stops suddenly. In cases of severe alcoholism, withdrawal can cause delirium tremens, or DTs. This condition produces hallucinations, seizures, and sometimes death. Medically supervised withdrawal can help an alcoholic to successfully stop drinking alcohol.

Fetal alcohol syndrome

Although alcohol can be damaging to anyone, unborn babies are particularly vulnerable to its harmful effects. When a pregnant woman drinks alcohol, alcohol passes from the mother to the developing fetus through the placenta, slowing the growth of fetal tissue. Brain tissue, which grows very quickly in developing fetuses, is particularly susceptible. With heavy drinking, fetal damage can be quite serious, resulting in a condition called fetal alcohol syndrome (FAS).

This syndrome includes physical, mental, and behavioral defects. Typically, babies born with FAS are smaller than normal. They also have smaller heads and some degree of mental retardation. As they grow up and start school, they tend to have trouble due to a short attention span and poor coordination. These children may also have trouble adjusting socially due to jittery or impulsive behavior. In some cases FAS children eventually catch up in their development and lead a normal life. In other cases, however, the damage is permanent.

Labels on alcoholic beverages include warnings to pregnant women. Public service announcements warn

FIGURE 34.25
The developing brain tissue of this child was damaged by alcohol prior to the child's birth.

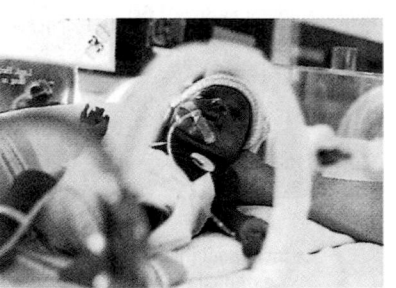

FACTS AND FIGURES

According to the U.S. Department of Education, alcohol is the leading drug problem among young people.

❶ The normal liver is smooth, dense and has normal amounts of fatty tissue. The alcohol-abused liver shows signs of scarring and a buildup of fatty tissue. The cirrhotic liver is significantly damaged by scarring and contains much fatty tissue.

future parents about the dangers of alcohol. Should more be done? What do you think would help solve the problem? ❷

TOBACCO

A pack of trouble

Because of the large number of smoking-related deaths each year, some consider nicotine to be the most deadly drug. A highly addictive stimulant, nicotine increases the heart rate and narrows blood vessels. Tobacco smoke contains many other harmful chemicals, such as carbon monoxide, hydrogen cyanide, ammonia gas, and tar. Tar is a thick, dark, sticky substance that is carcinogenic, or cancer-causing. All these substances can directly damage the respiratory and circulatory systems.

Smoking can paralyze or destroy the cilia that line respiratory structures. You may recall from Chapter 32 that cilia move the mucus that traps pathogens and particles out of the air passages. When the cilia are not working properly, mucus accumulates in the lungs, producing a "smoker's cough." Smoking eventually destroys the cilia completely.

Smoking is a recognized cause of lung cancer. Other cancers are also associated with tobacco use. For example, people who chew or sniff tobacco run a high risk of getting cancer of the mouth and throat. These cancers have

been detected even in teenagers.

Years of smoking can destroy the lungs' alveoli, causing emphysema. As scar tissue develops in the lungs, the alveoli lose their elasticity and exhaling becomes difficult. There is no cure for emphysema.

You may be surprised to know that heart attacks are the number-one cause of death among smokers. The narrowing of blood vessels caused by nicotine reduces the amount of blood that circulates throughout the body. The heart has to pump harder to force the blood through the system, so blood pressure rises.

Carbon monoxide, a by-product of smoking, complicates the work of the circulatory system by binding to hemoglobin at the sites used by oxygen and carbon dioxide. As a result, the blood delivers less oxygen to body tissues. During exercise, smokers tend to tire more easily than nonsmokers.

For people who quit smoking, the risk of heart attack returns to normal after about one year. However, quitting smoking is very difficult. Most people try to quit three to five times before they are successful. The addiction to nicotine and the habit of lighting and

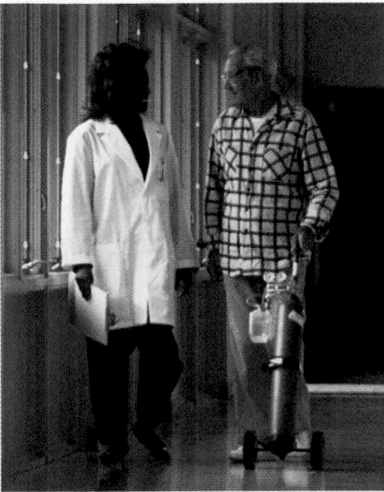

FIGURE 34.26
Emphysema results when scar tissue forms in the lungs. People with emphysema must often rely on oxygen tanks to breathe.

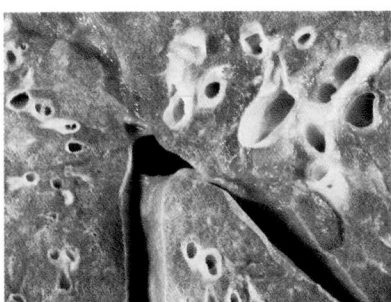 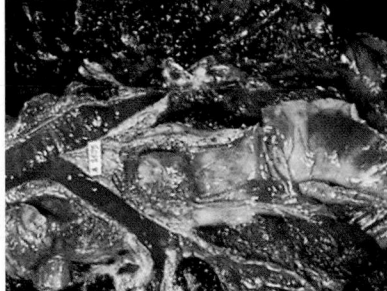

FIGURE 34.27
What differences do you see between the healthy lung tissue on the left and the lung tissue of a person who smoked cigarettes on the right? ❸

Chapter 34 Nervous Systems **843**

❷ Students may suggest support groups for pregnant women with alcohol problems.

❸ Healthy tissue is pink and alveolar walls are healthy. Smoker's lung is dark and alveolar walls are compressed.

In the Community

The name and location of programs that combat drug abuse may be found in a telephone directory. Most programs will probably be sponsored by community groups. Some groups may advertise, many do not.

3 ASSESS

Evaluate Understanding

Have students create a table in which they identify the health risks associated with misuse or abuse of over-the-counter, prescription, and each group of illegal drugs, as well as alcohol and tobacco. Check tables for accuracy.

Reteach

Write the following terms on the board as heads: *over-the-counter drugs, prescription drugs, illegal drugs, tobacco,* and *alcohol.* Have students define each group. Record their responses. Next, have volunteers list substances that belong in each group. Conclude the review with a discussion of the potential health problems associated with misuse or abuse of each type of substance.

 Finding the Main Idea and Supporting Details
To practice strategies for effective reading, use pages 73-74 in *Super Read!*

844

IN THE COMMUNITY
Drug Abuse Prevention

Find out if the town, city, or region where you live has organizations or programs aimed at preventing drug abuse. Find out what substance(s) each organization focuses on and what audience each organization targets. Do the programs operate through police or other law-enforcement agencies? Are the programs tied into community organizations? Do the programs advertise? Learn how the groups in your community work. Chart the approaches they use to change behavior. You can log on to *http://body_systems.biosurf.com* to find out more information on drug abuse prevention.

smoking a cigarette are a hard combination to break. No one ever regrets having stopped smoking, so if you do not smoke, do not start.

CARE OF YOUR NERVOUS SYSTEM
Helmet on and buckle up

FIGURE 34.28
What are the laws in your state about wearing helmets while biking or participating in other sports? **❶**

Your nervous system makes all your activities possible. So taking care of it is a good investment. Always wear a helmet when you ride a bike or a motorcycle, or when you are skateboarding or rollerblading. Fasten your seat belt whenever you ride in a car. Do not dive into water unless you know the water is deep enough to do so safely. If you participate in sports in which falling is likely, learn to fall safely.

Like other body systems, your nervous system benefits from proper food, rest, and exercise. Avoid abusing your body with drugs, including alcohol and tobacco. Also, make sure that you get enough sleep so that your brain can work at its peak performance level. Sleep deprivation affects memory and slows response time, which can lead to many kinds of accidents.

Protecting your sense organs is also important. Wear foam earplugs or other hearing protectors in noisy areas. To protect your eyes, wear protective goggles in the lab or workshop, and wear sunglasses while outside in bright sunlight. While working with chemicals or dust, wear a mask to protect your nose.

CHECKPOINT 34.5

1. Name three different disorders of the nervous system.
2. What are the harmful effects of alcohol and tobacco?
3. **Critical Thinking** Morphine is a prescription drug derived from opium. What type of drug is morphine? What are the effects of this type of drug?

Build on What You Know
4. What functions of the body could be affected if the liver is damaged by cirrhosis? *(Need to jog your memory? Revisit relevant concepts in Chapter 30, Section 30.2.)*

 What factors affect the health of the nervous system?

844   *Unit 8 Human Biology*

CHECKPOINT 34.5

1. Stroke, shock, Alzheimer disease, multiple sclerosis, polio, and injuries to sense organs
2. Alcohol depresses brain activity, damages the liver, and can cause death or injury from accidents or excessive consumption. Tobacco damages respiratory structures, narrows blood vessels, and interferes with the delivery of oxygen to body tissues.
3. **Comparing** Morphine is an opiate, or narcotic. It relieves pain and induces sleep, and it is highly addictive.
4. Liver damage would affect digestion and blood functions.

❶ Answers will vary.

Chapter 34 Review

 **THE BIG IDEA!**
34.1 Nervous systems control our detection of and response to the environment.
34.2–34.4 The human nervous system consists of the brain, spinal cord, nerves, and sensory organs.
34.5 The health of the nervous system can be affected by injury, disease, and substance abuse.

Sum It Up

Use the following summary to review the main concepts in this chapter.

34.1 Sensing and Control

- Nervous systems gather and respond to information from the environment.
- The peripheral nervous system (PNS) supplies data to the central nervous system (CNS); the CNS responds with instructions to the PNS.
- Neurons are cells that transmit nerve impulses.
- Glial cells protect and support neurons.

34.2 Nerves at Work

- During nerve impulse transmission, ions move across the neuron membrane.
- Chemicals carry messages across the synapse.
- Different types of neurons carry impulses to the CNS, from the CNS, and within the CNS.

34.3 Central and Peripheral Nervous Systems

- The spinal cord relays impulses between the PNS and the brain.
- The brain stem controls survival functions; the cerebellum coordinates muscle activity; the cerebrum controls conscious activities. Emotions, memory, and learning involve the limbic system.

- Some responses of the PNS are voluntary. Involuntary, or autonomic, PNS responses are controlled by opposing systems—the sympathetic and parasympathetic nervous systems—that function together to maintain homeostasis.

34.4 The Senses

- Receptors on the eye's retina and in the ear's cochlea change light and sound waves into nerve impulses, respectively.
- Chemoreceptors in taste buds and the nasal passages detect taste and smell.
- Skin has receptors for touch, temperature, and pain.

34.5 Nervous System Health and Substance Abuse

- Nerve tissue can be damaged by physical injury, a lack of oxygen, or disease.
- Drugs can speed up or slow down nerve impulses, alter perceptions, and damage organs.
- There are many health risks associated with alcohol and tobacco.

Use Terms and Concepts

Use each of the following words or terms in a complete sentence. If you need to review a meaning, turn to the page indicated.

ganglia (p. 822)
central nervous system (p. 823)
peripheral nervous system (p. 823)
neurons (p. 823)
glial cells (p. 824)
resting potential (p. 825)

action potential (p. 825)
synapses (p. 826)
sensory neurons (p. 826)
motor neurons (p. 827)
interneurons (p. 827)
reflex arc (p. 827)
brain stem (p. 829)
cerebellum (p. 829)

cerebrum (p. 829)
somatic nervous system (p. 831)
autonomic nervous system (p. 832)
sympathetic nervous system (p. 832)
parasympathetic nervous system (p. 832)

retina (p. 834)
cochlea (p. 835)
concussion (p. 838)
Alzheimer's disease (p. 839)
stimulants (p. 840)
depressants (p. 840)
hallucinogens (p. 840)
narcotics (p. 840)

Review the Big Ideas

Before students begin the Chapter Review, you may wish to discuss main concepts from the Big Ideas in Chapter 34. The function of the nervous system is to control the detection of and response to various environmental stimuli. In humans, the nervous system has two main parts: a central nervous system, consisting of the brain and spinal cord, and a peripheral nervous system, consisting of the network of nerves and the sense organs. The nervous system can be harmed by injury, disease, and the use of drugs, alcohol, and tobacco.

Answers

1. Alzheimer disease
2. depressants; stimulants
3. glial cells; neurons
4. cochlea; retina
5. cerebellum; brain stem; cerebrum
6. autonomic nervous system
7. concussion
8. True
9. False; parasympathetic nervous system
10. True
11. False; an automatic response
12. False; resting potential
13. True
14. False; hallucinogens
15. Stimulants speed up CNS activity; depressants slow down CNS activity.
16. Schwann cells form a myelin sheath that binds together and insulates nerve fibers; astrocytes supply nutrients to neurons and maintain a stable chemical environment.
17. Only autonomic activities are controlled in the brain stem; all voluntary activities are controlled by the cerebrum.
18. Sound waves (vibrate) → eardrum (vibrates) → stirrup (vibrates) → fluid in cochlea (vibrates) → hair cells (transmit impulses) → cochlear nerve
19. Parasympathetic nerves slow the heartbeat; sympathetic nerves speed up the heartbeat.
20. The iris controls the amount of light entering the eye, the retina contains the photoreceptors that convert light energy into electrical impulses; the optic nerve carries the impulses to the brain.
21. The resting potential is negative. When the positive

Use Your Word Power

COMPLETION Write the word or phrase that best completes each statement.

1. A loss of memory can be a key symptom of _____ .

2. Drugs that are _____ slow down impulses; drugs that are _____ speed up impulses.

3. Schwann cells and astrocytes are two kinds of _____ , which support and protect _____.

4. The _____ contains mechano-receptors; the _____ contains photoreceptors.

5. The _____ controls balance; the _____ controls breathing; the _____ controls speech.

6. Involuntary responses are controlled by the _____ .

7. A blow to the head can cause a(n) _____ .

TRUE-FALSE Write true if the statement is true. If the statement is false, replace the underlined word(s) to make the statement true.

8. Skeletal muscles are stimulated by the somatic nervous system.

9. Digestion is inhibited by the sympathetic nervous system.

10. Neurotransmitters carry messages across synapses.

11. The nerve pathway used for a voluntary response to a stimulus is a reflex arc.

12. The electrical charge across the membrane of a neuron prior to transmission is the action potential.

13. The brains of some invertebrates are clusters of nerve cells called ganglia.

14. Drugs such as LSD and mescaline are narcotics.

Show What You Know

15. What is the difference between a stimulant and a depressant?

16. Compare the functions of Schwann cells and astrocytes in the human nervous system.

17. What is the key difference between the functions of the cerebrum and the brain stem?

18. How do the structures in an ear change a sound wave into nerve impulses?

19. Give an example of how the sympathetic and parasympathetic nervous systems work together to maintain homeostasis.

20. What roles do the iris, retina, and optic nerve play in vision?

21. How does the flow of sodium and potassium ions across a neuron cell membrane affect the membrane potential?

22. What role does water play in the identification of tastes and smells?

23. **Make a Concept Map** As you walk by a plate of cookies, you smell them and decide to pick one up. Make a concept map to describe the interactions of the different parts of your nervous system that are involved in smelling the cookies and responding to this stimulus.

Take It Further

24. **Applying Concepts** Why are barbiturates and alcohol a life-threatening combination?

25. **Developing a Hypothesis** Acetylcholine is the neurotransmitter that relays signals between motor neurons and skeletal muscles. Muscles respond after acetylcholine binds to receptors on the muscles. The drug curare also binds to muscle receptors but cannot activate them. Hunters in South America have used curare on the tips of darts and arrows. What effect does curare have on an animal?

sodium ions flow into the cell, they create a positive potential; when the positive potassium ions flow out of the cell, they restore the negative potential.

22. Molecules must dissolve in watery saliva or in mucus before they are detected by taste buds or smell receptors.

23. Concepts maps should show: The nervous system is composed of the central nervous system, which consists of the brain and spinal cord, and the peripheral nervous system, which has sensory neurons, which go to a receptor that receive a stimulus, interneurons, and motor neurons, which go to a muscle that initiates the response.

24. Barbiturates and alcohol are both depressants.

26. Interpreting a Graph This graph is based on data from the U.S. Department of Health and Human Services. How often is alcohol involved in highway deaths? What percent of murders are alcohol related? What is the incidence of alcohol-related accidents at work?

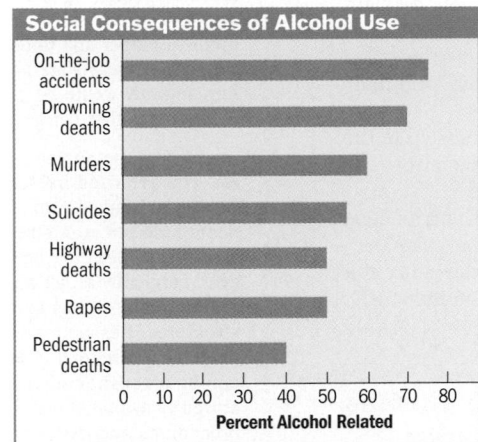

Social Consequences of Alcohol Use

Bar graph showing Percent Alcohol Related (x-axis, 0 to 80):
- On-the-job accidents
- Drowning deaths
- Murders
- Suicides
- Highway deaths
- Rapes
- Pedestrian deaths

27. Analyzing Data The following table shows the percent of brain neurons lost, on average, from different parts of the brain during aging. Which region of the brain shows the greatest loss of neurons? Which region shows the least? What functions could be affected by neuron loss in the cerebellum? In the hippocampus?

Neuron Loss and Aging	
Region of the Brain	**Percent Loss**
Cerebellum	25
Visual association area	50
Auditory association area	30–50
Hippocampus	30
Thalamus	0

28. Designing an Experiment What factors can affect the ability to learn? Do physical stresses such as hunger or lack of sleep have an effect on learning? What effect do distractions such as noise or music have on the ability to learn? Choose one factor, propose a hypothesis, and design an experiment to test your hypothesis.

29. Applying Concepts During an asthma attack, the respiratory passages become narrower. Which division of the nervous system should an asthma-treating drug target?

30. Making an Analogy Describe two characteristics that a neuron and an extension cord have in common. How do they differ?

Consider the Issues

31. Alternative Therapies Many people seek alternatives to conventional medicine to combat diseases or disorders. These therapies include ancient, traditional treatments, such as Chinese acupuncture, and many other nonconventional options. How can a consumer determine if an alternative treatment is safe and effective? What role should physicians play in evaluating alternative treatments?

Make New Connections

32. Biology and Language Speakers of English use words related to the senses in many descriptive phrases. For example, working hard may be described as keeping your "nose to the grindstone." Find as many of these phrases as you can and classify them according to each of the five senses.

33. Biology and History Report on the contributions to our knowledge of the nervous system made by Charles Sherrington, Joseph Erlanger, Edgar Adrian, Bernard Katz, A. F. Huxley, and Alan Hodgkin.

FAST-FORWARD TO CHAPTER 35

The nervous system provides an organism with information about its environment. Chapter 35 will describe the range of environments and the factors that organisms must adapt to in a given environment.

Chapter 34 Nervous Systems **847**

---

31. Consumers can contact their local health department or do research in the library or on the Internet to find out about alternative treatments

32. Vision is the sense most highly valued for metaphor as in "seeing is believing."

33. Students could also collect data about current researchers from news reports, periodicals, and the Internet.

---

25. Skeleton muscles in an animal poisoned by curare cannot be activated. The paralyzed animal dies when it stops breathing. (Doctors use small doses of curare to treat muscle spasms and to prevent contractions during surgery.)

26. 50 percent; 60 percent; 75 percent

27. Visual cortex; thalamus; balance and motion; memory and learning

28. Possible hypothesis: Subjects will learn better when not hungry/distracted.

29. Accept all logical answers.

30. Both the neuron and the electrical cord transmit electrical impulses and are surrounded by insulation. The extension cord can transmit a continuous flow of electrons; a neuron is dependent on neurotransmitters and nutrients.

Connect the Chapters

1. Alveoli increase surface area for gas exchange; villi increase surface area for the absorption of nutrients.
2. Both the muscles and the nerves are paired, with each member of the pair having an opposing effect.
3. The glial cells that support and protect neurons are connective tissue in the nervous system. Blood is connective tissue in the circulatory system.
4. Arthritis involves painful inflammation of joints. The inflammatory response is a nonspecific reaction of the immune system.
5. The liver breaks down drugs or toxins. The kidneys remove nitrogenous wastes, excess salts, and the products of liver detoxification. The lymph nodes filter intercellular fluid.
6. Both antibodies and protein hormones bind to molecules on target cell surfaces.
7. Motor neurons and sensory neurons carry impulses to and from the CNS; arteries and veins carry blood to and from the heart. Arteries and veins are connected by capillaries; motor and sensory neurons are connected by interneurons.

Connect the Units

8. Yes, energy is required to pump potassium ions back into the cell and sodium ions back out of the cell.
9. Answers will vary.
10. The enzyme reverse transcriptase transcribes viral RNA into viral DNA within T4 cells.

Unit 8 Review

THE BIG IDEA! Answering the following questions will help you to link ideas and grasp the core concepts.

Connect the Chapters

1. What key feature do the alveoli in lungs share with the villi in intestines? How does this feature support the functions of lungs and small intestines?
2. What do skeletal muscles and the motor nerves of the autonomic nervous system have in common?
3. Where can you find connective tissue in the nervous and circulatory systems?
4. Explain why drugs that suppress the immune system might be used in treating arthritis.
5. Compare the roles of the liver, kidneys, and lymph nodes in cleansing body fluids.
6. Describe a method used by both antibodies and protein hormones to accomplish their respective functions.
7. Compare the functions of the three types of blood vessels and the three types of neurons.

Connect the Units

8. Is active transport involved in nerve transmission? Explain.
9. What could fossils reveal about the skeletal, muscular, digestive, nervous, and reproductive systems?
10. Describe the first step in the replication of the retrovirus HIV by T4 cells.
11. What structures and functions do leaves and skin share?
12. Compare the respiratory systems of birds and humans, including the flow of air into the lungs.

Connect to Themes

13. **Unity and Diversity** Compare the role of antigens in blood transfusions and in the immune response.
14. **Energy** Describe how the differences in animals' excretory and respiratory systems are adaptations for life in different environments.
15. **Scale and Structure** Explain how the relative sizes of egg and sperm cells are related to their functions.

CRITIC'S CORNER

A.D.A.M.
The Inside Story
User's Guide

A.D.A.M. The Inside Story, is an excellent way to learn about the human body. The software allows one to explore any part of the body, from pectoral muscles to the skull, and to observe it from the front, back, or side. The software can also transform organs, muscles, and bone structures into 3-D figures, making it possible to observe the body on several levels simultaneously. I found this software gave me the freedom to explore what most interests me about the human body.

A CD-ROM REVIEW BY MAYA S. LEE MENLO PARK, CA

11. Answers should include descriptions of coverings, pores, and tissues.
12. A bird's respiratory system is unique in that it flows through the lungs in only one direction (from posterior air sacs.) The flow of air into the bird's lungs is continuous.

Connect to Themes

13. If the blood types in a transfusion do not match, the recipient's B leukocytes produce antibodies that bind to the foreign antigens on the surface of red blood cells from the donor's blood and cause the cells to clump, just as bacteria clump when antibodies produced by B lymphocytes bind to their antigens.

SPOTLIGHT ON CAREERS

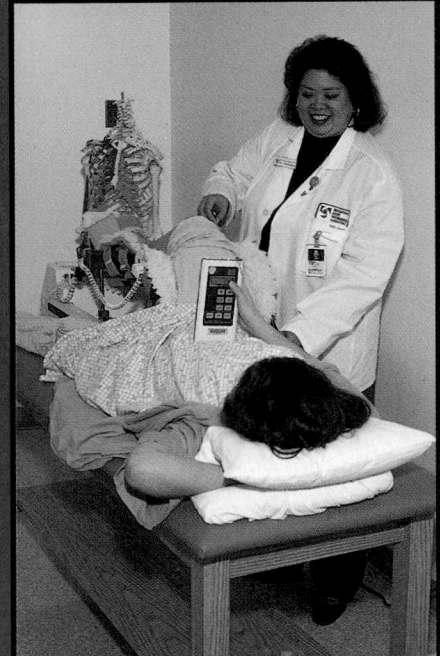

BARBARA ODAKA
Physical therapist and clinical supervisor
EDUCATION: B.S. in allied health sciences; certificate in physical therapy

"Biology is essential to anyone interested in a health career. It's important for a physical therapist to know about human development. We need to know how the body works normally, so someone with a disease or some kind of injury can be given the right kind of therapy. Most people come to a physical therapist for orthopedics after an injury, to regain the use of an injured limb, or to learn to walk again. We usually do manual therapy, using physical agents like heat, cold, and electricity. We also see cardiovascular patients to provide them with appropriate exercise programs to help them recuperate. These days, there's great research being done, making new therapies available. It's a challenge to keep up, but it's a good challenge . . . ."

bioSURF Visit the Internet site http://body_systems.biosurf.com to find out more about physical therapy.

JEAN DRISCOLL
Assistant coach
EDUCATION: B.S. in speech communication; M.S. in rehabilitation administration

"When I go on speaking tours, I talk about 'dreaming big and working hard.'"
—JEAN DRISCOLL

"I was born with spina bifida, which is an opening in the spine. . . . When I was growing up, for someone with a disability, fitness was never stressed. . . . I was recruited to play wheelchair basketball at the University of Illinois, and started doing racing just for fun. Then, when I started winning races, I got really interested in fitness. . . .The only muscles I have to work with are in my upper body, so I have to understand how the muscle groups work. . . . I do about 15–20 races per year, from track meet events to 10K races to marathons. . . . I work as an assistant to my coach, Marty Morse. I do administrative and coaching duties for him, and he trains me for races."

bioSURF Explore http://body_systems.biosurf.com for more information on biology careers.

Unit 8 Human Biology **849**

---

14. Students should describe adaptations in both terrestrial and aquatic animals. They should refer to sections 30.1 and 30.4 to answer the question.
15. Mature sperm cells are small and specialized for fast movement upstream through the female reproductive tract. The large egg cannot move on its own. The egg's cytoplasm sustains the zygote until the placenta forms.

Project Plans

1. Possible suggestions: artists study anatomy; beauticians need to know about skin, nails, and hair; a singer would be concerned with lung capacity.
2. Remind students that organ transplants are not devices. Devices include hip replacements and artificial limbs.
3. Job descriptions will vary.

SPOTLIGHT ON CAREERS

bioSURF Have students connect to the bioSurf address to learn about schools, educational programs, and scholarships that would prepare them for a career or occupation in a field related to human biology.

Consider These Careers

Careers involving health care are based on an understanding of the human body and its functions. Physicians, nurses, pharmacologists, nutritionists, physical therapists, optometrists, and even psychiatrists are just a few of the professionals involved in the care of the human body. Careers as paramedics or health-care administrators require less extensive training.

Plan for a Career

■ **Networking**
Employers are often reluctant to hire a "total stranger" because of the cost and risks involved in making the wrong hiring decision. Therefore, many employers prefer to choose candidates with whom they have had prior experience, either through professional contacts and organizations, or through other employees. Seminars, conferences, and other informal professional gatherings are an excellent way to establish a network of contacts. Have students research the professional organizations, clubs, and societies in your area that relate to their chosen fields. Find out about planned events for these groups in your area.

Unit Overview

The biosphere is home to a huge variety of organisms, all of which depend upon the resources in the biosphere to survive. The ecosystems that make up the biosphere are dynamic, evolving arenas that display an ability to change as well as to remain stable. As human populations grow, ecosystems become increasingly unstable and can lose their ability to sustain life. Steps are now being taken to slow the deterioration of the biosphere.

Unit Objectives

- Explain relationships between ecosystems and the biosphere
- Describe the flow of energy and some of the chemical cycles that take place within the biosphere
- Describe the relationships among populations within a community
- Discuss how humans interact with and affect the environment

Connect the Units

This unit provides a meaningful culmination to the study of life on Earth by exploring how Earth's organisms interact with each other to form the web of life. This unit could, however, be used as an introduction to the study of life by presenting the stage on which all of life's dramas are played. If this unit is presented first, it would be advisable to follow it with Unit 3: *Change and Diversity* to add meaning to the concepts of evolution and adaptive radiation that are critical to understanding ecosystem dynamics.

Which of these amazing statements about the environment are fact, and which are fiction?

Hit *or* Myth?

Some fishes do the work of **dentists.**

(Fact. They may not have gone to dentistry school, but wrasse fishes clean fungi and bacteria from the teeth and skin of larger fishes.)

Wetlands are not always wet.

(Fact. A wetland's dry cycle, which occurs in winter, does not completely remove moisture as a clothes dryer does, but it does remove enough to enable the wetland to absorb spring waters.)

The average amount of trash three Americans throw away in one year weighs nearly as much as a male **African elephant.**

(Fact. The average American throws away 1.85 tons of trash each year; the average African bull elephant weighs 6 tons.)

850 *Unit 9 Organisms and the Environment*

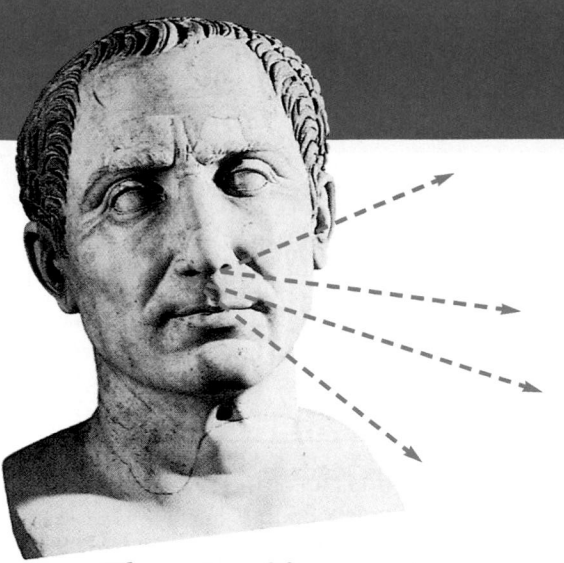

There is a 99 percent chance that some of the air you have inhaled contained a molecule from **Julius Caesar's last breath.**

(Fact. The molecules in air are part of chemical cycles that might have brought a molecule of 2000-year-old air to you.)

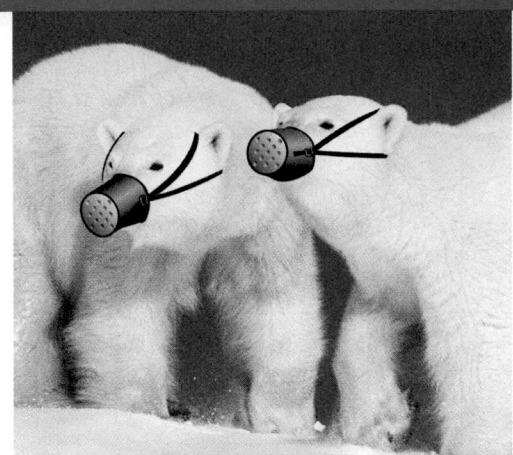

Only big cities have **smog.**

(Fiction. The wind can carry smog to remote areas. Some days, the smog in the Arctic rivals that of Los Angeles.)

All **deserts** are hot.

(Fiction. Deserts are characterized by lack of moisture, not high temperatures. For example, in the Great Basin Desert, temperatures range from -30° to 30° Celsius.)

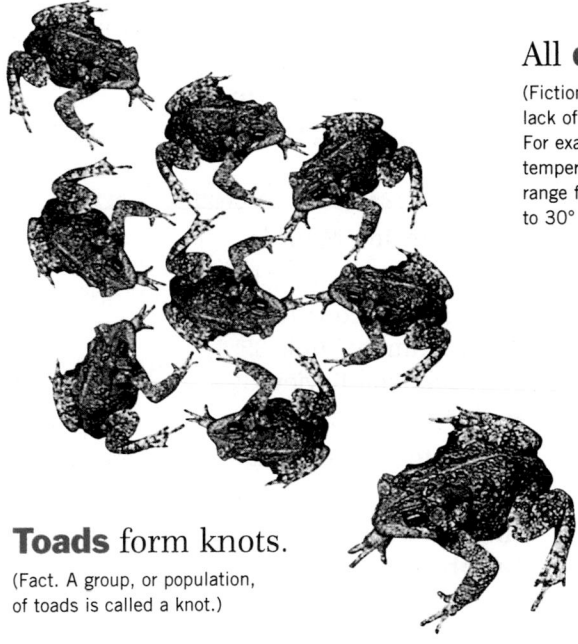

Toads form knots.

(Fact. A group, or population, of toads is called a knot.)

Unit 9 Organisms and the Environment **851**

Hit *or* Myth?

Use It

Review each of the statements with the class. Ask students to share their prior knowledge and misconceptions about each topic. Ask them to consider which sources of information on these topics are generally reliable and which may not be.

Link It

Chapter 35 links the characteristics of specific environments (wetlands, deserts) to their contributions to biodiversity. Chapters 36 and 37 link the concepts of species, populations, and communities to ecosystem structures (frogs). Chapter 38 explores the impact the growing human population has on the ecosystems and biodiversity of Earth (trash, smog).

Expand It

Cleaner wrasse fishes are not the only sea creatures that groom others. Cleaner shrimp, which remove dead skin tissues from other organisms, can be coaxed into giving people "manicures" by removing the cuticle at the base of fingernails.

Not all trash is garbage. About 50 to 60 percent of the trash generated by American cities could be used for fuel. Two metric tons of combustible wastes yield about as much energy as one metric ton of coal.

In addition to smog, volcanic eruptions like that of Mt. Pinatubo in the Philippines in 1990 can also send particles and pollutants high into the atmosphere, where they are transported by air currents around the world.

Chapter Objectives

Students will learn the main concepts of this chapter as they complete the following objectives.

- Identify the components of a biosphere
- Contrast populations, communities, and ecosystems
- Identify the factors that shape global and regional climates
- Explain the climate conditions that cause rain shadows
- Define the elements of a biome
- Compare land biomes
- Distinguish between the water biomes
- Describe the zones in the marine biome

Key Words

35.1 *ecology, biosphere, biotic factors, abiotic factors, population, community, ecosystem, habitat*

35.2 *climate, tropical zone, temperate zone, arctic zone, rain shadow, altitude*

35.3 *biome*

35.4 *wetlands, estuary*

The Opening Story

Have students discuss how they think the story relates to the content of this chapter. Elicit examples of organisms that are able to live in harsh environments and severe climates.

852

You can find out more about the biosphere by exploring the following Internet address:
http://ecology.biosurf.com

In this chapter . . .

FEATURES

Everyday Biology
- Making Soil
- Taking Water to the Cleaners

In the Community
Freshwater Field Day

 Issues in Biology
Help for Wetlands

LAB ZONES

Discover It!
- How Do Abiotic Factors Affect You

Do It!
- Modeling Seasons
- How Does Salt Water Affect Organisms?

Think About It!
- Predicting Weather in Your Biome

Investigate It!
- Testing the Water Capacity of Soils

852

HERE COMES THE RAIN

Every culture throughout history has valued rain. In an attempt to control rainfall, people from cultures native to North and South America, Europe, and Africa engaged in rituals. A rain dance in New Guinea included the use of long grasses, which were believed to pierce the sun's eyes, so that the sun would weep—making rain fall on Earth. In ancient Egypt, rain dances were memorialized in tomb paintings.

Rain is so valued because it determines climate, and climate affects the habitability of an area. Too little rain renders an area difficult to inhabit, as many organisms cannot survive the harsh conditions. Yet heavy rains can cause flooding, which may harm many organisms and destroy their habitats. Additional nonliving, or abiotic, factors that affect organisms in an environment are the amount of sunlight, the temperature, and the type of soil. How do these factors affect the organisms in a particular environment?

LAB ZONE Discover It!

How Do Abiotic Factors Affect You?

1. List several abiotic factors, such as rain and temperature.
2. Record how each factor affects your day-to-day activities. For example, if you live in an area that receives little rain, you may have to abide by water conservation laws.

Nonliving, or abiotic, factors determine your environment –for example, whether it is hot and dry, humid and tropical, or cold and snowy. Each environment has its own characteristics, to which its inhabitants are adapted. The variety of environments on Earth create its incredible biodiversity.

WRITE ABOUT IT!

In your science journal, write about the abiotic factors of your favorite climate. What do you like about each of these factors? What are some disadvantages?

Chapter 35 The Biosphere **853**

Opening Activities

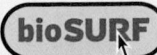 **bioSURF** If you have access to the Internet in your classroom or school, you may wish to have students connect to the address shown on page 852. You may also want to have students conduct net searches for information using key words related to this chapter. For example, they could search for entries under deserts, rain forests, the Everglades, or biodiversity.

LAB ZONE Discover It!

How Do Abiotic Factors Affect You? TEAM WORK

Before they begin the chapter, have students complete the activity as a homework assignment or in class. You may want to review the meaning of *abiotic* and identify other abiotic factors for students to consider.

WRITE ABOUT IT

Encourage students to illustrate their entries with drawings or photographs. Challenge them to name places that have the type of climate they prefer.

Rewind to Chapter 34

Briefly review the concepts learned in Chapter 34, *The Nervous System*. Ask:

- **How do think your senses, sensory receptors, and complex brain enhance your interaction with the environment?**

PORTFOLIO PREVIEW

Students should be encouraged to add to their portfolios as they work through this chapter. In addition to the *Write About It* opportunity, the following sections are excellent opportunities for portfolio entries:

- Section 35.1: *Characteristics of the Biosphere*
- Section 35.3: *Land Biomes*

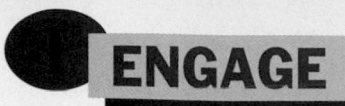

35.1 Characteristics of the Biosphere

What you'll learn

IDEAS
- To identify the components of a biosphere
- To contrast populations, communities, and ecosystems

WORDS
ecology, biosphere, biotic factors, abiotic factors, population, community, ecosystem, habitat

FIGURE 35.1
Earth is composed of a variety of regions. A computer compiled this cloudless image from several satellite photographs. What regions can you identify in this image? ❶

Not a typical office job
Ecologists are scientists who study environments all over the world, both in the water and on the land. This ecologist is studying an environment that is intermediate between land and water, called a marsh. She is especially interested in the organisms and food sources she may find in the water.

STUDYING ECOLOGY
Looking for life in all the right places

In the world of science, **ecology** is the study of organisms and their interactions with the environment. Biologists who specialize in this area are called ecologists. Ecologists, such as the one in the photograph above, work in every setting imaginable, from rain forests to prairie wetlands and from deserts to coral reefs.

There is no shortage of organisms for ecologists to study. Scientists have identified and classified more than 1.5 million different types of living things. How many millions more do you think await discovery? All these organisms live in a region of the Earth that extends from the darkest depths of the ocean floor to about 8 kilometers (km) into the atmosphere. This life-supporting region of Earth is called the **biosphere** (BY-uh-sfir). The biosphere includes all the land, water, and air in which organisms live.

Within Earth's biosphere are many different kinds of environments, including places as diverse as a bubbling

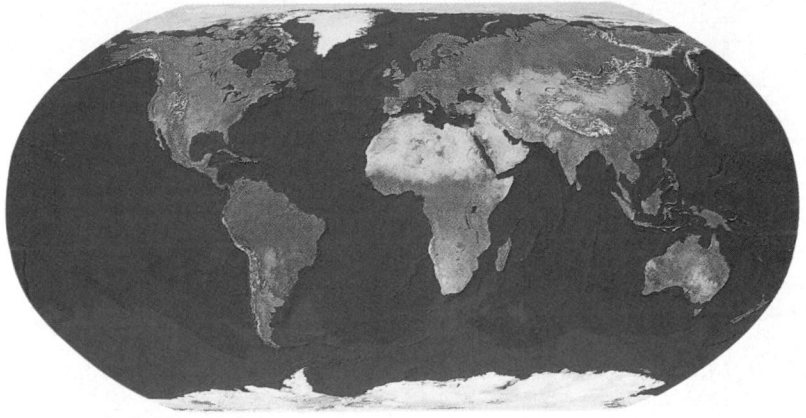

854

stream, a windswept mountain peak, and a vacant lot in a city. Although no two environments are exactly alike, every environment consists of both living and nonliving parts. The living parts of an environment are called **biotic** (by-OT-ic) **factors.** Examples of biotic factors are plants, animals, and other organisms. The nonliving parts of the environment are called **abiotic factors.** Abiotic factors include water, soil, light, temperature, wind, and physical space. Organisms obtain everything they need from the biosphere, and they depend on both biotic and abiotic factors to survive in their environments.

In Chapter 29 you learned that the human body has many levels of organization—cells, tissues, organs, and organ systems. The biosphere, too, has levels of organization—individuals, populations, communities, and ecosystems.

In the photos in *Figure* 35.2, you can identify the biotic and abiotic factors in the wildebeests' (WIL-duh-beests) environment. How does each factor affect the wildebeests? Could you learn about wildebeests by studying individual wildebeests? To get a more complete idea of how wildebeests interact with each other and their environment, you would probably study a group, or population, of wildebeests. A **population** consists of all the members of a single species that live in one area. A herd of wildebeests is a population, as is the grass growing in a field. What are some ways that the wildebeest population is interacting with its environment, as shown in ❷ *Figure* 35.2?

A population does not live alone in its environment. In any region of the biosphere, populations of many different organisms share a living space and interact with one another in a variety of ways. All the populations that live and interact in one environment make

up a **community.** How many members of the community can you identify in *Figure* 35.2? ❸

All the populations and abiotic factors in an area make up its **ecosystem.** An ecosystem can be a large area, such as a forest, a desert, or an ocean. It can also be a much smaller area, such as a sand dune, a quiet pond, or a backyard garden. What parts of an ecosystem can you identify in *Figure* 35.2? A healthy ecosystem usually includes a wide variety of species, a characteristic known as biodiversity. You will learn more about biodiversity in Chapter 36.

Like you, wildebeests also have a "home," or habitat. The type of environment in which a particular species lives is its **habitat.** Every species in a habitat has characteristics that enable it to function in the unique abiotic and biotic factors there. A habitat provides the members of a species with food, shelter, water, and whatever else they need to survive. What parts of the wildebeests' habitat are shown in *Figure* 35.2? ❺

FIGURE 35.2
The vulture (top) and wildebeests (bottom) belong to two of the many populations in this ecosystem (center). What abiotic factors can you see?

❹

EVERYDAY BIOLOGY

Making Soil

In a typical climate, it takes more than 2.5 centimeters (cm) of soil to be formed. In some climates, it may take hundreds of thousands of years to form 10 cm of soil!

Chapter 35 The Biosphere **855**

MEETING DIVERSE NEEDS

LEP Pair an LEP student with a native English speaker to create a visual illustrating the levels of organization within the biosphere. Tell them to include all terms in bold print in their visual. Encourage LEP students to record information in both English and their native language.

❶ Ocean, ice caps, and arid and tropical regions
❷ Wildebeests are eating grass and drinking water.
❸ Zebra, wildebeest, grass, vulture
❹ Water, soil, sunlight, arid climate
❺ Food, water, sunlight; open plain provides protection from enemies.

Use the Visual

Have students study Figure 35.2. Review the meaning of the terms *population, niches,* and *ecosystems.* Explain that a population is a group of organisms of the same species that live together in a particular location. A population's niche is defined by the role it plays in the environment, a role usually expressed in terms of feeding habits. Ask:

- **What is the niche of the buffalo?** (Consumer)
- **What is the niche of the grass?** (Producer)

Build Writing Skills

Have students work in small groups to select and study a nearby ecosystem, such as an aquarium, a park, garden, pond, or stream. Tell students to focus on interactions that occur between the living and nonliving parts of their ecosystem and prepare a group report. Encourage students to include drawings, diagrams, or photographs and label the abiotic and biotic factors shown. Provide time for groups to share their reports with the class.

Everyday Biology

Point out that different types of soil form in different environments. For example, deep soils form in warm, wet climates and shallow soils form in cool, dry areas. You may want to introduce the concept of soil erosion and discuss its causes. It is estimated that about 20 percent of the world's topsoil was lost to erosion between 1950 and 1990.

Earth Science

Earth scientists and environmentalists often speak of the Earth in terms of four spheres: the lithosphere, or land; the hydrosphere, or water; the atmosphere, the envelope of gases that surrounds Earth; and the biosphere, the parts of the other spheres that can support life.

Think Critically

Have students study Figure 35.3. Poll the class to see which of the abiotic factors pictured are cited in the lab activity on page 853. Ask:

■ **What do abiotic factors such as temperature, soil, water, and wind have in common?** (They are nonliving and relate to climate in some way.)

ASSESS

Evaluate Understanding

Write the objectives for this section on the board. Have students use the information from this section to write a paragraph that summarizes each objective. Review the summaries as a class.

Reteach

List the key words for the section on the board and review the definitions of each. With the class, use the terms to create a concept map to show the differences among populations, communities, and ecosystems, and the role that abiotic factors play in determining where in the biosphere organisms live.

FIGURE 35.3
Abiotic Factors

Water and oxygen ▶
Most living things cannot survive without water and oxygen. These two abiotic factors are both present in the waterfall.

Temperature ▲
Different organisms tolerate different temperature ranges. Some living things, such as the white spruce, can survive harsh environments, where temperatures are extreme.

◀ Wind
Wind affects weather. It shapes landforms (such as these sand dunes) and creates waves and currents that stir up nutrients in ponds, lakes, and oceans.

Fire ▶
Fire is a natural event that helps maintain conditions crucial for life in some ecosystems. After a fire sweeps across grasslands, grass plants quickly regrow, filling in the burned area before other types of plants can begin growing.

Soil ▲
Soils differ in texture, in the minerals and nutrients they contain, and in how well they hold water. Most land-dwelling organisms have adaptations that help them conserve water. The desert cacti shown here have a waxy coating that keeps them from drying out.

THE PHYSICAL ENVIRONMENT
Forces that shape life

As you just learned, the abiotic factors of an ecosystem include components such as light, water, temperature, oxygen, fire, wind, and soil. The degree to which these factors are present in an area affects the type and distribution of organisms that live in that area. The photographs above show examples of how abiotic factors affect ecosystems. How does sunlight affect a pond ecosystem? Why is fire sometimes beneficial to an ecosystem?

❶

856 *Unit 9 Organisms and the Environment*

CHECKPOINT 35.1

1. Identify the components that make up the biosphere.
2. Explain the difference between populations, communities, and ecosystems.
3. **Critical Thinking** How might fire be beneficial to the animals that live in a grassland?

Build on What You Know

4. How might changes in abiotic factors in an area lead to speciation? *(Need to jog your memory? Revisit relevant concepts in Chapter 10, Section 10.4.)*

CHECKPOINT 35.1

1. Land, water, and air in which organisms live
2. A population consists of just one species; a community, several different species; an ecosystem, communities and abiotic factors.
3. **Identifying cause and effect** A fire benefits animals that prey on other animals whose shelter is destroyed by fire.

4. Abiotic factors may cause an environmental change that isolates populations and results in gene pools so different that reproductive isolation and speciation occurs.

❶ Sunlight allows algae to photosynthesize, providing food for consumers. Fires can refurbish a habitat.

Testing the Water Capacity of Soils

WHAT YOU WILL DO Measure the water-holding capacity of three types of soil and estimate their rate of drainage

SKILLS YOU WILL USE Observing, measuring, collecting and recording data

WHAT YOU WILL NEED 3 funnels, filter paper, 3 glass beakers, a 100-mL graduated cylinder, grease pencil, sand, loam, clay, water

Propose a Hypothesis

Propose a hypothesis that predicts which type of soil holds the greatest amount of water and estimates the relative rate of drainage of each type.

Conduct Your Experiment

1 In your notebook, write the name of each soil type and record your observations of each, including the color.
2 Roll a small sample of each soil between your thumb and finger. In your notebook, describe the texture, or consistency, of each soil.
3 Line each of the three funnels with filter paper, and place each one in a glass beaker. **Caution:** Glass beakers are dangerous when broken.
4 Using a graduated cylinder, measure 40 mL of sand. Place the sand in one funnel, and use the grease pencil to label the glass beaker *Sand*.
5 Repeat step 2 for the clay and loam.

6 Use the graduated cylinder to pour 75 mL of water into each funnel.
7 Allow the water to drain for 15 minutes. Note the relative rates at which water drains through the samples. Record your observations.
8 Measure and record the volume of water in each beaker.
9 Calculate the water-holding capacity of each sample. Subtract the data from step 8 from the 75 mL of water added to each sample. Record your data.

Analyze Your Data

1 Make a graph of the data you collected.
2 Which sample had the highest water-holding capacity? The lowest?

3 Through which sample did water drain fastest? Slowest?

Draw Conclusions

Water moves quickly through permeable, or penetrable, soils. Which soil sample is the most permeable? The least permeable? Was your hypothesis correct? Why or why not?

Design a Related Experiment

Based on your observations and data, which type of soil might be best for growing crops? What other soil characteristics might influence crop growth? Design an investigation to answer one of these questions.

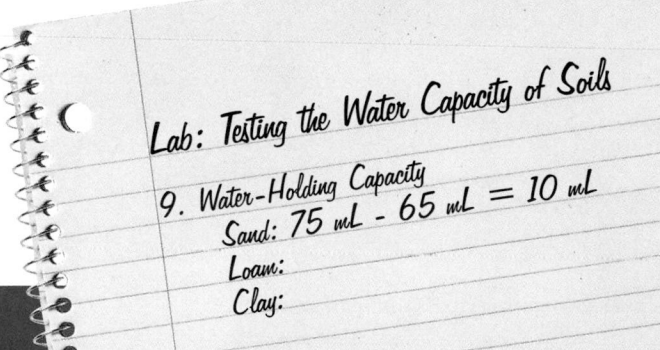

Lab: Testing the Water Capacity of Soils

9. Water-Holding Capacity
Sand: 75 mL - 65 mL = 10 mL

Loam:
Clay:

ENGAGE

Use the Visual

Have students study the photograph that opens the section. Explain that the conditions of daylight and darkness experienced at the North Pole result from the tilt of Earth on its axis. Demonstrate this phenomenon with a globe if possible. Ask:

■ **How do you think the conditions of daylight and darkness at the North Pole compare to those at the South Pole?** (They are identical but occur at opposite seasons.)

Check Prior Knowledge

To assess students' knowledge about climate, ask:

■ **Which abiotic factors do you think relate to climate?** (Temperature, wind, soil, sunlight, water)

Teacher Demo

Use a world map or globe to introduce the concept of latitude. Locate the equator and point out the lines of latitude. Explain that these imaginary lines, also called parallels, measure distance north or south of the equator in degrees. Call on volunteers to give the location in degrees of the following:

■ The equator (0°)
■ The North Pole (90°N)
■ The South Pole (90°S)

Tell students that in this section they will explore how latitude can be used to infer the climate of an area.

35.2 Climate

What you'll learn

IDEAS
• To identify the factors that shape global and regional climates
• To explain the climate conditions that cause rain shadows

WORDS
climate, tropical zone, temperate zone, arctic zone, rain shadow, altitude

Land of the midnight sun
If you lived at the North Pole, you would enjoy 24 hours of daylight every day during the summer. The sun never drops below the horizon. This phenomenon is shown in the time-lapse photo. During the winter, however, the sun never rises above the horizon, so you would have to get accustomed to several months of continual darkness.

GLOBAL CLIMATE

How's the weather?

Sunlight, water, temperature, and wind are all abiotic factors that affect the survival of organisms in an ecosystem. These factors also affect the climate. **Climate** is the typical weather pattern of an area over time.

Many different factors—especially temperature and precipitation—interact to shape global and regional climates. You will learn that climate plays a major role in determining how ecosystems are distributed throughout the biosphere.

Earth's primary source of heat is radiation from the sun—solar radiation. Because Earth is a sphere, however, different levels of solar radiation reach different parts of its curved surface. As you can see in *Figure 35.4*, the sun's rays strike the Earth most directly at the equator. Land and water areas near the equator receive more solar radiation—and heat—than other regions do.

Because Earth's axis is in a continuous cycle of tilting toward and away from the sun, the amount of solar radiation that reaches different parts of Earth's surface change throughout the year. This leads to variations in weather and climate. Seasonal changes in climate are most pronounced in areas farthest from the equator.

In June, the Northern Hemisphere is tilted toward the sun, and the Southern Hemisphere is tilted away. In the Northern Hemisphere, summer begins in June. There are more hours of daylight in summer, and the temperatures are higher. In the southern hemisphere, June marks the beginning of winter, with the daylight shorter and temperatures lower.

The latitude at the equator is 0°. As you move away from the equator, latitude increases and temperature decreases. Imagine

FIGURE 35.4
The sun's rays strike different regions of Earth at different angles, affecting climate zones. What zone do you live in?

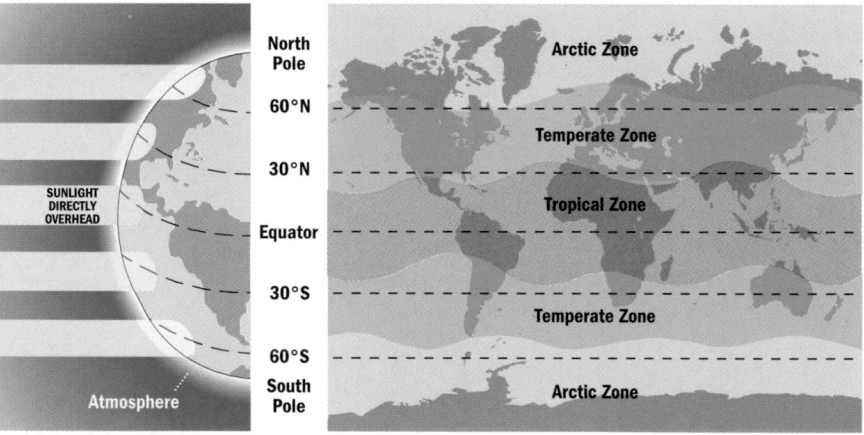

North Pole
60°N
30°N
Equator
30°S
60°S
South Pole

SUNLIGHT DIRECTLY OVERHEAD

Atmosphere

Arctic Zone
Temperate Zone
Tropical Zone
Temperate Zone
Arctic Zone

858 *Unit 9 Organisms and the Environment*

STUDENT RESOURCES

From the Teacher's Resource Package, use:
■ Section Review 35.2 and Activity Recordsheet 35-2 from Unit 9 Review Module

TECHNOLOGY RESOURCES

Relevant technology resources include:
■ Spanish Student Edition CD-ROM
■ Teacher's Resource Planner CD-ROM
■ Interactive Earth CD-ROM
■ Biology Alive! Video Series

you are traveling from the equator toward one of the poles. As you travel, you will cross several climate zones. At the equator, you are in the heart of the tropical zone. As you can see in *Figure 35.4*, the **tropical zone** is the region that extends from the equator to about 30° north and south latitudes.

Temperatures in most areas of the tropical zone are hot and fluctuate very little between summer and winter. As warm, moist air rises from equatorial regions, it cools. Clouds form and the moisture in the air falls back to Earth. The rain forests that grow in the tropical zone receive several meters of rain per year.

As you move north or south beyond the tropical zone, you enter the temperate zone. The general boundaries of the **temperate zone** extend from about 30° to about 60° north and south latitudes. Overall, temperatures are cooler than in the tropical zone, and they change with the seasons. Summers are warm to hot, and winters are cool to cold. During summer in the temperate zone, most precipitation falls as rain or drizzle. In winter, precipitation falls mainly as snow, sleet, and freezing rain.

Beyond 60° north or south latitude, you enter the **arctic zone.** At these high latitudes, summers are short and cool, and winters are long and severely cold. The poles are located at the northernmost and southernmost points in the arctic zones. At the poles, temperatures rarely get above freezing. All precipitation is frozen. Ice and snow cover exists year-round and can be very thick.

FIGURE 35.5

Same Latitude, Different Climate

San Diego and Dallas are located at the same latitude, yet they have very different climates. How do the climates of these two cities differ? Why? **❶**

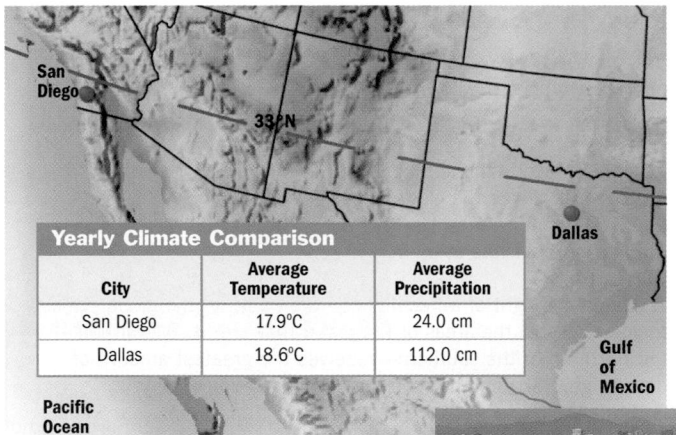

Yearly Climate Comparison		
City	Average Temperature	Average Precipitation
San Diego	17.9°C	24.0 cm
Dallas	18.6°C	112.0 cm

REGIONAL CLIMATE

Climate closer to home

Dallas, Texas, and San Diego, California, are at roughly the same latitude in the temperate zone. However, their climates are quite different. Why? Global climate patterns tell only part of the climate story. There are a variety of other factors—and three important ones—that can affect regional climate.

The distance to the nearest body of water is one factor that affects the

FIGURE 35.6

The rain-shadow effect is caused by mountain ranges.

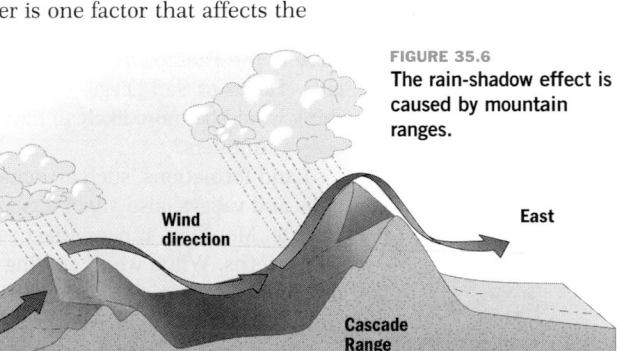

Chapter 35 The Biosphere **859**

TEACH

Class Activity

Provide students with an outline map of the United States, including Alaska and Hawaii. Have students identify the approximate location of each land biome as it is studied. Have students record the approximate latitudes between which each biome is located.

Use the Visual

Have students study Figure 35.8. Point out the climate graph which shows average temperatures and average precipitation. Tell students that the letters at the bottom of the graph indicate the months of the year. Call on a volunteer to demonstrate how to read a climate graph. Ask:

- **How would you describe the climate of the tundra?** (Long, cold winters; short, cool summers with little precipitation.)

Explain

Point out that the layer of frozen ground that characterizes the tundra is called permafrost. Permafrost prohibits plant growth by preventing the roots of plants from reaching into the soil and by keeping water in a frozen state that cannot be taken in by roots.

Use the Visual

Have students study Figure 35.9. Point out that the taiga begins where the tundra ends. Discuss the climate, landscape, and animals of the taiga.

FIGURE 35.8
Tundra

A tundra is cold and treeless, and most of the soil is permanently frozen. A thin layer of soil thaws briefly during short, cool summers. Winters are long, dark, and very cold. Where are tundras located? ❶

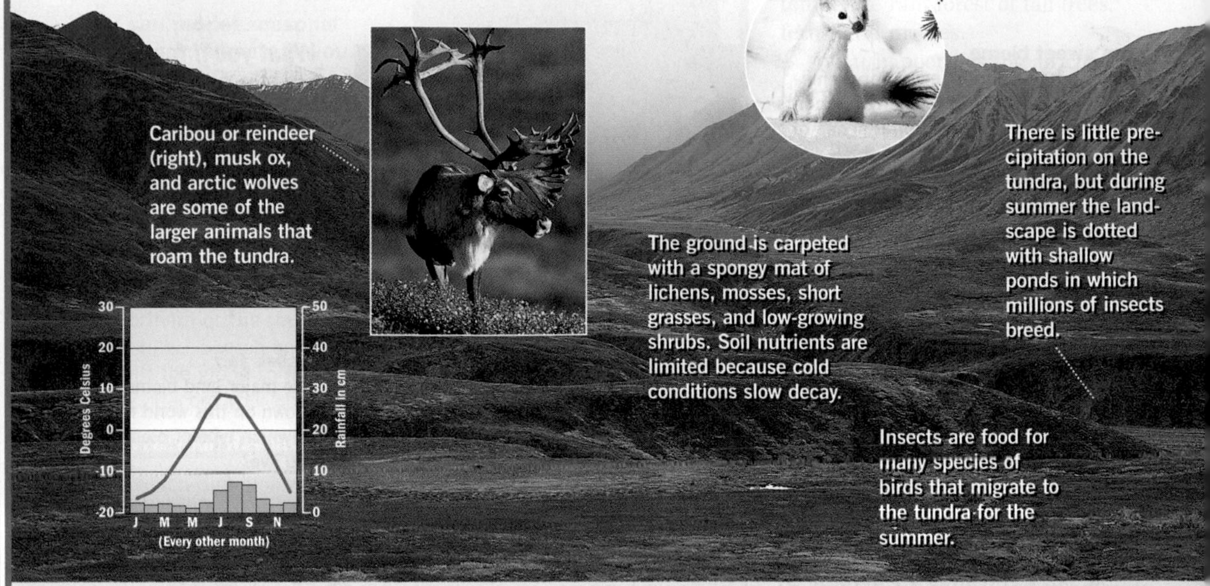

Caribou or reindeer (right), musk ox, and arctic wolves are some of the larger animals that roam the tundra.

The ground is carpeted with a spongy mat of lichens, mosses, short grasses, and low-growing shrubs. Soil nutrients are limited because cold conditions slow decay.

Weasels (below) prey on small rodents such as lemmings. Other lemming predators include snowy owls and arctic foxes.

There is little precipitation on the tundra, but during summer the landscape is dotted with shallow ponds in which millions of insects breed.

Insects are food for many species of birds that migrate to the tundra for the summer.

FIGURE 35.9
Taiga

The taiga (TY-guh) biome is located south of the tundra, at the northern edge of the temperate zone. Winters in the taiga are long and cold, and summers are relatively mild. How do taigas differ from tundras? 2

Perched in the trees, owls (above) and eagles keep a lookout for squirrels, rabbits (below), and small rodents.

Moose (above), elk, bears, and lynx are some of the large animals living in this biome.

Coniferous trees grow close together in taiga forests. On the forest floor, a dense mat of pine needles covers the acidic soil.

862   *Unit 9 Organisms and the Environment*

FACTS AND FIGURES

Climate conditions similar to those of the arctic exist at the tops of very high mountains. Such areas are often called alpine. The major difference between the two regions lies in the amount of moisture available.

❶ The tundra is located in the arctic zone.
❷ The taiga climate and soil can support trees such as conifers; plant life in the tundra consists of mosses and lichens.
❸ Tall deciduous trees
❹ Plants are drought-resistant; reptiles and insects have thick, watertight coverings.

FIGURE 35.10
Temperate Forest

Temperate forests grow where summers are pleasantly warm with frequent rains, and winters are somewhat cold. What type of trees make up a temperate forest? **3**

Tall deciduous trees, such as maple, beech, oak, hickory, and chestnut dominate this forest biome.

Black bears (right), deer, mice, and squirrels are common in temperate forests because berries and nuts are plentiful.

Blue jays (above) and dozens of species of birds flit through the trees. Snakes, salamanders, and frogs make their homes on the ground.

The leaf litter is an ideal habitat for a wide variety of insects, spiders, and worms.

The top layer of soil in a temperate forest is rich in minerals and humus.

Degrees Celsius / Rainfall in cm

J M M J S N (Every other month)

FIGURE 35.11
Chaparral

A chaparral (sha-puh-REL) is a warm region that has a rainy winter season, followed by a long dry summer. How do chaparral organisms adapt to these extremes in precipitation? **4**

Dense stands of tough, stunted plants such as shrub oak and manzanita (below) are drought-resistant.

Skunks (above), mice, deer, and birds like this roadrunner (left) live in chaparrals.

Reptiles, such as the lizard, and insects, have thick, watertight body coverings to help prevent dehydration.

Degrees Celsius / Rainfall in cm

J M M J S N (Every other month)

MULTICULTURAL PERSPECTIVE

Several Native American groups have settled in dry biomes. The Hopi live in northeastern Arizona where they farm and herd sheep. The Apache live on reservations in Arizona and New Mexico. The Zuni, known for their jewelry craft, live in villages in New Mexico.

MEETING DIVERSE NEEDS

Gifted Have students prepare a report comparing plants and animals that live in the same biome, but in different parts of the world, for example, grasslands in North and South America.

Use the Visual

Have students study Figure 35.10. After you discuss the major characteristics of the temperate forest biome, ask:

■ **How do the trees of a temperate forest differ from those of the taiga?** (Temperate forests have mostly tall deciduous trees; trees in the taiga are primarily members of the pine family.)

Explain

Highlight the seasonal changes in the plant and animal life of the temperate forest. For example, in the fall deciduous trees lose their leaves, some birds may migrate, and insects die in colder temperatures.

Teacher Demo

Show students leaves from deciduous trees and needles from pines. Discuss how each leaf type is adapted to the climate conditions of its biome.

Use the Visual

Have students study Figure 35.11. Discuss how the major traits of a chaparral differ from those of the temperate forest. Ask:

■ **Where in the United States would you find a chaparral?** (In the Southwest)

Language Arts

The origin of the word chaparral is the Spanish *chapparo,* "a dwarf evergreen oak." In the United States, thorny bushes have replaced what were largely evergreen oak trees.

Class Activity

After discussing the tropical rain forest divide the class into small groups. Provide each group with a large sheet of construction paper, colored markers, scissors, and old magazines. Instruct the students to divide the paper into three sections and label the sections: Taiga, Temperate Forest, and Tropical Rain Forest. Have students create a scene for each biome with cut-out photographs and/or original drawings. Remind them to include both plant and animal life in each scene.

Use the Visual

Have students study Figure 35.13. Ask:

- **How is a desert most similar to a tundra?** (Both areas receive minimal amounts of precipitation.)
- **Why is the Antarctic interior classified as a desert?** (It receives very little precipitation.)

Build Writing Skills

Have students select the biome in which they would most like to live and write a poem or short story describing what life in that biome would be like. Encourage students to retain scientific accuracy and meaning in their writing.

FIGURE 35.12
Tropical Rain Forest

Tropical rain forests are characterized by warm, wet weather, lush plant life, and diverse animal life. What abiotic factors contribute to this biodiversity? **1**

Tall trees with their leafy tops form a dense canopy about 50 m above the ground.

Rain forest soils are poor; most of the nutrients are in the vegetation. When leaves, animal waste, and dead organisms fall to the forest floor, they quickly decompose and the nutrients are recycled.

The diversity of plant life in rain forests is astounding. Ferns, vines, orchids, and other brilliantly colored flowers are everywhere.

Sloths (above), monkeys, eagles, and parrots are just a few of the animals that make their home in the canopy.

On the forest floor, leaf-cutter ants (left) and giant centipedes share space with peccaries and poison dart frogs.

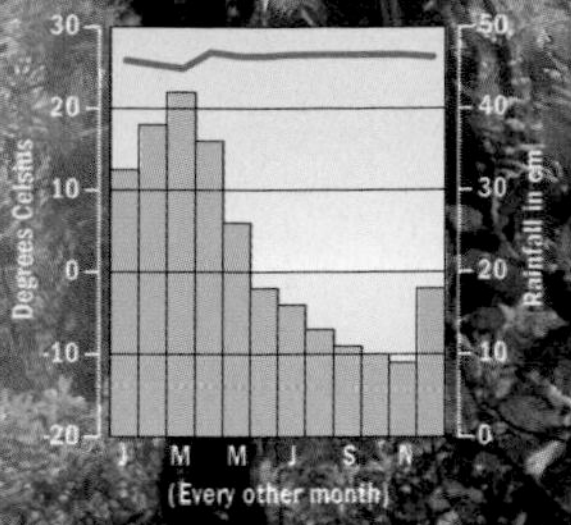

FIGURE 35.13
Desert

Too little precipitation creates deserts, arid regions with sparse plant life. Extremely dry, hot deserts may consist only of shifting sand dunes. How do desert plants conserve water? **2**

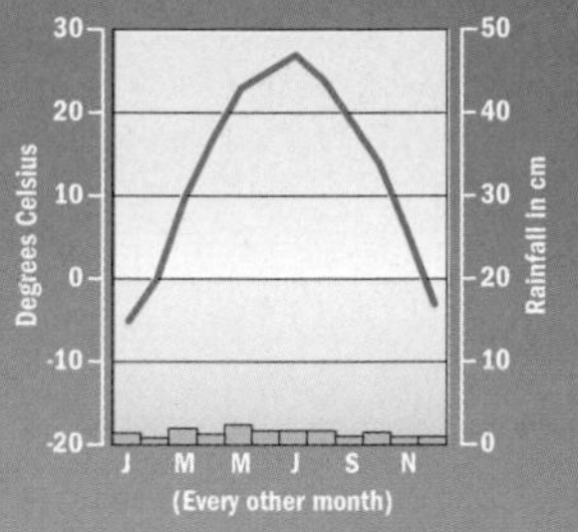

Small desert animals, such as gila monsters (below), must conserve water. Active only at night or early in the morning, they avoid the scorching daylight by hiding in rocky crevices.

Although most deserts are hot, some are cold. The interior of Antarctica is a cold polar desert that receives as little precipitation as the Sahara. However, it is covered with ice that melts very slowly because of the temperature.

A cactus has a thick, succulent stem in which water is stored. Sharp spines protect the cactus from animals.

Surprisingly, many desert soils are rich in nutrients and only need water to become productive.

MEETING DIVERSE NEEDS

LEP Encourage students to work with a partner to create a graphic comparing and contrasting the different land biomes in terms of climate, landscape, and animal life. Suggest students record information in both English and their native language.

❶ Sunlight, water, soil, temperature
❷ The plants store water in thick, succulent stems.

Grassland

Grasslands are widespread communities characterized by grasses and small plants. There are two kinds of grasslands: temperate grasslands (shown) and tropical savannas.

Long dry spells and occasional fires prevent the growth of most trees and shrubs, despite the presence of very rich soil.

Lush grass supports a great diversity of grazing animals, including antelopes (below).

Tropical savannas are generally warm year-round. Rather than winter and summer, savannas have alternating wet and dry seasons.

Large predators such as wolves and lions share their environment with many types of small mammals, such as the badger (below), birds, and insects.

In temperate grasslands (graph shown), summers are hot and winters are cold and windy.

Explain

Point out that grasslands are called prairies in North America. In South America, Asia, and Africa they are, respectively, pampas, steppes, and veldts.

LAB ZONE Think About It!

Predicting Weather in Your Biome

Analyze Your Data

1 Observations should justify answers.
2 Student predictions will be generally accurate.
3 Answers should be based on indigenous species.

CHECKPOINT 35.3

1. What are the elements of a biome?
2. Make a table that compares and contrasts the land biomes.
3. **Critical Thinking** Animals in hot climates have larger ears and longer, thinner legs than do similar species in colder climates. How might these adaptations enable the animals to survive in the different climates?

Build on What You Know

4. Choose one of the biomes and describe the niches that may be found there. *(Need to jog your memory? Revisit relevant concepts in Chapter 10, Section 10.1.)*

LAB ZONE Think About It! bioSURF

Predicting Weather in Your Biome

Biomes differ according to the amount of precipitation and range of temperatures. Research the average monthly temperature and precipitation your area receives over the year. Make a line-bar graph of your data.

Analyze Your Data

1 Based on your data, what type of biome do you live in?
2 Predict the weather for the next month, based on your graph. Observe the weather. Was your prediction correct?
3 How do the amount of precipitation and the temperature affect the organisms in your biome? How are these organisms adapted to the conditions in your biome?

3 ASSESS

Evaluate Understanding

Have students work in groups of seven. Provide each group with seven index cards. Have each group member choose a biome, write the name of the biome on one side of an index card, and list four characteristics on the other side. Tell each group to place its cards in a pile with the names face down. Have group members take turns selecting and naming the biome on a card.

Reteach

As a class, construct a table that compares the types of land biomes. Have students relate each biome location to its major climate conditions and location.

CHECKPOINT 35.3

1. Areas of similar climate which support similar ecosystems and contain certain types of organisms.
2. Tables should reflect differences in temperature, rainfall, plant and animal life.
3. **Making generalizations** Large ears and long, thin legs allow for efficient heat exchange with the environment because the blood vessels are near the surface. In cooler climates, thicker appendages with less surface area exposed are beneficial for conserving body heat.
4. Answers will vary depending on the biome chosen.

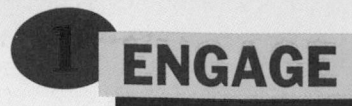

1 ENGAGE

Use the Visual

Have students study the photograph that opens the section. Ask:

- **To what other conditions must deep-ocean fish adapt?** (Cold temperatures, high pressure)

Check Prior Knowledge

To assess students' knowledge about biomes, ask:

- **What factors distinguish one land biome from another?** (Precipitation, temperature, plant and animal life)
- **What type of water habitats can you name?** (Likely responses are wetlands, lakes, ponds, rivers, oceans, marshes, swamps.)

Quick Activity

Display photographs or diagrams of different bodies of water, such as an ocean, a pond, a bay, an inlet, and a fjord. Ask students to identify the differences among the water bodies pictured. (They differ in size, depth, salt content, temperature, plant and animal life.) Tell students that in this section they will learn about the different ecosystems that make up the two water biomes on Earth.

SUPER READ! **Predicting** To practice strategies for effective reading, use pages 77-78 in *Super Read!*

866

35.4 Water Biomes

What you'll learn

IDEAS
- To distinguish between the water biomes
- To describe the zones in the marine biome

WORDS
wetlands, estuary

EVERYDAY BIOLOGY

Taking Water to the Cleaners

Wetland areas provide water storage and flood protection by soaking up rainwater like a sponge. They also function as natural water-treatment facilities by filtering out toxic chemicals and various pollutants.

Bring your own "chinlight"
This deep-ocean fish has a type of "flashlight" dangling from its chin. It lives in the total blackness of the ocean depths. Why light up the darkness? Deep-ocean fishes probably carry their own light, less for seeing than for being seen. The light may lure prey to a predator or signal a prospective mate.

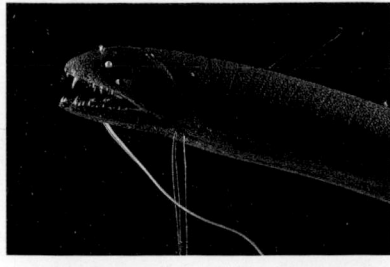

CHARACTERISTICS OF WATER BIOMES

It's a watery world

Water in all forms covers roughly 75 percent of Earth's surface. Consequently, most of the biosphere is composed of aquatic, or water, biomes. The two major water biomes are the freshwater biomes and the marine, or saltwater, biomes. Each biome contains ecosystems that are differentiated by abiotic factors such as light, temperature, and the amount of salt, oxygen, and nutrients in the water. Organisms that live in aquatic biomes have characteristics that enable them to live with these diverse and changing abiotic factors.

When ecologists study aquatic biomes, they examine specific zones within a particular system. In most large bodies of water there are three zones: photic, aphotic, and benthic.

The photic (light) zone is the uppermost portion of aquatic biomes through which light can penetrate to support photosynthesis. Beneath the photic zone is an aphotic (without light) zone where light does not penetrate. The bottom of a body of water is the benthic zone. The seafloor, a lake bottom, and a riverbed are all benthic zones.

FIGURE 35.17
Flowing Water

Problems facing organisms that live in flowing-water biomes include moving against the current and simply staying in one place. What adaptations might prevent animals that live in rivers and streams from being washed away? **1**

Moving water picks up sediment and carries it downstream. Where streams slow down or widen into rivers, sediment tends to settle out of the water.

Over long periods of time, flowing water can level mountains, cut deep canyons, and deposit enough sediment to create new landforms.

Insect larvae have tiny hooks that they use to attach to underwater objects.

Fishes such as salmon (left) and trout have streamlined bodies, allowing them to move through currents.

866 *Unit 9 Organisms and the Environment*

STUDENT RESOURCES

From the Teacher's Resource Package, use:
- Section Review 35.4, Activity Recordsheet 35-3, Vocabulary Review 35, Enrichment Topic 35-3, and Chapter 35 Tests from Unit 9 Review Module
- Lab 59: "Biomes of Life"

TECHNOLOGY RESOURCES

Relevant technology resources include:
- Spanish Student Edition CD-ROM
- Teacher's Resource Planner CD-ROM
- Interactive Earth CD-ROM
- Biology Alive! Video Series
- TestWorks CD-ROM: Chapter 35 Tests

FRESHWATER BIOMES

Go with the flow

Freshwater biomes include everything from cold mountain streams and muddy rivers to lakes and marshes. Many freshwater biomes undergo significant changes during a year, such as seasonal variations in water temperature or nutrient levels. The ability to adapt to changing conditions is a characteristic that many freshwater organisms have in order to survive.

Ecologists further divide freshwater biomes into three major categories: flowing-water biomes, standing-water biomes, and wetlands. Flowing-water biomes are rivers and streams in which currents are created. *Figure 35.17* shows some of the characteristics of this type of biome. Lakes and

---

IN THE COMMUNITY

Freshwater Field Day

Find a body of fresh water in, or near, your own neighborhood. What type of body of water is it—a lake, a pond, a river, or a stream? Where does the water come from? Is it a natural accumulation of water, or is it an artificial one, like an irrigation channel or a catch basin? If wading is permitted, use a dipnet or jar to collect and release small organisms. **Caution: Never go wading alone.** Make a chart of all the organisms you can find in the water. Can you make connections between the organisms and their surroundings? Do you think the types of organisms in the water might vary at different times of the year? Why? To learn more about freshwater resources, log on to *http://ecology.biosurf.com*.

FIGURE 35.18
Standing Water

Standing-water biomes include ponds and lakes. Ponds are smaller and usually shallower than lakes. How does light availability affect plant life in ponds and lakes? **2**

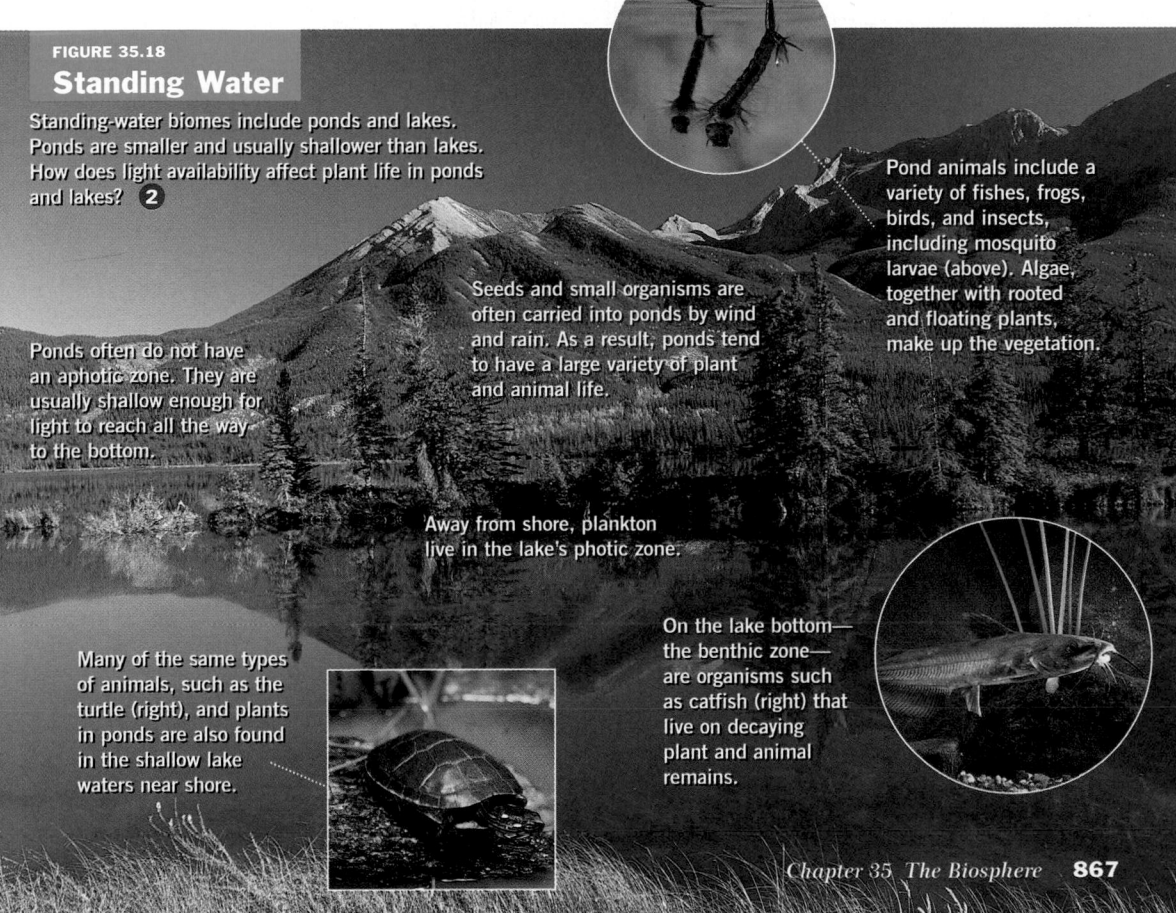

Ponds often do not have an aphotic zone. They are usually shallow enough for light to reach all the way to the bottom.

Seeds and small organisms are often carried into ponds by wind and rain. As a result, ponds tend to have a large variety of plant and animal life.

Pond animals include a variety of fishes, frogs, birds, and insects, including mosquito larvae (above). Algae, together with rooted and floating plants, make up the vegetation.

Away from shore, plankton live in the lake's photic zone.

Many of the same types of animals, such as the turtle (right), and plants in ponds are also found in the shallow lake waters near shore.

On the lake bottom—the benthic zone—are organisms such as catfish (right) that live on decaying plant and animal remains.

Chapter 35 The Biosphere **867**

MEETING DIVERSE NEEDS

At Risk Have students create a visual to compare and contrast the various types of water biomes. Suggest that students include captions for their visual that explain the major traits of each biome.

❶ Animals might have hooks or suckers to attach to plants or rocks.

❷ Large numbers of plants will grow in areas with available light, fewer plants where light is scarce.

---

2 TEACH

In the Community

Suggest students also refer to appropriate field guides to identify organisms and determine their role in the biome. Water sources will vary depending upon the biome explored and whether it is natural or artificial. Students should be able to cite interconnections between the organisms observed and recognize that different organisms live in different parts of the biome.

Literature

Bodies of water are the setting or the theme in a wide range of American literature. Examples include Ernest Hemingway's *The Old Man and the Sea*, James Michener's *Chesapeake,* and Barry Moser and Norman MacLean's *A River Runs Through It*. Have students share stories they have read that revolve around a body of water. Ask what aquatic plants or animals were part of the story.

Use the Visual

Have students study Figure 35.18. Ask:

- **What are the producers in a standing water biome?** (Algae, plants)
- **What type of organisms are found in the benthic zone?** (Decaying plants, animal remains, decomposers)

Use the Visual

Have students study Figure 35.19. Be sure students recognize that there are several types of wetlands. Ask:

- **What are three types of freshwater wetlands?** (Swamps, bogs, and marshes)

Use the Visual

Use Figure 35.20 to emphasize that not all wetlands are freshwater biomes. Point out that the salt water wetlands form along coastal regions. Ask:

- **What are two kinds of coastal wetlands?** (Salt marshes and mangrove swamps)

Explain

A bog is an area of spongy earth that was once a marsh or swamp. Bogs are often an indication that lake succession is taking place. Eventually the region may develop into a hardwood forest. In Canada, the wetland regions often identified as bogs in the United States, are usually called sloughs. Like bogs, such areas are often located in regions with cool climates.

 **STS**

Have students use the *Readers' Guide to Periodical Literature* or the Internet to find current articles about the Everglades. Suggest that they find out how the habitat is changing, which species are threatened, and what steps are being taken to restore the area to its natural state. Provide time for students to share their research with the class.

---

ponds are examples of standing-water biomes and their characteristics can be seen in *Figure 35.18* on page 867. A third freshwater biome is a wetland. **Wetlands** develop where fresh or salt water and land meet. Wetlands are categorized as either inland or coastal. Inland wetlands include marshes, swamps, and bogs. Coastal wetlands include mangrove swamps and salt marshes. You can see examples of these biomes in *Figure 35.19* and *Figure 35.20*.

ISSUES IN BIOLOGY

Help for wetlands

The Everglades in Florida was once the largest inland wetland in the continental United States. Agriculture and urban development led to the damming and draining of the natural waterways that ran through this wetland system. The effect on wildlife was devastating. Efforts now being made to restore this area to its natural state have been significantly successful.

Wildlife corridors have been established throughout the United States to protect endangered species. These corridors allow threatened species to travel between tracts of protected land, thereby increasing their range. Such increases in range result in better access to resources and reduce the threat of extinction. Ecologists have planned corridors in Florida, southern California, and the Pacific Northwest.

Some ecologists, however, think that these corridor plans are unjustifiable because there is little evidence of their effectiveness. Many ecologists emphasize the difficulty of studying complex ecological interactions in the field. To understand fully the importance of wildlife corridors, populations

FIGURE 35.19
Inland Wetland

A wetland is covered all or part of the time by water. Freshwater inland wetlands include marshes, swamps, and bogs.

Swamps such as the one shown here contain trees and shrubs, along with Spanish moss and water lilies.

American avocets (right) are one of the many species of wading birds in inland wetlands.

FIGURE 35.20
Coastal Wetland

Coastal wetlands are regions along the seacoast that are continually or periodically flooded with salt water.

Mangrove swamps, such as the one shown here, and salt marshes provide shelter to a variety of fishes, crabs, and shrimps.

Mudskippers (below) and fiddler crabs (right) are found in coastal wetlands.

MULTICULTURAL PERSPECTIVE

The only residents of the Everglades are several hundred Seminole Indians. These indigenous people and their habitat are protected by the government.

FIGURE 35.21
Estuary

Estuaries are areas where fresh water and salt water mix. They form where rivers containing large amounts of nutrient-rich sediment meet the sea and deposit the sediment.

The water in an estuary is brackish—never completely fresh, but less salty than sea water. Estuaries can support a large number of organisms because of their nutrient-rich environments.

Many kinds of fishes, mollusks, and crustaceans, such as this blue crab (left), live in estuaries. These organisms attract birds, such as the osprey (above) that feed on them.

in a large geographical area would have to be studied over long periods of time.

The mouth of a river is the place where a river empties into the ocean. Sediment—particles of rock and soil that are carried by a river—often settles near the river's mouth, making the region shallow. A shallow area where fresh water and salt water mix is called an **estuary** (ES-choo-ayr-ee). An estuary biome is shown in *Figure 35.21.*

THE MARINE BIOME
Pass the salt

More than 70 percent of Earth's surface is covered by the marine biome. Physical conditions within this biome vary tremendously. Light, temperature, and water pressure all change with depth. The salinity, or salt content, of the ocean also varies from place to place.

The organisms that inhabit the marine biome are remarkably

LAB ZONE **Do It!**

How Does Salt Water Affect Organisms?

What happens to your skin when you stay in the water a long time? Do salt water and fresh water affect your body the same way? You can find out how fresh water and salt water affect organisms if you . . .

Try This

1 Fill six identical glass jars with the same amount of tap water. Label three jars tap water, and three jars salt water. Put two spoonfuls of salt into each of the saltwater jars and stir.
2 Collect two small equal-sized pieces of apple, two raisins, and two grapes. Record the size and texture of each fruit sample.
3 Place one sample of each fruit in a jar of salt water and one sample of each in a jar of fresh water. Predict the effects of salt water and fresh water on each fruit.
4 Examine each sample after one hour. Record your observations and results in a data table. Be sure to record the size and texture of each fruit sample.

Analyze Your Results

1 What happened to the fruit? What might have caused the results?
2 What characteristics might an organism need to survive in a saltwater environment such as the ocean?

869

Think Critically

Discuss Figure 35.21 emphasizing that estuaries are diverse ecosystems that provide breeding grounds and nurseries for a wide variety of organisms. Ask:

- **Why is it important to protect estuaries from pollution and overuse?** (Pollution and overuse can deplete or kill populations of plants or animals. This loss creates an imbalance harmful to the remaining organisms.)

 Geography

The Chesapeake Bay is the largest estuary in the United States. Using a wall map, help students locate the Chesapeake Bay. Ask:

- **Name four rivers that flow into the Chesapeake Bay.** (Potomac, James, Rappahannock, and Susquehanna rivers)
- **What livelihoods do you think are supported by the Chesapeake Bay?** (Shipping, fishing, seafood industry, and recreation such as boating)

LAB ZONE **Do It!** TEAM WORK

How Does Salt Water Affect Organisms?

Analyze Your Results

1 Fruit in salt water shrivels, while fruit in freshwater swells. The result is due to osmosis.
2 Organisms need an adaptation for taking in water and excreting salt.

870

Teacher Demo

Display a jar filled with water where students can see it. Sprinkle some fish food flakes into the water and have students observe what happens. Tell students that the sinking flakes model how organisms in the aphotic zone are provided with food. The food "rains" down from upper ocean levels.

3 ASSESS

Evaluate Understanding

To assess students' understanding of water biomes, ask:

- **What abiotic factors differentiate ecosystems in water biomes?** (Light, temperature, salt content, oxygen, and nutrients)
- **What are three types of freshwater biomes? Give an example of each.** (Flowing-water: rivers and streams; standing-water: lakes and ponds; and wetlands: swamps and salt marshes)
- **In which ocean zone would you find most marine life?** (In the coastal zone)

Reteach

As a class, construct a graphic organizer that compares and contrasts the major features of each water biome discussed in this section. Have students copy the completed graphic. Then discuss how the zonation of lakes is similar to and different from that of oceans.

FIGURE 35.22
Marine Zones

The marine biome is a saltwater environment that includes the oceans and their shorelines. What characteristics enable organisms to live in the different marine zones? **1**

1 Intertidal zone
At the ocean's edge lies the intertidal zone. Organisms in this zone must survive extreme variation in both temperature and salinity. The organisms are repeatedly covered then exposed by the tides.

2 Neritic zone
The neritic zone lies over the continental shelf and is rich in mineral nutrients washed from the land. Light usually penetrates to the bottom of the neritic zone, allowing the growth of phytoplankton and algae.

3 Oceanic zone
In the oceanic zone, mineral nutrients are scarce. As a result, the populations of organisms are far less dense than in the neritic zone.

4 Photic zone
Here, light can penetrate ocean waters to a depth of about 200 m. The photic zone is home to phytoplankton, which are eaten by zooplankton, which are then eaten by larger animals, such as grunts (below), other fishes, and squids.

5 Aphotic zone
So little light penetrates this zone that photosynthesis cannot take place. Inhabitants live in complete darkness. Many deep-sea squids (below) and fishes make their own light.

6 Benthic zone
In the benthic zone are common bottom-dwelling organisms, such as sea stars, (left) shrimps, crabs, clams, worms, urchins, sponges, and sea anemones.

0 m
1000 m
5000 m
9000 m

diverse. And new species—especially from the deep sea—are being discovered continually. Although coastal zones make up only about 10 percent of the marine biome, they contain almost 90 percent of marine life. Coastal zones contain several distinct features.

The open ocean has several zones. The zones are classified according to water depth, presence of light, and distance from shore. You can locate each of the marine zones in *Figure* 35.22. Which zone **2** supports the most organisms? Why?

CHECKPOINT 35.4

1. How do freshwater biomes differ from marine biomes?
2. List and describe the zones in a marine biome.
3. **Critical Thinking** Predict how damming a river would affect an estuary at the river's mouth.

Build on What You Know

4. In which marine zones are heterotrophs located? Autotrophs? Explain your answers. *(Need to jog your memory? Review relevant concepts in Chapter 4, Section 4.1.)*

? What are the distinguishing characteristics of Earth's land and water biomes?

870 *Unit 9 Organisms and the Environment*

CHECKPOINT 35.4

1. Freshwater biomes have low levels of salts and minerals.
2. Students should describe the six zones outlined in Figure 35.22.
3. **Predicting** It would reduce the amount of freshwater reaching the estuary, increasing the concentration of salt and preventing many organisms from living there.
4. Heterotrophs: in all marine zones; photoautotrophs: in the photic zone where there is sunlight: chemoautotrophs: in the benthic zone near undersea vents

1 The ability to adapt to the temperature, salinity, sunlight, water pressure, and water movement of a particular zone

2 The photic zone, because sunlight is available

Chapter 35 Review

 **THE BIG IDEA!**

35.1–35.2 Life depends on the relationships between living and nonliving parts of the environment.

35.3–35.4 Regions of the biosphere have distinguishing characteristics.

Sum It Up

Use the following summary to review the main concepts in this chapter.

35.1 Characteristics of the Biosphere

- Ecologists study the interactions of organisms with their physical environments.
- Levels of organization in the biosphere increase in complexity from individuals to populations, communities, and ecosystems.
- Every environment is comprised of living (biotic) factors and nonliving (abiotic) factors.

35.2 Climate

- Temperature and precipitation are abiotic factors that distinguish climate patterns.
- Because Earth's surface is curved, the distribution of solar radiation is not uniform. Because Earth is tilted on its axis, the amount of radiation that reaches Earth varies by season.
- Earth can be divided into three large climate zones by latitude.
- The proximity to large bodies of water and the location of mountains affect regional climates.

35.3 Land Biomes

- Regions with similar climates support similar ecosystems.

- A tundra is a treeless plain with permanently frozen soil.
- The taiga biome has long, cold winters and relatively mild summers, which support conifers.
- Tall deciduous trees dominate the temperate forest biome.
- The chaparral's rainy seasons alternate with dry seasons to produce hardy, stunted plants.
- The humidity and warmth of tropical rain forests supports biodiversity.
- Plants and animals that live in arid deserts must be able to conserve water.
- Both temperate and tropical grasslands support diverse populations of grazing animals.

35.4 Water Biomes

- Most of Earth consists of aquatic biomes.
- Freshwater biomes include those with flowing water, those with standing water, and wetlands.
- Inland and coastal wetlands develop where freshwater or saltwater meets land.
- Marine zones are classified by the water depth, the presence of light, and the distance from shore.

Using Terms and Concepts

Use each of the following words in a complete sentence. If you need to review a meaning, turn to the page indicated.

ecology (p. 854)	ecosystem (p. 855)	rain shadow (p. 860)
biosphere (p. 854)	habitat (p. 855)	altitude (p.860)
biotic factors (p. 855)	climate (p. 858)	biome (p. 861)
abiotic factors (p. 855)	tropical zone (p. 859)	wetlands (p. 868)
population (p. 855)	temperate zone (p. 859)	estuary (p. 869)
community (p. 855)	arctic zone (p. 859)	

Review the Big Ideas

Before students begin the Chapter Review, you may wish to discuss the main concepts from the Big Ideas in Chapter 35. Point out that life depends upon both biotic factors, such as food, and abiotic factors, such as water, light, and temperature. Climate determines the abiotic factors present over time. Climate patterns can be distinguished by temperature and precipitation. Regions that share similar climates and ecosystems are called biomes. Most of the biosphere is made up of freshwater or saltwater biomes. Land biomes include the tundra, taiga, temperate forest, chaparral, tropical rain forest, grassland, and desert.

Chapter 35 The Biosphere **871**

Answers

1. climate
2. biotic and abiotic
3. biome
4. ecosystem
5. estuary
6. Ecology
7. Altitude
8. False; population
9. True
10. False; abiotic
11. True
12. True
13. False; tropical zone
14. True
15. As both factors increase, temperature decreases.
16. Both biomes have alternating wet and dry seasons. A chaparral is dominated by low–growing shrubs; grasslands, as their name implies, are dominated by grasses.
17. A lack of water
18. There is no change at the equator because the sun is directly overhead. At the North Pole, the daylight hours gradually increase from none in January to 24 hours at the end of June.
19. The neritic zone is rich in minerals; the oceanic zone is not.
20. Tropical rain forests are warm all year; temperate forests have relatively cold winters. The trees in the temperate forest are mainly deciduous.
21. Whether a benthic zone (the bottom of a body of water) is photic or aphotic depends on the depth of the water.
22. Accept all reasonable answers. Students may relate the following terms: aquatic biomes—freshwater and saltwater; freshwater— lake, pond, and river; lake and pond—standing water; river—flowing water;

Use Your Word Power

COMPLETION **Write the word or phrase that best completes each statement below.**

1. The _____ is the typical weather pattern in an area over time.

2. The environment consists of a unique set of _____ factors that support a specific species.

3. A large group of ecosystems that share similar conditions of temperature and precipitation is called a(n) _____.

4. All the communities and abiotic factors in a given area are a(n) _____.

5. The shallow area near the mouth of a river where freshwater and saltwater mix is called a(n) _____.

6. _____ is the study of organisms and their environments.

7. _____ is defined as height above sea level.

TRUE-FALSE **Write true if the statement is true. If the statement is false, replace the underlined word(s) to make the statement true.**

8. All the members of a species that live in a particular area are called a <u>community</u>.

9. The <u>tundra</u> is located in the arctic zone.

10. The amount of sunlight and oxygen are two of the <u>biotic</u> factors in marine environments.

11. The life-supporting region of Earth is called the <u>biosphere</u>.

12. A <u>rain shadow</u> forms on the eastern slopes of a mountain range.

13. Temperatures in the <u>temperate zone</u> vary little from season to season.

14. Mangrove swamps and salt marshes are examples of coastal <u>wetlands</u>.

Show What You Know

15. What characteristics do altitude and latitude have in common?

16. How is a tropical savanna similar to a chaparral? How are the two different?

17. What is the characteristic that cold deserts and hot deserts have in common?

18. How do the hours of available daylight change, from January to June at the equator? At the North Pole?

19. What is the primary difference between the neritic zone and the oceanic zone?

20. How does the climate in tropical rain forests and temperate forests differ? How do the trees in the temperate forest respond to the change in climate?

21. Explain how a benthic zone could be photic or aphotic.

22. **Make a Concept Map** Create a concept map that relates different climates and biomes.

Take It Further

23. **Developing a Hypothesis** Make a prediction about the degree of biodiversity at the boundary between two biomes.

24. **Applying Concepts** Suppose you had two locations: one 40° north of the equator, the other 40° south of the equator—and each at the same longitude. Would they have the same climate? Give reasons for your answer.

25. **Making an Analogy** A shadow occurs when an object blocks light from a surface, thereby "casting" a shadow. How is a light shadow similar to a rain shadow? Explain.

26. **Identifying Cause and Effect** Although the level of precipitation is low, most tundra ecosystems are very wet. What characteristic would explain this apparent contradiction?

---

saltwater—ocean; freshwater and saltwater—estuaries.

23. Answers will vary, but should reflect that the boundary might present a set of niches unavailable elsewhere in the biomes, which could increase biodiversity.

24. They may not have the same climate, as one location might be on land and the other in the ocean; one might be inland and one might be coastal; or one could be on the eastern or western slope of a mountain range.

25. Just as a light shadow is created by an object blocking light, a rain shadow is created by a mountain blocking rain from reaching its eastern, or leeward, slope.

27. Designing an Experiment Is there a minimum amount of precipitation that grass needs to survive? Do different species of grass need different amounts of water? How does the amount of precipitation affect the growth rate of grass? Does mowing a lawn affect the growth rate? Design an experiment to answer each of these questions.

28. Analyzing Data Graph the data below, using the x-axis for the location and the y-axis for the amount of rainfall. When labeling your locations, keep them in the order they appear in the table (Quinault nearest the origin and Spokane furthest from the origin).

Annual Rainfall in Washington State	
Location	**Rainfall (cm)**
Quinault	343
Sequim	43
Seattle	86
Snoqualimie Pass	257
Yakima	18
Spokane	38

29. Interpreting a Graph The locations in the table and your graph are listed in order from west to east. Washington has two mountain ranges—the Olympic Mountains near the coast and the inland Cascade Range. Use the information in your graph to describe where the locations are in relation to the mountains.

Consider the Issues

30. Wetlands or Paved Lands? Each year many wetlands are filled and paved over to provide land for homes and recreation. Although these actions provide valuable human resources, they also have their consequences. Wetlands are beneficial because they control pollution and flooding, and provide habitats for many organisms. What can be done to provide resources for humans while ensuring that wetlands are not completely destroyed?

Make New Connections

31. Biology and Cartoons Explain the joke in this cartoon. What did the artist need to know about biomes to create the cartoon? Use what you have learned in the chapter to create your own cartoon.

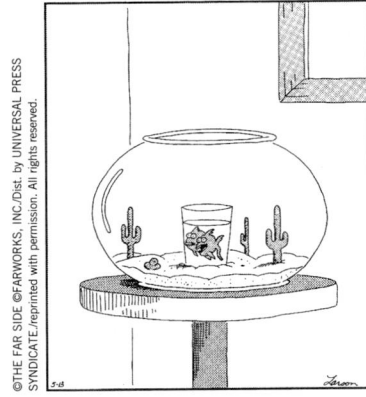

THE FAR SIDE By GARY LARSON

"I love the desert"

32. Biology and Physics When warm, moist air travels up and over a mountain range, clouds form. These clouds contain water in its liquid state. Look up *condensation*, and explain how water changes from the gaseous state to the liquid state. How does condensation affect the temperature at the top of a mountain?

33. Biology and Oceanography Research the Gulf Stream in the North Atlantic. What causes this warm ocean current? What is its effect on the climate of Iceland and Great Britain?

FAST-FORWARD TO CHAPTER 36

Chapter 35 focused on the abiotic factors that determine the location of communities. In Chapter 36, you will learn how both abiotic and biotic factors affect the survival of populations within communities.

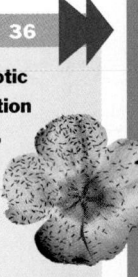

Chapter 35 The Biosphere **873**

33. Winds drive ocean currents. The path varies but generally flows from the equator along the east coast of North America. It moderates the climates of Iceland and Great Britain.

26. Because the ground is frozen, the water cannot drain.

27. Students could actually plant some grass seed and monitor its growth.

28. Check that graphs are correct in format and content.

29. The Olympic Mountains are east of Quinault and the Cascade Range is east of the Snoqualimie Pass.

30. Answers may include finding alternative places for development and replacing wetlands that are destroyed.

31. The fish is actually in a marine environment, not a desert. Check student cartoons for accuracy.

32. When water cools, it loses energy and changes into a liquid. The temperature at the top of mountain must be lower.

PLANNING GUIDE

Section	Student Activities/Features	Teacher's Resource Package
36.1 Population Growth **Objectives** ■ Define a population ■ Compare carrying capacity with exponential growth	**Lab Zone Discover It!** *Comparing Populations*, p. 875 **Lab Zone Think About It!** *Would You Work for Pennies?* p. 877 **Lab Zone Investigate It!** *Observing Population Growth*, p. 880	**Unit 9 Review Module** ■ Section Review 36.1 ■ Activity Recordsheet 36-1 **Consumer Applications** 36-1 **Issues and Decision Making** 36-1
36.2 Limits on Population Growth **Objectives** ■ Distinguish between exponential growth and a boom-and-bust curve ■ Compare and contrast limiting factors	**Everyday Biology** *Limits*, p. 883	**Unit 9 Review Module** ■ Section Review 36.2 ■ Interpreting Graphics 36 ■ Critical Thinking Exercise 36 **Issues and Decision Making** 36-2 **Interpreting and Developing Graphics** 106, 107, 108
36.3 Communities **Objectives** ■ Describe a community ■ Compare community interactions	**Lab Zone Do It!** *Analyzing Interactions in Your Community*, p. 886 **Everyday Biology** *Mutual Feelings*, p. 887 **In the Community** *What Is a Community?* p. 888 **STS: Issues in Biology** *Missing Members*, p. 889	**Unit 9 Review Module** ■ Section Review 36.3 ■ Activity Recordsheet 36-2 ■ Enrichment Topic 36-1 **Laboratory Manual** ■ Lab 60: "Sampling a Plant Community" ■ Lab 61: "Estimating Mobile Population Sizes"
36.4 Ecological Succession **Objectives** ■ Distinguish between modes of ecological succession ■ Describe the communities of ecological succession	**Lab Zone Do It!** *Studying Human Causes of Succession*, p. 892	**Unit 9 Review Module** ■ Section Review 36.4 ■ Activity Recordsheet 36-3 ■ Vocabulary Review 36 ■ Chapter 36 Tests **Spanish Reviews** Chapter 36

Technology Resources

Internet Connections

Within this chapter, you will see the **bioSURF** logo. If you and your students have access to the Internet, the following URL address will provide various Internet connections that are related to topics and features presented in this chapter:

http://ecology.biosurf.com

You can also find relevant chapter material at **The Biology Place** address:

http://www.biology.com

CD-ROMs

Biología: la telaraña de la vida,
   (Spanish Student Edition) Chapter 36
Teacher's Resource Planner, Chapter 36
   Supplements
TestWorks CD-ROM
- Chapter 36 Tests
Interactive Earth CD-ROM

Overhead Transparencies

- Population Growth Graphs, #88
- Population Cycle Graphs, #89

Videotapes

Biology Alive! Video Series
- The Continuity of Life Video
- Conflict and Cooperation Video
- Life's Fragile Balance Video
Rewind: The Web of Life Reteach Videos

Planning for Activities

STUDENT EDITION
Lab Zone
Discover It! p. 875
- a population of living things in your area (people, birds, grasses, or insects)

Lab Zone
Think About It! p. 877
- graph paper

Lab Zone
Investigate It! p. 880
- 6 empty baby-food jars with lids
- grease pencil
- graduated cylinder
- 10% molasses solution
- yeast solution
- dropper
- 6 microscope slides
- 6 coverslips
- microscope

Lab Zone Do It! p. 892
- vacant lot or abandoned farm field

TEACHER'S EDITION
Teacher Demo, p. 876
Carrying capacity
- beaker
- water
- dropper

Teacher Demo, p. 882
Density-dependent limiting factors
- marbles

Quick Activity, p. 885
Interactions between organisms
- photographs of animals interacting with their environment

Chapter Objectives

Students will learn the main concepts of this chapter as they complete the following objectives.

- Define population
- Compare carrying capacity with exponential growth
- Distinguish between exponential growth and a boom-and-bust curve
- Compare and contrast limiting factors
- Describe a community
- Compare community interactions
- Distinguish between modes of ecological succession
- Describe the communities of ecological succession

Key Words

36.1 *population, exponential growth, limiting factor, carrying capacity*

36.2 *density-dependent limiting factors, predation, density-independent limiting factors*

36.3 *community, symbiosis, mutualism, parasitism, commensalism*

36.4 *ecological succession, primary succession, pioneer community, climax community, secondary succession*

The Opening Story

Have students discuss how they think the story relates to the content of this chapter. Have them infer the scientific meaning of the term *community* and consider why ecologists study communities.

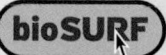

You can find out more about populations and communities by exploring the following Internet address:
http://biosurf.ecology.com

In this chapter . . .

FEATURES

Everyday Biology
- Limits
- Mutual Feelings

In the Community
What Is a Community?

 Issues in Biology
Missing Members

LAB ZONES

Discover It!
- Comparing Populations

Do It!
- Analyzing Interactions in Your Community
- Studying Human Causes of Succession

Think About It!
- Would You Work for Pennies?

Investigate It!
- Observing Population Growth

Little Dogs on the Prairie

On the Great Plains of the United States, many black-tailed prairie dogs live together in large groups. Prairie dogs build networks of underground tunnels that can be compared to towns. These "towns" consist of family units called coteries, which have neighboring territories with defined boundaries. Each coterie territory has several entrances, allowing quick access into and out of the protective tunnels. Prairie dogs spend much of their day above ground eating grass. When a predator is spotted, they warn each other, and the population scurries underground. Their system is so effective that a scientific research team witnessed only 22 successful attacks on prairie dogs in 73,000 hours of observation.

Other animals benefit from prairie-dog towns. As many as 171 different animal species have been associated with an underground prairie-dog town, and some of these animals use the tunnels as shelter. For example, the endangered black-footed ferret would be extinct if it were not for the shelter provided by prairie-dog towns. Scientists have concluded that prairie dogs and the animals that share their towns have a very social community. But what is a community, and what are the relationships in a community?

 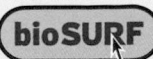 Discover It!

Comparing Populations

1. Observe a population of living things in your area. Populations to choose from can include people, birds, grasses, or insects. Estimate and record the size of the population.
2. What other living things interact with the population you have observed?
3. What abiotic factors affect this population?

Many different factors affect a population's size and growth. Changes in the environment can benefit some populations and harm others.

WRITE ABOUT IT!

Like many scientific terms, *community* has an everyday meaning in addition to its scientific definition. What does the word *community* mean to you? In your science journal, write about your community and how it affects your life.

875

Opening Activities

bioSURF If you have access to the Internet in your classroom or school, you may wish to have students connect to the address shown on page 874. You may also want to have students conduct a net search for information using key words such as population growth rate, population ecologists, or symbiosis.

LAB ZONE Discover It!

Comparing Populations

TEAM WORK

Write some of the students' population estimates on the board and discuss reasons for variations in data. Students may observe such interactions between species as predator/prey or parasitism. Abiotic factors will likely include air, water, temperature, and soil.

WRITE ABOUT IT

After students complete their journal entries, you may wish to have them discuss the different populations that make up their community.

REWIND to Chapter 35

Briefly review concepts learned in Chapter 35, *The Biosphere.* Ask:

■ **How do you think the study of the biosphere will help you understand changes that occur within populations and interactions between populations?**

PORTFOLIO PREVIEW

Students should be encouraged to add to their portfolios as they work through this chapter. In addition to the *Write About It* opportunity, the following sections are

excellent opportunities for portfolio entries:

■ Section 36.1: *Population Growth*
■ Section 36.3: *Communities*

36.1

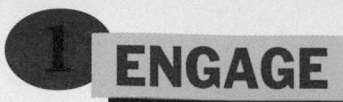

① ENGAGE

Consider the Big Idea

Have students read The Big Idea! at the top of the page. Explain that for a population to survive and grow, varied biological and environmental factors must be in balance.

Use the Visual

Have students study the photograph that opens the section. Explain that many animal species are identified by unique group names. Ask:

■ **What names do you use to refer to specific groups of animals?** (Examples include a flock of birds; a gaggle of geese, a herd of cattle.)

Check Prior Knowledge

To assess students' knowledge about the environment, ask:

■ **What are examples of abiotic and biotic factors?** (Abiotic: temperature, water, living space, soil; biotic: food supply, predators, disease organisms)

Teacher Demo

Fill a beaker almost to its top with water. Begin adding water to the beaker one drop at a time. Have students note the point when a drop of water causes the beaker to overflow. Explain that the beaker has exceeded its water-holding capacity. Tell students ecosystems also have a point at which they reach their capacity to support more organisms.

876

THE BIG IDEA! The size of a population is affected by living and nonliving factors. 36.1–36.2

36.1 Population Growth

What you'll learn

IDEAS
• To define a population
• To compare carrying capacity with exponential growth

WORDS
population, exponential growth, limiting factor, carrying capacity

FIGURE 36.1
How is a honeybee colony an example of a population? ①

Animal mobs
You may know that many fish make up a school, but did you know that a group of frogs is called an army? Other interesting names of groups of animals include a crash of rhinos, a mob of kangaroos, a smack of jellyfish, a drift of hogs, and a pod of whales. Birds also have unique group names: a murder of ravens, an exaltation of larks, and a parliament of owls.

STUDYING POPULATIONS

Getting the big picture

What comes to mind when you hear the word *population*? You are part of a population in your community. The school you attend also has a population.

A **population** is a group of organisms of the same species that live in a particular area. For example, the honeybees that live together

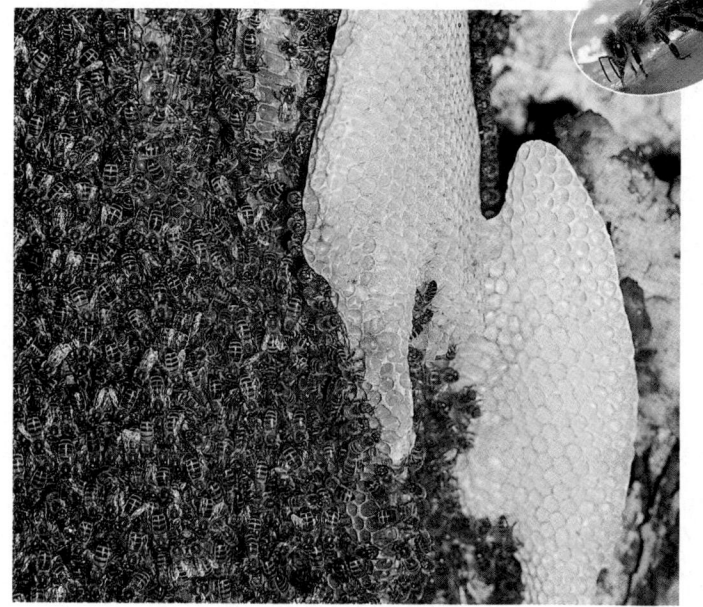

in a hive are members of the same species. All the honeybees in a hive make up a colony and a population.

During the course of a year, the size of a honeybee population may change dramatically. When flowers are blooming and food is plentiful, the colony may grow very quickly. Twenty, forty, or even sixty thousand bees may crowd together in the hive. During severe environmental conditions, however, the number of bees in the colony can decrease drastically. A cold winter or a mite infestation can kill thousands of bees.

Population ecology is the study of how and why populations change. In their research, ecologists try to determine what factors influence the size, density, distribution, and growth of various populations of organisms. Once the ecologists have identified the factors that affect a population, they can predict how that population may change in the future.

For populations to survive, many different environmental factors must be in balance. This balance can be upset by natural disasters. Think of what a prolonged drought can do to plant and animal populations in a forest or on a prairie. Human activities,

876 *Unit 9 Organisms and the Environment*

STUDENT RESOURCES

From the Teacher's Resource Package, use:
■ Section Review 36.1, and Activity Recordsheet 36-1 from Unit 9 Review Module
■ Consumer Applications 36-1
■ Issues and Decision Making 36-1

TECHNOLOGY RESOURCES

Relevant technology resources include:
■ Spanish Student Edition CD-ROM
■ Teacher's Resource Planner CD-ROM
■ Interactive Earth CD-ROM
■ Biology Alive! Video Series

such as pollution and habitat destruction, can also upset the balance of environmental factors that must exist in order for populations to survive.

Populations can change—sometimes permanently—as a result of human activities. For example, cod used to be abundant in the ocean off the coast of Newfoundland. But during the 1980s, the number of cod dropped dramatically due to overfishing. By the early 1990s, cod had all but disappeared. Studying these changes in populations can help people understand and reduce the negative impact of their activities.

EXPONENTIAL GROWTH

Growing by leaps and bounds

To understand how populations grow, think about what happens to a population under ideal conditions. Suppose you put a single bacterium in a nutrient-rich culture dish then incubate the culture under conditions ideal for bacterial growth. Each bacterium can divide every 20 minutes. How large would the population of bacteria be after one day?

The graph in *Figure 36.2* shows how a population of bacteria can increase in size. In the first 20 minutes, the single bacterium would divide to produce 2 bacteria. After 40 minutes, there would be 4 bacteria. After the first hour, there would be 8 bacteria. After 10 generations, there would be 1024 bacteria, and after 20 generations, 1,048,576 bacteria. After 72 generations—only 24 hours later— your culture dish would be teeming with 4.72×10^{21} bacteria!

The growth pattern of bacteria is an example of exponential (eks-poh-NEN-shul) growth. **Exponential growth** occurs when the rate of population growth in each new generation

Population Growth in Bacteria

Number of Generations	Number of Bacterial Cells
0	1
1	2
2	4
3	8
4	16
10	1024
20	1,048,576
72	4.72×10^{21}

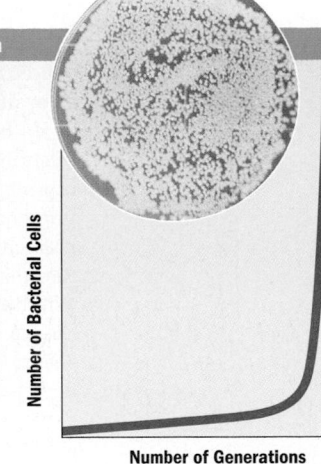

is a multiple of the previous generation. If you graph the exponential growth of a population, the result is a J-shaped curve, as shown in *Figure 36.2*.

The model of exponential growth in bacteria includes two assumptions. The first assumption is that no bacteria die, and the second is that all of the bacteria in the population reproduce. These assumptions make it possible for there to be a 100-percent

FIGURE 36.2
Bacterial growth occurs in an exponential, or J-shaped, curve. What assumptions are included in this growth curve? **2**

LAB ZONE **Think About It!** **bioSURF**

Would You Work for Pennies?

Would you rather have a job that paid $100 a week, or one that paid you one penny the first day, two pennies the second day, four pennies the third day, and so on for thirty days?

Analyzing the Information

1 Calculate the amount pay you would receive after thirty days for both methods of payment.
2 Make a graph to show your pay each day for the second method of payment. How does your graph compare with the graph of bacterial growth?
3 Which method of payment would you prefer? Explain your answer using your calculations and graph.

2 TEACH

Use the Visual

Have students study Figure 36.2. Emphasize that the J-shaped curve shown is typical of a curve showing exponential growth. Ask:

- **How does the population size change from one generation to the next?** (It doubles.)

LAB ZONE **Think About It!**

Would You Work for Pennies?

Provide students with graph paper. Suggest that they first construct a data table with two columns labeled *Day of the Month* and *Amount Paid.*

Analyzing the Information

1 After 30 days the student would earn approximately $400 if paid $100 a week; $5,368,709.11 if paid exponentially.
2 It is the same shape as the graph for bacterial growth, J-shaped.
3 Students are likely to prefer the exponential method of payment as they earn more money.

Math

After discussing population growth rate, ask:

- **What is the growth rate in a population that increases by 234 individuals every 3 years?** (78 individuals/year or 33 percent)

Social Studies

You can use the Irish potato famine of the 1840s as an example of how a biological factor affected the immigration and emigration of a human population. Explain to students that in the 1840s a funguslike protist destroyed much of the potato crop of Ireland, a food that was a staple for the country. To avoid starvation, many people *emigrated* from Ireland. A large percentage of Irish *immigrated* to the United States.

Build Writing Skills

Have students research current population figures for the United States in an almanac or on the Internet. Have them use the data they find to write an essay describing the predicted size and structure of the population of the United States by the year 2000.

❶ The curve in the graph in Figure 36.2 becomes steeper earlier.

increase in every generation. In other words, the population of bacteria doubles with every generation.

In nature, of course, not all of the offspring in a population survive to reproduce. Suppose a rabbit population begins with 100 rabbits. The population size of each new generation may increase by only 5 percent. Will this population growth produce an exponential growth curve? You can see in *Figure 36.3* that it will. But because the percentage increase in each rabbit generation is only 5 percent, compared to 100 percent in the bacteria, the curve looks different. It takes more generations for the growth curve of the rabbit population to become steep. Nevertheless, you can see that even a small percentage increase in the size of each generation can lead to exponential growth.

The total change in a population's size over time is its growth rate. You can calculate growth rate by using the following equation:

FIGURE 36.3
This graph shows the growth rate of a rabbit population. How does the shape of this graph differ from that in *Figure 36.2*? ❶

$$\text{Growth rate} = \frac{\text{Change in number of individuals}}{\text{Time period}}$$

Four factors play a role in growth rate: birth rate, immigration, death rate, and emigration. Immigration is the movement of organisms into an area occupied by an existing population. Emigration is the movement of organisms out of an area where a population is located. The combined effects of these four factors determine whether a population grows, shrinks, or stays the same size.

It is also possible to use the age structure of a population to make predictions about changes in population size. The age structure means the proportion of individuals in a population that are young, old, and in between. For example, what is the growth potential in a human population in which most people are over age 80? How about in one composed primarily of young adults? If most members of a population are young and able to reproduce, that population has the potential to grow rapidly. On the other hand, a population of mostly older individuals has less growth potential, and that potential may decrease as the death rate increases.

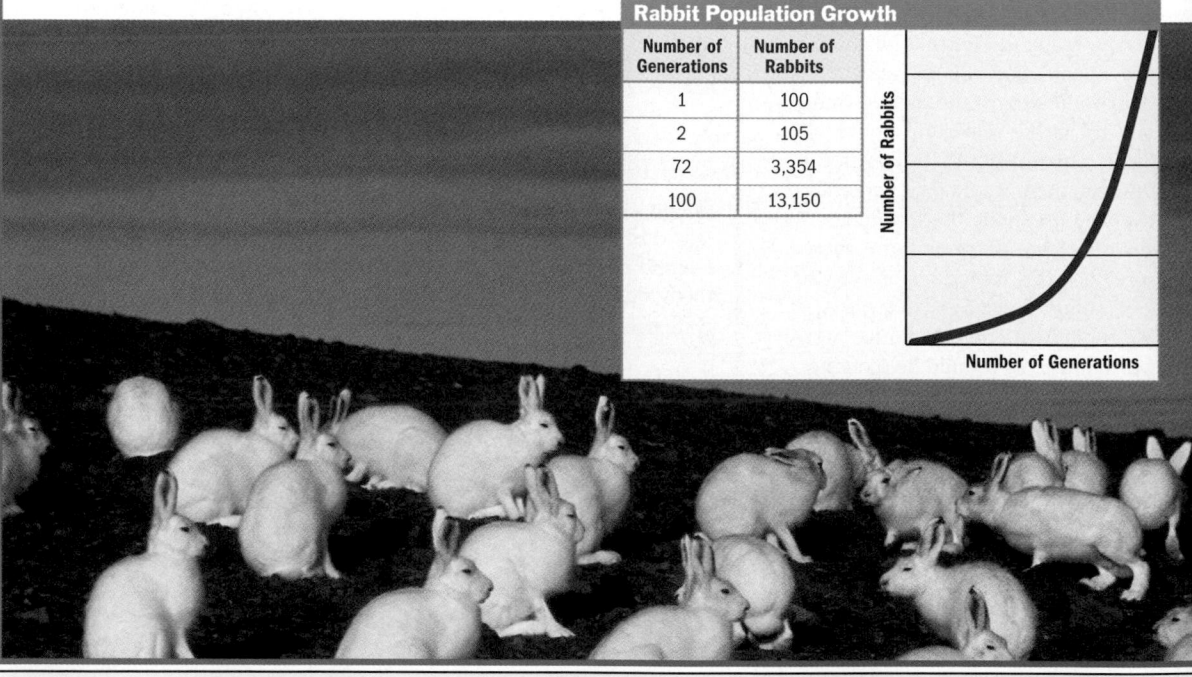

Rabbit Population Growth

Number of Generations	Number of Rabbits
1	100
2	105
72	3,354
100	13,150

Number of Rabbits / Number of Generations

MULTICULTURAL PERSPECTIVE

The Immigration Act of 1965 altered quotas favoring western Europe. By the 1980s, about 37 percent of all legal immigrants to the United States came from Asia and about 47 percent from Mexico, the Caribbean, and Latin America. The same patterns continued into the 1990s. It is predicted that by the year 2010 Hispanics will become the nation's largest minority group.

CARRYING CAPACITY

Exponential growth meets the real world

Study the graph of population growth in *Figure 36.4*. This graph shows the growth of a fruit fly population. Notice that the population first goes through a stage of exponential growth. But after a while, the population growth slows down. Eventually the number of fruit flies in the population levels off. Why does this happen?

As you may recall from Chapter 35, organisms obtain all of the biotic and abiotic resources they need from their environment. When a population first begins to grow, resources such as food, water, and living space are plentiful. The birth rate is high, the death rate is low, and the population increases exponentially. But as growth continues, the environment's resources are shared by more and more individuals. Eventually, some resources are in short supply and become limiting factors. A **limiting factor** is any biotic or abiotic resource in the environment that limits the size of a population.

Limiting factors determine an environment's carrying capacity. **Carrying capacity** is the number of individuals in a population that an environment can support over a relatively long period of time. The graph in *Figure 36.4* shows how carrying capacity works. Assume that food is a limiting factor. As food supplies dwindle, the birth rate drops and the death rate rises, causing population growth to slow down. Eventually, the population levels off as the carrying capacity of the environment is reached. When the birth rate and the death rate of the population become roughly equal, the population size stabilizes.

The growth pattern of the fruit fly population forms an S-shaped curve. This growth pattern is typical of many populations in nature. Population

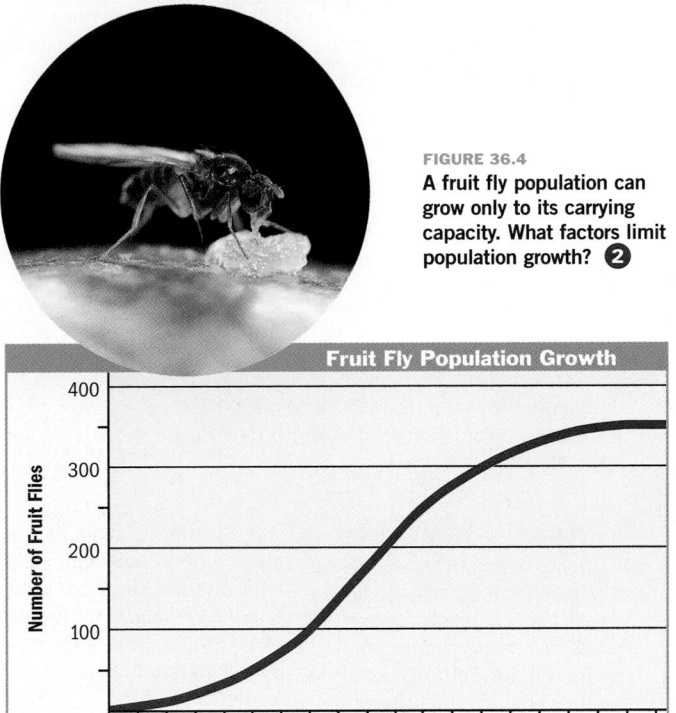

Fruit Fly Population Growth

growth is rapid at first, but then slows and levels off as the population reaches the environment's carrying capacity.

CHECKPOINT 36.1

1. What is a population? Give two examples of a population.
2. What is exponential growth? What causes a population to stop growing exponentially?
3. **Critical Thinking** How might a change in the water level of a river affect the fish populations living in the river?

Build on What You Know

4. Compare the factors that affect growth rate with the factors that affect the gene pool of a population. *(Need to jog your memory? Revisit relevant concepts in Chapter 10, Section 10.5.)*

Chapter 36 Populations and Communities **879**

CHECKPOINT 36.1

1. Group of organisms of the same species living in a particular area; a bee colony or whale pod.
2. The rate of population growth in each new generation is a multiple of the previous generation; competition for resources
3. **Identifying cause and effect** Water levels in the river may drop, changing the habitat of many fishes.

4. Immigration and emigration change the gene pool of a population. The gene pool is also affected by genetic mutations which may change the birth rate or death rate.

❷ Any biotic or abiotic factor that limits population size such as food supply, living space, disease organisms, and natural resources

Use the Visual

Have students study Figure 36.4. Ask:

- **How does the graph indicate that the environment has reached its carrying capacity for the population shown?** (The curve levels off.)

3 ASSESS

Evaluate Understanding

List the objectives for this section on the board. Have students work in pairs to provide the information requested in the objectives. Ask:

- **Describe a graph that reflects exponential growth.** (The line is J-shaped.)
- **What four factors affect growth rate?** (Birth rate, immigration, emigration, and death rate)
- **What does the term *carrying capacity* mean?** (The number of individuals in a population that an environment can support over time.)

Reteach

On the board, draw a graph with a J-shaped curve that levels off and one with a J-shaped curve that shows no leveling off. Have volunteers explain what each curve shows about population growth patterns. Use the graphs to review the concept of exponential growth and the factors that affect population growth.

TEAM WORK

Observing Population Growth

SAFETY FIRST!

Remind students of the proper procedures for handling and using the microscope. Advise students to handle the glass-ware with caution to avoid breakage.

Lab Prep and Planning

Day 1 requires 45 minutes; day 6 requires 30 minutes.

To prepare yeast, mix yeast with water as directed on the package. Do not add sugar. You may need to assist students in their first set of counts. Remind students that buds should count as individual cells. A yeast cell with a bud should be counted as two cells, not one.

Hypothesis Help

Students may wish to refer back to Chapter 16, Section 16.2 which presents information on yeast. Likely hypotheses will state that if resources are abundant, the population will show exponential growth. If resources become less abundant, then the population size will level off and eventually decrease, unless resources are replaced.

Lab Extension

Directed

Have students test varying concentrations of molasses by assigning each lab team a different concentration. At the end of one week, construct a class data table and have students graph the results. Have students conclude which concentration is optimal for growth.

Observing Population Growth

WHAT YOU WILL DO Observe the effect of a variable on a yeast cell population

SKILLS YOU WILL USE Observing, collecting and recording data, measuring, designing an experiment

WHAT YOU WILL NEED 6 empty baby-food jars with lids, grease pencil, graduated cylinder, 10% molasses solution, yeast solution, dropper, 6 microscope slides, 6 coverslips, microscope

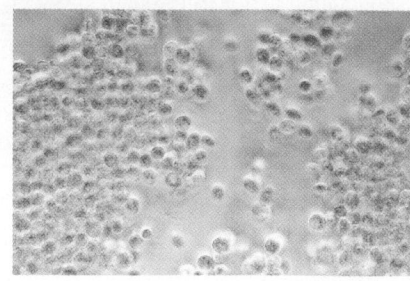

Propose a Hypothesis

Choose a variable (such as temperature, light, or food) that may change the growth rate of a yeast population. Propose a hypothesis about the effect of that variable on the growth of a yeast population.

Conduct Your Experiment

DAY 1

1 Label two jars *A*, two jars *B*, and two jars *C*. Then number each pair *1* and *2*. A1 and A2 are your control jars. Add 10 milliliters (mL) of molasses solution to each of your control jars. Add 10 mL of molasses solution or 10 mL of water to jars B1, B2, C1, and C2 depending on whether food is your chosen variable.

2 Stir the yeast solution with a dropper. Immediately transfer 10 drops of the yeast solution into each jar, then mix again.

3 Using a clean dropper, transfer one drop of the solution from jar A1, jar B1, and jar C1 onto slides with coverslips.

4 Observe the slides under a microscope at high power. Count the number of individual yeast cells in each of five different fields per slide. Buds also count as individual cells.

5 Make a table to record the five counts for each slide. Average the five counts for each slide and record your results. Empty and clean jars A1, B1, and C1 when you have completed this step.

6 Place jar A2 (the control) in a warm, dark place. Place jars B2 and C2 in places where you can test your chosen variables.

DAY 6

7 Repeat steps 3, 4, and 5 for jars A2, B2, and C2. Gently mix the yeast solution before transferring the drops to the slides. Record your data in the table.

Analyze Your Data

1 Make three line graphs to plot the changes in yeast cell populations A, B, and C.

2 Describe the shape of your graphs. How do these graphs differ? What do your graphs reveal about yeast population growth?

Draw Conclusions

How did your variable affect the rate of growth of the yeast population?

Design a Related Experiment

Design an experiment to test the effect of another variable on yeast population growth.

Lab: Observing Population Growth

5. Average Count per Slide
jar A1 average:
jar B1 average:
jar C1 average:

Analyze Your Data

1 Answers will vary depending on the variable; check graphs for clarity and format.
2 Students should describe their graphs not just in absolute numbers, but also in terms of the slope of the lines.

Draw Conclusions

Check students' conclusions.

36.2 Limits on Population Growth

Disappearance of the cliff dwellers
Between A.D. 1000 and 1300, the people of what is now the southwestern United States lived in cliff dwellings. These dwellings could house up to 1500 people and were constructed from stone, adobe, and timber. However, the cliff dwellers left their homes for unknown reasons—perhaps because of war or climate changes. What factors affect human populations today?

What you'll learn

IDEAS
• To distinguish between exponential growth and a boom-and-bust curve
• To compare and contrast limiting factors

WORDS
density-dependent limiting factors, predation, density-independent limiting factors

DENSITY-DEPENDENT LIMITING FACTORS

Too close for comfort

Limiting factors in the environment keep the population size in check in two ways: They either cause a decrease in the birth rate or an increase in the death rate. Some factors become limiting only when the population density—the number of organisms per unit of space—reaches a certain level. These factors are called **density-dependent limiting factors.**

One density-dependent limiting factor is living space. For example, mice that live together under stressful, crowded conditions often neglect their young. Neglected baby mice have a high death rate, and this limits population growth. Three other common density-dependent limiting factors are disease, competition, and predation.

Disease As a population becomes more dense, disease often limits growth. During the fourteenth century, for example, bubonic plague killed more than 25 million people in Europe. The disease spread through crowded villages and towns, killing people with frightening speed. In rural areas, however, where the human population was sparse, fewer

people contracted the disease. Today, bubonic plague is rare and treatable. What diseases affect the human population today? ❶

Competition You probably know what it is like to compete for something. Other organisms also compete with each other for resources. Competition is an interaction in which organisms try to obtain a share of the same limited resources. Animals compete for food, water, mates, and territories. Plants compete for water, minerals, pollinators, and sunlight. Within a population, competition for any resource is a density-dependent limiting factor.

FIGURE 36.5
This community watering hole is drying up. How is this change an example of a density-dependent limiting factor? ❷

881

❶ ENGAGE

Use the Visual

Have students study the photograph that opens the section. Explain that unlike other organisms, humans are able to alter their environments significantly to meet their needs. Ask:

■ **What are some environmental factors that humans cannot alter?** (Likely responses include amount of nonrenewable resources available, some disease organisms, and natural disasters.)

SUPER READ! **Identifying Cause and Effect** To practice strategies for effective reading, use pages 75-76 in *Super Read!*

❶ Answers may include AIDS, malaria, and cholera.
❷ The amount of water available is partially determined by the number of organisms using it.

Teacher Demo

Place ten marbles on a desk so they touch each other. Roll another marble into the group and have students observe how many of the original marbles move. Repeat the activity with the original marbles dispersed over a wider area. Challenge students to explain why the results differed in each trial. Relate responses to the idea of density-dependent limiting factors.

Use the Visual

Have students study Figure 36.6. Ask:

■ **What relationship does the graph suggest about hare and lynx populations?**
(Increases and decreases in the hare population are soon followed by similar changes in the lynx population.)

Clarify Misconceptions

Students often think that the term *predator* applies only to carnivores such as the lynx. Point out that all consumers are predators and all organisms eaten by consumers are prey. Some plants, bacteria, fungi, and protists can be considered predators.

FIGURE 36.6
Population Cycles

The graph (right) illustrates how the lynx population cycle changes as the snowshoe hare population fluctuates. The series of photos (below) illustrates why the size of the lynx population varies with the size of the hare population.

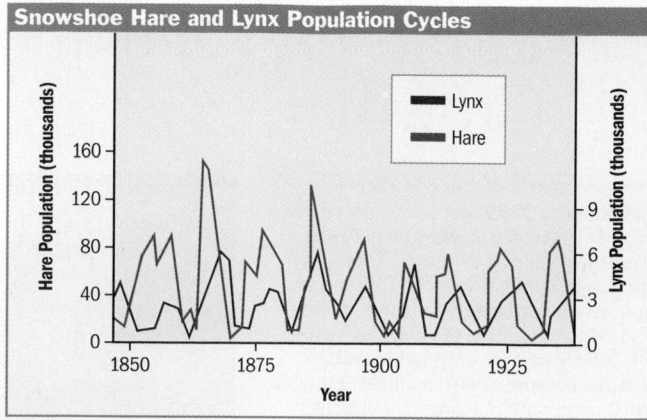

When population density increases, resources must be shared among more individuals.
Predation An interaction in which one species (a predator) feeds on another species (prey) is called **predation.** The lynx shown in *Figure 36.6* is a catlike predator of the northern forests that stalks and eats snowshoe hares. When snowshoe hares are plentiful, the lynx in the area are well fed, and many of their young survive. As a result, the lynx population grows. As the number of lynx increases, more snowshoe hares are killed and eaten, and the size of the snowshoe hare population decreases. As snowshoe hares become scarce, the lynx population will begin to decline as well.

Predation is a density-dependent limiting factor because its effects on a population change as the numbers of predators or prey increase or decrease.

In general, when a population grows beyond the carrying capacity of the environment, density-dependent limiting factors act to reduce the population. The population's size grows and shrinks, resulting in the cycles shown in *Figure 36.6.*

Changes in the size of predator-prey populations often occur in cycles. Determine the length of each population cycle shown in *Figure 36.6.* Can you explain the changes in hare and lynx populations? ❶

A similar interaction takes place between snowshoe hares and the plants they eat. When the snowshoe hare population increases, more plants are eaten, decreasing the plant population and the hares' food supply. Because there is less food available, the number of hares declines. With fewer hares around, the plant population increases and the cycle starts again.

Predator-prey relationships are a strong force in natural selection. Prey that escape predators can reproduce and pass on to their offspring traits that enabled them to escape. At the same time, predators that capture the most prey are likely to be stronger and to produce more offspring. Their offspring inherit traits that made their parents efficient predators. In this way, predators and their prey may coevolve.

882 *Unit 9 Organisms and the Environment*

Sight Impaired Recreate graphs using yarn or string of different textures to represent the curves. Students will be able to trace the curves and interpret the changes shown from the model.

❶ A rise in the hare population provides more food for the predator. The lynx population increases and the prey population decreases. With fewer prey, the predator population decreases, the hare population starts to increase, and the cycle begins again.

DENSITY-INDEPENDENT LIMITING FACTORS

Just bad luck

Some environmental factors can disrupt or destroy all sorts of populations. Factors that affect all populations in the same way, regardless of their density, are called **density-independent limiting factors.** Weather, seasonal cycles, natural disasters, and many human activities are density-independent limiting factors. These factors can cause growing or stable populations to collapse suddenly. For example, when Mount St. Helens erupted in 1980, many populations died within minutes.

Some density-independent disturbances happen regularly. In places where there are severe winters, large numbers of insects die every year. In some areas, periodic droughts wipe out entire grass populations.

Populations that live in areas of seasonal cold and drought seldom approach the environment's carrying capacity. Instead, they have a population growth pattern called a boom-and-bust curve. As you can see in *Figure 36.7*, a boom-and-bust curve represents a period of exponential growth followed by a sudden collapse of the population.

Environments are always changing, and most populations can adapt to a certain amount of change. Populations grow or shrink in response to changes in the environment until balance is restored.

Major upsets in the natural balance, however, can lead to extinction. Extinction occurs when populations cannot adapt to changing conditions in the environment. Human activities can upset the balance in natural systems so quickly that populations of organisms do not have time to adapt. Overhunting, overfishing, clear-cutting of forests, damming of rivers, and pollution all can lead to extinction. Although extinction can occur naturally, human activities have greatly accelerated the rate of extinction worldwide.

HUMAN POPULATION

Growing . . . growing . . .

In 1798 the English economist Thomas Malthus wrote that the human population was increasing at a much faster rate than its food supply. Malthus thought that population growth caused resource shortages that

EVERYDAY BIOLOGY

Limits

Some scientists hypothesize that Earth's total carrying capacity for humans is 15 to 20 billion people—three to four times the size of today's population. With current rates of growth, the human population could reach that size in 75 to 80 years.

FIGURE 36.7

Native to Australia, thrips are insects with a seasonal boom-and-bust cycle. The thrip's population peaks during the summer months of December and January. When would you find the fewest thrips per flower? ❷

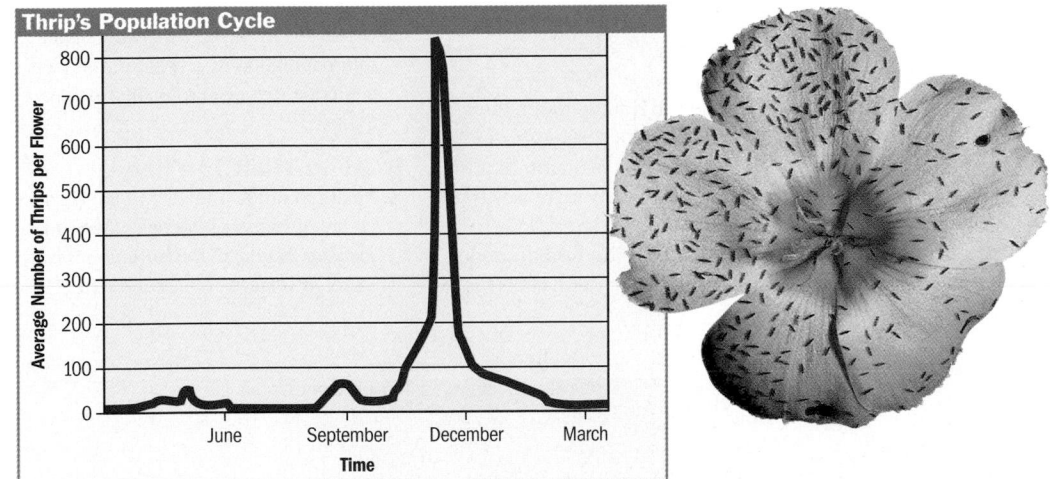

Thrip's Population Cycle

(Graph: Average Number of Thrips per Flower vs. Time, with months June, September, December, March marked. Population peaks near 800+ around December.)

Chapter 36 Populations and Communities **883**

Discuss

Explain to students that natural disasters such as volcanic eruptions and severe storms can sometimes kill almost all the organisms living in an area. Ask:

■ **Are natural disasters an example of a density-dependent or density-independent limiting factor? Explain.** (Because such disasters are not related to population density, they are density-independent limiting factors.)

Use the Visual

Have students study Figure 36.7. Point out that in a boom-and-bust curve, population size remains stable for a period of time, experiences exponential growth, and then shows a collapse. Emphasize that such growth patterns are an indication that density-independent factors are in play. Ask:

■ **What do you think causes the decrease in population from March through June?** (These are the fall and winter months in Australia. The colder weather may kill the thrips directly, or kill the plants the thrips eat.)

❷ In late fall and winter, March-August.

Everyday Biology

Have students work in small groups to prepare a report describing world population projections by the year 2020 Suggest that they use current almanacs, atlases, and other current references to find out what areas of the world are growing the fastest and what challenges current rates of growth pose for future generations.

ASSESS

Evaluate Understanding

To assess understanding of population growth patterns, have students compare conditions that produce a J-shaped curve with conditions that produce a boom-and-bust curve. Ask:

- **What conditions can lead to the extinction of populations of organisms?** (Natural disasters, seasonal cycles, and human activities that upset the balance of nature)

- **How would you describe the current human population growth rate?** (Human population is growing exponentially.)

Reteach

On the board, draw a J-shaped curve and a boom-and-bust curve. Have volunteers identify the types of curves shown. Then ask students to review the text to explain what each curve shows and the limiting factors associated with each curve.

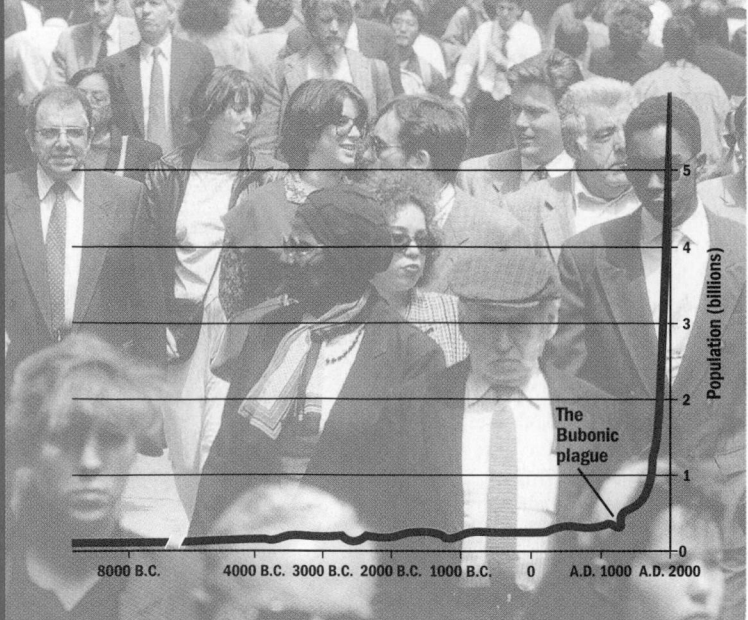

FIGURE 36.8
The human population is growing rapidly. What factors affect this growth curve? How does human population growth affect other populations? ❶

led to famines and wars. As you learned in Chapter 10, Charles Darwin later concluded that all populations could outgrow their resources.

How much has the human population increased over time? The J-shaped curve in *Figure 36.8* represents human population growth. As you can see, for thousands of years the population growth was very slow. Then, between 1650 and 1850, the population doubled—passing the one billion mark. And the population's doubling time is becoming shorter and shorter. After 1850 it took only 80 years for the population to double to 2 billion. It reached 4 billion just 45 years later. Population ecologists estimate that the human population now increases by 90 million people every year!

At the moment, the human population is growing exponentially. This rapid growth is due to the increasing gap between birth rates and death rates—far more people are born than die each year. Exponential growth of the human population cannot continue indefinitely. The same factors that limit population size for bacteria, lynx, or any other organism also apply to humans.

Population ecologists are not sure what the world's carrying capacity is for humans. They hope that population growth will level out in an S-shaped curve and become stable at some point. In the meantime, the expanding human population is placing huge demands on natural resources. As our population has grown, humans have developed medical, agricultural, and other technologies that enable more people to survive. Do you think there is a limit to our population? ❷

CHECKPOINT 36.2

1. What causes a boom-and-bust growth pattern? How is this pattern different from the growth patterns of the fly and bacteria discussed in Section 36.1?

2. Compare and contrast density-dependent limiting factors with density-independent limiting factors. Give examples of each.

3. **Critical Thinking** What will happen to a population of predators if there is a sudden increase in food for its prey? Explain.

Build on What You Know

4. Relate Malthus' theories to Darwin's theory of natural selection. *(Need to jog your memory? Revisit relevant concepts in Chapter 10, Section 10.2.)*

? What factors affect population size?

CHECKPOINT 36.2

1. Boom-and-bust is exponential growth followed by a sudden collapse in population. The bacteria are multiplying exponentially because they have not yet reached a limiting factor. The fly population grew exponentially at first, but leveled off as it reached the carrying capacity.

2. Density-dependent factors (living space), are limited when the population reaches a certain density. Density-independent factors (weather) affect all populations in the same way.

3. **Predicting** It will increase because the prey population will increase.

4. Malthus-population growth causes resource shortages; Darwin-individuals that "win" the competition for resources survive and reproduce.

THE BIG IDEA! How populations interact determines the structure and characteristics of a community. 36.3

36.3 Communities

Birds and beasts
African red-billed oxpeckers have a unique relationship with grazing animals. These birds eat ticks and other harmful insects found on rhinos, giraffes, and water buffalo. Not only are the grazers free of pests, but they also gain a built-in alarm system—the birds make noise when predators approach.

What you'll learn

IDEAS
• To describe a community
• To compare community interactions

WORDS
community, symbiosis, mutualism, parasitism, commensalism

ROLES IN THE COMMUNITY

All together

Picture a meadow full of tall grass and wildflowers. Honeybees flit from flower to flower. Dragonflies zoom around hunting for insects. Mice scurry through the grass looking for seeds. High overhead, a hawk circles. All the organisms living in and around this meadow form a community.

A **community** is a collection of populations that interact with each other in a given area. Populations in a community compete for resources, prey on one another, and interact in many other ways.

Different communities vary in the types of species they contain and in the abundance of each species. An Amazon rain forest community contains thousands of different kinds of plants and animals. Some species may be represented by only a handful of individuals, however. In contrast, a pine forest community in northern Canada might contain only a few dozen species, but most of those species would be very abundant. For example, there could be many thousands of individuals of one pine tree species.

In any community, each species is unique in what it does and in how it interacts with other community members and the physical environment. As you may recall from Chapter 10, the particular role that a population plays in its community is called its niche. In the meadow example, a honeybee population pollinates flowering plants. A population of mice eats seeds and is prey for other animals. Hawks are predators that feed on mice and other small animals.

A population's niche includes all its interactions with other species in its community, as well as interactions with abiotic parts of the community. Understanding a species' niche helps

FIGURE 36.9
The hawk and the mouse occupy different niches in the same community. What are their niches? ❸

36.3

① ENGAGE

Consider the Big Idea

Have students read The Big Idea! at the top of the page. Explain that a community can be characterized by the kinds and abundance of species it contains.

Use the Visual

Have students study the photograph and text that opens the section. Ask:

■ **How do the oxpeckers and grazing animals benefit from their relationship?** (The oxpeckers receive food, the grazing animals receive protection from predators, including parasites.)

Quick Activity

Display photographs of animals interacting with their environment. For each photograph, have students name the biotic and abiotic factors in the environment shown. Then ask students to describe possible interactions among different organisms living in the same environment. List student responses on the board. Have them add to the list of interactions as they complete the section.

❶ Availability of resources; can lead to their extinction
❷ Yes. Earth has limited resources.
❸ The mouse is a consumer of seeds and prey for the hawk, which is a predator.

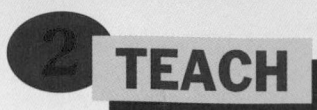

2 TEACH

Discuss

Students often confuse the terms *population* and *community* and the terms habitat and niche. Take a few minutes to review the meaning of these terms. Point out, as an example, that a *population* of trees has an address or *habitat* and a profession or *niche* in the *community* called a forest. Challenge students to provide other examples of how the terms are related.

LAB ZONE Do It! TEAM WORK

Analyzing Interactions in Your Community

To help students recognize that many microscopic organisms live in their home, you may wish to have them obtain carpet samples and examine them microscopically for the presence of mites. You may also wish to have students swab several surfaces and prepare cultures from the swabs. Growth occurring on the cultures will indicate the presence of bacteria or fungi.

Analyze Your Results

1 Students are likely to find that other animal species in their home rely on the human food supply.
2 Answers will vary depending on the species found.
3 Accept all logical responses. Encourage students to list any pest control devices used in the home.

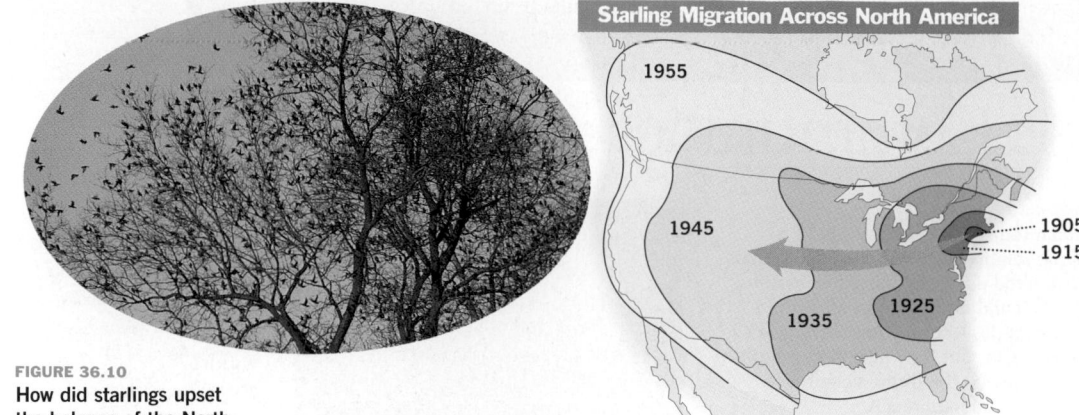

FIGURE 36.10
How did starlings upset the balance of the North American bird community? ❶

Starling Migration Across North America

ecologists predict how changing conditions might affect that species and other living organisms with which it interacts. How might plowing a meadow affect the niches of the different species living there? ❷

COMMUNITY INTERACTIONS

Tough competition

In any community, you will find organisms interacting in many different ways—so many, in fact, that studying

LAB ZONE Do It!

Analyzing Interactions in Your Community

The inside of your home is a dwelling place, not just for humans but for a whole community of species. You can investigate their interactions if you . . .

Try This

1 Make a list of organisms that can be found living in your house or apartment. Some may be invited, such as pets or houseplants. Others may be uninvited, such as insects or molds.
2 Make a table and record information about the food relationships among members in this community.

Analyze Your Results

1 What do the animals eat? Do they rely on the human food supply, or do they have their own sources of food?
2 Are there predators and prey in this community?
3 Describe how the community members compete for resources.

interactions can be a bit bewildering. But the interactions in a community fall into a few general categories.

As you read earlier in this chapter, most species in a community compete with other species for food, water, sunlight, nesting material—even places to perch or hide. Competition can occur between populations of different species or between members of the same species.

When a resource is in short supply, competition can become fierce. Sometimes foreign species move in and outcompete native species for limited resources. For example, 60 European starlings were released in New York City's Central Park in 1890. Now there are more than 200 million starlings in North America. Starlings compete with bluebirds, redheaded woodpeckers, flickers, and flycatchers for nesting sites. The growth in the starling population has had a negative impact on these native species.

Competition is not the only type of interaction between species. You have also read about predator-prey relationships. The lynx, for example, depends on the hare for survival. Can you suggest other examples of predator-prey relationships? ❸

Natural selection constantly acts to fine-tune predator-prey relationships.

❶ The increased starling population led to increased competition and many native bird populations decreased.
❷ The disturbance might destroy old niches and create new ones.
❸ Birds and insects, bobcats and rabbits, owls and mice, wolf and sheep

Many predators and prey have evolved sharp claws, teeth, and beaks. Prey have acquired defenses such as spines and shells. Both predators and prey have camouflaging body colors and patterns that make them less visible to each other.

Predator-prey relationships are one of the many types of interactions among populations. Another type of interaction, called **symbiosis,** occurs when one species lives in close association with another species over a period of time. There are three types of symbiotic relationships: mutualism, parasitism, and commensalism. What are some of the symbiotic relationships you read about in Units 4, 5, 6, and 7?

In **mutualism,** two species interact closely in a way that benefits both species. Honeybees and other insect pollinators have a mutualistic relationship with many flowers. Flowers attract bees with sweet nectar. As bees feed, they pick up pollen that they transfer to other flowers, pollinating them in the process.

Many animals, including cows and termites, have microorganisms in their digestive tracts. In this type of mutualism, the microorganisms help the host digest grass, wood, or other plant materials. In return, the microorganisms have a habitat with a constant food supply.

In **parasitism,** a parasite lives on or in another organism—its host. Parasites suck blood or obtain nutrients in some way from the host's body. Parasites may weaken their hosts, but they usually don't kill them like predators do. Parasites may live

Mutual Feelings

Humans have a symbiotic relationship with some bacteria. Bacteria on the skin can prevent infections by making the skin resistant to pathogens. Bacteria in the digestive system help break down food.

FIGURE 36.11
Symbiosis

How do these photographs represent the three types of symbiosis? ❹

Mutualism
The ants and acacia trees in Central and South America have an unusual mutualistic relationship. The ants live in the acacia's thorns and eat their leaves. The acacias benefit, too, because ants protect them from predators, and will even destroy other plants that shade the acacias from the sun.

Parasitism
Ticks (right), fleas, leeches, lice, and mites are examples of parasites that live outside the host, attached to skin or scales.

Commensalism
Barnacles and whales illustrate commensalism in an oceanic environment. Barnacles attach themselves to the skin of the whale. Barnacles obtain food by filtering the water. The movement of the whale through the water gives the attached barnacles a greater opportunity to encounter food. The presence of the barnacles does not harm the whale.

Chapter 36 Populations and Communities **887**

MEETING DIVERSE NEEDS

At Risk To help students understand the different types of symbiotic relationships that exist in nature, suggest that they work in pairs to create a visual, song, or poem that illustrates the similarities and differences among mutualism, commensalism, and parasitism.

❹ In each photograph, you can see how different organisms are interacting and affecting one another.

Everyday Biology

You may want to extend this feature with a discussion of other types of symbiotic relationships involving humans, such as parasitism. Ask students what type of interventions help prevent the spread of parasitic diseases. (Vaccines, sanitary living conditions, pest control)

Use the Visual

Have students study Figure 36.11. Ask:

- **How do both the ants and the acacia tree benefit from their relationship?** (The ants are provided with a home and food, the acacia is protected from predators by the ants.)
- **Which organism benefits in a parasitic relationship?** (The parasite)
- **How does the relationship between the clownfish and the sea anemone illustrate commensalism?** (The clownfish benefits from the relationship; the sea anemone neither benefits nor is harmed.)

Language Arts

The word *parasite* comes from the Greek *parasitos,* which means "one who eats at the table of another."

Build Writing Skills

Have students describe one of the three types of symbiotic relationships from the point of view of each organism involved.

Think Critically

After completing an explanation of parasitism, ask:

- **Is parasitism a density-dependent limiting factor or a density-independent limiting factor? Explain.** (Parasitism is a density-dependent limiting factor as parasites are most successful when they can spread easily in a crowded host population.)

- **How do predators differ from parasites?** (Predators kill and quickly eat their prey, parasites live off their host for a long time. Predators are usually larger than their prey; parasites are usually much smaller than their host.)

In the Community

Before students analyze their community, you may wish to review the concepts of food chains and food webs. Suggest that students work in pairs or in small groups and begin by designing a procedure for conducting and analyzing their research. Point out that interactions will vary depending upon the species observed, although some competition and feeding relationships will likely be evident.

FIGURE 36.12
Cheetahs are genetically very similar. How does this low genetic variability render them vulnerable to extinction? ❶

outside or inside a host's body. Parasites that live inside a host include tapeworms, pinworms, and liver flukes.

In **commensalism,** one organism benefits from the interaction, and the other organism is neither helped nor harmed. Barnacles that live on the skin of whales or sea turtles are examples of commensalism. Barnacles benefit because they are moved from place to place, increasing their access to food. The whales or sea turtles are not affected by the barnacles.

BALANCE IN A COMMUNITY
Everything in its place

An ecological community is a highly organized natural system in which all parts exist in a delicate balance. Every species occupies its own special niche. The complex interactions that take place between different species help maintain the balance and lead to stability in the community.

An important connection exists between biodiversity—the degree of species variety—and balance in ecological communities. To see this connection, compare a naturally diverse forest and a tree plantation.

In a forest, different species of trees grow side by side. Two spruce trees, for example, might be separated by a fir tree and several pines. If disease or insects attack a particular tree, neighboring trees of a different species may be resistant to the attack. In this way, species diversity in a forest acts as a natural barrier to the spread of disease or insect infestation.

In comparison, a tree plantation is more vulnerable to disease. All the trees are of the same species, so pests and disease spread from tree to tree much more easily.

Genetic diversity within populations is also important in maintaining ecological balance in a community. When a population of genetically diverse organisms is infected by a disease, some individuals will die, but others may survive because their different genetic makeup makes them more resistant to the disease. This is not the case in populations where all the organisms are genetically very similar, such as the cheetahs in *Figure 36.12.* A disease that affects one individual will most likely affect all the others. Species with low genetic variability are especially vulnerable to extinction.

Worldwide, between 10 and 200 species become extinct every day as a result of human activities. Adding or removing just one species from a community can have unpredictable and wide-ranging consequences.

The introduction of foreign species into existing communities is a global problem. Some introductions have been accidental, others intentional. In 1859, for example, two dozen rabbits were released into the Australian countryside. Within ten years, millions of rabbits had overrun the land.

The water hyacinth, a blue-flowered floating plant from South America, has been introduced into

---

Now that you have learned the scientific definition of a community, analyze your own community from a biological perspective. What different species occupy your community, and what niches do they occupy? How do the different species interact with each other? Draw a diagram that includes the different species in your community, and use arrows to indicate interactions. Do any species upset the balance of the community? Log on to *http://ecology.biosurf.com* to investigate other types of communities.

IN THE COMMUNITY
What Is a Community?

---

❶ A disease that affects one animal is likely to affect all the others.

FIGURE 36.13
These water hyacinths have overrun their water habitat. How have they upset the balance in the ecosystem? ❷

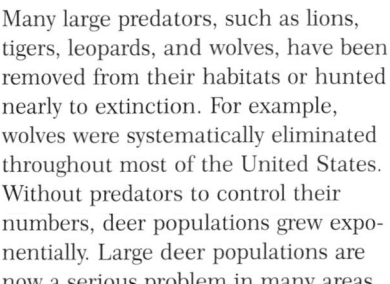

many countries. Once established, the water hyacinth's growth is almost unstoppable. You can see water hyacinths in *Figure 36.13*. They choke rivers, destroy lakes, and crowd out other species. Waterways in Florida and nearby states are overrun by water hyacinths, as is Lake Victoria in East Africa—Africa's largest lake. Can you think of other species that have upset ❸ the balance in an ecosystem?

ISSUES IN BIOLOGY

Missing members

Many large predators, such as lions, tigers, leopards, and wolves, have been removed from their habitats or hunted nearly to extinction. For example, wolves were systematically eliminated throughout most of the United States. Without predators to control their numbers, deer populations grew exponentially. Large deer populations are now a serious problem in many areas.

The deer destroy crops, damage trees and shrubs, and compete with other species for resources.

Wolves, bald eagles, and other predators are returning or being reintroduced into parts of their former ranges. In 1995 biologists released 29 gray wolves into Yellowstone National Park, the first phase of a program to restore wolf populations in the Rocky Mountains.

Some ranchers and area residents disagree with this reintroduction, as predators may kill pets or livestock. Human communities are working together to make predator reintroduction safe and successful for all.

FIGURE 36.14
Gray wolves have recently been released into the wild. How did their absence affect their community? ❹

CHECKPOINT 36.3

1. What is a community? Give two examples.
2. Describe three types of interactions in a community.
3. **Critical Thinking** Classify the relationship between oxpeckers and grazing animals as predator-prey, mutualism, parasitism, or commensalism. Explain.

Build on What You Know

4. What type of symbiosis can be found in lichens? *(Need to jog your memory? Revisit relevant concepts in Chapter 16, Section 16.3.)*

How are the structure and characteristics of a community determined?

STS

The methods used to protect and preserve endangered species, manage populations of wild organisms, and ensure the wise use of resources are forms of conservation. There are many positions in the field of conservation such as soil scientist, wildlife manager, or researcher. For more information about this field, students can write to the Forest Service, U.S. Department of Agriculture, P.O. Box 2417, Washington, DC 20013.

SUPER READ! **Identifying Cause and Effect** To practice strategies for effective reading, use pages 75-76 in *Super Read!*

③ ASSESS

Evaluate Understanding

Have students work in small groups to explain the relationship between populations and communities and to describe several types of interactions that occur within communities. Have students make sketches or diagrams to illustrate each type of interaction.

Reteach

As a class, develop a concept map illustrating the relationship among populations and communities and the types of interactions that occur in communities. Discuss the potential effects of each type of interaction.

CHECKPOINT 36.3

1. A community is a collection of populations that interact with each other in a given area, such as a rain forest.
2. Accept descriptions of predator-prey and symbiotic relationships
3. **Classifying** Mutualism; the oxpeckers find food such as insects, while the grazers are cleaned of parasites and alerted as danger approaches.

4. Commensalism. The fungi benefits from the algae and the algae is neither helped nor harmed.

❷ They choke out native species.
❸ The kudzu vine in the southeastern United States
❹ The prey population, or deer, grew exponentially and destroyed crops and trees.

THE BIG IDEA! Biotic and abiotic changes in a community alter the community structure. 36.4

① ENGAGE

Consider the Big Idea

Have students read The Big Idea! at the top of the page. Explain that change can create opportunities for new species to move into a community.

Use the Visual

Have students study the photograph that opens the section. Point out that phytoplankton are algae. Ask:

- **Why might an increase in the phytoplankton in an area bring about an increase in the number of fishes?** (Many fishes feed on phytoplankton or on other fishes that feed on phytoplankton.)

Quick Activity

Introduce the concept of succession by asking students to tell who becomes president of the United States should anything happen to the president. Record the names in correct order on the board. (Vice President, Speaker of the House, president pro tempore of the Senate, cabinet members according to rank, beginning with state, treasury, and defense.) Point out that this line of succession is dictated by law. Ask students what factors determine the line of succession in ecosystems. Tell students that in this section they will read about nature's way of replacing lost populations.

36.4 Ecological Succession

What you'll learn

IDEAS
- To distinguish between modes of ecological succession
- To describe the communities of ecological succession

WORDS
ecological succession, primary succession, pioneer community, climax community, secondary succession

FIGURE 36.15
Ecological succession has begun in this recently burned area. What new community will develop? ❶

Fertilizer for the sea
In 1995 a research ship dumped 450 kilograms of dissolved iron into the Pacific Ocean. Within weeks the area was filled with phytoplankton that use iron as a nutrient. Scientists hope that other community members will also increase—including species of fishes. How else might this ecosystem be affected?

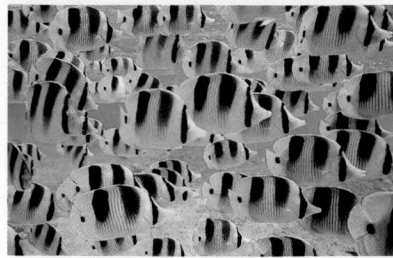

THE PROCESS OF SUCCESSION
Success in change

Change is a natural part of life in any ecological community. Competition for limited resources may eliminate one or more of a community's populations. Some populations may move to a new location, or a disease may wipe them out. Extreme weather or a natural disaster may drastically reduce some populations, yet enable others to thrive.

Whenever change occurs in a community, some habitats may be destroyed while new ones are created. For example, a forest fire might eliminate the habitats of some tree-dwelling birds. At the same time, however, the once-dark forest floor would be flooded with sunlight, creating a habitat suitable for grasses and small flowering plants. These plants could thrive in great numbers along with the animals, such as insects and rodents, that feed on them. Animals that feed on the rodents and insects, such as birds and large predators, could also move into the area.

In addition to fires, other natural disasters such as floods, earthquakes, and volcanic eruptions can destroy or alter niches. Wherever change occurs, opportunities arise for new species to move in and for new communities to develop. Over time, new communities of organisms may gradually replace existing ones in a process called **ecological succession.**

Natural disturbances can set the stage for ecological succession by emptying habitats that were previously occupied. Succession may occur as new species occupy the area and establish new niches. Human activities such as mining, logging, building, and farming can change environments and lead to ecological succession. Succession can also occur after humans have left an area. What might you observe during the first stages of ecological succession in a newly vacant lot? ❷

The barren slopes of a recently erupted volcano and an area of rock exposed by a recent landslide are places where primary succession

---

occurs. **Primary succession** occurs when communities begin to form where none existed before.

The first organisms to occupy an area undergoing primary succession are called pioneer species. A group of pioneer species eventually forms a **pioneer community.** As succession continues, a **climax community** becomes established. A climax community is one that has achieved relative stability and species diversity.

The interactions between the different species help keep the community stable. Unless disturbed by outside factors, such as a natural disaster, a climax community can remain stable for many generations.

Climax communities do not develop everywhere. Sometimes frequent disturbances prevent succession from proceeding beyond a certain point. In grasslands, for example, succession is continually occurring due to frequent fires.

A type of succession that occurs more rapidly than primary succession is secondary succession. **Secondary succession** occurs where a community has been cleared by a disturbance that did not destroy the soil. A vacant lot in a city, abandoned farmland, and a forest area where trees have been cut down are examples of places where secondary succession might occur.

ISLAND SUCCESSION

Colonists in a new land

How do new islands that form in the ocean, far from other lands, become populated with living things? In most cases, communities of organisms are slowly established on new islands through rare and "lucky" accidents. Seed pods can travel thousands of kilometers across the sea. Small animals and plants can be carried long distances on logs or floating debris.

FIGURE 36.16
Ecological Succession

During the establishment of a climax community, succession occurs in steps. In what biome is succession occurring here? ❸

Pioneer community
1 Lichens, which grow on bare rock, and other pioneer species form a pioneer community. Lichens produce acids that break down rock and begin the process of soil formation.

Growing grass
2 In time, enough soil accumulates to support the growth of grasses. As grasses grow and decompose season after season, the soil becomes deep enough for weeds and shrubs to grow.

Shallow trees
3 Over time, enough soil accumulates to support the growth of shallow-rooted trees, such as pines.

Climax community
4 In the shade of the pines, conditions may favor the growth of broadleaf trees such as maple and beech. As succession continues, a more stable community—a climax community—becomes established.

Chapter 36 Populations and Communities **891**

② TEACH

Use the Visual

Have students study Figure 36.16. Ask:

- **What is a pioneer community?** (The first organisms to occupy an area undergoing primary succession)
- **Name a pioneer organism.** (Lichens)
- **What is a climax community?** (The final stable community of organisms in a succession)

Explain

Make sure students understand that primary succession is a very slow process. Scientists estimate that primary succession from sand dunes to the climax beech-maple forest takes about 1000 years. Secondary succession, such as when a forest is cleared or burned, may take fewer than 100 years.

Apply

Have pairs or small groups of students conduct research to find out the sequence of events in lake succession or sand dune succession. Ask students to prepare diagrams that show the stages of ecological succession.

 Earth Science

Island biogeography combines information from the earth sciences and biology. Earth scientists are most interested in the events that lead to the formation of new islands. Biologists are concerned with how a new island becomes inhabited by organisms.

---

❶ A community that includes grasses and small flowering plants and insects and animals that feed on the plants. Eventually, the food chain will expand to include large predators.

❷ Answers may include the growth of weeds and grasses, the appearance of animals that live underground, such as moles

❸ A temperate forest

Studying Human Causes of Succession

Encourage students to photograph or videotape the areas they study. You may wish to divide the class into groups and assign a specific site to each group.

Analyze Your Results

1 Answers will vary depending on the site.
2 Answers will vary depending on locale.

Evaluate Understanding

Ask students to summarize the steps involved in the succession of an area that begins when an area is cleared by a volcanic eruption and ends with a hardwood forest. Review the summaries as a class.

Reteach

List the terms *pioneer community, climax community, pioneer organisms, lichens,* and *secondary succession* on the board. Have students create concept maps to show the relationships among the terms.

892

LAB ZONE Do It!   bioSURF

Studying Human Causes of Succession

Secondary succession often occurs after human disturbances. When lots, buildings, and farmland are abandoned, or large sections of forest are cleared, the soil is not destroyed and rapid succession results. You can observe secondary succession in action if you . . .

Try This

1 Find a vacant lot or abandoned farm or field in your community. Obtain permission to study the area.
2 Study the plants that have colonized the disturbed area. Compare these plants to the plants found in comparable areas, such as a park or working farmland. Record your observations.

Analyze Your Results

1 How tall are the plants in the disturbed area? Are they grasses and weeds, shrubs, or trees?
2 How does this plant community differ from those in the surrounding area? Describe your findings in terms of succession.

FIGURE 36.17
What factors determine the rate of island colonization? ❶

Insects and birds can be blown off course by storms and end up on a new island. New arrivals can carry seeds on their feet, fur, or feathers.

Two factors determine the rate of colonization and succession on an island: its distance from other land

 How do biotic and abiotic changes alter community structure?

892   *Unit 9 Organisms and the Environment*

---

and its size. If an island is close to other land, a colonizing plant or animal will more likely survive the short trip than if the island is far away. If an island is large, it is more likely that drifting plants and animals will wash ashore.

Organisms colonizing an island can find themselves without competitors or predators. Island populations often thrive and may evolve into new species. For example, recall from Chapter 10 that many finch species have evolved from a single common ancestor. While new species evolve on islands, their mainland relatives may become extinct. For this reason, islands are often home to species that do not exist anywhere else on Earth.

Any land area that is surrounded by a natural barrier can be thought of as an island. A desert oasis or a city park can be as isolated as an island. Island environments tend to be delicate and easily disturbed. New organisms can easily upset the balance of the island ecosystem.

CHECKPOINT 36.4

1. What is a climax community?
2. What are the similarities and differences between primary and secondary succession?
3. Critical Thinking In 1883 a volcanic eruption destroyed all life on the tropical island of Krakatoa in Indonesia. Describe how you think succession may have occurred on Krakatoa.

Build on What You Know

4. How do plants affect ecosystems in succession? *(Need to jog your memory? Revisit relevant concepts in Chapter 19, Section 19.2.)*

CHECKPOINT 36.4

1. One that has achieved stability and species diversity
2. Primary succession occurs where no community previously existed; secondary succession occurs where a previous community has been cleared.
3. **Applying** Seeds transported to the island by wind or water took root in the weathered volcanic rock. The accumulation of

soil favored the growth of larger shrubs and trees, which also supported animal life.

4. Plant roots break down rocks to form additional soil. Plants also provide food and habitat for many animals.

❶ The island's size and its distance from other land

Chapter 36 Review

THE BIG IDEA!
36.1–36.2 The size of a population is affected by living and nonliving factors.
36.3 How populations interact determines the structure and characteristics of a community.
36.4 Biotic and abiotic changes in a community alter the community structure.

Sum It Up

Use the following summary to review the main concepts in this chapter.

36.1 Population Growth

• If all individuals in a bacterial population survived and reproduced, the population would double in each generation. Even smaller percentage increases can lead to exponential growth.

• Four factors that affect growth rate are birth rate, death rate, immigration, and emigration.

• A population's carrying capacity is determined by limiting factors.

36.2 Limits on Population Growth

• Living space, disease, competition, and predation are density-dependent limiting factors. These factors reduce populations that have exceeded their carrying capacity.

• Seasonal climate changes, natural disasters, and human activity can affect populations regardless of their density. Seasonal changes can produce a boom-and-bust growth pattern. Major upsets can lead to species extinctions.

• The growth rate of the human population has increased dramatically in the last few centuries.

36.3 Communities

• In communities with a large number of species, some species may have few members. Where the number of species is limited, most of the species will have many members.

• Two species may have symbiotic relationships in which both species benefit, in which one species benefits while harming the other, or in which one species benefits without harming the other.

• Biodiversity and genetic diversity help maintain ecological balance in a community.

36.4 Ecological Succession

• Natural disasters, competition among species, and human activity can change environments and lead to ecological succession.

• The absence or presence of soil determines the type of succession that occurs in a disturbed habitat.

• Colonization and succession on islands often leads to speciation.

Review the Big Ideas

Before students begin the Chapter Review, you may wish to discuss main concepts from the Big Ideas in Chapter 36. Point out that the size of a population and changes in a community are affected by biotic and abiotic factors. Limits on population are determined by density-dependent factors such as disease, competition, and predation, and density-interdependent factors, such as weather, natural disasters, and human activities. Interactions among populations determine the characteristics of a community. Communities go through a process of succession from a pioneer community to a climax community.

Use Terms and Concepts

Use each of the following words or terms in a complete sentence. If you need to review a meaning, turn to the page indicated.

population (p. 876)
exponential growth (p. 877)
limiting factor (p. 879)
carrying capacity (p. 879)

density-dependent limiting factors (p. 881)
predation (p. 882)
density-independent limiting factors (p. 883)
community (p. 885)
symbiosis (p. 887)

mutualism (p. 887)
parasitism (p. 887)
commensalism (p. 888)
ecological succession (p. 890)
primary succession (p. 891)

pioneer community (p. 891)
climax community (p. 891)
secondary succession (p. 891)

Answers

1. predation
2. symbiosis
3. limiting factor
4. population
5. community
6. succession
7. carrying capacity
8. exponential growth
9. c
10. d
11. a
12. c
13. b
14. When the predator population exceeds the available prey, its size is reduced, which gives the prey population time to rebound.
15. The growth curve changes as the population reaches its carrying capacity.
16. Without large predators, deer populations grew exponentially, which caused serious damage to ecosystems.
17. A more youthful population is likely to have a higher birth rate; an older population, a higher death rate.
18. The forest fire both destroys some niches and creates others.
19. The disease will spread more rapidly when the hosts are crowded together.
20. Thrip populations thrive in the warm Australian summers and collapse in the cold winters.
21. A <u>community</u> is composed of many <u>populations</u>. During <u>ecological succession</u>, <u>populations</u> of lichens are pioneer species. These are gradually replaced by grasses and weeds and successively larger plants and animals until a mature <u>community</u> is established.

Use Your Word Power

COMPLETION Write the word or phrase that best completes each statement.

1. The interaction between a lynx and a snowshoe hare is an example of _____ .

2. Both parasitism and commensalism are examples of _____ .

3. Any resource that may be depleted is a(n) _____ .

4. A group of organisms of the same species that live in a particular area form a(n) _____ .

5. A(n) _____ in a tropical rain forest contains thousands of species.

6. The process in which new communities replace existing communities is called _____ .

7. The number of individuals that a population's environment can support is called its _____ .

8. When a population graph has a steep J-shaped curve, the population is experiencing _____ .

MULTIPLE CHOICE Choose the letter of the word or phrase that best completes each statement.

9. An example of a density-dependent limiting factor is (a) a killing frost; (b) a drought; (c) a tuberculosis epidemic; (d) a new dam.

10. A lifeless habitat can form a climax community by (a) secondary succession; (b) exponential growth; (c) competition; (d) primary succession.

11. An example of a density-independent limiting factor for human populations is (a) depletion of the ozone layer; (b) the cultivation of farmland; (c) an influenza epidemic; (d) the water available for irrigation.

12. In a pioneer community, one could find (a) shrubs; (b) trees; (c) lichens; (d) weeds.

13. The relationship between honeybees and flowers is an example of (a) parasitism; (b) mutualism; (c) commensalism; (d) predation.

Show What You Know

14. Explain why the changes in population size for a predator and its prey often occur in cycles.

15. What causes the growth curve of a population to change from a J-curve to an S-curve?

16. How were deer populations in North America affected by the removal of large predators?

17. How does the age structure of a population affect its growth rate?

18. How can a forest fire be both harmful and beneficial at the same time?

19. Explain why an infectious disease is classified as a density-dependent limiting factor.

20. Why do thrips experience a boom-and-bust growth pattern?

21. **Make a Concept Map** Create a concept map that shows the relationship among populations, communities, and ecological succession.

Take It Further

22. **Developing a Hypothesis** Temperate forests have more biodiversity than temperate grasslands. Tropical rain forests have more biodiversity than tropical grasslands. Propose an explanation for these differences.

23. **Designing an Experiment** As cattle graze in the grasslands of East Africa, they stir up insects living in the grass. Birds known as cattle egrets eat insects and capture more food when they hunt near the cattle than when they hunt on their own. Design an experiment that would determine if the relationship between cattle and egrets is mutualism, parasitism, or commensalism.

24. **Interpreting a Graph** Hawks prey on wood pigeons. The following graph compares the size of the pigeon population with the hawks' success rate. How does population size affect the hawks' success rate?

22. Because trees are more structurally complex, they offer a greater variety of habitats than do grasses.
23. The relationship is an example of commensalism. The cattle are neither helped nor harmed by the egrets. Experimental designs should include a field study and methods for recording observations.
24. The success rate for populations with fewer than 10 pigeons is 60–80 percent; the success rate for populations with more than 10 pigeons is less than 20 percent. As population size increases, the success rate decreases, perhaps because larger flocks react sooner to the hawk's approach.
25. Females and males are equally vulnera-

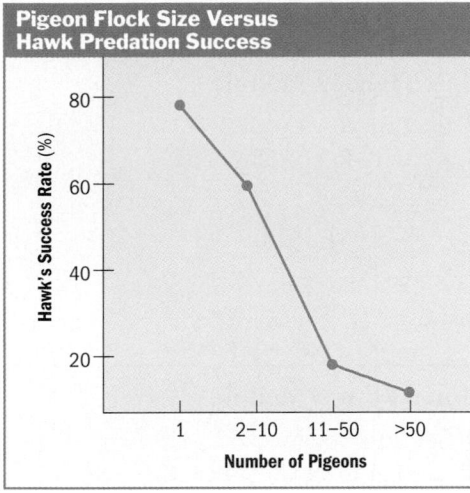

Pigeon Flock Size Versus Hawk Predation Success

Hawk's Success Rate (%) vs Number of Pigeons (1, 2–10, 11–50, >50)

25. Analyzing Data The table below shows death rates for red deer on Rhum Island in Scotland. The rates are the percent of each age group that die during the year. Female deer are capable of reproduction when they are 2–3 years old. How do the death rates change as the deer age? What happens to the death rates of female and male deer as they age? Propose an explanation for sex-specific differences.

Red Deer Death Rate		
Age	Females (%)	Males (%)
0–6 months	12.4	12.4
6–12 months	13.0	20.8
1 year	7.4	13.0
2 years	1.1	1.8
3–4 years	3.6	1.7
5–6 years	3.8	2.2
7–8 years	2.3	6.1
9–10 years	2.8	16.3
11–12 years	8.7	37.3

Consider the Issues

26. No Building Permit Like humans, beavers can have a major effect on their environment. When beavers cut down trees to build dams, they produce beaver ponds. Their activities can also increase the amount of seasonally flooded land in a neighborhood. Home owners who live near newly created beaver ponds may find their basements full of water. The neighbors whose properties are affected may suggest setting traps. Animal rights activists often object to the use of traps to control beavers. What would you do to address the problem?

Make New Connections

27. Biology and Art Identify a local site that was disturbed by a natural disaster such as a fire or earthquake. Make a drawing of the site as it looks today. Make a second drawing of what it might look like 10 years from now.

28. Biology and Social Studies Most communities in the United States do not produce all the resources they need to survive. For example, much of the food in local grocery stores is imported from other places. However, as the population of a town or city grows, the need for local resources increases. What resources might limit growth in your community? Can these resources be expanded?

FAST-FORWARD TO CHAPTER 37

As populations interact with one another, energy flows through the community. Chapter 37 will describe the flow of energy and chemicals through ecosystems.

ble in the first few months of life. The survival of female deers is fairly constant from age 2 to age 11. The death rate of male deers increases dramatically at maturity because of injuries sustained in fights over females during breeding season.
26. One alternative to trapping is to channel water away from residential areas.

27. Results will vary. Local libraries, newspaper morgues, and historical societies may have photographs.
28. Possible answers include water, living space, housing, schools, roads, electricity, fire stations, and hospital beds.

Section	Student Activities/Features	Teacher's Resource Package
37.1 Ecosystem Structure **Objectives** ■ Describe the flow of energy in an ecosystem ■ Distinguish between food chains and trophic levels ■ Explain the danger of biological magnification	**Lab Zone Discover It!** *Theorizing About How Organisms Interact,* p. 897 **Everyday Biology** *Our Food Chain,* p. 899 **Lab Zone Do It!** *How Do Decomposers Grow?* p. 900	**Unit 9 Review Module** ■ Section Review 37.1 ■ Activity Recordsheet 37-1
37.2 Energy Levels **Objectives** ■ Identify the relationships illustrated by an ecological pyramid ■ Define and illustrate a food web	**Lab Zone Think About It!** *Discovering Where Humans Belong in Energy Pyramids,* p. 903	**Unit 9 Review Module** ■ Section Review 37.2 ■ Interpreting Graphics 37 ■ Critical Thinking Exercise 37 **Consumer Applications** 37-1 **Interpreting and Developing Graphics** 109, 110
37.3 Chemical Cycles **Objectives** ■ Explain the importance of chemical cycles to an ecosystem ■ Describe the carbon cycle, the nitrogen cycle, and the water cycle	**STS: Environmental Awareness** *Gasoline-free Cars,* p. 907 **Everyday Biology** *Losing Lichens,* p. 908 **Lab Zone Do It!** *How Do Chemical Cycles Affect Ecosystems?* p. 909 **In the Community** *Beyond the Faucet,* p. 911 **Lab Zone Investigate It!** *Investigating the Water Cycle,* p. 912	**Unit 9 Review Module** ■ Section Review 37.3 ■ Activity Recordsheets 37-2 and 37-3 ■ Enrichment Topic 37-1 ■ Vocabulary Review 37 ■ Chapter 37 Tests **Laboratory Manual:** Lab 62: "Chemical Cycles in the Ecosystem" **Issues and Decision Making** 37-1 **Interpreting and Developing Graphics** 111 **Spanish Reviews** Chapter 37

Technology Resources

Internet Connections

Within this chapter, you will see the **bioSURF** logo. If you and your students have access to the Internet, the following URL address will provide various Internet connections that are related to topics and features presented in this chapter:

http://ecology.biosurf.com

You can also find relevant chapter material at **The Biology Place** address:

http://www.biology.com

CD-ROMs

Biología: la telaraña de la vida, (Spanish Student Edition) Chapter 37
Teacher's Resource Planner, Chapter 37 Supplements
TestWorks CD-ROM
- Chapter 37 Tests
Interactive Earth CD-ROM

Overhead Transparencies

- A Food Chain, #90
- Ecological Pyramids, #91
- Salt-Marsh Food Web, #92
- Carbon Cycle, #93
- Nitrogen Cycle, #94
- Water Cycle, #95

Videotapes

Biology Alive! Video Series
- The Domain of Life Video
- The Continuity of Life Video
- Life's Fragile Balance Video
Rewind: The Web of Life Reteach Videos

Planning for Activities

STUDENT EDITION
Lab Zone
Discover It! p. 897
- houseplant
- hand lens

Lab Zone Do It! p. 900
- 5 petri dishes (with lids)
- blotting paper
- hand lens
- grease pencil
- scissors
- shredded slice of bread
- Roquefort cheese
- piece of dill pickle
- orange wedge
- several grapes cut in half

Lab Zone Do It! p. 909
- dechlorinated water
- glass jar
- small fish
- aquatic plants
- soil or sand or gravel
- plants
- animals

Lab Zone
Investigate It! p. 912
- 4 large clear cups
- 2 15-cm squares of wax paper
- 2 strips of blue cobalt-chloride paper
- paper clip

- petroleum jelly
- 2 geranium plant leaves with stems
- tape

TEACHER'S EDITION
Quick Activity, p. 898
Trophic levels
- photographs of organisms in their natural environments obtaining food

Quick Activity, p. 902
Energy transfer from trophic levels
- photographs of different organisms living in a specific community or ecosystem

Teacher Demo, p. 908
Nitrogen compounds and plants
- guest speaker: farmer or gardener

Teacher Demo, p. 910
Where water comes from and where it drains
- glass of water

Class Activity, p. 910
Demonstrating water vapor
- small mirror

Chapter Objectives

Students will learn the main concepts of this chapter as they complete the following objectives.

- Describe the flow of energy in an ecosystem
- Distinguish between food chains and trophic levels
- Explain the danger of biological magnification
- Identify the relationships illustrated by an ecological pyramid
- Define and illustrate a food web
- Explain the importance of chemical cycles to an ecosystem
- Describe the carbon cycle, the nitrogen cycle, and the water cycle

Key Words

37.1 *autotroph, producers, heterotroph, consumers, food chain, trophic level, herbivore, carnivore, omnivore, scavenger, decomposer, biological magnification*

37.2 *biomass, ecological pyramid, food web*

37.3 *carbon cycle, fossil fuel, nitrogen cycle, nitrogen fixation, denitrification, water cycle*

The Opening Story

Have students discuss how they think the story relates to the content of this chapter. Review the meaning of the term *cycle* and the concept of a closed cycle. Have students speculate about what chemicals affect all of Earth's ecosystems.

CHAPTER 37

Ecosystem Dynamics

You can find out more about ecosystem dynamics by exploring the following Internet address:
http://ecology.biosurf.com

In this chapter . . .

FEATURES

Everyday Biology
- Our Food Chain
- Losing Lichens

In the Community
Beyond the Faucet

 Environmental Awareness
Gasoline-free Cars

LAB ZONES

Discover It!
- Theorizing About How Organisms Interact

Do It!
- How Do Decomposers Grow?
- How Do Chemical Cycles Affect Ecosystems?

Think About It!
- Discovering Where Humans Belong in Energy Pyramids

Investigate It!
- Investigating the Water Cycle

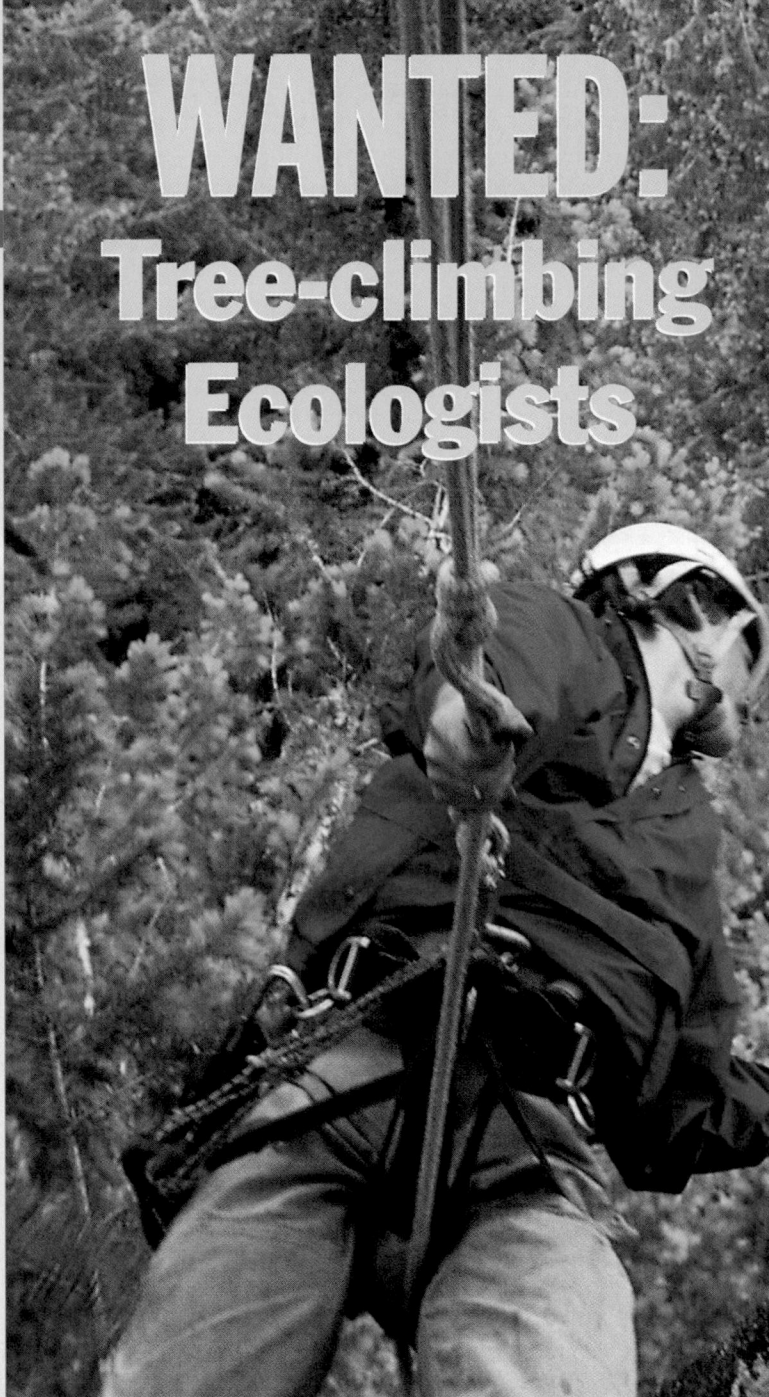

WANTED: Tree-climbing Ecologists

If you have ever climbed a tree, you could perform ecology research! In the early 1970s ecologists began exploring the treetops of ancient forests in the northwestern United States. But they had one important obstacle to overcome. The old Douglas firs, giant sequoias, and redwoods grow to 100 meters (m) tall, with the lowest branches looming 30 m above the forest floor.

Researchers developed a system of pulleys to make their way to the top of a forest, and there they discovered a previously unknown world. They found hundreds of new animal, plant, and fungal species and investigated how these organisms interacted with their environment. For example, ecologists discovered that the needles of these ancient trees block so much light that they lower the temperature of the ground and streams below. In these low stream temperatures, salmon thrive. Therefore, the loss of these ancient trees would result in a smaller salmon population—a surprising relationship. The treetops and their inhabitants also play an important role in the water and chemical cycles that affect the entire planet. What are these cycles, and what effect do they have on Earth's ecosystems?

LAB ZONE Discover It!

Theorizing About How Organisms Interact

You need a houseplant and a hand lens

1. Observe how the plant interacts with the environment. Using the hand lens, determine if any organisms inhabit the soil, stem, or leaves of the plant. Record your observations.
2. Using your knowledge of plants, theorize about the other interactions occurring among the plant, the air, and the light. How might these interactions be part of a cycle?

Every organism on Earth interacts with and changes its environment. Ecologists who study these interactions are researching ecosystem dynamics. What are some ways you change your environment?

WRITE ABOUT IT!

Select one of the biomes that you studied in Chapter 35. In your science journal, write a short story about an imaginary new organism in that biome. How does it affect the other organisms in the biome? How does it change the environment? Include biotic and abiotic factors in your story.

897

Opening Activities

bioSURF 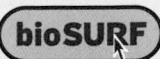 If you have access to the Internet in your classroom or school, you may wish to have students connect to the address shown on page 896. You may also want to have students conduct a net search for information using key words such as food webs, photosynthesis, fossil fuels, or solar energy.

LAB ZONE Discover It!

Theorizing About How Organisms Interact

TEAM WORK

Have students identify the houseplant and any other organisms they observe. Students should indicate that the plant carries out photosynthesis and respiration to survive, interacting with sunlight, carbon dioxide, and oxygen in the environment.

WRITE ABOUT IT

Encourage students to make an illustration of their new organism and write a caption explaining how the organism interacts with its environment. Check that the organism is suited to the chosen biome.

Rewind to Chapter 36

Briefly review with students concepts they learned in Chapter 36, *Populations and Communities*. Ask:

■ **How might populations and communities interact with their environments?**

1 ENGAGE

Consider the Big Idea

Have students read The Big Idea! at the top of the page. Point out that the flow of energy begins with the sun.

Use the Visual

Have students study the photograph that opens the section. Explain that most organisms get their energy from the sun, either directly or indirectly. Ask:

- **How is the energy obtained by the sunflowers passed to other organisms in the ecosystem?** (As food energy)

Check Prior Knowledge

To assess students' knowledge about food chains, ask:

- **What is energy?** (The ability to perform work)
- **Why are autotrophs classified as producers and heterotrophs classified as consumers?** (Autotrophs are able to produce food; heterotrophs cannot make their own food and must consume other organisms.)

Quick Activity

Display several photographs that show organisms in their natural environments obtaining food. Ask students to identify the producers, consumers, herbivores, and carnivores in the photographs. Discuss students' responses. Explain that the level at which an organism feeds in its environment is called a trophic level.

What you'll learn

IDEAS
- To describe the flow of energy in an ecosystem
- To distinguish between food chains and trophic levels
- To explain the danger of biological magnification

WORDS
autotroph, producers, heterotroph, consumers, food chain, trophic level, herbivore, carnivore, omnivore, scavenger, decomposer, biological magnification

FIGURE 37.1

How is the blackbird obtaining energy from the caterpillar? ❶

THE BIG IDEA!  In an ecosystem, the flow of energy moves in one direction. 37.1–37.2

37.1 Ecosystem Structure

You are my sunshine

At dawn, rays of golden summer sunshine spill across a field of sunflowers. Almost imperceptibly, the plants begin to move. Broad green leaves and yellow-rimmed flowers slowly turn toward their source of energy—the rising sun. The sun is the ultimate source of energy for nearly all of Earth's ecosystems.

ENERGY FOR LIFE

Pass it on

As sunlight pours down on the planet, plants and other photosynthetic organisms capture its radiant energy. They use the sun's energy to transform inorganic compounds into energy-rich organic compounds during photosynthesis. These photosynthetic organisms then use the energy stored in the organic compounds as food to fuel all of their life processes. This energy moves through the ecosystem as one organism consumes another for food. The flow of energy is one-way—moving from the sun through photosynthetic organisms, then through other organisms in the ecosystem.

A plant or other organism that converts the sun's energy or inorganic substances into energy-rich compounds is called an **autotroph**. Because autotrophs make food that is used by the entire community, they are also called **producers**. Algae in a pond, phytoplankton in the ocean, and grasses, shrubs, and trees on land are all producers in their ecosystems.

Although most of the producers in the biosphere are photosynthetic organisms, there are a few exceptions. As you learned in Chapter 14, chemosynthetic organisms use inorganic compounds, rather than sunlight, as sources of energy. Some types of chemosynthetic bacteria live around hydrothermal vents on the ocean floor. Chemosynthetic bacteria are the producers in these deep-sea communities, just as plants and algae are the producers in the sunlit world far above.

898 *Unit 9 Organisms and the Environment*

FOOD CHAINS AND TROPHIC LEVELS

Living links

Some of the energy captured by a producer is passed on to the organism that consumes it. Such an organism is called a **heterotroph.** It obtains energy and nutrients by consuming other organisms. Heterotrophs are the **consumers** in an ecosystem.

As an example, in a field of sunflowers, the sunflower plants are the producers. A consumer such as a caterpillar eats sunflower leaves. Another consumer such as a red-winged blackbird eats the caterpillar. Still another consumer, perhaps a fox, may eat the blackbird. Eventually, bacteria and fungi consume the remains of any dead organisms. This overall feeding pattern is an example of a food chain. A **food chain** models the

flow of energy through organisms in a community.

In the food chain shown in *Figure 37.2,* arrows show the energy flow from one organism to the next. For example, when the caterpillar eats the leaf, some of the energy and organic compounds stored in the leaf are transferred to the caterpillar. When the caterpillar is eaten by the red-winged blackbird, some of the energy and organic compounds from the caterpillar are transferred to the bird. This pattern continues through the food chain.

Notice that only some of the energy and matter is transferred each time one organism consumes another. At every link in a food chain, part of the energy is lost (as heat) to the environment. Because of energy loss, most food chains can support no more than four or five links.

EVERYDAY BIOLOGY

Our Food Chain

Most humans are part of a self-made food chain. We raise produce, such as grains and vegetables, and eat it ourselves or feed it to primary consumers. We, in turn, feed on the primary consumers. We depart from this pattern when we hunt, fish, or gather nuts and berries, all examples of consuming "wild" organisms.

FIGURE 37.2

A Food Chain

A food chain models the energy flow in a community. How do decomposers affect energy flow? ❷

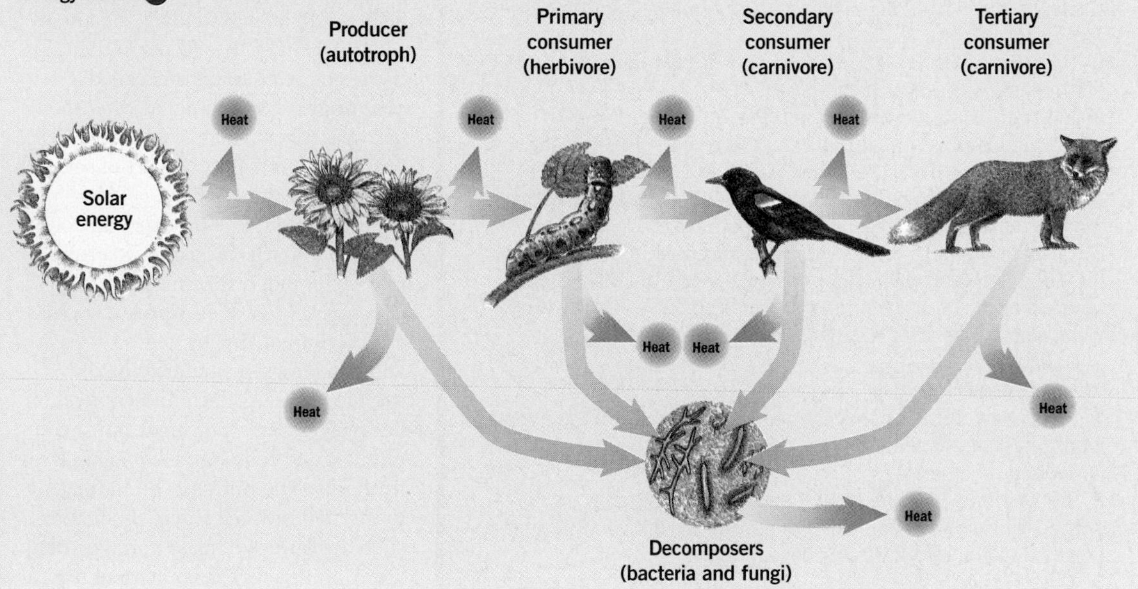

Producer (autotroph) — Primary consumer (herbivore) — Secondary consumer (carnivore) — Tertiary consumer (carnivore)

Solar energy

Heat

Decomposers (bacteria and fungi)

Chapter 37 Ecosystem Dynamics **899**

❶ The blackbird uses the caterpillar as food.

❷ Decomposers return nutrients to the environment for reuse.

② TEACH

✚ Language Arts

Explain to students that the term *trophic* comes from the Greek *trophikos,* which means "food" or "to feed." Ask:

■ **What other words relating to food chains use the suffix -*troph*?** (Likely responses include autotroph, heterotroph, and chemotroph.)

Discuss the meaning of each of these terms and ask students to suggest examples of organisms in each group.

Use the Visual

Have students study Figure 37.2. Ask:

■ **How do primary consumers differ from secondary consumers?** (Primary consumers are herbivores that feed directly on plants. Secondary consumers feed on organisms that have eaten plants.)

■ **Why is only some of the energy taken in by an organism in food available to the next trophic level?** (At each level, some energy is used by the organism or lost as heat.)

Everyday Biology

You may want to extend this feature by having students create a diagram or a flowchart tracing the energy from their last meal back to the sun.

Clarify Misconceptions

Students often believe that humans are herbivores when they eat plant products and carnivores when they eat meat products. Explain that humans, like other animals that eat both, are omnivores.

 Do It!

How Do Decomposers Grow?

Once dishes are covered, secure the covering with tape to avoid accidental openings. Have students sketch their observations every other day to illustrate changes over time.

Analyze Your Results

1 Students are likely to observe different colors, shapes, and textures.

2 Different decomposers may appear in each petri dish. Evidence of decomposition may be change in color, smell, and presence of moisture.

3 Decomposers break down complex organic materials into simpler nutrients and return these nutrients to the environment. The supply of nutrients would be depleted without decomposers and eventually all organisms in the ecosystem would die.

❶ The fox

Each step in the transfer of energy and matter in an ecological community is called a **trophic level** (TROH-fik). Producers such as plants form the community's first trophic level and are the base of all food chains. Primary consumers, which feed directly on producers, make up the second trophic level. In the sunflower-field food-chain example, the leaf-eating caterpillar is a primary consumer. A primary consumer that eats only plants is called an **herbivore**.

LAB ZONE Do It!

How Do Decomposers Grow?

You can find out which decomposers favor specific types of food if you . . .

Try This

1 Obtain five petri dishes (with lids), blotting paper, a hand lens, grease pencil, scissors, and the following foods: bread, Roquefort cheese, a piece of a dill pickle, an orange wedge, and several grapes cut in half.
2 Number the petri dishes #1 through 5. Line the bottoms of the petri dishes with moist blotting paper.
3 Moisten (don't soak) the bread. Place the bread in petri dish 1. Place the cheese in dish 2, the pickle in dish 3, the orange wedge in dish 4, and the grapes in dish 5.
4 Leave the uncovered dishes exposed for 24 hours. Then cover the petri dishes and place in a cool, dark place.
5 Observe the petri dishes every day for one or two weeks. Use the hand lens and record your observations of the dishes' contents. **Caution:** Do not remove lids from the dishes at any time. Wash your hands after handling petri dishes.

Analyze Your Results

1 How many different types of decomposers did you observe? What physical characteristics distinguished one type of decomposer from another?
2 Did you find that one type of decomposer can grow on different types of organic material? What evidence did you find that organic molecules were being decomposed?
3 Based on your observations, what is the role of decomposers in the food chain? How would an ecosystem differ if no decomposers were present?

The third and fourth trophic levels in a food chain are composed of carnivores. A **carnivore** is an organism that eats only meat. The third trophic level is composed of secondary consumers, which feed on primary consumers. The blackbird in our food-chain example is a secondary consumer. The fourth trophic level is composed of tertiary consumers, which feed on secondary consumers. Which animal in the sunflower-field example is a tertiary consumer? ❶

Some organisms can be part of more than one trophic level, depending on what they eat. For example, a fox that eats an insect-eating bird is a tertiary consumer. But that fox could also eat a primary consumer, such as a mouse or a rabbit. In that case, the fox would be a secondary consumer. Consumers called **omnivores,** such as bears and humans, eat both producers and other consumers. Because they eat all types of food, omnivores may act as primary, secondary, or tertiary consumers in an ecosystem. Can you describe a situation in which a bear would be a secondary consumer?

A consumer that feeds on the tissues of dead animals is called a **scavenger.** Depending on what they eat, scavengers such as vultures, crows, and ants may be part of several different trophic levels.

In addition to producers and consumers, every food chain has a third major group of organisms called decomposers. A **decomposer,** such as a bacterium or fungus, feeds on wastes and dead organic matter from all trophic levels. As decomposers feed on decaying matter, they break down complex organic compounds into simpler nutrients. The nutrients are returned to the soil or water, where producers such as plants and algae can use them again. In this way, decomposers recycle nutrients that are critically important to all members of the food chain.

MEETING DIVERSE NEEDS

Gifted Have students research how chemotrophic bacteria make food by using the energy in chemicals. Ask the students to find the chemical equation for this process and to show the equation, along with that for photosynthesis, in a diagram. Ask students to write captions explaining the similarities and differences between the two processes. Display the diagrams in class.

BIOLOGICAL MAGNIFICATION

A food chain's deadly links

You have just learned how energy moves from one organism to another in a food chain. But harmful substances can also move through food chains. DDT is one such substance.

Beginning in the late 1940s, the pesticide DDT was widely used to kill insects that spread disease and damaged crops. At first, the pesticide appeared to have no negative effects on other organisms. As time passed, however, people noticed that the populations of bald eagles and other large fish-eating birds were declining.

Ecologists discovered that DDT settled into the soil and got into the groundwater. Eventually, the DDT found its way into rivers and lakes, contaminating tiny planktonic organisms. Small fishes that ate the plankton stored DDT in their tissues. When larger fishes ate the contaminated fishes, they accumulated even higher concentrations of DDT in their tissues. This buildup of a pollutant in organisms at higher trophic levels in a food chain is called **biological magnification.**

When bald eagles ate the large contaminated fishes, they took DDT into their bodies. As a result of biological magnification, the DDT in the birds' tissues was ten million times the original concentration of DDT in the water and it interfered with the depositing of calcium in the shells of the eggs. The eggs' shells were thin and broke easily, so the eagle embryos inside did not survive. The eagle population began to decline, and this was one of the reasons DDT was banned in the United States in 1971. Although the populations of bald eagles and other affected birds have gradually recovered, DDT is still being used in some other countries.

FIGURE 37.3

Biological Magnification

Biological magnification can have devastating results. How did DDT affect the bald eagle populations? **❷**

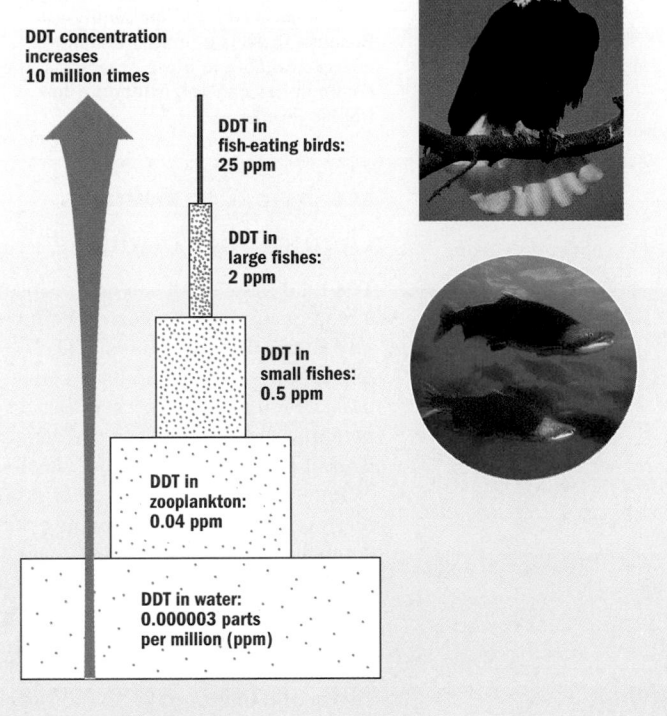

DDT concentration increases 10 million times

DDT in fish-eating birds: 25 ppm

DDT in large fishes: 2 ppm

DDT in small fishes: 0.5 ppm

DDT in zooplankton: 0.04 ppm

DDT in water: 0.000003 parts per million (ppm)

CHECKPOINT 37.1

1. Describe the flow of energy in an ecosystem.
2. What is a food chain? How does it relate to trophic levels?
3. Explain biological magnification and its dangers.
4. Critical Thinking Are you a primary, secondary, or tertiary consumer? Explain.

Build on What You Know

5. How is the energy from ingested food stored in the body of a consumer? *(Need to jog your memory? Revisit relevant concepts in Chapter 30, Section 30.3.)*

Chapter 37 Ecosystem Dynamics **901**

Use the Visual

Have students study Figure 37.3. Explain that unlike energy that decreases at each successive level of the food chain, the chemicals associated with biological magnification increase in concentration at each successive level of the food chain.

3  ASSESS

Evaluate Understanding

Draw a food chain on the board. Ask students to name the producers and consumers in the food chain. Call on a volunteer to draw arrows to show how energy flows from one organism to another. Ask:

■ **How does energy move in an ecosystem?** (In one direction from the producers to the consumers and then to the decomposers)

Reteach

On the board, restate the section objectives as main-idea statements. Have students review the text to suggest information that should be included beneath each statement. Guide them to use the key words in bold print. Write down their responses, adding information as needed and correcting any inaccurate information. Have students copy the completed outlines for use as a study tool.

CHECKPOINT 37.1

1. Energy flows from the sun, through photosynthetic organisms, to consumers.
2. It is a model of how energy flows through organisms in a community; each step in the transfer of energy or matter represents a trophic level.
3. It is the buildup of pollutants in the higher trophic levels of a food chain and can result in the loss or decline of species.
4. Applying All are acceptable, for example, primary-consume plants, secondary-consume beef, tertiary-consume fish.
5. It is stored as glycogen in the liver and muscles, and then as fat.

❷ The populations declined severely because most eggs broke and did not hatch.

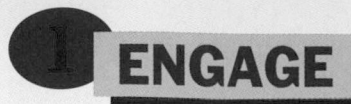

1 ENGAGE

Use the Visual

Have students study the photograph that opens the section. Explain that as energy decreases from one trophic level to the next, fewer organisms can be supported at each successive trophic level. Ask:

- **At which trophic level is the greatest amount of energy available?** (Producer)

Check Prior Knowledge

To assess students' knowledge about food chains, ask:
- **What kinds of organisms are always at the base of a food chain?** (Producers such as plants)
- **What is a primary consumer?** (An organism which feeds directly on producers)

Quick Activity

Show students photographs of different organisms living in a specific community or ecosystem. Call on a volunteer to arrange the photographs in order to illustrate how energy flows from one organism to another. Ask what trophic level each organism represents. Tell students that in this section they will find out why the transfer of energy from one level to another is not very efficient.

37.2 Energy Levels

What you'll learn

IDEAS
- To identify the relationships illustrated by an ecological pyramid
- To define and illustrate a food web

WORDS
biomass, ecological pyramid, food web

What kills killer whales?
Killer whales (right), eagles, and adult lions have no natural predators. Why are these animals the last stop in their food chains? The reason does not lie only in their ferocity and hunting ability. Because there is a limited amount of energy available to these organisms, their communities can only support a few trophic levels.

ECOLOGICAL PYRAMIDS

Community building

The total mass of all the organisms in a food chain or an ecological community is called the **biomass.** The biomass at each trophic level contains stored energy representing the potential food available to the organisms at the next trophic level. For example, the biomass of a community's producers contains energy-rich compounds and many other compounds that the producers make. When consumers eat the producers, they ingest both matter and energy. The consumers use this ingested energy and matter to build their own bodies and perform essential life functions.

The transfer of matter and energy from one trophic level to the next is not very efficient. Only a small fraction of the biomass from one trophic level moves on to the next. One reason for the inefficiency is that many of the organisms are not consumed by the organisms at the next trophic level. As a result, this energy is not available for transfer. A second reason is that some of the biomass at each trophic level consists of materials that consumers at the next level are not likely to eat: wood, bones, teeth, beaks, hooves, claws, and shells. Even if consumers do eat

these materials, they usually cannot digest them to release their stored energy.

A diagram called an **ecological pyramid** shows the relationships between producers and consumers at the trophic levels in an ecosystem. The energy available at each trophic level is about one-tenth the energy available from the trophic level below it. This pattern of energy transfer is sometimes called the 10 percent law.

FIGURE 37.4
Ecological Pyramids

These ecological pyramids represent the relationships between producers and consumers in three different ways. What pattern do all three pyramids share?

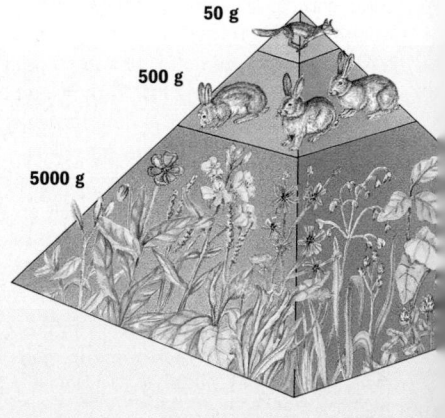

50 g
500 g
5000 g

STUDENT RESOURCES

From the Teacher's Resource Package, use:
- Section Review 37.2, Interpreting Graphics 37, and Critical Thinking Exercise 37 from Unit 9 Review Module
- Consumer Applications 37-1

TECHNOLOGY RESOURCES

Relevant technology resources include:
- Spanish Student Edition CD-ROM
- Teacher's Resource Planner CD-ROM
- Interactive Earth CD-ROM
- Biology Alive! Video Series

If the producers in the energy pyramid in *Figure 37.4* supply 200,000 kilocalories of energy, how many kilocalories will be passed on to each higher trophic level, assuming the 10 percent **❷** law applies?

In most food chains, fewer organisms occupy each higher trophic level. For example, a meadow is covered by a thick layer of grasses and other plants. These plants are the producers. The meadow has many primary consumers, including mice, seed-eating birds, and a variety of insects. But it has fewer secondary consumers, including robins, other insect-eating birds, and snakes. There are very few tertiary consumers, including hawks and bobcats, at the highest trophic level.

The number of organisms at each trophic level is proportional to the amount of biomass and energy available at the level below it. In fact, the biomass and energy from the producers at the lowest trophic level determine

the number of organisms a community can support. The more biomass and energy the producers supply, the larger the total number of organisms that the community can support.

LAB ZONE Think About It! bioSURF

Discovering Where Humans Belong in Energy Pyramids

Humans can be placed in many different energy pyramids. Draw the energy pyramids that would result from the following activities: humans consuming corn, consuming cattle, and consuming salmon.

Analyzing the Diagram

1 In which pyramid is the greatest amount of energy available to humans? In which activity is the least amount of energy available? Explain your answer, using percentages.

2 As the population grows, how might human diets be affected? Why?

Energy
An ecological pyramid can represent the energy contained in biomass. Organisms at each trophic level use some of this energy for their life processes, but much of it is lost as heat.

Number of organisms
An ecological pyramid can show the relative number of organisms at each trophic level. As you move up the pyramid, the number of organisms usually decreases.

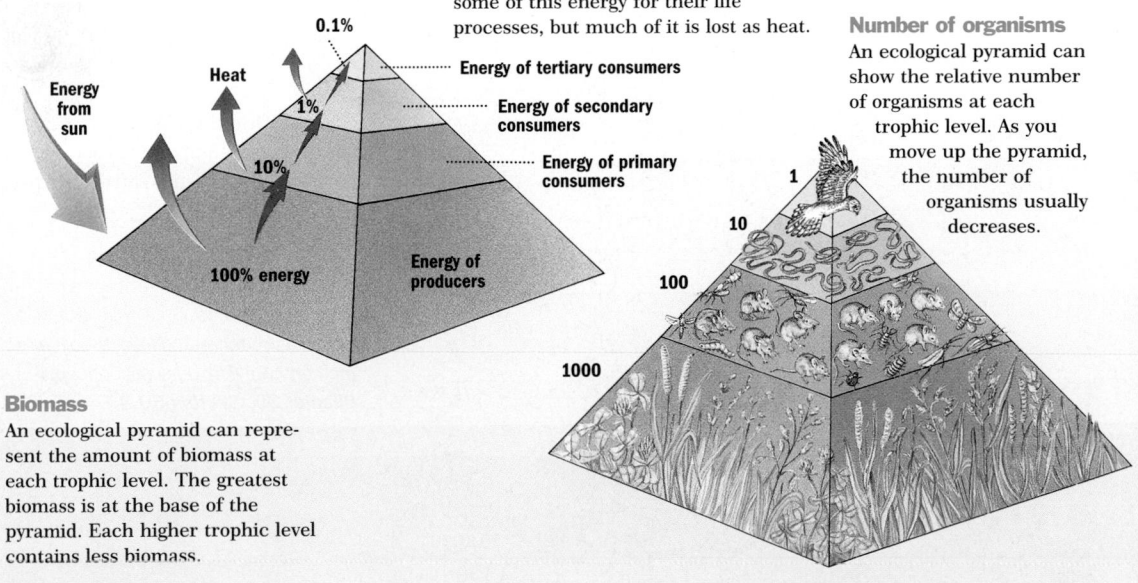

Biomass
An ecological pyramid can represent the amount of biomass at each trophic level. The greatest biomass is at the base of the pyramid. Each higher trophic level contains less biomass.

Chapter 37 Ecosystem Dynamics **903**

---

2 TEACH

✳ Math

Remind students that only 10 percent or one-tenth of energy is transferred from one feeding level to the next. Ask:

- **How many kilograms of squid would it take to support a 5 kg penguin?** (50 kg)
- **How many kilograms of shrimp-like krill would it take to support that much squid?** (500 kg)
- **How many kilograms of photosynthetic diatoms would it take to support that amount of krill?** (5000 kg, over 5 tons!)

LAB ZONE Think About It!

Discovering Where Humans Belong in Energy Pyramids

Analyzing the Diagram

1 Greatest: consuming corn; least: consuming salmon. By functioning as primary consumers (corn) 10 times more energy is available than when humans function as secondary consumers (cattle) and 100 times more than when humans are tertiary consumers (salmon).

2 Humans may be required to eat less meat in order to have enough energy available to more humans.

Evaluate Understanding

To assess students' understanding of energy levels and pyramids, direct them to Figure 37.5. Ask:

- **What organisms make up one food chain in the diagram?** (Possible response: algae, krill, duck, owl)
- **Where is the greatest biomass in the food web?** (In the producers)
- **How much energy is available at the primary consumer level compared to the producer level?** (10 percent)

Have students use the diagram to draw an ecological pyramid that indicates the change in biomass if 3 kg of biomass were available at the producer level.

Reteach

On the board, draw three pyramids, each having four levels. Have students use Figure 37.5 to name organisms that could be placed in each block in the pyramids and record their responses. Use the diagrams to review the types of information that can be shown in ecological pyramids and to review the 10 percent law.

FIGURE 37.5

The Salt-Marsh Food Web

This food web shows the energy flow in a salt-marsh community. Which organisms are herbivores? ❶

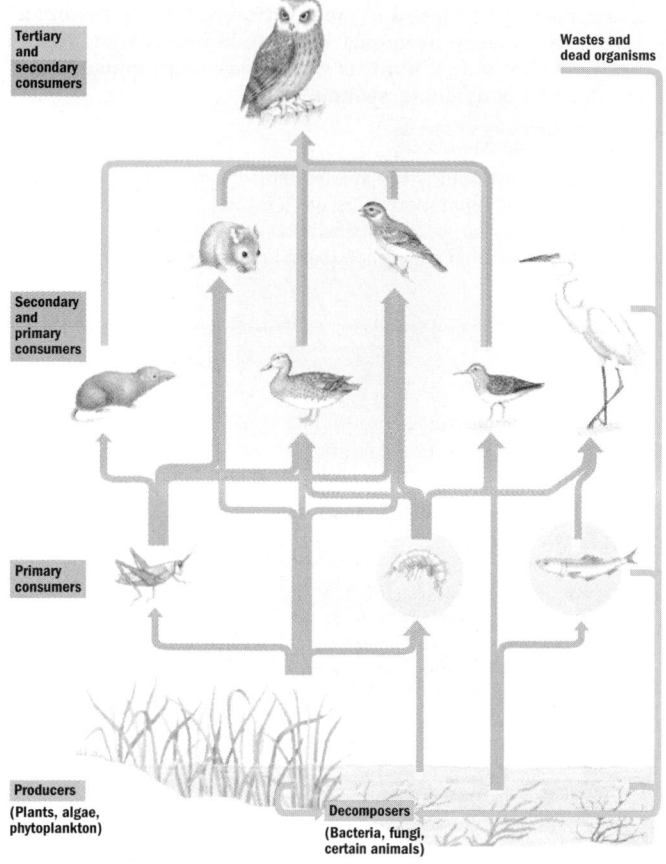

FOOD WEBS

Tying it all together

The feeding relationships in a community are far more complex than a simple food chain containing a few organisms. Most organisms in a community eat more than just one kind of food. If we look at how food chains combine to form a food web, a more complete picture emerges. A **food web** demonstrates the interconnectedness of food chains in a community or an ecosystem. An example of a food web in a salt marsh community is shown in *Figure* 37.5. Which organisms are the producers? ❷

Food webs in one community may be connected to food webs in others. For example, a river that meets the sea at a salt marsh may have flowed through forest and grassland communities. Organisms that move with the river may play a role in the food webs of each community the river meets.

CHECKPOINT 37.2

1. What types of organisms are always at the base of an ecological pyramid? At the top?
2. What is a food web? Draw a diagram of a food web that includes one producer, two primary consumers, two secondary consumers, and two decomposers.
3. **Critical Thinking** What would happen to a community if the biomass of producers increased greatly? Decreased greatly?

Build on What You Know

4. How could you estimate the number of kilocalories available in a given biomass of producers? *(Need to jog your memory? Revisit relevant concepts in Chapter 30, Section 30.3.)*

? **How does energy flow in an ecosystem?**

CHECKPOINT 37.2

1. Producers are at the base, secondary and tertiary consumers are at the top.
2. A food web models the interconnections between food chains in a community or ecosystem. Diagrams will vary.
3. **Predicting** If increased, the community could support more organisms at higher levels; if decreased, there would be fewer organisms in the community.
4. A calorimeter measures the number of kilocalories in a given biomass by measuring the amount of energy released while burning a sample.

❶ Grasshopper, shrimp, fish, some of the birds, mouse
❷ Algae, plants, phytoplankton

37.3 Chemical Cycles

Water, water everywhere
How much water do you use every day? Probably more than you think! Humans use water for drinking, cooking, washing, cleaning, agriculture, and watering lawns. Cities often use more water than the environment can supply. Water is involved in one of the chemical cycles essential to the ecosystem.

What you'll learn

IDEAS
• To explain the importance of chemical cycles to an ecosystem
• To describe the carbon cycle, the nitrogen cycle, and the water cycle

WORDS
carbon cycle, fossil fuel, nitrogen cycle, nitrogen fixation, denitrification, water cycle

CHEMICAL CYCLES

Recycled and reused

In any ecosystem, living organisms need energy and chemical nutrients. In the previous sections you learned about energy—how it enters an ecosystem and is captured by producers, and how it flows from one organism to another through the trophic levels in a food chain. At each step, energy is lost to the environment. Energy cannot be recycled; it must continually be replenished by the sun. As a result, the flow of energy through natural systems is a one-way process. Nutrients, on the other hand, do not move in one direction through an ecosystem.

Nutrients are the chemical elements and compounds that organisms must have to live and grow. Carbon, oxygen, and nitrogen are examples of nutrients. Unlike energy, nutrients are not constantly replenished from an outside source such as the sun. The supply of nutrients is limited, and they must be recycled in ecosystems again and again.

Sometimes nutrients cycle rapidly through an ecosystem. In a rain forest, for example, carbon in fallen leaves is rapidly cycled through the forest's complex food web. Other times, nutrients cycle very slowly and may be "tied up" in living organisms, in soil or rock, in the air, or in the oceans for long periods of time. For example, marine organisms deposit atoms of carbon in their shells, which eventually become limestone. The limestone may remain intact and undisturbed for millions of years.

Nutrients and water also cycle on a global scale. Earth's various nutrient

FIGURE 37.6
How do nutrients and energy flow in this terrarium? ❸

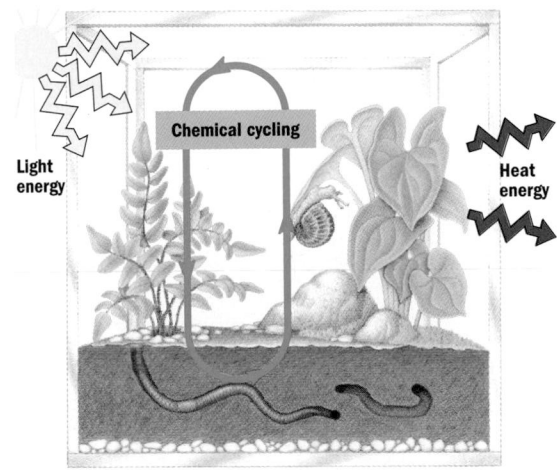

Chemical cycling

Light energy

Heat energy

Chapter 37 Ecosystem Dynamics **905**

STUDENT RESOURCES

From the Teacher's Resource Package, use:
■ Section Review 37.3, Activity Recordsheet 37-2 and 37-3, Enrichment Topic 37-1, Vocabulary Review 37, and Chapter 37 Tests from Unit 9 Review Module
■ Lab 62: "Chemical Cycles in the Ecosystem"
■ Issues and Decision Making 37-1

TECHNOLOGY RESOURCES

Relevant technology resources include:
■ Spanish Student Edition CD-ROM
■ Teacher's Resource Planner CD-ROM
■ Interactive Earth CD-ROM
■ Biology Alive! Video Series
■ TestWorks CD-ROM: Chapter 37 Tests

① ENGAGE

Consider the Big Idea

Have students read The Big Idea! at the top of the page. Point out that the limited supply of water and nutrients on Earth is constantly recycled.

Use the Visual

Have students study the photograph and read the text that opens the section. Ask:

■ **What are some ways people use water for recreation?** (Swimming, boating, fishing, skiing)

Check Prior Knowledge

To assess students' knowledge about chemistry, ask:

■ **What substances in photosynthesis and respiration contain carbon?** (Carbon dioxide and glucose)
■ **What is the most abundant element in the air?** (Nitrogen)

Quick Activity

Explain to students that the average person in the United States uses 300 L of water per day. Have students use this data to determine how much water their family uses on average in one day. Then ask them to calculate the weekly, monthly, and annual use of water for their family.

❸ From soil to plants, to consumers (worms and snails), to decomposers, which return nutrients to the soil.

2 TEACH

Use the Visual

Have students study the carbon cycle in Figure 37.7. Ask:

- **What are three ways in which carbon dioxide enters the atmosphere?** (Through burning of fossil fuels, as a by-product of animal respiration, and from the decomposition of dead material)
- **How is carbon dioxide removed from the atmosphere?** (Through photosynthesis by plants)

Clarify Misconceptions

Remind students that plants, like all living things, carry out respiratory functions. Point out that plants require energy to carry out cell functions just as other living things do and that this energy is provided through respiration. Instead of using lungs or gills, plants take in the oxygen through their stomata.

Explain

Point out that in aquatic ecosystems, the carbon dioxide needed for algae and plants to carry out photosynthesis is dissolved in the water. Similarly, the oxygen needed by aquatic organisms to carry out respiration is also dissolved in the water.

cycles are closely connected—what happens in one cycle can affect all the others. By studying Earth's complex nutrient cycles, we can gain a better understanding of how human activities impact them.

THE CARBON CYCLE

It's a gas

Organisms exchange carbon and oxygen with the air or water around them. These elements cycle mainly in the form of carbon dioxide gas (CO_2). Carbon dioxide moves from the air or water through living things, and back to the air or water again. The movement of carbon through the environment is called the **carbon cycle.** This cycle is illustrated in *Figure 37.7.*

How carbon cycles The driving forces behind the carbon cycle are the processes of photosynthesis and cellular respiration. Following are the chemical equations for both processes. Notice how each reaction depends on the products of the other.

Photosynthesis
$$6H_2O + 6CO_2 + energy \rightarrow C_6H_{12}O_6 + 6O_2$$

Respiration
$$C_6H_{12}O_6 + 6O_2 \rightarrow 6H_2O + 6CO_2 + energy$$

During photosynthesis, producers such as plants and algae take up CO_2 from the air or water around them. The producers use CO_2 and water (H_2O) to manufacture glucose ($C_6H_{12}O_6$), an energy-rich organic compound. During this reaction, oxygen (O_2) is released.

FIGURE 37.7
The Carbon Cycle

Photosynthesis and cellular respiration are the two main processes of the carbon cycle.

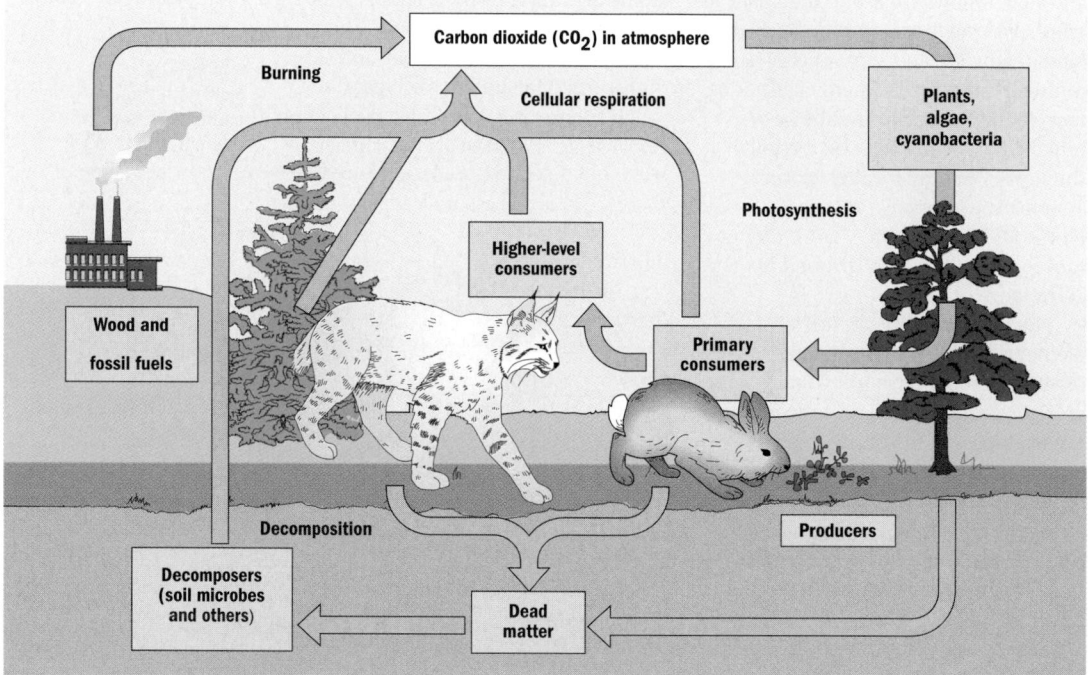

MEETING DIVERSE NEEDS

At Risk Suggest that students redraw the cycles shown in this section as flowcharts. Students can use their drawings as study tools to review the key concepts of the section.

LEP Pair LEP students with native English speakers. Check that students understand the meaning of the term *cycle.* Then have partners take turns tracing the cycles shown in Figures 37.7, 37.9, and 37.11.

Producers and consumers use glucose to fuel the process of cellular respiration. In cellular respiration, glucose breaks down as it undergoes a chemical reaction with O_2. The reaction releases energy and produces H_2O and CO_2. The CO_2 produced by the reaction is released into the air or water surrounding the organism. In other words, carbon and oxygen cycle through the environment, while photosynthesis and cellular respiration alternately build glucose and break it down. *Figure* 37.8 shows how carbon is stored in the carbon cycle.

Humans and the carbon cycle
Over the last few hundred years, humans have begun to interfere with the global carbon cycle. For example, people have cut down many forests around the world. Fewer forests means fewer trees and other plants that can absorb CO_2. Human activities are increasing the levels of CO_2 in the atmosphere. People have burned large amounts of fossil fuels for energy, releasing huge amounts of CO_2. A **fossil fuel** is an energy-rich compound formed from organic matter by a geological process.

There is evidence that increased levels of CO_2 may lead to changes in Earth's climate. These climate changes are possible because carbon dioxide in the atmosphere traps heat, as does glass in a greenhouse. If carbon dioxide levels continue to increase, global warming may occur. You will learn more about global warming and the greenhouse effect in Chapter 38.

ENVIRONMENTAL AWARENESS

Gasoline-free cars

In an effort to decrease fossil-fuel burning in automobiles and to reduce the amount of CO_2 released into the environment, scientists are developing

FIGURE 37.8
Carbon Storage

All carbon is not cycling through the environment at one time. Instead, some carbon is stored in various ways.

Organic compounds
1 Large amounts of carbon are stored in the organic compounds of trees. When the trees decay or are burned, the carbon is released as CO_2.

Fossil fuels
2 Fossil fuels—oil, coal, and natural gas—store carbon. Fossil fuels formed over millions of years as organisms were compressed by geological processes. When fossil fuels are burned, energy and CO_2 are released.

Limestone
3 Many marine organisms have calcium carbonate shells. When these organisms die, their shells sink and form carbon-rich sediments. Eventually, these sediments form limestone rock. When geological processes elevate and expose the limestone, it may break down and release stored carbon.

vehicles that are powered by alternative fuels. Among these alternative fuels are electricity and solar energy. The environmental advantage of these fuels is that they do not directly release CO_2.

Solar-powered cars run on electricity that is converted from the sun's energy and stored in batteries. Electric vehicles are powered by electricity stored in batteries, which are recharged by plugging them into electrical outlets. Many of these gasoline-free automobiles are in the early stages of development, and they continue to improve. One new electric sports car accelerates faster than most gas-powered cars and has a top speed of nearly 160 kilometers per hour (100 miles per hour). Best of all, it releases no CO_2!

Chapter 37 Ecosystem Dynamics **907**

Use the Visual

Have students study Figure 37.8. Ask:

- **Where is carbon stored in the environment?** (In organic compounds, fossil fuels, and limestone)
- **In addition to respiration and decomposition, what activities produce carbon dioxide?** (Burning of fossil fuels, the breakdown of limestone)

Earth Science

Climatologists, scientists who study atmospheric conditions, are concerned about the increased levels of carbon dioxide in the atmosphere. Carbon dioxide is a greenhouse gas, or a gas that absorbs infrared radiation. Increased levels of greenhouse gases prevent much of the heat radiated by Earth's surface from being transmitted back into space. As a result, a condition of higher atmospheric temperatures, called the greenhouse effect, may result.

STS

Students should recognize that gasoline-free cars are not necessarily pollution-free cars. For example, the batteries used in electric-powered cars contain lead. Have interested students research alternative fuels for cars and list the advantages and disadvantages of these fuels.

MULTICULTURAL PERSPECTIVE

Windmills are ancient inventions that were first used in the East and were used in Germany and the Netherlands by the twelfth century. In the past, windmills have been used to pump water and grind grain. In colonial America, windmills were used for farm work.

37.3

Everyday Biology

Display specimens or photographs of lichens. Explain that lichens are often found on rocks and tree bark. Lichens have three general patterns of growth—flat and crusty, bushy, and leafy. Lichens provide food for reindeer in the Lapp region of Scandinavia and also for people living in some areas of northern Africa and western Asia. Lichens are also used to make dyes, such as the dye in litmus paper.

✥ Chemistry

Point out that the nitrogen cycle is an example of a biogeochemical cycle. Such a cycle involves living organisms (bio), soil and rock (geo), and chemical substances (nitrogen compounds).

Use the Visual

Have students study Figure 37.9. Ask:

- **What are examples of decomposers?** (Bacteria and fungi)
- **How is nitrogen used in plants and animals?** (In amino acids and proteins)

Teacher Demo

Arrange for a farmer or gardener to speak to the class about the importance of nitrogen compounds to healthy plants. Ask the speaker to discuss how fertilizers are used to improve the nitrogen quality of soil.

❶ Ammonia, nitrates, and amino acids

908

Fixed on nitrogen

Losing Lichens

Lichens—combinations of fungi and algae or cyanobacteria— fix nitrogen in forests. However, lichens are easily killed by low levels of air pollution. In Europe and the Eastern United States, lichens are now almost nonexistent.

Air contains about 78 percent free-nitrogen gas (N_2). But N_2 must be converted into other compounds before it can be used by most living things. This conversion occurs during the **nitrogen cycle,** the pathway by which nitrogen moves through the environment. *Figure* 37.9 illustrates the nitrogen cycle.

How nitrogen cycles N_2 in the air is converted to usable nitrogen compounds in a process called **nitrogen fixation.** Lightning causes some nitrogen fixation by forming nitrogen oxides from nitrogen and oxygen in the air. But most nitrogen fixation is carried out by bacteria.

Some nitrogen-fixing bacteria live in soil or water. Others live in nodules on the roots of plants that belong to the legume family. Alfalfa, peanuts, soybeans, clover, and peas are all legumes that could support these bacteria.

Nitrogen-fixing bacteria convert N_2 to ammonia (NH_3), which quickly dissolves in water to produce ammonium ions (NH_4^+). Some plants can take up ammonium ions directly. Other plants can only take up nitrogen in the form of nitrates. Certain bacteria convert ammonium ions to nitrates in a two-step process. The nitrates can then be absorbed by the roots of plants.

Plants use the nitrogen compounds they absorb to make amino acids, proteins, and other needed substances. Animals get the nitrogen they need by

FIGURE 37.9
The Nitrogen Cycle

Nitrogen is converted into many compounds throughout the nitrogen cycle. What are some of these nitrogen compounds? ❶

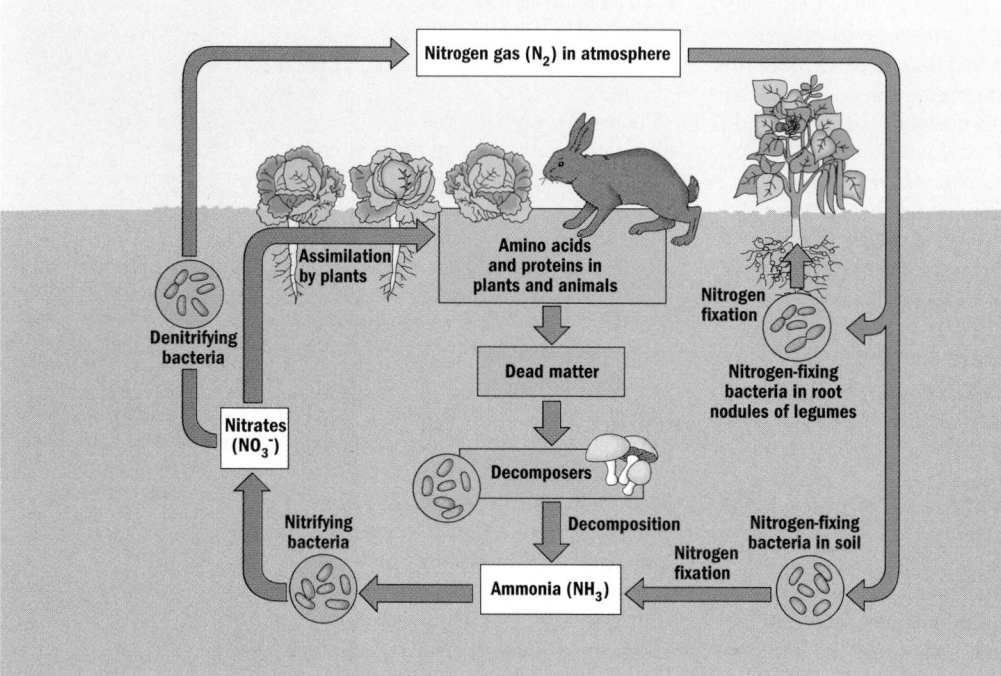

908 *Unit 9 Organisms and the Environment*

MULTICULTURAL PERSPECTIVE

Native Americans taught early European settlers to bury pieces of fish with the seeds of the corn they planted. According to tradition, this practice would ensure a good harvest. The practice worked because the fish acts as a fertilizer for the corn. Decomposers break down nitrogen compounds in the fish and release ammonia that remains in the soil for use by nitrifying bacteria. The soil ammonia and nitrates released by the bacteria are absorbed by the corn roots and used by the plant.

908

eating plants or the organisms that consume plants. All the amino acids that comprise your body's proteins contain the nitrogen you obtained by consuming other organisms or their products.

Decomposers play an important role in the nitrogen cycle. They break down nitrogen-containing animal wastes and the remains of dead organisms. The breakdown of these materials releases ammonia, which dissolves to produce ammonium ions. As just described, bacteria convert some ammonium ions to nitrates. Plants take up ammonium ions and nitrates, and the cycle starts over again. Another group of bacteria converts some of the ammonia and nitrates into free nitrogen gas. This process of returning nitrogen gas to the atmosphere is called **denitrification.**

Humans and the nitrogen cycle Human activities interfere with the nitrogen cycle in several ways. Many nitrogen compounds dissolve easily in water, so erosion and extensive irrigation can wash nitrogen out of the soil. Sewage and nitrogen-fertilizer runoff can add excess nitrogen to rivers, lakes, and ponds. When this happens, plants and algae can grow out of control, disrupting aquatic ecosystems.

Crop plants such as corn and cotton absorb nitrogen compounds from the soil as they grow. When the crops are harvested, the nitrogen they contain is removed from the environment. If crops are grown repeatedly in the same soil, the soil can quickly become nitrogen-depleted.

Farmers can use several strategies to return nitrogen to the soil. Crop rotation is an ancient and effective method of restoring nitrogen to farmland. Farmers rotate crops such as corn or cotton with soybeans or other legumes that support nitrogen-fixing bacteria in their roots. In modern

agriculture, however, farmers often replace lost nitrogen by adding commercially produced nitrogen fertilizers. Although the use of commercial fertilizers is effective, it is expensive. Large amounts of energy, usually from fossil fuels, are needed to make nitrogen fertilizers. What links can you see between the manufacture of nitrogen fertilizer and the carbon cycle? ❷

FIGURE 37.10
Excess nitrogen in bodies of water can spur plant and algae overgrowth. What can cause excess nitrogen to collect in a body of water? ❸

LAB ZONE **Do It!** **bioSURF**

How Do Chemical Cycles Affect Ecosystems?

Through various processes, resources in an ecosystem move back and forth between organisms and the environment. You can discover how if you . . .

Try This

1 Design and construct a model ecosystem. For example, you could model an aquatic ecosystem by using dechlorinated water, a glass jar, small fish, and aquatic plants. For any ecosystem, you must include soil or sand or gravel, plants, and animals.
2 Observe your ecosystem for one week and record any changes that occur.

Analyze Your Results

1 Describe a food chain in your ecosystem.
2 What chemical cycles did you observe? How did they affect your ecosystem?

Think Critically

After reviewing the steps in the nitrogen cycle, ask:

■ **How does the process of nitrogen-fixation compare to the process of denitrification?** (The processes are opposite. Nitrogen-fixation builds nitrogen compounds, while denitrification breaks apart nitrogen compounds.)

LAB ZONE **Do It!** **TEAM WORK**

How Do Chemical Cycles Affect Ecosystems?

You may want to have students do this lab after studying the water cycle. Students may choose from a variety of ecosystems, including saltwater, freshwater, and desert. Check that students have the appropriate amounts of food for the organisms. If students model an aquatic ecosystem, suggest that they monitor the pH and ammonia content of the water using commercially available kits designed for this purpose. Have students try to explain any changes in the values they observe.

Analyze Your Results

1 Answers will vary according to the ecosystem chosen.
2 Students are likely to observe the water cycle; evidence of nitrogen and carbon cycles may not be observable.

MEETING DIVERSE NEEDS

Gifted Have students conduct library research on the phosphorus cycle. Ask students to prepare a diagram that explains the cycle. Encourage students to present their diagrams to the class.

❷ The energy required to produce the fertilizers comes from fossil fuels. When fossil fuels are burned, carbon dioxide is released and enters the carbon cycle.
❸ Sewage and nitrogen fertilizer runoff

Teacher Demo

Turn on a faucet in class or display a glass of tap water. Have students speculate where the water comes from and where it drains. Tell students that the water they use for bathing, drinking, and cooking probably is pumped to their home from a reservoir or lake. Explain that the water entered the lake or reservoir as runoff or precipitation.

Class Activity

TEAM WORK

Divide the class into small groups. Provide each group with a small mirror, or have students use their own mirror. Tell students to hold the mirror close to their mouth and recite: *Horace the horse hulas in Hilo, Hawaii.* Have students observe what happens. Ask:

- **How does this activity relate to the water cycle?** (The water vapor that is released when people exhale is part of the cycle, moving water from a living thing to a nonliving part of the environment.)

Use the Visual

Have students study Figure 37.11. As a class, trace several of the paths that water may take as it moves through the environment. Ask:

- **How do plants contribute to the water cycle?** (Plants release water vapor to the air through transpiration.)

Puddle to cloud to rain

If you have ever noticed how quickly a puddle of water evaporates on a sunny day, you are already familiar with the water cycle. The **water cycle** is the continual movement of water from the Earth's surface to the atmosphere and back to the surface again. The water cycle is powered by solar energy, which causes evaporation. As you can see in *Figure 37.11,* water may take several paths as it moves through the environment.

How water cycles When water evaporates from oceans, lakes, or other bodies of water, it enters the atmosphere as a gas—water vapor. In the atmosphere, the water vapor cools and condenses to form clouds.

Eventually, clouds release the water they contain, and the water returns to Earth's surface as precipitation—rain, snow, hail, or sleet.

Water from precipitation may collect on the Earth's surface to form streams, rivers, and lakes. Most of the water eventually flows back to the ocean, carrying nutrients and sediments with it.

Some water, however, seeps into the ground instead of running off. It slowly percolates through soil and rock layers and is being filtered and purified along the way. Eventually, water moving down through the soil reaches groundwater deep beneath the surface. In some places, this water returns to the surface—bubbling up in clear, sparkling springs that fill wells, lakes, and ponds.

FIGURE 37.11

The Water Cycle

Solar radiation powers the water cycle. How does the water cycle affect the weather? **❶**

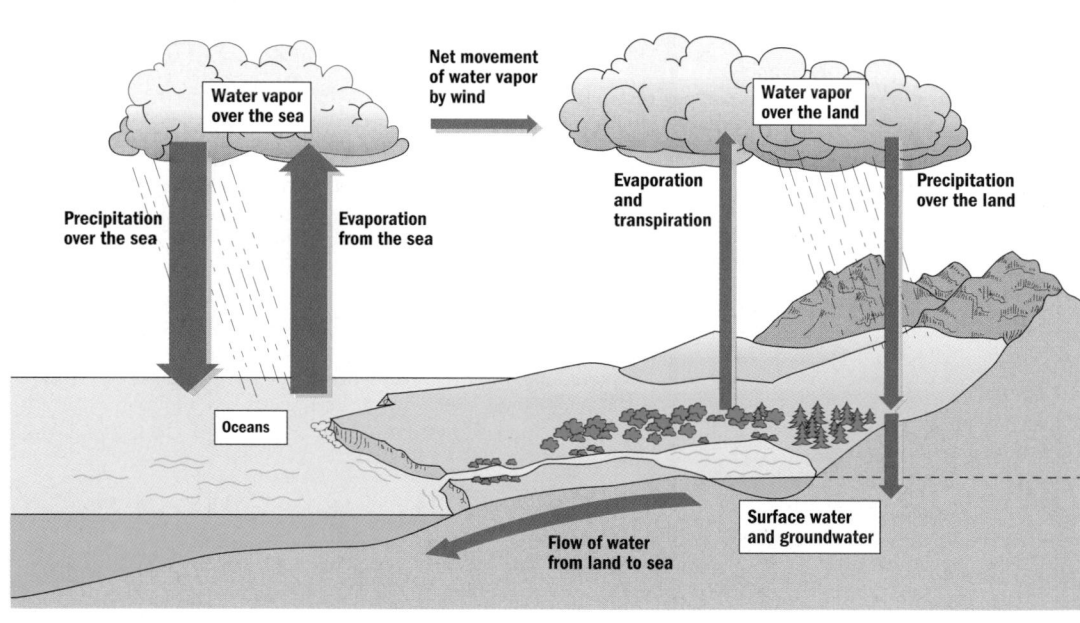

MEETING DIVERSE NEEDS

At Risk Have students work in small groups to develop a diorama, model, or diagram of the water cycle. Display the completed visuals in the class.

❶ Water vapor condenses to form clouds which then release the water as rain, snow, sleet, or hail.

Water cycles through living things as well as through the physical environment. For example, plants take up water through their root systems. Some of this water evaporates from plant leaves during transpiration. Animals also cycle water through their bodies. They take in water by eating and drinking, and they return some of the water to the environment when they perspire, urinate, or exhale water vapor.

Humans and the water cycle
Many human activities pollute water supplies. Chemicals, sewage, trash, and toxic wastes find their way into rivers, ponds, and lakes all over the world. Chemicals and toxic wastes contaminate groundwater. Deforestation can also affect the water cycle. For example, tropical rain forests transpire huge quantities of water up from the soil and into the atmosphere. When humans remove the trees and vegetation, this transpiration stops, and the land becomes susceptible to flooding and erosion. Soil and nutrients wash away, seriously changing the landscape.

FIGURE 37.12
Deforestation makes this tropical rain forest more susceptible to flooding. Why? What effect does the deforestation have? ❷

CHECKPOINT 37.3

1. How are chemical cycles important to an ecosystem?
2. Describe the carbon, nitrogen, and water cycles.
3. Critical Thinking Is water frozen in the polar ice caps during part of the water cycle? What might happen if the ice caps melted?

Build on What You Know

4. What step in cellular respiration produces carbon dioxide? What step in photosynthesis produces oxygen? *(Need to jog your memory? Revisit relevant concepts in Chapter 4, Section 4.2 and Section 4.3.)*

How are nutrients recycled in ecosystems?

Chapter 37 Ecosystem Dynamics **911**

CHECKPOINT 37.3

1. Because chemicals cannot be replenished, they must be recycled.
2. Students' answers should reflect the information in Figures 37.7, 37.9, and 37.11.
3. **Predicting** A relatively small amount of the water frozen in the polar ice caps can evaporate and become part of the water cycle. If the ice caps were to melt, sea level worldwide would increase.
4. The Krebs cycle produces carbon dioxide; oxygen is released during the light-dependent reactions.

❷ Deforestation removes the plants which absorb water and hold the soil in place, making the land more susceptible to flooding and erosion.

TEAM WORK Investigating the Water Cycle

SAFETY FIRST!

Instruct students to wash their hands after handling the cobalt chloride paper.

Lab Tips

Geranium plants can be grown from seed or may be purchased through a local nursery. If geraniums are not available in your area, substitute a different plant. Check the student set-ups to ensure that the plant leaves are not in direct contact with the cobalt chloride paper. As students make their observations, have them note whether any water is visible on the inside of the inverted cups.

Hypothesis Help

Students may refer to the diagram and text on page 910 to develop their hypotheses. Hypotheses should include the effects of transpiration and water storage in plants.

Lab Extension

Open Ended

Have students repeat the activity using different types of plants, including aloe or other succulents that are adapted to dry environments. Have students observe the plants daily for a one-week period and attempt to explain any differences they observe among the plants.

Time Required

- 50 minutes on first day
- 10 minutes on second day

Investigating the Water Cycle

WHAT YOU WILL DO Investigate the role of plants in the water cycle

SKILLS YOU WILL USE Controlling variables, observing, collecting and recording data

WHAT YOU WILL NEED 4 large clear cups, two 15-cm squares of waxed paper, 2 strips of blue cobalt-chloride paper, paper clip, petroleum jelly, 2 geranium-plant leaves with stems, tape

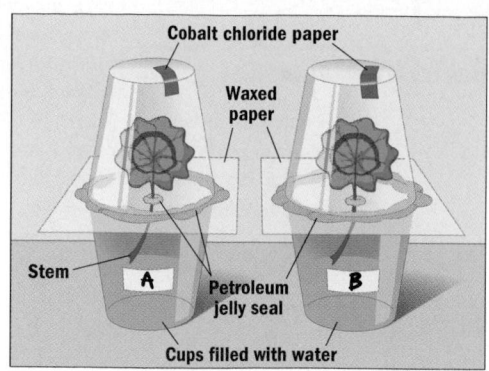

Propose a Hypothesis

Propose a hypothesis that explains the role of plants in the water cycle.

Conduct Your Experiment

1 Fill two cups (A and B) with water, and apply petroleum jelly to the rims.

2 Straighten the paper clip, and poke a hole in the center of each waxed paper square.

3 Insert a geranium-leaf stem through the hole in each waxed paper square. Apply petroleum jelly around each stem where it emerges from the waxed paper.

4 Apply a coat of petroleum jelly to both surfaces of one of the leaves.

5 Position the uncoated leaf over cup A. Gently press on the waxed paper so that it is held in place by the petroleum jelly around the rim. The stem should be in the water.

6 Repeat step 5 with the coated leaf and cup B. Be sure the stem is in the water.

7 Tape a piece of cobalt-chloride paper to the inside of each of the two other cups. Apply petroleum jelly around the rims of these cups.

8 Invert one of these cups over cup A and the other over cup B. Gently press them together. Do not allow the leaf to touch the cobalt-chloride paper.

9 Observe both setups for 10 minutes. After each minute,

record your observations in a data table, paying particular attention to the color of the cobalt chloride paper.

10 After 24 hours make your final observations and record them.

Analyze Your Data

1 What is the purpose of coating the leaf in setup B with petroleum jelly? Which setup is the control?

2 Did the color of either piece of chloride paper change? What does this change indicate?

3 What changes did you observe after 24 hours?

Draw Conclusions

1 How are green plants involved in the water cycle?

2 What is the plant process you observed in this experiment, and how might it affect local climates?

Design a Related Experiment

Design a related lab to determine the role of plants in the carbon cycle.

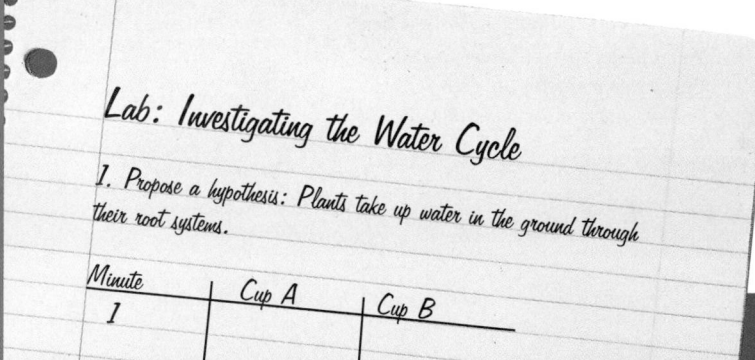

Lab: Investigating the Water Cycle

1. Propose a hypothesis: Plants take up water in the ground through their root systems.

Minute	Cup A	Cup B
1		

Analyze Your Data

1 The coating prevents transpiration; cup B is the control.

2 The cobalt chloride paper in cup A turns white, indicating that water vapor has come in contact with the paper.

3 Students should observe drops of moisture and a change in the color of the cobalt chloride paper.

Draw Conclusions

1 Plants absorb water through their roots and release water to the atmosphere during transpiration.

2 Respiration; Local climates may have an increase in humidity.

Chapter 37 Review

 THE BIG IDEA! 37.1–37.2 In an ecosystem, the flow of energy moves in one direction.
37.3 Nutrients are recycled in ecosystems.

Sum It Up

Use the following summary to review the main concepts in this chapter.

37.1 Ecosystem Structure

- Energy flows from the sun to autotrophs, which are consumed by heterotrophs. As energy is transferred in a food chain, some energy is lost as heat.
- Heterotrophs with varied diets can function at different trophic levels in different food chains.
- As decomposers feed on wastes and dead organisms, they recycle nutrients.
- When pollutants such as DDT move to higher levels in food chains, they become concentrated and their impact is magnified.

37.2 Energy Levels

- The transfer of matter and energy to higher trophic levels is inefficient. Only about 10 percent of energy is transferred between trophic levels.
- There are fewer organisms at higher trophic levels. The number of organisms at a given level depends on the biomass and energy supplied by the level below.
- Food webs show the connections between food chains in a community or an ecosystem.

37.3 Chemical Cycles

- Unlike energy, nutrients are not replenished by the sun. They must be recycled.
- Photosynthesis and cellular respiration are the processes responsible for the recycling of carbon and oxygen. Carbon also may be stored in organisms, fossil fuels, or limestone.
- The burning of fossil fuels and the destruction of forests interfere with the carbon cycle.
- Nitrogen must be converted into compounds by nitrogen-fixing bacteria before it can be used by other organisms. Decomposers release nitrogen from animal wastes and dead organisms.
- The nitrogen removed from the soil by plants can be restored through crop rotation or fertilizers. If nitrogen fertilizer or sewage is washed into a body of water, the water can become choked with overnourished plants and algae.
- Solar radiation evaporates water, which returns to Earth's surface as precipitation. Water also cycles through living organisms.
- Human activities can result in both surface and ground-water contamination.

Use Terms and Concepts

Use each of the following words or terms in a complete sentence. If you need to review a meaning, turn to the page indicated.

autotroph (p. 898)
producers (p. 898)
heterotroph (p. 899)
consumers (p. 899)
food chain (p. 899)
trophic level (p. 900)

herbivore (p. 900)
carnivore (p. 900)
omnivore (p. 900)
scavenger (p. 900)
decomposer (p. 900)
biological magnification
 (p. 901)

biomass (p. 902)
ecological pyramid
 (p. 902)
food web (p. 904)
carbon cycle (p. 906)
fossil fuel (p. 907)

nitrogen cycle (p. 908)
nitrogen fixation
 (p. 908)
denitrification (p. 909)
water cycle (p. 910)

Review the Big Ideas

Before students begin the Chapter Review, you may wish to discuss main concepts from the Big Ideas in Chapter 37. Point out that the flow of energy moves in one direction through an ecosystem. Energy generally moves from the sun to producers, from producers through the various levels of consumers, and then to decomposers. Unlike energy, nutrients such as water, carbon, oxygen, and nitrogen are constantly recycled through ecosystems.

Answers

1. biomass
2. food chain
3. carbon; nitrogen
4. trophic level
5. water cycle
6. herbivores; carnivores or omnivores
7. biological magnification
8. d
9. d
10. d
11. b
12. Both feed on dead organisms; decomposers return nutrients to the ecosystem.
13. Ecological pyramids provide information on relative size of populations, plus the energy and biomass available at a given trophic level.
14. Carbon is stored in glucose during photosynthesis and released from glucose during cellular respiration.
15. Energy is lost as heat at each link in the chain.
16. The bacteria convert nitrogen from the air into a form that can be used by the producers (plants).
17. Primary consumers are herbivores; secondary consumers are carnivores.
18. Biomass decreases at higher trophic levels.
19. Solar energy fuels evaporation of water and photosynthesis in producers.
20. Forests absorb carbon dioxide; through transpiration, forests return water to the atmosphere.
21. Answers will vary but students should include primary and secondary consumers as well as decomposers.
22. As the cool water sinks, it pushes up warmer water from the bottom, which carries up nutrients from

914

Use Your Word Power

COMPLETION Write the word or phrase that best completes each statement.

1. The primary consumers in an ecosystem have a smaller _____ than do the producers.

2. A(n) _____ provides a model of the flow of energy through a biological community.

3. Decomposers play a key role in the _____ and _____ cycles.

4. Primary consumers make up the second _____ in an ecological community.

5. Evaporation is one step in the _____ .

6. Consumers that eat only plants are _____ ; consumers that eat meat are _____ .

7. The buildup of pollutants in higher-level consumers is called _____ .

MULTIPLE CHOICE Choose the letter of the word or phrase that best completes each statement.

8. The number of organisms at each trophic level can be represented by (a) food chains; (b) biological magnifications; (c) food webs; (d) ecological pyramids.

9. Chemosynthetic bacteria are (a) autotrophs; (b) heterotrophs; (c) consumers; (d) producers.

10. The burning of fossil fuels produces some of the same end products as (a) photosynthesis; (b) nitrogen fixation; (c) denitrification; (d) cellular respiration.

11. Denitrifying bacteria are (a) scavengers; (b) decomposers; (c) producers; (d) omnivores.

Show What You Know

12. How are the roles of scavengers and decomposers similar? How are they different?

13. What information do ecological pyramids provide that is not provided by food chains and food webs?

14. What is the role of glucose in the carbon cycle?

15. Explain why the number of levels in a food chain is limited.

16. What is the relationship between producers and nitrogen-fixing bacteria?

17. What is the difference between a primary and secondary consumer?

18. What is the relationship between biomass and trophic level?

19. Describe how solar radiation affects the water cycle and ecological pyramids.

20. Why are forests included in the carbon and water cycles?

21. **Make a Concept Map** Create a concept map that shows the relationships between producers and consumers in an ecosystem of your choice.

Take It Further

22. **Developing a Hypothesis** In a lake, organisms sink to the bottom when they die. In temperate climates, the water at the lake surface cools in autumn. Why is it important for organisms living near the surface of temperate lakes that cool water is denser than warm water?

23. **Organizing and Classifying** In terms of trophic level, how would you classify a Venus-flytrap—a plant that traps insects? Explain.

24. **Applying Concepts** Apply what you have learned about biomass, energy, and ecological pyramids to the USDA food pyramid.

25. **Designing an Experiment** Design an experiment that would enable a cattle rancher to determine the average biomass required to produce a 1000-kilogram cow.

---

decomposing organisms.

23. A Venus's flytrap is both a first-level producer because it is an autotroph, and a third-level secondary consumer because it eats flies.

24. You need to eat larger portions of low-calorie foods to obtain the same energy.

25. The rancher could weigh cows after weaning and then again when the

animal reaches the desired weight. The rancher would need to weigh all feed eaten by the test animals.

26. Initially, the biomass increases sharply but gradually levels off; temperature and concentration of nutrients in soil. There is a limit to a plant's ability to absorb and transport water.

27. In ocean sediments; in the atmosphere

26. Interpreting a Graph The graph shows the effect of precipitation on the production of plant biomass. What happens to biomass as annual precipitation increases? What factors other than water might affect plant growth? Suggest reasons why the graph levels off at high levels of precipitation.

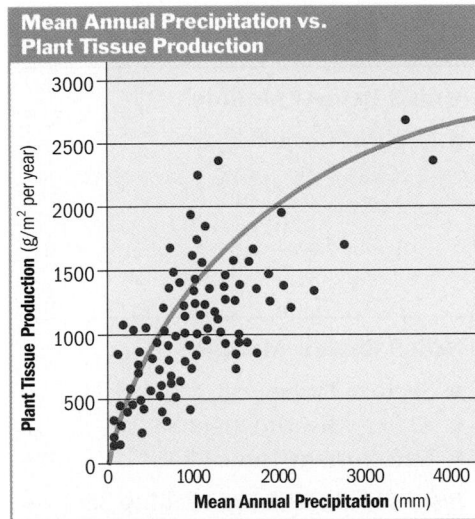

Mean Annual Precipitation vs. Plant Tissue Production

Plant Tissue Production (g/m² per year) vs. Mean Annual Precipitation (mm)

27. Analyzing Data Living organisms need phosphorus for structures such as cell membranes. The table below shows the distribution of available phosphorus in the global ecosystem. In which location is the most phosphorus stored? In which location is the least stored? Create a graph using these data.

Global Distribution of Phosphorus Storage	
Storage Location	Metric Tons
Atmosphere	2.8×10^3
Land organisms	3.0×10^9
Land	2.0×10^{12}
Shallow ocean water	2.71×10^9
Ocean organisms	1.38×10^8
Deep ocean water	8.71×10^{10}
Ocean sediments	4×10^{15}

Consider the Issues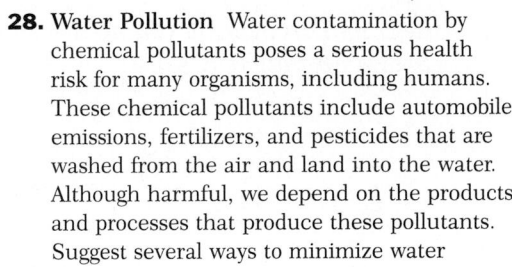

28. Water Pollution Water contamination by chemical pollutants poses a serious health risk for many organisms, including humans. These chemical pollutants include automobile emissions, fertilizers, and pesticides that are washed from the air and land into the water. Although harmful, we depend on the products and processes that produce these pollutants. Suggest several ways to minimize water pollution.

Make New Connections

29. Biology and Art Construct a food web with yourself at the center. Select foods that you enjoy eating and trace their energy back through the web. For example, if you drink milk, you would need to include a dairy cow in your web as well as the food eaten by the cow. Try to make as many connections as possible.

30. Biology and Economics Do a comparative study of cars that are fueled by gasoline and by electricity. How do the two car models compare in terms of initial cost, maintenance, speed, and range before refueling?

31. Biology and History Find a library or local historical society that keeps copies of old cookbooks. If possible, compare ingredient lists from recipes published about 100 years ago and today. Are any of the ingredients unfamiliar? How have the expectations about available foods changed over the century?

FAST-FORWARD TO CHAPTER 38 ▶▶

You now know that the water that organisms take in must not be polluted for the water cycle to be life sustaining. In Chapter 38, you will learn how humans affect the quality and quantity of all Earth's resources.

31. Students might want to ask a home economics teacher for help locating and interpreting recipes.

28. Answers may include the use of biological controls or genetically engineered plants instead of pesticides and crop rotation to reduce the amount of fertilizers. Car emissions can be reduced by using public transportation and car pooling. Cars which use alternative fuels may only substitute one pollutant for another.

29. If you have students who are strict vegetarians, you might suggest that they identify the crop pests that compete with them for food.

30. If there are no electric models being sold in your area, students could write to manufacturers or get data from automobile magazines. Students should include the cost of additional electricity resources.

PLANNING GUIDE

Section	Student Activities/Features	Teacher's Resource Package
38.1 Earth's Resources **Objectives** ■ Compare renewable and non-renewable resources ■ Identify the effects of human use of natural resources	**Lab Zone Discover It!** *Changing the Environment,* p. 917	**Unit 9 Review Module** ■ Section Review 38.1
38.2 Land in the Biosphere **Objectives** ■ Describe the processes that alter forests and soil ■ Appraise energy sources and waste buildup	**STS: Environmental Awareness** *Biodiversity,* p. 923 **Everyday Biology** *Natural Filters,* p. 923	**Unit 9 Review Module** ■ Section Review 38.2
38.3 Water in the Biosphere **Objectives** ■ Describe three different ways water can become polluted ■ Explain the modern sewage treatment process	**Lab Zone Do It!** *What Is the Quality of Local Water?* p. 925 **Everyday Biology** *Fluoride Inside,* p. 926	**Unit 9 Review Module** ■ Section Review 38.3 ■ Activity Recordsheet 38-1 ■ Enrichment Topic 38-1 **Issues and Decision Making** 38-1
38.4 Air in the Biosphere **Objectives** ■ Identify several sources of air pollution ■ Describe the cause and effects of acid rain, global warming, and ozone layer depletion	**Lab Zone Do It!** *Where Is Air Pollution?* p. 929	**Unit 9 Review Module** ■ Section Review 38.4 ■ Activity Recordsheet 38-2 ■ Interpreting Graphics 38 ■ Critical Thinking Exercise 38 ■ Enrichment Topic 38-2 **Laboratory Manual:** Lab 63: "The Effects of Acid Rain" **Interpreting and Developing Graphics** 112, 113, 114
38.5 Environmental Success Stories **Objectives** ■ Describe how humans have reversed some negative effects on the environment ■ Explain how humans can have a positive effect on the environment	**Lab Zone Think About It!** *Making Decisions About Land Use,* p. 933 **In the Community** *Your Success Story,* p. 934 **Lab Zone Investigate It!** *Recycling Paper,* p. 936	**Unit 9 Review Module** ■ Section Review 38.5 ■ Activity Recordsheet 38-3 ■ Vocabulary Review 38 ■ Chapter 38 Tests **Consumer Applications** 38-1 **Spanish Reviews** ■ Chapter 38 ■ Unit 9

Technology Resources

Internet Connections

Within this chapter, you will see the **bioSURF** logo. If you and your students have access to the Internet, the following URL address will provide various Internet connections that are related to topics and features presented in this chapter:

http://ecology.biosurf.com

You can also find relevant chapter material at **The Biology Place** address:

http://www.biology.com

CD-ROMs

Biología: la telaraña de la vida,
   (Spanish Student Edition) Chapter 38
Teacher's Resource Planner, Chapter 38
   Supplements
TestWorks CD-ROM
■ Chapter 38 Tests
Interactive Earth CD-ROM

Overhead Transparencies

■ The Greenhouse Effect, #96

Videotapes

Biology Alive! Video Series
■ Life's Fragile Balance Video
Rewind: The Web of Life Reteach Videos

Planning for Activities

STUDENT EDITION
Lab Zone Do It! p. 925
   ■ field trip to a river,
     stream, lake, or other
     water source near your
     school

Lab Zone Do It! p. 929
   ■ five microscope slides
   ■ petroleum jelly
   ■ five petri dishes with lids
   ■ hand lens

Lab Zone
Investigate It! p. 936
   ■ sheets of newspaper
   ■ large mixing bowl
   ■ eggbeater
   ■ water
   ■ liquid laundry starch
   ■ hand lens
   ■ large square pan
   ■ screen
   ■ 4 sheets of blotting paper
   ■ rolling pin

TEACHER'S EDITION
Quick Activity, p. 918
Recyclable vs. nonrecyclable
   ■ plastic and paper bags
   ■ Styrofoam cups and
     boxes
   ■ plastic bottles
   ■ coated milk cartons
   ■ aluminum cans

Quick Activity, p. 920
Simulating rainfall
   ■ dry potting soil
   ■ aluminum tray
   ■ spray bottle
   ■ water

Teacher Demo, p. 921
Sources of renewable energy
   ■ models demonstrating
     various renewable
     energy sources
   ■ pinwheel

   ■ water
   ■ radiometer
   ■ photovoltaic cell
   ■ solar-powered calcula-
     tors, flashlights, radios

Teacher Demo, p. 924
Toxins in soil
   ■ funnel
   ■ filter paper
   ■ soil
   ■ clear plastic container
     or empty 2-L beverage
     bottle
   ■ dropper
   ■ food coloring
   ■ water

Teacher Demo, p. 926
Representing "Earth's water"
   ■ 1-L graduated cylinder
   ■ water
   ■ beaker labeled "salt
     water"
   ■ beaker labeled "ice"

Teacher Demo, p. 926
*Water temperature in
ecosystems*
   ■ beaker
   ■ water
   ■ thermometer
   ■ boiling water

Teacher Demo, p. 928
*Demonstrating the green-
house effect*
   ■ thermometers
   ■ 2 containers of colored
     water
   ■ plastic wrap

Teacher Demo, p. 930
pH levels in water samples
   ■ rainwater
   ■ clean jars
   ■ distilled water
   ■ pH paper

Chapter Objectives

Students will learn the main concepts of this chapter as they complete the following objectives.

- Compare renewable and non-renewable resources
- Identify the effects of population growth on human use of natural resources
- Describe the processes that alter forests and soil
- Describe three different ways water can become polluted
- Identify several sources of air pollution
- Describe the effects of acid rain and global warming
- Describe how humans have reversed some negative effects on the environment
- Explain how humans can have a positive effect on the environment

Key Words

38.1 *renewable resource, non-renewable resource, sustainable development*

38.2 *soil erosion, desertification, deforestation, biodegradable, non-biodegradable*

38.4 *acid rain, greenhouse effect, global warming, chlorofluorocarbons*

The Opening Story

Have students discuss how they think the story relates to the content of this chapter. Challenge them to explain how obtaining natural resources may affect the environment of Alaska.

 Predicting To practice strategies for effective reading, use pages 77-78 in *Super Read!*

You can find out more about people and the environment by exploring the following Internet address:
http://ecology.biosurf.com

In this chapter . . .

FEATURES

Everyday Biology
- Natural Filters
- Fluoride Inside

In the Community
Your Success Story

 Environmental Awareness
Biodiversity

LAB ZONES

Discover It!
- Changing the Environment

Do It!
- What Is the Quality of Local Water?
- Where Is Air Pollution?

Think About It!
- Making Decisions About Land Use

Investigate It!
- Recycling Paper

SUPER READ!

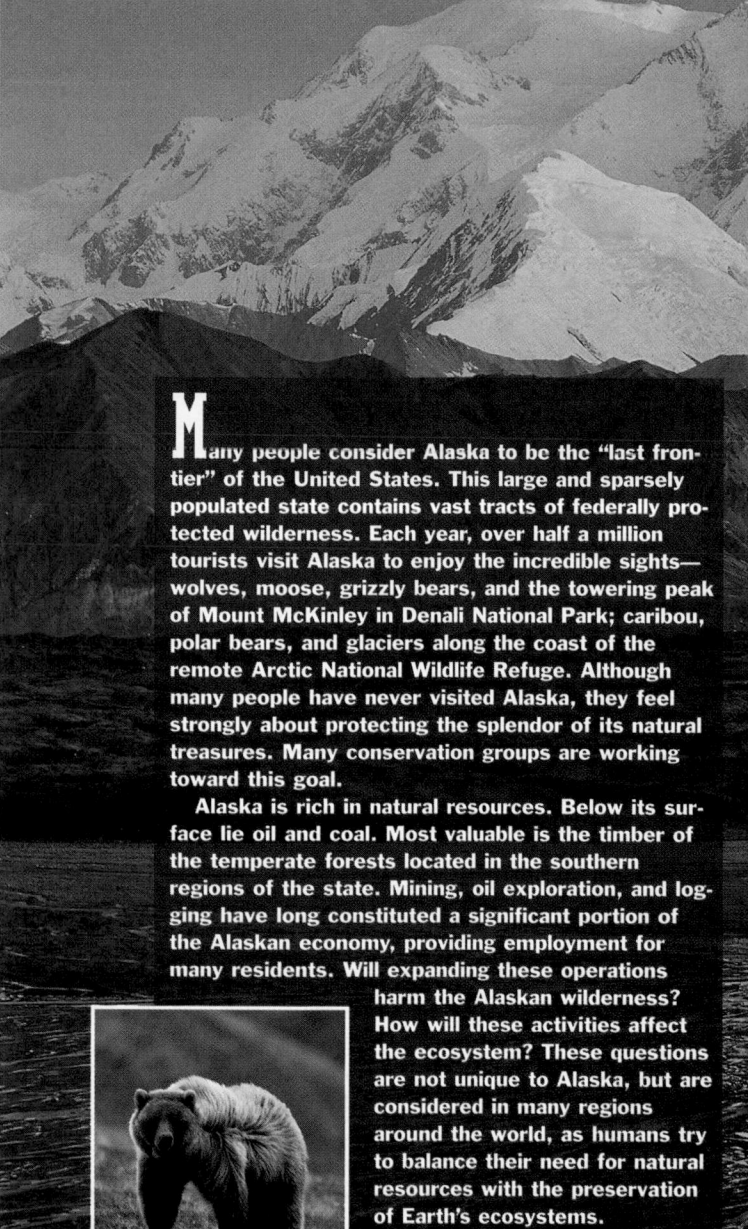

Many people consider Alaska to be the "last frontier" of the United States. This large and sparsely populated state contains vast tracts of federally protected wilderness. Each year, over half a million tourists visit Alaska to enjoy the incredible sights—wolves, moose, grizzly bears, and the towering peak of Mount McKinley in Denali National Park; caribou, polar bears, and glaciers along the coast of the remote Arctic National Wildlife Refuge. Although many people have never visited Alaska, they feel strongly about protecting the splendor of its natural treasures. Many conservation groups are working toward this goal.

Alaska is rich in natural resources. Below its surface lie oil and coal. Most valuable is the timber of the temperate forests located in the southern regions of the state. Mining, oil exploration, and logging have long constituted a significant portion of the Alaskan economy, providing employment for many residents. Will expanding these operations harm the Alaskan wilderness? How will these activities affect the ecosystem? These questions are not unique to Alaska, but are considered in many regions around the world, as humans try to balance their need for natural resources with the preservation of Earth's ecosystems.

The Last Frontier?

LAB ZONE Discover It!

Changing the Environment

1. Select a plant species and an animal species (not human) that live in your community.
2. On a sheet of paper, make three columns, one for the plant, one for the animal, and one for humans.
3. Under each column, list some characteristics of that species that help it to survive in its environment. Do these characteristics change the environment?

We humans are far more able to change our environment than other species. This ability can lead to conflicts about the use of natural resources and the protection of other species. How have these conflicts been resolved in your community? Do you agree or disagree with the methods of resolution?

WRITE ABOUT IT!

In your science journal, write about the ways that your environment has changed in the last year. What activities have you taken part in that might have contributed to the changes in your environment?

Opening Activities

bioSURF If you have access to the Internet in your classroom or school, you may wish to have students connect to the address shown on page 916. You may also want to have students conduct net searches for information using key words related to this chapter. For example, they could search for entries under ecology, natural resources, biodiversity, or endangered species.

LAB ZONE Discover It!

Changing the Environment

TEAM WORK

Before students begin this chapter, have them do the suggested activity as a class. Record selected responses on the board. Tell students to revisit this activity at the conclusion of the chapter to see if they would change any of their responses.

WRITE ABOUT IT!

Have students select a format and then begin their journal entries. Students may wish to write a descriptive essay, create a cartoon strip, or record their observations in chart form.

REWIND to Chapter 37

Briefly review concepts learned in Chapter 37, *Ecosystem Dynamics*. Ask:

- **What are some ways organisms interact with each other and with their environment?**

PORTFOLIO PREVIEW

Students should be encouraged to add to their portfolios as they work through this chapter. In addition to the *Write About It* opportunity, the following sections offer opportunities for portfolio entries:

- Section 38.1: *Earth's Resources*
- Section 38.3: *Water in the Biosphere*
- Section 38.5: *Environmental Success Stories*

ENGAGE

Consider the Big Idea

Have students read The Big Idea! at the top of the page. Explain that humans compete with all living things for a limited amount of natural resources.

Use the Visual

Have students study the photograph that opens the section. Point out that fuel is any source of heat or energy. Ask:

■ **What might be some benefits and drawbacks to using waste products as fuel?** (Benefits include reducing the accumulation of garbage and conserving other energy sources. Drawbacks include the release of pollutants into the environment when waste is burned.)

Quick Activity

Display in class a wide range of items used to package and carry food: plastic and paper bags, Styrofoam cups and boxes, plastic bottles, coated milk cartons, and aluminum cans. Have students identify which items are recyclable and which are not.

SUPER READ! **Predicting** To practice strategies for effective reading, use pages 77-78 in *Super Read!*

❶ Wind is constantly being generated by weather patterns.

❷ Sunlight, water, plants, and animals

918

What you'll learn

IDEAS
• To compare renewable and nonrenewable resources
• To identify the effects of human use of natural resources

WORDS
renewable resource, nonrenewable resource, sustainable development

SUPER READ!

FIGURE 38.1
Fossil fuels, such as oil, are nonrenewable resources. Wind is a renewable resource. Why?

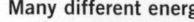

38.1 Earth's Resources

Wasting electricity?
Many different energy sources may be used in the future. Bacterial degradation of biological waste produces methane gas. Sawdust, old paper, tree bark, and sewage can be burned to produce electricity. Using waste products as fuel is nothing new. For example, dried cattle dung has long been a cooking fuel in south Asia.

TYPES OF NATURAL RESOURCES

Nature's bank

Humans, like all living things, need food, water, shelter, and space for survival. All of these needs are met by the natural resources of Earth. The quality of our natural resources is a major concern, because healthy soil, clean air, and drinkable water are essential for human survival. In addition, the quantity of resources available is critical.

When evaluating a natural resource, scientists consider whether or not it is replaceable. A **renewable resource** is a resource that can be replaced by natural processes. For example, oxygen in the air is a renewable resource because it is continuously replenished by plants and algae during photosynthesis. Trees are a renewable resource because new trees can grow after older trees are harvested. What are some other examples of renewable resources? ❷

Different time periods are needed to replenish different renewable resources. Oxygen is replaced continuously. Trees, on the other hand, can take hundreds of years to replace. Changing environmental conditions affect the rate of replenishment. When renewable resources are used faster than natural processes can replenish them, they are depleted.

There are only limited amounts of nonrenewable resources. A **nonrenewable resource** is a resource that cannot be replenished by natural processes. Fossil fuels and minerals such as copper are examples of nonrenewable resources. Many nonrenewable resources, such as fossil fuels, can be used only once. When these resources are depleted, they are gone forever. However, some nonrenewable resources can be used more than once. For example, the copper in electrical wires can be melted down and reused in other copper products.

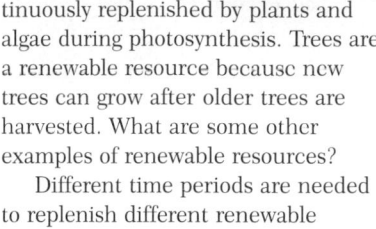

STUDENT RESOURCES

From the Teacher's Resource Package, use:
■ Section Review 38.1 from Unit 9 Review Module

TECHNOLOGY RESOURCES

Relevant technology resources include:
■ Spanish Student Edition CD-ROM
■ Teacher's Resource Planner CD-ROM
■ Interactive Earth CD-ROM
■ Biology Alive! Video Series

THE EFFECTS OF HUMAN USE

All used up

How are natural resources affected by human use? Human use of a natural resource greatly affects the quantity of the resource. **Sustainable development** means using renewable resources at a rate that does not deplete them. Renewable resources can be used over long periods of time if their short-term use is controlled. For example, farmers practice sustainable development by managing soil use to ensure that the soil will be fertile in the future. Switching from a nonrenewable resource to a renewable resource, such as from fossil fuels to wind power, is another example of sustainable development.

The quality of natural resources can also be changed by humans. The quality of drinking water depends on how people use water and dispose of waste. How is the quality of other natural resources affected by humans? ❸ Human use of natural resources can affect chemical cycles, food webs, biodiversity, and ecological succession. As you learned in Chapter 37, humans are part of an ecosystem. We have a dramatic effect on the ecological balance of our ecosystem.

The human effect on Earth's natural resources is proportional to the size of the population. For example, the exhaust fumes from one car might not be a problem. But when several million cars produce the same exhaust, it creates a harmful effect on air quality. Recall that the human population is growing exponentially, and scientists are uncertain about Earth's carrying capacity for humans. In order to meet the needs of a growing

population, humans must sustain both the quality and quantity of natural resources.

Behavioral adaptations enable humans to obtain the resources they need for survival. As you learned in Chapter 12, we are able to survive in most of Earth's ecological zones because of our ability to adapt to different environments. Most of these adaptations are behavioral, rather than physical, and behavior can be modified. The human capacity for changing behavior allows each of us to decide on the best way to use and preserve natural resources.

CHECKPOINT 38.1

1. Explain the difference between renewable and nonrenewable resources.

2. What are the effects of human use of natural resources?

3. Critical Thinking How could a lumber or fishing company practice sustainable development?

Build on What You Know

4. Why are fossil fuels a nonrenewable resource? *(Need to jog your memory? Revisit relevant concepts in Chapter 37, Section 37.3.)*

FIGURE 38.2
For decades, Spectacle Island was a city dump. Now the land is being restored and turned into a national park. How is Spectacle Island an example of humans restoring natural resources? ❹

How is the web of life affected by human use of natural resources? **?**

Chapter 38 People and the Environment **919**

CHECKPOINT 38.1

1. Renewable resources can be replenished by natural processes; nonrenewable resources cannot.
2. Human use affects the quantity and quality of natural resources.
3. **Applying** A lumber company could harvest trees at the same rate that new trees are planted. A fishing company's annual catch could be the same number of fish that are born in one year.
4. Fossil fuels take millions of years to form.

❸ The quality of air is affected by the use of fossil fuels; the quality of food grown depends on agricultural methods.

❹ Humans took an area that was not productive and turned it into one that could be used for recreation and preservation.

TEACH

Build Writing Skills

Ask students to write an article for their school or local newspaper describing how their lives would be different if the population of their community suddenly doubled.

ASSESS

Evaluate Understanding

To assess students' understanding of the key concepts of this section, ask:

■ **What are some examples of renewable and nonrenewable resources?** (Renewable—sun, trees, oxygen; nonrenewable—oil, coal, gas)

■ **What is sustainable development and how can it be encouraged?** (Using natural resources at a rate that does not deplete them; by controlling short-term use, using renewable resources, and changing human behaviors)

Reteach

On the board write the terms *renewable resources* and *nonrenewable resources*. Briefly, define each term. Show pictures or list a variety of natural resources. Have volunteers come to the board to list each resource beneath the appropriate head and to cite examples of how humans use the resource listed.

ENGAGE

Consider the Big Idea

Have students read The Big Idea! at the top of the page. Explain that land and its resources, clean water, and clean air are important to all parts of the web of life, including humans.

Use the Visual

Have students study the photograph that opens the section. Explain that plants and plant products are used in many different industries to benefit humans.

SUPER READ! **Identifying Cause and Effect** To practice strategies for effective reading, use pages 75-76 in *Super Read!*

Quick Activity **TEAM WORK**

Provide students working in small groups with dry potting soil in an aluminum tray and a spray bottle containing water. Instruct them to shape half the soil into a mound and use the spray bottle to simulate a heavy rainfall. Have students observe how the rainfall impacts the mound of soil. Next, have them shape the other half of the soil into stair steps and use the spray bottle to simulate heavy rainfall. Discuss what happened each time. Have volunteers explain how changing the shape of the soil helped protect it. (Make sure the soil is properly recycled after use.)

920

38.2 Land in the Biosphere

What you'll learn

IDEAS
• To describe the processes that alter forests and soil
• To appraise energy sources and waste buildup

WORDS
soil erosion, desertification, deforestation, biodegradable, nonbiodegradable

SUPER READ!

A rosy treatment

The rosy periwinkle, a flower found only in the tropical rain forests of Madagascar, is a source of two substances used in the treatment of Hodgkin's disease and other forms of cancer. Ecologists fear that the destruction of rain forests and other biomes may prevent the discovery of other species that have medicinal uses.

FORESTS, SOILS, AND MINERALS

A base for life

Land is essential for life on Earth. It provides resources and living space for many organisms, including humans. The soil that covers the land serves as a home for producers, decomposers, and burrowing animals. Forests and soil also provide a home for many populations. Humans depend on land for its valuable resources. For example, forests provide lumber for building materials. How do human activities ❷ affect these essential resources?

Poor farming and ranching practices can lead to soil erosion.

Soil erosion is the wearing away of surface soil by water and wind. In dry regions of the world, erosion and overgrazing can lead to desertification. **Desertification** is the reduction of a soil's ability to retain water and nutrients, both of which are essential for plant growth. Productive farms and grasslands can change into barren deserts because of desertification.

Many farmers and ranchers use techniques that protect the soil. Farmers reduce soil erosion with terracing, contour plowing, and reduced irrigation. Planting trees as windbreaks also slows soil erosion. Ranchers avoid overgrazing of land in an effort to stop desertification.

FIGURE 38.3
Fields terraced in this manner help prevent soil erosion (left). Recycling newspapers can help prevent deforestation (right). What effects do erosion and deforestation have on the biosphere? ❶

920 *Unit 9 Organisms and the Environment*

STUDENT RESOURCES

From the Teacher's Resource Package, use:
■ Section Review 38.2 from Unit 9 Review Module

TECHNOLOGY RESOURCES

Relevant technology resources include:
■ Spanish Student Edition CD-ROM
■ Teacher's Resource Planner CD-ROM
■ Interactive Earth CD-ROM
■ Biology Alive! Video Series

Human activities can also change forests. **Deforestation** is the removal of large numbers of trees from a forest. During deforestation many species lose their habitats. Because trees use carbon dioxide, deforestation can also contribute to the buildup of carbon dioxide in the air.

Deforestation is proceeding rapidly all over the world. An estimated 11 million hectares of tropical rain forest are cleared each year. Environmentally sensitive methods of lumber harvesting can help prevent deforestation. Everyone can help limit deforestation by recycling paper and choosing alternatives to wood products.

Minerals are mined for a variety of products used by humans. Unfortunately, mining of these valuable minerals can scar the landscape, destroy habitats, and pollute the air and water. Restoration of mining sites has reversed some of the damages. Newer, environmentally sensitive mining techniques are preventing future problems. Minerals are a nonrenewable resource. Recycling is an important method for conservation of key mineral resources. Aluminum, copper, and lead are now commonly recycled.

ENERGY

The power to live

Energy resources from the land—coal, oil, and natural gas—heat and light our homes, power our appliances, and run our vehicles. We rely on these energy sources because they are relatively accessible and inexpensive. But reliance on these fossil fuels is costly in terms of damage to our environment. Coal mining can cause severe soil erosion. Oil spills destroy plant and animal life. The burning of fossil fuels pollutes the air.

As you may know, fossil fuels are formed over a time period of millions of years from the remains of ancient

organisms. Some day the supplies of oil, coal, and natural gas will be depleted. Since fossil fuels are nonrenewable and can harm our environment, it is extremely important that renewable and environmentally safe energy sources be developed.

Solar energy is one of the most promising alternatives to fossil fuels. Simple, nonpolluting devices called photovoltaic cells can make electricity from sunlight almost anywhere the sun shines. However, solar energy technology is still relatively expensive.

Other alternatives to fossil fuels include nuclear energy, hydroelectric power, wind power, geothermal power, and tidal power. Each of these energy sources has advantages and disadvantages.

The raw materials for nuclear energy are essentially unlimited, and nuclear energy does not pollute the air. However, it produces dangerous radioactive waste that is difficult to dispose of. Hydroelectric power plants use moving water to generate electricity, requiring dams and reservoirs that flood plant and animal habitats. Wind drives windmills that can generate electricity on large "wind farms," but only a few locations have the steady winds needed for this technology. Geothermal energy,

FIGURE 38.4

The solar power generated by these solar panels is a renewable alternative to fossil fuels. What is the drawback of solar power?

Chapter 38 People and the Environment **921**

Teacher Demo

Exhibit models that demonstrate various renewable energy sources. Show a pinwheel and have a student blow on it to show wind power. Spray the pinwheel with water to show how water can move the wheel. Use a radiometer to illustrate how the energy of sunlight can be transformed into mechanical energy. Exhibit a photovoltaic cell and examples of products that use it, such as solar-powered calculators, flashlights, and radios. Discuss with students other sources of renewable energy that might be practical in their community.

Mathematics

Soil formation is a very slow process. Only about 2.5 cm of soil forms in an average area over a 100-year period. Ask:

- **About how much soil would form in the area in four years?** (.10 cm)

❶ Erosion removes valuable topsoil; deforestation eliminates important habitats and decreases the amount of breathable oxygen produced.

❷ Human demand determines how much lumber is needed; human carelessness can destroy a forest; different farming methods can either deplete or conserve topsoil.

❸ One of the major drawbacks to solar power is that installation costs are high.

MEETING DIVERSE NEEDS

LEP Encourage students to compile a picture dictionary illustrating the meaning of ecology-related terms such as: *solar energy, desertification, deforestation, biodegradable,* and *erosion.*

Gifted Have students choose an alternative energy source and prepare a report explaining the technology needed to make the energy source accessible to humans. Encourage students to include visuals with their report.

which comes from hot water or steam deep inside Earth, is available in only a few locations. Tidal or wave power also has limited availability. Other alternatives to fossil fuels are being studied in the hope they will help meet fuel needs.

WASTE

Reduce, reuse, recycle

The United States produces 19 percent of the world's solid waste. Most of the household solid waste ends up buried in landfills. Thousands of hectares of land are used for this purpose. What happens to the waste?

Some solid wastes, such as food scraps, leaves, and grass clippings, are biodegradable (BY-oh-dee-GRAY-duh-bul). **Biodegradable** wastes can be broken down and recycled by decomposers. **Nonbiodegradable** wastes, such as plastics, metals, and pesticides, cannot be broken down.

Unfortunately, very little decomposition takes place at a landfill. The wastes at a landfill are tightly packed and there is not enough oxygen for decomposers to survive. Chemical wastes buried in landfills can contaminate groundwater. In some places, solid wastes are burned in incinerators at very high temperatures. Although incinerators reduce waste volume, they are expensive to operate.

We can all take actions to help reduce the number and size of landfills. Reusing items and purchasing products with less packaging can keep household wastes to a minimum. Biodegradable wastes can be composted, or turned into a rich organic humus, and added to garden soil. Recycling paper, glass, certain plastics, and aluminum can reduce waste, and conserve valuable resources.

Some of the waste produced by industries such as manufacturing, mining, and agriculture is hazardous.

FIGURE 38.6
Landfills are now lined with clay and plastic to prevent soil and water contamination by waste materials.

FIGURE 38.5
In deep well injection, hazardous liquid wastes are pumped through lined pipes to rocks located far below water sources.

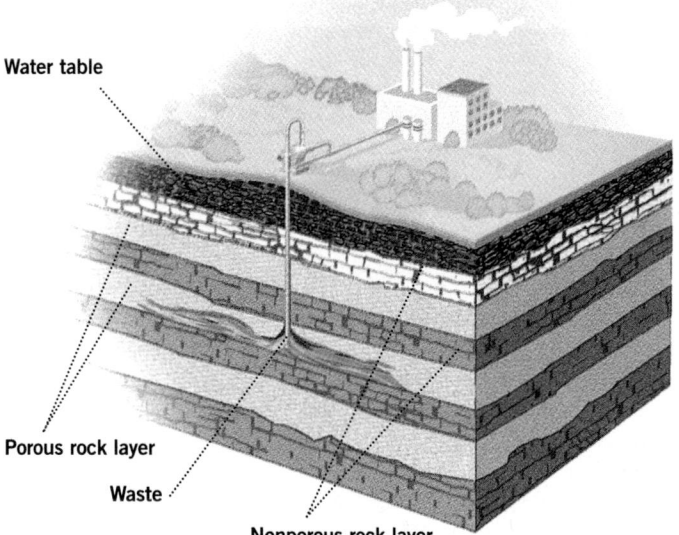

Water table

Porous rock layer

Waste

Nonporous rock layer

MULTICULTURAL PERSPECTIVE

Archaeologists have discovered that the ancient Maya (A.D. 1200) recycled broken pottery and grinding stones in building their temples. To reduce waste, they buried their dead with old, broken, and fake objects instead of using new pottery, ornaments, and tools.

Hazardous wastes may contain toxic or cancer-causing chemicals, heavy metals, or substances that are explosive, flammable, or corrosive. Strict government regulations exist to control disposal of hazardous wastes. These regulations protect humans and other living things in the environment.

Some hazardous wastes are stored far underground by deep well injection, as illustrated in *Figure 38.5*. In theory, deep well injection is safe. But if the stored wastes move in unpredictable ways, groundwater could be contaminated.

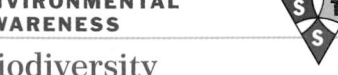

ENVIRONMENTAL AWARENESS

Biodiversity

Some human activities are changing Earth's environment. Some of these changes result in the extinction of other species and are causing an alarming decrease in biodiversity. You may recall from Chapter 36 that biodiversity is important for ecological stability. The ecological balance of an ecosystem—for example, our own—can be disrupted if biodiversity decreases rapidly.

In addition to maintaining ecological stability, the biodiversity of Earth is an important resource for humans. We depend on various species for foods, medicines, chemicals, and other useful materials. And only a fraction of the species on Earth have been studied. Cures for cancer and other diseases may exist in plants and animals that have not been discovered or analyzed.

Some of the ecosystems with the greatest biodiversity are most at risk. For example, tropical rain forests are home to between 50 and 90 percent of the total number of species on Earth. Other diverse ecosystems at risk include coral reefs, estuaries, wetlands, and temperate forests.

Habitat destruction is the greatest threat to biodiversity today. Cutting forests, filling in wetlands, and plowing up grasslands can destroy habitats. Pollution, commercial hunting, trade in exotic plants and animals, and introduction of foreign species also threaten biodiversity.

Steps are being taken to preserve biodiversity. Wildlife reserves and wilderness areas have been set aside in many countries. Laws such as the Endangered Species Act are being used to protect species and preserve habitats.

CHECKPOINT 38.2

1. Describe two processes that alter forests and soils.
2. What are some energy alternatives to fossil fuels? Explain the benefits of at least three alternatives.
3. **Critical Thinking** Explain why removing species from ecosystems is like "removing bricks from a wall."

Build on What You Know
4. Explain how genetic drift can affect biodiversity. *(Need to jog your memory? Revisit relevant concepts in Chapter 10, Section 10.5.)*

Chapter 38 People and the Environment **923**

FIGURE 38.7
Clearing the rain forest can provide new areas for people to live in and farm, but it also causes loss of biodiversity.

Natural Filters

Salt marshes are often targeted for draining and development because of their desirable coastal location. However, salt marshes have an important function—they can filter pollutants from coastal waters as effectively as waste-treatment plants.

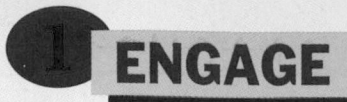

1 ENGAGE

Use the Visual

Have students study the photograph that opens the section. Explain that the process described in the opening text is called eutrophication. Ask:

- **Why would fertilizers that enter aquatic ecosystems encourage the growth of plankton?** (Plankton are plantlike protists that use nitrogen compounds to carry on growth processes.)

Teacher Demo

Place a funnel containing filter paper and soil atop a clear plastic container, such as an empty 2-L beverage bottle. While students observe, add a few drops of food coloring to the soil. Tell students the coloring represents a toxic substance. Next, pour water into the funnel, explaining that the water models rainwater. Have students observe the water that passes through the soil and into the container. Explain that just as the water carried the food coloring, rainwater can wash toxins deep into soil layers in a process called leaching. Explain that once in the soil, the toxins can kill soil organisms and also be carried into groundwater supplies.

❶ It adds soil to the mouth of the delta.

What you'll learn

IDEAS
- To describe three different ways water can become polluted
- To explain the modern sewage treatment process

When carp rule

Each year, the use of fossil fuels and fertilizers releases more than 272 million metric tons of nitrogen compounds into the biosphere. These compounds encourage the growth of plankton in lakes and rivers. Excessive plankton growth depletes the oxygen in water. Only certain fish, such as goldfish and carp, can survive in water with little oxygen.

SEDIMENT AND SEWAGE POLLUTION

Muddying the waters

Humans use water for drinking, cooking, and washing, and in agriculture, recreation, and industry. In addition, aquatic ecosystems provide food and much of the biodiversity on Earth. For these reasons, water pollution is a major concern today.

As you learned in the previous section, soil erosion is the carrying away of exposed soil by wind and water. The soil, or sediment, is carried from the land to streams, lakes, and other waterways. Rivers in the United States carry 3.6 billion metric tons of sediment per year.

Excessive sediment in waterways can harm or kill aquatic organisms. Small particles of sediment suspended in water block the light needed by aquatic plants for photosynthesis. Heavier particles settle to the bottom of lakes and rivers and bury bottom-dwelling organisms. In tropical regions, sediments that flow from rivers into the ocean can destroy coral reefs. You have learned that farming techniques such as contour plowing help prevent soil erosion. Avoiding soil erosion can prevent pollution of water.

Sewage is another major source of water pollution. In many parts of the world, raw untreated sewage is discharged directly into streams and lakes. Untreated sewage may contain disease-causing organisms that make the water unsafe to drink. In most developed nations, however, sewage is usually treated in some way before being discharged into waterways.

Basic sewage treatment involves filtering out debris and allowing solid materials to settle out. Next, bacterial decomposers are added to the mix. These bacteria break down most of the biodegradable wastes. The treated sewage, or sludge, passes on to sedimentation tanks, where the bacteria

FIGURE 38.8
This computer-enhanced satellite photograph shows how topsoil (green) is carried away by the Mississippi River and dumped into the Gulf of Mexico. How does this process affect the Mississippi delta? ❶

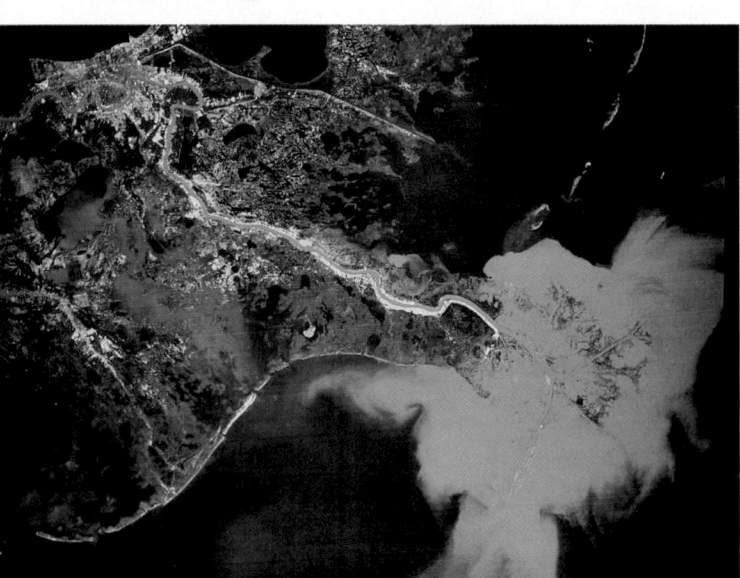

924   *Unit 9 Organisms and the Environment*

STUDENT RESOURCES

From the Teacher's Resource Package, use:
- Section Review 38.3, Activity Recordsheet 38-1, and Enrichment Topic 38-1 from Unit 9 Review Module

TECHNOLOGY RESOURCES

Relevant technology resources include:
- Spanish Student Edition CD-ROM
- Teacher's Resource Planner CD-ROM
- Interactive Earth CD-ROM
- Biology Alive! Video Series

FIGURE 38.9
Oil spills have devastating effects on many species. How did this 1989 oil spill in Alaska harm the species in this environment? ❷

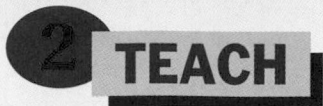
SUPER READ!

Build Writing Skills

Tell students to research the immediate and long-term effects of the *Exxon Valdez* oil spill and the cleanup efforts that followed. Have students write up their research as a script for a TV news special.

and sludge settle out. The sludge may eventually be burned, used as fertilizer, or dumped in landfills.

Advanced sewage treatment takes the process one step further by removing heavy metals and other chemicals, such as phosphates and nitrates. The result is clean water from which 95 percent of all pollutants have been removed. Chlorine is usually added to the treated water to kill any remaining bacteria and viruses.

CHEMICAL POLLUTION
Compound problems

Chemical pollutants from a variety of different sources can end up in the water supply. Mining and manufacturing wastes may contain toxic heavy metals, such as lead and mercury. Rainwater leaching through waste dumps can carry these substances into groundwater. Pesticides and fertilizers can enter waterways in runoff from agricultural lands. Organic compounds such as oil, plastics, detergents, and solvents wash into streams, rivers, and lakes through storm drains and sewers.

Oil spills are a major source of chemical pollution. For example, one

of the largest spills occurred in 1989 when the *Exxon Valdez* oil tanker accidentally released millions of liters of oil into the ocean near Alaska. Such large oil spills pollute the spill area for years, in spite of cleanup efforts. Smaller-scale oil spills occur frequently. Even more oil pollution

LAB ZONE Do It!

What Is the Quality of Local Water?

You can evaluate your local waterways and identify water pollution if you . . .

Try This

1 Take a field trip to a river, stream, lake, or other water source near your school.
2 Survey the site for water pollution. Make a table classifying the types of pollution you see.

Analyze Your Results

1 Try to identify the source of each pollutant. How might the pollutants affect the biome? The chemical cycles?
2 Write a short essay describing your observations. What can you do to help solve the problems you have identified?

LAB ZONE Do It! TEAM WORK

What Is the Quality of Local Water?

Remind students to get permission before attempting to study a water source located on private property. Check with local officials to determine if there are any hazardous wastes in the area studied. Encourage students to photograph or videotape the areas surveyed.

Analyze Your Results

1 Answers will vary according to the pollution found. Students should analyze the effect on all surrounding species, not just plants and animals, and on all chemical cycles, not just the water cycle.
2 Depending on the type of pollution observed, students may advocate picking up litter, building water treatment plants, improving drainage systems, or diverting sewage to another location.

❷ Oil coats bodies and interferes with life processes, destroys food supplies, and damages natural habitats.

SUPER READ! **Improving Vocabulary** To practice strategies for effective reading, use pages 79-80 in *Super Read!*

EVERYDAY BIOLOGY

Fluoride Inside

Many communities in the United States have fluoridated drinking water. Fluoride in water helps prevent tooth decay. Some communities add fluoride to their water supply, but other communities have naturally fluoridated water.

FIGURE 38.11

This tower at a nuclear power plant cools water before recycling it back to open water. How might warmer water adversely affect a freshwater biome? ❷

comes from waste oil spilled on land or into storm drains that empty into lakes and rivers.

Most chemical pollutants are toxic to humans and other species. Oil spills threaten water quality, destroy habitats, and kill wildlife. Compounds in pesticides and other industrial chemicals can disrupt the endocrine system. Sterility, birth defects, and rapidly declining reproductive rates have been linked to these chemical pollutants. As you learned in Chapter 37, some toxic chemicals become concentrated—and more deadly—through biological magnification.

Not all chemicals found in the water supply are harmful. Fluoride helps prevent tooth decay. In most cities, chlorine is used to purify drinking water and wastewater.

You can follow certain guidelines to help keep harmful chemicals out of your water supply. Limit the use of lawn and garden pesticides. Never pour oil, paint, or solvents down the drain, or throw pesticides or other toxic chemicals into the garbage. Instead, discard these substances at your community's household toxic-waste disposal center.

THERMAL POLLUTION

Turning up the heat

The release of heat into a body of water is called thermal pollution. Many industrial processes use large amounts of water for cooling, then release the heated water into rivers and lakes. Nuclear power plants use large amounts of water to cool reactors. Steel mills, oil refineries, and paper mills also use large amounts of water for cooling.

When heated water is released into lake and stream

FIGURE 38.10

These toxic chemicals are being handled in a responsible manner. Where can you safely dispose of such materials in your community? ❶

ecosystems, the temperature of the water increases. Temperature is a limiting factor in ecosystems. Each species has a particular range of temperatures in which it survives and reproduces best. Even a slight increase in the temperature of a river or lake can make the water uninhabitable for some species. They will die or move away to cooler waters.

Some types of fishes will not spawn in warmer-than-normal water, and some fish eggs will not hatch if the temperature is above a certain point. Warm water can also make many aquatic animals more vulnerable to disease, parasites, and the harmful effects of toxic chemicals.

Raising the water temperature lowers the water's oxygen content, because warm water holds less dissolved oxygen than cold water does. Low oxygen levels can harm fishes and other aquatic organisms or interfere with reproduction.

There are solutions to thermal pollution. Cooling towers like those in *Figure 38.11* allow heat from nuclear reactors and factories to dissipate in the air. Heated water from power plants and other industries can be pumped into artificial cooling ponds. After the

❶ Some communities have special toxic waste disposal days at specified locations. Other communities have designated places to dispose of certain kinds of toxic wastes.

❷ Warm water, introduced to cool freshwater systems, would upset the ecosystem balance and possibly do great harm to organisms living in this ecosystem.

water in the ponds has cooled down, it can be discharged safely into rivers and lakes.

BIODIVERSITY NEAR SHORE

No day at the beach

You may recall that biodiversity is an important feature in our environment. In waters near shore, biodiversity is abundant. For example, coral reefs are second only to tropical rain forests in the number of species found in a given area. Estuaries are nurseries for mollusks, fishes, and many other aquatic species. Because these wetland areas are near shorelines—and human populations—their biodiversity is particularly vulnerable to water pollution.

To survive, coral reefs need clear, shallow ocean waters. Sediment runoff can cloud the water, starving the coral by blocking the light to the symbiotic algae that live in coral tissues. Toxic chemicals in the water can kill coral or disrupt the coral ecosystem. Thermal pollution can cause coral to whiten and die. Strict environmental laws are helping to preserve some coral reefs, such as Australia's Great Barrier Reef.

Estuary ecosystems are vulnerable to pollutants carried by the rivers that flow into them. For example, pesticides and other toxic wastes have flowed into the Chesapeake Bay estuary for many years. High levels of nitrates and phosphates have led to algal blooms and oxygen depletion. Fish and crab populations, once sources of income for fishing fleets, have been devastated by pollution and disease. Oysters and other mollusks contain so many toxins that they are considered unsafe to eat. Restoration efforts are underway to improve the water quality in Chesapeake Bay.

The Everglades, a wetland area in south Florida, has been disrupted

and polluted for many years. A multimillion-dollar restoration project, which includes a huge water retention pond, has begun there. The pond will trap pollutants and release clean water into the wetlands, which are home to a wide variety of unique species.

FIGURE 38.12
Alligators and other species may benefit from efforts to preserve the Florida Everglades.

CHECKPOINT 38.3

1. Identify three types of water pollution. Where does each type come from?
2. Describe the process of modern sewage treatment. Explain the purpose of each step.
3. Critical Thinking What might happen if a container or pond holding hazardous waste were to rupture or leak?

Build on What You Know

4. What environmental factors make high levels of biodiversity possible in the waters near shore? *(Need to jog your memory? Revisit relevant concepts in Chapter 35, Section 35.4.)*

Chapter 38 People and the Environment **927**

Explain

Remind students that tropical rain forests are the most diverse land biomes on Earth. Tell students that coral reefs are sometimes called the "tropical rain forests of the sea" because these areas also have great biodiversity.

3 ASSESS

Evaluate Understanding

To assess students' understanding of water in the biosphere, ask:

■ **What are some ways in which chemical pollutants enter the water supply?** (Through dumping of industrial wastes, rainwater leaching, oil spills, and runoffs from agricultural lands treated with fertilizers and pesticides)

■ **What is thermal pollution?** (The release of heat into a body of water)

Reteach

As a class, develop a table that identifies the major causes of water pollution and their effects. Include in the table information on sediment, sewage, chemical pollution, and heat pollution. Review the completed table.

SUPER READ! **Identifying Cause and Effect** To practice strategies for effective reading, use pages 75-76 in *Super Read!*

CHECKPOINT 38.3

1. Thermal pollution: industrial processes; sediment: soil erosion; sewage: dumping untreated sewage into waterways
2. Filtering and settling removes solid material; bacteria break down biodegradable waste; sedimentation removes bacteria and sludge; advanced treatment removes heavy metals and other chemicals.

3. **Predicting** Hazardous waste could soak into the ground and contaminate groundwater. Plants in the area could be harmed by absorbing the wastes; they could in turn harm consumers.
4. Diversity of light, water temperature, salinity, water movement, and nutrient levels

Use the Visual

Have students study the photograph that opens the section. Explain that scientists have discovered that too much exposure to the ultraviolet (UV) rays of the sun causes skin cancer in humans.

Check Prior Knowledge

To assess students' knowledge of gases in the atmosphere, ask:

■ **How are the nutrients organisms need to live and grow recycled in ecosystems?**
(Through the processes involved in the carbon, nitrogen, and water cycles)

 Improving Vocabulary
To practice strategies for effective reading, use pages 79-80 in *Super Read!*

Teacher Demo

Place thermometers into two identical containers of colored water. Leave one container open to the air and cover the other with plastic wrap. Place both containers on a window sill that receives direct sunlight. Read out the temperatures of the two containers. Explain that the temperature difference results from the phenomenon known as the greenhouse effect, the trapping of heat near the Earth's surface.

38.4 Air in the Biosphere

What you'll learn

IDEAS
• To identify several sources of air pollution
• To describe the cause and effects of acid rain, global warming, and ozone layer depletion

WORDS
acid rain, greenhouse effect, global warming, chlorofluorocarbons

Dark shark
Humans are not the only animals who need protection from the burning effects of the sun. The sun darkens the skin of other animals, too. Researchers recently discovered that when hammerhead sharks were moved to water with increased light, their backs turned a deep brownish-black. Although sharks seem to have "tanning" ability, they do not seem to get skin cancer.

AIR QUALITY

Breathe free and easy

Take a deep breath and exhale. You probably do not think of air as a natural resource, but the gases in air (O_2, CO_2, N_2) are essential natural resources. Recall that the carbon cycle and the nitrogen cycle are both vital chemical cycles. Air is a renewable resource, but harmful substances in air can make it an unusable resource. Unfortunately, air pollution is a serious problem all over the world.

The main source of air pollution is the burning of fossil fuels. Smog (from the words SMoke and fOG) is a haze of pollutants that hangs in the air above many cities. Smog contains several harmful chemicals, including nitrogen dioxide, carbon monoxide, sulfur dioxide, and ozone. Smog also may contain particulates—tiny particles of soot, ash, or dust.

Volcanic eruptions are a natural source of air pollution. A major eruption, such as the 1991 eruption of Mount Pinatubo in the Philippines, releases large amounts of particulates. Particulates block sunlight and can cause a noticeable cooling of Earth's surface. Volcanoes also release chemical pollutants, such as sulfur dioxide.

Air pollution can cause respiratory problems, burning and watery eyes,

and increased susceptibility to disease. Permanent lung damage can result from breathing polluted air over a long period of time. Air pollution contributes to an estimated 50,000 deaths per year in the United States.

Industries can reduce air pollution by switching to fuels that emit fewer harmful substances. Pollution-control devices, such as scrubbers on smokestacks, can help reduce the amount of air pollution caused by industry. Scrubbers remove pollutants before they are released into the air. In the late 1960s, Japan's sulfur dioxide levels were some of the highest in the world. By installing scrubbers on industrial smokestacks, Japan was able to cut sulfur dioxide levels by 75 percent in just fifteen years.

The passing and enforcement of laws can also reduce air pollution. In the United States, the 1990 Clean Air Act Amendments set aggressive standards for reducing air pollution. For example, according to this legislation, by the year 2000 sulfur dioxide levels must be reduced to half of what they were in 1980.

You can help reduce pollution by reducing motor vehicle exhaust. Walk, bike, carpool, or use mass transit. At home, try to use less electricity—it is primarily produced by power plants that burn fossil fuels.

FIGURE 38.13

Idling commuters are adding to this city's smog problem. What is smog?

ACID PRECIPITATION

Deadly rain

Some air pollutants do more than irritate your eyes and lungs. The nitrogen dioxide and sulfur dioxide in smog dissolve in water to form nitric acid and sulfuric acid. These strong acids fall to earth as **acid rain.**

How acidic is acid rain? Normal rain is slightly acidic, with a pH of 5.0 to 5.6. Rain in some parts of the eastern United States has a pH close to 4.3. This decrease of about 1 on the pH scale means that rain is ten times more acidic than it should be! Some areas of the world receive acid rain with a pH of 2.3 or less, rain that is nearly a thousand times more acidic than normal.

Acid rain has damaged many ecosystems in North America, Europe, and Asia. Acid rain changes soil chemistry, disrupting chemical cycles. Some of the greatest effects of acid rain are seen in rivers and lakes. When snowpack formed from acid rain melts and flows into bodies of water, the organisms living in these rivers and lakes are often unable to survive the high acidity. The tissues of most organisms, including trees, are very sensitive to strong acid levels. Metal and limestone can also be damaged by

acid rain. Buildings, bridges, and statues are all vulnerable. Acid rain can cause these structures to weather quickly and fall apart. The most effective way to reduce acid rain is to reduce emissions of nitrogen dioxide and sulfur dioxide. Scientists predict

FIGURE 38.14
Acid rain can damage statues and destroy forests. How is acid rain formed?

LAB ZONE · Do It! · bioSURF

Where Is Air Pollution?

You can determine the numbers and types of air particulates in your school if you . . .

Try This

1 Obtain the following: five microscope slides, petroleum jelly, five petri dishes with lids, and a hand lens. Smear the center of each slide with a thin layer of petroleum jelly. Place each slide inside a petri dish, jelly side up.
2 Take four of the petri dishes to four different areas in your school. Remove the cover from each dish. Keep the fifth dish covered as a control.
3 Three to five days later, retrieve the slides. Examine the slides with a hand lens. Count the number of particulates on each slide and record your results.

Analyze Your Results

1 Identify five particulates that landed on the slides. Which of these would you classify as pollutants? Explain.
2 Describe the locations you chose. Which location showed the greatest number of air particulates? The least?

② TEACH

⊕ Chemistry

Help students understand how acid rain is formed by showing them the chemical equations. Begin with sulfur from smokestacks reacting with oxygen in the air to form sulfur trioxide: $2S + 3O_2 \rightarrow 2SO_3$. Sulfur trioxide reacts with water vapor to form sulfuric acid: $SO_3 + H_2O \rightarrow H_2SO_4$. Sulfur dioxide from burning coal reacts with water vapor to produce sulfurous acid: $SO_2 + H_2O \rightarrow H_2SO_3$.

LAB ZONE · Do It! · TEAM WORK

Where Is Air Pollution?

Notify school officials and custodial staff of this experiment. To reduce the amount of materials needed, have students work in groups of four or five. Before students begin, you may wish to have them observe common particulates with a compound microscope and sketch their observations. They can use their sketches to help them identify the particulates on their slides.

Analyze Your Results

Answers will vary. Some students may be alarmed at the results. You may want to encourage these students to investigate air quality at other locations for comparison or to investigate local regulations and the Clean Air Act.

that reducing air pollution caused by fossil-fuel consumption will result in the reduction of acid rain levels.

THE GREENHOUSE EFFECT

Heating up

Carbon dioxide (CO_2) and other gases in the atmosphere act like a blanket over Earth. They hold in heat from the sun that would otherwise radiate back into space. The trapping of heat in the atmosphere is the **greenhouse effect.** The greenhouse effect is a natural phenomenon that has warmed Earth enough to make life possible. Without it, Earth's surface temperature would average about –18°C.

CO_2 and other heat-trapping gases, such as methane (CH_4), are called greenhouse gases. The amount of CO_2 in Earth's atmosphere has increased more than 21 percent since the year 1750. This increase is a result of the burning of fossil fuels. As CO_2 levels increase in the atmosphere, the greenhouse effect gets stronger. The result may be **global warming,** an increase in Earth's average surface temperature.

If CO_2 levels keep increasing at the present rate, scientists hypothesize Earth's temperature may increase by 2°C to 4°C by the year 2050. Scientists predict that global warming of just a few degrees could bring about major climate changes. It could cause the oceans to warm and expand, raising sea levels by about 50 centimeters. If the polar ice caps melt, sea levels could rise by many meters, flooding

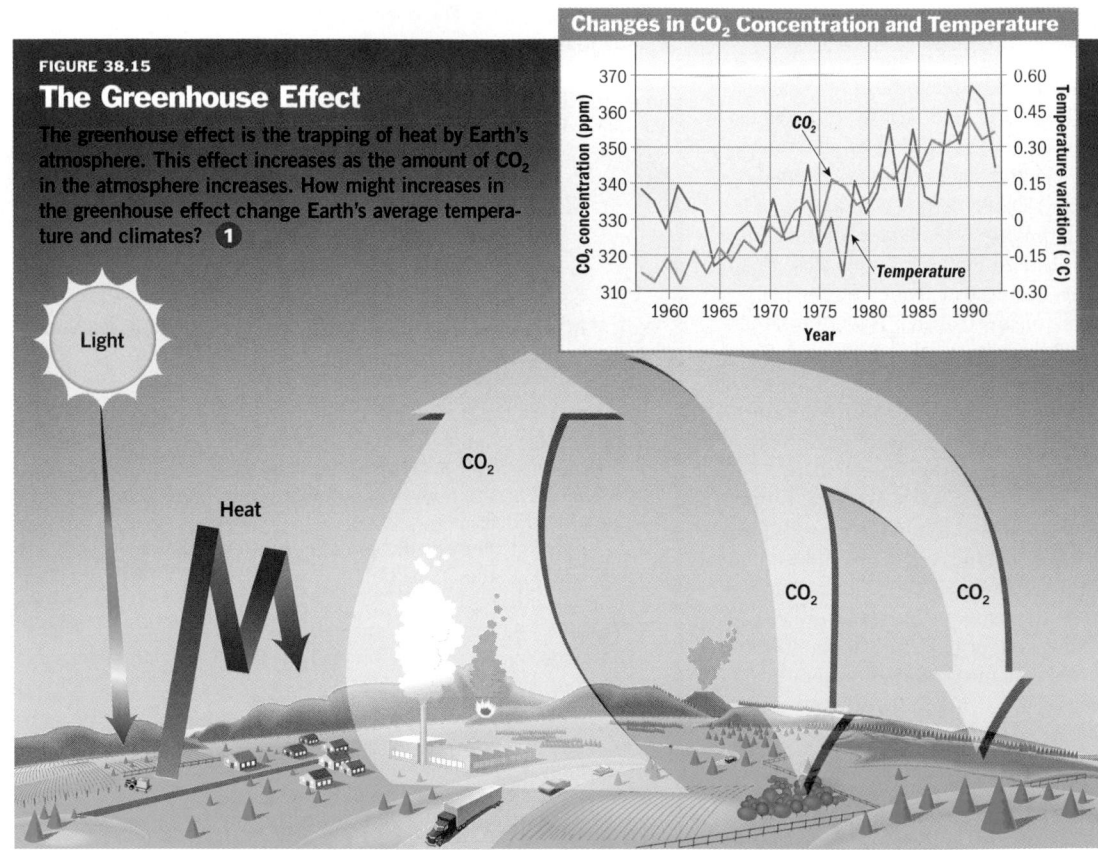

FIGURE 38.15

The Greenhouse Effect

The greenhouse effect is the trapping of heat by Earth's atmosphere. This effect increases as the amount of CO_2 in the atmosphere increases. How might increases in the greenhouse effect change Earth's average temperature and climates? ❶

Changes in CO_2 Concentration and Temperature

FACTS AND FIGURES

Swedish scientist Svante Arrhenius (1859-1927) was the first to use the term "greenhouse effect." However, the phenomenon was predicted as early as 1827 by French mathematician Joseph Fourier.

❶ Higher temperatures could increase evaporation, change precipitation patterns, disrupt climatic patterns needed for food production, speed up ice and snow melting, and increase the number of hurricanes and tornadoes.

coastal cities and causing low-lying islands to disappear. Global warming could change rainfall patterns and increase the amount of violent weather, such as hurricanes and tornadoes, that occurs.

Reducing the buildup of CO_2 and other greenhouse gases can prevent or slow global warming. This reduction can be accomplished by reducing the use of fossil fuels. Preserving forests can also help slow global warming. Recall that trees and plants remove CO_2 from the atmosphere.

THE OZONE LAYER

Saving the protective shield

Between 20 and 50 kilometers (km) above Earth, in a part of the atmosphere called the stratosphere, is a global sunscreen—the ozone layer. The ozone layer is a band of ozone molecules (O_3) that shields Earth from much of the sun's harmful ultraviolet (UV) radiation. Worldwide, the ozone layer is "thinning" as the total amount of ozone decreases. At certain times of year, enormous holes form in the ozone layer, particularly over Antarctica and the North Pole.

The main cause of the thinning of the ozone layer is a group of chlorine-containing chemicals known as **chlorofluorocarbons** (CLOR-oh-FLOR-oh-kar-bunz), or CFCs. These odorless, noncorrosive compounds were once widely used as propellants in aerosol cans and in the production of plastic foam. CFCs were also used as coolants in air conditioners, refrigerators, and freezers. In the lower atmosphere, CFCs are stable. But when CFCs are released into the environment, they are carried up into the stratosphere. In the stratosphere, they are bombarded by ultraviolet rays and they break apart. This process releases chlorine atoms that react with ozone and deplete the ozone layer.

Depletion of the ozone layer increases Earth's exposure to UV radiation. This exposure can cause cataracts and skin cancer. It may also decrease resistance to disease. In areas of the Southern Hemisphere where ozone depletion is severe, cases of skin cancer and cataracts are increasing. Increased UV radiation can lead to reductions in crop yields and disruptions of food webs.

CFCs have been banned in the United States and many other nations. Substitutes are being developed for some types of CFCs. However, CFCs persist in the atmosphere for many years. So even though CFC use has dropped dramatically, ozone destruction will continue for many years.

CHECKPOINT 38.4

1. What causes air pollution? Describe at least two sources.
2. What effects do acid rain, global warming, and ozone depletion have on the environment?
3. **Critical Thinking** What are the three types of invaluable natural resources? Why are they important?

Build on What You Know

4. How can ultraviolet radiation cause cancer? *(Need to jog your memory? Revisit relevant concepts in Chapter 8, Section 8.4.)*

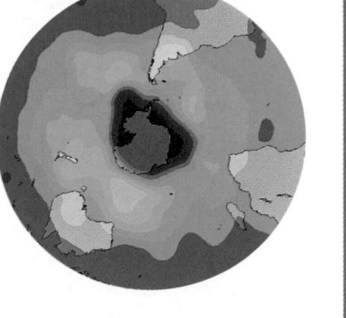

FIGURE 38.16
This computer-enhanced satellite image shows the ozone hole over Antarctica. What causes the ozone hole? ❷

Why are land, water, and air invaluable natural resources?

Chapter 38 People and the Environment **931**

Health

In addition to skin cancer, UV light has been linked to several kinds of eye disorders. People who spend a great deal of time outdoors are encouraged to wear sunglasses that have polarized lenses, which filter out some of the sun's harmful UV rays.

3 ASSESS

Evaluate Understanding

To assess students' understanding of the section, ask:

- **How does the burning of fossil fuels pollute the air?** (Burning fossil fuels sends harmful chemicals and particulates into the air.)
- **How is acid rain harmful?** (It damages trees and other plants, harms aquatic organisms, and can destroy statues and buildings made of limestone or metals.)
- **How is the greenhouse effect related to global warming?** (The greenhouse effect keeps high levels of carbon dioxide in the atmosphere, leading to global warming.)
- **Why is the depletion of the ozone layer a cause for concern?** (The ozone layer shields Earth from much of the sun's harmful UV radiation.)

Reteach

Work with students to develop a concept map describing the quality of air in the biosphere. Make sure that all the ideas and words listed on page 928 are included on the concept map.

CHECKPOINT 38.4

1. Smog from burning fossil fuels; volcanic eruptions
2. Acid rain can harm soil, water, and organisms. Global warming could cause major climate changes, disrupting ecosystems. Ozone depletion could cause increased exposure to UV radiation.
3. **Applying** Air, water, soil; air is vital for respiration; water is necessary for biological processes; plants grow in soil.
4. UV light can cause mutations in genes. If these genes control cell growth and specialization, cancer can result.

❷ CFCs in the stratosphere release chlorine atoms that react with ozone, depleting the ozone layer.

931

①ENGAGE

Consider the Big Idea

Have students read The Big Idea! at the top of the page. Explain that a knowledge of biology is crucial for finding solutions to environmental problems.

Use the Visual

Have students study the photograph that opens the section. Explain that breeding organisms in captivity is one way people are trying to save some species from extinction. Ask:

- **What other things might people do to save specific species from extinction?** (Likely responses: avoid destroying the habitats of organisms, limit hunting and trapping, use pesticides sparingly)

Quick Activity TEAM WORK

Divide the class into small groups. Have each group come up with a slogan for a bumper sticker, button, or T-shirt to encourage people to preserve and protect the biosphere. Have groups share their slogans.

SUPER READ! **Improving Vocabulary** To practice strategies for effective reading, use pages 79-80 in *Super Read!*

❶ DDT was banned; peregrine falcons were bred in captivity and then released into the wild.

THE BIG IDEA! Humans can affect the future of the biosphere in a positive way. 38.5

38.5 Environmental Success Stories

What you'll learn

IDEAS
- To describe how humans have reversed some negative effects on the environment
- To explain how humans can have a positive effect on the environment

Ferreting out black-footed ferrets
The black-footed ferret was once a common sight in America's western plains. Their habitat was destroyed, however, and the ferrets were considered extinct until 18 ferrets were found in the 1970s. Bred in captivity, black-footed ferrets now number in the hundreds and have been returned to their habitat in prairie-dog towns.

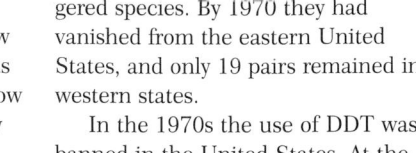

FIGURE 38.17
Peregrine falcons, such as this falcon living in Los Angeles, were a rare sight in the 1970s. They have since been brought back from the brink of extinction. How was this achieved? ❶

PEREGRINE FALCONS RETURN

Saved from extinction

In this chapter you have learned how humans' use of natural resources has changed our environment. People now realize that these changes frequently have negative effects on biodiversity, chemical cycles, food webs, and the stability of ecosystems. In recent years, many people have worked hard to avoid or reverse these negative effects on our environment. Some of this work has focused on alternative uses of natural resources—for example, recycling instead of disposing of waste. Other work has successfully restored damaged ecosystems, such as those of the black-footed ferrets and the peregrine falcons.

Peregrine falcons once hunted in the skies over much of North America. As predators at the top of a food chain, peregrine falcons ingested DDT, a pesticide that was present in the tissues of their prey. Due to biological magnification, the DDT became concentrated in the falcons' tissues. The DDT caused the falcons to lay eggs with very thin shells, which broke before hatching.

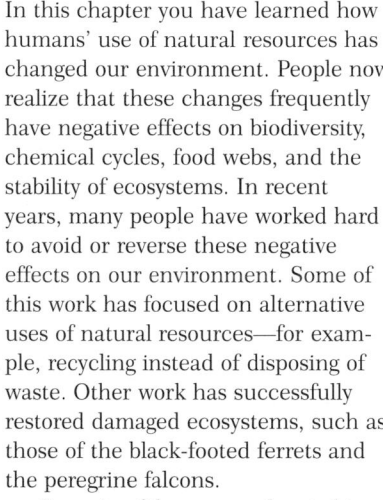

Unable to successfully reproduce, peregrine falcons became an endangered species. By 1970 they had vanished from the eastern United States, and only 19 pairs remained in western states.

In the 1970s the use of DDT was banned in the United States. At the same time, conservation groups began breeding peregrine falcons in captivity. When young falcons were old enough to survive on their own, they were released into the wild at selected sites all over the United States and Canada.

Gradually, the peregrine falcon population began to increase. By 1991, conservation groups stopped releasing captive-raised birds in the eastern United States. They were hopeful that the 90 or more pairs of falcons that had become established there would reproduce at a steady rate.

By 1996 more than 1000 breeding pairs of peregrine falcons were living in the continental United States. Not only did the birds make a remarkable comeback, but a surprising number have become adapted to big-city life. In the wild, peregrine falcons are

932 *Unit 9 Organisms and the Environment*

STUDENT RESOURCES

From the Teacher's Resource Package, use:
- Section Review 38.5, Activity Recordsheet 38-3, Vocabulary Review 38, and Chapter 38 Tests from Unit 9 Review Module
- Consumer Applications 38-1

TECHNOLOGY RESOURCES

Relevant technology resources include:
- Spanish Student Edition CD-ROM
- Teacher's Resource Planner CD-ROM
- Interactive Earth CD-ROM
- Biology Alive! Video Series
- TestWorks CD-ROM: Chapter 38 Tests

cliff-nesting birds. In cities, they nest on skyscrapers—hunting pigeons and starlings from high above the city streets. New York City alone has 15 nesting pairs of peregrine falcons. The successful return of the peregrine falcon has caused its status to be upgraded from endangered to threatened.

THE GREEN BELT MOVEMENT

Forests from seven trees

In 1977 a young Kenyan woman named Wangari Maathai planted seven trees in her nation's capital of Nairobi in honor of World Environment Day. She went on to found a nationwide reforestation program in Kenya called the Green Belt Movement.

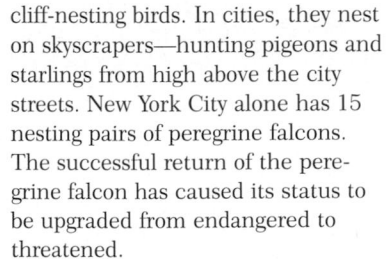

The Green Belt Movement has three main goals. The first goal is to halt erosion and desertification in rural Kenya. The second goal is to promote tree planting for firewood. The third goal is to educate people about environmental conservation and sustainable development.

Tree seedlings were made available to many villages, and women and children were paid a small fee to plant them. Tree nurseries were set up to raise more seedlings. People were educated about the causes and effects of ecological destruction, deforestation, and desertification.

Within 10 years the Green Belt Movement grew into a self-help community action program that involved 80,000 women and 500,000 children. By 1990 more than 10 million trees had been planted. The long-term goal is to plant one tree for each of Kenya's 27 million inhabitants.

In 1991 Wangari Maathai was awarded the Africa Prize for creating a successful program that combined community development with environmental protection. The Green Belt

Movement has helped thousands of people become self-reliant while protecting their environment. The success of the Green Belt Movement has led to the creation of similar reforestation programs in more than a dozen other African countries.

FIGURE 38.18
Wangari Maathai (left) began the Green Belt Movement in an effort to halt the desertification of Kenya.

SUPER READ!

LAB ZONE **Think About It!** **bioSURF**

Making Decisions About Land Use

The use of community-owned land can be a controversial issue. You can consider both arguments—development vs. open space—by walking around your community. Make a scale map of your neighborhood, shading the areas that are open spaces. Record the approximate percentage of land that is open space. In addition, do library research to determine what species, if any, would be affected by building on this open space.

Analyzing Your Results

1 If the open space in your neighborhood was chosen as the site of a much-needed community medical clinic, would you be in favor of or opposed to its development?
2 What would be the economic advantages of building a clinic on this site? What would be the economic disadvantages?
3 How would the community ecosystem be affected by building a clinic?

② TEACH

Discuss

You may wish to share with students information about Wangari Maathai's background. After completing high school in Kenya, she came to the United States to pursue her college education, receiving a B.S. degree in biology from Mount St. Scholastica College in Kansas. When she received her master's degree from the University of Pittsburgh she became the first woman in all of eastern and central Africa to obtain an advanced degree. Maathai later returned to her homeland, where she received a doctorate in veterinary medicine from the University of Nairobi.

SUPER READ! **Improving Vocabulary** To practice strategies for effective reading, use pages 79-80 in *Super Read!*

LAB ZONE **Think About It!**

Making Decisions About Land Use

Analyzing Your Results

You may wish to organize a debate between students who favor building the clinic and students who favor open space. Have students support their arguments with factual data they research.

MEETING DIVERSE NEEDS

Gifted Have students research and profile an environmental group or person working to preserve Earth's biodiversity. Have students prepare oral presentations to share with the class.

In the Community

Every state has some species that are considered threatened or endangered. Students who have access to the Internet can obtain a list of the threatened and endangered species in their state at the following Internet address:

http://nceet.snre.umich.edu

Suggest that interested students work together to start their own environmental awareness group at school or organize an Earth Day fair.

Build Writing Skills

Ask students to research a threatened or endangered species in their state. Have them write a "Letter to the Editor" in which they explain what individuals can do to help save the species from extinction.

Class Activity

TEAM WORK

Divide the class into groups. Have each group select an environmental problem of interest to them. The problem can be local, national, or global. Have group members work together to design a public information package that includes a poster, bumper sticker, a public service announcement, press release, or similar promotional materials.

IN THE COMMUNITY
Your Success Story

You can participate in environmental success stories in your own community. Find out if efforts are being made to restore a threatened habitat or to protect or reintroduce an endangered species. Environmental organizations such as the Audubon Society and the National Wildlife Federation, as well as outdoor recreation groups, will know where your help can make a difference to the environment. Keep a journal of your research and participation. You can access *http://ecology.biosurf.com* to find out about other inspiring environmental success stories.

COSTA RICA'S FORESTS

A catalog of 500,000

Costa Rica, sandwiched between Nicaragua and Panama, is a small Central American country about the size of West Virginia. Along Costa Rica's northwestern coast, in the lowlands of the Guanacaste National Park, lies one of the few remaining patches of tropical dry forest. Unlike a rain forest, a tropical dry forest consists of sparse, flat-topped trees and an understory of thorny shrubs. Tropical dry forests once stretched along the Pacific coast from Mexico to Panama. The small sections that remain are far more rare—and more endangered—than tropical rain forests.

Daniel Janzen, a professor of biology at the University of Pennsylvania, has devoted much of his life to protecting and restoring about 750 square km of tropical dry forest in the Guanacaste region. Since 1963, he and his wife have raised more than $10 million for the restoration project. Their project, like the Kenyan Green Belt Movement, has involved local people at every step of the way. Farmers living nearby were hired to sow tree seeds and to plant new tree seedlings. Education programs in local schools were designed to teach young people about the forest and how important it is to the region.

Much progress has been made in restoring Guanacaste's tropical dry forest. But it is a project that will probably take more than 100 years to complete. By involving the local people, including the children, the project can continue for the time it will take to restore the ecosystem. The rare ecosystem will continue to thrive under the care of the people who live in and around it.

In 1989 Professor Janzen also helped found the Costa Rican

FIGURE 38.19
This Costa Rican tropical dry forest may be more endangered than tropical rain forests. How do the rain forests and dry forests differ? ❶

---

❶ The rain forests differ in their vegetation. Have students refer to a photograph of a tropical rain forest on page 864 to compare the two forests.

❷ The inventory of biological resources and samples of various species will help pharmaceutical companies in their search for new medicines.

FIGURE 38.20
This rain forest preserve in Costa Rica is being cataloged for such diverse species as poison arrow frogs (below) and quetzal birds (left). Why are pharmaceutical companies interested in this project? ❷

National Biodiversity Institute (INBio). He recruited and trained hundreds of Costa Ricans to collect, identify, and store specimens of the country's approximately 500,000 species of plants and animals. The result of INBio's project will be a complete inventory of Costa Rica's biological resources—a catalog of the country's rich biodiversity.

Some of the organisms being collected may be sources of unique chemical compounds. These compounds may be used to create new medicines and other useful products. Recently, INBio signed an unusual contract with the world's largest pharmaceutical company. INBio agreed to supply the drug company with samples of plant and insect species from Costa Rican forests. If any compounds in those organisms are used to make new drugs or other products, the drug company agreed to return a percentage of the profits to

Costa Rica. There the money will be used to pay for other conservation projects and to protect the country's rich biodiversity.

CHECKPOINT 38.5

1. What human efforts have reversed the negative effects of humans on the environment?

2. What human efforts make it possible to preserve and protect the Earth's environments?

3. Critical Thinking What role does economic development play in environmental protection? How can it be successfully balanced with the needs of living things?

Build on What You Know

4. What have you learned about the interactions of living things with one another and with their environments? *(Need to jog your memory? Revisit relevant concepts in Chapters 1 through 38.)*

What type of effects can humans have on the biosphere? **?**

Chapter 38 People and the Environment **935**

❸ **ASSESS**

Evaluate Understanding

To assess students' understanding of environmental movements, ask:

- **What are some ways humans can have a positive impact on the future of the biosphere?** (By becoming involved in organizations that are trying to save threatened and endangered species, by practicing conservation to ensure that resources last, and by not polluting the environment)
- **Why do Earth's inhabitants form a web of life?** (Responses should reflect the idea that organisms interact with each other and with the abiotic parts of the environment. Since all organisms interact in some way with other organisms, a complex web of life is formed.)

Reteach

Rewrite the section objectives as questions on the board. As a class, discuss the information that is needed to answer each question. Have students cite specific examples to answer each question. Challenge students to describe other ways to protect the environment that were not addressed in the section.

CHECKPOINT 38.5

1. Breeding endangered species, tree planting, restoring forests

2. Educating people about conservation and sustainable development, banning the use of pesticides, and cataloging and respecting biodiversity

3. Making generalizations Economic development can deplete natural resources and conflict with environmental protection. Sustainable development aids economic development in the long run by preserving natural resources and it also helps meet the needs of living things.

4. All living things form the web of life and depend on the web and the environment for survival.

TEAM WORK Recycling Paper

SAFETY FIRST!

Have students cover their work area with newspapers and immediately clean up any spills that occur. Students should wear a laboratory coat or apron and safety goggles throughout the activity.

Hypothesis Help

Likely hypotheses will state that it is possible to recycle newspaper using simple techniques.

Lab Extension

Directed

Have students shred a sheet of newspaper and add it to a mixture of 300 mL of water and 300 mL of corn starch. Have them mix the ingredients with an eggbeater until the mixture (slurry) is cloudy and smooth, pour it into a square pan, and add water so that the slurry is 8-9 cm deep. Make sure they mix well to evenly distribute the fibers. Then have them dip the screen into the slurry at an angle and level it to rest on the bottom of the pan. Have them slosh the slurry back and forth over the screen. Students can then lift the screen slowly over the pan, letting most of the liquid drain. The screen should then be placed fiber-side up on a sheet of blotting paper, with another sheet of blotting paper on top. Tell students to repeat this step to blot out the liquid and use a rolling pin to squeeze out remaining liquid. Students can let the recycled paper dry between the blotters and then peel the blotters off when the paper is dry.

936

LAB ZONE Investigate It!

Recycling Paper

WHAT YOU WILL DO Develop a method of recycling paper

SKILLS YOU WILL USE Collecting and recording data, observing, estimating

WHAT YOU WILL NEED Sheets of newspaper, large mixing bowl, eggbeater, water, liquid laundry starch, hand lens, large square pan, screen, four sheets of blotting paper, rolling pin

Propose a Hypothesis

Propose a hypothesis about how paper is recycled. Develop a procedure using the materials listed. Consider the following information when developing your procedure: Liquid laundry starch acts as a glue, and the screen and rolling pin can be used to remove excess liquid.

Conduct Your Experiment

1 After planning your procedure, conduct your experiment. You may want to conduct the experiment more than once to determine the optimum proportion of the three ingredients: newspaper, water, and starch.
2 Use the hand lens to examine your paper mixture at different times throughout your experiment. Record your results.

Analyze Your Data

1 Why is liquid laundry starch needed in this process? Why is water needed?
2 Dense paper has many fibers arranged tightly together. Lighter-weight paper has fibers more loosely arranged. Was your recycled paper more or less dense than the original newspaper?

Draw Conclusions

1 Would you want to read a book that was printed on this type of recycled paper? Write a paragraph that describes how your recycled paper could be improved.
2 As a class, discuss the following question: Do you think you could use this process to recycle plastics?

Design a Related Experiment

Design a procedure for recycling another material that would result in more dense and less dense recycled paper.

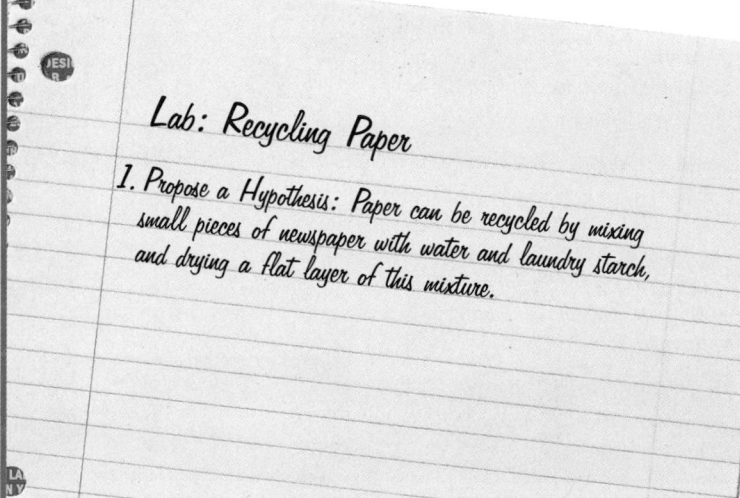

Lab: Recycling Paper

1. Propose a Hypothesis: Paper can be recycled by mixing small pieces of newspaper with water and laundry starch, and drying a flat layer of this mixture.

Analyze Your Data

1 The liquid laundry starch acts as a glue to hold the paper fibers together. The water acts to reduce and homogenize the newspaper fibers.
2 The paper is likely to be less dense than the original newspaper.

Draw Conclusions

1 Accept all reasonable responses.
2 Students are likely to conclude that this process would not be appropriate for recycling plastic. Have students discuss why this process would not work on plastic; for example, water could not break down plastic fibers as it does newspaper fibers.

Chapter 38 Review

 **THE BIG IDEA!**

38.1 Human use of essential natural resources can affect the web of life.
38.2–38.4 Land, water, and air are invaluable natural resources.
38.5 Humans can affect the future of the biosphere in a positive way.

Sum It Up

Use the following summary to review the main concepts in this chapter.

38.1 Earth's Resources

- Some of Earth's resources are renewable and can be replenished by natural processes. Other resources are limited and nonrenewable.
- In order to preserve natural resources, humans need to practice sustainable development—control the rate at which the resources are used.
- Humans are part of an ecosystem; we can change our behaviors to preserve the quality and quantity of Earth's natural resources.

38.2 Land in the Biosphere

- Farmers and ranchers need soils that retain water and nutrients.
- Paper recycling and careful lumber harvesting can help minimize deforestation.
- Mining nonrenewable mineral resources can destroy habitats and cause pollution.
- Each alternative to fossil fuels has advantages and disadvantages.
- Reducing solid wastes frees up the land used by landfills, which can threaten groundwater.
- Habitat destruction threatens biodiversity.

38.3 Water in the Biosphere

- Soil erosion contributes to water pollution, as does the release of untreated sewage.

- Chemical pollutants can threaten Earth's water supply. Oil spills are a major source of chemical pollution.
- Aquatic species are sensitive to thermal pollution. Coral reefs and estuaries are especially vulnerable to all forms of water pollution.

38.4 Air in the Biosphere

- Emission devices on cars and scrubbers on smokestacks help control air pollution.
- Acid rain damages ecosystems, changing soil chemicals; it also damages structures such as buildings.
- Reducing the level of greenhouse gases can help prevent or reduce global warming.
- CFCs damage the ozone layer, which protects organisms from UV radiation.

38.5 Environmental Success Stories

- The banning of DDT helped save peregrine falcons from extinction.
- The Green Belt Movement in Kenya is aimed at reforestation and helping to stop erosion and desertification.
- People in Costa Rica are working to save the endangered tropical dry forest.

Use Terms and Concepts

Use each of the following words or terms in a complete sentence. If you need to review a meaning, turn to the page indicated.

renewable resource (p. 918)
nonrenewable resource (p. 918)
sustainable development (p. 919)

soil erosion (p. 920)
desertification (p. 920)
deforestation (p. 921)
biodegradable (p. 922)
nonbiodegradable (p. 922)

acid rain (p. 929)
greenhouse effect (p. 930)
global warming (p. 930)
chlorofluorocarbons (p. 931)

Chapter 38 People and the Environment **937**

Review the Big Ideas

Before students begin the Chapter Review, you may wish to discuss main concepts from the Big Ideas in Chapter 38. All organisms on this planet, including humans, share Earth's resources, many of which are nonrenewable. For this reason, it is important for humans to use these resources wisely and avoid activities that pollute air and water. By practicing conservation and protecting the environment, humans can affect the future of the biosphere in a positive way and ensure that resources are available for all the organisms that interact to form a web of life.

Answers

1. nonbiodegradable
2. chlorofluorocarbons
3. sustainable development
4. deforestation
5. global warming
6. desertification
7. greenhouse effect
8. True
9. False; renewable
10. False; sulfur dioxide
11. True
12. True
13. Runoff may contain toxic chemicals such as pesticides as well as fertilizers, which can promote excess algae and plant growth.
14. Volcanoes release sulfur dioxide.
15. Suspended soil particles in water block sunlight. Particles that settle to the bottom can bury bottom-dwelling organisms.
16. Sea levels might rise and submerge land because the oceans might warm and expand and because water stored in polar ice caps might melt.
17. Tightly-packed wastes do not contain enough oxygen for decomposers to survive.
18. Bacteria decompose biodegradable waste.
19. Deforestation is the removal of large numbers of trees from a forest; desertification is the reduction of a soil's ability to support plant growth; soil erosion is the removal of soil by wind and water. Deforestation removes barriers to wind and roots, which can retain soil. Soil erosion is one cause of desertification.
20. CFCs will persist in the atmosphere for many years.
21. Answers will vary but students should note that

Use Your Word Power

MATCHING **Write the term from the list of key terms that best matches each of the phrases below.**

1. Wastes that cannot be recycled by natural processes.

2. Compounds that are capable of destroying ozone when released into the atmosphere.

3. The use of natural resources at a rate that does not deplete them.

4. A practice responsible for the destruction of many tropical habitats.

5. The predicted increase in Earth's average surface temperature.

6. The reduction in a soil's ability to retain water and nutrients.

7. The retention of atmospheric heat that would normally radiate back into space.

TRUE-FALSE **Write true if the statement is true. If the statement is false, replace the underlined word(s) to make the statement true.**

8. Recycling can help prevent <u>deforestation</u>.

9. Forests are <u>nonrenewable</u> resources.

10. Nitrogen oxide and <u>carbon dioxide</u> dissolve in water to form acid rain.

11. Contour plowing and terracing can help prevent <u>soil erosion</u>.

12. <u>Biodegradable wastes</u> can be composted to form humus.

Show What You Know

13. What danger does runoff from agricultural lands pose to living organisms?

14. How do volcanoes contribute to acid rain?

15. Describe an effect that soil erosion can have on aquatic organisms.

16. What effect might global warming have on coastal communities?

---

17. Explain why biodegradable wastes do not necessarily decompose at landfills.

18. What role do bacteria play at sewage treatment plants?

19. Describe the processes of deforestation, desertification, and soil erosion. What impact can these processes have on each other?

20. Explain why ozone destruction continues even though chlorofluorocarbons are banned.

21. **Make a Concept Map** Create a concept map that identifies different types of pollutants and shows how they affect air, water, and land.

Take It Further

22. **Applying Concepts** Gardeners who construct and keep a compost heap periodically turn over the materials in the pile. How does this action promote decomposition?

23. **Developing a Hypothesis** Ecologists are concerned about the effects of habitat fragmentation. For example, when land is cleared for agriculture or for homes, isolated sections of the original habitat may remain. How might fragmentation or a reduction in the size of an ecosystem affect its inhabitants?

24. **Applying Concepts** Explain why forest ecosystems can be described as a threatened habitat, despite the fact that trees are a renewable resource.

25. **Developing a Hypothesis** Different grades of coal contain different amounts of sulfur. Explain why burning low-sulfur coal can reduce acid rain.

26. **Designing an Experiment** Determine which commonly discarded items contribute most to the bulk of solid waste. Design an experiment to find out which of these bulky items are biodegradable and, if they are, how long they might take to degrade in a typical landfill.

---

pollutants such as pesticides affect more than one part of the environment.

22. Turning the pile aerates the heap, which facilitates decomposition. It also dissipates the heat produced by decomposition that has been building up in the center of the pile.

23. Species that need large territories would be endangered. For example,

bears could be killed crossing highways to expand their range. Smaller populations are subject to genetic drift and more vulnerable to environmental change.

24. Forest ecosystems contain many species other than trees.

25. Combustion of coal with sulfur produces sulfur dioxide, which dissolves in

27. Interpreting a Graph The graph below illustrates how thermal pollution might affect fish. What happens to the oxygen (O_2) consumption of fish as the temperature of the water rises? What happens to the O_2 content of the water as its temperature rises? Why might a fish become less active as the water temperature rises?

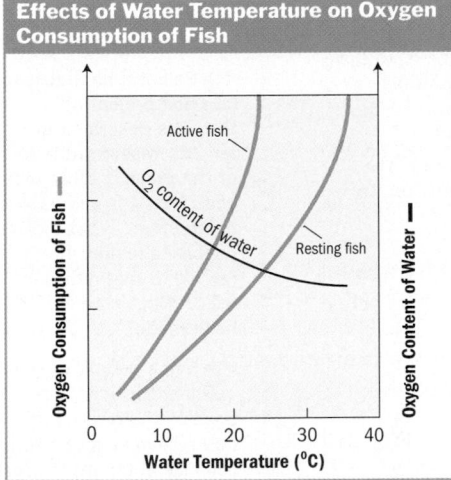

Effects of Water Temperature on Oxygen Consumption of Fish

Active fish

O_2 content of water

Resting fish

Oxygen Consumption of Fish →

Oxygen Content of Water →

Water Temperature (°C)
0   10   20   30   40

28. Analyzing Data The total biomass of primary producers on Earth, or net primary production, is about 132 petagrams. The table below shows amounts of primary production used by humans in several habitats. What is the total mass of primary production used by humans? What percent of Earth's net primary production does this represent? What percent of Earth's net primary production is available for all other species? How does the amount of primary production used by humans affect biodiversity?

Primary Producers Used by Humans

Habitat Category	Net Primary Production
Cultivated land	15.0
Grazing land	11.6
Forest land	13.6
Human-occupied areas	0.4

*Values are in petagrams (one petagram = 10^{15} grams)

Consider the Issues

29. Triage for Ecosystems After a disastrous occurrence, such as an earthquake or multi-car accident, doctors use a system called triage to treat the injured. They divide patients into three categories—those likely to recover without assistance, those most likely to benefit from medical treatment, and those whose injuries are most probably fatal. Could such a system be applied to ecosystems and species? Who could make the determinations? What criteria could they use?

Make New Connections

30. Biology and Literature Oklahoma during the Great Depression of the 1930s inspired John Steinbeck to write *The Grapes of Wrath*. Read Steinbeck's novel and find out how drought and soil erosion affected so many lives.

31. Biology and Government If your state periodically tests automobile emissions, visit a local testing center. Find out how often vehicles are tested. What equipment is used, and what does it measure? What are the criteria for passing the test? What happens when an automobile fails the test?

32. Biology and Anthropology Urban anthropologists study the lifestyle of city residents. One method of research includes analyzing their trash. What information might urban anthropologists be seeking? Investigate how anthropologists use waste products to research a community's lifestyle.

> **FAST-FORWARD**
>
> We are all a part of the web of life. In your continued studies and in your day-to-day activities, use what you have learned to strengthen and preserve the fragile connections and delicate strands that constitute the web of life.

consider how much reformation would be required and whether or not people would be willing to put forth the effort and resources to act.

30. Some students may have already read *The Grapes of Wrath*. You may wish to have a librarian suggest other fictional or nonfictional accounts that focus on the effects of environmental change.

31. If stickers are renewed on a monthly schedule, students should do their interviews in the middle of the month when the station will be less busy.

32. Anthropologists could get information on diet, clothing, health care, and forms of entertainment. Anthropologists are able to research lifestyles of past communities because nomadic ancestors often relocated when the refuse piles grew too large at a given site.

---

water to form sulfuric acid, which is part of acid rain.

26. Students could bury items in moist soil and periodically dig them up to note their condition.

27. The oxygen consumption increases; the oxygen content decreases; a resting fish requires less oxygen than an active fish.

28. Humans are directly using cultivated land and human-occupied areas: 15.4 petagrams or 38 percent of the total. Grazing land, which is often managed by humans, adds another 29 percent. Some forest land, the rest of the total, is also managed by humans.

29. Ecologists might need to identify keystone species, which would serve as bioindicators. They would have to

Connect the Chapters

1. Crop rotation replenishes nitrogen in the soil.
2. They might migrate, die out, or adapt.
3. Overgrazing, deforestation, and excess irrigation
4. Soil sediments suspended in water can block sunlight needed for photosynthesis.
5. Biomes that experience dramatic seasonal changes in temperature or precipitation
6. An S-shaped curve signifying a leveling out of growth would be better, because fewer resources would be required to sustain the population.
7. Density-independent: Any size population could be affected by pollution.

Connect the Units

8. Nitrogen is contained in proteins and in nucleic acids. It is returned to the environment in urine and by decomposers after death.
9. The greenhouse effect increases with the amount of atmospheric CO_2. During photosynthesis, plants use light energy to make glucose from CO_2 and H_2O, and they release O_2.
10. When inhaled, chemicals and solid particles in the air can irritate and damage the structure of respiratory system.

Connect to Themes

11. If soil has not been eroded, secondary succession will occur.
12. The non-native species might not have any natural predators. They would have an advantage when competing for the already-occupied niches.

940

Unit 9 Review

THE BIG IDEA! Answering the following questions will help you to link ideas and grasp the core concepts.

Connect the Chapters

1. How does crop rotation contribute to sustainable development?
2. Describe three ways in which nonhuman populations might respond to global warming.
3. What human activities might increase the range of desert biomes?
4. Explain how soil erosion could affect the photic zone in an aquatic biome.
5. In which types of biomes would a population be most likely to experience a boom-or-bust growth curve?
6. Which would be better for sustainable development: a human-population growth curve that is S-shaped or one that is J-shaped?
7. Are human activities that contribute to water pollution density-dependent or density-independent limiting factors? Explain your answer.

Connect the Units

8. What compounds in the human body contain nitrogen? How is nitrogen recycled from humans to the environment?
9. How is photosynthesis important in helping to reduce gases that contribute to the greenhouse effect?
10. How can poor air quality affect the human respiratory system?

Connect to Themes

11. **Patterns of Change/Cycles** Will primary or secondary succession occur in a habitat that has been deforested? Explain your answer.
12. **Stability and Equilibrium** How might introducing non-native species into an ecosystem affect native populations?
13. **Systems and Interactions** What effect does burning fossil fuels have on the carbon cycle and the water cycle?

project plans

1 Select one of the major latitude lines on a world map or globe. List at least six cities that are located on or near the latitude you have chosen. Include cities on at least two different continents. Make travel brochures that identify the cities' climates and biomes.

2 Select a habitat restoration project other than the ones described in Chapter 38. Research the history of the project. What factors contributed to the habitat's destruction? What motivated people to restore the habitat? What methods were used? What progress has been made?

3 Some people suggest that the way to deal with population growth and limited resources on Earth is to colonize outer space. Some think that the moon would be a good destination. As a class, research conditions on the moon. What resources would be available for human life? What resources would people need to transport from Earth?

CRITIC'S CORNER

Last Chance to See is a humorous account of Douglas Adams's worldwide travels to observe endangered species. The book does have a serious message: Unless we do something *NOW*, we may never see any of these animals—mountain gorillas, Komodo dragons, white rhinos, Yangtze river dolphins, and many others—again. I recommend this book to anyone who wants to know more about rare species and have a good laugh at the same time.

A BOOK REVIEW BY ANN K.D. MYERS ST. PAUL, MN

940

---

13. Combustion of fossil fuels increases carbon dioxide in the atmosphere that could lead to global warming. Nitrogen oxide and sulfur dioxide dissolve in water to form acid rain.

Project Plans

1. Students might want to repeat the project using longitude instead of latitude.

2. Students could pick a local effort or one that received national attention, such as the Hudson River cleanup.
3. Students could get an idea of what would be required for outer space colonization by researching the processes used by local groups to provide for people that have become homeless after a natural disaster, such as a flood, hurricane, or severe snow storm.

SPOTLIGHT ON CAREERS

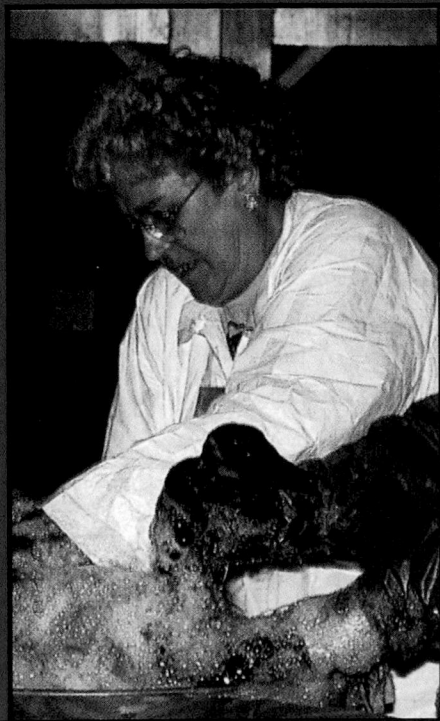

CAROL PADDEN
Chief conservation ranger
EDUCATION: M.S. in environmental science

❝My job is to care for town conservation land, including fields, wetlands, and about 90 miles (144 km) of hiking trails. Last summer we studied Flint's Pond, our drinking water supply. We look at whether ponds are affected by animals or humans—either from septic systems or road runoff.

I try to raise awareness about natural resources. For example, people who don't understand the ecology of water systems can damage our drinking supply. Any kind of wetland is valuable because it helps filter our water. We all need to understand how we effect the land and that our abuses may come back and affect us later.❞

(bioSURF) Visit *http://ecology.biosurf.com* to learn more about conservation of natural resources.

JOYCE PONSELL
Volunteer at a bird-rescue sanctuary
EDUCATION: B.A. in speech therapy; interested in bird watching and ecology

❝Before I retired, my job was to gather a team for cleanups. Now, I'm on the volunteer list. My volunteer work gives back to the wild.

Sometimes animals get hurt when nature and humans interact. Birds can be harmed by cars, by eating bugs or plants covered with pesticides, or by oil spills. We treat birds covered with oil. Oil is removed from feathers by washing them very gently.

We try to save each and every bird we find, no matter what species it is. For example, there are a lot of Canada geese on the East Coast and some people think they're a nuisance because they are noisy and can make a mess of ponds and golf courses. But all of the different shorebirds contribute to biodiversity, and all of them are a link in the chain of the ecosystem.❞

(bioSURF) Explore the Internet site *http://ecology.biosurf.com* to find out how communities protect the environment.

"We try to save each and every bird we find, no matter what species it is." — JOYCE PONSELL

Critic's Corner

Have students read the review of the book *Last Chance to See.* Ask if any students have read this book and ask them to share their opinion with the class. Encourage students to think about the finality of losing a rare species forever. You may wish to discuss the importance of preserving rare species of animals for future generations.

SPOTLIGHT ON CAREERS

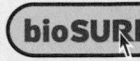 Have students connect to bioSurf to learn about schools, educational programs, and scholarships that would prepare them for a career or occupation in a field related to ecology.

Consider These Careers

Careers in environmental management are available to people with a wide range of educational backgrounds. Students can often find jobs in environmental restoration projects and fund raising activities. Careers such as naturalist, park ranger, environment technologist, and public educator require some specialized training. Scientists of all levels are employed in fields including agricultural research, meteorology, hydrology, geology, ecology, and environmental engineering.

Plan for a Career

■ **Following Through**
Many prospective job seekers assume that once they complete an interview, the process of employee selection is out of their hands. Actually, a follow-up phone call or correspondence can make a great deal of difference in the employer's final selection. Follow-up communication lets the employer know that you are enthusiastic and thorough. Have students compose a follow-up letter to be shared with the class. Encourage students to offer feedback on how an employer might view each letter, and suggest ways it might be improved.

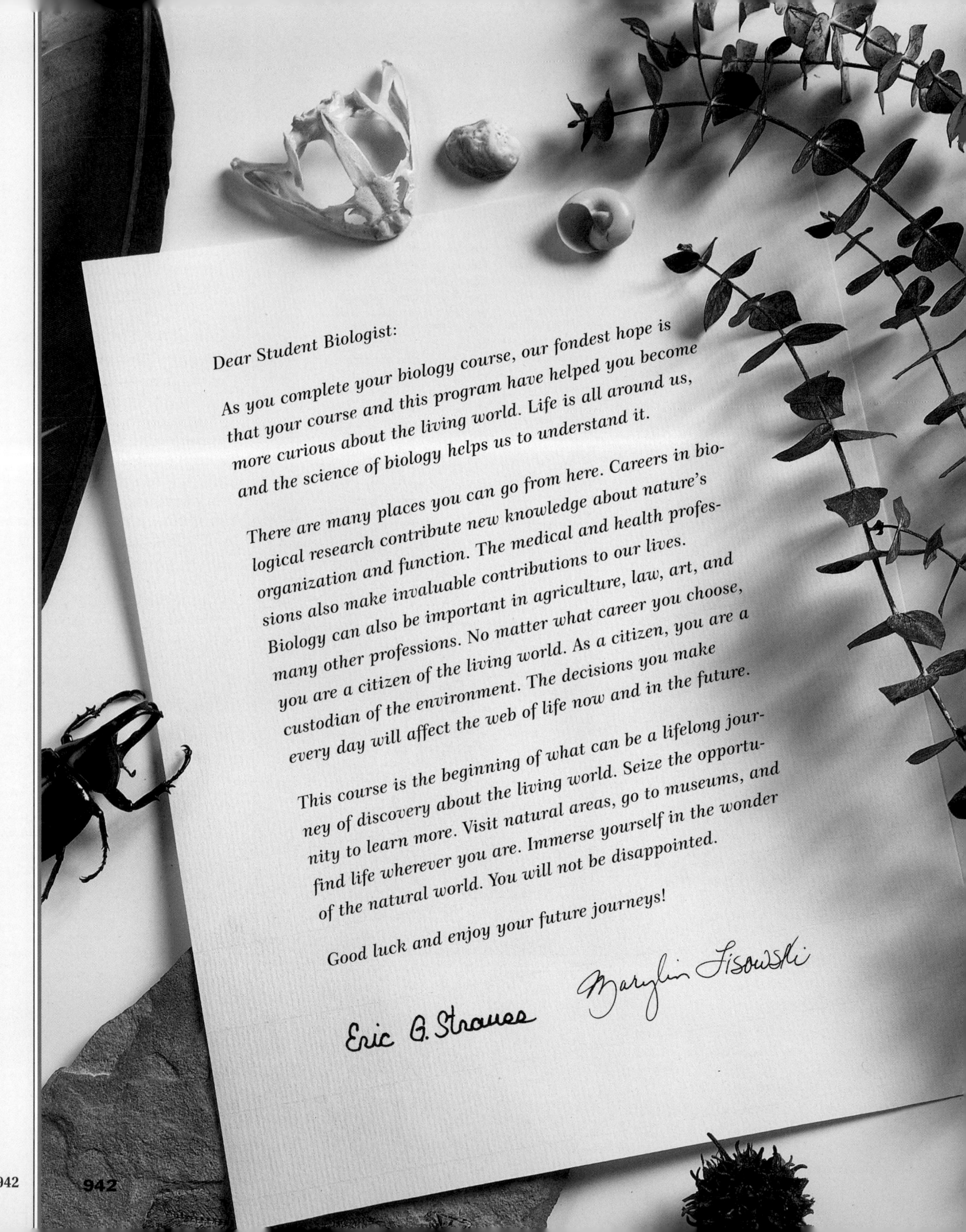

Dear Student Biologist:

As you complete your biology course, our fondest hope is that your course and this program have helped you become more curious about the living world. Life is all around us, and the science of biology helps us to understand it.

There are many places you can go from here. Careers in biological research contribute new knowledge about nature's organization and function. The medical and health professions also make invaluable contributions to our lives. Biology can also be important in agriculture, law, art, and many other professions. No matter what career you choose, you are a citizen of the living world. As a citizen, you are a custodian of the environment. The decisions you make every day will affect the web of life now and in the future.

This course is the beginning of what can be a lifelong journey of discovery about the living world. Seize the opportunity to learn more. Visit natural areas, go to museums, and find life wherever you are. Immerse yourself in the wonder of the natural world. You will not be disappointed.

Good luck and enjoy your future journeys!

Eric G. Strauss

Marylin Lisowski

Metric Conversions

Metric Units	Metric to English	English to Metric
LENGTH		
meter (m) = 100 cm	1 m = 3.28 ft	1 ft = 0.31 m
kilometer (km) = 1000 m	1 km = 0.62 mi	1 mi = 1.61 km
centimeter (cm) = 0.01 m	1 cm = 0.39 in	1 in = 2.54 cm
millimeter (mm) = 0.001 m	1 mm = 0.039 in	1 in = 25.4 mm
micrometer (μm) = 10^{-6} m	1 μm = 3.9 x 10^{-5} in	1 in = 25,400 μm
nanometer (nm) = 10^{-9} m	1nm=3.9 x 10^{-8} in	1 in = 2.54 x 10^7 nm
AREA		
square meter (m^2) = 10,000 cm^2	1 m^2 = 10.76 sq ft	1 sq ft = 0.09 m^2
square kilometer (km^2) = 10,000 m^2	1 km^2 = 0.39 sq mi	1 sq mi = 2.59 km^2
hectare (ha) = 10,000 m^2	1 ha = 2.47 acres	1 acre = 0.40 ha
square centimeter (cm^2) = 100 mm^2	1 cm^2 = 0.16 sq in	1 sq in = 6.45 cm^2
MASS		
gram (g) = 1000 mg	1 g = 0.04 oz	1 oz = 28.35 g
kilogram (kg) = 1000 g	1 kg = 2.21 lb	1 lb = 0.45 kg
milligram (mg) = 0.001 g	1 mg = 4×10^{-5} oz	1 oz = 28.350 mg
VOLUME (SOLIDS)		
cubic meter (m^3) = 1,000,000 cm^3	1 m^3 = 35.32 cu ft	1 cu ft = 0.03 m^3
cubic centimeter (cm^3) = 1000 mm^3	1 cm^3 = 0.06 cu in	1 cu in = 16.39 cm^3
VOLUME (LIQUIDS)		
liter (L) = 1000 mL	1 L = 1.06 qt 1 L = 0.27 gal	1 qt = 0.94 L 1 gal = 3.79 L
milliliter (mL) = 0.001 L	1 mL = 0.03 fluid oz	1 fluid oz = 29.57 mL

The Periodic Table

1

1 **H** Hydrogen 1.0079

1	.... Atomic Number
H	.... Symbol
Hydrogen	.... Element Name
1.0079	.... Atomic Mass

Alkali Metals	Alkaline earth metals	Transition Metals	Other Metals	Nonmetals	Noble Gases

1	2	3	4	5	6	7	8	9
3 **Li** Lithium 6.941	4 **Be** Beryllium 9.0122							
11 **Na** Sodium 22.990	12 **Mg** Magnesium 24.305							
19 **K** Potassium 39.098	20 **Ca** Calcium 40.08	21 **Sc** Scandium 44.956	22 **Ti** Titanium 47.90	23 **V** Vanadium 50.941	24 **Cr** Chromium 51.996	25 **Mn** Manganese 54.938	26 **Fe** Iron 55.847	27 **Co** Cobalt 58.933
37 **Rb** Rubidium 85.468	38 **Sr** Strontium 87.62	39 **Y** Yttrium 88.906	40 **Zr** Zirconium 91.22	41 **Nb** Niobium 92.906	42 **Mo** Molybdenum 95.94	43 **Tc** Technetium (97)	44 **Ru** Ruthenium 101.07	45 **Rh** Rhodium 102.91
55 **Cs** Cesium 132.91	56 **Ba** Barium 137.33	71 **Lu** Lutetium 174.97	72 **Hf** Hafnium 178.49	73 **Ta** Tantalum 180.95	74 **W** Tungsten 183.85	75 **Re** Rhenium 186.21	76 **Os** Osmium 190.2	77 **Ir** Iridium 192.22
87 **Fr** Francium (223)	88 **Ra** Radium 226.03	103 **Lr** Lawrencium (260)	104 **Rf** Rutherfordium (261)	105 **Db** Dubnium (262)	106 **Sg** Seaborgium (263)	107 **Bh** Bohrium (264)	108 **Hs** Hassium (265)	109 **Mt** Meitnerium (266)

57 **La** Lanthanum 138.91	58 **Ce** Cerium 140.12	59 **Pr** Praseodymium 140.12	60 **Nd** Neodymium 144.24	61 **Pm** Promethium (145)	62 **Sm** Samarium 150.4
89 **Ac** Actinum (227)	90 **Th** Thorium 232.04	91 **Pa** Protactinium 213.04	92 **U** Uranium 238.03	93 **Np** Neptunium 237.05	94 **Pu** Plutonium (244)

Inner transition elements

			13	14	15	16	17	18
								2 **He** Helium 4.0026
			5 **B** Boron 10.81	6 **C** Carbon 12.011	7 **N** Nitrogen 14.007	8 **O** Oxygen 15.999	9 **F** Fluorine 18.998	10 **Ne** Neon 20.179
10	11	12	13 **Al** Aluminum 26.982	14 **Si** Silicon 28.086	15 **P** Phosphorus 30.974	16 **S** Sulfur 32.06	17 **Cl** Chlorine 35.453	18 **Ar** Argon 39.948
28 **Ni** Nickel 58.71	29 **Cu** Copper 63.546	30 **Zn** Zinc 65.38	31 **Ga** Gallium 69.72	32 **Ge** Germanium 72.59	33 **As** Arsenic 74.922	34 **Se** Selenium 78.96	35 **Br** Bromine 79.904	36 **Kr** Krypton 83.80
46 **Pd** Palladium 106.4	47 **Ag** Silver 107.87	48 **Cd** Cadmium 112.41	49 **In** Indium 114.82	50 **Sn** Tin 118.69	51 **Sb** Antimony 121.75	52 **Te** Tellurium 127.60	53 **I** Iodine 126.90	54 **Xe** Xenon 131.30
78 **Pt** Platinum 195.09	79 **Au** Gold 196.97	80 **Hg** Mercury 200.59	81 **Tl** Thallium 204.37	82 **Pb** Lead 207.2	83 **Bi** Bismuth 208.98	84 **Po** Polonium (209)	85 **At** Astatine (210)	86 **Rn** Radon (222)
110 unnamed	111 unnamed	112 unnamed						

63 **Eu** Europium 151.96	64 **Gd** Gadolinium 157.25	65 **Tb** Terbium 158.93	66 **Dy** Dysprosium 162.50	67 **Ho** Holmium 164.93	68 **Er** Erbium 167.26	69 **Tm** Thulium 168.93	70 **Yb** Ytterbium 173.04
95 **Am** Americium (243)	96 **Cm** Curium (247)	97 **Bk** Berkelium (247)	98 **Cf** Californium (251)	99 **Es** Einsteinium (254)	100 **Fm** Fermium (257)	101 **Md** Mendelevium (258)	102 **No** Nobelium (259)

Laboratory Safety

A biology laboratory is an environment where exciting experiments and observations can occur. However, it is also an environment filled with dangerous materials and potential hazards. Following sensible safety precautions will help you create a positive laboratory experience. Read the following guidelines before you begin working in the laboratory, and periodically review these precautions throughout the year.

Safety Guidelines

1. Thoroughly read each laboratory procedure before entering the laboratory.

2. Know how to locate and use all safety equipment in the laboratory, including the first aid kit, fume hood, fire blanket, fire extinguisher, safety shower, and eye wash. Also, be able to locate the nearest exit in case of an emergency.

3. Do not engage in dangerous laboratory behavior such as horseplay or running.

4. Always wear safety goggles, unless otherwise instructed.

5. Wear an apron or a lab coat to protect your clothing.

6. Secure any loose-fitting clothing, and tie back long hair.

7. Never eat or drink in the laboratory.

8. Never taste, touch, or smell any chemicals unless instructed.

9. Thoroughly wash your hands before and after each laboratory activity.

10. Keep your work area clear of any unnecessary items.

11. Do not experiment with or mix any chemicals except as instructed during the prescribed laboratory activity. When combined, many chemicals in the laboratory can be explosive or otherwise dangerous.

12. Thoroughly wash all laboratory instruments before and after each use.

13. When using scissors or a scalpel, cut away from yourself and others.

14. When heating substances in a test tube, always slant and aim the mouth of the test tube away from yourself and others.

15. Clearly label all containers with the names of the materials you use during the activity.

16. Report all accidents, no matter how small, immediately to your instructor.

17. Never pick up broken glass with your hands. Sweep broken glass into a dustpan, and dispose of it in the broken glass container.

18. Never return unused chemicals to their original containers. Follow your instructor's directions for the proper disposal and cleanup of all unused materials.

19. Make sure all your materials are washed and put away. Clean your work area before leaving the laboratory.

20. Before leaving the laboratory, be certain that all Bunsen burners, gas outlets, and water faucets are turned off.

These symbols will draw your attention to specific potential hazards.

Safety Symbols

🐭	Live Animals	🌿	Plants
🔌	Electrical Safety	🧤	Hot Object
🦺	Protective Clothing	☠	Poison
🥽	Eye Protection	▨	Glassware
✂	Sharp Object		

Laboratory Skills

Use of a Compound Microscope

The microscope is an important tool in biology. The type of microscope common to most biology laboratories is the compound microscope. The compound microscope uses two lenses to magnify an image: the eyepiece, or ocular lens, and the objective lens.

Parts of a Microscope

Before you begin, locate the twelve main parts of a compound microscope in the diagram. Become familiar with each part and its specific function.

Eyepiece	**Body tube**
High-power objective	**Stage**
Low-power objective	**Stage clips**
Diaphragm	**Mirror**
Coarse adjustment	**Base**
Fine adjustment	**Arm**

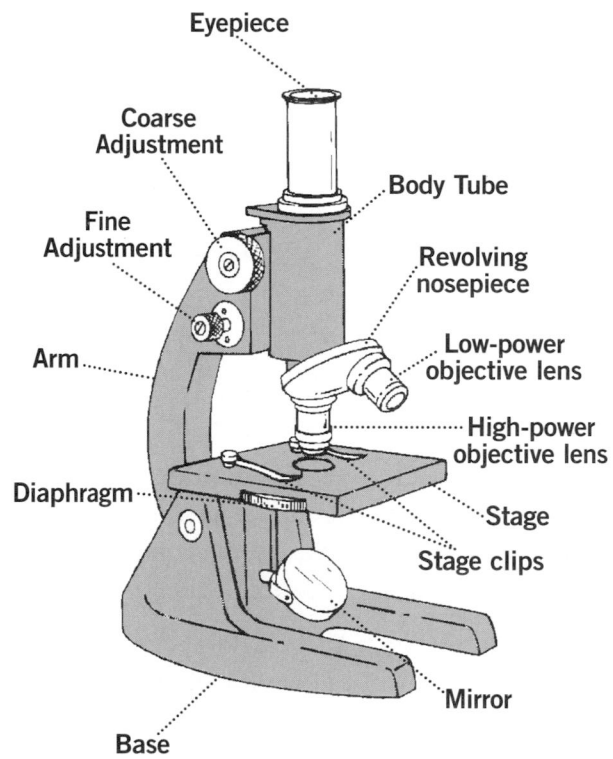

Using a Microscope

Follow these steps each time you use a microscope:

1. Carry the microscope to your table by holding the arm of the microscope with one hand while supporting its base with your other hand. Never carry a microscope with just one hand.

2. Carefully place the microscope on the table with the arm facing toward you.

3. If necessary, gently clean the lenses with lens paper. Do not touch the lenses with your fingers or regular tissue paper.

4. Determine the light source for your microscope. If the microscope has a lamp, plug it in and adjust the light to a comfortable level. If the microscope has a mirror, adjust the mirror to reflect light through the diaphragm. Never use direct sunlight as a light source when using a mirror, because it can damage your eyes.

5. Turn the revolving nosepiece until the low-power objective lens is in line with the body tube and the diaphragm. The lens should click into place.

6. Place a slide on the stage, and secure the slide with the stage clips. Make sure the specimen is directly in line with the light coming through the diaphragm. (See the next page for instructions on preparing slides.)

7. While watching from the side, not through the eyepiece, use the coarse adjustment to lower the objective toward the slide. Stop the objective just above, but not touching, the slide.

8. While looking through the eyepiece, slowly raise the objective with the coarse adjustment. When the specimen comes into view, turn the fine adjustment knob to focus sharply on the specimen. If you cannot find the specimen, repeat step 7.

947

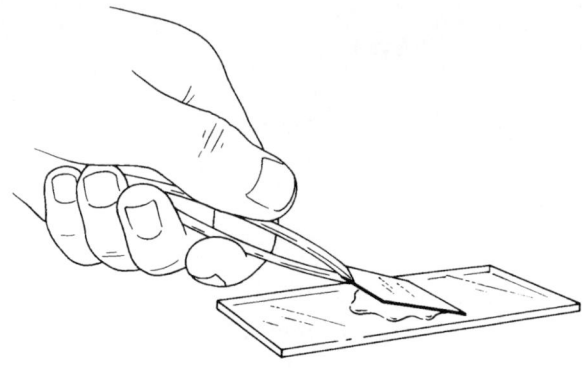

Preparing a Wet-Mount Slide

You can use a wet-mount slide to view a specimen through a compound microscope. Use the following steps to successfully prepare a wet-mount slide:

1. Obtain a slide and a coverslip. If necessary, clean each with lens paper. Use extreme care when cleaning coverslips, because they break easily.

2. Place the specimen you want to observe in the center of the slide. Using an eyedropper, place one drop of water on the specimen.

3. Holding the coverslip at a 45° angle (as shown above), touch its edge to the droplet of water. The water should spread evenly along the edge of the coverslip.

4. Slowly lower the coverslip over the specimen, avoiding air bubbles. If air bubbles become trapped under the coverslip, gently tap the coverslip with a pencil eraser until the bubbles disappear.

5. Remove excess water with a paper towel placed at the edge of the slide.

6. If the specimen begins to dry out over time, place another drop of water at the edge of the coverslip. Never lift the coverslip to add water.

Using a Triple-Beam Balance

There are many types of balances used to determine mass. However, the triple-beam balance is often used in biology laboratories. It can accurately measure the mass of an object to within 0.1 gram. Follow these steps every time you use the triple-beam balance:

1. Place the balance on a level surface.

2. Move all the weights to the left, and turn the adjustment screw so that the pointer rests at the zero mark.

3. Place the object to be measured on the pan.

4. Locate the beam with the heaviest weight. Slide the weight to the right until the pointer falls below the zero mark. Then slide the weight one notch to the left.

5. Locate the beam with the next-heaviest weight. Position the weight using the same procedure used in step 4.

6. Slide the lightest weight to the right until the pointer rests at zero. The mass of the object is the total of the masses shown on all three beams.

7. When measuring liquids, powders, and hot objects, place the substance in a container, rather than directly on the pan. To determine the mass of the substance, be sure to subtract the mass of the container from the total mass.

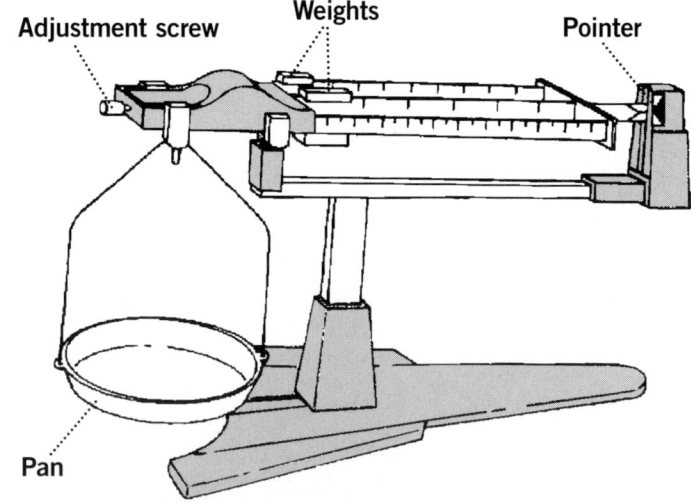

Adjustment screw   Weights   Pointer

Pan

Problem-Solving Skills
Observing and Interpreting

The scientific method involves making observations and interpreting them. An observation is something that can be made with the senses or with instruments that extend the senses. When conducting a scientific experiment, a scientist must be careful to observe the effects of only one variable at a time. A scientist must also repeat the experiment under the same set of conditions in order to confirm that there has been no error in observation.

An interpretation is a possible explanation of what might have produced the observations that were made. There are often several possible interpretations of the same set of observations. A scientist's task is to identify all the reasonable interpretations and then determine which interpretation is most probable.

Like all problem-solving tasks, observing and interpreting can be organized into a series of steps. Here are a few simple steps to help you:

- Think about the definitions of the words *observation* and *interpretation*.

- Divide the information given into small pieces.

- Apply the definitions of "observation" and "interpretion" to each piece of information.

- Look at the conditions under which the observations and interpretations were made. Decide whether the observations were made carefully and whether the interpretations are reasonable.

Everyday Applications

1. You check your mailbox and observe that it contains no mail. State two interpretations for this observation. How could you test each of your interpretations?

2. The kitchen flashlight does not light. State three ways to interpret this observation. What further observations might be useful?

Biology Applications

On a separate sheet of paper, identify the observations and interpretations in the following passage:

The Montero family notices that their lawn is turning brown. They suspect that the cause is insufficient water. To determine the cause, they divide the lawn into two sections. Section A is given an increased amount of water; section B is watered with the usual amount. After a few days, they also decide to add fertilizer to section A. Two weeks later, section A is green and section B is still brown. The Monteros decide that increased watering caused section A to turn green.

The Tran family has the same problem. They divide their lawn into three sections. Section A receives increased water, section B receives fertilizer and the usual amount of water, and section C is treated as usual. The Trans find that only section A becomes green; sections B and C remain brown. They, too, conclude that increased watering was the factor that improved the appearance of the lawn.

1. Which family was observing the results of two variables at one time?

2. Do you think the interpretations of both families are equally good? Why or why not?

3. Did both families use the correct procedures? How would you improve the experiments?

4. What other factors might have affected the experiments?

Lab Zone Applications

Practice the skills of observing and interpreting by doing these Lab Zone activities:

- **Think About It:** Analyzing Firefly Behavior, *Chapter 28, page 670*

- **Do It:** What Happens When You Exhale?, *Chapter 31, page 746*

Problem-Solving Skills
Analyzing

When people analyze information, they break it down into its parts and then determine how the parts relate to each other and to the whole. Analyzing helps to develop an understanding of how something works. When you analyze information rather than memorize it, you are more likely to remember the information and use it. Analyzing helps you to link new information to things you already know.

You can analyze many things—data, processes, diagrams, graphs, and more. When you are analyzing a subject that is complex, there are a few things to keep in mind. First, it is important to know the overall purpose of the subject you are analyzing. Once you understand the purpose, keep it in mind as you study the subject.

If the subject of your analysis has several parts, look at it one part at a time. Think about how each part contributes to the overall purpose. Also think about how the parts are related to one another.

After you have made observations, try to explain your subject aloud or in writing. If you truly understand the process, you will be able to explain it to someone else. If you are unable to explain the subject clearly, you should review your notes and repeat the process described below.

Here are a few simple steps to help you to analyze:

• Decide on the overall purpose of the subject.

• Break it down into parts.

• Review by explaining it in your own words aloud or on paper.

Everyday Applications

Your favorite music group has just released a new compact disc (CD), and you want to buy a copy. Some of the steps involved in your purchase are listed below, but they are not in the correct order. Place the steps in the correct order, and answer the accompanying questions.

A. Find out if your local music store has the CD in stock.

B. Pay for the CD.

C. Ride your bike to the store.

D. Check your wallet to see if you have enough money to buy the CD.

E. Find the CD in the store.

F. Ride your bike home.

G. Check the tires of your bike to make sure they are not flat.

H. Put the CD in your backpack.

1. Which step did you list first, and why?

2. What might have happened if you placed step H before step B?

3. What was the function of step G?

Biology Applications

Analyze the diagrams of photosynthesis described in Chapter 4 and answer the following questions:

1. What is the function of the Calvin cycle?

2. Why must the light-dependent reactions occur before the carbon-fixing reactions?

3. What is the function of light in photosynthesis? What would happen in the absence of light?

4. Could the light-dependent reactions occur in the absence of the Calvin cycle? Why or why not?

Lab Zone Applications

Practice the skill of analyzing by doing these Lab Zone activities:

• **Think About It:** Analyzing Tree Rings, *Chapter 18, page 439*

• **Think About It:** Determining the Age of a Fossil, *Chapter 11, page 265*

Problem-Solving Skills
Stating a Hypothesis

A hypothesis is an interpretation of observations. We all make hypotheses about things in our everyday lives. A scientist makes a hypothesis only after he or she has studied a problem and made observations. Next, the scientist analyzes his or her observations to find patterns and clues. If there are patterns in the data, the scientist uses his or her imagination and knowledge to think of possible explanations for all of the observations. These explanations are the hypotheses.

The best of the hypotheses are selected and tested in experiments that produce new observations or data. A hypothesis that is not consistent with the data must be rejected or changed.

The steps in stating a hypothesis can be summarized as follows:

- Collect all the data that appear to be related to the problem.

- Organize the information, and look for patterns.

- Make a list of explanations of the observations. Identify as many explanations as you can.

- Choose the explanation that is most consistent with all the available data. If two or more hypotheses seem to fit the data equally well, do not decide between them until more data can be collected.

Everyday Applications

You are packing for a camping trip and find that your flashlight does not light. In order to determine why the flashlight does not work, you make the following observations: The flashlight has the correct size and number of batteries; the flashlight worked last week when your younger brother was playing with it; the bulb does not appear broken.

1. Develop a hypothesis to explain why the flashlight does not work. Is your hypothesis consistent with all of your observations?

2. Suppose you also observed that the switch was left in the "on" position. How does this additional information affect your hypothesis?

Biology Applications

You are given the two Petri dishes shown below. Your teacher tells you that both dishes contain tobacco seedlings. The green seedlings in dish A were germinated in the light, and the white seedlings in dish B were germinated in darkness. Your teacher also tells you that there is a genetic condition called albinism in some plants. Plants with albinism cannot make chlorophyll and are therefore white.

 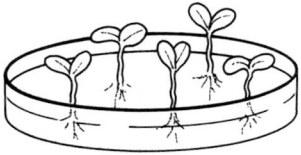

A   **B**

1. Form one or more hypotheses to explain the differences between the two sets of seedlings.

2. Another student says she would like to test her hypothesis by leaving both dishes in the light for a day. What do you think her hypothesis is?

3. After 24 hours in light, the plants in the two dishes are the same color. Use all the data you now have to choose the best hypothesis or to form a new hypothesis.

Lab Zone Applications

Practice the skill of stating a hypothesis by doing these Lab Zone activities:

• **Think About It:** Solving a Reproduction Puzzle, *Chapter 22, page 527*

• **Investigate It:** Does Temperature Affect Bacterial Growth?, *Chapter 14, page 339*

Problem-Solving Skills
Organizing and Classifying

Quite often, people must deal with large numbers of facts or objects. When dealing with a large collection of different things, it is important to organize and classify the items in the collection. Organizing and classifying make the items easier to find and to use.

When you organize and classify anything, you must first think about your purpose for doing so. Your reasons for organizing and classifying will determine the criteria you use. The most important criterion for organizing things is that the system makes sense to the person who uses the items. After the items are organized into groups according to the appropriate criteria, it may be necessary to form subgroups. Here again, the criterion is usefulness.

Here is a summary of the steps for classifying:

- Decide what your purpose is for classifying.

- Study the characteristics of the things to be classified. Decide on useful criteria for classifying.

- Go through the items, and place them in the appropriate groups.

- Decide if subgroups would be useful. If so, use the same process again.

Everyday Applications

Imagine you are organizing a kitchen that has a square cabinet under the sink, three drawers under the work counter, a shelf by the stove, and a tall, narrow closet by the entrance.

1. Where would you place each of the following items: broom, spice bottle, frying pan, knives, gloves?

2. What criteria did you use to determine where each item should be stored?

3. Name one other item that you would store with each of the four items listed.

Biology Applications

Imagine you are responsible for planning a zoo that will place the following animals in containments:

Lion	Rattlesnake
Alaskan king crab	Baboon
Jaguar	Parrot
Poison arrow frog	Walrus
Tsetse fly	Desert vulture
Collared lizard	Giraffe
Mako shark	Mexican tarantula
Pacific salmon	

1. The zoo is organized to group animals by ecosystems, such as the African plains, the Pacific coast, or the South American rain forests. Decide which animals you would place in neighboring containments.

2. The zoo decides to place the above animals into the following scientific groupings: Mammals, Reptiles, Fish, Amphibians, Birds, and Arthropods. Reorganize the animals on the list into these taxa.

3. Choose another biological charactertistic and group the animals according to your new characteristic. Groups may include predators and prey; herbivores, carnivores, and omnivores; large and small animals; and so on.

Lab Zone Applications

Practice the skills of organizing and classifying by doing these Lab Zone activities:

- **Do It:** Categorizing Plants, *Chapter 17, page 414*

- **Do It:** What is the Quality of Local Water?, *Chapter 38, page 917*

Problem-Solving Skills
Making a Concept Map

Through your study of biology, you will be presented with many new concepts. There are many ways to organize these concepts, but one of the most helpful ways is to create a concept map. In a concept map, ideas and concepts are expressed as words or phrases enclosed in circles. The circles are connected by lines that are accompanied by one or two words that describe the connection. Each main idea is linked to more specific concepts and examples. The following steps will help you to construct a concept map:

- Identify the main idea and concepts.

- Place the main idea at the top of the map and draw a circle around it. Draw lines to connect the main idea to the concepts, and circle each concept.

- Add linking words or phrases that explain the relationship between the circled concepts.

Do not be discouraged if you find concept mapping difficult at first. Remember, there is no one correct concept map for a topic. Your concept map will be correct if it shows the main ideas and general concepts and identifies the relationships among them.

Everyday Applications

The following concept map shows how to write an essay:

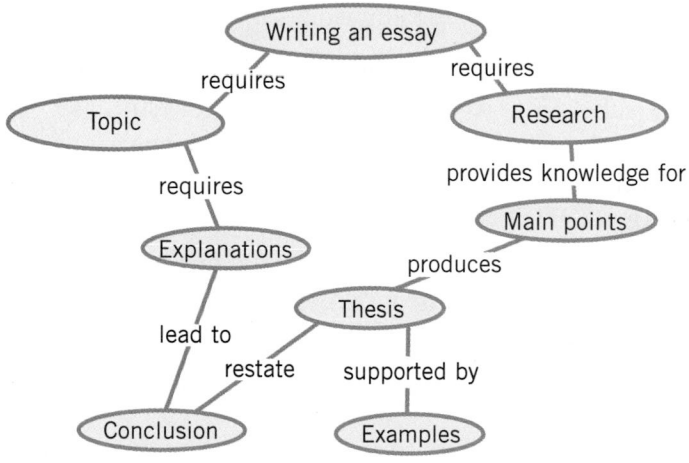

1. Where would you add quotations and a bibiography to the concept map? How would you link these concepts?

2. Create a concept map showing the organization of your classroom. Use the following terms in your concept map: teacher, students, desks, chalkboard, erasers, textbooks, bulletin board, computers, paper, principal, school building.

Biology Applications

The concept map below shows the relationships between the main idea–birds–and some general concepts and specific ideas about birds.

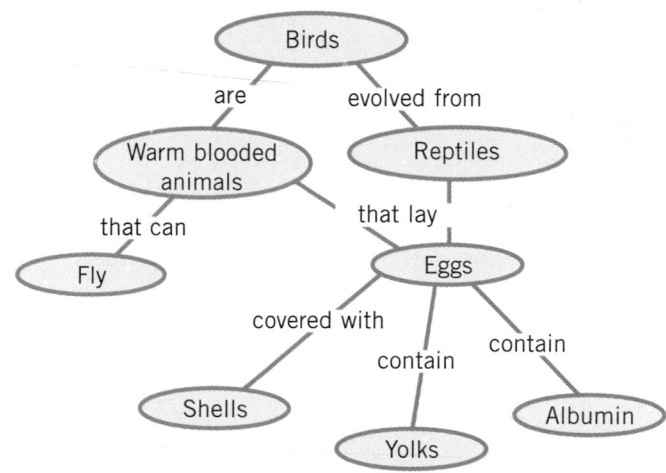

1. What organisms lay eggs? What do eggs contain?

2. Where and how would you add the following terms to the concept map above: wings, feathers, migrate.

Lab Zone Applications

Practice the skill of organizing concepts in other ways by doing these Lab Zone activities:

- **Think About It:** Constructing a Phylogenetic Tree, *Chapter 13, page 309*

- **Investigate It:** Using a Pedigree, *Chapter 6, page 146*

Problem-Solving Skills
Designing an Experiment

An experiment is designed test a hypothesis by investigating the effects of an experimental variable. Any factor that can influence the outcome of an experiment is a variable. Only one variable is analyzed in one experiment. All other variables are kept constant.

An experiment has two parts: the experimental setup and the control setup. In the experimental setup, the experimental variable is present. In the control setup, the experimental variable is missing or changed. The control setup is crucial to the experiment, because one cannot determine the effect of the experimental variable unless one can see what happens when it is changed or removed.

Here are some steps to follow when you design an experiment:

- Follow the procedure for stating an hypothesis (see page 951).
- Determine the variable you want to test.
- Set up an experiment to test your hypothesis.
- Devise an experimental setup and control setup.

Everyday Applications

A convenience store owner has recently purchased a soft-drink machine, but finds that soft-drink sales are slow. The owner hypothesizes that the reason for the slow sales is the location of the machine: a dark corner.

1. Design an experiment to test the store owner's hypothesis.
2. State two other hypotheses that could explain the slow sales.
3. Design an experiment to test each of the alternative hypotheses.

Biology Applications

Raj has an aquarium in which the water is heated to a constant temperature of 18°C. One day, the temperature control in the heater breaks, and the water rises to 22°C. Raj notices that the fishes appear more active than usual and seem to be breathing more rapidly.

Raj has a hypothesis, which he decides to test. He selects three fishes, places each fish in a beaker or water, and sets the beakers down in larger bowls of water. The bowls contain either warm water, ice water, or room-temperature water. During a 10-minute period Raj and several friends measure the water temperature in the beakers and count how many times per minute each fish breathes. After the experiment, the fish are returned to the tank unharmed. The data are organized on a table as shown.

Comparing Fish Breathing Rates						
	BOWL #1		BOWL #2		BOWL #3	
Min.	Temp. (°C)	Breaths (#/min.)	Temp. (°C)	Breaths (#/min.)	Temp. (°C)	Breaths (#/min.)
0	22°C	58	21°C	57	21°C	60
2	22°C	59	24°C	67	19°C	51
4	22°C	57	25°C	81	16°C	32
6	22°C	56	27°C	93	14°C	20
8	22°C	55	29°C	110	10°C	12
10	22°C	56	30°C	110	11°C	13

1. What hypothesis is Raj testing in this experiment?
2. What variable did Raj isolate?
3. Suppose Raj finds out that cold water can dissolve more oxygen than warm water can. Use this information to write a new hypothesis.

Lab Zone Applications

Practice the skill of designing an experiment by doing these Lab Zone activities:

- **Investigate It:** Designing a Scientific Experiment, *Chapter 1, page 26*
- **Investigate It:** Observing Population Growth, *Chapter 36, page 880*

Problem-Solving Skills
Making Analogies

If you are trying to understand a new idea, it sometimes helps to compare the new idea to something with which you are already familiar. Such a comparison is called an analogy. For example, you could compare an airplane to a bird. Both objects fly and they are similar in shape. Of course, an airplane and a bird are not alike in most ways. But they do have some similarities in structure that reflect their common functions. Like all analogies, the comparison between an airplane and a bird is limited by the differences between the two items.

Analogies are also often used in making models. Whenever you use an analogy to create a model, keep in mind the differences between the two objects. For example, an airplane might be useful if you are examining bird flight, but it would not be useful if you were planning to study bird songs.

Reasoning by analogy uses the skills of comparing and contrasting. It also uses the skill of analyzing, because finding a good analogy requires that you understand all the parts of the things you are comparing. Analogies can also help you understand new ideas because they help structure and focus your thinking. By understanding how things are alike, you can hypothesize about unknown features of the unfamiliar item. However, you must also remain aware of the ways that the items are different.

To make and use analogies, follow these steps:

- Look at the new concept or information, and think about its parts and its function.

- Think, "Is this like anything I already know about?" List anything you can think of, however silly, that seems like it might be similar.

- Try out each analogy. Identify the one that has the most similarities.

- Compare and contrast your analogy with the new concept. See how far you can take the analogy.

Everyday Applications

1. Develop an analogy between each word listed on the left and the word opposite it on the right. Explain the basis for each analogy.

Bird	**Factory**
Ship	**Theater**
Supermarket	**Airplane**

2. Choose four familiar nouns at random from the dictionary. Exchange your list with another student. From the list given to you by your classmate, find and explain as many analogies among the words as you can.

3. Explain the limitations of each analogy that you developed in questions 1 and 2.

Biology Applications

1. Use your comparing and contrasting skills to explain the following analogies:

    a. A cell is like a factory.

    b. A cell membrane is like a sieve.

    c. A circulatory system is like a railroad.

    d. The brain is like a telephone system.

    e. The xylem of a plant is like a straw.

2. Explain the limitations of each analogy used in question 1.

Lab Zone Applications

Practice the skill of making analogies by doing these Lab Zone Activities:

- **Think About It:** Modeling Fungal Growth, *Chapter 16, page 376*

- **Think About It:** From Milk to Wasp: Modeling Mutations, *Chapter 8, page 195*

Problem-Solving Skills
Making Generalizations

When people make generalizations, they draw conclusions about a broad category of things based on a number of experiences. Scientists make generalizations when they draw conclusions about the world based on the observations made in experiments. The scientist understands, however, that there are always possible exceptions to a generalization.

One way a generalization is helpful to a scientist is that it enables him or her to make predictions. Generalizations lead to assumptions, which form the basis of the prediction. Part of the purpose of conducting an experiment may be to test the generalization. The generalization, therefore, can be a starting point for developing a hypothesis.

To make useful generalizations, follow these steps:

- Collect all the related examples you can find of the situation you are studying.

- Analyze the examples and note patterns or similar parts.

- Make all the generalizations you can about the examples.

- List the significant exceptions to the generalizations you have made.

Everyday Applications

1. Finish the following statement: "Ten-year-olds always. . . ."

2. Now imagine you are 10 years old again, and that someone has just made the previous statement. Explain the reasons why the generalization would be unfair.

3. Make generalizations using examples in each of the following categories: cars, movies, sports, and shopping malls. Indicate whether you think each statement applies to all or most examples in each category.

Biology Applications

1. Suppose there is an animal called a glorpus. A male glorpus comes upon the territory of another male glorpus. Predict the behavior of the two male glorpuses during such an encounter.

   a. What assumptions did you make about the structure, lifestyle, and environment of the glorpuses?

   b. What generalizations did you use to predict the animals' behavior?

   c. If you were to find out that glorpuses are insects, would this information change your prediction? Why or why not?

2. One day, a stray cat appears at your doorstep. Because you like cats and do not like to see them suffer, you go to your kitchen and fill a bowl of milk for the cat. The cat sniffs the bowl, sits down, looks you in the eye and meows, but does not drink the milk.

   a. What generalizations inspired you to get the bowl of milk?

   b. What hypotheses can you make to explain the cat's lack of interest in the milk? List as many hypotheses as you can.

   c. State the generalizations you used to make the hypotheses. Do you think that using generalizations is a good way to make hypotheses? Explain your answer.

Lab Zone Applications

Practice the skill of making generalizations by doing these Lab Zone activities:

- **Think About It:** Finding Examples of Symmetry, *Chapter 21, page 510*

- **Investigate It:** Modeling Disease Transmission, *Chapter 32, page 776*

Classification of Organisms

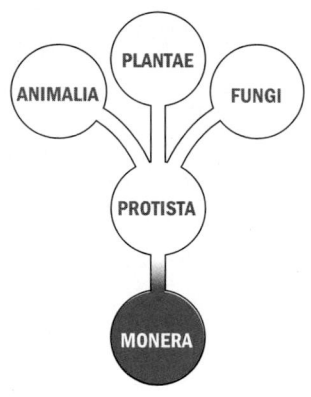

Kingdom: Monera

KEY CHARACTERISTICS: Prokaryotes; most unicellular, but some form filaments or clusters; reproduce asexually by binary fission, some species can exchange genetic information.

Category: Archaebacteria

KEY CHARACTERISTICS: Probably ancestral to other bacteria; most are anaerobic; live in harsh environments.

PHYLUM: METHANOGENS

KEY CHARACTERISTICS: Anaerobic; produce methane.
EXAMPLES: Bacteria found in swamps and in mammalian digestive tracts.

PHYLUM: THERMOPHILES

KEY CHARACTERISTIC: Live in hot, acidic environments.
EXAMPLE: *Sulfolobus*.

PHYLUM: EXTREME HALOPHILES

KEY CHARACTERISTIC: Live in extremely salty environments.
EXAMPLE: *Haloarcula marismortui*.

Category: Eubacteria

KEY CHARACTERISTICS: Known as "true bacteria"; includes heterotrophs and autotrophs; some are aerobic, some are anaerobic.

PHYLUM: GRAM-POSITIVE BACTERIA

KEY CHARACTERISTICS: Cell walls contain a thick layer of protein-sugar complex and a single layer of lipid molecules; many species form endospores.
EXAMPLES: *Staphylococcus, Streptococcus, Bacillus*.

PHYLUM: PROTEOBACTERIA

KEY CHARACTERISTICS: Unicellular eubacteria; many have flagella; some species play key role in nitrogen cycle.
EXAMPLES: *Rhizobium, Escherichia coli, Salmonella*.

PHYLUM: CYANOBACTERIA

KEY CHARACTERISTICS: Many have thick, gel-like cell walls; capable of photosynthesis; most live in freshwater environments.
EXAMPLES: *Oscillatoria, Gloeocapsa, Nostoc*.

PHYLUM: CHLAMYDIAS

KEY CHARACTERISTICS: Gram-negative; parasitic; limited metabolism.
EXAMPLE: *Chlamydia trachomatis*.

PHYLUM: SPIROCHETES

KEY CHARACTERISTICS: Spiral-shaped; capable of movement; free-living and parasitic species.
EXAMPLE: *Treponema pallidum*.

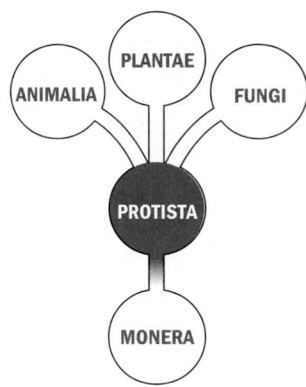

Kingdom: Protista

KEY CHARACTERISTICS: Eukaryotes; may be unicellular, colonial, or multicellular; can reproduce sexually or asexually.

Category: Protozoans

KEY CHARACTERISTICS: Heterotrophic; unicellular; animal-like; many parasitic; methods of reproduction are mostly asexual.

PHYLUM: SARCODINA

(Some classify these organisms into three phyla: Rhizopoda, Anthinopoda, and Foraminifera).
KEY CHARACTERISTICS: Have no definite shape; use pseudopodia for feeding and movement.
EXAMPLE: *Entamoeba histolytica* (causes amebic dysentery).

PHYLUM: ZOOFLAGELLATA

(Some call this phylum Zoomastigophora).
KEY CHARACTERISTICS: Most are unicellular; use flagella for movement.
EXAMPLES: *Trypanosoma, Trychonympha, Giardia*.

Classification of Organisms

PHYLUM: CILIOPHORA (CILIATES)
KEY CHARACTERISTICS: Most are unicellular; use cilia for movement; some reproduce sexually by conjugation; some reproduce asexually by binary fission.
EXAMPLES: *Paramecium, Vorticella, Didinium.*

PHYLUM: SPOROZOA
(Some classify these organisms into the phylum Apicomplexa).
KEY CHARACTERISTICS: Sessile; most are parasites, some species live inside other species in symbiotic relationships, individuals often change hosts throughout life cycle; reproduce in sexual and asexual stages.
EXAMPLES: *Plasmodium* (causes malaria), *Pneumocystis carinii* (causes AIDS-related pneumonia).

Category: Algae
KEY CHARACTERISTICS: Photosynthetic autotrophs; some are unicellular, many are multicellular; plantlike organisms, but all lack the distinct organs of true plants.

PHYLUM: CHRYSOPHYTA (DIATOMS)
(Some classify these organisms into the phylum Baccillariophyta).
KEY CHARACTERISTICS: Unicellular; cell walls made of glassy silicon with intricate patterns; contain yellow and brown photosynthetic pigments; motile; live in saltwater environments.
EXAMPLES: *Thallasiosina, Botrydium.*

PHYLUM: DINOFLAGELLATA (DINOFLAGELLATES)
KEY CHARACTERISTICS: Unicellular; cellulose plates provide unique shape; move using two flagella positioned at right angles to each other; most live in salt water; some species are bioluminescent.
EXAMPLES: *Gonyaulax* (causes "red tide"), *Noctilucans scintillans.*

PHYLUM: EUGLENOPHYTA (EUGLENOIDS)
KEY CHARACTERISTICS: Unicellular; contain a flexible protein covering; two flagella used for movement; reproduce by binary fission; most live in fresh water.
EXAMPLE: *Euglena.*

PHYLUM: CHLOROPHYTA (GREEN ALGAE)
KEY CHARACTERISTICS: Some are unicellular but most are multicellular; cell walls made of cellulose similar to plants; sessile; live in ponds, moist soils, and shallow ocean water.
EXAMPLES: *Volvox, Chlamydomonas, Ulva.*

PHYLUM: RHODOPHYTA (RED ALGAE)
KEY CHARACTERISTICS: Multicellular; contain special pigments that trap sunlight for photosynthesis in deep water; sessile; live in saltwater environments.
EXAMPLES: *Porphyra, Polysiphonia.*

PHYLUM: PHAEOPHYTA (BROWN ALGAE)
KEY CHARACTERISTICS: Large, multicellular; contain a brown photosynthetic pigment; reproduce by alternation of generations; sessile; most live in salt water.
EXAMPLES: *Fucus* (kelp), *Sargassum, Laminaria.*

Category: Molds
KEY CHARACTERISTICS: Unlike fungi, cell walls do not contain chitin; heterotrophs, usually decomposers; most use ameboid movement.

PHYLUM: MYXOMYCOTA (PLASMODIAL SLIME MOLDS)
KEY CHARACTERISTICS: Unicellular; multinucleated; under harsh conditions, form a spore-producing structure called a fruiting body.
EXAMPLE: *Physarum.*

PHYLUM: ACRASIOMYCOTA (CELLULAR SLIME MOLDS)
KEY CHARACTERISTICS: Unicellular; life cycle alternates between a spore-producing fruiting body form and a feeding form; live in fresh water, damp soil, or on decaying plant matter.

PHYLUM: OOMYCOTA (WATER MOLDS)
KEY CHARACTERISTICS: Unicellular; some species are parasitic and attack injured tissues; most live in fresh water.
EXAMPLE: *Phytophthora infestans* (causes potato blight).

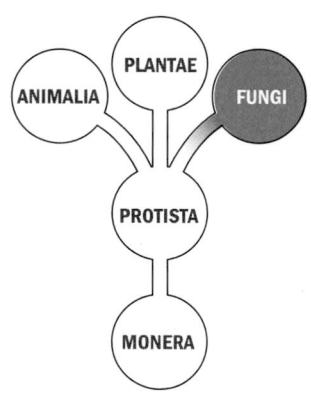

Kingdom: Fungi

KEY CHARACTERISTICS: Eukaryotes; mostly multicellular and multi-nucleated; cell walls contain chitin; body composed of hyphae; sessile; heterotrophic; reproduce sexually or asexually.

DIVISION: ZYGOMYCOTA (COMMON MOLDS)

KEY CHARACTERISTICS: Hyphae lack septa; decomposers of plant and animal matter; usually reproduce asexually by spore production, under harsher conditions most can reproduce sexually by producing zygospores; live in terrestrial environments.
EXAMPLES: *Rhizopus* (causes black bread mold), *Pilobolus*.

DIVISION: ASCOMYCOTA (SAC FUNGI)

KEY CHARACTERISTICS: Largest group of fungi; most are multicellular, yeast species are unicellular; species can be parasitic or free-living; reproduce sexually by forming ascospores in saclike ascus; reproduce asexually by forming spores at the ends of hyphae; yeasts reproduce asexually by budding.
EXAMPLES: Truffles, morels, yeasts.

DIVISION: BASIDIOMYCOTA (CLUB FUNGI)

KEY CHARACTERISTICS: Multicellular; incomplete septa in the hyphae; reproduce sexually by basidiospores formed in the basidium.
EXAMPLES: Bracket fungi, puff balls, rusts, smuts.

DIVISION: DEUTEROMYCOTA (IMPERFECT FUNGI)

KEY CHARACTERISTICS: Diverse group; only reproduce asexually by producing spores in specialized hyphae.
EXAMPLES: *Penicillium,* athlete's foot fungus, ringworm.

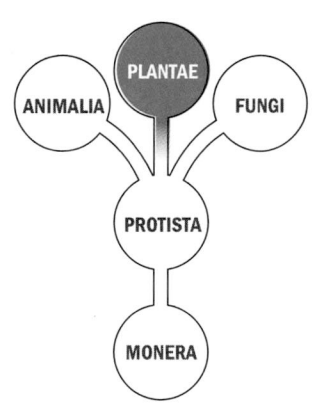

Kingdom: Plantae

KEY CHARACTERISTICS: Eukaryotes; multicellular; photosynthetic autotrophs with chlorophyll *a*, chlorophyll *b*, and other pigments contained in chloroplasts; sessile; cell walls contain cellulose; tissues organized into distinct organs; reproduce asexually by vegetative propagation, or sexually by alternation of generations; most species live in terrestrial environments.

DIVISION: BRYOPHYTA (MOSSES)

KEY CHARACTERISTICS: Nonvascular; reproduce by haploid spores; haploid gametophyte is dominant stage of life cycle; most live in damp terrestrial environments.
EXAMPLE: *Sphagnum* (peat moss).

DIVISION: HEPATOPHYTA (LIVERWORTS)

KEY CHARACTERISTICS: Nonvascular; reproduce by haploid spores; reproduce asexually by fragmentation and by gemmae; haploid gametophyte is dominant stage of life cycle; most live in damp terrestrial environments.

DIVISION: ANTHOCEROPHYTA (HORNWORTS)

KEY CHARACTERISTICS: Nonvascular; reproduce by haploid spores; haploid gametophyte is dominant stage of life cycle; sporophytes perform photosynthesis.

DIVISION: PSILOPHYTA

KEY CHARACTERISTICS: Vascular; branched stems; no true roots or leaves; reproduce by haploid spores; haploid gametophyte is dominant stage of life cycle; live in tropical environments.
EXAMPLE: *Psilotum nudum* (whisk fern).

DIVISION: LYCOPHYTA

KEY CHARACTERISTICS: Vascular; roots and leaves surround a single central taproot; diploid sporophyte is dominant stage of life cycle; reproduce by haploid and diploid spores; live in shady, damp terrestrial environments.
EXAMPLE: *Lycopodium* (club moss).

Classification of Organisms

DIVISION: SPHENOPHYTA (HORSETAILS)

KEY CHARACTERISTICS: Vascular; thick, hollow stem and scaly leaves; reproduce by haploid spores; sporophyte is dominant stage of life cycle.

EXAMPLE: *Equisetum.*

DIVISION: PTEROPHYTA (FERNS)

KEY CHARACTERISTICS: Highly developed vascular system; true roots, leaves, and stems; reproduce by spores; sporophyte is dominant stage of life cycle; most common seedless plant; live in tropical rain forests and moist woodlands.

EXAMPLES: *Polypodium, Azolla, Osmunda.*

Category: Seed Plants

KEY CHARACTERISTICS: Vascular plants; reproduce by seeds; water is not needed for fertilization; diploid sporophyte is dominant stage of life cycle.

Class: Monocotyledones (Monocots)

KEY CHARACTERISTICS: Seeds with one cotyledon; floral parts occur in multiples of three; leaves have parallel veins; most have fibrous roots.

EXAMPLES: Grasses, palm trees, corn, rice, wheat.

Class: Dicotyledones (Dicots)

KEY CHARACTERISTICS: Seeds with two cotyledons; floral parts occur in multiples of four or five; leaves have branching netlike veins; most have a taproot.

EXAMPLES: Fruit trees, roses, tulips, dandelions.

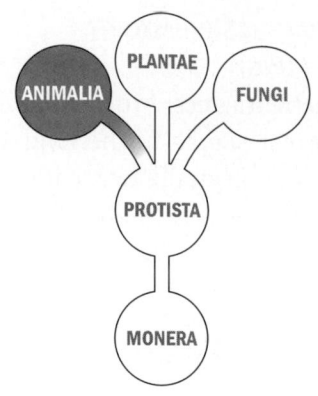

Kingdom: Animalia

KEY CHARACTERISTICS: Eukaryotes; cells lack cell walls; multicellular; most have radial or bilateral symmetry; heterotrophic; most are motile; most reproduce sexually with sperm and eggs; some reproduce asexually by budding or fragmentation.

PHYLUM: PORIFERA (SPONGES)

KEY CHARACTERISTICS: Internal skeleton made of spicules and spongin; two layers of porous tissue with no organ structure; filter-feeders; reproduce sexually or asexually; most live in saltwater environments.

PHYLUM: CNIDARIANS

KEY CHARACTERISTICS: Body consists of two tissue layers with a jellylike material in between; most have radial symmetry; two body forms, a sessile polyp and a free-floating medusa; tentacles with stinging cnidocytes; some species are colonial; most live in saltwater environments.

EXAMPLES: Jellyfish, coral, hydra.

PHYLUM: PLATYHELMINTHES (FLATWORMS)

KEY CHARACTERISTICS: Flat-bodied; acoelomates; digestive tract with one opening; bilateral symmetry; cephalization; parasitic and free-living forms.

EXAMPLES: Planarians, flukes, tapeworms.

PHYLUM: NEMATODA (ROUNDWORMS)

KEY CHARACTERISTICS: Long, slender bodies; pseudocoelomates; unsegmented; digestive tract with two openings; bilateral symmetry; cephalization; common in soil; many species are parasites.

EXAMPLES: *Trichinella spiralis, Ascaris,* pinworms, hookworms, vinegar worms.

PHYLUM: MOLLUSCA (MOLLUSKS)

KEY CHARACTERISTICS: Soft-bodied coelomates; some have shells; all have mantle, visceral mass, and muscular foot; most have open circulatory system; live in salt water, fresh water, or terrestrial environments.

EXAMPLES: Chitons, clams, snails, *Architeuthis* (giant squid), octopuses.

PHYLUM: ANNELIDA (SEGMENTED WORMS)

KEY CHARACTERISTICS: Segmented bodies; coelomates; most species have setae; closed circulatory system; well-developed nervous system.

EXAMPLES: Polychaetes, earthworms, leeches, sand worms.

PHYLUM: ARTHROPODA (ARTHROPODS)

KEY CHARACTERISTICS: Jointed legs or appendages; bilateral symmetry; exoskeleton contains chitin; open circulatory system; ventral nervous system.

EXAMPLES: Insects, spiders, lobsters, crabs.

PHYLUM: ECHINODERMATA (ECHINODERMS)

KEY CHARACTERISTICS: Deuterostomes; water vascular system used for movement, circulation, respiration, and excretion; spiny skin; radial symmetry in adult; bilateral symmetry in larva; live in saltwater environments.

EXAMPLE: Sea stars, brittle stars, sea urchins, sea cucumbers.

PHYLUM: CHORDATA (CHORDATES)

KEY CHARACTERISTICS: Notochord; gill slits; hollow, dorsal nerve tube; post-anal tail; nerve tube and notochord usually replaced by a vertebral column in adults.

Subphylum: Urochordata (Tunicates)

KEY CHARACTERISTICS: Soft, saclike body; no internal skeleton; sessile adult; motile larva; filter-feeders; live in saltwater environments.

EXAMPLES: Sea squirts, salps.

Subphylum: Cephalochordata (Lancelets)

KEY CHARACTERISTICS: No internal skeleton; transparent; thin, fish-like body; segmented; live in saltwater environments.

EXAMPLE: Amphioxus.

Subphylum: Vertebrata (Vertebrates)

KEY CHARACTERISTICS: Notochord develops into a spinal column enclosing dorsal nerve tube; internal skeleton usually made of bone; high degree of cephalization.

Class: Agnatha (Jawless Fishes)

KEY CHARACTERISTICS: Eel-like with smooth body; no scales; no jaws; round, sucking mouth; skeleton made of cartilage; two-chambered heart.

EXAMPLES: Hagfishes, lampreys.

Class: Chondrichthyes (Cartilaginous Fishes)

KEY CHARACTERISTICS: Skeleton made of cartilage; flexible jaw; rigid paired fins; body covered with scales; internal fertilization; two-chambered heart; most live in saltwater environments.

EXAMPLES: Rays, sharks, skates.

Class: Osteichthyes (Bony Fishes)

KEY CHARACTERISTICS: Bony skeleton; flexible jaw; flexible paired fins; air-filled swim bladder; two-chambered heart; live in saltwater and freshwater environments.

EXAMPLES: Salmon, tuna, carp, guppies, trout, bass.

Class: Amphibia (Amphibians)

KEY CHARACTERISTICS: Moist skin; most have lungs and a three-chambered heart; many undergo metamorphosis; most species have aquatic larval and terrestrial adult forms; external fertilization; water needed to reproduce.

EXAMPLES: Frogs, salamanders, newts.

Class: Reptilia (Reptiles)

KEY CHARACTERISTICS: Dry skin; body covered with scales; breathe through lungs; most have four limbs (except for snakes); internal fertilization; amniotic eggs with leathery shells.

EXAMPLES: Alligators, snakes, turtles, lizards.

Class: Aves (Birds)

KEY CHARACTERISTICS: Body covered with feathers; wings; lungs with one-way air flow; four-chambered heart; internal fertilization; eggs covered with hard shell; most species adapted for flight.

EXAMPLES: Ducks, penguins, sparrows, chickens.

Class: Mammalia (Mammals)

KEY CHARACTERISTICS: Body usually covered with hair or fur; four-chambered heart; highly developed brain; internal fertilization; young nourished by milk from the mother; extended period of parental care in many species.

EXAMPLES: Kangaroos, whales, bats, humans.

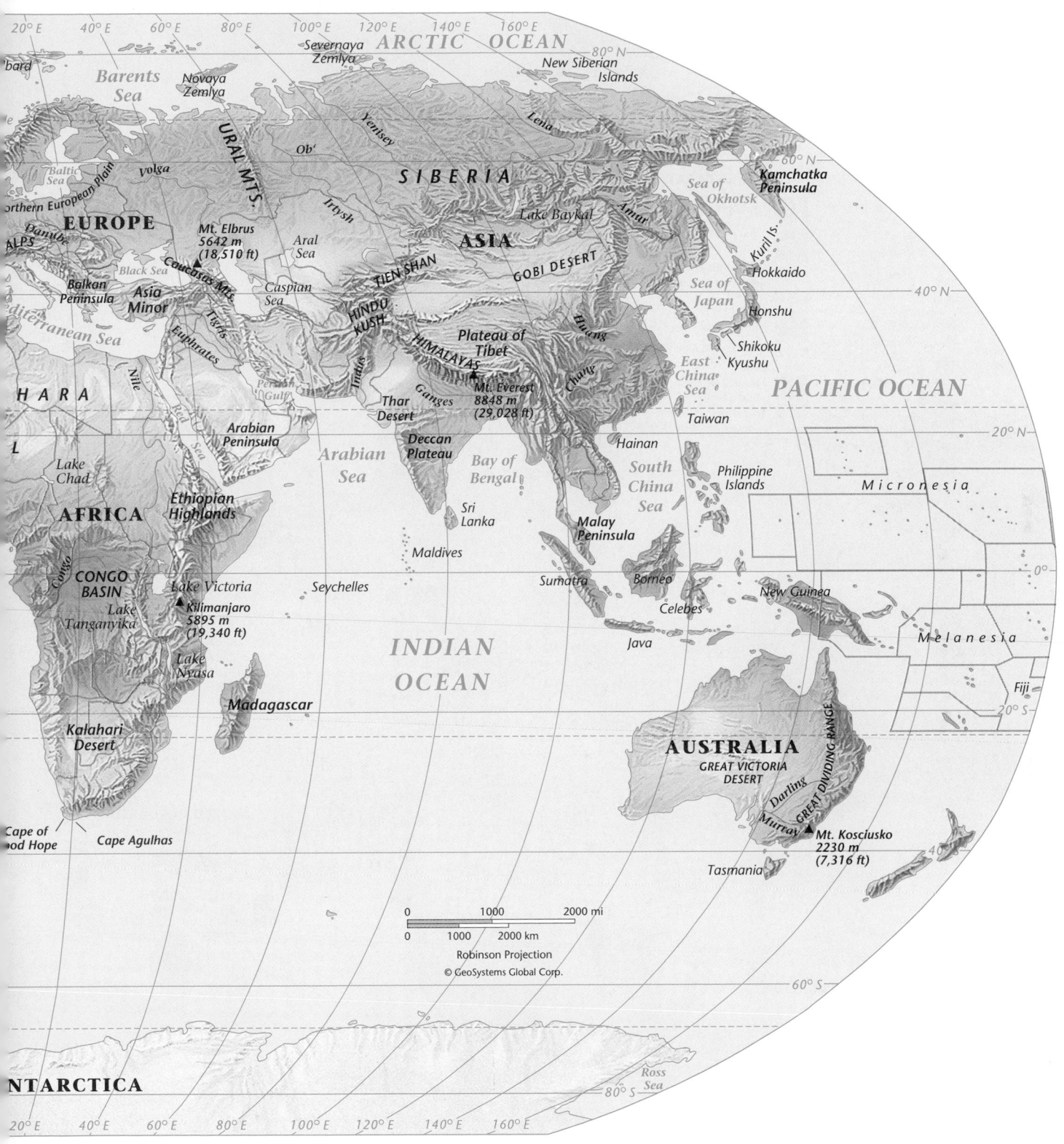

20° E 40° E 60° E 80° E 100° E 120° E 140° E 160° E

ARCTIC OCEAN

80° N

bard

Barents Sea

Severnaya Zemlya

Novaya Zemlya

New Siberian Islands

Kamchatka Peninsula

60° N

SIBERIA

Sea of Okhotsk

Kuril Is.

Baltic Sea

URAL MTS.

Yenisey

Lena

Amur

Volga

Ob'

ASIA

Lake Baykal

Northern European Plain

Irtysh

Aral Sea

Mt. Elbrus 5642 m (18,510 ft)

Hokkaido

EUROPE

Caspian Sea

TIEN SHAN

GOBI DESERT

Sea of Japan

40° N

ALPS

Danube

Caucasus Mts.

Honshu

Black Sea

HINDU KUSH

Shikoku Kyushu

Balkan Peninsula

Asia Minor

Tigris

Huang

East China Sea

PACIFIC OCEAN

diterranean Sea

Euphrates

Plateau of Tibet

HIMALAYAS

Chang

Nile

Persian Gulf

Indus

Ganges

Mt. Everest 8848 m (29,028 ft)

Taiwan

20° N

HARA

Thar Desert

Hainan

L

Arabian Peninsula

Arabian Sea

Deccan Plateau

South China Sea

Philippine Islands

Micronesia

Lake Chad

Bay of Bengal

AFRICA

Ethiopian Highlands

Sri Lanka

Malay Peninsula

Maldives

0°

CONGO BASIN

Lake Victoria

Seychelles

Sumatra

Borneo

New Guinea

Kilimanjaro 5895 m (19,340 ft)

Congo

Lake Tanganyika

Celebes

Melanesia

Java

INDIAN OCEAN

Lake Nyasa

Fiji

Madagascar

20° S

Kalahari Desert

AUSTRALIA

GREAT VICTORIA DESERT

GREAT DIVIDING RANGE

Cape of od Hope

Cape Agulhas

Darling

Murray

Mt. Kosciusko 2230 m (7,316 ft)

Tasmania

0 1000 2000 mi

0 1000 2000 km

Robinson Projection

© GeoSystems Global Corp.

60° S

NTARCTICA

Ross Sea

80° S

20° E 40° E 60° E 80° E 100° E 120° E 140° E 160° E

POPULATIONS OF MAJOR CITIES

Antigua & Barbuda
St. Johns   27,000

Bahamas
Nassau   172,000

Barbados
Bridgetown   6,000

Belize
Belize City   45,000
Belmopan   4,000

Canada   (metro)
Toronto   3,893,000
Montréal   3,127,000
Vancouver   1,603,000
Ottawa   921,000

Costa Rica   (metro)
San José   1,000,000

Cuba
Havana   2,119,000

Dominica
Roseau   16,000

Dominican Republic
Santo Domingo 2,400,000

El Salvador
San Salvador   423,000

Grenada
St. George's   30,000

Guatemala
Guatemala   1,676,000

Haiti
Port-au-Prince   690,000

Honduras
Tegucigalpa   608,000

Jamaica   (metro)
Kingston   587,000

Mexico   (metro)
Mexico City   20,000,000
Guadalajara   3,000,000
Monterrey   2,700,000

Nicaragua
Managua   1,000,000

Panama
Panamá   447,000

St. Kitts & Nevis
Basseterre   15,000

St. Lucia
Castries   45,000

St. Vincent & Grenadines
Kingstown   15,000

Trinidad & Tobago
Port of Spain   51,000

United States
New York   7,323,000
Los Angeles   3,485,000
Chicago   2,784,000
Houston   1,631,000
Philadelphia   1,586,000
San Diego   1,111,000
Detroit   1,028,000
Washington, D.C.   607,000

International comparability of city population
data is limited by various data inconsistencies.

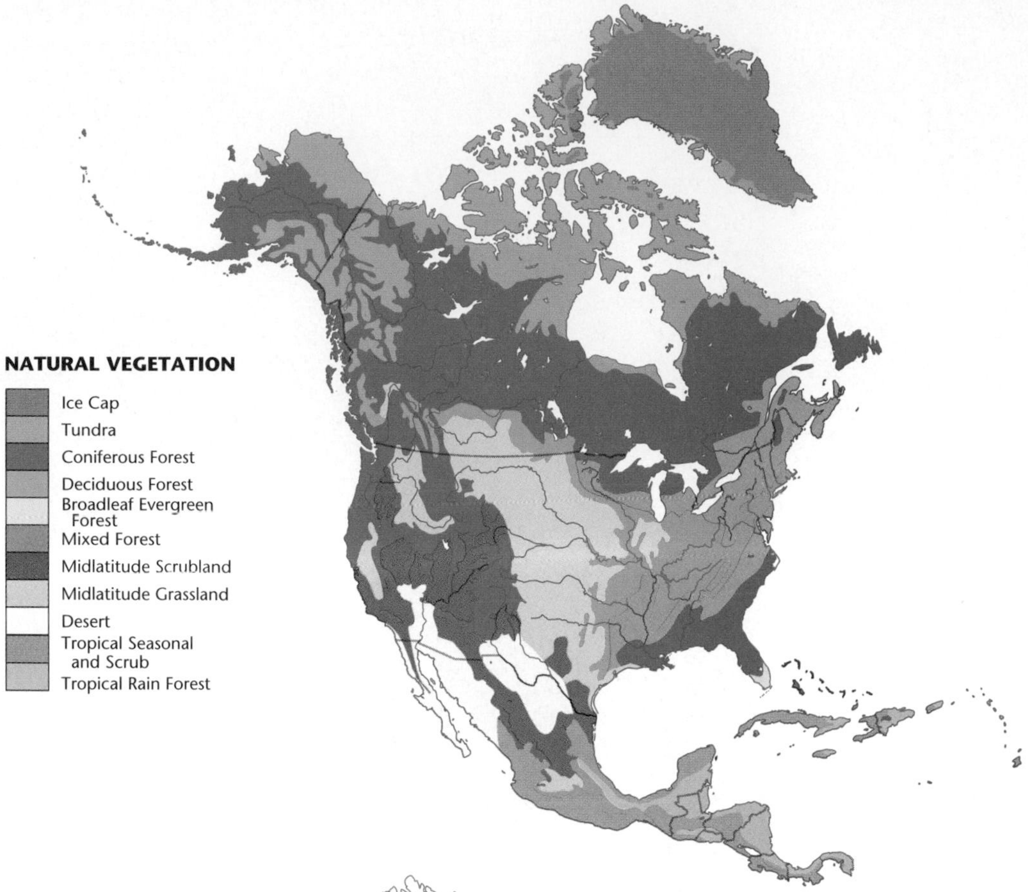

NATURAL VEGETATION

- Ice Cap
- Tundra
- Coniferous Forest
- Deciduous Forest
- Broadleaf Evergreen Forest
- Mixed Forest
- Midlatitude Scrubland
- Midlatitude Grassland
- Desert
- Tropical Seasonal and Scrub
- Tropical Rain Forest

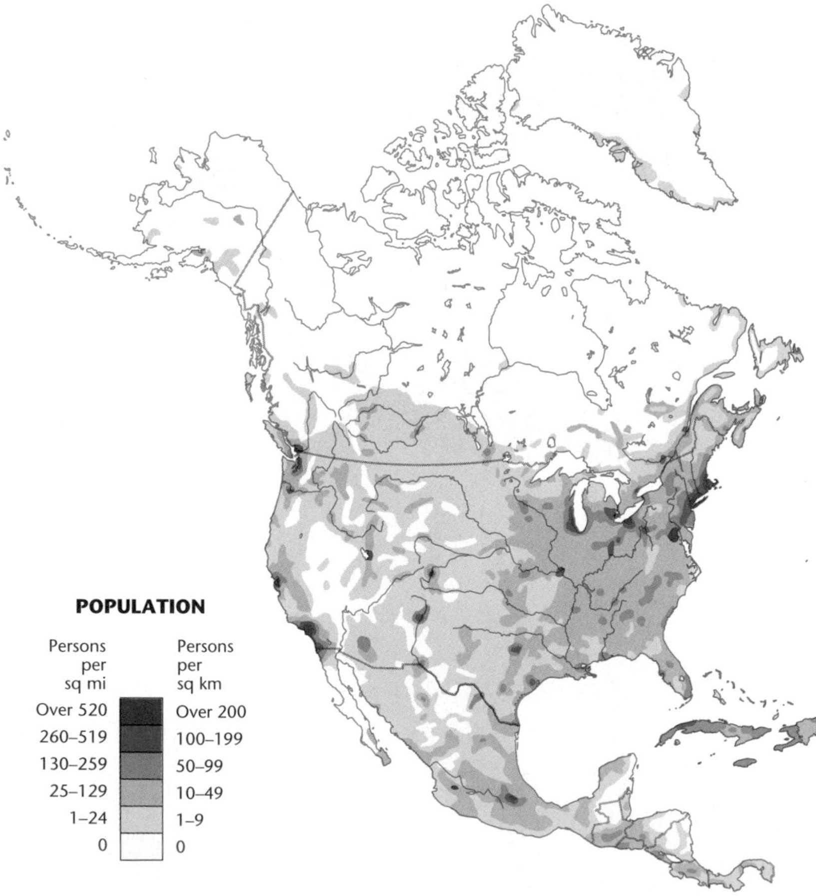

POPULATION

Persons per sq mi	Persons per sq km
Over 520	Over 200
260–519	100–199
130–259	50–99
25–129	10–49
1–24	1–9
0	0

WORLD POPULATION

Asia 61.0%
Europe 12.5%
Africa 12.4%
South America 5.6%
Oceania 0.5%
North America 8.0%

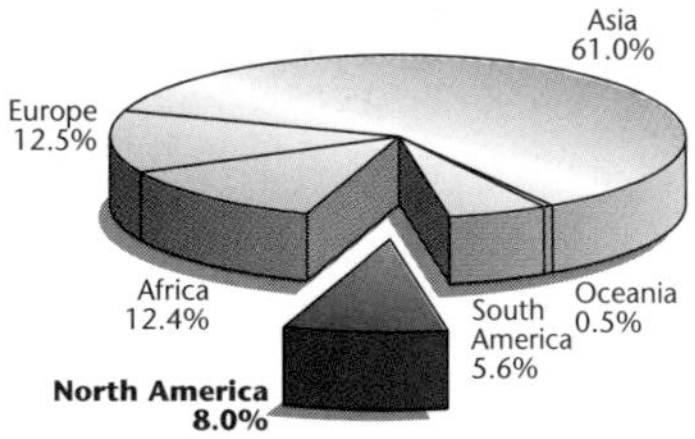

© GeoSystems Global Corp.

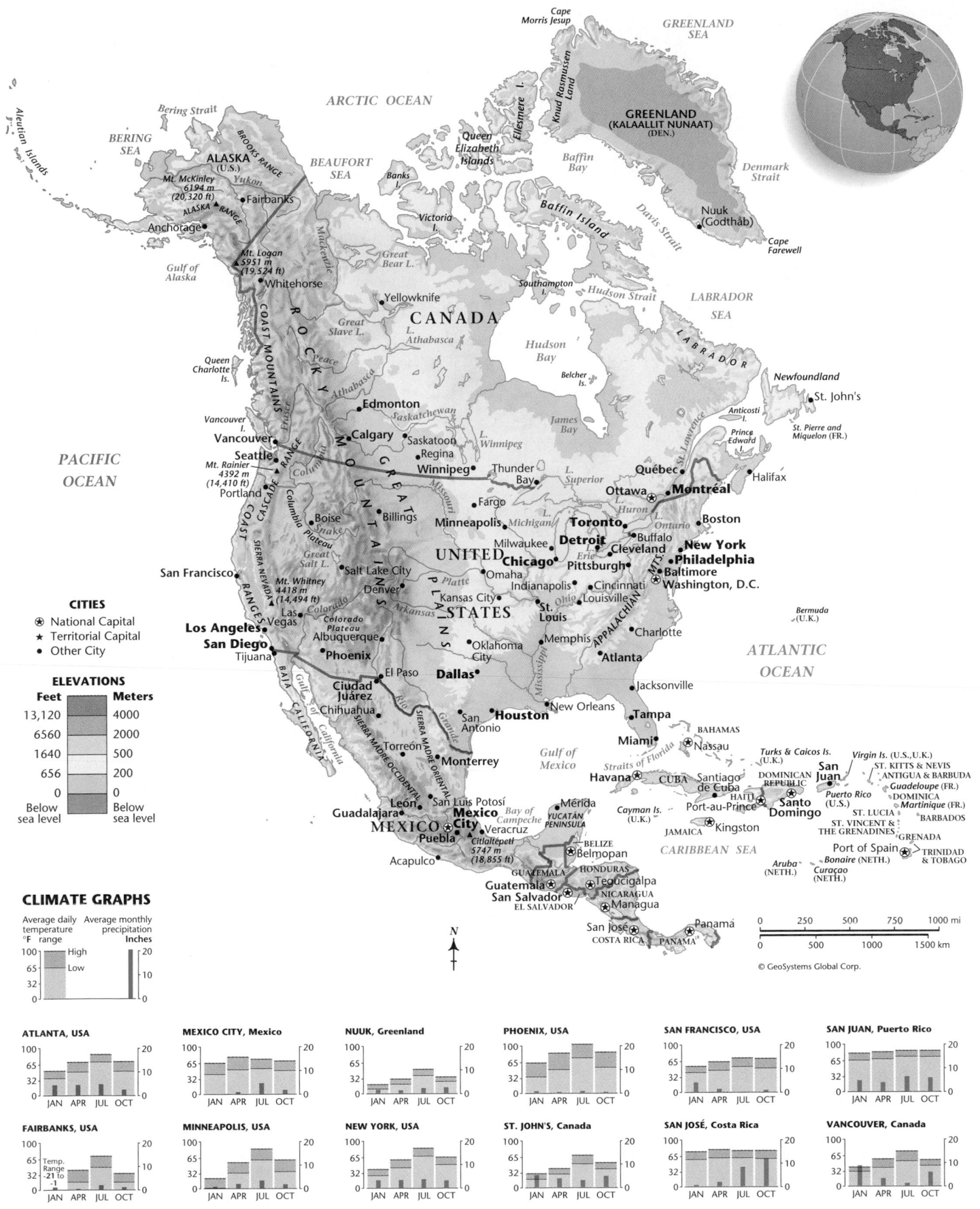

Cape
Morris Jesup

GREENLAND
SEA

ARCTIC OCEAN

BERING
SEA

Bering Strait

Aleutian Islands

ALASKA
(U.S.)
Mt. McKinley
6194 m
(20,320 ft)
Fairbanks

BROOKS RANGE

Yukon

ALASKA RANGE

Anchorage

Gulf of
Alaska

Mt. Logan
5951 m
(19,524 ft)
Whitehorse

PACIFIC
OCEAN

Queen
Charlotte Is.

Vancouver
I.

Vancouver

Seattle
Mt. Rainier
4392 m
(14,410 ft)
Portland

COAST RANGE

Columbia

Boise
Snake

CASCADE RANGE

COAST RANGES

San Francisco

SIERRA NEVADA

Mt. Whitney
4418 m
(14,494 ft)

Las
Vegas

Los Angeles
San Diego
Tijuana

BAJA CALIFORNIA

Gulf of California

SIERRA MADRE OCCIDENTAL

BEAUFORT
SEA

Banks
I.

Victoria
I.

Great
Bear L.

Yellowknife

Great
Slave L.

CANADA

Peace

Athabasca

L.
Athabasca

Edmonton

Calgary
Saskatoon
Regina

Winnipeg

Billings

ROCKY MOUNTAINS

Great
Salt L.

Salt Lake City
Denver

Colorado

Colorado
Plateau
Albuquerque

Phoenix

El Paso

Ciudad
Juárez
Chihuahua

Torreón

Monterrey

Rio Grande

SIERRA MADRE ORIENTAL

Queen
Elizabeth
Islands

Ellesmere I.

Knud Rasmussen
Land

GREENLAND
(KALAALLIT NUNAAT)
(DEN.)

Nuuk
(Godthåb)

Cape
Farewell

Denmark
Strait

Baffin
Bay

Davis Strait

Baffin Island

Southampton
I.

Hudson Strait

LABRADOR
SEA

Hudson
Bay

James
Bay

Belcher
Is.

LABRADOR

Newfoundland

St. John's

Anticosti
I.

St. Pierre and
Miquelon (FR.)

Prince
Edward I.

Halifax

Minneapolis

UNITED

STATES

Fargo

Missouri

L. Winnipeg

Thunder
Bay

L. Superior

L. Michigan

Milwaukee

Chicago

Omaha

Platte

Kansas City

Arkansas

Oklahoma
City

Dallas

San
Antonio

Houston

New Orleans

Gulf of
Mexico

GREAT PLAINS

Ottawa

Québec

Montréal

Boston

Toronto

Detroit
Buffalo
Cleveland

New York
Philadelphia

Pittsburgh
Baltimore
Washington, D.C.

L. Huron

L. Ontario

L. Erie

St.
Louis

Indianapolis

Cincinnati
Louisville

Ohio

Memphis

APPALACHIAN MTS.

Charlotte

Atlanta

Jacksonville

Tampa

Miami

Mississippi

St. Lawrence

Bermuda
(U.K.)

ATLANTIC
OCEAN

BAHAMAS

Nassau

Straits of Florida

Havana

CUBA

Santiago
de Cuba

Cayman Is.
(U.K.)

JAMAICA

Kingston

Turks & Caicos Is.
(U.K.)

HAITI

DOMINICAN
REPUBLIC

Port-au-Prince
Santo
Domingo

Puerto Rico
(U.S.)

San
Juan

Virgin Is. (U.S.,U.K.)
ST. KITTS & NEVIS
ANTIGUA & BARBUDA
Guadeloupe (FR.)
DOMINICA
Martinique (FR.)
ST. LUCIA
BARBADOS
ST. VINCENT &
THE GRENADINES
GRENADA

Port of Spain
TRINIDAD
& TOBAGO

Bonaire (NETH.)
Aruba
(NETH.)
Curaçao
(NETH.)

CARIBBEAN SEA

Guadalajara

León
San Luis Potosí

MEXICO

Mexico
City
Puebla

Acapulco

Veracruz

Citlaltépetl
5747 m
(18,855 ft)

Bay of
Campeche

Mérida

YUCATÁN
PENINSULA

BELIZE

Belmopan

GUATEMALA
Guatemala
San Salvador
EL SALVADOR

HONDURAS
Tegucigalpa

NICARAGUA
Managua

San José
COSTA RICA

PANAMA

Panamá

CITIES
⊛ National Capital
★ Territorial Capital
● Other City

ELEVATIONS
Feet	Meters
13,120	4000
6560	2000
1640	500
656	200
0	0
Below
sea level	Below
sea level

0   250   500   750   1000 mi
0   500   1000   1500 km

© GeoSystems Global Corp.

N

CLIMATE GRAPHS

Average daily
temperature
°F range
100
65
32
0
High
Low

Average monthly
precipitation
Inches
20
10
0

ATLANTA, USA

FAIRBANKS, USA
Temp.
Range
-21 to

MEXICO CITY, Mexico

MINNEAPOLIS, USA

NUUK, Greenland

NEW YORK, USA

PHOENIX, USA

ST. JOHN'S, Canada

SAN FRANCISCO, USA

SAN JOSÉ, Costa Rica

SAN JUAN, Puerto Rico

VANCOUVER, Canada

POPULATIONS OF MAJOR CITIES

Argentina
Buenos Aires	2,961,000
Córdoba	1,148,000
Rosario	895,000

Bolivia
La Paz	711,000
Santa Cruz	695,000
Sucre	131,000

Brazil
São Paulo	9,480,000
Rio de Janeiro	5,336,000
Salvador	2,056,000
Belo Horizonte	2,049,000
Fortaleza	1,758,000
Brasília	1,596,000
Recife	1,290,000
Curitiba	1,290,000
Pôrto Alegre	1,263,000
Belém	1,246,000
Manaus	1,011,000

Chile
Santiago	4,385,000
Concepción	306,000

Colombia | (metro)
Bogotá	3,975,000
Medellín	1,452,000
Cali	1,369,000
Barranquilla	917,000

Ecuador
Guayaquil	1,508,000
Quito	1,101,000

Falkland Islands
Stanley	1,200

French Guiana
Cayenne	41,000

Guyana
Georgetown	195,000

Paraguay
Asunción	502,000

Peru | (metro)
Lima	6,415,000
Arequipa	635,000
Trujillo	532,000

Suriname
Paramaribo	192,000

Uruguay
Montevideo	1,360,000

Venezuela
Caracas	1,825,000
Maracaibo	1,208,000
Valencia	903,000
Barquisimeto	603,000

International comparability of city population data is limited by various data inconsistencies.

NATURAL VEGETATION

- Unclassified Highlands
- Deciduous Forest
- Mixed Forest
- Midlatitude Scrubland
- Midlatitude Grassland
- Desert
- Tropical Seasonal and Scrub
- Tropical Rain Forest
- Tropical Savanna

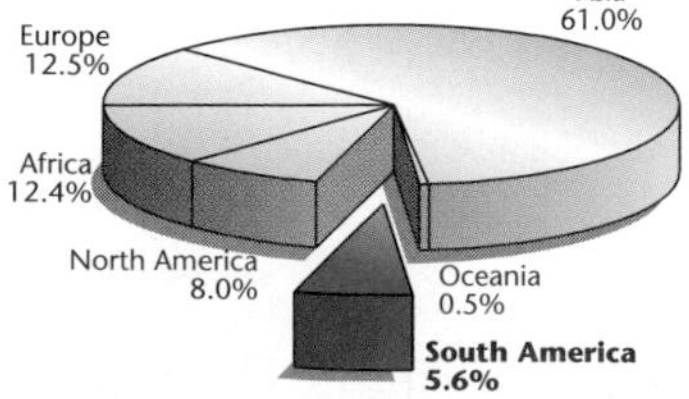

POPULATION

Persons per sq mi	Persons per sq km
Over 520	Over 200
260–519	100–199
130–259	50–99
25–129	10–49
1–24	1–9
0	0

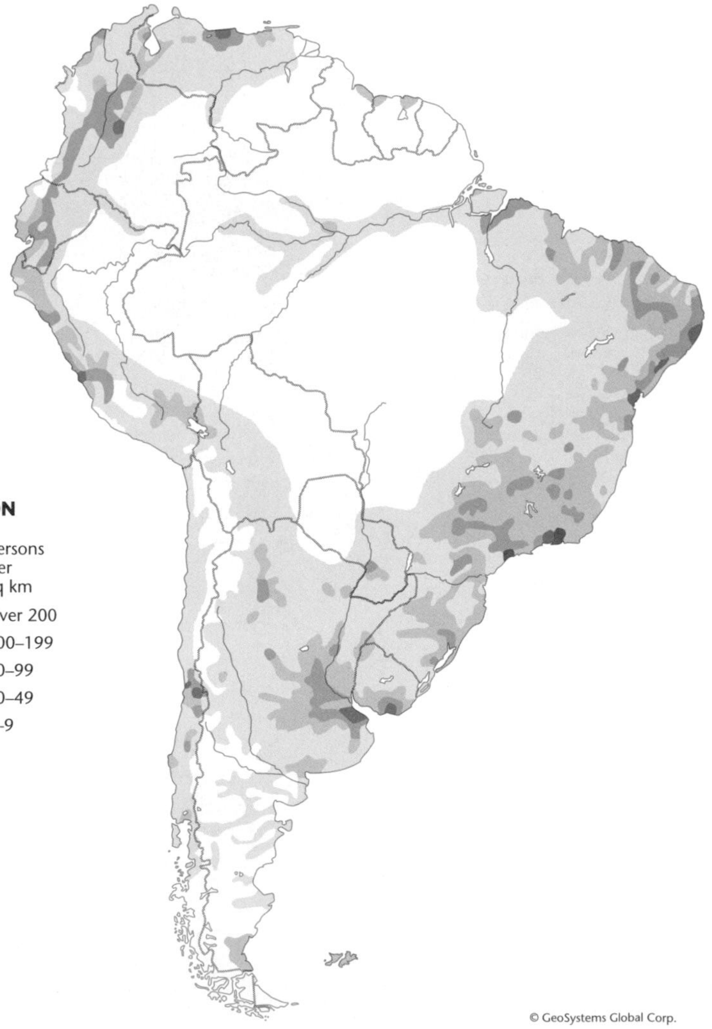

WORLD POPULATION

- Asia 61.0%
- Europe 12.5%
- Africa 12.4%
- North America 8.0%
- Oceania 0.5%
- South America 5.6%

© GeoSystems Global Corp.

CARIBBEAN SEA

Barranquilla
Cartagena
Maracaibo
Barquisimeto
Valencia
Caracas
Maracay
Cumaná
Maturín
Cúcuta
San Cristóbal
Bucaramanga
Medellín
Manizales
Pereira
Ibagué
★ Bogotá
Cali
Pasto

Ciudad
Bolívar
Ciudad Guayana

L. Maracaibo

VENEZUELA
GUIANA
GUYANA
SURINAME
FRENCH GUIANA (FR.)
Georgetown
Paramaribo
Cayenne

HIGHLANDS

ATLANTIC
OCEAN

COLOMBIA
LLANOS
Orinoco

Negro

Quito ⊗
ECUADOR
Guayaquil
Cuenca
Chimborazo
6267 m
(20,561 ft)

AMAZON

Iquitos

Manaus

SELVAS

Belém
Ilha
Marajó

Amazon

Fortaleza

PERU
Piura
Chiclayo
Trujillo
Chimbote
Huascarán
6768 m
(22,205 ft)
Pucallpa

BASIN

Juruá
Purús
Madeira

Pôrto Velho

Teresina
Natal

Recife
Maceió

Callao
Lima
Ica
Huancayo
Cuzco

BRAZIL

Tapajós
Xingu

Mamoré

Guaporé

BOLIVIA
MATO GROSSO
PLATEAU
Cuiabá

BRAZILIAN

Salvador

São Francisco

Tocantins

Araguaia

Arequipa
La Paz
Cochabamba
Santa Cruz
Oruro
⊗ Sucre
Potosí

Goiânia
⊗ Brasília

HIGHLANDS
Uberlândia
Belo Horizonte
Vitória

Arica
Iquique
ALTIPLANO
L. Poopó
Campo
Grande

Campinas

ATACAMA DESERT
Antofagasta
Salta

GRAN CHACO

PARAGUAY
Asunción ⊗
Ciudad
del Este

São Paulo
Santos
Rio de Janeiro
Curitiba

Pilcomayo
Paraná

San Miguel
de Tucumán
Ojos del Salado
6880 m
(22,572 ft)
Santiago
del Estero
Resistencia
Encarnación

Pôrto Alegre

Isla San Ambrosio
(CHILE)
Isla San Félix
(CHILE)

Aconcagua
6960 m
(22,834 ft)
CHILE
Córdoba
San Juan
Mendoza
Salto
Santa
Fe
Paysandú
URUGUAY
Rosario
Salto

Valparaíso
Santiago ⊗
Rancagua
Talca

Paraná
Uruguay

PAMPA

Buenos
Aires ⊗
Montevideo

Rio de la Plata

Islas Juan Fernández
(CHILE)

PACIFIC
OCEAN

ATLANTIC
OCEAN

Concepción
Temuco
Neuquén
Bahía Blanca

ARGENTINA
Mar del Plata

Puerto Montt
Chiloé

PATAGONIA

Península
Valdés

N

Archipiélago
de los Chonos
Península
Taitao

Comodoro Rivadavia

Falkland Is.
(Islas Malvinas)
(U.K.)
Stanley

Strait of
Magellan

Punta Arenas
Tierra del Fuego
Ushuaia
Cape Horn

CITIES
⊗ National Capital
★ Territorial Capital
• Other City

ELEVATIONS

Feet	Meters
13,120	4000
6560	2000
1640	500
656	200
0	0
Below sea level	Below sea level

0	250	500	750	1000 mi
0	250	500	750	1000	1250	1500 km

© GeoSystems Global Corp.

CLIMATE GRAPHS

Average daily
temperature
°F   range
Average monthly
precipitation
Inches

100		20
65	High	
32	Low	10
0		0

ASUNCIÓN, Paraguay

BUENOS AIRES, Argentina

CAYENNE, French Guiana

LIMA, Peru

PUNTA ARENAS, Chile

RIO DE JANEIRO, Brazil

BOGOTÁ, Colombia

CARACAS, Venezuela

LA PAZ, Bolivia

MANAUS, Brazil

RECIFE, Brazil

SANTIAGO, Chile

967

POPULATIONS OF MAJOR CITIES

Albania			**Luxembourg**	
Tiranë	244,000		Luxembourg	75,000
Andorra			**F.Y.R. Macedonia**	
Andorra la Vella	16,000		Skopje	393,000
Armenia			**Malta**	
Yerevan	1,254,000		Valletta	9,000
Austria			**Moldova**	
Vienna	1,539,000		Chişinău	667,000
Azerbaijan			**Monaco**	
Baku	1,149,000		Monaco	27,000
Belarus			**Netherlands**	
Minsk	1,613,000		Amsterdam	713,000
			Rotterdam	590,000
Belgium	(metro)		**Norway**	
Brussels	951,000		Oslo	465,000
Antwerp	465,000			
Bosnia and Herzegovina			**Poland**	
Sarajevo	416,000		Warsaw	1,654,000
			Łódź	847,000
Bulgaria			Kraków	751,000
Sofia	1,141,000		Wrocław	643,000
Croatia			**Portugal**	
Zagreb	704,000		Lisbon	678,000
Czech Republic			**Romania**	
Prague	1,212,000		Bucharest	2,064,000
Denmark			**Russia (European)**	
Copenhagen	617,000		Moscow	8,747,000
			St. Petersburg	4,437,000
Estonia			Nizh. Novgorod	1,441,000
Tallinn	478,000		Samara	1,239,000
			Kazan	1,104,000
Finland			Perm'	1,099,000
Helsinki	495,000		Ufa	1,097,000
			Rostov-na-Donu	1,027,000
France			Volgograd	1,006,000
Paris	2,152,000			
Marseille	800,000		**San Marino**	
Lyon	416,000		San Marino	3,000
Georgia			**Slovakia**	
Tbilisi	1,268,000		Bratislava	441,000
Germany			**Slovenia**	
Berlin	3,438,000		Ljubljana	277,000
Hamburg	1,661,000			
Munich	1,237,000		**Spain**	
Cologne	956,000		Madrid	2,991,000
Frankfurt	647,000		Barcelona	1,668,000
Essen	626,000		Valencia	719,000
Dortmund	600,000		Seville	654,000
Stuttgart	584,000			
Düsseldorf	577,000		**Sweden**	
Leipzig	508,000		Stockholm	679,000
Greece			**Switzerland**	
Athens	748,000		Zürich	342,000
			Bern	135,000
Hungary				
Budapest	2,017,000		**Turkey (European)**	
			İstanbul	6,620,000
Iceland				
Reykjavík	97,000		**Ukraine**	
			Kiev	2,643,000
Ireland			Kharkiv	1,622,000
Dublin	478,000		Dnipropetrov'sk	1,190,000
			Donets'k	1,121,000
Italy			Odesa	1,096,000
Rome	2,829,000			
Milan	1,549,000		**United Kingdom**	
Naples	1,208,000		London	6,803,000
Turin	1,060,000		Birmingham	995,000
Genoa	742,000		Leeds	706,000
Palermo	714,000		Glasgow	688,000
			Sheffield	520,000
Latvia			Liverpool	475,000
Riga	909,000		Edinburgh	439,000
			Manchester	433,000
Liechtenstein				
Vaduz	5,000		**Yugoslavia**	
			Belgrade	1,137,000
Lithuania				
Vilnius	591,000			

International comparability of city population data is limited by various data inconsistencies.

© GeoSystems Global Corp.

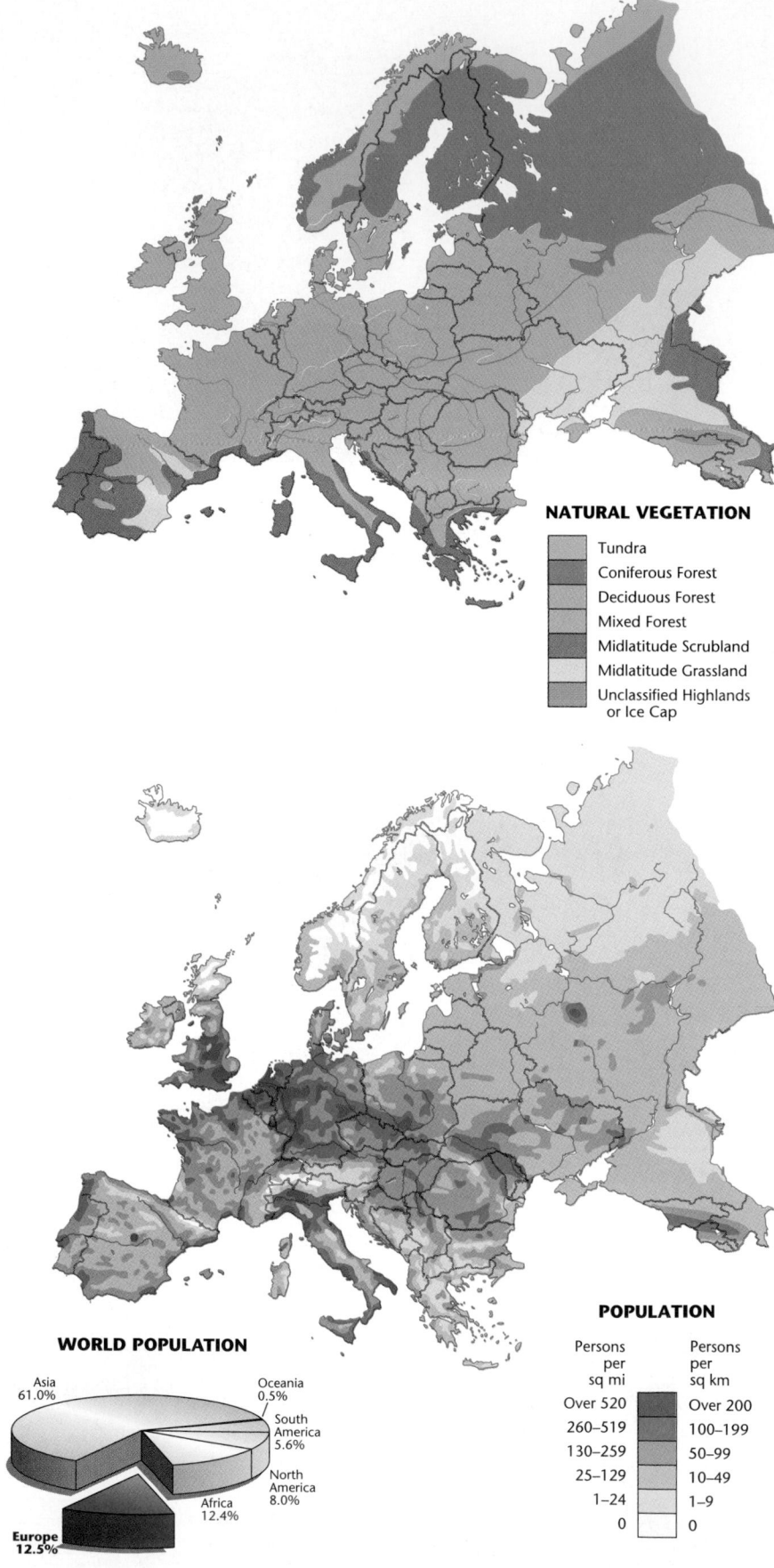

NATURAL VEGETATION

- Tundra
- Coniferous Forest
- Deciduous Forest
- Mixed Forest
- Midlatitude Scrubland
- Midlatitude Grassland
- Unclassified Highlands or Ice Cap

WORLD POPULATION

- Asia 61.0%
- Oceania 0.5%
- South America 5.6%
- North America 8.0%
- Africa 12.4%
- Europe 12.5%

POPULATION

Persons per sq mi	Persons per sq km
Over 520	Over 200
260–519	100–199
130–259	50–99
25–129	10–49
1–24	1–9
0	0

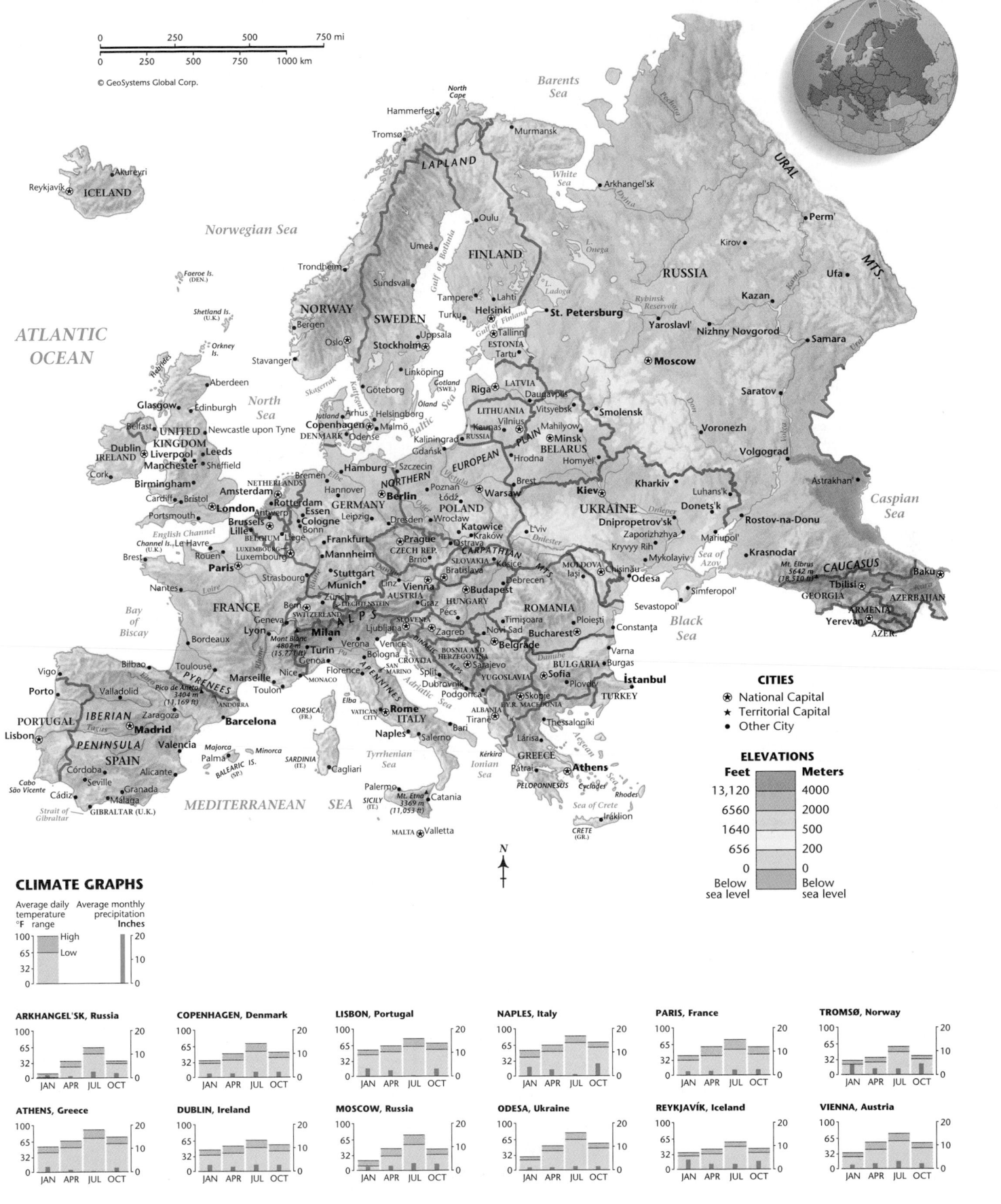

ATLANTIC
OCEAN

0 250 500 750 mi
0 250 500 750 1000 km
© GeoSystems Global Corp.

*Barents
Sea*

North
Cape

Hammerfest
Tromsø
Murmansk

LAPLAND

*White
Sea*

Arkhangel'sk

Akureyri
Reykjavík ⊛ ICELAND

Norwegian Sea

Oulu

FINLAND

RUSSIA

Perm'

*Faeroe Is.
(DEN.)*

Trondheim

Umeå

*L.
Onega*

Kirov

Ufa

*Shetland Is.
(U.K.)*

Bergen

SWEDEN

Sundsvall

Tampere

Lahti

*Rybinsk
Reservoir*

Kazan

Samara

Stavanger

Oslo

Stockholm

Uppsala

Turku Helsinki
ESTONIA

⊛ St. Petersburg

Yaroslavl'

Nizhny Novgorod

*Orkney
Is.*

⊛ Moscow

Saratov

Aberdeen

*North
Sea*

Göteborg

*Gotland
(SWE.)*

Tallinn

Tartu

Glasgow Edinburgh

Riga ⊛ LATVIA

Daugavpils

Vitsyebsk

Smolensk

Voronezh

Volgograd

Belfast UNITED
KINGDOM Newcastle upon Tyne

Copenhagen
DENMARK Malmö
Odense

Kaliningrad

LITHUANIA

Kaunas Vilnius

⊛ Minsk

Mahilyow

Astrakhan'

Dublin
IRELAND Liverpool Leeds

*Baltic
Sea*

Gdansk

EUROPEAN

BELARUS

Homyel'

Kharkiv

Rostov-na-Donu

*Caspian
Sea*

Cork

Birmingham

Sheffield

Bremen
Hamburg Szczecin
Poznan

Hrodna

Brest

Kiev ⊛

Luhans'k

Krasnodar

Cardiff Bristol

NETHERLANDS

Amsterdam

Berlin ⊛
GERMANY

NORTHERN

Warsaw

UKRAINE

Donets'k

CAUCASUS

Portsmouth

Rotterdam Essen
Antwerp Cologne
Leipzig Dresden Wroclaw Katowice

POLAND

Lódz

L'viv

Dnipropetrov'sk

Mariupol'

*Sea of
Azov*

Mt. Elbrus
5642 m
(18,510 ft)

London ⊛ Brussels
BELGIUM Bonn
Liège Frankfurt

Zaporizhzhya

Kryvyy Rih

Baku

English Channel

Lille

Prague

Kraków

Mykolayiv

*Channel Is.
(U.K.)* Le Havre

LUXEMBOURG
Luxembourg Mannheim

CZECH REP. Brno

SLOVAKIA Kosice

CARPATHIAN

MOLDOVA

Iasi Chisinau

Odesa

Simferopol'

Tbilisi

GEORGIA

AZERBAIJAN

Brest Rouen Paris ⊛ Strasbourg Stuttgart Munich

Vienna Bratislava

ARMENIA

Yerevan AZER.

Nantes

Bern

Zürich

LIECHTENSTEIN
AUSTRIA Graz

Budapest Debrecen

ROMANIA

Sevastopol'

*Black
Sea*

FRANCE

Geneva SWITZERLAND Ljubljana

HUNGARY

Pécs

Timisoara Ploiesti

Bucharest

Constanta

Bordeaux Lyon

Mont Blanc
4807 m
(15,771 ft) Milan Turin Verona Venice

SLOVENIA
Zagreb Novi Sad
CROATIA Belgrade

Varna

Bologna

Genoa

BOSNIA AND
HERZEGOVINA Sarajevo YUGOSLAVIA

Burgas

*Bay
of
Biscay*

Vigo Bilbao Toulouse Nice Florence

SAN
MARINO Split Dubrovnik Podgorica

BULGARIA Sofia ⊛ Plovdiv

Istanbul

Porto Valladolid Pico de Aneto
3404 m
(11,169 ft) Marseille Toulon MONACO

ANDORRA CORSICA
(FR.) Elba VATICAN
CITY Rome ⊛ ITALY

Skopje

F.Y.R. MACEDONIA

TURKEY

Thessaloniki

PORTUGAL

IBERIAN

Zaragoza Barcelona

PYRENEES

Bari

ALBANIA Tiranë

Lisbon ⊛ Madrid ⊛

Valencia

Majorca
Palma Minorca

SARDINIA
(IT.)

Naples ⊛ Salerno

Kérkira

GREECE

Lárisa

*Aegean
Sea*

Rhodes

SPAIN

PENINSULA

Córdoba

Alicante

BALEARIC IS.
(SP.)

Cagliari

Palermo

*Tyrrhenian
Sea*

Mt. Etna
3369 m
(11,053 ft)

*Ionian
Sea*

Pátrai

Athens ⊛

PELOPONNESUS

Cyclades

Cabo
São Vicente Seville Granada

Málaga

GIBRALTAR (U.K.)

*Strait of
Gibraltar*

MEDITERRANEAN   SEA

SICILY
(IT.) Catania

MALTA ⊙ Valletta

Sea of Crete

Iráklion

CRETE
(GR.)

N

CITIES

⊛ National Capital
★ Territorial Capital
● Other City

ELEVATIONS

Feet		Meters
13,120		4000
6560		2000
1640		500
656		200
0		0
Below
sea level		Below
sea level

CLIMATE GRAPHS

Average daily
temperature
°F   range

Average monthly
precipitation
Inches

100		High	20
65		Low	
32			10
0			0

ARKHANGEL'SK, Russia
COPENHAGEN, Denmark
LISBON, Portugal
NAPLES, Italy
PARIS, France
TROMSØ, Norway

ATHENS, Greece
DUBLIN, Ireland
MOSCOW, Russia
ODESA, Ukraine
REYKJAVÍK, Iceland
VIENNA, Austria

POPULATIONS OF MAJOR CITIES

Afghanistan			**Kyrgyzstan**	
Kabul	1,424,000		Bishkek	628,000
Bahrain			**Laos**	
Manama	151,000		Vientiane	377,000
Bangladesh	(metro)		**Lebanon**	
Dhaka	3,459,000		Beirut	475,000
Bhutan			**Malaysia**	
Thimphu	8,900		Kuala Lumpur	920,000
Brunei			**Maldives**	
Band. Seri Begawan	51,000		Male	55,000
Burma (Myanmar)			**Mongolia**	
Rangoon	2,513,000		Ulaanbaatar	536,000
Cambodia			**Nepal**	
Phnom Penh	800,000		Kathmandu	419,000
China			**Oman**	
Shanghai	7,500,000		Muscat	85,000
Beijing	5,700,000			
Tianjin	4,500,000		**Pakistan**	(metro)
Shenyang	3,600,000		Karachi	5,181,000
Wuhan	3,200,000		Lahore	2,953,000
Guangzhou	2,900,000		Faisalabad	1,104,000
Chongqing	2,700,000		Islamabad	204,000
Harbin	2,500,000			
Chengdu	2,500,000		**Philippines**	(metro)
Zibo	2,200,000		Manila	1,895,000
Xi'an	2,200,000			
Nanjing	2,091,000		**Qatar**	
			Doha	236,000
Cyprus	(metro)			
Nicosia	167,000		**Russia (Asian)**	
			Novosibirsk	1,442,000
India	(metro)		Yekaterinburg	1,371,000
Mumbai	12,572,000		Omsk	1,169,000
(Bombay)			Chelyabinsk	1,143,000
Calcutta	10,916,000		Krasnoyarsk	925,000
Delhi	8,375,000			
Chennai (Madras)	5,361,000		**Saudi Arabia**	
Hyderabad	4,280,000		Riyadh	1,300,000
Bangalore	4,087,000		Jiddah	1,200,000
Indonesia			**Singapore**	
Jakarta	8,200,000		Singapore	2,818,000
Surabaya	2,400,000			
Bandung	2,000,000		**Sri Lanka**	
Medan	1,700,000		Colombo	615,000
Iran			**Syria**	
Tehran	6,043,000		Damascus	1,451,000
Mashhad	1,464,000		Halab (Aleppo)	1,445,000
Iraq			**Taiwan**	
Baghdad	3,841,000		Taipei	1,770,000
Israel			**Tajikistan**	
Jerusalem	544,000		Dushanbe	602,000
Japan			**Thailand**	
Tokyo	8,164,000		Bangkok	5,876,000
Yokohama	3,220,000			
Osaka	2,624,000		**Turkey (Asian)**	
Nagoya	2,155,000		Ankara	2,559,000
Sapporo	1,672,000		İzmir	1,757,000
Kobe	1,477,000			
Kyoto	1,461,000		**Turkmenistan**	
Fukuoka	1,237,000		Ashgabat	407,000
Kawasaki	1,174,000			
Hiroshima	1,086,000		**United Arab Emirates**	
			Abu Dhabi	722,000
Jordan				
Amman	936,000		**Uzbekistan**	
			Tashkent	2,094,000
Kazakstan				
Almaty	1,147,000		**Vietnam**	
			Ho Chi Minh City	2,900,000
North Korea			Hanoi	1,090,000
P'yŏngyang	2,300,000			
			Yemen	(metro)
South Korea			Sana	427,000
Seoul	10,628,000			
Pusan	3,798,000			
Taegu	2,229,000			
Kuwait				
Kuwait	78,000			

International comparability of city population data is limited by various data inconsistencies.

NATURAL VEGETATION

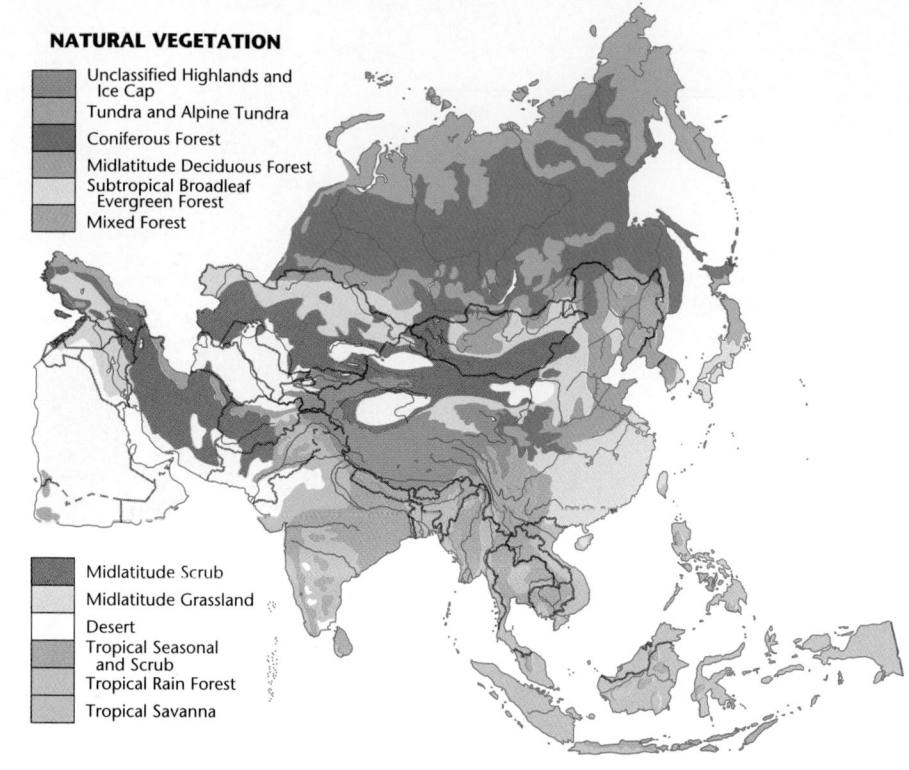

- Unclassified Highlands and Ice Cap
- Tundra and Alpine Tundra
- Coniferous Forest
- Midlatitude Deciduous Forest
- Subtropical Broadleaf Evergreen Forest
- Mixed Forest

- Midlatitude Scrub
- Midlatitude Grassland
- Desert
- Tropical Seasonal and Scrub
- Tropical Rain Forest
- Tropical Savanna

POPULATION

Persons per sq mi	Persons per sq km
Over 520	Over 200
260–519	100–199
130–259	50–99
25–129	10–49
1–24	1–9
0	0

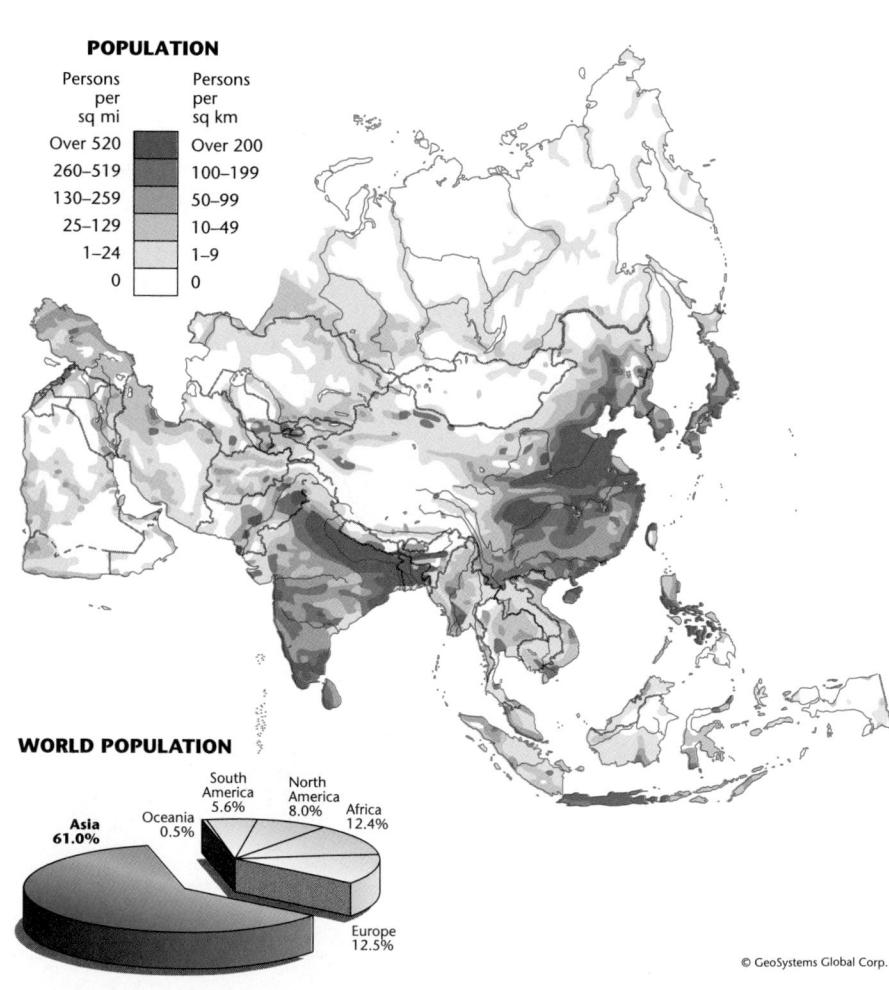

WORLD POPULATION

Asia 61.0%
Oceania 0.5%
South America 5.6%
North America 8.0%
Africa 12.4%
Europe 12.5%

© GeoSystems Global Corp.

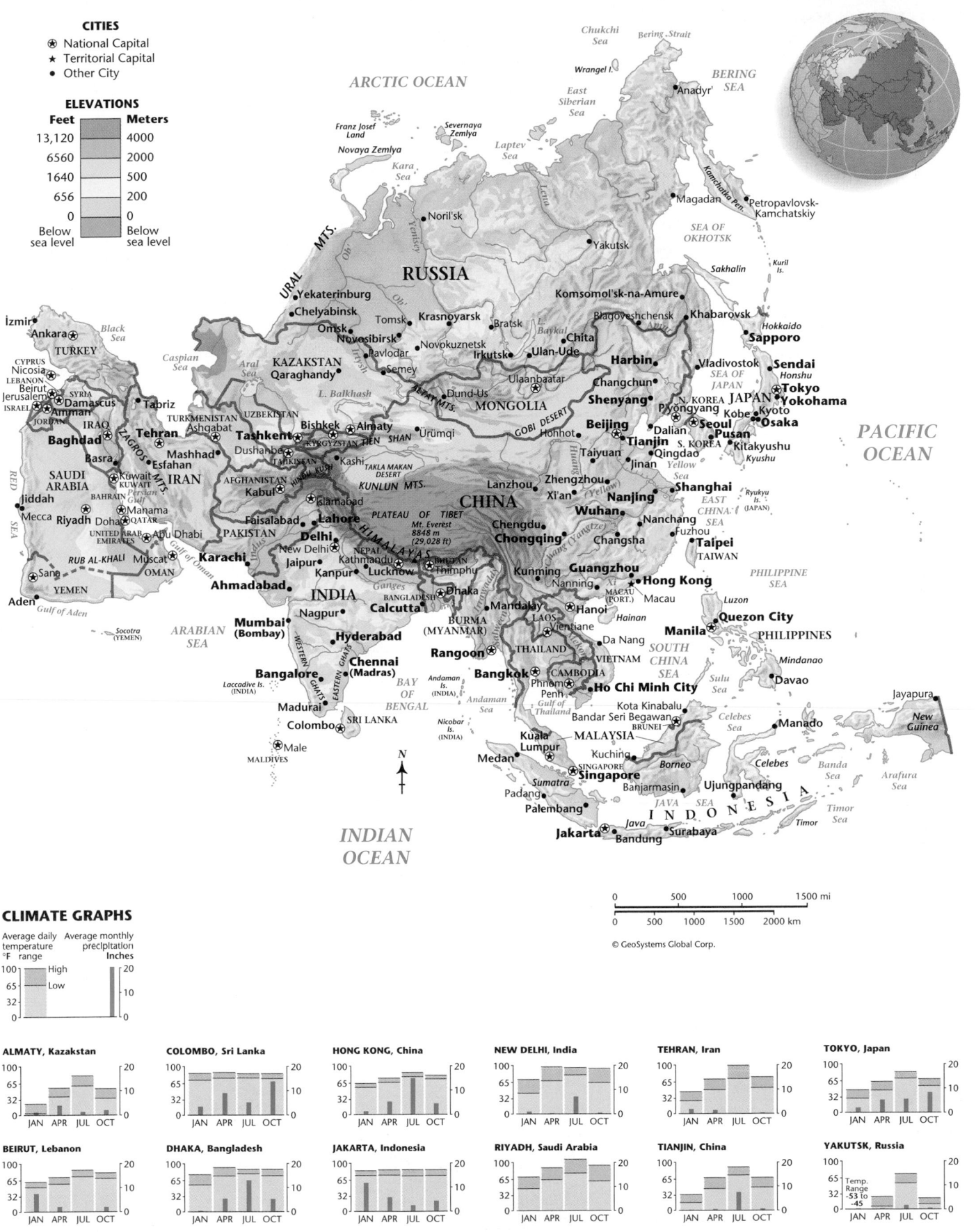

POPULATIONS OF MAJOR CITIES

Algeria
Algiers	1,483,000
Oran	590,000
Constantine	483,000

Angola
Luanda	1,100,000

Benin
Cotonou	402,000
Porto-Novo	144,000

Botswana
Gaborone	137,000

Burkina Faso
Ouagadougou	442,000

Burundi
Bujumbura	235,440

Cameroon
Douala	852,000
Yaoundé	700,000

Cape Verde
Praia	61,000

Central African Republic
Bangui	474,000

Chad
N'Djamena	687,000

Comoros
Moroni	(metro) 30,000

Congo
Brazzaville	596,000

Côte d'Ivoire
Abidjan	2,700,000
Yamoussoukro	107,000

Djibouti
Djibouti	(metro) 450,000

Egypt
Cairo	6,800,000
Alexandria	3,380,000
Port Said	460,000
Suez	388,000

Equatorial Guinea
Malabo	38,000

Eritrea
Asmara	358,000

Ethiopia
Addis Ababa	1,913,000

Gabon
Libreville	275,000

The Gambia
Banjul	40,000

Ghana
Accra	949,000

Guinea
Conakry	705,000

Guinea-Bissau
Bissau	138,000

Kenya
Nairobi	959,000
Mombasa	401,000

Lesotho
Maseru	109,000

Liberia
Monrovia	400,000

Libya
Tripoli	591,000

Madagascar
Antananarivo	802,000

Malawi
Blantyre	332,000
Lilongwe	234,000

Mali
Bamako	658,000

Mauritania
Nouakchott	550,000

Mauritius
Port Louis	142,000

Morocco
Casablanca	2,600,000
Fez	852,000
Rabat	556,000

Mozambique
Maputo	931,000

Namibia
Windhoek	114,000

Niger
Niamey	392,000

Nigeria
Lagos	1,300,000
Ibadan	1,300,000
Abuja	250,000

Rwanda
Kigali	237,000

São Tomé & Príncipe
São Tomé	43,000

Senegal
Dakar	1,700,000

Seychelles
Victoria	(metro) 24,000

Sierra Leone
Freetown	470,000

Somalia
Mogadishu	700,000

South Africa
Johannesburg	(metro) 1,900,000
Cape Town	1,900,000
Durban	1,100,000
Pretoria	1,000,000
Bloemfontein	270,000

Sudan
Khartoum	476,000

Swaziland
Mbabane	38,000

Tanzania
Dar es-Salaam	1,096,000

Togo
Lomé	600,000

Tunisia
Tunis	620,000

Uganda
Kampala	773,000

Western Sahara
Laayoune	90,000

Zaire
Kinshasa	3,800,000
Lubumbashi	739,000

Zambia
Lusaka	982,000

Zimbabwe
Harare	(metro) 1,200,000

International comparability of city population data is limited by various data inconsistencies.

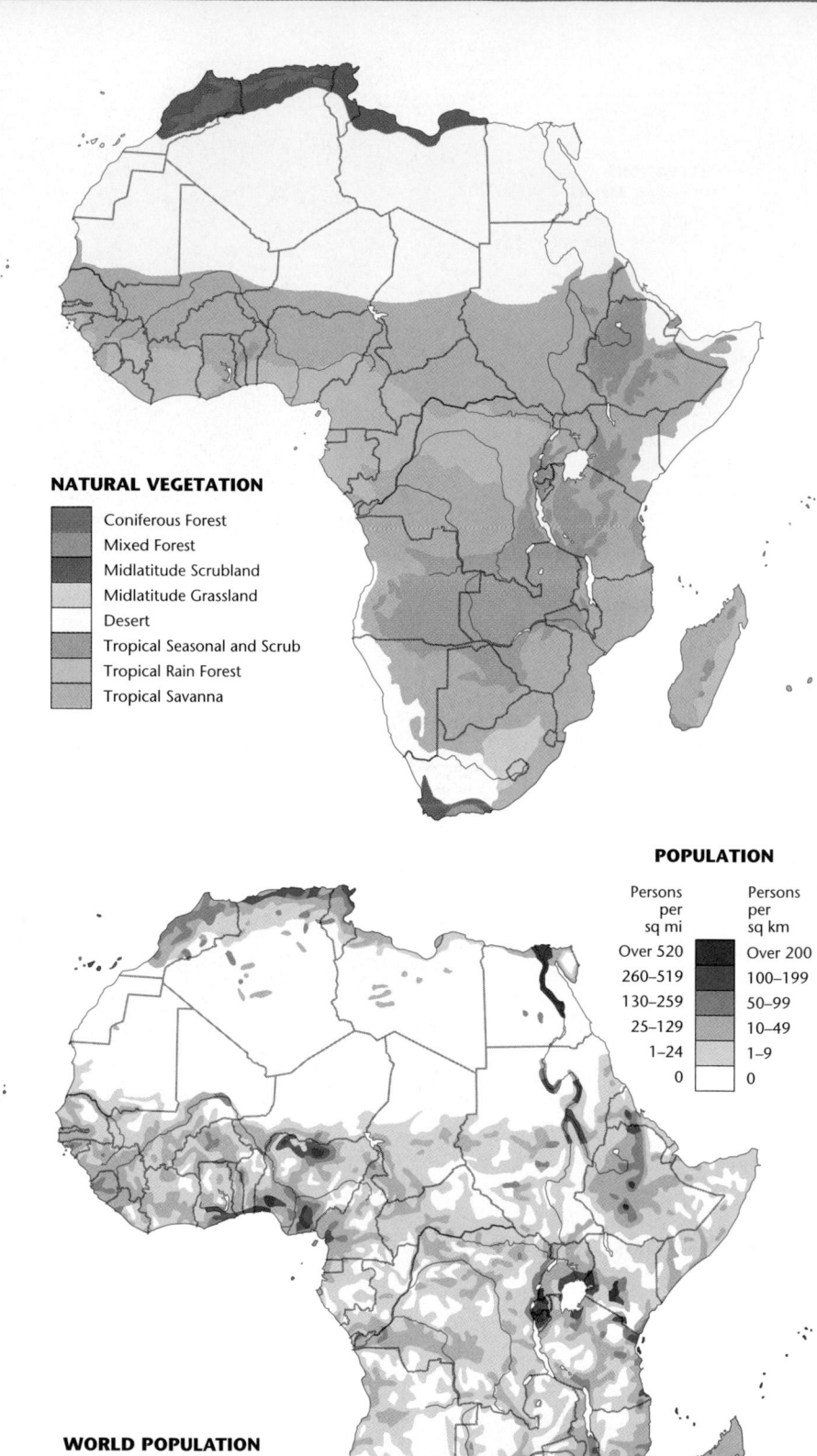

NATURAL VEGETATION

- Coniferous Forest
- Mixed Forest
- Midlatitude Scrubland
- Midlatitude Grassland
- Desert
- Tropical Seasonal and Scrub
- Tropical Rain Forest
- Tropical Savanna

POPULATION

Persons per sq mi	Persons per sq km
Over 520	Over 200
260–519	100–199
130–259	50–99
25–129	10–49
1–24	1–9
0	0

WORLD POPULATION

- Asia 61.0%
- Oceania 0.5%
- South America 5.6%
- North America 8.0%
- Africa 12.4%
- Europe 12.5%

© GeoSystems Global Corp.

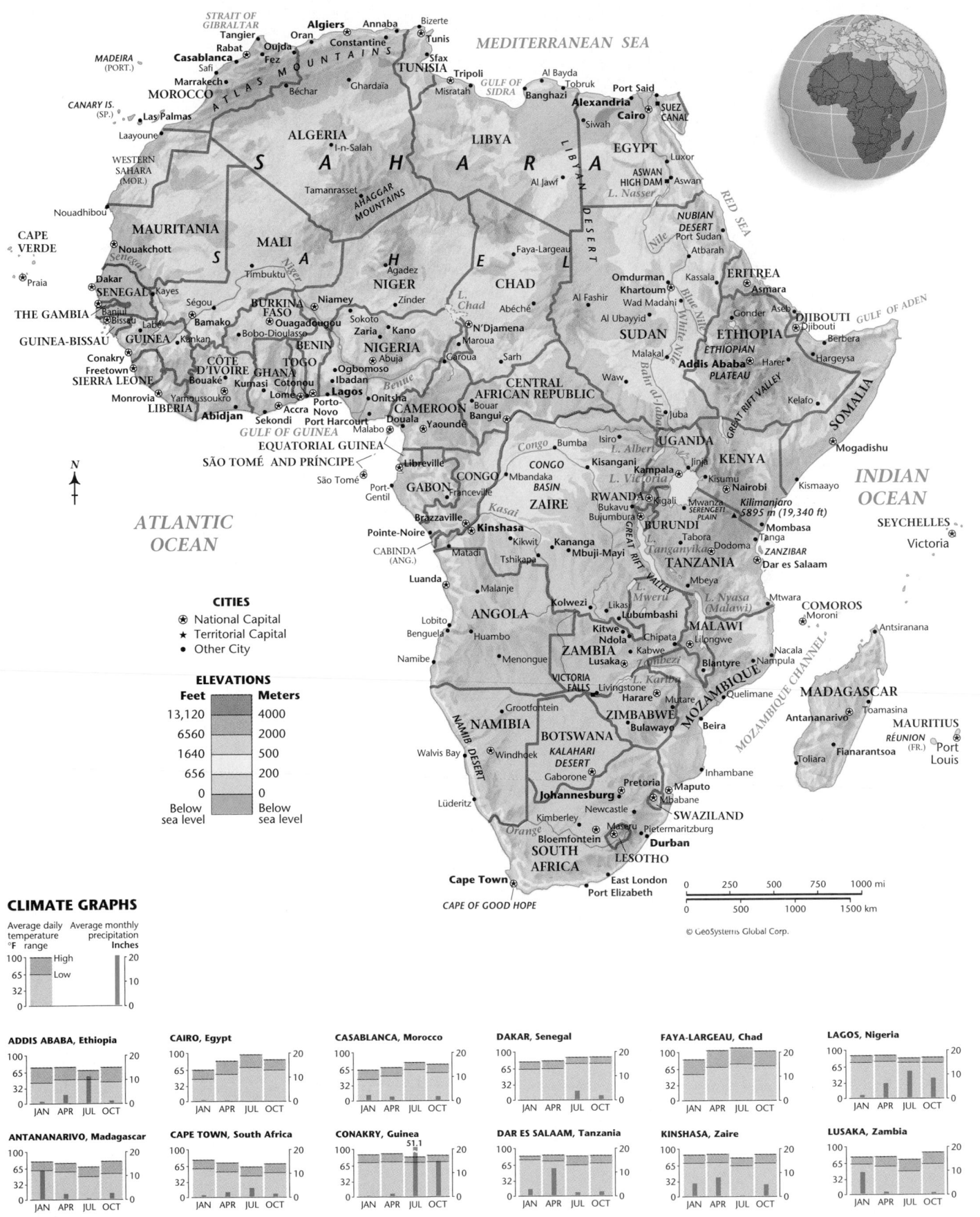

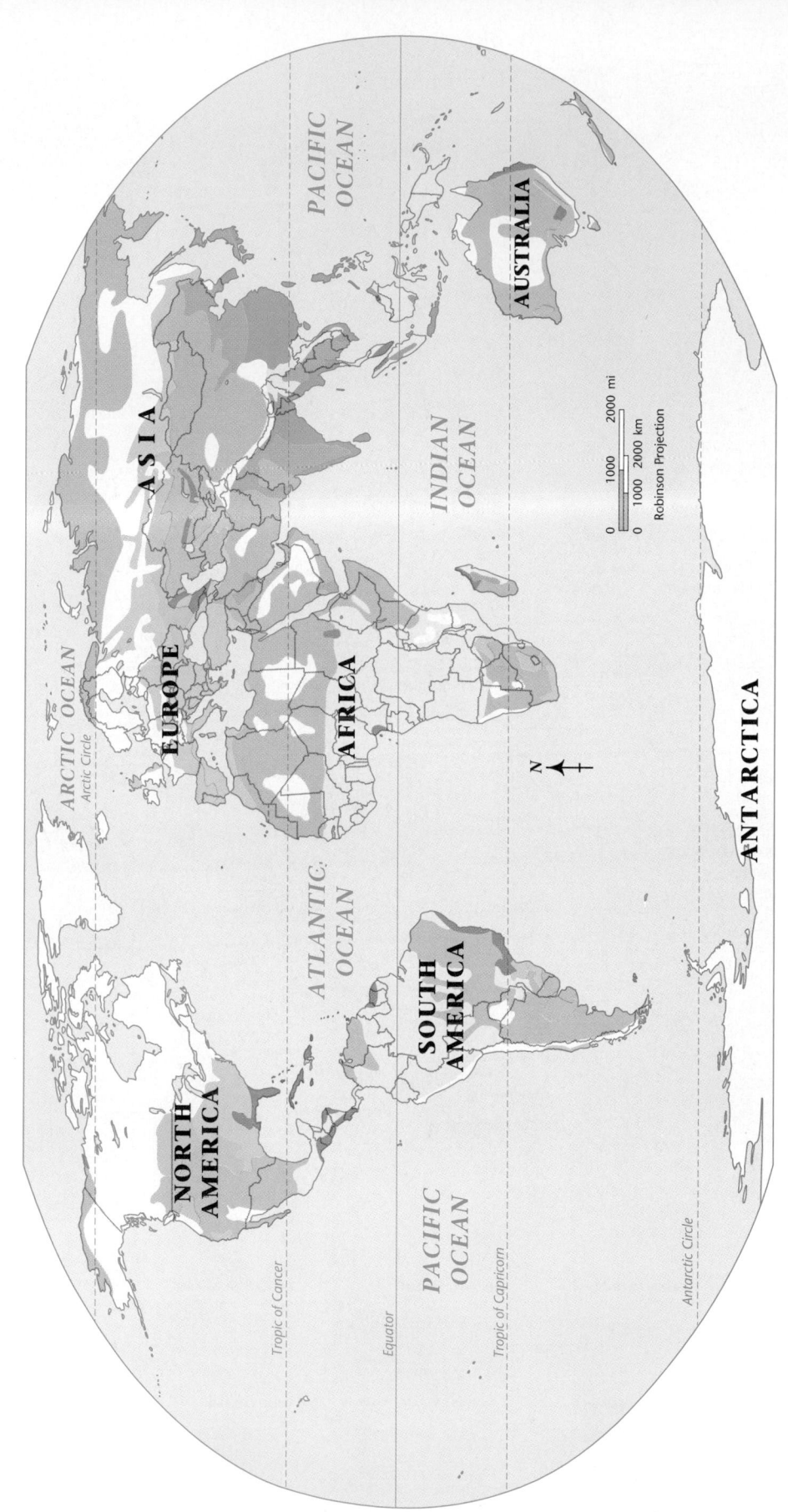

WORLD AGRICULTURE

Nomadic Herding

Primitive Cultivation and Gathering

Subsistence Rice Agriculture

Other Subsistence Agriculture

Mixed Crop/Livestock Farming

Livestock Raising

Grain Farming

Dairy Farming

Mediterranean Agriculture

Plantation Crops

Commercial Horticulture

Little or No Activity

© GeoSystems Global Corp.

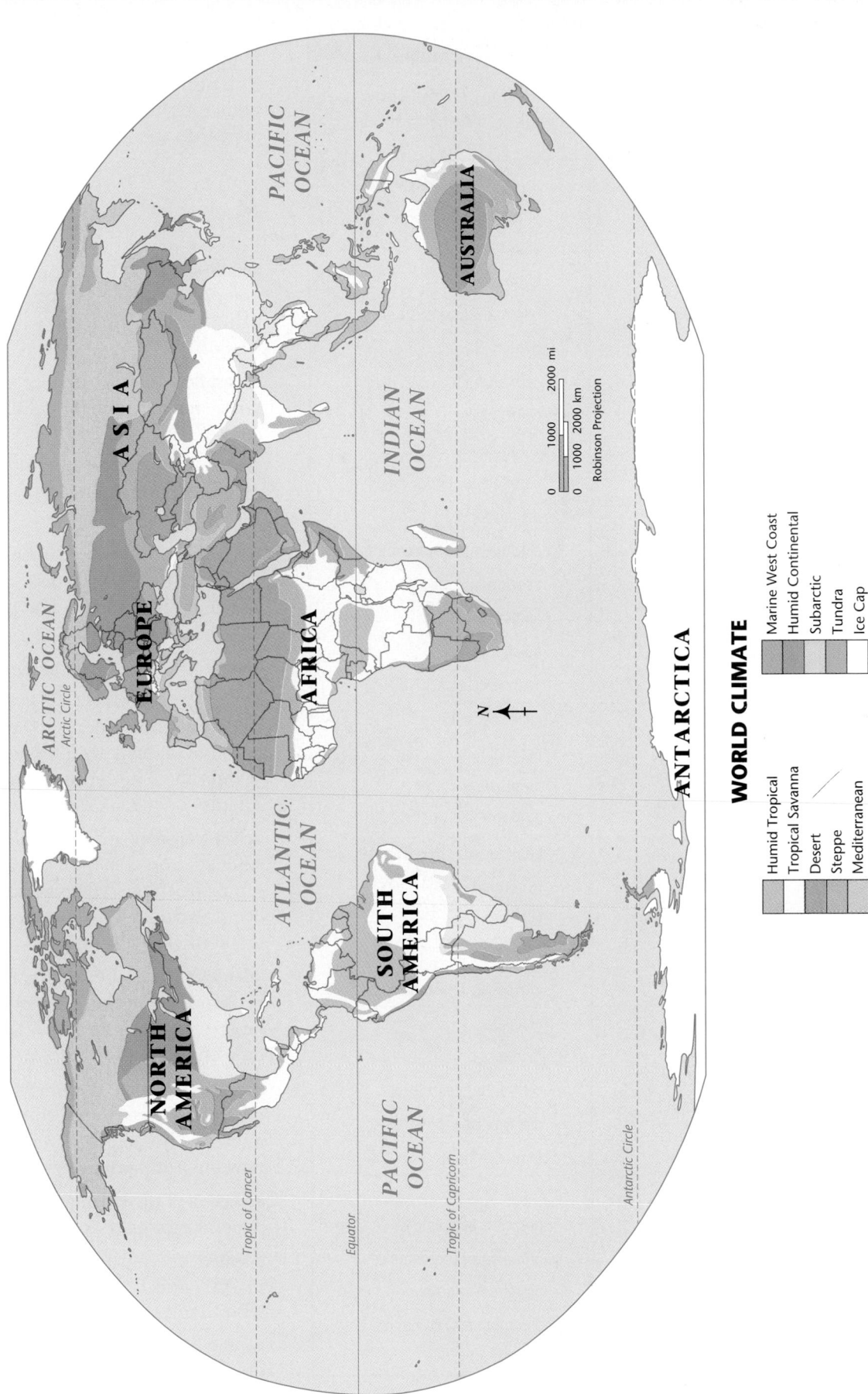

WORLD CLIMATE

	Humid Tropical		Marine West Coast
	Tropical Savanna		Humid Continental
	Desert		Subarctic
	Steppe		Tundra
	Mediterranean		Ice Cap
	Humid Subtropical		Highland

© GeoSystems Global Corp.

Vocabulary Preview

Learning new words can be a challenging part of biology. If you know what the parts of the words mean, however, your job is a lot easier.

Word Part	Meaning	Example
anti-	against	antibody
archae-	ancient, original	archaeologist
auto-	self	autotroph
bi-, di-	two, double	bilateral, disaccharide
bio-	life	biology
cephalo-	head	cephalization
chloro-	green	chlorophyll
chromo-	colored	chromosome
-cyte, cyto-	cell	amebocyte, endocytosis
-derm, derma-	skin, covering	echinoderm
ecto-, exo-	outer, external	ectothermic, exoskeleton
endo-	inner, internal	endodermis, endothermic
epi-	above, top layer	epidermis
eu-	true, modern	eukaryote
gastro-	stomach	gastrointestinal
-gen, gen-	make, produce	genetics, antigen
hemo-	blood	hemoglobin
herb-	plant	herbivore
hetero-	mixed, different	heterotroph
homo-, homeo-	same	homologous, homeostasis
hypo-	under, less	hypotonic
hyper-	over, more	hypertension
iso-	equivalent	isotonic
leuco-, leuko-	white	leucocyte, leukemia
-logy	study	ecology
mono-	one, single	monocot
-ped(e), -pod	foot, leg	centipede, gastropod
-phage, phago-	eat, engulf	macrophage, phagocyte
photo-	light	photosynthesis
-plasm	forming	cytoplasm
poly-	many	polymer, polyploidy
pro-, proto-	first, early	prokaryote, protostome
syn-	combine, together	protein synthesis
-some, soma-	body	chromosome, somatic
-troph	nutrition, feeding	phototrophic

Key terms are defined in the glossary to clarify their meaning in the text. The numbers following the definitions refer to pages on which terms appear in the text.

A

abiotic factor a nonliving part of an environment, such as water, soil, light, temperature, and wind (p. 855)

absorption the digestive process that takes small food molecules into the cells of the body (p. 720)

acid a compound that ionizes to release hydrogen ions (H^+) in water (p. 51)

acid rain nitric and sulfuric acid that fall to Earth as rain; strips the soil of valuable nutrients needed by trees and plants (p. 929)

actin the protein that makes up thin filaments in a myofibril (p. 708)

action potential a depolarization followed by a repolarization across the membrane of a neuron; a nerve impulse (p. 825)

active transport transport of a substance across a cell membrane requiring the use of energy; usually occurs against a concentration gradient (p. 72)

adaptation an inherited biological or behavioral trait that increases a population's chances for survival in a specific environment (p. 231)

adaptive radiation the emergence of diverse species from a common ancestor due to adaptation to many new environments (p. 243)

addiction a physical or psychological dependency on a drug (p. 839)

adenine one of the nitrogenous bases in DNA and RNA; a purine that pairs with thymine or uracil (p. 161)

aerobe an organism that uses oxygen during cellular respiration (p. 343)

albumin the liquid egg white that provides additional nutrients to the embryo (p. 637)

alcoholic fermentation a type of anaerobic respiration that converts pyruvate into carbon dioxide and ethanol (p. 94)

alga a plantlike photosynthetic protist (p. 358)

allantois a membrane that stores waste and provides the site for gas exchange in embryos (p. 622)

allele an alternate form of the same gene for a given trait (p. 133)

allele frequency the fraction of all genes for a particular trait that each allele represents in a given gene pool (p. 246)

allergy the response of the immune system to a normally harmless substance as if it were an antigen (p. 783)

alternation of generations the condition of an organism that alternates, or switches, from diploid ($2n$) spore-producing generations to haploid (n) gamete-producing generations (pp. 361, 412)

altitude the height above sea level (p. 860)

alveolus a tiny air sac of the lung where gas exchange between the circulatory and respiratory systems takes place (p. 747)

Alzheimer's disease a disease that causes the deterioration of the brain; characterized by memory loss, disorientation, or personality change (p. 839)

amebocyte a cell that shuttles nutrients and removes waste from other cells in a sponge (p. 504)

amniotic egg an egg that provides nourishment and protection for an embryo in a terrestrial environment by enclosing it in a shell with a fluid-filled membrane (p. 622)

amphibian a vertebrate adapted for living in water and on land (p. 605)

ampulla in echinoderms, a muscular sac that helps force water into and out of the tube feet (p. 573)

anaerobe an organism that does not use oxygen during cellular respiration (p. 343)

analogous structure characteristic shared by different species that is similar in function but not inherited from a common ancestor (p. 239)

anaphase the third phase of mitosis; replicated chromatids separate and move to opposite ends of the cell (p. 109)

anemia a condition in which a person's blood transports too little oxygen (p. 763)

angiosperm a flowering vascular plant that produces seeds enclosed in fruit (p. 415)

animal a eukaryotic multicellular heterotroph whose cells lack cell walls (p. 500)

annelid an earthworm, leech, or marine worm whose body is divided into segments (p. 536)

annual a plant that lives, reproduces, and dies in one year or one growing season (p. 416)

anorexia an eating disorder characterized by a refusal to eat coupled with a tendency to overexercise (p. 731)

anther the structure of the stamen that produces pollen (p. 463)

antheridium the male sperm-producing structure in bryophytes and pteridophytes (p. 476)

anthropoid a humanlike primate; monkeys, apes, and hominids are all anthropoids (p. 281)

antibody a disease-fighting protein produced in response to a specific antigen (p. 780)

anticodon the three-base sequence found on tRNA that binds to a complementary piece of mRNA during protein synthesis (p. 185)

antigen any substance that is identified by a macrophage as foreign to the body; induces the production of antibodies (p. 780)

aphotic zone an area in an aquatic biome in which light does not penetrate (p. 866)

appendicular skeleton the arm bones, leg bones, and bones of the pelvic girdle and shoulder areas; one of the two primary parts of the human skeleton (p. 698)

archaebacteria a group of monerans that live in extremely harsh environments (p. 340)

archegonium the female egg-producing structure in bryophytes and pteridophytes (p. 476)

arctic zone the region beyond 60° north or south latitude (p. 859)

arteriole the smallest of arteries (p. 757)

artery a blood vessel that carries blood away from the heart (p. 757)

arthritis a disease of the joints that causes inflammation and pain (p. 702)

artificial propagation the process whereby humans use asexual methods such as cutting, grafting, and tissue culturing to grow plants (p. 456)

artificial selection the breeding of a domesticated plant or animal to accentuate characteristics favorable to humans; also called selective breeding (pp. 206, 235)

ascus a saclike structure in which the spores of ascomycotes are contained (p. 381)

asexual reproduction the production of offspring by a single parent without combining genes from another individual (p. 105)

asthma a respiratory condition characterized by narrowed bronchial tubes; results in breathing difficulties (p. 752)

asymmetry without symmetry, irregular in shape (p. 509)

atherosclerosis a cardiovascular condition characterized by a narrowing of the arteries due to an accumulation of fat deposits (p. 762)

atom the smallest particle of an element that has the properties of the element (p. 38)

ATP (adenosine triphosphate) an energy-storing molecule used by most organisms (p. 82)

atrioventricular node a mass of nerve and muscle cells located in the septum between the atria; sends electrical signals to the ventricles, causing them to contract (p. 758)

atrium an upper chamber of the heart; receives incoming blood (p. 756)

autoimmune disease a disease in which the immune system attacks an organism's own tissues (p. 784)

autonomic nervous system a division of the peripheral nervous system; controls the activities of smooth muscles, organs, and glands (p. 832)

autosome any chromosome other than the sex chromosomes (p. 170)

autotroph an organism that produces its own food from inorganic compounds and sunlight (pp. 83, 898)

auxin a plant hormone that causes cells to elongate (p. 449)

axial skeleton the skull, vertebral column, and ribcage; one of the two primary pieces of the human skeleton (p. 698)

B

bacteriophage a type of virus that infects bacteria (pp. 159, 332)

bacterium a tiny prokaryotic organism from the kingdom Monera (p. 336)

base a compound that yields hydroxide ions (OH⁻) when dissolved in water (p. 51)

basidium the structure in which the spores of club fungi are produced (p. 382)

behavior the way an organism reacts to a change in its environment (p. 668)

benthic zone area at the bottom of an aquatic biome; seafloor, lake bottom, or riverbed (p. 866)

biennial a plant that completes its life cycle in two years (p. 416)

bilateral symmetry a body plan where the right and left halves of the body are approximate mirror images of each other when divided lengthwise down the central axis (p. 524)

bile a yellow-green liquid formed in the liver that contains cholesterol, pigments, bile salts, and other compounds (p. 728)

binary fission asexual reproduction in prokaryotes; a process in which the chromosome of a moneran replicates, after which the cell divides to form two identical cells (p. 338)

binocular vision the use of both eyes at once in overlapping fields so that objects appear to have depth (p. 282)

binomial nomenclature a system of identifying organisms by their genus and species names; the two-word naming scheme developed by Linnaeus (p. 304)

biodegradable substances that can be broken down and recycled by natural processes (p. 922)

biodiversity the degree of species variety and balance in an ecological community (p. 888)

biogenesis a theory that states that life arises from living things (pp. 5, 256)

bioindicator an organism or species whose health serves as an indicator of the health of the environment or ecosystem (p. 614)

biological magnification the buildup of pollutants in organisms at the higher trophic levels of a food chain (p. 901)

biomass the total mass of all organisms at a given trophic level within an ecosystem (p. 902)

biome a large group of similar ecosystems containing distinctive types of plants and other organisms; determined by the climate (p. 861)

bioremediation a general term used to describe the process of using microorganisms to help restore natural environmental conditions (p. 345)

biosphere the thin layer of air, land, and water that is home to all living things on Earth (pp. 4, 854)

biotic factor a living part of an environment, such as a plant, animal, or other organism (p. 855)

bipedal the ability to walk upright on two legs (p. 286)

blade the broad, flat photosynthetic surface of a leaf (p. 398)

blastopore an opening in an embryo that develops at the point where cells of the blastula move inward to form the cell layers of the gastrula (p. 503)

blastula a hollow ball of cells formed during embryonic development (p. 502)

blood a liquid tissue consisting of plasma and blood cells in suspension (p. 754)

blood vessel a tubular organ through which blood flows (p. 754)

B lymphocyte a white blood cell that produces antibodies (p. 780)

body symmetry the arrangement of body parts around a central point or plane (p. 503)

bone a hard connective tissue made up of living cells and minerals (p. 698)

boom-and-bust curve a population growth pattern characterized by exponential growth followed by a sudden collapse of the population (p. 883)

brain stem the part of the brain that connects the spinal cord to the rest of the brain (p. 829)

Broca's area the portion of the cerebral cortex that translates thoughts into speech and coordinates the muscles used for speaking (p. 830)

bronchiole a small tube branching from a bronchus (p. 747)

bronchitis a condition involving inflammation of bronchial tube membranes; results in increased production of mucus, making breathing difficult (p. 751)

bronchus a respiratory tube that leads to the lungs (p. 746)

bryophyte a nonvascular plant that belongs to the division Bryophyta; includes mosses, liverworts, and hornworts (p. 471)

budding a form of asexual reproduction that begins with the formation of a small budlike cell from a larger cell (p. 505)

bud scale a structure that forms in order to protect buds from cold and infection (p. 450)

bulimia an eating disorder characterized by first consuming a large amount of food and then purging this food from the system (p. 731)

C

calcium an element found in endoskeleton systems; hardens bone and is essential for muscle contraction and nerve impulse transmission (p. 698)

calorie the amount of heat energy needed to raise the temperature of 1 gram of water by 1 degree Celsius (pp. 95, 729)

calorimeter an instrument used to measure the energy value of food; measures the heat given off when a small sample of food is burned (p. 729)

Calvin cycle the process that uses NADPH and ATP to construct carbohydrates from carbon dioxide; the second stage of photosynthesis (p. 89)

cambium in plants, a type of lateral meristem tissue whose function is to produce new cells in plants (p. 438)

cancer uncontrolled, abnormal cell reproduction (p. 196)

canine a long, pointed tooth used for piercing and tearing (p. 649)

capillary a tiny, thin-walled blood vessel across which gases are exchanged (p. 757)

capsid the protein coat of a virus that surrounds the DNA or RNA (p. 326)

capsule the structure of a moss that forms haploid (n) spores by meiosis (p. 477)

carapace in crustaceans, a hard shield of chitin that covers the cephalothorax (p. 549)

carbohydrate an organic compound composed of carbon, hydrogen, and oxygen atoms; stores energy and provides shape or structure to organisms (p. 34)

carbon cycle a cycle that describes the movement of carbon and oxygen throughout the environment (p. 906)

carcinogen an agent that causes or tends to cause cancer (p. 198)

cardiac muscle the striated, involuntary muscle tissue that forms the heart (p. 707)

carnivore an animal that eats only other animals (p. 900)

carrier an individual who possesses a particular recessive trait but does not express it (p. 143)

carrier protein a special protein in the membrane that helps specific molecules cross the membrane (p. 73)

carrying capacity the maximum population size that a particular environment can support over time (p. 879)

cell the smallest unit of life capable of carrying out all of the functions of living things (p. 9)

cell cycle the period from one cell division to the start of the next cell division; the sequence of phases in the life cycle of a cell (p. 107)

cell-mediated immunity the response of the immune system to virus-infected body cells (p. 781)

cell membrane a thin layer of lipid and protein separating the cell's contents from the outside environment (p. 62)

cell theory the theory stating that cells are the basic unit of life, that all organisms are made of one or more cells, and that cells arise from existing cells (p. 60)

cellular respiration the process by which food molecules are broken down to release energy (p. 91)

cellulose organic compound made of long fibers, or chains, of glucose molecules; an important structural component of plant cell walls (p. 407)

cell wall a tough, rigid outer covering that provides a cell with protection and maintenance of its shape (p. 69)

central nervous system (CNS) the body's main control center; the brain and the spinal cord (p. 823)

centromere the point where sister chromatids are joined (p. 108)

cephalization the characteristic of a well-developed brain and a group of sensory organs located inside the head (pp. 592, 693)

cephalothorax the fused head and chest region in many arthropods to which legs and other appendages are attached (p. 549)

cereal the edible fruit or seed of grasses (p. 407)

cerebellum the second largest part of the brain; coordinates muscle activities (p. 829)

cerebrum the largest region of the human brain; responsible for all conscious, or voluntary, activity (p. 829)

chalaza in bird eggs, a ropelike strand of tissue that supports the albumin, which connects to the chorion (p. 637)

chaparral a warm biome characterized by a winter rainy season followed by a dry, hot summer (p. 863)

chelicerae the anterior appendage modified into pincers and fangs for food-gathering (p. 552)

chemical bond a force that holds two or more atoms together (p. 39)

chemical digestion a digestive process that breaks food down into smaller, simpler molecules (p. 720)

chemical reaction a reaction characterized by the breaking or forming of chemical bonds (p. 42)

chemoautotroph an organism that obtains energy from inorganic substances (p. 342)

chitin a tough, flexible carbohydrate that makes up the cell walls of fungi and the exoskeleton of arthropods (p. 374)

chlorofluorocarbon (CFC) a chlorine-containing chemical that causes the thinning of the ozone layer; can be discharged through aerosol sprays, air conditioners, and the production of plastic foam (p. 931)

chlorophyll an important group of photosynthetic pigments in plants and algae (p. 85)

chloroplast an organelle common in plants and algae that converts sunlight, carbon dioxide, and water into sugars during the process of photosynthesis; contains chlorophyll (pp. 69, 86)

chorion the outer membrane of an amniotic egg that provides a layer of protection and aids in regulating gas exchange (p. 623)

chromatin a thin, tangled bundle of DNA threads found in the nucleus of cells during interphase (p. 108)

chromosome a structure within a cell that contains a cell's genetic information (p. 64)

chromosome theory of heredity the theory stating that the material of inheritance is carried by genes on chromosomes (p. 134)

chyme a thick liquid made up of partially digested proteins, starches, acids, and undigested sugars and fats; food reduced to a soft pulp after about three hours in the stomach (p. 726)

ciliophoran a protozoan that is covered with cilia; also called ciliate (p. 357)

cilium a short, tiny, hairlike projection that is usually found in large numbers on the surface of cells; aids some eukaryotic cells in movement (pp. 68, 357)

circadian rhythm a rhythm that repeats approximately every 24 hours (p. 681)

class a group within a phylum in the classification system (p. 301)

classical conditioning the training of an animal to respond to a stimulus (p. 677)

climate the average weather pattern of an area over time (p. 858)

climax community an established community that encounters little ecological succession (p. 891)

cloaca in most vertebrates, a chamber where products of the digestive, excretory, and sometimes reproductive systems empty; not found in mammals (p. 606)

clone a product or offspring that is genetically identical to its parent (p. 455)

closed circulatory system a circulatory system in which blood travels through the body inside one continuous network of vessels (p. 534)

cochlea the fluid-filled structure of the inner ear that contains the mechanoreceptors needed for hearing (p. 835)

codominance a pattern of inheritance in which both alleles in a heterozygote are fully expressed (p. 149)

codon the sequence of three nitrogenous bases in mRNA or DNA (p. 184)

coelom in some animals, body cavity completely lined with mesoderm; it develops into the digestive tract and other internal organs (p. 532)

coevolution a process in which two or more populations that closely interact over an extended period of time adapt to one another (p. 243)

cohesion clinging together; shown in hydrogen bonds in water molecules; results in surface tension (p. 50)

collagen a protein made by the dermis layer of the skin; makes skin supple and strong (p. 711)

collar cell one of the flagellated cells lining the interior of a sponge; also called a choanocyte (p. 504)

colonizer the first organism to dwell in an uninhabited area (p. 452)

colony a group of similar cells or organisms living and growing together in close association (p. 353)

commensalism a relationship in which one organism benefits from an interaction and the other organism is neither helped nor harmed by it (p. 888)

community a collection of interacting populations within a given ecosystem; its organisms depend on each other for survival (pp. 855, 885)

compact bone dense bone found in shafts of long bones (p. 699)

companion cell a cell that controls the movement of substances through sieve tubes in plants (p. 431)

compensation point the amount of light a plant needs for photosynthesis to balance its energy use in cellular respiration (p. 425)

competition the struggle between organisms to obtain the same limited resource (p. 886)

compound two or more elements chemically combined in definite proportions (p. 37)

compound eyes multifaceted eyes with many separate lenses that combine to form a single mosaic image (p. 547)

concentration gradient the difference between the concentration of a particular molecule in one area and its concentration in a neighboring area (p. 73)

concussion a brain injury caused by a blow to the head (p. 838)

cone a photoreceptor that can distinguish colors but requires bright light (p. 834)

conjugation a form of sexual reproduction in which single-celled organisms exchange genetic material through cell-to-cell contact(p. 338)

connective tissue tissue that joins together body structures, providing protection and support (p. 692)

consumer a heterotroph (p. 899)

control setup in an experiment, all factors are exactly the same except for the change in the experimental variable (p. 22)

convergent evolution a process in which different species evolve with similar characteristics; often the result of living in a similar environment (p. 243)

cork cambium the tissue between the phloem and the epidermis that replaces the epidermis and cortex with cork (p. 438)

cotyledon a seed leaf in a plant's embryo; used as an organ for food storage (p. 460)

covalent bond a type of chemical bond formed when atoms share electrons (p. 40)

crop a storage area within the digestive tract of annelids and birds (pp. 537, 634)

crossing over the switching of genes between pairs of homologous chromosomes during meiosis I (p. 168)

cuticle a waxy, waterproof layer that coats the outer parts of a plant exposed to air and helps prevent evaporation (pp. 423, 470)

cyanobacteria a group of gram-negative monerans that perform photosynthesis (p. 342)

cytokinesis a step of eukaryotic cell division in which the cytoplasm divides creating two daughter cells (p. 108)

cytoplasm a jellylike substance made up primarily of water and the organelles suspended in it; the center for most of the cell's metabolic activity (p. 63)

cytosine one of four nitrogenous bases in DNA and RNA; a pyrimidine that pairs with guanine (p. 161)

cytoskeleton a network of fibers and tiny tubes throughout the cytoplasm; gives a cell support and helps it to maintain or change its shape (p. 64)

cytotoxic T cell also called killer T cell; an immune cell that produces a protein that ruptures the cell membrane of a specific target cell (p. 781)

D

decomposer an organism that breaks down dead organic materials into food (pp. 344, 900)

deforestation the removal of large numbers of trees from a forest (p. 920)

deletion the loss of a segment of DNA (p. 192)

denitrification the conversion of ammonia, nitrite, or nitrate into free nitrogen gas by bacteria (p. 909)

density-dependent limiting factor a factor that comes into operation only when the number of organisms per unit of space reaches a maximum level (p. 881)

density-independent limiting factor a factor that affects all populations regardless of their population density (p. 883)

depressant a drug that slows down the activity of the central nervous system (p. 840)

dermal tissue the outermost protective layers on leaves and stems (p. 410)

dermis the thick inner layer of the skin (p. 711)

desert an arid region with sparse plant and animal life; annual rainfall in a desert is usually less than 25 centimeters (p. 864)

desertification a process that occurs when a soil loses the ability to retain water and nutrients; can result from deforestation (p. 920)

deuterostome a coelomate whose blastopore develops into an anus; a mouth forms later at the opposite end of the digestive tube (p. 575)

diabetes mellitus a disorder in which the body is unable to control blood sugar levels (p. 801)

diaphragm a sheet of muscle below the lungs that separates the chest cavity from the abdomen; contracts during inhalation and relaxes during exhalation (pp. 650, 748)

diastole the part of the heart beat in which the heart muscle relaxes, enabling blood to flow into the atria and ventricles (p. 758)

diatom a type of alga lacking cilia and flagella, with a glasslike cell wall composed of silica (p. 359)

dichotomous key a guide designed to identify organisms; uses pairs of observable traits as a checklist to pinpoint the organism's identity (p. 313)

dicot an angiosperm whose embryo has two cotyledons (p. 460)

differentiation the development of cells into specialized shapes and functions (p. 105)

diffusion the random movement of molecules from an area of higher concentration (more molecules) to an area of lower concentration (fewer molecules) (p. 72)

digestion the process by which food is broken down by mechnical and chemical processes into smaller, usable molecules of chemical compounds (p. 725)

digestive system a system in humans and other animals that processes food (p. 720)

dinoflagellate a type of alga with two flagella that spin the cell in a corkscrew fashion (p. 358)

diploid referring to a cell having two sets of chromosomes ($2n$) (p. 114)

directional selection a change in the allele frequency of a population that occurs when an environmental change favors an extreme phenotype for a trait (p. 249)

disruptive selection a change in the allele frequency of a population that occurs when an environmental change is not favorable for the most common phenotype (p. 250)

divergent evolution a process in which once-related populations evolve independently; often occurs as the result of geographic isolation (p. 242)

division a major taxonomic group in the plant kingdom and fungi kingdom; equivalent to phylum in other kingdoms (pp. 301, 471)

DNA fingerprint the band patterns that form when DNA fragments are separated by gel electrophoresis (p. 210)

DNA polymerase an enzyme that assembles new strands of DNA during replication (p. 163)

dominant allele the expressed form of a trait that usually masks the recessive allele (p. 133)

dormancy a period of decreased activity that occurs because of structural and chemical changes in a plant (p. 450)

dorsal the back side of the body of an animal with bilateral symmetry (p. 693)

dorsal hollow nerve cord a nerve cord that is located on the back side of a chordate animal (p. 581)

double fertilization a process in angiosperms in which one sperm and egg form a zygote and a second sperm and two polar nuclei form an endosperm (p. 487)

double helix the twisted ladder shape of a DNA molecule formed by two strands of nulceotides (p. 161)

duplication a process that occurs when part of a chromosome breaks off and is incorporated into its homologous chromosome, giving that chromosome an extra copy of a DNA sequence (p. 193)

E

echinoderm a marine invertebrate with an endoskeleton, spiny skin, radial symmetry, and a water vascular system (p. 572)

echolocation the process some species use to find food and avoid objects in the dark; process using high-pitched sound waves to bounce off objects to determine their location (p. 661)

ecological pyramid a diagram that shows the relationships between producers and consumers at different trophic levels within an ecosystem (p. 902)

ecological succession a change in the community resulting in new populations of organisms gradually replacing existing ones (p. 890)

ecology the study of organisms and their interactions with their environment (p. 854)

ecosystem the combination of all the communities and abiotic factors in an environment (p. 855)

ectoderm in animals, the outer layer of embryonic tissue (p. 502)

ectopic pregnancy a pregnancy that occurs when a fertilized egg implants in the Fallopian tube instead of the uterus (p. 815)

ectotherm an animal whose body temperature is determined by its external environment (p. 593)

egestion the process of eliminating undigested food waste from an animal (p. 501)

egg a gamete produced by a female (p. 803)

electron a subatomic particle with a negative charge and a relatively small mass (p. 38)

electron transport the process by which energy is transferred from the electron carriers to ATP (p. 93)

element a substance that cannot be broken down by chemical processes into simpler substances (p. 37)

elongation the lengthening of the amino acid chain during protein synthesis (p. 184)

emigration the movement of organisms out of an area occupied by an existing population (p. 878)

endocrine gland a ductless gland that releases hormones directly into the blood (p. 794)

endocytosis a form of active transport in which a portion of the cell membrane surrounds outside particles and moves them into the cell (p. 76)

endoderm in animals, the inner layer of embryonic tissue (p. 502)

endometriosis a disease characterized by a scarring of the Fallopian tubes resulting in a blocking of an egg entering the uterus; parts of the uterine lining migrate outside the uterus (p. 815)

endoplasmic reticulum an extensive network of membranes that transports materials through a cell (p. 66)

endoskeleton a rigid framework inside an animal that provides support and protection (pp. 546, 697)

endospore a heat-resistant, thick-walled, inactive bacterial cell that develops when conditions are unfavorable (p. 337)

endosymbiosis the hypothesis that eukaryotic cells evolved when the prokaryotic ancestors of mitochondria and chloroplasts were engulfed by larger cells (p. 267)

endotherm an animal that uses food energy to maintain a constant body temperature (p. 593)

energy the ability to perform work (p. 46)

envelope the outer covering of viruses that infect animal cells; surrounds the capsid (p. 327)

enzyme a catalytic protein that speeds up the chemical reactions within an organism (p. 44)

epidermis the outer layer of skin that covers the human body and its organs (p. 711)

epiglottis a flap of elastic tissue forming a lid over the opening of the trachea; protects the larynx when you swallow (p. 746)

epithelial tissue the tissue that covers the body and its organs, includes skin and lining of organs (p. 692)

epoch a subdivision of a period on the geologic time scale (p. 268)

era the largest division of time on the geological time scale: Precambrian, Paleozoic, Mesozoic, and Cenozoic (p. 268)

esophagus the muscular tube that connects the pharynx and the stomach (p. 726)

estuary an area where fresh water and salt water mix; a coastal region that forms where a river meets the sea (p. 869)

eubacteria true bacteria; largest and most common group of monerans (p. 341)

eukaryote an organism whose cells have a nucleus surrounded by a nuclear membrane (p. 64)

evolution the changes in populations over long periods of time; the change within the gene pool of a population (p. 233)

excretion the process of eliminating nitrogen-containing waste products from a cell, organ, or organism (p. 501)

excretory system the system that removes nitrogen-containing wastes from the body (p. 733)

exocytosis a process in which wastes and cell products are secreted out of a cell through the cell membrane (p. 76)

exon the sections of DNA or RNA in eukaryotic cells that code for proteins; joined together during RNA splicing (p. 184)

exoskeleton a hard covering on the outside of an animal that provides support, protection, and a point of attachment for muscles (pp. 546, 697)

exponential growth a form of population growth in which the size of a population in each subsequent generation is a multiple of the previous generation (p. 877)

extensor a muscle that straightens a joint (p. 707)

extinction the destruction of a population because it cannot adapt to changing environmental conditions (p. 883)

F

facilitated diffusion the process of transporting molecules by carrier proteins during diffusion; requires no energy output (p. 73)

family the level below order in the classification system (p. 301)

feces an undigested solid waste matter formed inside the body (p. 727)

feedback control when the rate of a current process is controlled by the outcome of its previous cycle; functions within different systems throughout the body to maintain homeostasis (p. 799)

fermentation the extraction of a small amount of energy from pyruvate in the absence of oxygen; pyruvate is transformed into either alcohol or lactate (p. 94)

fetus a developing embryo (p. 810)

fibrin a substance created when clotting factors react with fibrinogen; forms strands that trap blood cells, creating a clot (p. 760)

fibrous root one of numerous extensively branched roots in a root system; it is efficient at preventing soil erosion (p. 401)

filament the structure of the stamen that supports the anther (p. 463)

filter-feeding a method of feeding in which organic matter and microscopic organisms are filtered from water (p. 504)

fixed-action pattern the mechanism for instinctive behavior triggered by an object or event (p. 672)

flagellum a long hairlike structure growing from a cell; it contracts in a whiplike motion and aids in the movement of organisms (pp. 68, 356)

flame cell a small bulblike structure that excretes water and chemical wastes (p. 525)

flexor a muscle that bends a joint (p. 707)

flower the reproductive structure of an angiosperm (pp. 402, 463)

food chain the pathway for the transfer of energy within an ecosystem; each organism provides food for the next higher organism (p. 899)

food web a web consisting of all interconnected food chains within an ecosystem (p. 904)

fossil the preserved remains or imprints of ancient organisms (p. 232)

fossil fuel an energy-rich compound formed from decayed plant matter (p. 907)

fragmentation a type of asexual reproduction that involves the growth of a new organism from a small piece that breaks off the parent organism (p. 477)

frameshift mutation the deletion or insertion of nucleotides that disrupts a codon (p. 193)

fruit a structure that develops from the ovary in a plant; houses and protects seeds (p. 403)

fruiting body the reproductive structure of fungi and funguslike protists; consists of a stalk that supports the structures in which spores are made (p. 379)

G

gallbladder a small saclike organ connected to the liver; concentrates and stores bile (p. 728)

gamete a specialized haploid (n) cell involved in sexual reproduction. (459)

gametophyte the haploid (n) phase of a plant life cycle; produces gametes (p. 459)

ganglion a cluster of nerve cells (p. 822)

gastrula the three-layered embryo formed during early development (p. 502)

gel electrophoresis a process used by researchers to break apart nucleic acids or proteins and sort the fragments by size (p. 209)

gemmae the tiny pieces of tissue that mosses produce to form new gametophytes (p. 477)

gemmule a dormant mass of amebocytes surrounded by protective layers of spicules; forms during adverse conditions (p. 506)

gene the unit of hereditary information that controls traits of a particular organism; located on a chromosome (p. 133)

gene cloning a process using genetic engineering to make copies of genes (p. 211)

gene mutation the errors within individual genes in a chromosome that occur during DNA replication (p. 193)

gene pool the combined genetic material of all the members of a given population (p. 246)

gene therapy a medical treatment that attempts to change a genome (p. 214)

genetic drift an accidental change in gene frequency that affects small populations only, as the result of chance instead of natural selection (p. 248)

genetic engineering the use of biochemical techniques to identify, study, and modify genes (p. 209)

genetic equilibrium a state of constant allele frequency in a population throughout generations (p. 246)

genetics the scientific study of heredity (p. 130)

genome the base sequence for all of the DNA in an organism (p. 173)

genotype an organism's genetic makeup (p. 134)

genus the level below family in the classification system; a group of closely related species (p. 301)

geotropism the growth of a plant in response to gravity (p. 446)

gestation period the length of time an embryo develops inside the mother's body (p. 652)

gill pouch a fold of tissue in the neck region in all vertebrate embryos (p. 240)

gill slit one of a pair of openings along the pharynx in many chordates (p. 581)

gizzard a digestive organ in annelids and birds that contains muscular walls to grind food (p. 634)

glial cell a nonconducting cell of the nervous system that protect, mechanically support, and assist the neurons (p. 824)

global warming an increase in Earth's average surface temperatures (p. 930)

glomerulus a group of capillaries in a nephron that allow fluid and wastes to seep out while blood and protein stay in (p. 736)

glucagon a hormone that raises the level of glucose in the blood (p. 799)

glycogen a carbohydrate in which animals store energy (p. 35)

glycolysis the process converting glucose to pyruvate; releases energy that can be stored as ATP (p. 92)

Golgi apparatus a membrane-bound organelle that packages and secretes products of the endoplasmic reticulum from the cell (p. 66)

gradualism a theory about the rate of evolution—that the small genetic changes accumulate in a population over long periods of time (p. 236)

grafting the process of inserting a piece of one plant into a slit in a second plant to make the two plants grow as one (p. 457)

grana the stacks of disc-shaped structures inside the chloroplast (p. 86)

grassland a biome with hot, humid summers coupled with cold winters; a large community characterized by grasses and small plants (p. 865)

greenhouse effect the heat-trapping action of gases in the atmosphere that may contribute to global warming (pp. 427, 930)

growth rate the total change in a population's size over time (p. 878)

guanine one of four nitrogenous bases in DNA and RNA; a purine that pairs with cytosine (p. 161)

gymnosperm a nonflowering vascular plant that produces seeds that lack a fruit (pp. 415, 481)

H

habitat the type of environment in which a particular species lives (p. 855)

habituation the process by which an animal learns to ignore an unimportant stimulus (p. 676)

half-life the time it takes for half of the atoms in a sample to undergo radioactive decay (p. 263)

hallucinogen a drug that affects the sensory perceptions of the central nervous system; LSD, PCP, and mescaline are hallucinogens (p. 840)

halophile archaebacteria that live in extremely salty environments (p. 341)

haploid referring to a cell having one set of chromosomes (n) (p. 114)

Hardy-Weinberg Principle the theory that states that if a population is not evolving, the allele frequencies in the population remain constant (p. 246)

Haversian canals the spaces in bone through which nerves and blood vessels pass (p. 699)

heart the main pump of the circulatory system (p. 754)

heartwood the dark-colored layers of xylem at the center of a tree that contain substances like gums, oils, resins, and tannins; its clogged cells are no longer able to carry water (p. 439)

helper T cell a white blood cell that stimulates the immune response at the onset of an infection (p. 781)

hemoglobin a large iron-containing protein in red blood cells that carries oxygen from the lungs to the rest of the body (p. 759)

herbaceous a nonwoody plant composed of a relatively soft green tissue covered with a thin protective layer (p. 400)

herbivore a consumer that only eats plants (p. 900)

hermaphrodite an organism that has functional male and female reproductive systems; capable of producing both eggs and sperm; not necessarily self-fertilizing (p. 506)

heterotroph an organism that cannot make its own food; obtains energy and nutrients by ingesting other organisms (pp. 84, 899)

heterozygous having two different alleles for a given trait (p. 135)

histamine a chemical released by injured cells that triggers an inflammatory response (p. 778)

HIV (human immunodeficiency virus) the virus that causes AIDS; attacks the human immune system and destroys the body's ability to fight infection (p. 785)

homeostasis the maintenance of a stable set of internal conditions within an organism (p. 47)

hominid a family that consists of humans and extinct humanlike primates (p. 286)

homologous pair a similar pair of chromosomes, one from the mother and one from the father (p. 115)

homologous structure a structure or characteristic with similar functions found in different species; thought to be inherited from common ancestors (p. 239)

homozygous having two identical alleles for a given trait (p. 135)

hormone an organic compound released by one part of an organism to affect another part of the organism (pp. 447, 794)

host an organism that shelters and nourishes another organism (p. 327)

humoral immunity the immune response to a disease occurring in bodily fluids (p. 780)

humus a part of soil formed by partially decayed plant material (p. 453)

hybrid an organism that receives different genetic information for a trait from each parent (p. 131)

hydrostatic skeleton a type of skeletal system in which the muscles are supported by a water-filled cavity (pp. 526, 696)

hypertension a disease that occurs when the force of blood pumping through blood vessels is too high (p. 763)

hyperthyroidism a disease characterized by a fast metabolism due to the thyroid gland producing too much thyroid hormone (p. 801)

hypertonic solution a solution having a higher concentration of solutes outside a cell than the concentration of solutes inside the cell (p. 74)

hypha a tiny filament filled with cytoplasm and nuclei that collectively form the body of a fungus (p. 374)

hypothalamus the part of the brain that controls basic body functions, such as blood pressure and body temperature (p. 796)

hypothesis a possible explanation for an event or a set of observations (p. 21)

hypothyrodism a disease characterized by the slowing of metabolism as a result of the thyroid gland not producing enough thyroid hormone (p. 801)

hypotonic solution a solution having a lower concentration of solutes outside the cell than the concentration of solutes inside the cell (p. 74)

I

immigration the movement of organisms into an area occupied by an existing population (p. 878)

implantation the process in which the embryo attaches to the uterine wall (p. 809)

imprinting the learning of a behavior that becomes the permanent response to a stimulus (p. 676)

inbreeding the crossing of parents that have similar genotypes (p. 206)

incisor a conelike tooth specialized for stripping and cutting (p. 649)

incomplete dominance a pattern of inheritance in which two alleles in a heterozygote are partially expressed (p. 148)

inflammatory response a nonspecific defense reaction to tissue damage caused by injury or infection; results in redness and swelling (p. 778)

innate behavior a behavior that is genetically determined, that is present and complete without the need for experience (p. 669)

instinct a complex pattern of innate behavior (p. 672)

insulin a hormone produced by the pancreas that causes glucose to move from the blood to the liver (p. 799)

integumentary system the name given to the skin, its surface glands, hair, and nails (p. 710)

interferon a protein that interferes with the replication of viruses (p. 779)

interneuron a neuron that conducts impulses within the central nervous system; connects with sensory neurons, motor neurons, or other interneurons (p. 827)

interphase the longest phase in the cell cycle, during which cells mature and chromosomes are duplicated (p. 107)

intron the sections of DNA or RNA in eukaryotic cells that do not code for proteins (p. 184)

inversion a process that occurs when part of a chromosome breaks off, turns around, and reattaches in the reverse order to the same chromosome (p. 193)

invertebrate an animal without a backbone (p. 503)

ion an atom that has lost or gained electrons (p. 38)

ionic bond a chemical bond formed between ions with opposite charges (p. 40)

isotonic solution a solution whose concentration is equal to the concentration of solutes inside the cell (p. 74)

isotope one of several atoms of the same element that have the same number of protons but different numbers of neutrons (p. 38)

J

joint the point where bones come together (p. 701)

K

karyotype a photograph showing an organism's chromosomes (p. 173)

keratin a protein that makes up skin, hair, feathers, and other animal coverings; insoluble in water (p. 710)

kidney the main organ of the excretory system that removes wastes from the blood and processes these wastes into urine (p. 735)

killer T cell a white blood cell that attacks an infected body cell by poking holes in the cell membrane; binds to a specific antigen on the surface of the infected cell (p. 781)

kingdom the broadest group in the classification system (p. 301)

Krebs cycle a series of oxidation reactions that break down pyruvate; the second phase of aerobic respiration (p. 92)

L

lactic acid fermentation a type of anaerobic respiration in which pyruvate is converted into lactic acid (p. 94)

large intestine the organ that absorbs water and water-soluble vitamins during digestion; also known as the colon (p. 727)

larynx the tube between the pharynx and the trachea containing vocal cords; also known as voice box (p. 747)

lateral line system the sensory organs in most fishes that are used to detect vibrations and water currents (p. 595)

Law of Dominance Mendel's law that states that if two alleles in a gene pair are different, then one allele can control the trait and the other one can be hidden (p. 136)

Law of Independent Assortment Mendel's law that states that gene pairs segregate into gametes randomly and independently of each other (p. 135)

Law of Segregation Mendel's law that states that each pair of genes segregates, or separates, during meiosis and each gamete contains one gene from each gene pair (p. 135)

leaf scar a structure that forms on a stem after a leaf drops (p. 450)

learned behavior a behavior that is acquired as a result of experience (p. 669)

learning a change in behavior that results from experience (p. 675)

leukemia a type of cancer affecting blood in which immature blood cells are produced (p. 763)

leukocytes also called white blood cells (p. 775)

lichen a symbiotic partnership between a fungus and a photosynthetic organism (p. 384)

ligament the connective tissue that joins bones (p. 701)

lignin a hard substance that strengthens cell walls, allowing cells to support additional weight (p. 470)

limiting factor any abiotic or biotic resource that limits the size of a population (p. 879)

linked genes genes located on the same chromosome (p. 167)

lipid an organic compound commonly referred to as fats and oils; tends to be insoluble in water (p. 35)

liver the largest organ inside the body; produces digestive fluids (p. 728)

lung a spongelike organ in which oxygen and carbon dioxide are exchanged (p. 745)

lungfish a fish that has both lungs and gills (p. 602)

lymph the fluid that collects inside the lymphatic vessels (p. 774)

lymphatic system the body system made of vessels, nodes, and organs that collect and clean the fluid around your cells (pp. 755, 774)

lymph node a mass of tissue through which the lymph ducts drain (p. 774)

lymphocyte a leucocyte involved in antibody production and other aspects of the body's specific defense system (p. 775)

lysogenic cycle a type of viral replication in which a virus does not immediately kill a host cell, because the viral DNA becomes incorporated into the host DNA (p. 328)

lysosome a small saclike organelle that contains digestive enzymes that help the cell break down large molecules of carbohydrates, proteins, and lipids (p. 66)

lytic cycle the viral replication process that rapidly kills a host cell by producing many new viruses (p. 328)

macrophage the largest phagocyte that has the ability to engulf hundreds of bacterial cells (p. 775)

Malpighian tubule an excretory organ in the abdomen of arachnids that filters wastes from body fluids (p. 552)

mammal an endothermic vertebrate with mammary glands (p. 648)

mammary gland a gland in females that secretes milk (p. 648)

mandible the jawlike appendage of crustaceans used to chew and crush food (p. 549)

mantle the soft outer tissue layer that, in many mollusks, secretes material to form an external shell (p. 530)

marrow a soft tissue that fills spaces within bone, stores fat, and produces red blood cells (p. 699)

marsupial a mammal producing offspring who initially develop internally but later develop in the mother's external pouch (p. 651)

mechanical digestion a digestive process that breaks food into small pieces without changing its chemical structure (p. 720)

medusa a usually motile, bell-shaped form of cnidarian with a mouth on the ventral surface and tentacles that point downward (p. 509)

meiosis reduction division of a cell; each daughter cell is haploid (n) (p. 114)

melanin the pigment that gives skin its color (p. 712)

menstrual cycle the female reproductive cycle that prepares the lining of the uterus to receive a fertilized egg or discharge an unfertilized egg (p. 807)

menstruation the release of the uterine lining and an unfertilized egg over a period of 5 to 7 days (p. 808)

meristem a growing tissue of a plant (p. 435)

mesoderm in animals, the middle layer of embryonic tissue between the ectoderm and the endoderm (p. 502)

mesophyll a plant tissue made of parenchyma cells; the part of a leaf where most photosynthesis takes place (p. 423)

metabolism the sum of all the chemical processes that occur within an organism (pp. 46, 729)

metamorphosis a series of changes undergone by young animals as they develop into adults (p. 559)

metaphase the second phase of mitosis; homologous chromosomes become arranged in the middle of the cell (p. 109)

methanogen a group of archaebacteria that live in oxygen-free environments and produce methane (p. 341)

microscope a system of lenses that produce an enlarged, focused image of an object (p. 59)

microsphere a bubblelike structure of water and proteins that is somewhat like a cellular membrane (p. 260)

mimicry an adaptation involving structural resemblance to another species or object (p. 562)

mitochondrion an organelle that changes energy found in food compounds into energy, or ATP, necessary to power the cell's functions; the site of cellular respiration (p. 66)

mitosis a step of eukaryotic cell division in which the nucleus divides into two nuclei (p. 108)

molar a broad, flattened tooth adapted for grinding and crushing; located behind the premolar (p. 649)

mold a funguslike protist that lives mostly in damp or watery places and acts as a decomposer (p. 362)

molting in animals, the process in which organisms periodically shed their exoskeleton, skin, or feathers (p. 546)

monocot an angiosperm with one cotyledon in each embryo (p. 460)

monomer a small organic molecule that acts as a building block for large molecules (p. 260)

monosomy a genetic condition in which the zygote receives only one copy of a particular chromosome instead of two (p. 175)

monotreme a mammal that reproduces by laying eggs (p. 651)

motile free-moving (p. 500)

motor neuron a neuron that conducts impulses away from the central nervous system and towards the cells involved in the response (p. 827)

mRNA (messenger RNA) a type of RNA that carries the genetic instructions for protein production from the DNA to the ribosome (p. 184)

multiple alleles the presence of more than two alleles for a gene in a population (p. 149)

muscle tissue tissue made of cells that contract in response to signals from the brain, resulting in movement (p. 692)

mutagen a factor in the environment that can cause mutations (p. 198)

mutation a change in the genes or nucleotides in DNA (p. 192)

mutualism a symbiotic relationship in which both organisms benefit (p. 887)

mycelium the mass of tangled, interwoven hyphae that form the body of a fungus (p. 375)

mycorrhiza a mutualistic association between a fungus and the roots of a plant (p. 385)

myelin sheath the protective wrapping of Schwann cells around an axon (p. 824)

myofibril a tiny structure in muscle, cylindrical in shape; many myofibrils comprise muscle fiber (p. 708)

myosin a protein that makes up a thick filament in a myofibril (p. 708)

N

narcotic any drug that relieves pain or induces sleep; opiates are narcotics (p. 840)

nastic movement a reversible plant response that occurs in the same way regardless of the direction of stimulus (p. 447)

natural killer cell a lymphocyte that attacks virus-infected body cells and causes the infected cells to burst; part of the body's nonspecific defense system (p. 779)

natural selection Charles Darwin's theory of a mechanism for evolution; organisms with traits favorable for their environment are more likely to survive, reproduce, and pass on the favorable traits to offspring (p. 236)

nematocyst a coiled filament with a tiny harpoonlike barb on the end, used by cnidarians to sting prey (p. 510)

nephridium an individual unit of the excretory system that excretes waste in earthworms (p. 536)

nephron the functional unit of the kidney that removes waste from the blood (p. 736)

nervous system a control system that enables the human body to gather information and respond quickly to internal and external changes (p. 822)

nervous tissue tissue composed of neurons and glial cells; carries information throughout the body (p. 693)

neuron a cell that can conduct nerve impulses through the body; the basic functional unit of the nervous system (p. 823)

neutron a subatomic particle located in the nucleus of the atom with about the same mass as a proton and no charge (p. 38)

New World monkeys a group of monkeys that evolved on the American continents; characteristics include broad, flat noses and prehensile tails (p. 281)

niche the specific role an organism plays within its community (p. 231)

nictitating membrane in frogs, a transparent membrane that covers the eyes (p. 605)

nitrogen cycle the pathway by which nitrogen moves through the environment (p. 908)

nitrogen fixation the conversion of atmospheric nitrogen gas into usable nitrogen compounds (p. 908)

nonbiodegradable cannot be broken down or recycled by natural processes (p. 922)

nondisjunction the failure of one or more homologous chromosome pairs to separate during cell division (p. 174)

nonrenewable resource a resource that cannot be replenished through natural processes (p. 918)

nonspecific defense the general cellular or chemical response of the immune system (p. 773)

nonvascular plant a plant lacking the tissues needed for transport and structural support (p. 413)

notochord a firm, flexible supporting rod located below the nerve cord (p. 581)

nucleic acid a large, complex DNA or RNA molecule that carries hereditary, or genetic, information (p. 36)

nucleolus a specialized organelle in the nucleus of cells; the site of ribosome production (p. 64)

nucleotide a part of a nucleic acid; consists of three parts: a five-carbon sugar, a phosphate group, and a nitrogen-containing base (p. 160)

nucleus the control center of a cell (p. 64)

nutrient a substance needed by the body for energy, growth, repair, or maintenance (p. 720)

O

Old World monkeys a group of monkeys that evolved on the African, Asian, and European continents; characteristics include long noses and short tails (p. 281)

omnivore a consumer that eats both producers and other consumers (p. 900)

oncogene a gene that has the ability to cause cancer (p. 196)

open circulatory system a circulatory system whose blood is enclosed in vessels in some places but flows freely over body tissues in other places (p. 530)

operant conditioning a type of training that involves environmental reward or punishment for certain accidental behaviors performed by an animal (p. 677)

operculum a protective flap of tissue that covers the gills in ray-finned fishes (p. 596)

opposable thumb a thumb that can be placed in the opposite direction from the other fingers (p. 281)

order a division of classes in the classification system (p. 301)

organ two or more different types of tissues that work together to perform a specific function (pp. 11, 693)

organic compound a compound that contains carbon; usually associated with living things (p. 37)

organism any living thing (p. 4)

osculum the opening at the top of a sponge where water leaves the body (p. 504)

osmosis the diffusion of water molecules across a semipermeable membrane (p. 73)

osteoblast a cell found in bones that produces new bone cells for growth and repair (p. 699)

osteoporosis a disease that causes bones to become brittle (p. 702)

ostracoderm an extinct fishlike animal without jaws and covered with bony plates; among the earliest known vertebrates (p. 593)

outbreeding the mating of distantly related organisms (p. 207)

ovarian cycle the cycle of changes that takes place in the ovary, including the maturation of the follicle and the release of the egg (p. 807)

ovary in a flower, the structure that contains maturing ovules and develops into a fruit; the female reproductive organ that releases eggs and produces the hormones estrogen and progesterone (pp. 463, 806)

ovulation the release of a mature egg from the ovary (p. 807)

ovule a structure in seed plants consisting of an egg inside protective cells; develops into a seed (pp. 463, 483)

ovum a mature egg cell in the female reproductive cycle (p. 807)

ozone layer the layer of the atmosphere composed of ozone molecules; shields Earth from ultraviolet radiation (p. 931)

P

paleontologist a scientist who studies ancient life through fossils (p. 232)

palmate a dicot leaf characterized by lobes radiating from a central point; resembles the fingers and palm of a hand (p. 399)

pancreas an organ involved in the digestive and endocrine systems; secretes the hormones insulin and glucagon (p. 728)

Pangaea the supercontinent once formed when the present world continents were connected (p. 271)

parapodium a paddlelike structure found on some annelids; used in respiration and/or locomotion (p. 538)

parasite an organism or virus that derives its nutrients by living in or on a host, eventually causing harm to the host (p. 329)

parasitism a symbiotic relationship between two organisms in which one species harms the other species (p. 887)

parasympathetic nervous system a division of the autonomic nervous system that controls body functions associated with rest and digestion (p. 832)

passive transport the movement of a substance across a cell membrane without the use of ATP energy (p. 72)

pathogen a substance or organism that causes an infectious disease in other organisms (p. 770)

peat bog a wet ecosystem formed by large mats of sphagnum moss in cold and temperate regions (p. 477)

pedigree a chart that shows how a trait is inherited throughout a family (p. 142)

pedipalp in arachnids, a specialized appendage that helps to hold and chew food (p. 553)

penis the male reproductive organ that delivers sperm during intercourse (p. 805)

perennial a plant that lives, reproduces, and continues to grow year after year (p. 416)

pericardium the double-walled sac surrounding the heart; covers, protects, and anchors the heart to the diaphragm and breast bone (p. 756)

period a subdivision of an era on the geologic time scale (p. 268)

periosteum the membrane covering bones in an endoskelcton (p. 699)

peripheral nervous system (PNS) a network of nerves that extend throughout the body and gather and deliver information to and from the central nervous system (p. 823)

peristalsis successive waves of smooth muscle contractions that move food along the digestive tract (p. 726)

petal the usually colorful, leaflike appendages on a flower that attract pollinators (p. 464)

petiole the stalk that connects a leaf to a stem (p. 399)

phagocyte a leucocyte that engulfs and digests unwanted cells and pathogens in a nonspecific manner (p. 775)

phagocytosis the process in which the cell membrane engulfs a food particle, or other solid substance, and brings it into the cell (p. 76)

pharynx in planarians, a muscular tube used to take in food; the tube in the human respiratory system located where the mouth and nose come together; throat (pp. 525, 746)

phenotype the outward expression of an allele or alleles (p. 135)

pheromone a chemical signal used by an insect or animal to communicate (pp. 48, 560)

phloem the vascular tissue that transports sugars and nutrients upward and downward in a plant (p. 410)

phospholipid a structural substance found in cell membranes (pp. 35, 62)

photic zone the area in an aquatic biome in which light can penetrate and support photosynthetic organisms (p. 866)

photoperiodism a plant response that is linked to day and night length (p. 449)

photoreceptor a receptor within the retina that responds to light energy (p. 834)

photosynthesis the process by which autotrophs convert sunlight into a usable form of energy (p. 85)

photosystem the light-collecting unit of a chloroplast (p. 86)

phototropism a response in which a plant grows towards the light (p. 446)

pH scale the standard measurement of the concentration of hydrogen ions (H^+) in a solution (p. 51)

phylogenetic tree the branching structure taxonomists use to compare relationships between taxa (p. 305)

phylum the level below kingdom in the classification system (p. 301)

phytochrome a blue pigment that controls photoperiodism and other responses, such as flowering, seed germination, and seasonal inactivity in plants (p. 450)

phytoplankton the algae component of plankton (p. 365)

pigment a molecule that absorbs certain wavelengths of light and reflects or transmits others (p. 85)

pinnate a featherlike dicot leaf characterized by smaller veins branching off a main central vein (p. 399)

pinocytosis a process in which the cell membrane encloses a droplet of fluid and its solutes and brings the droplet into the cell (p. 76)

pioneer community the first organisms to occupy an area previously uninhabited by its species (p. 891)

pistil the female structure of a flowering plant that produces eggs (p. 463)

pituitary gland an important endocrine gland that releases hormones that affect many body activities (p. 798)

placenta an organ through which materials are exchanged between the mother and the developing embryo (p. 810)

placental mammal a mammal whose offspring develop inside the mother's body until birth (p. 652)

plankton a collection of mostly microscopic organisms that float near the surface of oceans and lakes (p. 365)

planula a free-swimming, ciliated larva (p. 511)

plasma the thick yellowish fluid component of blood that suspends blood cells and other substances (p. 759)

plasmid a small circular piece of DNA found in bacteria; can serve as a vector in genetic engineering (pp. 211, 336)

plasmodium the feeding stage in the life cycle of a plasmodial slime mold (p. 362)

platelet a small membrane-bound cytoplasmic disk found in plasma; causes blood to clot (p. 760)

plate tectonics a theory that describes the movement of Earth's crustal plates relative to one another (p. 271)

pleiotropy a single gene that affects more than one trait (p. 150)

pneumonia a type of respiratory disease characterized by inflammation of alveoli; results in accumulation of fluid and debris in alveoli and decreased exchange of oxygen and carbon dioxide (p. 751)

point mutation the replacement of a single base pair in a gene (p. 194)

pollen the grains produced by the anther in a plant; the male gametophyte (p. 463)

pollination the transfer of pollen from a male plant part to a female plant part (pp. 402, 464)

pollinator the wind or an animal that carries pollen from plant to plant (p. 488)

polygenic trait a trait controlled by two or more gene pairs (p. 149)

polymer a large molecule composed of a string of monomers (p. 260)

polyp a sessile, tubelike form of cnidarian with a mouth on the dorsal surface and tentacles that point upward (p. 509)

polyploidy a genetic condition in which nondisjunction occurs in all the chromosome pairs; the organism has more than two sets of chromosomes (p. 176)

population a group of organisms of the same species living in a specific area (pp. 855, 876)

population ecology the study of how and why populations change and how those changes affect an environment (p. 876)

population genetics the study of genetic traits and changes in populations (p. 246)

post-anal tail a tail that extends beyond the anus (p. 581)

predation the interaction between organisms in which one species (the predator) captures and eats another species (the prey) (p. 882)

predator an organism that eats other organisms (p. 14)

prehensile tail a tail composed of many muscles that can be used to grip branches while climbing or swinging; characteristic of New World monkeys (p. 283)

premolar a broad, flattened tooth adapted for grinding and crushing; located in front of the molar (p. 649)

pressure-flow hypothesis an explanation of how sugar is transported throughout plant cells (p. 432)

prey an organism eaten by another organism (p. 14)

primary growth the elongation of plant stems and roots (p. 436)

primary immune response the initial response of the immune system to a new pathogen (p. 782)

primary shoot the first stem that emerges from a seed; forms the main stem and leaves (p. 436)

primary succession a process that occurs when a new community arises from a previously lifeless habitat (p. 891)

primate a group of mammals that includes all monkeys, apes, and humans (p. 280)

prion a carbohydrate-protein molecule that causes disease in animals (p. 333)

probability the likelihood of an event or the frequency of an occurrence (p. 138)

producer an autotroph that provides food for a community (p. 898)

prokaryote an organism whose cells do not contain a nucleus or membrane-bound organelles (pp. 64, 336)

promoter a section of DNA that serves as the binding site for the enzyme RNA polymerase (p. 190)

prophage a viral DNA segment that has become part of a host cell's chromosome (p. 328)

prophase the first stage of mitosis, during which the nuclear membrane and nucleolus disappear and chromatin condenses to form visible chromosomes (p. 109)

prosimian a small primate with large forward-facing eyes (p. 281)

protein a complex macromolecule composed of amino acids (p. 35)

protein synthesis the manufacture of proteins; the mechanism that translates an organism's genotype (the information stored in DNA) into its phenotype (the observed traits) (p. 182)

proton a subatomic particle with a positive charge and a relatively large mass (p. 38)

protostome a coelomate whose blastopore develops into a mouth (p. 575)

protozoan a protist with animal-like characteristics (p. 355)

pseudopod a lobe of extended cytoplasm used by sarcodinians for movement and capturing food (p. 356)

puberty a stage in humans between the ages of 10 and 13 when the sexual organs mature and secondary sexual characteristics develop (p. 813)

pulmonary circuit the circulatory loop that carries blood between the heart and lungs (p. 755)

punctuated equilibrium one theory about the rate of evolution—that species are stable for long periods of time followed by short periods of rapid genetic change (p. 237)

Punnett square a grid used to predict the outcome of breeding (p. 139)

purebred any organism that receives the same genetic information from each of its parents (p. 131)

pyrogen a chemical released by macrophages that causes fever by stimulating the hypothalamus to raise body temperature (p. 779)

R

radial symmetry the arrangement of body parts around a central axis in a shape similar to the spokes of a wheel (p. 509)

radioactive isotope an isotope in which the nucleus is highly unstable and breaks apart spontaneously, giving off energy in the form of radiation (p. 39)

radula a tonguelike organ in some mollusks that is used in feeding (p. 533)

rain shadow a region of low rainfall on the sheltered side of a mountain (p. 860)

reasoning thinking of a solution or drawing a conclusion from known information or observations (p. 677)

recessive allele the form of a trait that is typically masked by the dominant allele (p. 133)

recombinant DNA DNA containing fragments derived from different organisms (p. 211)

recombination the process by which new combinations of genes are passed on to offspring (p. 168)

red blood cell a cell that carries oxygen to all cells of the body (p. 759)

red bone marrow marrow producing blood cells (p. 699)

reflex a simple, innate, involuntary response to a specific stimulus; an automatic response to a change in the environment (pp. 672, 827)

reflex arc the pathway of neurons that carries the nerve impulses for an automatic, involuntary response to a stimulus (p. 827)

regeneration the process of growing back a lost body part (p. 379)

renewable resource a resource that can be replenished through natural processes (p. 918)

replication the process by which something makes copies of itself (pp. 107, 163)

repressor a protein that binds to DNA, turning the genes "off," or halting gene expression (p. 189)

respiration the overall process by which a body gets and uses oxygen and gets rid of carbon dioxide (p. 745)

response a reaction to a change (p. 668)

resting potential the electrical charge across the cell membrane of a neuron in the resting state (p. 825)

restriction enzyme the enzyme that "cuts," or breaks, DNA bonds at precise spots within the base sequence (p. 209)

retina the part of the eye that contains photoreceptors (p. 834)

retrovirus a virus containing an RNA core that replicates by first transcribing its RNA into DNA (p. 332)

reverse transcriptase an enzyme which transcribes viral RNA into viral DNA (p. 332)

rhizoid the part of a hypha that anchors a fungus to its nutrient source (p. 380)

rhizome an underground stem in vascular plants that produces shoots above the ground and roots below (p. 479)

ribosome an organelle that helps to assemble proteins from amino acids (p. 66)

ritual a series of communication behaviors performed the same way by all members of a population (p. 680)

RNA (ribonucleic acid) a single-stranded nucleic acid molecule; involved in protein synthesis; nitrogenous bases include cytosine, guanine, adenine, and uracil (p. 182)

RNA polymerase an enzyme that matches RNA bases with the complimentary bases on the DNA template; catalyzes transcription (p. 183)

RNA splicing a step in eukaryote protein synthesis in which introns are removed from mRNA; controls which genetic information leaves the nucleus (p. 184)

rod a photoreceptor in eyes that can function with very little light but cannot detect color (p. 834)

S

salivary gland a gland in the mouth that produces saliva (p. 725)

saprophyte a fungus that digests and absorbs nutrients from dead organisms (p. 376)

sapwood the outer, light-colored layers of secondary xylem that transport water (p. 439)

sarcodinian a protozoan that moves by extending lobes of cytoplasm (p. 355)

sarcomere a unit of layered thick and thin filaments; part of a myofibril (p. 708)

scavenger a consumer that feeds on the remains of dead organisms (p. 900)

scientific method a process that involves making predictions, designing an experiment that tests those predictions, making careful observations about that experiment, and interpreting those observations (p. 20)

sebaceous gland a gland usually found attached to hair follicles in the dermis that produces sebum (p. 712)

sebum an oily substance produced by glands in the dermis layer of the skin; keeps the dermis soft and flexible (p. 711)

secondary growth growth that makes the roots, stems, and branches of a seed plant wider (p. 437)

secondary immune response the rapid response of the immune system to a previously encountered pathogen (p. 782)

secondary succession the development of a new community in a previously occupied habitat (p. 891)

seed a reproductive structure consisting of a plant embryo and its stored food (pp. 402, 459)

selective breeding the breeding of organisms to produce specific traits in the offspring; also called artificial selection (pp. 206, 235)

self-fertilization the process in which an organism receives genetic information from one parent (p. 131)

semipermeable allowing only certain molecules to pass through membrane (p. 72)

sensory neuron a neuron that receives impulses from the environment and relays these messages towards the central nervous system (p. 826)

sepal a leaf at the base of the flower that covers the bud and protects the developing flower parts as they grow (p. 464)

septum a cross-wall that divides fungal hyphae into segments; thick wall of muscle separating right and left halves of the heart (pp. 375, 756)

sessile permanently attached to one spot (p. 500)

seta a bristlelike structure projecting from the body wall of many annelids; used in locomotion (p. 536)

sex chromosome a chromosome responsible for determining sex (p. 170)

sex-influenced trait an autosomal gene expressed differently in different sexes (p. 172)

sex-limited trait an autosomal gene expressed in only one sex (p. 172)

sex-linked gene a gene located on a sex chromosome (p. 170)

sexual reproduction the production of offspring by combining genetic material from two parent organisms (p. 106)

sieve plate in echinoderms, a cluster of openings in which water enters and leaves the body (p. 573)

sieve tube in plants, the tube formed by sieve tube elements stacked end to end (p. 431)

sieve tube element in plants, a cell present in phloem lacking ribosomes and nuclei; allows sap to move through sievelike end walls (p. 431)

sign stimulus an object, event, or behavior that signals a fixed-action pattern of behavior (p. 672)

sinoatrial node a mass of nerve and muscle cells located in the wall of the right atrium; sends electrical signals to the atria, causing them to contract (p. 758)

sister chromatid one of two identical copies of condensed genetic material attached at a point known as the centromere (p. 108)

skeletal muscle voluntary muscle tissue that enables the movement of the arms, legs, and other body parts (p. 706)

skeleton the framework of organs and connective tissues that supports the body, protects internal organs, and allows for movement (p. 696)

sliding filament theory a theory stating that skeletal muscles move because actin filaments travel towards each other during muscle contraction while myosin filaments remain constant (p. 708)

small intestine the organ between the stomach and the large intestine that completes the digestion and absorption of proteins and other nutrients (p. 726)

smog a haze of pollutants that hangs in the air; contains harmful chemicals and particulates (p. 928)

smooth muscle involuntary muscle tissue found in most internal organs (p. 706)

social insect an insect that lives in a colony where individual insects are structurally adapted to perform a specific job (p. 560)

soil erosion the slow destruction of land and topsoil by water and wind (p. 920)

solute the dissolved substance in a solution (p. 49)

solution a uniform mixture of two substances (p. 49)

solvent the dissolving substance in a solution (p. 49)

somatic nervous system a division of the peripheral nervous system that controls voluntary response (p. 831)

sorus a spore-containing structure on the underside of a fern leaf (p. 479)

speciation the evolution of one or more new species from a single ancestral species (p. 241)

species an interbreeding population of organisms that can produce healthy, fertile offspring (p. 230)

specific defense the cellular or chemical response of the immune system to a specific pathogen (p. 773)

sperm a small, motile gamete produced by males (p. 803)

spicule a tiny needlelike or starlike structure in a sponge made of silicon dioxide or calcium carbonate (p. 505)

spiracle a small external opening in the exoskeleton of arthropods through which air enters the respiratory system (p. 556)

spongin a network of protein fibers in a sponge (p. 504)

spongy bone bone tissue with many open spaces; found in ends of long bones and in middle parts of short, flat bones (p. 699)

spontaneous generation a theory stating that living organisms are produced from nonliving matter and ethers (pp. 4, 60)

sporangium a hollow reproductive structure that produces spores (p. 380)

spore a haploid (n) reproductive unit of plants that produces the gametophyte phase; its hard outer surface is specialized for dispersal (p. 379)

sporophyte the diploid (2n) phase of a plant life cycle that produces spores (p. 459)

sporozoan a spore-forming, parasitic protozoan (p. 357)

stamen the male structure of a flowering plant that produces pollen (p. 463)

steroid a group of lipids that provide structure and control functions for the cell (p. 35)

stigma the sticky structure of the pistil in which pollen grains land and germinate (p. 463)

stimulant a drug that increases the central nervous system's activity (p. 840)

stimulus an environmental condition to which an organism responds (pp. 446, 668)

stolon a hypha that connects groups of rhizoids in a plant or fungus (p. 380)

stoma a pore in the epidermis of a plant that allows for gas exchange (p. 423)

stomach a thick muscular sac with expandable walls that secretes acids and enzymes; it mechanically and chemically digests foods (p. 726)

strain smaller group of bacterial species within the classification system (p. 301)

striated muscle muscle characterized by narrow bands that are visible under a microscope; also known as skeletal muscle (p. 706)

stroke a blockage in one of the brain's blood vessels (p. 838)

stroma a gel-like matrix surrounding the thylakoids; the site of the sugar-producing reactions in photosynthesis (p. 86)

stromatolite a layered geological structure of fossilized bacteria and sediment (p. 266)

style the structure of the pistil connecting the stigma to the ovary (p. 463)

subcutaneous layer the layer of fat under skin layers that stores energy and insulates the body (p. 711)

substrate the reactant in an enzyme-catalyzed reaction (p. 44)

suppressor T cell a white blood cell that slows and then stops the immune response at the end of an infection (p. 781)

sustainable development using natural resources at a rate that does not deplete them (p. 919)

swim bladder in ray-finned fishes, a thin-walled sac that can inflate or deflate to regulate buoyancy (p. 594)

symbiosis a relationship in which two different organisms live in close association (pp. 344, 887)

sympathetic nervous system a division of the autonomic nervous system that controls the body's response to stressful situations (p. 832)

synapse a tiny gap between adjacent neurons and between neurons and effectors (p. 826)

systemic circuit the circulatory loop that transports oxygenated blood to the body and returns deoxygenated blood to the heart (p. 755)

systole the part of the heart beat in which the ventricles contract, pumping the blood out to the body (p. 758)

T

taiga a biome characterized by long, cold winters and short, relatively mild summers; its primary vegetation is spruce and fir (p. 862)

taproot in plants, single large central root with many smaller roots branching out from it (p. 401)

taxonomy the branch of biology that identifies, classifies, and names different types of organisms (p. 300)

telophase the final phase of mitosis in which new nuclear membranes form (p. 109)

temperate forest a biome characterized by warm summers and moderate winters, and approximately the same amount of precipitation in each of the four seasons; large deciduous forest community (p. 863)

temperate zone the region that extends from about 30° to about 60° north and south latitude (p. 859)

tendon connective tissue that attaches muscles to bones (p. 701)

test cross the cross of a homozygous recessive and an unknown genotype resulting in offspring with observable phenotypes (p. 141)

testes the male reproductive organs that produce sperm and the hormone testosterone (p. 804)

tetrad homologous chromosomes that pair up in a set of four chromatids during prophase I of meiosis (p. 168)

theory a hypothesis that is supported by many experiments done over a period of time (p. 23)

thermophile a group of archaebacteria that live in hot water environments (p. 341)

thigmotropism the growth of a plant in response to touch (p. 447)

thylakoid an individual disc-shaped structure within the chloroplast; contains chlorophyll and all other pigments necessary for photosynthesis (p. 86)

thymine one of four nitrogenous bases in DNA; a pyrimidine that pairs with adenine (p. 161)

tissue a group of similar cells that work together to perform a specific function (pp. 11, 692)

tissue culture the process of growing an entire plant from individual cells or from small pieces of leaf, stem, or root (p. 457)

T lymphocyte a white blood cell that participates in cell-mediated immune responses (p. 781)

toxin a poison (p. 730)

trachea the main passageway to the lungs; also called the windpipe (p. 746)

tracheid a long narrow cell found in xylem; forms a thick hollow cylinder that transports water (p. 430)

trait any characteristic that can be passed on from parents to offspring (p. 130)

transcription the process of transferring information from a strand of DNA to a strand of mRNA (p. 182)

transgenic organism a genetically engineered organism that has recombinant DNA from a different species added to its genome (p. 213)

translation the formation of an amino chain from the information provided by mRNA (p. 183)

translocation the process in which part of a chromosome breaks off and attaches to a different, nonhomologous chromosome (p. 193)

transpiration the evaporation of water from the parts of a plant exposed to air (p. 431)

trisomy a genetic condition in which the zygote receives three copies of a particular chromosome instead of two (p. 175)

tRNA (transfer RNA) a form of RNA that carries amino acids to the ribosome during protein synthesis (p. 184)

trophic level a step in the transfer of energy and matter within an ecological community (p. 900)

tropical rain forest a biome characterized by warm, wet weather, lush plant life, and diverse animal communities (p. 864)

tropical zone the region that extends from the equator to about 30° north and south latitudes (p. 859)

tropism the growth of a plant in a certain direction in response to a stimulus (pp. 446)

tube foot a hollow tube with a suction-producing cuplike end; located beneath an ampulla in echinoderms (p. 573)

tumor-suppressor gene a gene responsible for the control of cell reproduction; actions help prevent the growth of tumors (p. 197)

tundra a treeless permanently frozen biome in the arctic and subarctic regions (p. 862)

turgor the rigidity of a plant cell caused by osmotic pressure on the cell's membrane (p. 428)

tympanic membrane a circular structure behind a frog's eye that transmits sound waves to the inner ear (p. 606)

U

uniramian an arthropod that has a single pair of antennae, compound eyes, and highly specialized chewing mouthparts (p. 556)

uracil in RNA, the nitrogenous base that binds with the DNA base adenine (p. 183)

urine a yellow-colored liquid expelled from the body; contains wastes removed from the blood (p. 735)

uterus the female organ with muscular walls in which a fetus develops from a fertilized egg into an individual capable of surviving outside the mother's body (p. 806)

GLOSSARY

V

vaccination a process of injecting a person with a weakened or dead derivative of a pathogen; stimulates the immune system to produce and store special cells and proteins that will later destroy that type of pathogen if it ever enters the body (p. 335)

vaccine a medicine that contains dead or weakened pathogens that increases a person's immunity (p. 788)

vacuole a membrane-bound sac or compartment within plant cells that absorbs water or may store proteins, ions, and waste products (p. 70)

variable a factor that can change during the course of an experiment (p. 21)

variation a difference between members of the same population (pp. 119, 230)

vascular cambium the area located between the xylem and phloem; produces new xylem and phloem during the plant's secondary growth (p. 438)

vascular plant a plant, such as a tree, a vine, or grass, that has vascular tissue (p. 413)

vector a carrier of genetic material used in genetic engineering (p. 211)

vegetative reproduction the types of asexual reproduction that take place naturally in plants (p. 456)

vein in plants, the vascular bundle that transports water and food throughout a leaf; in animals, a blood vessel that returns blood from the tissues to the heart (pp. 399, 757)

ventral the front side of the body of an animal with bilateral symmetry (p. 693)

ventricle a lower chamber of the heart; pumps blood throughout the body (p. 756)

venule the smallest of veins (p. 757)

vertebrae the series of bones that form the backbone (p. 592)

vertebrate an animal with a backbone (pp. 503, 592)

vessel element in plants, the short wide cell in xylem with no end walls; transports water (p. 430)

vestigial structure a structure or characteristic that is unused but which is homologous with structures or characteristics in other species, suggesting common ancestry (p. 239)

villus a fingerlike projection on the intestinal wall that increases the surface area across which nutrients are absorbed (p. 727)

viroid a strand of pure RNA that causes disease in plants (p. 333)

virus a particle consisting of nucleic acid and a protein coat that causes disease in many organisms (p. 326)

vital capacity the largest volume of air that can be inhaled and exhaled (p. 748)

W

water cycle the continual movement of water from Earth's surface to the atmosphere and back to the surface again (p. 910)

water vascular system in echinoderms, a network of fluid-filled tubes that enable movement, feeding, and respiration (p. 573)

Wernicke's area the portion of the cerebral cortex that stores the information needed to understand language (p. 830)

wetland a region such as a bog, swamp, or marsh that is permanently or occasionally covered with water (p. 868)

white blood cell a cell that helps a body fight disease (p. 760)

X, Y, Z

xylem the vascular tissue that carries water and dissolved minerals from the roots to the leaves in a plant (p. 410)

yellow bone marrow marrow found in cavities within shafts of long bones; made mostly of fat cells (p. 699)

yolk the food source for a developing embryo (p. 622)

Z line an area of dense matter that separates sarcomeres in muscle tissue (p. 708)

zooflagellete a protozoan that moves by means of flagella (p. 356)

zygospore a thick-walled diploid fungal spore containing many nuclei; it is formed during sexual reproduction (p. 381)

INDEX

Note: **Bold** page number indicates a key word; *italicized* page number indicates a figure.

Acknowledgements

AA—Animals Animals; BA—Bonnier Alba; BC—Bruce Coleman, Inc.; CMS—Custom Medical Stock Photo; GL—Gamma Liaison; GH—Grant Heilman Photography, Inc.; IV—Innerspace Visions; MP—Minden Pictures; MYP—Mo Yung Productions; PA—Peter Arnold, Inc.; PR—Photo Researchers; PT—Phototake; SB—Stock Boston; TSA—Tom Stack & Assoc.; TSI—Tony Stone Images; VU—Visuals Unlimited

PHOTOGRAPHS

iiiB Art Wolfe/TSI; iiiT Norbert Wu/MYP; ixB Robin Kittrell Laughlin; ixC Robin Kittrell Laughlin; ixCR Robin Kittrell Laughlin; ixT Howard Hall/HHP; vBC The Institute of Greatly Endangered and Rare Species, Courtesy, Dr. Antle; vBL Pat Field/BC; vBR Rod Williams/BC; vCR Biophoto Assoc./PR; viBL Gerard Lacz/AA; viCR David M. Dennis/TSA; viT Anthony Mercieca/PR; viiBL Lee D. Simon/Science Source/PR; viiCR Hans Gelderblom/VU; viiiBL Jane Grushow/GH; viiiCL Allan Penn*; viiiT Runk/Schoenberger/GH; xBL Frans Lanting/MP; xBR Tom McHugh/PR; xT E. R. Degginger/PR; xi Dr. Dennis Kunkel/PT; xiiTL Dr. Dennis Kunkel/PT; xiiTR David M. Phillips/PR; xiiiB John Midgley/TSI; xiiiC Dr. Morley Read/Science Photo Library/PR; xiiiTC Alan Carey/PR; xiiiTL Alan Carey/PR; xiiiTR Alan Carey/PR

Chapter 1 1 Allan Penn*; 2–3 Robert & Linda Mitchell; 3BL Dr. Jeremy Burgess/Science Photo Library/PR; 3 TOP BAR E. R. Degginger/PR (firefly); Gustav W. Vergerber/VU (mite); Richard Walters/VU (snow); 4TR (AII79539) The Alchemist by Teniers, David the Elder (1582-1649), Palazzo Pitti, Florence/The Bridgeman Art Library, London; 6TL Richard Walters/VU; 6TR Runk/Schoenberger/GH; 7BC Cheryl Graham/TSI; 7BR E. R. Degginger/AA; 7TL Peter Salek/TSI; 7TR E. R. Degginger/PR; 8BL Raymond G. Barnes/TSI; 8BR Barry L. Runk/GH; 8TC CNRI/Science Photo Library/PR; 8TL Tracey Wheeler*; 10B C. C. Lockwood/AA; 10BL E. R. Degginger/PR; 10CL Michael P. Gadomski/PR; 10CR Cabisco/VU; 10TL NASA/GH; 10TR Dennis Drenner/VU; 12B Art Wolfe; 12T Leroy Simon/VU; 13B Runk/Schoenberger/GH; 13T Rene Sheret/TSI; 14B Kjell Sandved/PR; 14T Tom Brakefield/BC; 15BC L. J. Connor/VU; 15BR Gustav W. Vergerber/VU; 15T Gary Retherford/PR; 16BL Jim Balog/PR; 16BR PhotoDisc; 16CL Grant Heilman/GH; 16CR John D. Cunningham/VU; 17BL Larry Lefever/GH; 17BR John Elk III/BC; 17CL Grant Heilman/GH; 17CR Chip Henderson/TSI; 18 Peter Ziminski/VU; 19BL Jane Burton/BC; 19CL Gay Bumgarner/TSI; 19CR Frans Lanting/MP; 19R Tom McHugh/PR; 19T Bob Daemmrich/SB; 20TL Cabisco/VU; 20TR Fred Hossler/VU; 21 Len Rue Jr./BC; 24B Gregory G. Dimijian/PR; 24T Tracey Wheeler*; 25 Sherwood Landers/GL; 26 Allan Penn*

Unit 1 30BR Tracey Wheeler*; 30C Roland Birke/OKAPIA/PR; 30CL M. P. Kahl/DRK; 30TR Allan Penn*; 31B PhotoDisc; 31BL Kjell B. Sandved/VU; 31BR Jim Ballard/TSI; 31C David M. Phillips/VU; 31TR David Madison/BC; 124BL Courtesy, Carlos Contreras; 125B David Powers, 1995; 125T Jerry LeBlond, 1996

Chapter 2 32–33 David Thompson/Oxford Scientific Films/AA; 32C Harry Rogers/PR; 32TR Wolfgang Bayer/BC; 33 TOP BAR George I. Bernard/AA (pond skater); NASA (earth); 34–35 Barry L. Runk/GH; 34BR Barry L. Runk/GH; 34BL D. Wilder/TSA; 35BR Darwin Dale/PR; 36 Grant Heilman/GH; 37BR Michael Rosenfeld/TSI; 37C Dr. Dennis Kunkel/PT; 37TR F. Ruggeri/The Image Bank; 38 Dr. Mitsuo Ohtsuki/Science Photo Library/PR; 39B Hank Morgan/Science Source/PR; 40 Dr. Jeremy Burgess/Science Photo Library/PR; 42 John Gerlach/TSA; 43CR John D. Cunningham/VU; 43TC Thomas and Pat Leeson/PR; 43TL Bert Blokhuis/TSI; 43TR Allan Penn*; 45 Tracey Wheeler*; 46B Gunter Ziesler/PA; 46TR Stephen Dalton/AA; 47BR Ted Clutter/PR; 47T J. H. Robinson/AA; 48 Holt Studios Int'l./Nigel Cattlin/PR; 49 NASA; 49BC Allan Penn*; 49BL Allan Penn*; 49BR Allan Penn*; 50 John Shaw/TSA; 50BC George I. Bernard/AA; 50BL Liz Hymans/TSI; 50C George I. Bernard/AA; 50CL Dr. Jeremy Burgess/Science Photo Library/PR

Chapter 3 56–57 Dr. Gopal Murti/PT; 56C G. Covian/The Image Bank; 57C Art Montes de Oca/FPG; 57 TOP BAR Bruce Iverson/Science Photo Library/PR; 58TC Corbis-Bettmann; 58TR CNRI/Science Photo Library/PR; 59BC Kevin & Betty Collins/VU; 59TC Leonard Lessin/Peter Arnold Inc.; 59TL The Science Museum/Science & Society Picture Library; 60BL David M. Phillips/PR; 61 Courtesy, IBM; 61TR PhotoDisc; 62B VU; 62TR Bruce Iverson/Science Photo Library/PR; 63BR Dr. Dennis Kunkel/PT; 64 Alfred Pasieka/Science Photo Library/CMS; 65TL Institut Pasteur/CNRI/PT; 65TR Don Fawcett/Science Source/PR; 66 Proff. Motta, Correr & Nottola/University "La Sapienza", Rome/Science Photo Library/PR; 67BR K. G. Murti/VU; 67C VU; 68TL Karl Aufderheide/VU; 68TR David M. Phillips/VU; 69BL Dr. Dennis Kunkel/PT; 69BR Don Fawcett/Science Source/PR; 69TR George D. Dodge/BC; 71TC Runk/Schoenberger/GH; 71TR R. Calentine/VU; 72 Runk/Schoenberger/GH; 76 W. J. Johnson/VU

Chapter 4 80–81 Eric Crichton/BC; 80C John Cancalosi/DRK; 81 TOP BAR George B. Chapman/VU; 82 David E. Myers/TSI; 84 Betty Derig/PR; 85 Frans Lanting/TSI; 86BC George B. Chapman/VU; 86BL J. Michael Eichelberger/VU; 86CL Runk/Schoenberger/GH; 87 Tim Davis*; 90 Tracey Wheeler*; 91 Keith Porter/Science Source/PR; 94 David Madison/Duomo; 95 Phillip & Karen Smith/TSI; 96 Tracey Wheeler*; 97B K. & K. Ammann/BC; 97T Michael P. Gadomski/PR; 98 Will & Deni McIntyre/PR; 101 Jason Burns/Ace/PT

Chapter 5 102–103 Art Wolfe/TSI; 102C Clem Haagner/PR; 103 (grass background) Alan Pitcairn/GH; 103 TOP BAR Kent Wood; 104BC Biophoto Assoc./Science Source/PR; 104C Grant Heilman/GH; 104CL Thomas Dressler/DRK; 104TR Gerry Ellis/Ellis Nature Photography; 105 Glenn M. Oliver/VU; 106BC Kent Wood; 107 John D. Cunningham/VU; 108 Gunther F. Bahr/AFIP/TSI; 110BR John D. Cunningham/VU; 110TR M. Abbey/VU; 111L John D. Cunningham/VU; 112 Jason Burns/Ace/PT; 113

Carolina Biological Supply/PT; 114 Oxford Scientific Films/Michael Fogden/AA; 115 CNRI/Science Photo Library/PR; 118 Francois Gohier/PR; 123 CNRI/Science Photo Library/PR; 124BR SimLife ® and © 1992, SimEarth ® and © 1992 Maxis Inc. All Rights Reserved.

Unit 2 126–127 Tracey Wheeler*; 126BL Peter Menzel; 126CR Gary John Norman/TSI; 126T PhotoDisc, photo manipulation by John Scott; 127CR James Gerholdt/PA; 127TL James King-Holmes/Science Photo Library/PR; 224BL Courtesy, Stacie Simmons; 224BR; Reprinted with permission of Scribner, a Division of Simon & Schuster from THE DOUBLE HELIX by James D. Watson. Jacket design Jeanyee Wong. Copyright (c) 1968 James D. Watson. 225B Robert Campagna, Courtesy Cornell College; 225T Los Angeles Times. Reprinted by permission.

Chapter 6 128–129 Wayne R. Bilenduke/TSI; 129 TOP BAR Jack M. Bostrack/VU; 130BR Erich Lessing/Art Resource, NY; 130TR Telegraph Colour Library/FPG; 131BR Image Select/Art Resource, NY; 131CR Dwight Kuhn; 132 Mary Evans Picture Library; 134BL Biophoto Assoc./PR; 134TR Jack M. Bostrack/VU; 135 B. Everett Webb; 138 J. D. Schwalm/Stock South; 142BL Ashley Morrison/Uniphoto, Inc.; 142CL Patricia J. Bruno/Positive Images; 142TR Michael Krasowitz/FPG; 143CR CNRI/Science Photo Library/PR; 143TL SIU/PR; 143TR Courtesy, Dr. Eugene J. Mark/Massachusetts General Hospital; 144BR Courtesy, Dr. Jean Paul G. Vonsattel/Massachusetts General Hospital; 144BL CNRI/Science Photo Library/PR; 144TL Nancy M. Hamilton/PR; 145 Peter Menzel/SB; 147 Courtesy, Dr. Erick Greene; 148 CMS; 149 Allan Penn*; 150 Dr. Dennis Kunkel/PT; 150BR Dan McCoy/Rainbow; 150TL Stanley Flegler/VU; 151 R. J. Erwin/PR; 152 Paul Merideth/TSI; 155 Charles Neal/SuperStock

Chapter 7 156C S.N.S./Sipa Press; 156–157 SYGMA; 157 TOP BAR CNRI/Science Photo Library/PR; 158TR Martin Rotker/PT; 160 Dan McCoy/Rainbow; 160TR from "The Double Helix" by J.D. Watson/Cold Spring Harbor Laboratory Archives; 161BR A. Barrington Brown/Science Source/PR; 161CR Science Photo Library/PR; 161TR PR; 162 Dr. Gopal Murti/Science Photo Library/PR; 164 Tracey Wheeler*; 165 Gerard Lacz/AA; 170BL Biophoto Assoc./PR; 170CL Biophoto Assoc./PR; 170TR Visusal Unlimited; 171 Runk/Schoenberger/GH; 172BL L. West/BC; 172BR L. West/BC; 172TR Bill Ballenberg; 173B CNRI/Science Photo Library/PR; 173T Jeff Greenberg/VU; 174 Shahn Kermani/GL; 175 Jeff Greenberg/VU; 179 Chanan

Chapter 8 180–181 Allan Penn*; 181 TOP BAR David Scharf; 182 Stephen J. Krasemann/PR; 186L Tracey Wheeler*; 186TR Kiselva D. Fawcett/VU; 188B Reprinted with permission from Dr. Bjorn Reino Olsen/Harvard Medical School/1996 American Association for the Advancement of Science; 188T Reprinted with permission from Dr. Lee Niswander (Memorial Sloan Kettering Cancer Institute) 1996 American Association for the Advancement of Science; 191B Professors P. M. Motta, P. M. Andrews, K. R. Porter & J. Vial/Science Photo Library/PR; 191C Steven E. Sutton/Duomo; 191CL Prof. P. Motta/Dept. of Anatomy/University "La Sapienza" Rome/Science Photo Library/PR; 191CR David M. Phillips/VU; 191TL CNRI/Science Photo Library/PR; 191TR Andrew Syred/Science Photo Library/PR; 192BL Kent Wood; 192TR Chanan; 193CL David Scharf; 193TL David Scharf; 193TR Horticultural Photography; 196BC J. Croyle/CMS; 196BL Courtesy, Dr. Bruce Rosen/Massachusetts General Hospital; 196T Corbis-Bettmann; 198BL Heidi Bradner, Courtesy of Dr. Robert Baker /Texas Tech University; 198BR Sovfoto/Eastfoto; 199 Ernest Manewal/FPG; 200CL Grant Le Duc/SB; 200T Franklin Viola; 203 Jon Gordon/PT

Chapter 9 204 Roger/Viollet/GL; 205 Vlastimir Shone/GL; 205 TOP BAR CMS (electrophoresis, left); Jon Gordon/PT (microinjection); Michael Skott/The Image Bank (cat); NIH/CMS (electrophoresis, right); 206BC VU; 206BL David Cavagnaro/PA; 206BR Holt Studios Int'l./Nigel Cattlin/PR; 206T Mitch Kezar/TSI; 207BC Barbara Von Hoffmann/TSA; 207TC Michael Skott/The Image Bank; 207TL Jean-Michel Labat/Jacana/PR; 207TR Victoria Hurst/TSA; 208C The Institute of Greatly Endangered and Rare Species, Courtesy, Dr. Antle; 208TL Pat Field/BC; 208TR Rod Williams/BC; 209 Kjell Sandved/PR; 211BL NIH/CMS; 211CR Courtesy,The Whitehead Institute; 213BC Rick Browne/SB; 213BR Michael P. Gadomski/PR; 213CR Christi Carter/Grant Heilman; 213T Courtesy, Dr. Daniel Smith, University of Akron; 214 Jon Gordon/PT; 215 Professor P. M. Motta, G. Macchiarelli, S. A. Nottola/Science Photo Library/CMS; 216B Tracey Wheeler*, posters courtesy of The Whitehead Institute; 216TL SIU/VU; 217TL Peter Menzel; 217TR Science Photo Library/CMS; 219B SIU/PA; 219T Dan McCoy/Rainbow; 223BR Kenneth W. Fink/BC; 223TR Drawing by Gahan Wilson; The New Yorker Magazine, Inc.

Unit 3 226BL Francois Gohier/PR; 226BR Tracey Wheeler*; 226TL Frank Rossotto/Stocktrek; 226TR Charles Shotwell; 227BR Tracey Wheeler*; 227CL Keren Su/TSI; 227CR Robin Kittrell Laughlin; 227TL Francois Gohier/PR; 227TR M. P. Kahl/PR; 320BL Courtesy, Dana Denson; 320BR Inherit The Wind © 1960 United Artists Pictures, Inc. All Rights Reserved. Still courtesy of MGM Consumer Products. 321B The Field Museum, photo by John Weinstein, neg # GN 88096; 321T Courtesy, Conneticut College

Chapter 10 228–229Barry L. Runk/GH; 229BRby permission of the Syndics of Cambridge University Library; 229TL The Granger Collection, New York; 229 TOP BAR David M. Dennis/TSA; 230BL Zig Leszczynski/AA; 230CL Darrell Gulin/TSI; 230T Rudie Kuiter/1985 Discover Magazine; 231BC Kim Taylor/BC; 231BL Tom Brakefield/BC; 232BL Jeff Foott/TSA; 233BR Archive Photos; 233C Science Photo Library/PR; 233CR Illustrated London News/Archive Photos; 233TC Michio Hoshino/MP; 234BL Norman Owen Tomalin/BC; 234BR Tim Davis/PR; 235CL Jane Grushow/GH; 235CR Michael P. Gadomski/PR; 235T Frank T. Awbrey/VU; 235TL Norm Thomas/PR; 235TR John Colwell/GH; 236B Karl Ammann/BC; 236T William & Marcia Levy/PR; 238T David M. Dennis/TSA; 239BR Kenneth W. Fink/PR; 239CR John D. Cunningham/VU; 240CL Petit Format/Nestle/Science Source/PR; 240TL Lennart Nilsson/BA; 241BC G. C. Kelley/PR; 241BR Douglas Faulkner/PR; 241CR Charlie Ott/PR; 241TC Dieter & Mary Plage/BC; 241TL Corbis-Bettmann; 242BL Gerard Lacz/AA; 242BR Gerard Lacz/PA; 242TL Bryn Campbell/TSI; 242TR Stephen

J. Krasemann/PR; 243CR Anthony Mercieca/PR; 243TR Clayton Fogle/TSI; 244CL Frans Lanting/MP; 244CR Tui De Roy/BC; 244T Alan Root/Okapia/PR; 244TC Allan Root/BC; 244TL Tui De Roy/BC; 244TR Tui De Roy/BC; 245 Tracey Wheeler*; 246 World Perspectives; 247 Gordon Langsbury/BC; 248TL Grant Heilman/GH; 248TR Janis Burger/BC; 250 Kim Taylor/BC; 253 Kim Taylor/BC

Chapter 11 254–255 Sigurgeir Jónasson; 255 TOP BAR D. Cavagnaro/VU (fossils); Paul Berger/TSI (lava); Sidney Fox/VU (microspheres); 256B Michael Collier/SB; 256CL Tony Freeman/PhotoEdit; 256TR NASA; 259 NASA; 260 Paul Berger/TSI; 261 Sidney Fox/VU; 263B Michael H. Black/BC; 263TL NASA; 265BL J. Cancalosi/TSA; 265C John Reader/Science Photo Library/PR; 265TL S. M. Awramik, U. of California/Biological Photo Service; 265TR Stanley M. Awramik, U. of California/Biological Photo Service; 268 Gerry Ellis/Ellis Nature Photography; 269CR Kim Taylor/BC; 270 D. Cavagnaro/VU; 273 Tracey Wheeler*; 277 Ron Austing/PR

Chapter 12 278–279 John Reader/Science Photo Library/PR; 279 Courtesy, Dr. Richard L. Hay, University of Illinois; 279C John Reader/Science Photo Library/PR; 279 TOP BAR David L. Brill (point, skull); Robert Frerck/TSI (cave painting); Ron Austing/PR (loris); 280TL Warren Garst/TSA; 281BL Gerry Ellis/Ellis Nature Photography; 281TL Gerard Lacz/AA; 282BC Mickey Gibson/AA; 282C Compost/Visage/PA; 282T Ron Austing/PR; 283 Art Wolfe/TSI; 284CL Gerry Ellis/Ellis Nature Photography; 284CR Gregory G. Dimijian/PR; 284TC George H. Harrison/GH; 284TR Akira Uchiyama/PR; 286TR John Reader/Science Photo Library/PR; 289 David L. Brill; 290TR Robert Frerck/TSI; 291TC David L. Brill; 291TL David L. Brill; 291TR E. R. Degginger/PR; 292 David L. Brill; 294 Corbis-Bettmann

Chapter 13 298–299 The Granger Collection, New York; 298BC Norbert Wu/MYP; 298C New Zealand Herald; 299 TOP BAR James D. Watt/Earthviews (dolphin); Mickey Gibson/AA (monkey); Robin Kittrell Laughlin (fly); 300 Bob Daemmrich/SB; 304BL E. R. Degginger/AA; 304TR Gary W. Carter/VU; 305T Barth Schorre/BC; 308B James D. Watt/Earthviews; 308C G. Soury/Jacana/PR; 309TC Norman Owen Tomalin/BC; 309TL Tim Davis/PR; 309TR Norman Owen Tomalin/BC; 311CR Yngve Rakke/The Image Bank; 313BR E. R. Degginger/AA; 313CL Robin Kittrell Laughlin; 313CR Stephen Dalton/PR; 313TL 1995 Discover Magazine; 314 Stewart Westmorland/TSI; 314 Tracey Wheeler*; 315 Michael Newman/PhotoEdit; 315BC Drawing: Karen Phillipps/93/World Wildlife Fund; 315BL David Hulse, Courtesy, World Wildlife Fund; 316 Tracey Wheeler*

Unit 4 322BL Jerry Sarapochiello/BC; 322CL C. P. Hickman/VU; 322TR Peter Cade/TSI; 323BL Tracey Wheeler*; 323CR Flip Nicklin/MP; 323TR Allan Penn; 392BL Courtesy, Nora Cannick; 392BR *The Hot Zone* by Richard Preston, copyright © Random House, Inc. 393B Wayne & Karen Brown; 393T Dr. Kimberly J. Holding

Chapter 14 324–325 Ted Horowitz/Stock Market; 324C AP/Wide World; 325CR Dr. Gopal Murti/Science Photo Library/PR; 325 TOP BAR R. Kessel-G. Shih/VU; 326B Lee D. Simon/Science Source/PR; 326T Courtesy, Center for Disease Control; 329 Lennart Nilsson/BA; 330CL Runk/Schoenberger/GH; 330CR Lee D. Simon/Science Source/PR; 330TR Biophoto Assoc./Science Source/PR; 331BL Hans Gelderblom/VU; 331BR Barry Dowsett/Science Photo Library/PR; 331BR Science Source/PR; 334 Karl Ammann/BC; 335CR Courtesy of March of Dimes; 335TR UPI/Corbis-Bettmann; 336 Dr. Tony Brain & David Parker/Science Photo Library/PR; 337B Dr. T. J. Beveridge/Biological Photo Service; 337TR Pamela McTurk/Science Photo Library/PR; 338B James A. Sullivan, Quill Graphics; 338BL James A. Sullivan, Quill Graphics; 338CL James A. Sullivan, Quill Graphics; 338TC CNRI/Science Photo Library/PR; 338TL James A. Sullivan, Quill Graphics; 338TR Dr. Dennis Kunkel/PT; 339 Dr. E Buttone/PA; 340B Breck P. Kent/AA; 340T Norbert Wu/MYP; 341 Paul W. Johnson/Biological Photo Service; 342BC M. Abbey/PR; 342BL David M. Phillips/VU; 342BR Dr. Rosalind King/Science Photo Library/PR; 342CL R. Kessel-G. Shih/VU; 342TL David M. Phillips/VU; 343TC Courtesy, Dr. Wayne Carmichael; 343TL Science Photo Library/PR; 344BL David M. Phillips/VU; 344C Courtesy of Exxon; 344TR Randy Brandon/Sipa Press; 346BC Lawrence Migdale/PR; 346TR Charles O'Rear/Westlight; 349 Runk/Schoenberger/GH

Chapter 15 350–351 Gregory G. Dimijian/PR; 351BC Steve Raymer/National Geographic Image Collection; TOP BAR Chuck Davis/TSI (giant kelp); 351 David M. Phillips/VU (gonyaulux); 352 Chuck Davis/TSI; 354 VU; 355B Roger Klocek/VU; 355CR Eric Grave/PT; 355TL G. Tortoli/PR; 356TL K. Jeon/VU; 356TR Eric Grave/Science Source/PR; 357TL Michael Abbey/PR; 357TR Robert Becker, Ph.D./CMS; 358B Courtesy, Dr. P. Hargraves; 358CL David M. Phillips/VU; 358TR NASA; 359BC Biophoto Assoc./Science Source/PR; 359TC Dr. Anne Smith/Science Photo Library/PR; 359TL Carolina Biological Supply Company/PT; 360–361 Gregory Ochocki/PR; 360BC T. A. Wiewandt; 360BL Runk/Schoenberger/GH; 360C Cabisco/VU; 360CL Andrew Martinez/PR; 360TL William Dentler/TSI; 361BR William Jorgensen/VU; 362B Matt Meadows/PA; 362T Bill Beatty/VU; 363BC Cabisco/VU; 363BL Cabisco/VU; 363CL Cabisco/VU; 363TR Dwight Kuhn; 365B Jen & Des Bartlett/BC; 365T Thia Konig/TSI; 366B F. Pedrick/The Image Works; 366CL Kevin Schafer/PA; 366CR Andrew Syred/Science Photo Library/PR; 366TR Holt Studios Int'l./Nigel Cattlin/PR; 368TL Dick Poe/VU; 368TR Tracey Wheeler*; 371BR Scott Camazine/PR

Chapter 16 372TC M. Viardi Jacana/PR; 372–373 Bruno Barbey/Magnum Photos, Inc.; 373 TOP BAR David Cavagnaro/PA (morels); David Scharf (athlete's foot mold); Phil A. Dotson/PR (club fungus); 374BC Michael Fogden/BC; 374BL Kirtley-Perkins/VU; 374T C. B. & D. W. Frith/BC; 375C Dick Poe/VU; 376 L. E. Gilbert, Univ. of TX, Austin/Biological Photo Service; 377B Hans Reinhard/BC; 377T Jack M. Bostrack/VU; 378BC Adrian Davies/BC; 378BL David M. Phillips/VU; 378T Scott Camazine/PR; 379BC Phil A. Dotson/PR; 379BL Michael Fogden/BC; 379CL Astrid & Hanns-Frieder/Science Photo Library/PR; 380 Eric Grave/PR; 381CR S. Flegler/VU; 381TR David Cavagnaro/PA; 382 Steve Solum/BC; 383 David Scharf; 384BL Courtney Milne/Earth Vision; 384T Dan Lamont; 385BR James W. Richardson/VU; 385CR Holt Studios Int'l./Nigel Cattlin/PR; 385TC R. Roncadori/VU; 385TR John D. Cunningham/VU; 386 Rannels/GH; 387TC St. Mary's Hospital Medical School/Science Photo Library/PR; 387TR Holt Studios Int'l./Nigel Cattlin/PR; 388 Tim Davis*; 391B Runk/Schoenberger/GH; 391T Dick Poe/VU

Unit 5 394 Allan Penn* (sunglasses); 394BR Art Wolfe/TSI; 394TL Allan Penn* (flower); 394TR AP/Wide World; 395BC Dr. Wm. M. Harlow/PR; 395BL Leonard Lee Rue/BC; 395BR Scott Camazine/PR; 395TL Allan Penn* (utensils); 395TL Fletcher & Baylis/PR (flower); 395TR Ray Ellis/PR (lotus); 395TR Tracey Wheeler* (bulb base); 494BL Courtesy, Lily Fossner; 494BR SimLife ® and © 1992, SimEarth ® and © Maxis Inc. All Rights Reserved. 495B John Coletti; 495T S. G. Sprague

Chapter 17 396C Grant Heilman/GH; 396–397 David Muench; 397 TOP BAR Jacques Jangous Brazil-Mato Grosso Pantanal/PR (water hyacinth); Runk/Schoenberger/GH (leaves); 398 J. C. Carton/BC; 398B Allan Penn*; 399BC Runk/Schoenberger/GH; 399BL Runk/Schoenberger/GH; 399BR Runk/Schoenberger/GH; 399C Allan Penn*; 399CL Runk/Schoenberger/GH; 400BC Michael P. Gadomski/PR; 400BL Jane Grushow/GH; 400BR John D. Cunningham/VU; 401B Rod Planck/TSI; 401T Michael P. Gadomski/BC; 402B Alan Pitcairn/GH; 402BR Allan Penn*; 402CL Holt Studios Int'l./Nigel Cattlin/PR; 403 John Barr/GL; 404 Allan Penn*; 405BL Grant Heilman/GH; 405BR Darrell Gulin/TSI; 405CL Wesley Bocxe/PR; 405CR Tom Ulrich/TSI; 405T Jacques Jangous Brazil-Mato Grosso Pantanal/PR; 407 Jack Stein Grove/TSA; 408 Tracey Wheeler*; 409B John Bova/PR; 409TL Carole Elies/TSI; 409TR Michael P. Gadomski/BC; 411B Grant Heilman/GH; 411T Leonard Lee Rue/BC; 413B Jeff Foott/BC; 413T David Matherly/VU; 415BL Lefever/Grushow/GH; 415BR TSI; 415CL TSI; 415CR Lefever/Grushow/GH; 416 Gerald & Buff Corsi/VU; 419C Runk/Schoenberger/GH; 419CL Runk/Schoenberger/GH; 419CR Erich Lessing/Art Resource, NY

Chapter 18 420–421 Jack Dermid/PR; 421 TOP BAR Christi Carter/GH (mimosa pudica); Dr. Dennis Kunkel/PT (stomata); R. G. Kessel-C. Y. Shih/VU (xylem); Ted Vaughan/GH (begonia); 422C John D. Cunningham/VU; 422T Ted Vaughan/GH; 423 Dr. Dennis Kunkel/PT; 424BL Alan Pitcairn/GH; 424BR Bruce M. Herman/PR; 427 Will Owens; 428BC Cabisco/VU; 428TC Christi Carter/GH; 428TR Christi Carter/GH; 429BL Wendell Metzen/BC; 429CR Tracey Wheeler*; 429TC Runk/Schoenberger/GH; 429TL Runk/Schoenberger/GH; 429TR Tracey Wheeler*; 430BC R. G. Kessel-C. Y. Shih/VU; 430BR George J. Wilder/VU; 431 Runk/Schoenberger/GH; 434 Tracey Wheeler*; 435 Runk/Schoenberger/GH; 436BC Runk/Rannels/GH; 436BR M. I. Walker/PR; 439BC Ed. Reschke/PA; 439BL Ed. Reschke/PA; 440 Figure from Story Told by a Fallen Redwood, by Emanuel Fritz. Reproduced by permission of Save-the-Redwoods League.; 443 Runk/Schoenberger/GH

Chapter 19 444C Hugh Rose/VU; 444–445 Hans Reinhard/BC; 445 TOP BAR Alan L. Detrick/PR (rose); John Shaw/BC (aspen); Kim Taylor/BC (venus fly trap); 446B Runk/Schoenberger/GH; 446T G. A. Maclean/Oxford Scientific Films; 447 Kim Taylor/BC; 447BR Kim Taylor/BC; 447T Tracey Wheeler*; 451 Stephen P. Parker; 452BC Grant Heilman/GH; 452BL McCutcheon/VU; 452BR Grant Heilman/GH; 452T Robert Dunne/BC; 453 Robert Carr/BC; 454TC Michael Fogden/PR; 454TL Carol Hughes/BC; 455BC John Shaw/BC; 455BL David Overcash/BC; 455T Runk/Schoenberger/GH; 456 Renee Lynn*; 456TC Tracey Wheeler*; 456TC Tracey Wheeler*; 456TL Allan Penn*; 458B Alan L. Detrick/PR; 458T A. Henderson/Photo NATS; 462 Tracey Wheeler*; 463 Sean Morris/Oxford Scientific Films; 464 Robert Carr/BC; 467CR Tate Gallery, London/Art Resource, NY

Chapter 20 468–469 James Martin/TSI; 469CL Raphael Gaillarde/GL; 469 TOP BAR David Sieren/VU (cone); Gary Holscher/TSI (apple blossoms); Jack Dermid/PR (marsh); Wm. S. Ormerod/VU (moss); 470 Joe McDonald/BC; 471 All Rights Reserved, Photo Archives, Denver Museum of Natural History, Photo by Rick Wicker, DMNH cat # 5849; 473BL Jack Dermid/PR; 473BR Bill Bachman/PR; 474 Lefever/Grushow/GH; 475BC John M. Trager/VU; 475BR Brian Enting/PR; 475CR Wm. S. Ormerod/VU; 475T Jen & Des Bartlett/BC; 477 Farrell Grehan/PR; 478BC Jim Zipp/PR; 478BL Jacques Jangoux/TSI; 478CL Doug Plummer/PR; 478T George Holton/PR; 479 Art Wolfe/TSI; 480 Ken Wagner/VU; 481BC David Sieren/VU; 481BR E. R. Degginger/BC; 481C David Sieren/VU; 481CR S. Nielsen/BC; 482 Leonard Lee Rue/BC; 483 Stan W. Elems/VU; 484CL James P. Rowan/DRK; 484TL Bob & Clara Calhoun/BC; 484TR S. J. Krasemann/PR; 485BC Jane Grushow/GH; 485BR Gary Holscher/TSI; 485C Allan Penn*; 485CR Allan Penn*; 485T Larry Lefever/GH; 488 Steve & Dave Maslowski/PR; 489 C. Brad Simmons/BC; 493 Stephen Frink/WaterHouse

Unit 6 496CL Jane Burton/BC; 496TR Peter Menzel; 496BR Stephen J. Krasemann/PR; 496BL Michael Smith/PR; 496TCR Peter Menzel; 496CR Peter Menzel; 496C Tracey Wheeler*; 497TL Robert C. Hermes/PR; 497CR R. N. Mariscal/BC; 497BR Bucky Reeves/National Audubon Society/PR; 497BL Carson Baldwin Jr./AA; 497TR Allan Penn*; 586BL Courtesy, Abby Greenbaum; 586BR *Sea of Cortez*, courtesy of Paul P. Appel, Publisher; 587B Doug Perrine/IV; 587T Nance S. Trueworthy

Chapter 21 498BR Norbert Wu/MYP; 498–499 Stephen Frink/WaterHouse; 499 TOP BAR Franklin Viola (reef); Norbert Wu/MYP (jelly); 500B Franklin Viola; 500T Doug Perrine/IV; 501B Robin Kittrell Laughlin; 501T Thomas Zimmermann/TSI; 504B Stephen Frink/WaterHouse; 504T Norbert Wu/MYP; 505C Stephen Frink/WaterHouse; 506B Franklin Viola; 506T Stephen Frink/WaterHouse; 507 Stephen Frink/WaterHouse; 508BC Stephen Frink/WaterHouse; 508BL Stephen Frink/WaterHouse; 508BR Norbert Wu/MYP; 508C Daniel W. Gotshall; 509BL Ronald L. Sefton/BC; 509BR Neil McDaniel/PR; 509T Howard Hall/HHP; 511CR Doug Perrine/Norbert Wu/MYP; 511T Mike Waters/WaterHouse; 513 Ron & Valerie Taylor/BC; 514B Norbert Wu/MYP; 514T M. I. Walker/Science Source/PR; 515B Neil McDaniel/PR; 515TL Norbert Wu/MYP; 516–517 Franklin Viola; 516T Fred McConnaughey/PR; 517CR Paul Chesley/TSI; 518 Gareth Hopson*; 521 Norbert Wu/MYP

1014

L. Carson/CMS; 807BR C. Edelmann/La Villette/PR; 807CR C. Edelmann/La Villette/PR; 807TR C. Edelmann/La Villette/PR; 809 Bruce Ayres/TSI; 811 Lennart Nilsson/BA; 812 CMS; 813 Lawrence Migdale/SB; 814B Jay Syverson/SB; 814T TSI; 815BR Dr. Tony Brain/Science Photo Library/PR; 815CR CNRI/Science Photo Library/PR; 815T Lennart Nilsson/BA; 816 Tracey Wheeler*

Chapter 34 820–821 Gary Yeowell/TSI; 821B Gary Yeowell/TSI; 821 TOP BAR David M. Phillips/PR; 822 Pascal Quittemelle/SB; 824 David M. Phillips/PR; 825 CNRI/PT; 828 Michael Newman/PhotoEdit; 830 Hank Morgan/Science Source/PR; 833 Tim Davis*; 834TR Jerome Tisne/TSI; 838BL Biophoto Assoc./Science Source/PR; 838CL R. C. Eager/PR; 838TR Allan Penn*; 839 David Chambers/TSI; 840BC Lefever/Grushow/GH; 840BL M. Viardi Jacana/PR; 840BR Phil Schermeister/TSI; 840CL Wesley Bocxe/PR; 841 Mark Reinstein/GL; 842B Yoav Levy/PT; 842T A. Glauberman/Science Source/PR; 843BL Joseph R. Siebert/CMS; 843BR Martin Rotker/PT; 843T Jeff Zaruba/AllStock; 844B Linc Cornell/SB; 844T Bob Daemmrich/SB; 847 Tom Van Sant/Geosphere Project,Santa Monica/Science Photo Library/PR

Unit 9 850BL Peter Cade/TSI; 850BR James Balog/TSI; 850CL Phil Degginger/BC; 850TR Bill Wood/BC; 851BL E. R. Degginger/BC; 851BR John Kieffer/PA; 851TL SEF/Art Resource, NY; 851TR Johnny Johnson/TSI; 940BL Courtesy, Ann Myers; 940BR "From Last Chance to See" by Douglas Adams and Mark Carwardine. ©1990 by Serias Productions Ltd. Reprinted by Permission of Harmony Books, a division of Crown Publishers, Inc.; 941B John Coletti; 941T Tri-State Bird Rescue

Chapter 35 852–853 Henry Gonzalez/BC; 853B Jean-Paul Manceau/TSI (leopards); 853 TOP BAR Frank Siteman/TSI (fish); Gregory G. Dimijian/PR (ant); Norbert Wu/TSI (sloth); Jean-Paul Manceau/TSI (desert); 854B Tom Van Sant/Geosphere Project,Santa Monica/Science Photo Library/PR; 854T Mark Burnett/PR; 855CR Manoj Shah/TSI; 855TC R.S. Virdee/GH; 855TR Tim Davis/PR; 856BL Grant Heilman/GH; 856BR Jen & Des Bartlett/BC; 856C John Beatty/TSI; 856TL Schafer & Hill/PA; 856TR E. R. Degginger/BC; 858T Arnulf Husmo/TSI; 859BR J. Messerschmidt/BC; 859TR James Blank/BC; 860 Tracey Wheeler*; 861 Jane Grushow/GH; 862B Charlie Ott/PR; 862BL Mark Newman/PR; 862BR Michael Giannechini/PR; 862C Scott Nielsen/BC; 862T Arthur C. Smith III/GH; 862TC Kim Heacox/TSI; 862TR W. Lankinen/BC; 863B Danilo S. Donadoni/BC; 863BC Larry Brock/TSA; 863BL Robert E. Daemmrich/TSI; 863BR John R. MacGregor/PA; 863T Michael Busselle/TSI; 863TC Michio Hoshino/MP; 863TR Steve & Dave Maslowski/PR; 864B Jean-Paul Manceau/TSI; 864BL Kim Heacox/Petet Arnold, Inc.; 864BR Gary Meszaros/BC; 864T Art Wolfe/TSI; 864TL Gregory G. Dimijian/PR; 864TR Norbert Wu/TSI; 865C Art Wolfe; 865CL William Felger/GH; 865T John Shaw/BC; 866B John Shaw/TSA; 866BL Dan Guravich/PR; 866T Peter David/Planet Earth Pictures; 867B Grant Heilman/GH; 867BL Runk/Schoenberger/GH; 867BR Runk/Schoenberger/GH; 867C John Shaw/BC; 868B Tom Tietz/TSI; 868BC Runk/Schoenberger/GH; 868BL Randy Wells/TSI; 868BR Jeff Foott/BC; 868CR Patricio Robles Gil/BC; 869C John Gerlach/AA; 869T M. E. Warren/PR; 869TR Fritz Polking/PA; 870CL Randy Morse/TSA; 870CR Tom McHugh/Steinhart Aquarium/PR; 870T Scott Blackman/TSA; 870TR Frank Siteman/TSI; 873 Dr. Morley Read/Science Photo Library/PR; 873CR THE FAR SIDE © FARWORKS, INC./Dist. by UNIVERSAL PRESS SYNDICATE. /reprinted with permission. All rights reserved.

Chapter 36 874–875 Erwin & Peggy Bauer/BC; 875 TOP BAR Art Wolfe/TSI (butterflyfish); Tim Davis/TSI (cheetahs); Leonard Lee Rue III/PR (starlings); 876BL Jane Burton/BC; 876C Kim Taylor/BC; 876TR Hans Reinhard/BC; 877 M. Gabridge/VU; 878B Jim Brandenburg/MP; 879TC Kim Taylor/BC; 880 Kent Wood; 881B Clem Haagner/BC; 881T Frank Siteman/TSI; 882 Alan Carey/PR; 883 Dr. Morley Read/Science Photo Library/PR; 884 Jim Pickerell/TSI; 885B Allan Blank/BC; 885T Art Wolfe; 886 Leonard Lee Rue III/PR; 887BC Francois Gohier/PR; 887BL Robert & Linda Mitchell; 887CR L. West/PR; 888 Tim Davis/TSI; 889C Victoria McCormick/AA; 889CR Lynn M. Stone/DRK; 889T Alan L. Detrick/PR; 889TC Mark N. Boulton/PR; 890B Arthur C. Smith III/GH; 890T Art Wolfe/TSI; 891B Michael Busselle/TSI; 891C Grant Heilman/GH; 891CR Michael P. Gadomski/PR; 891T Grant Heilman/GH; 892 Sylvain Grandadam/TSI

Chapter 37 896–897 Gary Braasch; 897BL Richard Alan Wood/AA; 897BR Gary Braasch; 897 TOP BAR Brandon Cole/MYP (salmon); Grant Heilman/GH (sunflowers); 898B Joe McDonald/BC; 898T Grant Heilman/GH; 901CR Brandon Cole/MYP; 901TR Steve Bly/TSI; 902 Francios Gohier/PR; 905 Jerry Howard/SB; 907C Charlie Ott/PR; 907CR Albert J. Copley/VU; 907TR Grant Heilman/GH; 909 Grant Heilman/GH; 911B Ohlt Studios International/PR; 911T Lawrence Migdale/PR; 915 Richard Parker/PR

Chapter 38 916BC Johnny Johnson/DRK; 916–917 Larry Ulrich/TSI; 917 TOP BAR Billy Hustace/TSI (wind turbine); Johnny Johnson/DRK (grizzly); Larry Ulrich/TSI (mountains); 918BC Billy Hustace/TSI; 918BL Ken Graham/TSI; 918TR Ned Therrien/VU; 919 Courtesy, Central Artery/Tunnel Project, photo by Louis Martin; 920BL John Midgley/TSI; 920BR Ed Degginger/BC; 920TR Richard Parker/PR; 921 Torin Boyd/GL; 922 J. Sarapochiello/BC; 923 Sue Cunningham/TSI; 924BL VU; 924TR Joe Munroe/PR; 925BR John Chiasson/GL; 925TL John S. Lough/VU; 925TR John S. Lough/VU; 926BL Carolyn Schaefer/GL; 926TR Joseph Sohm/TSI; 927 Guido Cozzi/BC; 928BL Ed Pritchard/TSI; 928TR Ron & Valerie Taylor/BC; 929TL Runk/Schoenberger/GH; 929TR Oliver Strewe/TSI; 931 NOAA/Science Photo Library/PR; 932BL Galen Rowell/Mountain Light; 932TR Marty Stouffer/AA; 933 Wendy Stone/GL; 934BL Jack Swenson/Wildlife Collection; 934TR Bob Daemmrich/SB; 935C Michael Fogden/BC; 935R Stephen J. Krasemann/PR; 935TL Michael Fogden/BC; 936 Jose Azel/Aurora; 939 NASA; 942 Allan Penn*

* Photographed expressly for Scott Foresman-Addison Wesley.